Collins

Spanish

Dictionary
& Grammar

HarperCollins Publishers
Westerhill Road
Bishopbriggs
Glasgow
G64 2QT

Seventh Edition 2014

Reprint 10 9 8 7 6 5 4 3 2 1 0

© HarperCollins Publishers 1997, 2000,
2004, 2006, 2008, 2010, 2014

ISBN 978-0-00-748436-2

www.collinsdictionary.com
www.collins.co.uk

A catalogue record for this book is
available from the British Library

Typeset by Davidson Publishing Solutions

Printed in India by Gopsons Papers Ltd

Acknowledgements
We would like to thank those authors
and publishers who kindly gave
permission for copyright material to be
used in the Collins Corpus. We would also
like to thank Times Newspapers Ltd for
providing valuable data.

EDITOR
Susie Beattie

CONTRIBUTORS
José A. Gálvez
Val McNulty
Helen Newstead
José María Ruiz Vaca

TECHNICAL SUPPORT
Thomas Callan
Agnieszka Urbanowicz
Dave Wark

FOR THE PUBLISHER
Gerry Breslin
Catherine Love
Evelyn Sword

Contributors to the previous edition
Gaëlle Amiot-Cadey, Jeremy Butterfield,
José Miguel Galván Déniz, Teresa Álvarez
García, Genevieve Gerrard, Mike González,
Sharon Hunter, Ana Cristina Llompart,
Tracy Lomas, Caitlin McMahon,
Enrique González Sandinero, Brian Steel

Índice de materias

Contents

Introduction

You may be starting Spanish for the first time, or you may wish to extend your knowledge of the language. Perhaps you want to read and study Spanish books, newspapers and magazines, or perhaps simply have a conversation with Spanish speakers. Whatever the reason, whether you're a student, a tourist or want to use Spanish for business, this is the ideal book to help you understand and communicate. This modern, user-friendly dictionary gives priority to everyday vocabulary and the language of current affairs, business, computing and tourism, and, as in all Collins dictionaries, the emphasis is firmly placed on contemporary language and expressions.

How to use the dictionary

Below you will find an outline of how information is presented in your dictionary. Our aim is to give you the maximum amount of detail in the clearest and most helpful way.

Entries

A typical entry in your dictionary will be made up of the following elements:

Phonetic transcription

Phonetics appear in square brackets immediately after the headword. They are shown using the International Phonetic Alphabet (IPA), and a complete list of the symbols used in this system can be found on page x. The pronunciation given is for Castilian Spanish except where a word is solely used in Latin America, when we give the Latin American pronunciation. A further guide to the differences in types of Spanish pronunciation is given on page x.

Grammatical information

All words belong to one of the following parts of speech: noun, verb, adjective, adverb, pronoun, article, conjunction, preposition, abbreviation. Nouns can be singular or plural and, in Spanish, masculine or feminine. Verbs can be transitive, intransitive, reflexive or impersonal: on the Spanish side, each verb is followed by a bold number, which corresponds to verb tables on pages xiii-xiv. Parts of speech appear in SMALL CAPS immediately after the phonetic spelling of the headword. The gender of the translation also appears in *italics* immediately following the key element of the translation, except where this is a regular masculine singular noun ending in "o", or a regular feminine singular noun ending in "a".

Often a word can have more than one part of speech. Just as the English word **chemical** can be an adjective or a noun, the Spanish word **conocido** can be an adjective ("(well-) known") or a noun ("acquaintance"). In the same way the verb **to walk** is sometimes transitive, ie it takes an object ("to walk the dog") and sometimes intransitive, ie it doesn't take an object ("to walk to school"). To help you find the meaning you are looking for quickly and for clarity of presentation, the different part of speech categories are separated by a solid black triangle ▸.

Meaning divisions

Most words have more than one meaning. Take, for example, **punch** which can be, amongst other things, a blow with the fist or an object used for making holes. Other words are translated differently depending on the context in which they are used. The transitive verb **to put on**, for example, can be translated by "ponerse", "encender" etc depending on *what* it is you are putting on. To help you select the most appropriate translation in every context, entries are divided according to meaning. Each different meaning is introduced by an "indicator" in *italics* and in brackets. Thus, the examples given above will be shown as follows:

> **punch** [pʌntʃ] N (*blow*) golpe *m*, puñetazo; (*tool*) punzón *m*

Likewise, some words can have a different meaning when used to talk about a specific subject area or field. For example **bishop**, which in a religious context means a high-ranking clergyman, is also the name of a chess piece. To show English speakers which translation to use, we have added "subject field labels" in brackets, in this case (*Chess*):

> **bishop** ['bɪʃəp] N obispo; (*Chess*) alfil *m*

Field labels are often shortened to save space. You will find a complete list of abbreviations used in the dictionary on pages viii and ix.

Translations

Most English words have a direct translation in Spanish and vice versa, as shown in the examples given above. Sometimes, however, no exact equivalent exists in the target language. In such cases we have given an approximate equivalent, indicated by the sign ≈. An example is **Health Service**, the Spanish equivalent of which is "Insalud". There is no exact equivalent since the bodies in the two countries are quite different:

> **Health Service** N (*BRIT*) servicio de salud pública, ≈ Insalud *m* (*SP*)

On occasion it is impossible to find even an approximate equivalent. This may be the case, for example, with the names of types of food:

> **fabada** [fa'βaða] NF *bean and sausage stew*

Here the translation (which doesn't exist) is replaced by an explanation. For increased clarity, the explanation, or "gloss", is shown in *italics*.

It is often the case that a word, or a particular meaning of a word, cannot be translated in isolation. The translation of **Dutch**, for example, is "holandés/esa". However, the phrase **to go Dutch** is rendered by "pagar cada uno lo suyo". Even an expression as simple as **washing powder** needs a separate translation since it translates as "detergente (en polvo)", not "polvo para lavar". This is where your dictionary will prove to be particularly informative and useful since it contains an abundance of compounds, phrases and idiomatic expressions.

Levels of formality and familiarity

In English you instinctively know when to say **I'm broke** or **I'm a bit short of cash** and when to say **I don't have any money**. When you are trying to understand someone who is speaking Spanish, however, or when you yourself try to speak Spanish, it is important to know what is polite and what is less so, and what you can say in a relaxed situation but not in a formal context. To help you with this, on the Spanish-English side we have added the label (*fam*) to show that a Spanish meaning or expression is colloquial, while those meanings or expressions which are vulgar are given an exclamation mark (*fam!*), warning you they can cause serious offence. Note also that on the English-Spanish side, translations which are vulgar are followed by an exclamation mark in brackets.

Keywords

Words labelled in the text as KEYWORDS, such as **have** and **do** or their Spanish equivalents **tener** and **hacer**, have been given special treatment because they form the basic elements of the language. This extra help will ensure that you know how to use these complex words with confidence.

Cultural information

Entries which appear next to a fading vertical bar explain aspects of culture in Spanish and English-speaking countries. Subject areas covered include politics, education, media and national festivals.

Spanish alphabetical order

In 1994 the **Real Academia Española** and the Spanish American language academies jointly decided to stop treating CH and LL as separate letters in Spanish, thereby bringing it into line with European spelling norms. This means that **chapa** and **lluvia** will appear in letters C and L respectively. Of course, it should also be remembered that words like **cancha** and **callar**, with **ch** and **ll** in the middle of the words, will also have changed places alphabetically, now being found after **cáncer** and **cáliz** respectively. Spanish, however still has one more letter than English with Ñ treated separately, between N and O.

Abreviaturas   Abbreviations

abreviatura	AB(B)R	abbreviation
adjetivo, locución adjetiva	ADJ	adjective, adjectival phrase
administración, lenguaje administrativo	Admin	administration
adverbio, locución adverbial	ADV	adverb, adverbial phrase
agricultura	Agr	agriculture
alguien	algn	
anatomía	Anat	anatomy
arquitectura	Arq, Arch	architecture
astrología, astronomía	Astro	astrology, astronomy
el automóvil	Aut(o)	automobiles
aviación, viajes en avión	Aviat	flying, air travel
biología	Bio(l)	biology
botánica, flores	Bot	botany
inglés británico	BRIT	British English
química	Chem	chemistry
cine	Cine	cinema
comercio, finanzas, banca	Com(m)	commerce, finance, banking
informática	Comput	computing
conjunción	CONJ	conjunction
construcción	Constr	building
compuesto	CPD	compound element
cocina	Culin	cookery
economía	Econ	economics
electricidad, electrónica	Elec	electricity, electronics
enseñanza, sistema escolar	Escol	schooling, schools
España	Esp	Spain
especialmente	esp	especially
exclamación, interjección	EXCL	exclamation, interjection
femenino	f	feminine
lenguaje familiar (! vulgar)	fam (!)	colloquial usage (! particularly offensive)
ferrocarril	Ferro	railways
uso figurado	fig	figurative use
fotografía	Foto	photography
(verbo inglés) del cual la partícula es inseparable	FUS	(phrasal verb) where the particle is inseparable
generalmente	gen	generally
geografía, geología	Geo	geography, geology
geometría	Geom	geometry
uso familiar	inf(!)	informal usage (! particularly offensive)
informática	Inform	computing
invariable	inv	invariable
irregular	irreg	irregular
lo jurídico	Jur	law
América Latina	LAm	Latin America
gramática, lingüística	Ling	grammar, linguistics
literatura	Lit	literature

masculino	*m*	masculine
matemáticas	*Mat(h)*	mathematics
medicina	*Med*	medical term, medicine
masculino/femenino	*m/f*	masculine/feminine
lo militar, el ejército	*Mil*	military matters
música	*Mus*	music
sustantivo	N	noun
navegación, náutica	*Naut*	sailing, navigation
sustantivo no empleado en el plural	*no pl*	collective (uncountable) noun, not used in plural
sustantivo numérico	NUM	numeral noun
complemento	*obj*	(grammatical) object
	o.s.	oneself
peyorativo	*pey, pej*	derogatory, pejorative
fotografía	*Phot*	photography
fisiología	*Physiol*	physiology
plural	*pl*	plural
política	*Pol*	politics
participio de pasado	*pp*	past participle
prefijo	PREF	prefix
preposición	PREP	preposition
pronombre	PRON	pronoun
psicología, psiquiatría	*Psico, Psych*	psychology, psychiatry
tiempo pasado	*pt*	past tense
ferrocarril	*Rail*	railways
religión, lo eclesiástico	*Rel*	religion, church service
alguien	*sb*	somebody
enseñanza, sistema escolar	*Scol*	schooling, schools
singular	*sg*	singular
España	*SP*	Spain
algo	*sth*	something
subjuntivo	*subjun*	subjunctive
sujeto	*su(b)j*	(grammatical) subject
sufijo	*suff*	suffix
tauromaquia	*Taur*	bullfighting
también	*tb*	also
teatro	*Teat*	
técnica, tecnología	*Tec(h)*	technical term, technology
telecomunicaciones	*Telec, Tel*	telecommunications
	Theat	theatre
imprenta, tipografía	*Tip, Typ*	typography, printing
televisión	TV	television
sistema universitario	*Univ*	universities
inglés norteamericano	*US*	American English
verbo	VB	verb
verbo intransitivo	VI	intransitive verb
verbo pronominal	VR	reflexive verb
verbo transitivo	VT	transitive verb
zoología, animales	*Zool*	zoology
marca registrada	®	registered trademark
indica un equivalente cultural	≈	introduces a cultural equivalent

Spanish pronunciation

Consonants

b	[b]	See notes on v below	*bomba*
	[β]		*labor*
c	[k]	c before *a, o* or *u* is pronounced as in *cat*	*caja*
ce, ci	[θe, θi]	c before *e* or *i* is pronounced as in *thin* and as *s*	*cero, cielo*
	[se, si']	in *sin* in Latin America and parts of Spain	*vocero, noticiero*
ch	[tʃ]	*ch* is pronounced as *ch* in *chair*	*chiste*
d	[d]	at the beginning of a word or after *l* or *n*,	*danés*
	[ð]	*d* is pronounced as in English. In any other position it is like *th* in *the*	*ciudad*
g	[g]	g before *a, o* or *u* is pronounced as in *gap* if	*gafas, guerra*
	[ɤ]	at the beginning of a word or after *n*. In other positions the sound is softened.	*paga*
ge, gi	[xe, xi]	g before *e* or *i* is pronounced similar to *ch* in Scottish lo*ch*	*gente, girar*
h		*h* is always silent in Spanish	*haber*
j	[x]	*j* is pronounced like *ch* in Scottish lo*ch*	*jugar*
ll	[ʎ]	*ll* is pronounced like the *lli* in mi*lli*on	*talle*
ñ	[ɲ]	*ñ* is pronounced like the *ni* in o*ni*on	*niño*
q	[k]	*q* is pronounced as *k* in *king*	*que*
r, rr	[r]	*r* is always pronounced in Spanish, unlike	*quitar*
	[rr]	the *r* in dancer. *rr* and *r* at the beginning of a word are trilled, like a Scottish *r*	*garra*
s	[s]	*s* is usually pronounced as in *pass*, but before	*quizás*
	[z]	*b, d, g, l, m* or *n* it is pronounced as in *rose*	*isla*
v	[b]	*v* is pronounced something like *b*. At the	*vía*
	[β]	beginning of a word or after *m* or *n* it is pronounced as *b* in *boy*. In any other position it is pronounced with the lips in position to pronounce *b* of *boy*, but not meeting	*dividir*
w	[b]	pronounced either like Spanish *b*, or like	*wáter*
	[w]	English *w*	*whiskey*

z	[θ]	z is pronounced as *th* in *th*in and as *s* in *s*in in	tena*z*
	[sˈ]	Latin America and parts of Spain	i*z*ada
	[ks]	x is pronounced as in to*x*in except in informal	tó*x*ico
	[s]	Spanish or at the beginning of a word	*x*enofobia

f, k, l, m, n, p and *t* are pronounced as in English
ˈ Only shown in Latin American entries.

Vowels

a	[a]	Not as long as *a* in f*a*r. When followed by a consonant in the same syllable (ie in a closed syllable), as in am*a*nte, the *a* is short as in b*a*t	p*a*ta
e	[e]	like *e* in th*e*y. In a closed syllable, as in g*e*nte, the *e* is short as in p*e*t	m*e*
i	[i]	as in m*ea*n or mach*i*ne	p*i*no
o	[o]	as in l*o*cal. In a closed syllable, as in c*o*ntrol, the *o* is short as in c*o*t	l*o*
u	[u]	As in r*u*le. It is silent after *q*, and in *gue, gui*, unless marked *güe, güi* eg antig*ü*edad, when it is pronounced like *w* in *w*olf	l*u*nes

Semi-vowels

| i, y | [j] | pronounced like *y* in *y*es | b*i*en, h*i*elo, *y*unta |
| u | [w] | unstressed *u* between consonant and vowel is pronounced like *w* in *w*ell. See also notes on *u* above | h*u*evo, f*u*ente, antig*ü*edad |

Diphthongs

ai, ay	[ai]	as *i* in r*i*de	b*ai*le
au	[au]	as *ou* in sh*ou*t	*au*to
ei, ey	[ei]	as *ey* in gr*ey*	bu*ey*
eu	[eu]	both elements pronounced independently [e] + [u]	d*eu*da
oi, oy	[oi]	as *oy* in t*oy*	h*oy*

Stress

The rules of stress in Spanish are as follows:

(a)   when a word ends in a vowel or in *n* or *s*, the second last syllable is stressed: pa*ta*ta, pa*ta*tas, *co*me, *co*men

(b)   when a word ends in a consonant other than *n* or *s*, the stress falls on the last syllable: pa*red*, ha*blar*

(c)   when the rules set out in (a) and (b) are not applied, an acute accent appears over the stressed vowel: común, geografía, inglés

In the phonetic transcription, the symbol ['] precedes the syllable on which the stress falls.

In general, we give the pronunciation of each entry in square brackets after the word in question.

Spanish irregular verbs

1 Gerund **2** Imperative **3** Present **4** Preterite **5** Future **6** Present subjunctive
7 Imperfect subjunctive **8** Past participle **9** Imperfect

Etc indicates that the irregular root is used for all persons of the tense, e.g. **oír: 6** oiga, oigas, oigamos, oigáis, oigan

1a HABLAR 1 hablando **2** habla, hablad **3** hablo, hablas, habla, hablamos, habláis, hablan **4** hablé, hablaste, habló, hablamos, hablasteis, hablaron **5** hablaré, hablarás, hablará, hablaremos, hablaréis, hablarán **6** hable, hables, hable, hablemos, habléis, hablen **7** hablara, hablaras, hablara, habláramos, hablarais, hablaran **8** hablado **9** hablaba, hablabas, hablaba, hablábamos, hablabais, hablaban

1b cambiar 2 cambia **3** cambio *etc* **6** cambie *etc*

1c enviar 2 envía **3** envío, envías, envía, envíen **6** envíe, envíes, envíe, envíen

1d evacuar 2 evacua **3** evacuo *etc* **6** evacue *etc*

1e situar 2 sitúa **3** sitúo, sitúas, sitúa, sitúen **6** sitúe, sitúes, sitúe, sitúen

1f cruzar 4 crucé **6** cruce *etc*

1g picar 4 piqué **6** pique *etc*

1h pagar 4 pagué **6** pague *etc*

1i averiguar 4 averigüé **6** averigüe *etc*

1j cerrar 2 cierra **3** cierro, cierras, cierra, cierran **6** cierre, cierres, cierre, cierren

1k errar 2 yerra **3** yerro, yerras, yerra, yerran **6** yerre, yerres, yerre, yerren

1l contar 2 cuenta **3** cuento, cuentas, cuenta, cuentan **6** cuente, cuentes, cuente, cuenten

1m degollar 2 degüella **3** degüello, degüellas, degüella, degüellan **6** degüelle, degüelles, degüelle, degüellen

1n jugar 2 juega **3** juego, juegas, juega, jueguen **6** juegue, juegues, juegue, jueguen

1o ESTAR 2 está **3** estoy, estás, está, están **4** estuve, estuviste, estuvo, estuvimos, estuvisteis, estuvieron **6** esté, estés, esté, estén **7** estuviera *etc*

1p andar 4 anduve *etc* **7** anduviera *etc*

1q dar 3 doy **4** di, diste, dio, dimos, disteis, dieron **7** diera *etc*

2a COMER 1 comiendo **2** come, comed **3** como, comes, come, comemos, coméis, comen **4** comí, comiste, comió, comimos, comisteis, comieron **5** comeré, comerás, comerá, comeremos, comeréis, comerán **6** coma, comas, coma, comamos, comáis, coman **7** comiera, comieras, comiera, comiéramos, comierais, comieran **8** comido **9** comía, comías, comía, comíamos, comíais, comían

2b vencer 3 venzo **6** venza *etc*

2c coger 3 cojo **6** coja *etc*

2d parecer 3 parezco **6** parezca *etc*

2e leer 1 leyendo **4** leyó, leyeron **7** leyera *etc*

2f tañer 1 tañendo **4** tañó, tañeron

2g perder 2 pierde **3** pierdo, pierdes, pierde, pierden **6** pierda, pierdas, pierda, pierdan

2h mover 2 mueve **3** muevo, mueves, mueve, mueven **6** mueva, muevas, mueva, muevan

2i oler 2 huele **3** huelo, hueles, huele, huelen **6** huela, huelas, huela, huelan

2j HABER 3 he, has, ha, hemos, han **4** hube, hubiste, hubo, hubimos, hubisteis, hubieron **5** habré *etc* **6** haya *etc* **7** hubiera *etc*

2k tener 2 ten **3** tengo, tienes, tiene, tienen **4** tuve, tuviste, tuvo, tuvimos, tuvisteis, tuvieron **5** tendré *etc* **6** tenga *etc* **7** tuviera *etc*

2l caber 3 quepo **4** cupe, cupiste, cupo, cupimos, cupisteis, cupieron **5** cabré *etc* **6** quepa *etc* **7** cupiera *etc*

2m saber 3 sé **4** supe, supiste, supo, supimos, supisteis, supieron **5** sabré *etc* **6** sepa *etc* **7** supiera *etc*

2n caer 1 cayendo **3** caigo **4** cayó, cayeron **6** caiga *etc* **7** cayera *etc*

2o traer 1 trayendo **3** traigo **4** traje, trajiste, trajo, trajimos, trajisteis, trajeron **6** traiga *etc* **7** trajera *etc*

2p valer 2 vale **3** valgo **5** valdré *etc* **6** valga *etc*

2q poner 2 pon **3** pongo **4** puse, pusiste, puso, pusimos, pusisteis, pusieron **5** pondré *etc* **6** ponga *etc* **7** pusiera *etc* **8** puesto

2r hacer 2 haz **3** hago **4** hice, hiciste, hizo, hicimos, hicisteis, hicieron **5** haré *etc* **6** haga *etc* **7** hiciera *etc* **8** hecho

2s poder 1 pudiendo **2** puede **3** puedo, puedes, puede, pueden **4** pude, pudiste, pudo, pudimos, pudisteis, pudieron **5** podré *etc* **6** pueda, puedas, pueda, puedan **7** pudiera *etc*

2t querer 2 quiere **3** quiero, quieres, quiere, quieren **4** quise, quisiste, quiso, quisimos, quisisteis, quisieron **5** querré *etc* **6** quiera, quieras, quiera, quieran **7** quisiera *etc*

2u ver 3 veo **6** vea *etc* **8** visto **9** veía *etc*

2v SER 2 sé **3** soy, eres, es, somos, sois, son **4** fui, fuiste, fue, fuimos, fuisteis, fueron **6** sea *etc* **7** fuera *etc* **9** era, eras, era, éramos, erais, eran

2w placer 3 plazco **6** plazca *etc*

2x yacer 2 yace or yaz **3** yazco or yazgo **6** yazca or yazga *etc*

2y roer 1 royendo **3** roo or roigo **7** royó, royeron, **6** roa or roiga *etc* **7** royera *etc*

3a VIVIR 1 viviendo **2** vive, vivid **3** vivo, vives, vive, vivimos, vivís, viven **4** viví, viviste, vivió, vivimos, vivisteis, vivieron **5** viviré, vivirás, vivirá, viviremos, viviréis, vivirán **6** viva, vivas, viva, vivamos, viváis, vivan **7** viviera, vivieras, viviera, viviéramos, vivierais, vivieran **8** vivido **9** vivía, vivías, vivía, vivíamos, vivías, vivían

3b esparcir 3 esparzo **6** esparza *etc*

3c dirigir 3 dirijo **6** dirija *etc*

3d distinguir 3 distingo **6** distinga *etc*

3e delinquir 3 delinco **6** delinca *etc*

3f lucir 3 luzco **6** luzca *etc*

3g instruir 1 instruyendo **2** instruye **3** instruyo, instruyes, instruye, instruyen **4** instruyó, instruyeron **6** instruya *etc* **7** instruyera *etc*

3h gruñir 1 gruñendo **4** gruñó, gruñeron

3i sentir 1 sintiendo **2** siente **3** siento, sientes, siente, sienten **4** sintió, sintieron **6** sienta, sientas, sienta, sintamos, sintáis, sientan **7** sintiera *etc*

3j dormir 1 durmiendo **2** duerme **3** duermo, duermes, duerme, duermen **4** durmió, durmieron **6** duerma, duermas, duerma, durmamos, durmáis, duerman **7** durmiera *etc*

3k pedir 1 pidiendo **2** pide **3** pido, pides, pide, piden **4** pidió, pidieron **6** pida *etc* **7** pidiera *etc*

3l reír 2 ríe **3** río, ríes, ríe, ríen **4** reí, rieron **6** ría, rías, ría, riamos, riáis, rían **7** riera *etc*

3m erguir 1 irguiendo **2** yergue **3** yergo, yergues, yergue, yerguen **6** irguió, irguieron **7** irguiera *etc*

3n reducir 3 reduzco **5** reduje *etc* **6** reduzca *etc* **7** redujera *etc*

3o decir 2 di **3** digo **4** dije, dijiste, dijo, dijimos, dijisteis, dijeron **5** diré *etc* **6** diga *etc* **7** dijera *etc* **8** dicho

3p oír 1 oyendo **2** oye **3** oigo, oyes, oye, oyen **4** oyó, oyeron **6** oiga *etc* **7** oyera *etc*

3q salir 2 sal **3** salgo **5** saldré *etc* **6** salga *etc*

3r venir 2 ven **3** vengo, vienes, viene, vienen **4** vine, viniste, vino, vinimos, vinisteis, vinieron **5** vendré *etc* **6** venga *etc* **7** viniera *etc*

3s ir 1 yendo **2** ve **3** voy, vas, va, vamos, vais, van **4** fui, fuiste, fue, fuimos, fuisteis, fueron **6** vaya, vayas, vaya, vayamos, vayáis, vayan **7** fuera *etc* **9** iba, ibas, iba, íbamos, ibais, iban

Números

Numbers

uno (un, una)*	1	one
dos	2	two
tres	3	three
cuatro	4	four
cinco	5	five
seis	6	six
siete	7	seven
ocho	8	eight
nueve	9	nine
diez	10	ten
once	11	eleven
doce	12	twelve
trece	13	thirteen
catorce	14	fourteen
quince	15	fifteen
dieciséis	16	sixteen
diecisiete	17	seventeen
dieciocho	18	eighteen
diecinueve	19	nineteen
veinte	20	twenty
veintiuno(-un, -una)*	21	twenty-one
veintidós	22	twenty-two
treinta	30	thirty
treinta y uno(un, una)*	31	thirty-one
treinta y dos	32	thirty-two
cuarenta	40	forty
cincuenta	50	fifty
sesenta	60	sixty
setenta	70	seventy
ochenta	80	eighty
noventa	90	ninety
cien(ciento)**	100	a hundred, one hundred
ciento uno(un, una)*	101	a hundred and one
ciento dos	102	a hundred and two
ciento cincuenta y seis	156	a hundred and fifty-six
doscientos(-as)	200	two hundred
trescientos(-as)	300	three hundred
quinientos(-as)	500	five hundred
mil	1,000	a thousand
mil tres	1,003	a thousand and three
dos mil	2,000	two thousand
un millón	1,000,000	a million

*'uno' (+ 'veintiuno' etc) agrees in gender (but not number) with its noun: **treinta y una personas**; the masculine form is shortened to 'un' unless it stands alone: **veintiún caballos, veintiuno**.

'ciento' is used in compound numbers, except when it multiplies: **ciento diez, but **cien mil**. 'Cien' is used before nouns: **cien hombres, cien casas**.

Números

primero (primer, primera) 1°, 1er/1^a, 1^{era}
segundo(-a) 2°/2^a
tercero (tercer, tercera) 3°, 3er/3^a, 3^{era}
cuarto(-a) 4°/4^a
quinto(-a)
sexto(-a)
séptimo(-a)
octavo(-a)
noveno(-a); nono(-a)
décimo(-a)
undécimo(-a)
duodécimo(-a)
decimotercero(-a)
decimocuarto(-a)
decimoquinto(-a)
decimosexto(-a)
decimoséptimo(-a)
decimoctavo(-a)
decimonoveno(-a)
vigésimo(-a)
vigésimo(-a) primero(-a)
vigésimo(-a) segundo(-a)
trigésimo(-a)
trigésimo(-a) primero(-a)
trigésimo(-a) segundo(-a)
cuadragésimo(-a)
quincuagésimo(-a)
sexagésimo(-a)
septuagésimo(-a)
octogésimo(-a)
nonagésimo(-a)
centésimo(-a)
centésimo(-a) primero(-a)
milésimo(-a)

Numbers

first, 1st
second, 2nd
third, 3rd
fourth, 4th
fifth, 5th
sixth, 6th
seventh
eighth
ninth
tenth
eleventh
twelfth
thirteenth
fourteenth
fifteenth
sixteenth
seventeenth
eighteenth
nineteenth
twentieth
twenty-first
twenty-second
thirtieth
thirty-first
thirty-second
fortieth
fiftieth
sixtieth
seventieth
eightieth
ninetieth
hundredth
hundred-and-first
thousandth

La hora

¿qué hora es?
es la una
son las cuatro
medianoche, las doce de la noche
la una (de la madrugada)
la una y cinco
la una y diez
la una y cuarto, la una quince
la una y veinticinco
la una y media, la una treinta
las dos menos veinticinco,
   la una treinta y cinco
las dos menos veinte, la una cuarenta
las dos menos cuarto,
   la una cuarenta y cinco
las dos menos diez, la una cincuenta
mediodía, las doce (de la mañana)
   la dos (de la tarde)
two o'clock (in the afternoon)
la siete (de la tarde), seven o'clock
   (in the evening)

¿a qué hora?
a medianoche
a las siete
a la una
en veinte minutos
hace diez minutos

The time

what time is it?
it's one o'clock
it's four o'clock
midnight
one o'clock (in the morning), one (a.m.)
five past one
ten past one
a quarter past one, one fifteen
twenty-five past one, one twenty-five
half past one, one thirty
twenty-five to two, one thirty-five

twenty to two, one forty
a quarter to two, one forty-five

ten to two, one fifty
twelve o'clock, midday, noon

two (p.m.)
seven (p.m.)

at what time?
at midnight
at seven o'clock
at one o'clock
in twenty minutes
ten minutes ago

La fecha

hoy
mañana
pasado mañana
ayer
antes de ayer, anteayer
la víspera
el día siguiente
la mañana
la tarde
esta mañana
esta tarde
ayer por la mañana
ayer por la tarde

The date

today
tomorrow
the day after tomorrow
yesterday
the day before yesterday
the day before, the previous day
the next *or* following day
morning
evening
this morning
this evening, this afternoon
yesterday morning
yesterday evening

mañana por la mañana	tomorrow morning
mañana por la tarde	tomorrow evening, tomorrow afternoon
en la noche del sábado al domingo	during Saturday night, during the night of Saturday to Sunday
vendrá el sábado	he's coming on Saturday
los sábados	on Saturdays
todos los sábados	every Saturday
el sábado pasado	last Saturday
el sábado que viene, el próximo sábado	next Saturday
del sábado en ocho días	a week on Saturday
del sábado en quince días	a fortnight or two weeks on Saturday
de lunes a sábado	from Monday to Saturday
todos las días	every day
una vez a la semana	once a week
una vez al mes	once a month
dos veces a la semana	twice a week
hace una semana u ocho días	a week ago
hace quince días	a fortnight or two weeks ago
el año pasado	last year
dentro de dos días	in two days
dentro de ocho días o una semana	in a week
dentro de quince días	in a fortnight or two weeks
el mes que viene, el próximo mes	next month
el año que viene, el próximo año	next year
¿a qué o a cuántos estamos?	*what day is it?*
el 1/22 octubre de 2013	the 1st/22nd of October 2013, October 1st/22nd 2013
en 2013	in 2013
mil novecientos noventa y cinco	nineteen ninety-five
44 a. de J.C.	44 BC
14 d. de J.C.	14 AD
en el (siglo) XIX	in the nineteenth century
en los años treinta	in the thirties
érase una vez ...	once upon a time ...

Aa

A, a [a] NF (*letra*) A, a; **A de Antonio** A for Andrew (*Brit*) o Able (*US*)

(PALABRA CLAVE)

a [a] PREP (**a** + **el** = **al**) **1** (*dirección*) to; **fueron a Madrid/Grecia** they went to Madrid/Greece; **me voy a casa** I'm going home

2 (*distancia*): **está a 15 km de aquí** it's 15 km from here

3 (*posición*): **estar a la mesa** to be at table; **al lado de** next to, beside; **a la derecha/izquierda** on the right/left; *ver tb* **puerta**

4 (*tiempo*): **a las 10/a medianoche** at 10/ midnight; **¿a qué hora?** (at) what time?; **a la mañana siguiente** the following morning; **a los pocos días** after a few days; **estamos a 9 de julio** it's the 9th of July; **a los 24 años** at the age of 24; **ocho horas al día** eight hours a day; **al año/a la semana** (*Am*) a year/week later

5 (*manera*): **a la francesa** the French way; **a caballo** on horseback; **a oscuras** in the dark; **a rayas** striped; **le echaron a patadas** they kicked him out

6 (*medio, instrumento*): **a lápiz** in pencil; **a mano** by hand; **cocina a gas** gas stove

7 (*razón*): **a dos euros el kilo** at two euros a kilo; **a más de 50 km por hora** at more than 50 km per hour; **poco a poco** little by little

8 (*dativo*): **se lo di a él** I gave it to him; **se lo compré a él** I bought it from him

9 (*complemento directo*): **vi al policía** I saw the policeman

10 (*tras ciertos verbos*): **voy a verle** I'm going to see him; **empezó a trabajar** he started working o to work; **sabe a queso** it tastes of cheese

11 (+ *infin*): **al verle, le reconocí inmediatamente** when I saw him I recognized him at once; **el camino a recorrer** the distance we *etc* have to travel; **¡a callar!** keep quiet!; **¡a comer!** let's eat!

12: **a que: ¡a que llueve!** I bet it's going to rain!; **¿a qué viene eso?** what's the

meaning of this?; **¿a que sí va a venir?** he IS coming, isn't he?; **¿a que no lo haces?** — **¡a que sí!** bet you don't do it! — yes, I WILL!

A. ABR (*Escol*: = *aprobado*) pass

AA NFPL ABR = **Aerolíneas Argentinas**

AA EE ABR (= *Asuntos Exteriores*): **Min. de ~** ≈ FO (*Brit*)

ab. ABR (= *abril*) Apr.

abad, esa [a'βað, 'ðesa] NM/F abbot (abbess)

abadía [aβa'ðia] NF abbey

abajo [a'βaxo] ADV (*situación*) (down) below, underneath; (*en edificio*) downstairs; (*dirección*) down, downwards; **~ de** *prep* below, under; **el piso de ~** the downstairs flat; **la parte de ~** the lower part; **¡~ el gobierno!** down with the government!; **cuesta/río ~** downhill/downstream; **de arriba ~** from top to bottom; **el ~ firmante** the undersigned; **más ~** lower o further down

abalance *etc* [aβa'lanθe] VB *ver* **abalanzarse**

abalanzarse [aβalan'θarse] /**1f**/ VR: **~ sobre** o **contra** to throw o.s. at

abalear [aβale'ar] /**1a**/ VT (*Am fam*) to shoot

abalorios [aβa'lorjos] NMPL (*chucherías*) trinkets

abanderado, -a [aβande'raðo, a] NM/F (*portaestandarte*) standard bearer; (*de un movimiento*) champion, leader; (*Am*: *linier*) linesman, assistant referee

abandonado, -a [aβando'naðo, a] ADJ derelict; (*desatendido*) abandoned; (*desierto*) deserted; (*descuidado*) neglected

abandonar [aβando'nar] /**1a**/ VT to leave; (*persona*) to abandon, desert; (*cosa*) to abandon, leave behind; (*descuidar*) to neglect; (*renunciar a*) to give up; (*Inform*) to quit; **abandonarse** VR: **abandonarse a** to abandon o.s. to; **abandonarse al alcohol** to take to drink

abandono [aβan'dono] NM (*acto*) desertion, abandonment; (*estado*) abandon, neglect; (*renuncia*) withdrawal, retirement; **ganar por ~** to win by default

abanicar [aβani'kar] /**1g**/ vт to fan

abanico [aβa'niko] nm fan; (*Naut*) derrick; **en ~** fan-shaped

abanique *etc* [aβa'nike] vв *ver* **abanicar**

abaratar [aβara'tar] /**1a**/ vт to lower the price of ▶ vi, **abaratarse** vr to go o come down in price

abarcar [aβar'kar] /**1g**/ vт to include, embrace; (*contener*) to comprise; (*Am*) to monopolize; **quien mucho abarca poco aprieta** don't bite off more than you can chew

abarque *etc* [a'βarke] vв *ver* **abarcar**

abarrotado, -a [aβarro'taðo, a] adj packed; **~ de** packed o bursting with

abarrotar [aβarro'tar] /**1a**/ vт (*local, estadio, teatro*) to fill, pack

abarrote [aβa'rrote] nm packing; **abarrotes** nmpl (*Am*) groceries; **tienda de abarrotes** (*Am*) grocery store

abarrotería [aβarrote'ria] nf (*Am*) grocery store

abarrotero, -a [aβarro'tero, a] nm/f (*Am*) grocer

abastecedor, a [aβasteθe'ðor, a] adj supplying ▶ nm/f supplier

abastecer [aβaste'θer] /**2d**/ vт: **~ (de)** to supply (with)

abastecimiento [aβasteθi'mjento] nm supply

abastezca *etc* [aβas'teθka] vв *ver* **abastecer**

abasto [a'βasto] nm supply; (*abundancia*) abundance; **no dar ~ a algo** not to be able to cope with sth

abatible [aβa'tiβle] adj: **asiento ~** tip-up seat; (*Auto*) reclining seat

abatido, -a [aβa'tiðo, a] adj dejected, downcast; **estar muy ~** to be very depressed

abatimiento [aβati'mjento] nm (*depresión*) dejection, depression

abatir [aβa'tir] /**3a**/ vт (*muro*) to demolish; (*pájaro*) to shoot o bring down; (*fig*) to depress; **abatirse** vr to get depressed; **abatirse sobre** to swoop o pounce on

abdicación [aβðika'θjon] nf abdication

abdicar [aβði'kar] /**1g**/ vi to abdicate; **~ en algn** to abdicate in favour of sb

abdique *etc* [aβ'ðike] vв *ver* **abdicar**

abdomen [aβ'ðomen] nm abdomen

abdominal [aβðomi'nal] adj abdominal ▶ nm: **abdominales** abdominals, stomach muscles; (*Deporte: tb*: **ejercicios abdominales**) sit-ups

abecedario [aβeθe'ðarjo] nm alphabet

abedul [aβe'ðul] nm birch

abeja [a'βexa] nf bee; (*fig: hormiguita*) hard worker

abejorro [aβe'xorro] nm bumblebee

aberración [aβerra'θjon] nf aberration

aberrante [aβe'rrante] adj (*disparatado*) ridiculous

abertura [aβer'tura] nf = **apertura**

abertzale [aβer'tʃale] adj, nmf Basque nationalist

abeto [a'βeto] nm fir

abierto, -a [a'βjerto, a] pp de **abrir** ▶ adj open; (*fig: carácter*) frank

abigarrado, -a [aβiɣa'rraðo, a] adj multicoloured; (*fig*) motley

abismal [aβis'mal] adj (*fig*) vast, enormous

abismar [aβis'mar] /**1a**/ vт to humble, cast down; **abismarse** vr to sink; (*Am*) to be amazed; **abismarse en** (*fig*) to be plunged into

abismo [a'βismo] nm abyss; **de sus ideas a las mías hay un ~** our views are worlds apart

abjurar [aβxu'rar] /**1a**/ vт to abjure, forswear ▶ vi: **~ de** to abjure, forswear

ablandar [aβlan'dar] /**1a**/ vт to soften; (*conmover*) to touch; (*Culin*) to tenderize ▶ vi, **ablandarse** vr to get softer

abnegación [aβneɣa'θjon] nf self-denial

abnegado, -a [aβne'ɣaðo, a] adj self-sacrificing

abobado, -a [aβo'βaðo, a] adj silly

abobamiento [aβoβa'mjento] nm (*asombro*) bewilderment

abocado, -a [aβo'kaðo, a] adj: **verse ~ al desastre** to be heading for disaster

abochornar [aβotʃor'nar] /**1a**/ vт to embarrass; **abochornarse** vr to get flustered; (*Bot*) to wilt; **abochornarse de** to get embarrassed about

abofetear [aβofete'ar] /**1a**/ vт to slap (in the face)

abogacía [aβoɣa'θia] nf legal profession; (*ejercicio*) practice of the law

abogado, -a [aβo'ɣaðo, a] nm/f lawyer; (*notario*) solicitor; (*asesor*) counsel; (*en tribunal*) barrister, advocate, attorney (*US*); **~ defensor** defence lawyer (*Brit*), defense attorney (*US*); **~ del diablo** devil's advocate

abogar [aβo'ɣar] /**1h**/ vi: **~ por** to plead for; (*fig*) to advocate

abogue *etc* [a'βoɣe] vв *ver* **abogar**

abolengo [aβo'lengo] nm ancestry, lineage

abolición [aβoli'θjon] nf abolition

abolir [aβo'lir] vт to abolish; (*cancelar*) to cancel

abolladura [aβoʎa'ðura] nf dent

abollar [aβo'ʎar] /**1a**/ vт to dent

abombarse [aβom'barse] /**1a**/ (*Am*) vr to go bad

abominable [aβomi'naβle] adj abominable

abominación [aβomina'θjon] nf abomination

abonado, -a [aβo'naðo, a] adj (*deuda*) paid(-up) ▶ nm/f subscriber

abonar [aβo'nar] /**1a**/ vt to pay; (*deuda*) to settle; (*terreno*) to fertilize; (*idea*) to endorse; **abonarse** vr to subscribe; **~ dinero en una cuenta** to pay money into an account, credit money to an account

abono [a'βono] nm payment; fertilizer; subscription

abordable [aβor'ðaβle] adj (*persona*) approachable

abordar [aβor'ðar] /**1a**/ vt (*barco*) to board; (*asunto*) to broach; (*individuo*) to approach

aborigen [aβo'rixen] nmf aborigine

aborrecer [aβorre'θer] /**2d**/ vt to hate, loathe

aborrezca *etc* [aβo'rreθka] vb *ver* **aborrecer**

abortar [aβor'tar] /**1a**/ vi (*malparir*) to have a miscarriage; (*deliberadamente*) to have an abortion

aborto [a'βorto] nm miscarriage; abortion

abotagado, -a [aβota'ɣaðo, a] adj swollen

abotonar [aβoto'nar] /**1a**/ vt to button (up), do up

abovedado, -a [aβoβe'ðaðo, a] adj vaulted, domed

abr. abr (= *abril*) Apr.

abrace *etc* [a'βraθe] vb *ver* **abrazar**

abrasar [aβra'sar] /**1a**/ vt to burn (up); (*Agr*) to dry up, parch

abrazadera [aβraθa'ðera] nf bracket

abrazar [aβra'θar] /**1f**/ vt to embrace, hug; **abrazarse** vr to embrace, hug each other

abrazo [a'βraθo] nm embrace, hug; **un ~** (*en carta*) with best wishes

abrebotellas [aβreβo'teʎas] nm inv bottle opener

abrecartas [aβre'kartas] nm inv letter opener

abrelatas [aβre'latas] nm inv tin (*Brit*) o can (*US*) opener

abrevadero [aβreβa'ðero] nm watering place

abreviar [aβre'βjar] /**1b**/ vt to abbreviate; (*texto*) to abridge; (*plazo*) to reduce ▶ vi: **bueno, para ~** well, to cut a long story short

abreviatura [aβreβja'tura] nf abbreviation

abridor [aβri'ðor] nm (*de botellas*) bottle opener; (*de latas*) tin (*Brit*) o can (*US*) opener

abrigador, a [aβriɣa'ðor, a] adj (*Am*) warm

abrigar [aβri'ɣar] /**1h**/ vt (*proteger*) to shelter; (*suj: ropa*) to keep warm; (*fig*) to cherish; **abrigarse** vr (*con ropa*) to cover (o.s.) up; **abrigarse (de)** to take shelter (from), protect o.s. (from); **¡abrígate bien!** wrap up well!

abrigo [a'βriɣo] nm (*prenda*) coat, overcoat; (*lugar protegido*) shelter; **al ~ de** in the shelter of

abrigue *etc* [a'βriɣe] vb *ver* **abrigar**

abril [a'βril] nm April; *ver tb* **julio**

abrillantador [aβriʎanta'ðor] nm polish

abrillantar [aβriʎan'tar] /**1a**/ vt (*pulir*) to polish; (*fig*) to enhance

abrir [a'βrir] /**3a**/ vt to open (up); (*camino etc*) to open up; (*apetito*) to whet; (*lista*) to head

▶ vi to open; **abrirse** vr to open (up); (*extenderse*) to open out; (*cielo*) to clear; **~ un negocio** to start up a business; **en un ~ y cerrar de ojos** in the twinkling of an eye; **abrirse paso** to find o force a way through

abrochar [aβro'tʃar] /**1a**/ vt (*con botones*) to button (up); (*zapato, con broche*) to do up; **abrocharse** vr: **abrocharse los zapatos** to tie one's shoelaces

abrogación [aβroɣa'θjon] nf repeal

abrogar [aβro'ɣar] /**1h**/ vt to repeal

abrumador, a [aβruma'ðor, a] adj (*mayoría*) overwhelming

abrumar [aβru'mar] /**1a**/ vt to overwhelm; (*sobrecargar*) to weigh down

abrupto, -a [a'βrupto, a] adj abrupt; (*empinado*) steep

absceso [aβs'θeso] nm abscess

absentismo [aβsen'tismo] nm (*de obreros*) absenteeism

absolución [aβsolu'θjon] nf (*Rel*) absolution; (*Jur*) acquittal

absoluto, -a [aβso'luto, a] adj absolute; (*total*) utter, complete; **en ~** *adv* not at all

absolver [aβsol'βer] /**2h**/ vt to absolve; (*Jur*) to pardon; (: *acusado*) to acquit

absorbente [aβsor'βente] adj absorbent; (*interesante*) absorbing, interesting; (*exigente*) demanding

absorber [aβsor'βer] /**2a**/ vt to absorb; (*embeber*) to soak up; **absorberse** vr to become absorbed

absorción [aβsor'θjon] nf absorption; (*Com*) takeover

absorto, -a [aβ'sorto, a] pp *de* **absorber** ▶ adj absorbed, engrossed

abstemio, -a [aβs'temjo, a] adj teetotal

abstención [aβsten'θjon] nf abstention

abstendré *etc* [aβsten'dre] vb *ver* **abstenerse**

abstenerse [aβste'nerse] /**2k**/ vr: **~ (de)** to abstain o refrain (from)

abstenga *etc* [aβs'tenga] vb *ver* **abstenerse**

abstinencia [aβsti'nenθja] nf abstinence; (*ayuno*) fasting

abstracción [aβstrak'θjon] nf abstraction

abstracto, -a [aβ'strakto, a] adj abstract; **en ~** in the abstract

abstraer [aβstra'er] /**2o**/ vt to abstract; **abstraerse** vr to be o become absorbed

abstraído, -a [aβstra'iðo, a] adj absent-minded

abstraiga *etc* [aβs'traiɣa], **abstraje** *etc* [aβs'traxe], **abstrayendo** *etc* [aβstra'jendo] vb *ver* **abstraer**

abstuve *etc* [aβs'tuβe] vb *ver* **abstenerse**

absuelto [aβ'swelto] pp *de* **absolver**

absurdo, -a [aβ'surðo, a] adj absurd ▶ nm absurdity; **lo ~ es que ...** the ridiculous thing is that ...

abuchear [aβutʃe'ar] /**1a**/ vt to boo

abucheo [aβu'tʃeo] NM booing; **ganarse un ~** (de *Teat*) to be booed

abuela [a'βwela] NF grandmother; **¡cuéntaselo a tu ~!** (*fam!*) do you think I was born yesterday? (*fam*); **no tener/necesitar ~** (*fam*) to be full of o.s./blow one's own trumpet

abuelita [aβwe'lita] NF granny

abuelo [a'βwelo] NM grandfather; (*antepasado*) ancestor; **abuelos** NMPL grandparents

abulense [aβu'lense] ADJ of Ávila ▶ NMF native o inhabitant of Ávila

abulia [a'βulja] NF lethargy

abúlico, -a [a'βuliko, a] ADJ lethargic

abultado, -a [aβul'taðo, a] ADJ bulky

abultar [aβul'tar] /**1a**/ vt to enlarge; (*aumentar*) to increase; (*fig*) to exaggerate ▶ vi to be bulky

abundancia [aβun'danθja] NF: **una ~ de** plenty of; **en ~** in abundance

abundante [aβun'dante] ADJ abundant, plentiful

abundar [aβun'dar] /**1a**/ vi to abound, be plentiful; **~ en una opinión** to share an opinion

aburguesarse [aβurɣe'sarse] /**1a**/ vr to become middle-class

aburrido, -a [aβu'rriðo, a] ADJ (*hastiado*) bored; (*que aburre*) boring

aburrimiento [aβurri'mjento] NM boredom, tedium

aburrir [aβu'rrir] /**3a**/ vt to bore; **aburrirse** vr to be bored, get bored; **aburrirse como una almeja** *u* **ostra** to be bored stiff

abusado, -a [aβu'saðo, a] ADJ (*Am fam: astuto*) sharp, cunning ▶ EXCL: **¡~!** (*inv*) look out!, careful!

abusar [aβu'sar] /**1a**/ vi to go too far; **~ de** to abuse

abusivo, -a [aβu'siβo, a] ADJ (*precio*) exorbitant

abuso [a'βuso] NM abuse; **~ de confianza** betrayal of trust

abyecto, -a [aβ'jekto, a] ADJ wretched, abject

a. C. ABR (= *antes de Cristo*) B.C.

a/c ABR (= *al cuidado de*) c/o; (= *a cuenta*) on account

acá [a'ka] ADV (*lugar*) here; **pasearse de ~ para allá** to walk up and down; **¡vente para ~!** come over here!; **¿de cuándo ~?** since when?

acabado, -a [aka'βaðo, a] ADJ finished, complete; (*perfecto*) perfect; (*agotado*) worn out; (*fig*) masterly ▶ NM finish

acabar [aka'βar] /**1a**/ vt (*llevar a su fin*) to finish, complete; (*consumir*) to use up; (*rematar*) to finish off ▶ vi to finish, end; (*morir*) to die; **acabarse** vr to finish, stop; (*terminarse*) to be over; (*agotarse*) to run out; **~ con** to put an end to; **~ mal** to come to a sticky end; **esto acabará conmigo** this will be the end of me; **~ de llegar** to have just arrived; **acababa de hacerlo** I had just done it; **~ haciendo** o **por hacer algo** to end up (by) doing sth; **¡se acabó!** (*¡basta!*) that's enough!; (*se terminó*) it's all over!; **se me acabó el tabaco** I ran out of cigarettes

acabose [aka'βose] NM: **esto es el ~** this is the last straw

acacia [a'kaθja] NF acacia

academia [aka'ðemja] NF academy; (*Escol*) private school; **~ de idiomas** language school; ver tb **colegio**

académico, -a [aka'ðemiko, a] ADJ academic

acaecer [akae'θer] /**2d**/ vi to happen, occur

acaezca etc [aka'eθka] vB ver **acaecer**

acallar [aka'ʎar] /**1a**/ vt (*silenciar*) to silence; (*calmar*) to pacify

acalorado, -a [akalo'raðo, a] ADJ (*discusión*) heated

acalorarse [akalo'rarse] /**1a**/ vr (*fig*) to get heated

acampada [akam'paða] NF: **ir de ~** to go camping

acampanado, -a [akampa'naðo, a] ADJ flared

acampar [akam'par] /**1a**/ vi to camp

acanalado, -a [akana'laðo, a] ADJ (*hierro*) corrugated

acanalar [akana'lar] /**1a**/ vt to groove; (*ondular*) to corrugate

acantilado [akanti'laðo] NM cliff

acaparador, a [akapara'ðor, a] NM/F monopolizer

acaparar [akapa'rar] /**1a**/ vt to monopolize; (*acumular*) to hoard

acápite [a'kapite] NM (*Am*) paragraph; **punto ~** full stop, new paragraph

acaramelado, -a [akarame'laðo, a] ADJ (*Culin*) toffee-coated; (*fig*) sugary

acariciar [akari'θjar] /**1b**/ vt to caress; (*esperanza*) to cherish

acarrear [akarre'ar] /**1a**/ vt to transport; (*fig*) to cause, result in; **le acarreó muchos disgustos** it brought him lots of problems

acaso [a'kaso] ADV perhaps, maybe ▶ NM chance; **¿~ es mi culpa?** (*Am fam*) what makes you think it's my fault?; **(por) si ~** (just) in case

acatamiento [akata'mjento] NM respect; (*de la ley*) observance

acatar [aka'tar] /**1a**/ vt to respect; (*ley*) to obey, observe

acatarrarse [akata'rrarse] /**1a**/ vr to catch a cold

acaudalado, -a [akauða'laðo, a] ADJ well-off

acaudillar [akauði'ʎar] /**1a**/ vt to lead, command

acceder [akθe'ðer] /**2a**/ vi to accede, agree; **~ a** (petición etc) to agree to; (tener acceso a) to have access to; (Inform) to access

accesible [akθe'siβle] ADJ accessible; **~ a** open to

accésit [ak'θesit] (pl **accésits** [ak'θesits]) NM consolation prize

acceso [ak'θeso] NM access, entry; (camino) access road; (Med) attack, fit; (de cólera) fit; (Pol) accession; (Inform) access; **~ aleatorio/ directo/secuencial** o **en serie** (Inform) random/direct/sequential o serial access; **de ~ múltiple** multi-access

accesorio, -a [akθe'sorjo, a] ADJ accessory ▸ NM accessory; **accesorios** NMPL (Auto) accessories, extras; (Teat) props

accidentado, -a [akθiðen'taðo, a] ADJ uneven; (montañoso) hilly; (azaroso) eventful ▸ NM/F accident victim

accidental [akθiðen'tal] ADJ accidental; (empleo) temporary

accidentarse [akθiðen'tarse] /**1a**/ VR to have an accident

accidente [akθi'ðente] NM accident; **por ~** by chance; **accidentes** NMPL (de terreno) unevenness sg, roughness sg; **~ laboral** o **de trabajo/de tráfico** industrial/road o traffic accident

acción [ak'θjon] NF action; (acto) action, act; (Teat) plot; (Com) share; (Jur) action, lawsuit; **capital en acciones** share capital; **~ liberada/ordinaria/preferente** fully-paid/ordinary/preference share

accionamiento [akθjona'mjento] NM (de máquina) operation

accionar [akθjo'nar] /**1a**/ VT to work, operate; (ejecutar) to activate

accionista [akθjo'nista] NMF shareholder

acebo [a'θeβo] NM holly; (árbol) holly tree

acechanza [aθe'tʃanθa] NF = **acecho**

acechar [aθe'tʃar] /**1a**/ VT to spy on; (aguardar) to lie in wait for

acecho [a'θetʃo] NM: **estar al ~ (de)** to lie in wait (for)

acedera [aθe'ðera] NF sorrel

aceitar [aθei'tar] /**1a**/ VT to oil, lubricate

aceite [a'θeite] NM oil; **~ de girasol/oliva** sunflower/olive oil; **~ de hígado de bacalao** cod-liver oil

aceitera [aθei'tera] NF oilcan

aceitoso, -a [aθei'toso, a] ADJ oily

aceituna [aθei'tuna] NF olive; **~ rellena** stuffed olive

aceitunado, -a [aθeitu'naðo, a] ADJ olive cpd; **de tez aceitunada** olive-skinned

acelerador [aθelera'ðor] NM accelerator

acelerar [aθele'rar] /**1a**/ VT to accelerate; **acelerarse** VR to hurry

acelga [a'θelɣa] NF chard, beet

acendrado, -a [aθen'draðo, a] ADJ: **de ~ carácter español** typically Spanish

acendrar [aθen'drar] /**1a**/ VT to purify

acento [a'θento] NM accent; (acentuación) stress; **~ cerrado** strong o thick accent

acentuar [aθen'twar] /**1e**/ VT to accent; to stress; (fig) to accentuate

acepción [aθep'θjon] NF meaning

aceptable [aθep'taβle] ADJ acceptable

aceptación [aθepta'θjon] NF acceptance; (aprobación) approval

aceptar [aθep'tar] /**1a**/ VT to accept; (aprobar) to approve; **~ hacer algo** to agree to do sth

acequia [a'θekja] NF irrigation ditch

acera [a'θera] NF pavement (Brit), sidewalk (US)

acerado, -a [aθe'raðo, a] ADJ steel; (afilado) sharp; (fig: duro) steely; (: mordaz) biting

acerbo, -a [a'θerβo, a] ADJ bitter; (fig) harsh

acerca [a'θerka]: **~ de** prep about, concerning

acercar [aθer'kar] /**1g**/ VT to bring o move nearer; **acercarse** VR to approach, come near

acerico [aθe'riko] NM pincushion

acero [a'θero] NM steel; **~ inoxidable** stainless steel

acerque etc [a'θerke] VB ver **acercar**

acérrimo, -a [a'θerrimo, a] ADJ (partidario) staunch; (enemigo) bitter

acertado, -a [aθer'taðo, a] ADJ correct; (apropiado) apt; (sensato) sensible

acertar [aθer'tar] /**1j**/ VT (blanco) to hit; (solución) to get right; (adivinar) to guess ▸ VI to get it right, be right; **~ a** to manage to; **~ con** to happen o hit on

acertijo [aθer'tixo] NM riddle, puzzle

acervo [a'θerβo] NM heap; **~ común** undivided estate

achacar [atʃa'kar] /**1g**/ VT to attribute

achacoso, -a [atʃa'koso, a] ADJ sickly

achantar [atʃan'tar] /**1a**/ VT (fam) to scare, frighten; **achantarse** VR to back down

achaque etc [a'tʃake] VB ver **achacar** ▸ NM ailment

achatar [atʃa'tar] /**1a**/ VT to flatten

achicar [atʃi'kar] /**1g**/ VT to reduce; (humillar) to humiliate; (Naut) to bale out; **achicarse** VR (ropa) to shrink; (fig) to humble o.s.

achicharrar [atʃitʃa'rrar] /**1a**/ VT to scorch, burn

achichincle [atʃi'tʃinkle] NMF (Am fam) minion

achicoria [atʃi'korja] NF chicory

achinado, -a [atʃi'naðo, a] ADJ (ojos) slanting; (Am) half-caste

achique etc [a'tʃike] VB ver **achicar**

acholado, -a [atʃo'laðo, a] ADJ (Am) half-caste

achuchar [atʃu'tʃar] /**1a**/ VT to crush

achuchón [atʃu'tʃon] NM shove; **tener un ~** (Med) to be poorly

5

achuras [a'tʃuras] NF (*Am Culin*) offal

aciago, -a [a'θjaɣo, a] ADJ ill-fated, fateful

acicalar [aθika'lar] /**1a**/ VT to polish; (*adornar*) to bedeck; **acicalarse** VR to get dressed up

acicate [aθi'kate] NM spur; (*fig*) incentive

acidez [aθi'ðeθ] NF acidity

ácido, -a ['aθiðo, a] ADJ sour, acid ▶ NM acid; (*fam: droga*) LSD

aciertoetc [a'θjerto] VB *ver* **acertar** ▶ NM success; (*buen paso*) wise move; (*solución*) solution; (*habilidad*) skill, ability; (*al adivinar*) good guess; **fue un ~ suyo** it was a sensible choice on his part

acitronar [aθitro'nar] /**1a**/ (*Am*) VT (*fam*) to brown

aclamación [aklama'θjon] NF acclamation; (*aplausos*) applause

aclamar [akla'mar] /**1a**/ VT to acclaim; (*aplaudir*) to applaud

aclaración [aklara'θjon] NF clarification, explanation

aclarar [akla'rar] /**1a**/ VT to clarify, explain; (*ropa*) to rinse ▶ VI to clear up; **aclararse** VR (*suj: persona: explicarse*) to understand; (*fig: asunto*) to become clear; **aclararse la garganta** to clear one's throat

aclaratorio, -a [aklara'torjo, a] ADJ explanatory

aclimatación [aklimata'θjon] NF acclimatization

aclimatar [aklima'tar] /**1a**/ VT to acclimatize; **aclimatarse** VR to become o get acclimatized; **aclimatarse a algo** to get used to sth

acné [ak'ne] NM acne

ACNUR NM ABR (= *Alto Comisionado de las Naciones Unidas para los Refugiados*) UNHCR nf

acobardar [akoβar'ðar] /**1a**/ VT to daunt, intimidate; **acobardarse** VR (*atemorizarse*) to be intimidated; (*echarse atrás*): **acobardarse (ante)** to shrink back (from)

acodarse [ako'ðarse] /**1a**/ VR: **~ en** to lean on

acogedor, a [akoxe'ðor, a] ADJ welcoming; (*hospitalario*) hospitable

acoger [ako'xer] /**2c**/ VT to welcome; (*abrigar*) to shelter; **acogerse** VR to take refuge; **acogerse a** (*pretexto*) to take refuge in; (*ley*) to resort to

acogida [ako'xiða] NF reception; refuge

acojaetc [a'koxa] VB *ver* **acoger**

acojonante [akoxo'nante] ADJ (*Esp fam*) tremendous

acolchar [akol'tʃar] /**1a**/ VT to pad; (*fig*) to cushion

acólito [a'kolito] NM (*Rel*) acolyte; (*fig*) minion

acomedido, -a [akome'ðiðo, a] (*Am*) ADJ helpful, obliging

acometer [akome'ter] /**2a**/ VT to attack; (*emprender*) to undertake

acometida [akome'tiða] NF attack, assault

acomodado, -a [akomo'ðaðo, a] ADJ (*persona*) well-to-do

acomodador, a [akomoða'ðor, a] NM/F usher(ette)

acomodar [akomo'ðar] /**1a**/ VT to adjust; (*alojar*) to accommodate; **acomodarse** VR to conform; (*instalarse*) to install o.s.; (*adaptarse*) to adapt o.s.; **acomodarse (a)** to adapt (to); **¡acomódese a su gusto!** make yourself comfortable!

acomodaticio, -a [akomoða'tiθjo, a] ADJ (*complaciente*) accommodating, obliging; (*manejable*) pliable

acompañamiento [akompaɲa'mjento] NM (*Mus*) accompaniment

acompañante, -a [akompa'ɲante, a] NM/F companion

acompañar [akompa'ɲar] /**1a**/ VT to accompany, go with; (*documentos*) to enclose; **¿quieres que te acompañe?** do you want me to come with you?; **~ a algn a la puerta** to see sb to the door o out; **le acompaño en el sentimiento** please accept my condolences

acompasar [akompa'sar] /**1a**/ VT (*Mus*) to mark the rhythm of

acomplejado, -a [akomple'xaðo, a] ADJ neurotic

acomplejar [akomple'xar] /**1a**/ VT to give a complex to; **acomplejarse** VR: **acomplejarse (con)** to get a complex (about)

acondicionado, -a [akondiθjo'naðo, a] ADJ (*Tec*) in good condition

acondicionador [akondiθjona'ðor] NM conditioner

acondicionar [akondiθjo'nar] /**1a**/ VT to get ready, prepare; (*pelo*) to condition

acongojar [akongo'xar] /**1a**/ VT to distress, grieve

aconsejable [akonse'xaβle] ADJ advisable

aconsejar [akonse'xar] /**1a**/ VT to advise, counsel; **~ a algn hacer** o **que haga algo** to advise sb to do sth; **aconsejarse** VR: **aconsejarse con** o **de** to consult

acontecer [akonte'θer] /**2d**/ VI to happen, occur

acontecimiento [akonteθi'mjento] NM event

acontezcaetc [akon'teθka] VB *ver* **acontecer**

acopiar [ako'pjar] /**1b**/ VT (*recoger*) to gather; (*Com*) to buy up

acopio [a'kopjo] NM store, stock

acoplador [akopla'ðor] NM: **~ acústico** (*Inform*) acoustic coupler

acoplamiento [akopla'mjento] NM coupling, joint

acoplar [ako'plar] /**1a**/ VT to fit; (*Elec*) to connect; (*vagones*) to couple

acoquinar [akoki'nar] /**1a**/ VT to scare; **acoquinarse** VR to get scared

acorazado, -a [akoraˈθaðo, a] ADJ armour-plated, armoured ▶ NM battleship

acordar [akorˈðar] /1l/ VT (*resolver*) to agree, resolve; (*recordar*) to remind; **acordarse** VR to agree; ~ **hacer algo** to agree to do sth; **acordarse (de algo)** to remember (sth)

acorde [aˈkorðe] ADJ (*Mus*) harmonious ▶ NM chord; ~ **con** (*medidas etc*) in keeping with

acordeón [akorðeˈon] NM accordion

acordonado, -a [akorðoˈnaðo, a] ADJ (*calle*) cordoned-off

acorralar [akorraˈlar] /1a/ VT to round up, corral; (*fig*) to intimidate

acortar [akorˈtar] /1a/ VT to shorten; (*duración*) to cut short; (*cantidad*) to reduce; **acortarse** VR to become shorter

acosar [akoˈsar] /1a/ VT to pursue relentlessly; (*fig*) to hound, pester; ~ **a algn a preguntas** to pester sb with questions

acoso [aˈkoso] NM relentless pursuit; (*fig*) harassment; ~ **escolar** bullying; ~ **sexual** sexual harassment

acostar [akosˈtar] /1l/ VT (*en cama*) to put to bed; (*en suelo*) to lay down; (*barco*) to bring alongside; **acostarse** VR to go to bed; to lie down; **acostarse con algn** to sleep with sb

acostumbrado, -a [akostumˈbraðo, a] ADJ (*habitual*) usual; **estar ~ a (hacer) algo** to be used to (doing) sth

acostumbrar [akostumˈbrar] /1a/ VT: ~ **a algn a algo** to get sb used to sth ▶ VI: ~ **(a hacer algo)** to be in the habit (of doing sth); **acostumbrarse** VR: **acostumbrarse a** to get used to

acotación [akotaˈθjon] NF (*apunte*) marginal note; (*Geo*) elevation mark; (*de límite*) boundary mark; (*Teat*) stage direction

acotamiento [akotaˈmjento] NM (*AM*) hard shoulder (*BRIT*), berm (*US*)

acotar [akoˈtar] /1a/ VT (*terreno*) to mark out; (*fig*) to limit; (*caza*) to protect

acotejar [akoteˈxar] /1a/ VT (*AM*) to put in order, arrange

ácrata [ˈakrata] ADJ, NMF anarchist

acre [ˈakre] ADJ (*sabor*) sharp, bitter; (*olor*) acrid; (*fig*) biting ▶ NM acre

acrecentar [akreθenˈtar] /1j/ VT to increase, augment

acreciente *etc* [akreˈθjente] VB *ver* **acrecentar**

acreditado, -a [akreðiˈtaðo, a] ADJ (*Pol*) accredited; (*Com*): **una casa acreditada** a reputable firm

acreditar [akreðiˈtar] /1a/ VT (*garantizar*) to vouch for, guarantee; (*autorizar*) to authorize; (*dar prueba de*) to prove; (*Com: abonar*) to credit; (*embajador*) to accredit; **acreditarse** VR to become famous; (*demostrar valía*) to prove one's worth; **acreditarse de** to get a reputation for

acreedor, a [akreeˈðor, a] ADJ: ~ **a** worthy of ▶ NM/F creditor; ~ **común/diferido/con garantía** (*Com*) unsecured/deferred/secured creditor

acribillar [akriβiˈʎar] /1a/ VT: ~ **a balazos** to riddle with bullets

acrimonia [akriˈmonja], **acritud** [akriˈtuð] NF acrimony

acrobacia [akroˈβaθja] NF acrobatics; ~ **aérea** aerobatics

acróbata [aˈkroβata] NMF acrobat

acta [ˈakta] NF certificate; (*de comisión*) minutes *pl*, record; ~ **de nacimiento/matrimonio** birth/marriage certificate; ~ **notarial** affidavit; **levantar ~** (*Jur*) to make a formal statement *o* deposition

actitud [aktiˈtuð] NF attitude; (*postura*) posture; **adoptar una ~ firme** to take a firm stand

activar [aktiˈβar] /1a/ VT to activate; (*acelerar*) to speed up

actividad [aktiβiˈðað] NF activity; **estar en plena ~** to be in full swing

activo, -a [akˈtiβo, a] ADJ active; (*vivo*) lively ▶ NM (*Com*) assets *pl*; ~ **y pasivo** assets and liabilities; ~ **circulante/fijo/inmaterial/invisible** (*Com*) current/fixed/intangible/invisible assets; ~ **realizable** liquid assets; **activos congelados** *o* **bloqueados** frozen assets; ~ **tóxico** toxic asset; **estar en ~** (*Mil*) to be on active service

acto [ˈakto] NM act, action; (*ceremonia*) ceremony; (*Teat*) act; **en el ~** immediately; **hacer ~ de presencia** (*asistir*) to attend (formally)

actor [akˈtor] NM actor; (*Jur*) plaintiff ▶ ADJ: **parte actora** prosecution

actora [akˈtora] ADJ: **parte ~** prosecution; (*demandante*) plaintiff

actriz [akˈtriθ] NF actress

actuación [aktwaˈθjon] NF action; (*comportamiento*) conduct, behaviour; (*Jur*) proceedings *pl*; (*desempeño*) performance

actual [akˈtwal] ADJ present(-day), current; **el 6 del ~** the 6th of this month

actualice *etc* [aktwaˈliθe] VB *ver* **actualizar**

actualidad [aktwaliˈðað] NF present; **actualidades** NFPL (*noticias*) news *sg*; **ser de gran ~** to be current; **en la ~** at present; (*hoy día*) nowadays, at present

actualización [aktwaliθaˈθjon] NF updating, modernization

actualizar [aktwaliˈθar] /1f/ VT to update, modernize

actualmente [aktwalˈmente] ADV at present; (*hoy día*) nowadays

actuar [akˈtwar] /1e/ VI (*obrar*) to work, operate; (*actor*) to act, perform ▶ VT to work, operate; ~ **de** to act as

7

actuario, -a [ak'twarjo, a] NM/F clerk; (*Com*) actuary

acuarela [akwa'rela] NF watercolour

acuario [a'kwarjo] NM aquarium; **A~** (*Astro*) Aquarius

acuartelar [akwarte'lar] /**1a**/ VT (*Mil*: *alojar*) to quarter

acuático, -a [a'kwatiko, a] ADJ aquatic

acuchillar [akutʃi'ʎar] /**1a**/ VT (*Tec*) to plane (down), smooth

acuciar [aku'θjar] /**1b**/ VT to urge on

acuclillarse [akukli'ʎarse] /**1a**/ VR to crouch down

ACUDE [a'kuðe] NF ABR = **Asociación de Consumidores y Usuarios de España**

acudir [aku'ðir] /**3a**/ VI to attend, turn up; (*ir*) to go; **~ a** to turn to; **~ en ayuda de** to go to the aid of; **~ a una cita** to keep an appointment; **~ a una llamada** to answer a call; **no tener a quién ~** to have nobody to turn to

acuerdo [a'kwerðo] VB *ver* **acordar** ▶ NM agreement; (*Pol*) resolution; **~ de pago respectivo** (*Com*) knock-for-knock agreement; **A~ general sobre aranceles aduaneros y comercio** (*Com*) General Agreement on Tariffs and Trade; **tomar un ~** to pass a resolution; **¡de ~!** agreed!; **de ~ con** (*persona*) in agreement with; (*acción*, *documento*) in accordance with; **de común** by common consent; **estar de ~** (*persona*) to agree; **llegar a un ~** to come to an understanding

acueste *etc* [a'kweste] VB *ver* **acostar**

acullá [aku'ʎa] ADV over there

acumular [akumu'lar] /**1a**/ VT to accumulate, collect

acunar [aku'nar] /**1a**/ VT to rock (to sleep)

acuñar [aku'ɲar] /**1a**/ VT (*moneda*) to mint; (*frase*) to coin

acuoso, -a [a'kwoso, a] ADJ watery

acupuntura [akupun'tura] NF acupuncture

acurrucarse [akurru'karse] /**1g**/ VR to crouch; (*ovillarse*) to curl up

acurruque *etc* [aku'rruke] VB *ver* **acurrucarse**

acusación [akusa'θjon] NF accusation

acusado, -a [aku'saðo, a] ADJ (*Jur*) accused; (*marcado*) marked; (*acento*) strong

acusar [aku'sar] /**1a**/ VT to accuse; (*revelar*) to reveal; (*denunciar*) to denounce; (*emoción*) to show; **acusarse** VR: **acusarse (de)** to confess (to); **~ recibo** to acknowledge receipt; **su rostro acusó extrañeza** his face registered surprise

acuse [a'kuse] NM: **~ de recibo** acknowledgement of receipt

acústico, -a [a'kustiko, a] ADJ acoustic ▶ NF (*de una sala etc*) acoustics *pl*; (*ciencia*) acoustics *sg*

ADA ['aða] NF ABR (*Esp*: = *Ayuda del Automovilista*) ≈ AA, RAC (*Brit*), AAA (*US*)

adagio [a'ðaxjo] NM adage; (*Mus*) adagio

adalid [aða'lið] NM leader, champion

adaptación [aðapta'θjon] NF adaptation

adaptador [aðapta'ðor] NM (*Elec*) adapter; **~ universal** universal adapter

adaptar [aðap'tar] /**1a**/ VT to adapt; (*acomodar*) to fit; (*convertir*): **~ (para)** to convert (to)

adecentar [aðeθen'tar] /**1a**/ VT to tidy up

adecuado, -a [aðe'kwaðo, a] ADJ (*apto*) suitable; (*oportuno*) appropriate; **el hombre ~ para el puesto** the right man for the job

adecuar [aðe'kwar] /**1d**/ VT (*adaptar*) to adapt; (*hacer apto*) to make suitable

adefesio [aðe'fesjo] NM (*fam*): **estaba hecha un ~** she looked a sight

a. de J.C. ABR (= *antes de Jesucristo*) B.C.

adelantado, -a [aðelan'taðo, a] ADJ advanced; (*reloj*) fast; **pagar por ~** to pay in advance

adelantamiento [aðelanta'mjento] NM advance, advancement; (*Auto*) overtaking

adelantar [aðelan'tar] /**1a**/ VT to move forward; (*avanzar*) to advance; (*acelerar*) to speed up; (*Auto*) to overtake ▶ VI (*ir delante*) to go ahead; (*progresar*) to improve; **adelantarse** VR (*tomar la delantera*: *corredor*) to move forward; **adelantarse a** to get ahead of sb; **adelantarse a los deseos de algn** to anticipate sb's wishes

adelante [aðe'lante] ADV forward(s), onward(s), ahead ▶ EXCL come in!; **de hoy en ~** from now on; **más ~** later on; (*más allá*) further on

adelanto [aðe'lanto] NM advance; (*mejora*) improvement; (*progreso*) progress; (*dinero*) advance; **los adelantos de la ciencia** the advances of science

adelgace *etc* [aðel'ɣaθe] VB *ver* **adelgazar**

adelgazar [aðelɣa'θar] /**1f**/ VT to thin (down); (*afilar*) to taper ▶ VI to get thin; (*con régimen*) to slim down, lose weight

ademán [aðe'man] NM gesture; **ademanes** NMPL manners; **en ~ de** as if to

además [aðe'mas] ADV besides; (*por otra parte*) moreover; (*también*) also; **~ de** besides, in addition to

ADENA [a'ðena] NF ABR (*Esp*: = *Asociación para la Defensa de la Naturaleza*) *organization for nature conservation*

adentrarse [aðen'trarse] /**1a**/ VR: **~ en** to go into, get inside; (*penetrar*) to penetrate (into)

adentro [a'ðentro] ADV inside, in ▶ NM: **dijo para sus adentros** he said to himself; **mar ~** out at sea; **tierra ~** inland

adepto, -a [a'ðepto, a] NM/F supporter

aderece *etc* [aðe'reθe] VB *ver* **aderezar**

aderezar [aðere'θar] /**1f**/ VT (*ensalada*) to dress; (*comida*) to season

aderezo [aðe'reθo] NM dressing; seasoning

adeudar [aðeu'ðar] /**1a**/ VT to owe; **adeudarse** VR to run into debt; **~ una suma en una cuenta** to debit an account with a sum

adherirse [aðe'rirse] /**3i**/ VR: **~ a** to adhere to; (*partido*) to join; (*fig*) to follow

adhesión [aðe'sjon] NF adhesion; (*fig*) adherence

adhesivo, -a [aðe'siβo, a] ADJ adhesive ▸ NM sticker

adhiera *etc* [a'ðjera], **adhiriendo** *etc* [aði'rjendo] VB *ver* **adherirse**

adicción [aðik'θjon] NF addiction

adición [aði'θjon] NF addition

adicional [aðiθjo'nal] ADJ additional; (*Inform*) add-on

adicionar [aðiθjo'nar] /**1a**/ VT to add

adicto, -a [a'ðikto, a] ADJ: **~ a** (*droga etc*) addicted to; (*dedicado*) devoted to ▸ NM/F supporter, follower; (*toxicómano etc*) addict

adiestrar [aðjes'trar] /**1a**/ VT to train, teach; (*conducir*) to guide, lead; **adiestrarse** VR to practise; (*aprender*) to train o.s.

adinerado, -a [aðine'raðo, a] ADJ wealthy

adiós [a'ðjos] EXCL (*para despedirse*) goodbye!, cheerio!; (*al pasar*) hello!

aditivo [aði'tiβo] NM additive

adivinanza [aðiβi'nanθa] NF riddle

adivinar [aðiβi'nar] /**1a**/ VT (*profetizar*) to prophesy; (*conjeturar*) to guess

adivino, -a [aði'βino, a] NM/F fortune-teller

adj. ABR (= *adjunto*) encl; (= *adjetivo*) adj

adjetivo [aðxe'tiβo] NM adjective

adjudicación [aðxuðika'θjon] NF award; (*Com*) adjudication

adjudicar [aðxuði'kar] /**1g**/ VT to award; **adjudicarse** VR: **adjudicarse algo** to appropriate sth

adjudique *etc* [aðxu'ðike] VB *ver* **adjudicar**

adjuntar [aðxun'tar] /**1a**/ VT to attach, enclose

adjunto, -a [að'xunto, a] ADJ attached, enclosed ▸ NM/F assistant

adminículo [aðmi'nikulo] NM gadget

administración [aðministra'θjon] NF administration; (*dirección*) management; **~ pública** civil service; **A~ de Correos** General Post Office

administrador, a [aðministra'ðor, a] NM/F administrator; manager(ess)

administrar [aðminis'trar] /**1a**/ VT to administer

administrativo, -a [aðministra'tiβo, a] ADJ administrative

admirable [aðmi'raβle] ADJ admirable

admiración [aðmira'θjon] NF admiration; (*asombro*) wonder; (*Ling*) exclamation mark

admirar [aðmi'rar] /**1a**/ VT to admire; (*extrañar*) to surprise; **admirarse** VR to be surprised; **se admiró de saberlo** he was amazed to hear it; **no es de ~ que** ... it's not surprising that ...

admisible [aðmi'siβle] ADJ admissible

admisión [aðmi'sjon] NF admission; (*reconocimiento*) acceptance

admitir [aðmi'tir] /**3a**/ VT to admit; (*aceptar*) to accept; (*dudas*) to leave room for; **esto no admite demora** this must be dealt with immediately

admón. ABR (= *administración*) admin

admonición [aðmoni'θjon] NF warning

ADN NM ABR (= *ácido desoxirribonucleico*) DNA

adobar [aðo'βar] /**1a**/ VT (*preparar*) to prepare; (*cocinar*) to season

adobe [a'ðoβe] NM adobe, sun-dried brick

adocenado, -a [aðoθe'naðo, a] ADJ (*fam*) mediocre

adoctrinar [aðoktri'nar] /**1a**/ VT to indoctrinate

adolecer [aðole'θer] /**2d**/ VI: **~ de** to suffer from

adolescente [aðoles'θente] NMF adolescent, teenager ▸ ADJ adolescent, teenage

adolezca *etc* [aðo'leθka] VB *ver* **adolecer**

adonde CONJ (to) where

adónde [a'ðonde] ADV = **dónde**

adondequiera [aðonde'kjera] ADV wherever

adopción [aðop'θjon] NF adoption

adoptar [aðop'tar] /**1a**/ VT to adopt

adoptivo, -a [aðop'tiβo, a] ADJ (*padres*) adoptive; (*hijo*) adopted

adoquín [aðo'kin] NM paving stone

adorar [aðo'rar] /**1a**/ VT to adore

adormecer [aðorme'θer] /**2d**/ VT to put to sleep; **adormecerse** VR to become sleepy; (*dormirse*) to fall asleep

adormezca *etc* [aðor'meθka] VB *ver* **adormecer**

adormilarse [aðormi'larse] /**1a**/ VR to doze

adornar [aðor'nar] /**1a**/ VT to adorn

adorno [a'ðorno] NM (*objeto*) ornament; (*decoración*) decoration, adornment

adosado, -a [aðo'saðo, a] ADJ (*casa*) semidetached

adosar [aðo'sar] /**1a**/ (AM) VT (*adjuntar*) to attach, enclose (*with a letter*)

adquiera *etc* [að'kjera] VB *ver* **adquirir**

adquirir [aðki'rir] /**3i**/ VT to acquire, obtain

adquisición [aðkisi'θjon] NF acquisition; (*compra*) purchase

adrede [a'ðreðe] ADV on purpose

Adriático [að'rjatiko] NM: **el (Mar) ~** the Adriatic (Sea)

adscribir [aðskri'βir] /**3a**/ VT to appoint; **estuvo adscrito al servicio de** ... he was attached to ...

adscrito [að'skrito] PP *de* **adscribir**

ADSL NM ABR ADSL

aduana [a'ðwana] NF customs *pl*; (*impuesto*) (customs) duty

aduanero, -a [aðwa'nero, a] ADJ customs *cpd* ▶ NM/F customs officer

aducir [aðu'θir] /**3n**/ VT to adduce; (*dar como prueba*) to offer as proof

adueñarse [aðwe'ɲarse] /**1a**/ VR: ~ **de** to take possession of

adulación [aðula'θjon] NF flattery

adular [aðu'lar] /**1a**/ VT to flatter

adulterar [aðulte'rar] /**1a**/ VT to adulterate ▶ VI to commit adultery

adulterio [aðul'terjo] NM adultery

adúltero, -a [a'ðultero, a] ADJ adulterous ▶ NM/F adulterer/adulteress

adulto, -a [a'ðulto, a] ADJ, NM/F adult

adusto, -a [a'ðusto, a] ADJ stern; (*austero*) austere

aduzca *etc* [a'ðuθka] VB *ver* **aducir**

advenedizo, -a [aðβene'ðiθo, a] NM/F upstart

advenimiento [aðβeni'mjento] NM arrival; (*al trono*) accession

adverbio [að'βerβjo] NM adverb

adversario, -a [aðβer'sarjo, a] NM/F adversary

adversidad [aðβersi'ðað] NF adversity; (*contratiempo*) setback

adverso, -a [að'βerso, a] ADJ adverse; (*suerte*) bad

advertencia [aðβer'tenθja] NF warning; (*prefacio*) preface, foreword

advertir [aðβer'tir] /**3i**/ VT (*observar*) to notice; (*avisar*): ~ **a algn de** to warn sb about *o* of

Adviento [að'βjento] NM Advent

advierta *etc* [að'βjerta], **advirtiendo** *etc* [aðβir'tjendo] VB *ver* **advertir**

adyacente [aðja'θente] ADJ adjacent

aéreo, -a [a'ereo, a] ADJ aerial; (*tráfico*) air *cpd*

aerobic [ae'roβik] NM, (AM) **aerobics** [ae'roβiks] NMPL aerobics *sg*

aerodeslizador [aeroðesliθa'ðor] NM hovercraft

aerodinámico, -a [aeroði'namiko, a] ADJ aerodynamic

aeródromo [ae'roðromo] NM aerodrome

aerograma [aero'ɣrama] NM airmail letter

aeromodelismo [aeromoðe'lismo] NM model aircraft making, aeromodelling

aeromozo, -a [aero'moθo, a] NM/F (AM) flight attendant, air steward(ess)

aeronáutica [aero'nautika] NF aeronautics *sg*

aeronáutico, -a [aero'nautiko, a] ADJ aeronautical

aeronave [aero'naβe] NM spaceship

aeroplano [aero'plano] NM aeroplane

aeropuerto [aero'pwerto] NM airport

aerosol [aero'sol] NM aerosol, spray

a/f ABR (= *a favor*) in favour

afabilidad [afaβili'ðað] NF affability, pleasantness

afable [a'faβle] ADJ affable, pleasant

afamado, -a [afa'maðo, a] ADJ famous

afán [a'fan] NM hard work; (*deseo*) desire; **con** ~ keenly

afanador, a [afana'ðor, a] NM/F (AM) (*de limpieza*) cleaner

afanar [afa'nar] /**1a**/ VT to harass; (*fam*) to pinch; **afanarse** VR: **afanarse por** to strive to

afanoso, -a [afa'noso, a] ADJ (*trabajo*) hard; (*trabajador*) industrious

AFE ['afe] NF ABR (= *Asociación de Futbolistas Españoles*) ≈ FA

afear [afe'ar] /**1a**/ VT to disfigure

afección [afek'θjon] NF affection; (*Med*) disease

afectación [afekta'θjon] NF affectation

afectado, -a [afek'taðo, a] ADJ affected

afectar [afek'tar] /**1a**/ VT to affect, have an effect on; (AM: *dañar*) to hurt; **por lo que afecta a esto** as far as this is concerned

afectísimo, -a [afek'tisimo, a] ADJ affectionate; **suyo** ~ yours truly

afectivo, -a [afek'tiβo, a] ADJ (*problema etc*) emotional

afecto, -a [a'fekto, a] ADJ: ~ **a** fond of; (*Jur*) subject to ▶ NM affection; **tenerle** ~ **a algn** to be fond of sb

afectuoso, -a [afek'twoso, a] ADJ affectionate

afeitar [afei'tar] /**1a**/ VT to shave; **afeitarse** VR to shave

afeminado, -a [afemi'naðo, a] ADJ effeminate

aferrar [afe'rrar] /**1j**/ VT to moor; (*fig*) to grasp ▶ VI to moor; **aferrarse** VR (*agarrarse*) to cling on; **aferrarse a un principio** to stick to a principle; **aferrarse a una esperanza** to cling to a hope

Afganistán [afɣanis'tan] NM Afghanistan

afgano, -a [af'ɣano, a] ADJ, NM/F Afghan

afiance *etc* [a'fjanθe] VB *ver* **afianzar**

afianzamiento [afjanθa'mjento] NM strengthening; security

afianzar [afjan'θar] /**1f**/ VT to strengthen, secure; **afianzarse** VR to steady o.s.; (*establecerse*) to become established

afiche [a'fitʃe] NM (AM) poster

afición [afi'θjon] NF: ~ **a** fondness *o* liking for; **la** ~ the fans *pl*; **pinto por** ~ I paint as a hobby

aficionado, -a [afiθjo'naðo, a] ADJ keen, enthusiastic; (*no profesional*) amateur ▶ NM/F enthusiast, fan; amateur; **ser** ~ **a algo** to be very keen on *o* fond of sth

aficionar [afiθjo'nar] /**1a**/ VT: ~ **a algn a algo** to make sb like sth; **aficionarse** VR: **aficionarse a algo** to grow fond of sth

afilado, -a [afiˈlaðo, a] ADJ sharp

afilador [afilaˈðor] NM knife grinder

afilalápices [afilaˈlapiθes] NM INV pencil sharpener

afilar [afiˈlar] /**1a**/ VT to sharpen; **afilarse** VR (cara) to grow thin

afiliación [afiljaˈθjon] NF (de sindicatos) membership

afiliado, -a [afiˈljaðo, a] ADJ subsidiary
▶ NM/F affiliate

afiliarse [afiˈljarse] /**1b**/ VR to affiliate

afín [aˈfin] ADJ (parecido) similar; (conexo) related

afinar [afiˈnar] /**1a**/ VT (Tec) to refine; (Mus) to tune ▶ VI (tocar) to play in tune; (cantar) to sing in tune

afincarse [afinˈkarse] /**1g**/ VR to settle

afinidad [afiniˈðað] NF affinity; (parentesco) relationship; **por ~** by marriage

afirmación [afirmaˈθjon] NF affirmation

afirmar [afirˈmar] /**1a**/ VT to affirm, state; (sostener) to strengthen; **afirmarse** VR (recuperar el equilibrio) to steady o.s.; **afirmarse en lo dicho** to stand by what one has said

afirmativo, -a [afirmaˈtiβo, a] ADJ affirmative

aflicción [aflikˈθjon] NF affliction; (dolor) grief

afligir [afliˈxir] /**3c**/ VT to afflict; (apenar) to distress; **afligirse** VR: **afligirse (por o con o de)** to grieve (about o at); **no te aflijas tanto** you must not let it affect you like this

aflija etc [aˈflixa] VB ver **afligir**

aflojar [afloˈxar] /**1a**/ VT to slacken; (desatar) to loosen, undo; (relajar) to relax ▶ VI (amainar) to drop; (bajar) to go down; **aflojarse** VR to relax

aflorar [afloˈrar] /**1a**/ VI (Geo, fig) to come to the surface, emerge

afluencia [afluˈenθja] NF flow

afluente [afluˈente] ADJ flowing ▶ NM (Geo) tributary

afluir [afluˈir] /**3g**/ VI to flow

afluya etc [aˈfluja], **afluyendo** etc [afluˈjendo] VB ver **afluir**

afmo., -a. ABR (= afectísimo/a suyo/a) Yours

afónico, -a [aˈfoniko, a] ADJ: **estar ~** to have a sore throat; to have lost one's voice

aforar [afoˈrar] /**1a**/ VT (Tec) to gauge; (fig) to value

aforo [aˈforo] NM (Tec) gauging; (de teatro etc) capacity; **el teatro tiene un ~ de 2,000** the theatre can seat 2,000

afortunadamente [afortunaðaˈmente] ADV fortunately, luckily

afortunado, -a [afortuˈnaðo, a] ADJ fortunate, lucky

afrancesado, -a [afranθeˈsaðo, a] ADJ francophile; (pey) Frenchified

afrenta [aˈfrenta] NF affront, insult; (deshonra) dishonour (BRIT), dishonor (US), shame

afrentoso, -a [afrenˈtoso, a] ADJ insulting; shameful

África [ˈafrika] NF Africa; **~ del Sur** South Africa

africano, -a [afriˈkano, a] ADJ, NM/F African

afrontar [afronˈtar] /**1a**/ VT to confront; (poner cara a cara) to bring face to face

afrutado, -a [afruˈtaðo, a] ADJ fruity

after [ˈafter] (pl **afters** o **~**) NM, **afterhours** [ˈafterauars] NM INV after-hours club

afuera [aˈfwera] ADV out, outside; **por ~** on the outside; **afueras** NFPL outskirts

ag. ABR (= agosto) Aug.

agachar [aɣaˈtʃar] /**1a**/ VT to bend, bow; **agacharse** VR to stoop, bend

agalla [aˈɣaʎa] NF (Zool) gill; **agallas** NFPL (Med) tonsillitis sg; (Anat) tonsils; **tener agallas** (fam) to have guts

agarradera [aɣarraˈðera] NF, (AM)

agarradero [aɣarraˈðero] NM handle; **agarraderas** NFPL pull sg, influence sg

agarrado, -a [aɣaˈrraðo, a] ADJ mean, stingy

agarrar [aɣaˈrrar] /**1a**/ VT to grasp, grab; (AM: tomar) to take, catch; (recoger) to pick up ▶ VI (planta) to take root; **agarrarse** VR to hold on (tightly); (meterse uno con otro) to grapple (with each other); **agarrársela con algn** (AM) to pick on sb; **agarró y se fue** (esp AM fam) he upped and went

agarrotar [aɣarroˈtar] /**1a**/ VT (lío) to tie tightly; (persona) to squeeze tightly; (reo) to garrotte; **agarrotarse** VR (motor) to seize up; (Med) to stiffen

agasajar [aɣasaˈxar] /**1a**/ VT to treat well, fête

agave [aˈɣaβe] NF agave

agazapar [aɣaθaˈpar] /**1a**/ VT (coger) to grab hold of; **agazaparse** VR (agacharse) to crouch down

agencia [aˈxenθja] NF agency; **~ de créditos/ publicidad/viajes** credit/advertising/travel agency; **~ inmobiliaria** estate agent's (office) (BRIT), real estate office (US); **~ matrimonial** marriage bureau

agenciar [axenˈθjar] /**1b**/ VT to bring about; **agenciarse** VR to look after o.s.; **agenciarse algo** to get hold of sth

agenda [aˈxenda] NF diary; **~ electrónica** PDA; **~ telefónica** telephone directory

agente [aˈxente] NMF agent; (tb: **agente de policía**) policeman/policewoman; **~ de bolsa** stockbroker; **~ de negocios** (Com) business agent; **~ de seguros** insurance broker; **~ de tránsito** (AM) traffic cop; **~ de viajes** travel agent; **~ inmobiliario** estate agent (BRIT), realtor (US); **agentes sociales** social partners

ágil ['axil] ADJ agile, nimble

agilidad [axili'ðað] NF agility, nimbleness

agilizar [axili'θar] /1f/ VT (*trámites*) to speed up

agiotista [axjo'tista] (*AM*) NMF (*usurero*) usurer

agitación [axita'θjon] NF (*de mano etc*) shaking, waving; (*de líquido etc*) stirring; agitation

agitado, -a [axi'aðo, a] ADJ hectic; (*viaje*) bumpy

agitar [axi'tar] /1a/ VT to wave, shake; (*líquido*) to stir; (*fig*) to stir up, excite; **agitarse** VR to get excited; (*inquietarse*) to get worried o upset

aglomeración [aɣlomera'θjon] NF: **~ de tráfico/gente** traffic jam/mass of people

aglomerar [aɣlome'rar] /1a/ VT, **aglomerarse** VR to crowd together

agnóstico, -a [aɣ'nostiko, a] ADJ, NM/F agnostic

agobiante [aɣo'βjante] ADJ (*calor*) oppressive

agobiar [aɣo'βjar] /1b/ VT to weigh down; (*oprimir*) to oppress; (*cargar*) to burden; **sentirse agobiado por** to be overwhelmed by

agobio [a'ɣoβjo] NM (*peso*) burden; (*fig*) oppressiveness

agolpamiento [aɣolpa'mjento] NM crush

agolparse [aɣol'parse] /1a/ VR to crowd together

agonía [aɣo'nia] NF death throes pl; (*fig*) agony, anguish

agonice *etc* [aɣo'niθe] VB *ver* **agonizar**

agonizante [aɣoni'θante] ADJ dying

agonizar [aɣoni'θar] /1f/ VI to be dying

agorero, -a [aɣo'rero, a] ADJ ominous ▶ NM/F soothsayer; **ave agorera** bird of ill omen

agostar [aɣo'star] /1a/ VT (*quemar*) to parch; (*fig*) to wither

agosto [a'ɣosto] NM August; (*fig*) harvest; **hacer su ~** to make one's pile; *ver tb* **julio**

agotado, -a [aɣo'taðo, a] ADJ (*persona*) exhausted; (*acabado*) finished; (*Com*) sold out; (: *libros*) out of print; (*pila*) flat

agotador, a [aɣota'ðor, a] ADJ exhausting

agotamiento [aɣota'mjento] NM exhaustion

agotar [aɣo'tar] /1a/ VT to exhaust; (*consumir*) to drain; (*recursos*) to use up, deplete; **agotarse** VR to be exhausted; (*acabarse*) to run out; (*libro*) to go out of print

agraciado, -a [aɣra'θjaðo, a] ADJ (*atractivo*) attractive; (*en sorteo etc*) lucky

agraciar [aɣra'θjar] /1b/ VT (*Jur*) to pardon; (*con premio*) to reward; (*hacer más atractivo*) to make more attractive

agradable [aɣra'ðaβle] ADJ pleasant, nice

agradar [aɣra'ðar] /1a/ VT, VI to please; **él me agrada** I like him; **agradarse** VR to like each other

agradecer [aɣraðe'θer] /2d/ VT to thank; (*favor etc*) to be grateful for; **le agradecería me enviara …** I would be grateful if you would send me …; **agradecerse** VR: **¡se agradece!** much obliged!

agradecido, -a [aɣraðe'θiðo, a] ADJ grateful; **¡muy ~!** thanks a lot!

agradecimiento [aɣraðeθi'mjento] NM thanks pl; gratitude

agradezca *etc* [aɣra'ðeθka] VB *ver* **agradecer**

agrado [a'ɣraðo] NM: **ser de tu** *etc* **~** to be to your *etc* liking

agrandar [aɣran'dar] /1a/ VT to enlarge; (*fig*) to exaggerate; **agrandarse** VR to get bigger

agrario, -a [a'ɣrarjo, a] ADJ agrarian, land cpd; (*política*) agricultural, farming cpd

agravante [aɣra'βante] ADJ aggravating ▶ NM O F complication; **con el** or **la ~ de que …** with the further difficulty that …

agravar [aɣra'βar] /1a/ VT (*pesar sobre*) to make heavier; (*irritar*) to aggravate; **agravarse** VR to worsen, get worse

agraviar [aɣra'βjar] /1b/ VT to offend; (*ser injusto con*) to wrong; **agraviarse** VR to take offence

agravio [a'ɣraβjo] NM offence; wrong; (*Jur*) grievance

agraz [a'ɣraθ] NM (*uva*) sour grape; **en ~** (*fig*) immature

agredir [aɣre'ðir] /3a/ VT to attack

agregado [aɣre'ɣaðo] NM aggregate; (*persona*) attaché; (*profesor*) assistant professor; **A~** = teacher (*who is not head of department*)

agregar [aɣre'ɣar] /1h/ VT to gather; (*añadir*) to add; (*persona*) to appoint

agregue *etc* [a'ɣreɣe] VB *ver* **agregar**

agresión [aɣre'sjon] NF aggression; (*ataque*) attack

agresivo, -a [aɣre'siβo, a] ADJ aggressive

agreste [a'ɣreste] ADJ (*rural*) rural; (*fig*) rough

agriar [a'ɣrjar] VT (*fig*) to (turn) sour; **agriarse** VR to turn sour

agrícola [a'ɣrikola] ADJ farming cpd, agricultural

agricultor, a [aɣrikul'tor, a] NM/F farmer

agricultura [aɣrikul'tura] NF agriculture, farming

agridulce [aɣri'ðulθe] ADJ bittersweet; (*Culin*) sweet and sour

agrietarse [aɣrje'tarse] /1a/ VR to crack; (*la piel*) to chap

agrimensor, a [aɣrimen'sor, a] NM/F surveyor

agringado, -a [aɣrin'gaðo, a] ADJ gringolike

agrio, -a ['aɣrjo, a] ADJ bitter

agronomía [aɣrono'mia] NF agronomy, agriculture

agrónomo, -a [a'ɣronomo, a] NM/F agronomist, agricultural expert

agropecuario, -a [aɣrope'kwarjo, a] ADJ farming *cpd*, agricultural

agrupación [aɣrupa'θjon] NF group; (*acto*) grouping

agrupar [aɣru'par] /**1a**/ VT to group; (*Inform*) to block; **agruparse** VR (*Pol*) to form a group; (*juntarse*) to gather

agua ['aɣwa] NF water; (*Naut*) wake; (*Arq*) slope of a roof; **aguas** NFPL (*de joya*) sparkle *sg*; (*Med*) water *sg*, urine *sg*; (*Naut*) waters; **aguas abajo/arriba** downstream/upstream; **~ bendita/destilada/potable** holy/distilled/drinking water; **~ caliente** hot water; **~ corriente** running water; **~ de colonia** eau de cologne; **~ mineral (con/sin gas)** (fizzy/non-fizzy) mineral water; **~ oxigenada** hydrogen peroxide; **aguas jurisdiccionales** territorial waters; **aguas mayores** excrement *sg*; **~ pasada no mueve molino** it's no use crying over spilt milk; **estar con el ~ al cuello** to be up to one's neck; **venir como ~ de mayo** to be a godsend

aguacate [aɣwa'kate] NM avocado (pear)

aguacero [aɣwa'θero] NM (heavy) shower, downpour

aguachirle [aɣwa'tʃirle] NM (*bebida*) slops *pl*

aguado, -a [a'ɣwaðo, a] ADJ watery, watered down ▶ NF (*Agr*) watering place; (*Naut*) water supply; (*Arte*) watercolour

aguafiestas [aɣwa'fjestas] NMF spoilsport

aguafuerte [aɣwa'fwerte] NF etching

aguaitar [aɣwai'tar] /**1a**/ VT (*AM*) to watch

aguamiel [aɣwa'mjel] (*AM*) NF fermented maguey *o* agave juice

aguanieve [aɣwa'njeβe] NF sleet

aguantable [aɣwan'taβle] ADJ bearable, tolerable

aguantar [aɣwan'tar] /**1a**/ VT to bear, put up with; (*sostener*) to hold up ▶ VI to last; **aguantarse** VR to restrain o.s.; **no sé cómo aguanta** I don't know how he can take it

aguante [a'ɣwante] NM (*paciencia*) patience; (*resistencia*) endurance; (*Deporte*) stamina

aguar [a'ɣwar] /**1i**/ VT to water down; (*fig*): **~ la fiesta a algn** to spoil sb's fun

aguardar [aɣwar'ðar] /**1a**/ VT to wait for

aguardentoso, -a [aɣwarðen'toso, a] ADJ (*pey: voz*) husky, gruff

aguardiente [aɣwar'ðjente] NM brandy, liquor

aguarrás [aɣwa'rras] NM turpentine

aguaviva [aɣwa'βiβa] (*RPL*) NF jellyfish

aguce *etc* [a'ɣuθe] VB *ver* **aguzar**

agudeza [aɣu'ðeθa] NF sharpness; (*ingenio*) wit

agudice *etc* [aɣu'ðiθe] VB *ver* **agudizar**

agudizar [aɣuði'θar] /**1f**/ VT to sharpen; (*crisis*) to make worse; **agudizarse** VR to worsen, deteriorate

agudo, -a [a'ɣuðo, a] ADJ sharp; (*voz*) high-pitched, piercing; (*dolor, enfermedad*) acute

agüe *etc* ['aɣwe] VB *ver* **aguar**

agüero [a'ɣwero] NM: **buen/mal ~** good/bad omen; **ser de buen ~** to augur well; **pájaro de mal ~** bird of ill omen

aguerrido, -a [aɣe'rriðo, a] ADJ hardened; (*fig*) experienced

aguijar [aɣi'xar] /**1a**/ VT to goad; (*incitar*) to urge on ▶ VI to hurry along

aguijón [aɣi'xon] NM sting; (*fig*) spur

aguijonear [aɣixone'ar] /**1a**/ VT = **aguijar**

águila ['aɣila] NF eagle; (*fig*) genius

aguileño, -a [aɣi'leɲo, a] ADJ (*nariz*) aquiline; (*rostro*) sharp-featured

aguinaldo [aɣi'naldo] NM Christmas box

aguja [a'ɣuxa] NF needle; (*de reloj*) hand; (*Arq*) spire; (*Tec*) firing-pin; **agujas** NFPL (*Zool*) ribs; (*Ferro*) points

agujerear [aɣuxere'ar] /**1a**/ VT to make holes in; (*penetrar*) to pierce

agujero [aɣu'xero] NM hole; (*Com*) deficit

agujetas [aɣu'xetas] NFPL stitch *sg*; (*rigidez*) stiffness *sg*

aguzar [aɣu'θar] /**1f**/ VT to sharpen; (*fig*) to incite; **~ el oído** to prick up one's ears

aherrumbrarse [aerrum'brarse] /**1a**/ VR to get rusty

ahí [a'i] ADV there; (*allá*) over there; **de ~ que** so that, with the result that; **~ llega** here he comes; **por ~** (*dirección*) that way; **¡hasta ~ hemos llegado!** so it has come to this!; **¡~ va!** (*objeto*) here it comes!; (*individuo*) there he goes!; **~ donde le ve** as sure as he's standing there; **200 o por ~** 200 or so

ahijado, -a [ai'xaðo, a] NM/F godson(-daughter)

ahijar [ai'xar] /**1a**/ VT: **~ algo a algn** (*fig*) to attribute sth to sb

ahínco [a'inko] NM earnestness; **con ~** eagerly

ahíto, -a [a'ito, a] ADJ: **estoy ~** I'm full up

ahogado, -a [ao'ɣaðo, a] ADJ (*en agua*) drowned; (*emoción*) pent-up; (*grito*) muffled

ahogar [ao'ɣar] /**1h**/ VT (*en agua*) to drown; (*asfixiar*) to suffocate, smother; (*fuego*) to put out; **ahogarse** VR (*en agua*) to drown; (*por asfixia*) to suffocate

ahogo [a'oɣo] NM (*Med*) breathlessness; (*fig*) distress; (*económico*) financial difficulty

ahogue *etc* [a'oɣe] VB *ver* **ahogar**

ahondar [aon'dar] /**1a**/ VT to deepen, make deeper; (*fig*) to study thoroughly ▶ VI: **~ en** to study thoroughly

ahora [a'ora] ADV now; (*hace poco*) a moment ago, just now; (*dentro de poco*) in a moment; **~ voy** I'm coming; **~ mismo** right now; **~ bien** now then; **por ~** for the present

ahorcado, -a [aor'kaðo, a] NM/F hanged person

ahorcar [aor'kar] /**1g**/ VT to hang; **ahorcarse** VR to hang o.s.

ahorita [ao'rita], **ahoritita** [aori'tita] ADV (*esp Am fam: en este momento*) right now; (: *hace poco*) just now; (: *dentro de poco*) in a minute

ahorque *etc* [a'orke] VB *ver* **ahorcar**

ahorrar [ao'rrar] /**1a**/ VT (*dinero*) to save; (*esfuerzos*) to save, avoid; **ahorrarse** VR: **ahorrarse molestias** to save o.s. trouble

ahorrativo, -a [aorra'tiβo, a] ADJ thrifty

ahorro [a'orro] NM (*acto*) saving; (*frugalidad*) thrift; **ahorros** NMPL (*dinero*) savings

ahuecar [awe'kar] /**1g**/ VT to hollow (out); (*voz*) to deepen ▶ VI: **¡ahueca!** (*fam*) beat it! (*fam*); **ahuecarse** VR to give o.s. airs

ahueque *etc* [a'weke] VB *ver* **ahuecar**

ahumar [au'mar] /**1a**/ VT to smoke, cure; (*llenar de humo*) to fill with smoke ▶ VI to smoke; **ahumarse** VR to fill with smoke

ahuyentar [aujen'tar] /**1a**/ VT to drive off, frighten off; (*fig*) to dispel

AI NF ABR (= *Amnistía Internacional*) AI

aimara [ai'mara], **aimará** [aima'ra] ADJ, NMF Aymara

aindiado, -a [aindi'aðo, a] ADJ (*Am*) Indian-like

airado, -a [ai'raðo, a] ADJ angry

airar [ai'rar] /**1a**/ VT to anger; **airarse** VR to get angry

aire ['aire] NM air; (*viento*) wind; (*corriente*) draught; (*Mus*) tune; **aires** NMPL: **darse aires** to give o.s. airs; **al ~ libre** in the open air; **~ climatizado** o **acondicionado** air conditioning; **tener ~ de** to look like; **estar de buen/mal ~** to be in a good/bad mood; **estar en el ~** (*Radio*) to be on the air; (*fig*) to be up in the air

airear [aire'ar] /**1a**/ VT to ventilate; (*fig: asunto*) to air; **airearse** VR to get some fresh air

airoso, -a [ai'roso, a] ADJ windy; draughty; (*fig*) graceful

aislado, -a [ais'laðo, a] ADJ (*remoto*) isolated; (*incomunicado*) cut off; (*Elec*) insulated

aislante [ais'lante] NM (*Elec*) insulator

aislar [ais'lar] /**1a**/ VT to isolate; (*Elec*) to insulate; **aislarse** VR to cut o.s. off

ajar [a'xar] /**1a**/ VT to spoil; (*fig*) to abuse; **ajarse** VR to get crumpled; (*fig: piel*) to get wrinkled

ajardinado, -a [axarði'naðo, a] ADJ landscaped

ajedrez [axe'ðreθ] NM chess

ajenjo [a'xenxo] NM (*bebida*) absinth(e)

ajeno, -a [a'xeno, a] ADJ (*que pertenece a otro*) somebody else's; **~ a** foreign to; **~ de** free from, devoid of; **por razones ajenas a nuestra voluntad** for reasons beyond our control

ajetreado, -a [axetre'aðo, a] ADJ busy

ajetrearse [axetre'arse] /**1a**/ VR (*atarearse*) to bustle about; (*fatigarse*) to tire o.s. out

ajetreo [axe'treo] NM bustle

ají [a'xi] NM chil(l)i, red pepper; (*salsa*) chil(l)i sauce

ajiaco [axi'ako] NM (*Am*) potato and chil(l)i stew

ajilimoje [axili'moxe] NM sauce of garlic and pepper; **ajilimojes** NMPL (*fam*) odds and ends

ajillo [a'xiʎo] NM: **gambas al ~** garlic prawns

ajo ['axo] NM garlic; **~ porro** o **puerro** leek; **(tieso) como un ~** (*fam*) snobbish; **estar en el ~** to be mixed up in it

ajorca [a'xorka] NF bracelet

ajuar [a'xwar] NM household furnishings *pl*; (*de novia*) trousseau; (*de niño*) layette

ajustado, -a [axus'taðo, a] ADJ (*tornillo*) tight; (*cálculo*) right; (*ropa*) tight(-fitting); (*Deporte: resultado*) close

ajustar [axus'tar] /**1a**/ VT (*adaptar*) to adjust; (*encajar*) to fit; (*Tec*) to engage; (*Tip*) to make up; (*apretar*) to tighten; (*concertar*) to agree (on); (*reconciliar*) to reconcile; (*cuenta, deudas*) to settle ▶ VI to fit; **ajustarse** VR: **ajustarse a** (*precio etc*) to be in keeping with, fit in with; **~ las cuentas a algn** to get even with sb

ajuste [a'xuste] NM adjustment; (*Costura*) fitting; (*acuerdo*) compromise; (*de cuenta*) settlement

al [al] (= *a + el*) *ver* **a**

ala ['ala] NF wing; (*de sombrero*) brim; (*futbolista*) winger; **~ delta** hang-glider; **andar con el ~ caída** to be downcast; **cortar las alas a algn** to clip sb's wings; **dar alas a algn** to encourage sb

alabanza [ala'βanθa] NF praise

alabar [ala'βar] /**1a**/ VT to praise

alacena [ala'θena] NF cupboard (*Brit*), closet (*US*)

alacrán [ala'kran] NM scorpion

ALADI [a'laði] NF ABR = **Asociación Latinoamericana de Integración**

alado, -a [a'laðo, a] ADJ winged

ALALC [a'lalk] NF ABR (= *Asociación Latinoamericana de Libre Comercio*) LAFTA

alambicado, -a [alambi'kaðo, a] ADJ distilled; (*fig*) affected

alambicar [alambi'kar] /**1g**/ VT to distil

alambique *etc* [alam'bike] VB *ver* **alambicar** ▶ NM still

alambrada [alam'braða] NF, **alambrado** [alam'braðo] NM wire fence; (*red*) wire netting

alambre [a'lambre] NM wire; **~ de púas** barbed wire

alambrista [alam'brista] NMF tightrope walker

a

alameda [alaˈmeða] NF (*plantío*) poplar grove; (*lugar de paseo*) avenue, boulevard

álamo [ˈalamo] NM poplar; **~ temblón** aspen

alano [aˈlano] NM mastiff

alarde [aˈlarðe] NM show, display; **hacer ~ de** to boast of

alardear [alarðeˈar] /**1a**/ VI to boast

alargador [alarɣaˈðor] NM extension cable *o* lead

alargar [alarˈɣar] /**1h**/ VT to lengthen, extend; (*paso*) to hasten; (*brazo*) to stretch out; (*cuerda*) to pay out; (*conversación*) to spin out; **alargarse** VR to get longer

alargue *etc* [aˈlarɣe] VB *ver* **alargar**

alarido [alaˈriðo] NM shriek

alarma [aˈlarma] NF alarm; **voz de ~** warning note; **dar la ~** to raise the alarm; **~ de incendios** fire alarm

alarmante [alarˈmante] ADJ alarming

alarmar [alarˈmar] /**1a**/ VT to alarm; **alarmarse** VR to get alarmed

alavés, -esa [alaˈβes, esa] ADJ of Álava ▶ NM/F native *o* inhabitant of Álava

alazán [alaˈθan] NM sorrel

alba [ˈalβa] NF dawn

albacea [alβaˈθea] NMF executor (executrix)

albaceteño, -a [alβaθeˈteɲo, a] ADJ of Albacete ▶ NM/F native *o* inhabitant of Albacete

albahaca [alˈβaka] NF (*Bot*) basil

Albania [alˈβanja] NF Albania

albañal [alβaˈɲal] NM drain, sewer

albañil [alβaˈɲil] NM bricklayer; (*cantero*) mason

albarán [alβaˈran] NM (*Com*) delivery note, invoice

albarda [alˈβarða] NF packsaddle

albaricoque [alβariˈkoke] NM apricot

albedrío [alβeˈðrio] NM: **libre ~** free will

alberca [alˈβerka] NF reservoir; (*Am*) swimming pool

albergar [alβerˈɣar] /**1h**/ VT to shelter; (*esperanza*) to cherish; **albergarse** VR (*refugiarse*) to shelter; (*alojarse*) to lodge

albergue [alˈβerɣe] VB *ver* **albergar** ▶ NM shelter, refuge; **~ juvenil** youth hostel

albis [ˈalβis] ADV: **quedarse en ~** not to have a clue

albóndiga [alˈβondiɣa] NF meatball

albor [alˈβor] NM whiteness; (*amanecer*) dawn

alborada [alβoˈraða] NF dawn; (*diana*) reveille

alborear [alβoreˈar] /**1a**/ VI to dawn

albornoz [alβorˈnoθ] NM (*de los árabes*) burnous; (*para el baño*) bathrobe

alboroce *etc* [alβoˈroθe] VB *ver* **alborozar**

alborotar [alβoroˈtar] /**1a**/ VI to make a row ▶ VT to agitate, stir up; **alborotarse** VR to get excited; (*mar*) to get rough

alboroto [alβoˈroto] NM row, uproar

alborozar [alβoroˈθar] /**1f**/ VT to gladden; **alborozarse** VR to rejoice, be overjoyed

alborozo [alβoˈroθo] NM joy

albricias [alˈβriθjas] NFPL: **¡~!** good news!

álbum [ˈalβum] (*pl* **álbums** *o* **álbumes**) NM album; **~ de recortes** scrapbook

albumen [alˈβumen] NM egg white, albumen

albur [alˈβur] (*Am*) NM (*juego de palabras*) pun; (*doble sentido*) double entendre

alcabala [alkaˈβala] NF (*Am*) roadblock

alcachofa [alkaˈtʃofa] NF (*globe*) artichoke; (*Tip*) golf ball; (*de ducha*) shower head

alcahueta [alkaˈweta] NF procuress

alcahuete [alkaˈwete] NM pimp

alcalde, -esa [alˈkalde, alkalˈdesa] NM/F mayor(ess)

alcaldía [alkalˈdia] NF mayoralty; (*lugar*) mayor's office

álcali [ˈalkali] NM (*Química*) alkali

alcance [alˈkanθe] VB *ver* **alcanzar** ▶ NM (*Mil, Radio*) range; (*fig*) scope; (*Com*) adverse balance, deficit; **estar al/fuera del ~ de algn** to be within/beyond sb's reach; (*fig*) to be within sb's powers/over sb's head; **de gran ~** (*Mil*) long-range; (*fig*) far-reaching

alcancía [alkanˈθia] (*Am*) NF (*para ahorrar*) money box; (*para colectas*) collection box

alcanfor [alkanˈfor] NM camphor

alcantarilla [alkantaˈriʎa] NF (*de aguas cloacales*) sewer; (*en la calle*) gutter

alcanzar [alkanˈθar] /**1f**/ VT (*algo: con la mano, el pie*) to reach; (*alguien: en el camino etc*) to catch up (with); (*autobús*) to catch; (*suj: bala*) to hit, strike ▶ VI (*ser suficiente*) to be enough; **~ algo a algn** to hand sth to sb; **alcánzame la sal, por favor** pass the salt please; **~ a hacer** to manage to do

alcaparra [alkaˈparra] NF (*Bot*) caper

alcatraz [alkaˈtraθ] NM gannet

alcayata [alkaˈjata] NF hook

alcázar [alˈkaθar] NM fortress; (*Naut*) quarter-deck

alce *etc* [ˈalθe] VB *ver* **alzar**

alcista [alˈθista] NM speculator ▶ ADJ (*Com, Econ*): **mercado ~** bull market; **la tendencia ~** the upward trend

alcoba [alˈkoβa] NF bedroom

alcohol [alˈkol] NM alcohol; **no bebe ~** he doesn't drink (alcohol); **~ metílico** methylated spirits *pl* (*BRIT*), wood alcohol (*US*)

alcoholemia [alkooˈlemja] NF blood alcohol level; **prueba de la ~** breath test

alcoholice *etc* [alkoˈliθe] VB *ver* **alcoholizarse**

alcohólico, -a [alˈkoliko, a] ADJ, NM/F alcoholic

alcoholímetro [alkoˈlimetro] NM Breathalyser®, drunkometer (*US*)

alcoholismo [alko'lismo] NM alcoholism

alcoholizarse [alkoli'θarse] /1f/ VR to become an alcoholic

alcornoque [alkor'noke] NM cork tree; (fam) idiot

alcotana [alko'tana] NF pickaxe; (Deporte) ice-axe

alcurnia [al'kurnja] NF lineage

alcuza [al'kusa] NF (Am) cruet

aldaba [al'daβa] NF (door) knocker

aldea [al'dea] NF village

aldeano, -a [alde'ano, a] ADJ village cpd
▶ NM/F villager

ale ['ale] EXCL come on!, let's go!

aleación [alea'θjon] NF alloy

aleatorio, -a [alea'torjo, a] ADJ random, contingent; **acceso ~** (Inform) random access

aleccionador, a [alekθjona'ðor, a] ADJ instructive

aleccionar [alekθjo'nar] /1a/ VT to instruct; (adiestrar) to train

aledaño, -a [ale'ðaɲo, a] ADJ: **~ a** bordering on
▶ NM: **aledaños** outskirts

alegación [aleɣa'θjon] NF allegation

alegar [ale'ɣar] /1h/ VT (dificultad etc) to plead; (Jur) to allege ▶ VI to argue; **~ que ...** to give as an excuse that ...

alegato [ale'ɣato] NM (Jur) allegation; (escrito) indictment; (declaración) statement; (Am) argument

alegoría [aleɣo'ria] NF allegory

alegrar [ale'ɣrar] /1a/ VT (causar alegría) to cheer (up); (fuego) to poke; (fiesta) to liven up; **alegrarse** VR (fam) to get merry o tight; **alegrarse de** to be glad about

alegre [a'leɣre] ADJ happy, cheerful; (fam) merry, tight; (chiste) risqué, blue

alegría [ale'ɣria] NF happiness; merriment; **~ vital** joie de vivre

alegrón [ale'ɣron] NM (fig) sudden joy

alegue etc [a'leɣe] VB ver **alegar**

alejamiento [alexa'mjento] NM removal; (distancia) remoteness

alejar [ale'xar] /1a/ VT to move away, remove; (fig) to estrange; **alejarse** VR to move away

alelado, -a [ale'laðo, a] ADJ (bobo) foolish

alelar [ale'lar] /1a/ VT to bewilder

aleluya [ale'luja] NM (canto) hallelujah

alemán, -ana [ale'man, ana] ADJ, NM/F German ▶ NM (lengua) German

Alemania [ale'manja] NF Germany

alentador, a [alenta'ðor, a] ADJ encouraging

alentar [alen'tar] /1j/ VT to encourage

alergia [a'lerxja] NF allergy

alero [a'lero] NM (de tejado) eaves pl; (de foca, Deporte) flipper; (Auto) mudguard

alerta [a'lerta] ADJ INV, NM alert

aleta [a'leta] NF (de pez) fin; (de ave) wing; (de foca, Deporte) flipper; (de coche) mudguard

aletargar [aletar'ɣar] /1h/ VT to make drowsy; (entumecer) to make numb; **aletargarse** VR to grow drowsy; to become numb

aletargue etc [ale'tarɣe] VB ver **aletargar**

aletear [alete'ar] /1a/ VI to flutter; (ave) to flap its wings; (individuo) to wave one's arms

alevín [ale'βin] NM fry, young fish

alevosía [aleβo'sia] NF treachery

alfabetización [alfaβetiθa'θjon] NF: **campaña de ~** literacy campaign

alfabeto [alfa'βeto] NM alphabet

alfajor [alfa'xor] NM (Esp: polvorón) cake eaten at Christmas time

alfalfa [al'falfa] NF alfalfa, lucerne

alfaque [al'fake] NM (Naut) bar, sandbank

alfar [al'far] NM (taller) potter's workshop; (arcilla) clay

alfarería [alfare'ria] NF pottery; (tienda) pottery shop

alfarero, -a [alfa'rero, a] NM/F potter

alféizar [al'feiθar] NM window-sill

alférez [al'fereθ] NM (Mil) second lieutenant; (Naut) ensign

alfil [al'fil] NM (Ajedrez) bishop

alfiler [alfi'ler] NM pin; (broche) clip; (pinza) clothes peg (BRIT) o pin (US); **~ de gancho** (Am) safety pin; **prendido con alfileres** shaky

alfiletero [alfile'tero] NM needle case

alfombra [al'fombra] NF carpet; (más pequeña) rug

alfombrar [alfom'brar] /1a/ VT to carpet

alfombrilla [alfom'briʎa] NF rug, mat; (Inform) mouse mat o pad

alforja [al'forxa] NF saddlebag

alforza [al'forθa] NF pleat

algarabía [alɣara'βia] NF (fam) gibberish; (griterío) hullabaloo

algarada [alɣa'raða] NF outcry; **hacer** o **levantar una ~** to kick up a tremendous fuss

Algarbe [al'ɣarβe] NM: **el ~** the Algarve

algarroba [alɣa'rroβa] NF carob

algarrobo [alɣa'rroβo] NM carob tree

algas ['alɣas] NFPL seaweed sg

algazara [alɣa'θara] NF din, uproar

álgebra ['alxeβra] NF algebra

álgido, -a ['alxiðo, a] ADJ icy; (momento etc) crucial, decisive

algo ['alɣo] PRON something; (en frases interrogativas) anything ▶ ADV somewhat, rather; **¿~ más?** anything else?; (en tienda) is that all?; **por ~ será** there must be some reason for it; **es ~ difícil** it's a bit awkward

algodón [alɣo'ðon] NM cotton; (planta) cotton plant; **~ de azúcar** candy floss (BRIT), cotton candy (US); **~ hidrófilo** cotton wool (BRIT), absorbent cotton (US)

algodonero, -a [alɣoðo'nero, a] ADJ cotton cpd
▶ NM/F cotton grower ▶ NM cotton plant

algoritmo [alɣo'ritmo] NM algorithm

alguacil [alɣwa'θil] NM bailiff; (*Taur*) mounted official

alguien ['alɣjen] PRON someone, somebody; (*en frases interrogativas*) anyone, anybody

alguno, -a [al'ɣuno, a] ADJ (*antes de n msg* **algún**) some; (*después de n*): **no tiene talento** ~ he has no talent, he doesn't have any talent ▸ PRON (*alguien*) someone, somebody; **algún que otro libro** some book or other; **algún día iré** I'll go one o some day; **sin interés** ~ without the slightest interest; **~ que otro** an occasional one; **algunos piensan** some (people) think; **~ de ellos** one of them

alhaja [a'laxa] NF jewel; (*tesoro*) precious object, treasure

alhelí [ale'li] NM wallflower, stock

aliado, -a [a'ljaðo, a] ADJ allied

alianza [a'ljanθa] NF (*Pol etc*) alliance; (*anillo*) wedding ring

aliar [a'ljar] /**1c**/ VT to ally; **aliarse** VR to form an alliance

alias ['aljas] ADV alias

alicaído, -a [alika'iðo, a] ADJ (*Med*) weak; (*fig*) depressed

alicantino, -a [alikan'tino, a] ADJ of Alicante ▸ NM/F native o inhabitant of Alicante

alicatado [alika'taðo] (*Esp*) NM tiling

alicatar [alika'tar] /**1a**/ VT to tile

alicate [ali'kate] NM, **alicates** [ali'kates] NMPL pliers *pl*; **~(s) de uñas** nail clippers

aliciente [ali'θjente] NM incentive; (*atracción*) attraction

alienación [aljena'θjon] NF alienation

aliento [a'ljento] VB *ver* **alentar** ▸ NM breath; (*respiración*) breathing; **sin ~** breathless; **de un ~** in one breath; (*fig*) in one go

aligerar [alixe'rar] /**1a**/ VT to lighten; (*reducir*) to shorten; (*aliviar*) to alleviate; (*mitigar*) to ease; (*paso*) to quicken

alijo [a'lixo] NM (*Naut: descarga*) unloading; (: *contrabando*) consignment (of smuggled goods)

alimaña [ali'maɲa] NF pest

alimentación [alimenta'θjon] NF (*comida*) food; (*acción*) feeding; (*tienda*) grocer's (shop); **~ continua** (*en fotocopiadora etc*) stream feed

alimentador [alimenta'ðor] NM: **~ de papel** sheet-feeder

alimentar [alimen'tar] /**1a**/ VT to feed; (*nutrir*) to nourish; **alimentarse** VR: **alimentarse (de)** to feed (on)

alimenticio, -a [alimen'tiθjo, a] ADJ food *cpd*; (*nutritivo*) nourishing, nutritious

alimento [ali'mento] NM food; (*nutrición*) nourishment; **alimentos** NMPL (*Jur*) alimony *sg*; **alimentos transgénicos** GM foods

alimón [ali'mon]: **al ~** adv jointly, together

alineación [alinea'θjon] NF alignment; (*Deporte*) line-up

alineado, -a [aline'aðo, a] ADJ (*Tip*): **(no) ~** (un)justified; **~ a la izquierda/derecha** ranged left/right

alinear [aline'ar] /**1a**/ VT to align; (*Tip*) to justify; (*Deporte*) to select, pick; **alinearse** VR to line up; **alinearse en** to fall in with

aliñar [ali'ɲar] /**1a**/ VT (*Culin*) to season; (: *ensalada*) to dress

aliño [a'liɲo] NM (*Culin*) dressing

alioli [ali'oli] NM garlic mayonnaise

alisar [ali'sar] /**1a**/ VT to smooth

aliso [a'liso] NM alder

alistamiento [alista'mjento] NM recruitment

alistar [alis'tar] /**1a**/ VT to recruit; **alistarse** VR to enlist; (*inscribirse*) to enrol; (*Am: prepararse*) to get ready

aliviar [ali'βjar] /**1b**/ VT (*carga*) to lighten; (*persona*) to relieve; (*dolor*) to relieve, alleviate

alivio [a'liβjo] NM alleviation, relief; **~ de luto** half-mourning

aljibe [al'xiβe] NM cistern

allá [a'ʎa] ADV (*lugar*) there; (*por ahí*) over there; (*tiempo*) then; **~ abajo** down there; **más ~** further on; **más ~ de** beyond; **¡~ tú!** that's your problem!

allanamiento [aʎana'mjento] NM (*Am Policía*) raid, search; **~ de morada** breaking and entering

allanar [aʎa'nar] /**1a**/ VT to flatten, level (out); (*igualar*) to smooth (out); (*fig*) to subdue; (*Jur*) to burgle, break into; (*Am Policía*) to raid, search; **allanarse** VR to fall down; **allanarse a** to submit to, accept

allegado, -a [aʎe'ɣaðo, a] ADJ near, close ▸ NM/F relation

allende [a'ʎende] ADV on the other side ▸ PREP: **~ los mares** beyond the seas

allí [a'ʎi] ADV there; **~ mismo** right there; **por ~** over there; (*por ese camino*) that way

alma ['alma] NF soul; (*persona*) person; (*Tec*) core; **se le cayó el ~ a los pies** he became very disheartened; **entregar el ~** to pass away; **estar con el ~ en la boca** to be scared to death; **lo siento en el ~** I am truly sorry; **tener el ~ en un hilo** to have one's heart in one's mouth; **estar como ~ en pena** to suffer; **ir como ~ que lleva el diablo** to go at breakneck speed

almacén [alma'θen] NM (*depósito*) warehouse, store; (*Mil*) magazine; (*Am*) grocer's shop, food store, grocery store (*US*); **(grandes) almacenes** NMPL department store *sg*; **~ depositario** (*Com*) depository

almacenaje [almaθe'naxe] NM storage; **~ secundario** backup storage

almacenamiento [almaθena'mjento] NM
(*Inform*) storage; **~ temporal en disco** disk
spooling

almacenar [almaθe'nar] /**1a**/ VT to store, put
in storage; (*Inform*) to store; (*proveerse*) to
stock up with

almacenero [almaθe'nero] NM
warehouseman; (*Am*) grocer, shopkeeper

almanaque [alma'nake] NM almanac

almeja [al'mexa] NF clam

almenas [al'menas] NFPL battlements

almendra [al'mendra] NF almond

almendro [al'mendro] NM almond tree

almeriense [alme'rjense] ADJ of Almería
▸ NMF native o inhabitant of Almería

almiar [al'mjar] NM haystack

almíbar [al'miβar] NM syrup

almidón [almi'ðon] NM starch

almidonado, -a [almiðo'naðo, a] ADJ starched

almidonar [almiðo'nar] /**1a**/ VT to starch

almirantazgo [almiran'taθγo] NM
admiralty

almirante [almi'rante] NM admiral

almirez [almi'reθ] NM mortar

almizcle [al'miθkle] NM musk

almizclero [almiθ'klero] NM musk deer

almohada [almo'aða] NF pillow; (*funda*)
pillowcase

almohadilla [almoa'ðiʎa] NF cushion;
(*Tec*) pad; (*Am*) pincushion; (*Inform*) hash
key, hashtag

almohadillado, -a [almoaði'ʎaðo, a] ADJ
(*acolchado*) padded

almohadón [almoa'ðon] NM large pillow

almorcé [almor'θe], **almorcemos** *etc*
[almor'θemos] VB *ver* **almorzar**

almorranas [almo'rranas] NFPL piles,
haemorrhoids (*Brit*), hemorrhoids (*US*)

almorzar [almor'θar] /**1f, 1l**/ VT: **~ una
tortilla** to have an omelette for lunch ▸ VI
to (have) lunch

almuerce *etc* [al'mwerθe] VB *ver* **almorzar**

almuerzo [al'mwerθo] VB *ver* **almorzar** ▸ NM
lunch

aló [a'lo] EXCL (*esp Am Telec*) hello!

alocado, -a [alo'kaðo, a] ADJ crazy

alojamiento [aloxa'mjento] NM lodging(s)
(*pl*); (*viviendas*) housing

alojar [alo'xar] /**1a**/ VT to lodge; **alojarse** VR:
alojarse en to stay at; (*bala*) to lodge in

alondra [a'londra] NF lark, skylark

alpaca [al'paka] NF alpaca

alpargata [alpar'γata] NF rope-soled shoe,
espadrille

Alpes ['alpes] NMPL: **los ~** the Alps

alpinismo [alpi'nismo] NM mountaineering,
climbing

alpinista [alpi'nista] NMF mountaineer,
climber

alpino, -a [al'pino, a] ADJ alpine

alpiste [al'piste] NM (*semillas*) birdseed;
(*Am fam: dinero*) dough; (*fam: alcohol*) booze

alquería [alke'ria] NF farmhouse

alquilar [alki'lar] /**1a**/ VT (*suj: propietario:
inmuebles*) to let, rent (out); (*: coche*) to hire out;
(*: TV*) to rent (out); (*suj: alquilador: inmuebles,
TV*) to rent; (*: coche*) to hire; **"se alquila
casa"** "house to let (*Brit*) o for rent (*US*)"

alquiler [alki'ler] NM renting; letting;
hiring; (*arriendo*) rent; hire charge; **de ~** for
hire; **~ de automóviles** car hire

alquimia [al'kimja] NF alchemy

alquitrán [alki'tran] NM tar

alrededor [alreðe'ðor] ADV around, about;
alrededores NMPL surroundings; **~ de** *prep*
around, about; **mirar a su ~** to look (round)
about one

Alsacia [al'saθja] NF Alsace

alta ['alta] NF (certificate of) discharge; **dar
a algn de ~** to discharge sb; **darse de ~** (*Mil*)
to join, enrol; (*Deporte*) to declare o.s. fit

altanería [altane'ria] NF haughtiness,
arrogance

altanero, -a [alta'nero, a] ADJ haughty,
arrogant

altar [al'tar] NM altar

altavoz [alta'βoθ] NM loudspeaker;
(*amplificador*) amplifier

alteración [altera'θjon] NF alteration;
(*alboroto*) disturbance; **~ del orden público**
breach of the peace

alterar [alte'rar] /**1a**/ VT to alter; to disturb;
alterarse VR (*persona*) to get upset

altercado [alter'kaðo] NM argument

alternar [alter'nar] /**1a**/ VT to alternate ▸ VI
to alternate; (*turnar*) to take turns;
alternarse VR to alternate; (*turnar*) to take
turns; **~ con** to mix with

alternativo, -a [alterna'tiβo, a] ADJ
alternative; (*alterno*) alternating ▸ NF
alternative; (*elección*) choice; **alternativas**
NFPL ups and downs; **tomar la alternativa**
(*Taur*) to become a fully-qualified bullfighter

alterno, -a [al'terno, a] ADJ (*Bot, Mat*)
alternate; (*Elec*) alternating

Alteza [al'teθa] NF (*tratamiento*) Highness

altibajos [alti'βaxos] NMPL ups and downs

altillo [al'tiʎo] NM (*Geo*) small hill; (*Am*) attic

altiplanicie [altipla'niθje] NF, **altiplano**
[alti'plano] NM high plateau

altisonante [altiso'nante] ADJ high-flown,
high-sounding

altitud [alti'tuð] NF height; (*Aviat, Geo*)
altitude; **a una ~ de** at a height of

altivez [alti'βeθ] NF haughtiness, arrogance

altivo, -a [al'tiβo, a] ADJ haughty, arrogant

alto, -a ['alto, a] ADJ high; (*persona*) tall;
(*sonido*) high, sharp; (*noble*) high, lofty;

(*Geo, clase*) upper ▸ NM halt; (*Mus*) alto; (*Geo*) hill; (*AM*) pile ▸ ADV (*estar*) high; (*hablar*) loud, loudly ▸ EXCL halt!; **la pared tiene dos metros de** ~ the wall is two metres high; **en alta mar** on the high seas; **en voz alta** in a loud voice; **las altas horas de la noche** the small (*BRIT*) o wee (*US*) hours; **en lo ~ de** at the top of; **pasar por** ~ to overlook; **altos y bajos** ups and downs; **poner la radio más** ~ to turn the radio up; **¡más ~, por favor!** louder, please!

altoparlante [altopar'lante] NM (*AM*) loudspeaker

altramuz [altra'muθ] NM lupin

altruismo [al'truismo] NM altruism

altura [al'tura] NF height; (*Naut*) depth; (*Geo*) latitude; **la pared tiene 1.80 de** ~ the wall is 1 metre 80 (cm) high; **a estas alturas** at this stage; **a esta ~ del año** at this time of the year; **estar a la ~ de las circunstancias** to rise to the occasion; **ha sido un partido de gran** ~ it has been a terrific match

alubia [a'luβja] NF bean; (*judía verde*) French bean; (*judía blanca*) cannellini bean

alucinación [aluθina'θjon] NF hallucination

alucinante [aluθi'nante] ADJ (*fam: estupendo*) great, super

alucinar [aluθi'nar] /1a/ VI to hallucinate ▸ VT to deceive; (*fascinar*) to fascinate

alud [a'luð] NM avalanche; (*fig*) flood

aludir [alu'ðir] /3a/ VI: ~ a to allude to; **darse por aludido** to take the hint; **no te des por aludido** don't take it personally

alumbrado [alum'braðo] NM lighting

alumbramiento [alumbra'mjento] NM lighting; (*Med*) childbirth, delivery

alumbrar [alum'brar] /1a/ VT to light (up) ▸ VI (*iluminar*) to give light; (*Med*) to give birth

aluminio [alu'minjo] NM aluminium (*BRIT*), aluminum (*US*)

alumnado [alum'naðo] NM (*Univ*) student body; (*Escol*) pupils pl

alumno, -a [a'lumno, a] NM/F pupil, student

alunice *etc* [alu'niθe] VB ver **alunizar**

alunizar [aluni'θar] /1f/ VI to land on the moon

alusión [alu'sjon] NF allusion

alusivo, -a [alu'siβo, a] ADJ allusive

aluvión [alu'βjon] NM (*Geo*) alluvium; (*fig*) flood; ~ **de improperios** torrent of abuse

alvéolo [al'βeolo] NM (*Anat*) alveolus; (*fig*) network

alverja [al'βerxa] NF (*AM*) pea

alza [ˈalθa] NF rise; (*Mil*) sight; **alzas fijas/graduables** fixed/adjustable sights; **al** o **en** ~ (*precio*) rising; **jugar al** ~ to speculate on a rising o bull market; **cotizarse** o **estar en** ~ to be rising

alzado, -a [al'θaðo, a] ADJ (*gen*) raised; (*Com: precio*) fixed; (: *quiebra*) fraudulent; **por un** tanto ~ for a lump sum ▸ NF (*de caballos*) height; (*Jur*) appeal

alzamiento [alθa'mjento] NM (*aumento*) rise, increase; (*acción*) lifting, raising; (*mejor postura*) higher bid; (*rebelión*) rising; (*Com*) fraudulent bankruptcy

alzar [al'θar] /1f/ VT to lift (up); (*precio, muro*) to raise; (*cuello de abrigo*) to turn up; (*Agr*) to gather in; (*Tip*) to gather; **alzarse** VR to get up, rise; (*rebelarse*) to revolt; (*Com*) to go fraudulently bankrupt; (*Jur*) to appeal; **alzarse con el premio** to carry off the prize

a.m. ABR (*AM*: = *ante meridiem*) a.m.

ama [ˈama] NF lady of the house; (*dueña*) owner; (*institutriz*) governess; (*madre adoptiva*) foster mother; ~ **de casa** housewife; ~ **de cría** o **de leche** wet-nurse; ~ **de llaves** housekeeper

amabilidad [amaβili'ðað] NF kindness; (*simpatía*) niceness

amabilísimo, -a [amaβi'lisimo, a] ADJ SUPERLATIVO *de* **amable**

amable [a'maβle] ADJ kind; nice; **es usted muy** ~ that's very kind of you

amaestrado, -a [amaes'traðo, a] ADJ (*animal*) trained; (: *en circo etc*) performing

amaestrar [amaes'trar] /1a/ VT to train

amagar [ama'ɣar] /1h/ VT, VI to threaten

amago [a'maɣo] NM threat; (*gesto*) threatening gesture; (*Med*) symptom

amague *etc* [a'maɣe] VB ver **amagar**

amainar [amai'nar] /1a/ VT (*Naut*) to lower, take in; (*fig*) to calm ▸ VI (*viento*) to die down; **amainarse** VR to drop, die down; **el viento amaina** the wind is dropping

amalgama [amal'ɣama] NF amalgam

amalgamar [amalɣa'mar] /1a/ VT to amalgamate; (*combinar*) to combine, mix

amamantar [amaman'tar] /1a/ VT to suckle, nurse

amancebarse [amanθe'βarse] /1a/ VR (*pareja*) to live together

amanecer [amane'θer] /2d/ VI to dawn; (*fig*) to appear, begin to show ▸ NM dawn; ~ **afiebrado** to wake up with a fever

amanerado, -a [amane'raðo, a] ADJ affected

amanezca *etc* [ama'neθka] VB ver **amanecer**

amansar [aman'sar] /1a/ VT to tame; (*persona*) to subdue; **amansarse** VR (*persona*) to calm down

amante [a'mante] ADJ: ~ **de** fond of ▸ NMF lover

amanuense [ama'nwense] NM (*escribiente*) scribe; (*copista*) copyist; (*Pol*) secretary

amañar [ama'ɲar] /1a/ VT (*gen*) to do skilfully; (*pey: resultado*) to alter

amaño [a'maɲo] NM (*habilidad*) skill; **amaños** NMPL (*Tec*) tools; (*fig*) tricks

amapola [ama'pola] NF poppy

amar [a'mar] /**1a**/ VT to love

amargado, -a [amar'ɣaðo, a] ADJ bitter; embittered

amargar [amar'ɣar] /**1h**/ VT to make bitter; (fig) to embitter; **amargarse** VR to become embittered

amargo, -a [a'marɣo, a] ADJ bitter

amargor [amar'ɣor] NM (sabor) bitterness; (fig) grief

amargue etc [a'marɣe] VB ver **amargar**

amargura [amar'ɣura] NF = **amargor**

amarillento, -a [amari'ʎento, a] ADJ yellowish; (tez) sallow

amarillismo [amari'ʎismo] NM (de prensa) sensationalist journalism

amarillo, -a [ama'riʎo, a] ADJ, NM yellow

amarra [a'marra] NF (Naut) mooring line; **amarras** NFPL (fig) protection sg; **tener buenas amarras** to have good connections; **soltar amarras** (Naut) to set sail

amarrado, -a [ama'rraðo, a] ADJ (AM fam) mean, stingy

amarrar [ama'rrar] /**1a**/ VT to moor; (sujetar) to tie up

amartillar [amarti'ʎar] /**1a**/ VT (fusil) to cock

amasar [ama'sar] /**1a**/ VT (masa) to knead; (mezclar) to mix, prepare; (confeccionar) to concoct

amasijo [ama'sixo] NM kneading; mixing; (fig) hotchpotch

amateur ['amatur] NMF amateur

amatista [ama'tista] NF amethyst

amazacotado, -a [amaθako'taðo, a] ADJ (terreno, arroz etc) lumpy

amazona [ama'θona] NF horsewoman

Amazonas [ama'θonas] NM: **el (río)** ~ the Amazon

ambages [am'baxes] NMPL: **sin** ~ in plain language

ámbar ['ambar] NM amber

Amberes [am'beres] NM Antwerp

ambición [ambi'θjon] NF ambition

ambicionar [ambiθjo'nar] /**1a**/ VT to aspire to

ambicioso, -a [ambi'θjoso, a] ADJ ambitious

ambidextro, -a [ambi'ðekstro, a] ADJ ambidextrous

ambientación [ambjenta'θjon] NF (Cine, Lit etc) setting; (Radio etc) sound effects pl

ambientador [ambjenta'ðor] NM air freshener

ambientar [ambjen'tar] /**1a**/ VT (gen) to give an atmosphere to; (Lit etc) to set

ambiente [am'bjente] NM (tb fig) atmosphere; (medio) environment; (AM) room

ambigüedad [ambiɣwe'ðað] NF ambiguity

ambiguo, -a [am'biɣwo, a] ADJ ambiguous

ámbito ['ambito] NM (campo) field; (fig) scope

ambos, -as ['ambos, as] ADJ PL, PRON PL both

ambulancia [ambu'lanθja] NF ambulance

ambulante [ambu'lante] ADJ travelling, itinerant; (biblioteca) mobile

ambulatorio [ambula'torio] NM state health-service clinic

ameba [a'meβa] NF amoeba

amedrentar [ameðren'tar] /**1a**/ VT to scare

amén [a'men] EXCL amen; ~ **de** prep besides, in addition to; **en un decir** ~ in the twinkling of an eye; **decir** ~ **a todo** to have no mind of one's own

amenace etc [ame'naθe] VB ver **amenazar**

amenaza [ame'naθa] NF threat

amenazar [amena'θar] /**1f**/ VT to threaten ▶ VI: ~ **con hacer** to threaten to do

amenidad [ameni'ðað] NF pleasantness

ameno, -a [a'meno, a] ADJ pleasant

América [a'merika] NF (continente) America, the Americas; (EEUU) America; (Hispanoamérica) Latin o South America; ~ **del Norte/del Sur** North/South America; ~ **Central/Latina** Central/Latin America

americanismo [amerika'nismo] NM Americanism

americano, -a [ameri'kano, a] ADJ, NM/F American; Latin o South American ▶ NF (abrigo) coat; (chaqueta) jacket

americe etc [ame'riθe] VB ver **amerizar**

amerindio, -a [ame'rindjo, a] ADJ, NM/F Amerindian, American Indian

amerizaje [ameri'θaxe] NM (Aviat) landing (on the sea)

amerizar [ameri'θar] /**1f**/ VI (Aviat) to land (on the sea)

ametralladora [ametraʎa'ðora] NF machine gun

amianto [a'mjanto] NM asbestos

amigable [ami'ɣaβle] ADJ friendly

amígdala [a'miɣðala] NF tonsil

amigdalitis [amiɣða'litis] NF tonsillitis

amigo, -a [a'miɣo, a] ADJ friendly ▶ NM/F friend; (amante) lover; ~ **de lo ajeno** thief; ~ **corresponsal** penfriend; **hacerse amigos** to become friends; **ser ~ de** to like, be fond of; **ser muy amigos** to be close friends

amigote [ami'ɣote] NM mate (BRIT), buddy

amilanar [amila'nar] /**1a**/ VT to scare; **amilanarse** VR to get scared

aminorar [amino'rar] /**1a**/ VT to diminish; (reducir) to reduce; ~ **la marcha** to slow down

amistad [amis'tað] NF friendship; **amistades** NFPL (amigos) friends

amistoso, -a [ami'stoso, a] ADJ friendly

amnesia [am'nesja] NF amnesia

amnistía [amnis'tia] NF amnesty

amnistiar [amni'stjar] /**1c**/ VT to amnesty, grant an amnesty to

amo ['amo] NM owner; (jefe) boss

amodorrarse [amoðo'rrarse] /**1a**/ VR to get sleepy

amolar [amo'lar] /**1l**/ vt to annoy; (*MÉXICO fam*) to ruin, damage

amoldar [amol'dar] /**1a**/ vt to mould; (*adaptar*) to adapt

amonestación [amonesta'θjon] nf warning; **amonestaciones** nfpl marriage banns

amonestar [amone'star] /**1a**/ vt to warn; (*Rel*) to publish the banns of

amoniaco [amo'njako] nm ammonia

amontonar [amonto'nar] /**1a**/ vt to collect, pile up; **amontonarse** vr (*gente*) to crowd together; (*acumularse*) to pile up; (*datos*) to accumulate; (*desastres*) to come one on top of another

amor [a'mor] nm love; (*amante*) lover; **hacer el ~** to make love; **~ interesado** love; **~ propio** self-respect; **por (el) ~ de Dios** for God's sake; **estar al ~ de la lumbre** to be close to the fire

amoratado, -a [amora'taðo, a] adj purple, blue with cold; (*con cardenales*) bruised

amordace etc [amor'ðaθe] vb ver **amordazar**

amordazar [amorða'θar] /**1f**/ vt to muzzle; (*fig*) to gag

amorfo, -a [a'morfo, a] adj amorphous, shapeless

amorío [amo'rio] nm (*fam*) love affair

amoroso, -a [amo'roso, a] adj affectionate, loving

amortajar [amorta'xar] /**1a**/ vt (*fig*) to shroud

amortice etc [amor'tiθe] vb ver **amortizar**

amortiguador [amortiɣwa'ðor] nm shock absorber; (*parachoques*) bumper; (*silenciador*) silencer; **amortiguadores** nmpl (*Auto*) suspension sg

amortiguar [amorti'ɣwar] /**1i**/ vt to deaden; (*ruido*) to muffle; (*color*) to soften

amortigüe etc [amor'tiɣwe] vb ver **amortiguar**

amortización [amortiθa'θjon] nf redemption; repayment; (*Com*) capital allowance

amortizar [amorti'θar] /**1f**/ vt (*Econ: bono*) to redeem; (: *capital*) to write off; (: *préstamo*) to pay off

amoscarse [amos'karse] /**1g**/ vr to get cross

amosque etc [a'moske] vb ver **amoscarse**

amotinar [amoti'nar] /**1a**/ vt to stir up, incite (to riot); **amotinarse** vr to mutiny

amparar [ampa'rar] /**1a**/ vt to protect; **ampararse** vr to seek protection; (*de la lluvia etc*) to shelter

amparo [am'paro] nm help, protection; **al ~ de** under the protection of

amperímetro [ampe'rimetro] nm ammeter

amperio [am'perjo] nm ampère, amp

ampliable [am'pljaβle] adj (*Inform*) expandable

ampliación [amplja'θjon] nf enlargement; (*extensión*) extension

ampliar [am'pljar] /**1c**/ vt to enlarge; to extend

amplificación [amplifika'θjon] nf enlargement

amplificador [amplifika'ðor] nm amplifier

amplificar [amplifi'kar] /**1g**/ vt to amplify

amplifique etc [ampli'fike] vb ver **amplificar**

amplio, -a ['ampljo, a] adj spacious; (*falda etc*) full; (*extenso*) extensive; (*ancho*) wide

amplitud [ampli'tuð] nf spaciousness; extent; (*fig*) amplitude; **~ de miras** broadmindedness; **de gran ~** far-reaching

ampolla [am'poʎa] nf blister; (*Med*) ampoule

ampolleta [ampo'ʎeta] nf (*Am*) (light) bulb

ampuloso, -a [ampu'loso, a] adj bombastic, pompous

amputar [ampu'tar] /**1a**/ vt to cut off, amputate

amueblar [amwe'βlar] /**1a**/ vt to furnish

amuleto [amu'leto] nm (lucky) charm

amurallar [amura'ʎar] /**1a**/ vt to wall up o in

anacarado, -a [anaka'raðo, a] adj mother-of-pearl cpd

anacardo [ana'karðo] nm cashew (nut)

anaconda [ana'konda] nf anaconda

anacronismo [anakro'nismo] nm anachronism

ánade ['anaðe] nm duck

anagrama [ana'ɣrama] nm anagram

anales [a'nales] nmpl annals

analfabetismo [analfaβe'tismo] nm illiteracy

analfabeto, -a [analfa'βeto, a] adj, nm/f illiterate

analgésico [anal'xesiko] nm painkiller, analgesic

analice etc [ana'liθe] vb ver **analizar**

análisis [a'nalisis] nm inv analysis; **~ de costos-beneficios** cost-benefit analysis; **~ de mercados** market research; **~ de sangre** blood test

analista [ana'lista] nmf (*gen*) analyst; (*Pol, Historia*) chronicler; **~ de sistemas** (*Inform*) systems analyst

analizar [anali'θar] /**1f**/ vt to analyse

analogía [analo'xia] nf analogy; **por ~ con** on the analogy of

analógico, -a [ana'loxiko, a] adj (*Inform*) analog; (*reloj*) analogue (BRIT), analog (US)

análogo, -a [a'naloɣo, a] adj analogous, similar

ananá [ana'na], **ananás** [ana'nas] nm pineapple

anaquel [ana'kel] nm shelf

anaranjado, -a [anaran'xaðo, a] adj orange(-coloured)

anarquía [anar'kia] nf anarchy

anarquismo [anar'kismo] NM anarchism
anarquista [anar'kista] NMF anarchist
anatematice etc [anatema'tiθe] VB ver **anatematizar**
anatematizar [anatemati'θar] /**1f**/ VT (Rel) to anathematize; (fig) to curse
anatomía [anato'mia] NF anatomy
anca ['anka] NF rump, haunch; **ancas** NFPL (fam) behind sg; **llevar a algn en ancas** to carry sb behind one
ancestral [anθes'tral] ADJ (costumbre) age-old
ancho, -a ['antʃo, a] ADJ wide; (falda) full; (fig) liberal ▶ NM width; (Ferro) gauge; **le viene muy ~ el cargo** (fig) the job is too much for him; **ponerse ~** to get conceited; **quedarse tan ~** to go on as if nothing had happened; **estar a sus anchas** to be at one's ease
anchoa [an'tʃoa] NF anchovy
anchura [an'tʃura] NF width; (amplitud) wideness
anchuroso, -a [antʃu'roso, a] ADJ wide
anciano, -a [an'θjano, a] ADJ old, aged ▶ NM/F old man/woman ▶ NM elder
ancla ['ankla] NF anchor; **levar anclas** to weigh anchor
ancladero [ankla'ðero] NM anchorage
anclar [an'klar] /**1a**/ VI to (drop) anchor
andadas [an'daðas] NFPL (aventuras) adventures; **volver a las ~** to backslide
andaderas [anda'ðeras] NFPL baby-walker sg
andadura [anda'ðura] NF gait; (de caballo) pace
Andalucía [andalu'θia] NF Andalusia
andaluz, a [anda'luθ, a] ADJ, NM/F Andalusian
andamiaje [anda'mjaxe], **andamio** [an'damjo] NM scaffold(ing)
andanada [anda'naða] NF (fig) reprimand; **soltarle a algn una ~** to give sb a rocket
andante [an'dante] ADJ: **caballero ~** knight errant
andar [an'dar] /**1p**/ VT to go, cover, travel ▶ VI to go, walk, travel; (funcionar) to go, work; (estar) to be ▶ NM walk, gait, pace; **andarse** VR (irse) to go away o off; **~ a pie/a caballo/en bicicleta** to go on foot/on horseback/by bicycle; **¡anda!** (sorpresa) go on!; **anda en** o **por los 40** he's about 40; **¿en qué andas?** what are you up to?; **andamos mal de dinero/tiempo** we're badly off for money/we're short of time; **andarse por las ramas** to beat about the bush; **no andarse con rodeos** to call a spade a spade (fam); **todo se andará** all in good time; **anda por aquí** it's round here somewhere; **~ haciendo algo** to be doing sth
andariego, -a [anda'rjeɣo, a] ADJ fond of travelling
andas ['andas] NFPL stretcher sg

andén [an'den] NM (Ferro) platform; (Naut) quayside; (Am: acera) pavement (BRIT), sidewalk (US)
Andes ['andes] NMPL: **los ~** the Andes
andinismo [andin'ismo] NM (Am) mountaineering, climbing
andino, -a [an'dino, a] ADJ Andean, of the Andes
Andorra [an'dorra] NF Andorra
andrajo [an'draxo] NM rag
andrajoso, -a [andra'xoso, a] ADJ ragged
andurriales [andu'rrjales] NMPL out-of-the-way place sg, the sticks; **en esos ~** in that godforsaken spot
anduve [an'duβe], **anduviera** etc [andu'βjera] VB ver **andar**
anécdota [a'nekðota] NF anecdote, story
anegar [ane'ɣar] /**1h**/ VT to flood; (ahogar) to drown; **anegarse** VR to drown; (hundirse) to sink
anegue etc [a'neɣe] VB ver **anegar**
anejo, -a [a'nexo, a] ADJ attached ▶ NM (Arq) annexe
anemia [a'nemja] NF anaemia
anestesia [anes'tesja] NF anaesthetic; **~ general/local** general/local anaesthetic
anestesiar [aneste'sjar] /**1b**/ VT to anaesthetize (BRIT), anesthetize (US)
anestésico [anes'tesiko] NM anaesthetic
anexar [anek'sar] /**1a**/ VT to annex; (documento) to attach; (Inform) to append
anexión [anek'sjon] NF, **anexionamiento** [aneksjona'mjento] NM annexation
anexionar [aneksjo'nar] /**1a**/ VT to annex; **anexionarse** VR: **anexionarse un país** to annex a country
anexo, -a [a'nekso, a] ADJ attached ▶ NM annexe
anfetamina [anfeta'mina] NF amphetamine
anfibio, -a [an'fiβjo, a] ADJ amphibious ▶ NM amphibian
anfiteatro [anfite'atro] NM amphitheatre; (Teat) dress circle
anfitrión, -ona [anfi'trjon, ona] NM/F host(ess)
ánfora ['anfora] NF (cántaro) amphora; (Am Pol) ballot box
ángel ['anxel] NM angel; **~ de la guarda** guardian angel; **tener ~** to have charm
Ángeles ['anxeles] NMPL: **los ~** Los Angeles
angélico, -a [an'xeliko, a], **angelical** [anxeli'kal] ADJ angelic(al)
angina [an'xina] NF (Med) inflammation of the throat; **~ de pecho** angina; **tener anginas** to have tonsillitis, have a sore throat
anglicano, -a [angli'kano, a] ADJ, NM/F Anglican

anglicismo [angli'θismo] NM anglicism
anglosajón, -ona [anglosa'xon, 'xona] ADJ, NM/F Anglo-Saxon
Angola [an'gola] NF Angola
angoleño, -a [ango'leɲo, a] ADJ, NM/F Angolan
angosto, -a [an'gosto, a] ADJ narrow
anguila [an'gila] NF eel; **anguilas** NFPL slipway sg
angula [an'gula] NF elver, baby eel
ángulo ['angulo] NM angle; (esquina) corner; (curva) bend
angustia [an'gustja] NF anguish
angustiar [angus'tjar] /1b/ VT to distress, grieve; **angustiarse** VR: **angustiarse (por)** to be distressed (at o on account of)
anhelante [ane'lante] ADJ eager; (deseoso) longing
anhelar [ane'lar] /1a/ VT to be eager for; (desear) to long for, desire ▶ VI to pant, gasp
anhelo [a'nelo] NM eagerness; desire
anhídrido [a'niðriðo] NM: ~ **carbónico** carbon dioxide
anidar [ani'ðar] /1a/ VT (acoger) to take in, shelter ▶ VI to nest; (fig) to make one's home
anilina [ani'lina] NF aniline
anilla [a'niʎa] NF ring; (las) **anillas** (Deporte) the rings
anillo [a'niʎo] NM ring; ~ **de boda** wedding ring; ~ **de compromiso** engagement ring; **venir como ~ al dedo** to suit to a tee
ánima ['anima] NF soul; **las ánimas** the Angelus (bell) sg
animación [anima'θjon] NF liveliness; (vitalidad) life; (actividad) bustle
animado, -a [ani'maðo, a] ADJ (vivo) lively; (vivaz) animated; (concurrido) bustling; (alegre) in high spirits; **dibujos animados** cartoon sg
animador, a [anima'ðor, a] NM/F (TV) host(ess), compère ▶ NF (Deporte) cheerleader
animadversión [animaðβer'sjon] NF ill-will, antagonism
animal [ani'mal] ADJ animal; (fig) stupid ▶ NM animal; (fig) fool; (bestia) brute
animalada [anima'laða] NF (gen) silly thing (to do o say); (ultraje) disgrace
animar [ani'mar] /1a/ VT (Bio) to animate, give life to; (fig) to liven up, brighten up, cheer up; (estimular) to stimulate; **animarse** VR to cheer up, feel encouraged; (decidirse) to make up one's mind
ánimo ['animo] NM (alma) soul; (mente) mind; (valentía) courage ▶ EXCL cheer up!; **cobrar ~** to take heart; **dar ~(s) a** to encourage
animoso, -a [ani'moso, a] ADJ brave; (vivo) lively
aniñado, -a [ani'ɲaðo, a] ADJ (facción) childlike; (carácter) childish

aniquilar [aniki'lar] /1a/ VT to annihilate, destroy
anís [a'nis] NM (grano) aniseed; (licor) anisette
aniversario [aniβer'sarjo] NM anniversary
Ankara [an'kara] NF Ankara
ano ['ano] NM anus
anoche [a'notʃe] ADV last night; **antes de ~** the night before last
anochecer [anotʃe'θer] /2d/ VI to get dark ▶ NM nightfall, dark; **al ~** at nightfall
anochezca etc [ano'tʃeθka] VB ver **anochecer**
anodino, -a [ano'ðino, a] ADJ dull, anodyne
anomalía [anoma'lia] NF anomaly
anonadado, -a [anona'ðaðo, a] ADJ: **estar ~** to be stunned
anonimato [anoni'mato] NM anonymity
anónimo, -a [a'nonimo, a] ADJ anonymous; (Com) limited ▶ NM (carta) anonymous letter; (: maliciosa) poison-pen letter
anorak [ano'rak] (pl **anoraks**) NM anorak
anorexia [ano'reksja] NF anorexia
anormal [anor'mal] ADJ abnormal
anotación [anota'θjon] NF note; annotation
anotar [ano'tar] /1a/ VT to note down; (comentar) to annotate
anquilosado, -a [ankilo'saðo, a] ADJ (fig) stale, out of date
anquilosamiento [ankilosa'mjento] NM (fig) paralysis, stagnation
ansia ['ansja] NF anxiety; (añoranza) yearning
ansiar [an'sjar] /1b/ VT to long for
ansiedad [ansje'ðað] NF anxiety
ansioso, -a [an'sjoso, a] ADJ anxious; (anhelante) eager; ~ **de** o **por algo** greedy for sth
antagónico, -a [anta'ɣoniko, a] ADJ antagonistic; (opuesto) contrasting
antagonista [antaɣo'nista] NMF antagonist
antaño [an'taɲo] ADV in years gone by, long ago
Antártico [an'tartiko] NM: **el (océano) ~** the Antarctic (Ocean)
Antártida [an'tartiða] NF Antarctica
ante ['ante] PREP before, in the presence of; (encarado con) faced with ▶ NM (piel) suede; ~ **todo** above all
anteanoche [antea'notʃe] ADV the night before last
anteayer [antea'jer] ADV the day before yesterday
antebrazo [ante'βraθo] NM forearm
antecámara [ante'kamara] NF (Arq) anteroom; (antesala) waiting room; (Pol) lobby
antecedente [anteθe'ðente] ADJ previous ▶ NM antecedent; **antecedentes** NMPL (profesionales) background sg; **antecedentes penales** criminal record; **no tener antecedentes** to have a clean record;

anteceder [anteθe'ðer] /**2a**/ VT to precede, go before

antecesor, a [anteθe'sor, a] NM/F predecessor

antedicho, -a [ante'ðitʃo, a] ADJ aforementioned

antelación [antela'θjon] NF: **con ~** in advance

antemano [ante'mano]: **de ~** *adv* beforehand, in advance

antena [an'tena] NF antenna; (*de televisión etc*) aerial; **~ de telefonía móvil** mobile phone mast (*BRIT*), cell tower (*US*); **~ parabólica** satellite dish

antenoche [ante'notʃe] ADV (*AM*) the night before last

anteojeras [anteo'xeras] NFPL blinkers (*BRIT*), blinders (*US*)

anteojo [ante'oxo] NM eyeglass; **anteojos** NMPL (*esp AM*) glasses, spectacles

antepasados [antepa'saðos] NMPL ancestors

antepecho [ante'petʃo] NM guardrail, parapet; (*repisa*) ledge, sill

antepondré *etc* [antepon'dre] VB *ver* **anteponer**

anteponer [antepo'ner] /**2q**/ VT to place in front of; (*fig*) to prefer

anteponga *etc* [ante'ponɣa] VB *ver* **anteponer**

anteproyecto [antepro'jekto] NM preliminary sketch; (*fig*) blueprint; (*Pol*): **~ de ley** draft bill

antepuesto, -a [ante'pwesto, a] PP *de* **anteponer**

antepuse *etc* [ante'puse] VB *ver* **anteponer**

anterior [ante'rjor] ADJ preceding, previous

anterioridad [anterjori'ðað] NF: **con ~ a** prior to, before

anteriormente [anterjor'mente] ADV previously, before

antes ['antes] ADV sooner; (*primero*) first; (*con anterioridad*) before; (*hace tiempo*) previously, once; (*más bien*) rather ▸ PREP: **~ de** before ▸ CONJ: **~ (de) que** before; **~ bien** (but) rather; **dos días ~** two days before *o* previously; **mucho/poco ~** long/shortly before; **~ muerto que esclavo** better dead than enslaved; **no quiso venir ~** she didn't want to come any earlier; **tomo el avión ~ que el barco** I take the plane rather than the boat; **~ de** *o* **que nada** (*en el tiempo*) first of all; (*indicando preferencia*) above all; **~ que yo** before me; **cuanto ~, lo ~ posible** as soon as possible; **cuanto ~ mejor** the sooner the better

antesala [ante'sala] NF anteroom

antiadherente [antiaðe'rente] ADJ non-stick

antiaéreo, -a [antia'ereo, a] ADJ anti-aircraft

antialcohólico, -a [antial'koliko, a] ADJ: **centro ~** (*Med*) detoxification unit

antibalas [anti'βalas] ADJ INV: **chaleco ~** bulletproof jacket

antibiótico [anti'βjotiko] NM antibiotic

anticaspa [anti'kaspa] ADJ INV anti-dandruff *cpd*

anticiclón [antiθi'klon] NM (*Meteorología*) anti-cyclone

anticipación [antiθipa'θjon] NF anticipation; **con 10 minutos de ~** 10 minutes early

anticipado, -a [antiθi'paðo, a] ADJ (in) advance; **por ~** in advance

anticipar [antiθi'par] /**1a**/ VT to anticipate; (*adelantar*) to bring forward; (*Com*) to advance; **anticiparse** VR: **anticiparse a su época** to be ahead of one's time

anticipo [anti'θipo] NM (*Com*) advance; *ver tb* **anticipación**

anticonceptivo, -a [antikonθep'tiβo, a] ADJ, NM contraceptive; **métodos anticonceptivos** methods of birth control

anticongelante [antikonxe'lante] NM antifreeze

anticonstitucional [antikonstituθjo'nal] ADJ unconstitutional

anticuado, -a [anti'kwaðo, a] ADJ out-of-date, old-fashioned; (*desusado*) obsolete

anticuario [anti'kwarjo] NM antique dealer

anticuerpo [anti'kwerpo] NM (*Med*) antibody

antidemocrático, -a [antiðemo'kratiko, a] ADJ undemocratic

antideportivo, -a [antiðepor'tiβo, a] ADJ unsporting

antidepresivo [antiðepre'siβo] NM antidepressant

antideslumbrante [antiðeslum'brante] ADJ (*Inform*) anti-dazzle

antidoping [anti'ðopin] ADJ INV anti-drug; **control ~** drugs test

antídoto [an'tiðoto] NM antidote

antidroga [anti'ðroɣa] ADJ INV anti-drug; **brigada ~** drug squad

antiestético, -a [anties'tetiko, a] ADJ unsightly

antifaz [anti'faθ] NM mask; (*velo*) veil

antigás [anti'gas] ADJ INV: **careta ~** gas mask

antiglobalización [antiglobaliθa'θjon] NF anti-globalization; **manifestantes ~** anti-globalization protesters

antiglobalizador, a [antiglobaliθa'ðor, a] ADJ anti-globalization *cpd*

antigualla [anti'ɣwaʎa] NF antique; (*reliquia*) relic; **antiguallas** NFPL old things

antiguamente [antiɣwa'mente] ADV formerly; (*hace mucho tiempo*) long ago

antigüedad [antiɣwe'ðað] NF antiquity; (*artículo*) antique; (*rango*) seniority

antiguo, -a [an'tiɣwo, a] ADJ old, ancient; (*que fue*) former; **a la antigua** in the old-fashioned way

antihigiénico, -a [anti'xjeniko, a] ADJ unhygienic

antihistamínico, -a [antista'miniko, a] ADJ, NM antihistamine

antiinflacionista [antinflaθjo'nista] ADJ anti-inflationary, counter-inflationary

antillano, -a [anti'ʎano, a] ADJ, NM/F West Indian

Antillas [an'tiʎas] NFPL: **las ~** the West Indies, the Antilles; **el mar de las ~** the Caribbean Sea

antílope [an'tilope] NM antelope

antimonopolios [antimono'poljos] ADJ INV: **ley ~** anti-trust law

antinatural [antinatu'ral] ADJ unnatural

antiparras [anti'parras] NFPL (*fam*) specs

antipatía [antipa'tia] NF antipathy, dislike

antipático, -a [anti'patiko, a] ADJ disagreeable, unpleasant

Antípodas [an'tipoðas] NFPL: **las ~** the Antipodes

antiquísimo, -a [anti'kisimo, a] ADJ ancient

antirreglamentario, -a [antirreɣlamen'tarjo, a] ADJ (*gen*) unlawful; (*Pol etc*) unconstitutional

antirrobo [anti'rroβo] NM (*tb*: **dispositivo antirrobo**: *para casas etc*) burglar alarm; (*: para coches*) car alarm ▶ ADJ INV (*alarma etc*) anti-theft

antisemita [antise'mita] ADJ anti-Semitic ▶ NMF anti-Semite

antiséptico, -a [anti'septiko, a] ADJ antiseptic ▶ NM antiseptic

antisistema [antisis'tema] ADJ INV anticapitalist

antiterrorismo [antiterro'rismo] NM counterterrorism

antiterrorista [antiterro'rista] ADJ antiterrorist, counterterrorist; **la lucha ~** the fight against terrorism

antítesis [an'titesis] NF INV antithesis

antivírico, -a [anti'βiriko, a] ADJ (*Med*) antiviral

antivirus [anti'birus] NM INV (*Inform*) antivirus program

antojadizo, -a [antoxa'ðiθo, a] ADJ capricious

antojarse [anto'xarse] /1a/ VR (*desear*): **se me antoja comprarlo** I have a mind to buy it; (*pensar*): **se me antoja que ...** I have a feeling that ...

antojo [an'toxo] NM caprice, whim; (*rosa*) birthmark; (*lunar*) mole; **hacer a su ~** to do as one pleases

antología [antolo'xia] NF anthology

antonomasia [antono'masja] NF: **por ~** par excellence

antorcha [an'tortʃa] NF torch

antro ['antro] NM cavern; **~ de corrupción** (*fig*) den of iniquity

antropófago, -a [antro'pofaɣo, a] ADJ, NM/F cannibal

antropología [antropolo'xia] NF anthropology

antropólogo, -a [antro'poloɣo, a] NM/F anthropologist

anual [a'nwal] ADJ annual

anualidad [anwali'ðað] NF annuity, annual payment; **~ vitalicia** life annuity

anuario [a'nwarjo] NM yearbook

anublado, -a [anu'βlaðo, a] ADJ overcast

anudar [anu'ðar] /1a/ VT to knot, tie; (*unir*) to join; **anudarse** VR to get tied up; **se me anudó la voz** I got a lump in my throat

anulación [anula'θjon] NF (*de un matrimonio*) annulment; (*cancelación*) cancellation; (*de una ley*) repeal

anular [anu'lar] /1a/ VT (*contrato*) to annul, cancel; (*suscripción*) to cancel; (*ley*) to repeal ▶ NM ring finger

anunciación [anunθja'θjon] NF announcement; **A~** (*Rel*) Annunciation

anunciante [anun'θjante] NMF (*Com*) advertiser

anunciar [anun'θjar] /1b/ VT to announce; (*proclamar*) to proclaim; (*Com*) to advertise

anuncio [a'nunθjo] NM announcement; (*señal*) sign; (*Com*) advertisement; (*cartel*) poster; (*Teat*) bill; **anuncios por palabras** classified ads

anverso [am'berso] NM obverse

anzuelo [an'θwelo] NM hook; (*para pescar*) fish hook; **tragar el ~** to swallow the bait

añadido [aɲa'ðiðo] NM addition

añadidura [aɲaði'ðura] NF addition, extra; **por ~** besides, in addition

añadir [aɲa'ðir] /3a/ VT to add

añejo, -a [a'ɲexo, a] ADJ old; (*vino*) mature; (*jamón*) well-cured

añicos [a'ɲikos] NMPL: **hacer ~** to smash, shatter; **hacerse ~** to smash, shatter

añil [a'ɲil] NM (*Bot, color*) indigo

año ['aɲo] NM year; **¡Feliz A~ Nuevo!** Happy New Year!; **tener 15 años** to be 15 (years old); **los años 80** the eighties; **~ bisiesto/ escolar/fiscal/sabático** leap/school/tax/ sabbatical year; **~ fiscal** fiscal o tax year; **estar de buen ~** to be in good shape; **en el ~ de la nana** in the year dot; **el ~ que viene** next year

añoranza [aɲo'ranθa] NF nostalgia; (*anhelo*) longing

añorar [aɲo'rar] /1a/ VT to long for

añoso, -a [a'ɲoso, a] ADJ ancient, old

aovado, -a [ao'βaðo, a] ADJ oval

aovar [ao'βar] /1a/ VI to lay eggs

apa ['apa] EXCL (*Am*) goodness me!, good gracious!

apabullar [apaβu'ʎar] /**1a**/ VT (*lit, fig*) to crush

apacentar [apaθen'tar] /**1j**/ VT to pasture, graze

apacible [apa'θiβle] ADJ gentle, mild

apaciente *etc* [apa'θjente] VB *ver* **apacentar**

apaciguar [apaθi'ɣwar] /**1i**/ VT to pacify, calm (down)

apacigüe *etc* [apa'θiɣwe] VB *ver* **apaciguar**

apadrinar [apaðri'nar] /**1a**/ VT to sponsor, support; (*Rel: niño*) to be godfather to

apagado, -a [apa'ɣaðo, a] ADJ (*volcán*) extinct; (*color*) dull; (*voz*) quiet; (*sonido*) muted, muffled; (*persona: apático*) listless; **estar ~** (*fuego, luz*) to be out; (*radio, TV etc*) to be off

apagar [apa'ɣar] /**1h**/ VT to put out; (*color*) to tone down; (*sonido*) to silence, muffle; (*sed*) to quench; (*Elec, Radio, TV*) to turn off; (*Inform*) to toggle off; **apagarse** VR (*luz, fuego*) to go out; (*sonido*) to die away; (*pasión*) to wither; **~ el sistema** (*Inform*) to close *o* shut down

apagón [apa'ɣon] NM blackout, power cut

apague *etc* [apa'ɣe] VB *ver* **apagar**

apaisado, -a [apai'saðo, a] ADJ (*papel*) landscape *cpd*

apalabrar [apala'βrar] /**1a**/ VT to agree to; (*obrero*) to engage

Apalaches [apa'latʃes] NMPL: (**Montes**) **~** Appalachians

apalear [apale'ar] /**1a**/ VT to beat, thrash; (*Agr*) to winnow

apantallar [apanta'ʎar] /**1a**/ VT (*Am*) to impress

apañado, -a [apa'ɲaðo, a] ADJ (*mañoso*) resourceful; (*arreglado*) tidy; (*útil*) handy

apañar [apa'ɲar] /**1a**/ VT to pick up; (*asir*) to take hold of, grasp; (*reparar*) to mend, patch up; **apañarse** VR to manage, get along; **apañárselas por su cuenta** to look after number one (*fam*)

apaño [a'paɲo] NM (*Costura*) patch; (*maña*) skill; **esto no tiene ~** there's no answer to this one

apapachar [apapa'tʃar] /**1a**/ VT (*Am fam*) to cuddle, hug

aparador [apara'ðor] NM sideboard; (*Am: escaparate*) shop window

aparato [apa'rato] NM apparatus; (*máquina*) machine; (*doméstico*) appliance; (*boato*) ostentation; (*Inform*) device; **al ~** (*Telec*) speaking; **~ de facsímil** facsimile (machine), fax; **~ respiratorio** respiratory system; **~ digestivo** digestive system; **aparatos de mando** (*Aviat etc*) controls

aparatoso, -a [apara'toso, a] ADJ showy, ostentatious

aparcamiento [aparka'mjento] NM car park (*Brit*), parking lot (*US*); **~ disuasorio** park and ride

aparcar [apar'kar] /**1g**/ VT, VI to park

aparear [apare'ar] /**1a**/ VT (*objetos*) to pair, match; (*animales*) to mate; **aparearse** VR to form a pair; to mate

aparecer [apare'θer] /**2d**/ VI to appear; **aparecerse** VR to appear; **apareció borracho** he turned up drunk

aparejado, -a [apare'xaðo, a] ADJ fit, suitable; **ir ~ con** to go hand in hand with; **llevar** *o* **traer ~** to involve

aparejador, a [aparexa'ðor, a] NM/F (*Arq*) quantity surveyor

aparejar [apare'xar] /**1a**/ VT to prepare; (*caballo*) to saddle, harness; (*Naut*) to fit out, rig out

aparejo [apa'rexo] NM preparation; (*de caballo*) harness; (*Naut*) rigging; (*de poleas*) block and tackle

aparentar [aparen'tar] /**1a**/ VT (*edad*) to look; (*fingir*): **~ tristeza** to pretend to be sad

aparente [apa'rente] ADJ apparent; (*adecuado*) suitable

aparezca *etc* [apa'reθka] VB *ver* **aparecer**

aparición [apari'θjon] NF appearance; (*de libro*) publication; (*de fantasma*) apparition

apariencia [apa'rjenθja] NF (outward) appearance; **en ~** outwardly, seemingly

aparque *etc* [a'parke] VB *ver* **aparcar**

apartado, -a [apar'taðo, a] ADJ separate; (*lejano*) remote ▶ NM (*tipográfico*) paragraph; **~ de correos** (*Esp*), **~ postal** (*Am*) post office box

apartamento [aparta'mento] NM apartment, flat (*Brit*)

apartamiento [aparta'mjento] NM separation; (*aislamiento*) remoteness; (*Am*) apartment, flat (*Brit*)

apartar [apar'tar] /**1a**/ VT to separate; (*quitar*) to remove; (*Minería*) to extract; **apartarse** VR (*separarse*) to separate, part; (*irse*) to move away; (*mantenerse aparte*) to keep away

aparte [a'parte] ADV (*separadamente*) separately; (*además*) besides ▶ PREP: **~ de** apart from ▶ NM (*Teat*) aside; (*tipográfico*) new paragraph; **"punto y ~"** "new paragraph"

aparthotel [aparto'tel] NM serviced apartments

apasionado, -a [apasjo'naðo, a] ADJ passionate; (*pey*) biassed, prejudiced ▶ NM/F admirer

apasionante [apasjo'nante] ADJ exciting

apasionar [apasjo'nar] /**1a**/ VT to excite; **apasionarse** VR to get excited; **le apasiona el fútbol** she's crazy about football

apatía [apa'tia] NF apathy

apático, -a [a'patiko, a] ADJ apathetic

apátrida [a'patriða] ADJ stateless

Apdo. NM ABR (= *Apartado (de Correos)*) P.O. Box

apeadero [apea'ðero] NM halt, stopping place

apearse [ape'arse] /**1a**/ VR (*jinete*) to dismount; (*bajarse*) to get down o out; (*de coche*) to get out, alight; **no ~ del burro** to refuse to climb down

apechugar [apetʃu'ɣar] /**1h**/ VI: **~ con algo** to face up to sth

apechugue *etc* [ape'tʃuɣe] VB *ver* **apechugar**

apedrear [apeðre'ar] /**1a**/ VT to stone

apegarse [ape'ɣarse] /**1h**/ VR: **~ a** to become attached to

apego [a'peɣo] NM attachment, devotion

apegue *etc* [a'peɣe] VB *ver* **apegarse**

apelación [apela'θjon] NF appeal

apelar [ape'lar] /**1a**/ VI to appeal; **~ a** (*fig*) to resort to

apelativo [apela'tiβo] NM (*Ling*) appellative; (*Am*) surname

apellidar [apeʎi'ðar] /**1a**/ VT to call, name; **apellidarse** VR: **se apellida Pérez** her (sur)name's Pérez

apellido [ape'ʎiðo] NM surname; *see note*

> In the Spanish-speaking world most people use two *apellidos*, the first being their father's first surname, and the second their mother's first surname: eg the children of Juan García López, married to Carmen Pérez Rodríguez would have as their surname García Pérez. Married women retain their own surname(s) and sometimes add their husband's first surname on to theirs: eg Carmen Pérez de García. She could also be referred to as (la) Señora de García. In Latin America it is usual for the second surname to be shortened to an initial in correspondence eg: Juan García L.

apelmazado, -a [apelma'θaðo, a] ADJ compact, solid

apelotonar [apeloto'nar] /**1a**/ VT to roll into a ball; **apelotonarse** VR (*gente*) to crowd together

apenar [ape'nar] /**1a**/ VT to grieve, trouble; (*Am: avergonzar*) to embarrass; **apenarse** VR to grieve; (*Am: avergonzarse*) to be embarrassed

apenas [a'penas] ADV scarcely, hardly ▶ CONJ as soon as, no sooner

apéndice [a'pendiθe] NM appendix

apendicitis [apendi'θitis] NF appendicitis

Apeninos [ape'ninos] NMPL Apennines

apercibimiento [aperθiβi'mjento] NM (*aviso*) warning

apercibir [aperθi'βir] /**3a**/ VT to prepare; (*avisar*) to warn; (*Jur*) to summon; (*Am*) to notice, see; **apercibirse** VR to get ready; **apercibirse de** to notice

aperitivo [aperi'tiβo] NM (*bebida*) aperitif; (*comida*) appetizer

apero [a'pero] NM (*Agr*) implement; **aperos** NMPL farm equipment *sg*

apertura [aper'tura] NF (*gen*) opening; (*Pol*) openness, liberalization; (*Teat etc*) beginning; **~ de un juicio hipotecario** (*Com*) foreclosure

aperturismo [apertu'rismo] NM (*Pol*) (policy of) liberalization

apesadumbrar [apesaðum'brar] /**1a**/ VT to grieve, sadden; **apesadumbrarse** VR to distress o.s.

apestar [apes'tar] /**1a**/ VT to infect ▶ VI: **~ (a)** to stink (of)

apestoso, -a [apes'toso, a] ADJ (*hediondo*) stinking; (*asqueroso*) sickening

apetecer [apete'θer] /**2d**/ VT: **¿te apetece una tortilla?** do you fancy an omelette?

apetecible [apete'θiβle] ADJ desirable; (*comida*) appetizing

apetezca *etc* [ape'teθka] VB *ver* **apetecer**

apetito [ape'tito] NM appetite

apetitoso, -a [apeti'toso, a] ADJ (*gustoso*) appetizing; (*fig*) tempting

apiadarse [apja'ðarse] /**1a**/ VR: **~ de** to take pity on

ápice ['apiθe] NM apex; (*fig*) whit, iota; **ni un ~** not a whit; **no ceder un ~** not to budge an inch

apicultor, a [apikul'tor, a] NM/F beekeeper, apiarist

apicultura [apikul'tura] NF beekeeping

apiladora [apila'ðora] NF (*para máquina impresora*) stacker

apilar [api'lar] /**1a**/ VT to pile o heap up; **apilarse** VR to pile up

apiñado, -a [api'ɲaðo, a] ADJ (*apretado*) packed

apiñar [api'ɲar] /**1a**/ VT to crowd; **apiñarse** VR to crowd o press together

apio ['apjo] NM celery

apisonadora [apisona'ðora] NF (*máquina*) steamroller

aplacar [apla'kar] /**1g**/ VT to placate; **aplacarse** VR to calm down

aplace *etc* [a'plaθe] VB *ver* **aplazar**

aplanamiento [aplana'mjento] NM smoothing, levelling

aplanar [apla'nar] /**1a**/ VT to smooth, level; (*allanar*) to roll flat, flatten; **aplanarse** VR (*edificio*) to collapse; (*persona*) to get discouraged

aplaque *etc* [a'plake] VB *ver* **aplacar**

aplastante [aplas'tante] ADJ overwhelming; (*lógica*) compelling

aplastar [aplas'tar] /**1a**/ VT to squash (flat); (*fig*) to crush

aplatanarse [aplata'narse] /**1a**/ VR to get lethargic

27

aplaudir [aplau'ðir] /**3a**/ vt to applaud

aplauso [a'plauso] nm applause; (fig) approval, acclaim

aplazamiento [aplaθa'mjento] nm postponement

aplazar [apla'θar] /**1f**/ vt to postpone, defer

aplicación [aplika'θjon] nf application; (para móvil, internet) app; (esfuerzo) effort; **aplicaciones de gestión** business applications

aplicado, -a [apli'kaðo, a] adj diligent, hard-working

aplicar [apli'kar] /**1g**/ vt (ejecutar) to apply; (poner en vigor) to put into effect; (esfuerzos) to devote; **aplicarse** vr to apply o.s.

aplique etc [a'plike] vb ver **aplicar** ▶ nm wall light o lamp

aplomo [a'plomo] nm aplomb, self-assurance

apocado, -a [apo'kaðo, a] adj timid

apocamiento [apoka'mjento] nm timidity; (depresión) depression

apocarse [apo'karse] /**1g**/ vr to feel small o humiliated

apocopar [apoko'par] /**1a**/ vt (Ling) to shorten

apócope [a'pokope] nf apocopation; **gran es ~ de grande** "gran" is the shortened form of "grande"

apócrifo, -a [a'pokrifo, a] adj apocryphal

apodar [apo'ðar] /**1a**/ vt to nickname

apoderado [apoðe'raðo] nm agent, representative

apoderar [apoðe'rar] /**1a**/ vt to authorize, empower; (Jur) to grant (a) power of attorney to; **apoderarse** vr: **apoderarse de** to take possession of

apodo [a'poðo] nm nickname

apogeo [apo'xeo] nm peak, summit

apolillado, -a [apoli'ʎaðo, a] adj moth-eaten

apolillarse [apoli'ʎarse] /**1a**/ vr to get moth-eaten

apología [apolo'xia] nf eulogy; (defensa) defence

apoltronarse [apoltro'narse] /**1a**/ vr to get lazy

apoplejía [apople'xia] nf apoplexy, stroke

apoque etc [a'poke] vb ver **apocarse**

apoquinar [apoki'nar] /**1a**/ vt (fam) to cough up, fork out

aporrear [aporre'ar] /**1a**/ vt to beat (up)

aportación [aporta'θjon] nf contribution

aportar [apor'tar] /**1a**/ vt to contribute ▶ vi to reach port; **aportarse** vr (Am: llegar) to arrive, come

aposentar [aposen'tar] /**1a**/ vt to lodge, put up

aposento [apo'sento] nm lodging; (habitación) room

apósito [a'posito] nm (Med) dressing

aposta [a'posta] adv deliberately, on purpose

apostar [apos'tar] /**1a, 1l**/ vt to bet, stake; (tropas etc) to station, post ▶ vi to bet

apostatar [aposta'tar] /**1a**/ (Rel) to apostatize; (fig) to change sides

a posteriori [aposte'rjori] adv at a later date o stage; (Filosofía) a posteriori

apostilla [apos'tiʎa] nf note, comment

apóstol [a'postol] nm apostle

apóstrofo [a'postrofo] nm apostrophe

apostura [apos'tura] nf neatness, elegance

apoteósico, -a [apote'osiko, a] adj tremendous

apoyar [apo'jar] /**1a**/ vt to lean, rest; (fig) to support, back; **apoyarse** vr: **apoyarse en** to lean on

apoyo [a'pojo] nm support, backing

apreciable [apre'θjaβle] adj considerable; (fig) esteemed

apreciación [apreθja'θjon] nf appreciation; (Com) valuation

apreciar [apre'θjar] /**1b**/ vt to evaluate, assess; (Com) to appreciate, value; (persona) to respect; (tamaño) to gauge, assess; (detalles) to notice ▶ vi (Econ) to appreciate

aprecio [a'preθjo] nm valuation, estimate; (fig) appreciation

aprehender [apreen'der] /**2a**/ vt to apprehend, detain; (ver) to see, observe

aprehensión [apreen'sjon] nf detention, capture

apremiante [apre'mjante] adj urgent, pressing

apremiar [apre'mjar] /**1b**/ vt to compel, force ▶ vi to be urgent, press

apremio [a'premjo] nm urgency; **~ de pago** demand note

aprender [apren'der] /**2a**/ vt, vi to learn; **~ a conducir** to learn to drive; **aprenderse** vr: **aprenderse algo de memoria** to learn sth (off) by heart

aprendiz, a [apren'diθ, a] nm/f apprentice; (principiante) learner, trainee; **~ de comercio** business trainee

aprendizaje [aprendi'θaxe] nm apprenticeship

aprensión [apren'sjon] nm apprehension, fear

aprensivo, -a [apren'siβo, a] adj apprehensive

apresar [apre'sar] /**1a**/ vt to seize; (capturar) to capture

aprestar [apres'tar] /**1a**/ vt to prepare, get ready; (Tec) to prime, size; **aprestarse** vr to get ready

apresto [a'presto] nm (gen) preparation; (sustancia) size

apresurado, -a [apresu'raðo, a] adj hurried, hasty

apresuramiento [apresura'mjento] NM hurry, haste

apresurar [apresu'rar] /**1a**/ VT to hurry, accelerate; **apresurarse** VR to hurry, make haste; **me apresuré a sugerir que ...** I hastily suggested that ...

apretado, -a [apre'taðo, a] ADJ tight; (*escritura*) cramped

apretar [apre'tar] /**1j**/ VT to squeeze, press; (*mano*) to clasp; (*dientes*) to grit; (*Tec*) to tighten; (*presionar*) to press together, pack ▶ VI to be too tight; **apretarse** VR to crowd together; **~ la mano a algn** to shake sb's hand; **~ el paso** to quicken one's step

apretón [apre'ton] NM squeeze; **~ de manos** handshake

aprieto [a'prjeto] VB *ver* **apretar** ▶ NM squeeze; (*dificultad*) difficulty, predicament; **estar en un ~** to be in a fix; **ayudar a algn a salir de un ~** to help sb out of trouble

a priori [apri'ori] ADV beforehand; (*Filosofía*) a priori

aprisa [a'prisa] ADV quickly, hurriedly

aprisionar [aprisjo'nar] /**1a**/ VT to imprison

aprobación [aproβa'θjon] NF approval

aprobado [apro'βaðo] NM (*nota*) pass mark

aprobar [apro'βar] /**1l**/ VT to approve (of); (*examen, materia*) to pass ▶ VI to pass

apropiación [apropja'θjon] NF appropriation

apropiado, -a [apro'pjaðo, a] ADJ appropriate, suitable

apropiarse [apro'pjarse] /**1b**/ VR: **~ de** to appropriate

aprovechado, -a [aproβe'tʃaðo, a] ADJ industrious, hardworking; (*económico*) thrifty; (*pey*) unscrupulous

aprovechamiento [aproβetʃa'mjento] NM use, exploitation

aprovechar [aproβe'tʃar] /**1a**/ VT to use; (*explotar*) to exploit; (*experiencia*) to profit from; (*oferta, oportunidad*) to take advantage of ▶ VI to progress, improve; **aprovecharse** VR: **aprovecharse de** to make use of; (*pey*) to take advantage of; **¡que aproveche!** enjoy your meal!

aprovisionar [aproβisjo'nar] /**1a**/ VT to supply

aproximación [aproksima'θjon] NF approximation; (*de lotería*) consolation prize

aproximadamente [aproksimaða'mente] ADV approximately

aproximado, -a [aproksi'maðo, a] ADJ approximate

aproximar [aproksi'mar] /**1a**/ VT to bring nearer; **aproximarse** VR to come near, approach

apruebe *etc* [a'prweβe] VB *ver* **aprobar**

aptitud [apti'tuð] NF aptitude; (*capacidad*) ability; **~ para los negocios** business sense

apto, -a ['apto, a] ADJ (*hábil*) capable; (*apropiado*): **~ (para)** fit (for), suitable (for); **~/no ~ para menores** (*Cine*) suitable/ unsuitable for children

apuesto, -a [a'pwesto, a] VB *ver* **apostar** ▶ ADJ neat, elegant ▶ NF bet, wager

apuntador [apunta'ðor] NM prompter

apuntalar [apunta'lar] /**1a**/ VT to prop up

apuntar [apun'tar] /**1a**/ VT (*con arma*) to aim at; (*con dedo*) to point at *o* to; (*anotar*) to note (down); (*datos*) to record; (*Teat*) to prompt; **apuntarse** VR (*Deporte: tanto, victoria*) to score; (*Escol*) to enrol; **~ una cantidad en la cuenta de algn** to charge a sum to sb's account; **apuntarse en un curso** to enrol on a course; **¡yo me apunto!** count me in!

apunte [a'punte] NM note; (*Teat: voz*) prompt; (*: texto*) prompt book

apuñalar [apuɲa'lar] /**1a**/ VT to stab

apurado, -a [apu'raðo, a] ADJ needy; (*difícil*) difficult; (*peligroso*) dangerous; (*Am: con prisa*) hurried, rushed; **estar en una situación apurada** to be in a tight spot; **estar ~** to be in a hurry

apurar [apu'rar] /**1a**/ VT (*agotar*) to drain; (*recursos*) to use up; (*molestar*) to annoy; **apurarse** VR (*preocuparse*) to worry; (*esp Am: darse prisa*) to hurry

apuro [a'puro] NM (*aprieto*) fix, jam; (*escasez*) want, hardship; (*vergüenza*) embarrassment; (*Am: prisa*) haste, urgency

aquejado, -a [ake'xaðo, a] ADJ: **~ de** (*Med*) afflicted by

aquejar [ake'xar] /**1a**/ VT (*afligir*) to distress; **le aqueja una grave enfermedad** he suffers from a serious disease

aquel, aquella, aquellos, -as [a'kel, a'keʎa, a'keʎos, as] ADJ that, those *pl* ▶ PRON that (one), those (ones) *pl*

aquél, aquélla, aquéllos, -as [a'kel, a'keʎa, a'keʎos, as] PRON that (one), those (ones) *pl*

aquello [a'keʎo] PRON that, that business

aquí [a'ki] ADV (*lugar*) here; (*tiempo*) now; **~ arriba** up here; **~ mismo** right here; **~ yace** here lies; **de ~ a siete días** a week from now

aquietar [akje'tar] /**1a**/ VT to quieten (down), calm (down)

Aquisgrán [akis'ɣran] NM Aachen, Aix-la-Chapelle

A.R. ABR (= *Alteza Real*) R.H.

ara ['ara] NF (*altar*) altar; **en aras de** for the sake of

árabe ['araβe] ADJ Arab, Arabian, Arabic ▶ NMF Arab ▶ NM (*Ling*) Arabic

Arabia [a'raβja] NF Arabia; **~ Saudí** *o* **Saudita** Saudi Arabia

arábigo, -a [a'raβiɣo, a] ADJ Arab, Arabian, Arabic

arácnido [a'rakniðo] NM arachnid

arado [a'raðo] NM plough

Aragón [ara'ɣon] NM Aragon

aragonés, -esa [araɣo'nes, esa] ADJ, NM/F Aragonese ▶ NM (Ling) Aragonese

arancel [aran'θel] NM tariff, duty; **~ de aduanas** (customs) duty

arandela [aran'dela] NF (Tec) washer; (chorrera) frill

araña [a'raɲa] NF (Zool) spider; (lámpara) chandelier

arañar [ara'ɲar] /1a/ VT to scratch

arañazo [ara'ɲaθo] NM scratch

arar [a'rar] /1a/ VT to plough, till

araucano, -a [arau'kano, a] ADJ, NM/F Araucanian

arbitraje [arβi'traxe] NM arbitration

arbitrar [arβi'trar] /1a/ VT to arbitrate in; (recursos) to bring together; (Deporte) to referee ▶ VI to arbitrate

arbitrariedad [arβitrarje'ðað] NF arbitrariness; (acto) arbitrary act

arbitrario, -a [arβi'trarjo, a] ADJ arbitrary

arbitrio [ar'βitrjo] NM free will; (Jur) adjudication, decision; **dejar al ~ de algn** to leave to sb's discretion

árbitro ['arβitro] NM arbitrator; (Deporte) referee; (Tenis) umpire

árbol ['arβol] NM (Bot) tree; (Naut) mast; (Tec) axle, shaft; **~ de Navidad** Christmas tree

arbolado, -a [arβo'laðo, a] ADJ wooded; (camino) tree-lined ▶ NM woodland

arboladura [arβola'ðura] NF rigging

arbolar [arβo'lar] /1a/ VT to hoist, raise

arboleda [arβo'leða] NF grove, plantation

arbusto [ar'βusto] NM bush, shrub

arca ['arka] NF chest, box; **A~ de la Alianza** Ark of the Covenant; **A~ de Noé** Noah's Ark

arcada [ar'kaða] NF arcade; (de puente) arch, span; **arcadas** NFPL (náuseas) retching sg

arcaico, -a [ar'kaiko, a] ADJ archaic

arce ['arθe] NM maple tree

arcén [ar'θen] NM (de autopista) hard shoulder; (de carretera) verge

archiconocido, -a [artʃikono'θiðo, a] ADJ extremely well-known

archipiélago [artʃi'pjelaɣo] NM archipelago

archisabido, -a [artʃisa'βiðo, a] ADJ extremely well-known

archivador [artʃiβa'ðor] NM filing cabinet; **~ colgante** suspension file

archivar [artʃi'βar] /1a/ VT to file (away); (Inform) to archive

archivo [ar'tʃiβo] NM archive(s) pl; (Inform) file; **A~ Nacional** Public Record Office; **archivos policíacos** police files; **nombre de ~** (Inform) filename; **~ adjunto** (Inform) attachment; **~ de seguridad** (Inform) backup file

arcilla [ar'θiʎa] NF clay

arco ['arko] NM arch; (Mat) arc; (Mil, Mus) bow; (Am Deporte) goal; **~ iris** rainbow

arcón [ar'kon] NM large chest

arder [ar'ðer] /2a/ VT, VI to burn; **~ sin llama** to smoulder; **estar que arde** (persona) to fume

ardid [ar'ðið] NM ploy, trick

ardiente [ar'ðjente] ADJ ardent

ardilla [ar'ðiʎa] NF squirrel

ardor [ar'ðor] NM (calor) heat, warmth; (fig) ardour; **~ de estómago** heartburn

ardoroso, -a [arðo'roso, a] ADJ passionate

arduo, -a ['arðwo, a] ADJ arduous

área ['area] NF area; (Deporte) penalty area

arena [a'rena] NF sand; (de una lucha) arena

arenal [are'nal] NM (terreno arenoso) sandy area; (arena movediza) quicksand

arenga [a'renga] NF (fam) sermon

arengar [aren'gar] /1h/ VT to harangue

arengue etc [a'renge] VB ver **arengar**

arenillas [are'niʎas] NFPL (Med) stones

arenisca [are'niska] NF sandstone; (cascajo) grit

arenoso, -a [are'noso, a] ADJ sandy

arenque [a'renke] NM herring

arepa [a'repa] NF (Am) corn pancake

arete [a'rete] NM (Am) earring

argamasa [arɣa'masa] NF mortar, plaster

Argel [ar'xel] N Algiers

Argelia [ar'xelja] NF Algeria

argelino, -a [arxe'lino, a] ADJ, NM/F Algerian

Argentina [arxen'tina] NF: **(la) ~** Argentina, the Argentine

argentino, -a [arxen'tino, a] ADJ Argentinian; (de plata) silvery ▶ NM/F Argentinian

argolla [ar'ɣoʎa] NF (large) ring; (Am: de matrimonio) wedding ring

argot [ar'ɣo] NM (pl **argots** [ar'ɣo, ar'ɣos]) slang

argucia [ar'ɣuθja] NF subtlety, sophistry

argüir [ar'ɣwir] /3g/ VT to deduce; (discutir) to argue; (indicar) to indicate, imply; (censurar) to reproach ▶ VI to argue

argumentación [arɣumenta'θjon] NF (line of) argument

argumentar [arɣumen'tar] /1a/ VT, VI to argue

argumento [arɣu'mento] NM argument; (razonamiento) reasoning; (de novela etc) plot; (Cine, TV) storyline

arguyendo etc [arɣu'jendo] VB ver **argüir**

aria ['arja] NF aria

aridez [ari'ðeθ] NF aridity, dryness

árido, -a ['ariðo, a] ADJ arid, dry; **áridos** NMPL dry goods

Aries ['arjes] NM Aries

ariete [a'rjete] NM battering ram

ario, -a ['arjo, a] ADJ Aryan

arisco, -a [a'risko, a] ADJ surly; (*insociable*) unsociable

aristocracia [aristo'kraθja] NF aristocracy

aristócrata [aris'tokrata] NMF aristocrat

aristocrático, -a [aristo'kratiko, a] ADJ aristocratic

aritmética [arit'metika] NF arithmetic

aritmético, -a [arit'metiko, a] ADJ arithmetic(al) ▶ NM/F arithmetician

arma ['arma] NF arm; **armas** NFPL arms; **~ blanca** blade, knife; (*espada*) sword; **~ de doble filo** double-edged sword; **~ de fuego** firearm; **armas cortas** small arms; **armas de destrucción masiva** weapons of mass destruction; **rendir las armas** to lay down one's arms; **ser de armas tomar** to be somebody to be reckoned with

armada [ar'maða] NF armada; (*flota*) fleet; *ver tb* **armado**

armadillo [arma'ðiʎo] NM armadillo

armado, -a [ar'maðo, a] ADJ armed; (*Tec*) reinforced

armador [arma'ðor] NM (*Naut*) shipowner

armadura [arma'ðura] NF (*Mil*) armour; (*Tec*) framework; (*Zool*) skeleton; (*Física*) armature

armamentista [armamen'tista], **armamentístico, -a** [armamen'tistiko, a] ADJ arms *cpd*

armamento [arma'mento] NM armament; (*Naut*) fitting-out

armar [ar'mar] /1a/ VT (*soldado*) to arm; (*máquina*) to assemble; (*navío*) to fit out; **armarla, ~ un lío** to start a row, kick up a fuss; **armarse** VR: **armarse de valor** to summon up one's courage

armario [ar'marjo] NM wardrobe; (*de cocina, baño*) cupboard; **~ empotrado** built-in cupboard; **salir del ~** to come out (of the closet)

armatoste [arma'toste] NM (*mueble*) monstrosity; (*máquina*) contraption

armazón [arma'θon] NM O F body, chassis; (*de mueble etc*) frame; (*Arq*) skeleton

Armenia [ar'menja] NF Armenia

armería [arme'ria] NF (*museo*) military museum; (*tienda*) gunsmith's

armiño [ar'miɲo] NM stoat; (*piel*) ermine

armisticio [armis'tiθjo] NM armistice

armonía [armo'nia] NF harmony

armónica [ar'monika] NF harmonica; *ver tb* **armónico**

armonice *etc* [armo'niθe] VB *ver* **armonizar**

armónico, -a [ar'moniko, a] ADJ harmonic

armonioso, -a [armo'njoso, a] ADJ harmonious

armonizar [armoni'θar] /1f/ VT to harmonize; (*diferencias*) to reconcile ▶ VI to harmonize; **~ con** (*fig*) to be in keeping with; (*colores*) to tone in with

arnés [ar'nes] NM armour; **arneses** NMPL harness *sg*

aro ['aro] NM ring; (*tejo*) quoit; (*Am: pendiente*) earring; **entrar por el ~** to give in

aroma [a'roma] NM aroma

aromaterapia [aromate'rapja] NF aromatherapy

aromático, -a [aro'matiko, a] ADJ aromatic

arpa ['arpa] NF harp

arpegio [ar'pexjo] NM (*Mus*) arpeggio

arpía [ar'pia] NF (*fig*) shrew

arpillera [arpi'ʎera] NF sacking, sackcloth

arpón [ar'pon] NM harpoon

arquear [arke'ar] /1a/ VT to arch, bend; **arquearse** VR to arch, bend

arqueo [ar'keo] NM (*gen*) arching; (*Naut*) tonnage

arqueología [arkeolo'xia] NF archaeology

arqueológico, -a [arkeo'loxiko, a] ADJ archaeological

arqueólogo, -a [arke'oloɣo, a] NM/F archaeologist

arquero [ar'kero] NM archer, bowman; (*Am Deporte*) goalkeeper

arquetipo [arke'tipo] NM archetype

arquitecto, -a [arki'tekto, a] NM/F architect; **~ paisajista** O **de jardines** landscape gardener

arquitectónico, -a [arkitek'toniko, a] ADJ architectural

arquitectura [arkitek'tura] NF architecture

arrabal [arra'βal] NM suburb; (*Am*) slum; **arrabales** NMPL (*afueras*) outskirts

arrabalero, -a [arraβa'lero, a] ADJ (*fig*) common, coarse

arracimarse [arraθi'marse] /1a/ VR to cluster together

arraigado, -a [arrai'ɣaðo, a] ADJ deep-rooted; (*fig*) established

arraigar [arrai'ɣar] /1h/ VI to take root; **arraigarse** VR (*persona*) to settle

arraigo [a'rraiɣo] NM (*raíces*) roots *pl*; (*bienes*) property; (*influencia*) hold; **hombre de ~** man of property

arraigue *etc* [a'rraiɣe] VB *ver* **arraigar**

arrancada [arran'kaða] NF (*arranque*) sudden start

arrancar [arran'kar] /1g/ VT (*sacar*) to extract, pull out; (*arrebatar*) to snatch (away); (*pedazo*) to tear off; (*página*) to rip out; (*suspiro*) to heave; (*Auto*) to start; (*Inform*) to boot; (*fig*) to extract ▶ VI (*Auto, máquina*) to start; (*ponerse en marcha*) to get going; **~ información a algn** to extract information from sb; **~ de** to stem from

arranque *etc* [a'rranke] VB *ver* **arrancar** ▶ NM sudden start; (*Auto*) start; (*fig*) fit, outburst

arras ['arras] NFPL pledge *sg*, security *sg*

arrasar [arra'sar] /1a/ VT (*aplanar*) to level, flatten; (*destruir*) to demolish

arrastrado, -a [arras'traðo, a] ADJ poor, wretched

arrastrador [arrastra'ðor] NM (*en máquina impresora*) tractor

arrastrar [arras'trar] /**1a**/ VT to drag (along); (*fig*) to drag down, degrade; (*suj: agua, viento*) to carry away ▶ VI to drag, trail on the ground; **arrastrarse** VR to crawl; (*fig*) to grovel; **llevar algo arrastrado** to drag sth along

arrastre [a'rrastre] NM drag, dragging; (*Deporte*) crawl; **estar para el ~** (*fig*) to have had it

array [a'rrai] NM (*Inform*) array; **~ empaquetado** (*Inform*) packed array

arrayán [arra'jan] NM myrtle

arre ['arre] EXCL gee up!

arrear [arre'ar] /**1a**/ VT to drive on, urge on ▶ VI to hurry along

arrebañar [arreβa'ɲar] /**1a**/ VT (*juntar*) to scrape together

arrebatado, -a [arreβa'taðo, a] ADJ rash, impetuous; (*repentino*) sudden, hasty

arrebatar [arreβa'tar] /**1a**/ VT to snatch (away), seize; (*fig*) to captivate; **arrebatarse** VR to get carried away, get excited

arrebato [arre'βato] NM fit of rage, fury; (*éxtasis*) rapture; **en un ~ de cólera** in an outburst of anger

arrebolar [arreβo'lar] /**1a**/ VT to redden; **arrebolarse** VR (*enrojecer*) to blush

arrebujar [arreβu'xar] /**1a**/ VT (*objetos*) to jumble together; **arrebujarse** VR to wrap o.s. up

arrechar [arre'tʃar] /**1a**/ (*AM*) VT to arouse, excite; **arrecharse** VR to become aroused

arrechucho [arre'tʃutʃo] NM (*Med*) turn

arreciar [arre'θjar] /**1b**/ VI to get worse; (*viento*) to get stronger

arrecife [arre'θife] NM reef

arredrar [arre'ðrar] /**1a**/ VT (*hacer retirarse*) to drive back; **arredrarse** VR (*apartarse*) to draw back; **arredrarse ante algo** to shrink away from sth

arreglado, -a [arre'ɣlaðo, a] ADJ (*ordenado*) neat, orderly; (*moderado*) moderate, reasonable

arreglar [arre'ɣlar] /**1a**/ VT (*poner orden*) to tidy up; (*algo roto*) to fix, repair; (*problema*) to solve; **arreglarse** VR to reach an understanding; **arreglárselas** (*fam*) to get by, manage

arreglo [a'rreɣlo] NM settlement; (*orden*) order; (*acuerdo*) agreement; (*Mus*) arrangement, setting; (*Inform*) array; **con ~ a** in accordance with; **llegar a un ~** to reach a compromise

arrellanarse [arreʎa'narse] /**1a**/ VR to sprawl; **~ en el asiento** to lie back in one's chair

arremangar [arreman'gar] /**1h**/ VT to roll up, turn up; **arremangarse** VR to roll up one's sleeves

arremangue *etc* [arre'mange] VB *ver* **arremangar**

arremeter [arreme'ter] /**2a**/ VT to attack, assault ▶ VI: **~ contra algn** to attack sb

arremetida [arreme'tiða] NF assault

arremolinarse [arremoli'narse] /**1a**/ VR to crowd around, mill around; (*corriente*) to swirl, eddy

arrendador, a [arrenda'ðor, a] NM/F landlord/lady

arrendamiento [arrenda'mjento] NM letting; (*el alquilar*) hiring; (*contrato*) lease; (*alquiler*) rent

arrendar [arren'dar] /**1j**/ VT to let; to hire; to lease; to rent

arrendatario, -a [arrenda'tarjo, a] NM/F tenant

arreos [a'rreos] NMPL (*de caballo*) harness *sg*, trappings

arrepentido, -a [arrepen'tiðo, a] NM/F (*Pol*) reformed terrorist

arrepentimiento [arrepenti'mjento] NM regret, repentance

arrepentirse [arrepen'tirse] /**3i**/ VR to repent; **~ de (haber hecho) algo** to regret (doing) sth

arrepienta *etc* [arre'pjenta], **arrepintiendo** *etc* [arrepin'tjendo] VB *ver* **arrepentirse**

arrestar [arres'tar] /**1a**/ VT to arrest; (*encarcelar*) to imprison

arresto [a'rresto] NM arrest; (*Mil*) detention; (*audacia*) boldness, daring; **~ domiciliario** house arrest

arriar [a'rrjar] /**1c**/ VT (*velas*) to haul down; (*bandera*) to lower, strike; (*un cable*) to pay out

arriate [a'rrjate] NM (*Bot*) bed; (*camino*) road

(**PALABRA CLAVE**)

arriba [a'rriβa] ADV **1** (*posición*) above; **desde arriba** from above; **arriba del todo** at the very top, right on top; **Juan está arriba** Juan is upstairs; **lo arriba mencionado** the aforementioned; **aquí/allí arriba** up here/there; **está hasta arriba de trabajo** (*fam*) he's up to his eyes in work (*fam*)

2 (*dirección*) up, upwards; **más arriba** higher *o* further up; **calle arriba** up the street

3: **de arriba abajo** from top to bottom; **mirar a algn de arriba abajo** to look sb up and down

4: **para arriba: de 50 euros para arriba** from 50 euros up(wards); **de la cintura (para) arriba** from the waist up

▶ ADJ: **de arriba: el piso de arriba** the upstairs flat (*BRIT*) *o* apartment; **la parte de arriba** the top *o* upper part

► PREP: **arriba de** (Am: *por encima de*) above; **arriba de 200 dólares** more than 200 dollars ► EXCL: **¡arriba!** up!; **¡manos arriba!** hands up!; **¡arriba España!** long live Spain!

arribar [arri'βar] /**1a**/ VI to put into port; (*esp* Am: *llegar*) to arrive

arribista [arri'βista] NMF parvenu(e), upstart

arribo [a'rriβo] NM (*esp Am*) arrival

arriendo *etc* [a'rrjendo] VB *ver* **arrendar** ► NM = **arrendamiento**

arriero [a'rrjero] NM muleteer

arriesgado, -a [arrjes'ɣaðo, a] ADJ (*peligroso*) risky; (*audaz*) bold, daring

arriesgar [arrjes'ɣar] /**1h**/ VT to risk; (*poner en peligro*) to endanger; **arriesgarse** VR to take a risk

arriesgue *etc* [a'rrjesɣe] VB *ver* **arriesgar**

arrimar [arri'mar] /**1a**/ VT (*acercar*) to bring close; (*poner de lado*) to set aside; **arrimarse** VR to come close o closer; **arrimarse a** to lean on; (*fig*) to keep company with; (*buscar ayuda*) to seek the protection of; **arrímate a mí** cuddle up to me

arrinconado, -a [arrinko'naðo, a] ADJ forgotten, neglected

arrinconar [arrinko'nar] /**1a**/ VT (*colocar*) to put in a corner; (*enemigo*) to corner; (*fig*) to put on one side; (*abandonar*) to push aside

arriscado, -a [arris'kaðo, a] ADJ (*Geo*) craggy; (*fig*) bold, resolute

arroba [a'rroβa] NF (*peso*) 25 pounds; (*Inform: en dirección electrónica*) at sign, @; **tiene talento por arrobas** he has loads o bags of talent

arrobado, -a [arro'βaðo, a] ADJ entranced, enchanted

arrobamiento [arroβa'mjento] NM ecstasy

arrobar [arro'βar] /**1a**/ VT to enchant; **arrobarse** VR to be enraptured; (*místico*) to go into a trance

arrodillarse [arroði'ʎarse] /**1a**/ VR to kneel (down)

arrogancia [arro'ɣanθja] NF arrogance

arrogante [arro'ɣante] ADJ arrogant

arrojar [arro'xar] /**1a**/ VT to throw, hurl; (*humo*) to emit, give out; (*Com*) to yield, produce; **arrojarse** VR to throw o hurl o.s.

arrojo [a'rroxo] NM daring

arrollador, a [arroʎa'ðor, a] ADJ crushing, overwhelming

arrollar [arro'ʎar] /**1a**/ VT (*enrollar*) to roll up; (*suj: inundación*) to wash away; (*Auto*) to run over; (*Deporte*) to crush

arropar [arro'par] /**1a**/ VT to cover (up), wrap up; **arroparse** VR to wrap o.s. up

arrostrar [arros'trar] /**1a**/ VT to face (up to); **arrostrarse** VR: **arrostrarse con algn** to face up to sb

arroyo [a'rrojo] NM stream; (*de la calle*) gutter; **poner a algn en el ~** to turn sb onto the streets

arroz [a'rroθ] NM rice; **~ con leche** rice pudding

arrozal [arro'θal] NM paddy field

arruga [a'rruɣa] NF fold; (*de cara*) wrinkle; (*de vestido*) crease

arrugar [arru'ɣar] /**1h**/ VT to fold; to wrinkle; to crease; **arrugarse** VR to get wrinkled; to get creased

arrugue *etc* [a'rruɣe] VB *ver* **arrugar**

arruinar [arrwi'nar] /**1a**/ VT to ruin, wreck; **arruinarse** VR to be ruined

arrullar [arru'ʎar] /**1a**/ VI to coo ► VT to lull to sleep

arrumaco [arru'mako] NM (*caricia*) caress; (*halago*) piece of flattery

arrumbar [arrum'bar] /**1a**/ VT (*objeto*) to discard; (*individuo*) to silence

arrurruz [arru'rruθ] NM arrowroot

arsenal [arse'nal] NM naval dockyard; (*Mil*) arsenal

arsénico [ar'seniko] NM arsenic

arte ['arte] NM (*gen m en sg, f en pl*) art; (*maña*) skill, guile; **artes** NFPL arts; **por ~ de magia** (as if) by magic; **no tener ~ ni parte en algo** to have nothing whatsoever to do with sth; **Bellas Artes** Fine Art *sg*; **artes y oficios** arts and crafts

artefacto [arte'fakto] NM appliance; (*Arqueología*) artefact

arteria [ar'terja] NF artery

arterial [arte'rjal] ADJ arterial; (*presión*) blood *cpd*

arterioesclerosis [arterjoeskle'rosis], **arteriosclerosis** [arterjoskle'rosis] NF INV hardening of the arteries, arteriosclerosis

artesa [ar'tesa] NF trough

artesanía [artesa'nia] NF craftsmanship; (*artículos*) handicrafts *pl*

artesano, -a [arte'sano, a] NM/F artisan, craftsman/woman

ártico, -a ['artiko, a] ADJ Arctic ► NM: **el (océano) Á~** the Arctic (Ocean)

articulación [artikula'θjon] NF articulation; (*Med, Tec*) joint

articulado, -a [artiku'laðo, a] ADJ articulated; jointed

articular [artiku'lar] /**1a**/ VT to articulate; to join together

articulista [artiku'lista] NMF columnist, contributor (to a newspaper)

artículo [ar'tikulo] NM article; (*cosa*) thing, article; (*TV*) feature, report; **~ de fondo** leader, editorial; **artículos** NMPL goods; **artículos de marca** (*Com*) proprietary goods; **artículos de escritorio** stationery

artífice [ar'tifiθe] NMF artist, craftsman; (*fig*) architect

artificial [artifi'θjal] ADJ artificial

artificio [arti'fiθjo] NM art, skill; (*artesanía*) craftsmanship; (*astucia*) cunning

artillería [artiʎe'ria] NF artillery

artillero [arti'ʎero] NM artilleryman, gunner

artilugio [arti'luxjo] NM gadget

artimaña [arti'maɲa] NF trap, snare; (*astucia*) cunning

artista [ar'tista] NMF (*pintor*) artist, painter; (*Teat*) artist, artiste; **~ de cine** film actor/ actress

artístico, -a [ar'tistiko, a] ADJ artistic

artritis [ar'tritis] NF arthritis

artrosis [ar'trosis] NF osteoarthritis

arveja [ar'βexa] NF (*Am*) pea

Arz. ABR (= *Arzobispo*) Abp

arzobispo [arθo'βispo] NM archbishop

as [as] NM ace; **as del fútbol** star player

asa ['asa] NF handle; (*fig*) lever

asado [a'saðo] NM roast (meat); (*Am: barbacoa*) barbecue

> Traditional Latin American barbecues, especially in the River Plate area, are celebrated in the open air around a large grill which is used to grill mainly beef and various kinds of spicy pork sausage. They are usually very common during the summer and can go on for several days.

asador [asa'ðor] NM (*varilla*) spit; (*aparato*) spit roaster

asadura, asaduras [asa'ðura(s)] NF, NFPL entrails *pl*, offal *sg*; (*Culin*) chitterlings *pl*

asaetear [asaete'ar] /**1a**/ VT (*fig*) to bother

asalariado, -a [asala'rjaðo, a] ADJ paid, wage-earning, salaried ▶ NM/F wage earner

asaltador, a [asalta'ðor, a], **asaltante** [asal'tante] NM/F assailant

asaltar [asal'tar] /**1a**/ VT to attack, assault; (*fig*) to assail

asalto [a'salto] NM attack, assault; (*Deporte*) round

asamblea [asam'blea] NF assembly; (*reunión*) meeting

asar [a'sar] /**1a**/ VT to roast; **~ al horno/a la parrilla** to bake/grill; **asarse** VR (*fig*): **me aso de calor** I'm roasting; **aquí se asa uno vivo** it's boiling hot here

asbesto [as'βesto] NM asbestos

ascendencia [asθen'denθja] NF ancestry; (*Am: influencia*) ascendancy; **de ~ francesa** of French origin

ascender [asθen'der] /**2g**/ VI (*subir*) to ascend, rise; (*ser promovido*) to gain promotion ▶ VT to promote; **~ a** to amount to

ascendiente [asθen'djente] NM influence ▶ NMF ancestor

ascensión [asθen'sjon] NF ascent; **la A~** the Ascension

ascenso [as'θenso] NM ascent; (*promoción*) promotion

ascensor [asθen'sor] NM lift (*BRIT*), elevator (*US*)

ascético, -a [as'θetiko, a] ADJ ascetic

ascienda *etc* [as'θjenda] VB *ver* **ascender**

asco ['asko] NM: **el ajo me da ~** I hate *o* loathe garlic; **hacer ascos de algo** to turn up one's nose at sth; **estar hecho un ~** to be filthy; **poner a algn de ~** to call sb all sorts of names *o* every name under the sun; **¡qué ~!** how revolting *o* disgusting!

ascua ['askwa] NF ember; **arrimar el ~ a su sardina** to look after number one; **estar en ascuas** to be on tenterhooks

aseado, -a [ase'aðo, a] ADJ clean; (*arreglado*) tidy; (*pulcro*) smart

asear [ase'ar] /**1a**/ VT (*lavar*) to wash; (*ordenar*) to tidy (up)

asechanza [ase'tʃanθa] NF trap, snare

asediar [ase'ðjar] /**1b**/ VT (*Mil*) to besiege, lay siege to; (*fig*) to chase, pester

asedio [a'seðjo] NM siege; (*Com*) run

asegurado, a [aseɣu'raðo, a] ADJ insured

asegurador, -a [aseɣura'ðor, a] NM/F insurer

asegurar [aseɣu'rar] /**1a**/ VT (*consolidar*) to secure, fasten; (*dar garantía de*) to guarantee; (*preservar*) to safeguard; (*afirmar, dar por cierto*) to assure, affirm; (*tranquilizar*) to reassure; (*hacer un seguro*) to insure; **asegurarse** VR to assure o.s., make sure

asemejarse [aseme'xarse] /**1a**/ VR to be alike; **~ a** to be like, resemble

asentado, -a [asen'taðo, a] ADJ established, settled

asentar [asen'tar] /**1j**/ VT (*sentar*) to seat, sit down; (*poner*) to place, establish; (*alisar*) to level, smooth down *o* out; (*anotar*) to note down ▶ VI to be suitable, suit

asentimiento [asenti'mjento] NM assent, agreement

asentir [asen'tir] /**3i**/ VI to assent, agree; **~ con la cabeza** to nod (one's head)

aseo [a'seo] NM cleanliness; **aseos** NMPL toilet *sg* (*BRIT*), cloakroom *sg* (*BRIT*), restroom *sg* (*US*)

aséptico, -a [a'septiko, a] ADJ germ-free, free from infection

asequible [ase'kiβle] ADJ (*precio*) reasonable; (*meta*) attainable; (*persona*) approachable

aserradero [aserra'ðero] NM sawmill

aserrar [ase'rrar] /**1j**/ VT to saw

asesinar [asesi'nar] /**1a**/ VT to murder; (*Pol*) to assassinate

asesinato [asesi'nato] NM murder; assassination

asesino, -a [ase'sino, a] NM/F murderer, killer; (*Pol*) assassin

asesor, a [ase'sor, a] NM/F adviser,
consultant; (Com) assessor, consultant;
~ **administrativo** management consultant
asesorar [aseso'rar] /**1a**/ VT (Jur) to advise,
give legal advice to; (Com) to act as
consultant to; **asesorarse** VR: **asesorarse
con** o **de** to take advice from, consult
asesoría [aseso'ria] NF (cargo) consultancy;
(oficina) consultant's office
asestar [ases'tar] /**1a**/ VT (golpe) to deal; (arma)
to aim; (tiro) to fire
aseverar [aseβe'rar] /**1a**/ VT to assert
asfaltado, -a [asfal'taðo, a] ADJ asphalted
▸ NM (pavimento) asphalt
asfalto [as'falto] NM asphalt
asfixia [as'fiksja] NF asphyxia, suffocation
asfixiar [asfik'sjar] /**1b**/ VT to asphyxiate,
suffocate; **asfixiarse** VR to be asphyxiated,
suffocate
asga etc ['asɣa] VB ver **asir**
así [a'si] ADV (de esta manera) in this way, like
this, thus; (aunque) although; (tan pronto
como) as soon as; ~ **que** so; ~ **como** as well as;
~ **y todo** even so; ¿**no es ~?** isn't it?, didn't
you? etc; ~ **de grande** this big; ¡~ **sea!** so be
it!; ~ **es la vida** such is life, that's life
Asia ['asja] NF Asia
asiático, -a [a'sjatiko, a] ADJ, NM/F Asian,
Asiatic
asidero [asi'ðero] NM handle
asiduidad [asiðwi'ðað] NF assiduousness
asiduo, -a [a'siðwo, a] ADJ assiduous;
(frecuente) frequent ▸ NM/F regular (customer)
asiento [a'sjento] VB ver **asentar; asentir**
▸ NM (mueble) seat, chair; (de coche, en tribunal
etc) seat; (localidad) seat, place; (fundamento)
site; ~ **delantero/trasero** front/back seat
asierre etc [a'sjerre] VB ver **aserrar**
asignación [asiɣna'θjon] NF (atribución)
assignment; (reparto) allocation; (sueldo)
salary; (Com) allowance; ~ (**semanal**)
(weekly) pocket money; ~ **de presupuesto**
budget appropriation
asignar [asiɣ'nar] /**1a**/ VT to assign, allocate
asignatura [asiɣna'tura] NF subject; (curso)
course; ~ **pendiente** (fig) matter pending
asilado, -a [asi'laðo, a] NM/F refugee
asilo [a'silo] NM (refugio) asylum, refuge;
(establecimiento) home, institution; ~ **político**
political asylum
asimilación [asimila'θjon] NF assimilation
asimilar [asimi'lar] /**1a**/ VT to assimilate
asimismo [asi'mismo] ADV in the same way,
likewise
asintiendo etc [asin'tjendo] VB ver **asentir**
asir [a'sir] VT to seize, grasp; **asirse** VR to take
hold; **asirse a** o **de** to seize
asistencia [asis'tenθja] NF presence; (Teat)
audience; (Med) attendance; (ayuda)

assistance; ~ **social** social o welfare work;
~ **en carretera** roadside assistance
asistente, -a [asis'tente, a] NM/F assistant
▸ NM (Mil) orderly ▸ NF daily help; **los
asistentes** those present; ~ **social** social
worker
asistido, -a [asis'tiðo, a] ADJ (Auto: dirección)
power-assisted; ~ **por ordenador**
computer-assisted
asistir [asis'tir] /**3a**/ VT to assist, help ▸ VI:
~ **a** to attend, be present at
asma ['asma] NF asthma
asno ['asno] NM donkey; (fig) ass
asociación [asoθja'θjon] NF association;
(Com) partnership
asociado, -a [aso'θjaðo, a] ADJ associate
▸ NM/F associate; (Com) partner
asociar [aso'θjar] /**1b**/ VT to associate;
asociarse VR to become partners
asolar [aso'lar] /**1a**/ VT to destroy
asolear [asole'ar] /**1a**/ VT to put in the sun;
asolearse VR to sunbathe
asomar [aso'mar] /**1a**/ VT to show, stick out
▸ VI to appear; **asomarse** VR to appear, show
up; ~ **la cabeza por la ventana** to put one's
head out of the window
asombrar [asom'brar] /**1a**/ VT to amaze,
astonish; **asombrarse** VR: **asombrarse (de)**
(sorprenderse) to be amazed (at); (asustarse) to
be frightened (at)
asombro [a'sombro] NM amazement,
astonishment; (susto) fright
asombroso, -a [asom'broso, a] ADJ amazing,
astonishing
asomo [a'somo] NM hint, sign; **ni por** ~ by
no means
asonancia [aso'nanθja] NF (Lit) assonance;
(fig) connection; **no tener** ~ **con** to bear no
relation to
asorocharse [asoro't∫arse] /**1a**/ VR (AM) to get
mountain sickness
aspa ['aspa] NF (cruz) cross; (de molino) sail;
en ~ X-shaped
aspaviento [aspa'βjento] NM exaggerated
display of feeling; (fam) fuss
aspecto [as'pekto] NM (apariencia) look,
appearance; (fig) aspect; **bajo ese** ~ from
that point of view
aspereza [aspe're θa] NF roughness; (de fruta)
sharpness; (de carácter) surliness
áspero, -a ['aspero, a] ADJ (al tacto) rough;
(al gusto) sharp, sour; (voz) harsh
aspersión [asper'sjon] NF sprinkling; (Agr)
spraying
aspersor [asper'sor] NM sprinkler
aspiración [aspira'θjon] NF breath,
inhalation; (Mus) short pause; **aspiraciones**
NFPL (ambiciones) aspirations
aspirador [aspira'ðor] NM = **aspiradora**

aspiradora [aspira'ðora] NF vacuum cleaner, Hoover®

aspirante [aspi'rante] NMF (*candidato*) candidate; (*Deporte*) contender

aspirar [aspi'rar] /**1a**/ VT to breathe in ▶ VI: **~ a** to aspire to

aspirina [aspi'rina] NF aspirin

asquear [aske'ar] /**1a**/ VT to sicken ▶ VI to be sickening; **asquearse** VR to feel disgusted

asquerosidad [askerosi'ðað] NF (*suciedad*) filth; (*dicho*) obscenity; (*faena*) dirty trick

asqueroso, -a [aske'roso, a] ADJ disgusting, sickening

asta ['asta] NF lance; (*arpón*) spear; (*mango*) shaft, handle; (*Zool*) horn; **a media ~** at half mast

astado, -a [as'taðo, a] ADJ horned ▶ NM bull

asterisco [aste'risko] NM asterisk

asteroide [aste'roiðe] NM asteroid

astigmatismo [astiɣma'tismo] NM astigmatism

astilla [as'tiʎa] NF splinter; (*pedacito*) chip; **astillas** NFPL (*leña*) firewood *sg*

astillarse [asti'ʎarse] /**1a**/ VR to splinter; (*fig*) to shatter

astillero [asti'ʎero] NM shipyard

astringente [astrin'xente] ADJ, NM astringent

astro ['astro] NM star

astrología [astrolo'xia] NF astrology

astrólogo, -a [as'troloɣo, a] NM/F astrologer

astronauta [astro'nauta] NMF astronaut

astronave [astro'naβe] NM spaceship

astronomía [astrono'mia] NF astronomy

astronómico, -a [astro'nomiko, a] ADJ (*tb fig*) astronomical

astrónomo, -a [as'tronomo, a] NM/F astronomer

astroso, -a [as'troso, a] ADJ (*desaliñado*) untidy; (*vil*) contemptible

astucia [as'tuθja] NF astuteness; (*destreza*) clever trick

asturiano, -a [astu'rjano, a] ADJ, NM/F Asturian

Asturias [as'turjas] NFPL Asturias; **Príncipe de ~** crown prince

astuto, -a [as'tuto, a] ADJ astute; (*taimado*) cunning

asueto [a'sweto] NM holiday; (*tiempo libre*) time off; **día de ~** day off; **tarde de ~** (*trabajo*) afternoon off; (*Escol*) half-holiday

asumir [asu'mir] /**3a**/ VT to assume

asunción [asun'θjon] NF assumption; (*Rel*): **A~** Assumption

asunto [a'sunto] NM (*tema*) matter, subject; (*negocio*) business; **¡eso es ~ mío!** that's my business!; **asuntos exteriores** foreign affairs; **asuntos a tratar** agenda *sg*

asustadizo, -a [asusta'ðiθo, a] ADJ easily frightened

asustar [asus'tar] /**1a**/ VT to frighten; **asustarse** VR to be/become frightened

atacante [ata'kante] NMF attacker

atacar [ata'kar] /**1g**/ VT to attack

atadura [ata'ðura] NF bond, tie

atajar [ata'xar] /**1a**/ VT (*enfermedad, mal*) to stop; (*ruta de fuga*) to cut off; (*discurso*) to interrupt ▶ VI (*persona*) to take a short cut

atajo [a'taxo] NM short cut; (*Deporte*) tackle

atalaya [ata'laja] NF watchtower

atañer [ata'ɲer] VI: **~ a** to concern; **en lo que atañe a eso** with regard to that

ataque *etc* [a'take] VB *ver* **atacar** ▶ NM attack; **~ cardíaco** heart attack

atar [a'tar] /**1a**/ VT to tie, tie up; **~ la lengua a algn** (*fig*) to silence sb

atarantado, -a [ataran'taðo, a] ADJ (*Am: aturdido*) dazed

atardecer [ataɾðe'θer] /**2d**/ VI to get dark ▶ NM evening; (*crepúsculo*) dusk

atardezca *etc* [ataɾ'ðeθka] VB *ver* **atardecer**

atareado, -a [atare'aðo, a] ADJ busy

atascar [atas'kar] /**1g**/ VT to clog up; (*obstruir*) to jam; (*fig*) to hinder; **atascarse** VR to stall; (*cañería*) to get blocked up; (*fig*) to get bogged down; (*en discurso*) to dry up

atasco [a'tasko] NM obstruction; (*Auto*) traffic jam

atasque *etc* [a'taske] VB *ver* **atascar**

ataúd [ata'uð] NM coffin

ataviar [ata'βjar] /**1c**/ VT to deck, array; **ataviarse** VR to dress up

atavío [ata'βio] NM attire, dress; **atavíos** NMPL finery *sg*

ateísmo [ate'ismo] NM atheism

atemorice *etc* [atemo'riθe] VB *ver* **atemorizar**

atemorizar [atemori'θar] /**1f**/ VT to frighten, scare; **atemorizarse** VR to get frightened *o* scared

Atenas [a'tenas] NF Athens

atención [aten'θjon] NF attention; (*bondad*) kindness ▶ EXCL (be) careful!, look out!; **en ~ a esto** in view of this

atender [aten'der] /**2g**/ VT to attend to, look after; (*Tec*) to service; (*enfermo*) to care for; (*ruego*) to comply with; (*Telec*) to answer ▶ VI to pay attention; **~ a** to attend to; (*detalles*) to take care of

atendré *etc* [aten'dre] VB *ver* **atenerse**

atenerse [ate'nerse] /**2k**/ VR: **~ a** to abide by, adhere to

atenga *etc* [a'tenga] VB *ver* **atenerse**

ateniense [ate'njense] ADJ, NMF Athenian

atentado [aten'taðo] NM crime, illegal act; (*asalto*) assault; (*tb*: **atentado terrorista**) terrorist attack; **~ contra la vida de algn** attempt on sb's life; **~ golpista** attempted coup; **~ suicida** suicide bombing, suicide attack

atentamente [atenta'mente] ADV: **Le saluda ~** Yours faithfully

atentar [aten'tar] /**1a**/ VI: **~ a** o **contra** to commit an outrage against

atento, -a [a'tento, a] ADJ attentive, observant; (*cortés*) polite, thoughtful; **estar ~ a** (*explicación*) to pay attention to; **su atenta (carta)** (*Com*) your letter

atenuante [ate'nwante] ADJ: **circunstancias atenuantes** extenuating o mitigating circumstances ▶ NF: **atenuantes** extenuating o mitigating circumstances

atenuar [ate'nwar] /**1e**/ VT to attenuate; (*disminuir*) to lessen, minimize

ateo, -a [a'teo, a] ADJ atheistic ▶ NM/F atheist

aterciopelado, -a [aterθjope'laðo, a] ADJ velvety

aterido, -a [ate'riðo, a] ADJ: **~ de frío** frozen stiff

aterrador, a [aterra'ðor, a] ADJ frightening

aterrar [ate'rrar] /**1a**/ VT to frighten; (*aterrorizar*) to terrify; **aterrarse** VR to be frightened; to be terrified

aterrice etc [ate'rriθe] VB ver **aterrizar**

aterrizaje [aterri'θaxe] NM landing; **~ forzoso** emergency o forced landing

aterrizar [aterri'θar] /**1f**/ VI to land

aterrorice etc [aterro'riθe] VB ver **aterrorizar**

aterrorizar [aterrori'θar] /**1f**/ VT to terrify

atesorar [ateso'rar] /**1a**/ VT to hoard, store up

atestado, -a [ates'taðo, a] ADJ packed ▶ NM (*Jur*) affidavit

atestar [ates'tar] /**1a, 1j**/ VT to pack, stuff; (*Jur*) to attest, testify to

atestiguar [atesti'ɣwar] /**1i**/ VT to testify to, bear witness to

atestigüe etc [ates'tiɣwe] VB ver **atestiguar**

atiborrar [atiβo'rrar] /**1a**/ VT to fill, stuff; **atiborrarse** VR to stuff o.s.

atice etc [a'tiθe] VB ver **atizar**

ático ['atiko] NM (*desván*) attic; **~ de lujo** penthouse flat

atienda etc [a'tjenda] VB ver **atender**

atildar [atil'dar] /**1a**/ VT to criticize; (*Tip*) to put a tilde over; **atildarse** VR to spruce o.s. up

atinado, -a [ati'naðo, a] ADJ correct; (*sensato*) wise, sensible

atinar [ati'nar] /**1a**/ VI (*acertar*) to be right; **~ con** o **en** (*solución*) to hit upon; **~ al blanco** to hit the target; (*fig*) to be right; **~ a hacer** to manage to do

atípico, -a [a'tipiko, a] ADJ atypical

atiplado, -a [ati'plaðo, a] ADJ (*voz*) high-pitched

atisbar [atis'βar] /**1a**/ VT to spy on; (*echar ojeada*) to peep at

atizar [ati'θar] /**1f**/ VT to poke; (*horno etc*) to stoke; (*fig*) to stir up, rouse

atlántico, -a [at'lantiko, a] ADJ Atlantic ▶ NM: **el (océano) A~** the Atlantic (Ocean)

atlas ['atlas] NM INV atlas

atleta [at'leta] NMF athlete

atlético, -a [at'letiko, a] ADJ athletic

atletismo [atle'tismo] NM athletics sg

atmósfera [at'mosfera] NF atmosphere

atmosférico, -a [atmos'feriko, a] ADJ atmospheric

atol [a'tol], **atole** [a'tole] NM (*Am*) cornflour drink

atolladero [atoʎa'ðero] NM: **estar en un ~** to be in a jam

atollarse [ato'ʎarse] /**1a**/ VR to get stuck; (*fig*) to get into a jam

atolondrado, -a [atolon'draðo, a] ADJ scatterbrained

atolondramiento [atolondra'mjento] NM bewilderment; (*insensatez*) silliness

atómico, -a [a'tomiko, a] ADJ atomic

atomizador [atomiθa'ðor] NM atomizer

átomo ['atomo] NM atom

atónito, -a [a'tonito, a] ADJ astonished, amazed

atontado, -a [aton'taðo, a] ADJ stunned; (*bobo*) silly, daft

atontar [aton'tar] /**1a**/ VT to stun; **atontarse** VR to become confused

atorar [ato'rar] /**1a**/ VT to obstruct; **atorarse** VR (*atragantarse*) to choke

atormentar [atormen'tar] /**1a**/ VT to torture; (*molestar*) to torment; (*acosar*) to plague, harass

atornillar [atorni'ʎar] /**1a**/ VT to screw on o down

atorón [ato'ron] NM (*Am*) traffic jam

atosigar [atosi'ɣar] /**1h**/ VT to harass, pester

atosigue etc [ato'siɣe] VB ver **atosigar**

atrabiliario, -a [atraβi'ljarjo, a] ADJ bad-tempered

atracadero [atraka'ðero] NM pier

atracador, a [atraka'ðor, a] NM/F robber

atracar [atra'kar] /**1g**/ VT (*Naut*) to moor; (*robar*) to hold up, rob ▶ VI to moor; **atracarse** VR: **atracarse (de)** to stuff o.s. (with)

atracción [atrak'θjon] NF attraction

atraco [a'trako] NM holdup, robbery

atracón [atra'kon] NM: **darse** o **pegarse un ~ (de)** (*fam*) to stuff o.s. (with)

atractivo, -a [atrak'tiβo, a] ADJ attractive ▶ NM appeal; (*belleza*) attractiveness

atraer [atra'er] /**2o**/ VT to attract; **dejarse ~ por** to be tempted by

atragantarse [atraɣan'tarse] /**1a**/ VR: **~ (con algo)** to choke (on sth); **se me ha atragantado el chico ese/el inglés** I can't stand that boy/English

atraiga etc [a'traiɣa], **atraje** etc [a'traxe] VB ver **atraer**

atrancar [atran'kar] /**1g**/ VT (*con tranca, barra*) to bar, bolt

atranqueetc [a'tranke] VB ver **atrancar**

atrapar [atra'par] /**1a**/ VT to trap; (resfriado etc) to catch

atraqueetc [a'trake] VB ver **atracar**

atrás [a'tras] ADV (movimiento) back(wards); (lugar) behind; (tiempo) previously; **ir hacia ~** to go back(wards); to go to the rear; **estar ~** to be behind o at the back

atrasado, -a [atra'saðo, a] ADJ slow; (pago) overdue, late; (país) backward

atrasar [atra'sar] /**1a**/ VI to be slow; **atrasarse** VR to stay behind; (tren) to be o run late; (llegar tarde) to be late

atraso [a'traso] NM slowness; lateness, delay; (de país) backwardness; **atrasos** NMPL (Com) arrears

atravesado, -a [atraβe'saðo, a] ADJ: **un tronco ~ en la carretera** a tree trunk lying across the road

atravesar [atraβe'sar] /**1j**/ VT (cruzar) to cross (over); (traspasar) to pierce; (período) to go through; (poner al través) to lay o put across; **atravesarse** VR to come in between; (intervenir) to interfere

atravieseetc [atra'βjese] VB ver **atravesar**

atrayendo [atra'jendo] VB ver **atraer**

atrayente [atra'jente] ADJ attractive

atreverse [atre'βerse] /**2a**/ VR to dare; (insolentarse) to be insolent

atrevido, -a [atre'βiðo, a] ADJ daring; insolent

atrevimiento [atreβi'mjento] NM daring; insolence

atribución [atriβu'θjon] NF (Lit) attribution; **atribuciones** NFPL (Pol) powers, functions; (Admin) responsibilities

atribuir [atriβu'ir] /**3g**/ VT to attribute; (funciones) to confer

atribular [atriβu'lar] /**1a**/ VT to afflict, distress

atributo [atri'βuto] NM attribute

atribuyaetc [atri'βuja], **atribuyendo**etc [atriβu'jendo] VB ver **atribuir**

atril [a'tril] NM (para libro) lectern; (Mus) music stand

atrincherarse [atrintʃe'rarse] /**1a**/ VR (Mil) to dig (o.s.) in; **~ en** (fig) to hide behind

atrio ['atrjo] NM (Rel) porch

atrocidad [atroθi'ðað] NF atrocity, outrage

atrofiado, -a [atro'fjaðo, a] ADJ (extremidad) withered

atrofiarse [atro'fjarse] /**1b**/ VR (tb fig) to atrophy

atronador, a [atrona'ðor, a] ADJ deafening

atropellar [atrope'ʎar] /**1a**/ VT (derribar) to knock over o down; (empujar) to push (aside); (Auto) to run over o down; (agraviar) to insult; **atropellarse** VR to act hastily

atropello [atro'peʎo] NM (Auto) accident; (empujón) push; (agravio) wrong; (atrocidad) outrage

atroz [a'troθ] ADJ atrocious, awful

A.T.S. NMF (= Ayudante Técnico Sanitario) nurse

attrezzo [a'treθo] NM props pl

atuendo [a'twendo] NM attire

atufar [atu'far] /**1a**/ VT (suj: olor) to overcome; (molestar) to irritate; **atufarse** VR (fig) to get cross

atún [a'tun] NM tuna, tunny

aturdir [atur'ðir] /**3a**/ VT to stun; (suj: ruido) to deafen; (fig) to dumbfound, bewilder

aturrullar /**1a**/, **aturullar** /**1a**/ [atur(r)u'ʎar] VT to bewilder

atusar [atu'sar] /**1a**/ VT (cortar) to trim; (alisar) to smooth (down)

atuveetc [a'tuβe] VB ver **atenerse**

audacia [au'ðaθja] NF boldness, audacity

audaz [au'ðaθ] ADJ bold, audacious

audible [au'ðiβle] ADJ audible

audición [auði'θjon] NF hearing; (Teat) audition; **~ radiofónica** radio concert

audiencia [au'ðjenθja] NF audience; (Jur) high court; (Pol): **~ pública** public inquiry

audífono [au'ðifono] NM (para sordos) hearing aid

audiovisual [auðjoβi'swal] ADJ audio-visual

auditivo, -a [auði'tiβo, a] ADJ hearing cpd; (conducto, nervio) auditory

auditor [auði'tor] NM (Jur) judge advocate; (Com) auditor

auditoría [auðito'ria] NF audit; (profesión) auditing

auditorio [auði'torjo] NM audience; (sala) auditorium

auge ['auxe] NM boom; (clímax) climax; (Econ) expansion; **estar en ~** to thrive

augurar [auɣu'rar] /**1a**/ VT to predict; (presagiar) to portend

augurio [au'ɣurjo] NM omen

aula ['aula] NF classroom; (en universidad etc) lecture room

aullar [au'ʎar] /**1a**/ VI to howl, yell

aullido [au'ʎiðo] NM howl, yell

aumentar [aumen'tar] /**1a**/ VT to increase; (precios) to put up; (producción) to step up; (con microscopio, anteojos) to magnify ▶ VI to increase, be on the increase

aumento [au'mento] NM increase; rise

aun [a'un] ADV even; **~ así** even so; **~ más** even o yet more

aún [a'un] ADV still, yet; **~ está aquí** he's still here; **~ no lo sabemos** we don't know yet; **¿no ha venido ~?** hasn't she come yet?

aunque [a'unke] CONJ though, although, even though

aúpa [a'upa] EXCL up!, come on!; (fam): **una función de ~** a slap-up do; **una paliza de ~** a good hiding

aupar [au'par] /**1a**/ VT (levantar) to help up; (fig) to praise

aura ['aura] NF (*atmósfera*) aura
aureola [aure'ola] NF halo
auricular [auriku'lar] NM (*Telec*) earpiece, receiver; **auriculares** NMPL (*cascos*) headphones
aurora [au'rora] NF dawn; **~ boreal(is)** northern lights *pl*
auscultar [auskul'tar] /**1a**/ VT (*Med: pecho*) to listen to, sound
ausencia [au'senθja] NF absence
ausentarse [ausen'tarse] /**1a**/ VR to go away; (*por poco tiempo*) to go out
ausente [au'sente] ADJ absent ▶ NMF (*Escol*) absentee; (*Jur*) missing person
auspiciar [auspi'sjar] /**1b**/ VT (*AM*) to back, sponsor
auspicios [aus'piθjos] NMPL auspices; (*protección*) protection *sg*
austeridad [austeri'ðað] NF austerity
austero, -a [aus'tero, a] ADJ austere
austral [aus'tral] ADJ southern ▶ NM *monetary unit of Argentina (1985-1991)*
Australia [aus'tralja] NF Australia
australiano, -a [austra'ljano, a] ADJ, NM/F Australian
Austria ['austrja] NF Austria
austriaco, -a [aus'trjako, a], **austríaco, -a** [aus'triako, a] ADJ Austrian ▶ NM/F Austrian
autenticar [autenti'kar] /**1g**/ VT to authenticate
auténtico, -a [au'tentiko, a] ADJ authentic
autentificar [autentifi'kar] /**1g**/ VT to authenticate
autentique*etc* [auten'tike] VB *ver* **autenticar**
auto ['auto] NM (*coche*) car; (*Jur*) edict, decree; (*: orden*) writ; **autos** NMPL (*Jur*) proceedings; (*: acta*) court record *sg*; **~ de comparecencia** summons, subpoena; **~ de ejecución** writ of execution
autoadhesivo, -a [autoaðe'siβo, a] ADJ self-adhesive; (*sobre*) self-sealing
autoalimentación [autoalimenta'θjon] NF (*Inform*): **~ de hojas** automatic paper feed
autobiografía [autoβjoɣra'fia] NF autobiography
autobomba [auto'bomba] NM (*RPL*) fire engine
autobronceador, a [autoβronθea'ðor, a] ADJ (self-)tanning
autobús [auto'βus] NM bus; **~ de línea** long-distance coach
autocar [auto'kar] NM coach (*BRIT*), (*passenger*) bus (*US*); **~ de línea** intercity coach *or* bus
autocomprobación [autokomproβa'θjon] NF (*Inform*) self-test
autóctono, -a [au'toktono, a] ADJ native, indigenous
autodefensa [autoðe'fensa] NF self-defence

autodeterminación [autoðetermina'θjon] NF self-determination
autodidacta [autoði'ðakta] ADJ self-taught ▶ NMF: **ser un(a) ~** to be self-taught
autoescuela [autoes'kwela] NF (*ESP*) driving school
autofinanciado, -a [autofinan'θjaðo, a] ADJ self-financing
autogestión [autoxes'tjon] NF self-management
autógrafo [au'toɣrafo] NM autograph
automación [automa'θjon] NF = **automatización**
autómata [au'tomata] NM automaton
automáticamente [auto'matikamente] ADV automatically
automatice*etc* [automa'tiθe] VB *ver* **automatizar**
automático, -a [auto'matiko, a] ADJ automatic ▶ NM press stud
automatización [automatiθa'θjon] NF: **~ de fábricas** factory automation; **~ de oficinas** office automation
automatizar [automati'θar] /**1f**/ VT to automate
automontable [automon'taβle] ADJ self-assembly
automotor, -triz [automo'tor, 'triθ] ADJ self-propelled ▶ NM diesel train
automóvil [auto'moβil] NM (motor) car (*BRIT*), automobile (*US*)
automovilismo [automoβi'lismo] NM (*actividad*) motoring; (*Deporte*) motor racing
automovilista [automoβi'lista] NMF motorist, driver
automovilístico, -a [automoβi'listiko, a] ADJ (*industria*) car *cpd*
autonomía [autono'mia] NF autonomy; (*ESP Pol*) autonomy, self-government; (*: comunidad*) autonomous region
autonómico, -a [auto'nomiko, a] ADJ (*ESP Pol*) relating to autonomy, autonomous; **gobierno ~** autonomous government
autónomo, -a [au'tonomo, a] ADJ autonomous; (*Inform*) stand-alone, offline
autopista [auto'pista] NF motorway (*BRIT*), freeway (*US*); **~ de cuota** (*AM*) *o* **peaje** (*ESP*) toll (*BRIT*) *o* turnpike (*US*) road
autopsia [au'topsja] NF post-mortem, autopsy
autor, a [au'tor, a] NM/F author; **los autores del atentado** those responsible for the attack
autorice*etc* [auto'riθe] VB *ver* **autorizar**
autoridad [autori'ðað] NF authority; **~ local** local authority
autoritario, -a [autori'tarjo, a] ADJ authoritarian
autorización [autoriθa'θjon] NF authorization

autorizado, -a [autori'θaðo, a] ADJ authorized; (aprobado) approved

autorizar [autori'θar] /**1f**/ VT to authorize; to approve

autorretrato [autorre'trato] NM self-portrait

autoservicio [autoser'βiθjo] NM (tienda) self-service shop o store; (restaurante) self-service restaurant

autostop [auto'stop] NM hitch-hiking; **hacer ~** to hitch-hike

autostopista [autosto'pista] NMF hitch-hiker

autosuficiencia [autosufi'θjenθja] NF self-sufficiency

autosuficiente [autosufi'θjente] ADJ self-sufficient; (pey) smug

autosugestión [autosuxes'tjon] NF autosuggestion

autovía [auto'βia] NF ≈ dual carriageway (BRIT), ≈ divided highway (US)

auxiliar [auksi'ljar] /**1b**/ VT to help ▶ NMF assistant

auxilio [auk'siljo] NM assistance, help; **primeros auxilios** first aid sg

Av ABR (= Avenida) Av(e)

a/v ABR (Com: = a vista) at sight

aval [a'βal] NM guarantee; (persona) guarantor

avalancha [aβa'lantʃa] NF avalanche

avalar [aβa'lar] /**1a**/ VT (Com etc) to underwrite; (fig) to endorse

avalista [aβa'lista] NM (Com) endorser

avance [a'βanθe] VB ver **avanzar** ▶ NM advance; (pago) advance payment; (Cine) trailer

avanzado, -a [aβan'θaðo, a] ADJ advanced; **de edad avanzada, ~ de edad** elderly

avanzar [aβan'θar] /**1f**/ VT, VI to advance

avaricia [aβa'riθja] NF avarice, greed

avaricioso, -a [aβari'θjoso, a] ADJ avaricious, greedy

avaro, -a [a'βaro, a] ADJ miserly, mean ▶ NM/F miser

avasallar [aβasa'ʎar] /**1a**/ VT to subdue, subjugate

avatar [aβa'tar] NM change; **avatares** ups and downs

Avda ABR (= Avenida) Av(e)

AVE ['aβe] NM ABR (= Alta Velocidad Española) ≈ bullet train

ave ['aβe] NF bird; **~ de rapiña** bird of prey

avecinarse [aβeθi'narse] /**1a**/ VR (tormenta, fig) to approach, be on the way

avejentar [aβexen'tar] /**1a**/ VT, VI, **avejentarse** VR to age

avellana [aβe'ʎana] NF hazelnut

avellano [aβe'ʎano] NM hazel tree

avemaría [aβema'ria] NM Hail Mary, Ave Maria

avena [a'βena] NF oats pl

avendré etc [aβen'dre], **avenga** etc [a'βenga] VB ver **avenir**

avenida [aβe'niða] NF (calle) avenue

avenir [aβe'nir] /**3a**/ VT to reconcile; **avenirse** VR to come to an agreement, reach a compromise

aventado, -a [aβen'taðo, a] ADJ (AM) daring

aventajado, -a [aβenta'xaðo, a] ADJ outstanding

aventajar [aβenta'xar] /**1a**/ VT (sobrepasar) to surpass, outstrip

aventar [aβen'tar] /**1j**/ VT to fan, blow; (grano) to winnow; (AM fam: echar) to chuck out

aventón [aβen'ton] NM (AM) push; **pedir ~** to hitch a lift, hitch a ride (US)

aventura [aβen'tura] NF adventure; **~ sentimental** love affair

aventurado, -a [aβentu'raðo, a] ADJ risky

aventurar [aβentu'rar] /**1a**/ VT to risk; **aventurarse** VR to dare; **aventurarse a hacer algo** to venture to do sth

aventurero, -a [aβentu'rero, a] ADJ adventurous

avergoncé [aβerɣon'θe], **avergoncemos** etc [aβerɣon'θemos] VB ver **avergonzar**

avergonzar [aβerɣon'θar] /**1f, 1l**/ VT to shame; (desconcertar) to embarrass; **avergonzarse** VR to be ashamed; to be embarrassed

avergüence etc [aβer'ɣwenθe] VB ver **avergonzar**

avería [aβe'ria] NF (Tec) breakdown, fault

averiado, -a [aβe'rjaðo, a] ADJ broken-down; "~" "out of order"

averiar [aβe'rjar] /**1c**/ VT to break; **averiarse** VR to break down

averiguación [aβeriɣwa'θjon] NF investigation

averiguar [aβeri'ɣwar] /**1i**/ VT to investigate; (descubrir) to find out, ascertain

averigüe etc [aβe'riɣwe] VB ver **averiguar**

aversión [aβer'sjon] NF aversion, dislike; **cobrar ~ a** to take a strong dislike to

avestruz [aβes'truθ] NM ostrich

aviación [aβja'θjon] NF aviation; (fuerzas aéreas) air force

aviado, -a [a'βjaðo, a] ADJ: **estar ~** to be in a mess

aviador, a [aβja'ðor, a] NM/F aviator, airman/ woman

aviar [a'βjar] /**1c**/ VT to prepare, get ready

avícola [a'βikola] ADJ poultry cpd

avicultura [aβikul'tura] NF poultry farming

avidez [aβi'ðeθ] NF avidity, eagerness

ávido, -a ['aβiðo, a] ADJ avid, eager

aviente etc [a'βjente] VB ver **aventar**

avieso, -a [a'βjeso, a] ADJ (torcido) distorted; (perverso) wicked

avinagrado, -a [aβina'ɣraðo, a] ADJ sour, acid

avinagrarse [aβina'ɣrarse] /**1a**/ VR to go o turn sour

avine etc [a'βine] VB ver **avenir**

Aviñón [aβi'ɲon] NM Avignon

avío [a'βio] NM preparation; **avíos** NMPL gear sg, kit sg

avión [a'βjon] NM aeroplane; (ave) martin; ~ **de reacción** jet (plane); **por** ~ (Correos) by air mail

avioneta [aβjo'neta] NF light aircraft

avisar [aβi'sar] /**1a**/ VT (advertir) to warn, notify; (informar) to tell; (aconsejar) to advise, counsel

aviso [a'βiso] NM warning; (noticia) notice; (Com) demand note; (Inform) prompt; ~ **escrito** notice in writing; **sin previo** ~ without warning; **estar sobre** ~ to be on the look-out

avispa [a'βispa] NF wasp

avispado, -a [aβis'paðo, a] ADJ sharp, clever

avispero [aβis'pero] NM wasp's nest

avispón [aβis'pon] NM hornet

avistar [aβis'tar] /**1a**/ VT to sight, spot

avitaminosis [aβitami'nosis] NF INV vitamin deficiency

avituallar [aβitwa'ʎar] /**1a**/ VT to supply with food

avivar [aβi'βar] /**1a**/ VT to strengthen, intensify; **avivarse** VR to revive, acquire new life

avizor [aβi'θor] ADJ: **estar ojo** ~ to be on the alert

avizorar [aβiθo'rar] /**1a**/ VT to spy on

axila [ak'sila] NF armpit

axioma [ak'sjoma] NM axiom

ay [ai] EXCL (dolor) ow!, ouch!; (aflicción) oh!, oh dear!; **¡ay de mí!** poor me!

aya ['aja] NF governess; (niñera) nanny

ayer [a'jer] ADV, NM yesterday; **antes de** ~ the day before yesterday; ~ **por la tarde** yesterday afternoon/evening; ~ **mismo** only yesterday

aymara, aymará [ai'mara, aima'ra] ADJ, NMF Aymara

ayo ['ajo] NM tutor

ayote [a'jote] NM (Am) pumpkin

Ayto. ABR = **ayuntamiento**

ayuda [a'juða] NF help, assistance; (Med) enema ▶ NM page; ~ **humanitaria** humanitarian aid

ayudante, -a [aju'ðante, a] NM/F assistant, helper; (Escol) assistant; (Mil) adjutant

ayudar [aju'ðar] /**1a**/ VT to help, assist

ayunar [aju'nar] /**1a**/ VI to fast

ayunas [a'junas] NFPL: **estar en** ~ (no haber comido) to be fasting; (ignorar) to be in the dark

ayuno [a'juno] NM fast; fasting

ayuntamiento [ajunta'mjento] NM (consejo) town/city council; (edificio) town/ city hall; (cópula) sexual intercourse

azabache [aθa'βatʃe] NM jet

azada [a'θaða] NF hoe

azafata [aθa'fata] NF air hostess (BRIT) o stewardess

azafate [asa'fate] NM (Am) tray

azafrán [aθa'fran] NM saffron

azahar [aθa'ar] NM orange/lemon blossom

azalea [aθa'lea] NF azalea

azar [a'θar] NM (casualidad) chance, fate; (desgracia) misfortune, accident; **por** ~ by chance; **al** ~ at random

azaroso, -a [aθa'roso, a] ADJ (arriesgado) risky; (vida) eventful

Azerbaiyán [aθerba'jan] NM Azerbaijan

azerbaiyano, -a [aθerba'jano, a], **azerí** [aθe'ri] ADJ, NM/F Azerbaijani, Azeri

azogue [a'θoɣe] NM mercury

azor [a'θor] NM goshawk

azoramiento [aθora'mjento] NM alarm; (confusión) confusion

azorar [aθo'rar] /**1a**/ VT to alarm; **azorarse** VR to get alarmed

Azores [a'θores] NFPL: **las (Islas)** ~ the Azores

azotaina [aθo'taina] NF beating

azotar [aθo'tar] /**1a**/ VT to whip, beat; (pegar) to spank

azote [a'θote] NM (látigo) whip; (latigazo) lash, stroke; (en las nalgas) spank; (calamidad) calamity

azotea [aθo'tea] NF (flat) roof

azteca [aθ'teka] ADJ, NMF Aztec

azúcar [a'θukar] NM sugar

azucarado, -a [aθuka'raðo, a] ADJ sugary, sweet

azucarero, -a [aθuka'rero, a] ADJ sugar cpd ▶ NM sugar bowl

azuce etc [a'θuθe] VB ver **azuzar**

azucena [aθu'θena] NF white lily

azufre [a'θufre] NM sulphur

azul [a'θul] ADJ, NM blue; ~ **celeste/marino** sky/navy blue

azulejo [aθu'lexo] NM tile

azulgrana [aθul'ɣrana] ADJ INV of Barcelona Football Club ▶ NM: **los A**~ the Barcelona F.C. players o team

azuzar [aθu'θar] /**1f**/ VT to incite, egg on

Bb

B, b [(*Esp*) be, (*Am*) be'larɣa] NF (*letra*) B, b; **B de Barcelona** B for Benjamin (*Brit*) o Baker (*US*)

B.A. ABR (= *Buenos Aires*) B.A.

baba ['baβa] NF spittle, saliva; **se le caía la ~** (*fig*) he was thrilled to bits

babear [baβe'ar] /**1a**/ VI (*echar saliva*) to slobber; (*niño*) to dribble; (*fig*) to drool, slaver

babel [ba'βel] NM O F bedlam

babero [ba'βero] NM bib

Babia ['baβja] NF: **estar en ~** to be daydreaming

bable ['baβle] NM Asturian (dialect)

babor [ba'βor] NM port (side); **a ~** to port

babosada [baβo'saða] NF: **decir babosadas** (*Am fam*) to talk rubbish

baboso, -a [ba'βoso, a] ADJ slobbering; (*Zool*) slimy; (*Am*) silly ► NM/F (*Am*) fool

babucha [ba'βutʃa] NF slipper

baca ['baka] NF (*Auto*) luggage o roof rack

bacalao [baka'lao] NM cod(fish)

bacanal [baka'nal] NF orgy

bache ['batʃe] NM pothole, rut; (*fig*) bad patch

bachillerato [batʃiʎe'rato] NM *two-year advanced secondary school course*; *ver tb* **sistema educativo**

bacilo [ba'θilo] NM bacillus, germ

bacinica [baθi'nika], **bacinilla** [baθi'niʎa] NF potty

bacteria [bak'terja] NF bacterium, germ

bacteriológico, -a [bakterjo'loxiko, a] ADJ bacteriological; **guerra bacteriológica** germ warfare

báculo ['bakulo] NM stick, staff; (*fig*) support

badajo [ba'ðaxo] NM clapper (*of a bell*)

bádminton ['baðminton] NM badminton

bafle ['bafle], **baffle** ['baffle] NM (*Elec*) speaker

bagaje [ba'ɣaxe] NM baggage; (*fig*) background

bagatela [baɣa'tela] NF trinket, trifle

Bahama [ba'ama]: **las (Islas) ~, las Bahamas** *nfpl* the Bahamas

bahía [ba'ia] NF bay

bailar [bai'lar] /**1a**/ VT, VI to dance

bailarín, -ina [baila'rin, ina] NM/F dancer; (*de ballet*) ballet dancer

baile ['baile] NM dance; (*formal*) ball

baja ['baxa] NF drop, fall; (*Econ*) slump; (*Mil*) casualty; (*paro*) redundancy; **dar de ~** (*soldado*) to discharge; (*empleado*) to dismiss, sack; **darse de ~** (*retirarse*) to drop out; (*Med*) to go sick; (*dimitir*) to resign; **estar de ~** (*enfermo*) to be off sick; (*Bolsa*) to be dropping o falling; **jugar a la ~** (*Econ*) to speculate on a fall in prices; *ver tb* **bajo**

bajada [ba'xaða] NF descent; (*camino*) slope; (*de aguas*) ebb

bajamar [baxa'mar] NF low tide

bajar [ba'xar] /**1a**/ VI to go o come down; (*temperatura, precios*) to drop, fall ► VT (*cabeza*) to bow; (*escalera*) to go o come down; (*radio etc*) to turn down; (*precio, voz*) to lower; (*llevar abajo*) to take down; **bajarse** VR (*de vehículo*) to get out; (*de autobús*) to get off; **~ de** (*coche*) to get out of; (*autobús*) to get off; **bajarle los humos a algn** (*fig*) to cut sb down to size; **bajarse algo de Internet** to download sth from the internet

bajeza [ba'xeθa] NF baseness; (*una bajeza*) vile deed

bajío [ba'xio] NM shoal, sandbank; (*Am*) lowlands *pl*

bajista [ba'xista] NMF (*Mus*) bassist ► ADJ (*Bolsa*) bear *cpd*

bajo, -a ['baxo, a] ADJ (*terreno*) low(-lying); (*mueble, número, precio*) low; (*piso*) ground *cpd*; (*de estatura*) small, short; (*color*) pale; (*sonido*) faint, soft, low; (*voz, tono*) deep; (*metal*) base; (*humilde*) low, humble ► ADV (*hablar*) softly, quietly; (*volar*) low ► PREP under, below, underneath ► NM (*Mus*) bass; **hablar en voz baja** to whisper; **~ la lluvia** in the rain

bajón [ba'xon] NM fall, drop

bajura [ba'xura] NF: **pesca de ~** coastal fishing

bakalao [baka'lao] NM (*Mus*) rave music

bala ['bala] NF bullet; **~ de goma** plastic bullet

balacear [balaθe'ar] /**1a**/ VT (*Am*) to shoot
balacera [bala'sera] NF (*Am*) shoot-out
balada [ba'laða] NF ballad
baladí [bala'ði] ADJ trivial
baladronada [balaðro'naða] NF (*dicho*) boast, brag; (*hecho*) piece of bravado
balance [ba'lanθe] NM (*Com*) balance; (: *libro*) balance sheet; (: *cuenta general*) stocktaking; **~ de comprobación** trial balance; **~ consolidado** consolidated balance sheet; **hacer ~** to take stock
balancear [balanθe'ar] /**1a**/ VT to balance ▶ VI to swing (to and fro); (*vacilar*) to hesitate; **balancearse** VR to swing (to and fro); (*vacilar*) to hesitate
balanceo [balan'θeo] NM swinging
balandro [ba'landro] NM yacht
balanza [ba'lanθa] NF scales *pl*, balance; **~ comercial** balance of trade; **~ de pagos/de poder(es)** balance of payments/of power; (*Astro*) **B~** Libra
balar [ba'lar] /**1a**/ VI to bleat
balaustrada [balaus'traða] NF balustrade; (*pasamanos*) banister
balazo [ba'laθo] NM (*tiro*) shot; (*herida*) bullet wound
balboa [bal'βoa] NF *Panamanian currency unit*
balbucear [balβuθe'ar] /**1a**/ VI, VT to stammer, stutter
balbuceo [balβu'θeo] NM stammering, stuttering
balbucir [balβu'θir] /**3f**/ VI, VT to stammer, stutter
Balcanes [bal'kanes] NMPL: **los (Montes) ~** the Balkans, the Balkan Mountains; **la Península de los ~** the Balkan Peninsula
balcánico, -a [bal'kaniko, a] ADJ Balkan
balcón [bal'kon] NM balcony
balda ['balda] NF (*estante*) shelf
baldar [bal'dar] /**1a**/ VT to cripple; (*agotar*) to exhaust
balde ['balde] NM (*esp Am*) bucket, pail; **de ~** *adv* (for) free, for nothing; **en ~** *adv* in vain
baldío, -a [bal'dio, a] ADJ uncultivated; (*terreno*) waste; (*inútil*) vain ▶ NM wasteland
baldosa [bal'dosa] NF (*azulejo*) floor tile; (*grande*) flagstone
baldosín [baldo'sin] NM tile
balear [bale'ar] /**1a**/ ADJ Balearic, of the Balearic Islands ▶ NMF native *o* inhabitant of the Balearic Islands ▶ VT (*Am*) to shoot (at)
Baleares [bale'ares] NFPL: **las (Islas) ~** the Balearics, the Balearic Islands
balero [ba'lero] NM (*Am*: *juguete*) cup-and-ball toy
balido [ba'liðo] NM bleat, bleating
balín [ba'lin] NM pellet; **balines** NMPL buckshot *sg*
balística [ba'listika] NF ballistics *pl*

baliza [ba'liθa] NF (*Aviat*) beacon; (*Naut*) buoy
ballena [ba'ʎena] NF whale
ballenero, -a [baʎe'nero, a] ADJ: **industria ballenera** whaling industry ▶ NM (*pescador*) whaler; (*barco*) whaling ship
ballesta [ba'ʎesta] NF crossbow; (*Auto*) spring
ballet [ba'le] (*pl* **ballets** [ba'les]) NM ballet
balneario, -a [balne'arjo, a] ADJ: **estación balnearia** (bathing) resort ▶ NM spa, health resort; (*Am*: *en la costa*) seaside resort
balompié [balom'pje] NM football
balón [ba'lon] NM ball
baloncesto [balon'θesto] NM basketball
balonmano [balon'mano] NM handball
balonred [balon'reð] NM netball
balonvolea [balombo'lea] NM volleyball
balsa ['balsa] NF raft; (*Bot*) balsa wood
bálsamo ['balsamo] NM balsam, balm
balsón [bal'son] NM (*Am*) swamp, bog
báltico, -a ['baltiko, a] ADJ Baltic; **el (Mar) B~** the Baltic (Sea)
baluarte [ba'lwarte] NM bastion, bulwark
bambolearse [bambole'arse] /**1a**/ VR to swing, sway; (*silla*) to wobble
bamboleo [bambo'leo] NM swinging, swaying; wobbling
bambú [bam'bu] NM bamboo
banal [ba'nal] ADJ banal, trivial
banana [ba'nana] NF (*Am*) banana
bananal [bana'nal] NM (*Am*) banana plantation
banano [ba'nano] NM (*Am*) banana tree; (*fruta*) banana
banasta [ba'nasta] NF large basket, hamper
banca ['banka] NF (*asiento*) bench; (*Com*) banking
bancario, -a [ban'karjo, a] ADJ banking *cpd*, bank *cpd*; **giro ~** bank draft
bancarrota [banka'rrota] NF bankruptcy; **declararse en** *o* **hacer ~** to go bankrupt
banco ['banko] NM bench; (*Escol*) desk; (*Com*) bank; (*Geo*) stratum; **~ comercial** *o* **mercantil** commercial bank; **~ por acciones** joint-stock bank; **~ de crédito/de ahorros** credit/savings bank; **~ de arena** sandbank; **~ de datos** (*Inform*) data bank; **~ de hielo** iceberg
banda ['banda] NF band; (*cinta*) ribbon; (*pandilla*) gang; (*Mus*) brass band; (*Naut*) side, edge; **la ~ ancha** broadband; **~ gástrica** gastric band; **la B~ Oriental** Uruguay; **~ sonora** soundtrack; **~ transportadora** conveyor belt
bandada [ban'daða] NF (*de pájaros*) flock; (*de peces*) shoal
bandazo [ban'daθo] NM: **dar bandazos** (*coche*) to veer from side to side

bandeja [ban'dexa] NF tray; **~ de entrada/salida** in-tray/out-tray

bandera [ban'dera] NF *(de tela)* flag; *(estandarte)* banner; **izar la ~** to hoist the flag

banderilla [bande'riʎa] NF banderilla; *(tapa)* savoury appetizer *(served on a cocktail stick)*

banderín [bande'rin] NM pennant, small flag

banderola [bande'rola] NF *(Mil)* pennant

bandido [ban'diðo] NM bandit

bando ['bando] NM *(edicto)* edict, proclamation; *(facción)* faction; **pasar al otro ~** to change sides; **los bandos** *(Rel)* the banns

bandolera [bando'lera] NF: **llevar en ~** to wear across one's chest; **bolsa de ~** shoulder bag

bandolero [bando'lero] NM bandit, brigand

bandoneón [bandone'on] NM *(Am)* large accordion

banquero [ban'kero] NM banker

banqueta [ban'keta] NF stool; *(Am: acera)* pavement *(Brit)*, sidewalk *(US)*

banquete [ban'kete] NM banquet; *(para convidados)* formal dinner; **~ de boda** wedding reception

banquillo [ban'kiʎo] NM *(Jur)* dock, prisoner's bench; *(banco)* bench; *(para los pies)* footstool

banquina [ban'kina] NF *(RPL)* hard shoulder *(Brit)*, berm *(US)*

bañadera [baɲa'ðera] NF *(Am)* bath(tub)

bañado [ba'ɲaðo] NM *(Am)* swamp

bañador [baɲa'ðor] NM swimming costume *(Brit)*, bathing suit *(US)*

bañar [ba'ɲar] /1a/ VT *(niño)* to bath, bathe; *(objeto)* to dip; *(de barniz)* to coat; **bañarse** VR *(en el mar)* to bathe, swim; *(en la bañera)* to have a bath

bañera [ba'ɲera] NF *(Esp)* bath(tub)

bañero, -a [ba'ɲero, a] NM/F lifeguard ▶ NF bath(tub)

bañista [ba'ɲista] NMF bather

baño ['baɲo] NM *(en bañera)* bath; *(en río, mar)* dip, swim; *(cuarto)* bathroom; *(bañera)* bath(tub); *(capa)* coating; **darse o tomar un ~** *(en bañera)* to have o take a bath; *(en mar, piscina)* to have a swim; **~ María** bain-marie

baptista [bap'tista] NMF Baptist

baqueano, -a [bake'ano, a], **baquiano, -a** [baki'ano, a] NM/F *(Am)* guide

baqueta [ba'keta] NF *(Mus)* drumstick

bar [bar] NM bar

barahúnda [bara'unda] NF uproar, hubbub

baraja [ba'raxa] NF pack (of cards); *see note*

> The *baraja española* is the traditional Spanish deck of cards and differs from a standard poker deck. The four *palos* (suits) are *oros* (golden coins), *copas* (goblets), *espadas* (swords), and *bastos* ("clubs", but not like the clubs in a poker pack). Every suit has 9 numbered cards, although for certain games only 7 are used, and 3 face cards: *sota* (Jack), *caballo* (queen) and *rey* (king).

barajar [bara'xar] /1a/ VT *(naipes)* to shuffle; *(fig)* to jumble up

baranda [ba'randa], **barandilla** [baran'diʎa] NF rail, railing

barata [ba'rata] NF *(Am)* (bargain) sale

baratija [bara'tixa] NF trinket; *(fig)* trifle; **baratijas** NFPL *(Com)* cheap goods

baratillo [bara'tiʎo] NM *(tienda)* junk shop; *(subasta)* bargain sale; *(conjunto de cosas)* second-hand goods pl

barato, -a [ba'rato, a] ADJ cheap ▶ ADV cheap, cheaply

baratura [bara'tura] NF cheapness

baraúnda [bara'unda] NF = **barahúnda**

barba ['barβa] NF *(mentón)* chin; *(pelo)* beard; **tener ~** to be unshaven; **hacer algo en las barbas de algn** to do sth under sb's very nose; **reírse en las barbas de algn** to laugh in sb's face

barbacoa [barβa'koa] NF *(parrilla)* barbecue; *(carne)* barbecued meat

barbaridad [barβari'ðað] NF barbarity; *(acto)* barbarism; *(atrocidad)* outrage; **una ~ de** *(fam)* loads of; **¡qué ~!** *(fam)* how awful!; **cuesta una ~** *(fam)* it costs a fortune

barbarie [bar'βarje] NF, **barbarismo** [barβa'rismo] NM barbarism; *(crueldad)* barbarity

bárbaro, -a ['barβaro, a] ADJ barbarous, cruel; *(grosero)* rough, uncouth ▶ NM/F barbarian ▶ ADV: **lo pasamos ~** *(fam)* we had a great time; **¡qué ~!** *(fam)* how marvellous!; **un éxito ~** *(fam)* a terrific success; **es un tipo ~** *(fam)* he's a great bloke

barbecho [bar'βetʃo] NM fallow land

barbero [bar'βero] NM barber, hairdresser

barbilampiño, a [barβilam'piɲo, a] ADJ smooth-faced; *(fig)* inexperienced

barbilla [bar'βiʎa] NF chin, tip of the chin

barbitúrico [barβi'turiko] NM barbiturate

barbo ['barβo] NM: **~ de mar** red mullet

barbotar [barβo'tar] /1a/, **barbotear** [barβote'ar] /1a/ VT, VI to mutter, mumble

barbudo, -a [bar'βuðo, a] ADJ bearded

barbullar [barβu'ʎar] /1a/ VI to jabber away

barca ['barka] NF *(small)* boat; **~ pesquera** fishing boat; **~ de pasaje** ferry

barcaza [bar'kaθa] NF barge; **~ de desembarco** landing craft

Barcelona [barθe'lona] NF Barcelona

barcelonés, -esa [barθelo'nes, esa] ADJ of o from Barcelona ▶ NM/F native o inhabitant of Barcelona

barco ['barko] NM boat; (*buque*) ship; (*Com etc*) vessel; ~ **de carga** cargo boat; ~ **de guerra** warship; ~ **de vela** sailing ship; **ir en** ~ to go by boat

barda ['barða] NF (*AM: de madera*) fence

baremo [ba'remo] NM scale; (*tabla de cuentas*) ready reckoner

barítono [ba'ritono] NM baritone

barman ['barman] NM barman

Barna ABR = **Barcelona**

barnice *etc* [bar'niθe] VB *ver* **barnizar**

barniz [bar'niθ] NM varnish; (*en la loza*) glaze; (*fig*) veneer

barnizar [barni'θar] /1f/ VT to varnish; (*loza*) to glaze

barómetro [ba'rometro] NM barometer

barón [ba'ron] NM baron

baronesa [baro'nesa] NF baroness

barquero [bar'kero] NM boatman

barquilla [bar'kiʎa] NF (*Naut*) log

barquillo [bar'kiʎo] NM cone, cornet

barra ['barra] NF bar, rod; (*Jur*) rail; (: *banquillo*) dock; (*de un bar, café*) bar; (*de pan*) French loaf; (*palanca*) lever; ~ **de carmín** o **de labios** lipstick; ~ **de herramientas** (*Inform*) toolbar; ~ **de espaciado** (*Inform*) space bar; ~ **inversa** backslash; ~ **libre** free bar; **no pararse en barras** to stick o stop at nothing

barrabasada [barraβa'saða] NF (piece of) mischief

barraca [ba'rraka] NF hut, cabin; (*en Valencia*) thatched farmhouse; (*en feria*) booth

barracón [barra'kon] NM (*caseta*) big hut

barragana [barra'ɣana] NF concubine

barranca [ba'rranka] NF ravine, gully

barranco [ba'rranko] NM ravine; (*fig*) difficulty

barrena [ba'rrena] NF drill

barrenar [barre'nar] /1a/ VT to drill (through), bore

barrendero, -a [barren'dero, a] NM/F street-sweeper

barreno [ba'rreno] NM large drill

barreño [ba'rreɲo] NM washing-up bowl

barrer [ba'rrer] /2a/ VT to sweep; (*quitar*) to sweep away; (*Mil, Naut*) to sweep, rake (with gunfire) ▸ VI to sweep up

barrera [ba'rrera] NF barrier; (*Mil*) barricade; (*Ferro*) crossing gate; **poner barreras a** to hinder; ~ **arancelaria** (*Com*) tariff barrier; ~ **comercial** (*Com*) trade barrier

barriada [ba'rrjaða] NF quarter, district

barricada [barri'kaða] NF barricade

barrida [ba'rriða] NF, **barrido** [ba'rriðo] NM sweep, sweeping

barriga [ba'rriɣa] NF belly; (*panza*) paunch; (*vientre*) guts *pl*; **echar** ~ to get middle-age spread

barrigón, -ona [barri'ɣon, ona], **barrigudo, -a** [barri'ɣuðo, a] ADJ potbellied

barril [ba'rril] NM barrel, cask; **cerveza de** ~ draught beer

barrio ['barrjo] NM (*vecindad*) area, neighborhood (*US*); (*en las afueras*) suburb; **barrios bajos** poor quarter *sg*; ~ **chino** red-light district

barriobajero, -a [barrjobβa'xero, a] ADJ (*vulgar*) common

barro ['barro] NM (*lodo*) mud; (*objetos*) earthenware; (*Med*) pimple

barroco, -a [ba'rroko, a] ADJ Baroque; (*fig*) elaborate ▸ NM Baroque

barrote [ba'rrote] NM (*de ventana etc*) bar

barruntar [barrun'tar] /1a/ VT (*conjeturar*) to guess; (*presentir*) to suspect

barrunto [ba'rrunto] NM guess; suspicion

bartola [bar'tola] NF: **tirarse a la** ~ to take it easy, be lazy

bártulos ['bartulos] NMPL things, belongings

barullo [ba'ruʎo] NM row, uproar

basa ['basa] NF (*Arq*) base

basamento [basa'mento] NM base, plinth

basar [ba'sar] /1a/ VT to base; **basarse** VR: **basarse en** to be based on

basca ['baska] NF nausea

báscula ['baskula] NF (platform) scales *pl*

base ['base] NF base; **a** ~ **de** on the basis of, based on; (*mediante*) by means of; **a** ~ **de bien** in abundance; ~ **de conocimiento** knowledge base; ~ **de datos** database

básico, -a ['basiko, a] ADJ basic

Basilea [basi'lea] NF Basle

basílica [ba'silika] NF basilica

basilisco [basi'lisko] NM (*AM*) iguana; **estar hecho un** ~ to be hopping mad

basket, básquet ['basket] NM basketball

básquetbol ['basketbol] NM (*AM*) basketball

bastante [bas'tante] ADJ **1** (*suficiente*) enough; **bastante dinero** enough o sufficient money; **bastantes libros** enough books **2** (*valor intensivo*): **bastante gente** quite a lot of people; **tener bastante calor** to be rather hot; **hace bastante tiempo que ocurrió** it happened quite o rather a long time ago ▸ ADV: **bastante bueno/malo** quite good/ rather bad; **bastante rico** pretty rich; (**lo**) **bastante inteligente (como) para hacer algo** clever enough o sufficiently clever to do sth; **voy a tardar bastante** I'm going to be a while o quite some time

bastar [bas'tar] /1a/ VI to be enough o sufficient; **bastarse** VR to be self-sufficient;

~ para to be enough to; **¡basta!** (that's) enough!

bastardilla [bastar'ðiʎa] NF italics pl

bastardo, -a [bas'tarðo, a] ADJ, NM/F bastard

bastidor [basti'ðor] NM frame; (de coche) chassis; (Arte) stretcher; (Teat) wing; **entre bastidores** behind the scenes

basto, -a ['basto, a] ADJ coarse, rough ▶ NM: **bastos** (Naipes) one of the suits in the Spanish card deck; ver tb **baraja española**

bastón [bas'ton] NM stick, staff; (para pasear) walking stick; **~ de mando** baton

bastonazo [basto'naθo] NM blow with a stick

bastoncillo [baston'θiʎo] NM (tb: **bastoncillo de algodón**) cotton bud

basura [ba'sura] NF rubbish, refuse (BRIT), garbage (US) ▶ ADJ: **comida/televisión ~** junk food/TV

basurero [basu'rero] NM (hombre) dustman (BRIT), garbage collector o man (US); (lugar) rubbish dump; (cubo) (rubbish) bin (BRIT), trash can (US)

bata ['bata] NF (gen) dressing gown; (cubretodo) smock, overall; (Med, Tec etc) lab(oratory) coat

batacazo [bata'kaθo] NM bump

batalla [ba'taʎa] NF battle; **de ~** for everyday use; **~ campal** pitched battle

batallar [bata'ʎar] /1a/ VI to fight

batallón [bata'ʎon] NM battalion

batata [ba'tata] NF (Am Culin) sweet potato

bate ['bate] NM (Deporte) bat

batea [ba'tea] NF (Am) washing trough

bateador [batea'ðor] NM (Deporte) batter, batsman

batería [bate'ria] NF battery; (Mus) drums pl; (Teat) footlights pl; **~ de cocina** kitchen utensils pl

batiburrillo [batiβu'rriʎo] NM hotchpotch

batido, -a [ba'tiðo, a] ADJ (camino) beaten, well-trodden ▶ NM (Culin) batter; **~ (de leche)** milk shake ▶ NF (Am) (police) raid

batidora [bati'ðora] NF beater, mixer; **~ eléctrica** food mixer, blender

batir [ba'tir] /3a/ VT to beat, strike; (vencer) to beat, defeat; (revolver) to beat, mix; (pelo) to back-comb; **batirse** VR to fight; **~ palmas** to clap, applaud

baturro, -a [ba'turro, a] NM/F Aragonese peasant

batuta [ba'tuta] NF baton; **llevar la ~** (fig) to be the boss

baudio ['bauðjo] NM (Inform) baud

baúl [ba'ul] NM trunk; (Am Auto) boot (BRIT), trunk (US)

bautice etc [bau'tiθe] VB ver **bautizar**

bautismo [bau'tismo] NM baptism, christening

bautista [bau'tista] ADJ, NMF Baptist

bautizar [bauti'θar] /1f/ VT to baptize, christen; (fam: diluir) to water down; (dar apodo) to dub

bautizo [bau'tiθo] NM baptism, christening

bávaro, -a ['baβaro, a] ADJ, NM/F Bavarian

Baviera [ba'βjera] NF Bavaria

baya [baja] NF berry; ver tb **bayo**

bayeta [ba'jeta] NF (trapo) floor cloth; (Am: pañal) nappy (BRIT), diaper (US)

bayo, -a ['bajo, a] ADJ bay

bayoneta [bajo'neta] NF bayonet

baza [baθa] NF trick; **meter ~** to butt in

bazar [ba'θar] NM bazaar

bazo ['baθo] NM spleen

bazofia [ba'θofja] NF pigswill (BRIT), hogwash (US); (libro etc) trash

BCE NM ABR (= Banco Central Europeo) ECB

be [be] NF name of the letter B; **be chica/grande** (Am) V/B; **be larga** (Am) B

beatificar [beatifi'kar] /1g/ VT to beatify

beato, -a [be'ato, a] ADJ blessed; (piadoso) pious

bebé [be'βe] (pl **bebés** [be'βes]), (Am) **bebe** ['beβe] (pl **bebes** ['beβes]) NM baby; **~ de diseño** designer baby

bebedero [beβe'ðero] NM (para animales) drinking trough; (Am: para personas) drinking fountain

bebedizo, -a [beβe'ðiθo, a] ADJ drinkable ▶ NM potion

bebedor, a [beβe'ðor, a] ADJ hard-drinking

bebé-probeta [be'βe-pro'βeta] (pl **bebés-probeta**) NM test-tube baby

beber [be'βer] /2a/ VT, VI to drink; **~ a sorbos/tragos** to sip/gulp; **se lo bebió todo** he drank it all up

bebido, -a [be'βiðo, a] ADJ drunk ▶ NF drink; **bebida energética** energy drink

beca ['beka] NF grant, scholarship

becado, -a [be'kaðo, a] NM/F = **becario**

becario, -a [be'karjo, a] NM/F scholarship holder, grant holder; (en prácticas laborales) intern

becerro [be'θerro] NM yearling calf

bechamel [betʃa'mel] NF = **besamel**

becuadro [be'kwaðro] NM (Mus) natural sign

bedel [be'ðel] NM porter, janitor; (Univ) porter

beduino, -a [be'ðwino, a] ADJ, NM/F Bedouin

befarse [be'farse] /1a/ VR: **~ de algo** to scoff at sth

beige ['beix], **beis** ['beis] ADJ, NM beige

béisbol ['beisβol] NM baseball

bejuco [be'juko] NM (Am) reed, liana

beldad [bel'dað] NF beauty

Belén [be'len] NM Bethlehem; **belén** (de Navidad) nativity scene, crib

belga ['belɣa] ADJ, NMF Belgian

Bélgica ['belxika] NF Belgium

Belgrado [bel'ɣraðo] NM Belgrade

Belice [be'liθe] NM Belize

bélico, -a ['beliko, a] ADJ (*actitud*) warlike

belicoso, -a [beli'koso, a] ADJ (*guerrero*) warlike; (*agresivo*) aggressive, bellicose

beligerante [belixe'rante] ADJ belligerent

bellaco, -a [be'ʎako, a] ADJ sly, cunning ▶ NM villain, rogue

belladona [beʎa'ðona] NF deadly nightshade

bellaquería [beʎake'ria] NF (*acción*) dirty trick; (*calidad*) wickedness

belleza [be'ʎeθa] NF beauty

bello, -a ['beʎo, a] ADJ beautiful, lovely; **Bellas Artes** Fine Art *sg*

bellota [be'ʎota] NF acorn

bemol [be'mol] NM (*Mus*) flat; **esto tiene bemoles** (*fam*) this is a tough one

bencina [ben'sina] NF (*Am: gasolina*) petrol (*BRIT*), gas (*US*)

bendecir [bende'θir] /3o/ VT to bless; **~ la mesa** to say grace

bendición [bendi'θjon] NF blessing

bendiga *etc* [ben'diɣa], **bendije** *etc* [ben'dixe] VB *ver* **bendecir**

bendito, -a [ben'dito, a] PP *de* **bendecir** ▶ ADJ (*santo*) blessed; (*agua*) holy; (*afortunado*) lucky; (*feliz*) happy; (*sencillo*) simple ▶ NM/F simple soul; **¡~ sea Dios!** thank goodness!; **es un ~** he's sweet; **dormir como un ~** to sleep like a log

benedictino, -a [beneðik'tino, a] ADJ, NM Benedictine

benefactor, a [benefak'tor, a] NM/F benefactor/benefactress

beneficencia [benefi'θenθja] NF charity

beneficiar [benefi'θjar] /1b/ VT to benefit, be of benefit to; **beneficiarse** VR to benefit, profit

beneficiario, -a [benefi'θjarjo, a] NM/F beneficiary; (*de cheque*) payee

beneficio [bene'fiθjo] NM (*bien*) benefit, advantage; (*Com*) profit, gain; **a ~ de** for the benefit of; **en ~ propio** to one's own advantage; **~ bruto/neto** gross/net profit; **~ por acción** earnings *pl* per share

beneficioso, -a [benefi'θjoso, a] ADJ beneficial

benéfico, -a [be'nefiko, a] ADJ charitable; **sociedad benéfica** charity (organization)

benemérito, -a [bene'merito, a] ADJ meritorious ▶ NF: **la Benemérita** (*ESP*) the Civil Guard; *ver tb* **guardia**

beneplácito [bene'plaθito] NM approval, consent

benevolencia [beneβo'lenθja] NF benevolence, kindness

benévolo, -a [be'neβolo, a] ADJ benevolent, kind

Bengala [ben'gala] NF Bengal; **el Golfo de ~** the Bay of Bengal

bengala [ben'gala] NF (*Mil*) flare; (*fuego*) Bengal light; (*materia*) rattan

bengalí [benga'li] ADJ, NMF Bengali

benignidad [beniɣni'ðað] NF (*afabilidad*) kindness; (*suavidad*) mildness

benigno, -a [be'niɣno, a] ADJ kind; (*suave*) mild; (*Med: tumor*) benign, non-malignant

benjamín [benxa'min] NM youngest child

beodo, -a [be'oðo, a] ADJ drunk ▶ NM/F drunkard

berberecho [berβe'retʃo] NM cockle

berenjena [beren'xena] NF aubergine (*BRIT*), eggplant (*US*)

berenjenal [berenxe'nal] NM (*Agr*) aubergine bed; (*fig*) mess; **en buen ~ nos hemos metido** we've got ourselves into a fine mess

bergantín [berɣan'tin] NM brig(antine)

Berlín [ber'lin] NM Berlin

berlinés, -esa [berli'nes, esa] ADJ of o from Berlin ▶ NM/F Berliner

berlinesa [berli'nesa] NF (*Am*) doughnut, donut (*US*)

bermejo, -a [ber'mexo, a] ADJ red

bermellón [berme'ʎon] NM vermilion

bermudas [ber'muðas] NFPL Bermuda shorts

berrear [berre'ar] /1a/ VI to bellow, low

berrido [be'rriðo] NM bellow(ing)

berrinche [be'rrintʃe] NM (*fam*) temper, tantrum

berro ['berro] NM watercress

berza ['berθa] NF cabbage; **~ lombarda** red cabbage

besamel [besa'mel], **besamela** [besa'mela] NF (*Culin*) white sauce, bechamel sauce

besar [be'sar] /1a/ VT to kiss; (*fig: tocar*) to graze; **besarse** VR to kiss (one another)

beso ['beso] NM kiss

bestia ['bestja] NF beast, animal; (*fig*) idiot; **~ de carga** beast of burden; **¡~!** you idiot!; **¡no seas ~!** (*bruto*) don't be such a brute!; (*idiota*) don't be such an idiot!

bestial [bes'tjal] ADJ bestial; (*fam*) terrific

bestialidad [bestjali'ðað] NF bestiality; (*fam*) stupidity

besugo [be'suɣo] NM sea bream; (*fam*) idiot

besuguera [besu'ɣera] NF (*Culin*) fish pan

besuquear [besuke'ar] /1a/ VT to cover with kisses; **besuquearse** VR to kiss and cuddle

betabel [beta'bel] NM (*Am*) beetroot (*BRIT*), beet (*US*)

bético, -a ['betiko, a] ADJ Andalusian

betún [be'tun] NM shoe polish; (*Química*) bitumen, asphalt

Bib. ABR = **biblioteca**

biberón [biβe'ron] NM feeding bottle

Biblia ['biβlja] NF Bible

bíblico, -a ['biβliko, a] ADJ biblical
bibliografía [biβljoɣra'fia] NF bibliography
biblioteca [biβljo'teka] NF library; (*estantes*) bookcase, bookshelves *pl*; **~ de consulta** reference library
bibliotecario, -a [biβljote'karjo, a] NM/F librarian
B.I.C. [bik] NF ABR (= *Brigada de Investigación Criminal*) ≈ CID (BRIT), FBI (US)
bicarbonato [bikarβo'nato] NM bicarbonate
bíceps ['biθeps] NM INV biceps
bicho ['bitʃo] NM (*animal*) small animal; (*sabandija*) bug, insect; (*Taur*) bull; **~ raro** (*fam*) queer fish
bici ['biθi] NF (*fam*) bike
bicicleta [biθi'kleta] NF bicycle, cycle; **ir en ~** to cycle; **~ estática/de montaña** exercise/mountain bike
bicoca [bi'koka] NF (ESP *fam*) cushy job
bidé [bi'ðe] NM bidet
bidireccional [biðirekθjo'nal] ADJ bidirectional
bidón [bi'ðon] NM (*grande*) drum; (*pequeño*) can
Bielorrusia [bjelo'rrusja] NF Belarus, Byelorussia
bielorruso, -a [bjelo'rruso, a] ADJ, NM/F Belarussian, Belorussian ▶ NM (*Ling*) Belarussian, Belorussian

(PALABRA CLAVE)

bien [bjen] NM **1** (*bienestar*) good; **te lo digo por tu bien** I'm telling you for your own good; **el bien y el mal** good and evil
2 (*posesión*): **bienes** NMPL goods; **bienes de consumo/equipo** consumer/capital goods; **bienes inmuebles** *o* **raíces/bienes muebles** real estate *sg*/personal property *sg*
▶ ADV **1** (*de manera satisfactoria, correcta etc*) well; **trabaja/come bien** she works/eats well; **contestó bien** he answered correctly; **oler bien** to smell nice *o* good; **me siento bien** I feel fine; **no me siento bien** I don't feel very well; **se está bien aquí** it's nice here
2: **hiciste bien en llamarme** you were right to call me
3 (*valor intensivo*) very; **un cuarto bien caliente** a nice warm room; **bien de veces** lots of times; **bien se ve que …** it's quite clear that …
4: **estar bien**: **estoy muy bien aquí** I feel very happy here; **te está bien la falda** (*ser la talla*) the skirt fits you; (*sentar*) the skirt suits you; **el libro está muy bien** the book is really good; **está bien que vengan** it's all right for them to come; **¡está bien! lo haré** oh all right, I'll do it; **ya está bien de quejas** that's quite enough complaining; **¿te encuentras bien?** are you all right?

5 (*de buena gana*): **yo bien que iría pero …** I'd gladly go but …
▶ EXCL: **¡bien!** (*aprobación*) OK!; **¡muy bien!** well done!; **¡qué bien!** great!; **bien, gracias, ¿y usted?** fine thanks, and you?
▶ ADJ INV: **niño bien** rich kid; **gente bien** posh people
▶ CONJ **1**: **bien … bien**: **bien en coche bien en tren** either by car or by train
2: **no bien** (*esp* AM): **no bien llegue te llamaré** as soon as I arrive I'll call you
3: **si bien** even though; *ver tb* **más**

bienal [bje'nal] ADJ biennial
bienaventurado, -a [bjenaβentu'raðo, a] ADJ (*feliz*) happy; (*afortunado*) fortunate; (*Rel*) blessed
bienestar [bjenes'tar] NM well-being; **estado de ~** welfare state
bienhechor, a [bjene'tʃor, a] ADJ beneficent ▶ NM/F benefactor/benefactress
bienio [bjenjo] NM two-year period
bienvenido, -a [bjembe'niðo, a] ADJ welcome ▶ EXCL welcome! ▶ NF welcome; **dar la bienvenida a algn** to welcome sb
bies ['bjes] NM: **falda al ~** bias-cut skirt; **cortar al ~** to cut on the bias
bifásico, -a [bi'fasiko, a] ADJ (*Elec*) two-phase
bife ['bife] NM (AM) steak
bifocal [bifo'kal] ADJ bifocal
bifurcación [bifurka'θjon] NF fork; (*Ferro*, *Inform*) branch
bifurcarse [bifur'karse] **/1g/** VR to fork
bigamia [bi'ɣamja] NF bigamy
bígamo, -a ['biɣamo, a] ADJ bigamous ▶ NM/F bigamist
bígaro ['biɣaro] NM winkle
bigote [bi'ɣote] NM (*tb*: **bigotes**) moustache
bigotudo, -a [biɣo'tuðo, a] ADJ with a big moustache
bigudí [biɣu'ði] NM (hair-)curler
bikini [bi'kini] NM bikini; (*Culin*) toasted cheese and ham sandwich
bilateral [bilate'ral] ADJ bilateral
bilbaíno, -a [bilβa'ino, a] ADJ of *o* from Bilbao ▶ NM/F native *o* inhabitant of Bilbao
bilingüe [bi'lingwe] ADJ bilingual
bilis ['bilis] NF INV bile
billar [bi'ʎar] NM billiards *sg*; **billares** NMPL (*lugar*) billiard hall; (*galería de atracciones*) amusement arcade; **~ americano** pool
billete [bi'ʎete] NM ticket; (*de banco*) banknote (BRIT), bill (US); (*carta*) note; **~ de ida** *o* **sencillo** single (BRIT) *o* one-way (US) ticket; **~ de ida y vuelta** return (BRIT) *o* round-trip (US) ticket; **~ electrónico** e-ticket; **sacar (un) ~** to get a ticket; **un ~ de cinco libras** a five-pound note
billetera [biʎe'tera] NF, **billetero** [biʎe'tero] NM wallet

billón [bi'ʎon] NM billion
bimensual [bimen'swal] ADJ twice monthly
bimestral [bimes'tral] ADJ bimonthly
bimestre [bi'mestre] NM two-month period
bimotor, a [bimo'tor, a] ADJ twin-engined
▶ NM twin-engined plane
binario, -a [bi'narjo, a] ADJ (*Inform*) binary
bingo ['bingo] NM (*juego*) bingo; (*sala*) bingo hall
binóculo [bi'nokulo] NM pince-nez
binomio [bi'nomjo] NM (*Mat*) binomial
biocarburante [biokarβu'rante],
biocombustible [biokombus'tiβle] NM biofuel
biodegradable [bioðeɣra'ðaβle] ADJ biodegradable
biodiésel [bio'disel] NM biodiesel
biodiversidad [bioðiβersi'ðað] NF biodiversity
biografía [bjoɣra'fia] NF biography
biográfico, -a [bio'ɣrafiko, a] ADJ biographical
biógrafo, -a [bi'oɣrafo, a] NM/F biographer
biología [biolo'xia] NF biology
biológico, -a [bio'loxiko, a] ADJ biological; (*cultivo, producto*) organic; **guerra biológica** biological warfare
biólogo, -a [bi'oloɣo, a] NM/F biologist
biombo ['bjombo] NM (folding) screen
biométrico, -a [bio'metriko, a] ADJ biometric
biopsia [bi'opsja] NF biopsy
bioquímico, -a [bio'kimiko, a] ADJ biochemical ▶ NM/F biochemist ▶ NF biochemistry
biosfera [bios'fera] NF biosphere
bioterrorismo [bioterro'rismo] NM bioterrorism
bióxido [bi'oksiðo] NM dioxide
bipartidismo [biparti'ðismo] NM (*Pol*) two-party system
biquini [bi'kini] NM = **bikini**
birlar [bir'lar] /**1a**/ VT (*fam*) to pinch
birlibirloque [birliβir'loke] NM: **por arte de ~** (as if) by magic
Birmania [bir'manja] NF Burma
birmano, -a [bir'mano, a] ADJ, NM/F Burmese
birome [bi'rome] NF (*AM*) ballpoint (pen)
birrete [bi'rrete] NM (*Jur*) judge's cap
birria ['birrja] NF (*fam*): **ser una ~** (*película, libro*) to be rubbish; **ir hecho una ~** to be *o* look a sight
bis [bis] EXCL encore! ▶ NM encore ▶ ADV (*dos veces*) twice; **viven en el 27 ~** they live at 27a
bisabuelo, -a [bisa'βwelo, a] NM/F great-grandfather/mother; **bisabuelos** NMPL great-grandparents
bisagra [bi'saɣra] NF hinge
bisbisar [bisβi'sar] /**1a**/, **bisbisear** [bisβise'ar] /**1a**/ VT to mutter, mumble

bisbiseo [bisβi'seo] NM muttering
biselar [bise'lar] /**1a**/ VT to bevel
bisexual [bisek'swal] ADJ, NMF bisexual
bisiesto [bi'sjesto] ADJ: **año ~** leap year
bisnieto, -a [bis'njeto, a] NM/F great-grandson/daughter; **bisnietos** NMPL great-grandchildren
bisonte [bi'sonte] NM bison
bisoñé [biso'ɲe] NM toupée
bisoño, -a [bi'soɲo, a] ADJ green, inexperienced
bistec [bis'tek], **bisté** [bis'te] NM steak
bisturí [bistu'ri] NM scalpel
bisutería [bisute'ria] NF imitation *o* costume jewellery
bit [bit] NM (*Inform*) bit; **~ de parada** stop bit; **~ de paridad** parity bit
bitácora [bi'takora] NF: **cuaderno de ~** logbook, ship's log
bizantino, -a [biθan'tino, a] ADJ Byzantine; (*fig*) pointless
bizarría [biθa'rria] NF (*valor*) bravery; (*generosidad*) generosity
bizarro, -a [bi'θarro, a] ADJ brave; generous
bizco, -a ['biθko, a] ADJ cross-eyed
bizcocho [biθ'kotʃo] NM (*Culin*) sponge cake
biznieto, -a [biθ'njeto, a] NM/F = **bisnieto**
bizquear [biθke'ar] /**1a**/ VI to squint
blanco, -a ['blanko, a] ADJ white ▶ NM/F white man/woman, white ▶ NM (*color*) white; (*en texto*) blank; (*Mil, fig*) target ▶ NF (*Mus*) minim; **en ~** blank; **cheque en ~** blank cheque; **votar en ~** to spoil one's vote; **quedarse en ~** to be disappointed; **noche en ~** sleepless night; **ser el ~ de las burlas** to be the butt of jokes; **estar sin blanca** to be broke
blancura [blan'kura] NF whiteness
blandengue [blan'denge] ADJ (*fam*) soft, weak
blandir [blan'dir] VT to brandish
blando, -a ['blando, a] ADJ soft; (*tierno*) tender, gentle; (*carácter*) mild; (*fam*) cowardly ▶ NM/F (*Pol etc*) soft-liner
blandura [blan'dura] NF softness; tenderness; mildness
blanqueador [blankea'ðor] NM (*AM*) bleach
blanquear [blanke'ar] /**1a**/ VT to whiten; (*fachada*) to whitewash; (*paño*) to bleach; (*dinero*) to launder ▶ VI to turn white
blanquecino, -a [blanke'θino, a] ADJ whitish
blanqueo [blan'keo] NM (*de pared*) whitewashing; (*de dinero*) laundering
blanquillo [blan'kiʎo] NM (*AM, CAM*) egg
blasfemar [blasfe'mar] /**1a**/ VI to blaspheme; (*fig*) to curse
blasfemia [blas'femja] NF blasphemy
blasfemo, -a [blas'femo, a] ADJ blasphemous ▶ NM/F blasphemer

b

blasón [bla'son] NM coat of arms; (*fig*) honour

blasonar [blaso'nar] /**1a**/ VT to emblazon ▶ VI to boast, brag

bledo ['bleðo] NM: **(no) me importa un ~** I couldn't care less

blindado, -a [blin'daðo, a] ADJ (*Mil*) armour-plated; (*antibalas*) bulletproof; **coche** *o* (*AM*) **carro ~** armoured car; **puertas blindadas** security doors

blindaje [blin'daxe] NM armour, armour-plating

bloc [blok] (*pl* **blocs** [blos]) NM writing pad; (*Escol*) jotter; **~ de dibujos** sketch pad

blof [blof] NM (*AM*) bluff

blofear [blofe'ar] /**1a**/ VI (*AM*) to bluff

blog [bloɣ] (*pl* **blogs**) NM blog

blogging ['bloɣin] NM blogging

blogosfera [bloɣos'fera] NF blogosphere

bloguear [bloɣe'ar] /**1a**/ VI to blog

bloguero, -a [blo'ɣero, a] NM/F blogger

bloque ['bloke] NM (*tb Inform*) block; (*Pol*) bloc; **~ de cilindros** cylinder block

bloquear [bloke'ar] /**1a**/ VT (*Naut etc*) to blockade; (*aislar*) to cut off; (*Com, Econ*) to freeze; **fondos bloqueados** frozen assets

bloqueo [blo'keo] NM blockade; (*Com*) freezing, blocking; **~ mental** mental block

bluejean [blu'jin] NM (*AM*) jeans *pl*, denims *pl*

blusa ['blusa] NF blouse

B.° ABR (*Finanzas*: = *banco*) bank; (*Com*: = *beneficiario*) beneficiary

boa ['boa] NF boa

boato [bo'ato] NM show, ostentation

bobada [bo'βaða] NF foolish action (*o* statement); **decir bobadas** to talk nonsense

bobalicón, -ona [boβali'kon, ona] ADJ utterly stupid

bobería [boβe'ria] NF = **bobada**

bobina [bo'βina] NF (*Tec*) bobbin; (*Foto*) spool; (*Elec*) coil, winding

bobo, -a ['boβo, a] ADJ (*tonto*) daft, silly; (*cándido*) naïve ▶ NM/F fool, idiot ▶ NM (*Teat*) clown, funny man

boca ['boka] NF mouth; (*de crustáceo*) pincer; (*de cañón*) muzzle; (*entrada*) mouth, entrance; **bocas** NFPL (*de río*) mouth *sg*; **~ abajo/arriba** face down/up; **a ~ jarro** point-blank; **se me hace la ~ agua** my mouth is watering; **todo salió a pedir de ~** it all turned out perfectly; **en ~ de** (*esp AM*) according to; **la cosa anda de ~ en ~** the story is going the rounds; **¡cállate la ~!** (*fam*) shut up!; **quedarse con la ~ abierta** to be dumbfounded; **no abrir la ~** to keep quiet; **~ de incendios** hydrant; **~ del estómago** pit of the stomach; **~ de metro** tube (*BRIT*) *o* subway (*US*) entrance

bocacalle [boka'kaʎe] NF side street; **la primera ~** the first turning *o* street

bocadillo [boka'ðiʎo] NM sandwich

bocado [bo'kaðo] NM mouthful, bite; (*de caballo*) bridle; **~ de Adán** Adam's apple

bocajarro [boka'xarro]: **a ~** *adv* (*Mil*) at point-blank range; **decir algo a ~** to say sth bluntly

bocanada [boka'naða] NF (*de vino*) mouthful, swallow; (*de aire*) gust, puff

bocata [bo'kata] NM (*fam*) sandwich

bocazas [bo'kaθas] NMF (*fam*) bigmouth

boceto [bo'θeto] NM sketch, outline

bocha ['botʃa] NF bowl; **bochas** NFPL bowls *sg*

bochinche [bo'tʃintʃe] NM (*fam*) uproar

bochorno [bo'tʃorno] NM (*vergüenza*) embarrassment; (*calor*): **hace ~** it's very muggy

bochornoso, -a [botʃor'noso, a] ADJ muggy; embarrassing

bocina [bo'θina] NF (*Mus*) trumpet; (*Auto*) horn; (*para hablar*) megaphone; **tocar la ~** (*Auto*) to sound *o* blow one's horn

bocinazo [boθi'naθo] NM (*Auto*) toot

bocio [bo'θjo] NM (*Med*) goitre

boda ['boða] NF (*tb*: **bodas**) wedding, marriage; (*fiesta*) wedding reception; **bodas de plata/de oro** silver/golden wedding *sg*

bodega [bo'ðeɣa] NF (*de vino*) (wine) cellar; (*bar*) bar; (*restaurante*) restaurant; (*depósito*) storeroom; (*de barco*) hold

bodegón [boðe'ɣon] NM (*Arte*) still life

bodrio [bo'ðrio] NM: **el libro es un ~** the book is awful *o* rubbish

B.O.E. ['boe] NM ABR = **Boletín Oficial del Estado**

bofe ['bofe] NM (*tb*: **bofes**: *de res*) lights *pl*; **echar los bofes** to slave (away)

bofetada [bofe'taða] NF slap (in the face); **dar de bofetadas a algn** to punch sb

bofetón [bofe'ton] NM = **bofetada**

boga ['boɣa] NF: **en ~** in vogue

bogar [bo'ɣar] /**1h**/ VI (*remar*) to row; (*navegar*) to sail

bogavante [boɣa'βante] NM (*Naut*) stroke, first rower; (*Zool*) lobster

Bogotá [boɣo'ta] N Bogota

bogotano, -a [boɣo'tano, a] ADJ of *o* from Bogota ▶ NM/F native *o* inhabitant of Bogota

bogue *etc* ['boɣe] VB *ver* **bogar**

bohemio, -a [bo'emjo, a] ADJ, NM/F Bohemian

bohío [bo'io] NM (*AM*) shack, hut

boicot [boi'ko(t)] (*pl* **boicots**) NM boycott

boicotear [boikote'ar] /**1a**/ VT to boycott

boicoteo [boiko'teo] NM boycott

bóiler ['boiler] NM (*AM*) boiler

boina ['boina] NF beret

bola ['bola] NF ball; (*canica*) marble; (*Naipes*) (grand) slam; (*betún*) shoe polish; (*mentira*) tale, story; **bolas** NFPL (*AM*) bolas; **~ de billar** billiard ball; **~ de nieve** snowball

bolchevique [bolt∫e'βike] ADJ, NMF Bolshevik

boleadoras [bolea'ðoras] NFPL (*Am*) bolas *sg*

bolear [bole'ar] /**1a**/ VT (*Am: zapatos*) to polish, shine

bolera [bo'lera] NF skittle *o* bowling alley

bolero, -a [bo'lero, a] NM bolero ▸ NM/F (*Am: limpiabotas*) shoeshine boy/girl

boleta [bo'leta] NF (*Am: permiso*) pass, permit; (: *de rifa*) ticket; (: *recibo*) receipt; (: *para votar*) ballot; **~ de calificaciones** report card

boletería [bolete'ria] NF (*Am*) ticket office

boletero, -a [bole'tero, a] NM/F (*Am*) ticket seller

boletín [bole'tin] NM bulletin; (*periódico*) journal, review; **~ escolar** (*Esp*) school report; **~ de noticias** news bulletin; **~ de pedido** application form; **~ de precios** price list; **~ de prensa** press release; *see note*

> The *Boletín Oficial del Estado*, abbreviated to *BOE*, is the official government record of all laws and resolutions passed by *las Cortes* (Spanish Parliament). It is widely consulted, mainly because it also publishes the announcements for the *oposiciones* (public competitive examinations).

boleto [bo'leto] NM (*esp Am*) ticket; **~ de apuestas** betting slip; **~ de ida y vuelta** (*Am*) round-trip ticket; **~ electrónico** (*Am*) e-ticket; **~ redondo** (*Am*) round-trip ticket

boli ['boli] NM Biro®

boliche [bo'lit∫e] NM (*bola*) jack; (*juego*) bowls *sg*; (*lugar*) bowling alley; (*Am: tienda*) small grocery store

bólido ['boliðo] NM meteorite; (*Auto*) racing car

bolígrafo [bo'liɣrafo] NM ball-point pen, Biro®

bolilla [bo'liʎa] NF (*Am*) topic

bolillo [bo'liʎo] NM (*Costura*) bobbin (for lacemaking); (*Am*) (bread) roll

bolita [bo'lita] NF (*Am*) marble

bolívar [bo'liβar] NM *monetary unit of Venezuela*

Bolivia [bo'liβja] NF Bolivia

boliviano, -a [boli'βjano, a] ADJ, NM/F Bolivian

bollería [boʎe'ria] NF cakes *pl* and pastries *pl*

bollo ['boʎo] NM (*de pan*) roll; (*dulce*) scone; (*chichón*) bump, lump; (*abolladura*) dent; **bollos** NMPL (*Am*) troubles

bolo ['bolo] NM skittle; (*píldora*) (large) pill; **(juego de) bolos** skittles *sg*

Bolonia [bo'lonja] NF Bologna

bolsa ['bolsa] NF (*cartera*) purse; (*saco*) bag; (*Am*) pocket; (*de mujer*) handbag; (*Anat*) cavity, sac; (*Com*) stock exchange; (*Minería*) pocket; **~ de agua caliente** hot water bottle; **~ de aire** air pocket; **~ de (la) basura** bin-liner; **~ de dormir** (*Am*) sleeping bag; **~ de papel** paper bag; **~ de plástico** plastic (*o* carrier)

bag; **~ de la compra** shopping bag; **"B~ de la propiedad"** "Property Mart"; **~ de trabajo** employment bureau; **jugar a la ~** to play the market

bolsillo [bol'siʎo] NM pocket; (*cartera*) purse; **de ~** pocket *cpd*; **meterse a algn en el ~** to get sb eating out of one's hand

bolsista [bol'sista] NMF stockbroker

bolso ['bolso] NM (*bolsa*) bag; (*de mujer*) handbag

boludo, -a [bo'luðo, a] (*Am fam!*) ADJ stupid ▸ NM/F prat (*fam!*)

bomba ['bomba] NF (*Mil*) bomb; (*Tec*) pump; (*Am: borrachera*) drunkenness ▸ ADJ (*fam*): **noticia ~** bombshell ▸ ADV (*fam*): **pasarlo ~** to have a great time; **~ atómica/de humo/de retardo** atomic/smoke/time bomb; **~ de gasolina** petrol pump; **~ de incendios** fire engine

bombacha [bom'bat∫a] NF (*Am*) panties *pl*

bombacho, -a [bom'bat∫o, a] ADJ baggy

bombardear [bombarðe'ar] /**1a**/ VT to bombard; (*Mil*) to bomb

bombardeo [bombar'ðeo] NM bombardment; bombing

bombardero [bombar'ðero] NM bomber

bombazo [bom'baθo] NM (*Am: explosión*) explosion; (*fam: notición*) bombshell; (: *éxito*) smash hit

bombear [bombe'ar] /**1a**/ VT (*agua*) to pump (out *o* up); (*Mil*) to bomb; (*Fútbol*) to lob; **bombearse** VR to warp

bombero [bom'bero] NM fireman; **(cuerpo de) bomberos** fire brigade

bombilla [bom'biʎa] NF (*Esp*), **bombillo** [bom'biʎo] NM (*Am*) (light) bulb

bombín [bom'bin] NM bowler hat

bombita [bom'bita] NF (*Am*) (light) bulb

bombo ['bombo] NM (*Mus*) bass drum; (*Tec*) drum; (*fam*) exaggerated praise; **hacer algo a ~ y platillo** to make a great song and dance about sth; **tengo la cabeza hecha un ~** I've got a splitting headache

bombón [bom'bon] NM chocolate; (*Am: de caramelo*) marshmallow; (*belleza*) gem

bombona [bom'bona] NF: **~ de butano** gas cylinder

bombonería [bombone'ria] NF sweetshop

bonachón, -ona [bona't∫on, ona] ADJ good-natured

bonaerense [bonae'rense] ADJ of *o* from Buenos Aires ▸ NMF native *o* inhabitant of Buenos Aires

bonancible [bonan'θiβle] ADJ (*tiempo*) fair, calm

bonanza [bo'nanθa] NF (*Naut*) fair weather; (*fig*) bonanza; (*Minería*) rich pocket *o* vein

bondad [bon'dað] NF goodness, kindness; **tenga la ~ de** (please) be good enough to

bondadoso, -a [bonda'ðoso, a] ADJ good, kind

bongo ['bonɣo] NM large canoe

boniato [bo'njato] NM sweet potato, yam

bonificación [bonifika'θjon] NF (Com) allowance, discount; (pago) bonus; (Deporte) extra points pl

bonito, -a [bo'nito, a] ADJ (lindo) pretty; (agradable) nice ▸ ADV (Am fam) well ▸ NM (atún) tuna (fish)

bono ['bono] NM voucher; (Finanzas) bond; **~ de billetes de metro** booklet of metro tickets; **~ del Tesoro** treasury bill

bonobús [bono'βus] NM (Esp) bus pass

Bono Loto, bonoloto [bono'loto] NM O F (Esp) state-run weekly lottery; ver tb **lotería**

boom [bum] (pl **booms** [bums]) NM boom

boquear [boke'ar] /1a/ VI to gasp

boquerón [boke'ron] NM (pez) (kind of) anchovy; (agujero) large hole

boquete [bo'kete] NM gap, hole

boquiabierto, -a [bokia'βjerto, a] ADJ open-mouthed (in astonishment); **quedarse ~** to be amazed o flabbergasted

boquilla [bo'kiʎa] NF (de riego) nozzle; (de cigarro) cigarette holder; (Mus) mouthpiece

borbollar [borβo'ʎar] /1a/, **borbollear** [borβoʎe'ar] /1a/ VI to bubble

borbollón [borβo'ʎon] NM bubbling; **hablar a borbollones** to gabble; **salir a borbollones** (agua) to gush out

borbotar [borβo'tar] /1a/ VI = **borbollar**

borbotón [borβo'ton] NM: **salir a borbotones** to gush out

borda ['borða] NF (Naut) gunwale, rail; **echar o tirar algo por la ~** to throw sth overboard

bordado [bor'ðaðo] NM embroidery

bordar [bor'ðar] /1a/ VT to embroider

borde ['borðe] NM edge, border; (de camino etc) side; (en la costura) hem; **al ~ de** (fig) on the verge o brink of ▸ ADJ: **ser ~** (Esp fam) to be rude

bordear [borðe'ar] /1a/ VT to border

bordillo [bor'ðiʎo] NM kerb (Brit), curb (US)

bordo ['borðo] NM (Naut) side; **a ~** on board

Borgoña [bor'ɣoɲa] NF Burgundy

borgoña [bor'ɣoɲa] NM burgundy

boricua [bo'rikwa], **borinqueño, -a** [borin'keɲo, a] ADJ, NM/F Puerto Rican

borla ['borla] NF (gen) tassel; (de gorro) pompon

borlote [bor'lote] NM (Am) row, uproar

borra ['borra] NF (pelusa) fluff; (sedimento) sediment

borrachera [borra'tʃera] NF (ebriedad) drunkenness; (orgía) spree, binge

borracho, -a [bo'rratʃo, a] ADJ drunk ▸ NM/F (que bebe mucho) drunkard, drunk; (temporalmente) drunk, drunk man/woman ▸ NM (Culin) cake soaked in liqueur or spirit

borrador [borra'ðor] NM (escritura) first draft, rough sketch; (cuaderno) scribbling pad; (goma) rubber (Brit), eraser; (Com) daybook; (para pizarra) duster; **hacer un nuevo ~ de** (Com) to redraft

borrar [bo'rrar] /1a/ VT to erase, rub out; (tachar) to delete; (cinta) to wipe out; (Inform: archivo) to delete, erase; (Pol etc: eliminar) to deal with

borrasca [bo'rraska] NF (Meteorología) storm

borrascoso, -a [borras'koso, a] ADJ stormy

borrego, -a [bo'rreɣo, a] NM/F lamb; (oveja) sheep; (fig) simpleton ▸ NM (Am fam) false rumour

borricada [borri'kaða] NF foolish action/statement

borrico, -a [bo'rriko, a] NM donkey; (fig) stupid man ▸ NF she-donkey; (fig) stupid woman

borrón [bo'rron] NM (mancha) stain; **~ y cuenta nueva** let bygones be bygones

borroso, -a [bo'rroso, a] ADJ vague, unclear; (escritura) illegible; (escrito) smudgy; (Foto) blurred

Bósforo ['bosforo] NM: **el (Estrecho del) ~** the Bosp(h)orus

Bosnia ['bosnja] NF Bosnia

bosnio, -a ['bosnjo, a] ADJ, NM/F Bosnian

bosque ['boske] NM wood; (grande) forest

bosquejar [boske'xar] /1a/ VT to sketch

bosquejo [bos'kexo] NM sketch

bosta ['bosta] NF dung, manure

bostece etc [bos'teθe] VB ver **bostezar**

bostezar [boste'θar] /1f/ VI to yawn

bostezo [bos'teθo] NM yawn

bota ['bota] NF (calzado) boot; (de vino) leather wine bottle; **botas de agua** o **goma** Wellingtons; **ponerse las botas** (fam) to strike it rich

botadura [bota'ðura] NF launching

botanas [bo'tanas] NFPL (Am) hors d'œuvres

botánico, -a [bo'taniko, a] ADJ botanical ▸ NM/F botanist ▸ NF botany

botar [bo'tar] /1a/ VT to throw, hurl; (Naut) to launch; (esp Am fam) to throw out ▸ VI to bounce

botarate [bota'rate] NM (imbécil) idiot

bote ['bote] NM (salto) bounce; (golpe) thrust; (vasija) tin, can; (embarcación) boat; (Am pey: cárcel) jail; **de ~ en ~** packed, jammed full; **~ salvavidas** lifeboat; **dar un ~** to jump; **dar botes** (Auto etc) to bump; **~ de la basura** (Am) dustbin (Brit), trash can (US)

botella [bo'teʎa] NF bottle; **~ de vino** (contenido) bottle of wine; (recipiente) wine bottle

botellero [bote'ʎero] NM wine rack

botellín [bote'ʎin] NM small bottle

botellón [bote'ʎon] NM (*Esp fam*) outdoor drinking session (*involving groups of young people*)

botica [bo'tika] NF chemist's (shop) (*Brit*), pharmacy

boticario, -a [boti'karjo, a] NM/F chemist (*Brit*), pharmacist

botijo [bo'tixo] NM (earthenware) jug; (*tren*) excursion train

botín [bo'tin] NM (*calzado*) half boot; (*polaina*) spat; (*Mil*) booty; (*de ladrón*) loot

botiquín [boti'kin] NM (*armario*) medicine chest; (*portátil*) first-aid kit

botón [bo'ton] NM button; (*Bot*) bud; (*de florete*) tip; **~ de arranque** (*Auto etc*) starter; **~ de oro** buttercup; **pulsar el ~** to press the button

botones [bo'tones] NM INV bellboy, bellhop (*US*)

botulismo [botu'lismo] NM botulism, food poisoning

bóveda ['boβeða] NF (*Arq*) vault

bovino, -a [bo'βino, a] ADJ bovine; (*Agr*): **ganado ~** cattle

box [boks] NM (*Am*) boxing

boxeador [boksea'ðor] NM boxer

boxear [bokse'ar] /1a/ VI to box

boxeo [bok'seo] NM boxing

boya ['boja] NF (*Naut*) buoy; (*flotador*) float

boyante [bo'jante] ADJ (*Naut*) buoyant; (*feliz*) buoyant; (*próspero*) prosperous

bozal [bo'θal] NM (*de caballo*) halter; (*de perro*) muzzle

bozo ['boθo] NM (*pelusa*) fuzz; (*boca*) mouth

bracear [braθe'ar] /1a/ VI (*agitar los brazos*) to wave one's arms

bracero [bra'θero] NM labourer; (*en el campo*) farmhand

braga ['braɣa] NF (*cuerda*) sling, rope; (*de bebé*) nappy, diaper (*US*); **bragas** NFPL (*de mujer*) panties

braguero [bra'ɣero] NM (*Med*) truss

bragueta [bra'ɣeta] NF fly (*Brit*), flies pl (*Brit*), zipper (*US*)

braguetazo [braɣe'taθo] NM marriage of convenience

braille [breil] NM braille

bramante [bra'mante] NM twine, string

bramar [bra'mar] /1a/ VI to bellow, roar

bramido [bra'miðo] NM bellow, roar

branquias ['brankjas] NFPL gills

brasa ['brasa] NF live o hot coal; **carne a la ~** grilled meat; **dar la ~** (*fam*: *dar la lata, molestar*) to be a pain (*fam*); **dar la ~ a algn** to go on at sb (*fam*); **¡deja de darme la ~!** stop going on at me! (*fam*)

brasero [bra'sero] NM brazier; (*Am*: *chimenea*) fireplace

brasier [bra'sjer] NM (*Am*) bra

Brasil [bra'sil] NM: **(el) ~** Brazil

brasileño, -a [brasi'leɲo, a] ADJ, NM/F Brazilian

brassier [bra'sjer] NM (*Am*) ver **brasier**

bravata [bra'βata] NF boast

braveza [bra'βeθa] NF (*valor*) bravery; (*ferocidad*) ferocity

bravío, -a [bra'βio, a] ADJ wild; (*feroz*) fierce

bravo, -a ['braβo, a] ADJ (*valiente*) brave; (*bueno*) fine, splendid; (*feroz*) ferocious; (*salvaje*) wild; (*mar etc*) rough, stormy; (*Culin*) hot, spicy ▶ EXCL bravo!

bravucón, -ona [braβu'kon, ona] ADJ swaggering ▶ NM/F braggart

bravura [bra'βura] NF bravery; ferocity; (*pey*) boast

braza ['braθa] NF fathom; **nadar a la ~** to swim (the) breast-stroke

brazada [bra'θaða] NF stroke

brazalete [braθa'lete] NM (*pulsera*) bracelet; (*banda*) armband

brazo ['braθo] NM arm; (*Zool*) foreleg; (*Bot*) limb, branch; **brazos** NMPL (*braceros*) hands, workers; **~ derecho** (*fig*) right-hand man; **a ~ partido** hand-to-hand; **cogidos** *etc* **del ~** arm in arm; **no dar su ~ a torcer** not to give way easily; **huelga de brazos caídos** sit-down strike

brea ['brea] NF pitch, tar

brebaje [bre'βaxe] NM potion

brecha ['bretʃa] NF (*hoyo, vacío*) gap, opening; (*Mil, fig*) breach

brécol ['brekol] NM broccoli

brega ['breɣa] NF (*lucha*) struggle; (*trabajo*) hard work

bregar [bre'ɣar] /1h/ VI (*luchar*) to struggle; (*trabajar mucho*) to slog away

bregue *etc* ['breɣe] VB ver **bregar**

breña ['breɲa] NF rough ground

Bretaña [bre'taɲa] NF Brittany

brete ['brete] NM (*cepo*) shackles pl; (*fig*) predicament; **estar en un ~** to be in a jam

breteles [bre'teles] NMPL (*Am*) straps

bretón, -ona [bre'ton, ona] ADJ, NM/F Breton

breva ['breβa] NF (*Bot*) early fig; (*puro*) flat cigar; **¡no caerá esa ~!** no such luck!

breve ['breβe] ADJ short, brief; **en ~** (*pronto*) shortly; (*en pocas palabras*) in short ▶ NF (*Mus*) breve

brevedad [breβe'ðað] NF brevity, shortness; **con o a la mayor ~** as soon as possible

breviario [bre'βjarjo] NM (*Rel*) breviary

brezal [bre'θal] NM moor(land), heath

brezo [bre'θo] NM heather

bribón, -ona [bri'βon, ona] ADJ idle, lazy ▶ NM/F (*vagabundo*) vagabond; (*pícaro*) rascal, rogue

bricolaje [briko'laxe] NM do-it-yourself, DIY

brida ['briða] NF bridle, rein; (*Tec*) clamp; **a toda ~** at top speed

bridge [brɪtʃ] NM (*Naipes*) bridge

brigada [bri'ɣaða] NF (*unidad*) brigade; (*trabajadores*) squad, gang ▸ NM ≈ sergeant major

brigadier [briɣa'ðjer] NM brigadier(-general)

brillante [bri'ʎante] ADJ brilliant; (*color*) bright; (*joya*) sparkling ▸ NM diamond

brillantez [briʎan'teθ] NF (*de color etc*) brightness; (*fig*) brilliance

brillar [bri'ʎar] /1a/ VI (*tb fig*) to shine; (*joyas*) to sparkle; ~ **por su ausencia** to be conspicuous by one's absence

brillo ['briʎo] NM shine; (*brillantez*) brilliance; (*fig*) splendour; **sacar ~ a** to polish

brilloso, -a [bri'ʎoso, a] ADJ (*Am*) = **brillante**

brincar [brin'kar] /1g/ VI to skip about, hop about, jump about; **está que brinca** he's hopping mad

brinco ['brinko] NM jump, leap; **a brincos** by fits and starts; **de un ~** at one bound

brindar [brin'dar] /1a/ VI: ~ **a** o **por** to drink (a toast) to ▸ VT to offer, present; **brindarse** VR: **brindarse a hacer algo** to offer to do sth; **le brinda la ocasión de** it offers o affords him the opportunity to

brindis ['brindis] NM INV toast; (*Taur*) (ceremony of) dedication

brinque *etc* ['brinke] VB *ver* **brincar**

brío ['brio] NM spirit, dash

brioso, -a [bri'oso, a] ADJ spirited, dashing

brisa ['brisa] NF breeze

británico, -a [bri'taniko, a] ADJ British ▸ NM/F Briton, British person; **los británicos** the British

brizna ['briθna] NF (*hebra*) strand, thread; (*de hierba*) blade; (*de tabaco*) leaf; (*trozo*) piece

broca ['broka] NF (*Costura*) bobbin; (*Tec*) drill bit; (*clavo*) tack

brocado [bro'kaðo] NM brocade

brocal [bro'kal] NM rim

brocha ['brotʃa] NF (large) paintbrush; ~ **de afeitar** shaving brush; **pintor de ~ gorda** painter and decorator; (*fig*) poor painter

brochazo [bro'tʃaθo] NM brush-stroke; **a grandes brochazos** (*fig*) in general terms

broche ['brotʃe] NM brooch

broma ['broma] NF joke; (*inocentada*) practical joke; **en ~** in fun, as a joke; **gastar una ~ a algn** to play a joke on sb; **tomar algo a ~** to take sth as a joke; ~ **pesada** practical joke

bromear [brome'ar] /1a/ VI to joke

bromista [bro'mista] ADJ fond of joking ▸ NMF joker, wag

bromuro [bro'muro] NM bromide

bronca ['bronka] NF row; (*regañada*) ticking-off; **armar una ~** to kick up a fuss; **echar una ~ a algn** to tell sb off

bronce ['bronθe] NM bronze; (*latón*) brass

bronceado, -a [bronθe'aðo, a] ADJ bronze *cpd*; (*por el sol*) tanned ▸ NM (sun)tan; (*Tec*) bronzing

bronceador [bronθea'ðor] NM suntan lotion

broncearse [bronθe'arse] /1a/ VR to get a suntan

bronco, -a ['bronko, a] ADJ (*manera*) rude, surly; (*voz*) harsh

bronquios ['bronkjos] NMPL bronchial tubes

bronquitis [bron'kitis] NF INV bronchitis

brotar [bro'tar] /1a/ VT (*tierra*) to produce ▸ VI (*Bot*) to sprout; (*aguas*) to gush (forth); (*lágrimas*) to well up; (*Med*) to break out

brote ['brote] NM (*Bot*) shoot; (*Med, fig*) outbreak

broza ['broθa] NF (*Bot*) dead leaves *pl*; (*fig*) rubbish

bruces ['bruθes]: **de ~** *adv*: **caer** o **dar de ~** to fall headlong, fall flat

bruja ['bruxa] NF witch

Brujas ['bruxas] NF Bruges

brujería [bruxe'ria] NF witchcraft

brujo ['bruxo] NM wizard, magician

brújula ['bruxula] NF compass

bruma ['bruma] NF mist

brumoso, -a [bru'moso, a] ADJ misty

bruñendo *etc* [bru'ɲendo] VB *ver* **bruñir**

bruñido [bru'ɲiðo] NM polish

bruñir [bru'ɲir] /3h/ VT to polish

brusco, -a ['brusko, a] ADJ (*súbito*) sudden; (*áspero*) brusque

Bruselas [bru'selas] NF Brussels

brusquedad [bruske'ðað] NF suddenness; brusqueness

brutal [bru'tal] ADJ brutal

brutalidad [brutali'ðað] NF brutality

bruto, -a ['bruto, a] ADJ (*idiota*) stupid; (*bestial*) brutish; (*peso*) gross ▸ NM brute; **a la bruta**, **a lo ~** roughly; **en ~** raw, unworked

Bs. ABR = **bolívares**

Bs.As. ABR = **Buenos Aires**

bucal [bu'kal] ADJ oral; **por vía ~** orally

bucanero [buka'nero] NM buccaneer

bucear [buθe'ar] /1a/ VI to dive ▸ VT to explore

buceo [bu'θeo] NM diving; (*fig*) investigation

buche ['butʃe] NM (*de ave*) crop; (*Zool*) maw; (*fam*) belly

bucle ['bukle] NM curl; (*Inform*) loop

budín [bu'ðin] NM pudding

budismo [bu'ðismo] NM Buddhism

budista [bu'ðista] ADJ, NMF Buddhist

buen [bwen] ADJ *ver* **bueno**

buenamente [bwena'mente] ADV (*fácilmente*) easily; (*voluntariamente*) willingly

buenaventura [bwenaβen'tura] NF (*suerte*) good luck; (*adivinación*) fortune; **decir** o **echar la ~ a algn** to tell sb's fortune

buenmozo [bwen'moθo] ADJ (*Am*) handsome

bueno, -a ['bweno, a] (*antes de nmsg* **buen**) ADJ
1 (*excelente etc*) good; **es un libro bueno**, **es un buen libro** it's a good book; **hace bueno**, **hace buen tiempo** the weather is fine, it is fine; **es buena persona** he's a good sort; **el bueno de Paco** good old Paco; **fue muy bueno conmigo** he was very nice o kind to me; **ya está bueno** he's fine now
2 (*apropiado*): **ser bueno para** to be good for; **creo que vamos por buen camino** I think we're on the right track
3 (*irónico*): **le di un buen rapapolvo** I gave him a good o real ticking off; **¡buen conductor estás hecho!** some driver o a fine driver you are!; **¡estaría bueno que ...!** a fine thing it would be if ...!
4 (*atractivo, sabroso*): **está bueno este bizcocho** this sponge is delicious; **Julio está muy bueno** (*fam*) Julio's gorgeous
5 (*saludos*): **¡buen día!**, (*AM*) **¡buenos días!** (good) morning!; **¡buenas (tardes)!** good afternoon!; (*más tarde*) good evening!; **¡buenas noches!** good night!
6 (*Med*) well
7 (*otras locuciones*): **estar de buenas** to be in a good mood; **por las buenas o por las malas** by hook or by crook; **de buenas a primeras** all of a sudden
8 (*grande*) good, big; **un buen número de ...** a good number of ...; **un buen trozo de ...** a nice big piece of ...
▶ EXCL: **¡bueno!** all right!; **bueno, ¿y qué?** well, so what?; **bueno, lo que pasa es que ...** well, the thing is ...; **pero ¡bueno!** well, I like that!; **bueno, pues ...** right, (then) ...

Buenos Aires [bweno'saires] NM Buenos Aires
buey [bwei] NM ox
búfalo ['bufalo] NM buffalo
bufanda [bu'fanda] NF scarf
bufar [bu'far] /1a/ VI to snort
bufete [bu'fete] NM (*despacho de abogado*) lawyer's office; **establecer su ~** to set up in legal practice
buffer ['bufer] NM (*Inform*) buffer
bufón [bu'fon] NM clown
bufonada [bufo'naða] NF (*dicho*) jest; (*hecho*) piece of buffoonery; (*Teat*) farce
buhardilla [buar'ðiʎa] NF attic
búho ['buo] NM owl; (*fig*) hermit, recluse
buhonero [buo'nero] NM pedlar
buitre ['bwitre] NM vulture
bujía [bu'xia] NF (*vela*) candle; (*Elec*) candle (power); (*Auto*) spark plug
bula ['bula] NF (*papal*) bull
bulbo ['bulβo] NM (*Bot*) bulb
bulevar [bule'βar] NM boulevard

Bulgaria [bul'ɣarja] NF Bulgaria
búlgaro, -a ['bulɣaro, a] ADJ, NM/F Bulgarian
bulimia [bu'limja] NF bulimia
bulla ['buʎa] NF (*ruido*) uproar; (*de gente*) crowd; **armar** o **meter ~** to kick up a row
bullendo *etc* [bu'ʎendo] VB *ver* **bullir**
bullicio [bu'ʎiθjo] NM (*ruido*) uproar; (*movimiento*) bustle
bullicioso, -a [buʎi'θjoso, a] ADJ (*ruidoso*) noisy; (*calle*) busy; (*situación*) turbulent
bullir [bu'ʎir] /3h/ VI (*hervir*) to boil; (*burbujear*) to bubble; (*moverse*) to move, stir; (*insectos*) to swarm; **~ de** (*fig*) to teem o seethe with
bulo ['bulo] NM false rumour
bulto ['bulto] NM (*paquete*) package; (*fardo*) bundle; (*tamaño*) size, bulkiness; (*Med*) swelling, lump; (*silueta*) vague shape; (*estatua*) bust, statue; **hacer ~** to take up space; **escurrir el ~** to make o.s. scarce; (*fig*) to dodge the issue
buñuelo [bu'ɲwelo] NM ≈ doughnut, ≈ donut (US); (*fruta de sartén*) fritter
buque ['buke] NM ship, vessel; **~ de guerra** warship; **~ mercante** merchant ship; **~ de vela** sailing ship
burbuja [bur'βuxa] NF bubble; **hacer burbujas** to bubble; (*gaseosa*) to fizz
burbujear [burβuxe'ar] /1a/ VI to bubble
burdel [bur'ðel] NM brothel
Burdeos [bur'ðeos] NM Bordeaux
burdo, -a ['burðo, a] ADJ coarse, rough
burgalés, -esa [burɣa'les, esa] ADJ of o from Burgos ▶ NM/F native o inhabitant of Burgos
burgués, -esa [bur'ɣes, esa] ADJ middle-class, bourgeois; **pequeño ~** lower middle-class; (*Pol, pey*) petty bourgeois
burguesía [burɣe'sia] NF middle class, bourgeoisie
burla ['burla] NF (*mofa*) gibe; (*broma*) joke; (*engaño*) trick; **hacer ~ de** to make fun of
burladero [burla'ðero] NM (*bullfighter's*) refuge
burlador, a [burla'ðor, a] ADJ mocking ▶ NM/F mocker; (*bromista*) joker ▶ NM (*libertino*) seducer
burlar [bur'lar] /1a/ VT (*engañar*) to deceive; (*seducir*) to seduce ▶ VI to joke; **burlarse** VR to joke; **burlarse de** to make fun of
burlesco, -a [bur'lesko, a] ADJ burlesque
burlón, -ona [bur'lon, ona] ADJ mocking
buró [bu'ro] NM bureau
burocracia [buro'kraθja] NF bureaucracy
burócrata [bu'rokrata] NMF bureaucrat
buromática [buro'matika] NF office automation
burrada [bu'rraða] NF stupid act; **decir burradas** to talk nonsense; **hacer burradas** to act stupid; **una ~** (*ESP: mucho*) a (hell of a) lot

burro, -a ['burro, a] NM/F (*Zool*) donkey;
(*fig*) ass, idiot ▶ ADJ stupid; **caerse del ~**
to realise one's mistake; **no ver tres en
un ~** to be as blind as a bat
bursátil [bur'satil] ADJ stock-exchange *cpd*
bus [bus] NM bus
busca ['buska] NF search, hunt ▶ NM bleeper,
pager; **en ~ de** in search of
buscador, a [buska'ðor, a] NM/F searcher
▶ NM (*Internet*) search engine
buscapiés [buska'pjes] NM INV jumping jack
(*BRIT*), firecracker (*US*)
buscapleitos [buska'pleitos] NMF
troublemaker
buscar [bus'kar] /**1g**/ VT to look for; (*objeto
perdido*) to have a look for; (*beneficio*) to seek;
(*enemigo*) to seek out; (*traer*) to bring, fetch;
(*provocar*) to provoke; (*Inform*) to search ▶ VI to
look, search, seek; **ven a buscarme a la
oficina** come and pick me up at the office;
buscarle 3 o 4 pies al gato to split hairs;
"~ y reemplazar" (*Inform*) "search and

replace"; **se busca secretaria** secretary
wanted; **se la buscó** he asked for it
buscavidas [buska'βiðas] NMF snooper;
(*persona ambiciosa*) go-getter
buscona [bus'kona] NF whore
busilis [bu'silis] NM INV (*fam*) snag
busque *etc* ['buske] VB *ver* **buscar**
búsqueda ['buskeða] NF = **busca**
busto ['busto] NM (*Anat, Arte*) bust
butaca [bu'taka] NF armchair; (*de cine, teatro*)
stall, seat
butano [bu'tano] NM butane (gas);
bombona de ~ gas cylinder
butifarra [buti'farra] NF Catalan sausage
buzo ['buθo] NM diver; (*AM: chandal*)
tracksuit
buzón [bu'θon] NM (*gen*) letter box; (*en la calle*)
pillar box (*BRIT*); (*Telec*) mailbox; **echar al ~**
to post; **~ de entrada** (*Inform*) inbox; **~ de
salida** (*Inform*) outbox
buzonear [buθone'ar] /**1a**/ VT to leaflet
byte [bait] NM (*Inform*) byte

Cc

C, c [θe, (esp Am) se] NF (letra) C, c; **C de Carmen** C for Charlie
C. ABR (= centígrado) C.; (= compañía) Co
c. ABR (= capítulo) ch
C/ ABR (= calle) St, Rd
c/ ABR (Com: = cuenta) a/c
ca [ka] EXCL not a bit of it!
c.a. ABR (= corriente alterna) A.C.
cabal [ka'βal] ADJ (exacto) exact; (correcto) right, proper; (acabado) finished, complete; **cabales** NMPL: **estar en sus cabales** to be in one's right mind
cábala ['kaβala] NF (Rel) cab(b)ala; (fig) cabal, intrigue; **cábalas** NFPL guess sg, supposition sg; **hacer cábalas** to guess
cabalgadura [kaβalγa'ðura] NF mount, horse
cabalgar [kaβal'γar] /1h/ VT, VI to ride
cabalgata [kaβal'γata] NF procession; ver tb **Reyes Magos**
cabalgue etc [ka'βalγe] VB ver **cabalgar**
cabalístico, -a [kaβa'listiko, a] ADJ (fig) mysterious
caballa [ka'βaʎa] NF mackerel
caballeresco, -a [kaβaʎe'resko, a] ADJ noble, chivalrous
caballería [kaβaʎe'ria] NF mount; (Mil) cavalry
caballeriza [kaβaʎe'riθa] NF stable
caballerizo [kaβaʎe'riθo] NM groom, stableman
caballero [kaβa'ʎero] NM gentleman; (de la orden de caballería) knight; (trato directo) sir; **"Caballeros"** "Gents"
caballerosidad [kaβaʎerosi'ðað] NF chivalry
caballete [kaβa'ʎete] NM (Agr) ridge; (Arte) easel; (Tec) trestle
caballito [kaβa'ʎito] NM (caballo pequeño) small horse, pony; (juguete) rocking horse; **caballitos** NMPL merry-go-round sg; ~ **de mar** seahorse; ~ **del diablo** dragonfly
caballo [ka'βaʎo] NM horse; (Ajedrez) knight; (Naipes) ≈ queen; **ir en** ~ to ride; ~ **de carreras** racehorse; ~ **de vapor** o **de fuerza**

horsepower; **es su** ~ **de batalla** it's his hobby-horse; ~ **blanco** (Com) backer; ver tb **baraja española**
cabaña [ka'βaɲa] NF (casita) hut, cabin
cabaré, cabaret [kaβa're] (pl **cabarés** o **cabarets** [kaβa'res]) NM cabaret
cabecear [kaβeθe'ar] /1a/ VT, VI to nod
cabecera [kaβe'θera] NF (gen) head; (de distrito) chief town; (de cama) headboard; (Imprenta) headline
cabecilla [kaβe'θiʎa] NM ringleader
cabellera [kaβe'ʎera] NF (head of) hair; (de cometa) tail
cabello [ka'βeʎo] NM (tb: **cabellos**) hair sg; ~ **de ángel** confectionery and pastry filling made of pumpkin and syrup
cabelludo [kaβe'ʎuðo] ADJ ver **cuero**
caber [ka'βer] /2l/ VI (entrar) to fit, go; **caben tres más** there's room for three more; **cabe preguntar si...** one might ask whether...; **cabe que venga más tarde** he may come later
cabestrillo [kaβes'triʎo] NM sling
cabestro [ka'βestro] NM halter
cabeza [ka'βeθa] NF head; (Pol) chief, leader; ~ **de ajo** bulb of garlic; ~ **de familia** head of the household; ~ **rapada** skinhead; **caer de** ~ to fall head first; **sentar la** ~ to settle down; ~ **de lectura/escritura** read/write head; ~ **impresora** o **de impresión** printhead
cabezada [kaβe'θaða] NF (golpe) butt; **dar una** ~ to nod off
cabezal [kaβe'θal] NM: ~ **impresor** print head
cabezazo [kaβe'θaθo] NM (golpe) headbutt; (Fútbol) header
cabezón, -ona [kaβe'θon, ona] ADJ with a big head; (vino) heady; (obstinado) pig-headed
cabezota [kaβe'θota] ADJ INV obstinate, stubborn
cabezudo, -a [kaβe'θuðo, a] ADJ with a big head; (obstinado) obstinate, stubborn

cabida [ka'βiða] NF space; **dar ~ a** to make room for; **tener ~ para** to have room for

cabildo [ka'βildo] NM (de iglesia) chapter; (Pol) town council

cabina [ka'βina] NF cabin; (de avión) cockpit; (de camión) cab; **~ telefónica** (tele)phone box (BRIT) o booth

cabizbajo, -a [kaβiθ'βaxo, a] ADJ crestfallen, dejected

cable ['kaβle] NM cable; (de aparato) lead; **~ aéreo** (Elec) overhead cable; **conectar con ~** (Inform) to hardwire

cabo ['kaβo] NM (de objeto) end, extremity; (Mil) corporal; (Naut) rope, cable; (Geo) cape; (Tec) thread; **al ~ de tres días** after three days; **de ~ a rabo** o **~** from beginning to end; (libro: leer) from cover to cover; **llevar a ~** to carry out; **atar cabos** to tie up the loose ends; **C~ de Buena Esperanza** Cape of Good Hope; **C~ de Hornos** Cape Horn; **las Islas de C~ Verde** the Cape Verde Islands

cabra ['kaβra] NF goat; **estar como una ~** (fam) to be nuts

cabré etc [ka'βre] VB ver **caber**

cabrear [kaβre'ar] /1a/ VT to annoy; **cabrearse** VR (enfadarse) to fly off the handle

cabrío, -a [ka'βrio, a] ADJ goatish; **macho ~** (he-)goat, billy goat

cabriola [ka'βrjola] NF caper

cabritilla [kaβri'tiʎa] NF kid, kidskin

cabrito [ka'βrito] NM kid

cabrón [ka'βron] NM cuckold; (fam!) bastard (fam!)

cabronada [kaβro'naða] NF (fam!): **hacer una ~ a algn** to be a bastard to sb

caca ['kaka] NF (palabra de niños) pooh ▶ EXCL: **no toques, ¡~!** don't touch, it's dirty!

cacahuete [kaka'wete] NM (ESP) peanut

cacao [ka'kao] NM cocoa; (Bot) cacao

cacarear [kakare'ar] /1a/ VI (persona) to boast; (gallo) to cluck; (gallo) to crow

cacarizo, -a [kaka'riθo, a] ADJ (AM) pockmarked

cacatúa [kaka'tua] NF cockatoo

cacereño, -a [kaθe'reɲo, a] ADJ of o from Cáceres ▶ NM/F native o inhabitant of Cáceres

cacería [kaθe'ria] NF hunt

cacerola [kaθe'rola] NF pan, saucepan

cacha ['katʃa] NF (mango) handle; (nalga) buttock

cachalote [katʃa'lote] NM sperm whale

cacharro [ka'tʃarro] NM (cazo) pot; (cerámica) piece of pottery; (fam) useless object; **cacharros** NMPL pots and pans

cachear [katʃe'ar] /1a/ VT to search, frisk

cachemir [katʃe'mir] NM cashmere

cacheo [ka'tʃeo] NM searching, frisking

cachetada [katʃe'taða] NF (AM fam: bofetada) slap

cachete [ka'tʃete] NM (Anat) cheek; (bofetada) slap (in the face)

cachimba [ka'tʃimba] NF, **cachimbo** [ka'tʃimbo] NM (AM) pipe

cachiporra [katʃi'porra] NF truncheon

cachivache [katʃi'βatʃe] NM piece of junk; **cachivaches** NMPL trash sg, junk sg

cacho ['katʃo] NM (small) bit; (AM: cuerno) horn

cachondearse [katʃonde'arse] /1a/ VR: **~ de algn** to tease sb

cachondeo [katʃon'deo] NM (ESP fam) farce, joke; (guasa) laugh

cachondo, -a [ka'tʃondo, a] ADJ (Zool) on heat; (caliente) randy, sexy; (gracioso) funny

cachorro, -a [ka'tʃorro, a] NM/F (de perro) pup, puppy; (de león) cub

cachucha [ka'tʃutʃa] (MÉXICO fam) NF cap

cacique [ka'θike] NM chief, local ruler; (Pol) local party boss; (fig) despot

caco ['kako] NM pickpocket

cacofonía [kakofo'nia] NF cacophony

cacto ['kakto] NM, **cactus** ['kaktus] NM INV cactus

cada [kaða] ADJ INV each; (antes de número) every; **~ día** each day, every day; **~ dos días** every other day; **~ uno/a** each one, every one; **~ vez más/menos** more and more/less and less; **~ vez que ...** whenever, every time (that) ...; **uno de ~ diez** one out of every ten; **¿~ cuánto?** how often?

cadalso [ka'ðalso] NM scaffold

cadáver [ka'ðaβer] NM (dead) body, corpse

cadavérico, -a [kaða'βeriko, a] ADJ cadaverous; (pálido) deathly pale

cadena [ka'ðena] NF chain; (TV) channel; **reacción en ~** chain reaction; **trabajo en ~** assembly line work; **~ midi/mini** (Mus) midi/mini system; **~ montañosa** mountain range; **~ perpetua** (Jur) life imprisonment; **~ de caracteres** (Inform) character string

cadencia [ka'ðenθja] NF cadence, rhythm

cadera [ka'ðera] NF hip

cadete [ka'ðete] NM cadet

Cádiz ['kaðiθ] NM Cadiz

caducar [kaðu'kar] /1g/ VI to expire

caducidad [kaðuθi'ðað] NF: **fecha de ~** expiry date; (de comida) sell-by date

caduco, -a [ka'ðuko, a] ADJ (idea etc) outdated, outmoded; **de hoja caduca** deciduous

caduque etc [ka'ðuke] VB ver **caducar**

caer [ka'er] /2n/ VI to fall; (premio) to go; (sitio) to be, lie; (pago) to fall due; **caerse** VR to fall (down); **dejar ~** to drop; **estar al ~** to be due to happen; (persona) to be about to arrive; **me cae bien/mal** I like/don't like him; **~ en la cuenta** to catch on; **su cumpleaños cae en**

viernes her birthday falls on a Friday; **se me ha caído el guante** I've dropped my glove

café [ka'fe] (pl **cafés** [ka'fes]) NM (bebida, planta) coffee; (lugar) café ▶ ADJ (color) brown; **~ con leche** white coffee; **~ solo**, **~ negro** (Am) (small) black coffee

cafeína [kafe'ina] NF caffein(e)

cafetal [kafe'tal] NM coffee plantation

cafetera [kafe'tera] NF ver **cafetero**

cafetería [kafete'ria] NF cafe

cafetero, -a [kafe'tero, a] ADJ coffee cpd ▶ NF coffee pot; **ser muy ~** to be a coffee addict

cafishio [ka'fiʃjo] NM (Am) pimp

cafre ['kafre] NMF: **como cafres** (fig) like savages

cagalera [kaɣa'lera] NF (fam!): **tener ~** to have the runs

cagar [ka'ɣar] /1h/ (fam!) VT to shit (fam!); (fig) to bungle, mess up ▶ VI to have a shit (fam!); **cagarse** VR: ¡**me cago en diez** etc! Christ! (fam!)

cague etc ['kaɣe] VB ver **cagar**

caído, -a [ka'iðo, a] ADJ fallen; (Inform) down ▶ NF fall; (declive) slope; (disminución) fall, drop; **~ del cielo** out of the blue; **la caída del sol** at sunset; **sufrir una caída** to have a fall

caiga etc ['kaiɣa] VB ver **caer**

caimán [kai'man] NM alligator

Cairo ['kairo] NM: **el ~** Cairo

caja ['kaxa] NF box; (ataúd) coffin, casket (US); (para reloj) case; (de ascensor) shaft; (Com) cash box; (Econ) fund; (donde se hacen los pagos) cashdesk; (en supermercado) checkout, till; (Tip) case; (de parking) pay station; **~ de ahorros** savings bank; **~ de cambios** gearbox; **~ de fusibles** fuse box; **~ fuerte** o **de caudales** safe, strongbox; **ingresar en ~** to be paid in

cajero, -a [ka'xero, a] NM/F cashier; (en banco) (bank) teller ▶ NM: **~ automático** cash dispenser, automatic telling machine, ATM

cajetilla [kaxe'tiʎa] NF (de cigarrillos) packet

cajista [ka'xista] NMF typesetter

cajón [ka'xon] NM big box; (de mueble) drawer

cajuela [kax'wela] NF (México Auto) boot (Brit), trunk (US)

cal [kal] NF lime; **cerrar algo a ~ y canto** to shut sth firmly

cal. ABR (= caloría(s)) cal. (= calorie(s))

cala ['kala] NF (Geo) cove, inlet; (de barco) hold

calabacín [kalaβa'θin] NM (Bot) baby marrow; (: más pequeño) courgette (Brit), zucchini (US)

calabacita [kalaβa'θita] (Am) NF courgette (Brit), zucchini (US)

calabaza [kala'βaθa] NF (Bot) pumpkin; **dar calabazas a** (candidato) to fail

calabozo [kala'βoθo] NM (cárcel) prison; (celda) cell

calado, -a [ka'laðo, a] ADJ (prenda) lace cpd ▶ NM (Tec) fretwork; (Naut) draught ▶ NF (de cigarrillo) puff; **estar ~ (hasta los huesos)** to be soaked (to the skin)

calamar [kala'mar] NM squid

calambre [ka'lambre] NM (Elec) shock; (tb: **calambres**) cramp

calamidad [kalami'ðað] NF calamity, disaster; (persona): **es una ~** he's a dead loss

calamina [kala'mina] NF calamine

cálamo ['kalamo] NM (Bot) stem; (Mus) reed

calaña [ka'laɲa] NF model, pattern; (fig) nature, stamp

calar [ka'lar] /1a/ VT to soak, drench; (penetrar) to pierce, penetrate; (comprender) to see through; (vela, red) to lower; **calarse** VR (Auto) to stall; **calarse las gafas** to stick one's glasses on

calavera [kala'βera] NF skull

calcañal [kalka'ɲal], **calcañar** [kalka'ɲar] NM heel

calcar [kal'kar] /1g/ VT (reproducir) to trace; (imitar) to copy

calce etc ['kalθe] VB ver **calzar**

cal. cen. ABR = **calefacción central**

calceta [kal'θeta] NF (knee-length) stocking; **hacer ~** to knit

calcetín [kalθe'tin] NM sock

calcinar [kalθi'nar] /1a/ VT to burn, blacken

calcio ['kalθjo] NM calcium

calco ['kalko] NM tracing

calcomanía [kalkoma'nia] NF transfer

calculador, a [kalkula'ðor, a] ADJ calculating ▶ NF calculator

calcular [kalku'lar] /1a/ VT (Mat) to calculate, compute; **~ que ...** to reckon that ...

cálculo ['kalkulo] NM calculation; (Med) (gall)stone; (Mat) calculus; **~ de costo** costing; **~ diferencial** differential calculus; **obrar con mucho ~** to act cautiously

caldear [kalde'ar] /1a/ VT to warm (up), heat (up); (metales) to weld

caldera [kal'dera] NF boiler

calderero [kalde'rero] NM boilermaker

calderilla [kalde'riʎa] NF (moneda) small change

caldero [kal'dero] NM small boiler

caldo ['kaldo] NM stock; (consomé) consommé; **~ de cultivo** (Bio) culture medium; **poner a ~ a algn** to tear sb off a strip; **los caldos jerezanos** sherries

caldoso, -a [kal'doso, a] ADJ (guisado) juicy; (sopa) thin

calé [ka'le] ADJ gipsy cpd

calefacción [kalefak'θjon] NF heating; **~ central** central heating

calefón [kale'fon] NM (RPL) boiler

caleidoscopio [kaleiðos'kopjo] NM
kaleidoscope

calendario [kalen'darjo] NM calendar

calentador [kalenta'ðor] NM heater

calentamiento [kalenta'mjento] NM
(*Deporte*) warm-up; **~ global** global warming

calentar [kalen'tar] /**1j**/ VT to heat (up); (*fam:
excitar*) to turn on; (*Am: enfurecer*) to anger;
calentarse VR to heat up, warm up; (*fig:
discusión etc*) to get heated

calentón, -ona [kalen'ton, ona] (*RPL fam*) ADJ
(*sexualmente*) horny, randy (BRIT)

calentura [kalen'tura] NF (*Med*) fever, (high)
temperature; (*de boca*) mouth sore

calenturiento, -a [kalentu'rjento, a] ADJ
(*mente*) overactive

calesita [kale'sita] NF (*Am*) merry-go-round,
carousel

calibrar [kali'βrar] /**1a**/ VT to gauge,
measure

calibre [ka'liβre] NM (*de cañón*) calibre, bore;
(*diámetro*) diameter; (*fig*) calibre

calidad [kali'ðað] NF quality; **de ~** quality
cpd; **~ de borrador** (*Inform*) draft quality;
~ de carta o **de correspondencia** (*Inform*)
letter quality; **~ texto** (*Inform*) text quality;
~ de vida quality of life; **en ~ de** in the
capacity of

cálido, -a ['kaliðo, a] ADJ hot; (*fig*) warm

caliente [ka'ljente] VB ver **calentar** ▶ ADJ hot;
(*fig*) fiery; (*disputa*) heated; (*fam: cachondo*)
randy

califa [ka'lifa] NM caliph

calificación [kalifika'θjon] NF qualification;
(*de alumno*) grade, mark; **~ de sobresaliente**
first-class mark

calificado, -a [kalifi'kado, a] ADJ (*Am:
competente*) qualified; (*: obrero*) skilled

calificar [kalifi'kar] /**1g**/ VT to qualify;
(*alumno*) to grade, mark; **~ de** to describe as

calificativo, -a [kalifika'tiβo, a] ADJ
qualifying ▶ NM qualifier, epithet

califique *etc* [kali'fike] VB ver **calificar**

californiano, -a [kalifor'njano, a] ADJ, NM/F
Californian

caligrafía [kaliɣra'fia] NF calligraphy

calima [ka'lima] NF (*cerca del mar*) mist

calina [ka'lina] NF haze

cáliz ['kaliθ] NM (*Bot*) calyx; (*Rel*) chalice

caliza [ka'liθa] NF limestone

callado, -a [ka'ʎaðo, a] ADJ quiet, silent

callar [ka'ʎar] /**1a**/ VT (*asunto delicado*) to keep
quiet about, say nothing about; (*persona,
oposición*) to silence ▶ VI to keep quiet, be
silent; (*dejar de hablar*) to stop talking;
callarse VR to keep quiet, be silent; (*dejar de
hablar*) to stop talking; **¡calla!** be quiet!;
¡cállate!, ¡cállese! shut up!; **¡cállate la boca!**
shut your mouth!

calle ['kaʎe] NF street; (*Deporte*) lane; **~ arriba/
abajo** up/down the street; **~ de sentido único**
one-way street; **~ mayor** (*Esp*) high (BRIT) o
main (*US*) street; **~ peatonal** pedestrianized
o pedestrian street; **~ principal** (*Am*) high
(BRIT) o main (*US*) street; **poner a algn (de
patitas) en la ~** to kick sb out

calleja [ka'ʎexa] NF alley, narrow street

callejear [kaʎexe'ar] /**1a**/ VI to wander
(about) the streets

callejero, -a [kaʎe'xero, a] ADJ street *cpd* ▶ NM
street map

callejón [kaʎe'xon] NM alley, passage; (*Geo*)
narrow pass; **~ sin salida** cul-de-sac; (*fig*)
blind alley

callejuela [kaʎe'xwela] NF side-street, alley

callista [ka'ʎista] NMF chiropodist

callo ['kaʎo] NM callus; (*en el pie*) corn; **callos**
NMPL (*Culin*) tripe *sg*

callosidad [kaʎosi'ðað] NF (*de pie*) corn;
(*de mano*) callus

calloso, -a [ka'ʎoso, a] ADJ horny, rough

calma ['kalma] NF calm; (*pachorra*) slowness;
(*Com, Econ*) calm, lull; **~ chicha** dead calm;
¡~!, ¡con ~! take it easy!

calmante [kal'mante] ADJ soothing ▶ NM
sedative, tranquillizer

calmar [kal'mar] /**1a**/ VT to calm, calm down;
(*dolor*) to relieve; **calmarse** VR (*tempestad*) to
abate; (*mente etc*) to become calm

calmoso, -a [kal'moso, a] ADJ calm, quiet

caló [ka'lo] NM (*de gitanos*) gipsy language,
Romany; (*argot*) slang

calor [ka'lor] NM heat; (*calor agradable*)
warmth; **entrar en ~** to get warm; **tener ~**
to be o feel hot

caloría [kalo'ria] NF calorie

calorífero, -a [kalo'rifero, a] ADJ heat-
producing, heat-giving ▶ NM heating
system

calque *etc* ['kalke] VB ver **calcar**

calumnia [ka'lumnja] NF slander; (*por escrito*)
libel

calumniar [kalum'njar] /**1b**/ VT to slander;
to libel

calumnioso, -a [kalum'njoso, a] ADJ
slanderous; libellous

caluroso, -a [kalu'roso, a] ADJ hot; (*sin exceso*)
warm; (*fig*) enthusiastic

calva ['kalβa] NF bald patch; (*en bosque*)
clearing

calvario [kal'βarjo] NM stations *pl* of the
cross; (*fig*) cross, heavy burden

calvicie [kal'βiθje] NF baldness

calvo, -a ['kalβo, a] ADJ bald; (*terreno*) bare,
barren; (*tejido*) threadbare ▶ NM bald man

calza ['kalθa] NF wedge, chock

calzado, -a [kal'θaðo, a] ADJ shod ▶ NM
footwear ▶ NF roadway, highway

calzador [kalθa'ðor] NM shoehorn
calzar [kal'θar] /**1f**/ VT (zapatos etc) to wear; (un mueble) to put a wedge under; (Tec: rueda etc) to scotch; **calzarse** VR: **calzarse los zapatos** to put on one's shoes; **¿qué (número) calza?** what size do you take?
calzón [kal'θon] NM (tb: **calzones**) shorts pl; (Am: de hombre) pants pl; (: de mujer) panties pl
calzoncillos [kalθon'θiλos] NMPL underpants
cama ['kama] NF bed; (Geo) stratum; **~ individual/de matrimonio** single/double bed; **hacer la ~** to make the bed; **guardar ~** to be ill in bed
camada [ka'maða] NF litter; (de personas) gang, band
camafeo [kama'feo] NM cameo
camaleón [kamale'on] NM chameleon
cámara ['kamara] NF (Pol etc) chamber; (habitación) room; (sala) hall; (Cine) cine camera; (fotográfica) camera; **~ de aire** inner tube; **~ alta/baja** upper/lower house; **~ de circuito cerrado de televisión** CCTV camera; **~ de comercio** chamber of commerce; **~ de control de velocidad** speed camera; **~ digital** digital camera; **~ de gas** gas chamber; **~ de vídeo** video camera; **a ~ lenta** in slow motion; **~ frigorífica** cold-storage room
camarada [kama'raða] NM comrade, companion
camaradería [kamaraðe'ria] NF comradeship
camarero, -a [kama'rero, a] NM waiter ▶ NF (en restaurante) waitress; (en casa, hotel) maid
camarilla [kama'riλa] NF (clan) clique; (Pol) lobby
camarín [kama'rin] NM (Teat) dressing room
camarógrafo, -a [kama'rografo, a] NM/F (Am) cameraman/camerawoman
camarón [kama'ron] NM shrimp
camarote [kama'rote] NM (Naut) cabin
cambiable [kam'bjaβle] ADJ (variable) changeable, variable; (intercambiable) interchangeable
cambiante [kam'bjante] ADJ variable
cambiar [kam'bjar] /**1b**/ VT to change; (trocar) to exchange ▷ VI to change; **cambiarse** VR (mudarse) to move; (de ropa) to change; **~ de idea** u **opinión** to change one's mind; **cambiarse de ropa** to change (one's clothes)
cambiazo [kam'bjaθo] NM: **dar el ~ a algn** to swindle sb
cambio ['kambjo] NM change; (trueque) exchange; (Com) rate of exchange; (oficina) bureau de change; (dinero menudo) small change; **a ~ de** in return o exchange for; **en ~** on the other hand; (en lugar de eso) instead;

~ climático climate change; **~ de divisas** (Com) foreign exchange; **~ de línea** (Inform) line feed; **~ de página** (Inform) form feed; **~ a término** (Com) forward exchange; **~ de velocidades** gear lever; **~ de vía** points pl
cambista [kam'bista] NM (Com) exchange broker
Camboya [kam'boja] NF Cambodia, Kampuchea
camboyano, -a [kambo'jano, a] ADJ, NM/F Cambodian, Kampuchean
camelar [kame'lar] /**1a**/ VT (con mujer) to flirt with; (persuadir) to sweet-talk
camelia [ka'melia] NF camellia
camello [ka'meλo] NM camel; (fam: traficante) pusher
camelo [ka'melo] NM: **me huele a ~** it smells fishy
camerino [kame'rino] NM (Teat) dressing room
camilla [ka'miλa] NF (Med) stretcher
caminante [kami'nante] NMF traveller
caminar [kami'nar] /**1a**/ VI (marchar) to walk, go; (viajar) to travel, journey ▶ VT (recorrer) to cover, travel
caminata [kami'nata] NF long walk; (por el campo) hike
camino [ka'mino] NM way, road; (sendero) track; **a medio ~** halfway (there); **en el ~** on the way, en route; **~ de** on the way to; **~ particular** private road; **~ vecinal** country road; **Caminos, Canales y Puertos** (Univ) Civil Engineering; **ir por buen ~** (fig) to be on the right track; **C~ de Santiago** Way of St James; see note

> The Camino de Santiago is a medieval pilgrim route stretching from the Pyrenees to Santiago de Compostela in north-west Spain, where tradition has it the body of the Apostle James is buried. Nowadays it is a popular tourist route as well as a religious one. The concha (cockleshell) is a symbol of the Camino de Santiago, because it is said that when St James's body was found it was covered in shells.

camión [ka'mjon] NM lorry, truck (US); (Am: autobús) bus; **~ cisterna** tanker; **~ de la basura** dustcart, refuse lorry; **~ de mudanzas** removal (BRIT) o moving (US) van; **~ de bomberos** fire engine
camionero [kamjo'nero] NM lorry o truck (US) driver, trucker (esp US)
camioneta [kamjo'neta] NF van, small truck
camionista [kamjo'nista] NMF (Am) lorry o truck driver
camisa [ka'misa] NF shirt; (Bot) skin; **~ de dormir** nightdress; **~ de fuerza** straitjacket
camisería [kamise'ria] NF outfitter's (shop)

camiseta [kami'seta] NF tee-shirt; (*ropa interior*) vest; (*de deportista*) top

camisón [kami'son] NM nightdress, nightgown

camomila [kamo'mila] NF camomile

camorra [ka'morra] NF: **armar ~** to kick up a row; **buscar ~** to look for trouble

camorrista [kamo'rrista] NMF thug

camote [ka'mote] NM (*AM*) sweet potato; (*bulbo*) tuber, bulb; (*fam: enamoramiento*) crush

campal [kam'pal] ADJ: **batalla ~** pitched battle

campamento [kampa'mento] NM camp

campana [kam'pana] NF bell

campanada [kampa'naða] NF peal

campanario [kampa'narjo] NM belfry

campanilla [kampa'niʎa] NF (*campana*) small bell

campante [kam'pante] ADJ: **siguió tan ~** he went on as if nothing had happened

campaña [kam'paɲa] NF (*Mil, Pol*) campaign; **hacer ~ (en pro de/contra)** to campaign (for/against); **~ de venta** sales campaign; **~ electoral** election campaign

campechano, -a [kampe'tʃano, a] ADJ (*franco*) open

campeón, -ona [kampe'on, ona] NM/F champion

campeonato [kampeo'nato] NM championship

cámper ['kamper] NM o F (*AM*) caravan (*BRIT*), trailer (*US*)

campera [kam'pera] NF (*RPL*) anorak

campesino, -a [kampe'sino, a] ADJ country *cpd*, rural; (*gente*) peasant *cpd* ▶ NM/F countryman/woman; (*agricultor*) farmer

campestre [kam'pestre] ADJ country *cpd*, rural

camping ['kampin] NM camping; (*lugar*) campsite; **ir de** o **hacer ~** to go camping

campiña [kam'piɲa] NF countryside

campista [kam'pista] NMF camper

campo ['kampo] NM (*fuera de la ciudad*) country, countryside; (*Agr, Elec, Inform*) field; (*de fútbol*) pitch; (*de golf*) course; (*Mil*) camp; **~ de batalla** battlefield; **~ de minas** minefield; **~ petrolífero** oilfield; **~ visual** field of vision; **~ de concentración/de internación/de trabajo** concentration/internment/labour camp; **~ de deportes** sports ground, playing field

camposanto [kampo'santo] NM cemetery

campus ['kampus] NM INV (*Univ*) campus

camuflaje [kamu'flaxe] NM camouflage

camuflar [kamu'flar] /1a/ VT to camouflage

can [kan] NM dog, mutt (*fam*)

cana ['kana] NF *ver* **cano**

Canadá [kana'ða] NM Canada

canadiense [kana'ðjense] ADJ, NMF Canadian ▶ NF fur-lined jacket

canal [ka'nal] NM canal; (*Geo*) channel, strait; (*de televisión*) channel; (*de tejado*) gutter; **C~ de la Mancha** English Channel; **C~ de Panamá** Panama Canal

canaleta [kana'leta] NF (*AM: de tejado*) gutter

canalice etc [kana'liθe] VB *ver* **canalizar**

canalizar [kanali'θar] /1f/ VT to channel

canalla [ka'naʎa] NF rabble, mob ▶ NM swine

canallada [kana'ʎaða] NF (*hecho*) dirty trick

canalón [kana'lon] NM (*conducto vertical*) drainpipe; (*del tejado*) gutter; **canalones** NMPL (*Culin*) cannelloni

canapé [kana'pe] (*pl* **canapés** [kana'pes]) NM sofa, settee; (*Culin*) canapé

Canarias [ka'narjas] NFPL: **las (Islas) ~** the Canaries, the Canary Isles

canario, -a [ka'narjo, a] ADJ of o from the Canary Isles ▶ NM/F native o inhabitant of the Canary Isles ▶ NM (*Zool*) canary

canasta [ka'nasta] NF (*round*) basket

canastilla [kanas'tiʎa] NF small basket; (*de niño*) layette

canasto [ka'nasto] NM large basket

cancela [kan'θela] NF (*wrought-iron*) gate

cancelación [kanθela'θjon] NF cancellation

cancelar [kanθe'lar] /1a/ VT to cancel; (*una deuda*) to write off

cáncer ['kanθer] NM (*Med*) cancer; **C~** (*Astro*) Cancer

cancerígeno, -a [kanθe'rixeno, a] ADJ carcinogenic

cancha ['kantʃa] NF (*de baloncesto, tenis etc*) court; (*AM: de fútbol etc*) pitch; **~ de tenis** (*AM*) tennis court

canciller [kanθi'ʎer] NM chancellor; **C~** (*AM*) Foreign Minister, ≈ Foreign Secretary (*BRIT*)

Cancillería [kansiʎe'ria] NF (*AM*) Foreign Ministry, ≈ Foreign Office (*BRIT*)

canción [kan'θjon] NF song; **~ de cuna** lullaby

cancionero [kanθjo'nero] NM song book

candado [kan'daðo] NM padlock

candela [kan'dela] NF candle

candelabro [kande'laβro] NM candelabra

candelero [kande'lero] NM (*para vela*) candlestick; (*de aceite*) oil lamp

candente [kan'dente] ADJ red-hot; (*tema*) burning

candidato, -a [kandi'ðato, a] NM/F candidate; (*para puesto*) applicant

candidatura [kandiða'tura] NF candidature

candidez [kandi'ðeθ] NF (*sencillez*) simplicity; (*simpleza*) naiveté

cándido, -a ['kandiðo, a] ADJ simple; naive

candil [kan'dil] NM oil lamp

candilejas [kandi'lexas] NFPL (*Teat*) footlights

candor [kan'dor] NM (*sinceridad*) frankness; (*inocencia*) innocence

canela [ka'nela] NF cinnamon

canelo [ka'nelo] NM: **hacer el ~** to act the fool

canelones [kane'lones] NMPL cannelloni

cangrejo [kan'grexo] NM crab

canguro [kan'guro] NM (*Zool*) kangaroo; (*de niños*) baby-sitter; **hacer de ~** to baby-sit

caníbal [ka'niβal] ADJ, NMF cannibal

canica [ka'nika] NF marble

caniche [ka'nitʃe] NM poodle

canícula [ka'nikula] NF midsummer heat

canijo, -a [ka'nixo, a] ADJ frail, sickly

canilla [ka'niʎa] NF (*Tec*) bobbin; (*AM*) tap (*BRIT*), faucet (*US*)

canino, -a [ka'nino, a] ADJ canine ▶ NM canine (tooth)

canje [kan'xe] NM exchange; (*trueque*) swap

canjear [kanxe'ar] /1a/ VT to exchange; (*trocar*) to swap

cano, -a ['kano, a] ADJ grey-haired, white-haired ▶ NF (*tb*: **canas**) white o grey hair; **tener canas** to be going grey

canoa [ka'noa] NF canoe

canon ['kanon] NM canon; (*pensión*) rent; (*Com*) tax

canonice *etc* [kano'niθe] VB *ver* **canonizar**

canónico, -a [ka'noniko, a] ADJ: **derecho ~** canon law

canónigo [ka'noniɣo] NM canon

canonizar [kanoni'θar] /1f/ VT to canonize

canoro, -a [ka'noro, a] ADJ melodious

canoso, -a [ka'noso, a] ADJ (*pelo*) grey (*BRIT*), gray (*US*); (*persona*) grey-haired

cansado, -a [kan'saðo, a] ADJ tired, weary; (*tedioso*) tedious, boring; **estoy ~ de hacerlo** I'm sick of doing it

cansancio [kan'sanθjo] NM tiredness, fatigue

cansar [kan'sar] /1a/ VT (*fatigar*) to tire, tire out; (*aburrir*) to bore; (*fastidiar*) to bother; **cansarse** VR to tire, get tired; (*aburrirse*) to get bored

cantábrico, -a [kan'taβriko, a] ADJ Cantabrian; **Mar C~** Bay of Biscay; **(Montes) Cantábricos, Cordillera Cantábrica** Cantabrian Mountains

cántabro, -a ['kantaβro, a] ADJ, NM/F Cantabrian

cantante [kan'tante] ADJ singing ▶ NMF singer

cantaor, a [kanta'or, a] NM/F Flamenco singer

cantar [kan'tar] /1a/ VT to sing ▶ VI to sing; (*insecto*) to chirp; (*rechinar*) to squeak; (*fam*: *criminal*) to squeal ▶ NM (*acción*) singing; (*canción*) song; (*poema*) poem; **~ a algn las cuarenta** to tell sb a few home truths; **~ a dos voces** to sing a duet

cántara ['kantara] NF large pitcher

cántaro ['kantaro] NM pitcher, jug; **llover a cántaros** to rain cats and dogs

cantautor, a [kantau'tor, a] NM/F singer-songwriter

cante ['kante] NM *Andalusian folk song*; **~ jondo** flamenco singing

cantera [kan'tera] NF quarry

cantero [kan'tero] NM (*AM*: *arriate*) border

cántico ['kantiko] NM (*Rel*) canticle; (*fig*) song

cantidad [kanti'ðað] NF quantity, amount; (*Econ*) sum ▶ ADV (*fam*) a lot; **~ alzada** lump sum; **~ de** lots of

cantilena [kanti'lena] NF = **cantinela**

cantimplora [kantim'plora] NF water bottle, canteen

cantina [kan'tina] NF canteen; (*de estación*) buffet; (*esp AM*) bar

cantinela [kanti'nela] NF ballad, song

cantinero, -a [kanti'nero, a] NM/F (*AM*) barman/barmaid, bartender (*US*)

canto ['kanto] NM singing; (*canción*) song; (*borde*) edge, rim; (*de un cuchillo*) back; **~ rodado** boulder

cantón [kan'ton] NM canton

cantor, a [kan'tor, a] NM/F singer

canturrear [kanturre'ar] /1a/ VI to sing softly

canutas [ka'nutas] NFPL: **pasarlas ~** (*fam*) to have a rough time (of it)

canuto [ka'nuto] NM (*tubo*) small tube; (*fam*: *porro*) joint

caña ['kaɲa] NF (*Bot*: *tallo*) stem, stalk; (: *carrizo*) reed; (*de cerveza*) glass of beer; (*Anat*) shinbone; (*AM*: *aguardiente*) cane liquor; **~ de azúcar** sugar cane; **~ de pescar** fishing rod

cañada [ka'ɲaða] NF (*entre dos montañas*) gully, ravine; (*camino*) cattle track

cáñamo ['kaɲamo] NM (*Bot*) hemp

cañaveral [kaɲaβe'ral] NM (*Bot*) reedbed; (*Agr*) sugar-cane field

cañería [kaɲe'ria] NF piping; (*tubo*) pipe

caño ['kaɲo] NM (*tubo*) tube, pipe; (*de aguas servidas*) sewer; (*Mus*) pipe; (*Naut*) navigation channel; (*de fuente*) jet

cañón [ka'ɲon] NM (*Mil*) cannon; (*de fusil*) barrel; (*Geo*) canyon, gorge

cañonazo [kaɲo'naθo] NM (*Mil*) gunshot

cañonera [kaɲo'nera] NF (*tb*: **lancha cañonera**) gunboat

caoba [ka'oβa] NF mahogany

caos ['kaos] NM chaos

caótico, -a [ka'otiko, a] ADJ chaotic

cap. ABR (= *capítulo*) ch.

C.A.P. NM ABR (= *Certificado de Aptitud Pedagógica*) teaching certificate

capa ['kapa] NF cloak, cape; (*Culin*) coating; (*Geo*) layer, stratum; (*de pintura*) coat; **de ~ y**

espada cloak-and-dagger; **so ~ de** under the pretext of; **~ de ozono** ozone layer; **capas sociales** social groups

capacho [ka'patʃo] NM wicker basket

capacidad [kapaθi'ðað] NF (*medida*) capacity; (*aptitud*) capacity, ability; **una sala con ~ para 900** a hall seating 900; **~ adquisitiva** purchasing power

capacitación [kapaθita'θjon] NF training

capacitar [kapaθi'tar] /1a/ VT: **~ a algn para algo** to qualify sb for sth; (*Tec*) to train sb for sth; **capacitarse** VR: **capacitarse para algo** to qualify for sth

capar [ka'par] /1a/ VT to castrate, geld

caparazón [kapara'θon] NM (*Zool*) shell

capataz [kapa'taθ] NM foreman, charge hand

capaz [ka'paθ] ADJ able, capable; (*amplio*) capacious, roomy; **es ~ que venga mañana** (*Am*) he'll probably come tomorrow

capcioso, -a [kap'θjoso, a] ADJ wily, deceitful; **pregunta capciosa** trick question

capea [ka'pea] NF (*Taur*) bullfight with young bulls

capear [kape'ar] /1a/ VT (*dificultades*) to dodge; **~ el temporal** to weather the storm

capellán [kape'ʎan] NM chaplain; (*sacerdote*) priest

caperuza [kape'ruθa] NF hood; (*de bolígrafo*) cap

capi ['kapi] NF (*esp Am fam*) capital (city)

capicúa [kapi'kua] ADJ INV (*número, fecha*) reversible ▶ NF *reversible number, e.g.* 1441

capilar [kapi'lar] ADJ hair cpd

capilla [ka'piʎa] NF chapel

capital [kapi'tal] ADJ capital ▶ NM (*Com*) capital ▶ NF (*de nación*) capital (city); (*tb:* **capital de provincia**) provincial capital, ≈ county town; **~ activo/en acciones** working/share o equity capital; **~ arriesgado** venture capital; **~ autorizado** o **social** authorised capital; **~ emitido** issued capital; **~ improductivo** idle money; **~ invertido** o **utilizado** capital employed; **~ pagado** paid-up capital; **~ de riesgo** risk capital; **~ social** equity o share capital; **inversión de capitales** capital investment; *ver tb* **provincia**

capitalice *etc* [kapita'liθe] VB *ver* **capitalizar**

capitalino, -a [kapita'lino, a] ADJ (*Am*) of o from the capital ▶ NM/F native o inhabitant of the capital

capitalismo [kapita'lismo] NM capitalism

capitalista [kapita'lista] ADJ, NMF capitalist

capitalizar [kapitali'θar] /1f/ VT to capitalize

capitán [kapi'tan] NM captain; (*fig*) leader

capitana [kapi'tana] NF flagship

capitanear [kapitane'ar] /1a/ VT to captain

capitanía [kapita'nia] NF captaincy

capitel [kapi'tel] NM (*Arq*) capital

capitolio [kapi'toljo] NM capitol

capitulación [kapitula'θjon] NF (*rendición*) capitulation, surrender; (*acuerdo*) agreement, pact; **capitulaciones matrimoniales** marriage contract *sg*

capitular [kapitu'lar] /1a/ VI to come to terms, make an agreement; (*Mil*) to surrender

capítulo [ka'pitulo] NM chapter

capo [ka'po] NM drugs baron

capó [ka'po] NM (*Auto*) bonnet (*Brit*), hood (*US*)

capón [ka'pon] NM (*gallo*) capon

caporal [kapo'ral] NM chief, leader

capota [ka'pota] NF (*de mujer*) bonnet; (*Auto*) hood (*Brit*), top (*US*)

capote [ka'pote] NM (*abrigo: de militar*) greatcoat; (*: de torero*) cloak

capricho [ka'pritʃo] NM whim, caprice

caprichoso, -a [kapri'tʃoso, a] ADJ capricious

Capricornio [kapri'kornjo] NM Capricorn

cápsula ['kapsula] NF capsule; **~ espacial** space capsule

captar [kap'tar] /1a/ VT (*comprender*) to understand; (*Radio*) to pick up; (*atención, apoyo*) to attract

captura [kap'tura] NF capture; (*Jur*) arrest; **~ de pantalla** screenshot

capturar [kaptu'rar] /1a/ VT to capture; (*Jur*) to arrest; (*datos*) to input

capucha [ka'putʃa] NF hood, cowl

capuchón [kapu'tʃon] NM (*Esp: de bolígrafo*) cap

capullo [ka'puʎo] NM (*Zool*) cocoon; (*Bot*) bud; (*fam!*) idiot

caqui ['kaki] NM khaki

cara ['kara] NF (*Anat, de moneda*) face; (*aspecto*) appearance; (*de disco*) side; (*fig*) boldness; (*descaro*) cheek, nerve ▶ PREP: **~ a** facing; **de ~ a** opposite, facing; **dar la ~ to** face the consequences; **echar algo en ~ a algn** to reproach sb for sth; **¿~ o cruz?** heads or tails?; **¡qué ~ más dura!** what a nerve!; **de una ~** (*disquete*) single-sided

carabina [kara'βina] NF carbine, rifle; (*persona*) chaperone

carabinero [karaβi'nero] NM (*de aduana*) customs officer; (*Am*) gendarme

Caracas [ka'rakas] NF Caracas

caracol [kara'kol] NM (*Zool*) snail; (*concha*) (sea)shell; **escalera de ~** spiral staircase

caracolear [karakole'ar] /1a/ VI (*caballo*) to prance about

carácter [ka'rakter] (*pl* **caracteres** [karak'teres]) NM character; **caracteres de imprenta** (*Tip*) type(face) *sg*; **~ libre** (*Inform*) wildcard character; **tener buen/mal ~** to be good-natured/bad tempered

caracterice *etc* [karakte'riθe] VB *ver* **caracterizar**

característico, -a [karakte'ristiko, a] ADJ characteristic ► NF characteristic

caracterizar [karakteri'θar] /**1f**/ VT (*distinguir*) to characterize, typify; (*honrar*) to confer a distinction on

caradura [kara'ðura] NMF cheeky person; **es un ~** he's got a nerve

carajillo [kara'xiʎo] NM *black coffee with brandy*

carajo [ka'raxo] NM (*espAm fam!*): **¡~!** shit! (*fam!*); **¡qué ~!** what the hell!; **me importa un ~** I don't give a damn

caramba [ka'ramba] EXCL well!, good gracious!

carámbano [ka'rambano] NM icicle

carambola [karam'bola] NF: **por ~** by a fluke

caramelo [kara'melo] NM (*dulce*) sweet; (*azúcar fundido*) caramel

carantoñas [karan'toɲas] NFPL: **hacer ~ a algn** to (try to) butter sb up

caraqueño, -a [kara'keɲo, a] ADJ of o from Caracas ► NM/F native o inhabitant of Caracas

carátula [ka'ratula] NF (*máscara*) mask; (*Teat*): **la ~** the stage

caravana [kara'βana] NF caravan; (*fig*) group; (*de autos*) tailback

carbo ['karβo] NM (*fam*: = *carbohidrato*) carb

carbón [kar'βon] NM coal; **~ de leña** charcoal; **papel ~** carbon paper

carbonatado, -a [karβona'taðo, a] ADJ carbonated

carbonato [karβo'nato] NM carbonate; **~ sódico** sodium carbonate

carboncillo [karβon'θiʎo] NM (*Arte*) charcoal

carbonice *etc* [karβo'niθe] VB *ver* **carbonizar**

carbonilla [karβo'niʎa] NF coal dust

carbonizar [karβoni'θar] /**1f**/ VT to carbonize; (*quemar*) to char; **quedar carbonizado** (*Elec*) to be electrocuted

carbono [kar'βono] NM carbon; **~ neutral** carbon-neutral

carburador [karβura'ðor] NM carburettor

carburante [karβu'rante] NM fuel

carca ['karka] ADJ, NMF reactionary

carcajada [karka'xaða] NF (loud) laugh, guffaw

carcajearse [karkaxe'arse] /**1a**/ VR to roar with laughter

cárcel ['karθel] NF prison, jail; (*Tec*) clamp

carcelero, -a [karθe'lero, a] ADJ prison *cpd* ► NM/F warder

carcoma [kar'koma] NF woodworm

carcomer [karko'mer] /**2a**/ VT to bore into, eat into; (*fig*) to undermine; **carcomerse** VR to become worm-eaten; (*fig*) to decay

carcomido, -a [karko'miðo, a] ADJ worm-eaten; (*fig*) rotten

cardar [kar'ðar] /**1a**/ VT (*Tec*) to card, comb; (*pelo*) to backcomb

cardenal [karðe'nal] NM (*Rel*) cardinal; (*Med*) bruise

cárdeno, -a ['karðeno, a] ADJ purple; (*lívido*) livid

cardiaco, -a [kar'ðjako, a], **cardíaco, a** [kar'ðiako, a] ADJ cardiac; (*ataque*) heart *cpd*

cardinal [karði'nal] ADJ cardinal

cardiólogo, -a [kar'ðj'oloɣo, a] NM/F cardiologist

cardo ['karðo] NM thistle

carear [kare'ar] /**1a**/ VT to bring face to face; (*comparar*) to compare; **carearse** VR to come face to face, meet

carecer [kare'θer] /**2d**/ VI: **~ de** to lack, be in need of

carencia [ka'renθja] NF lack; (*escasez*) shortage; (*Med*) deficiency

carente [ka'rente] ADJ: **~ de** lacking in, devoid of

carestía [kares'tia] NF (*escasez*) scarcity, shortage; (*Com*) high cost; **época de ~** period of shortage

careta [ka'reta] NF mask

carey [ka'rei] NM (*tortuga*) turtle; (*concha*) tortoiseshell

carezca *etc* [ka'reθka] VB *ver* **carecer**

carga ['karɣa] NF (*peso, Elec*) load; (*de barco*) cargo, freight; (*Finanzas*) tax, duty; (*Mil*) charge; (*Inform*) loading; (*obligación, responsabilidad*) duty, obligation; **~ aérea** (*Com*) air cargo; **~ útil** (*Com*) payload; **la ~ fiscal** the tax burden

cargadero [karɣa'ðero] NM goods platform, loading bay

cargado, -a [kar'ɣaðo, a] ADJ loaded; (*Elec*) live; (*café, té*) strong; (*cielo*) overcast

cargador, a [karɣa'ðor, a] NM/F loader; (*Naut*) docker ► NM (*Inform*): **~ de discos** disk pack; (*Telec: del móvil*) charger

cargamento [karɣa'mento] NM (*acción*) loading; (*mercancías*) load, cargo

cargante [kar'ɣante] ADJ (*persona*) trying

cargar [kar'ɣar] /**1h**/ VT (*barco, arma*) to load; (*Elec*) to charge; (*impuesto*) to impose; (*Com: algo en cuenta*) to charge, debit; (*Mil: enemigo*) to charge; (*Inform*) to load ► VI (*Auto*) to load (up); (*inclinarse*) to lean; **~ con** to pick up, carry away; (*peso, tb fig*) to shoulder, bear; **cargarse** VR (*fam: estropear*) to break; (: *matar*) to bump off; (*Elec*) to become charged

cargo ['karɣo] NM (*Com etc*) charge, debit; (*puesto*) post, office; (*responsabilidad*) duty, obligation; (*fig*) weight, burden; (*Jur*) charge; **altos cargos** high-ranking officials; **una cantidad en ~ a algn** a sum chargeable to sb; **hacerse ~ de** to take charge of o responsibility for

cargue etc ['karɣe] VB ver **cargar**

carguero [kar'ɣero] NM freighter, cargo boat; (avión) freight plane

Caribe [ka'riβe] NM: **el ~** the Caribbean; **del ~** Caribbean

caribeño, -a [kari'βeɲo, a] ADJ Caribbean

caricatura [karika'tura] NF caricature

caricia [ka'riθja] NF caress; (a animal) pat, stroke

caridad [kari'ðað] NF charity

caries ['karjes] NF INV (Med) tooth decay

cariño [ka'riɲo] NM affection, love; (caricia) caress; (en carta) love ...; **tener ~ a** to be fond of

cariñoso, -a [kari'ɲoso, a] ADJ affectionate

carioca [ka'rjoka] ADJ (AM) of o from Rio de Janeiro ▶ NMF native o inhabitant of Rio de Janeiro

carisma [ka'risma] NM charisma

carismático, -a [karis'matiko, a] ADJ charismatic

caritativo, -a [karita'tiβo, a] ADJ charitable

cariz [ka'riθ] NM: **tener o tomar buen/mal ~** to look good/bad

carmesí [karme'si] ADJ, NM crimson

carmín [kar'min] NM (color) carmine; (tb: **carmín de labios**) lipstick

carnal [kar'nal] ADJ carnal; **primo ~** first cousin

carnaval [karna'βal] NM carnival; see note

The 3 days before miércoles de ceniza (Ash Wednesday), when fasting traditionally starts, are the time for carnaval, an exuberant celebration which dates back to pre-Christian times. Although in decline during the Franco years, the carnaval has grown in popularity recently in Spain, Cádiz and Tenerife being particularly well-known for their celebrations. El martes de carnaval (Shrove Tuesday) is the biggest day, with colourful street parades, fancy dress, fireworks and a general party atmosphere.

carne ['karne] NF flesh; (Culin) meat; **se me pone la ~ de gallina sólo verlo** I get the creeps just seeing it; **~ de cerdo/de cordero/de ternera/de vaca** pork/lamb/veal/beef; **~ molida** (AM), **~ picada** (ESP) mince (BRIT), ground meat (US); **~ de gallina** (fig) gooseflesh

carné [kar'ne] (pl **carnés**) NM: **~ de conducir** driving licence (BRIT), driver's license (US); **~ de identidad** identity card; **~ de socio** membership card; ver tb **Documento Nacional de Identidad**

carnero [kar'nero] NM sheep, ram; (carne) mutton

carnet [kar'ne] (pl **carnets** [kar'nes]) NM (ESP) = **carné**

carnicería [karniθe'ria] NF butcher's (shop); (fig: matanza) carnage, slaughter

carnicero, -a [karni'θero, a] ADJ carnivorous ▶ NM/F (tb fig) butcher ▶ NM carnivore

carnívoro, -a [kar'niβoro, a] ADJ carnivorous ▶ NM carnivore

carnoso, -a [kar'noso, a] ADJ beefy, fat

caro, -a ['karo, a] ADJ dear; (Com) dear, expensive ▶ ADV dear, dearly; **vender ~** to sell at a high price

carpa ['karpa] NF (pez) carp; (de circo) big top; (AM: de camping) tent

carpeta [kar'peta] NF folder, file

carpintería [karpinte'ria] NF carpentry, joinery

carpintero [karpin'tero] NM carpenter; **pájaro ~** woodpecker

carraca [ka'rraka] NF (Deporte) rattle

carraspear [karraspe'ar] /1a/ VI (aclararse la garganta) to clear one's throat

carraspera [karras'pera] NF hoarseness

carrera [ka'rrera] NF (acción) run(ning); (espacio recorrido) run; (certamen) race; (trayecto) course; (profesión) career; (Escol, Univ) course; (de taxi) ride; (en medias) ladder; **a la ~** at (full) speed; **caballo de ~(s)** racehorse; **~ de obstáculos** (Deporte) steeplechase; **~ de armamentos** arms race

carrerilla [karre'riʎa] NF: **decir algo de ~** to reel sth off; **tomar ~** to get up speed

carreta [ka'rreta] NF wagon, cart

carrete [ka'rrete] NM reel, spool; (Tec) coil

carretera [karre'tera] NF (main) road, highway; **~ nacional** ≈ A road (BRIT), ≈ state highway (US); **~ de circunvalación** ring road

carretilla [karre'tiʎa] NF trolley; (Agr) (wheel)barrow

carril [ka'rril] NM furrow; (de autopista) lane; (Ferro) rail

carril bici [karil'βiθi] (pl **carriles bici** [kariles'βiθi]) NM cycle lane, bikeway (US)

carrillo [ka'rriʎo] NM (Anat) cheek; (Tec) pulley

carrito [ka'rrito] NM trolley, cart (US); **~ de la compra** (tb Inform) shopping trolley, shopping cart (US)

carro ['karro] NM cart, wagon; (Mil) tank; (AM: coche) car; (Tip) carriage; **~ blindado** armoured car; **~ patrulla** (AM) patrol o panda (BRIT) car

carrocería [karroθe'ria] NF body, bodywork no pl (BRIT)

carroña [ka'rroɲa] NF carrion no pl

carroza [ka'rroθa] NF (vehículo) coach ▶ NMF (fam) old fogey

carruaje [ka'rrwaxe] NM carriage

carrusel [karru'sel] NM merry-go-round, roundabout (BRIT)

carta ['karta] NF letter; (Culin) menu; (naipe) card; (mapa) map; (Jur) document; **~ de crédito** credit card; **~ de crédito documentaria** (Com) documentary letter of credit; **~ de crédito irrevocable** (Com) irrevocable letter of credit; **~ certificada/ urgente** registered/special delivery letter; **~ marítima** chart; **~ de pedido** (Com) order; **~ verde** (Auto) green card; **~ de vinos** wine list; **echar una ~ al correo** to post a letter; **echar las cartas a algn** to tell sb's fortune

cartabón [karta'βon] NM set square

cartearse [karte'arse] /1a/ VR to correspond

cartel [kar'tel] NM (anuncio) poster, placard; (Escol) wall chart; (Com) cartel

cartelera [karte'lera] NF hoarding, billboard; (en periódico etc) listings pl, entertainments guide; **"en ~"** "showing"

cartera [kar'tera] NF (de bolsillo) wallet; (de colegial, cobrador) satchel; (Am: de señora) handbag (BRIT), purse (US); (para documentos) briefcase; (Com) portfolio; **ministro sin ~** (Pol) minister without portfolio; **ocupa la ~ de Agricultura** he is Minister of Agriculture; **~ de pedidos** (Com) order book; **efectos en ~** (Econ) holdings

carterista [karte'rista] NMF pickpocket

cartero [kar'tero] NM postman

cartílago [kar'tilaɣo] NM cartilage

cartilla [kar'tiʎa] NF (Escol) primer, first reading book; **~ de ahorros** savings book

cartografía [kartoɣra'fia] NF cartography

cartón [kar'ton] NM cardboard; **~ piedra** papier-mâché

cartucho [kar'tutʃo] NM (Mil) cartridge; (bolsita) paper cone; **~ de datos** (Inform) data cartridge; **~ de tinta** ink cartridge

cartulina [kartu'lina] NF fine cardboard, card

CASA ['kasa] NF ABR (Esp Aviat) **= Construcciones Aeronáuticas S.A.**

casa ['kasa] NF house; (hogar) home; (edificio) building; (Com) firm, company; **~ consistorial** town hall; **~ de huéspedes** boarding house; **~ de socorro** first aid post; **~ de citas** (fam) brothel; **~ independiente** detached house; **~ rural** (de alquiler) holiday cottage; (pensión) rural B&B; **~ rodante** (RPL) caravan (BRIT), trailer (US); **en ~** at home; **ir a ~** to go home; **salir de ~** to go out; (para siempre) to leave home; **echar la ~ por la ventana** (gastar) to spare no expense; ver tb **hotel**

casadero, -a [kasa'ðero, a] ADJ marriageable

casado, -a [ka'saðo, a] ADJ married ▶ NM/F married man/woman

casamiento [kasa'mjento] NM marriage, wedding

casar [ka'sar] /1a/ VT to marry; (Jur) to quash, annul; **casarse** VR to marry, get married;

casarse por lo civil to have a civil wedding, get married in a registry office (BRIT)

cascabel [kaska'βel] NM (small) bell; (Zool) rattlesnake

cascada [kas'kaða] NF waterfall

cascajo [kas'kaxo] NM gravel, stone chippings pl

cascanueces [kaska'nweθes] NM INV nutcracker sg; **un ~** a pair of nutcrackers

cascar [kas'kar] /1g/ VT to split; (nuez) to crack ▶ VI to chatter; **cascarse** VR to crack, split, break (open)

cáscara ['kaskara] NF (de huevo, fruta seca) shell; (de fruta) skin; (de limón) peel

cascarón [kaska'ron] NM (broken) eggshell

cascarrabias [kaska'rraβjas] NMF (fam) hothead

casco ['kasko] NM (de bombero, soldado) helmet; (cráneo) skull; (Naut: de barco) hull; (Zool: de caballo) hoof; (botella) empty bottle; (de ciudad): **el ~ antiguo** the old part; **el ~ urbano** the town centre; **los cascos azules** the UN peace-keeping force, the blue helmets

cascote [kas'kote] NM piece of rubble; **cascotes** NMPL rubble sg

caserío [kase'rio] NM hamlet, group of houses; (casa) farmhouse

casero, -a [ka'sero, a] ADJ (pan etc) home-made; (persona): **ser muy ~** to be home-loving ▶ NM/F (propietario) landlord/lady; (Com) house agent; **"comida casera"** "home cooking"

caserón [kase'ron] NM large (ramshackle) house

caseta [ka'seta] NF hut; (para bañista) cubicle; (de feria) stall

casete [ka'sete] NM O F cassette; **~ digital** digital audio tape, DAT

casi ['kasi] ADV almost; **~ nunca** hardly ever, almost never; **~ nada** next to nothing; **~ te caes** you almost o nearly fell

casilla [ka'siʎa] NF (casita) hut, cabin; (Teat) box office; (para cartas) pigeonhole; (Ajedrez) square; **C~ postal** o **de Correo(s)** (AM) P.O. Box; **sacar a algn de sus casillas** to drive sb round the bend (fam), make sb lose his temper

casillero [kasi'ʎero] NM (para cartas) pigeonholes pl

casino [ka'sino] NM club; (de juego) casino

caso ['kaso] NM case; (suceso) event; **en ~ de ...** in case of ...; **el ~ es que** the fact is that; **en el mejor de los casos** at best; **en ese ~** in that case; **en todo ~** in any case; **en último ~** as a last resort; **hacer ~ a** to pay attention to; **hacer ~ omiso de** to fail to mention, pass over; **hacer** o **venir al ~** to be relevant

caspa ['kaspa] NF dandruff

Caspio ['kaspjo] ADJ: **Mar** ~ Caspian Sea

casque etc ['kaske] = ver **cascar**

casquillo [kas'kiʎo] NM (de bombilla) fitting; (de bala) cartridge case

cassette [ka'set] NM O F = **casete**

casta ['kasta] NF caste; (raza) breed

castaña [kas'taɲa] NF ver **castaño**

castañetear [kastaɲete'ar] /1a/ VI (dientes) to chatter

castaño, -a [kas'taɲo, a] ADJ chestnut(-coloured), brown ▶ NM chestnut tree ▶ NF chestnut; (fam: golpe) punch; ~ **de Indias** horse chestnut tree

castañuelas [kasta'ɲwelas] NFPL castanets

castellano, -a [kaste'ʎano, a] ADJ Castilian; (fam) Spanish ▶ NM/F Castilian; (fam) Spaniard ▶ NM (Ling) Castilian, Spanish; see note

> The term *castellano* is now the most widely used term in Spain and Spanish America to refer to the Spanish language, since *español* is too closely associated with Spain as a nation. Of course some people maintain that *castellano* should only refer to the type of Spanish spoken in Castilla.

castellonense [kasteʎo'nense] ADJ of o from Castellón de la Plana ▶ NMF native o inhabitant of Castellón de la Plana

castidad [kasti'ðað] NF chastity, purity

castigar [kasti'ɣar] /1h/ VT to punish; (Deporte) to penalize; (afligir) to afflict

castigo [kas'tiɣo] NM punishment; (Deporte) penalty

castigue etc [kas'tiɣe] VB ver **castigar**

Castilla [kas'tiʎa] NF Castile

castillo [kas'tiʎo] NM castle

castizo, -a [kas'tiθo, a] ADJ (Ling) pure; (de buena casta) purebred, pedigree; (auténtico) genuine

casto, -a ['kasto, a] ADJ chaste, pure

castor [kas'tor] NM beaver

castrar [kas'trar] /1a/ VT to castrate; (gato) to doctor; (Bot) to prune

castrense [kas'trense] ADJ army cpd, military

casual [ka'swal] ADJ chance, accidental

casualidad [kaswali'ðað] NF chance, accident; (combinación de circunstancias) coincidence; **da la ~ de que ...** it (just) so happens that ...; **¡qué ~!** what a coincidence!

casualmente [kaswal'mente] ADV by chance

cataclismo [kata'klismo] NM cataclysm

catador [kata'ðor] NM taster

catadura [kata'ðura] NF (aspecto) looks pl

catalán, -ana [kata'lan, ana] ADJ, NM/F Catalan ▶ NM (Ling) Catalan; ver tb **lenguas cooficiales**

catalejo [kata'lexo] NM telescope

catalizador [kataliθa'ðor] NM catalyst; (Auto) catalytic converter

catalogar [katalo'ɣar] /1h/ VT to catalogue; ~ **(de)** (fig) to classify as

catálogo [ka'taloɣo] NM catalogue

catalogue etc [kata'loɣe] VB ver **catalogar**

Cataluña [kata'luɲa] NF Catalonia

cataplasma [kata'plasma] NF (Med) poultice

catapulta [kata'pulta] NF catapult

catar [ka'tar] /1a/ VT to taste, sample

catarata [kata'rata] NF (Geo) (water)fall; (Med) cataract

catarro [ka'tarro] NM catarrh; (constipado) cold

catarsis [ka'tarsis] NF catharsis

catastro [ka'tastro] NM property register

catástrofe [ka'tastrofe] NF catastrophe

catear [kate'ar] /1a/ VT (fam: examen, alumno) to fail

catecismo [kate'θismo] NM catechism

cátedra ['kateðra] NF (Univ) chair, professorship; (Escol) principal teacher's post; **sentar ~ sobre un argumento** to take one's stand on an argument

catedral [kate'ðral] NF cathedral

catedrático, -a [kate'ðratiko, a] NM/F professor; (Escol) principal teacher

categoría [kateɣo'ria] NF category; (rango) rank, standing; (calidad) quality; **de ~** (hotel) top-class; **de baja ~** (oficial) low-ranking; **de segunda ~** second-rate; **no tiene ~** he has no standing

categórico, -a [kate'ɣoriko, a] ADJ categorical

catequesis [kate'kesis] NF catechism lessons

caterva [ka'terβa] NF throng, crowd

cateto, -a [ka'teto, a] NM/F yokel

cátodo ['katoðo] NM cathode

catolicismo [katoli'θismo] NM Catholicism

católico, -a [ka'toliko, a] ADJ, NM/F Catholic

catorce [ka'torθe] NUM fourteen

catre ['katre] NM camp bed (BRIT), cot (US); (fam) pit

Cáucaso ['kaukaso] NM Caucasus

cauce ['kauθe] NM (de río) riverbed; (fig) channel

caucho ['kautʃo] NM rubber; (AM: llanta) tyre

caución [kau'θjon] NF bail

caucionar [kauθjo'nar] /1a/ VT (Jur) to bail (out), go bail for

caudal [kau'ðal] NM (de río) volume, flow; (fortuna) wealth; (abundancia) abundance

caudaloso, -a [kauða'loso, a] ADJ (río) large; (persona) wealthy, rich

caudillaje [kauði'ʎaxe] NM leadership

caudillo [kau'ðiʎo] NM leader, chief

causa ['kausa] NF cause; (razón) reason; (Jur) lawsuit, case; **a o por ~ de** because of, on account of

causar [kau'sar] /1a/ VT to cause

cáustico, -a ['kaustiko, a] ADJ caustic

cautela [kau'tela] NF caution, cautiousness

cauteloso, -a [kaute'loso, a] ADJ cautious, wary

cautivar [kauti'βar] /**1a**/ VT to capture; (fig) to captivate

cautiverio [kauti'βerjo] NM, **cautividad** [kautiβi'ðað] NF captivity

cautivo, -a [kau'tiβo, a] ADJ, NM/F captive

cauto, -a ['kauto, a] ADJ cautious, careful

cava ['kaβa] NF (bodega) (wine) cellar ▶ NM (vino) champagne-type wine

cavar [ka'βar] /**1a**/ VT to dig; (Agr) to dig over

caverna [ka'βerna] NF cave, cavern

cavernoso, -a [kaβer'noso, a] ADJ cavernous; (voz) resounding

caviar [ka'βjar] NM caviar(e)

cavidad [kaβi'ðað] NF cavity

cavilación [kaβila'θjon] NF deep thought

cavilar [kaβi'lar] /**1a**/ VT to ponder

cayado [ka'jaðo] NM (de pastor) crook; (de obispo) crozier

cayendo etc [ka'jendo] VB ver **caer**

caza ['kaθa] NF (acción: gen) hunting; (: con fusil) shooting; (una caza) hunt, chase; (animales) game; **coto de ~** hunting estate ▶ NM (Aviat) fighter; **ir de ~** to go hunting; **~ mayor** game hunting

cazabe [ka'saβe] NM (Am) cassava bread o flour

cazador, a [kaθa'ðor, a] NM/F hunter/huntress ▶ NF jacket

cazaejecutivos [kaθaexeku'tiβos] NM INV (Com) headhunter

cazar [ka'θar] /**1f**/ VT to hunt; (perseguir) to chase; (prender) to catch; **cazarlas al vuelo** to be pretty sharp

cazasubmarinos [kaθasuβma'rinos] NM INV (Naut) destroyer; (Aviat) anti-submarine craft

cazo ['kaθo] NM saucepan

cazuela [ka'θwela] NF (vasija) pan; (guisado) casserole

cazurro, -a [ka'θurro, a] ADJ surly

CC ABR (= compensación de carbono) carbon offsetting ▶ NM ABR (Pol: = Comité Central) Central Committee

c/c. ABR (Com: = cuenta corriente) current account

CCAA ABR (ESP) = **Comunidades Autónomas**

CCI NF ABR (Com: = Cámara de Comercio Internacional) ICC

CC.OO. NF PL ABR = **Comisiones Obreras**

CD NM ABR (= compact disc) CD; (Pol: = Cuerpo Diplomático) CD (= Diplomatic Corps)

c/d ABR (= en casa de) c/o, care of

CDN NM ABR (= Centro Dramático Nacional) ≈ RADA (BRIT)

CD-ROM [θeðe'rom] NM ABR CD-ROM

CE NM ABR (= Consejo de Europa) Council of Europe ▶ NF ABR (= Comunidad Europea) EC

cebada [θe'βaða] NF barley

cebar [θe'βar] /**1a**/ VT (animal) to fatten (up); (anzuelo) to bait; (Mil, Tec) to prime; **cebarse en** to vent one's fury on, take it out on

cebo ['θeβo] NM (gen: para animales) feed, food; (para peces, fig) bait; (de arma) charge

cebolla [θe'βoʎa] NF onion

cebolleta [θeβo'ʎeta] NF spring onion

cebollino [θeβo'ʎino] NM spring onion

cebón, -ona [θe'βon, ona] ADJ fat, fattened

cebra ['θeβra] NF zebra; **paso de ~** zebra crossing

CECA ['θeka] NF ABR (= Comunidad Europea del Carbón y del Acero) ECSC

ceca ['θeka] NF: **andar** o **ir de la ~ a la Meca** to chase about all over the place

cecear [θeθe'ar] /**1a**/ VI to lisp

ceceo [θe'θeo] NM lisp

cecina [θe'θina] NF cured o smoked meat

cedazo [θe'ðaθo] NM sieve

ceder [θe'ðer] /**2a**/ VT (entregar) to hand over; (renunciar a) to give up, part with ▶ VI (renunciar) to give in, yield; (disminuir) to diminish, decline; (romperse) to give way; (viento) to drop; (fiebre etc) to abate; **"ceda el paso"** (Auto) "give way"

cederom [θeðe'rom] NM CD-ROM

cedro ['θeðro] NM cedar

cédula [θe'ðula] NF certificate, document; **~ de identidad** (Am) identity card; **~ electoral** (Am) ballot; **~ en blanco** blank cheque; ver tb **Documento Nacional de Identidad**

cegar [θe'ɣar] /**1h, 1j**/ VT to blind; (tubería etc) to block up, stop up ▶ VI to go blind; **cegarse** VR: **cegarse (de)** to be blinded (by)

cegué etc [θe'ɣe] VB ver **cegar**

ceguemos etc [θe'ɣemos] VB ver **cegar**

ceguera [θe'ɣera] NF blindness

CEI NF ABR (= Comunidad de Estados Independientes) CIS

Ceilán [θei'lan] NM Ceylon, Sri Lanka

ceja ['θexa] NF eyebrow; **cejas pobladas** bushy eyebrows; **arquear las cejas** to raise one's eyebrows; **fruncir las cejas** to frown

cejar [θe'xar] /**1a**/ VI (fig) to back down; **no ~** to keep it up, stick at it

cejijunto, -a [θexi'xunto, a] ADJ with bushy eyebrows; (fig) scowling

celada [θe'laða] NF ambush, trap

celador, a [θela'ðor, a] NM/F (de edificio) watchman; (de museo etc) attendant; (de cárcel) warder

celda ['θelda] NF cell

celebérrimo, -a [θele'βerrimo, a] ADJ SUPERLATIVO *de* **célebre**

celebración [θeleβra'θjon] NF celebration

celebrar [θele'βrar] /**1a**/ VT to celebrate; (*alabar*) to praise ▶ VI to be glad; **celebrarse** VR to occur, take place

célebre ['θeleβre] ADJ famous

celebridad [θeleβri'ðað] NF fame; (*persona*) celebrity

celeridad [θeleri'ðað] NF: **con ~** promptly

celeste [θe'leste] ADJ sky-blue; (*cuerpo etc*) heavenly ▶ NM sky blue

celestial [θeles'tjal] ADJ celestial, heavenly

celibato [θeli'βato] NM celibacy

célibe ['θeliβe] ADJ, NMF celibate

celo¹ ['θelo] NM zeal; (*Rel*) fervour; (*pey*) envy; **celos** NMPL jealousy *sg*; **dar celos a algn** to make sb jealous; **tener celos de algn** to be jealous of sb; **en ~** (*animales*) on heat

celo²® ['θelo] NM Sellotape®

celofán [θelo'fan] NM Cellophane®

celosía [θelo'sia] NF lattice (window)

celoso, -a [θe'loso, a] ADJ (*envidioso*) jealous; (*trabajador*) zealous; (*desconfiado*) suspicious

celta ['θelta] ADJ Celtic ▶ NMF Celt

célula ['θelula] NF cell

celular [θelu'lar] NM (*Am*) mobile (phone) (*Brit*), cellphone (*US*) ▶ ADJ: **tejido ~** cell tissue

celulitis [θelu'litis] NF (*enfermedad*) cellulitis; (*grasa*) cellulite

celuloide [θelu'loiðe] NM celluloid

celulosa [θelu'losa] NF cellulose

cementerio [θemen'terjo] NM cemetery, graveyard; **~ de coches** scrap yard

cemento [θe'mento] NM cement; (*hormigón*) concrete; (*Am: cola*) glue

CEN NM ABR (*Esp*) = **Consejo de Economía Nacional**

cena ['θena] NF evening meal, dinner

cenagal [θena'ɣal] NM bog, quagmire

cenar [θe'nar] /**1a**/ VT to have for dinner, dine on ▶ VI to have dinner, dine

cencerro [θen'θerro] NM cowbell; **estar como un ~** (*fam*) to be round the bend

cenicero [θeni'θero] NM ashtray

ceniciento, -a [θeni'θjento, a] ADJ ash-coloured, ashen

cenit [θe'nit] NM zenith

ceniza [θe'niθa] NF ash, ashes *pl*

censar [θen'sar] /**1a**/ VT to take a census of

censo ['θenso] NM census; **~ electoral** electoral roll

censor [θen'sor] NM censor; **~ de cuentas** (*Com*) auditor; **~ jurado de cuentas** chartered (*Brit*) *o* certified public (*US*) accountant

censura [θen'sura] NF (*Pol*) censorship; (*moral*) censure, criticism

censurable [θensu'raβle] ADJ reprehensible

censurar [θensu'rar] /**1a**/ VT (*idea*) to censure; (*cortar: película*) to censor

centavo [θen'taβo] NM hundredth (part); (*Am*) cent

centella [θen'teʎa] NF spark

centellear [θenteʎe'ar] /**1a**/ VI (*metal*) to gleam; (*estrella*) to twinkle; (*fig*) to sparkle

centelleo [θente'ʎeo] NM gleam(ing); twinkling; sparkling

centena [θen'tena] NF hundred

centenar [θente'nar] NM hundred

centenario, -a [θente'narjo, a] ADJ hundred-year-old ▶ NM centenary; **ser ~** to be one hundred years old

centeno [θen'teno] NM rye

centésimo, -a [θen'tesimo, a] ADJ, NM hundredth

centígrado [θen'tiɣraðo] ADJ centigrade

centigramo [θenti'ɣramo] NM centigramme

centilitro [θenti'litro] NM centilitre (*Brit*), centiliter (*US*)

centímetro [θen'timetro] NM centimetre (*Brit*), centimeter (*US*)

céntimo ['θentimo] NM cent

centinela [θenti'nela] NM sentry, guard

centollo, -a [θen'toʎo, a] NM/F large (*o* spider) crab

central [θen'tral] ADJ central ▶ NF head office; (*Tec*) plant; (*Telec*) exchange; **~ eléctrica** power station; **~ nuclear** nuclear power station; **~ telefónica** telephone exchange

centralice *etc* [θentra'liθe] VB *ver* **centralizar**

centralita [θentra'lita] NF switchboard

centralización [θentraliθa'θjon] NF centralization

centralizar [θentrali'θar] /**1f**/ VT to centralize

centrar [θen'trar] /**1a**/ VT to centre

céntrico, -a ['θentriko, a] ADJ central

centrifugar [θentrifu'ɣar] /**1h**/ VT (*ropa*) to spin-dry

centrífugo, -a [θent'rifuɣo, a] ADJ centrifugal

centrifugue *etc* [θentri'fuɣe] VB *ver* **centrifugar**

centrista [θen'trista] ADJ centre *cpd*

centro ['θentro] NM centre; **ser de ~** (*Pol*) to be a moderate; **~ de acogida (para niños)** children's home; **~ de beneficios** (*Com*) profit centre; **~ cívico** community centre; **~ comercial** shopping centre; **~ de informática** computer centre; **~ (de determinación) de costos** (*Com*) cost centre; **~ delantero** (*Deporte*) centre forward; **~ de atención al cliente** call centre; **~ de salud** health centre; **~ docente** teaching institution; **~ escolar** school; **~ juvenil** youth club; **~ social** community centre;

~ turístico (*lugar muy visitado*) tourist centre; **~ urbano** urban area, city

centroafricano, -a [θentroafri'kano, a] ADJ: **la República Centroafricana** the Central African Republic

centroamericano, -a [θentroameri'kano, a] ADJ, NM/F Central American

centrocampista [θentrokam'pista] NMF (*Deporte*) midfielder

ceñido, -a [θe'niðo, a] ADJ tight

ceñir [θe'nir] VT (*rodear*) to encircle, surround; (*ajustar*) to fit (tightly); (*apretar*) to tighten; **ceñirse** VR: **ceñirse algo** to put sth on; **ceñirse al asunto** to stick to the matter in hand

ceño ['θeno] NM frown, scowl; **fruncir el ~** to frown, knit one's brow

CEOE NF ABR (= *Confederación Española de Organizaciones Empresariales*) ≈ CBI (BRIT)

cepa ['θepa] NF (*de vid, fig*) stock; (*Bio*) strain

CEPAL [θe'pal] NF ABR (= *Comisión Económica de las Naciones Unidas para la América Latina*) ECLA

cepillar [θepi'ʎar] /1a/ VT to brush; (*madera*) to plane (down)

cepillo [θe'piʎo] NM brush; (*para madera*) plane; (*Rel*) poor box, alms box; **~ de dientes** toothbrush

cepo ['θepo] NM (*de caza*) trap

CEPSA ['θepsa] NF ABR (*Com*) = **Compañía Española de Petróleos, S.A.**

CEPYME NF ABR = **Confederación Española de la Pequeña y Mediana Empresa**

cera ['θera] NF wax; **~ de abejas** beeswax

cerámica [θe'ramika] NF pottery; (*arte*) ceramics *sg*

ceramista [θera'mista] NMF potter

cerbatana [θerβa'tana] NF blowpipe

cerca ['θerka] NF fence ► ADV near, nearby, close; **por aquí ~** nearby ► PREP: **~ de** (*cantidad*) nearly, about; (*distancia*) near, close to

cercado [θer'kaðo] NM enclosure

cercanía [θerka'nia] NF nearness, closeness; **cercanías** NFPL outskirts, suburbs; **tren de cercanías** commuter o local train

cercano, -a [θer'kano, a] ADJ close, near; (*pueblo etc*) nearby; **C~ Oriente** Near East

cercar [θer'kar] /1g/ VT to fence in; (*rodear*) to surround

cerciorar [θerθjo'rar] /1a/ VT (*asegurar*) to assure; **cerciorarse** VR: **cerciorarse (de)** (*descubrir*) to find out (about); (*asegurarse*) to make sure (of)

cerco ['θerko] NM (*Agr*) enclosure; (*Am*) fence; (*Mil*) siege

cerda ['θerða] NF (*de cepillo*) bristle; (*Zool*) sow

cerdada [θer'ðaða] NF (*fam*): **hacer una ~ a algn** to play a dirty trick on sb

Cerdeña [θer'ðena] NF Sardinia

cerdo ['θerðo] NM pig; **carne de ~** pork

cereal [θere'al] NM cereal; **cereales** NMPL cereals, grain *sg*

cerebral [θere'βral] ADJ (*tb fig*) cerebral; (*tumor*) brain *cpd*

cerebro [θe'reβro] NM brain; (*fig*) brains *pl*; **ser un ~** (*fig*) to be brilliant

ceremonia [θere'monja] NF ceremony; **reunión de ~** formal meeting; **hablar sin ~** to speak plainly

ceremonial [θeremo'njal] ADJ, NM ceremonial

ceremonioso, -a [θeremo'njoso, a] ADJ ceremonious; (*cumplido*) formal

cereza [θe'reθa] NF cherry

cerezo [θe'reθo] NM cherry tree

cerilla [θe'riʎa] NF, **cerillo** [se'riʎo] NM (*Am*) match

cerner [θer'ner] /2g/ VT to sift, sieve; **cernerse** VR to hover

cero ['θero] NM nothing, zero; (*Deporte*) nil; **8 grados bajo ~** 8 degrees below zero; **a partir de ~** from scratch

cerque *etc* ['θerke] VB *ver* **cercar**

cerquillo [θer'kiʎo] NM (*Am*) fringe (BRIT), bangs *pl* (US)

cerrado, -a [θe'rraðo, a] ADJ closed, shut; (*con llave*) locked; (*tiempo*) cloudy, overcast; (*curva*) sharp; (*acento*) thick, broad; **a puerta cerrada** (*Jur*) in camera

cerradura [θerra'ðura] NF (*acción*) closing; (*mecanismo*) lock

cerrajería [θerraxe'ria] NF locksmith's craft; (*tienda*) locksmith's (shop)

cerrajero, -a [θerra'xero, a] NM/F locksmith

cerrar [θe'rrar] /1j/ VT to close, shut; (*paso, carretera*) to close; (*grifo*) to turn off; (*trato, cuenta, negocio*) to close ► VI to close, shut; (*la noche*) to come down; **cerrarse** VR to close, shut; (*herida*) to heal; **~ con llave** to lock; **~ el sistema** (*Inform*) to close o shut down the system; **~ un trato** to strike a bargain

cerro ['θerro] NM hill; **andar por las cerros de Úbeda** to wander from the point, digress

cerrojo [θe'rroxo] NM (*herramienta*) bolt; (*de puerta*) latch

certamen [θer'tamen] NM competition, contest

certero, -a [θer'tero, a] ADJ accurate

certeza [θer'teθa], **certidumbre** [θerti'ðumbre] NF certainty

certidumbre [θerti'ðumβre] NF = **certeza**

certificación [θertifika'θjon] NF certification; (*Jur*) affidavit

certificado, -a [θertifi'kaðo, a] ADJ certified; (*Correos*) registered ► NM certificate; **~ médico** medical certificate

certificar [θertifi'kar] /1g/ VT (*asegurar, atestar*) to certify

certifique etc [θerti'fike] vb ver **certificar**

cervatillo [θerβa'tiʎo] NM fawn

cervecería [θerβeθe'ria] NF (fábrica) brewery; (taberna) public house, pub

cerveza [θer'βeθa] NF beer; **~ de barril** draught beer

cervical [θerβi'kal] ADJ cervical

cerviz [θer'βiθ] NF nape of the neck

cesación [θesa'θjon] NF cessation, suspension

cesante [θe'sante] ADJ redundant; (Am) unemployed; (ministro) outgoing; (diplomático) recalled ▶ NMF redundant worker

cesantía [θesan'tia] NF (Am) unemployment

cesar [θe'sar] /1a/ vi to cease, stop; (de un trabajo) to leave ▶ vt (en el trabajo) to dismiss; (alto cargo) to remove from office

cesárea [θe'sarea] NF Caesarean (section)

cese ['θese] NM (de trabajo) dismissal; (de pago) suspension

CESID [θe'siδ] NM ABR (Esp: = Centro Superior de Investigación de la Defensa Nacional) military intelligence service

cesión [θe'sjon] NF: **~ de bienes** surrender of property

césped ['θespeδ] NM grass, lawn

cesta ['θesta] NF basket

cesto ['θesto] NM (large) basket, hamper

cetrería [θetre'ria] NF falconry

cetrino, -a [θe'trino, a] ADJ (tez) sallow

cetro ['θetro] NM sceptre

Ceuta [θe'uta] NF Ceuta

ceutí [θeu'ti] ADJ of o from Ceuta ▶ NMF native o inhabitant of Ceuta

C.F. NM ABR (= Club de Fútbol) F.C.

CFC NM ABR (= clorofluorocarbono) CFC

cfr. ABR (= confróntese, compárese) cf

cg ABR (= centígramo) cg

CGPJ NM ABR (= Consejo General del Poder Judicial) governing body of Spanish legal system

CGS NF ABR (GUATEMALA, EL SALVADOR) = **Confederación General de Sindicatos**

CGT NF ABR (COLOMBIA, MÉXICO, NICARAGUA, ESP) = **Confederación General de Trabajadores**; (ARGENTINA) = **Confederación General del Trabajo**

Ch, ch [tʃe] NF former letter in the Spanish alphabet

chabacano, -a [tʃaβa'kano, a] ADJ vulgar, coarse

chabola [tʃa'βola] NF shack; **barriada** or **barrio de chabolas** shanty town

chabolismo [tʃaβo'lismo] NM: **el problema del ~** the problem of substandard housing, the shanty town problem

chacal [tʃa'kal] NM jackal

chacarero [tʃaka'rero] NM (Am) small farmer

chacha ['tʃatʃa] NF (fam) maid

cháchara ['tʃatʃara] NF chatter; **estar de ~** to chatter away

chacra ['tʃakra] NF (Am) smallholding

chafa ['tʃafa] ADJ (Am fam) useless, dud

chafar [tʃa'far] /1a/ vt (aplastar) to crush, flatten; (arruinar) to ruin

chaflán [tʃa'flan] NM (Tec) bevel

chal [tʃal] NM shawl

chalado, -a [tʃa'laδo, a] ADJ (fam) crazy

chalé [tʃa'le] (pl **chalés** [tʃa'les]) NM = **chalet**

chaleco [tʃa'leko] NM waistcoat, vest (US); **~ antibalas** bulletproof vest; **~ salvavidas** life jacket; **~ de seguridad, ~ reflectante** (Auto) high-visibility vest

chalet [tʃa'le] (pl **chalets** [tʃa'les]) NM villa, = detached house; **~ adosado** semi-detached house

chalupa [tʃa'lupa] NF launch, boat

chamaco, -a [tʃa'mako, a] NM/F (Am) kid

chamarra [tʃa'marra] NF sheepskin jacket; (Am: poncho) blanket

champán [tʃam'pan], **champaña** [tʃam'paɲa] NM champagne

champiñón [tʃampi'non] NM mushroom

champú [tʃam'pu] (pl **champús** o **champúes**) NM shampoo

chamuscar [tʃamus'kar] /1g/ vt to scorch, singe

chamusque etc [tʃa'muske] vb ver **chamuscar**

chamusquina [tʃamus'kina] NF singeing

chance ['tʃanθe] NM o F (Am) chance, opportunity

chanchada [tʃan'tʃaδa] NF (Am fam) dirty trick

chancho, -a ['tʃantʃo, a] NM/F (Am) pig

chanchullo [tʃan'tʃuʎo] NM (fam) fiddle, wangle

chancla ['tʃankla], **chancleta** [tʃan'kleta] NF flip-flop; (zapato viejo) old shoe

chandal [tʃan'dal] NM tracksuit; **~ (de Tactel®)** shellsuit

chantaje [tʃan'taxe] NM blackmail; **hacer ~ a uno** to blackmail sb

chanza ['tʃanθa] NF joke

chao [tʃao] EXCL (fam) cheerio

chapa ['tʃapa] NF (de metal) plate, sheet; (de madera) board, panel; (de botella) bottle top; (insignia) (lapel) badge; (Am Auto: tb: **chapa de matrícula**) number (BRIT) o license (US) plate; (Am: cerradura) lock; **de 3 chapas** (madera) 3-ply

chapado, -a [tʃa'paδo, a] ADJ (metal) plated; (muebles etc) finished; **~ en oro** gold-plated

chaparro, -a [tʃa'parro, a] ADJ squat; (Am: bajito) short

chaparrón [tʃapa'rron] NM downpour, cloudburst

chaperón, -ona [tʃape'ron, ona] NM/F (Am): **hacer de ~** to play gooseberry

chapotear [tʃapote'ar] /**1a**/ VT to sponge down ▶ VI (*fam*) to splash about

chapucero, -a [tʃapu'θero, a] ADJ rough, crude ▶ NM/F bungler

chapulín [tʃapu'lin] NM (*Am*) grasshopper

chapurrar [tʃapurr'ar] /**1a**/, **chapurrear** [tʃapurre'ar] /**1a**/ VT (*idioma*) to speak badly

chapuza [tʃa'puθa] NF botched job

chapuzón [tʃapu'θon] NM: **darse un ~** to go for a dip

chaqué [tʃa'ke] NM morning coat

chaqueta [tʃa'keta] NF jacket; **cambiar la ~** (*fig*) to change sides

chaquetón [tʃake'ton] NM (three-quarter-length) coat

charca ['tʃarka] NF pond, pool

charco ['tʃarko] NM pool, puddle

charcutería [tʃarkute'ria] NF (*tienda*) shop selling chiefly pork meat products; (*productos*) cooked pork meats *pl*

charla ['tʃarla] NF talk, chat; (*conferencia*) lecture

charlar [tʃar'lar] /**1a**/ VI to talk, chat

charlatán, -ana [tʃarla'tan, ana] NM/F chatterbox; (*estafador*) trickster

charol¹ [tʃa'rol] NM varnish; (*cuero*) patent leather

charol² [tʃa'rol] NM, **charola** [tʃa'rola] NF (*Am*) tray

charqui ['tʃarki] NM (*Am*) dried beef, jerky (*US*)

charro, -a ['tʃarro, a] ADJ Salamancan; (*Am*) Mexican; (*ropa*) loud, gaudy; (*costumbres*) traditional ▶ NM/F Salamancan ▶ NM (*vaquero*) typical Mexican

chárter ['tʃarter] ADJ INV: **vuelo ~** charter flight

chascarrillo [tʃaska'rriʎo] NM (*fam*) funny story

chasco ['tʃasko] NM (*broma*) trick, joke; (*desengaño*) disappointment

chasis ['tʃasis] NM INV (*Auto*) chassis; (*Foto*) plate holder

chasquear [tʃaske'ar] /**1a**/ VT (*látigo*) to crack; (*lengua*) to click

chasquido [tʃas'kiðo] NM (*de lengua*) click; (*de látigo*) crack

chat [tʃat] NM (*Internet*) chat room

chatarra [tʃa'tarra] NF scrap (metal)

chatear [tʃate'ar] /**1a**/ VI (*Internet*) to chat

chatero, -a [tʃa'tero, a] ADJ chat *cpd* ▶ NM/F chat-room user

chato, -a ['tʃato, a] ADJ flat; (*nariz*) snub ▶ NM wine tumbler; **beber unos chatos** to have a few drinks

chau [tʃau], **chaucito** [tʃau'sito] EXCL (*fam*) cheerio

chaucha ['tʃautʃa] (*Am*) NF runner (*Brit*) o pole (*US*) bean

chauvinismo [tʃoβi'nismo] NM chauvinism

chauvinista [tʃoβi'nista] ADJ, NMF chauvinist

chaval, a [tʃa'βal, a] NM/F kid (*fam*), lad/lass

chavo, -a ['tʃaβo, a] NM/F (*Am fam*) guy/girl

checar [tʃe'kar] /**1g**/ VT (*Am*): **~ tarjeta** (*al entrar*) to clock in o on; (*al salir*) to clock off o out

checo, -a ['tʃeko, a] ADJ, NM/F Czech ▶ NM (*Ling*) Czech; **la República Checa** the Czech Republic

checo(e)slovaco, -a [tʃeko(e)slo'βako, a] ADJ, NM/F (*Historia*) Czech, Czechoslovak

Checo(e)slovaquia [tʃeko(e)slo'βakja] NF (*Historia*) Czechoslovakia

chepa ['tʃepa] NF hump

cheque ['tʃeke] NM cheque (*Brit*), check (*US*); **cobrar un ~** to cash a cheque; **~ abierto/en blanco/cruzado** open/blank/crossed cheque; **~ al portador** cheque payable to bearer; **~ de viajero** traveller's cheque

chequeo [tʃe'keo] NM (*Med*) check-up; (*Auto*) service

chequera [tʃe'kera] NF (*Am*) chequebook (*Brit*), checkbook (*US*)

chévere ['tʃeβere] ADJ (*Am*) great, fabulous (*fam*)

chicano, -a [tʃi'kano, a] ADJ, NM/F chicano, Mexican-American

chicha ['tʃitʃa] NF (*Am*) maize liquor

chícharo ['tʃitʃaro] NM (*Am*) pea

chicharra [tʃi'tʃarra] NF harvest bug, cicada

chicharrón [tʃitʃa'rron] NM (pork) crackling

chichón [tʃi'tʃon] NM bump, lump

chicle ['tʃikle] NM chewing gum

chico, -a ['tʃiko, a] ADJ small, little ▶ NM/F child; (*muchacho*) boy; (*muchacha*) girl

chicote [tʃi'kote] NM (*Am*) whip

chiflado, -a [tʃi'flaðo, a] ADJ (*fam*) crazy, round the bend ▶ NM/F nutcase

chiflar [tʃi'flar] /**1a**/ VT to hiss, boo ▶ VI (*esp Am*) to whistle

chilango, -a [tʃi'lango, a] ADJ (*Am*) of o from Mexico City

Chile ['tʃile] NM Chile

chile ['tʃile] NM chilli pepper

chileno, -a [tʃi'leno, a] ADJ, NM/F Chilean

chillar [tʃi'ʎar] /**1a**/ VI (*persona*) to yell, scream; (*animal salvaje*) to howl; (*cerdo*) to squeal; (*puerta*) to creak

chillido [tʃi'ʎiðo] NM (*de persona*) yell, scream; (*de animal*) howl; (*de frenos*) screech(ing)

chillón, -ona [tʃi'ʎon, ona] ADJ (*niño*) noisy; (*color*) loud, gaudy

chimenea [tʃime'nea] NF chimney; (*hogar*) fireplace

chimpancé [tʃimpan'θe] (*pl* **chimpancés** [tʃimpan'θes]) NM chimpanzee

China ['tʃina] NF: **(la) ~** China

china ['tʃina] NF pebble

chinchar [tʃin'tʃar] /**1a**/ (fam) VT to pester, annoy; **chincharse** VR to get cross; **¡chínchate!** tough!

chinche ['tʃintʃe] NF bug; (Tec) drawing pin (BRIT), thumbtack (US) ▶ NMF nuisance, pest

chincheta [tʃin'tʃeta] NF drawing pin (BRIT), thumbtack (US)

chinchorro [tʃin'tʃorro] NM (AM) hammock

chingado, -a [tʃin'gaðo, a] ADJ (esp AM fam!) lousy, bloody (fam!); **hijo de la chingada** bastard (fam!), son of a bitch (US fam!)

chingar [tʃin'gar] /**1h**/ VT (AM fam!) to fuck (up) (fam!), screw (up) (fam!); **chingarse** VR (AM: emborracharse) to get pissed (BRIT), get plastered (; (: fracasar) to fail

chingue etc ['tʃinge] VB ver **chingar**

chino, -a ['tʃino, a] ADJ, NM/F Chinese ▶ NM (Ling) Chinese; (Culin) chinois, conical strainer

chip [tʃip] NM (Inform) chip

chipirón [tʃipi'ron] NM squid

Chipre ['tʃipre] NF Cyprus

chipriota [tʃi'prjota], **chipriote** [tʃi'prjote] ADJ Cypriot, Cyprian ▶ NMF Cypriot

chiquillada [tʃiki'ʎaða] NF childish prank; (AM: chiquillos) kids pl

chiquillo, -a [tʃi'kiʎo, a] NM/F kid (fam), youngster, child

chiquito, -a [tʃi'kito, a] ADJ very small, tiny ▶ NM/F kid (fam)

chirigota [tʃiri'ɣota] NF joke

chirimbolo [tʃirim'bolo] NM thingummyjig (fam)

chirimoya [tʃiri'moja] NF custard apple

chiringuito [tʃirin'gito] NM small open-air bar

chiripa [tʃi'ripa] NF fluke; **por** ~ by chance

chirona [tʃi'rona], (AM) **chirola** [tʃi'rola] NF (fam) clink, jail

chirriar [tʃi'rrjar] /**1b**/ VI (goznes) to creak, squeak; (pájaros) to chirp, sing

chirrido [tʃi'rriðo] NM creak(ing), squeak(ing); (de pájaro) chirp(ing)

chis [tʃis] EXCL sh!

chisme ['tʃisme] NM (habladurías) piece of gossip; (fam: objeto) thingummyjig

chismoso, -a [tʃis'moso, a] ADJ gossiping ▶ NM/F gossip

chispa ['tʃispa] NF spark; (fig) sparkle; (ingenio) wit; (fam) drunkenness

chispeante [tʃispe'ante] ADJ (tb fig) sparkling

chispear [tʃispe'ar] /**1a**/ VI to spark; (lloviznar) to drizzle

chisporrotear [tʃisporrote'ar] /**1a**/ VI (fuego) to throw out sparks; (leña) to crackle; (aceite) to hiss, splutter

chistar [tʃistar] /**1a**/ VI: **no** ~ not to say a word

chiste ['tʃiste] NM joke, funny story; ~ **verde** blue joke

chistera [tʃis'tera] NF top hat

chistoso, -a [tʃis'toso, a] ADJ (gracioso) funny, amusing; (bromista) witty

chivarse [tʃi'βarse] /**1a**/ VR (fam) to grass

chivatazo [tʃiβa'taθo] NM (fam) tip-off; **dar** ~ to inform

chivo, -a ['tʃiβo, a] NM/F (billy/nanny-)goat; ~ **expiatorio** scapegoat

chocante [tʃo'kante] ADJ startling; (extraño) odd; (ofensivo) shocking

chocar [tʃo'kar] /**1g**/ VI (coches etc) to collide, crash; (Mil, fig) to clash ▶ VT to shock; (sorprender) to startle; ~ **con** to collide with; (fig) to run into, run up against; **¡chócala!** (fam) put it there!

chochear [tʃotʃe'ar] /**1a**/ VI to dodder, be senile

chocho, -a ['tʃotʃo, a] ADJ doddering, senile; (fig) soft, doting

choclo ['tʃoklo] (AM) NM (grano) sweetcorn; (mazorca) corn on the cob

chocolate [tʃoko'late] ADJ chocolate ▶ NM chocolate; (fam) dope, marijuana

chocolatería [tʃokolate'ria] NF chocolate factory (o shop)

chocolatina [tʃokola'tina] NF chocolate

chófer ['tʃofer], (esp AM) **chofer** [tʃo'fer] NM driver

chollo ['tʃoʎo] NM (fam) bargain, snip

chomba ['tʃomba], **chompa** ['tʃompa] NF (AM) jumper, sweater

chopo ['tʃopo] NM black poplar

choque ['tʃoke] VB ver **chocar** ▶ NM (impacto) impact; (golpe) jolt; (Auto) crash; (fig) conflict; ~ **frontal** head-on collision

chorizo [tʃo'riθo] NM hard pork sausage (type of salami); (ladrón) crook

chorra ['tʃorra] NF luck

chorrada [tʃo'rraða] NF (fam): **¡es una ~!** that's crap! (fam!); **decir chorradas** to talk crap (fam!)

chorrear [tʃorre'ar] /**1a**/ VT to pour ▶ VI to gush (out), spout (out); (gotear) to drip, trickle

chorreras [tʃo'rreras] NFPL (adorno) frill sg

chorro ['tʃorro] NM jet; (caudalito) dribble, trickle; (fig) stream; **salir a chorros** to gush forth; **con propulsión a ~** jet-propelled

chotearse [tʃote'arse] /**1a**/ VR to joke

choto ['tʃoto] NM (cabrito) kid

chovinismo [tʃoβi'nismo] NM = **chauvinismo**

chovinista [tʃoβi'nista] ADJ, NMF = **chauvinista**

choza ['tʃoθa] NF hut, shack

chubasco [tʃu'βasko] NM squall

chubasquero [tʃuβas'kero] NM cagoule, raincoat

chuche ['tʃutʃe] NF (fam) sweetie (BRIT fam), candy (US)

chuchería [tʃutʃe'ria] NF trinket

chucho ['tʃutʃo] NM (Zool) mongrel

chufa ['tʃufa] NF chufa, earth almond, tiger nut; **horchata de chufas** drink made from chufas

chuleta [tʃu'leta] NF chop, cutlet; (Escol fam) crib

chulo, -a ['tʃulo, a] ADJ (encantador) charming; (aire) proud; (pey) fresh; (fam: estupendo) great, fantastic ▶ NM (pícaro) rascal; (madrileño) working-class person from Madrid; (rufián: tb: **chulo de putas**) pimp

chumbera [tʃum'bera] NF prickly pear

chungo, -a ['tʃungo, a] (fam) ADJ lousy ▶ NF: **estar de chunga** to be in a merry mood

chupa ['tʃupa] NF (fam) jacket

chupado, -a [tʃu'paðo, a] ADJ (delgado) skinny, gaunt; **está ~** (fam) it's simple, it's dead easy

chupaleta [tʃupa'leta] NF (Am) lollipop

chupar [tʃu'par] /1a/ VT to suck; (absorber) to absorb; **chuparse** VR to grow thin; **para chuparse los dedos** mouthwatering

chupatintas [tʃupa'tintas] NM INV penpusher

chupe ['tʃupe] NM (Am) stew

chupete [tʃu'pete] NM dummy (BRIT), pacifier (US)

chupetín [tʃupe'tin] NF (Am) lollipop

chupetón [tʃupe'ton] NM suck

chupito [tʃu'pito] NM (fam) shot

chupón [tʃu'pon] NM (piruleta) lollipop; (Am: chupete) dummy (BRIT), pacifier (US)

churrasco [tʃu'rrasko] NM (Am) barbecue, barbecued meat

churrería [tʃurre'ria] NF stall or shop which sells "churros"

churrete [tʃu'rrete] NM grease spot

churretón [tʃurre'ton] NM stain

churrigueresco, -a [tʃurrige'resko, a] ADJ (Arq) baroque; (fig) excessively ornate

churro, -a ['tʃurro, a] ADJ coarse ▶ NM (Culin) (type of) fritter; see note; (chapuza) botch, mess

Churros, long fritters made with flour and water, are very popular in much of Spain and are often eaten with thick hot chocolate, either for breakfast or as a snack. In Madrid, they eat a thicker variety of churro called porra.

churruscar [tʃurrus'kar] /1g/ VT to fry crisp

churrusque etc [tʃu'rruske] VB ver **churruscar**

churumbel [tʃurum'bel] NM (fam) kid

chus [tʃus] EXCL: **no decir ni ~ ni mus** not to say a word

chusco, -a ['tʃusko, a] ADJ funny

chusma ['tʃusma] NF rabble, mob

chutar [tʃu'tar] /1a/ VI (Deporte) to shoot (at goal); **esto va que chuta** it's going fine

chuzo ['tʃuθo] NM: **llueve a chuzos, llueven chuzos de punta** it's raining cats and dogs

C.I. NM ABR = **coeficiente intelectual**; **coeficiente de inteligencia**

Cía ABR (= compañía) Co.

cianuro [θja'nuro] NM cyanide

ciática ['θjatika] NF sciatica

ciberacoso [θiβera'koso] NM cyberbullying

ciberataque [θiβera'take] NM cyber attack

cibercafé [θiβerka'fe] NM cybercafé

ciberespacio [θiβeres'paθjo] NM cyberspace

cibernauta [θiβer'nauta] NMF cybernaut

cibernética [θiβer'netika] NF cybernetics sg

ciberseguridad [θiβerseɣuri'ðað] NF cybersecurity

ciberterrorista [θiβerterro'rista] NMF cyberterrorist

cicatrice etc [θika'triθe] VB ver **cicatrizar**

cicatriz [θika'triθ] NF scar

cicatrizar [θikatri'θar] /1f/ VT to heal; **cicatrizarse** VR to heal (up), form a scar

cíclico, -a ['θikliko, a] ADJ cyclical

ciclismo [θi'klismo] NM cycling

ciclista [θi'klista] ADJ cycle cpd ▶ NMF cyclist

ciclo ['θiklo] NM cycle

ciclomotor [θiklomo'tor] NM moped

ciclón [θi'klon] NM cyclone

cicloturismo [θiklotu'rismo] NM touring by bicycle

cicuta [θi'kuta] NF hemlock

ciego, -a ['θjeɣo, a] VB ver **cegar** ▶ ADJ blind ▶ NM/F blind man/woman; **a ciegas** blindly; **me puse ciega mariscos** (fam) I stuffed myself with seafood

ciegue etc ['θjeɣe] VB ver **cegar**

cielo ['θjelo] NM sky; (Rel) heaven; (Arq: tb: **cielo raso**) ceiling; **¡cielos!** good heavens!; **ver el ~ abierto** to see one's chance

ciempiés [θjem'pjes] NM INV centipede

cien [θjen] NUM ver **ciento**

ciénaga ['θjenaɣa] NF marsh, swamp

ciencia ['θjenθja] NF science; **ciencias** NFPL science sg; **saber algo a ~ cierta** to know sth for certain

ciencia-ficción ['θjenθjafik'θjon] NF science fiction

cieno ['θjeno] NM mud, mire

científico, -a [θjen'tifiko, a] ADJ scientific ▶ NM/F scientist

ciento ['θjento], **cien** NUM hundred; **pagar al 10 por ~** to pay at 10 per cent

cierne etc ['θjerne] VB ver **cerner** ▶ NM: **en ~** in blossom; **en ~(s)** (fig) in its infancy

cierre ['θjerre] NM closing, shutting; (con llave) locking; (Radio, TV) close-down; **~ de cremallera** zip (fastener); **precios de ~** (Bolsa) closing prices; **~ del sistema** (Inform) system shutdown

cierro etc VB ver **cerrar**

cierto, -a ['θjerto, a] ADJ sure, certain; (*un tal*) a certain; (*correcto*) right, correct; **~ hombre** a certain man; **ciertas personas** certain *o* some people; **sí, es ~** yes, that's correct; **por ~** by the way; **lo ~ es que …** the fact is that …; **estar en lo ~** to be right

ciervo ['θjerβo] NM (*Zool*) deer; (: *macho*) stag

cierzo ['θjerθo] NM north wind

CIES NM ABR = **Consejo Interamericano Económico y Social**

cifra ['θifra] NF number, figure; (*cantidad*) number, quantity; (*secreta*) code; **~ global** lump sum; **~ de negocios** (*Com*) turnover; **en cifras redondas** in round figures; **~ de referencia** (*Com*) bench mark; **~ de ventas** (*Com*) sales figures

cifrado, -a [θi'fraðo, a] ADJ in code

cifrar [θi'frar] /**1a**/ VT to code, write in code; (*resumir*) to abridge; (*calcular*) to reckon

cigala [θi'ɣala] NF Norway lobster

cigarra [θi'ɣarra] NF cicada

cigarrera [θiɣa'rrera] NF cigar case

cigarrillo [θiɣa'rriʎo] NM cigarette

cigarro [θi'ɣarro] NM cigarette; (*puro*) cigar

cigüeña [θi'ɣweɲa] NF stork

cilíndrico, -a [θi'lindriko, a] ADJ cylindrical

cilindro [θi'lindro] NM cylinder

cima ['θima] NF (*de montaña*) top, peak; (*de árbol*) top; (*fig*) height

címbalo ['θimbalo] NM cymbal

cimbrear [θimbre'ar] /**1a**/ VT to brandish; **cimbrearse** VR to sway

cimentar [θimen'tar] /**1j**/ VT to lay the foundations of; (*fig: reforzar*) to strengthen; (: *fundar*) to found

cimiento [θi'mjento] VB *ver* **cimentar** ▶ NM foundation

cinc [θink] NM zinc

cincel [θin'θel] NM chisel

cincelar [θinθe'lar] /**1a**/ VT to chisel

cincha ['θintʃa] NF girth, saddle strap

cincho ['θintʃo] NM sash, belt

cinco ['θinko] NUM five; (*fecha*) fifth; **las ~** five o'clock; **no estar en sus ~** (*fam*) to be off one's rocker

cincuenta [θin'kwenta] NUM fifty

cincuentón, -ona [θinkwen'ton, ona] ADJ, NM/F fifty-year-old

cine ['θine] NM cinema; **el ~ mudo** silent films *pl*; **hacer ~** to make films

cineasta [θine'asta] NMF (*director de cine*) film-maker *o* director

cine-club ['θine'klub] NM film club

cinéfilo, -a [θi'nefilo, a] NM/F film buff

cinematográfico, -a [θinemato'ɣrafiko, a] ADJ cine-, film *cpd*

cínico, -a ['θiniko, a] ADJ cynical; (*descarado*) shameless ▶ NM/F cynic

cinismo [θi'nismo] NM cynicism

cinta ['θinta] NF band, strip; (*de tela*) ribbon; (*película*) reel; (*de máquina de escribir*) ribbon; (*métrica*) tape measure; (*magnetofónica*) tape; **~ adhesiva** sticky tape; **~ aislante** insulating tape; **~ de vídeo** videotape; **~ de carbón** carbon ribbon; **~ magnética** (*Inform*) magnetic tape; **~ métrica** tape measure; **~ de múltiples impactos** (*en impresora*) multistrike ribbon; **~ de tela** (*para máquina de escribir*) fabric ribbon; **~ transportadora** conveyor belt

cinto ['θinto] NM belt, girdle

cintura [θin'tura] NF waist; (*medida*) waistline

cinturón [θintu'ron] NM belt; (*fig*) belt, zone; **~ salvavidas** lifebelt; **~ de seguridad** safety belt

ciña *etc* ['θiɲa], **ciñendo** *etc* [θi'ɲendo] VB *ver* **ceñir**

ciprés [θi'pres] NM cypress (tree)

circo ['θirko] NM circus

circuito [θir'kwito] NM circuit; (*Deporte*) lap; **TV por ~ cerrado** closed-circuit TV; **~ experimental** (*Inform*) breadboard; **~ impreso** printed circuit; **~ lógico** (*Inform*) logical circuit

circulación [θirkula'θjon] NF circulation; (*Auto*) traffic; **"cerrado a la ~ rodada"** "closed to vehicles"

circular [θirku'lar] /**1a**/ ADJ, NF circular ▶ VT to circulate ▶ VI to circulate; (*dinero*) to be in circulation; (*Auto*) to drive; (*autobús*) to run; **"circule por la derecha"** "keep (to the) right"

círculo ['θirkulo] NM circle; (*centro*) clubhouse; (*Pol*) political group; **~ vicioso** vicious circle

circuncidar [θirkunθi'dar] /**1a**/ VT to circumcise

circunciso, -a [θirkun'θiso, a] PP *de* **circuncidar**

circundante [θirkun'dante] ADJ surrounding

circundar [θirkun'dar] /**1a**/ VT to surround

circunferencia [θirkunfe'renθja] NF circumference

circunloquio [θirkun'lokjo] NM circumlocution

circunscribir [θirkunskri'βir] /**3a**/ VT to circumscribe; **circunscribirse** VR to be limited

circunscripción [θirkunskrip'θjon] NF division; (*Pol*) constituency

circunscrito [θirkuns'krito] PP *de* **circunscribir**

circunspección [θirkunspek'θjon] NF circumspection, caution

circunspecto, -a [θirkuns'pekto, a] ADJ circumspect, cautious

circunstancia [θirkuns'tanθja] NF circumstance; **circunstancias agravantes/extenuantes** aggravating/extenuating circumstances; **estar a la altura de las circunstancias** to rise to the occasion

circunvalación [θirkumbala'θjon] NF: **carretera de ~** ring road

cirio ['θirjo] NM (wax) candle

cirrosis [θi'rrosis] NF cirrhosis (of the liver)

ciruela [θi'rwela] NF plum; **~ pasa** prune

ciruelo [θi'rwelo] NM plum tree

cirugía [θiru'xia] NF surgery; **~ estética o plástica** plastic surgery

cirujano [θiru'xano] NM surgeon

cisco ['θisko] NM: **armar un ~** to kick up a row; **estar hecho ~** to be a wreck

cisma ['θisma] NM schism; (Pol etc) split

cisne ['θisne] NM swan; **canto de ~** swan song

cisterna [θis'terna] NF cistern, tank

cistitis [θis'titis] NF cystitis

cita ['θita] NF appointment, meeting; (de novios) date; (referencia) quotation; **acudir/faltar a una ~** to turn up for/miss an appointment

citación [θita'θjon] NF (Jur) summons sg

citadino, -a [sita'ðino, a] ADJ (AM) urban ▶ NM/F urban o city dweller

citar [θi'tar] /1a/ VT to make an appointment with, arrange to meet; (Jur) to summons; (un autor, texto) to quote; **citarse** VR: **citarse con algn** to arrange to meet sb; **se citaron en el cine** they arranged to meet at the cinema

cítara ['θitara] NF zither

citología [θitolo'xia] NF smear test

cítrico, -a ['θitriko, a] ADJ citric ▶ NM: **cítricos** citrus fruits

CiU NM ABR (Pol) = **Convergència i Unió**

ciudad [θju'ðað] NF town; (capital de país etc) city; **~ universitaria** university campus; **C~ del Cabo** Cape Town; **la C~ Condal** Barcelona

ciudadanía [θjuðaða'nia] NF citizenship

ciudadano, -a [θjuða'ðano, a] ADJ civic ▶ NM/F citizen

ciudadrealeño, -a [θjuðaðrea'leɲo, a] ADJ of o from Ciudad Real ▶ NM/F native o inhabitant of Ciudad Real

cívico, -a ['θiβiko, a] ADJ civic; (fig) public-spirited

civil [θi'βil] ADJ civil ▶ NM (guardia) policeman

civilice etc [θiβi'liθe] VB ver **civilizar**

civilización [θiβiliθa'θjon] NF civilization

civilizar [θiβili'θar] /1f/ VT to civilize

civismo [θi'βismo] NM public spirit

cizaña [θi'θaɲa] NF (fig) discord; **sembrar ~** to sow discord

cl ABR (= centilitro) cl.

clamar [kla'mar] /1a/ VT to clamour for, cry out for ▶ VI to cry out, clamour

clamor [kla'mor] NM (grito) cry, shout; (fig) clamour, protest

clamoroso, -a [klamo'roso, a] ADJ (éxito etc) resounding

clan [klan] NM clan; (de gángsters) gang

clandestinidad [klandestini'ðað] NF secrecy

clandestino, -a [klandes'tino, a] ADJ clandestine; (Pol) underground

clara ['klara] NF (de huevo) egg white

claraboya [klara'βoja] NF skylight

clarear [klare'ar] /1a/ VI (el día) to dawn; (el cielo) to clear up, brighten up; **clearearse** VR to be transparent

clarete [kla'rete] NM rosé (wine)

claridad [klari'ðað] NF (del día) brightness; (de estilo) clarity

clarificar [klarifi'kar] /1g/ VT to clarify

clarifique etc [klari'fike] VB ver **clarificar**

clarín [kla'rin] NM bugle

clarinete [klari'nete] NM clarinet

clarividencia [klariβi'ðenθja] NF clairvoyance; (fig) far-sightedness

claro, -a ['klaro, a] ADJ clear; (luminoso) bright; (color) light; (evidente) clear, evident; (poco espeso) thin ▶ NM (en bosque) clearing ▶ ADV clearly ▶ EXCL: **¡~ que sí!** of course!; **¡~ que no!** of course not!; **hablar ~** (fig) to speak plainly; **a las claras** openly; **no sacamos nada en ~** we couldn't get anything definite

clase ['klase] NF class; (tipo) kind, sort; (Escol etc) class; (: aula) classroom; **~ alta/media/obrera** upper/middle/working class; **dar clases** to teach; **clases particulares** private lessons o tuition sg

clásico, -a ['klasiko, a] ADJ classical; (fig) classic

clasificable [klasifi'kaβle] ADJ classifiable

clasificación [klasifika'θjon] NF classification; (Deporte) league (table); (Com) ratings pl

clasificador [klasifika'ðor] NM filing cabinet

clasificar [klasifi'kar] /1g/ VT to classify; (Inform) to sort; **clasificarse** VR (Deporte: en torneo) to qualify

clasifique etc [klasi'fike] VB ver **clasificar**

clasista [kla'sista] ADJ (fam: actitud) snobbish

claudicar [klauði'kar] /1g/ VI (fig) to back down

claudique etc [klau'ðike] VB ver **claudicar**

claustro ['klaustro] NM cloister; (Univ) staff; (junta) senate

claustrofobia [klaustro'foβja] NF claustrophobia

cláusula ['klausula] NF clause; **~ de exclusión** (Com) exclusion clause

clausura [klau'sura] NF closing, closure

clausurar [klausu'rar] /1a/ VT (congreso etc) to close, bring to a close; (Pol etc) to adjourn; (cerrar) to close (down)

clavado, -a [kla'βaðo, a] ADJ nailed ▶ EXCL exactly!, precisely!

clavar [kla'βar] /1a/ VT (tablas etc) to nail (together); (con alfiler) to pin; (clavo) to hammer in; (cuchillo) to stick, thrust; (mirada) to fix; (fam: estafar) to cheat

clave ['klaβe] NF key; (Mus) clef ▶ ADJ INV key cpd; **~ de acceso** password; **~ lada** (AM) dialling (BRIT) o area (US) code

clavel [kla'βel] NM carnation

clavicémbalo [klaβi'θembalo] NM harpsichord

clavicordio [klaβikor'ðjo] NM clavichord

clavícula [kla'βikula] NF collar bone

clavija [kla'βixa] NF peg, pin; (Mus) peg; (Elec) plug

clavo ['klaβo] NM (de metal) nail; (Bot) clove; **dar en el ~** (fig) to hit the nail on the head

claxon ['klakson] (pl **claxons**) NM horn; **tocar el ~** to sound one's horn

clemencia [kle'menθja] NF mercy, clemency

clemente [kle'mente] ADJ merciful, clement

cleptómano, -a [klep'tomano, a] NM/F kleptomaniac

clerical [kleri'kal] ADJ clerical

clérigo ['kleriɣo] NM priest, clergyman

clero ['klero] NM clergy

clic [klik] NM click; **hacer ~/doble ~ en algo** to click/double-click on sth

clicar [kli'kar] /1a/ VI (Inform) to click; **clica en el icono** click on the icon; **~ dos veces** to double-click

cliché [kli'tʃe] NM cliché; (Tip) stencil; (Foto) negative

cliente, -a ['kljente, a] NM/F client, customer

clientela [kljen'tela] NF clientele, customers pl; (Com) goodwill; (Med) patients pl

clima ['klima] NM climate

climatizado, -a [klimati'θaðo, a] ADJ air-conditioned

clímax ['klimaks] NM INV climax

clínico, -a ['kliniko, a] ADJ clinical ▶ NF clinic; (particular) private hospital

clip [klip] (pl **clips** [klis]) NM paper clip

cliquear [klike'ar] /1a/ VI (Inform) to click; **cliquea en el icono** click on the icon

clítoris ['klitoris] NM INV clitoris

cloaca [klo'aka] NF sewer, drain

clonación [klona'θjon] NF cloning

clonar [klo'nar] /1a/ VT to clone

clorhídrico, -a [klo'riðriko, a] ADJ hydrochloric

cloro ['kloro] NM chlorine

clorofila [kloro'fila] NF chlorophyl(l)

cloroformo [kloro'formo] NM chloroform

cloruro [klo'ruro] NM chloride; **~ sódico** sodium chloride

club [klub] (pl **clubs** [klus] o **clubes** ['kluβes]) NM club; **~ de jóvenes** youth club; **~ nocturno** night club

cm ABR (= centímetro) cm

C.N.T. NF ABR (ESP: = Confederación Nacional de Trabajo) Anarchist Union Confederation; (AM) **= Confederación Nacional de Trabajadores**

coacción [koak'θjon] NF coercion, compulsion

coaccionar [koakθjo'nar] /1a/ VT to coerce, compel

coagular [koaɣu'lar] /1a/ VT, **coagularse** VR (sangre) to clot; (leche) to curdle

coágulo [ko'aɣulo] NM clot

coalición [koali'θjon] NF coalition

coartada [koar'taða] NF alibi

coartar [koar'tar] /1a/ VT to limit, restrict

coba ['koβa] NF: **dar ~ a algn** (adular) to suck up to sb

cobarde [ko'βarðe] ADJ cowardly ▶ NMF coward

cobardía [koβar'ðia] NF cowardice

cobaya [ko'βaja] NF guinea pig

cobertizo [koβer'tiθo] NM shelter

cobertor [koβer'tor] NM bedspread

cobertura [koβer'tura] NF cover; (Com) coverage; **~ de dividendo** (Com) dividend cover; **no tengo ~** (Telec) I can't get a signal

cobija [ko'βixa] NF (AM) blanket

cobijar [koβi'xar] /1a/ VT (cubrir) to cover; (abrigar) to shelter; **cobijarse** VR to take shelter

cobijo [ko'βixo] NM shelter

cobra ['koβra] NF cobra

cobrador, a [koβra'ðor, a] NM/F (de autobús) conductor/conductress; (de impuestos, gas) collector

cobrar [ko'βrar] /1a/ VT (cheque) to cash; (sueldo) to collect, draw; (objeto) to recover; (precio) to charge; (deuda) to collect ▶ VI to be paid; **cobrarse** VR to recover, get on well; **cóbrese al entregar** cash on delivery (COD) (BRIT), collect on delivery (COD) (US); **a ~** (Com) receivable; **cantidades por ~** sums due; **¿me cobra, por favor?** (en tienda) how much do I owe you?; (en restaurante) can I have the bill, please?

cobre ['koβre] NM copper; (AM fam) cent; **cobres** NMPL (Mus) brass instruments

cobrizo, -a [ko'βriθo, a] ADJ coppery

cobro ['koβro] NM (de cheque) cashing; (pago) payment; **presentar al ~** to cash; ver tb **llamada**

coca ['koka] NF coca; (droga) coke

cocaína [koka'ina] NF cocaine

cocainómano, -a [kokai'nomano, a] NM/F cocaine addict

cocción [kok'θjon] NF (Culin) cooking; (el hervir) boiling

cocear [koθe'ar] /1a/ VI to kick

cocer [ko'θer] /2b, 2h/ VT, VI to cook; (en agua) to boil; (en horno) to bake

coche ['kotʃe] NM (*Auto*) car, automobile (*US*); (*de tren, de caballos*) coach, carriage; (*para niños*) pram (*BRIT*), baby carriage (*US*); **ir en** ~ to drive; ~ **de bomberos** fire engine; ~ **celular** police van, patrol wagon (*US*); ~ **(comedor)** (*Ferro*) (dining) car; ~ **de carreras** racing car; ~-**escuela** learner car; ~ **fúnebre** hearse

coche-bomba ['kotʃe'βomba] (*pl* **coches-bomba**) NM car bomb

coche-cama ['kotʃe'kama] (*pl* **coches-cama**) NM (*Ferro*) sleeping car, sleeper

coche-escuela ['kotʃees'kwela] NM INV learner car

cochera [ko'tʃera] NF garage; (*de autobuses, trenes*) depot

coche-restaurante ['kotʃerestau'rante] (*pl* **coches-restaurante**) NM (*Ferro*) dining-car, diner

cochinada [kotʃi'naða] NF dirty trick

cochinillo [kotʃi'niʎo] NM piglet, suckling pig

cochino, -a [ko'tʃino, a] ADJ filthy, dirty ▸ NM/F pig

cocido, -a [ko'θiðo, a] ADJ boiled; (*fam*) plastered ▸ NM stew

cociente [ko'θjente] NM quotient

cocina [ko'θina] NF kitchen; (*aparato*) cooker, stove; (*actividad*) cookery; ~ **casera** home cooking; ~ **eléctrica** electric cooker; ~ **francesa** French cuisine; ~ **de gas** gas cooker

cocinar [koθi'nar] /1a/ VT, VI to cook

cocinero, -a [koθi'nero, a] NM/F cook

coco ['koko] NM coconut; (*fantasma*) bogeyman; (*fam: cabeza*) nut; **comer el** ~ **a algn** (*fam*) to brainwash sb

cocodrilo [koko'ðrilo] NM crocodile

cocotero [koko'tero] NM coconut palm

cóctel ['koktel] NM (*bebida*) cocktail; (*reunión*) cocktail party; ~ **Molotov** Molotov cocktail, petrol bomb

coctelera [kokte'lera] NF cocktail shaker

cod. ABR (= *código*) code

codazo [ko'ðaθo] NM: **dar un** ~ **a algn** to nudge sb

codear [koðe'ar] /1a/ VI to elbow, jostle; **codearse** VR: **codearse con** to rub shoulders with

códice ['koðiθe] NM manuscript, codex

codicia [ko'ðiθja] NF greed; (*fig*) lust

codiciar [koði'θjar] /1b/ VT to covet

codicioso, -a [koði'θjoso, a] ADJ covetous

codificador [koðifika'ðor] NM (*Inform*) encoder; ~ **digital** digitizer

codificar [koðifi'kar] /1g/ VT (*mensaje*) to (en)code; (*leyes*) to codify

código ['koðiɣo] NM code; ~ **de barras** (*Com*) bar code; ~ **binario** binary code; ~ **de caracteres** (*Inform*) character code; ~ **de (la)**

circulación highway code; ~ **de la zona** (*Am*) dialling (*BRIT*) o area (*US*) code; ~ **postal** postcode; ~ **civil** common law; ~ **de control** (*Inform*) control code; ~ **máquina** (*Inform*) machine code; ~ **militar** military law; ~ **de operación** (*Inform*) operational o machine code; ~ **penal** penal code; ~ **de práctica** code of practice

codillo [ko'ðiʎo] NM (*Zool*) knee; (*Tec*) elbow (joint)

codo ['koðo] NM (*Anat, de tubo*) elbow; (*Zool*) knee; **hablar por los codos** to talk nineteen to the dozen

codorniz [koðor'niθ] NF quail

coeficiente [koefi'θjente] NM (*Mat*) coefficient; (*Econ etc*) rate; ~ **intelectual** o **de inteligencia** I.Q.

coerción [koer'θjon] NF coercion

coercitivo, -a [koerθi'tiβo, a] ADJ coercive

coetáneo, -a [koe'taneo, a] NM/F: **coetáneos** contemporaries

coexistencia [koeksis'tenθja] NF coexistence

coexistir [koeksis'tir] /3a/ VI to coexist

cofia ['kofja] NF (*de enfermera*) (white) cap

cofradía [kofra'ðia] NF brotherhood, fraternity; *ver tb* **semana**

cofre ['kofre] NM (*baúl*) trunk; (*de joyas*) box; (*de dinero*) chest; (*Am Auto*) bonnet (*BRIT*), hood (*US*)

cogedor [koxe'ðor] NM dustpan

coger [ko'xer] /2c/ VT (*ESP*) to take (hold of); (: *objeto caído*) to pick up; (: *frutas*) to pick, harvest; (: *resfriado, ladrón, pelota*) to catch; (*AM fam!*) to lay (*fam!*) ▸ VI: ~ **por el buen camino** to take the right road; **cogerse** VR (*el dedo*) to catch; ~ **a algn desprevenido** to take sb unawares; **cogerse a algo** to get hold of sth

cogida [ko'xiða] NF gathering, harvesting; (*de peces*) catch; (*Taur*) goring

cognitivo, -a [koɣni'tiβo, a] ADJ cognitive

cogollo [ko'ɣoʎo] NM (*de lechuga*) heart; (*fig*) core, nucleus

cogorza [ko'ɣorθa] NF (*fam*): **agarrar una** ~ to get smashed

cogote [ko'ɣote] NM back o nape of the neck

cohabitar [koaβi'tar] /1a/ VI to live together, cohabit

cohecho [ko'etʃo] NM (*acción*) bribery; (*soborno*) bribe

coherencia [koe'renθja] NF coherence

coherente [koe'rente] ADJ coherent

cohesión [koe'sjon] NF cohesion

cohete [ko'ete] NM rocket

cohibido, -a [koi'βiðo, a] ADJ (*Psico*) inhibited; (*tímido*) shy; **sentirse** ~ to feel embarrassed

cohibir [koi'βir] /3a/ VT to restrain, restrict; **cohibirse** VR to feel inhibited

COI NM ABR (= *Comité Olímpico Internacional*) IOC

coima ['koima] NF (*Am fam*) bribe

coincidencia [koinθi'ðenθja] NF coincidence

coincidir [koinθi'ðir] /**3a**/ VI (*en idea*) to coincide, agree; (*en lugar*) to coincide

coito ['koito] NM intercourse, coitus

coja *etc* VB *ver* **coger**

cojear [koxe'ar] /**1a**/ VI (*persona*) to limp, hobble; (*mueble*) to wobble, rock

cojera [ko'xera] NF lameness; (*andar cojo*) limp

cojín [ko'xin] NM cushion

cojinete [koxi'nete] NM small cushion, pad; (*Tec*) (ball) bearing

cojo, -a ['koxo, a] VB *ver* **coger** ▶ ADJ (*que no puede andar*) lame, crippled; (*mueble*) wobbly ▶ NM/F lame person, cripple

cojón [ko'xon] NM (*fam!*) ball (*fam!*), testicle; **¡cojones!** shit! (*fam!*)

cojonudo, -a [koxo'nuðo, a] ADJ (*Esp fam*) great, fantastic

col [kol] NF cabbage; **coles de Bruselas** Brussels sprouts

cola ['kola] NF tail; (*de gente*) queue; (*lugar*) end, last place; (*para pegar*) glue, gum; (*de vestido*) train; **hacer ~** to queue (up)

colaboración [kolaβora'θjon] NF (*gen*) collaboration; (*en periódico*) contribution

colaborador, a [kolaβora'ðor, a] NM/F collaborator; contributor

colaborar [kolaβo'rar] /**1a**/ VI to collaborate

colación [kola'θjon] NF: **sacar a ~** to bring up

colado, -a [ko'laðo, a] ADJ (*metal*) cast ▶ NF: **hacer la colada** to do the washing

colador [kola'ðor] NM (*de té*) strainer; (*para verduras etc*) colander

colapsar [kolap'sar] /**1a**/ VT (*tráfico etc*) to bring to a standstill

colapso [ko'lapso] NM collapse; **~ nervioso** nervous breakdown

colar [ko'lar] /**1l**/ VT (*líquido*) to strain off; (*metal*) to cast ▶ VI to ooze, seep (through); **colarse** VR to jump the queue; (*en mitin*) to sneak in; (*equivocarse*) to slip up; **colarse en** to get into without paying; (*en una fiesta*) to gatecrash

colateral [kolate'ral] NM collateral

colcha ['koltʃa] NF bedspread

colchón [kol'tʃon] NM mattress; **~ inflable** air bed, inflatable mattress

colchoneta [koltʃo'neta] NF (*en gimnasio*) mat; **~ hinchable** air bed, inflatable mattress

colear [kole'ar] /**1a**/ VI (*perro*) to wag its tail

colección [kolek'θjon] NF collection

coleccionar [kolekθjo'nar] /**1a**/ VT to collect

coleccionista [kolekθjo'nista] NMF collector

colecta [ko'lekta] NF collection

colectivo, -a [kolek'tiβo, a] ADJ collective, joint ▶ NM (*Am: autobús*) (small) bus; (*: taxi*) collective taxi

colector [kolek'tor] NM collector; (*sumidero*) sewer

colega [ko'leɣa] NMF colleague; (*Esp: amigo*) mate

colegiado, -a [kole'xjaðo, a] ADJ (*profesional*) registered ▶ NM/F referee

colegial, a [kole'xjal, a] ADJ (*Escol etc*) school cpd, college cpd ▶ NM/F schoolboy/girl

colegio [ko'lexjo] NM college; (*escuela*) school; (*de abogados etc*) association; **~ de internos** boarding school; **ir al ~** to go to school; **~ electoral** polling station; **~ mayor** (*Esp*) hall of residence; *see note*

> A **colegio** is often a private primary or secondary school. In the state system it means a primary school although these are also called **escuela**. State secondary schools are called **institutos**. Extracurricular subjects, such as computing or foreign languages, are offered in private schools called **academias**.

colegir [kole'xir] /**3c, 3k**/ VT (*juntar*) to collect, gather; (*deducir*) to infer, conclude

cólera ['kolera] NF (*ira*) anger; **montar en ~** to get angry ▶ NM (*Med*) cholera

colérico, -a [ko'leriko, a] ADJ angry, furious

colesterol [koleste'rol] NM cholesterol

coleta [ko'leta] NF pigtail

coletazo [kole'taθo] NM: **dar un ~** (*animal*) to flap its tail; **los últimos coletazos** death throes

coletilla [kole'tiʎa] NF (*en carta*) postscript; (*en conversación*) filler phrase

colgado, -a [kol'ɣaðo, a] PP *de* **colgar** ▶ ADJ hanging; (*ahorcado*) hanged; **dejar ~ a algn** to let sb down

colgajo [kol'ɣaxo] NM tatter

colgante [kol'ɣante] ADJ hanging; *ver* **puente** ▶ NM (*joya*) pendant

colgar [kol'ɣar] /**1h, 1l**/ VT to hang (up); (*tender: ropa*) to hang out ▶ VI to hang; (*teléfono*) to hang up; **no cuelgue** please hold

colgué [kol'ɣe]**, colguemos** *etc* [kol'ɣemos] VB *ver* **colgar**

colibrí [koli'βri] NM hummingbird

cólico ['koliko] NM colic

coliflor [koli'flor] NF cauliflower

coligiendo *etc* [koli'xjenðo] VB *ver* **colegir**

colija *etc* [ko'lixa] VB *ver* **colegir**

colilla [ko'liʎa] NF cigarette end, butt

colina [ko'lina] NF hill

colindante [kolin'dante] ADJ adjacent, neighbouring

colindar [kolin'dar] /**1a**/ VI to adjoin, be adjacent

colisión [koli'sjon] NF collision; **~ frontal** head-on crash

colitis [ko'litis] NF INV: **tener ~** to have diarrhoea

collar [ko'ʎar] NM necklace; (de perro) collar

colmado, -a [kol'maðo, a] ADJ full ▶ NM grocer's (shop) (BRIT), grocery store (US)

colmar [kol'mar] /1a/ VT to fill to the brim; (fig) to fulfil, realize

colmena [kol'mena] NF beehive

colmillo [kol'miʎo] NM (diente) eye tooth; (de elefante) tusk; (de perro) fang

colmo ['kolmo] NM height, summit; **para ~ de desgracias** to cap it all; **¡eso es ya el ~!** that's beyond a joke!

colocación [koloka'θjon] NF (acto) placing; (empleo) job, position; (situación) place, position; (Com) placement

colocar [kolo'kar] /1g/ VT to place, put, position; (poner en empleo) to find a job for; **~ dinero** to invest money; **colocarse** VR to place o.s.; (conseguir trabajo) to find a job

colofón [kolo'fon] NM: **como ~ de las conversaciones** as a sequel to o following the talks

Colombia [ko'lombja] NF Colombia

colombiano, -a [kolom'bjano, a] ADJ, NM/F Colombian

colon ['kolon] NM colon

colón [ko'lon] NM (AM) monetary unit of Costa Rica and El Salvador

Colonia [ko'lonja] NF Cologne

colonia [ko'lonja] NF colony; (de casas) housing estate; (agua de colonia) cologne; **~ escolar** summer camp (for schoolchildren); **~ proletaria** (AM) shantytown

colonice etc [kolo'niθe] VB ver **colonizar**

colonización [koloniθa'θjon] NF colonization

colonizador, a [koloniθa'ðor, a] ADJ colonizing ▶ NM/F colonist, settler

colonizar [koloni'θar] /1f/ VT to colonize

colono [ko'lono] NM (Pol) colonist, settler; (Agr) tenant farmer

coloque etc [ko'loke] VB ver **colocar**

coloquial [kolo'kjal] ADJ colloquial

coloquio [ko'lokjo] NM conversation; (congreso) conference

color [ko'lor] NM colour; **a todo ~** in full colour; **verlo todo ~ de rosa** to see everything through rose-coloured spectacles; **le salieron los colores** she blushed

colorado, -a [kolo'raðo, a] ADJ (rojo) red; (AM: chiste) rude, blue; **ponerse ~** to blush

colorante [kolo'rante] NM colouring (matter)

colorar [kolo'rar] /1a/ VT to colour; (teñir) to dye

colorear [kolore'ar] /1a/ VT to colour

colorete [kolo'rete] NM blusher

colorido [kolo'riðo] NM colour(ing)

coloso [ko'loso] NM colossus

columbrar [kolum'brar] /1a/ VT to glimpse, spy

columna [ko'lumna] NF column; (pilar) pillar; (apoyo) support; **~ blindada** (Mil) armoured column; **~ vertebral** spine, spinal column; (fig) backbone

columpiar [kolum'pjar] /1b/ VT to swing; **columpiarse** VR to swing

columpio [ko'lumpjo] NM swing

colza ['kolθa] NF rape; **aceite de ~** rapeseed oil

coma ['koma] NF comma ▶ NM (Med) coma

comadre [ko'maðre] NF (madrina) godmother; (vecina) neighbour; (chismosa) gossip

comadrear [komaðre'ar] /1a/ VI (esp AM) to gossip

comadreja [koma'ðrexa] NF weasel

comadrona [koma'ðrona] NF midwife

comal [ko'mal] NM (AM) griddle

comandancia [koman'danθja] NF command

comandante [koman'dante] NM commandant; (grado) major

comandar [koman'dar] /1a/ VT to command

comando [ko'mando] NM (Mil: mando) command; (: grupo) commando unit; (Inform) command; **~ de búsqueda** search command

comarca [ko'marka] NF region; ver tb **provincia**

comarcal [komar'kal] ADJ local

comba ['komba] NF (curva) curve; (en viga) warp; (cuerda) skipping rope; **saltar a la ~** to skip

combar [kom'bar] /1a/ VT to bend, curve

combate [kom'bate] NM fight; (fig) battle; **fuera de ~** out of action

combatiente [komba'tjente] NM combatant

combatir [komba'tir] /3a/ VT to fight, combat

combatividad [kombatiβi'ðað] NF (actitud) fighting spirit; (agresividad) aggressiveness

combativo, -a [komba'tiβo, a] ADJ full of fight

combi ['kombi] NM fridge-freezer

combinación [kombina'θjon] NF combination; (Química) compound; (bebida) cocktail; (plan) scheme, setup; (prenda) slip

combinado, -a [kombi'naðo, a] ADJ: **plato ~** main course served with vegetables

combinar [kombi'nar] /1a/ VT to combine; (colores) to match

combustible [kombus'tiβle] NM fuel

combustión [kombus'tjon] NF combustion

comedia [ko'meðja] NF comedy; (Teat) play, drama; (fig) farce

comediante [kome'ðjante] NMF (comic) actor/actress

81

comedido, -a [kome'ðiðo, a] ADJ moderate

comedirse [kome'ðirse] /**3k**/ vr to behave moderately; (*ser cortés*) to be courteous

comedor, a [kome'ðor, a] NM/F (*persona*) glutton ▸ NM (*habitación*) dining room; (*restaurante*) restaurant; (*cantina*) canteen

comencé [komen'θe], **comencemos** *etc* [komen'θemos] VB ver **comenzar**

comensal [komen'sal] NMF fellow guest/diner

comentar [komen'tar] /**1a**/ VT to comment on; (*fam*) to discuss; **comentó que ...** he made the comment that ...

comentario [komen'tarjo] NM comment, remark; (*Lit*) commentary; **comentarios** NMPL gossip *sg*; **dar lugar a comentarios** to cause gossip

comentarista [komenta'rista] NMF commentator

comenzar [komen'θar] /**1f, 1j**/ VT, VI to begin, start, commence; **~ a hacer algo** to begin *o* start doing *o* to do sth

comer [ko'mer] /**2a**/ VT to eat; (*Damas, Ajedrez*) to take, capture ▸ VI to eat; (*almorzar*) to have lunch; **comerse** VR to eat up; (*párrafo etc*) to skip; **~ el coco a** (*fam*) to brainwash; **¡a ~!** food's ready!

comercial [komer'θjal] ADJ commercial; (*relativo al negocio*) business *cpd*

comercializar [komerθjali'θar] /**1f**/ VT (*producto*) to market; (*pey*) to commercialize

comerciante [komer'θjante] NMF trader, merchant; (*tendero*) shopkeeper; **~ exclusivo** (*Com*) sole trader

comerciar [komer'θjar] /**1b**/ VI to trade, do business

comercio [ko'merθjo] NM commerce, trade; (*tienda*) shop, store; (*negocio*) business; (*grandes empresas*) big business; (*fig*) dealings *pl*; **~ autorizado** (*Com*) licensed trade; **~ electrónico** e-commerce; **~ exterior** foreign trade

comestible [komes'tiβle] ADJ eatable, edible ▸ NM: **comestibles** food *sg*, foodstuffs; (*Com*) groceries

cometa [ko'meta] NM comet ▸ NF kite

cometer [kome'ter] /**2a**/ VT to commit

cometido [kome'tiðo] NM (*misión*) task, assignment; (*deber*) commitment

comezón [kome'θon] NF itch, itching

cómic ['komik] (*pl* **cómics** ['komiks]) NM comic

comicios [ko'miθjos] NMPL elections; (*voto*) voting *sg*

cómico, -a ['komiko, a] ADJ comic(al) ▸ NM/F comedian; (*de teatro*) (comic) actor/actress

comida [ko'miða] VB ver **comedirse** ▸ NF (*alimento*) food; (*almuerzo, cena*) meal; (*de mediodía*) lunch; (*Am*) dinner; **~ basura** junk food; **~ chatarra** (*Am*) junk food

comidilla [komi'ðiʎa] NF: **ser la ~ del barrio** *o* **pueblo** to be the talk of the town

comience *etc* [ko'mjenθe] VB ver **comenzar**

comienzo [ko'mjenθo] VB ver **comenzar** ▸ NM beginning, start; **dar ~ a un acto** to begin a ceremony; **~ del archivo** (*Inform*) top-of-file

comillas [ko'miʎas] NFPL quotation marks

comilón, -ona [komi'lon, ona] ADJ greedy ▸ NF (*fam*) blow-out

comino [ko'mino] NM cumin (seed); **no me importa un ~** I don't give a damn!

comisaría [komisa'ria] NF police station, precinct (*US*); (*Mil*) commissariat

comisario [komi'sarjo] NM (*Mil etc*) commissary; (*Pol*) commissar

comisión [komi'sjon] NF (*Com: pago*) commission, rake-off (*fam*); (*: junta*) board; (*encargo*) assignment; **~ mixta/permanente** joint/standing committee; **Comisiones Obreras** (*Esp*) former Communist Union Confederation

comisura [komi'sura] NF: **~ de los labios** corner of the mouth

comité [komi'te] (*pl* **comités** [komi'tes]) NM committee; **~ de empresa** works council

comitiva [komi'tiβa] NF suite, retinue

como ['komo] ADV as; (*tal como*) like; (*aproximadamente*) about, approximately ▸ CONJ (*ya que, puesto que*) as, since; (*en seguida que*) as soon as; (*si: +subjun*) if; **¡~ no!** of course!; **~ no lo haga hoy** unless he does it today; **~ si** as if; **es tan alto ~ ancho** it is as high as it is wide

cómo ['komo] ADV how?, why? ▸ EXCL what?, I beg your pardon? ▸ NM: **el ~ y el porqué** the whys and wherefores; **¿~ está Ud?** how are you?; **¿~ no?** why not?; **¡~ no!** (*esp Am*) of course!; **¿~ son?** what are they like?

cómoda ['komoða] NF chest of drawers

comodidad [komoði'ðað] NF comfort; **venga a su ~** come at your convenience

comodín [komo'ðin] NM joker; (*Inform*) wild card; **símbolo ~** wild-card character

cómodo, -a ['komoðo, a] ADJ comfortable; (*práctico, de fácil uso*) convenient

comodón, -ona [komo'ðon, -ona] ADJ comfort-loving ▸ NM/F: **ser un(a) ~/ona** to like one's home comforts

comoquiera [komo'kjera] CONJ: **~ que** (*+subjun*) in whatever way; **~ que sea eso** however that may be

comp. ABR (= *compárese*) cp

compact [kom'pakt] (*pl* **compacts**) NM (*tb*: **compact disc**) compact disk

compacto, -a [kom'pakto, a] ADJ compact

compadecer [kompaðe'θer] /**2d**/ VT to pity, be sorry for; **compadecerse** VR: **compadecerse de** to pity, be sorry for

compadezca etc [kompa'ðeθka] VB ver
compadecer

compadre [kom'paðre] NM (padrino)
godfather; (espAm: amigo) friend, pal

compaginar [kompaxi'nar] /1a/ VT: **~ A con
B** to bring A into line with B; **compaginarse**
VR: **compaginarse con** to tally with, square
with

compañerismo [kompaɲe'rismo] NM
comradeship

compañero, -a [kompa'ɲero, a] NM/F
companion; (novio) boyfriend/girlfriend;
~ de clase classmate

compañía [kompa'ɲia] NF company;
~ afiliada associated company;
~ concesionaria franchiser; **~ (no)
cotizable** (un)listed company;
~ inversionista investment trust; **hacer ~ a
algn** to keep sb company

comparación [kompara'θjon] NF
comparison; **en ~ con** in comparison with

comparar [kompa'rar] /1a/ VT to compare

comparativo, -a [kompara'tiβo, a] ADJ
comparative

comparecencia [kompare'θenθja] NF (Jur)
appearance (in court); **orden de ~**
summons sg

comparecer [kompare'θer] /2d/ VI to appear
(in court)

comparezca etc [kompa're θka] VB ver
comparecer

comparsa [kom'parsa] NMF extra

compartim(i)ento [komparti'm(j)ento] NM
(Ferro) compartment; (de mueble, cajón)
section; **compartimento estanco** (fig)
watertight compartment

compartir [kompar'tir] /3a/ VT to share;
(dinero, comida etc) to divide (up), share (out)

compás [kom'pas] NM (Mus) beat, rhythm;
(Mat) compasses pl; (Naut etc) compass; **al ~**
in time

compasión [kompa'sjon] NF compassion,
pity

compasivo, -a [kompa'siβo, a] ADJ
compassionate

compatibilidad [kompatiβili'ðað] NF (tb
Inform) compatibility

compatible [kompa'tiβle] ADJ compatible

compatriota [kompa'trjota] NMF
compatriot, fellow countryman/woman

compendiar [kompen'djar] /1b/ VT to
summarize; (libro) to abridge

compendio [kom'pendjo] NM summary;
abridgement

compenetración [kompenetra'θjon] NF (fig)
mutual understanding

compenetrarse [kompene'trarse] /1a/ VR to
be in tune; (fig): **~ (muy) bien** to get on (very)
well together

compensación [kompensa'θjon] NF
compensation; (Jur) damages pl; (Com)
clearing; **~ (de emisiones) de carbono**
(crédito) carbon offset; (sistema) carbon
offsetting

compensar [kompen'sar] /1a/ VT to
compensate; (pérdida) to make up for

competencia [kompe'tenθja] NF
(incumbencia) domain, field; (Com) receipt;
(Jur, habilidad) competence; (rivalidad)
competition

competente [kompe'tente] ADJ (Jur, persona)
competent; (conveniente) suitable

competer [kompe'ter] /2a/ VI: **~ a** to be the
responsibility of, fall to

competición [kompeti'θjon] NF competition

competidor, a [kompeti'ðor, a] NM/F
competitor

competir [kompe'tir] /3k/ VI to compete

competitivo, -a [kompeti'tiβo, a] ADJ
competitive

compilación [kompila'θjon] NF
compilation; **tiempo de ~** (Inform) compile
time

compilador [kompila'ðor] NM compiler

compilar [kompi'lar] /1a/ VT to compile

compinche [kom'pintʃe] NMF (Am fam) mate,
buddy (US)

compita etc [kom'pita] VB ver **competir**

complacencia [kompla'θenθja] NF (placer)
pleasure; (satisfacción) satisfaction; (buena
voluntad) willingness

complacer [kompla'θer] /2w/ VT to please;
complacerse VR to be pleased

complaciente [kompla'θjente] ADJ kind,
obliging, helpful

complazca etc [kom'plaθka] VB ver
complacer

complejo, -a [kom'plexo, a] ADJ, NM complex

complementario, -a [komplemen'tarjo, a]
ADJ complementary

complemento [komple'mento] NM (de moda,
diseño) accessory; (Ling) complement

completar [komple'tar] /1a/ VT to complete

completo, -a [kom'pleto, a] ADJ complete;
(perfecto) perfect; (lleno) full ▶ NM full
complement

complexión [komple'ksjon] NF constitution

complicación [komplika'θjon] NF
complication

complicado, -a [kompli'kaðo, a] ADJ
complicated; **estar ~ en** to be mixed up in

complicar [kompli'kar] /1g/ VT to complicate

cómplice ['kompliθe] NMF accomplice

complique etc [kom'plike] VB ver **complicar**

complot [kom'plo(t)] (pl **complots**
[kom'plos]) NM plot; (conspiración) conspiracy

compondré etc [kompon'dre] VB ver
componer

componenda [kompo'nenda] NF compromise; (pey) shady deal

componente [kompo'nente] ADJ, NM component

componer [kompo'ner] /2q/ VT to make up, put together; (Mus, Lit, Imprenta) to compose; (algo roto) to mend, repair; (adornar) to adorn; (arreglar) to arrange; (reconciliar) to reconcile; **componerse** VR: **componerse de** to consist of; **componérselas para hacer algo** to manage to do sth

componga etc [kom'ponga] VB ver **componer**

comportamiento [komporta'mjento] NM behaviour, conduct

comportarse [kompor'tarse] /1a/ VR to behave

composición [komposi'θjon] NF composition

compositor, a [komposi'tor, a] NM/F composer

compostelano, -a [komposte'lano, a] ADJ of o from Santiago de Compostela ▶ NM/F native o inhabitant of Santiago de Compostela

compostura [kompos'tura] NF (reparación) mending, repair; (composición) composition; (acuerdo) agreement; (actitud) composure

compota [kom'pota] NF compote, preserve

compra ['kompra] NF purchase; **compras** NFPL purchases, shopping sg; **hacer la ~/ir de compras** to go the/go shopping; **~ a granel** (Com) bulk buying; **~ proteccionista** (Com) support buying

comprador, a [kompra'ðor, a] NM/F buyer, purchaser

comprar [kom'prar] /1a/ VT to buy, purchase; **~ deudas** (Com) to factor

compraventa [kompra'βenta] NF (Jur) contract of sale

comprender [kompren'der] /2a/ VT to understand; (incluir) to comprise, include

comprensible [kompren'siβle] ADJ understandable

comprensión [kompren'sjon] NF understanding; (totalidad) comprehensiveness

comprensivo, -a [kompren'siβo, a] ADJ comprehensive; (actitud) understanding

compresa [kom'presa] NF compress; (higiénica) sanitary towel (BRIT) o napkin (US)

compresión [kompre'sjon] NF compression

comprimido, -a [kompri'miðo, a] ADJ compressed ▶ NM (Med) pill, tablet; **en caracteres comprimidos** (Tip) condensed

comprimir [kompri'mir] /3a/ VT to compress; (fig) to control; (Inform) to compress, zip

comprobación [komproβa'θjon] NF: **~ general de cuentas** (Com) general audit

comprobante [kompro'βante] NM proof; (Com) voucher; **~ (de pago)** receipt; **~ de compra** proof of purchase

comprobar [kompro'βar] /1l/ VT to check; (probar) to prove; (Tec) to check, test

comprometedor, a [kompromete'ðor, a] ADJ compromising

comprometer [komprome'ter] /2a/ VT to compromise; (exponer) to endanger; **comprometerse** VR to compromise o.s.; (involucrarse) to get involved

comprometido, -a [komprome'tiðo, a] ADJ (situación) awkward; (escritor etc) committed

compromiso [kompro'miso] NM (obligación) obligation; (cita) engagement, date; (cometido) commitment; (convenio) agreement; (dificultad) awkward situation; **libre de ~** (Com) without obligation

comprueba etc [kom'prweβa] VB ver **comprobar**

compuerta [kom'pwerta] NF (en canal) sluice, floodgate; (Inform) gate

compuesto, -a [kom'pwesto, a] PP de **componer** ▶ ADJ: **~ de** composed of, made up of ▶ NM compound; (Med) preparation

compulsar [kompul'sar] /1a/ VT (cotejar) to collate, compare; (Jur) to make an attested copy of

compulsivo, -a [kompul'siβo, a] ADJ compulsive

compungido, -a [kompun'xiðo, a] ADJ remorseful

compuse etc [kom'puse] VB ver **componer**

computación [komputa'θjon] NF computing; **~ en (la) nube** cloud computing

computador [komputa'ðor] NM, **computadora** [komputa'ðora] NF computer; **~ central** mainframe computer; **~ especializado** dedicated computer; **~ personal** personal computer

computar [kompu'tar] /1a/ VT to calculate, compute

cómputo ['komputo] NM calculation

comulgar [komul'ɣar] /1h/ VI to receive communion

comulgue etc [ko'mulɣe] VB ver **comulgar**

común [ko'mun] ADJ (gen) common; (corriente) ordinary; **por lo ~** generally ▶ NM: **el ~** the community

comuna [ko'muna] NF commune; (AM) district

comunicación [komunika'θjon] NF communication; (informe) report

comunicado [komuni'kaðo] NM announcement; **~ de prensa** press release

comunicar [komuni'kar] /1g/ VT to communicate; (Arq) to connect ▶ VI to communicate; to send a report;

comunicarse VR to communicate; **está comunicando** (*Telec*) the line's engaged (*BRIT*) *o* busy (*US*)

comunicativo, -a [komunika'tiβo, a] ADJ communicative

comunidad [komuni'ðað] NF community; **~ autónoma** (*ESP*) autonomous region; **~ de vecinos** residents' association; *see note*

> The 1978 Constitution provides for a degree of self-government for the 19 regions, called *comunidades autónomas* or *autonomías*. Some, such as Catalonia and the Basque Country, with their own language, history and culture, have long felt separate from the rest of Spain. This explains why some of the *autonomías* have more devolved powers than others, in all matters except foreign affairs and national defence. The regions are: Andalucía, Aragón, Asturias, Islas Baleares, Canarias, Cantabria, Castilla y León, Castilla-La Mancha, Cataluña, Extremadura, Galicia, Madrid, Murcia, Navarra, País Vasco, La Rioja, Comunidad Valenciana, Ceuta, Melilla.

comunión [komu'njon] NF communion

comunique *etc* [komu'nike] VB *ver* **comunicar**

comunismo [komu'nismo] NM communism

comunista [komu'nista] ADJ, NMF communist

comunitario, -a [komuni'tarjo, a] ADJ (*de la* CE) Community *cpd*, EC *cpd*

PALABRA CLAVE

con [kon] PREP **1** (*medio, compañía, modo*) with; **comer con cuchara** to eat with a spoon; **café con leche** white coffee; **estoy con un catarro** I've got a cold; **pasear con algn** to go for a walk with sb; **con habilidad** skilfully

2 (*a pesar de*): **con todo, merece nuestros respetos** all the same *o* even so, he deserves our respect

3 (*para con*): **es muy bueno para con los niños** he's very good with (the) children

4 (+ *infin*): **con llegar tan tarde se quedó sin comer** by arriving *o* because he arrived so late he missed out on eating; **con estudiar un poco apruebas** with a bit of studying you should pass

5 (*queja*): **¡con las ganas que tenía de ir!** and I really wanted to go (too)!

▶ CONJ: **con que: será suficiente con que le escribas** it will be enough if you write to her

conato [ko'nato] NM attempt; **~ de robo** attempted robbery

cóncavo, -a ['konkaβo, a] ADJ concave

concebir [konθe'βir] /**3k**/ VT to conceive; (*imaginar*) to imagine ▶ VI to conceive

conceder [konθe'ðer] /**2a**/ VT to concede

concejal, a [konθe'xal, a] NM/F town councillor

concejo [kon'θexo] NM council

concentración [konθentra'θjon] NF concentration

concentrar [konθen'trar] /**1a**/ VT to concentrate; **concentrarse** VR to concentrate

concéntrico, -a [kon'θentriko, a] ADJ concentric

concepción [konθep'θjon] NF conception

concepto [kon'θepto] NM concept; **por ~ de** as, by way of; **tener buen ~ de algn** to think highly of sb; **bajo ningún ~** under no circumstances

conceptuar [konθep'twar] /**1e**/ VT to judge

concernir [konθer'nir] VI to concern; **en lo que concierne a ...** with regard to ...; **en lo que a mí concierne** as far as I'm concerned

concertar [konθer'tar] /**1j**/ VT (*entrevista*) to arrange; (*precio*) to agree; (*esfuerzos*) to coordinate; (*Mus*) to harmonize ▶ VI to harmonize, be in tune

concesión [konθe'sjon] NF concession; (*Com: fabricación*) licence

concesionario, -a [konθesjo'narjo, a] NM/F (*Com*) (licensed) dealer, agent, concessionaire; (: *de venta*) franchisee; (: *de transportes etc*) contractor

concha ['kontʃa] NF shell; (*AM fam!*) cunt (*fam!*)

conchabarse [kontʃa'βarse] /**1a**/ VR: **~ contra** to gang up on

conciencia [kon'θjenθja] NF (*moral*) conscience; (*conocimiento*) awareness; **libertad de ~** freedom of worship; **tener/tomar ~ de** to be/become aware of; **tener la ~ limpia** *o* **tranquila** to have a clear conscience; **tener plena ~ de** to be fully aware of

concienciar [konθjen'θjar] /**1b**/ VT to make aware; **concienciarse** VR to become aware

concienzudo, -a [konθjen'θuðo, a] ADJ conscientious

concierne *etc* [kon'θjerne] VB *ver* **concernir**

concierto [kon'θjerto] VB *ver* **concertar** ▶ NM concert; (*obra*) concerto

conciliación [konθilja'θjon] NF conciliation

conciliar [konθi'ljar] /**1b**/ VT to reconcile ▶ ADJ (*Rel*) council *cpd*; **~ el sueño** to get to sleep

concilio [kon'θiljo] NM council

concisión [konθi'sjon] NF conciseness

conciso, -a [kon'θiso, a] ADJ concise

conciudadano, -a [konθjuða'ðano, a] NM/F fellow citizen

concluir [konklu'ir] /**3g**/ VT (*acabar*) to conclude; (*inferir*) to infer, deduce ▶ VI, **concluirse** VR to conclude; **todo ha concluido** it's all over

conclusión [konklu'sjon] NF conclusion; **llegar a la ~ de que ...** to come to the conclusion that ...

concluya *etc* [kon'kluja] VB *ver* **concluir**

concluyente [konklu'jente] ADJ (*prueba, información*) conclusive

concordancia [konkor'ðanθja] NF agreement

concordar [konkor'ðar] /**1l**/ VT to reconcile ▶ VI to agree, tally

concordia [kon'korðja] NF harmony

concretamente [konkreta'mente] ADV specifically, to be exact

concretar [konkre'tar] /**1a**/ VT to make concrete, make more specific; (*problema*) to pinpoint; **concretarse** VR to become more definite

concreto, -a [kon'kreto, a] ADJ, NM (AM) concrete; **en ~** (*en resumen*) to sum up; (*específicamente*) specifically; **no hay nada en ~** there's nothing definite

concubina [konku'ßina] NF concubine

concuerde *etc* [kon'kwerðe] VB *ver* **concordar**

concupiscencia [konkupis'θenθja] NF (*avaricia*) greed; (*lujuria*) lustfulness

concurrencia [konku'rrenθja] NF turnout

concurrido, -a [konku'rriðo, a] ADJ (*calle*) busy; (*local, reunión*) crowded

concurrir [konku'rrir] /**3a**/ VI (*juntarse: ríos*) to meet, come together; (: *personas*) to gather, meet

concursante [konkur'sante] NM competitor

concursar [konkur'sar] /**1a**/ VI to compete

concurso [kon'kurso] NM (*de público*) crowd; (*Escol, Deporte, competición*) competition; (*Com*) invitation to tender; (*examen*) open competition; (*TV etc*) quiz; (*ayuda*) help, cooperation

condado [kon'daðo] NM county

condal [kon'dal] ADJ: **la ciudad ~** Barcelona

conde ['konde] NM count

condecoración [kondekora'θjon] NF (*Mil*) medal, decoration

condecorar [kondeko'rar] /**1a**/ VT to decorate

condena [kon'dena] NF sentence; **cumplir una ~** to serve a sentence

condenación [kondena'θjon] NF condemnation; (*Rel*) damnation

condenado, -a [konde'naðo, a] ADJ (*Jur*) condemned; (*fam: maldito*) damned ▶ NM/F (*Jur*) convicted person

condenar [konde'nar] /**1a**/ VT to condemn; (*Jur*) to convict; **condenarse** VR (*Jur*) to confess (one's guilt); (*Rel*) to be damned

condensar [konden'sar] /**1a**/ VT to condense

condesa [kon'desa] NF countess

condescendencia [kondesθen'denθja] NF condescension; **aceptar algo por ~** to accept sth so as not to hurt feelings

condescender [kondesθen'der] /**2g**/ VI to acquiesce, comply

condescienda *etc* [kondes'θjenda] VB *ver* **condescender**

condición [kondi'θjon] NF (*gen*) condition; (*rango*) social class; **condiciones** NFPL (*cualidades*) qualities; (*estado*) condition; **a ~ de que ...** on condition that ...; **las condiciones del contrato** the terms of the contract; **condiciones de trabajo** working conditions; **condiciones de venta** conditions of sale

condicional [kondiθjo'nal] ADJ conditional

condicionamiento [kondiθjona'mjento] NM conditioning

condicionar [kondiθjo'nar] /**1a**/ VT (*acondicionar*) to condition; **~ algo a algo** to make sth conditional *o* dependent on sth

condimento [kondi'mento] NM seasoning

condiscípulo, -a [kondis'θipulo, a] NM/F fellow student

condolerse [kondo'lerse] /**2h**/ VR to sympathize

condominio [kondo'minjo] NM (*Com*) joint ownership; (*AM*) condominium, apartment

condón [kon'don] NM condom

condonar [kondo'nar] /**1a**/ VT (*Jur: reo*) to reprieve; (*Com: deuda*) to cancel

cóndor ['kondor] NM condor

conducente [kondu'θente] ADJ: **~ a** conducive to, leading to

conducir [kondu'θir] /**3n**/ VT to take, convey; (*Elec etc*) to carry; (*Auto*) to drive; (*negocio*) to manage ▶ VI to drive; (*fig*) to lead; **conducirse** VR to behave

conducta [kon'dukta] NF conduct, behaviour

conducto [kon'dukto] NM pipe, tube; (*fig*) channel; (*Elec*) lead; **por ~ de** through

conductor, a [konduk'tor, a] ADJ leading, guiding ▶ NM (*Física*) conductor; (*de vehículo*) driver

conduela *etc* [kon'dwela] VB *ver* **condolerse**

conduje *etc* [kon'duxe] VB *ver* **conducir**

conduzco *etc* [kon'duθko] VB *ver* **conducir**

conectado, -a [konek'taðo, a] ADJ (*Elec*) connected, plugged in; (*Inform*) on-line

conectar [konek'tar] /**1a**/ VT to connect (up); (*enchufar*) plug in; (*Inform*) to toggle on; **conectarse** VR (*Inform*) to log in *or* on

conejillo [kone'xiʎo] NM: **~ de Indias** guinea pig

conejo [ko'nexo] NM rabbit

conexión [konek'sjon] NF connection; (*Inform*) logging in *or* on

confabularse [konfaβu'larse] /**1a**/ VR: ~ **(para hacer algo)** to plot o conspire (to do sth)

confección [konfek'θjon] NF (*preparación*) preparation, making-up; (*industria*) clothing industry; (*producto*) article; **de** ~ (*ropa*) off-the-peg

confeccionar [konfekθjo'nar] /**1a**/ VT to make (up)

confederación [konfeðera'θjon] NF confederation

conferencia [konfe'renθja] NF conference; (*lección*) lecture; (*Telec*) call; ~ **de cobro revertido** (*Telec*) reversed-charge (BRIT) o collect (US) call; ~ **cumbre** summit (conference); ~ **de prensa** press conference

conferenciante [konferen'θjante] NMF lecturer

conferir [konfe'rir] /**3i**/ VT to award

confesar [konfe'sar] /**1j**/ VT (*admitir*) to confess, admit; (*error*) to acknowledge; (*crimen*) to own up to

confesión [konfe'sjon] NF confession

confesionario [konfesjo'narjo] NM confessional

confeso, -a [kon'feso, a] ADJ (*Jur etc*) self-confessed

confeti [kon'feti] NM confetti

confiado, -a [kon'fjaðo, a] ADJ (*crédulo*) trusting; (*seguro*) confident; (*presumido*) conceited, vain

confianza [kon'fjanθa] NF trust; (*aliento, confidencia*) confidence; (*familiaridad*) intimacy, familiarity; (*pey*) vanity, conceit; **margen de** ~ credibility gap; **tener** ~ **con algn** to be on close terms with sb

confiar [kon'fjar] /**1c**/ VT to entrust ▶ VI (*fiarse*) to trust; (*contar con*) to rely; **confiarse** VR to put one's trust in; ~ **en algn** to trust sb; ~ **en que** ... to hope that ...

confidencia [konfi'ðenθja] NF confidence

confidencial [konfiðen'θjal] ADJ confidential

confidente [konfi'ðente] NMF confidant/ confidante; (*policial*) informer

confiera *etc* [kon'fjera] VB *ver* **conferir**

confiese *etc* [kon'fjese] VB *ver* **confesar**

configuración [konfiɣura'θjon] NF (*tb Inform*) configuration; **la** ~ **del terreno** the lie of the land; ~ **de bits** (*Inform*) bit pattern

configurar [konfiɣu'rar] /**1a**/ VT to shape, form

confín [kon'fin] NM limit; **confines** NMPL confines, limits

confinar [konfi'nar] /**1a**/ VI to confine; (*desterrar*) to banish

confiriendo *etc* [konfi'rjendo] VB *ver* **conferir**

confirmación [konfirma'θjon] NF confirmation; (*Rel*) Confirmation

confirmar [konfir'mar] /**1a**/ VT to confirm; (*Jur etc*) to corroborate; **la excepción confirma la regla** the exception proves the rule

confiscar [konfis'kar] /**1g**/ VT to confiscate

confisque *etc* [kon'fiske] VB *ver* **confiscar**

confitado, -a [konfi'taðo, a] ADJ: **fruta confitada** crystallized fruit

confite [kon'fite] NM sweet (BRIT), candy (US)

confitería [konfite'ria] NF confectionery; (*tienda*) confectioner's (shop)

confitura [konfi'tura] NF jam

conflagración [konflaɣra'θjon] NF conflagration

conflictivo, -a [konflik'tiβo, a] ADJ (*asunto, propuesta*) controversial; (*país, situación*) troubled

conflicto [kon'flikto] NM conflict; (*fig*) clash; (: *dificultad*): **estar en un** ~ to be in a jam; ~ **laboral** labour dispute

confluir [konflu'ir] /**3g**/ VI (*ríos etc*) to meet; (*gente*) to gather

confluya *etc* [kon'fluja] VB *ver* **confluir**

conformar [konfor'mar] /**1a**/ VT to shape, fashion ▶ VI to agree; **conformarse** VR to conform; (*resignarse*) to resign o.s.; **conformarse con algo** to be happy with sth

conforme [kon'forme] ADJ alike, similar; (*correspondiente*): ~ **con** in line with; (*de acuerdo*) agreed, in agreement; (*satisfecho*) satisfied ▶ ADV as ▶ EXCL agreed! ▶ NM agreement ▶ PREP: ~ **a** in accordance with; **estar conformes (con algo)** to be in agreement (with sth); **quedarse** ~ **(con algo)** to be satisfied (with sth)

conformidad [konformi'ðað] NF (*semejanza*) similarity; (*acuerdo*) agreement; (*resignación*) resignation; **de/en** ~ **con** in accordance with; **dar su** ~ to consent

conformismo [konfor'mismo] NM conformism

conformista [konfor'mista] NMF conformist

confort [kon'for] (*pl* **conforts** [kon'for(t)s]) NM comfort

confortable [konfor'taβle] ADJ comfortable

confortar [konfor'tar] /**1a**/ VT to comfort

confraternidad [konfraterni'ðað] NF brotherhood; **espíritu de** ~ feeling of unity

confraternizar [konfraterni'θar] /**1f**/ VI to fraternize

confrontación [konfronta'θjon] NF confrontation

confrontar [konfron'tar] /**1a**/ VT to confront; (*dos personas*) to bring face to face; (*cotejar*) to compare ▶ VI to border

confundir [konfun'dir] /**3a**/ VT (*borrar*) to blur; (*equivocar*) to mistake, confuse; (*mezclar*) to mix; (*turbar*) to confuse; **confundirse** VR *(hacerse borroso)* to become blurred; *(turbarse)* to get confused; *(equivocarse)* to make a mistake; *(mezclarse)* to mix

confusión [konfu'sjon] NF confusion

confusionismo [konfusjo'nismo] NM confusion, uncertainty

confuso, -a [kon'fuso, a] ADJ *(gen)* confused; *(recuerdo)* hazy; *(estilo)* obscure

congelación [konxela'θjon] NF freezing; **~ de créditos** credit freeze

congelado, -a [konxe'laðo, a] ADJ frozen ▶ NM: **congelados** frozen food *sg o* foods

congelador [konxela'ðor] NM freezer, deep freeze

congelar [konxe'lar] /**1a**/ VT to freeze; **congelarse** VR *(sangre, grasa)* to congeal

congénere [kon'xenere] NMF: **sus congéneres** his peers

congeniar [konxe'njar] /**1b**/ VI to get on *(BRIT)* o along *(US)* (well)

congénito, -a [kon'xenito, a] ADJ congenital

congestión [konxes'tjon] NF congestion

congestionado, -a [konxestjo'naðo, a] ADJ congested

congestionar [konxestjo'nar] /**1a**/ VT to congest; **congestionarse** VR to become congested; **se le congestionó la cara** his face became flushed

conglomerado [konglome'raðo] NM conglomerate

Congo ['kongo] NM: **el ~** the Congo

congoja [kon'goxa] NF distress, grief

congraciarse [kongra'θjarse] /**1b**/ VR to ingratiate o.s.

congratular [kongratu'lar] /**1a**/ VT to congratulate

congregación [kongreɣa'θjon] NF congregation

congregar [kongre'ɣar] /**1h**/ VT to gather together; **congregarse** VR to gather together

congregue *etc* [kon'greɣe] VB *ver* **congregar**

congresista [kongre'sista] NMF delegate, congressman/woman

congreso [kon'greso] NM congress; **C~ de los Diputados** *(ESP Pol)* ≈ House of Commons *(BRIT)*, House of Representatives *(US)*; *ver tb* **corte**

congrio ['kongrjo] NM conger (eel)

congruente [kon'grwente] ADJ congruent, congruous

conífera [ko'nifera] NF conifer

conjetura [konxe'tura] NF guess; *(Com)* guesstimate

conjeturar [konxetu'rar] /**1a**/ VT to guess

conjugación [konxuɣa'θjon] NF conjugation

conjugar [konxu'ɣar] /**1h**/ VT to combine, fit together; *(Ling)* to conjugate

conjugue *etc* [kon'xuɣe] VB *ver* **conjugar**

conjunción [konxun'θjon] NF conjunction

conjuntivitis [konxunti'βitis] NF conjunctivitis

conjunto, -a [kon'xunto, a] ADJ joint, united ▶ NM whole; *(Mus)* band; *(de ropa)* ensemble; *(Inform)* set; **en ~** as a whole; **~ integrado de programas** *(Inform)* integrated software suite

conjura [kon'xura] NF plot, conspiracy

conjurar [konxu'rar] /**1a**/ VT *(Rel)* to exorcise; *(peligro)* to ward off ▶ VI to plot

conjuro [kon'xuro] NM spell

conllevar [konʎe'βar] /**1a**/ VT to bear; *(implicar)* to imply, involve

conmemoración [konmemora'θjon] NF commemoration

conmemorar [konmemo'rar] /**1a**/ VT to commemorate

conmigo [kon'miɣo] PRON with me

conminar [konmi'nar] /**1a**/ VT to threaten

conmiseración [konmisera'θjon] NF pity, commiseration

conmoción [konmo'θjon] NF shock; *(Pol)* disturbance; *(fig)* upheaval; **~ cerebral** *(Med)* concussion

conmovedor, a [konmoβe'ðor, a] ADJ touching, moving; *(emocionante)* exciting

conmover [konmo'βer] /**2h**/ VT to shake, disturb; *(fig)* to move; **conmoverse** VR *(fig)* to be moved

conmueva *etc* [kon'mweβa] VB *ver* **conmover**

conmutación [konmuta'θjon] NF *(Inform)* switching; **~ de mensajes** message switching; **~ por paquetes** packet switching

conmutador [konmuta'ðor] NM switch; *(AM Telec)* switchboard; *(: central)* telephone exchange

conmutar [konmu'tar] /**1a**/ VT *(Jur)* to commute

connivencia [konni'βenθja] NF: **estar en ~ con** to be in collusion with

connotación [konnota'θjon] NF connotation

cono ['kono] NM cone; **C~ Sur** Southern Cone

conocedor, a [konoθe'ðor, a] ADJ expert, knowledgeable ▶ NM/F expert, connoisseur

conocer [kono'θer] /**2d**/ VT to know; *(por primera vez)* to meet, get to know; *(entender)* to know about; *(reconocer)* to recognize; **conocerse** VR *(una persona)* to know o.s.; *(dos personas)* to (get to) know each other; **~ a algn de vista** to know sb by sight; **darse a ~** *(presentarse)* to make o.s. known; **se conoce que ...** *(parece)* apparently ...

conocido, -a [kono'θiðo, a] ADJ (well-)known ▶ NM/F acquaintance

conocimiento [konoθi'mjento] NM knowledge; *(Med)* consciousness; *(Naut: tb:* **conocimiento de embarque***)* bill of lading; **conocimientos** NMPL (*personas*) acquaintances; (*saber*) knowledge *sg*; **hablar con ~ de causa** to speak from experience; **~ (de embarque) aéreo** (*Com*) air waybill

conozco *etc* [ko'noθko] VB *ver* **conocer**

conque ['konke] CONJ and so, so then

conquense [kon'kense] ADJ of *o* from Cuenca ▶ NMF native *o* inhabitant of Cuenca

conquista [kon'kista] NF conquest

conquistador, a [konkista'ðor, a] ADJ conquering ▶ NM conqueror

conquistar [konkis'tar] /1a/ VT (*Mil*) to conquer; (*puesto, simpatía*) to win; (*enamorar*) to win the heart of

consabido, -a [konsa'βiðo, a] ADJ (*frase etc*) old; (*pey*): **las consabidas excusas** the same old excuses

consagrado, -a [konsa'ɣraðo, a] ADJ (*Rel*) consecrated; (*actor*) established

consagrar [konsa'ɣrar] /1a/ VT (*Rel*) to consecrate; (*fig*) to devote

consciente [kons'θjente] ADJ conscious; **ser** *o* **estar ~ de** to be aware of

consecución [konseku'θjon] NF acquisition; (*de fin*) attainment

consecuencia [konse'kwenθja] NF consequence, outcome; (*firmeza*) consistency; **de ~** of importance

consecuente [konse'kwente] ADJ consistent

consecutivo, -a [konseku'tiβo, a] ADJ consecutive

conseguir [konse'ɣir] /3d, 3k/ VT to get, obtain; (*sus fines*) to attain

consejería [konsexe'ria] NF (*Pol*) ministry (*in a regional government*)

consejero, -a [konse'xero, a] NM/F adviser, consultant; (*Pol*) minister (*in a regional government*); (*Com*) director; (*en comisión*) member

consejo [kon'sexo] NM advice; (*Pol*) council; (*Com*) board; **un ~** a piece of advice; **~ de administración** board of directors; **~ de guerra** court-martial; **~ de ministros** cabinet meeting; **C~ de Europa** Council of Europe

consenso [kon'senso] NM consensus

consentido, -a [konsen'tiðo, a] ADJ (*mimado*) spoiled

consentimiento [konsenti'mjento] NM consent

consentir [konsen'tir] /3i/ VT (*permitir, tolerar*) to consent to; (*mimar*) to pamper, spoil; (*aguantar*) to put up with ▶ VI to agree, consent; **~ que algn haga algo** to allow sb to do sth

conserje [kon'serxe] NM caretaker; (*portero*) porter

conserva [kon'serβa] NF: **en ~** (*alimentos*) tinned (BRIT), canned; **conservas** NFPL (*tb*:

conservas alimenticias) tinned (BRIT) *o* canned foods

conservación [konserβa'θjon] NF conservation; (*de alimentos, vida*) preservation

conservador, a [konserβa'ðor, a] ADJ (*Pol*) conservative ▶ NM/F conservative

conservadurismo [konserβaðu'rismo] NM (*Pol etc*) conservatism

conservante [konser'βante] NM preservative

conservar [konser'βar] /1a/ VT (*gen*) to preserve; (*recursos*) to conserve, keep; (*alimentos, vida*) to preserve; **conservarse** VR to survive

conservatorio [konserβa'torjo] NM (*Mus*) conservatoire, conservatory; (*Am*) greenhouse

considerable [konsiðe'raβle] ADJ considerable

consideración [konsiðera'θjon] NF consideration; (*estimación*) respect; **de ~** important; **De mi** *o* **nuestra (mayor) ~** (*Am*) Dear Sir(s) *o* Madam; **tomar en ~** to take into account

considerado, -a [konsiðe'raðo, a] ADJ (*atento*) considerate; (*respetado*) respected

considerar [konsiðe'rar] /1a/ VT (*gen*) to consider; (*meditar*) to think about; (*tener en cuenta*) to take into account

consienta *etc* [kon'sjenta] VB *ver* **consentir**

consigna [kon'siɣna] NF (*orden*) order, instruction; (*para equipajes*) left-luggage office (BRIT), checkroom (US)

consignación [konsiɣna'θjon] NF consignment; **~ de créditos** allocation of credits

consignador [konsiɣna'ðor] NM (*Com*) consignor

consignar [konsiɣ'nar] /1a/ VT (*Com*) to send; (*créditos*) to allocate

consignatario, -a [konsiɣna'tarjo, a] NM/F (*Com*) consignee

consigo [kon'siɣo] VB *ver* **conseguir** ▶ PRON (*m*) with him; (*f*) with her; (*usted*) with you; (*reflexivo*) with o.s.

consiguiendo *etc* [konsi'ɣjendo] VB *ver* **conseguir**

consiguiente [konsi'ɣjente] ADJ consequent; **por ~** and so, therefore, consequently

consintiendo *etc* [konsin'tjendo] VB *ver* **consentir**

consistente [konsis'tente] ADJ consistent; (*sólido*) solid, firm; (*válido*) sound; **~ en** consisting of

consistir [konsis'tir] /3a/ VI: **~ en** (*componerse de*) to consist of; (*ser resultado de*) to be due to

consola [kon'sola] NF console, control panel; (*mueble*) console table; **~ de juegos** games console; **~ de mandos** (*Inform*) control console; **~ de visualización** visual display console

consolación [konsola'θjon] NF consolation

consolar [konso'lar] /1l/ VT to console

consolidar [konsoli'ðar] /1a/ VT to consolidate

consomé [konso'me] (*pl* **consomés** [konso'mes]) NM consommé, clear soup

consonancia [konso'nanθja] NF harmony; **en ~ con** in accordance with

consonante [konso'nante] ADJ consonant, harmonious ▶ NF consonant

consorcio [kon'sorθjo] NM (*Com*) consortium, syndicate

consorte [kon'sorte] NMF consort

conspicuo, -a [kons'pikwo, a] ADJ conspicuous

conspiración [konspira'θjon] NF conspiracy

conspirador, a [konspira'ðor, a] NM/F conspirator

conspirar [konspi'rar] /1a/ VI to conspire

constancia [kons'tanθja] NF (*gen*) constancy; (*certeza*) certainly; **dejar ~ de algo** to put sth on record

constante [kons'tante] ADJ, NF constant

constar [kons'tar] /1a/ VI (*evidenciarse*) to be clear *o* evident; **~ (en)** to appear (in); **~ de** to consist of; **hacer ~** to put on record; **me consta que ...** I have evidence that ...; **que conste que lo hice por ti** believe me, I did it for your own good

constatar [konsta'tar] /1a/ VT (*controlar*) to check; (*observar*) to note

constelación [konstela'θjon] NF constellation

consternación [konsterna'θjon] NF consternation

constipado, -a [konsti'paðo, a] ADJ: **estar ~** to have a cold ▶ NM cold

constiparse [konsti'parse] /1a/ VR to catch a cold

constitución [konstitu'θjon] NF constitution; **Día de la C~** (*ESP*) Constitution Day (*6th December*)

constitucional [konstituθjo'nal] ADJ constitutional

constituir [konstitu'ir] /3g/ VT (*formar, componer*) to constitute, make up; (*fundar, erigir, ordenar*) to constitute, establish; (*ser*) to be; **constituirse** VR (*Pol etc: cuerpo*) to be composed; (: *fundarse*) to be established

constitutivo, -a [konstitu'tiβo, a] ADJ constitutive, constituent

constituya *etc* [konsti'tuja] VB *ver* **constituir**

constituyente [konstitu'jente] ADJ constituent

constreñir [konstre'ɲir] VT (*obligar*) to compel, oblige; (*restringir*) to restrict

constriño *etc* [kons'triɲo], **constriñendo** *etc* [konstri'ɲendo] VB *ver* **constreñir**

construcción [konstruk'θjon] NF construction, building

constructivo, -a [konstruk'tiβo, a] ADJ constructive

constructor, a [konstruk'tor, a] NM/F builder

construir [konstru'ir] /3g/ VT to build, construct

construyendo *etc* [konstru'jendo] VB *ver* **construir**

consuelo [kon'swelo] VB *ver* **consolar** ▶ NM consolation, solace

consuetudinario, -a [konswetuði'narjo, a] ADJ customary; **derecho ~** common law

cónsul ['konsul] NM consul

consulado [konsu'laðo] NM (*sede*) consulate; (*cargo*) consulship

consulta [kon'sulta] NF consultation; (*Med: consultorio*) consulting room; (*Inform*) enquiry; **horas de ~** (*Med*) surgery hours; **obra de ~** reference book

consultar [konsul'tar] /1a/ VT to consult; **~ un archivo** (*Inform*) to interrogate a file; **~ algo con algn** to discuss sth with sb

consultor, a [konsul'tor, a] NM: **~ en dirección de empresas** management consultant

consultorio [konsul'torjo] NM (*Med*) surgery

consumado, -a [konsu'maðo, a] ADJ perfect; (*bribón*) out-and-out

consumar [konsu'mar] /1a/ VT to complete, carry out; (*crimen*) to commit; (*sentencia*) to carry out

consumición [konsumi'θjon] NF consumption; (*bebida*) drink; (*comida*) food; **~ mínima** cover charge

consumido, -a [konsu'miðo, a] ADJ (*flaco*) skinny

consumidor, a [konsumi'ðor, a] NM/F consumer

consumir [konsu'mir] /3a/ VT to consume; **consumirse** VR to be consumed; (*persona*) to waste away

consumismo [konsu'mismo] NM (*Com*) consumerism

consumo [kon'sumo] NM consumption; **bienes de ~** consumer goods

contabilice *etc* [kontaβi'liθe] VB *ver* **contabilizar**

contabilidad [kontaβili'ðað] NF accounting, book-keeping; (*profesión*) accountancy; (*Com*): **~ analítica** variable costing; **~ de costos** cost accounting; **~ de doble partida** double-entry book-keeping; **~ de gestión** management accounting; **~ por partida simple** single-entry book-keeping

contabilizar [kontaβi'liθar] /1f/ VT to enter in the accounts

contable [kon'taβle] NMF bookkeeper; (*licenciado*) accountant; **~ de costos** (*Com*) cost accountant

contactar [kontak'tar] /**1a**/ VI: **~ con algn** to contact sb

contacto [kon'takto] NM contact; (*Auto*) ignition; **lentes de ~** contact lenses; **estar en ~ con** to be in touch with

contado, -a [kon'taðo, a] ADJ: **contados** (*escasos*) numbered, scarce, few ▸ NM: **al ~** for cash; **pagar al ~** to pay (in) cash; **precio al ~** cash price

contador [konta'ðor] NM (*aparato*) meter; (*Am: contable*) accountant

contaduría [kontaðu'ria] NF accountant's office

contagiar [konta'xjar] /**1b**/ VT (*enfermedad*) to pass on, transmit; (*persona*) to infect; **contagiarse** VR to become infected

contagio [kon'taxjo] NM infection

contagioso, -a [konta'xjoso, a] ADJ infectious; (*fig*) catching

contaminación [kontamina'θjon] NF (*gen*) contamination; (*del ambiente etc*) pollution

contaminar [kontami'nar] /**1a**/ VT (*gen*) to contaminate; (*aire, agua*) to pollute; (*fig*) to taint

contante [kon'tante] ADJ: **dinero ~ (y sonante)** hard cash

contar [kon'tar] /**1l**/ VT (*páginas, dinero*) to count; (*anécdota etc*) to tell ▸ VI to count; **contarse** VR to be counted, figure; **~ con** to rely on, count on; **sin ~** not to mention; **le cuento entre mis amigos** I reckon him among my friends

contemplación [kontempla'θjon] NF contemplation; **no andarse con contemplaciones** not to stand on ceremony

contemplar [kontem'plar] /**1a**/ VT to contemplate; (*mirar*) to look at

contemporáneo, -a [kontempo'raneo, a] ADJ, NM/F contemporary

contemporizar [kontempori'θar] /**1f**/ VI: **~ con** to keep in with

contención [konten'θjon] NF (*Jur*) suit; **muro de ~** retaining wall

contencioso, -a [konten'θjoso, a] ADJ (*Jur etc*) contentious ▸ NM (*Pol*) conflict, dispute

contender [konten'der] /**2g**/ VI to contend; (*en un concurso*) to compete

contendiente [konten'djente] NMF contestant

contendrá *etc* [konten'dra] VB *ver* **contener**

contenedor [kontene'ðor] NM container; (*de escombros*) skip; **~ de (la) basura** wheelie-bin (*BRIT*); **~ de vidrio** bottle bank

contener [konte'ner] /**2k**/ VT to contain, hold; (*risa etc*) to hold back, contain; **contenerse** VR to control o restrain o.s.

contenga *etc* [kon'tenga] VB *ver* **contener**

contenido, -a [konte'niðo, a] ADJ (*moderado*) restrained; (*risa etc*) suppressed ▸ NM contents *pl*, content

contentar [konten'tar] /**1a**/ VT (*satisfacer*) to satisfy; (*complacer*) to please; (*Com*) to endorse; **contentarse** VR to be satisfied

contento, -a [kon'tento, a] ADJ contented, content; (*alegre*) pleased; (*feliz*) happy

contestación [kontesta'θjon] NF answer, reply; **~ a la demanda** (*Jur*) defence plea

contestador [kontesta'ðor] NM: **~ automático** answering machine

contestar [kontes'tar] /**1a**/ VT to answer (back), reply; (*Jur*) to corroborate, confirm

contestatario, -a [kontesta'tarjo, a] ADJ anti-establishment, nonconformist

contexto [kon'teksto] NM context

contienda [kon'tjenda] NF contest, struggle

contiene *etc* [kon'tjene] VB *ver* **contener**

contigo [kon'tiɣo] PRON with you

contiguo, -a [kon'tiɣwo, a] ADJ (*de al lado*) next; (*vecino*) adjacent, adjoining

continental [kontinen'tal] ADJ continental

continente [konti'nente] ADJ, NM continent

contingencia [kontin'xenθja] NF contingency; (*riesgo*) risk; (*posibilidad*) eventuality

contingente [kontin'xente] ADJ contingent ▸ NM contingent; (*Com*) quota

continuación [kontinwa'θjon] NF continuation; **a ~** then, next

continuamente [kon'tinwamente] ADV (*sin interrupción*) continuously; (*a todas horas*) constantly

continuar [konti'nwar] /**1e**/ VT to continue, go on with; (*reanudar*) to resume ▸ VI to continue, go on; **~ hablando** to continue talking o to talk

continuidad [kontinwi'ðað] NF continuity

continuo, -a [kon'tinwo, a] ADJ (*sin interrupción*) continuous; (*acción perseverante*) continual

contonearse [kontone'arse] /**1a**/ VR (*hombre*) to swagger; (*mujer*) to swing one's hips

contorno [kon'torno] NM outline; (*Geo*) contour; **contornos** NMPL neighbourhood *sg*, surrounding area *sg*

contorsión [kontor'sjon] NF contortion

contra ['kontra] PREP against; (*Com: giro*) on ▸ ADV against ▸ ADJ, NMF (*Pol: fam*) counter-revolutionary ▸ NM con ▸ NF: **la C~ (nicaragüense)** the Contras *pl*

contraalmirante [kontraalmi'rante] NM rear admiral

contraanálisis [kontraa'nalisis] NM follow-up test, countertest

contraataque [kontraa'take] NM counterattack

contrabajo [kontra'βaxo] NM double bass

contrabandista [kontraβan'dista] NMF smuggler

contrabando [kontra'βando] NM (*acción*) smuggling; (*mercancías*) contraband; **~ de armas** gun-running

contracción [kontrak'θjon] NF contraction

contrachapado [kontratʃa'paðo] NM plywood

contracorriente [kontrako'rrjente] NF cross-current

contradecir [kontraðe'θir] /**3o**/ VT to contradict

contradicción [kontraðik'θjon] NF contradiction; **espíritu de ~** contrariness

contradicho [kontra'ðitʃo] PP *de* **contradecir**

contradiciendo *etc* [kontraði'θjendo] VB *ver* **contradecir**

contradictorio, -a [kontraðik'torjo, a] ADJ contradictory

contradiga *etc* [kontra'ðiɣa], **contradije** [kontra'ðixe], **contradirá** *etc* [kontraði'ra] VB *ver* **contradecir**

contraer [kontra'er] /**2o**/ VT to contract; (*hábito*) to acquire; (*limitar*) to restrict; **contraerse** VR to contract; (*limitarse*) to limit o.s.

contraespionaje [kontraespjo'naxe] NM counter-espionage

contrafuerte [kontra'fwerte] NM (*Arq*) buttress

contragolpe [kontra'ɣolpe] NM backlash

contrahacer [kontraa'θer] /**2r**/ VB (*copiar*) to copy, imitate; (*moneda*) to counterfeit; (*documento*) to forge, fake; (*libro*) to pirate

contrahaga *etc* [kontra'aɣa], **contraharé** *etc* [kontraa're] VB *ver* **contrahacer**

contrahecho, -a [kontra'etʃo, a] PP *de* **contrahacer** ▶ ADJ fake; (*Anat*) hunchbacked

contrahice *etc* [kontra'iθe] VB *ver* **contrahacer**

contraiga *etc* [kon'traiɣa] VB *ver* **contraer**

contraindicaciones [kontraindika'θjones] NFPL (*Med*) contraindications

contraje *etc* [kon'traxe] VB *ver* **contraer**

contralor [kontra'lor] NM (*Am*) government accounting inspector

contraluz [kontra'luθ] NM O F view against the light; (*Foto etc*) back lighting; **a ~** against the light

contramaestre [kontrama'estre] NM foreman

contraofensiva [kontraofen'siβa] NF counteroffensive

contraorden [kontra'orðen] NF counter-order, countermand

contrapartida [kontrapar'tiða] NF (*Com*) balancing entry; **como ~ (de)** in return (for), as o in compensation (for)

contrapelo [kontra'pelo]: **a ~** *adv* the wrong way

contrapesar [kontrape'sar] /**1a**/ VT to counterbalance; (*fig*) to offset

contrapeso [kontra'peso] NM counterweight; (*fig*) counterbalance; (*Com*) makeweight

contrapondré *etc* [kontrapon'dre] VB *ver* **contraponer**

contraponer [kontrapo'ner] /**2q**/ VT (*cotejar*) to compare; (*oponer*) to oppose

contraponga *etc* [kontra'ponga] VB *ver* **contraponer**

contraportada [kontrapor'taða] NF (*de revista*) back cover

contraproducente [kontraproðu'θente] ADJ counterproductive

contrapuesto [kontra'pwesto] PP *de* **contraponer**

contrapunto [kontra'punto] NM counterpoint

contrapuse *etc* [kontra'puse] VB *ver* **contraponer**

contrariar [kontra'rjar] /**1c**/ VT (*oponerse*) to oppose; (*poner obstáculo*) to impede; (*enfadar*) to vex

contrariedad [kontrarje'ðað] NF (*oposición*) opposition; (*obstáculo*) obstacle, setback; (*disgusto*) vexation, annoyance

contrario, -a [kon'trarjo, a] ADJ contrary; (*persona*) opposed; (*sentido, lado*) opposite ▶ NM/F enemy, adversary; (*Deporte*) opponent; **al ~**, **por el ~** on the contrary; **de lo ~** otherwise

Contrarreforma [kontrarre'forma] NF Counter-Reformation

contrarreloj [kontrarre'lo(x)] NF (*tb*: **prueba contrarreloj**) time trial

contrarrestar [kontrarres'tar] /**1a**/ VT to counteract

contrarrevolución [kontrarreβolu'θjon] NF counter-revolution

contrasentido [kontrasen'tiðo] NM contradiction; **es un ~ que él ...** it doesn't make sense for him to ...

contraseña [kontra'seɲa] NF countersign; (*frase*) password

contrastar [kontras'tar] /**1a**/ VT to verify ▶ VI to contrast

contraste [kon'traste] NM contrast

contrata [kon'trata] NF (*Jur*) written contract; (*empleo*) hiring

contratar [kontra'tar] /**1a**/ VT (*firmar un acuerdo para*) to contract for; (*empleados, obreros*) to hire, engage; (*Deporte*) to sign up; **contratarse** VR to sign on

contratiempo [kontra'tjempo] NM (*revés*) setback; (*accidente*) mishap; **a ~** (*Mus*) off-beat

contratista [kontra'tista] NMF contractor

contrato [kon'trato] NM contract; **~ de compraventa** contract of sale; **~ a precio fijo** fixed-price contract; **~ a término** forward contract; **~ de trabajo** contract of employment o service

contravalor [kontraβa'lor] NM exchange value

contravención [kontraβen'θjon] NF contravention, violation

contravendré etc [kontraβen'dre], **contravenga** etc [kontra'βenga] VB ver **contravenir**

contravenir [kontraβe'nir] /3r/ VI: **~ a** to contravene, violate

contraventana [kontraβen'tana] NF shutter

contraviene etc [kontra'βjene], **contraviniendo** etc [kontraβi'njendo] VB ver **contravenir**

contrayendo [kontra'jendo] VB ver **contraer**

contribución [kontriβu'θjon] NF (municipal etc) tax; (ayuda) contribution; **exento de contribuciones** tax-free

contribuir [kontriβu'ir] /3g/ VT, VI to contribute; (Com) to pay (in taxes)

contribuyendo etc [kontriβu'jendo] VB ver **contribuir**

contribuyente [kontriβu'jente] NMF (Com) taxpayer; (que ayuda) contributor

contrincante [kontrin'kante] NM opponent, rival

control [kon'trol] NM control; (inspección) inspection, check; (Com): **~ de calidad** quality control; **~ de cambios** exchange control; **~ de costos** cost control; **~ de créditos** credit control; **~ de existencias** stock control; **~ de precios** price control; **~ de pasaportes** passport inspection

controlador, a [kontrola'ðor, a] NM/F controller; **~ aéreo** air-traffic controller

controlar [kontro'lar] /1a/ VT to control; to inspect, check; (Com) to audit

controversia [kontro'βersja] NF controversy

contubernio [kontu'βernjo] NM ring, conspiracy

contumaz [kontu'maθ] ADJ obstinate, stubbornly disobedient

contundente [kontun'dente] ADJ (prueba) conclusive; (fig: argumento) convincing; **instrumento ~** blunt instrument

contusión [kontu'sjon] NF bruise

contuve etc [kon'tuβe] VB ver **contener**

convalecencia [kombale'θenθja] NF convalescence

convalecer [kombale'θer] /2d/ VI to convalesce, get better

convaleciente [kombale'θjente] ADJ, NMF convalescent

convalezca etc [komba'leθka] VB ver **convalecer**

convalidar [kombali'ðar] /1a/ VT (título) to recognize

convencer [komben'θer] /2b/ VT to convince; (persuadir) to persuade

convencimiento [kombenθi'mjento] NM (acción) convincing; (persuasión) persuasion; (certidumbre) conviction; **tener el ~ de que ...** to be convinced that ...

convención [komben'θjon] NF convention

convencional [kombenθjo'nal] ADJ conventional

convendré etc [komben'dre], **convenga** etc [kom'benga] VB ver **convenir**

conveniencia [kombe'njenθja] NF suitability; (conformidad) agreement; (utilidad, provecho) usefulness; **conveniencias** NFPL conventions; (Com) property sg; **ser de la ~ de algn** to suit sb

conveniente [kombe'njente] ADJ suitable; (útil) useful; (correcto) fit, proper; (aconsejable) advisable

convenio [kom'benjo] NM agreement, treaty; **~ de nivel crítico** threshold agreement

convenir [kombe'nir] /3r/ VI (estar de acuerdo) to agree; (ser conveniente) to suit, be suitable; **"sueldo a ~"** "salary to be agreed"; **conviene recordar que ...** it should be remembered that ...

convento [kom'bento] NM monastery; (de monjas) convent

convenza etc [kom'benθa] VB ver **convencer**

convergencia [komber'xenθja] NF convergence

converger [komber'xer] /2c/, **convergir** [komber'xir] /3c/ VI to converge; **sus esfuerzos convergen a un fin común** their efforts are directed towards the same objective

converja etc [kom'berxa] VB ver **converger**

conversación [kombersa'θjon] NF conversation

conversar [komber'sar] /1a/ VI to talk, converse

conversión [komber'sjon] NF conversion

converso, -a [kom'berso, a] NM/F convert

convertir [komber'tir] /3i/ VT to convert; (transformar) to transform, turn; (Com) to (ex)change; **convertirse** VR (Rel) to convert

convexo, -a [kom'bekso, a] ADJ convex

convicción [kombik'θjon] NF conviction

convicto, -a [kom'bikto, a] ADJ convicted; (condenado) condemned

convidado, -a [kombi'ðaðo, a] NM/F guest

convidar [kombi'ðar] /1a/ VT to invite; **~ a algn a una cerveza** to buy sb a beer

conviene etc [kom'bjene] VB ver **convenir**

convierta etc [kom'bjerta] VB ver **convertir**
convincente [kombin'θente] ADJ convincing
conviniendo etc [kombi'njendo] VB ver **convenir**
convirtiendo etc [kombir'tjendo] VB ver **convertir**
convite [kom'bite] NM invitation; (banquete) banquet
convivencia [kombi'βenθja] NF coexistence, living together
convivir [kombi'βir] /3a/ VI to live together; (Pol) to coexist
convocar [kombo'kar] /1g/ VT to summon, call (together)
convocatoria [komboka'torja] NF summons sg; (anuncio) notice of meeting; (Escol) examination session
convoque etc [kom'boke] VB ver **convocar**
convoy [kom'boj] NM (Ferro) train
convulsión [kombul'sjon] NF convulsion; (Pol etc) upheaval
conyugal [konju'ɣal] ADJ conjugal; **vida ~** married life
cónyuge ['konjuxe] NMF spouse, partner
coña ['koɲa] NF (fam!): **tomar algo a ~** to take sth as a joke
coñac ['koɲa(k)] (pl **coñacs** ['koɲas]) NM cognac, brandy
coñazo [ko'ɲaθo] NM (fam) pain; **dar el ~** to be a real pain
coño ['koɲo] (fam!) NM cunt (fam!); (Am pey) Spaniard ▶ EXCL (enfado) shit (fam!); (sorpresa) bloody hell (fam!); **¡qué ~!** what a pain in the arse! (fam!)
cookie ['kuki] NF (Inform) cookie
cool [kul] ADJ (fam) cool
cooperación [koopera'θjon] NF cooperation
cooperar [koope'rar] /1a/ VI to cooperate
cooperativo, -a [koopera'tiβo, a] ADJ cooperative ▶ NF cooperative
coordenada [koorðe'naða] NF (Mat) coordinate; **coordenadas** NFPL (fig) guidelines, framework sg
coordinación [koorðina'θjon] NF coordination
coordinador, a [koorðina'ðor, a] NM/F coordinator ▶ NF coordinating committee
coordinar [koorði'nar] /1a/ VT to coordinate
copa ['kopa] NF (tb Deporte) cup; (vaso) glass; (de árbol) top; (de sombrero) crown; **copas** NFPL (Naipes) one of the suits in the Spanish card deck; (**tomar una**) ~ (to have a) drink; **ir de copas** to go out for a drink; ver tb **baraja española**
copar [ko'par] /1a/ VT (puestos) to monopolize
coparticipación [kopartiθipa'θjon] NF (Com) co-ownership
COPE NF ABR (= Cadena de Ondas Populares Españolas) Spanish radio network

Copenhague [kope'naxe] N Copenhagen
copete [ko'pete] NM tuft (of hair); **de alto ~** aristocratic, upper-crust (fam)
copia ['kopja] NF copy; (Arte) replica; (Com etc) duplicate; (Inform): ~ **impresa** hard copy; ~ **de respaldo** o **de seguridad** backup copy; **hacer ~ de seguridad** to back up; ~ **de trabajo** working copy
copiadora [kopja'ðora] NF photocopier; ~ **al alcohol** spirit duplicator
copiar [ko'pjar] /1b/ VT to copy; ~ **al pie de la letra** to copy word for word
copiloto [kopi'loto] NM (Aviat) co-pilot; (Auto) co-driver
copioso, -a [ko'pjoso, a] ADJ copious, plentiful
copita [ko'pita] NF (small) glass; (Golf) tee
copla ['kopla] NF verse; (canción) (popular) song
copo ['kopo] NM: **copos de maíz** cornflakes; ~ **de nieve** snowflake
coprocesador [koproθesa'ðor] NM (Inform) co-processor
coproducción [koproðuk'θjon] NF (Cine etc) joint production
copropietarios [kopropje'tarjos] NMPL (Com) joint owners
cópula ['kopula] NF copulation
copular [kopu'lar] /1a/ VI to copulate
coqueta [ko'keta] ADJ flirtatious, coquettish ▶ NF (mujer) flirt
coquetear [kokete'ar] /1a/ VI to flirt
coraje [ko'raxe] NM courage; (ánimo) spirit; (ira) anger
coral [ko'ral] ADJ choral ▶ NF choir ▶ NM (Zool) coral
Corán [ko'ran] NM: **el ~** the Koran
coraza [ko'raθa] NF (armadura) armour; (blindaje) armour-plating
corazón [kora'θon] NM heart; (Bot) core; **corazones** NMPL (Naipes) hearts; **de buen ~** kind-hearted; **de todo ~** wholeheartedly; **estar mal del ~** to have heart trouble
corazonada [koraθo'naða] NF impulse; (presentimiento) presentiment, hunch
corbata [kor'βata] NF tie
corbeta [kor'βeta] NF corvette
Córcega ['korθeɣa] NF Corsica
corcel [kor'θel] NM steed
corchea [kor'tʃea] NF quaver
corchete [kor'tʃete] NM catch, clasp; **corchetes** NMPL (Tip) square brackets
corcho ['kortʃo] NM cork; (Pesca) float
corcovado, -a [korko'βaðo, a] ADJ hunchbacked ▶ NM/F hunchback
cordel [kor'ðel] NM cord, line
cordero [kor'ðero] NM lamb; (piel) lambskin
cordial [kor'ðjal] ADJ cordial ▶ NM cordial, tonic

cordialidad [korðjali'ðað] NF warmth, cordiality

cordillera [korði'ʎera] NF range (of mountains)

Córdoba ['korðoβa] NF Cordova

cordobés, -esa [korðo'βes, esa] ADJ, NM/F Cordovan

cordón [kor'ðon] NM (*cuerda*) cord, string; (*de zapatos*) lace; (*Elec*) flex, wire (*US*); (*Mil etc*) cordon; **~ umbilical** umbilical cord

cordura [kor'ðura] NF (*Med*) sanity; (*fig*) good sense; **con ~** (*obrar, hablar*) sensibly

Corea [ko'rea] NF Korea; **~ del Norte/Sur** North/South Korea

coreano, -a [kore'ano, a] ADJ, NM/F Korean

corear [kore'ar] /**1a**/ VT to chorus

coreografía [koreoɣra'fia] NF choreography

corista [ko'rista] NF (*Teat etc*) chorus girl

cornada [kor'naða] NF (*Taur etc*) butt, goring

córner ['korner] (*pl* **córners** ['korners]) NM corner (kick)

corneta [kor'neta] NF bugle

cornisa [kor'nisa] NF cornice

Cornualles [kor'nwaʎes] NM Cornwall

cornudo, -a [kor'nuðo, a] ADJ (*Zool*) horned; (*marido*) cuckolded

coro ['koro] NM chorus; (*conjunto de cantores*) choir

corolario [koro'larjo] NM corollary

corona [ko'rona] NF crown; (*de flores*) garland

coronación [korona'θjon] NF coronation

coronar [koro'nar] /**1a**/ VT to crown

coronel [koro'nel] NM colonel

coronilla [koro'niʎa] NF (*Anat*) crown (of the head); **estar hasta la ~ (de)** to be utterly fed up (with)

corpiño [korpiɲo] NM bodice; (*AM: sostén*) bra

corporación [korpora'θjon] NF corporation

corporal [korpo'ral] ADJ corporal, bodily

corporativo, -a [korpora'tiβo, a] ADJ corporate

corpulento, -a [korpu'lento, a] ADJ (*persona*) heavily-built

corral [ko'rral] NM (*patio*) farmyard; (*Agr: de aves*) poultry yard; (*redil*) pen

correa [ko'rrea] NF strap; (*cinturón*) belt; (*de perro*) lead, leash; **~ transportadora** conveyor belt; **~ del ventilador** (*Auto*) fan belt

correaje [korre'axe] NM (*Agr*) harness

corrección [korrek'θjon] NF correction; (*reprensión*) rebuke; (*cortesía*) good manners; (*Inform*): **~ por líneas** line editing; **~ en pantalla** screen editing; **~ (de pruebas)** (*Tip*) proofreading

correccional [korrekθjo'nal] NM reformatory

correcto, -a [ko'rrekto, a] ADJ correct; (*persona*) well-mannered

corrector, a [korrek'tor, a] NM/F: **~ de pruebas** proofreader

corredera [korre'ðera] NF: **puerta de ~** sliding door

corredizo, -a [korre'ðiθo, a] ADJ (*puerta etc*) sliding; (*nudo*) running

corredor, a [korre'ðor, a] ADJ running; (*rápido*) fast ► NM/F (*Deporte*) runner ► NM (*pasillo*) corridor; (*balcón corrido*) gallery; (*Com*) agent, broker; **~ de bienes raíces** real-estate broker; **~ de bolsa** stockbroker; **~ de seguros** insurance broker

corregir [korre'xir] /**3c, 3k**/ VT (*error*) to correct; (*amonestar, reprender*) to rebuke, reprimand; **corregirse** VR to reform

correo [ko'rreo] NM post, mail; (*persona*) courier; **Correos** NMPL Post Office *sg*; **~ aéreo** airmail; **~ basura** (*por carta*) junk mail; (*por Internet*) spam; **~ certificado** registered mail; **~ electrónico** email, electronic mail; **~ urgente** special delivery; **~ web** webmail; **a vuelta de ~** by return (of post)

correr [ko'rrer] /**2a**/ VT to run; (*viajar*) to cover, travel; (*riesgo*) to run; (*aventura*) to have; (*cortinas*) to draw; (*cerrojo*) to shoot ► VI to run; (*líquido*) to run, flow; (*rumor*) to go round; **correrse** VR to slide, move; (*colores*) to run; (*fam: tener orgasmo*) to come; **echar a ~** to break into a run; **~ con los gastos** to pay the expenses; **eso corre de mi cuenta** I'll take care of that

correspondencia [korrespon'denθja] NF correspondence; (*Ferro*) connection; (*reciprocidad*) return; **~ directa** (*Com*) direct mail

corresponder [korrespon'der] /**2a**/ VI to correspond; (*convenir*) to be suitable; (*pertenecer*) to belong; (*tocar*) to concern; (*favor*) to repay; **corresponderse** VR (*por escrito*) to correspond; (*amarse*) to love one another; **"a quien corresponda"** "to whom it may concern"

correspondiente [korrespon'djente] ADJ corresponding; (*respectivo*) respective

corresponsal [korrespon'sal] NMF (*newspaper*) correspondent; (*Com*) agent

corretaje [korre'taxe] NM (*Com*) brokerage

corretear [korrete'ar] /**1a**/ VI to loiter

corrido, -a [ko'rriðo, a] ADJ (*avergonzado*) abashed; (*fluido*) fluent ► NF run, dash; (*de toros*) bullfight; **de ~** fluently; **tres noches corridas** three nights running; **un kilo ~** a good kilo

corriente [ko'rrjente] ADJ (*agua*) running; (*fig*) flowing; (*dinero, cuenta etc*) current; (*común*) ordinary, normal ► NF current; (*fig: tendencia*) course ► NM current month; **~ de aire** draught; **~ eléctrica** electric current; **las corrientes modernas del arte** modern trends in art; **estar al ~ de** to be informed about

corrigiendo *etc* [korri'xjendo] VB *ver* **corregir**

corrija *etc* [ko'rrixa] VB *ver* **corregir**

corrillo [ko'rriʎo] NM ring, circle (of people); (*fig*) clique

corro ['korro] NM ring, circle (of people); (*baile*) ring-a-ring-a-roses; **la gente hizo ~** the people formed a ring

corroborar [korroβo'rar] /1a/ VT to corroborate

corroer [korro'er] /2a/ VT (*tb fig*) to corrode, eat away; (*Geo*) to erode

corromper [korrom'per] /2a/ VT (*madera*) to rot; (*fig*) to corrupt

corrompido, -a [korrom'piðo, a] ADJ corrupt

corrosivo, -a [korro'siβo, a] ADJ corrosive

corroyendo *etc* [korro'jendo] VB *ver* **corroer**

corrupción [korrup'θjon] NF rot, decay; (*fig*) corruption

corrupto, -a [ko'rrupto, a] ADJ corrupt

corsario [kor'sarjo] NM privateer, corsair

corsé [kor'se] NM corset

corso, -a ['korso, a] ADJ, NM/F Corsican

cortacésped [korta'θespeð] NM lawn mower

cortado, -a [kor'taðo, a] ADJ (*con cuchillo*) cut; (*leche*) sour; (*confuso*) confused; (*desconcertado*) embarrassed; (*tímido*) shy ▶ NM coffee with a little milk

cortadora [korta'ðora] NF cutter, slicer

cortadura [korta'ðura] NF cut

cortafuegos [korta'fweɣos] NM INV (*en el bosque*) firebreak, fire lane (US); (*Internet*) firewall

cortalápices [korta'lapiθes] NM INV (pencil) sharpener

cortante [kor'tante] ADJ (*viento*) biting; (*frío*) bitter

cortapisa [korta'pisa] NF (*restricción*) restriction; (*traba*) snag

cortar [kor'tar] /1a/ VT to cut; (*suministro*) to cut off; (*un pasaje*) to cut out; (*comunicación, teléfono*) to cut off ▶ VI to cut; (*Am Telec*) to hang up; **cortarse** VR (*turbarse*) to become embarrassed; (*leche*) to turn, curdle; **~ por lo sano** to settle things once and for all; **cortarse el pelo** to have one's hair cut; **se cortó la línea** *o* **el teléfono** I got cut off

cortauñas [korta'uɲas] NM INV nail clippers *pl*

corte ['korte] NM cut, cutting; (*filo*) edge; (*de tela*) piece, length; (*Costura*) tailoring ▶ NF (*real*) (royal) court; **~ y confección** dressmaking; **~ de corriente** *o* **luz** power cut; **~ de pelo** haircut; **me da ~ pedírselo** I'm embarrassed to ask him for it; **¡qué ~ le di!** I left him with no comeback!; **C~ Internacional de Justicia** International Court of Justice; **las Cortes** the Spanish Parliament *sg*; **hacer la ~ a** to woo, court; *see note*

> The Spanish Parliament, *Las Cortes (Españolas)*, has a Lower and an Upper Chamber, the *Congreso de los Diputados* and the *Senado* respectively. Members of Parliament are called *diputados* and are elected in national elections by proportional representation. Some Senate members, *senadores*, are chosen by being voted in during national elections and others are appointed by the regional parliaments.

cortejar [korte'xar] /1a/ VT to court

cortejo [kor'texo] NM entourage; **~ fúnebre** funeral procession, cortège

cortés [kor'tes] ADJ courteous, polite

cortesano, -a [korte'sano, a] ADJ courtly

cortesía [korte'sia] NF courtesy

corteza [kor'teθa] NF (*de árbol*) bark; (*de pan*) crust; (*de fruta*) peel, skin; (*de queso*) rind

cortijo [kor'tixo] NM (*ESP*) farm, farmhouse

cortina [kor'tina] NF curtain; **~ de humo** smoke screen

corto, -a ['korto, a] ADJ (*breve*) short; (*tímido*) bashful; **~ de luces** not very bright; **~ de oído** hard of hearing; **~ de vista** short-sighted; **estar ~ de fondos** to be short of funds

cortocircuito [kortoθir'kwito] NM short-circuit

cortometraje [kortome'traxe] NM (*Cine*) short

Coruña [ko'ruɲa] NF: **La ~** Corunna

coruñés, -esa [koru'ɲes, esa] ADJ of *o* from Corunna ▶ NM/F native *o* inhabitant of Corunna

corvo, -a ['korβo, a] ADJ curved; (*nariz*) hooked ▶ NF back of knee

cosa ['kosa] NF thing; (*asunto*) affair; **~ de** about; **eso es ~ mía** that's my business; **es poca ~** it's not important; **¡qué ~ más rara!** how strange!

cosaco, -a [ko'sako, a] ADJ, NM/F Cossack

coscorrón [kosko'rron] NM bump on the head

cosecha [ko'setʃa] NF (*Agr*) harvest; (*acto*) harvesting; (*de vino*) vintage; (*producción*) yield

cosechadora [kosetʃa'ðora] NF combine harvester

cosechar [kose'tʃar] /1a/ VT to harvest, gather (in)

coser [ko'ser] /2a/ VT to sew; (*Med*) to stitch (up)

cosido [ko'siðo] NM sewing

cosmético, -a [kos'metiko, a] ADJ, NM cosmetic ▶ NF cosmetics *pl*

cosmopolita [kosmopo'lita] ADJ cosmopolitan

cosmos ['kosmos] NM cosmos

coso ['koso] NM bullring

cosquillas [kos'kiʎas] NFPL: **hacer ~** to tickle; **tener ~** to be ticklish

cosquilleo [koski'ʎeo] NM tickling (sensation)

costa ['kosta] NF (Geo) coast; **C~ Brava** Costa Brava; **C~ Cantábrica** Cantabrian Coast; **C~ de Marfil** Ivory Coast; **C~ del Sol** Costa del Sol; **a ~** (Com) at cost; **a ~ de** at the expense of; **a toda ~** at any price

costado [kos'taðo] NM side; **de ~** (dormir) on one's side; **español por los 4 costados** Spanish through and through

costal [kos'tal] NM sack

costalada [kosta'laða] NF bad fall

costanera [kosta'nera] NF (Am) promenade, sea front

costar [kos'tar] /1l/ VT (valer) to cost; **me cuesta hablarle** I find it hard to talk to him; **¿cuánto cuesta?** how much does it cost?

Costa Rica [kosta'rika] NF Costa Rica

costarricense [kostarri'θense], **costarriqueño, -a** [kostarri'keɲo, a] ADJ, NM/F Costa Rican

coste ['koste] NM (Com): **~ promedio** average cost; **costes fijos** fixed costs

costear [koste'ar] /1a/ VT to pay for; (Com etc) to finance; (Naut) to sail along the coast of; **costearse** VR (negocio) to pay for itself, cover its costs

costeño, -a [kos'teɲo, a] ADJ coastal

costero [kos'tero, a] ADJ coastal, coast cpd

costilla [kos'tiʎa] NF rib; (Culin) cutlet

costo ['kosto] NM cost, price; **~ directo** direct cost; **~ de expedición** shipping charges; **~ de sustitución** replacement cost; **~ unitario** unit cost; **~ de la vida** cost of living

costoso, -a [kos'toso, a] ADJ costly, expensive

costra ['kostra] NF (corteza) crust; (Med) scab

costumbre [kos'tumbre] NF custom, habit; **como de ~** as usual

costura [kos'tura] NF sewing, needlework; (confección) dressmaking; (zurcido) seam

costurera [kostu'rera] NF dressmaker

costurero [kostu'rero] NM sewing box o case

cota ['kota] NF (Geo) height above sea level; (fig) height

cotarro [ko'tarro] NM: **dirigir el ~** (fam) to rule the roost

cotejar [kote'xar] /1a/ VT to compare

cotejo [ko'texo] NM comparison

cotice etc [ko'tiθe] VB ver **cotizar**

cotidiano, -a [koti'ðjano, a] ADJ daily, day to day

cotilla [ko'tiʎa] NF busybody, gossip

cotillear [kotiʎe'ar] /1a/ VI to gossip

cotilleo [koti'ʎeo] NM gossip(ing)

cotización [kotiθa'θjon] NF (Com) quotation, price; (de club) dues pl

cotizado, -a [koti'θaðo, a] ADJ (fig) highly-prized

cotizar [koti'θar] /1f/ VT (Com) to quote, price; **cotizarse** VR (fig) to be highly prized; **cotizarse a** to sell at, fetch; (Bolsa) to stand at, be quoted at

coto ['koto] NM (terreno cercado) enclosure; (de caza) reserve; (Com) price-fixing agreement; **poner ~ a** to put a stop to

cotorra [ko'torra] NF (Zool: loro) parrot; (fam: persona) windbag

coyote [ko'jote] NM coyote, prairie wolf

coyuntura [kojun'tura] NF (Anat) joint; (fig) juncture, occasion; **esperar una ~ favorable** to await a favourable moment

coz [koθ] NF kick

CP NM ABR (= computador personal) PC

C.P. ABR (Esp) = **Caja Postal**

C.P.A. NF ABR (= Caja Postal de Ahorros) Post Office Savings Bank

CP/M NM ABR (= Programa de control para microprocesadores) CP/M

CPN NM ABR (Esp) = **Cuerpo de la Policía Nacional**

cps ABR (= caracteres por segundo) c.p.s.

crac [krak] NM (Econ) crash

crack [krak] NM (droga) crack

cráneo ['kraneo] NM skull, cranium

crápula ['krapula] NF drunkenness

cráter ['krater] NM crater

crayón [kra'jon] NM (Am: lápiz) (coloured) pencil; (cera) crayon

creación [krea'θjon] NF creation

creador, a [krea'ðor, a] ADJ creative ▶ NM/F creator

crear [kre'ar] /1a/ VT to create, make; (originar) to originate; (Inform: archivo) to create; **crearse** VR (comité etc) to be set up

creativo, -a [krea'tiβo, a] ADJ creative

crecer [kre'θer] /2d/ VI to grow; (precio) to rise; **crecerse** VR (engreírse) to get cocky

creces ['kreθes]: **con ~** adv amply, fully

crecido, -a [kre'θiðo, a] ADJ (persona, planta) full-grown; (cantidad) large ▶ NF (de río) spate, flood

creciente [kre'θjente] ADJ growing; (cantidad) increasing; (luna) crescent ▶ NM crescent

crecimiento [kreθi'mjento] NM growth; (aumento) increase; (Com) rise

credencial [kreðen'θjal] NF (Am: tarjeta) card; **credenciales** NFPL credentials; **~ de socio** (Am) membership card

crédito ['kreðito] NM credit; **a ~** on credit; **dar ~ a** to believe (in); **~ al consumidor** consumer credit; **~ rotativo o renovable** revolving credit

credo ['kreðo] NM creed

crédulo, -a ['kreðulo, a] ADJ credulous

creencia [kre'enθja] NF belief

creer [kre'er] /2e/ VT, VI to think, believe; (*considerar*) to think, consider; **creerse** VR to believe o.s. (to be); ~ **en** to believe in; **creo que sí/no** I think/don't think so; **¡ya lo creo!** I should think so!

creíble [kre'iβle] ADJ credible, believable

creído, -a [kre'iðo, a] ADJ (*engreído*) conceited

crema ['krema] ADJ INV cream (coloured) ▶ NF cream; (*natillas*) custard; ~ **batida** (*Am*) whipped cream; ~ **pastelera** (confectioner's) custard; **la ~ de la sociedad** the cream of society

cremallera [krema'ʎera] NF zip (fastener) (*Brit*), zipper (*US*)

crematorio [krema'torjo] NM crematorium (*Brit*), crematory (*US*)

cremoso, -a [kre'moso, a] ADJ creamy

crepe ['krepe] NF (*Esp*) pancake

crepitar [krepi'tar] /1a/ VI (*fuego*) to crackle

crepúsculo [kre'puskulo] NM twilight, dusk

crespo, -a ['krespo, a] ADJ (*pelo*) curly

crespón [kres'pon] NM crêpe

cresta ['kresta] NF (*Geo*, *Zool*) crest

Creta ['kreta] NF Crete

cretino, -a [kre'tino, a] ADJ cretinous ▶ NM/F cretin

creyendo *etc* [kre'jendo] VB *ver* **creer**

creyente [kre'jente] NMF believer

creyó *etc* [kre'jo] VB *ver* **creer**

crezca *etc* ['kreθka] VB *ver* **crecer**

cría ['kria] VB *ver* **criar** ▶ NF (*de animales*) rearing, breeding; (*animal*) young; *ver tb* **crío**

criada [kri'aða] NF *ver* **criado**

criadero [kria'ðero] NM nursery; (*Zool*) breeding place

criadillas [kria'ðiʎas] NFPL (*Culin*) bull's (*o* sheep's) testicles

criado, -a [kri'aðo, a] NM servant ▶ NF servant, maid

criador [kria'ðor] NM breeder

crianza [kri'anθa] NF rearing, breeding; (*fig*) breeding; (*Med*) lactation

criar [kri'ar] /1c/ VT (*amamantar*) to suckle, feed; (*educar*) to bring up; (*producir*) to grow, produce; (*animales*) to breed; **criarse** VR to grow (up); ~ **cuervos** to nourish a viper in one's bosom; **Dios los cría y ellos se juntan** birds of a feather flock together

criatura [kria'tura] NF creature; (*niño*) baby, (small) child

criba ['kriβa] NF sieve

cribar [kri'βar] /1a/ VT to sieve

crimen ['krimen] NM crime; ~ **pasional** crime of passion

criminal [krimi'nal] ADJ, NMF criminal

crin [krin] NF (*tb*: **crines**) mane

crío, -a ['krio, a] NM/F (*fam*: *chico*) kid ▶ NF (*de animales*) rearing, breeding; (*animal*) young

criollo, -a [kri'oʎo, a] ADJ (*gen*) Creole; (*Am*) native (to America), national ▶ NM/F (*gen*) Creole; (*Am*) native American

cripta ['kripta] NF crypt

crisis ['krisis] NF INV crisis; ~ **nerviosa** nervous breakdown

crisma ['krisma] NF: **romperle la ~ a algn** (*fam*) to knock sb's block off

crismas ['krismas] NM INV (*Esp*) Christmas card

crisol [kri'sol] NM (*Tec*) crucible; (*fig*) melting pot

crispación [krispa'θjon] NF tension

crispar [kris'par] /1a/ VT to cause to contract; (*nervios*) to set on edge

cristal [kris'tal] NM crystal; (*de ventana*) glass, pane; (*lente*) lens; **de ~** glass *cpd*; ~ **ahumado/tallado** smoked/cut glass

cristalería [kristale'ria] NF (*tienda*) glassware shop; (*objetos*) glassware

cristalice *etc* [krista'liθe] VB *ver* **cristalizar**

cristalino, -a [krista'lino, a] ADJ crystalline; (*fig*) clear ▶ NM lens of the eye

cristalizar [kristali'θar] /1f/ VT, VI to crystallize

cristiandad [kristjan'dað] NF, **cristianismo** [kristja'nismo] NM Christianity

cristianismo [kristja'nismo] NM Christianity

cristiano, -a [kris'tjano, a] ADJ, NM/F Christian; **hablar en ~** to speak proper Spanish; (*fig*) to speak clearly

Cristo ['kristo] NM (*dios*) Christ; (*crucifijo*) crucifix

Cristóbal [kris'toβal] NM: ~ **Colón** Christopher Columbus

criterio [kri'terjo] NM criterion; (*juicio*) judgement; (*enfoque*) attitude, approach; (*punto de vista*) view, opinion; ~ **de clasificación** (*Inform*) sort criterion

criticar [kriti'kar] /1g/ VT to criticize

crítico, -a ['kritiko, a] ADJ critical ▶ NM critic ▶ NF criticism; (*Teat etc*) review, notice; **la crítica** the critics *pl*

critique *etc* [kri'tike] VB *ver* **criticar**

Croacia [kro'aθja] NF Croatia

croar [kro'ar] /1a/ VI to croak

croata [kro'ata] ADJ, NMF Croat(ian) ▶ NM (*Ling*) Croat(ian)

croissant, croissant [krwa'san] NM croissant

crol ['krol] NM crawl

cromado [kro'maðo] NM chromium plating, chrome

cromo ['kromo] NM chrome; (*Tip*) coloured print

cromosoma [kromo'soma] NM chromosome

crónico, -a ['kroniko, a] ADJ chronic ▶ NF chronicle, account; (*de periódico*) feature, article

cronología [kronolo'xia] NF chronology

cronológico, -a [krono'loxiko, a] ADJ chronological

cronometraje [kronome'traxe] NM timing

cronometrar [kronome'trar] /**1a**/ VT to time

cronómetro [kro'nometro] NM (*Deporte*) stopwatch; (*Tec etc*) chronometer

croqueta [kro'keta] NF croquette, rissole

croquis ['krokis] NM INV sketch

cruce ['kruθe] VB *ver* **cruzar** ▶ NM (*para peatones*) crossing; (*de carreteras*) crossroads; (*Auto etc*) junction, intersection; (*Bio: proceso*) crossbreeding; **luces de** ~ dipped headlights

crucero [kru'θero] NM (*Naut: barco*) cruise ship; (: *viaje*) cruise

crucial [kru'θjal] ADJ crucial

crucificar [kruθifi'kar] /**1g**/ VT to crucify; (*fig*) to torment

crucifijo [kruθi'fixo] NM crucifix

crucifique *etc* [kruθi'fike] VB *ver* **crucificar**

crucigrama [kruθi'ɣrama] NM crossword (puzzle)

cruda ['kruða] NF (*Am fam*) hangover

crudeza [kru'ðeθa] NF (*rigor*) harshness; (*aspereza*) crudeness

crudo, -a ['kruðo, a] ADJ raw; (*no maduro*) unripe; (*petróleo*) crude; (*rudo, cruel*) cruel; (*agua*) hard; (*clima etc*) harsh ▶ NM crude (oil)

cruel [krwel] ADJ cruel

crueldad [krwel'ðað] NF cruelty

cruento, -a ['krwento, a] ADJ bloody

crujido [kru'xiðo] NM (*de madera etc*) creak

crujiente [kru'xjente] ADJ (*galleta etc*) crunchy

crujir [kru'xir] /**3a**/ VI (*madera etc*) to creak; (*dedos*) to crack; (*dientes*) to grind; (*nieve, arena*) to crunch

cruz [kruθ] NF cross; (*de moneda*) tails *sg*; (*fig*) burden; ~ **gamada** swastika; **C~ Roja** Red Cross

cruzado, -a [kru'θaðo, a] ADJ crossed ▶ NM crusader ▶ NF crusade

cruzar [kru'θar] /**1f**/ VT to cross; (*palabras*) to exchange; **cruzarse** VR (*líneas etc*) to cross, intersect; (*personas*) to pass each other; **cruzarse de brazos** to fold one's arms; (*fig*) not to lift a finger to help; **cruzarse con algn en la calle** to pass sb in the street

CSIC [θe'sik] NM ABR (*Esp Escol*) = **Consejo Superior de Investigaciones Científicas**

cta., c.ta NF ABR (= *cuenta*) a/c

cta. cto. ABR (= *carta de crédito*) L.C.

cte. ABR = **corriente**; (= *de los corrientes*) inst.

CTNE NF ABR (*Telec*) = **Compañía Telefónica Nacional de España**

c/u ABR (= *cada uno*) ea

cuaco ['kwako] NM (*Am*) nag

cuaderno [kwa'ðerno] NM notebook; (*de escuela*) exercise book; (*Naut*) logbook

cuadra ['kwaðra] NF (*caballeriza*) stable; (*Am*) (city) block

cuadrado, -a [kwa'ðraðo, a] ADJ square ▶ NM (*Mat*) square

cuadragésimo, -a [kwaðra'xesimo, a] NUM fortieth

cuadrángulo [kwa'ðrangulo] NM quadrangle

cuadrante [kwa'ðrante] NM quadrant

cuadrar [kwa'ðrar] /**1a**/ VT to square; (*Tip*) to justify ▶ VI: ~ **con** (*cuenta*) to square with, tally with; **cuadrarse** VR (*soldado*) to stand to attention; ~ **por la derecha/izquierda** to right-/left-justify

cuadrícula [kwa'ðrikula] NF (*Tip etc*) grid, ruled squares

cuadriculado, -a [kwaðriku'laðo, a] ADJ: **papel** ~ squared o graph paper

cuadrilátero [kwaðri'latero] NM (*Deporte*) boxing ring; (*Mat*) quadrilateral

cuadrilla [kwa'ðriʎa] NF (*de amigos*) party, group; (*de delincuentes*) gang; (*de obreros*) team

cuadro ['kwaðro] NM square; (*Arte*) painting; (*Teat*) scene; (*diagrama: tb*: **cuadro sinóptico**) chart, table, diagram; (*Deporte, Med*) team; (*Pol*) executive; ~ **de mandos** control panel; **a cuadros** check *cpd*; **tela a cuadros** checked (*Brit*) o chequered (*US*) material

cuadruplicarse [kwaðrupli'karse] /**1g**/ VR to quadruple

cuádruplo, -a ['kwaðruplo, a], **cuádruple** ['kwaðruple] ADJ quadruple

cuajado, -a [kwa'xaðo, a] ADJ: ~ **de** (*fig*) full of ▶ NF (*de leche*) curd

cuajar [kwa'xar] /**1a**/ VT to thicken; (*leche*) to curdle; (*sangre*) to congeal; (*adornar*) to adorn; (*Culin*) to set ▶ VI (*nieve*) to lie; (*fig*) to become set, become established; (*idea*) to be received, be acceptable; **cuajarse** VR to curdle; to congeal; (*llenarse*) to fill up

cuajo ['kwaxo] NM: **de** ~ (*arrancar*) by the roots; (*cortar*) completely; **arrancar algo de** ~ to tear sth out by its roots

cual [kwal] ADV like, as ▶ PRON: **el** ~ *etc* which; (*persona: sujeto*) who; (*persona: objeto*) whom; (*relativo*) which ▶ ADJ such as; **allá cada** ~ every man to his own taste; **son a** ~ **más gandul** each is as idle as the other; **cada** ~ each one; **tal** ~ just as it is

cuál [kwal] PRON INTERROGATIVO which (one), what

cualesquier [kwales'kjer], **cualesquiera** [kwales'kjera] ADJ PL, PRON PL *de* **cualquier**

cualidad [kwali'ðað] NF quality

cualificado, -a [kwalifi'kaðo, a] ADJ (*obrero*) skilled, qualified

cualquier [kwal'kjer], **cualquiera** [kwal'kjera] (*pl* **cualesquier(a)**) ADJ any ▸ PRON anybody, anyone; (*quienquiera*) whoever; **en ~ momento** any time; **~ día/ libro** any day/book; **en ~ parte** anywhere; **cualquiera que sea** whichever it is; (*persona*) whoever it is; **un coche cualquiera servirá** any car will do; **no es un hombre cualquiera** he isn't just anybody; **eso cualquiera lo sabe hacer** anybody can do that; **es un cualquiera** he's a nobody

cuán [kwan] ADV how

cuando ['kwando] ADV when; (*aún si*) if, even if ▸ CONJ (*puesto que*) since ▸ PREP: **yo, ~ niño** ... when I was a child *o* as a child I ...; **~ no sea así** even if it is not so; **~ más** at (the) most; **~ menos** at least; **~ no** if not, otherwise; **de ~ en ~** from time to time; **ven ~ quieras** come when(ever) you like

cuándo ['kwando] ADV when; **¿desde ~?**, **¿de ~ acá?** since when?

cuantía [kwan'tia] NF (*importe: de pérdidas, deuda, daños*) extent; (*importancia*) importance

cuantioso, -a [kwan'tjoso, a] ADJ substantial

(PALABRA CLAVE)

cuanto, -a ['kwanto, a] ADJ **1** (*todo*): **tiene todo cuanto desea** he's got everything he wants; **le daremos cuantos ejemplares necesite** we'll give him as many copies as *o* all the copies he needs; **cuantos hombres la ven** all the men who see her

2: **unos cuantos**: **había unos cuantos periodistas** there were (quite) a few journalists

3 (+ *más*): **cuanto más vino bebas peor te sentirás** the more wine you drink the worse you'll feel; **cuantos más, mejor** the more the merrier

▸ PRON: **tiene cuanto desea** he has everything he wants; **tome cuanto/ cuantos quiera** take as much/many as you want

▸ ADV: **en cuanto**: **en cuanto profesor** as a teacher; **en cuanto a mí** as for me; *ver tb* **antes**

▸ CONJ **1**: **cuanto más gana menos gasta** the more he earns the less he spends; **cuanto más joven se es más se es confiado** the younger you are the more trusting you are

2: **en cuanto**: **en cuanto llegue/llegué** as soon as I arrive/arrived

cuánto, -a ['kwanto, a] ADJ (*exclamación*) what a lot of; (*interrogativo: sg*) how much?; (: *pl*) how many? ▸ PRON, ADV how; (*interrogativo: sg*) how much?; (: *pl*) how many?

▸ EXCL: **¡~ me alegro!** I'm so glad!; **¡cuánta gente!** what a lot of people!; **¿~ tiempo?** how long?; **¿~ cuesta?** how much does it cost?; **¿a cuántos estamos?** what's the date?; **¿~ hay de aquí a Bilbao?** how far is it from here to Bilbao?; **Señor no sé cuántos** Mr. So-and-So

cuarenta [kwa'renta] NUM forty

cuarentena [kwaren'tena] NF (*Med etc*) quarantine; (*conjunto*) forty(-odd)

cuarentón, -ona [kwaren'ton, ona] ADJ forty-year-old, fortyish ▸ NM/F person of about forty

cuaresma [kwa'resma] NF Lent

cuarta ['kwarta] NF *ver* **cuarto**

cuartear [kwarte'ar] /**1a**/ VT to quarter; (*dividir*) to divide up; **cuartearse** VR to crack, split

cuartel [kwar'tel] NM (*de ciudad*) quarter, district; (*Mil*) barracks *pl*; **~ de bomberos** (*Am*) fire station; **~ general** headquarters *pl*

cuartelazo [kwarte'laθo] NM coup, military uprising

cuarteto [kwar'teto] NM quartet

cuartilla [kwar'tiʎa] NF (*hoja*) sheet (of paper); **cuartillas** NFPL (*Tip*) copy *sg*

cuarto, -a ['kwarto, a] ADJ fourth ▸ NM (*Mat*) quarter, fourth; (*habitación*) room ▸ NF (*Mat*) quarter, fourth; (*palmo*) span; **~ de baño** bathroom; **~ de estar** living room; **~ de hora** quarter (of an) hour; **~ de kilo** quarter kilo; **cuartos de final** quarter finals; **no tener un ~** to be broke (*fam*)

cuarzo ['kwarθo] NM quartz

cuatrero [kwa'trero] NM (*Am*) rustler, stock thief

cuatrimestre [kwatri'mestre] NM four-month period

cuatro ['kwatro] NUM four; **las ~** four o'clock; **el ~ de octubre** (on) the fourth of October; *ver tb* **seis**

cuatrocientos, -as [kwatro'θjentos, as] NUM four hundred; *ver tb* **seiscientos**

Cuba ['kuβa] NF Cuba

cuba ['kuβa] NF cask, barrel; **estar como una ~** (*fam*) to be sloshed

cubalibre [kuβa'liβre] NM (white) rum and coke®

cubano, -a [ku'βano, a] ADJ, NM/F Cuban

cubata [ku'βata] NM = **cubalibre**

cubertería [kuβerte'ria] NF cutlery

cubeta [ku'βeta] NF (*balde*) bucket, tub

cúbico, -a ['kuβiko, a] ADJ cubic

cubierto, -a [ku'βjerto, a] PP *de* **cubrir** ▸ ADJ covered; (*cielo*) overcast ▸ NM cover; (*en la mesa*) place ▸ NF cover, covering; (*neumático*) tyre; (*Naut*) deck; **cubiertos** NMPL cutlery *sg*; **a ~** under cover; **a ~ de** covered with *o* in; **precio del ~** cover charge

cubil [ku'βil] NM den
cubilete [kuβi'lete] NM (en juegos) cup
cubito [ku'βito] NM: ~ **de hielo** ice cube
cubo ['kuβo] NM cube; (balde) bucket, tub; (Tec) drum; ~ **de (la) basura** dustbin (BRIT), trash can (US)
cubrecama [kuβre'kama] NM bedspread
cubrir [ku'βrir] /3a/ VT to cover; (vacante) to fill; (Bio) to mate with; (gastos) to meet; **cubrirse** VR (cielo) to become overcast; (Com: gastos) to be met o paid; (: deuda) to be covered; ~ **las formas** to keep up appearances; **lo cubrieron las aguas** the waters closed over it; **el agua casi me cubría** I was almost out of my depth
cucaracha [kuka'ratʃa] NF cockroach
cuchara [ku'tʃara] NF spoon; (Tec) scoop
cucharada [kutʃa'raða] NF spoonful; ~ **colmada** heaped spoonful
cucharadita [kutʃara'ðita] NF teaspoonful
cucharilla [kutʃa'riʎa] NF teaspoon
cucharita [kutʃa'rita] NF teaspoon
cucharón [kutʃa'ron] NM ladle
cuchichear [kutʃitʃe'ar] /1a/ VI to whisper
cuchicheo [kutʃi'tʃeo] NM whispering
cuchilla [ku'tʃiʎa] NF (large) knife; (de arma blanca) blade; ~ **de afeitar** razor blade; **pasar a ~** to put to the sword
cuchillada [kutʃi'ʎaða] NF (golpe) stab; (herida) knife o stab wound
cuchillo [ku'tʃiʎo] NM knife
cuchitril [kutʃi'tril] NM hovel; (habitación etc) pigsty
cuclillas [ku'kliʎas] NFPL: **en ~** squatting
cuco, -a ['kuko, a] ADJ pretty; (astuto) sharp ▶ NM cuckoo
cucurucho [kuku'rutʃo] NM paper cone, cornet
cueca ['kweka] NF Chilean national dance
cuece etc ['kweθe] VB ver **cocer**
cuele etc ['kwele] VB ver **colar**
cuelgue etc ['kwelɣe] VB ver **colgar**
cuello ['kweʎo] NM (Anat) neck; (de vestido, camisa) collar
cuenca ['kwenka] NF (Anat) eye socket; (Geo: valle) bowl, deep valley; (: fluvial) basin
cuenco ['kwenko] NM (earthenware) bowl
cuenta ['kwenta] VB ver **contar** ▶ NF (cálculo) count, counting; (en café, restaurante) bill (BRIT), check (US); (Com) account; (de collar) bead; (fig) account; **a fin de cuentas** in the end; **en resumidas cuentas** in short; **caer en la ~** to catch on; **dar ~ a algn de sus actos** to account to sb for one's actions; **darse ~ de** to realize; **tener en ~** to bear in mind; **echar cuentas** to take stock; ~ **atrás** countdown; ~ **corriente/de ahorros/a plazo (fijo)** current/savings/deposit account; ~ **de caja** cash account; ~ **de**

capital capital account; ~ **por cobrar** account receivable; ~ **de correo** (Internet) email account; ~ **de crédito** credit o loan account; ~ **de gastos e ingresos** income and expenditure account; ~ **por pagar** account payable; **abonar una cantidad en ~ a algn** to credit a sum to sb's account; **ajustar** o **liquidar una ~** to settle an account; **pasar la ~** to send the bill
cuentagotas [kwenta'ɣotas] NM INV (Med) dropper; **a** o **con ~** (fam: fig) drop by drop, bit by bit
cuentakilómetros [kwentaki'lometros] NM INV (de distancias) ≈ milometer, clock; (velocímetro) speedometer
cuentista [kwen'tista] NMF gossip; (Lit) short-story writer
cuento ['kwento] VB ver **contar** ▶ NM story; (Lit) short story; ~ **chino** tall story; ~ **de hadas** fairy tale o story; **es el ~ de nunca acabar** it's an endless business; **eso no viene a ~** that's irrelevant
cuerda ['kwerða] NF rope; (hilo) string; (de reloj) spring; (Mus: de violín etc) string; (Mat) chord; (Anat) cord; ~ **floja** tightrope; **cuerdas vocales** vocal cords; **dar ~ a un reloj** to wind up a clock
cuerdo, -a ['kwerðo, a] ADJ sane; (prudente) wise, sensible
cuerear [kwere'ar] /1a/ VT (AM) to skin
cuerno ['kwerno] NM (Zool: gen) horn; (: de ciervo) antler; **poner los cuernos a** (fam) to cuckold; **saber a ~ quemado** to leave a nasty taste
cuero ['kwero] NM (Zool) skin, hide; (Tec) leather; **en cueros** stark naked; ~ **cabelludo** scalp
cuerpo ['kwerpo] NM body; (cadáver) corpse; (fig) main part; ~ **de bomberos** fire brigade; ~ **diplomático** diplomatic corps; **luchar ~ a ~** to fight hand-to-hand; **tomar ~** (plan etc) to take shape
cuervo ['kwerβo] NM (Zool) raven, crow; ver **criar**
cuesta ['kwesta] VB ver **costar** ▶ NF slope; (en camino etc) hill; ~ **arriba/abajo** uphill/downhill; **a cuestas** on one's back
cueste etc ['kweste] VB ver **costar**
cuestión [kwes'tjon] NF matter, question, issue; (riña) quarrel, dispute; **eso es otra ~** that's another matter
cuestionar [kwestjo'nar] /1a/ VT to question
cuestionario [kwestjo'narjo] NM questionnaire
cuete ['kwete] ADJ (AM fam) drunk ▶ NM (cohete) rocket; (fam: embriaguez) drunkenness; (Culin) steak
cueva ['kweβa] NF cave
cueza etc ['kweθa] VB ver **cocer**

cuidado [kwi'ðaðo] NM care, carefulness; (*preocupación*) care, worry ▶ EXCL careful!, look out!; **eso me tiene sin ~** I'm not worried about that

cuidadoso, -a [kwiða'ðoso, a] ADJ careful; (*preocupado*) anxious

cuidar [kwi'ðar] /1a/ VT (*Med*) to care for; (*ocuparse de*) to take care of, look after; (*detalles*) to pay attention to ▶ VI: **~ de** to take care of, look after; **cuidarse** VR to look after o.s.; **cuidarse de hacer algo** to take care to do sth

cuita ['kwita] NF (*preocupación*) worry, trouble; (*pena*) grief

culata [ku'lata] NF (*de fusil*) butt

culatazo [kula'taθo] NM kick, recoil

culebra [ku'leβra] NF snake; **~ de cascabel** rattlesnake

culebrear [kuleβre'ar] /1a/ VI to wriggle along; (*río*) to meander

culebrón [kule'βron] NM (*fam*) soap (opera)

culinario, -a [kuli'narjo, a] ADJ culinary, cooking *cpd*

culminación [kulmina'θjon] NF culmination

culminante [kulmi'nante] ADJ: **momento ~** climax, highlight, highspot

culminar [kulmi'nar] /1a/ VI to culminate

culo ['kulo] NM (*fam: asentaderas*) bottom, backside, bum (BRIT); (: *ano*) arse(hole) (BRIT fam!), ass(hole) (US fam!); (*de vaso*) bottom

culpa ['kulpa] NF fault; (*Jur*) guilt; **culpas** NFPL sins; **por ~ de** through, because of; **echar la ~ a algn** to blame sb for sth; **tener la ~ (de)** to be to blame (for)

culpabilidad [kulpaβili'ðað] NF guilt

culpable [kul'paβle] ADJ guilty ▶ NMF culprit; **confesarse ~** to plead guilty; **declarar ~ a algn** to find sb guilty

culpar [kul'par] /1a/ VT to blame; (*acusar*) to accuse

cultivadora [kultiβa'ðora] NF cultivator

cultivar [kulti'βar] /1a/ VT to cultivate; (*cosecha*) to raise; (*talento*) to develop

cultivo [kul'tiβo] NM (*acto*) cultivation; (*plantas*) crop; (*Bio*) culture; **~ transgénico** GM crop

culto, -a ['kulto, a] ADJ (*cultivado*) cultivated; (*que tiene cultura*) cultured, educated ▶ NM (*homenaje*) worship; (*religión*) cult; (*Pol etc*) cult

cultura [kul'tura] NF culture

cultural [kultu'ral] ADJ cultural

culturismo [kultu'rismo] NM body-building

cumbia ['kumbja] NF *popular Colombian dance*

cumbre ['kumbre] NF summit, top; (*fig*) top, height; **conferencia (en la) ~** summit (conference)

cumpleaños [kumple'aɲos] NM INV birthday

cumplido, -a [kum'pliðo, a] ADJ complete, perfect; (*abundante*) plentiful; (*cortés*) courteous ▶ NM compliment; **visita de ~** courtesy call

cumplidor, a [kumpli'ðor, a] ADJ reliable

cumplimentar [kumplimen'tar] /1a/ VT to congratulate; (*órdenes*) to carry out

cumplimiento [kumpli'mjento] NM (*de un deber*) fulfilment, execution, performance; (*acabamiento*) completion; (*Com*) expiry, end

cumplir [kum'plir] /3a/ VT (*orden*) to carry out, obey; (*promesa*) to carry out, fulfil; (*condena*) to serve; (*años*) to reach, attain ▶ VI (*pago*) to fall due; (*plazo*) to expire; **cumplirse** VR (*plazo*) to expire; (*plan etc*) to be fulfilled; (*vaticinio*) to come true; **hoy cumple dieciocho años** he is eighteen today; **~ con** (*deber*) to carry out, fulfil

cúmulo ['kumulo] NM (*montón*) heap; (*nube*) cumulus

cuna ['kuna] NF cradle, cot; **canción de ~** lullaby

cundir [kun'dir] /3a/ VI (*noticia, rumor, pánico*) to spread; (*rendir*) to go a long way

cuneta [ku'neta] NF ditch

cuña ['kuɲa] NF (*Tec*) wedge; (*Com*) advertising spot; (*Med*) bedpan; **tener cuñas** to have influence

cuñado, -a [ku'ɲaðo, a] NM/F brother-/sister-in-law

cuño ['kuɲo] NM (*Tec*) die-stamp; (*fig*) stamp

cuota ['kwota] NF (*parte proporcional*) share; (*cotización*) fee, dues *pl*; **~ inicial** (*Com*) down payment

cupe *etc* ['kupe] VB *ver* **caber**

cupiera *etc* [ku'pjera] VB *ver* **caber**

cupo *etc* ['kupo] VB *ver* **caber** ▶ NM quota, share; (*Com*): **~ de importación** import quota; **~ de ventas** sales quota

cupón [ku'pon] NM coupon; **~ de la ONCE** o **de los ciegos** ONCE lottery ticket; *ver tb* **lotería**

cúpula ['kupula] NF (*Arq*) dome

cura ['kura] NF (*curación*) cure; (*método curativo*) treatment ▶ NM priest; **~ de emergencia** emergency treatment

curación [kura'θjon] NF cure; (*acción*) curing

curado, -a [ku'raðo, a] ADJ (*Culin*) cured; (*pieles*) tanned

curandero, -a [kuran'dero, a] NM/F healer; (*pey*) quack

curar [ku'rar] /1a/ VT (*Med: herida*) to treat, dress; (: *enfermo*) to cure; (*Culin*) to cure, salt; (*cuero*) to tan ▶ VI, **curarse** VR to get well, recover

curda ['kurða] (*fam*) NM drunk ▶ NF: **agarrar una/estar ~** to get/be sloshed

curiosear [kurjose'ar] /1a/ VT to glance at, look over ▶ VI to look round, wander round; (*explorar*) to poke about

curiosidad [kurjosi'ðað] NF curiosity
curioso, -a [ku'rjoso, a] ADJ curious; (*aseado*) neat ▶ NM/F bystander, onlooker; **¡qué ~!** how odd!
curita [ku'rita] NF (*AM*) sticking plaster
currante [ku'rrante] NMF (*fam*) worker
currar [ku'rrar] /**1a**/, **currelar** [kurre'lar] /**1a**/ VI (*fam*) to work
currículo [ku'rrikulo], **currículum** [ku'rrikulum] NM curriculum vitae
curro ['kurro] NM (*fam*) work, job
cursar [kur'sar] /**1a**/ VT (*Escol*) to study
cursi ['kursi] ADJ (*fam*) pretentious; (: *amanerado*) affected
cursilada [kursi'laða] NF: **¡qué ~!** how tacky!
cursilería [kursile'ria] NF (*vulgaridad*) bad taste; (*amaneramiento*) affectation
cursillo [kur'siʎo] NM short course
cursiva [kur'siβa] NF italics pl
curso ['kurso] NM (*dirección*) course; (*fig*) progress; (*Escol*) school year; (*Univ*) academic year; **en ~** (*año*) current; (*proceso*) going on, under way; **moneda de ~ legal** legal tender
cursor [kur'sor] NM (*Inform*) cursor; (*Tec*) slide
curtido, -a [kur'tiðo, a] ADJ (*cara etc*) weather-beaten; (*fig: persona*) experienced

curtir [kur'tir] /**3a**/ VT (*piel*) to tan; (*fig*) to harden
curul [ku'rul] NM (*AM: escaño*) seat
curvo, -a ['kurβo, a] ADJ (*gen*) curved; (*torcido*) bent ▶ NF (*gen*) curve, bend; **curva de rentabilidad** (*Com*) break-even chart
cúspide ['kuspiðe] NF (*Geo*) summit, peak; (*fig*) top, pinnacle
custodia [kus'toðja] NF (*cuidado*) safekeeping; (*Jur*) custody
custodiar [kusto'ðjar] /**1b**/ VT (*conservar*) to keep, take care of; (*vigilar*) to guard
custodio [kus'toðjo] NM guardian, keeper
cutáneo, -a [ku'taneo, a] ADJ skin cpd
cutícula [ku'tikula] NF cuticle
cutis ['kutis] NM INV skin, complexion
cutre ['kutre] ADJ (*fam: lugar*) grotty; (: *persona*) naff
cuyo, -a ['kujo, a] PRON (*de quien*) whose; (*de que*) whose, of which; **la señora en cuya casa me hospedé** the lady in whose house I stayed; **el asunto cuyos detalles conoces** the affair the details of which you know; **por ~ motivo** for which reason; **en ~ caso** in which case

C.V. ABR (= *Curriculum Vitae*) CV; (= *caballos de vapor*) H.P.

Dd

D, d [de] NF (letra) D, d; **D de Dolores** D for David (BRIT), D for Dog (US)

D. ABR (= Don) Esq

D.ª ABR = **doña**

dactilar [dakti'lar] ADJ: **huellas dactilares** fingerprints

dactilógrafo, -a [dakti'loɣrafo, a] NM/F typist

dádiva ['daðiβa] NF (donación) donation; (regalo) gift

dadivoso, -a [daði'βoso, a] ADJ generous

dado, -a ['daðo, a] PP de **dar** ▶ NM die; **dados** NMPL dice ▶ ADJ: **en un momento ~** at a certain point; **ser ~ a (hacer algo)** to be very fond of (doing sth); **~ que** conj given that

daga ['daɣa] NF dagger

daltónico, -a [dal'toniko, a] ADJ colour-blind

daltonismo [dalto'nismo] NM colour blindness

dama ['dama] NF (gen) lady; (Ajedrez) queen; **damas** NFPL draughts; **primera ~** (Teat) leading lady; (Pol) president's wife, first lady (US); **~ de honor** (de reina) lady-in-waiting; (de novia) bridesmaid

damasco [da'masko] NM (tela) damask; (AM: árbol) apricot tree; (: fruta) apricot

damnificado, -a [damnifi'kaðo, a] NM/F: **los damnificados** the victims

damnificar [damnifi'kar] /1g/ VT to harm; (persona) to injure

damnifique etc [damni'fike] VB ver **damnificar**

dance etc ['danθe] VB ver **danzar**

danés, -esa [da'nes, esa] ADJ Danish ▶ NM/F Dane ▶ NM (Ling) Danish

Danubio [da'nuβjo] NM Danube

danza ['danθa] NF (gen) dancing; (una danza) dance

danzar [dan'θar] /1f/ VT, VI to dance

danzarín, -ina [danθa'rin, ina] NM/F dancer

dañar [da'ɲar] /1a/ VT (objeto) to damage; (persona) to hurt; (estropear) to spoil; **dañarse** VR (objeto) to get damaged

dañino, -a [da'ɲino, a] ADJ harmful

daño ['daɲo] NM (a un objeto) damage; (a una persona) harm, injury; **daños y perjuicios** (Jur) damages; **hacer ~ a** to damage; (persona) to hurt, injure; **hacerse ~** to hurt o.s.

dañoso, -a [da'ɲoso, a] ADJ harmful

DAO ABR (= Diseño Asistido por Ordenador) CAD

(PALABRA CLAVE)

dar [dar] **/1q/** VT **1** (gen) to give; (obra de teatro) to put on; (film) to show; (fiesta) to have; **dar algo a algn** to give sb sth o sth to sb; **dar una patada a algn/algo** to kick sb/sth, give sb/ sth a kick; **dar un susto a algn** to give sb a fright; **dar de beber a algn** to give sb a drink; **dar de comer** to feed

2 (producir: intereses) to yield; (: fruta) to produce

3 (locuciones + n): **da gusto escucharlo** it's a pleasure to listen to him; **me da pena/asco** it frightens/sickens me; ver tb **paseo**

4 (+ n: = perífrasis de verbo): **me da asco** it sickens me

5 (considerar): **dar algo por descontado/ entendido** to take sth for granted/as read; **dar algo por concluido** to consider sth finished; **lo dieron por desaparecido** they gave him up as lost

6 (hora): **el reloj dio las seis** the clock struck six (o'clock)

7: **me da lo mismo** it's all the same to me; ver tb **igual; más**

8: ¡**y dale!** (¡otra vez!) not again!; **estar/seguir dale que dale** o **dale que te pego** o (AM) **dale y dale** to go/keep on and on

▶ VI **1**: **dar a** (habitación) to overlook, look on to; (accionar: botón etc) to press, hit

2: **dar con: dimos con él dos horas más tarde** we came across him two hours later; **al final di con la solución** I eventually came up with the answer

3: **dar en** (blanco, suelo) to hit; **el sol me da en la cara** the sun is shining (right) in my face

4: **dar de sí** (zapatos etc) to stretch, give

5: **dar para** to be enough for; **nuestro presupuesto no da para más** our budget's really tight
6: **dar por**: **le ha dado por estudiar música** now he's into studying music
7: **dar que hablar** to set people talking; **una película que da que pensar** a thought-provoking film
darse VR **1**: **darse un baño** to have a bath; **darse un golpe** to hit o.s.
2: **darse por vencido** to give up; **con eso me doy por satisfecho** I'd settle for that
3 (*ocurrir*): **se han dado muchos casos** there have been a lot of cases
4: **darse a**: **se ha dado a la bebida** he's taken to drinking
5: **se me dan bien/mal las ciencias** I'm good/bad at science
6: **dárselas de**: **se las da de experto** he fancies himself *o* poses as an expert

dardo ['darðo] NM dart
dársena ['darsena] NF (*Naut*) dock
datar [da'tar] /**1a**/ VI: ~ **de** to date from
dátil ['datil] NM date
dativo [da'tiβo] NM (*Ling*) dative
dato ['dato] NM fact, piece of information; (*Mat*) datum; **datos** NMPL (*Inform*) data; **datos de entrada/salida** input/output data; **datos personales** personal details
dcha. ABR (= *derecha*) ɪ (= *right*)
d. de C. ABR (= *después de Cristo*) A.D. (= *Anno Domini*)

(PALABRA CLAVE)

de [de] PREP (**de** + **el** = **del**) **1** (*posesión, pertenencia*) of; **la casa de Isabel/mis padres** Isabel's/my parents' house; **es de ellos/ella** it's theirs/hers; **un libro de Unamuno** a book by Unamuno
2 (*origen, distancia, con números*) from; **soy de Gijón** I'm from Gijón; **de 8 a 20** from 8 to 20; **5 metros de largo** 5 metres long; **salir del cine** to go out of *o* leave the cinema; **de ... en ...** from ... to ...; **de 2 en 2** 2 by 2, 2 at a time; **9 de cada 10** 9 out of every 10
3 (*valor descriptivo*): **una copa de vino** a glass of wine; **una silla de madera** a wooden chair; **la mesa de la cocina** the kitchen table; **un viaje de dos días** a two-day journey; **un billete de 50 euros** a 50-euro note; **un niño de tres años** a three-year-old (child); **una máquina de coser** a sewing machine; **la ciudad de Madrid** the city of Madrid; **el tonto de Juan** that idiot Juan; **ir vestido de gris** to be dressed in grey; **la niña del vestido azul** the girl in the blue dress; **la chica del pelo largo** the girl with long hair; **trabaja de profesora** she works

as a teacher; **de lado** sideways; **de atrás/delante** rear/front
4 (*hora: tiempo*): **a las 8 de la mañana** at 8 o'clock in the morning; **de día/noche** by day/night; **de hoy en ocho días** a week from now; **de niño era gordo** as a child he was fat
5 (*comparaciones*): **más/menos de cien personas** more/less than a hundred people; **el más caro de la tienda** the most expensive in the shop; **menos/más de lo esperado** less/more than expected
6 (*causa*): **del calor** from the heat; **de puro tonto** out of sheer stupidity
7 (*tema*) about; **clases de inglés** English classes; **¿sabes algo de él?** do you know anything about him?; **un libro de física** a physics book
8 (*adj + de + infin*): **fácil de entender** easy to understand
9 (*oraciones pasivas*): **fue respetado de todos** he was loved by all
10 (*condicional + infin*) if; **de ser posible** if possible; **de no terminarlo hoy** if I *etc* don't finish it today

dé [de] VB *ver* **dar**
deambular [deambu'lar] /**1a**/ VI to stroll, wander
debajo [de'βaxo] ADV underneath; ~ **de** below, under; **por** ~ **de** beneath
debate [de'βate] NM debate
debatir [deβa'tir] /**3a**/ VT to debate; **debatirse** VR to struggle
debe ['deβe] NM (*en cuenta*) debit side; ~ **y haber** debit and credit
deber [de'βer] /**2a**/ NM duty ▶ VT to owe ▶ VI: **debe** (**de**) it must, it should; **deberse** VR: **deberse a** to be owing *o* due to; **deberes** NMPL (*Escol*) homework *sg*; **debo hacerlo** I must do it; **debe de ir** he should go; **¿qué** *o* **cuánto le debo?** how much is it?
debidamente [deβiða'mente] ADV properly; (*rellenar*) duly
debido, -a [de'βiðo, a] ADJ proper, due; ~ **a** due to, because of; **en debida forma** duly
débil ['deβil] ADJ weak; (*persona: físicamente*) feeble; (*salud*) poor; (*voz, ruido*) faint; (*luz*) dim
debilidad [deβili'ðað] NF weakness; feebleness; dimness; **tener** ~ **por algn** to have a soft spot for sb
debilitar [deβili'tar] /**1a**/ VT to weaken; **debilitarse** VR to grow weak
débito [de'βito] NM debit; (*deuda*) debt; ~ **bancario** (*Am*) direct debit (*Brit*) *o* billing (*US*)
debutante [deβu'tante] NMF beginner
debutar [deβu'tar] /**1a**/ VI to make one's debut

década ['dekaða] NF decade
decadencia [deka'ðenθja] NF (estado) decadence; (proceso) decline, decay
decadente [deka'ðente] ADJ decadent
decaer [deka'er] /2n/ VI (declinar) to decline; (debilitarse) to weaken; (salud) to fail; (negocio) to fall off
decaído, -a [deka'iðo, a] ADJ: **estar ~** (persona) to be down
decaiga etc [de'kaiɣa] VB ver **decaer**
decaimiento [dekai'mjento] NM (declinación) decline; (desaliento) discouragement; (Med: depresión) depression
decanato [deka'nato] NM (cargo) deanship; (despacho) dean's office
decano, -a [de'kano, a] NM/F (Univ etc) dean; (de grupo) senior member
decantar [dekan'tar] /1a/ VT (vino) to decant
decapitar [dekapi'tar] /1a/ VT to behead
decayendo etc [deka'jendo] VB ver **decaer**
decena [de'θena] NF: **una ~** ten (or so)
decencia [de'θenθja] NF (modestia) modesty; (honestidad) respectability
decenio [de'θenjo] NM decade
decente [de'θente] ADJ decent
decepción [deθep'θjon] NF disappointment
decepcionante [deθepθjo'nante] ADJ disappointing
decepcionar [deθepθjo'nar] /1a/ VT to disappoint
decibelio [deθi'βeljo] NM decibel
decidido, -a [deθi'ðiðo, a] ADJ decided; (resuelto) resolute
decidir [deθi'ðir] /3a/ VT (persuadir) to convince, persuade; (resolver) to decide ▶ VI to decide; **decidirse** VR: **decidirse a** to make up one's mind to; **decidirse por** to decide o settle on, choose
decimal [deθi'mal] ADJ, NM decimal
décimo, -a ['deθimo, a] NUM tenth ▶ NF (Mat) tenth; **tiene unas décimas de fiebre** he has a slight temperature
decimoctavo, -a [deθimok'taβo, a] NUM eighteenth; ver tb **sexto**
decimocuarto, -a [deθimo'kwarto, a] NUM fourteenth; ver tb **sexto**
decimonoveno, -a [deθimono'βeno, a] NUM nineteenth; ver tb **sexto**
decimoquinto, -a [deθimo'kinto, a] NUM fifteenth; ver tb **sexto**
decimoséptimo, -a [deθimo'septimo, a] NUM seventeenth; ver tb **sexto**
decimosexto, -a [deθimo'seksto, a] NUM sixteenth; ver tb **sexto**
decimotercero, -a [deθimoter'θero, a] NUM thirteenth; ver tb **sexto**
decir [de'θir] /3o/ VT (expresar) to say; (contar) to tell; (hablar) to speak; (indicar) to show; (revelar) to reveal; (fam: nombrar) to call ▶ NM

saying; **decirse** VR: **se dice** it is said, they say; (se cuenta) the story goes; **¿cómo se dice en inglés "cursi"?** what's the English for "cursi"?; **~ para** o **entre sí** to say to o.s.; **~ por ~** to talk for talking's sake; **dar que ~ (a la gente)** to make people talk; **querer ~** to mean; **es ~** that is to say, namely; **ni que ~ tiene que ...** it goes without saying that ...; **como quien dice** so to speak; **¡quién lo diría!** would you believe it!; **el qué dirán** gossip; **¡diga!, ¡dígame!** (en tienda etc) can I help you?; (Telec) hello?; **le dije que fuera más tarde** I told her to go later; **es un ~** it's just a phrase
decisión [deθi'sjon] NF decision; (firmeza) decisiveness; (voluntad) determination
decisivo, -a [deθi'siβo, a] ADJ decisive
declamar [dekla'mar] /1a/ VT, VI to declaim; (versos etc) to recite
declaración [deklara'θjon] NF (manifestación) statement; (de amor) declaration; (explicación) explanation; (Jur: testimonio) evidence; **~ de derechos** (Pol) bill of rights; **~ de impuestos** (Com) tax return; **~ de ingresos** o **de la renta** income tax return; **~ jurada** affidavit; **~ falsa** (Jur) misrepresentation
declarar [dekla'rar] /1a/ VT to declare ▶ VI to declare; (Jur) to testify; **declararse** VR (a una chica) to propose; (guerra, incendio) to break out; **~ culpable/inocente a algn** to find sb guilty/not guilty; **declararse culpable/inocente** to plead guilty/not guilty
declinación [deklina'θjon] NF (decaimiento) decline; (Ling) declension
declinar [dekli'nar] /1a/ VT (gen, Ling) to decline; (Jur) to reject ▶ VI (el día) to draw to a close
declive [de'kliβe] NM (cuesta) slope; (inclinación) incline; (fig) decline; (Com: tb: **declive económico**) slump
decodificador [dekoðifika'ðor] NM (Inform) decoder
decolorarse [dekolo'rarse] /1a/ VR to become discoloured
decomisar [dekomi'sar] /1a/ VT to seize, confiscate
decomiso [deko'miso] NM seizure
decoración [dekora'θjon] NF decoration; (Teat) scenery, set; **~ de escaparates** window dressing
decorado [deko'raðo] NM (Cine, Teat) scenery, set
decorador, a [dekora'ðor, a] NM/F (de interiores) (interior) decorator; (Teat) stage o set designer
decorar [deko'rar] /1a/ VT to decorate
decorativo, -a [dekora'tiβo, a] ADJ ornamental, decorative
decoro [de'koro] NM (respeto) respect; (dignidad) decency; (recato) propriety

decoroso, -a [deko'roso, a] ADJ (*decente*)
decent; (*modesto*) modest; (*digno*) proper

decrecer [dekre'θer] /**2d**/ VI to decrease,
diminish; (*nivel de agua*) to go down; (*días*) to
draw in

decrépito, -a [de'krepito, a] ADJ decrepit

decretar [dekre'tar] /**1a**/ VT to decree

decreto [de'kreto] NM decree; (*Pol*) act

decreto-ley [dekreto'lei] (*pl* **decretos-leyes**)
NM decree

decrezca *etc* [de'kreθka] VB *ver* **decrecer**

decúbito [de'kuβito] NM (*Med*): **~ prono/
supino** prone/supine position

dedal [de'ðal] NM thimble

dedalera [deða'lera] NF foxglove

dédalo ['deðalo] NM (*laberinto*) labyrinth; (*fig*)
tangle, mess

dedicación [deðika'θjon] NF dedication; **con
~ exclusiva** *o* **plena** full-time

dedicar [deði'kar] /**1g**/ VT (*libro*) to dedicate;
(*tiempo, dinero*) to devote; (*palabras: decir,
consagrar*) to dedicate, devote; **dedicarse** VR:
dedicarse a (hacer algo) to devote o.s. to
(doing sth); (*carrera, estudio*) to go in for (doing
sth), take up (doing sth); **¿a qué se dedica
usted?** what do you do (for a living)?

dedicatoria [deðika'torja] NF (*de libro*)
dedication

dedillo [de'ðiʎo] NM: **saber algo al ~** to have
sth at one's fingertips

dedique *etc* [de'ðike] VB *ver* **dedicar**

dedo ['deðo] NM finger; (*de vino etc*) drop;
~ (del pie) toe; **~ anular** ring finger;
~ índice index finger; **~ mayor** *o* **cordial**
middle finger; **~ meñique** little finger;
~ pulgar thumb; **contar con los dedos** to
count on one's fingers; **comerse los dedos**
to get very impatient; **entrar a ~** to get a job
by pulling strings; **hacer ~** (*fam*) to hitch (a
lift); **poner el ~ en la llaga** to put one's
finger on it; **no tiene dos dedos de frente**
he's pretty dim

deducción [deðuk'θjon] NF deduction

deducir [deðu'θir] /**3n**/ VT (*concluir*) to deduce,
infer; (*Com*) to deduct

deduje *etc* [de'ðuxe], **dedujera** *etc*
[deðu'xera], **deduzca** *etc* [de'ðuθka] VB *ver*
deducir

defección [defek'θjon] NF defection,
desertion

defecto [de'fekto] NM defect, flaw; (*de cara*)
imperfection; **~ de pronunciación** speech
defect; **por ~** (*Inform*) default; **~ latente**
(*Com*) latent defect

defectuoso, -a [defek'twoso, a] ADJ defective,
faulty

defender [defen'der] /**2g**/ VT to defend;
(*ideas*) to uphold; (*causa*) to champion;
(*amigos*) to stand up for; **defenderse** VR to

defend o.s.; **defenderse bien** to give a good
account of o.s.; **me defiendo en inglés** (*fig*)
I can get by in English

defendible [defen'diβle] ADJ defensible

defensa [de'fensa] NF defence; (*Naut*) fender
▶ NM (*Deporte*) defender, back; **en ~ propia** in
self-defence

defensivo, -a [defen'siβo, a] ADJ defensive
▶ NF: **a la defensiva** on the defensive

defensor, -a [defen'sor, a] ADJ defending
▶ NM/F (*abogado defensor*) defending counsel;
(*protector*) protector; **~ del pueblo** (*Esp*)
≈ ombudsman

deferente [defe'rente] ADJ deferential

deferir [defe'rir] /**3k**/ VT (*Jur*) to refer, delegate
▶ VI: **~ a** to defer to

deficiencia [defi'θjenθja] NF deficiency

deficiente [defi'θjente] ADJ (*defectuoso*)
defective; **~ en** lacking *o* deficient in ▶ NMF:
ser un ~ mental to be mentally
handicapped

déficit ['defiθit] (*pl* **déficits**) NM (*Com*) deficit;
(*fig*) lack, shortage; **~ presupuestario**
budget deficit

deficitario, -a [defiθi'tarjo, a] ADJ (*Com*) in
deficit; (*: empresa*) loss-making

defienda *etc* [de'fjenda] VB *ver* **defender**

defiera *etc* [de'fjera] VB *ver* **deferir**

definición [defini'θjon] NF definition;
(*Inform: de pantalla*) resolution

definido, -a [defi'niðo, a] ADJ (*tb Ling*)
definite; **bien ~** well *o* clearly defined;
~ por el usuario (*Inform*) user-defined

definir [defi'nir] /**3a**/ VT (*determinar*) to
determine, establish; (*decidir, Inform*) to
define; (*aclarar*) to clarify

definitivo, -a [defini'tiβo, a] ADJ (*edición, texto*)
definitive; (*fecha*) definite; **en definitiva**
definitively; (*en conclusión*) finally; (*en resumen*)
in short

defiriendo *etc* [defi'rjendo] VB *ver* **deferir**

deflacionario, -a [deflaθjo'narjo, a],
deflacionista [deflaθjo'nista] ADJ
deflationary

deflector [deflek'tor] NM (*Tec*) baffle

deforestación [deforesta'θjon] NF
deforestation

deformación [deforma'θjon] NF (*alteración*)
deformation; (*Radio etc*) distortion

deformar [defor'mar] /**1a**/ VT (*gen*) to deform;
deformarse VR to become deformed

deforme [de'forme] ADJ (*informe*) deformed;
(*feo*) ugly; (*mal hecho*) misshapen

deformidad [deformi'ðað] NF (*forma anormal*)
deformity; (*fig: defecto*) (moral) shortcoming

defraudar [defrau'ðar] /**1a**/ VT (*decepcionar*) to
disappoint; (*estafar*) to cheat, to defraud;
~ impuestos to evade tax

defunción [defun'θjon] NF death, demise

degeneración [dexenera'θjon] NF (*de las células*) degeneration; (*moral*) degeneracy

degenerar [dexene'rar] /**1a**/ VI to degenerate; (*empeorar*) to get worse

deglutir [deɣlu'tir] /**3a**/ VT, VI to swallow

degolladero [deɣoʎa'ðero] NM (*Anat*) throat; (*cadalso*) scaffold; (*matadero*) slaughterhouse

degollar [deɣo'ʎar] /**1m**/ VT to slaughter

degradar [deɣra'ðar] /**1a**/ VT to debase, degrade; (*Inform: datos*) to corrupt; **degradarse** VR to demean o.s.

degüelle *etc* [de'ɣweʎe] VB *ver* **degollar**

degustación [deɣusta'θjon] NF sampling, tasting

deificar [deifi'kar] /**1g**/ VT (*persona*) to deify

deifique *etc* [dei'fike] VB *ver* **deificar**

dejadez [dexa'ðeθ] NF (*negligencia*) neglect; (*descuido*) untidiness, carelessness

dejado, -a [de'xaðo, a] ADJ (*desaliñado*) slovenly; (*negligente*) careless; (*indolente*) lazy

dejar [de'xar] /**1a**/ VT (*gen*) to leave; (*permitir*) to allow, let; (*abandonar*) to abandon, forsake; (*actividad, empleo*) to give up; (*beneficios*) to produce, yield ▶ VI: **~ de** (*parar*) to stop; (*no hacer*) to fail to; **dejarse** VR (*abandonarse*) to let o.s. go; **no puedo ~ de fumar** I can't give up smoking; **no dejes de visitarlos** don't fail to visit them; **no dejes de comprar un billete** make sure you buy a ticket; **~ a un lado** to leave o set aside; **~ caer** to drop; **~ entrar/salir** to let in/out; **~ pasar** to let through; **¡déjalo!** (*no te preocupes*) don't worry about it; **te dejo en tu casa** I'll drop you off at your place; **deja mucho que desear** it leaves a lot to be desired; **dejarse persuadir** to allow o.s. to o let o.s. be persuaded; **¡déjate de tonterías!** stop messing about!

deje ['dexe] NM (trace of) accent

dejo ['dexo] NM (*Ling*) accent

del [del] (= *de* + *el*) *ver* **de**

del. ABR (*Admin*: = *Delegación*) district office

delantal [delan'tal] NM apron

delante [de'lante] ADV in front; (*enfrente*) opposite; (*adelante*) ahead ▶ PREP: **~ de** in front of, before; **la parte de ~** the front part; **estando otros ~** with others present

delantero, -a [delan'tero, a] ADJ front; (*patas de animal*) fore ▶ NM (*Deporte*) forward, striker ▶ NF (*de vestido, casa etc*) front part; (*Teat*) front row; (*Deporte*) forward line; **llevar la delantera (a algn)** to be ahead (of sb)

delatar [dela'tar] /**1a**/ VT to inform on o against, betray; **los delató a la policía** he reported them to the police

delator, -a [dela'tor, a] NM/F informer

delegación [deleɣa'θjon] NF (*acción: delegados*) delegation; (*Com: oficina*) district office, branch; **~ de poderes** (*Pol*) devolution; **~ de policía** (*Am*) police station

delegado, -a [dele'ɣaðo, a] NM/F delegate; (*Com*) agent

delegar [dele'ɣar] /**1h**/ VT to delegate

delegue *etc* [de'leɣe] VB *ver* **delegar**

deleitar [delei'tar] /**1a**/ VT to delight; **deleitarse** VR: **deleitarse con** o **en** to delight in, take pleasure in

deleite [de'leite] NM delight, pleasure

deletrear [deletre'ar] /**1a**/ VT (*tb fig*) to spell (out)

deletreo [dele'treo] NM spelling; (*fig*) interpretation, decipherment

deleznable [deleθ'naβle] ADJ (*frágil*) fragile; (*fig: malo*) poor; (: *excusa*) feeble

delfín [del'fin] NM dolphin

delgadez [delɣa'ðeθ] NF thinness, slimness

delgado, -a [del'ɣaðo, a] ADJ thin; (*persona*) slim, thin; (*tierra*) poor; (*tela etc*) light, delicate ▶ ADV: **hilar (muy) ~** (*fig*) to split hairs

deliberación [deliβera'θjon] NF deliberation

deliberar [deliβe'rar] /**1a**/ VT to debate, discuss ▶ VI to deliberate

delicadeza [delika'ðeθa] NF delicacy; (*refinamiento, sutileza*) refinement

delicado, -a [deli'kaðo, a] ADJ delicate; (*sensible*) sensitive; (*rasgos*) dainty; (*gusto*) refined; (*situación: difícil*) tricky; (: *violento*) embarrassing; (*punto, tema*) sore; (*persona: difícil de contentar*) hard to please; (: *sensible*) touchy, hypersensitive; (: *atento*) considerate

delicia [de'liθja] NF delight

delicioso, -a [deli'θjoso, a] ADJ (*gracioso*) delightful; (*exquisito*) delicious

delictivo, -a [delik'tiβo, a] ADJ criminal *cpd*

delimitar [delimi'tar] /**1a**/ VT to delimit; (*función, responsabilidades*) to define

delincuencia [delin'kwenθja] NF: **~ juvenil** juvenile delinquency; **cifras de la ~** crime rate

delincuente [delin'kwente] NMF delinquent; (*criminal*) criminal; **~ sin antecedentes** first offender; **~ habitual** hardened criminal

delineante [deline'ante] NMF draughtsman (draughtswoman); (*US*) draftsman (draftswoman)

delinear [deline'ar] /**1a**/ VT to delineate; (*dibujo*) to draw; (*contornos, fig*) to outline; **~ un proyecto** to outline a project

delinquir [delin'kir] /**3e**/ VI to commit an offence

delirante [deli'rante] ADJ delirious

delirar [deli'rar] /**1a**/ VI to be delirious, rave; (*fig: desatinar*) to talk nonsense

delirio [de'lirjo] NM (*Med*) delirium; (*palabras insensatas*) ravings *pl*; **~ de grandeza**

megalomania; **~ de persecución** persecution mania; **con ~** (*fam*) madly; **¡fue el ~!** (*fam*) it was great!

delito [de'lito] NM (*gen*) crime; (*infracción*) offence

delta ['delta] NM delta

demacrado, -a [dema'kraðo, a] ADJ emaciated; **estar ~** to look pale and drawn, be wasted away

demagogia [dema'ɣoxja] NF demagogy, demagoguery

demagogo, -a [dema'ɣoɣo, a] NM/F demagogue

demanda [de'manda] NF (*pedido, Com*) demand; (*petición*) request; (*pregunta*) inquiry; (*reivindicación*) claim; (*Jur*) action, lawsuit; (*Teat*) call; (*Elec*) load; **~ de pago** demand for payment; **escribir en ~ de ayuda** to write asking for help; **entablar ~** (*Jur*) to sue; **presentar ~ de divorcio** to sue for divorce; **~ final** final demand; **~ indirecta** derived demand; **~ de mercado** market demand

demandado, -a [deman'daðo, a] NM/F defendant; (*en divorcio*) respondent

demandante [deman'dante] NMF claimant; (*Jur*) plaintiff

demandar [deman'dar] /**1a**/ VT (*gen*) to demand; (*Jur*) to sue, file a lawsuit against, start proceedings against; **~ a algn por calumnia/daños y perjuicios** to sue sb for libel/damages

demarcación [demarka'θjon] NF (*de terreno*) demarcation

demás [de'mas] ADJ: **los ~ niños** the other children, the remaining children ▶ PRON: **los/las ~** the others, the rest (of them); **lo ~** the rest (of it); **por ~** moreover; (*en vano*) in vain; **y ~** etcetera

demasía [dema'sia] NF (*exceso*) excess, surplus; **comer en ~** to eat to excess

demasiado, -a [dema'sjaðo, a] ADJ: **~ vino** too much wine ▶ ADV (*antes de adj, adv*) too; **demasiados libros** too many books; **¡es ~!** it's too much!; **es ~ pesado para levantarlo** it is too heavy to lift; **~ lo sé** I know it only too well; **hace ~ calor** it's too hot; **~ despacio** too slowly; **demasiados** too many

demencia [de'menθja] NF (*locura*) madness

demencial [demen'θjal] ADJ crazy

demente [de'mente] ADJ mad, insane ▶ NMF lunatic

democracia [demo'kraθja] NF democracy

demócrata [de'mokrata] NMF democrat

democratacristiano, -a [demokratakris'tjano, a], **democristiano, -a** [demokris'tjano, a] ADJ, NM/F Christian Democrat

democrático, -a [demo'kratiko, a] ADJ democratic

demográfico, -a [demo'ɣrafiko, a] ADJ demographic, population *cpd*; **la explosión demográfica** the population explosion

demoledor, a [demole'ðor, a] ADJ (*fig: argumento*) overwhelming; (: *ataque*) shattering

demoler [demo'ler] /**2h**/ VT to demolish; (*edificio*) to pull down

demolición [demoli'θjon] NF demolition

demonio [de'monjo] NM devil, demon; **¡demonios!** hell!, damn!; **¿cómo demonios?** how the hell?; **¿qué demonios será?** what the devil can it be?; **¿dónde ~ lo habré dejado?** where the devil can I have left it?; **tener el ~ en el cuerpo** (*no parar*) to be always on the go

demora [de'mora] NF delay

demorar [demo'rar] /**1a**/ VT (*retardar*) to delay, hold back; (*dilatar*) to hold up ▶ VI to linger, stay on; **demorarse** VR to linger, stay on; (*retrasarse*) to take a long time; **demorarse en hacer algo** (*esp Am*) to take time doing sth

demos ['demos] VB *ver* **dar**

demostración [demostra'θjon] NF (*gen*) demonstration; (*de cariño, fuerza*) show; (*de teorema*) proof; (*de amistad*) gesture; (*de cólera, gimnasia*) display; **~ comercial** commercial exhibition

demostrar [demos'trar] /**1l**/ VT (*probar*) to prove; (*mostrar*) to show; (*manifestar*) to demonstrate

demostrativo, -a [demostra'tiβo, a] ADJ demonstrative

demudado, -a [demu'ðaðo, a] ADJ (*rostro*) pale; (*fig*) upset; **tener el rostro ~** to look pale

demudar [demu'ðar] /**1a**/ VT to change, alter; **demudarse** VR (*expresión*) to alter; (*perder color*) to change colour

demuela *etc* [de'mwela] VB *ver* **demoler**

demuestre *etc* [de'mwestre] VB *ver* **demostrar**

den [den] VB *ver* **dar**

denegación [deneɣa'θjon] NF refusal

denegar [dene'ɣar] /**1h, 1j**/ VT (*rechazar*) to refuse; (*negar*) to deny; (*Jur*) to reject

denegué [dene'ɣe], **deneguemos** *etc* [dene'ɣemos], **deniego** *etc* [de'njeɣo], **deniegue** *etc* [de'njeɣe] VB *ver* **denegar**

dengue ['denɣe] NM dengue *o* breakbone fever

denigrante [deni'ɣrante] ADJ (*injurioso*) insulting; (*deshonroso*) degrading

denigrar [deni'ɣrar] /**1a**/ VT (*desacreditar*) to denigrate; (*injuriar*) to insult

denodado, -a [deno'ðaðo, a] ADJ bold, brave

denominación [denomina'θjon] NF (*acto*)
naming; (*clase*) denomination; *see note*

The *denominación de origen*, often
abbreviated to D.O., is a prestigious
product classification given to
designated regions by the awarding body,
the *Consejo Regulador de la Denominación de
Origen*, when their produce meets the
required quality and production
standards. It is often associated with
manchego cheeses and many of the wines
from the Rioja and Ribera de Duero
regions.

denominador [denomina'ðor] NM: **~ común**
common denominator

denostar [denos'tar] /**1l**/ VT to insult

denotar [deno'tar] /**1a**/ VT (*indicar*) to indicate,
denote

densidad [densi'ðað] NF (*Física*) density; (*fig*)
thickness

denso, -a ['denso, a] ADJ (*apretado*) solid;
(*espeso, pastoso*) thick, dense; (*fig*) heavy

dentado, -a [den'taðo, a] ADJ (*rueda*) cogged;
(*filo*) jagged; (*sello*) perforated; (*Bot*) dentate

dentadura [denta'ðura] NF (set of) teeth *pl*;
~ postiza false teeth *pl*

dental [den'tal] ADJ dental

dentellada [dente'ʎaða] NF (*mordisco*) bite,
nip; (*señal*) tooth mark; **partir algo a
dentelladas** to sever sth with one's teeth

dentera [den'tera] NF (*sensación desagradable*)
the shivers *pl*; (*grima*): **dar ~ a algn** to set sb's
teeth on edge

dentición [denti'θjon] NF (*acto*) teething;
(*Anat*) dentition; **estar con la ~** to be
teething

dentífrico, -a [den'tifriko, a] ADJ dental,
tooth *cpd* ▶ NM toothpaste; **pasta dentífrica**
toothpaste

dentista [den'tista] NMF dentist

dentro ['dentro] ADV inside ▶ PREP: **~ de** in,
inside, within; **por ~** (on the) inside; **allí ~**
in there; **mirar por ~** to look inside; **~ de lo
posible** as far as possible; **~ de todo** all in
all; **~ de tres meses** within three months

denuedo [de'nweðo] NM boldness, daring

denuesto [de'nwesto] NM insult

denuncia [de'nunθja] NF (*delación*)
denunciation; (*acusación*) accusation; (*de
accidente*) report; **hacer o poner una ~** to
report an incident to the police

denunciable [denun'θjaβle] ADJ indictable,
punishable

denunciante [denun'θjante] NMF accuser;
(*delator*) informer

denunciar [denun'θjar] /**1b**/ VT to report;
(*delatar*) to inform on *o* against

Dep. ABR (= *Departamento*) Dept.; (= *Depósito*)
dep.

deparar [depa'rar] /**1a**/ VT (*brindar*) to provide
o furnish with; (*futuro, destino*) to have in
store for; **los placeres que el viaje nos
deparó** the pleasures which the trip
afforded us

departamento [departa'mento] NM (*sección*)
department, section; (*AM: piso*) flat (*BRIT*),
apartment (*US*); (*distrito*) department,
province; **~ de envíos** (*Com*) dispatch
department; **~ de máquinas** (*Naut*) engine
room

departir [depar'tir] /**3a**/ VI to talk, converse

dependencia [depen'denθja] NF
dependence; (*Pol*) dependency; (*Com*) office,
section; (*sucursal*) branch office; (*Arq: cuarto*)
room; **dependencias** NFPL outbuildings

depender [depen'der] /**2a**/ VI: **~ de** to depend
on; (*contar con*) to rely on; (*autoridad*) to be
under, be answerable to; **depende** it (all)
depends; **no depende de mí** it's not up to
to me

dependienta [depen'djenta] NF
saleswoman, shop assistant

dependiente [depen'djente] ADJ dependent
▶ NM salesman, shop assistant

depilación [depila'θjon] NF hair removal

depilar [depi'lar] /**1a**/ VT (*con cera: piernas*) to
wax; (*cejas*) to pluck

depilatorio, -a [depila'torjo, a] ADJ depilatory
▶ NM hair remover

deplorable [deplo'raβle] ADJ deplorable

deplorar [deplo'rar] /**1a**/ VT to deplore

depondré *etc* [depon'dre] VB *ver* **deponer**

deponer [depo'ner] /**2q**/ VT (*armas*) to lay
down; (*rey*) to depose; (*gobernante*) to oust;
(*ministro*) to remove from office ▶ VI (*Jur*)
to give evidence; (*declarar*) to make a
statement

deponga *etc* [de'ponga] VB *ver* **deponer**

deportación [deporta'θjon] NF deportation

deportar [depor'tar] /**1a**/ VT to deport

deporte [de'porte] NM sport; **hacer ~** to play
sports

deportista [depor'tista] ADJ sports *cpd* ▶ NMF
sportsman(-woman)

deportivo, -a [depor'tiβo, a] ADJ (*club,
periódico*) sports *cpd* ▶ NM sports car

deposición [deposi'θjon] NF (*de funcionario etc*)
removal from office; (*Jur: testimonio*) evidence

depositante [deposi'tante] NMF depositor

depositar [deposi'tar] /**1a**/ VT (*dinero*) to
deposit; (*mercaderías*) to put away, store;
depositarse VR to settle; **~ la confianza en
algn** to place one's trust in sb

depositario, -a [deposi'tarjo, a] NM/F
trustee; **~ judicial** official receiver

depósito [de'posito] NM (*gen*) deposit; (*de
mercaderías*) warehouse, store; (*de animales,
coches*) pound; (*de agua, gasolina etc*) tank;

(*en retrete*) cistern; ~ **afianzado** bonded warehouse; ~ **bancario** bank deposit; ~ **de cadáveres** mortuary; ~ **de maderas** timber yard; ~ **de suministro** feeder bin

depravar [depra'βar] /**1a**/ VT to deprave, corrupt; **depravarse** VR to become depraved

depreciación [depreθja'θjon] NF depreciation

depreciar [depre'θjar] /**1b**/ VT to depreciate, reduce the value of; **depreciarse** VR to depreciate, lose value

depredador, a [depreða'ðor, a] (*Zool*) ADJ predatory ▶ NM predator

depredar [depre'ðar] /**1a**/ VT to pillage

depresión [depre'sjon] NF (*gen*, *Med*) depression; (*hueco*) hollow; (*en horizonte*, *camino*) dip; (*merma*) drop; (*Econ*) slump, recession; ~ **nerviosa** nervous breakdown

deprimente [depri'mente] ADJ depressing

deprimido, -a [depri'miðo, a] ADJ depressed

deprimir [depri'mir] /**3a**/ VT to depress; **deprimirse** VR (*persona*) to become depressed

deprisa [de'prisa] ADV quickly, hurriedly

depuesto [de'pwesto] PP *de* **deponer**

depuración [depura'θjon] NF purification; (*Pol*) purge

depurador [depura'ðor] NM purifier

depuradora [depura'ðora] NF (*de agua*) water-treatment plant; (*tb*: **depuradora de aguas residuales**) sewage farm

depurar [depu'rar] /**1a**/ VT to purify; (*purgar*) to purge

depuse *etc* [de'puse] VB *ver* **deponer**

der., der.° ABR (= *derecho*) r

der., der.ª ABR (= *derecha*) r

derecha [de'retʃa] NF *ver* **derecho**

derechazo [dere'tʃaθo] NM (*Boxeo*) right; (*Tenis*) forehand drive; (*Taur*) *a pass with the cape*

derechista [dere'tʃista] (*Pol*) ADJ right-wing ▶ NMF right-winger

derecho, -a [de'retʃo, a] ADJ right, right-hand ▶ NM (*privilegio*) right; (*título*) claim, title; (*lado*) right(-hand) side; (*leyes*) law ▶ NF right(-hand) side; (*Pol*) right ▶ ADV straight, directly; **derechos** NMPL dues; (*profesionales*) fees; (*impuestos*) taxes; (*de autor*) royalties; **la(s) derecha(s)** (*Pol*) the Right; **derechos civiles** civil rights; **derechos de patente** patent rights; **derechos portuarios** (*Com*) harbour dues; ~ **de propiedad literaria** copyright; ~ **de timbre** (*Com*) stamp duty; ~ **de votar** right to vote; ~ **a voto** voting right; **Facultad de D~** Faculty of Law; **a derechas** rightly, correctly; **de derechas** (*Pol*) right-wing; **"reservados todos los derechos"** "all rights reserved"; **¡no hay ~!** it's not fair!; **tener ~ a** to have a right to; **a la derecha** on the right; (*dirección*) to

the right; **siga todo** ~ carry *o* (*Brit*) go straight on

deriva [de'riβa] NF: **ir** *o* **estar a la** ~ to drift, be adrift

derivación [deriβa'θjon] NF derivation

derivado, -a [deri'βaðo, a] ADJ derived ▶ NM (*Ling*) derivative; (*Industria*, *Química*) by-product

derivar [deri'βar] /**1a**/ VT to derive; (*desviar*) to direct ▶ VI to derive, be derived; (*Naut*) to drift; **derivarse** VR to derive, be derived; ~**(se) de** (*consecuencia*) to spring from

dermatólogo, -a [derma'toloɣo, a] NM/F dermatologist

dérmico, -a ['dermiko, a] ADJ skin *cpd*

dermoprotector, a [dermoprotek'tor, a] ADJ protective

derogación [deroɣa'θjon] NF repeal

derogar [dero'ɣar] /**1h**/ VT (*ley*) to repeal; (*contrato*) to revoke

derogue *etc* [de'roɣe] VB *ver* **derogar**

derramamiento [derrama'mjento] NM (*dispersión*) spilling; (*fig*) squandering; ~ **de sangre** bloodshed

derramar [derra'mar] /**1a**/ VT to spill; (*verter*) to pour out; (*esparcir*) to scatter; **derramarse** VR to pour out; ~ **lágrimas** to weep

derrame [de'rrame] NM (*de líquido*) spilling; (*de sangre*) shedding; (*de tubo etc*) overflow; (*pérdida*) leakage; (*Med*) discharge; (*declive*) slope; ~ **cerebral** brain haemorrhage; ~ **sinovial** water on the knee

derrapar [derra'par] /**1a**/ VI to skid

derredor [derre'ðor] ADV: **al** *o* **en** ~ **de** around, about

derrengado, -a [derren'gaðo, a] ADJ (*torcido*) bent; (*cojo*) crippled; **estar** ~ (*fig*) to ache all over; **dejar** ~ **a algn** (*fig*) to wear sb out

derretido, -a [derre'tiðo, a] ADJ melted; (*metal*) molten; **estar** ~ **por algn** (*fig*) to be crazy about sb

derretir [derre'tir] /**3k**/ VT (*gen*) to melt; (*nieve*) to thaw; (*fig*) to squander; **derretirse** VR to melt

derribar [derri'βar] /**1a**/ VT to knock down; (*construcción*) to demolish; (*persona*, *gobierno*, *político*) to bring down

derribo [de'rriβo] NM (*de edificio*) demolition; (*Lucha*) throw; (*Aviat*) shooting down; (*Pol*) overthrow; **derribos** NMPL rubble *sg*, debris *sg*

derrita *etc* [de'rrita] VB *ver* **derretir**

derrocar [derro'kar] /**1g**/ VT (*gobierno*) to bring down, overthrow; (*ministro*) to oust

derrochador, a [derrotʃa'ðor, a] ADJ, NM/F spendthrift

derrochar [derro'tʃar] /**1a**/ VT (*dinero*, *recursos*) to squander; (*energía*, *salud*) to be bursting with *o* full of

derroche [de'rrotʃe] NM (*despilfarro*) waste, squandering; (*exceso*) extravagance; **con un ~ de buen gusto** with a fine display of good taste

derroqueetc [de'rroke] VB ver **derrocar**

derrota [de'rrota] NF (*Naut*) course; (*Mil*) defeat, rout; **sufrir una grave ~** (*fig*) to suffer a grave setback

derrotar [derro'tar] /**1a**/ VT (*gen*) to defeat

derrotero [derro'tero] NM (*rumbo*) course; **tomar otro ~** (*fig*) to adopt a different course

derrotista [derro'tista] ADJ, NMF defeatist

derruir [derru'ir] /**3g**/ VT to demolish, tear down

derrumbamiento [derrumba'mjento] NM (*caída*) plunge; (*demolición*) demolition; (*desplome*) collapse; **~ de tierra** landslide

derrumbar [derrum'bar] /**1a**/ VT to throw down; (*despeñar*) to fling o hurl down; (*edificio*) to knock down; (*volcar*) to upset; **derrumbarse** VR (*hundirse*) to collapse; (: *techo*) to fall in, cave in; (*fig*: *esperanzas*) to collapse

derrumbe [de'rrumbe] NM
= **derrumbamiento**

derruyendoetc [derru'jendo] VB ver **derruir**

des [des] VB ver **dar**

desabastecido, -a [desaβaste'θiðo, a] ADJ: **estar ~ de algo** to be short of o out of sth

desabotonar [desaβoto'nar] /**1a**/ VT to unbutton, undo ▶ VI (*flores*) to blossom; **desabotonarse** VR to come undone

desabrido, -a [desa'βriðo, a] ADJ (*comida*) insipid, tasteless; (*persona*: *soso*) dull; (: *antipático*) rude, surly; (*respuesta*) sharp; (*tiempo*) unpleasant

desabrigado, -a [desaβri'ɣaðo, a] ADJ (*sin abrigo*) not sufficiently protected; (*fig*) exposed

desabrigar [desaβri'ɣar] /**1h**/ VT (*quitar ropa a*) to remove the clothing of; (*descubrir*) to uncover; (*fig*) to deprive of protection; **desabrigarse** VR: **me desabrigué en la cama** the bedclothes came off

desabrigueetc [desa'βriɣe] VB ver **desabrigar**

desabrochar [desaβro'tʃar] /**1a**/ VT (*botones, broches*) to undo, unfasten; **desabrocharse** VR (*ropa etc*) to come undone

desacatar [desaka'tar] /**1a**/ VT (*ley*) to disobey

desacato [desa'kato] NM (*falta de respeto*) disrespect; (*Jur*) contempt

desacertado, -a [desaθer'taðo, a] ADJ (*equivocado*) mistaken; (*inoportuno*) unwise

desacierto [desa'θjerto] NM (*error*) mistake, error; (*dicho*) unfortunate remark

desaconsejable [desakonse'xaβle] ADJ inadvisable

desaconsejado, -a [desakonse'xaðo, a] ADJ ill-advised

desaconsejar [desakonse'xar] /**1a**/ VT: **~ algo a algn** to advise sb against sth

desacoplar [desako'plar] /**1a**/ VT (*Elec*) to disconnect; (*Tec*) to take apart

desacorde [desa'korðe] ADJ (*Mus*) discordant; (*fig*: *opiniones*) conflicting; **estar ~ con algo** to disagree with sth

desacreditar [desakreði'tar] /**1a**/ VT (*desprestigiar*) to discredit, bring into disrepute; (*denigrar*) to run down

desactivar [desakti'βar] /**1a**/ VT to deactivate; (*bomba*) to defuse

desacuerdo [desa'kwerðo] NM (*conflicto*) disagreement, discord; (*error*) error, blunder; **en ~** out of keeping

desafiante [desa'fjante] ADJ (*insolente*) defiant; (*retador*) challenging ▶ NMF challenger

desafiar [desa'fjar] /**1c**/ VT (*retar*) to challenge; (*enfrentarse a*) to defy

desafilado, -a [desafi'laðo, a] ADJ blunt

desafinado, -a [desafi'naðo, a] ADJ: **estar ~** to be out of tune

desafinar [desafi'nar] /**1a**/ VI to be out of tune; **desafinarse** VR to go out of tune

desafío [desa'fio] NM (*reto*) challenge; (*combate*) duel; (*resistencia*) defiance

desaforadamente [desaforaða'mente] ADV: **gritar ~** to shout one's head off

desaforado, -a [desafo'raðo, a] ADJ (*grito*) ear-splitting; (*comportamiento*) outrageous

desafortunadamente [desafortunaða'mente] ADV unfortunately

desafortunado, -a [desafortu'naðo, a] ADJ (*desgraciado*) unfortunate, unlucky

desagradable [desaɣra'ðaβle] ADJ (*fastidioso, enojoso*) unpleasant; (*irritante*) disagreeable; **ser ~ con algn** to be rude to sb

desagradar [desaɣra'ðar] /**1a**/ VI (*disgustar*) to displease; (*molestar*) to bother

desagradecido, -a [desaɣraðe'θiðo, a] ADJ ungrateful

desagrado [desa'ɣraðo] NM (*disgusto*) displeasure; (*contrariedad*) dissatisfaction; **con ~** unwillingly

desagraviar [desaɣra'βjar] /**1b**/ VT to make amends to

desagravio [desa'ɣraβjo] NM (*satisfacción*) amends; (*compensación*) compensation

desaguadero [desaɣwa'ðero] NM drain

desagüe [de'saɣwe] NM (*de un líquido*) drainage; (*cañería*: tb: **tubo de desagüe**) drainpipe; (*salida*) outlet, drain

desaguisado, -a [desaɣi'saðo, a] ADJ illegal ▶ NM outrage

desahogado, -a [desao'ɣaðo, a] ADJ (*holgado*) comfortable; (*espacioso*) roomy

desahogar [desao'ɣar] /**1h**/ VT (*aliviar*) to ease, relieve; (*ira*) to vent; **desahogarse** VR (*distenderse*) to relax; (*desfogarse*) to let off steam (*fam*); (*confesarse*) to confess, get sth off one's chest (*fam*)

desahogo [desa'oɣo] NM (*alivio*) relief; (*comodidad*) comfort, ease; **vivir con ~** to be comfortably off

desahogue*etc* [desa'oɣe] VB *ver* **desahogar**

desahuciado, -a [desau'θjaðo, a] ADJ hopeless

desahuciar [desau'θjar] /1b/ VT (*enfermo*) to give up hope for; (*inquilino*) to evict

desahucio [de'sauθjo] NM eviction

desairado, -a [desai'raðo, a] ADJ (*menospreciado*) disregarded; (*desgarbado*) shabby; (*sin éxito*) unsuccessful; **quedar ~** to come off badly

desairar [desai'rar] /1a/ VT (*menospreciar*) to slight, snub; (*cosa*) to disregard; (*Com*) to default on

desaire [des'aire] NM (*menosprecio*) slight; (*falta de garbo*) unattractiveness; **dar** *o* **hacer un ~ a algn** to offend sb; **¿me va usted a hacer ese ~?** I won't take no for an answer!

desajustar [desaxus'tar] /1a/ VT (*desarreglar*) to disarrange; (*desconcertar*) to throw off balance; (*fig: planes*) to upset; **desajustarse** VR to get out of order; (*aflojarse*) to loosen

desajuste [desa'xuste] NM (*de máquina*) disorder; (*avería*) breakdown; (*situación*) imbalance; (*desacuerdo*) disagreement

desalentador, -a [desalenta'ðor, a] ADJ discouraging

desalentar [desalen'tar] /1j/ VT (*desanimar*) to discourage; **desalentarse** VR to get discouraged

desaliento*etc* [desa'ljento] VB *ver* **desalentar**
▶ NM discouragement; (*abatimiento*) depression

desaliñado, -a [desali'ɲaðo, a] ADJ (*descuidado*) slovenly; (*raído*) shabby; (*desordenado*) untidy; (*negligente*) careless

desaliño [desa'liɲo] NM (*descuido*) slovenliness; (*negligencia*) carelessness

desalmado, -a [desal'maðo, a] ADJ (*cruel*) cruel, heartless

desalojar [desalo'xar] /1a/ VT (*gen*) to remove, expel; (*expulsar, echar*) to eject; (*abandonar*) to move out of ▶ VI to move out; **la policía desalojó el local** the police cleared people out of the place

desalquilar [desalki'lar] /1a/ VT to vacate, move out; **desalquilarse** VR to become vacant

desamarrar [desama'rrar] /1a/ VT to untie; (*Naut*) to cast off

desamor [desa'mor] NM (*frialdad*) indifference; (*odio*) dislike

desamparado, -a [desampa'raðo, a] ADJ (*persona*) helpless; (*lugar: expuesto*) exposed; (: *desierto*) deserted

desamparar [desampa'rar] /1a/ VT (*abandonar*) to desert, abandon; (*Jur*) to leave defenceless; (*barco*) to abandon

desamparo [desam'paro] NM (*acto*) desertion; (*estado*) helplessness

desamueblado, -a [desamwe'βlaðo, a] ADJ unfurnished

desandar [desan'dar] /1p/ VT: ~ **lo andado** *o* **el camino** to retrace one's steps

desanduve*etc* [desan'duβe], **desanduviera** *etc* [desandu'βjera] VB *ver* **desandar**

desangelado, -a [desanxe'laðo, a] ADJ (*habitación, edificio*) lifeless

desangrar [desan'grar] /1a/ VT to bleed; (*fig: persona*) to bleed dry; (*lago*) to drain; **desangrarse** VR to lose a lot of blood; (*morir*) to bleed to death

desanimado, -a [desani'maðo, a] ADJ (*persona*) downhearted; (*espectáculo, fiesta*) dull

desanimar [desani'mar] /1a/ VT (*desalentar*) to discourage; (*deprimir*) to depress; **desanimarse** VR to lose heart

desánimo [de'sanimo] NM despondency; (*abatimiento*) dejection; (*falta de animación*) dullness

desanudar [desanu'ðar] /1a/ VT to untie; (*fig*) to clear up

desapacible [desapa'θiβle] ADJ unpleasant

desaparecer [desapare'θer] /2d/ VI to disappear; (*el sol, la luz*) to vanish; (*desaparecer de vista*) to drop out of sight; (*efectos, señales*) to wear off ▶ VT (*esp Am: Pol*) to cause to disappear; (: *eufemismo*) to murder

desaparecido, -a [desapare'θiðo, a] ADJ missing; (*especie*) extinct ▶ NM/F (*Am Pol*) kidnapped *o* missing person

desaparezca*etc* [desapa'reθka] VB *ver* **desaparecer**

desaparición [desapari'θjon] NF disappearance; (*de especie etc*) extinction

desapasionado, -a [desapasjo'naðo, a] ADJ dispassionate, impartial

desapego [desa'peɣo] NM (*frialdad*) coolness; (*distancia*) detachment

desapercibido, -a [desaperθi'βiðo, a] ADJ unnoticed; (*desprevenido*) unprepared; **pasar ~** to go unnoticed

desaplicado, -a [desapli'kaðo, a] ADJ slack, lazy

desaprensivo, -a [desapren'siβo, a] ADJ unscrupulous

desaprobar [desapro'βar] /1l/ VT (*reprobar*) to disapprove of; (*condenar*) to condemn; (*no consentir*) to reject

desaprovechado, -a [desaproβe'tʃaðo, a] ADJ (*oportunidad, tiempo*) wasted; (*estudiante*) slack

desaprovechar [desaproβe'tʃar] /1a/ VT to waste; (*talento*) not to use to the full ▶ VI (*perder terreno*) to lose ground

desapruebe *etc* [desa'prweβe] VB *ver*
desaprobar

desarmador [desarma'ðor] NM (*AM*)
screwdriver

desarmar [desar'mar] /**1a**/ VT (*Mil, fig*) to
disarm; (*Tec*) to take apart, dismantle

desarme [de'sarme] NM disarmament

desarraigado, -a [desarrai'ɣaðo, a] ADJ
(*persona*) without roots, rootless

desarraigar [desarrai'ɣar] /**1h**/ VT to uproot;
(*fig: costumbre*) to root out; (: *persona*) to banish

desarraigo [desa'rraiɣo] NM uprooting

desarraigue *etc* [desa'rraiɣe] VB *ver*
desarraigar

desarrapado, -a [desarra'paðo, a] ADJ
ragged; (**de aspecto**) ~ shabby

desarreglado, -a [desarre'ɣlaðo, a] ADJ
(*desordenado*) disorderly, untidy; (*hábitos*)
irregular

desarreglar [desarre'ɣlar] /**1a**/ VT to mess up;
(*desordenar*) to disarrange; (*trastocar*) to upset,
disturb

desarreglo [desa'rreɣlo] NM (*de casa, persona*)
untidiness; (*desorden*) disorder; (*Tec*) trouble;
(*Med*) upset; **viven en el mayor ~** they live in
complete chaos

desarrollado, -a [desarro'ʎaðo, a] ADJ
developed

desarrollar [desarro'ʎar] /**1a**/ VT (*gen*) to
develop; (*extender*) to unfold; (*teoría*) to
explain; **desarrollarse** VR to develop; (*ocurrir*)
to take place; (*extenderse*) to open (out); (*film*)
to develop; (*fig*) to grow; (*tener lugar*) to take
place; **aquí desarrollan un trabajo muy
importante** they carry on *o* out very
important work here; **la acción se
desarrolla en Roma** (*Cine etc*) the scene is
set in Rome

desarrollo [desa'rroʎo] NM development;
(*de acontecimientos*) unfolding; (*de industria,
mercado*) expansion, growth; **país en vías de
~** developing country; **la industria está en
pleno ~** industry is expanding steadily;
~ sostenible sustainable development

desarrugar [desarru'ɣar] /**1h**/ VT (*alisar*) to
smooth (out); (*ropa*) to remove the creases
from

desarrugue *etc* [desa'rruɣe] VB *ver*
desarrugar

desarticulado, -a [desartiku'laðo, a] ADJ
disjointed

desarticular [desartiku'lar] /**1a**/ VT (*huesos*) to
dislocate, put out of joint; (*objeto*) to take
apart; (*grupo terrorista etc*) to break up

desaseado, -a [desase'aðo, a] ADJ (*sucio*) dirty;
(*desaliñado*) untidy

desaseo [desa'seo] NM (*suciedad*) dirtiness;
(*desarreglo*) untidiness

desasga *etc* [de'sasɣa] VB *ver* **desasir**

desasir [desa'sir] /**3a**/ VT to loosen; **desasirse**
VR to extricate o.s.; **desasirse de** to let go,
give up

desasosegar [desasose'ɣar] /**1h, 1j**/ VT
(*inquietar*) to disturb, make uneasy;
desasosegarse VR to become uneasy

desasosegué [desasose'ɣe],
desasoseguemos *etc* [desasose'ɣemos] VB
ver **desasosegar**

desasosiego *etc* [desaso'sjeɣo] VB *ver*
desasosegar ▶ NM (*intranquilidad*)
uneasiness, restlessness; (*ansiedad*) anxiety;
(*Pol etc*) unrest

desasosiegue *etc* [desaso'sjeɣe] VB *ver*
desasosegar

desastrado, -a [desas'traðo, a] ADJ (*desaliñado*)
shabby; (*sucio*) dirty

desastre [de'sastre] NM disaster; **¡un ~!** how
awful!; **la función fue un ~** the show was a
shambles

desastroso, -a [desas'troso, a] ADJ
disastrous

desatado, -a [desa'taðo, a] ADJ (*desligado*)
untied; (*violento*) violent, wild

desatar [desa'tar] /**1a**/ VT (*nudo*) to untie;
(*paquete*) to undo; (*perro, odio*) to unleash;
(*misterio*) to solve; (*separar*) to detach;
desatarse VR (*zapatos*) to come untied;
(*tormenta*) to break; (*perder control de sí mismo*) to
lose self-control; **desatarse en injurias** to
pour out a stream of insults

desatascar [desatas'kar] /**1g**/ VT (*cañería*) to
unblock, clear

desatasque *etc* [desa'taske] VB *ver*
desatascar

desatención [desaten'θjon] NF (*descuido*)
inattention; (*distracción*) absent-mindedness

desatender [desaten'der] /**2g**/ VT (*no prestar
atención a*) to disregard; (*abandonar*) to neglect

desatento, -a [desa'tento, a] ADJ (*distraído*)
inattentive; (*descortés*) discourteous

desatienda *etc* [desa'tjenda] VB *ver*
desatender

desatinado, -a [desati'naðo, a] ADJ foolish,
silly

desatino [desa'tino] NM (*idiotez*) foolishness,
folly; (*error*) blunder; **desatinos** NMPL
nonsense *sg*; **¡qué ~!** how silly!, what
rubbish!

desatornillar [desatorni'ʎar] /**1a**/ VT to
unscrew

desatrancar [desatran'kar] /**1g**/ VT (*puerta*) to
unbolt; (*cañería*) to unblock

desatranque *etc* [desa'tranke] VB *ver*
desatrancar

desautorice *etc* [desauto'riθe] VB *ver*
desautorizar

desautorizado, -a [desautori'θaðo, a] ADJ
unauthorized

desautorizar [desautori'θar] /**1f**/ VT (*oficial*) to deprive of authority; (*informe*) to deny

desavendré *etc* [desaβen'dre] VB *ver* **desavenir**

desavenencia [desaβe'nenθja] NF (*desacuerdo*) disagreement; (*discrepancia*) quarrel

desavenga *etc* [desa'βenga] VB *ver* **desavenir**

desavenido, -a [desaβe'niðo, a] ADJ (*opuesto*) contrary; (*reñido*) in disagreement; **ellos están desavenidos** they are at odds

desavenir [desaβe'nir] /**3r**/ VT (*enemistar*) to make trouble between; **desavenirse** VR to fall out

desaventajado, -a [desaβenta'xaðo, a] ADJ (*inferior*) inferior; (*poco ventajoso*) disadvantageous

desaviene *etc* [desa'βjene], **desaviniendo** *etc* [desaβi'njendo] VB *ver* **desavenir**

desayunar [desaju'nar] /**1a**/ VI to have breakfast ▶ VT to have for breakfast; ~ **café** to have coffee for breakfast; ~ **con algo** (*fig*) to get the first news of sth

desayuno [desa'juno] NM breakfast

desazón [desa'θon] NF (*angustia*) anxiety; (*Med*) discomfort; (*fig*) annoyance

desazonar [desaθo'nar] /**1a**/ VT (*fig*) to annoy, upset; **desazonarse** VR (*enojarse*) to be annoyed; (*preocuparse*) to worry, be anxious

desbancar [desβan'kar] /**1g**/ VT (*quitar el puesto a*) to oust; (*suplantar*) to supplant (in sb's affections)

desbandada [desβan'daða] NF rush; ~ **general** mass exodus; **a la ~** in disorder

desbandarse [desβan'darse] /**1a**/ VR (*Mil*) to disband; (*fig*) to flee in disorder

desbanque *etc* [des'βanke] VB *ver* **desbancar**

desbarajuste [desβara'xuste] NM confusion, disorder; **¡qué ~!** what a mess!

desbaratar [desβara'tar] /**1a**/ VT (*gen*) to mess up; (*plan*) to spoil; (*deshacer, destruir*) to ruin ▶ VI to talk nonsense; **desbaratarse** VR (*máquina*) to break down; (*persona: irritarse*) to fly off the handle (*fam*)

desbarrar [desβa'rrar] /**1a**/ VI to talk nonsense

desbloquear [desβloke'ar] /**1a**/ VT (*negociaciones, tráfico*) to get going again; (*Com: cuenta*) to unfreeze

desbocado, -a [desβo'kaðo, a] ADJ (*caballo*) runaway; (*herramienta*) worn

desbocar [desβo'kar] /**1g**/ VT (*vasija*) to break the rim of; **desbocarse** VR (*caballo*) to bolt; (*persona: soltar injurias*) to let out a stream of insults

desboque *etc* [des'βoke] VB *ver* **desbocar**

desbordamiento [desβorða'mjento] NM (*de río*) overflowing; (*Inform*) overflow; (*de cólera*) outburst; (*de entusiasmo*) upsurge

desbordar [desβor'ðar] /**1a**/ VT (*sobrepasar*) to go beyond; (*exceder*) to exceed ▶ VI, **desbordarse** VR (*líquido, río*) to overflow; (*entusiasmo*) to erupt; (*persona: exaltarse*) to get carried away

desbravar [desβra'βar] /**1a**/ VT (*caballo*) to break in; (*animal*) to tame

descabalgar [deskaβal'ɣar] /**1h**/ VI to dismount

descabalgue *etc* [deska'βalɣe] VB *ver* **descabalgar**

descabellado, -a [deskaβe'ʎaðo, a] ADJ (*disparatado*) wild, crazy; (*insensato*) preposterous

descabellar [deskaβe'ʎar] /**1a**/ VT to ruffle; (*Taur: toro*) to give the coup de grace to

descabezado, -a [deskaβe'θaðo, a] ADJ (*sin cabeza*) headless; (*insensato*) wild

descafeinado, -a [deskafei'naðo, a] ADJ decaffeinated ▶ NM decaffeinated coffee, de-caff

descalabrar [deskala'βrar] /**1a**/ VT to smash; (*persona*) to hit; (: *en la cabeza*) to hit on the head; (*Naut*) to cripple; (*dañar*) to harm, damage; **descalabrarse** VR to hurt one's head

descalabro [deska'laβro] NM blow; (*desgracia*) misfortune

descalce *etc* [des'kalθe] VB *ver* **descalzar**

descalificación [deskalifika'θjon] NF disqualification; **descalificaciones** NFPL discrediting *sg*

descalificar [deskalifi'kar] /**1g**/ VT to disqualify; (*desacreditar*) to discredit

descalifique *etc* [deskali'fike] VB *ver* **descalificar**

descalzar [deskal'θar] /**1f**/ VT (*zapato*) to take off; (*persona*) to take the shoes off

descalzo, -a [des'kalθo, a] ADJ barefoot(ed); (*fig*) destitute; **estar (con los pies) ~(s)** to be barefooted

descambiar [deskam'bjar] /**1b**/ VT to exchange

descaminado, -a [deskami'naðo, a] ADJ (*equivocado*) on the wrong road; (*fig*) misguided; **en eso no anda usted muy ~** you're not far wrong there

descamisado, -a [deskami'saðo, a] ADJ bare-chested

descampado [deskam'paðo] NM open space, piece of empty ground; **comer al ~** to eat in the open air

descansado, -a [deskan'saðo, a] ADJ (*gen*) rested; (*que tranquiliza*) restful

descansar [deskan'sar] /**1a**/ VT (*gen*) to rest; (*apoyar*): ~ **(sobre)** to lean (on) ▶ VI to rest, have a rest; (*echarse*) to lie down; (*cadáver, restos*) to lie; **¡que usted descanse!** sleep well!; ~ **en** (*argumento*) to be based on

descansillo [deskan'siʎo] NM (*de escalera*)
landing

descanso [des'kanso] NM (*reposo*) rest; (*alivio*)
relief; (*pausa*) break; (*Deporte*) interval, half
time; **día de ~** day off; **~ de enfermedad/
maternidad** sick/maternity leave; **tomarse
unos días de ~** to take a few days' leave o rest

descapitalizado, -a [deskapitali'θaðo, a] ADJ
undercapitalized

descapotable [deskapo'taβle] NM (*tb:* **coche
descapotable**) convertible

descarado, -a [deska'raðo, a] ADJ (*sin
vergüenza*) shameless; (*insolente*) cheeky

descarga [des'karɣa] NF (*Arq, Elec, Mil*)
discharge; (*Naut*) unloading; (*Inform*)
download

descargable [deskar'ɣaβle] ADJ
downloadable

descargador [deskarɣa'ðor] NM (*de barcos*)
docker

descargar [deskar'ɣar] /**1h**/ VT to unload;
(*golpe*) to let fly; (*arma*) to fire; (*Elec*) to
discharge; (*pila*) to run down; (*conciencia*) to
relieve; (*Com*) to take up; (*persona: de una
obligación*) to release; (*: de una deuda*) to free;
(*Jur*) to clear ▶ VI (*río*): **~ (en)** to flow (into);
descargarse VR to unburden o.s.;
descargarse de algo to get rid of sth;
descargarse algo de Internet to download
sth from the internet

descargo [des'karɣo] NM (*de obligación*)
release; (*Com: recibo*) receipt; (*: de deuda*)
discharge; (*Jur*) evidence; **~ de una
acusación** acquittal on a charge

descargue *etc* [des'karɣe] VB *ver* **descargar**

descarnado, -a [deskar'naðo, a] ADJ scrawny;
(*fig*) bare; (*estilo*) straightforward

descaro [des'karo] NM nerve

descarriar [deska'rrjar] /**1c**/ VT (*descaminar*) to
misdirect; (*fig*) to lead astray; **descarriarse**
VR (*perderse*) to lose one's way; (*separarse*) to
stray; (*pervertirse*) to err, go astray

descarrilamiento [deskarrila'mjento] NM
(*de tren*) derailment

descarrilar [deskarri'lar] /**1a**/ VI to be
derailed

descartable [deskar'taβle] ADJ (*Inform*)
temporary

descartar [deskar'tar] /**1a**/ VT (*rechazar*) to
reject; (*eliminar*) to rule out; **descartarse** VR
(*Naipes*) to discard; **descartarse de** to shirk

descascarar [deskaska'rar] /**1a**/ VT (*naranja,
limón*) to peel; (*nueces, huevo duro*) to shell;
descascararse VR to peel (off)

descascarillado, -a [deskaskari'ʎaðo, a] ADJ
(*paredes*) peeling

descendencia [desθen'denθja] NF (*origen*)
origin, descent; (*hijos*) offspring; **morir sin
dejar ~** to die without issue

descendente [desθen'dente] ADJ (*cantidad*)
diminishing; (*Inform*) top-down

descender [desθen'der] /**2g**/ VT (*bajar: escalera*)
to go down ▶ VI to descend; (*temperatura, nivel*)
to fall, drop; (*líquido*) to run; (*cortina etc*) to
hang; (*fuerzas, persona*) to fail, get weak; **~ de**
to be descended from

descendiente [desθen'djente] NMF
descendant

descenso [des'θenso] NM descent; (*de
temperatura*) drop; (*de producción*) downturn;
(*de calidad*) decline; (*Minería*) collapse; (*bajada*)
slope; (*fig: decadencia*) decline; (*de empleado etc*)
demotion

descentrado, -a [desθen'traðo, a] ADJ (*pieza de
una máquina*) off-centre; (*rueda*) out of true;
(*persona*) bewildered; (*desequilibrado*)
unbalanced; (*problema*) out of focus; **todavía
está algo ~** he is still somewhat out of touch

descentralice *etc* [desθentra'liθe] VB *ver*
descentralizar

descentralizar [desθentrali'θar] /**1f**/ VT to
decentralize

descerrajar [desθerra'xar] /**1a**/ VT (*puerta*) to
break open

descienda *etc* [des'θjenda] VB *ver* **descender**

descifrable [desθi'fraβle] ADJ (*gen*)
decipherable; (*letra*) legible

descifrar [desθi'frar] /**1a**/ VT (*escritura*) to
decipher; (*mensaje*) to decode; (*problema*) to
puzzle out; (*misterio*) to solve

descocado, -a [desko'kaðo, a] ADJ (*descarado*)
cheeky; (*desvergonzado*) brazen

descoco [des'koko] NM (*descaro*) cheek;
(*atrevimiento*) brazenness

descodificador [deskoðifika'ðor] NM
decoder

descodificar [deskoðifi'kar] /**1g**/ VT to decode

descolgar [deskol'ɣar] /**1h, 1l**/ VT (*bajar*) to
take down; (*desde una posición alta*) to lower;
(*de una pared etc*) to unhook; (*teléfono*) to pick
up; **descolgarse** VR to let o.s. down;
descolgarse por (*bajar escurriéndose*) to slip
down; (*pared*) to climb down; **dejó el
teléfono descolgado** he left the phone off
the hook

descolgué [deskol'ɣe], **descolguemos** *etc*
[deskol'ɣemos] VB *ver* **descolgar**

descollar [desko'ʎar] /**1l**/ VI (*sobresalir*) to
stand out; (*montaña etc*) to rise; **la obra que
más descuella de las suyas** his most
outstanding work

descolocado, -a [desko'lokaðo, a] ADJ: **estar
~** (*cosa*) to be out of place; (*criada*) to be
unemployed

descolorido, -a [deskolo'riðo, a] ADJ (*color,
tela*) faded; (*pálido*) pale; (*fig: estilo*) colourless

descompaginar [deskompaxi'nar] /**1a**/ VT
(*desordenar*) to disarrange, mess up

descompasado, -a [deskompa'saðo, a] ADJ
(*sin proporción*) out of all proportion; (*excesivo*)
excessive; (*hora*) unearthly

descompensar [deskompen'sar] /**1a**/ VT to
unbalance

descompondré *etc* [deskompon'dre] VB *ver*
descomponer

descomponer [deskompo'ner] /**2q**/ VT
(*gen, Ling, Mat*) to break down; (*desordenar*) to
disarrange, disturb; (*materia orgánica*) to rot,
decompose; (*Tec*) to put out of order;
(*facciones*) to distort; (*estómago etc*) to upset;
(*planes*) to mess up; (*persona: molestar*) to
upset; (: *irritar*) to annoy; **descomponerse** VR
(*corromperse*) to rot, decompose; (*estómago*) to
get upset; (*el tiempo*) to change (for the
worse); (*Tec*) to break down

descomponga *etc* [deskom'ponga] VB *ver*
descomponer

descomposición [deskomposi'θjon] NF
(*de un objeto*) breakdown; (*de fruta etc*)
decomposition; (*putrefacción*) rotting;
(*de cara*) distortion; **~ de vientre** (*Med*)
stomach upset, diarrhoea, diarrhea (US)

descompostura [deskompos'tura] NF (*Tec*)
breakdown, fault; (*desorganización*)
disorganization; (*desorden*) untidiness; (*Am:
diarrea*) diarrhoea, diarrhea (US)

descompuesto, -a [deskom'pwesto, a] PP
de **descomponer** ▸ ADJ (*corrompido*)
decomposed; (*roto*) broken (down)

descompuse *etc* [deskom'puse] VB *ver*
descomponer

descomunal [deskomu'nal] ADJ (*enorme*)
huge; (*fam: excelente*) fantastic

desconcertado, -a [deskonθer'taðo, a] ADJ
disconcerted, bewildered

desconcertar [deskonθer'tar] /**1j**/ VT
(*confundir*) to baffle; (*incomodar*) to upset, put
out; (*orden*) to disturb; **desconcertarse** VR
(*turbarse*) to be upset; (*confundirse*) to be
bewildered

desconchado, -a [deskon'tʃaðo, a] ADJ
(*pintura*) peeling

desconchar [deskon'tʃar] /**1a**/ VT (*pared*) to
strip off; (*loza*) to chip off

desconcierto *etc* [deskon'θjerto] VB *ver*
desconcertar ▸ NM (*gen*) disorder;
(*desorientación*) uncertainty; (*inquietud*)
uneasiness; (*confusión*) bewilderment

desconectado, -a [deskonek'taðo, a] ADJ
(*Elec*) disconnected, switched off; (*Inform*)
offline; **estar ~ de** (*fig*) to have no contact
with

desconectar [deskonek'tar] /**1a**/ VT to
disconnect; (*desenchufar*) to unplug; (*radio,
televisión*) to switch off; (*Inform*) to toggle off

desconfiado, -a [deskon'fjaðo, a] ADJ
suspicious

desconfianza [deskon'fjanθa] NF distrust

desconfiar [deskon'fjar] /**1c**/ VI to be
distrustful; **~ de** (*sospechar*) to mistrust,
suspect; (*no tener confianza en*) to have no faith
o confidence in; **desconfío de ello** I doubt it;
desconfíe de las imitaciones (*Com*) beware
of imitations

desconforme [deskon'forme] ADJ
= **disconforme**

descongelar [deskonxe'lar] /**1a**/ VT (*nevera*)
to defrost; (*comida*) to thaw; (*Auto*) to
de-ice; (*Com, Pol*) to unfreeze

descongestionar [deskonxestjo'nar] /**1a**/ VT
(*cabeza, tráfico*) to clear; (*calle, ciudad*) to relieve
congestion in; (*fig: despejar*) to clear

desconocer [deskono'θer] /**2d**/ VT (*ignorar*)
not to know, be ignorant of; (*no aceptar*) to
deny; (*repudiar*) to disown

desconocido, -a [deskono'θiðo, a] ADJ
unknown; (*que no se conoce*) unfamiliar; (*no
reconocido*) unrecognized ▸ NM/F stranger;
(*recién llegado*) newcomer; **está ~** he is hardly
recognizable

desconocimiento [deskonoθi'mjento] NM
(*falta de conocimientos*) ignorance; (*repudio*)
disregard

desconozca *etc* [desko'noθka] VB *ver*
desconocer

desconsiderado, -a [deskonsiðe'raðo, a] ADJ
inconsiderate; (*insensible*) thoughtless

desconsolado, -a [deskonso'laðo, a] ADJ
(*afligido*) disconsolate; (*cara*) sad; (*desanimado*)
dejected

desconsolar [deskonso'lar] /**1l**/ VT to distress;
desconsolarse VR to despair

desconsuelo [deskon'swelo] VB *ver*
desconsolar ▸ NM (*tristeza*) distress;
(*desesperación*) despair

descontado, -a [deskon'taðo, a] ADJ: **por ~** of
course; **dar por ~ (que)** to take it for granted
(that)

descontar [deskon'tar] /**1l**/ VT (*deducir*) to take
away, deduct; (*rebajar*) to discount

descontento, -a [deskon'tento, a] ADJ
dissatisfied ▸ NM dissatisfaction, discontent

descontrol [deskon'trol] NM (*fam*) lack of
control

descontrolado, -a [deskontro'laðo, a] ADJ
uncontrolled

descontrolarse [deskontro'larse] /**1a**/ VR
(*persona*) to lose control

desconvenir [deskombe'nir] /**3s**/ VI (*personas*)
to disagree; (*no corresponder*) not to fit; (*no
convenir*) to be inconvenient

desconvocar [deskombo'kar] /**1g**/ VT to call
off

descorazonar [deskoraθo'nar] /**1a**/ VT to
discourage, dishearten; **descorazonarse** VR
to get discouraged, lose heart

descorchador [deskortʃaˈðor] NM corkscrew

descorchar [deskorˈtʃar] /**1a**/ VT to uncork, open

descorrer [deskoˈrrer] /**2a**/ VT (*cortina, cerrojo*) to draw back; (*velo*) to remove

descortés [deskorˈtes] ADJ (*mal educado*) discourteous; (*grosero*) rude

descortesía [deskorteˈsia] NF discourtesy; (*grosería*) rudeness

descoser [deskoˈser] /**2a**/ VT to unstitch; **descoserse** VR to come apart (at the seams); (*fam: descubrir un secreto*) to blurt out a secret; **descoserse de risa** to split one's sides laughing

descosido, -a [deskoˈsiðo, a] ADJ (*costura*) unstitched; (*desordenado*) disjointed ▸ NM: **como un ~** (*obrar*) wildly; (*beber, comer*) to excess; (*estudiar*) like mad

descoyuntar [deskojunˈtar] /**1a**/ VT (*Anat*) to dislocate; (*hechos*) to twist; **descoyuntarse** VR: **descoyuntarse un hueso** (*Anat*) to put a bone out of joint; **descoyuntarse de risa** (*fam*) to split one's sides laughing; **estar descoyuntado** (*persona*) to be double-jointed

descrédito [desˈkreðito] NM discredit; **caer en ~** to fall into disrepute; **ir en ~ de** to be to the discredit of

descreído, -a [deskreˈiðo, a] ADJ (*incrédulo*) incredulous; (*falto de fe*) unbelieving

descremado, -a [deskreˈmaðo, a] ADJ skimmed

descremar [deskreˈmar] /**1a**/ VT (*leche*) to skim

describir [deskriˈβir] /**3a**/ VT to describe

descripción [deskripˈθjon] NF description

descrito [desˈkrito] PP de **describir**

descuajar [deskwaˈxar] /**1a**/ VT (*disolver*) to melt; (*planta*) to pull out by the roots; (*extirpar*) to eradicate, wipe out; (*desanimar*) to dishearten

descuajaringarse [deskwaxarinˈgarse] /**1h**/ VR to fall to bits

descuajaringue etc [deskwaxaˈringe] VB ver **descuajaringarse**

descuartice etc [deskwarˈtiθe] VB ver **descuartizar**

descuartizar [deskwartiˈθar] /**1f**/ VT (*animal*) to carve up, cut up; (*fig: hacer pedazos*) to tear apart

descubierto, -a [deskuˈβjerto, a] PP de **descubrir** ▸ ADJ uncovered, bare; (*persona*) bare-headed; (*cielo*) clear; (*coche*) open; (*campo*) treeless ▸ NM (*lugar*) open space; (*Com: en el presupuesto*) shortage; (: *bancario*) overdraft; **al ~** in the open; **poner al ~** to lay bare; **quedar al ~** to be exposed; **estar en ~** to be overdrawn

descubridor, a [deskuβriˈðor, a] NM/F discoverer

descubrimiento [deskuβriˈmjento] NM (*hallazgo*) discovery; (*de criminal, fraude*) detection; (*revelación*) revelation; (*de secreto etc*) disclosure; (*de estatua etc*) unveiling

descubrir [deskuˈβrir] /**3a**/ VT to discover, find; (*petróleo*) to strike; (*inaugurar*) to unveil; (*vislumbrar*) to detect; (*sacar a la luz: crimen*) to bring to light; (*revelar*) to reveal, show; (*poner al descubierto*) to expose to view; (*naipes*) to lay down; (*quitar la tapa de*) to uncover; (*cacerola*) to take the lid off; (*enterarse de: causa, solución*) to find out; (*divisar*) to see, make out; (*delatar*) to give away, betray; **descubrirse** VR to reveal o.s.; (*quitarse sombrero*) to take off one's hat; (*confesar*) to confess; (*fig: salir a la luz*) to come out o to light

descuelga etc [desˈkwelɣa], **descuelgue** etc [desˈkwelɣe] VB ver **descolgar**

descuelle etc [desˈkweʎe] VB ver **descollar**

descuento [desˈkwento] VB ver **descontar** ▸ NM discount; **~ del 3%** 3% off; **con ~** at a discount; **~ por pago al contado** (*Com*) cash discount; **~ por volumen de compras** (*Com*) volume discount

descuidado, -a [deskwiˈðaðo, a] ADJ (*sin cuidado*) careless; (*desordenado*) untidy; (*olvidadizo*) forgetful; (*dejado*) neglected; (*desprevenido*) unprepared

descuidar [deskwiˈðar] /**1a**/ VT (*dejar*) to neglect; (*olvidar*) to overlook ▸ VI, **descuidarse** VR (*distraerse*) to be careless; (*estar desaliñado*) to let o.s. go; (*desprevenirse*) to drop one's guard; **¡descuida!** don't worry!

descuido [desˈkwiðo] NM (*dejadez*) carelessness; (*olvido*) negligence; (*un descuido*) oversight; **al ~** casually; (*sin cuidado*) carelessly; **al menor ~** if my etc attention wanders for a minute; **con ~** thoughtlessly; **por ~** by an oversight

(PALABRA CLAVE)

desde [ˈdesðe] PREP **1** (*lugar*) from; **desde Burgos hasta mi casa hay 30 km** it's 30 km from Burgos to my house; **desde lejos** from a distance

2 (*posición*): **hablaba desde el balcón** she was speaking from the balcony

3 (*tiempo: + adv, n*): **desde ahora** from now on; **desde entonces/la boda** since then/the wedding; **desde niño** since I etc was a child; **desde tres años atrás** since three years ago

4 (*tiempo: + vb*) since; for; **nos conocemos desde 1988/desde hace 20 años** we've known each other since 1988/for 20 years; **no lo veo desde 2005/desde hace 5 años** I haven't seen him since 2005/for 5 years; **¿desde cuándo vives aquí?** how long have you lived here?

5 (*gama*): **desde los más lujosos hasta los**

más económicos from the most luxurious to the most reasonably priced
6: **desde luego (que no)** of course (not) ► CONJ: **desde que: desde que recuerdo** for as long as I can remember; **desde que llegó no ha salido** he hasn't been out since he arrived

desdecir [desðe'θir] /**3o**/ VI: ~ **de** (*no merecer*) to be unworthy of; (*no corresponder*) to clash with; **desdecirse** VR: **desdecirse de** to go back on

desdén [des'ðen] NM scorn

desdentado, -a [desðen'taðo, a] ADJ toothless

desdeñable [desðe'naβle] ADJ contemptible; **nada** ~ far from negligible, considerable

desdeñar [desðe'nar] /**1a**/ VT (*despreciar*) to scorn

desdeñoso, -a [desðe'noso, a] ADJ scornful

desdibujar [desðiβu'xar] /**1a**/ VT to blur (the outlines of); **desdibujarse** VR to get blurred, fade (away); **el recuerdo se ha desdibujado** the memory has become blurred

desdicha [des'ðitʃa] NF (*desgracia*) misfortune; (*infelicidad*) unhappiness

desdichado, -a [desði'tʃaðo, a] ADJ (*sin suerte*) unlucky; (*infeliz*) unhappy; (*día*) ill-fated ► NM/F (*pobre desgraciado*) poor devil

desdicho, -a [des'ðitʃo, a] PP *de* **desdecir** ► NF (*desgracia*) misfortune; (*infelicidad*) unhappiness

desdiciendo *etc* [desði'θjendo] VB *ver* **desdecir**

desdiga *etc* [des'ðiɣa], **desdije** *etc* [des'dixe] VB *ver* **desdecir**

desdoblado, -a [desðo'βlaðo, a] ADJ (*personalidad*) split

desdoblar [desðo'βlar] /**1a**/ VT (*extender*) to spread out; (*desplegar*) to unfold

deseable [dese'aβle] ADJ desirable

desear [dese'ar] /**1a**/ VT to want, desire, wish for; **¿qué desea la señora?** (*tienda etc*) what can I do for you, madam?; **estoy deseando que esto termine** I'm longing for this to finish

desecar [dese'kar] /**1g**/ VT, **desecarse** VR to dry up

desechable [dese'tʃaβle] ADJ (*envase etc*) disposable

desechar [dese'tʃar] /**1a**/ VT (*basura*) to throw out o away; (*ideas*) to reject, discard; (*miedo*) to cast aside; (*plan*) to drop

desecho [de'setʃo] NM (*desprecio*) contempt; (*lo peor*) dregs pl; **desechos** NMPL rubbish sg, waste sg; **de** ~ (*hierro*) scrap; (*producto*) waste; (*ropa*) cast-off

desembalar [desemba'lar] /**1a**/ VT to unpack

desembarace *etc* [desemba'raθe] VB *ver* **desembarazar**

desembarazado, -a [desembara'θaðo, a] ADJ (*libre*) clear, free; (*desenvuelto*) free and easy

desembarazar [desembara'θar] /**1f**/ VT (*desocupar*) to clear; (*desenredar*) to free; **desembarazarse** VR: **desembarazarse de** to free o.s. of, get rid of

desembarazo [desemba'raθo] NM (*acto*) clearing; (*AM: parto*) birth; (*desenfado*) ease

desembarcadero [desembarka'ðero] NM quay

desembarcar [desembar'kar] /**1g**/ VT (*personas*) to land; (*mercancías etc*) to unload ► VI (*de barco, avión*) to disembark

desembarco [desem'barko] NM landing

desembargar [desembar'ɣar] /**1h**/ VT (*gen*) to free; (*Jur*) to remove the embargo on

desembargue *etc* [desem'βarɣe] VB *ver* **desembargar**

desembarque *etc* [desem'barke] VB *ver* **desembarcar** ► NM disembarkation; (*de pasajeros*) landing; (*de mercancías*) unloading

desembocadura [desemboka'ðura] NF (*de río*) mouth; (*de calle*) opening

desembocar [desembo'kar] /**1g**/ VI: ~ **en** to flow into; (*fig*) to result in

desemboce *etc* [desem'boθe] VB *ver* **desembozar**

desembolsar [desembol'sar] /**1a**/ VT (*pagar*) to pay out; (*gastar*) to lay out

desembolso [desem'bolso] NM payment

desemboque *etc* [desem'boke] VB *ver* **desembocar**

desembozar [desembo'θar] /**1f**/ VT to unmask

desembragar [desembra'ɣar] /**1h**/ VT (*Tec*) to disengage, release ► VI (*Auto*) to declutch

desembrague *etc* [desem'βraɣe] VB *ver* **desembragar**

desembrollar [desembro'ʎar] /**1a**/ VT (*madeja*) to unravel; (*asunto, malentendido*) to sort out

desembuchar [desembu'tʃar] /**1a**/ VT to disgorge; (*fig*) to come out with ► VI (*confesar*) to spill the beans (*fam*) ► **¡desembucha!** out with it!

desemejante [deseme'xante] ADJ dissimilar; ~ **de** different from, unlike

desemejanza [deseme'xanθa] NF dissimilarity

desempacar [desempa'kar] /**1g**/ VT (*esp AM*) to unpack

desempañar [desempa'nar] /**1a**/ VT (*cristal*) to clean, demist

desempaque *etc* [desem'pake] VB *ver* **desempacar**

desempaquetar [desempake'tar] /**1a**/ VT (*regalo*) to unwrap; (*mercancía*) to unpack

desempatar [desempa'tar] /**1a**/ vi to break a tie; **volvieron a jugar para ~** they held a play-off

desempate [desem'pate] nm (*Fútbol*) replay, play-off; (*Tenis*) tie-break(er)

desempeñar [desempe'ɲar] /**1a**/ vt (*cargo*) to hold; (*papel*) to play; (*deber, función*) to perform, carry out; (*lo empeñado*) to redeem; **desempeñarse** vr to get out of debt; **~ un papel** (*fig*) to play (a role)

desempeño [desem'peɲo] nm occupation; (*de lo empeñado*) redeeming; **de mucho ~** very capable

desempleado, -a [desemple'aðo, a] adj unemployed, out of work ▶ nm/f unemployed person

desempleo [desem'pleo] nm unemployment

desempolvar [desempol'βar] /**1a**/ vt (*muebles etc*) to dust; (*lo olvidado*) to revive

desencadenar [desenkaðe'nar] /**1a**/ vt to unchain; (*ira*) to unleash; (*provocar*) to cause, set off; **desencadenarse** vr to break loose; (*tormenta*) to burst; (*guerra*) to break out; **se desencadenó una lucha violenta** a violent struggle ensued

desencajar [desenka'xar] /**1a**/ vt (*hueso*) to put out of joint; (*mandíbula*) to dislocate; (*mecanismo, pieza*) to disconnect, disengage

desencantar [desenkan'tar] /**1a**/ vt to disillusion, disenchant

desencanto [desen'kanto] nm disillusionment, disenchantment

desenchufar [desentʃu'far] /**1a**/ vt to unplug, disconnect

desenfadado, -a [desenfa'ðaðo, a] adj (*desenvuelto*) uninhibited; (*descarado*) forward; (*en el vestir*) casual

desenfado [desen'faðo] nm (*libertad*) freedom; (*comportamiento*) free and easy manner; (*descaro*) forwardness; (*desenvoltura*) self-confidence

desenfocado, -a [desenfo'kaðo, a] adj (*Foto*) out of focus

desenfrenado, -a [desenfre'naðo, a] adj (*descontrolado*) uncontrolled; (*inmoderado*) unbridled

desenfrenarse [desenfre'narse] /**1a**/ vr (*persona: desmandarse*) to lose all self-control; (*multitud*) to run riot; (*tempestad*) to burst; (*viento*) to rage

desenfreno [desen'freno] nm (*vicio*) wildness; (*falta de control*) lack of self-control; (*de pasiones*) unleashing

desenganchar [desengan'tʃar] /**1a**/ vt (*gen*) to unhook; (*Ferro*) to uncouple; (*Tec*) to disengage

desengañar [desenga'ɲar] /**1a**/ vt to disillusion; (*abrir los ojos a*) to open the eyes of; **desengañarse** vr to become disillusioned; **¡desengáñate!** don't you believe it!

desengaño [desen'gaɲo] nm disillusionment; (*decepción*) disappointment; (*sufrir un ~ amoroso* to be disappointed in love

desengrasar [desengra'sar] /**1a**/ vt to degrease

desenlace *etc* [desen'laθe] vb ver **desenlazar**
▶ nm outcome; (*Lit*) ending

desenlazar [desenla'θar] /**1f**/ vt (*desatar*) to untie; (*problema*) to solve; (*aclarar: asunto*) to unravel; **desenlazarse** vr (*desatarse*) to come undone; (*Lit*) to end

desenmarañar [desenmara'ɲar] /**1a**/ vt (*fig*) to unravel

desenmascarar [desenmaska'rar] /**1a**/ vt to unmask, expose

desenredar [desenre'ðar] /**1a**/ vt (*pelo*) to untangle; (*problema*) to sort out

desenrollar [desenro'ʎar] /**1a**/ vt to unroll, unwind

desenroscar [desenros'kar] /**1g**/ vt (*tornillo etc*) to unscrew

desenrosque *etc* [desen'roske] vb ver **desenroscar**

desentenderse [desenten'derse] /**2g**/ vr: **~ de** to pretend not to know about; (*apartarse*) to have nothing to do with

desentendido, -a [desenten'diðo, a] adj: **hacerse el ~** to pretend not to notice; **se hizo el ~** he didn't take the hint

desenterrar [desente'rrar] /**1j**/ vt to exhume; (*tesoro, fig*) to unearth, dig up

desentierre *etc* [desen'tjerre] vb ver **desenterrar**

desentonar [desento'nar] /**1a**/ vi (*Mus*) to sing (*o play*) out of tune; (*no encajar*) to be out of place; (*color*) to clash

desentorpecer [desentorpe'θer] /**2d**/ vt (*miembro*) to stretch; (*fam: persona*) to polish up

desentorpezca *etc* [desentor'peθka] vb ver **desentorpecer**

desentrañar [desentra'ɲar] /**1a**/ vt (*misterio*) to unravel

desentrenado, -a [desentre'naðo, a] adj out of training

desentumecer [desentume'θer] /**2d**/ vt (*pierna etc*) to stretch; (*Deporte*) to loosen up

desentumezca *etc* [desentu'meθka] vb ver **desentumecer**

desenvainar [desembai'nar] /**1a**/ vt (*espada*) to draw, unsheathe

desenvoltura [desembol'tura] nf (*libertad, gracia*) ease; (*descaro*) free and easy manner; (*al hablar*) fluency

desenvolver [desembol'βer] /**2h**/ vt (*paquete*) to unwrap; (*fig*) to develop; **desenvolverse**

VR (*desarrollarse*) to unfold, develop; (*suceder*) to go off; (*prosperar*) to prosper; (*arreglárselas*) to cope

desenvolvimiento [desembolβi'mjento] NM (*desarrollo*) development; (*de idea*) exposition

desenvuelto, -a [desem'bwelto, a] PP *de* **desenvolver** ▸ ADJ (*suelto*) easy; (*desenfadado*) confident; (*al hablar*) fluent; (*pey*) forward

desenvuelva *etc* [desem'buelβa] VB *ver* **desenvolver**

deseo [de'seo] NM desire, wish; ~ **de saber** thirst for knowledge; **buen** ~ good intentions *pl*; **arder en deseos de algo** to yearn for sth

deseoso, -a [dese'oso, a] ADJ: **estar** ~ **de hacer** to be anxious to do

deseque *etc* [de'seke] VB *ver* **desecar**

desequilibrado, -a [desekili'βraðo, a] ADJ unbalanced ▸ NM/F unbalanced person; ~ **mental** mentally disturbed person

desequilibrar [desekili'βrar] /1a/ VT (*mente*) to unbalance; (*objeto*) to throw out of balance; (*persona*) to throw off balance

desequilibrio [deseki'liβrio] NM (*mental*) unbalance; (*entre cantidades*) imbalance; (*Med*) unbalanced mental condition

desertar [deser'tar] /1a/ VT (*Jur: derecho de apelación*) to forfeit ▸ VI to desert; ~ **de sus deberes** to neglect one's duties

desértico, -a [de'sertiko, a] ADJ desert *cpd*; (*vacío*) deserted

desertor, a [deser'tor, a] NM/F deserter

desesperación [desespera'θjon] NF desperation, despair; (*irritación*) fury; **es una** ~ it's maddening; **es una ~ tener que ...** it's infuriating to have to ...

desesperado, -a [desespe'raðo, a] ADJ (*persona: sin esperanza*) desperate; (*caso, situación*) hopeless; (*esfuerzo*) furious ▸ NM: **como un** ~ like mad ▸ NF: **hacer algo a la desesperada** to do sth as a last resort *o* in desperation

desesperance *etc* [desespe'ranθe] VB *ver* **desesperanzar**

desesperante [desespe'rante] ADJ (*exasperante*) infuriating; (*persona*) hopeless

desesperanzar [desesperan'θar] /1f/ VT to drive to despair; **desesperanzarse** VR to lose hope, despair

desesperar [desespe'rar] /1a/ VT to drive to despair; (*exasperar*) to drive to distraction ▸ VI: ~ **de** to despair of; **desesperarse** VR to despair, lose hope

desespero [deses'pero] NM (*AM*) despair

desestabilice *etc* [desestaβi'liθe] VB *ver* **desestabilizar**

desestabilizar [desestaβili'θar] /1f/ VT to destabilize

desestimar [desesti'mar] /1a/ VT (*menospreciar*) to have a low opinion of; (*rechazar*) to reject

desfachatez [desfatʃa'teθ] NF (*insolencia*) impudence; (*descaro*) rudeness

desfalco [des'falko] NM embezzlement

desfallecer [desfaʎe'θer] /2d/ VI (*perder las fuerzas*) to become weak; (*desvanecerse*) to faint

desfallecido, -a [desfaʎe'θiðo, a] ADJ (*débil*) weak

desfallezca *etc* [desfa'ʎeθka] VB *ver* **desfallecer**

desfasado, -a [desfa'saðo, a] ADJ (*anticuado*) old-fashioned; (*Tec*) out of phase

desfasar [desfa'sar] /1a/ VT to phase out

desfase [des'fase] NM (*diferencia*) gap

desfavorable [desfaβo'raβle] ADJ unfavourable

desfavorecer [desfaβore'θer] /2d/ VT (*sentar mal*) not to suit

desfavorezca *etc* [desfaβo'reθka] VB *ver* **desfavorecer**

desfiguración [desfiɣura'θjon] NF, **desfiguramiento** [desfiɣura'mjento] NM (*de persona*) disfigurement; (*de monumento*) defacement; (*Foto*) blurring

desfigurar [desfiɣu'rar] /1a/ VT (*cara*) to disfigure; (*cuerpo*) to deform; (*cuadro, monumento*) to deface; (*Foto*) to blur; (*sentido*) to twist; (*suceso*) to misrepresent

desfiladero [desfila'ðero] NM gorge, defile

desfilar [desfi'lar] /1a/ VI to parade; **desfilaron ante el general** they marched past the general

desfile [des'file] NM procession; (*Mil*) parade; ~ **de modelos** fashion show

desflorar [desflo'rar] /1a/ VT (*mujer*) to deflower; (*arruinar*) to tarnish; (*asunto*) to touch on

desfogar [desfo'ɣar] /1h/ VT (*fig*) to vent ▸ VI (*Naut: tormenta*) to burst; **desfogarse** VR (*fig*) to let off steam

desfogue *etc* [des'foɣe] VB *ver* **desfogar**

desgajar [desɣa'xar] /1a/ VT (*arrancar*) to tear off; (*romper*) to break off; (*naranja*) to split into segments; **desgajarse** VR to come off

desgana [des'ɣana] NF (*falta de apetito*) loss of appetite; (*renuencia*) unwillingness; **hacer algo a** ~ to do sth unwillingly

desganado, -a [desɣa'naðo, a] ADJ: **estar** ~ (*sin apetito*) to have no appetite; (*sin entusiasmo*) to have lost interest

desgañitarse [desɣaɲi'tarse] /1a/ VR to shout o.s. hoarse

desgarbado, -a [desɣar'βaðo, a] ADJ (*sin gracia*) clumsy, ungainly

desgarrador, a [desɣarra'ðor, a] ADJ heartrending

desgarrar [desɣa'rrar] /1a/ VT to tear (up); (*fig*) to shatter

desgarro [des'ɣarro] NM (*en tela*) tear; (*aflicción*) grief; (*descaro*) impudence

desgastar [desɣas'tar] /**1a**/ VT (*deteriorar*) to wear away *o* down; (*estropear*) to spoil; **desgastarse** VR to get worn out

desgaste [des'ɣaste] NM wear (and tear); (*de roca*) erosion; (*de cuerda*) fraying; (*de metal*) corrosion; ~ **económico** drain on one's resources

desglosar [desɣlo'sar] /**1a**/ VT to detach; (*factura*) to break down

desgobernar [desɣoβer'nar] /**1j**/ VB (*Pol*) to misgovern, misrule; (*asunto*) to handle badly; (*Anat*) to dislocate

desgobierno *etc* [desɣo'βjerno] VB *ver* **desgobernar** ▸ NM (*Pol*) misgovernment, misrule

desgracia [des'ɣraθja] NF misfortune; (*accidente*) accident; (*vergüenza*) disgrace; (*contratiempo*) setback; **por** ~ unfortunately; **en el accidente no hay que lamentar desgracias personales** there were no casualties in the accident; **caer en** ~ to fall from grace; **tener la** ~ **de** to be unlucky enough to

desgraciadamente [desɣraθjaða'mente] ADV unfortunately

desgraciado, -a [desɣra'θjaðo, a] ADJ (*sin suerte*) unlucky, unfortunate; (*miserable*) wretched; (*infeliz*) miserable ▸ NM/F (*malvado*) swine; (*infeliz*) poor creature; **¡esa radio desgraciada!** (*esp Am*) that lousy radio!

desgraciar [desɣra'θjar] /**1b**/ VT (*estropear*) to spoil; (*ofender*) to displease

desgranar [desɣra'nar] /**1a**/ VT (*trigo*) to thresh; (*guisantes*) to shell; ~ **un racimo** to pick the grapes from a bunch; ~ **mentiras** to come out with a string of lies

desgravación [desɣraβa'θjon] NF (*Com*): ~ **de impuestos** tax relief; ~ **personal** personal allowance

desgravar [desɣra'βar] /**1a**/ VT (*producto*) to reduce the tax *o* duty on

desgreñado, -a [desɣre'ɲaðo, a] ADJ dishevelled

desguace [des'ɣwaθe] NM (*de coches*) scrapping; (*lugar*) scrapyard

desguazar [desɣwa'θar] /**1f**/ VT (*coche*) to scrap

deshabitado, -a [desaβi'taðo, a] ADJ uninhabited

deshabitar [desaβi'tar] /**1a**/ VT (*casa*) to leave empty; (*despoblar*) to depopulate

deshacer [desa'θer] /**2r**/ VT (*lo hecho*) to undo, unmake; (*proyectos: arruinar*) to spoil; (*casa*) to break up; (*Tec*) to take apart; (*enemigo*) to defeat; (*diluir*) to melt; (*contrato*) to break; (*intriga*) to solve; (*cama*) to strip; (*maleta*) to unpack; (*paquete*) to unwrap; (*nudo*) to untie; (*costura*) to unpick; **deshacerse** VR (*desatarse*) to come undone; (*estropearse*) to be spoiled; (*descomponerse*) to fall to pieces; (*disolverse*) to melt; (*despedazarse*) to come apart *o* undone; **deshacerse de** to get rid of; (*Com*) to dump, unload; **deshacerse en** (*cumplidos, elogios*) to be lavish with; **deshacerse en lágrimas** to burst into tears; **deshacerse por algo** to be crazy about sth

deshaga *etc* [de'saɣa], **desharé** *etc* [desa're] VB *ver* **deshacer**

desharrapado, -a [desarra'paðo, a] ADJ = **desarrapado**

deshecho, -a [de'setʃo, a] PP *de* **deshacer** ▸ ADJ (*lazo, nudo*) undone; (*roto*) smashed; (*despedazado*) in pieces; (*cama*) unmade; (*Med: persona*) weak, emaciated; (: *salud*) broken; **estoy** ~ I'm shattered

deshelar [dese'lar] /**1j**/ VT (*cañería*) to thaw; (*heladera*) to defrost

desheredar [desere'ðar] /**1a**/ VT to disinherit

deshice *etc* [de'siθe] VB *ver* **deshacer**

deshidratación [desiðrata'θjon] NF dehydration

deshidratar [desiðra'tar] /**1a**/ VT to dehydrate

deshielo [des'jelo] VB *ver* **deshelar** ▸ NM thaw

deshilachar [desila'tʃar] /**1a**/ VT, **deshilacharse** VR to fray

deshilar [desi'lar] /**1a**/ VT (*tela*) to unravel

deshilvanado, -a [desilβa'naðo, a] ADJ (*fig*) disjointed, incoherent

deshinchar [desin'tʃar] /**1a**/ VT (*neumático*) to let down; (*herida etc*) to reduce (the swelling of); **deshincharse** VR (*neumático*) to go flat; (*hinchazón*) to go down

deshojar [deso'xar] /**1a**/ VT (*árbol*) to strip the leaves off; (*flor*) to pull the petals off; **deshojarse** VR to lose its leaves *etc*

deshollinar [desoʎi'nar] /**1a**/ VT (*chimenea*) to sweep

deshonesto, -a [deso'nesto, a] ADJ (*no honrado*) dishonest; (*indecente*) indecent

deshonor [deso'nor] NM dishonour, disgrace; (*un deshonor*) insult, affront

deshonra [de'sonra] NF (*deshonor*) dishonour; (*vergüenza*) shame

deshonrar [deson'rar] /**1a**/ VT to dishonour

deshonroso, -a [deson'roso, a] ADJ dishonourable, disgraceful

deshora [de'sora]: **a** ~ *adv* at the wrong time; (*llegar*) unexpectedly; (*acostarse*) at some unearthly hour

deshuesadero [deswesa'ðero] NM (*Am*) junkyard

deshuesar [deswe'sar] /**1a**/ VT (*carne*) to bone; (*fruta*) to stone

desidia [de'siðja] NF (*pereza*) idleness

desierto, -a [de'sjerto, a] ADJ (*casa, calle, negocio*) deserted; (*paisaje*) bleak ▶ NM desert

designación [desiɣna'θjon] NF (*para un cargo*) appointment; (*nombre*) designation

designar [desiɣ'nar] /**1a**/ VT (*nombrar*) to designate; (*indicar*) to fix

designio [de'siɣnjo] NM plan; **con el ~ de** with the intention of

desigual [desi'ɣwal] ADJ (*lucha*) unequal; (*diferente*) different; (*terreno*) uneven; (*tratamiento*) unfair; (*cambiadizo: tiempo*) changeable; (: *carácter*) unpredictable

desigualdad [desiɣwal'ðað] NF (*Econ, Pol*) inequality; (*de carácter, tiempo*) unpredictability; (*de escritura*) unevenness; (*de terreno*) roughness

desilusión [desilu'sjon] NF disillusionment; (*decepción*) disappointment

desilusionar [desilusjo'nar] /**1a**/ VT to disillusion; (*decepcionar*) to disappoint; **desilusionarse** VR to become disillusioned

desinencia [desi'nenθja] NF (*Ling*) ending

desinfectar [desinfek'tar] /**1a**/ VT to disinfect

desinfestar [desinfes'tar] /**1a**/ VT to decontaminate

desinflación [desinfla'θjon] NF (*Com*) disinflation

desinflar [desin'flar] /**1a**/ VT to deflate; **desinflarse** VR (*neumático*) to go down o flat

desinstalar [desinsta'lar] VT uninstall

desintegración [desinteɣra'θjon] NF disintegration; **~ nuclear** nuclear fission

desintegrar [desinte'ɣrar] /**1a**/ VT (*gen*) to disintegrate; (*átomo*) to split; (*grupo*) to break up; **desintegrarse** VR to disintegrate; to split; to break up

desinterés [desinte'res] NM (*desgana*) lack of interest; (*altruismo*) unselfishness

desinteresado, -a [desintere'saðo, a] ADJ (*imparcial*) disinterested; (*altruista*) unselfish

desintoxicar [desintoksi'kar] /**1g**/ VT to detoxify; **desintoxicarse** VR (*drogadicto*) to undergo detoxification; **desintoxicarse de** (*rutina, trabajo*) to get away from

desintoxique *etc* [desintok'sike] VB *ver* **desintoxicar**

desistir [desis'tir] /**3a**/ VI (*renunciar*) to stop, desist; **~ de** (*empresa*) to give up; (*derecho*) to waive

deslavazado, -a [deslaβa'θaðo, a] ADJ (*lacio*) limp; (*desteñido*) faded; (*insípido*) colourless; (*incoherente*) disjointed

desleal [desle'al] ADJ (*infiel*) disloyal; (*Com: competencia*) unfair

deslealtad [desleal'tað] NF disloyalty

desleído, -a [desle'iðo, a] ADJ weak, woolly

desleír [desle'ir] /**3l**/ VT (*líquido*) to dilute; (*sólido*) to dissolve

deslenguado, -a [deslen'gwaðo, a] ADJ (*grosero*) foul-mouthed

deslía *etc* [des'lia] VB *ver* **desleír**

desliar [des'ljar] /**1c**/ VT (*desatar*) to untie; (*paquete*) to open; **desliarse** VR to come undone

deslice *etc* [des'liθe] VB *ver* **deslizar**

desliendo *etc* [desli'endo] VB *ver* **desleír**

desligar [desli'ɣar] /**1h**/ VT (*desatar*) to untie, undo; (*separar*) to separate; **desligarse** VR (*de un compromiso*) to extricate o.s.

desligue *etc* [des'liɣe] VB *ver* **desligar**

deslindar [deslin'dar] /**1a**/ VT (*señalar las lindes de*) to mark out, fix the boundaries of; (*fig*) to define

desliz [des'liθ] NM (*fig*) lapse; **~ de lengua** slip of the tongue; **cometer un ~** to slip up

deslizar [desli'θar] /**1f**/ VT to slip, slide; **deslizarse** VR (*escurrirse: persona*) to slip, slide; (: *coche*) to skid; (*aguas mansas*) to flow gently; (*error*) to creep in; (*tiempo*) to pass; (*persona: irse*) to slip away; **deslizarse en un cuarto** to slip into a room

deslomar [deslo'mar] /**1a**/ VT (*romper el lomo de*) to break the back of; (*fig*) to wear out; **deslomarse** VR (*fig, fam*) to work one's guts out

deslucido, -a [deslu'θiðo, a] ADJ dull; (*torpe*) awkward, graceless; (*deslustrado*) tarnished; (*fracasado*) unsuccessful; **quedar ~** to make a poor impression

deslucir [deslu'θir] /**3f**/ VT (*deslustrar*) to tarnish; (*estropear*) to spoil, ruin; (*persona*) to discredit; **la lluvia deslució el acto** the rain ruined the ceremony

deslumbrar [deslum'brar] /**1a**/ VT (*con la luz*) to dazzle; (*cegar*) to blind; (*impresionar*) to dazzle; (*dejar perplejo a*) to puzzle, confuse

deslustrar [deslus'trar] /**1a**/ VT (*vidrio*) to frost; (*quitar lustre a*) to dull; (*reputación*) to sully

desluzca *etc* [des'luθka] VB *ver* **deslucir**

desmadrarse [desma'ðrarse] /**1a**/ VR (*fam: descontrolarse*) to run wild; (: *divertirse*) to let one's hair down

desmadre [des'maðre] NM (*fam: desorganización*) chaos; (: *jaleo*) commotion

desmán [des'man] NM (*exceso*) outrage; (*abuso de poder*) abuse

desmandarse [desman'darse] /**1a**/ VR (*portarse mal*) to behave badly; (*excederse*) to get out of hand; (*caballo*) to bolt

desmano [des'mano]: **a ~** *adv*: **me coge** o **pilla a ~** it's out of my way

desmantelar [desmante'lar] /**1a**/ VT (*deshacer*) to dismantle; (*casa*) to strip; (*organización*) to disband; (*Mil*) to raze; (*andamio*) to take down; (*Naut*) to unrig

desmaquillador [desmakiʎa'ðor] NM make-up remover

desmaquillarse [desmaki'ʎarse] /**1a**/ VR to take off one's make-up

desmarcarse [desmar'karse] /**1g**/ VR: ~ **de** (*Deporte*) to get clear of; (*fig*) to distance o.s. from

desmayado, -a [desma'jaðo, a] ADJ (*sin sentido*) unconscious; (*carácter*) dull; (*débil*) faint, weak; (*color*) pale

desmayar [desma'jar] /**1a**/ VI to lose heart; **desmayarse** VR (*Med*) to faint

desmayo [des'majo] NM (*Med: acto*) faint; (: *estado*) unconsciousness; (: *depresión*) dejection; (*de voz*) faltering; **sufrir un ~** to have a fainting fit

desmedido, -a [desme'ðiðo, a] ADJ excessive; (*ambición*) boundless

desmejorado, -a [desmexo'raðo, a] ADJ: **está muy desmejorada** (*Med*) she's not looking too well

desmejorar [desmexo'rar] /**1a**/ VT (*dañar*) to impair, spoil; (*Med*) to weaken

desmembración [desmembra'θjon] NF dismemberment; (*fig*) break-up

desmembrar [desmem'brar] /**1j**/ VT (*Med*) to dismember; (*fig*) to separate

desmemoriado, -a [desmemo'rjaðo, a] ADJ forgetful, absent-minded

desmentir [desmen'tir] /**3i**/ VT (*contradecir*) to contradict; (*refutar*) to deny; (*rumor*) to scotch ▶ VI: ~ **de** to refute; **desmentirse** VR to contradict o.s.

desmenuce *etc* [desme'nuθe] VB *ver* **desmenuzar**

desmenuzar [desmenu'θar] /**1f**/ VT (*deshacer*) to crumble; (*carne*) to chop; (*examinar*) to examine closely

desmerecer [desmere'θer] /**2d**/ VT to be unworthy of ▶ VI (*deteriorarse*) to deteriorate

desmerezca *etc* [desme'reθka] VB *ver* **desmerecer**

desmesurado, -a [desmesu'raðo, a] ADJ (*desmedido*) disproportionate; (*enorme*) enormous; (*ambición*) boundless; (*descarado*) insolent

desmiembre *etc* [des'mjembre] VB *ver* **desmembrar**

desmienta *etc* [des'mjenta] VB *ver* **desmentir**

desmigajar [desmiɣa'xar] /**1a**/, **desmigar** [desmi'ɣar] /**1h**/ VT to crumble

desmigue *etc* [des'miɣe] VB *ver* **desmigajar**

desmilitarice *etc* [desmilita'riθe] VB *ver* **desmilitarizar**

desmilitarizar [desmilitari'θar] /**1f**/ VT to demilitarize

desmintiendo *etc* [desmin'tjendo] VB *ver* **desmentir**

desmochar [desmo'tʃar] /**1a**/ VT (*árbol*) to lop; (*texto*) to cut, hack about

desmontable [desmon'taβle] ADJ (*que se quita*) detachable; (*en compartimientos*) sectional; (*que se puede plegar etc*) collapsible, folding

desmontar [desmon'tar] /**1a**/ VT (*deshacer*) to dismantle; (*motor*) to strip down; (*máquina*) to take apart; (*escopeta*) to uncock; (*tienda de campaña*) to take down; (*tierra*) to level; (*quitar los árboles a*) to clear; (*jinete*) to throw ▶ VI to dismount

desmonte [des'monte] NM (*de tierra*) levelling; (*de árboles*) clearing; (*terreno*) levelled ground; (*Ferro*) cutting

desmoralice *etc* [desmora'liθe] VB *ver* **desmoralizar**

desmoralizador, a [desmoraliθa'ðor, a] ADJ demoralizing

desmoralizar [desmorali'θar] /**1f**/ VT to demoralize

desmoronado, -a [desmoro'naðo, a] ADJ (*casa, edificio*) dilapidated

desmoronamiento [desmorona'mjento] NM (*tb fig*) crumbling

desmoronar [desmoro'nar] /**1a**/ VT to wear away, erode; **desmoronarse** VR (*edificio, dique*) to collapse; (*economía*) to decline

desmovilice *etc* [desmoβi'liθe] VB *ver* **desmovilizar**

desmovilizar [desmoβili'θar] /**1f**/ VT to demobilize

desnacionalización [desnaθjonaliθa'θjon] NF denationalization

desnacionalizado, -a [desnaθjonali'θaðo, a] ADJ (*industria*) denationalized; (*persona*) stateless

desnatado, -a [desna'taðo, a] ADJ (*leche*) skimmed; (*yogur, queso*) low-fat

desnatar [desna'tar] /**1a**/ VT (*leche*) to skim; **leche sin ~** whole milk

desnaturalice *etc* [desnatura'liθe] VB *ver* **desnaturalizar**

desnaturalizado, -a [desnaturali'θaðo, a] ADJ (*persona*) unnatural; **alcohol ~** methylated spirits

desnaturalizar [desnaturali'θar] /**1f**/ VT (*Química*) to denature; (*corromper*) to pervert; (*sentido de algo*) to distort; **desnaturalizarse** VR (*perder la nacionalidad*) to give up one's nationality

desnivel [desni'βel] NM (*de terreno*) unevenness; (*Pol*) inequality; (*diferencia*) difference

desnivelar [desniβe'lar] /**1a**/ VT (*terreno*) to make uneven; (*fig: desequilibrar*) to unbalance; (*balanza*) to tip

desnuclearizado, -a [desnukleari'θaðo, a] ADJ: **región desnuclearizada** nuclear-free zone

desnudar [desnu'ðar] /**1a**/ VT (*desvestir*) to undress; (*despojar*) to strip; **desnudarse** VR (*desvestirse*) to get undressed

desnudez [desnu'ðeθ] NF (*de persona*) nudity; (*fig*) bareness

desnudo, -a [des'nuðo, a] ADJ (*cuerpo*) naked; (*árbol, brazo*) bare; (*paisaje*) flat; (*estilo*) unadorned; (*verdad*) plain ▶ NM nude; **~ de** devoid o bereft of; **la retrató al ~** he painted her in the nude; **poner al ~** to lay bare

desnutrición [desnutri'θjon] NF malnutrition

desnutrido, -a [desnu'triðo, a] ADJ undernourished

desobedecer [desoβeðe'θer] /**2d**/ VT, VI to disobey

desobedezca *etc* [desoβe'ðeθka] VB *ver* **desobedecer**

desobediencia [desoβe'ðjenθja] NF disobedience

desobediente [desoβe'ðjente] ADJ disobedient

desocupación [desokupa'θjon] NF (*AM*) unemployment

desocupado, -a [desoku'paðo, a] ADJ at leisure; (*desempleado*) unemployed; (*deshabitado*) empty, vacant

desocupar [desoku'par] /**1a**/ VT to vacate; **desocuparse** VR (*quedar libre*) to be free; **se ha desocupado aquella mesa** that table's free now

desodorante [desoðo'rante] NM deodorant

desoiga *etc* [de'soiɣa] VB *ver* **desoír**

desoír [deso'ir] /**3p**/ VT to ignore, disregard

desolación [desola'θjon] NF (*de lugar*) desolation; (*fig*) grief

desolar [deso'lar] /**1a**/ VT to ruin, lay waste

desollar [deso'ʎar] /**1l**/ VT (*quitar la piel a*) to skin; (*criticar*): **~ vivo a** to criticize unmercifully

desorbitado, -a [desorβi'taðo, a] ADJ (*excesivo: ambición*) boundless; (*: deseos*) excessive; (*: precio*) exorbitant; **con los ojos desorbitados** pop-eyed

desorbitar [desorβi'tar] /**1a**/ VT (*exagerar*) to exaggerate; (*interpretar mal*) to misinterpret; **desorbitarse** VR (*persona*) to lose one's sense of proportion; (*asunto*) to get out of hand

desorden [de'sorðen] NM confusion; (*de casa, cuarto*) mess; (*político*) disorder; **desórdenes** NMPL (*alborotos*) disturbances; (*excesos*) excesses; **en ~** (*gente*) in confusion

desordenado, -a [desorðe'naðo, a] ADJ (*habitación, persona*) untidy; (*objetos revueltos*) in a mess, jumbled; (*conducta*) disorderly

desordenar [desorðe'nar] /**1a**/ VT (*gen*) to disarrange; (*pelo*) to mess up; (*cuarto*) to make a mess in; (*causar confusión a*) to throw into confusion

desorganice *etc* [desorɣa'niθe] VB *ver* **desorganizar**

desorganización [desorɣaniθa'θjon] NF (*de persona*) disorganization; (*en empresa, oficina*) disorder, chaos

desorganizar [desorɣani'θar] /**1f**/ VT to disorganize

desorientar [desorjen'tar] /**1a**/ VT (*extraviar*) to mislead; (*confundir, desconcertar*) to confuse; **desorientarse** VR (*perderse*) to lose one's way

desovar [deso'βar] /**1l**/ VI (*peces*) to spawn; (*insectos*) to lay eggs

desoyendo *etc* [deso'jendo] VB *ver* **desoír**

despabilado, -a [despaβi'laðo, a] ADJ (*despierto*) wide-awake; (*fig*) alert, sharp

despabilar [despaβi'lar] /**1a**/ VT (*despertar*) to wake up; (*fig: persona*) to liven up; (*trabajo*) to get through quickly ▶ VI, **despabilarse** VR to wake up; (*fig*) to get a move on

despachar [despa'tʃar] /**1a**/ VT (*negocio*) to do, complete; (*resolver: problema*) to settle; (*: correspondencia*) to deal with; (*fam: comida*) to polish off; (*: bebida*) to knock back; (*enviar*) to send, dispatch; (*vender*) to sell, deal in; (*Com: cliente*) to attend to; (*: billete*) to issue; (*mandar ir*) to send away ▶ VI (*decidirse*) to get things settled; (*apresurarse*) to hurry up; **despacharse** VR to finish off; (*apresurarse*) to hurry up; **despacharse de algo** to get rid of sth; **despacharse a su gusto con algn** to give sb a piece of one's mind; **¿quién despacha?** is anybody serving?

despacho [des'patʃo] NM (*oficina*) office; (*: en una casa*) study; (*de paquetes*) dispatch; (*Com: venta*) sale (of goods); (*: comunicación*) message; **~ de billetes** o (*AM*) **boletos** booking office; **~ de localidades** box office; **géneros sin ~** unsaleable goods; **tener buen ~** to find a ready sale

despachurrar [despatʃu'rrar] /**1a**/ VT (*aplastar*) to crush; (*persona*) to flatten

despacio [des'paθjo] ADV (*lentamente*) slowly; (*esp AM: en voz baja*) softly; **¡~!** take it easy!

despacito [despa'θito] ADV (*fam*) slowly; (*suavemente*) softly

despampanante [despampa'nante] ADJ (*fam: chica*) stunning

desparejado, -a [despare'xaðo, a] ADJ odd

desparpajo [despar'paxo] NM (*desenvoltura*) self-confidence; (*pey*) nerve

desparramar [desparra'mar] /**1a**/ VT (*esparcir*) to scatter; (*líquido*) to spill

despatarrarse [despata'rrarse] /**1a**/ VR (*abrir las piernas*) to open one's legs wide; (*caerse*) to tumble; (*fig*) to be flabbergasted

despavorido, -a [despaβo'riðo, a] ADJ terrified

despecho [des'petʃo] NM spite; **a ~ de** in spite of; **por ~** out of (sheer) spite

despectivo, -a [despek'tiβo, a] ADJ (*despreciativo*) derogatory; (*Ling*) pejorative

despedace *etc* [despe'ðaθe] VB *ver* **despedazar**

despedazar [despeða'θar] /**1f**/ VT to tear to pieces

despedida [despe'ðiða] NF (*adiós*) goodbye, farewell; (*antes de viaje*) send-off; (*en carta*) closing formula; (*de obrero*) sacking; (*Inform*) logout; **cena/función de ~** farewell dinner/performance; **regalo de ~** parting gift; **~ de soltero/soltera** stag/hen party

despedir [despe'ðir] /**3k**/ VT (*visita*) to see off, show out; (*empleado*) to dismiss; (*inquilino*) to evict; (*objeto*) to hurl; (*olor etc*) to give out o off; **despedirse** VR (*dejar un empleo*) to give up one's job; (*Inform*) to log out o off; **despedirse de** to say goodbye to; **se despidieron** they said goodbye to each other

despegado, -a [despe'ɣaðo, a] ADJ (*separado*) detached; (*persona: poco afectuoso*) cold, indifferent ▶ NM/F: **es un ~** he has cut himself off from his family

despegar [despe'ɣar] /**1h**/ VT to unstick; (*sobre*) to open ▶ VI (*avión*) to take off; (*cohete*) to blast off; **despegarse** VR to come loose, come unstuck; **sin ~ los labios** without uttering a word

despego [des'peɣo] NM detachment

despegue *etc* [des'peɣe] VB *ver* **despegar** ▶ NM takeoff; (*de cohete*) blast-off

despeinado, -a [despei'naðo, a] ADJ dishevelled, unkempt

despeinar [despei'nar] /**1a**/ VT (*pelo*) to ruffle; **¡me has despeinado todo!** you've completely ruined my hairdo!

despejado, -a [despe'xaðo, a] ADJ (*lugar*) clear, free; (*cielo*) clear; (*persona*) wide-awake, bright

despejar [despe'xar] /**1a**/ VT (*gen*) to clear; (*misterio*) to clarify, clear up; (*Mat: incógnita*) to find ▶ VI (*el tiempo*) to clear; **despejarse** VR (*tiempo, cielo*) to clear (up); (*misterio*) to become clearer; (*cabeza*) to clear; **¡despejen!** (*moverse*) move along!; (*salirse*) everybody out!

despeje [des'pexe] NM (*Deporte*) clearance

despellejar [despeʎe'xar] /**1a**/ VT (*animal*) to skin; (*criticar*) to criticize unmercifully; (*fam: arruinar*) to fleece

despelotarse [despelo'tarse] /**1a**/ VR (*fam*) to strip off; (*fig*) to let one's hair down

despelote [despe'lote] NM (*AM fam: lío*) mess; **¡qué o vaya ~!** what a riot o laugh!

despenalizar [despenali'θar] /**1f**/ VT to decriminalize

despensa [des'pensa] NF (*armario*) larder; (*Naut*) storeroom; (*provisión de comestibles*) stock of food

despeñadero [despeɲa'ðero] NM (*Geo*) cliff, precipice

despeñar [despe'ɲar] /**1a**/ VT (*arrojar*) to fling down; **despeñarse** VR to fling o.s. down; (*caer*) to fall headlong; (*coche*) to tumble over

desperdiciar [desperði'θjar] /**1b**/ VT (*comida, tiempo*) to waste; (*oportunidad*) to throw away

desperdicio [desper'ðiθjo] NM (*despilfarro*) squandering; (*residuo*) waste; **desperdicios** NMPL (*basura*) rubbish *sg*, refuse *sg*, garbage *sg* (*US*); (*residuos*) waste *sg*; **desperdicios de cocina** kitchen scraps; **el libro no tiene ~** the book is excellent from beginning to end

desperdigar [desperði'ɣar] /**1h**/ VT (*esparcir*) to scatter; (*energía*) to dissipate; **desperdigarse** VR to scatter

desperdigue *etc* [desper'ðiɣe] VB *ver* **desperdigar**

desperece *etc* [despe'reθe] VB *ver* **desperezarse**

desperezarse [despere'θarse] /**1f**/ VR to stretch

desperfecto [desper'fekto] NM (*deterioro*) slight damage; (*defecto*) flaw, imperfection

despertador [desperta'ðor] NM alarm clock; **~ de viaje** travelling clock

despertar [desper'tar] /**1j**/ VT (*persona*) to wake up; (*recuerdos*) to revive; (*esperanzas*) to raise; (*sentimiento*) to arouse ▶ VI to awaken, wake up; **despertarse** VR to awaken, wake up ▶ NM awakening; **despertarse a la realidad** to wake up to reality

despiadado a [despja'ðaðo, a] ADJ (*ataque*) merciless; (*persona*) heartless

despido *etc* [des'piðo] VB *ver* **despedir** ▶ NM dismissal, sacking; **~ improcedente** o **injustificado** wrongful dismissal; **~ injusto** unfair dismissal; **~ libre** right to hire and fire; **~ voluntario** voluntary redundancy

despierto, -a [des'pjerto, a] PP *de* **despertar** ▶ ADJ awake; (*fig*) sharp, alert

despilfarrar [despilfa'rrar] /**1a**/ VT (*gen*) to waste; (*dinero*) to squander

despilfarro [despil'farro] NM (*derroche*) squandering; (*lujo desmedido*) extravagance

despintar [despin'tar] /**1a**/ VT (*quitar pintura a*) to take the paint off; (*hechos*) to distort ▶ VI: **A no despinta a B** A is in no way inferior to B; **despintarse** VR (*desteñir*) to fade

despiojar [despjo'xar] /**1a**/ VT to delouse

despistado, -a [despis'taðo, a] ADJ (*distraído*) vague, absent-minded; (*poco práctico*) unpractical; (*confuso*) confused; (*desorientado*) off the track ▶ NM/F (*persona distraída*) scatterbrain, absent-minded person

despistar [despis'tar] /**1a**/ VT to throw off the track o scent; (*fig*) to mislead, confuse; **despistarse** VR to take the wrong road; (*fig*) to become confused

despiste [des'piste] NM (*Auto etc*) swerve; (*error*) slip; (*distracción*) absent-mindedness; **un ~** a mistake *o* slip; **tiene un terrible ~** he's terribly absent-minded

desplace *etc* [des'plaθe] VB *ver* **desplazar**

desplante [des'plante] NM: **hacer un ~ a algn** to be rude to sb

desplazado, -a [despla'θaðo, a] ADJ (*pieza*) wrongly placed ▶ NM/F (*inadaptado*) misfit; **sentirse un poco ~** to feel rather out of place

desplazamiento [desplaθa'mjento] NM displacement; (*viaje*) journey; (*de opinión, votos*) shift, swing; (*Inform*) scrolling; **~ hacia arriba/abajo** (*Inform*) scroll up/down

desplazar [despla'θar] /1f/ VT (*gen*) to move; (*Física, Naut, Tec*) to displace; (*tropas*) to transfer; (*suplantar*) to take the place of; (*fig*) to oust; (*Inform*) to scroll; **desplazarse** VR (*persona, vehículo*) to travel, go; (*objeto*) to move, shift; (*votos, opinión*) to shift, swing

desplegable [desple'ɣaβle] ADJ (*libro, tb Inform*) pop-up

desplegar [desple'ɣar] /1h, 1j/ VT (*tela, papel*) to unfold, open out; (*bandera*) to unfurl; (*alas*) to spread; (*Mil*) to deploy; (*manifestar*) to display

desplegué [desple'ɣe], **despleguemos** *etc* [desple'ɣemos] VB *ver* **desplegar**

despliegue *etc* [des'pljeɣe] VB *ver* **desplegar** ▶ NM unfolding, opening; deployment, display

desplomarse [desplo'marse] /1a/ VR (*edificio, gobierno, persona*) to collapse; (*derrumbarse*) to topple over; (*precios*) to slump; **se ha desplomado el techo** the ceiling has fallen in

desplumar [desplu'mar] /1a/ VT (*ave*) to pluck; (*fam: estafar*) to fleece

despoblado, -a [despo'βlaðo, a] ADJ (*sin habitantes*) uninhabited; (*con pocos habitantes*) depopulated; (*con insuficientes habitantes*) underpopulated ▶ NM deserted spot

despojar [despo'xar] /1a/ VT (*a alguien: de sus bienes*) to divest of, deprive of; (*casa*) to strip, leave bare; (*de su cargo*) to strip of; **despojarse** VR (*desnudarse*) to undress; **despojarse de** (*ropa, hojas*) to shed; (*poderes*) to relinquish

despojo [des'poxo] NM (*acto*) plundering; (*objetos*) plunder, loot; **despojos** NMPL (*de ave, res*) offal *sg*

desposado, -a [despo'saðo, a] ADJ, NM/F newly-wed

desposar [despo'sar] /1a/ VT (*sacerdote: pareja*) to marry; **desposarse** VR (*casarse*) to marry, get married

desposeer [despose'er] /2e/ VT (*despojar*) to dispossess; **~ a algn de su autoridad** to strip sb of his authority

desposeído, -a [despose'iðo, a] NM/F: **los desposeídos** the have-nots

desposeyendo *etc* [despose'jendo] VB *ver* **desposeer**

desposorios [despo'sorjos] NMPL (*esponsales*) betrothal *sg*; (*boda*) marriage ceremony *sg*

déspota ['despota] NMF despot

despotismo [despo'tismo] NM despotism

despotricar [despotri'kar] /1g/ VI: **~ contra** to moan *o* complain about

despotrique *etc* [despo'trike] VB *ver* **despotricar**

despreciable [despre'θjaβle] ADJ (*moralmente*) despicable; (*objeto*) worthless; (*cantidad*) negligible

despreciar [despre'θjar] /1b/ VT (*desdeñar*) to despise, scorn; (*afrentar*) to slight

despreciativo, -a [despreθja'tiβo, a] ADJ (*observación, tono*) scornful, contemptuous; (*comentario*) derogatory

desprecio [des'preθjo] NM scorn, contempt; slight

desprender [despren'der] /2a/ VT (*soltar*) to loosen; (*separar*) to separate; (*desatar*) to unfasten; (*olor*) to give off; **desprenderse** VR (*botón: caerse*) to fall off; (*broche*) to come unfastened; (*olor, perfume*) to be given off; **desprenderse de** to follow from; **desprenderse de algo** (*ceder*) to give sth up; (*desembarazarse*) to get rid of sth; **desprenderse de algo que ...** to draw from sth that ...; **se desprende que ...** it transpires that ...

desprendido, -a [despren'dido, a] ADJ (*pieza*) loose; (*sin abrochar*) unfastened; (*desinteresado*) disinterested; (*generoso*) generous

desprendimiento [desprendi'mjento] NM (*gen*) loosening; (*generosidad*) disinterestedness; (*indiferencia*) detachment; (*de gas*) leak; (*de tierra, rocas*) landslide; **~ de retina** detachment of the retina

despreocupado, -a [despreoku'paðo, a] ADJ (*sin preocupación*) unworried, unconcerned; (*tranquilo*) nonchalant; (*en el vestir*) casual; (*negligente*) careless

despreocuparse [despreoku'parse] /1a/ VR to be carefree, not to worry; (*dejar de inquietarse*) to stop worrying; (*ser indiferente*) to be unconcerned; **~ de** to have no interest in

desprestigiar [despresti'xjar] /1b/ VT (*criticar*) to run down, disparage; (*desacreditar*) to discredit

desprestigio [despres'tixjo] NM (*denigración*) disparagement; (*impopularidad*) unpopularity

desprevenido, -a [despreβe'niðo, a] ADJ (*no preparado*) unprepared, unready; **coger** (*ESP*) *o* **agarrar** (*AM*) **a algn ~** to catch sb unawares

desproporción [despropor'θjon] NF disproportion, lack of proportion

desproporcionado, -a [desproporθjo'naðo, a] ADJ disproportionate, out of proportion

despropósito [despro'posito] NM (*salida de tono*) irrelevant remark; (*disparate*) piece of nonsense

desprovisto, -a [despro'βisto, a] ADJ: ~ **de** devoid of; **estar ~ de** to lack

después [des'pwes] ADV afterwards, later; (*desde entonces*) since (then); (*próximo paso*) next ▶ PREP: ~ **de** (*tiempo*) after, since; (*orden*) next (to) ▶ CONJ: ~ **(de) que** after; **poco ~** soon after; **un año ~** a year later; **~ se debatió el tema** next the matter was discussed; **~ de comer** after lunch; **~ de corregido el texto** after the text had been corrected; **~ de esa fecha** (*pasado*) since that date; (*futuro*) from o after that date; **~ de todo** after all; **~ de verlo** after seeing it, after I *etc* saw it; **mi nombre está ~ del tuyo** my name comes next to yours; **~ (de) que lo escribí** after o since I wrote it, after writing it

despuntar [despun'tar] /1a/ VT (*lápiz*) to blunt ▶ VI (*Bot: plantas*) to sprout; (: *flores*) to bud; (*alba*) to break; (*día*) to dawn; (*persona: descollar*) to stand out

desquiciado, -a [deski'θjaðo, a] ADJ deranged

desquiciar [deski'θjar] /1b/ VT (*puerta*) to take off its hinges; (*descomponer*) to upset; (*persona: turbar*) to disturb; (: *volver loco a*) to unhinge

desquitarse [deski'tarse] /1a/ VR to obtain satisfaction; (*Com*) to recover a debt; (*fig: vengarse de*) to get one's own back; **~ de una pérdida** to make up for a loss

desquite [des'kite] NM (*satisfacción*) satisfaction; (*venganza*) revenge

Dest. ABR = **destinatario**

destacado, -a [desta'kaðo, a] ADJ outstanding

destacamento [destaka'mento] NM (*Mil*) detachment

destacar [desta'kar] /1g/ VT (*Arte: hacer resaltar*) to make stand out; (: *subrayar*) to emphasize, point up; (*Mil*) to detach, detail; (*Inform*) to highlight ▶ VI (*resaltarse*) to stand out; (*persona*) to be outstanding o exceptional; **destacarse** VR (*resaltarse*) to stand out; (*persona*) to be outstanding o exceptional; **quiero ~ que...** I wish to emphasize that...; **~(se) contra** o **en** o **sobre** to stand out o be outlined against

destajo [des'taxo] NM: **a ~** (*por pieza*) by the job; (*con afán*) eagerly; **trabajar a ~** to do piecework; (*fig*) to work one's fingers to the bone

destapar [desta'par] /1a/ VT (*botella*) to open; (*cacerola*) to take the lid off; (*descubrir*) to uncover; **destaparse** VR (*descubrirse*) to get uncovered; (*revelarse*) to reveal one's true character

destape [des'tape] NM nudity; (*fig*) permissiveness; **el ~ español** *the process of liberalization in Spain after Franco's death*

destaque *etc* [des'take] VB *ver* **destacar**

destartalado, -a [destarta'laðo, a] ADJ (*desordenado*) untidy; (*casa etc: grande*) rambling; (: *ruinoso*) tumbledown

destellar [deste'ʎar] /1a/ VI (*diamante*) to sparkle; (*metal*) to glint; (*estrella*) to twinkle

destello [des'teʎo] NM (*de diamante*) sparkle; (*de metal*) glint; (*de estrella*) twinkle; (*de faro*) signal light; **no tiene un ~ de verdad** there's not a grain of truth in it

destemplado, -a [destem'plaðo, a] ADJ (*Mus*) out of tune; (*voz*) harsh; (*Med*) out of sorts; (*Meteorología*) unpleasant, nasty

destemplar [destem'plar] /1a/ VT (*Mus*) to put out of tune; (*alterar*) to upset; **destemplarse** VR (*Mus*) to lose its pitch; (*descomponerse*) to get out of order; (*persona: irritarse*) to get upset; (*Med*) to get out of sorts

desteñir [deste'ɲir] VT, VI to fade; **desteñirse** VR to fade; **esta tela no destiñe** this fabric will not run

desternillarse [desterni'ʎarse] /1a/ VR: ~ **de risa** to split one's sides laughing

desterrado, -a [deste'rraðo, a] NM/F (*exiliado*) exile

desterrar [deste'rrar] /1j/ VT (*exiliar*) to exile; (*fig*) to banish, dismiss

destetar [deste'tar] /1a/ VT to wean

destiempo [des'tjempo]: **a ~** *adv* at the wrong time

destierro *etc* [des'tjerro] VB *ver* **desterrar** ▶ NM exile; **vivir en el ~** to live in exile

destilar [desti'lar] /1a/ VT to distil; (*pus, sangre*) to ooze; (*fig: rebosar*) to exude; (: *revelar*) to reveal ▶ VI (*gotear*) to drip

destilería [destile'ria] NF distillery; **~ de petróleo** oil refinery

destinar [desti'nar] /1a/ VT (*funcionario*) to appoint, assign; (*fondos*) to set aside; **es un libro destinado a los niños** it is a book (intended o meant) for children; **una carta que viene destinada a usted** a letter for you, a letter addressed to you

destinatario, -a [destina'tarjo, a] NM/F addressee; (*Com*) payee

destino [des'tino] NM (*suerte*) destiny; (*de viajero*) destination; (*función*) use; (*puesto*) post, placement; **~ público** public appointment; **salir con ~ a** to leave for; **con ~ a Londres** (*avión, barco*) (bound) for London; (*carta*) to London

destiña *etc* [des'tiɲa], **destiñendo** *etc* [desti'ɲenðo] VB *ver* **desteñir**

destitución [destitu'θjon] NF dismissal, removal

destituir [destitu'ir] /3g/ VT (*despedir*) to dismiss; (: *ministro, funcionario*) to remove from office

destituyendoetc [destitu'jendo] vb ver **destituir**

destornillador [destorniʎa'ðor] NM screwdriver

destornillar [destorni'ʎar] /1a/ vт (tornillo) to unscrew; **destornillarse** vR to unscrew

destreza [des'treθa] NF (habilidad) skill; (maña) dexterity

destripar [destri'par] /1a/ vт (animal) to gut; (reventar) to mangle

destroceetc [des'stroθe] vb ver **destrozar**

destronar [destro'nar] /1a/ vт (rey) to dethrone; (fig) to overthrow

destroncar [destron'kar] /1h/ vт (árbol) to chop off, lop; (proyectos) to ruin; (discurso) to interrupt

destronqueetc [des'tronke] vb ver **destroncar**

destrozar [destro'θar] /1f/ vт (romper) to smash, break (up); (estropear) to ruin; (nervios) to shatter; **~ a algn en una discusión** to crush sb in an argument

destrozo [des'troθo] NM (acción) destruction; (desastre) smashing; **destrozos** NMPL (pedazos) pieces; (daños) havoc sg

destrucción [destruk'θjon] NF destruction

destructor, a [destruk'tor, a] ADJ destructive ▶ NM (Naut) destroyer

destruir [destru'ir] /3g/ vт to destroy; (casa) to demolish; (equilibrio) to upset; (proyecto) to spoil; (esperanzas) to dash; (argumento) to demolish

destruyendoetc [destru'jendo] vb ver **destruir**

desuelleetc [de'sweʎe] vb ver **desollar**

desunión [desu'njon] NF (separación) separation; (discordia) disunity

desunir [desu'nir] /3a/ vт to separate; (Tec) to disconnect; (fig) to cause a quarrel o rift between

desuso [de'suso] NM disuse; **caer en ~** to fall into disuse, become obsolete; **una expresión caída en ~** an obsolete expression

desvaído, -a [desβa'iðo, a] ADJ (color) pale; (contorno) blurred

desvalido, -a [desβa'liðo, a] ADJ (desprotegido) destitute; (sin fuerzas) helpless; **niños desvalidos** waifs and strays

desvalijar [desβali'xar] /1a/ vт (persona) to rob; (casa, tienda) to burgle; (coche) to break into

desvaloriceetc [desβalo'riθe] vb ver **desvalorizar**

desvalorizar [desβalori'θar] /1f/ vт to devalue

desván [des'βan] NM attic

desvanecer [desβane'θer] /2d/ vт (disipar) to dispel; (recuerdo, temor) to banish; (borrar) to blur; **desvanecerse** vR (humo etc) to vanish, disappear; (duda) to be dispelled; (color) to fade; (recuerdo, sonido) to fade away; (Med) to pass out

desvanecido, -a [desβane'θiðo, a] ADJ (Med) faint; **caer ~** to fall in a faint

desvanecimiento [desβaneθi'mjento] NM (desaparición) disappearance; (de dudas) dispelling; (de colores) fading; (evaporación) evaporation; (Med) fainting fit

desvanezcaetc [desβa'neθka] vb ver **desvanecer**

desvariar [desβa'rjar] /1c/ vı (enfermo) to be delirious; (delirar) to talk nonsense

desvarío [desβa'rio] NM delirium; (desatino) absurdity; **desvaríos** NMPL ravings

desvelar [desβe'lar] /1a/ vт to keep awake; **desvelarse** vR (no poder dormir) to stay awake; (vigilar) to be vigilant o watchful; **desvelarse por algo** (inquietarse) to be anxious about sth; (poner gran cuidado) to take great care over sth

desvelo [des'βelo] NM lack of sleep; (insomnio) sleeplessness; (fig) vigilance; **desvelos** NMPL (preocupación) anxiety sg, effort sg

desvencijado, -a [desβenθi'xaðo, a] ADJ (silla) rickety; (máquina) broken-down

desvencijar [desβenθi'xar] /1a/ vт (romper) to break; (soltar) to loosen; (persona: agotar) to exhaust; **desvencijarse** vR to come apart

desventaja [desβen'taxa] NF disadvantage; (inconveniente) drawback

desventajoso, -a [desβenta'xoso, a] ADJ disadvantageous, unfavourable

desventura [desβen'tura] NF misfortune

desventurado, -a [desβentu'raðo, a] ADJ (desgraciado) unfortunate; (de poca suerte) ill-fated

desvergonzado, -a [desβeryon'θaðo, a] ADJ (sin vergüenza) shameless; (descarado) insolent ▶ NM/F shameless person

desvergüenza [desβer'ɣwenθa] NF (descaro) shamelessness; (insolencia) impudence; (mala conducta) effrontery; **esto es una ~** this is disgraceful; **¡qué ~!** what a nerve!

desvestir [desβes'tir] /3k/ vт to undress; **desvestirse** vR to undress

desviación [desβja'θjon] NF deviation; (Auto: rodeo) diversion, detour; (: carretera de circunvalación) ring road (BRIT), circular route (US); **~ de la circulación** traffic diversion; **es una ~ de sus principios** it is a departure from his usual principles

desviar [des'βjar] /1c/ vт to turn aside; (balón, flecha, golpe) to deflect; (pregunta) to parry; (ojos) to avert, turn away; (río) to alter the course of; (navío) to divert, re-route; (conversación) to sidetrack; **desviarse** vR (apartarse del camino) to turn aside; (: barco) to go off course; (Auto: dar un rodeo) to make a detour; **desviarse de un tema** to get away from the point

desvincular [desβinku'lar] /**1a**/ VT to free, release; **desvincularse** VR (*aislarse*) to be cut off; (*alejarse*) to cut o.s. off

desvío [des'βio] VB *ver* **desviar** ▶ NM (*desviación*) detour, diversion; (*fig*) indifference

desvirgar [desβir'γar] /**1h**/ VT to deflower

desvirtuar [desβir'twar] /**1e**/ VT (*estropear*) to spoil; (*argumento, razonamiento*) to detract from; (*efecto*) to counteract; (*sentido*) to distort; **desvirtuarse** VR to spoil

desvistiendo *etc* [desβis'tjendo] VB *ver* **desvestir**

desvitalizar [desβitali'θar] /**1f**/ VT (*nervio*) to numb

desvivirse [desβi'βirse] /**3a**/ VR: ~ **por** to long for, crave for; ~ **por los amigos** to do anything for one's friends

detalladamente [detaʎaða'mente] ADV (*en detalle*) in detail; (*extensamente*) at great length

detallar [deta'ʎar] /**1a**/ VT to detail; (*asunto por asunto*) to itemize

detalle [de'taʎe] NM detail; (*fig*) gesture, token; **al** ~ in detail; (*Com*) retail *cpd*; **comercio al** ~ retail trade; **vender al** ~ to sell retail; **no pierde** ~ he doesn't miss a trick; **me observaba sin perder** ~ he watched my every move; **tiene muchos detalles** she is very considerate

detallista [deta'ʎista] NMF retailer ▶ ADJ (*meticuloso*) meticulous; **comercio** ~ retail trade

detectar [detek'tar] /**1a**/ VT to detect

detective [detek'tiβe] NMF detective; ~ **privado** private detective

detector [detek'tor] NM (*Naut, Tec etc*) detector; ~ **de mentiras/de minas** lie/mine detector

detención [deten'θjon] NF (*acción*) stopping; (*estancamiento*) stoppage; (*retraso*) holdup, delay; (*Jur: arresto*) arrest; (: *prisión*) detention; (: *cuidado*) care; ~ **de juego** (*Deporte*) stoppage of play; ~ **ilegal** unlawful detention

detendré *etc* [deten'dre] VB *ver* **detener**

detener [dete'ner] /**2k**/ VT (*gen*) to stop; (*Jur: arrestar*) to arrest; (: *encarcelar*) to detain; (*objeto*) to keep; (*retrasar*) to hold up, delay; (*aliento*) to hold; **detenerse** VR to stop; **detenerse en** (*demorarse*) to delay over, linger over

detenga *etc* [de'tenga] VB *ver* **detener**

detenidamente [deteniða'mente] ADV (*minuciosamente*) carefully; (*extensamente*) at great length

detenido, -a [dete'niðo, a] ADJ (*arrestado*) under arrest; (*minucioso*) detailed; (*examen*) thorough; (*tímido*) timid ▶ NM/F person under arrest, prisoner

detenimiento [deteni'mjento] NM care; **con** ~ thoroughly; (*observar, considerar*) carefully

detentar [deten'tar] /**1a**/ VT to hold; (*sin derecho: título*) to hold unlawfully; (: *puesto*) to occupy unlawfully

detergente [deter'xente] ADJ, NM detergent

deteriorado, -a [deterjo'raðo, a] ADJ (*estropeado*) damaged; (*desgastado*) worn

deteriorar [deterjo'rar] /**1a**/ VT to spoil, damage; **deteriorarse** VR to deteriorate

deterioro [dete'rjoro] NM deterioration

determinación [determina'θjon] NF (*empeño*) determination; (*decisión*) decision; (*de fecha, precio*) settling, fixing

determinado, -a [determi'naðo, a] ADJ (*preciso*) certain; (*Ling: artículo*) definite; (*persona: resuelto*) determined; **un día** ~ on a certain day; **no hay ningún tema** ~ there is no particular theme

determinar [determi'nar] /**1a**/ VT (*plazo*) to fix; (*precio*) to settle; (*daños, impuestos*) to assess; (*pleito*) to decide; (*causar*) to cause; **determinarse** VR to decide; **el reglamento determina que ...** the rules lay it down *or* state that ...; **aquello determinó la caída del gobierno** that brought about the fall of the government; **esto le determinó** this decided him

detestable [detes'taβle] ADJ (*persona*) hateful; (*acto*) detestable

detestar [detes'tar] /**1a**/ VT to detest

detonación [detona'θjon] NF detonation; (*sonido*) explosion

detonante [deto'nante] NM (*fig*) trigger

detonar [deto'nar] /**1a**/ VI to detonate

detractor, a [detrak'tor, a] ADJ disparaging ▶ NM/F detractor

detrás [de'tras] ADV (*tb*: **por detrás**) behind; (*atrás*) at the back ▶ PREP: ~ **de** behind; **por** ~ **de algn** (*fig*) behind sb's back; **salir de** ~ to come out from behind; **por** ~ behind

detrasito [detra'sito] ADV (*Am fam*) behind

detrimento [detri'mento] NM: **en** ~ **de** to the detriment of

detuve *etc* [de'tuβe] VB *ver* **detener**

deuda [de'uða] NF (*condición*) indebtedness, debt; (*cantidad*) debt; ~ **a largo plazo** long-term debt; ~ **exterior/pública** foreign/national debt; ~ **incobrable** *o* **morosa** bad debt; **deudas activas/pasivas** assets/liabilities; **contraer deudas** to get into debt

deudor, a [deu'ðor, a] NM/F debtor; ~ **hipotecario** mortgager; ~ **moroso** slow payer

devaluación [deβalwa'θjon] NF devaluation

devaluar [deβalu'ar] /**1e**/ VT to devalue

devanar [deβa'nar] /**1a**/ VT (*hilo*) to wind; **devanarse** VR: **devanarse los sesos** to rack one's brains

devaneo [deβa'neo] NM (*Med*) delirium; (*desatino*) nonsense; (*fruslería*) idle pursuit; (*amorío*) flirtation

devastar [deβas'tar] /1a/ VT (*destruir*) to devastate

devendré *etc* [deβen'dre], **devenga** *etc* [de'βenga] VB *ver* **devenir**

devengar [deβen'gar] /1h/ VT (*salario: ganar*) to earn; (: *tener que cobrar*) to be due; (*intereses*) to bring in, accrue, earn

devengue *etc* [de'βenge] VB *ver* **devengar**

devenir [deβe'nir] /3r/ VI: ~ **en** to become, turn into ▶ NM (*movimiento progresivo*) process of development; (*transformación*) transformation

deveras [de'βeras] NF INV (*Am*): **un amigo de (a)** ~ a true o real friend

deviene *etc* [de'βjene], **deviniendo** *etc* [deβi'njendo] VB *ver* **devenir**

devoción [deβo'θjon] NF devotion; (*afición*) strong attachment

devolución [deβolu'θjon] NF (*reenvío*) return, sending back; (*reembolso*) repayment; (*Jur*) devolution

devolver [deβol'βer] /2h/ VT to return; (*lo extraviado, prestado*) to give back; (*a su sitio*) to put back; (*carta al correo*) to send back; (*Com*) to repay, refund; (*visita, la palabra*) to return; (*salud, vista*) to restore; (*fam: vomitar*) to throw up ▶ VI (*fam*) to be sick; **devolverse** VR (*Am*) to return; ~ **mal por bien** to return ill for good; ~ **la pelota a algn** to give sb tit for tat

devorar [deβo'rar] /1a/ VT to devour; (*comer ávidamente*) to gobble up; (*fig: fortuna*) to run through; **todo lo devoró el fuego** the fire consumed everything; **le devoran los celos** he is consumed with jealousy

devoto, -a [de'βoto, a] ADJ (*Rel: persona*) devout; (: *obra*) devotional; (*amigo*): ~ **(de algn)** devoted (to sb) ▶ NM/F admirer; **los devotos** NMPL (*Rel*) the faithful; **su muy ~ servidor** your devoted servant

devuelto [de'βwelto], **devuelva** *etc* [de'βwelβa] VB *ver* **devolver**

D.F. ABR (*México*) = **Distrito Federal**

dg ABR (= *decigramo*) dg

D.G. ABR = **Dirección General**; (= *Director General*) DG

DGT NF ABR = **Dirección General de Tráfico**; **Dirección General de Turismo**

di [di] VB *ver* **dar; decir**

día ['dia] NM day; ~ **de asueto** day off; ~ **feriado** (*Am*) o **festivo** (public) holiday; ~ **hábil/inhábil** working/non-working day; ~ **lunes** (*Am*) Monday; ~ **lectivo** teaching day; ~ **libre** day off; **D~ de Reyes** Epiphany (*6 January*); **D~ de la Independencia** Independence Day; **¿qué ~ es?** what's the date?; **estar/poner al ~** to be/keep up to date; **el ~ de hoy/de mañana** today/tomorrow; **el ~ menos pensado** when you least expect it; **al ~ siguiente** on the following day; **todos los días** every day; **un ~ sí y otro no** every other day; **vivir al ~** to live from hand to mouth; **de ~** during the day, by day; **es de ~** it's daylight; **del ~** (*estilos*) fashionable; (*menú*) today's; **de un ~ para otro** any day now; **en pleno ~** in full daylight; **en su ~** in due time; **¡hasta otro ~!** so long!

diabetes [dja'betes] NF diabetes *sg*

diabético, -a [dja'betiko, a] ADJ, NM/F diabetic

diablo ['djaβlo] NM (*tb fig*) devil; **pobre ~** poor devil; **hace un frío de todos los diablos** it's hellishly cold

diablura [dja'βlura] NF prank; (*travesura*) mischief

diabólico, -a [dja'βoliko, a] ADJ diabolical

diadema [dja'ðema] NF (*para el pelo*) Alice band, headband; (*joya*) tiara

diáfano, -a ['djafano, a] ADJ (*tela*) diaphanous; (*agua*) crystal-clear; (*espacio*) open-plan

diafragma [dja'fraɣma] NM diaphragm

diagnosis [djaɣ'nosis] NF INV, **diagnóstico** [djaɣ'nostiko] NM diagnosis

diagnosticar [djaɣnosti'kar] /1g/ VT to diagnose

diagnóstico [djaɣ'nostiko] NM = **diagnosis**

diagonal [djaɣo'nal] ADJ diagonal ▶ NF (*Mat*) diagonal; **en** ~ diagonally

diagrama [dja'ɣrama] NM diagram; ~ **de barras** (*Com*) bar chart; ~ **de dispersión** (*Com*) scatter diagram; ~ **de flujo** (*Inform*) flowchart

dial [di'al] NM dial

dialecto [dja'lekto] NM dialect

dialogar [djalo'ɣar] /1h/ VT to write in dialogue form ▶ VI (*conversar*) to have a conversation; ~ **con** (*Pol*) to hold talks with

diálogo ['djaloɣo] NM dialogue

dialogue *etc* [dja'loɣe] VB *ver* **dialogar**

diamante [dja'mante] NM diamond

diametralmente [djametral'mente] ADV diametrically; ~ **opuesto a** diametrically opposed to

diámetro [di'ametro] NM diameter; ~ **de giro** (*Auto*) turning circle; **faros de gran** ~ wide-angle headlights

diana ['djana] NF (*Mil*) reveille; (*de blanco*) centre, bull's-eye

diantre ['djantre] NM: **¡~!** (*fam*) oh hell!

diapasón [djapa'son] NM (*instrumento*) tuning fork; (*de violín etc*) fingerboard; (*de voz*) tone

diapositiva [djaposi'tiβa] NF (*Foto*) slide, transparency

diario, -a ['djarjo, a] ADJ daily ▶ NM newspaper; (*libro diario*) diary; (: *Com*) daybook; (*Com: gastos*) daily expenses; ~ **de navegación** (*Naut*) logbook; ~ **hablado** (*Radio*) news (bulletin); ~ **de sesiones** parliamentary report; **a** ~ daily; **de** o **para** ~ everyday

diarrea [dja'rrea] NF diarrhoea

diatriba [dja'triβa] NF diatribe, tirade

dibujante [diβu'xante] NMF (*de bosquejos*) sketcher; (*de dibujos animados*) cartoonist; (*de moda*) designer; ~ **de publicidad** commercial artist

dibujar [diβu'xar] /1a/ VT to draw, sketch; **dibujarse** VR (*emoción*) to show; **dibujarse contra** to be outlined against

dibujo [di'βuxo] NM drawing; (*Tec*) design; (*en papel, tela*) pattern; (*en periódico*) cartoon; (*fig*) description; **dibujos animados** cartoons; ~ **del natural** drawing from life

dic., dic.ᵉ ABR (= *diciembre*) Dec.; *ver tb* **julio**

diccionario [dikθjo'narjo] NM dictionary

dice *etc* VB *ver* **decir**

dicharachero, -a [ditʃara'tʃero, a] ADJ talkative ▶ NM/F (*con ingenio*) wit; (*parlanchín*) chatterbox

dicho, -a ['ditʃo, a] PP *de* **decir** ▶ ADJ (*susodicho*) aforementioned ▶ NM saying; (*proverbio*) proverb; (*ocurrencia*) bright remark ▶ NF (*buena suerte*) good luck; **mejor** ~ rather; ~ **y hecho** no sooner said than done

dichoso, -a [di'tʃoso, a] ADJ (*feliz*) happy; (*afortunado*) lucky; **¡aquel ~ coche!** (*fam*) that blessed car!

diciembre [di'θjembre] NM December; *ver tb* **julio**

diciendo *etc* [di'θjendo] VB *ver* **decir**

dictado [dik'taðo] NM dictation; **escribir al** ~ to take dictation; **los dictados de la conciencia** (*fig*) the dictates of conscience

dictador [dikta'ðor] NM dictator

dictadura [dikta'ðura] NF dictatorship

dictáfono® [dik'tafono] NM Dictaphone®

dictamen [dik'tamen] NM (*opinión*) opinion; (*informe*) report; ~ **contable** auditor's report; ~ **facultativo** (*Med*) medical report

dictar [dik'tar] /1a/ VT (*carta*) to dictate; (*Jur: sentencia*) to pass; (*decreto*) to issue; (*Am: clase*) to give; (: *conferencia*) to deliver

didáctico, -a [di'ðaktiko, a] ADJ didactic; (*material*) teaching *cpd*; (*juguete*) educational

diecinueve [djeθinu'eβe] NUM nineteen; (*fecha*) nineteenth; *ver tb* **seis**

dieciochesco, -a [djeθio'tʃesko, a] ADJ eighteenth-century

dieciocho [djeθi'otʃo] NUM eighteen; (*fecha*) eighteenth; *ver tb* **seis**

dieciséis [djeθi'seis] NUM sixteen; (*fecha*) sixteenth; *ver tb* **seis**

diecisiete [djeθi'sjete] NUM seventeen; (*fecha*) seventeenth; *ver tb* **seis**

diente ['djente] NM (*Anat, Tec*) tooth; (*Zool*) fang; (: *de elefante*) tusk; (*de ajo*) clove; ~ **de león** dandelion; **dientes postizos** false teeth; **enseñar los dientes** (*fig*) to show one's claws; **hablar entre dientes** to mutter, mumble; **hincar el** ~ **en** (*comida*) to bite into

diera *etc* ['djera] VB *ver* **dar**

diéresis [di'eresis] NF diaeresis

dieron ['djeron] VB *ver* **dar**

diesel ['disel] ADJ: **motor** ~ diesel engine

diestro, -a ['djestro, a] ADJ (*derecho*) right; (*hábil*) skilful; (: *con las manos*) handy ▶ NM (*Taur*) matador ▶ NF right hand; **a** ~ **y siniestro** (*sin método*) wildly

dieta ['djeta] NF diet; **dietas** NFPL expenses; **estar a** ~ to be on a diet

dietético, -a [dje'tetiko, a] ADJ dietetic ▶ NM/F dietician ▶ NF dietetics *sg*

dietista [dje'tista] NMF dietician

diez [djeθ] NUM ten; (*fecha*) tenth; **hacer las** ~ **de últimas** (*Naipes*) to sweep the board; *ver tb* **seis**

diezmar [djeθ'mar] /1a/ VT to decimate

difamación [difama'θjon] NF slander; libel

difamar [difa'mar] /1a/ VT (*Jur: hablando*) to slander; (: *por escrito*) to libel

difamatorio, -a [difama'torjo, a] ADJ slanderous; libellous

diferencia [dife'renθja] NF difference; **a** ~ **de** unlike; **hacer** ~ **entre** to make a distinction between; ~ **salarial** (*Com*) wage differential

diferencial [diferen'θjal] NM (*Auto*) differential

diferenciar [diferen'θjar] /1b/ VT to differentiate between ▶ VI to differ; **diferenciarse** VR to differ, be different; (*distinguirse*) to distinguish o.s.

diferente [dife'rente] ADJ different

diferido [dife'riðo] NM: **en** ~ (*TV etc*) recorded

diferir [dife'rir] /3i/ VT to defer

difícil [di'fiθil] ADJ difficult; (*tiempos, vida*) hard; (*situación*) delicate; **es un hombre** ~ he's a difficult man to get on with

difícilmente [di'fiθilmente] ADV (*con dificultad*) with difficulty; (*apenas*) hardly

dificultad [difikul'tað] NF difficulty; (*problema*) trouble; (*objeción*) objection

dificultar [difikul'tar] /1a/ VT (*complicar*) to complicate, make difficult; (*estorbar*) to obstruct; **las restricciones dificultan el comercio** the restrictions hinder trade

dificultoso, -a [difikul'toso, a] ADJ (*difícil*) difficult, hard; (*fam: cara*) odd, ugly; (*persona: exigente*) fussy

difiera *etc* [di'fjera], **difiriendo** *etc* [difi'rjendo] VB *ver* **diferir**

difuminar [difumiˈnar] /**1a**/ VT to blur
difundir [difunˈdir] /**3a**/ VT (calor, luz) to
diffuse; (Radio) to broadcast; **difundirse** VR
to spread (out); **~ una noticia** to spread a
piece of news
difunto, -a [diˈfunto, a] ADJ dead, deceased
▶ NM/F deceased (person); **el ~** the deceased
difusión [difuˈsjon] NF (de calor, luz) diffusion;
(de noticia, teoría) dissemination; (de programa)
broadcasting; (programa) broadcast
difuso, -a [diˈfuso, a] ADJ (luz) diffused;
(conocimientos) widespread; (estilo, explicación)
wordy
diga etc [ˈdiɣa] VB ver **decir**
digerir [dixeˈrir] /**3i**/ VT to digest; (fig) to
absorb; (reflexionar sobre) to think over
digestión [dixesˈtjon] NF digestion; **corte
de ~** indigestion
digestivo, -a [dixesˈtiβo, a] ADJ digestive
▶ NM (bebida) liqueur, digestif
digiera etc [diˈxjera], **digiriendo** etc
[dixiˈrjenðo] VB ver **digerir**
digital [dixiˈtal] ADJ (Inform) digital; (dactilar)
finger cpd ▶ NF (Bot) foxglove; (droga)
digitalis
digitalizador [dixitaliθaˈðor] NM (Inform)
digitizer
dignarse [diɣˈnarse] /**1a**/ VR to deign to
dignidad [diɣniˈðað] NF dignity; (honra)
honour; (rango) rank; (persona) dignitary;
herir la ~ de algn to hurt sb's pride
dignificar [diɣnifiˈkar] /**1g**/ VT to dignify
dignifique etc [diɣniˈfike] VB ver **dignificar**
digno, -a [ˈdiɣno, a] ADJ worthy; (persona:
honesto) honourable; **~ de elogio**
praiseworthy; **~ de mención** worth
mentioning; **es ~ de verse** it is worth
seeing; **poco ~** unworthy
digo etc VB ver **decir**
digresión [diɣreˈsjon] NF digression
dije etc [ˈdixe], **dijera** etc [diˈxera] VB ver **decir**
dilación [dilaˈθjon] NF delay; **sin ~** without
delay, immediately
dilapidar [dilapiˈðar] /**1a**/ VT to squander,
waste
dilatación [dilataˈθjon] NF (expansión)
dilation
dilatado, -a [dilaˈtaðo, a] ADJ dilated; (período)
long drawn-out; (extenso) extensive
dilatar [dilaˈtar] /**1a**/ VT (gen) to dilate;
(prolongar) to prolong; (aplazar) to delay;
dilatarse VR (pupila etc) to dilate; (agua) to
expand
dilema [diˈlema] NM dilemma
diligencia [diliˈxenθja] NF diligence; (rapidez)
speed; (ocupación) errand, job; (carruaje)
stagecoach; **diligencias** NFPL (Jur)
formalities; **diligencias judiciales** judicial
proceedings; **diligencias previas** inquest sg

diligente [diliˈxente] ADJ diligent; **poco ~**
slack
dilucidar [diluθiˈðar] /**1a**/ VT (aclarar) to
elucidate, clarify; (misterio) to clear up
diluir [diluˈir] /**3g**/ VT to dilute; (aguar, fig) to
water down
diluviar [diluˈβjar] /**1b**/ VI to pour with rain
diluvio [diˈluβjo] NM deluge, flood; **un ~ de
cartas** (fig) a flood of letters
diluyendo etc [diluˈjendo] VB ver **diluir**
dimanar [dimaˈnar] /**1a**/ VI: **~ de** to arise o
spring from
dimensión [dimenˈsjon] NF dimension;
dimensiones NFPL size sg; **tomar las
dimensiones de** to take the measurements
of
dimes [ˈdimes] NMPL: **andar en ~ y diretes
con algn** to bicker o squabble with sb
diminutivo [diminuˈtiβo] NM diminutive
diminuto, -a [dimiˈnuto, a] ADJ tiny,
diminutive
dimisión [dimiˈsjon] NF resignation
dimitir [dimiˈtir] /**3a**/ VT (cargo) to give up;
(despedir) to sack ▶ VI to resign
dimos [ˈdimos] VB ver **dar**
Dinamarca [dinaˈmarka] NF Denmark
dinamarqués, -esa [dinamarˈkes, esa] ADJ
Danish ▶ NM/F Dane ▶ NM (Ling) Danish
dinámico, -a [diˈnamiko, a] ADJ dynamic
▶ NF dynamics sg
dinamita [dinaˈmita] NF dynamite
dinamitar [dinamiˈtar] /**1a**/ VT to dynamite
dinamo [diˈnamo], (Am) **dínamo** [ˈdinamo]
NF dynamo
dinastía [dinasˈtia] NF dynasty
dineral [dineˈral] NM fortune
dinero [diˈnero] NM money; (dinero en
circulación) currency; **~ caro** (Com) dear
money; **~ contante (y sonante)** hard cash;
~ de curso legal legal tender; **~ efectivo** o
metálico cash, ready cash; **~ suelto** (loose)
change; **es hombre de ~** he is a man of
means; **andar mal de ~** to be short of
money; **ganar ~ a espuertas** to make
money hand over fist
dinosaurio [dinoˈsaurjo] NM dinosaur
dintel [dinˈtel] NM lintel; (umbral) threshold
diñar [diˈɲar] /**1a**/ VT (fam) to give; **diñarla** to
kick the bucket
dio [djo] VB ver **dar**
diócesis [ˈdjoθesis] NF INV diocese
dios [djos] NM god; **D~** God; **D~ mediante**
God willing; **a D~ gracias** thank heaven; **a
la buena de D~** any old how; **una de D~ es
Cristo** an almighty row; **D~ los cría y ellos
se juntan** birds of a feather flock together;
como D~ manda as is proper; **¡D~ mío!** (oh)
my God!; **¡por D~!** for God's sake!; **¡válgame
D~!** bless my soul!

diosa ['djosa] NF goddess

Dip. ABR (= *Diputación*) ≈ CC

diploma [di'ploma] NM diploma

diplomacia [diplo'maθja] NF diplomacy; *(fig)* tact

diplomado, -a [diplo'maðo, a] ADJ qualified ▶ NM/F holder of a diploma; *(Univ)* graduate; *ver tb* **licenciado**

diplomático, -a [diplo'matiko, a] ADJ *(cuerpo)* diplomatic; *(que tiene tacto)* tactful ▶ NM/F diplomat

diptongo [dip'tongo] NM diphthong

diputación [diputa'θjon] NF deputation; *(tb:* **diputación provincial**) ≈ county council; **~ permanente** *(Pol)* standing committee

diputado, -a [dipu'taðo, a] NM/F delegate; *(Pol)* ≈ member of parliament *(Brit)*, ≈ representative *(US)*; *ver tb* **cortes**

dique ['dike] NM dyke; *(rompeolas)* breakwater; **~ de contención** dam

Dir. ABR = **dirección**; (= *director*) Mgr

diré *etc* [di're] VB *ver* **decir**

dirección [direk'θjon] NF direction; *(fig: tendencia)* trend; *(señas, tb Inform)* address; *(Auto)* steering; *(gerencia)* management; *(de periódico)* editorship; *(en escuela)* headship; *(Pol)* leadership; *(junta)* board of directors; *(despacho)* director's/manager's/headmaster's/editor's office; **~ administrativa** office management; **~ asistida** power-assisted steering; **D~ General de Seguridad/Turismo** State Security/Tourist Office; **"~ única"** "one-way street"; **"~ prohibida"** "no entry"; **tomar la ~ de una empresa** to take over the running of a company

direccional [direkθjo'nal] NF *(Am Auto)* indicator

direccionamiento [direkθjona'mjento] NM *(Inform)* addressing

directa [di'rekta] NF *(Auto)* top gear

directivo, -a [direk'tiβo, a] ADJ *(junta)* managing; *(función)* administrative ▶ NM/F *(Com)* manager ▶ NF *(norma)* directive; *(tb:* **junta directiva**) board of directors

directo, -a [di'rekto, a] ADJ direct; *(línea)* straight; *(inmediato)* immediate; *(tren)* through; *(TV)* live; **programa en ~** live programme; **transmitir en ~** to broadcast live

director, a [direk'tor, a] ADJ leading ▶ NM/F director; *(Escol)* head (teacher) *(Brit)*, principal *(US)*; *(gerente)* manager/manageress; *(de compañía)* president; *(jefe)* head; *(Prensa)* editor; *(de prisión)* governor; *(Mus)* conductor; **~ adjunto** assistant manager; **~ de cine** film director; **~ comercial** marketing manager; **~ ejecutivo** executive director; **~ de**

empresa company director; **~ general** general manager; **~ gerente** managing director; **~ de sucursal** branch manager

directorio [direk'torjo] NM *(Inform)* directory; *(Am: telefónico)* phone book

directrices [direk'triθes] NFPL guidelines

dirigente [diri'xente] ADJ leading ▶ NMF *(Pol)* leader; **los dirigentes del partido** the party leaders

dirigible [diri'xiβle] ADJ *(Aviat, Naut)* steerable ▶ NM airship

dirigir [diri'xir] /3c/ VT to direct; *(acusación)* to level; *(carta)* to address; *(obra de teatro, película)* to direct; *(Mus)* to conduct; *(comercio)* to manage; *(expedición)* to lead; *(sublevación)* to head; *(periódico)* to edit; *(guiar)* to guide; **dirigirse** VR: **dirigirse a** to go towards, make one's way towards; *(hablar con)* to speak to; **dirigirse a algn solicitando algo** to apply to sb for sth; **"diríjase a …"** "apply to …"

dirigismo [diri'xismo] NM management, control; **~ estatal** state control

dirija *etc* [di'rixa] VB *ver* **dirigir**

dirimir [diri'mir] /3a/ VT *(contrato, matrimonio)* to dissolve

discado [dis'kaðo] NM: **~ automático** autodial

discernir [disθer'nir] /3k/ VT to discern ▶ VI to distinguish

discierna *etc* [dis'θjerna] VB *ver* **discernir**

disciplina [disθi'plina] NF discipline

disciplinar [disθipli'nar] /1a/ VT to discipline; *(enseñar)* to school; *(Mil)* to drill; *(azotar)* to whip

discípulo, -a [dis'θipulo, a] NM/F disciple; *(seguidor)* follower; *(Escol)* pupil

Discman® ['diskman] NM Discman®, personal CD player

disco ['disko] NM disc *(Brit)*, disk *(US)*; *(Deporte)* discus; *(Telec)* dial; *(Auto: semáforo)* light; *(Mus)* record; *(Inform)* disk; **~ de arranque** boot disk; **~ compacto** compact disc; **~ de densidad sencilla/doble** single/double density disk; **~ de larga duración** long-playing record (LP); **~ flexible** *o* **floppy** floppy disk; **~ de freno** brake disc; **~ maestro** master disk; **~ de reserva** backup disk; **~ rígido** hard disk; **~ de una cara/dos caras** single-/double-sided disk; **~ virtual** RAM disk

discóbolo [dis'koβolo] NM discus thrower

discográfico, -a [disko'ɣrafiko, a] ADJ record *cpd*; **casa discográfica** record company; **sello ~** label

díscolo, -a ['diskolo, a] ADJ *(rebelde)* unruly

disconforme [diskon'forme] ADJ differing; **estar ~ (con)** to be in disagreement (with)

discontinuo, -a [diskon'tinwo, a] ADJ discontinuous; *(Auto: línea)* broken

discordar [diskor'ðar] /**1l**/ vi (*Mus*) to be out of tune; (*estar en desacuerdo*) to disagree; (*colores, opiniones*) to clash

discorde [dis'korðe] ADJ (*sonido*) discordant; (*opiniones*) clashing

discordia [dis'korðja] NF discord

discoteca [disko'teka] NF disco(theque)

discreción [diskre'θjon] NF discretion; (*reserva*) prudence; **¡a ~!** (*Mil*) stand easy!; **añadir azúcar a ~** (*Culin*) add sugar to taste; **comer a ~** to eat as much as one wishes

discrecional [diskreθjo'nal] ADJ (*facultativo*) discretionary; **parada ~** request stop

discrepancia [diskre'panθja] NF (*diferencia*) discrepancy; (*desacuerdo*) disagreement

discrepante [diskre'pante] ADJ divergent; **hubo varias voces discrepantes** there were some dissenting voices

discrepar [diskre'par] /**1a**/ vi to disagree

discreto, -a [dis'kreto, a] ADJ (*diplomático*) discreet; (*sensato*) sensible; (*reservado*) quiet; (*sobrio*) sober; (*mediano*) fair, fairly good; **le daremos un plazo ~** we'll allow him a reasonable time

discriminación [diskrimina'θjon] NF discrimination

discriminar [diskrimi'nar] /**1a**/ vt to discriminate against; (*diferenciar*) to discriminate between

discuerde *etc* [dis'kwerðe] vB *ver* **discordar**

disculpa [dis'kulpa] NF excuse; (*pedir perdón*) apology; **pedir disculpas a/por** to apologize to/for

disculpar [diskul'par] /**1a**/ vt to excuse, pardon; **disculparse** vR to excuse o.s.; to apologize

discurrir [disku'rrir] /**3a**/ vt to contrive, think up ▶ vi (*pensar, reflexionar*) to think, meditate; (*recorrer*) to roam, wander; (*río*) to flow; (*el tiempo*) to pass, flow by

discurso [dis'kurso] NM speech; **~ de clausura** closing speech; **pronunciar un ~** to make a speech; **en el ~ del tiempo** with the passage of time

discusión [disku'sjon] NF (*diálogo*) discussion; (*riña*) argument; **tener una ~** to have an argument

discutible [disku'tiβle] ADJ debatable; **de mérito ~** of dubious worth

discutido, -a [disku'tiðo, a] ADJ controversial

discutir [disku'tir] /**3a**/ vt (*debatir*) to discuss; (*pelear*) to argue about; (*contradecir*) to argue against ▶ vi to discuss; (*disputar*) to argue; **~ de política** to argue about politics; **¡no discutas!** don't argue!

disecar [dise'kar] /**1g**/ vt (*para conservar*: *animal*) to stuff; (: *planta*) to dry

diseminar [disemi'nar] /**1a**/ vt to disseminate, spread

disentir [disen'tir] /**3i**/ vi to dissent, disagree

diseñador, a [diseɲa'dor, a] NM/F designer

diseñar [dise'ɲar] /**1a**/ vt, vi to design

diseño [di'seɲo] NM (*Tec*) design; (*Arte*) drawing; (*Costura*) pattern; **de ~ italiano** Italian-designed; **~ asistido por ordenador** computer-assisted design, CAD

diseque *etc* [di'seke] vB *ver* **disecar**

disertar [diser'tar] /**1a**/ vi to speak

disfrace *etc* [dis'fraθe] vB *ver* **disfrazar**

disfraz [dis'fraθ] NM (*máscara*) disguise; (*traje*) fancy dress; (*excusa*) pretext; **bajo el ~ de** under the cloak of

disfrazado, -a [disfra'θaðo, a] ADJ disguised; **ir ~ de** to masquerade as

disfrazar [disfra'θar] /**1f**/ vt to disguise; **disfrazarse** vR to dress (o.s.) up; **disfrazarse de** to disguise o.s. as

disfrutar [disfru'tar] /**1a**/ vt to enjoy ▶ vi to enjoy o.s.; **¡que disfrutes!** have a good time!; **~ de** to enjoy, possess; **~ de buena salud** to enjoy good health

disfrute [dis'frute] NM (*goce*) enjoyment; (*aprovechamiento*) use

disgregar [disɣre'ɣar] /**1h**/ vt (*desintegrar*) to disintegrate; (*manifestantes*) to disperse; **disgregarse** vR to disintegrate, break up

disgregue *etc* [dis'ɣreɣe] vB *ver* **disgregar**

disgustar [disɣus'tar] /**1a**/ vt (*no gustar*) to displease; (*contrariar, enojar*) to annoy; to upset; **disgustarse** vR to get upset; (*dos personas*) to fall out; **estaba muy disgustado con el asunto** he was very upset about the affair

disgusto [dis'ɣusto] NM (*repugnancia*) disgust; (*contrariedad*) annoyance; (*desagrado*) displeasure; (*tristeza*) grief; (*riña*) quarrel; (*desgracia*) misfortune; **hacer algo a ~** to do sth unwillingly; **matar a algn a disgustos** to drive sb to distraction

disidente [disi'ðente] NM dissident

disienta *etc* [di'sjenta] vB *ver* **disentir**

disimulado, -a [disimu'laðo, a] ADJ (*solapado*) furtive, underhand; (*oculto*) covert; **hacerse el ~** to pretend not to notice

disimular [disimu'lar] /**1a**/ vt (*ocultar*) to hide, conceal ▶ vi to dissemble

disimulo [disi'mulo] NM (*fingimiento*) dissimulation; **con ~** cunningly

disipar [disi'par] /**1a**/ vt (*duda, temor*) to dispel; (*esperanza*) to destroy; (*fortuna*) to squander; **disiparse** vR (*nubes*) to vanish; (*dudas*) to be dispelled; (*indisciplinarse*) to dissipate

diskette [dis'ket] NM (*Inform*) diskette, floppy disk

dislate [dis'late] NM (*absurdo*) absurdity; **dislates** NMPL nonsense *sg*

dislexia [dis'leksja] NF dyslexia

dislocar [dislo'kar] /**1g**/ VT (*gen*) to dislocate; (*tobillo*) to sprain; **dislocarse** VR (*articulación*) to sprain, dislocate

disloque *etc* [dis'loke] VB *ver* **dislocar** ▶ NM: **es el ~** (*fam*) it's the last straw

disminución [disminu'θjon] NF decrease, reduction

disminuido, -a [disminu'iðo, a] NM/F: **~ mental/físico** mentally/physically-handicapped person

disminuir [disminu'ir] /**3g**/ VT to decrease, diminish; (*estrechar*) to lessen; (*temperatura*) to lower; (*gastos, raciones*) to cut down; (*dolor*) to relieve; (*autoridad, prestigio*) to weaken; (*entusiasmo*) to damp ▶ VI (*días*) to grow shorter; (*precios, temperatura*) to drop, fall; (*velocidad*) to slacken; (*población*) to decrease; (*beneficios, número*) to fall off; (*memoria, vista*) to fail

disminuyendo *etc* [disminu'jendo] VB *ver* **disminuir**

disociar [diso'θjar] /**1b**/ VT to disassociate; **disociarse** VR to disassociate o.s.

disoluble [diso'luβle] ADJ soluble

disolución [disolu'θjon] NF (*acto*) dissolution; (*Química*) solution; (*Com*) liquidation; (*moral*) dissoluteness

disoluto, -a [diso'luto, a] ADJ dissolute

disolvente [disol'βente] NM solvent, thinner

disolver [disol'βer] /**2h**/ VT (*gen*) to dissolve; (*manifestación*) to break up; **disolverse** VR to dissolve; (*Com*) to go into liquidation

disonar [diso'nar] /**1l**/ VB (*Mus*) to be out of tune; (*no armonizar*) to lack harmony; **~ con** to be out of keeping with, clash with

dispar [dis'par] ADJ (*distinto*) different; (*irregular*) uneven

disparado, -a [dispa'raðo, a] ADJ: **entrar ~** to shoot in; **salir ~** to shoot out; **ir ~** to go like mad

disparador [dispara'ðor] NM (*de arma*) trigger; (*Foto, Tec*) release; **~ atómico** aerosol; **~ de bombas** bomb release

disparar [dispa'rar] /**1a**/ VT, VI to shoot, fire; **dispararse** VR (*arma de fuego*) to go off; (*persona: marcharse*) to rush off; (: *enojarse*) to lose control; (*caballo*) to bolt

disparatado, -a [dispara'taðo, a] ADJ crazy

disparate [dispa'rate] NM (*tontería*) foolish remark; (*error*) blunder; **decir disparates** to talk nonsense; **¡qué ~!** how absurd!; **costar un ~** to cost a hell of a lot

disparo [dis'paro] NM shot; (*acto*) firing; **disparos** NMPL shooting *sg*, exchange *sg* of shots, shots; **~ inicial** (*de cohete*) blast-off

dispendio [dis'pendjo] NM waste

dispensar [dispen'sar] /**1a**/ VT to dispense; (*ayuda*) to give; (*honores*) to grant; (*disculpar*) to excuse; **¡usted dispense!** I beg your pardon!; **~ a algn de hacer algo** to excuse sb from doing sth

dispensario [dispen'sarjo] NM (*clínica*) community clinic; (*de hospital*) outpatients' department

dispersar [disper'sar] /**1a**/ VT to disperse; (*manifestación*) to break up; **dispersarse** VR to scatter

disperso, -a [dis'perso, a] ADJ scattered

displicencia [displi'θenθja] NF (*mal humor*) peevishness; (*desgana*) lack of enthusiasm

displicente [displi'θente] ADJ (*malhumorado*) peevish; (*poco entusiasta*) unenthusiastic

dispondré *etc* [dispon'dre] VB *ver* **disponer**

disponer [dispo'ner] /**2q**/ VT (*arreglar*) to arrange; (*ordenar*) to put in order; (*preparar*) to prepare, get ready ▶ VI: **~ de** to have, own; **disponerse** VR: **disponerse para** to prepare to, prepare for; **la ley dispone que ...** the law provides that ...; **no puede ~ de esos bienes** she cannot dispose of those properties

disponga *etc* [dis'ponga] VB *ver* **disponer**

disponibilidad [disponiβili'ðað] NF availability; **disponibilidades** NFPL (*Com*) resources, financial assets

disponible [dispo'niβle] ADJ available; (*tiempo*) spare; (*dinero*) on hand

disposición [disposi'θjon] NF arrangement, disposition; (*voluntad*) willingness; (*de casa, Inform*) layout; (*ley*) order; (*cláusula*) provision; (*aptitud*) aptitude; **~ de ánimo** attitude of mind; **última ~** last will and testament; **a la ~ de** at the disposal of; **a su ~** at your service

dispositivo [disposi'tiβo] NM device, mechanism; **~ de alimentación** hopper; **~ de almacenaje** storage device; **~ periférico** peripheral (device); **~ de seguridad** safety catch; (*fig*) security measure

dispuesto, -a [dis'pwesto, a] PP *de* **disponer** ▶ ADJ (*arreglado*) arranged; (*preparado*) disposed; (*persona: dinámico*) bright; **estar ~/poco ~ a hacer algo** to be inclined/reluctant to do sth

dispuse *etc* [dis'puse] VB *ver* **disponer**

disputa [dis'puta] NF (*discusión*) dispute, argument; (*controversia*) controversy

disputar [dispu'tar] /**1a**/ VT (*discutir*) to dispute, question; (*contender*) to contend for; (*carrera*) to compete in ▶ VI to argue

disquete [dis'kete] NM (*Inform*) diskette, floppy disk

disquetera [diske'tera] NF disk drive

Dist. ABR (= *Distrito*) dist.

distancia [dis'tanθja] NF distance; (*de tiempo*) interval; **~ de parada** braking distance; **~ del suelo** (*Auto etc*) height off the ground;

a gran o **a larga** ~ long-distance;
mantenerse a ~ to keep one's distance; (*fig*)
to remain aloof; **guardar las distancias** to
keep one's distance

distanciado, -a [distan'θjaðo, a] ADJ (*remoto*)
remote; (*fig: alejado*) far apart; **estamos
distanciados en ideas** our ideas are poles
apart

distanciamiento [distanθja'mjento] NM
(*acto*) spacing out; (*estado*) remoteness; (*fig*)
distance

distanciar [distan'θjar] /**1b**/ VT to space out;
distanciarse VR to become estranged

distante [dis'tante] ADJ distant

distar [dis'tar] /**1a**/ VI: **dista 5 km de aquí** it
is 5 km from here; **¿dista mucho?** is it far?;
dista mucho de la verdad it's very far from
the truth

diste ['diste], **disteis** ['disteis] VB *ver* **dar**

distensión [disten'sjon] NF distension;
(*Pol*) détente; ~ **muscular** (*Med*) muscular
strain

distinción [distin'θjon] NF distinction;
(*elegancia*) elegance; (*honor*) honour; **a** ~ **de**
unlike; **sin** ~ indiscriminately; **sin** ~ **de
edades** irrespective of age

distinga etc [dis'tinga] VB *ver* **distinguir**

distinguido, -a [distin'giðo, a] ADJ
distinguished; (*famoso*) prominent,
well-known; (*elegante*) elegant

distinguir [distin'gir] /**3d**/ VT to distinguish;
(*divisar*) to make out; (*escoger*) to single out;
(*caracterizar*) to mark out; **distinguirse** VR to
be distinguished; (*destacarse*) to distinguish
o.s.; **a lo lejos no se distingue** it's not
visible from a distance

distintivo, -a [distin'tiβo, a] ADJ distinctive;
(*signo*) distinguishing ▶ NM (*de policía etc*)
badge; (*fig*) characteristic

distinto, -a [dis'tinto, a] ADJ different; (*claro*)
clear; **distintos** several, various

distorsión [distor'sjon] NF (*Anat*) twisting;
(*Radio etc*) distortion

distorsionar [distorsjo'nar] /**1a**/ VT, VI to
distort

distracción [distrak'θjon] NF distraction;
(*pasatiempo*) hobby, pastime; (*olvido*)
absent-mindedness, distraction

distraer [distra'er] /**2o**/ VT (*atención*) to
distract; (*divertir*) to amuse; (*fondos*) to
embezzle ▶ VI to be relaxing; **distraerse** VR
(*entretenerse*) to amuse o.s.; (*perder la
concentración*) to allow one's attention to
wander; ~ **a algn de su pensamiento** to
divert sb from his train of thought; **el
pescar distrae** fishing is a relaxation

distraído, -a [distra'iðo, a] ADJ (*gen*)
absent-minded; (*desatento*) inattentive;
(*entretenido*) amusing ▶ NM: **hacerse el** ~

to pretend not to notice; **con aire** ~ idly; **me
miró distraída** she gave me a casual glance

distraiga etc [dis'traiɣa], **distraje** etc
[dis'traxe], **distrajera** etc [distra'xera],
distrayendo [distra'jendo] VB *ver* **distraer**

distribución [distriβu'θjon] NF distribution;
(*entrega*) delivery; (*en estadística*) distribution,
incidence; (*Arq*) layout; ~ **de premios** prize
giving; **la** ~ **de los impuestos** the incidence
of taxes

distribuidor, a [distriβui'ðor, a] NM/F
(*persona: gen*) distributor; (*: Correos*) sorter;
(*: Com*) dealer, agent; **su** ~ **habitual** your
regular dealer

distribuir [distriβu'ir] /**3g**/ VT to distribute;
(*prospectos*) to hand out; (*cartas*) to deliver;
(*trabajo*) to allocate; (*premios*) to award;
(*dividendos*) to pay; (*peso*) to distribute; (*Arq*)
to plan

distribuyendo etc [distriβu'jendo] VB *ver*
distribuir

distrito [dis'trito] NM (*sector, territorio*) region;
(*barrio*) district; ~ **electoral** constituency;
~ **postal** postal district; **D~ Federal** (*Am*)
Federal District

disturbio [dis'turβjo] NM disturbance;
(*desorden*) riot; **los disturbios** NMPL the
troubles

disuadir [diswa'ðir] /**3a**/ VT to dissuade

disuasión [diswa'sjon] NF dissuasion; (*Mil*)
deterrent; ~ **nuclear** nuclear deterrent

disuasivo, -a [diswa'siβo, a] ADJ dissuasive;
arma disuasiva deterrent

disuasorio, -a [diswa'sorjo, a] ADJ = **disuasivo**

disuelto [di'swelto] PP *de* **disolver**

disuelva etc [di'swelβa] VB *ver* **disolver**

disuene etc [di'swene] VB *ver* **disonar**

disyuntiva [disjun'tiβa] NF (*dilema*) dilemma

DIU ['diu] NM ABR (= *dispositivo intrauterino*) IUD

diurno, -a ['djurno, a] ADJ day *cpd*, diurnal

diva ['diβa] NF prima donna

divagar [diβa'ɣar] /**1h**/ VI (*desviarse*) to digress

divague etc [di'βaɣe] VB *ver* **divagar**

diván [di'βan] NM divan

divergencia [diβer'xenθja] NF divergence

divergir [diβer'xir] /**3c**/ VI (*líneas*) to diverge;
(*opiniones*) to differ; (*personas*) to disagree

diverja etc [di'βerxa] VB *ver* **divergir**

diversidad [diβersi'ðað] NF diversity, variety

diversificación [diβersifika'θjon] NF (*Com*)
diversification

diversificar [diβersifi'kar] /**1g**/ VT to diversify

diversifique etc [diβersi'fike] VB *ver*
diversificar

diversión [diβer'sjon] NF (*gen*)
entertainment; (*actividad*) hobby, pastime

diverso, -a [di'βerso, a] ADJ diverse; (*diferente*)
different ▶ NM: **diversos** (*Com*) sundries;
diversos libros several books

divertido, -a [diβer'tiðo, a] ADJ (chiste) amusing, funny; (fiesta etc) enjoyable; (película, libro) entertaining; **está ~** (irónico) this is going to be fun

divertir [diβer'tir] /3i/ VT (entretener, recrear) to amuse, entertain; **divertirse** VR (pasarlo bien) to have a good time; (distraerse) to amuse o.s.

dividendo [diβi'ðendo] NM (Com) dividend, dividends; **~ definitivo** final dividend; **dividendos por acción** earnings per share

dividir [diβi'ðir] /3a/ VT (gen) to divide; (separar) to separate; (distribuir) to distribute, share out

divierta etc [di'βjerta] VB ver **divertir**

divinidad [diβini'ðað] NF (esencia divina) divinity; **la D~** God

divino, -a [di'βino, a] ADJ divine; (fig) lovely

divirtiendo etc [diβir'tjendo] VB ver **divertir**

divisa [di'βisa] NF (emblema) emblem, badge; **divisas** NFPL currency sg; (Com) foreign exchange sg; **control de divisas** exchange control; **~ de reserva** reserve currency

divisar [diβi'sar] /1a/ VT to make out, distinguish

división [diβi'sjon] NF division; (de partido) split; (de país) partition

divisorio, -a [diβi'sorjo, a] ADJ (línea) dividing; **línea divisoria de las aguas** watershed

divorciado, -a [diβor'θjaðo, a] ADJ divorced; (opinión) split ▶ NM/F divorcé(e)

divorciar [diβor'θjar] /1b/ VT to divorce; **divorciarse** VR to get divorced

divorcio [di'βorθjo] NM divorce; (fig) split

divulgación [diβulɣa'θjon] NF (difusión) spreading; (popularización) popularization

divulgar [diβul'ɣar] /1h/ VT (desparramar) to spread; (popularizar) to popularize; (hacer circular) to divulge, circulate; **divulgarse** VR (secreto) to leak out; (rumor) to get about

divulgue etc [di'βulɣe] VB ver **divulgar**

dizque ['diske] ADV (Am fam) apparently

Dls, dls ABR (Am) = **dólares**

dm ABR (= decímetro) dm

DNI NM ABR (ESP) = **Documento Nacional de Identidad**

> The Documento Nacional de Identidad is a Spanish ID card which must be carried at all times and produced on request for the police. It contains the holder's photo, fingerprints and personal details. It is also known as the DNI or carnet de identidad.

Dña. ABR (= Doña) Mrs

do [do] NM (Mus) C

D.O. ABR = **Denominación de Origen**; ver **denominación**

dobladillo [doβla'ðiλo] NM (de vestido) hem; (de pantalón: vuelta) turn-up (BRIT), cuff (US)

doblaje [do'βlaxe] NM (Cine) dubbing

doblar [do'βlar] /1a/ VT to double; (papel) to fold; (caño) to bend; (la esquina) to turn, go round; (film) to dub ▶ VI to turn; (campana) to toll; **doblarse** VR (plegarse) to fold (up), crease; (encorvarse) to bend; **~ a la derecha/izquierda** to turn right/left

doble ['doβle] ADJ (gen) double; (de dos aspectos) dual; (cuerda) thick; (fig) two-faced ▶ NM double ▶ NMF (Teat) double, stand-in; **dobles** NMPL (Deporte) doubles sg; **~ o nada** double or quits; **~ página** double-page spread; **con ~ sentido** with a double meaning; **el ~** twice the quantity o as much; **su sueldo es el ~ del mío** his salary is twice (as much as) mine; (Inform) **~ cara** double-sided; **~ densidad** double density; **~ espacio** double spacing

doblegar [doβle'ɣar] /1h/ VT to fold, crease; **doblegarse** VR to yield

doblegue etc [do'βleɣe] VB ver **doblegar**

doblez [do'βleθ] NM (pliegue) fold, hem ▶ NF (falsedad) duplicity

doc. ABR (= docena) doz.; (= documento) doc.

doce ['doθe] NUM twelve; (fecha) twelfth; **las ~** twelve o'clock; ver tb **seis**

docena [do'θena] NF dozen; **por docenas** by the dozen

docente [do'θente] ADJ: **personal ~** teaching staff; **centro ~** educational institution

dócil ['doθil] ADJ (pasivo) docile; (manso) gentle; (obediente) obedient

docto, -a ['dokto, a] ADJ learned, erudite ▶ NM/F scholar

doctor, a [dok'tor, a] NM/F doctor; **~ en filosofía** Doctor of Philosophy

doctorado [dokto'raðo] NM doctorate

doctorarse [dokto'rarse] /1a/ VR to get a doctorate

doctrina [dok'trina] NF doctrine, teaching

documentación [dokumenta'θjon] NF documentation; (de identidad etc) papers pl

documental [dokumen'tal] ADJ, NM documentary

documentar [dokumen'tar] /1a/ VT to document; **documentarse** VR to gather information

documento [doku'mento] NM (certificado) document; (Jur) exhibit; **documentos** NMPL papers; **~ adjunto** (Inform) attachment; **~ justificativo** voucher; **D~ Nacional de Identidad** national identity card; ver tb **DNI**

dogma ['doɣma] NM dogma

dogmático, -a [doɣ'matiko, a] ADJ dogmatic

dogo ['doɣo] NM bulldog

dólar ['dolar] NM dollar

dolencia [do'lenθja] NF (achaque) ailment; (dolor) ache

doler [do'ler] /2h/ VT, VI to hurt; (fig) to grieve; **dolerse** VR (de su situación) to grieve, feel sorry;

(*de las desgracias ajenas*) to sympathize; (*quejarse*) to complain; **me duele el brazo** my arm hurts; **no me duele el dinero** I don't mind about the money; **¡ahí le duele!** you've put your finger on it!

doliente [do'ljente] ADJ (*enfermo*) sick; (*dolorido*) aching; (*triste*) sorrowful; **la familia ~** the bereaved family

dolor [do'lor] NM pain; (*fig*) grief, sorrow; **~ de cabeza** headache; **~ de estómago** stomach ache; **~ de oídos** earache; **~ sordo** dull ache

dolorido, -a [dolo'riðo, a] ADJ (*Med*) sore; **la parte dolorida** the part which hurts

doloroso, -a [dolo'roso, a] ADJ (*Med*) painful; (*fig*) distressing

dom. ABR (= *domingo*) Sun.

domar [do'mar] /**1a**/ VT to tame

domesticado, -a [domesti'kaðo, a] ADJ (*amansado*) tame

domesticar [domesti'kar] /**1g**/ VT to tame

doméstico, -a [do'mestiko, a] ADJ domestic; (*vida, servicio*) home; (*tareas*) household; (*animal*) tame, pet ▶ NM/F servant; **economía doméstica** home economy; **gastos domésticos** household expenses

domestique etc [domes'tike] VB ver **domesticar**

domiciliación [domiθilja'θjon] NF: **~ de pagos** (*Com*) direct debit

domiciliar [domiθi'ljar] /**1b**/ VT to domicile; **domiciliarse** VR to take up (one's) residence

domiciliario, -a [domiθi'ljarjo, a] ADJ: **arresto ~** house arrest

domicilio [domi'θiljo] NM home; **~ particular** private residence; **~ social** (*Com*) head office, registered office; **servicio a ~** delivery service; **sin ~ fijo** of no fixed abode

dominante [domi'nante] ADJ dominant; (*persona*) domineering

dominar [domi'nar] /**1a**/ VT (*gen*) to dominate; (*países*) to rule over; (*adversario*) to overpower; (*caballo, nervios, emoción*) to control; (*incendio, epidemia*) to bring under control; (*idiomas*) to be fluent in ▶ VI to dominate, prevail; **dominarse** VR to control o.s.

domingo [do'mingo] NM Sunday; **D~ de Ramos** Palm Sunday; **D~ de Resurrección** Easter Sunday; ver tb **sábado**; **Semana Santa**

dominguero, -a [domin'gero, a] ADJ Sunday cpd

dominical [domini'kal] ADJ Sunday cpd; **periódico ~** Sunday newspaper

dominicano, -a [domini'kano, a] ADJ, NM/F Dominican

dominio [do'minjo] NM (*tierras*) domain; (*Pol*) dominion; (*autoridad*) power, authority; (*supremacía*) supremacy; (*de las*

pasiones) grip, hold; (*de idioma*) command; **ser del ~ público** to be widely known

dominó [domi'no] NM (*pieza*) domino; (*juego*) dominoes

don [don] NM (*talento*) gift; **D~ Juan Gómez** Mr Juan Gómez, Juan Gómez Esq. (BRIT); **tener ~ de gentes** to know how to handle people; **~ de lenguas** gift for languages; **~ de mando** (qualities of) leadership; **~ de palabra** gift of the gab; see note

> *Don* or *doña* is a term used before someone's first name – eg Don Diego, Doña Inés – when showing respect or being polite to someone of a superior social standing or to an older person. It is becoming somewhat rare, but it does however continue to be used with names and surnames in official documents and in correspondence: eg Sr. D. Pedro Rodríguez Hernández, Sra. Dña. Inés Rodríguez Hernández.

dona ['dona] NF (*AM*) doughnut, donut (*US*)

donación [dona'θjon] NF donation

donaire [do'naire] NM charm

donante [do'nante] NMF donor; **~ de sangre** blood donor

donar [do'nar] /**1a**/ VT to donate

donativo [dona'tiβo] NM donation

doncella [don'θeʎa] NF (*criada*) maid

donde ['donde] ADV where ▶ PREP: **el coche está allí ~ el farol** the car is over there by the lamppost o where the lamppost is; **por ~** through which; **a ~** to where, to which; **en ~** where, in which; **es a ~ vamos nosotros** that's where we're going

dónde ['donde] ADV INTERROGATIVO where?; **¿a ~ vas?** where are you going (to)?; **¿de ~ vienes?** where have you been?; **¿en ~?** where?; **¿por ~?** where?, whereabouts?; **¿por ~ se va al estadio?** how do you get to the stadium?

dondequiera [donde'kjera] ADV anywhere ▶ CONJ: **~ que** wherever; **por ~** everywhere, all over the place

donostiarra [donos'tjarra] ADJ of o from San Sebastián ▶ NMF native o inhabitant of San Sebastián

donut® [do'nut] NM (*ESP*) doughnut, donut (*US*)

doña ['dona] NF: **~ Alicia** Alicia; **D~ Carmen Gómez** Mrs Carmen Gómez; ver tb **don**

dopar [do'par] /**1a**/ VT to dope, drug

doping ['dopin] NM doping, drugging

doquier [do'kjer] ADV: **por ~** all over, everywhere

dorado, -a [do'raðo, a] ADJ (*color*) golden; (*Tec*) gilt

dorar [do'rar] /**1a**/ VT (*Tec*) to gild; (*Culin*) to brown, cook lightly; **~ la píldora** to sweeten the pill

dormilón, -ona [dormi'lon, ona] ADJ fond of sleeping ▶ NM/F sleepyhead

dormir [dor'mir] /**3j**/ VT: ~ **la siesta** to have an afternoon nap ▶ VI to sleep; **dormirse** VR (*persona, brazo, pierna*) to fall asleep; **dormirla** (*fam*) to sleep it off; ~ **la mona** (*fam*) to sleep off a hangover; ~ **como un lirón** *o* **tronco** to sleep like a log; ~ **a pierna suelta** to sleep soundly

dormitar [dormi'tar] /**1a**/ VI to doze

dormitorio [dormi'torjo] NM bedroom; ~ **común** dormitory

dorsal [dor'sal] ADJ dorsal ▶ NM (*Deporte*) number

dorso ['dorso] NM (*de mano*) back; (*de hoja*) other side; **escribir algo al** ~ to write sth on the back; **"véase al ~"** "see other side", "please turn over"

DOS NM ABR (= *sistema operativo de disco*) DOS

dos [dos] NUM two; (*fecha*) second; **los** ~ the two of them, both of them; **cada** ~ **por tres** every five minutes; **de** ~ **en** ~ in twos; **estamos a** ~ (*Tenis*) the score is deuce; *ver tb* **seis**

doscientos, -as [dos'θjentos, as] NUM two hundred

dosel [do'sel] NM canopy

dosificar [dosifi'kar] /**1g**/ VT (*Culin, Med, Química*) to measure out; (*no derrochar*) to be sparing with

dosifique *etc* [dosi'fike] VB *ver* **dosificar**

dosis ['dosis] NF INV dose, dosage

dossier [do'sjer] NM dossier, file

dotación [dota'θjon] NF (*acto, dinero*) endowment; (*plantilla*) staff; (*Naut*) crew; **la** ~ **es insuficiente** we are understaffed

dotado, -a [do'taðo, a] ADJ gifted; ~ **de** (*persona*) endowed with; (*máquina*) equipped with

dotar [do'tar] /**1a**/ VT to endow; (*Tec*) to fit; (*barco*) to man; (*oficina*) to staff

dote ['dote] NF (*de novia*) dowry; **dotes** NFPL (*talentos*) gifts

doy [doj] VB *ver* **dar**

Dpto. ABR (= *Departamento*) dept.

Dr., Dra. ABR (= *Doctor, Doctora*) Dr

draga ['draɣa] NF dredge

dragado [dra'ɣaðo] NM dredging

dragar [dra'ɣar] /**1h**/ VT to dredge; (*minas*) to sweep

dragón [dra'ɣon] NM dragon

drague *etc* ['draɣe] VB *ver* **dragar**

drama ['drama] NM drama; (*obra*) play

dramático, -a [dra'matiko, a] ADJ dramatic ▶ NM/F dramatist; (*actor*) actor; **obra dramática** play

dramaturgo, -a [drama'turɣo, a] NM/F dramatist, playwright

dramón [dra'mon] NM (*Teat*) melodrama; **¡qué ~!** what a scene!

drástico, -a ['drastiko, a] ADJ drastic

drenaje [dre'naxe] NM drainage

drenar [dre'nar] /**1a**/ VT to drain

droga ['droɣa] NF drug; (*Deporte*) dope; **el problema de la** ~ the drug problem

drogadicto, -a [droɣa'ðikto, a] NM/F drug addict

drogar [dro'ɣar] /**1h**/ VT to drug; (*Deporte*) to dope; **drogarse** VR to take drugs

drogodependencia [droɣoðepen'denθja] NF drug addiction

drogue *etc* ['droɣe] VB *ver* **drogar**

droguería [droɣe'ria] NF ≈ hardware shop (*Brit*) *o* store (*US*)

dromedario [drome'ðarjo] NM dromedary

Dto. ABR = **descuento**

Dtor., Dtora. ABR (= *Director, Directora*) Dir.

ducado [du'kaðo] NM duchy, dukedom

ducha ['dutʃa] NF (*baño*) shower; (*Med*) douche

ducharse [du'tʃarse] /**1a**/ VR to take a shower

ducho, -a ['dutʃo, a] ADJ: ~ **en** (*experimentado*) experienced in; (*hábil*) skilled at

dúctil ['duktil] ADJ (*metal*) ductile; (*persona*) easily influenced

duda ['duða] NF doubt; **sin** ~ no doubt, doubtless; **¡sin ~!** of course!; **no cabe** ~ there is no doubt about it; **no le quepa** ~ make no mistake about it; **no quiero poner en** ~ **su conducta** I don't want to call his behaviour into question; **sacar a algn de la** ~ to settle sb's doubts; **tengo una** ~ I have a query

dudar [du'ðar] /**1a**/ VT to doubt ▶ VI to doubt, have doubts; ~ **acerca de algo** to be uncertain about sth; **dudó en comprarlo** he hesitated to buy it; **dudan que sea verdad** they doubt whether *o* if it's true

dudoso, -a [du'ðoso, a] ADJ (*incierto*) hesitant; (*sospechoso*) doubtful; (*conducta*) dubious

duela *etc* VB *ver* **doler**

duelo ['dwelo] VB *ver* **doler** ▶ NM (*combate*) duel; (*luto*) mourning; **batirse en** ~ to fight a duel

duende ['dwende] NM imp, goblin; **tiene** ~ he's got real soul

dueño, -a ['dweɲo, a] NM/F (*propietario*) owner; (*de pensión, taberna*) landlord (-lady); (*de casa, perro*) master (mistress); (*empresario*) employer; **ser** ~ **de sí mismo** to have self-control; (*libre*) to be one's own boss; **eres** ~ **de hacer como te parezca** you're free to do as you think fit; **hacerse** ~ **de una situación** to take command of a situation

duerma *etc* ['dwerma] VB *ver* **dormir**

duermevela [dwerme'βela] NF (*fam*) nap, snooze

Duero ['dwero] NM Douro

dulce ['dulθe] ADJ sweet; (*carácter, clima*) gentle, mild ▶ ADV gently, softly ▶ NM sweet

dulcería [dulθe'ria] NF (*Am*) confectioner's (shop)

dulcificar [dulθifi'kar] /**1g**/ VT (*fig*) to soften

dulcifique*etc* [dulθi'fike] VB *ver* **dulcificar**

dulzón, -ona [dul'θon, ona] ADJ (*alimento*) sickly-sweet, too sweet; (*canción etc*) gooey

dulzura [dul'θura] NF sweetness; (*ternura*) gentleness

duna ['duna] NF dune

Dunquerque [dun'kerke] NM Dunkirk

dúo ['duo] NM duet, duo

duodécimo, -a [duo'deθimo, a] ADJ twelfth; *ver tb* **sexto**

dup., dup.^{do} ABR (= *duplicado*) duplicated

dúplex ['dupleks] NM INV (*piso*) duplex (apartment); (*Telec*) link-up; (*Inform*): **~ integral** full duplex

duplicar [dupli'kar] /**1g**/ VT (*hacer el doble de*) to duplicate; (*cantidad*) to double; **duplicarse** VR to double

duplique*etc* [du'plike] VB *ver* **duplicar**

duque ['duke] NM duke

duquesa [du'kesa] NF duchess

durable [du'raβle] ADJ durable

duración [dura'θjon] NF (*de película, disco etc*) length; (*de pila etc*) life; (*curso: de acontecimientos etc*) duration; **~ media de la vida** average life expectancy; **de larga ~**

(*enfermedad*) lengthy; (*pila*) long-life; (*disco*) long-playing; **de poca ~** short

duradero, -a [dura'ðero, a] ADJ (*tela*) hard-wearing; (*fe, paz*) lasting

durante [du'rante] ADV during; **~ toda la noche** all night long; **habló ~ una hora** he spoke for an hour

durar [du'rar] /**1a**/ VI (*permanecer*) to last; (*recuerdo*) to remain; (*ropa*) to wear (well)

durazno [du'rasno] NM (*Am: fruta*) peach; (*: árbol*) peach tree

durex ['dureks] NM (*Am: tira adhesiva*) Sellotape® (*Brit*), Scotch tape® (*US*)

dureza [du'reθa] NF (*cualidad*) hardness; (*de carácter*) toughness

durmiendo*etc* [dur'mjendo] VB *ver* **dormir**

durmiente [dur'mjente] ADJ sleeping ▶ NMF sleeper

duro, -a ['duro, a] ADJ hard; (*carácter*) tough; (*pan*) stale; (*cuello, puerta*) stiff; (*clima, luz*) harsh ▶ ADV hard ▶ NM (*moneda*) five peseta coin; **el sector ~ del partido** the hardliners *pl* in the party; **ser ~ con algn** to be tough with *o* hard on sb; **~ de mollera** (*torpe*) dense; **~ de oído** hard of hearing; **trabajar ~** to work hard; **estar sin un ~** to be broke

DVD NM ABR (= *disco de vídeo digital*) DVD

Ee

E, e [e] NF (letra) E, e; **E de Enrique** E for Edward (BRIT) o Easy (US)

E ABR (= este) E

e [e] CONJ (delante de i- e hi- pero no hie-) and; ver tb **y**

e/ ABR (Com: = envío) shpt.

EA ABR = **Ejército del Aire**

EAU NMPL ABR (= Emiratos Árabes Unidos) UAE

ebanista [eβa'nista] NMF cabinetmaker

ébano ['eβano] NM ebony

ebrio, -a ['eβrjo, a] ADJ drunk

Ebro ['eβro] NM Ebro

ebullición [eβuʎi'θjon] NF boiling; **punto de ~** boiling point

e-card ['ikard] NF e-card

eccema [ek'θema] NM (Med) eczema

echar [e'tʃar] /**1a**/ VT to throw; (agua, vino) to pour (out); (Culin) to put in, add; (dientes) to cut; (discurso) to give; (empleado: despedir) to fire, sack; (hojas) to sprout; (cartas) to post; (humo) to emit, give out; (reprimenda) to deal out; (cuenta) to make up; (freno) to put on ▶ VI: **~ a correr** to start running o to run, break into a run; **echarse** VR to lie down; **~ llave a** to lock (up); **~ abajo** (gobierno) to overthrow; (edificio) to demolish; **~ mano a** to lay hands on; **~ una mano a algn** (ayudar) to give sb a hand; **~ la buenaventura a algn** to tell sb's fortune; **~ la culpa a** to lay the blame on; **~ de menos** to miss; **~ una mirada a** to give a look; **~ sangre** to bleed; **~ a llorar** to burst into tears; **~ a reír** to burst out laughing; **echarse atrás** to throw o.s. back(wards); (fig) to back out; **echarse una novia** to get o.s. a girlfriend; **echarse una siestecita** to have a nap

echarpe [e'tʃarpe] NM (woman's) stole

eclesiástico, -a [ekle'sjastiko, a] ADJ ecclesiastical; (autoridades etc) church cpd ▶ NM clergyman

eclipsar [eklip'sar] /**1a**/ VT to eclipse; (fig) to outshine, overshadow

eclipse [e'klipse] NM eclipse

eco ['eko] NM echo; **encontrar un ~ en** to produce a response from; **hacerse ~ de una opinión** to echo an opinion; **tener ~** to catch on

ecografía [ekoɣra'fia] NF ultrasound

ecología [ekolo'xia] NF ecology

ecológico, -a [eko'loxiko, a] ADJ ecological; (producto, método) environmentally-friendly; (agricultura) organic

ecologista [ekolo'xista] ADJ environmental, conservation cpd ▶ NMF environmentalist

economato [ekono'mato] NM cooperative store

economía [ekono'mia] NF (sistema) economy; (carrera) economics; (cualidad) thrift; **~ dirigida** planned economy; **~ doméstica** housekeeping; **~ de mercado** market economy; **~ mixta** mixed economy; **~ sumergida** black economy; **hacer economías** to economize; **economías de escala** economies of scale

economice etc [ekono'miθe] VB ver **economizar**

económico, -a [eko'nomiko, a] ADJ (barato) cheap, economical; (persona) thrifty; (Com: año etc) financial; (: situación) economic

economista [ekono'mista] NMF economist

economizar [ekonomi'θar] /**1f**/ VT to economize on ▶ VI (ahorrar) to save up; (pey) to be miserly

ecosistema [ekosis'tema] NM ecosystem

ecu ['eku] NM ecu

ecuación [ekwa'θjon] NF equation

Ecuador [ekwa'ðor] NM Ecuador

ecuador [ekwa'ðor] NM equator

ecuánime [e'kwanime] ADJ (carácter) level-headed; (estado) calm

ecuatorial [ekwato'rjal] ADJ equatorial

ecuatoriano, -a [ekwato'rjano, a] ADJ, NM/F Ecuador(i)an

ecuestre [e'kwestre] ADJ equestrian

eczema [ek'θema] NM = **eccema**

ed. ABR (= edición) ed.

edad [e'ðað] NF age; **¿qué ~ tienes?** how old are you?; **tiene ocho años de ~** he is eight (years old); **de corta ~** young; **ser de ~ mediana/avanzada** to be middle-aged/ getting on; **ser mayor de ~** to be of age; **llegar a mayor ~** to come of age; **ser menor de ~** to be under age; **la E~ Media** the Middle Ages; **la E~ de Oro** the Golden Age

Edén [e'ðen] NM Eden

edición [eði'θjon] NF (*acto*) publication; (*ejemplar*) edition; **"al cerrar la ~"** (*Tip*) "stop press"

edicto [e'ðikto] NM edict, proclamation

edificante [eðifi'kante] ADJ edifying

edificar [eðifi'kar] /**1g**/ VT, VI (*Arq*) to build

edificio [eði'fiθjo] NM building; (*fig*) edifice, structure

edifique *etc* [eði'fike] VB *ver* **edificar**

Edimburgo [eðim'burɣo] NM Edinburgh

editar [eði'tar] /**1a**/ VT (*publicar*) to publish; (*preparar textos, tb Inform*) to edit

editor, a [eði'tor, a] NM/F (*que publica*) publisher; (*redactor*) editor ▶ ADJ: **casa ~** publishing company

editorial [eðito'rjal] ADJ editorial ▶ NM leading article, editorial; (*tb:* **casa editorial**) publisher

editorialista [eðitorja'lista] NMF leader-writer

edredón [eðre'ðon] NM eiderdown, quilt; **~ nórdico** continental quilt, duvet

educación [eðuka'θjon] NF education; (*crianza*) upbringing; (*modales*) (good) manners *pl*; (*formación*) training; **sin ~** ill-mannered; **¡qué falta de ~!** how rude!

educado, -a [eðu'kaðo, a] ADJ well-mannered; **mal ~** ill-mannered

educar [eðu'kar] /**1g**/ VT to educate; (*criar*) to bring up; (*voz*) to train

educativo, -a [eðuka'tiβo, a] ADJ educational; (*política*) education *cpd*

eduque *etc* [e'ðuke] VB *ver* **educar**

EE.UU. NMPL ABR (= *Estados Unidos*) USA

efectista [efek'tista] ADJ sensationalist

efectivamente [efektiβa'mente] ADV (*como respuesta*) exactly, precisely; (*verdaderamente*) really; (*de hecho*) in fact

efectivo, -a [efek'tiβo, a] ADJ effective; (*real*) actual, real ▶ NM: **pagar en ~** to pay (in) cash; **hacer ~ un cheque** to cash a cheque

efecto [e'fekto] NM effect, result; (*objetivo*) purpose, end; **efectos** NMPL (*personales*) effects; (*bienes*) goods; (*Com*) assets; (*Econ*) bills, securities; **~ invernadero** greenhouse effect; **efectos de consumo** consumer goods; **efectos a cobrar** bills receivable; **efectos especiales** special effects; **efectos personales** personal effects; **efectos secundarios** side effects; **efectos sonoros** sound effects; **hacer** *o* **surtir ~** to have the desired effect; **hacer ~** (*impresionar*) to make

an impression; **llevar algo a ~** to carry sth out; **en ~** in fact; (*respuesta*) exactly, indeed

efectuar [efek'twar] /**1e**/ VT to carry out; (*viaje*) to make

efervescente [eferβes'θente] ADJ (*bebida*) fizzy, bubbly

eficacia [efi'kaθja] NF (*de persona*) efficiency; (*de medicamento etc*) effectiveness

eficaz [efi'kaθ] ADJ (*persona*) efficient; (*acción*) effective

eficiencia [efi'θjenθja] NF efficiency

eficiente [efi'θjente] ADJ efficient

efigie [e'fixje] NF effigy

efímero, -a [e'fimero, a] ADJ ephemeral

EFTA SIGLA F = **Asociación Europea de Libre Comercio**

efusión [efu'sjon] NF outpouring; (*en el trato*) warmth; **con ~** effusively

efusivo, -a [efu'siβo, a] ADJ effusive; **mis más efusivas gracias** my warmest thanks

EGB NF ABR (*Esp Escol*) = *Educación General Básica*) primary education for six- to fourteen-year olds

Egeo [e'xeo] NM: **(Mar) ~** Aegean (Sea)

egipcio, -a [e'xipθjo, a] ADJ, NM/F Egyptian

Egipto [e'xipto] NM Egypt

egocéntrico, -a [eɣo'θentriko, a] ADJ self-centred

egoísmo [eɣo'ismo] NM egoism

egoísta [eɣo'ista] ADJ egoistical, selfish ▶ NMF egoist

ególatra [e'ɣolatra] ADJ big-headed

egregio, -a [e'ɣrexjo, a] ADJ eminent, distinguished

egresado, -a [eɣre'saðo, a] NM/F (*Am*) graduate

egresar [eɣre'sar] /**1a**/ VI (*Am*) to graduate

eh [e] EXCL hey!, hi!

Eire ['eire] NM Eire

ej. ABR (= *ejemplo*) eg

eje ['exe] NM (*Geo, Mat*) axis; (*Pol, fig*) axis, main line; (*de rueda*) axle; (*de máquina*) shaft, spindle

ejecución [exeku'θjon] NF execution; (*cumplimiento*) fulfilment; (*actuación*) performance; (*Jur: embargo de deudor*) attachment

ejecutar [exeku'tar] /**1a**/ VT to execute, carry out; (*matar*) to execute; (*cumplir*) to fulfil; (*Mus*) to perform; (*Jur: embargar*) to attach, distrain; (*deseos*) to fulfil; (*Inform*) to run

ejecutivo, -a [exeku'tiβo, a] ADJ, NM/F executive; **el (poder) ~** the executive (power)

ejecutor [exeku'tor] NM (*tb:* **ejecutor testamentario**) executor

ejecutoria [exeku'torja] NF (*Jur*) final judgment

ejemplar [exem'plar] ADJ exemplary ▶ NM example; (*Zool*) specimen; (*de libro*) copy;

(*de periódico*) number, issue; **~ de regalo** complimentary copy; **sin ~** unprecedented

ejemplificar [exemplifiˈkar] /**1g**/ VT to exemplify, illustrate

ejemplifique *etc* [exempliˈfike] VB *ver* **ejemplificar**

ejemplo [eˈxemplo] NM example; (*caso*) instance; **por ~** for example; **dar ~** to set an example

ejercer [exerˈθer] /**2b**/ VT to exercise; (*funciones*) to perform; (*negocio*) to manage; (*influencia*) to exert; (*un oficio*) to practise; (*poder*) to wield ▶ VI: **~ de** to practise as

ejercicio [exerˈθiθjo] NM exercise; (*Mil*) drill; (*Com*) fiscal o financial year; (*período*) tenure; **~ acrobático** (*Aviat*) stunt; **~ comercial** business year; **ejercicios espirituales** (*Rel*) retreat *sg*; **hacer ~** to take exercise

ejercitar [exerθiˈtar] /**1a**/ VT to exercise; (*Mil*) to drill

ejército [eˈxerθito] NM army; **E~ del Aire/de Tierra** Air Force/Army; **~ de ocupación** army of occupation; **~ permanente** standing army; **entrar en el ~** to join the army, join up

ejerza *etc* [eˈxerθa] VB *ver* **ejercer**

ejote [eˈxote] NM (*Am*) green bean

(PALABRA CLAVE)

el [el] (*fem* **la**, *neutro* **lo**, *pl* **los**, *pl* **las**) ARTÍCULO DEFINIDO **1** the; **el libro/la mesa/los estudiantes/las flores** the book/table/students/flowers; **me gusta el fútbol** I like football; **está en la cama** she's in bed
2 (*con nombre abstracto o propio: no se traduce*) **el amor/la juventud** love/youth; **el Conde Drácula** Count Dracula
3 (*posesión: se traduce a menudo por adj posesivo*): **romperse el brazo** to break one's arm; **levantó la mano** he put his hand up; **se puso el sombrero** she put her hat on
4 (*valor descriptivo*): **tener la boca grande/los ojos azules** to have a big mouth/blue eyes
5 (*con días*) on; **me iré el viernes** I'll leave on Friday; **los domingos suelo ir a nadar** on Sundays I generally go swimming
6 (*lo + adj*): **lo difícil/caro** what is difficult/expensive; (*cuán*): **no se da cuenta de lo pesado que es** he doesn't realize how boring he is
▶ PRON DEMOSTRATIVO **1**: **mi libro y el de usted** my book and yours; **las de Pepe son mejores** Pepe's are better; **no la(s) blanca(s) sino la(s) gris(es)** not the white one(s) but the grey one(s)
2: **lo de: lo de ayer** what happened yesterday; **lo de las facturas** that business about the invoices
▶ PRON RELATIVO **1**: **el que** *etc* (*indef*): **el (los)**

que quiera(n) que se vaya(n) anyone who wants to can leave; **llévese el/la que más le guste** take the one you like best; (*def*): **el que compré ayer** the one I bought yesterday; **los que se van** those who leave
2: **lo que: lo que pienso yo/más me gusta** what I think/like most
▶ CONJ: **el que: el que lo diga** the fact that he says so; **el que sea tan vago me molesta** his being so lazy bothers me
▶ EXCL: **¡el susto que me diste!** what a fright you gave me!
▶ PRON PERSONAL **1** (*persona: m*) him; (*: f*) her; (*: pl*) them; **lo/las veo** I can see him/them
2 (*animal, cosa: sg*) it; (*: pl*) them; **lo** (o **la**) **veo** I can see it; **los** (o **las**) **veo** I can see them
3: **lo** (*como sustituto de frase*): **no lo sabía** I didn't know; **ya lo entiendo** I understand now

él [el] PRON (*persona*) he; (*cosa*) it; (*después de prep: persona*) him; (*: cosa*) it; **mis libros y los de él** my books and his

elaboración [elaβoraˈθjon] NF (*producción*) manufacture; **~ de presupuestos** (*Com*) budgeting

elaborar [elaβoˈrar] /**1a**/ VT (*producto*) to make, manufacture; (*preparar*) to prepare; (*madera, metal etc*) to work; (*proyecto etc*) to work on o out

elasticidad [elastiθiˈðað] NF elasticity

elástico, -a [eˈlastiko, a] ADJ elastic; (*flexible*) flexible ▶ NM elastic; (*gomita*) elastic band

elección [elekˈθjon] NF election; (*selección*) choice, selection; **elecciones parciales** by-election *sg*; **elecciones generales** general election *sg*

electo, -a [eˈlekto, a] ADJ elect; **el presidente ~** the president-elect

electorado [elektoˈraðo] NM electorate, voters *pl*

electoral [elektoˈral] ADJ electoral

electrice *etc* [elekˈtriθe] VB *ver* **electrizar**

electricidad [elektriθiˈðað] NF electricity

electricista [elektriˈθista] NMF electrician

eléctrico, -a [eˈlektriko, a] ADJ electric

electrificar [elektrifiˈkar] /**1g**/ VT to electrify

electrizar [elektriˈθar] /**1f**/ VT (*Ferro, fig*) to electrify

electro... [elektro] PREF electro...

electrocardiograma [elektrokarðjoˈɣrama] NM electrocardiogram

electrocución [elektrokuˈθjon] NF electrocution

electrocutar [elektrokuˈtar] /**1a**/ VT to electrocute

electrodo [elekˈtroðo] NM electrode

electrodomésticos [elektroðoˈmestikos] NMPL (electrical) household appliances; (*Com*) white goods

electroimán [elektroi'man] NM
electromagnet

electromagnético, -a [elektromaɣ'netiko, a] ADJ electromagnetic

electrón [elek'tron] NM electron

electrónico, -a [elek'troniko, a] ADJ electronic ▶ NF electronics *sg*

electrotecnia [elektro'teknja] NF electrical engineering

electrotécnico, -a [elektro'tekniko, a] NM/F electrical engineer

electrotren [elektro'tren] NM express electric train

elefante [ele'fante] NM elephant

elegancia [ele'ɣanθja] NF elegance, grace; (*estilo*) stylishness

elegante [ele'ɣante] ADJ elegant, graceful; (*estiloso*) stylish, fashionable; (*traje etc*) smart; (*decoración*) tasteful

elegía [ele'xia] NF elegy

elegir [ele'xir] /**3c, 3k**/ VT (*escoger*) to choose, select; (*optar*) to opt for; (*presidente*) to elect

elemental [elemen'tal] ADJ (*claro, obvio*) elementary; (*fundamental*) elemental, fundamental

elemento [ele'mento] NM element; (*fig*) ingredient; (*AM*) person, individual; (*tipo raro*) odd person; (*de pila*) cell; **elementos** NMPL elements, rudiments; **estar en su ~** to be in one's element; **vino a verle un ~** someone came to see you

elenco [e'lenko] NM catalogue, list; (*Teat*) cast; (*AM: equipo*) team

elepé [ele'pe] NM LP

elevación [eleβa'θjon] NF elevation; (*acto*) raising, lifting; (*de precios*) rise; (*Geo etc*) height, altitude

elevado, -a [ele'βaðo, a] PP *de* **elevar** ▶ ADJ high

elevador [eleβa'ðor] NM (*AM*) lift (*BRIT*), elevator (*US*)

elevar [ele'βar] /**1a**/ VT to raise, lift (up); (*precio*) to put up; (*producción*) to step up; (*informe etc*) to present; **elevarse** VR (*edificio*) to rise; (*precios*) to go up; (*transportarse, enajenarse*) to get carried away; **la cantidad se eleva a ...** the total amounts to ...

eligiendo *etc* [eli'xjenðo], **elija** *etc* [e'lixa] VB *ver* **elegir**

eliminar [elimi'nar] /**1a**/ VT to eliminate, remove; (*olor, persona*) to get rid of; (*Deporte*) to eliminate, knock out

eliminatoria [elimina'torja] NF heat, preliminary (round)

elite [e'lite], **élite** ['elite] NF elite, élite

elitista [eli'tista] ADJ elitist

elixir [elik'sir] NM elixir; (*tb*: **elixir bucal**) mouthwash

ella ['eʎa] PRON (*persona*) she; (*cosa*) it; (*después de prep: persona*) her; (: *cosa*) it; **de ~** hers

ellas ['eʎas] PRON *ver* **ellos**

ello ['eʎo] PRON NEUTRO it; **es por ~ que ...** that's why ...

ellos, -as ['eʎos, as] PRON PERSONAL PL they; (*después de prep*) them; **de ~** theirs

elocuencia [elo'kwenθja] NF eloquence

elocuente [elo'kwente] ADJ eloquent; (*fig*) significant; **un dato ~** a fact which speaks for itself

elogiar [elo'xjar] /**1b**/ VT to praise, eulogize

elogio [e'loxjo] NM praise; **queda por encima de todo ~** it's beyond praise; **hacer ~ de** to sing the praises of

elote [e'lote] NM (*AM*) corn on the cob

El Salvador NM El Salvador

eludir [elu'ðir] /**3a**/ VT (*evitar*) to avoid, evade; (*escapar*) to escape, elude

E.M. ABR (*Mil*) = **Estado Mayor**

Em.ª ABR (= *Eminencia*) Mgr

email ['imeil] NM (*gen*) email *m*; (*dirección*) email address; **mandar un ~ a algn** to email sb, send sb an email

emanar [ema'nar] /**1a**/ VI: **~ de** to emanate from, come from; (*derivar de*) to originate in

emancipar [emanθi'par] /**1a**/ VT to emancipate; **emanciparse** VR to become emancipated, free o.s.

embadurnar [embaður'nar] /**1a**/ VT to smear

embajada [emba'xaða] NF embassy

embajador, a [embaxa'ðor, a] NM/F ambassador (ambassadress)

embaladura [embala'ðura] NF, (*AM*)
embalaje [emba'laxe] NM packing

embalar [emba'lar] /**1a**/ VT (*envolver*) to parcel, wrap (up); (*envasar*) to package ▶ VI to sprint; **embalarse** VR to go fast

embalsamar [embalsa'mar] /**1a**/ VT to embalm

embalsar [embal'sar] /**1a**/ VT (*río*) to dam (up); (*agua*) to retain

embalse [em'balse] NM (*presa*) dam; (*lago*) reservoir

embarace *etc* [emba'raθe] VB *ver* **embarazar**

embarazada [embara'θaða] ADJ F pregnant ▶ NF pregnant woman

embarazar [embara'θar] /**1f**/ VT to obstruct, hamper; **embarazarse** VR (*aturdirse*) to become embarrassed; (*confundirse*) to get into a mess

embarazo [emba'raθo] NM (*de mujer*) pregnancy; (*impedimento*) obstacle, obstruction; (*timidez*) embarrassment

embarazoso, -a [embara'θoso, a] ADJ (*molesto*) awkward; (*violento*) embarrassing

embarcación [embarka'θjon] NF (*barco*) boat, craft; (*acto*) embarkation; **~ de arrastre** trawler; **~ de cabotaje** coasting vessel

embarcadero [embarka'ðero] NM pier, landing stage

embarcar [embar'kar] /**1g**/ VT (*cargamento*) to ship, stow; (*persona*) to embark, put on board; (*fig*): ~ **a algn en una empresa** to involve sb in an undertaking; **embarcarse** VR to embark, go on board; (*marinero*) to sign on; (*Am: en tren etc*) to get on, get in

embargar [embar'ɣar] /**1h**/ VT (*frenar*) to restrain; (*sentidos*) to overpower; (*Jur*) to seize, impound

embargo [em'barɣo] NM (*Jur*) seizure; (*Com etc*) embargo; **sin ~** still, however, nonetheless

embargue *etc* [em'barɣe] VB *ver* **embargar**

embarque *etc* [em'barke] VB *ver* **embarcar** ▶ NM shipment, loading

embarrancar [embarran'kar] /**1g**/ VT, VI (*Naut*) to run aground; (*Auto etc*) to run into a ditch

embarranque *etc* [emba'rranke] VB *ver* **embarrancar**

embarrullar [embarru'ʎar] /**1a**/ VT to make a mess of

embate [em'bate] NM (*de mar, viento*) beating, violence

embaucador, a [embauka'ðor, a] NM/F (*estafador*) trickster; (*impostor*) impostor

embaucar [embau'kar] /**1g**/ VT to trick, fool

embauque *etc* [em'bauke] VB *ver* **embaucar**

embeber [embe'βer] /**2a**/ VT (*absorber*) to absorb, soak up; (*empapar*) to saturate ▶ VI to shrink; **embeberse** VR: **embeberse en un libro** to be engrossed *o* absorbed in a book

embelesado, -a [embele'saðo, a] ADJ spellbound

embelesar [embele'sar] /**1a**/ VT to enchant; **embelesarse** VR: **embelesarse (con)** to be enchanted (by)

embellecer [embeʎe'θer] /**2d**/ VT to embellish, beautify

embellezca *etc* [embe'ʎeθka] VB *ver* **embellecer**

embestida [embes'tiða] NF attack, onslaught; (*carga*) charge

embestir [embes'tir] /**3k**/ VT to attack, assault; to charge, attack ▶ VI to attack

embistiendo *etc* [embis'tjendo] VB *ver* **embestir**

emblanquecer [emblanke'θer] /**2d**/ VT to whiten, bleach; **emblanquecerse** VR to turn white

emblanquezca *etc* [emblan'keθka] VB *ver* **emblanquecer**

emblema [em'blema] NM emblem

embobado, -a [embo'βaðo, a] ADJ (*atontado*) stunned, bewildered

embobar [embo'βar] /**1a**/ VT (*asombrar*) to amaze; (*fascinar*) to fascinate; **embobarse** VR: **embobarse con** *o* **de** *o* **en** to be amazed at; to be fascinated by

embocadura [emboka'ðura] NF narrow entrance; (*de río*) mouth; (*Mus*) mouthpiece

embolado [embo'laðo] NM (*Teat*) bit part, minor role; (*fam*) trick

embolia [em'bolja] NF (*Med*) clot, embolism; **~ cerebral** clot on the brain

émbolo ['embolo] NM (*Auto*) piston

embolsar [embol'sar] /**1a**/ VT to pocket

emboquillado, -a [emboki'ʎaðo, a] ADJ (*cigarrillo*) tipped, filter *cpd*

emborrachar [emborra'tʃar] /**1a**/ VT to make drunk, intoxicate; **emborracharse** VR to get drunk

emboscada [embos'kaða] NF (*celada*) ambush

embotar [embo'tar] /**1a**/ VT to blunt, dull; **embotarse** VR (*adormecerse*) to go numb

embotellamiento [emboteʎa'mjento] NM (*Auto*) traffic jam

embotellar [embote'ʎar] /**1a**/ VT to bottle; **embotellarse** VR (*circulación*) to get into a jam

embozo [em'boθo] NM muffler, mask; (*de sábana*) turnover

embragar [embra'ɣar] /**1h**/ VT (*Auto, Tec*) to engage; (*partes*) to connect ▶ VI to let in the clutch

embrague [em'braɣe] VB *ver* **embragar** ▶ NM (*tb*: **pedal de embrague**) clutch

embravecer [embraβe'θer] /**2d**/ VT to enrage, infuriate; **embravecerse** VR to become furious; (*mar*) to get rough; (*tormenta*) to rage

embravecido, -a [embraβe'θiðo, a] ADJ (*mar*) rough; (*persona*) furious

embriagador, a [embrjaɣa'ðor, a] ADJ intoxicating

embriagar [embrja'ɣar] /**1h**/ VT (*emborrachar*) to make drunk; (*alegrar*) to delight; **embriagarse** VR (*emborracharse*) to get drunk

embriague *etc* [em'brjaɣe] VB *ver* **embriagar**

embriaguez [embrja'ɣeθ] NF (*borrachera*) drunkenness

embrión [em'brjon] NM embryo

embrionario, -a [embrjo'narjo, a] ADJ embryonic

embrollar [embro'ʎar] /**1a**/ VT (*asunto*) to confuse, complicate; (*persona*) to involve, embroil; **embrollarse** VR (*confundirse*) to get into a muddle *o* mess

embrollo [em'broʎo] NM (*enredo*) muddle, confusion; (*aprieto*) fix, jam

embromado, -a [embro'maðo, a] ADJ (*Am fam*) tricky, difficult

embromar [embro'mar] /**1a**/ VT (*burlarse de*) to tease, make fun of; (*Am fam: molestar*) to annoy

embrujado, -a [embru'xaðo, a] ADJ (*persona*) bewitched; **casa embrujada** haunted house

embrujo [em'bruxo] NM (*de mirada etc*) charm, magic

embrutecer [embrute'θer] /**2d**/ VT (*atontar*) to stupefy; **embrutecerse** VR to be stupefied

embrutezca *etc* [embru'teθka] VB *ver* **embrutecer**

embudo [em'buðo] NM funnel

embuste [em'buste] NM trick; (*mentira*) lie; (*humorístico*) fib

embustero, -a [embus'tero, a] ADJ lying, deceitful ▶ NM/F (*tramposo*) cheat; (*mentiroso*) liar; (*humorístico*) fibber

embutido [embu'tiðo] NM (*Culin*) sausage; (*Tec*) inlay

embutir [embu'tir] /**3a**/ VT to insert; (*Tec*) to inlay; (*llenar*) to pack tight, cram

emergencia [emer'xenθja] NF emergency; (*surgimiento*) emergence

emergente [emer'xente] ADJ resultant, consequent; (*nación*) emergent; (*Inform*) pop-up *cpd*; **menú/ventana** ~ pop-up menu/window

emerger [emer'xer] /**2c**/ VI to emerge, appear

emeritense [emeri'tense] ADJ of *o* from Mérida ▶ NMF native *o* inhabitant of Mérida

emerja *etc* [e'merxa] VB *ver* **emerger**

emigración [emiɣra'θjon] NF emigration; (*de pájaros*) migration

emigrado, -a [emi'ɣraðo, a] NM/F emigrant; (*Pol etc*) émigré(e)

emigrante [emi'ɣrante] ADJ, NMF emigrant

emigrar [emi'ɣrar] /**1a**/ VI (*personas*) to emigrate; (*pájaros*) to migrate

eminencia [emi'nenθja] NF eminence; (*en títulos*): **Su E~** His Eminence; **Vuestra E~** Your Eminence

eminente [emi'nente] ADJ eminent, distinguished; (*elevado*) high

emisario [emi'sarjo] NM emissary

emisión [emi'sjon] NF (*acto*) emission; (*Com etc*) issue; (*Radio, TV: acto*) broadcasting; (*: programa*) broadcast, programme, program (*US*); ~ **de acciones** (*Com*) share issue; ~ **gratuita de acciones** (*Com*) rights issue; ~ **de valores** (*Com*) flotation

emisor, a [emi'sor, a] NM transmitter ▶ NF radio *o* broadcasting station

emitir [emi'tir] /**3a**/ VT (*olor etc*) to emit, give off; (*moneda etc*) to issue; (*opinión*) to express; (*voto*) to cast; (*señal*) to send out; (*Radio*) to broadcast; ~ **una señal sonora** to beep

emoción [emo'θjon] NF emotion; (*excitación*) excitement; (*sentimiento*) feeling; ¡**qué ~**! how exciting!; (*irónico*) what a thrill!

emocionado, -a [emoθjo'naðo, a] ADJ deeply moved, stirred

emocionante [emoθjo'nante] ADJ (*excitante*) exciting, thrilling

emocionar [emoθjo'nar] /**1a**/ VT (*excitar*) to excite, thrill; (*conmover*) to move, touch; (*impresionar*) to impress; **emocionarse** VR to get excited

emoticón [emoti'kon], **emoticono** [emoti'kono] NM smiley, emoticon

emotivo, -a [emo'tiβo, a] ADJ emotional

empacar [empa'kar] /**1g**/ VT (*gen*) to pack; (*en caja*) to bale, crate

empacharse [empa'tʃarse] /**1a**/ VR (*Med*) to get indigestion

empacho [em'patʃo] NM (*Med*) indigestion; (*fig*) embarrassment

empadronamiento [empaðrona'mjento] NM census; (*de electores*) electoral register

empadronarse [empaðro'narse] /**1a**/ VR (*Pol: como elector*) to register

empalagar [empala'ɣar] /**1h**/ VT (*comida*) to cloy; (*hartar*) to pall on ▶ VI to pall

empalagoso, -a [empala'ɣoso, a] ADJ cloying; (*fig*) tiresome

empalague *etc* [empa'laɣe] VB *ver* **empalagar**

empalizada [empali'θaða] NF fence; (*Mil*) palisade

empalmar [empal'mar] /**1a**/ VT to join, connect ▶ VI (*dos caminos*) to meet, join

empalme [em'palme] NM joint, connection; (*de vías*) junction; (*de trenes*) connection

empanada [empa'naða] NF pie, pasty

empanar [empa'nar] /**1a**/ VT (*Culin*) to cook *o* roll in breadcrumbs *o* pastry

empantanarse [empanta'narse] /**1a**/ VR to get swamped; (*fig*) to get bogged down

empañarse [empa'ɲarse] /**1a**/ VR (*nublarse*) to get misty, steam up

empapar [empa'par] /**1a**/ VT (*mojar*) to soak, saturate; (*absorber*) to soak up, absorb; **empaparse** VR: **empaparse de** to soak up

empapelar [empape'lar] /**1a**/ VT (*paredes*) to paper

empaque *etc* [em'pake] VB *ver* **empacar**

empaquetar [empake'tar] /**1a**/ VT to pack, parcel up; (*Com*) to package

emparedado [empare'ðaðo] NM sandwich

emparejar [empare'xar] /**1a**/ VT to pair ▶ VI to catch up

emparentar [emparen'tar] /**1j**/ VI: ~ **con** to marry into

empariente *etc* [empa'rjente] VB *ver* **emparentar**

empastar [empas'tar] /**1a**/ VT (*embadurnar*) to paste; (*diente*) to fill

empaste [em'paste] NM (*de diente*) filling

empatar [empa'tar] /**1a**/ VI to draw, tie; **empataron a dos** they drew two-all

empate [em'pate] NM draw, tie; **un ~ a cero** a no-score draw

empecé [empe'θe], **empecemos** *etc* [empe'θemos] VB *ver* **empezar**

empecinado, -a [empeθi'naðo, a] ADJ stubborn

empedernido, -a [empeðer'niðo, a] ADJ hard, heartless; (*fijado*) hardened, inveterate; **un fumador ~** a heavy smoker

empedrado, -a [empe'ðraðo, a] ADJ paved ▶ NM paving

empedrar [empe'ðrar] /**1j**/ VT to pave

empeine [em'peine] NM (*de pie, zapato*) instep

empellón [empe'ʎon] NM push, shove; **abrirse paso a empellones** to push o shove one's way past o through

empeñado, -a [empe'ɲaðo, a] ADJ (*persona*) determined; (*objeto*) pawned

empeñar [empe'ɲar] /**1a**/ VT (*objeto*) to pawn, pledge; (*persona*) to compel; **empeñarse** VR (*obligarse*) to bind o.s., pledge o.s.; (*endeudarse*) to get into debt; **empeñarse en hacer** to be set on doing, be determined to do

empeño [em'peɲo] NM (*determinación*) determination; (*cosa prendada*) pledge; **casa de empeños** pawnshop; **con ~** insistently; (*con celo*) eagerly; **tener ~ en hacer algo** to be bent on doing sth

empeoramiento [empeora'mjento] NM worsening

empeorar [empeo'rar] /**1a**/ VT to make worse, worsen ▶ VI to get worse, deteriorate

empequeñecer [empekeɲe'θer] /**2d**/ VT to dwarf; (*fig*) to belittle

empequeñezca *etc* [empeke'ɲeθka] VB *ver* **empequeñecer**

emperador [empera'ðor] NM emperor

emperatriz [empera'triθ] NF empress

emperrarse [empe'rrarse] /**1a**/ VR to get stubborn; **~ en algo** to persist in sth

empezar [empe'θar] /**1f, 1j**/ VT, VI to begin, start; **empezó a llover** it started to rain; **bueno, para ~** well, to start with

empiece *etc* [em'pjeθe] VB *ver* **empezar**

empiedre *etc* [em'pjeðre] VB *ver* **empedrar**

empiezo *etc* [em'pjeθo] VB *ver* **empezar**

empinado, -a [empi'naðo, a] ADJ steep

empinar [empi'nar] /**1a**/ VT to raise; (*botella*) to tip up; **empinarse** VR (*persona*) to stand on tiptoe; (*animal*) to rear up; (*camino*) to climb steeply; **~ el codo** to booze (*fam*)

empingorotado, -a [empingoro'taðo, a] ADJ (*fam*) stuck-up

empírico, -a [em'piriko, a] ADJ empirical

emplace *etc* [em'plaθe] VB *ver* **emplazar**

emplaste [em'plaste], **emplasto** [em'plasto] NM (*Med*) plaster

emplasto [em'plasto] NM (*Med*) plaster

emplazamiento [emplaθa'mjento] NM site, location; (*Jur*) summons *sg*

emplazar [empla'θar] /**1f**/ VT (*ubicar*) to site, place, locate; (*Jur*) to summons; (*convocar*) to summon

empleado, -a [emple'aðo, a] NM/F (*gen*) employee; (*de banco etc*) clerk; **~ público** civil servant

emplear [emple'ar] /**1a**/ VT (*usar*) to use, employ; (*dar trabajo a*) to employ; **emplearse** VR (*conseguir trabajo*) to be employed; (*ocuparse*) to occupy o.s.; **~ mal el tiempo** to waste time; **¡te está bien empleado!** it serves you right!

empleo [em'pleo] NM (*puesto*) job; (*puestos: colectivamente*) employment; (*uso*) use, employment; **"modo de ~"** "instructions for use"

emplumar [emplu'mar] /**1a**/ VT (*estafar*) to swindle

empobrecer [empoβre'θer] /**2d**/ VT to impoverish; **empobrecerse** VR to become poor o impoverished

empobrecimiento [empoβreθi'mjento] NM impoverishment

empobrezca *etc* [empo'βreθka] VB *ver* **empobrecer**

empollar [empo'ʎar] /**1a**/ VT to incubate; (*Escol: fam*) to swot (up) ▶ VI (*gallina*) to brood; (*Escol: fam*) to swot

empollón, -ona [empo'ʎon, ona] NM/F (*Escol: fam*) swot

empolvar [empol'βar] /**1a**/ VT (*cara*) to powder; **empolvarse** VR to powder one's face; (*superficie*) to get dusty

emponzoñar [emponθo'ɲar] /**1a**/ VT (*esp fig*) to poison

emporio [em'porjo] NM emporium, trading centre; (*Am: gran almacén*) department store

empotrado, -a [empo'traðo, a] ADJ (*armario etc*) built-in

empotrar [empo'trar] /**1a**/ VT to embed; (*armario etc*) to build in

emprendedor, a [emprende'ðor, a] ADJ enterprising

emprender [empren'der] /**2a**/ VT to undertake; (*empezar*) to begin, embark on; (*acometer*) to tackle, take on; **~ marcha a** to set out for

empresa [em'presa] NF enterprise; (*Com: sociedad*) firm, company; (: *negocio*) business; (*esp Teat*) management; **~ filial** (*Com*) affiliated company; **~ matriz** (*Com*) parent company

empresarial [empresa'rjal] ADJ (*función, clase*) managerial; **sector ~** business sector

empresariales [empresa'rjales] NFPL business studies

empresario, -a [empre'sarjo, a] NM/F (*Com*) businessman(-woman), entrepreneur; (*Tec*) manager; (*Mus: de ópera etc*) impresario; **~ de pompas fúnebres** undertaker (*Brit*), mortician (*US*)

empréstito [em'prestito] NM (public) loan; (*Com*) loan capital

empujar [empu'xar] /**1a**/ VT to push, shove
empuje [em'puxe] NM thrust; (*presión*)
pressure; (*fig*) vigour, drive
empujón [empu'xon] NM push, shove;
abrirse paso a empujones to shove one's
way through
empuñadura [empuɲa'ðura] NF (*de espada*)
hilt; (*de herramienta etc*) handle
empuñar [empu'ɲar] /**1a**/ VT (*asir*) to grasp,
take (firm) hold of; **~ las armas** (*fig*) to take
up arms
emulación [emula'θjon] NF emulation
emular [emu'lar] /**1a**/ VT to emulate; (*rivalizar*)
to rival
émulo, -a ['emulo, a] NM/F rival, competitor
emulsión [emul'sjon] NF emulsion

(PALABRA CLAVE)

en [en] PREP **1** (*posición*) in; (*: sobre*) on; **está en
el cajón** it's in the drawer; **en Argentina/
La Paz** in Argentina/La Paz; **en el colegio/la
oficina** at school/the office; **en casa** at
home; **está en el suelo/quinto piso** it's on
the floor/the fifth floor; **en el periódico** in
the paper
2 (*dirección*) into; **entró en el aula** she went
into the classroom; **meter algo en el bolso**
to put sth into one's bag; **ir de puerta en
puerta** to go from door to door
3 (*tiempo*) in; on; **en 1605/3 semanas/
invierno** in 1605/3 weeks/winter; **en (el
mes de) enero** in (the month of) January;
en aquella ocasión/época on that occasion/
at that time
4 (*precio*) for; **lo vendió en 20 dólares** he sold
it for 20 dollars
5 (*diferencia*) by; **reducir/aumentar en una
tercera parte/un 20 por ciento** to reduce/
increase by a third/20 per cent
6 (*manera: forma*): **en avión/autobús** by
plane/bus; **escrito en inglés** written in
English; **en serio** seriously; **en espiral/
círculo** in a spiral/circle
7 (*después de vb que indica gastar etc*) on; **han
cobrado demasiado en dietas** they've
charged too much to expenses; **se le va la
mitad del sueldo en comida** half his salary
goes on food
8 (*tema: ocupación*): **experto en la materia**
expert on the subject; **trabaja en la
construcción** he works in the building
industry
9 (*adj + en + infin*): **lento en reaccionar** slow to
react

enagua(s) [ena'ɣwa(s)] NF(PL) (*esp AM*)
petticoat *sg*, underskirt *sg*
enajenación [enaxena'θjon] NF,
enajenamiento [enaxena'mjento] NM

alienation; (*tb*: **enajenación mental**) mental
derangement; (*fig*: *distracción*) absent-
mindedness; (: *embelesamiento*) rapture,
trance
enajenar [enaxe'nar] /**1a**/ VT to alienate; (*fig*)
to carry away
enamorado, -a [enamo'raðo, a] ADJ in love
▶ NM/F lover; **estar ~ (de)** to be in love (with)
enamorar [enamo'rar] /**1a**/ VT to win the love
of; **enamorarse** VR: **enamorarse (de)** to fall
in love (with)
enano, -a [e'nano, a] ADJ tiny, dwarf ▶ NM/F
dwarf; (*pey*) runt
enarbolar [enarβo'lar] /**1a**/ VT (*bandera etc*) to
hoist; (*espada etc*) to brandish
enardecer [enarðe'θer] /**2d**/ VT (*pasiones*) to
fire, inflame; (*persona*) to fill with
enthusiasm; **enardecerse** VR to get excited;
enardecerse por to get enthusiastic about
enardezca *etc* [enar'deθka] VB *ver* **enardecer**
encabece *etc* [enka'βeθe] VB *ver* **encabezar**
encabezado [enkaβe'θaðo] NM (*Com*) header
encabezamiento [enkaβeθa'mjento] NM
(*de carta*) heading; (*Com*) billhead, letterhead;
(*de periódico*) headline; (*preámbulo*) foreword,
preface; **~ normal** (*Tip etc*) running head
encabezar [enkaβe'θar] /**1f**/ VT (*movimiento,
revolución*) to lead, head; (*lista*) to head; (*carta*)
to put a heading to; (*libro*) to entitle
encadenar [enkaðe'nar] /**1a**/ VT to chain
(together); (*poner grilletes a*) to shackle
encajar [enka'xar] /**1a**/ VT (*meter a la fuerza*) to
push in; (*máquina etc*) to house; (*partes*) to
join; (*fam*: *golpe*) to give, deal; (*entremeter*) to
insert; (*ajustar*): **~ en** to fit (into) ▶ VI to fit
(well); (*fig*: *corresponder a*) to match; **encajarse**
VR: **encajarse en un sillón** to squeeze into
a chair
encaje [en'kaxe] NM (*labor*) lace
encajonar [enkaxo'nar] /**1a**/ VT to box (up),
put in a box
encalar [enka'lar] /**1a**/ VT (*pared*) to
whitewash
encallar [enka'ʎar] /**1a**/ VI (*Naut*) to run
aground
encaminado, -a [enkami'naðo, a] ADJ:
medidas encaminadas a … measures
designed to o aimed at …
encaminar [enkami'nar] /**1a**/ VT to direct,
send; **encaminarse**: **encaminarse a** to
set out for; **~ por** (*expedición etc*) to route via
encandilar [enkandi'lar] /**1a**/ VT to dazzle;
(*persona*) to daze, bewilder
encanecer [enkane'θer] /**2d**/ VI, **encanecerse**
VR (*pelo*) to go grey
encanezca *etc* [enka'neθka] VB *ver* **encanecer**
encantado, -a [enkan'taðo, a] ADJ (*hechizado*)
bewitched; (*muy contento*) delighted; **¡~!** how
do you do!, pleased to meet you

e

encantador, a [enkanta'ðor, a] ADJ
charming, lovely ▶ NM/F magician,
enchanter (enchantress)

encantar [enkan'tar] /**1a**/ VT to charm,
delight; (*cautivar*) to fascinate; (*hechizar*) to
bewitch, cast a spell on; **me encanta eso** I
love that

encanto [en'kanto] NM (*magia*) spell, charm;
(*fig*) charm, delight; (*expresión de ternura*)
sweetheart; **como por ~** as if by magic

encapotado, -a [enkapo'taðo, a] ADJ (*cielo*)
overcast

encapricharse [enkapri'tʃarse] /**1a**/ VR: **se ha
encaprichado con ir** he's taken it into his
head to go; **se ha encaprichado** he's
digging his heels in

encaramar [enkara'mar] /**1a**/ VT (*subir*) to
raise, lift up; **encaramarse** VR (*subir*) to
perch; **encaramarse a** (*árbol etc*) to climb

encararse [enka'rarse] /**1a**/ VR: **~ o con** to
confront, come face to face with

encarcelar [enkarθe'lar] /**1a**/ VT to imprison,
jail

encarecer [enkare'θer] /**2d**/ VT to put up the
price of ▶ VI, **encarecerse** VR to get dearer

encarecidamente [enkareθiða'mente] ADV
earnestly

encarecimiento [enkareθi'mjento] NM
price increase

encarezca *etc* [enka're θka] VB *ver* **encarecer**

encargado, -a [enkar'ɣaðo, a] ADJ in charge
▶ NM/F agent, representative; (*responsable*)
person in charge

encargar [enkar'ɣar] /**1h**/ VT to entrust; (*Com*)
to order; (*recomendar*) to urge, recommend;
encargarse VR: **encargarse de** to look after,
take charge of; **~ algo a algn** to put sb in
charge of sth

encargo [en'karɣo] NM (*pedido*) assignment,
job; (*responsabilidad*) responsibility;
(*recomendación*) recommendation; (*Com*)
order

encargue *etc* [en'karɣe] VB *ver* **encargar**

encariñarse [enkari'ɲarse] /**1a**/ VR: **~ con** to
grow fond of, get attached to

encarnación [enkarna'θjon] NF incarnation,
embodiment

encarnado, -a [enkar'naðo, a] ADJ (*color*) red;
ponerse ~ to blush

encarnar [enkar'nar] /**1a**/ VT to personify;
(*Teat: papel*) to play ▶ VI (*Rel etc*) to become
incarnate

encarnizado, -a [enkarni'θaðo, a] ADJ (*lucha*)
bloody, fierce

encarrilar [enkarri'lar] /**1a**/ VT (*tren*) to put
back on the rails; (*fig*) to correct, put on the
right track

encasillar [enkasi'ʎar] /**1a**/ VT (*Teat*) to
typecast; (*clasificar: pey*) to pigeonhole

encasquetar [enkaske'tar] /**1a**/ VT (*sombrero*)
to pull down *o* on; **encasquetarse** VR:
encasquetarse el sombrero to pull one's
hat down *o* on; **~ algo a algn** to offload sth
onto sb

encauce *etc* [en'kauθe] VB *ver* **encauzar**

encausar [enkau'sar] /**1a**/ VT to prosecute,
sue

encauzar [enkau'θar] /**1f**/ VT to channel; (*fig*)
to direct

encendedor [enθende'ðor] NM lighter

encender [enθen'der] /**2g**/ VT (*con fuego*) to
light; (*incendiar*) to set fire to; (*luz, radio*) to
put on, switch on; (*Inform*) to toggle on,
switch on; (*avivar: pasiones etc*) to inflame;
(*despertar: entusiasmo*) to arouse; (: *odio*) to
awaken; **encenderse** VR to catch fire;
(*excitarse*) to get excited; (*de cólera*) to flare up;
(*el rostro*) to blush

encendidamente [enθendiða'mente] ADV
passionately

encendido, -a [enθen'diðo, a] ADJ alight;
(*aparato*) (switched) on; (*mejillas*) glowing;
(*cara: por el vino etc*) flushed; (*mirada*)
passionate ▶ NM (*Auto*) ignition; (*de faroles*)
lighting

encerado, -a [enθe'raðo, a] ADJ (*suelo*) waxed,
polished ▶ NM (*Escol*) blackboard; (*hule*)
oilcloth

encerar [enθe'rar] /**1a**/ VT (*suelo*) to wax,
polish

encerrar [enθe'rrar] /**1j**/ VT (*confinar*) to shut
in *o* up; (*con llave*) to lock in *o* up; (*comprender,
incluir*) to include, contain; **encerrarse** VR to
shut *o* lock o.s. up *o* in

encerrona [enθe'rrona] NF trap

encestar [enθes'tar] /**1a**/ VI to score a basket

encharcado, -a [entʃar'kaðo, a] ADJ (*terreno*)
flooded

encharcar [entʃar'kar] /**1g**/ VT to swamp,
flood; **encharcarse** VR to become flooded

encharque *etc* [en'tʃarke] VB *ver* **encharcar**

enchufado, -a [entʃu'faðo, a] NM/F (*fam*)
well-connected person

enchufar [entʃu'far] /**1a**/ VT (*Elec*) to plug in;
(*Tec*) to connect, fit together; (*Com*) to merge

enchufe [en'tʃufe] NM (*Elec: clavija*) plug;
(: *toma*) socket; (*de dos tubos*) joint,
connection; (*fam: influencia*) contact,
connection; (: *puesto*) cushy job; **~ de clavija**
jack plug; **tiene un ~ en el ministerio** he
can pull strings at the ministry

encía [en'θia] NF (*Anat*) gum

enciclopedia [enθiklo'peðja] NF
encyclopaedia

encienda *etc* [en'θjenda] VB *ver* **encender**

encierro *etc* [en'θjerro] VB *ver* **encerrar** ▶ NM
shutting in *o* up; (*calabozo*) prison; (*Agr*) pen;
(*Taur*) penning

encima [en'θima] ADV (*sobre*) above, over; (*además*) besides; **~ de** (*en*) on, on top of; (*sobre*) above, over; (*además de*) besides, on top of; **por ~ de** over; **¿llevas dinero ~?** have you (got) any money on you?; **se me vino ~** it took me by surprise

encina [en'θina] NF (holm) oak

encinta [en'θinta] ADJ F pregnant

enclave [en'klaβe] NM enclave

enclenque [en'klenke] ADJ weak, sickly

encoger [enko'xer] /**2c**/ VT (*gen*) to shrink, contract; (*fig: asustar*) to scare; (:*desanimar*) to discourage; **encogerse** VR to shrink, contract; (*fig*) to cringe; **encogerse de hombros** to shrug one's shoulders

encoja *etc* [en'koxa] VB *ver* **encoger**

encolar [enko'lar] /**1a**/ VT (*engomar*) to glue, paste; (*pegar*) to stick down

encolerice *etc* [enkole'riθe] VB *ver* **encolerizar**

encolerizar [enkoleri'θar] /**1f**/ VT to anger, provoke; **encolerizarse** VR to get angry

encomendar [enkomen'dar] /**1j**/ VT to entrust, commend; **encomendarse** VR: **encomendarse a** to put one's trust in

encomiar [enko'mjar] /**1b**/ VT to praise, pay tribute to

encomienda *etc* [enko'mjenda] VB *ver* **encomendar** ▶ NF (*encargo*) charge, commission; (*elogio*) tribute; (*Am*) parcel, package; **~ postal** (*Am: servicio*) parcel post

encomio [en'komjo] NM praise, tribute

encono [en'kono] NM (*rencor*) rancour, spite

encontrado, -a [enkon'traðo, a] ADJ (*contrario*) contrary, conflicting; (*hostil*) hostile

encontrar [enkon'trar] /**1l**/ VT (*hallar*) to find; (*inesperadamente*) to meet, run into; **encontrarse** VR to meet (each other); (*situarse*) to be (situated); (*persona*) to find o.s., be; (*entrar en conflicto*) to crash, collide; **encontrarse con** to meet; **encontrarse bien (de salud)** to feel well; **no se encuentra aquí en este momento** he's not in at the moment

encontronazo [enkontro'naθo] NM collision, crash

encorvar [enkor'βar] /**1a**/ VT to curve; (*inclinar*) to bend (down); **encorvarse** VR to bend down, bend over

encrespado, -a [enkres'paðo, a] ADJ (*pelo*) curly; (*mar*) rough

encrespar [enkres'par] /**1a**/ VT (*cabellos*) to curl; (*fig*) to anger, irritate; **encresparse** VR (*el mar*) to get rough; (*fig*) to get cross *o* irritated

encriptar [enkrip'tar] VT encrypt

encrucijada [enkruθi'xaða] NF crossroads *sg*; (*empalme*) junction

encuadernación [enkwaðerna'θjon] NF binding; (*taller*) binder's

encuadernador, a [enkwaðerna'ðor, a] NM/F bookbinder

encuadrar [enkwa'ðrar] /**1a**/ VT (*retrato*) to frame; (*ajustar*) to fit, insert; (*encerrar*) to contain

encubierto [enku'βjerto] PP *de* **encubrir**

encubrir [enku'βrir] /**3a**/ VT (*ocultar*) to hide, conceal; (*criminal*) to harbour, shelter; (*ayudar*) to be an accomplice in

encuentro *etc* [en'kwentro] VB *ver* **encontrar** ▶ NM (*de personas*) meeting; (*Auto etc*) collision, crash; (*Deporte*) match, game; (*Mil*) encounter

encuerado, -a [enkwe'raðo, a] ADJ (*Am*) nude, naked

encuesta [en'kwesta] NF inquiry, investigation; (*sondeo*) public opinion poll; **~ judicial** post-mortem

encumbrado, -a [enkum'braðo, a] ADJ eminent, distinguished

encumbrar [enkum'brar] /**1a**/ VT (*persona*) to exalt; **encumbrarse** VR (*fig*) to become conceited

endeble [en'deβle] ADJ (*argumento, excusa, persona*) weak

endémico, -a [en'demiko, a] ADJ endemic

endemoniado, -a [endemo'njaðo, a] ADJ possessed (of the devil); (*travieso*) devilish

enderece *etc* [ende're θe] VB *ver* **enderezar**

enderezar [endere'θar] /**1f**/ VT (*poner derecho*) to straighten (out); (:*verticalmente*) to set upright; (*fig*) to straighten *o* sort out; (*dirigir*) to direct; **enderezarse** VR (*persona sentada*) to sit up straight

endeudarse [endeu'ðarse] /**1a**/ VR to get into debt

endiablado, -a [endja'βlaðo, a] ADJ devilish, diabolical; (*humorístico*) mischievous

endibia [en'diβja] NF endive

endilgar [endil'γar] /**1h**/ VT (*fam*): **~ algo a algn** to lumber sb with sth; **~ un sermón a algn** to give sb a lecture

endilgue *etc* [en'dilγe] VB *ver* **endilgar**

endiñar [endi'ɲar] /**1a**/ VT: **~ algo a algn** to land sth on sb

endomingarse [endomin'garse] /**1h**/ VR to dress up, put on one's best clothes

endomingue *etc* [endo'minge] VB *ver* **endomingarse**

endosar [endo'sar] /**1a**/ VT (*cheque etc*) to endorse

endulce *etc* [en'dulθe] VB *ver* **endulzar**

endulzar [endul'θar] /**1f**/ VT to sweeten; (*suavizar*) to soften

endurecer [endure'θer] /**2d**/ VT to harden; **endurecerse** VR to harden, grow hard

endurecido, -a [endure'θiðo, a] ADJ (*duro*) hard; (*fig*) hardy, tough; **estar ~ a algo** to be hardened *o* used to sth

endurezca etc [endu're0ka] VB ver **endurecer**

ene. ABR (= enero) Jan.; ver tb **julio**

enema [e'nema] NM (Med) enema

enemigo, -a [ene'miɣo, a] ADJ enemy, hostile ▶ NM/F enemy ▶ NF enmity, hostility; **ser ~ de** (persona) to dislike; (tendencia) to be inimical to

enemistad [enemis'taδ] NF enmity

enemistar [enemis'tar] /1a/ VT to make enemies of, cause a rift between; **enemistarse** VR to become enemies; (amigos) to fall out

energético, -a [ener'xetiko, a] ADJ: **política energética** energy policy

energía [ener'xia] NF (vigor) energy, drive; (empuje) push; (Tec, Elec) energy, power; **~ atómica/eléctrica/eólica** atomic/electric/wind power; **~ solar** solar energy o power; **energías renovables** renewable energy sources

enérgico, -a [e'nerxiko, a] ADJ (gen) energetic; (ataque) vigorous; (ejercicio) strenuous; (medida) bold; (voz, modales) forceful

energúmeno, -a [ener'yumeno, a] NM/F madman(-woman); **ponerse como un ~ con algn** to get furious with sb

enero [e'nero] NM January; ver tb **julio**

enervar [ener'βar] /1a/ VT (poner nervioso a) to get on sb's nerves

enésimo, -a [e'nesimo, a] ADJ (Mat) nth; **por enésima vez** (fig) for the umpteenth time

enfadado, -a [enfa'δaδo, a] ADJ angry, annoyed

enfadar [enfa'δar] /1a/ VT to anger, annoy; **enfadarse** VR to get angry o annoyed

enfado [en'faδo] NM (enojo) anger, annoyance; (disgusto) trouble, bother

énfasis ['enfasis] NM emphasis, stress; **poner ~ en** to stress

enfático, -a [en'fatiko, a] ADJ emphatic

enfatizado, -a [enfati'θaδo, a] ADJ: **en caracteres enfatizados** (Inform) emphasized

enfermar [enfer'mar] /1a/ VT to make ill ▶ VI to fall ill, be taken ill; **su actitud me enferma** his attitude makes me sick; **~ del corazón** to develop heart trouble

enfermedad [enferme'δaδ] NF illness; **~ venérea** venereal disease

enfermera [enfer'mera] NF ver **enfermero**

enfermería [enferme'ria] NF infirmary; (de colegio etc) sick bay

enfermero, -a [enfer'mero, a] NM (male) nurse ▶ NF nurse; **enfermera jefa** matron

enfermizo, -a [enfer'miθo, a] ADJ (persona) sickly, unhealthy; (fig) unhealthy

enfermo, -a [en'fermo, a] ADJ ill, sick ▶ NM/F invalid, sick person; (en hospital) patient; **caer** o **ponerse ~** to fall ill

enfilar [enfi'lar] /1a/ VT (aguja) to thread; (calle) to go down

enflaquecer [enflake'θer] /2d/ VT (adelgazar) to make thin; (debilitar) to weaken

enflaquezca etc [enfla'keθka] VB ver **enflaquecer**

enfocar [enfo'kar] /1g/ VT (foto etc) to focus; (problema etc) to consider, look at

enfoque etc [en'foke] VB ver **enfocar** ▶ NM focus; (acto) focusing; (óptica) approach

enfrascado, -a [enfras'kaδo, a] ADJ: **estar ~ en algo** (fig) to be wrapped up in sth

enfrascarse [enfras'karse] /1g/ VR: **~ en un libro** to bury o.s. in a book

enfrasque etc [en'fraske] VB ver **enfrascarse**

enfrentamiento [enfrenta'mjento] NM confrontation

enfrentar [enfren'tar] /1a/ VT (peligro) to face (up to), confront; (oponer) to bring face to face; **enfrentarse** VR (dos personas) to face o confront each other; (Deporte: dos equipos) to meet; **enfrentarse a** o **con** to face up to, confront

enfrente [en'frente] ADV opposite; **~ de** opposite, facing; **la casa de ~** the house opposite, the house across the street

enfriamiento [enfria'mjento] NM chilling, refrigeration; (Med) cold, chill

enfriar [enfri'ar] /1c/ VT (alimentos) to cool, chill; (algo caliente) to cool down; (habitación) to air, freshen; (entusiasmo) to dampen; **enfriarse** VR to cool down; (Med) to catch a chill; (amistad) to cool

enfurecer [enfure'θer] /2d/ VT to enrage, madden; **enfurecerse** VR to become furious, fly into a rage; (mar) to get rough

enfurezca etc [enfu'reθka] VB ver **enfurecer**

engalanar [engala'nar] /1a/ VT (adornar) to adorn; (ciudad) to decorate; **engalanarse** VR to get dressed up

enganchar [engan'tʃar] /1a/ VT to hook; (ropa) to hang up; (dos vagones) to hitch up; (Tec) to couple, connect; (Mil) to recruit; (fam: atraer: persona) to rope into; **engancharse** VR (Mil) to enlist, join up; **engancharse (a)** (drogas) to get hooked (on)

enganche [en'gantʃe] NM hook; (Tec) coupling, connection; (acto) hooking (up); (Mil) recruitment, enlistment; (Am: depósito) deposit

engañar [enga'ɲar] /1a/ VT to deceive; (estafar) to cheat, swindle ▶ VI: **las apariencias engañan** appearances are deceptive; **engañarse** VR (equivocarse) to be wrong; (a sí mismo) to deceive o kid o.s.; **engaña a su mujer** he's unfaithful to o cheats on his wife

engaño [en'gaɲo] NM deceit; (estafa) trick, swindle; (error) mistake, misunderstanding; (ilusión) delusion

engañoso, -a [enga'ɲoso, a] ADJ (tramposo) crooked; (mentiroso) dishonest, deceitful; (aspecto) deceptive; (consejo) misleading

engarce etc [en'garθe] VB ver **engarzar**

engarzar [engar'θar] /**1f**/ VT (joya) to set, mount; (fig) to link, connect

engatusar [engatu'sar] /**1a**/ VT (fam) to coax

engendrar [enxen'drar] /**1a**/ VT to breed; (procrear) to beget; (fig) to cause, produce

engendro [en'xendro] NM (Bio) foetus; (fig) monstrosity; (: idea) brainchild

englobar [englo'βar] /**1a**/ VT (comprender) to include, comprise; (incluir) to lump together

engomar [engo'mar] /**1a**/ VT to glue, stick

engordar [engor'ðar] /**1a**/ VT to fatten ▶ VI to get fat, put on weight

engorro [en'gorro] NM bother, nuisance

engorroso, -a [engo'rroso, a] ADJ bothersome, trying

engranaje [engra'naxe] NM (Auto) gear; (juego) gears pl

engrandecer [engrande'θer] /**2d**/ VT to enlarge, magnify; (alabar) to praise, speak highly of; (exagerar) to exaggerate

engrandezca etc [engran'deθka] VB ver **engrandecer**

engrasar [engra'sar] /**1a**/ VT (Tec: poner grasa) to grease; (: lubricar) to lubricate, oil; (manchar) to make greasy

engrase [en'grase] NM greasing, lubrication

engreído, -a [engre'iðo, a] ADJ vain, conceited

engrosar [engro'sar] /**1l**/ VT (ensanchar) to enlarge; (aumentar) to increase; (hinchar) to swell

engrudo [en'gruðo] NM paste

engruese etc [en'grwese] VB ver **engrosar**

engullir [engu'ʎir] /**3a, 3h**/ VT to gobble, gulp (down)

enhebrar [ene'βrar] /**1a**/ VT to thread

enhiesto, -a [e'njesto, a] ADJ (derecho) erect; (bandera) raised; (edificio) lofty

enhorabuena [enora'βwena] EXCL: ¡~! congratulations! ▶ NF: **dar la ~ a** to congratulate

enigma [e'niɣma] NM enigma; (problema) puzzle; (misterio) mystery

enigmático, -a [eniɣ'matiko, a] ADJ enigmatic

enjabonar [enxaβo'nar] /**1a**/ VT to soap; (barba) to lather; (fam: adular) to soft-soap; (: regañar) to tick off

enjalbegar [enxalβe'ɣar] /**1h**/ VT (pared) to whitewash

enjalbegue etc [enxal'βeɣe] VB ver **enjalbegar**

enjambre [en'xamβre] NM swarm

enjaular [enxau'lar] /**1a**/ VT to (put in a) cage; (fam) to jail, lock up

enjuagar [enxwa'ɣar] /**1h**/ VT (ropa) to rinse (out)

enjuague etc [en'xwaɣe] VB ver **enjuagar** ▶ NM (Med) mouthwash; (de ropa) rinse, rinsing

enjugar [enxu'ɣar] /**1h**/ VT to wipe (off); (lágrimas) to dry; (déficit) to wipe out

enjugue etc [en'xuɣe] VB ver **enjugar**

enjuiciar [enxwi'θjar] /**1b**/ VT (Jur: procesar) to prosecute, try; (fig) to judge

enjuto, -a [en'xuto, a] ADJ dry, dried up; (fig) lean, skinny

enlace [en'laθe] VB ver **enlazar** ▶ NM link, connection; (relación) relationship; (tb: **enlace matrimonial**) marriage; (de trenes) connection; **~ de datos** data link; **~ sindical** shop steward; **~ telefónico** telephone link-up

enlatado, -a [enla'taðo, a] ADJ (alimentos, productos) tinned, canned

enlazar [enla'θar] /**1f**/ VT (unir con lazos) to bind together; (atar) to tie; (conectar) to link, connect; (AM) to lasso

enlodar [enlo'ðar] /**1a**/ VT to cover in mud; (fig: manchar) to stain; (: rebajar) to debase

enloquecer [enloke'θer] /**2d**/ VT to drive mad ▶ VI to go mad

enloquezca etc [enlo'keθka] VB ver **enloquecer**

enlutado, -a [enlu'taðo, a] ADJ (persona) in mourning

enlutar [enlu'tar] /**1a**/ VT to dress in mourning; **enlutarse** VR to go into mourning

enmarañar [enmara'ɲar] /**1a**/ VT (enredar) to tangle up, entangle; (complicar) to complicate; (confundir) to confuse; **enmarañarse** VR (enredarse) to become entangled; (confundirse) to get confused

enmarcar [enmar'kar] /**1g**/ VT (cuadro) to frame; (fig) to provide a setting for

enmarque etc [en'marke] VB ver **enmarcar**

enmascarar [enmaska'rar] /**1a**/ VT to mask; (intenciones) to disguise; **enmascararse** VR to put on a mask

enmendar [enmen'dar] /**1j**/ VT to emend, correct; (constitución etc) to amend; (comportamiento) to reform; **enmendarse** VR to reform, mend one's ways

enmienda [en'mjenda] VB ver **enmendar** ▶ NF correction; amendment; reform

enmohecerse [enmoe'θerse] /**2d**/ VR (metal) to rust, go rusty; (muro, plantas) to go mouldy

enmohezca etc [enmo'eθka] VB ver **enmohecerse**

enmudecer [enmuðe'θer] /**2d**/ VT to silence ▶ VI (perder el habla) to fall silent; (guardar silencio) to remain silent; (por miedo) to be struck dumb

enmudezca etc [enmu'ðeθka] VB ver **enmudecer**

ennegrecer [enneɣre'θer] /**2d**/ VT (poner negro) to blacken; (oscurecer) to darken; **ennegrecerse** VR to turn black; (oscurecerse) to get dark, darken

ennegrezca etc [enne'ɣreθka] VB ver
ennegrecer

ennoblecer [ennoβle'θer] /**2d**/ VT to ennoble

ennoblezca etc [enno'βleθka] VB ver
ennoblecer

en.° ABR (= enero) Jan.

enojadizo, -a [enoxa'ðiθo, a] ADJ irritable,
short-tempered

enojado, -a [eno'xaðo, a] ADJ (Am) angry

enojar [eno'xar] /**1a**/ (esp Am) (encolerizar) to
anger; (disgustar) to annoy, upset; **enojarse**
VR to get angry; to get annoyed

enojo [e'noxo] NM (esp Am: cólera) anger;
(irritación) annoyance; **enojos** NMPL trials,
problems

enojoso, -a [eno'xoso, a] ADJ annoying

enorgullecerse [enorɣuʎe'θerse] /**2d**/ VR to
be proud; ~ **de** to pride o.s. on, be proud of

enorgullezca etc [enorɣu'ʎeθka] VB ver
enorgullecerse

enorme [e'norme] ADJ enormous, huge; (fig)
monstrous

enormidad [enormi'ðað] NF hugeness,
immensity

enraice etc [en'raiθe] VB ver **enraizar**

enraizar [enrai'θar] /**1f**/ VI to take root

enrarecido, -a [enrare'θiðo, a] ADJ rarefied

enredadera [enreða'ðera] NF (Bot) creeper,
climbing plant

enredar [enre'ðar] /**1a**/ VT (cables, hilos etc) to
tangle (up), entangle; (situación) to complicate,
confuse; (meter cizaña) to sow discord among
o between; (implicar) to embroil, implicate;
enredarse VR to get entangled, get tangled
(up); (situación) to get complicated; (persona)
to get embroiled; (Am fam) to meddle

enredo [en'reðo] NM (maraña) tangle;
(confusión) mix-up, confusion; (intriga)
intrigue; (apuro) jam; (amorío) love affair

enrejado [enre'xaðo] NM grating; (de ventana)
lattice; (en jardín) trellis

enrevesado, -a [enreβe'saðo, a] ADJ (asunto)
complicated, involved

enriquecer [enrike'θer] /**2d**/ VT to make rich;
(fig) to enrich; **enriquecerse** VR to get rich

enriquezca etc [enri'keθka] VB ver **enriquecer**

enrojecer [enroxe'θer] /**2d**/ VT to redden ▸ VI
(persona) to blush; **enrojecerse** VR to blush

enrojezca etc [enro'xeθka] VB ver **enrojecer**

enrolar [enro'lar] /**1a**/ VT (Mil) to enlist;
(reclutar) to recruit; **enrolarse** VR (Mil) to join
up; (afiliarse) to enrol, sign on

enrollar [enro'ʎar] /**1a**/ VT to roll (up), wind
(up); **enrollarse** VR: **enrollarse con algn** to
get involved with sb

enroque [en'roke] NM (Ajedrez) castling

enroscar [enros'kar] /**1g**/ VT (torcer, doblar) to
twist; (arrollar) to coil (round), wind; (tornillo,
rosca) to screw in; **enroscarse** VR to coil, wind

enrosque etc [en'roske] VB ver **enroscar**

ensalada [ensa'laða] NF salad; (lío) mix-up

ensaladilla [ensala'ðiʎa] NF (tb: **ensaladilla
rusa**) ≈ Russian salad

ensalce etc [en'salθe] VB ver **ensalzar**

ensalzar [ensal'θar] /**1f**/ VT (alabar) to praise,
extol; (exaltar) to exalt

ensamblador [ensambla'ðor] NM (Inform)
assembler

ensambladura [ensambla'ðura] NF,
ensamblaje [ensam'blaxe] NM assembly;
(Tec) joint

ensamblar [ensam'blar] /**1a**/ VT (montar) to
assemble; (madera etc) to join

ensanchar [ensan'tʃar] /**1a**/ VT (hacer más
ancho) to widen; (agrandar) to enlarge,
expand; (Costura) to let out; **ensancharse** VR
to get wider, expand; (pey) to give o.s. airs

ensanche [en'santʃe] NM (de calle) widening;
(de negocio) expansion

ensangrentado, -a [ensangren'taðo, a] ADJ
bloodstained, covered with blood

ensangrentar [ensangren'tar] /**1j**/ VT to
stain with blood

ensangriente etc [ensan'grjente] VB ver
ensangrentar

ensañarse [ensa'ɲarse] /**1a**/ VR: ~ **con** to treat
brutally

ensartar [ensar'tar] /**1a**/ VT (gen) to string
(together); (carne) to spit, skewer

ensayar [ensa'jar] /**1a**/ VT to test, try (out);
(Teat) to rehearse

ensayista [ensa'jista] NMF essayist

ensayo [en'sajo] NM test, trial; (Química)
experiment; (Teat) rehearsal; (Deporte) try;
(Escol, Lit) essay; **pedido de ~** (Com) trial
order; **~ general** (Teat) dress rehearsal; (Mus)
full rehearsal

enseguida [ense'ɣuiða] ADV at once, right
away; **~ termino** I've nearly finished, I
shan't be long now

ensenada [ense'naða] NF inlet, cove

enseña [en'seɲa] NF ensign, standard

enseñante [ense'ɲante] NMF teacher

enseñanza [ense'ɲanθa] NF (educación)
education; (acción) teaching; (doctrina)
teaching, doctrine; **~ primaria/
secundaria/superior** primary/secondary/
higher education

enseñar [ense'ɲar] /**1a**/ VT (educar) to teach;
(instruir) to teach, instruct; (mostrar, señalar)
to show

enseres [en'seres] NMPL belongings

ensillar [ensi'ʎar] /**1a**/ VT to saddle (up)

ensimismarse [ensimis'marse] /**1a**/ VR
(abstraerse) to become lost in thought; (estar
absorto) to be lost in thought; (Am) to become
conceited

ensopar [enso'par] /**1a**/ VT (Am) to soak

ensordecer [ensorðe'θer] **/2d/** vt to deafen
  ▶ vi to go deaf

ensordezca etc [ensor'ðeθka] vb ver
  ensordecer

ensortijado, -a [ensorti'xaðo, a] ADJ (pelo) curly

ensuciar [ensu'θjar] **/1b/** vt (manchar) to dirty,
  soil; (fig) to defile; **ensuciarse** vr (mancharse)
  to get dirty; (bebé) to dirty one's nappy

ensueño [en'sweɲo] NM (sueño) dream,
  fantasy; (ilusión) illusion; (soñando despierto)
  daydream; **de ~** dream-like

entablado [enta'βlaðo] NM (piso) floorboards
  pl; (armazón) boarding

entablar [enta'βlar] **/1a/** vt (recubrir) to board
  (up); (Ajedrez, Damas) to set up; (conversación)
  to strike up; (Jur) to draw

entablillar [entaβli'ʎar] **/1a/** vt (Med) to (put
  in a) splint

entallado, -a [enta'ʎaðo, a] ADJ waisted

entallar [enta'ʎar] **/1a/** vt (traje) to tailor ▶ vi:
  el traje entalla bien the suit fits well

ente ['ente] NM (organización) body,
  organization; (compañía) company; (fam:
  persona) odd character; (ser) being; **~ público**
  (Esp) state(-owned) body

entender [enten'der] **/2g/** vt (comprender) to
  understand; (darse cuenta) to realize; (querer
  decir) to mean ▶ vi to understand; (creer) to
  think, believe ▶ NM: **a mi ~** in my opinion;
  entenderse vr (comprenderse) to be
  understood; (2 personas) to get on together;
  (ponerse de acuerdo) to agree, reach an
  agreement; **~ de** to know all about; **~ algo
  de** to know a little about; **~ en** to deal with,
  have to do with; **dar a ~ que ...** to lead to
  believe that ...; **entenderse mal** to get on
  badly; **¿entiendes?** (do you) understand?

entendido, -a [enten'diðo, a] ADJ (comprendido)
  understood; (hábil) skilled; (inteligente)
  knowledgeable ▶ NM/F (experto) expert
  ▶ EXCL agreed!

entendimiento [entendi'mjento] NM
  (comprensión) understanding; (inteligencia)
  mind, intellect; (juicio) judgement

enterado, -a [ente'raðo, a] ADJ well-
  informed; **estar ~ de** to know about, be
  aware of; **no darse por ~** to pretend not to
  understand

enteramente [entera'mente] ADV entirely,
  completely

enterar [ente'rar] **/1a/** vt (informar) to inform,
  tell; **enterarse** vr to find out, get to know;
  para que te enteres ... (fam) for your
  information ...

entereza [ente'reθa] NF (totalidad) entirety;
  (fig: de carácter) strength of mind; (honradez)
  integrity

enterito [ente'rito] NM (AM) boiler suit (BRIT),
  overalls (US)

enternecedor, a [enterneθe'ðor, a] ADJ
  touching

enternecer [enterne'θer] **/2d/** vt (ablandar) to
  soften; (apiadar) to touch, move;
  enternecerse vr to be touched, be moved

enternezca etc [enter'neθka] vb ver
  enternecer

entero, -a [en'tero, a] ADJ (total) whole, entire;
  (fig: recto) honest; (: firme) firm, resolute ▶ NM
  (Mat) integer; (Com: punto) point; (AM: pago)
  payment; **las acciones han subido dos
  enteros** the shares have gone up two points

enterrador [enterra'ðor] NM gravedigger

enterrar [ente'rrar] **/1j/** vt to bury; (fig) to
  forget

entibiar [enti'βjar] **/1b/** vt (enfriar) to cool;
  (calentar) to warm; **entibiarse** vr (fig) to cool

entidad [enti'ðað] NF (empresa) firm,
  company; (organismo) body; (sociedad) society;
  (Filosofía) entity

entienda etc [en'tjenda] vb ver **entender**

entierro [en'tjerro] vb ver **enterrar** ▶ NM
  (acción) burial; (funeral) funeral

entomología [entomolo'xia] NF entomology

entomólogo, -a [ento'moloɣo, a] NM/F
  entomologist

entonación [entona'θjon] NF (Ling)
  intonation; (fig) conceit

entonar [ento'nar] **/1a/** vt (canción) to intone;
  (colores) to tone; (Med) to tone up ▶ vi to be in
  tune; **entonarse** vr (engreírse) to give o.s. airs

entonces [en'tonθes] ADV then, at that time;
  desde ~ since then; **en aquel ~** at that time;
  (pues) ~ and so; **el ~ embajador de España**
  the then Spanish ambassador

entornar [entor'nar] **/1a/** vt (puerta, ventana)
  to half close, leave ajar; (los ojos) to screw up

entorno [en'torno] NM setting,
  environment; **~ de redes** (Inform) network
  environment

entorpecer [entorpe'θer] **/2d/** vt
  (entendimiento) to dull; (impedir) to obstruct,
  hinder; (: tránsito) to slow down, delay

entorpezca etc [entor'peθka] vb ver
  entorpecer

entrado, -a [en'traðo, a] ADJ: **~ en años**
  elderly; **(una vez) ~ el verano** in the
  summer(time), when summer comes ▶ NF
  (acción) entry, access; (sitio) entrance, way in;
  (principio) beginning; (Com) receipts pl,
  takings pl; (Culin) entrée; (Deporte) innings
  sg; (Teat) house, audience; (para el cine etc)
  ticket; (Inform) input; **entradas** NFPL (Econ)
  income sg; **entradas brutas** gross receipts;
  entradas y salidas (Com) income and
  expenditure; **entrada de aire** (Tec) air
  intake o inlet; **de entrada** from the out~
  "entrada gratis" "admission free";
  entradas he's losing his hair

entramparse [entram'parse] /**1a**/ VR to get into debt

entrante [en'trante] ADJ next, coming; (*Pol*) incoming ▶ NM inlet; (*Culin*) starter; **entrantes** NMPL starters; **mes/año ~** next month/year

entraña [en'traɲa] NF (*fig: centro*) heart, core; (*raíz*) root; **entrañas** NFPL (*Anat*) entrails; (*fig*) heart *sg*

entrañable [entra'ɲaβle] ADJ (*amigo*) dear; (*recuerdo*) fond; (*acto*) intimate

entrañar [entra'ɲar] /**1a**/ VT to entail

entrar [en'trar] /**1a**/ VT (*introducir*) to bring in; (*persona*) to show in; (*Inform*) to input ▶ VI (*meterse*) to go *o* come in, enter; (*comenzar*): **~ diciendo** to begin by saying; **entré en** *o* **a la casa** (*Am*) I went into the house; **le entraron ganas de reír** he felt a sudden urge to laugh; **me entró sed/sueño** I started to feel thirsty/sleepy; **no me entra** I can't get the hang of it

entre ['entre] PREP (*dos*) between; (*en medio de*) among(st); (*por*): **se abrieron paso ~ la multitud** they forced their way through the crowd; **~ una cosa y otra** what with one thing and another; **~ más estudia más aprende** (*Am*) the more he studies the more he learns

entreabierto [entrea'βjerto] PP *de* **entreabrir**

entreabrir [entrea'βrir] /**3a**/ VT to half-open, open halfway

entreacto [entre'akto] NM interval

entrecano, -a [entre'kano, a] ADJ greying; **ser ~** (*persona*) to be going grey

entrecejo [entre'θexo] NM: **fruncir el ~** to frown

entrechocar [entretʃo'kar] /**1g**/ VI (*dientes*) to chatter

entrechoque *etc* [entre'tʃoke] VB *ver* **entrechocar**

entrecomillado, -a [entrekomi'ʎaðo, a] ADJ in inverted commas

entrecortado, -a [entrekor'taðo, a] ADJ (*respiración*) laboured, difficult; (*habla*) faltering

entrecot [entre'ko(t)] NM (*Culin*) sirloin steak

entrecruce *etc* [entre'kruθe] VB *ver* **entrecruzarse**

entrecruzarse [entrekru'θarse] /**1f**/ VR (*Bio*) to interbreed

entredicho [entre'ðitʃo] NM (*Jur*) injunction; **poner en ~** to cast doubt on; **estar en ~** to be in doubt

entrega [en'treɣa] NF (*de mercancías*) delivery; (*de premios*) presentation; (*de novela etc*) instalment; **"~ a domicilio"** "door-to-door delivery service"

entregar [entre'ɣar] /**1h**/ VT (*dar*) to hand (over), deliver; (*ejercicios*) to hand in;

entregarse VR (*rendirse*) to surrender, give in, submit; **entregarse a** (*dedicarse*) to devote *o.s.* to; **a ~** (*Com*) to be supplied

entregue *etc* [en'treɣe] VB *ver* **entregar**

entrelace *etc* [entre'laθe] VB *ver* **entrelazar**

entrelazar [entrela'θar] /**1f**/ VT to entwine

entremedias [entre'meðjas] ADV (*en medio*) in between, halfway

entremeses [entre'meses] NMPL hors d'œuvres

entremeter [entreme'ter] /**2a**/ VT to insert, put in; **entremeterse** VR to meddle, interfere

entremetido, -a [entreme'tiðo, a] ADJ meddling, interfering

entremezclar [entremeθ'klar] /**1a**/ VT to intermingle; **entremezclarse** VR to intermingle

entrenador, a [entrena'ðor, a] NM/F trainer, coach

entrenamiento [entrena'mjento] NM training

entrenar [entre'nar] /**1a**/ VT (*Deporte*) to train; (*caballo*) to exercise ▶ VI, **entrenarse** VR to train

entrepierna [entre'pjerna] NF (*tb*: **entrepiernas**) crotch, crutch

entresacar [entresa'kar] /**1g**/ VT to pick out, select

entresaque *etc* [entresa'sake] VB *ver* **entresacar**

entresuelo [entre'swelo] NM mezzanine, entresol; (*Teat*) dress *o* first circle

entretanto [entre'tanto] ADV meanwhile, meantime

entretecho [entre'tetʃo] NM (*Am*) attic

entretejer [entrete'xer] /**2a**/ VT to interweave

entretela [entre'tela] NF (*de ropa*) interlining; **entretelas** NFPL heartstrings

entretención [entreten'sjon] NF (*Am*) entertainment

entretendré *etc* [entreten'dre] VB *ver* **entretener**

entretener [entrete'ner] /**2k**/ VT (*divertir*) to entertain, amuse; (*detener*) to hold up, delay; (*mantener*) to maintain; **entretenerse** VR (*divertirse*) to amuse *o.s.*; (*retrasarse*) to delay, linger; **no le entretengo más** I won't keep you any longer

entretenga *etc* [entre'tenga] VB *ver* **entretener**

entretenido, -a [entrete'niðo, a] ADJ entertaining, amusing

entretenimiento [entreteni'mjento] NM entertainment, amusement; (*mantenimiento*) upkeep, maintenance

entretiempo [entre'tjempo] NM: **ropa de ~** *clothes for spring and autumn*

entretiene *etc* [entre'tjene], **entretuve** *etc* [entre'tuβe] VB *ver* **entretener**

entreveía *etc* [entreβe'ia] VB *ver* **entrever**

entrever [entre'βer] /**2u**/ VT to glimpse, catch a glimpse of

entrevista [entre'βista] NF interview

entrevistador, a [entreβista'ðor, a] NM/F interviewer

entrevistar [entreβis'tar] /**1a**/ VT to interview; **entrevistarse** VR: **entrevistarse con** to have an interview with, see; **el ministro se entrevistó con el Rey ayer** the minister had an audience with the King yesterday

entrevisto [entre'βisto] PP *de* **entrever**

entristecer [entriste'θer] /**2d**/ VT to sadden, grieve; **entristecerse** VR to grow sad

entristezca *etc* [entris'teθka] VB *ver* **entristecer**

entrometerse [entrome'terse] /**2a**/ VR: ~ **(en)** to interfere (in *o* with)

entrometido, -a [entrome'tiðo, a] ADJ interfering, meddlesome

entroncar [entron'kar] /**1g**/ VI to be connected *o* related

entronque *etc* [en'tronke] VB *ver* **entroncar**

entuerto [en'twerto] NM wrong, injustice; **entuertos** NMPL (*Med*) afterpains

entumecer [entume'θer] /**2d**/ VT to numb, benumb; **entumecerse** VR (*por el frío*) to go *o* become numb

entumecido, -a [entume'θiðo, a] ADJ numb, stiff

entumezca *etc* [entu'meθka] VB *ver* **entumecer**

enturbiar [entur'βjar] /**1b**/ VT (*el agua*) to make cloudy; (*fig*) to confuse; **enturbiarse** VR (*oscurecerse*) to become cloudy; (*fig*) to get confused, become obscure

entusiasmar [entusjas'mar] /**1a**/ VT to excite, fill with enthusiasm; (*gustar mucho*) to delight; **entusiasmarse** VR: **entusiasmarse con** *o* **por** to get enthusiastic *o* excited about

entusiasmo [entu'sjasmo] NM enthusiasm; (*excitación*) excitement

entusiasta [entu'sjasta] ADJ enthusiastic ▶ NMF enthusiast

enumerar [enume'rar] /**1a**/ VT to enumerate

enunciación [enunθja'θjon] NF, **enunciado** [enun'θjaðo] NM enunciation; (*declaración*) declaration, statement

enunciar [enun'θjar] /**1b**/ VT to enunciate; to declare, state

envainar [embai'nar] /**1a**/ VT to sheathe

envalentonar [embalento'nar] /**1a**/ VT to give courage to; **envalentonarse** VR (*pey*: *jactarse*) to boast, brag

envanecer [embane'θer] /**2d**/ VT to make conceited; **envanecerse** VR to grow conceited

envanezca *etc* [emba'neθka] VB *ver* **envanecer**

envasar [emba'sar] /**1a**/ VT (*empaquetar*) to pack, wrap; (*enfrascar*) to bottle; (*enlatar*) to can; (*embolsar*) to pocket

envase [em'base] NM packing, wrapping; bottling; canning; pocketing; (*recipiente*) container; (*paquete*) package; (*botella*) bottle; (*lata*) tin (BRIT), can

envejecer [embexe'θer] /**2d**/ VT to make old, age ▶ VI (*volverse viejo*) to grow old; (*parecer viejo*) to age

envejecido, -a [embexe'θiðo, a] ADJ old, aged; (*de aspecto*) old-looking

envejezca *etc* [embe'xeθka] VB *ver* **envejecer**

envenenar [embene'nar] /**1a**/ VT to poison; (*fig*) to embitter

envergadura [emberɣa'ðura] NF (*expansión*) expanse; (*Naut*) breadth; (*fig*) scope; **un programa de gran ~** a wide-ranging programme

envés [em'bes] NM (*de tela*) back, wrong side

enviado, -a [em'bjaðo, a] NM/F (*Pol*) envoy; ~ **especial** (*de periódico*, TV) special correspondent

enviar [em'bjar] /**1c**/ VT to send; ~ **un mensaje a algn** (*por móvil*) to text sb, send sb a text message

enviciar [embi'θjar] /**1b**/ VT to corrupt ▶ VI (*trabajo etc*) to be addictive; **enviciarse** VR: **enviciarse (con** *o* **en)** to get addicted (to)

envidia [em'biðja] NF envy; **tener ~ a** to envy, be jealous of

envidiar [embi'ðjar] /**1b**/ VT (*desear*) to envy; (*tener celos de*) to be jealous of

envidioso, -a [embi'ðjoso, a] ADJ envious, jealous

envío [em'bio] NM (*acción*) sending; (*de mercancías*) consignment; (*de dinero*) remittance; (*en barco*) shipment; **gastos de ~** postage and packing; ~ **contra reembolso** COD shipment

enviudar [embju'ðar] /**1d**/ VI to be widowed

envoltorio [embol'torjo] NM package

envoltura [embol'tura] NF (*cobertura*) cover; (*embalaje*) wrapper, wrapping

envolver [embol'βer] /**2h**/ VT to wrap (up); (*cubrir*) to cover; (*enemigo*) to surround; (*implicar*) to involve, implicate

envuelto [em'bwelto], **envuelva** *etc* [em'bwelβa] VB *ver* **envolver**

enyesar [enje'sar] /**1a**/ VT (*pared*) to plaster; (*Med*) to put in plaster

enzarzarse [enθar'θarse] /**1f**/ VR: ~ **en algo** to get mixed up in sth; (*disputa*) to get involved in sth

epa ['epa], (*AM*) **épale** ['epale] EXCL hey!, wow!

E.P.D. ABR (= *en paz descanse*) RIP

epicentro [epi'θentro] NM epicentre
épico, -a ['epiko, a] ADJ epic ▶ NF epic (poetry)
epidemia [epi'ðemja] NF epidemic
epidémico, -a [epi'ðemiko, a] ADJ epidemic
epidermis [epi'ðermis] NF epidermis
epifanía [epifa'nia] NF Epiphany
epilepsia [epi'lepsja] NF epilepsy
epiléptico, -a [epi'leptiko, a] ADJ, NM/F epileptic
epílogo [e'piloɣo] NM epilogue
episcopado [episko'paðo] NM (cargo) bishopric; (obispos) bishops pl (collectively)
episodio [epi'soðjo] NM episode; (suceso) incident
epístola [e'pistola] NF epistle
epitafio [epi'tafjo] NM epitaph
epíteto [e'piteto] NM epithet
época ['epoka] NF period, time; (temporada) season; (Historia) age, epoch; **hacer ~** to be epoch-making
equidad [eki'ðað] NF equity, fairness
equilibrar [ekili'βrar] /1a/ VT to balance
equilibrio [eki'liβrjo] NM balance, equilibrium; **mantener/perder el ~** to keep/lose one's balance; **~ político** balance of power
equilibrista [ekili'βrista] NMF (funámbulo) tightrope walker; (acróbata) acrobat
equinoccio [eki'nokθjo] NM equinox
equipaje [eki'paxe] NM luggage (BRIT), baggage (US); (de máquinas) plant; (turbinas etc) set; **~ de caza** hunting gear; **~ de música** music centre; **~ físico** (Inform) hardware; **~ médico** medical team
equipar [eki'par] /1a/ VT (proveer) to equip
equiparar [ekipa'rar] /1a/ VT (igualar) to put on the same level; (comparar): **~ con** to compare with; **equipararse** VR: **equipararse con** to be on a level with
equipo [e'kipo] NM (conjunto de cosas) equipment; (Deporte, grupo) team; (de obreros) shift; (de máquinas) plant; (turbinas etc) set; **~ de caza** hunting gear; **~ de música** music centre; **~ físico** (Inform) hardware; **~ médico** medical team
equis ['ekis] NF (the letter) X
equitación [ekita'θjon] NF (acto) riding; (arte) horsemanship
equitativo, -a [ekita'tiβo, a] ADJ equitable, fair
equivaldré etc [ekiβal'dre] VB ver **equivaler**
equivalencia [ekiβa'lenθja] NF equivalence
equivalente [ekiβa'lente] ADJ, NM equivalent
equivaler [ekiβa'ler] /2p/ VI: **~ a** to be equivalent o equal to; (en rango) to rank as
equivalga etc [eki'βalɣa] VB ver **equivaler**
equivocación [ekiβoka'θjon] NF mistake, error; (malentendido) misunderstanding
equivocado, -a [ekiβo'kaðo, a] ADJ wrong, mistaken
equivocarse [ekiβo'karse] /1g/ VR to be wrong, make a mistake; **~ de camino** to take the wrong road

equívoco, -a [e'kiβoko, a] ADJ (dudoso) suspect; (ambiguo) ambiguous ▶ NM ambiguity; (malentendido) misunderstanding
equivoque etc [eki'βoke] VB ver **equivocarse**
era ['era] VB ver **ser** ▶ NF era, age; (Agr) threshing floor
erais ['erais], **éramos** ['eramos], **eran** ['eran] VB ver **ser**
erario [e'rarjo] NM exchequer, treasury
eras ['eras], **eres** ['eres] VB ver **ser**
e-reader ['irider] NM e-reader
erección [erek'θjon] NF erection
ergonomía [erɣono'mia] NF ergonomics sg, human engineering
erguir [er'ɣir] /3m/ VT to raise, lift; (poner derecho) to straighten; **erguirse** VR to straighten up
erice etc [e'riθe] VB ver **erizarse**
erigir [eri'xir] /3c/ VT to erect, build; **erigirse** VR: **erigirse en** to set o.s. up as
erija etc [e'rixa] VB ver **erigir**
erizado, -a [eri'θaðo, a] ADJ bristly
erizarse [eri'θarse] /1f/ VR (pelo: de perro) to bristle; (: de persona) to stand on end
erizo [e'riθo] NM hedgehog; **~ de mar** sea urchin
ermita [er'mita] NF hermitage
ermitaño, -a [ermi'taɲo, a] NM/F hermit
erosión [ero'sjon] NF erosion
erosionar [erosjo'nar] /1a/ VT to erode
erótico, -a [e'rotiko, a] ADJ erotic
erotismo [ero'tismo] NM eroticism
erradicar [erraði'kar] /1g/ VT to eradicate
erradique etc [erra'ðike] VB ver **erradicar**
errado, -a [e'rraðo, a] ADJ mistaken, wrong
errante [e'rrante] ADJ wandering, errant
errar [e'rrar] /1k/ VI (vagar) to wander, roam; (equivocarse) to be mistaken ▶ VT: **~ el camino** to take the wrong road; **~ el tiro** to miss
errata [e'rrata] NF misprint
erre ['erre] NF (the letter) R; **~ que ~** stubbornly
erróneo, -a [e'rroneo, a] ADJ (equivocado) wrong, mistaken; (falso) false, untrue
error [e'rror] NM error, mistake; (Inform) bug; **~ de imprenta** misprint; **~ de lectura/escritura** (Inform) read/write error; **~ sintáctico** syntax error; **~ judicial** miscarriage of justice
Ertzaintza [er'tʃantʃa] NF Basque police; ver tb **policía**
eructar [eruk'tar] /1a/ VT to belch, burp
eructo [e'rukto] NM belch
erudición [eruði'θjon] NF erudition, learning
erudito, -a [eru'ðito, a] ADJ erudite, learned ▶ NM/F scholar; **los eruditos en esta materia** the experts in this field

erupción [erup'θjon] NF eruption; (Med) rash; (de violencia) outbreak; (de ira) outburst

es [es] VB ver **ser**

E/S ABR (Inform: = entrada/salida) I/O

esa ['esa], **esas** ['esas] ADJ DEMOSTRATIVO, PRON ver **ese**

ésa ['esa], **ésas** ['esas] PRON ver **ése**

esbelto, -a [es'βelto, a] ADJ slim, slender

esbirro [es'βirro] NM henchman

esbozar [esβo'θar] /1f/ VT to sketch, outline

esbozo [es'βoθo] NM sketch, outline

escabeche [eska'βetʃe] NM brine; (de aceitunas etc) pickle; **en ~** pickled

escabechina [eskaβe'tʃina] NF (batalla) massacre; **hacer una ~** (Escol) to fail a lot of students

escabroso, -a [eska'βroso, a] ADJ (accidentado) rough, uneven; (fig) tough, difficult; (: atrevido) risqué

escabullirse [eskaβu'ʎirse] /3a/ VR to slip away; (largarse) to clear out

escacharrar [eskatʃa'rrar] /1a/ VT (fam) to break; **escacharrarse** VR to get broken

escafandra [eska'fandra] NF (buzo) diving suit; (escafandra espacial) spacesuit

escala [es'kala] NF (proporción, Mus) scale; (de mano) ladder; (Aviat) stopover; (de colores etc) range; **~ de tiempo** time scale; **~ de sueldos** salary scale; **una investigación a ~ nacional** a nationwide inquiry; **reproducir a ~** to reproduce to scale; **hacer ~ en** (gen) to stop off at o call in at; (Aviat) to stop over in

escalada [eska'laða] NF (de montaña) climb; (de pared) scaling

escalafón [eskala'fon] NM (escala de salarios) salary scale, wage scale

escalar [eska'lar] /1a/ VT to climb, scale ▶ VI (Mil, Pol) to escalate

escaldar [eskal'dar] /1a/ VT (quemar) to scald; (escarmentar) to teach a lesson

escalera [eska'lera] NF stairs pl, staircase; (escala) ladder; (Naipes) run; (de camión) tailboard; **~ mecánica** escalator; **~ de caracol** spiral staircase; **~ de incendios** fire escape

escalerilla [eskale'riʎa] NF (de avión) steps pl

escalfar [eskal'far] /1a/ VT (huevos) to poach

escalinata [eskali'nata] NF staircase

escalofriante [eskalo'frjante] ADJ chilling

escalofrío [eskalo'frio] NM (Med) chill; **escalofríos** NMPL (fig) shivers

escalón [eska'lon] NM step, stair; (de escalera) rung; (fig: paso) step; (al éxito) ladder

escalonar [eskalo'nar] /1a/ VT to spread out; (tierra) to terrace; (horas de trabajo) to stagger

escalope [eska'lope] NM (Culin) escalope

escama [es'kama] NF (de pez, serpiente) scale; (de jabón) flake; (fig) resentment

escamar [eska'mar] /1a/ VT (pez) to scale; (producir recelo) to make wary

escamotear [eskamote'ar] /1a/ VT (fam: robar) to lift, swipe; (hacer desaparecer) to make disappear

escampar [eskam'par] /1a/ VB IMPERSONAL to stop raining

escanciar [eskan'θjar] /1b/ VT (vino) to pour (out)

escandalice etc [eskanda'liθe] VB ver **escandalizar**

escandalizar [eskandali'θar] /1f/ VT to scandalize, shock; **escandalizarse** VR to be shocked; (ofenderse) to be offended

escándalo [es'kandalo] NM scandal; (alboroto, tumulto) row, uproar; **armar un ~** to make a scene; **¡es un ~!** it's outrageous!

escandaloso, -a [eskanda'loso, a] ADJ scandalous, shocking; (risa) hearty; (niño) noisy

Escandinavia [eskandi'naβja] NF Scandinavia

escandinavo, -a [eskandi'naβo, a] ADJ, NM/F Scandinavian

escanear [eskane'ar] /1a/ VT to scan

escaneo [es'kaneo] NM scanning

escáner [es'kaner] NM scanner

escaño [es'kaɲo] NM bench; (Pol) seat

escapada [eska'paða] NF (huida) escape, flight; (Deporte) breakaway; (viaje) quick trip

escapar [eska'par] /1a/ VI (gen) to escape, run away; (Deporte) to break away; **escaparse** VR to escape, get away; (agua, gas, noticias) to leak (out); **se me escapa su nombre** his name escapes me

escaparate [eskapa'rate] NM shop window; (Com) showcase; **ir de escaparates** to go window shopping

escapatoria [eskapa'torja] NF: **no tener ~** (fig) to have no way out

escape [es'kape] NM (huida) escape; (de agua, gas) leak; (de motor) exhaust; **salir a ~** to rush out

escapismo [eska'pismo] NM escapism

escaquearse [eskake'arse] /1a/ VR (fam) to duck out

escarabajo [eskara'βaxo] NM beetle

escaramuza [eskara'muθa] NF skirmish; (fig) brush

escarbar [eskar'βar] /1a/ VT (gallina) to scratch; (fig) to inquire into, investigate

escarceos [eskar'θeos] NMPL: **en sus ~ con la política** in his occasional forays into politics; **~ amorosos** love affairs

escarcha [es'kartʃa] NF frost

escarchado, -a [eskar'tʃaðo, a] ADJ (Culin: fruta) crystallized

escarlata [eskar'lata] ADJ INV scarlet

escarlatina [eskarla'tina] NF scarlet fever

escarmentar [eskarmen'tar] /**1j**/ VT to punish severely ▶ VI to learn one's lesson; **¡para que escarmientes!** that'll teach you!

escarmiento etc [eskar'mjento] VB ver **escarmentar** ▶ NM (ejemplo) lesson; (castigo) punishment

escarnio [es'karnjo] NM mockery; (injuria) insult

escarola [eska'rola] NF (Bot) endive

escarpado, -a [eskar'paðo, a] ADJ (pendiente) sheer, steep; (rocas) craggy

escasamente [eskasa'mente] ADV (insuficientemente) scantily; (apenas) scarcely

escasear [eskase'ar] /**1a**/ VI to be scarce

escasez [eska'seθ] NF (falta) shortage, scarcity; (pobreza) poverty; **vivir con ~** to live on the breadline

escaso, -a [es'kaso, a] ADJ (poco) scarce; (raro) rare; (ralo) thin, sparse; (limitado) limited; (recursos) scanty; (público) sparse; (posibilidad) slim; (visibilidad) poor

escatimar [eskati'mar] /**1a**/ VT (limitar) to skimp (on), be sparing with; **no ~ esfuerzos (para)** to spare no effort (to)

escayola [eska'jola] NF plaster

escayolar [eskajo'lar] /**1a**/ VT to put in plaster

escena [es'θena] NF scene; (decorado) scenery; (escenario) stage; **poner en ~** to put on

escenario [esθe'narjo] NM (Teat) stage; (Cine) set; (fig) scene; **el ~ del crimen** the scene of the crime; **el ~ político** the political scene

escenografía [esθenoɣra'fia] NF set o stage design

escepticismo [esθepti'θismo] NM scepticism

escéptico, -a [es'θeptiko, a] ADJ sceptical ▶ NM/F sceptic

escindir [esθin'dir] /**3a**/ VT to split; **escindirse** VR (facción) to split off; **escindirse en** to split into

escisión [esθi'sjon] NF (Med) excision; (fig, Pol) split; **~ nuclear** nuclear fission

esclarecer [esklare'θer] /**2d**/ VT (iluminar) to light up, illuminate; (misterio, problema) to shed light on

esclarezca etc [eskla're θka] VB ver **esclarecer**

esclavice etc [eskla'βiθe] VB ver **esclavizar**

esclavitud [esklaβi'tuð] NF slavery

esclavizar [esklaβi'θar] /**1f**/ VT to enslave

esclavo, -a [es'klaβo, a] NM/F slave

esclusa [es'klusa] NF (de canal) lock; (compuerta) floodgate

escoba [es'koβa] NF broom; **pasar la ~** to sweep up

escobazo [esko'βaθo] NM (golpe) blow with a broom; **echar a algn a escobazos** to kick sb out

escobilla [esko'βiʎa] NF brush

escocer [esko'θer] /**2b, 2h**/ VI to burn, sting; **escocerse** VR to chafe, get chafed

escocés, -esa [esko'θes, esa] ADJ Scottish; (whisky) Scotch ▶ NM/F Scotsman(-woman), Scot ▶ NM (Ling) Scots sg; **tela escocesa** tartan

Escocia [es'koθja] NF Scotland

escoger [esko'xer] /**2c**/ VT to choose, pick, select

escogido, -a [esko'xiðo, a] ADJ chosen, selected; (calidad) choice, select; (persona): **ser muy ~** to be very fussy

escoja etc [es'koxa] VB ver **escoger**

escolar [esko'lar] ADJ school cpd ▶ NMF schoolboy(-girl), pupil

escolaridad [eskolari'ðað] NF schooling; **libro de ~** school record

escolarización [eskolariθa'θjon] NF: **~ obligatoria** compulsory education

escolarizado, -a [eskolari'θaðo, a] ADJ, NM/F: **los escolarizados** those in o attending school

escollo [es'koʎo] NM (arrecife) reef, rock; (fig) pitfall

escolta [es'kolta] NF escort

escoltar [eskol'tar] /**1a**/ VT to escort; (proteger) to guard

escombros [es'kombros] NMPL (basura) rubbish sg; (restos) debris sg

esconder [eskon'der] /**2a**/ VT to hide, conceal; **esconderse** VR to hide

escondidas [eskon'diðas] NFPL (AM) hide-and-seek sg; **a ~** secretly; **hacer algo a ~ de algn** to do sth behind sb's back

escondite [eskon'dite] NM hiding place; (juego) hide-and-seek

escondrijo [eskon'drixo] NM hiding place, hideout

escopeta [esko'peta] NF shotgun; **~ de aire comprimido** air gun

escoria [es'korja] NF (desecho mineral) slag; (fig) scum, dregs pl

Escorpio [es'korpjo] NM (Astro) Scorpio

escorpión [eskor'pjon] NM scorpion

escotado, -a [esko'taðo, a] ADJ low-cut

escotar [esko'tar] /**1a**/ VT (vestido: ajustar) to cut to fit; (cuello) to cut low

escote [es'kote] NM (de vestido) low neck; **pagar a ~** to share the expenses

escotilla [esko'tiʎa] NF (Naut) hatchway

escotillón [eskoti'ʎon] NM trapdoor

escozor [esko'θor] NM (dolor) sting(ing)

escribano, -a [eskri'βano, a], **escribiente** [eskri'βjente] NM/F clerk; (secretario judicial) court o lawyer's clerk

escribible [eskri'βiβle] ADJ writable

escribir [eskri'βir] /**3a**/ VT, VI to write; **~ a máquina** to type; **¿cómo se escribe?** how do you spell it?

escrito, -a [es'krito, a] PP de **escribir** ▶ ADJ written, in writing; (examen) written

▶ NM (*documento*) document; (*manuscrito*) text, manuscript; **por ~** in writing

escritor, a [eskri'tor, a] NM/F writer

escritorio [eskri'torjo] NM desk; (*oficina*) office; (*Inform*) desktop

escritura [eskri'tura] NF (*acción*) writing; (*caligrafía*) (hand)writing; (*Jur*: *documento*) deed; (*Com*) indenture; **~ de propiedad** title deed; **Sagrada E~** (Holy) Scripture; **~ social** articles *pl* of association

escroto [es'kroto] NM scrotum

escrúpulo [es'krupulo] NM scruple; (*minuciosidad*) scrupulousness

escrupuloso, -a [eskrupu'loso, a] ADJ scrupulous

escrutar [eskru'tar] /1a/ VT to scrutinize, examine; (*votos*) to count

escrutinio [eskru'tinjo] NM (*examen atento*) scrutiny; (*Pol*: *recuento de votos*) count(ing)

escuadra [es'kwaðra] NF (*Tec*) square; (*Mil etc*) squad; (*Naut*) squadron; (*de coches etc*) fleet

escuadrilla [eskwa'ðriʎa] NF (*de aviones*) squadron; (*Am*: *de obreros*) gang

escuadrón [eskwa'ðron] NM squadron

escuálido, -a [es'kwaliðo, a] ADJ skinny, scraggy; (*sucio*) squalid

escucha [es'kutʃa] NF (*acción*) listening ▶ NM (*Telec*: *sistema*) monitor; (: *oyente*) listener; **estar a la ~** to listen in; **estar de ~** to spy; **escuchas telefónicas** (phone-)tapping *sg*

escuchar [esku'tʃar] /1a/ VT to listen to; (*consejo*) to heed; (*esp Am*: *oír*) to hear ▶ VI to listen; **escucharse** VR: **se escucha muy mal** (*Telec*) it's a very bad line

escudarse [esku'ðarse] /1a/ VR: **~ en** (*fig*) to hide behind

escudería [eskuðe'ria] NF: **la ~ Ferrari** the Ferrari team

escudero [esku'ðero] NM squire

escudilla [esku'ðiʎa] NF bowl, basin

escudo [es'kuðo] NM shield; **~ de armas** coat of arms

escudriñar [eskuðri'ɲar] /1a/ VT (*examinar*) to investigate, scrutinize; (*mirar de lejos*) to scan

escuece *etc* [es'kweθe] VB *ver* **escocer**

escuela [es'kwela] NF (*tb fig*) school; **~ normal** teacher training college; **~ técnica superior** university offering five-year courses in engineering and technical subjects; **~ universitaria** university offering three-year diploma courses; **~ de párvulos** kindergarten; **~ de artes y oficios** (*Esp*) ≈ technical college; **~ de choferes** (*Am*) driving school; **~ de manejo** (*Am*) driving school; *ver tb* **colegio**

escueto, -a [es'kweto, a] ADJ plain; (*estilo*) simple; (*explicación*) concise

escueza *etc* [es'kweθa] VB *ver* **escocer**

escuincle [es'kwinkle] NM (*Am fam*) kid

esculpir [eskul'pir] /3a/ VT to sculpt; (*grabar*) to engrave; (*tallar*) to carve

escultor, a [eskul'tor, a] NM/F sculptor

escultura [eskul'tura] NF sculpture

escupidera [eskupi'ðera] NF spittoon

escupir [esku'pir] /3a/ VT to spit (out) ▶ VI to spit

escupitajo [eskupi'taxo] NM (*fam*) gob of spit

escurreplatos [eskurre'platos] NM INV plate rack

escurridero [eskurri'ðero] NM (*Am*) draining board (*Brit*), drainboard (*US*)

escurridizo, -a [eskurri'ðiθo, a] ADJ slippery

escurridor [eskurri'ðor] NM colander

escurrir [esku'rrir] /3a/ VT (*ropa*) to wring out; (*verduras, platos*) to drain ▶ VI (*los líquidos*) to drip; **escurrirse** VR (*secarse*) to drain; (*resbalarse*) to slip, slide; (*escaparse*) to slip away

ese[1] ['ese] NF (the letter) S; **hacer eses** (*carretera*) to zigzag; (*borracho*) to reel about

ese[2] ['ese], **esa** ['esa], **esos** ['esos], **esas** ['esas] ADJ DEMOSTRATIVO that *sg*, those *pl* ▶ PRON that (one) *sg*, those (ones) *pl*

ése ['ese], **ésa** ['esa], **ésos** ['esos], **ésas** ['esas] PRON that (one) *sg*, those (ones) *pl*; **~ ... éste ...** the former ... the latter ...; **¡no me vengas con ésas!** don't give me any more of that nonsense!

esencia [e'senθja] NF essence

esencial [esen'θjal] ADJ essential; (*principal*) chief; **lo ~** the main thing

esfera [es'fera] NF sphere; (*de reloj*) face; **~ de acción** scope; **~ terrestre** globe

esférico, -a [es'feriko, a] ADJ spherical

esfinge [es'finxe] NF sphinx

esforcé [esfor'θe], **esforcemos** *etc* [esfor'θemos] VB *ver* **esforzarse**

esforzado, -a [esfor'θaðo, a] ADJ (*enérgico*) energetic, vigorous

esforzarse [esfor'θarse] /1f, 1l/ VR to exert o.s., make an effort

esfuerce *etc* [es'fwerθe] VB *ver* **esforzarse**

esfuerzo [es'fwerθo] VB *ver* **esforzarse** ▶ NM effort; **sin ~** effortlessly

esfumarse [esfu'marse] /1a/ VR (*apoyo, esperanzas*) to fade away; (*persona*) to vanish

esgrima [es'ɣrima] NF fencing

esgrimidor [esɣrimi'ðor] NM fencer

esgrimir [esɣri'mir] /3a/ VT (*arma*) to brandish; (*argumento*) to use ▶ VI to fence

esguince [es'ɣinθe] NM (*Med*) sprain

eslabón [esla'βon] NM link; **~ perdido** (*Bio, fig*) missing link

eslabonar [eslaβo'nar] /1a/ VT to link, connect

eslálom [es'lalom] NM slalom

eslavo, -a [es'laβo, a] ADJ Slav, Slavonic ▶ NM/F Slav ▶ NM (*Ling*) Slavonic

eslip [es'lip] NM pants pl (BRIT), briefs pl

eslogan [es'loɣan] NM (pl **eslogans**) slogan

eslora [es'lora] NF (Naut) length

eslovaco, -a [eslo'βako, a] ADJ, NM/F Slovak, Slovakian ▶ NM (Ling) Slovak, Slovakian

Eslovaquia [eslo'βakja] NF Slovakia

Eslovenia [eslo'βenja] NF Slovenia

esloveno, -a [eslo'βeno, a] ADJ, NM/F Slovene, Slovenian ▶ NM (Ling) Slovene, Slovenian

esmaltar [esmal'tar] /**1a**/ VT to enamel

esmalte [es'malte] NM enamel; **~ de uñas** nail varnish o polish

esmerado, -a [esme'raðo, a] ADJ careful, neat

esmeralda [esme'ralda] NF emerald

esmerarse [esme'rarse] /**1a**/ VR (aplicarse) to take great pains, exercise great care; (afanarse) to work hard; (hacer lo mejor) to do one's best

esmero [es'mero] NM (great) care

esmirriado, -a [esmi'rrjaðo, a] ADJ puny

esmoquin [es'mokin] NM dinner jacket (BRIT), tuxedo (US)

esnob [es'nob] ADJ INV (persona) snobbish; (coche etc) posh ▶ NMF snob

esnobismo [esno'βismo] NM snobbery

eso ['eso] PRON that, that thing o matter; **~ de su coche** that business about his car; **~ de ir al cine** all that about going to the cinema; **a ~ de las cinco** at about five o'clock; **en ~** thereupon, at that point; **por ~** therefore; **~ es** that's it; **nada de ~** far from it; **¡~ sí que es vida!** now this is really living!; **por ~ te lo dije** that's why I told you; **y ~ que llovía** in spite of the fact it was raining

esófago [e'sofaɣo] NM (Anat) oesophagus

esos ['esos] ADJ DEMOSTRATIVO ver **ese**

ésos ['esos] PRON ver **ése**

esotérico, -a [eso'teriko, a] ADJ esoteric

esp. ABR (= español) Sp., Span.;
= **especialmente**

espabilado, -a [espaβi'laðo, a] ADJ quick-witted

espabilar [espaβi'lar] /**1a**/ VT, **espabilarse** VR
= **despabilar**

espachurrar [espatʃu'rrar] /**1a**/ VT to squash; **espachurrarse** VR to get squashed

espaciado [espa'θjaðo] NM (Inform) spacing

espacial [espa'θjal] ADJ (del espacio) space cpd

espaciar [espa'θjar] /**1b**/ VT to space (out)

espacio [es'paθjo] NM space; (Mus) interval; (Radio, TV) programme, program (US); **el ~** space; **ocupar mucho ~** to take up a lot of room; **a dos espacios**, **a doble ~** (Tip) double-spaced; **por ~ de** during, for; **~ aéreo/exterior** air/outer space

espacioso, -a [espa'θjoso, a] ADJ spacious, roomy

espada [es'paða] NF sword ▶ NM swordsman; (Taur) matador; **espadas** NFPL (Naipes) one of the suits in the Spanish card deck; **estar entre la ~ y la pared** to be between the devil and the deep blue sea; ver tb **baraja española**

espadachín [espaða'tʃin] NM (esgrimidor) skilled swordsman

espaguetis [espa'ɣetis] NMPL spaghetti sg

espalda [es'palda] NF (gen) back; (Natación) backstroke; **espaldas** nfpl (hombros) shoulders; **a espaldas de algn** behind sb's back; **estar de espaldas** to have one's back turned; **tenderse de espaldas** to lie (down) on one's back; **volver la ~ a algn** to cold-shoulder sb

espaldarazo [espalda'raθo] NM (tb fig) slap on the back

espaldilla [espal'ðiʎa] NF shoulder blade

espantadizo, -a [espanta'ðiθo, a] ADJ timid, easily frightened

espantajo [espan'taxo] NM,

espantapájaros [espanta'paxaros] NM INV scarecrow

espantar [espan'tar] /**1a**/ VT (asustar) to frighten, scare; (ahuyentar) to frighten off; (asombrar) to horrify, appal; **espantarse** VR to get frightened o scared; to be appalled

espanto [es'panto] NM (susto) fright; (terror) terror; (asombro) astonishment; **¡qué ~!** how awful!

espantoso, -a [espan'toso, a] ADJ frightening, terrifying; (ruido) dreadful

España [es'paɲa] NF Spain; **la ~ de pandereta** touristy Spain

español, a [espa'ɲol, a] ADJ Spanish ▶ NM/F Spaniard ▶ NM (Ling) Spanish; ver tb **castellano**

españolice etc [espaɲo'liθe] VB ver **españolizar**

españolizar [espaɲoli'θar] /**1f**/ VT to make Spanish, Hispanicize; **españolizarse** VR to adopt Spanish ways

esparadrapo [espara'ðrapo] NM surgical tape

esparcido, -a [espar'θiðo, a] ADJ scattered

esparcimiento [esparθi'mjento] NM (dispersión) spreading; (derramamiento) scattering; (fig) cheerfulness

esparcir [espar'θir] /**3b**/ VT to spread; (derramar) to scatter; **esparcirse** VR to spread (out); to scatter; (divertirse) to enjoy o.s.

espárrago [es'parraɣo] NM (tb: **espárragos**) asparagus; **estar hecho un ~** to be as thin as a rake; **¡vete a freír espárragos!** (fam) go to hell!

esparto [es'parto] NM esparto (grass)

esparza etc [es'parθa] VB ver **esparcir**

espasmo [es'pasmo] NM spasm

espátula [es'patula] NF (Med) spatula; (Arte) palette knife; (Culin) fish slice

especia [es'peθja] NF spice

especial [espe'θjal] ADJ special

especialidad [espeθjali'ðað] NF speciality, specialty (US); (Escol: ramo) specialism

especialista [espeθja'lista] NMF specialist; (Cine) stuntman(-woman)

especializado, -a [espeθjali'θaðo, a] ADJ specialized; (obrero) skilled

especialmente [espeθjal'mente] ADV particularly, especially

especie [es'peθje] NF (Bio) species; (clase) kind, sort; **pagar en ~** to pay in kind

especificar [espeθifi'kar] /1g/ VT to specify

específico, -a [espe'θifiko, a] ADJ specific

especifique etc [espeθi'fike] VB ver **especificar**

espécimen [es'peθimen] (pl **especímenes**) NM specimen

espectáculo [espek'takulo] NM (gen) spectacle; (Teat etc) show; (función) performance; **dar un ~** to make a scene

espectador, a [espekta'ðor, a] NM/F spectator; (de incidente) onlooker; **los espectadores** NMPL (Teat) the audience sg

espectro [es'pektro] NM ghost; (fig) spectre

especulación [espekula'θjon] NF speculation; **~ bursátil** speculation on the Stock Market

especular [espeku'lar] /1a/ VT, VI to speculate

especulativo, -a [espekula'tiβo, a] ADJ speculative

espejismo [espe'xismo] NM mirage

espejo [es'pexo] NM mirror; (fig) model; **~ retrovisor** rear-view mirror; **mirarse al ~** to look (at o.s.) in the mirror

espeleología [espeleolo'xia] NF potholing

espeluznante [espeluθ'nante] ADJ horrifying, hair-raising

espera [es'pera] NF (pausa, intervalo) wait; (Jur: plazo) respite; **en ~ de** waiting for; (con expectativa) expecting; **en ~ de su contestación** awaiting your reply

esperance etc [espe'ranθe] VB ver **esperanzar**

esperanza [espe'ranθa] NF (confianza) hope; (expectativa) expectation; **hay pocas esperanzas de que venga** there is little prospect of his coming; **~ de vida** life expectancy

esperanzador, a [esperanθa'ðor, a] ADJ hopeful, encouraging

esperanzar [esperan'θar] /1f/ VT to give hope to

esperar [espe'rar] /1a/ VT (aguardar) to wait for; (tener expectativa de) to expect; (desear) to hope for ▶ VI to wait; to expect; to hope; **esperarse** VR: **como podía esperarse** as was to be expected; **hacer ~ a algn** to keep sb waiting; **ir a ~ a algn** to go and meet sb; **~ un bebé** to be expecting (a baby)

esperma [es'perma] NF sperm

espermatozoide [espermato'θoiðe] NM spermatozoid

esperpento [esper'pento] NM (persona) sight (fam); (disparate) (piece of) nonsense

espesar [espe'sar] /1a/ VT to thicken; **espesarse** VR to thicken, get thicker

espeso, -a [es'peso, a] ADJ thick; (bosque) dense; (nieve) deep; (sucio) dirty

espesor [espe'sor] NM thickness; (de nieve) depth

espesura [espe'sura] NF (de bosque) thicket

espetar [espe'tar] /1a/ VT (reto, sermón) to give

espía [es'pia] NMF spy

espiar [espi'ar] /1c/ VT (observar) to spy on ▶ VI: **~ para** to spy for

espiga [es'piɣa] NF (Bot: de trigo etc) ear; (: de flores) spike

espigado, -a [espi'ɣaðo, a] ADJ (Bot) ripe; (fig) tall, slender

espigón [espi'ɣon] NM (Bot) ear; (Naut) breakwater

espina [es'pina] NF thorn; (de pez) bone; **~ dorsal** (Anat) spine; **me da mala ~** I don't like the look of it

espinaca [espi'naka] NF (tb: **espinacas**) spinach

espinar [espi'nar] NM (matorral) thicket

espinazo [espi'naθo] NM spine, backbone

espinilla [espi'niʎa] NF (Anat: tibia) shin(bone); (: en la piel) blackhead

espino [es'pino] NM hawthorn

espinoso, -a [espi'noso, a] ADJ (planta) thorny, prickly; (fig) bony; (asunto) difficult; (problema) knotty

espionaje [espjo'naxe] NM spying, espionage

espiral [espi'ral] ADJ, NF spiral; **la ~ inflacionista** the inflationary spiral

espirar [espi'rar] /1a/ VT, VI to breathe out, exhale

espiritista [espiri'tista] ADJ, NMF spiritualist

espíritu [es'piritu] NM spirit; (mente) mind; (inteligencia) intelligence; (Rel) spirit, soul; **E~ Santo** Holy Ghost; **con ~ amplio** with an open mind

espiritual [espiri'twal] ADJ spiritual

espita [es'pita] NF tap (BRIT), faucet (US)

esplendidez [esplendi'ðeθ] NF (abundancia) lavishness; (magnificencia) splendour

espléndido, -a [es'plendiðo, a] ADJ (magnífico) magnificent, splendid; (generoso) generous, lavish

esplendor [esplen'dor] NM splendour

espliego [es'pljeɣo] NM lavender

espolear [espole'ar] /1a/ VT to spur on

espoleta [espo'leta] NF (de bomba) fuse

espolvorear [espolβore'ar] /1a/ VT to dust, sprinkle

esponja [es'ponxa] NF sponge; (fig) sponger

esponjoso, -a [espon'xoso, a] ADJ spongy
esponsales [espon'sales] NMPL betrothal *sg*
espontaneidad [espontanei'ðað] NF
  spontaneity
espontáneo, -a [espon'taneo, a] ADJ
  spontaneous; (*improvisado*) impromptu;
  (*persona*) natural
espora [es'pora] NF spore
esporádico, -a [espo'raðiko, a] ADJ sporadic
esposa [es'posa] NF ver **esposo**
esposar [espo'sar] /**1a**/ VT to handcuff
esposo, -a [es'poso, a] NM husband ▸ NF
  wife; **esposas** NFPL handcuffs
espray [es'prai] NM spray
espuela [es'pwela] NF spur; (*fam: trago*) one
  for the road
espuerta [es'pwerta] NF basket, pannier
espuma [es'puma] NF foam; (*de cerveza*)
  froth, head; (*de jabón*) lather; (*de olas*) surf;
  ~ de afeitar shaving foam
espumadera [espuma'ðera] NF skimmer
espumarajo [espuma'raxo] NM froth, foam;
  echar espumarajos (de rabia) to splutter
  with rage
espumoso, -a [espu'moso, a] ADJ frothy,
  foamy; (*vino*) sparkling
esputo [es'puto] NM (*de saliva*) spit; (*Med*)
  sputum
esqueje [es'kexe] NM (*Bot*) cutting
esquela [es'kela] NF: **~ mortuoria**
  announcement of death
esquelético, -a [eske'letiko, a] ADJ (*fam*) skinny
esqueleto [eske'leto] NM skeleton; (*lo
  esencial*) bare bones (of a matter); **en ~**
  unfinished
esquema [es'kema] NM (*diagrama*) diagram;
  (*dibujo*) plan; (*plan*) scheme; (*Filosofía*) schema
esquemático, -a [eske'matiko, a] ADJ
  schematic; **un resumen ~** a brief outline
esquí [es'ki] (*pl* **esquís**) NM (*objeto*) ski;
  (*deporte*) skiing; **~ acuático** water-skiing;
  hacer ~ to go skiing
esquiador, a [eskja'ðor, a] NM/F skier
esquiar [es'kjar] /**1c**/ VI to ski
esquila [es'kila] NF (*campanilla*) small bell;
  (*cencerro*) cowbell
esquilar [eski'lar] /**1a**/ VT to shear
esquimal [eski'mal] ADJ, NMF Eskimo
esquina [es'kina] NF corner; **doblar la ~** to
  turn the corner
esquinazo [eski'naθo] NM: **dar ~ a algn** to
  give sb the slip
esquirla [es'kirla] NF splinter
esquirol [eski'rol] NM (*Esp*) strikebreaker,
  blackleg
esquivar [eski'βar] /**1a**/ VT to avoid; (*evadir*) to
  dodge, elude
esquivo, -a [es'kiβo, a] ADJ (*altanero*) aloof;
  (*desdeñoso*) scornful, disdainful

esquizofrenia [eskiθo'frenja] NF
  schizophrenia
esta ['esta] ADJ DEMOSTRATIVO, PRON ver **este²**
está [es'ta] VB ver **estar**
ésta ['esta] PRON ver **éste**
estabilice *etc* [estaβi'liθe] VB ver **estabilizar**
estabilidad [estaβili'ðað] NF stability
estabilización [estaβiliθa'θjon] NF (*Com*)
  stabilization
estabilizador, a [estabiliθa'ðor, a] ADJ (*Foto*)
  antishake
estabilizar [estaβili'θar] /**1f**/ VT to stabilize;
  (*fijar*) to make steady; (*precios*) to peg;
  estabilizarse VR to become stable
estable [es'taβle] ADJ stable
establecer [estaβle'θer] /**2d**/ VT to establish;
  (*fundar*) to set up; (*colonos*) to settle; (*récord*) to
  set (up); **establecerse** VR to establish o.s.;
  (*echar raíces*) to settle (down); (*Com*) to start up
establecimiento [estaβleθi'mjento] NM
  establishment; (*fundación*) institution; (*de
  negocio*) start-up; (*de colonias*) settlement; (*local*)
  establishment; **~ comercial** business house
establezca *etc* [esta'βleθka] VB ver **establecer**
establo [es'taβlo] NM (*Agr*) stall; (*para vacas*)
  cowshed; (*para caballos*) stable; (*esp Am*) barn
estaca [es'taka] NF stake, post; (*de tienda de
  campaña*) peg
estacada [esta'kaða] NF (*cerca*) fence,
  fencing; (*palenque*) stockade; **dejar a algn en
  la ~** to leave sb in the lurch
estación [esta'θjon] NF station; (*del año*)
  season; **~ de autobuses/ferrocarril** bus/
  railway station; **~ balnearia (de turistas)**
  seaside resort; **~ de servicio** service station;
  ~ terminal terminus; **~ de trabajo** (*Com*)
  work station; **~ transmisora** transmitter;
  ~ de visualización display unit
estacionamiento [estaθjona'mjento] NM
  (*Auto*) parking; (*Mil*) stationing
estacionar [estaθjo'nar] /**1a**/ VT (*Auto*) to
  park; (*Mil*) to station
estacionario, -a [estaθjo'narjo, a] ADJ
  stationary; (*Com: mercado*) slack
estada [es'taða], **estadía** [esta'ðia] NF (*Am*)
  stay
estadio [es'taðjo] NM (*fase*) stage, phase;
  (*Deporte*) stadium
estadista [esta'ðista] NM (*Pol*) statesman;
  (*Estadística*) statistician
estadística [esta'ðistika] NF (*una estadística*)
  figure, statistic; (*ciencia*) statistics *sg*
estado [es'taðo] NM (*Pol: condición*) state;
  ~ civil marital status; **~ de ánimo** state of
  mind; **~ de cuenta(s)** bank statement,
  statement of accounts; **~ de excepción** (*Pol*)
  state of emergency; **~ financiero** (*Com*)
  financial statement; **~ mayor** (*Mil*) staff;
  ~ de pérdidas y ganancias (*Com*) profit and

loss statement, operating statement; **Estados Unidos (EE.UU.)** United States (of America) (USA); **estar en ~ (de buena esperanza)** to be pregnant

estadounidense [estaðouni'ðense] ADJ United States cpd, American ▶ NMF United States citizen, American

estafa [es'tafa] NF swindle, trick; (Com etc) racket

estafar [esta'far] /1a/ VT to swindle, defraud

estafeta [esta'feta] NF (oficina de correos) post office; **~ diplomática** diplomatic bag

estáis VB ver **estar**

estalactita [estalak'tita] NF stalactite

estalagmita [estalaɣ'mita] NF stalagmite

estallar [esta'ʎar] /1a/ VI to burst; (bomba) to explode, go off; (volcán) to erupt; (vidrio) to shatter; (látigo) to crack; (epidemia, guerra, rebelión) to break out; **~ en llanto** to burst into tears

estallido [esta'ʎiðo] NM explosion; (de látigo, trueno) crack; (fig) outbreak

estambre [es'tambre] NM (tela) worsted; (Bot) stamen

Estambul [estam'bul] NM Istanbul

estamento [esta'mento] NM (social) class

estampa [es'tampa] NF (impresión, imprenta) print, engraving; (imagen, figura: de persona) appearance

estampado, -a [estam'paðo, a] ADJ printed ▶ NM (dibujo) print; (impresión) printing

estampar [estam'par] /1a/ VT (imprimir) to print; (marcar) to stamp; (metal) to engrave; (poner sello en) to stamp; (fig) to stamp, imprint

estampida [estam'piða] NF stampede

estampido [estam'piðo] NM bang, report

estampilla [estam'piʎa] NF (sello de goma) (rubber) stamp; (Am) (postage) stamp

están [es'tan] VB ver **estar**

estancado, -a [estan'kaðo, a] ADJ (agua) stagnant

estancamiento [estanka'mjento] NM stagnation

estancar [estan'kar] /1g/ VT (aguas) to hold up, hold back; (Com) to monopolize; (fig) to block, hold up; **estancarse** VR to stagnate

estancia [es'tanθja] NF (permanencia) stay; (sala) room; (Am) farm, ranch

estanciero [estan'sjero] NM (Am) farmer, rancher

estanco, -a [es'tanko, a] ADJ watertight ▶ NM tobacconist's (shop); see note

> Cigarettes, tobacco, postage stamps and official forms are all sold under state monopoly and usually through a shop called an *estanco*. Tobacco products are also sold in *quioscos* and bars but are generally more expensive. The number of *estanco* licences is regulated by the state.

estándar [es'tandar] ADJ, NM standard

estandarice etc [estanda'riθe] VB ver **estandarizar**

estandarizar [estandari'θar] /1f/ VT to standardize

estandarte [estan'darte] NM banner, standard

estanque [es'tanke] VB ver **estancar** ▶ NM (lago) pool, pond; (Agr) reservoir

estanquero, -a [estan'kero, a] NM/F tobacconist

estante [es'tante] NM (armario) rack, stand; (biblioteca) bookcase; (anaquel) shelf; (Am) prop

estantería [estante'ria] NF shelving, shelves pl

estaño [es'taɲo] NM tin

PALABRA CLAVE

estar [es'tar] /1o/ VI **1** (posición) to be; **está en la plaza** it's in the square; **¿está Juan?** is Juan in?; **estamos a 30 km de Junín** we're 30 km from Junín

2 (+ adj o adv: estado) to be; **estar enfermo** to be ill; **está muy elegante** he's looking very smart; **estar lejos** to be far (away); **¿cómo estás?** how are you keeping?

3 (+ gerundio) to be; **estoy leyendo** I'm reading

4 (uso pasivo): **está condenado a muerte** he's been condemned to death; **está envasado en ...** it's packed in ...

5: **estar a: ¿a cuántos estamos?** what's the date today?; **estamos a 9 de mayo** it's the 9th of May; **las manzanas están a 1,50 euros** apples are (selling at) 1.5 euros; **estamos a 25 grados** it's 25 degrees today

6 (locuciones): **¿estamos?** (¿de acuerdo?) okay?; (¿listo?) ready?; **¡ya está bien!** that's enough!; **¿está la comida?** is dinner ready?; **¡ya está! ¡ya estuvo!** (Am) that's it!

7: **estar con: está con gripe** he's got (the) flu

8: **estar de: estar de vacaciones/viaje** to be on holiday/away o on a trip; **está de camarero** he's working as a waiter

9: **estar para: está para salir** he's about to leave; **no estoy para bromas** I'm not in the mood for jokes

10: **estar por** (propuesta etc) to be in favour of; (persona etc) to support, side with; **está por limpiar** it still has to be cleaned; **¡estoy por dejarlo!** I think I'm going to leave this!

11: **estar sin: estar sin dinero** to have no money; **está sin terminar** it isn't finished yet

12 (+ que): **está que rabia** (fam) he's hopping mad (fam); **estoy que me caigo de sueño** I'm terribly sleepy, I can't keep my eyes open

estarse VR: **se estuvo en la cama toda la tarde** he stayed in bed all afternoon; **¡estate quieto!** stop fidgeting!

estárter [es'tarter] NM (*Auto*) choke

estas ['estas] ADJ DEMOSTRATIVO, PRON *ver* **este¹**

estás [es'tas] VB *ver* **estar**

éstas ['estas] PRON *ver* **éste**

estatal [esta'tal] ADJ state *cpd*

estático, -a [es'tatiko, a] ADJ static

estatua [es'tatwa] NF statue

estatura [esta'tura] NF stature, height

estatus [es'tatus] NM INV status

estatutario, -a [estatu'tarjo, a] ADJ statutory

estatuto [esta'tuto] NM (*Jur*) statute; (*de ciudad*) bye-law; (*de comité*) rule; **estatutos sociales** (*Com*) articles of association

este¹ ['este] ADJ (*lado*) east; (*dirección*) easterly ▶ NM east; **en la parte del ~** in the eastern part

este² ['este], **esta** [esta], **estos** ['estos], **estas** ['estas] ADJ DEMOSTRATIVO this *sg*, these *pl*; (*Am: como muletilla*) er, um ▶ PRON this (one) *sg*, these (ones) *pl*

esté [es'te] VB *ver* **estar**

éste ['este], **ésta** [esta], **éstos** ['estos], **éstas** ['estas] PRON this (one) *sg*, these (ones) *pl*; **ése ... ~ ...** the former ... the latter ...

estela [es'tela] NF wake, wash; (*fig*) trail

estelar [este'lar] ADJ (*Astro*) stellar; (*Teat*) star *cpd*

estén [es'ten] VB *ver* **estar**

estenografía [estenoɣra'fia] NF shorthand

estentóreo, -a [esten'toreo, a] ADJ (*sonido*) strident; (*voz*) booming

estepa [es'tepa] NF (*Geo*) steppe

estera [es'tera] NF (*alfombra*) mat; (*tejido*) matting

estercolero [esterko'lero] NM manure heap, dunghill

estéreo [es'tereo] ADJ INV, NM stereo

estereofónico, -a [estereo'foniko, a] ADJ stereophonic

estereotipar [estereoti'par] /**1a**/ VT to stereotype

estereotipo [estereo'tipo] NM stereotype

estéril [es'teril] ADJ sterile, barren; (*fig*) vain, futile

esterilice *etc* [esteri'liθe] VB *ver* **esterilizar**

esterilizar [esterili'θar] /**1f**/ VT to sterilize

esterilla [este'riʎa] NF (*alfombrilla*) small mat

esterlina [ester'lina] ADJ: **libra ~** pound sterling

esternón [ester'non] NM breastbone

estero [es'tero] NM (*Am*) swamp

estertor [ester'tor] NM death rattle

estés [es'tes] VB *ver* **estar**

esteta [es'teta] NMF aesthete

esteticienne [esteti'θjen] NF beautician

estético, -a [es'tetiko, a] ADJ aesthetic ▶ NF aesthetics *sg*

estetoscopio [estetos'kopjo] NM stethoscope

estibador [estiβa'ðor] NM stevedore

estibar [esti'βar] /**1a**/ VT (*Naut*) to stow

estiércol [es'tjerkol] NM dung, manure

estigma [es'tiɣma] NM stigma

estigmatice *etc* [estiɣma'tiθe] VB *ver* **estigmatizar**

estigmatizar [estiɣmati'θar] /**1f**/ VT to stigmatize

estilarse [esti'larse] /**1a**/ VR (*estar de moda*) to be in fashion; (*usarse*) to be used

estilice *etc* [esti'liθe] VB *ver* **estilizar**

estilizar [estili'θar] /**1f**/ VT to stylize; (*Tec*) to design

estilo [es'tilo] NM style; (*Tec*) stylus; (*Natación*) stroke; **~ de vida** lifestyle; **al ~ de** in the style of; **algo por el ~** something along those lines

estilográfica [estilo'ɣrafika] NF fountain pen

estima [es'tima] NF esteem, respect

estimación [estima'θjon] NF (*evaluación*) estimation; (*aprecio, afecto*) esteem, regard

estimado, -a [esti'maðo, a] ADJ esteemed; **"E~ Señor"** "Dear Sir"

estimar [esti'mar] /**1a**/ VT (*evaluar*) to estimate; (*valorar*) to value; (*apreciar*) to esteem, respect; (*pensar, considerar*) to think, reckon

estimulante [estimu'lante] ADJ stimulating ▶ NM stimulant

estimular [estimu'lar] /**1a**/ VT to stimulate; (*excitar*) to excite; (*animar*) to encourage

estímulo [es'timulo] NM stimulus; (*ánimo*) encouragement

estío [es'tio] NM summer

estipendio [esti'pendjo] NM salary; (*Com*) stipend

estipulación [estipula'θjon] NF stipulation, condition

estipular [estipu'lar] /**1a**/ VT to stipulate

estirado, -a [esti'raðo, a] ADJ (*tenso*) (stretched *o* drawn) tight; (*fig: persona*) stiff, pompous; (*engreído*) stuck-up

estirar [esti'rar] /**1a**/ VT to stretch; (*dinero, suma etc*) to stretch out; (*cuello*) to crane; (*discurso*) to spin out; **~ la pata** (*fam*) to kick the bucket; **estirarse** VR to stretch

estirón [esti'ron] NM pull, tug; (*crecimiento*) spurt, sudden growth; **dar un ~** (*niño*) to shoot up

estirpe [es'tirpe] NF stock, lineage

estival [esti'βal] ADJ summer *cpd*

esto ['esto] PRON this, this thing *o* matter; (*como muletilla*) er, um; **~ de la boda** this business about the wedding; **en ~** at this *o* that point; **por ~** for this reason

estocada [esto'kaða] NF (*acción*) stab; (*Taur*) death blow

Estocolmo [esto'kolmo] NM Stockholm

estofa [es'tofa] NF: **de baja ~** poor-quality

estofado [esto'faðo] NM stew

estofar [esto'far] /**1a**/ VT (*bordar*) to quilt; (*Culin*) to stew

estoico, -a [es'toiko, a] ADJ (*Filosofía*) stoic(al); (*fig*) cold, indifferent

estomacal [estoma'kal] ADJ stomach *cpd*; **trastorno ~** stomach upset

estómago [es'tomaɣo] NM stomach; **tener ~** to be thick-skinned

Estonia [es'tonja] NF Estonia

estonio, -a [es'tonjo, a] ADJ, NM/F Estonian ▶ NM (*Ling*) Estonian

estoque [es'toke] NM rapier, sword

estorbar [estor'βar] /**1a**/ VT to hinder, obstruct; (*fig*) to bother, disturb ▶ VI to be in the way

estorbo [es'torβo] NM (*molestia*) bother, nuisance; (*obstáculo*) hindrance, obstacle

estornino [estor'nino] NM starling

estornudar [estornu'ðar] /**1a**/ VI to sneeze

estornudo [estor'nuðo] NM sneeze

estos ['estos] ADJ DEMOSTRATIVO *ver* **este²**

éstos ['estos] PRON *ver* **éste**

estoy [es'toi] VB *ver* **estar**

estrabismo [estra'βismo] NM squint

estrado [es'traðo] NM (*tarima*) platform; (*Mus*) bandstand; **estrados** NMPL law courts

estrafalario, -a [estrafa'larjo, a] ADJ odd, eccentric; (*desarreglado*) slovenly, sloppy

estrago [es'traɣo] NM ruin, destruction; **hacer estragos en** to wreak havoc among

estragón [estra'ɣon] NM (*Culin*) tarragon

estrambótico, -a [estram'botiko, a] ADJ odd, eccentric; (*peinado, ropa*) outlandish

estrangulación [estrangula'θjon] NF strangulation

estrangulador, -a [estrangula'ðor, a] NM/F strangler ▶ NM (*Tec*) throttle; (*Auto*) choke

estrangulamiento [estrangula'mjento] NM (*Auto*) bottleneck

estrangular [estrangu'lar] /**1a**/ VT (*persona*) to strangle; (*Med*) to strangulate

estraperlista [estraper'lista] NMF black marketeer

estraperlo [estra'perlo] NM black market

estratagema [estrata'xema] NF (*Mil*) stratagem; (*astucia*) cunning

estratega [estra'teɣa] NMF strategist

estrategia [estra'texja] NF strategy

estratégico, -a [estra'texiko, a] ADJ strategic

estratificar [estratifi'kar] /**1g**/ VT to stratify

estratifique *etc* [estrati'fike] VB *ver* **estratificar**

estrato [es'trato] NM stratum, layer

estratosfera [estratos'fera] NF stratosphere

estrechar [estre'tʃar] /**1a**/ VT (*reducir*) to narrow; (*vestido*) to take in; (*persona*) to hug, embrace; **estrecharse** VR (*reducirse*) to narrow, grow narrow; (*2 personas*) to embrace; **~ la mano** to shake hands

estrechez [estre'tʃeθ] NF narrowness; (*de ropa*) tightness; (*intimidad*) intimacy; (*Com*) want o shortage of money; **estrecheces** NFPL financial difficulties

estrecho, -a [es'tretʃo, a] ADJ narrow; (*apretado*) tight; (*íntimo*) close, intimate; (*miserable*) mean ▶ NM strait; **~ de miras** narrow-minded; **E~ de Gibraltar** Straits of Gibraltar

estrella [es'treʎa] NF star; **~ fugaz** shooting star; **~ de mar** starfish; **tener (buena)/mala ~** to be lucky/unlucky

estrellado, -a [estre'ʎaðo, a] ADJ (*forma*) star-shaped; (*cielo*) starry; (*huevos*) fried

estrellar [estre'ʎar] /**1a**/ VT (*hacer añicos*) to smash (to pieces); (*huevos*) to fry; **estrellarse** VR to smash; (*chocarse*) to crash; (*fracasar*) to fail

estrellato [estre'ʎato] NM stardom

estremecer [estreme'θer] /**2d**/ VT to shake; **estremecerse** VR to shake, tremble; **~ de** (*horror*) to shudder with; (*frío*) to shiver with

estremecimiento [estremeθi'mjento] NM (*temblor*) trembling, shaking

estremezca *etc* [estre'meθka] VB *ver* **estremecer**

estrenar [estre'nar] /**1a**/ VT (*vestido*) to wear for the first time; (*casa*) to move into; (*película, obra de teatro*) to première; **estrenarse** VR (*persona*) to make one's début; (*película*) to have its première; (*Teat*) to open

estreno [es'treno] NM (*primer uso*) first use; (*Cine etc*) première

estreñido, -a [estre'ɲiðo, a] ADJ constipated

estreñimiento [estreɲi'mjento] NM constipation

estreñir [estre'ɲir] VT to constipate

estrépito [es'trepito] NM noise, racket; (*fig*) fuss

estrepitoso, -a [estrepi'toso, a] ADJ noisy; (*fiesta*) rowdy

estrés [es'tres] NM stress

estresante [estre'sante] ADJ stressful

estría [es'tria] NF groove; **estrías (en el cutis)** stretchmarks

estribación [estriβa'θjon] NF (*Geo*) spur; **estribaciones** NFPL foothills

estribar [estri'βar] /**1a**/ VI (*Arq*): **~ en** to rest on, be supported by; **la dificultad estriba en el texto** the difficulty lies in the text

estribillo [estri'βiʎo] NM (*Lit*) refrain; (*Mus*) chorus

estribo [es'triβo] NM (*de jinete*) stirrup; (*de coche, tren*) step; (*de puente*) support; (*Geo*) spur; **perder los estribos** to fly off the handle

estribor [estri'βor] NM (*Naut*) starboard

estricnina [estrik'nina] NF strychnine

estricto, -a [es'trikto, a] ADJ (*riguroso*) strict; (*severo*) severe

estridente [estri'ðente] ADJ (*color*) loud; (*voz*) raucous

estro ['estro] NM inspiration

estrofa [es'trofa] NF verse

estropajo [estro'paxo] NM scourer

estropeado, -a [estrope'aðo, a] ADJ: **está ~** it's not working

estropear [estrope'ar] /1a/ VT (*arruinar*) to spoil; (*dañar*) to damage; (: *máquina*) to break; **estropearse** VR (*objeto*) to get damaged; (*coche*) to break down; (*la piel etc*) to be ruined

estropicio [estro'piθjo] NM (*rotura*) breakage; (*efectos*) harmful effects *pl*

estructura [estruk'tura] NF structure

estruendo [es'trwendo] NM (*ruido*) racket, din; (*fig: alboroto*) uproar, turmoil

estrujar [estru'xar] /1a/ VT (*apretar*) to squeeze; (*aplastar*) to crush; (*fig*) to drain, bleed

estuario [es'twarjo] NM estuary

estuche [es'tutʃe] NM box, case

estudiante [estu'ðjante] NMF student

estudiantil [estuðjan'til] ADJ INV student *cpd*

estudiantina [estuðjan'tina] NF student music group

estudiar [estu'ðjar] /1b/ VT to study; (*propuesta*) to think about o over; **~ para abogado** to study to become a lawyer

estudio [es'tuðjo] NM study; (*encuesta*) research; (*proyecto*) plan; (*piso*) studio flat; (*Cine, Arte, Radio*) studio; **estudios** NMPL studies; (*erudición*) learning *sg*; **cursar** o **hacer estudios** to study; **~ de casos prácticos** case study; **~ de desplazamientos y tiempos** (*Com*) time and motion study; **estudios de motivación** motivational research *sg*; **~ del trabajo** (*Com*) work study; **~ de viabilidad** (*Com*) feasibility study

estudioso, -a [estu'ðjoso, a] ADJ studious

estufa [es'tufa] NF heater, fire

estulticia [estul'tiθja] NF foolishness

estupefaciente [estupefa'θjente] ADJ, NM narcotic

estupefacto, -a [estupe'fakto, a] ADJ speechless, thunderstruck

estupendamente [estupenda'mente] ADV (*fam*): **estoy ~** I feel great; **le salió ~** he did it very well

estupendo, -a [estu'pendo, a] ADJ wonderful, terrific; (*fam*) great; **¡~!** that's great!, fantastic!

estupidez [estupi'ðeθ] NF (*torpeza*) stupidity; (*acto*) stupid thing (to do); **fue una ~ mía** that was a silly thing for me to do o say

estúpido, -a [es'tupiðo, a] ADJ stupid, silly

estupor [estu'por] NM stupor; (*fig*) astonishment, amazement

estupro [es'tupro] NM rape

estuve *etc* [es'tuβe], **estuviera** *etc* [estu'βjera] VB *ver* **estar**

esvástica [es'βastika] NF swastika

ET ABR = **Ejército de Tierra**

ETA ['eta] NF ABR (*Pol: = Euskadi Ta Askatasuna*) ETA

etapa [e'tapa] NF (*de viaje*) stage; (*Deporte*) leg; (*parada*) stopping place; (*fig*) stage, phase; **por etapas** gradually, in stages

etarra [e'tarra] ADJ ETA *cpd* ▶ NMF member of ETA

etc. ABR (= *etcétera*) etc

etcétera [et'θetera] ADV etcetera

etéreo, -a [e'tereo, a] ADJ ethereal

eternice *etc* [eter'niθe] VB *ver* **eternizarse**

eternidad [eterni'ðað] NF eternity

eternizarse [eterni'θarse] /1f/ VR: **~ en hacer algo** to take ages to do sth

eterno, -a [e'terno, a] ADJ eternal, everlasting; (*despectivo*) never-ending

ético, -a ['etiko, a] ADJ ethical ▶ NF ethics

etimología [etimolo'xia] NF etymology

etiqueta [eti'keta] NF (*modales*) etiquette; (*rótulo*) label, tag; **de ~** formal

etnia ['etnja] NF ethnic group

étnico, -a ['etniko, a] ADJ ethnic

ETS SIGLA F (= *Enfermedad de Transmisión Sexual*) STD

EU(A) NMPL ABR (*esp Am*: = *Estados Unidos (de América)*) US(A)

eucalipto [euka'lipto] NM eucalyptus

Eucaristía [eukaris'tia] NF Eucharist

eufemismo [eufe'mismo] NM euphemism

euforia [eu'forja] NF euphoria

eufórico, -a [eu'foriko, a] ADJ euphoric

eunuco [eu'nuko] NM eunuch

euro ['euro] NM (*moneda*) euro

eurodiputado, -a [euroðipu'taðo, a] NM/F Euro MP, MEP

Eurolandia [euro'landja] NF Euroland

Europa [eu'ropa] NF Europe

europeice *etc* [euro'peiθe] VB *ver* **europeizar**

europeizar [europei'θar] /1f/ VT to Europeanize; **europeizarse** /1f/ VR to become Europeanized

europeo, -a [euro'peo, a] ADJ, NM/F European

Eurotúnel [euro'tunel] NM (*estructura*) Channel Tunnel

eurozona [euro'θona] NF Eurozone

Euskadi [eus'kaði] NM the Basque Provinces *pl*

euskera, eusquera [eus'kera] NM (*Ling*) Basque; *ver tb* **lengua**

eutanasia [euta'nasja] NF euthanasia

evacuación [eβakwa'θjon] NF evacuation

evacuar [eβa'kwar] /1d/ VT to evacuate

evadir [eβa'ðir] /3a/ VT to evade, avoid;
 evadirse VR to escape

evaluación [eβalwa'θjon] NF evaluation,
 assessment

evaluar [eβa'lwar] /1e/ VT to evaluate, assess

evangélico, -a [eβan'xeliko, a] ADJ
 evangelical

evangelio [eβan'xeljo] NM gospel

evaporación [eβapora'θjon] NF evaporation

evaporar [eβapo'rar] /1a/ VT to evaporate;
 evaporarse VR to vanish

evasión [eβa'sjon] NF escape, flight; (fig)
 evasion; ~ fiscal o tributaria tax evasion;
 ~ de capitales flight of capital

evasivo, -a [eβa'siβo, a] ADJ evasive,
 non-committal ▶ NF (pretexto) excuse;
 contestar con evasivas to avoid giving a
 straight answer

evento [e'βento] NM event; (eventualidad)
 eventuality

eventual [eβen'twal] ADJ possible,
 conditional (upon circumstances);
 (trabajador) casual, temporary

Everest [eβe'rest] NM: el (Monte) ~ (Mount)
 Everest

evidencia [eβi'ðenθja] NF evidence, proof;
 poner en ~ to make clear; ponerse en ~
 (persona) to show o.s. up

evidenciar [eβiðen'θjar] /1b/ VT (hacer patente)
 to make evident; (probar) to prove, show;
 evidenciarse VR to be evident

evidente [eβi'ðente] ADJ obvious, clear,
 evident

evitar [eβi'tar] /1a/ VT (evadir) to avoid;
 (impedir) to prevent; (peligro) to escape;
 (molestia) to save; (tentación) to shun; ~ hacer
 algo to avoid doing sth; si puedo evitarlo if
 I can help it

evocador, a [eβoka'ðor, a] ADJ (sugestivo)
 evocative

evocar [eβo'kar] /1g/ VT to evoke, call forth

evolución [eβolu'θjon] NF (desarrollo)
 evolution, development; (cambio) change;
 (Mil) manoeuvre

evolucionar [eβoluθjo'nar] /1a/ VI to evolve;
 (Mil, Aviat) to manoeuvre

evoque etc [e'βoke] VB ver evocar

ex [eks] ADJ ex-; el ex ministro the former
 minister, the ex-minister

exabrupto [eksa'βrupto] NM interjection

exacción [eksak'θjon] NF (acto) exaction;
 (de impuestos) demand

exacerbar [eksaθer'βar] /1a/ VT to irritate,
 annoy

exactamente [eksakta'mente] ADV exactly

exactitud [eksakti'tuð] NF exactness;
 (precisión) accuracy; (puntualidad) punctuality

exacto, -a [ek'sakto, a] ADJ exact; accurate;
 punctual; ¡~! exactly!; eso no es del todo ~

that's not quite right; para ser ~ to be
 precise

exageración [eksaxera'θjon] NF
 exaggeration

exagerado, -a [eksaxe'raðo, a] ADJ (relato)
 exaggerated; (precio) excessive; (persona)
 over-demonstrative; (gesto) theatrical

exagerar [eksaxe'rar] /1a/ VT to exaggerate;
 (exceder) to overdo

exaltado, -a [eksal'taðo, a] ADJ (apasionado)
 over-excited, worked up; (exagerado)
 extreme; (fanático) hot-headed; (discurso)
 impassioned ▶ NM/F (fanático) hothead;
 (Pol) extremist

exaltar [eksal'tar] /1a/ VT to exalt, glorify;
 exaltarse VR (excitarse) to get excited o
 worked up

examen [ek'samen] NM examination; (de
 problema) consideration; ~ de (encuesta)
 inquiry into; ~ de conducir driving test;
 ~ de ingreso entrance examination;
 ~ eliminatorio qualifying examination

examinar [eksami'nar] /1a/ VT to examine;
 (poner a prueba) to test; (inspeccionar) to inspect;
 examinarse VR to be examined, take an
 examination

exánime [ek'sanime] ADJ lifeless; (fig)
 exhausted

exasperar [eksaspe'rar] /1a/ VT to exasperate;
 exasperarse VR to get exasperated, lose
 patience

Exc.ª ABR = Excelencia

excarcelar [ekskarθe'lar] /1a/ VT to release
 (from prison)

excavador, a [ekskaβa'ðor, a] NM/F (persona)
 excavator ▶ NF (Tec) digger

excavar [ekska'βar] /1a/ VT to excavate, dig
 (out)

excedencia [eksθe'ðenθja] NF (Mil) leave;
 (Escol) sabbatical; estar en ~ to be on leave;
 pedir o solicitar la ~ to ask for leave

excedente [eksθe'ðente] ADJ, NM excess,
 surplus

exceder [eksθe'ðer] /2a/ VT to exceed,
 surpass; excederse VR (extralimitarse) to go
 too far; (sobrepasarse) to excel o.s.

excelencia [eksθe'lenθja] NF excellence;
 E~ Excellency; por ~ par excellence

excelente [eksθe'lente] ADJ excellent

excelso, -a [eks'θelso, a] ADJ lofty, sublime

excentricidad [eksθentriθi'ðað] NF
 eccentricity

excéntrico, -a [eks'θentriko, a] ADJ, NM/F
 eccentric

excepción [eksθep'θjon] NF exception; a ~
 de with the exception of, except for; la ~
 confirma la regla the exception proves the
 rule

excepcional [eksθepθjo'nal] ADJ exceptional

excepto [eks'θepto] ADV excepting, except (for)

exceptuar [eksθep'twar] /1e/ VT to except, exclude

excesivo, -a [eksθe'siβo, a] ADJ excessive

exceso [eks'θeso] NM excess; (Com) surplus; **~ de equipaje/peso** excess luggage/weight; **~ de velocidad** speeding; **en o por ~** excessively

excitación [eksθita'θjon] NF (sensación) excitement; (acción) excitation

excitado, -a [eksθi'taðo, a] ADJ excited; (emociones) aroused

excitante [eksθi'tante] ADJ exciting; (Med) stimulating ▶ NM stimulant

excitar [eksθi'tar] /1a/ VT to excite; (incitar) to urge; (emoción) to stir up; (esperanzas) to raise; (pasión) to arouse; **excitarse** VR to get excited

exclamación [eksklama'θjon] NF exclamation

exclamar [ekskla'mar] /1a/ VI to exclaim; **exclamarse** VR: **exclamarse (contra)** to complain (about)

excluir [eksklu'ir] /3g/ VT to exclude; (dejar fuera) to shut out; (solución) to reject; (posibilidad) to rule out

exclusión [eksklu'sjon] NF exclusion

exclusiva [eksklu'siβa] NF ver **exclusivo**

exclusive [eksklu'siβe] PREP exclusive of, not counting

exclusivo, -a [eksklu'siβo, a] ADJ exclusive ▶ NF (Prensa) exclusive, scoop; (Com) sole right o agency; **derecho ~** sole o exclusive right

excluyendo etc [eksklu'jendo] VB ver **excluir**

Excma. ABR (= Excelentísima) courtesy title

Excmo. ABR (= Excelentísimo) courtesy title

excombatiente [ekskomba'tjente] NM ex-serviceman, war veteran (US)

excomulgar [ekskomul'ɣar] /1h/ VT (Rel) to excommunicate

excomulgue etc [eksko'mulɣe] VB ver **excomulgar**

excomunión [ekskomu'njon] NF excommunication

excoriar [eksko'rjar] /1b/ VT to flay, skin

excremento [ekskre'mento] NM excrement

exculpar [ekskul'par] /1a/ VT to exonerate; (Jur) to acquit; **exculparse** VR to exonerate o.s.

excursión [ekskur'sjon] NF excursion, outing; **ir de ~** to go (off) on a trip

excursionista [ekskursjo'nista] NMF (turista) sightseer

excusa [eks'kusa] NF excuse; (disculpa) apology; **presentar sus excusas** to excuse o.s.

excusado, -a [eksku'saðo, a] ADJ unnecessary; (disculpado) excused, forgiven

excusar [eksku'sar] /1a/ VT to excuse; (evitar) to avoid, prevent; **excusarse** VR (disculparse) to apologize

execrable [ekse'kraβle] ADJ appalling

exención [eksen'θjon] NF exemption

exento, -a [ek'sento, a] PP de **eximir** ▶ ADJ exempt

exequias [ek'sekjas] NFPL funeral rites

exfoliar [eksfo'ljar] /1b/ VT to exfoliate

exhalación [eksala'θjon] NF (del aire) exhalation; (de vapor) fumes pl, vapour; (rayo) shooting star; **salir como una ~** to shoot out

exhalar [eksa'lar] /1a/ VT to exhale, breathe out; (olor etc) to give off; (suspiro) to breathe, heave

exhaustivo, -a [eksaus'tiβo, a] ADJ (análisis) thorough; (estudio) exhaustive

exhausto, -a [ek'sausto, a] ADJ exhausted, worn-out

exhibición [eksiβi'θjon] NF exhibition; (demostración) display, show; (de película) showing; (de equipo) performance

exhibicionista [eksiβiθjo'nista] ADJ, NMF exhibitionist

exhibir [eksi'βir] /3a/ VT (cuadros) to exhibit; (colección) to display, show; (artículos) to display; (pasaporte) to show; (película) to screen; (mostrar con orgullo) to show off; **exhibirse** VR (mostrarse en público) to show o.s. off; (fam: indecentemente) to expose o.s.

exhortación [eksorta'θjon] NF exhortation

exhortar [eksor'tar] /1a/ VT: **~ a** to exhort to

exhumar [eksu'mar] /1a/ VT to exhume

exigencia [eksi'xenθja] NF demand, requirement

exigente [eksi'xente] ADJ demanding; (profesor) strict; **ser ~ con algn** to be hard on sb

exigir [eksi'xir] /3c/ VT (gen) to demand, require; (impuestos) to exact, levy; **~ el pago** to demand payment

exiguo, -a [ek'siɣwo, a] ADJ (cantidad) meagre; (objeto) tiny

exija etc [ek'sixa] VB ver **exigir**

exiliado, -a [eksi'ljaðo, a] ADJ exiled, in exile ▶ NM/F exile

exiliar [eksi'ljar] /1b/ VT to exile; **exiliarse** VR to go into exile

exilio [ek'siljo] NM exile

eximio, -a [ek'simjo, a] ADJ (eminente) distinguished, eminent

eximir [eksi'mir] /3a/ VT to exempt

existencia [eksis'tenθja] NF existence; **existencias** NFPL stock sg; **~ de mercancías** (Com) stock-in-trade; **tener en ~** to have in stock; **amargar la ~ a algn** to make sb's life a misery

existir [eksis'tir] /3a/ VI to exist, be

éxito ['eksito] NM (*resultado*) result, outcome; (*triunfo*) success; (*Mus, Teat*) hit; **~ editorial** bestseller; **~ rotundo** smash hit; **tener ~** to be successful

exitoso, -a [eksi'toso, a] ADJ (*esp Am*) successful

éxodo ['eksoðo] NM exodus; **el ~ rural** the drift from the land

ex oficio [ekso'fiθjo] ADJ, ADV ex officio

exonerar [eksone'rar] /**1a**/ VT to exonerate; **~ de una obligación** to free from an obligation

exorbitante [eksorβi'tante] ADJ (*precio*) exorbitant; (*cantidad*) excessive

exorcice *etc* [eksor'θiθe] VB *ver* **exorcizar**

exorcismo [eksor'θismo] NM exorcism

exorcizar [eksorθi'θar] /**1f**/ VT to exorcize

exótico, -a [ek'sotiko, a] ADJ exotic

expandido, -a [ekspan'diðo, a] ADJ: **en caracteres expandidos** (*Inform*) double width

expandir [ekspan'dir] /**3a**/ VT to expand; (*Com*) to expand, enlarge; **expandirse** VR to expand, spread

expansión [ekspan'sjon] NF expansion; (*recreo*) relaxation; **la ~ económica** economic growth; **economía en ~** expanding economy

expansionarse [ekspansjo'narse] /**1a**/ VR (*dilatarse*) to expand; (*recrearse*) to relax

expansivo, -a [ekspan'siβo, a] ADJ expansive; (*efusivo*) communicative; **onda expansiva** shock wave

expatriado, -a [ekspa'trjaðo, a] NM/F (*emigrado*) expatriate; (*exiliado*) exile

expatriarse [ekspa'trjarse] /**1b**/ VR to emigrate; (*Pol*) to go into exile

expectación [ekspekta'θjon] NF (*esperanza*) expectation; (*ilusión*) excitement

expectativa [ekspekta'tiβa] NF (*espera*) expectation; (*perspectiva*) prospect; **~ de vida** life expectancy; **estar a la ~** to wait and see (what will happen)

expedición [ekspeði'θjon] NF (*excursión*) expedition; **gastos de ~** shipping charges

expedientar [ekspeðjen'tar] /**1a**/ VT to open a file on; (*funcionario*) to discipline, start disciplinary proceedings against

expediente [ekspe'ðjente] NM expedient; (*Jur: procedimiento*) action, proceedings *pl*; (: *papeles*) dossier, file, record; **~ judicial** court proceedings *pl*; **~ académico** (student's) record

expedir [ekspe'ðir] /**3k**/ VT (*despachar*) to send, forward; (*pasaporte*) to issue; (*cheque*) to make out

expedito, -a [ekspe'ðito, a] ADJ (*libre*) clear, free

expeler [ekspe'ler] /**2a**/ VT to expel, eject

expendedor, a [ekspende'ðor, a] NM/F (*vendedor*) dealer; (*Teat*) ticket agent ▸ NM (*aparato*) (vending) machine; **~ de cigarrillos** cigarette machine

expendeduría [ekspendedu'ria] NF (*estanco*) tobacconist's (shop) (BRIT), cigar store (US)

expendio [eks'pendjo] NM (*Am*) small shop (BRIT) o store (US)

expensas [eks'pensas] NFPL (*Jur*) costs; **a ~ de** at the expense of

experiencia [ekspe'rjenθja] NF experience

experimentado, -a [eksperimen'taðo, a] ADJ experienced

experimentar [eksperimen'tar] /**1a**/ VT (*en laboratorio*) to experiment with; (*probar*) to test, try out; (*notar, observar*) to experience; (*deterioro, pérdida*) to suffer; (*aumento*) to show; (*sensación*) to feel

experimento [eksperi'mento] NM experiment

experto, -a [eks'perto, a] ADJ expert ▸ NM/F expert

expiar [ekspi'ar] /**1c**/ VT to atone for

expida *etc* [eks'piða] VB *ver* **expedir**

expirar [ekspi'rar] /**1a**/ VI to expire

explanada [ekspla'naða] NF (*paseo*) esplanade; (*a orillas del mar*) promenade

explayarse [ekspla'jarse] /**1a**/ VR (*en discurso*) to speak at length; **~ con algn** to confide in sb

explicación [eksplika'θjon] NF explanation

explicar [ekspli'kar] /**1g**/ VT to explain; (*teoría*) to expound; (*Univ*) to lecture in; **explicarse** VR to explain (o.s.); **no me lo explico** I can't understand it

explícito, -a [eks'pliθito, a] ADJ explicit

explique *etc* [eks'plike] VB *ver* **explicar**

exploración [eksplora'θjon] NF exploration; (*Mil*) reconnaissance

explorador, a [eksplora'ðor, a] NM/F (*pionero*) explorer; (*Mil*) scout ▸ NM (*Med*) probe; (*radar*) (radar) scanner

explorar [eksplo'rar] /**1a**/ VT to explore; (*Med*) to probe; (*radar*) to scan

explosión [eksplo'sjon] NF explosion

explosivo, -a [eksplo'siβo, a] ADJ explosive

explotación [eksplota'θjon] NF exploitation; (*de planta etc*) running; (*de mina*) working; (*de recurso*) development; **~ minera** mine; **gastos de ~** operating costs

explotar [eksplo'tar] /**1a**/ VT to exploit; (*planta*) to run, operate; (*mina*) to work ▸ VI (*bomba etc*) to explode, go off

expondré *etc* [ekspon'dre] VB *ver* **exponer**

exponer [ekspo'ner] /**2q**/ VT to expose; (*cuadro*) to display; (*vida*) to risk; (*idea*) to explain; (*teoría*) to expound; (*hechos*) to set out; **exponerse** VR: **exponerse a (hacer) algo** to run the risk of (doing) sth

exponga etc [eks'ponga] VB ver **exponer**

exportación [eksporta'θjon] NF (acción) export; (mercancías) exports pl

exportador, a [eksporta'ðor, a] ADJ (país) exporting ▶ NM/F exporter

exportar [ekspor'tar] /**1a**/ VT to export

exposición [eksposi'θjon] NF (gen) exposure; (de arte) show, exhibition; (Com) display; (feria) show, fair; (explicación) explanation; (de teoría) exposition; (narración) account, statement

exprés [eks'pres] ADJ INV (café) espresso ▶ NM (Ferro) express (train)

expresamente [ekspresa'mente] ADV (decir) clearly; (concretamente) expressly; (a propósito) on purpose

expresar [ekspre'sar] /**1a**/ VT to express; (redactar) to phrase, put; (emoción) to show; **expresarse** VR to express o.s.; (dato) to be stated; **como abajo se expresa** as stated below

expresión [ekspre'sjon] NF expression; **~ familiar** colloquialism

expresivo, -a [ekspre'siβo, a] ADJ expressive; (cariñoso) affectionate

expreso, -a [eks'preso, a] ADJ (explícito) express; (claro) specific, clear; (tren) fast ▶ NM (Ferro) fast train

express [eks'pres] ADV (AM): **enviar algo ~** to send sth special delivery

exprimidor [eksprimi'ðor] NM (lemon) squeezer

exprimir [ekspri'mir] /**3a**/ VT (fruta) to squeeze; (zumo) to squeeze out

ex profeso [ekspro'feso] ADV expressly

expropiar [ekspro'pjar] /**1b**/ VT to expropriate

expuesto, -a [eks'pwesto, a] PP de **exponer** ▶ ADJ exposed; (cuadro etc) on show, on display; **según lo ~ arriba** according to what has been stated above

expulsar [ekspul'sar] /**1a**/ VT (echar) to eject, throw out; (alumno) to expel; (despedir) to sack, fire; (Deporte) to send off

expulsión [ekspul'sjon] NF expulsion; sending-off

expurgar [ekspur'ɣar] /**1h**/ VT to expurgate

expuse etc [eks'puse] VB ver **exponer**

exquisito, -a [ekski'sito, a] ADJ exquisite; (comida) delicious; (afectado) affected

Ext. ABR (= Exterior) ext.; (= Extensión) ext.

éxtasis ['ekstasis] NM (tb droga) ecstasy

extemporáneo, -a [ekstempo'raneo, a] ADJ unseasonal

extender [eksten'der] /**2g**/ VT to extend; (los brazos) to stretch out, hold out; (mapa, tela) to spread (out), open (out); (mantequilla) to spread; (certificado) to issue; (cheque, recibo) to make out; (documento) to draw up; **extenderse** VR to extend; (terreno) to stretch o spread (out); (persona: en el suelo) to stretch out; (: en el tiempo) to extend, last; (costumbre, epidemia) to spread; (guerra) to escalate; **extenderse sobre un tema** to enlarge on a subject

extendido, -a [eksten'diðo, a] ADJ (abierto) spread out, open; (brazos) outstretched; (costumbre etc) widespread

extensible [eksten'siβle] ADJ extending

extensión [eksten'sjon] NF (de terreno, mar) expanse, stretch; (Mus) range; (de conocimientos) extent; (de programa) scope; (de tiempo) length, duration; (Telec) extension; **~ de plazo** (Com) extension; **en toda la ~ de la palabra** in every sense of the word; **de ~** (Inform) add-on

extenso, -a [eks'tenso, a] ADJ extensive

extenuar [ekste'nwar] /**1e**/ VT (debilitar) to weaken

exterior [ekste'rjor] ADJ (de fuera) external; (afuera) outside, exterior; (apariencia) outward; (deuda, relaciones) foreign ▶ NM exterior, outside; (aspecto) outward appearance; (Deporte) wing(er); (países extranjeros) abroad; **asuntos exteriores** foreign affairs; **al ~** outwardly, on the outside; **en el ~** abroad; **noticias del ~** foreign o overseas news

exteriorice etc [eksterjo'riθe] VB ver **exteriorizar**

exteriorizar [eksterjori'θar] /**1f**/ VT (emociones) to show, reveal

exteriormente [eksterjor'mente] ADV outwardly

exterminar [ekstermi'nar] /**1a**/ VT to exterminate

exterminio [ekster'minjo] NM extermination

externo, -a [eks'terno, a] ADJ (exterior) external, outside; (superficial) outward ▶ NM/F day pupil

extienda etc [eks'tjenda] VB ver **extender**

extinción [ekstin'θjon] NF extinction

extinga etc [eks'tinga] VB ver **extinguir**

extinguido, -a [ekstin'giðo, a] ADJ (animal, volcán) extinct; (fuego) out, extinguished

extinguir [ekstin'gir] /**3d**/ VT (fuego) to extinguish, put out; (raza, población) to wipe out; **extinguirse** VR (fuego) to go out; (Bio) to die out, become extinct

extinto, -a [eks'tinto, a] ADJ extinct

extintor [ekstin'tor] NM (fire) extinguisher

extirpar [ekstir'par] /**1a**/ VT (vicios) to eradicate, stamp out; (Med) to remove (surgically)

extorsión [ekstor'sjon] NF blackmail

extra ['ekstra] ADJ INV (tiempo) extra; (vino) vintage; (chocolate) good-quality; (gasolina) high-octane ▶ NMF extra ▶ NM extra; (bono) bonus; (periódico) special edition

extracción [ekstrak'θjon] NF extraction; (*en lotería*) draw; (*de carbón*) mining

extracto [eks'trakto] NM extract

extractor [ekstrak'tor] NM (*tb:* **extractor de humos**) extractor fan

extradición [ekstraði'θjon] NF extradition

extraditar [ekstraði'tar] /**1a**/ VT to extradite

extraer [ekstra'er] /**2o**/ VT to extract, take out

extraescolar [ekstraesko'lar] ADJ: **actividad ~** extracurricular activity

extrafino, -a [ekstra'fino, a] ADJ extra-fine; **azúcar ~** caster sugar

extraiga *etc* [eks'traiɣa], **extraje** *etc* [eks'traxe], **extrajera** *etc* [ekstra'xera] VB *ver* **extraer**

extralimitarse [ekstralimi'tarse] /**1a**/ VR to go too far

extranjerismo [ekstranxe'rismo] NM foreign word *o* phrase *etc*

extranjero, -a [ekstran'xero, a] ADJ foreign ▶ NM/F foreigner ▶ NM foreign countries *pl*; **en el ~** abroad

extrañamiento [ekstraɲa'mjento] NM estrangement

extrañar [ekstra'ɲar] /**1a**/ VT (*sorprender*) to find strange *o* odd; (*echar de menos*) to miss; **extrañarse** VR (*sorprenderse*) to be amazed, be surprised; (*distanciarse*) to become estranged, grow apart; **me extraña** I'm surprised

extrañeza [ekstra'ɲeθa] NF (*rareza*) strangeness, oddness; (*asombro*) amazement, surprise

extraño, -a [eks'traɲo, a] ADJ (*extranjero*) foreign; (*raro, sorprendente*) strange, odd

extraoficial [ekstraofi'θjal] ADJ unofficial, informal

extraordinario, -a [ekstraorði'narjo, a] ADJ extraordinary; (*edición, número*) special ▶ NM (*de periódico*) special edition; **horas extraordinarias** overtime *sg*

extrarradio [ekstra'rraðjo] NM suburbs *pl*

extrasensorial [ekstrasenso'rjal] ADJ: **percepción ~** extrasensory perception

extraterrestre [ekstrate'rrestre] ADJ of *o* from outer space ▶ NMF creature from outer space

extravagancia [ekstraβa'ɣanθja] NF oddness; outlandishness; (*rareza*)

peculiarity; **extravagancias** NFPL (*tonterías*) nonsense *sg*

extravagante [ekstraβa'ɣante] ADJ (*excéntrico*) eccentric; (*estrafalario*) outlandish

extraviado, -a [ekstra'βjaðo, a] ADJ lost, missing

extraviar [ekstra'βjar] /**1c**/ VT to mislead, misdirect; (*perder*) to lose, misplace; **extraviarse** VR to lose one's way, get lost; (*objeto*) to go missing, be mislaid

extravío [ekstra'βio] NM loss; (*fig*) misconduct

extrayendo [ekstra'jendo] VB *ver* **extraer**

extremado, -a [ekstre'maðo, a] ADJ extreme, excessive

Extremadura [ekstrema'ðura] NF Estremadura

extremar [ekstre'mar] /**1a**/ VT to carry to extremes; **extremarse** VR to do one's utmost, make every effort

extremaunción [ekstremaun'θjon] NF extreme unction, last rites *pl*

extremidad [ekstremi'ðað] NF (*punta*) extremity; (*fila*) edge; **extremidades** NFPL (*Anat*) extremities

extremista [ekstre'mista] ADJ, NMF extremist

extremo, -a [eks'tremo, a] ADJ extreme; (*más alejado*) furthest; (*último*) last ▶ NM end; (*situación*) extreme; **E~ Oriente** Far East; **en último ~** as a last resort; **pasar de un ~ a otro** (*fig*) to go from one extreme to the other; **con ~** in the extreme; **la extrema derecha** (*Pol*) the far right; **~ derecho/izquierdo** (*Deporte*) outside right/left

extrínseco, -a [eks'trinseko, a] ADJ extrinsic

extrovertido, -a [ekstroβer'tiðo, a] ADJ extrovert, outgoing ▶ NM/F extrovert

exuberancia [eksuβe'ranθja] NF exuberance

exuberante [eksuβe'rante] ADJ exuberant; (*fig*) luxuriant, lush

exudar [eksu'ðar] /**1a**/ VT, VI to exude

exultar [eksul'tar] /**1a**/ VI: **~ (en)** to exult (in); (*pey*) to gloat (over)

exvoto [eks'βoto] NM votive offering

eyaculación [ejakula'θjon] NF ejaculation

eyacular [ejaku'lar] /**1a**/ VT, VI to ejaculate

Ff

F, f ['efe] NF (*letra*) F, f; **F de Francia** F for
Frederick (*BRIT*), F for Fox (*US*)

fa [fa] NM (*Mus*) F

f.ᵃ ABR (*Com*: = *factura*) Inv.

fabada [fa'βaða] NF *bean and sausage stew*

fábrica ['faβrika] NF factory; **~ de moneda**
mint; **marca de ~** trademark; **precio de ~**
factory price

fabricación [faβrika'θjon] NF (*manufactura*)
manufacture; (*producción*) production; **de ~
casera** home-made; **de ~ nacional** home
produced; **~ en serie** mass production

fabricante [faβri'kante] NMF manufacturer

fabricar [faβri'kar] /**1g**/ VT (*manufacturar*) to
manufacture, make; (*construir*) to build;
(*cuento*) to fabricate, devise; **~ en serie** to
mass-produce

fabril [fa'βril] ADJ: **industria ~**
manufacturing industry

fabrique *etc* [fa'βrike] VB *ver* **fabricar**

fábula ['faβula] NF (*cuento*) fable; (*chisme*)
rumour; (*mentira*) fib

fabuloso, -a [faβu'loso, a] ADJ fabulous,
fantastic

facción [fak'θjon] NF (*Pol*) faction; **facciones**
NFPL (*del rostro*) features

Facebook® [ˈfeisβuk] M Facebook®

faceta [fa'θeta] NF facet

facha ['fatʃa] (*fam*) NMF fascist, right-wing
extremist ▶ NF (*aspecto*) look; (*cara*) face;
¡qué ~ tienes! you look a sight!

fachada [fa'tʃaða] NF (*Arq*) façade, front; (*Tip*)
title page; (*fig*) façade, outward show

facial [fa'θjal] ADJ facial

fácil ['faθil] ADJ (*simple*) easy; (*sencillo*) simple,
straightforward; (*probable*) likely; (*respuesta*)
facile; **~ de usar** (*Inform*) user-friendly

facilidad [faθili'ðað] NF (*capacidad*) ease;
(*sencillez*) simplicity; (*de palabra*) fluency;
facilidades NFPL facilities; **"facilidades de
pago"** (*Com*) "credit facilities", "payment
terms"

facilitar [faθili'tar] /**1a**/ VT (*hacer fácil*) to make
easy; (*proporcionar*) to provide; (*documento*) to

issue; **le agradecería me facilitara ...**
I would be grateful if you could let me
have ...

fácilmente ['faθilmente] ADV easily

facsímil [fak'simil] NM (*documento*) facsimile;
enviar por ~ to fax

factible [fak'tiβle] ADJ feasible

factor [fak'tor] NM factor; (*Com*) agent;
(*Ferro*) freight clerk

factoría [fakto'ria] NF (*Com*: *fábrica*) factory

factura [fak'tura] NF (*cuenta*) bill; (*nota de
pago*) invoice; (*hechura*) manufacture;
presentar ~ a to invoice

facturación [faktura'θjon] NF (*Com*)
invoicing; (: *ventas*) turnover; **~ de equipajes**
luggage check-in; **~ online** online check-in

facturar [faktu'rar] /**1a**/ VT (*Com*) to invoice,
charge for; (*Aviat*) to check in; (*equipaje*) to
register, check (*US*)

facultad [fakul'tað] NF (*aptitud, Escol etc*)
faculty; (*poder*) power

facultativo, -a [fakulta'tiβo, a] ADJ optional;
(*de un oficio*) professional; **prescripción
facultativa** medical prescription

FAD NM ABR (*ESP*) = **Fondo de Ayuda al
Desarrollo**

faena [fa'ena] NF (*trabajo*) work; (*quehacer*)
task, job; **faenas domésticas** housework *sg*

faenar [fae'nar] /**1a**/ VI to fish

fagot [fa'yot] NM (*Mus*) bassoon

faisán [fai'san] NM pheasant

faja ['faxa] NF (*para la cintura*) sash; (*de mujer*)
corset; (*de tierra*) strip

fajo ['faxo] NM (*de papeles*) bundle; (*de billetes*)
role, wad

falange [fa'lanxe] NF: **la F~** (*Pol*) the Falange

falda ['falda] NF (*prenda de vestir*) skirt; (*Geo*)
foothill; **~ pantalón** culottes *pl*, split skirt;
~ escocesa kilt

fálico, -a ['faliko, a] ADJ phallic

falla ['faʎa] NF (*defecto*) fault, flaw; **~ humana**
(*AM*) human error

fallar [fa'ʎar] /**1a**/ VT (*Jur*) to pronounce
sentence on; (*Naipes*) to trump ▶ VI (*memoria*)

to fail; (*plan*) to go wrong; (*motor*) to miss; **~ a algn** to let sb down

Fallas ['faʎas] NFPL *see note*

> In the week of the 19th of March (the feast of St Joseph, San José), Valencia honours its patron saint with a spectacular *fiesta* called *las Fallas*. The *Fallas* are huge sculptures, made of wood, cardboard, paper and cloth, depicting famous politicians and other targets for ridicule, which are set alight and burned by the *falleros*, members of the competing local groups who have just spent months preparing them.

fallecer [faʎe'θer] /**2d**/ VI to pass away, die

fallecido, -a [faʎe'θiðo, a] ADJ late ▸ NM/F deceased

fallecimiento [faʎeθi'mjento] NM decease, demise

fallero, -a [fa'ʎero, a] NM/F maker of "Fallas"

fallezca etc [fa'ʎeθka] VB ver **fallecer**

fallido, -a [fa'ʎiðo, a] ADJ vain; (*intento*) frustrated, unsuccessful

fallo ['faʎo] NM (*Jur*) verdict, ruling; (*decisión*) decision; (*de jurado*) findings; (*fracaso*) failure; (*Deporte*) miss; (*Inform*) bug; **~ cardíaco** heart failure; **~ humano** (ESP) human error

falo ['falo] NM phallus

falsear [false'ar] /**1a**/ VT to falsify; (*firma etc*) to forge ▸ VI (*Mus*) to be out of tune

falsedad [false'ðað] NF falseness; (*hipocresía*) hypocrisy; (*mentira*) falsehood

falsificación [falsifika'θjon] NF (*acto*) falsification; (*objeto*) forgery

falsificar [falsifi'kar] /**1g**/ VT (*firma etc*) to forge; (*voto etc*) to rig; (*moneda*) to counterfeit

falsifique etc [falsi'fike] VB ver **falsificar**

falso, -a ['falso, a] ADJ false; (*erróneo*) wrong, mistaken; (*firma, documento*) forged; (*moneda etc*) fake; **en ~** falsely; **dar un paso en ~** to trip; (*fig*) to take a false step

falta ['falta] NF (*defecto*) fault, flaw; (*privación*) lack, want; (*ausencia*) absence; (*carencia*) shortage; (*equivocación*) mistake; (*Jur*) default; (*Deporte*) foul; (*Tenis*) fault; **~ de ortografía** spelling mistake; **~ de respeto** disrespect; **echar en ~** to miss; **hacer ~ hacer algo** to be necessary to do sth; **me hace ~ una pluma** I need a pen; **~ de educación** bad manners pl; **~ de ortografía** spelling mistake; **sin ~** without fail; **por ~ de** through o for lack of

faltar [fal'tar] /**1a**/ VI (*escasear*) to be lacking, be wanting; (*ausentarse*) to be absent, be missing; **¿falta algo?** is anything missing?; **falta mucho todavía** there's plenty of time yet; **¿falta mucho?** is there long to go?; **faltan dos horas para llegar** there are two

hours to go till arrival; **~ (al respeto) a algn** to be disrespectful to sb; **~ a una cita** to miss an appointment; **~ a la verdad** to lie; **¡no faltaba más!** (*no hay de qué*) don't mention it!

falto, -a ['falto, a] ADJ (*desposeído*) deficient, lacking; (*necesitado*) poor, wretched; **estar ~ de** to be short of

fama ['fama] NF (*renombre*) fame; (*reputación*) reputation

famélico, -a [fa'meliko, a] ADJ starving

familia [fa'milja] NF family; **~ numerosa** large family; **~ política** in-laws pl

familiar [fami'ljar] ADJ (*relativo a la familia*) family cpd; (*conocido, informal*) familiar; (*estilo*) informal; (*Ling*) colloquial ▸ NMF relative, relation

familiarice etc [familja'riθe] VB ver **familiarizarse**

familiaridad [familjari'ðað] NF familiarity; (*informalidad*) homeliness

familiarizarse [familjari'θarse] /**1f**/ VR: **~ con** to familiarize o.s. with

famoso, -a [fa'moso, a] ADJ famous ▸ NM/F celebrity

fan [fan] (*pl* **fans** [fans]) NM fan

fanático, -a [fa'natiko, a] ADJ fanatical ▸ NM/F fanatic; (*Cine, Deporte etc*) fan

fanatismo [fana'tismo] NM fanaticism

fanfarrón, -ona [fanfa'rron, ona] ADJ boastful; (*pey*) showy

fanfarronear [fanfarrone'ar] /**1a**/ VI to boast

fango ['fango] NM mud

fangoso, -a [fan'goso, a] ADJ muddy

fantasear [fantase'ar] /**1a**/ VI to fantasize; **~ con una idea** to toy with an idea

fantasía [fanta'sia] NF fantasy, imagination; (*Mus*) fantasia; (*capricho*) whim; **joyas de ~** imitation jewellery sg

fantasma [fan'tasma] NM (*espectro*) ghost, apparition; (*presumido*) show-off

fantástico, -a [fan'tastiko, a] ADJ (*irreal, fam*) fantastic

fanzine [fan'θine] NM fanzine

FAO ['fao] NF ABR (= *Organización de las Naciones Unidas para la Agricultura y la Alimentación*) FAO

faquir [fa'kir] NM fakir

faraón [fara'on] NM Pharaoh

faraónico, -a [fara'oniko, a] ADJ Pharaonic; (*fig*) grandiose

fardar [far'ðar] /**1a**/ VI to show off; **~ de** to boast about

fardo ['farðo] NM bundle; (*fig*) burden

faringe [fa'rinxe] NF pharynx

faringitis [farin'xitis] NF pharyngitis

farmacéutico, -a [farma'θeutiko, a] ADJ pharmaceutical ▸ NM/F chemist (BRIT), pharmacist

farmacia [far'maθja] NF (*ciencia*) pharmacy; (*tienda*) chemist's (shop) (BRIT), pharmacy,

f

drugstore (*US*); **~ de turno** duty chemist; **~ de guardia** all-night chemist

fármaco ['farmako] NM medicine, drug

faro ['faro] NM (*Naut: torre*) lighthouse; (*: señal*) beacon; (*Auto*) headlamp; **faros antiniebla** fog lamps; **faros delanteros/traseros** headlights/rear lights

farol [fa'rol] NM (*luz*) lantern, lamp; (*Ferro*) headlamp; (*poste*) lamppost; **echarse un ~** (*fam*) to show off

farola [fa'rola] NF street lamp (*BRIT*) o light (*US*), lamppost

farra ['farra] NF (*AM fam*) party; **ir de ~** to go on a binge

farruco, -a [fa'rruko, a] ADJ (*fam*): **estar** o **ponerse ~** to get aggressive

farsa ['farsa] NF farce

farsante [far'sante] NMF fraud, fake

fascículo [fas'θikulo] NM part, instalment (*BRIT*), installment (*US*)

fascinante [fasθi'nante] ADJ fascinating

fascinar [fasθi'nar] /**1a**/ VT to fascinate; (*encantar*) to captivate

fascismo [fas'θismo] NM fascism

fascista [fas'θista] ADJ, NMF fascist

fase ['fase] NF phase

fashion ['faʃon] ADJ (*fam*) trendy

fastidiar [fasti'ðjar] /**1b**/ VT (*disgustar*) to annoy, bother; (*estropear*) to spoil; **fastidiarse** VR (*disgustarse*) to get annoyed o cross; **¡no fastidies!** you're joking!; **¡que se fastidie!** (*fam*) he'll just have to put up with it!

fastidio [fas'tiðjo] NM (*disgusto*) annoyance

fastidioso, -a [fasti'ðjoso, a] ADJ (*molesto*) annoying

fastuoso, -a [fas'twoso, a] ADJ (*espléndido*) magnificent; (*banquete etc*) lavish

fatal [fa'tal] ADJ (*gen*) fatal; (*desgraciado*) ill-fated; (*fam: malo, pésimo*) awful ▶ ADV terribly; **lo pasó ~** he had a terrible time (of it)

fatalidad [fatali'ðað] NF (*destino*) fate; (*mala suerte*) misfortune

fatídico, -a [fa'tiðiko, a] ADJ fateful

fatiga [fa'tiɣa] NF (*cansancio*) fatigue, weariness; **fatigas** NFPL hardships

fatigar [fati'ɣar] /**1h**/ VT to tire, weary; **fatigarse** VR to get tired

fatigoso, -a [fati'ɣoso, a] ADJ (*que cansa*) tiring

fatigue *etc* [fa'tiɣe] VB *ver* **fatigar**

fatuo, -a ['fatwo, a] ADJ (*vano*) fatuous; (*presuntuoso*) conceited

fauces ['fauθes] NFPL (*Anat*) gullet *sg*; (*fam*) jaws

fauna ['fauna] NF fauna

favor [fa'βor] NM favour (*BRIT*), favor (*US*); **haga el ~ de ...** would you be so good as to ..., kindly ...; **por ~** please; **a ~** in favo(u)r; **a ~ de** in favo(u)r of; (*Com*) to the order of

favorable [faβo'raβle] ADJ favourable (*BRIT*), favorable (*US*); (*condiciones etc*) advantageous

favorecer [faβore'θer] /**2d**/ VT to favour (*BRIT*), favor (*US*); (*amparar*) to help; (*vestido etc*) to become, flatter; **este peinado le favorece** this hairstyle suits him

favorezca *etc* [faβo'reθka] VB *ver* **favorecer**

favorito, -a [faβo'rito, a] ADJ, NM/F favourite (*BRIT*), favorite (*US*)

fax [faks] NM INV fax; **mandar por ~** to fax

faz [faθ] NF face; **la ~ de la tierra** the face of the earth

FBI NM ABR FBI

F.C., f.c. ABR = **ferrocarril**; (= *Fútbol Club*) FC

FE NF ABR = **Falange Española**

fe [fe] NF (*Rel*) faith; (*confianza*) belief; (*documento*) certificate; **de buena fe** (*Jur*) bona fide; **prestar fe a** to believe, credit; **actuar con buena/mala fe** to act in good/bad faith; **dar fe de** to bear witness to; **fe de erratas** errata

fealdad [feal'dað] NF ugliness

feb., feb.º ABR (= *febrero*) Feb.

febrero [fe'βrero] NM February; *ver tb* **julio**

febril [fe'βril] ADJ feverish; (*movido*) hectic

fecha ['fetʃa] NF date; **~ límite** o **tope** closing o last date; **~ límite de venta** (*de alimentos*) sell-by date; **~ de caducidad** (*de alimentos*) sell-by date; (*de contrato*) expiry date; **con ~ adelantada** postdated; **en ~ próxima** soon; **hasta la ~** to date, so far; **~ de vencimiento** (*Com*) due date; **~ de vigencia** (*Com*) effective date

fechar [fe'tʃar] /**1a**/ VT to date

fechoría [fetʃo'ria] NF misdeed

fécula ['fekula] NF starch

fecundación [fekunda'θjon] NF fertilization; **~ in vitro** in vitro fertilization, I.V.F.

fecundar [fekun'dar] /**1a**/ VT (*generar*) to fertilize, make fertile

fecundidad [fekundi'ðað] NF fertility; (*fig*) productiveness

fecundo, -a [fe'kundo, a] ADJ (*fértil*) fertile; (*fig*) prolific; (*productivo*) productive

FED NM ABR (= *Fondo Europeo de Desarrollo*) EDF

FEDER NM ABR (= *Fondo Europeo de Desarrollo Regional*) ERDF

federación [feðera'θjon] NF federation

federal [feðe'ral] ADJ federal

federalismo [feðera'lismo] NM federalism

FEF NF ABR (= *Federación Española de Fútbol*) Spanish Football Federation

felicidad [feliθi'ðað] NF (*satisfacción, contento*) happiness; **felicidades** NFPL best wishes, congratulations; (*en cumpleaños*) happy birthday

felicitación [feliθita'θjon] NF (*tarjeta*) greetings card; **felicitaciones** NFPL (*enhorabuena*) congratulations; ~ **navideña** o **de Navidad** Christmas Greetings

felicitar [feliθi'tar] /**1a**/ VT to congratulate

feligrés, -esa [feli'ɣres, esa] NM/F parishioner

felino, -a [fe'lino, a] ADJ cat-like; (*Zool*) feline ▶ NM feline

feliz [fe'liθ] ADJ (*contento*) happy; (*afortunado*) lucky

felonía [felo'nia] NF felony, crime

felpa ['felpa] NF (*terciopelo*) plush; (*toalla*) towelling

felpudo [fel'puðo] NM doormat

femenino, -a [feme'nino, a] ADJ feminine; (*Zool etc*) female ▶ NM (*Ling*) feminine

feminismo [femi'nismo] NM feminism

feminista [femi'nista] ADJ, NM feminist

fenomenal [fenome'nal] ADJ phenomenal; (*fam*) great, terrific

fenómeno [fe'nomeno] NM phenomenon; (*fig*) freak, accident ▶ ADV: **lo pasamos ~** we had a great time ▶ EXCL great!, marvellous!

feo, -a ['feo, a] ADJ (*gen*) ugly; (*desagradable*) bad, nasty ▶ NM insult; **hacer un ~ a algn** to offend sb; **más ~ que Picio** as ugly as sin

féretro ['feretro] NM (*ataúd*) coffin; (*sarcófago*) bier

feria ['ferja] NF (*gen*) fair; (*Am: mercado*) market; (*descanso*) holiday, rest day; (*Am: cambio*) small change; ~ **comercial** trade fair; ~ **de muestras** trade show

feriado, -a [fe'rjaðo, a] (*Am*) ADJ: **día ~** (public) holiday ▶ NM (public) holiday

fermentar [fermen'tar] /**1a**/ VI to ferment

fermento [fer'mento] NM leaven, leavening

ferocidad [feroθi'ðað] NF fierceness, ferocity

ferocísimo, -a [fero'θisimo, a] ADJ SUPERLATIVO *de* **feroz**

feroz [fe'roθ] ADJ (*cruel*) cruel; (*salvaje*) fierce

férreo, -a ['ferreo, a] ADJ iron *cpd*; (*Tec*) ferrous; (*fig*) (of) iron

ferretería [ferrete'ria] NF (*tienda*) ironmonger's (shop) (*Brit*), hardware store

ferretero [ferre'tero] NM ironmonger

ferrocarril [ferroka'rril] NM railway, railroad (*US*); ~ **de vía estrecha/única** narrow-gauge/single-track railway o line

ferroviario, -a [ferroβja'rjo, a] ADJ rail *cpd*, railway *cpd* (*Brit*), railroad *cpd* (*US*) ▶ NM: **ferroviarios** railway (*Brit*) o railroad (*US*) workers

ferry ['ferri] (*pl* **ferrys** o **ferries**) NM ferry

fértil ['fertil] ADJ (*productivo*) fertile; (*rico*) rich

fertilice *etc* [ferti'liθe] VB *ver* **fertilizar**

fertilidad [fertili'ðað] NF (*gen*) fertility; (*productividad*) fruitfulness

fertilizante [fertili'θante] NM fertilizer

fertilizar [fertili'θar] /**1f**/ VT to fertilize

ferviente [fer'βjente] ADJ fervent

fervor [fer'βor] NM fervour (*Brit*), fervor (*US*)

fervoroso, -a [ferβo'roso, a] ADJ fervent

festejar [feste'xar] /**1a**/ VT (*agasajar*) to wine and dine, fête; (*galantear*) to court; (*celebrar*) to celebrate

festejo [fes'texo] NM (*diversión*) entertainment; (*galanteo*) courtship; (*fiesta*) celebration; **festejos** NMPL (*fiestas*) festivals

festín [fes'tin] NM feast, banquet

festival [festi'βal] NM festival

festividad [festiβi'ðað] NF festivity

festivo, -a [fes'tiβo, a] ADJ (*de fiesta*) festive; (*fig*) witty; (*Cine, Lit*) humorous; **día ~** holiday

fetiche [fe'titʃe] NM fetish

fetichista [feti'tʃista] ADJ fetishistic ▶ NM/F fetishist

fétido, -a ['fetiðo, a] ADJ (*hediondo*) foul-smelling

feto ['feto] NM foetus; (*fam*) monster

F.E.V.E. NF ABR (= *Ferrocarriles Españoles de Vía Estrecha*) Spanish narrow-gauge railways

FF.AA. NFPL ABR (*Mil*) = **Fuerzas Armadas**

FF.CC. NMPL ABR (= *Ferrocarriles*) *ver* **ferrocarril**

fiable [fi'aβle] ADJ (*persona*) trustworthy; (*máquina*) reliable

fiado [fi'aðo] NM: **comprar al ~** to buy on credit; **en ~** on bail

fiador, a [fia'ðor, a] NM/F (*Jur*) surety, guarantor; (*Com*) backer; **salir ~ por algn** to stand bail for sb

fiambre ['fjambre] ADJ (*Culin*) served cold ▶ NM (*Culin*) cold meat (*Brit*), cold cut (*US*); (*fam*) corpse, stiff

fiambrera [fjam'brera] NF ≈ lunch box, ≈ dinner pail (*US*)

fianza ['fjanθa] NF surety; (*Jur*): **libertad bajo ~** release on bail

fiar [fi'ar] /**1c**/ VT (*salir garante de*) to guarantee; (*Jur*) to stand bail o bond (*US*) for; (*vender a crédito*) to sell on credit; (*secreto*) to confide ▶ VI: ~ **(de)** to trust (in); **ser de ~** to be trustworthy; **fiarse** VR: **fiarse de** to trust (in), rely on; **fiarse de algn** to rely on sb

fiasco ['fjasko] NM fiasco

fibra ['fiβra] NF fibre (*Brit*), fiber (*US*); (*fig*) vigour (*Brit*), vigor (*US*); ~ **óptica** (*Inform*) optical fibre (*Brit*) o fiber (*US*)

ficción [fik'θjon] NF fiction

ficha ['fitʃa] NF (*Telec*) token; (*en juegos*) counter, marker; (*en casino*) chip; (*Com, Econ*) tally, check (*US*); (*Inform*) file; (*tarjeta*) (index) card; (*Elec*) plug; (*en hotel*) registration form; ~ **policíaca** police dossier

fichaje [fi'tʃaxe] NM signing(-up)

fichar [fi'tʃar] /**1a**/ VT (*archivar*) to file, index; (*Deporte*) to sign (up) ▶ VI (*deportista*) to sign (up); (*obrero*) to clock in o on; **estar fichado** to have a record

fichero [fi'tʃero] NM card index; (*archivo*) filing cabinet; (*Com*) box file; (*Inform*) file, archive; (*de policía*) criminal records; ~ **activo** (*Inform*) active file; ~ **archivado** (*Inform*) archived file; ~ **indexado** (*Inform*) index file; ~ **de reserva** (*Inform*) backup file; ~ **de tarjetas** card index; **nombre de** ~ filename

ficticio, -a [fik'tiθjo, a] ADJ (*imaginario*) fictitious; (*falso*) fabricated

ficus ['fikus] NM INV (*Bot*) rubber plant

fidedigno, -a [fiðe'ðiɣno, a] ADJ reliable

fideicomiso [fiðeiko'miso] NM (*Com*) trust

fidelidad [fiðeli'ðað] NF (*lealtad*) fidelity, loyalty; (*exactitud: de dato etc*) accuracy; **alta** ~ high fidelity, hi-fi

fidelísimo, -a [fiðe'lisimo, a] ADJ SUPERLATIVO *de* **fiel**

fideos [fi'ðeos] NMPL noodles

fiduciario, -a [fiðu'θjarjo, a] NM/F fiduciary

fiebre ['fjeβre] NF (*Med*) fever; (*fig*) fever, excitement; ~ **amarilla/del heno** yellow/hay fever; ~ **palúdica** malaria; **tener** ~ to have a temperature; ~ **aftosa** foot-and-mouth disease

fiel [fjel] ADJ (*leal*) faithful, loyal; (*fiable*) reliable; (*exacto*) accurate ▶ NM (*aguja*) needle, pointer; **los fieles** NMPL the faithful

fieltro ['fjeltro] NM felt

fiera ['fjera] NF *ver* **fiero**

fiereza [fje'reθa] NF (*Zool*) wildness; (*bravura*) fierceness

fiero, -a ['fjero, a] ADJ (*cruel*) cruel; (*feroz*) fierce; (*duro*) harsh ▶ NM/F (*fig*) fiend ▶ NF (*animal feroz*) wild animal *o* beast; (*fig*) dragon

fierro ['fjerro] NM (*Am*) iron

fiesta ['fjesta] NF party; (*de pueblo*) festival; **la** ~ **nacional** bullfighting; (**día de**) ~ (public) holiday; **mañana es** ~ it's a holiday tomorrow; ~ **mayor** annual festival; ~ **patria** (*Am*) independence day; ~ **de guardar** (*Rel*) day of obligation; *see note*

| Fiestas can be official public holidays (such as the *Día de la Constitución*), or special holidays for each *comunidad autónoma*, many of which are religious feast days. All over Spain there are also special local *fiestas* for a patron saint or the Virgin Mary. These often last several days and can include religious processions, carnival parades, bullfights, dancing and feasts of typical local produce.

FIFA NF ABR (= *Federación Internacional de Fútbol Asociación*) FIFA

figura [fi'ɣura] NF (*gen*) figure; (*forma, imagen*) shape, form; (*Naipes*) face card

figurado, -a [fiɣu'raðo, a] ADJ figurative

figurante [fiɣu'rante] NMF (*Teat*) walk-on part; (*Cine*) extra

figurar [fiɣu'rar] /1a/ VT (*representar*) to represent; (*fingir*) to feign ▶ VI to figure; **figurarse** VR (*imaginarse*) to imagine; (*suponer*) to suppose; **ya me lo figuraba** I thought as much

fijador [fixa'ðor] NM (*Foto etc*) fixative; (*de pelo*) gel

fijar [fi'xar] /1a/ VT (*gen*) to fix; (*cartel*) to post, put up; (*estampilla*) to affix, stick (on); (*pelo*) to set; (*fig*) to settle (on), decide; **fijarse** VR: **fijarse en** to notice; **¡fíjate!** just imagine!; **¿te fijas?** see what I mean?

fijo, -a ['fixo, a] ADJ (*gen*) fixed; (*firme*) firm; (*permanente*) permanent; (*trabajo*) steady; (*colorfast*) fast ▶ ADV: **mirar** ~ to stare; **teléfono** ~ landline

fila ['fila] NF row; (*Mil*) rank; (*cadena*) line; (*en marcha*) file; ~ **india** single file; **ponerse en** ~ to line up, get into line; **primera** ~ front row

filántropo, -a [fi'lantropo, a] NM/F philanthropist

filarmónico, a [filar'moniko, a] ADJ, NF philharmonic

filatelia [fila'telja] NF philately, stamp collecting

filatelista [filate'lista] NMF philatelist, stamp collector

filete [fi'lete] NM (*de carne*) fillet steak; (*de cerdo*) tenderloin; (*pescado*) fillet; (*Mecánica: rosca*) thread

filiación [filja'θjon] NF (*Pol etc*) affiliation; (*señas*) particulars *pl*; (*Mil, Policía*) records *pl*

filial [fi'ljal] ADJ filial ▶ NF subsidiary; (*sucursal*) branch

Filipinas [fili'pinas] NFPL: **las (Islas)** ~ the Philippines

filipino, -a [fili'pino, a] ADJ, NM/F Philippine

film [film] (*pl* **films**) NM = **filme**

filmación [filma'θjon] NF filming, shooting

filmar [fil'mar] /1a/ VT to film, shoot

filme ['filme] NM film, movie (*US*)

filmoteca [filmo'teka] NF film library

filo ['filo] NM (*gen*) edge; **sacar** ~ **a** to sharpen; **al** ~ **del mediodía** at about midday; **de doble** ~ double-edged

filología [filolo'xia] NF philology; ~ **inglesa** (*Univ*) English Studies

filólogo, -a [fi'loloɣo, a] NM/F philologist

filón [fi'lon] NM (*Minería*) vein, lode; (*fig*) gold mine

filoso, -a [fi'loso, a] ADJ (*Am*) sharp

filosofía [filoso'fia] NF philosophy

filosófico, -a [filo'sofiko, a] ADJ philosophic(al)

filósofo, -a [fi'losofo, a] NM/F philosopher

filtración [filtra'θjon] NF (*Tec*) filtration; (*Inform*) sorting; (*fig: de fondos*) misappropriation; (*de datos*) leak

filtrar [fil'trar] /**1a**/ VT, VI to filter, strain; (*información*) to leak; **filtrarse** VR to filter; (*fig: dinero*) to dwindle

filtro ['filtro] NM (*Tec, utensilio*) filter

filudo, -a [fi'luðo, a] ADJ (*Am*) sharp

fin [fin] NM end; (*objetivo*) aim, purpose; **al ~ y al cabo** when all's said and done; **a ~ de** in order to; **a ~ de cuentas** at the end of the day; **por ~** finally; **en ~** (*resumiendo*) in short; **¡en ~!** (*resignación*) oh, well!; **~ de archivo** (*Inform*) end-of-file; **~ de semana** weekend; **sin ~** endless(ly)

final [fi'nal] ADJ final ▶ NM end, conclusion ▶ NF (*Deporte*) final; **al ~** in the end; **a finales de** at the end of

finalice *etc* [fina'liθe] VB *ver* **finalizar**

finalidad [finali'ðað] NF finality; (*propósito*) purpose, aim

finalista [fina'lista] NMF finalist

finalizar [finali'θar] /**1f**/ VT to end, finish ▶ VI to end, come to an end; **~ la sesión** (*Inform*) to log out o off

financiación [finanθja'θjon] NF financing

financiar [finan'θjar] /**1b**/ VT to finance

financiero, -a [finan'θjero, a] ADJ financial ▶ NM/F financier

financista [finan'sista] NMF (*Am*) financier

finanzas [fi'nanθas] NFPL finances

finca ['finka] NF (*casa de recreo*) house in the country; (*Esp: bien inmueble*) property, land; (*Am: granja*) farm

finde ['finde] NM ABR (*fam*: = *fin de semana*) weekend

fineza [fi'neθa] NF (*cualidad*) fineness; (*de modales*) refinement

fingir [fin'xir] /**3c**/ VT (*simular*) to simulate, feign; (*pretextar*) to sham, fake ▶ VI (*aparentar*) to pretend; **fingirse** VR: **fingirse dormido** to pretend to be asleep

finiquitar [finiki'tar] /**1a**/ VT (*Econ: cuenta*) to settle and close

Finisterre [finis'terre] NM: **el cabo de ~** Cape Finisterre

finja *etc* ['finxa] VB *ver* **fingir**

finlandés, -esa [finlan'des, esa] ADJ Finnish ▶ NM/F Finn ▶ NM (*Ling*) Finnish

Finlandia [fin'landja] NF Finland

fino, -a ['fino, a] ADJ fine; (*delgado*) slender; (*de buenas maneras*) polite, refined; (*inteligente*) shrewd; (*punta*) sharp; (*gusto*) discriminating; (*oído*) sharp; (*jerez*) fino, dry ▶ NM (*jerez*) dry sherry

finura [fi'nura] NF (*calidad*) fineness; (*cortesía*) politeness; (*elegancia*) elegance; (*agudeza*) shrewdness

firma ['firma] NF signature; (*Com*) firm, company

firmamento [firma'mento] NM firmament

firmante [fir'mante] ADJ, NMF signatory; **los**

abajo firmantes the undersigned

firmar [fir'mar] /**1a**/ VT to sign; **~ un contrato** (*Com: colocarse*) to sign on; **firmado y sellado** signed and sealed

firme ['firme] ADJ firm; (*estable*) stable; (*sólido*) solid; (*constante*) steady; (*decidido*) resolute; (*duro*) hard ▶ NM road (surface); **¡firmes!** (*Mil*) attention!; **oferta en ~** (*Com*) firm offer

firmemente [firme'mente] ADV firmly

firmeza [fir'meθa] NF firmness; (*constancia*) steadiness; (*solidez*) solidity

fiscal [fis'kal] ADJ fiscal ▶ NM (*Jur*) public prosecutor, ≈ district attorney (*US*); **año ~** tax o fiscal year

fiscalice *etc* [fiska'liθe] VB *ver* **fiscalizar**

fiscalizar [fiskali'θar] /**1f**/ VT (*controlar*) to control; (*registrar*) to inspect (officially); (*fig*) to criticize

fisco ['fisko] NM (*hacienda*) treasury, exchequer; **declarar algo al ~** to declare sth for tax purposes

fisgar [fis'ɣar] /**1h**/ VT to pry into

fisgón, -ona [fis'ɣon, ona] ADJ nosey

fisgonear [fisɣone'ar] /**1a**/ VT to poke one's nose into ▶ VI to pry, spy

fisgue *etc* ['fisɣe] VB *ver* **fisgar**

físico, -a ['fisiko, a] ADJ physical ▶ NM physique; (*aspecto*) appearance, looks *pl* ▶ NM/F physicist ▶ NF physics *sg*

fisioterapeuta [fisjotera'peuta] NMF physiotherapist

fisioterapia [fisjote'rapja] NF physiotherapy

fisioterapista [fisjotera'pista] NMF (*Am*) physiotherapist

fisonomía [fisono'mia] NF physiognomy, features *pl*

fisonomista [fisono'mista] NMF: **ser buen ~** to have a good memory for faces

fisura [fi'sura] NF crack; (*Med*) fracture

flaccidez [flakθi'ðeθ], **flacidez** [flaθi'ðeθ] NF softness, flabbiness

fláccido, -a ['flakθiðo, a], **flácido, -a** ['flakθiðo, a] ADJ flabby

flaco, -a ['flako, a] ADJ (*muy delgado*) skinny, thin; (*débil*) weak, feeble

flagrante [fla'ɣrante] ADJ flagrant

flama ['flama] NF (*Am*) flame

flamable [fla'maβle] ADJ (*Am*) flammable

flamante [fla'mante] ADJ (*fam*) brilliant; (: *nuevo*) brand-new

flamear [flame'ar] /**1a**/ VT (*Culin*) to flambé

flamenco, -a [fla'menko, a] ADJ (*de Flandes*) Flemish; (*baile, música*) flamenco ▶ NM/F Fleming; **los flamencos** the Flemish ▶ NM (*Ling*) Flemish; (*baile, música*) flamenco; (*Zool*) flamingo

flamingo [fla'mingo] NM (*Am*) flamingo

flan [flan] NM creme caramel

flanco ['flanko] NM side; (*Mil*) flank
Flandes ['flandes] NM Flanders
flanquear [flanke'ar] /**1a**/ VT to flank; (*Mil*) to outflank
flaquear [flake'ar] /**1a**/ VI (*debilitarse*) to weaken; (*persona*) to slack
flaqueza [fla'keθa] NF (*delgadez*) thinness, leanness; (*fig*) weakness
flaquísimo, -a [fla'kisimo, a] ADJ SUPERLATIVO *de* **flaco**
flash [flaʃ, flas] (*pl* **flashes**) NM (*Foto*) flash; (*Inform*): **~ drive** flash drive
flato ['flato] NM: **el** (*o* **un**) **~** the (*o* a) stitch
flauta ['flauta] (*Mus*) NF flute ▶ NMF flautist, flute player; **¡la gran ~!** (*Am*) my God!; **hijo de la gran ~** (*Am fam!*) bastard (*fam!*), son of a bitch (*US fam!*)
flecha ['fletʃa] NF arrow
flechazo [fle'tʃaθo] NM (*acción*) bowshot; (*fam*): **fue un ~** it was love at first sight
fleco ['fleko] NM fringe
flema ['flema] NF phlegm
flemático, -a [fle'matiko, a] ADJ phlegmatic; (*tono etc*) matter-of-fact
flemón [fle'mon] NM (*Med*) gumboil
flequillo [fle'kiʎo] NM (*de pelo*) fringe, bangs (*US*)
fletar [fle'tar] /**1a**/ VT (*Com*) to charter; (*embarcar*) to load; (*Auto*) to lease(-purchase)
flete ['flete] NM (*carga*) freight; (*alquiler*) charter; (*precio*) freightage; **~ debido** (*Com*) freight forward; **~ sobre compras** (*Com*) freight inward
flexible [flek'siβle] ADJ flexible; (*individuo*) compliant
flexión [flek'sjon] NF (*Deporte*) bend; (: *en el suelo*) press-up
flexo ['flekso] NM adjustable table lamp
flipper ['fliper] NM pinball machine
flirtear [flirte'ar] /**1a**/ VI to flirt
FLN NM ABR (*Pol*: *Esp*, *Perú*, *Venezuela*: = *Frente de Liberación Nacional*) political party
flojear [floxe'ar] /**1a**/ VI (*piernas*: *al andar*) to give way; (*alumno*) to do badly; (*cosecha, mercado*) to be poor
flojera [flo'xera] NF (*Am*) laziness; **me da ~** I can't be bothered
flojo, -a ['floxo, a] ADJ (*gen*) loose; (*sin fuerzas*) limp; (*débil*) weak; (*viento*) light; (*bebida*) weak; (*trabajo*) poor; (*actitud*) slack; (*precio*) low; (*Com*: *mercado*) dull, slack; (*Am*) lazy
flor [flor] NF flower; (*piropo*) compliment; **la ~ y nata de la sociedad** (*fig*) the cream of society; **en la ~ de la vida** in the prime of life; **a ~ de** on the surface of
flora ['flora] NF flora
florecer [flore'θer] /**2d**/ VI (*Bot*) to flower, bloom; (*fig*) to flourish
floreciente [flore'θjente] ADJ (*Bot*) in flower, flowering; (*fig*) thriving

Florencia [flo'renθja] NF Florence
florería [flore'ria] NF (*Am*) florist's (shop)
florero [flo'rero] NM vase
florezca *etc* [flo'reθka] VB *ver* **florecer**
florista [flo'rista] NMF florist
floristería [floriste'ria] NF florist's (shop)
flota ['flota] NF fleet
flotación [flota'θjon] NF (*Com*) flotation
flotador [flota'ðor] NM (*gen*) float; (*para nadar*) rubber ring; (*de cisterna*) ballcock
flotante [flo'tante] ADJ floating; (*Inform*): **de coma ~** floating-point
flotar [flo'tar] /**1a**/ VI to float
flote ['flote] NM: **a ~** afloat; **salir a ~** (*fig*) to get back on one's feet
FLS NM ABR (*Pol*: *Nicaragua*) = **Frente de Liberación Sandinista**
fluctuación [fluktwa'θjon] NF fluctuation
fluctuante [fluk'twante] ADJ fluctuating
fluctuar [fluk'twar] /**1e**/ VI (*oscilar*) to fluctuate
fluidez [flui'ðeθ] NF fluidity; (*fig*) fluency
fluido, -a ['flwiðo, a] ADJ fluid; (*lenguaje*) fluent; (*estilo*) smooth ▶ NM (*líquido*) fluid
fluir [flu'ir] /**3g**/ VI to flow
flujo ['fluxo] NM flow; (*Pol*) swing; (*Naut*) rising tide; **~ y reflujo** ebb and flow; **~ de sangre** (*Med*) haemorrhage (*Brit*), hemorrhage (*US*); **~ positivo/negativo de efectivo** (*Com*) positive/negative cash flow
flúor ['fluor] NM fluorine; (*en dentífrico*) fluoride
fluorescente [flwores'θente] ADJ fluorescent ▶ NM (*tb*: **tubo fluorescente**) fluorescent tube
fluoruro [flwo'ruro] NM fluoride
fluvial [fluβi'al] ADJ (*navegación, cuenca*) fluvial, river *cpd*
fluyendo *etc* [flu'jendo] VB *ver* **fluir**
FM NF ABR (= *Frecuencia Modulada*) FM
FMI NM ABR (= *Fondo Monetario Internacional*) IMF
F.N. NF ABR (*Esp Pol*) = **Fuerza Nueva** ▶ NM ABR = **Frente Nacional**
f.º ABR (= *folio*) fo., fol.
fobia ['fobja] NF phobia; **~ a las alturas** fear of heights
foca ['foka] NF seal
foco ['foko] NM focus; (*centro*) focal point; (*fuente*) source; (*de incendio*) seat; (*Elec*) floodlight; (*Teat*) spotlight; (*Am*) (light) bulb, light
fofo, -a ['fofo, a] ADJ (*esponjoso*) soft, spongy; (*músculo*) flabby
fogata [fo'ɣata] NF (*hoguera*) bonfire
fogón [fo'ɣon] NM (*de cocina*) ring, burner
fogoso, -a [fo'ɣoso, a] ADJ spirited
foja ['foxa] NF (*Am*) sheet (of paper); **~ de servicios** record (file)

fol. ABR (= *folio*) fo., fol.

folder, fólder ['folder] NM (*Am*) folder

folio ['foljo] NM folio; (*hoja*) sheet (of paper), page

folklore [fol'klore] NM folklore

folklórico, -a [fol'kloriko, a] ADJ traditional

follaje [fo'ʎaxe] NM foliage

follar [fo'ʎar] /**1l**/ VT, VI (*fam!*) to fuck (*fam!*)

folletinesco, -a [foʎetin'esko, a] ADJ melodramatic

folleto [fo'ʎeto] NM pamphlet; (*Com*) brochure; (*prospecto*) leaflet; (*Escol etc*) handout

follón [fo'ʎon] NM (*fam: lío*) mess; (: *conmoción*) fuss, rumpus, shindy; **armar un ~** to kick up a fuss; **se armó un ~** there was a hell of a row

fomentar [fomen'tar] /**1a**/ VT (*Med*) to foment; (*fig: promover*) to promote, foster; (*odio etc*) to stir up

fomento [fo'mento] NM (*fig: ayuda*) fostering; (*promoción*) promotion

fonda ['fonda] NF ≈ boarding house; *vertb* **hotel**

fondear [fonde'ar] /**1a**/ VT (*Naut: sondear*) to sound; (*barco*) to search

fondo ['fondo] NM (*de caja etc*) bottom; (*medida*) depth; (*de coche, sala*) back; (*Arte etc*) background; (*reserva*) fund; (*fig: carácter*) nature; **fondos** NMPL (*Com*) funds, resources; **~ de escritorio** (*Inform*) wallpaper; **F~ Monetario Internacional** International Monetary Fund; **~ del mar** sea bed o floor; **una investigación a ~** a thorough investigation; **en el ~** at bottom, deep down; **tener buen ~** to be good-natured

fonética [fo'netika] NF phonetics *sg*

fono ['fono] NM (*Am*) telephone (number)

fonobuzón [fonoβu'θon] NM voice mail

fonógrafo [fo'noɣrafo] NM (*esp Am*) gramophone, phonograph (*US*)

fonología [fonolo'xia] NF phonology

fontanería [fontane'ria] NF plumbing

fontanero [fonta'nero] NM plumber

footing ['futin] NM jogging; **hacer ~** to jog

F.O.P. [fop] NFPL ABR (*Esp*) = **Fuerza del Orden Público**

forajido [fora'xiðo] NM outlaw

foráneo, -a [fo'raneo, a] ADJ foreign ▶ NM/F outsider

forastero, -a [foras'tero, a] NM/F stranger

forcé [for'θe] *ver* **forzar**

forcejear [forθexe'ar] /**1a**/ VI (*luchar*) to struggle

forcemos *etc* [for'θemos] VB *ver* **forzar**

fórceps ['forθeps] NM INV forceps *pl*

forense [fo'rense] ADJ forensic ▶ NMF pathologist

forestal [fores'tal] ADJ forest *cpd*

forjar [for'xar] /**1a**/ VT to forge; (*formar*) to form

forma ['forma] NF (*figura*) form, shape; (*molde*) mould, pattern; (*Med*) fitness; (*método*) way, means; **estar en ~** to be fit; **~ de pago** (*Com*) method of payment; **las formas** the conventions; **de ~ que ...** so that ...; **de todas formas** in any case

formación [forma'θjon] NF (*gen*) formation; (*enseñanza*) training; **~ profesional** vocational training; **~ fuera del trabajo** off-the-job training; **~ en el trabajo** o **sobre la práctica** on-the-job training

formal [for'mal] ADJ (*gen*) formal; (*fig: persona*) serious; (: *de fiar*) reliable; (: *conducta*) steady

formalice *etc* [forma'liθe] VB *ver* **formalizar**

formalidad [formali'ðað] NF formality; seriousness; reliability; steadiness

formalizar [formali'θar] /**1f**/ VT (*Jur*) to formalize; (*plan*) to draw up; (*situación*) to put in order, regularize; **formalizarse** VR (*situación*) to be put in order, be regularized

formar [for'mar] /**1a**/ VT (*componer*) to form, shape; (*constituir*) to make up, constitute; (*Escol*) to train, educate ▶ VI (*Mil*) to fall in; (*Deporte*) to line up; **formarse** VR (*Escol*) to be trained (o educated); (*cobrar forma*) to form, take form; (*desarrollarse*) to develop

formatear [formate'ar] /**1a**/ VT (*Inform*) to format

formateo [forma'teo] NM (*Inform*) formatting

formato [for'mato] NM (*Inform*) format; **sin ~** (*disco, texto*) unformatted; **~ de registro** record format

formidable [formi'ðaβle] ADJ (*temible*) formidable; (*asombroso*) tremendous

fórmula ['formula] NF formula

formular [formu'lar] /**1a**/ VT (*queja*) to lodge; (*petición*) to draw up; (*pregunta*) to pose, formulate; (*idea*) to formulate

formulario [formu'larjo] NM form; **~ de solicitud/de pedido** (*Com*) application/order form; **llenar un ~** to fill in a form; **~ continuo desplegable** ▶ (*Inform*) fanfold paper

fornicar [forni'kar] /**1g**/ VI to fornicate

fornido, -a [for'niðo, a] ADJ well-built

fornique *etc* [for'nike] VB *ver* **fornicar**

foro ['foro] NM (*gen*) forum; (*Jur*) court; **~ de debate/discusión** (*Internet*) discussion forum, message board

forofo, -a [fo'rofo, a] NM/F fan

FORPPA ['forpa] NM ABR (*Esp*) = **Fondo de Ordenación y Regulación de Productos y Precios Agrarios**

FORPRONU [for'pronu] NF ABR (= *Fuerza de Protección de las Naciones Unidas*) UNPROFOR

forrado, -a [fo'rraðo, a] ADJ (*ropa*) lined; (*fam*) well-heeled

forrar [fo'rrar] /**1a**/ VT (abrigo) to line; (libro) to cover; (coche) to upholster; **forrarse** VR (fam) to line one's pockets

forro ['forro] NM (de cuaderno) cover; (costura) lining; (de sillón) upholstery; ~ **polar** fleece

fortalecer [fortale'θer] /**2d**/ VT to strengthen; **fortalecerse** VR to fortify o.s.; (opinión etc) to become stronger

fortaleza [forta'leθa] NF (Mil) fortress, stronghold; (fuerza) strength; (determinación) resolution

fortalezca etc [forta'leθka] VB ver **fortalecer**

fortificar [fortifi'kar] /**1g**/ VT to fortify; (fig) to strengthen

fortifique etc [forti'fike] VB ver **fortificar**

fortísimo, -a [for'tisimo, a] ADJ SUPERLATIVO de **fuerte**

fortuito, -a [for'twito, a] ADJ accidental, chance cpd

fortuna [for'tuna] NF (suerte) fortune, (good) luck; (riqueza) fortune, wealth

forzar [for'θar] /**1f, 1l**/ VT (puerta) to force (open); (compeler) to compel; (violar) to rape; (ojos etc) to strain

forzoso, -a [for'θoso, a] ADJ necessary; (inevitable) inescapable; (obligatorio) compulsory

forzudo, -a [for'θuðo, a] ADJ burly

fosa ['fosa] NF (sepultura) grave; (en tierra) pit; (Med) cavity; **fosas nasales** nostrils

fosfato [fos'fato] NM phosphate

fosforescente [fosfores'θente] ADJ phosphorescent

fósforo ['fosforo] NM (Química) phosphorus; (esp Am: cerilla) match

fósil ['fosil] ADJ fossil, fossilized ▶ NM fossil

foso ['foso] NM ditch; (Teat) pit; (Auto): ~ **de reconocimiento** inspection pit

foto ['foto] NF photo, snap(shot); **sacar una** ~ to take a photo o picture; ~ **(de) carné** passport(-size) photo

fotocopia [foto'kopja] NF photocopy

fotocopiadora [fotokopja'ðora] NF photocopier

fotocopiar [fotoko'pjar] /**1b**/ VT to photocopy

fotogénico, -a [foto'xeniko, a] ADJ photogenic

fotografía [fotoɣra'fia] NF (arte) photography; (una fotografía) photograph

fotografiar [fotoɣra'fjar] /**1c**/ VT to photograph

fotógrafo, -a [fo'toɣrafo, a] NM/F photographer

fotomatón [fotoma'ton] NM (cabina) photo booth

fotómetro [fo'tometro] NM (Foto) light meter

fotonovela [fotono'βela] NF photo-story

foulard [fu'lar] NM (head)scarf

FP NF ABR (Esp Escol, Com) = **Formación Profesional** ▶ NM ABR (Pol) = **Frente Popular**

FPLP NM ABR (Pol: = Frente Popular para la Liberación de Palestina) PFLP

Fr. ABR (= Fray) Fr.

fra. ABR = **factura**

frac [frak] (pl **fracs** o **fraques** ['frakes]) NM dress coat, tails

fracasar [fraka'sar] /**1a**/ VI (gen) to fail; (plan etc) to fall through

fracaso [fra'kaso] NM (desgracia, revés) failure; (de negociaciones etc) collapse, breakdown

fracción [frak'θjon] NF fraction; (Pol) faction, splinter group

fraccionamiento [fraksjona'mjento] NM (Am) housing estate

fractura [frak'tura] NF fracture, break

fragancia [fra'ɣanθja] NF (olor) fragrance, perfume

fragante [fra'ɣante] ADJ fragrant, scented

fraganti [fra'ɣanti]: **in** ▶ adv: **coger a algn in** ~ to catch sb red-handed

fragata [fra'ɣata] NF frigate

frágil ['fraxil] ADJ (débil) fragile; (Com) breakable; (fig) frail, delicate

fragilidad [fraxili'ðað] NF fragility; (de persona) frailty

fragmento [fraɣ'mento] NM fragment; (pedazo) piece; (de discurso) excerpt; (de canción) snatch

fragor [fra'ɣor] NM (ruido intenso) din

fragua ['fraɣwa] NF forge

fraguar [fra'ɣwar] /**1i**/ VT to forge; (fig) to concoct ▶ VI to harden

fragüe etc ['fraɣwe] VB ver **fraguar**

fraile ['fraile] NM (Rel) friar; (: monje) monk

frambuesa [fram'bwesa] NF raspberry

francés, -esa [fran'θes, esa] ADJ French ▶ NM/F Frenchman(-woman) ▶ NM (Ling) French

Francia ['franθja] NF France

franco, -a ['franko, a] ADJ (cándido) frank, open; (Com: exento) free ▶ NM (moneda) franc; ~ **de derechos** duty-free; ~ **al costado del buque** (Com) free alongside ship; ~ **puesto sobre vagón** (Com) free on rail; ~ **a bordo** free on board

francotirador, a [frankotira'ðor, a] NM/F sniper

franela [fra'nela] NF flannel

franja ['franxa] NF fringe; (de uniforme) stripe; (de tierra etc) strip

franquear [franke'ar] /**1a**/ VT (camino) to clear; (carta, paquete) to frank, stamp; (obstáculo) to overcome; (Com etc) to free, exempt

franqueo [fran'keo] NM postage

franqueza [fran'keθa] NF frankness

franquicia [fran'kiθja] NF exemption; ~ **aduanera** exemption from customs duties

franquismo [fran'kismo] NM: **el ~** (*sistema*) the Franco system; (*período*) the Franco years; *see note*

> The political reign and style of government of Francisco Franco (from the end of the Spanish Civil War in 1939 until his death in 1975) are commonly called *franquismo*. He was a powerful, authoritarian, right-wing dictator, who promoted a traditional, Catholic and self-sufficient country. From the 1960s Spain gradually opened its doors to the international community, coinciding with a rise in economic growth and internal political opposition. On his death Spain became a democratic constitutional monarchy.

franquista [fran'kista] ADJ pro-Franco ▶ NMF supporter of Franco

frasco ['frasko] NM bottle, flask; **~ al vacío** (vacuum) flask

frase ['frase] NF sentence; (*locución*) phrase, expression; **~ hecha** set phrase; (*pey*) stock phrase

fraternal [frater'nal] ADJ brotherly, fraternal

fraterno, -a [fra'terno, a] ADJ brotherly, fraternal

fraude ['frauðe] NM (*cualidad*) dishonesty; (*acto*) fraud, swindle

fraudulento, -a [frauðu'lento, a] ADJ fraudulent

frazada [fra'saða] NF (*AM*) blanket

frecuencia [fre'kwenθja] NF frequency; **con ~** frequently, often; **~ de red** (*Inform*) mains frequency; **~ del reloj** (*Inform*) clock speed; **~ telefónica** voice frequency

frecuentar [frekwen'tar] /**1a**/ VT (*lugar*) to frequent; (*persona*) to see frequently o often; **~ la buena sociedad** to mix in high society

frecuente [fre'kwente] ADJ frequent; (*costumbre*) common; (*vicio*) rife

fregadero [freɣa'ðero] NM (kitchen) sink

fregado, -a [fre'ɣaðo, a] ADJ (*AM fam!*) damn, bloody (*fam!*)

fregar [fre'ɣar] /**1h, 1j**/ VT (*frotar*) to scrub; (*platos*) to wash (up); (*AM fam: fastidiar*) to annoy; (: *malograr*) to screw up

fregón, -ona [fre'ɣon, ona] ADJ = **fregado** ▶ NF (*utensilio*) mop; (*pey: sirvienta*) skivvy

fregué [fre'ɣe], **freguemos** etc [fre'ɣemos] VB ver **fregar**

freidora [frei'ðora] NF deep-fat fryer

freír [fre'ir] /**3l**/ VT to fry

fréjol ['frexol] NM = **frijol**

frenar [fre'nar] /**1a**/ VT to brake; (*fig*) to check

frenazo [fre'naθo] NM: **dar un ~** to brake sharply

frenesí [frene'si] NM frenzy

frenético, -a [fre'netiko, a] ADJ frantic; **ponerse ~** to lose one's head

freno ['freno] NM (*Tec, Auto*) brake; (*de cabalgadura*) bit; (*fig*) check; **~ de mano** handbrake

frente ['frente] NM (*Arq, Mil, Pol*) front; (*de objeto*) front part ▶ NF forehead, brow; **~ de batalla** battle front; **hacer ~ común con algn** to make common cause with sb; **~ a** in front of; (*en situación opuesta a*) opposite; **chocar de ~** to crash head-on; **hacer ~ a** to face up to

fresa ['fresa] NF (*ESP: fruta*) strawberry; (*de dentista*) drill

fresco, -a ['fresko, a] ADJ (*nuevo*) fresh; (*huevo*) newly-laid; (*frío*) cool; (*fam: descarado*) cheeky, bad-mannered ▶ NM (*aire*) fresh air; (*Arte*) fresco; (*AM: bebida*) fruit juice o drink ▶ NM/F (*fam*) shameless person; (: *persona insolente*) impudent person; **tomar el ~** to get some fresh air; **ser un(a) ~/a** to have a nerve; **¡qué ~!** what a cheek!

frescor [fres'kor] NM freshness

frescura [fres'kura] NF freshness; (*descaro*) cheek, nerve; (*calma*) calmness

fresno ['fresno] NM ash (tree)

fresón [fre'son] NM strawberry

frialdad [frjal'dað] NF (*gen*) coldness; (*indiferencia*) indifference

fricción [frik'θjon] NF (*gen*) friction; (*acto*) rub(bing); (*Med*) massage; (*Pol, fig etc*) friction, trouble

friega etc ['frjeɣa], **friegue** etc ['frjeɣe] VB ver **fregar**

friendo etc [fri'endo] VB ver **freír**

frigidez [frixi'ðeθ] NF frigidity

frígido, -a ['frixiðo, a] ADJ frigid

frigo ['friɣo] NM fridge

frigorífico, -a [friɣo'rifiko, a] ADJ refrigerating ▶ NM refrigerator; (*camión*) freezer lorry o truck (*US*); **instalación frigorífica** cold-storage plant

frijol [fri'xol], **fríjol** ['frixol] NM kidney bean

friki (*fam*) ADJ weird (*fam*) ▶ NMF weirdo (*fam*); **me pasó una cosa muy ~** something really weird (*fam*) happened to me; **¡qué tío más ~!** what a weirdo! (*fam*)

frío [fri'o] VB ver **freír**

frío, -a ['frio, a] VB ver **freír** ▶ ADJ cold; (*fig: indiferente*) unmoved, indifferent; (*poco entusiasta*) chilly ▶ NM cold(ness); indifference; **hace ~** it's cold; **tener ~** to be cold; **¡qué ~!** how cold it is!

friolento, -a [frjo'lento, a] (*AM*), **friolero, -a** [frjo'lero, a] ADJ sensitive to cold

frito, -a ['frito, a] PP de **freír** ▶ ADJ fried ▶ NM fry; **fritos** NMPL fried food; **me trae ~ ese hombre** I'm sick and tired of that man; **fritos variados** mixed grill

frívolo, -a ['friβolo, a] ADJ frivolous

frondoso, -a [fron'doso, a] ADJ leafy

frontal [fron'tal] ADJ frontal ▶ NM: **choque ~** head-on collision

frontera [fron'tera] NF frontier; (*línea divisoria*) border; (*zona*) frontier area

fronterizo, -a [fronte'riθo, a] ADJ frontier *cpd*; (*contiguo*) bordering

frontón [fron'ton] NM (*Deporte: cancha*) pelota court; (: *juego*) pelota

frotar [fro'tar] /1a/ VT to rub; (*fósforo*) to strike; **frotarse** VR: **frotarse las manos** to rub one's hands

fructífero, -a [fruk'tifero, a] ADJ productive, fruitful

frugal [fru'ɣal] ADJ frugal

fruncir [frun'θir] /3b/ VT to pucker; (*Costura*) to gather; (*ceño*) to frown; (*labios*) to purse; **~ el ceño** to knit one's brow

frunza *etc* ['frunθa] VB *ver* **fruncir**

frustración [frustra'θjon] NF frustration

frustrar [frus'trar] /1a/ VT to frustrate; **frustrarse** VR to be frustrated; (*plan etc*) to fail

fruta ['fruta] NF fruit

frutal [fru'tal] ADJ fruit-bearing, fruit *cpd* ▶ NM: **(árbol) ~** fruit tree

frutería [frute'ria] NF fruit shop

frutero, -a [fru'tero, a] ADJ fruit *cpd* ▶ NM/F fruiterer ▶ NM fruit dish *o* bowl

frutilla [fru'tiʎa] NF (*Am*) strawberry

fruto ['fruto] NM (*Bot*) fruit; (*fig: resultado*) result, outcome; (: *beneficio*) benefit; **frutos secos** nuts and dried fruit

FSLN NM ABR (*Pol: NICARAGUA*) = **Frente Sandinista de Liberación Nacional**

fucsia ['fuksja] NF fuchsia

fue [fwe] VB *ver* **ser; ir**

fuego ['fweɣo] NM (*gen*) fire; (*Culin: gas*) burner, ring; (*Mil*) fire; (*fig: pasión*) fire, passion; **~ amigo** friendly fire; **fuegos artificiales** *o* **de artificio** fireworks; **prender ~ a** to set fire to; **a ~ lento** on a low flame *o* gas; **¡alto el ~!** cease fire!; **estar entre dos fuegos** to be in the crossfire; **¿tienes ~?** have you (got) a light?

fuelle ['fweʎe] NM bellows *pl*

fueloil [fuel'oil] NM paraffin (*BRIT*), kerosene (*US*)

fuente ['fwente] NF fountain; (*manantial, fig*) spring; (*origen*) source; (*plato*) large dish; **~ de alimentación** (*Inform*) power supply; **de ~ desconocida/fidedigna** from an unknown/reliable source

fuera ['fwera] VB *ver* **ser; ir** ▶ ADV out(side); (*en otra parte*) away; (*excepto, salvo*) except, save ▶ PREP: **~ de** outside; (*fig*) besides; **~ de alcance** out of reach; **~ de combate** out of action; (*boxeo*) knocked out; **~ de sí**

beside o.s.; **por ~** (on the) outside; **los de ~** strangers, newcomers; **estar ~** (*en el extranjero*) to be abroad

fuera-borda [fwera'βorða] NM INV (*barco*) speedboat; (*motor*) outboard engine *o* motor

fuerce *etc* ['fwerθe] VB *ver* **forzar**

fuereño, -a [fwe'reɲo, a] NM/F (*Am*) outsider

fuero ['fwero] NM (*carta municipal*) municipal charter; (*leyes locales*) local *o* regional law code; (*privilegio*) privilege; (*autoridad*) jurisdiction; (*fig*): **en mi** *etc* **~ interno …** in my *etc* heart of hearts …, deep down …

fuerte ['fwerte] ADJ strong; (*golpe*) hard; (*ruido*) loud; (*comida*) rich; (*lluvia*) heavy; (*dolor*) intense ▶ ADV strongly; hard; loud(ly) ▶ NM (*Mil*) fort, strongpoint; **ser ~ en** (*fig*) to be good at; **el canto no es mi ~** singing is not my strong point

fuerza ['fwerθa] VB *ver* **forzar** ▶ NF (*fortaleza*) strength; (*Tec, Elec*) power; (*coacción*) force; (*violencia*) violence; (*Mil: tb*: **fuerzas**) forces *pl*; **~ de arrastre** (*Tec*) pulling power; **~ de brazos** manpower; **~ mayor** force majeure; **~ bruta** brute force; **fuerzas armadas (FF. AA.)** armed forces; **~ del orden público (F.O.P.)** police (forces); **fuerzas aéreas** air force *sg*; **~ vital** vitality; **a ~ de** by (dint of); **cobrar fuerzas** to recover one's strength; **tener fuerzas para** to have the strength to; **hacer algo a la ~** to be forced to do sth; **con ~ legal** (*Com*) legally binding; **a la ~** forcibly, by force; **por ~** of necessity; **~ de voluntad** willpower

fuete ['fwete] NM (*Am*) whip

fuga ['fuɣa] NF (*huida*) flight, escape; (*de enamorados*) elopement; (*de gas etc*) leak; **~ de cerebros** (*fig*) brain drain

fugarse [fu'ɣarse] /1h/ VR to flee, escape

fugaz [fu'ɣaθ] ADJ fleeting

fugitivo, -a [fuxi'tiβo, a] ADJ fugitive, fleeing ▶ NM/F fugitive

fugue *etc* ['fuɣe] VB *ver* **fugarse**

fui *etc* [fwi] VB *ver* **ser; ir**

fulano, -a [fu'lano, a] NM/F so-and-so, what's-his-name

fulgor [ful'ɣor] NM brilliance

fulminante [fulmi'nante] ADJ (*pólvora*) fulminating; (*fig: mirada*) withering; (*Med*) sudden, serious; (*fam*) terrific, tremendous; (*éxito, golpe*) sudden; **ataque ~** stroke

fulminar [fulmi'nar] /1a/ VT: **caer fulminado por un rayo** to be struck down by lightning; **~ a algn con la mirada** to look daggers at sb

fumador, a [fuma'ðor, a] NM/F smoker; **no ~** non-smoker

fumar [fu'mar] /1a/ VT, VI to smoke; **fumarse** VR (*disipar*) to squander; **~ en pipa** to smoke a pipe

fumigar [fumi'ɣar] /**1h**/ vt to fumigate
funámbulo, -a [fu'nambulo, a], NM/F
funambulista [funambu'lista] NMF
tightrope walker
función [fun'θjon] NF function; (*de puesto*)
duties pl; (*Teat etc*) show; **entrar en
funciones** to take up one's duties; ~ **de
tarde/de noche** matinée/evening
performance
funcional [funθjo'nal] ADJ functional
funcionamiento [funθjona'mjento] NM
functioning; (*Tec*) working; **en** ~ (*Com*) on
stream; **entrar en** ~ to come into operation
funcionar [funθjo'nar] /**1a**/ vi (*gen*) to
function; (*máquina*) to work; **"no funciona"**
"out of order"
funcionario, -a [funθjo'narjo, a] NM/F
official; (*público*) civil servant
funda ['funda] NF (*gen*) cover; (*de almohada*)
pillowcase; ~ **protectora del disco** (*Inform*)
disk-jacket
fundación [funda'θjon] NF foundation
fundado, -a [fun'daðo, a] ADJ (*justificado*)
well-founded
fundamental [fundamen'tal] ADJ
fundamental, basic
fundamentalismo [fundamenta'lismo] NM
fundamentalism
fundamentalista [fundamenta'lista] ADJ,
NMF fundamentalist
fundamentar [fundamen'tar] /**1a**/ vt (*poner
base*) to lay the foundations of; (*establecer*) to
found; (*fig*) to base
fundamento [funda'mento] NM (*base*)
foundation; (*razón*) grounds pl; **eso carece
de** ~ that is groundless
fundar [fun'dar] /**1a**/ vt to found; (*crear*) to set
up; (*fig: basar*): ~ **(en)** to base *o* found (on);
fundarse VR: **fundarse en** to be founded on
fundición [fundi'θjon] NF (*acción*) smelting;
(*fábrica*) foundry; (*Tip*) font
fundir [fun'dir] /**3a**/ vt (*gen*) to fuse; (*metal*) to
smelt, melt down; (*nieve etc*) to melt; (*Com*) to
merge; (*estatua*) to cast; **fundirse** VR (*colores etc*)
to merge, blend; (*unirse*) to fuse together; (*Elec:
fusible, lámpara etc*) to blow; (*nieve etc*) to melt

fúnebre ['funeβre] ADJ funeral *cpd*, funereal
funeral [fune'ral] NM funeral
funeraria [fune'rarja] NF undertaker's
(BRIT), mortician's (US)
funesto, -a [fu'nesto, a] ADJ ill-fated;
(*desastroso*) fatal
fungir [fun'xir] /**3c**/ vi: ~ **de** (AM) to act as
funicular [funiku'lar] NM (*tren*) funicular;
(*teleférico*) cable car
furgón [fur'ɣon] NM wagon
furgoneta [furɣo'neta] NF (*Auto, Com*)
(transit) van (BRIT), pickup (truck) (US)
furia ['furja] NF (*ira*) fury; (*violencia*) violence
furibundo, -a [furi'βundo, a] ADJ furious
furioso, -a [fu'rjoso, a] ADJ (*iracundo*)
furious; (*violento*) violent
furor [fu'ror] NM (*cólera*) rage; (*pasión*) frenzy,
passion; **hacer** ~ to be a sensation
furtivo, -a [fur'tiβo, a] ADJ furtive ▶ NM
poacher
furúnculo [fu'runkulo] NM (*Med*) boil
fuselaje [fuse'laxe] NM fuselage
fusible [fu'siβle] NM fuse
fusil [fu'sil] NM rifle
fusilamiento [fusila'mjento] NM (*Jur*)
execution by firing squad
fusilar [fusi'lar] /**1a**/ vt to shoot
fusión [fu'sjon] NF (*gen*) melting; (*unión*)
fusion; (*Com*) merger, amalgamation
fusionar [fusjo'nar] /**1a**/ vt to fuse (together);
(*Com*) to merge; **fusionarse** VR (*Com*) to
merge, amalgamate
fusta ['fusta] NF (*látigo*) riding crop
fútbol ['futβol] NM football (BRIT), soccer (US);
~ **americano** American football (BRIT),
football (US); ~ **sala** indoor football (BRIT) *o*
soccer (US)
futbolín [futβo'lin] NM table football
futbolista [futβo'lista] NMF footballer
fútil ['futil] ADJ trifling
futilidad [futili'ðað], **futileza** [futi'leθa] NF
triviality
futón [fu'ton] NM futon
futuro, -a [fu'turo, a] ADJ future ▶ NM future;
(*Ling*) future tense; **futuros** NMPL (*Com*)
futures

f

G, g [xe] NF (*letra*) G, g; **G de Gerona** G for George

gabacho, -a [gaˈβatʃo, a] ADJ Pyrenean; (*fam*) Frenchified ▶ NM/F Pyrenean villager; (*fam*) Frenchy

gabán [gaˈβan] NM overcoat

gabardina [gaβarˈðina] NF (*tela*) gabardine; (*prenda*) raincoat

gabinete [gaβiˈnete] NM (*Pol*) cabinet; (*estudio*) study; (*de abogados etc*) office; **~ de consulta/ de lectura** consulting/reading room

gacela [gaˈθela] NF gazelle

gaceta [gaˈθeta] NF gazette

gacetilla [gaθeˈtiʎa] NF (*en periódico*) news in brief; (*de personalidades*) gossip column

gachas [ˈgatʃas] NFPL porridge *sg*

gacho, -a [ˈgatʃo, a] ADJ (*encorvado*) bent down; (*orejas*) drooping

gaditano, -a [gaðiˈtano, a] ADJ of o from Cadiz ▶ NM/F native o inhabitant of Cadiz

gaélico, -a [gaˈeliko, a] ADJ Gaelic ▶ NM/F Gael ▶ NM (*Ling*) Gaelic

gafar [gaˈfar] /**1a**/ VT (*fam: traer mala suerte*) to put a jinx on

gafas [ˈgafas] NFPL glasses; **~ oscuras** dark glasses; **~ de sol** sunglasses

gafe [ˈgafe] ADJ: **ser ~** to be jinxed ▶ NM (*fam*) jinx

gaita [ˈgaita] NF flute; (*tb:* **gaita gallega**) bagpipes *pl*; (*dificultad*) bother; (*cosa engorrosa*) tough job

gajes [ˈgaxes] NMPL (*salario*) pay *sg*; **los ~ del oficio** occupational hazards; **~ y emolumentos** perquisites

gajo [ˈgaxo] NM (*gen*) bunch; (*de árbol*) bough; (*de naranja*) segment

gala [ˈgala] NF full dress; (*fig: lo mejor*) cream, flower; **galas** NFPL finery *sg*; **estar de ~** to be in one's best clothes; **hacer ~ de** to display, show off; **tener algo a ~** to be proud of sth

galaico, -a [gaˈlaiko, a] ADJ Galician

galán [gaˈlan] NM lover, gallant; (*hombre atractivo*) ladies' man; (*Teat*): **primer ~** leading man

galante [gaˈlante] ADJ gallant; (*atento*) charming; (*cortés*) polite

galantear [galanteˈar] /**1a**/ VT (*hacer la corte a*) to court, woo

galanteo [galanˈteo] NM (*coqueteo*) flirting; (*de pretendiente*) wooing

galantería [galanteˈria] NF (*caballerosidad*) gallantry; (*cumplido*) politeness; (*piropo*) compliment

galápago [gaˈlapaɣo] NM (*Zool*) turtle, sea/ freshwater turtle (*US*)

galardón [galarˈðon] NM award, prize

galardonar [galarðoˈnar] /**1a**/ VT (*premiar*) to reward; (*una obra*) to award a prize for

galaxia [gaˈlaksja] NF galaxy

galbana [galˈβana] NF (*pereza*) sloth, laziness

galeote [galeˈote] NM galley slave

galera [gaˈlera] NF (*nave*) galley; (*carro*) wagon; (*Med*) hospital ward; (*Tip*) galley

galería [galeˈria] NF (*gen*) gallery; (*balcón*) veranda(h); (*de casa*) corridor; (*fam: público*) audience; **~ secreta** secret passage; **~ comercial** shopping mall

Gales [ˈgales] NM: **(el País de) ~** Wales

galés, -esa [gaˈles, esa] ADJ Welsh ▶ NM/F Welshman(-woman) ▶ NM (*Ling*) Welsh

galgo, -a [ˈgalɣo, a] NM/F greyhound

Galia [ˈgalja] NF Gaul

Galicia [gaˈliθja] NF Galicia

galicismo [galiˈθismo] NM gallicism

Galilea [galiˈlea] NF Galilee

galimatías [galimaˈtias] NM INV (*asunto*) rigmarole; (*lenguaje*) gibberish, nonsense

gallardía [gaʎarˈðia] NF (*galantería*) dash; (*gracia*) gracefulness; (*valor*) bravery; (*elegancia*) elegance; (*nobleza*) nobleness

gallego, -a [gaˈʎeɣo, a] ADJ Galician; (*Am pey*) Spanish ▶ NM/F Galician; (*Am pey*) Spaniard ▶ NM (*Ling*) Galician; *ver tb* **lengua**

galleta [gaˈʎeta] NF biscuit (*Brit*), cookie (*US*); (*fam: bofetada*) whack, slap

gallina [gaˈʎina] NF hen ▶ NM (*fam*) chicken; **~ ciega** blind man's buff; **~ llueca** broody hen

gallinazo [gaʎi'naso] NM (AM) turkey buzzard

gallinero [gaʎi'nero] NM (criadero) henhouse; (Teat) gods sg, top gallery; (voces) hubbub

gallo ['gaʎo] NM cock, rooster; (Mus) false o wrong note; (cambio de voz) break in the voice; **en menos que canta un ~** in an instant

galo, -a ['galo, a] ADJ Gallic; (= francés) French ▶ NM/F Gaul

galón [ga'lon] NM (Costura) braid; (Mil) stripe; (medida) gallon

galopante [galo'pante] ADJ galloping

galopar [galo'par] /**1a**/ VI to gallop

galope [ga'lope] NM gallop; **al ~** (fig) in great haste; **a ~ tendido** at full gallop

galvanice etc [galβa'niθe] VB ver **galvanizar**

galvanizar [galβani'θar] /**1f**/ VT to galvanize

gama ['gama] NF (Mus) scale; (fig) range; (Zool) doe

gamba ['gamba] NF prawn (BRIT), shrimp (US)

gamberrada [gambe'rraða] NF act of hooliganism

gamberro, -a [gam'berro, a] NM/F hooligan, lout

gamo ['gamo] NM (Zool) buck

gamuza [ga'muθa] NF chamois; (bayeta) duster; (AM: piel) suede

gana ['gana] NF (deseo) desire, wish; (apetito) appetite; (voluntad) will; (añoranza) longing; **de buena ~** willingly; **de mala ~** reluctantly; **me da ganas de** I feel like, I want to; **tener ganas de** to feel like; **no me da la (real) ~** I (really) don't feel like it; **son ganas de molestar** they're just trying to be awkward

ganadería [ganaðe'ria] NF (ganado) livestock; (ganado vacuno) cattle pl; (cría, comercio) cattle raising

ganadero, -a [gana'ðero, a] ADJ stock cpd ▶ NM/F (hacendado) rancher

ganado [ga'naðo] NM livestock; **~ caballar/ cabrío** horses pl/goats pl; **~ lanar** u **ovejuno** sheep pl; **~ porcino/vacuno** pigs pl/cattle pl

ganador, -a [gana'ðor, a] ADJ winning ▶ NM/F winner; (Econ) earner

ganancia [ga'nanθja] NF (lo ganado) gain; (aumento) increase; (beneficio) profit; **ganancias** NFPL (ingresos) earnings; (beneficios) profit sg, winnings; **ganancias y pérdidas** profit and loss; **~ bruta/líquida** gross/net profit; **ganancias de capital** capital gains; **sacar ~ de** to draw profit from

ganapán [gana'pan] NM (obrero casual) odd-job man; (individuo tosco) lout

ganar [ga'nar] /**1a**/ VT (obtener) to get, obtain; (sacar ventaja) to gain; (Com) to earn; (Deporte, premio) to win; (derrotar) to beat; (alcanzar) to reach; (Mil: objetivo) to take; (: apoyo) to gain, win ▶ VI (Deporte) to win; **ganarse** VR: **ganarse la vida** to earn one's living; **se lo**

ha ganado he deserves it; **~ tiempo** to gain time

ganchillo [gan'tʃiʎo] NM (para croché) crochet hook; (arte) crochet

gancho ['gantʃo] NM (gen) hook; (colgador) hanger; (pey: revendedor) tout; (fam: atractivo) sex appeal; (Boxeo: golpe) hook

gandul, -a [gan'dul, a] ADJ, NM/F good-for-nothing, layabout

ganga ['ganga] NF (cosa) bargain; (chollo) cushy job

Ganges ['ganxes] NM: **el (Río) ~** the Ganges

ganglio ['gangljo] NM (Anat) ganglion; (Med) swelling

gangrena [gan'grena] NF gangrene

gansada [gan'saða] NF (fam) stupid thing (to do)

ganso, -a ['ganso, a] NM/F (Zool) gander (goose); (fam) idiot

Gante ['gante] NM Ghent

ganzúa [gan'θua] NF skeleton key ▶ NMF burglar

gañán [ga'ɲan] NM farmhand, farm labourer

garabatear [garaβate'ar] /**1a**/ VT to scribble, scrawl

garabato [gara'βato] NM (gancho) hook; (garfio) grappling iron; (escritura) scrawl, scribble; (fam) sex appeal

garaje [ga'raxe] NM garage

garajista [gara'xista] NMF mechanic

garante [ga'rante] ADJ responsible ▶ NMF guarantor

garantía [garan'tia] NF guarantee; (seguridad) pledge; (compromiso) undertaking; (Jur: caución) warranty; **de máxima ~** absolutely guaranteed; **~ de trabajo** job security

garantice etc [garan'tiθe] VB ver **garantizar**

garantizar [garanti'θar] /**1f**/ VT (hacerse responsable de) to vouch for; (asegurar) to guarantee

garbanzo [gar'βanθo] NM chickpea

garbeo [gar'βeo] NM: **darse un ~** to go for a walk

garbo ['garβo] NM grace, elegance; (desenvoltura) jauntiness; (de mujer) glamour; **andar con ~** to walk gracefully

garboso, -a [gar'βoso, a] ADJ graceful, elegant

garete [ga'rete] NM: **irse al ~** to go to the dogs

garfio ['garfjo] NM grappling iron; (gancho) hook; (Alpinismo) climbing iron

gargajo [gar'ɣaxo] NM phlegm, sputum

garganta [gar'ɣanta] NF (interna) throat; (externa, de botella) neck; (Geo: barranco) ravine; (: desfiladero) narrow pass

gargantilla [garɣan'tiʎa] NF necklace

gárgara ['garɣara] NF gargle, gargling; **hacer gárgaras** to gargle; **¡vete a hacer gárgaras!** (fam) go to blazes!

gargarear [garɣare'ar] /**1a**/ VI (*Am*) to gargle
gárgola ['garɣola] NF gargoyle
garita [ga'rita] NF cabin, hut; (*Mil*) sentry box; (*puesto de vigilancia*) lookout post
garito [ga'rito] NM (*lugar*) gaming house *o* den
garra ['garra] NF (*de gato, Tec*) claw; (*de ave*) talon; (*fam*) hand, paw; (*fig: de canción etc*) bite; **caer en las garras de algn** to fall into sb's clutches
garrafa [ga'rrafa] NF carafe, decanter
garrafal [garra'fal] ADJ enormous, terrific; (*error*) terrible
garrapata [garra'pata] NF (*Zool*) tick
garrotazo [garro'taθo] NM blow with a stick *o* club
garrote [ga'rrote] NM (*palo*) stick; (*porra*) club, cudgel; (*suplicio*) garrotte
garza ['garθa] NF heron
gas [gas] NM gas; (*vapores*) fumes *pl*; **gases de escape** exhaust (fumes); **gases lacrimógenos** tear gas *sg*
gasa ['gasa] NF gauze; (*de pañal*) nappy liner
gaseoso, -a [gase'oso, a] ADJ gassy, fizzy ▶ NF lemonade, pop (*fam*)
gasoducto [gaso'ðukto] NM gas pipeline
gasoil [ga'soil], **gasóleo** [ga'soleo] NM diesel (oil)
gasolina [gaso'lina] NF petrol, gas(oline) (*US*); **~ sin plomo** unleaded petrol
gasolinera [gasoli'nera] NF petrol (*Brit*) *o* gas (*US*) station
gastado, -a [gas'taðo, a] ADJ (*dinero*) spent; (*ropa*) worn out; (*usado: frase etc*) trite
gastar [gas'tar] /**1a**/ VT (*dinero, tiempo*) to spend; (*consumir*) to use (up), consume; (*desperdiciar*) to waste; (*llevar*) to wear; **gastarse** VR to wear out; (*terminarse*) to run out; (*estropearse*) to waste; **~ en** to spend on; **~ bromas** to crack jokes; **¿qué número gastas?** what size (shoe) do you take?
gasto ['gasto] NM (*desembolso*) expenditure, spending; (*cantidad gastada*) outlay, expense; (*consumo, uso*) use; (*desgaste*) waste; **gastos** NMPL (*desembolsos*) expenses; (*cargos*) charges, costs; **~ corriente** (*Com*) revenue expenditure; **~ fijo** (*Com*) fixed charge; **gastos bancarios** bank charges; **gastos corrientes** running expenses; **gastos de distribución** (*Com*) distribution costs; **gastos generales** overheads; **gastos de mantenimiento** maintenance expenses; **gastos operacionales** operating costs; **gastos de tramitación** (*Com*) handling charge *sg*; **gastos vencidos** (*Com*) accrued charges; **cubrir gastos** to cover expenses; **meterse en gastos** to incur expense
gastronomía [gastrono'mia] NF gastronomy

gata ['gata] NF (*Zool*) she-cat; **andar a gatas** to go on all fours
gatear [gate'ar] /**1a**/ VI (*andar a gatas*) to go on all fours
gatillo [ga'tiʎo] NM (*de arma de fuego*) trigger; (*de dentista*) forceps
gato ['gato] NM (*Zool*) cat; (*Tec*) jack; **~ de Angora** Angora cat; **~ montés** wildcat; **dar a algn ~ por liebre** to take sb in; **aquí hay ~ encerrado** there's something fishy here; **andar a gatas** to go on all fours
GATT [gat] SIGLA M (= *Acuerdo General sobre Aranceles Aduaneros y Comercio*) GATT
gatuno, -a [ga'tuno, a] ADJ feline
gaucho, -a ['gautʃo, a] ADJ, NM/F gaucho

> Gauchos are the herdsmen or riders of the Southern Cone plains. Although popularly associated with Argentine folklore, *gauchos* belong equally to the cattle-raising areas of Southern Brazil and Uruguay. *Gauchos'* traditions and clothing reflect their mixed ancestry and cultural roots. Their baggy trousers are Arabic in origin, while the horse and guitar are inherited from the Spanish conquistadors; the poncho, maté and *boleadoras* (strips of leather weighted at either end with stones) form part of the Indian tradition.

gaveta [ga'βeta] NF drawer
gavilán [ga'βi'lan] NM sparrowhawk
gavilla [ga'βiʎa] NF sheaf
gaviota [ga'βjota] NF seagull
gay [ge] ADJ, NM gay, homosexual
gazapo [ga'θapo] NM young rabbit
gaznate [gaθ'nate] NM (*pescuezo*) gullet; (*garganta*) windpipe
gazpacho [gaθ'patʃo] NM gazpacho
gel [xel] NM gel; **~ de baño/ducha** bath/ shower gel
gelatina [xela'tina] NF jelly; (*polvos etc*) gelatine
gema ['xema] NF gem
gemelo, -a [xe'melo, a] ADJ, NM/F twin; **gemelos** NMPL (*de camisa*) cufflinks; **gemelos de campo** field glasses, binoculars; **gemelos de teatro** opera glasses
gemido [xe'miðo] NM (*quejido*) moan, groan; (*lamento*) wail, howl
Géminis ['xeminis] NM (*Astro*) Gemini
gemir [xe'mir] /**3k**/ VI (*quejarse*) to moan, groan; (*animal*) to whine; (*viento*) to howl
gen [xen] NM gene
gen. ABR (*Ling*) = **género**; **genitivo**
gendarme [xen'darme] NM (*Am*) policeman
genealogía [xenealo'xia] NF genealogy
generación [xenera'θjon] NF generation; **primera/segunda/tercera/cuarta ~** (*Inform*) first/second/third/fourth generation

generado, -a [xeneˈraðo, a] ADJ (*Inform*): ~ **por ordenador** computer generated

generador [xeneraˈðor] NM generator; ~ **de programas** (*Inform*) program generator

general [xeneˈral] ADJ general; (*común*) common; (*pey: corriente*) rife; (*frecuente*) usual ▶ NM general; ~ **de brigada/de división** brigadier-/major-general; **por lo** o **en** ~ in general

generalice etc [xeneraˈliθe] VB ver **generalizar**

generalidad [xeneraliˈðað] NF generality

Generalitat [jeneraliˈtat] NF *regional government of Catalonia*; ~ **Valenciana** *regional government of Valencia*

generalización [xeneraliθaˈθjon] NF generalization

generalizar [xeneraliˈθar] /**1f**/ VT to generalize; **generalizarse** VR to become generalized, spread; (*difundirse*) to become widely known

generalmente [xeneralˈmente] ADV generally

generar [xeneˈrar] /**1a**/ VT to generate

genérico, -a [xeˈneriko, a] ADJ generic

género [ˈxenero] NM (*clase*) kind, sort; (*tipo*) type; (*Bio*) genus; (*Ling*) gender; (*Com*) material; **géneros** NMPL (*productos*) goods; ~ **humano** human race; ~ **chico** (*zarzuela*) Spanish operetta; **géneros de punto** knitwear sg

generosidad [xenerosiˈðað] NF generosity

generoso, -a [xeneˈroso, a] ADJ generous

genético, -a [xeˈnetiko, a] ADJ genetic ▶ NF genetics sg

genial [xeˈnjal] ADJ inspired; (*idea*) brilliant; (*estupendo*) wonderful; (*afable*) genial

genialidad [xenjaliˈðað] NF (*singularidad*) genius; (*acto genial*) stroke of genius; **es una** ~ **suya** it's one of his brilliant ideas

genio [ˈxenjo] NM (*carácter*) nature, disposition; (*humor*) temper; (*facultad creadora*) genius; **mal** ~ bad temper; ~ **vivo** quick o hot temper; **de mal** ~ bad-tempered

genital [xeniˈtal] ADJ genital ▶ NM: **genitales** genitals, genital organs

genitivo [xeniˈtiβo] NM (*Ling*) genitive

genocidio [xenoˈθiðjo] NM genocide

Génova [ˈxenoβa] NF Genoa

genovés, -esa [xenoˈβes, esa] ADJ, NM/F Genoese

gente [ˈxente] NF (*personas*) people pl; (*raza*) race; (*nación*) nation; (*parientes*) relatives pl; ~ **bien/baja** posh/lower-class people pl; ~ **menuda** (*niños*) children pl; **es buena** ~ (*fam: esp Am*) he's a good sort; **una** ~ **como usted** (*Am*) a person like you

gentil [xenˈtil] ADJ (*elegante*) graceful; (*encantador*) charming; (*Rel*) gentile

gentileza [xentiˈleθa] NF grace; charm; (*cortesía*) courtesy; **por** ~ **de** by courtesy of

gentilicio, -a [xentiˈliθjo, a] ADJ (*familiar*) family cpd

gentío [xenˈtio] NM crowd, throng

gentuza [xenˈtuθa] NF (*pey: plebe*) rabble; (: *chusma*) riffraff

genuflexión [xenuflekˈsjon] NF genuflexion

genuino, -a [xeˈnwino, a] ADJ genuine

GEO [ˈxeo] NMPL ABR (*Esp*: = *Grupos Especiales de Operaciones*) *Special Police Units used in anti-terrorist operations etc*

geografía [xeoɣraˈfia] NF geography

geográfico, -a [xeoˈɣrafiko, a] ADJ geographic(al)

geología [xeoloˈxia] NF geology

geólogo, -a [xeˈoloɣo, a] NM/F geologist

geometría [xeomeˈtria] NF geometry

geométrico, -a [xeoˈmetriko, a] ADJ geometric(al)

Georgia [xeˈorxja] NF Georgia

georgiano, -a [xeorˈxjano, a] ADJ, NM/F Georgian ▶ NM (*Ling*) Georgian

geranio [xeˈranjo] NM (*Bot*) geranium

gerencia [xeˈrenθja] NF management; (*cargo*) post of manager; (*oficina*) manager's office

gerente [xeˈrente] NMF (*supervisor*) manager; (*jefe*) director

geriatría [xerjaˈtria] NF (*Med*) geriatrics sg

geriátrico, -a [xerˈjatriko, a] ADJ geriatric

germano, -a [xerˈmano, a] ADJ German, Germanic ▶ NM/F German

germen [ˈxermen] NM germ

germinar [xermiˈnar] /**1a**/ VI to germinate; (*brotar*) to sprout

gerundense [xerunˈdense] ADJ of o from Gerona ▶ NMF native o inhabitant of Gerona

gerundio [xeˈrundjo] NM (*Ling*) gerund

gestación [xestaˈθjon] NF gestation

gesticulación [xestikulaˈθjon] NF (*ademán*) gesticulation; (*mueca*) grimace

gesticular [xestikuˈlar] /**1a**/ VI (*con ademanes*) to gesticulate; (*con muecas*) to make faces

gestión [xesˈtjon] NF management; (*diligencia, acción*) negotiation; **hacer las gestiones preliminares** to do the groundwork; ~ **de cartera** (*Com*) portfolio management; ~ **financiera** (*Com*) financial management; ~ **interna** (*Inform*) housekeeping; ~ **de personal** personnel management; ~ **de riesgos** (*Com*) risk management

gestionar [xestjoˈnar] /**1a**/ VT (*tratar de arreglar*) to try to arrange; (*llevar*) to manage

gesto [ˈxesto] NM (*mueca*) grimace; (*ademán*) gesture; **hacer gestos** to make faces

gestor, a [xesˈtor, a] ADJ managing ▶ NM/F manager; (*promotor*) promoter; (*agente*) business agent

g

gestoría [xesto'ria] NF *agency undertaking business with government departments, insurance companies etc*

Gibraltar [xiβral'tar] NM Gibraltar

gibraltareño, -a [xiβralta'reɲo, a] ADJ *of o from* Gibraltar, Gibraltarian ▶ NM/F Gibraltarian

giga ['xiɣa] NM ABR gig (= *gigabyte*)

gigabyte ['xiɣaβait] NM gigabyte

gigante [xi'ɣante] ADJ, NMF giant

gigantesco, -a [xiɣan'tesko, a] ADJ gigantic

gijonés, -esa [xixo'nes, esa] ADJ *of o from* Gijón ▶ NM/F *native o inhabitant of Gijón*

gilipollas [xili'poʎas] (*fam*) ADJ INV daft ▶ NMF berk (*BRIT*), jerk (*esp US*)

gilipollez [xilipo'ʎeθ] NF (*fam*): **es una ~** that's a load of crap (*fam!*); **decir gilipolleces** to talk crap (*fam!*)

gima *etc* ['xima] VB *ver* **gemir**

gimnasia [xim'nasja] NF gymnastics *pl*; **confundir la ~ con la magnesia** to get things mixed up

gimnasio [xim'nasjo] NM gym(nasium)

gimnasta [xim'nasta] NMF gymnast

gimnástica [xim'nastika] NF gymnastics *sg*

gimotear [ximote'ar] /1a/ VI to whine, whimper; (*lloriquear*) to snivel

Ginebra [xi'neβra] N Geneva

ginebra [xi'neβra] NF gin

ginecología [xinekolo'xia] NF gyn(a)ecology

ginecológico, -a [xineko'loxiko, a] ADJ gyn(a)ecological

ginecólogo, -a [xine'koloɣo, a] NM/F gyn(a)ecologist

gira ['xira] NF tour, trip

girar [xi'rar] /1a/ VT (*dar la vuelta*) to turn (around); (: *rápidamente*) to spin; (*Com: giro postal*) to draw; (*comerciar: letra de cambio*) to issue ▶ VI to turn (round); (*dar vueltas*) to rotate; (*rápido*) to spin; **la conversación giraba en torno a las elecciones** the conversation centred on the election; **~ en descubierto** to overdraw

girasol [xira'sol] NM sunflower

giratorio, -a [xira'torjo, a] ADJ (*gen*) revolving; (*puente*) swing *cpd*; (*silla*) swivel *cpd*

giro ['xiro] NM (*movimiento*) turn, revolution; (*Ling*) expression; (*Com*) draft; (*de sucesos*) trend, course; **~ bancario** bank draft, bank giro; **~ de existencias** (*Com*) stock turnover; **~ postal** money order

gis [xis] NM (*Am*) chalk

gitano, -a [xi'tano, a] ADJ, NM/F gypsy

glacial [gla'θjal] ADJ icy, freezing

glaciar [gla'θjar] NM glacier

glándula ['glandula] NF (*Anat, Bot*) gland

glicerina [gliθe'rina] NF (*Tec*) glycerin(e)

global [glo'βal] ADJ (*en conjunto*) global; (*completo*) total; (*investigación*) full; (*suma*) lump *cpd*

globalización [gloβaliθa'θjon] NF globalization

globo ['gloβo] NM (*esfera*) globe, sphere; (*aeróstato, juguete*) balloon

glóbulo ['gloβulo] NM globule; (*Anat*) corpuscle; **~ blanco/rojo** white/red corpuscle

gloria ['glorja] NF glory; (*fig*) delight; (*delicia*) bliss

glorieta [glo'rjeta] NF (*de jardín*) bower, arbour, arbor (*US*); (*Auto*) roundabout (*BRIT*), traffic circle (*US*); (*plaza redonda*) circus; (*cruce*) junction

glorificar [glorifi'kar] /1g/ VT (*enaltecer*) to glorify, praise

glorifique *etc* [glori'fike] VB *ver* **glorificar**

glorioso, -a [glo'rjoso, a] ADJ glorious

glosa ['glosa] NF comment; (*explicación*) gloss

glosar [glo'sar] /1a/ VT (*comentar*) to comment on

glosario [glo'sarjo] NM glossary

glotón, -ona [glo'ton, ona] ADJ gluttonous, greedy ▶ NM/F glutton

glotonería [glotone'ria] NF gluttony, greed

glucosa [glu'kosa] NF glucose

glúteo ['gluteo] NM (*fam: nalga*) buttock

G.N. ABR (*NICARAGUA, PANAMA*: = *Guardia Nacional*) police

gnomo ['nomo] NM gnome

gobernación [goβerna'θjon] NF government, governing; (*Pol*) Provincial Governor's office; **Ministro de la G~** Minister of the Interior, Home Secretary (*BRIT*)

gobernador, -a [goβerna'ðor, a] ADJ governing ▶ NM/F governor

gobernanta [goβer'nanta] NF (*esp Am: niñera*) governess

gobernante [goβer'nante] ADJ governing ▶ NM ruler, governor ▶ NF (*en hotel etc*) housekeeper

gobernar [goβer'nar] /1j/ VT (*dirigir*) to guide, direct; (*Pol*) to rule, govern ▶ VI to govern; (*Naut*) to steer; **~ mal** to misgovern

gobierno [go'βjerno] VB *ver* **gobernar** ▶ NM (*Pol*) government; (*gestión*) management; (*dirección*) guidance, direction; (*Naut*) steering; (*puesto*) governorship

goce *etc* ['goθe] VB *ver* **gozar** ▶ NM enjoyment

godo, -a ['goðo, a] NM/F Goth; (*Am pey*) Spaniard

gol [gol] NM goal

golear [gole'ar] /1a/ VT (*marcar*) to score a goal against

golf [golf] NM golf

golfo, -a ['golfo, a] NM/F (*pilluelo*) street urchin; (*vagabundo*) tramp; (*gorrón*) loafer; (*gamberro*) lout ▶ NM (*Geo*) gulf ▶ NF (*fam: prostituta*) slut, whore, hooker (*US*)

golondrina [golon'drina] NF swallow

golosina [golo'sina] NF titbit; (*dulce*) sweet

goloso, -a [go'loso, a] ADJ sweet-toothed; (*fam: glotón*) greedy

golpe ['golpe] NM blow; (*de puño*) punch; (*de mano*) smack; (*de remo*) stroke; (*Fútbol*) kick; (*Tenis etc*) hit, shot; (*mala suerte*) misfortune; (*fam: atraco*) job, heist (*US*); (*fig: choque*) clash; **no dar** ~ to be bone idle; **de un** ~ with one blow; **de** ~ suddenly; ~ **(de estado)** coup (d'état); ~ **de gracia** coup de grâce (*tb fig*); ~ **de fortuna/maestro** stroke of luck/genius; **cerrar una puerta de** ~ to slam a door

golpear [golpe'ar] /1a/ VT, VI to strike, knock; (*asestar*) to beat; (*de puño*) to punch; (*golpetear*) to tap; (*mesa*) to bang

golpista [gol'pista] ADJ: **intentona** ~ coup attempt ▶ NMF participant in a coup (d'état)

golpiza [gol'pisa] NF: **dar una** ~ **a algn** (*AM*) to beat sb up

goma ['goma] NF (*caucho*) rubber; (*elástico*) elastic; (*tira*) rubber o elastic (*BRIT*) band; (*fam: preservativo*) condom; (*droga*) hashish; (*explosivo*) plastic explosive; ~ **(de borrar)** eraser, rubber (*BRIT*); ~ **de mascar** chewing gum; ~ **de pegar** gum, glue; ~ **espuma** foam rubber

goma-espuma [gomaes'puma] NF foam rubber

gomina [go'mina] NF hair gel

gomita [go'mita] NF rubber o elastic (*BRIT*) band

góndola ['gondola] NF (*barco*) gondola; (*de tren*) goods wagon

Google® ['gugel] NM Google®

gordo, -a ['gorðo, a] ADJ (*gen*) fat; (*persona*) plump; (*agua*) hard; (*fam*) enormous ▶ NM/F fat man o woman; **el (premio)** ~ (*en lotería*) first prize; **¡~!** (*fam*) fatty!

gordura [gor'ðura] NF fat; (*corpulencia*) fatness, stoutness

gorgojo [gor'ɣoxo] NM (*insecto*) grub

gorgorito [gorɣ'rito] NM (*gorjeo*) trill, warble

gorila [go'rila] NM gorilla; (*fam*) tough, thug; (*guardaespaldas*) bodyguard

gorjear [gorxe'ar] /1a/ VI to twitter, chirp

gorjeo [gor'xeo] NM twittering, chirping

gorra ['gorra] NF (*gen*) cap; (*de niño*) bonnet; (*militar*) bearskin; ~ **de montar/de paño/de punto/de visera** riding/cloth/knitted/peaked cap; **andar** o **ir** o **vivir de** ~ to sponge, scrounge; **entrar de** ~ (*fam*) to gatecrash

gorrión [go'rrjon] NM sparrow

gorro ['gorro] NM cap; (*de niño, mujer*) bonnet; **estoy hasta el** ~ I am fed up

gorrón, -ona [go'rron, ona] NM pebble; (*Tec*) pivot ▶ NM/F scrounger

gorronear [gorrone'ar] /1a/ VI (*fam*) to sponge, scrounge

gota ['gota] NF (*gen*) drop; (*de pintura*) blob; (*de sudor*) bead; (*Med*) gout; ~ **a** ~ drop by drop; **caer a gotas** to drip

gotear [gote'ar] /1a/ VI to drip; (*escurrir*) to trickle; (*salirse*) to leak; (*cirio*) to gutter; (*lloviznar*) to drizzle

gotera [go'tera] NF leak

gótico, -a ['gotiko, a] ADJ Gothic

gozar [go'θar] /1f/ VI to enjoy o.s.; ~ **de** (*disfrutar*) to enjoy; (*poseer*) to possess; ~ **de buena salud** to enjoy good health

gozne ['goθne] NM hinge

gozo ['goθo] NM (*alegría*) joy; (*placer*) pleasure; **¡mi** ~ **en el pozo!** that's torn it!, just my luck!

g.p. NM ABR (= *giro postal*) m.o.

GPS NM ABR (= *global positioning system*) GPS

gr. ABR (= *gramo(s)*) g

grabación [graβa'θjon] NF recording

grabado, -a [gra'βaðo, a] ADJ (*Mus*) recorded; (*en cinta*) taped, on tape ▶ NM print, engraving; ~ **al agua fuerte** etching; ~ **al aguatinta** aquatint; ~ **en cobre** copperplate; ~ **en madera** woodcut; ~ **rupestre** rock carving

grabador, -a [graβa'ðor, a] NM/F engraver ▶ NF tape-recorder; **grabadora de CD/DVD** CD/DVD writer

grabar [gra'βar] /1a/ VT to engrave; (*discos, cintas*) to record; (*impresionar*) to impress

gracejo [gra'θexo] NM (*ingenio*) wit, humour; (*elegancia*) grace

gracia ['graθja] NF (*encanto*) grace, gracefulness; (*Rel*) grace; (*chiste*) joke; (*humor*) humour, wit; **¡muchas gracias!** thanks very much!; **gracias a** thanks to; **tener** ~ (*chiste etc*) to be funny; **¡qué** ~**!** how funny!; (*irónico*) what a nerve!; **no me hace** ~ (*broma*) it's not funny; (*plan*) I am not too keen; **con gracias anticipadas/repetidas** thanking you in advance/again; **dar las gracias a algn por algo** to thank sb for sth

grácil ['graθil] ADJ (*sutil*) graceful; (*delgado*) slender; (*delicado*) delicate

gracioso, -a [gra'θjoso, a] ADJ (*garboso*) graceful; (*chistoso*) funny; (*cómico*) comical; (*agudo*) witty; (*título*) gracious ▶ NM/F (*Teat*) comic character, fool; **su graciosa Majestad** His/Her Gracious Majesty

grada ['graða] NF (*de escalera*) step; (*de anfiteatro*) tier, row; **gradas** NFPL (*de estadio*) terraces

gradación [graða'θjon] NF gradation; (*serie*) graded series

gradería [graðe'ria] NF (*gradas*) (flight of) steps *pl*; (*de anfiteatro*) tiers *pl*, rows *pl*; ~ **cubierta** covered stand

grado ['graðo] NM degree; (*etapa*) stage, step; (*nivel*) rate; (*de parentesco*) order of lineage; (*de aceite, vino*) grade; (*grada*) step; (*Escol*) class, year, grade (US); (Univ) degree; (Ling) degree of comparison; (Mil) rank; **de buen ~** willingly; **en sumo ~, en ~ superlativo** in the highest degree; **~ centígrado/Fahrenheit** degree centigrade/Fahrenheit

graduación [graðwa'θjon] NF (acto) gradation; (clasificación) rating; (del alcohol) proof, strength; (Escol) graduation; (Mil) rank; **de alta ~** high-ranking

gradual [gra'ðwal] ADJ gradual

graduar [gra'ðwar] /1e/ VT (gen) to graduate; (medir) to gauge; (Tec) to calibrate; (Univ) to confer a degree on; (Mil) to commission; **graduarse** VR to graduate; **graduarse la vista** to have one's eyes tested

grafía [gra'fia] NF (escritura) writing; (ortografía) spelling

gráfico, -a ['grafiko, a] ADJ graphic; (fig: vívido) vivid, lively ▶ NM diagram ▶ NF graph; **gráficos** NMPL (tb Inform) graphics; **~ de barras** (Com) bar chart; **~ de sectores** o **de tarta** (Com) pie chart; **gráficos empresariales** (Com) business graphics

grafito [gra'fito] NM (Tec) graphite, black lead

grafología [grafolo'xia] NF graphology

gragea [gra'xea] NF (Med) pill; (caramelo) dragée

grajo ['graxo] NM rook

Gral. ABR (Mil: = General) Gen.

gramático, -a [gra'matiko, a] NM/F (persona) grammarian ▶ NF grammar

gramo ['gramo] NM gramme (BRIT), gram (US)

gran [gran] ADJ ver **grande**

grana ['grana] NF (Bot) seedling; (color) scarlet; **ponerse como la ~** to go as red as a beetroot

granada [gra'naða] NF pomegranate; (Mil) grenade; **~ de mano** hand grenade; **~ de metralla** shrapnel shell

granadilla [grana'ðiʎa] NF (Am) passion fruit

granadino, -a [grana'ðino, a] ADJ of o from Granada ▶ NM/F native o inhabitant of Granada ▶ NF grenadine

granar [gra'nar] /1a/ VI to seed

granate [gra'nate] ADJ INV maroon ▶ NM garnet; (color) maroon

Gran Bretaña [grambre'taɲa] NF Great Britain

Gran Canaria [granka'narja] NF Grand Canary

grancanario, -a [granka'narjo, a] ADJ of o from Grand Canary ▶ NM/F native o inhabitant of Grand Canary

grande ['grande], **gran** (antes de nmsg) ADJ (de tamaño) big, large; (alto) tall; (distinguido) great; (impresionante) grand ▶ NM grandee; **¿cómo es de ~?** how big is it?, what size is it?; **pasarlo en ~** to have a tremendous time

grandeza [gran'deθa] NF greatness; (tamaño) bigness; (esplendor) grandness; (nobleza) nobility

grandioso, -a [gran'djoso, a] ADJ magnificent, grand

grandullón, -ona [granðu'ʎon, ona] ADJ oversized

granel [gra'nel] NM (montón) heap; **a ~** (Com) in bulk

granero [gra'nero] NM granary, barn

granice etc [gra'niθe] VB ver **granizar**

granito [gra'nito] NM (Agr) small grain; (roca) granite

granizada [grani'θaða] NF hailstorm; (fig) hail; **una ~ de balas** a hail of bullets

granizado [grani'θaðo] NM iced drink; **~ de café** iced coffee

granizar [grani'θar] /1f/ VI to hail

granizo [gra'niθo] NM hail

granja ['granxa] NF (gen) farm; **~ avícola** chicken o poultry farm

granjear [granxe'ar] /1a/ VT (cobrar) to earn; (ganar) to win; (avanzar) to gain; **granjearse** VR (amistad etc) to gain for o.s.

granjero, -a [gran'xero, a] NM/F farmer

grano ['grano] NM grain; (semilla) seed; (baya) berry; (Med) pimple, spot; (partícula) particle; (punto) speck; **granos** NMPL cereals; **~ de café** coffee bean; **ir al ~** to get to the point

granuja [gra'nuxa] NM rogue; (golfillo) urchin

grapa ['grapa] NF staple; (Tec) clamp; (sujetador) clip, fastener; (Arq) cramp

grapadora [grapa'ðora] NF stapler

GRAPO ['grapo] NM ABR (Esp Pol) = **Grupo de Resistencia Antifascista Primero de Octubre**

grasa ['grasa] NF ver **graso**

grasiento, -a [gra'sjento, a] ADJ greasy; (de aceite) oily; (mugriento) filthy

graso, -a ['graso, a] ADJ fatty; (aceitoso) greasy, oily ▶ NF (gen) grease; (de cocina) fat, lard; (sebo) suet; (mugre) filth; (Auto) oil; (lubricante) grease; **grasa de ballena** blubber; **grasa de pescado** fish oil

grasoso, -a [gra'soso, a] ADJ (Am) greasy, sticky

gratificación [gratifika'θjon] NF (propina) tip; (aguinaldo) gratuity; (bono) bonus; (recompensa) reward

gratificar [gratifi'kar] /1g/ VT (dar propina) to tip; (premiar) to reward; **"se gratificará"** "a reward is offered"

gratifique etc [grati'fike] VB ver **gratificar**

gratinar [grati'nar] /1a/ VT to cook au gratin

gratis ['gratis] ADV free, for nothing

gratitud [grati'tuð] NF gratitude

grato, -a ['grato, a] ADJ (agradable) pleasant, agreeable; (bienvenido) welcome; **nos es ~**

informarle que ... we are pleased to inform you that ...

gratuito, -a [gra'twito, a] ADJ (*gratis*) free; (*sin razón*) gratuitous; (*acusación*) unfounded

grava ['graβa] NF (*guijos*) gravel; (*piedra molida*) crushed stone; (*en carreteras*) road metal

gravamen [gra'βamen] NM (*carga*) burden; (*impuesto*) tax; **libre de ~** (*Econ*) free from encumbrances

gravar [gra'βar] /1a/ VT to burden; (*Com*) to tax; (*Econ*) to assess for tax; **~ con impuestos** to burden with taxes

grave ['graβe] ADJ heavy; (*fig, Med*) grave, serious; (*importante*) important; (*herida*) severe; (*Mus*) low, deep; (*Ling: acento*) grave; **estar ~** to be seriously ill

gravedad [graβe'ðað] NF gravity; (*fig*) seriousness; (*grandeza*) importance; (*dignidad*) dignity; (*Mus*) depth

grávido, -a ['graβiðo, a] ADJ (*preñada*) pregnant

gravilla [gra'βiʎa] NF gravel

gravitación [graβita'θjon] NF gravitation

gravitar [graβi'tar] /1a/ VI to gravitate; **~ sobre** to rest on

gravoso, -a [gra'βoso, a] ADJ (*pesado*) burdensome; (*costoso*) costly

graznar [graθ'nar] /1a/ VI (*cuervo*) to squawk; (*pato*) to quack; (*hablar ronco*) to croak

graznido [graθ'niðo] NM squawk; croak

Grecia ['greθja] NF Greece

gregario, -a [gre'ɣarjo, a] ADJ gregarious; **instinto ~** herd instinct

gremio ['gremjo] NM trade, industry; (*asociación*) professional association, guild

greña ['greɲa] NF (*cabellos*) shock of hair; (*maraña*) tangle; **andar a la ~** to bicker, squabble

greñudo, -a [gre'ɲuðo, a] ADJ (*persona*) dishevelled; (*pelo*) tangled

gresca ['greska] NF uproar; (*trifulca*) row

griego, -a ['grjeɣo, a] ADJ Greek, Grecian ▶ NM/F Greek ▶ NM (*Ling*) Greek

grieta ['grjeta] NF crack; (*hendidura*) chink; (*quiebra*) crevice; (*Med*) chap; (*Pol*) rift

grifa ['grifa] NF (*fam: droga*) marijuana

grifo ['grifo] NM tap (BRIT), faucet (US); (*Am*) petrol (BRIT) o gas (US) station

grilletes [gri'ʎetes] NMPL fetters, shackles

grillo ['griʎo] NM (*Zool*) cricket; (*Bot*) shoot; **grillos** NMPL shackles, irons

grima ['grima] NF (*horror*) loathing; (*desagrado*) reluctance; (*desazón*) uneasiness; **me da ~** it makes me sick

gringo, -a ['gringo, a] (*Am fam, pey*) ADJ (*norteamericano*) Yankee; (*idioma*) foreign; (*extranjero*) foreign ▶ NM/F foreigner; Yank

gripa ['gripa] NF (*Am*) flu, influenza

gripe ['gripe] NF flu, influenza; **~ A** swine flu; **~ porcina** swine flu; **~ aviar** bird flu

gris [gris] ADJ grey

grisáceo, -a [gri'saθeo, a] ADJ greyish

grisoso, -a [gri'soso, a] ADJ (*Am*) greyish, grayish (*esp US*)

gritar [gri'tar] /1a/ VT, VI to shout, yell; **¡no grites!** stop shouting!

grito ['grito] NM shout, yell; (*de horror*) scream; **a ~ pelado** at the top of one's voice; **poner el ~ en el cielo** to scream blue murder; **es el último ~** (*de moda*) it's all the rage

groenlandés, -esa [groenlan'des, esa] ADJ Greenland *cpd* ▶ NM/F Greenlander

Groenlandia [groen'landja] NF Greenland

grosella [gro'seʎa] NF (red)currant; **~ negra** blackcurrant

grosería [grose'ria] NF (*actitud*) rudeness; (*comentario*) vulgar comment; (*palabrota*) swearword

grosero, -a [gro'sero, a] ADJ (*poco cortés*) rude, bad-mannered; (*ordinario*) vulgar, crude

grosor [gro'sor] NM thickness

grotesco, -a [gro'tesko, a] ADJ grotesque; (*absurdo*) bizarre

grúa ['grua] NF (*Tec*) crane; (*de petróleo*) derrick; **~ corrediza** o **móvil/de pescante/puente/de torre** travelling/jib/overhead/tower crane

grueso, -a ['grweso, a] ADJ thick; (*persona*) stout; (*calidad*) coarse ▶ NM bulk; (*espesor*) thickness; (*densidad*) density; (*de gente*) main body, mass; **el ~ de** the bulk of

grulla ['gruʎa] NF (*Zool*) crane

grumete [gru'mete] NM (*Naut*) cabin o ship's boy

grumo ['grumo] NM (*coágulo*) clot, lump; (*masa*) dollop

gruñido [gru'ɲiðo] NM grunt, growl; (*fig*) grumble

gruñir [gru'ɲir] /3h/ VI (*animal*) to grunt, growl; (*fam*) to grumble

gruñón, -ona [gru'ɲon, ona] ADJ grumpy ▶ NM/F grumbler

grupa ['grupa] NF (*Zool*) rump

grupo ['grupo] NM group; (*Tec*) unit, set; (*de árboles*) cluster; **~ sanguíneo** blood group; **~ de presión** pressure group

gruta ['gruta] NF grotto

Gta. ABR (*Auto*) = **glorieta**

guaca ['gwaka] NF Indian tomb

guacamole [gwaka'mole] NM (*Am*) avocado salad

guachimán [gwatʃi'man] NM (*Am*) night watchman

guacho, -a ['gwatʃo, a] NM/F (*Am*) homeless child

guadalajareño, -a [gwaðalaxa'reɲo, a] ADJ of o from Guadalajara ▶ NM/F native o inhabitant of Guadalajara

Guadalquivir [gwaðalki'βir] NM: **el (Río) ~** the Guadalquivir

guadaña [gwa'ðaɲa] NF scythe

guadañar [gwaða'ɲar] /**1a**/ VT to scythe, mow

Guadiana [gwa'ðjana] NM: **el (Río) ~** the Guadiana

guagua ['gwaɣwa] NF (AM, CANARIAS) bus; (AM: criatura) baby

guajolote [gwaxo'lote] NM (AM) turkey

guano ['gwano] NM guano

guantada [gwan'taða] NF, **guantazo** [gwan'taθo] NM slap

guante ['gwante] NM glove; **guantes de goma** rubber gloves; **se ajusta como un ~** it fits like a glove; **echar el ~ a algn** to catch hold of sb; (fig: policía) to catch sb

guantera [gwan'tera] NF glove compartment

guapo, -a ['gwapo, a] ADJ good-looking; (mujer) pretty, attractive; (hombre) handsome; (elegante) smart ▸ NM lover, gallant; (AM fam) tough guy, bully

guaraní [gwara'ni] ADJ, NMF Guarani ▸ NM (moneda) monetary unit of Paraguay

guarapo [gwa'rapo] NM (AM) fermented cane juice

guarda ['gwarða] NMF (persona) warden, keeper ▸ NF (acto) guarding; (custodia) custody; (Tip) flyleaf, endpaper; **~ forestal** game warden; **~ jurado** (armed) security guard

guardaagujas [gwarda'ɣuxas] NM INV (Ferro) switchman

guardabarros [gwarða'βarros] NM INV mudguard (BRIT), fender (US)

guardabosques [gwarda'βoskes] NM INV gamekeeper

guardacoches [gwarða'kotʃes] NMF (celador) parking attendant

guardacostas [gwarða'kostas] NM INV coastguard vessel ▸ NMF guardian, protector

guardador, a [gwarða'ðor, a] ADJ protective; (tacaño) mean, stingy ▸ NM/F guardian, protector

guardaespaldas [gwardaes'paldas] NMF bodyguard

guardagujas [gwarda'ɣuxas] NM INV = **guardaagujas**

guardameta [gwarða'meta] NM goalkeeper

guardapolvo [gwarda'polβo] NM dust cover; (prenda de vestir) overalls pl

guardar [gwar'ðar] /**1a**/ VT (gen) to keep; (vigilar) to guard, watch over; (conservar) to put away; (dinero: ahorrar) to save; (promesa etc) to keep; (ley) to observe; (rencor) to bear, harbour; (Inform: archivo) to save; **guardarse** VR (preservarse) to protect o.s.; **guardarse de algo** (evitar) to avoid sth; (abstenerse) to refrain

from sth; **guardarse de hacer algo** to be careful not to do sth; **guardársela a algn** to have it in for sb; **~ cama** to stay in bed

guardarropa [gwarða'rropa] NM (armario) wardrobe; (en establecimiento público) cloakroom

guardería [gwarðe'ria] NF nursery

guardia ['gwarðja] NF (Mil) guard; (cuidado) care, custody ▸ NMF guard; (policía) policeman(-woman); **estar de ~** to be on guard; **montar ~** to mount guard; **la G~ Civil** the Civil Guard; **~ municipal** o **urbana** municipal police; **un ~ civil** a Civil Guard(sman); **un(a) ~ nacional** a policeman(-woman); **~ urbano** traffic policeman; see note

> The *Guardia Civil* is a branch of the *Ejército de Tierra* (Army) run along military lines, which fulfils a policing role outside large urban communities and is under the joint control of the Spanish Ministry of Defence and the Ministry of the Interior. It is also known as *La Benemérita*.

guardián, -ana [gwar'ðjan, ana] NM/F (gen) guardian, keeper

guarecer [gware'θer] /**2d**/ VT (proteger) to protect; (abrigar) to shelter; **guarecerse** VR to take refuge

guarezca etc [gwa'reθka] VB ver **guarecer**

guarida [gwa'riða] NF (de animal) den, lair; (de persona) haunt, hideout; (refugio) refuge

guarnecer [gwarne'θer] /**2d**/ VT (equipar) to provide; (adornar) to adorn; (Tec) to reinforce

guarnezca etc [gwar'neθka] VB ver **guarnecer**

guarnición [gwarni'θjon] NF (de vestimenta) trimming; (de piedra) mount; (Culin) garnish; (arneses) harness; (Mil) garrison

guarrada [gwa'rraða] (fam) NF (cosa sucia) dirty mess; (acto o dicho obsceno) obscenity; **hacer una ~ a algn** to do the dirty on sb

guarrería [gwarre'ria] NF = **guarrada**

guarro, -a ['gwarro, a] NM/F (fam) pig; (fig) dirty o slovenly person

guasa ['gwasa] NF joke; **con** o **de ~** jokingly, in fun

guasón, -ona [gwa'son, ona] ADJ witty; (bromista) joking ▸ NM/F wit; joker

Guatemala [gwate'mala] NF Guatemala

guatemalteco, -a [gwatemal'teko, a] ADJ, NM/F Guatemalan

guateque [gwa'teke] NM (fiesta) party

guay [gwai] ADJ (fam) super, great

guayaba [gwa'jaβa] NF (Bot) guava

Guayana [gwa'jana] NF Guyana, Guiana

gubernamental [guβernamen'tal], **gubernativo, -a** [guβerna'tiβo, a] ADJ governmental

guedeja [ge'ðexa] NF long hair

güero, -a ['gwero, a] ADJ (AM) blond(e)

guerra ['gerra] NF war; (*arte*) warfare; (*pelea*) struggle; ~ **atómica/bacteriológica/ nuclear/de guerrillas** atomic/germ/ nuclear/guerrilla warfare; **Primera/ Segunda G~ Mundial** First/Second World War; ~ **de precios** (*Com*) price war; ~ **civil/ fría** civil/cold war; ~ **a muerte** fight to the death; **de** ~ military, war *cpd*; **estar en** ~ to be at war; **dar** ~ to be a nuisance; **dar** ~ **a algn** to give s.o. a lot of bother

guerrear [gerre'ar] /**1a**/ VI to wage war

guerrero, -a [ge'rrero, a] ADJ fighting; (*carácter*) warlike ▶ NM/F warrior

guerrilla [ge'rriʎa] NF guerrilla warfare; (*tropas*) guerrilla band *o* group

guerrillero, -a [gerri'ʎero, a] NM/F guerrilla (fighter); (*contra invasor*) partisan

gueto ['geto] NM ghetto

guía ['gia] VB ver **guiar** ▶ NMF (*persona*) guide ▶ NF (*libro*) guidebook; (*manual*) handbook; ~ **de ferrocarriles** railway timetable; ~ **telefónica** telephone directory; ~ **del turista/del viajero** tourist/traveller's guide

guiar [gi'ar] /**1c**/ VT to guide, direct; (*dirigir*) to lead; (*orientar*) to advise; (*Auto*) to steer; **guiarse** VR: **guiarse por** to be guided by

guijarro [gi'xarro] NM pebble

guillotina [giʎo'tina] NF guillotine

guinda ['ginda] NF morello cherry; (*licor*) cherry liqueur

guindar [gin'dar] /**1a**/ VT to hoist; (*fam: robar*) to nick

guindilla [gin'diʎa] NF chil(l)i pepper

Guinea [gi'nea] NF Guinea

guineo, -a [gi'neo, a] ADJ Guinea *cpd*, Guinean ▶ NM/F Guinean

guiñapo [gi'ɲapo] NM (*harapo*) rag; (*persona*) rogue

guiñar [gi'ɲar] /**1a**/ VI to wink

guiño ['giɲo] NM (*parpadeo*) wink; (*muecas*) grimace; **hacer guiños a** (*enamorados*) to make eyes at

guiñol [gi'ɲol] NM (*Teat*) puppet theatre

guión [gi'on] NM (*Ling*) hyphen, dash; (*esquema*) summary, outline; (*Cine*) script

guionista [gjo'nista] NMF scriptwriter

guipuzcoano, -a [gipuθko'ano, a] ADJ of *o* from Guipúzcoa ▶ NM/F native *o* inhabitant of Guipúzcoa

guiri ['giri] NMF (*fam, pey*) foreigner

guirigay [giri'gai] NM (*griterío*) uproar; (*confusión*) chaos

guirnalda [gir'nalda] NF garland

guisa ['gisa] NF: **a ~ de** as, like

guisado [gi'saðo] NM stew

guisante [gi'sante] NM pea

guisar [gi'sar] /**1a**/ VT, VI to cook; (*fig*) to arrange

guiso ['giso] NM cooked dish

guita ['gita] NF twine; (*fam: dinero*) dough

guitarra [gi'tarra] NF guitar

guitarrista [gita'rrista] NMF guitarist

gula ['gula] NF gluttony, greed

gusano [gu'sano] NM maggot, worm; (*de mariposa, polilla*) caterpillar; (*lombriz*) earthworm; (*fig*) worm; (*ser despreciable*) creep; ~ **de seda** silk-worm

gustar [gus'tar] /**1a**/ VT to taste, sample ▶ VI to please, be pleasing; ~ **de algo** to like *o* enjoy sth; **me gustan las uvas** I like grapes; **le gusta nadar** she likes *o* enjoys swimming; **¿gusta usted?** would you like some?; **como usted guste** as you wish

gusto ['gusto] NM (*sentido, sabor*) taste; (*agrado*) liking; (*placer*) pleasure; **tiene un ~ amargo** it has a bitter taste; **tener buen ~** to have good taste; **sobre gustos no hay nada escrito** there's no accounting for tastes; **de buen/mal ~** in good/bad taste; **sentirse a ~** to feel at ease; **¡mucho** *o* **tanto ~ (en conocerle)!** how do you do?, pleased to meet you; **el ~ es mío** the pleasure is mine; **tomar ~ a** to take a liking to; **con ~** willingly, gladly

gustoso, -a [gus'toso, a] ADJ (*sabroso*) tasty; (*agradable*) pleasant; (*con voluntad*) willing, glad; **lo hizo ~** he did it gladly

gutural [gutu'ral] ADJ guttural

guyanés, -esa [gwaja'nes, esa] ADJ, NM/F Guyanese

Hh

H, h ['atʃe] NF (*letra*) H, h; **H de Historia** H for Harry (*BRIT*) o How (*US*)

H. ABR (*Química*: = *Hidrógeno*) H; (= *Hectárea(s)*) ha.

h. ABR (= *hora(s)*) h., hr(s). ▶ NMPL ABR (= *habitantes*) pop.

ha¹ [a] VB *ver* **haber**

ha² ABR (= *Hectárea(s)*) ha.

haba ['aβa] NF bean; **son habas contadas** it goes without saying; **en todas partes cuecen habas** it's the same (story) the whole world over

Habana [a'βana] NF: **la ~** Havana

habanero, -a [aβa'nero, a] ADJ of o from Havana ▶ NM/F native o inhabitant of Havana ▶ NF (*Mus*) habanera

habano [a'βano] NM Havana cigar

habeas corpus [a'βeas'korpus] NM (*Jur*) habeas corpus

habéis VB *ver* **haber**

(PALABRA CLAVE)

haber [a'βer] /2j/ VB AUXILIAR **1** (*tiempos compuestos*) to have; **había comido** I have/had eaten; **antes/después de haberlo visto** before seeing/after seeing o having seen it; **si lo hubiera sabido habría ido** if I had known I would have gone

2: **¡haberlo dicho antes!** you should have said so before!; **¿habrase visto (cosa igual)?** have you ever seen anything like it?

3: **haber de: he de hacerlo** I must do it; **ha de llegar mañana** it should arrive tomorrow

▶ VB IMPERSONAL **1** (*existencia*: sg) there is; (: pl) there are; **hay un hermano/dos hermanos** there is one brother/there are two brothers; **¿cuánto hay de aquí a Sucre?** how far is it from here to Sucre?; **habrá unos 4 grados** it must be about 4 degrees; **no hay quien te entienda** there's no understanding you

2 (*obligación*): **hay que hacer algo** something must be done; **hay que apuntarlo para acordarse** you have to write it down to remember

3: **¡hay que ver!** well I never!

4: **¡no hay de qué!**, (*AM*) **¡no hay por qué!** don't mention it!, not at all!

5: **¿qué hay?** (*¿qué pasa?*) what's up?, what's the matter?; (*¿qué tal?*) how's it going?

haberse VB IMPERSONAL: **habérselas con algn** to have it out with sb

▶ VT: **he aquí unas sugerencias** here are some suggestions; **todos los inventos habidos y por haber** all inventions present and future; **en el encuentro habido ayer** in yesterday's game

▶ NM (*en cuenta*) credit side

haberes NMPL assets; **¿cuánto tengo en el haber?** how much do I have in my account?; **tiene varias novelas en su haber** he has several novels to his credit

habichuela [aβi'tʃwela] NF kidney bean

hábil ['aβil] ADJ (*listo*) clever, smart; (*capaz*) fit, capable; (*experto*) expert; **día ~** working day

habilidad [aβili'ðað] NF (*gen*) skill, ability; (*inteligencia*) cleverness; (*destreza*) expertness, expertise; (*Jur*) competence; **~ (para)** fitness (for); **tener ~ manual** to be clever with one's hands

habilitación [aβilita'θjon] NF qualification; (*colocación de muebles*) fitting out; (*financiamiento*) financing; (*oficina*) paymaster's office

habilitado [aβili'taðo] NM paymaster

habilitar [aβili'tar] /1a/ VT to qualify; (*autorizar*) to authorize; (*capacitar*) to enable; (*dar instrumentos*) to equip; (*financiar*) to finance

hábilmente [aβil'mente] ADV skilfully, expertly

habitable [aβi'taβle] ADJ inhabitable

habitación [aβita'θjon] NF (*cuarto*) room; (*casa*) dwelling, abode; (*Bio: morada*) habitat; **~ sencilla o individual** single room; **~ doble o de matrimonio** double room

habitante [aβi'tante] NMF inhabitant

habitar [aβi'tar] /1a/ VT (*residir en*) to inhabit; (*ocupar*) to occupy ▶ VI to live

hábitat ['aβitat] (*pl* **hábitats** ['aβitats]) NM habitat

hábito ['aβito] NM habit; **tener el ~ de hacer algo** to be in the habit of doing sth

habitual [aβi'twal] ADJ habitual

habituar [aβi'twar] /**1e**/ VT to accustom; **habituarse** VR: **habituarse a** to get used to

habla ['aβla] NF (*capacidad de hablar*) speech; (*idioma*) language; (*dialecto*) dialect; **perder el ~** to become speechless; **de ~ francesa** French-speaking; **estar al ~** to be in contact; (*Telec*) to be on the line; **¡González al ~!** (*Telec*) Gonzalez speaking!

hablador, a [aβla'ðor, a] ADJ talkative ▶ NM/F chatterbox

habladuría [aβlaðu'ria] NF rumour; **habladurías** NFPL gossip *sg*

hablante [a'βlante] ADJ speaking ▶ NMF speaker

hablar [a'βlar] /**1a**/ VT to speak, talk ▶ VI to speak; **hablarse** VR to speak to each other; **~ con** to speak to; **¡hable!**, **¡puede ~!** (*Telec*) you're through!; **de eso ni ~** no way, that's out of the question; **~ alto/bajo/claro** to speak loudly/quietly/plainly *o* bluntly; **~ de** to speak of *o* about; **"se habla inglés"** "English spoken here"; **no se hablan** they are not on speaking terms

habré *etc* [a'βre] VB *ver* **haber**

hacedor, a [aθe'ðor, a] NM/F maker

hacendado, -a [aθen'daðo, a] ADJ property-owning ▶ NM/F (*Am*) rancher, farmer; (*terrateniente*) large landowner

hacendoso, -a [aθen'doso, a] ADJ industrious, hard-working

(PALABRA CLAVE)

hacer [a'θer] /**2r**/ VT **1** (*fabricar, producir, conseguir*) to make; **hacer una película/un ruido** to make a film/noise; **el guisado lo hice yo** I made *o* cooked the stew; **hacer amigos** to make friends

2 (*ejecutar: trabajo etc*) to do; **hacer la colada** to do the washing; **hacer la comida** to do the cooking; **¿qué haces?** what are you doing?; **¡eso está hecho!** you've got it!; **hacer el tonto/indio** to act the fool/clown; **hacer el malo** *o* **el papel del malo** (*Teat*) to play the villain

3 (*estudios, algunos deportes*) to do; **hacer español/económicas** to do *o* study Spanish/economics; **hacer yoga/gimnasia** to do yoga/go to the gym

4 (*transformar, incidir en*): **esto lo hará más difícil** this will make it more difficult; **salirte hará sentir mejor** going out will make you feel better; **te hace más joven** it makes you look younger

5 (*cálculo*): **2 y 2 hacen 4** 2 and 2 make 4; **éste hace 100** this one makes 100

6 (+ *sub*): **esto hará que ganemos** this will make us win; **harás que no quiera venir** you'll stop him wanting to come

7 (*como sustituto de vb*) to do; **él bebió y yo hice lo mismo** he drank and I did likewise

8: **no hace más que criticar** all he does is criticize

▶ VB SEMI-AUXILIAR (+ *infin*) **1** (*directo*): **les hice venir** I made *o* had them come; **hacer trabajar a los demás** to get others to work

2 (*por intermedio de otros*): **hacer reparar algo** to get sth repaired

▶ VI **1**: **haz como que no lo sabes** act as if you don't know; **hiciste bien en decírmelo** you were right to tell me

2 (*ser apropiado*): **si os hace** if it's alright with you

3: **hacer de**: **hacer de madre para uno** to be like a mother to sb; (*Teat*): **hacer de Otelo** to play Othello; **la tabla hace de mesa** the board does as a table

▶ VB IMPERSONAL **1**: **hace calor/frío** it's hot/cold; *ver tb* **bueno**; **sol**; **tiempo**

2 (*tiempo*): **hace tres años** three years ago; **hace un mes que voy/no voy** I've been going/I haven't been for a month; **no le veo desde hace mucho** I haven't seen him for a long time

3: **¿cómo has hecho para llegar tan rápido?** how did you manage to get here so quickly?

hacerse VR **1** (*volverse*) to become; **se hicieron amigos** they became friends; **hacerse viejo** to get *o* grow old; **se hace tarde** it's getting late

2: **hacerse algo**: **me hice un traje** I got a suit made

3 (*acostumbrarse*): **hacerse a** to get used to; **hacerse a la idea** to get used to the idea

4: **se hace con huevos y leche** it's made out of eggs and milk; **eso no se hace** that's not done

5 (*obtener*): **hacerse de** *o* **con algo** to get hold of sth

6 (*fingirse*): **hacerse el sordo/sueco** to turn a deaf ear/pretend not to notice

hacha ['atʃa] NF axe; (*antorcha*) torch

hachazo [a'tʃaθo] NM axe blow

hache ['atʃe] NF (the letter) H; **llámele usted ~** call it what you will

hachís [a'tʃis] NM hashish

hacia ['aθja] PREP (*en dirección de*) towards; (*cerca de*) near; (*actitud*) towards; **~ adelante/atrás** forwards/backwards; **~ arriba/abajo** up(wards)/down(wards); **~ mediodía** about noon

hacienda [a'θjenda] NF (*propiedad*) property; (*finca*) farm; (*Am*) ranch; **~ pública** public finance; **(Ministerio de) H~** Exchequer (BRIT), Treasury Department (US)

hacinar [aθi'nar] /**1a**/ VT to pile (up); (Agr) to stack; (fig) to overcrowd

hada ['aða] NF fairy; **~ madrina** fairy godmother

hado ['aðo] NM fate, destiny

haga etc ['aɣa] VB ver **hacer**

Haití [ai'ti] NM Haiti

haitiano, -a [ai'tjano, a] ADJ, NM/F Haitian

hala ['ala] EXCL (vamos) come on!; (anda) get on with it!

halagar [ala'ɣar] /**1h**/ VT (lisonjear) to flatter

halago [a'laɣo] NM (adulación) flattery

halague etc [a'laɣe] VB ver **halagar**

halagüeño, -a [ala'ɣweɲo, a] ADJ flattering

halcón [al'kon] NM falcon, hawk

hálito ['alito] NM breath

halitosis [ali'tosis] NF halitosis, bad breath

hallar [a'ʎar] /**1a**/ VT (gen) to find; (descubrir) to discover; (toparse con) to run into; **hallarse** VR to be (situated); (encontrarse) to find o.s.; **se halla fuera** he is away; **no se halla** he feels out of place

hallazgo [a'ʎaθɣo] NM discovery; (cosa) find

halo ['alo] NM halo

halógeno, -a [a'loxeno, a] ADJ: **faro ~** halogen lamp

halterofilia [altero'filja] NF weightlifting

hamaca [a'maka] NF hammock

hambre ['ambre] NF hunger; (carencia) famine; (inanición) starvation; (fig) longing; **tener ~** to be hungry; **¡me muero de ~!** I'm starving!

hambriento, -a [am'brjento, a] ADJ hungry, starving ▸ NM/F starving person; **los hambrientos** the hungry; **~ de** hungry o longing for

hambruna [am'bruna] NF famine

Hamburgo [am'burɣo] NM Hamburg

hamburguesa [ambur'ɣesa] NF hamburger, burger

hamburguesería [amburɣese'ria] NF burger bar

hampa ['ampa] NF underworld

hampón [am'pon] NM thug

hámster ['xamster] NM hamster

han [an] VB ver **haber**

haragán, -ana [ara'ɣan, ana] ADJ, NM/F good-for-nothing

haraganear [araɣane'ar] /**1a**/ VI to idle, loaf about

harapiento, -a [ara'pjento, a] ADJ tattered, in rags

harapo [a'rapo] NM rag

hardware ['xardwer] NM (Inform) hardware

haré etc [a're] VB ver **hacer**

harén [a'ren] NM harem

harina [a'rina] NF flour; **~ de maíz** cornflour (BRIT), cornstarch (US); **~ de trigo** wheat flour; **eso es ~ de otro costal** that's another kettle of fish

harinero, -a [ari'nero, a] NM/F flour merchant

harinoso, -a [ari'noso, a] ADJ floury

hartar [ar'tar] /**1a**/ VT to satiate, glut; (fig) to tire, sicken; **hartarse** VR (de comida) to fill o.s., gorge o.s.; (cansarse) **hartarse de** to get fed up with

hartazgo [ar'taθɣo] NM surfeit, glut

harto, -a ['arto, a] ADJ (lleno) full; (cansado) fed up ▸ ADV (bastante) enough; (muy) very; **estar ~ de** to be fed up with; **¡estoy ~ de decírtelo!** I'm sick and tired of telling you (so)!

hartura [ar'tura] NF (exceso) surfeit; (abundancia) abundance; (satisfacción) satisfaction

has¹ [as] VB ver **haber**

has² ABR (= Hectáreas) ha.

hashtag [xas'taɣ] NM (Inform) hashtag

hasta ['asta] ADV even ▸ PREP (alcanzando a) as far as, up/down to; (de tiempo: a tal hora) till, until; (: antes de) before ▸ CONJ: **~ que** until; **~ luego** o **ahora/el sábado** see you soon/on Saturday; **~ pronto** see you soon; **~ la fecha** (up) to date; **~ nueva orden** until further notice; **~ en Valencia hiela a veces** even in Valencia it freezes sometimes

hastiar [as'tjar] /**1c**/ VT (gen) to weary; (aburrir) to bore; **hastiarse** VR: **hastiarse de** to get fed up with

hastío [as'tio] NM weariness; boredom

hatajo [a'taxo] NM: **un ~ de gamberros** a bunch of hooligans

hatillo [a'tiʎo] NM belongings pl, kit; (montón) bundle, heap

Hawai [a'wai] NM (tb: **las Islas Hawai**) Hawaii

hawaianas [awa'janas] NFPL (esp Am) flip-flops (BRIT), thongs

hawaiano, -a [awa'jano, a] ADJ, NM/F Hawaian

hay [ai] VB ver **haber**

Haya ['aja] NF: **la ~** The Hague

haya etc ['aja] VB ver **haber** ▸ NF beech tree

hayal [a'jal] NM beech grove

haz [aθ] VB ver **hacer** ▸ NM bundle, bunch; (rayo: de luz) beam ▸ NF: **~ de la tierra** face of the earth

hazaña [a'θaɲa] NF feat, exploit; **sería una ~** it would be a great achievement

hazmerreír [aθmerre'ir] NM INV laughing stock

he [e] VB ver **haber** ▸ ADV: **he aquí** here is, here are; **he aquí por qué ...** that is why ...

hebilla [e'βiʎa] NF buckle, clasp

hebra ['eβra] NF thread; (Bot: fibra) fibre, grain

hebreo, -a [e'βreo, a] ADJ, NM/F Hebrew ▸ NM (*Ling*) Hebrew

Hébridas ['eβriðas] NFPL: **las ~** the Hebrides

hechice *etc* [e'tʃiθe] VB *ver* **hechizar**

hechicero, -a [etʃi'θero, a] NM/F sorcerer (sorceress)

hechizar [etʃi'θar] /**1f**/ VT to cast a spell on, bewitch

hechizo [e'tʃiθo] NM witchcraft, magic; (*acto de magia*) spell, charm

hecho, -a ['etʃo, a] PP *de* **hacer** ▸ ADJ complete; (*maduro*) mature; (*carne*) done; (*Costura*) ready-to-wear ▸ NM deed, act; (*dato*) fact; (*cuestión*) matter; (*suceso*) event ▸ EXCL agreed!, done!; **¡bien ~!** well done!; **de ~** in fact, as a matter of fact; (*Pol etc: adj, adv*) de facto; **de ~ y de derecho** de facto and de jure; **~ a la medida** made-to-measure; **a lo ~, pecho** it's no use crying over spilt milk; **el ~ es que ...** the fact is that ...

hechura [e'tʃura] NF making, creation; (*producto*) product; (*forma*) form, shape; (*de persona*) build; (*Tec*) craftsmanship

hectárea [ek'tarea] NF hectare

heder [e'ðer] /**2g**/ VI to stink, smell; (*fig*) to be unbearable

hediondez [eðjon'deθ] NF stench, stink; (*cosa*) stinking thing

hediondo, -a [e'ðjondo, a] ADJ stinking

hedor [e'ðor] NM stench

hegemonía [exemo'nia] NF hegemony

helada [e'laða] NF frost

heladera [ela'ðera] NF (*Am: refrigerador*) refrigerator

heladería [elaðe'ria] NF ice-cream stall (*o* parlour)

helado, -a [e'laðo, a] ADJ frozen; (*glacial*) icy; (*fig*) chilly, cold ▸ NM ice-cream; **dejar ~ a algn** to dumbfound sb

helador, a [ela'ðor, a] ADJ (*viento etc*) icy, freezing

helar [e'lar] /**1j**/ VT to freeze, ice (up); (*dejar atónito*) to amaze ▸ VI to freeze; **helarse** VR to freeze; (*Aviat, Ferro etc*) to ice (up), freeze up

helecho [e'letʃo] NM bracken, fern

helénico, -a [e'leniko, a] ADJ Hellenic, Greek

heleno, -a [e'leno, a] NM/F Hellene, Greek

hélice ['eliθe] NF spiral; (*Tec*) propeller; (*Mat*) helix

helicóptero [eli'koptero] NM helicopter

helio ['eljo] NM helium

helmántico, -a [el'mantiko, a] ADJ of *o* from Salamanca

helvético, -a [el'βetiko, a] ADJ, NM/F Swiss

hematoma [ema'toma] NM bruise

hembra ['embra] NF (*Bot, Zool*) female; (*mujer*) woman; (*Tec*) nut; **un elefante ~** a she-elephant

hemeroteca [emero'teka] NF newspaper library

hemiciclo [emi'θiklo] NM: **el ~** (*Pol*) the floor

hemisferio [emis'ferjo] NM hemisphere

hemofilia [emo'filja] NF haemophilia (*BRIT*), hemophilia (*US*)

hemorragia [emo'rraxja] NF haemorrhage (*BRIT*), hemorrhage (*US*)

hemorroides [emo'rroiðes] NFPL haemorrhoids (*BRIT*), hemorrhoids (*US*)

hemos ['emos] VB *ver* **haber**

henar [e'nar] NM meadow, hayfield

henchir [en'tʃir] /**3h**/ VT to fill, stuff; **henchirse** VR (*llenarse de comida*) to stuff o.s. (with food); (*inflarse*) to swell (up)

Hendaya [en'daja] NF Hendaye

hender [en'der] /**2g**/ VT to cleave, split

hendidura [endi'ðura] NF crack, split; (*Geo*) fissure

henequén [ene'ken] NM (*Am*) henequen

heno ['eno] NM hay

hepatitis [epa'titis] NF INV hepatitis

herbario, -a [er'βarjo, a] ADJ herbal ▸ NM (*colección*) herbarium; (*especialista*) herbalist; (*botánico*) botanist

herbicida [erβi'θiða] NM weedkiller

herbívoro, -a [er'βiβoro, a] ADJ herbivorous

herboristería [erβoriste'ria] NF herbalist's shop

heredad [ere'ðað] NF landed property; (*granja*) farm

heredar [ere'ðar] /**1a**/ VT to inherit

heredero, -a [ere'ðero, a] NM/F heir(ess); **~ del trono** heir to the throne

hereditario, -a [ereði'tarjo, a] ADJ hereditary

hereje [e'rexe] NMF heretic

herejía [ere'xia] NF heresy

herencia [e'renθja] NF inheritance; (*fig*) heritage; (*Bio*) heredity

herético, -a [e'retiko, a] ADJ heretical

herido, -a [e'riðo, a] ADJ injured, wounded; (*fig*) offended ▸ NM/F casualty ▸ NF wound, injury

herir [e'rir] /**3i**/ VT to wound, injure; (*fig*) to offend; (*conmover*) to touch, move

hermana [er'mana] NF *ver* **hermano**

hermanación [ermana'θjon] NF (*de ciudades*) twinning

hermanado, -a [erma'naðo, a] PP *de* **hermanar** ▸ ADJ (*ciudad*) twinned

hermanar [erma'nar] /**1a**/ VT to match; (*unir*) to join; (*ciudades*) to twin

hermanastro, -a [erma'nastro, a] NM/F stepbrother(-sister)

hermandad [erman'dað] NF brotherhood; (*de mujeres*) sisterhood; (*sindicato etc*) association

hermano, -a [er'mano, a] ADJ similar ▸ NM brother ▸ NF sister; **~ gemelo** twin brother;

h

199

~ político brother-in-law; **~ primo** first cousin; **mis hermanos** my brothers, my brothers and sisters; **hermana política** sister-in-law

hermético, -a [er'metiko, a] ADJ hermetic; (fig) watertight

hermoso, -a [er'moso, a] ADJ beautiful, lovely; (estupendo) splendid; (guapo) handsome

hermosura [ermo'sura] NF beauty; (de hombre) handsomeness

hernia ['ernja] NF hernia, rupture; **~ discal** slipped disc

herniarse [er'njarse] /**1b**/ VR to rupture o.s.; (fig) to break one's back

héroe ['eroe] NM hero

heroicidad [eroiθi'ðað] NF heroism; (una heroicidad) heroic deed

heroico, -a [e'roiko, a] ADJ heroic

heroína [ero'ina] NF (mujer) heroine; (droga) heroin

heroinómano, -a [eroi'nomano, a] NM/F heroin addict

heroísmo [ero'ismo] NM heroism

herpes ['erpes] NMPL o NFPL (Med: gen) herpes sg; (: de la piel) shingles sg

herradura [erra'ðura] NF horseshoe

herraje [e'rraxe] NM (trabajos) ironwork

herramienta [erra'mjenta] NF tool

herrería [erre'ria] NF smithy; (Tec) forge

herrero [e'rrero] NM blacksmith

herrumbre [e'rrumbre] NF rust

herrumbroso, -a [errum'broso, a] ADJ rusty

hervidero [erβi'ðero] NM (fig) swarm; (Pol etc) hotbed

hervir [er'βir] /**3i**/ VI to boil; (burbujear) to bubble; (fig): **~ de** to teem with; **~ a fuego lento** to simmer

hervor [er'βor] NM boiling; (fig) ardour, fervour

heterogéneo, -a [etero'xeneo, a] ADJ heterogeneous

heterosexual [eterosek'swal] ADJ, NMF heterosexual

hez [eθ] NF (tb: **heces**) dregs pl

hibernar [iβer'nar] /**1a**/ VI to hibernate

híbrido, -a ['iβriðo, a] ADJ hybrid

hice etc ['iθe] VB ver **hacer**

hidalgo, -a [i'ðalɣo, a] ADJ noble; (honrado) honourable (BRIT), honorable (US) ▶ NM/F noble(man-woman))

hidratante [iðra'tante] ADJ: **crema ~** moisturizing cream, moisturizer

hidratar [iðra'tar] /**1a**/ VT to moisturize

hidrato [i'ðrato] NM hydrate; **~ de carbono** carbohydrate

hidráulico, -a [i'ðrauliko, a] ADJ hydraulic ▶ NF hydraulics sg

hidro... [iðro] PREF hydro..., water-...

hidroavión [iðroa'βjon] NM seaplane

hidrodeslizador [iðrodesliθa'ðor] NM hovercraft

hidroeléctrico, -a [iðroe'lektriko, a] ADJ hydroelectric

hidrófilo, -a [i'ðrofilo, a] ADJ absorbent; **algodón ~** cotton wool (BRIT), absorbent cotton (US)

hidrofobia [iðro'foβja] NF hydrophobia, rabies

hidrófugo, -a [i'ðrofuɣo, a] ADJ damp-proof

hidrógeno [i'ðroxeno] NM hydrogen

hieda etc ['jeða] VB ver **heder**

hiedra ['jeðra] NF ivy

hiel [jel] NF gall, bile; (fig) bitterness

hielo ['jelo] VB ver **helar** ▶ NM (gen) ice; (escarcha) frost; (fig) coldness, reserve; **romper el ~** (fig) to break the ice

hiena ['jena] NF (Zool) hyena

hiera etc ['jera] VB ver **herir**

hierba ['jerβa] NF (pasto) grass; (Culin, Med: planta) herb; **mala ~** weed; (fig) evil influence

hierbabuena [jerβa'βwena] NF mint

hierro ['jerro] NM (metal) iron; (objeto) iron object; **~ acanalado** corrugated iron; **~ colado** o **fundido** cast iron; **de ~** iron cpd

hierva etc ['jerβa] VB ver **hervir**

hígado ['iɣaðo] NM liver; **hígados** NMPL (fig) guts; **echar los hígados** to wear o.s. out

higiene [i'xjene] NF hygiene

higiénico, -a [i'xjeniko, a] ADJ hygienic

higo ['iɣo] NM fig; **~ seco** dried fig; **~ chumbo** prickly pear; **de higos a brevas** once in a blue moon

higuera [i'ɣera] NF fig tree

hijastro, -a [i'xastro, a] NM/F stepson(-daughter)

hijo, -a ['ixo, a] NM/F son (daughter), child; (uso vocativo) dear; **hijos** NMPL children, sons and daughters; **sin hijos** childless; **~/hija político/a** son-/daughter-in-law; **~ pródigo** prodigal son; **~ adoptivo** adopted child; **~ de papá/mamá** daddy's/mummy's boy; **~ de puta** (fam!) bastard (fam!), son of a bitch (fam!); **~ único** only child; **cada ~ de vecino** any Tom, Dick or Harry

hilacha [i'latʃa] NF ravelled thread; **~ de acero** steel wool

hilado, -a [i'laðo, a] ADJ spun

hilandero, -a [ilan'dero, a] NM/F spinner

hilar [i'lar] /**1a**/ VT to spin; (fig) to reason, infer; **~ delgado** to split hairs

hilera [i'lera] NF row, file

hilo ['ilo] NM thread; (Bot) fibre; (tela) linen; (de metal) wire; (de agua) trickle, thin stream; (de luz) beam, ray; (de conversación) thread, theme; (de pensamientos) train; **~ dental** dental floss; **colgar de un ~** (fig) to hang by a thread; **traje de ~** linen suit

hilvanar [ilβa'nar] /**1a**/ VT (Costura) to tack (BRIT), baste (US); (fig) to do hurriedly

Himalaya [ima'laja] NM: **el ~, los Montes ~** the Himalayas

himno ['imno] NM hymn; **~ nacional** national anthem

hincapié [inka'pje] NM: **hacer ~ en** to emphasize, stress

hincar [in'kar] /**1g**/ VT to drive (in), thrust (in); (diente) to sink; **hincarse** VR: **hincarse de rodillas** (esp AM) to kneel down

hincha ['intʃa] NMF (fam: Deporte) fan

hinchado, -a [in'tʃaðo, a] ADJ (gen) swollen; (persona) pompous ▶ NF (group of) supporters o fans

hinchar [in'tʃar] /**1a**/ VT (gen) to swell; (inflar) to blow up, inflate; (fig) to exaggerate; **hincharse** VR (inflarse) to swell up; (fam: llenarse) to stuff o.s.; (fig) to get conceited; **hincharse de reír** to have a good laugh

hinchazón [intʃa'θon] NF (Med) swelling; (protuberancia) bump, lump; (altivez) arrogance

hindú [in'du] ADJ, NMF Hindu

hinojo [i'noxo] NM fennel

hinque etc ['inke] VB ver **hincar**

hipar [i'par] /**1a**/ VI to hiccup

hiper... [iper] PREF hyper...

hiperactivo, -a [iperak'tiβo, a] ADJ hyperactive

hipermercado [ipermer'kaðo] NM hypermarket, superstore

hipersensible [ipersen'siβle] ADJ hypersensitive

hipertensión [iperten'sjon] NF high blood pressure, hypertension

hípico, -a ['ipiko, a] ADJ horse cpd, equine; **club ~** riding club

hipnosis [ip'nosis] NF INV hypnosis

hipnotice etc [ipno'tiθe] VB ver **hipnotizar**

hipnotismo [ipno'tismo] NM hypnotism

hipnotizar [ipnoti'θar] /**1f**/ VT to hypnotize

hipo ['ipo] NM hiccups pl; **quitar el ~ a algn** to cure sb's hiccups

hipocondría [ipokon'dria] NF hypochondria

hipocondríaco, -a [ipokon'driako, a] ADJ, NM/F hypochondriac

hipocresía [ipokre'sia] NF hypocrisy

hipócrita [i'pokrita] ADJ hypocritical ▶ NMF hypocrite

hipodérmico, -a [ipo'ðermiko, a] ADJ: **aguja hipodérmica** hypodermic needle

hipódromo [i'poðromo] NM racetrack

hipopótamo [ipo'potamo] NM hippopotamus

hipoteca [ipo'teka] NF mortgage; **redimir una ~** to pay off a mortgage

hipotecar [ipote'kar] /**1g**/ VT to mortgage; (fig) to jeopardize

hipotecario, -a [ipote'karjo, a] ADJ mortgage cpd

hipótesis [i'potesis] NF INV hypothesis; **es una ~ (nada más)** that's just a theory

hipotético, -a [ipo'tetiko, a] ADJ hypothetic(al)

hiriendo etc [i'rjendo] VB ver **herir**

hiriente [i'rjente] ADJ offensive, wounding

hirsuto, -a [ir'suto, a] ADJ hairy

hirviendo etc [ir'βjendo] VB ver **hervir**

hisopo [i'sopo] NM (Rel) sprinkler; (Bot) hyssop; (de algodón) swab

hispánico, -a [is'paniko, a] ADJ Hispanic, Spanish

hispanidad [ispani'ðað] NF (cualidad) Spanishness; (Pol) Spanish o Hispanic world

hispanista [ispa'nista] NMF (Univ etc) Hispan(ic)ist

hispano, -a [is'pano, a] ADJ Hispanic, Spanish, Hispano- ▶ NM/F Spaniard

Hispanoamérica [ispanoa'merika] NF Spanish o Latin America

hispanoamericano, -a [ispanoameri'kano, a] ADJ, NM/F Spanish o Latin American

hispanohablante [ispanoa'βlante], **hispanoparlante** [ispanopar'lante] ADJ Spanish-speaking

histeria [is'terja] NF hysteria

histérico, -a [is'teriko, a] ADJ hysterical

histerismo [iste'rismo] NM (Med) hysteria; (fig) hysterics

histograma [isto'ɣrama] NM histogram

historia [is'torja] NF history; (cuento) story, tale; **historias** NFPL (chismes) gossip sg; **dejarse de historias** to come to the point; **pasar a la ~** to go down in history

historiador, a [istorja'ðor, a] NM/F historian

historial [isto'rjal] NM record; (profesional) curriculum vitae, C.V., résumé (US); (Med) case history

histórico, -a [is'toriko, a] ADJ historical; (fig) historic

historieta [isto'rjeta] NF tale, anecdote; (de dibujos) comic strip

histrionismo [istrjo'nismo] NM (Teat) acting; (fig) histrionics pl

hito ['ito] NM (fig) landmark; (objetivo) goal, target; (fig) milestone

hizo ['iθo] VB ver **hacer**

Hna., Hnas. ABR (= Hermana(s)) Sr(s).

Hno., Hnos. ABR (= Hermano(s)) Bro(s).

hocico [o'θiko] NM snout; (fig) grimace

hockey ['xoki] NM hockey; **~ sobre hielo** ice hockey

hogar [o'ɣar] NM fireplace, hearth; (casa) home; (vida familiar) home life

hogareño, -a [oɣa'reɲo, a] ADJ home cpd; (persona) home-loving

hogaza [o'ɣaθa] NF (de pan) large loaf

hoguera [o'ɣera] NF (gen) bonfire; (para herejes) stake

hoja ['oxa] NF (gen) leaf; (de flor) petal; (de hierba) blade; (de papel) sheet; (página) page; (formulario) form; (de puerta) leaf; ~ **de afeitar** razor blade; ~ **de cálculo electrónica** spreadsheet; ~ **informativa** leaflet, handout; ~ **de ruta** road map; ~ **de solicitud** application form; ~ **de trabajo** (Inform) worksheet; **de ~ ancha** broad-leaved; **de ~ caduca/perenne** deciduous/evergreen

hojalata [oxa'lata] NF tin(plate)

hojaldre [o'xaldre] NM (Culin) puff pastry

hojarasca [oxa'raska] NF (hojas) dead o fallen leaves pl; (fig) rubbish

hojear [oxe'ar] /1a/ VT to leaf through, turn the pages of

hojuela [o'xwela] NF (AM) flake

hola ['ola] EXCL hello!

Holanda [o'landa] NF Holland

holandés, -esa [olan'des, esa] ADJ Dutch ▶ NM/F Dutchman(-woman); **los holandeses** the Dutch ▶ NM (Ling) Dutch

holgado, -a [ol'ɣaðo, a] ADJ loose, baggy; (rico) well-to-do

holgar [ol'ɣar] /1h, 1l/ VI (descansar) to rest; (sobrar) to be superfluous; **huelga decir que** it goes without saying that

holgazán, -ana [olɣa'θan, ana] ADJ idle, lazy ▶ NM/F loafer

holgazanear [olɣaθane'ar] /1a/ VI to laze o loaf around

holgura [ol'ɣura] NF looseness, bagginess; (Tec) play, free movement; (vida) comfortable living, luxury

hollar [o'ʎar] /1l/ VT to tread (on), trample

hollín [o'ʎin] NM soot

hombre ['ombre] NM man; (raza humana): **el ~** man(kind) ▶ EXCL (para énfasis) man, old chap; **¡sí ~!** (claro) of course!; ~ **de negocios** businessman; ~**-rana** frogman; ~ **de bien** o **pro** honest man; ~ **de confianza** right-hand man; ~ **de estado** statesman; **el ~ medio** the average man

hombrera [om'brera] NF shoulder strap

hombro ['ombro] NM shoulder; **arrimar el ~** to lend a hand; **encogerse de hombros** to shrug one's shoulders

hombruno, -a [om'bruno, a] ADJ mannish

homenaje [ome'naxe] NM (gen) homage; (tributo) tribute; **un partido ~** a benefit match

homeopatía [omeopa'tia] NF hom(o)eopathy

homeopático, -a [omeo'patiko, a] ADJ hom(o)eopathic

homicida [omi'θiða] ADJ homicidal ▶ NMF murderer

homicidio [omi'θiðjo] NM murder, homicide; (involuntario) manslaughter

homologación [omoloɣa'θjon] NF (de sueldo, condiciones) parity

homologar [omolo'ɣar] /1h/ VT (Com) to standardize; (Escol) to officially approve; (Deporte) to officially recognize; (sueldos) to equalize

homólogo, -a [o'moloɣo, a] NM/F counterpart, opposite number

homónimo [o'monimo] NM (tocayo) namesake

homosexual [omosek'swal] ADJ, NMF homosexual

honda ['onda] NF (RPL) catapult

hondo, -a ['ondo, a] ADJ deep; **lo ~** the depth(s) (pl), the bottom; **con ~ pesar** with deep regret

hondonada [ondo'naða] NF hollow, depression; (cañón) ravine; (Geo) lowland

hondura [on'dura] NF depth, profundity

Honduras [on'duras] NF Honduras

hondureño, -a [ondu'reno, a] ADJ, NM/F Honduran

honestidad [onesti'ðað] NF purity, chastity; (decencia) decency

honesto, -a [o'nesto, a] ADJ chaste, decent, honest; (justo) just

hongo ['ongo] NM (Bot: gen) fungus; (: comestible) mushroom; (: venenoso) toadstool; (sombrero) bowler (hat) (BRIT), derby (US); **hongos del pie** foot rot sg, athlete's foot sg

honor [o'nor] NM (gen) honour (BRIT), honor (US); (gloria) glory; ~ **profesional** professional etiquette; **en ~ a la verdad** to be fair

honorable [ono'raβle] ADJ honourable (BRIT), honorable (US)

honorario, -a [ono'rarjo, a] ADJ honorary ▶ NM: **honorarios** fees

honorífico, -a [ono'rifiko, a] ADJ honourable (BRIT), honorable (US); **mención honorífica** hono(u)rable mention

honra ['onra] NF (gen) honour (BRIT), honor (US); (renombre) good name; **honras fúnebres** funeral rites; **tener algo a mucha ~** to be proud of sth

honradez [onra'ðeθ] NF honesty; (de persona) integrity

honrado, -a [on'raðo, a] ADJ honest, upright

honrar [on'rar] /1a/ VT to honour (BRIT) o honor (US); **honrarse** VR: **honrarse con algo/de hacer algo** to be honoured by sth/to do sth

honroso, -a [on'roso, a] ADJ (honrado) honourable (BRIT) o honorable (US); (respetado) respectable

hora ['ora] NF hour; (tiempo) time; **¿qué ~ es?** what time is it?; **¿a qué ~?** at what time?; **media ~** half an hour; **a la ~ de comer/del**

recreo at lunchtime/at playtime; **a primera** ~ first thing (in the morning); **a última** ~ at the last moment; **"última ~"** "breaking news"; **noticias de última** ~ last-minute news; **a altas horas** in the small hours; **a la** ~ **en punto** on the dot; **¡a buena ~!** about time, too!; **en mala** ~ unluckily; **pedir** ~ to make an appointment; **dar la** ~ to strike the hour; **poner el reloj en** ~ to set one's watch; **horas de oficina/de trabajo** office/working hours; **horas de visita** visiting times; **horas extras** o **extraordinarias** overtime sg; **horas pico** (AM) rush o peak hours; **horas punta** rush hours; **no ver la ~ de** to look forward to; **¡ya era ~!** and about time too!

horadar [ora'ðar] /**1a**/ VT to drill, bore

horario, -a [o'rarjo, a] ADJ hourly, hour cpd ▶ NM timetable; ~ **comercial** business hours

horca ['orka] NF gallows sg; (Agr) pitchfork

horcajadas [orka'xaðas]: **a** ~ adv astride

horchata [or'tʃata] NF tiger nut milk

horda ['orða] NF horde

horizontal [oriθon'tal] ADJ horizontal

horizonte [ori'θonte] NM horizon

horma ['orma] NF mould; ~ **(de calzado)** last; ~ **de sombrero** hat block

hormiga [or'miɣa] NF ant; **hormigas** NFPL (Med) pins and needles

hormigón [ormi'ɣon] NM concrete; ~ **armado/pretensado** reinforced/prestressed concrete

hormigonera [ormiɣon'era] NF cement mixer

hormigueo [ormi'ɣeo] NM (comezón) itch; (fig) uneasiness

hormiguero [ormi'ɣero] NM (Zool) ants' nest; **era un** ~ it was swarming with people

hormona [or'mona] NF hormone

hornada [or'naða] NF batch of loaves (etc)

hornillo [or'niʎo] NM (cocina) portable stove; ~ **de gas** gas ring

horno ['orno] NM (Culin) oven; (Tec) furnace; (para cerámica) kiln; ~ **microondas** microwave (oven); **alto** ~ blast furnace; ~ **crematorio** crematorium

horóscopo [o'roskopo] NM horoscope

horquilla [or'kiʎa] NF hairpin; (Agr) pitchfork

horrendo, -a [o'rrendo, a] ADJ horrendous, frightful

horrible [o'rriβle] ADJ horrible, dreadful

horripilante [orripi'lante] ADJ hair-raising, horrifying

horripilar [orripi'lar] /**1a**/ VT: ~ **a algn** to horrify sb; **horripilarse** VR to be horrified

horror [o'rror] NM horror, dread; (atrocidad) atrocity; **¡qué ~!** (fam) how awful!; **estudia horrores** he studies a hell of a lot

horrorice etc [orro'riθe] VB ver **horrorizar**

horrorizar [orrori'θar] /**1f**/ VT to horrify, frighten; **horrorizarse** VR to be horrified

horroroso, -a [orro'roso, a] ADJ horrifying, ghastly

hortaliza [orta'liθa] NF vegetable

hortelano, -a [orte'lano, a] NM/F (market) gardener

hortera [or'tera] ADJ (fam) tacky

horterada [orte'raða] NF (fam): **es una** ~ it's really naff

hortícola [or'tikola] ADJ horticultural

horticultura [ortikul'tura] NF horticulture

hortofrutícola [ortofru'tikola] ADJ fruit and vegetable cpd

hosco, -a ['osko, a] ADJ dark; (persona) sullen, gloomy

hospedaje [ospe'ðaxe] NM (cost of) board and lodging

hospedar [ospe'ðar] /**1a**/ VT to put up; **hospedarse** VR: **hospedarse (con/en)** to stay o lodge (with/at)

hospedería [ospeðe'ria] NF (edificio) inn; (habitación) guest room

hospicio [os'piθjo] NM (para niños) orphanage

hospital [ospi'tal] NM hospital

hospitalario, -a [ospita'larjo, a] ADJ (acogedor) hospitable

hospitalice etc [ospita'liθe] VB ver **hospitalizar**

hospitalidad [ospitali'ðað] NF hospitality

hospitalizar [ospitali'θar] /**1f**/ VT to send o take to hospital, hospitalize

hosquedad [oske'ðað] NF sullenness

hostal [os'tal] NM small hotel; ver tb **hotel**

hostelería [ostele'ria] NF hotel business o trade

hostia ['ostja] NF (Rel) host, consecrated wafer; (fam: golpe) whack, punch ▶ EXCL: **¡~(s)!** (fam!) damn!

hostigar [osti'ɣar] /**1h**/ VT to whip; (fig) to harass, pester

hostigue etc [os'tiɣe] VB ver **hostigar**

hostil [os'til] ADJ hostile

hostilidad [ostili'ðað] NF hostility

hotdog [ot'doɡ] NM (AM) hot dog

hotel [o'tel] NM hotel; see note

> In Spain you can choose from the following categories of accommodation, in descending order of quality and price: hotel (from 5 stars to 1), hostal, pensión, casa de huéspedes, fonda. Quality can vary widely even within these categories. The State also runs luxury hotels called paradores, which are usually sited in places of particular historical interest and are often historic buildings themselves.

hotelero, -a [ote'lero, a] ADJ hotel cpd ▶ NM/F hotelier

hoy [oi] ADV (*este día*) today; (*en la actualidad*) now(adays) ▶ NM present time; **~ (en) día** now(adays); **el día de ~**, **~ día** (*AM*) this very day; **~ por ~** right now; **de ~ en ocho días** a week today; **de ~ en adelante** from now on

hoya ['oja] NF pit; (*sepulcro*) grave; (*Geo*) valley

hoyo ['ojo] NM hole, pit; (*tumba*) grave; (*Golf*) hole; (*Med*) pockmark

hoyuelo [oj'welo] NM dimple

hoz [oθ] NF sickle

hube *etc* ['uβe] VB *ver* **haber**

hucha ['utʃa] NF money box

hueco, -a ['weko, a] ADJ (*vacío*) hollow, empty; (*resonante*) booming; (*sonido*) resonant; (*persona*) conceited; (*estilo*) pompous ▶ NM hollow, cavity; (*agujero*) hole; (*de escalera*) well; (*de ascensor*) shaft; (*vacante*) vacancy; **~ de la mano** hollow of the hand

huela *etc* ['wela] VB *ver* **oler**

huelga ['welɣa] VB *ver* **holgar** ▶ NF strike; **declararse en ~** to go on strike, come out on strike; **~ general** general strike; **~ de hambre** hunger strike; **~ oficial** official strike

huelgue *etc* ['welɣe] VB *ver* **holgar**

huelguista [wel'ɣista] NMF striker

huella ['weʎa] NF (*acto de pisar, pisada*) tread(ing); (*marca del paso*) footprint, footstep; (: *de animal, máquina*) track; **~ de carbono** carbon footprint; **~ dactilar** o **digital** fingerprint; **sin dejar ~** without leaving a trace

huelo *etc* VB *ver* **oler**

huérfano, -a ['werfano, a] ADJ orphan(ed); (*fig*) unprotected ▶ NM/F orphan

huerta ['werta] NF market garden (*BRIT*), truck farm (*US*); (*de Murcia, Valencia*) irrigated region

huerto ['werto] NM kitchen garden; (*de árboles frutales*) orchard

hueso ['weso] NM (*Anat*) bone; (*de fruta*) stone, pit (*US*); **sin ~** (*carne*) boned; **estar en los huesos** to be nothing but skin and bone; **ser un ~** (*profesor*) to be terribly strict; **un ~ duro de roer** a hard nut to crack

huesoso, -a [we'soso, a] ADJ (*esp AM*) bony

huésped, a ['wespeð, a] NM/F (*invitado*) guest; (*habitante*) resident; (*anfitrión*) host(ess)

huesudo, -a [we'suðo, a] ADJ bony, big-boned

huevas ['weβas] NFPL eggs, roe *sg*; (*AM fam!*) balls (*fam!*)

huevera [we'βera] NF eggcup

huevo ['weβo] NM egg; (*fam!*) ball (*fam!*), testicle; **~ duro/escalfado/estrellado** o **frito/pasado por agua** hard-boiled/ poached/fried/soft-boiled egg; **huevos revueltos** scrambled eggs; **~ tibio** (*AM*) soft-boiled egg; **me costó un ~** (*fam!*) it was hard work; **tener huevos** (*fam!*) to have guts

huevón, -ona [we'βon, ona] NM/F (*AM fam!*) stupid bastard (*fam!*), stupid idiot

huida [u'iða] NF escape, flight; **~ de capitales** (*Com*) flight of capital

huidizo, -a [ui'ðiθo, a] ADJ (*tímido*) shy; (*pasajero*) fleeting

huir [u'ir] **/3g/** VT (*escapar*) to flee, escape; (*evadir*) to avoid ▶ VI to flee, run away

hule ['ule] NM (*encerado*) oilskin; (*esp AM*) rubber

hulera [u'lera] NF (*AM*) catapult

hulla ['uʎa] NF bituminous coal

humanice *etc* [uma'niθe] VB *ver* **humanizar**

humanidad [umani'ðað] NF (*género humano*) man(kind); (*cualidad*) humanity; (*fam: gordura*) corpulence

humanitario, -a [umani'tarjo, a] ADJ humanitarian; (*benévolo*) humane

humanizar [umani'θar] **/1f/** VT to humanize; **humanizarse** VR to become more human

humano, -a [u'mano, a] ADJ (*gen*) human; (*humanitario*) humane ▶ NM human; **ser ~** human being

humareda [uma'reða] NF cloud of smoke

humeante [ume'ante] ADJ smoking, smoky

humedad [ume'ðað] NF (*del clima*) humidity; (*de pared etc*) dampness; **a prueba de ~** damp-proof

humedecer [umeðe'θer] **/2d/** VT to moisten, wet; **humedecerse** VR to get wet

humedezca *etc* [ume'ðeθka] VB *ver* **humedecer**

húmedo, -a ['umeðo, a] ADJ (*mojado*) damp, wet; (*tiempo etc*) humid

humildad [umil'dað] NF humility, humbleness

humilde [u'milde] ADJ humble, modest; (*clase etc*) low, modest

humillación [umiʎa'θjon] NF humiliation

humillante [umi'ʎante] ADJ humiliating

humillar [umi'ʎar] **/1a/** VT to humiliate; **humillarse** VR to humble o.s., grovel

humo ['umo] NM (*de fuego*) smoke; (*gas nocivo*) fumes *pl*; (*vapor*) steam, vapour; **humos** NMPL (*fig*) conceit *sg*; **irse todo en ~** (*fig*) to vanish without trace; **bajar los humos a algn** to take sb down a peg or two

humor [u'mor] NM (*disposición*) mood, temper; (*lo que divierte*) humour; **de buen/mal ~** in a good/bad mood

humorismo [umo'rismo] NM humour

humorista [umo'rista] NMF comic

humorístico, -a [umo'ristiko, a] ADJ funny, humorous

hundimiento [undi'mjento] NM (*gen*) sinking; (*colapso*) collapse

hundir [un'dir] **/3a/** VT to sink; (*edificio, plan*) to ruin, destroy; **hundirse** VR to sink, collapse; (*fig: arruinarse*) to be ruined;

(*desaparecer*) to disappear; **se hundió la economía** the economy collapsed; **se hundieron los precios** prices slumped

húngaro, -a [ˈungaro, a] ADJ, NM/F Hungarian ▶ NM (*Ling*) Hungarian, Magyar

Hungría [unˈgria] NF Hungary

huracán [uraˈkan] NM hurricane

huraño, -a [uˈraɲo, a] ADJ shy; (*antisocial*) unsociable

hurgar [urˈɣar] /1h/ VT to poke, jab; (*remover*) to stir (up); **hurgarse** VR: **hurgarse (las narices)** to pick one's nose

hurgonear [urɣoneˈar] /1a/ VT to poke

hurgue etc [ˈurɣe] VB ver **hurgar**

hurón [uˈron] NM (*Zool*) ferret

hurra [ˈurra] EXCL hurray!, hurrah!

hurtadillas [urtaˈðiʎas]: **a ~** adv stealthily, on the sly

hurtar [urˈtar] /1a/ VT to steal; **hurtarse** VR to hide, keep out of the way

hurto [ˈurto] NM theft, stealing; (*lo robado*) (piece of) stolen property, loot

husmear [usmeˈar] /1a/ VT (*oler*) to sniff out, scent; (*fam*) to pry into ▶ VI to smell bad

huso [ˈuso] NM (*Tec*) spindle; (*de torno*) drum

huy [ˈui] EXCL (*dolor*) ow!, ouch!; (*sorpresa*) well!; (*alivio*) phew!; **¡~, perdona!** oops, sorry!

huyendo etc [uˈjendo] VB ver **huir**

huyo etc VB ver **huir**

h

I i

I, i [i] NF (*letra*) I, i; **I de Inés** I for Isaac (BRIT) o Item (US)

IA ABR = **inteligencia artificial**

iba *etc* ['iβa] VB *ver* **ir**

Iberia [i'βerja] NF Iberia

ibérico, -a [i'βeriko, a] ADJ Iberian; **la Península ibérica** the Iberian Peninsula

ibero, -a [i'βero, a], **íbero, -a** ['iβero, a] ADJ, NM/F Iberian

iberoamericano, -a [iβeroameri'kano, a] ADJ, NM/F Latin American

íbice ['iβiθe] NM ibex

ibicenco, -a [iβi'θenko, a] ADJ of o from Ibiza ▶ NM/F native o inhabitant of Ibiza

Ibiza [i'βiθa] NF Ibiza

ice *etc* ['iθe] VB *ver* **izar**

iceberg [iθe'βer] NM iceberg

ICONA [i'kona] NM ABR (ESP) = **Instituto Nacional para la Conservación de la Naturaleza**

icono [i'kono] NM (*tb Inform*) icon

iconoclasta [ikono'klasta] ADJ iconoclastic ▶ NMF iconoclast

ictericia [ikte'riθja] NF jaundice

I+D NF ABR (= *Investigación y Desarrollo*) R&D

íd. ABR = **ídem**

ida ['iða] NF going, departure; **~ y vuelta** round trip, return; **idas y venidas** comings and goings

IDE ['iðe] NF ABR (= *Iniciativa de Defensa Estratégica*) SDI

idea [i'ðea] NF idea; (*impresión*) opinion; (*propósito*) intention; **~ genial** brilliant idea; **a mala ~** out of spite; **no tengo la menor ~** I haven't a clue

ideal [iðe'al] ADJ, NM ideal

idealice *etc* [iðea'liθe] VB *ver* **idealizar**

idealista [iðea'lista] ADJ idealistic ▶ NMF idealist

idealizar [iðeali'θar] /1f/ VT to idealize

idear [iðe'ar] /1a/ VT to think up; (*aparato*) to invent; (*viaje*) to plan

ídem ['iðem] PRON ditto

idéntico, -a [i'ðentiko, a] ADJ identical

identidad [iðenti'ðað] NF identity; **~ corporativa** corporate identity o image

identificación [iðentifika'θjon] NF identification

identificador de llamadas [iðentifika'ðor-] NM caller ID

identificar [iðentifi'kar] /1g/ VT to identify; **identificarse** VR: **identificarse con** to identify with

identifique *etc* [iðenti'fike] VB *ver* **identificar**

ideología [iðeolo'xia] NF ideology

ideológico, -a [iðeo'loxiko, a] ADJ ideological

idílico, -a [i'ðiliko, a] ADJ idyllic

idilio [i'ðiljo] NM love affair

idioma [i'ðjoma] NM language

idiomático, -a [iðjo'matiko, a] ADJ idiomatic

idiota [i'ðjota] ADJ idiotic ▶ NMF idiot

idiotez [iðjo'teθ] NF idiocy

idolatrar [iðola'trar] /1a/ VT (*fig*) to idolize

ídolo ['iðolo] NM (*tb fig*) idol

idoneidad [iðonei'ðað] NF suitability; (*capacidad*) aptitude

idóneo, -a [i'ðoneo, a] ADJ suitable

I.E.S. NM ABR = **Instituto de Enseñanza Secundaria**

iglesia [i'ɣlesja] NF church; **~ parroquial** parish church; **¡con la ~ hemos topado!** now we're really up against it!

iglú [i'ɣlu] NM igloo; (*contenedor*) bottle bank

IGME NM ABR = **Instituto Geográfico y Minero**

ignición [iɣni'θjon] NF ignition

ignominia [iɣno'minja] NF ignominy

ignominioso, -a [iɣnomi'njoso, a] ADJ ignominious

ignorado, -a [iɣno'raðo, a] ADJ unknown; (*dato*) obscure

ignorancia [iɣno'ranθja] NF ignorance; **por ~** through ignorance

ignorante [iɣno'rante] ADJ ignorant, uninformed ▶ NMF ignoramus

ignorar [iɣno'rar] /1a/ VT not to know, be ignorant of; (*no hacer caso a*) to ignore; **ignoramos su paradero** we don't know his whereabouts

ignoto, -a [iɣ'noto, a] ADJ unknown

igual [i'ɣwal] ADJ equal; (*similar*) like, similar; (*mismo*) (the) same; (*constante*) constant; (*temperatura*) even ▶ NMF, CONJ equal; **al ~ que** *prep* like, just like; **~ que** the same as; **sin ~** peerless; **me da o es ~** I don't care, it makes no difference; **no tener ~** to be unrivalled; **son iguales** they're the same

iguala [i'ɣwala] NF equalization; (*Com*) agreement

igualada [iɣwa'laða] NF equalizer

igualar [iɣwa'lar] /**1a**/ VT (*gen*) to equalize, make equal; (*terreno*) to make even; (*allanar, nivelar*) to level (off); (*Com*) to agree upon; **igualarse** VR (*platos de balanza*) to balance out; **igualarse (a)** (*equivaler*) to be equal (to)

igualdad [iɣwal'dað] NF equality; (*similaridad*) sameness; (*uniformidad*) uniformity; **en ~ de condiciones** on an equal basis

igualmente [iɣwal'mente] ADV equally; (*también*) also, likewise ▶ EXCL the same to you!

iguana [i'ɣwana] NF iguana

ikurriña [iku'rriɲa] NF Basque flag

ilegal [ile'ɣal] ADJ illegal

ilegitimidad [ilexitimi'ðað] NF illegitimacy

ilegítimo, -a [ile'xitimo, a] ADJ illegitimate

ileso, -a [i'leso, a] ADJ unhurt, unharmed

ilícito, -a [i'liθito, a] ADJ illicit

ilimitado, -a [ilimi'taðo, a] ADJ unlimited

Ilma., Ilmo. ABR (= *Ilustrísima, Ilustrísimo*) *courtesy title*

ilógico, -a [i'loxiko, a] ADJ illogical

iluminación [ilumina'θjon] NF illumination; (*alumbrado*) lighting; (*fig*) enlightenment

iluminar [ilumi'nar] /**1a**/ VT to illuminate, light (up); (*fig*) to enlighten

ilusión [ilu'sjon] NF illusion; (*quimera*) delusion; (*esperanza*) hope; (*emoción*) excitement, thrill; **hacerse ilusiones** to build up one's hopes; **no te hagas ilusiones** don't build up your hopes o get too excited

ilusionado, -a [ilusjo'naðo, a] ADJ excited

ilusionar [ilusjo'nar] /**1a**/ VT: **~ a algn** (*falsamente*) to build up sb's hopes ▶ VI: **le ilusiona ir de vacaciones** he's looking forward to going on holiday; **ilusionarse** VR (*falsamente*) to build up one's hopes; (*entusiasmarse*) to get excited; **me ilusiona mucho el viaje** I'm really excited about the trip

ilusionista [ilusjo'nista] NMF conjurer

iluso, -a [i'luso, a] ADJ gullible, easily deceived ▶ NM/F dreamer, visionary

ilusorio, -a [ilu'sorjo, a] ADJ (*de ilusión*) illusory, deceptive; (*esperanza*) vain

ilustración [ilustra'θjon] NF illustration; (*saber*) learning, erudition; **la I~** the Enlightenment

ilustrado, -a [ilus'traðo, a] ADJ illustrated; learned

ilustrar [ilus'trar] /**1a**/ VT to illustrate; (*instruir*) to instruct; (*explicar*) to explain, make clear; **ilustrarse** VR to acquire knowledge

ilustre [i'lustre] ADJ famous, illustrious

imagen [i'maxen] NF (*gen*) image; (*dibujo, TV*) picture; (*Rel*) statue; **ser la viva ~ de** to be the spitting o living image of; **a su ~** in one's own image

imaginación [imaxina'θjon] NF imagination; (*fig*) fancy; **ni por ~** on no account; **no se me pasó por la ~ que ...** it never even occurred to me that ...

imaginar [imaxi'nar] /**1a**/ VT (*gen*) to imagine; (*idear*) to think up; (*suponer*) to suppose; **imaginarse** VR to imagine; **¡imagínate!** just imagine!, just fancy!; **imagínese que ...** suppose that ...; **me imagino que sí** I should think so

imaginario, -a [imaxi'narjo, a] ADJ imaginary

imaginativo, -a [imaxina'tiβo, a] ADJ imaginative ▶ NF imagination

imán [i'man] NM magnet

imanar [ima'nar] /**1a**/, **imantar** [ima'ntar] /**1a**/ VT to magnetize

imbécil [im'beθil] NMF imbecile, idiot

imbecilidad [imbeθili'ðað] NF imbecility, stupidity

imberbe [im'berβe] ADJ beardless

imborrable [imbo'rraβle] ADJ indelible; (*inolvidable*) unforgettable

imbuir [imbu'ir] /**3g**/ VI to imbue

imbuyendo *etc* [imbu'jendo] VB *ver* **imbuir**

imitación [imita'θjon] NF imitation; (*parodia*) mimicry; **a ~ de** in imitation of; **desconfíe de las imitaciones** (*Com*) beware of copies o imitations

imitador, a [imita'ðor, a] ADJ imitative ▶ NM/F imitator; (*Teat*) mimic

imitar [imi'tar] /**1a**/ VT to imitate; (*parodiar, remedar*) to mimic, ape; (*copiar*) to follow

impaciencia [impa'θjenθja] NF impatience

impacientar [impaθjen'tar] /**1a**/ VT to make impatient; (*enfadar*) to irritate; **impacientarse** VR to get impatient; (*inquietarse*) to fret

impaciente [impa'θjente] ADJ impatient; (*nervioso*) anxious

impacto [im'pakto] NM impact; (*esp Am fig*) shock

impagado, -a [impa'ɣaðo, a] ADJ unpaid, still to be paid

impar [im'par] ADJ odd ▶ NM odd number

imparable [impa'raβle] ADJ unstoppable
imparcial [impar'θjal] ADJ impartial, fair
imparcialidad [imparθjali'ðað] NF impartiality, fairness
impartir [impar'tir] /3a/ VT to impart, give
impasible [impa'siβle] ADJ impassive
impávido, -a [im'paβiðo, a] ADJ fearless, intrepid
IMPE ['impe] NM ABR (Esp, Com) = **Instituto de la Mediana y Pequeña Empresa**
impecable [impe'kaβle] ADJ impeccable
impedido, -a [impe'ðiðo, a] ADJ: **estar ~** to be an invalid ▶ NM/F: **ser un ~ físico** to be an invalid
impedimento [impeði'mento] NM impediment, obstacle
impedir [impe'ðir] /3k/ VT (obstruir) to impede, obstruct; (estorbar) to prevent; **~ a algn hacer** o **que algn haga algo** to prevent sb (from) doing sth; **~ el tráfico** to block the traffic
impeler [impe'ler] /2a/ VT to drive, propel; (fig) to impel
impenetrabilidad [impenetraβili'ðað] NF impenetrability
impenetrable [impene'traβle] ADJ impenetrable; (fig) incomprehensible
impensable [impen'saβle] ADJ unthinkable
impepinable [impepi'naβle] ADJ (fam) certain, inevitable
imperante [impe'rante] ADJ prevailing
imperar [impe'rar] /1a/ VI (reinar) to rule, reign; (fig) to prevail, reign; (precio) to be current
imperativo, -a [impera'tiβo, a] ADJ (persona) imperious; (urgente, Ling) imperative
imperceptible [imperθep'tiβle] ADJ imperceptible
imperdible [imper'ðiβle] NM safety pin
imperdonable [imperðo'naβle] ADJ unforgivable, inexcusable
imperecedero, -a [impereθe'ðero, a] ADJ undying
imperfección [imperfek'θjon] NF imperfection; (falla) flaw, fault
imperfecto, -a [imper'fekto, a] ADJ faulty, imperfect ▶ NM (Ling) imperfect tense
imperial [impe'rjal] ADJ imperial
imperialismo [imperja'lismo] NM imperialism
imperialista [imperja'lista] ADJ imperialist(ic) ▶ NMF imperialist
impericia [impe'riθja] NF (torpeza) unskilfulness; (inexperiencia) inexperience
imperio [im'perjo] NM empire; (autoridad) rule, authority; (fig) pride, haughtiness; **vale un ~** (fig) it's worth a fortune
imperioso, -a [impe'rjoso, a] ADJ imperious; (urgente) urgent; (imperativo) imperative

impermeable [imperme'aβle] ADJ (a prueba de agua) waterproof ▶ NM raincoat, mac (BRIT)
impersonal [imperso'nal] ADJ impersonal
impertérrito, -a [imper'territo, a] ADJ undaunted
impertinencia [imperti'nenθja] NF impertinence
impertinente [imperti'nente] ADJ impertinent
imperturbable [impertur'βaβle] ADJ imperturbable; (sereno) unruffled; (impasible) impassive
ímpetu ['impetu] NM (impulso) impetus, impulse; (impetuosidad) impetuosity; (violencia) violence
impetuosidad [impetwosi'ðað] NF impetuousness; (violencia) violence
impetuoso, -a [impe'twoso, a] ADJ impetuous; (río) rushing; (acto) hasty
impida etc [im'piða] VB ver **impedir**
impío, -a [im'pio, a] ADJ impious, ungodly; (cruel) cruel, pitiless
implacable [impla'kaβle] ADJ implacable, relentless
implantación [implanta'θjon] NF introduction; (Bio) implantation
implantar [implan'tar] /1a/ VT (costumbre) to introduce; (Bio) to implant; **implantarse** VR to be introduced
implemento [imple'mento] NM (Am) tool, implement
implicar [impli'kar] /1g/ VT to involve; (entrañar) to imply; **esto no implica que ...** this does not mean that ...
implícito, -a [im'pliθito, a] ADJ (tácito) implicit; (sobreentendido) implied
implique etc [im'plike] VB ver **implicar**
implorar [implo'rar] /1a/ VT to beg, implore
impondré etc [impon'dre] VB ver **imponer**
imponente [impo'nente] ADJ (impresionante) impressive, imposing; (solemne) grand ▶ NMF (Com) depositor
imponer [impo'ner] /2q/ VT (gen) to impose; (tarea) to set; (exigir) to exact; (miedo) to inspire; (Com) to deposit; **imponerse** VR to assert o.s.; (prevalecer) to prevail; (costumbre) to grow up; **imponerse un deber** to assume a duty
imponga etc [im'ponga] VB ver **imponer**
imponible [impo'niβle] ADJ (Com) taxable, subject to tax; (importación) dutiable, subject to duty; **no ~** tax-free, tax-exempt (US)
impopular [impopu'lar] ADJ unpopular
importación [importa'θjon] NF (acto) importing; (mercancías) imports pl
importancia [impor'tanθja] NF importance; (valor) value, significance; (extensión) size, magnitude; **no dar ~ a** to consider unimportant; (fig) to make light of; **no tiene ~** it's nothing

importante [impor'tante] ADJ important; valuable, significant

importar [impor'tar] /1a/ VT (del extranjero) to import; (costar) to amount to; (implicar) to involve ▶ VI to be important, matter; **me importa un rábano** or **un bledo** I couldn't care less, I don't give a damn; **¿le importa que fume?** do you mind if I smoke?; **¿te importa prestármelo?** would you mind lending it to me?; **¿qué importa?** what difference does it make?; **no importa** it doesn't matter; **no le importa** he doesn't care, it doesn't bother him; **"no importa precio"** "cost no object"

importe [im'porte] NM (cantidad) amount; (valor) value

importunar [importu'nar] /1a/ VT to bother, pester

importuno, -a [impor'tuno, a] ADJ (inoportuno, molesto) inopportune; (indiscreto) troublesome

imposibilidad [imposiβili'ðað] NF impossibility; **mi ~ para hacerlo** my inability to do it

imposibilitado, -a [imposiβili'taðo, a] ADJ: **verse ~ para hacer algo** to be unable to do sth

imposibilitar [imposiβili'tar] /1a/ VT to make impossible, prevent

imposible [impo'siβle] ADJ impossible; (insoportable) unbearable, intolerable; **es ~** it's out of the question; **es ~ de predecir** it's impossible to forecast o predict

imposición [imposi'θjon] NF imposition; (Com) tax; (inversión) deposit; **efectuar una ~** to make a deposit

impostor, a [impos'tor, a] NM/F impostor

impostura [impos'tura] NF fraud, imposture

impotencia [impo'tenθja] NF impotence

impotente [impo'tente] ADJ impotent

impracticable [imprakti'kaβle] ADJ (irrealizable) impracticable; (intransitable) impassable

imprecar [impre'kar] /1g/ VI to curse

imprecisión [impreθi'sjon] NF lack of precision, vagueness

impreciso, -a [impre'θiso, a] ADJ imprecise, vague

impredecible [impreðe'θiβle], **impredictible** [impreðik'tiβle] ADJ unpredictable

impregnar [impreɣ'nar] /1a/ VT to impregnate; (fig) to pervade; **impregnarse** VR to become impregnated

imprenta [im'prenta] NF (acto) printing; (aparato) press; (casa) printer's; (letra) print

impreque etc [im'preke] VB ver **imprecar**

imprescindible [impresθin'diβle] ADJ essential, vital

impresión [impre'sjon] NF impression; (Imprenta) printing; (edición) edition; (Foto) print; (marca) imprint; **~ digital** fingerprint

impresionable [impresjo'naβle] ADJ (sensible) impressionable

impresionado, -a [impresjo'naðo, a] ADJ impressed; (Foto) exposed

impresionante [impresjo'nante] ADJ impressive; (tremendo) tremendous; (maravilloso) great, marvellous

impresionar [impresjo'nar] /1a/ VT (conmover) to move; (afectar) to impress, strike; (película fotográfica) to expose; **impresionarse** VR to be impressed; (conmoverse) to be moved

impresionista [impresjo'nista] ADJ impressionist(ic); (Arte) impressionist ▶ NMF impressionist

impreso, -a [im'preso, a] PP de **imprimir** ▶ ADJ printed ▶ NM printed paper/book etc; **impresos** NMPL printed matter sg; **~ de solicitud** application form

impresora [impre'sora] NF (Inform) printer; **~ de chorro de tinta** ink-jet printer; **~ (por) láser** laser printer; **~ de línea** line printer; **~ de matriz (de agujas)** dot-matrix printer; **~ de rueda** o **de margarita** daisy-wheel printer

imprevisible [impreβi'siβle] ADJ unforeseeable; (individuo) unpredictable

imprevisión [impreβi'sjon] NF short-sightedness; (irreflexión) thoughtlessness

imprevisto, -a [impre'βisto, a] ADJ unforeseen; (inesperado) unexpected ▶ NM: **imprevistos** (dinero) incidentals, unforeseen expenses

imprimir [impri'mir] /3a/ VT to stamp; (textos) to print; (Inform) to output, print out

improbabilidad [improβaβili'ðað] NF improbability, unlikelihood

improbable [impro'βaβle] ADJ improbable; (inverosímil) unlikely

improcedente [improθe'ðente] ADJ inappropriate; (Jur) inadmissible

improductivo, -a [improðuk'tiβo, a] ADJ unproductive

impronunciable [impronun'θjaβle] ADJ unpronounceable

improperio [impro'perjo] NM insult; **improperios** NMPL abuse sg

impropiedad [impropje'ðað] NF impropriety (of language)

impropio, -a [im'propjo, a] ADJ improper; (inadecuado) inappropriate

improvisación [improβisa'θjon] NF improvisation

improvisado, -a [improβi'saðo, a] ADJ improvised, impromptu

improvisar [improβi'sar] /**1a**/ VT to improvise; (*comida*) to rustle up ▶ VI to improvise; (*Mus*) to extemporize; (*Teat etc*) to ad-lib

improviso [impro'βiso] ADV: **de ~** unexpectedly, suddenly; (*Mus etc*) impromptu

imprudencia [impru'ðenθja] NF imprudence; (*indiscreción*) indiscretion; (*descuido*) carelessness

imprudente [impru'ðente] ADJ unwise, imprudent; (*indiscreto*) indiscreet

Impte. ABR (= *Importe*) amt.

impúdico, -a [im'puðiko, a] ADJ shameless; (*lujurioso*) lecherous

impudor [impu'ðor] NM shamelessness; (*lujuria*) lechery

impuesto, -a [im'pwesto, a] PP *de* **imponer** ▶ ADJ imposed ▶ NM tax; **anterior al ~** pre-tax; **sujeto a ~** taxable; **~ ambiental** green tax, environmental tax; **~ de lujo** luxury tax; **~ de plusvalía** capital gains tax; **~ sobre la propiedad** property tax; **~ sobre la renta** income tax; **~ sobre la renta de las personas físicas (IRPF)** personal income tax; **~ sobre la riqueza** wealth tax; **~ de transferencia de capital** capital transfer tax; **~ de venta** sales tax; **~ sobre el valor añadido (IVA)** value added tax (VAT)

impugnar [impuɣ'nar] /**1a**/ VT to oppose, contest; (*refutar*) to refute, impugn

impulsar [impul'sar] /**1a**/ VT to drive; (*promover*) to promote, stimulate

impulsivo, -a [impul'siβo, a] ADJ impulsive

impulso [im'pulso] NM impulse; (*fuerza, empuje*) thrust, drive; (*fig: sentimiento*) urge, impulse; **a impulsos del miedo** driven on by fear

impune [im'pune] ADJ unpunished

impunemente [impune'mente] ADV with impunity

impureza [impu'reθa] NF impurity; (*fig*) lewdness

impuro, -a [im'puro, a] ADJ impure; lewd

impuse *etc* [im'puse] VB *ver* **imponer**

imputación [imputa'θjon] NF imputation

imputar [impu'tar] /**1a**/ VT: **~ a** to attribute to, impute to

inabordable [inaβor'ðaβle] ADJ unapproachable

inacabable [inaka'βaβle] ADJ (*infinito*) endless; (*interminable*) interminable

inaccesible [inakθe'siβle] ADJ inaccessible; (*fig: precio*) beyond one's reach, prohibitive; (*individuo*) aloof

inacción [inak'θjon] NF inactivity

inaceptable [inaθep'taβle] ADJ unacceptable

inactividad [inaktiβi'ðað] NF inactivity; (*Com*) dullness

inactivo, -a [inak'tiβo, a] ADJ inactive; (*Com*) dull; (*población*) non-working

inadaptación [inaðapta'θjon] NF maladjustment

inadaptado, -a [inaðap'taðo, a] ADJ maladjusted ▶ NM/F misfit

inadecuado, -a [inaðe'kwaðo, a] ADJ (*insuficiente*) inadequate; (*inapto*) unsuitable

inadmisible [inaðmi'siβle] ADJ inadmissible

inadvertido, -a [inaðβer'tiðo, a] ADJ (*no visto*) unnoticed

inagotable [inaɣo'taβle] ADJ inexhaustible

inaguantable [inaɣwan'taβle] ADJ unbearable

inalámbrico, -a [ina'lambriko, a] ADJ cordless, wireless

inalcanzable [inalkan'θaβle] ADJ unattainable

inalterable [inalte'raβle] ADJ immutable, unchangeable

inamovible [inamo'βiβle] ADJ fixed, immovable; (*Tec*) undetachable

inanición [inani'θjon] NF starvation

inanimado, -a [inani'maðo, a] ADJ inanimate

inapelable [inape'laβle] ADJ (*Jur*) unappealable; (*fig*) irremediable

inapetencia [inape'tenθja] NF lack of appetite

inaplicable [inapli'kaβle] ADJ not applicable

inapreciable [inapre'θjaβle] ADJ invaluable

inarrugable [inarru'ɣaβle] ADJ crease-resistant

inasequible [inase'kiβle] ADJ unattainable

inaudito, -a [inau'ðito, a] ADJ unheard-of

inauguración [inauɣura'θjon] NF inauguration; (*de exposición*) opening

inaugurar [inauɣu'rar] /**1a**/ VT to inaugurate; (*exposición*) to open

I.N.B.A. ABR (*Am*) = **Instituto Nacional de Bellas Artes**

inca ['inka] NMF Inca

INCAE [in'kae] NM ABR = **Instituto Centroamericano de Administración de Empresas**

incaico, -a [in'kaiko, a] ADJ Inca

incalculable [inkalku'laβle] ADJ incalculable

incandescente [inkandes'θente] ADJ incandescent

incansable [inkan'saβle] ADJ tireless, untiring

incapacidad [inkapaθi'ðað] NF incapacity; (*incompetencia*) incompetence; **~ física/mental** physical/mental disability

incapacitar [inkapaθi'tar] /**1a**/ VT (*inhabilitar*) to incapacitate, handicap; (*descalificar*) to disqualify

incapaz [inka'paθ] ADJ incapable; **~ de hacer algo** unable to do sth

incautación [inkauta'θjon] NF seizure, confiscation

incautarse – incondicional

incautarse [inkau'tarse] /**1a**/ VR: **~ de** to seize, confiscate

incauto, -a [in'kauto, a] ADJ (*imprudente*) incautious, unwary

incendiar [inθen'djar] /**1b**/ VT to set fire to; (*fig*) to inflame; **incendiarse** VR to catch fire

incendiario, -a [inθen'djarjo, a] ADJ incendiary ▶ NM/F fire-raiser, arsonist

incendio [in'θendjo] NM fire; **~ intencionado** arson

incentivo [inθen'tiβo] NM incentive

incertidumbre [inθerti'ðumbre] NF (*inseguridad*) uncertainty; (*duda*) doubt

incesante [inθe'sante] ADJ incessant

incesto [in'θesto] NM incest

incidencia [inθi'ðenθja] NF (*Mat*) incidence; (*fig*) effect

incidente [inθi'ðente] NM incident

incidir [inθi'ðir] /**3a**/ VI: **~ en** (*influir*) to influence; (*afectar*) to affect; **~ en un error** to be mistaken

incienso [in'θjenso] NM incense

incierto, -a [in'θjerto, a] ADJ uncertain

incineración [inθinera'θjon] NF incineration; (*de cadáveres*) cremation

incinerar [inθine'rar] /**1a**/ VT to burn; (*cadáveres*) to cremate

incipiente [inθi'pjente] ADJ incipient

incisión [inθi'sjon] NF incision

incisivo, -a [inθi'siβo, a] ADJ sharp, cutting; (*fig*) incisive

inciso [in'θiso] NM (*Ling*) clause, sentence; (*coma*) comma; (*Jur*) subsection

incitante [inθi'tante] ADJ (*estimulante*) exciting; (*provocativo*) provocative

incitar [inθi'tar] /**1a**/ VT to incite, rouse

incivil [inθi'βil] ADJ rude, uncivil

inclemencia [inkle'menθja] NF (*severidad*) harshness, severity; (*del tiempo*) inclemency

inclemente [inkle'mente] ADJ harsh, severe; inclement

inclinación [inklina'θjon] NF (*gen*) inclination; (*de tierras*) slope, incline; (*de cabeza*) nod, bow; (*fig*) leaning, bent

inclinado, -a [inkli'naðo, a] ADJ (*objeto*) leaning; (*superficie*) sloping

inclinar [inkli'nar] /**1a**/ VT to incline; (*cabeza*) to nod, bow; **inclinarse** VR to lean, slope; (*en reverencia*) to bow; (*encorvarse*) to stoop; **inclinarse a** (*parecerse*) to take after, resemble; **inclinarse ante** to bow down to; **me inclino a pensar que ...** I'm inclined to think that ...

incluir [inklu'ir] /**3g**/ VT to include; (*incorporar*) to incorporate; (*meter*) to enclose; **todo incluido** (*Com*) inclusive, all-in

inclusive [inklu'siβe] ADV inclusive ▶ PREP including

incluso, -a [in'kluso, a] ADJ included ▶ ADV inclusively; (*hasta*) even

incluyendo *etc* [inklu'jendo] VB *ver* **incluir**

incobrable [inko'βraβle] ADJ irrecoverable; (*deuda*) bad

incógnita [in'koɣnita] NF (*Mat*) unknown quantity; (*fig*) mystery

incógnito [in'koɣnito] NM: **de ~** incognito

incoherencia [inkoe'renθja] NF incoherence; (*falta de conexión*) disconnectedness

incoherente [inkoe'rente] ADJ incoherent

incoloro, -a [inko'loro, a] ADJ colourless

incólume [in'kolume] ADJ safe; (*indemne*) unhurt, unharmed

incombustible [inkombus'tiβle] ADJ (*gen*) fire-resistant; (*telas*) fireproof

incomodar [inkomo'ðar] /**1a**/ VT to inconvenience; (*molestar*) to bother, trouble; (*fastidiar*) to annoy; **incomodarse** VR to put o.s. out; (*fastidiarse*) to get annoyed; **no se incomode** don't bother

incomodidad [inkomoði'ðað] NF inconvenience; (*fastidio, enojo*) annoyance; (*de vivienda*) discomfort

incómodo, -a [in'komoðo, a] ADJ (*inconfortable*) uncomfortable; (*molesto*) annoying; (*inconveniente*) inconvenient; **sentirse ~** to feel ill at ease

incomparable [inkompa'raβle] ADJ incomparable

incomparecencia [inkompare'θenθja] NF (*Jur etc*) failure to appear

incompatible [inkompa'tiβle] ADJ incompatible

incompetencia [inkompe'tenθja] NF incompetence

incompetente [inkompe'tente] ADJ incompetent

incompleto, -a [inkom'pleto, a] ADJ incomplete, unfinished

incomprendido, -a [inkompren'diðo, a] ADJ misunderstood

incomprensible [inkompren'siβle] ADJ incomprehensible

incomunicado, -a [inkomuni'kaðo, a] ADJ (*aislado*) cut off, isolated; (*confinado*) in solitary confinement

incomunicar [inkomuni'kar] /**1g**/ VT (*gen*) to cut off; (*preso*) to put into solitary confinement; **incomunicarse** VR (*fam*) to go into one's shell

incomunique *etc* [inkomu'nike] VB *ver* **incomunicar**

inconcebible [inkonθe'βiβle] ADJ inconceivable

inconcluso, -a [inkon'kluso, a] ADJ (*inacabado*) unfinished

incondicional [inkondiθjo'nal] ADJ unconditional; (*apoyo*) wholehearted; (*partidario*) staunch

inconexo, -a [inko'nekso, a] ADJ unconnected; (*desunido*) disconnected; (*incoherente*) incoherent

inconfeso, -a [inkon'feso, a] ADJ unconfessed; **un homosexual ~** a closet homosexual

inconformista [inkonfor'mista] ADJ, NMF nonconformist

inconfundible [inkonfun'diβle] ADJ unmistakable

incongruente [inkon'grwente] ADJ incongruous

inconmensurable [inkonmensu'raβle] ADJ immeasurable, vast

inconsciencia [inkons'θjenθja] NF unconsciousness; (*fig*) thoughtlessness

inconsciente [inkons'θjente] ADJ unconscious; thoughtless; (*ignorante*) unaware; (*involuntario*) unwitting

inconsecuencia [inkonse'kwenθja] NF inconsistency

inconsecuente [inkonse'kwente] ADJ inconsistent

inconsiderado, -a [inkonsiðe'raðo, a] ADJ inconsiderate

inconsistente [inkonsis'tente] ADJ inconsistent; (*Culin*) lumpy; (*endeble*) weak; (*tela*) flimsy

inconstancia [inkons'tanθja] NF inconstancy; (*de tiempo*) changeability; (*capricho*) fickleness

inconstante [inkons'tante] ADJ inconstant; changeable; fickle

incontable [inkon'taβle] ADJ countless, innumerable

incontestable [inkontes'taβle] ADJ unanswerable; (*innegable*) undeniable

incontinencia [inkonti'nenθja] NF incontinence

incontrolado, -a [inkontro'laðo, a] ADJ uncontrolled

incontrovertible [inkontroβer'tiβle] ADJ undeniable, incontrovertible

inconveniencia [inkombe'njenθja] NF unsuitability, inappropriateness; (*falta de cortesía*) impoliteness

inconveniente [inkombe'njente] ADJ unsuitable; impolite ▶ NM obstacle; (*desventaja*) disadvantage; **el ~ es que ...** the trouble is that ...; **no hay ~ en** o **para hacer eso** there is no objection to doing that; **no tengo ~** I don't mind

incordiar [inkor'ðjar] /**1b**/ VT (*fam*) to hassle

incorporación [inkorpora'θjon] NF incorporation; (*fig*) inclusion

incorporado, -a [inkorpo'raðo, a] ADJ (*Tec*) built-in

incorporar [inkorpo'rar] /**1a**/ VT to incorporate; (*abarcar*) to embody;

(*Culin*) to mix; **incorporarse** VR to sit up; **incorporarse a** to join

incorrección [inkorrek'θjon] NF incorrectness, inaccuracy; (*descortesía*) bad-mannered behaviour

incorrecto, -a [inko'rrekto, a] ADJ incorrect, wrong; (*comportamiento*) bad-mannered

incorregible [inkorre'xiβle] ADJ incorrigible

incorruptible [inkorrup'tiβle] ADJ incorruptible

incorrupto, -a [inko'rrupto, a] ADJ uncorrupted; (*fig*) pure

incredulidad [inkreðuli'ðað] NF incredulity; (*escepticismo*) scepticism

incrédulo, -a [in'kreðulo, a] ADJ incredulous, unbelieving; sceptical

increíble [inkre'iβle] ADJ incredible

incrementar [inkremen'tar] /**1a**/ VT (*aumentar*) to increase; (*alzar*) to raise; **incrementarse** VR to increase

incremento [inkre'mento] NM increment; (*aumento*) rise, increase; **~ de precio** rise in price

increpar [inkre'par] /**1a**/ VT to reprimand

incriminar [inkrimi'nar] /**1a**/ VT (*Jur*) to incriminate

incruento, -a [in'krwento, a] ADJ bloodless

incrustar [inkrus'tar] /**1a**/ VT to incrust; (*piedras: en joya*) to inlay; (*fig*) to graft; (*Tec*) to set

incubar [inku'βar] /**1a**/ VT to incubate; (*fig*) to hatch

incuestionable [inkwestjo'naβle] ADJ unchallengeable

inculcar [inkul'kar] /**1g**/ VT to inculcate

inculpar [inkul'par] /**1a**/ VT: **~ de** (*acusar*) to accuse of; (*achacar, atribuir*) to charge with, blame for

inculque *etc* [in'kulke] VB *ver* **inculcar**

inculto, -a [in'kulto, a] ADJ (*persona*) uneducated, uncultured; (*fig: grosero*) uncouth ▶ NM/F ignoramus

incumbencia [inkum'benθja] NF obligation; **no es de mi ~** it is not my field

incumbir [inkum'bir] /**3a**/ VI: **~ a** to be incumbent upon; **no me incumbe a mí** it is no concern of mine

incumplimiento [inkumpli'mjento] NM non-fulfilment; (*Com*) repudiation; **~ de contrato** breach of contract; **por ~** by default

incurable [inku'raβle] ADJ (*enfermedad*) incurable; (*paciente*) incurably ill

incurrir [inku'rrir] /**3a**/ VI: **~ en** to incur; (*crimen*) to commit; **~ en un error** to make a mistake

indagación [indaɣa'θjon] NF investigation; (*búsqueda*) search; (*Jur*) inquest

indagar [inda'ɣar] /**1h**/ VT to investigate; to search; (*averiguar*) to ascertain

indague *etc* [in'daɣe] VB *ver* **indagar**

indebido, -a [inde'βiðo, a] ADJ undue; (*dicho*) improper

indecencia [inde'θenθja] NF indecency; (*dicho*) obscenity

indecente [inde'θente] ADJ indecent, improper; (*lascivo*) obscene

indecible [inde'θiβle] ADJ unspeakable; (*indescriptible*) indescribable

indeciso, -a [inde'θiso, a] ADJ (*por decidir*) undecided; (*vacilante*) hesitant

indefenso, -a [inde'fenso, a] ADJ defenceless

indefinido, -a [indefi'niðo, a] ADJ indefinite; (*vago*) vague, undefined

indeleble [inde'leβle] ADJ indelible

indemne [in'demne] ADJ (*objeto*) undamaged; (*persona*) unharmed, unhurt

indemnice *etc* [indem'niθe] VB *ver* **indemnizar**

indemnización [indemniθa'θjon] NF (*acto*) indemnification; (*suma*) indemnity; **~ por cese** redundancy payment; **~ por despido** severance pay; **doble ~** double indemnity

indemnizar [indemni'θar] /**1f**/ VT to indemnify; (*compensar*) to compensate

independencia [indepen'denθja] NF independence

independice *etc* [indepen'diθe] VB *ver* **independizar**

independiente [indepen'djente] ADJ (*libre*) independent; (*autónomo*) self-sufficient; (*Inform*) stand-alone

independizar [independi'θar] /**1f**/ VT to make independent; **independizarse** VR to become independent

indescifrable [indesθi'fraβle] ADJ (*Mil*: *código*) indecipherable; (*fig*: *misterio*) impenetrable

indeseable [indese'aβle] ADJ, NMF undesirable

indeterminado, -a [indetermi'naðo, a] ADJ (*tb Ling*) indefinite; (*desconocido*) indeterminate

India ['indja] NF: **la ~** India

indiano, -a [in'djano, a] ADJ (Spanish-)American ▶ NM *Spaniard who has made good in America*

indicación [indika'θjon] NF indication; (*dato*) piece of information; (*señal*) sign; (*sugerencia*) suggestion, hint; **indicaciones** NFPL (*Com*) instructions

indicado, -a [indi'kaðo, a] ADJ (*momento, método*) right; (*tratamiento*) appropriate; (*solución*) likely

indicador [indika'ðor] NM indicator; (*Tec*) gauge, meter; (*aguja*) hand, pointer; (*de carretera*) road sign; **~ de encendido** (*Inform*) power-on indicator

indicar [indi'kar] /**1g**/ VT (*mostrar*) to indicate, show; (*suj*: *termómetro etc*) to read, register; (*señalar*) to point to

indicativo, -a [indika'tiβo, a] ADJ indicative ▶ NM (*Radio*) call sign; **~ de nacionalidad** (*Auto*) national identification plate

índice ['indiθe] NM index; (*catálogo*) catalogue; (*Anat*) index finger, forefinger; **~ del coste de (la) vida** cost-of-living index; **~ de crédito** credit rating; **~ de materias** table of contents; **~ de natalidad** birth rate; **~ de precios al por menor (IPM)** (*Com*) retail price index (RPI)

indicio [in'diθjo] NM indication, sign; (*en pesquisa etc*) clue

indiferencia [indife'renθja] NF indifference; (*apatía*) apathy

indiferente [indife'rente] ADJ indifferent; **me es ~** it makes no difference to me

indígena [in'dixena] ADJ indigenous, native ▶ NMF native

indigencia [indi'xenθja] NF poverty, need

indigenista [indixe'nista] (*Am*) ADJ pro-Indian ▶ NMF (*estudiante*) student of Indian cultures; (*Pol etc*) promoter of Indian cultures

indigestar [indixes'tar] /**1a**/ VT to cause indigestion to; **indigestarse** VR to get indigestion

indigestión [indixes'tjon] NF indigestion

indigesto, -a [indi'xesto, a] ADJ undigested; (*indigerible*) indigestible; (*fig*) turgid

indignación [indiɣna'θjon] NF indignation

indignante [indiɣ'nante] ADJ outrageous, infuriating

indignar [indiɣ'nar] /**1a**/ VT to anger, make indignant; **indignarse** VR: **indignarse por** to get indignant about

indigno, -a [in'diɣno, a] ADJ (*despreciable*) low, contemptible; (*inmerecido*) unworthy

indio, -a ['indjo, a] ADJ, NM/F Indian

indique *etc* [in'dike] VB *ver* **indicar**

indirecto, -a [indi'rekto, a] ADJ indirect ▶ NF insinuation, innuendo; (*sugerencia*) hint

indisciplina [indisθi'plina] NF (*gen*) lack of discipline; (*Mil*) insubordination

indiscreción [indiskre'θjon] NF (*imprudencia*) indiscretion; (*irreflexión*) tactlessness; (*acto*) gaffe, faux pas; **..., si no es ~** ..., if I may say so

indiscreto, -a [indis'kreto, a] ADJ indiscreet

indiscriminado, -a [indiskrimi'naðo, a] ADJ indiscriminate

indiscutible [indisku'tiβle] ADJ indisputable, unquestionable

indispensable [indispen'saβle] ADJ indispensable, essential

indispondré *etc* [indispon'dre] VB *ver* **indisponer**

indisponer [indispo'ner] /**2q**/ VT to spoil, upset; (*salud*) to make ill; **indisponerse** VR to fall ill; **indisponerse con algn** to fall out with sb

indisponga *etc* [indis'ponga] VB *ver* **indisponer**
indisposición [indisposi'θjon] NF
indisposition; (*desgana*) unwillingness
indispuesto, -a [indis'pwesto, a] PP *de*
indisponer ▶ ADJ (*enfermo*) unwell,
indisposed; **sentirse ~** to feel unwell *o*
indisposed
indispuse *etc* [indis'puse] VB *ver* **indisponer**
indistinto, -a [indis'tinto, a] ADJ indistinct;
(*vago*) vague
individual [indiβi'ðwal] ADJ individual;
(*habitación*) single ▶ NM (*Deporte*) singles *sg*
individuo, -a [indi'βiðwo, a] ADJ individual
▶ NM individual
Indochina [indo'tʃina] NF Indochina
indocumentado, -a [indokumen'taðo, a] ADJ
without identity papers
indoeuropeo, -a [indoeuro'peo, a] ADJ, NM/F
Indo-European
índole ['indole] NF (*naturaleza*) nature; (*clase*)
sort, kind
indolencia [indo'lenθja] NF indolence,
laziness
indoloro, -a [in'doloro, a] ADJ painless
indomable [indo'maβle] ADJ (*animal*)
untameable; (*espíritu*) indomitable
indómito, -a [in'domito, a] ADJ indomitable
Indonesia [indo'nesja] NF Indonesia
indonesio, -a [indo'nesjo, a] ADJ, NM/F
Indonesian
inducción [induk'θjon] NF (*Filosofía, Elec*)
induction; **por ~** by induction
inducir [indu'θir] /**3n**/ VT to induce; (*inferir*) to
infer; (*persuadir*) to persuade; **~ a algn en el
error** to mislead sb
indudable [indu'ðaβle] ADJ undoubted;
(*incuestionable*) unquestionable; **es ~ que ...**
there is no doubt that ...
indulgencia [indul'xenθja] NF indulgence;
(*Jur etc*) leniency; **proceder sin ~ contra** to
proceed ruthlessly against
indultar [indul'tar] /**1a**/ VT (*perdonar*) to
pardon, reprieve; (*librar de pago*) to exempt
indulto [in'dulto] NM pardon; exemption
indumentaria [indumen'tarja] NF (*ropa*)
clothing, dress
industria [in'dustrja] NF industry; (*habilidad*)
skill; **~ agropecuaria** farming and fishing;
~ pesada heavy industry; **~ petrolífera** oil
industry
industrial [indus'trjal] ADJ industrial ▶ NMF
industrialist
industrializar [industrjali'θar] /**1f**/ VT to
industrialize; **industrializarse** VR to become
industrialized
INE ['ine] NM ABR (*ESP*) = **Instituto Nacional
de Estadística**
inédito, -a [i'neðito, a] ADJ (*libro*)
unpublished; (*nuevo*) new

inefable [ine'faβle] ADJ ineffable,
indescribable
ineficacia [inefi'kaθja] NF (*de medida*)
ineffectiveness; (*de proceso*) inefficiency
ineficaz [inefi'kaθ] ADJ (*inútil*) ineffective;
(*ineficiente*) inefficient
ineludible [inelu'ðiβle] ADJ inescapable,
unavoidable
INEM [i'nem] NM ABR (*ESP*: = *Instituto Nacional
de Empleo*) ≈ Department of Employment
(*BRIT*)
INEN [i'nen] NM ABR (*MÉXICO*) = **Instituto
Nacional de Energía Nuclear**
inenarrable [inena'rraβle] ADJ inexpressible
ineptitud [inepti'tuð] NF ineptitude,
incompetence
inepto, -a [i'nepto, a] ADJ inept, incompetent
inequívoco, -a [ine'kiβoko, a] ADJ
unequivocal; (*inconfundible*) unmistakable
inercia [i'nerθja] NF inertia; (*pasividad*)
passivity
inerme [i'nerme] ADJ (*sin armas*) unarmed;
(*indefenso*) defenceless
inerte [i'nerte] ADJ inert; (*inmóvil*) motionless
inescrutable [ineskru'taβle] ADJ inscrutable
inesperado, -a [inespe'raðo, a] ADJ
unexpected, unforeseen
inestable [ines'taβle] ADJ unstable
inestimable [inesti'maβle] ADJ inestimable;
de valor ~ invaluable
inevitable [ineβi'taβle] ADJ inevitable
inexactitud [ineksakti'tuð] NF inaccuracy
inexacto, -a [inek'sakto, a] ADJ inaccurate;
(*falso*) untrue
inexistente [ineksis'tente] ADJ non-existent
inexorable [inekso'raβle] ADJ inexorable
inexperiencia [inekspe'rjenθja] NF
inexperience, lack of experience
inexperto, -a [ineks'perto, a] ADJ (*novato*)
inexperienced
inexplicable [inekspli'kaβle] ADJ
inexplicable
inexpresable [inekspre'saβle] ADJ
inexpressible
inexpresivo, -a [inekspre'siβo, a] ADJ
inexpressive; (*ojos*) dull; (*cara*) wooden
inexpugnable [inekspuɣ'naβle] ADJ (*Mil*)
impregnable; (*fig*) firm
infalible [infa'liβle] ADJ infallible;
(*indefectible*) certain, sure; (*plan*) foolproof
infame [in'fame] ADJ infamous
infamia [in'famja] NF infamy; (*deshonra*)
disgrace
infancia [in'fanθja] NF infancy, childhood;
jardín de ~ nursery school
infanta [in'fanta] NF (*hija del rey*) infanta,
princess
infante [in'fante] NM (*hijo del rey*) infante,
prince

infantería [infante'ria] NF infantry

infantil [infan'til] ADJ child's, children's; *(pueril, aniñado)* infantile; *(cándido)* childlike

infarto [in'farto] NM *(tb:* **infarto de miocardio***)* heart attack; ~ **cerebral** stroke

infatigable [infati'ɣaβle] ADJ tireless, untiring

infección [infek'θjon] NF infection

infeccioso, -a [infek'θjoso, a] ADJ infectious

infectar [infek'tar] /1a/ VT to infect; **infectarse** VR: **infectarse (de)** *(tb fig)* to become infected (with)

infecundidad [infekundi'ðað] NF *(de tierra)* infertility, barrenness; *(de mujer)* sterility

infecundo, -a [infe'kundo, a] ADJ infertile, barren; sterile

infeliz [infe'liθ] ADJ *(desgraciado)* unhappy, wretched; *(inocente)* gullible ▶ NMF *(desgraciado)* wretch; *(inocentón)* simpleton

inferior [infe'rjor] ADJ inferior; *(situación, Mat)* lower ▶ NMF inferior, subordinate; **cualquier número ~ a nueve** any number less than o under o below nine; **una cantidad ~** a lesser quantity

inferioridad [inferjori'ðað] NF inferiority; **estar en ~ de condiciones** to be at a disadvantage

inferir [infe'rir] /3i/ VT *(deducir)* to infer, deduce; *(causar)* to cause

infernal [infer'nal] ADJ infernal

infértil [in'fertil] ADJ infertile

infestar [infes'tar] /1a/ VT to infest

infidelidad [infiðeli'ðað] NF infidelity, unfaithfulness

infiel [in'fjel] ADJ unfaithful, disloyal; *(falso)* inaccurate ▶ NMF infidel, unbeliever

infiera *etc* [in'fjera] VB *ver* **inferir**

infierno [in'fjerno] NM hell; **¡vete al ~!** go to hell; **está en el quinto ~** it's at the back of beyond

infiltrar [infil'trar] /1a/ VT to infiltrate; **infiltrarse** VR to infiltrate; **infiltrarse en** to infiltrate in(to); *(persona)* to work one's way in(to)

ínfimo, -a ['infimo, a] ADJ *(vil)* vile, mean; *(más bajo)* lowest; *(peor)* worst; *(miserable)* wretched

infinidad [infini'ðað] NF infinity; *(abundancia)* great quantity; ~ **de** vast numbers of; ~ **de veces** countless times

infinitivo [infini'tiβo] NM infinitive

infinito, -a [infi'nito, a] ADJ infinite; *(fig)* boundless ▶ ADV infinitely ▶ NM infinite; *(Mat)* infinity; **hasta lo ~** ad infinitum

infiriendo *etc* [infi'rjendo] VB *ver* **inferir**

inflación [infla'θjon] NF *(hinchazón)* swelling; *(monetaria)* inflation; *(fig)* conceit

inflacionario, -a [inflaθjo'narjo, a] ADJ inflationary

inflacionismo [inflaθjo'nismo] NM *(Econ)* inflation

inflacionista [inflaθjo'nista] ADJ inflationary

inflamable [infla'maβle] ADJ flammable

inflamar [infla'mar] /1a/ VT to set on fire; *(Med, fig)* to inflame; **inflamarse** VR to catch fire; to become inflamed

inflar [in'flar] /1a/ VT *(hinchar)* to inflate, blow up; *(fig)* to exaggerate; **inflarse** VR to swell (up); *(fig)* to get conceited

inflexible [inflek'siβle] ADJ inflexible; *(fig)* unbending

infligir [infli'xir] /3c/ VT to inflict

inflija *etc* [in'flixa] VB *ver* **infligir**

influencia [influ'wenθja] NF influence

influenciar [influwen'θjar] /1b/ VT to influence

influir [influ'ir] /3g/ VT to influence ▶ VI to have influence, carry weight; ~ **en** o **sobre** to influence, affect; *(contribuir a)* to have a hand in

influjo [in'fluxo] NM influence; ~ **de capitales** *(Econ etc)* capital influx

influya *etc* VB *ver* **influir**

influyente [influ'jente] ADJ influential

información [informa'θjon] NF information; *(noticias)* news sg; *(informe)* report; *(Inform: datos)* data; *(Jur)* inquiry; **I~** *(oficina)* information desk; *(Telec)* Directory Enquiries (BRIT), Directory Assistance (US); *(mostrador)* Information Desk; **una ~** a piece of information; **abrir una ~** *(Jur)* to begin proceedings; ~ **deportiva** *(en periódico)* sports section

informal [infor'mal] ADJ informal

informante [infor'mante] NMF informant

informar [infor'mar] /1a/ VT *(gen)* to inform; *(revelar)* to reveal, make known ▶ VI *(Jur)* to plead; *(denunciar)* to inform; *(dar cuenta de)* to report on; **informarse** VR to find out; **informarse de** to inquire into

informática [infor'matika] NF *ver* **informático**

informatice *etc* [informa'tiθe] VB *ver* **informatizar**

informático, -a [infor'matiko, a] ADJ computer *cpd* ▶ NF *(Tec)* information technology; computing; *(Escol)* computer science o studies; ~ **de gestión** commercial computing

informativo, -a [informa'tiβo, a] ADJ *(libro)* informative; *(folleto)* information *cpd*; *(Radio, TV)* news *cpd* ▶ NM *(Radio, TV)* news programme

informatización [informatiθa'θjon] NF computerization

informatizar [informati'θar] /1f/ VT to computerize

215

informe [in'forme] ADJ shapeless ▶ NM report; (*dictamen*) statement; (*Mil*) briefing; (*Jur*) plea; **informes** NMPL information *sg*; (*datos*) data; ~ **anual** annual report; ~ **del juez** summing-up

infortunio [infor'tunjo] NM misfortune

infracción [infrak'θjon] NF infraction, infringement; (*Auto*) offence

infraestructura [infraestruk'tura] NF infrastructure

in fraganti [infra'ɣanti] ADV: **pillar a algn ~** to catch sb red-handed

infranqueable [infranke'aβle] ADJ impassable; (*fig*) insurmountable

infrarrojo, -a [infra'rroxo, a] ADJ infrared

infravalorar [infraβalo'rar] /**1a**/ VT to undervalue; (*Finanzas*) to underestimate

infringir [infrin'xir] /**3c**/ VT to infringe, contravene

infrinja *etc* [in'frinxa] VB *ver* **infringir**

infructuoso, -a [infruk'twoso, a] ADJ fruitless, unsuccessful

infundado, -a [infun'daðo, a] ADJ groundless, unfounded

infundir [infun'dir] /**3a**/ VT to infuse, instil; ~ **ánimo a algn** to encourage sb; ~ **miedo a algn** to intimidate sb

infusión [infu'sjon] NF infusion; ~ **de manzanilla** camomile tea

Ing. ABR (*AM*) = **ingeniero**

ingeniar [inxe'njar] /**1a**/ VT to think up, devise; **ingeniarse** VR to manage; **ingeniarse para** to manage to

ingeniería [inxenje'ria] NF engineering; ~ **genética** genetic engineering; ~ **de sistemas** (*Inform*) systems engineering

ingeniero, -a [inxe'njero, a] NM/F engineer; (*AM*) courtesy title; ~ **de sonido** sound engineer; ~ **de caminos** civil engineer

ingenio [in'xenjo] NM (*talento*) talent; (*agudeza*) wit; (*habilidad*) ingenuity, inventiveness; (*Tec*): ~ **azucarero** sugar refinery

ingenioso, -a [inxe'njoso, a] ADJ ingenious, clever; (*divertido*) witty

ingente [in'xente] ADJ huge, enormous

ingenuidad [inxenwi'ðað] NF ingenuousness; (*sencillez*) simplicity

ingenuo, -a [in'xenwo, a] ADJ ingenuous

ingerir [inxe'rir] /**3i**/ VT to ingest; (*tragar*) to swallow; (*consumir*) to consume

ingiera *etc* [in'xjera], **ingiriendo** *etc* [inxi'rjenðo] VB *ver* **ingerir**

Inglaterra [ingla'terra] NF England

ingle ['ingle] NF groin

inglés, -esa [in'gles, esa] ADJ English ▶ NM/F Englishman(-woman) ▶ NM (*Ling*) English; **los ingleses** the English

ingratitud [ingrati'tuð] NF ingratitude

ingrato, -a [in'grato, a] ADJ ungrateful; (*tarea*) thankless

ingravidez [ingraβi'ðeθ] NF weightlessness

ingrediente [ingre'ðjente] NM ingredient; **ingredientes** NMPL (*AM*: *tapas*) titbits

ingresar [ingre'sar] /**1a**/ VT (*dinero*) to deposit ▶ VI to come o go in; ~ **a** (*esp AM*) to enter; ~ **en** (*club*) to join; (*Mil, Escol*) to enrol in; ~ **en el hospital** to go into hospital

ingreso [in'greso] NM (*entrada*) entry; (: *en hospital etc*) admission; (*Mil, Escol*) enrolment; **ingresos** NMPL (*dinero*) income *sg*; (: *Com*) takings *pl*; ~ **gravable** taxable income *sg*; **ingresos accesorios** fringe benefits; **ingresos brutos** gross receipts; **ingresos devengados** earned income *sg*; **ingresos exentos de impuestos** non-taxable income *sg*; **ingresos personales disponibles** disposable personal income *sg*

íngrimo, -a ['ingrimo, a] ADJ (*AM*: *tb*: **íngrimo y solo**) all alone

inhábil [i'naβil] ADJ unskilful, clumsy

inhabilitar [inaβili'tar] /**1a**/ VT (*Pol, Med*): ~ **a algn (para hacer algo)** to disqualify sb (from doing sth)

inhabitable [inaβi'taβle] ADJ uninhabitable

inhabituado, -a [inaβi'twaðo, a] ADJ unaccustomed

inhalador [inala'ðor] NM (*Med*) inhaler

inhalar [ina'lar] /**1a**/ VT to inhale

inherente [ine'rente] ADJ inherent

inhibición [iniβi'θjon] NF inhibition

inhibir [ini'βir] /**3a**/ VT to inhibit; (*Rel*) to restrain; **inhibirse** VR to keep out

inhospitalario, -a [inospita'larjo, a], **inhóspito, -a** [i'nospito, a] ADJ inhospitable

inhóspito, -a [i'nospito, a] ADJ (*región, paisaje*) inhospitable

inhumación [inuma'θjon] NF burial, interment

inhumano, -a [inu'mano, a] ADJ inhuman

INI ['ini] NM ABR = **Instituto Nacional de Industria**

inicial [ini'θjal] ADJ, NF initial

inicialice *etc* [iniθja'liθe] VB *ver* **inicializar**

inicializar [iniθjali'θar] /**1f**/ VT (*Inform*) to initialize

iniciar [ini'θjar] /**1b**/ VT (*persona*) to initiate; (*empezar*) to begin, commence; (*conversación*) to start up; ~ **a algn en un secreto** to let sb into a secret; ~ **la sesión** (*Inform*) to log in o on

iniciativa [iniθja'tiβa] NF initiative; (*liderazgo*) leadership; ~ **privada** private enterprise

inicio [i'niθjo] NM start, beginning

inicuo, -a [i'nikwo, a] ADJ iniquitous

inigualado, -a [iniɣwa'laðo, a] ADJ unequalled

ininteligible [ininteli'xiβle] ADJ
unintelligible

ininterrumpido, -a [ininterrum'piðo, a] ADJ
uninterrupted; (*proceso*) continuous;
(*progreso*) steady

injerencia [inxe'renθja] NF interference

injertar [inxer'tar] /**1a**/ VT to graft

injerto [in'xerto] NM graft; ~ **de piel** skin
graft

injuria [in'xurja] NF (*agravio, ofensa*) offence;
(*insulto*) insult; **injurias** NFPL abuse *sg*

injuriar [inxu'rjar] /**1b**/ VT to insult

injurioso, -a [inxu'rjoso, a] ADJ offensive;
insulting

injusticia [inxus'tiθja] NF injustice,
unfairness; **con ~** unjustly

injusto, -a [in'xusto, a] ADJ unjust, unfair

inmaculado, -a [inmaku'laðo, a] ADJ
immaculate, spotless

inmadurez [inmaðu're θ] NF immaturity

inmaduro, -a [inma'ðuro, a] ADJ immature;
(*fruta*) unripe

inmediaciones [inmeða'θjones] NFPL
neighbourhood *sg*, environs

inmediatamente [in meðjata'mente] ADV
immediately

inmediatez [inmeðja'teθ] NF immediacy

inmediato, -a [inme'ðjato, a] ADJ immediate;
(*contiguo*) adjoining; (*rápido*) prompt;
(*próximo*) neighbouring, next; **de ~** (*esp AM*)
immediately

inmejorable [inmexo'raβle] ADJ
unsurpassable; (*precio*) unbeatable

inmemorable [inmemo'raβle], **inmemorial**
[inmemo'rjal] ADJ immemorial

inmenso, -a [in'menso, a] ADJ immense,
huge

inmerecido, -a [inmere'θiðo, a] ADJ
undeserved

inmersión [inmer'sjon] NF immersion;
(*buzo*) dive

inmigración [inmiɣra'θjon] NF immigration

inmigrante [inmi'ɣrante] ADJ, NMF
immigrant

inminente [inmi'nente] ADJ imminent,
impending

inmiscuirse [inmisku'irse] /**3g**/ VR to
interfere, meddle

inmiscuyendo *etc* [inmisku'jendo] VB *ver*
inmiscuirse

inmobiliario, -a [inmoβi'ljarjo, a] ADJ
real-estate *cpd*, property *cpd* ▸ NF estate
agency

inmolar [inmo'lar] /**1a**/ VT to immolate,
sacrifice

inmoral [inmo'ral] ADJ immoral

inmortal [inmor'tal] ADJ immortal

inmortalice *etc* [inmorta'liθe] VB *ver*
inmortalizar

inmortalizar [inmortali'θar] /**1f**/ VT to
immortalize

inmotivado, -a [inmoti'βaðo, a] ADJ
motiveless; (*sospecha*) groundless

inmóvil [in'moβil] ADJ immobile

inmovilizar [inmoβili'θar] /**1f**/ VT to
immobilize; (*paralizar*) to paralyse:
inmovilizarse VR: **se le inmovilizó la pierna**
her leg was paralysed

inmueble [in'mweβle] ADJ: **bienes
inmuebles** real estate *sg*, landed property *sg*
▸ NM property

inmundicia [inmun'diθja] NF filth

inmundo, -a [in'mundo, a] ADJ filthy

inmune [in'mune] ADJ: ~ **(a)** (*Med*) immune
(to)

inmunidad [inmuni'ðað] NF immunity;
(*fisco*) exemption; ~ **diplomática/
parlamentaria** diplomatic/
parliamentary immunity

inmunitario, -a [inmuni'tarjo, a] ADJ:
sistema ~ immune system

inmunización [inmuniθa'θjon] NF
immunization

inmunizar [inmuni'θar] /**1f**/ VT to immunize

inmutable [inmu'taβle] ADJ immutable;
permaneció ~ he didn't flinch

inmutarse [inmu'tarse] /**1a**/ VR to turn pale;
no se inmutó he didn't turn a hair; **siguió
sin ~** he carried on unperturbed

innato, -a [in'nato, a] ADJ innate

innecesario, -a [inneθe'sarjo, a] ADJ
unnecessary

innegable [inne'ɣaβle] ADJ undeniable

innoble [in'noβle] ADJ ignoble

innovación [innoβa'θjon] NF innovation

innovador, a [innoβa'ðor, a] ADJ innovatory,
innovative ▸ NM/F innovator

innovar [inno'βar] /**1a**/ VT to introduce

innumerable [innume'raβle] ADJ countless

inocencia [ino'θenθja] NF innocence

inocentada [inoθen'taða] NF practical joke

inocente [ino'θente] ADJ (*ingenuo*) naive,
innocent; (*no culpable*) innocent; (*sin malicia*)
harmless ▸ NM/F simpleton; **día de los
(Santos) Inocentes** ≈ April Fools' Day;
see note

> The 28th December, *el día de los (Santos)
> Inocentes*, is when the Church
> commemorates the story of Herod's
> slaughter of the innocent children of
> Judea in the time of Christ. On this day
> Spaniards play *inocentadas* (practical
> jokes) on each other, much like our April
> Fools' Day pranks, eg typically sticking a
> *monigote* (cut-out paper figure) on
> someone's back, or broadcasting unlikely
> news stories.

inocuidad [inokwi'ðað] NF harmlessness

inocular [inoku'lar] /**1a**/ VT to inoculate

inocuo, -a [i'nokwo, a] ADJ (*sustancia*) harmless

inodoro, -a [ino'ðoro, a] ADJ odourless ▶ NM toilet (*BRIT*), lavatory (*BRIT*), washroom (*US*)

inofensivo, -a [inofen'siβo, a] ADJ inoffensive

inolvidable [inolβi'ðaβle] ADJ unforgettable

inoperante [inope'rante] ADJ ineffective

inopinado, -a [inopi'naðo, a] ADJ unexpected

inoportuno, -a [inopor'tuno, a] ADJ untimely; (*molesto*) inconvenient; (*inapropiado*) inappropriate

inoxidable [inoksi'ðaβle] ADJ stainless; **acero ~** stainless steel

inquebrantable [inkeβran'taβle] ADJ unbreakable; (*fig*) unshakeable

inquiera *etc* [in'kjera] VB *ver* **inquirir**

inquietante [inkje'tante] ADJ worrying

inquietar [inkje'tar] /**1a**/ VT to worry, trouble; **inquietarse** VR to worry, get upset

inquieto, -a [in'kjeto, a] ADJ anxious, worried; **estar ~ por** to be worried about

inquietud [inkje'tuð] NF anxiety, worry

inquilino, -a [inki'lino, a] NM/F tenant; (*Com*) lessee

inquiriendo *etc* [inki'rjendo] VB *ver* **inquirir**

inquirir [inki'rir] /**3i**/ VT to enquire into, investigate

insaciable [insa'θjaβle] ADJ insatiable

insalubre [insa'luβre] ADJ unhealthy; (*condiciones*) insanitary

INSALUD [insa'luð] NM ABR (*ESP*) = **Instituto Nacional de la Salud**

insano, -a [in'sano, a] ADJ (*loco*) insane; (*malsano*) unhealthy

insatisfacción [insatisfak'θjon] NF dissatisfaction

insatisfecho, -a [insatis'fetʃo, a] ADJ (*condición*) unsatisfied; (*estado de ánimo*) dissatisfied

inscribir [inskri'βir] /**3a**/ VT to inscribe; (*en lista*) to put; (*en censo*) to register; **inscribirse** VR to register; (*Escol etc*) to enrol

inscripción [inskrip'θjon] NF inscription; (*Escol etc*) enrolment; (*en censo*) registration

inscrito [ins'krito] PP *de* **inscribir**

insecticida [insekti'θiða] NM insecticide

insecto [in'sekto] NM insect

inseguridad [inseɣuri'ðað] NF insecurity; **~ ciudadana** lack of safety in the streets

inseguro, -a [inse'ɣuro, a] ADJ insecure; (*inconstante*) unsteady; (*incierto*) uncertain

inseminación [insemina'θjon] NF: **~ artificial** artificial insemination (A.I.)

inseminar [insemi'nar] /**1a**/ VT to inseminate, fertilize

insensato, -a [insen'sato, a] ADJ foolish, stupid

insensibilice *etc* [insensiβi'liθe] VB *ver* **insensibilizar**

insensibilidad [insensiβili'ðað] NF (*gen*) insensitivity; (*dureza de corazón*) callousness

insensibilizar [insensiβili'θar] /**1f**/ VT to desensitize; (*Med*) to anaesthetize (*BRIT*), anesthetize (*US*); (*eufemismo*) to knock out o unconscious

insensible [insen'siβle] ADJ (*gen*) insensitive; (*movimiento*) imperceptible; (*sin sensación*) numb

inseparable [insepa'raβle] ADJ inseparable

INSERSO [in'serso] NM ABR (= *Instituto Nacional de Servicios Sociales*) branch of social services

insertar [inser'tar] /**1a**/ VT to insert

inservible [inser'βiβle] ADJ useless

insidioso, -a [insi'ðjoso, a] ADJ insidious

insigne [in'siɣne] ADJ distinguished; (*famoso*) notable

insignia [in'siɣnja] NF (*señal distintiva*) badge; (*estandarte*) flag

insignificante [insiɣnifi'kante] ADJ insignificant

insinuar [insi'nwar] /**1e**/ VT to insinuate, imply; **insinuarse** VR: **insinuarse con algn** to ingratiate o.s. with sb

insípido, -a [in'sipiðo, a] ADJ insipid

insistencia [insis'tenθja] NF insistence

insistir [insis'tir] /**3a**/ VI to insist; **~ en algo** to insist on sth; (*enfatizar*) to stress sth

in situ [in'situ] ADV on the spot, in situ

insobornable [insoβor'naβle] ADJ incorruptible

insociable [inso'θjaβle] ADJ unsociable

insolación [insola'θjon] NF (*Med*) sunstroke

insolencia [inso'lenθja] NF insolence

insolente [inso'lente] ADJ insolent

insólito, -a [in'solito, a] ADJ unusual

insoluble [inso'luβle] ADJ insoluble

insolvencia [insol'βenθja] NF insolvency

insomne [in'somne] ADJ sleepless ▶ NMF insomniac

insomnio [in'somnjo] NM insomnia

insondable [inson'daβle] ADJ bottomless

insonorización [insonoriθa'θjon] NF soundproofing

insonorizado, -a [insonori'θaðo, a] ADJ (*cuarto etc*) soundproof

insoportable [insopor'taβle] ADJ unbearable

insoslayable [insosla'jaβle] ADJ unavoidable

insospechado, -a [insospe'tʃaðo, a] ADJ (*inesperado*) unexpected

insostenible [insoste'niβle] ADJ untenable

inspección [inspek'θjon] NF inspection, check; **I~** inspectorate; **~ técnica (de vehículos)** ≈ MOT (test) (*BRIT*)

inspeccionar [inspekθjo'nar] /**1a**/ VT (*examinar*) to inspect, examine; (*controlar*) to check

inspector, a [inspek'tor, a] NM/F inspector
inspectorado [inspekto'raðo] NM inspectorate
inspiración [inspira'θjon] NF inspiration
inspirador, a [inspira'ðor, a] ADJ inspiring
inspirar [inspi'rar] /**1a**/ VT to inspire; (Med) to inhale; **inspirarse** VR: **inspirarse en** to be inspired by
instalación [instala'θjon] NF (equipo) fittings pl, equipment; **~ eléctrica** wiring
instalar [insta'lar] /**1a**/ VT (establecer) to instal; (erguir) to set up, erect; **instalarse** VR to establish o.s.; (en una vivienda) to move into
instancia [ins'tanθja] NF (solicitud) application; (ruego) request; (Jur) petition; **a ~ de** at the request of; **en última ~** as a last resort
instantáneo, -a [instan'taneo, a] ADJ instantaneous ▶ NF snap(shot); **café ~** instant coffee
instante [ins'tante] NM instant, moment; **al ~** right now; **en un ~** in a flash
instar [ins'tar] /**1a**/ VT to press, urge
instaurar [instau'rar] /**1a**/ VT (costumbre) to establish; (normas, sistema) to bring in, introduce; (gobierno) to install
instigador, a [instiɣa'ðor, a] NM/F instigator; **~ de un delito** (Jur) accessory before the fact
instigar [insti'ɣar] /**1h**/ VT to instigate
instigue etc [ins'tiɣe] VB ver **instigar**
instintivo, -a [instin'tiβo, a] ADJ instinctive
instinto [ins'tinto] NM instinct; **por ~** instinctively
institución [institu'θjon] NF institution, establishment; **~ benéfica** charitable foundation
instituir [institu'ir] /**3g**/ VT to establish; (fundar) to found
instituto [insti'tuto] NM (gen) institute; **I~ Nacional de Enseñanza** (Esp) ≈ comprehensive (BRIT) o high (US) school; **I~ Nacional de Industria (INI)** (Esp Com) ≈ National Enterprise Board (BRIT)
institutriz [institu'triθ] NF governess
instituyendo etc [institu'jendo] VB ver **instituir**
instrucción [instruk'θjon] NF instruction; (enseñanza) education, teaching; (Jur) proceedings pl; (Mil) training; (Deporte) coaching; (conocimientos) knowledge; (Inform) statement; **instrucciones para el uso** directions for use; **instrucciones de funcionamiento** operating instructions
instructivo, -a [instruk'tiβo, a] ADJ instructive
instructor [instruk'tor] NM instructor; **~ de fitness** fitness instructor
instruir [instru'ir] /**3g**/ VT (gen) to instruct; (enseñar) to teach, educate; (Jur: proceso) to prepare, draw up; **instruirse** VR to learn, teach o.s.
instrumento [instru'mento] NM (gen, Mus) instrument; (herramienta) tool, implement; (Com) indenture; (Jur) legal document; **~ de percusión/cuerda/viento** percussion/string(ed)/wind instrument
instruyendo etc [instru'jendo] VB ver **instruir**
insubordinarse [insuβorði'narse] /**1a**/ VR to rebel
insuficiencia [insufi'θjenθja] NF (carencia) lack; (inadecuación) inadequacy; **~ cardíaca/renal** heart/kidney failure
insuficiente [insufi'θjente] ADJ (gen) insufficient; (Escol: nota) D, fail
insufrible [insu'friβle] ADJ insufferable
insular [insu'lar] ADJ insular
insulina [insu'lina] NF insulin
insulso, -a [in'sulso, a] ADJ insipid; (fig) dull
insultar [insul'tar] /**1a**/ VT to insult
insulto [in'sulto] NM insult
insumisión [insumi'sjon] NF refusal to do military service or community service
insumiso, -a [insu'miso, a] ADJ (rebelde) rebellious ▶ NM/F (Pol) person who refuses to do military service or community service; ver tb **mili**
insuperable [insupe'raβle] ADJ (excelente) unsurpassable; (problema etc) insurmountable
insurgente [insur'xente] ADJ, NMF insurgent
insurrección [insurrek'θjon] NF insurrection, rebellion
insustituible [insusti'twiβle] ADJ irreplaceable
intachable [inta'tʃaβle] ADJ irreproachable
intacto, -a [in'takto, a] ADJ (sin tocar) untouched; (entero) intact
integrado, -a [inte'ɣraðo, a] ADJ (Inform): **circuito ~** integrated circuit
integral [inte'ɣral] ADJ integral; (completo) complete; (Tec) built-in; **pan ~** wholemeal bread
integrante [inte'ɣrante] ADJ integral ▶ NMF member
integrar [inte'ɣrar] /**1a**/ VT to make up, compose; (Mat, fig) to integrate
integridad [inteɣri'ðað] NF wholeness; (carácter, tb Inform) integrity; **en su ~** completely
integrismo [inte'ɣrismo] NM fundamentalism
integrista [inte'ɣrista] ADJ, NMF fundamentalist
íntegro, -a ['inteɣro, a] ADJ whole, entire; (texto) uncut, unabridged; (honrado) honest
intelectual [intelek'twal] ADJ, NMF intellectual
intelectualidad [intelektwali'ðað] NF intelligentsia, intellectuals pl

inteligencia [inteli'xenθja] NF intelligence; (*ingenio*) ability; **~ artificial** artificial intelligence

inteligente [inteli'xente] ADJ intelligent

inteligible [inteli'xiβle] ADJ intelligible

intemperancia [intempe'ranθja] NF excess, intemperance

intemperie [intem'perje] NF: **a la ~** outdoors, out in the open, exposed to the elements

intempestivo, -a [intempes'tiβo, a] ADJ untimely

intención [inten'θjon] NF intention, purpose; **con segundas intenciones** maliciously; **con ~** deliberately

intencionado, -a [intenθjo'naðo, a] ADJ deliberate; **bien ~** well-meaning; **mal ~** ill-disposed, hostile

intendencia [inten'denθja] NF management, administration; (*Mil*: *tb*: **cuerpo de intendencia**) ≈ service corps

intensidad [intensi'ðað] NF (*gen*) intensity; (*Elec, Tec*) strength; (*de recuerdo*) vividness; **llover con ~** to rain hard

intensificar [intensifi'kar] /1g/ VT, **intensificarse** VR to intensify

intensifique *etc* [intensi'fike] VB *ver* **intensificar**

intensivo, -a [inten'siβo, a] ADJ intensive; **curso ~** crash course

intenso, -a [in'tenso, a] ADJ intense; (*impresión*) vivid; (*sentimiento*) profound, deep

intentar [inten'tar] /1a/ VT (*tratar*) to try, attempt

intento [in'tento] NM (*intención*) intention, purpose; (*tentativa*) attempt

intentona [inten'tona] NF (*Pol*) attempted coup

interaccionar [interakθjo'nar] /1a/ VI (*Inform*) to interact

interactivo, -a [interak'tiβo, a] ADJ interactive; (*Inform*): **computación interactiva** interactive computing

intercalación [interkala'θjon] NF (*Inform*) merging

intercalar [interka'lar] /1a/ VT to insert; (*Inform*: *archivos, texto*) to merge

intercambiable [interkam'bjaβle] ADJ interchangeable

intercambio [interkam'bjo] NM (*canje*) exchange; (*trueque*) swap

interceder [interθe'ðer] /2a/ VI to intercede

interceptar [interθep'tar] /1a/ VT to intercept, cut off; (*Auto*) to hold up

interceptor [interθep'tor] NM interceptor; (*Tec*) trap

intercesión [interθe'sjon] NF intercession

interés [inte'res] NM (*gen, Com*) interest; (*importancia*) concern; (*parte*) share, part; (*pey*) self-interest; **~ compuesto** compound interest; **~ simple** simple interest; **con un ~ del 9 por ciento** at an interest of 9%; **dar a ~** to lend at interest; **tener ~ en** (*Com*) to hold a share in; **intereses acumulados** accrued interest *sg*; **intereses por cobrar** interest receivable *sg*; **intereses creados** vested interests; **intereses por pagar** interest payable *sg*

interesado, -a [intere'saðo, a] ADJ interested; (*prejuiciado*) prejudiced; (*pey*) mercenary, self-seeking ▶ NM/F person concerned; (*firmante*) the undersigned

interesante [intere'sante] ADJ interesting

interesar [intere'sar] /1a/ VT to interest, be of interest to ▶ VI to interest, be of interest; (*importar*) to be important; **interesarse** VR: **interesarse en** *o* **por** to take an interest in; **no me interesan los toros** bullfighting does not appeal to me

interestatal [interesta'tal] ADJ inter-state

interface [inter'faθe], **interfase** [inter'fase] NM (*Inform*) interface; **~ hombre/máquina/ por menús** man/machine/menu interface

interfaz [inter'faθ] NM = **interface**

interferencia [interfe'renθja] NF interference

interferir [interfe'rir] /3i/ VT to interfere with; (*Telec*) to jam ▶ VI to interfere

interfiera *etc* [inter'fjera], **interfiriendo** *etc* [interfi'rjendo] VB *ver* **interferir**

interfón [inter'fon] NM (*AM*) = **interfono**

interfono [inter'fono] NM intercom, entry phone

ínterin ['interin] ADV meanwhile ▶ NM interim; **en el ~** in the meantime

interino, -a [inte'rino, a] ADJ temporary; (*empleado etc*) provisional ▶ NM/F temporary holder of a post; (*Med*) locum; (*Escol*) supply teacher; (*Teat*) stand-in

interior [inte'rjor] ADJ inner, inside; (*Com*) domestic, internal ▶ NM interior, inside; (*fig*) soul, mind; (*Deporte*) inside forward; **Ministerio del I~** ≈ Home Office (*BRIT*), ≈ Department of the Interior (*US*); **dije para mí ~** I said to myself

interjección [interxek'θjon] NF interjection

interlínea [inter'linea] NF (*Inform*) line feed

interlocutor, a [interloku'tor, a] NM/F speaker; (*al teléfono*) person at the other end (of the line); **mi ~** the person I was speaking to

intermediario, -a [interme'ðjarjo, a] ADJ (*mediador*) mediating ▶ NM/F intermediary, go-between; (*mediador*) mediator

intermedio, -a [inter'meðjo, a] ADJ intermediate; (*tiempo*) intervening ▶ NM interval; (*Pol*) recess

interminable [intermi'naβle] ADJ endless, interminable

intermitente [intermi'tente] ADJ
intermittent ▸ NM (*Auto*) indicator
internacional [internaθjo'nal] ADJ
international
internado [inter'naðo] NM boarding school
internamiento [interna'mjento] NM
internment
internar [inter'nar] /**1a**/ VT to intern; (*en un manicomio*) to commit; **internarse** VR
(*penetrar*) to penetrate; **internarse en** to go
into *o* right inside; **internarse en un estudio** to study a subject in depth
internauta [inter'nauta] NMF web surfer,
internet user
Internet [inter'net] NM O F internet, Internet
interno, -a [in'terno, a] ADJ internal, interior;
(*Pol etc*) domestic ▸ NM/F (*alumno*) boarder
interpelación [interpela'θjon] NF appeal,
plea
interpelar [interpe'lar] /**1a**/ VT (*rogar*) to
implore; (*hablar*) to speak to; (*Pol*) to ask for
explanations, question formally
interpondré *etc* [interpon'dre] VB *ver*
interponer
interponer [interpo'ner] /**2q**/ VT to
interpose, put in; **interponerse** VR to
intervene
interponga *etc* [inter'ponga] VB *ver*
interponer
interposición [interposi'θjon] NF insertion
interpretación [interpreta'θjon] NF
interpretation; (*Mus, Teat*) performance;
mala ~ misinterpretation
interpretar [interpre'tar] /**1a**/ VT to
interpret; (*Teat, Mus*) to perform, play
intérprete [in'terprete] NMF (*Ling*)
interpreter, translator; (*Mus, Teat*)
performer, artist(e)
interpuesto [inter'pwesto], **interpuse** *etc*
[inter'puse] VB *ver* **interponer**
interrogación [interroɣa'θjon] NF
interrogation; (*Ling: tb:* **signo de
interrogación**) question mark; (*Telec*)
polling
interrogante [interro'ɣante] ADJ
questioning ▸ NM question mark; (*fig*)
question mark, query
interrogar [interro'ɣar] /**1h**/ VT to
interrogate, question
interrogatorio [interroɣa'torjo] NM
interrogation; (*Mil*) debriefing; (*Jur*)
examination
interrogue *etc* [inte'rroɣe] VB *ver* **interrogar**
interrumpir [interrum'pir] /**3a**/ VT to
interrupt; (*vacaciones*) to cut short; (*servicio*)
to cut off; (*tráfico*) to block
interrupción [interrup'θjon] NF
interruption
interruptor [interrup'tor] NM (*Elec*) switch

intersección [intersek'θjon] NF
intersection; (*Auto*) junction
interurbano, -a [interur'βano, a] ADJ inter
city; (*Telec*) long-distance
intervalo [inter'βalo] NM interval; (*descanso*)
break; **a intervalos** at intervals, every now
and then
intervención [interβen'θjon] NF supervision;
(*Com*) audit(ing); (*Med*) operation; (*Telec*)
tapping; (*participación*) intervention;
~ quirúrgica surgical operation; **la política
de no ~** the policy of non-intervention
intervencionista [interβenθjo'nista] ADJ:
no ~ (*Com*) laissez-faire
intervendré *etc* [interβen'dre], **intervenga**
etc [inter'βenga] VB *ver* **intervenir**
intervenir [interβe'nir] /**3r**/ VT (*controlar*) to
control, supervise; (*Com*) to audit; (*Med*) to
operate on; (*Telec*) to tap ▸ VI (*participar*) to
take part, participate; (*mediar*) to intervene
interventor, a [interβen'tor, a] NM/F
inspector; (*Com*) auditor
interviniendo *etc* [interβi'njendo] VB *ver*
intervenir
interviú [inter'βju] NF interview
intestino [intes'tino] NM intestine
inti ['inti] NM *monetary unit of Peru*
intimar [inti'mar] /**1a**/ VT to intimate,
announce; (*mandar*) to order ▸ VI to become
friendly
intimidad [intimi'ðað] NF intimacy;
(*familiaridad*) familiarity; (*vida privada*) private
life; (*Jur*) privacy
intimidar [intimi'ðar] /**1a**/ VT to intimidate,
scare
íntimo, -a ['intimo, a] ADJ intimate;
(*pensamientos*) innermost; (*vida*) personal,
private; **una boda íntima** a quiet wedding
intolerable [intole'raβle] ADJ intolerable,
unbearable
intolerancia [intole'ranθja] NF intolerance
intoxicación [intoksika'θjon] NF poisoning;
~ alimenticia food poisoning
intraducible [intraðu'θiβle] ADJ
untranslatable
intranet [intra'net] NF intranet
intranquilice *etc* [intranki'liθe] VB *ver*
intranquilizarse
intranquilizarse [intrankili'θarse] /**1f**/ VR to
get worried *o* anxious
intranquilo, -a [intran'kilo, a] ADJ worried
intranscendente [intransθen'dente] ADJ
unimportant
intransferible [intransfe'riβle] ADJ not
transferable
intransigente [intransi'xente] ADJ
intransigent
intransitable [intransi'taβle] ADJ
impassable

intransitivo, -a [intransi'tiβo, a] ADJ intransitive

intratable [intra'taβle] ADJ (*problema*) intractable; (*dificultad*) awkward; (*individuo*) unsociable

intrepidez [intrepi'ðeθ] NF courage, bravery

intrépido, -a [in'trepiðo, a] ADJ intrepid, fearless

intriga [in'triɣa] NF intrigue; (*plan*) plot

intrigar [intri'ɣar] /**1h**/ VT, VI to intrigue

intrigue *etc* [in'triɣe] VB *ver* **intrigar**

intrincado, -a [intrin'kaðo, a] ADJ intricate

intrínseco, -a [in'trinseko, a] ADJ intrinsic

introducción [introðuk'θjon] NF introduction; (*de libro*) foreword; (*Inform*) input

introducir [introðu'θir] /**3n**/ VT (*gen*) to introduce; (*moneda*) to insert; (*Inform*) to input, enter

introduje *etc* [intro'ðuxe], **introduzca** *etc* [intro'ðuθka] VB *ver* **introducir**

intromisión [intromi'sjon] NF interference, meddling

introvertido, -a [introβer'tiðo, a] ADJ, NM/F introvert

intruso, -a [in'truso, a] ADJ intrusive ▶ NM/F intruder

intuición [intwi'θjon] NF intuition

intuir [intu'ir] /**3g**/ VT to know by intuition, intuit

intuyendo *etc* [intu'jendo] VB *ver* **intuir**

inundación [inunda'θjon] NF flood(ing)

inundar [inun'dar] /**1a**/ VT to flood; (*fig*) to swamp, inundate

inusitado, -a [inusi'taðo, a] ADJ unusual

inútil [i'nutil] ADJ useless; (*esfuerzo*) vain, fruitless

inutilice *etc* [inuti'liθe] VB *ver* **inutilizar**

inutilidad [inutili'ðað] NF uselessness

inutilizar [inutili'θar] /**1f**/ VT to make unusable, put out of action; (*incapacitar*) to disable; **inutilizarse** VR to become useless

invadir [imba'ðir] /**3a**/ VT to invade

invalidar [imbali'ðar] /**1a**/ VT to invalidate

invalidez [imbali'ðeθ] NF (*Med*) disablement; (*Jur*) invalidity

inválido, -a [im'baliðo, a] ADJ invalid; (*Jur*) null and void ▶ NM/F invalid

invariable [imba'rjaβle] ADJ invariable

invasión [imba'sjon] NF invasion

invasor, a [imba'sor, a] ADJ invading ▶ NM/F invader

invencible [imben'θiβle] ADJ invincible; (*timidez, miedo*) unsurmountable

invención [imben'θjon] NF invention

inventar [imben'tar] /**1a**/ VT to invent

inventario [imben'tarjo] NM inventory; (*Com*) stocktaking

inventiva [imben'tiβa] NF inventiveness

invento [im'bento] NM invention; (*fig*) brainchild; (*pey*) silly idea

inventor, a [imben'tor, a] NM/F inventor

invernadero [imberna'ðero] NM greenhouse

invernal [imber'nal] ADJ wintry, winter *cpd*

invernar [imber'nar] /**1j**/ VI (*Zool*) to hibernate

inverosímil [imbero'simil] ADJ implausible

inversión [imber'sjon] NF (*Com*) investment; **~ de capitales** capital investment; **inversiones extranjeras** foreign investment *sg*

inverso, a [im'berso, a] ADJ inverse, opposite; **en el orden ~** in reverse order; **a la inversa** inversely, the other way round

inversor, -a [imber'sor, a] NM/F (*Com*) investor

invertebrado, -a [imberte'βraðo, a] ADJ, NM invertebrate

invertido, -a [imber'tiðo, a] ADJ inverted; (*al revés*) reversed; (*homosexual*) homosexual ▶ NM/F homosexual

invertir [imber'tir] /**3i**/ VT (*Com*) to invest; (*volcar*) to turn upside down; (*tiempo etc*) to spend

investigación [imbestiɣa'θjon] NF investigation; (*indagación*) inquiry; (*Univ*) research; **~ y desarrollo** (*Com*) research and development (R & D); **~ de los medios de publicidad** media research; **~ del mercado** market research

investigador, a [imbestiɣa'ðor, a] NM/F investigator; (*Univ*) research fellow

investigar [imbesti'ɣar] /**1h**/ VT to investigate; (*estudiar*) to do research into

investigue *etc* [imbes'tiɣe] VB *ver* **investigar**

investir [imbes'tir] /**3k**/ VT: **~ a algn con algo** to confer sth on sb; **fue investido Doctor Honoris Causa** he was awarded an honorary doctorate

invicto, -a [im'bikto, a] ADJ unconquered

invidente [imbi'ðente] ADJ sightless ▶ NMF blind person; **los invidentes** the sightless

invierno [im'bjerno] NM winter

invierta *etc* [im'bjerta] VB *ver* **invertir**

inviolabilidad [imbjolaβili'ðað] NF inviolability; **~ parlamentaria** parliamentary immunity

invirtiendo *etc* [imbir'tjendo] VB *ver* **invertir**

invisible [imbi'siβle] ADJ invisible; **exportaciones/importaciones invisibles** invisible exports/imports

invitación [imbita'θjon] NF invitation

invitado, -a [imbi'taðo, a] NM/F guest

invitar [imbi'tar] /**1a**/ VT to invite; (*incitar*) to entice; **~ a algn a hacer algo** to invite sb to do sth; **~ a algo** to pay for sth; **nos invitó a cenar fuera** she took us out for dinner; **invito yo** it's on me

in vitro [im'bitro] ADV in vitro
invocar [imbo'kar] /**1g**/ VT to invoke, call on
involucrar [imbolu'krar] /**1a**/ VT: ~ **algo en un discurso** to bring something irrelevant into a discussion; ~ **a algn en algo** to involve sb in sth; **involucrarse** VR (*interesarse*) to get involved
involuntario, -a [imbolun'tarjo, a] ADJ involuntary; (*ofensa etc*) unintentional
invoque *etc* [im'boke] VB *ver* **invocar**
inyección [injek'θjon] NF injection
inyectar [injek'tar] /**1a**/ VT to inject
ión [i'on] NM ion
IPC NM ABR (*ESP*: = *índice de precios al consumo*) CPI
IPM NM ABR (= *índice de precios al por menor*) RPI
iPod® ['ipoð] (*pl* **iPods**) NM iPod®

(PALABRA CLAVE)

ir [ir] /**3s**/ VI **1** to go; (*a pie*) to walk; (*viajar*) to travel; **ir caminando** to walk; **fui en tren** I went *o* travelled by train; **voy a la calle** I'm going out; **ir en coche/en bicicleta** to drive/cycle; **ir a pie** to walk, go on foot; **ir de pesca** to go fishing; ¡(**ahora**) **voy!** (I'm just) coming!
2: **ir (a) por**: **ir (a) por el médico** to fetch the doctor
3 (*progresar: persona, cosa*) to go; **el trabajo va muy bien** work is going very well; **¿cómo te va?** how are things going?; **me va muy bien** I'm getting on very well; **le fue fatal** it went awfully badly for him
4 (*funcionar*): **el coche no va muy bien** the car isn't running very well
5 (*sentar*): **me va estupendamente** (*ropa, color*) it suits me really well; (*medicamento*) it works really well for me; **ir bien con algo** to go well with sth; **te va estupendamente ese color** that colour suits you fantastically well
6 (*aspecto*): **iba muy bien vestido** he was very well dressed; **ir con zapatos negros** to wear black shoes
7 (*locuciones*): **¿vino? — ¡que va!** did he come? — of course not!; **vamos, no llores** come on, don't cry; **¡vaya coche!** (*admiración*) what a car!, that's some car!; (*desprecio*) that's a terrible car!; **¡vaya!** (*regular*) so so; (*desagrado*) come on!; **¡vamos!** come on!; **¡que le vaya bien!** (*adiós*) take care!
8: **no vaya a ser**: **tienes que correr, no vaya a ser que pierdas el tren** you'll have to run so as not to miss the train
9: **no me** *etc* **va ni me viene** I *etc* don't care
▶ VB AUXILIAR **1**: **ir a**: **voy/iba a hacerlo hoy** I am/was going to do it today
2 (+ *gerundio*): **iba anocheciendo** it was getting dark; **todo se me iba aclarando** everything was gradually becoming clearer to me

3 (+ *pp = pasivo*): **van vendidos 300 ejemplares** 300 copies have been sold so far
irse VR **1**: **¿por dónde se va al zoológico?** which is the way to the zoo?
2 (*marcharse*) to leave; **ya se habrán ido** they must already have left *o* gone; **¡vámonos!**, **¡nos fuimos!** (*AM*) let's go!; **¡vete!** go away!; **¡vete a saber!** your guess is as good as mine!, who knows!

IRA ['ira] NM ABR (= *Irish Republican Army*) IRA
ira ['ira] NF anger, rage
iracundo, -a [ira'kundo, a] ADJ irascible
Irak [i'rak] NM = **Iraq**
irakí ADJ, NMF Iraqui
Irán [i'ran] NM Iran
iraní [ira'ni] ADJ, NMF Iranian
Iraq [i'rak] NM Iraq
iraquí [ira'ki] ADJ, NMF Iraqi
irascible [iras'θiβle] ADJ irascible
irguiendo *etc* [ir'ɣjendo] VB *ver* **erguir**
iris ['iris] NM INV (*arco iris*) rainbow; (*Anat*) iris
Irlanda [ir'landa] NF Ireland; ~ **del Norte** Northern Ireland, Ulster
irlandés, -esa [irlan'des, esa] ADJ Irish
▶ NM/F Irishman(-woman) ▶ NM (*Ling*) Gaelic, Irish; **los irlandeses** NMPL the Irish
ironía [iro'nia] NF irony
irónico, -a [i'roniko, a] ADJ ironic(al)
IRPF NM ABR (*ESP*) = **impuesto sobre la renta de las personas físicas**
irracional [irraθjo'nal] ADJ irrational
irrazonable [irraθo'naβle] ADJ unreasonable
irreal [irre'al] ADJ unreal
irrealizable [irreali'θaβle] ADJ (*gen*) unrealizable; (*meta*) unrealistic
irrebatible [irreβa'tiβle] ADJ irrefutable
irreconocible [irrekono'θiβle] ADJ unrecognizable
irrecuperable [irrekupe'raβle] ADJ irrecoverable, irretrievable
irreembolsable [irreembol'saβle] ADJ (*Com*) non-returnable
irreflexión [irreflek'sjon] NF thoughtlessness; (*ímpetu*) rashness
irregular [irreɣu'lar] ADJ irregular; (*situación*) abnormal, anomalous; **margen izquierdo/derecho** ~ (*texto*) ragged left/right (margin)
irregularidad [irreɣulari'ðað] NF irregularity
irremediable [irreme'ðjaβle] ADJ irremediable; (*vicio*) incurable
irreparable [irrepa'raβle] ADJ (*daños*) irreparable; (*pérdida*) irrecoverable
irreprochable [irrepro'tʃaβle] ADJ irreproachable
irresistible [irresis'tiβle] ADJ irresistible
irresoluto, -a [irreso'luto, a] ADJ irresolute, hesitant; (*sin resolver*) unresolved

irrespetuoso, -a [irrespe'twoso, a] ADJ disrespectful

irresponsable [irrespon'saβle] ADJ irresponsible

irreverente [irreβe'rente] ADJ disrespectful

irreversible [irreβer'siβle] ADJ irreversible

irrevocable [irreβo'kaβle] ADJ irrevocable

irrigar [irri'γar] /**1h**/ VT to irrigate

irrigue etc [i'rriγe] VB ver **irrigar**

irrisorio, -a [irri'sorjo, a] ADJ derisory, ridiculous; (precio) bargain cpd

irritación [irrita'θjon] NF irritation

irritar [irri'tar] /**1a**/ VT to irritate, annoy; **irritarse** VR to get angry, lose one's temper

irrompible [irrom'piβle] ADJ unbreakable

irrumpir [irrum'pir] /**3a**/ VI: ~ **en** to burst o rush into

irrupción [irrup'θjon] NF irruption; (invasión) invasion

IRTP NM ABR (Esp: = impuesto sobre el rendimiento del trabajo personal) ≈ PAYE

ISBN NM ABR (= International Standard Book Number) ISBN

isla ['isla] NF (Geo) island; **Islas Británicas** British Isles; **Islas Filipinas/Malvinas/Canarias** Philippines/Falklands/Canaries

Islam [is'lam] NM Islam

islámico, -a [is'lamiko, a] ADJ Islamic

islandés, -esa [islan'des, esa] ADJ Icelandic ▶ NM/F Icelander ▶ NM (Ling) Icelandic

Islandia [is'landja] NF Iceland

isleño, -a [is'leɲo, a] ADJ island cpd ▶ NM/F islander

islote [is'lote] NM small island

isotónico, -a [iso'toniko, a] ADJ isotonic

isótopo [i'sotopo] NM isotope

Israel [isra'el] NM Israel

israelí [israe'li] ADJ, NMF Israeli

istmo ['istmo] NM isthmus; **el I~ de Panamá** the Isthmus of Panama

Italia [i'talja] NF Italy

italiano, -a [ita'ljano, a] ADJ, NM/F Italian ▶ NM (Ling) Italian

itinerante [itine'rante] ADJ travelling; (embajador) roving

itinerario [itine'rarjo] NM itinerary, route

ITV NF ABR (= Inspección Técnica de Vehículos) ≈ MOT (test)

IVA ['iβa] NM ABR (Esp Com: = Impuesto sobre el Valor Añadido) VAT

IVP NM ABR = **Instituto Venezolano de Petroquímica**

izada [i'saða] NF (Am) lifting, raising

izar [i'θar] /**1f**/ VT to hoist

izda., izq.ª ABR (= izquierda) L, l

izdo., izq.º ABR (= izquierdo) L, l

izquierda [iθ'kjerða] NF ver **izquierdo**

izquierdista [iθkjer'ðista] ADJ leftist, left-wing ▶ NMF left-winger, leftist

izquierdo, -a [iθ'kjerðo, a] ADJ left ▶ NF left; (Pol) left (wing); **a la izquierda** on the left; (torcer etc) (to the) left; **es un cero a la izquierda** (fam) he is a nonentity; **conducción por la izquierda** left-hand drive

J j

J, j ['xota] NF (letra) J, j; **J de José** J for Jack
(BRIT) o Jig (US)

J ABR (= julio(s)) J

jabalí [xaβa'li] NM wild boar

jabalina [xaβa'lina] NF javelin

jabato, -a [xa'βato, a] ADJ brave, bold ▶ NM
young wild boar

jabón [xa'βon] NM soap; (fam: adulación)
flattery; **~ de afeitar** shaving soap; **~ de
tocador** toilet soap; **dar ~ a algn** to
soft-soap sb

jabonar [xaβo'nar] /1a/ VT to soap

jaca ['xaka] NF pony

jacal [xa'kal] NM (AM) shack

jacinto [xa'θinto] NM hyacinth

jactancia [xak'tanθja] NF boasting,
boastfulness

jactarse [xak'tarse] /1a/ VR: **~ (de)** to boast o
brag (about o of)

jadear [xaðe'ar] /1a/ VI to pant, gasp for
breath

jadeo [xa'ðeo] NM panting, gasping

jaguar [xa'ɣwar] NM jaguar

jaiba ['xaiβa] NF (AM) crab

jalar [xa'lar] /1a/ VT (AM) to pull

jalbegue [xal'βeɣe] NM whitewash

jalea [xa'lea] NF jelly

jaleo [xa'leo] NM racket, uproar; **armar un ~**
to kick up a racket

jalón [xa'lon] NM (AM) tug

jalonar [xalo'nar] /1a/ VT to stake out; (fig) to
mark

Jamaica [xa'maika] NF Jamaica

jamaicano, -a [xamai'kano, a] ADJ, NM/F
Jamaican

jamás [xa'mas] ADV never, not … ever;
(interrogativo) ever; **¿~ se vio tal cosa?** did you
ever see such a thing?

jamón [xa'mon] NM ham; **~ (de) York**
boiled ham; **~ dulce/serrano** boiled/cured
ham

Japón [xa'pon] NM: **el ~** Japan

japonés, -esa [xapo'nes, esa] ADJ, NM/F
Japanese ▶ NM (Ling) Japanese

jaque ['xake] NM: **~ mate** checkmate

jaqueca [xa'keka] NF (very bad) headache,
migraine

jarabe [xa'raβe] NM syrup; **~ para la tos**
cough syrup o mixture

jarana [xa'rana] NF (juerga) spree (fam);
andar/ir de ~ to be/go on a spree

jarcia ['xarθja] NF (Naut) ropes pl, rigging

jardín [xar'ðin] NM garden; **~ botánico**
botanical garden; **~ de (la) infancia** (ESP) o
de niños (AM) o **infantil** kindergarten,
nursery school

jardinaje [xarði'naxe] NM gardening

jardinería [xarðine'ria] NF gardening

jardinero, -a [xarði'nero, a] NM/F gardener

jarra ['xarra] NF jar; (jarro) jug; (de leche)
churn; (de cerveza) mug; **de o en jarras** with
arms akimbo

jarro ['xarro] NM jug

jarrón [xa'rron] NM vase; (Arqueología) urn

jaspeado, -a [xaspe'ado, a] ADJ mottled,
speckled

jaula ['xaula] NF cage; (embalaje) crate

jauría [xau'ria] NF pack of hounds

jazmín [xaθ'min] NM jasmine

J. C. ABR = **Jesucristo**

jeans [jins, dʒins] NMPL (AM) jeans, denims;
unos ~ a pair of jeans

jeep® [jip] (pl **jeeps** [jips]) NM jeep®

jefa ['xefa] NF ver **jefe**

jefatura [xefa'tura] NF (liderazgo) leadership;
(sede) central office; **J~ de la aviación civil**
≈ Civil Aviation Authority; **~ de policía**
police headquarters sg

jefazo [xe'faθo] NM bigwig

jefe, -a ['xefe, a] NM/F (gen) chief, head;
(patrón) boss; (Pol) leader; (Com)
manager(ess); **~ de camareros** head waiter;
~ de cocina chef; **~ ejecutivo** (Com) chief
executive; **~ de estación** stationmaster;
~ de estado head of state; **~ de oficina** (Com)
office manager; **~ de producción** (Com)
production manager; **~ supremo**
commander-in-chief; **~ de estudios** (Escol)

director of studies; **~ de gobierno** head of government; **ser el ~** (fig) to be the boss

JEN [xen] NF ABR (*ESP*) = **Junta de Energía Nuclear**

jengibre [xen'xiβre] NM ginger

jeque ['xeke] NM sheik(h)

jerarquía [xerar'kia] NF (*orden*) hierarchy; (*rango*) rank

jerárquico, -a [xe'rarkiko, a] ADJ hierarchic(al)

jerez [xe'reθ] NM sherry; **J~ de la Frontera** Jerez

jerezano, -a [xere'θano, a] ADJ of o from Jerez ▸ NM/F native o inhabitant of Jerez

jerga ['xerɣa] NF (*tela*) coarse cloth; (*lenguaje*) jargon; **~ informática** computer jargon

jerigonza [xeri'ɣonθa] NF (*jerga*) jargon, slang; (*galimatías*) nonsense, gibberish

jeringa [xe'ringa] NF syringe; (*Am*) annoyance, bother; **~ de engrase** grease gun

jeringar [xerin'gar] /**1h**/ VT to annoy, bother

jeringue etc [xe'ringe] VB ver **jeringar**

jeringuilla [xerin'guiʎa] NF syringe

jeroglífico [xero'ɣlifiko] NM hieroglyphic

jersey [xer'sei] (*pl* **jerseys**) NM jersey, pullover, jumper

Jerusalén [xerusa'len] N Jerusalem

Jesucristo [xesu'kristo] NM Jesus Christ

jesuita [xe'swita] ADJ, NM Jesuit

Jesús [xe'sus] NM Jesus; **¡~!** good heavens!; (*al estornudar*) bless you!

jet [jet] (*pl* **jets** [jet]) NM jet (plane) ▸ NF: **la ~** the jet set

jeta ['xeta] NF (*Zool*) snout; (*fam: cara*) mug; **¡que ~ tienes!** (*fam: insolencia*) you've got a nerve!

jíbaro, -a ['xiβaro, a] ADJ, NM/F Jíbaro (Indian)

jícara ['xikara] NF small cup

jiennense [xjen'nense] ADJ of o from Jaén ▸ NMF native o inhabitant of Jaén

jilguero [xil'ɣero] NM goldfinch

jinete, -a [xi'nete, a] NM/F horseman(-woman)

jipijapa [xipi'xapa] NM (*Am*) straw hat

jira ['xira] NF (*de tela*) strip; (*excursión*) picnic

jirafa [xi'rafa] NF giraffe

jirón [xi'ron] NM rag, shred

jitomate [xito'mate] NM (*Am*) tomato

JJ.OO. NMPL ABR = **Juegos Olímpicos**

jocosidad [xokosi'ðað] NF humour; (*chiste*) joke

jocoso, -a [xo'koso, a] ADJ humorous, jocular

joder [xo'ðer] /**2a**/ (*fam!*) VT to fuck (*fam!*), screw (*fam!*); (*fig: fastidiar*) to piss off (*fam!*), bug; **joderse** VR (*fracasar*) to fail; **¡~!** damn it!; **se jodió todo** everything was ruined

jodido, -a [xo'ðiðo, a] ADJ (*fam!: difícil*) awkward; **estoy ~** I'm knackered

jofaina [xo'faina] NF washbasin

jogging ['joɣin] NM (*Am*) tracksuit (*Brit*), sweat suit (*US*)

jojoba [xo'xoβa] NF jojoba

jolgorio [xol'ɣorjo] NM (*juerga*) fun, revelry

jonrón [xon'ron] NM home run

Jordania [xor'ðanja] NF Jordan

jornada [xor'naða] NF (*viaje de un día*) day's journey; (*camino o viaje entero*) journey; (*día de trabajo*) working day; **~ de 8 horas** 8-hour day; (**trabajar a**) **~ partida** (to work a) split shift

jornal [xor'nal] NM (day's) wage

jornalero, -a [xorna'lero, a] NM/F (day) labourer

joroba [xo'roβa] NF hump

jorobado, -a [xoro'βaðo, a] ADJ hunchbacked ▸ NM/F hunchback

jorobar [xoro'βar] /**1a**/ VT to annoy, pester, bother; **jorobarse** VR to get cross; **¡hay que jorobarse!** to hell with it!; **esto me joroba!** ¡I'm fed up with this!

jota ['xota] NF letter J; (*danza*) Aragonese dance; (*fam*) jot, iota; **no saber ni ~** to have no idea

joven ['xoβen] ADJ young ▸ NM young man, youth ▸ NF young woman, girl

jovencito, -a [xoβen'θito, a] NM/F youngster

jovial [xo'βjal] ADJ cheerful, jolly

jovialidad [xoβjali'ðað] NF cheerfulness

joya ['xoja] NF jewel, gem; (*fig: persona*) gem; **joyas de fantasía** imitation jewellery sg

joyería [xoje'ria] NF (*joyas*) jewellery; (*tienda*) jeweller's (shop)

joyero [xo'jero] NM (*persona*) jeweller; (*caja*) jewel case

Juan [xwan] NM: **Noche de San ~** ver **noche**

juanete [xwa'nete] NM (*del pie*) bunion

jubilación [xuβila'θjon] NF (*retiro*) retirement

jubilado, -a [xuβi'lado, a] ADJ retired ▸ NM/F retired person, pensioner (*Brit*), senior citizen

jubilar [xuβi'lar] /**1a**/ VT to pension off, retire; (*fam*) to discard; **jubilarse** VR to retire

jubileo [xuβi'leo] NM jubilee

júbilo ['xuβilo] NM joy, rejoicing

jubiloso, -a [xuβi'loso, a] ADJ jubilant

judaísmo [xuða'ismo] NM Judaism

judía [xu'ðia] NF ver **judío**

judicatura [xuðika'tura] NF (*cargo de juez*) office of judge; (*cuerpo de jueces*) judiciary

judicial [xuði'θjal] ADJ judicial

judío, -a [xu'ðio, a] ADJ Jewish ▸ NM Jew ▸ NF Jewess, Jewish woman; (*Culin*) bean; **judía blanca** haricot bean; **judía verde** French o string bean

judo ['juðo] NM judo

juego ['xweɣo] VB ver **jugar** ▸ NM (*gen*) play; (*pasatiempo, partido*) game; (*en casino*) gambling; (*deporte*) sport; (*conjunto*) set;

(*herramientas*) kit; **~ de azar** game of chance;
~ de café coffee set; **~ de caracteres** (*Inform*)
font; **~ limpio/sucio** fair/foul o dirty play;
~ de mesa board game; **~ de palabras** pun,
play on words; **Juegos Olímpicos** Olympic
Games; **~ de programas** (*Inform*) suite of
programs; **fuera de ~** (*Deporte: persona*)
offside; (*: pelota*) out of play; **por ~** in fun,
for fun

juegue *etc* ['xweɣe] VB *ver* **jugar**

juerga ['xwerɣa] NF binge; (*fiesta*) party;
ir de ~ to go out on a binge

juerguista [xwer'ɣista] NMF reveller

jueves ['xweβes] NM INV Thursday; *ver tb*
sábado

juez [xweθ] NMF judge; (*Tenis*) umpire; **~ de
instrucción** examining magistrate; **~ de
línea** linesman; **~ de paz** justice of the
peace; **~ de salida** starter

jueza [xweθa] NF judge

jugada [xu'ɣaða] NF play; **buena ~** good
move (o shot o stroke) *etc*

jugador, a [xuɣa'ðor, a] NM/F player; (*en
casino*) gambler

jugar [xu'ɣar] /**1h, 1n**/ VT to play; (*en casino*) to
gamble; (*apostar*) to bet ▶ VI to play; to
gamble; (*Com*) to speculate; **jugarse** VR to
gamble (away); **~ al fútbol** to play football;
¡me la han jugado! (*fam*) I've been had!;
¿quién juega? whose move is it?; **jugarse el
todo por el todo** to stake one's all, go for
bust

jugarreta [xuɣa'rreta] NF (*mala jugada*) bad
move; (*trampa*) dirty trick; **hacer una ~ a
algn** to play a dirty trick on sb

juglar [xu'ɣlar] NM minstrel

jugo ['xuɣo] NM (*Bot, de fruta*) juice; (*fig*)
essence, substance; **~ de naranja** (*esp Am*)
orange juice

jugoso, -a [xu'ɣoso, a] ADJ juicy; (*fig*)
substantial, important

jugué [xu'ɣe], **juguemos** *etc* [xu'ɣemos] VB
ver **jugar**

juguete [xu'ɣete] NM toy

juguetear [xuɣete'ar] /**1a**/ VI to play

juguetería [xuɣete'ria] NF toyshop

juguetón, -ona [xuɣe'ton, ona] ADJ playful

juicio ['xwiθjo] NM judgement; (*sana razón*)
sanity, reason; (*opinión*) opinion; (*Jur: proceso*)
trial; **estar fuera de ~** to be out of one's
mind; **a mi ~** in my opinion

juicioso, -a [xwi'θjoso, a] ADJ wise, sensible

JUJEM [xu'xem] NF ABR (*Esp Mil*) = **Junta de
Jefes del Estado Mayor**

jul. ABR (= *julio*) Jul.

julio ['xuljo] NM July; **el uno** o **el primero
de ~** the first of July; **en el mes de ~**
during July; **en ~ del año que viene**
in July of next year

jumento, -a [xu'mento, a] NM/F donkey

jumper ['dʒumper] NM (*Am*) pinafore dress
(*Brit*), jumper (*US*)

jun. ABR (= *junio*) Jun.

junco ['xunko] NM rush, reed

jungla ['xungla] NF jungle

junio ['xunjo] NM June; *ver tb* **julio**

junta ['xunta] NF *ver* **junto**

juntar [xun'tar] /**1a**/ VT to join, unite;
(*maquinaria*) to assemble, put together;
(*dinero*) to collect; **juntarse** VR to join, meet;
(*reunirse: personas*) to meet, assemble;
(*arrimarse*) to approach, draw closer;
juntarse con algn to join sb

junto, -a ['xunto, a] ADJ joined; (*unido*) united;
(*anexo*) near, close; (*contiguo, próximo*) next,
adjacent ▶ NF (*asamblea*) meeting, assembly;
(*comité, consejo*) board, council, committee;
(*Mil, Pol*) junta; (*articulación*) joint ▶ ADV: **todo
~** all at once ▶ PREP: **~ a** near (to), next to;
juntos together; **~ con** (together) with;
junta constitutiva (*Com*) statutory
meeting; **junta directiva** (*Com*) board of
management; **junta general
extraordinaria** (*Com*) extraordinary general
meeting

juntura [xun'tura] NF (*punto de unión*) join,
junction; (*articulación*) joint

jura ['xura] NF oath, pledge; **~ de bandera**
(ceremony of taking the) oath of allegiance

jurado [xu'raðo] NM (*Jur: individuo*) juror;
(*: grupo*) jury; (*de concurso: grupo*) panel (of
judges); (*: individuo*) member of a panel

juramentar [xuramen'tar] /**1a**/ VT to swear
in, administer the oath to; **juramentarse** VR
to be sworn in, take the oath

juramento [xura'mento] NM oath;
(*maldición*) oath, curse; **bajo ~** on oath;
prestar ~ to take the oath; **tomar ~ a** to
swear in, administer the oath to

jurar [xu'rar] /**1a**/ VT, VI to swear; **~ en falso** to
commit perjury; **jurárselas a algn** to have
it in for sb

jurídico, -a [xu'riðiko, a] ADJ legal, juridical

jurisdicción [xurisðik'θjon] NF (*poder,
autoridad*) jurisdiction; (*territorio*) district

jurisprudencia [xurispru'ðenθja] NF
jurisprudence

jurista [xu'rista] NMF jurist

justamente [xusta'mente] ADV justly, fairly;
(*precisamente*) just, exactly

justicia [xus'tiθja] NF justice; (*equidad*)
fairness, justice; **de ~** deservedly

justiciero, -a [xusti'θjero, a] ADJ just,
righteous

justificable [xustifi'kaβle] ADJ justifiable

justificación [xustifika'θjon] NF
justification; **~ automática** (*Inform*)
automatic justification

justificado, -a [xustifi'kaðo, a] ADJ (*Tip*): **(no) ~** (un)justified

justificante [xustifi'kante] NM voucher; **~ médico** sick note

justificar [xustifi'kar] /**1g**/ VT (*tb Tip*) to justify; (*probar*) to verify

justifique*etc* [xusti'fike] VB *ver* **justificar**

justo, -a ['xusto, a] ADJ (*equitativo*) just, fair, right; (*preciso*) exact, correct; (*ajustado*) tight
▸ ADV (*precisamente*) exactly, precisely; (*apenas a tiempo*) just in time; **¡~!** that's it!, correct!; **llegaste muy ~** you just made it; **vivir muy ~** to be hard up

juvenil [xuβe'nil] ADJ youthful

juventud [xuβen'tuð] NF (*adolescencia*) youth; (*jóvenes*) young people *pl*

juzgado [xuθ'yaðo] NM tribunal; (*Jur*) court

juzgar [xuθ'yar] /**1h**/ VT to judge; **a ~ por ...** to judge by ..., judging by ...; **~ mal** to misjudge; **júzguelo usted mismo** see for yourself

Kk

K, k [ka] NF (*letra*) K, k; **K de Kilo** K for King
K ABR (= 1.000) K; (*Inform*: = 1.024) K
Kampuchea [kampu'tʃea] NF Kampuchea
karaoke [kara'oke] NM karaoke
kárate ['karate], **karate** [ka'rate] NM karate
Kazajstán [kaθaxs'tan] NM Kazakhstan
k/c. ABR (= *kilociclos*) kc.
Kenia ['kenja] NF Kenya
keniata [ke'njata] ADJ, NMF Kenyan
kepí, kepis [ke'pi, 'kepis] NM (*esp Am*) kepi, military hat
kerosene [kero'sene] NM kerosene
Kg, kg ABR (= *kilogramo(s)*) K, kg
KGB SIGLA M KGB
kilate [ki'late] NM = **quilate**
kilo ['kilo] NM kilo
kilobyte ['kiloβait] NM (*Inform*) kilobyte
kilogramo [kilo'ɣramo] NM kilogramme (*Brit*), kilogram (*US*)
kilolitro [kilo'litro] NM kilolitre (*Brit*), kiloliter (*US*)
kilometraje [kilome'traxe] NM distance in kilometres, ≈ mileage
kilométrico, -a [kilo'metriko, a] ADJ kilometric; (*fam*) very long; (**billete**) ~ (*Ferro*) mileage ticket
kilómetro [ki'lometro] NM kilometre (*Brit*), kilometer (*US*)
kiloocteto [kilook'teto] NM (*Inform*) kilobyte
kilovatio [kilo'βatjo] NM kilowatt
kiosco ['kjosko] NM = **quiosco**
Kirguizistán [kirɣiθis'tan] NM Kirghizia
kiwi ['kiwi] NM kiwi (fruit)
kleenex® [kli'neks] NM paper handkerchief, tissue
km ABR (= *kilómetro(s)*) km
km/h ABR (= *kilómetros por hora*) km/h
knock-out ['nokau], **K.O.** ['kao] NM knockout; (*golpe*) knockout blow; **dejar** *o* **poner a algn** ~ to knock sb out
kosovar, a [koso'βar, a] ADJ Kosovan
Kosovo [koso'βo] NM Kosovo
k.p.h. ABR (= *kilómetros por hora*) km/h
kurdo, -a ['kurðo, a] ADJ Kurdish ▶ NM/F Kurd ▶ NM (*Ling*) Kurdish
kuwaití [kuβai'ti] ADJ, NMF Kuwaiti
kv ABR (= *kilovatio*) kw
kv/h ABR (= *kilovatios-hora*) kw-h

k

Ll

L, l ['ele] NF (*letra*) L, l; **L de Lorenzo** L for Lucy (*Brit*) o Love (*US*)
l ABR (= *litro(s)*) l; (= *libro*) bk
L/ ABR (*Com*) = **letra**
la [la] ARTÍCULO DEFINIDO FSG the ▶ PRON her; (*en relación a usted*) you; (*en relación a una cosa*) it ▶ NM (*Mus*) A; **está en la cárcel** he's in jail; **la del sombrero rojo** the woman/girl/one in the red hat
laberinto [laβe'rinto] NM labyrinth
labia ['laβja] NF fluency; (*pey*) glibness; **tener mucha ~** to have the gift of the gab
labial [la'βjal] ADJ labial
labio ['laβjo] NM lip; (*de vasija etc*) edge, rim; **~ inferior/superior** lower/upper lip
labor [la'βor] NF labour; (*Agr*) farm work; (*tarea*) job, task; (*Costura*) needlework, sewing; (*punto*) knitting; **~ de equipo** teamwork; **~ de ganchillo** crochet; **labores domésticas** o **del hogar** household chores
laborable [laβo'raβle] ADJ (*Agr*) workable; **día ~** working day
laboral [laβo'ral] ADJ (*accidente, conflictividad*) industrial; (*jornada*) working; (*derecho, relaciones*) labour *cpd*
laboralista [laβora'lista] ADJ: **abogado ~** labour lawyer
laborar [laβo'rar] /1a/ VI to work
laboratorio [laβora'torjo] NM laboratory
laborioso, -a [laβo'rjoso, a] ADJ (*persona*) hard-working; (*trabajo*) tough
laborista [laβo'rista] (*Pol*) ADJ: **Partido L~** Labour Party ▶ NMF Labour Party member o supporter
labrado, -a [la'βraðo, a] ADJ worked; (*madera*) carved; (*metal*) wrought ▶ NM (*Agr*) cultivated field
Labrador [laβra'ðor] NM Labrador
labrador, a [laβra'ðor, a] ADJ farming *cpd* ▶ NM/F farmer
labranza [la'βranθa] NF (*Agr*) cultivation
labrar [la'βrar] /1a/ VT to work; (*madera etc*) to carve; (*fig*) to cause, bring about
labriego, -a [la'βrjeɣo, a] NM/F peasant

laca ['laka] NF lacquer; (*de pelo*) hairspray; **~ de uñas** nail varnish
lacayo [la'kajo] NM lackey
lacerar [laθe'rar] /1a/ VT to lacerate
lacio, -a ['laθjo, a] ADJ (*pelo*) lank, straight
lacón [la'kon] NM shoulder of pork
lacónico, -a [la'koniko, a] ADJ laconic
lacra ['lakra] NF (*defecto*) blemish; **~ social** social disgrace
lacrar [la'krar] /1a/ VT (*cerrar*) to seal (with sealing wax)
lacre ['lakre] NM sealing wax
lacrimógeno, -a [lakri'moxeno, a] ADJ (*fig*) sentimental; **gas ~** tear gas
lacrimoso, -a [lakri'moso, a] ADJ tearful
lactancia [lak'tanθja] NF lactation, breast-feeding
lactar [lak'tar] /1a/ VT, VI to suckle, breast-feed
lácteo, -a ['lakteo, a] ADJ: **productos lácteos** dairy products
ladear [laðe'ar] /1a/ VT to tip, tilt ▶ VI to tilt; **ladearse** VR to lean; (*Deporte*) to swerve; (*Aviat*) to bank, turn
ladera [la'ðera] NF slope
ladino, -a [la'ðino, a] ADJ cunning
lado ['laðo] NM (*gen*) side; (*fig*) protection; (*Mil*) flank; **~ izquierdo** left(-hand) side; **~ a ~** side by side; **al ~ de** next to, beside; **hacerse a un ~** to stand aside; **poner de ~** to put on its side; **poner a un ~** to put aside; **me da de ~** I don't care; **por un ~ ..., por otro ~ ...** on the one hand ..., on the other (hand) ...; **por todos lados** on all sides, all round (*Brit*)
ladrar [la'ðrar] /1a/ VI to bark
ladrido [la'ðriðo] NM bark, barking
ladrillo [la'ðriʎo] NM (*gen*) brick; (*azulejo*) tile; (*fam: negocio*) real estate (business)
ladrón, -ona [la'ðron, ona] NM/F thief
lagar [la'ɣar] NM (wine/oil) press
lagartija [laɣar'tixa] NF (small) lizard, wall lizard
lagarto [la'ɣarto] NM (*Zool*) lizard; (*Am*) alligator

lago ['laɣo] NM lake

Lagos ['laɣos] NM Lagos

lágrima ['laɣrima] NF tear

lagrimal [laɣri'mal] NM (inner) corner of the eye

lagrimear [laɣrime'ar] /**1a**/ VI to weep; (ojos) to water

laguna [la'ɣuna] NF (lago) lagoon; (en escrito, conocimientos) gap

laico, -a ['laiko, a] ADJ lay ▶ NM/F layman(-woman)

laja ['laxa] NF rock

lamber [lam'ber] /**2a**/ VT (Am) to lick

lambiscón, -ona [lambis'kon, ona] ADJ flattering ▶ NM/F flatterer

lameculos [lame'kulos] NMF (fam) arselicker (fam!), crawler

lamentable [lamen'taβle] ADJ lamentable, regrettable; (miserable) pitiful

lamentación [lamenta'θjon] NF lamentation; **ahora no sirven lamentaciones** it's no good crying over spilt milk

lamentar [lamen'tar] /**1a**/ VT (sentir) to regret; (deplorar) to lament; **lamentarse** VR to lament; **lo lamento mucho** I'm very sorry

lamento [la'mento] NM lament

lamer [la'mer] /**2a**/ VT to lick

lámina ['lamina] NF (plancha delgada) sheet; (para estampar, estampa) plate; (grabado) engraving

laminar [lami'nar] /**1a**/ VT (en libro) to laminate; (Tec) to roll

lámpara ['lampara] NF lamp; ~ **de alcohol/gas** spirit/gas lamp; ~ **de pie** standard lamp

lamparilla [lampa'riʎa] NF night-light

lamparón [lampa'ron] NM (Med) scrofula; (mancha) (large) grease spot

lampiño, -a [lam'piɲo, a] ADJ (sin pelo) hairless

lana ['lana] NF wool; (tela) woollen (BRIT) o woolen (US) cloth; (Am fam: dinero) dough; **(hecho) de** ~ wool cpd

lance etc ['lanθe] VB ver **lanzar** ▶ NM (golpe) stroke; (suceso) event, incident

lanceta [lan'seta] NF (Am) sting

lancha ['lantʃa] NF launch; ~ **motora** motorboat; ~ **de pesca** fishing boat; ~ **salvavidas/torpedera** lifeboat/torpedo boat; ~ **neumática** rubber dinghy

lanero, -a [la'nero, a] ADJ wool cpd

langosta [lan'gosta] NF (insecto) locust; (crustáceo) lobster; (: de río) crayfish

langostino [langos'tino] NM prawn; (de agua dulce) crayfish

languidecer [langiðe'θer] /**2d**/ VI to languish

languidez [langi'ðeθ] NF languor

languidezca etc [langi'ðeθka] VB ver **languidecer**

lánguido, -a ['langiðo, a] ADJ (gen) languid; (sin energía) listless

lanilla [la'niʎa] NF nap; (tela) thin flannel cloth

lanolina [lano'lina] NF lanolin(e)

lanudo, -a [la'nuðo, a] ADJ woolly, fleecy

lanza ['lanθa] NF (arma) lance, spear; **medir lanzas** to cross swords

lanzacohetes [lanθako'etes] NM INV rocket launcher

lanzadera [lanθa'ðera] NF shuttle

lanzado, -a [lan'θaðo, a] ADJ (atrevido) forward; (decidido) determined; **ir** ~ (rápido) to fly along

lanzallamas [lanθa'ʎamas] NM INV flamethrower

lanzamiento [lanθa'mjento] NM (gen) throwing; (Naut, Com) launch, launching; ~ **de pesos** putting the shot

lanzar [lan'θar] /**1f**/ VT (gen) to throw; (con violencia) to fling; (Deporte: pelota) to bowl, pitch (US); (Naut, Com) to launch; (Jur) to evict; (grito) to give, utter; **lanzarse** VR to throw o.s. (fig) to take the plunge; **lanzarse a** (fig) to embark upon

Lanzarote [lanθa'rote] NM Lanzarote

lanzatorpedos [lanθator'peðos] NM INV torpedo tube

lapa ['lapa] NF limpet

La Paz NF La Paz

lapicero [lapi'θero] NM (lápiz) pencil; (Am: portaminas) propelling (BRIT) o mechanical (US) pencil; (: bolígrafo) ballpoint pen, Biro®

lápida ['lapiða] NF stone; ~ **conmemorativa** memorial stone; ~ **mortuoria** headstone

lapidar [lapi'ðar] /**1a**/ VT to stone; (Tec) to polish, lap

lapidario, -a [lapi'ðarjo, a] ADJ, NM lapidary

lápiz ['lapiθ] NM pencil; ~ **de color** coloured pencil; ~ **de labios** lipstick; ~ **de ojos** eyebrow pencil; ~ **óptico** o **luminoso** light pen

lapón, -ona [la'pon, ona] ADJ Lapp ▶ NM/F Laplander, Lapp ▶ NM (Ling) Lapp

Laponia [la'ponja] NF Lapland

lapso ['lapso] NM lapse; (error) error; ~ **de tiempo** interval of time

lapsus ['lapsus] NM INV error, mistake

LAR [lar] NF ABR (ESP Jur) = **Ley de Arrendamientos Rústicos**

largamente [larɣa'mente] ADV for a long time; (relatar) at length

largar [lar'ɣar] /**1h**/ VT (soltar) to release; (aflojar) to loosen; (lanzar) to launch; (fam) to let fly; (velas) to unfurl; (Am) to throw; **largarse** VR (fam) to beat it; **largarse a** (Am) to start to

largo, -a ['larɣo, a] ADJ (longitud) long; (tiempo) lengthy; (persona: alta) tall; (: fig) generous ▶ NM length; (Mus) largo; **dos años largos** two long years; **a** ~ **plazo** in the long term; **tiene nueve metros de** ~ it is nine metres long; **a lo ~** (*posición*) lengthways; **a lo ~ de** along; (*tiempo*) all through, throughout; **a la larga** in the long run; **me dio largas con una promesa** she put me off with a promise; **¡~ de aquí!** (*fam*) clear off!

largometraje [larɣome'traxe] NM full-length o feature film

largue *etc* ['larɣe] VB ver **largar**

larguero [lar'ɣero] NM (*Arq*) main beam, chief support; (*de puerta*) jamb; (*Deporte*) crossbar; (*de cama*) bolster

largueza [lar'ɣeθa] NF generosity

larguirucho, -a [larɣi'rutʃo, a] ADJ lanky, gangling

larguísimo, -a [lar'ɣisimo, a] ADJ SUPERLATIVO *de* **largo**

largura [lar'ɣura] NF length

laringe [la'rinxe] NF larynx

laringitis [larin'xitis] NF laryngitis

larva ['larβa] NF larva

las [las] ARTÍCULO DEFINIDO FPL the ▶ PRON them; **~ que cantan** the ones/women/girls who sing

lasaña [la'saɲa] NF lasagne, lasagna

lasca ['laska] NF chip of stone

lascivia [las'θiβja] NF lewdness; (*lujuria*) lust; (*fig*) playfulness

lascivo, -a [las'θiβo, a] ADJ lewd

láser ['laser] NM laser

Las Palmas NF Las Palmas

lástima ['lastima] NF (*pena*) pity; **dar ~** to be pitiful; **es una ~ que** it's a pity that; **¡qué ~!** what a pity!; **estar hecho una ~** to be a sorry sight

lastimar [lasti'mar] /1a/ VT (*herir*) to wound; (*ofender*) to offend; **lastimarse** VR to hurt o.s.

lastimero, -a [lasti'mero, a] ADJ pitiful, pathetic

lastre ['lastre] NM (*Tec*, *Naut*) ballast; (*fig*) dead weight

lata ['lata] NF (*metal*) tin; (*envase*) tin, can; (*fam*) nuisance; **en ~** tinned; **dar (la) ~** to be a nuisance

latente [la'tente] ADJ latent

lateral [late'ral] ADJ side, lateral ▶ NM (*Teat*) wings *pl*

latido [la'tiðo] NM (*del corazón*) beat; (*de herida*) throb(bing)

latifundio [lati'fundjo] NM large estate

latifundista [latifun'dista] NMF owner of a large estate

latigazo [lati'ɣaθo] NM (*golpe*) lash; (*sonido*) crack; (*fig: regaño*) dressing-down

látigo ['latiɣo] NM whip

latiguillo [lati'ɣiʎo] NM (*Teat*) hamming

latín [la'tin] NM Latin; **saber (mucho) ~** (*fam*) to be pretty sharp

latinajo [lati'naxo] NM dog Latin; **echar latinajos** to come out with Latin words

latino, -a [la'tino, a] ADJ Latin

Latinoamérica [latinoa'merika] NF Latin America

latinoamericano, -a [latinoameri'kano, a] ADJ, NM/F Latin American

latir [la'tir] /3a/ VI (*corazón*, *pulso*) to beat

latitud [lati'tuð] NF (*Geo*) latitude; (*fig*) breadth, extent

lato, -a ['lato, a] ADJ broad

latón [la'ton] NM brass

latoso, -a [la'toso, a] ADJ (*molesto*) annoying; (*aburrido*) boring

latrocinio [latro'θinjo] NM robbery

LAU NF ABR (*Esp Jur*) = **Ley de Arrendamientos Urbanos**

laúd [la'uð] NM lute

laudatorio, -a [lauða'torjo, a] ADJ laudatory

laudo ['lauðo] NM (*Jur*) decision, finding

laurear [laure'ar] /1a/ VT to honour, reward

laurel [lau'rel] NM (*Bot*) laurel; (*Culin*) bay

Lausana [lau'sana] NF Lausanne

lava ['laβa] NF lava

lavable [la'βaβle] ADJ washable

lavabo [la'βaβo] NM (*jofaina*) washbasin; (*retrete*) lavatory (*Brit*), toilet (*Brit*), washroom (*US*)

lavadero [laβa'ðero] NM laundry

lavado [la'βaðo] NM washing; (*de ropa*) wash, laundry; (*Arte*) wash; **~ de cerebro** brainwashing; **~ en seco** dry-cleaning

lavadora [laβa'ðora] NF washing machine

lavanda [la'βanda] NF lavender

lavandería [laβande'ria] NF laundry; **~ automática** launderette

lavaparabrisas [laβapara'βrisas] NM INV windscreen washer

lavaplatos [laβa'platos] NM INV dishwasher

lavar [la'βar] /1a/ VT to wash; (*borrar*) to wipe away; **lavarse** VR to wash o.s.; **lavarse las manos** to wash one's hands; (*fig*) to wash one's hands of it; **lavarse los dientes** to brush one's teeth; **~ y marcar** (*pelo*) to shampoo and set; **~ en seco** to dry-clean; **~ los platos** to wash the dishes

lavarropas [laβa'rropas] NM INV (*RPL*) washing machine

lavativa [laβa'tiβa] NF (*Med*) enema

lavavajillas [laβaβa'xiʎas] NM INV dishwasher

laxante [lak'sante] NM laxative

laxitud [laksi'tuð] NF laxity, slackness

lazada [la'θaða] NF bow

lazarillo [laθa'riʎo] NM: **perro de ~** guide dog

lazo ['laθo] NM knot; (*lazada*) bow; (*para animales*) lasso; (*trampa*) snare; (*vínculo*) tie; **~ corredizo** slipknot

lb ABR = **libra**

lbs ABR = **libras**

L/C ABR (= *Letra de Crédito*) B/E
Lda., Ldo. ABR = **Licenciada, o**
le [le] PRON (*directo*) him (*o* her); (: *en relación a usted*) you; (*indirecto*) to him (*o* her *o* it); (: *a usted*) to you
leal [le'al] ADJ loyal
lealtad [leal'taθ] NF loyalty
lebrel [le'βrel] NM greyhound
lección [lek'θjon] NF lesson; **~ práctica** object lesson; **dar lecciones** to teach, give lessons; **dar una ~ a algn** (*fig*) to teach sb a lesson
leche ['letʃe] NF milk; (*fam!*) semen, spunk (*fam!*); **dar una ~ a algn** (*fam*) to belt sb; **estar de mala ~** (*fam*) to be in a foul mood; **tener mala ~** (*fam*) to be a nasty piece of work; **~ condensada/en polvo** condensed/powdered milk; **~ desnatada** skimmed milk; **~ de magnesia** milk of magnesia; **¡~!** hell!
lechera [le'tʃera] NF *ver* **lechero**
lechería [letʃe'ria] NF dairy
lechero, -a [le'tʃero, a] ADJ milk *cpd* ▶ NM milkman ▶ NF (*vendedora*) milkwoman; (*recipiente*) milk pan; (*para servir*) milk churn
lecho ['letʃo] NM (*cama, de río*) bed; (*Geo*) layer; **~ mortuorio** deathbed
lechón [le'tʃon] NM sucking (*BRIT*) *o* suckling (*US*) pig
lechoso, -a [le'tʃoso, a] ADJ milky
lechuga [le'tʃuɣa] NF lettuce
lechuza [le'tʃuθa] NF (barn) owl
lectivo, -a [lek'tiβo, a] ADJ (*horas*) teaching *cpd*; **año** *o* **curso ~** (*Escol*) school year; (*Univ*) academic year
lector, a [lek'tor, a] NM/F reader; (*Escol, Univ*) (*conversation*) assistant ▶ NM: **~ de discos compactos** CD player; **~ óptico de caracteres** (*Inform*) optical character reader ▶ NF: **~ de fichas** (*Inform*) card reader; **~ de libros electrónicos** e-reader, eReader
lectura [lek'tura] NF reading; **~ de marcas sensibles** (*Inform*) mark sensing
leer [le'er] /2e/ VT to read; **~ entre líneas** to read between the lines
legación [leɣa'θjon] NF legation
legado [le'ɣaðo] NM (*don*) bequest; (*herencia*) legacy; (*enviado*) legate
legajo [le'ɣaxo] NM file, bundle (of papers)
legal [le'ɣal] ADJ legal, lawful; (*persona*) trustworthy
legalice *etc* [leɣa'liθe] VB *ver* **legalizar**
legalidad [leɣali'ðað] NF legality
legalizar [leɣali'θar] /1f/ VT to legalize; (*documento*) to authenticate
legaña [le'ɣaɲa] NF sleep (*in eyes*)
legar [le'ɣar] /1h/ VT to bequeath, leave
legatario, -a [leɣa'tarjo, a] NM/F legatee
legendario, -a [lexen'darjo, a] ADJ legendary

legible [le'xiβle] ADJ legible; **~ por máquina** (*Inform*) machine-readable
legión [le'xjon] NF legion
legionario, -a [lexjo'narjo, a] ADJ legionary ▶ NM legionnaire
legislación [lexisla'θjon] NF legislation; (*leyes*) laws *pl*; **~ antimonopolio** (*Com*) anti-trust legislation
legislar [lexis'lar] /1a/ VT to legislate
legislativo, -a [lexisla'tiβo, a] ADJ: **(elecciones) legislativas** = general election
legislatura [lexisla'tura] NF (*Pol*) period of office
legitimar [lexiti'mar] /1a/ VT to legitimize
legítimo, -a [le'xitimo, a] ADJ (*genuino*) authentic; (*legal*) legitimate, rightful
lego, -a ['leɣo, a] ADJ (*Rel*) secular; (*ignorante*) ignorant ▶ NM layman
legua ['leɣwa] NF league; **se ve** (*o* **nota**) **a la ~** you can tell (it) a mile off
legue *etc* ['leɣe] VB *ver* **legar**
leguleyo [leɣu'lejo] NM (*pey*) petty *o* shyster (*US*) lawyer
legumbres [le'ɣumbres] NFPL pulses
leído, -a [le'iðo, a] ADJ well-read
lejanía [lexa'nia] NF distance
lejano, -a [le'xano, a] ADJ far-off; (*en el tiempo*) distant; (*fig*) remote; **L~ Oriente** Far East
lejía [le'xia] NF bleach
lejísimos [le'xisimos] ADV a long, long way
lejos ['lexos] ADV far, far away; **a lo ~** in the distance; **de** *o* **desde ~** from a distance; **está muy ~** it's a long way (away); **¿está ~?** is it far?; **~ de** *prep* far from
lelo, -a ['lelo, a] ADJ silly ▶ NM/F idiot
lema ['lema] NM motto; (*Pol*) slogan
lencería [lenθe'ria] NF (*telas*) linen, drapery; (*ropa interior*) lingerie
lendakari [lenda'kari] NM *head of the Basque Autonomous Government*
lengua ['lengwa] NF tongue; (*Ling*) language; **~ materna** mother tongue; **~ de tierra** (*Geo*) spit *o* tongue of land; **dar a la ~** to chatter; **morderse la ~** to hold one's tongue; **sacar la ~ a algn** (*fig*) to cock a snook at sb; *see note*

> Under the Spanish constitution *lenguas cooficiales* or *oficiales* enjoy the same status as *castellano* in those regions which have retained their own distinct language, ie in Galicia, *gallego*; in the Basque Country, *euskera*; in Catalonia and the Balearic Islands, *catalán*. The regional governments actively promote their own language through the media and the education system. Of the three regions with their own language, Catalonia has the highest number of people who speak the *lengua cooficial*.

lenguado [len'gwaðo] NM sole

lenguaje [len'gwaxe] NM language; (*forma de hablar*) (mode of) speech; **~ comercial** business language; **~ ensamblador** *o* **de alto nivel** (*Inform*) high-level language; **~ máquina** (*Inform*) machine language; **~ original** source language; **~ periodístico** journalese; **~ de programación** (*Inform*) programming language; **en ~ llano** ≈ in plain English

lenguaraz [lengwa'raθ] ADJ talkative; (*pey*) foul-mouthed

lengüeta [len'gweta] NF (*Anat*) epiglottis; (*de zapatos*) tongue; (*Mus*) reed

lenidad [leni'ðað] NF lenience

Leningrado [lenin'graðo] NM Leningrad

lente ['lente] NM *o* F lens; (*lupa*) magnifying glass; **lentes** NMPL glasses; **lentes bifocales/de sol** (*Am*) bifocals/sunglasses; **lentes de contacto** contact lenses; **lentes progresivas** varifocal lenses

lenteja [len'texa] NF lentil

lentejuela [lente'xwela] NF sequin

lentilla [len'tiʎa] NF contact lens

lentitud [lenti'tuð] NF slowness; **con ~** slowly

lento, -a ['lento, a] ADJ slow

leña ['leɲa] NF firewood; **dar ~ a** to thrash; **echar ~ al fuego** to add fuel to the flames

leñador, a [leɲa'ðor, a] NM/F woodcutter

leño ['leɲo] NM (*trozo de árbol*) log; (*madera*) timber; (*fig*) blockhead

Leo ['leo] NM (*Astro*) Leo

león [le'on] NM lion; **~ marino** sea lion

leona [le'ona] NF lioness

leonera [leo'nera] NF (*jaula*) lion's cage; **parece una ~** it's shockingly dirty

leonés, -esa [leo'nes, esa] ADJ, NM/F Leonese ▶ NM (*Ling*) Leonese

leonino, -a [leo'nino, a] ADJ leonine

leopardo [leo'parðo] NM leopard

leotardos [leo'tarðos] NMPL tights

lepra ['lepra] NF leprosy

leprosería [leprose'ria] NF leper colony

leproso, -a [le'proso, a] NM/F leper

lerdo, -a ['lerðo, a] ADJ (*lento*) slow; (*patoso*) clumsy

leridano, -a [leri'ðano, a] ADJ of *o* from Lérida ▶ NM/F native *o* inhabitant of Lérida

les [les] PRON (*directo*) them; (: *en relación a ustedes*) you; (*indirecto*) to them; (: *a ustedes*) to you

lesbiana [les'βjana] ADJ, NF lesbian

lesión [le'sjon] NF wound, lesion; (*Deporte*) injury

lesionado, -a [lesjo'naðo, a] ADJ injured ▶ NM/F injured person

lesionar [lesjo'nar] /**1a**/ VT (*dañar*) to hurt; (*herir*) to wound; **lesionarse** VR to get hurt

letal [le'tal] ADJ lethal

letanía [leta'nia] NF litany; (*retahíla*) long list

letárgico, -a [le'tarxiko, a] ADJ lethargic

letargo [le'taryo] NM lethargy

letón, -ona [le'ton, ona] ADJ, NM/F Latvian ▶ NM (*Ling*) Latvian

Letonia [le'tonja] NF Latvia

letra ['letra] NF letter; (*escritura*) handwriting; (*Com*) letter, bill, draft; (*Mus*) lyrics *pl*; **letras** NFPL (*Univ*) arts; **~ bastardilla/negrilla** italics *pl*/bold type; **~ de cambio** bill of exchange; **~ de imprenta** print; **~ inicial/mayúscula/ minúscula** initial/capital/small letter; **lo tomó al pie de la ~** he took it literally; **~ bancaria** (*Com*) bank draft; **~ de patente** (*Com*) letters patent *pl*; **escribir cuatro letras a algn** to drop a line to sb

letrado, -a [le'traðo, a] ADJ learned; (*fam*) pedantic ▶ NM/F lawyer

letrero [le'trero] NM (*cartel*) sign; (*etiqueta*) label

letrina [le'trina] NF latrine

leucemia [leu'θemja] NF leukaemia

leucocito [leuko'θito] NM white blood cell, leucocyte

leva ['leβa] NF (*Naut*) weighing anchor; (*Mil*) levy; (*Tec*) lever

levadizo, -a [leβa'ðiθo, a] ADJ: **puente ~** drawbridge

levadura [leβa'ðura] NF yeast, leaven; **~ de cerveza** brewer's yeast

levantamiento [leβanta'mjento] NM raising, lifting; (*rebelión*) revolt, rising; (*Geo*) survey; **~ de pesos** weightlifting

levantar [leβan'tar] /**1a**/ VT (*gen*) to raise; (*del suelo*) to pick up; (*hacia arriba*) to lift (up); (*plan*) to make, draw up; (*mesa*) to clear; (*campamento*) to strike; (*fig*) to cheer up, hearten; **levantarse** VR to get up; (*enderezarse*) to straighten up; (*rebelarse*) to rebel; (*sesión*) to be adjourned; (*niebla*) to lift; (*viento*) to rise; **levantarse (de la cama)** to get up, get out of bed; **~ el ánimo** to cheer up

levante [le'βante] NM east; (*viento*) east wind; **el L~** region of Spain extending along the coast from Castellón to Murcia

levantino, -a [leβan'tino, a] ADJ of *o* from the Levante ▶ NM/F: **los levantinos** the people of the Levante

levar [le'βar] /**1a**/ VT, VI: **~ (anclas)** to weigh anchor

leve ['leβe] ADJ light; (*fig*) trivial; (*mínimo*) slight

levedad [leβe'ðað] NF lightness; (*fig*) levity

levita [le'βita] NF frock coat

léxico, -a ['leksiko, a] ADJ lexical ▶ NM (*vocabulario*) vocabulary; (*Ling*) lexicon

ley [lei] NF (*gen*) law; (*metal*) standard; **decreto-~** decree law; **de buena ~** (*fig*) genuine; **según la ~** in accordance with the law, by law, in law

leyenda [le'jenda] NF legend; (*Tip*) inscription

leyendo *etc* [le'jendo] VB *ver* **leer**

leyó *etc* VB *ver* **leer**

LGBT ABR (= *lesbianas, gays, bisexuales y transexuales*) LGBT

liar [li'ar] /**1c**/ VT to tie (up); (*unir*) to bind; (*envolver*) to wrap (up); (*enredar*) to confuse; (*cigarrillo*) to roll; **liarse** VR (*fam*) to get involved; (*confundirse*) to get mixed up; **liarse a palos** to get involved in a fight

lib. ABR (= *libro*) bk.

libanés, -esa [liβa'nes, esa] ADJ, NM/F Lebanese

Líbano ['liβano] NM: **el ~** the Lebanon

libar [li'βar] /**1a**/ VT to suck

libelo [li'βelo] NM satire, lampoon; (*Jur*) petition

libélula [li'βelula] NF dragonfly

liberación [liβera'θjon] NF liberation; (*de la cárcel*) release

liberado, -a [liβe'raðo, a] ADJ liberated; (*Com*) paid-up, paid-in (*US*)

liberal [liβe'ral] ADJ, NMF liberal

liberar [liβe'rar] /**1a**/ VT to liberate

libertad [liβer'tað] NF liberty, freedom; **~ de asociación/de culto/de prensa/de comercio/de palabra** freedom of association/of worship/of the press/of trade/ of speech; **~ condicional** probation; **~ bajo palabra** parole; **~ bajo fianza** bail; **estar en ~** to be free; **poner a algn en ~** to set sb free

libertador, a [liβerta'ðor, a] ADJ liberating ▶ NM/F liberator; **El L~** (*Am*) The Liberator

libertar [liβer'tar] /**1a**/ VT (*preso*) to set free; (*de una obligación*) to release; (*eximir*) to exempt

libertinaje [liβerti'naxe] NM licentiousness

libertino, -a [liβer'tino, a] ADJ permissive ▶ NM/F permissive person

Libia ['liβja] NF Libya

libidinoso, -a [liβiði'noso, a] ADJ lustful; (*viejo*) lecherous

libido [li'βiðo] NF libido

libio, -a ['liβjo, a] ADJ, NM/F Libyan

libra ['liβra] NF pound; **L~** (*Astro*) Libra; **~ esterlina** pound sterling

librador, a [liβra'ðor, a] NM/F drawer

libramiento [liβra'mjento] (*Am*) NM ring road (*Brit*), beltway (*US*)

libranza [li'βranθa] NF (*Com*) draft; (*letra de cambio*) bill of exchange

librar [li'βrar] /**1a**/ VT (*de peligro*) to save; (*batalla*) to wage, fight; (*de impuestos*) to exempt; (*cheque*) to make out; (*Jur*) to exempt; **librarse** VR: **librarse de** to escape from, free o.s. from; **de buena nos hemos librado** we're well out of that

libre ['liβre] ADJ (*gen*) free; (*lugar*) unoccupied; (*tiempo*) spare; (*asiento*) vacant; (*de deudas*) free of debts; (*Com*): **~ a bordo** free on board; **~ de franqueo** post-free; **~ de impuestos** free of tax; **tiro ~** free kick; **los 100 metros ~** the 100 metres freestyle (race); **al aire ~** in the open air; **¿estás ~?** are you free?

librecambio [liβre'kambjo] NM free trade

librecambista [liβrekam'bista] ADJ free-trade *cpd* ▶ NM free-trader

librería [liβre'ria] NF (*tienda*) bookshop; (*estante*) bookcase; **~ de ocasión** secondhand bookshop

librero, -a [li'βrero, a] NM/F bookseller

libreta [li'βreta] NF notebook; (*pan*) one-pound loaf; **~ de ahorros** savings book

libro ['liβro] NM book; **~ de actas** minute book; **~ de bolsillo** paperback; **~ de cabecera** bedside book; **~ de caja** (*Com*) cashbook; **~ de caja auxiliar** (*Com*) petty cash book; **~ de cocina** cookery book (*Brit*), cookbook (*US*); **~ de consulta** reference book; **~ de cuentas** account book; **~ de cuentos** storybook; **~ de cheques** cheque (*Brit*) o check (*US*) book; **~ de entradas y salidas** (*Com*) daybook; **~ de honor** visitors' book; **~ diario** journal; **~ electrónico** e-book; **~ mayor** (*Com*) general ledger; **~ de reclamaciones** complaints book; **~ de texto** textbook

Lic. ABR = **Licenciado, a**

licencia [li'θenθja] NF (*gen*) licence; (*permiso*) permission; **~ por enfermedad** sick leave; **~ con goce de sueldo** (*Am*) paid leave; **~ de armas/de caza** gun/game licence; **~ de exportación** (*Com*) export licence; **~ poética** poetic licence

licenciado, -a [liθen'θjaðo, a] ADJ licensed ▶ NM/F graduate; **L~ en Filosofía y Letras** ≈ Bachelor of Arts; *see note*

> When students finished University after an average of five years they used to receive the degree of *licenciado*. If the course was only three years, they were awarded the degree of *diplomado*. Now the average length of a university degree or *grado* is four years, like the rest of Europe. *Cursos de posgrado*, postgraduate courses, are becoming increasingly popular, especially one-year specialist courses called *masters*.

licenciar [liθen'θjar] /**1b**/ VT (*empleado*) to dismiss; (*permitir*) to permit, allow; (*soldado*) to discharge; (*estudiante*) to confer a degree upon; **licenciarse** VR: **licenciarse en derecho** to graduate in law; **licenciarse en letras** to get an arts degree

licenciatura [liθenθja'tura] NF (*título*) degree; (*estudios*) degree course

licencioso, -a [liθen'θjoso, a] ADJ licentious

liceo [li'θeo] NM (*espAm*) (high) school

licitación [liθita'θjon] NF bidding; (*oferta*) tender, offer

licitador [liθita'ðor] NM bidder

licitar [liθi'tar] /**1a**/ VT to bid for ▸ VI to bid

lícito, -a ['liθito, a] ADJ (*legal*) lawful; (*justo*) fair, just; (*permisible*) permissible

licor [li'kor] NM spirits *pl* (*BRIT*), liquor (*US*); (*con hierbas etc*) liqueur

licra® ['likra] NF Lycra®

licuadora [likwa'ðora] NF blender

licuar [li'kwar] /**1d**/ VT to liquidize

lid [lið] NF combat; (*fig*) controversy

líder ['liðer] NMF leader

liderazgo [liðe'raθγo], **liderato** [liðe'rato] NM leadership

lidia ['liðja] NF bullfighting; (*una lidia*) bullfight; **toros de ~** fighting bulls

lidiar [li'ðjar] /**1b**/ VT, VI to fight

liebre ['ljeβre] NF hare; **dar gato por ~** to con

Lieja ['ljexa] NF Liège

lienzo ['ljenθo] NM linen; (*Arte*) canvas; (*Arq*) wall

lifting ['liftin] NM facelift

liga ['liγa] NF (*de medias*) garter, suspender; (*confederación*) league; (*Am: gomita*) rubber band

ligadura [liγa'ðura] NF bond, tie; (*Med, Mus*) ligature

ligamento [liγa'mento] NM (*Anat*) ligament; (*atadura*) tie; (*unión*) bond

ligar [li'γar] /**1h**/ VT (*atar*) to tie; (*unir*) to join; (*Med*) to bind up; (*Mus*) to slur; (*fam*) to get off with, pick up ▸ VI to mix, blend; (*fam*) to get off with sb; (: *2 personas*) to get off with one another; **ligarse** VR (*fig*) to commit o.s.; **(él) liga mucho** (*fam*) he pulls a lot of women; **~ con** (*fam*) to get off with, pick up; **ligarse a algn** to get off with *o* pick up sb

ligereza [lixe'reθa] NF lightness; (*rapidez*) swiftness; (*agilidad*) agility; (*superficialidad*) flippancy

ligero, -a [li'xero, a] ADJ (*de peso*) light; (*tela*) thin; (*rápido*) swift, quick; (*ágil*) agile, nimble; (*de importancia*) slight; (*de carácter*) flippant, superficial ▸ ADV quickly, swiftly; **a la ligera** superficially; **juzgar a la ligera** to jump to conclusions

light ['lait] ADJ INV (*cigarrillo*) low-tar; (*comida*) diet *cpd*

ligón [li'γon] NM (*fam*) Romeo

ligue *etc* ['liγe] VB *ver* **ligar** ▸ NMF boyfriend (girlfriend) ▸ NM (*persona*) pick-up

liguero [li'γero] NM suspender (*BRIT*) *o* garter (*US*) belt

lija ['lixa] NF (*Zool*) dogfish; **(papel de) ~** sandpaper

lijar [li'xar] /**1a**/ VT to sand

lila ['lila] ADJ INV, NF lilac ▸ NM (*fam*) twit

lima ['lima] NF file; (*Bot*) lime; **~ de uñas** nail file; **comer como una ~** to eat like a horse

limar [li'mar] /**1a**/ VT to file; (*alisar*) to smooth over; (*fig*) to polish up

limbo ['limbo] NM (*Rel*) limbo; **estar en el ~** to be on another planet

limitación [limita'θjon] NF limitation, limit; **~ de velocidad** speed limit

limitado, -a [limi'taðo, a] ADJ limited; **sociedad limitada** (*Com*) limited company

limitar [limi'tar] /**1a**/ VT to limit; (*reducir*) to reduce, cut down ▸ VI: **~ con** to border on; **limitarse** VR: **limitarse a** to limit *o* confine o.s. to

límite ['limite] NM (*gen*) limit; (*fin*) end; (*frontera*) border; **como** ~ at (the) most; (*fecha*) at the latest; **no tener límites** to know no bounds; **~ de crédito** (*Com*) credit limit; **~ de página** (*Inform*) page break; **~ de velocidad** speed limit

limítrofe [li'mitrofe] ADJ bordering, neighbouring

limón [li'mon] NM lemon ▸ ADJ: **amarillo ~** lemon-yellow

limonada [limo'naða] NF lemonade

limonero [limo'nero] NM lemon tree

limosna [li'mosna] NF alms *pl*; **pedir ~** to beg; **vivir de ~** to live on charity

limpiabotas [limpja'βotas] NMF bootblack (*BRIT*), shoeshine boy/girl

limpiacristales [limpjakris'tales] NM INV (*detergente*) window cleaner

limpiador, a [limpja'ðor, a] ADJ cleaning, cleansing ▸ NM/F cleaner ▸ NM (*Am*) = **limpiaparabrisas**

limpiaparabrisas [limpjapara'βrisas] NM INV windscreen (*BRIT*) *o* windshield (*US*) wiper

limpiar [lim'pjar] /**1b**/ VT to clean; (*con trapo*) to wipe; (*quitar*) to wipe away; (*zapatos*) to shine, polish; (*casa*) to tidy up; (*Inform*) to debug; (*fig*) to clean up; (: *purificar*) to cleanse, purify; (*Mil*) to mop up; **~ en seco** to dry-clean

limpieza [lim'pjeθa] NF (*estado*) cleanliness; (*acto*) cleaning; (: *de las calles*) cleansing; (: *de zapatos*) polishing; (*habilidad*) skill; (*fig: Policía*) clean-up; (*pureza*) purity; (*Mil*): **operación de ~** mopping-up operation; **~ étnica** ethnic cleansing; **~ en seco** dry cleaning

limpio, -a ['limpjo, a] ADJ clean; (*moralmente*) pure; (*ordenado*) tidy; (*despejado*) clear; (*Com*) clear, net; (*fam*) honest ▸ ADV: **jugar ~** to play fair; **pasar a ~** to make a fair copy; **sacar algo en ~** to get benefit from sth; **~ de** free from

linaje [li'naxe] NM lineage, family

linaza [li'naθa] NF linseed; **aceite de ~** linseed oil

lince ['linθe] NM lynx; **ser un ~** (fig: observador) to be very observant (: astuto) to be shrewd

linchar [lin'tʃar] /**1a**/ VT to lynch

lindante [lin'dante] ADJ adjoining; **~ con** bordering on

lindar [lin'dar] /**1a**/ VI to adjoin; **~ con** to border on; (Arq) to abut on

linde ['linde] NM O F boundary

lindero, -a [lin'dero, a] ADJ adjoining ▶ NM boundary

lindo, -a ['lindo, a] ADJ pretty, lovely ▶ ADV (esp AM fam) nicely, very well; **canta muy ~** (AM) he sings beautifully; **se divertían de lo ~** they enjoyed themselves enormously

línea ['linea] NF (gen, moral, Pol etc) line; (talle) figure; (Inform): **en ~** on line; **fuera de ~** off line; **~ de estado** status line; **~ de formato** format line; **~ aérea** airline; **~ de alto el fuego** ceasefire line; **~ de fuego** firing line; **~ de meta** goal line; (de carrera) finishing line; **~ de montaje** assembly line; **~ discontinua** (Auto) broken line; **~ dura** (Pol) hard line; **~ recta** straight line; **la ~ de 2013** (moda) the 2013 look

lineal [line'al] ADJ linear

lingote [lin'gote] NM ingot

lingüista [lin'gwista] NMF linguist

lingüística [lin'gwistika] NF linguistics sg

linimento [lini'mento] NM liniment

lino ['lino] NM linen; (Bot) flax

linóleo [li'noleo] NM lino, linoleum

linterna [lin'terna] NF lantern, lamp; **~ eléctrica** o **a pilas** torch (BRIT), flashlight (US)

lío ['lio] NM bundle; (desorden) muddle, mess; (fam: follón) fuss; (: relación amorosa) affair; **armar un ~** to make a fuss; **meterse en un ~** to get into a jam; **tener un ~ con algn** to be having an affair with sb

lipotimia [lipo'timja] NF blackout

liquen ['liken] NM lichen

liquidación [likiða'θjon] NF liquidation; (de cuenta) settlement; **venta de ~** clearance sale

liquidar [liki'ðar] /**1a**/ VT (Química) to liquefy; (Com) to liquidate; (deudas) to pay off; (empresa) to wind up; **~ a algn** to bump sb off, rub sb out (fam)

liquidez [liki'ðeθ] NF liquidity

líquido, -a ['likiðo, a] ADJ liquid; (ganancia) net ▶ NM liquid; (Com: efectivo) ready cash o money; (: ganancia) net amount o profit; **~ imponible** net taxable income

lira ['lira] NF (Mus) lyre; (moneda) lira

lírico, -a ['liriko, a] ADJ lyrical

lirio ['lirjo] NM (Bot) iris

lirismo [li'rismo] NM lyricism; (sentimentalismo) sentimentality

lirón [li'ron] NM (Zool) dormouse; (fig) sleepyhead

Lisboa [lis'βoa] NF Lisbon

lisboeta [lisβo'eta] ADJ of o from Lisbon ▶ NMF native o inhabitant of Lisbon

lisiado, -a [li'sjaðo, a] ADJ injured ▶ NM/F cripple

lisiar [li'sjar] /**1b**/ VT to maim; **lisiarse** VR to injure o.s.

liso, -a ['liso, a] ADJ (terreno) flat; (cabello) straight; (superficie) even; (tela) plain; **lisa y llanamente** in plain language, plainly

lisonja [li'sonxa] NF flattery

lisonjear [lisonxe'ar] /**1a**/ VT to flatter; (fig) to please

lisonjero, -a [lison'xero, a] ADJ flattering; (agradable) gratifying, pleasing ▶ NM/F flatterer

lista ['lista] NF list; (en escuela) school register; (de libros) catalogue; (tb: **lista de correos**) poste restante, general delivery (US); (tb: **lista de platos**) menu; (tb: **lista de precios**) price list; **pasar ~** to call the roll; (Escol) to call the register; **~ de direcciones** mailing list; **~ electoral** electoral roll; **~ de espera** waiting list; **tela a listas** striped material

listado, -a [lis'taðo, a] ADJ striped ▶ NM (Com, Inform) listing; **~ paginado** (Inform) paged listing

listar [lis'tar] /**1a**/ VT (Inform) to list

listo, -a ['listo, a] ADJ (perspicaz) smart, clever; (preparado) ready; **~ para usar** ready-to-use; **¿estás ~?** are you ready?; **pasarse de ~** to be too clever by half

listón [lis'ton] NM (de tela) ribbon; (de madera, metal) strip

litera [li'tera] NF (en barco, tren) berth; (en dormitorio) bunk, bunk bed

literal [lite'ral] ADJ literal

literario, -a [lite'rarjo, a] ADJ literary

literato, -a [lite'rato, a] ADJ literary ▶ NM/F writer

literatura [litera'tura] NF literature

litigante [liti'ɣante] NMF litigant, claimant

litigar [liti'ɣar] /**1h**/ VT to fight ▶ VI (Jur) to go to law; (fig) to dispute, argue

litigio [li'tixjo] NM (Jur) lawsuit; (fig): **en ~ con** in dispute with

litigue etc [li'tiɣe] VB ver **litigar**

litografía [litoɣra'fia] NF lithography; (una litografía) lithograph

litoral [lito'ral] ADJ coastal ▶ NM coast, seaboard

litro ['litro] NM litre, liter (US)

Lituania [li'twanja] NF Lithuania

lituano, -a [li'twano, a] ADJ, NM/F Lithuanian ▶ NM (Ling) Lithuanian

liturgia [li'turxja] NF liturgy

liviano, -a [li'βjano, a] ADJ (*persona*) fickle; (*cosa, objeto*) trivial; (*AM*) light

lívido, -a ['liβiðo, a] ADJ livid

living ['liβin] (*pl* **livings**) NM (*esp AM*) sitting room

Ll, ll ['eʎe] NF *former letter in the Spanish alphabet*

llaga ['ʎaɣa] NF wound

llagar [ʎa'ɣar] /**1h**/ VT to make sore; (*herir*) to wound

llague etc ['ʎaɣe] VB ver **llagar**

llama ['ʎama] NF flame; (*fig*) passion; (*Zool*) llama; **en llamas** burning, ablaze

llamada [ʎa'maða] NF call; (*a la puerta*) knock; (*: al timbre*) ring; **~ a cobro revertido** reverse-charge call; **~ al orden** call to order; **~ de atención** warning; **~ a pie de página** reference note; **~ a procedimiento** (*Inform*) procedure call; **~ interurbana** trunk call; **~ metropolitana, ~ local** local call; **~ por cobrar** (*AM*) reverse-charge call

llamado [ʎa'maðo] NM (*AM*) (telephone) call; (*llamamiento*) appeal, call

llamamiento [ʎama'mjento] NM call; **hacer un ~ a algn para que haga algo** to appeal to sb to do sth

llamar [ʎa'mar] /**1a**/ VT to call; (*convocar*) to summon; (*invocar*) to invoke; (*atraer con gesto*) to beckon; (*atención*) to attract; (*Telec: tb:* **llamar por teléfono**) to call, ring up, telephone; (*Mil*) to call up ▸ VI (*por teléfono*) to phone; (*a la puerta*) to knock (o ring); (*por señas*) to beckon; **llamarse** VR to be called, be named; **¿cómo se llama usted?** what's your name?; **¿quién llama?** (*Telec*) who's calling?, who's that?; **no me llama la atención** (*fam*) I don't fancy it

llamarada [ʎama'raða] NF (*llamas*) blaze; (*rubor*) flush; (*fig*) flare-up

llamativo, -a [ʎama'tiβo, a] ADJ showy; (*color*) loud

llamear [ʎame'ar] /**1a**/ VI to blaze

llanamente [ʎana'mente] ADV (*lisamente*) smoothly; (*sin ostentaciones*) plainly; (*sinceramente*) frankly; ver tb **liso**

llaneza [ʎa'neθa] NF (*gen*) simplicity; (*honestidad*) straightforwardness, frankness

llano, -a ['ʎano, a] ADJ (*superficie*) flat; (*persona*) straightforward; (*estilo*) clear ▸ NM plain, flat ground

llanta ['ʎanta] NF (wheel) rim; (*AM*: *neumático*) tyre; (*: cámara*) (inner) tube; **~ de repuesto** (*AM*) spare tyre

llanto ['ʎanto] NM weeping; (*fig*) lamentation; (*canción*) dirge, lament

llanura [ʎa'nura] NF (*lisura*) flatness, smoothness; (*Geo*) plain

llave ['ʎaβe] NF key; (*de gas, agua*) tap (*BRIT*), faucet (*US*); (*Mecánica*) spanner; (*de la luz*) switch; (*Mus*) key; **~ inglesa** monkey wrench; **~ maestra** master key; **~ de contacto, ~ de encendido** (*AM Auto*) ignition key; **~ de paso** stopcock; **echar ~ a** to lock up

llavero [ʎa'βero] NM keyring

llavín [ʎa'βin] NM latchkey

llegada [ʎe'ɣaða] NF arrival

llegar [ʎe'ɣar] /**1h**/ VT to bring up, bring over ▸ VT to arrive; (*bastar*) to be enough; **llegarse** VR: **llegarse a** to approach; **~ a** (*alcanzar*) to reach; (*lograr*) to manage to, succeed in; **~ a saber** to find out; **~ a ser famoso/el jefe** to become famous/the boss; **~ a las manos** to come to blows; **~ a las manos de** to come into the hands of; **no llegues tarde** don't be late; **esta cuerda no llega** this rope isn't long enough

llegue etc ['ʎeɣe] VB ver **llegar**

llenar [ʎe'nar] /**1a**/ VT to fill; (*superficie*) to cover; (*espacio, tiempo*) to fill, take up; (*formulario*) to fill in o out; (*fig*) to heap; **llenarse** VR to fill (up); **llenarse de** (*fam*) to stuff o.s. with

lleno, -a ['ʎeno, a] ADJ full, filled; (*repleto*) full up ▸ NM (*abundancia*) abundance; (*Teat*) full house; **dar de ~ contra un muro** to hit a wall head-on

llevadero, -a [ʎeβa'ðero, a] ADJ bearable, tolerable

llevar [ʎe'βar] /**1a**/ VT to take; (*ropa*) to wear; (*cargar*) to carry; (*quitar*) to take away; (*en coche*) to drive; (*transportar*) to transport; (*ruta*) to follow, keep to; (*traer: dinero*) to carry; (*conducir*) to lead; (*Mat*) to carry; (*aguantar*) to bear; (*negocio*) to conduct, direct; to manage ▸ VI (*suj: camino etc*): **~ a** to lead to; **llevarse** VR to carry off, take away; **llevamos dos días aquí** we have been here for two days; **él me lleva dos años** he's two years older than me; **~ adelante** (*fig*) to carry forward; **~ por delante a uno** (*en coche etc*) to run sb over; (*fig*) to ride roughshod over sb; **~ la ventaja** to be winning o in the lead; **~ los libros** (*Com*) to keep the books; **llevo las de perder** I'm likely to lose; **no las lleva todas consigo** he's not all there; **nos llevó a cenar fuera** she took us out for a meal; **llevarse a uno por delante** (*atropellar*) to run sb over; **llevarse bien** to get on well (together)

llorar [ʎo'rar] /**1a**/ VT to cry, weep ▸ VI to cry, weep; (*ojos*) to water; **~ a moco tendido** to sob one's heart out; **~ de risa** to cry with laughter

lloriquear [ʎorike'ar] /**1a**/ VI to snivel, whimper

lloro ['ʎoro] NM crying, weeping

llorón, -ona [ʎo'ron, ona] ADJ tearful ▸ NM/F cry-baby

lloroso, -a [ʎo'roso, a] ADJ (*gen*) weeping, tearful; (*triste*) sad, sorrowful

llover [ʎo'βer] /**2h**/ vi to rain; ~ **a cántaros** o **a cubos** o **a mares** to rain cats and dogs, pour (down); **ser una cosa llovida del cielo** to be a godsend; **llueve sobre mojado** it never rains but it pours

llovizna [ʎo'βiθna] NF drizzle

lloviznar [ʎoβiθ'nar] /**1a**/ vi to drizzle

llueve etc ['ʎweβe] vb ver **llover**

lluvia ['ʎuβja] NF rain; (cantidad) rainfall; (fig: de balas etc) hail, shower; ~ **radioactiva** radioactive fallout; **día de** ~ rainy day; **una ~ de regalos** a shower of gifts

lluvioso, -a [ʎu'βjoso, a] ADJ rainy

lo [lo] ARTÍCULO DEFINIDO NEUTRO: **lo bueno** the good (thing) ▶ PRON (en relación a una persona) him; (en relación a una cosa) it; **lo mío** what is mine; **lo difícil es que ...** the difficult thing about it is that ...; **no saben lo aburrido que es** they don't know how boring it is; **viste a lo americano** he dresses in the American style; **lo de** that matter of; **lo que** what, that which; **toma lo que quieras** take what(ever) you want; **lo que sea** whatever; **¡toma lo que he dicho!** I stand by what I said!; ver tb **el**

loa ['loa] NF praise

loable [lo'aβle] ADJ praiseworthy

LOAPA [lo'apa] NF ABR (Esp Jur) = **Ley Orgánica de Armonización del Proceso Autónomo**

loar [lo'ar] /**1a**/ vt to praise

lobato [lo'βato] NM (Zool) wolf cub

lobo ['loβo] NM wolf; ~ **de mar** (fig) sea dog; ~ **marino** seal

lóbrego, -a ['loβreɣo, a] ADJ dark; (fig) gloomy

lóbulo ['loβulo] NM lobe

LOC NM ABR (= lector óptico de caracteres) OCR

local [lo'kal] ADJ local ▶ NM place, site; (oficinas) premises pl

localice etc [loka'liθe] vb ver **localizar**

localidad [lokali'ðað] NF (barrio) locality; (lugar) location; (Teat) seat, ticket

localizador NM (de un vuelo) booking reference, reservation code

localizar [lokali'θar] /**1f**/ vt (ubicar) to locate, find; (encontrar) to find, track down; (restringir) to localize; (situar) to place

loción [lo'θjon] NF lotion, wash

loco, -a ['loko, a] ADJ mad; (fig) wild, mad ▶ NM/F lunatic, madman(-woman); ~ **de atar**, ~ **de remate**, ~ **rematado** raving mad; **a lo ~** without rhyme or reason; **ando ~ con el examen** the exam is driving me crazy; **estar ~ con** o **por algo/por algn** to be mad about sth/sb; **estar ~ de alegría** to be overjoyed o over the moon

locomoción [lokomo'θjon] NF locomotion

locomotora [lokomo'tora] NF engine, locomotive

locuaz [lo'kwaθ] ADJ loquacious, talkative

locución [loku'θjon] NF expression

locura [lo'kura] NF madness; (acto) crazy act

locutor, a [loku'tor, a] NM/F (Radio) announcer; (comentarista) commentator; (TV) newscaster, newsreader

locutorio [loku'torjo] NM (Telec) telephone box o booth; (negocio) shop or internet café providing telephone services

lodo ['lodo] NM mud

logia ['loxja] NF (Mil, de masones) lodge; (Arq) loggia

lógico, -a ['loxiko, a] ADJ logical; (correcto) natural; (razonable) reasonable ▶ NM logician ▶ NF logic; **es ~ que ...** it stands to reason that ...; **ser de una lógica aplastante** to be as clear as day

login ['loxin] NM login

logístico, -a [lo'xistiko, a] ADJ logistical ▶ NF logistics pl

logotipo [loɣo'tipo] NM logo

logrado, -a [lo'ɣraðo, a] PP de **lograr** ▶ ADJ (interpretación, reproducción) polished, excellent

lograr [lo'ɣrar] /**1a**/ vt (obtener) to get, obtain; (conseguir) to achieve, attain; ~ **hacer** to manage to do; ~ **que algn venga** to manage to get sb to come; ~ **acceso a** (Inform) to access

logro ['loɣro] NM achievement, success; (Com) profit

logroñés, -esa [loɣro'ɲes, esa] ADJ of o from Logroño ▶ NM/F native o inhabitant of Logroño

Loira ['loira] NM Loire

lóker ['loker] NM (Am) locker

loma ['loma] NF hillock, low ridge

Lombardía [lombar'ðia] NF Lombardy

lombriz [lom'briθ] NF (earth)worm

lomo ['lomo] NM (de animal) back; (Culin: de cerdo) pork loin; (: de vaca) rib steak; (de libro) spine

lona ['lona] NF canvas

loncha ['lontʃa] NF = **lonja**

lonche ['lontʃe] NM (Am) lunch

lonchería [lontʃe'ria] NF (Am) snack bar, diner (US)

londinense [londi'nense] ADJ London cpd, of o from London ▶ NMF Londoner

Londres ['londres] NM London

longaniza [longa'niθa] NF pork sausage

longevidad [lonxeβi'ðað] NF longevity

longitud [lonxi'tuð] NF length; (Geo) longitude; **tener tres metros de** ~ to be three metres long; ~ **de onda** wavelength; **salto de** ~ long jump

longitudinal [lonxituði'nal] ADJ longitudinal

lonja ['lonxa] NF slice; (de tocino) rasher; (Com) market, exchange; ~ **de pescado** fish market

lontananza [lonta'nanθa] NF background;
en ~ far away, in the distance

Lorena [lo'rena] NF Lorraine

loro ['loro] NM parrot

los [los] ARTÍCULO DEFINIDO MPL the ▶ PRON
them; (*en relación a ustedes*) you; **mis libros y
~ tuyos** my books and yours

losa ['losa] NF stone; **~ sepulcral** gravestone

lote ['lote] NM portion, share; (*Com*) lot;
(*Inform*) batch

lotería [lote'ria] NF lottery; (*juego*) lotto; **le
tocó la ~** he won a big prize in the lottery;
(*fig*) he struck lucky; **~ nacional** national
lottery; **~ primitiva** (*Esp*) *type of state-run
lottery; see note*

> Millions of euros are spent every year
> on *loterías*, lotteries. There is the weekly
> *Lotería Nacional* which is very popular
> especially at Christmas. Other weekly
> lotteries are the *Bono Loto* and the (*Lotería*)
> *Primitiva*. One of the most famous
> lotteries is run by the wealthy and
> influential society for the blind, *la ONCE*,
> and the form is called *el cupón de la ONCE* or
> *el cupón de los ciegos*.

lotero, -a [lo'tero, a] NM/F seller of lottery
tickets

Lovaina [lo'βaina] NF Louvain

loza ['loθa] NF crockery; **~ fina** china

lozanía [loθa'nia] NF (*lujo*) luxuriance

lozano, -a [lo'θano, a] ADJ luxuriant;
(*animado*) lively

LSD SIGLA M (= *Dietilamida del Acido Lisérgico*) LSD

lubina [lu'βina] NF (*Zool*) sea bass

lubricante [luβri'kante] ADJ, NM lubricant

lubricar [luβri'kar] /**1g**/, **lubrificar**
[luβrifi'kar] /**1a**/ VT to lubricate

lubrique *etc* [lu'βrike] VB *ver* **lubricar**

lucense [lu'θense] ADJ of *o* from Lugo ▶ NMF
native *o* inhabitant of Lugo

Lucerna [lu'θerna] NF Lucerne

lucero [lu'θero] NM (*Astro*) bright star;
(*fig*) brilliance; **~ del alba/de la tarde**
morning/evening star

luces ['luθes] NFPL *de* **luz**

lucha ['lutʃa] NF fight, struggle; **~ de clases**
class struggle; **~ libre** wrestling

luchar [lu'tʃar] /**1a**/ VI to fight

lucidez [luθi'ðeθ] NF lucidity

lucido, -a [lu'θiðo, a] ADJ (*espléndido*) splendid,
brilliant; (*elegante*) elegant; (*exitoso*) successful

lúcido, -a ['luθiðo, a] ADJ (*persona*) lucid;
(*mente*) logical; (*idea*) crystal-clear

luciérnaga [lu'θjernaɣa] NF glow-worm

lucimiento [luθi'mjento] NM (*brillo*)
brilliance; (*éxito*) success

lucio ['luθjo] NM (*Zool*) pike

lucir [lu'θir] /**3f**/ VT to illuminate, light
(up); (*ostentar*) to show off ▶ VI (*brillar*) to
shine; (*Am*: *parecer*) to look, seem; **lucirse** VR
(*irónico*) to make a fool of o.s.; (*presumir*) to
show off; **la casa luce limpia** the house
looks clean

lucrativo, -a [lukra'tiβo, a] ADJ lucrative,
profitable; **institución no lucrativa** non
profit-making institution

lucro ['lukro] NM profit, gain; **lucros y
daños** (*Com*) profit and loss *sg*

luctuoso, -a [luk'twoso, a] ADJ mournful

lúdico, -a ['luðiko, a] ADJ playful; (*actividad*)
recreational

ludopatía [luðopa'tia] NF addiction to
gambling (*o* videogames)

luego ['lweɣo] ADV (*después*) next; (*más tarde*)
later, afterwards; (*Am fam*: *en seguida*) at once,
immediately; **desde ~** of course; **¡hasta ~!**
see you later!, so long!; **¿y ~?** what next?

lugar [lu'ɣar] NM place; (*sitio*) spot; (*pueblo*)
village, town; **en ~ de** instead of; **en primer
~** in the first place, firstly; **dar ~ a** to give rise
to; **hacer ~** to make room; **fuera de ~** out of
place; **sin ~ a dudas** without doubt,
undoubtedly; **tener ~** to take place;
~ común commonplace; **yo en su ~** if I were
him; **no hay ~ para preocupaciones** there
is no cause for concern

lugareño, -a [luɣa'reɲo, a] ADJ village *cpd*
▶ NM/F villager

lugarteniente [luɣarte'njente] NM deputy

lúgubre ['luɣuβre] ADJ mournful

lujo ['luxo] NM luxury; (*fig*) profusion,
abundance; **de ~** luxury *cpd*, de luxe

lujoso, -a [lu'xoso, a] ADJ luxurious

lujuria [lu'xurja] NF lust

lumbago [lum'baɣo] NM lumbago

lumbre ['lumbre] NF (*luz*) light; (*fuego*) fire;
cerca de la ~ near the fire, at the fireside;
¿tienes ~? (*para cigarro*) have you got a light?

lumbrera [lum'brera] NF luminary; (*fig*)
leading light

luminoso, -a [lumi'noso, a] ADJ luminous,
shining; (*idea*) bright, brilliant

luna ['luna] NF moon; (*vidrio*: *escaparate*) plate
glass; (: *de un espejo*) glass; (: *de gafas*) lens; (*fig*)
crescent; **~ creciente/llena/menguante/
nueva** crescent/full/waning/new moon;
~ de miel honeymoon; **estar en la ~** to have
one's head in the clouds

lunar [lu'nar] ADJ lunar ▶ NM (*Anat*) mole;
tela a lunares spotted material

lunes ['lunes] NM INV Monday; *ver tb* **sábado**

luneta [lu'neta] NF lens

lupa ['lupa] NF magnifying glass

lusitano, -a [lusi'tano, a], **luso, -a** ['luso, a]
ADJ, NM/F Portuguese

lustrador [lustra'ðor] NM (*Am*) bootblack

lustrar [lus'trar] /**1a**/ VT (*esp Am*: *mueble*) to
polish; (*zapatos*) to shine

lustre ['lustre] NM polish; (*fig*) lustre; **dar ~ a** to polish
lustro ['lustro] NM period of five years
lustroso, -a [lus'troso, a] ADJ shining
luterano, -a [lute'rano, a] ADJ Lutheran
luto ['luto] NM mourning; (*congoja*) grief, sorrow; **llevar el** *o* **vestirse de ~** to be in mourning
luxación [luksa'θjon] NF (*Med*) dislocation; **tener una ~ de tobillo** to have a dislocated ankle
Luxemburgo [luksem'burɣo] NM Luxembourg
luz [luθ] (*pl* **luces**) NF (*tb fig*) light; (*fam*) electricity; **dar a ~ un niño** to give birth to a child; **sacar a la ~** to bring to light; **dar la ~** to switch on the light; **encender** (*Esp*) *o* **prender** (*Am*)/**apagar la ~** to switch the light on/off; **les cortaron la ~** their (electricity) supply was cut off; **a la ~ de** in the light of; **a todas luces** by any reckoning; **hacer la ~ sobre** to shed light on; **tener pocas luces** to be dim *o* stupid; **~ de la luna/del sol** *o* **solar** moonlight/sunlight; **~ eléctrica** electric light; **~ roja/verde** red/green light; **~ de cruce** (*Auto*) dipped headlight; **~ de freno** brake light; **~ intermitente/trasera** flashing/rear light; **luces de tráfico** traffic lights; **el Siglo de las Luces** the Age of Enlightenment; **traje de luces** bullfighter's costume

Mm

M, m ['eme] NF (*letra*) M, m; **M de Madrid** M for Mike

m ABR (= *metro(s)*) m; (= *minuto(s)*) min., m; (= *masculino*) m., masc

M. ABR (*Ferro*) = **metro**; (= *mujer*) F

M.ª ABR = **María**

macabro, -a [ma'kaβro, a] ADJ macabre

macaco [ma'kako] NM (*Zool*) rhesus monkey; (*fam*) runt, squirt

macana [ma'kana] NF (*Am: porra*) club; (: *mentira*) lie, fib; (: *tontería*) piece of nonsense

macanudo, -a [maka'nuðo, a] ADJ (*Am fam*) great

macarra [ma'karra] NM (*fam*) thug

macarrones [maka'rrones] NMPL macaroni *sg*

Macedonia [maθe'ðonja] NF Macedonia

macedonia [maθe'ðonja] NF: ~ **de frutas** fruit salad

macedonio, -a [maθe'ðonjo, a] ADJ, NM/F Macedonian ▶ NM (*Ling*) Macedonian

macerar [maθe'rar] /1a/ VT (*Culin*) to soak, macerate; **macerarse** VR to soak, soften

maceta [ma'θeta] NF (*de flores*) pot of flowers; (*para plantas*) flowerpot

macetero [maθe'tero] NM flowerpot stand *o* holder

machacar [matʃa'kar] /1g/ VT to crush, pound; (*moler*) to grind (up); (*aplastar*) to mash ▶ VI (*insistir*) to go on, keep on

machacón, -ona [matʃa'kon, ona] ADJ (*pesado*) tiresome; (*insistente*) insistent; (*monótono*) monotonous

machamartillo [matʃamar'tiλo] NM: **a ~** *adv*: **creer a ~** (*firmemente*) to believe, firmly

machaque *etc* [ma'tʃake] VB *ver* **machacar**

machete [ma'tʃete] NM machete, (large) knife

machetear [matʃete'ar] /1a/ VT (*Am*) to swot (*Brit*), grind away (*US*)

machismo [ma'tʃismo] NM sexism; male chauvinism

machista [ma'tʃista] ADJ, NM sexist; male chauvinist

macho ['matʃo] ADJ male; (*fig*) virile ▶ NM male; (*fig*) he-man, tough guy (*US*); (*Tec: perno*) pin, peg; (*Elec*) pin, plug; (*Costura*) hook

macilento, -a [maθi'lento, a] ADJ (*pálido*) pale; (*ojeroso*) haggard

macizo, -a [ma'θiθo, a] ADJ (*grande*) massive; (*fuerte, sólido*) solid ▶ NM mass, chunk; (*Geo*) massif

macramé [makra'me] NM macramé

macrobiótico, -a [makro'βjotiko, a] ADJ macrobiotic

macrocomando [makroko'mando] NM (*Inform*) macro (command)

macroeconomía [makroekono'mia] NF (*Com*) macroeconomics *sg*

mácula ['makula] NF stain, blemish

macuto [ma'kuto] NM (*Mil*) knapsack

Madagascar [maðaɣas'kar] NM Madagascar

madeja [ma'ðexa] NF (*de lana*) skein, hank; (*de pelo*) mass, mop

madera [ma'ðera] NF wood; (*fig*) nature, character; (: *aptitud*) aptitude; **una ~** a piece of wood; **~ contrachapada** *o* **laminada** plywood; **tiene buena ~** he's made of solid stuff; **tiene ~ de futbolista** he's got the makings of a footballer

maderaje [maðe'raxe], **maderamen** [maðe'ramen] NM timber; (*trabajo*) woodwork, timbering

maderero [maðe'rero] NM timber merchant

madero [ma'ðero] NM beam; (*fig*) ship

madrastra [ma'ðrastra] NF stepmother

madre ['maðre] ADJ mother *cpd*; (*Am*) tremendous ▶ NF mother; (*de vino etc*) dregs *pl*; ~ **adoptiva/política/soltera** foster mother/mother-in-law/unmarried mother; **la M~ Patria** the Mother Country; **sin ~** motherless; **¡~ mía!** oh dear!; **¡tu ~!** (*fam!*) fuck off! (*fam!*); **salirse de ~** (*río*) to burst its banks; (*persona*) to lose all self-control

madreperla [maðre'perla] NF mother-of-pearl

madreselva [maðre'selβa] NF honeysuckle

Madrid [ma'ðrið] N Madrid

madriguera [maðri'ɣera] NF burrow

madrileño, -a [maðri'leɲo, a] ADJ of o from Madrid ▸ NM/F native o inhabitant of Madrid

Madriles [ma'ðriles] NMPL: **Los ~** (fam) Madrid sg

madrina [ma'ðrina] NF godmother; (Arq) prop, shore; (Tec) brace; **~ de boda** bridesmaid

madroño [ma'ðroɲo] NM (Bot) strawberry tree, arbutus

madrugada [maðru'ɣaða] NF early morning, small hours; (alba) dawn, daybreak; **a las cuatro de la ~** at four o'clock in the morning

madrugador, a [maðruɣa'ðor, a] ADJ early-rising

madrugar [maðru'ɣar] /1h/ VI to get up early; (fig) to get ahead

madrugue etc [ma'ðruɣe] VB ver **madrugar**

madurar [maðu'rar] /1a/ VT, VI (fruta) to ripen; (fig) to mature

madurez [maðu're θ] NF ripeness; (fig) maturity

maduro, -a [ma'ðuro, a] ADJ ripe; (fig) mature; **poco ~** unripe

MAE NM ABR (ESP Pol) = **Ministerio de Asuntos Exteriores**

maestra [ma'estra] NF ver **maestro**

maestría [maes'tria] NF mastery; (habilidad) skill, expertise; (AM) Master's Degree

maestro, -a [ma'estro, a] ADJ masterly; (perito) skilled, expert; (principal) main; (educado) trained ▸ NM/F master/mistress; (profesor) teacher ▸ NM (autoridad) authority; (Mus) maestro; (experto) master; (obrero) skilled workman; **~ albañil** master mason; **~ de obras** foreman

mafia ['mafja] NF mafia; **la M~** the Mafia

mafioso [ma'fjoso] NM gangster

Magallanes [maɣa'ʎanes] NM: **Estrecho de ~** Strait of Magellan

magdalena [maɣða'lena] NF fairy cake

magia ['maxja] NF magic

mágico, -a ['maxiko, a] ADJ magic(al) ▸ NM/F magician

magisterio [maxis'terjo] NM (enseñanza) teaching; (profesión) teaching profession; (maestros) teachers pl

magistrado [maxis'traðo] NM magistrate; **Primer M~** (AM) President, Prime Minister

magistral [maxis'tral] ADJ magisterial; (fig) masterly

magistratura [maxistra'tura] NF magistracy; **M~ del Trabajo** (ESP) ≈ Industrial Tribunal

magnánimo, -a [maɣ'nanimo, a] ADJ magnanimous

magnate [maɣ'nate] NM magnate, tycoon; **~ de la prensa** press baron

magnesio [maɣ'nesjo] NM (Química) magnesium

magnetice etc [maɣne'tiθe] VB ver **magnetizar**

magnético, -a [maɣ'netiko, a] ADJ magnetic

magnetismo [maɣne'tismo] NM magnetism

magnetizar [maɣneti'θar] /1f/ VT to magnetize

magnetofón [maɣneto'fon], **magnetófono** [maɣne'tofono] NM tape recorder

magnetofónico, -a [maɣneto'foniko, a] ADJ: **cinta magnetofónica** recording tape

magnicidio [maɣni'θiðjo] NM assassination (of an important person)

magnífico, -a [maɣ'nifiko, a] ADJ splendid, magnificent

magnitud [maɣni'tuð] NF magnitude

mago, -a ['maɣo, a] NM/F magician, wizard; **los Reyes Magos** the Magi, the Three Wise Men; ver tb **Reyes Magos**

magrear [maɣre'ar] /1a/ VT (fam) to touch up

magro, -a ['maɣro, a] ADJ (persona) thin, lean; (carne) lean

maguey [ma'ɣei] NM (Bot) agave

magulladura [maɣuʎa'ðura] NF bruise

magullar [maɣu'ʎar] /1a/ VT (amoratar) to bruise; (dañar) to damage; (fam: golpear) to bash, beat

Maguncia [ma'ɣunθja] NF Mainz

mahometano, -a [maome'tano, a] ADJ Mohammedan

mahonesa [mao'nesa] NF mayonnaise

maicena [mai'θena] NF cornflour, corn starch (US)

mail [meil] NM (fam) email

maillot [ma'jot] NM swimming costume; (Deporte) vest

maître ['metre] NM head waiter

maíz [ma'iθ] NM maize (BRIT), corn (US); sweet corn

maizal [mai'θal] NM maize field, cornfield

majadero, -a [maxa'ðero, a] ADJ silly, stupid

majar [ma'xar] /1a/ VT to crush, grind

majareta [maxa'reta] ADJ (fam) cracked, potty

majestad [maxes'tað] NF majesty; **Su M~** His/Her Majesty; **(Vuestra) M~** Your Majesty

majestuoso, -a [maxes'twoso, a] ADJ majestic

majo, -a ['maxo, a] ADJ nice; (guapo) attractive, good-looking; (elegante) smart

mal [mal] ADV badly; (equivocadamente) wrongly; (con dificultad) with difficulty ▸ ADJ = **malo** ▸ NM evil; (desgracia) misfortune; (daño) harm, damage; (Med) illness ▸ CONJ: **~ que le pese** whether he likes it or not; **me entendió ~** he misunderstood me; **hablar ~ de algn** to speak ill of sb; **huele ~** it smells bad; **ir de ~ en peor** to go from bad to worse; **oigo/veo ~** I can't hear/see very well; **si ~ no recuerdo** if my memory serves me right; **¡menos ~!** just as well!; **~ que bien** rightly or wrongly; **no hay ~ que por bien no venga** every cloud has a silver lining; **~ de ojo** evil eye

malabarismo [mala'β'rismo] NM juggling

malabarista [malaβa'rista] NMF juggler

malaconsejado, -a [malakonse'xaðo, a] ADJ ill-advised

malacostumbrado, -a [malakostum'braðo, a] ADJ (*consentido*) spoiled

malacostumbrar [malakostum'brar] /**1a**/ VT: **~ a algn** to get sb into bad habits

malagueño, -a [mala'ɣeɲo, a] ADJ of o from Málaga ▸ NM/F native o inhabitant of Málaga

Malaisia [ma'laisja] NF Malaysia

malaria [ma'larja] NF malaria

Malasia [ma'lasja] NF Malaysia

malavenido, -a [malaβe'niðo, a] ADJ incompatible

malayo, -a [ma'lajo, a] ADJ Malay(an) ▸ NM/F Malay ▸ NM (*Ling*) Malay

Malaysia [ma'laisja] NF Malaysia

malcarado, -a [malka'raðo, a] ADJ ugly, grim-faced

malcriado, -a [mal'krjaðo, a] ADJ (*consentido*) spoiled

malcriar [mal'krjar] /**1c**/ VT to spoil, pamper

maldad [mal'dað] NF evil, wickedness

maldecir [malde'θir] /**3o**/ VT to curse ▸ VI: **~ de** to speak ill of

maldiciendo *etc* [maldi'θjendo] VB *ver* **maldecir**

maldición [maldi'θjon] NF curse; **¡~!** curse it!, damn!

maldiga *etc* [mal'diɣa], **maldije** *etc* [mal'dixe] VB *ver* **maldecir**

maldito, -a [mal'dito, a] ADJ (*condenado*) damned; (*perverso*) wicked ▸ NM: **el ~** the devil; **¡~ sea!** damn it!; **no le hace ~ (el) caso** he doesn't take a blind bit of notice

maleable [male'aβle] ADJ malleable

maleante [male'ante] ADJ wicked ▸ NMF criminal, crook

malecón [male'kon] NM pier, jetty; (*rompeolas*) breakwater; (*Am: paseo*) sea front, promenade

maledicencia [maleði'θenθja] NF slander, scandal

maleducado, -a [maleðu'kaðo, a] ADJ bad-mannered, rude

maleficio [male'fiθjo] NM curse, spell

malentendido [malenten'diðo] NM misunderstanding

malestar [males'tar] NM (*gen*) discomfort; (*enfermedad*) indisposition; (*fig: inquietud*)

uneasiness; (*Pol*) unrest; **siento un ~ en el estómago** my stomach is upset

maleta [ma'leta] NF case, suitcase; (*Auto*) boot (*BRIT*), trunk (*US*); **hacer la ~** to pack

maletera [male'tera] NF (*Am Auto*) boot (*BRIT*), trunk (*US*)

maletero [male'tero] NM (*Auto*) boot (*BRIT*), trunk (*US*); (*persona*) porter

maletín [male'tin] NM small case, bag; (*portafolio*) briefcase

malevolencia [maleβo'lenθja] NF malice, spite

malévolo, -a [ma'leβolo, a] ADJ malicious, spiteful

maleza [ma'leθa] NF (*malas hierbas*) weeds pl; (*arbustos*) thicket

malgache [mal'ɣatʃe] ADJ of o from Madagascar ▸ NMF native o inhabitant of Madagascar

malgastar [malɣas'tar] /**1a**/ VT (*tiempo, dinero*) to waste; (*recursos*) to squander; (*salud*) to ruin

malhaya [ma'laja] EXCL (*esp Am fam!*) damn (it)! (*fam!*); **¡~ sea/sean!** damn it/them! (*fam!*)

malhechor, a [male'tʃor, a] NM/F delinquent; (*criminal*) criminal

malherido, -a [male'riðo, a] ADJ badly injured

malhumorado, -a [malumo'raðo, a] ADJ bad-tempered

malicia [ma'liθja] NF (*maldad*) wickedness; (*astucia*) slyness, guile; (*mala intención*) malice, spite; (*carácter travieso*) mischievousness

malicioso, -a [mali'θjoso, a] ADJ (*malintencionado*) malicious, spiteful; (*pícaro*) mischievous; (*astuto*) sly, crafty; (*malo*) wicked, evil

malignidad [maliɣni'ðað] NF (*Med*) malignancy; (*malicia*) malice

maligno, -a [ma'liɣno, a] ADJ evil; (*dañino*) pernicious, harmful; (*malévolo*) malicious; (*Med*) malignant ▸ NM: **el ~** the devil

malintencionado, -a [malintenθjo'naðo, a] ADJ (*comentario*) hostile; (*persona*) malicious

malla ['maʎa] NF (*de una red*) mesh; (*red*) network; (*Am: de baño*) swimsuit; (*de ballet, gimnasia*) leotard; **mallas** NFPL tights; **~ de alambre** wire mesh

Mallorca [ma'ʎorka] NF Majorca

mallorquín, -ina [maʎor'kin, ina] ADJ, NM/F Majorcan ▸ NM (*Ling*) Majorcan

malnutrido, -a [malnu'triðo, a] ADJ undernourished

malo, -a ['malo, a] ADJ (**mal** *antes de nmsg*) bad; (*calidad*) poor; (*falso*) false; (*espantoso*) dreadful; (*niño*) naughty ▸ NM/F villain ▸ NM (*Cine: fam*) bad guy ▸ NF spell of bad luck; **estar ~** to be ill; **andar a malas con**

algn to be on bad terms with sb; **estar de malas** (*mal humor*) to be in a bad mood; **lo ~ es que ...** the trouble is that ...

malograr [malo'ɣrar] /**1a**/ VT to spoil; (*plan*) to upset; (*ocasión*) to waste; **malograrse** VR (*plan etc*) to fail, come to grief; (*persona*) to die before one's time

maloliente [malo'ljente] ADJ stinking, smelly

malparado, -a [malpa'raðo, a] ADJ: **salir ~ to** come off badly

malpensado, -a [malpen'saðo, a] ADJ nasty

malquerencia [malke'renθja] NF dislike

malquistar [malkis'tar] /**1a**/ VT: **~ a dos personas** to cause a rift between two people; **malquistarse** VR to fall out

malsano, -a [mal'sano, a] ADJ unhealthy

malsonante [malso'nante] ADJ (*palabra*) nasty, rude

Malta ['malta] NF Malta

malta ['malta] NF malt

malteada [malte'aða] NF (*AM*) milk shake

maltés, -esa [mal'tes, esa] ADJ, NM/F Maltese

maltraer [maltra'er] /**2o**/ VT (*abusar*) to insult, abuse; (*maltratar*) to ill-treat

maltratar [maltra'tar] /**1a**/ VT to ill-treat, mistreat

maltrecho, -a [mal'tretʃo, a] ADJ battered, damaged

malva ['malβa] NF mallow; **~ loca** hollyhock; **(de color de) ~** mauve

malvado, -a [mal'βaðo, a] ADJ evil, villainous

malvavisco [malβa'βisko] NM marshmallow

malvender [malβen'der] /**2a**/ VT to sell off cheap *o* at a loss

malversación [malβersa'θjon] NF embezzlement, misappropriation

malversar [malβer'sar] /**1a**/ VT to embezzle, misappropriate

Malvinas [mal'βinas] NFPL: **Islas ~** Falkland Islands

malware ['malwer] NM malware

mama ['mama] (*pl* **mamás**) NF (*de animal*) teat; (*de mujer*) breast

mamá [ma'ma] NF (*fam*) mum, mummy

mamacita [mama'sita] NF (*AM fam*) mum, mummy

mamadera [mama'dera] NF (*AM*) baby's bottle

mamagrande [mama'grande] NF (*AM*) grandmother

mamar [ma'mar] /**1a**/ VT (*pecho*) to suck; (*fig*) to absorb, assimilate ▶ VI to suck; **dar de ~** to (breast-)feed; (*animal*) to suckle

mamarracho [mama'rratʃo] NM sight, mess

mambo ['mambo] NF (*Mus*) mambo

mameluco [mameluko] (*AM*) NM dungarees *pl* (*BRIT*), overalls *pl* (*US*)

mamífero, -a [ma'mifero, a] ADJ mammalian, mammal *cpd* ▶ NM mammal

mamón, -ona [ma'mon, ona] ADJ small, baby *cpd* ▶ NM/F small baby; (*fam!*) wanker (*fam!*)

mamotreto [mamo'treto] NM hefty volume; (*fam*) whacking great thing

mampara [mam'para] NF (*entre habitaciones*) partition; (*biombo*) screen

mamporro [mam'porro] NM (*fam*): **dar un ~ a** to clout

mampostería [mamposte'ria] NF masonry

mamut [ma'mut] NM mammoth

maná [ma'na] NM manna

manada [ma'naða] NF (*Zool*) herd; (: *de leones*) pride; (: *de lobos*) pack; **llegaron en manadas** (*fam*) they came in droves

Managua [ma'naɣwa] N Managua

manantial [manan'tjal] NM spring; (*fuente*) fountain; (*fig*) source

manar [ma'nar] /**1a**/ VT to run with, flow with ▶ VI to run, flow; (*abundar*) to abound

manaza [ma'naθa] NF big hand

manazas [ma'naθas] NMF: **ser un manazas** to be clumsy

mancebo [man'θeβo] NM (*joven*) young man

mancha ['mantʃa] NF stain, mark; (*de tinta*) blot; (*de vegetación*) patch; (*imperfección*) stain, blemish, blot; (*boceto*) sketch, outline; **la M~** La Mancha

manchado, -a [man'tʃaðo, a] ADJ (*sucio*) dirty; (*animal*) spotted; (*ave*) speckled; (*de tinta*) smudged

manchar [man'tʃar] /**1a**/ VT to stain, mark; (*Zool*) to patch; (*ensuciar*) to soil, dirty; **mancharse** VR to get dirty; (*fig*) to dirty one's hands

manchego, -a [man'tʃeɣo, a] ADJ of *o* from La Mancha ▶ NM/F native *o* inhabitant of La Mancha

mancilla [man'θiʎa] NF stain, blemish

mancillar [manθi'ʎar] /**1a**/ VT to stain, sully

manco, -a ['manko, a] ADJ (*de un brazo*) one-armed; (*de una mano*) one-handed; (*fig*) defective, faulty; **no ser ~** to be useful *o* active

mancomunar [mankomu'nar] /**1a**/ VT to unite, bring together; (*recursos*) to pool; (*Jur*) to make jointly responsible

mancomunidad [mankomuni'ðað] NF union, association; (*comunidad*) community; (*Jur*) joint responsibility

mandado [man'daðo] NM (*orden*) order; (*recado*) commission, errand

mandamás [manda'mas] ADJ, NMF boss; **ser un ~** to be very bossy

mandamiento [manda'mjento] NM (*orden*) order, command; (*Rel*) commandment; **~ judicial** warrant

mandar [man'dar] /**1a**/ VT (*ordenar*) to order; (*dirigir*) to lead, command; (*país*) to rule over; (*enviar*) to send; (*pedir*) to order, ask for ▶ VI to be in charge; (*pey*) to be bossy; **mandarse** VR:

m

mandarse mudar (*Am fam*) to go away, clear off; **¿mande?** pardon?, excuse me? (*US*); **¿manda usted algo más?** is there anything else?; **~ a algn a paseo** o **a la porra** to tell sb to go to hell; **se lo mandaremos por correo** we'll post it to you; **~ hacer un traje** to have a suit made

mandarín [manda'rin] NM petty bureaucrat

mandarina [manda'rina] NF (*fruta*) tangerine, mandarin (orange)

mandatario, -a [manda'tarjo, a] NM/F (*representante*) agent; **primer ~** (*esp Am*) head of state

mandato [man'dato] NM (*orden*) order; (*Pol: período*) term of office; (*: territorio*) mandate; **~ judicial** (search) warrant

mandíbula [man'diβula] NF jaw

mandil [man'dil] NM (*delantal*) apron

Mandinga [man'dinɣa] NM (*Am*) Devil

mandioca [man'djoka] NF cassava

mando ['mando] NM (*Mil*) command; (*de país*) rule; (*el primer lugar*) lead; (*Pol*) term of office; (*Tec*) control; **~ a la izquierda** left-hand drive; **los altos mandos** the high command *sg*; **~ por botón** push-button control; **~ a distancia** remote control; **al ~ de** in charge of; **tomar el ~** to take the lead

mandolina [mando'lina] NF mandolin(e)

mandón, -ona [man'don, ona] ADJ bossy, domineering

manecilla [mane'θiʎa] NF (*Tec*) pointer; (*de reloj*) hand

manejable [mane'xaβle] ADJ manageable; (*fácil de usar*) handy

manejar [mane'xar] /1a/ VT to manage; (*máquina*) to work, operate; (*caballo etc*) to handle; (*casa*) to run, manage; (*Am Auto*) to drive ▶ VI (*Am Auto*) to drive; **manejarse** VR (*comportarse*) to act, behave; (*arreglárselas*) to manage; **"~ con cuidado"** "handle with care"

manejo [ma'nexo] NM (*de bicicleta*) handling; (*de negocio*) management, running; (*Auto*) driving; (*facilidad de trato*) ease, confidence; (*de idioma*) command; **manejos** NMPL intrigues; **tengo ~ del francés** I have a good command of French

manera [ma'nera] NF way, manner, fashion; (*Arte, Lit etc: estilo*) manner, style; **maneras** NFPL (*modales*) manners; **su ~ de ser** the way he is; (*aire*) his manner; **de mala ~** (*fam*) badly, unwillingly; **de ninguna ~** no way, by no means; **de otra ~** otherwise; **de todas maneras** at any rate; **en gran ~** to a large extent; **a mi ~ de ver** in my view; **no hay ~ de persuadirle** there's no way of convincing him

manga ['manga] NF (*de camisa*) sleeve; (*de riego*) hose; **de ~ corta/larga** short-/long-sleeved; **andar ~ por hombro** (*desorden*)

to be topsy-turvy; **tener ~ ancha** to be easy-going

mangante [man'gante] ADJ (*descarado*) brazen ▶ NM (*mendigo*) beggar

mangar [man'gar] /1h/ VT (*unir*) to plug in; (*fam: birlar*) to pinch, nick, swipe; (*mendigar*) to beg

mango ['mango] NM handle; (*Bot*) mango; **~ de escoba** broomstick

mangonear [mangone'ar] /1a/ VT to boss about ▶ VI to be bossy

mangue *etc* ['mange] VB *ver* **mangar**

manguera [man'gera] NF (*de riego*) hose; (*tubo*) pipe; **~ de incendios** fire hose

maní [ma'ni] (*pl* **maníes** o **manises**) NM (*Am: cacahuete*) peanut; (*: planta*) groundnut plant

manía [ma'nia] NF (*Med*) mania; (*fig: moda*) rage, craze; (*disgusto*) dislike; (*malicia*) spite; **tiene manías** she's a bit fussy; **coger ~ a algn** to take a dislike to sb; **tener ~ a algn** to dislike sb

maníaco, -a [ma'niako, a] ADJ maniac(al) ▶ NM/F maniac

maniatar [manja'tar] /1a/ VT to tie the hands of

maniático, -a [ma'njatiko, a] ADJ maniac(al); (*loco*) crazy; (*tiquismiquis*) fussy ▶ NM/F maniac

manicomio [mani'komjo] NM mental hospital (*Brit*), insane asylum (*US*)

manicuro, -a [mani'kuro, a] NM/F manicurist ▶ NF manicure

manido, -a [ma'niðo, a] ADJ (*tema etc*) trite, stale

manifestación [manifesta'θjon] NF (*declaración*) statement, declaration; (*demostración*) show, display; (*Pol*) demonstration; (*concentración*) mass meeting

manifestante [manifes'tante] NMF demonstrator

manifestar [manifes'tar] /1j/ VT to show, manifest; (*declarar*) to state, declare; **manifestarse** VR to show, become apparent; (*Pol: desfilar*) to demonstrate; (*: reunirse*) to hold a mass meeting

manifiesto, -a [mani'fjesto, a] VB *ver* **manifestar** ▶ ADJ clear, manifest ▶ NM manifesto; (*Anat, Naut*) manifest; **poner algo de ~** (*aclarar*) to make sth clear; (*revelar*) to reveal sth; **quedar ~** to be plain o clear

manija [ma'nixa] NF handle

manilla [ma'niʎa] NF (*de reloj*) hand; (*Am*) handle, lever; **manillas (de hierro)** *nfpl* handcuffs

manillar [mani'ʎar] NM handlebars *pl*

maniobra [ma'njoβra] NF manœuvring; (*manejo*) handling; (*fig: movimiento*) manœuvre, move; (*: estratagema*) trick, stratagem; **maniobras** NFPL manœuvres

maniobrar [manioˈβrar] /**1a**/ VT to manœuvre; *(manejar)* to handle ▸ VI to manœuvre

manipulación [manipulaˈθjon] NF manipulation; *(Com)* handling

manipular [manipuˈlar] /**1a**/ VT to manipulate; *(manejar)* to handle

maniquí [maniˈki] NMF model ▸ NM dummy

manirroto, -a [maniˈrroto, a] ADJ lavish, extravagant ▸ NM/F spendthrift

manita [maˈnita] NF little hand; **manitas de plata** artistic hands

manitas [maˈnitas] ADJ INV good with one's hands ▸ NMF: **ser un ~** to be very good with one's hands

manito [maˈnito] NM *(AM: en conversación)* mate *(fam)*, chum

manivela [maniˈβela] NF crank

manjar [manˈxar] NM *(tasty)* dish

mano¹ [ˈmano] NF hand; *(Zool)* foot, paw; *(de pintura)* coat; *(serie)* lot, series; **a ~** by hand; **a ~ derecha/izquierda** on *(o* to) the right(-hand side)/left(-hand side); **a manos llenas** lavishly, generously; **hecho a ~** handmade; **robo a ~ armada** armed robbery; **darse la(s) ~(s)** to shake hands; **de primera ~** (at) first hand; **de segunda ~** (at) second hand; **echar ~ de** to make use of; **echar una ~** to lend a hand; **echar una ~ a** to lay hands on; **está en tus manos** it's up to you; **estrechar la ~ a algn** to shake sb's hand; **~ de obra** labour, manpower; **~ de santo** sure remedy; **¡manos a la obra!** to work!; **manos libres** hands-free; **Pedro es mi ~ derecha** Pedro is my right-hand man; **se le fue la ~** his hand slipped; *(fig)* he went too far; **traer** *o* **llevar algo entre manos** to deal *o* be busy with sth

mano² [ˈmano] NM *(Am fam)* friend, mate

manojo [maˈnoxo] NM handful, bunch; **~ de llaves** bunch of keys

manómetro [maˈnometro] NM *(pressure)* gauge

manopla [maˈnopla] NF *(paño)* flannel; **manoplas** NFPL mittens

manoseado, -a [manoseˈaðo, a] ADJ well-worn

manosear [manoseˈar] /**1a**/ VT *(tocar)* to handle, touch; *(desordenar)* to mess up, rumple; *(insistir en)* to overwork; *(acariciar)* to caress, fondle; *(pey: persona)* to feel *o* touch up

manos libres [ˈmanos ˈliβres] ADJ INV *(teléfono, dispositivo)* hands-free ▸ NM INV hands-free kit

manotazo [manoˈtaθo] NM slap, smack

mansalva [manˈsalβa]: **a ~** adv indiscriminately

mansedumbre [manseˈðumbre] NF gentleness, meekness; *(de animal)* tameness

mansión [manˈsjon] NF mansion

manso, -a [ˈmanso, a] ADJ gentle, mild; *(animal)* tame

manta [ˈmanta] NF blanket; *(Am)* poncho

manteca [manˈteka] NF fat; *(Am)* butter; **~ de cacahuete/cacao** peanut/cocoa butter; **~ de cerdo** lard

mantecado [manteˈkaðo] NM *(Esp: dulce navideño)* Christmas sweet made from flour, almonds and lard; *(helado)* ice cream

mantecoso, -a [manteˈkoso, a] ADJ fat, greasy; **queso ~** soft cheese

mantel [manˈtel] NM tablecloth

mantelería [manteleˈria] NF table linen

mantendré *etc* [mantenˈdre] VB *ver* **mantener**

mantener [manteˈner] /**2k**/ VT to support, maintain; *(alimentar)* to sustain; *(conservar)* to keep; *(Tec)* to maintain, service; **mantenerse** VR *(seguir de pie)* to be still standing; *(no ceder)* to hold one's ground; *(subsistir)* to sustain o.s., keep going; **~ algo en equilibrio** to keep sth balanced; **mantenerse a distancia** to keep one's distance; **mantenerse firme** to hold one's ground

mantenga *etc* [manˈtenga] VB *ver* **mantener**

mantenimiento [manteniˈmjento] NM maintenance; sustenance; *(sustento)* support

mantequería [mantekeˈria] NF *(ultramarinos)* grocer's (shop)

mantequilla [manteˈkiʎa] NF butter

mantilla [manˈtiʎa] NF mantilla; **mantillas** NFPL baby clothes; **estar en mantillas** *(persona)* to be terribly innocent; *(proyecto)* to be in its infancy

manto [ˈmanto] NM *(capa)* cloak; *(de ceremonia)* robe, gown

mantón [manˈton] NM shawl

mantuve *etc* [manˈtuβe] VB *ver* **mantener**

manual [maˈnwal] ADJ manual ▸ NM manual, handbook; **habilidad ~** manual skill

manubrio [maˈnuβrio] NM *(Am Auto)* steering wheel

manufactura [manufakˈtura] NF manufacture; *(fábrica)* factory

manufacturado, -a [manufaktuˈraðo, a] ADJ manufactured

manuscrito, -a [manusˈkrito, a] ADJ handwritten ▸ NM manuscript

manutención [manutenˈθjon] NF maintenance; *(sustento)* support

manzana [manˈθana] NF apple; *(Arq)* block; **~ de la discordia** *(fig)* bone of contention

manzanal [manθaˈnal] NM apple orchard

manzanilla [manθaˈniʎa] NF *(planta)* camomile; *(infusión)* camomile tea; *(vino)* manzanilla

m

manzano [man'θano] NM apple tree

maña ['maɲa] NF (*destreza*) skill; (*pey*) guile; (*ardid*) trick; **con ~** craftily

mañana [ma'ɲana] ADV tomorrow ▸ NM future ▸ NF morning; **de** *o* **por la ~** in the morning; **¡hasta ~!** see you tomorrow!; **pasado ~** the day after tomorrow; **~ por la ~** tomorrow morning

mañanero, -a [maɲa'nero, a] ADJ early-rising

maño, -a ['maɲo, a] ADJ Aragonese ▸ NM/F native *o* inhabitant of Aragon

mañoso, -a [ma'ɲoso, a] ADJ (*hábil*) skilful; (*astuto*) smart, clever

mapa ['mapa] NM map

maple ['maple] NM (*AM*) maple

mapuche [ma'putʃe] ADJ, NMF Mapuche, Araucanian

maqueta [ma'keta] NF (scale) model

maquiavélico, -a [makja'βeliko, a] ADJ Machiavellian

maquillador, a [makiʎa'ðor, a] NM/F (*Teat etc*) make-up artist ▸ NF (*AM Com*) bonded assembly plant

maquillaje [maki'ʎaxe] NM make-up; (*acto*) making up

maquillar [maki'ʎar] /1a/ VT to make up; **maquillarse** VR to put on (some) make-up

máquina ['makina] NF machine; (*de tren*) locomotive, engine; (*Foto*) camera; (*AM: coche*) car; (*fig*) machinery; (: *proyecto*) plan, project; **a toda ~** at full speed; **escrito a ~** typewritten; **~ de afeitar** electric razor; **~ de coser** sewing machine; **~ de escribir** typewriter; **~ fotográfica** camera; **~ de coser/lavar** sewing/washing machine; **~ de facsímil** facsimile (machine), fax; **~ de franqueo** franking machine; **~ tragaperras** fruit machine; (*Com*) slot machine

maquinación [makina'θjon] NF machination, plot

maquinal [maki'nal] ADJ (*fig*) mechanical, automatic

maquinar [maki'nar] /1a/ VT, VI to plot

maquinaria [maki'narja] NF (*máquinas*) machinery; (*mecanismo*) mechanism, works *pl*

maquinilla [maki'niʎa] NF small machine; (*torno*) winch; **~ de afeitar** razor; **~ eléctrica** electric razor

maquinista [maki'nista] NMF (*Ferro*) engine driver (*BRIT*), engineer (*US*); (*Tec*) operator; (*Naut*) engineer

mar [mar] NM sea; **~ de fondo** groundswell; **~ llena** high tide; **~ adentro** *o* **afuera** out at sea; **en alta ~** on the high seas; **por ~** by sea *o* boat; **hacerse a la ~** to put to sea; **a mares** in abundance; **un ~ de** lots of; **es la ~ de guapa** she is ever so pretty; **el M~ Negro/Báltico** the Black/Baltic Sea; **el M~ Muerto/**

Rojo the Dead/Red Sea; **el M~ del Norte** the North Sea

mar. ABR (= *marzo*) Mar.

maraca [ma'raka] NF maraca

maraña [ma'raɲa] NF (*maleza*) thicket; (*confusión*) tangle

maravilla [mara'βiʎa] NF marvel, wonder; (*Bot*) marigold; **hacer maravillas** to work wonders; **a (las mil) maravillas** wonderfully well

maravillar [maraβi'ʎar] /1a/ VT to astonish, amaze; **maravillarse** VR to be astonished, be amazed

maravilloso, -a [maraβi'ʎoso, a] ADJ wonderful, marvellous

marbellí [marβe'ʎi] ADJ of *o* from Marbella ▸ NMF native *o* inhabitant of Marbella

marca ['marka] NF mark; (*sello*) stamp; (*Com*) make, brand; (*de ganado*) brand; (: *acto*) branding; (*Naut*) seamark; (: *boya*) marker; (*Deporte*) record; **de ~** excellent, outstanding; **~ de fábrica** trademark; **~ propia** own brand; **~ registrada** registered trademark

marcación [marka'θjon] NF (*Telec*): **~ automática** autodial

marcado, -a [mar'kaðo, a] ADJ marked, strong

marcador [marka'ðor] NM marker; (*rotulador*) marker (pen); (*de libro*) bookmark; (*Deporte*) scoreboard; (: *persona*) scorer

marcapasos [marka'pasos] NM INV pacemaker

marcar [mar'kar] /1g/ VT to mark; (*número de teléfono*) to dial; (*gol*) to score; (*números*) to record, keep a tally of; (*el pelo*) to set; (*ganado*) to brand; (*suj: termómetro*) to read, register; (: *reloj*) to show; (*tarea*) to assign; (*Com*) to put a price on ▸ VI (*Deporte*) to score; (*Telec*) to dial; **mi reloj marca las dos** it's two o'clock by my watch; **~ el compás** (*Mus*) to keep time; **~ el paso** (*Mil*) to mark time

marcha ['martʃa] NF march; (*Deporte*) walk; (*Tec*) running, working; (*Auto*) gear; (*velocidad*) speed; (*fig*) progress; (*curso*) course; **dar ~ atrás** to reverse, put into reverse; **estar en ~** to be under way, be in motion; **hacer algo sobre la ~** to do sth as you *etc* go along; **poner en ~** to put into gear; **ponerse en ~** to start, get going; **a marchas forzadas** (*fig*) with all speed; **¡en ~!** (*Mil*) forward march!; (*fig*) let's go!; **"~ moderada"** (*Auto*) "drive slowly"; **que tiene** *o* **de mucha ~** (*fam*) very lively

marchante, -a [mar'tʃante, a] NM/F dealer, merchant

marchar [mar'tʃar] /1a/ VI (*ir*) to go; (*funcionar*) to work, go; (*fig*) to go, proceed; **marcharse** VR to go (away), leave; **todo marcha bien** everything is going well

marchitar [martʃi'tar] /**1a**/ vt to wither, dry up; **marchitarse** vr (*Bot*) to wither; (*fig*) to fade away

marchito, -a [mar'tʃito, a] ADJ withered, faded; (*fig*) in decline

marchoso, -a [mar'tʃoso, a] ADJ (*fam: animado*) lively; (: *moderno*) modern

marcial [mar'θjal] ADJ martial, military

marciano, -a [mar'θjano, a] ADJ Martian, of o from Mars

marco ['marko] NM frame; (*Deporte*) goalposts pl; (*moneda*) mark; (*fig*) setting; (: *contexto*) framework; **~ de chimenea** mantelpiece

marea [ma'rea] NF tide; (*llovizna*) drizzle; **~ alta/baja** high/low tide; **~ negra** oil slick

mareado, -a [mare'aðo, a] ADJ: **estar ~** (*con náuseas*) to feel sick; (*aturdido*) to feel dizzy

marear [mare'ar] /**1a**/ vt (*fig: irritar*) to annoy, upset; (*Med*): **~ a algn** to make sb feel sick; **marearse** vr (*tener náuseas*) to feel sick; (*desvanecerse*) to feel faint; (*aturdirse*) to feel dizzy; (*fam: emborracharse*) to get tipsy

marejada [mare'xaða] NF (*Naut*) swell, heavy sea

maremágnum [mare'maɣnum] NM (*fig*) ocean, abundance

maremoto [mare'moto] NM tidal wave

mareo [ma'reo] NM (*náusea*) sick feeling; (*en viaje*) travel sickness; (*aturdimiento*) dizziness; (*fam: lata*) nuisance

marfil [mar'fil] NM ivory

margarina [marɣa'rina] NF margarine

margarita [marɣa'rita] NF (*Bot*) daisy; (**rueda**) **~** (*en máquina impresora*) daisy wheel

margen ['marxen] NM (*borde*) edge, border; (*fig*) margin, space ▶ NF (*de río etc*) bank; **~ de beneficio** o **de ganancia** profit margin; **~ comercial** mark-up; **~ de confianza** credibility gap; **dar ~ para** to give an opportunity for; **dejar a algn al ~** to leave sb out (in the cold); **mantenerse al ~** to keep out (of things); **al ~ de lo que digas** despite what you say

marginado, -a [marxi'naðo, a] NM/F outcast

marginal [marxi'nal] ADJ (*tema, error*) minor; (*grupo*) fringe cpd; (*anotación*) marginal

marginar [marxi'nar] /**1a**/ vt to exclude; (*socialmente*) to marginalize, ostracize

maría [ma'ria] NF (*fam: mujer*) housewife

mariachi [ma'rjatʃi] NM (*música*) mariachi music; (*grupo*) mariachi band; (*persona*) mariachi musician

> Mariachi music is the musical style most characteristic of Mexico. From the state of Jalisco in the 19th century, this music spread rapidly throughout the country, until each region had its own particular style of the mariachi "sound". A mariachi

band can be made up of several singers, up to eight violins, two trumpets, guitars, a *vihuela* (an old form of guitar), and a harp. The dance associated with this music is called the *zapateado*.

marica [ma'rika] NM (*fam*) sissy; (*homosexual*) queer

Maricastaña [marikas'taɲa] NF: **en los días** o **en tiempos de ~** way back, in the good old days

maricón [mari'kon] NM (*fam*) queer

marido [ma'riðo] NM husband

marihuana [mari'wana] NF marijuana, cannabis

marimacho [mari'matʃo] NF (*fam*) mannish woman

marimorena [marimo'rena] NF fuss, row; **armar una ~** to kick up a row

marina [ma'rina] NF navy; **~ mercante** merchant navy

marinero, -a [mari'nero, a] ADJ sea cpd; (*barco*) seaworthy ▶ NM sailor, seaman

marino, -a [ma'rino, a] ADJ sea cpd, marine ▶ NM sailor; **~ de agua dulce/de cubierta/ de primera** landlubber/deckhand/able seaman

marioneta [marjo'neta] NF puppet

mariposa [mari'posa] NF butterfly

mariposear [maripose'ar] /**1a**/ vi (*revolotear*) to flutter about; (*ser inconstante*) to be fickle; (*coquetear*) to flirt

mariquita [mari'kita] NM (*fam*) sissy; (*homosexual*) queer ▶ NF (*Zool*) ladybird (BRIT), ladybug (US)

marisco [ma'risko] NM (*tb*: **mariscos**) shellfish, seafood

marisma [ma'risma] NF marsh, swamp

marisquería [mariske'ria] NF shellfish bar, seafood restaurant

marítimo, -a [ma'ritimo, a] ADJ sea cpd, maritime

marmita [mar'mita] NF pot

mármol ['marmol] NM marble

marmóreo, -a [mar'moreo, a] ADJ marble

marmota [mar'mota] NF (*Zool*) marmot; (*fig*) sleepyhead

maroma [ma'roma] NF rope

marque etc ['marke] VB ver **marcar**

marqués, -esa [mar'kes, esa] NM/F marquis/ marchioness

marquesina [marke'sina] NF (*de parada*) bus-shelter

marquetería [markete'ria] NF marquetry, inlaid work

marranada [marra'naða] NF (*fam*): **es una ~** that's disgusting; **hacer una ~ a algn** to do the dirty on sb

marrano, -a [ma'rrano, a] ADJ filthy, dirty ▶ NM (*Zool*) pig; (*malo*) swine; (*sucio*) dirty pig

m

marras ['marras]: **de ~** *adv*: **es el problema de ~** it's the same old problem
marrón [ma'rron] ADJ brown
marroquí [marro'ki] ADJ, NMF Moroccan
▶ NM Morocco (leather)
Marruecos [ma'rrwekos] NM Morocco
marta ['marta] NF (*animal*) (pine) marten; (*piel*) sable
Marte ['marte] NM Mars
martes ['martes] NM INV Tuesday; **~ de carnaval** Shrove Tuesday; *ver tb* **carnaval**; **sábado; ~ y trece** ≈ Friday 13th

> According to Spanish superstition Tuesday is an unlucky day, even more so if it falls on the 13th of the month.

martillar [marti'ʎar] /**1a**/, **martillear** [martiʎe'ar] /**1a**/ VT to hammer
martilleo [marti'ʎeo] NM hammering
martillo [mar'tiʎo] NM hammer; (*de presidente de asamblea, comité*) gavel; **~ neumático** pneumatic drill (BRIT), jackhammer (US)
Martinica [marti'nika] NF Martinique
mártir ['martir] NMF martyr
martirice *etc* [marti'riθe] VB *ver* **martirizar**
martirio [mar'tirjo] NM martyrdom; (*fig*) torture, torment
martirizar [martiri'θar] /**1f**/ VT (*Rel*) to martyr; (*fig*) to torture, torment
maruja [ma'ruxa] NF (*fam*) = **maría**
marxismo [mark'sismo] NM Marxism
marxista [mark'sista] ADJ, NMF Marxist
marzo ['marθo] NM March; **11 de ~** *the Madrid train bombings of 11 March 2004 (also 11-M)*; *ver tb* **julio**
mas [mas] CONJ but

(PALABRA CLAVE)

más [mas] ADJ, ADV **1**: **más (que/de)** (*compar*) more (than), ...+ er (than); **más grande/inteligente** bigger/more intelligent; **trabaja más (que yo)** he works more (than me); **más de seis** more than six; **es más de medianoche** it's after midnight; **durar más** to last longer; *ver tb* **cada**
2 (*superl*): **el más** the most, ...+ est; **el más grande/inteligente (de)** the biggest/most intelligent (in)
3 (*negativo*): **no tengo más dinero** I haven't got any more money; **no viene más por aquí** he doesn't come round here any more; **no sé más** I don't know any more, that's all I know
4 (*adicional*): **un kilómetro más** one more kilometre; **no le veo más solución que ...** I see no other solution than to ...; **¿algo más?** anything else?; (*en tienda*) will that be all?; **¿quién más?** anybody else?
5 (*+ adj: valor intensivo*): **¡qué perro más sucio!** what a filthy dog!; **¡es más tonto!** he's so stupid!
6 (*locuciones*): **más o menos** more or less; **los más** most people; **es más** in fact, furthermore; **más bien** rather; **¡qué más da!** what does it matter!; *ver tb* **no**
7: **por más: por más que lo intento** no matter how much o hard I try; **por más que quisiera ayudar** much as I should like to help
8: **de más: veo que aquí estoy de más** I can see I'm not needed here; **tenemos uno de más** we've got one extra
9 (*Am*): **no más** only, just; **ayer no más** just yesterday
▶ PREP: **2 más 2 son 4** 2 and o plus 2 are 4
▶ NM INV: **este trabajo tiene sus más y sus menos** this job's got its good points and its bad points

masa ['masa] NF (*mezcla*) dough; (*volumen*) volume, mass; (*Física*) mass; **en ~** en masse; **las masas** (*Pol*) the masses
masacrar [masa'krar] /**1a**/ VT to massacre
masacre [ma'sakre] NF massacre
masaje [ma'saxe] NM massage; **dar ~ a** to massage
masajista [masa'xista] NMF masseur/masseuse
mascar [mas'kar] /**1g**/ VT, VI to chew; (*fig*) to mumble, mutter
máscara ['maskara] NF (*tb Inform*) mask
▶ NMF masked person; **~ antigás** gas mask
mascarada [maska'raða] NF masquerade
mascarilla [maska'riʎa] NF mask; (*vaciado*) deathmask; (*de maquillaje*) face pack
mascarón [maska'ron] NM large mask; **~ de proa** figurehead
mascota [mas'kota] NF mascot
masculino, -a [masku'lino, a] ADJ masculine; (*Bio*) male ▶ NM (*Ling*) masculine
mascullar [masku'ʎar] /**1a**/ VT to mumble, mutter
masía [ma'sia] NF farmhouse
masificación [masifika'θjon] NF overcrowding
masilla [ma'siʎa] NF putty
masivo, -a [ma'siβo, a] ADJ (*en masa*) mass
masón [ma'son] NM (free)mason
masonería [masone'ria] NF (free)masonry
masoquista [maso'kista] ADJ masochistic
▶ NMF masochist
masque *etc* ['maske] VB *ver* **mascar**
mastectomía [mastekto'mia] NF mastectomy
máster ['master] (*pl* **masters** ['masters]) NM master's degree; *ver tb* **licenciado**
masticar [masti'kar] /**1g**/ VT to chew; (*fig*) to ponder over

mástil ['mastil] NM (*de navío*) mast; (*de guitarra*) neck

mastín [mas'tin] NM mastiff

mastique *etc* [mas'tike] VB *ver* **masticar**

masturbación [masturβa'θjon] NF masturbation

masturbarse [mastur'βarse] /**1a**/ VR to masturbate

Mat. ABR = **matemáticas**

mata ['mata] NF (*arbusto*) bush, shrub; (*de hierbas*) tuft; (*campo*) field; (*manojo*) tuft, blade; **matas** NFPL scrub *sg*; **~ de pelo** mop of hair; **a salto de ~** (*día a día*) from day to day; (*al azar*) haphazardly

matadero [mata'ðero] NM slaughterhouse, abattoir

matador, a [mata'ðor, a] ADJ killing ▶ NM/F killer ▶ NM (*Taur*) matador, bullfighter

matamoscas [mata'moskas] NM INV (*palo*) fly swat

matanza [ma'tanθa] NF slaughter

matar [ma'tar] /**1a**/ VT to kill; (*tiempo, pelota*) to kill ▶ VI to kill; **matarse** VR (*suicidarse*) to kill o.s., commit suicide; (*morir*) to be o get killed; (*gastarse*) to wear o.s. out; **~ el hambre** to stave off hunger; **~ a algn a disgustos** to make sb's life a misery; **matarlas callando** to go about things slyly; **matarse trabajando** to kill o.s. with work; **matarse por hacer algo** to struggle to do sth

matarife [mata'rife] NM slaughterman

matasanos [mata'sanos] NM INV quack

matasellos [mata'seʎos] NM INV postmark

mate ['mate] ADJ (*sin brillo: color*) dull, matt ▶ NM (*en ajedrez*) (check)mate; (*Am: hierba*) maté; (: *vasija*) gourd

matemáticas [mate'matikas] NFPL mathematics

matemático, -a [mate'matiko, a] ADJ mathematical ▶ NM/F mathematician

materia [ma'terja] NF (*gen*) matter; (*Tec*) material; (*Escol*) subject; **en ~ de** on the subject of; (*en cuanto a*) as regards; **~ prima** raw material; **entrar en ~** to get down to business

material [mate'rjal] ADJ material; (*dolor*) physical; (*real*) real; (*literal*) literal ▶ NM material; (*Tec*) equipment; **~ de construcción** building material; **materiales de derribo** rubble *sg*

materialismo [materja'lismo] NM materialism

materialista [materja'lista] ADJ materialist(ic)

materialmente [materjal'mente] ADV materially; (*fig*) absolutely

maternal [mater'nal] ADJ motherly, maternal

maternidad [materni'ðað] NF motherhood, maternity

materno, -a [ma'terno, a] ADJ maternal; (*lengua*) mother *cpd*

matice *etc* [ma'tiθe] VB *ver* **matizar**

matinal [mati'nal] ADJ morning *cpd*

matiz [ma'tiθ] NM shade; (*de sentido*) shade, nuance; (*de ironía etc*) touch

matizar [mati'θar] /**1f**/ VT (*variar*) to vary; (*Arte*) to blend; **~ de** to tinge with

matón [ma'ton] NM bully

matorral [mato'rral] NM thicket

matraca [ma'traka] NF rattle; (*fam*) nuisance

matraz [ma'traθ] NM (*Química*) flask

matriarcado [matrjar'kaðo] NM matriarchy

matrícula [ma'trikula] NF (*registro*) register; (*Escol: inscripción*) registration; (*Auto*) registration number; (: *placa*) number plate; **~ de honor** (*Univ*) top marks in a subject at university

matricular [matriku'lar] /**1a**/ VT to register, enrol

matrimonial [matrimo'njal] ADJ matrimonial

matrimonio [matri'monjo] NM (*pareja*) (married) couple; (*acto*) marriage; **~ civil/ clandestino** civil/secret marriage; **contraer ~ (con)** to marry

matriz [ma'triθ] NF (*Anat*) womb; (*Tec*) mould; (*Mat*) matrix; **casa ~** (*Com*) head office

matrona [ma'trona] NF (*mujer de edad*) matron; (*comadrona*) midwife

matufia [ma'tufja] NF (*Am fam*) put-up job

matutino, -a [matu'tino, a] ADJ morning *cpd*

maula ['maula] ADJ (*persona*) good-for-nothing ▶ NMF (*vago*) idler, slacker ▶ NF (*persona*) dead loss (*fam*)

maullar [mau'ʎar] /**1a**/ VI to mew, miaow

maullido [mau'ʎiðo] NM mew(ing), miaow(ing)

Mauricio [mau'riθjo] NM Mauritius

Mauritania [mauri'tanja] NF Mauritania

mausoleo [mauso'leo] NM mausoleum

max. ABR (= *máximo*) max.

maxilar [maksi'lar] NM jaw(bone)

máxima ['maksima] NF *ver* **máximo**

máxime ['maksime] ADV especially

máximo, -a ['maksimo, a] ADJ maximum; (*más alto*) highest; (*más grande*) greatest ▶ NM maximum ▶ NF maxim; **~ jefe** o **líder** (*Am*) President, leader; **como ~** at most; **al ~** to the utmost

maya ['maja] ADJ Mayan ▶ NMF Maya(n)

mayo ['majo] NM May; *ver tb* **julio**

mayonesa [majo'nesa] NF mayonnaise

mayor [ma'jor] ADJ main, chief; (*adulto*) grown-up, adult; (*Jur*) of age; (*de edad avanzada*) elderly; (*Mus*) major; (*comparativo*):

de tamaño) bigger; (: *de edad*) older; (*superlativo: de tamaño*) biggest; (*tb fig*) greatest; (: *de edad*) oldest ▶ NM chief, boss; (*adulto*) adult; **mayores** NMPL (*antepasados*) ancestors; grown-ups; **al por ~** wholesale; **~ de edad** adult; **llegar a mayores** to get out of hand

mayoral [majo'ral] NM foreman

mayordomo [major'ðomo] NM butler

mayoreo [majo'reo] NM (*AM*) wholesale (trade)

mayoría [majo'ria] NF majority, greater part; **en la ~ de los casos** in most cases; **en su ~** on the whole

mayorista [majo'rista] NMF wholesaler

mayoritario, -a [majori'tarjo, a] ADJ majority *cpd*; **gobierno ~** majority government

mayúsculo, -a [ma'juskulo, a] ADJ (*fig*) big, tremendous ▶ NF capital (letter); **mayúsculas** NFPL capitals; (*Tip*) upper case *sg*

maza ['maθa] NF (*arma*) mace; (*Deporte*) bat; (*Polo*) stick

mazacote [maθa'kote] NM hard mass; (*Culin*) dry doughy food; (*Arte, Lit etc*) mess, hotchpotch

mazapán [maθa'pan] NM marzipan

mazmorra [maθ'morra] NF dungeon

mazo ['maθo] NM (*martillo*) mallet; (*de mortero*) pestle; (*de flores*) bunch; (*Deporte*) bat

mazorca [ma'θorka] NF (*Bot*) spike; (*de maíz*) cob, ear

Mb ABR (= *megabyte*) Mb

MCAC NM ABR = **Mercado Común de la América Central**

m.c.d. ABR (= *mínimo común denominador*) lcd

MCI NM ABR = **Mercado Común Iberoamericano**

m.c.m. ABR = **mínimo común múltiplo**

me [me] PRON (*directo*) me; (*indirecto*) (to) me; (*reflexivo*) (to) myself; **¡dámelo!** give it to me!; **me lo compró** (*de mí*) he bought it from me; (*para mí*) he bought it for me

meandro [me'andro] NM meander

mear [me'ar] /**1a**/ (*fam*) VT to piss on (*fam!*) ▶ VI to pee, piss (*fam!*), have a piss (*fam!*); **mearse** VR to wet o.s.

Meca ['meka] NF: **La ~** Mecca

mecánica [me'kanika] NF *ver* **mecánico**

mecanice *etc* [meka'niθe] VB *ver* **mecanizar**

mecánico, -a [me'kaniko, a] ADJ mechanical; (*repetitivo*) repetitive ▶ NM/F mechanic ▶ NF (*estudio*) mechanics *sg*; (*mecanismo*) mechanism

mecanismo [meka'nismo] NM mechanism; (*engranaje*) gear

mecanizar [mekani'θar] /**1f**/ VT to mechanize

mecanografía [mekanoɣra'fia] NF typewriting

mecanografiado, -a [mekanoɣra'fjaðo, a] ADJ typewritten ▶ NM typescript

mecanógrafo, -a [meka'noɣrafo, a] NM/F (*copy*) typist

mecate [me'kate] NM (*AM*) rope

mecedor [mese'ðor] NM (*AM*), **mecedora** [meθe'ðora] NF rocking chair

mecenas [me'θenas] NM INV patron

mecenazgo [meθe'naθɣo] NM patronage

mecer [me'θer] /**2b**/ VT (*cuna*) to rock; **mecerse** VR to rock; (*rama*) to sway

mecha ['metʃa] NF (*de vela*) wick; (*de bomba*) fuse; **a toda ~** at full speed; **ponerse mechas** to streak one's hair

mechero [me'tʃero] NM (*cigarette*) lighter

mechón [me'tʃon] NM (*gen*) tuft; (*manojo*) bundle; (*de pelo*) lock

medalla [me'ðaʎa] NF medal

media ['meðja] NF *ver* **medio**

mediación [meða'θjon] NF mediation; **por ~ de** through

mediado, -a [me'ðjaðo, a] ADJ half-full; (*trabajo*) half-completed; **a mediados de** in the middle of, halfway through

medianamente [meðjana'mente] ADV (*moderadamente*) moderately, fairly; (*regularmente*) moderately well

mediano, -a [me'ðjano, a] ADJ (*regular*) medium, average; (*mediocre*) mediocre ▶ NF (*Auto*) central reservation, median (*US*); (**de tamaño**) **~** medium-sized

medianoche [meðja'notʃe] NF midnight

mediante [me'ðjante] ADV by (means of), through

mediar [me'ðjar] /**1b**/ VI (*tiempo*) to elapse; (*interceder*) to mediate, intervene; (*existir*) to exist; **media el hecho de que ...** there is the fact that ...

medicación [meðika'θjon] NF medication, treatment

medicamento [meðika'mento] NM medicine, drug

medicina [meði'θina] NF medicine

medicinal [meðiθi'nal] ADJ medicinal

medición [meði'θjon] NF measurement

médico, -a ['meðiko, a] ADJ medical ▶ NM/F doctor; **~ de cabecera** family doctor; **~ pediatra** paediatrician; **~ residente** house physician, intern (*US*)

medida [me'ðiða] NF measure; (*medición*) measurement; (*de camisa, zapato etc*) size, fitting; (*moderación*) moderation, prudence; **en cierta/gran ~** up to a point/to a great extent; **un traje a la ~** a made-to-measure suit; **~ de cuello** collar size; **a ~ de** in proportion to; (*de acuerdo con*) in keeping with; **con ~** with restraint; **sin ~** immoderately; **a ~ que ...** (at the same time) as ...; **tomar medidas** to take steps

medidor [meði'ðor] NM (AM) meter

medieval [meðje'βal] ADJ medieval

medio, -a ['meðjo, a] ADJ half (a); (punto) mid, middle; (promedio) average ▶ ADV half-; (esp AM: un tanto) rather, quite ▶ NM (centro) middle, centre; (método) means, way; (ambiente) environment ▶ NF (prenda de vestir) stocking; (AM) sock; (promedio) average; **medias** NFPL tights; **media hora** half an hour; **~ litro** half a litre; **las tres y media** half past three; **M~ Oriente** Middle East; **a ~ camino** halfway (there); **~ dormido** asleep; **~ enojado** (esp AM) rather annoyed; **lo dejó a medios** he left it half-done; **ir a medios** to go fifty-fifty; **~ de transporte** means of transport; **a ~ terminar** half finished; **en ~** in the middle; (entre) in between; **por ~ de** by (means of), through; **en los medios financieros** in financial circles; **encontrarse en su ~** to be in one's element; **~ ambiente** environment; **~ circulante** (Com) money supply; ver tb **medios**

medioambiental [meðjoambjen'tal] ADJ environmental

mediocre [me'ðjokre] ADJ middling, average; (pey) mediocre

mediocridad [meðjokri'ðað] NF middling quality; (pey) mediocrity

mediodía [meðjo'ðia] NM midday, noon

mediopensionista [meðjopensjo'nista] NMF day boy (girl)

medios ['meðjos] NMPL means, resources; **los ~ de comunicación** the media; **los ~ sociales** social media

medir [me'ðir] /3k/ VT (gen) to measure ▶ VI to measure; **medirse** VR (moderarse) to be moderate, act with restraint; **¿cuánto mides? — mido 1.50 m** how tall are you? — I am 1.50 m tall

meditabundo, -a [meðita'βundo, a] ADJ pensive

meditar [meði'tar] /1a/ VT to ponder, think over, meditate on; (planear) to think out ▶ VI to ponder, think, meditate

mediterráneo, -a [meðite'rraneo, a] ADJ Mediterranean ▶ NM: **el (mar) M~** the Mediterranean (Sea)

medrar [me'ðrar] /1a/ VI to increase, grow; (mejorar) to improve; (prosperar) to prosper, thrive; (animal, planta etc) to grow

medroso, -a [me'ðroso, a] ADJ fearful, timid

médula ['meðula] NF (Anat) marrow; (Bot) pith; **~ espinal** spinal cord; **hasta la ~** (fig) to the core

medusa [me'ðusa] NF (ESP) jellyfish

megabyte ['meɣaβait] NM (Inform) megabyte

megafonía [meɣafo'nia] NF PA o public address system

megáfono [me'ɣafono] NM megaphone

megalomanía [meɣaloma'nia] NF megalomania

megalómano, -a [meɣa'lomano, a] NM/F megalomaniac

megaocteto [meɣaok'teto] NM (Inform) megabyte

megapíxel [meɣa'piksel] (pl **megapixels** o **megapíxeles**) NM megapixel

mejicano, -a [mexi'kano, a] ADJ, NM/F Mexican

Méjico ['mexiko] NM Mexico

mejilla [me'xiʎa] NF cheek

mejillón [mexi'ʎon] NM mussel

mejor [me'xor] ADJ, ADV (comparativo) better; (superlativo) best; **lo ~** the best thing; **lo ~ de la vida** the prime of life; **a lo ~** probably; (quizá) maybe; **~ dicho** rather; **tanto ~** so much the better; **es el ~ de todos** he's the best of all

mejora [me'xora] NF, **mejoramiento** [mexora'mjento] NM improvement

mejorar [mexo'rar] /1a/ VT to improve, make better ▶ VI to improve, get better; (Com) to do well, prosper; **mejorarse** VR to improve, get better; **~ a** to be better than; **los negocios mejoran** business is picking up

mejoría [mexo'ria] NF improvement; (restablecimiento) recovery

mejunje [me'xunxe] NM (pey) concoction

melancolía [melanko'lia] NF melancholy

melancólico, -a [melan'koliko, a] ADJ (triste) sad, melancholy; (soñador) dreamy

melena [me'lena] NF (de persona) long hair; (Zool) mane

melillense [meli'ʎense] ADJ of o from Melilla ▶ NMF native o inhabitant of Melilla

mella ['meʎa] NF (rotura) notch, nick; **hacer ~** (fig) to make an impression

mellizo, -a [me'ʎiθo, a] ADJ, NM/F twin

melocotón [meloko'ton] NM (ESP) peach

melodía [melo'ðia] NF melody; (tonada) tune; (de móvil) ringtone

melodrama [melo'ðrama] NM melodrama

melodramático, -a [meloðra'matiko, a] ADJ melodramatic

melón [me'lon] NM melon

melopea [melo'pea] NF (fam): **tener una ~** to be sloshed

meloso, -a [me'loso, a] ADJ honeyed, sweet; (empalagoso) sickly, cloying; (voz) sweet; (zalamero) smooth

membrana [mem'brana] NF membrane

membrete [mem'brete] NM letterhead; **papel con ~** headed notepaper

membrillo [mem'briʎo] NM quince; **carne de ~** quince jelly

memo, -a ['memo, a] ADJ silly, stupid ▶ NM/F idiot

memorable [memo'raβle] ADJ memorable
memorándum [memo'randum] NM (*libro*)
notebook; (*comunicación*) memorandum
memoria [me'morja] NF (*gen*) memory;
(*artículo*) (learned) paper; **memorias** NFPL
(*de autor*) memoirs; **~ anual** annual report;
aprender algo de ~ to learn sth by heart;
si tengo buena ~ if my memory serves me
right; **venir a la ~** to come to mind; (*Inform*)
~ auxiliar backing storage; **~ de acceso
aleatorio** random access memory, RAM;
~ del teclado keyboard memory; **~ fija**
read-only memory, ROM; **~ flash** flash drive
memorice *etc* [memo'riθe] VB *ver* **memorizar**
memorizar [memori'θar] /**1f**/ VT to memorize
menaje [me'naxe] NM (*muebles*) furniture;
(*tb:* **artículos de menaje**) household items *pl*;
~ de cocina kitchenware
mención [men'θjon] NF mention; **digno de
~** noteworthy; **hacer ~ de** to mention
mencionar [menθjo'nar] /**1a**/ VT to mention;
(*nombrar*) to name; **sin ~ ...** let alone ...
mendicidad [mendiθi'ðað] NF begging
mendigar [mendi'ɣar] /**1h**/ VT to beg (for)
mendigo, -a [men'diɣo, a] NM/F beggar
mendigue *etc* [men'diɣe] VB *ver* **mendigar**
mendrugo [men'druɣo] NM crust
menear [mene'ar] /**1a**/ VT to move; (*cola*) to
wag; (*cadera*) to swing; (*fig*) to handle;
menearse VR to shake; (*balancearse*) to sway;
(*moverse*) to move; (*fig*) to get a move on
menester [menes'ter] NM (*necesidad*)
necessity; **menesteres** NMPL (*deberes*) duties;
es ~ hacer algo it is necessary to do sth, sth
must be done
menestra [me'nestra] NF: **~ de verduras**
vegetable stew
mengano, -a [men'gano, a] NM/F Mr (*o* Mrs *o*
Miss) So-and-so
mengua ['mengwa] NF (*disminución*) decrease;
(*falta*) lack; (*pobreza*) poverty; (*fig*) discredit;
en ~ de to the detriment of
menguante [men'gwante] ADJ decreasing,
diminishing; (*luna*) waning; (*marea*) ebb *cpd*
menguar [men'gwar] /**1i**/ VT to lessen,
diminish; (*fig*) to discredit ▶ VI to diminish,
decrease; (*fig*) to decline
mengüe *etc* ['mengwe] VB *ver* **menguar**
menopausia [meno'pausja] NF menopause
menor [me'nor] ADJ (*más pequeño: comparativo*)
smaller; (: *número*) less, lesser; (: *superlativo*)
smallest; (: *número*) least; (*más joven:
comparativo*) younger; (: *superlativo*) youngest;
(*Mus*) minor ▶ NMF (*joven*) young person,
juvenile; **Juanito es ~ que Pepe** Juanito is
younger than Pepe; **ella es la ~ de todas** she
is the youngest of all; **no tengo la ~ idea** I
haven't the faintest idea; **al por ~** retail;
~ de edad minor

Menorca [me'norka] NF Minorca
menorquín, -ina [menor'kin, ina] ADJ, NM/F
Minorcan

(PALABRA CLAVE)

menos [menos] ADJ **1** (*compar*): **menos (que/
de)** (*cantidad*) less (than); (*número*) fewer
(than); **con menos entusiasmo** with less
enthusiasm; **menos gente** fewer people; *ver
tb* **cada**
2 (*superl*): **es el que menos culpa tiene** he is
the least to blame; **donde menos
problemas hay** where there are fewest
problems
▶ ADV **1** (*compar*): **menos (que/de)** less (than);
me gusta menos que el otro I like it less
than the other one; **menos de cinco** less
than five; **menos de lo que piensas** less
than you think
2 (*superl*): **es el menos listo (de su clase)**
he's the least bright (in his class); **de todas
ellas es la que menos me agrada** out of all
of them she's the one I like least; **(por) lo
menos** at (the very) least; **es lo menos que
puedo hacer** it's the least I can do; **lo
menos posible** as little as possible
3 (*locuciones*): **no quiero verlo y menos
visitarlo** I don't want to see him let alone
visit him; **tenemos siete (de) menos** we're
seven short; **eso es lo de menos** that's the
least of it; **¡todo menos eso!** anything but
that!; **al/por lo menos** at (the very) least;
si al menos if only; **¡menos mal!** thank
goodness!
▶ PREP except; (*cifras*) minus; **todos menos
él** everyone except (for) him; **5 menos 2** 5
minus 2; **las 7 menos 20** (*hora*) 20 to 7
▶ CONJ: **a menos que: a menos que venga
mañana** unless he comes tomorrow

menoscabar [menoska'βar] /**1a**/ VT (*estropear*)
to damage, harm; (*fig*) to discredit
menospreciar [menospre'θjar] /**1b**/ VT to
underrate, undervalue; (*despreciar*) to scorn,
despise
menosprecio [menos'preθjo] NM
(*subestimación*) underrating, undervaluation;
(*desdén*) scorn, contempt
mensaje [men'saxe] NM message; **enviar un
~ a algn** (*por móvil*) to text sb, send sb a text
message; **~ de error** (*Inform*) error message;
~ de texto text message; **~ electrónico**
email
mensajero, -a [mensa'xero, a] NM/F
messenger
menso, -a ['menso, a] ADJ (*AM fam*) stupid
menstruación [menstrwa'θjon] NF
menstruation
menstruar [mens'trwar] /**1e**/ VI to menstruate

mensual [men'swal] ADJ monthly; **10 euros mensuales** 10 euros a month

mensualidad [menswali'ðað] NF (*salario*) monthly salary; (*Com*) monthly payment o instalment

menta ['menta] NF mint

mentado, -a [men'taðo, a] ADJ (*mencionado*) aforementioned; (*famoso*) well-known ▶ NF: **hacerle una mentada a algn** (*AM fam*) to (seriously) insult sb

mental [men'tal] ADJ mental

mentalidad [mentali'ðað] NF mentality

mentalizar [mentali'θar] /**1f**/ VT (*sensibilizar*) to make aware; (*convencer*) to convince; (*preparar mentalmente*) to prepare mentally; **mentalizarse** VR (*concienciarse*) to become aware; (*prepararse mentalmente*) to prepare o.s. mentally; **mentalizarse (de)** to get used to the idea (of); **mentalizarse de que ...** (*convencerse*) to get it into one's head that ...

mentar [men'tar] /**1j**/ VT to mention, name; **~ la madre a algn** to swear at sb

mente ['mente] NF mind; (*inteligencia*) intelligence; **no tengo en ~ hacer eso** it is not my intention to do that

mentecato, -a [mente'kato, a] ADJ silly, stupid ▶ NM/F fool, idiot

mentir [men'tir] /**3i**/ VI to lie; **¡miento!** sorry, I'm wrong!

mentira [men'tira] NF (*una mentira*) lie; (*acto*) lying; (*invención*) fiction; **~ piadosa** white lie; **una ~ como una casa** a whopping great lie (*fam*); **parece ~ que ...** it seems incredible that ..., I can't believe that ...

mentiroso, -a [menti'roso, a] ADJ lying; (*falso*) deceptive ▶ NM/F liar

mentís [men'tis] NM INV denial; (*tb*: **dar el mentís a**) to deny

mentón [men'ton] NM chin

menú [me'nu] NM (*tb Inform*) menu; (*tb*: **menú del día**) set meal; **~ turístico** tourist menu; **guiado por ~** (*Inform*) menu-driven

menudear [menuðe'ar] /**1a**/ VT (*repetir*) to repeat frequently ▶ VI (*ser frecuente*) to be frequent; (*detallar*) to go into great detail

menudencia [menu'ðenθja] NF (*bagatela*) trifle; **menudencias** NFPL odds and ends; (*Culin*) giblets

menudeo [menu'ðeo] NM retail sales pl

menudillos [menu'ðiʎos] NMPL giblets

menudo, -a [me'nuðo, a] ADJ (*pequeño*) small, tiny; (*sin importancia*) petty, insignificant; **¡~ negocio!** (*fam*) some deal!; **a ~** often, frequently

meñique [me'ɲike] NM little finger

meollo [me'oʎo] NM (*fig*) essence, core

mequetrefe [meke'trefe] NM good-for-nothing, whippersnapper

mercader [merka'ðer] NM merchant

mercadería [merkaðe'ria] NF commodity; **mercaderías** NFPL goods, merchandise sg

mercadillo [merka'ðiʎo] NM (*ESP*) flea market

mercado [mer'kaðo] NM market; **~ en baja** falling market; **M~ Común** Common Market; **~ de demanda/de oferta** seller's/buyer's market; **~ laboral** labour market; **~ objetivo** target market; **~ de productos básicos** commodity market; **~ de pulgas** (*AM*) flea market; **~ de valores** stock market; **~ exterior/interior** o **nacional/libre** overseas/home/free market

mercancía [merkan'θia] NF commodity; **mercancías** NFPL goods, merchandise sg; goods train, freight train (*US*); **mercancías en depósito** bonded goods; **mercancías perecederas** perishable goods

mercantil [merkan'til] ADJ mercantile, commercial

mercenario, -a [merθe'narjo, a] ADJ, NM mercenary

mercería [merθe'ria] NF (*artículos*) haberdashery (*BRIT*), notions pl (*US*); (*tienda*) haberdasher's shop (*BRIT*), drapery (*BRIT*), notions store (*US*)

Mercosur [merko'sur] NM ABR (*ARGENTINA, BRASIL, PARAGUAY, URUGUAY*) = **Mercado Común del Sur**

mercurio [mer'kurjo] NM mercury

merecedor, a [mereθe'ðor, a] ADJ deserving; **~ de confianza** trustworthy

merecer [mere'θer] /**2d**/ VT to deserve, merit ▶ VI to be deserving, be worthy; **merece la pena** it's worthwhile

merecido, -a [mere'θiðo, a] ADJ (well) deserved; **llevarse su ~** to get one's deserts

merendar [meren'dar] /**1j**/ VT to have for tea ▶ VI to have tea; (*en el campo*) to have a picnic

merendero [meren'dero] NM (open-air) café; (*en el campo*) picnic spot

merengue [me'renge] NM meringue

merezca etc [me'reθka] VB ver **merecer**

meridiano [meri'ðjano] NM (*Astro, Geo*) meridian; **la explicación es de una claridad meridiana** the explanation is as clear as day

meridional [meriðjo'nal] ADJ Southern ▶ NMF Southerner

merienda [me'rjenda] VB ver **merendar** ▶ NF (light) tea, afternoon snack; (*de campo*) picnic; **~ de negros** free-for-all

mérito ['merito] NM merit; (*valor*) worth, value; **hacer méritos** to make a good impression; **restar ~ a** to detract from

meritorio, -a [meri'torjo, a] ADJ deserving

merluza [mer'luθa] NF hake; **coger una ~** (*fam*) to get sozzled

merma ['merma] NF decrease; (*pérdida*) wastage

mermar [mer'mar] /1a/ VT to reduce, lessen ▸ VI to decrease, dwindle

mermelada [merme'laða] NF jam; **~ de naranja** marmalade

mero, -a ['mero, a] ADJ mere, simple; (Am fam) very ▸ ADV (Am) just, right ▸ NM (Zool) grouper; **el ~** (Am fam) the boss

merodear [meroðe'ar] /1a/ VI (Mil) to maraud; (de noche) to prowl (about); (curiosear) to snoop around

mes [mes] NM month; (salario) month's pay; **el ~ corriente** this o the current month

mesa ['mesa] NF table; (de trabajo) desk; (Com) counter; (en mitin) platform; (Geo) plateau; (Arq) landing; **~ de noche/de tijera/de operaciones** u **operatoria** bedside/folding/operating table; **~ electoral** officials in charge of a polling station; **~ redonda** (reunión) round table; **~ digitalizadora** (Inform) graph pad; **~ directiva** board; **~ y cama** bed and board; **poner/quitar la ~** to lay/clear the table

mesarse [me'sarse] /1a/ VR: **~ el pelo** o **los cabellos** to tear one's hair

mesero, -a [me'sero, a] NM/F (Am) waiter (waitress)

meseta [me'seta] NF (Geo) tableland; (Arq) landing

mesilla [me'siʎa], **mesita** [me'sita] NF: **~ de noche** bedside table

mesón [me'son] NM inn

mestizo, -a [mes'tiθo, a] ADJ mixed-race; (Zool) crossbred ▸ NM/F person of mixed race

mesura [me'sura] NF (calma) calm; (moderación) moderation, restraint; (cortesía) courtesy

mesurar [mesu'rar] /1a/ VT (contener) to restrain; **mesurarse** VR to restrain o.s.

meta ['meta] NF goal; (de carrera) finish; (fig) goal, aim, objective

metabolismo [metaβo'lismo] NM metabolism

metafísico, -a [meta'fisiko, a] ADJ metaphysical ▸ NF metaphysics sg

metáfora [me'tafora] NF metaphor

metafórico, -a [meta'foriko, a] ADJ metaphorical

metal [me'tal] NM (materia) metal; (Mus) brass

metálico, -a [me'taliko, a] ADJ metallic; (de metal) metal ▸ NM (dinero contante) cash

metalurgia [meta'lurxja] NF metallurgy

metalúrgico, -a [meta'lurxiko, a] ADJ metallurgic(al); **industria metalúrgica** engineering industry

metamorfosear [metamorfose'ar] /1a/ VT: **~ (en)** to metamorphose o transform (into)

metamorfosis [metamor'fosis] NF INV metamorphosis, transformation

metedura [mete'ðura] NF: **~ de pata** (fam) blunder

meteorito [meteo'rito] NM meteorite

meteoro [mete'oro] NM meteor

meteorología [meteorolo'xia] NF meteorology

meteorólogo, -a [meteo'roloɣo, a] NM/F meteorologist; (Radio, TV) weather reporter

meter [me'ter] /2a/ VT (colocar) to put, place; (introducir) to put in, insert; (involucrar) to involve; (causar) to make, cause; **meterse** VR: **meterse en** to go into, enter; (fig) to interfere in, meddle in; **meterse a** to start; **meterse a escritor** to become a writer; **meterse con algn** to provoke sb, pick a quarrel with sb; **~ prisa a algn** to hurry sb up

meticuloso, -a [metiku'loso, a] ADJ meticulous, thorough

metido, -a [me'tiðo, a] ADJ: **estar muy ~ en un asunto** to be deeply involved in a matter; **~ en años** elderly; **~ en carnes** plump

metódico, -a [me'toðiko, a] ADJ methodical

metodismo [meto'ðismo] NM Methodism

método ['metoðo] NM method

metodología [metoðolo'xia] NF methodology

metomentodo [metomen'toðo] NM INV meddler, busybody

metraje [me'traxe] NM (Cine) length; **cinta de largo/corto ~** full-length film/short

metralla [me'traʎa] NF shrapnel

metralleta [metra'ʎeta] NF sub-machine-gun

métrico, -a ['metriko, a] ADJ metric ▸ NF metrics pl; **cinta métrica** tape measure

metro ['metro] NM metre; (tren: tb: **metropolitano**) underground (Brit), subway (US); (instrumento) rule; **~ cuadrado/cúbico** square/cubic metre

metrópoli [me'tropoli], **metrópolis** [me'tropolis] NF (ciudad) metropolis; (colonial) mother country

metrosexual [metrosexu'al] ADJ, NM metrosexual

mexicano, -a [mexi'kano, a] ADJ, NM/F (Am) Mexican

México ['mexiko] NM (Am) Mexico; **Ciudad de ~** Mexico City

mezcla ['meθkla] NF mixture; (fig) blend

mezclar [meθ'klar] /1a/ VT to mix (up); (armonizar) to blend; (combinar) to merge; **mezclarse** VR to mix, mingle; **~ en** to get mixed up in, get involved in

mezcolanza [meθko'lanθa] NF hotchpotch, jumble

mezquindad [meθkin'dað] NF (cicatería) meanness; (miras estrechas) pettiness; (acto) mean action

mezquino, -a [meθ'kino, a] ADJ (cicatero) mean ▸ NM/F (avaro) mean person; (miserable) petty individual

mezquita [meθ'kita] NF mosque

mg ABR (= *miligramo(s)*) mg

mi [mi] ADJ POSESIVO my ▶ NM (*Mus*) E

mí [mi] PRON me, myself; **¿y a mí qué?** so what?

mía ['mia] PRON *ver* **mío**

miaja ['mjaxa] NF crumb; **ni una ~** (*fig*) not the least little bit

miau [mjau] NM miaow

michelín [mitʃe'lin] NM (*fam*) spare tyre

mico ['miko] NM monkey

micro ['mikro] NM (*Radio*) mike, microphone; (*Am: pequeño*) minibus; (*: grande*) coach, bus

microbio [mi'kroβjo] NM microbe

microblog [mikro'βloɣ] NM microblog

microbús [mikro'βus] NM minibus

microchip [mikro'tʃip] NM microchip

microcomputador [mikrokomputa'ðor] NM, **microcomputadora** [mikrokomputa'ðora] NF micro(computer)

microeconomía [mikroekono'mia] NF microeconomics *sg*

microficha [mikro'fitʃa] NF microfiche

microfilm [mikro'film] (*pl* **microfilms** [mikro'films]) NM microfilm

micrófono [mi'krofono] NM microphone

microinformática [mikroinfor'matika] NF microcomputing

micrómetro [mi'krometro] NM micrometer

microonda [mikro'onda] NF, **microondas** [mikro'ondas] NM INV microwave; (**horno**) **microondas** microwave (oven)

microordenador [mikroordena'ðor] NM microcomputer

micropastilla [mikropas'tiʎa], **microplaqueta** [mikropla'keta] NF (*Inform*) chip, wafer

microplaquita [mikropla'kita] NF: **~ de silicio** silicon chip

microprocesador [mikroproθesa'ðor] NM microprocessor

microscópico, -a [mikros'kopiko, a] ADJ microscopic

microscopio [mikros'kopjo] NM microscope

midiendo *etc* [mi'ðjendo] VB *ver* **medir**

miedo ['mjeðo] NM fear; (*nerviosismo*) apprehension, nervousness; **meter ~ a** to scare, frighten; **tener ~ to** be afraid; **de ~** wonderful, marvellous; **¡qué ~!** (*fam*) how awful!; **me da ~** it scares me; **hace un frío de ~** (*fam*) it's terribly cold

miedoso, -a [mje'ðoso, a] ADJ fearful, timid

miel [mjel] NF honey; **no hay ~ sin hiel** there's no rose without a thorn

miembro ['mjembro] NM limb; (*socio*) member; (*de institución*) fellow; **~ viril** penis

mientes *etc* ['mjentes] VB *ver* **mentar; mentir** ▶ NFPL: **no parar ~ en** to pay no attention to; **traer a las ~** to recall

mientras ['mjentras] CONJ while; (*duración*) as long as ▶ ADV meanwhile; **~ (que)** whereas; **~ tanto** meanwhile; **~ más tiene, más quiere** the more he has, the more he wants

miércoles ['mjerkoles] NM INV Wednesday; **~ de ceniza** Ash Wednesday; *ver tb* **carnaval; sábado**

mierda ['mjerða] NF (*fam!*) shit (*fam!*), crap (*fam!*); (*fig*) filth, dirt; **¡vete a la ~!** go to hell!

mies [mjes] NF (ripe) corn, wheat, grain

miga ['miɣa] NF crumb; (*fig: meollo*) essence; **hacer buenas migas** (*fam*) to get on well; **esto tiene su ~** there's more to this than meets the eye

migaja [mi'ɣaxa] NF: **una ~** (*un poquito*) a little; **migajas** NFPL (*pey*) crumbs; left-overs

migración [miɣra'θjon] NF migration

migratorio, -a [miɣra'torjo, a] ADJ migratory

mil [mil] NUM thousand; **dos ~ libras** two thousand pounds

milagro [mi'laɣro] NM miracle; **hacer milagros** (*fig*) to work wonders

milagroso, -a [mila'ɣroso, a] ADJ miraculous

Milán [mi'lan] NM Milan

milenario, -a [mile'narjo, a] ADJ millennial; (*fig*) very ancient

milenio [mi'lenjo] NM millennium

milésima [mi'lesima] NF (*de segundo*) thousandth

milésimo, -a [mi'lesimo, a] NUM thousandth

mileurista NMF *person earning around a thousand euros or less* ▶ ADJ *of (around) a thousand euros*; **un ~ no puede comprar ese piso** no one on a salary of a thousand euros could afford that flat; **un sueldo ~** a salary of (around) a thousand euros

mili ['mili] NF: **hacer la ~** (*fam*) to do one's military service

milicia [mi'liθja] NF (*Mil*) militia; (*servicio militar*) military service

miligramo [mili'ɣramo] NM milligram

milímetro [mi'limetro] NM millimetre (*Brit*), millimeter (*US*)

militante [mili'tante] ADJ militant

militar [mili'tar] /**1a**/ ADJ military ▶ NM/F soldier ▶ VI to serve in the army; (*fig*) to militate, fight

militarismo [milita'rismo] NM militarism

mill. ABR = **millón**; (= *millones*) M

milla ['miʎa] NF mile; **~ marina** nautical mile

millar [mi'ʎar] NUM thousand; **a millares** in thousands

millón [mi'ʎon] NUM million

millonario, -a [miʎo'narjo, a] NM/F millionaire

millonésimo, -a [miʎo'nesimo, a] NUM millionth

m

milusos [mi'lusos] NM INV (*Am*) odd-job man

mimado, -a [mi'maðo, a] ADJ spoiled

mimar [mi'mar] /**1a**/ VT to spoil, pamper

mimbre ['mimbre] NM wicker; **de ~** wicker *cpd*, wickerwork

mimetismo [mime'tismo] NM mimicry

mímica ['mimika] NF (*para comunicarse*) sign language; (*imitación*) mimicry

mimo ['mimo] NM (*caricia*) caress; (*de niño*) spoiling; (*Teat*) mime; (: *actor*) mime artist

mina ['mina] NF mine; (*pozo*) shaft; (*de lápiz*) lead refill; **hullera** o **- de carbón** coal mine

minar [mi'nar] /**1a**/ VT to mine; (*fig*) to undermine

mineral [mine'ral] ADJ mineral ▸ NM (*Geo*) mineral; (*mena*) ore

minería [mine'ria] NF mining

minero, -a [mi'nero, a] ADJ mining *cpd* ▸ NM/F miner

miniatura [minja'tura] ADJ INV, NF miniature

minicadena [minika'ðena] NF (*Mus*) mini hi-fi

minicomputador [minikomputa'ðor] NM minicomputer

MiniDisc® [mini'disk] NM MiniDisc®

minidisco [mini'ðisko] NM diskette

minifalda [mini'falda] NF miniskirt

minifundio [mini'fundjo] NM smallholding, small farm

minimizar [minimi'θar] /**1f**/ VT to minimize

mínimo, -a ['minimo, a] ADJ minimum; (*insignificante*) minimal ▸ NM minimum; **precio/salario ~** minimum price/wage; **lo ~ que pueden hacer** the least they can do

minino, -a [mi'nino, a] NM/F (*fam*) puss, pussy

ministerio [minis'terjo] NM ministry (*BRIT*), department (*US*); **M~ de Asuntos Exteriores** Foreign Office (*BRIT*), State Department (*US*); **M~ de Comercio e Industria** Department of Trade and Industry; **M~ de (la) Gobernación** o **del Interior** ≈ Home Office (*BRIT*), Ministry of the Interior; **M~ de Hacienda** Treasury (*BRIT*), Treasury Department (*US*)

ministro, -a [mi'nistro, a] NM/F minister, secretary (*esp US*); **M~ de Hacienda** Chancellor of the Exchequer, Secretary of the Treasury (*US*); **M~ de (la) Gobernación** o **del Interior** ≈ Home Secretary (*BRIT*), Secretary of the Interior (*US*)

minoría [mino'ria] NF minority

minorista [mino'rista] NM retailer

mintiendo *etc* [min'tjendo] VB *ver* **mentir**

minucia [mi'nuθja] NF (*detalle insignificante*) trifle; (*bagatela*) mere nothing

minuciosidad [minuθjosi'ðað] NF (*meticulosidad*) thoroughness, meticulousness

minucioso, -a [minu'θjoso, a] ADJ thorough, meticulous; (*prolijo*) very detailed

minúsculo, -a [mi'nuskulo, a] ADJ tiny, minute ▸ NF small letter; **minúsculas** NFPL (*Tip*) lower case *sg*

minusvalía [minusβa'lia] NF physical handicap; (*Com*) depreciation, capital loss

minusválido, -a [minus'βaliðo, a] ADJ (*physically*) handicapped o disabled ▸ NM/F disabled person

minuta [mi'nuta] NF (*de comida*) menu; (*de abogado etc*) fee

minutero [minu'tero] NM minute hand

minuto [mi'nuto] NM minute

Miño ['miɲo] NM: **el (río) ~** the Miño

mío, -a ['mio, a] ADJ, PRON: **el ~** mine; **un amigo ~** a friend of mine; **lo ~** what is mine; **los míos** my people, my relations

miope ['mjope] ADJ short-sighted

miopía [mjo'pia] NF near- o short-sightedness

MIR [mir] NM ABR (*Pol*) = **Movimiento de Izquierda Revolucionaria**; (*ESP Med*) = **Médico Interno y Residente**

mira ['mira] NF (*de arma*) sight(s) *pl*; (*fig*) aim, intention; **de amplias/estrechas miras** broad-/narrow-minded

mirada [mi'raða] NF look, glance; (*expresión*) look, expression; **~ de soslayo** sidelong glance; **~ fija** stare, gaze; **~ perdida** distant look; **clavar la ~ en** to stare at; **echar una ~ a** to glance at; **levantar/bajar la ~** to look up/down; **resistir la ~ de algn** to stare sb out

mirado, -a [mi'raðo, a] ADJ (*sensato*) sensible; (*considerado*) considerate; **bien/mal ~** well/not well thought of; **bien ~ ...** all things considered ...

mirador [mira'ðor] NM viewpoint, vantage point

miramiento [mira'mjento] NM (*consideración*) considerateness; **tratar sin miramientos a algn** to ride roughshod over sb

mirar [mi'rar] /**1a**/ VT to look at; (*observar*) to watch; (*considerar*) to consider, think over; (*vigilar, cuidar*) to watch, look after ▸ VI to look; (*Arq*) to face; **mirarse** VR (*dos personas*) to look at each other; **~ algo/a algn de reojo** o **de través** to look askance at sth/sb; **~ algo/a algn por encima del hombro** to look down on sth/sb; **~ bien/mal** to think highly of/have a poor opinion of; **~ fijamente** to stare o gaze at; **~ por** (*fig*) to look after; **~ por la ventana** to look out of the window; **mirarse al espejo** to look at o.s. in the mirror; **mirarse a los ojos** to look into each other's eyes

mirilla [mi'riʎa] NF (*agujero*) spyhole, peephole

mirlo ['mirlo] NM blackbird

misa ['misa] NF mass; ~ **del gallo** midnight mass (*on Christmas Eve*); ~ **de difuntos** requiem mass; **como en** ~ in dead silence; **estos datos van a** ~ (*fig*) these facts are utterly trustworthy

misántropo [mi'santropo] NM misanthrope, misanthropist

miscelánea [misθe'lanea] NF miscellany

miserable [mise'raβle] ADJ (*avaro*) mean, stingy; (*nimio*) miserable, paltry; (*lugar*) squalid; (*fam*) vile, despicable ▶ NMF (*malvado*) rogue

miseria [mi'serja] NF misery; (*pobreza*) poverty; (*tacañería*) meanness, stinginess; (*condiciones*) squalor; **una** ~ a pittance

misericordia [miseri'korðja] NF (*compasión*) compassion, pity; (*perdón*) forgiveness, mercy

misil [mi'sil] NM missile

misión [mi'sjon] NF mission; (*tarea*) job, duty; (*Pol*) assignment; **misiones** NFPL (*Rel*) overseas missions

misionero, -a [misjo'nero, a] NM/F missionary

mismamente [misma'mente] ADV (*fam: sólo*) only, just

mismísimo, -a [mis'misimo, a] ADJ SUPERLATIVO selfsame, very (same)

mismo, -a ['mismo, a] ADJ (*semejante*) same; (*después de pronombre*) -self; (*para énfasis*) very ▶ ADV **aquí/ayer/hoy** ~ right here/only yesterday/this very day ▶ CONJ: **lo** ~ **que** just like, just as; **por lo** ~ for the same reason; **el** ~ **traje** the same suit; **en ese** ~ **momento** at that very moment; **vino el** ~ **Ministro** the Minister himself came; **yo** ~ **lo vi** I saw it myself; **lo hizo por sí** ~ he did it by himself; **lo** ~ the same (thing); **da lo** ~ it's all the same; **quedamos en las mismas** we're no further forward; **ahora** ~ right now

misógino, -a [mi'soxino, a] NM misogynist ▶ ADJ misogynistic, misogynist

miss [mis] NF beauty queen

misterio [mis'terjo] NM mystery; (*lo secreto*) secrecy

misterioso, -a [miste'rjoso, a] ADJ mysterious; (*inexplicable*) puzzling

misticismo [misti'θismo] NM mysticism

místico, -a ['mistiko, a] ADJ mystic(al) ▶ NM/F mystic ▶ NF mysticism

mitad [mi'tað] NF (*medio*) half; (*centro*) middle; ~ **(y)** ~ half-and-half; (*fig*) yes and no; **a** ~ **de precio** (at) half-price; **en** *o* **a** ~ **del camino** halfway along the road; **cortar por la** ~ to cut through the middle

mítico, -a ['mitiko, a] ADJ mythical

mitigar [miti'yar] /**1h**/ VT to mitigate; (*dolor*) to relieve; (*sed*) to quench; (*ira*) to appease; (*preocupación*) to allay; (*soledad*) to alleviate

mitigue *etc* [mi'tiɣe] VB *ver* **mitigar**

mitin ['mitin] NM (*esp Pol*) meeting

mito ['mito] NM myth

mitología [mitolo'xia] NF mythology

mitológico, -a [mito'loxiko, a] ADJ mythological

mixto, -a ['miksto, a] ADJ mixed; (*comité*) joint

ml ABR (= *mililitro(s)*) ml

mm ABR (= *milímetro(s)*) mm

MMS NM ABR (= *multimedia message service*) MMS *m*

M.N., m/n ABR (*Am Econ*) = **moneda nacional**

M.° ABR (*Pol*: = *Ministerio*) Min

m/o ABR (*Com*) = **mi orden**

mobiliario [moβi'ljarjo] NM furniture

mocasín [moka'sin] NM moccasin

mocedad [moθe'ðað] NF youth

mochila [mo'tʃila] NF rucksack (BRIT), backpack

moción [mo'θjon] NF motion; ~ **compuesta** (*Pol*) composite motion

moco ['moko] NM mucus; **mocos** NMPL (*fam*) snot; **limpiarse los mocos** to blow one's nose; **no es** ~ **de pavo** it's no trifle

mocoso, -a [mo'koso, a] ADJ snivelling; (*fig*) ill-bred ▶ NM/F (*fam*) brat

moda ['moða] NF fashion; (*estilo*) style; **de** *o* **a la** ~ in fashion, fashionable; **pasado de** ~ out of fashion; **vestido a la última** ~ trendily dressed

modal [mo'ðal] ADJ modal; **modales** NMPL manners

modalidad [moðali'ðað] NF (*clase*) kind, variety; (*manera*) way; (*Inform*) mode; ~ **de texto** (*Inform*) text mode

modelar [moðe'lar] /**1a**/ VT to model

modelo [mo'ðelo] ADJ INV model ▶ NMF model ▶ NM (*patrón*) pattern; (*norma*) standard

módem ['moðem] NM (*Inform*) modem

moderado, -a [moðe'raðo, a] ADJ moderate

moderar [moðe'rar] /**1a**/ VT to moderate; (*violencia*) to restrain, control; (*velocidad*) to reduce; **moderarse** VR to restrain o.s., control o.s.

modernice *etc* [moðer'niθe] VB *ver* **modernizar**

modernizar [moðerni'θar] /**1f**/ VT to modernize; (*Inform*) to upgrade

moderno, -a [mo'ðerno, a] ADJ modern; (*actual*) present-day; (*equipo etc*) up-to-date

modestia [mo'ðestja] NF modesty

modesto, -a [mo'ðesto, a] ADJ modest

módico, -a ['moðiko, a] ADJ moderate, reasonable

modificar [moðifi'kar] /**1g**/ VT to modify

modifique *etc* [moði'fike] VB *ver* **modificar**

modismo [mo'ðismo] NM idiom

modisto, -a [mo'ðisto, a] NM/F (*diseñador*) couturier, designer; (*que confecciona*) dressmaker

modo ['moðo] NM (*manera, forma*) way, manner; (*Inform, Mus*) mode; (*Ling*) mood; **modos** NMPL manners; **"~ de empleo"** "instructions for use"; **~ de gobierno** form of government; **a ~ de** like; **de este ~** in this way; **de ningún ~** in no way; **de todos modos** at any rate; **de un ~ u otro** (in) one way or another

modorra [mo'ðorra] NF drowsiness

modoso, -a [mo'ðoso, a] ADJ (*educado*) quiet, well-mannered

modulación [moðula'θjon] NF modulation; **~ de frecuencia** (*Radio*) frequency modulation, FM

módulo ['moðulo] NM module; (*de mueble*) unit

mofarse [mo'farse] /1a/ VR: **~ de** to mock, scoff at

mofle ['mofle] NM (*Am*) silencer (*Brit*), muffler (*US*)

moflete [mo'flete] NM fat cheek, chubby cheek

mogollón [moɣo'ʎon] (*fam*) NM: **~ de discos** *etc* loads of records *etc* ▶ ADV: **un ~** a hell of a lot

mohín [mo'in] NM (*mueca*) (wry) face; (*pucheros*) pout

mohíno, -a [mo'ino, a] ADJ (*triste*) gloomy, depressed; (*enojado*) sulky

moho ['moo] NM (*Bot*) mould, mildew; (*en metal*) rust

mohoso, -a [mo'oso, a] ADJ mouldy; rusty

mojado, -a [mo'xaðo, a] ADJ wet; (*húmedo*) damp; (*empapado*) drenched

mojar [mo'xar] /1a/ VT to wet; (*humedecer*) to damp(en), moisten; (*calar*) to soak; **mojarse** VR to get wet; **~ el pan en el café** to dip *o* dunk one's bread in one's coffee

mojigato, -a [moxi'ɣato, a] ADJ (*hipócrita*) hypocritical; (*santurrón*) sanctimonious; (*gazmoño*) prudish ▶ NM/F hypocrite; sanctimonious person; prude

mojón [mo'xon] NM (*hito*) landmark; (*en un camino*) signpost; (*tb*: **mojón kilométrico**) milestone

mol. ABR (= *molécula*) mol

molar [mo'lar] /1a/ NM molar ▶ VT (*fam*): **lo que más me mola es …** what I'm really into is …; **¿te mola un cigarrillo?** do you fancy a smoke?

molcajete [molka'xete] (*Am*) NM mortar

Moldavia [mol'ðaβja], **Moldova** [mol'ðoβa] NF Moldavia, Moldova

moldavo, -a [mol'ðaβo, a] ADJ, NM/F Moldavian, Moldovan

molde ['molde] NM mould; (*vaciado*) cast; (*de costura*) pattern; (*fig*) model

moldeado [molde'aðo] PP *de* **moldear** ▶ NM soft perm

moldear [molde'ar] /1a/ VT to mould; (*en yeso etc*) to cast

mole ['mole] NF mass, bulk; (*edificio*) pile

molécula [mo'lekula] NF molecule

moler [mo'ler] /2h/ VT to grind, crush; (*pulverizar*) to pound; (*trigo etc*) to mill; (*cansar*) to tire out, exhaust; **~ a algn a palos** to give sb a beating

molestar [moles'tar] /1a/ VT to bother; (*fastidiar*) to annoy; (*incomodar*) to inconvenience, put out; (*perturbar*) to trouble, upset ▶ VI to be a nuisance; **molestarse** VR to bother; (*incomodarse*) to go to a lot of trouble; (*ofenderse*) to take offence; **¿le molesta el ruido?** do you mind the noise?; **siento molestarle** I'm sorry to trouble you

molestia [mo'lestja] NF bother, trouble; (*incomodidad*) inconvenience; (*Med*) discomfort; **es una ~** it's a nuisance; **no es ninguna ~** it's no trouble at all

molesto, -a [mo'lesto, a] ADJ (*que fastidia*) annoying; (*incómodo*) inconvenient; (*inquieto*) uncomfortable, ill at ease; (*enfadado*) annoyed; **estar ~** (*Med*) to be in some discomfort; **estar ~ con algn** (*fig*) to be cross with sb; **me sentí ~** I felt embarrassed

molido, -a [mo'liðo, a] ADJ (*machacado*) ground; (*pulverizado*) powdered; **estar ~** (*fig*) to be exhausted *o* dead beat

molinero [moli'nero] NM miller

molinillo [moli'niʎo] NM hand mill; **~ de carne/café** mincer/coffee grinder

molino [mo'lino] NM (*edificio*) mill; (*máquina*) grinder

mollera [mo'ʎera] NF (*Anat*) crown of the head; (*fam: seso*) brains *pl*; **duro de ~** (*estúpido*) thick

Molucas [mo'lukas] NFPL: **las (Islas) ~** the Moluccas, the Molucca Islands

molusco [mo'lusko] NM mollusc

momentáneo, -a [momen'taneo, a] ADJ momentary

momento [mo'mento] NM (*gen*) moment; (*Tec*) momentum; **de ~** at the moment, for the moment; **en ese ~** at that moment, just then; **por el ~** for the time being

momia ['momja] NF mummy

mona ['mona] NF *ver* **mono**

Mónaco ['monako] NM Monaco

monada [mo'naða] NF (*gracia*) charming habit; (*cosa primorosa*) lovely thing; (*chica*) pretty girl; **¡qué ~!** isn't it cute?

monaguillo [mona'ɣiʎo] NM altar boy

monarca [mo'narka] NMF monarch, ruler

monarquía [monar'kia] NF monarchy

monárquico, -a [mo'narkiko, a] NM/F royalist, monarchist

monasterio [monas'terjo] NM monastery

Moncloa [mon'kloa] NF: **la ~** *official residence of the Spanish Prime Minister*

monda ['monda] NF (*poda*) pruning; (: *de árbol*) lopping; (: *de fruta*) peeling; (*cáscara*) skin; **¡es la ~!** (*fam: fantástico*) it's great!; (: *el colmo*) it's the limit!; (: *es gracioso*) he's a knockout!

mondadientes [monda'ðjentes] NM INV toothpick

mondar [mon'dar] /**1a**/ VT (*limpiar*) to clean; (*pelar*) to peel; **mondarse** VR: **mondarse de risa** (*fam*) to split one's sides laughing

mondongo [mon'dongo] NM (*AM*) tripe

moneda [mo'neða] NF (*tipo de dinero*) currency, money; (*pieza*) coin; **una ~ de 50 céntimos** a 50-cent coin; **~ de curso legal** legal tender; **~ extranjera** foreign exchange; **~ única** single currency; **es ~ corriente** (*fig*) it's common knowledge

monedero [mone'ðero] NM purse

monegasco, -a [mone'yasko, a] ADJ of o from Monaco, Monegasque ► NM/F Monegasque

monetario, -a [mone'tarjo, a] ADJ monetary, financial

monetarista [moneta'rista] ADJ, NMF monetarist

mongólico, -a [mon'goliko, a] ADJ, NM/F Mongol

monigote [moni'yote] NM (*dibujo*) doodle; (*de papel*) cut-out figure; (*pey*) wimp; *ver tb* **inocente**

monitor, a [moni'tor, a] NM/F instructor, coach ► NM (*TV*) set; (*Inform*) monitor; **~ en color** colour monitor

monja ['monxa] NF nun

monje ['monxe] NM monk

mono, -a ['mono, a] ADJ (*bonito*) lovely, pretty; (*gracioso*) nice, charming ► NM/F monkey, ape ► NM dungarees *pl*; (*traje de faena*) overalls *pl*; (*fam: de drogadicto*) cold turkey; **una chica muy mona** a very pretty girl; **dormir la ~** to sleep it off

monóculo [mo'nokulo] NM monocle

monografía [monoyra'fia] NF monograph

monolingüe [mono'lingwe] ADJ monolingual

monólogo [mo'noloyo] NM monologue

monomando [mono'mando] NM (*tb:* **grifo monomando**) mixer tap

monoparental [monoparen'tal] ADJ: **familia ~** single-parent family

monopatín [monopa'tin] NM skateboard

monopolice *etc* [monopo'liθe] VB *ver* **monopolizar**

monopolio [mono'poljo] NM monopoly; **~ total** absolute monopoly

monopolista [monopo'lista] ADJ, NMF monopolist

monopolizar [monopoli'θar] /**1f**/ VT to monopolize

monosílabo, -a [mono'silaβo, a] ADJ monosyllabic ► NM monosyllable

monotonía [monoto'nia] NF (*sonido*) monotone; (*fig*) monotony

monótono, -a [mo'notono, a] ADJ monotonous

mono-usuario, -a [monou'swarjo, a] ADJ (*Inform*) single-user

monóxido [mo'noksiðo] NM monoxide; **~ de carbono** carbon monoxide

Mons. ABR (*Rel*) = **monseñor**

monseñor [monse'ɲor] NM monsignor

monserga [mon'serγa] NF (*lenguaje confuso*) gibberish; (*tonterías*) drivel

monstruo ['monstrwo] NM monster ► ADJ INV fantastic

monstruoso, -a [mons'trwoso, a] ADJ monstrous

monta ['monta] NF total, sum; **de poca ~** unimportant, of little account

montacargas [monta'karγas] NM INV service lift (*BRIT*), freight elevator (*US*)

montador [monta'ðor] NM (*para montar*) mounting block; (*profesión*) fitter; (*Cine*) film editor

montaje [mon'taxe] NM assembly; (*organización*) fitting up; (*Teat*) décor; (*Cine*) montage

montante [mon'tante] NM (*poste*) upright; (*soporte*) stanchion; (*Arq: de puerta*) transom; (: *de ventana*) mullion; (*suma*) amount, total

montaña [mon'taɲa] NF (*monte*) mountain; (*sierra*) mountains *pl*, mountainous area; (*AM: selva*) forest; **~ rusa** roller coaster

montañero, -a [monta'ɲero, a] ADJ mountain *cpd* ► NM/F mountaineer, climber

montañés, -esa [monta'ɲes, esa] ADJ mountain *cpd*; (*de Santander*) of o from the Santander region ► NM/F highlander; native o inhabitant of the Santander region

montañismo [monta'ɲismo] NM mountaineering, climbing

montañoso, -a [monta'ɲoso, a] ADJ mountainous

montar [mon'tar] /**1a**/ VT (*subir a*) to mount, get on; (*caballo etc*) to ride; (*Tec*) to assemble, put together; (*negocio*) to set up; (*colocar*) to lift on to; (*Cine: película*) to edit; (*Teat: obra*) to stage, put on; (*Culin: batir*) to whip, beat ► VI to mount, get on; (*sobresalir*) to overlap; **~ en bicicleta** to ride a bicycle; **~ en cólera** to get angry; **~ a caballo** to ride, go horseriding; **~ un número** o **numerito** to make a scene; **tanto monta** it makes no odds

montaraz [monta'raθ] ADJ mountain *cpd*, highland *cpd*; (*pey*) uncivilized

monte ['monte] NM (*montaña*) mountain; (*bosque*) woodland; (*área sin cultivar*) wild area, wild country; **~ de piedad** pawnshop; **~ alto** forest; **~ bajo** scrub(land)

montera [mon'tera] NF (*sombrero*) cloth cap; (*de torero*) bullfighter's hat

monto ['monto] NM total, amount

montón [mon'ton] NM heap, pile; **un ~ de** (*fig*) heaps of, lots of; **a montones** by the score, galore

montura [mon'tura] NF (*cabalgadura*) mount; (*silla*) saddle; (*arreos*) harness; (*de joya*) mounting; (*de gafas*) frame

monumental [monumen'tal] ADJ (*tb fig*) monumental; **zona ~** area of historical interest

monumento [monu'mento] NM monument; (*de conmemoración*) memorial

monzón [mon'θon] NM monsoon

moña ['moɲa] NF hair ribbon

moño ['moɲo] NM (*de pelo*) bun; **estar hasta el ~** (*fam*) to be fed up to the back teeth

MOPTMA NM ABR = **Ministerio de Obras Públicas, Transporte y Medio Ambiente**

moqueta [mo'keta] NF fitted carpet

moquillo [mo'kiʎo] NM (*enfermedad*) distemper

mora ['mora] NF (*Bot*) mulberry; (*: zarzamora*) blackberry; (*Com*): **en ~** in arrears

morado, -a [mo'raðo, a] ADJ purple, violet ▶ NM bruise ▶ NF (*casa*) dwelling, abode; **pasarlas moradas** to have a tough time of it

moral [mo'ral] ADJ moral ▶ NF (*ética*) ethics *pl*; (*moralidad*) morals *pl*, morality; (*ánimo*) morale; **tener baja la ~** to be in low spirits

moraleja [mora'lexa] NF moral

moralice *etc* [mora'liθe] VB *ver* **moralizar**

moralidad [morali'ðað] NF morals *pl*, morality

moralizar [morali'θar] /**1f**/ VT to moralize

morar [mo'rar] /**1a**/ VI to live, dwell

moratón [mora'ton] NM bruise

moratoria [mora'torja] NF moratorium

morbo ['morβo] NM (*fam*) morbid pleasure

morbosidad [morβosi'ðað] NF morbidity

morboso, -a [mor'βoso, a] ADJ morbid

morcilla [mor'θiʎa] NF blood sausage, ≈ black pudding (*Brit*)

mordaz [mor'ðaθ] ADJ (*crítica*) biting, scathing

mordaza [mor'ðaθa] NF (*para la boca*) gag; (*Tec*) clamp

morder [mor'ðer] /**2h**/ VT to bite; (*mordisquear*) to nibble; (*fig: consumir*) to eat away, eat into ▶ VI, **morderse** VR to bite; **está que muerde** he's hopping mad; **morderse la lengua** to hold one's tongue

mordida [mor'ðiða] NF (*Am fam*) bribe

mordisco [mor'ðisko] NM bite

mordisquear [morðiske'ar] /**1a**/ VT to nibble at

moreno, -a [mo'reno, a] ADJ (*color*) (dark) brown; (*de tez*) dark; (*de pelo moreno*) dark-haired; (*negro*) black ▶ NM/F (*de tez*) dark-skinned man/woman; (*de pelo*) dark-haired man/woman

morfina [mor'fina] NF morphine

morfinómano, -a [morfi'nomano, a] ADJ addicted to hard drugs ▶ NM/F drug addict

morgue ['morɣe] NF (*Am*) mortuary (*Brit*), morgue (*US*)

moribundo, -a [mori'βundo, a] ADJ dying ▶ NM/F dying person

morir [mo'rir] /**3j**/ VI to die; (*fuego*) to die down; (*luz*) to go out; **morirse** VR to die; (*fig*) to be dying; (*Ferro etc: vías*) to end; (*: calle*) to come out; **fue muerto a tiros/en un accidente** he was shot (dead)/was killed in an accident; **~ de frío/hambre** to die of cold/starve to death; **¡me muero de hambre!** (*fig*) I'm starving!; **morirse por algo** to be dying for sth; **morirse por algn** to be crazy about sb

mormón, -ona [mor'mon, ona] NM/F Mormon

moro, -a ['moro, a] ADJ Moorish ▶ NM/F Moor; **¡hay moros en la costa!** watch out!

moroso, -a [mo'roso, a] ADJ (*lento*) slow ▶ NM/F (*Com*) bad debtor, defaulter; **deudor ~** (*Com*) slow payer

morral [mo'rral] NM haversack

morriña [mo'rriɲa] NF homesickness; **tener ~** to be homesick

morro ['morro] NM (*Zool*) snout, nose; (*Auto, Aviat*) nose; (*fam: labio*) (thick) lip; **beber a ~** to drink from the bottle; **caer de ~** to nosedive; **estar de morros (con algn)** to be in a bad mood (with sb); **tener ~** to have a nerve

morrocotudo, -a [morroko'tuðo, a] ADJ (*fam: fantástico*) smashing; (*riña, golpe*) tremendous; (*fuerte*) strong; (*pesado*) heavy; (*difícil*) awkward

morsa ['morsa] NF walrus

morse ['morse] NM Morse (code)

mortadela [morta'ðela] NF mortadella, bologna sausage

mortaja [mor'taxa] NF shroud; (*Tec*) mortise; (*Am*) cigarette paper

mortal [mor'tal] ADJ mortal; (*golpe*) deadly

mortalidad [mortali'ðað], **mortandad** [mortan'dað] NF mortality

mortecino, -a [morte'θino, a] ADJ (*débil*) weak; (*luz*) dim; (*color*) dull

mortero [mor'tero] NM mortar

mortífero, -a [mor'tifero, a] ADJ deadly, lethal

mortificar [mortifi'kar] /**1g**/ VT to mortify; (*atormentar*) to torment

mortifique *etc* [morti'fike] VB *ver* **mortificar**

mortuorio, -a [mor'tworjo, a] ADJ mortuary, death *cpd*

Mosa ['mosa] NM: **el (Río)** ~ the Meuse

mosaico [mo'saiko] NM mosaic

mosca ['moska] NF fly; **por si las moscas** just in case; **estar** ~ (*desconfiar*) to smell a rat; **tener la** ~ **en** o **detrás de la oreja** to be wary

moscovita [mosko'βita] ADJ Muscovite, Moscow *cpd* ▶ NMF Muscovite

Moscú [mos'ku] NM Moscow

mosquear [moske'ar] /**1a**/ (*fam*) VT (*hacer sospechar*) to make suspicious; (*fastidiar*) to annoy; **mosquearse** VR (*enfadarse*) to get annoyed; (*ofenderse*) to take offence

mosquita [mos'kita] NF: **parece una** ~ **muerta** he looks as though butter wouldn't melt in his mouth

mosquitero [moski'tero] NM mosquito net

mosquito [mos'kito] NM mosquito

Mossos ['mosos] NMPL: ~ **d'Esquadra** Catalan police; *ver tb* **policía**

mostaza [mos'taθa] NF mustard

mosto ['mosto] NM unfermented grape juice

mostrador [mostra'ðor] NM (*de tienda*) counter; (*de café*) bar

mostrar [mos'trar] /**1l**/ VT to show; (*exhibir*) to display, exhibit; (*explicar*) to explain; **mostrarse** VR: **mostrarse amable** to be kind; to prove to be kind; **no se muestra muy inteligente** he doesn't seem (to be) very intelligent; ~ **en pantalla** (*Inform*) to display

mota ['mota] NF speck, tiny piece; (*en diseño*) dot

mote ['mote] NM (*apodo*) nickname

motín [mo'tin] NM (*del pueblo*) revolt, rising; (*del ejército*) mutiny

motivación [motiβa'θjon] NF motivation

motivar [moti'βar] /**1a**/ VT (*causar*) to cause, motivate; (*explicar*) to explain, justify

motivo [mo'tiβo] NM motive, reason; (*Arte, Mus*) motif; **con** ~ **de** (*debido a*) because of; (*en ocasión de*) on the occasion of; (*con el fin de*) in order to; **sin** ~ for no reason at all

moto ['moto], **motocicleta** [motoθi'kleta] NF motorbike (BRIT), motorcycle

motociclista [motoθi'klista] NMF motorcyclist, biker

motoneta [moto'neta] NF (AM) (*motor*) scooter

motor, a [mo'tor, a] ADJ (*Tec*) motive; (*Anat*) motor ▶ NM motor, engine ▶ NF motorboat; ~ **a chorro** o **de reacción/de explosión** jet engine/internal combustion engine; ~ **de búsqueda** (*Internet*) search engine

motorismo [moto'rismo] NM motorcycling

motorista [moto'rista] NMF (*esp AM*: *automovilista*) motorist; (: *motociclista*) motorcyclist

motorizado, -a [motori'θaðo, a] ADJ motorized

motosierra [moto'sjerra] NF mechanical saw

motriz [mo'triθ] ADJ: **fuerza** ~ motive power; (*fig*) driving force

movedizo, -a [moβe'ðiθo, a] ADJ (*inseguro*) unsteady; (*fig*) unsettled, changeable; (*persona*) fickle

mover [mo'βer] /**2h**/ VT to move; (*cambiar de lugar*) to shift; (*cabeza: para negar*) to shake; (: *para asentir*) to nod; (*accionar*) to drive; (*fig*) to cause, provoke; **moverse** VR to move; (*mar*) to get rough; (*viento*) to rise; (*fig: apurarse*) to get a move on; (: *transformarse*) to be on the move

movible [mo'βiβle] ADJ (*no fijo*) movable; (*móvil*) mobile; (*cambiadizo*) changeable

movido, -a [mo'βiðo, a] ADJ (*Foto*) blurred; (*persona: activo*) active; (*mar*) rough; (*día*) hectic ▶ NF move; **la movida madrileña** the Madrid scene

móvil [mo'βil] ADJ mobile; (*pieza de máquina*) moving; (*mueble*) movable ▶ NM (*motivo*) motive; (*teléfono*) mobile, cellphone (US)

movilice *etc* [moβi'liθe] VB *ver* **movilizar**

movilidad [moβili'ðað] NF mobility

movilizar [moβili'θar] /**1f**/ VT to mobilize

movimiento [moβi'mjento] NM (*gen, Lit, Pol*) movement; (*Tec*) motion; (*actividad*) activity; (*Mus*) tempo; **el M~** the Falangist Movement; ~ **de bloques** (*Inform*) block move; ~ **de mercancías** (*Com*) turnover, volume of business; ~ **obrero/sindical** workers'/trade union movement; ~ **sísmico** earth tremor

Mozambique [moθam'bike] NM Mozambique

mozambiqueño, -a [moθambi'keɲo, a] ADJ, NM/F Mozambican

mozo, -a ['moθo, a] ADJ (*joven*) young; (*soltero*) single, unmarried ▶ NM/F (*joven*) youth, young man (girl); (*camarero*) waiter; (*camarera*) waitress; ~ **de estación** porter

MP3 NM MP3; **reproductor (de)** ~ MP3 player

mucama [mu'kama] NF (AM) maid

muchacho, -a [mu'tʃatʃo, a] NM/F (*niño*) boy/ girl; (*criado*) servant/servant o maid

muchedumbre [mutʃe'ðumbre] NF crowd

muchísimo, -a [mu'tʃisimo, a] ADJ SUPERLATIVO *de* **mucho** lots and lots of, ever so much ▶ ADV ever so much

---

(PALABRA CLAVE)

mucho, -a ['mutʃo, a] ADJ **1** (*cantidad*) a lot of, much; (*número*) lots of, a lot of, many; **mucho dinero** a lot of money; **hace mucho calor** it's very hot; **muchas amigas** lots o a lot of o many friends

2 (*sg: fam*): **ésta es mucha casa para él** this house is much too big for him;

había mucho borracho there were a lot o lots of drunks

▶ PRON: **tengo mucho que hacer** I've got a lot to do; **muchos dicen que …** a lot of people say that …; ver tb **tener**

▶ ADV **1**: **me gusta mucho** I like it a lot o very much; **lo siento mucho** I'm very sorry; **come mucho** he eats a lot; **trabaja mucho** he works hard; **¿te vas a quedar mucho?** are you going to be staying long?; **mucho más/menos** much o a lot more/less **2** (respuesta) very; **¿estás cansado? — ¡mucho!** are you tired? — very! **3** (locuciones): **como mucho** at (the) most; **el mejor con mucho** by far the best; **¡ni mucho menos!** far from it!; **no es rico ni mucho menos** he's far from being rich **4**: **por mucho que**: **por mucho que le creas** however much o no matter how much you believe him

muda ['muða] NF (de ropa) change of clothing; (Zool) moult; (de serpiente) slough
mudanza [mu'ðanθa] NF (cambio) change; (de casa) move; **estar de ~** to be moving
mudar [mu'ðar] /**1a**/ VT to change; (Zool) to shed ▶ VI to change; **mudarse** VR (la ropa) to change; **mudarse de casa** to move house
mudo, -a ['muðo, a] ADJ dumb; (callado: película) silent; (Ling: letra) mute; (: consonante) voiceless; **quedarse ~ (de)** (fig) to be dumb with; **quedarse ~ de asombro** to be speechless
mueble ['mweβle] NM piece of furniture; **muebles** NMPL furniture sg
mueble-bar [mweβle'βar] NM cocktail cabinet
mueca ['mweka] NF face, grimace; **hacer muecas a** to make faces at
muela ['mwela] VB ver **moler** ▶ NF (diente) tooth; (: de atrás) back tooth; (de molino) millstone; (de afilar) grindstone; **~ del juicio** wisdom tooth
muelle ['mweʎe] ADJ (blando) soft; (fig) soft, easy ▶ NM spring; (Naut) wharf; (malecón) pier
muera etc ['mwera] VB ver **morir**
muerda etc ['mwerða] VB ver **morder**
muermo ['mwermo] NM (fam) wimp
muerte ['mwerte] NF death; (homicidio) murder; **dar ~ a** to kill; **de mala ~** (fam) lousy, rotten; **es la ~** (fam) it's deadly boring
muerto, -a ['mwerto, a] PP de **morir** ▶ ADJ dead; (color) dull ▶ NM/F dead man(-woman); (difunto) deceased; (cadáver) corpse; **echar el ~ a algn** to carry the can; **cargar con el ~** (fam) to pass the buck; **hacer el ~** (nadando) to float; **estar ~ de**

cansancio to be dead tired; **Día de los Muertos** (Am) All Souls' Day

All Souls' Day (or "Day of the Dead") in Mexico coincides with All Saints' Day, which is celebrated in the Catholic countries of Latin America on November 1st and 2nd. All Souls' Day is actually a celebration which begins in the evening of October 31st and continues until November 2nd. It is a combination of the Catholic tradition of honouring the Christian saints and martyrs, and the ancient Mexican or Aztec traditions, in which death was not something sinister. For this reason all the dead are honoured by bringing offerings of food, flowers and candles to the cemetery.

muesca ['mweska] NF nick
muestra ['mwestra] VB ver **mostrar** ▶ NF (señal) indication, sign; (demostración) demonstration; (prueba) proof; (estadística) sample; (modelo) model, pattern; (testimonio) token; **dar muestras de** to show signs of; **~ al azar** (Com) random sample
muestrario [mwes'trarjo] NM collection of samples; (exposición) showcase
muestreo [mwes'treo] NM sample, sampling
muestro etc VB ver **mostrar**
muevo etc ['mweβa] VB ver **mover**
mugir [mu'xir] /**3c**/ VI (vaca) to moo
mugre ['muɣre] NF dirt, filth, muck
mugriento, -a [mu'ɣrjento, a] ADJ dirty, filthy, mucky
mugroso, -a [muɣ'roso, a] ADJ (Am) filthy, grubby
muja etc ['muxa] VB ver **mugir**
mujer [mu'xer] NF woman; (esposa) wife
mujeriego [muxe'rjeɣo] NM womaniser
mula ['mula] NF mule
mulato, -a [mu'lato, a] ADJ, NM/F mulatto
muleta [mu'leta] NF (para andar) crutch; (Taur) stick with red cape attached
muletilla [mule'tiʎa] NF (palabra) pet word, tag; (de cómico) catch phrase
mullido, -a [mu'ʎiðo, a] ADJ (cama) soft; (hierba) soft, springy
multa ['multa] NF fine; **echar** o **poner una ~ a** to fine
multar [mul'tar] /**1a**/ VT to fine; (Deporte) to penalize
multiacceso [multjak'θeso] ADJ (Inform) multi-access
multicines [multi'θine] NMPL multiscreen cinema
multicolor [multiko'lor] ADJ multicoloured
multimillonario, -a [multimiʎo'narjo, a] ADJ (contrato) multimillion pound o dollar cpd ▶ NM/F multimillionaire/-millionairess

multinacional [multinaθjo'nal] ADJ, NF multinational

múltiple ['multiple] ADJ multiple, many pl, numerous; **de tarea** ~ (*Inform*) multitasking; **de usuario** ~ (*Inform*) multi-user

multiplicar [multipli'kar] /**1g**/ VT (*Mat*) to multiply; (*fig*) to increase; **multiplicarse** VR (*Bio*) to multiply; (*fig*) to be everywhere at once

multiplique etc [multi'plike] VB ver **multiplicar**

múltiplo ['multiplo] ADJ, NM multiple

multitud [multi'tuð] NF (*muchedumbre*) crowd; ~ **de** lots of

multitudinario, -a [multituði'narjo, a] ADJ (*numeroso*) multitudinous; (*de masas*) mass cpd

mundanal [munda'nal] ADJ worldly; **alejarse del ~ ruido** to get away from it all

mundano, -a [mun'dano, a] ADJ worldly; (*de moda*) fashionable

mundial [mun'djal] ADJ world-wide, universal; (*guerra, récord*) world cpd

mundialización [mundjaliθa'θjon] NF globalization

mundialmente [mundjal'mente] ADV worldwide; ~ **famoso** world-famous

mundo ['mundo] NM world; (*ámbito*) world, circle; **el otro** ~ the next world; **el ~ del espectáculo** show business; **todo el** ~ everybody; **tener** ~ to be experienced, know one's way around; **el ~ es un pañuelo** it's a small world; **no es nada del otro** ~ it's nothing special; **se le cayó el ~ (encima)** his world fell apart

Munich ['munitʃ] NM Munich

munición [muni'θjon] NF (*Mil: provisiones*) stores pl, supplies pl; (: *de armas*) ammunition

municipal [muniθi'pal] ADJ (*elección*) municipal; (*concejo*) town cpd, local; (*piscina etc*) public ▶ NM (*guardia*) policeman

municipio [muni'θipjo] NM (*ayuntamiento*) town council, corporation; (*territorio administrativo*) town, municipality

muñeca [mu'ɲeka] NF (*Anat*) wrist; (*juguete*) doll

muñeco [mu'ɲeko] NM (*figura*) figure; (*marioneta*) puppet; (*fig*) puppet, pawn; (*niño*) pretty little boy; ~ **de nieve** snowman

muñequera [muɲe'kera] NF wristband

muñón [mu'ɲon] NM (*Anat*) stump

mural [mu'ral] ADJ mural, wall cpd ▶ NM mural

muralla [mu'raʎa] NF (*city*) walls pl

murciano, -a [mur'θjano, a] ADJ of o from Murcia ▶ NM/F native o inhabitant of Murcia

murciélago [mur'θjelaɣo] NM bat

murga ['murɣa] NF (*banda*) band of street musicians; **dar la** ~ to be a nuisance

murmullo [mur'muʎo] NM murmur(ing); (*cuchicheo*) whispering; (*de arroyo*) murmur, rippling; (*de hojas, viento*) rustle, rustling; (*ruido confuso*) hum(ming)

murmuración [murmura'θjon] NF gossip; (*críticas*) backbiting

murmurador, a [murmura'ðor, a] ADJ gossiping; (*criticón*) backbiting ▶ NM/F gossip; backbiter

murmurar [murmu'rar] /**1a**/ VI to murmur, whisper; (*criticar*) to criticize; (*cotillear*) to gossip

muro ['muro] NM wall; ~ **de contención** retaining wall

mus [mus] NM *card game*

musaraña [musa'raɲa] NF (*Zool*) shrew; (*insecto*) creepy-crawly; **pensar en las musarañas** to daydream

muscular [musku'lar] ADJ muscular

músculo ['muskulo] NM muscle

musculoso, -a [musku'loso, a] ADJ muscular

museo [mu'seo] NM museum; ~ **de arte** o **de pintura** art gallery; ~ **de cera** waxworks

musgo ['musɣo] NM moss

musical [musi'kal] ADJ, NM musical

músico, -a ['musiko, a] ADJ musical ▶ NM/F musician ▶ NF music; **irse con la música a otra parte** to clear off

musitar [musi'tar] /**1a**/ VT, VI to mutter, mumble

muslo ['muslo] NM thigh; (*de pollo*) leg, drumstick

mustio, -a ['mustjo, a] ADJ (*persona*) depressed, gloomy; (*planta*) faded, withered

musulmán, -ana [musul'man, ana] NM/F Moslem, Muslim

mutación [muta'θjon] NF (*Bio*) mutation; (*cambio*) (sudden) change

mutilar [muti'lar] /**1a**/ VT to mutilate; (*a una persona*) to maim

mutis ['mutis] NM INV (*Teat*) exit; **hacer** ~ (*Teat: retirarse*) to exit, go off; (*fig*) to say nothing

mutismo [mu'tismo] NM silence

mutualidad [mutwali'ðað] NF (*reciprocidad*) mutual character; (*asociación*) friendly o benefit (US) society

mutuamente [mutwa'mente] ADV mutually

mutuo, -a ['mutwo, a] ADJ mutual

muy [mwi] ADV very; (*demasiado*) too; **M~ Señor mío** Dear Sir; ~ **bien** (*de acuerdo*) all right; ~ **de noche** very late at night; **eso es** ~ **de él** that's just like him; **eso es** ~ **español** that's typically Spanish

m

Nn

N, n ['ene] NF (*letra*) N, n; **N de Navarra** N for Nellie (*BRIT*) o Nan (*US*)

N ABR (= *norte*) N

N. ABR (= *noviembre*) Nov; = **carretera nacional**; (*AM*: = *moneda nacional*) local currency; **le entregaron sólo N.$2.000** they only gave him $2000 pesos

n. ABR (*Ling*: = *nombre*) n; = **nacido, a**

n/ ABR = **nuestro, a**

N.ª ABR = **Nuestra Señora**

nabo ['naβo] NM turnip

nácar ['nakar] NM mother-of-pearl

nacer [na'θer] /**2d**/ VI to be born; (*huevo*) to hatch; (*vegetal*) to sprout; (*río*) to rise; (*fig*) to begin, originate, have its origins; **nací en Barcelona** I was born in Barcelona; **nació para poeta** he was born to be a poet; **nadie nace enseñado** we all have to learn; **nació una sospecha en su mente** a suspicion formed in her mind

nacido, -a [na'θiðo, a] ADJ born; **recién ~** newborn

naciente [na'θjente] ADJ new, emerging; (*sol*) rising

nacimiento [naθi'mjento] NM birth; (*fig*) birth, origin; (*de Navidad*) Nativity; (*linaje*) descent, family; (*de río*) source; **ciego de ~** blind from birth

nación [na'θjon] NF nation; (*pueblo*) people; **Naciones Unidas** United Nations

nacional [naθjo'nal] ADJ national; (*Com, Econ*) domestic, home *cpd*

nacionalice *etc* [naθjona'liθe] VB ver **nacionalizar**

nacionalidad [naθjonali'ðað] NF nationality; (*ESP, Pol*) autonomous region

nacionalismo [naθjona'lismo] NM nationalism

nacionalista [naθjona'lista] ADJ, NMF nationalist

nacionalizar [naθjonali'θar] /**1f**/ VT to nationalize; **nacionalizarse** VR (*persona*) to become naturalized

nada ['naða] PRON nothing ▶ ADV not at all, in no way ▶ NF nothingness; **no decir ~ (más)** to say nothing (else), not to say anything (else); **¡~ más!** that's all; **de ~** don't mention it; **~ de eso** nothing of the kind; **antes de ~** right away; **como si ~** as if it didn't matter; **no ha sido ~** it's nothing; **la ~** the void

nadador, a [naða'ðor, a] NM/F swimmer

nadar [na'ðar] /**1a**/ VI to swim; **~ en la abundancia** (*fig*) to be rolling in money

nadie ['naðje] PRON nobody, no-one; **~ habló** nobody spoke; **no había ~** there was nobody there, there wasn't anybody there; **es un don ~** he's a nobody o nonentity

nadita [na'ðita] (*esp AM fam*) = **nada**

nado ['naðo]: **a ~** *adv*: **pasar a ~** to swim across

nafta ['nafta] NF (*AM*) petrol (*BRIT*), gas(oline) (*US*)

naftalina [nafta'lina] NF: **bolas de ~** mothballs

náhuatl ['nawatl] ADJ, NM Nahuatl

naipe ['naipe] NM (*playing*) card; **naipes** NMPL cards

nal. ABR (= *nacional*) nat

nalgas ['nalɣas] NFPL buttocks

nalguear [nalɣe'ar] /**1a**/ VT (*AM, CAM*) to spank

Namibia [na'miβja] NF Namibia

nana ['nana] NF lullaby

napias ['napjas] NFPL (*fam*) conk *sg*

Nápoles ['napoles] NF Naples

napolitano, -a [napoli'tano, a] ADJ *of o* from Naples, Neapolitan ▶ NM/F Neapolitan

naranja [na'ranxa] ADJ INV, NF orange; **media ~** (*fam*) better half; **¡naranjas de la China!** nonsense!

naranjada [naran'xaða] NF orangeade

naranjo [na'ranxo] NM orange tree

Narbona [nar'βona] NF Narbonne

narcisista [narθi'sista] ADJ narcissistic

narciso [nar'θiso] NM narcissus

narcotice *etc* [narko'tiθe] VB ver **narcotizar**

narcótico, -a [nar'kotiko, a] ADJ, NM narcotic

narcotizar [narkoti'θar] /**1f**/ vt to drug

narcotraficante [narkotrafi'kante] NMF narcotics o drug trafficker

narcotráfico [narko'trafiko] NM narcotics o drug trafficking

nardo ['narðo] NM lily

narices [na'riθes] NFPL ver **nariz**

narigón, -ona [nari'ɣon, ona], **narigudo, -a** [nari'ɣuðo, a] ADJ big-nosed

nariz [na'riθ] NF nose; **narices** NFPL nostrils; **¡narices!** (fam) rubbish!; **delante de las narices de algn** under one's (very) nose; **estar hasta las narices** to be completely fed up; **meter las narices en algo** to poke one's nose into sth; **~ chata/respingona** snub/turned-up nose

narración [narra'θjon] NF narration

narrador, a [narra'ðor, a] NM/F narrator

narrar [na'rrar] /**1a**/ vt to narrate, recount

narrativo, -a [narra'tiβo, a] ADJ narrative ▶ NF narrative, story

nasal [na'sal] ADJ nasal

nata ['nata] NF cream (tb fig); (en leche cocida etc) skin; **~ batida** whipped cream

natación [nata'θjon] NF swimming

natal [na'tal] ADJ natal; (país) native; **ciudad ~** home town

natalicio [nata'liθjo] NM birthday

natalidad [natali'ðað] NF birth rate

natillas [na'tiʎas] NFPL (egg) custard sg

natividad [natiβi'ðað] NF nativity

nativo, -a [na'tiβo, a] ADJ, NM/F native

nato, -a ['nato, a] ADJ born; **un músico ~** a born musician

natural [natu'ral] ADJ natural; (fruta etc) fresh ▶ NMF native ▶ NM disposition, temperament; **buen ~** good nature; **fruta al ~** fruit in its own juice

naturaleza [natura'leθa] NF nature; (género) nature, kind; **~ muerta** still life

naturalice etc [natura'liθe] VB ver **naturalizarse**

naturalidad [naturali'ðað] NF naturalness

naturalización [naturaliθa'θjon] NF naturalization

naturalizarse [naturali'θarse] /**1f**/ VR to become naturalized; (aclimatarse) to become acclimatized

naturalmente [natural'mente] ADV naturally; (de modo natural) in a natural way; **¡~!** of course!

naturista [natu'rista] ADJ (Med) naturopathic ▶ NMF naturopath

naufragar [naufra'ɣar] /**1h**/ vi (barco) to sink; (gente) to be shipwrecked; (fig) to fail

naufragio [nau'fraxjo] NM shipwreck

náufrago, -a ['naufraɣo, a] NM/F castaway, shipwrecked person

naufrague etc [nau'fraɣe] VB ver **naufragar**

náusea ['nausea] NF nausea; **me da náuseas** it makes me feel sick

nauseabundo, -a [nausea'βundo, a] ADJ nauseating, sickening

náutico, -a ['nautiko, a] ADJ nautical; **club ~** sailing o yacht club ▶ NF navigation, seamanship

navaja [na'βaxa] NF (cortaplumas) clasp knife (BRIT), penknife; **~ (de afeitar)** razor

navajazo [naβa'xaθo] NM (herida) gash; (acto) slash

naval [na'βal] ADJ (Mil) naval; **construcción ~** shipbuilding; **sector ~** shipbuilding industry

Navarra [na'βarra] NF Navarre

navarro, -a [na'βarro, a] ADJ of o from Navarre, Navarrese ▶ NM/F Navarrese ▶ NM (Ling) Navarrese

nave ['naβe] NF (barco) ship, vessel; (Arq) nave; **~ espacial** spaceship; **quemar las naves** to burn one's boats; **~ industrial** factory premises pl

navegación [naβeɣa'θjon] NF navigation; (viaje) sea journey; **~ aérea** air traffic; **~ costera** coastal shipping; **~ fluvial** river navigation

navegador [naβeɣa'ðor] NM (Inform) browser; (de coche) sat nav

navegante [naβe'ɣante] NMF navigator

navegar [naβe'ɣar] /**1h**/ vi (barco) to sail; (avión) to fly ▶ vt to sail; to fly; (dirigir el rumbo de) to navigate; **~ por Internet** to surf the Net

navegue etc [na'βeɣe] VB ver **navegar**

Navidad [naβi'ðað] NF Christmas; **Navidades** NFPL Christmas time sg; **día de ~** Christmas Day; **por Navidades** at Christmas (time); **¡Feliz ~!** Merry Christmas!

navideño, -a [naβi'ðeɲo, a] ADJ Christmas cpd

navío [na'βio] NM ship

nazca etc VB ver **nacer**

nazi ['naθi] ADJ, NMF Nazi

nazismo [na'θismo] NM Nazism

N. de la R. ABR (= nota de la redacción) editor's note

N. de la T./del T. ABR (= nota de la traductora/del traductor) translator's note

NE ABR (= nor(d)este) NE

neblina [ne'βlina] NF mist

nebuloso, -a [neβu'loso, a] ADJ foggy; (calinoso) misty; (indefinido) nebulous, vague ▶ NF nebula

necedad [neθe'ðað] NF foolishness; (una necedad) foolish act

necesario, -a [neθe'sarjo, a] ADJ necessary; **si fuera o fuese ~** if need(s) be

neceser [neθe'ser] NM toilet bag; (bolsa grande) holdall

necesidad [neθesi'ðað] NF need; (*lo inevitable*) necessity; (*miseria*) poverty, need; **en caso de ~** in case of need *o* emergency; **hacer sus necesidades** to relieve o.s.

necesitado, -a [neθesi'taðo, a] ADJ needy, poor; **~ de** in need of

necesitar [neθesi'tar] /**1a**/ VT to need, require ▶ VI: **~ de** to have need of; **necesitarse** VR to be needed; (*en anuncios*) **"necesitase coche"** "car wanted"

necio, -a ['neθjo, a] ADJ foolish ▶ NM/F fool

necrología [nekrolo'xia] NF obituary

necrópolis [ne'kropolis] NF INV cemetery

néctar ['nektar] NM nectar

nectarina [nekta'rina] NF nectarine

neerlandés, -esa [neerlan'des, esa] ADJ Dutch ▶ NM/F Dutchman(-woman) ▶ NM (*Ling*) Dutch; **los neerlandeses** the Dutch

nefando, -a [ne'fando, a] ADJ unspeakable

nefasto, -a [ne'fasto, a] ADJ ill-fated, unlucky

negación [neɣa'θjon] NF negation; (*Ling*) negative; (*rechazo*) refusal, denial

negado, -a [ne'ɣaðo, a] ADJ: **~ para** inept at, unfitted for

negar [ne'ɣar] /**1h, 1j**/ VT (*renegar, rechazar*) to refuse; (*prohibir*) to refuse, deny; (*desmentir*) to deny; **negarse** VR: **negarse a hacer algo** to refuse to do sth

negativo, -a [neɣa'tiβo, a] ADJ negative ▶ NM (*Foto*) negative; (*Mat*) minus ▶ NF (*gen*) negative; (*rechazo*) refusal, denial; **negativa rotunda** flat refusal

negligencia [neɣli'xenθja] NF negligence

negligente [neɣli'xente] ADJ negligent

negociable [neɣo'θjaβle] ADJ negotiable

negociación [neɣoθja'θjon] NF negotiation

negociado [neɣo'θjaðo] NM department, section

negociante [neɣo'θjante] NMF businessman(-woman)

negociar [neɣo'θjar] /**1b**/ VT, VI to negotiate; **~ en** to deal in, trade in

negocio [ne'ɣoθjo] NM (*Com*) business; (*asunto*) affair, business; (*operación comercial*) deal, transaction; (*Am*) shop, store; (*lugar*) place of business; **los negocios** business *sg*; **hacer ~** to do business; **el ~ del libro** the book trade; **~ autorizado** licensed trade; **hombre de negocios** businessman; **~ sucio** shady deal; **hacer un buen ~** to pull off a profitable deal; **¡mal ~!** it looks bad!

negra ['neɣra] NF (*Mus*) crotchet; *ver tb* **negro**

negrita [ne'ɣrita] NF (*Tip*) bold face; **en ~** in bold (type)

negro, -a ['neɣro, a] ADJ black; (*suerte*) awful, atrocious; (*humor etc*) sad; (*lúgubre*) gloomy ▶ NM (*color*) black ▶ NM/F black person ▶ NF (*Mus*) crotchet; **~ como la boca del lobo** pitch-black; **estoy ~ con esto** I'm getting desperate about it; **ponerse ~** (*fam*) to get cross

negrura [ne'ɣrura] NF blackness

negué [ne'ɣe], **neguemos** *etc* [ne'ɣemos] VB *ver* **negar**

nene, -a ['nene, a] NM/F baby, small child

nenúfar [ne'nufar] NM water lily

neologismo [neolo'xismo] NM neologism

neón [ne'on] NM neon; **luces/lámpara de ~** neon lights/lamp

neoyorquino, -a [neojor'kino, a] ADJ New York *cpd* ▶ NM/F New Yorker

neozelandés, -esa [neoθelan'des, esa] ADJ New Zealand *cpd* ▶ NM/F New Zealander

nepotismo [nepo'tismo] NM nepotism

nervio ['nerβjo] NM (*Anat*) nerve; (: *tendón*) tendon; (*fig*) vigour; (*Tec*) rib; **crispar los nervios a algn**, **poner los nervios de punta a algn** to get on sb's nerves

nerviosismo [nerβjo'sismo] NM nervousness, nerves *pl*

nervioso, -a [ner'βjoso, a] ADJ nervous; (*sensible*) nervy, highly-strung; (*impaciente*) restless; **¡no te pongas ~!** take it easy!

nervudo, -a [ner'βuðo, a] ADJ tough; (*mano*) sinewy

netiqueta [neti'keta] NF netiquette

neto, -a ['neto, a] ADJ clear; (*limpio*) clean; (*Com*) net

neumático, -a [neu'matiko, a] ADJ pneumatic ▶ NM (*Esp*) tyre (*Brit*), tire (*US*); **~ de recambio** spare tyre

neumonía [neumo'nia] NF pneumonia; **~ asiática** SARS

neura ['neura] NF (*fam: obsesión*) obsession

neuralgia [neu'ralxja] NF neuralgia

neurálgico, -a [neu'ralxiko, a] ADJ neuralgic; (*fig: centro*) nerve *cpd*

neurastenia [neuras'tenja] NF neurasthenia; (*fig*) excitability

neurasténico, -a [neuras'teniko, a] ADJ neurasthenic; excitable

neurólogo, -a [neu'roloɣo, a] NM/F neurologist

neurona [neu'rona] NF neuron

neurosis [neu'rosis] NF INV neurosis

neurótico, -a [neu'rotiko, a] ADJ, NM/F neurotic

neutral [neu'tral] ADJ neutral

neutralice *etc* [neutra'liθe] VB *ver* **neutralizar**

neutralizar [neutrali'θar] /**1f**/ VT to neutralize; (*contrarrestar*) to counteract

neutro, -a ['neutro, a] ADJ (*Bio, Ling*) neuter

neutrón [neu'tron] NM neutron

nevado, -a [ne'βaðo, a] ADJ snow-covered; (*montaña*) snow-capped; (*fig*) snowy, snow-white ▶ NF (*tormenta*) snowstorm; (*caída de nieve*) snowfall

nevar [ne'βar] /**1j**/ vi to snow ▶ vt (fig) to whiten

nevera [ne'βera] nf (Esp) refrigerator (Brit), icebox (US)

nevería [neβe'ria] nf (Am) ice-cream parlour

nevisca [ne'βiska] nf flurry of snow

nexo ['nekso] nm link, connection

n/f abr (Com) = **nuestro favor**

ni [ni] conj nor, neither; (tb: **ni siquiera**) not even; **ni que** not even if; **ni blanco ni negro** neither white nor black; **ni el uno ni el otro** neither one nor the other

Nicaragua [nika'raɣwa] nf Nicaragua

nicaragüense [nikara'ɣwense] adj, nmf Nicaraguan

nicho ['nitʃo] nm niche

nick [nik] nm (Internet) nickname, user name, nick

nicotina [niko'tina] nf nicotine

nido ['niðo] nm nest; (fig) hiding place; **~ de ladrones** den of thieves

niebla ['njeβla] nf fog; (neblina) mist; **hay ~** it is foggy

niego etc ['njeɣo], **niegue** etc ['njeɣe] vb ver **negar**

nieto, -a ['njeto, a] nm/f grandson/granddaughter; **nietos** nmpl grandchildren

nieve ['njeβe] vb ver **nevar** ▶ nf snow; (Am) ice cream; **copo de ~** snowflake

N.I.F. nm abr (= Número de Identificación Fiscal) ID number used for tax purposes

Nigeria [ni'xerja] nf Nigeria

nigeriano, -a [nixe'rjano, a] adj, nm/f Nigerian

nigromancia [niɣro'manθja] nf necromancy, black magic

nihilista [nii'lista] adj nihilistic ▶ nmf nihilist

Nilo ['nilo] nm: **el (Río) ~** the Nile

nimbo ['nimbo] nm (aureola) halo; (nube) nimbus

nimiedad [nimje'ðað] nf smallmindedness; (trivialidad) triviality; (una nimiedad) trifle, tiny detail

nimio, -a ['nimjo, a] adj trivial, insignificant

ninfa ['ninfa] nf nymph

ninfómana [nin'fomana] nf nymphomaniac

ningún [nin'gun] adj ver **ninguno**

ninguno, -a [nin'guno, a] adj (antes de nmsg **ningún**) no ▶ pron (nadie) nobody; (ni uno) none, not one; (ni uno ni otro) neither; **de ninguna manera** by no means, not at all; **no voy a ninguna parte** I'm not going anywhere

niña ['nina] nf ver **niño**

niñera [ni'nera] nf nursemaid, nanny

niñería [nine'ria] nf childish act

niñez [ni'neθ] nf childhood; (infancia) infancy

niño, -a ['nino, a] adj (joven) young; (inmaduro) immature ▶ nm (chico) boy, child ▶ nf girl, child; (Anat) pupil; **los niños** the children; **~ bien** rich kid; **~ expósito** foundling; **~ de pecho** babe-in-arms; **~ prodigio** child prodigy; **de ~** as a child; **ser el ~ mimado de algn** to be sb's pet; **ser la niña de los ojos de algn** to be the apple of sb's eye

nipón, -ona [ni'pon, ona] adj, nm/f Japanese; **los nipones** the Japanese

níquel ['nikel] nm nickel

niquelar [nike'lar] /**1a**/ vt (Tec) to nickel-plate

níspero ['nispero] nm medlar

nitidez [niti'ðeθ] nf (claridad) clarity; (: de atmósfera) brightness; (: de imagen) sharpness

nítido, -a [ni'tiðo, a] adj bright; (fig) pure; (imagen) clear, sharp

nitrato [ni'trato] nm nitrate

nitrógeno [ni'troxeno] nm nitrogen

nitroglicerina [nitroɣliθe'rina] nf nitroglycerine

nivel [ni'βel] nm (Geo) level; (norma) level, standard; (altura) height; **~ de aceite** oil level; **~ de aire** spirit level; **~ de vida** standard of living; **al ~ de** on a level with, at the same height as; (fig) on a par with; **a 900 m sobre el ~ del mar** at 900 m above sea level

nivelado, -a [niβe'laðo, a] adj level, flat; (Tec) flush

nivelar [niβe'lar] /**1a**/ vt to level out; (fig) to even up; (Com) to balance

Niza ['niθa] nf Nice

n/l. abr (Com) = **nuestra letra**

NNE abr (= nornordeste) NNE

NNO abr (= nornoroeste) NNW

NN. UU. nfpl abr (= Naciones Unidas) UN sg

N.º abr (= número) No

NO abr (= noroeste) NW

no [no] adv no; (con verbo) not ▶ excl no!; **no tengo nada** I don't have anything, I have nothing; **no es el mío** it's not mine; **ahora no** not now; **¿no lo sabes?** don't you know?; **no mucho** not much; **no bien termine, lo entregaré** as soon as I finish I'll hand it over; **ayer no más** just yesterday; **¡pase no más!** come in!; **¡a que no lo sabes!** I bet you don't know!; **¡cómo no!** of course!; **pacto de no agresión** non-aggression pact; **los países no alineados** the non-aligned countries; **el no va más** the ultimate; **la no intervención** non-intervention

n/o abr (Com) = **nuestra orden**

noble ['noβle] adj, nmf noble; **los nobles** the nobility sg

nobleza [no'βleθa] nf nobility

noche ['notʃe] nf night, night-time; (la tarde) evening; (fig) darkness; **de ~, por la ~** at night; **ayer por la ~** last night; **esta ~**

tonight; **(en) toda la** ~ all night; **hacer ~ en un sitio** to spend the night in a place; **se hace de** ~ it's getting dark; **es de** ~ it's dark; **N~ de San Juan** *see note*

> The *Noche de San Juan* is a *fiesta* which takes place on 23rd or 24th June, around the time of the summer solstice, and which has taken the place of ancient pagan festivals. Traditionally, fire plays a major part in these festivities, with celebrations and dancing taking place around bonfires in towns and villages.

Nochebuena [notʃe'βwena] NF Christmas Eve; *see note*

> On *Nochebuena* in Spanish homes there is normally a large supper when family members come from all over to be together. The more religiously inclined attend *la misa del gallo* at midnight. The tradition of receiving Christmas presents from Santa Claus is becoming more and more widespread and gradually replacing the tradition of *los Reyes Magos* (the Three Wise Men) on the 6th of January.

Nochevieja [notʃe'βjexa] NF New Year's Eve; *ver tb* **uva**

noción [no'θjon] NF notion; **nociones** NFPL elements, rudiments

nocivo, -a [no'θiβo, a] ADJ harmful

noctambulismo [noktambu'lismo] NM sleepwalking

noctámbulo, -a [nok'tambulo, a] NM/F sleepwalker

nocturno, -a [nok'turno, a] ADJ (*de la noche*) nocturnal, night *cpd*; (*de la tarde*) evening *cpd* ▶ NM nocturne

Noé [no'e] NM Noah

nogal [no'ɣal] NM walnut tree; (*madera*) walnut

nómada ['nomaða] ADJ nomadic ▶ NMF nomad

nomás [no'mas] (*Am*) ADV (*gen*) just; (*tan sólo*) only ▶ CONJ (*en cuanto*): ~ **se fue se acordó** no sooner had she left than she remembered; **así** ~ (*fam*) just like that; **ayer** ~ only yesterday

nombramiento [nombra'mjento] NM naming; (*para un empleo*) appointment; (*Pol etc*) nomination; (*Mil*) commission

nombrar [nom'brar] /**1a**/ VT (*gen*) to name; (*mencionar*) to mention; (*designar*) to appoint, nominate; (*Mil*) to commission

nombre ['nombre] NM name; (*sustantivo*) noun; (*fama*) renown; ~ **y apellidos** name in full; **poner** ~ **a** to call, name; ~ **común/propio** common/proper noun; ~ **de pila/de soltera** Christian/maiden name; ~ **de fichero** (*Inform*) file name; **en** ~ **de** in the name of, on behalf of; **sin** ~ nameless;

su conducta no tiene ~ his behaviour is utterly despicable

nomenclatura [nomenkla'tura] NF nomenclature

nomeolvides [nomeol'βiðes] NM INV forget-me-not

nómina ['nomina] NF (*lista*) list; (*Com: tb:* **nóminas**) payroll; (*hoja*) payslip

nominal [nomi'nal] ADJ nominal; (*valor*) face *cpd*; (*Ling*) noun *cpd*, substantival

nominar [nomi'nar] /**1a**/ VT to nominate

nominativo, -a [nomina'tiβo, a] ADJ (*Ling*) nominative; (*Com*): **un cheque** ~ **a X** a cheque made out to X

non [non] ADJ odd, uneven ▶ NM odd number; **pares y nones** odds and evens

nonagésimo, -a [nona'xesimo, a] NUM ninetieth

nono, -a ['nono, a] NUM ninth

nordeste [nor'ðeste] ADJ north-east, north-eastern, north-easterly ▶ NM north-east; (*viento*) north-east wind, north-easterly

nórdico, -a ['norðiko, a] ADJ (*del norte*) northern, northerly; (*escandinavo*) Nordic, Norse ▶ NM/F northerner; (*escandinavo*) Norseman/-woman ▶ NM (*Ling*) Norse

noreste [no'reste] ADJ, NM = **nordeste**

noria ['norja] NF (*Agr*) waterwheel; (*de feria*) big (*BRIT*) o Ferris (*US*) wheel

norma ['norma] NF standard, norm, rule; (*patrón*) pattern; (*método*) method

normal [nor'mal] ADJ (*corriente*) normal; (*habitual*) usual, natural; (*Tec*) standard; **Escuela N~** teacher training college; **(gasolina)** ~ two-star petrol

normalice *etc* [norma'liθe] VB *ver* **normalizar**

normalidad [normali'ðað] NF normality

normalización [normaliθa'θjon] NF (*Com*) standardization

normalizar [normali'θar] /**1f**/ VT (*reglamentar*) to normalize; (*Com, Tec*) to standardize; **normalizarse** VR to return to normal

normalmente [normal'mente] ADV (*con normalidad*) normally; (*habitualmente*) usually

Normandía [norman'dia] NF Normandy

normando, -a [nor'mando, a] ADJ, NM/F Norman

normativo, -a [norma'tiβo, a] ADJ: **es** ~ **en todos los coches nuevos** it is standard in all new cars ▶ NF rules *pl*, regulations *pl*

noroeste [noro'este] ADJ north-west, north-western, north-westerly ▶ NM north-west; (*viento*) north-west wind, north-westerly

norte ['norte] ADJ north, northern, northerly ▶ NM north; (*fig*) guide

Norteamérica [nortea'merika] NF North America

norteamericano, -a [norteameri'kano, a] ADJ, NM/F (North) American

norteño, -a [nor'teɲo, a] ADJ northern ▶ NM/F northerner

Noruega [no'rweɣa] NF Norway

noruego, -a [no'rweɣo, a] ADJ, NM/F Norwegian ▶ NM (Ling) Norwegian

nos [nos] PRON (directo) us; (indirecto) (to) us; (reflexivo) (to) ourselves; (recíproco) (to) each other; **ayer ~ levantamos a las siete** we got up at seven yesterday

nosocomio [noso'komjo] NM (Am) hospital

nosotros, -as [no'sotros, as] PRON (sujeto) we; (después de prep) us; **~ (mismos)** ourselves

nostalgia [nos'talxja] NF nostalgia, homesickness

nostálgico, -a [nos'talxiko, a] ADJ nostalgic, homesick

nota ['nota] NF note; (Escol) mark; (de fin de año) report; (Univ etc) footnote; (Com) account; **~ de aviso** advice note; **~ de crédito/débito** credit/debit note; **~ de gastos** expenses claim; **~ de sociedad** gossip column; **tomar notas** to take notes

notable [no'taβle] ADJ noteworthy, notable; (Escol etc) outstanding ▶ NMF notable

notar [no'tar] /1a/ VT to notice, note; (percibir) to feel; (ver) to see; **notarse** VR to be obvious; **se nota que …** one observes that …

notaría [nota'ria] NF (profesión) profession of notary; (despacho) notary's office

notarial [nota'rjal] ADJ (estilo) legal; **acta ~** affidavit

notario [no'tarjo] NM notary; (abogado) solicitor

noticia [no'tiθja] NF (información) piece of news; (TV etc) news item; **las noticias** the news sg; **según nuestras noticias** according to our information; **tener noticias de algn** to hear from sb

noticiario [noti'θjarjo] NM (Cine) newsreel; (TV) news bulletin

noticiero [noti'θjero] NM newspaper, gazette; (Am: tb: **noticiero telediario**) news bulletin

notificación [notifika'θjon] NF notification

notificar [notifi'kar] /1g/ VT to notify, inform

notifique etc [noti'fike] VB ver **notificar**

notoriedad [notorje'ðað] NF fame, renown

notorio, -a [no'torjo, a] ADJ (público) well-known; (evidente) obvious

nov. ABR (= noviembre) Nov.

novatada [noβa'taða] NF (burla) teasing, hazing (US); **pagar la ~** to learn the hard way

novato, -a [no'βato, a] ADJ inexperienced ▶ NM/F beginner, novice

novecientos, -as [noβe'θjentos, as] NUM nine hundred

novedad [noβe'ðað] NF (calidad de nuevo) newness, novelty; (noticia) piece of news; (cambio) change, (new) development; (sorpresa) surprise; **novedades** NFPL (noticia) latest (news) sg

novedoso, -a [noβe'ðoso, a] ADJ novel

novel [no'βel] ADJ new; (inexperto) inexperienced ▶ NMF beginner

novela [no'βela] NF novel; **~ policíaca** detective story

novelero, -a [noβe'lero, a] ADJ highly imaginative

novelesco, -a [noβe'lesko, a] ADJ fictional; (romántico) romantic; (fantástico) fantastic

novelista [noβe'lista] NMF novelist

novelística [noβe'listika] NF: **la ~** fiction, the novel

noveno, -a [no'βeno, a] NUM ninth

noventa [no'βenta] NUM ninety

novia ['noβja] NF ver **novio**

noviazgo [no'βjaθɣo] NM engagement

novicio, -a [no'βiθjo, a] NM/F novice

noviembre [no'βjembre] NM November; ver tb **julio**

novilla [no'βiʎa] NF heifer

novillada [noβi'ʎaða] NF (Taur) bullfight with young bulls

novillero [noβi'ʎero] NM novice bullfighter

novillo [no'βiʎo] NM young bull, bullock; **hacer novillos** (fam) to play truant (BRIT) o hooky (US)

novio, -a ['noβjo, a] NM/F boyfriend/girlfriend; (prometido) fiancé/fiancée; (recién casado) bridegroom/bride; **los novios** the newly-weds

novísimo, -a [no'βisimo, a] ADJ SUPERLATIVO de **nuevo**

NPI NM ABR (Inform: = número personal de identificación) PIN

N. S. ABR = **Nuestro Señor**

ns/nc ABR = **no sabe(n)/no contesta(n)**

ntra., ntro. ABR = **nuestra, nuestro**

Ntro. Sr. ABR = **Nuestro Señor**

NU NFPL ABR (= Naciones Unidas) UN sg

nubarrón [nuβa'rron] NM storm cloud

nube ['nuβe] NF cloud; (Med: ocular) cloud, film; (fig) mass; **una ~ de críticas** a storm of criticism; **los precios están por las nubes** prices are sky-high; **estar en las nubes** to be away with the fairies

nublado, -a [nu'βlaðo, a] ADJ cloudy ▶ NM storm cloud

nublar [nu'βlar] /1a/ VT (oscurecer) to darken; (confundir) to cloud; **nublarse** VR to cloud over

nuboso, -a [nu'βoso, a] ADJ cloudy

nuca ['nuka] NF nape of the neck

nuclear [nukle'ar] ADJ nuclear

nuclearizado, -a [nukleari'θaðo, a] ADJ: **países nuclearizados** countries possessing nuclear weapons

núcleo ['nukleo] NM (centro) core; (Física) nucleus; **~ urbano** city centre

nudillo [nu'ðiʎo] NM knuckle

nudista [nu'dista] ADJ, NMF nudist

nudo ['nuðo] NM knot; (*unión*) bond; (*de problema*) crux; (*Ferro*) junction; (*fig*) lump; **~ corredizo** slipknot; **con un ~ en la garganta** with a lump in one's throat

nudoso, -a [nu'ðoso, a] ADJ knotty; (*tronco*) gnarled; (*bastón*) knobbly

nueces ['nweθes] NFPL *de* **nuez**

nuera ['nwera] NF daughter-in-law

nuestro, -a ['nwestro, a] ADJ POSESIVO our ▶ PRON ours; **~ padre** our father; **un amigo ~** a friend of ours; **es el ~** it's ours; **los nuestros** our people; (*Deporte*) our o the local team o side

nueva ['nweβa] NF *ver* **nuevo**

Nueva Escocia NF Nova Scotia

nuevamente [nweβa'mente] ADV (*otra vez*) again; (*de nuevo*) anew

Nueva York [-'jork] NF New York

Nueva Zelanda [-θe'landa], **Nueva Zelandia** [-θe'landja] NF New Zealand

nueve ['nweβe] NUM nine

nuevo, -a ['nweβo, a] ADJ (*gen*) new ▶ NF piece of news; **¿qué hay de ~?** (*fam*) what's new?; **de ~** again

Nuevo México NM New Mexico

nuez [nweθ] (*pl* **nueces**) NF nut; (*del nogal*) walnut; **~ de Adán** Adam's apple; **~ moscada** nutmeg

nulidad [nuli'ðað] NF (*incapacidad*) incompetence; (*abolición*) nullity; (*individuo*) nonentity; **es una ~** he's a dead loss

nulo, -a ['nulo, a] ADJ (*inepto, torpe*) useless; (*inválido*) (null and) void; (*Deporte*) drawn, tied

núm. ABR (= *número*) no.

numen ['numen] NM inspiration

numeración [numera'θjon] NF (*cifras*) numbers *pl*; (*arábiga, romana etc*) numerals *pl*; **~ de línea** (*Inform*) line numbering

numerador [numera'ðor] NM (*Mat*) numerator

numeral [nume'ral] NM numeral

numerar [nume'rar] /**1a**/ VT to number; **numerarse** VR (*Mil etc*) to number off

numerario, -a [nume'rarjo, a] ADJ numerary; **profesor ~** permanent o tenured member of teaching staff ▶ NM hard cash

numérico, -a [nu'meriko, a] ADJ numerical

número ['numero] NM (*gen*) number; (*tamaño: de zapato*) size; (*ejemplar: de diario*) number, issue; (*Teat etc*) turn, act, number; **sin ~** numberless, unnumbered; **~ binario** (*Inform*) binary number; **~ de matrícula/de teléfono** registration/telephone number; **~ personal de identificación** (*Inform etc*) personal identification number; **~ impar/par** odd/even number; **~ romano** Roman numeral; **~ de serie** (*Com*) serial number; **~ atrasado** back number

numeroso, -a [nume'roso, a] ADJ numerous; **familia numerosa** large family

numerus ['numerus] NM: **~ clausus** (*Univ*) restricted o selective entry

nunca ['nunka] ADV (*jamás*) never; (*con verbo negativo*) ever; **~ lo pensé** I never thought it; **no viene ~** he never comes; **~ más** never again; **más que ~** more than ever

nuncio ['nunθjo] NM (*Rel*) nuncio

nupcial [nup'θjal] ADJ wedding *cpd*

nupcias ['nupθjas] NFPL wedding *sg*, nuptials

nutria ['nutrja] NF otter

nutrición [nutri'θjon] NF nutrition

nutrido, -a [nu'triðo, a] ADJ (*alimentado*) nourished; (*fig: grande*) large; (*abundante*) abundant; **mal ~** undernourished; **~ de** full of

nutrir [nu'trir] /**3a**/ VT (*alimentar*) to nourish; (*dar de comer*) to feed; (*fig*) to strengthen

nutritivo, -a [nutri'tiβo, a] ADJ nourishing, nutritious

nylon [ni'lon] NM nylon

Ññ   Oo

Ñ, ñ ['eɲe] NF (letra) Ñ ñ
ñango, -a ['ɲaŋgo, a] ADJ (AM) puny
ñapa ['ɲapa] NF (AM) extra
ñata ['ɲata] NF (AM fam) nose; *ver tb* **ñato**
ñato, -a ['ɲato, a] ADJ (AM) snub-nosed
ñoñería [ɲoɲe'ria], **ñoñez** [ɲo'ɲeθ]

NF insipidness
ñoño, -a ['ɲoɲo, a] ADJ (tonto) silly,
stupid; (soso) insipid; (débil: persona)
spineless; (ESP: película, novela)
sentimental
ñoquis ['ɲokis] NMPL (Culin) gnocchi

Oo

O, o [o] NF (*letra*) O, o; **O de Oviedo** O for Oliver (*BRIT*) o Oboe (*US*)

O ABR (= *oeste*) W

o [o] CONJ or; **o ... o** either ... or; **o sea** that is

ó [o] CONJ (*en números para evitar confusión*) or; **cinco ó seis** five or six

o/ NM (*Com*: = *orden*) o

OACI NF ABR (= *Organización de la Aviación Civil Internacional*) ICAO

oasis [o'asis] NM INV oasis

obcecado, -a [oβθe'kaðo, a] ADJ blind; (*terco*) stubborn

obcecarse [oβθe'karse] /**1g**/ VR to become obsessed; **~ en hacer** to insist on doing

obceque *etc* [oβ'θeke] VB *ver* **obcecarse**

obedecer [oβeðe'θer] /**2d**/ VT to obey; **~ a** (*Med etc*) to yield to; (*fig*) **~ a ..., ~ al hecho de que ...** to be due to ..., arise from ...

obedezca *etc* [oβe'ðeθka] VB *ver* **obedecer**

obediencia [oβe'ðjenθja] NF obedience

obediente [oβe'ðjente] ADJ obedient

obertura [oβer'tura] NF overture

obesidad [oβesi'ðað] NF obesity

obeso, -a [o'βeso, a] ADJ obese

óbice ['oβiθe] NM obstacle, impediment

obispado [oβis'paðo] NM bishopric

obispo [o'βispo] NM bishop

óbito ['oβito] NM demise

obituario [oβi'twarjo] NM (*Am*) obituary

objeción [oβxe'θjon] NF objection; **hacer una ~, poner objeciones** to raise objections, object

objetar [oβxe'tar] /**1a**/ VT, VI to object

objetivo, -a [oβxe'tiβo, a] ADJ objective ▶ NM objective; (*fig*) aim; (*Foto*) lens

objeto [oβ'xeto] NM (*cosa*) object; (*fin*) aim

objetor, a [oβxe'tor, a] NM/F objector; **~ de conciencia** conscientious objector; *ver tb* **mili**

oblea [o'βlea] NF (*Rel, fig*) wafer

oblicuo, -a [o'βlikwo, a] ADJ oblique; (*mirada*) sidelong

obligación [oβliɣa'θjon] NF obligation; (*Com*) bond, debenture

obligar [oβli'ɣar] /**1h**/ VT to force; **obligarse VR: obligarse a** to commit o.s. to

obligatorio, -a [oβliɣa'torjo, a] ADJ compulsory, obligatory

obligue *etc* [o'βliɣe] VB *ver* **obligar**

Ob.º ABR (= *Obispo*) Bp

oboe [o'βoe] NM oboe; (*músico*) oboist

Ob.Pº ABR = **obispo**

obra ['oβra] NF work; (*producción*) piece of work; (*Arq*) construction, building; (*libro*) book; (*Mus*) opus; (*Teat*) play; **~ de arte** work of art; **~ maestra** masterpiece; **~ de consulta** reference book; **obras completas** complete works; **~ benéfica** charity; **"obras"** (*en carretera*) "men at work"; **obras públicas** public works; **por ~ de** thanks to (the efforts of); **obras son amores y no buenas razones** actions speak louder than words

obrar [o'βrar] /**1a**/ VT to work; (*tener efecto*) to have an effect on ▶ VI to act, behave; (*tener efecto*) to have an effect; **la carta obra en su poder** the letter is in his/her possession

obr. cit. ABR (= *obra citada*) op. cit.

obrero, -a [o'βrero, a] ADJ working; (*movimiento*) labour *cpd*; **clase obrera** working class ▶ NM/F (*gen*) worker; (*sin oficio*) labourer

obscenidad [oβsθeni'ðað] NF obscenity

obsceno, -a [oβs'θeno, a] ADJ obscene

obscu... PREF = **oscu...**

obsequiar [oβse'kjar] /**1b**/ VT (*ofrecer*) to present; (*agasajar*) to make a fuss of, lavish attention on

obsequio [oβ'sekjo] NM (*regalo*) gift; (*cortesía*) courtesy, attention

obsequioso, -a [oβse'kjoso, a] ADJ attentive

observación [oβserβa'θjon] NF observation; (*reflexión*) remark; (*objeción*) objection

observador, a [oβserβa'ðor, a] ADJ observant ▶ NM/F observer

observancia [oβser'βanθja] NF observance

observar [oβser'βar] /**1a**/ VT to observe; (*notar*) to notice; (*leyes*) to observe, respect;

(reglas) to abide by; **observarse** VR to keep to, observe

observatorio [oβserβa'torjo] NM observatory; **~ del tiempo** weather station

obsesión [oβse'sjon] NF obsession

obsesionar [oβsesjo'nar] /**1a**/ VT to obsess

obsesivo, -a [obse'siβo, a] ADJ obsessive

obseso, -a [oβ'seso, a] NM/F *(sexual)* sex maniac

obsolescencia [oβsoles'θenθja] NF: **~ incorporada** *(Com)* built-in obsolescence

obsoleto, -a [oβso'leto, a] ADJ obsolete

obstaculice *etc* [oβstaku'liθe] VB *ver* **obstaculizar**

obstaculizar [oβstakuli'θar] /**1f**/ VT *(dificultar)* to hinder, hamper

obstáculo [oβs'takulo] NM *(gen)* obstacle; *(impedimento)* hindrance, drawback

obstante [oβs'tante]: **no ~** *adv* nevertheless; *(de todos modos)* all the same ▶ PREP in spite of

obstetra [oβs'tetra] NMF obstetrician

obstetricia [oβste'triθja] NF obstetrics *sg*

obstinado, -a [oβsti'naðo, a] ADJ *(gen)* obstinate; *(terco)* stubborn

obstinarse [oβsti'narse] /**1a**/ VR to be obstinate; **~ en** to persist in

obstrucción [oβstruk'θjon] NF obstruction

obstruir [oβstru'ir] /**3g**/ VT to obstruct; *(bloquear)* to block; *(estorbar)* to hinder

obstruyendo *etc* [oβstru'jendo] VB *ver* **obstruir**

obtención [oβten'θjon] NF *(Com)* procurement

obtendré *etc* [oβten'dre] VB *ver* **obtener**

obtener [oβte'ner] /**2k**/ VT *(conseguir)* to obtain; *(ganar)* to gain; *(premio)* to win

obtenga *etc* [oβ'tenga] VB *ver* **obtener**

obturación [oβtura'θjon] NF plugging, stopping; *(Foto)*: **velocidad de ~** shutter speed

obturador [oβtura'ðor] NM *(Foto)* shutter

obtuso, -a [oβ'tuso, a] ADJ *(filo)* blunt; *(Mat, fig)* obtuse

obtuve *etc* [oβ'tuβe] VB *ver* **obtener**

obús [o'βus] NM *(Mil)* shell

obviar [oβ'βjar] /**1c**/ VT to obviate, remove

obvio, -a ['oββjo, a] ADJ obvious

oca ['oka] NF goose; *(tb:* **juego de la oca***)* ≈ snakes and ladders

ocasión [oka'sjon] NF *(oportunidad)* opportunity, chance; *(momento)* occasion, time; *(causa)* cause; **de ~** secondhand; **con ~ de** on the occasion of; **en algunas ocasiones** sometimes; **aprovechar la ~** to seize one's opportunity

ocasionar [okasjo'nar] /**1a**/ VT to cause

ocaso [o'kaso] NM sunset; *(fig)* decline

occidental [okθiðen'tal] ADJ western ▶ NMF westerner ▶ NM west

occidente [okθi'ðente] NM west; **el O~** the West

occiso, -a [ok'θiso, a] NM/F: **el ~** the deceased; *(de asesinato)* the victim

O.C.D.E. NF ABR (= *Organización de Cooperación y Desarrollo Económicos*) OECD

océano [o'θeano] NM ocean; **el ~ Índico** the Indian Ocean

ochenta [o'tʃenta] NUM eighty

ocho ['otʃo] NUM eight; *(fecha)* eighth; **~ días** a week; **dentro de ~ días** within a week

ochocientos, -as [otʃo'θjentos, as] NUM eight hundred

OCI ['oθi] NF ABR (Pol: VENEZUELA, PERÚ) = **Oficina Central de Información**

ocio ['oθjo] NM *(tiempo)* leisure; *(pey)* idleness; **"guía del ~"** "what's on"

ociosidad [oθjosi'ðað] NF idleness

ocioso, -a [o'θjoso, a] ADJ *(inactivo)* idle; *(inútil)* useless

oct. ABR (= *octubre*) Oct.

octanaje [okta'naxe] NM: **de alto ~** high octane

octano [ok'tano] NM octane

octavilla [okta'βiʎa] NF leaflet, pamphlet

octavo, -a [ok'taβo, a] NUM eighth

octeto [ok'teto] NM *(Inform)* byte

octogenario, -a [oktoxe'narjo, a] ADJ, NM/F octogenarian

octubre [ok'tuβre] NM October; *ver tb* **julio**

OCU ['oku] NF ABR (ESP: = *Organización de Consumidores y Usuarios*) ≈ Consumers' Association

ocular [oku'lar] ADJ ocular, eye *cpd*; **testigo ~** eyewitness

oculista [oku'lista] NMF oculist

ocultar [okul'tar] /**1a**/ VT *(esconder)* to hide; *(callar)* to conceal; *(disfrazar)* to screen; **ocultarse** VR to hide (o.s.); **ocultarse a la vista** to keep out of sight

oculto, -a [o'kulto, a] ADJ hidden; *(fig)* secret

ocupación [okupa'θjon] NF occupation; *(tenencia)* occupancy

ocupado, -a [oku'paðo, a] ADJ *(persona)* busy; *(plaza)* occupied, taken; *(teléfono)* engaged; **¿está ocupada la silla?** is that seat taken?

ocupar [oku'par] /**1a**/ VT *(gen)* to occupy; *(puesto)* to hold, fill; *(individuo)* to engage; *(obreros)* to employ; *(confiscar)* to seize; **ocuparse** VR: **ocuparse de** o **en** to concern o.s. with; *(cuidar)* to look after; **ocuparse de lo suyo** to mind one's own business

ocurrencia [oku'rrenθja] NF *(ocasión)* occurrence; *(agudeza)* witticism; *(idea)* bright idea

ocurrir [oku'rrir] /**3a**/ VI to happen; **ocurrirse** VR: **se me ocurrió que ...** it occurred to me that ...; **¿se te ocurre algo?** can you think of o come up with anything?; **¿qué ocurre?** what's going on?

oda ['oða] NF ode

ODECA [o'ðeka] NF ABR = **Organización de Estados Centroamericanos**

odiar [o'ðjar] /**1b**/ VT to hate

odio ['oðjo] NM (gen) hate, hatred; (disgusto) dislike

odioso, -a [o'ðjoso, a] ADJ (gen) hateful; (malo) nasty

odisea [oði'sea] NF odyssey

odontología [oðontolo'xia] NF dentistry, dental surgery

odontólogo, -a [oðon'toloγo, a] NM/F dentist, dental surgeon

odre ['oðre] NM wineskin

O.E.A. NF ABR (= Organización de Estados Americanos) O.A.S.

OECE NF ABR (= Organización Europea de Cooperación Económica) OEEC

OELA [o'ela] NF ABR = **Organización de Estados Latinoamericanos**

oeste [o'este] NM west; **una película del ~** a western

ofender [ofen'der] /**2a**/ VT (agraviar) to offend; (insultar) to insult; **ofenderse** VR to take offence

ofensa [o'fensa] NF offence; (insulto) slight

ofensivo, -a [ofen'siβo, a] ADJ (insultante) insulting; (Mil) offensive ▶ NF offensive

oferta [o'ferta] NF offer; (propuesta) proposal; (para contrato) bid, tender; **la ~ y la demanda** supply and demand; **artículos en ~** goods on offer; **~ excedentaria** (Com) excess supply; **~ monetaria** money supply; **~ pública de adquisición (OPA)** (Com) takeover bid; **ofertas de trabajo** (en periódicos) situations vacant column

offset ['ofset] NM offset

oficial [ofi'θjal] ADJ official ▶ NM official; (Mil) officer

oficialista [ofisja'lista] ADJ (AM) (pro-) government; **el candidato ~** the governing party's candidate

oficiar [ofi'θjar] /**1b**/ VT to inform officially ▶ VI (Rel) to officiate

oficina [ofi'θina] NF office; **~ de correos** post office; **~ de empleo** employment agency; **~ de información** information bureau; **~ de objetos perdidos** lost property office (BRIT), lost-and-found department (US); **~ de turismo** tourist office; **~ principal** (Com) head office, main branch

oficinista [ofiθi'nista] NMF clerk; **los oficinistas** white-collar workers

oficio [o'fiθjo] NM (profesión) profession; (puesto) post; (Rel) service; (función) function; (comunicado) official letter; **ser del ~** to be an old hand; **tener mucho ~** to have a lot of experience; **~ de difuntos** funeral service; **de ~** officially

oficioso, -a [ofi'θjoso, a] ADJ (pey) officious; (no oficial) unofficial, informal

ofimática [ofi'matika] NF office automation

ofrecer [ofre'θer] /**2d**/ VT (dar) to offer; (proponer) to propose; **ofrecerse** VR (persona) to offer o.s., volunteer; (situación) to present itself; **¿qué se le ofrece?, ¿se le ofrece algo?** what can I do for you?, can I get you anything?

ofrecimiento [ofreθi'mjento] NM offer, offering

ofrendar [ofren'dar] /**1a**/ VT to offer, contribute

ofrezca etc [o'freθka] VB ver **ofrecer**

oftalmología [oftalmolo'xia] NF ophthalmology

oftalmólogo, -a [oftal'moloγo, a] NM/F ophthalmologist

ofuscación [ofuska'θjon] NF, **ofuscamiento** [ofuska'mjento] NM (fig) bewilderment

ofuscar [ofus'kar] /**1g**/ VT (confundir) to bewilder; (enceguecer) **de ~** to dazzle, blind

ofusque etc [o'fuske] VB ver **ofuscar**

ogro ['oγro] NM ogre

OIC NF ABR (Com) = **Organización Interamericana del Café**; **Organización Internacional del Comercio**

oída [o'iða] NF: **de oídas** by hearsay

oído [o'iðo] NM (Anat, Mus) ear; (sentido) hearing; **~ interno** inner ear; **de ~** by ear; **apenas pude dar crédito a mis oídos** I could scarcely believe my ears; **hacer oídos sordos a** to turn a deaf ear to

OIEA NM ABR (= Organismo Internacional de Energía Atómica) IAEA

oigo etc VB ver **oír**

OIR [o'ir] NF ABR (= Organización Internacional para los Refugiados) IRO; = **Organización Internacional de Radiodifusión**

oír [o'ir] /**3p**/ VT (gen) to hear; (esp AM: escuchar) to listen to; **¡oye!** (sorpresa) I say!, say! (US); **¡oiga!** excuse me!; (Telec) hullo?; **~ misa** to attend mass; **como quien oye llover** without paying (the slightest) attention

O.I.T. NF ABR (= Organización Internacional del Trabajo) ILO

ojal [o'xal] NM buttonhole

ojalá [oxa'la] EXCL if only (it were so)!, some hope! ▶ CONJ if only...!, would that...!; **~ que venga hoy** I hope he comes today; **¡~ pudiera!** I wish I could!

ojeada [oxe'aða] NF glance; **echar una ~ a** to take a quick look at

ojera [o'xera] NF: **tener ojeras** to have bags under one's eyes

ojeriza [oxe'riθa] NF ill-will; **tener ~ a** to have a grudge against, have it in for

ojeroso, -a [oxe'roso, a] ADJ haggard

ojete [o'xete] NM eye(let)

ojo ['oxo] NM eye; (*de puente*) span; (*de cerradura*) keyhole ▸ EXCL careful!; **tener ~ para** to have an eye for; **ojos saltones** bulging o goggle eyes; **~ de buey** porthole; **~ por ~** an eye for an eye; **en un abrir y cerrar de ojos** in the twinkling of an eye; **a ojos vistas** openly; (*crecer etc*) before one's (very) eyes; **a ~ (de buen cubero)** roughly; **ojos que no ven, corazón que no siente** out of sight, out of mind; **ser el ~ derecho de algn** (*fig*) to be the apple of sb's eye

okey ['okei] EXCL (*AM*) O.K.

okupa [o'kupa] NMF (*fam*) squatter

OL ABR (= *onda larga*) LW, long wave

ola ['ola] NF wave; **~ de calor/frío** heatwave/cold spell; **la nueva ~** the latest fashion; (*Cine, Mus*) (the) new wave

OLADE [o'laðe] NF ABR = **Organización Latinoamericana de Energía**

olé [o'le] EXCL bravo!, olé!

oleada [ole'aða] NF big wave, swell; (*fig*) wave

oleaje [ole'axe] NM swell

óleo ['oleo] NM oil

oleoducto [oleo'ðukto] NM (oil) pipeline

oler [o'ler] /2i/ VT (*gen*) to smell; (*inquirir*) to pry into; (*fig: sospechar*) to sniff out ▸ VI to smell; **~ a** to smell of; **huele mal** it smells bad, it stinks

olfatear [olfate'ar] /1a/ VT to smell; (*fig: sospechar*) to sniff out; (*inquirir*) to pry into

olfato [ol'fato] NM sense of smell

oligarquía [oliɣar'kia] NF oligarchy

olimpiada [olim'piaða] NF: **la ~** o **las olimpiadas** the Olympics

olímpicamente [o'limpikamente] ADV: **pasar ~ de algo** to totally ignore sth

olímpico, -a [o'limpiko, a] ADJ Olympian; (*deportes*) Olympic

oliva [o'liβa] NF (*aceituna*) olive; **aceite de ~** olive oil

olivar [oli'βar] NM olive grove o plantation

olivo [o'liβo] NM olive tree

olla ['oʎa] NF pan; (*para hervir agua*) kettle; (*comida*) stew; **~ a presión** pressure cooker; **~ podrida** *type of Spanish stew*

olmo ['olmo] NM elm (tree)

olor [o'lor] NM smell

oloroso, -a [olo'roso, a] ADJ scented

OLP NF ABR (= *Organización para la Liberación de Palestina*) PLO

olvidadizo, -a [olβiða'ðiθo, a] ADJ (*desmemoriado*) forgetful; (*distraído*) absent-minded

olvidar [olβi'ðar] /1a/ VT to forget; (*omitir*) to omit; (*abandonar*) to leave behind; **olvidarse** VR (*fig*) to forget o.s.; **se me olvidó** I forgot

olvido [ol'βiðo] NM oblivion; (*acto*) oversight; (*descuido*) slip; (*despiste*) forgetfulness; **caer en el ~** to fall into oblivion

O.M. ABR (= *onda media*) MW, medium wave; (*Pol*) = **Orden Ministerial**; (= *Oriente Medio*) Middle East

ombligo [om'bliɣo] NM navel

omelette [ome'lete] NF (*AM*) omelet(te)

OMI NF ABR (= *Organización Marítima Internacional*) IMO

ominoso, -a [omi'noso, a] ADJ ominous

omisión [omi'sjon] NF (*abstención*) omission; (*descuido*) neglect

omiso, -a [o'miso, a] ADJ: **hacer caso ~ de** to ignore, pass over

omitir [omi'tir] /3a/ VT to leave o miss out, omit

ómnibus ['omniβus] NM (*AM*) bus

omnipotente [omnipo'tente] ADJ omnipotent

omnipresente [omnipre'sente] ADJ omnipresent

omnívoro, -a [om'niβoro, a] ADJ omnivorous

omoplato [omo'plato], **omóplato** [o'moplato] NM shoulder-blade

OMS NF ABR (= *Organización Mundial de la Salud*) WHO

ONCE ['onθe] NF ABR (= *Organización Nacional de Ciegos Españoles*) charity for the blind

once ['onθe] NUM eleven; **onces** NFPL tea break *sg*

onda ['onda] NF wave; **~ corta/larga/media** short/long/medium wave; **ondas acústicas/hertzianas** acoustic/Hertzian waves; **~ sonora** sound wave

ondear [onde'ar] /1a/ VI to wave; (*tener ondas*) to be wavy; (*agua*) to ripple; **ondearse** VR to swing, sway

ondulación [ondula'θjon] NF undulation

ondulado, -a [ondu'laðo, a] ADJ wavy ▸ NM wave

ondulante [ondu'lante] ADJ undulating

ondular [ondu'lar] /1a/ VT (*el pelo*) to wave ▸ VI, **ondularse** VR to undulate

oneroso, -a [one'roso, a] ADJ onerous

ONG NF ABR (= *organización no gubernamental*) NGO

onomástico, -a [ono'mastiko, a] ADJ: **fiesta onomástica** saint's day ▸ NM saint's day

ONU ['onu] NF ABR (= *Organización de las Naciones Unidas*) UN

onubense [onu'βense] ADJ of o from Huelva ▸ NMF native o inhabitant of Huelva

ONUDI [o'nuði] NF ABR (= *Organización de las Naciones Unidas para el Desarrollo Industrial*) UNIDO (= *United Nations Industrial Development Organization*)

onza ['onθa] NF ounce

O.P. NFPL ABR = **Obras Públicas**; (*Com*) = **Oficina Principal**

OPA ['opa] NF ABR (= *Oferta Pública de Adquisición*) takeover bid

opaco, -a [o'pako, a] ADJ opaque; (*fig*) dull
ópalo ['opalo] NM opal
opción [op'θjon] NF (*gen*) option; (*derecho*) right, option; **no hay ~** there is no alternative
opcional [opθjo'nal] ADJ optional
O.P.E.P. [o'pep] NF ABR (= *Organización de Países Exportadores de Petróleo*) OPEC
ópera ['opera] NF opera; **~ bufa** *o* **cómica** comic opera
operación [opera'θjon] NF (*gen*) operation; (*Com*) transaction, deal; **~ a plazo** (*Com*) forward transaction; **operaciones accesorias** (*Inform*) housekeeping; **operaciones a término** (*Com*) futures
operador, a [opera'ðor, a] NM/F operator; (*Cine: proyección*) projectionist; (*: rodaje*) cameraman
operar [ope'rar] /**1a**/ VT (*producir*) to produce, bring about; (*Med*) to operate on ▶ VI (*Com*) to operate, deal; **operarse** VR to occur; (*Med*) to have an operation; **se han operado grandes cambios** great changes have been made *o* have taken place
operario, -a [ope'rarjo, a] NM/F worker
opereta [ope'reta] NF operetta
opinar [opi'nar] /**1a**/ VT (*estimar*) to think ▶ VI (*enjuiciar*) to give one's opinion; **~ bien de** to think well of
opinión [opi'njon] NF (*creencia*) belief; (*criterio*) opinion; **la ~ pública** public opinion
opio ['opjo] NM opium
opíparo, -a [o'piparo, a] ADJ sumptuous
opondré *etc* [opon'dre] VB *ver* **oponer**
oponente [opo'nente] NMF opponent
oponer [opo'ner] /**2q**/ VT (*resistencia*) to put up, offer; (*negativa*) to raise; **oponerse** VR (*objetar*) to object; (*estar frente a frente*) to be opposed; (*dos personas*) to oppose each other; **~ A a B** to set A against B; **me opongo a pensar que ...** I refuse to believe *o* think that ...
oponga *etc* [o'ponga] VB *ver* **oponer**
Oporto [o'porto] NM Oporto
oporto [o'porto] NM port
oportunidad [oportuni'ðað] NF (*ocasión*) opportunity; (*posibilidad*) chance
oportunismo [oportu'nismo] NM opportunism
oportunista [oportu'nista] NMF opportunist; (*infección*) opportunistic
oportuno, -a [opor'tuno, a] ADJ (*en su tiempo*) opportune, timely; (*respuesta*) suitable; **en el momento ~** at the right moment
oposición [oposi'θjon] NF opposition; **oposiciones** NFPL (*Escol*) public examinations; **ganar un puesto por oposiciones** to win a post by public competitive examination; **hacer oposiciones a**, **presentarse a unas**

oposiciones a to sit a competitive examination for; *see note*

> The *oposiciones* are exams that are held nationally and locally for posts in the public sector, state education, the judiciary etc. These posts are permanent and the number of candidates is high so the exams are tough. The candidates, *opositores*, have to study a great number of subjects relating to their field and also the Constitution. People can spend years studying and resitting exams.

opositar [oposi'tar] /**1a**/ VI to sit a public entrance examination
opositor, -a [oposi'tor, a] NM/F (*Admin*) candidate to a public examination; (*adversario*) opponent; **~ (a)** candidate (for)
opresión [opre'sjon] NF oppression
opresivo, -a [opre'siβo, a] ADJ oppressive
opresor, a [opre'sor, a] NM/F oppressor
oprimir [opri'mir] /**3a**/ VT to squeeze; (*asir*) to grasp; (*pulsar*) to press; (*fig*) to oppress
optar [op'tar] /**1a**/ VI (*elegir*) to choose; **~ a** *o* **por** to opt for
optativo, -a [opta'tiβo, a] ADJ optional
óptico, -a ['optiko, a] ADJ optic(al) ▶ NM/F optician ▶ NF (*ciencia*) optics *sg*; (*tienda*) optician's; (*fig*) viewpoint; **desde esta óptica** from this point of view
optimismo [opti'mismo] NM optimism
optimista [opti'mista] NMF optimist
óptimo, -a ['optimo, a] ADJ (*el mejor*) very best
opuesto, -a [o'pwesto, a] PP *de* **oponer** ▶ ADJ (*contrario*) opposite; (*antagónico*) opposing
opulencia [opu'lenθja] NF opulence
opulento, -a [opu'lento, a] ADJ opulent
opuse *etc* [o'puse] VB *ver* **oponer**
ora ['ora] ADV: **~ tú ~ yo** now you, now me
oración [ora'θjon] NF (*Rel*) prayer; (*Ling*) sentence
oráculo [o'rakulo] NM oracle
orador, a [ora'ðor, a] NM/F orator; (*conferenciante*) speaker
oral [o'ral] ADJ oral; **por vía ~** (*Med*) orally
orangután [orangu'tan] NM orang-utan
orar [o'rar] /**1a**/ VI (*Rel*) to pray
oratoria [ora'torja] NF oratory
orbe ['orβe] NM orb, sphere; (*fig*) world; **en todo el ~** all over the globe
órbita ['orβita] NF orbit; (*Anat: ocular*) (eye-)socket
orden ['orðen] NM (*colocación*) order ▶ NF (*mandato*) order; (*Inform*) command; **~ público** public order, law and order; **del ~ de** (*números*) about; **de primer ~** first-rate; **en ~ de prioridad** in order of priority; **~ bancaria** banker's order; **una ~ de compra** (*Com*) a purchase order; **el ~ del día** the agenda; **eso ahora está a la ~ del día**

that is now the order of the day; **a la ~ de usted** at your service; **dar la ~ de hacer algo** to give the order to do sth

ordenación [orðena'θjon] NF (*estado*) order; (*acto*) ordering; (*Rel*) ordination

ordenado, -a [orðe'naðo, a] ADJ (*metódico*) methodical; (*arreglado*) orderly

ordenador [orðena'ðor] NM computer; **~ central** mainframe computer; **~ de gestión** business computer; **~ portátil** laptop (computer); **~ de sobremesa** desktop computer

ordenamiento [orðena'mjento] NM legislation

ordenanza [orðe'nanθa] NF ordinance; **ordenanzas municipales** by-laws ▶ NM (*Com etc*) messenger; (*Mil*) orderly; (*bedel*) porter

ordenar [orðe'nar] /1a/ VT (*mandar*) to order; (*poner orden*) to put in order, arrange; **ordenarse** VR (*Rel*) to be ordained

ordeñadora [orðeɲa'ðora] NF milking machine

ordeñar [orðe'ɲar] /1a/ VT to milk

ordinariez [orðina'rjeθ] NF (*cualidad*) coarseness, vulgarity; (*una ordinariez*) coarse remark o joke *etc*

ordinario, -a [orði'narjo, a] ADJ (*común*) ordinary, usual; (*vulgar*) vulgar, common

ordinograma [orðino'ɣrama] NM flowchart

orear [ore'ar] /1a/ VT to air; **orearse** VR (*ropa*) to air

orégano [o'reɣano] NM oregano

oreja [o'rexa] NF ear; (*Mecánica*) lug, flange

orensano, -a [oren'sano, a] ADJ of o from Orense ▶ NM/F native o inhabitant of Orense

orfanato [orfa'nato], **orfanatorio** [orfana'torjo] NM orphanage

orfandad [orfan'dað] NF orphanhood

orfebre [or'feβre] NM gold-/silversmith

orfebrería [orfeβre'ria] NF gold/silver work

orfelinato [orfeli'nato] NM orphanage

orfeón [orfe'on] NM (*Mus*) choral society

organice *etc* [orɣa'niθe] VB *ver* **organizar**

orgánico, -a [or'ɣaniko, a] ADJ organic

organigrama [orɣani'ɣrama] NM flow chart; (*de organización*) organization chart

organillo [orɣa'niʎo] NM barrel organ

organismo [orɣa'nismo] NM (*Bio*) organism; (*Pol*) organization; **O~ Internacional de Energía Atómica** International Atomic Energy Agency

organista [orɣa'nista] NMF organist

organización [orɣaniθa'θjon] NF organization; **O~ de las Naciones Unidas (ONU)** United Nations Organization; **O~ del Tratado del Atlántico Norte (OTAN)** North Atlantic Treaty Organization (NATO)

organizador, a [orɣaniθa'ðor, a] ADJ organizing; **el comité ~** the organizing committee ▶ NM/F organizer

organizar [orɣani'θar] /1f/ VT to organize

órgano ['orɣano] NM organ

orgasmo [or'ɣasmo] NM orgasm

orgía [or'xia] NF orgy

orgullo [or'ɣuʎo] NM (*altanería*) pride; (*autorrespeto*) self-respect

orgulloso, -a [orɣu'ʎoso, a] ADJ (*gen*) proud; (*altanero*) haughty

orientación [orjenta'θjon] NF (*posición*) position; (*dirección*) direction; **~ profesional** occupational guidance

oriental [orjen'tal] ADJ oriental; (*región etc*) eastern ▶ NMF oriental

orientar [orjen'tar] /1a/ VT (*situar*) to orientate; (*señalar*) to point; (*dirigir*) to direct; (*guiar*) to guide; **orientarse** VR to get one's bearings; (*decidirse*) to decide on a course of action

oriente [o'rjente] NM east; **el O~** the East, the Orient; **Cercano/Medio/Lejano O~** Near/Middle/Far East

orificio [ori'fiθjo] NM hole; (*Anat*) orifice

origen [o'rixen] NM origin; (*nacimiento*) lineage, birth; **dar ~ a** to cause, give rise to

original [orixi'nal] ADJ (*nuevo*) original; (*extraño*) odd, strange ▶ NM original; (*Tip*) manuscript (copy)

originalidad [orixinali'ðað] NF originality

originar [orixi'nar] /1a/ VT to start, cause; **originarse** VR to originate

originario, -a [orixi'narjo, a] ADJ (*nativo*) native; (*primordial*) original; **ser ~ de** to originate from; **país ~** country of origin

orilla [o'riʎa] NF (*borde*) border; (*de río*) bank; (*de bosque, tela*) edge; (*de mar*) shore; **a orillas de** on the banks of

orillar [ori'ʎar] /1a/ VT (*bordear*) to skirt, go round; (*Costura*) to edge; (*resolver*) to wind up; (*tocar: asunto*) to touch briefly on; (: *dificultad*) to avoid

orín [o'rin] NM rust

orina [o'rina] NF urine

orinal [ori'nal] NM (chamber) pot

orinar [ori'nar] /1a/ VI to urinate; **orinarse** VR to wet o.s.

orines [o'rines] NMPL urine *sg*

oriundo, -a [o'rjundo, a] ADJ: **~ de** native of

orla ['orla] NF edge, border; (*Escol*) graduation photograph

ornamentar [ornamen'tar] /1a/ VT (*adornar, ataviar*) to adorn; (*revestir*) to bedeck

ornar [or'nar] /1a/ VT to adorn

ornitología [ornitolo'xia] NF ornithology, bird watching

ornitólogo, -a [orni'toloɣo, a] NM/F ornithologist

O

oro ['oro] NM gold; **~ en barras** gold ingots; **de ~** gold, golden; **no es ~ todo lo que reluce** all that glitters is not gold; **hacerse de ~** to make a fortune; *ver tb* **oros**

orondo, -a [o'rondo, a] ADJ (*vasija*) rounded; (*individuo*) smug, self-satisfied

oropel [oro'pel] NM tinsel

oros ['oros] NMPL (*Naipes*) *one of the suits in the Spanish card deck*; *ver tb* **baraja española**

orquesta [or'kesta] NF orchestra; **~ de cámara/sinfónica** chamber/symphony orchestra; **~ de jazz** jazz band

orquestar [orkes'tar] /**1a**/ VT to orchestrate

orquídea [or'kiðea] NF orchid

ortiga [or'tiɣa] NF nettle

ortodoncia [orto'ðonθja] NF orthodontics *sg*

ortodoxo, -a [orto'ðokso, a] ADJ orthodox

ortografía [ortoɣra'fia] NF spelling

ortopedia [orto'peðja] NF orthop(a)edics *sg*

ortopédico, -a [orto'peðiko, a] ADJ orthop(a)edic

oruga [o'ruɣa] NF caterpillar

orujo [o'ruxo] NM *type of strong grape liqueur made from grape pressings*

orzuelo [or'θwelo] NM (*Med*) stye

os [os] PRON (*gen*) you; (*a vosotros*) (to) you; (*reflexivo*) (to) yourselves; (*mutuo*) (to) each other; **vosotros os laváis** you wash yourselves; **¡callaos!** (*fam*) shut up!

osa ['osa] NF (she-)bear; **O~ Mayor/Menor** Great/Little Bear, Ursa Major/Minor

osadía [osa'ðia] NF daring; (*descaro*) impudence

osamenta [osa'menta] NF skeleton

osar [o'sar] /**1a**/ VI to dare

oscense [os'θense] ADJ of o from Huesca
▶ NMF native o inhabitant of Huesca

oscilación [osθila'θjon] NF (*movimiento*) oscillation; (*fluctuación*) fluctuation; (*vacilación*) hesitation; (*de columpio*) swinging, movement to and fro

oscilar [osθi'lar] /**1a**/ VI to oscillate; (*precio, peso, temperatura*) to fluctuate; (*dudar*) to hesitate

ósculo ['oskulo] NM kiss

oscurecer [oskure'θer] /**2d**/ VT to darken
▶ VI to grow dark; **oscurecerse** VR to grow o get dark

oscurezca *etc* [osku'reθka] VB *ver* **oscurecer**

oscuridad [oskuri'ðað] NF obscurity; (*tinieblas*) darkness

oscuro, -a [os'kuro, a] ADJ dark; (*fig*) obscure; (*indefinido*) confused; (*cielo*) overcast, cloudy; (*futuro etc*) uncertain; **a oscuras** in the dark

óseo, -a ['oseo, a] ADJ bony; (*Med etc*) bone *cpd*

oso ['oso] NM bear; **~ blanco/gris/pardo** polar/grizzly/brown bear; **~ de peluche** teddy bear; **~ hormiguero** anteater; **hacer el ~** to play the fool

Ostende [os'tende] NM Ostend

ostensible [osten'siβle] ADJ obvious

ostensiblemente [ostensiβle'mente] ADV perceptibly, visibly

ostentación [ostenta'θjon] NF (*gen*) ostentation; (*acto*) display

ostentar [osten'tar] /**1a**/ VT (*gen*) to show; (*pey*) to flaunt, show off; (*poseer*) to have, possess

ostentoso, -a [osten'toso, a] ADJ ostentatious, showy

osteópata [oste'opata] NMF osteopath

ostión [os'tjon] NM (*Am*) = **ostra**

ostra ['ostra] NF oyster ▶ EXCL: **¡ostras!** (*fam*) sugar!

ostracismo [ostra'θismo] NM ostracism

OTAN ['otan] NF ABR (= *Organización del Tratado del Atlántico Norte*) NATO

OTASE [o'tase] NF ABR (= *Organización del Tratado del Sudeste Asiático*) SEATO

otear [ote'ar] /**1a**/ VT to observe; (*fig*) to look into

otero [o'tero] NM low hill, hillock

otitis [o'titis] NF earache

otoñal [oto'ɲal] ADJ autumnal

otoño [o'toɲo] NM autumn, fall (*US*)

otorgamiento [otorɣa'mjento] NM conferring, granting; (*Jur*) execution

otorgar [otor'ɣar] /**1h**/ VT (*conceder*) to concede; (*dar*) to grant; (*poderes*) to confer; (*premio*) to award

otorgue *etc* [o'torɣe] VB *ver* **otorgar**

otorrinolaringólogo, -a [otorrinolarin'go loɣo, a] NM/F (*Med: tb*: **otorrino**) ear, nose and throat specialist

PALABRA CLAVE

otro, -a ['otro, a] ADJ **1** (*distinto: sg*) another; (*: pl*) other; **otra cosa/persona** something/ someone else; **con otros amigos** with other o different friends; **a/en otra parte** elsewhere, somewhere else
2 (*adicional*): **tráigame otro café (más), por favor** can I have another coffee please; **otros 10 días más** another 10 days
▶ PRON **1** (*sg*) another one; **el otro** the other one; **¡otra!** (*Mus*) more!; **de otro** somebody o someone else's; **que lo haga otro** let somebody o someone else do it; **ni uno ni otro** neither one nor the other
2 (*pl*): **(los) otros** (the) others
3 (*recíproco*): **se odian (la) una a (la) otra** they hate one another o each other
4: **otro tanto**: **comer otro tanto** to eat the same o as much again; **recibió una decena de telegramas y otras tantas llamadas** he got about ten telegrams and as many calls

otrora [o'trora] ADV formerly; **el ~ señor del país** the one-time ruler of the country

OUA NF ABR (= *Organización de la Unidad Africana*) OAU

ovación [oβa'θjon] NF ovation

ovacionar [oβaθjo'nar] /**1a**/ VT to cheer

oval [o'βal], **ovalado, -a** [oβa'laðo, a] ADJ oval

óvalo ['oβalo] NM oval

ovario [o'βarjo] NM ovary

oveja [o'βexa] NF sheep; ~ **negra** (*fig*) black sheep (of the family)

overol [oβe'rol] NM (*Am*) overalls *pl*

ovetense [oβe'tense] ADJ of *o* from Oviedo ▸ NMF native *o* inhabitant of Oviedo

ovillo [o'βiʎo] NM (*de lana*) ball; (*fig*) tangle; **hacerse un ~** to curl up (into a ball)

OVNI ['oβni] NM ABR (= *objeto volante (o volador) no identificado*) UFO

ovulación [oβula'θjon] NF ovulation

óvulo ['oβulo] NM ovum

oxidación [oksiða'θjon] NF rusting

oxidar [oksi'ðar] /**1a**/ VT to rust; **oxidarse** VR to go rusty; (*Tec*) to oxidize

óxido ['oksiðo] NM oxide

oxigenado, -a [oksixe'naðo, a] ADJ (*Química*) oxygenated; (*pelo*) bleached

oxigenar [oksixe'nar] /**1a**/ VT to oxygenate; **oxigenarse** VR to become oxygenated; (*fam*) to get some fresh air

oxígeno [ok'sixeno] NM oxygen

oyendo *etc* [o'jendo] VB *ver* **oír**

oyente [o'jente] NMF listener, hearer; (*Escol*) unregistered *o* occasional student

oyes *etc* VB *ver* **oír**

ozono [o'θono] NM ozone

O

Pp

P, p [pe] NF (*letra*) P, p; **P de Pamplona** P for Peter

P ABR (*Rel*: = *padre*) Fr.; (= *pregunta*) Q; = **papa**

p. ABR (= *página*) p; (*Costura*) = **punto**

p.a. ABR = **por autorización; por ausencia**

pabellón [paβe'ʎon] NM bell tent; (*Arq*) pavilion; (*de hospital etc*) block, section; (*bandera*) flag; **~ de conveniencia** (*Com*) flag of convenience; **~ de la oreja** outer ear

pábilo ['paβilo] NM wick

pábulo ['paβulo] NM food; **dar ~ a** to feed, encourage

PAC NF ABR (= *Política Agrícola Común*) CAP

pacense [pa'θense] ADJ of *o* from Badajoz ▶ NMF native *o* inhabitant of Badajoz

paceño, -a [pa'θeɲo, a] ADJ of *o* from La Paz ▶ NM/F native *o* inhabitant of La Paz

pacer [pa'θer] /2d/ VI to graze ▶ VT to graze on

pachá [pa'tʃa] NM: **vivir como un ~** to live like a king

pachanguero, -a [patʃan'gero, a] ADJ (*pey: música*) *noisy and catchy*

pachorra [pa'tʃorra] NF (*indolencia*) slowness; (*tranquilidad*) calmness

pachucho, -a [pa'tʃutʃo, a] ADJ (*fruta*) overripe; (*persona*) off-colour, poorly

paciencia [pa'θjenθja] NF patience; **¡~!** be patient!; **¡~ y barajar!** don't give up!; **perder la ~** to lose one's temper

paciente [pa'θjente] ADJ, NMF patient

pacificación [paθifika'θjon] NF pacification

pacificar [paθifi'kar] /1g/ VT to pacify; (*tranquilizar*) to calm

pacífico, -a [pa'θifiko, a] ADJ peaceful; (*persona*) peaceable; (*existencia*) peaceful; **el (océano) P~** the Pacific (Ocean)

pacifique *etc* [paθi'fike] VB *ver* **pacificar**

pacifismo [paθi'fismo] NM pacifism

pacifista [paθi'fista] NMF pacifist

pack [pak] NM (*de yogures, latas*) pack; (*de vacaciones*) package

pacotilla [pako'tiʎa] NF trash; **de ~** shoddy

pactar [pak'tar] /1a/ VT to agree to, agree on ▶ VI to come to an agreement

pacto ['pakto] NM (*tratado*) pact; (*acuerdo*) agreement

padecer [paðe'θer] /2d/ VT (*sufrir*) to suffer; (*soportar*) to endure, put up with; (*ser víctima de*) to be a victim of ▶ VI: **~ de** to suffer from

padecimiento [paðeθi'mjento] NM suffering

pádel ['paðel] NM paddle tennis

padezca *etc* [pa'ðeθka] VB *ver* **padecer**

padrastro [pa'ðrastro] NM stepfather

padre ['paðre] NM father ▶ ADJ (*fam*): **un éxito ~** a tremendous success; **padres** NMPL parents; **~ espiritual** confessor; **P~ Nuestro** Lord's Prayer; **~ político** father-in-law; **García ~** García senior; **¡tu ~!** (*fam!*) up yours! (*fam!*)

padrino [pa'ðrino] NM godfather; (*fig*) sponsor, patron; **padrinos** NMPL godparents; **~ de boda** best man

padrón [pa'ðron] NM (*censo*) census, roll; (*de socios*) register

padrote [pa'ðrote] NM (*Am fam*) pimp

paella [pa'eʎa] NF paella, *dish of rice with meat, shellfish etc*

pág(s). ABR (= *página(s)*) p(p)

paga ['paɣa] NF (*dinero pagado*) payment; (*sueldo*) pay, wages *pl*

pagadero, -a [paɣa'ðero, a] ADJ payable; **~ a la entrega/a plazos** payable on delivery/in instalments

pagano, -a [pa'ɣano, a] ADJ, NM/F pagan, heathen

pagar [pa'ɣar] /1h/ VT (*gen*) to pay; (*las compras, crimen*) to pay for; (*deuda*) to pay (off); (*fig: favor*) to repay ▶ VI to pay; **pagarse** VR: **pagarse con algo** to be content with sth; **~ al contado/a plazos** to pay (in) cash/in instalments; **¡me las pagarás!** I'll get you for this!

pagaré [paɣa're] NM IOU

página ['paxina] NF page; **~ de inicio** (*Inform*) home page; **~ personal** (*Internet*) personal web page; **~ web** (*Internet*) web page; **páginas amarillas** Yellow Pages®

paginación [paxina'θjon] NF (*Inform*, *Tip*) pagination

paginar [paxi'nar] /**1a**/ VT (*Inform*, *Tip*) to paginate

pago ['paɣo] NM (*dinero*) payment; (*fig*) return; ~ **anticipado/a cuenta/a la entrega/en especie/inicial** advance payment/payment on account/cash on delivery/payment in kind/down payment; ~ **a título gracioso** ex gratia payment; **en ~ de** in return for

pague *etc* ['paɣe] VB *ver* **pagar**

paila ['paila] NF (*Am*) frying pan

país [pa'is] NM (*gen*) country; (*región*) land; **los Países Bajos** the Low Countries; **el P~ Vasco** the Basque Country

paisaje [pai'saxe] NM countryside, landscape; (*vista*) scenery

paisano, -a [pai'sano, a] ADJ of the same country ▶ NM/F (*compatriota*) fellow countryman(-woman); **vestir de ~** (*soldado*) to be in civilian clothes; (*guardia*) to be in plain clothes

paja ['paxa] NF straw; (*fig*) trash, rubbish; (*en libro*, *ensayo*) padding, waffle; **riñeron por un quítame allá esas pajas** they quarrelled over a trifle

pajar [pa'xar] NM hay loft

pajarita [paxa'rita] NF bow tie

pájaro ['paxaro] NM bird; (*fam*: *astuto*) clever fellow; **tener la cabeza a pájaros** to be featherbrained; ~ **carpintero** woodpecker

pajita [pa'xita] NF (drinking) straw

pajizo, -a [pa'xiθo, a] ADJ (*de paja*) straw *cpd*; (*techo*) thatched; (*color*) straw-coloured

pakistaní [pakista'ni] ADJ, NM F Pakistani

pala ['pala] NF (*de mango largo*) spade; (*de mango corto*) shovel; (*raqueta etc*) bat; (: *de tenis*) racquet; (*Culin*) slice; ~ **matamoscas** fly swat; ~ **mecánica** power shovel

palabra [pa'laβra] NF (*gen*, *promesa*) word; (*facultad*) (power of) speech; (*derecho de hablar*) right to speak; **faltar a su ~** to go back on one's word; **quedarse con la ~ en la boca** to stop short; **tomar la ~** (*en reunión*, *comité etc*) to speak, take the floor; **pedir la ~** to ask to be allowed to speak; **tener la ~** to have the floor; **no encuentro palabras para expresarme** words fail me

palabrería [palaβre'ria] NF hot air

palabrota [pala'βrota] NF swearword

palacio [pa'laθjo] NM palace; (*mansión*) mansion, large house; ~ **de justicia** courthouse; ~ **municipal** town/city hall

palada [pa'laða] NF shovelful, spadeful; (*de remo*) stroke

paladar [pala'ðar] NM palate

paladear [palaðe'ar] /**1a**/ VT to taste

palanca [pa'lanka] NF lever; (*fig*) pull, influence; ~ **de cambio** (*Auto*) gear lever, gearshift (*US*); ~ **de freno** (*Auto*) brake lever; ~ **de gobierno** *o* **de control** (*Inform*) joystick

palangana [palan'gana] NF washbasin

palco ['palko] NM box

palenque [pa'lenke] NM (*cerca*) stockade, fence; (*área*) arena, enclosure; (*de gallos*) pit

palentino, -a [palen'tino, a] ADJ of *o* from Palencia ▶ NM/F native *o* inhabitant of Palencia

paleolítico, -a [paleo'litiko, a] ADJ palaeolithic (*Brit*), paleolithic (*US*)

paleontología [paleonto'xia] NF palaeontology (*Brit*), paleontology (*US*)

Palestina [pales'tina] NF Palestine

palestino, -a [pales'tino, a] ADJ, NM/F Palestinian

palestra [pa'lestra] NF: **salir** *o* **saltar a la ~** to come into the spotlight

paleto, -a [pa'leto, a] NM/F yokel, hick (*US*) ▶ NF (*pala*) small shovel; (*Arte*) palette; (*Anat*) shoulder blade; (*Deporte*: *de ping-pong*) bat; (*Am*: *helado*) ice lolly (*Brit*), Popsicle® (*US*)

paliar [pa'ljar] /**1b**/ VT (*mitigar*) to mitigate; (*disfrazar*) to conceal

paliativo [palja'tiβo] NM palliative

palidecer [paliðe'θer] /**2d**/ VI to turn pale

palidez [pali'ðeθ] NF paleness

palidezca *etc* [pali'ðeθka] VB *ver* **palidecer**

pálido, -a ['paliðo, a] ADJ pale

palillo [pa'liʎo] NM small stick; (*para dientes*) toothpick; **palillos (chinos)** chopsticks; **estar hecho un ~** to be as thin as a rake

palio ['paljo] NM canopy

palique [pa'like] NM: **estar de ~** (*fam*) to have a chat

paliza [pa'liθa] NF beating, thrashing; **dar** *o* **propinar** (*fam*) **una ~ a algn** to give sb a thrashing

palma ['palma] NF (*Anat*) palm; (*árbol*) palm tree; **batir** *o* **dar palmas** to clap, applaud; **llevarse la ~** to triumph, win

palmada [pal'maða] NF slap; **palmadas** NFPL clapping *sg*, applause *sg*

Palma de Mallorca NF Palma

palmar [pal'mar] /**1a**/ VI (*tb*: **palmarla**) to die, kick the bucket

palmarés [palma'res] NM (*lista*) list of winners; (*historial*) track record

palmear [palme'ar] /**1a**/ VI to clap

palmera [pal'mera] NF (*Bot*) palm tree

palmero, -a [pal'mero, a] ADJ of the island of Palma ▶ NM/F native *o* inhabitant of the island of Palma

palmo ['palmo] NM (*medida*) span; (*fig*) small amount; ~ **a ~** inch by inch

palmotear [palmote'ar] /**1a**/ VI to clap, applaud

palmoteo [palmo'teo] NM clapping, applause

palo ['palo] NM stick; (*poste*) post, pole; (*mango*) handle, shaft; (*golpe*) blow, hit; (*de golf*) club; (*de béisbol*) bat; (*Naut*) mast; (*Naipes*) suit; **vermut a ~ seco** straight vermouth; **de tal ~ tal astilla** like father like son

paloma [pa'loma] NF dove, pigeon; **~ mensajera** carrier o homing pigeon

palomilla [palo'miʎa] NF moth; (*Tec: tuerca*) wing nut; (: *soporte*) bracket

palomitas [palo'mitas] NFPL popcorn *sg*

palpable [pal'paβle] ADJ palpable; (*fig*) tangible

palpar [pal'par] /1a/ VT to touch, feel

palpitación [palpita'θjon] NF palpitation

palpitante [palpi'tante] ADJ palpitating; (*fig*) burning

palpitar [palpi'tar] /1a/ VI to palpitate; (*latir*) to beat

palta ['palta] NF (*AM*) avocado

palúdico, -a [pa'luðiko, a] ADJ marshy

paludismo [palu'ðismo] NM malaria

palurdo, -a [pa'lurðo, a] ADJ coarse, uncouth ▶ NM/F yokel, hick (*US*)

pamela [pa'mela] NF sun hat

pampa ['pampa] NF (*AM*) pampa(s), prairie

pamplinas [pam'plinas] NFPL nonsense *sg*

pamplonés, -esa [pamplo'nes, esa], **pamplonica** [pamplo'nika] ADJ of o from Pamplona ▶ NM/F native o inhabitant of Pamplona

pan [pan] NM bread; (*una barra*) loaf; **~ de molde** sliced loaf; **~ integral** wholemeal bread; **~ rallado** breadcrumbs *pl*; **~ tostado** toast; **eso es ~ comido** it's a cinch; **llamar al ~ ~ y al vino vino** to call a spade a spade

pana ['pana] NF corduroy

panadería [panaðe'ria] NF baker's (shop)

panadero, -a [pana'ðero, a] NM/F baker

panal [pa'nal] NM honeycomb

Panamá [pana'ma] NM Panama

panameño, -a [pana'meɲo, a] ADJ Panamanian

pancarta [pan'karta] NF placard, banner

panceta [pan'θeta] NF bacon

pancho, -a ['pantʃo, a] ADJ: **estar tan ~** to remain perfectly calm ▶ NM (*AM*) hot dog

pancito [pan'sito] NM (*AM*) (bread) roll

páncreas ['pankreas] NM pancreas

panda ['panda] NM panda ▶ NF gang

pandemia [pan'demja] NF pandemic

pandereta [pande'reta] NF tambourine

pandilla [pan'diʎa] NF set, group; (*de criminales*) gang; (*pey*) clique

pando, -a ['pando, a] ADJ sagging

panecillo [pane'θiʎo] NM (bread) roll

panel [pa'nel] NM panel; **~ acústico** acoustic screen; **~ solar** solar panel

panera [pa'nera] NF bread basket

panfleto [pan'fleto] NM (*Pol etc*) pamphlet; lampoon

pánico ['paniko] NM panic

panificadora [panifika'ðora] NF bakery

panorama [pano'rama] NM panorama; (*vista*) view

panqué [pan'ke], **panqueque** [pan'keke] NM (*AM*) pancake

pantaletas [panta'letas] NFPL (*AM*) panties

pantalla [pan'taʎa] NF (*de cine*) screen; (*de lámpara*) lampshade; (*Inform*) screen, display; **servir de ~ a** to be a blind for; **~ de ayuda** help screen; **~ de cristal líquido** liquid crystal display; **~ de plasma** plasma screen; **~ plana** flatscreen; **~ táctil** touch screen

pantalón, pantalones [panta'lon(es)] NM(PL) trousers *pl*, pants *pl* (*US*); **pantalones cortos** shorts *pl*; **pantalones vaqueros** jeans *pl*

pantano [pan'tano] NM (*ciénaga*) marsh, swamp; (*depósito: de agua*) reservoir; (*fig*) jam, fix, difficulty

panteón [pante'on] NM (*monumento*) pantheon

pantera [pan'tera] NF panther

pantimedias [panti'meðjas] NFPL (*AM*) = **pantis**

pantis ['pantis] NMPL tights (*BRIT*), pantyhose (*US*)

pantomima [panto'mima] NF pantomime

pantorrilla [panto'rriʎa] NF calf (of the leg)

pants [pants] NMPL (*AM*) tracksuit (*BRIT*), sweat suit (*US*)

pantufla [pan'tufla] NF slipper

panty(s) ['panti(s)] NM(PL) tights (*BRIT*), pantyhose (*US*)

panza ['panθa] NF belly, paunch

panzón, -ona [pan'θon, ona], **panzudo, -a** [pan'θuðo, a] ADJ fat, potbellied

pañal [pa'ɲal] NM nappy, diaper (*US*); (*fig*) early stages, infancy *sg*; **estar todavía en pañales** to be still wet behind the ears

pañería [paɲe'ria] NF (*artículos*) drapery; (*tienda*) draper's (shop), dry-goods store (*US*)

paño ['paɲo] NM (*tela*) cloth; (*pedazo de tela*) (piece of) cloth; (*trapo*) duster, rag; **~ de cocina** dishcloth; **~ higiénico** sanitary towel; **paños menores** underclothes; **paños calientes** (*fig*) half-measures; **no andarse con paños calientes** to pull no punches

pañuelo [pa'ɲwelo] NM handkerchief, hanky (*fam*); (*para la cabeza*) (head)scarf

papa ['papa] NF (*AM: patata*) potato ▶ NM: **el P~** the Pope; **papas fritas** (*AM*) French fries, chips (*BRIT*); (*de bolsa*) crisps (*BRIT*), potato chips (*US*)

papá [pa'pa] NM (pl **papás**) (fam) dad, daddy, pop (US); **papás** NMPL parents; **hijo de ~** Hooray Henry (fam)

papada [pa'paða] NF double chin

papagayo [papa'ɣajo] NM parrot

papalote [papa'lote] NM (AM) kite

papanatas [papa'natas] NM INV (fam) sucker, simpleton

paparrucha [papa'rrutʃa] NF (tontería) piece of nonsense

papaya [pa'paja] NF papaya

papear [pape'ar] /1a/ VT, VI (fam) to eat

papel [pa'pel] NM (gen) paper; (hoja de papel) sheet of paper; (Teat) part, role; **papeles** NMPL identification papers; **~ de calco/carbón/de cartas** tracing paper/carbon paper/stationery; **~ continuo** (Inform) continuous stationery; **~ de arroz/envolver/fumar** rice/wrapping/cigarette paper; **~ de aluminio/lija** tinfoil/sandpaper; **~ del o de pagos al Estado** government bonds pl; **~ higiénico** toilet paper; **~ moneda** paper money; **~ plegado (en abanico o en acordeón)** fanfold paper; **~ pintado** wallpaper; **~ secante** blotting paper; **~ térmico** thermal paper

papeleo [pape'leo] NM red tape

papelera [pape'lera] NF (cesto) wastepaper basket; (escritorio) desk; **~ de reciclaje** (Inform) wastebasket

papelería [papele'ria] NF (tienda) stationer's (shop)

papeleta [pape'leta] NF (pedazo de papel) slip o bit of paper; (Pol) ballot paper; (Escol) report; **¡vaya ~!** this is a tough one!

paperas [pa'peras] NFPL mumps sg

papilla [pa'piʎa] NF (de bebé) baby food; (pey) mush; **estar hecho ~** to be dog-tired

paquete [pa'kete] NM (caja) packet; (bulto) parcel; (AM fam) nuisance, bore; (Inform) package (of software); (de vacaciones) package tour; **~ de aplicaciones** (Inform) applications package; **~ integrado** (Inform) integrated package; **~ de gestión integrado** combined management suite; **paquetes postales** parcel post sg

paquistaní [pakista'ni] = **pakistaní**

par [par] ADJ (igual) like, equal; (Mat) even ▶ NM equal; (de guantes) pair; (de veces) couple; (título) peer; (Golf, Com) par ▶ NF par; **pares o nones** odds or evens; **abrir de ~ en ~** to open wide; **a la ~** par; **sobre/bajo la ~** above/below par

para ['para] PREP for; **no es ~ comer** it's not for eating; **decir ~ sí** to say to o.s.; **¿~ qué lo quieres?** what do you want it for?; **se casaron ~ separarse otra vez** they married only to separate again; **~ entonces** by then o that time; **lo tendré ~ mañana** I'll have it

for tomorrow; **ir ~ casa** to go home, head for home; **~ profesor es muy estúpido** he's very stupid for a teacher; **¿quién es usted ~ gritar así?** who are you to shout like that?; **tengo bastante ~ vivir** I have enough to live on

parabellum [paraβe'lum] NM (automatic) pistol

parabién [para'βjen] NM congratulations pl

parábola [pa'raβola] NF parable; (Mat) parabola

parabólica [para'βolika] NF (tb: **antena parabólica**) satellite dish

parabrisas [para'βrisas] NM INV windscreen, windshield (US)

paracaídas [paraka'iðas] NM INV parachute

paracaidista [parakai'ðista] NMF parachutist; (Mil) paratrooper

parachoques [para'tʃokes] NM INV bumper, fender (US); shock absorber

parada [pa'raða] NF ver **parado**

paradero [para'ðero] NM stopping-place; (situación) whereabouts

parado, -a [pa'raðo, a] ADJ (persona) motionless, standing still; (fábrica) closed, at a standstill; (coche) stopped; (AM: de pie) standing (up); (sin empleo) unemployed, idle; (confuso) confused ▶ NF (gen) stop; (acto) stopping; (de industria) shutdown, stoppage; (lugar) stopping-place; **salir bien ~** to come off well; **parada de autobús** bus stop; **parada discrecional** request stop; **parada en seco** sudden stop; **parada de taxis** taxi rank

paradoja [para'ðoxa] NF paradox

paradójico, -a [para'ðoxiko, a] ADJ paradoxical

parador [para'ðor] NM (ESP) (luxury) hotel (owned by the state)

parafrasear [parafrase'ar] /1a/ VT to paraphrase

paráfrasis [pa'rafrasis] NF INV paraphrase

paragolpes [para'golpes] NM INV (AM Auto) bumper, fender (US)

paraguas [pa'raɣwas] NM INV umbrella

Paraguay [para'ɣwai] NM Paraguay

paraguayo, -a [para'ɣwajo, a] ADJ, NM/F Paraguayan

paraíso [para'iso] NM paradise, heaven; **~ fiscal** (Com) tax haven

paraje [pa'raxe] NM place, spot

paralelo, -a [para'lelo, a] ADJ, NM parallel; **en ~** (Elec, Inform) (in) parallel

paralice etc [para'liθe] VB ver **paralizar**

parálisis [pa'ralisis] NF INV paralysis; **~ cerebral** cerebral palsy; **~ progresiva** creeping paralysis

paralítico, -a [para'litiko, a] ADJ, NM/F paralytic

paralizar [parali'θar] /**1f**/ VT to paralyse; **paralizarse** VR to become paralysed; (*fig*) to come to a standstill

parámetro [pa'rametro] NM parameter

paramilitar [paramili'tar] ADJ paramilitary

páramo ['paramo] NM bleak plateau

parangón [paran'gon] NM: **sin ~** incomparable

paraninfo [para'ninfo] NM (*Escol*) assembly hall

paranoia [para'noia] NF paranoia

paranoico, -a [para'noiko, a] ADJ, NM/F paranoid

paranormal [paranor'mal] ADJ paranormal

parapente [para'pente] NM (*deporte*) paragliding; (*aparato*) paraglider

parapetarse [parape'tarse] /**1a**/ VR to shelter

parapléjico, -a [para'plexiko, a] ADJ, NM/F paraplegic

parar [pa'rar] /**1a**/ VT to stop; (*progreso etc*) to check, halt; (*golpe*) to ward off ▶ VI to stop; (*hospedarse*) to stay, put up; **pararse** VR to stop; (*AM*) to stand up; **no ~ de hacer algo** to keep on doing sth; **ha parado de llover** it has stopped raining; **van a ~ en la comisaría** they're going to end up in the police station; **no sabemos en qué va a ~ todo esto** we don't know where all this is going to end; **pararse a hacer algo** to stop to do sth; **pararse en** to pay attention to

pararrayos [para'rrajos] NM INV lightning conductor

parásito, -a [pa'rasito, a] NM/F parasite

parasol [para'sol] NM parasol, sunshade

parcela [par'θela] NF plot, piece of ground, smallholding

parche ['partʃe] NM patch

parchís [par'tʃis] NM ludo

parcial [par'θjal] ADJ (*pago*) part-; (*eclipse*) partial; (*juez*) prejudiced, biased; (*Pol*) partisan

parcialidad [parθjali'ðað] NF (*prejuicio*) prejudice, bias

parco, -a ['parko, a] ADJ (*frugal*) sparing; (*moderado*) moderate

pardillo, -a [par'ðiʎo, a] ADJ (*pey*) provincial ▶ NM/F (*pey*) country bumpkin ▶ NM (*Zool*) linnet

pardo, -a ['parðo, a] ADJ (*color*) brown; (*cielo*) overcast; (*voz*) flat, dull

parear [pare'ar] /**1a**/ VT (*juntar, hacer par*) to match, put together; (*calcetines*) to put into pairs; (*Bio*) to mate, pair

parecer [pare'θer] /**2d**/ NM (*opinión*) opinion, view; (*aspecto*) looks pl ▶ VI (*tener apariencia*) to seem, look; (*asemejarse*) to look like, seem like; (*aparecer, llegar*) to appear; **parecerse** VR to look alike, resemble each other; **según parece** evidently, apparently; **parecerse a** to look like, resemble; **al ~** apparently; **me parece que** I think (that), it seems to me that

parecido, -a [pare'θiðo, a] ADJ similar ▶ NM similarity, likeness, resemblance; **~ a** like, similar to; **bien ~** good-looking, nice-looking

pared [pa'reð] NF wall; **~ divisoria/medianera** dividing/party wall; **subirse por las paredes** (*fam*) to go up the wall

paredón [pare'ðon] NM: **llevar a algn al ~** to put sb up against a wall, shoot sb

parejo, -a [pa'rexo, a] ADJ (*igual*) equal; (*liso*) smooth, even ▶ NF (*dos*) pair; (: *de personas*) couple; (*el otro: de un par*) other one (of a pair); (: *persona*) partner; (*de Guardias*) Civil Guard patrol

parentela [paren'tela] NF relations pl

parentesco [paren'tesko] NM relationship

paréntesis [pa'rentesis] NM INV parenthesis; (*digresión*) digression; (*en escrito*) bracket

parezco etc VB ver **parecer**

parida [pa'riða] NF: **~ mental** (*fam*) dumb idea

paridad [pari'ðað] NF (*Econ*) parity

pariente, -a [pa'rjente, a] NM/F relative, relation

parihuela [pari'wela] NF stretcher

paripé [pari'pe] NM: **hacer el ~** to put on an act

parir [pa'rir] /**3a**/ VT to give birth to ▶ VI (*mujer*) to give birth, have a baby; (*yegua*) to foal; (*vaca*) to calve

París [pa'ris] NM Paris

parisiense [pari'sjense] ADJ, NMF Parisian

paritario, -a [pari'tarjo, a] ADJ equal

parka ['parka] NF (*AM*) anorak

parking ['parkin] NM car park, parking lot (*US*)

parlamentar [parlamen'tar] /**1a**/ VI (*negociar*) to parley

parlamentario, -a [parlamen'tarjo, a] ADJ parliamentary ▶ NM/F member of parliament

parlamento [parla'mento] NM (*Pol*) parliament; (*Jur*) speech

parlanchín, -ina [parlan'tʃin, ina] ADJ loose-tongued, indiscreet ▶ NM/F chatterbox

parlante [par'lante] NM (*AM*) loudspeaker

parlar [par'lar] /**1a**/ VI to chatter (away)

parlotear [parlote'ar] /**1a**/ VI to chatter, prattle

parloteo [parlo'teo] NM chatter, prattle

paro ['paro] NM (*huelga*) stoppage (of work), strike; (*desempleo*) unemployment; **~ cardiaco** cardiac arrest; **estar en ~** (*ESP*) to be unemployed; **subsidio de ~** unemployment benefit; **hay ~ en la**

industria work in the industry is at a standstill; **~ del sistema** (*Inform*) system shutdown

parodia [pa'roðja] NF parody

parodiar [paro'ðjar] /**1b**/ VT to parody

parpadear [parpaðe'ar] /**1a**/ VI (*los ojos*) to blink; (*luz*) to flicker

parpadeo [parpa'ðeo] NM (*de ojos*) blinking, winking; (*de luz*) flickering

párpado ['parpaðo] NM eyelid

parque ['parke] NM (*lugar verde*) park; (*Am: munición*) ammunition; **~ de atracciones/de bomberos** fairground/fire station; **~ infantil/temático/zoológico** playground/theme park/zoo

parqué, parquet [par'ke] NM parquet

parqueadero [parkea'ðero] NM (*Am*) car park, parking lot (*US*)

parquímetro [par'kimetro] NM parking meter

parra ['parra] NF grapevine

párrafo ['parrafo] NM paragraph; **echar un ~** (*fam*) to have a chat

parranda [pa'rranda] NF (*fam*) spree, binge

parrilla [pa'rriʎa] NF (*Culin*) grill; (*Am Auto*) roof-rack; **~ (de salida)** (*Auto*) starting grid; **(carne a la)** ~ grilled meat, barbecue

parrillada [parri'ʎaða] NF barbecue

párroco ['parroko] NM parish priest

parroquia [pa'rrokja] NF parish; (*iglesia*) parish church; (*Com*) clientele, customers *pl*

parroquiano, -a [parro'kjano, a] NM/F parishioner; client, customer

parsimonia [parsi'monja] NF (*frugalidad*) sparingness; (*calma*) deliberateness; **con ~** calmly

parte ['parte] NM message; (*informe*) report ▶ NF part; (*lado, cara*) side; (*de reparto*) share; (*Jur*) party; **en alguna ~ de Europa** somewhere in Europe; **en cualquier ~** anywhere; **por ahí no se va a ninguna ~** that leads nowhere; (*fig*) this is getting us nowhere; **en o por todas partes** everywhere; **en gran ~** to a large extent; **la mayor ~ de los españoles** most Spaniards; **de algún tiempo a esta ~** for some time past; **de ~ de algn** on sb's behalf; **¿de ~ de quién?** (*Telec*) who is speaking?; **por ~ de** on the part of; **yo por mi ~** I for my part; **por una ~ ... por otra ~** on the one hand, ... on the other (hand); **dar ~ a algn** to report to sb; **tomar ~** to take part; **~ meteorológico** weather forecast o report

partera [par'tera] NF midwife

parterre [par'terre] NM (flower)bed

partición [parti'θjon] NF division, sharing-out; (*Pol*) partition

participación [partiθipa'θjon] NF (*acto*) participation, taking part; (*parte*) share;

(*Com*) share, stock (*US*); (*de lotería*) (share in a) lottery ticket; (*aviso*) notice, notification; **~ en los beneficios** profit-sharing; **~ minoritaria** minority interest

participante [partiθi'pante] NMF participant

participar [partiθi'par] /**1a**/ VT to notify, inform ▶ VI to take part, participate; **~ en una empresa** (*Com*) to invest in an enterprise; **le participo que ...** I have to tell you that ...

partícipe [par'tiθipe] NMF participant; **hacer ~ a algn de algo** to inform sb of sth

participio [parti'θipjo] NM participle; **~ de pasado/presente** past/present participle

partícula [par'tikula] NF particle

particular [partiku'lar] ADJ (*especial*) particular, special; (*individual, personal*) private, personal ▶ NM (*punto, asunto*) particular, point; (*individuo*) individual; **tiene coche ~** he has a car of his own; **no dijo mucho sobre el ~** he didn't say much about the matter

particularice *etc* [partikula'riθe] VB *ver* **particularizar**

particularidad [partikulari'ðað] NF peculiarity; **tiene la ~ de que ...** one of its special features is (that) ...

particularizar [partikulari'θar] /**1f**/ VT to distinguish; (*especificar*) to specify; (*detallar*) to give details about

partida [par'tiða] NF (*salida*) departure; (*Com*) entry, item; (*juego*) game; (*grupo, bando*) band, group; **mala ~** dirty trick; **~ de nacimiento/matrimonio/defunción** birth/marriage/death certificate; **echar una ~** to have a game

partidario, -a [parti'ðarjo, a] ADJ partisan ▶ NM/F (*Deporte*) supporter; (*Pol*) partisan

partidismo [parti'ðismo] NM (*Jur*) partisanship, bias; (*Pol*) party politics

partido [par'tiðo] NM (*Pol*) party; (*encuentro*) game, match; (*apoyo*) support; (*equipo*) team; **~ amistoso** (*Deporte*) friendly (game); **~ de fútbol** football match; **sacar ~ de** to profit from, benefit from; **tomar ~** to take sides

partir [par'tir] /**3a**/ VT (*dividir*) to split, divide; (*compartir, distribuir*) to share (out), distribute; (*romper*) to break open, split open; (*rebanada*) to cut (off) ▶ VI (*ponerse en camino*) to set off, set out; **partirse** VR to crack o split o break (in two *etc*); **a ~ de** (*starting*) from; **partirse de risa** to split one's sides (laughing)

partitura [parti'tura] NF score

parto ['parto] NM birth, delivery; (*fig*) product, creation; **estar de ~** to be in labour

parvulario [parβu'larjo] NM nursery school, kindergarten

párvulo, -a ['parβulo, a] NM/F infant

287

pasa ['pasa] NF *ver* **paso**
pasable [pa'saβle] ADJ passable
pasacintas [pasa'θintas] NM (*Am*) cassette player
pasada [pa'saða] NF *ver* **pasado**
pasadizo [pasa'ðiθo] NM (*pasillo*) passage, corridor; (*callejuela*) alley
pasado, -a [pa'saðo, a] ADJ past; (*malo: comida, fruta*) bad; (*muy cocido*) overdone; (*anticuado*) out of date ▶ NM past; (*Ling*) past (tense) ▶ NF passing, passage; (*acción de pulir*) rub, polish; ~ **mañana** the day after tomorrow; **el mes** ~ last month; **pasados dos días** after two days; **lo** ~, ~ let bygones be bygones; ~ **de moda** old-fashioned; ~ **por agua** (*huevo*) boiled; **estar** ~ **de vueltas** *o* **de rosca** (*grifo, tuerca*) to be worn; **de pasada** in passing, incidentally; **una mala pasada** a dirty trick
pasador [pasa'ðor] NM (*gen*) bolt; (*de pelo*) slide; (*horquilla*) grip; **pasadores** NMPL (*Am: cordones*) shoelaces
pasaje [pa'saxe] NM (*gen*) passage; (*pago de viaje*) fare; (*los pasajeros*) passengers *pl*; (*pasillo*) passageway
pasajero, -a [pasa'xero, a] ADJ passing; (*situación, estado*) temporary; (*amor, enfermedad*) brief; (*ave*) migratory ▶ NM/F passenger; (*viajero*) traveller
pasamanos [pasa'manos] NM INV rail, handrail; (*de escalera*) banister
pasamontañas [pasamon'taɲas] NM INV balaclava (helmet)
pasaporte [pasa'porte] NM passport
pasar [pa'sar] /**1a**/ VT (*gen*) to pass; (*tiempo*) to spend; (*durezas*) to suffer, endure; (*noticia*) to give, pass on; (*película*) to show; (*persona*) to take, conduct; (*río*) to cross; (*barrera*) to pass through; (*falta*) to overlook, tolerate; (*contrincante*) to surpass, do better than; (*coche*) to overtake; (*contrabando*) to smuggle (in/out); (*enfermedad*) to give, infect with ▶ VI (*gen*) to pass, go; (*terminarse*) to be over; (*ocurrir*) to happen; **pasarse** VR (*efectos*) to pass, be over; (*flores*) to fade; (*comida*) to go bad, go off; (*fig*) to overdo it, go too far *o* over the top; ~ **la aspiradora** to do the vacuuming *or* hoovering, hoover; ~ **de** to go beyond, exceed; **¡pase!** come in!; **nos hicieron** ~ they showed us in; ~ **por** to fetch; ~ **por alto** to skip; ~ **por una crisis** to go through a crisis; **se hace** ~ **por médico** he passes himself off as a doctor; **pasarlo bien/bomba** *o* **de maravilla** to have a good/great time; **¡que lo pases bien!** have a good time!; **pasarse al enemigo** to go over to the enemy; **pasarse de la raya** to go too far; **¡no te pases!** don't try me!; **se me pasó** I forgot; **se me pasó el turno** I missed my turn; **no se**

le pasa nada nothing escapes him, he misses nothing; **ya se te pasará** you'll get over it; **¿qué pasa?** what's happening?, what's going on?, what's up?; **¿qué te pasa?** what's wrong?; **¡cómo pasa el tiempo!** time just flies!; **pase lo que pase** come what may; **el autobús pasa por nuestra casa** the bus goes past our house
pasarela [pasa'rela] NF footbridge; (*en barco*) gangway
pasatiempo [pasa'tjempo] NM pastime, hobby; (*distracción*) amusement
Pascua, pascua ['paskwa] NF: ~ (**de Resurrección**) Easter; **Pascuas** NFPL Christmas time *sg*; ~ **de Navidad** Christmas; **¡felices Pascuas!** Merry Christmas!; **de Pascuas a Ramos** once in a blue moon; **hacer la** ~ **a** (*fam*) to annoy, bug
pase ['pase] NM pass; (*Cine*) performance, showing; (*Com*) permit; (*Jur*) licence; ~ **de diapositivas** slide show
pasear [pase'ar] /**1a**/ VT to take for a walk; (*exhibir*) to parade, show off ▶ VI to walk, go for a walk; **pasearse** VR to walk, go for a walk; ~ **en coche** to go for a drive
paseo [pa'seo] NM (*distancia corta*) (short) walk, stroll; (*avenida*) avenue; ~ **marítimo** promenade; **dar un** ~ to go for a walk; ~ **en bicicleta** (bike) ride; ~ **en barco** boat trip; **mandar a algn a** ~ to tell sb to go to blazes; **¡vete a** ~! get lost!
pasillo [pa'siʎo] NM passage, corridor
pasión [pa'sjon] NF passion
pasional [pasjo'nal] ADJ passionate; **crimen** ~ crime of passion
pasivo, -a [pa'siβo, a] ADJ passive; (*inactivo*) inactive ▶ NM (*Com*) liabilities *pl*, debts *pl*; (*de cuenta*) debit side; ~ **circulante** current liabilities
pasma ['pasma] NM (*fam*) cop
pasmado, -a [pas'maðo, a] ADJ (*asombrado*) astonished; (*atontado*) bewildered
pasmar [pas'mar] /**1a**/ VT (*asombrar*) to amaze, astonish; **pasmarse** VR to be amazed *o* astonished
pasmo ['pasmo] NM amazement, astonishment; (*fig*) wonder, marvel
pasmoso, -a [pas'moso, a] ADJ amazing, astonishing
paso, -a ['paso, a] ADJ dried ▶ NM (*gen, de baile*) step; (*modo de andar*) walk; (*huella*) footprint; (*rapidez*) speed, pace, rate; (*camino accesible*) way through, passage; (*cruce*) crossing; (*pasaje*) passing, passage; (*Rel*) religious float or sculpture; (*Geo*) pass; (*estrecho*) strait; (*fig*) step, measure; (*apuro*) difficulty ▶ NF raisin; **pasa de Corinto/de Esmirna** currant/sultana; ~ **a** step by step; **a ese** ~ (*fig*) at that rate; **salir al** ~ **de** *o* **a** to waylay; **salir del** ~

to get out of trouble; **dar un ~ en falso** to trip; (*fig*) to take a false step; **estar de ~** to be passing through; **~ atrás** step backwards; (*fig*) backward step; **~ elevado/subterráneo** flyover/subway, underpass (*US*); **prohibido el ~** no entry; **ceda el ~** give way; **~ a nivel** (*Ferro*) level-crossing; **~ (de) cebra** (*Esp*) zebra crossing; **~ de peatones** pedestrian crossing; **~ elevado** flyover; *ver tb* **Semana Santa**

pasota [pa'sota] ADJ, NMF (*fam*) ≈ dropout; **ser un (tipo) ~** to be a bit of a dropout; (*ser indiferente*) not to care about anything

pasotismo [paso'tismo] NM underground o alternative culture

pasta ['pasta] NF (*gen*) paste; (*Culin: masa*) dough; (: *de bizcochos etc*) pastry; (*fam*) money, dough; (*encuadernación*) hardback; **pastas** NFPL (*bizcochos*) pastries, small cakes; (*espaguetis etc*) pasta *sg*; **~ de dientes** o **dentífrica** toothpaste; **~ de madera** wood pulp

pastar [pas'tar] /1a/ VT, VI to graze

pastel [pas'tel] NM (*dulce*) cake; (*Arte*) pastel; (*fig*) plot; **pasteles** NMPL pastry *sg*, confectionery *sg*; **~ de carne** meat pie

pastelería [pastele'ria] NF cake shop, pastry shop

pasteurizado, -a [pasteuri'θaðo, a] ADJ pasteurized

pastilla [pas'tiʎa] NF (*de jabón, chocolate*) cake, bar; (*píldora*) tablet, pill

pastizal [pasti'θal] NM pasture

pasto ['pasto] NM (*hierba*) grass; (*lugar*) pasture, field; (*fig*) food, nourishment

pastor, a [pas'tor, a] NM/F shepherd(ess) ▶ NM clergyman, pastor; (*Zool*) sheepdog; **~ alemán** Alsatian

pastoso, -a [pas'toso, a] ADJ (*material*) doughy, pasty; (*lengua*) furry; (*voz*) mellow

pat. ABR (= *patente*) pat

pata ['pata] NF (*pierna*) leg; (*pie*) foot; (*de muebles*) leg; **patas arriba** upside down; **a cuatro patas** on all fours; **meter la ~** to put one's foot in it; **~ de cabra** (*Tec*) crowbar; **patas de gallo** crow's feet; **metedura de ~** (*fam*) gaffe; **tener buena/mala ~** to be lucky/unlucky

patada [pa'taða] NF stamp; (*puntapié*) kick; **a patadas** (*muchos*) in abundance; (*trato*) roughly; **echar a algn a patadas** to kick sb out

patagón, -ona [pata'ɣon, ona] ADJ, NM/F Patagonian

Patagonia [pata'ɣonja] NF: **la ~** Patagonia

patalear [patale'ar] /1a/ VI to stamp one's feet

pataleo [pata'leo] NM stamping

patán [pa'tan] NM rustic, yokel

patata [pa'tata] NF potato; **patatas fritas** o **a la española** chips, French fries; (*de bolsa*) crisps; **ni ~** (*fam*) nothing at all; **no entendió ni ~** he didn't understand a single word

paté [pa'te] NM pâté

patear [pate'ar] /1a/ VT (*pisar*) to stamp on, trample (on); (*pegar con el pie*) to kick ▶ VI to stamp (with rage), stamp one's foot

patentar [paten'tar] /1a/ VT to patent

patente [pa'tente] ADJ obvious, evident; (*Com*) patent ▶ NF patent

patera [pa'tera] NF boat

paternal [pater'nal] ADJ fatherly, paternal

paternalista [paterna'lista] ADJ (*tono, actitud etc*) patronizing

paternidad [paterni'ðað] NF fatherhood, parenthood; (*Jur*) paternity

paterno, -a [pa'terno, a] ADJ paternal

patético, -a [pa'tetiko, a] ADJ pathetic, moving

patíbulo [pa'tiβulo] NM scaffold, gallows *sg*

patilla [pa'tiʎa] NF (*de gafas*) sidepiece; **patillas** NFPL sideburns

patín [pa'tin] NM skate; (*de tobogán*) runner; **patines de hielo** ice skates; **patines de ruedas** rollerskates

patinaje [pati'naxe] NM skating

patinar [pati'nar] /1a/ VI to skate; (*resbalarse*) to skid, slip; (*fam*) to slip up, blunder

patinazo [pati'naθo] NM (*Auto*) skid; **dar un ~** (*fam*) to blunder

patineta [pati'neta] NF (*patinete*) scooter; (*Am: monopatín*) skateboard

patinete [pati'nete] NM scooter

patio ['patjo] NM (*de casa*) patio, courtyard; **~ de recreo** playground

pato ['pato] NM duck; **pagar el ~** (*fam*) to take the blame, carry the can

patológico, -a [pato'loxiko, a] ADJ pathological

patoso, -a [pa'toso, a] ADJ awkward, clumsy

patotero [pato'tero] NM (*Am*) hooligan, lout

patraña [pa'traɲa] NF story, fib

patria ['patrja] NF native land, mother country; **~ chica** home town

patrimonio [patri'monjo] NM inheritance; (*fig*) heritage; (*Com*) net worth

patriota [pa'trjota] NMF patriot

patriotero, -a [patrjo'tero, a] ADJ chauvinistic

patriótico, -a [pa'trjotiko, a] ADJ patriotic

patriotismo [patrjo'tismo] NM patriotism

patrocinador, a [patroθina'ðor, a] NM/F sponsor

patrocinar [patroθi'nar] /1a/ VT to sponsor; (*apoyar*) to back, support

patrocinio [patro'θinjo] NM sponsorship; backing, support

P

patrón, -ona [pa'tron, ona] NM/F (*jefe*) boss, chief, master (mistress); (*propietario*) landlord(-lady); (*Rel*) patron saint ▸ NM (*Costura*) pattern; (*Tec*) standard; ~ **oro** gold standard

patronal [patro'nal] ADJ: **la clase ~** management; **cierre ~** lockout

patronato [patro'nato] NM sponsorship; (*acto*) patronage; (*Com*) employers' association; (*fundación*) trust; **el ~ de turismo** the tourist board

patrulla [pa'truʎa] NF patrol

patrullar [patru'ʎar] /**1a**/ VI to patrol

paulatino, -a [paula'tino, a] ADJ gradual, slow

paupérrimo, -a [pau'perrimo, a] ADJ very poor, poverty-stricken

pausa ['pausa] NF pause; (*intervalo*) break; (*interrupción*) interruption; (*Tec: en videograbadora*) hold; **con ~** slowly

pausado, -a [pau'saðo, a] ADJ slow, deliberate

pauta ['pauta] NF line, guide line

pava ['paβa] NF (*Am*) kettle

pavimento [paβi'mento] NM (*Arq*) flooring; (*de losa*) pavement, paving

pavo ['paβo] NM turkey; (*necio*) silly thing, idiot; ~ **real** peacock; **¡no seas ~!** don't be silly!

pavonearse [paβone'arse] /**1a**/ VR to swagger, show off

pavor [pa'βor] NM dread, terror

payasada [paja'saða] NF ridiculous thing (to do); **payasadas** NFPL clowning *sg*

payaso, -a [pa'jaso, a] NM/F clown

payo, -a ['pajo, a] ADJ, NM/F non-gipsy

paz [paθ] NF peace; (*tranquilidad*) peacefulness, tranquillity; **dejar a algn en ~** to leave sb alone *o* in peace; **hacer las paces** to make peace; (*fig*) to make up; **¡déjame en ~!** leave me alone!; **¡haya ~!** stop it!

pazca *etc* ['paθka] VB *ver* **pacer**

PC NM ABR (*Pol*: = *Partido Comunista*) CP ▸ NM PC, personal computer

P.C.E. NM ABR = **Partido Comunista de España**

PCL NF ABR (= *pantalla de cristal líquido*) LCD

P.D. ABR (= *posdata*) P.S.

pdo. ABR (= *pasado*) ult.

peaje [pe'axe] NM toll; **autopista de ~** toll motorway, turnpike (*US*)

peatón [pea'ton] NM pedestrian; **paso de peatones** pedestrian crossing, crosswalk (*US*)

peatonal [peato'nal] ADJ pedestrian

peca ['peka] NF freckle

pecado [pe'kaðo] NM sin

pecador, a [peka'ðor, a] ADJ sinful ▸ NM/F sinner

pecaminoso, -a [pekami'noso, a] ADJ sinful

pecar [pe'kar] /**1g**/ VI (*Rel*) to sin; (*fig*): ~ **de generoso** to be too generous

pecera [pe'θera] NF fish tank; (*redonda*) goldfish bowl

pecho ['petʃo] NM (*Anat*) chest; (*de mujer*) breast(s *pl*), bosom; (*corazón*) heart, breast; (*valor*) courage, spirit; **dar el ~ a** to breast-feed; **tomar algo a ~** to take sth to heart; **no le cabía en el ~** he was bursting with happiness

pechuga [pe'tʃuɣa] NF breast

pecoso, -a [pe'koso, a] ADJ freckled

peculiar [peku'ljar] ADJ special, peculiar; (*característico*) typical, characteristic

peculiaridad [pekuljari'ðað] NF peculiarity; special feature, characteristic

pedagogía [peðaɣo'ɣia] NF education

pedagogo [peða'ɣoɣo] NM pedagogue, teacher

pedal [pe'ðal] NM pedal; ~ **de embrague** clutch (pedal); ~ **de freno** footbrake

pedalear [peðale'ar] /**1a**/ VI to pedal

pédalo ['peðalo] NM pedalo, pedal boat

pedante [pe'ðante] ADJ pedantic ▸ NMF pedant

pedantería [peðante'ria] NF pedantry

pedazo [pe'ðaθo] NM piece, bit; **hacerse pedazos** to fall to pieces; (*romperse*) to smash, shatter; **un ~ de pan** a scrap of bread; (*fig*) a terribly nice person

pedernal [peðer'nal] NM flint

pedestal [peðes'tal] NM base; **tener/poner a algn en un ~** to put sb on a pedestal

pedestre [pe'ðestre] ADJ pedestrian; **carrera ~** foot race

pediatra [pe'ðjatra] NMF paediatrician (*Brit*), pediatrician (*US*)

pediatría [peðja'tria] NF paediatrics *sg* (*Brit*), pediatrics *sg* (*US*)

pedicuro, -a [peði'kuro, a] NM/F chiropodist (*Brit*), podiatrist (*US*)

pedido [pe'ðiðo] NM (*Com*) order; (*petición*) request; **pedidos en cartera** (*Com*) backlog *sg*

pedigrí [peði'ɣri] NM pedigree

pedir [pe'ðir] /**3k**/ VT to ask for, request; (*comida, Com: mandar*) to order; (*exigir: precio*) to ask; (*necesitar*) to need, demand, require ▸ VI to ask; ~ **prestado** to borrow; ~ **disculpas** to apologize; **me pidió que cerrara la puerta** he asked me to shut the door; **¿cuánto piden por el coche?** how much are they asking for the car?

pedo ['peðo] (*fam*) ADJ INV: **estar ~** to be pissed (*fam!*) ▸ NM fart (*fam!*)

pedrada [pe'ðraða] NF throw of a stone; (*golpe*) blow from a stone; **herir a algn de una ~** to hit sb with a stone

pedrea [pe'ðrea] NF (*granizada*) hailstorm; (*de lotería*) minor prizes

pedrisco [pe'ðrisko] NM (*granizo*) hail; (*granizada*) hailstorm

Pedro ['peðro] NM Peter; **entrar como ~ por su casa** to come in as if one owned the place

pega ['peɣa] NF (*dificultad*) snag; **de ~** false, dud; **poner pegas** to raise objections

pegadizo, -a [peɣa'ðiθo, a] ADJ (*canción etc*) catchy

pegajoso, -a [peɣa'xoso, a] ADJ sticky, adhesive

pegamento [peɣa'mento] NM gum, glue

pegar [pe'ɣar] /**1h**/ VT (*papel, sellos*) to stick (on); (*con cola*) to glue; (*cartel*) to post, stick up; (*coser*) to sew (on); (*unir: partes*) to join, fix together; (*Inform*) to paste; (*Med*) to give, infect with; (*dar: golpe*) to give, deal ▶ VI (*adherirse*) to stick, adhere; (*Inform*) to paste; (*ir juntos: colores*) to match, go together; (*golpear*) to hit; (*quemar: el sol*) to strike hot, burn; **pegarse** VR (*gen*) to stick; (*dos personas*) to hit each other, fight; **pegarle a algo** to be a great one for sth; **~ un grito** to let out a yell; **~ un salto** to jump (with fright); **~ fuego** to catch fire; **~ en** to touch; **pegarse un tiro** to shoot o.s.; **no pega** that doesn't seem right; **ese sombrero no pega con el abrigo** that hat doesn't go with the coat

pegatina [peɣa'tina] NF (*Pol etc*) sticker

pego ['peɣo] NM: **dar el ~** (*pasar por verdadero*) to look like the real thing

pegote [pe'ɣote] NM (*fam*) eyesore, sight; (*fig*) patch, ugly mend; **tirarse pegotes** (*fam*) to come on strong

pegue *etc* ['peɣe] VB *ver* **pegar**

peinado [pei'naðo] NM (*en peluquería*) hairdo; (*estilo*) hairstyle

peinar [pei'nar] /**1a**/ VT to comb sb's hair; (*con un cierto estilo*) to style; **peinarse** VR to comb one's hair

peine ['peine] NM comb

peineta [pei'neta] NF ornamental comb

p.ej. ABR (= *por ejemplo*) e.g.

Pekín [pe'kin] N Peking, Beijing

pela ['pela] NF (*Esp fam*) peseta; *ver tb* **pelas**

pelado, -a [pe'laðo, a] ADJ (*cabeza*) shorn; (*fruta*) peeled; (*campo, fig*) bare; (*fam: sin dinero*) broke

pelaje [pe'laxe] NM (*Zool*) fur, coat; (*fig*) appearance

pelambre [pe'lambre] NM long hair, mop

pelar [pe'lar] /**1a**/ VT (*fruta, patatas*) to peel; (*cortar el pelo a*) to cut the hair of; (*quitar la piel: animal*) to skin; (: *ave*) to pluck; (: *habas etc*) to shell; **pelarse** VR (*la piel*) to peel off; **voy a pelarme** I'm going to get my hair cut; **corre que se las pela** (*fam*) he runs like nobody's business

pelas ['pelas] NFPL (*Esp fam*) dough

peldaño [pel'daɲo] NM step; (*de escalera portátil*) rung

pelea [pe'lea] NF (*lucha*) fight; (*discusión*) quarrel, row

peleado, -a [pele'aðo, a] ADJ: **estar ~ (con algn)** to have fallen out (with sb)

pelear [pele'ar] /**1a**/ VI to fight; **pelearse** VR to fight; (*reñir*) to fall out, quarrel

pelela [pe'lela] NF (*Am*) potty

pelele [pe'lele] NM (*figura*) guy, dummy; (*fig*) puppet

peletería [pelete'ria] NF furrier's, fur shop

peliagudo, -a [pelja'ɣuðo, a] ADJ tricky

pelícano [pe'likano] NM pelican

película [pe'likula] NF (*Cine*) film, movie (*US*); (*cobertura ligera*) film, thin covering; (*Foto: rollo*) roll *o* reel of film; **~ de dibujos (animados)** cartoon film; **~ muda** silent film; **de ~** (*fam*) astonishing, out of this world

peligrar [peli'ɣrar] /**1a**/ VI to be in danger

peligro [pe'liɣro] NM danger; (*riesgo*) risk; **"~ de muerte"** "danger"; **correr ~ de** to be in danger of, run the risk of; **con ~ de la vida** at the risk of one's life

peligrosidad [peliɣrosi'ðað] NF danger, riskiness

peligroso, -a [peli'ɣroso, a] ADJ dangerous; risky

pelirrojo, -a [peli'rroxo, a] ADJ red-haired, red-headed ▶ NM/F redhead

pellejo [pe'ʎexo] NM (*de animal*) skin, hide; **salvar el ~** to save one's skin

pellizcar [peʎiθ'kar] /**1g**/ VT to pinch, nip

pellizco [pe'ʎiθko] NM pinch

pellizque *etc* [pe'ʎiθke] VB *ver* **pellizcar**

pelma ['pelma] NMF, **pelmazo, -a** [pel'maθo, a] NM/F (*fam*) pain (in the neck)

pelo ['pelo] NM (*cabellos*) hair; (*de barba, bigote*) whisker; (*de animal: piel*) fur, coat; (*de perro etc*) hair, coat; (*de ave*) down; (*de tejido*) nap; (*Tec*) fibre; **a ~** bareheaded; (*desnudo*) naked; **al ~** just right; **venir al ~** to be exactly what one needs; **un hombre de ~ en pecho** a brave man; **por los pelos** by the skin of one's teeth; **escaparse por un ~** to have a close shave; **se me pusieron los pelos de punta** my hair stood on end; **no tener pelos en la lengua** to be outspoken, not mince words; **con pelos y señales** in minute detail; **tomar el ~ a algn** to pull sb's leg

pelón, -ona [pe'lon, ona] ADJ hairless, bald

pelota [pe'lota] NF ball; (*fam: cabeza*) nut (*fam*); **en ~(s)** stark naked; **~ vasca** pelota; **devolver la ~ a algn** (*fig*) to turn the tables on sb; **hacer la ~ (a algn)** to creep (to sb)

pelotera [pelo'tera] NF (*fam*) barney

pelotón [pelo'ton] NM (*Mil*) squad, detachment

peluca [pe'luka] NF wig

peluche [pe'lutʃe] NM: **muñeco de** ~ soft toy

peludo, -a [pe'luðo, a] ADJ hairy, shaggy

peluquería [peluke'ria] NF hairdresser's; (*para hombres*) barber's (shop)

peluquero, -a [pelu'kero, a] NM/F hairdresser; barber

peluquín [pelu'kin] NM toupée

pelusa [pe'lusa] NF (*Bot*) down; (*Costura*) fluff

pelvis ['pelβis] NF pelvis

PEMEX [pe'meks] NM ABR = **Petróleos Mexicanos**

PEN [pen] NM ABR (*ESP*) = **Plan Energético Nacional**; (*ARGENTINA*) = **Poder Ejecutivo Nacional**

pena ['pena] NF (*congoja*) grief, sadness; (*remordimiento*) regret; (*dificultad*) trouble; (*dolor*) pain; (*AM: vergüenza*) shame; (*Jur*) sentence; (*Deporte*) penalty; ~ **capital** capital punishment; ~ **de muerte** death penalty; ~ **pecuniaria** fine; **merecer** o **valer la** ~ to be worthwhile; **a duras penas** with great difficulty; **so** ~ **de** on pain of; **me dan** ~ I feel sorry for them; **¿no te da** ~ **hacerlo?** (*AM*) aren't you embarrassed doing that?; **¡qué** ~! what a shame o pity!

penal [pe'nal] ADJ penal ▶ NM (*cárcel*) prison

penalidad [penali'ðað] NF (*problema, dificultad*) trouble, hardship; (*Jur*) penalty, punishment; **penalidades** NFPL trouble *sg*, hardship *sg*

penalizar [penali'θar] /**1f**/ VT to penalize

penalti, penalty [pe'nalti] (*pl* **penalties** o **penaltys**) NM (*Deporte*) penalty (kick)

penar [pe'nar] /**1a**/ VT to penalize; (*castigar*) to punish ▶ VI to suffer

pendejo, -a [pen'dexo, a] NM/F (*AM fam!*) wanker (*BRIT fam!*), jerk (*US fam!*)

pender [pen'der] /**2a**/ VI (*colgar*) to hang; (*Jur*) to be pending

pendiente [pen'djente] ADJ pending, unsettled ▶ NM earring ▶ NF hill, slope; **tener una asignatura** ~ to have to resit a subject

pendón [pen'don] NM banner, standard

péndulo ['pendulo] NM pendulum

pene ['pene] NM penis

penene [pe'nene] NMF = **PNN**

penetración [penetra'θjon] NF (*acto*) penetration; (*agudeza*) sharpness, insight

penetrante [pene'trante] ADJ (*herida*) deep; (*persona, arma*) sharp; (*sonido*) penetrating, piercing; (*mirada*) searching; (*viento, ironía*) biting

penetrar [pene'trar] /**1a**/ VT to penetrate, pierce; (*entender*) to grasp ▶ VI to penetrate, go in; (*entrar*) to enter; (*líquido*) to soak in; (*emoción*) to pierce

penicilina [peniθi'lina] NF penicillin

península [pe'ninsula] NF peninsula; **P~ Ibérica** Iberian Peninsula

peninsular [peninsu'lar] ADJ peninsular

penique [pe'nike] NM penny; **peniques** NMPL pence

penitencia [peni'tenθja] NF (*remordimiento*) penitence; (*castigo*) penance; **en** ~ as a penance

penitencial [peniten'θjal] ADJ penitential

penitenciaría [penitenθja'ria] NF prison, penitentiary

penitenciario, -a [peniten'θjarjo, a] ADJ prison *cpd*

penoso, -a [pe'noso, a] ADJ laborious, difficult; (*lamentable*) distressing

pensado, -a [pen'saðo, a] ADJ: **bien/mal** ~ well intentioned/cynical; **en el momento menos** ~ when least expected

pensador, a [pensa'ðor, a] NM/F thinker

pensamiento [pensa'mjento] NM (*gen*) thought; (*mente*) mind; (*idea*) idea; (*Bot*) pansy; **no se le pasó por el** ~ it never occurred to him

pensar [pen'sar] /**1j**/ VT to think; (*considerar*) to think over, think out; (*proponerse*) to intend, plan, propose; (*imaginarse*) to think up, invent ▶ VI to think; ~ **en** to think of o about; (*anhelar*) to aim at, aspire to; **dar que** ~ **a algn** to give sb food for thought

pensativo, -a [pensa'tiβo, a] ADJ thoughtful, pensive

pensión [pen'sjon] NF (*casa*) ≈ guest house; (*dinero*) pension; (*cama y comida*) board and lodging; ~ **de jubilación** retirement pension; ~ **escalada** graduated pension; ~ **completa** full board; **media** ~ half board

pensionista [pensjo'nista] NMF (*jubilado*) (old-age) pensioner; (*el que vive en una pensión*) lodger; (*Escol*) boarder

pentágono [pen'taɣono] NM pentagon; **el P~** the Pentagon

pentagrama [penta'ɣrama] NM (*Mus*) stave, staff

penúltimo, -a [pe'nultimo, a] ADJ penultimate, second last

penumbra [pe'numbra] NF half-light, semi-darkness

penuria [pe'nurja] NF shortage, want

peña ['peɲa] NF (*roca*) rock; (*acantilado*) cliff, crag; (*grupo*) group, circle; (*AM: club*) folk club; (*Deporte*) supporters' club

peñasco [pe'ɲasko] NM large rock, boulder

peñón [pe'ɲon] NM crag; **el P~** the Rock (of Gibraltar)

peón [pe'on] NM labourer; (*AM*) farm labourer, farmhand; (*Tec*) spindle, shaft; (*Ajedrez*) pawn

peonza [pe'onθa] NF spinning top

peor [pe'or] ADJ (*comparativo*) worse; (*superlativo*) worst ▶ ADV (*comparativo*) worse; (*superlativo*) worst; **de mal en ~** from bad to worse; **tanto ~** so much the worse; **A es ~ que B** A is worse than B; **Z es el ~ de todos** Z is the worst of all

pepenar [pepe'nar] /1a/ VI (AM) to sift through rubbish o garbage

pepinillo [pepi'niʎo] NM gherkin

pepino [pe'pino] NM cucumber; **(no) me importa un ~** I don't care one bit

pepita [pe'pita] NF (*Bot*) pip; (*Minería*) nugget

pepito [pe'pito] NM (*ESP*: *tb*: **pepito de ternera**) steak sandwich

peque *etc* ['peke] VB *ver* **pecar**

pequeñez [peke'ɲeθ] NF smallness, littleness; (*trivialidad*) trifle, triviality

pequeño, -a [pe'keɲo, a] ADJ small, little; (*cifra*) small, low; (*bajo*) short; **~ burgués** lower middle-class

pequinés, -esa [peki'nes, esa] ADJ, NM/F Pekinese

pera ['pera] ADJ INV classy; **niño ~** spoiled upper-class brat ▶ NF pear; **eso es pedir peras al olmo** that's asking the impossible

peral [pe'ral] NM pear tree

percance [per'kanθe] NM setback, misfortune

per cápita [per'kapita] ADJ: **renta ~** per capita income

percatarse [perka'tarse] /1a/ VR: **~ de** to notice, take note of

percebe [per'θeβe] NM (*Zool*) barnacle; (*fam*) idiot

percepción [perθep'θjon] NF (*vista*) perception; (*idea*) notion, idea; (*Com*) collection

perceptible [perθep'tiβle] ADJ perceptible, noticeable; (*Com*) payable, receivable

percha ['pertʃa] NF (*poste*) pole, support; (*gancho*) peg; (*de abrigos*) coat stand; (*colgador*) coat hanger; (*ganchos*) coat hooks *pl*; (*de ave*) perch

perchero [per'tʃero] NM clothes rack

percibir [perθi'βir] /3a/ VT to perceive, notice; (*ver*) to see; (*peligro etc*) to sense; (*Com*) to earn, receive, get

percusión [perku'sjon] NF percussion

percusor [perku'sor], **percutor** [perku'tor] NM (*Tec*) hammer; (*de arma*) firing pin

perdedor, a [perðe'ðor, a] ADJ losing ▶ NM/F loser

perder [per'ðer] /2g/ VT to lose; (*tiempo, palabras*) to waste; (*oportunidad*) to lose, miss; (*tren*) to miss ▶ VI to lose; **perderse** VR (*extraviarse*) to get lost; (*desaparecer*) to disappear, be lost to view; (*arruinarse*) to be ruined; **echar a ~** (*comida*) to spoil, ruin; (*oportunidad*) to waste; **tener buen ~** to be a good loser; **¡no te lo pierdas!** don't miss it!; **he perdido la costumbre** I have got out of the habit

perdición [perði'θjon] NF perdition; (*fig*) ruin

pérdida ['perðiða] NF loss; (*de tiempo*) waste; (*Com*) net loss; **pérdidas** NFPL (*Com*) losses; **¡no tiene ~!** you can't go wrong!; **~ contable** (*Com*) book loss

perdido, -a [per'ðiðo, a] ADJ lost; **estar ~ por** to be crazy about; **es un caso ~** he is a hopeless case

perdigón [perði'ɣon] NM pellet

perdiz [per'ðiθ] NF partridge

perdón [per'ðon] NM (*disculpa*) pardon, forgiveness; (*clemencia*) mercy; **¡~!** sorry!, I beg your pardon!; **con ~** if I may, if you don't mind

perdonar [perðo'nar] /1a/ VT to pardon, forgive; (*la vida*) to spare; (*excusar*) to exempt, excuse ▶ VI to pardon, forgive; **¡perdone (usted)!** sorry!, I beg your pardon!; **perdone, pero me parece que …** excuse me, but I think …

perdurable [perðu'raβle] ADJ lasting; (*eterno*) everlasting

perdurar [perðu'rar] /1a/ VI (*resistir*) to last, endure; (*seguir existiendo*) to stand, still exist

perecedero, -a [pereθe'ðero, a] ADJ perishable

perecer [pere'θer] /2d/ VI to perish, die

peregrinación [pereɣrina'θjon] NF (*Rel*) pilgrimage

peregrino, -a [pere'ɣrino, a] ADJ (*extraño*) strange; (*singular*) rare ▶ NM/F pilgrim

perejil [pere'xil] NM parsley

perenne [pe'renne] ADJ perennial

perentorio, -a [peren'torjo, a] ADJ (*urgente*) urgent; (*terminante*) peremptory; (*fijo*) set, fixed

pereza [pe'reθa] NF (*flojera*) laziness; (*lentitud*) sloth, slowness

perezca *etc* [pe'reθka] VB *ver* **perecer**

perezoso, -a [pere'θoso, a] ADJ lazy; slow, sluggish

perfección [perfek'θjon] NF perfection; **a la ~** to perfection

perfeccionar [perfekθjo'nar] /1a/ VT to perfect; (*mejorar*) to improve; (*acabar*) to complete, finish

perfectamente [perfekta'mente] ADV perfectly

perfecto, -a [per'fekto, a] ADJ perfect ▶ NM (*Ling*) perfect (tense)

perfidia [per'fiðja] NF perfidy, treachery

pérfido, -a ['perfiðo, a] ADJ perfidious, treacherous

P

293

perfil [per'fil] NM (*parte lateral*) profile; (*silueta*) silhouette, outline; (*Tec*) (*cross*) section; **perfiles** NMPL (*fig*) features; social graces; **~ del cliente** (*Com*) customer profile; **en ~** from the side, in profile

perfilado, -a [perfi'laðo, a] ADJ (*bien formado*) well-shaped; (*largo: cara*) long

perfilar [perfi'lar] /1a/ VT (*trazar*) to outline; (*dar carácter a*) to shape, give character to; **perfilarse** VR: **perfilarse (en)** to be silhouetted (against); **el proyecto se va perfilando** the project is taking shape

perforación [perfora'θjon] NF perforation; (*con taladro*) drilling

perforadora [perfora'ðora] NF drill; (*tb:* **perforadora de fichas**) card-punch

perforar [perfo'rar] /1a/ VT to perforate; (*agujero*) to drill, bore; (*papel*) to punch a hole in ▶ VI to drill, bore

perfumar [perfu'mar] /1a/ VT to scent, perfume

perfume [per'fume] NM perfume, scent

perfumería [perfume'ria] NF perfume shop

pergamino [perɣa'mino] NM parchment

pericia [pe'riθja] NF skill, expertise

periferia [peri'ferja] NF periphery; (*de ciudad*) outskirts *pl*

periférico, -a [peri'feriko, a] ADJ peripheral ▶ NM (*Inform*) peripheral; (*Am Auto*) ring road (*Brit*), beltway (*US*); **barrio ~** outlying district

perilla [pe'riʎa] NF (*barba*) goatee; (*Am: de puerta*) doorknob, door handle

perímetro [pe'rimetro] NM perimeter

periódico, -a [pe'rjoðiko, a] ADJ periodic(al) ▶ NM (*news*)paper; **~ dominical** Sunday (*news*)paper

periodismo [perjo'ðismo] NM journalism

periodista [perjo'ðista] NMF journalist

periodístico, -a [perjo'ðistiko, a] ADJ journalistic

periodo [pe'rjoðo], **período** [pe'rioðo] NM period; **~ contable** (*Com*) accounting period

peripecias [peri'peθjas] NFPL adventures

peripuesto, -a [peri'pwesto, a] ADJ dressed up; **tan ~** all dressed up (to the nines)

periquito [peri'kito] NM budgerigar, budgie (*fam*)

perito, -a [pe'rito, a] ADJ (*experto*) expert; (*diestro*) skilled, skilful ▶ NM/F expert; skilled worker; (*técnico*) technician

perjudicar [perxuði'kar] /1g/ VT (*gen*) to damage, harm; (*fig*) to prejudice

perjudicial [perxuði'θjal] ADJ damaging, harmful; (*en detrimento*) detrimental

perjudique *etc* [perxu'ðike] VB *ver* **perjudicar**

perjuicio [per'xwiθjo] NM damage, harm; **en/sin ~ de** to the detriment of/without prejudice to

perjurar [perxu'rar] /1a/ VI to commit perjury

perla ['perla] NF pearl; **me viene de perlas** it suits me fine

permanecer [permane'θer] /2d/ VI (*quedarse*) to stay, remain; (*seguir*) to continue to be

permanencia [perma'nenθja] NF (*duración*) permanence; (*estancia*) stay

permanente [perma'nente] ADJ (*que queda*) permanent; (*constante*) constant; (*comisión etc*) standing ▶ NF perm; **hacerse una ~** to have one's hair permed

permanezca *etc* [perma'neθka] VB *ver* **permanecer**

permisible [permi'siβle] ADJ permissible, allowable

permiso [per'miso] NM permission; (*licencia*) permit, licence (*Brit*), license (*US*); **con ~** excuse me; **estar de ~** (*Mil*) to be on leave; **~ de conducir** o **conductor** driving licence (*Brit*), driver's license (*US*); **~ de exportación/importación** export/import licence; **~ por asuntos familiares** compassionate leave; **~ por enfermedad** (*Am*) sick leave

permitir [permi'tir] /3a/ VT to permit, allow; **permitirse** VR: **permitirse algo** to allow o.s. sth; **no me puedo ~ ese lujo** I can't afford that; **¿me permite?** may I?; **si lo permite el tiempo** weather permitting

permuta [per'muta] NF exchange

permutar [permu'tar] /1a/ VT to switch, exchange; **~ destinos con algn** to swap o exchange jobs with sb

pernera [per'nera] NF trouser leg

pernicioso, -a [perni'θjoso, a] ADJ (*maligno, Med*) pernicious; (*persona*) wicked

perno ['perno] NM bolt

pernoctar [pernok'tar] /1a/ VI to stay for the night

pero ['pero] CONJ but; (*aún*) yet ▶ NM (*defecto*) flaw, defect; (*reparo*) objection; **¡no hay ~ que valga!** there are no buts about it

perogrullada [peroɣru'ʎaða] NF platitude, truism

perol [pe'rol] NM, **perola** [pe'rola] NF pan

peronista [pero'nista] ADJ, NMF Peronist

perorata [pero'rata] NF long-winded speech

perpendicular [perpendiku'lar] ADJ perpendicular; **el camino es ~ al río** the road is at right angles to the river

perpetrar [perpe'trar] /1a/ VT to perpetrate

perpetuamente [perpetwa'mente] ADV perpetually

perpetuar [perpe'twar] /1e/ VT to perpetuate

perpetuo, -a [per'petwo, a] ADJ perpetual; (*Jur etc: condena*) life *cpd*

Perpiñán [perpi'ɲan] NM Perpignan

perplejo, -a [per'plexo, a] ADJ perplexed, bewildered

perra ['perra] NF (Zool) bitch; (fam: dinero) money; (: manía) mania, crazy idea; (: rabieta) tantrum; **estar sin una** ~ to be flat broke

perrera [pe'rrera] NF kennel

perrito [pe'rrito] NM (tb: **perrito caliente**) hot dog

perro ['perro] NM dog; ~ **caliente** hot dog; "~ **peligroso**" "beware of the dog"; **ser ~ viejo** to be an old hand; **tiempo de perros** filthy weather; ~ **que ladra no muerde** his bark is worse than his bite

persa ['persa] ADJ, NMF Persian ▶ NM (Ling) Persian

persecución [perseku'θjon] NF pursuit, hunt, chase; (Rel, Pol) persecution

perseguir [perse'ɣir] /3d, 3k/ VT to pursue, hunt; (cortejar) to chase after; (molestar) to pester, annoy; (Rel, Pol) to persecute; (Jur) to prosecute

perseverante [perseβe'rante] ADJ persevering, persistent

perseverar [perseβe'rar] /1a/ VI to persevere, persist; ~ **en** to persevere in, persist with

persiana [per'sjana] NF (Venetian) blind

persiga etc [per'siɣa] VB ver **perseguir**

persignarse [persiɣ'narse] VR to cross o.s.

persiguiendo etc [persi'ɣjendo] VB ver **perseguir**

persistente [persis'tente] ADJ persistent

persistir [persis'tir] /3a/ VI to persist

persona [per'sona] NF person; **10 personas** 10 people; ~ **mayor** elderly person; **tercera** ~ third party; (Ling) third person; **en** ~ in person o the flesh; **por** ~ a head; **es buena** ~ he's a good sort

personaje [perso'naxe] NM important person, celebrity; (Teat) character

personal [perso'nal] ADJ (particular) personal; (para una persona) single, for one person ▶ NM (plantilla) personnel, staff; (Naut) crew; (fam: gente) people

personalidad [personali'ðað] NF personality; (Jur) status

personalizar [personali'θar] /1f/ VT to personalize ▶ VI (al hablar) to name names

personarse [perso'narse] /1a/ VR to appear in person; ~ **en** to present o.s. at, report to

personero, -a [perso'nero, a] NM/F (Am) (government) official

personificar [personifi'kar] /1g/ VT to personify

personifique etc [personi'fike] VB ver **personificar**

perspectiva [perspek'tiβa] NF perspective; (vista, panorama) view, panorama; (posibilidad futura) outlook, prospect; **tener algo en** ~ to have sth in view

perspicacia [perspi'kaθja] NF discernment, perspicacity

perspicaz [perspi'kaθ] ADJ shrewd

persuadir [perswa'ðir] /3a/ VT (gen) to persuade; (convencer) to convince; **persuadirse** VR to become convinced

persuasión [perswa'sjon] NF (acto) persuasion; (convicción) conviction

persuasivo, -a [perwa'siβo, a] ADJ persuasive; convincing

pertenecer [pertene'θer] /2d/ VI: ~ **a** to belong to; (fig) to concern

perteneciente [pertene'θjente] ADJ: ~ **a** belonging to

pertenencia [perte'nenθja] NF ownership; **pertenencias** NFPL possessions, property sg

pertenezca etc [perte'neθka] VB ver **pertenecer**

pértiga ['pertiɣa] NF pole; **salto de** ~ pole vault

pertinaz [perti'naθ] ADJ (persistente) persistent; (terco) obstinate

pertinente [perti'nente] ADJ relevant, pertinent; (apropiado) appropriate; ~ **a** concerning, relevant to

pertrechar [pertre'tʃar] /1a/ VT (gen) to supply; (Mil) to supply with ammunition and stores; **pertrecharse** VR: **pertrecharse de algo** to provide o.s. with sth

pertrechos [per'tretʃos] NMPL (gen) implements; (Mil) supplies and stores

perturbación [perturβa'θjon] NF (Pol) disturbance; (Med) upset, disturbance; ~ **del orden público** breach of the peace

perturbador, a [perturβa'ðor, a] ADJ (que perturba) perturbing, disturbing; (subversivo) subversive

perturbar [pertur'βar] /1a/ VT (el orden) to disturb; (Med) to upset, disturb; (mentalmente) to perturb

Perú [pe'ru] NM: **el** ~ Peru

peruano, -a [pe'rwano, a] ADJ, NM/F Peruvian

perversión [perβer'sjon] NF perversion

perverso, -a [perβerso, a] ADJ perverse; (depravado) depraved

pervertido, -a [perβer'tiðo, a] ADJ perverted ▶ NM/F pervert

pervertir [perβer'tir] /3i/ VT to pervert, corrupt

pervierta etc [per'βjerta], **pervirtiendo** etc [perβir'tjendo] VB ver **pervertir**

pesa ['pesa] NF weight; (Deporte) shot

pesadez [pesa'ðeθ] NF (calidad de pesado) heaviness; (lentitud) slowness; (aburrimiento) tediousness; **es una** ~ **tener que ...** it's a bind having to ...

pesadilla [pesa'ðiʎa] NF nightmare, bad dream; (fig) worry, obsession

pesado, -a [pe'saðo, a] ADJ (gen) heavy; (lento) slow; (difícil, duro) tough, hard; (aburrido) tedious, boring; (bochornoso) sultry ▶ NM/F bore; **tener el estómago ~** to feel bloated; **¡no seas ~!** come off it!

pesadumbre [pesa'ðumbre] NF grief, sorrow

pésame ['pesame] NM expression of condolence, message of sympathy; **dar el ~** to express one's condolences

pesar [pe'sar] /1a/ VT to weigh; (fig) to weigh heavily on; (afligir) to grieve ▶ VI to weigh; (ser pesado) to weigh a lot, be heavy; (fig: opinión) to carry weight ▶ NM (sentimiento) regret; (pena) grief, sorrow; **no pesa mucho** it's not very heavy; **a ~ de (que)** in spite of, despite; **no me pesa haberlo hecho** I'm not sorry I did it

pesca ['peska] NF (acto) fishing; (cantidad de pescado) catch; **~ de altura/en bajura** deep sea/coastal fishing; **ir de ~** to go fishing

pescadería [peskaðe'ria] NF fish shop, fishmonger's

pescadilla [peska'ðiʎa] NF whiting

pescado [pes'kaðo] NM fish

pescador, a [peska'ðor, a] NM/F fisherman(-woman)

pescar [pes'kar] /1g/ VT (coger) to catch; (tratar de coger) to fish for; (fam: lograr) to get hold of, land; (conseguir: trabajo) to manage to get; (sorprender) to catch unawares ▶ VI to fish, go fishing

pescuezo [pes'kweθo] NM neck

pese ['pese] PREP: **~ a** despite, in spite of

pesebre [pe'seβre] NM manger

peseta [pe'seta] NF peseta

pesetero, -a [pese'tero, a] ADJ money-grubbing

pesimismo [pesi'mismo] NM pessimism

pesimista [pesi'mista] ADJ pessimistic ▶ NM/F pessimist

pésimo, -a ['pesimo, a] ADJ awful, dreadful

peso ['peso] NM weight; (balanza) scales pl; (AM Com) monetary unit; (moneda) peso; (Deporte) shot; **~ bruto/neto** gross/net weight; **~ mosca/pesado** fly-/heavyweight; **de poco ~** light(weight); **levantamiento de pesos** weightlifting; **vender a ~** to sell by weight; **argumento de ~** weighty argument; **eso cae por su propio ~** that goes without saying

pesque etc ['peske] VB ver **pescar**

pesquero, -a [pes'kero, a] ADJ fishing cpd

pesquisa [pes'kisa] NF inquiry, investigation

pestaña [pes'taɲa] NF (Anat) eyelash; (borde) rim

pestañear [pestaɲe'ar] /1a/ VI to blink

peste ['peste] NF plague; (fig) nuisance; (mal olor) stink, stench; **~ negra** Black Death; **echar pestes de algn** to slag sb off (fam)

pesticida [pesti'θiða] NM pesticide

pestilencia [pesti'lenθja] NF (mal olor) stink, stench

pestillo [pes'tiʎo] NM bolt, latch; (cerrojo) catch; (picaporte) (door) handle

petaca [pe'taka] NF (de cigarrillos) cigarette case; (de pipa) tobacco pouch; (AM: maleta) suitcase

pétalo ['petalo] NM petal

petanca [pe'tanka] NF a game in which metal bowls are thrown at a target bowl

petardo [pe'tarðo] NM firework, firecracker

petición [peti'θjon] NF (pedido) request, plea; (memorial) petition; (Jur) plea; **a ~ de** at the request of; **~ de aumento de salarios** wage demand o claim

petirrojo [peti'rroxo] NM robin

peto ['peto] NM dungarees pl, overalls pl (US); (corpiño) bodice; (Taur) horse's padding

pétreo, -a ['petreo, a] ADJ stony, rocky

petrificar [petrifi'kar] /1g/ VT to petrify

petrifique etc [petri'fike] VB ver **petrificar**

petrodólar [petro'ðolar] NM petrodollar

petróleo [pe'troleo] NM oil, petroleum

petrolero, -a [petro'lero, a] ADJ petroleum cpd ▶ NM (Com) oil man; (buque) (oil) tanker

PETROVEN [petro'ben] NM ABR = **Petróleos de Venezuela**

petulancia [petu'lanθja] NF (insolencia) vanity, opinionated nature

peyorativo, -a [pejora'tiβo, a] ADJ pejorative

pez [peθ] NM fish; **~ de colores** goldfish; **~ espada** swordfish; **estar como el ~ en el agua** to feel completely at home

pezón [pe'θon] NM teat, nipple

pezuña [pe'θuɲa] NF hoof

Photoshop® [foto'sop] NM Photoshop®

piadoso, -a [pja'ðoso, a] ADJ (devoto) pious, devout; (misericordioso) kind, merciful

Piamonte [pja'monte] NM Piedmont

pianista [pja'nista] NMF pianist

piano ['pjano] NM piano; **~ de cola** grand piano

piar [pjar] /1c/ VI to cheep

piara ['pjara] NF (manada) herd, drove

PIB NM ABR (ESP Com: = Producto Interior Bruto) GDP

pibe, -a ['piβe, a] NM/F (AM) boy (girl), kid, child

pica ['pika] NF (Mil) pike; (Taur) goad; **poner una ~ en Flandes** to bring off something difficult

picadero [pika'ðero] NM riding school

picadillo [pika'ðiʎo] NM mince, minced meat

picado, -a [pi'kaðo, a] ADJ pricked, punctured; (Culin) minced, chopped; (mar) choppy; (diente) bad; (tabaco) cut; (enfadado) cross

picador [pika'ðor] NM (*Taur*) picador; (*minero*) faceworker

picadora [pika'ðora] NF mincer

picadura [pika'ðura] NF (*pinchazo*) puncture; (*de abeja*) sting; (*de mosquito*) bite; (*tabaco picado*) cut tobacco

picana [pi'kana] (*AM*) NF (*Agr*) cattle prod; (*Pol: para tortura*) electric prod

picante [pi'kante] ADJ (*comida, sabor*) hot; (*comentario*) racy, spicy

picaporte [pika'porte] NM (*tirador*) handle; (*pestillo*) latch

picar [pi'kar] /**1g**/ VT (*agujerear, perforar*) to prick, puncture; (*billete*) to punch, clip; (*abeja*) to sting; (*mosquito, serpiente*) to bite; (*Culin*) to mince, chop; (*persona*) to nibble (at); (*incitar*) to incite, goad; (*dañar, irritar*) to annoy, bother; (*quemar: lengua*) to burn, sting ▶ VI (*pez*) to bite, take the bait; (*el sol*) to burn, scorch; (*abeja, Med*) to sting; (*mosquito*) to bite; **picarse** VR (*agriarse*) to turn sour, go off; (*mar*) to get choppy; (*ofenderse*) to take offence; **me pican los ojos** my eyes sting; **me pica el brazo** my arm itches

picardía [pikar'ðia] NF villainy; (*astucia*) slyness, craftiness; (*una picardía*) dirty trick; (*palabra*) rude/bad word o expression

picaresco, -a [pika'resko, a] ADJ (*travieso*) roguish, rascally; (*Lit*) picaresque

pícaro, -a ['pikaro, a] ADJ (*malicioso*) villainous; (*travieso*) mischievous ▶ NM (*astuto*) sly sort; (*sinvergüenza*) rascal, scoundrel

picazón [pika'θon] NF (*comezón*) itch; (*ardor*) sting(ing feeling); (*remordimiento*) pang of conscience

pichi ['pitʃi] NM (*ESP*) pinafore dress (*BRIT*), jumper (*US*)

pichón, -ona [pi'tʃon, ona] NM (*de paloma*) young pigeon ▶ NM/F (*apelativo*) darling, dearest

pico ['piko] NM (*de ave*) beak; (*punta aguda*) peak, sharp point; (*Tec*) pick, pickaxe; (*Geo*) peak, summit; (*labia*) talkativeness; **no abrir el ~** to keep quiet; **~ parásito** (*Elec*) spike; **y ~** and a bit; **las seis y ~** six and a bit; **son las tres y ~** it's just after three; **tiene 50 libros y ~** he has 50-odd books; **me costó un ~** it cost me quite a bit

picor [pi'kor] NM itch; (*ardor*) sting(ing feeling)

picoso, -a [pi'koso, a] (*AM*) ADJ (*comida*) hot

picota [pi'kota] NF pillory; **poner a algn en la ~** (*fig*) to ridicule sb

picotada [piko'taða] NF, **picotazo** [piko'taθo] NM (*de pájaro*) peck; (*de insecto*) sting, bite

picotear [pikote'ar] /**1a**/ VT to peck ▶ VI to nibble, pick

pictórico, -a [pik'toriko, a] ADJ pictorial; **tiene dotes pictóricas** she has a talent for painting

picudo, -a [pi'kuðo, a] ADJ pointed, with a point

pidiendo *etc* [pi'ðjendo] VB *ver* **pedir**

pidió *etc* VB *ver* **pedir**

pido *etc* VB *ver* **pedir**

pie [pje] (*pl* **pies**) NM (*gen, Mat*) foot; (*de cama, página, escalera*) foot, bottom; (*Teat*) cue; (*fig: motivo*) motive, basis; (: *fundamento*) foothold; **pies planos** flat feet; **ir a ~** to go on foot, walk; **estar de ~** to be standing (up); **ponerse de ~** to stand up; **al ~ de la letra** (*citar*) literally, verbatim; (*copiar*) exactly, word for word; **de pies a cabeza** from head to foot; **en ~ de guerra** on a war footing; **sin pies ni cabeza** pointless, absurd; **dar ~ a** to give cause for; **hacer ~** (*en el agua*) to touch (the) bottom; **no dar ~ con bola** to be no good at anything; **saber de qué ~ cojea algn** to know sb's weak spots

piedad [pje'ðað] NF (*lástima*) pity, compassion; (*clemencia*) mercy; (*devoción*) piety, devotion; **tener ~ de** to take pity on

piedra ['pjeðra] NF stone; (*roca*) rock; (*de mechero*) flint; (*Meteorología*) hailstone; **primera ~** foundation stone; **~ de afilar** grindstone; **~ arenisca/caliza** sand-/limestone; **~ preciosa** precious stone

piel [pjel] NF (*Anat*) skin; (*Zool*) skin, hide; (*de oso*) fur; (*cuero*) leather; (*Bot*) skin, peel ▶ NMF: **~ roja** redskin

pienso *etc* ['pjenso] VB *ver* **pensar** ▶ NM (*Agr*) feed

piercing ['pjersiŋ] NM piercing

pierdo *etc* ['pjerðo] VB *ver* **perder**

pierna ['pjerna] NF leg; **en piernas** bare-legged

pieza ['pjeθa] NF piece; (*esp AM: habitación*) room; (*Mus*) piece, composition; (*Teat*) work, play; **~ de recambio** o **repuesto** spare (part), extra (*US*); **~ de ropa** article of clothing; **quedarse de una ~** to be dumbfounded

pigmento [piɣ'mento] NM pigment

pigmeo, -a [piɣ'meo, a] ADJ, NM/F pigmy

pijama [pi'xama] NM pyjamas *pl*

pijo, -a ['pixo, a] NM/F (*fam*) upper-class twit

pijotada [pixo'taða] NF nuisance

pila ['pila] NF (*Elec*) battery; (*montón*) heap, pile; (*de fuente*) sink; (*Rel: tb:* **pila bautismal**) font; **nombre de ~** Christian o first name; **tengo una ~ de cosas que hacer** (*fam*) I have heaps o stacks of things to do

pilar [pi'lar] NM pillar; (*de puente*) pier; (*fig*) prop, mainstay

píldora ['pildora] NF pill; **la ~ (anticonceptiva)** the pill; **tragarse la ~** to be taken in

pileta [pi'leta] NF basin, bowl; (AM: *de cocina*) sink; (: *piscina*) swimming pool

pillaje [pi'ʎaxe] NM pillage, plunder

pillar [pi'ʎar] /1a/ VT (*saquear*) to pillage, plunder; (*fam: coger*) to catch; (: *agarrar*) to grasp, seize; (: *entender*) to grasp, catch on to; (*suj: coche etc*) to run over; **pillarse** VR: **pillarse un dedo con la puerta** to catch one's finger in the door; ~ **un resfriado** (*fam*) to catch a cold

pillo, -a ['piʎo, a] ADJ villainous; (*astuto*) sly, crafty ▶ NM/F rascal, rogue, scoundrel

pilón [pi'lon] NM pillar, post; (*Elec*) pylon; (*bebedero*) drinking trough; (*de fuente*) basin

pilotar [pilo'tar] /1a/ VT (*avión*) to pilot; (*barco*) to steer

piloto [pi'loto] NM pilot; (*de aparato*) (pilot) light; (*Auto*) rear light, tail light; (*conductor*) driver ▶ ADJ INV: **planta** ~ pilot plant; **luz** ~ side light; ~ **automático** automatic pilot

piltrafa [pil'trafa] NF (*carne*) poor quality meat; (*fig*) worthless object; (: *individuo*) wretch

pimentón [pimen'ton] NM (*polvo*) paprika

pimienta [pi'mjenta] NF pepper

pimiento [pi'mjento] NM pepper, pimiento

pimpante [pim'pante] ADJ (*encantador*) charming; (*tb*: **tan pimpante**) smug, self-satisfied

PIN NM ABR (*Esp Com: = Producto Interior Neto*) net domestic product

pin [pin] (*pl* **pins** [pins]) NM badge

pinacoteca [pinako'teka] NF art gallery

pinar [pi'nar] NM pinewood

pincel [pin'θel] NM paintbrush

pincelada [pinθe'laða] NF brushstroke; **última** ~ (*fig*) finishing touch

pinchadiscos [pintʃa'diskos] NMF disc jockey, DJ

pinchar [pin'tʃar] /1a/ VT (*perforar*) to prick, pierce; (*neumático*) to puncture; (*incitar*) to prod; (*Inform*) to click ▶ VI (*Mus: fam*) to be DJ; **pincharse** VR (*con droga*) to inject o.s.; (*neumático*) to burst, puncture; **no ~ ni cortar** (*fam*) to cut no ice; **tener un neumático pinchado** to have a puncture *o* a flat tyre

pinchazo [pin'tʃaθo] NM (*perforación*) prick; (*de llanta*) puncture, flat (US); (*fig*) prod

pinche ['pintʃe] NM (*de cocina*) kitchen boy, scullion

pinchito [pin'tʃito] NM shish kebab

pincho ['pintʃo] NM point; (*aguijón*) spike; (*Culin*) savoury (snack); (*Inform*) dongle; ~ **moruno** shish kebab; ~ **de tortilla** small slice of omelette

ping-pong ['pimpon] NM table tennis

pingüe ['pingwe] ADJ (*cosecha*) bumper *cpd*; (*negocio*) lucrative

pingüino [pin'gwino] NM penguin

pinitos [pi'nitos] NMPL: **hacer sus primeros** ~ to take one's first steps

pino ['pino] NM pine (tree); **vivir en el quinto** ~ to live at the back of beyond

pinta ['pinta] NF spot; (*gota*) spot, drop; (*aspecto*) appearance, look(s) *pl*; (*medida*) pint; **tener buena** ~ to look good, look well; **por la** ~ by the look of it

pintado, -a [pin'taðo, a] ADJ spotted; (*de muchos colores*) colourful ▶ NF piece of political graffiti; **pintadas** NFPL political graffiti *sg*; **me sienta que ni** ~, **me viene que ni** ~ it suits me a treat

pintalabios [pinta'laβjos] NM INV (*Esp*) lipstick

pintar [pin'tar] /1a/ VT to paint ▶ VI to paint; (*fam*) to count, be important; **pintarse** VR to put on make-up; **pintárselas solo para hacer algo** to manage to do sth by o.s.; **no pinta nada** (*fam*) he has no say

pintor, a [pin'tor, a] NM/F painter; ~ **de brocha gorda** house painter; (*fig*) bad painter

pintoresco, -a [pinto'resko, a] ADJ picturesque

pintura [pin'tura] NF painting; ~ **a la acuarela** watercolour; ~ **al óleo** oil painting; ~ **rupestre** cave painting

pinza ['pinθa] NF (*Zool*) claw; (*para colgar ropa*) clothes peg, clothespin (US); (*Tec*) pincers *pl*; **pinzas** NFPL (*para depilar*) tweezers

piña ['piɲa] NF (*fruto del pino*) pine cone; (*fruta*) pineapple; (*fig*) group

piñata [pi'ɲata] NF piñata (*figurine hung up at parties to be beaten with sticks until sweets or presents fall out*)

piñón [pi'ɲon] NM (*Bot*) pine nut; (*Tec*) pinion

pío, -a ['pio, a] ADJ (*devoto*) pious, devout; (*misericordioso*) merciful ▶ NM: **no decir ni** ~ not to breathe a word

piojo ['pjoxo] NM louse

piojoso, -a [pjo'xoso, a] ADJ lousy; (*sucio*) dirty

piolet [pjo'le] (*pl* **piolets**) NM ice axe

pionero, -a [pjo'nero, a] ADJ pioneering ▶ NM/F pioneer

pipa ['pipa] NF pipe; (*Bot*) seed, pip; (*de girasol*) sunflower seed

pipí [pi'pi] NM (*fam*): **hacer** ~ to have a wee(-wee)

pipiolo [pi'pjolo] NM youngster; (*novato*) novice, greenhorn

pique ['pike] VB *ver* picar ▶ NM (*resentimiento*) pique, resentment; (*rivalidad*) rivalry, competition; **irse a** ~ to sink; (*familia*) to be ruined; **tener un** ~ **con algn** to have a grudge against sb

piqueta [pi'keta] NF pick(axe)

piquete [pi'kete] NM (*agujerito*) small hole; (*Mil*) squad, party; (*de obreros*) picket; (*AM: de insecto*) bite; ~ **secundario** secondary picket

pirado, -a [pi'raðo, a] ADJ (fam) round the bend ▸ NM/F nutter

piragua [pi'raɣwa] NF canoe

piragüismo [pira'ɣwismo] NM (Deporte) canoeing

pirámide [pi'ramiðe] NF pyramid

piraña [pi'raɲa] NF piranha

pirarse [pi'rarse] /1a/ VR (tb: **pirárselas**: largarse) to beat it (fam); (: Escol) to cut class

pirata [pi'rata] ADJ: **edición/disco ~** pirate edition/bootleg record ▸ NM pirate; (tb: **pirata informático**) hacker

pirenaico, -a [pire'naiko, a] ADJ Pyrenean

Pirineo(s) [piri'neo(s)] NM(PL) Pyrenees pl

pirómano, -a [pi'romano, a] NM/F (Psico) pyromaniac; (Jur) arsonist

piropo [pi'ropo] NM compliment, (piece of) flattery; **echar piropos a** to make flirtatious remarks to

pirueta [pi'rweta] NF pirouette

piruleta [piru'leta] NF lollipop

pirulí [piru'li] NM lollipop

pis [pis] NM (fam) pee; **hacer ~** to have a pee; (para niños) to wee-wee

pisada [pi'saða] NF (paso) footstep; (huella) footprint

pisar [pi'sar] /1a/ VT (caminar sobre) to walk on, tread on; (apretar con el pie) to press; (fig) to trample on, walk all over ▸ VI to tread, step, walk; **~ el acelerador** to step on the accelerator; **~ fuerte** (fig) to act determinedly

piscifactoría [pisθifakto'ria] NF fish farm

piscina [pis'θina] NF swimming pool; **~ de bolas** ball pool, ball pit

Piscis [pis'θis] NM (Astro) Pisces

piso [piso] NM (suelo: de edificio) floor; (Am) ground; (apartamento) flat, apartment; **primer ~** (Esp) first o second (US) floor; (Am) ground o first (US) floor

pisotear [pisote'ar] /1a/ VT to trample (on o underfoot); (fig: humillar) to trample on

pisotón [piso'ton] NM (con el pie) stamp

pista [pista] NF track, trail; (indicio) clue; (Inform) track; **~ de auditoría** (Com) audit trail; **~ de aterrizaje** runway; **~ de baile** dance floor; **~ de tenis** tennis court; **~ de hielo** ice rink; **estar sobre la ~ de algn** to be on sb's trail

pisto [pisto] NM (Culin) ratatouille; **darse ~** (fam) to show off

pistola [pis'tola] NF pistol; (Tec) spray-gun

pistolero, -a [pisto'lero, a] NM/F gunman, gangster ▸ NF holster

pistón [pis'ton] NM (Tec) piston; (Mus) key

pitar [pi'tar] /1a/ VT (hacer sonar) to blow; (partido) to referee; (rechiflar) to whistle at, boo; (actor, obra) to hiss ▸ VI to whistle; (Auto) to sound o toot one's horn; (Am) to smoke; **salir pitando** to beat it

pitido [pi'tiðo] NM whistle; (sonido agudo) beep; (sonido corto) pip

pitillera [piti'ʎera] NF cigarette case

pitillo [pi'tiʎo] NM cigarette

pito [pito] NM whistle; (de coche) horn; (cigarrillo) cigarette; (fam: de marihuana) joint; (fam!) prick (fam!); **me importa un ~** I don't care two hoots

pitón [pi'ton] NM (Zool) python

pitonisa [pito'nisa] NF fortune-teller

pitorrearse [pitorre'arse] /1a/ VR: **~ de** to scoff at, make fun of

pitorreo [pito'rreo] NM joke, laugh; **estar de ~** to be in a joking mood

píxel [piksel] NM (Inform) pixel

piyama [pi'jama] NM (Am) pyjamas pl, pajamas pl (US)

pizarra [pi'θarra] NF (piedra) slate; (encerado) blackboard; **~ blanca** whiteboard; **~ interactiva** interactive whiteboard

pizarrón [piθa'rron] NM (Am) blackboard

pizca [piθka] NF pinch, spot; (fig) spot, speck, trace; **ni ~** not a bit

pizza [pitsa] NF pizza

placa [plaka] NF plate; (Med) dental plate; (distintivo) badge; **~ de matrícula** number plate; **~ madre** (Inform) mother board

placaje [pla'kaxe] NM tackle

placard [pla'kar] NM (Am) built-in cupboard, (clothes) closet (US)

placenta [pla'θenta] NF placenta; (tras el parto) afterbirth

placentero, -a [plaθen'tero, a] ADJ pleasant, agreeable

placer [pla'θer] /2w/ NM pleasure ▸ VT to please; **a ~** at one's pleasure

plácido, -a [plaθiðo, a] ADJ placid

plafón [pla'fon] NM (Am) ceiling

plaga [plaɣa] NF (Zool) pest; (Med) plague; (fig) swarm; (: abundancia) abundance

plagar [pla'ɣar] /1h/ VT to infest, plague; (llenar) to fill; **plagado de** riddled with; **han plagado la ciudad de carteles** they have plastered the town with posters

plagiar [pla'gjar] /1b/ VT to plagiarize; (Am) to kidnap

plagiario, -a [pla'gjario, a] NM/F plagiarist; (Am) kidnapper

plagio [plaxjo] NM plagiarism; (Am) kidnap

plague etc [plaɣe] VB ver **plagar**

plan [plan] NM (esquema, proyecto) plan; (idea, intento) idea, intention; (de curso) programme; **~ cotizable de jubilación** contributory pension scheme; **~ de estudios** curriculum, syllabus; **~ de incentivos** (Com) incentive scheme; **tener ~** (fam) to have a date; **tener un ~** (fam) to have an affair; **en ~ de cachondeo** for a laugh; **en ~ económico** (fam) on the cheap; **vamos en**

p

~ de turismo we're going as tourists; **si te pones en ese ~ ...** if that's your attitude ...

plana ['plana] NF ver **plano**

plancha ['plantʃa] NF (*para planchar*) iron; (*rótulo*) plate, sheet; (*Naut*) gangway; (*Culin*) grill; **pescado a la ~** grilled fish; **~ de pelo** straighteners; **a la ~** (*Culin*) grilled

planchado, -a [plan'tʃaðo, a] ADJ (*ropa*) ironed; (*traje*) pressed ▶ NM ironing

planchar [plan'tʃar] /**1a**/ VT to iron ▶ VI to do the ironing

planeador [planea'ðor] NM glider

planear [plane'ar] /**1a**/ VT to plan ▶ VI to glide

planeta [pla'neta] NM planet

planetario, -a [plane'tarjo, a] ADJ planetary ▶ NM planetarium

planicie [pla'niθje] NF plain

planificación [planifika'θjon] NF planning; **~ corporativa** (*Com*) corporate planning; **~ familiar** family planning; **diagrama de ~** (*Com*) planner

planilla [pla'niʎa] NF (*Am*) form

plano, -a ['plano, a] ADJ flat, level, even; (*liso*) smooth ▶ NM (*Mat, Tec, Aviat*) plane; (*Foto*) shot; (*Arq*) plan; (*Geo*) map; (*de ciudad*) map, street plan ▶ NF sheet of paper, page; (*Tec*) trowel; **primer ~** close-up; **caer de ~** to fall flat; **rechazar algo de ~** to turn sth down flat; **le daba el sol de ~** (*fig*) the sun shone directly on it; **en primera plana** on the front page; **plana mayor** staff

planta ['planta] NF (*Bot, Tec*) plant; (*Anat*) sole of the foot, foot; (*piso*) floor; (*Am: personal*) staff; **~ baja** ground floor

plantación [planta'θjon] NF (*Agr*) plantation; (*acto*) planting

plantar [plan'tar] /**1a**/ VT (*Bot*) to plant; (*puesto*) to put in; (*levantar*) to erect, set up; **plantarse** VR to stand firm; **~ a algn en la calle** to chuck sb out; **dejar plantado a algn** (*fam*) to stand sb up; **plantarse en** to reach, get to

plantear [plante'ar] /**1a**/ VT (*problema*) to pose; (*dificultad*) to raise; **se lo plantearé** I'll put it to him

plantel [plan'tel] NM (*fig*) group, set

plantilla [plan'tiʎa] NF (*de zapato*) insole; (*personal*) personnel; **ser de ~** to be on the staff

plantío [plan'tio] NM (*acto*) planting; (*lugar*) plot, bed, patch

plantón [plan'ton] NM (*Mil*) guard, sentry; (*fam*) long wait; **dar (un) ~ a algn** to stand sb up

plañir [pla'ɲir] /**3h**/ VI to mourn

plasma ['plasma] NM plasma

plasmar [plas'mar] /**1a**/ VT (*dar forma*) to mould, shape; (*representar*) to represent ▶ VI: **~ en** to take the form of

plasta ['plasta] NF soft mass, lump; (*desastre*) botch, mess ▶ NMF (*Esp fam*) bore ▶ ADJ (*Esp fam*) boring

plasticidad [plastiθi'ðað] NF (*fig*) expressiveness

plástico, -a ['plastiko, a] ADJ plastic ▶ NF (art of) sculpture, modelling ▶ NM plastic

plastificar [plastifi'kar] /**1g**/ VT (*documento*) to laminate

plastifique etc [plasti'fike] VB ver **plastificar**

Plastilina® [plasti'lina] NF Plasticine®

plata ['plata] NF (*metal*) silver; (*cosas hechas de plata*) silverware; (*Am*) cash, dough (*fam*); **hablar en ~** to speak bluntly o frankly

plataforma [plata'forma] NF platform; **~ de lanzamiento/perforación** launch(ing) pad/drilling rig

plátano ['platano] NM (*fruta*) banana; (*árbol*) plane tree; banana tree

platea [pla'tea] NF (*Teat*) pit

plateado, -a [plate'aðo, a] ADJ silver; (*Tec*) silver-plated

platense [pla'tense] (*fam*) = **rioplatense**

plática ['platika] NF (*Am*) talk, chat; (*Rel*) sermon

platicar [plati'kar] /**1g**/ VI (*Am*) to talk, chat

platillo [pla'tiʎo] NM saucer; (*de limosnas*) collecting bowl; **platillos** NMPL cymbals; **~ volador** o **volante** flying saucer; **pasar el ~** to pass the hat round

platina [pla'tina] NF (*Mus*) tape deck

platino [pla'tino] NM platinum; **platinos** NMPL (*Auto*) (contact) points

platique etc [pla'tike] VB ver **platicar**

plato ['plato] NM plate, dish; (*parte de comida*) course; (*guiso*) dish; **~ frutero/sopero** fruit/ soup dish; **primer ~** first course; **~ combinado** set main course (*served on one plate*); **~ fuerte** main course; **pagar los platos rotos** (*fam*) to carry the can (*fam*)

plató [pla'to] NM set

platónico, -a [pla'toniko, a] ADJ platonic

playa ['plaja] NF beach; (*costa*) seaside; **~ de estacionamiento** (*Am*) car park

playero, -a [pla'jero, a] ADJ beach *cpd* ▶ NF (*Am: camiseta*) T-shirt; **playeras** NFPL canvas shoes; (*Tenis*) tennis shoes

plaza ['plaθa] NF square; (*mercado*) market(place); (*sitio*) room, space; (*en vehículo*) seat, place; (*colocación*) post, job; **~ de abastos** food market; **~ mayor** main square; **~ de toros** bullring; **hacer la ~** to do the daily shopping; **reservar una ~** to reserve a seat; **el hotel tiene 100 plazas** the hotel has 100 beds

plazca etc ['plaθka] VB ver **placer**

plazo ['plaθo] NM (*lapso de tiempo*) time, period, term; (*fecha de vencimiento*) expiry date; (*pago parcial*) instalment; **a corto/**

largo ~ short-/long-term; **comprar a plazos** to buy on hire purchase, pay for in instalments; **nos dan un ~ de ocho días** they allow us a week

plazoleta [plaθo'leta], **plazuela** [pla'θwela] NF small square

pleamar [plea'mar] NF high tide

plebe ['pleβe] NF: **la ~** the common people *pl*, the masses *pl*; *(pey)* the plebs *pl*

plebeyo, -a [ple'βejo, a] ADJ plebeian; *(pey)* coarse, common

plebiscito [pleβis'θito] NM plebiscite

pleca ['pleka] NF *(Inform)* backslash

plegable [ple'ɣaβle] ADJ pliable; *(silla)* folding

plegar [ple'ɣar] /**1h, 1j**/ VT *(doblar)* to fold, bend; *(Costura)* to pleat; **plegarse** VR to yield, submit

plegaria [ple'ɣarja] NF *(oración)* prayer

plegué [ple'ɣe], **pleguemos** *etc* [ple'ɣemos] VB *ver* **plegar**

pleitear [pleite'ar] /**1a**/ VI *(Jur)* to plead, conduct a lawsuit; *(litigar)* to go to law

pleito ['pleito] NM *(Jur)* lawsuit, case; *(fig)* dispute, feud; **pleitos** NMPL litigation *sg*; **entablar ~** to bring an action *o* a lawsuit; **poner ~** to sue

plenario, -a [ple'narjo, a] ADJ plenary, full

plenilunio [pleni'lunjo] NM full moon

plenitud [pleni'tuð] NF plenitude, fullness; *(abundancia)* abundance

pleno, -a ['pleno, a] ADJ full; *(completo)* complete ▶ NM plenum; **en ~** as a whole; *(por unanimidad)* unanimously; **en ~ día** in broad daylight; **en ~ verano** at the height of summer; **en plena cara** full in the face

pletina NF *(Mus)* tape deck

pleuresía [pleure'sia] NF pleurisy

plexiglás [pleksi'ɣlas] NM acrylic

pliego ['pljeɣo] VB *ver* **plegar** ▶ NM *(hoja)* sheet (of paper); *(carta)* sealed letter/document; **~ de condiciones** details *pl*, specifications *pl*

pliegue ['pljeɣe] VB *ver* **plegar** ▶ NM fold, crease; *(de vestido)* pleat

plisado [pli'saðo] NM pleating

plomería [plome'ria] NF *(Am)* plumbing

plomero, -a [plo'mero, a] NM/F *(Am)* plumber

plomizo, -a [plo'miθo, a] ADJ leaden, lead-coloured

plomo ['plomo] NM *(metal)* lead; *(Elec)* fuse; **sin ~** unleaded; **caer a ~** to fall heavily *o* flat

pluma ['pluma] NF *(Zool)* feather; *(para escribir)*: **~ (estilográfica)** ink pen; **~ fuente** *(Am)* fountain pen

plumazo [plu'maθo] NM *(lit, fig)* stroke of the pen

plumero [plu'mero] NM *(quitapolvos)* feather duster; **ya te veo el ~** I know what you're up to

plumón [plu'mon] NM *(de ave)* down; *(Am)* felt-tip pen

plural [plu'ral] ADJ plural ▶ NM: **en ~** in the plural

pluralidad [plurali'ðað] NF plurality; **una ~ de votos** a majority of votes

pluriempleo [pluriem'pleo] NM having more than one job

plus [plus] NM bonus

plusmarquista [plusmar'kista] NMF *(Deporte)* record holder

plusvalía [plusβa'lia] NF *(mayor valor)* appreciation, added value; *(Com)* goodwill

plutocracia [pluto'kraθja] NF plutocracy

PM NF ABR *(Mil: = Policía Militar)* MP

p.m. ABR *(= post meridiem)* p.m.; *(= por minuto)* per minute

PMA NM ABR *(= Programa Mundial de Alimentos)* World Food Programme

P.M.A. NM ABR = **peso máximo autorizado**

pmo. ABR *(= próximo)* prox.

PN NF ABR *(Mil: = Policía Naval)* Naval Police

PNB NM ABR *(Esp Com: = Producto Nacional Bruto)* GNP

P.N.D. NM ABR *(Escol: = personal no docente)* non-teaching staff

PNN [pe'nene] NMF *(= profesor(a) no numerario(-a))* untenured teacher ▶ NM ABR *(Esp Com: = Producto Nacional Neto)* net national product

PNUD NM ABR *(= Programa de las Naciones Unidas para el Desarrollo)* United Nations Development Programme

PNV NM ABR *(Esp Pol)* = **Partido Nacionalista Vasco**

P.° ABR *(= Paseo)* Av(e).

p.o. ABR = **por orden**

población [poβla'θjon] NF population; *(pueblo, ciudad)* town, city; **~ activa** working population

poblado, -a [po'βlaðo, a] ADJ inhabited; *(barba)* thick; *(cejas)* bushy ▶ NM *(aldea)* village; *(pueblo)* (small) town; **~ de** *(lleno de)* filled with; **densamente ~** densely populated

poblador, a [poβla'ðor, a] NM/F settler, colonist

poblar [po'βlar] /**1l**/ VT *(colonizar)* to colonize; *(fundar)* to found; *(habitar)* to inhabit; **poblarse** VR: **poblarse de** to fill up with; *(irse cubriendo)* to become covered with

pobre ['poβre] ADJ poor ▶ NMF poor person; *(mendigo)* beggar; **los pobres** the poor; **¡~!** poor thing!; **~ diablo** *(fig)* poor wretch *o* devil

pobreza [po'βreθa] NF poverty; **~ energética** fuel poverty

pocho, -a ['potʃo, a] ADJ *(flor, color)* faded, discoloured; *(persona)* pale; *(fruta)* overripe; *(deprimido)* depressed

pocilga [po'θilɣa] NF pigsty
pocillo [po'siʎo] NM (AM) coffee cup
pócima ['poθima], **poción** [po'θjon] NF
  potion; (brebaje) concoction, nasty drink

(PALABRA CLAVE)

poco, -a ['poko, a] ADJ **1** (sg) little, not much;
  poco tiempo little o not much time; **de
  poco interés** of little interest, not very
  interesting; **poca cosa** not much
  2 (pl) few, not many; **unos pocos** a few,
  some; **pocos niños comen lo que les
  conviene** few children eat what they should
  ▶ ADV **1** little, not much; **cuesta poco** it
  doesn't cost much; **poco más o menos**
  more or less
  2 (+ adj: negativo, antónimo): **poco amable/
  inteligente** not very nice/intelligent
  3: **por poco me caigo** I almost fell
  4 (tiempo): **poco después** soon after that;
  dentro de poco shortly; **hace poco** a short
  time ago, not long ago; **a poco de haberse
  casado** shortly after getting married
  5: **poco a poco** little by little
  6 (AM): **¿a poco no está divino?** isn't it just
  divine?; **de a poco** gradually
  ▶ NM a little, a bit; **un poco triste/de
  dinero** a little sad/money

poda ['poða] NF (acto) pruning; (temporada)
  pruning season
podar [po'ðar] /1a/ VT to prune
podcast ['poðkast] NM podcast
podcastear [poðkaste'ar] /1a/ VI to podcast
podenco [po'ðenko] NM hound

(PALABRA CLAVE)

poder [po'ðer] /2s/ VI **1** (capacidad) can, be able
  to; **no puedo hacerlo** I can't do it, I'm
  unable to do it
  2 (permiso) can, may, be allowed to; **¿se puede?**
  may I (o we)?; **puedes irte ahora** you may go
  now; **no se puede fumar en este hospital**
  smoking is not allowed in this hospital
  3 (posibilidad) may, might, could; **puede
  llegar mañana** he may o might arrive
  tomorrow; **pudiste haberte hecho daño**
  you might o could have hurt yourself;
  ¡podías habérmelo dicho antes! you might
  have told me before!
  4: **puede (ser)** perhaps; **puede que lo sepa
  Tomás** Tomás may o might know
  5: **¡no puedo más!** I've had enough!; **no
  pude menos que dejarlo** I couldn't help but
  leave it; **es tonto a más no poder** he's as
  stupid as they come
  6: **poder con**: **no puedo con este crío** this
  kid's too much for me; **¿puedes con eso?**
  can you manage that?

7: **él me puede** (fam) he's stronger than me
  ▶ NM power; **el poder** the Government;
  poder adquisitivo purchasing power;
  detentar u **ocupar** o **estar en el poder** to be
  in power o office; **estar** u **obrar en poder de**
  to be in the hands o possession of; **por
  poder(es)** by proxy; **poder judicial**
  judiciary

poderío [poðe'rio] NM power; (autoridad)
  authority
poderoso, -a [poðe'roso, a] ADJ powerful
podio ['poðjo] NM podium
pódium ['poðjum] = **podio**
podólogo, -a [po'ðoloɣo, a] NM/F chiropodist
  (BRIT), podiatrist (US)
podré etc [po'ðre] VB ver **poder**
podrido, -a [po'ðriðo, a] ADJ rotten, bad; (fig)
  rotten, corrupt
podrir [po'ðrir] = **pudrir**
poema [po'ema] NM poem
poesía [poe'sia] NF poetry
poeta [po'eta] NM poet
poético, -a [po'etiko, a] ADJ poetic(al)
poetisa [poe'tisa] NF (woman) poet
póker ['poker] NM poker
polaco, -a [po'lako, a] ADJ Polish ▶ NM/F Pole
  ▶ NM (Ling) Polish
polar [po'lar] ADJ polar
polarice etc [pola'riθe] VB ver **polarizar**
polaridad [polari'ðað] NF polarity
polarizar [polari'θar] /1f/ VT to polarize
polea [po'lea] NF pulley
polémica [po'lemika] NF polemics sg; (una
  polémica) controversy
polemice etc [pole'miθe] VB ver **polemizar**
polémico, -a [po'lemiko, a] ADJ polemic(al)
polemizar [polemi'θar] /1f/ VI argue
polen ['polen] NM pollen
poleo [po'leo] NM pennyroyal
poli ['poli] NM (fam) cop (fam) ▶ NF: **la ~** the
  cops pl (fam)
policía [poli'θia] NMF policeman(-woman)
  ▶ NF police; see note

  There are two branches of the police,
  both armed: the policía nacional, in charge
  of national security and public order in
  general, and the policía municipal, with
  duties of regulating traffic and policing
  the local community. Catalonia and the
  Basque Country have their own police
  forces, the Mossos d'Esquadra and the
  Ertzaintza respectively.

policíaco, -a [poli'θiako, a] ADJ police cpd;
  novela policíaca detective story
policial [poli'θjal] ADJ police cpd
polideportivo [poliðepor'tiβo] NM sports
  centre
poliéster [poli'ester] NM polyester

polietileno [polieti'leno] NM polythene (BRIT), polyethylene (US)

polifacético, -a [polifa'θetiko, a] ADJ (persona, talento) many-sided, versatile

poligamia [poli'ɣamja] NF polygamy

polígamo, -a [po'liɣamo, a] ADJ polygamous ▶ NM polygamist

polígono [po'liɣono] NM (Mat) polygon; (solar) building lot; (zona) area; (residencial) housing estate; ~ **industrial** industrial estate

polígrafo [po'liɣrafo] NM polygraph

polilla [po'liʎa] NF moth

Polinesia [poli'nesja] NF Polynesia

polinesio, -a [poli'nesjo, a] ADJ, NM/F Polynesian

polio [po'ljo] NF polio

Polisario [poli'sarjo] NM ABR (Pol: tb: **Frente Polisario**) = **Frente Político de Liberación del Sáhara y Río de Oro**

politécnico [poli'tekniko] NM polytechnic

político, -a [po'litiko, a] ADJ political; (discreto) tactful; (pariente) in-law ▶ NM/F politician ▶ NF politics sg; (económica, agraria) policy; **padre** ~ father-in-law; **política exterior/de ingresos y precios** foreign/prices and incomes policy

póliza [po'liθa] NF certificate, voucher; (impuesto) tax o fiscal stamp; ~ **de seguro(s)** insurance policy

polizón [poli'θon] NM (Aviat, Naut) stowaway

pollera [po'ʎera] NF (criadero) hencoop; (AM) skirt, overskirt

pollería [poʎe'ria] NF poulterer's (shop)

pollo [po'ʎo] NM chicken; (joven) young man; (señorito) playboy; ~ **asado** roast chicken

polo [po'lo] NM (Geo, Elec) pole; (helado) ice lolly (BRIT), Popsicle® (US); (Deporte) polo; (suéter) polo-neck; **P~ Norte/Sur** North/South Pole; **esto es el ~ opuesto de lo que dijo antes** this is the exact opposite of what he said before

Polonia [po'lonja] NF Poland

poltrona [pol'trona] NF reclining chair, easy chair

polución [polu'θjon] NF pollution; ~ **ambiental** environmental pollution

polvera [pol'βera] NF powder compact

polvo [po'lβo] NM dust; (Química, Culin, Med) powder; (fam!) screw (fam!); **polvos** NMPL (maquillaje) powder sg; **en** ~ powdered; ~ **de talco** talcum powder; **estar hecho** ~ to be worn out o exhausted; **hacer algo** ~ to smash sth; **hacer** ~ **a algn** to shatter sb; ver tb **polvos**

pólvora [po'lβora] NF gunpowder; (fuegos artificiales) fireworks pl; **propagarse como la** ~ (noticia) to spread like wildfire

polvoriento, -a [polβo'rjento, a] ADJ (superficie) dusty; (sustancia) powdery

polvorín [polβo'rin] NM (fig) powder keg

polvorosa [polβo'rosa] ADJ (fam): **poner pies en** ~ to beat it

polvos ['polβos] NMPL powder sg

polvoso, -a [pol'βoso, a] ADJ (AM) dusty

pomada [po'maða] NF cream

pomelo [po'melo] NM grapefruit

pómez ['pomeθ] NF: **piedra** ~ pumice stone

pomo ['pomo] NM knob, handle

pompa ['pompa] NF (burbuja) bubble; (bomba) pump; (esplendor) pomp, splendour; **pompas fúnebres** funeral sg

pomposo, -a [pom'poso, a] ADJ splendid, magnificent; (pey) pompous

pómulo ['pomulo] NM cheekbone

pon [pon] VB ver **poner**

ponchadura [pontʃa'dura] NF (AM) puncture (BRIT), flat (US)

ponchar [pon'tʃar] /**1a**/ VT (AM: llanta) to puncture

ponche ['pontʃe] NM punch

poncho ['pontʃo] NM (AM) poncho, cape

ponderar [ponde'rar] /**1a**/ VT (considerar) to weigh up, consider; (elogiar) to praise highly, speak in praise of

pondré etc [pon'dre] VB ver **poner**

ponencia [po'nenθja] NF (exposición) (learned) paper, communication; (informe) report

(PALABRA CLAVE)

poner [po'ner] /**2q**/ VT **1** to put; (colocar) to place, set; (ropa) to put on; (problema, la mesa) to set; (interés) to show; (telegrama) to send; (obra de teatro) to put on; (película) to show; **ponlo más alto** turn it up; **¿qué ponen en el Excelsior?** what's on at the Excelsior?; **poner algo a secar** to put sth (out) to dry; **¡no pongas esa cara!** don't look at me like that!

2 (tienda) to open; (instalar: gas etc) to put in; (radio, TV) to switch o turn on

3 (suponer): **pongamos que ...** let's suppose that ...

4 (contribuir): **el gobierno ha puesto otro millón** the government has contributed another million

5 (Telec): **póngame con el Sr. López** can you put me through to Mr. López?

6: **poner de: le han puesto de director general** they've appointed him general manager

7 (+ adj) to make; **me estás poniendo nerviosa** you're making me nervous

8 (dar nombre): **al hijo le pusieron Diego** they called their son Diego

9 (estar escrito) to say; **¿qué pone aquí?** what does it say here?

▶ VI (gallina) to lay

ponerse VR **1** (colocarse): **se puso a mi lado** he came and stood beside me; **tú ponte en esa**

silla you go and sit on that chair; **ponerse en camino** to set off

2 (*vestido, cosméticos*) to put on; **¿por qué no te pones el vestido nuevo?** why don't you put on *o* wear your new dress?

3 (*sol*) to set

4 (*+ adj*) to get, become; **ponerse enfermo/ gordo/triste** to get ill/fat/sad; **se puso muy serio** he got very serious; **después de lavarla la tela se puso azul** after washing it the material turned blue; **¡no te pongas así!** don't be like that!; **ponerse cómodo** to make o.s. comfortable

5: **ponerse a**: **se puso a llorar** he started to cry; **tienes que ponerte a estudiar** you must get down to studying; **ponerse a bien con algn** to make it up with sb; **ponerse a mal con algn** to get on the wrong side of sb

6 (*Am*): **se me pone que ...** it seems to me that ..., I think that ...

pongo *etc* ['pongo] vb *ver* **poner**

poniente [po'njente] nm west; (*viento*) west wind

pontevedrés, -esa [ponteβe'ðres, esa] adj of *o* from Pontevedra ▸ nm/f native *o* inhabitant of Pontevedra

pontificado [pontifi'kaðo] nm papacy, pontificate

pontífice [pon'tifiθe] nm pope, pontiff; **el Sumo P~** His Holiness the Pope

pontón [pon'ton] nm pontoon

ponzoña [pon'θoɲa] nf poison, venom

ponzoñoso, -a [ponθo'ɲoso, a] adj poisonous, venomous

pop [pop] adj inv, nm (*Mus*) pop

popa ['popa] nf stern; **a ~** astern, abaft; **de ~ a proa** fore and aft

popote [po'pote] nm (*Am*) straw

popular [popu'lar] adj popular; (*del pueblo*) of the people

popularice *etc* [popula'riθe] vb *ver* **popularizarse**

popularidad [populari'ðað] nf popularity

popularizarse [populari'θarse] /**1f**/ vr to become popular

poquísimo, -a [po'kisimo, a] adj superlativo *de* **poco** very little, very few *pl*; (*casi nada*) hardly any

poquito [po'kito] nm: **un ~** a little bit ▸ adv a little, a bit; **a poquitos** bit by bit

por [por] prep **1** (*objetivo*) for; **luchar por la patria** to fight for one's country; **hazlo por mí** do it for my sake

2 (*+ infin*): **por no llegar tarde** so as not to arrive late; **por citar unos ejemplos** to give a few examples

3 (*causa*) out of, because of; **no es por eso** that's not the reason; **por escasez de fondos** through *o* for lack of funds

4 (*tiempo*): **por la mañana/noche** in the morning/at night; **se queda por una semana** she's staying (for) a week

5 (*lugar*): **pasar por Madrid** to pass through Madrid; **ir a Guayaquil por Quito** to go to Guayaquil via Quito; **caminar por la calle** to walk along the street; **por allí** over there; **se va por ahí** we have to go that way; **¿hay un banco por aquí?** is there a bank near here?; **¿por dónde?** which way?; **está por el norte** it's somewhere in the north; **por todo el país** throughout the country

6 (*cambio: precio*): **te doy uno nuevo por el que tienes** I'll give you a new one (in return) for the one you've got; **lo vendí por 15 dólares** I sold it for 15 dollars

7 (*valor distributivo*): **30 euros por hora/ cabeza** 30 euros an *o* per hour/a *o* per head; **10 por ciento** 10 per cent; **80 (kms) por hora** 80 (kilómetros) an *o* per hour

8 (*modo, medio*) by; **por correo/avión** by post/ air; **día por día** day by day; **por orden** in order; **entrar por la entrada principal** to go in through the main entrance

9 (*agente*) by; **hecho por él** done by him; **"dirigido por"** "directed by"

10: **10 por 10 son 100** 10 times 10 is 100

11 (*en lugar de*): **vino él por su jefe** he came instead of his boss

12: **por mí que revienten** as far as I'm concerned they can drop dead

13 (*evidencia*): **por lo que dicen** judging by *o* from what they say

14: **estar/quedar por hacer** to be still *o* remain to be done

15: **por (muy) difícil que sea** however hard it is *o* may be; **por más que lo intente** no matter how *o* however hard I try

16: **por qué** why; **¿por qué?** why?; **¿por qué no?** why not?; **¿por?** (*fam*) why (do you ask)?

porcelana [porθe'lana] nf porcelain; (*china*) china

porcentaje [porθen'taxe] nm percentage; **~ de actividad** (*Inform*) hit rate

porche ['portʃe] nm (*de una plaza*) arcade; (*de casa*) porch

porción [por'θjon] nf (*parte*) portion, share; (*cantidad*) quantity, amount

pordiosero, -a [porðjo'sero, a] nm/f beggar

porfía [por'fia] nf persistence; (*terquedad*) obstinacy

porfiado, -a [por'fjaðo, a] adj persistent; obstinate

porfiar [por'fjar] /**1c**/ vi to persist, insist; (*disputar*) to argue stubbornly

pormenor [porme'nor] NM detail, particular

pormenorice etc [pormeno'riθe] VB ver **pormenorizar**

pormenorizar [pormenori'θar] /**1f**/ VT to (set out in) detail ▶ VI to go into detail

porno ['porno] ADJ INV porno ▶ NM porn

pornografía [pornoɣra'fia] NF pornography

poro ['poro] NM pore

pororó [poro'ro] NM (AM) popcorn

poroso, -a [po'roso, a] ADJ porous

poroto [po'roto] NM (AM) kidney bean

porque ['porke] CONJ (a causa de) because; (ya que) since; (con el fin de) so that, in order that; **~ sí** because I feel like it

porqué [por'ke] NM reason, cause

porquería [porke'ria] NF (suciedad) filth, muck, dirt; (acción) dirty trick; (objeto) small thing, trifle; (fig) rubbish

porqueriza [porke'riθa] NF pigsty

porra ['porra] NF (arma) stick, club; (cachiporra) truncheon; **¡porras!** oh heck!; **¡vete a la ~!** go to heck!

porrazo [po'rraθo] NM (golpe) blow; (caída) bump; **de un ~** in one go

porro ['porro] NM (fam: droga) joint

porrón [po'rron] NM glass wine jar with a long spout

portaaviones [port(a)a'βjones] NM INV aircraft carrier

portada [por'taða] NF (Tip) title page; (: de revista) cover

portador, a [porta'ðor, a] NM/F carrier, bearer; (Com) bearer, payee; (Med) carrier; **ser ~ del virus del sida** to be HIV-positive

portaequipajes [portaeki'paxes] NM INV boot (BRIT), trunk (US); (baca) luggage rack

portafolio [porta'foljo], **portafolios** [porta'foljos] NM (AM) briefcase; **~(s) de inversiones** (Com) investment portfolio

portal [por'tal] NM (entrada) vestibule, hall; (pórtico) porch, doorway; (puerta de entrada) main door; (Deporte) goal; (Internet) portal; **portales** NMPL arcade sg

portaligas [porta'liɣas] NM INV (AM) suspender belt

portamaletas [portama'letas] NM INV (Auto: maletero) boot; (: baca) roof rack

portamonedas [portamo'neðas] NM INV (AM) purse

portar [por'tar] /**1a**/ VT to carry, bear; **portarse** VR to behave, conduct o.s.; **portarse mal** to misbehave; **se portó muy bien conmigo** he treated me very well

portátil [por'tatil] ADJ portable; **(ordenador) ~** laptop (computer)

portaviones [porta'βjones] NM INV aircraft carrier

portavoz [porta'βoθ] NMF spokesman(-woman)

portazo [por'taθo] NM: **dar un ~** to slam the door

porte ['porte] NM (Com) transport; (precio) transport charges pl; (Correos) postage; **~ debido** (Com) carriage forward; **~ pagado** (Com) carriage paid, post-paid

portento [por'tento] NM marvel, wonder

portentoso, -a [porten'toso, a] ADJ marvellous, extraordinary

porteño, -a [por'teɲo, a] ADJ of o from Buenos Aires ▶ NM/F native o inhabitant of Buenos Aires

portería [porte'ria] NF (oficina) porter's office; (gol) goal

portero, -a [por'tero, a] NM/F porter; (conserje) caretaker; (ujier) doorman; (Deporte) goalkeeper; **~ automático** (ESP) entry phone

pórtico ['portiko] NM (porche) portico, porch; (fig) gateway; (arcada) arcade

portilla [por'tiʎa] NF, **portillo** [por'tiʎo] NM gate

portorriqueño, -a [portorri'keɲo, a] ADJ, NM/F Puerto Rican

portuario, -a [por'twarjo, a] ADJ (del puerto) port cpd, harbour cpd; (del muelle) dock cpd; **trabajador ~** docker

Portugal [portu'ɣal] NM Portugal

portugués, -esa [portu'ɣes, esa] ADJ, NM/F Portuguese ▶ NM (Ling) Portuguese

porvenir [porβe'nir] NM future

pos [pos]: **en ~ de** prep after, in pursuit of

posada [po'saða] NF (refugio) shelter, lodging; (mesón) guest house; **dar ~ a** to give shelter to, take in

posaderas [posa'ðeras] NFPL backside sg, buttocks

posar [po'sar] /**1a**/ VT (en el suelo) to lay down, put down; (la mano) to place, put gently ▶ VI to sit, pose; **posarse** VR to settle; (pájaro) to perch; (avión) to land, come down

posavasos [posa'basos] NM INV coaster; (para cerveza) beermat

posdata [pos'ðata] NF postscript

pose ['pose] NF (Arte, afectación) pose

poseedor, a [posee'ðor, a] NM/F owner, possessor; (de récord, puesto) holder

poseer [pose'er] /**2e**/ VT to have, possess, own; (ventaja) to enjoy; (récord, puesto) to hold

poseído, -a [pose'iðo, a] ADJ possessed; **estar muy ~ de** to be very vain about

posesión [pose'sjon] NF possession; **tomar ~ (de)** to take over

posesionarse [posesjo'narse] /**1a**/ VR: **~ de** to take possession of, take over

posesivo, -a [pose'siβo, a] ADJ possessive

poseyendo etc [pose'jendo] VB ver **poseer**

posgrado [pos'ɣraðo] NM = **postgrado**

posgraduado, -a [posɣra'ðwaðo, a] ADJ, NM/F = **postgraduado**

P

posguerra [pos'ɣerra] NF = **postguerra**
posibilidad [posiβili'ðað] NF possibility;
(*oportunidad*) chance
posibilitar [posiβili'tar] /**1a**/ VT to make
possible, permit; (*hacer factible*) to make
feasible
posible [po'siβle] ADJ possible; (*factible*)
feasible ▶ NM: **posibles** means; (*bienes*)
funds, assets; **de ser ~** if possible; **en** o
dentro de lo ~ as far as possible; **lo antes ~**
as quickly as possible
posición [posi'θjon] NF (*gen*) position; (*rango
social*) status
positivo, -a [posi'tiβo, a] ADJ positive ▶ NF
(*Foto*) print
poso ['poso] NM sediment; (*heces*) dregs *pl*
posoperatorio, -a [posopera'torjo, a] ADJ, NM
= **postoperatorio**
posponer [pospo'ner] /**2q**/ VT (*relegar*) to put
behind o below; (*aplazar*) to postpone
posponga *etc* [pos'poŋga], **pospuesto**
[pos'pwesto], **pospuse** *etc* [pos'puse] VB *ver*
posponer
post [post] (*pl* **posts**) NM (*en sitio web*) post
posta ['posta] NF (*de caballos*) relay, team;
a ~ on purpose, deliberately
postal [pos'tal] ADJ postal ▶ NF postcard
poste ['poste] NM (*de telégrafos*) post, pole;
(*columna*) pillar
póster ['poster] (*pl* **posters** ['posters]) NM
poster
postergar [poster'ɣar] /**1h**/ VT (*esp Am*) to put
off, postpone, delay
postergue *etc* [pos'terɣe] VB *ver* **postergar**
posteridad [posteri'ðað] NF posterity
posterior [poste'rjor] ADJ back, rear;
(*siguiente*) following, subsequent; (*más tarde*)
later; **ser ~ a** to be later than
posterioridad [posterjori'ðað] NF: **con ~**
later, subsequently
postgrado [post'ɣraðo] NM: **curso de ~**
postgraduate course
postgraduado, -a [postɣra'ðwaðo, a] ADJ,
NM/F postgraduate
postguerra [post'ɣerra] NF postwar period;
en la ~ after the war
postigo [pos'tiɣo] NM (*portillo*) postern;
(*contraventana*) shutter
postín [pos'tin] NM (*fam*) elegance; **de ~**
posh; **darse ~** to show off
postizo, -a [pos'tiθo, a] ADJ false, artificial;
(*sonrisa*) false, phoney ▶ NM hairpiece
postoperatorio, -a [postopera'torjo, a] ADJ
postoperative ▶ NM postoperative period
postor, a [pos'tor, a] NM/F bidder; **mejor ~**
highest bidder
postrado, -a [pos'traðo, a] ADJ prostrate
postrar [pos'trar] /**1a**/ VT (*derribar*) to cast
down, overthrow; (*humillar*) to humble;

(*Med*) to weaken, exhaust; **postrarse** VR to
prostrate o.s.
postre ['postre] NM sweet, dessert ▶ NF: **a la ~**
in the end, when all is said and done; **para ~**
(*fam*) to crown it all; **llegar a los postres** (*fig*)
to come too late
postrero, -a [pos'trero, a] ADJ (*antes de nmsg*
postrer) (*último*) last; (*que viene detrás*) rear
postrimerías [postrime'rias] NFPL final
stages
postulado [postu'laðo] NM postulate
postulante [postu'lante] NMF petitioner;
(*Rel*) postulant
póstumo, -a ['postumo, a] ADJ posthumous
postura [pos'tura] NF (*del cuerpo*) posture,
position; (*fig*) attitude, position
post-venta [pos'βenta] ADJ (*Com*) after-sales
potable [po'taβle] ADJ drinkable; **agua ~**
drinking water
potaje [po'taxe] NM thick vegetable soup
pote ['pote] NM pot, jar
potencia [po'tenθja] NF power; (*capacidad*)
capacity; **~ (en caballos)** horsepower; **en ~**
potential, in the making; **las grandes
potencias** the great powers
potencial [poten'θjal] ADJ, NM potential
potenciar [poten'θjar] /**1b**/ VT (*promover*) to
promote; (*fortalecer*) to boost
potente [po'tente] ADJ powerful
potestad [potes'tað] NF authority; **patria ~**
paternal authority
potosí [poto'si] NM fortune; **cuesta un ~** it
costs the earth
potra ['potra] NF (*Zool*) filly; **tener ~** to be
lucky
potro ['potro] NM (*Zool*) colt; (*Deporte*)
vaulting horse
pozo ['poθo] NM well; (*de río*) deep pool;
(*de mina*) shaft; **~ negro** cesspool; **ser un
~ de ciencia** (*fig*) to be deeply learned
PP ABR (= *por poderes*) pp; (= *porte pagado*)
carriage paid ▶ NM ABR = **Partido Popular**
p.p. ABR = **por poderes**
p.p.m. ABR (= *palabras por minuto*) wpm
práctica ['praktika] NF *ver* **práctico**
practicable [prakti'kaβle] ADJ practicable;
(*camino*) passable, usable
prácticamente ['praktikamente] ADV
practically
practicante [prakti'kante] NMF (*Med*:
ayudante de doctor) medical assistant;
(: *enfermero*) nurse; (*el que practica algo*)
practitioner ▶ ADJ practising
practicar [prakti'kar] /**1g**/ VT to practise;
(*deporte*) to go in for, play; (*ejecutar*) to carry
out, perform
práctico, -a ['praktiko, a] ADJ (*gen*)
practical; (*conveniente*) handy; (*instruido*:
persona) skilled, expert ▶ NF practice;

(*método*) method; (*arte, capacidad*) skill; **en la práctica** in practice

practique *etc* [prak'tike] VB *ver* **practicar**

pradera [pra'ðera] NF meadow; (*de Canadá*) prairie

prado ['praðo] NM (*campo*) meadow, field; (*pastizal*) pasture; (AM) lawn

Praga ['praɣa] NF Prague

pragmático, -a [praɣ'matiko, a] ADJ pragmatic

preámbulo [pre'ambulo] NM preamble, introduction; **decir algo sin preámbulos** to say sth without beating about the bush

precalentamiento [prekalenta'mjento] NM (*Deporte*) warm-up

precalentar [prekalen'tar] /**1j**/ VT to preheat

precaliente *etc* [preka'ljente] VB *ver* **precalentar**

precario, -a [pre'karjo, a] ADJ precarious

precaución [prekau'θjon] NF (*medida preventiva*) preventive measure, precaution; (*prudencia*) caution, wariness

precaver [preka'βer] /**2a**/ VT to guard against; (*impedir*) to forestall; **precaverse** VR: **precaverse de** o **contra algo** to (be on one's) guard against sth

precavido, -a [preka'βiðo, a] ADJ cautious, wary

precedencia [preθe'ðenθja] NF precedence; (*prioridad*) priority; (*superioridad*) greater importance, superiority

precedente [preθe'ðente] ADJ preceding; (*anterior*) former ▶ NM precedent; **sin ~(s)** unprecedented; **establecer** o **sentar un ~** to establish o set a precedent

preceder [preθe'ðer] /**2a**/ VT, VI to precede, go/come before

precepto [pre'θepto] NM precept

preceptor [preθep'tor] NM (*maestro*) teacher; (: *particular*) tutor

preciado, -a [pre'θjaðo, a] ADJ (*estimado*) esteemed, valuable

preciar [pre'θjar] /**1b**/ VT to esteem, value; **preciarse** VR to boast; **preciarse de** to pride o.s. on

precintar [preθin'tar] /**1a**/ VT (*local*) to seal off; (*producto*) to seal

precinto [pre'θinto] NM (Com: *tb*: **precinto de garantía**) seal

precio ['preθjo] NM (*de mercado*) price; (*costo*) cost; (*valor*) value, worth; (*de viaje*) fare; **~ de coste** o **de cobertura** cost price; **~ al contado** cash price; **~ al detalle** o **al por menor** retail price; **~ al detallista** trade price; **~ de entrega inmediata** spot price; **~ de oferta** offer price, bargain price; **~ de salida** upset price; **~ tope** top price; **~ unitario** unit price; **no tener ~** (*fig*) to be priceless; **"no importa ~"** "cost no object"

preciosidad [preθjosi'ðað] NF (*valor*) (high) value, (great) worth; (*encanto*) charm; (*cosa bonita*) beautiful thing; **es una ~** it's lovely, it's really beautiful

precioso, -a [pre'θjoso, a] ADJ precious; (*de mucho valor*) valuable; (*fam*) lovely, beautiful

precipicio [preθi'pjθjo] NM cliff, precipice; (*fig*) abyss

precipitación [preθipita'θjon] NF (*prisa*) haste; (*lluvia*) rainfall; (*Química*) precipitation

precipitado, -a [preθipi'taðo, a] ADJ hasty, rash; (*salida*) hasty, sudden ▶ NM (*Química*) precipitate

precipitar [preθipi'tar] /**1a**/ VT (*arrojar*) to hurl, throw; (*apresurar*) to hasten; (*acelerar*) to speed up, accelerate; (*Química*) to precipitate; **precipitarse** VR to throw o.s.; (*apresurarse*) to rush; (*actuar sin pensar*) to act rashly; **precipitarse hacia** to rush towards

precisado, -a [preθi'saðo, a] ADJ: **verse ~ a hacer algo** to be obliged to do sth

precisamente [preθisa'mente] ADV precisely; (*justo*) precisely, exactly, just; **~ por eso** for that very reason; **~ fue él quien lo dijo** as a matter of fact he said it; **no es eso ~** it's not really that

precisar [preθi'sar] /**1a**/ VT (*necesitar*) to need, require; (*fijar*) to determine exactly, fix; (*especificar*) to specify; (*señalar*) to pinpoint

precisión [preθi'sjon] NF (*exactitud*) precision

preciso, -a [pre'θiso, a] ADJ (*exacto*) precise; (*necesario*) necessary, essential; (*estilo, lenguaje*) concise; **es ~ que lo hagas** you must do it

precocidad [prekoθi'ðað] NF precociousness, precocity

preconcebido, -a [prekonθe'βiðo, a] ADJ preconceived

preconice *etc* [preko'niθe] VB *ver* **preconizar**

preconizar [prekoni'θar] /**1f**/ VT (*aconsejar*) to advise; (*prever*) to foresee

precoz [pre'koθ] ADJ (*persona*) precocious; (*calvicie*) premature

precursor, a [prekur'sor, a] NM/F precursor

predecesor, a [preðeθe'sor, a] NM/F predecessor

predecir [preðe'θir] /**3o**/ VT to predict, foretell, forecast

predestinado, -a [preðesti'naðo, a] ADJ predestined

predeterminar [preðetermi'nar] /**1a**/ VT to predetermine

predicado [preði'kaðo] NM predicate

predicador, a [preðika'ðor, a] NM/F preacher

predicar [preði'kar] /**1g**/ VT, VI to preach

predicción [preðik'θjon] NF prediction; (*pronóstico*) forecast; **~ del tiempo** weather forecast(ing)

P

predicho [preˈðitʃo], **prediga** etc [preˈðiɣa], **predije** etc [preˈðixe] VB ver **predecir**
predilecto, -a [preðiˈlekto, a] ADJ favourite
predique etc [preˈðike] VB ver **predicar**
prediré etc [preðiˈre] VB ver **predecir**
predispondré etc [preðispoˈndre] VB ver **predisponer**
predisponer [preðispoˈner] /2q/ VT to predispose; (pey) to prejudice
predisponga etc [preðisˈponga] VB ver **predisponer**
predisposición [preðisposiˈθjon] NF predisposition, inclination; (prejuicio) prejudice, bias; (Med) tendency
predispuesto [preðisˈpwesto], **predispuse** etc [preðisˈpuse] VB ver **predisponer**
predominante [preðomiˈnante] ADJ predominant; (preponderante) prevailing; (interés) controlling
predominar [preðomiˈnar] /1a/ VT to dominate ▶ VI to predominate; (prevalecer) to prevail
predominio [preðoˈminjo] NM predominance
preescolar [preeskoˈlar] ADJ preschool
preestreno [preesˈtreno] NM preview, press view
prefabricado, -a [prefaβriˈkaðo, a] ADJ prefabricated
prefacio [preˈfaθjo] NM preface
preferencia [prefeˈrenθja] NF preference; **de ~** preferably, for preference; **localidad de ~** reserved seat
preferible [prefeˈriβle] ADJ preferable
preferido, -a [prefeˈriðo, a] ADJ, NM/F favourite, favorite (US)
preferir [prefeˈrir] /3i/ VT to prefer
prefiero etc [preˈfjero] VB ver **preferir**
prefijo [preˈfixo] NM prefix; (Telec) (dialling) code
prefiriendo etc [prefiˈrjendo] VB ver **preferir**
pregón [preˈɣon] NM proclamation, announcement
pregonar [preɣoˈnar] /1a/ VT to proclaim, announce; (mercancía) to hawk
pregonero [preɣoˈnero] NM town crier
pregunta [preˈɣunta] NF question; **~ capciosa** catch question; **hacer una ~** to ask a question; **preguntas frecuentes** FAQs, frequently asked questions
preguntar [preɣunˈtar] /1a/ VT to ask; (cuestionar) to question ▶ VI to ask; **preguntarse** VR to wonder; **~ por algn** to ask for sb; **~ por la salud de algn** to ask after sb's health
preguntón, -ona [preɣunˈton, ona] ADJ inquisitive
prehistórico, -a [preisˈtoriko, a] ADJ prehistoric

prejuicio [preˈxwiθjo] NM prejudgement; (preconcepción) preconception; (pey) prejudice, bias
prejuzgar [prexuθˈɣar] /1h/ VT (predisponerse) to prejudge
prejuzgue etc [preˈxuθɣe] VB ver **prejuzgar**
preliminar [prelimiˈnar] ADJ, NM preliminary
preludio [preˈluðjo] NM (Mus, fig) prelude
premamá [premaˈma] ADJ: **vestido ~** maternity dress
prematrimonial [prematrimoˈnjal] ADJ: **relaciones prematrimoniales** premarital sex
prematuro, -a [premaˈturo, a] ADJ premature
premeditación [premeðitaˈθjon] NF premeditation
premeditado, -a [premeðiˈtaðo, a] ADJ premeditated, deliberate; (intencionado) wilful
premeditar [premeðiˈtar] /1a/ VT to premeditate
premiar [preˈmjar] /1b/ VT to reward; (en un concurso) to give a prize to
premio [ˈpremjo] NM reward; prize; (Com) premium; **~ gordo** first prize
premisa [preˈmisa] NF premise
premonición [premoniˈθjon] NF premonition
premura [preˈmura] NF (prisa) haste, urgency
prenatal [prenaˈtal] ADJ antenatal, prenatal
prenda [ˈprenda] NF (de ropa) garment, article of clothing; (garantía) pledge; (fam) darling!; **prendas** NFPL talents, gifts; **dejar algo en ~** to pawn sth; **no soltar ~** to give nothing away; (fig) not to say a word
prendar [prenˈdar] /1a/ VT to captivate, enchant; **prendarse de algo** to fall in love with sth
prendedor [prendeˈðor] NM brooch
prender [prenˈder] /2a/ VT (captar) to catch, capture; (detener) to arrest; (coser) to pin, attach; (sujetar) to fasten; (AM) to switch on ▶ VI to catch; (arraigar) to take root; **prenderse** VR (encenderse) to catch fire
prendido, -a [prenˈdiðo, a] ADJ (AM: luz) on
prensa [ˈprensa] NF press; **la P~** the press; **tener mala ~** to have o get a bad press; **la ~ nacional** the national press
prensar [prenˈsar] /1a/ VT to press
preñado, -a [preˈɲaðo, a] ADJ (mujer) pregnant; **~ de** pregnant with, full of
preocupación [preokupaˈθjon] NF worry, concern; (ansiedad) anxiety
preocupado, -a [preokuˈpaðo, a] ADJ worried, concerned
preocupar [preokuˈpar] /1a/ VT to worry; **preocuparse** VR to worry; **preocuparse de**

algo (*hacerse cargo de algo*) to take care of sth; **preocuparse por algo** to worry about sth

preparación [prepara'θjon] NF (*acto*) preparation; (*estado*) preparedness, readiness; (*entrenamiento*) training

preparado, -a [prepa'raðo, a] ADJ (*dispuesto*) prepared; (*Culin*) ready (to serve) ▶ NM (*Med*) preparation; **¡preparados, listos, ya!** ready, steady, go!

preparar [prepa'rar] /**1a**/ VT (*disponer*) to prepare, get ready; (*Tec: tratar*) to prepare, process, treat; (*entrenar*) to teach, train; **prepararse** VR: **prepararse a** o **para hacer algo** to prepare o get ready to do sth

preparativo, -a [prepara'tiβo, a] ADJ preparatory, preliminary; **preparativos** NMPL preparations

preparatoria [prepara'torja] NF (*Am*) sixth form college (*Brit*), senior high school (*US*)

preposición [preposi'θjon] NF preposition

prepotencia [prepo'tenθja] NF abuse of power; (*Pol*) high-handedness; (*soberbia*) arrogance

prepotente [prepo'tente] ADJ (*Pol*) high-handed; (*soberbio*) arrogant

prerrogativa [prerroɣa'tiβa] NF prerogative, privilege

presa ['presa] NF (*cosa apresada*) catch; (*víctima*) victim; (*de animal*) prey; (*de agua*) dam; **hacer ~ en** to clutch (on to), seize; **ser ~ de** (*fig*) to be a prey to

presagiar [presa'xjar] /**1b**/ VT to presage

presagio [pre'saxjo] NM omen

presbítero [pres'βitero] NM priest

prescindir [presθin'dir] /**3a**/ VI: **~ de** (*privarse de*) to do without, go without; (*descartar*) to dispense with; **no podemos ~ de él** we can't manage without him

prescribir [preskri'βir] /**3a**/ VT to prescribe

prescripción [preskrip'θjon] NF prescription; **~ facultativa** medical prescription

prescrito [pres'krito] PP *de* **prescribir**

preseleccionar [preselekθjo'nar] /**1a**/ VT (*Deporte*) to seed

presencia [pre'senθja] NF presence; **en ~ de** in the presence of

presencial [presen'θjal] ADJ: **testigo ~** eyewitness

presenciar [presen'θjar] /**1b**/ VT to be present at; (*asistir a*) to attend; (*ver*) to see, witness

presentación [presenta'θjon] NF presentation; (*introducción*) introduction

presentador, a [presenta'ðor, a] NM/F compère

presentar [presen'tar] /**1a**/ VT to present; (*ofrecer*) to offer; (*mostrar*) to show, display; (*renuncia*) to tender; (*moción*) to propose; (*a una persona*) to introduce; **presentarse** VR (*llegar inesperadamente*) to appear, turn up;

(*ofrecerse: como candidato*) to run, stand; (*aparecer*) to show, appear; (*solicitar empleo*) to apply; **~ al cobro** (*Com*) to present for payment; **presentarse a la policía** to report to the police

presente [pre'sente] ADJ present ▶ NM present; (*Ling*) present (tense); (*regalo*) gift; **los presentes** those present; **hacer ~** to state, declare; **tener ~** to remember, bear in mind; **la carta ~, la ~** this letter

presentimiento [presenti'mjento] NM premonition, presentiment

presentir [presen'tir] /**3i**/ VT to have a premonition of

preservación [preserβa'θjon] NF protection, preservation

preservar [preser'βar] /**1a**/ VT to protect, preserve

preservativo [preserβa'tiβo] NM sheath, condom

presidencia [presi'ðenθja] NF presidency; (*de comité*) chairmanship; **ocupar la ~** to preside, be in o take the chair

presidente [presi'ðente] NMF president; (*de comité*) chairman(-woman); (*en parlamento*) speaker; (*Jur*) presiding magistrate

presidiario [presi'ðjarjo] NM convict

presidio [pre'siðjo] NM prison, penitentiary

presidir [presi'ðir] /**3a**/ VT (*dirigir*) to preside at, preside over; (: *comité*) to take the chair at; (*dominar*) to dominate, rule ▶ VI to preside; to take the chair

presienta *etc* [pre'sjenta], **presintiendo** *etc* [presin'tjendo] VB *ver* **presentir**

presión [pre'sjon] NF pressure; **~ atmosférica** atmospheric o air pressure; **~ arterial** o **sanguínea** blood pressure; **a ~** under pressure

presionar [presjo'nar] /**1a**/ VT to press; (*botón*) to push, press; (*fig*) to press, put pressure on ▶ VI: **~ para** o **por** to press for

preso, -a ['preso, a] ADJ: **estar ~ de terror** o **pánico** to be panic-stricken ▶ NM/F prisoner; **tomar** o **llevar ~ a algn** to arrest sb, take sb prisoner

prestación [presta'θjon] NF (*aportación*) lending; (*Inform*) capability; (*servicio*) service; (*subsidio*) benefit; **prestaciones** NFPL (*Auto*) performance features; **~ de juramento** oath-taking; **~ personal** obligatory service; **P~ Social Sustitutoria** community service for conscientious objectors

prestado, -a [pres'taðo, a] ADJ on loan; **dar algo ~** to lend sth; **pedir ~** to borrow

prestamista [presta'mista] NMF moneylender

préstamo ['prestamo] NM loan; **~ con garantía** loan against collateral; **~ hipotecario** mortgage

prestar [pres'tar] /**1a**/ VT to lend, loan; (*atención*) to pay; (*ayuda*) to give; (*servicio*) to do, render; (*juramento*) to take, swear; **prestarse** VR (*ofrecerse*) to offer o volunteer

prestatario, -a [presta'tarjo, a] NM/F borrower

presteza [pres'teθa] NF speed, promptness

prestidigitador [prestiðixita'ðor] NM conjurer

prestigio [pres'tixjo] NM prestige; (*reputación*) face; (*renombre*) good name

prestigioso, -a [presti'xjoso, a] ADJ (*honorable*) prestigious; (*famoso, renombrado*) renowned, famous

presto, -a ['presto, a] ADJ (*rápido*) quick, prompt; (*dispuesto*) ready ▶ ADV at once, right away

presumido, -a [presu'miðo, a] ADJ conceited

presumir [presu'mir] /**3a**/ VT to presume ▶ VI (*darse aires*) to be conceited; **según cabe ~** as may be presumed, presumably; **~ de listo** to think o.s. very smart

presunción [presun'θjon] NF presumption; (*sospecha*) suspicion; (*vanidad*) conceit

presunto, -a [pre'sunto, a] ADJ (*supuesto*) supposed, presumed; (*así llamado*) so-called

presuntuoso, -a [presun'twoso, a] ADJ conceited, presumptuous

presupondré *etc* [presupon'dre] VB *ver* **presuponer**

presuponer [presupo'ner] /**2q**/ VT to presuppose

presuponga *etc* [presu'ponga] VB *ver* **presuponer**

presupuestar [presupwes'tar] /**1a**/ VI to budget ▶ VT: **~ algo** to budget for sth

presupuestario, -a [presupwes'tarjo, a] ADJ (*Finanzas*) budgetary, budget *cpd*

presupuesto [presu'pwesto] PP *de* **presuponer** ▶ NM (*Finanzas*) budget; (*estimación: de costo*) estimate; **asignación de ~** (*Com*) budget appropriation

presupuse *etc* [presu'puse] VB *ver* **presuponer**

presuroso, -a [presu'roso, a] ADJ (*rápido*) quick, speedy; (*que tiene prisa*) hasty

pretencioso, -a [preten'θjoso, a] ADJ pretentious

pretender [preten'der] /**2a**/ VT (*intentar*) to try to, seek to; (*reivindicar*) to claim; (*buscar*) to seek, try for; (*cortejar*) to woo, court; **~ que** to expect that; **¿qué pretende usted?** what are you after?

pretendiente [preten'djente] NMF (*candidato*) candidate, applicant; (*amante*) suitor; (*al trono*) pretender

pretensión [preten'sjon] NF (*aspiración*) aspiration; (*reivindicación*) claim; (*orgullo*) pretension

pretérito, -a [pre'terito, a] ADJ (*Ling*) past; (*fig*) past, former

pretextar [preteks'tar] /**1a**/ VT to plead, use as an excuse

pretexto [pre'teksto] NM pretext; (*excusa*) excuse; **so ~ de** under pretext of

pretil [pre'til] NM (*valla*) parapet; (*baranda*) handrail

prevalecer [preβale'θer] /**2d**/ VI to prevail

prevaleciente [preβale'θjente] ADJ prevailing, prevalent

prevalezca *etc* [preβa'leθka] VB *ver* **prevalecer**

prevención [preβen'θjon] NF (*preparación*) preparation; (*estado*) preparedness, readiness; (*medida*) prevention; (*previsión*) foresight, forethought; (*precaución*) precaution

prevendré *etc* [preβen'dre], **prevenga** *etc* [pre'βenga] VB *ver* **prevenir**

prevenido, -a [preβe'niðo, a] ADJ prepared, ready; (*cauteloso*) cautious; **estar ~** (*preparado*) to be ready; **ser ~** (*cuidadoso*) to be cautious; **hombre ~ vale por dos** forewarned is forearmed

prevenir [preβe'nir] /**3r**/ VT (*impedir*) to prevent; (*prever*) to foresee, anticipate; (*predisponer*) to prejudice, bias; (*avisar*) to warn; (*preparar*) to prepare, get ready; **prevenirse** VR to get ready, prepare; **prevenirse contra** to take precautions against

preventivo, -a [preβen'tiβo, a] ADJ preventive, precautionary

prever [pre'βer] /**2u**/ VT to foresee; (*anticipar*) to anticipate

previniendo *etc* [preβi'njendo] VB *ver* **prevenir**

previo, -a ['preβjo, a] ADJ (*anterior*) previous, prior; (*preliminar*) preliminary ▶ PREP: **~ acuerdo de los otros** subject to the agreement of the others; **~ pago de los derechos** on payment of the fees

previsible [preβi'siβle] ADJ foreseeable

previsión [preβi'sjon] NF (*perspicacia*) foresight; (*predicción*) forecast; (*prudencia*) caution; **~ de ventas** (*Com*) sales forecast

previsor, a [preβi'sor, a] ADJ (*precavido*) far-sighted; (*prudente*) thoughtful

previsto, -a [pre'βisto, a] PP *de* **prever** ▶ ADJ anticipated, forecast

P.R.I. ['pri] NM ABR (*Am*: = *Partido Revolucionario Institucional*) *Mexican political party*

prieto, -a ['prjeto, a] ADJ (*oscuro*) dark; (*Am*) dark(-skinned); (*fig*) mean; (*comprimido*) tight, compressed

prima ['prima] NF *ver* **primo**

primacía [prima'θia] NF primacy

primar [pri'mar] /**1a**/ VI (*tener primacía*) to occupy first place; **~ sobre** to have priority over

primario, -a [pri'marjo, a] ADJ primary
▶ NF primary education
primavera [prima'βera] NF (temporada)
spring; (período) springtime; **P~ árabe** Arab
Spring, Arab Awakening
primaveral [primaβe'ral] ADJ spring cpd,
springlike
Primer Ministro [pri'mer-] NM Prime
Minister
primero, -a [pri'mero, a] ADJ (antes de nmsg
primer) first; (fig) prime; (anterior) former;
(básico) fundamental ▶ ADV first; (más bien)
sooner, rather ▶ NF (Auto) first gear; (Ferro)
first class; **de primera** (fam) first-class,
first-rate; **de buenas a primeras** suddenly;
primera dama (Teat) leading lady; **primera
plana** front page
primicia [pri'miθja] NF (Prensa) scoop;
primicias NFPL (tb fig) first fruits
primitivo, -a [primi'tiβo, a] ADJ primitive;
(original) original; (Com: acción) ordinary ▶ NF:
(Lotería) **Primitiva** weekly state-run lottery;
ver tb **lotería**
primo, -a ['primo, a] ADJ (Mat) prime ▶ NM/F
cousin; (fam) fool, idiot ▶ NF (Com) bonus;
(de seguro) premium; (a la exportación) subsidy;
~ hermano first cousin; **materias primas**
raw materials; **hacer el ~** to be taken for a ride
primogénito, -a [primo'xenito, a] ADJ
first-born
primor [pri'mor] NM (cuidado) care; **es un ~**
it's lovely
primordial [primor'ðjal] ADJ basic,
fundamental
primoroso, -a [primo'roso, a] ADJ exquisite,
fine
princesa [prin'θesa] NF princess
principado [prinθi'paðo] NM principality
principal [prinθi'pal] ADJ principal, main;
(más destacado) foremost; (piso) first, second
(US); (Inform) foreground ▶ NM (jefe) chief,
principal
príncipe ['prinθipe] NM prince; **~ heredero**
crown prince; **P~ de Asturias** King's son and
heir to the Spanish throne; **~ de Gales** (tela)
check
principiante [prinθi'pjante] NMF beginner;
(novato) novice
principio [prin'θipjo] NM (comienzo)
beginning, start; (origen) origin; (base)
rudiment, basic idea; (moral) principle;
a principios de at the beginning of; **desde
el ~** from the first; **en un ~** at first
pringar [prin'gar] /1h/ VT (Culin: pan) to dip;
(ensuciar) to dirty; **pringarse** VR to get
splashed o soiled; **~ a algn en un asunto**
(fam) to involve sb in a matter
pringoso, -a [prin'goso, a] ADJ greasy;
(pegajoso) sticky

pringue ['pringe] VB ver **pringar** ▶ NM (grasa)
grease, fat, dripping
prioridad [priori'ðað] NF priority; (Auto)
right of way
prioritario, -a [priori'tarjo, a] ADJ (Inform)
foreground
prisa ['prisa] NF (apresuramiento) hurry, haste;
(rapidez) speed; (urgencia) (sense of) urgency;
a o de ~ quickly; **correr ~** to be urgent;
darse ~ to hurry up; **estar de o tener ~** to be
in a hurry
prisión [pri'sjon] NF (cárcel) prison; (período de
cárcel) imprisonment
prisionero, -a [prisjo'nero, a] NM/F prisoner
prismáticos [pris'matikos] NMPL binoculars
privación [priβa'θjon] NF deprivation; (falta)
want, privation; **privaciones** NFPL
hardships, privations
privado, -a [pri'βaðo, a] ADJ (particular)
private; (Pol: favorito) favourite (BRIT), favorite
(US); **en ~** privately, in private; **"~ y
confidencial"** "private and confidential"
privar [pri'βar] /1a/ VT to deprive; **privarse**
VR: **privarse de** (abstenerse de) to deprive o.s.
of; (renunciar a) to give up
privativo, -a [priβa'tiβo, a] ADJ exclusive
privatizar [priβati'θar] /1f/ VT to privatize
privilegiado, -a [priβile'xjaðo, a] ADJ
privileged; (memoria) very good ▶ NM/F
(afortunado) privileged person
privilegiar [priβile'xjar] /1b/ VT to grant a
privilege to; (favorecer) to favour
privilegio [priβi'lexjo] NM privilege;
(concesión) concession
pro [pro] NM o F profit, advantage ▶ PREP:
asociación ~ ciegos association for the
blind ▶ PREF: **~ soviético/americano**
pro-Soviet/-American; **en ~ de** on behalf of,
for; **los pros y los contras** the pros and cons
proa ['proa] NF (Naut) bow, prow; **de ~** bow
cpd, fore; ver tb **popa**
probabilidad [proβaβili'ðað] NF probability,
likelihood; (oportunidad, posibilidad) chance,
prospect
probable [pro'βaβle] ADJ probable, likely;
es ~ que (+ subjun) it is probable o likely that;
es ~ que no venga he probably won't come
probador [proβa'ðor] NM (persona) taster (of
wine etc); (en una tienda) fitting room
probar [pro'βar] /1l/ VT (demostrar) to prove;
(someter a prueba) to test, try out; (ropa) to try
on; (comida) to taste ▶ VI to try; **probarse** VR:
probarse un traje to try on a suit
probeta [pro'βeta] NF test tube
problema [pro'βlema] NM problem
procaz [pro'kaθ] ADJ insolent, impudent
procedencia [proθe'ðenθja] NF (principio)
source, origin; (lugar de salida) point of
departure

P

procedente [proθe'ðente] ADJ (*razonable*) reasonable; (*conforme a derecho*) proper, fitting; ~ **de** coming from, originating in

proceder [proθe'ðer] /**2a**/ VI (*avanzar*) to proceed; (*actuar*) to act; (*ser correcto*) to be right (and proper), be fitting ▶ NM (*comportamiento*) behaviour, conduct; **no procede obrar así** it is not right to act like that; ~ **de** to come from, originate in

procedimiento [proθeði'mjento] NM procedure; (*proceso*) process; (*método*) means, method; (*trámite*) proceedings *pl*

prócer ['proθer] NM (*persona eminente*) worthy; (*líder*) great man, leader; (*esp Am*) national hero

procesado, -a [proθe'saðo, a] NM/F accused (person)

procesador [proθesa'ðor] NM: ~ **de textos** (*Inform*) word processor

procesamiento [proθesa'mjento] NM (*Inform*) processing; ~ **de datos** data processing; ~ **por lotes** batch processing; ~ **solapado** multiprogramming; ~ **de textos** word processing

procesar [proθe'sar] /**1a**/ VT to try, put on trial; (*Inform*) to process

procesión [proθe'sjon] NF procession; **la ~ va por dentro** he keeps his troubles to himself

proceso [pro'θeso] NM process; (*Jur*) trial; (*lapso*) course (of time); (*Inform*): ~ **(automático) de datos** (automatic) data processing; ~ **no prioritario** background process; ~ **por pasadas** batch processing; ~ **en tiempo real** real-time programming

proclama [pro'klama] NF (*acto*) proclamation; (*cartel*) poster

proclamar [prokla'mar] /**1a**/ VT to proclaim

proclive [pro'kliβe] ADJ: ~ **(a)** inclined *o* prone (to)

procreación [prokrea'θjon] NF procreation

procrear [prokre'ar] /**1a**/ VT, VI to procreate

procurador, a [prokura'ðor, a] NM/F attorney, solicitor

procurar [proku'rar] /**1a**/ VT (*intentar*) to try, endeavour; (*conseguir*) to get, obtain; (*asegurar*) to secure; (*producir*) to produce

prodigar [proði'ɣar] /**1h**/ VT to lavish; **prodigarse** VR: **prodigarse en** to be lavish with

prodigio [pro'ðixjo] NM prodigy; (*milagro*) wonder, marvel; **niño ~** child prodigy

prodigioso, -a [proði'xjoso, a] ADJ prodigious, marvellous

pródigo, -a ['proðiɣo, a] ADJ (*rico*) rich, productive; **hijo ~** prodigal son

producción [proðuk'θjon] NF production; (*suma de productos*) output; (*producto*) product; ~ **en serie** mass production

producir [proðu'θir] /**3n**/ VT to produce; (*generar*) to cause, bring about; (*impresión*) to give; (*Com: interés*) to bear; **producirse** VR (*cambio*) to come about, happen; (*hacerse*) to be produced, be made; (*estallar*) to break out; (*accidente*) to take place; (*problema etc*) to arise

productividad [proðuktiβi'ðað] NF productivity

productivo, -a [proðuk'tiβo, a] ADJ productive; (*provechoso*) profitable

producto [pro'ðukto] NM (*resultado*) product; (*producción*) production; ~ **alimenticio** foodstuff; ~ **(nacional) bruto** gross (national) product; ~ **interior bruto** gross domestic product

productor, a [proðuk'tor, a] ADJ productive, producing ▶ NM/F producer

produje [pro'ðuxe], **produjera** [proðu'xera], **produzca** etc [pro'ðuθka] VB ver **producir**

proeza [pro'eθa] NF exploit, feat

profanar [profa'nar] /**1a**/ VT to desecrate, profane

profano, -a [pro'fano, a] ADJ profane ▶ NM/F (*inexperto*) layman(-woman); **soy ~ en música** I don't know anything about music

profecía [profe'θia] NF prophecy

proferir [profe'rir] /**3i**/ VT (*palabra, sonido*) to utter; (*injuria*) to hurl, let fly

profesar [profe'sar] /**1a**/ VT (*declarar*) to profess; (*practicar*) to practise

profesión [profe'sjon] NF profession; (*en formulario*) occupation; (*confesión*) avowal; **abogado de ~, de ~ abogado** a lawyer by profession

profesional [profesjo'nal] ADJ professional

profesor, a [profe'sor, a] NM/F teacher; (*instructor*) instructor; ~ **de universidad** lecturer; ~ **adjunto** assistant lecturer, associate professor (*US*)

profesorado [profeso'raðo] NM (*profesión*) teaching profession; (*cuerpo*) teaching staff, faculty (*US*); (*cargo*) professorship

profeta [pro'feta] NMF prophet

profetice etc [profe'tiθe] VB ver **profetizar**

profetizar [profeti'θar] /**1f**/ VT, VI to prophesy

profiera etc [pro'fjera], **profiriendo** etc [profi'rjendo] VB ver **proferir**

profilaxis [profi'laksis] NF INV prevention

prófugo, -a ['profuɣo, a] NM/F fugitive; (*desertor*) deserter

profundice etc [profun'diθe] VB ver **profundizar**

profundidad [profundi'ðað] NF depth; **tener una ~ de 30 cm** to be 30 cm deep

profundizar [profundi'θar] /**1f**/ (*fig*) VT to go into deeply, study in depth ▶ VI: ~ **en** to go into deeply

profundo, -a [pro'fundo, a] ADJ deep; (misterio, pensador) profound; **poco ~** shallow

profusión [profu'sjon] NF (abundancia) profusion; (prodigalidad) wealth

progenie [pro'xenje] NF offspring

progenitor [proxeni'tor] NM ancestor; **progenitores** NMPL (fam) parents

programa [pro'ɣrama] NM programme; (Inform) program; **~ de estudios** curriculum, syllabus; **~ verificador de ortografía** (Inform) spelling checker

programación [proɣrama'θjon] NF (Inform) programming; **~ estructurada** structured programming

programador, a [proɣrama'ðor, a] NM/F (computer) programmer; **~ de aplicaciones** applications programmer

programar [proɣra'mar] /1a/ VT (Inform) to program

progre ['proɣre] ADJ (fam) liberal

progresar [proɣre'sar] /1a/ VI to progress, make progress

progresión [proɣres'jon] NF: **~ geométrica/aritmética** geometric/arithmetic progression

progresista [proɣre'sista] ADJ, NMF progressive

progresivo, -a [proɣre'siβo, a] ADJ progressive; (gradual) gradual; (continuo) continuous

progreso [pro'ɣreso] NM (tb: **progresos**) progress; **hacer progresos** to progress, advance

prohibición [proiβi'θjon] NF prohibition, ban; **levantar la ~ de** to remove the ban on

prohibir [proi'βir] /3a/ VT to prohibit, ban, forbid; **se prohíbe fumar** no smoking; **"prohibido el paso"** "no entry"

prohibitivo, -a [proiβi'tiβo, a] ADJ prohibitive

prójimo, -a ['proximo, a] NM fellow man ▸ NM/F (vecino) neighbour

prole ['prole] NF (descendencia) offspring

proletariado [proleta'rjaðo] NM proletariat

proletario, -a [prole'tarjo, a] ADJ, NM/F proletarian

proliferación [prolifera'θjon] NF proliferation; **~ de armas nucleares** spread of nuclear arms

proliferar [prolife'rar] /1a/ VI to proliferate

prolífico, -a [pro'lifiko, a] ADJ prolific

prolijo, -a [pro'lixo, a] ADJ long-winded, tedious; (Am) neat

prólogo ['proloɣo] NM prologue; (preámbulo) preface, introduction

prolongación [prolonga'θjon] NF extension

prolongado, -a [prolon'gaðo, a] ADJ (largo) long; (alargado) lengthy

prolongar [prolon'gar] /1h/ VT (gen) to extend; (en el tiempo) to prolong; (calle, tubo) to make longer, extend; **prolongarse** VR (alargarse) to extend, go on

prolongue etc [pro'longe] VB ver **prolongar**

prom. ABR (= promedio) av.

promedio [pro'meðjo] NM average; (de distancia) middle, mid-point

promesa [pro'mesa] NF promise ▸ ADJ: **jugador ~** promising player; **faltar a una ~** to break a promise

prometer [prome'ter] /2a/ VT to promise ▸ VI to show promise; **prometerse** VR (dos personas) to get engaged

prometido, -a [prome'tiðo, a] ADJ promised; engaged ▸ NM/F fiancé (fiancée)

prominente [promi'nente] ADJ prominent

promiscuidad [promiskwi'ðað] NF promiscuity

promiscuo, -a [pro'miskwo, a] ADJ promiscuous

promoción [promo'θjon] NF promotion; (año) class, year; **~ por correspondencia directa** (Com) direct mailshot; **~ de ventas** sales promotion o drive

promocionar [promoθjo'nar] /1a/ VT (Com: dar publicidad) to promote

promontorio [promon'torjo] NM promontory

promotor [promo'tor] NM promoter; (instigador) instigator

promover [promo'βer] /2h/ VT to promote; (causar) to cause; (juicio) to bring; (motín) to instigate, stir up

promueva etc [pro'mweβa] VB ver **promover**

promulgar [promul'ɣar] /1h/ VT to promulgate; (fig) to proclaim

promulgue etc [pro'mulɣe] VB ver **promulgar**

pronombre [pro'nombre] NM pronoun

pronosticar [pronosti'kar] /1g/ VT to predict, foretell, forecast

pronóstico [pro'nostiko] NM prediction, forecast; (profecía) omen; (Med: diagnóstico) prognosis; **de ~ leve** slight, not serious; **~ del tiempo** weather forecast

pronostique etc [pronos'tike] VB ver **pronosticar**

prontitud [pronti'tuð] NF speed, quickness

pronto, -a ['pronto, a] ADJ (rápido) prompt, quick; (preparado) ready ▸ ADV quickly, promptly; (en seguida) at once, right away; (dentro de poco) soon; (temprano) early ▸ NM urge, sudden feeling; **tener prontos de enojo** to be quick-tempered; **al ~** at first; **de ~** suddenly; **tiene unos prontos muy malos** he gets ratty all of a sudden (fam); **¡hasta ~!** see you soon!; **lo más ~ posible** as soon as possible; **por lo ~** meanwhile, for the present; **tan ~ como** as soon as

pronunciación [pronunθja'θjon] NF
pronunciation

pronunciado, -a [pronun'θjaðo, a] ADJ
(marcado) pronounced; *(curva etc)* sharp;
(facciones) marked

pronunciamiento [pronunθja'mjento] NM
(rebelión) insurrection

pronunciar [pronun'θjar] /**1b**/ VT to
pronounce; *(discurso)* to make, deliver; *(Jur:
sentencia)* to pass, pronounce; **pronunciarse**
VR to revolt, rise, rebel; *(declararse)* to declare
o.s.; **pronunciarse sobre** to pronounce on

propagación [propaɣa'θjon] NF
propagation; *(difusión)* spread(ing)

propaganda [propa'ɣanda] NF *(política)*
propaganda; *(comercial)* advertising; **hacer ~
de** *(Com)* to advertise

propagar [propa'ɣar] /**1h**/ VT to propagate;
(difundir) to spread, disseminate; **propagarse**
VR *(Bio)* to propagate; *(fig)* to spread

propague etc [pro'paɣe] VB ver **propagar**

propalar [propa'lar] /**1a**/ VT *(divulgar)* to
divulge; *(publicar)* to publish an account of

propano [pro'pano] NM propane

propasarse [propa'sarse] /**1a**/ VR *(excederse)* to
go too far; *(sexualmente)* to take liberties

propensión [propen'sjon] NF inclination,
propensity

propenso, -a [pro'penso, a] ADJ: **~ a** prone *o*
inclined to; **ser ~ a hacer algo** to be inclined
o have a tendency to do sth

propiamente [propja'mente] ADV properly;
(realmente) really, exactly; **~ dicho** real, true

propicio, -a [pro'piθjo, a] ADJ favourable,
propitious

propiedad [propje'ðað] NF property;
(posesión) possession, ownership;
(conveniencia) suitability; *(exactitud)* accuracy;
~ particular private property; **~ pública**
(Com) public ownership; **ceder algo a algn
en ~** to transfer to sb the full rights over sth

propietario, -a [propje'tarjo, a] NM/F owner,
proprietor

propina [pro'pina] NF tip; **dar algo de ~** to
give something extra

propinar [propi'nar] /**1a**/ VT *(golpe)* to strike;
(azotes) to give

propio, -a ['propjo, a] ADJ own, of one's own;
(característico) characteristic, typical;
(conveniente) proper; *(mismo)* selfsame, very;
el ~ ministro the minister himself; **¿tienes
casa propia?** have you a house of your own?;
eso es muy ~ de él that's just like him;
tiene un olor muy ~ it has a smell of its own

propondré etc [propon'dre] VB ver **proponer**

proponente [propo'nente] NM proposer,
mover

proponer [propo'ner] /**2q**/ VT to propose, put
forward; *(candidato)* to propose, nominate;

(problema) to pose; **proponerse** VR to propose,
plan, intend

proponga etc [pro'ponga] VB ver **proponer**

proporción [propor'θjon] NF proportion;
(Mat) ratio; *(razón, porcentaje)* rate;
proporciones NFPL dimensions *(fig)*; size *sg*;
en ~ con in proportion to

proporcionado, -a [proporθjo'naðo, a] ADJ
proportionate; *(regular)* medium, middling;
(justo) just right; **bien ~** well-proportioned

proporcional [proporθjo'nal] ADJ
proportional; **~ a** proportional to

proporcionar [proporθjo'nar] /**1a**/ VT *(dar)* to
give, supply, provide; **esto le proporciona
una renta anual de ...** this brings him in a
yearly income of ...

proposición [proposi'θjon] NF proposition;
(propuesta) proposal

propósito [pro'posito] NM *(intención)* purpose;
(intento) aim, intention ▸ ADV: **a ~** by the way,
incidentally; *(a posta)* on purpose,
deliberately; **a ~ de** about, with regard to

propuesto, -a [pro'pwesto, a] PP de **proponer**
▸ NF proposal

propugnar [propuɣ'nar] /**1a**/ VT to uphold

propulsar [propul'sar] /**1a**/ VT to drive,
propel; *(fig)* to promote, encourage

propulsión [propul'sjon] NF propulsion;
~ a chorro *o* **por reacción** jet propulsion

propuse etc [pro'puse] VB ver **proponer**

prorrata [pro'rrata] NF *(porción)* share, quota,
prorate *(US)* ▸ ADV *(Com)* pro rata

prorratear [prorrate'ar] /**1a**/ VT *(dividir)* to
share out, prorate *(US)*

prórroga ['prorroɣa] NF *(gen)* extension; *(Jur)*
stay; *(Com)* deferment; *(Deporte)* extra time

prorrogable [prorro'ɣaβle] ADJ which can be
extended

prorrogar [prorro'ɣar] /**1h**/ VT *(período)* to
extend; *(decisión)* to defer, postpone

prorrogue etc [pro'rroɣe] VB ver **prorrogar**

prorrumpir [prorrum'pir] /**3a**/ VI to burst
forth, break out; **~ en gritos** to start
shouting; **~ en lágrimas** to burst into tears

prosa ['prosa] NF prose

prosaico, -a [pro'saiko, a] ADJ prosaic, dull

proscribir [proskri'βir] /**3a**/ VT to prohibit, ban;
(desterrar) to exile, banish; *(partido)* to proscribe

proscripción [proskrip'θjon] NF *(prohibition)*
prohibition *(frm)*, ban; *(de partido)*
proscription; *(destierro)* banishment

proscrito, -a [pros'krito, a] PP de **proscribir**
▸ ADJ *(prohibido)* banned; *(desterrado)* outlawed
▸ NM/F *(exilado)* exile; *(bandido)* outlaw

prosecución [proseku'θjon] NF
continuation; *(persecución)* pursuit

proseguir [prose'ɣir] /**3d, 3k**/ VT to continue,
carry on, proceed with; *(investigación, estudio)*
to pursue ▸ VI to continue, go on

prosiga etc [pro'siɣa], **prosiguiendo** etc [prosi'ɣjenðo] vb ver **proseguir**

prosista [pro'sista] NMF (escritor) prose writer

prospección [prospek'θjon] NF exploration; (del petróleo, del oro) prospecting

prospecto [pros'pekto] NM prospectus; (folleto) leaflet, sheet of instructions

prosperar [prospe'rar] /1a/ vi to prosper, thrive, flourish

prosperidad [prosperi'ðað] NF prosperity; (éxito) success

próspero, -a ['prospero, a] ADJ prosperous, thriving; (que tiene éxito) successful

prostíbulo [pros'tiβulo] NM brothel

prostitución [prostitu'θjon] NF prostitution

prostituir [prosti'twir] /3g/ vt to prostitute; **prostituirse** vr to prostitute o.s., become a prostitute

prostituta [prosti'tuta] NF prostitute

prostituyendo etc [prostitu'jendo] vb ver **prostituir**

protagonice etc [protaɣo'niθe] vb ver **protagonizar**

protagonista [protaɣo'nista] NMF protagonist; (Lit: personaje) main character, hero/heroine

protagonizar [protaɣoni'θar] /1f/ vt to head, take the chief role in

protección [protek'θjon] NF protection

proteccionismo [protekθjo'nismo] NM (Com) protectionism

protector, a [protek'tor, a] ADJ protective, protecting; (tono) patronizing ▶ NM/F protector; (bienhechor) patron; (de la tradición) guardian

proteger [prote'xer] /2c/ vt to protect; **~ contra grabación** o **contra escritura** (Inform) to write-protect

protegido, -a [prote'xiðo, a] NM/F protégé (protégée)

proteína [prote'ina] NF protein

proteja etc [pro'texa] vb ver **proteger**

prótesis ['protesis] NF (Med) prosthesis

protesta [pro'testa] NF protest; (declaración) protestation

protestante [protes'tante] ADJ Protestant

protestar [protes'tar] /1a/ vt to protest, declare; (fe) to protest ▶ vi to protest; (objetar) to object; **cheque protestado por falta de fondos** cheque referred to drawer

protocolo [proto'kolo] NM protocol; **sin protocolos** (formalismo) informal(ly)

protón [pro'ton] NM proton

prototipo [proto'tipo] NM prototype; (ideal) model

protuberancia [protuβe'ranθja] NF protuberance

prov. ABR (= provincia) prov.

provecho [pro'βetʃo] NM advantage, benefit; (Finanzas) profit; **¡buen ~!** bon appétit!; **en ~ de** to the benefit of; **sacar ~ de** to benefit from, profit by

provechoso, -a [proβe'tʃoso, a] ADJ (ventajoso) advantageous; (beneficioso) beneficial, useful; (Finanzas: lucrativo) profitable

proveedor, a [proβee'ðor, a] NM/F (abastecedor) supplier; (distribuidor) dealer; **~ de (acceso a) Internet** Internet Service Provider

proveer [proβe'er] /2e/ vt to provide, supply; (preparar) to provide, get ready; (vacante) to fill; (negocio) to transact, dispatch ▶ vi: **~ a** to provide for; **proveerse** vr: **proveerse de** to provide o.s. with

provendré etc [proβen'dre], **provenga** etc [pro'βenga] vb ver **provenir**

provenir [proβe'nir] /3r/ vi: **~ de** to come from

Provenza [pro'βenθa] NF Provence

proverbial [proβer'βjal] ADJ proverbial; (fig) notorious

proverbio [pro'βerβjo] NM proverb

proveyendo etc [proβe'jendo] vb ver **proveer**

providencia [proβi'ðenθja] NF providence; (previsión) foresight; **providencias** NFPL measures, steps

provincia [pro'βinθja] NF province; (Esp Admin) ≈ county, ≈ region (Scot); **un pueblo de ~(s)** a country town; see note

> Spain is divided up into 55 administrative provincias, including the islands, and territories in North Africa. Each one has a capital de provincia, which generally bears the same name. Provincias are grouped by geography, history and culture into comunidades autónomas. It should be noted that the term comarca normally has a purely geographical function in Spanish, but in Catalonia it designates administrative boundaries.

provinciano, -a [proβin'θjano, a] ADJ provincial; (del campo) country cpd

proviniendo etc [proβi'njendo] vb ver **provenir**

provisión [proβi'sjon] NF provision; (abastecimiento) provision, supply; (medida) measure, step

provisional [proβisjo'nal] ADJ provisional

provisorio, -a [proβi'sorjo, a] ADJ (esp Am) provisional

provisto, -a [pro'βisto, a] ADJ: **~ de** provided o supplied with; (que tiene) having, possessing

provocación [proβoka'θjon] NF provocation

provocador, a [proβoka'ðor, a] ADJ provocative, provoking

P

provocar [proβo'kar] /**1g**/ VT to provoke; (*alentar*) to tempt, invite; (*causar*) to bring about, lead to; (*promover*) to promote; (*estimular*) to rouse, stir, stimulate; (*protesta, explosión*) to cause, spark off; (*AM*): **¿te provoca un café?** would you like a coffee?

provocativo, -a [proβoka'tiβo, a] ADJ provocative

provoque *etc* [pro'βoke] VB *ver* **provocar**

proxeneta [prokse'neta] NMF go-between; (*de prostitutas*) pimp (procuress)

próximamente [proksima'mente] ADV shortly, soon

proximidad [proksimi'ðað] NF closeness, proximity

próximo, -a ['proksimo, a] ADJ near, close; (*vecino*) neighbouring; (*el que viene*) next; **en fecha próxima** at an early date; **el mes ~** next month

proyección [projek'θjon] NF projection; (*Cine*) showing; (*diapositiva*) slide, transparency; (*influencia*) influence; **el tiempo de ~ es de 35 minutos** the film runs for 35 minutes

proyectar [projek'tar] /**1a**/ VT (*objeto*) to hurl, throw; (*luz*) to cast, shed; (*Cine*) to screen, show; (*planear*) to plan

proyectil [projek'til] NM projectile, missile; **~ (tele)dirigido** guided missile

proyecto [pro'jekto] NM plan; (*idea*) project; (*estimación de coste*) detailed estimate; **tener algo en ~** to be planning sth; **~ de ley** (*Pol*) bill

proyector [projek'tor] NM (*Cine*) projector

prudencia [pru'ðenθja] NF (*sabiduría*) wisdom, prudence; (*cautela*) care

prudente [pru'ðente] ADJ sensible, wise, prudent; (*cauteloso*) careful

prueba ['prweβa] VB *ver* **probar** ▶ NF proof; (*ensayo*) test, trial; (*cantidad*) taste, sample; (*saboreo*) testing, sampling; (*de ropa*) fitting; (*Deporte*) event; **a ~** on trial; (*Com*) on approval; **a ~ de** proof against; **a ~ de agua/fuego** waterproof/fireproof; **~ de capacitación** (*Com*) proficiency test; **~ de fuego** (*fig*) acid test; **~ de vallas** hurdles; **someter a ~** to put to the test; **¿tiene usted ~ de ello?** can you prove it?, do you have proof?

prurito [pru'rito] NM itch; (*de bebé*) nappy rash; (*anhelo*) urge

psico... [siko] PREF psycho...

psicoanálisis [sikoa'nalisis] NM psychoanalysis

psicoanalista [sikoana'lista] NMF psychoanalyst

psicología [sikolo'xia] NF psychology

psicológico, -a [siko'loxiko, a] ADJ psychological

psicólogo, -a [si'koloɣo, a] NM/F psychologist

psicópata [si'kopata] NMF psychopath

psicosis [si'kosis] NF INV psychosis

psicosomático, -a [sikoso'matiko, a] ADJ psychosomatic

psicoterapia [sikote'rapja] NF psychotherapy

psiquiatra [si'kjatra] NMF psychiatrist

psiquiátrico, -a [si'kjatriko, a] ADJ psychiatric ▶ NM mental hospital

psíquico, -a ['sikiko, a] ADJ psychic(al)

PSOE [pe'soe] NM ABR = **Partido Socialista Obrero Español**

PSS NF ABR (= *Prestación Social Sustitutoria*) community service for conscientious objectors

Pta. ABR (*Geo*: = *Punta*) Pt.

pta(s) ABR (*Historia*) = **peseta**

pts ABR (*Historia*) = **pesetas**

púa ['pua] NF sharp point; (*Bot, Zool*) prickle, spine; (*para guitarra*) plectrum; **alambre de púas** barbed wire

pub [puβ/paβ/paf] NM bar

púber, a ['puβer, a] ADJ, NM/F adolescent

pubertad [puβer'tað] NF puberty

publicación [puβlika'θjon] NF publication

publicar [puβli'kar] /**1g**/ VT (*editar*) to publish; (*hacer público*) to publicize; (*divulgar*) to make public, divulge

publicidad [puβliθi'ðað] NF publicity; (*Com*) advertising; **dar ~ a** to publicize, give publicity to; **~ gráfica** display advertising; **~ en el punto de venta** point-of-sale advertising

publicitar [puβliθi'tar] /**1a**/ VT to publicize

publicitario, -a [puβliθi'tarjo, a] ADJ publicity *cpd*; advertising *cpd*

público, -a ['puβliko, a] ADJ public ▶ NM public; (*Teat etc*) audience; (*Deporte*) spectators *pl*, crowd; (*en restaurantes etc*) clients *pl*; **el gran ~** the general public; **hacer ~** to publish; (*difundir*) to disclose; **~ objetivo** (*Com*) target audience

publique *etc* [pu'βlike] VB *ver* **publicar**

pucherazo [putʃe'raθo] NM (*fraude*) electoral fiddle; **dar ~** to rig an election

puchero [pu'tʃero] NM (*Culin*: *olla*) cooking pot; (: *guiso*) stew; **hacer pucheros** to pout

pucho ['putʃo] (*AM fam*) NM cigarette, fag (*BRIT*)

pude *etc* VB *ver* **poder**

pudibundo, -a [puði'βundo, a] ADJ bashful

púdico, -a ['puðiko, a] ADJ modest; (*pudibundo*) bashful

pudiendo *etc* [pu'ðjendo] VB *ver* **poder**

pudiente [pu'ðjente] ADJ (*opulento*) wealthy; (*poderoso*) powerful

pudiera *etc* VB *ver* **poder**

pudín [pu'ðin] NM pudding

pudor [pu'ðor] NM modesty; (*vergüenza*) (sense of) shame

pudoroso, -a [puðo'roso, a] ADJ (*modesto*) modest; (*casto*) chaste

pudrir [pu'ðrir] /**3a**/ VT to rot; (*fam*) to upset, annoy; **pudrirse** VR to rot, decay; (*fig*) to rot, languish

pueblerino, -a [pweβle'rino, a] ADJ (*lugareño*) small-town *cpd*; (*persona*) rustic, provincial ▶ NM/F (*aldeano*) country person

pueblo ['pweβlo] VB ver **poblar** ▶ NM people; (*nación*) nation; (*aldea*) village; (*plebe*) common people; (*población pequeña*) small town, country town

puedo etc ['pweðo] VB ver **poder**

puente ['pwente] NM (*gen*) bridge; (*Naut: tb:* **puente de mando**) bridge; (: *cubierta*) deck; **~ aéreo** shuttle service; **~ colgante** suspension bridge; **~ levadizo** drawbridge; **hacer ~** (*fam*) to take a long weekend

> When a public holiday in Spain falls on a Tuesday or Thursday it is common practice for employers to make the Monday or Friday a holiday as well and to give everyone a four-day weekend. This is known as *hacer puente*. When a named public holiday such as the *Día de la Constitución* falls on a Tuesday or Thursday, people refer to the whole holiday period as e.g. the *puente de la Constitución*.

puenting ['pwentin] NM bungee jumping

puerco, -a ['pwerko, a] ADJ (*sucio*) dirty, filthy; (*obsceno*) disgusting ▶ NM/F pig (sow); **~ espín** porcupine

pueril [pwe'ril] ADJ childish

puerro ['pwerro] NM leek

puerta ['pwerta] NF door; (*de jardín*) gate; (*portal*) doorway; (*fig*) gateway; (*gol*) goal; (*Inform*) port; **a la ~** at the door; **a ~ cerrada** behind closed doors; **~ corredera/giratoria** sliding/swing o revolving door; **~ principal/ trasera o de servicio** front/back door; **~ (de transmisión en) paralelo/serie** (*Inform*) parallel/serial port; **tomar la ~** (*fam*) to leave

puerto ['pwerto] NM (*tb Inform*) port; (*de mar*) seaport; (*paso*) pass; (*fig*) haven, refuge; **llegar a ~** (*fig*) to get over a difficulty

Puerto Rico [pwerto'riko] NM Puerto Rico

puertorriqueño, -a [pwertorri'keɲo, a] ADJ, NM/F Puerto Rican

pues [pwes] ADV (*entonces*) then; (*¡entonces!*) well, well then; (*así que*) so ▶ CONJ (*porque*) since; **¡~ sí!** yes!, certainly!; **~ ... no sé** well ... I don't know

puesto, -a ['pwesto, a] PP *de* **poner** ▶ ADJ dressed ▶ NM (*lugar, posición*) place; (*trabajo*) post, job; (*Mil*) post; (*Com*) stall; (*quiosco*) kiosk ▶ CONJ: **~ que** since, as ▶ NF (*apuesta*) bet, stake; **tener algo ~** to have sth on, be wearing sth; **~ de mercado** market stall; **~ de policía** police station; **~ de socorro** first aid post; **puesta en escena** staging; **puesta al día** updating; **puesta en marcha** starting; **puesta a punto** fine tuning; **puesta del sol** sunset; **puesta a cero** (*Inform*) reset

púgil ['puxil] NM boxer

pugna ['puɣna] NF battle, conflict

pugnar [puɣ'nar] /**1a**/ VI (*luchar*) to struggle, fight; (*pelear*) to fight

puja ['puxa] NF (*esfuerzo*) attempt; (*en una subasta*) bid

pujante [pu'xante] ADJ strong, vigorous

pujar [pu'xar] /**1a**/ VT (*precio*) to raise, push up ▶ VI (*en licitación*) to bid, bid up; (*fig: esforzarse*) to struggle, strain

pulcro, -a ['pulkro, a] ADJ neat, tidy

pulga ['pulɣa] NF flea; **tener malas pulgas** to be short-tempered

pulgada [pul'ɣaða] NF inch

pulgar [pul'ɣar] NM thumb

pulgón [pul'ɣon] NM plant louse, greenfly

pulir [pu'lir] /**3a**/ VT to polish; (*alisar*) to smooth; (*fig*) to polish up, touch up

pulla ['puʎa] NF cutting remark

pulmón [pul'mon] NM lung; **a pleno ~** (*respirar*) deeply; (*gritar*) at the top of one's voice; **~ de acero** iron lung

pulmonía [pulmo'nia] NF pneumonia

pulpa ['pulpa] NF pulp; (*de fruta*) flesh, soft part

pulpería [pulpe'ria] NF (*Am*) small grocery store

púlpito ['pulpito] NM pulpit

pulpo ['pulpo] NM octopus

pulque ['pulke] NM pulque

> Pulque is a thick, white, alcoholic drink which is very popular in Mexico. In ancient times it was considered sacred by the Aztecs. It is produced by fermenting the juice of the *maguey*, a Mexican cactus similar to the agave. It can be drunk by itself or mixed with fruit or vegetable juice.

pulsación [pulsa'θjon] NF beat, pulsation; (*Anat*) throb(bing); (*en máquina de escribir*) tap; (*de pianista, mecanógrafo*) touch; **~ de una tecla** (*Inform*) keystroke; **~ doble** (*Inform*) strikeover; **pulsaciones** pulse rate

pulsador [pulsa'ðor] NM button, push button

pulsar [pul'sar] /**1a**/ VT (*tecla*) to touch, tap; (*Mus*) to play; (*botón*) to press, push ▶ VI to pulsate; (*latir*) to beat, throb

pulsera [pul'sera] NF bracelet; **reloj de ~** wristwatch

pulso ['pulso] NM (*Med*) pulse; (*fuerza*) strength; (*firmeza*) steadiness, steady hand;

P

hacer algo a ~ to do sth unaided o by one's own efforts

pulular [pulu'lar] /**1a**/ VI (estar plagado): ~ **(de)** to swarm (with)

pulverice etc [pulβe'riθe] VB ver **pulverizar**

pulverizador [pulβeriθa'ðor] NM spray, spray gun

pulverizar [pulβeri'θar] /**1f**/ VT to pulverize; (líquido) to spray

puna ['puna] NF (Am Med) mountain sickness

punce etc ['punθe] VB ver **punzar**

punción [pun'θjon] NF (Med) puncture

pundonor [pundo'nor] NM (dignidad) self-respect

punición [puni'θjon] NF punishment

punitivo, -a [puni'tiβo, a] ADJ punitive

punki ['punki] ADJ, NM F punk

punta ['punta] NF point, tip; (extremidad) end; (promontorio) headland; (Costura) corner; (Tec) small nail; (fig) touch, trace; **horas puntas** peak hours, rush hours; **sacar** ~ **a** to sharpen; **de** ~ on end; **de** ~ **a** ~ from one end to the other; **estar de** ~ to be edgy; **ir de** ~ **en blanco** to be all dressed up to the nines; **tener algo en la** ~ **de la lengua** to have sth on the tip of one's tongue; **se le pusieron los pelos de** ~ her hair stood on end

puntada [pun'taða] NF (Costura) stitch

puntal [pun'tal] NM prop, support

puntapié [punta'pje] (pl **puntapiés**) NM kick; **echar a algn a puntapiés** to kick sb out

punteado, -a [punte'aðo, a] ADJ (moteado) dotted; (diseño) of dots ▶ NM (Mus) twang

puntear [punte'ar] /**1a**/ VT to tick, mark; (Mus) to pluck

puntería [punte'ria] NF (de arma) aim, aiming; (destreza) marksmanship

puntero, -a [pun'tero, a] ADJ leading ▶ NM (señal, Inform) pointer; (dirigente) leader

puntiagudo, -a [puntja'ɣuðo, a] ADJ sharp, pointed

puntilla [pun'tiʎa] NF (Tec) tack, braid; (Costura) lace edging; **(andar) de puntillas** (to walk) on tiptoe

puntilloso, -a [punti'ʎoso, a] ADJ (pundonoroso) punctilious; (susceptible) touchy

punto ['punto] NM (gen) point; (señal diminuta) spot, dot; (lugar) spot, place; (momento) point, moment; (en un examen) mark; (tema) item; (Costura) stitch; (Inform: impresora) pitch; (: pantalla) pixel; **a** ~ ready; **estar a** ~ **de** to be on the point of o about to; **llegar a** ~ to come just at the right moment; **al** ~ at once; **en** ~ on the dot; **estar en su** ~ (Culin) to be done to a turn; **hasta cierto** ~ to some extent; **hacer** ~ to knit; **poner un motor en** ~ to tune an engine; ~ **de partida/de congelación/de fusión** starting/freezing/melting point; ~ **de vista** point of view, viewpoint; ~ **muerto**

dead centre; (Auto) neutral (gear); **puntos a tratar** matters to be discussed, agenda sg; ~ **final** full stop; **dos puntos** colon; ~ **y coma** semicolon; ~ **acápite** (Am) full stop, new paragraph; ~ **de interrogación** question mark; **puntos suspensivos** suspension points; ~ **de equilibrio/de pedido** (Com) breakeven/reorder point; ~ **inicial** o **de partida** (Inform) home; ~ **de referencia/de venta** (Com) benchmark point/point-of-sale

puntocom [punto'kom] NF INV, ADJ INV dotcom, dot.com

puntuación [puntwa'θjon] NF punctuation; (puntos: en examen) mark(s) pl; (: Deporte) score

puntual [pun'twal] ADJ (a tiempo) punctual; (cálculo) exact, accurate; (informe) reliable

puntualice etc [puntwa'liθe] VB ver **puntualizar**

puntualidad [puntwali'ðað] NF (de llegada) punctuality; (exactitud) exactness, accuracy; (fiabilidad) reliability

puntualizar [puntwali'θar] /**1f**/ VT to fix, specify

puntuar [pun'twar] /**1e**/ VT (Ling, Tip) to punctuate; (examen) to mark ▶ VI (Deporte) to score, count

punzada [pun'θaða] NF (puntura) prick; (Med) stitch; (dolor) twinge (of pain)

punzante [pun'θante] ADJ (dolor) shooting, sharp; (herramienta) sharp; (comentario) biting

punzar [pun'θar] /**1f**/ VT to prick, pierce ▶ VI to shoot, stab

punzón [pun'θon] NM (Tec) punch

puñado [pu'ɲaðo] NM handful (tb fig); **a puñados** by handfuls

puñal [pu'ɲal] NM dagger

puñalada [puɲa'laða] NF stab

puñeta [pu'ɲeta] NF: **¡~!**, **¡qué ~(s)!** (fam!) hell!; **mandar a algn a hacer puñetas** (fam) to tell sb to go to hell

puñetazo [puɲe'taθo] NM punch

puño ['puɲo] NM (Anat) fist; (cantidad) fistful, handful; (Costura) cuff; (de herramienta) handle; **como un** ~ (verdad) obvious; (palpable) tangible, visible; **de** ~ **y letra del poeta** in the poet's own handwriting

pupila [pu'pila] NF (Anat) pupil

pupitre [pu'pitre] NM desk

puré [pu're] (pl **purés**) NM purée; (sopa) (thick) soup; ~ **de patatas**, (Esp) ~ **de papas** (Am) mashed potatoes; **estar hecho** ~ (fig) to be knackered

pureza [pu'reθa] NF purity

purga ['purɣa] NF purge

purgante [pur'ɣante] ADJ, NM purgative

purgar [pur'ɣar] /**1h**/ VT to purge; (Pol: depurar) to purge, liquidate; **purgarse** VR (Med) to take a purge

purgatorio [purɣa'torjo] NM purgatory

purgue etc ['purɣe] VB ver **purgar**
purificar [purifi'kar] /1g/ VT to purify; (refinar) to refine
purifique etc [puri'fike] VB ver **purificar**
puritano, -a [puri'tano, a] ADJ (actitud) puritanical; (iglesia, tradición) puritan ▶ NM/F puritan
puro, -a ['puro, a] ADJ pure; (depurado) unadulterated; (oro) solid; (cielo) clear; (verdad) simple, plain ▶ ADV: **de ~ cansado** out of sheer tiredness ▶ NM cigar; **por pura casualidad** by sheer chance
púrpura ['purpura] NF purple
purpúreo, -a [pur'pureo, a] ADJ purple
pus [pus] NM pus
puse etc ['puse] VB ver **poner**

pusiera etc VB ver **poder**
pústula ['pustula] NF pimple, sore
puta ['puta] NF whore, prostitute
putada [pu'taða] NF (fam!): **hacer una ~ a algn** to play a dirty trick on sb; **¡qué ~!** what a pain in the arse! (fam!)
putería [pute'ria] NF (prostitución) prostitution; (prostíbulo) brothel
putrefacción [putrefak'θjon] NF rotting, putrefaction
pútrido, -a ['putriðo, a] ADJ rotten
puzzle ['puθle] NM puzzle
PVP ABR (Esp: = Precio Venta al Público) ≈ RRP
PYME ['pime] NF ABR (= Pequeña y Mediana Empresa) SME
Pza ABR = **plaza**

P

Qq

Q, q [ku] NF (*letra*) Q, q; **Q de Querido** Q for Queen

q.e.p.d. ABR (= *que en paz descanse*) R.I.P

qm ABR = **quintal métrico**; **quintales métricos**

qts. ABR = **quilates**

(PALABRA CLAVE)

que [ke] CONJ **1** (*con oración subordinada: muchas veces no se traduce*) that; **dijo que vendría** he said (that) he would come; **espero que lo encuentres** I hope (that) you find it; **dile que me llame** ask him to call me; *ver tb* **el**

2 (*en oración independiente*): **¡que entre!** send him in; **¡que aproveche!** enjoy your meal!; **¡que se mejore tu padre!** I hope your father gets better; **¡que lo haga él!** he can do it!; (*orden*) get him to do it!

3 (*enfático*): **¿me quieres? — ¡que sí!** do you love me? — of course!; **te digo que sí** I'm telling you

4 (*consecutivo: muchas veces no se traduce*) that; **es tan grande que no lo puedo levantar** it's so big (that) I can't lift it

5 (*comparaciones*) than; **yo que tú/él** if I were you/him; *ver tb* **más**; **menos**

6 (*valor disyuntivo*): **que le guste o no** whether he likes it or not; **que venga o que no venga** whether he comes or not

7 (*porque*): **no puedo, que tengo que quedarme en casa** I can't, I've got to stay in

8: **siguió toca que toca** he kept on playing ▶ PRON **1** (*cosa*) that, which; (: +*prep*) which; **el sombrero que te compraste** the hat (that *o* which) you bought; **la cama en que dormí** the bed (that *o* which) I slept in; **el día (en) que ella nació** the day (when) she was born

2 (*persona: suj*) that, who; (: *objeto*) that, whom; **el amigo que me acompañó al museo** the friend that *o* who went to the museum with me; **la chica que invité** the girl (that *o* whom) I invited

qué [ke] ADJ what?, which? ▶ PRON what?; **¡~ divertido/asco!** how funny/revolting!; **¡~ día más espléndido!** what a glorious day!; **¿~ edad tienes?** how old are you?; **¿de ~ me hablas?** what are you saying to me?; **¿~ tal?** how are you?, how are things?; **¿~ hay (de nuevo)?** what's new?; **¿~ más?** anything else?

quebrada [ke'βraða] NF *ver* **quebrado**

quebradero [keβra'ðero] NM: **~ de cabeza** headache, worry

quebradizo, -a [keβra'ðiθo, a] ADJ fragile; (*persona*) frail

quebrado, -a [ke'βraðo, a] ADJ (*roto*) broken; (*terreno*) rough, uneven ▶ NM/F bankrupt ▶ NM (*Mat*) fraction ▶ NF ravine; **~ rehabilitado** discharged bankrupt

quebradura [keβra'ðura] NF (*fisura*) fissure; (*Med*) rupture

quebrantamiento [keβranta'mjento] NM (*acto*) breaking; (*de ley*) violation; (*estado*) exhaustion

quebrantar [keβran'tar] /**1a**/ VT (*infringir*) to violate, transgress; **quebrantarse** VR (*persona*) to fail in health

quebranto [ke'βranto] NM damage, harm; (*decaimiento*) exhaustion; (*dolor*) grief, pain

quebrar [ke'βrar] /**1j**/ VT to break, smash ▶ VI to go bankrupt; **quebrarse** VR to break, get broken; (*Med*) to be ruptured

quechua ['ketʃua] ADJ, NMF Quechua

queda ['keða] NF: **(toque de) ~** curfew

quedar [ke'ðar] /**1a**/ VI to stay, remain; (*encontrarse*) to be; (*restar*) to remain, be left; **quedarse** VR to remain, stay (behind); **~ en** (*acordar*) to agree on/to; (*acabar siendo*) to end up as; **~ por hacer** to be still to be done; **~ ciego/mudo** to be left blind/dumb; **no te queda bien ese vestido** that dress doesn't suit you; **quedamos a las seis** we agreed to meet at six; **eso queda muy lejos** that's a long way (away); **nos quedan 12 kilómetros para llegar al pueblo** there are still 12 km before we get to the village;

no queda otra there's no alternative;
quedarse (con) algo to keep sth; **quedarse
con algn** (*fam*) to swindle sb; **quedarse en
nada** to come to nothing o nought;
quedarse frito (*fam*) to fall asleep, to crash
out; **quedarse sin** to run out of

quedo, -a ['keðo, a] ADJ still ▶ ADV softly,
gently

quehacer [kea'θer] NM task, job;
quehaceres (domésticos) household
chores

queja ['kexa] NF complaint

quejarse [ke'xarse] /1a/ VR (*enfermo*) to moan,
groan; (*protestar*) to complain; **~ de que ...**
to complain (about the fact) that ...

quejica [ke'xika] ADJ grumpy, complaining
▶ NMF grumbler, whinger

quejido [ke'xiðo] NM moan

quejoso, -a [ke'xoso, a] ADJ complaining

quema ['kema] NF fire; (*combustión*) burning

quemado, -a [ke'maðo, a] ADJ burnt; (*irritado*)
annoyed

quemadura [kema'ðura] NF burn, scald; (*de
sol*) sunburn; (*de fusible*) blow-out

quemar [ke'mar] /1a/ VT to burn; (*fig:
malgastar*) to burn up, squander; (*Com: precios*)
to slash, cut; (*fastidiar*) to annoy, bug ▶ VI to
be burning hot; **quemarse** VR (*consumirse*) to
burn (up); (*del sol*) to get sunburnt

quemarropa [kema'rropa]: **a ~** *adv*
point-blank

quemazón [kema'θon] NF burn; (*calor*)
intense heat; (*sensación*) itch

quena ['kena] NF (*Am*) Indian flute

quepo *etc* ['kepo] VB *ver* **caber**

querella [ke'reʎa] NF (*Jur*) charge; (*disputa*)
dispute

querellarse [kere'ʎarse] /1a/ VR to file a
complaint

querencia [ke'renθja] NF (*Zool*) homing
instinct; (*fig*) homesickness

(PALABRA CLAVE)

querer [ke'rer] /2t/ VT **1** (*desear*) to want;
quiero más dinero I want more money;
quisiera o **querría un té** I'd like a tea; **sin
querer** unintentionally; **quiero ayudar/
que vayas** I want to help/you to go; **como
usted quiera** as you wish, as you please;
ven cuando quieras come when you like;
lo hizo sin querer he didn't mean to do it;
no quiero I don't want to; **le pedí que me
dejara ir pero no quiso** I asked him to let
me go but he refused

2 (*preguntas: para pedir u ofrecer algo*): **¿quiere
abrir la ventana?** could you open the
window?; **¿quieres echarme una mano?**
can you give me a hand?; **¿quiere un café?**
would you like some coffee?

3 (*amar*) to love; **te quiero** I love you; **no
estoy enamorado, pero la quiero mucho**
I'm not in love, but I'm very fond of her

4 (*requerir*): **esta planta quiere más luz** this
plant needs more light

5: **querer decir** to mean; **¿qué quieres
decir?** what do you mean?

querido, -a [ke'riðo, a] ADJ dear ▶ NM/F
darling; (*amante*) lover; **nuestra querida
patria** our beloved country

querosén [kero'sen], **querosene** [kero'sene]
NM (*Am*) kerosene, paraffin

querré *etc* [ke'rre] VB *ver* **querer**

quesería [kese'ria] NF dairy; (*fábrica*) cheese
factory

quesero, -a [ke'sero, a] ADJ: **la industria
quesera** the cheese industry ▶ NM/F
cheesemaker ▶ NF cheese dish

queso ['keso] NM cheese; **~ rallado** grated
cheese; **~ crema** (*Am*), **~ de untar** (*Esp*)
cream cheese; **~ manchego** *sheep's milk cheese
made in La Mancha*; **dárselas con ~ a algn**
(*fam*) to take sb in

quetzal [ket'sal] NM *monetary unit of Guatemala*

quicio ['kiθjo] NM hinge; **estar fuera de ~** to
be beside o.s.; **sacar a algn de ~** to drive sb
up the wall

quid [kið] NM gist, crux; **dar en el ~** to hit the
nail on the head

quiebra ['kjeβra] NF break, split; (*Com*)
bankruptcy; (*Econ*) slump

quiebro *etc* ['kjeβro] VB *ver* **quebrar** ▶ NM (*del
cuerpo*) swerve

quien [kjen] PRON RELATIVO (*suj*) who;
(*complemento*) whom; (*indefinido*): **~ dice
eso es tonto** whoever says that is a fool;
hay ~ piensa que there are those who think
that; **no hay ~ lo haga** no-one will do it;
~ más, ~ menos tiene sus problemas
everybody has problems

quién [kjen] PRON INTERROGATIVO who;
(*complemento*) whom; **¿~ es?** who is it?, who's
there?; (*Telec*) who's calling?

quienquiera [kjen'kjera] (*pl* **quienesquiera**)
PRON whoever

quiero *etc* ['kjero] VB *ver* **querer**

quieto, -a ['kjeto, a] ADJ still; (*carácter*) placid;
¡estate ~! keep still!

quietud [kje'tuð] NF stillness

quijada [ki'xaða] NF jaw, jawbone

quijote [ki'xote] NM dreamer; **Don Q~** Don
Quixote

quil. ABR = **quilates**

quilate [ki'late] NM carat

quilla ['kiʎa] NF keel

quilo ... ['kilo] = **kilo...**

quimera [ki'mera] NF (*sueño*) pipe dream

quimérico, -a [ki'meriko, a] ADJ fantastic

q

químico, -a ['kimiko, a] ADJ chemical ▶ NM/F chemist ▶ NF chemistry
quimioterapia [kimiote'rapia] NF chemotherapy
quina ['kina] NF quinine
quincalla [kin'kaʎa] NF hardware, ironmongery (BRIT)
quincallería [kinkaʎe'ria] NF ironmonger's (shop), hardware store (US)
quince ['kinθe] NUM fifteen; ~ **días** a fortnight
quinceañero, -a [kinθea'ɲero, a] ADJ fifteen-year-old; (adolescente) teenage ▶ NM/F fifteen-year-old; (adolescente) teenager
quincena [kin'θena] NF fortnight; (pago) fortnightly pay
quincenal [kinθe'nal] ADJ fortnightly
quincuagésimo, -a [kinkwa'xesimo, a] NUM fiftieth
quiniela [ki'njela] NF football pools pl; **quinielas** NFPL pools coupon sg
quinientos, -as [ki'njentos, as] NUM five hundred
quinina [ki'nina] NF quinine
quinqué [kin'ke] NM oil lamp
quinquenal [kinke'nal] ADJ five-year cpd
quinqui ['kinki] NM delinquent
quinta ['kinta] NF ver **quinto**
quintaesencia [kintae'senθja] NF quintessence
quintal [kin'tal] NM (CASTILLA: peso) = 46kg; ~ **métrico** = 100kg
quinteto [kin'teto] NM quintet
quinto, -a ['kinto, a] ADJ fifth ▶ NM (Mil) conscript, draftee ▶ NF country house; (Mil) call-up, draft
quíntuplo, -a [kin'tuplo, a] ADJ quintuple, five-fold

quiosco ['kjosko] NM (de música) bandstand; (de periódicos) news stand (also selling sweets, cigarettes etc)
quirófano [ki'rofano] NM operating theatre
quiromancia [kiro'manθja] NF palmistry
quirúrgico, -a [ki'rurxiko, a] ADJ surgical
quise etc ['kise] VB ver **querer**
quisiera etc VB ver **querer**
quisque ['kiske] PRON (fam): **cada** o **todo** ~ (absolutely) everyone
quisquilloso [kiski'ʎoso, a] ADJ (susceptible) touchy; (meticuloso) pernickety
quiste ['kiste] NM cyst
quitaesmalte [kitaes'malte] NM nail polish remover
quitamanchas [kita'mantʃas] NM INV stain remover
quitanieves [kita'njeβes] NM INV snowplough (BRIT), snowplow (US)
quitar [ki'tar] /1a/ VT to remove, take away; (ropa) to take off; (dolor) to relieve; (vida) to take; (valor) to reduce; (hurtar) to remove, steal ▶ VI: ¡**quita de ahí**! get away!; **quitarse** VR to withdraw; (mancha) to come off o out; (ropa) to take off; **me quita mucho tiempo** it takes up a lot of my time; **el café me quita el sueño** coffee stops me sleeping; ~ **de en medio a algn** to get rid of sb; **quitarse algo de encima** to get rid of sth; **quitarse del tabaco** to give up smoking; **se quitó el sombrero** he took off his hat
quitasol [kita'sol] NM sunshade (BRIT), parasol
quite ['kite] NM (en esgrima) parry; (evasión) dodge; **estar al** ~ to be ready to go to sb's aid
Quito ['kito] N Quito
quizá(s) [ki'θa(s)] ADV perhaps, maybe
quórum ['kworum] (pl **quórums** ['kworum]) NM quorum

Rr

R, r ['erre] NF (letra) R, r; **R de Ramón** R for Robert (BRIT) o Roger (US)

R. ABR (Rel) = **real**; **reverendo**; **remite**, **remitente**; **río**

rabadilla [raβa'ðiʎa] NF base of the spine

rábano ['raβano] NM radish; **me importa un ~** I don't give a damn

rabia ['raβja] NF (Med) rabies sg; (fig: ira) fury, rage; **¡qué ~!** isn't it infuriating!; **me da ~** it maddens me; **tener ~ a algn** to have a grudge against sb

rabiar [ra'βjar] /1b/ VI to have rabies; to rage, be furious; **~ por algo** to long for sth

rabieta [ra'βjeta] NF tantrum, fit of temper

rabino [ra'βino] NM rabbi

rabioso, -a [ra'βjoso, a] ADJ rabid; (fig) furious

rabo ['raβo] NM tail

racanear [rakane'ar] /1a/ VI (fam) to skive

rácano ['rakano] NM (fam) slacker, skiver

RACE ['raθe] NM ABR (= Real Automóvil Club de España) ≈ RAC

racha ['ratʃa] NF gust of wind; (serie) string, series; **buena/mala ~** spell of good/bad luck

racial [ra'θjal] ADJ racial, race cpd

racimo [ra'θimo] NM bunch

raciocinio [raθjo'θinjo] NM reason; (razonamiento) reasoning

ración [ra'θjon] NF portion; **raciones** NFPL rations

racional [raθjo'nal] ADJ (razonable) reasonable; (lógico) rational

racionalice etc [raθjona'liθe] VB ver **racionalizar**

racionalizar [raθjonali'θar] /1f/ VT to rationalize; (Com) to streamline

racionamiento [raθjona'mjento] NM (Com) rationing

racionar [raθjo'nar] /1a/ VT to ration (out)

racismo [ra'θismo] NM racialism, racism

racista [ra'θista] ADJ, NMF racist

radar [ra'ðar] NM radar

radiación [raðja'θjon] NF radiation; (Telec) broadcasting

radiactividad [raðjaktiβi'ðað] NF radioactivity

radiactivo, -a [raðjak'tiβo, a] ADJ radioactive

radiado, -a [ra'ðjaðo, a] ADJ radio cpd, broadcast

radiador [raðja'ðor] NM radiator

radial [ra'ðjal] ADJ (AM) radio cpd

radiante [ra'ðjante] ADJ radiant

radiar [ra'ðjar] /1b/ VT to radiate; (Telec) to broadcast; (Med) to give radiotherapy to

radical [raði'kal] ADJ, NMF radical ▶ NM (Ling) root; (Mat) square-root sign

radicar [raði'kar] /1g/ VI to take root; **~ en** (dificultad, problema) to lie in; (solución) to consist in; **radicarse** VR to establish o.s., put down (one's) roots

radio ['raðjo] NF radio; (aparato) radio (set) ▶ NM (Mat) radius; (AM) radio; (Química) radium; **~ de acción** extent of one's authority, sphere of influence

radioactividad [raðjoaktiβi'ðað] NF radioactivity

radioactivo, -a [raðjoak'tiβo, a] ADJ radioactive

radioaficionado, -a [raðjoafiθjo'naðo, a] NM/F radio ham

radiocasete [raðjoka'sete] NM radiocassette (player)

radiodifusión [raðjodifu'sjon] NF broadcasting

radioemisora [raðjoemi'sora] NF transmitter, radio station

radiofónico, -a [raðjo'foniko, a] ADJ radio cpd

radiografía [raðjoɣra'fia] NF X-ray

radiólogo, -a [ra'ðjoloɣo, a] NM/F radiologist

radionovela [raðjono'βela] NF radio series

radiotaxi [raðjo'taksi] NM radio taxi

radioterapia [raðjote'rapja] NF radiotherapy

radioyente [raðjo'jente] NMF listener

radique etc [ra'ðike] VB ver **radicar**

RAE ['rae] NF ABR (= Real Academia Española) ver **real**

ráfaga ['rafaɣa] NF gust; (de luz) flash; (de tiros) burst

raído, -a [ra'iðo, a] ADJ (*ropa*) threadbare; (*persona*) shabby

raigambre [rai'ɣambre] NF (*Bot*) roots pl; (*fig*) tradition

raíz [ra'iθ] (pl **raíces**) NF root; **~ cuadrada** square root; **a ~ de** as a result of; (*después de*) immediately after

raja ['raxa] NF (*de melón etc*) slice; (*hendidura*) slit, split; (*grieta*) crack

rajar [ra'xar] /1a/ VT to split; (*fam*) to slash; **rajarse** VR to split, crack; **rajarse de** to back out of

rajatabla [raxa'taβla]: **a ~** adv (*estrictamente*) strictly, to the letter

RAL ABR (*Inform*) = **red de área local**

ralea [ra'lea] NF (*pey*) kind, sort

ralentí [ra'lenti] NM (*TV etc*) slow motion; (*Auto*) neutral; **al ~** in slow motion; (*Auto*) ticking over

rallador [raʎa'ðor] NM grater

rallar [ra'ʎar] /1a/ VT to grate

ralo, -a ['ralo, a] ADJ thin, sparse

RAM [ram] NF ABR (= *random access memory*) RAM

rama ['rama] NF bough, branch; **andarse por las ramas** (*fig: fam*) to beat about the bush

ramaje [ra'maje] NM branches pl, foliage

ramal [ra'mal] NM (*de cuerda*) strand; (*Ferro*) branch line; (*Auto*) branch (road)

rambla ['rambla] NF (*avenida*) avenue

ramera [ra'mera] NF whore, hooker (*US*)

ramificación [ramifika'θjon] NF ramification

ramificarse [ramifi'karse] /1g/ VR to branch out

ramifique etc [rami'fike] VB ver **ramificarse**

ramillete [rami'ʎete] NM bouquet; (*fig*) select group

ramo ['ramo] NM branch, twig; (*sección*) department, section; (*sector*) field, sector

rampa ['rampa] NF ramp; **~ de acceso** entrance ramp

ramplón, -ona [ram'plon, ona] ADJ uncouth, coarse

rana ['rana] NF frog; **salto de ~** leapfrog; **cuando las ranas críen pelos** when pigs fly

ranchero [ran'tʃero] NM (*Am*) rancher; (*pequeño propietario*) smallholder

rancho ['rantʃo] NM (*Mil*) food; (*Am: grande*) ranch; (*: pequeño*) small farm

rancio, -a ['ranθjo, a] ADJ (*comestibles*) stale, rancid; (*vino*) aged, mellow; (*fig*) ancient

rango ['rango] NM rank; (*prestigio*) standing

ranura [ra'nura] NF groove; (*de teléfono etc*) slot; **~ de expansión** (*Inform*) expansion slot

rap [rap] NM (*Mus*) rap

rapacidad [rapaθi'ðað] NF rapacity

rapapolvo [rapa'polβo] NM: **echar un ~ a algn** to give sb a ticking off

rapar [ra'par] /1a/ VT to shave; (*los cabellos*) to crop

rapaz [ra'paθ] ADJ (*Zool*) predatory ▶ NM young boy

rape ['rape] NM quick shave; (*pez*) monkfish; **al ~** cropped

rapé [ra'pe] NM snuff

rapel [ra'pel] NM = **rappel**

rápidamente ['rapiðarmente] ADV quickly

rapidez [rapi'ðeθ] NF speed, rapidity

rápido, -a ['rapiðo, a] ADJ fast, quick ▶ ADV quickly ▶ NM (*Ferro*) express; **rápidos** NMPL rapids

rapiña [ra'piɲa] NF robbery; **ave de ~** bird of prey

rappel [ra'pel] NM (*Deporte*) abseiling

raptar [rap'tar] /1a/ VT to kidnap

rapto ['rapto] NM kidnapping; (*impulso*) sudden impulse; (*éxtasis*) ecstasy, rapture

raqueta [ra'keta] NF racket

raquítico, -a [ra'kitiko, a] ADJ stunted; (*fig*) poor, inadequate

raquitismo [raki'tismo] NM rickets sg

raramente [rara'mente] ADV rarely

rareza [ra'reθa] NF rarity; (*fig*) eccentricity

raro, -a ['raro, a] ADJ (*poco común*) rare; (*extraño*) odd, strange; (*excepcional*) remarkable; **¡qué ~!** how (very) odd!; **¡(qué) cosa más rara!** how strange!

ras [ras] NM: **a ~** level with; **a ~ de tierra** at ground level

rasar [ra'sar] /1a/ VT to level

rascacielos [raska'θjelos] NM INV skyscraper

rascar [ras'kar] /1g/ VT (*con las uñas etc*) to scratch; (*raspar*) to scrape; **rascarse** VR to scratch (o.s.)

rasgar [ras'ɣar] /1h/ VT to tear, rip (up)

rasgo ['rasɣo] NM (*con pluma*) stroke; **rasgos** NMPL features, characteristics; **a grandes rasgos** in outline, broadly

rasgue etc ['rasɣe] VB ver **rasgar**

rasguear [rasɣe'ar] /1a/ VT (*Mus*) to strum

rasguñar [rasɣu'ɲar] /1a/ VT to scratch; (*bosquejar*) to sketch

rasguño [ras'ɣuɲo] NM scratch

raso, -a ['raso, a] ADJ (*liso*) flat, level; (*a baja altura*) very low ▶ NM satin; (*campo llano*) flat country; **cielo ~** clear sky; **al ~** in the open

raspado [ras'paðo] NM (*Med*) scrape

raspador [raspa'ðor] NM scraper

raspadura [raspa'ðura] NF (*acto*) scrape, scraping; (*marca*) scratch; **raspaduras** NFPL (*de papel etc*) scrapings

raspar [ras'par] /1a/ VT to scrape; (*arañar*) to scratch; (*limar*) to file ▶ VI (*manos*) to be rough; (*vino*) to be sharp, have a rough taste

rasque etc ['raske] VB ver **rascar**

rastra ['rastra] NF (*Agr*) rake; **a rastras** by dragging; (*fig*) unwillingly

rastreador [rastrea'ðor] NM tracker; **~ de minas** minesweeper

rastrear [rastre'ar] /**1a**/ VT (*seguir*) to track; (*minas*) to sweep

rastrero, -a [ras'trero, a] ADJ (*Bot, Zool*) creeping; (*fig*) despicable, mean

rastrillar [rastri'ʎar] /**1a**/ VT to rake

rastrillo [ras'triʎo] NM rake; (*Am*) safety razor

rastro ['rastro] NM (*Agr*) rake; (*pista*) track, trail; (*vestigio*) trace; (*mercado*) flea market; **el R~** *the Madrid flea market*; **perder el ~** to lose the scent; **desaparecer sin ~** to vanish without trace

rastrojo [ras'troxo] NM stubble

rasurado [rasu'raðo] NM (*Am*) shaving

rasurador [rasura'ðor] NM, (*Am*)
rasuradora [rasura'ðora] NF electric shaver o razor

rasurar [rasu'rar] /**1a**/ VT (*Am*) to shave; **rasurarse** VR to shave

rata ['rata] NF rat

ratear [rate'ar] /**1a**/ VT (*robar*) to steal

ratero, -a [ra'tero, a] ADJ light-fingered
▶ NM/F (*carterista*) pickpocket; (*ladrón*) petty thief; (*Am: de casas*) burglar

ratificar [ratifi'kar] /**1g**/ VT to ratify

ratifique *etc* [rati'fike] VB *ver* **ratificar**

rato ['rato] NM while, short time; **a ratos** from time to time; **al poco ~** shortly after, soon afterwards; **ratos libres** o **de ocio** free o leisure time *sg*; **hay para ~** there's still a long way to go; **pasar el ~** to kill time; **pasar un buen/mal ~** to have a good/rough time

ratón [ra'ton] NM (*tb Inform*) mouse

ratonera [rato'nera] NF mousetrap

RAU NF ABR (= *República Árabe Unida*) UAR

raudal [rau'ðal] NM torrent; **a raudales** in abundance; **entrar a raudales** to pour in

raya ['raja] NF line; (*marca*) scratch; (*en tela*) stripe; (*puntuación*) dash; (*de pelo*) parting; (*límite*) boundary; (*pez*) ray; **a rayas** striped; **pasarse de la ~** to overstep the mark; **tener a ~** to keep in check

rayado, -a [ra'jaðo, a] ADJ (*papel*) ruled; (*tela, diseño*) striped

rayar [ra'jar] /**1a**/ VT to line; to scratch; (*subrayar*) to underline ▶ VI: **~ en** o **con** to border on; **al ~ el alba** at first light; **~ a algn** (*fam*) to do sb's head in (*fam*); **está siempre rayándome con esa historia** he's doing my head in with that business (*fam*)

rayo ['rajo] NM (*del sol*) ray, beam; (*de luz*) shaft; (*en una tormenta*) (flash of) lightning; **~ solar** o **de sol** sunbeam; **rayos infrarrojos** infrared rays; **rayos X** X-rays; **como un ~** like a shot; **la noticia cayó como un ~** the news was a bombshell; **pasar como un ~** to flash past

raza ['raθa] NF race; (*de animal*) breed; **~ humana** human race; **de pura ~** (*caballo*) thoroughbred; (*perro etc*) pedigree

razón [ra'θon] NF reason; (*justicia*) right, justice; (*razonamiento*) reasoning; (*motivo*) reason, motive; (*proporción*) rate; (*Mat*) ratio; **a ~ de 10 cada día** at the rate of 10 a day; **"~: ..."** "inquiries to ..."; **en ~ de** with regard to; **perder la ~** to go out of one's mind; **dar ~ a algn** to agree that sb is right; **dar ~ de** to give an account of, report on; **tener/no tener ~** to be right/wrong; **~ directa/inversa** direct/inverse proportion; **~ de ser** raison d'être

razonable [raθo'naβle] ADJ reasonable; (*justo, moderado*) fair

razonado, -a [raθo'naðo, a] ADJ (*Com: cuenta etc*) itemized

razonamiento [raθona'mjento] NM (*juicio*) judgement; (*argumento*) reasoning

razonar [raθo'nar] /**1a**/ VT, VI to reason, argue

RDA NF ABR (*Historia*: = *República Democrática Alemana*) *ver* **república**

Rdo. ABR (*Rel*: = *Reverendo*) Rev

RDSI NF ABR (= *Red Digital de Servicios Integrados*) ISDN

re [re] NM (*Mus*) D

reabierto [rea'βjerto] PP *de* **reabrir**

reabrir [rea'βrir] /**3a**/ VT, **reabrirse** VR to reopen

reacción [reak'θjon] NF reaction; **avión a ~** jet plane; **~ en cadena** chain reaction

reaccionar [reakθjo'nar] /**1a**/ VI to react

reaccionario, -a [reakθjo'narjo, a] ADJ reactionary

reacio, -a [re'aθjo, a] ADJ stubborn; **ser** o **estar ~ a** to be opposed to

reactivar [reakti'βar] /**1a**/ VT to reactivate; (*economía*) revitalize; **reactivarse** VR (*economía*) to be on the upturn

reactor [reak'tor] NM reactor; (*avión*) jet plane; **~ nuclear** nuclear reactor

readaptación [reaðapta'θjon] NF: **~ profesional** industrial retraining

readmitir [reaðmi'tir] /**3a**/ VT to readmit

reafirmar [reafir'mar] /**1a**/ VT to reaffirm

reagrupar [reaɣru'par] /**1a**/ VT to regroup

reajustar [reaxus'tar] /**1a**/ VT (*Inform*) to reset

reajuste [rea'xuste] NM readjustment; **~ salarial** wage increase; **~ de plantilla** rationalization

real [re'al] ADJ real; (*del rey, fig*) royal; (*espléndido*) grand ▶ NM (*de feria*) fairground; **la R~ Academia Española** *see note*

> The *Real Academia Española* (RAE) is the regulatory body for the Spanish language in Spain and was founded in 1713. It produces dictionaries and grammars bearing its own name, and is considered

the authority on the language, although it has been criticized for being too conservative. In 1994, along with the Spanish American *academias*, it approved a change to the Spanish alphabet, no longer treating "ch" and "ll" as separate letters. "ñ" continues to be treated separately.

realce *etc* [re'alθe] vb *ver* **realzar** ▶ NM (*Tec*) embossing; **poner de ~** to emphasize

real-decreto [re'alde'kreto] (*pl* **reales-decretos**) NM royal decree

realeza [rea'leθa] NF royalty

realice *etc* [rea'liθe] vb *ver* **realizar**

realidad [reali'ðað] NF reality; (*verdad*) truth; **~ virtual** virtual reality; **en ~** in fact

realismo [rea'lismo] NM realism

realista [rea'lista] NMF realist

realización [realiθa'θjon] NF fulfilment, realization; (*Com*) selling up (*BRIT*), conversion into money (*US*); **~ de plusvalías** profit-taking

realizador, a [realiθa'ðor, a] NM/F film-maker; (*TV etc*) producer

realizar [reali'θar] /**1f**/ VT (*objetivo*) to achieve; (*plan*) to carry out; (*viaje*) to make, undertake; (*Com*) to realize; **realizarse** VR to come about, come true; **realizarse como persona** to fulfil one's aims in life

realmente [real'mente] ADV really, actually

realojar [realo'xar] /**1a**/ VT to rehouse

realquilar [realki'lar] /**1a**/ VT (*subarrendar*) to sublet; (*alquilar de nuevo*) to relet

realzar [real'θar] /**1f**/ VT (*Tec*) to raise; (*embellecer*) to enhance; (*acentuar*) to highlight

reanimar [reani'mar] /**1a**/ VT to revive; (*alentar*) to encourage; **reanimarse** VR to revive

reanudar [reanu'ðar] /**1a**/ VT (*renovar*) to renew; (*historia, viaje*) to resume

reaparición [reapari'θjon] NF reappearance; (*vuelta*) return

reapertura [reaper'tura] NF reopening

rearme [re'arme] NM rearmament

reata [re'ata] NF (*AM*) lasso

reavivar [reaβi'βar] /**1a**/ VT (*persona*) to revive; (*fig*) to rekindle

rebaja [re'βaxa] NF reduction, lowering; (*Com*) discount; **rebajas** NFPL (*Com*) sale; **"grandes rebajas"** "big reductions", "sale"

rebajar [reβa'xar] /**1a**/ VT (*bajar*) to lower; (*reducir*) to reduce; (*precio*) to cut; (*disminuir*) to lessen; (*humillar*) to humble; **rebajarse** VR: **rebajarse a hacer algo** to stoop to doing sth

rebanada [reβa'naða] NF slice

rebañar [reβa'ɲar] /**1a**/ VT (*comida*) to scrape up; (*plato*) to scrape clean

rebaño [re'βaɲo] NM herd; (*de ovejas*) flock

rebasar [reβa'sar] /**1a**/ VT (*tb*: **rebasar de**) to exceed; (*Auto*) to overtake

rebatir [reβa'tir] /**3a**/ VT to refute; (*rebajar*) to reduce; (*ataque*) to repel

rebato [re'βato] NM alarm; (*ataque*) surprise attack; **llamar** *o* **tocar a ~** (*fig*) to sound the alarm

rebeca [re'βeka] NF cardigan

rebelarse [reβe'larse] /**1a**/ VR to rebel, revolt

rebelde [re'βelde] ADJ rebellious; (*niño*) unruly ▶ NMF rebel; **ser ~ a** to be in revolt against, rebel against

rebeldía [reβel'dia] NF rebelliousness; (*desobediencia*) disobedience; (*Jur*) default

rebelión [reβe'ljon] NF rebellion

rebenque [re'βenke] NM (*AM*) whip

reblandecer [reβlande'θer] /**2d**/ VT to soften

reblandezca *etc* [reβlan'deθka] vb *ver* **reblandecer**

rebobinar [reβoβi'nar] /**1a**/ VT to rewind

reboce *etc* [re'βoθe] vb *ver* **rebozar**

rebosante [reβo'sante] ADJ: **~ de** (*fig*) brimming *o* overflowing with

rebosar [reβo'sar] /**1a**/ VI to overflow; (*abundar*) to abound, be plentiful; **~ de salud** to be bursting *o* brimming with health

rebotar [reβo'tar] /**1a**/ VT to bounce; (*rechazar*) to repel ▶ VI (*pelota*) to bounce; (*bala*) to ricochet

rebote [re'βote] NM rebound; **de ~** on the rebound

rebozado, -a [reβo'θaðo, a] ADJ (*Culin*) fried in batter *o* breadcrumbs *o* flour

rebozar [reβo'θar] /**1f**/ VT to wrap up; (*Culin*) to fry in batter *etc*

rebozo [reβo'θo] NM: **sin ~** openly

rebuscado, -a [reβus'kaðo, a] ADJ (*amanerado*) affected; (*palabra*) recherché; (*idea*) far-fetched

rebuscar [reβus'kar] /**1g**/ VI (*en bolsillo, cajón*) to fish; (*en habitación*) to search high and low

rebuznar [reβuθ'nar] /**1a**/ VI to bray

recabar [reka'βar] /**1a**/ VT (*obtener*) to manage to get; **~ fondos** to collect money

recadero [reka'ðero] NM messenger

recado [re'kaðo] NM message; (*encargo*) errand; **dejar/tomar un ~** (*Telec*) to leave/take a message

recaer [reka'er] /**2n**/ VI to relapse; **~ en** to fall to *o* on; (*criminal etc*) to fall back into, relapse into; (*premio*) to go to

recaída [reka'iða] NF relapse

recaiga *etc* [re'kaiɣa] vb *ver* **recaer**

recalcar [rekal'kar] /**1g**/ VT (*fig*) to stress, emphasize

recalcitrante [rekalθi'trante] ADJ recalcitrant

recalentamiento [rekalenta'mjento] NM: **~ global** global warming

recalentar [rekalen'tar] /**1j**/ VT (*comida*) to warm up, reheat; (*demasiado*) to overheat; **recalentarse** VR to overheat, get too hot

recaliente *etc* [reka'ljente] VB *ver* **recalentar**

recalque *etc* [re'kalke] VB *ver* **recalcar**

recámara [re'kamara] NF side room; (*AM*) bedroom

recamarera [rekama'rera] NF (*AM*) maid

recambio [re'kambjo] NM spare; (*de pluma*) refill; **piezas de ~** spares

recapacitar [rekapaθi'tar] /**1a**/ VI to reflect

recapitular [rekapitu'lar] /**1a**/ VT to recap

recargable [rekar'ɣaβle] ADJ (*batería, pila*) rechargeable; (*mechero, pluma*) refillable

recargado, -a [rekar'ɣaðo, a] ADJ overloaded; (*exagerado*) over-elaborate

recargar [rekar'ɣar] /**1h**/ VT to overload; (*batería*) to recharge; (*mechero, pluma*) to refill; (*tarjeta de teléfono*) to top up

recargo [re'karɣo] NM surcharge; (*aumento*) increase

recargue *etc* [re'karɣe] VB *ver* **recargar**

recatado, -a [reka'taðo, a] ADJ (*modesto*) modest, demure; (*prudente*) cautious

recato [re'kato] NM (*modestia*) modesty, demureness; (*cautela*) caution

recauchutado, -a [rekautʃu'taðo, a] ADJ remould *cpd*

recaudación [rekauða'θjon] NF (*acción*) collection; (*cantidad*) takings *pl*; (*en deporte*) gate; (*oficina*) tax office

recaudador, a [rekauða'ðor, a] NM/F tax collector

recaudar [rekau'ðar] /**1a**/ VT to collect

recaudo [re'kauðo] NM: **estar a buen ~** to be in safekeeping; **poner algo a buen ~** to put sth in a safe place

recayendo *etc* [reka'jendo] VB *ver* **recaer**

rece *etc* ['reθe] VB *ver* **rezar**

recelar [reθe'lar] /**1a**/ VT: **~ que** (*sospechar*) to suspect that; (*temer*) to fear that ▶ VI: **~(se) de** to distrust

recelo [re'θelo] NM distrust, suspicion

receloso, -a [reθe'loso, a] ADJ distrustful, suspicious

recepción [reθep'θjon] NF reception; (*acto de recibir*) receipt

recepcionista [reθepθjo'nista] NMF receptionist

receptáculo [reθep'takulo] NM receptacle

receptivo, -a [reθep'tiβo, a] ADJ receptive

receptor, a [reθep'tor, a] NM/F recipient ▶ NM (*Telec*) receiver; **descolgar el ~** to pick up the receiver

recesión [reθe'sjon] NF (*Com*) recession

receta [re'θeta] NF (*Culin*) recipe; (*Med*) prescription

recetar [reθe'tar] /**1a**/ VT to prescribe

rechace *etc* [re'tʃaθe] VB *ver* **rechazar**

rechazar [retʃa'θar] /**1f**/ VT to repel, drive back; (*idea*) to reject; (*oferta*) to turn down

rechazo [re'tʃaθo] NM (*de propuesta, tb Med: de un órgano*) rejection; (*rebote*) rebound; (*de fusil*) recoil

rechifla [re'tʃifla] NF hissing, booing; (*fig*) derision

rechinar [retʃi'nar] /**1a**/ VI to creak; (*dientes*) to grind; (*máquina*) to clank, clatter; (*metal seco*) to grate; (*motor*) to hum

rechistar [retʃis'tar] /**1a**/ VI: **sin ~** without complaint

rechoncho, -a [re'tʃontʃo, a] ADJ (*fam*) stocky, thickset (*BRIT*), heavy-set (*US*)

rechupete [retʃu'pete]: **de ~** *adv* (*comida*) delicious

recibidor [reθiβi'ðor] NM entrance hall

recibimiento [reθiβi'mjento] NM reception, welcome

recibir [reθi'βir] /**3a**/ VT to receive; (*dar la bienvenida*) to welcome; (*salir al encuentro de*) to go and meet ▶ VI to entertain; **recibirse** VR: **recibirse de** to qualify as

recibo [re'θiβo] NM receipt; **acusar ~ de** to acknowledge receipt of

reciclable [reθi'klaβle] ADJ recyclable

reciclaje [reθi'klaxe] NM recycling; (*de trabajadores*) retraining; **cursos de ~** refresher courses

reciclar [reθi'klar] /**1a**/ VT to recycle; (*trabajador*) to retrain

recién [re'θjen] ADV recently, newly; (*AM*) just, recently; **~ casado** newly-wed; **el ~ llegado** the newcomer; **el ~ nacido** the newborn child; **~ a las seis** only at six o'clock

reciente [re'θjente] ADJ recent; (*fresco*) fresh

recientemente [reθjente'mente] ADV recently

recinto [re'θinto] NM enclosure; (*área*) area, place

recio, -a ['reθjo, a] ADJ strong, tough; (*voz*) loud ▶ ADV hard; loud(ly)

recipiente [reθi'pjente] NM (*objeto*) container, receptacle; (*persona*) recipient

reciprocidad [reθiproθi'ðað] NF reciprocity

recíproco, -a [re'θiproko, a] ADJ reciprocal

recital [reθi'tal] NM (*Mus*) recital; (*Lit*) reading

recitar [reθi'tar] /**1a**/ VT to recite

reclamación [reklama'θjon] NF claim, demand; (*queja*) complaint; **libro de reclamaciones** complaints book; **~ salarial** pay claim

reclamar [rekla'mar] /**1a**/ VT to claim, demand ▶ VI: **~ contra** to complain about; **~ a algn en justicia** to take sb to court

reclamo [re'klamo] NM (*anuncio*) advertisement; (*tentación*) attraction

r

reclinar [rekli'nar] /**1a**/ VT to recline, lean; **reclinarse** VR to lean back

recluir [reklu'ir] /**3g**/ VT to intern, confine

reclusión [reklu'sjon] NF (*prisión*) prison; (*refugio*) seclusion; ~ **perpetua** life imprisonment

recluso, -a [re'kluso, a] ADJ imprisoned; **población reclusa** prison population ▶ NM/F (*solitario*) recluse; (*Jur*) prisoner

recluta [re'kluta] NMF recruit ▶ NF recruitment

reclutamiento [rekluta'mjento] NM recruitment

reclutar [reklu'tar] /**1a**/ VT (*datos*) to collect; (*dinero*) to collect up

recluyendo etc [reklu'jendo] VB ver **recluir**

recobrar [reko'βrar] /**1a**/ VT (*recuperar*) to recover; (*rescatar*) to get back; (*ciudad*) to recapture; (*tiempo*) to make up (for); **recobrarse** VR to recover

recochineo [rekotʃi'neo] NM (*fam*) mickey-taking

recodo [re'koðo] NM (*de río, camino*) bend

recogedor, a [rekoxe'ðor, a] NM dustpan ▶ NM/F picker, harvester

recoger [reko'xer] /**2c**/ VT to collect; (*Agr*) to harvest; (*fruta*) to pick; (*levantar*) to pick up; (*juntar*) to gather; (*pasar a buscar*) to come for, get; (*dar asilo*) to give shelter to; (*faldas*) to gather up; (*mangas*) to roll up; (*pelo*) to put up; **recogerse** VR (*retirarse*) to retire; **me recogieron en la estación** they picked me up at the station

recogido, -a [reko'xiðo, a] ADJ (*lugar*) quiet, secluded; (*pequeño*) small ▶ NF (*Correos*) collection; (*Agr*) harvest; **recogida de datos** (*Inform*) data capture

recogimiento [rekoxi'mjento] NM collection; (*Agr*) harvesting

recoja etc [re'koxa] VB ver **recoger**

recolección [rekolek'θjon] NF (*Agr*) harvesting; (*colecta*) collection

recomencé [rekomen'θe], **recomencemos** etc [rekomen'θemos] VB ver **recomenzar**

recomendable [rekomen'daβle] ADJ recommendable; **poco** ~ inadvisable

recomendación [rekomenda'θjon] NF (*sugerencia*) suggestion, recommendation; (*referencia*) reference; **carta de** ~ **para** letter of introduction to

recomendar [rekomen'dar] /**1j**/ VT to suggest, recommend; (*confiar*) to entrust

recomenzar [rekomen'θar] /**1f, 1j**/ VT, VI to begin again, recommence

recomience etc [reko'mjenθe] VB ver **recomenzar**

recomiende etc [reko'mjende] VB ver **recomendar**

recomienzo etc [reko'mjenθo] VB ver **recomenzar**

recompensa [rekom'pensa] NF reward, recompense; (*compensación*): ~ **(de una pérdida)** compensation (for a loss); **como** o **en** ~ **por** in return for

recompensar [rekompen'sar] /**1a**/ VT to reward, recompense

recompondré etc [rekompon'dre] VB ver **recomponer**

recomponer [rekompo'ner] /**2q**/ VT to mend; (*Inform: texto*) to reformat

recomponga etc [rekom'ponga], **recompuesto** [rekom'pwesto], **recompuse** etc [rekom'puse] VB ver **recomponer**

reconciliación [rekonθilja'θjon] NF reconciliation

reconciliar [rekonθi'ljar] /**1b**/ VT to reconcile; **reconciliarse** VR to become reconciled

recóndito, -a [re'kondito, a] ADJ (*lugar*) hidden, secret

reconfortar [rekonfor'tar] /**1a**/ VT to comfort

reconocer [rekono'θer] /**2d**/ VT to recognize; (*registrar*) to search; (*Med*) to examine; ~ **los hechos** to face the facts

reconocido, -a [rekono'θiðo, a] ADJ recognized; (*agradecido*) grateful

reconocimiento [rekonoθi'mjento] NM recognition; (*registro*) search; (*inspección*) examination; (*gratitud*) gratitude; (*confesión*) admission; ~ **óptico de caracteres** (*Inform*) optical character recognition; ~ **de la voz** (*Inform*) speech recognition

reconozca etc [reko'noθka] VB ver **reconocer**

reconquista [rekon'kista] NF reconquest; **la R~** the Reconquest (of Spain)

reconquistar [rekonkis'tar] /**1a**/ VT (*Mil*) to reconquer; (*fig*) to recover, win back

reconstituyente [rekonstitu'jente] NM tonic

reconstruir [rekonstru'ir] /**3g**/ VT to reconstruct

reconstruyendo etc [rekonstru'jendo] VB ver **reconstruir**

reconversión [rekomber'sjon] NF restructuring, reorganization; (*tb*: **reconversión industrial**) rationalization

recopilación [rekopila'θjon] NF (*resumen*) summary; (*compilación*) compilation

recopilar [rekopi'lar] /**1a**/ VT to compile

récord ['rekorð] ADJ INV record; **cifras** ~ record figures ▶ NM (*pl* **récords** o **records**) record; **batir el** ~ to break the record

recordar [rekor'ðar] /**1l**/ VT (*acordarse de*) to remember; (*traer a la memoria*) to recall; (*recordar a otro*) to remind ▶ VI to remember; **recuérdale que me debe cinco dólares** remind him that he owes me five dollars; **que yo recuerde** as far as I can remember; **creo** ~, **si mal no recuerdo** if my memory serves me right

recordatorio [rekorða'torjo] NM (*de fallecimiento*) in memoriam card; (*de bautizo, comunión*) commemorative card

recorrer [reko'rrer] /**2a**/ VT (*país*) to cross, travel through; (*distancia*) to cover; (*registrar*) to search; (*repasar*) to look over

recorrido [reko'rriðo] NM run, journey; **tren de largo** ~ main-line o inter-city (BRIT) train

recortado, -a [rekor'taðo, a] ADJ uneven, irregular

recortar [rekor'tar] /**1a**/ VT (*papel*) to cut out; (*el pelo*) to trim; (*dibujar*) to draw in outline; **recortarse** VR to stand out, be silhouetted

recorte [re'korte] NM (*acción, de prensa*) cutting; (*de telas, chapas*) trimming; ~ **presupuestario** budget cut; ~ **salarial** wage cut

recostado, -a [rekos'taðo, a] ADJ leaning; **estar** ~ to be lying down

recostar [rekos'tar] /**1l**/ VT to lean; **recostarse** VR to lie down

recoveco [reko'βeko] NM (*de camino, río etc*) bend; (*en casa*) cubbyhole

recreación [rekrea'θjon] NF recreation

recrear [rekre'ar] /**1a**/ VT (*entretener*) to entertain; (*volver a crear*) to recreate

recreativo, -a [rekrea'tiβo, a] ADJ recreational

recreo [re'kreo] NM recreation; (*Escol*) break, playtime

recriminar [rekrimi'nar] /**1a**/ VT to reproach ▶ VI to recriminate; **recriminarse** VR to reproach each other

recrudecer [rekruðe'θer] /**2d**/ VT, VI to worsen; **recrudecerse** VR to worsen

recrudecimiento [rekruðeθi'mjento] NM upsurge

recrudezca *etc* [rekru'ðeθka] VB *ver* **recrudecer**

recta ['rekta] NF *ver* **recto**

rectangular [rektangu'lar] ADJ rectangular

rectángulo, -a [rek'tangulo, a] ADJ rectangular ▶ NM rectangle

rectificable [rektifi'kaβle] ADJ rectifiable; **fácilmente** ~ easily rectified

rectificación [rektifika'θjon] NF correction

rectificar [rektifi'kar] /**1g**/ VT to rectify; (*volverse recto*) to straighten ▶ VI to correct o.s.

rectifique *etc* [rekti'fike] VB *ver* **rectificar**

rectitud [rekti'tuð] NF straightness; (*fig*) rectitude

recto, -a ['rekto, a] ADJ straight; (*persona*) honest, upright; (*estricto*) strict; (*juez*) fair; (*juicio*) sound ▶ NM rectum; (*Atletismo*) straight ▶ NF straight line; **siga todo** ~ go straight on; **en el sentido** ~ **de la palabra** in the proper sense of the word; **recta final** o **de llegada** home straight

rector, a [rek'tor, a] ADJ governing ▶ NM/F

head, chief; (*Escol*) rector, president (US)

rectorado [rekto'raðo] NM (*cargo*) rectorship, presidency (US); (*oficina*) rector's office

recuadro [re'kwaðro] NM box; (*Tip*) inset

recubrir [reku'βir] /**3a**/ VT: ~ **(con)** (*pintura, crema*) to cover (with)

recuento [re'kwento] NM inventory; **hacer el** ~ **de** to count o reckon up

recuerdo [re'kwerðo] VB *ver* **recordar** ▶ NM souvenir; **recuerdos** NMPL memories; **¡recuerdos a tu madre!** give my regards to your mother!; **"R~ de Mallorca"** "a present from Majorca"; **contar los recuerdos** to reminisce

recueste *etc* [re'kweste] VB *ver* **recostar**

recular [reku'lar] /**1a**/ VI to back down

recuperable [rekupe'raβle] ADJ recoverable

recuperación [rekupera'θjon] NF recovery; ~ **de datos** (*Inform*) data retrieval

recuperar [rekupe'rar] /**1a**/ VT to recover; (*tiempo*) to make up; (*Inform*) to retrieve; **recuperarse** VR to recuperate

recurrir [reku'rrir] /**3a**/ VI (*Jur*) to appeal; ~ **a** to resort to; (*persona*) to turn to

recurso [re'kurso] NM resort; (*medio*) means pl, resource; (*Jur*) appeal; **como último** ~ as a last resort; **recursos económicos** economic resources; **recursos naturales** natural resources

recusar [reku'sar] /**1a**/ VT to reject, refuse

red [reð] NF net, mesh; (*Ferro, Inform*) network; (*Elec, de agua*) mains, supply system; (*de tiendas*) chain; (*trampa*) trap; **la R~** (*Internet*) the Net; **estar conectado con la** ~ to be connected to the mains; ~ **de transmisión** (*Inform*) data network; ~ **local** (*Inform*) local area network; **redes sociales** social networks; (*páginas web*) social networking sites

redacción [reðak'θjon] NF (*acción*) writing; (*Escol*) essay, composition; (*limpieza de texto*) editing; (*personal*) editorial staff

redactar [reðak'tar] /**1a**/ VT to draw up, draft; (*periódico, Inform*) to edit

redactor, a [reðak'tor, a] NM/F writer; (*en periódico*) editor

redada [re'ðaða] NF (*Pesca*) cast, throw; (*fig*) catch; ~ **policial** police raid, round-up

rededor [reðe'ðor] NM: **al** o **en** ~ around, round about

redención [reðen'θjon] NF redemption

redentor, a [reðen'tor, a] ADJ redeeming ▶ NM/F (*Com*) redeemer

redescubierto [reðesku'βjerto] PP *de* **redescubrir**

redescubrir [reðesku'βrir] /**3a**/ VT to rediscover

redesignar [reðesiɣ'nar] /**1a**/ VT (*Inform*) to rename

redicho, -a [re'ðitʃo, a] ADJ affected
redil [re'ðil] NM sheepfold
redimir [reði'mir] /**3a**/ VT to redeem; (*rehén*) to ransom
redistribución [reðistriβu'θjon] NF (*Com*) redeployment
rédito ['reðito] NM interest, yield
redoblar [reðo'βlar] /**1a**/ VT to redouble ▸ VI (*tambor*) to roll
redoble [re'ðoβle] NM (*Mus*) drumroll, drumbeat; (*de trueno*) roll
redomado, -a [reðo'maðo, a] ADJ (*astuto*) sly, crafty; (*perfecto*) utter
redonda [re'ðonda] NF *ver* **redondo**
redondear [reðonde'ar] /**1a**/ VT to round, round off; (*cifra*) to round up
redondel [reðon'del] NM (*círculo*) circle; (*Taur*) bullring, arena; (*Auto*) roundabout
redondo, -a [re'ðondo, a] ADJ (*circular*) round; (*completo*) complete ▸ NF: **a la redonda** around, round about; **en muchas millas a la redonda** for many miles around; **rehusar en ~** to give a flat refusal
reducción [reðuk'θjon] NF reduction; **~ del activo** (*Com*) divestment; **~ de precios** (*Com*) price-cutting
reducido, -a [reðu'θiðo, a] ADJ reduced; (*limitado*) limited; (*pequeño*) small; **quedar ~ a** to be reduced to
reducir [reðu'θir] /**3n**/ VT to reduce, limit; (*someter*) to bring under control; **reducirse** VR to diminish; (*Mat*) **~ (a)** to reduce (to), convert (into); **~ las millas a kilómetros** to convert miles into kilometres; **reducirse a** (*fig*) to come o boil down to
reducto [re'ðukto] NM redoubt
reduje *etc* [re'ðuxe] VB *ver* **reducir**
redundancia [reðun'danθja] NF redundancy
reduzca *etc* [re'ðuθka] VB *ver* **reducir**
reedición [re(e)ði'θjon] NF reissue
reeditar [re(e)ði'tar] /**1a**/ VT to reissue
reelección [re(e)lek'θjon] NF re-election
reelegir [re(e)le'xir] /**3c, 3k**/ VT to re-elect
reembolsable [re(e)mbol'saβle] ADJ (*Com*) redeemable, refundable
reembolsar [re(e)mbol'sar] /**1a**/ VT (*persona*) to reimburse; (*dinero*) to repay, pay back; (*depósito*) to refund
reembolso [re(e)m'bolso] NM reimbursement; refund; **enviar algo contra ~** to send sth cash on delivery; **contra ~ del flete** freight forward; **~ fiscal** tax rebate
reemplace *etc* [re(e)m'plaθe] VB *ver* **reemplazar**
reemplazar [re(e)mpla'θar] /**1f**/ VT to replace
reemplazo [re(e)m'plaθo] NM replacement; **de ~** (*Mil*) reserve
reencuentro [re(e)n'kwentro] NM reunion

reengancharse [re(e)ngan'tʃarse] /**1a**/ VR (*Mil*) to re-enlist
reescribible [reeskri'βiβle] ADJ rewritable
reestreno [re(e)s'treno] NM rerun
reestructurar [re(e)struktu'rar] /**1a**/ VT to restructure
reexportación [re(e)ksporta'θjon] NF (*Com*) re-export
reexportar [re(e)kspor'tar] /**1a**/ VT (*Com*) to re-export
REF NM ABR (*Esp Econ*) = **Régimen Económico Fiscal**
Ref.ª ABR (= *referencia*) ref
refacción [refak'θjon] NF (*Am*) repair(s); **refacciones** NFPL (*piezas de repuesto*) spare parts
referencia [refe'renθja] NF reference; **con ~ a** with reference to; **hacer ~ a** to refer o allude to; **~ comercial** (*Com*) trade reference
referéndum [refe'rendum] (*pl* **referéndums**) NM referendum
referente [refe'rente] ADJ: **~ a** concerning, relating to
réferi ['referi] NMF (*Am*) referee
referir [refe'rir] /**3i**/ VT (*contar*) to tell, recount; (*relacionar*) to refer, relate; **referirse** VR: **referirse a** to refer to; **~ al lector a un apéndice** to refer the reader to an appendix; **~ a** (*Com*) to convert into; **por lo que se refiere a eso** as for that, as regards that
refiera *etc* [re'fjera] VB *ver* **referir**
refilón [refi'lon]: **de ~** *adv* obliquely; **mirar a algn de ~** to look out of the corner of one's eye at sb
refinado, -a [refi'naðo, a] ADJ refined
refinamiento [refina'mjento] NM refinement; **~ por pasos** (*Inform*) stepwise refinement
refinar [refi'nar] /**1a**/ VT to refine
refinería [refine'ria] NF refinery
refiriendo *etc* [refi'rjendo] VB *ver* **referir**
reflector [reflek'tor] NM reflector; (*Elec*) spotlight; (*Aviat, Mil*) searchlight
reflejar [refle'xar] /**1a**/ VT to reflect; **reflejarse** VR to be reflected
reflejo, -a [re'flexo, a] ADJ reflected; (*movimiento*) reflex ▸ NM reflection; (*Anat*) reflex; **reflejos** *nmpl* (*en el pelo*) highlights; **tiene el pelo castaño con reflejos rubios** she has chestnut hair with blond streaks
reflexión [reflek'sjon] NF reflection
reflexionar [refleksjo'nar] /**1a**/ VT to reflect on ▸ VI to reflect; (*detenerse*) to pause (to think); **¡reflexione!** you think it over!
reflexivo, -a [reflek'siβo, a] ADJ thoughtful; (*Ling*) reflexive
refluir [reflu'ir] /**3g**/ VI to flow back
reflujo [re'fluxo] NM ebb
refluyendo *etc* [reflu'jendo] VB *ver* **refluir**

reforcé [refor'θe], **reforcemos** *etc*
[refor'θemos] VB *ver* **reforzar**

reforma [re'forma] NF reform; *(Arq etc)*
repair; **~ agraria** agrarian reform

reformar [refor'mar] /**1a**/ VT to reform;
(modificar) to change, alter; *(texto)* to revise;
(Arq) to repair; **reformarse** VR to mend one's
ways

reformatear [reformate'ar] /**1a**/ VT *(Inform:
disco)* to reformat

reformatorio [reforma'torjo] NM
reformatory; **~ de menores** remand home

reformista [refor'mista] ADJ, NMF reformist

reforzamiento [reforθa'mjento] NM
reinforcement

reforzar [refor'θar] /**1f, 1l**/ VT to strengthen;
(Arq) to reinforce; *(fig)* to encourage

refractario, -a [refrak'tarjo, a] ADJ *(Tec)*
heat-resistant; **ser ~ a una reforma** to
resist *o* be opposed to a reform

refrán [re'fran] NM proverb, saying

refregar [refre'ɣar] /**1h, 1j**/ VT to scrub

refrenar [refre'nar] /**1a**/ VT to check, restrain

refrendar [refren'dar] /**1a**/ VT *(firma)* to
endorse, countersign; *(ley)* to approve

refrescante [refres'kante] ADJ refreshing,
cooling

refrescar [refres'kar] /**1g**/ VT to refresh ▶ VI to
cool down; **refrescarse** VR to get cooler;
(tomar aire fresco) to go out for a breath of fresh
air; *(beber)* to have a drink

refresco [re'fresko] NM soft drink, cool drink;
"refrescos" "refreshments"

refresque *etc* [re'freske] VB *ver* **refrescar**

refriega *etc* [re'frjeɣa] VB *ver* **refregar** ▶ NF
scuffle, brawl

refriegue *etc* [re'frjeɣe] VB *ver* **refregar**

refrigeración [refrixera'θjon] NF
refrigeration; *(de casa)* air-conditioning

refrigerado, -a [refrixe'raðo, a] ADJ cooled;
(sala) air-conditioned

refrigerador [refrixera'ðor] NM, *(Am)*
refrigeradora [refrixera'ðora] NF
refrigerator, icebox *(US)*

refrigerar [refrixe'rar] /**1a**/ VT to refrigerate;
(sala) to air-condition

refrito [re'frito] NM *(Culin)*: **un ~ de cebolla y
tomate** sautéed onions and tomatoes; **un ~**
(fig) a rehash

refuerce *etc* [re'fwerθe] VB *ver* **reforzar**

refuerzo *etc* [re'fwerθo] VB *ver* **reforzar** ▶ NM
reinforcement; *(Tec)* support

refugiado, -a [refu'xjaðo, a] NM/F refugee

refugiarse [refu'xjarse] /**1b**/ VR to take
refuge, shelter

refugio [re'fuxjo] NM refuge; *(protección)*
shelter; *(Auto)* street *o* traffic island;
~ alpino *o* **de montaña** mountain hut;
~ subterráneo *(Mil)* underground shelter

refulgencia [reful'xenθja] NF brilliance

refulgir [reful'xir] /**3c**/ VI to shine, be dazzling

refulja *etc* [re'fulxa] VB *ver* **refulgir**

refundir [refun'dir] /**3a**/ VT to recast; *(escrito
etc)* to adapt, rewrite

refunfuñar [refunfu'ɲar] /**1a**/ VI to grunt,
growl; *(quejarse)* to grumble

refunfuñón, -ona [refunfu'ɲon, ona] *(fam)*
ADJ grumpy ▶ NM/F grouch

refutación [refuta'θjon] NF refutation

refutar [refu'tar] /**1a**/ VT to refute

regadera [reɣa'ðera] NF watering can; *(Am)*
shower; **estar como una ~** *(fam)* to be as
mad as a hatter

regadío [reɣa'ðio] NM irrigated land

regalado, -a [reɣa'laðo, a] ADJ comfortable,
luxurious; *(gratis)* free, for nothing; **lo tuvo
~** it was handed to him on a plate

regalar [reɣa'lar] /**1a**/ VT *(dar)* to give (as a
present); *(entregar)* to give away; *(mimar)* to
pamper, make a fuss of; **regalarse** VR to treat
o.s. to

regalía [reɣa'lia] NF privilege, prerogative;
(Com) bonus; *(de autor)* royalty

regaliz [reɣa'liθ] NM liquorice

regalo [re'ɣalo] NM *(obsequio)* gift, present;
(gusto) pleasure; *(comodidad)* comfort

regañadientes [reɣaɲa'ðjentes]: **a ~** *adv*
reluctantly

regañar [reɣa'ɲar] /**1a**/ VT to scold ▶ VI to
grumble; *(dos personas)* to fall out, quarrel

regañón, -ona [reɣa'ɲon, ona] ADJ nagging

regar [re'ɣar] /**1h, 1j**/ VT to water, irrigate;
(fig) to scatter, sprinkle

regata [re'ɣata] NF *(Naut)* race

regatear [reɣate'ar] /**1a**/ VT *(Com)* to bargain
over; *(escatimar)* to be mean with ▶ VI to
bargain, haggle; *(Deporte)* to dribble; **no ~
esfuerzos** to spare no effort

regateo [reɣa'teo] NM bargaining; *(Deporte)*
dribbling; *(con el cuerpo)* swerve, dodge

regazo [re'ɣaθo] NM lap

regencia [re'xenθja] NF regency

regeneración [rexenera'θjon] NF
regeneration

regenerar [rexene'rar] /**1a**/ VT to regenerate

regentar [rexen'tar] /**1a**/ VT to direct,
manage; *(puesto)* to hold in an acting
capacity; *(negocio)* to be in charge of

regente, -a [re'xente, a] ADJ *(príncipe)* regent;
(director) managing ▶ NM *(Com)* manager;
(Pol) regent

régimen ['reximen] *(pl* **regímenes**
[re'ximenes]*)* NM regime; *(reinado)* rule;
(Med) diet; *(reglas)* (set of) rules *pl*; *(manera
de vivir)* lifestyle; **estar a ~** to be on a diet

regimiento [rexi'mjento] NM regiment

regio, -a ['rexjo, a] ADJ royal, regal; *(fig:
suntuoso)* splendid; *(Am fam)* great, terrific

región [re'xjon] NF region; (*área*) area

regional [rexjo'nal] ADJ regional

regir [re'xir] /**3c, 3k**/ VT to govern, rule; (*dirigir*) to manage, run; (*Econ, Jur, Ling*) to govern ▶ VI to apply, be in force

registrador [rexistra'ðor] NM registrar, recorder

registrar [rexis'trar] /**1a**/ VT (*buscar*) to search; (*en cajón*) to look through; (*inspeccionar*) to inspect; (*anotar*) to register, record; (*Inform*) to log; (*Mus*) to record; **registrarse** VR to register; (*ocurrir*) to happen

registro [re'xistro] NM (*acto*) registration; (*Mus, libro*) register; (*lista*) list, record; (*Inform*) record; (*inspección*) inspection, search; **~ civil** registry office; **~ electoral** voting register; **~ de la propiedad** land registry (office)

regla ['reɣla] NF (*ley*) rule, regulation; (*de medir*) ruler, rule; (*Med: período*) period; **en ~** in order; (*regla científica*) law, principle; **no hay ~ sin excepción** every rule has its exception

reglamentación [reɣlamenta'θjon] NF (*acto*) regulation; (*lista*) rules *pl*

reglamentar [reɣlamen'tar] /**1a**/ VT to regulate

reglamentario, -a [reɣlamen'tarjo, a] ADJ statutory; **en la forma reglamentaria** in the properly established way

reglamento [reɣla'mento] NM rules *pl*, regulations *pl*; **~ del tráfico** highway code

reglar [re'ɣlar] /**1a**/ VT (*acciones*) to regulate; **reglarse** VR: **reglarse por** to be guided by

regocijarse [reɣoθi'xarse] /**1a**/ VR: **~ de** *o* **por** to rejoice at, be glad about

regocijo [reɣo'θixo] NM joy, happiness

regodearse [reɣoðe'arse] /**1a**/ VR to be glad, be delighted; (*pey*): **~ con** *o* **en** to gloat over

regodeo [reɣo'ðeo] NM delight; (*pey*) perverse pleasure

regrabadora [regraβa'ðora] NF rewriter; **~ de DVD** DVD rewriter

regresar [reɣre'sar] /**1a**/ VI to come/go back, return; **regresarse** VR (*Am*) to return

regresivo, -a [reɣre'siβo, a] ADJ backward; (*fig*) regressive

regreso [re'ɣreso] NM return; **estar de ~** to be back, be home

regué [re'ɣe], **reguemos** *etc* [re'ɣemos] VB *ver* **regar**

reguero [re'ɣero] NM (*de sangre*) trickle; (*de humo*) trail

regulación [reɣula'θjon] NF regulation; (*Tec*) adjustment; (*control*) control; **~ de empleo** redundancies *pl*; **~ del tráfico** traffic control

regulador [reɣula'ðor] NM (*Tec*) regulator; (*de radio etc*) knob, control

regular [reɣu'lar] /**1a**/ ADJ regular; (*normal*) normal, usual; (*común*) ordinary; (*organizado*) regular, orderly; (*mediano*) average; (*fam*) not bad, so-so ▶ ADV: **estar ~** to be so-so *o* all right ▶ VT (*controlar*) to control, regulate; (*Tec*) to adjust; **por lo ~** as a rule

regularice *etc* [reɣula'riθe] VB *ver* **regularizar**

regularidad [reɣulari'ðað] NF regularity; **con ~** regularly

regularizar [reɣulari'θar] /**1f**/ VT to regularize

regusto [re'ɣusto] NM aftertaste

rehabilitación [reaβilita'θjon] NF rehabilitation; (*Arq*) restoration

rehabilitar [reaβili'tar] /**1a**/ VT to rehabilitate; (*Arq*) to restore; (*reintegrar*) to reinstate

rehacer [rea'θer] /**2r**/ VT (*reparar*) to mend, repair; (*volver a hacer*) to redo, repeat; **rehacerse** VR (*Med*) to recover

rehaga *etc* [re'aɣa], **reharé** *etc* [rea're], **rehaz** [re'aθ], **rehecho** [re'etʃo] VB *ver* **rehacer**

rehén [re'en] NMF hostage

rehice *etc* [re'iθe], **rehizo** [re'iθo] VB *ver* **rehacer**

rehogar [reo'ɣar] /**1h**/ VT to sauté, toss in oil

rehuir [reu'ir] /**3g**/ VT to avoid, shun

rehusar [reu'sar] /**1a**/ VT, VI to refuse

rehuyendo *etc* [reu'jendo] VB *ver* **rehuir**

reina ['reina] NF queen

reinado [rei'naðo] NM reign

reinante [rei'nante] ADJ (*fig*) prevailing

reinar [rei'nar] /**1a**/ VI to reign; (*fig: prevalecer*) to prevail, be general

reincidir [reinθi'ðir] /**3a**/ VI to relapse; (*criminal*) to repeat an offence

reincorporarse [reinkorpo'rarse] /**1a**/ VR: **~ a** to rejoin

reinicializar [reiniθjali'θar] /**1f**/ VT (*Inform*) to reset

reino ['reino] NM kingdom; **~ animal/vegetal** animal/plant kingdom; **el R~ Unido** the United Kingdom

reinserción [reinser'θjon] NF rehabilitation

reinsertar [reinser'tar] /**1a**/ VT to rehabilitate

reintegración [reinteɣra'θjon] NF (*Com*) reinstatement

reintegrar [reinte'ɣrar] /**1a**/ VT (*reconstituir*) to reconstruct; (*persona*) to reinstate; (*dinero*) to refund, pay back; **reintegrarse** VR: **reintegrarse a** to return to

reintegro [rein'teɣro] NM refund, reimbursement; (*en banco*) withdrawal

reír [re'ir] VI to laugh; **reírse** VR to laugh; **reírse de** to laugh at

reiterado, -a [reite'raðo, a] ADJ repeated

reiterar [reite'rar] /**1a**/ VT to reiterate; (*repetir*) to repeat

reivindicación [reiβindika'θjon] NF (*demanda*) claim, demand; (*justificación*) vindication

reivindicar [reiβindi'kar] /**1g**/ VT to claim

reivindique *etc* [reiβin'dike] VB *ver* **reivindicar**

reja ['rexa] NF (*de ventana*) grille, bars *pl*; (*en la calle*) grating

rejilla [re'xiʎa] NF grating, grille; (*muebles*) wickerwork; (*de ventilación*) vent; (*de coche etc*) luggage rack

rejoneador [rexonea'ðor] NM mounted bullfighter

rejuvenecer [rexuβene'θer] /**2d**/ VT, VI to rejuvenate

rejuvenezca *etc* [rexuβe'neθka] VB *ver* **rejuvenecer**

relación [rela'θjon] NF relation, relationship; (*Mat*) ratio; (*lista*) list; (*narración*) report; **~ costo-efectivo** *o* **costo-rendimiento** (*Com*) cost-effectiveness; **relaciones** NFPL (*enchufes*) influential friends, connections; **relaciones carnales** sexual relations; **relaciones comerciales** business connections; **relaciones empresariales/ humanas** industrial/human relations; **relaciones laborales/públicas** labour/ public relations; **con ~ a, en ~ con** in relation to; **estar en** *o* **tener buenas relaciones con** to be on good terms with

relacionar [relaθjo'nar] /**1a**/ VT to relate, connect; **relacionarse** VR to be connected *o* linked

relajación [relaxa'θjon] NF relaxation

relajado, -a [rela'xaðo, a] ADJ (*disoluto*) loose; (*cómodo*) relaxed; (*Med*) ruptured

relajante [rela'xante] ADJ relaxing; (*Med*) sedative

relajar [rela'xar] /**1a**/ VT to relax; **relajarse** VR to relax

relamerse [rela'merse] /**2a**/ VR to lick one's lips

relamido, -a [rela'miðo, a] ADJ (*pulcro*) overdressed; (*afectado*) affected

relámpago [re'lampaɣo] NM flash of lightning ▶ ADJ lightning *cpd*; **como un ~** as quick as lightning, in a flash; **visita/huelga ~** lightning visit/strike

relampaguear [relampaɣe'ar] /**1a**/ VI to flash

relanzar [relan'θar] /**1f**/ VT to relaunch

relatar [rela'tar] /**1a**/ VT to tell, relate

relatividad [relatiβi'ðað] NF relativity

relativo, -a [rela'tiβo, a] ADJ relative; **en lo ~ a** concerning

relato [re'lato] NM (*narración*) story, tale

relax [re'las] NM rest; **"R~"** (*en anuncio*) "Personal services"

relegar [rele'ɣar] /**1h**/ VT to relegate; **~ algo al olvido** to banish sth from one's mind

relegue *etc* [re'leɣe] VB *ver* **relegar**

relevante [rele'βante] ADJ eminent, outstanding

relevar [rele'βar] /**1a**/ VT (*sustituir*) to relieve;

relevarse VR to relay; **~ a algn de un cargo** to relieve sb of his post

relevo [re'leβo] NM relief; **carrera de relevos** relay race; **coger** *o* **tomar el ~** to take over, stand in

relieve [re'ljeβe] NM (*Arte, Tec*) relief; (*fig*) prominence, importance; **bajo ~** bas-relief; **un personaje de ~** an important man; **dar ~ a** to highlight

religión [reli'xjon] NF religion

religioso, -a [reli'xjoso, a] ADJ religious ▶ NM/F monk/nun

relinchar [relin'tʃar] /**1a**/ VI to neigh

relincho [re'lintʃo] NM neigh; (*acto*) neighing

reliquia [re'likja] NF relic; **~ de familia** heirloom

rellano [re'ʎano] NM (*Arq*) landing

rellenar [reʎe'nar] /**1a**/ VT (*llenar*) to fill up; (*Culin*) to stuff; (*Costura*) to pad; (*formulario etc*) to fill in *o* out

relleno, -a [re'ʎeno, a] ADJ full up; (*Culin*) stuffed ▶ NM stuffing; (*de tapicería*) padding

reloj [re'lo(x)] NM clock; **poner el ~ (en hora)** to set one's watch *o* the clock; **~ de pie** grandfather clock; **~ (de pulsera)** (wrist)watch; **~ de sol** sundial; **~ despertador** alarm (clock); **~ digital** digital watch; **como un ~** like clockwork; **contra (el) ~** against the clock

relojería [reloxe'ria] NF (*tienda*) watchmaker's (shop); **aparato de ~** clockwork; **bomba de ~** time bomb

relojero, -a [relo'xero, a] NM/F clockmaker; watchmaker

reluciente [relu'θjente] ADJ brilliant, shining

relucir [relu'θir] /**3f**/ VI to shine; (*fig*) to excel; **sacar algo a ~** to show sth off

relumbrante [relum'brante] ADJ dazzling

relumbrar [relum'brar] /**1a**/ VI to dazzle, shine brilliantly

reluzca *etc* [re'luθka] VB *ver* **relucir**

remachar [rema'tʃar] /**1a**/ VT to rivet; (*fig*) to hammer home, drive home

remache [re'matʃe] NM rivet

remanente [rema'nente] NM remainder; (*Com*) balance; (*de producto*) surplus

remangar [reman'gar] /**1h**/ VT to roll up; **remangarse** VR to roll one's sleeves up

remanso [re'manso] NM pool

remar [re'mar] /**1a**/ VI to row

rematado, -a [rema'taðo, a] ADJ complete, utter; **es un loco ~** he's a raving lunatic

rematar [rema'tar] /**1a**/ VT to finish off; (*animal*) to put out of its misery; (*Com*) to sell off cheap ▶ VI to end, finish off; (*Deporte*) to shoot

remate [re'mate] NM end, finish; (*punta*) tip; (*Deporte*) shot; (*Arq*) top; (*Com*) auction sale;

r

de o **para ~** to crown it all (BRIT), to top it off

remedar [reme'ðar] /**1a**/ VT to imitate

remediable [reme'ðjaβle] ADJ: **fácilmente ~** easily remedied

remediar [reme'ðjar] /**1b**/ VT (gen) to remedy; (subsanar) to make good, repair; (evitar) to avoid; **sin poder remediarlo** without being able to prevent it

remedio [re'meðjo] NM remedy; (alivio) relief, help; (Jur) recourse, remedy; **poner ~ a** to correct, stop; **no tener más ~** to have no alternative; **¡qué ~!** there's no choice!; **como último ~** as a last resort; **sin ~** inevitable; (Med) hopeless

remedo [re'meðo] NM imitation; (pey) parody

remendar [remen'dar] /**1j**/ VT to repair; (con parche) to patch; (fig) to correct

remesa [re'mesa] NF remittance; (Com) shipment

remiendo etc [re'mjendo] VB ver **remendar** ▶ NM mend; (con parche) patch; (cosido) darn; (fig) correction

remilgado, -a [remil'ɣaðo, a] ADJ prim; (afectado) affected

remilgo [re'milɣo] NM primness; (afectación) affectation

reminiscencia [reminis'θenθja] NF reminiscence

remirar [remi'rar] /**1a**/ VT (volver a mirar) to look at again; (examinar) to look hard at

remisión [remi'sjon] NF (acto) sending, shipment; (Rel) forgiveness, remission; **sin ~** hopelessly

remiso, -a [re'miso, a] ADJ slack, slow

remite [re'mite] NM (en sobre) name and address of sender

remitente [remi'tente] NMF (Correos) sender

remitir [remi'tir] /**3a**/ VT to remit, send ▶ VI to slacken; (en carta): **remite: X** sender: X

remo ['remo] NM (de barco) oar; (Deporte) rowing; **cruzar un río a ~** to row across a river

remoce etc [re'moθe] VB ver **remozar**

remodelación [remodela'θjon] NF (Pol): **~ del gobierno** cabinet reshuffle

remojar [remo'xar] /**1a**/ VT to steep, soak; (galleta etc) to dip, dunk; (fam) to celebrate with a drink

remojo [re'moxo] NM steeping, soaking; (por la lluvia) drenching, soaking; **dejar la ropa en ~** to leave clothes to soak

remojón [remo'xon] NM soaking; **darse un ~** (fam) to go (in) for a dip

remolacha [remo'latʃa] NF beet, beetroot (BRIT)

remolcador [remolka'ðor] NM (Naut) tug; (Auto) breakdown lorry

remolcar [remol'kar] /**1g**/ VT to tow

remolino [remo'lino] NM eddy; (de agua) whirlpool; (de viento) whirlwind; (de gente) crowd

remolón, -ona [remo'lon, ona] ADJ lazy ▶ NM/F slacker, shirker

remolque [re'molke] VB ver **remolcar** ▶ NM tow, towing; (cuerda) towrope; **llevar a ~** to tow

remontar [remon'tar] /**1a**/ VT to mend; (obstáculo) to negotiate, get over; **remontarse** VR to soar; **remontarse a** (Com) to amount to; (en tiempo) to go back to, date from; **~ el vuelo** to soar

rémora ['remora] NF hindrance

remorder [remor'ðer] /**2h**/ VT to distress, disturb; **remorderle la conciencia a algn** to have a guilty conscience

remordimiento [remorði'mjento] NM remorse

remotamente [remota'mente] ADV vaguely

remoto, -a [re'moto, a] ADJ remote

remover [remo'βer] /**2h**/ VT to stir; (tierra) to turn over; (objetos) to move round

remozar [remo'θar] /**1f**/ VT (Arq) to refurbish; (fig) to brighten o polish up

remuerda etc [re'mwerða] VB ver **remorder**

remueva etc [re'mweβa] VB ver **remover**

remuneración [remunera'θjon] NF remuneration

remunerado, -a [remune'raðo, a] ADJ: **trabajo bien/mal ~** well-/badly-paid job

remunerar [remune'rar] /**1a**/ VT to remunerate; (premiar) to reward

renacer [rena'θer] /**2d**/ VI to be reborn; (fig) to revive

renacimiento [renaθi'mjento] NM rebirth; **el R~** the Renaissance

renacuajo [rena'kwaxo] NM (Zool) tadpole

renal [re'nal] ADJ renal, kidney cpd

Renania [re'nanja] NF Rhineland

renazca etc [re'naθka] VB ver **renacer**

rencilla [ren'θiʎa] NF quarrel; **rencillas** NFPL bickering sg

rencor [ren'kor] NM rancour, bitterness; (resentimiento) ill feeling, resentment; **guardar ~ a** to have a grudge against

rencoroso, -a [renko'roso, a] ADJ spiteful

rendición [rendi'θjon] NF surrender

rendido, -a [ren'diðo, a] ADJ (sumiso) submissive; (agotado) worn-out, exhausted; (enamorado) devoted

rendija [ren'dixa] NF (hendidura) crack; (abertura) aperture; (fig) rift, split; (Jur) loophole

rendimiento [rendi'mjento] NM (producción) output; (Com) yield, profit(s) nf; (Tec, Com) efficiency; **~ de capital** (Com) return on capital

rendir [ren'dir] /**3k**/ VT (*vencer*) to defeat; (*producir*) to produce; (*dar beneficio*) to yield; (*agotar*) to exhaust ▸ VI to pay; (*Com*) to yield; **rendirse** VR (*someterse*) to surrender; (*ceder*) to yield; (*cansarse*) to wear o.s. out; **~ homenaje** o **culto a** to pay homage to; **el negocio no rinde** the business doesn't pay

renegado, -a [rene'ɣaðo, a] ADJ, NM/F renegade

renegar [rene'ɣar] /**1h, 1j**/ VT (*negar*) to deny vigorously ▸ VI (*blasfemar*) to blaspheme; **~ de** (*renunciar*) to renounce; (*quejarse*) to complain about

renegué [rene'ɣe], **reneguemos** *etc* [rene'ɣemos] VB *ver* **renegar**

RENFE ['renfe] NF ABR (*Esp Ferro*) = **Red Nacional de Ferrocarriles Españoles**

renglón [ren'glon] NM (*línea*) line; (*Com*) item, article; **a ~ seguido** immediately after

rengo, -a ['rengo, a] ADJ (*Am*) lame

reniego *etc* [re'njeɣo], **reniegue** *etc* [re'njeɣe] VB *ver* **renegar**

reno ['reno] NM reindeer

renombrado, -a [renom'braðo, a] ADJ renowned

renombre [re'nombre] NM renown

renovable [reno'βaβle] ADJ renewable

renovación [renoβa'θjon] NF (*de contrato*) renewal; (*Arq*) renovation

renovar [reno'βar] /**1l**/ VT (*contrato*) to renew; (*Arq*) to renovate; (*sala*) to redecorate

renquear [renke'ar] /**1a**/ VI to limp; (*fam*) to get along, scrape by

renta ['renta] NF (*ingresos*) income; (*beneficio*) profit; (*alquiler*) rent; **~ gravable** o **imponible** taxable income; **~ nacional (bruta)** (gross) national income; **~ no salarial** unearned income; **~ sobre el terreno** (*Com*) ground rent; **~ vitalicia** annuity; **política de rentas** incomes policy; **vivir de sus rentas** to live on one's private income

rentabilizar [rentaβili'θar] /**1f**/ VT to make profitable

rentable [ren'taβle] ADJ profitable; **no ~** unprofitable

rentar [ren'tar] /**1a**/ VT to produce, yield; (*Am*) to rent

rentista [ren'tista] NMF (*accionista*) shareholder (*Brit*), stockholder (*US*)

renuencia [re'nwenθja] NF reluctance

renuente [re'nwente] ADJ reluctant

renueve *etc* [re'nweβe] VB *ver* **renovar**

renuncia [re'nunθja] NF resignation

renunciar [renun'θjar] /**1b**/ VT to renounce, give up ▸ VI to resign; **~ a** (*tabaco, alcohol etc*) to give up; (*oferta, oportunidad*) to turn down; (*puesto*) to resign; **~ a hacer algo** to give up doing sth

reñido, -a [re'niðo, a] ADJ (*batalla*) bitter, hard-fought; **estar ~ con algn** to be on bad terms with sb; **está ~ con su familia** he has fallen out with his family

reñir [re'nir] /**3h, 3k**/ VT (*regañar*) to scold ▸ VI (*estar peleado*) to quarrel, fall out; (*combatir*) to fight

reo ['reo] NMF culprit, offender; (*Jur*) accused

reojo [re'oxo]: **de ~** ADV out of the corner of one's eye

reorganice *etc* [reorɣa'niθe] VB *ver* **reorganizar**

reorganizar [reorɣani'θar] /**1f**/ VT to reorganize

Rep. ABR = **república**

reparación [repara'θjon] NF (*acto*) mending, repairing; (*Tec*) repair; (*fig*) amends, reparation; **"reparaciones en el acto"** "repairs while you wait"

reparador, -a [repara'ðor, a] ADJ refreshing; (*comida*) fortifying ▸ NM repairer

reparar [repa'rar] /**1a**/ VT to repair; (*fig*) to make amends for; (*suerte*) to retrieve; (*observar*) to observe ▸ VI: **~ en** (*darse cuenta de*) to notice; (*poner atención en*) to pay attention to; **sin ~ en los gastos** regardless of the cost

reparo [re'paro] NM (*advertencia*) observation; (*duda*) doubt; (*dificultad*) difficulty; (*escrúpulo*) scruple, qualm; **poner reparos (a)** to raise objections (to); (*criticar*) to criticize; **no tuvo ~ en hacerlo** he did not hesitate to do it

repartición [reparti'θjon] NF distribution; (*división*) division

repartidor, a [reparti'ðor, a] NM/F distributor; **~ de leche** milkman

repartir [repar'tir] /**3a**/ VT to distribute, share out; (*Com, Correos*) to deliver; (*Mil*) to partition; (*libros*) to give out; (*comida*) to serve out; (*Naipes*) to deal

reparto [re'parto] NM distribution; (*Com, Correos*) delivery; (*Teat, Cine*) cast; (*Am: urbanización*) housing estate (*Brit*), real estate development (*US*); **"~ a domicilio"** "home delivery service"

repasar [repa'sar] /**1a**/ VT (*Escol*) to revise; (*Mecánica*) to check, overhaul; (*Costura*) to mend

repaso [re'paso] NM revision; (*Mecánica*) overhaul, checkup; (*Costura*) mending; **~ general** servicing, general overhaul; **curso de ~** refresher course

repatriar [repa'trjar] /**1b**/ VT to repatriate; **repatriarse** VR to return home

repecho [re'petʃo] NM steep incline

repelente [repe'lente] ADJ repellent, repulsive

repeler [repe'ler] /**2a**/ VT to repel; (*idea, oferta*) to reject

repensar [repen'sar] /**1j**/ VT to reconsider

r

repente [re'pente] NM sudden movement; (*fig*) impulse; **de ~** suddenly; **~ de ira** fit of anger

repentice *etc* [repen'tiθe] VB *ver* **repentizar**

repentino, -a [repen'tino, a] ADJ sudden; (*imprevisto*) unexpected

repentizar [repenti'θar] /**1f**/ VI (*Mus*) to sight-read

repercusión [reperku'sjon] NF repercussion; **de amplia** *o* **ancha ~** far-reaching

repercutir [reperku'tir] /**3a**/ VI (*objeto*) to rebound; (*sonido*) to echo; **~ en** (*fig*) to have repercussions *o* effects on

repertorio [reper'torjo] NM list; (*Teat*) repertoire

repesca [re'peska] NF (*Escol: fam*) resit

repetición [repeti'θjon] NF repetition

repetido, -a [repe'tiðo, a] ADJ repeated; **repetidas veces** repeatedly

repetir [repe'tir] /**3k**/ VT to repeat; (*plato*) to have a second helping of; (*Teat*) to give as an encore, sing *etc* again ▶ VI to repeat; (*sabor*) to come back; **repetirse** VR to repeat o.s.; (*suceso*) to recur

repetitivo, -a [repeti'tiβo, a] ADJ repetitive, repetitious

repicar [repi'kar] /**1g**/ VI (*campanas*) to ring (out)

repiense *etc* [re'pjense] VB *ver* **repensar**

repipi [re'pipi] ADJ la-di-da ▶ NF: **es una ~** she's a little madam

repique [re'pike] VB *ver* **repicar** ▶ NM pealing, ringing

repiqueteo [repike'teo] NM pealing; (*de tambor*) drumming

repisa [re'pisa] NF ledge, shelf; **~ de chimenea** mantelpiece; **~ de ventana** windowsill

repito *etc* [re'pito] VB *ver* **repetir**

replantear [replante'ar] /**1a**/ VT (*cuestión pública*) to readdress; (*problema personal*) to reconsider; (*en reunión*) to raise again; **replantearse** VR: **replantearse algo** to reconsider sth

replegarse [reple'ɣarse] /**1h, 1j**/ VR to fall back, retreat

replegué [reple'ɣe], **repleguemos** *etc* [reple'ɣemos] VB *ver* **replegarse**

repleto, -a [re'pleto, a] ADJ replete, full up; **~ de** filled *o* crammed with

réplica ['replika] NF answer; (*Arte*) replica; **derecho de ~** right of *o* to reply

replicar [repli'kar] /**1g**/ VI to answer; (*objetar*) to argue, answer back

repliego *etc* [re'pljeɣo] VB *ver* **replegarse**

repliegue [re'pljeɣe] VB *ver* **replegarse** ▶ NM (*Mil*) withdrawal

replique *etc* [re'plike] VB *ver* **replicar**

repoblación [repoβla'θjon] NF repopulation; (*de río*) restocking; **~ forestal** reafforestation

repoblar [repo'βlar] /**1l**/ VT to repopulate; to restock; (*con árboles*) to reafforest

repollito [repo'ʎito] NM (*Am*): **repollitos de Bruselas** (Brussels) sprouts

repollo [re'poʎo] NM cabbage

repondré *etc* [repon'dre] VB *ver* **reponer**

reponer [repo'ner] /**2q**/ VT to replace, put back; (*máquina*) to re-set; (*Teat*) to revive; **reponerse** VR to recover; **~ que** to reply that

reponga *etc* [re'ponga] VB *ver* **reponer**

reportaje [repor'taxe] NM report, article; **~ gráfico** illustrated report

reportar [repor'tar] /**1a**/ VT (*traer*) to bring, carry; (*conseguir*) to obtain; (*fig*) to check; **reportarse** VR (*contenerse*) to control o.s.; (*calmarse*) to calm down; **la cosa no le reportó sino disgustos** the affair brought him nothing but trouble

reportero, -a [repor'tero, a] NM/F reporter; **~ gráfico/a** news photographer

reposacabezas [reposaka'βeθas] NM INV headrest

reposado, -a [repo'saðo, a] ADJ (*descansado*) restful; (*tranquilo*) calm

reposar [repo'sar] /**1a**/ VI to rest, repose; (*muerto*) to lie, rest

reposición [reposi'θjon] NF replacement; (*Cine*) second showing; (*Teat*) revival

reposo [re'poso] NM rest

repostar [repos'tar] /**1a**/ VT to replenish; (*Auto*) to fill up (with petrol *o* gasoline)

repostería [reposte'ria] NF (*arte*) confectionery, pastry-making; (*tienda*) confectioner's (shop)

repostero, -a [repos'tero, a] NM/F confectioner

reprender [repren'der] /**2a**/ VT to reprimand; (*niño*) to scold

reprensión [repren'sjon] NF rebuke, reprimand; (*de niño*) telling-off, scolding

represa [re'presa] NF dam; (*lago artificial*) lake, pool

represalia [repre'salja] NF reprisal; **tomar represalias** to take reprisals, retaliate

representación [representa'θjon] NF representation; (*Teat*) performance; **en ~ de** representing; **por ~** by proxy

representante [represen'tante] NM/F (*Pol, Com*) representative; (*Teat*) performer

representar [represen'tar] /**1a**/ VT to represent; (*significar*) to mean; (*Teat*) to perform; (*edad*) to look; **representarse** VR to imagine; **tal acto representaría la guerra** such an act would mean war

representativo, -a [representa'tiβo, a] ADJ representative

represión [repre'sjon] NF repression

represivo, -a [repre'siβo, a] ADJ repressive

reprimenda [repri'menda] NF reprimand, rebuke

reprimir [repri'mir] /3a/ VT to repress; **reprimirse** VR: **reprimirse de hacer algo** to stop o.s. from doing sth

reprobación [reproβa'θjon] NF reproval; (*culpa*) blame

reprobar [repro'βar] /1l/ VT to censure, reprove

réprobo, -a ['reproβo, a] NM/F reprobate

reprochar [repro'tʃar] /1a/ VT to reproach; (*censurar*) to condemn, censure

reproche [re'protʃe] NM reproach

reproducción [reproðuk'θjon] NF reproduction

reproducir [reproðu'θir] /3n/ VT to reproduce; **reproducirse** VR to breed; (*situación*) to recur

reproductor, a [reproðuk'tor, a] ADJ reproductive ▶ NM: **~ de CD** CD player; **~ MP3/MP4** MP3/MP4 player

reproduje [repro'ðuxe], **reprodujera** etc [reproðu'xera], **reproduzca** etc [repro'duθka] VB ver **reproducir**

repruebe etc [re'prweβe] VB ver **reprobar**

reptar [rep'tar] /1a/ VI to creep, crawl

reptil [rep'til] NM reptile

república [re'puβlika] NF republic; **R~ Dominicana** Dominican Republic; **R~ Federal Alemana (RFA)** Federal Republic of Germany

republicano, -a [repuβli'kano, a] ADJ, NM/F republican

repudiar [repu'ðjar] /1b/ VT to repudiate; (*fe*) to renounce

repudio [re'puðjo] NM repudiation

repueble etc [re'pweβle] VB ver **repoblar**

repuesto [re'pwesto] PP de **reponer** ▶ NM (*pieza de recambio*) spare (part); (*abastecimiento*) supply; **rueda de ~** spare wheel; **y llevamos otro de ~** and we have another as a spare o in reserve

repugnancia [repuɣ'nanθja] NF repugnance

repugnante [repuɣ'nante] ADJ repugnant, repulsive

repugnar [repuɣ'nar] /1a/ VT to disgust ▶ VI, **repugnarse** VR (*contradecirse*) to contradict each other

repujar [repu'xar] /1a/ VT to emboss

repulsa [re'pulsa] NF rebuff

repulsión [repul'sjon] NF repulsion, aversion

repulsivo, -a [repul'siβo, a] ADJ repulsive

repuse etc [re'puse] VB ver **reponer**

reputación [reputa'θjon] NF reputation

reputar [repu'tar] /1a/ VT to consider, deem

requemado, -a [reke'maðo, a] ADJ (*quemado*) scorched; (*bronceado*) tanned

requemar [reke'mar] /1a/ VT (*quemar*) to scorch; (*secar*) to parch; (*Culin*) to overdo, burn; (*la lengua*) to burn, sting

requerimiento [rekeri'mjento] NM request; (*demanda*) demand; (*Jur*) summons

requerir [reke'rir] /3i/ VT (*pedir*) to ask, request; (*exigir*) to require; (*ordenar*) to call for; (*llamar*) to send for, summon

requesón [reke'son] NM whey cheese (*similar to ricotta*)

requete... [rekete] PREF extremely

requiebro [re'kjeβro] NM (*piropo*) compliment, flirtatious remark

réquiem ['rekjem] NM requiem

requiera etc [re'kjera], **requiriendo** etc [reki'rjendo] VB ver **requerir**

requisa [re'kisa] NF (*inspección*) survey, inspection; (*Mil*) requisition

requisar [reki'sar] /1a/ VT (*Mil*) to requisition; (*confiscar*) to seize, confiscate

requisito [reki'sito] NM requirement, requisite; **~ previo** prerequisite; **tener los requisitos para un cargo** to have the essential qualifications for a post

res [res] NF beast, animal

resabio [re'saβjo] NM (*maña*) vice, bad habit; (*dejo*) (unpleasant) aftertaste

resaca [re'saka] NF (*en el mar*) undertow, undercurrent; (*fig*) backlash; (*fam*) hangover

resaltar [resal'tar] /1a/ VI to project, stick out; (*fig*) to stand out

resarcir [resar'θir] /3b/ VT to compensate; (*pagar*) to repay; **resarcirse** VR to make up for; **~ a algn una pérdida** to compensate sb for a loss; **~ a algn de una cantidad** to repay sb a sum

resarza etc [re'sarθa] VB ver **resarcir**

resbalada [resβa'laða] NF (Am) slip

resbaladero [resβala'ðero] NM (Am) slide

resbaladizo, -a [resβala'ðiθo, a] ADJ slippery

resbalar [resβa'lar] /1a/ VI to slip, slide; (*fig*) to slip (up); **resbalarse** VR to slip, slide; (*fig*) to slip (up); **le resbalaban las lágrimas por las mejillas** tears were trickling down his cheeks

resbalón [resβa'lon] NM (*acción*) slip; (*deslizamiento*) slide; (*fig*) slip

rescatar [reska'tar] /1a/ VT (*salvar*) to save, rescue; (*objeto*) to get back, recover; (*cautivos*) to ransom

rescate [res'kate] NM rescue; (*de objeto*) recovery; (*Com*) bailout; **pagar un ~** to pay a ransom

rescindir [resθin'dir] /3a/ VT (*contrato*) to annul, rescind

rescisión [resθi'sjon] NF cancellation

rescoldo [res'koldo] NM embers pl

resecar [rese'kar] /1g/ VT to dry off, dry thoroughly; (*Med*) to cut out, remove; **resecarse** VR to dry up

reseco, -a [re'seko, a] ADJ very dry; (*fig*) skinny

r

resentido, -a [resen'tiðo, a] ADJ resentful;
es un ~ he's bitter

resentimiento [resenti'mjento] NM
resentment, bitterness

resentirse [resen'tirse] /3i/ VR (*debilitarse*:
persona) to suffer; **~ con** to resent; **~ de** (*sufrir
las consecuencias de*) to feel the effects of; **~ de** o
por algo to resent sth, be bitter about sth

reseña [re'seɲa] NF (*cuenta*) account; (*informe*)
report; (*Lit*) review

reseñar [rese'ɲar] /1a/ VT to describe; (*Lit*) to
review

reseque *etc* [re'seke] VB *ver* **resecar**

reserva [re'serβa] NF reserve; (*reservación*)
reservation; **a ~ de que** ... unless ...; **con
toda ~** in strictest confidence; **de ~** spare;
tener algo de ~ to have sth in reserve; **~ de
indios** Indian reservation; (*Com*) **~ para
amortización** depreciation allowance; **~ de
caja** o **en efectivo** cash reserves; **reservas
del Estado** government stock; **reservas en
oro** gold reserves

reservación [reserβa'θjon] NF (*Am*)
reservation

reservado, -a [reser'βaðo, a] ADJ reserved;
(*retraído*) cold, distant ▶ NM private room;
(*Ferro*) reserved compartment

reservar [reser'βar] /1a/ VT (*guardar*) to keep;
(*Ferro, Teat etc*) to reserve, book; **reservarse** VR
to save o.s.; (*callar*) to keep to o.s.; **~ con
exceso** to overbook

resfriado [res'frjaðo] NM cold

resfriarse [res'frjarse] /1c/ VR to cool off;
(*Med*) to catch (a) cold

resfrío [res'frio] NM (*esp Am*) cold

resguardar [resɣwar'ðar] /1a/ VT to protect,
shield; **resguardarse** VR: **resguardarse de**
to guard against

resguardo [res'ɣwarðo] NM defence; (*vale*)
voucher; (*recibo*) receipt, slip

residencia [resi'ðenθja] NF residence; (*Univ*)
hall of residence; **~ para ancianos** o
jubilados residential home, old people's
home

residencial [resiðen'θjal] ADJ residential
▶ NF (*urbanización*) housing estate (*Brit*), real
estate development (*US*)

residente [resi'ðente] ADJ, NMF resident

residir [resi'ðir] /3a/ VI to reside, live; **~ en** to
reside o lie in; (*consistir en*) to consist of

residual [resi'ðwal] ADJ residual; **aguas
residuales** sewage

residuo [re'siðwo] NM residue; **residuos
atmosféricos** o **radiactivos** fallout *sg*

resienta *etc* [re'sjenta] VB *ver* **resentirse**

resignación [resiɣna'θjon] NF resignation

resignarse [resiɣ'narse] /1a/ VR: **~ a** o **con** to
resign o.s. to, be resigned to

resina [re'sina] NF resin

resintiendo *etc* [resin'tjendo] VB *ver*
resentirse

resistencia [resis'tenθja] NF (*dureza*)
endurance, strength; (*oposición, Elec*)
resistance; **la R~** (*Mil*) the Resistance

resistente [resis'tente] ADJ strong, hardy;
(*Tec*) resistant; **~ al calor** heat-resistant

resistir [resis'tir] /3a/ VT (*soportar*) to bear;
(*oponerse a*) to resist, oppose; (*aguantar*) to put
up with ▶ VI to resist; (*aguantar*) to last,
endure; **resistirse** VR: **resistirse a** to refuse
to, resist; **no puedo ~ este frío** I can't bear o
stand this cold; **me resisto a creerlo** I
refuse to believe it; **se le resiste la química**
chemistry escapes her

resol [re'sol] NM glare of the sun

resollar [reso'ʎar] /1l/ VI to breathe noisily,
wheeze

resolución [resolu'θjon] NF resolution;
(*decisión*) decision; (*moción*) motion;
~ judicial legal ruling; **tomar una ~** to take
a decision

resoluto, -a [reso'luto, a] ADJ resolute

resolver [resol'βer] /2h/ VT to resolve;
(*solucionar*) to solve, resolve; (*decidir*) to decide,
settle; **resolverse** VR to make up one's mind

resonancia [reso'nanθja] NF (*del sonido*)
resonance; (*repercusión*) repercussion; (*fig*)
wide effect, impact

resonante [reso'nante] ADJ resonant,
resounding; (*fig*) tremendous

resonar [reso'nar] /1l/ VI to ring, echo

resoplar [reso'plar] /1a/ VI to snort; (*por
cansancio*) to puff

resoplido [reso'pliðo] NM heavy breathing

resorte [re'sorte] NM spring; (*fig*) lever

resortera [resor'tera] NF (*Am*) catapult

respaldar [respal'dar] /1a/ VT to back (up),
support; (*Inform*) to back up; **respaldarse** VR
to lean back; **respaldarse con** o **en** (*fig*) to
take one's stand on

respaldo [res'paldo] NM (*de sillón*) back; (*fig*)
support, backing

respectivo, -a [respek'tiβo, a] ADJ respective;
en lo ~ a with regard to

respecto [res'pekto] NM: **al ~** on this matter;
con ~ a, **~ de** with regard to, in relation to

respetable [respe'taβle] ADJ respectable

respetar [respe'tar] /1a/ VT to respect

respeto [res'peto] NM respect; (*acatamiento*)
deference; **respetos** NMPL respects; **por ~ a**
out of consideration for; **presentar sus
respetos a** to pay one's respects to

respetuoso, -a [respe'twoso, a] ADJ
respectful

respingo [res'pingo] NM start, jump

respiración [respira'θjon] NF breathing;
(*Med*) respiration; (*ventilación*) ventilation;
~ asistida artificial respiration (*by machine*)

respirar [respi'rar] /**1a**/ VT, VI to breathe; **no dejar ~ a algn** to keep on at sb; **estuvo escuchándole sin ~** he listened to him in complete silence

respiratorio, -a [respira'torjo, a] ADJ respiratory

respiro [res'piro] NM breathing; (*fig: descanso*) respite, rest; (*Com*) period of grace

resplandecer [resplande'θer] /**2d**/ VI to shine

resplandeciente [resplande'θjente] ADJ resplendent, shining

resplandezca etc [resplan'deθka] VB ver **resplandecer**

resplandor [resplan'dor] NM brilliance, brightness; (*del fuego*) blaze

responder [respon'der] /**2a**/ VT to answer ▶ VI to answer; (*fig*) to respond; (*pey*) to answer back; (*corresponder*) to correspond; **~ a** (*situación etc*) to respond to; **~ a una pregunta** to answer a question; **~ a una descripción** to fit a description; **~ de** o **por** to answer for

respondón, -ona [respon'don, ona] ADJ cheeky

responsabilice etc [responsaβi'liθe] VB ver **responsabilizarse**

responsabilidad [responsaβili'ðað] NF responsibility; **bajo mi ~** on my authority; **~ ilimitada** (*Com*) unlimited liability

responsabilizarse [responsaβili'θarse] /**1f**/ VR to make o.s. responsible, take charge

responsable [respon'sable] ADJ responsible; **la persona ~** the person in charge; **hacerse ~ de algo** to assume responsibility for sth

respuesta [res'pwesta] NF answer, reply; (*reacción*) response

resquebrajar [reskeβra'xar] /**1a**/ VT to crack, split; **resquebrajarse** VR to crack, split

resquemor [reske'mor] NM resentment

resquicio [res'kiθjo] NM chink; (*hendidura*) crack

resta ['resta] NF (*Mat*) remainder

restablecer [restaβle'θer] /**2d**/ VT to re-establish, restore; **restablecerse** VR to recover

restablecimiento [restaβleθi'mjento] NM re-establishment; (*restauración*) restoration; (*Med*) recovery

restablezca etc [resta'βleθka] VB ver **restablecer**

restallar [resta'ʎar] /**1a**/ VI to crack

restante [res'tante] ADJ remaining; **lo ~** the remainder; **los restantes** the rest, those left (over)

restar [res'tar] /**1a**/ VT (*Mat*) to subtract; (*descontar*) to deduct; (*fig*) to take away ▶ VI to remain, be left

restauración [restaura'θjon] NF restoration

restaurador, a [restaura'ðor, a] NM/F (*persona*) restorer

restaurante [restau'rante] NM restaurant

restaurar [restau'rar] /**1a**/ VT to restore

restitución [restitu'θjon] NF return, restitution

restituir [restitu'ir] /**3g**/ VT (*devolver*) to return, give back; (*rehabilitar*) to restore

restituyendo etc [restitu'jendo] VB ver **restituir**

resto ['resto] NM (*residuo*) rest, remainder; (*apuesta*) stake; **restos** NMPL remains; (*Culin*) leftovers, scraps; **restos mortales** mortal remains

restorán [resto'ran] NM (*Am*) restaurant

restregar [restre'ɣar] /**1h, 1j**/ VT to scrub, rub

restregué [restre'ɣe], **restreguemos** etc [restre'ɣemos] VB ver **restregar**

restricción [restrik'θjon] NF restriction; **sin ~ de** without restrictions on o as to; **hablar sin restricciones** to talk freely

restrictivo, -a [restrik'tiβo, a] ADJ restrictive

restriego etc [res'trjeɣo], **restriegue** etc [res'trjeɣe] VB ver **restregar**

restringir [restrin'xir] /**3c**/ VT to restrict, limit

restrinja etc [res'trinxa] VB ver **restringir**

resucitar [resuθi'tar] /**1a**/ VT, VI to resuscitate, revive

resuello etc [re'sweʎo] VB ver **resollar** ▶ NM (*aliento*) breath

resuelto, -a [re'swelto, a] PP de **resolver** ▶ ADJ resolute, determined; **estar ~ a algo** to be set on sth; **estar ~ a hacer algo** to be determined to do sth

resuelva etc [re'swelβa] VB ver **resolver**

resuene etc [re'swene] VB ver **resonar**

resulta [re'sulta] NF result; **de resultas de** as a result of

resultado [resul'taðo] NM result; (*conclusión*) outcome; **resultados** NMPL (*Inform*) output sg; **dar ~** to produce results

resultante [resul'tante] ADJ resulting, resultant

resultar [resul'tar] /**1a**/ VI (*ser*) to be; (*llegar a ser*) to turn out to be; (*salir bien*) to turn out well; (*seguir*) to ensue; **~ a** (*Com*) to amount to; **~ de** to stem from; **~ en** to result in, produce; **resulta que ...** (*en consecuencia*) it follows that ...; (*parece que*) it seems that ...; **el conductor resultó muerto** the driver was killed; **no resultó** it didn't work o come off; **me resulta difícil hacerlo** it's difficult for me to do it

resumen [re'sumen] NM summary, résumé; **en ~** in short

resumir [resu'mir] /**3a**/ VT to sum up; (*condensar*) to summarize; (*cortar*) to abridge, cut down; **resumirse** VR: **la situación se resume en pocas palabras** the situation can be summed up in a few words

r

resurgir [resur'xir] /**3c**/ VI (*reaparecer*) to reappear

resurrección [resurrek'θjon] NF resurrection

retablo [re'taβlo] NM altarpiece

retaguardia [reta'ɣwarðja] NF rearguard

retahíla [reta'ila] NF series, string; (*de injurias*) volley, stream

retal [re'tal] NM remnant

retar [re'tar] /**1a**/ VT (*gen*) to challenge; (*desafiar*) to defy, dare

retardar [retar'ðar] /**1a**/ VT (*demorar*) to delay; (*hacer más lento*) to slow down; (*retener*) to hold back

retardo [re'tarðo] NM delay

retazo [re'taθo] NM snippet (BRIT), fragment

RETD NF ABR (*Esp Telec*) = **Red Especial de Transmisión de Datos**

rete ... ['rete] PREF very, extremely

retén [re'ten] NM (*AM*) roadblock, checkpoint

retención [reten'θjon] NF retention; (*de pago*) deduction; (*tráfico*) hold-up; **~ fiscal** deduction for tax purposes; **~ de llamadas** (*Telec*) hold facility

retendré *etc* [reten'dre] VB *ver* **retener**

retener [rete'ner] /**2k**/ VT (*guardar*) to retain, keep; (*intereses*) to withhold

retenga *etc* [re'tenga] VB *ver* **retener**

reticencia [reti'θenθja] NF (*insinuación*) insinuation, (*malevolent*) suggestion; (*verdad a medias*) half-truth

reticente [reti'θente] ADJ (*insinuador*) insinuating; (*engañoso*) deceptive; (*postura*) reluctant; **ser ~ a hacer algo** to be reluctant *o* unwilling to do sth

retiene *etc* [re'tjene] VB *ver* **retener**

retina [re'tina] NF retina

retintín [retin'tin] NM jangle, jingle; **decir algo con ~** to say sth sarcastically

retirado, -a [reti'raðo, a] ADJ (*lugar*) remote; (*vida*) quiet; (*jubilado*) retired ▶ NF (*Mil*) retreat; (*de dinero*) withdrawal; (*de embajador*) recall; **batirse en retirada** to retreat

retirar [reti'rar] /**1a**/ VT to withdraw; (*la mano*) to draw back; (*quitar*) to remove; (*dinero*) to take out, withdraw; (*jubilar*) to retire, pension off; **retirarse** VR to retreat, withdraw; (*jubilarse*) to retire; (*acostarse*) to retire, go to bed

retiro [re'tiro] NM retreat; (*jubilación, tb Deporte*) retirement; (*pago*) pension; (*lugar*) quiet place

reto ['reto] NM dare, challenge

retocar [reto'kar] /**1g**/ VT (*fotografía*) to touch up, retouch

retoce *etc* [re'toθe] VB *ver* **retozar**

retoño [re'toɲo] NM sprout, shoot; (*fig*) offspring, child

retoque [re'toke] VB *ver* **retocar** ▶ NM retouching

retorcer [retor'θer] /**2b, 2h**/ VT to twist; (*argumento*) to turn, twist; (*manos, lavado*) to wring; **retorcerse** VR to become twisted; (*persona*) to writhe; **retorcerse de dolor** to writhe in *o* squirm with pain

retorcido, -a [retor'θiðo, a] ADJ (*tb fig*) twisted

retorcijón [retorθi'xon] NM (*AM*: *tb*: **retorcijón de tripas**) stomach cramp

retorcimiento [retorθi'mjento] NM twist, twisting; (*fig*) deviousness

retórico, -a [re'toriko, a] ADJ rhetorical; (*pey*) affected, windy ▶ NF rhetoric; (*pey*) affectedness

retornable [retor'naβle] ADJ returnable

retornar [retor'nar] /**1a**/ VT to return, give back ▶ VI to return, go/come back

retorno [re'torno] NM return; **~ del carro** (*Inform, Tip*) carriage return

retortero [retor'tero] NM: **andar al ~** to bustle about, have heaps of things to do; **andar al ~ por algn** to be madly in love with sb

retortijón [retorti'xon] NM twist, twisting; **~ de tripas** stomach cramp

retorzamos *etc* [retor'θamos] VB *ver* **retorcer**

retozar [reto'θar] /**1f**/ VI (*juguetear*) to frolic, romp; (*saltar*) to gambol

retozón, -ona [reto'θon, ona] ADJ playful

retracción [retrak'θjon] NF retraction

retractarse [retrak'tarse] /**1a**/ VR to retract; **me retracto** I take that back

retraerse [retra'erse] /**2o**/ VR to retreat, withdraw

retraído, -a [retra'iðo, a] ADJ shy, retiring

retraiga *etc* [re'traiɣa] VB *ver* **retraerse**

retraimiento [retrai'mjento] NM retirement; (*timidez*) shyness

retraje *etc* [re'traxe], **retrajera** *etc* [retra'xera] VB *ver* **retraerse**

retransmisión [retransmi'sjon] NF repeat (broadcast)

retransmitir [retransmi'tir] /**3a**/ VT (*mensaje*) to relay; (*TV etc*) to repeat, retransmit; (*: en vivo*) to broadcast live

retrasado, -a [retra'saðo, a] ADJ late; (*mentalmente*) backward; (*país etc*) backward, underdeveloped; **estar ~** (*reloj*) to be slow; (*persona, industria*) to be *o* lag behind

retrasar [retra'sar] /**1a**/ VT (*demorar*) to postpone, put off; (*retardar*) to slow down ▶ VI (*atrasarse*) to be late; (*reloj*) to be slow; (*producción*) to fall (off); (*quedarse atrás*) to lag behind; **retrasarse** VR to be late; to be slow; to fall (off); to lag behind

retraso [re'traso] NM (*demora*) delay; (*lentitud*) slowness; (*tardanza*) lateness; (*atraso*) backwardness; **retrasos** NMPL (*Com*) arrears; (*deudas*) deficit *sg*, debts; **llegar con ~** to arrive late; **llegar con 25 minutos de ~** to be

25 minutes late; **llevo un ~ de seis semanas** I'm six weeks behind (with my work *etc*); **~ mental** mental deficiency

retratar [retra'tar] /**1a**/ VT (*Arte*) to paint the portrait of; (*fotografiar*) to photograph; (*fig*) to depict, describe; **retratarse** VR (*en cuadro*) to have one's portrait painted; (*en fotografía*) to have one's photograph taken

retratista [retra'tista] NMF (*Arte*) (portrait) painter; (*Foto*) photographer

retrato [re'trato] NM portrait; (*Foto*) photograph; (*descripción*) portrayal, depiction; (*fig*) likeness; **ser el vivo ~ de** to be the spitting image of

retrato-robot [re'tratoro'βo(t)] (*pl* **retratos-robot**) NM Identikit® picture

retrayendo *etc* [retra'jendo] VB *ver* **retraerse**

retreta [re'treta] NF retreat

retrete [re'trete] NM toilet

retribución [retriβu'θjon] NF (*recompensa*) reward; (*pago*) pay, payment

retribuir [retriβu'ir] /**3g**/ VT (*recompensar*) to reward; (*pagar*) to pay

retribuyendo *etc* [retriβu'jendo] VB *ver* **retribuir**

retro... [retro] PREF retro...

retroactivo, -a [retroak'tiβo, a] ADJ retroactive, retrospective; **dar efecto ~ a un pago** to backdate a payment

retroalimentación [retroalimenta'θjon] NF (*Inform*) feedback

retroceder [retroθe'ðer] /**2a**/ VI (*echarse atrás*) to move back(wards); (*fig*) to back down; **no ~ to** stand firm; **la policía hizo ~ a la multitud** the police forced the crowd back

retroceso [retro'θeso] NM backward movement; (*Med*) relapse; (*Com*) recession, depression; (*fig*) backing down

retrógrado, -a [re'troɣraðo, a] ADJ retrograde, retrogressive; (*Pol*) reactionary

retropropulsión [retropropul'sjon] NF jet propulsion

retrospectivo, -a [retrospek'tiβo, a] ADJ retrospective; **mirada retrospectiva** backward glance

retrovisor [retroβi'sor] NM rear-view mirror

retuerce *etc* [re'twerθe], **retuerza** *etc* [re'twerθa] VB *ver* **retorcer**

retuit [re'twit] NM (*en Twitter*) retweet

retuitear [retwite'ar] VT (*en Twitter*) retweet

retumbante [retum'bante] ADJ resounding

retumbar [retum'bar] /**1a**/ VI to echo, resound; (*continuamente*) to reverberate

retuve *etc* [re'tuβe] VB *ver* **retener**

reuma ['reuma] NM rheumatism

reumático, -a [reu'matiko, a] ADJ rheumatic

reumatismo [reuma'tismo] NM rheumatism

reunificar [reunifi'kar] /**1g**/ VT to reunify

reunifique *etc* [reuni'fike] VB *ver* **reunificar**

reunión [reu'njon] NF (*asamblea*) meeting; (*fiesta*) party; **~ en la cumbre** summit meeting; **~ de ventas** (*Com*) sales meeting

reunir [reu'nir] /**3a**/ VT (*juntar*) to reunite, join (together); (*recoger*) to gather (together); (*personas*) to bring o get together; (*cualidades*) to combine; **reunirse** VR (*personas: en asamblea*) to meet, gather; **reunió a sus amigos para discutirlo** he got his friends together to talk it over

reválida [re'βaliða] NF (*Escol*) final examination

revalidar [reβali'ðar] /**1a**/ VT (*ratificar*) to confirm, ratify

revalorar [reβalo'rar] /**1a**/ VT to revalue, reassess

revalorización [reβaloriθa'θjon], **revaloración** [reβalora'θjon] NF revaluation; (*Econ*) reassessment

revalorizar [reβalori'θar] /**1f**/ VT to revalue, reassess

revancha [re'βantʃa] NF revenge; (*Deporte*) return match; (*Boxeo*) return fight

revelación [reβela'θjon] NF revelation

revelado [reβe'laðo] NM developing

revelador, a [reβela'ðor, a] ADJ revealing

revelar [reβe'lar] /**1a**/ VT to reveal; (*secreto*) to disclose; (*mostrar*) to show; (*Foto*) to develop

revendedor, a [reβende'ðor, a] NM/F retailer; (*pey*) ticket tout

revendré *etc* [reβen'dre], **revenga** *etc* [re'βenga] VB *ver* **revenirse**

revenirse [reβe'nirse] /**3r**/ VR to shrink; (*comida*) to go bad o off; (*vino*) to sour; (*Culin*) to get tough

reventa [re'βenta] NF resale; (*especulación*) speculation; (*de entradas*) touting

reventar [reβen'tar] /**1j**/ VT to burst, explode; (*molestar*) to annoy, rile ▶ VI, **reventarse** VR (*estallar*) to burst, explode; **me revienta tener que ponérmelo** I hate having to wear it; **~ de** (*fig*) to be bursting with; **~ por** to be bursting to

reventón [reβen'ton] NM (*Auto*) blow-out (*BRIT*), flat (*US*)

reverberación [reβerβera'θjon] NF reverberation

reverberar [reβerβe'rar] /**1a**/ VI (*luz*) to play, be reflected; (*superficie*) to shimmer; (*nieve*) to glare; (*sonido*) to reverberate

reverbero [reβer'βero] NM play; shimmer, shine; glare; reverberation

reverencia [reβe'renθja] NF reverence; (*inclinación*) bow

reverenciar [reβeren'θjar] /**1b**/ VT to revere

reverendo, -a [reβe'rendo, a] ADJ reverend; (*fam*) big, awful; **un ~ imbécil** an awful idiot

reverente [reβe'rente] ADJ reverent

r

reversa [re'βersa] NF (*Am*) (reverse) gear
reversible [reβer'siβle] ADJ reversible
reverso [re'βerso] NM back, other side; (*de moneda*) reverse
revertir [reβer'tir] /3i/ VI to revert; ~ **en beneficio de** to be to the advantage of; ~ **en perjuicio de** to be to the detriment of
revés [re'βes] NM back, wrong side; (*fig*) reverse, setback; (*Deporte*) backhand; **al** ~ the wrong way round; (*de arriba abajo*) upside down; (*ropa*) inside out; **y al** ~ and vice versa; **volver algo del** ~ to turn sth round; (*ropa*) to turn sth inside out; **los reveses de la fortuna** the blows of fate
revestir [reβes'tir] /3k/ VT (*poner*) to put on; (*cubrir*) to cover, coat; (*cualidad*) to have, possess; **revestirse** VR (*Rel*) to put on one's vestments; (*ponerse*) to put on; ~ **con** o **de** to arm o.s. with; **el acto revestía gran solemnidad** the ceremony had great dignity
reviejo, -a [re'βjexo, a] ADJ very old, ancient
reviene *etc* [re'βjene] VB *ver* **revenirse**
reviente *etc* [re'βjente] VB *ver* **reventar**
revierta *etc* [re'βjerta] VB *ver* **revertir**
reviniendo *etc* [reβi'njendo] VB *ver* **revenirse**
revirtiendo *etc* [reβir'tjendo] VB *ver* **revertir**
revisar [reβi'sar] /1a/ VT (*examinar*) to check; (*texto etc*) to revise; (*Jur*) to review
revisión [reβi'sjon] NF revision; ~ **aduanera** customs inspection; ~ **de cuentas** audit; ~ **salarial** wage review
revisor, a [reβi'sor, a] NM/F inspector; (*Ferro*) ticket collector; ~ **de cuentas** auditor
revista [re'βista] VB *ver* **revestir** ▶ NF magazine, review; (*Teat*) revue; (*inspección*) inspection; ~ **literaria** literary review; ~ **de libros** book reviews (page); ~ **del corazón** *magazine featuring celebrity gossip and real-life romance stories*; **pasar ~ a** to review, inspect
revivir [reβi'βir] /3a/ VT (*recordar*) to revive memories of ▶ VI to revive
revocación [reβoka'θjon] NF repeal
revocar [reβo'kar] /1g/ VT (*decisión*) to revoke; (*Arq*) to plaster
revolcar [reβol'kar] /1g, 1l/ VT to knock down, send flying; **revolcarse** VR to roll about
revolcón [reβol'kon] NM tumble
revolotear [reβolote'ar] /1a/ VI to flutter
revoloteo [reβolo'teo] NM fluttering
revolqué [reβol'ke], **revolquemos** *etc* [reβol'kemos] VB *ver* **revolcar**
revoltijo [reβol'tixo] NM mess, jumble
revoltoso, -a [reβol'toso, a] ADJ (*travieso*) naughty, unruly
revolución [reβolu'θjon] NF revolution
revolucionar [reβoluθjo'nar] /1a/ VT to revolutionize
revolucionario, -a [reβoluθjo'narjo, a] ADJ, NM/F revolutionary

revolver [reβol'βer] /2h/ VT (*desordenar*) to disturb, mess up; (*agitar*) to shake; (*líquido*) to stir; (*mover*) to move about; (*Pol*) to stir up ▶ VI: ~ **en** to go through, rummage (about) in; **revolverse** VR (*en cama*) to toss and turn; (*Meteorología*) to break, turn stormy; **revolverse contra** to turn on o against; **han revuelto toda la casa** they've turned the whole house upside down
revólver [re'βolβer] NM revolver
revoque *etc* [re'βoke] VB *ver* **revocar**
revuelco *etc* [re'βwelko] VB *ver* **revolcar**
revuelo [re'βwelo] NM fluttering; (*fig*) commotion; **armar** o **levantar un gran** ~ to cause a great stir
revuelque *etc* [re'βwelke] VB *ver* **revolcar**
revuelto, -a [re'βwelto, a] PP *de* **revolver** ▶ ADJ (*mezclado*) mixed-up, in disorder; (*mar*) rough; (*tiempo*) unsettled ▶ NF (*motín*) revolt; (*agitación*) commotion; **todo estaba ~** everything was in disorder o was topsy-turvy
revuelva *etc* [re'βwelβa] VB *ver* **revolver**
revulsivo [reβul'siβo] NM: **servir de ~** to have a salutary effect
rey [rei] NM king; **Día de Reyes** Twelfth Night; **los Reyes Magos** the Three Wise Men, the Magi; **los Reyes** the King and Queen; *ver tb* **baraja española**; *see note*

The night before the 6th of January (the Epiphany), which is a holiday in Spain, children go to bed expecting *los Reyes Magos*, the Three Wise Men who visited the baby Jesus, to bring them presents. Twelfth night processions, known as *cabalgatas*, take place that evening, when 3 people dressed as *los Reyes Magos* arrive in the town by land or sea to the delight of the children.

reyerta [re'jerta] NF quarrel, brawl
rezagado, -a [reθa'ɣaðo, a] ADJ: **quedar ~** to be left behind; (*estar retrasado*) to be late, be behind ▶ NM/F straggler
rezagar [reθa'ɣar] /1h/ VT (*dejar atrás*) to leave behind; (*retrasar*) to delay, postpone; **rezagarse** VR (*atrasarse*) to fall behind
rezague *etc* [re'θaɣe] VB *ver* **rezagar**
rezar [re'θar] /1f/ VI to pray; ~ **con** (*fam*) to concern, have to do with
rezo ['reθo] NM prayer
rezongar [reθon'gar] /1h/ VI to grumble; (*murmurar*) to mutter; (*refunfuñar*) to growl
rezongue *etc* [re'θoŋge] VB *ver* **rezongar**
rezumar [reθu'mar] /1a/ VT to ooze ▶ VI to leak; **rezumarse** VR to leak out
RFA NF ABR (= *República Federal Alemana*) *ver* **república**
RFEF NF ABR (= *Real Federación Española de Fútbol*) Spanish Football Federation

RI ABR = **regimiento de infantería**

ría ['ria] NF estuary

riachuelo [rja'tʃwelo] NM stream

riada [ri'aða] NF flood

ribera [ri'βera] NF (*de río*) bank; (: *área*) riverside

ribete [ri'βete] NM (*de vestido*) border; (*fig*) addition

ribetear [riβete'ar] /**1a**/ VT to edge, border

rice *etc* ['riθe] VB *ver* **rizar**

ricino [ri'θino] NM: **aceite de ~** castor oil

rico, -a ['riko, a] ADJ (*adinerado*) rich, wealthy; (*lujoso*) luxurious; (*comida*) delicious; (*niño*) lovely, cute ▶ NM/F rich person; **nuevo ~** nouveau riche

rictus ['riktus] NM (*mueca*) sneer, grin; **~ de amargura** bitter smile

ridiculez [riðiku'leθ] NF absurdity

ridiculice *etc* [riðiku'liθe] VB *ver* **ridiculizar**

ridiculizar [riðikuli'θar] /**1f**/ VT to ridicule

ridículo, -a [ri'ðikulo, a] ADJ ridiculous; **hacer el ~** to make a fool of o.s.; **poner a algn en ~** to make a fool of sb; **ponerse en ~** to make a fool of o.s.

riego ['rjeɣo] VB *ver* **regar** ▶ NM (*aspersión*) watering; (*irrigación*) irrigation; **~ sanguíneo** blood flow *o* circulation

riegue *etc* ['rjeɣe] VB *ver* **regar**

riel [rjel] NM rail

rienda ['rjenda] NF rein; (*fig*) restraint, moderating influence; **dar ~ suelta a** to give free rein to; **llevar las riendas** to be in charge

riendo ['rjendo] VB *ver* **reír**

riesgo ['rjesɣo] NM risk; **seguro a** *o* **contra todo ~** comprehensive insurance; **~ para la salud** health hazard; **correr el ~ de** to run the risk of

Rif [rif] NM Rif(f)

rifa ['rifa] NF (*lotería*) raffle

rifar [ri'far] /**1a**/ VT to raffle

rifeño, -a [ri'feɲo, a] ADJ of the Rif(f), Rif(f)ian ▶ NM/F Rif(f)ian, Rif(f)

rifle ['rifle] NM rifle

rigidez [rixi'ðeθ] NF rigidity, stiffness; (*fig*) strictness

rígido, -a ['rixiðo, a] ADJ rigid, stiff; (*moralmente*) strict, inflexible; (*cara*) wooden, expressionless

rigiendo *etc* [ri'xjendo] VB *ver* **regir**

rigor [ri'ɣor] NM strictness, rigour; (*dureza*) toughness; (*inclemencia*) harshness; (*meticulosidad*) accuracy; **el ~ del verano** the hottest part of the summer; **con todo ~ científico** with scientific precision; **de ~** de rigueur, essential; **después de los saludos de ~** after the inevitable greetings

riguroso, -a [riɣu'roso, a] ADJ rigorous; (*Meteorología*) harsh; (*severo*) severe

rija *etc* ['rixa] VB *ver* **regir** ▶ NF quarrel

rima ['rima] NF rhyme; **rimas** NFPL verse *sg*; **~ imperfecta** assonance; **~ rimando** (*fam*) merrily

rimar [ri'mar] /**1a**/ VI to rhyme

rimbombante [rimbom'bante] ADJ (*fig*) pompous

rímel, rimmel ['rimel] NM mascara

rimero [ri'mero] NM stack, pile

rímmel ['rimel] NM = **rímel**

Rin [rin] NM Rhine

rin [rin] NM (*AM*) (wheel) rim

rincón [rin'kon] NM corner (*inside*)

rindiendo *etc* [rin'djendo] VB *ver* **rendir**

ring [riŋ] NM (*Boxeo*) ring

rinoceronte [rinoθe'ronte] NM rhinoceros

riña ['riɲa] NF (*disputa*) argument; (*pelea*) brawl

riñendo *etc* [ri'ɲendo] VB *ver* **reñir**

riñón [ri'ɲon] NM kidney; **me costó un ~** (*fam*) it cost me an arm and a leg; **tener riñones** to have guts

rio [ri'o] VB *ver* **reír**

río ['rio] VB *ver* **reír** ▶ NM river; (*fig*) torrent, stream; **~ abajo/arriba** downstream/ upstream; **cuando el ~ suena, agua lleva** there's no smoke without fire; **R~ de la Plata** River Plate

Río de Janeiro ['rioðexa'neiro] NM Rio de Janeiro

Río de la Plata ['rioðela'plata] NM Rio de la Plata, River Plate

rioja [ri'oxa] NM rioja wine ▶ NF: **La R~** La Rioja

riojano, -a [rjo'xano, a] ADJ, NM/F Riojan

rioplatense [riopla'tense] ADJ of *o* from the River Plate region ▶ NMF native *o* inhabitant of the River Plate region

riqueza [ri'keθa] NF wealth, riches *pl*; (*cualidad*) richness

risa ['risa] NF laughter; (*una risa*) laugh; **¡qué ~!** what a laugh!; **caerse** *o* **morirse de ~** to split one's sides laughing, die laughing; **tomar algo a ~** to laugh sth off

risco ['risko] NM crag, cliff

risible [ri'siβle] ADJ ludicrous, laughable

risotada [riso'taða] NF guffaw, loud laugh

ristra ['ristra] NF string

ristre ['ristre] NM: **en ~** at the ready

risueño, -a [ri'sweɲo, a] ADJ (*sonriente*) smiling; (*contento*) cheerful

ritmo ['ritmo] NM rhythm; **a ~ lento** slowly; **trabajar a ~ lento** to go slow; **~ cardíaco** heart rate

rito ['rito] NM rite

ritual [ri'twal] ADJ, NM ritual

rival [ri'βal] ADJ, NMF rival

rivalice *etc* [riβa'liθe] VB *ver* **rivalizar**

rivalidad [riβali'ðað] NF rivalry, competition

r

343

rivalizar [riβali'θar] /**1f**/ vi: ~ **con** to rival, vie with

rizado, -a [ri'θaðo, a] ADJ (*pelo*) curly; (*superficie*) ridged; (*terreno*) undulating; (*mar*) choppy ▸ NM curls *pl*

rizar [ri'θar] /**1f**/ vt to curl; **rizarse** vr (*el pelo*) to curl; (*agua*) to ripple; (*el mar*) to become choppy

rizo ['riθo] NM curl; (*en agua*) ripple

Rma. ABR (= *Reverendísima*) *courtesy title*

Rmo. ABR (= *Reverendísimo*) Rt. Rev.

RNE NF ABR = **Radio Nacional de España**

R. O. ABR (= *Real Orden*) royal order

robar [ro'βar] /**1a**/ vt to rob; (*objeto*) to steal; (*casa etc*) to break into; (*Naipes*) to draw; (*atención*) to steal, capture; (*paciencia*) to exhaust

roble ['roβle] NM oak

robledal [roβle'ðal], **robledo** [ro'βleðo] NM oakwood

robo ['roβo] NM robbery, theft; (*objeto robado*) stolen article *o* goods *pl*; **¡esto es un ~!** this is daylight robbery!

robot [ro'βo(t)] (*pl* **robots**) ADJ, NM robot ▸ NM (*tb*: **robot de cocina**) food processor

robótica [ro'βotika] NF robotics *sg*

robustecer [roβuste'θer] /**2d**/ vt to strengthen

robustezca *etc* [roβus'teθka] VB *ver* **robustecer**

robusto, -a [ro'βusto, a] ADJ robust, strong

ROC ABR (*Inform*: = *reconocimiento óptico de caracteres*) OCR

roca ['roka] NF rock; **la R~** the Rock (of Gibraltar)

roce ['roθe] VB *ver* **rozar** ▸ NM rub, rubbing; (*caricia*) brush; (*Tec*) friction; (*en la piel*) graze; **tener ~ con** to have a brush with

rociar [ro'θjar] /**1c**/ vt to sprinkle, spray

rocín [ro'θin] NM nag, hack

rocío [ro'θio] NM dew

rock [rok] ADJ INV, NM (*Mus*) rock *cpd*

rockero, -a [ro'kero, a] ADJ rock *cpd* ▸ NM/F rocker

rocola [ro'kola] NF (*Am*) jukebox

rocoso, -a [ro'koso, a] ADJ rocky

rodaballo [roða'baʎo] NM turbot

rodado, -a [ro'ðaðo, a] ADJ (*con ruedas*) wheeled ▸ NF rut

rodaja [ro'ðaxa] NF (*raja*) slice

rodaje [ro'ðaxe] NM (*Cine*) shooting, filming; (*Auto*): **en ~** running in

rodamiento [roða'mjento] NM (*Auto*) tread

Ródano ['roðano] NM Rhône

rodar [ro'ðar] /**1l**/ vt (*vehículo*) to wheel (along); (*escalera*) to roll down; (*viajar por*) to travel (over) ▸ vi to roll; (*coche*) to go, run; (*Cine*) to shoot, film; (*persona*) to move about (from place to place), drift; **echarlo todo a ~** (*fig*) to mess it all up

Rodas ['roðas] NF Rhodes

rodear [roðe'ar] /**1a**/ vt to surround ▸ vi to go round; **rodearse** vr: **rodearse de amigos** to surround o.s. with friends

rodeo [ro'ðeo] NM (*ruta indirecta*) long way round, roundabout way; (*desvío*) detour; (*evasión*) evasion; (*Am*) rodeo; **dejarse de rodeos** to talk straight; **hablar sin rodeos** to come to the point, speak plainly

rodilla [ro'ðiʎa] NF knee; **de rodillas** kneeling; **ponerse de rodillas** to kneel (down)

rodillo [ro'ðiʎo] NM roller; (*Culin*) rolling-pin; (*en máquina de escribir, impresora*) platen

rododendro [roðo'ðendro] NM rhododendron

roedor, a [roe'ðor, a] ADJ gnawing ▸ NM rodent

roer [ro'er] /**2y**/ vt (*masticar*) to gnaw; (*corroer, fig*) to corrode

rogar [ro'ɣar] /**1h, 1l**/ vt (*pedir*) to beg, ask for ▸ vi (*suplicar*) to beg, plead; **rogarse** vr: **se ruega no fumar** please do not smoke; **~ que** (+ *subjun*) to ask to ...; **ruegue a este señor que nos deje en paz** please ask this gentleman to leave us alone; **no se hace de ~** he doesn't have to be asked twice

rogué [ro'ɣe], **roguemos** *etc* [ro'ɣemos] VB *ver* **rogar**

rojizo, -a [ro'xiθo, a] ADJ reddish

rojo, -a ['roxo, a] ADJ red ▸ NM red (colour); (*Pol*) red; **ponerse ~** to turn red, blush; **al ~ vivo** red-hot

rol [rol] NM list, roll; (*esp Am*: *papel*) role

rollito [ro'ʎito] NM (*tb*: **rollito de primavera**) spring roll

rollizo, -a [ro'ʎiθo, a] ADJ (*objeto*) cylindrical; (*persona*) plump

rollo, -a ['roʎo, a] ADJ (*fam*) boring, tedious ▸ NM roll; (*de cuerda*) coil; (*de madera*) log; (*fam*) bore; (*discurso*) boring speech; **¡qué ~!** what a carry-on!; **la conferencia fue un ~** the lecture was a big drag

ROM [rom] NF ABR (= *memoria de sólo lectura*) ROM

Roma ['roma] NF Rome; **por todas partes se va a ~** all roads lead to Rome

romance [ro'manθe] NM (*amoroso*) romance; (*Ling*) Romance language; (*Lit*) ballad; **hablar en ~** to speak plainly

románico, -a [ro'maniko, a] ADJ, NM Romanesque

romano, -a [ro'mano, a] ADJ Roman, of Rome ▸ NM/F Roman; **a la romana** in batter

romanticismo [romanti'θismo] NM romanticism

romántico, -a [ro'mantiko, a] ADJ romantic

rombo ['rombo] NM (*Mat*) rhombus; (*diseño*) diamond; (*Tip*) lozenge

romería [rome'ria] NF (*Rel*) pilgrimage; (*excursión*) trip, outing; *see note*

> Originally a pilgrimage to a shrine or church to express devotion to Our Lady or a local Saint, the *romería* has also become a rural *fiesta* which accompanies the pilgrimage. People come from all over to attend, bringing their own food and drink, and spend the day in celebration.

romero, -a [ro'mero, a] NM/F pilgrim ▶ NM rosemary

romo, -a ['romo, a] ADJ blunt; (*fig*) dull

rompecabezas [rompeka'βeθas] NM INV riddle, puzzle; (*juego*) jigsaw (puzzle)

rompehielos [rompe'jelos] NM INV icebreaker

rompehuelgas [rompe'welɣas] NM INV (*Am*) strikebreaker, scab

rompeolas [rompe'olas] NM INV breakwater

romper [rom'per] /**2a**/ VT to break; (*hacer pedazos*) to smash; (*papel, tela etc*) to tear, rip; (*relaciones*) to break off ▶ VI (*olas*) to break; (*sol, diente*) to break through; ~ **un contrato** to break a contract; ~ **a** to start (suddenly) to; ~ **a llorar** to burst into tears; ~ **con algn** to fall out with sb; **ha roto con su novio** she has broken up with her fiancé

rompimiento [rompi'mjento] NM (*acto*) breaking; (*fig*) break; (*quiebra*) crack; ~ **de relaciones** breaking off of relations

ron [ron] NM rum

roncar [ron'kar] /**1g**/ VI (*al dormir*) to snore; (*animal*) to roar

roncha ['rontʃa] NF (*cardenal*) bruise; (*hinchazón*) swelling

ronco, -a ['ronko, a] ADJ (*afónico*) hoarse; (*áspero*) raucous

ronda ['ronda] NF (*de bebidas etc*) round; (*patrulla*) patrol; (*de naipes*) hand, game; **ir de** ~ to do one's round

rondar [ron'dar] /**1a**/ VT to patrol; (*a una persona*) to hang round; (*molestar*) to harass; (*a una chica*) to court ▶ VI to patrol; (*fig*) to prowl round; (*Mus*) to go serenading

rondeño, -a [ron'deɲo, a] ADJ of *o* from Ronda ▶ NM/F native *o* inhabitant of Ronda

ronque *etc* ['ronke] VB *ver* **roncar**

ronquido [ron'kiðo] NM snore, snoring

ronronear [ronrone'ar] /**1a**/ VI to purr

ronroneo [ronro'neo] NM purr

roña ['roɲa] NF (*en veterinaria*) mange; (*mugre*) dirt, grime; (*óxido*) rust

roñica [ro'ɲika] NMF (*fam*) skinflint

roñoso, -a [ro'ɲoso, a] ADJ (*mugriento*) filthy; (*tacaño*) mean

ropa ['ropa] NF clothes *pl*, clothing; ~ **blanca** linen; ~ **de cama** bed linen; ~ **de color** coloureds *pl*; ~ **interior** underwear; ~ **lavada** *o* **para lavar** washing; ~ **planchada** ironing;

~ **sucia** dirty clothes *pl*, dirty washing; ~ **usada** secondhand clothes

ropaje [ro'paxe] NM gown, robes *pl*

ropero [ro'pero] NM linen cupboard; (*guardarropa*) wardrobe

rosa ['rosa] ADJ INV pink ▶ NF rose; (*Anat*) red birthmark; ~ **de los vientos** the compass; **estar como una** ~ to feel as fresh as a daisy; **(color) de** ~ pink

rosado, -a [ro'saðo, a] ADJ pink ▶ NM rosé

rosal [ro'sal] NM rosebush

rosaleda [rosa'leða] NF rose bed *o* garden

rosario [ro'sarjo] NM (*Rel*) rosary; (*fig: serie*) string; **rezar el** ~ to say the rosary

rosbif [ros'βif] NM roast beef

rosca ['roska] NF (*de tornillo*) thread; (*de humo*) coil, spiral; (*pan, postre*) ring-shaped roll/ pastry; **hacer la** ~ **a algn** (*fam*) to suck up to sb; **pasarse de** ~ (*fig*) to go too far

Rosellón [rose'ʎon] NM Roussillon

rosetón [rose'ton] NM rosette; (*Arq*) rose window

rosquilla [ros'kiʎa] NF ring-shaped cake; (*de humo*) ring

rosticería [rostise'ria] NF (*Am*) roast chicken shop

rostro ['rostro] NM (*cara*) face; (*fig*) cheek

rotación [rota'θjon] NF rotation; ~ **de cultivos** crop rotation

rotativo, -a [rota'tiβo, a] ADJ rotary ▶ NM newspaper

roto, -a ['roto, a] PP *de* **romper** ▶ ADJ broken; (*en pedazos*) smashed; (*tela, papel*) torn; (*vida*) shattered ▶ NM (*en vestido*) hole, tear

rotonda [ro'tonda] NF roundabout

rótula ['rotula] NF kneecap; (*Tec*) ball-and-socket joint

rotulador [rotula'ðor] NM felt-tip pen

rotular [rotu'lar] /**1a**/ VT (*carta, documento*) to head, entitle; (*objeto*) to label

rótulo ['rotulo] NM (*título*) heading, title; (*etiqueta*) label; (*letrero*) sign

rotundamente [rotunda'mente] ADV (*negar*) flatly; (*responder, afirmar*) emphatically

rotundo, -a [ro'tundo, a] ADJ round; (*enfático*) emphatic

rotura [ro'tura] NF (*rompimiento*) breaking; (*Med*) fracture

roturar [rotu'rar] /**1a**/ VT to plough

roulotte [ru'lote] NF caravan (*Brit*), trailer (*US*)

rozado, -a [ro'θaðo, a] ADJ worn

rozadura [roθa'ðura] NF abrasion, graze

rozar [ro'θar] /**1f**/ VT (*frotar*) to rub; (*arañar*) to scratch; (*ensuciar*) to dirty; (*Med*) to graze; (*tocar ligeramente*) to shave, skim; (*fig*) to touch *o* border on; **rozarse** VR to rub (together); ~ **con** (*fam*) to rub shoulders with

Rte. ABR = **remite; remitente**

RTVE NF ABR (TV) = **Radiotelevisión Española**
Ruán [ru'an] NM Rouen
rubéola [ru'βeola] NF German measles, rubella
rubí [ru'βi] NM ruby; (de reloj) jewel
rubio, -a ['ruβjo, a] ADJ fair-haired, blond(e) ▶ NM/F blond/blonde; **tabaco** ~ Virginia tobacco; (**cerveza**) **rubia** lager
rubor [ru'βor] NM (sonrojo) blush; (timidez) bashfulness
ruborice etc [ruβo'riθe] VB ver **ruborizarse**
ruborizarse [ruβori'θarse] /1f/ VR to blush
ruboroso, -a [ruβo'roso, a] ADJ blushing
rúbrica ['ruβrika] NF (título) title, heading; (de la firma) flourish; **bajo la ~ de** under the heading of
rubricar [ruβri'kar] /1g/ VT (firmar) to sign with a flourish; (concluir) to sign and seal
rubrique etc [ru'βrike] VB ver **rubricar**
rudeza [ru'ðeθa] NF (tosquedad) coarseness; (sencillez) simplicity
rudimentario, -a [ruðimen'tarjo, a] ADJ rudimentary, basic
rudo, -a ['ruðo, a] ADJ (sin pulir) unpolished; (grosero) coarse; (violento) violent; (sencillo) simple
rueda ['rweða] NF wheel; (círculo) ring, circle; (rodaja) slice, round; (en impresora etc) sprocket; ~ **de auxilio** (AM) spare tyre; ~ **delantera/trasera/de repuesto** front/back/spare wheel; ~ **impresora** (Inform) print wheel; ~ **de prensa** press conference; ~ **gigante** (AM) big (BRIT) o Ferris (US) wheel
ruedo ['rweðo] VB ver **rodar** ▶ NM (contorno) edge, border; (de vestido) hem; (círculo) circle; (Taur) arena, bullring; (esterilla) (round) mat
ruego etc ['rweɣo] VB ver **rogar** ▶ NM request; **a** ~ **de** at the request of; **"ruegos y preguntas"** "question and answer session"
ruegue etc ['rweɣe] VB ver **rogar**
rufián [ru'fjan] NM scoundrel
rugby ['ruɣβi] NM rugby
rugido [ru'xiðo] NM roar
rugir [ru'xir] /3c/ VI to roar; (toro) to bellow; (estómago) to rumble
rugoso, -a [ru'ɣoso, a] ADJ (arrugado) wrinkled; (áspero) rough; (desigual) ridged
ruibarbo [rwi'βarβo] NM rhubarb
ruido ['rwiðo] NM noise; (sonido) sound; (alboroto) racket, row; (escándalo) commotion, rumpus; ~ **de fondo** background noise; **hacer** o **meter** ~ to cause a stir
ruidoso, -a [rwi'ðoso, a] ADJ noisy, loud; (fig) sensational
ruin [rwin] ADJ contemptible, mean

ruina ['rwina] NF ruin; (hundimiento) collapse; (de persona) ruin, downfall; **estar hecho una** ~ to be a wreck; **la empresa lo llevó a la** ~ the venture ruined him (financially)
ruindad [rwin'dað] NF lowness, meanness; (acto) low o mean act
ruinoso, -a [rwi'noso, a] ADJ ruinous; (destartalado) dilapidated, tumbledown; (Com) disastrous
ruiseñor [rwise'ɲor] NM nightingale
ruja etc ['ruxa] VB ver **rugir**
rulero [ru'lero] NM (AM) roller
ruleta [ru'leta] NF roulette
rulo ['rulo] NM (para el pelo) curler
rulot [ru'lot], **rulote** [ru'lote] NF caravan (BRIT), trailer (US)
Rumania [ru'manja] NF Rumania
rumano, -a [ru'mano, a] ADJ, NM/F Rumanian
rumba ['rumba] NF rumba
rumbo ['rumbo] NM (ruta) route, direction; (ángulo de dirección) course, bearing; (fig) course of events; **con** ~ **a** in the direction of; **ir con** ~ **a** to be heading for; (Naut) to be bound for
rumboso, -a [rum'boso, a] ADJ (generoso) generous
rumiante [ru'mjante] NM ruminant
rumiar [ru'mjar] /1b/ VT to chew; (fig) to chew over ▶ VI to chew the cud
rumor [ru'mor] NM (ruido sordo) low sound; (murmuración) murmur, buzz
rumorearse [rumore'arse] /1a/ VR: **se rumorea que** it is rumoured that
rumoroso, -a [rumo'roso, a] ADJ full of sounds; (arroyo) murmuring
runrún [run'run] NM (de voces) murmur, sound of voices; (fig) rumour; (de una máquina) whirr
rupestre [ru'pestre] ADJ rock cpd; **pintura** ~ cave painting
ruptura [rup'tura] NF (gen) rupture; (disputa) split; (de contrato) breach; (de relaciones) breaking-off
rural [ru'ral] ADJ rural
Rusia ['rusja] NF Russia
ruso, -a ['ruso, a] ADJ, NM/F Russian ▶ NM (Ling) Russian
rústico, -a ['rustiko, a] ADJ rustic; (ordinario) coarse, uncouth ▶ NM/F yokel ▶ NF: **libro en rústica** paperback (book)
ruta ['ruta] NF route
rutina [ru'tina] NF routine; ~ **diaria** daily routine; **por** ~ as a matter of course
rutinario, -a [ruti'narjo, a] ADJ routine

Ss

S, s ['ese] NF (*letra*) S, s; **S de Santander** S for Sugar

S ABR (= *san; santo, a*) St.; (= *sur*) S

s. ABR (*tb:* **S.**) (= *siglo*) c.; (= *siguiente*) foll.

s/ ABR (*Com*) = **su; sus**

S.ª ABR (= *Sierra*) Mts

S.A. ABR (= *Sociedad Anónima*) Ltd., Inc. (*US*); (= *Su Alteza*) H.H.

sáb. ABR (= *sábado*) Sat.

sábado ['saβaðo] NM Saturday; (*de los judíos*) Sabbath; **del ~ en ocho días** a week on Saturday; **un ~ sí y otro no, cada dos sábados** every other Saturday; **S~ Santo** Holy Saturday; *ver tb* **Semana Santa**

sabana [sa'βana] NF savannah

sábana ['saβana] NF sheet; **se le pegan las sábanas** he can't get up in the morning

sabandija [saβan'dixa] NF (*bicho*) bug; (*fig*) louse

sabañón [saβa'ɲon] NM chilblain

sabático, -a [sa'βatiko, a] ADJ (*Rel, Univ*) sabbatical

sabelotodo [saβelo'toðo] NMF know-all

saber [sa'βer] /2m/ VT to know; (*llegar a conocer*) to find out, learn; (*tener capacidad de*) to know how to ▶ VI: **~ a** to taste of, taste like ▶ NM knowledge, learning; **saberse** VR: **se sabe que ...** it is known that ...; **no se sabe** nobody knows; **a ~** namely; **¿sabes conducir/nadar?** can you drive/swim?; **¿sabes francés?** do you o can you speak French?; **~ de memoria** to know by heart; **lo sé** I know; **hacer ~** to inform, let know; **que yo sepa** as far as I know; **vete** o **anda a ~** your guess is as good as mine, who knows!; **¿sabe?** (*fam*) you know (what I mean)?; **le sabe mal que otro la saque a bailar** it upsets him that anybody else should ask her to dance

sabido, -a [sa'βiðo, a] ADJ (*consabido*) well-known; **como es ~** as we all know

sabiduría [saβiðu'ria] NF (*conocimientos*) wisdom; (*instrucción*) learning; **~ popular** folklore

sabiendas [sa'βjendas]: **a ~** adv knowingly; **a ~ de que ...** knowing full well that ...

sabihondo, -a [sa'βjondo, a] ADJ, NM/F know-all, know-it-all (*US*)

sabio, -a ['saβjo, a] ADJ (*docto*) learned; (*prudente*) wise, sensible

sablazo [sa'βlaθo] NM (*herida*) sword wound; (*fam*) sponging; **dar un ~ a algn** to tap sb for money

sable [sa'βle] NM sabre

sabor [sa'βor] NM taste, flavour; (*fig*) flavour; **sin ~** flavourless

saborear [saβore'ar] /1a/ VT to taste, savour; (*fig*) to relish

sabotaje [saβo'taxe] NM sabotage

saboteador, a [saβotea'ðor, a] NM/F saboteur

sabotear [saβote'ar] /1a/ VT to sabotage

Saboya [sa'βoja] NF Savoy

sabré *etc* [sa'βre] VB *ver* **saber**

sabroso, -a [sa'βroso, a] ADJ tasty; (*fig: fam*) racy, salty

saca ['saka] NF big sack; **~ de correo(s)** mailbag; (*Com*) withdrawal

sacacorchos [saka'kortʃos] NM INV corkscrew

sacapuntas [saka'puntas] NM INV pencil sharpener

sacar [sa'kar] /1g/ VT to take out; (*fig: extraer*) to get (out); (*quitar*) to remove, get out; (*hacer salir*) to bring out; (*fondos: de cuenta*) to draw out, withdraw; (*obtener: legado etc*) to get; (*demostrar*) to show; (*conclusión*) to draw; (*novela etc*) to publish, bring out; (*ropa*) to take off; (*obra*) to make; (*premio*) to receive; (*entradas*) to get; (*Tenis*) to serve; (*Fútbol*) to put into play; **~ adelante** (*niño*) to bring up; (*negocio*) to carry on, go on with; **~ a algn a bailar** to get sb up to dance; **~ a algn de sí** to infuriate sb; **~ una foto** to take a photo, **~ la lengua** to stick out one's tongue; **~ buenas/malas notas** to get good/bad marks

sacarina [saka'rina] NF saccharin(e)

sacerdote [saθer'ðote] NM priest

s

saciar [sa'θjar] /**1b**/ VT (*hartar*) to satiate; (*fig*) to satisfy; **saciarse** VR (*de comida*) to get full up; (*fig*) to be satisfied

saciedad [saθje'ðað] NF satiety; **hasta la ~** (*comer*) one's fill; (*repetir*) ad nauseam

saco ['sako] NM bag; (*grande*) sack; (*contenido*) bagful; (*Am: chaqueta*) jacket; **~ de dormir** sleeping bag

sacramento [sakra'mento] NM sacrament

sacrificar [sakrifi'kar] /**1g**/ VT to sacrifice; (*animal*) to slaughter; (*perro etc*) to put to sleep; **sacrificarse** VR to sacrifice o.s.

sacrificio [sakri'fiθjo] NM sacrifice

sacrifique *etc* [sakri'fike] VB *ver* **sacrificar**

sacrilegio [sakri'lexjo] NM sacrilege

sacrílego, -a [sa'krileɣo, a] ADJ sacrilegious

sacristán [sakris'tan] NM verger

sacristía [sakris'tia] NF sacristy

sacro, -a ['sakro, a] ADJ sacred

sacudida [saku'ðiða] NF (*agitación*) shake, shaking; (*sacudimiento*) jolt, bump; (*fig*) violent change; (*Pol*) upheaval; **~ eléctrica** electric shock

sacudir [saku'ðir] /**3a**/ VT to shake; (*golpear*) to hit; (*ala*) to flap; (*alfombra*) to beat; **~ a algn** (*fam*) to belt sb

S.A. de C.V. ABR (*Am*: = *Sociedad Anónima de Capital Variable*) ≈ PLC (*Brit*), ≈ Corp (*US*), ≈ Inc. (*US*)

sádico, -a ['saðiko, a] ADJ sadistic ▶ NM/F sadist

sadismo [sa'ðismo] NM sadism

sadomasoquismo [saðomaso'kismo] NM sadomasochism, S & M

sadomasoquista [saðomaso'kista] ADJ sadomasochistic ▶ NMF sadomasochist

saeta [sa'eta] NF (*flecha*) arrow; (*Mus*) sacred song in flamenco style

safari [sa'fari] NM safari

sagacidad [saɣaθi'ðað] NF shrewdness, cleverness

sagaz [sa'ɣaθ] ADJ shrewd, clever

Sagitario [saxi'tarjo] NM (*Astro*) Sagittarius

sagrado, -a [sa'ɣraðo, a] ADJ sacred, holy

Sáhara ['saara] NM: **el ~** the Sahara (desert)

saharaui [saxa'rawi] ADJ Saharan ▶ NMF native o inhabitant of the Sahara

sajón, -ona [sa'xon, 'xona] ADJ, NM/F Saxon

Sajonia [sa'xonja] NF Saxony

sal [sal] VB *ver* **salir** ▶ NF salt; (*gracia*) wit; (*encanto*) charm; **sales de baño** bath salts; **~ gorda** o **de cocina** kitchen o cooking salt

sala ['sala] NF (*cuarto grande*) large room; (*tb*: **sala de estar**) living room; (*Teat*) house, auditorium; (*de hospital*) ward; **~ de apelación** court; **~ de conferencias** lecture hall; **~ de espera** waiting room; **~ de embarque** departure lounge; **~ de estar** living room; **~ de juntas** (*Com*) boardroom;

~ VIP (*en aeropuerto, discoteca*) VIP lounge

salado, -a [sa'laðo, a] ADJ salty; (*fig*) witty, amusing; **agua salada** salt water

salar [sa'lar] /**1a**/ VT to salt, add salt to

salariado, -a [sala'rjaðo, a] ADJ (*empleado*) salaried

salarial [sala'rjal] ADJ (*aumento, revisión*) wage *cpd*, salary *cpd*, pay *cpd*

salario [sa'larjo] NM wage, pay

salchicha [sal'tʃitʃa] NF (*pork*) sausage

salchichón [saltʃi'tʃon] NM (salami-type) sausage

saldar [sal'dar] /**1a**/ VT to pay; (*vender*) to sell off; (*fig*) to settle, resolve

saldo ['saldo] NM (*pago*) settlement; (*de una cuenta*) balance; (*lo restante*) remnant(s) (*pl*), remainder; (*de móvil*) credit; **saldos** NMPL (*en tienda*) sale; (*Com*) **~ anterior** balance brought forward; **~ acreedor/deudor** o **pasivo** credit/debit balance; **~ final** final balance

saldré *etc* [sal'dre] VB *ver* **salir**

salero [sa'lero] NM salt cellar; (*ingenio*) wit; (*encanto*) charm

salgo *etc* ['salɣo] VB *ver* **salir**

salida [sa'liða] NF (*puerta etc*) exit, way out; (*acto*) leaving, going out; (*de tren, Aviat*) departure; (*Com, Tec*) output, production; (*fig*) way out; (*resultado*) outcome; (*Com: oportunidad*) opening; (*Geo, válvula*) outlet; (*de gas*) leak; (*ocurrencia*) joke; **calle sin ~** cul-de-sac; **~ de baño** (*Am*) bathrobe; **a la ~ del teatro** after the theatre; **dar la ~** (*Deporte*) to give the starting signal; **~ de incendios** fire escape; **~ impresa** (*Inform*) hard copy; **no hay ~** there's no way out of it; **no tenemos otra ~** we have no option; **tener salidas** to be witty

salido, -a [sa'liðo, a] ADJ (*fam*) randy

saliente [sa'ljente] ADJ (*Arq*) projecting; (*sol*) rising; (*fig*) outstanding

salina [sa'lina] NF salt mine; **salinas** NFPL saltworks *sg*

PALABRA CLAVE

salir [sa'lir] /**3q**/ VI **1** (*persona*) to come o go out; (*tren, avión*) to leave; **Juan ha salido** Juan has gone out; **salió de la cocina** he came out of the kitchen; **salimos de Madrid a las ocho** we left Madrid at eight (o'clock); **salió corriendo (del cuarto)** he ran out (of the room); **salir de un apuro** to get out of a jam **2** (*pelo*) to grow; (*diente*) to come through; (*disco, libro*) to come out; (*planta, número de lotería*) to come up; **salir a la superficie** to come to the surface; **anoche salió en la tele** she appeared o was on TV last night; **salió en todos los periódicos** it was in all the papers; **le salió un trabajo** he got a job

3 (*resultar*): **la muchacha nos salió muy trabajadora** the girl turned out to be a very hard worker; **la comida te ha salido exquisita** the food was delicious; **sale muy caro** it's very expensive; **la entrevista que hice me salió bien/mal** the interview I did turned out *o* went well/badly; **nos salió a 50 euros cada una** it worked out at 50 euros each; **no salen las cuentas** it doesn't work out *o* add up; **salir ganando** to come out on top; **salir perdiendo** to lose out
4 (*Deporte*) to start; (*Naipes*) to lead
5: **salir con algn** to go out with sb
6: **salir adelante**: **no sé como haré para salir adelante** I don't know how I'll get by
salirse VR **1** (*líquido*) to spill; (*animal*) to escape
2 (*desviarse*): **salirse de la carretera** to leave *o* go off the road; **salirse de lo normal** to be unusual; **salirse del tema** to get off the point
3: **salirse con la suya** to get one's own way

saliva [sa'liβa] NF saliva
salivadera [saliβa'ðera] NF (*Am*) spittoon
salmantino, -a [salman'tino, a] ADJ of *o* from Salamanca ▶ NM/F native *o* inhabitant of Salamanca
salmo ['salmo] NM psalm
salmón [sal'mon] NM salmon
salmonete [salmo'nete] NM red mullet
salmuera [sal'mwera] NF pickle, brine
salón [sa'lon] NM (*de casa*) living-room, lounge; (*muebles*) lounge suite; **~ de belleza** beauty parlour; **~ de baile** dance hall; **~ de actos/sesiones** assembly hall
salpicadera [salpika'ðera] NF (*Am*) mudguard (BRIT), fender (US)
salpicadero [salpika'ðero] NM (*Auto*) dashboard
salpicar [salpi'kar] /**1g**/ VT (*de barro, pintura*) to splash; (*rociar*) to sprinkle, spatter; (*esparcir*) to scatter
salpicón [salpi'kon] NM (*acto*) splashing; (*Culin*) meat *o* fish salad; (*tb*: **salpicón de marisco**) seafood salad
salpimentar [salpimen'tar] /**1a**/ VT (*Culin*) to season
salpique *etc* [sal'pike] VB *ver* **salpicar**
salsa ['salsa] NF sauce; (*con carne asada*) gravy; (*fig*) spice; **~ mayonesa** mayonnaise; **estar en su ~** (*fam*) to be in one's element
saltamontes [salta'montes] NM INV grasshopper
saltar [sal'tar] /**1a**/ VT to jump (over), leap (over); (*dejar de lado*) to skip, miss out ▶ VI to jump, leap; (*pelota*) to bounce; (*al aire*) to fly up; (*quebrarse*) to break; (*al agua*) to dive; (*fig*) to explode, blow up; (*botón*) to come off; (*corcho*) to pop out; **saltarse** VR (*omitir*) to skip, miss; **salta a la vista** it's obvious; **saltarse**

todas las reglas to break all the rules
salteado, -a [salte'aðo, a] ADJ (*Culin*) sauté(ed)
salteador [saltea'ðor] NM (*tb*: **salteador de caminos**) highwayman
saltear [salte'ar] /**1a**/ VT (*robar*) to rob (in a holdup); (*asaltar*) to assault, attack; (*Culin*) to sauté
saltimbanqui [saltim'banki] NMF acrobat
salto ['salto] NM jump, leap; (*al agua*) dive; **a saltos** by jumping; **~ de agua** waterfall; **~ de altura** high jump; **~ de cama** negligee; **~ mortal** somersault; (*Inform*) **~ de línea** line feed; **~ de línea automático** wordwrap; **~ de página** formfeed
saltón, -ona [sal'ton, ona] ADJ (*ojos*) bulging, popping; (*dientes*) protruding
salubre [sa'luβre] ADJ healthy, salubrious
salud [sa'luð] NF health; **estar bien/mal de ~** to be in good/poor health; **¡(a su) ~!** cheers!, good health!; **beber a la ~ de** to drink (to) the health of
saludable [salu'ðaβle] ADJ (*de buena salud*) healthy; (*provechoso*) good, beneficial
saludar [salu'ðar] /**1a**/ VT to greet; (*Mil*) to salute; **ir a ~ a algn** to drop in to see sb; **salude de mi parte a X** give my regards to X; **le saluda atentamente** (*en carta*) yours faithfully
saludo [sa'luðo] NM greeting; **saludos** (*en carta*) best wishes, regards; **un ~ afectuoso** *o* **cordial** yours sincerely
salva ['salβa] NF (*Mil*) salvo; **una ~ de aplausos** thunderous applause
salvación [salβa'θjon] NF salvation; (*rescate*) rescue
salvado [sal'βaðo] NM bran
salvador [salβa'ðor] NM rescuer, saviour; **el S~** (*Rel*) the Saviour; **El S~** (*Geo*) El Salvador; **San S~** San Salvador
salvadoreño, -a [salβaðo'reɲo, a] ADJ, NM/F Salvadoran, Salvadorian
salvaguardar [salβaɣwar'ðar] /**1a**/ VT to safeguard; (*Inform*) to back up, make a backup copy of
salvajada [salβa'xaða] NF savage deed, atrocity
salvaje [sal'βaxe] ADJ wild; (*tribu*) savage
salvajismo [salβa'xismo] NM savagery
salvamanteles [salβaman'teles] NM INV table mat
salvamento [salβa'mento] NM (*acción*) rescue; (*de naufragio*) salvage; **~ y socorrismo** life-saving
salvapantallas [salβapan'taʎas] NM INV screensaver
salvar [sal'βar] /**1a**/ VT (*rescatar*) to save, rescue; (*resolver*) to overcome, resolve; (*cubrir distancias*) to cover, travel; (*hacer excepción*) to except, exclude; (*un barco*) to salvage;

S

salvarse VR to save o.s., escape; **¡sálvese el que pueda!** every man for himself!

salvavidas [salβa'βiðas] ADJ INV: **bote/ chaleco/cinturón** ~ lifeboat/lifejacket/ lifebelt

salvedad [salβe'ðað] NF reservation, qualification; **con la ~ de que ...** with the proviso that ...

salvia ['salβja] NF sage

salvo, -a ['salβo, a] ADJ safe ▶ PREP except (for), save; ~ **error u omisión** (Com) errors and omissions excepted; **a ~** out of danger; ~ **que** unless

salvoconducto [salβokon'dukto] NM safe-conduct

samba ['samba] NF samba

san [san] N (apócope de **santo**) saint; ~ **Juan** St. John; ver tb **noche**

sanar [sa'nar] /1a/ VT (herida) to heal; (persona) to cure ▶ VI (persona) to get well, recover; (herida) to heal

sanatorio [sana'torjo] NM sanatorium

sanción [san'θjon] NF sanction

sancionar [sanθjo'nar] /1a/ VT to sanction

sancochado, -a [sanko'tʃaðo, a] ADJ (Am Culin) underdone, rare

sancocho [san'kotʃo] NM (Am) stew

sandalia [san'dalja] NF sandal

sándalo ['sandalo] NM sandal(wood)

sandez [san'deθ] NF (cualidad) foolishness; (acción) stupid thing; **decir sandeces** to talk nonsense

sandía [san'dia] NF watermelon

sandinista [sandi'nista] ADJ, NMF Sandinist(a)

sándwich ['sandwitʃ] (pl **sándwichs** o **sandwiches**) NM sandwich

saneamiento [sanea'mjento] NM sanitation

sanear [sane'ar] /1a/ VT to drain; (indemnizar) to compensate; (Econ) to reorganize

Sanfermines [sanfer'mines] NMPL festivities in celebration of San Fermín

The Sanfermines are a week of fiestas in Pamplona, the capital of Navarre, made famous by Ernest Hemingway. From the 7th of July, the feast of San Fermín, crowds of mainly young people take to the streets drinking, singing and dancing. Early in the morning bulls are released along the narrow streets leading to the bullring, and people risk serious injury by running out in front of them.

sangrar [san'grar] /1a/ VT, VI to bleed; (texto) to indent

sangre ['sangre] NF blood; ~ **fría** sangfroid; **a ~ fría** in cold blood

sangría [san'gria] NF (Med) bleeding; (Culin)

sangria (sweetened drink of red wine with fruit), ≈ fruit cup

sangriento, -a [san'grjento, a] ADJ bloody

sanguijuela [sangi'xwela] NF (Zool, fig) leech

sanguinario, -a [sangi'narjo, a] ADJ bloodthirsty

sanguíneo, -a [san'gineo, a] ADJ blood cpd

sanidad [sani'ðað] NF sanitation; (calidad de sano) health, healthiness; ~ **pública** public health (department)

San Isidro [sani'sidro] NM patron saint of Madrid

San Isidro is the patron saint of Madrid, and gives his name to the week-long festivities which take place around the 15th May. Originally an 18th-century trade fair, the San Isidro celebrations now include music, dance, a famous romería, theatre and bullfighting.

sanitario, -a [sani'tarjo, a] ADJ sanitary; (de la salud) health cpd; **sanitarios** NMPL toilets (BRIT), restroom sg (US)

San Marino [sanma'rino] NM: **(La República de)** ~ San Marino

sano, -a ['sano, a] ADJ healthy; (sin daños) sound; (comida) wholesome; (entero) whole, intact; ~ **y salvo** safe and sound

santanderino, -a [santande'rino, a] ADJ of o from Santander ▶ NM/F native o inhabitant of Santander

Santiago [san'tjaɣo] NM: ~ **(de Chile)** Santiago

santiamén [santja'men] NM: **en un** ~ in no time at all

santidad [santi'ðað] NF holiness, sanctity

santificar [santifi'kar] /1g/ VT to sanctify

santifique etc [santi'fike] VB ver **santificar**

santiguarse [santi'ɣwarse] /1i/ VR to make the sign of the cross

santigüe etc [san'tiɣwe] VB ver **santiguarse**

santo, -a ['santo, a] ADJ holy; (fig) wonderful, miraculous ▶ NM/F saint ▶ NM saint's day; **hacer su santa voluntad** to do as one jolly well pleases; **¿a ~ de qué ...?** why on earth ...?; **se le fue el ~ al cielo** he forgot what he was about to say; ~ **y seña** password; see note

As well as celebrating their birthday, Spaniards have traditionally celebrated el santo, their Saint's day, when the Saint they were called after at birth, eg San Pedro or la Virgen de los Dolores, is honoured in the Christian calendar.

santuario [san'twarjo] NM sanctuary, shrine

saña ['saɲa] NF rage, fury

sapo ['sapo] NM toad

saque ['sake] VB ver **sacar** ▶ NM (Tenis) service, serve; (Fútbol) throw-in; ~ **inicial** kick-off; ~ **de esquina** corner (kick); **tener buen** ~ to eat heartily

saquear [sake'ar] /**1a**/ VT (*Mil*) to sack; (*robar*) to loot, plunder; (*fig*) to ransack

saqueo [sa'keo] NM sacking; looting, plundering; ransacking

S.A.R. ABR (= *Su Alteza Real*) HRH

sarampión [saram'pjon] NM measles *sg*

sarape [sa'rape] NM (*AM*) blanket

sarcasmo [sar'kasmo] NM sarcasm

sarcástico, -a [sar'kastiko, a] ADJ sarcastic

sarcófago [sar'kofaɣo] NM sarcophagus

sardina [sar'ðina] NF sardine

sardo, -a ['sarðo, a] ADJ, NM/F Sardinian

sardónico, -a [sar'ðoniko, a] ADJ sardonic; (*irónico*) ironical, sarcastic

sargento [sar'xento] NM sergeant

sarmiento [sar'mjento] NM vine shoot

sarna ['sarna] NF itch; (*Med*) scabies

sarpullido [sarpu'ʎiðo] NM (*Med*) rash

sarro ['sarro] NM deposit; (*en dientes*) tartar, plaque

sarta ['sarta] NF (*fig*): **una ~ de mentiras** a pack of lies

sartén [sar'ten] NF frying pan; **tener la ~ por el mango** to rule the roost

sastre ['sastre] NM tailor

sastrería [sastre'ria] NF (*arte*) tailoring; (*tienda*) tailor's (shop)

Satanás [sata'nas] NM Satan

satélite [sa'telite] NM satellite

satinado, -a [sati'naðo, a] ADJ glossy ▶ NM gloss, shine

sátira ['satira] NF satire

satírico, -a [sa'tiriko, a] ADJ satiric(al)

sátiro ['satiro] NM (*Mitología*) satyr; (*fig*) sex maniac

satisfacción [satisfak'θjon] NF satisfaction

satisfacer [satisfa'θer] /**2r**/ VT to satisfy; (*gastos*) to meet; (*deuda*) to pay; (*Com: letra de cambio*) to honour (*BRIT*), honor (*US*); (*: pérdida*) to make good; **satisfacerse** VR to satisfy o.s., be satisfied; (*vengarse*) to take revenge

satisfaga *etc* [satis'faɣa], **satisfaré** *etc* [satisfa're] VB *ver* **satisfacer**

satisfecho, -a [satis'fetʃo, a] PP *de* **satisfacer** ▶ ADJ satisfied; (*contento*) content(ed), happy; (*tb*: **satisfecho de sí mismo**) self-satisfied, smug

satisfice *etc* [satis'fiθe] VB *ver* **satisfacer**

saturación [satura'θjon] NF saturation; **llegar a la ~** to reach saturation point

saturar [satu'rar] /**1a**/ VT to saturate; **saturarse** VR (*mercado, aeropuerto*) to reach saturation point; **¡estoy saturado de tanta televisión!** I can't take any more television!

sauce ['sauθe] NM willow; **~ llorón** weeping willow

saúco [sa'uko] NM (*Bot*) elder

saudí [sau'ði] ADJ, NMF Saudi

sauna ['sauna] NF sauna

savia ['saβja] NF sap

saxo ['sakso] NM sax

saxofón [sakso'fon] NM saxophone

saya ['saja] NF (*falda*) skirt; (*enagua*) petticoat

sayo ['sajo] NM smock

sazón [sa'θon] NF (*de fruta*) ripeness; **a la ~** then, at that time

sazonado, -a [saθo'naðo, a] ADJ (*fruta*) ripe; (*Culin*) flavoured, seasoned

sazonar [saθo'nar] /**1a**/ VT to ripen; (*Culin*) to flavour, season

s/c ABR (*Com*: = *su casa*) your firm; (= *su cuenta*) your account

scooter [e'skuter] NF (*ESP*) scooter

Scotch® [skotʃ] NM (*AM*) Sellotape® (*BRIT*), Scotch tape® (*US*)

screenshot [es'krinʃot] NM screenshot

SE ABR (= *sudeste*) SE

(PALABRA CLAVE)

se [se] PRON **1** (*reflexivo*: *sg*: *m*) himself; (*: f*) herself; (*: pl*) themselves; (*: cosa*) itself; (*: de usted*) yourself; (*: de ustedes*) yourselves; (*: indefinido*) oneself; **se mira en el espejo** he looks at himself in the mirror; **¡siéntese!** sit down!; **se durmió** he fell asleep; **se está preparando** she's getting (herself) ready (*para usos léxicos del pron ver el vb en cuestión, p. ej.* **arrepentirse**)

2 (*como complemento indirecto*) to him; to her; to them; to it; to you; **se lo dije ayer** (*a usted*) I told you yesterday; **se compró un sombrero** he bought himself a hat; **se rompió la pierna** he broke his leg; **cortarse el pelo** to get one's hair cut; (*uno mismo*) to cut one's hair; **se comió un pastel** he ate a cake

3 (*uso recíproco*) each other, one another; **se miraron (el uno al otro)** they looked at each other *o* one another

4 (*en oraciones pasivas*): **se han vendido muchos libros** a lot of books have been sold; **"se vende coche"** "car for sale"

5 (*impers*): **se dice que** people say that, it is said that; **allí se come muy bien** the food there is very good, you can eat very well there

sé [se] VB *ver* **saber**; **ser**

sea *etc* ['sea] VB *ver* **ser**

SEAT ['seat] NF ABR = **Sociedad Española de Automóviles de Turismo**

sebo ['seβo] NM fat, grease

Sec. ABR (= *Secretario*) Sec

seca ['seka] NF *ver* **seco**

secado [se'kaðo] NM drying; **~ a mano** blow-dry

secador [seka'ðor] NM: **~ para el pelo** hairdryer

secadora [seka'ðora] NF tumble dryer;
~ **centrífuga** spin-dryer

secano [se'kano] NM (*Agr*: *tb*: **tierra de secano**) dry land *o* region; **cultivo de** ~ dry farming

secante [se'kante] ADJ (*viento*) drying ▸ NM blotting paper

secar [se'kar] /**1g**/ VT to dry; (*superficie*) to wipe dry; (*frente, suelo*) to mop; (*líquido*) to mop up; (*tinta*) to blot; **secarse** VR to dry (off); (*río, planta*) to dry up

sección [sek'θjon] NF section; (*Com*) department; ~ **deportiva** (*en periódico*) sports page(s)

seco, -a ['seko, a] ADJ dry; (*fruta*) dried; (*persona: magro*) thin, skinny; (*carácter*) cold; (*antipático*) disagreeable; (*respuesta*) sharp, curt ▸ NF dry season; **habrá pan a secas** there will be just bread; **decir algo a secas** to say sth curtly; **parar en** ~ to stop dead

secreción [sekre'θjon] NF secretion

secretaría [sekreta'ria] NF secretariat; (*oficina*) secretary's office

secretariado [sekreta'rjaðo] NM (*oficina*) secretariat; (*cargo*) secretaryship; (*curso*) secretarial course

secretario, -a [sekre'tarjo, a] NM/F secretary; ~ **adjunto** (*Com*) assistant secretary

secreto, -a [se'kreto, a] ADJ secret; (*información*) confidential; (*persona*) secretive ▸ NM secret; (*calidad*) secrecy

secta ['sekta] NF sect

sectario, -a [sek'tarjo, a] ADJ sectarian

sector [sek'tor] NM (*tb Inform*) sector; (*de opinión*) section; (*fig: campo*) area, field; ~ **privado/público** (*Com, Econ*) private/public sector

secuela [se'kwela] NF consequence

secuencia [se'kwenθja] NF sequence

secuestrar [sekwes'trar] /**1a**/ VT to kidnap; (*avión*) to hijack; (*bienes*) to seize, confiscate

secuestro [se'kwestro] NM (*de persona*) kidnapping; (*de avión*) hijack; (*Jur: de cargamento, propiedad*) seizure, confiscation

secular [seku'lar] ADJ secular

secundar [sekun'dar] /**1a**/ VT to second, support

secundario, -a [sekun'darjo, a] ADJ secondary; (*carretera*) side *cpd*; (*Inform*) background *cpd* ▸ NF secondary education

sed [seð] NF thirst; (*fig*) thirst, craving; **tener** ~ to be thirsty

seda ['seða] NF silk; ~ **dental** dental floss

sedal [se'ðal] NM fishing line

sedán [se'ðan] NM (*Am*) saloon (*Brit*), sedan (*US*)

sedante [se'ðante] NM sedative

sede ['seðe] NF (*de gobierno*) seat; (*de compañía*) headquarters *pl*, head office; **Santa S**~ Holy See

sedentario, -a [seðen'tarjo, a] ADJ sedentary

SEDIC [se'ðik] NF ABR = **Sociedad Española de Documentación e Información Científica**

sedición [seði'θjon] NF sedition

sediento, -a [se'ðjento, a] ADJ thirsty

sedimentar [seðimen'tar] /**1a**/ VT to deposit; **sedimentarse** VR to settle

sedimento [seði'mento] NM sediment

sedoso, -a [se'ðoso, a] ADJ silky, silken

seducción [seðuk'θjon] NF seduction

seducir [seðu'θir] /**3n**/ VT to seduce; (*sobornar*) to bribe; (*cautivar*) to charm, fascinate; (*atraer*) to attract

seductor, a [seðuk'tor, a] ADJ (*sexualmente*) seductive; (*cautivador: persona*) charming; (: *idea*) tempting; (*engañoso*) deceptive, misleading ▸ NM/F seducer

seduje *etc* [se'ðuxe], **seduzca** *etc* [se'ðuθka] VB *ver* **seducir**

sefardí [sefar'ði], **sefardita** [sefar'ðita] ADJ Sephardi(c) ▸ NMF Sephardi

segador, a [seɣa'ðor, a] NM/F (*persona*) harvester ▸ NF (*Tec*) mower, reaper

segadora-trilladora [seɣa'ðoratriʎa'ðora] NF combine harvester

segar [se'ɣar] /**1h, 1j**/ VT (*mies*) to reap, cut; (*hierba*) to mow, cut; (*esperanzas*) to ruin

seglar [se'ɣlar] ADJ secular, lay

segoviano, -a [seɣo'βjano, a] ADJ of *o* from Segovia ▸ NM/F native *o* inhabitant of Segovia

segregación [seɣreɣa'θjon] NF segregation; ~ **racial** racial segregation

segregar [seɣre'ɣar] /**1h**/ VT to segregate, separate

segregue *etc* [se'ɣreɣe] VB *ver* **segregar**

segué [se'ɣe], **seguemos** *etc* [se'ɣemos] VB *ver* **segar**

seguidamente [seɣiða'mente] ADV (*sin parar*) without a break; (*inmediatamente después*) immediately after

seguido, -a [se'ɣiðo, a] ADJ (*continuo*) continuous, unbroken; (*recto*) straight ▸ ADV (*directo*) straight (on); (*después*) after; (*Am*: *a menudo*) often ▸ NF: **en seguida** at once, right away; **cinco días seguidos** five days running, five days in a row; **en seguida termino** I've nearly finished, I shan't be long now

seguidor, a [seɣi'ðor, a] NM/F follower

seguimiento [seɣi'mjento] NM chase, pursuit; (*continuación*) continuation

seguir [se'ɣir] /**3d, 3k**/ VT to follow; (*venir después*) to follow on, come after; (*proseguir*) to continue; (*perseguir*) to chase, pursue; (*indicio*) to follow up; (*mujer*) to court ▸ VI (*gen*) to follow; (*continuar*) to continue, carry *o* go on;

seguirse VR to follow; **a ~** to be continued; **sigo sin comprender** I still don't understand; **sigue lloviendo** it's still raining; **sigue** (en carta) P.T.O.; (en libro, TV) continued; **"hágase ~"** "please forward"; **¡siga!** (AM: pase) come in!

según [se'ɣun] PREP according to ▸ ADV: **~ (y conforme)** it all depends ▸ CONJ as; **~ esté el tiempo** depending on the weather; **~ me consta** as far as I know; **está ~ lo dejaste** it is just as you left it

segundo, -a [se'ɣundo, a] ADJ second; (en discurso) secondly ▸ NM (gen, medida de tiempo) second; (piso) second floor ▸ NF (sentido) second meaning; **~ (de a bordo)** (Naut) first mate; **segunda (clase)** (Ferro) second class; **segunda (marcha)** (Auto) second (gear); **de segunda mano** second hand

seguramente [seɣura'mente] ADV surely; (con certeza) for sure, with certainty; (probablemente) probably; **¿lo va a comprar? — ~** is he going to buy it? — I should think so

seguridad [seɣuri'ðað] NF safety; (del estado, de casa etc) security; (certidumbre) certainty; (confianza) confidence; (estabilidad) stability; **~ social** social security; **~ contra incendios** fire precautions pl; **~ en sí mismo** (self-)confidence; **~ cibernética** cybersecurity

seguro, -a [se'ɣuro, a] ADJ (cierto) sure, certain; (fiel) trustworthy; (libre de peligro) safe; (bien defendido, firme) secure; (datos etc) reliable; (fecha) firm ▸ ADV for sure, certainly ▸ NM (dispositivo) safety device; (de cerradura) tumbler; (de arma) safety catch; (Com) insurance; **~ contra accidentes/incendios** fire/accident insurance; **~ contra terceros/a todo riesgo** third party/comprehensive insurance; **~ dotal con beneficios** with-profits endowment assurance; **S~ de Enfermedad** ≈ National Insurance; **~ marítimo** marine insurance; **~ mixto** endowment assurance; **~ temporal** term insurance; **~ de vida** life insurance; **seguros sociales** social security sg

seis [seis] NUM six; **~ mil** six thousand; **tiene ~ años** she is six (years old); **unos ~** about six; **hoy es el ~** today is the sixth

seiscientos, -as [seis'θjentos, as] NUM six hundred

seísmo [se'ismo] NM tremor, earthquake

SELA SIGLA M = **Sistema Económico Latinoamericano**

selección [selek'θjon] NF selection; **~ múltiple** multiple choice; **~ nacional** (Deporte) national team

seleccionador, a [selekθjona'ðor, a] NM/F (Deporte) selector

seleccionar [selekθjo'nar] /1a/ VT to pick, choose, select

selectividad [selektiβi'ðað] NF (Univ) entrance examination

selecto, -a [se'lekto, a] ADJ select, choice; (escogido) selected

sellado, -a [se'ʎaðo, a] ADJ (documento oficial) sealed; (pasaporte) stamped

sellar [se'ʎar] /1a/ VT (documento oficial) to seal; (pasaporte, visado) to stamp; (marcar) to brand; (pacto, labios) to seal

sello ['seʎo] NM stamp; (precinto) seal; (fig: tb: **sello distintivo**) hallmark; **~ fiscal** revenue stamp; **sellos de prima** (Com) trading stamps

selva ['selβa] NF (bosque) forest, woods pl; (jungla) jungle; **la S~ Negra** the Black Forest

S.Em. ABR = **Su Eminencia**

semáforo [se'maforo] NM (Auto) traffic lights pl; (Ferro) signal

semana [se'mana] NF week; **~ inglesa** five-day (working) week; **~ laboral** working week; **S~ Santa** Holy Week; **entre ~** during the week; see note

> Semana Santa is a holiday in Spain. All regions take Viernes Santo, Good Friday, Sábado Santo, Holy Saturday, and Domingo de Resurrección, Easter Sunday. Other holidays at this time vary according to each region. There are spectacular procesiones all over the country, with members of cofradías (brotherhoods) dressing in hooded robes and parading their pasos (religious floats or sculptures) through the streets. Seville has the most renowned celebrations, on account of the religious fervour shown by the locals.

semanal [sema'nal] ADJ weekly

semanario [sema'narjo] NM weekly (magazine)

semántica [se'mantika] NF semantics sg

semblante [sem'blante] NM face; (fig) look

sembrar [sem'brar] /1j/ VT to sow; (objetos) to sprinkle, scatter about; (noticias etc) to spread

semejante [seme'xante] ADJ (parecido) similar; (tal) such; **semejantes** alike, similar ▸ NM fellow man, fellow creature; **son muy semejantes** they are very much alike; **nunca hizo cosa ~** he never did such a thing

semejanza [seme'xanθa] NF similarity, resemblance; **a ~ de** like, as

semejar [seme'xar] /1a/ VI to seem like, resemble; **semejarse** VR to look alike, be similar

semen ['semen] NM semen

semental [semen'tal] NM (macho) stud

sementera [semen'tera] NF (acto) sowing; (temporada) seedtime; (tierra) sown land

semestral [semes'tral] ADJ half-yearly, bi-annual

353

semestre [se'mestre] NM period of six months; (*Univ*) semester; (*Com*) half-yearly payment

semicírculo [semi'θirkulo] NM semicircle

semiconductor [semikonduk'tor] NM semiconductor

semiconsciente [semikons'θjente] ADJ semiconscious

semidesnatado, -a [semiðesna'taðo, a] ADJ semi-skimmed

semifinal [semifi'nal] NF semifinal

semiinconsciente [semi(i)nkons'θjente] ADJ semiconscious

semilla [se'miʎa] NF seed

semillero [semi'ʎero] NM (*Agr etc*) seedbed; (*fig*) hotbed

seminario [semi'narjo] NM (*Rel*) seminary; (*Escol*) seminar; **~ web** (*Inform*) webinar

semiseco [semi'seko] NM medium-dry

semita [se'mita] ADJ Semitic ▶ NMF Semite

sémola ['semola] NF semolina

sempiterno, -a [sempi'terno, a] ADJ everlasting

Sena ['sena] NM: **el ~** the (river) Seine

senado [se'naðo] NM senate; *ver tb* **las Cortes**

senador, a [sena'ðor, a] NM/F senator

sencillez [senθi'ʎeθ] NF simplicity; (*de persona*) naturalness

sencillo, -a [sen'θiʎo, a] ADJ simple; (*carácter*) natural, unaffected; (*billete*) single ▶ NM (*disco*) single; (*Am*) small change

senda ['senda] NF, **sendero** [sen'dero] NM path, track; **Sendero Luminoso** the Shining Path (guerrilla movement)

senderismo [sende'rismo] NM hiking

sendero [sen'dero] NM path, track

sendos, -as ['sendos, as] ADJ PL: **les dio ~ golpes** he hit both of them

senil [se'nil] ADJ senile

seno ['seno] NM (*Anat*) bosom, bust; (*fig*) bosom; **senos** NMPL breasts; **~ materno** womb

sensación [sensa'θjon] NF sensation; (*sentido*) sense; (*sentimiento*) feeling; **causar o hacer ~** to cause a sensation

sensacional [sensaθjo'nal] ADJ sensational

sensatez [sensa'teθ] NF common sense

sensato, -a [sen'sato, a] ADJ sensible

sensibilidad [sensiβili'ðað] NF sensitivity; (*para el arte*) feel

sensibilizar [sensiβili'θar] /1f/ VT: **~ a la población/opinión pública** to raise public awareness

sensible [sen'sible] ADJ sensitive; (*apreciable*) perceptible, appreciable; (*pérdida*) considerable

sensiblero, -a [sensi'βlero, a] ADJ sentimental, slushy

sensitivo, -a [sensi'tiβo, a] ADJ sense *cpd*

sensor [sen'sor] NM: **~ de fin de papel** paper out sensor

sensorial [senso'rjal] ADJ sensory

sensual [sen'swal] ADJ sensual

sentado, -a [sen'taðo, a] ADJ (*establecido*) settled; (*carácter*) sensible ▶ NF sitting; (*Pol*) sit-in, sit-down protest; **dar por ~** to take for granted, assume; **dejar algo ~** to establish sth firmly; **estar ~** to sit, be sitting (down); **de una sentada** at one sitting

sentar [sen'tar] /1j/ VT to sit, seat; (*fig*) to establish ▶ VI (*vestido*) to suit; (*alimento*): **~ bien/mal a** to agree/disagree with; **sentarse** VR (*persona*) to sit, sit down; (*el tiempo*) to settle (down); (*los depósitos*) to settle; **¡siéntese!** (do) sit down, take a seat

sentencia [sen'tenθja] NF (*máxima*) maxim, saying; (*Jur*) sentence; **~ de muerte** death sentence

sentenciar [senten'θjar] /1b/ VT to sentence

sentido, -a [sen'tiðo, a] ADJ (*pérdida*) regrettable; (*carácter*) sensitive ▶ NM sense; (*sentimiento*) feeling; (*significado*) sense, meaning; (*dirección*) direction; **mi más ~ pésame** my deepest sympathy; **~ del humor** sense of humour; **~ común** common sense; **en el buen ~ de la palabra** in the best sense of the word; **sin ~** meaningless; **tener ~** to make sense; **~ único** one-way (street)

sentimental [sentimen'tal] ADJ sentimental; **vida ~** love life

sentimiento [senti'mjento] NM (*emoción*) feeling, emotion; (*sentido*) sense; (*pesar*) regret, sorrow

sentir [sen'tir] /3i/ VT to feel; (*percibir*) to perceive, sense; (*esp Am*): **oír** to hear; (*lamentar*) to regret, be sorry for; (*música etc*) to have a feeling for ▶ VI to feel; (*lamentarse*) to feel sorry ▶ NM opinion, judgement; **sentirse** VR to feel; **lo siento** I'm sorry; **sentirse mejor/mal** to feel better/ill; **sentirse como en su casa** to feel at home

seña ['sena] NF sign; (*Mil*) password; **señas** NFPL address *sg*; **señas personales** personal description *sg*; **por más señas** moreover; **dar señas de** to show signs of

señal [se'nal] NF sign; (*síntoma*) symptom; (*indicio*) indication; (*Ferro, Telec*) signal; (*marca*) mark; (*Com*) deposit; (*Inform*) marker, mark; **en ~ de** as a token of, as a sign of; **dar señales de** to show signs of; **~ de auxilio/de peligro** distress/danger signal; **~ de llamada** ringing tone; **~ para marcar** dialling tone

señalado, -a [sena'laðo, a] ADJ (*persona*) distinguished; (*pey*) notorious

señalar [sena'lar] /1a/ VT to mark; (*indicar*) to point out, indicate; (*significar*) to denote;

(*referirse a*) to allude to; (*fijar*) to fix, settle; (*pey*) to criticize

señalice *etc* [seɲaˈliθe] VB *ver* **señalizar**

señalización [seɲaliθaˈθjon] NF signposting; signals *pl*

señalizar [seɲaliˈθar] /**1f**/ VT (*Auto*) to put up road signs on; (*Ferro*) to put signals on; (*Auto*: *ruta*): **está bien señalizada** it's well signposted

señas [ˈseɲas] NFPL *ver* **seña**

señor, a [seˈɲor, a] ADJ (*fam*) lordly ▶ NM (*hombre*) man; (*caballero*) gentleman; (*dueño*) owner, master; (*trato: antes de nombre propio*) Mr; (: *hablando directamente*) sir ▶ NF (*dama*) lady; (*trato: antes de nombre propio*) Mrs; (: *hablando directamente*) madam; (*esposa*) wife; **los señores González** Mr and Mrs González; **S~ Don Jacinto Benavente** (*en sobre*) Mr J. Benavente, J. Benavente Esq.; **S~ Director ...** (*de periódico*) Dear Sir ...; **~ juez** my lord, your worship (*US*); **~ Presidente** Mr Chairman *o* President; **Muy ~ mío** Dear Sir; **Muy señores nuestros** Dear Sirs; **Nuestro S~** (*Rel*) Our Lord; **¿está la ~?** is the lady of the house in?; **la ~ de Smith** Mrs Smith; **Nuestra S~** (*Rel*) Our Lady

señoría [seɲoˈria] NF rule; **su** *o* **vuestra S~** your *o* his/her lordship/ladyship

señorío [seɲoˈrio] NM manor; (*fig*) rule

señorita [seɲoˈrita] NF (*gen*) Miss; (*mujer joven*) young lady; (*maestra*) schoolteacher

señorito [seɲoˈrito] NM young gentleman; (*lenguaje de criados*) master; (*pey*) toff

señuelo [seˈɲwelo] NM decoy

Sep. ABR (= *septiembre*) Sept

sepa *etc* [ˈsepa] VB *ver* **saber**

separable [sepaˈraβle] ADJ separable; (*Tec*) detachable

separación [separaˈθjon] NF separation; (*división*) division; (*distancia*) gap, distance; **~ de bienes** division of property

separado, -a [sepaˈraðo, a] ADJ separate; (*Tec*) detached; **vive ~ de su mujer** he is separated from his wife; **por ~** separately

separador [separaˈðor] NM (*Inform*) delimiter

separadora [separaˈðora] NF: **~ de hojas** burster

separar [sepaˈrar] /**1a**/ VT to separate; (*silla (de la mesa)*) to move away; (*Tec: pieza*) to detach; (: *persona: de un cargo*) to remove, dismiss; (*dividir*) to divide; **separarse** VR (*parte*) to come away; (*partes*) to come apart; (*persona*) to leave, go away; (*matrimonio*) to separate

separata [sepaˈrata] NF offprint

separatismo [separaˈtismo] NM (*Pol*) separatism

sepelio [seˈpeljo] NM burial, interment

sepia [ˈsepja] NF cuttlefish

Sept. ABR (= *septiembre*) Sept.

septentrional [septentrjoˈnal] ADJ north *cpd*, northern

septiembre [sepˈtjembre] NM September; *ver tb* **julio**

séptimo, -a [ˈseptimo, a] ADJ, NM seventh

septuagésimo, -a [septwaˈxesimo, a] ADJ seventieth

sepulcral [sepulˈkral] ADJ sepulchral; (*fig*) gloomy, dismal; (*silencio, atmósfera*) deadly

sepulcro [seˈpulkro] NM tomb, grave, sepulchre

sepultar [sepulˈtar] /**1a**/ VT to bury; (*en accidente*) to trap; **quedaron sepultados en la caverna** they were trapped in the cave

sepultura [sepulˈtura] NF (*acto*) burial; (*tumba*) grave, tomb; **dar ~ a** to bury; **recibir ~** to be buried

sepulturero, -a [sepultuˈrero, a] NM/F gravedigger

seque *etc* [ˈseke] VB *ver* **secar**

sequedad [sekeˈðað] NF dryness; (*fig*) brusqueness, curtness

sequía [seˈkia] NF drought

séquito [ˈsekito] NM (*de rey etc*) retinue; (*Pol*) followers *pl*

SER NF ABR (*Radio*: = *Sociedad Española de Radiodifusión*) Spanish radio network

(PALABRA CLAVE)

ser [ser] /**2v**/ VI **1** (*descripción, identidad*) to be; **es médica/muy alta** she's a doctor/very tall; **su familia es de Cuzco** his family is from Cuzco; **ser de madera** to be made of wood; **soy Ana** I'm Ana; (*por teléfono*) it's Ana

2 (*propiedad*): **es de Joaquín** it's Joaquín's, it belongs to Joaquín

3 (*horas: fechas: números*): **es la una** it's one o'clock; **son las seis y media** it's half-past six; **es el 1 de junio** it's the first of June; **somos/son seis** there are six of us/ them; **2 y 2 son 4** 2 and 2 are *o* make 4

4 (*suceso*): **¿qué ha sido eso?** what was that?; **la fiesta es en mi casa** the party's at my house; **¿qué será de mí?** what will become of me?; **"érase una vez ..."** "once upon a time ..."

5 (*en oraciones pasivas*): **ha sido descubierto ya** it's already been discovered

6: **es de esperar que ...** it is to be hoped *o* I *etc* hope that ...

7 (*locuciones con subjun*): **o sea** that is to say; **sea él sea su hermana** either him or his sister; **tengo que irme, no sea que mis hijos estén esperándome** I have to go in case my children are waiting for me

8: **a** *o* **de no ser por él ...** but for him ...

9: **a no ser que: a no ser que tenga uno ya** unless he's got one already

▶ NM being; **ser humano** human being; **ser vivo** living creature

Serbia ['serβja] NF Serbia

serbio, -a ['serβjo, a] ADJ Serbian ▶ NM/F Serb

serenarse [sere'narse] /**1a**/ VR to calm down; (*mar*) to grow calm; (*tiempo*) to clear up

serenidad [sereni'ðað] NF calmness

sereno, -a [se'reno, a] ADJ (*persona*) calm, unruffled; (*tiempo*) fine, settled; (*ambiente*) calm, peaceful ▶ NM night watchman

serial [se'rjal] NM serial

serie ['serje] NF series; (*cadena*) sequence, succession; (*TV etc*) serial; (*de inyecciones*) course; **fuera de** ~ out of order; (*fig*) special, out of the ordinary; **fabricación en** ~ mass production; (*Inform*) **interface/impresora en** ~ serial interface/printer

seriedad [serje'ðað] NF seriousness; (*formalidad*) reliability; (*de crisis*) gravity, seriousness

serigrafía [seriɣra'fia] NF silk screen printing

serio, -a ['serjo, a] ADJ serious; (*fiable: persona*) reliable, dependable; **poco** ~ (*actitud*) undignified; (*carácter*) unreliable; **en** ~ seriously

sermón [ser'mon] NM (*Rel*) sermon

sermonear [sermone'ar] /**1a**/ VT (*fam*) to lecture ▶ VI to sermonize

seropositivo, -a [seroposi'tiβo, a] ADJ HIV-positive

serpentear [serpente'ar] /**1a**/ VI to wriggle; (*camino, río*) to wind, snake

serpentina [serpen'tina] NF streamer

serpiente [ser'pjente] NF snake; ~ **boa** boa constrictor; ~ **de cascabel** rattlesnake

serranía [serra'nia] NF mountainous area

serrano, -a [se'rrano, a] ADJ highland *cpd*, hill *cpd* ▶ NM/F highlander

serrar [se'rrar] /**1j**/ VT to saw

serrín [se'rrin] NM sawdust

serrucho [se'rrutʃo] NM handsaw

Servia ['serβja] NF Serbia

service ['serβis] NM (*Am Auto*) service

servicial [serβi'θjal] ADJ helpful, obliging

servicio [ser'βiθjo] NM service; (*Culin etc*) set; **servicios** NMPL toilet(s); **estar de** ~ to be on duty; ~ **aduanero** *o* **de aduana** customs service; ~ **a domicilio** home delivery service; ~ **incluido** (*en hotel etc*) service charge included; ~ **militar** military service; ~ **público** (*Com*) public utility

servidor, a [serβi'ðor, a] NM/F servant ▶ NM (*Inform*) server; **su seguro** ~ **(s.s.s.)** yours faithfully; **un** ~ (*el que habla o escribe*) your humble servant

servidumbre [serβi'ðumbre] NF (*sujeción*) servitude; (*criados*) servants *pl*, staff

servil [ser'βil] ADJ servile

servilleta [serβi'ʎeta] NF serviette, napkin

servilletero [serβiʎe'tero] NM (*aro*) napkin ring

servir [ser'βir] /**3k**/ VT to serve; (*comida*) to serve out *o* up; (*Tenis etc*) to serve ▶ VI to serve; (*camarero*) to serve, wait; (*tener utilidad*) to be of use, be useful; **servirse** VR to serve *o* help o.s.; **¿en qué puedo servirle?** how can I help you?; ~ **vino a algn** to pour out wine for sb; ~ **de guía** to act *o* serve as a guide; **no sirve para nada** it's no use at all; **servirse de algo** to make use of sth, use sth; **sírvase pasar** please come in

sesenta [se'senta] NUM sixty

sesentón, -ona [sesen'ton, ona] ADJ, NM/F sixty-year-old

sesgado, -a [ses'ɣaðo, a] ADJ slanted, slanting

sesgo ['sesɣo] NM slant; (*fig*) slant, twist

sesión [se'sjon] NF (*Pol*) session, sitting; (*Cine*) showing; (*Teat*) performance; **abrir/ levantar la** ~ to open/close *o* adjourn the meeting; **la segunda** ~ the second house

seso ['seso] NM brain; (*fig*) intelligence; **sesos** NMPL (*Culin*) brains; **devanarse los sesos** to rack one's brains

sesudo, -a [se'suðo, a] ADJ sensible, wise

set [set] (*pl* **sets** [sets]) NM (*Tenis*) set

Set. ABR (= *setiembre*) Sept.

seta ['seta] NF mushroom; ~ **venenosa** toadstool

setecientos, -as [sete'θjentos, as] NUM seven hundred

setenta [se'tenta] NUM seventy

setiembre [se'tjembre] NM = **septiembre**; *ver tb* **julio**

seto ['seto] NM fence; ~ **vivo** hedge

seudo... [seuðo] PREF pseudo...

seudónimo [seu'ðonimo] NM pseudonym

Seúl [se'ul] NM Seoul

s.e.u.o. ABR (= *salvo error u omisión*) E & O E

severidad [seβeri'ðað] NF severity

severo, -a [se'βero, a] ADJ severe; (*disciplina*) strict; (*frío*) bitter

Sevilla [se'βiʎa] NF Seville

sevillano, -a [seβi'ʎano, a] ADJ of *o* from Seville ▶ NM/F native *o* inhabitant of Seville

sexagenario, -a [seksaxe'narjo, a] ADJ sixty-year-old ▶ NM/F person in his/her sixties

sexagésimo, -a [seksa'xesimo, a] NUM sixtieth

S.Exc. ABR = **Su Excelencia**

sexo ['sekso] NM sex; **el** ~ **femenino/ masculino** the female/male sex

sexto, -a ['seksto, a] NUM sixth; **Juan S~** John the Sixth

sexual [sek'swal] ADJ sexual; **vida** ~ sex life

sexualidad [sekswali'ðað] NF sexuality

s.f. ABR (= *sin fecha*) no date

s/f ABR (*Com*: = *su favor*) your favour

sgte(s). ABR (= *siguiente*) foll.

si [si] CONJ if; (*en pregunta indirecta*) if, whether ▶ NM (*Mus*) B; **si ... si ...** whether ... or ...; **me pregunto si ...** I wonder if *o* whether ...; **si no** if not, otherwise; **¡si fuera verdad!** if only it were true!; **por si viene** in case he comes

sí [si] ADV yes ▶ NM consent ▶ PRON (*uso impersonal*) oneself; (*sg: m*) himself; (: *f*) herself; (: *de cosa*) itself; (: *de usted*) yourself; (*pl*) themselves; (: *de ustedes*) yourselves; (: *recíproco*) each other; **él no quiere pero yo sí** he doesn't want to but I do; **ella sí vendrá** she will certainly come, she is sure to come; **claro que sí** of course; **creo que sí** I think so; **porque sí** because that's the way it is; (*porque lo digo yo*) because I say so; **¡sí que lo es!** I'll say it is!; **¡eso sí que no!** never!; **se ríe de sí misma** she laughs at herself; **cambiaron una mirada entre sí** they gave each other a look; **de por sí** in itself

siamés, -esa [sja'mes, esa] ADJ, NM/F Siamese

sibarita [siβa'rita] ADJ sybaritic ▶ NMF sybarite

sicario [si'karjo] NM hired killer

Sicilia [si'θilja] NF Sicily

siciliano, -a [siθi'ljano, a] ADJ, NM/F Sicilian ▶ NM (*Ling*) Sicilian

SIDA ['siða] NM ABR (= *síndrome de inmunodeficiencia adquirida*) AIDS

siderurgia [siðe'rurxja] NF iron and steel industry

siderúrgico, -a [siðe'rurxiko, a] ADJ iron and steel *cpd*

sidra ['siðra] NF cider

siega *etc* ['sjeɣa] VB *ver* **segar** ▶ NF (*el cosechar*) reaping; (*el segar*) mowing; (*época*) harvest (time)

siegue *etc* ['sjeɣe] VB *ver* **segar**

siembra ['sjembra] VB *ver* **sembrar** ▶ NF sowing

siempre ['sjempre] ADV always; (*todo el tiempo*) all the time; (*AM: así y todo*) still ▶ CONJ: **~ que ...** (+*indic*) whenever ...; (+ *subjun*) provided that ...; **es lo de ~** it's the same old story; **como ~** as usual; **para ~** forever; **~ me voy mañana** (*AM*) I'm still leaving tomorrow

sien [sjen] NF (*Anat*) temple

siento *etc* ['sjento] VB *ver* **sentar**; **sentir**

sierra ['sjerra] VB *ver* **serrar** ▶ NF (*Tec*) saw; (*Geo*) mountain range; **S~ Leona** Sierra Leone

siervo, -a ['sjerβo, a] NM/F slave

siesta ['sjesta] NF siesta, nap; **dormir la** *o* **echarse una** *o* **tomar una ~** to have an afternoon nap *o* a doze

siete ['sjete] NUM seven ▶ EXCL (*AM fam*): **¡la gran ~!** wow!, hell!; **hijo de la gran ~** (*fam!*) bastard (*fam!*), son of a bitch (*US fam!*)

sífilis ['sifilis] NF syphilis

sifón [si'fon] NM syphon; **whisky con ~** whisky and soda

siga *etc* ['siɣa] VB *ver* **seguir**

sigilo [si'xilo] NM secrecy; (*discreción*) discretion

sigla ['siɣla] NF initial, abbreviation

siglo ['siɣlo] NM century; (*fig*) age; **S~ de las Luces** Age of Enlightenment; **S~ de Oro** Golden Age

significación [siɣnifika'θjon] NF significance

significado [siɣnifi'kaðo] NM significance; (*de palabra etc*) meaning

significar [siɣnifi'kar] /**1g**/ VT to mean, signify; (*notificar*) to make known, express

significativo, -a [siɣnifika'tiβo, a] ADJ significant

signifique *etc* [siɣni'fike] VB *ver* **significar**

signo ['siɣno] NM sign; **~ de admiración** *o* **exclamación** exclamation mark; **~ igual** equals sign; **~ de interrogación** question mark; **~ de más/de menos** plus/minus sign; **signos de puntuación** punctuation marks

sigo *etc* VB *ver* **seguir**

siguiendo *etc* [si'ɣjendo] VB *ver* **seguir**

siguiente [si'ɣjente] ADJ following; (*próximo*) next

siguió *etc* VB *ver* **seguir**

sílaba ['silaβa] NF syllable

silbar [sil'βar] /**1a**/ VT, VI to whistle; (*silbato*) to blow; (*Teat etc*) to hiss

silbato [sil'βato] NM (*instrumento*) whistle

silbido [sil'βiðo] NM whistle, whistling; (*abucheo*) hiss

silenciador [silenθja'ðor] NM silencer

silenciar [silen'θjar] /**1b**/ VT (*persona*) to silence; (*escándalo*) to hush up

silencio [si'lenθjo] NM silence, quiet; **en el ~ más absoluto** in dead silence; **guardar ~** to keep silent

silencioso, -a [silen'θjoso, a] ADJ silent, quiet

sílfide ['silfiðe] NF sylph

silicio [si'liθjo] NM silicon

silla ['siʎa] NF (*asiento*) chair; (*tb*: **silla de montar**) saddle; **~ de ruedas** wheelchair

sillería [siʎe'ria] NF (*asientos*) chairs *pl*, set of chairs; (*Rel*) choir stalls *pl*; (*taller*) chairmaker's workshop

sillín [si'ʎin] NM saddle, seat

sillón [si'ʎon] NM armchair, easy chair

silueta [si'lweta] NF silhouette; (*de edificio*) outline; (*figura*) figure

silvestre [sil'βestre] ADJ (*Bot*) wild; (*fig*) rustic, rural

sima ['sima] NF abyss, chasm

simbolice etc [simbo'liθe] VB ver **simbolizar**
simbólico, -a [sim'boliko, a] ADJ symbolic(al)
simbolizar [simboli'θar] /**1f**/ VT to symbolize
símbolo ['simbolo] NM symbol; **~ gráfico** (*Inform*) icon
simetría [sime'tria] NF symmetry
simétrico, -a [si'metriko, a] ADJ symmetrical
simiente [si'mjente] NF seed
similar [simi'lar] ADJ similar
similitud [simili'tuð] NF similarity, resemblance
simio ['simjo] NM ape
simpatía [simpa'tia] NF liking; (*afecto*) affection; (*amabilidad*) kindness; (*de ambiente*) friendliness; (*de persona, lugar*) charm, attractiveness; (*solidaridad*) mutual support, solidarity; **tener ~ a** to like; **la famosa ~ andaluza** that well-known Andalusian charm
simpatice etc [simpa'tiθe] VB ver **simpatizar**
simpático, -a [sim'patiko, a] ADJ nice, pleasant; (*bondadoso*) kind; **no le hemos caído muy simpáticos** she didn't much take to us
simpatiquísimo, -a [simpati'kisimo, a] ADJ SUPERLATIVO *de* **simpático** ever so nice; ever so kind
simpatizante [simpati'θante] NMF sympathizer
simpatizar [simpati'θar] /**1f**/ VI: **~ con** to get on well with
simple ['simple] ADJ simple; (*elemental*) simple, easy; (*mero*) mere; (*puro*) pure, sheer ▶ NMF simpleton; **un ~ soldado** an ordinary soldier
simpleza [sim'pleθa] NF simpleness; (*necedad*) silly thing
simplicidad [simpliθi'ðað] NF simplicity
simplificar [simplifi'kar] /**1g**/ VT to simplify
simplifique etc [simpli'fike] VB ver **simplificar**
simplón, -ona [sim'plon, ona] ADJ simple, gullible ▶ NM/F simple soul
simposio [sim'posjo] NM symposium
simulacro [simu'lakro] NM (*apariencia*) semblance; (*fingimiento*) sham
simular [simu'lar] /**1a**/ VT to simulate; (*fingir*) to feign, sham
simultanear [simultane'ar] /**1a**/ VT: **~ dos cosas** to do two things simultaneously
simultáneo, -a [simul'taneo, a] ADJ simultaneous
sin [sin] PREP without; (*a no ser por*) but for ▶ CONJ: **~ que** (+*subjun*) without; **~ decir nada** without a word; **~ verlo yo** without my seeing it; **platos ~ lavar** unwashed *o* dirty dishes; **la ropa está ~ lavar** the clothes are unwashed; **~ que lo sepa él** without his knowing; **~ embargo** however
sinagoga [sina'ɣoɣa] NF synagogue

Sinaí [sina'i] NM: **El ~** Sinai, the Sinai Peninsula; **el Monte ~** Mount Sinai
sinceridad [sinθeri'ðað] NF sincerity
sincero, -a [sin'θero, a] ADJ sincere; (*persona*) genuine; (*opinión*) frank; (*felicitaciones*) heartfelt
síncope ['sinkope] NM (*desmayo*) blackout; **~ cardíaco** (*Med*) heart failure
sincronice etc [sinkro'niθe] VB ver **sincronizar**
sincronizar [sinkroni'θar] /**1f**/ VT to synchronize
sindical [sindi'kal] ADJ union *cpd*, trade-union *cpd*
sindicalista [sindika'lista] ADJ trade-union *cpd* ▶ NMF trade unionist
sindicar [sindi'kar] /**1g**/ VT (*obreros*) to organize, unionize; **sindicarse** VR (*obrero*) to join a union
sindicato [sindi'kato] NM (*de trabajadores*) trade(s) *o* labor (*US*) union; (*de negociantes*) syndicate
sindique etc [sin'dike] VB ver **sindicar**
síndrome ['sindrome] NM syndrome; **~ de abstinencia** withdrawal symptoms; **~ de la clase turista** economy-class syndrome
sine qua non [sine'kwanon] ADJ: **condición ~** sine qua non
sinfín [sin'fin] NM: **un ~ de** a great many, no end of
sinfonía [sinfo'nia] NF symphony
sinfónico, -a [sin'foniko, a] ADJ (*música*) symphonic; **orquesta sinfónica** symphony orchestra
Singapur [singa'pur] NM Singapore
singular [singu'lar] ADJ singular; (*fig*) outstanding, exceptional; (*pey*) peculiar, odd ▶ NM (*Ling*) singular; **en ~** in the singular
singularice etc [singula'riθe] VB ver **singularizar**
singularidad [singulari'ðað] NF singularity, peculiarity
singularizar [singulari'θar] /**1f**/ VT to single out; **singularizarse** VR to distinguish o.s., stand out
siniestro, -a [si'njestro, a] ADJ left; (*fig*) sinister ▶ NM (*accidente*) accident; (*desastre*) natural disaster
sinnúmero [sin'numero] NM = **sinfín**
sino ['sino] NM fate, destiny ▶ CONJ (*pero*) but; (*salvo*) except, save; **no son 8 ~ 9** there are not 8 but 9; **todos ~ él** all except him
sinónimo, -a [si'nonimo, a] ADJ synonymous ▶ NM synonym
sinrazón [sinra'θon] NF wrong, injustice
sinsabor [sinsa'βor] NM (*molestia*) trouble; (*dolor*) sorrow; (*preocupación*) uneasiness
sintaxis [sin'taksis] NF syntax
síntesis ['sintesis] NF INV synthesis
sintetice etc [sinte'tiθe] VB ver **sintetizar**

sintético, -a [sin'tetiko, a] ADJ synthetic
sintetizador [sinteti θa'ðor] NM synthesizer
sintetizar [sinteti'θar] /**1f**/ VT to synthesize
sintiendo etc [sin'tjendo] VB ver **sentir**
sintió VB ver **sentir**
síntoma ['sintoma] NM symptom
sintomático, -a [sinto'matiko, a] ADJ symptomatic
sintonía [sinto'nia] NF (Radio) tuning; (melodía) signature tune
sintonice etc [sinto'niθe] VB ver **sintonizar**
sintonizador [sintoniθa'ðor] NM (Radio) tuner
sintonizar [sintoni'θar] /**1f**/ VT (Radio) to tune (in) to, pick up
sinuoso, -a [si'nwoso, a] ADJ (camino) winding; (rumbo) devious
sinvergüenza [simber'γwenθa] NMF rogue, scoundrel; **¡es un ~!** he's got a nerve!
sionismo [sjo'nismo] NM Zionism
siquiera [si'kjera] CONJ even if, even though ▶ ADV (esp AM) at least; **ni ~** not even; **~ bebe algo** at least drink something
sirena [si'rena] NF siren, mermaid; (bocina) siren, hooter
Siria ['sirja] NF Syria
sirio, -a ['sirjo, a] ADJ, NM/F Syrian
sirviendo etc [sir'βjendo] VB ver **servir**
sirviente, -a [sir'βjente, a] NM/F servant
sirvo etc VB ver **servir**
sisa ['sisa] NF petty theft; (Costura) dart; (sobaquera) armhole
sisar [si'sar] /**1a**/ VT (robar) to thieve; (Costura) to take in
sisear [sise'ar] /**1a**/ VT, VI to hiss
sísmico, -a ['sismiko, a] ADJ: **movimiento ~** earthquake
sismógrafo [sis'moγrafo] NM seismograph
sistema [sis'tema] NM system; (método) method; **~ binario** (Inform) binary system; **~ de alerta inmediata** early-warning system; **~ de facturación** (Com) invoicing system; **~ de fondo fijo** (Com) imprest system; **~ de lógica compartida** (Inform) shared logic system; **~ educativo** educational system; **~ experto** expert system; **~ impositivo** o **tributario** taxation, tax system; **~ métrico** metric system; **~ operativo (en disco)** (Inform) (disk-based) operating system
sistemático, -a [siste'matiko, a] ADJ systematic
sitiar [si'tjar] /**1b**/ VT to besiege, lay siege to
sitio ['sitjo] NM (lugar) place; (espacio) room, space; (Mil) siege; **~ de taxis** (AM: parada) taxi stand o rank (BRIT); **~ web** website; **¿hay ~?** is there any room?; **hay ~ de sobra** there's plenty of room
situación [sitwa'θjon] NF situation,

position; (estatus) position, standing
situado, -a [si'twaðo, a] ADJ situated, placed; **estar ~** (Com) to be financially secure
situar [si'twar] /**1e**/ VT to place, put; (edificio) to locate, situate
S.L. ABR (Com: = Sociedad Limitada) Ltd
slip [es'lip] (pl **slips**) NM pants pl, briefs pl
slot [es'lot] (pl **slots**) NM: **~ de expansión** expansion slot
S.M. ABR (= Su Majestad) HM
SME NM ABR (= Sistema Monetario Europeo) EMS; **(mecanismo de cambios del) ~** ERM
smoking [(e)'smokin] (pl **smokings**) NM dinner jacket (BRIT), tuxedo (US)
SMS NM (mensaje) text (message), SMS (message)
s/n ABR (= sin número) no number
snob [es'nob] = **esnob**
snowboard [es'nouβor] NM snowboarding; **tabla de ~** snowboard
SO ABR (= suroeste) SW
so [so] EXCL whoa!; **¡so burro!** you idiot! ▶ PREP under
s/o ABR (Com: = su orden) your order
sobaco [so'βako] NM armpit
sobado, -a [so'βaðo, a] ADJ (ropa) worn; (arrugado) crumpled; (libro) well-thumbed; (Culin: bizcocho) short
sobar [so'βar] /**1a**/ VT (tela) to finger; (ropa) to rumple, mess up; (músculos) to rub, massage; (comida) to play around with
soberanía [soβera'nia] NF sovereignty
soberano, -a [soβe'rano, a] ADJ sovereign; (fig) supreme ▶ NM/F sovereign; **los soberanos** the king and queen
soberbio, -a [so'βerβjo, a] ADJ (orgulloso) proud; (altanero) haughty, arrogant; (magnífico) magnificent, superb ▶ NF (orgullo) pride; (altanería) haughtiness, arrogance; (magnificencia) magnificence
sobornar [soβor'nar] /**1a**/ VT to bribe
soborno [so'βorno] NM (un soborno) bribe; (el soborno) bribery
sobra ['soβra] NF excess, surplus; **sobras** NFPL leftovers, scraps; **de ~** surplus, extra; **lo sé de ~** I'm only too aware of it; **tengo de ~** I've more than enough
sobradamente [soβraða'mente] ADV amply; (saber) only too well
sobrado, -a [so'βraðo, a] ADJ (más que suficiente) more than enough; (superfluo) excessive ▶ ADV too, exceedingly; **sobradas veces** repeatedly
sobrante [so'βrante] ADJ remaining, extra ▶ NM surplus, remainder
sobrar [so'βrar] /**1a**/ VT to exceed, surpass ▶ VI (tener de más) to be more than enough; (quedar) to remain, be left (over)
sobrasada [soβra'saða] NF ≈ sausage spread

s

sobre ['soβre] PREP (gen) on; (encima) on (top of); (por encima de, arriba de) over, above; (más que) more than; (además) in addition to, besides; (alrededor de) about; (porcentaje) in, out of; (tema) about, on ▶ NM envelope; ~ **todo** above all; **3 ~ 100** 3 in a 100, 3 out of every 100; **un libro ~ Tirso** a book about Tirso; ~ **de ventanilla** window envelope

sobrecama [soβre'kama] NF bedspread

sobrecapitalice etc [soβrekapita'liθe] VB ver **sobrecapitalizar**

sobrecapitalizar [soβrekapitali'θar] /1f/ VI to overcapitalize

sobrecargar [soβrekar'ɣar] /1h/ VT (camión) to overload; (Com) to surcharge

sobrecargue etc [soβre'karɣe] VB ver **sobrecargar**

sobrecoger [soβreko'xer] /2c/ VT (sobresaltar) to startle; (asustar) to scare; **sobrecogerse** VR (sobresaltarse) to be startled; (asustarse) to get scared; (quedar impresionado) **sobrecogerse (de)** to be overawed (by)

sobrecoja etc [soβre'koxa] VB ver **sobrecoger**

sobredosis [soβre'ðosis] NF INV overdose

sobreentender [soβreenten'der] /2g/ VT to understand; (adivinar) to deduce, infer; **sobreentenderse** VR: **se sobreentiende que ... it is implied that ...**

sobreescribir [soβreeskri'βir] /3a/ VT (Inform) to overwrite

sobreestimar [soβreesti'mar] /1a/ VT to overestimate

sobregiro [soβre'xiro] NM (Com) overdraft

sobrehumano, -a [soβreu'mano, a] ADJ superhuman

sobreimprimir [soβreimpri'mir] /3a/ VT (Com) to merge

sobrellevar [soβreʎe'βar] /1a/ VT (fig) to bear, endure

sobremanera [soβrema'nera] ADV exceedingly

sobremesa [soβre'mesa] NF (después de comer) sitting on after a meal; (Inform) desktop; **durante la ~** after dinner; **conversación de ~** table talk

sobremodo [soβre'moðo] ADV very much, enormously

sobrenatural [soβrenatu'ral] ADJ supernatural

sobrenombre [soβre'nombre] NM nickname

sobrentender [soβrenten'der] /2g/ VT = **sobreentender**

sobrepasar [soβrepa'sar] /1a/ VT to exceed, surpass

sobrepondré etc [soβrepon'dre] VB ver **sobreponer**

sobreponer [soβrepo'ner] /2q/ VT (poner encima) to put on top; (añadir) to add; **sobreponerse** VR: **sobreponerse a** to overcome

sobreponga etc [soβre'ponga] VB ver **sobreponer**

sobreprima [soβre'prima] NF (Com) loading

sobreproducción [soβreproðuk'θjon] NF overproduction

sobrepuesto [soβre'pwesto], **sobrepuse** etc [soβre'puse] VB ver **sobreponer**

sobresaldré etc [soβresal'dre], **sobresalga** etc [soβresal'ɣa] VB ver **sobresalir**

sobresaliente [soβresa'ljente] ADJ projecting; (fig) outstanding, excellent; (Univ etc) first class ▶ NM (Univ etc) first class (mark), distinction

sobresalir [soβresa'lir] /3q/ VI to project, jut out; (fig) to stand out, excel

sobresaltar [soβresal'tar] /1a/ VT (asustar) to scare, frighten; (sobrecoger) to startle

sobresalto [soβre'salto] NM (movimiento) start; (susto) scare; (turbación) sudden shock

sobrescribir [soβreskri'βir] /3a/ VT = **sobreescribir**

sobreseer [soβrese'er] /2e/ VT: ~ **una causa** (Jur) to stop a case

sobrestadía [soβresta'ðia] NF (Com) demurrage

sobrestimar [soβresti'mar] /1a/ VT = **sobreestimar**

sobretensión [soβreten'sjon] NF (Elec): ~ **transitoria** surge

sobretiempo [soβre'tjempo] NM (Am) overtime

sobretodo [soβre'toðo] NM overcoat

sobrevendré etc [soβreβen'dre], **sobrevenga** etc [soβre'βenga] VB ver **sobrevenir**

sobrevenir [soβreβe'nir] /3r/ VI (ocurrir) to happen (unexpectedly); (resultar) to follow, ensue

sobreviene etc [soβre'βjene], **sobrevine** etc [soβre'βine] VB ver **sobrevenir**

sobreviviente [soβreβi'βjente] ADJ surviving ▶ NMF survivor

sobrevivir [soβreβi'βir] /3a/ VI to survive; (persona) to outlive; (objeto etc) to outlast

sobrevolar [soβreβo'lar] /1l/ VT to fly over

sobrevuele etc [soβre'βwele] VB ver **sobrevolar**

sobriedad [soβrje'ðað] NF sobriety, soberness; (moderación) moderation, restraint

sobrino, -a [so'βrino, a] NM/F nephew/niece

sobrio, -a ['soβrjo, a] ADJ sober; (moderado) moderate, restrained

socarrón, -ona [soka'rron, ona] ADJ (sarcástico) sarcastic, ironic(al)

socavar [soka'βar] /1a/ VT to undermine; (excavar) to dig underneath o below

socavón [soka'βon] NM (en mina) gallery; (hueco) hollow; (en la calle) hole

sociable [so'θjaβle] ADJ (*persona*) sociable, friendly; (*animal*) social

social [so'θjal] ADJ social; (*Com*) company *cpd*

socialdemócrata [soθjalde'mokrata] ADJ social-democratic ▶ NMF social democrat

socialice *etc* [soθja'liθe] VB *ver* **socializar**

socialista [soθja'lista] ADJ, NMF socialist

socializar [soθjali'θar] /**1f**/ VT to socialize

sociedad [soθje'ðað] NF society; (*Com*) company; ~ **de ahorro y préstamo** savings and loan society; ~ **anónima (S.A.)** limited company (Ltd) (BRIT), incorporated company (Inc) (US); ~ **de beneficiencia** friendly society (BRIT), benefit association (US); ~ **de cartera** investment trust; ~ **comanditaria** (*Com*) co-ownership; ~ **conjunta** (*Com*) joint venture; ~ **de consumo** consumer society; ~ **inmobiliaria** building society (BRIT), savings and loan (society) (US); ~ **de responsabilidad limitada** (*Com*) private limited company

socio, -a ['soθjo, a] NM/F (*miembro*) member; (*Com*) partner; ~ **activo** active partner; ~ **capitalista** o **comanditario** sleeping o silent (US) partner

socioeconómico, -a [soθjoeko'nomiko, a] ADJ socio-economic

sociología [soθjolo'xia] NF sociology

sociólogo, -a [so'θjoloɣo, a] NM/F sociologist

socorrer [soko'rrer] /**2a**/ VT to help

socorrido, -a [soko'rriðo, a] ADJ (*tienda*) well-stocked; (*útil*) handy; (*persona*) helpful

socorrismo [soko'rrismo] NM life-saving

socorrista [soko'rrista] NMF first aider; (*en piscina, playa*) lifeguard

socorro [so'korro] NM (*ayuda*) help, aid; (*Mil*) relief; **¡~!** help!

soda ['soða] NF (*sosa*) soda; (*bebida*) soda (water)

sódico, -a ['soðiko, a] ADJ sodium *cpd*

soez [so'eθ] ADJ dirty, obscene

sofá [so'fa] NM sofa, settee

sofá-cama [so'fakama] NM studio couch, sofa bed

Sofia ['sofja] NF Sofia

sofisticación [sofistika'θjon] NF sophistication

sofisticado, -a [sofisti'kaðo, a] ADJ sophisticated

sofocado, -a [sofo'kaðo, a] ADJ: **estar ~** (*fig*) to be out of breath; (*ahogarse*) to feel stifled

sofocar [sofo'kar] /**1g**/ VT to suffocate; (*apagar*) to smother, put out; **sofocarse** VR to suffocate; (*fig*) to blush, feel embarrassed

sofoco [so'foko] NM suffocation; (*azoro*) embarrassment

sofocón [sofo'kon] NM: **llevarse** o **pasar un ~** to have a sudden shock

sofreír [sofre'ir] /**3l**/ VT to fry lightly

sofría *etc* [so'fria], **sofriendo** *etc* [so'frjendo], **sofrito** [so'frito] VB *ver* **sofreír**

soft ['sof], **software** ['sofwer] NM (*Inform*) software

soga ['soɣa] NF rope

sois [sois] VB *ver* **ser**

soja ['soxa] NF soya

sojuzgar [soxuθ'ɣar] /**1h**/ VT to subdue, rule despotically

sojuzgue *etc* [so'xuθɣe] VB *ver* **sojuzgar**

sol [sol] NM sun; (*luz*) sunshine, sunlight; (*Mus*) G; ~ **naciente/poniente** rising/setting sun; **tomar el ~** to sunbathe; **hace ~** it is sunny

solace *etc* [so'laθe] VB *ver* **solazar**

solamente [sola'mente] ADV only, just

solapa [so'lapa] NF (*de chaqueta*) lapel; (*de libro*) jacket

solapado, -a [sola'paðo, a] ADJ (*intenciones*) underhand; (*gestos, movimiento*) sly

solar [so'lar] ADJ solar, sun *cpd* ▶ NM (*terreno*) plot (of ground); (*local*) undeveloped site

solaz [so'laθ] NM recreation, relaxation

solazar [sola'θar] /**1f**/ VT (*divertir*) to amuse; **solazarse** VR to enjoy o.s., relax

soldada [sol'daða] NF pay

soldado [sol'daðo] NM soldier; ~ **raso** private

soldador [solda'ðor] NM soldering iron; (*persona*) welder

soldar [sol'dar] /**1l**/ VT to solder, weld; (*unir*) to join, unite

soleado, -a [sole'aðo, a] ADJ sunny

soledad [sole'ðað] NF solitude; (*estado infeliz*) loneliness

solemne [so'lemne] ADJ solemn; (*tontería*) utter; (*error*) complete

solemnidad [solemni'ðað] NF solemnity

soler [so'ler] VI to be in the habit of, be accustomed to; **suele salir a las ocho** she usually goes out at 8 o'clock; **solíamos ir todos los años** we used to go every year

solera [so'lera] NF (*tradición*) tradition; **vino de ~** vintage wine

solfeo [sol'feo] NM sol-fa, singing of scales; **ir a clases de ~** to take singing lessons

solicitar [soliθi'tar] /**1a**/ VT (*permiso*) to ask for, seek; (*puesto*) to apply for; (*votos*) to canvass for; (*atención*) to attract; (*persona*) to pursue, chase after

solícito, -a [so'liθito, a] ADJ (*diligente*) diligent; (*cuidadoso*) careful

solicitud [soliθi'tuð] NF (*calidad*) great care; (*petición*) request; (*a un puesto*) application

solidaridad [soliðari'ðað] NF solidarity; **por ~ con** (*Pol etc*) out of o in solidarity with

solidario, -a [soli'ðarjo, a] ADJ (*participación*) joint, common; (*compromiso*) mutually binding; **hacerse ~ de** to declare one's solidarity with

S

solidarizarse [soliðari'θarse] /**1f**/ vr: ~ **con algn** to support sb, sympathize with sb
solidez [soli'ðeθ] nf solidity
sólido, -a ['soliðo, a] adj solid; (*Tec*) solidly made; (*bien construido*) well built
soliloquio [soli'lokjo] nm soliloquy
solista [so'lista] nmf soloist
solitario, -a [soli'tarjo, a] adj (*persona*) lonely, solitary; (*lugar*) lonely, desolate ▶ nm/f (*reclusa*) recluse; (*en la sociedad*) loner ▶ nm solitaire ▶ nf tapeworm
soliviantar [soliβjan'tar] /**1a**/ vt to stir up, rouse (to revolt); (*enojar*) to anger; (*sacar de quicio*) to exasperate
solloce *etc* [so'ʎoθe] vb *ver* **sollozar**
sollozar [soʎo'θar] /**1f**/ vi to sob
sollozo [so'ʎoθo] nm sob
solo¹, -a ['solo, a] adj (*único*) single, sole; (*sin compañía*) alone; (*Mus*) solo; (*solitario*) lonely; **hay una sola dificultad** there is just one difficulty; **a solas** alone, by o.s.
solo², sólo ['solo] adv only, just; (*exclusivamente*) solely; **tan** ~ only just
solomillo [solo'miʎo] nm sirloin
solsticio [sols'tiθjo] nm solstice
soltar [sol'tar] /**1l**/ vt (*dejar ir*) to let go of; (*desprender*) to unfasten, loosen; (*librar*) to release, set free; (*amarras*) to cast off; (*Auto: freno etc*) to release; (*: suspiro*) to heave; (*: risa etc*) to let out; **soltarse** vr (*desanudarse*) to come undone; (*desprenderse*) to come off; (*adquirir destreza*) to become expert; (*en idioma*) to become fluent
soltero, -a [sol'tero, a] adj single, unmarried ▶ nm bachelor ▶ nf single woman, spinster
solterón [solte'ron] nm confirmed bachelor
solterona [solte'rona] nf spinster, maiden lady; (*pey*) old maid
soltura [sol'tura] nf looseness, slackness; (*de los miembros*) agility, ease of movement; (*en el hablar*) fluency, ease
soluble [so'luβle] adj (*Química*) soluble; (*problema*) solvable; ~ **en agua** soluble in water
solución [solu'θjon] nf solution; ~ **de continuidad** break in continuity
solucionar [soluθjo'nar] /**1a**/ vt (*problema*) to solve; (*asunto*) to settle, resolve
solvencia [sol'βenθja] nf (*Com: estado*) solvency; (*: acción*) settlement, payment
solventar [solβen'tar] /**1a**/ vt (*pagar*) to settle, pay; (*resolver*) to resolve
solvente [sol'βente] adj solvent, free of debt
Somalia [so'malja] nf Somalia
sombra ['sombra] nf shadow; (*como protección*) shade; **sombras** nfpl darkness *sg*, shadows; **sin ~ de duda** without a shadow of doubt; **tener buena/mala ~** (*suerte*) to be lucky/unlucky; (*carácter*) to be likeable/disagreeable

sombrero [som'brero] nm hat; ~ **hongo** bowler (hat), derby (*US*); ~ **de copa** o **de pelo** (*Am*) top hat
sombrilla [som'briʎa] nf parasol, sunshade
sombrío, -a [som'brio, a] adj (*oscuro*) dark; (*fig*) sombre, sad; (*persona*) gloomy
somero, -a [so'mero, a] adj superficial
someter [some'ter] /**2a**/ vt (*país*) to conquer; (*persona*) to subject to one's will; (*informe*) to present, submit; **someterse** vr to give in, yield, submit; ~ **a** to subject to; **someterse a** to submit to; **someterse a una operación** to undergo an operation
sometimiento [someti'mjento] nm (*estado*) submission; (*acción*) presentation
somier [so'mjer] (*pl* **somiers**) nm spring mattress
somnífero [som'nifero] nm sleeping pill o tablet
somnolencia [somno'lenθja] nf sleepiness, drowsiness
somos ['somos] vb *ver* **ser**
son [son] vb *ver* **ser** ▶ nm sound; **en ~ de broma** as a joke
sonado, -a [so'naðo, a] adj (*comentado*) talked-of; (*famoso*) famous; (*Com: pey*) hyped(-up)
sonaja [so'naxa] nf (*Am*) = **sonajero**
sonajero [sona'xero] nm (baby's) rattle
sonambulismo [sonambu'lismo] nm sleepwalking
sonámbulo, -a [so'nambulo, a] nm/f sleepwalker
sonar [so'nar] /**1l**/ vt (*campana*) to ring; (*trompeta, sirena*) to blow ▶ vi to sound; (*hacer ruido*) to make a noise; (*Ling*) to be sounded, be pronounced; (*ser conocido*) to sound familiar; (*campana*) to ring; (*reloj*) to strike, chime; **sonarse** vr: **sonarse (la nariz)** to blow one's nose; **es un nombre que suena** it's a name that's in the news; **me suena ese nombre** that name rings a bell
sonda ['sonda] nf (*Naut*) sounding; (*Tec*) bore, drill; (*Med*) probe
sondear [sonde'ar] /**1a**/ vt (*Med*) to probe, sound; (*Naut*) to sound; (*Tec*) to bore (into), drill; (*fig: persona, intenciones*) to sound out
sondeo [son'deo] nm (*Med, Naut*) sounding; (*Tec*) boring, drilling; (*encuesta*) poll, enquiry; ~ **de la opinión pública** public opinion poll
sónico, -a ['soniko, a] adj sonic, sound *cpd*
sonido [so'niðo] nm sound
sonoro, -a [so'noro, a] adj sonorous; (*resonante*) loud, resonant; (*Ling*) voiced; **efectos sonoros** sound effects
sonreír [sonre'ir] /**3l**/ vi to smile; **sonreírse** vr to smile
sonría *etc* [son'ria], **sonriendo** *etc* [son'rjendo] vb *ver* **sonreír**

sonriente [son'rjente] ADJ smiling

sonrisa [son'risa] NF smile

sonrojar [sonro'xar] /**1a**/ VT to make sb blush; **sonrojarse** VR: **sonrojarse (de)** to blush (at)

sonrojo [son'roxo] NM blush

sonsacar [sonsa'kar] /**1g**/ VT to wheedle, coax; ~ **a algn** to pump sb for information

sonsaque etc [son'sake] VB ver **sonsacar**

sonsonete [sonso'nete] NM (golpecitos) tap(ping); (voz monótona) monotonous delivery, singsong (voice)

soñador, a [soɲa'ðor, a] NM/F dreamer

soñar [so'ɲar] /**1l**/ VT, VI to dream; ~ **con** to dream about o of; **soñé contigo anoche** I dreamed about you last night

soñoliento, -a [soɲo'ljento, a] ADJ sleepy, drowsy

sopa ['sopa] NF soup; ~ **de fideos** noodle soup

sopero, -a [so'pero, a] ADJ (plato, cuchara) soup cpd ▶ NM soup plate ▶ NF soup tureen

sopesar [sope'sar] /**1a**/ VT to try the weight of; (fig) to weigh up

sopetón [sope'ton] NM: **de** ~ suddenly, unexpectedly

soplar [so'plar] /**1a**/ VT (polvo) to blow away, blow off; (inflar) to blow up; (vela) to blow out; (ayudar a recordar) to prompt; (birlar) to nick; (delatar) to split on ▶ VI to blow; (delatar) to squeal; (beber) to booze, bend the elbow

soplete [so'plete] NM blowlamp; ~ **soldador** welding torch

soplo ['soplo] NM blow, puff; (de viento) puff, gust

soplón, -ona [so'plon, ona] NM/F (fam: chismoso) telltale; (: de policía) informer, grass

soponcio [so'ponθjo] NM dizzy spell

sopor [so'por] NM drowsiness

soporífero, -a [sopo'rifero, a] ADJ sleep-inducing; (fig) soporific ▶ NM sleeping pill

soportable [sopor'taβle] ADJ bearable

soportal [sopor'tal] NM porch; **soportales** NMPL arcade sg

soportar [sopor'tar] /**1a**/ VT to bear, carry; (fig) to bear, put up with

soporte [so'porte] NM support; (fig) pillar, support; (Inform) medium; ~ **de entrada/salida** input/output medium

soprano [so'prano] NF soprano

sor [sor] NF: **S~ María** Sister Mary

sorber [sor'βer] /**2a**/ VT (chupar) to sip; (inhalar) to sniff, inhale; (absorber) to soak up, absorb

sorbete [sor'βete] NM iced fruit drink

sorbo ['sorβo] NM (trago) gulp, swallow; (chupada) sip; **beber a sorbos** to sip

sordera [sor'ðera] NF deafness

sórdido, -a ['sorðiðo, a] ADJ dirty, squalid

sordo, -a ['sorðo, a] ADJ (persona) deaf; (ruido) dull; (Ling) voiceless ▶ NM/F deaf person; **quedarse** ~ to go deaf

sordomudo, -a [sorðo'muðo, a] ADJ deaf and dumb ▶ NM/F deaf-mute

soriano, -a [so'rjano, a] ADJ of o from Soria ▶ NM/F native o inhabitant of Soria

sorna ['sorna] NF (malicia) slyness; (tono burlón) sarcastic tone

soroche [so'rotʃe] NM (Am Med) mountain sickness

sorprendente [sorpren'dente] ADJ surprising

sorprender [sorpren'der] /**2a**/ VT to surprise; (asombrar) to amaze; (sobresaltar) to startle; (coger desprevenido) to catch unawares; **sorprenderse** VR: **sorprenderse (de)** to be surprised o amazed (at)

sorpresa [sor'presa] NF surprise

sorpresivo, -a [sorpre'siβo, a] ADJ (Am) surprising; (imprevisto) sudden

sortear [sorte'ar] /**1a**/ VT to draw lots for; (rifar) to raffle; (dificultad) to dodge, avoid

sorteo [sor'teo] NM (en lotería) draw; (rifa) raffle

sortija [sor'tixa] NF ring; (rizo) ringlet, curl

sortilegio [sorti'lexjo] NM (hechicería) sorcery; (hechizo) spell

SOS SIGLA M SOS

sosegado, -a [sose'ɣaðo, a] ADJ quiet, calm

sosegar [sose'ɣar] /**1h, 1j**/ VT to quieten, calm; (el ánimo) to reassure ▶ VI to rest

sosegué [sose'ɣe], **soseguemos** etc [sose'ɣemos] VB ver **sosegar**

sosiego [so'sjeɣo] VB ver **sosegar** ▶ NM quiet(ness), calm(ness)

sosiegue etc [so'sjeɣe] VB ver **sosegar**

soslayar [sosla'jar] /**1a**/ VT (preguntas) to get round

soslayo [sos'lajo]: **de** ~ adv obliquely, sideways; **mirar de** ~ to look out of the corner of one's eye (at)

soso, -a ['soso, a] ADJ (Culin) tasteless; (fig) dull, uninteresting

sospecha [sos'petʃa] NF suspicion

sospechar [sospe'tʃar] /**1a**/ VT to suspect ▶ VI: ~ **de** to be suspicious of

sospechoso, -a [sospe'tʃoso, a] ADJ suspicious; (testimonio, opinión) suspect ▶ NM/F suspect

sostén [sos'ten] NM (apoyo) support; (sujetador) bra; (alimentación) sustenance, food

sostendré etc [sosten'dre] VB ver **sostener**

sostener [soste'ner] /**2k**/ VT to support; (mantener) to keep up, maintain; (alimentar) to sustain, keep going; **sostenerse** VR to support o.s.; (seguir) to continue, remain

sostenga etc [sos'tenga] VB ver **sostener**

sostenido, -a [soste'niðo, a] ADJ continuous, sustained; (*prolongado*) prolonged; (*Mus*) sharp ▶ NM (*Mus*) sharp

sostuve *etc* [sos'tuβe] VB *ver* **sostener**

sota ['sota] NF (*Naipes*) ≈ jack; *ver tb* **baraja española**

sotana [so'tana] NF (*Rel*) cassock

sótano ['sotano] NM basement

sotavento [sota'βento] NM (*Naut*) lee, leeward

soterrar [sote'rrar] /**1j**/ VT to bury; (*esconder*) to hide away

sotierre *etc* [so'tjerre] VB *ver* **soterrar**

soviético, -a [so'βjetiko, a] ADJ, NM/F Soviet; **los soviéticos** the Soviets, the Russians

soy [soi] VB *ver* **ser**

soya ['soja] NF (*Am*) soya (bean)

SP ABR (*Auto*) = **servicio público**

SPM NM ABR (= *síndrome premenstrual*) PMS

spooling [es'pulin] NM (*Inform*) spooling

sport [es'por(t)] NM sport

spot [es'pot] (*pl* **spots**) NM (*publicitario*) ad

spyware [es'paiwer] NM spyware

squash [es'kwas] NM (*Deporte*) squash

Sr. ABR (= *Señor*) Mr

Sra. ABR (= *Señora*) Mrs

Sras. ABR (= *Señoras*) Mrs

S.R.C. ABR (= *se ruega contestación*) R.S.V.P.

Sres., Srs. ABR (= *Señores*) Messrs

Sri Lanka [sri'lanka] NM Sri Lanka

Srta. ABR = **señorita**

SS ABR = **Santos**; (= *Santas*) SS

ss. ABR (= *siguientes*) foll

S.S. ABR (*Rel*: = *Su Santidad*) H.H.; = **Seguridad Social**

SSE ABR (= *sursudeste*) SSE

SS.MM. ABR (= *Sus Majestades*) Their Royal Highnesses

SSO ABR (= *sursudoeste*) SSW

Sta. ABR (= *Santa*) St; (= *Señorita*) Miss

stand [es'tan] (*pl* **stands** [es'tan(s)]) NM (*Com*) stand

stárter [es'tarter] NM (*Auto*) self-starter, starting motor

statu quo [es'tatu'kuo], **status quo** [es'tatus'kuo] NM status quo

status ['status, es'tatus] NM INV status

Sto. ABR (= *Santo*) St

stop [es'top] (*pl* **stops** [es'top(s)]) NM (*Auto*) stop sign

su [su] PRON (*de él*) his; (*de ella*) her; (*de una cosa*) its; (*de ellos, ellas*) their; (*de usted, ustedes*) your

suave ['swaβe] ADJ gentle; (*superficie*) smooth; (*trabajo*) easy; (*música, voz*) soft, sweet; (*clima, sabor*) mild

suavice *etc* [swa'βiθe] VB *ver* **suavizar**

suavidad [swaβi'ðað] NF gentleness; (*de superficie*) smoothness; (*de música*) softness, sweetness

suavizante [swaβi'θante] NM (*de ropa*) softener; (*del pelo*) conditioner

suavizar [swaβi'θar] /**1f**/ VT to soften; (*quitar la aspereza*) to smooth (out); (*pendiente*) to ease; (*colores*) to tone down; (*carácter*) to mellow; (*dureza*) to temper

subalimentado, -a [suβalimen'taðo, a] ADJ undernourished

subalterno, -a [suβal'terno, a] ADJ (*importancia*) secondary; (*personal*) minor, auxiliary ▶ NM subordinate

subarrendar [suβarren'dar] /**1j**/ VT (*Com*) to lease back

subarriendo [suβa'rrjendo] NM (*Com*) leaseback

subasta [su'βasta] NF auction; **poner en** o **sacar a pública ~** to put up for public auction; **~ a la rebaja** Dutch auction

subastador, a [suβasta'ðor, a] NM/F auctioneer

subastar [suβas'tar] /**1a**/ VT to auction (off)

subcampeón, -ona [suβkampe'on, ona] NM/F runner-up

subconsciente [suβkons'θjente] ADJ subconscious

subcontratar [suβkontra'tar] /**1a**/ VT (*Com*) to subcontract

subcontrato [suβkon'trato] NM (*Com*) subcontract

subdesarrollado, -a [suβðesarro'ʎaðo, a] ADJ underdeveloped

subdesarrollo [suβðesa'rroʎo] NM underdevelopment

subdirector, a [suβðirek'tor, a] NM/F assistant o deputy manager

subdirectorio [suβðirek'torjo] NM (*Inform*) subdirectory

súbdito, -a ['suβðito, a] NM/F subject

subdividir [suβðiβi'ðir] /**3a**/ VT to subdivide

subempleo [suβem'pleo] NM underemployment

subestimar [suβesti'mar] /**1a**/ VT to underestimate, underrate

subido, -a [su'βiðo, a] ADJ (*color*) bright, strong; (*precio*) high ▶ NF (*de montaña etc*) ascent, climb; (*de precio*) rise, increase; (*pendiente*) slope, hill

subíndice [su'βindiθe] NM (*Inform, Tip*) subscript

subir [su'βir] /**3a**/ VT (*objeto*) to raise, lift up; (*cuesta, calle*) to go up; (*colina, montaña*) to climb; (*precio*) to raise, put up; (*empleado etc*) to promote ▶ VI to go/come up; (*a un coche*) to get in; (*a un autobús, tren*) to get on; (*precio*) to rise, go up; (*en el empleo*) to be promoted; (*río, marea*) to rise; **subirse** VR to get up, climb; **subirse a un coche** to get in(to) a car

súbito, -a ['suβito, a] ADJ (*repentino*) sudden; (*imprevisto*) unexpected

subjetivo, -a [suβxe'tiβo, a] ADJ subjective
subjuntivo [suβxun'tiβo] NM subjunctive (mood)
sublevación [suβleβa'θjon] NF revolt, rising
sublevar [suβle'βar] /1a/ VT to rouse to revolt; **sublevarse** VR to revolt, rise
sublimar [suβli'mar] /1a/ VT (persona) to exalt; (deseos etc) to sublimate
sublime [su'βlime] ADJ sublime
subliminal [suβlimi'nal] ADJ subliminal
submarinismo [suβmari'nismo] NM scuba diving
submarinista [suβmari'nista] NMF underwater explorer
submarino, -a [suβma'rino, a] ADJ underwater ▶ NM submarine
subnormal [suβnor'mal] ADJ subnormal ▶ NMF subnormal person
suboficial [suβofi'θjal] NM non-commissioned officer
subordinado, -a [suβorði'naðo, a] ADJ, NM/F subordinate
subproducto [suβpro'ðukto] NM by-product
subrayado [suβra'jaðo] NM underlining
subrayar [suβra'jar] /1a/ VT to underline; (recalcar) to underline, emphasize
subrepticio, -a [suβrep'tiθjo, a] ADJ surreptitious
subrutina [suβru'tina] NF (Inform) subroutine
subsanar [suβsa'nar] /1a/ VT (reparar) to rectify; (perdonar) to excuse; (sobreponerse a) to overcome
subscribir [suβskri'βir] /3a/ VT = **suscribir**
subscrito [suβs'krito] PP de **subscribir**
subsecretario, -a [suβsekre'tarjo, a] NM/F undersecretary, assistant secretary
subsidiariedad [suβsiðjarie'ðað] NF (Pol) subsidiarity
subsidiario, -a [suβsi'ðjarjo, a] ADJ subsidiary
subsidio [suβ'siðjo] NM (ayuda) aid, financial help; (subvención) subsidy, grant; (de enfermedad, paro etc) benefit, allowance
subsistencia [suβsis'tenθja] NF subsistence
subsistir [suβsis'tir] /3a/ VI to subsist; (vivir) to live; (sobrevivir) to survive, endure
subsuelo [suβ'swelo] NM subsoil
subte ['suβte] NM (RPL) underground (Brit), subway (US)
subterfugio [suβter'fuxjo] NM subterfuge
subterráneo, -a [suβte'rraneo, a] ADJ underground, subterranean ▶ NM underpass, underground passage; (Am) underground railway, subway (US)
subtitulado, -a [suβtitu'laðo, a] ADJ subtitled
subtítulo [suβ'titulo] NM subtitle, subheading
suburbano, -a [suβur'βano, a] ADJ suburban

suburbio [su'βurβjo] NM (barrio) slum quarter; (afueras) suburbs pl
subvención [suββen'θjon] NF subsidy, subvention, grant; ~ **estatal** state subsidy o support; ~ **para la inversión** (Com) investment grant
subvencionar [suββenθjo'nar] /1a/ VT to subsidize
subversión [suββer'sjon] NF subversion
subversivo, -a [suββer'siβo, a] ADJ subversive
subyacente [suβja'θente] ADJ underlying
subyugar [suβju'ɣar] /1h/ VT (país) to subjugate, subdue; (enemigo) to overpower; (voluntad) to dominate
subyugue etc [sub'juɣe] VB ver **subyugar**
succión [suk'θjon] NF suction
succionar [sukθjo'nar] /1a/ VT (sorber) to suck; (Tec) to absorb, soak up
sucedáneo, -a [suθe'ðaneo, a] ADJ substitute ▶ NM substitute (food)
suceder [suθe'ðer] /2a/ VI to happen; ~ a (seguir) to succeed, follow; **lo que sucede es que ...** the fact is that ...; ~ **al trono** to succeed to the throne
sucesión [suθe'sjon] NF succession; (serie) sequence, series; (hijos) issue, offspring
sucesivamente [suθesiβa'mente] ADV: **y así ~** and so on
sucesivo, -a [suθe'siβo, a] ADJ successive, following; **en lo ~** in future, from now on
suceso [su'θeso] NM (hecho) event, happening; (incidente) incident
sucesor, a [suθe'sor, a] NM/F successor; (heredero) heir/heiress
suciedad [suθje'ðað] NF (estado) dirtiness; (mugre) dirt, filth
sucinto, -a [su'θinto, a] ADJ (conciso) succinct, concise
sucio, -a [su'θjo, a] ADJ dirty; (mugriento) grimy; (manchado) grubby; (borroso) smudged; (conciencia) bad; (conducta) vile; (táctica) dirty, unfair
Sucre ['sukre] N Sucre
sucre ['sukre] NM Ecuadorean monetary unit
suculento, -a [suku'lento, a] ADJ (sabroso) tasty; (jugoso) succulent
sucumbir [sukum'bir] /3a/ VI to succumb
sucursal [sukur'sal] NF branch (office); (filial) subsidiary
sudadera [suða'ðera] NF sweatshirt
Sudáfrica [su'ðafrika] NF South Africa
sudafricano, -a [suðafri'kano, a] ADJ, NM/F South African
Sudamérica [suða'merika] NF South America
sudamericano, -a [suðameri'kano, a] ADJ, NM/F South American
sudanés, -esa [suða'nes, esa] ADJ, NM/F Sudanese

S

sudar [su'ðar] /**1a**/ VT, VI to sweat; (*Bot*) to ooze, give out o off
sudeste [su'ðeste] ADJ south-east(ern); (*rumbo, viento*) south-easterly ▸ NM south-east; (*viento*) south-east wind
sudoeste [suðo'este] ADJ south-west(ern); (*rumbo, viento*) south-westerly ▸ NM south-west; (*viento*) south-west wind
sudoku [su'doku] NM sudoku
sudor [su'ðor] NM sweat
sudoroso, -a [suðo'roso, a] ADJ sweaty, sweating
Suecia ['sweθja] NF Sweden
sueco, -a ['sweko, a] ADJ Swedish ▸ NM/F Swede ▸ NM (*Ling*) Swedish; **hacerse el ~** to pretend not to hear o understand
suegro, -a ['sweɣro, a] NM/F father-/mother-in-law; **los suegros** one's in-laws
suela ['swela] NF (*de zapato, tb pescado*) sole
sueldo ['sweldo] VB ver **soldar** ▸ NM pay, wage(s) (*pl*)
suelo ['swelo] VB ver **soler** ▸ NM (*tierra*) ground; (*de casa*) floor
suelto, -a ['swelto, a] VB ver **soltar** ▸ ADJ loose; (*libre*) free; (*separado*) detached; (*ágil*) quick, agile; (*fue corre*) fluent, flowing ▸ NM (loose) change, small change; **está muy ~ en inglés** he is very good at o fluent in English
suene etc ['swene] VB ver **sonar**
sueñito [swe'ɲito] NM (*Am*) nap
sueño ['sweɲo] VB ver **soñar** ▸ NM sleep; (*somnolencia*) sleepiness, drowsiness; (*lo soñado, fig*) dream; **~ pesado o profundo** deep o heavy sleep; **tener ~** to be sleepy
suero ['swero] NM (*Med*) serum; (*de leche*) whey
suerte ['swerte] NF (*fortuna*) luck; (*azar*) chance; (*destino*) fate, destiny; (*condición*) lot; (*género*) sort, kind; **lo echaron a suertes** they drew lots o tossed up for it; **tener ~** to be lucky; **de otra ~** otherwise, if not; **de ~ que** so that, in such a way that
suéter ['sweter] (*pl* **suéters**) NM sweater
suficiencia [sufi'θjenθja] NF (*cabida*) sufficiency; (*idoneidad*) suitability; (*aptitud*) adequacy
suficiente [sufi'θjente] ADJ enough, sufficient ▸ NM (*Escol*) pass
sufijo [su'fixo] NM suffix
sufragar [sufra'ɣar] /**1h**/ VT (*ayudar*) to help; (*gastos*) to meet; (*proyecto*) to pay for
sufragio [su'fraxjo] NM (*voto*) vote; (*derecho de voto*) suffrage
sufrague etc [su'fraɣe] VB ver **sufragar**
sufrido, -a [su'friðo, a] ADJ (*de carácter fuerte*) tough; (*paciente*) long-suffering, patient; (*tela*) hard-wearing; (*color*) that does not show the dirt; (*marido*) complaisant
sufrimiento [sufri'mjento] NM suffering

sufrir [su'frir] /**3a**/ VT (*padecer*) to suffer; (*soportar*) to bear, stand, put up with; (*apoyar*) to hold up, support ▸ VI to suffer
sugerencia [suxe'renθja] NF suggestion
sugerir [suxe'rir] /**3i**/ VT to suggest; (*sutilmente*) to hint; (*idea: incitar*) to prompt
sugestión [suxes'tjon] NF suggestion; (*sutil*) hint; (*poder*) hypnotic power
sugestionar [suxestjo'nar] /**1a**/ VT to influence
sugestivo, -a [suxes'tiβo, a] ADJ stimulating; (*atractivo*) attractive; (*fascinante*) fascinating
sugiera etc [su'xjera], **sugiriendo** etc [suxi'rjendo] VB ver **sugerir**
suicida [sui'θiða] ADJ suicidal ▸ NMF suicidal person; (*muerto*) suicide, person who has committed suicide
suicidarse [suiθi'ðarse] /**1a**/ VR to commit suicide, kill o.s.
suicidio [sui'θiðjo] NM suicide
Suiza ['swiθa] NF Switzerland
suizo, -a ['swiθo, a] ADJ, NM/F Swiss ▸ NM sugared bun
sujeción [suxe'θjon] NF subjection
sujetador [suxeta'ðor] NM fastener, clip; (*prenda femenina*) bra, brassiere
sujetapapeles [suxetapa'peles] NM INV paper clip
sujetar [suxe'tar] /**1a**/ VT (*fijar*) to fasten; (*detener*) to hold down; (*fig*) to subject, subjugate; (*pelo etc*) to keep o hold in place; (*papeles*) to fasten together; **sujetarse** VR to subject o.s.
sujeto, -a [su'xeto, a] ADJ fastened, secure ▸ NM subject; (*individuo*) individual; (*fam: tipo*) fellow, character, type, guy (*US*); **~ a** subject to
sulfurar [sulfu'rar] /**1a**/ VT (*Tec*) to sulphurate; (*sacar de quicio*) to annoy; **sulfurarse** VR (*enojarse*) to get riled, see red, blow up
sulfuro [sul'furo] NM sulphide
suma ['suma] NF (*cantidad*) total, sum; (*de dinero*) sum; (*acto*) adding (up), addition; **en ~** in short; **~ y sigue** (*Com*) carry forward
sumador [suma'ðor] NM (*Inform*) adder
sumamente [suma'mente] ADV extremely, exceedingly
sumar [su'mar] /**1a**/ VT to add (up); (*reunir*) to collect, gather ▸ VI to add up
sumario, -a [su'marjo, a] ADJ brief, concise ▸ NM summary
sumergir [sumer'xir] /**3c**/ VT to submerge; (*hundir*) to sink; (*bañar*) to immerse, dip; **sumergirse** VR (*hundirse*) to sink beneath the surface
sumerja etc [su'merxa] VB ver **sumergir**
sumidero [sumi'ðero] NM drain, sewer; (*Tec*) sump

suministrador, a [suministra'ðor, a] NM/F
supplier

suministrar [suminis'trar] /**1a**/ VT to supply,
provide

suministro [sumi'nistro] NM supply; (*acto*)
supplying, providing

sumir [su'mir] /**3a**/ VT to sink, submerge; (*fig*)
to plunge; **sumirse** VR (*objeto*) to sink;
sumirse en el estudio to become absorbed
in one's studies

sumisión [sumi'sjon] NF (*acto*) submission;
(*calidad*) submissiveness, docility

sumiso, -a [su'miso, a] ADJ submissive, docile

súmmum ['sumum] NM INV (*fig*) height

sumo, -a ['sumo, a] ADJ great, extreme;
(*mayor*) highest, supreme ▶ NM sumo
(wrestling); **a lo ~** at most

suntuoso, -a [sun'twoso, a] ADJ sumptuous,
magnificent; (*lujoso*) lavish

sup. ABR (= *superior*) sup

supe *etc* ['supe] VB *ver* **saber**

supeditar [supeði'tar] /**1a**/ VT to subordinate;
(*sojuzgar*) to subdue; (*oprimir*) to oppress;
supeditarse VR: **supeditarse a** to subject o.s.
to

súper ['super] ADJ (*fam*) super, great ▶ NF
(*gasolina*) four-star (petrol)

super... [super] PREF super..., over...

superable [supe'raβle] ADJ (*dificultad*)
surmountable; (*tarea*) that can be performed

superación [supera'θjon] NF (*tb*: **superación
personal**) self-improvement

superar [supe'rar] /**1a**/ VT (*sobreponerse a*) to
overcome; (*rebasar*) to surpass, do better
than; (*pasar*) to go beyond; (*marca, récord*) to
break; (*etapa: dejar atrás*) to get past;
superarse VR to excel o.s.

superávit [supe'raβit] (*pl* **superávits**) NM
surplus

superbueno, a [super'bweno, a] ADJ great,
fantastic

superchería [supertʃe'ria] NF fraud, trick,
swindle

superficial [superfi'θjal] ADJ superficial;
(*medida*) surface *cpd*

superficie [super'fiθje] NF surface; (*área*)
area; **grandes superficies** (*Com*) superstores

superfluo, -a [su'perflwo, a] ADJ superfluous

superíndice [supe'rindiθe] NM (*Inform, Tip*)
superscript

superintendente [superinten'dente] NMF
supervisor, superintendent

superior [supe'rjor] ADJ (*piso, clase*) upper;
(*temperatura, número, nivel*) higher; (*mejor:
calidad, producto*) superior, better ▶ NMF
superior

superiora [supe'rjora] NF (*Rel*) mother
superior

superioridad [superjori'ðað] NF superiority

superlativo, -a [superla'tiβo, a] ADJ, NM
superlative

supermercado [supermer'kaðo] NM
supermarket

superpoblación [superpoβla'θjon] NF
overpopulation; (*congestionamiento*)
overcrowding

superponer [superpo'ner] /**2q**/ VT to
superimpose; (*Inform*) to overstrike

superposición [superposi'θjon] NF (*en
impresora*) overstrike

superpotencia [superpo'tenθja] NF
superpower, great power

superproducción [superproðuk'θjon] NF
overproduction

supersónico, -a [super'soniko, a] ADJ
supersonic

superstición [supersti'θjon] NF superstition

supersticioso, -a [supersti'θjoso, a] ADJ
superstitious

supervisar [superβi'sar] /**1a**/ VT to supervise;
(*Com*) to superintend

supervisor, a [superβi'sor, a] NM/F
supervisor

supervivencia [superβi'βenθja] NF survival

superviviente [superβi'βjente] ADJ
surviving ▶ NMF survivor

supiera *etc* VB *ver* **saber**

suplantar [suplan'tar] /**1a**/ VT (*persona*) to
supplant; (*hacerse pasar por otro*) to take the
place of

suplementario, -a [suplemen'tarjo, a] ADJ
supplementary

suplemento [suple'mento] NM supplement

suplencia [su'plenθja] NF substitution,
replacement; (*etapa*) period during which
one deputizes *etc*

suplente [su'plente] ADJ substitute;
(*disponible*) reserve ▶ NMF substitute

supletorio, -a [suple'torjo, a] ADJ
supplementary; (*adicional*) extra ▶ NM
supplement; **mesa supletoria** spare table;
teléfono ~ extension

súplica ['suplika] NF request; (*Rel*)
supplication; (*Jur: instancia*) petition;
súplicas NFPL entreaties

suplicar [supli'kar] /**1g**/ VT (*cosa*) to beg (for),
plead for; (*persona*) to beg, plead with; (*Jur*)
to appeal to, petition

suplicio [su'pliθjo] NM torture; (*tormento*)
torment; (*emoción*) anguish; (*experiencia
penosa*) ordeal

suplique *etc* [su'plike] VB *ver* **suplicar**

suplir [su'plir] /**3a**/ VT (*compensar*) to make
good, make up for; (*reemplazar*) to replace,
substitute ▶ VI: **~ a** to take the place of,
substitute for

supo *etc* ['supo] VB *ver* **saber**

supondré *etc* [supon'dre] VB *ver* **suponer**

suponer [supo'ner] /**2q**/ VT to suppose; (*significar*) to mean; (*acarrear*) to involve ▶ VI to count, have authority; **era de ~ que ...** it was to be expected that ...

suponga *etc* [su'ponga] VB *ver* **suponer**

suposición [suposi'θjon] NF supposition

supositorio [suposi'torjo] NM suppository

supremacía [suprema'θia] NF supremacy

supremo, -a [su'premo, a] ADJ supreme

supresión [supre'sjon] NF suppression; (*de derecho*) abolition; (*de dificultad*) removal; (*de palabra etc*) deletion; (*de restricción*) cancellation, lifting

suprimir [supri'mir] /**3a**/ VT to suppress; (*derecho, costumbre*) to abolish; (*dificultad*) to remove; (*palabra etc, Inform*) to delete; (*restricción*) to cancel, lift

supuestamente [supwesta'mente] ADV supposedly

supuesto, -a [su'pwesto, a] PP *de* **suponer** ▶ ADJ (*hipotético*) supposed; (*falso*) false ▶ NM assumption, hypothesis ▶ CONJ: **~ que** since; **dar por ~ algo** to take sth for granted; **por ~** of course

supurar [supu'rar] /**1a**/ VI to fester, suppurate

supuse *etc* [su'puse] VB *ver* **suponer**

sur [sur] ADJ southern; (*rumbo*) southerly ▶ NM south; (*viento*) south wind

Suráfrica *etc* [su'rafrika] = **Sudáfrica** *etc*

Suramérica *etc* [sura'merika] = **Sudamérica** *etc*

suramericano, -a [surameri'kano, a] ADJ South American ▶ NM/F South American

surcar [sur'kar] /**1g**/ VT to plough; (*superficie*) to cut, score

surco ['surko] NM (*en metal, disco*) groove; (*Agr*) furrow

surcoreano, -a [surkore'ano, a] ADJ, NM/F South Korean

sureño, -a [su'reno, a] ADJ southern ▶ NM/F southerner

sureste [su'reste] = **sudeste**

surf [surf] NM surfing

surfear [surfe'ar] /**1a**/ VT: **~ por Internet** to surf the internet

surgir [sur'xir] /**3c**/ VI to arise, emerge; (*dificultad*) to come up, crop up

surja *etc* ['surxa] VB *ver* **surgir**

suroeste [suro'este] NM south-west

surque *etc* ['surke] VB *ver* **surcar**

surrealismo [surrea'lismo] NM surrealism

surrealista [surrea'lista] ADJ, NMF surrealist

surtido, -a [sur'tiðo, a] ADJ mixed, assorted ▶ NM (*selección*) selection, assortment; (*abastecimiento*) supply, stock

surtidor [surti'ðor] NM (*chorro*) jet, spout; (*fuente*) fountain; **~ de gasolina** petrol (BRIT) *o* gas (US) pump

surtir [sur'tir] /**3a**/ VT to supply, provide; (*efecto*) to have, produce ▶ VI to spout, spurt;

surtirse VR: **surtirse de** to provide o.s. with

susceptible [susθep'tiβle] ADJ susceptible; (*sensible*) sensitive; **~ de** capable of

suscitar [susθi'tar] /**1a**/ VT to cause, provoke; (*discusión*) to start; (*duda, problema*) to raise; (*interés, sospechas*) to arouse

suscribir [suskri'βir] /**3a**/ VT (*firmar*) to sign; (*respaldar*) to subscribe to, endorse; (*Com: acciones*) to take out an option on; **suscribirse** VR to subscribe; **~ a algn a una revista** to take out a subscription to a journal for sb

suscripción [suskrip'θjon] NF subscription

suscrito, -a [sus'krito, a] PP *de* **suscribir** ▶ ADJ: **~ en exceso** oversubscribed

sushi ['suʃi] NM sushi

susodicho, -a [suso'ditʃo, a] ADJ above-mentioned

suspender [suspen'der] /**2a**/ VT (*objeto*) to hang (up), suspend; (*trabajo*) to stop, suspend; (*Escol*) to fail; (*interrumpir*) to adjourn; (*atrasar*) to postpone

suspense [sus'pense] NM suspense; **película/novela de ~** thriller

suspensión [suspen'sjon] NF suspension; (*fig*) stoppage, suspension; (*Jur*) stay; **~ de fuego** *o* **de hostilidades** ceasefire, cessation of hostilities; **~ de pagos** suspension of payments

suspensivo, -a [suspen'siβo, a] ADJ: **puntos suspensivos** dots, suspension points

suspenso, -a [sus'penso, a] ADJ hanging, suspended; (*Escol*) failed ▶ NM (*Escol*) fail(ure); **quedar** *o* **estar en ~** to be pending; **película** *o* **novela de ~** (AM) thriller

suspicacia [suspi'kaθja] NF suspicion, mistrust

suspicaz [suspi'kaθ] ADJ suspicious, distrustful

suspirar [suspi'rar] /**1a**/ VI to sigh

suspiro [sus'piro] NM sigh

sustancia [sus'tanθja] NF substance; **~ gris** (*Anat*) grey matter; **sin ~** lacking in substance, shallow

sustancial [sustan'θjal] ADJ substantial

sustancioso, -a [sustan'θjoso, a] ADJ substantial; (*discurso*) solid

sustantivo, -a [sustan'tiβo, a] ADJ substantive; (*Ling*) substantival, noun *cpd* ▶ NM noun, substantive

sustentar [susten'tar] /**1a**/ VT (*alimentar*) to sustain, nourish; (*objeto*) to hold up, support; (*idea, teoría*) to maintain, uphold; (*fig*) to sustain, keep going

sustento [sus'tento] NM support; (*alimento*) sustenance, food

sustituir [sustitu'ir] /**3g**/ VT to substitute, replace

sustituto, -a [susti'tuto, a] NM/F substitute, replacement

sustituyendo *etc* [sustitu'jendo] VB *ver*
sustituir

susto ['susto] NM fright, scare; **dar un ~ a
algn** to give sb a fright; **darse** *o* **pegarse un
~** *(fam)* to get a fright

sustraer [sustra'er] /2p/ VT to remove, take
away; *(Mat)* to subtract

sustraiga *etc* [sus'traiɣa], **sustraje** *etc*
[sus'traxe] VB *ver* **sustraer**

sustrato [sus'trato] NM substratum

sustrayendo *etc* [sustra'jendo] VB *ver* **sustraer**

susurrar [susu'rrar] /1a/ VI to whisper

susurro [su'surro] NM whisper

sutil [su'til] ADJ *(aroma)* subtle; *(tenue)* thin;
(hilo, hebra) fine; *(olor)* delicate; *(brisa)* gentle;
(diferencia) fine, subtle; *(inteligencia)* sharp,
keen

sutileza [suti'leθa] NF subtlety;
(delgadez) thinness; *(delicadeza)* delicacy;

(agudeza) keenness

sutura [su'tura] NF suture

suturar [sutu'rar] /1a/ VT to suture; *(juntar
con puntos)* to stitch

suyo, -a ['sujo, a] ADJ *(con artículo o después del
verbo* ser: *de él)* his; *(: de ella)* hers; *(: de ellos,
ellas)* theirs; *(: de usted, ustedes)* yours; *(después
de un nombre: de él)* of his; *(: de ella)* of hers; *(: de
ellos, ellas)* of theirs; *(: de usted, ustedes)* of yours;
lo ~ (what is) his; *(su parte)* his share, what he
deserves; **los suyos** *(su familia)* one's family *o*
relations; *(sus partidarios)* one's own people *o*
supporters; **~ afectísimo** *(en carta)* yours
faithfully *o* sincerely; **de ~** in itself; **eso es
muy ~** that's just like him; **hacer de las
suyas** to get up to one's old tricks; **ir a la
suya, ir a lo ~** to go one's own way; **salirse
con la suya** to get one's way; **un amigo ~**
a friend of his (*o* hers *o* theirs *o* yours)

S

Tt

T, t [te] NF (letra) T, t; **T de Tarragona** T for Tommy

t ABR = **tonelada**

T. ABR (= Teléfon; Telégrafo) tel.; (Com) = **tarifa; tasa**

t. ABR (= tomo(s)) vol(s)

Tabacalera [taβaka'lera] NF former Spanish state tobacco monopoly

tabaco [ta'βako] NM tobacco; (fam) cigarettes pl

tábano ['taβano] NM horsefly

tabaquería [tabake'ria] NF tobacconist's (BRIT), cigar store (US)

tabarra [ta'βarra] NF (fam) nuisance; **dar la ~** to be a pain in the neck

taberna [ta'βerna] NF bar

tabernero, -a [taβer'nero, a] NM/F (encargado) publican; (camarero) barman/barmaid

tabique [ta'βike] NM (pared) thin wall; (para dividir) partition

tabla ['taβla] NF (de madera) plank; (estante) shelf; (de anuncios) board; (lista, catálogo) list; (de vestido) pleat; (Arte) panel; **tablas** NFPL (Taur, Teat) boards; **estar o quedar en tablas** to draw; **~ de consulta** (Inform) lookup table

tablado [ta'βlaðo] NM (plataforma) platform; (suelo) plank floor; (Teat) stage

tablao [ta'βlao] NM (tb: **tablao flamenco**) flamenco show

tablero [ta'βlero] NM (de madera) plank, board; (pizarra) blackboard; (de ajedrez, damas) board; (Auto) dashboard; **~ de gráficos** (Inform) graph pad; **~ de mandos** (Am Auto) dashboard

tableta [ta'βleta] NF (Med) tablet; (de chocolate) bar; (Inform) tablet (computer)

tablilla [ta'βliʎa] NF small board; (Med) splint

tablón [ta'βlon] NM (de suelo) plank; (de techo) beam; (de anuncios) notice board

tabú [ta'βu] NM taboo

tabulación [taβula'θjon] NF (Inform) tab(bing)

tabulador [taβula'ðor] NM (Inform, Tip) tab

tabuladora [taβula'ðora] NF: **~ eléctrica** electric accounting machine

tabular [taβu'lar] /**1a**/ VT to tabulate; (Inform) to tab

taburete [taβu'rete] NM stool

tacaño, -a [ta'kaɲo, a] ADJ (avaro) mean; (astuto) crafty

tacha ['tatʃa] NF (defecto) flaw, defect; (Tec) stud; **poner ~ a** to find fault with; **sin ~** flawless

tachar [ta'tʃar] /**1a**/ VT (borrar) to cross out; (corregir) to correct; (criticar) to criticize; **~ de** to accuse of

tacho ['tatʃo] NM (Am) bucket, pail; **~ de la basura** rubbish bin (BRIT), trash can (US)

tachón [ta'tʃon] NM erasure; (tachadura) crossing-out; (Tec) ornamental stud; (Costura) trimming

tachuela [ta'tʃwela] NF (clavo) tack

tácito, -a ['taθito, a] ADJ tacit; (acuerdo) unspoken; (Ling) understood; (ley) unwritten

taciturno, -a [taθi'turno, a] ADJ (callado) silent; (malhumorado) sullen

taco ['tako] NM (Billar) cue; (libro de billetes) book; (manojo de billetes) wad; (Am) heel; (tarugo) peg; (fam: bocado) snack; (: palabrota) swear word; (: trago de vino) swig; (México) filled tortilla; **armarse o hacerse un ~** to get into a mess

tacógrafo [ta'koɣrafo] NM (Com) tachograph

tacón [ta'kon] NM heel; **de ~ alto** high-heeled

taconear [takone'ar] /**1a**/ VI (dar golpecitos) to tap with one's heels; (Mil etc) to click one's heels

taconeo [tako'neo] NM (heel) tapping o clicking

táctico, -a ['taktiko, a] ADJ tactical ▸ NF tactics pl

tacto ['takto] NM touch; (acción) touching; (fig) tact

TAE NF ABR (= tasa anual equivalente) APR

tafetán [tafe'tan] NM taffeta; **tafetanes** NMPL (*fam*) frills; **~ adhesivo** o **inglés** sticking plaster

tafilete [tafi'lete] NM morocco leather

tahona [ta'ona] NF (*panadería*) bakery; (*molino*) flour mill

tahúr [ta'ur] NM gambler; (*pey*) cheat

tailandés, -esa [tailan'des, esa] ADJ, NM/F Thai ▶ NM (*Ling*) Thai

Tailandia [tai'landja] NF Thailand

taimado, -a [tai'maðo, a] ADJ (*astuto*) sly; (*resentido*) sullen

taita ['taita] NM dad, daddy

tajada [ta'xaða] NF slice; (*fam*) rake-off; **sacar ~** to get one's share

tajante [ta'xante] ADJ sharp; (*negativa*) emphatic; **es una persona ~** he's an emphatic person

tajar [ta'xar] /**1a**/ VT to cut, slice

Tajo ['taxo] NM Tagus

tajo ['taxo] NM (*corte*) cut; (*filo*) cutting edge; (*Geo*) cleft

tal [tal] ADJ such; **un ~ García** a man called García; **~ vez** perhaps ▶ PRON (*persona*) someone, such a one; (*cosa*) something, such a thing; **~ como** such as; **~ para cual** tit for tat; (*dos iguales*) two of a kind; **hablábamos de que si ~ si cual** we were talking about this, that and the other ▶ ADV: **~ como** (*igual*) just as; **~ cual** (*como es*) just as it is; **~ el padre, cual el hijo** like father, like son; **¿qué ~?** how are things?; **¿qué ~ te gusta?** how do you like it? ▶ CONJ: **con ~ (de) que** provided that

tala ['tala] NF (*de árboles*) tree felling

taladradora [talaðra'ðora] NF drill; **~ neumática** pneumatic drill

taladrar [tala'ðrar] /**1a**/ VT to drill; (*fig: ruido*) to pierce

taladro [ta'laðro] NM (*gen*) drill; (*hoyo*) drill hole; **~ neumático** pneumatic drill

talante [ta'lante] NM (*humor*) mood; (*voluntad*) will, willingness

talar [ta'lar] /**1a**/ VT to fell, cut down; (*fig*) to devastate

talco ['talko] NM (*polvos*) talcum powder; (*Minería*) talc

talega [ta'leɣa] NF sack

talego [ta'leɣo] NM sack; **tener ~** (*fam*) to have money

talento [ta'lento] NM talent; (*capacidad*) ability; (*don*) gift

Talgo ['talɣo] NM ABR (= *tren articulado ligero Goicoechea Oriol*) high-speed train

talidomida [taliðo'miða] NM thalidomide

talismán [talis'man] NM talisman

talla ['taʎa] NF (*estatura, fig, Med*) height, stature; (*de ropa*) size, fitting; (*palo*) measuring rod; (*Arte: de madera*) carving;

(: *de piedra*) sculpture

tallado, -a [ta'ʎaðo, a] ADJ carved ▶ NM (*de madera*) carving; (*de piedra*) sculpture

tallar [ta'ʎar] /**1a**/ VT (*trabajar*) to work, carve; (*grabar*) to engrave; (*medir*) to measure; (*repartir*) to deal ▶ VI to deal

tallarín [taʎa'rin] NM noodle

talle ['taʎe] NM (*Anat*) waist; (*medida*) size; (*física*) build; (: *de mujer*) figure; (*fig*) appearance; **de ~ esbelto** with a slim figure

taller [ta'ʎer] NM (*Tec*) workshop; (*fábrica*) factory; (*Auto*) garage; (*de artista*) studio

tallo ['taʎo] NM (*de planta*) stem; (*de hierba*) blade; (*brote*) shoot; (*col*) cabbage; (*Culin*) candied peel

talmente [tal'mente] ADV (*de esta forma*) in such a way; (*hasta tal punto*) to such an extent; (*exactamente*) exactly

talón [ta'lon] NM (*gen*) heel; (*Com*) counterfoil; (*cheque*) cheque (BRIT), check (US); (*Tec*) rim; **~ de Aquiles** Achilles heel

talonario [talo'narjo] NM (*de cheques*) chequebook (BRIT), checkbook (US); (*de billetes*) book of tickets; (*de recibos*) receipt book

tamaño, -a [ta'maɲo, a] ADJ (*tan grande*) such a big; (*tan pequeño*) such a small ▶ NM size; **de ~ natural** full-size; **¿de qué ~ es?** what size is it?

tamarindo [tama'rindo] NM tamarind

tambaleante [tambale'ante] ADJ (*persona*) staggering; (*mueble*) wobbly; (*vehículo*) swaying

tambalearse [tambale'arse] /**1a**/ VR (*persona*) to stagger; (*mueble*) to wobble; (*vehículo*) to sway

también [tam'bjen] ADV (*igualmente*) also, too, as well; (*además*) besides; **estoy cansado — yo ~** I'm tired — so am I o me too

tambor [tam'bor] NM drum; (*Anat*) eardrum; **~ del freno** brake drum; **~ magnético** (*Inform*) magnetic drum

tamboril [tambo'ril] NM small drum

tamborilear [tamborile'ar] /**1a**/ VI (*Mus*) to drum; (*con los dedos*) to drum with one's fingers

tamborilero [tambori'lero] NM drummer

Támesis ['tamesis] NM Thames

tamice *etc* [ta'miθe] VB *ver* **tamizar**

tamiz [ta'miθ] NM sieve

tamizar [tami'θar] /**1f**/ VT to sieve

tampoco [tam'poko] ADV nor, neither; **yo ~ lo compré** I didn't buy it either

tampón [tam'pon] NM plug; (*Med*) tampon

tan [tan] ADV so; **~ es así que** so much so that; **¡qué cosa ~ rara!** how strange!; **no es una idea ~ buena** it is not such a good idea

tanatorio [tana'torjo] NM (*privado*) funeral home o parlour; (*público*) mortuary

tanda ['tanda] NF (gen) series; (de inyecciones) course; (juego) set; (turno) shift; (grupo) gang

tándem ['tandem] NM tandem; (Pol) duo

tanga ['tanga] NM (bikini) tanga; (ropa interior) tanga briefs

tangente [tan'xente] NF tangent; **salirse por la ~** to go off at a tangent

Tánger ['tanxer] N Tangier

tangerina [tanxe'rina] NF (Am) tangerine

tangerino, -a [tanxe'rino, a] ADJ of o from Tangier ▶ NM/F native o inhabitant of Tangier

tangible [tan'xiβle] ADJ tangible

tango ['tango] NM tango

tanino [ta'nino] NM tannin

tankini [tan'kini] NM tankini

tanque ['tanke] NM (gen) tank; (Auto, Naut) tanker

tanqueta [tan'keta] NF (Mil) small tank, armoured vehicle

tantear [tante'ar] /1a/ VT (calcular) to reckon (up); (medir) to take the measure of; (probar) to test, try out; (tomar la medida: persona) to take the measurements of; (considerar) to weigh up; (persona: opinión) to sound out ▶ VI (Deporte) to score

tanteo [tan'teo] NM (cálculo aproximado) (rough) calculation; (prueba) test, trial; (Deporte) scoring; (adivinanzas) guesswork; **al ~** by trial and error

tantísimo, -a [tan'tisimo, a] ADJ so much; **tantísimos** so many

tanto, -a ['tanto, a] ADJ (cantidad) so much, as much; **tantos** so many, as many; **20 y tantos** 20-odd
▶ ADV (cantidad) so much, as much; (tiempo) so long, as long; **tanto tú como yo** both you and I; **tanto como eso** as much as that; **tanto más ... cuanto que** it's all the more ... because; **tanto mejor/peor** so much the better/the worse; **tanto si viene como si va** whether he comes or whether he goes; **tanto es así que** so much so that; **por tanto, por lo tanto** therefore; **me he vuelto ronco de o con tanto hablar** I have become hoarse with so much talking
▶ CONJ: **con tanto que** provided (that); **en tanto que** while; **hasta tanto (que)** until such time as
▶ NM **1** (punto) point
2 (gol) goal
3 (locuciones): **tanto alzado** agreed price; **tanto por ciento** percentage; **al tanto** up to date; **estar al tanto de los acontecimientos** to be fully abreast of events; **al tanto de que** because of the fact that

▶ PRON: **cada uno paga tanto** each one pays so much; **uno de tantos** one of many; **a tantos de agosto** on such and such a day in August; **entre tanto** meanwhile

tañer [ta'ɲer] /2f/ VT (Mus) to play; (campana) to ring

T/año ABR = **toneladas por año**

TAO NF ABR (= traducción asistida por ordenador) MAT

tapa ['tapa] NF (de caja, olla) lid; (de botella) top; (de libro) cover; (de comida) snack

tapacubos [tapa'kuβos] NM INV hub cap

tapadera [tapa'ðera] NF lid, cover

tapado [ta'paðo] NM (Am: abrigo) coat

tapar [ta'par] /1a/ VT (cubrir) to cover; (envolver) to wrap o cover up; (la vista) to obstruct; (persona, falta) to conceal; (Am) to fill; **taparse** VR to wrap o.s. up

taparrabo [tapa'rraβo] NM loincloth

tapete [ta'pete] NM table cover; **estar sobre el ~** (fig) to be under discussion

tapia ['tapja] NF (garden) wall

tapiar [ta'pjar] /1b/ VT to wall in

tapice etc [ta'piθe] VB ver **tapizar**

tapicería [tapiθe'ria] NF tapestry; (para muebles) upholstery; (tienda) upholsterer's (shop)

tapicero, -a [tapi'θero, a] NM/F (de muebles) upholsterer

tapiz [ta'piθ] NM (alfombra) carpet; (tela tejida) tapestry

tapizar [tapi'θar] /1f/ VT (pared) to wallpaper; (suelo) to carpet; (muebles) to upholster

tapón [ta'pon] NM (de botella) top; (corcho) stopper; (Tec) plug; (Med) tampon; **~ de rosca** o **de tuerca** screw-top

taponar [tapo'nar] /1a/ VT (botella) to cork; (tubería) to block

taponazo [tapo'naθo] NM (de tapón) pop

tapujo [ta'puxo] NM (embozo) muffler; (engaño) deceit; **sin tapujos** honestly

taquigrafía [takiɣra'fia] NF shorthand

taquígrafo, -a [ta'kiɣrafo, a] NM/F shorthand writer, stenographer (US)

taquilla [ta'kiʎa] NF (de estación etc) booking office; (de teatro) box office; (suma recogida) takings pl; (archivador) filing cabinet

taquillero, -a [taki'ʎero, a] ADJ: **función taquillera** box office success ▶ NM/F ticket clerk

taquimecanografía [takimekanoɣra'fia] NF shorthand and typing

taquímetro [ta'kimetro] NM speedometer; (de control) tachymeter

tara ['tara] NF (defecto) defect; (Com) tare

tarado, -a [ta'raðo, a] ADJ (Com) defective, imperfect; (idiota) stupid; (loco) crazy, nuts ▶ NM/F idiot, cretin

tarántula [ta'rantula] NF tarantula

tararear [tarare'ar] /**1a**/ VI to hum

tardanza [tar'ðanθa] NF (demora) delay; (lentitud) slowness

tardar [tar'ðar] /**1a**/ VI (tomar tiempo) to take a long time; (llegar tarde) to be late; (demorar) to delay; **¿tarda mucho el tren?** does the train take long?; **a más ~** at the (very) latest; **~ en hacer algo** to be slow o take a long time to do sth; **no tardes en venir** come soon, come before long

tarde ['tarðe] ADV (hora) late; (fuera de tiempo) too late ▶ NF (de día) afternoon; (de noche) evening; **~ o temprano** sooner or later; **de ~ en ~** from time to time; **¡buenas tardes!** (de día) good afternoon!; (de noche) good evening!; **a o por la ~** in the afternoon; in the evening

tardío, -a [tar'ðio, a] ADJ (retrasado) late; (lento) slow (to arrive)

tardo, -a ['tarðo, a] ADJ (lento) slow; (torpe) dull; **~ de oído** hard of hearing

tarea [ta'rea] NF task; **tareas** NFPL (Escol) homework sg; **~ de ocasión** chore

tarifa [ta'rifa] NF (lista de precios) price list; (Com) tariff; **~ básica** basic rate; **~ completa** all-in cost; **~ a destajo** piece rate; **~ doble** double time

tarima [ta'rima] NF (plataforma) platform

tarjeta [tar'xeta] NF card; **~ postal/de crédito/de Navidad** postcard/credit card/ Christmas card; **~ de circuitos** (Inform) circuit board; **~ cliente** loyalty card; **~ comercial** (Com) calling card; **~ dinero** cash card; **~ gráficos** (Inform) graphics card; **~ monedero** electronic purse o wallet; **~ de embarque** boarding pass; **~ de memoria** memory card; **~ prepago** top-up card; **~ SIM** SIM card

tarot [ta'rot] NM tarot

tarraconense [tarrako'nense] ADJ of o from Tarragona ▶ NMF native o inhabitant of Tarragona

tarro ['tarro] NM jar, pot

tarta ['tarta] NF (pastel) cake; (torta) tart

tartajear [tartaxe'ar] /**1a**/ VI to stammer

tartamudear [tartamuðe'ar] /**1a**/ VI to stutter, stammer

tartamudo, -a [tarta'muðo, a] ADJ stuttering, stammering ▶ NM/F stutterer, stammerer

tartárico, -a [tar'tariko, a] ADJ: **ácido ~** tartaric acid

tártaro, -a ['tartaro, a] ADJ: **salsa tártara** tartar(e) sauce ▶ NM Tartar; (Química) tartar

tarugo, -a [ta'ruɣo, a] ADJ stupid ▶ NM (de madera) lump

tarumba [ta'rumba] ADJ (confuso) confused

tasa ['tasa] NF (precio) (fixed) price, rate; (valoración) valuation; (medida, norma) measure, standard; **~ básica** (Com) basic rate; **~ de cambio** exchange rate; **de ~ cero** (Com) zero-rated; **tasas de aeropuerto** airport tax; **~ de crecimiento** growth rate; **~ de interés/de nacimiento** rate of interest/ birth rate; **~ de rendimiento** (Com) rate of return; **tasas universitarias** university fees

tasación [tasa'θjon] NF assessment, valuation; (fig) appraisal

tasador, a [tasa'ðor, a] NM/F valuer; (Com: de impuestos) assessor

tasar [ta'sar] /**1a**/ VT (arreglar el precio) to fix a price for; (valorar) to value, assess; (limitar) to limit

tasca ['taska] NF (fam) pub

tata ['tata] NM (fam) dad(dy) ▶ NF (niñera) nanny, maid

tatarabuelo, -a [tatara'βwelo, a] NM/F great-great-grandfather/mother; **los tatarabuelos** one's great-great-grandparents

tatuaje [ta'twaxe] NM (dibujo) tattoo; (acto) tattooing

tatuar [ta'twar] /**1d**/ VT to tattoo

taumaturgo [tauma'turɣo] NM miracle-worker

taurino, -a [tau'rino, a] ADJ bullfighting cpd

Tauro ['tauro] NM Taurus

tauromaquia [tauro'makja] NF (art of) bullfighting

tautología [tautolo'xia] NF tautology

taxativo, -a [taksa'tiβo, a] ADJ (restringido) limited; (sentido) specific

taxi ['taksi] NM taxi

taxidermia [taksi'ðermja] NF taxidermy

taxímetro [tak'simetro] NM taximeter

taxista [tak'sista] NMF taxi driver

Tayikistán [tajikis'tan] NM Tajikistan

taza ['taθa] NF cup; (de retrete) bowl; **~ para café** coffee cup; **~ de café** cup of coffee

tazón [ta'θon] NM mug, large cup; (escudilla) basin

TCI NF ABR (= tarjeta de circuito impreso) PCB

te [te] PRON (complemento de objeto) you; (complemento indirecto) (to) you; (reflexivo) (to) yourself; **¿te duele mucho el brazo?** does your arm hurt a lot?; **te equivocas** you're wrong; **¡cálmate!** calm yourself!

té [te] (pl **tés**) NM tea; (reunión) tea party

tea ['tea] NF (antorcha) torch

teatral [tea'tral] ADJ theatre cpd; (fig) theatrical

teatro [te'atro] NM theatre; (Lit) plays pl, drama; **el ~** (carrera) the theatre, acting; **~ de aficionados/de variedades** amateur/ variety theatre, vaudeville theater (US); **hacer ~** (fig) to make a fuss

tebeo [te'βeo] NM children's comic

techado [te'tʃaðo] NM (*techo*) roof; **bajo ~** under cover

techo ['tetʃo] NM (*externo*) roof; (*interno*) ceiling

techumbre [te'tʃumbre] NF roof

tecla ['tekla] NF (*Inform, Mus, Tip*) key; (*Inform*): **~ de anulación/de borrar** cancel/delete key; **~ de control/de edición** control/edit key; **~ con flecha** arrow key; **~ programable** user-defined key; **~ de retorno/de tabulación** return/tab key; **~ del cursor** cursor key; **teclas de control direccional del cursor** cursor control keys

teclado [te'klaðo] NM (*tb Inform*) keyboard; **~ numérico** (*Inform*) numeric keypad

teclear [tekle'ar] /**1a**/ VI to strum; (*fam*) to drum ▶ VT (*Inform*) to key (in), type in, keyboard

tecleo [te'kleo] NM (*Mus: sonido*) strumming; (*: forma de tocar*) fingering; (*fam*) drumming

tecnicismo [tekni'θismo] NM (*carácter técnico*) technical nature; (*Ling*) technical term

técnico, -a ['tekniko, a] ADJ technical ▶ NM/F technician; (*experto*) expert ▶ NF (*procedimientos*) technique; (*tecnología*) technology; (*arte, oficio*) craft

tecnicolor [tekniko'lor] NM Technicolor®

tecnócrata [tek'nokrata] NMF technocrat

tecnología [teknolo'xia] NF technology; **~ de estado sólido** (*Inform*) solid-state technology; **~ de la información** information technology; **~ limpia** clean technology

tecnológico, -a [tekno'loxiko, a] ADJ technological

tecnólogo, -a [tek'noloɣo, a] NM/F technologist

tecolote [teko'lote] NM (*Am*) owl

tedio ['teðjo] NM (*aburrimiento*) boredom; (*apatía*) apathy; (*fastidio*) depression

tedioso, -a [te'ðjoso, a] ADJ boring; (*cansado*) wearisome, tedious

Teherán [tee'ran] NM Teheran

teja ['texa] NF (*azulejo*) tile; (*Bot*) lime (tree)

tejado [te'xaðo] NM (tiled) roof

tejano, -a [te'xano, a] ADJ, NM/F Texan ▶ NMPL: **tejanos** (*vaqueros*) jeans

Tejas ['texas] NM Texas

tejemaneje [texema'nexe] NM (*actividad*) bustle; (*lío*) fuss, to-do; (*intriga*) intrigue

tejer [te'xer] /**2a**/ VT to weave; (*tela de araña*) to spin; (*Am*) to knit; (*fig*) to fabricate ▶ VI: **~ y destejer** to chop and change

tejido [te'xiðo] NM fabric; (*estofa, tela*) (knitted) material; (*telaraña*) web; (*Anat*) tissue; (*textura*) texture

tejo ['texo] NM (*Bot*) yew (tree)

tel. ABR (= *teléfono*) tel.

tela ['tela] NF (*material*) material; (*de fruta, en líquido*) skin; (*del ojo*) film; **hay ~ para rato** there's lots to talk about; **poner en ~ de juicio** to (call in) question; **~ de araña** cobweb, spider's web

telar [te'lar] NM (*máquina*) loom; (*de teatro*) gridiron; **telares** NMPL textile mill *sg*

telaraña [tela'raɲa] NF cobweb, spider's web

tele ['tele] NF (*fam*) TV

tele... [tele] PREF tele...

telebasura [teleβa'sura] NF trash TV

telecargar [telekar'ɣar] /**1h**/ VT (*Inform*) to download

telecomunicación [telekomunika'θjon] NF telecommunication

teleconferencia [telekonfe'renθja] NF (*reunión*) teleconference; (*sistema*) teleconferencing

telecontrol [telekon'trol] NM remote control

telecopiadora [telekopja'ðora] NF: **~ facsímil** fax copier

telediario [tele'ðjarjo] NM television news

teledifusión [teleðifu'sjon] NF (television) broadcast

teledirigido, -a [teleðiri'xiðo, a] ADJ remote-controlled

teléf. ABR (= *teléfono*) tel.

teleférico [tele'feriko] NM (*tren*) cable-railway; (*de esquí*) ski-lift

telefilm [tele'film], **telefilme** [tele'filme] NM TV film

telefonazo [telefo'naθo] NM (*fam*) telephone call; **te daré un ~** I'll give you a ring

telefonear [telefone'ar] /**1a**/ VI to telephone

telefónicamente [tele'fonikamente] ADV by (tele)phone

telefónico, -a [tele'foniko, a] ADJ telephone *cpd* ▶ NF: **Telefónica** (*Esp*) Spanish national telephone company, ≈ British Telecom

telefonillo [telefo'niʎo] NM (*de puerta*) intercom

telefonista [telefo'nista] NMF telephonist

teléfono [te'lefono] NM (tele)phone; **~ móvil** mobile phone; **está hablando por ~** he's on the phone; **llamar a algn por ~** to ring sb (up) *o* phone sb (up); **~ celular** (*Am*) mobile phone; **~ con cámara** camera phone; **~ inalámbrico** cordless phone

telefoto [tele'foto] NF telephoto

telegrafía [teleɣra'fia] NF telegraphy

telégrafo [te'leɣrafo] NM telegraph; (*fam: persona*) telegraph boy

telegrama [tele'ɣrama] NM telegram

teleimpresor [teleimpre'sor] NM teleprinter

telemática [tele'matika] NF telematics *sg*

telémetro [te'lemetro] NM rangefinder

telenovela [teleno'βela] NF soap (opera)

teleobjetivo [teleobxe'tiβo] NM telephoto lens

telepatía [telepa'tia] NF telepathy

telepático, -a [tele'patiko, a] ADJ telepathic

teleproceso [telepro'θeso] NM teleprocessing

telerrealidad [telerreali'ðað] NF reality TV

telescópico, -a [tele'skopiko, a] ADJ telescopic

telescopio [tele'skopjo] NM telescope

telesilla [tele'siʎa] NM chairlift

telespectador, a [telespekta'ðor, a] NM/F viewer

telesquí [teles'ki] NM ski-lift

teletarjeta [teletar'xeta] NF phonecard

teletex [tele'teks], **teletexto** [tele'teksto] NM teletext

teletipista [teleti'pista] NMF teletypist

teletipo [tele'tipo] NM teletype(writer)

teletrabajador, a [teletraβaxa'ðor, a] NM/F teleworker

teletrabajo [teletra'βaxo] NM teleworking

televentas [tele'βentas] NFPL telesales

televidente [teleβi'ðente] NMF viewer

televisar [teleβi'sar] /1a/ VT to televise

televisión [teleβi'sjon] NF television; **~ en color/por satélite** colour/satellite television; **~ digital** digital television

televisivo, -a [teleβi'siβo, a] ADJ television cpd

televisor [teleβi'sor] NM television set

télex ['teleks] NM telex; **máquina ~** telex (machine); **enviar por ~** to telex

telón [te'lon] NM curtain; **~ de boca/ seguridad** front/safety curtain; **~ de acero** (Pol) iron curtain; **~ de fondo** backcloth, background

telonero, -a [telo'nero, a] NM/F support act; **los teloneros** (Mus) the support band

tema ['tema] NM (asunto) subject, topic; (Mus) theme; **temas de actualidad** current affairs ▶ NF (obsesión) obsession; (manía) ill-will; **tener ~ a algn** to have a grudge against sb

temario [te'marjo] NM (Escol) set of topics; (de una conferencia) agenda

temático, -a [te'matiko, a] ADJ thematic ▶ NF subject matter

tembladera [tembla'ðera] NF shaking; (Am) quagmire

temblar [tem'blar] /1j/ VI to shake, tremble; (de frío) to shiver

tembleque [tem'bleke] ADJ shaking ▶ NM shaking

temblón, -ona [tem'blon, ona] ADJ shaking

temblor [tem'blor] NM trembling; (de tierra) earthquake

tembloroso, -a [temblo'roso, a] ADJ trembling

temer [te'mer] /2a/ VT to fear ▶ VI to be afraid; **temo que Juan llegue tarde** I am afraid Juan may be late

temerario, -a [teme'rarjo, a] ADJ (imprudente) rash; (descuidado) reckless; (arbitrario) hasty

temeridad [temeri'ðað] NF (imprudencia) rashness; (audacia) boldness

temeroso, -a [teme'roso, a] ADJ (miedoso) fearful; (que inspira temor) frightful

temible [te'miβle] ADJ fearsome

temor [te'mor] NM (miedo) fear; (duda) suspicion

témpano ['tempano] NM (Mus) kettledrum; **~ de hielo** ice floe

temperamento [tempera'mento] NM temperament; **tener ~** to be temperamental

temperar [tempe'rar] /1a/ VT to temper, moderate

temperatura [tempera'tura] NF temperature

tempestad [tempes'tað] NF storm; **~ en un vaso de agua** (fig) storm in a teacup

tempestuoso, -a [tempes'twoso, a] ADJ stormy

templado, -a [tem'plaðo, a] ADJ (agua) lukewarm; (clima) mild; (Mus) in tune, well-tuned; (moderado) moderate

templanza [tem'planθa] NF moderation; (en el beber) abstemiousness; (del clima) mildness

templar [tem'plar] /1a/ VT (moderar) to moderate; (furia) to restrain; (calor) to reduce; (solución) to dilute; (afinar) to tune (up); (acero) to temper; (tuerca) to tighten up ▶ VI to moderate; **templarse** VR to be restrained

temple ['temple] NM (humor) mood; (coraje) courage; (ajuste) tempering; (afinación) tuning; (pintura) tempera

templo ['templo] NM (iglesia) church; (pagano etc) temple; **~ metodista** Methodist chapel

temporada [tempo'raða] NF time, period; (estación, social, Deporte) season; **en plena ~** at the height of the season

temporal [tempo'ral] ADJ (no permanente) temporary; (Rel) temporal ▶ NM storm

temporario, -a [tempo'rarjo, a] ADJ (Am) temporary

tempranero, -a [tempra'nero, a] ADJ (Bot) early; (persona) early-rising

temprano, -a [tem'prano, a] ADJ early ▶ ADV early; (demasiado pronto) too soon, too early; **lo más ~ posible** as soon as possible

ten [ten] VB ver **tener**

tenaces [te'naθes] ADJ PL ver **tenaz**

tenacidad [tenaθi'ðað] NF (gen) tenacity; (dureza) toughness; (terquedad) stubbornness

tenacillas [tena'θiʎas] NFPL (gen) tongs; (para el pelo) curling tongs; (Med) forceps

tenaz [te'naθ] ADJ (material) tough; (persona) tenacious; (pegajoso) sticky; (terco) stubborn

tenaza(s) [te'naθa(s)] NF(PL) (Med) forceps; (Tec) pliers; (Zool) pincers

tendal [ten'dal] NM awning

tendedero [tende'ðero] NM (para ropa) drying-place; (cuerda) clothes line

tendencia [ten'denθja] NF tendency; (proceso) trend; **~ imperante** prevailing tendency; **~ del mercado** run of the market; **tener ~ a** to tend o have a tendency to

tendenciosidad [tendenθjosi'ðað] NF tendentiousness

tendencioso, -a [tenden'θjoso, a] ADJ tendentious

tender [ten'der] **/2g/** VT (extender) to spread out; (ropa) to hang out; (vía férrea, cable) to lay; (cuerda) to stretch; (trampa) to set ▶ VI to tend; **tenderse** VR to lie down; (fig: dejarse llevar) to let o.s. go; (: dejar ir) to let things go; **~ la cama/la mesa** (AM) to make the bed/lay the table

ténder ['tender] NM (Ferro) tender

tenderete [tende'rete] NM (puesto) stall; (carretilla) barrow; (exposición) display of goods

tendero, -a [ten'dero, a] NM/F shopkeeper

tendido, -a [ten'diðo, a] ADJ (acostado) lying down, flat; (colgado) hanging ▶ NM (ropa) washing; (Taur) front rows pl of seats; (colocación) laying; (Arq: enyesado) coat of plaster; **a galope ~** flat out

tendón [ten'don] NM tendon

tendré etc [ten'dre] VB ver **tener**

tenducho [ten'dutʃo] NM small dirty shop

tenebroso, -a [tene'βroso, a] ADJ (oscuro) dark; (fig) gloomy; (siniestro) sinister

tenedor [tene'ðor] NM (Culin) fork; (poseedor) holder; **~ de libros** book-keeper; **~ de acciones** shareholder; **~ de póliza** policyholder

teneduría [teneðu'ria] NF keeping; **~ de libros** book-keeping

tenencia [te'nenθja] NF (de casa) tenancy; (de oficio) tenure; (de propiedad) possession; **~ asegurada** security of tenure; **~ ilícita de armas** illegal possession of weapons

(PALABRA CLAVE)

tener [te'ner] **/2k/** VT **1** (poseer: gen) to have; (: en la mano) to hold; **¿tienes un boli?** have you got a pen?; **va a tener un niño** she's going to have a baby; **tiene los ojos azules** he's got blue eyes; **¡ten** o **tenga!, ¡aquí tienes** o **tiene!** here you are!

2 (edad, medidas) to be; **tiene siete años** she's seven (years old); **tiene 15 cm de largo** it's 15 cm long

3 (sentimientos, sensaciones): **tener sed/ hambre/frío/calor** to be thirsty/hungry/ cold/hot; **tener celos** to be jealous; **tener cuidado** to be careful; **tener razón** to be right; **tener suerte** to be lucky

4 (considerar): **lo tengo por brillante** I consider him to be brilliant; **tener en**

mucho a algn to think very highly of sb

5 (+ pp): **tengo terminada ya la mitad del trabajo** I've done half the work already; **tenía el sombrero puesto** he had his hat on; **tenía pensado llamarte** I had been thinking of phoning you; **nos tiene hartos** we're fed up with him; **me ha tenido tres horas esperando** he kept me waiting three hours

6: **tener que hacer algo** to have to do sth; **tengo que acabar este trabajo hoy** I have to finish this job today

7: **¿qué tienes, estás enfermo?** what's the matter with you, are you ill?

8 (locuciones): **¿conque ésas tenemos?** so it's like that, then?; **no las tengo todas conmigo** I'm a bit unsure (about it); **lo tiene difícil** he'll have a hard job

tenerse VR **1**: **tenerse en pie** to stand up

2: **tenerse por** to think o.s.; **se tiene por un gran cantante** he thinks himself a great singer

tengo etc ['tengo] VB ver **tener**

tenia ['tenja] NF tapeworm

teniente [te'njente] NM lieutenant; (ayudante) deputy; **~ coronel** lieutenant colonel

tenis ['tenis] NM tennis; **~ de mesa** table tennis

tenista [te'nista] NMF tennis player

tenor [te'nor] NM (tono) tone; (sentido) meaning; (Mus) tenor; **a ~ de** on the lines of

tenorio [te'norjo] NM (fam) ladykiller, Don Juan

tensar [ten'sar] **/1a/** VT to tauten; (arco) to draw

tensión [ten'sjon] NF tension; (Tec) stress; (Med): **~ arterial** blood pressure; **~ nerviosa** nervous strain; **tener la ~ alta** to have high blood pressure

tenso, -a ['tenso, a] ADJ tense; (relaciones) strained

tentación [tenta'θjon] NF temptation

tentáculo [ten'takulo] NM tentacle

tentador, a [tenta'ðor, a] ADJ tempting ▶ NM/F tempter/temptress

tentar [ten'tar] **/1j/** VT (tocar) to touch, feel; (seducir) to tempt; (atraer) to attract; (probar) to try (out); (Med) to probe; **~ hacer algo** to try to do sth

tentativa [tenta'tiβa] NF attempt; **~ de asesinato** attempted murder

tentempié [tentem'pje] NM (fam) snack

tenue ['tenwe] ADJ (delgado) thin, slender; (alambre) fine; (insustancial) tenuous; (sonido) faint; (neblina) light; (lazo, vínculo) slight

teñir [te'ɲir] VT to dye; (fig) to tinge; **teñirse** VR to dye; **teñirse el pelo** to dye one's hair

teología [teolo'xia] NF theology

teólogo, -a [te'oloɣo, a] NM/F theologist, theologian

teorema [teo'rema] NM theorem

teoría [teo'ria] NF theory; **en ~** in theory

teóricamente [te'orikamente] ADV theoretically

teorice etc [teo'riθe] VB ver **teorizar**

teórico, -a [te'oriko, a] ADJ theoretic(al) ▸ NM/F theoretician, theorist

teorizar [teori'θar] /**1f**/ VI to theorize

tequila [te'kila] NM o F tequila

TER [ter] NM ABR (Ferro) = **tren español rápido**

terapeuta [tera'peuta] NMF therapist

terapéutico, -a [tera'peutiko, a] ADJ therapeutic(al) ▸ NF therapeutics sg

terapia [te'rapja] NF therapy; **~ laboral** occupational therapy

tercer [ter'θer] ADJ ver **tercero**

tercermundista [terθermun'dista] ADJ Third World cpd

tercero, -a [ter'θero, a], **tercer** (antes de nmsg) ADJ third ▸ NM (árbitro) mediator; (Jur) third party

terceto [ter'θeto] NM trio

terciado, -a [ter'θjaðo, a] ADJ slanting; **azúcar ~** brown sugar

terciar [ter'θjar] /**1b**/ VT (Mat) to divide into three; (inclinarse) to slope; (llevar) to wear across one's chest ▸ VI (participar) to take part; (hacer de árbitro) to mediate; **terciarse** VR to arise

terciario, -a [ter'θjarjo, a] ADJ tertiary

tercio [ter'θjo] NM third

terciopelo [terθjo'pelo] NM velvet

terco, -a ['terko, a] ADJ obstinate, stubborn; (material) tough

tergal® [ter'ɣal] NM Terylene®, Dacron® (US)

tergiversación [terxiβersa'θjon] NF (deformación) distortion; (evasivas) prevarication

tergiversar [terxiβer'sar] /**1a**/ VT to distort ▸ VI to prevaricate

termal [ter'mal] ADJ thermal

termas ['termas] NFPL hot springs

térmico, -a ['termiko, a] ADJ thermic, thermal, heat cpd

terminación [termina'θjon] NF (final) end; (conclusión) conclusion, ending

terminal [termi'nal] ADJ terminal ▸ NM (Elec, Inform) terminal ▸ NF (Aviat, Ferro) terminal; **un ~ conversacional** an interactive terminal; **un ~ de pantalla** a visual display unit

terminante [termi'nante] ADJ (final) final, definitive; (tajante) categorical

terminantemente [terminante'mente] ADV: **~ prohibido** strictly forbidden

terminar [termi'nar] /**1a**/ VT (completar) to complete, finish; (concluir) to end ▸ VI (llegar a su fin) to end; (parar) to stop; (acabar) to finish; **terminarse** VR to come to an end; **~ por hacer algo** to end up (by) doing sth

término ['termino] NM end, conclusion; (parada) terminus; (límite) boundary; (en discusión) point; (Ling, Com) term; **~ medio** average; (fig) middle way; **en otros términos** in other words; **en último ~** (a fin de cuentas) in the last analysis; (como último recurso) as a last resort; **~ medio** average; (fig) middle way; **en términos de** in terms of; **según los términos del contrato** according to the terms of the contract

terminología [terminolo'xia] NF terminology

termita [ter'mita] NF termite

termo® ['termo] NM Thermos® (flask)

termodinámico, -a [termoði'namiko, a] ADJ thermodynamic ▸ NF thermodynamics sg

termoimpresora [termoimpre'sora] NF thermal printer

termómetro [ter'mometro] NM thermometer

termonuclear [termonukle'ar] ADJ thermonuclear

termostato [termos'tato] NM thermostat

ternero, -a [ter'nero, a] NM/F (animal) calf ▸ NF (carne) veal, beef

terneza [ter'neθa] NF tenderness

ternilla [ter'niʎa] NF gristle; (cartílago) cartilage

terno ['terno] NM (traje) three-piece suit; (conjunto) set of three

ternura [ter'nura] NF (trato) tenderness; (palabra) endearment; (cariño) fondness

terquedad [terke'ðað] NF obstinacy; (dureza) harshness

terrado [te'rraðo] NM terrace

Terranova [terra'noβa] NF Newfoundland

terraplén [terra'plen] NM (Agr) terrace; (Ferro) embankment; (Mil) rampart; (cuesta) slope

terráqueo, -a [te'rrakeo, a] ADJ: **globo ~** globe

terrateniente [terrate'njente] NM landowner

terraza [te'rraθa] NF (balcón) balcony; (techo) flat roof; (Agr) terrace

terremoto [terre'moto] NM earthquake

terrenal [terre'nal] ADJ earthly

terreno, -a [te'rreno, a] ADJ (de la tierra) earthly, worldly ▸ NM (tierra) land; (parcela) plot; (suelo) soil; (fig) field; **un ~** a piece of land; **sobre el ~** on the spot; **ceder/perder ~** to give/lose ground; **preparar el ~ (a)** (fig) to pave the way (for)

terrestre [te'rrestre] ADJ terrestrial; (ruta) land cpd

terrible [te'rriβle] ADJ (espantoso) terrible; (aterrador) dreadful; (tremendo) awful

t

territorial [territo'rjal] ADJ territorial
territorio [terri'torjo] NM territory; **~ bajo
mandato** mandated territory
terrón [te'rron] NM (de azúcar) lump; (de tierra)
clod, lump; **terrones** NMPL land sg
terror [te'rror] NM terror
terrorífico, -a [terro'rifiko, a] ADJ terrifying
terrorismo [terro'rismo] NM terrorism
terrorista [terro'rista] ADJ, NMF terrorist;
~ suicida suicide bomber
terroso, -a [te'rroso, a] ADJ earthy
terruño [te'rruɲo] NM (pedazo) clod; (parcela)
plot; (fig) native soil; **apego al ~** attachment
to one's native soil
terso, -a ['terso, a] ADJ (liso) smooth; (pulido)
polished; (fig: estilo) flowing
tersura [ter'sura] NF smoothness; (brillo)
shine
tertulia [ter'tulja] NF (reunión informal) social
gathering; (grupo) group, circle; (sala)
clubroom; **~ literaria** literary circle
tesina [te'sina] NF dissertation
tesis ['tesis] NF INV thesis
tesón [te'son] NM (firmeza) firmness;
(tenacidad) tenacity
tesorería [tesore'ria] NF treasurership
tesorero, -a [teso'rero, a] NM/F treasurer
tesoro [te'soro] NM treasure; (Com, Pol)
treasury; **T~ público** (Pol) Exchequer
test [tes(t)] (pl **tests** [tes(t)]) NM test
testaferro [testa'ferro] NM figurehead
testamentaría [testamenta'ria] NF
execution of a will
testamentario, -a [testamen'tarjo, a] ADJ
testamentary ▶ NM/F executor/executrix
testamento [testa'mento] NM will; **~ vital**
living will
testar [tes'tar] /1a/ VI to make a will
testarada [testa'raða] NF, **testarazo**
[testa'raθo] NM: **darse una ~ o un testarazo**
(fam) to bump one's head
testarudo, -a [testa'ruðo, a] ADJ stubborn
testículo [tes'tikulo] NM testicle
testificar [testifi'kar] /1g/ VT to testify; (fig)
to attest ▶ VI to give evidence
testifique etc [testi'fike] VB ver **testificar**
testigo [tes'tiɣo] NMF witness; **~ de cargo/
descargo** witness for the prosecution/
defence; **~ ocular** eye witness; **poner a algn
por ~** to cite sb as a witness
testimonial [testimo'njal] ADJ (prueba)
testimonial; (gesto) token
testimoniar [testimo'njar] /1b/ VT to testify
to; (fig) to show
testimonio [testi'monjo] NM testimony; **en
~ de** as a token o mark of; **falso ~** perjured
evidence, false witness
teta ['teta] NF (de biberón) teat; (Anat) nipple;
(: fam) breast; (fam!) tit (fam!)

tétanos ['tetanos] NM tetanus
tetera [te'tera] NF teapot; **~ eléctrica**
(electric) kettle
tetilla [te'tiʎa] NF (Anat) nipple; (de biberón)
teat
tétrico, -a ['tetriko, a] ADJ gloomy, dismal
textear [tekste'ar] /1a/ VT (Am) to text
textil [teks'til] ADJ textile
texto ['teksto] NM text
textual [teks'twal] ADJ textual; **palabras
textuales** exact words
textura [teks'tura] NF (de tejido) texture; (de
mineral) structure
tez [teθ] NF (cutis) complexion; (color)
colouring
tfno. ABR (= teléfono) tel.
ti [ti] PRON you; (reflexivo) yourself
tía ['tia] NF (pariente) aunt; (fam: mujer) girl
Tibet [ti'βet] NM: **El ~** Tibet
tibetano, -a [tiβe'tano, a] ADJ, NM/F Tibetan
▶ NM (Ling) Tibetan
tibia ['tiβja] NF tibia
tibieza [ti'βjeθa] NF (temperatura) tepidness;
(fig) coolness
tibio, -a ['tiβjo, a] ADJ lukewarm, tepid
tiburón [tiβu'ron] NM shark
tic [tik] NM (ruido) click; (de reloj) tick;
~ nervioso (Med) nervous tic
tico, -a ['tiko, a] ADJ, NM/F (Am fam) Costa
Rican
tictac [tik'tak] NM (de reloj) tick tock
tiemble etc ['tjemble] VB ver **temblar**
tiempo ['tjempo] NM (gen) time; (época,
período) age, period; (Meteorología) weather;
(Ling) tense; (edad) age; (de juego) half; **a ~** in
time; **a un o al mismo ~** at the same time;
al poco ~ very soon (after); **andando el ~** in
due course; **cada cierto ~** every so often;
con ~ in time; **con el ~** eventually; **se quedó
poco ~** he didn't stay very long; **hace poco ~**
not long ago; **mucho ~** a long time; **de ~ en
~** from time to time; **en mis tiempos** in my
time; **en los buenos tiempos** in the good
old days; **hace buen/mal ~** the weather is
fine/bad; **estar a ~** to be in time; **hace ~**
some time ago; **hacer ~** to while away the
time; **¿qué ~ tiene?** how old is he?; **motor
de 2 tiempos** two-stroke engine;
~ compartido (Inform) time sharing; **~ de
ejecución** (Inform) run time; **~ inactivo**
(Com) downtime; **~ libre** spare time; **~ de
paro** (Com) idle time; **a ~ partido** (trabajar)
part-time; **~ preferencial** (Com) prime time;
en ~ real (Inform) real time; **primer ~** first
half
tienda ['tjenda] VB ver **tender** ▶ NF shop; (más
grande) store; (Naut) awning; **~ de campaña**
tent; **~ de comestibles** grocer's (shop)
(Brit), grocery (store) (US)

tiene etc ['tjene] VB ver **tener**

tienta ['tjenta] VB ver **tentar** ▶ NF (Med) probe; (fig) tact; **andar a tientas** to grope one's way along

tiento etc ['tjento] VB ver **tentar** ▶ NM (tacto) touch; (precaución) wariness; (pulso) steady hand; (Zool) feeler, tentacle

tierno, -a ['tjerno, a] ADJ (blando, dulce) tender; (fresco) fresh

tierra ['tjerra] NF earth; (suelo) soil; (mundo) world; (país) country, land; (Elec) earth, ground (US); ~ **adentro** inland; ~ **natal** native land; **echar ~ a un asunto** to hush an affair up; **no es de estas tierras** he's not from these parts; **la T~ Santa** the Holy Land

tieso, -a ['tjeso, a] ADJ (rígido) rigid; (duro) stiff; (fig: testarudo) stubborn; (fam: orgulloso) conceited ▶ ADV strongly

tiesto ['tjesto] NM flowerpot; (pedazo) piece of pottery

tifoidea [tifoi'ðea] NF typhoid

tifón [ti'fon] NM (huracán) typhoon; (de mar) tidal wave

tifus ['tifus] NM typhus; ~ **icteroides** yellow fever

tigre ['tiɣre] NM tiger; (Am) jaguar

TIJ SIGLA M (= Tribunal Internacional de Justicia) ICJ

tijera [ti'xera] NF (utensilio) (pair of) scissors pl; (Zool) claw; (persona) gossip; **de** ~ folding; **tijeras** NFPL scissors; (para plantas) shears; **unas tijeras** a pair of scissors

tijeretear [tixerete'ar] /1a/ VT to snip ▶ VI (fig) to meddle

tila ['tila] NF (Bot) lime tree; (Culin) lime flower tea

tildar [til'dar] /1a/ VT: ~ **de** to brand as

tilde ['tilde] NF (defecto) defect; (trivialidad) triviality; (Tip) tilde

tilín [ti'lin] NM tinkle

tilo ['tilo] NM lime tree

timador, a [tima'ðor, a] NM/F swindler

timar [ti'mar] /1a/ VT (robar) to steal; (estafar) to swindle; (persona) to con; **timarse** VR (fam): **timarse con algn** to make eyes at sb

timbal [tim'bal] NM small drum

timbrar [tim'brar] /1a/ VT to stamp; (sellar) to seal; (carta) to postmark

timbrazo [tim'braθo] NM ring; **dar un** ~ to ring the bell

timbre ['timbre] NM (sello) stamp; (campanilla) bell; (tono) timbre; (Com) stamp duty

timidez [timi'ðeθ] NF shyness

tímido, -a ['timiðo, a] ADJ shy, timid

timo ['timo] NM swindle; **dar un** ~ **a algn** to swindle sb

timón [ti'mon] NM helm, rudder; (Am) steering wheel; **coger el** ~ (fig) to take charge

timonel [timo'nel] NM helmsman

timorato, -a [timo'rato, a] ADJ God-fearing; (mojigato) sanctimonious

tímpano ['timpano] NM (Anat) eardrum; (Mus) small drum

tina ['tina] NF tub; (Am: baño) bath(tub)

tinaja [ti'naxa] NF large earthen jar

tinerfeño, -a [tiner'feɲo, a] ADJ of o from Tenerife ▶ NM/F native o inhabitant of Tenerife

tinglado [tiŋ'glaðo] NM (cobertizo) shed; (fig: truco) trick; (intriga) intrigue; **armar un** ~ to lay a plot

tinieblas [ti'njeβlas] NFPL darkness sg; (sombras) shadows; **estamos en** ~ **sobre sus proyectos** (fig) we are in the dark about his plans

tino ['tino] NM (habilidad) skill; (Mil) marksmanship; (juicio) insight; (moderación) moderation; **sin** ~ immoderately; **coger el** ~ to get the feel o hang of it

tinta ['tinta] NF ink; (Tec) dye; (Arte) colour; ~ **china** Indian ink; **tintas** NFPL (fig) shades; **medias tintas** (fig) half measures; **saber algo de buena** ~ to have sth on good authority

tinte ['tinte] NM dye; (acto) dyeing; (fig) tinge; (barniz) veneer

tintero [tin'tero] NM inkwell; **se le quedó en el** ~ he clean forgot about it

tintinear [tintine'ar] /1a/ VT to tinkle

tinto, -a ['tinto, a] ADJ (teñido) dyed; (manchado) stained ▶ NM red wine

tintorera [tinto'rera] NF shark

tintorería [tintore'ria] NF dry cleaner's

tintorero [tinto'rero] NM dry cleaner('s)

tintura [tin'tura] NF (acto) dyeing; (Química) dye; (farmacéutico) tincture

tiña etc ['tiɲa] VB ver **teñir** ▶ NF (Med) ringworm

tío ['tio] NM (pariente) uncle; (fam: hombre) bloke, guy (US)

tiovivo [tio'βiβo] NM merry-go-round

típico, -a ['tipiko, a] ADJ typical; (pintoresco) picturesque

tiple ['tiple] NM soprano (voice) ▶ NF soprano

tipo ['tipo] NM (clase) type, kind; (norma) norm; (patrón) pattern; (fam: hombre) fellow, bloke, guy (US); (Anat) build; (: de mujer) figure; (Imprenta) type; ~ **bancario/de descuento** bank/discount rate; ~ **de interés** interest rate; ~ **de interés vigente** (Com) standard rate; ~ **de cambio** exchange rate; ~ **base** (Com) base rate; ~ **a término** (Com) forward rate; **dos tipos sospechosos** two suspicious characters; ~ **de letra** (Inform, Tip) typeface; ~ **de datos** (Inform) data type

tipografía [tipoɣra'fia] NF (tipo) printing; (lugar) printing press

tipográfico, -a [tipo'ɣrafiko, a] ADJ printing

t

tipógrafo, -a [ti'poɣrafo, a] NM/F printer

tique, tíquet ['tike] (pl **~(t)s** ['tikes]) NM ticket; (en tienda) cash slip

tiquismiquis [tikis'mikis] NM fussy person ▶ NMPL (querellas) squabbling sg; (escrúpulos) silly scruples

TIR SIGLA MPL = **Transportes internacionales por carretera**

tira ['tira] NF strip; (fig) abundance ▶ NM: **~ y afloja** give and take; **la ~ de ...** (fam) lots of ...

tirabuzón [tiraβu'θon] NM corkscrew; (rizo) curl

tirachinas [tira'tʃinas] NM INV catapult

tiradero [tira'ðero] NM (AM) rubbish dump

tirado, -a [ti'raðo, a] ADJ (barato) dirt-cheap; (fam: fácil) very easy ▶ NF (acto) cast, throw; (distancia) distance; (serie) series; (Tip) printing, edition; **de una tirada** at one go; **está ~** (fam) it's a cinch

tirador, a [tira'ðor, a] NM/F (persona) shooter ▶ NM (mango) handle; (Elec) flex; **~ certero** sniper

tiralíneas [tira'lineas] NM INV ruling-pen

tiranía [tira'nia] NF tyranny

tiránico, -a [ti'raniko, a] ADJ tyrannical

tiranizar [tirani'θar] /1f/ VT (pueblo, empleado) to tyrannize

tirano, -a [ti'rano, a] ADJ tyrannical ▶ NM/F tyrant

tirante [ti'rante] ADJ (cuerda) tight, taut; (relaciones) strained ▶ NM (Arq) brace; (Tec) stay; (correa) shoulder strap; **tirantes** NMPL braces, suspenders (US)

tirantez [tiran'teθ] NF tightness; (fig) tension

tirar [ti'rar] /1a/ VT to throw; (volcar) to upset; (derribar) to knock down o over; (tiro) to fire; (cohete) to launch; (bomba) to drop; (edificio) to pull down; (desechar) to throw out o away; (disipar) to squander; (imprimir) to print; (dar: golpe) to deal ▶ VI (disparar) to shoot; (dar un tirón) to pull; (fig) to draw; (interesar) to appeal; (fam: andar) to go; (tender a) to tend to; (Deporte) to shoot; **tirarse** VR to throw o.s.; (fig) to demean o.s.; (fam!) to screw (fam!); **~ abajo** to bring down, destroy; **tira más a su padre** he takes more after his father; **~ de algo** to pull o tug (on) sth; **ir tirando** to manage; **~ a la derecha** to turn o go right; **a todo ~** at the most

tirita [ti'rita] NF (sticking) plaster, Band-Aid® (US)

tiritar [tiri'tar] /1a/ VI to shiver

tiritona [tiri'tona] NF shivering (fit)

tiro ['tiro] NM (lanzamiento) throw; (disparo) shot; (tiroteo) shooting; (Deporte) shot; (Tenis, Golf) drive; (alcance) range; (de escalera) flight (of stairs); (golpe) blow; (engaño) hoax; **~ al blanco** target practice; **caballo de ~**

cart-horse; **andar de tiros largos** to be all dressed up; **al ~** (AM) at once; **de a ~** (AM fam) completely; **se pegó un ~** he shot himself; **le salió el ~ por la culata** it backfired on him

tiroides [ti'roiðes] NM INV thyroid

Tirol [ti'rol] NM: **El ~** the Tyrol

tirolés, -esa [tiro'les, esa] ADJ, NM/F Tyrolean

tirón [ti'ron] NM (sacudida) pull, tug; **de un ~** in one go; **dar un ~ a** to pull at, tug at

tirotear [tirote'ar] /1a/ VT to shoot at; **tirotearse** VR to exchange shots

tiroteo [tiro'teo] NM exchange of shots, shooting; (escaramuza) skirmish

tirria ['tirrja] NF: **tener ~ a algn** to have a grudge against sb

tísico, -a ['tisiko, a] ADJ, NM/F consumptive

tisis ['tisis] NF consumption, tuberculosis

tít. ABR = **título**

titánico, -a [ti'taniko, a] ADJ titanic

títere ['titere] NM puppet; **no dejar ~ con cabeza** to turn everything upside-down

titilar [titi'lar] /1a/ VI (luz, estrella) to twinkle; (párpado) to flutter

titiritero, -a [titiri'tero, a] NM/F (acróbata) acrobat; (malabarista) juggler

titubeante [tituβe'ante] ADJ (inestable) shaky, tottering; (farfullante) stammering; (dudoso) hesitant

titubear [tituβe'ar] /1a/ VI to stagger; (balbucear) to stammer; (vacilar) to hesitate

titubeo [titu'βeo] NM staggering; (balbuceo) stammering; (vacilación) hesitation

titulado, -a [titu'laðo, a] ADJ (libro) entitled; (persona) titled

titular [titu'lar] /1a/ ADJ titular ▶ NM/F (de oficina) occupant; (de pasaporte) holder ▶ NM headline ▶ VT to title; **titularse** VR to be entitled

título ['titulo] NM (gen) title; (de diario) headline; (certificado) professional qualification; (universitario) university degree; (Com) bond; (fig) right; **títulos** NMPL qualifications; **a ~ de** by way of; (en calidad de) in the capacity of; **a ~ de curiosidad** as a matter of interest; **~ de propiedad** title deed; **títulos convertibles de interés fijo** (Com) convertible loan stock sg

tiza ['tiθa] NF chalk; **una ~** a piece of chalk

tizna ['tiθna] NF grime

tiznar [tiθ'nar] /1a/ VT to blacken; (manchar) to smudge, stain; (fig) to tarnish

tizón [ti'θon], **tizo** ['tiθo] NM brand; (fig) stain

TLC NM ABR (= Tratado de Libre Comercio) NAFTA

Tm. ABR = **tonelada(s) métrica(s)**

TNT SIGLA M (= trinitrotolueno) TNT

toalla [to'aʎa] NF towel

tobillo [to'βiʎo] NM ankle

tobogán [toβo'ɣan] NM toboggan;

(*resbaladilla*) slide, chute; (*montaña rusa*) roller-coaster

toca ['toka] NF headdress

tocadiscos [toka'ðiskos] NM INV record player

tocado, -a [to'kaðo, a] ADJ (*fruta etc*) rotten; (*fam*) touched ▶ NM headdress; **estar ~ de la cabeza** (*fam*) to be weak in the head

tocador [toka'ðor] NM (*mueble*) dressing table; (*cuarto*) boudoir; (*neceser*) toilet case; (*fam*) ladies' room

tocante [to'kante]: **~ a** prep with regard to; **en lo ~ a** as for, so far as concerns

tocar [to'kar] /1g/ VT to touch; (*sentir*) to feel; (*con la mano*) to handle; (*Mus*) to play; (*campana*) to ring; (*tambor*) to beat; (*trompeta*) to blow; (*topar con*) to run into, strike; (*referirse a*) to allude to; (*estar emparentado con*) to be related to ▶ VI (*a la puerta*) to knock (on *o* at the door); (*ser el turno*) to fall to, be the turn of; (*ser hora*) to be due; (*atañer*) to concern; **tocarse** VR (*cubrirse la cabeza*) to cover one's head; (*tener contacto*) to touch (each other); **tocarle a algn** to fall to sb's lot; **~ en** (*Naut*) to call at; **por lo que a mí me toca** as far as I am concerned; **te toca a ti** it's your turn; **esto toca en la locura** this verges on madness

tocateja [toka'texa]: **a ~** adv (*fam*) in readies

tocayo, -a [to'kajo, a] NM/F namesake

tocino [to'θino] NM (bacon) fat; **~ de panceta** bacon

todavía [toða'βia] ADV (*aun*) even; (*aún*) still, yet; **~ más** yet *o* still more; **~ no** not yet; **~ en 1970** as late as 1970; **está lloviendo ~** it's still raining

toditito, -a [toði'tito, a], **todito, -a** [to'ðito, a] ADJ (*AM fam*) (absolutely) all

todo, -a ['toðo, a] ADJ **1** (*sg*) all; **toda la carne** all the meat; **toda la noche** all night, the whole night; **todo el libro** the whole book; **toda una botella** a whole bottle; **todo lo contrario** quite the opposite; **está toda sucia** she's all dirty; **a toda velocidad** at full speed; **por todo el país** throughout the whole country; **es todo un hombre** he's every inch a man; **soy todo oídos** I'm all ears

2 (*pl*) all; every; **todos los libros** all the books; **todas las noches** every night; **todos los que quieran salir** all those who want to leave; **todos vosotros** all of you

▶ PRON **1** everything, all; **todos** everyone, everybody; **lo sabemos todo** we know everything; **todos querían más tiempo** everybody *o* everyone wanted more time; **nos marchamos todos** all of us left;

corriendo y todo, no llegaron a tiempo even though they ran, they still didn't arrive in time

2 (*con preposición*): **a pesar de todo** even so, in spite of everything; **con todo él me sigue gustando** even so I still like him; **le llamaron de todo** they called him all the names under the sun; **no me agrada del todo** I don't entirely like it

▶ ADV all; **vaya todo seguido** keep straight on *o* ahead

▶ NM: **como un todo** as a whole; **arriba del todo** at the very top; **todo a cien** ≈ pound store (*BRIT*), ≈ dollar store (*US*)

todopoderoso, -a [toðopoðe'roso, a] ADJ all-powerful; (*Rel*) almighty

todoterreno [toðote'rreno] NM (*tb*: **vehículo todoterreno**) four-wheel drive, SUV (*esp US*)

toga ['toɣa] NF toga; (*Escol*) gown

Tokio ['tokjo] N Tokyo

toldo ['toldo] NM (*para el sol*) sunshade; (*en tienda*) marquee; (*fig*) pride

tole ['tole] NM (*fam*) commotion

toledano, -a [tole'ðano, a] ADJ of *o* from Toledo ▶ NM/F native *o* inhabitant of Toledo

tolerable [tole'raβle] ADJ tolerable

tolerancia [tole'ranθja] NF tolerance

tolerante [tole'rante] ADJ tolerant; (*sociedad*) liberal; (*fig*) open-minded

tolerar [tole'rar] /1a/ VT to tolerate; (*resistir*) to endure

Tolón [to'lon] NM Toulon

toma ['toma] NF (*gen*) taking; (*Med*) dose; (*Elec*: *tb*: **toma de corriente**) socket; (*Mecánica*) inlet; **~ de posesión** (*por presidente*) taking up office; **~ de tierra** (*Elec*) earth (wire), ground (wire) (*US*); (*Aviat*) landing

tomacorriente [tomako'rrjente] NM (*AM*) socket

tomadura [toma'ðura] NF: **~ de pelo** hoax

tomar [to'mar] /1a/ VT (*gen, Cine, Foto, TV*) to take; (*actitud*) to adopt; (*aspecto*) to take on; (*notas*) to take down; (*beber*) to drink ▶ VI to take; (*AM*) to drink; **tomarse** VR to take; **tomarse por** to consider o.s. to be; **¡toma!** here you are!; **~ asiento** to sit down; **~ a algn por loco** to think sb mad; **~ a bien/a mal** to take well/badly; **~ en serio** to take seriously; **~ el pelo a algn** to pull sb's leg; **tomarla con algn** to pick a quarrel with sb; **~ el sol** to sunbathe; **~ por escrito** to write down; **toma y daca** give and take

tomate [to'mate] NM tomato

tomatera [toma'tera] NF tomato plant

tomavistas [toma'βistas] NM INV movie camera

tomillo [to'miʎo] NM thyme

tomo ['tomo] NM (*libro*) volume; (*fig*) importance

ton [ton] ABR = **tonelada** ▶ NM: **sin ~ ni son** without rhyme or reason

tonada [to'naða] NF tune

tonalidad [tonali'ðað] NF tone

tonel [to'nel] NM barrel

tonelada [tone'laða] NF ton; **~(s) métrica(s)** metric ton(s)

tonelaje [tone'laxe] NM tonnage

tonelero [tone'lero] NM cooper

tongo ['tongo] NM (*Deporte*) fix

tónico, -a ['toniko, a] ADJ tonic ▶ NM (*Med*) tonic ▶ NF (*Mus*) tonic; (*fig*) keynote

tonificador, a [tonifika'ðor, a], **tonificante** [tonifi'kante] ADJ invigorating, stimulating

tonificar [tonifi'kar] /**1g**/ VT to tone up

tonifique *etc* [toni'fike] VB *ver* **tonificar**

tonillo [to'niʎo] NM monotonous voice

tono ['tono] NM (*Mus*) tone; (*altura*) pitch; (*color*) shade; **fuera de ~** inappropriate; **~ de llamada** ringtone; **~ de marcar** (*Telec*) dialling tone; **darse ~** to put on airs

tontear [tonte'ar] /**1a**/ VI (*fam*) to fool about; (*enamorados*) to flirt

tontería [tonte'ria] NF (*estupidez*) foolishness; (*una tontería*) silly thing; **tonterías** NFPL rubbish *sg*, nonsense *sg*

tonto, -a ['tonto, a] ADJ stupid; (*ridículo*) silly ▶ NM/F fool; (*payaso*) clown; **a tontas y a locas** anyhow; **hacer(se) el ~** to act the fool

topacio [to'paθjo] NM topaz

topar [to'par] /**1a**/ VT (*tropezar*) to bump into; (*encontrar*) to find, come across; (*cabra etc*) to butt ▶ VI: **~ contra** *o* **en** to run into; **~ con** to run up against; **el problema topa en eso** that's where the problem lies

tope ['tope] ADJ maximum ▶ NM (*fin*) end; (*límite*) limit; (*Ferro*) buffer; (*Auto*) bumper; **al ~** end to end; **fecha ~** closing date; **precio ~** top price; **sueldo ~** maximum salary; **~ de tabulación** tab stop

tópico, -a ['topiko, a] ADJ topical; (*Med*) local ▶ NM platitude, cliché; **de uso ~** for external application

topo ['topo] NM (*Zool*) mole; (*fig*) blunderer

topografía [topoɣra'fia] NF topography

topógrafo, -a [to'poɣrafo, a] NM/F topographer; (*agrimensor*) surveyor

toponimia [topo'nimja] NF place names *pl*; (*estudio*) study of place names

toque *etc* ['toke] VB *ver* **tocar** ▶ NM touch; (*Mus*) beat; (*de campana*) chime, ring; (*Mil*) bugle call; (*fig*) crux; **dar un ~ a** to test; **dar el último ~ a** to put the final touch to; **~ de queda** curfew

toqué *etc* VB *ver* **tocar**

toquetear [tokete'ar] /**1a**/ VT to finger; (*fam!*) to touch up

toquilla [to'kiʎa] NF (*pañuelo*) headscarf; (*chal*) shawl

tórax ['toraks] NM INV thorax

torbellino [torbe'ʎino] NM whirlwind; (*fig*) whirl

torcedura [torθe'ðura] NF twist; (*Med*) sprain

torcer [tor'θer] /**2b, 2h**/ VT to twist; (*la esquina*) to turn; (*Med*) to sprain; (*cuerda*) to plait; (*ropa, manos*) to wring; (*persona*) to corrupt; (*sentido*) to distort ▶ VI (*cambiar de dirección*) to turn; (*desviar*) to turn off; **torcerse** VR to twist; (*doblar*) to bend; (*desviarse*) to go astray; (*fracasar*) to go wrong; **~ el gesto** to scowl; **torcerse un pie** to twist one's foot; **el coche torció a la derecha** the car turned right

torcido, -a [tor'θiðo, a] ADJ twisted; (*fig*) crooked ▶ NM curl

tordo, -a ['torðo, a] ADJ dappled ▶ NM thrush

torear [tore'ar] /**1a**/ VT (*fig: evadir*) to dodge; (*jugar con*) to tease; (*toro*) to fight ▶ VI to fight bulls

toreo [to'reo] NM bullfighting

torero, -a [to'rero, a] NM/F bullfighter

toril [to'ril] NM bullpen

tormenta [tor'menta] NF storm; (*fig: confusión*) turmoil

tormento [tor'mento] NM torture; (*fig*) anguish

tormentoso, -a [tormen'toso, a] ADJ stormy

tornar [tor'nar] /**1a**/ VT (*devolver*) to return, give back; (*transformar*) to transform ▶ VI to go back; **tornarse** VR (*ponerse*) to become; (*volver*) to return

tornasol [torna'sol] NM (*Bot*) sunflower; **papel ~** litmus paper

tornasolado, -a [tornaso'laðo, a] ADJ (*brillante*) iridescent; (*reluciente*) shimmering

torneo [tor'neo] NM tournament

tornero, -a [tor'nero, a] NM/F machinist

tornillo [tor'niʎo] NM screw; **apretar los tornillos a algn** to apply pressure on sb; **le falta un ~** (*fam*) he's got a screw loose

torniquete [torni'kete] NM (*puerta*) turnstile; (*Med*) tourniquet

torno ['torno] NM (*Tec: grúa*) winch; (*: de carpintero*) lathe; (*tambor*) drum; **~ de banco** vice, vise (*US*); **en ~ (a)** round, about

toro ['toro] NM bull; (*fam*) he-man; **los toros** bullfighting *sg*

toronja [to'ronxa] NF grapefruit

torpe ['torpe] ADJ (*poco hábil*) clumsy, awkward; (*movimiento*) sluggish; (*necio*) dim; (*lento*) slow; (*indecente*) crude; (*no honrado*) dishonest

torpedo [tor'peðo] NM torpedo

torpemente [torpe'mente] ADV (*sin destreza*) clumsily; (*lentamente*) slowly

torpeza [tor'peθa] NF (*falta de agilidad*) clumsiness; (*lentitud*) slowness; (*rigidez*) stiffness; (*error*) mistake; (*crudeza*) obscenity

torre ['torre] NF tower; (*de petróleo*) derrick; (*de electricidad*) pylon; (*Ajedrez*) rook; (*Aviat, Mil, Naut*) turret; **~ de telefonía móvil** mobile phone mast (*BRIT*); cell tower (*US*)

torrefacto, -a [torre'fakto, a] ADJ roasted; **café ~** high roast coffee

torrencial [torren'θjal] ADJ torrential

torrente [to'rrente] NM torrent

tórrido, -a ['torriðo, a] ADJ torrid

torrija [to'rrixa] NF fried bread; **torrijas** French toast *sg*

torsión [tor'sjon] NF twisting

torso ['torso] NM torso

torta ['torta] NF cake; (*fam*) slap; **~ de huevos** (*AM*) omelette; **no entendió ni ~** he didn't understand a word of it

tortazo [tor'taθo] NM (*bofetada*) slap; (*de coche*) crash

tortícolis [tor'tikolis] NM INV stiff neck

tortilla [tor'tiʎa] NF omelette; (*AM*) maize pancake; **~ francesa/española** plain/potato omelette; **cambiar o volver la ~ a algn** to turn the tables on sb

tortillera [torti'ʎera] NF (*fam!*) lesbian

tórtola ['tortola] NF turtledove

tortuga [tor'tuɣa] NF tortoise; **~ marina** turtle

tortuoso, -a [tor'twoso, a] ADJ winding

tortura [tor'tura] NF torture

torturar [tortu'rar] /1a/ VT to torture

torvo, -a ['torβo, a] ADJ grim, fierce

torzamos *etc* [tor'θamos] VB *ver* **torcer**

tos [tos] NF INV cough; **~ ferina** whooping cough

Toscana [tos'kana] NF: **La ~** Tuscany

tosco, -a ['tosko, a] ADJ coarse

toser [to'ser] /2a/ VI to cough; **no hay quien le tosa** he's in a class by himself

tostado, -a [tos'taðo, a] ADJ toasted; (*por el sol*) dark brown; (*piel*) tanned ▶ NF (*pan*) piece of toast; **tostadas** NFPL toast *sg*

tostador [tosta'ðor] NM, **tostadora** [tosta'ðora] NF toaster

tostar [tos'tar] /1l/ VT to toast; (*café*) to roast; (*al sol*) to tan; **tostarse** VR to get brown

tostón [tos'ton] NM: **ser un ~** to be a drag

total [to'tal] ADJ total ▶ ADV in short; (*al fin y al cabo*) when all is said and done ▶ NM total; **en ~** in all; **~ que** to cut a long story short; **~ de comprobación** (*Inform*) hash total; **~ debe/haber** (*Com*) debit/assets total

totalidad [totali'ðað] NF whole

totalitario, -a [totali'tarjo, a] ADJ totalitarian

totalmente [to'talmente] ADV totally

tóxico, -a ['toksiko, a] ADJ toxic ▶ NM poison

toxicómano, -a [toksi'komano, a] ADJ addicted to drugs ▶ NM/F drug addict

toxina [to'ksina] NF toxin

tozudo, -a [to'θuðo, a] ADJ obstinate

traba ['traβa] NF bond, tie; (*cadena*) fetter; **poner trabas a** to restrain

trabajador, a [traβaxa'ðor, a] NM/F worker ▶ ADJ hard-working; **~ autónomo o por cuenta propia** self-employed person

trabajar [traβa'xar] /1a/ VT to work; (*arar*) to till; (*empeñarse en*) to work at; (*empujar: persona*) to push; (*convencer*) to persuade ▶ VI to work; (*esforzarse*) to strive; **¡a ~!** let's get to work!; **~ por hacer algo** to strive to do sth

trabajo [tra'βaxo] NM work; (*tarea*) task; (*Pol*) labour; (*fig*) effort; **tomarse el ~ de** to take the trouble to; **~ por turnos/a destajo** shift work/piecework; **~ en equipo** teamwork; **~ en proceso** (*Com*) work-in-progress; **trabajos forzados** hard labour *sg*

trabajoso, -a [traβa'xoso, a] ADJ hard; (*Med*) pale

trabalenguas [traβa'lengwas] NM INV tongue twister

trabar [tra'βar] /1a/ VT (*juntar*) to join, unite; (*atar*) to tie down, fetter; (*agarrar*) to seize; (*amistad*) to strike up; **trabarse** VR to become entangled; (*reñir*) to squabble; **se le traba la lengua** he gets tongue-tied

trabazón [traβa'θon] NF (*Tec*) joining, assembly; (*fig*) bond, link

trabucar [traβu'kar] /1g/ VT (*confundir*) to confuse, mix up; (*palabras*) to misplace

trabuque *etc* [tra'βuke] VB *ver* **trabucar**

tracción [trak'θjon] NF traction; **~ delantera/trasera** front-wheel/rear-wheel drive

trace *etc* ['traθe] VB *ver* **trazar**

tractor [trak'tor] NM tractor

trad. ABR (= *traducido*) trans

tradición [traði'θjon] NF tradition

tradicional [traðiθjo'nal] ADJ traditional

traducción [traðuk'θjon] NF translation; **~ asistida por ordenador** computer-assisted translation

traducible [traðu'θiβle] ADJ translatable

traducir [traðu'θir] /3n/ VT to translate; **traducirse** VR: **traducirse en** (*fig*) to entail, result in

traductor, a [traðuk'tor, a] NM/F translator

traduzca *etc* [tra'ðuθka] VB *ver* **traducir**

traer [tra'er] /2o/ VT to bring; (*llevar*) to carry; (*ropa*) to wear; (*incluir*) to carry; (*fig*) to cause; **traerse** VR: **traerse algo** to be up to sth; **traerse bien/mal** to dress well/badly; **traérselas** to be annoying; **~ consigo** to involve, entail; **es un problema que se las trae** it's a difficult problem

traficante [trafi'kante] NMF trader, dealer

traficar [trafi'kar] /1g/ VI to trade; **~ con** (*pey*) to deal illegally in

tráfico ['trafiko] NM (Com) trade; (Auto) traffic

trafique etc [tra'fike] VB ver **traficar**

tragaderas [traɣa'ðeras] NFPL (garganta) throat sg, gullet sg; (credulidad) gullibility sg

tragaluz [traɣa'luθ] NM skylight

tragamonedas [traɣamo'neðas] NM INV, **tragaperras** [traɣa'perras] NM INV slot machine

tragar [tra'ɣar] /1h/ VT to swallow; (devorar) to devour, bolt down; **tragarse** VR to swallow; (tierra) to absorb, soak up; **no lo puedo ~** (persona) I can't stand him

tragedia [tra'xeðja] NF tragedy

trágico, -a ['traxiko, a] ADJ tragic

trago ['traɣo] NM (de líquido) drink; (comido de golpe) gulp; (fam: de bebida) swig; (desgracia) blow; **echar un ~** to have a drink; **~ amargo** (fig) hard time

trague etc ['traɣe] VB ver **tragar**

traición [trai'θjon] NF treachery; (Jur) treason; (una traición) act of treachery

traicionar [traiθjo'nar] /1a/ VT to betray

traicionero, -a [traiθjo'nero, a] = **traidor**

traída [tra'iða] NF carrying; **~ de aguas** water supply

traidor, a [trai'ðor, a] ADJ treacherous ▶ NM/F traitor

traigo etc ['traiɣo] VB ver **traer**

trailer ['trailer] (pl **trailers** ['trailer(s)]) NM trailer

traje ['traxe] VB ver **traer** ▶ NM (gen) dress; (de hombre) suit; (traje típico) costume; (fig) garb; **~ de baño** swimsuit; **~ de luces** bullfighter's costume; **~ hecho a la medida** made-to-measure suit

trajera etc [tra'xera] VB ver **traer**

trajín [tra'xin] NM haulage; (fam: movimiento) bustle; **trajines** NMPL goings-on

trajinar [traxi'nar] /1a/ VT (llevar) to carry, transport ▶ VI (moverse) to bustle about; (viajar) to travel around

trama ['trama] NF (fig) link; (: intriga) plot; (de tejido) weft

tramar [tra'mar] /1a/ VT to plot; (Tec) to weave; **tramarse** VR (fig): **algo se está tramando** there's something going on

tramitar [trami'tar] /1a/ VT (asunto) to transact; (negociar) to negotiate; (manejar) to handle

trámite ['tramite] NM (paso) step; (Jur) transaction; **trámites** NMPL (burocracia) paperwork sg, procedures; (Jur) proceedings

tramo ['tramo] NM (de tierra) plot; (de escalera) flight; (de vía) section

tramoya [tra'moja] NF (Teat) piece of stage machinery; (fig) trick

tramoyista [tramo'jista] NMF scene shifter; (fig) trickster

trampa ['trampa] NF trap; (en el suelo) trapdoor; (prestidigitación) conjuring trick; (engaño) trick; (fam) fiddle; **caer en la ~** to fall into the trap; **hacer trampas** (trampear) to cheat

trampear [trampe'ar] /1a/ VT, VI to cheat

trampilla [tram'piʎa] NF trap, hatchway

trampolín [trampo'lin] NM trampoline; (de piscina etc) diving board

tramposo, -a [tram'poso, a] ADJ crooked, cheating ▶ NM/F crook, cheat

tranca ['tranka] NF (palo) stick; (viga) beam; (de puerta, ventana) bar; (borrachera) binge; **a trancas y barrancas** with great difficulty

trancar [tran'kar] /1g/ VT to bar ▶ VI to stride along

trancazo [tran'kaθo] NM (golpe) blow

trance ['tranθe] NM (momento difícil) difficult moment; (situación crítica) critical situation; (estado de hipnosis) trance; **estar en ~ de muerte** to be at death's door

tranco ['tranko] NM stride

tranque etc ['tranke] VB ver **trancar**

tranquilamente [tran'kilamente] ADV (sin preocupaciones: leer, trabajar) peacefully; (sin enfadarse: hablar, discutir) calmly

tranquilice etc [tranki'liθe] VB ver **tranquilizar**

tranquilidad [trankili'ðað] NF (calma) calmness, stillness; (paz) peacefulness

tranquilizador, a [trankiliθa'ðor, a] ADJ (música) soothing; (hecho) reassuring

tranquilizante [trankili'θante] NM tranquillizer

tranquilizar [trankili'θar] /1f/ VT (calmar) to calm (down); (asegurar) to reassure; **tranquilizarse** VR to calm down

tranquilo, -a [tran'kilo, a] ADJ (calmado) calm; (apacible) peaceful; (mar) calm; (mente) untroubled

Trans. ABR (Com) = **transferencia**

transacción [transak'θjon] NF transaction

transar [tran'sar] /1a/ VI (Am) = **transigir**

transatlántico, -a [transat'lantiko, a] ADJ transatlantic ▶ NM (ocean) liner

transbordador [transβorða'ðor] NM ferry

transbordar [transβor'ðar] /1a/ VT to transfer; **transbordarse** VR to change

transbordo [trans'borðo] NM transfer; **hacer ~** to change (trains)

transcender [transθen'der] /2g/ VT = **trascender**

transcribir [transkri'βir] /3a/ VT to transcribe

transcurrir [transku'rrir] /3a/ VI (tiempo) to pass; (hecho) to turn out

transcurso [trans'kurso] NM passing, lapse; **~ del tiempo** lapse (of time); **en el ~ de ocho días** in the course of a week

transeúnte [transe'unte] ADJ transient ▶ NMF passer-by

transexual [transe'kswal] ADJ, NMF transsexual

transferencia [transfe'renθja] NF transference; (*Com*) transfer; **~ bancaria** banker's order; **~ de crédito** (*Com*) credit transfer; **~ electrónica de fondos** (*Com*) electronic funds transfer

transferir [transfe'rir] /3i/ VT to transfer; (*aplazar*) to postpone

transfiera *etc* [trans'fjera] VB *ver* **transferir**

transfigurar [transfiɣu'rar] /1a/ VT to transfigure

transfiriendo *etc* [transfi'rjendo] VB *ver* **transferir**

transformación [transforma'θjon] NF transformation

transformador [transforma'ðor] NM transformer

transformar [transfor'mar] /1a/ VT to transform; (*convertir*) to convert

tránsfuga ['transfuɣa] NMF (*Mil*) deserter; (*Pol*) turncoat

transfusión [transfu'sjon] NF (*tb:* **transfusión de sangre**) (blood) transfusion

transgénico, -a [trans'xeniko, a] ADJ genetically modified

transgredir [transɣre'dir] /3a/ VT to transgress

transgresión [transɣre'sjon] NF transgression

transición [transi'θjon] NF transition; **período de ~** transitional period

transido, -a [tran'siðo, a] ADJ overcome; **~ de angustia** beset with anxiety; **~ de dolor** racked with pain

transigir [transi'xir] /3c/ VI to compromise; (*ceder*) to make concessions

transija *etc* [tran'sixa] VB *ver* **transigir**

Transilvania [transil'βanja] NF Transylvania

transistor [transis'tor] NM transistor

transitable [transi'taβle] ADJ (*camino*) passable

transitar [transi'tar] /1a/ VI to go (from place to place)

transitivo, -a [transi'tiβo, a] ADJ transitive

tránsito ['transito] NM transit; (*Auto*) traffic; (*parada*) stop; **horas de máximo ~** rush hours; **"se prohíbe el ~"** "no thoroughfare"

transitorio, -a [transi'torjo, a] ADJ transitory

transmisión [transmi'sjon] NF (*Radio, TV*) transmission, broadcast(ing); (*transferencia*) transfer; **~ en circuito** hookup; **~ en directo/exterior** live/outside broadcast; **~ de datos (en paralelo/en serie)** (*Inform*) (parallel/serial) data transfer *o* transmission; **plena/media ~ bidireccional** (*Inform*) full/half duplex

transmitir [transmi'tir] /3a/ VT to transmit; (*Radio, TV*) to broadcast; (*enfermedad*) to give, pass on

transparencia [transpa'renθja] NF transparency; (*claridad*) clearness, clarity; (*diapositiva*) slide

transparentar [transparen'tar] /1a/ VT to reveal ▶ VI to be transparent

transparente [transpa'rente] ADJ transparent; (*aire*) clear; (*ligero*) diaphanous ▶ NM curtain

transpirar [transpi'rar] /1a/ VI to perspire; (*fig*) to transpire

transpondré *etc* [transpon'dre] VB *ver* **transponer**

transponer [transpo'ner] /2q/ VT to transpose; (*cambiar de sitio*) to move about ▶ VI (*desaparecer*) to disappear; (*ir más allá*) to go beyond; **transponerse** VR to change places; (*ocultarse*) to hide; (*sol*) to go down

transponga *etc* [trans'ponga] VB *ver* **transponer**

transportador [transporta'ðor] NM (*Mecánica*): **~ de correa** belt conveyor

transportar [transpor'tar] /1a/ VT to transport; (*llevar*) to carry

transporte [trans'porte] NM transport; (*Com*) haulage; **Ministerio de Transportes** Ministry of Transport

transpuesto [trans'pwesto], **transpuse** *etc* [trans'puse] VB *ver* **transponer**

transversal [transβer'sal] ADJ transverse, cross ▶ NF (*tb:* **calle transversal**) cross street

transversalmente [transβersal'mente] ADV obliquely

tranvía [tram'bia] NM tram, streetcar (*US*)

trapeador [trapea'ðor] NM (*Am*) mop

trapear [trape'ar] /1a/ VT (*Am*) to mop

trapecio [tra'peθjo] NM trapeze

trapecista [trape'θista] NMF trapeze artist

trapero, -a [tra'pero, a] NM/F ragman

trapicheos [trapi'tʃeos] NMPL (*fam*) schemes, fiddles

trapisonda [trapi'sonda] NF (*jaleo*) row; (*estafa*) swindle

trapo ['trapo] NM (*tela*) rag; (*de cocina*) cloth; **trapos** NMPL (*fam: de mujer*) clothes, dresses; **a todo ~** under full sail; **soltar el ~** (*llorar*) to burst into tears

tráquea ['trakea] NF trachea, windpipe

traqueteo [trake'teo] NM (*crujido*) crack; (*golpeteo*) rattling

tras [tras] PREP (*detrás*) behind; (*después*) after; **~ de** besides; **día ~ día** day after day; **uno ~ otro** one after the other

trasatlántico [trasat'lantiko] NM (*barco*) (cabin) cruiser

trascendencia [trasθen'denθja] NF (*importancia*) importance; (*en filosofía*) transcendence

trascendental [trasθenden'tal] ADJ important; transcendental

385

trascender [trasθen'der] /**2g**/ vi (*oler*) to smell; (*noticias*) to come out, leak out; (*sucesos, sentimientos*) to spread, have a wide effect; ~ **a** (*afectar*) to reach, have an effect on; (*olera*) to smack of; **en su novela todo trascienda a romanticismo** everything in his novel smacks of romanticism

trascienda *etc* [tras'θjenda] vb *ver* **trascender**

trasegar [trase'ɣar] /**1h, 1j**/ vt (*mover*) to move about; (*vino*) to decant

trasegué [trase'ɣe], **traseguemos** *etc* [trase'ɣemos] vb *ver* **trasegar**

trasero, -a [tra'sero, a] adj back, rear ▶ nm (*Anat*) bottom; **traseros** nmpl ancestors

trasfondo [tras'fondo] nm background

trasgo ['trasɣo] nm (*duende*) goblin

trasgredir [trasɣre'ðir] /**3a**/ vt to contravene

trashumante [trasu'mante] adj migrating

trasiego *etc* [tra'sjeɣo] vb *ver* **trasegar** ▶ nm (*cambiar de sitio*) move, switch; (*de vino*) decanting; (*trastorno*) upset

trasiegue *etc* [tra'sjeɣe] vb *ver* **trasegar**

trasladar [trasla'ðar] /**1a**/ vt to move; (*persona*) to transfer; (*postergar*) to postpone; (*copiar*) to copy; (*interpretar*) to interpret; **trasladarse** vr (*irse*) to go; (*mudarse*) to move; **trasladarse a otro puesto** to move to a new job

traslado [tras'laðo] nm move; (*mudanza*) move, removal; (*de persona*) transfer; (*copia*) copy; ~ **de bloque** (*Inform*) block move, cut-and-paste

traslucir [traslu'θir] /**3f**/ vt to show; **traslucirse** vr to be translucent; (*fig*) to be revealed

trasluz [tras'luθ] nm reflected light; **al ~** against o up to the light

trasluzca *etc* [tras'luθka] vb *ver* **traslucir**

trasmano [tras'mano]: **a ~** adv (*fuera de alcance*) out of reach; (*apartado*) out of the way

trasnochado, -a [trasno'tʃaðo, a] adj dated

trasnochador, a [trasnotʃa'ðor, a] adj given to staying up late ▶ nm/f (*fig*) night owl

trasnochar [trasno'tʃar] /**1a**/ vi (*acostarse tarde*) to stay up late; (*no dormir*) to have a sleepless night; (*pasar la noche*) to stay the night

traspapelar [traspape'lar] /**1a**/ vt (*documento, carta*) to mislay, misplace

traspasar [traspa'sar] /**1a**/ vt (*bala*) to pierce, go through; (*propiedad*) to sell, transfer; (*calle*) to cross over; (*límites*) to go beyond; (*ley*) to break; **"traspaso negocio"** "business for sale"

traspaso [tras'paso] nm (*venta*) transfer, sale; (*fig*) anguish

traspié [tras'pje] (*pl* **traspiés**) nm (*caída*) stumble; (*tropezón*) trip; (*fig*) blunder

trasplantar [trasplan'tar] /**1a**/ vt to transplant

trasplante [tras'plante] nm transplant

traspuesto, -a [tras'pwesto, a] adj: **quedarse ~** to doze off

trastada [tras'taða] nf (*fam*) prank

trastazo [tras'taθo] nm (*fam*) bump; **darse un ~** (*persona*) to bump o.s.; (*en coche*) to have a bump

traste ['traste] nm (*Mus*) fret; **dar al ~ con algo** to ruin sth; **ir al ~** to fall through

trastero [tras'tero] nm lumber room

trastienda [tras'tjenda] nf back room (*of shop*); **obtener algo por la ~** to get sth by underhand means

trasto ['trasto] nm (*mueble*) piece of furniture; (*tarro viejo*) old pot; (*pey: cosa*) piece of junk; (: *persona*) dead loss; **trastos** nmpl (*Teat*) scenery *sg*; **tirar los trastos a la cabeza** to have a blazing row

trastocar [trasto'kar] /**1g, 1l**/ vt (*papeles*) to mix up

trastornado, -a [trastor'naðo, a] adj (*loco*) mad; (*agitado*) crazy

trastornar [trastor'nar] /**1a**/ vt to overturn, upset; (*fig: ideas*) to confuse; (: *nervios*) to shatter; (: *persona*) to drive crazy; **trastornarse** vr (*plan*) to fall through; (*volverse loco*) to go mad o crazy

trastorno [tras'torno] nm (*acto*) overturning; (*confusión*) confusion; (*Pol*) disturbance, upheaval; (*Med*) upset; ~ **estomacal** stomach upset; ~ **mental** mental disorder, breakdown

trasunto [tra'sunto] nm copy

trasvase [tras'βase] nm (*de río*) diversion

tratable [tra'taβle] adj friendly

tratado [tra'taðo] nm (*Pol*) treaty; (*Com*) agreement; (*Lit*) treatise

tratamiento [trata'mjento] nm treatment; (*Tec*) processing; (*de problema*) handling; ~ **de datos** (*Inform*) data processing; ~ **de gráficos** (*Inform*) graphics; ~ **de márgenes** margin settings; ~ **de textos** (*Inform*) word processing; ~ **por lotes** (*Inform*) batch processing; ~ **de tú** familiar address

tratante [tra'tante] nmf dealer, merchandiser

tratar [tra'tar] /**1a**/ vt (*ocuparse de*) to treat; (*manejar, Tec*) to handle; (*Inform*) to process; (*Med*) to treat; (*dirigirse a: persona*) to address ▶ vi: ~ **de** (*hablar sobre*) to deal with, be about; (*intentar*) to try to; **tratarse** vr to treat each other; ~ **con** (*Com*) to trade in; (*negociar con*) to negotiate with; (*tener tratos con*) to have dealings with; **se trata de la nueva piscina** it's about the new pool; **¿de qué se trata?** what's it about?

trato ['trato] nm dealings *pl*; (*relaciones*) relationship; (*comportamiento*) manner; (*Com, Jur*) agreement, contract; (*título*) (form of) address; **de ~ agradable** pleasant; **de fácil ~** easy to get on with; **~ equitativo** fair deal; **¡~ hecho!** it's a deal!; **malos tratos** ill-treatment *sg*

trauma ['trauma] NM trauma

traumático, -a [trau'matiko, a] ADJ traumatic

través [tra'βes] NM (*contratiempo*) reverse; **al ~** across, crossways; **a ~ de** across; (*sobre*) over; (*por*) through; **de ~** across; (*de lado*) sideways

travesaño [traβe'saɲo] NM (*Arq*) crossbeam; (*Deporte*) crossbar

travesía [traβe'sia] NF (*calle*) cross-street; (*Naut*) crossing

travesti [tra'βesti] NMF transvestite

travesura [traβe'sura] NF (*broma*) prank; (*ingenio*) wit

travieso, -a [tra'βjeso, a] ADJ (*niño*) naughty; (*adulto*) restless; (*ingenioso*) witty ▶ NF crossing; (*Arq*) crossbeam; (*Ferro*) sleeper

trayecto [tra'jekto] NM (*ruta*) road, way; (*viaje*) journey; (*tramo*) stretch; (*curso*) course; **final del ~** end of the line

trayectoria [trajek'torja] NF trajectory; (*desarrollo*) development; (*fig*) path; **la ~ actual del partido** the party's present line

trayendo *etc* [tra'jendo] VB *ver* **traer**

traza ['traθa] NF (*Arq*) plan, design; (*aspecto*) looks *pl*; (*señal*) sign; (*engaño*) trick; (*habilidad*) skill; (*Inform*) trace

trazado, -a [tra'θaðo, a] ADJ: **bien ~** shapely, well-formed ▶ NM (*Arq*) plan, design; (*fig*) outline; (*de carretera etc*) line, route

trazador [traθa'ðor] NM plotter; **~ plano** flatbed plotter

trazar [tra'θar] /1f/ VT (*Arq*) to plan; (*Arte*) to sketch; (*fig*) to trace; (*hacer: itinerario*) to plot; (*plan*) to draw up

trazo ['traθo] NM (*línea*) line; (*bosquejo*) sketch; **trazos** NMPL (*de cara*) lines, features

TRB ABR = **toneladas de registro bruto**

trébol ['treβol] NM (*Bot*) clover; **tréboles** NMPL (*Naipes*) clubs

trece ['treθe] NUM thirteen; **estar en sus ~** to stand firm

trecho ['tretʃo] NM (*distancia*) distance; (*de tiempo*) while; (*fam*) piece; **de ~ en ~** at intervals

tregua ['treɣwa] NF (*Mil*) truce; (*fig*) lull, respite; **sin ~** without respite

treinta ['treinta] NUM thirty

treintena [trein'tena] NF (about) thirty

tremendo, -a [tre'mendo, a] ADJ (*terrible*) terrible; (*imponente: cosa*) imposing; (*fam: fabuloso*) tremendous; (*divertido*) entertaining

trémulo, -a ['tremulo, a] ADJ quivering; (*luz*) flickering

tren [tren] NM (*Ferro*) train; **~ de aterrizaje** undercarriage; **~ directo/expreso/(de)**

mercancías/de pasajeros/suplementario through/fast/goods *o* freight/passenger/ relief train; **~ de cercanías** suburban train; **~ de vida** way of life

trenca ['trenka] NF duffel coat

trence *etc* ['trenθe] VB *ver* **trenzar**

trenza ['trenθa] NF (*de pelo*) plait

trenzar [tren'θar] /1f/ VT (*el pelo*) to plait ▶ VI (*en baile*) to weave in and out; **trenzarse** VR (*Am*) to become involved

trepa ['trepa] NF (*subida*) climb; (*ardid*) trick

trepador, a [trepa'ðor, a] NM/F (*fam*): **ser un(a) ~(a)** to be on the make ▶ NF (*Bot*) climber

trepar [tre'par] /1a/ VT, VI to climb; (*Tec*) to drill

trepidación [trepiða'θjon] NF shaking, vibration

trepidar [trepi'ðar] /1a/ VI to shake, vibrate

tres [tres] NUM three; (*fecha*) third; **las ~** three o'clock

trescientos, -as [tres'θjentos, as] NUM three hundred

tresillo [tre'siʎo] NM three-piece suite; (*Mus*) triplet

treta ['treta] NF (*Com etc*) gimmick; (*fig*) trick

tri ... [tri] PREF tri..., three-...

tríada ['triaða] NF triad

triangular [trjangu'lar] ADJ triangular

triángulo [tri'angulo] NM triangle

tribal [tri'βal] ADJ tribal

tribu ['triβu] NF tribe

tribuna [tri'βuna] NF (*plataforma*) platform; (*Deporte*) stand; (*fig*) public speaking; **~ de la prensa** press box; **~ del acusado** (*Jur*) dock; **~ del jurado** jury box

tribunal [triβu'nal] NM (*en juicio*) court; (*comisión, fig*) tribunal; (*Escol: examinadores*) board of examiners; **T~ Supremo** High Court, Supreme Court (*US*); **T~ de Justicia de las Comunidades Europeas** European Court of Justice; **~ popular** jury

tributar [triβu'tar] /1a/ VT to pay; (*las gracias*) to give; (*cariño*) to show

tributario, -a [triβu'tarjo, a] ADJ (*Geo, Pol*) tributary *cpd*; (*Econ*) tax *cpd*, taxation *cpd* ▶ NM (*Geo*) tributary ▶ NM/F (*Com*) taxpayer; **sistema ~** tax system

tributo [tri'βuto] NM (*Com*) tax

triciclo [tri'θiklo] NM tricycle

tricornio [tri'kornjo] NM three-cornered hat

tricota [tri'kota] NF (*Am*) knitted sweater

tricotar [triko'tar] /1a/ VI to knit

tridimensional [triðimensjo'nal] ADJ three-dimensional

trienal [trje'nal] ADJ three-year

trifulca [tri'fulka] NF (*fam*) row, shindy

trigal [tri'ɣal] NM wheat field

trigésimo, -a [tri'xesimo, a] NUM thirtieth

trigo ['triɣo] NM wheat; **trigos** NMPL wheat field(s) nf

trigueño, -a [tri'ɣeɲo, a] ADJ (pelo) corn-coloured; (piel) olive-skinned

trillado, -a [tri'ʎaðo, a] ADJ threshed; (fig) trite, hackneyed

trilladora [triʎa'ðora] NF threshing machine

trillar [tri'ʎar] /1a/ VT (Agr) to thresh; (fig) to frequent

trillizos, -as [tri'ʎiθos, as] NMPL/NFPL triplets

trilogía [trilo'xia] NF trilogy

trimestral [trimes'tral] ADJ quarterly; (Escol) termly

trimestre [tri'mestre] NM (Escol) term; (Com) quarter, financial period; (: pago) quarterly payment

trinar [tri'nar] /1a/ VI (Mus) to trill; (ave) to sing, warble; (rabiar) to fume, be angry; **está que trina** he's hopping mad

trincar [trin'kar] /1g/ VT (atar) to tie up; (Naut) to lash; (agarrar) to pinion

trinchante [trin'tʃante] NM (para cortar carne) carving knife; (tenedor) meat fork

trinchar [trin'tʃar] /1a/ VT to carve

trinchera [trin'tʃera] NF (fosa) trench; (para vía) cutting; (impermeable) trench-coat

trineo [tri'neo] NM sledge

trinidad [trini'ðað] NF trio; (Rel): **la T~** the Trinity

trino ['trino] NM trill

trinque etc ['trinke] VB ver **trincar**

trinquete [trin'kete] NM (Tec) pawl; (Naut) foremast

trío ['trio] NM trio

tripa ['tripa] NF (Anat) intestine; (fam) belly; **tripas** NFPL (Anat) insides; (Culin) tripe sg; **tener mucha ~** to be fat; **me duelen las tripas** I have a stomach ache

tripartito, -a [tripar'tito, a] ADJ tripartite

triple ['triple] ADJ triple; (tres veces) threefold

triplicado, -a [tripli'kaðo, a] ADJ: **por ~** in triplicate

triplicar [tripli'kar] /1g/ VT to treble

triplo, -a ['triplo, a] ADJ = **triple**

trípode ['tripoðe] NM tripod

Trípoli ['tripoli] NM Tripoli

tríptico ['triptiko] NM (Arte) triptych; (documento) three-part document

tripulación [tripula'θjon] NF crew

tripulante [tripu'lante] NMF crewman/woman

tripular [tripu'lar] /1a/ VT (barco) to man; (Auto) to drive

triquiñuela [triki'ɲwela] NF trick

tris [tris] NM crack; **en un ~** in an instant; **estar en un ~ de hacer algo** to be within an inch of doing sth

triste ['triste] ADJ (afligido) sad; (sombrío) melancholy, gloomy; (desolado) desolate; (lamentable) sorry, miserable; (viejo) old; (único) single; **no queda sino un ~ penique** there's just one miserable penny left

tristeza [tris'teθa] NF (aflicción) sadness; (melancolía) melancholy; (de lugar) desolation; (pena) misery

tristón, -ona [tris'ton, ona] ADJ sad, downhearted

trituradora [tritura'ðora] NF shredder

triturar [tritu'rar] /1a/ VT (moler) to grind; (mascar) to chew; (documentos) to shred

triunfador, a [triunfa'ðor, a] ADJ triumphant; (ganador) winning ▶ NM/F winner

triunfal [triun'fal] ADJ triumphant; (arco) triumphal

triunfante [triun'fante] ADJ triumphant; (ganador) winning

triunfar [triun'far] /1a/ VI (tener éxito) to triumph; (ganar) to win; (Naipes) to be trumps; **triunfan corazones** hearts are trumps; **~ en la vida** to succeed in life

triunfo [tri'unfo] NM triumph; (Naipes) trump

trivial [tri'βjal] ADJ trivial

trivialice etc [triβja'liθe] VB ver **trivializar**

trivializar [triβjali'θar] /1f/ VT to minimize, play down

triza ['triθa] NF bit, piece; **hacer algo trizas** to smash sth to bits; (papel) to tear sth to shreds

trocar [tro'kar] /1g, 1l/ VT (Com) to exchange; (dinero, de lugar) to change; (palabras) to exchange; (confundir) to confuse; **trocarse** VR (confundirse) to get mixed up; (transformarse) **trocarse (en)** to change (into)

trocear [troθe'ar] /1a/ VT to cut up

trocha ['trotʃa] NF (sendero) by-path; (atajo) short cut

troche ['trotʃe]: **a ~ y moche** adv helter-skelter, pell-mell

trofeo [tro'feo] NM (premio) trophy

trola ['trola] NF (fam) fib

troll [trol] NM (Internet) troll

tromba ['tromba] NF whirlwind; **~ de agua** downpour

trombón [trom'bon] NM trombone

trombosis [trom'bosis] NF INV thrombosis

trompa ['trompa] NF (Mus) horn; (de elefante) trunk; (trompo) humming top; (hocico) snout; (Anat) tube, duct ▶ NM (Mus) horn player; **~ de Falopio** Fallopian tube; **cogerse una ~** (fam) to get tight

trompada [trom'paða] NF, **trompazo** [trom'paθo] NM (choque) bump, bang; (puñetazo) punch

trompeta [trom'peta] NF trumpet; (clarín) bugle ▶ NM trumpeter

trompetilla [trompe'tiʎa] NF ear trumpet

trompicón [trompi'kon]: **a trompicones** *adv* in fits and starts

trompo ['trompo] NM spinning top

trompón [trom'pon] NM bump

tronado, -a [tro'naðo, a] ADJ broken-down

tronar [tro'nar] /**1l**/ VT (*AM*) to shoot, execute; (: *examen*) to flunk ▶ VI to thunder; (*fig*) to rage; (*fam*) to go broke

tronchar [tron'tʃar] /**1a**/ VT (*árbol*) to chop down; (*fig: vida*) to cut short; (*esperanza*) to shatter; (*persona*) to tire out; **troncharse** VR to fall down; **troncharse de risa** to split one's sides with laughter

tronco ['tronko] NM (*de árbol, Anat*) trunk; (*de planta*) stem; **estar hecho un ~** to be sound asleep

tronera [tro'nera] NF (*Mil*) loophole; (*Arq*) small window

trono ['trono] NM throne

tropa ['tropa] NF (*Mil*) troop; (*soldados*) soldiers *pl*; (*soldados rasos*) ranks *pl*; (*gentío*) mob

tropecé [trope'θe], **tropecemos** *etc* [trope'θemos] VB *ver* **tropezar**

tropel [tro'pel] NM (*muchedumbre*) crowd; (*prisa*) rush; (*montón*) throng; **acudir** (*etc*) **en ~** to come (*etc*) in a mad rush

tropelía [trope'lia] NM outrage

tropezar [trope'θar] /**1f, 1j**/ VI to trip, stumble; (*fig*) to slip up; **tropezarse** VR (*dos personas*) to run into each other; **~ con** (*encontrar*) to run into; (*topar con*) to bump into

tropezón [trope'θon] NM trip; (*fig*) blunder; (*traspié*): **dar un ~** to trip

tropical [tropi'kal] ADJ tropical

trópico ['tropiko] NM tropic

tropiece *etc* [tro'pjeθe] VB *ver* **tropezar**

tropiezo *etc* [tro'pjeθo] VB *ver* **tropezar** ▶ NM (*error*) slip, blunder; (*desgracia*) misfortune; (*revés*) setback; (*obstáculo*) snag; (*discusión*) quarrel

troqué [tro'ke], **troquemos** *etc* [tro'kemos] VB *ver* **trocar**

trotamundos [trota'mundos] NM INV globetrotter

trotar [tro'tar] /**1a**/ VI to trot; (*viajar*) to travel about

trote ['trote] NM trot; (*fam*) travelling; **de mucho ~** hard-wearing

Troya ['troja] NF Troy; **aquí fue ~** now there's nothing but ruins

trozar [tro'θar] /**1f**/ VT (*AM*) to cut up, cut into pieces

trozo ['troθo] NM bit, piece; (*Lit, Mus*) passage; **a trozos** in bits

trucha ['trutʃa] NF (*pez*) trout; (*Tec*) crane

truco ['truko] NM (*habilidad*) knack; (*engaño*) trick; (*Cine*) trick effect *o* photography; **trucos** NMPL billiards *sg*; **~ publicitario** advertising gimmick

trueco *etc* ['trweko] VB *ver* **trocar**

trueno ['trweno] VB *ver* **tronar** ▶ NM (*gen*) thunder; (*estampido*) boom; (: *de arma*) bang

trueque ['trweke] VB *ver* **trocar** ▶ NM exchange; (*Com*) barter

trufa ['trufa] NF (*Bot*) truffle; (*fig: fam*) fib

truhán, -ana [tru'an, ana] NM/F rogue

truncado, -a [trun'kaðo, a] ADJ truncated

truncar [trun'kar] /**1g**/ VT (*cortar*) to truncate; (*la vida etc*) to cut short; (*el desarrollo*) to stunt

trunque *etc* ['trunke] VB *ver* **truncar**

Tte. ABR (= *Teniente*) Lt.

tu [tu] ADJ your

tú [tu] PRON you

tubérculo [tu'βerkulo] NM (*Bot*) tuber

tuberculosis [tuβerku'losis] NF INV tuberculosis

tubería [tuβe'ria] NF pipes *pl*, piping; (*conducto*) pipeline

tubo ['tuβo] NM tube, pipe; **~ de desagüe** drainpipe; **~ de ensayo** test-tube; **~ de escape** exhaust (pipe); **~ digestivo** alimentary canal

tuerca ['twerka] NF (*Tec*) nut

tuerce *etc* ['twerθe] VB *ver* **torcer**

tuerto, -a ['twerto, a] ADJ (*torcido*) twisted; (*ciego*) blind in one eye ▶ NM/F one-eyed person ▶ NM (*ofensa*) wrong; **a tuertas** upside-down

tuerza *etc* ['twerθa] VB *ver* **torcer**

tueste *etc* ['tweste] VB *ver* **tostar**

tuétano ['twetano] NM (*Anat: médula*) marrow; (*Bot*) pith; **hasta los tuétanos** through and through, utterly

tufo ['tufo] NM vapour; (*fig: pey*) stench

tugurio [tu'ɣurjo] NM slum

tuit M (*Inform*) tweet; Twitter® message

tuitear [tuite'ar] VT, VI to tweet ▶ VB (*Inform*) to tweet

tul [tul] NM tulle

tulipán [tuli'pan] NM tulip

tullido, -a [tu'ʎiðo, a] ADJ crippled; (*cansado*) exhausted

tumba ['tumba] NF (*sepultura*) tomb; (*sacudida*) shake; (*voltereta*) somersault; **ser (como) una ~** to keep one's mouth shut

tumbar [tum'bar] /**1a**/ VT to knock down; (*doblar*) to knock over; (*fam: suj: olor*) to overpower ▶ VI to fall down; **tumbarse** VR (*echarse*) to lie down; (*extenderse*) to stretch out

tumbo ['tumbo] NM (*caída*) fall; (*de vehículo*) jolt; (*momento crítico*) critical moment; **dar tumbos** to stagger

tumbona [tum'bona] NF (*butaca*) easy chair; (*de playa: para acostarse*) lounger; (: *para sentarse*) deckchair (*BRIT*), beach chair (*US*)

tumor [tu'mor] NM tumour

tumulto [tu'multo] NM turmoil; (*Pol: motín*) riot

t

tuna ['tuna] NF (*Mus*) student music group; *ver tb* **tuno**; *see note*

> A *tuna* is made up of university students, or quite often former students, who dress up in costumes from the *Edad de Oro*, the Spanish Golden Age. These musical troupes go through the town playing their guitars, lutes and tambourines and serenade the young ladies in the halls of residence, or make impromptu appearances at weddings or parties singing traditional Spanish songs for a few coins.

tunante [tu'nante] ADJ rascally ▶ NM rogue, villain; **¡~!** you villain!

tunda ['tunda] NF (*de tela*) shearing; (*de golpes*) beating

tundir [tun'dir] /3a/ VT (*tela*) to shear; (*hierba*) to mow; (*fig*) to exhaust; (*fam: golpear*) to beat

tunecino, -a [tune'θino, a] ADJ, NM/F Tunisian

túnel ['tunel] NM tunnel

Túnez ['tuneθ] NM Tunis

túnica ['tunika] NF tunic; (*vestido largo*) long dress; (*Anat, Bot*) tunic

Tunicia [tu'niθja] NF Tunisia

tuning ['tunin] NM (*Auto*) car styling, modding (*fam*)

tuno, -a ['tuno, a] NM/F (*fam*) rogue ▶ NM (*Mus*) member of a "tuna"; *ver* **tuna**

tuntún [tun'tun] **al ~** ADV thoughtlessly

tupamaro, -a [tupa'maro, a] ADJ, NM/F (*AM*) urban guerrilla

tupé [tu'pe] NM quiff

tupí [tu'pi], **tupí-guaraní** [tupigwara'ni] ADJ, NMF Tupi-Guarani

tupido, -a [tu'piðo, a] ADJ (*denso*) dense; (*fig: torpe*) dim; (*tela*) close-woven

turba ['turβa] NF (*combustible*) turf; (*muchedumbre*) crowd

turbación [turβa'θjon] NF (*molestia*) disturbance; (*preocupación*) worry

turbado, -a [tur'βaðo, a] ADJ (*molesto*) disturbed; (*preocupado*) worried

turbante [tur'βante] NM turban

turbar [tur'βar] /1a/ VT (*molestar*) to disturb; (*incomodar*) to upset; **turbarse** VR to be disturbed

turbina [tur'βina] NF turbine

turbio, -a [tur'βjo, a] ADJ (*agua etc*) cloudy; (*vista*) dim, blurred; (*tema*) unclear, confused; (*negocio*) shady ▶ ADV indistinctly

turbión [tur'βjon] NF downpour; (*fig*) shower, hail

turbo ['turβo] ADJ INV turbo(-charged) ▶ NM (*tb coche*) turbo

turbulencia [turβu'lenθja] NF turbulence; (*fig*) restlessness

turbulento, -a [turβu'lento, a] ADJ turbulent; (*fig: intranquilo*) restless; (*ruidoso*) noisy

turco, -a ['turko, a] ADJ Turkish ▶ NM/F Turk ▶ NM (*Ling*) Turkish

Turena [tu'rena] NF Touraine

turgente [tur'xente], **túrgido, a** ['turxiðo, a] ADJ (*tirante*) turgid, swollen

Turín [tu'rin] NM Turin

turismo [tu'rismo] NM tourism; (*coche*) saloon car; **hacer ~** to go travelling (abroad)

turista [tu'rista] NMF tourist; (*visitante*) sightseer

turístico, -a [tu'ristiko, a] ADJ tourist *cpd*

Turkmenistán [turkmeni'stan] NM Turkmenistan

turnarse [tur'narse] /1a/ VR to take (it in) turns

turno ['turno] NM (*de trabajo*) shift; (*oportunidad, orden de prioridad*) opportunity; (*Deporte etc*) turn; **es su ~** it's his turn (next); **~ de día/de noche** day/night shift

turolense [turo'lense] ADJ of o from Teruel ▶ NMF native o inhabitant of Teruel

turquesa [tur'kesa] NF turquoise

Turquía [tur'kia] NF Turkey

turrón [tu'rron] NM (*dulce*) nougat; (*fam*) sinecure, cushy job o number

tute ['tute] NM (*Naipes*) card game; **darse un ~** to break one's back

tutear [tute'ar] /1a/ VT to address as familiar "tú"; **tutearse** VR to be on familiar terms

tutela [tu'tela] NF (*legal*) guardianship; (*instrucción*) guidance; **estar bajo la ~ de** (*fig*) to be under the protection of

tutelar [tute'lar] /1a/ ADJ tutelary ▶ VT to protect

tutor, a [tu'tor, a] NM/F (*legal*) guardian; (*Escol*) tutor; **~ de curso** form master/mistress

tuve *etc* ['tuβe] VB *ver* **tener**

tuviera *etc* VB *ver* **tener**

tuyo, -a ['tujo, a] ADJ yours, of yours ▶ PRON yours; **un amigo ~** a friend of yours; **los tuyos** (*fam*) your relations, your family

TV NF ABR (= *televisión*) TV

TVE NF ABR = **Televisión Española**

tweet [twit] (*pl* **tweets**) NM (*en Twitter*) tweet

Uu

U, u [u] NF (letra) U, u; **viraje en U** U-turn; **U de Ulises** U for Uncle

u [u] CONJ or

u. ABR = **unidad**

ubérrimo, -a [u'βerrimo, a] ADJ very rich, fertile

ubicación [uβika'θjon] NF (esp Am) place, position, location

ubicado, -a [uβi'kaðo, a] ADJ (esp Am) situated

ubicar [uβi'kar] /1g/ VT (esp Am) to place, situate; (: encontrar) to find; **ubicarse** VR to be situated, be located

ubicuo, -a [u'βikwo, a] ADJ ubiquitous

ubique etc [u'βike] VB ver **ubicar**

ubre ['uβre] NF udder

UCI ['uθi] SIGLA F (= Unidad de Cuidados Intensivos) ICU

Ucrania [u'kranja] NF Ukraine

ucraniano, -a [ukra'njano, a] ADJ, NM/F Ukrainian ▶ NM (Ling) Ukrainian

ucranio [u'kranjo] NM (Ling) Ukrainian

Ud(s) ABR = **usted**

UDV SIGLA F = **Unidad de Despliegue Visual**

UE NF ABR (= Unión Europea) EU

UEFA [w'efa] NF ABR (= Unión de Asociaciones de Fútbol Europeo) UEFA

UEO NF ABR (= Unión Europea Occidental) WEU

UEP NF ABR = **Unión Europea de Pagos**

UER SIGLA F = **Unión Europea de Radiodifusión**

uf [uf] EXCL (cansancio) phew!; (repugnancia) ugh!

ufanarse [ufa'narse] /1a/ VR to boast; **~ de** to pride o.s. on

ufano, -a [u'fano, a] ADJ (arrogante) arrogant; (presumido) conceited

UGT NF ABR ver **Unión General de Trabajadores**

UIT SIGLA F = **Unión Internacional de Telecomunicaciones**

ujier [u'xjer] NM usher; (portero) doorkeeper

úlcera ['ulθera] NF ulcer

ulcerar [ulθe'rar] /1a/ VT to make sore; **ulcerarse** VR to ulcerate

ulterior [ulte'rjor] ADJ (más allá) farther, further; (subsecuente, siguiente) subsequent

ulteriormente [ulterjor'mente] ADV later, subsequently

últimamente ['ultimamente] ADV (recientemente) lately, recently; (finalmente) finally; (como último recurso) as a last resort

ultimar [ulti'mar] /1a/ VT to finish; (finalizar) to finalize; (Am: matar) to kill

ultimátum [ulti'matum] NM (pl ultimátums) ultimatum

último, -a ['ultimo, a] ADJ last; (más reciente) latest, most recent; (más bajo) bottom; (más alto) top; (fig) final, extreme; **en las últimas** on one's last legs; **por ~** finally

ultra ['ultra] ADJ ultra ▶ NMF extreme right-winger

ultracongelar [ultrakonxe'lar] /1a/ VT to deep-freeze

ultraderecha [ultraðe'retʃa] NF extreme right (wing)

ultrajar [ultra'xar] /1a/ VT (escandalizar) to outrage; (insultar) to insult, abuse

ultraje [ul'traxe] NM outrage; insult

ultraligero [ultrali'xero] NM microlight (BRIT), microlite (US)

ultramar [ultra'mar] NM: **de** o **en ~** abroad, overseas; **los países de ~** the overseas countries

ultramarino, -a [ultrama'rino, a] ADJ overseas, foreign ▶ NM: **ultramarinos** groceries; **tienda de ultramarinos** grocer's (shop)

ultranza [ul'tranθa] **a ~** ADV to the death; (a toda costa) at all costs; (completo) outright; (Pol etc) out-and-out, extreme; **un nacionalista a ~** a rabid nationalist

ultrarrojo, -a [ultra'rroxo, a] ADJ = **infrarrojo**

ultrasónico, -a [ultra'soniko, a] ADJ ultrasonic

ultratumba [ultra'tumba] NF: **la vida de ~** the next life; **una voz de ~** a ghostly voice

ultravioleta [ultraβjo'leta] ADJ INV ultraviolet

u

ulular [ulu'lar] /**1a**/ vi to howl; (búho) to hoot
umbilical [umbili'kal] ADJ: **cordón ~** umbilical cord
umbral [um'bral] NM (gen) threshold; **~ de rentabilidad** (Com) break-even point
umbrío, -a [um'brio, a] ADJ shady
UME NF ABR (= Unión Monetaria y Económica) EMU

PALABRA CLAVE

un, una [un, 'una] ARTÍCULO INDEFINIDO
1 a; (antes de vocal) an; **una mujer/naranja** a woman/an orange
2: **unos/unas**: **hay unos regalos para ti** there are some presents for you; **hay unas cervezas en la nevera** there are some beers in the fridge; ver tb **uno**
3 (enfático): **¡hace un frío!** it's so cold!; **¡tiene una casa!** he's got some house!

U.N.A.M. ['unam] NF ABR = **Universidad Nacional Autónoma de México**
unánime [u'nanime] ADJ unanimous
unanimidad [unanimi'ðað] NF unanimity; **por ~** unanimously
unción [un'θjon] NF anointing
uncir [un'θir] /**3b**/ vt to yoke
undécimo, -a [un'deθimo, a] ADJ, NM/F eleventh
UNED [u'ned] NF ABR (Esp Univ: = Universidad Nacional de Enseñanza a Distancia) ≈ Open University (BRIT)
UNEF [u'nef] SIGLA F = **Fuerzas de Urgencia de las Naciones Unidas**
UNESCO, Unesco [u'nesko] SIGLA F (= United Nations Educational, Scientific and Cultural Organization) UNESCO
ungir [un'xir] /**3c**/ vt to rub with ointment; (Rel) to anoint
ungüento [un'gwento] NM ointment; (fig) salve, balm
únicamente ['unikamente] ADV solely; (solamente) only
UNICEF, Unicef [uni'θef] SIGLA F (= United Nations International Children's Emergency Fund) ≈ UNICEF
unicidad [uniθi'ðað] NF uniqueness
único, -a ['uniko, a] ADJ only; (solo) sole, single; (sin par) unique; **hijo ~** only child
unidad [uni'ðað] NF unity; (Tec) unit; **~ móvil** (TV) mobile unit; (Inform) **~ central** system unit, central processing unit; **~ de control** control unit; **~ de disco** disk drive; **~ de disco duro** hard drive; **~ de entrada/salida** input/output device; **~ de información** data item; **~ de presentación visual** o **de visualización** visual display unit; **~ periférica** peripheral device; **~ procesadora central** central processing unit

unido, -a [u'niðo, a] ADJ joined, linked; (fig) united
unifamiliar [unifamil'jar] ADJ: **vivienda ~** single-family home
unificar [unifi'kar] /**1g**/ vt to unite, unify
unifique etc [uni'fike] VB ver **unificar**
uniformado, -a [unifor'maðo, a] ADJ uniformed, in uniform
uniformar [unifor'mar] /**1a**/ vt to make uniform; (persona) to put into uniform; (Tec) to standardize
uniforme [uni'forme] ADJ uniform, equal; (superficie) even ▶ NM uniform
uniformidad [uniformi'ðað] NF uniformity; (llaneza) levelness, evenness
unilateral [unilate'ral] ADJ unilateral
unión [u'njon] NF (gen) union; (acto) uniting, joining; (calidad) unity; (Tec) joint; (fig) closeness, togetherness; **en ~ con** (together) with, accompanied by; **~ aduanera** customs union; **U~ General de Trabajadores** (Esp) Socialist Union Confederation; **U~ Europea** European Union; **la U~ Soviética** the Soviet Union; **punto de ~** (Tec) junction
unir [u'nir] /**3a**/ vt (juntar) to join, unite; (atar) to tie, fasten; (combinar) to combine ▶ vi (ingredientes) to mix well; **unirse** VR to join together, unite; (empresas) to merge; **les une una fuerte simpatía** they are bound by (a) strong affection; **unirse en matrimonio** to marry
unisex [uni'seks] ADJ INV unisex
unísono [u'nisono] NM: **al ~** in unison
unitario, -a [uni'tarjo, a] ADJ unitary; (Rel) Unitarian ▶ NM/F (Rel) Unitarian
universal [uniβer'sal] ADJ universal; (mundial) world cpd; **historia ~** world history
universidad [uniβersi'ðað] NF university; **~ laboral** polytechnic, poly
universitario, -a [uniβersi'tarjo, a] ADJ university cpd ▶ NM/F (profesor) lecturer; (estudiante) (university) student; (graduado) graduate
universo [uni'βerso] NM universe
unja etc ['unxa] VB ver **ungir**

PALABRA CLAVE

uno, -a ['uno, a] ADJ one; **es todo uno** it's all one and the same; **unos pocos** a few; **unos cien** about a hundred
▶ PRON **1** one; **quiero uno solo** I only want one; **uno de ellos** one of them; **una de dos** either one or the other; **no doy una hoy** I can't do anything right today
2 (alguien) somebody, someone; **conozco a uno que se te parece** I know somebody o someone who looks like you; **unos querían quedarse** some (people) wanted to stay
3 (impersonal) one; **uno mismo** oneself; **uno**

nunca sabe qué hacer one never knows what to do

4: **unos ... otros ...** some ... others; **una y otra son muy agradables** they're both very nice; **(los) uno(s) a (los) otro(s)** each other, one another

▶ NF one; **es la una** it's one o'clock

▶ NUM (number) one; **el día uno** the first; *ver tb* **un**

untar [un'tar] /**1a**/ VT (*gen*) to rub; (*mantequilla*) to spread; (*engrasar*) to grease, oil; (*Med*) to rub (with ointment); (*fig*) to bribe; **untarse** VR (*fig*) to be crooked; **~ el pan con mantequilla** to spread butter on one's bread

unto ['unto] NM animal fat; (*Med*) ointment

unza *etc* ['unθa] VB *ver* **uncir**

uña ['uɲa] NF (*Anat*) nail; (*del pie*) toenail; (*garra*) claw; (*casco*) hoof; (*arrancaclavos*) claw; **ser ~ y carne** to be as thick as thieves; **enseñar** *o* **mostrar** *o* **sacar las uñas** to show one's claws

UOE NF ABR (*Esp Mil*) = **Unidad de Operaciones Especiales**

UPA NF ABR = **Unión Panamericana**

UPC NF ABR (= *unidad procesadora central*) CPU

uperizado, -a [uperi'θaðo, a] ADJ: **leche uperizada** UHT milk

Urales [u'rales] NMPL (*tb:* **Montes Urales**) Urals

uralita® [ura'lita] NF corrugated asbestos cement

uranio [u'ranjo] NM uranium

urbanidad [urβani'ðað] NF courtesy, politeness

urbanismo [urβa'nismo] NM town planning

urbanista [urβa'nista] NMF town planner

urbanización [urβaniθa'θjon] NF (*colonia, barrio*) estate, housing scheme

urbanizar [urβani'θar] /**1f**/ VT (*zona*) to develop, urbanize

urbano, -a [ur'βano, a] ADJ (*de ciudad*) urban, town *cpd*; (*cortés*) courteous, polite

urbe ['urβe] NF large city, metropolis

urdimbre [ur'ðimbre] NF (*de tejido*) warp; (*intriga*) intrigue

urdir [ur'ðir] /**3a**/ VT to warp; (*fig*) to plot, contrive

urgencia [ur'xenθja] NF urgency; (*prisa*) haste, rush; (*emergencia*) emergency; **salida de ~** emergency exit; **servicios de ~** emergency services; **"Urgencias"** "Accident & Emergency", "Casualty"

urgente [ur'xente] ADJ urgent; (*insistente*) insistent; **carta ~** registered (*Brit*) *o* special delivery (*US*) letter

urgir [ur'xir] /**3c**/ VI to be urgent; **me urge** I'm in a hurry for it; **me urge terminarlo** I must finish it as soon as I can

urinario, -a [uri'narjo, a] ADJ urinary ▶ NM urinal, public lavatory, comfort station (*US*)

urja *etc* [urxa] VB *ver* **urgir**

urna ['urna] NF urn; (*Pol*) ballot box; **acudir a las urnas** (*fig: persona*) to (go and) vote (: *gobierno*) to go to the country

urología [urolo'xia] NF urology

urólogo, -a [u'roloɣo, a] NM/F urologist

urraca [u'rraka] NF magpie

URSS NF ABR (*Historia*: = *Unión de Repúblicas Socialistas Soviéticas*) USSR

Uruguay [uru'ɣwai] NM Uruguay

uruguayo, -a [uru'ɣwajo, a] ADJ, NM/F Uruguayan

usado, -a [u'saðo, a] ADJ (*gen*) used; (*ropa etc*) worn; **muy ~** worn out; (*de segunda mano*) secondhand

usanza [u'sanθa] NF custom, usage

usar [u'sar] /**1a**/ VT to use; (*ropa*) to wear; (*tener costumbre*) to be in the habit of ▶ VI: **~ de** to make use of; **usarse** VR to be used; (*ropa*) to be worn *o* in fashion

USO ['uso] NF ABR (*Esp*: = *Unión Sindical Obrera*) *workers' union*

uso ['uso] NM use; (*Mecánica etc*) wear; (*costumbre*) usage, custom; (*moda*) fashion; **al ~** in keeping with custom; **al ~ de** in the style of; **de ~ externo** (*Med*) for external use; **estar en el ~ de la palabra** to be speaking, have the floor; **~ y desgaste** (*Com*) wear and tear; **~ compartido de archivos** (*Inform*) file sharing

usted [us'teð] PRON (*sg formal: abr* **Ud** *o* **Vd**) you *sg*; **ustedes** (*pl formal: abr* **Uds** *o* **Vds**) you *pl*; (*Am frm, tb fam*) you *pl*

usual [u'swal] ADJ usual

usuario, -a [usw'arjo, a] NM/F user; **~ final** (*Com*) end user

usufructo [usu'frukto] NM use; **~ vitalicio (de)** life interest (in)

usura [u'sura] NF usury

usurero, -a [usu'rero, a] NM/F usurer

usurpar [usur'par] /**1a**/ VT to usurp

utensilio [uten'siljo] NM tool; (*Culin*) utensil

útero ['utero] NM uterus, womb

útil ['util] ADJ useful; (*servible*) usable, serviceable ▶ NM tool; **día ~** working day, weekday; **es muy ~ tenerlo aquí cerca** it's very handy having it here close by

utilice *etc* [uti'liθe] VB *ver* **utilizar**

utilidad [utili'ðað] NF usefulness, utility; (*Com*) profit; **utilidades líquidas** net profit *sg*

utilitario [utili'tarjo] NM (*Inform*) utility

utilizar [utili'θar] /**1f**/ VT to use, utilize; (*explotar*) to harness

utopía [uto'pia] NF Utopia

utópico, -a [u'topiko, a] ADJ Utopian

UVA SIGLA MPL (= *ultravioleta*) UV, UVA

u

uva ['uβa] NF grape; **~ pasa** raisin; **~ de Corinto** currant; **estar de mala ~** to be in a bad mood; *see note*

> In Spain *las uvas* play a big part on New Years' Eve (*Nochevieja*), when on the stroke of midnight people from every part of Spain, at home, in restaurants, in open spaces and in public squares eat a grape for each stroke of the clock – especially the one at Puerta del Sol in Madrid. It is said to bring luck for the following year.

uve ['uβe] NF *name of the letter V*; **en forma de ~** V-shaped; **~ doble** *name of the letter W*

UVI ['uβi] NF ABR (*ESP Med: = unidad de vigilancia intensiva*) ICU

Vv

V, v [(Esp) 'uβe, (Am) be'korta, be'tʃika] NF
(letra) V, v; **V de Valencia** V for Victor
V. ABR = **usted**; (= *visto*) approved, passed
v. ABR (= *voltio*) v; (*Lit*: = *verso*) v; (= *ver, véase*) v.
va [ba] VB *ver* **ir**
vaca ['baka] NF (*animal*) cow; (*carne*) beef;
(*cuero*) cowhide; **vacas flacas/gordas** (*fig*)
bad/good times
vacaciones [baka'θjones] NFPL holiday(s);
estar/irse o **marcharse de** ~ to be/go (away)
on holiday
vacante [ba'kante] ADJ vacant, empty ▸ NF
vacancy
vaciado, -a [ba'θjaðo, a] ADJ (*hecho en molde*)
cast in a mould; (*hueco*) hollow ▸ NM cast,
mould(ing)
vaciar [ba'θjar] /1c/ VT to empty (out);
(*ahuecar*) to hollow out; (*moldear*) to cast;
(*Inform*) to dump ▸ VI (*río*): ~ **en** to flow into;
vaciarse VR to empty; (*fig*) to blab, spill the
beans
vaciedad [baθje'ðað] NF emptiness
vacilación [baθila'θjon] NF hesitation
vacilante [baθi'lante] ADJ unsteady; (*habla*)
faltering; (*luz*) flickering; (*fig*) hesitant
vacilar [baθi'lar] /1a/ VI (*dudar*) to hesitate,
waver; (*mueble*) to be unsteady; (*persona: al
andar*) to stagger, stumble; (: *al hablar*) to
falter; (*memoria*) to fail; (*luz*) to flicker;
(*esp Am: divertirse*) to have a great time
vacilón [baθi'lon] NM (*esp Am*): **estar** o **ir de** ~
to have a great time
vacío, -a [ba'θio, a] ADJ empty; (*puesto*)
vacant; (*desocupado*) idle; (*vano*) (*charla
etc*) light, superficial ▸ NM emptiness;
(*Física*) vacuum; (*un vacío*) (empty) space;
hacer el ~ **a algn** to send sb to Coventry
vacuna [ba'kuna] NF vaccine
vacunar [baku'nar] /1a/ VT to vaccinate;
vacunarse VR to get vaccinated
vacuno, -a [ba'kuno, a] ADJ bovine;
ganado ~ cattle
vacuo, -a ['bakwo, a] ADJ empty
vadear [baðe'ar] /1a/ VT (*río*) to ford;

(*problema*) to overcome; (*persona*) to sound out
vado ['baðo] NM ford; (*solución*) solution;
(*descanso*) respite; **"~ permanente"** "keep
clear"
vagabundo, -a [baɣa'βundo, a] ADJ
wandering; (*pey*) vagrant ▸ NM/F (*errante*)
wanderer; (*vago*) tramp, bum (*US*)
vagamente [baɣa'mente] ADV vaguely
vagancia [ba'ɣanθja] NF (*pereza*) idleness,
laziness; (*vagabundeo*) vagrancy
vagar [ba'ɣar] /1h/ VI to wander; (*pasear*) to
saunter up and down; (*no hacer nada*) to idle
▸ NM leisure
vagido [ba'xiðo] NM wail
vagina [ba'xina] NF vagina
vago, -a ['baɣo, a] ADJ vague; (*perezoso*) lazy;
(*ambulante*) wandering ▸ NM/F (*vagabundo*)
tramp, bum (*US*); (*perezoso*) lazybones *sg*, idler
vagón [ba'ɣon] NM (*de pasajeros*) carriage;
(*de mercancías*) wagon; ~ **cama/restaurante**
sleeping/dining car
vague *etc* ['baɣe] VB *ver* **vagar**
vaguear [baɣe'ar] /1a/ VI to laze around
vaguedad [baɣe'ðað] NF vagueness
vahído [ba'iðo] NM dizzy spell
vaho ['bao] NM (*vapor*) vapour, steam; (*olor*)
smell; (*respiración*) breath; **vahos** NMPL (*Med*)
inhalation *sg*
vaina ['baina] NF sheath ▸ NM (*Am*) nuisance
vainilla [bai'niʎa] NF vanilla
vainita [bai'nita] NF (*Am*) green o French bean
vais [bais] VB *ver* **ir**
vaivén [bai'βen] NM to-and-fro movement;
(*de tránsito*) coming and going; **vaivenes**
NMPL (*fig*) ups and downs
vajilla [ba'xiʎa] NF crockery, dishes *pl*; (*una
vajilla*) service; ~ **de porcelana** chinaware
val [bal], **valdré** *etc* [bal'dre] VB *ver* **valer**
valdré *etc* VB *ver* **valer**
vale ['bale] NM voucher; (*recibo*) receipt;
(*pagaré*) IOU; ~ **de regalo** gift voucher o token
valedero, -a [bale'ðero, a] ADJ valid
valenciano, -a [balen'θjano, a] ADJ, NM/F
Valencian ▸ NM (*Ling*) Valencian

valentía [balen'tia] NF courage, bravery; (*pey*) boastfulness; (*acción*) heroic deed

valentísimo, -a [balen'tisimo, a] ADJ SUPERLATIVO *de* **valiente** very brave, courageous

valentón, -ona [balen'ton, ona] ADJ blustering

valer [ba'ler] /**2p**/ VT to be worth; (*Mat*) to equal; (*costar*) to cost; (*amparar*) to aid, protect ▶ VI (*ser útil*) to be useful; (*ser válido*) to be valid; **valerse** VR, NM to take care of o.s.; worth, value; ~ **la pena** to be worthwhile; **¿vale?** O.K.?; **¡vale!** (*¡basta!*) that'll do!; **¡eso no vale!** that doesn't count!; **no vale nada** it's no good; (*mercancía*) it's worthless; (*argumento*) it's no use; **no vale para nada** he's no good at all; **más vale tarde que nunca** better late than never; **más vale que nos vayamos** we'd better go; **valerse de** to make use of, take advantage of; **valerse por sí mismo** to help o manage by o.s.; **¡eso a mí no me vale!** (*AM fam: no importa*) I couldn't care less about that

valeroso, -a [bale'roso, a] ADJ brave, valiant

valgo *etc* ['balɣo] VB *ver* **valer**

valía [ba'lia] NF worth; **de gran ~** (*objeto*) very valuable

validar [bali'ðar] /**1a**/ VT to validate; (*Pol*) to ratify

validez [bali'ðeθ] NF validity; **dar ~ a** to validate

válido, -a ['baliðo, a] ADJ valid

valiente [ba'ljente] ADJ brave, valiant; (*audaz*) bold; (*pey*) boastful; (*con ironía*) fine, wonderful ▶ NM brave man/woman

valija [ba'lixa] NF (*AM*) case, suitcase; (*mochila*) satchel; (*Correos*) mailbag; **~ diplomática** diplomatic bag

valioso, -a [ba'ljoso, a] ADJ valuable; (*rico*) wealthy

valla ['baʎa] NF fence; (*Deporte*) hurdle; (*fig*) barrier; **~ publicitaria** hoarding (*esp* BRIT), billboard (*esp US*)

vallar [ba'ʎar] /**1a**/ VT to fence in

valle ['baʎe] NM valley, vale

vallisoletano, -a [baʎisole'tano, a] ADJ of o from Valladolid ▶ NM/F native o inhabitant of Valladolid

valor [ba'lor] NM value, worth; (*precio*) price; (*valentía*) valour, courage; (*importancia*) importance; (*cara*) nerve, cheek (*fam*); **sin ~** worthless; **~ adquisitivo** o **de compra** purchasing power; **dar ~ a** to attach importance to; **quitar ~ a** to minimize the importance of; (*Com*) **~ según balance** book value; **~ comercial** o **de mercado** market value; **~ contable/desglosado** asset/break-up value; **~ de escasez** scarcity value; **~ intrínseco** intrinsic value; **~ a la par** par

value; **~ neto** net worth; **~ de rescate/de sustitución** surrender/replacement value; *ver tb* **valores**

valoración [balora'θjon] NF valuation

valorar [balo'rar] /**1a**/ VT to value; (*tasar*) to price; (*fig*) to assess

valores [ba'lores] NMPL (*Com*) securities; **~ en cartera** o **habidos** investments

vals [bals] NM waltz

válvula ['balβula] NF valve

vamos ['bamos] VB *ver* **ir**

vampiro, -iresa [bam'piro, i'resa] NM/F vampire ▶ NF (*Cine*) vamp, femme fatale

van [ban] VB *ver* **ir**

vanagloriarse [banaɣlo'rjarse] /**1b**/ VR to boast

vandalismo [banda'lismo] NM vandalism

vándalo, -a ['bandalo, a] NM/F vandal

vanguardia [ban'gwardja] NF vanguard; **de ~** (*Arte*) avant-garde; **estar en** o **ir a la ~ de** (*fig*) to be in the forefront of

vanguardista [bangwar'ðista] ADJ avant-garde

vanidad [bani'ðað] NF vanity; (*inutilidad*) futility; (*irrealidad*) unreality

vanidoso, -a [bani'ðoso, a] ADJ vain, conceited

vano, -a ['bano, a] ADJ (*irreal*) unreal; (*irracional*) unreasonable; (*inútil*) vain, useless; (*persona*) vain, conceited; (*frívolo*) frivolous

vapor [ba'por] NM vapour; (*vaho*) steam; (*de gas*) fumes pl; (*neblina*) mist; **vapores** NMPL (*Med*) hysterics; **al ~** (*Culin*) steamed; **~ de agua** water vapour

vaporice *etc* [bapo'riθe] VB *ver* **vaporizar**

vaporizador [baporiθa'ðor] NM (*de perfume etc*) spray

vaporizar [bapori'θar] /**1f**/ VT to vaporize; (*perfume*) to spray

vaporoso, -a [bapo'roso, a] ADJ vaporous; (*vahoso*) steamy; (*tela*) light, airy

vapulear [bapule'ar] /**1a**/ VT to thrash; (*fig*) to slate

vaquería [bake'ria] NF dairy

vaquero, -a [ba'kero, a] ADJ cattle *cpd* ▶ NM cowboy; **vaqueros** NMPL jeans

vaquilla [ba'kiʎa] NF heifer

vara ['bara] NF stick, pole; (*Tec*) rod; **~ mágica** magic wand

varado, -a [ba'raðo, a] ADJ (*Naut*) stranded; **estar ~** to be aground

varar [ba'rar] /**1a**/ VT to beach ▶ VI, **vararse** VR to be beached

varear [bare'ar] /**1a**/ VT to hit, beat; (*frutas*) to knock down (with poles)

variable [ba'rjaβle] ADJ, NF (*tb Inform*) variable

variación [barja'θjon] NF variation; **sin ~** unchanged

variado, -a [baˈrjaðo, a] ADJ varied; *(dulces, galletas)* assorted; **entremeses variados** a selection of starters

variante [baˈrjante] ADJ variant ▶ NF *(alternativa)* alternative; *(Auto)* bypass

variar [baˈrjar] /**1c**/ VT *(cambiar)* to change; *(poner variedad)* to vary; *(modificar)* to modify; *(cambiar de posición)* to switch around ▶ VI to vary; ~ **de** to differ from; ~ **de opinión** to change one's mind; **para** ~ just for a change

varicela [bariˈθela] NF chicken pox

varices [baˈriθes] NFPL varicose veins

variedad [barjeˈðað] NF variety

varilla [baˈriʎa] NF stick; *(Bot)* twig; *(Tec)* rod; *(de rueda)* spoke; ~ **mágica** magic wand

vario, -a [ˈbarjo, a] ADJ *(variado)* varied; *(multicolor)* motley; *(cambiable)* changeable; **varios** various, several

variopinto, -a [barjoˈpinto, a] ADJ diverse; **un público** ~ a mixed audience

varita [baˈrita] NF: ~ **mágica** magic wand

varón [baˈron] NM male, man

varonil [baroˈnil] ADJ manly

Varsovia [barˈsoβja] NF Warsaw

vas [bas] VB ver **ir**

vasco, -a [ˈbasko, a], **vascongado, -a** [baskonˈgaðo, a] ADJ, NM/F Basque ▶ NM *(Ling)* Basque ▶ NFPL: **las Vascongadas** the Basque Country *sg*

vascuence [basˈkwenθe] NM *(Ling)* Basque

vasectomía [basektoˈmia] NF vasectomy

vaselina [baseˈlina] NF Vaseline®

vasija [baˈsixa] NF (earthenware) vessel

vaso [ˈbaso] NM glass, tumbler; *(Anat)* vessel; *(cantidad)* glass(ful); ~ **de vino** glass of wine; ~ **para vino** wineglass

vástago [ˈbastaɣo] NM *(Bot)* shoot; *(Tec)* rod; *(fig)* offspring

vasto, -a [ˈbasto, a] ADJ vast, huge

váter [ˈbater] NM lavatory, W.C.

Vaticano [batiˈkano] NM: **el** ~ the Vatican; **la Ciudad del** ~ the Vatican City

vaticinar [batiθiˈnar] /**1a**/ VT to prophesy, predict

vaticinio [batiˈθinjo] NM prophecy

vatio [ˈbatjo] NM *(Elec)* watt

vaya *etc* [ˈbaja] VB ver **ir**

Vd ABR = **usted**

Vda. ABR (= *viuda*) ver **viudo**

Vds ABR = **ustedes**; ver **usted**

ve [be] VB ver **ir**; **ver**

vea *etc* [ˈbea] VB ver **ver**

vecinal [beθiˈnal] ADJ *(camino, impuesto etc)* local

vecindad [beθinˈdað] NF, **vecindario** [beθinˈdarjo] NM neighbourhood; *(habitantes)* residents *pl*

vecino, -a [beˈθino, a] ADJ neighbouring ▶ NM/F neighbour; *(residente)* resident; **somos vecinos** we live next door to one another

vector [bekˈtor] NM vector

veda [ˈbeða] NF prohibition; *(temporada)* close season

vedado [beˈðaðo] NM preserve

vedar [beˈðar] /**1a**/ VT *(prohibir)* to ban, prohibit; *(idea, plan)* to veto; *(impedir)* to stop, prevent

vedette [beˈðet] NF *(Teat, Cine)* star(let)

vega [ˈbeɣa] NF fertile plain o valley

vegetación [bexetaˈθjon] NF vegetation

vegetal [bexeˈtal] ADJ, NM vegetable

vegetar [bexeˈtar] /**1a**/ VI to vegetate

vegetariano, -a [bexetaˈrjano, a] ADJ, NM/F vegetarian

vegetativo, -a [bexetaˈtiβo, a] ADJ vegetative

vehemencia [beeˈmenθja] NF *(insistencia)* vehemence; *(pasión)* passion; *(fervor)* fervour; *(violencia)* violence

vehemente [beeˈmente] ADJ vehement; passionate; fervent; violent

vehículo [beˈikulo] NM vehicle; *(Med)* carrier; ~ **de servicio público** public service vehicle; ~ **espacial** spacecraft

veía *etc* VB ver **ver**

veinte [ˈbeinte] NUM twenty; *(orden, fecha)* twentieth; **el siglo** ~ the twentieth century

veintena [beinˈtena] NF: **una** ~ (about) twenty, a score

vejación [bexaˈθjon] NF vexation; *(humillación)* humiliation

vejamen [beˈxamen] NM satire

vejar [beˈxar] /**1a**/ VT *(irritar)* to annoy, vex; *(humillar)* to humiliate

vejatorio, -a [bexaˈtorjo, a] ADJ humiliating, degrading

vejez [beˈxeθ] NF old age

vejiga [beˈxiɣa] NF *(Anat)* bladder

vela [ˈbela] NF *(de cera)* candle; *(Naut)* sail; *(insomnio)* sleeplessness; *(vigilia)* vigil; *(Mil)* sentry duty; *(fam)* snot; **a toda** ~ *(Naut)* under full sail; **estar a dos velas** *(fam)* to be skint; **pasar la noche en** ~ to have a sleepless night

velado, -a [beˈlaðo, a] ADJ veiled; *(sonido)* muffled; *(Foto)* blurred ▶ NF soirée

velador [belaˈðor] NM watchman; *(candelero)* candlestick; *(Am)* bedside table

velar [beˈlar] /**1a**/ VT *(vigilar)* to keep watch over; *(cubrir)* to veil ▶ VI to stay awake; ~ **por** to watch over, look after

velatorio [belaˈtorjo] NM *(funeral)* wake

veleidad [beleiˈðað] NF *(ligereza)* fickleness; *(capricho)* whim

velero [beˈlero] NM *(Naut)* sailing ship; *(Aviat)* glider

veleta [beˈleta] NMF fickle person ▶ NF weather vane

V

veliz [be'lis] NM (*AM*) suitcase
vello ['beʎo] NM down, fuzz
vellón [be'ʎon] NM fleece
velloso, -a [be'ʎoso, a] ADJ fuzzy
velludo, -a [be'ʎuðo, a] ADJ shaggy ▶ NM plush, velvet
velo ['belo] NM veil; **~ de paladar** (*Anat*) soft palate
velocidad [beloθi'ðað] NF speed; (*Tec*) rate, pace, velocity; (*Mecánica, Auto*) gear; **¿a qué ~?** how fast?; **de alta ~** high-speed; **cobrar ~** to pick up *o* gather speed; **meter la segunda ~** to change into second gear; **~ máxima de impresión** (*Inform*) maximum print speed
velocímetro [belo'θimetro] NM speedometer
velódromo [be'loðromo] NM cycle track
velorio [be'lorjo] NM (*AM*) (funeral) wake
veloz [be'loθ] ADJ fast, swift
ven [ben] VB ver **venir**
vena ['bena] NF vein; (*fig*) vein, disposition; (*Geo*) seam, vein
venablo [be'naβlo] NM javelin
venado [be'naðo] NM deer; (*Culin*) venison
venal [be'nal] ADJ (*Anat*) venous; (*pey*) venal
venalidad [benali'ðað] NF venality
vencedor, a [benθe'ðor, a] ADJ victorious ▶ NM/F victor, winner
vencer [ben'θer] /2b/ VT (*dominar*) to defeat, beat; (*derrotar*) to vanquish; (*superar, controlar*) to overcome, master ▶ VI (*triunfar*) to win (through), triumph; (*pago*) to fall due; (*plazo*) to expire; **dejarse ~** to yield, give in
vencido, -a [ben'θiðo, a] ADJ (*derrotado*) defeated, beaten; (*Com*) payable, due ▶ ADV: **pagar ~** to pay in arrears; **le pagan por meses vencidos** he is paid at the end of the month; **darse por ~** to give up
vencimiento [benθi'mjento] NM collapse; (*Com: de plazo*) expiration; **a su ~** when it falls due
venda ['benda] NF bandage
vendaje [ben'daxe] NM bandage, dressing
vendar [ben'dar] /1a/ VT to bandage; **~ los ojos** to blindfold
vendaval [benda'βal] NM (*viento*) gale; (*huracán*) hurricane
vendedor, a [bende'ðor, a] NM/F seller; **~ ambulante** hawker, pedlar (*BRIT*), peddler (*US*)
vender [ben'der] /2a/ VT to sell; (*comerciar*) to market; (*traicionar*) to sell out, betray; **venderse** VR (*estar a la venta*) to be on sale; **~ al contado/al por mayor/al por menor/ a plazos** to sell for cash/wholesale/retail/on credit; **"se vende"** "for sale"; **"véndese coche"** "car for sale"; **~ al descubierto** to sell short
vendimia [ben'dimja] NF grape harvest; **la ~ de 1993** the 1993 vintage

vendimiar [bendi'mjar] /1b/ VI to pick grapes
vendré *etc* [ben'dre] VB ver **venir**
Venecia [be'neθja] NF Venice
veneciano, -a [bene'θjano, a] ADJ, NM/F Venetian
veneno [be'neno] NM poison; (*de serpiente*) venom
venenoso, -a [bene'noso, a] ADJ poisonous; venomous
venerable [bene'raβle] ADJ venerable
veneración [benera'θjon] NF veneration
venerar [bene'rar] /1a/ VT (*respetar*) to revere; (*reconocer*) to venerate; (*adorar*) to worship
venéreo, -a [be'nereo, a] ADJ venereal; **enfermedad venérea** venereal disease
venezolano, -a [beneθo'lano, a] ADJ, NM/F Venezuelan
Venezuela [bene'θwela] NF Venezuela
venga *etc* ['benga] VB ver **venir**
vengador, a [benga'ðor, a] ADJ avenging ▶ NM/F avenger
venganza [ben'ganθa] NF vengeance, revenge
vengar [ben'gar] /1h/ VT to avenge; **vengarse** VR to take revenge
vengativo, -a [benga'tiβo, a] ADJ (*persona*) vindictive
vengo *etc* VB ver **venir**
vengue *etc* ['benge] VB ver **vengar**
venia ['benja] NF (*perdón*) pardon; (*permiso*) consent; **con su ~** by your leave
venial [be'njal] ADJ venial
venida [be'niða] NF (*llegada*) arrival; (*regreso*) return; (*fig*) rashness
venidero, -a [beni'ðero, a] ADJ coming, future; **en lo ~** in (the) future
venir [be'nir] /3r/ VI to come; (*llegar*) to arrive; (*ocurrir*) to happen; **venirse** VR: **venirse abajo** to collapse; **~ a menos** (*persona*) to lose status; (*empresa*) to go downhill; **~ bien** to be suitable, come just right; (*ropa, gusto*) to suit; **~ mal** to be unsuitable *o* inconvenient, come awkwardly; **el año que viene** next year; **¡ven acá!** come (over) here!; **¡venga!** (*fam*) come on!
venta ['benta] NF (*Com*) sale; (*posada*) inn; **~ a plazos** hire purchase; **"en ~"** "for sale"; **~ al contado/al por mayor/al por menor** *o* **al detalle** cash sale/wholesale/retail; **~ a domicilio** door-to-door selling; **~ y arrendamiento al vendedor** sale and lease back; **~ de liquidación** clearance sale; **estar de *o* en ~** to be (up) for sale *o* on the market; **ventas brutas** gross sales; **ventas a término** forward sales
ventaja [ben'taxa] NF advantage; **llevar la ~** (*en carrera*) to be leading *o* ahead
ventajoso, -a [benta'xoso, a] ADJ advantageous

ventana [ben'tana] NF window; **~ de guillotina/galería** sash/bay window; **~ de la nariz** nostril

ventanilla [venta'niʎa] NF (*de taquilla, tb Inform*) window

ventearse [bente'arse] /**1a**/ VR (*romperse*) to crack; (*Anat*) to break wind

ventilación [bentila'θjon] NF ventilation; (*corriente*) draught; (*fig*) airing

ventilador [bentila'ðor] NM ventilator; (*eléctrico*) fan

ventilar [benti'lar] /**1a**/ VT to ventilate; (*poner a secar*) to put out to dry; (*fig*) to air, discuss

ventisca [ben'tiska] NF blizzard

ventisquero [bentis'kero] NM snowdrift

ventolera [bento'lera] NF (*ráfaga*) gust of wind; (*idea*) whim, wild idea; **le dio la ~ de comprarlo** he had a sudden notion to buy it

ventosear [bentose'ar] /**1a**/ VI to break wind

ventosidad [bentosi'ðað] NF flatulence

ventoso, -a [ben'toso, a] ADJ windy ▶ NF (*Zool*) sucker; (*instrumento*) suction pad

ventrículo [ben'trikulo] NM ventricle

ventrílocuo, -a [ben'trilokwo, a] NM/F ventriloquist

ventriloquia [bentri'lokja] NF ventriloquism

ventura [ben'tura] NF (*felicidad*) happiness; (*buena suerte*) luck; (*destino*) fortune; **a la (buena) ~** at random

venturoso, -a [bentu'roso, a] ADJ happy; (*afortunado*) lucky, fortunate

venza *etc* ['benθa] VB *ver* **vencer**

veo *etc* VB *ver* **ver**

ver [ber] /**2u**/ VT, VI to see; (*mirar*) to look at, watch; (*investigar*) to look into; (*entender*) to see, understand ▶ NM looks *pl*, appearance; **verse** VR (*encontrarse*) to meet; (*dejarse ver*) to be seen; (*hallarse: en un apuro*) to find o.s., be **a ~** let's see; **a ~ si ...** I wonder if ...; **por lo que veo** apparently; **dejarse ~** to become apparent; **no tener nada que ~ con** to have nothing to do with; **a mi modo de ~** as I see it; **merece verse** it's worth seeing; **no lo veo** I can't see it; **¡nos vemos!** see you (later)!; **¡hábrase visto!** did you ever! (*fam*); **¡viera(n) o hubiera(n) visto qué casa!** (*Am fam*) if only you'd seen the house!, what a house!; **ya se ve que ...** it is obvious that ...; **si te vi no me acuerdo** they *etc* just don't want to know; **ya veremos** we'll see

vera ['bera] NF edge, verge; (*de río*) bank; **a la ~ de** near, next to

veracidad [beraθi'ðað] NF truthfulness

veraneante [berane'ante] NMF holidaymaker, (summer) vacationer (US)

veranear [berane'ar] /**1a**/ VI to spend the summer

veraneo [bera'neo] NM summer holiday; **estar de ~** to be away on (one's summer) holiday; **lugar de ~** holiday resort

veraniego, -a [bera'njeɣo, a] ADJ summer *cpd*

verano [be'rano] NM summer

veras ['beras] NFPL truth *sg*; **de ~** really, truly; **esto va de ~** this is serious

veraz [be'raθ] ADJ truthful

verbal [ber'βal] ADJ verbal; (*mensaje etc*) oral

verbena [ber'βena] NF street party; (*baile*) open-air dance

verbigracia [berβi'ɣraθja] ADV for example

verbo ['berβo] NM verb

verborrea [berβo'rrea] NF verbosity, verbal diarrhoea

verboso, -a [ber'βoso, a] ADJ verbose

verdad [ber'ðað] NF (*lo verídico*) truth; (*fiabilidad*) reliability ▶ ADV really; **¿~?, ¿no es ~?**, **¿no es ~?** isn't it?, aren't you?, don't you? *etc*; **de ~** *adj* real, proper; **a decir ~**, **no quiero** to tell (you) the truth, I don't want to; **la pura ~** the plain truth

verdaderamente [berðaðera'mente] ADV really, indeed, truly

verdadero, -a [berða'ðero, a] ADJ (*veraz*) true, truthful; (*fiable*) reliable; (*fig*) real

verde ['berðe] ADJ green; (*fruta etc*) green, unripe; (*chiste etc*) blue, smutty, dirty ▶ NM green; **viejo ~** dirty old man; **poner ~ a algn** to give sb a dressing-down

verdear [berðe'ar] /**1a**/, **verdecer** [berðe'θer] /**2d**/ VI to turn green

verdezca *etc* [ber'ðeθka] VB *ver* **verdear**

verdor [ber'ðor] NM (*lo verde*) greenness; (*Bot*) verdure; (*fig*) youthful vigour

verdugo [ber'ðuɣo] NM executioner; (*Bot*) shoot; (*cardenal*) weal

verdulería [berðule'ria] NF greengrocer's (shop)

verdulero, -a [berðu'lero, a] NM/F greengrocer

verdura [ber'ðura] NF greenness; **verduras** NFPL (*Culin*) greens

vereda [be'reða] NF path; (*Am*) pavement, sidewalk (US); **meter a algn en ~** to bring sb into line

veredicto [bere'ðikto] NM verdict

vergel [ber'xel] NM lush garden

vergonzoso, -a [berɣon'θoso, a] ADJ shameful; (*tímido*) timid, bashful

vergüenza [ber'ɣwenθa] NF shame, sense of shame; (*timidez*) bashfulness; (*pudor*) modesty; **tener ~** to be ashamed; **me da ~ decírselo** I feel too shy *o* it embarrasses me to tell him; **¡qué ~!** (*de situación*) what a disgrace!; (*a persona*) shame on you!

vericueto [beri'kweto] NM rough track

verídico, -a [be'riðiko, a] ADJ true, truthful

V

verificar [berifi'kar] /**1a**/ VT to check; (*corroborar: tb Inform*) to verify; (*testamento*) to prove; (*llevar a cabo*) to carry out; **verificarse** VR to occur, happen; (*mitin etc*) to be held; (*profecía etc*) to come o prove true

verifique *etc* [beri'fike] VB *ver* **verificar**

verja ['berxa] NF (*cancela*) iron gate; (*cerca*) railing(s); (*rejado*) grating

vermut [ber'mu] (*pl* **vermuts**) NM vermouth ▶ NF (*esp Am*) matinée

verosímil [bero'simil] ADJ likely, probable; (*relato*) credible

verosimilitud [berosimili'tuð] NF likeliness, probability

verruga [be'rruɣa] NF wart

versado, -a [ber'saðo, a] ADJ: ~ **en** versed in

Versalles [ber'saʎes] NM Versailles

versar [ber'sar] /**1a**/ VI to go round, turn; ~ **sobre** to deal with, be about

versátil [ber'satil] ADJ versatile

versículo [ber'sikulo] NM (*Rel*) verse

versión [ber'sjon] NF version; (*traducción*) translation

verso ['berso] NM verse; **un** ~ a line of poetry; ~ **libre/suelto** free/blank verse

vértebra ['berteβra] NF vertebra

vertebrado, -a [berte'βraðo, a] ADJ, NM/F vertebrate

vertebral [berte'βral] ADJ vertebral; **columna** ~ spine

vertedero [berte'ðero] NM rubbish dump, tip

verter [ber'ter] /**2g**/ VT (*vaciar*) to empty, pour (out); (*sin querer*) to spill; (*basura*) to dump ▶ VI to flow

vertical [berti'kal] ADJ vertical; (*postura, piano etc*) upright ▶ NF vertical

vértice ['bertiθe] NM vertex, apex

vertidos [ber'tiðos] NMPL waste *sg*

vertiente [ber'tjente] NF slope; (*fig*) aspect

vertiginoso, -a [bertixi'noso, a] ADJ giddy, dizzy

vértigo ['bertiɣo] NM vertigo; (*mareo*) dizziness; (*actividad*) intense activity; **de** ~ (*fam: velocidad*) giddy; (*: ruido*) tremendous; (*: talento*) fantastic

vesícula [be'sikula] NF blister; ~ **biliar** gall bladder

vespa® ['bespa] NF (*motor*) scooter

vespertino, -a [besper'tino, a] ADJ evening *cpd*

vespino® [bes'pino] NM O F ≈ moped

vestíbulo [bes'tiβulo] NM hall; (*de teatro*) foyer

vestido [bes'tiðo] NM (*ropa*) clothes *pl*, clothing; (*de mujer*) dress, frock

vestidor [besti'ðor] NM (*Am Deporte*) changing (*Brit*) o locker (*US*) room

vestigio [bes'tixjo] NM (*trazo*) trace;

(*señal*) sign; **vestigios** NMPL remains

vestimenta [besti'menta] NF clothing

vestir [bes'tir] /**3k**/ VT (*poner: ropa*) to put on; (*llevar: ropa*) to wear; (*cubrir*) to clothe, cover; (*pagar: la ropa*) to clothe, pay for the clothing of; (*sastre*) to make clothes for ▶ VI (*ponerse: ropa*) to dress; (*verse bien*) to look good; **vestirse** VR to get dressed, dress o.s.; **traje de** ~ (*formal*) formal suit; **estar vestido de** to be dressed o clad in; (*como disfraz*) to be dressed as

vestuario [bes'twarjo] NM clothes *pl*, wardrobe; (*Teat: para actores*) dressing room; (*: para público*) cloakroom; (*Deporte*) changing room

Vesubio [be'suβjo] NM Vesuvius

veta ['beta] NF (*vena*) vein, seam; (*raya*) streak; (*de madera*) grain

vetar [be'tar] /**1a**/ VT to veto

veterano, -a [bete'rano, a] ADJ, NM/F veteran

veterinario, -a [beteri'narjo, a] NM/F vet(erinary surgeon) ▶ NF veterinary science

veto ['beto] NM veto

vetusto, -a [be'tusto, a] ADJ ancient

vez [beθ] NF time; (*turno*) turn; **a la** ~ **que** at the same time as; **a su** ~ in its turn; **cada** ~ **más/menos** more and more/less and less; **una** ~ once; **dos veces** twice; **de una** ~ in one go; **de una** ~ **para siempre** once and for all; **en** ~ **de** instead of; **a veces** sometimes; **otra** ~ again; **una y otra** ~ repeatedly; **muchas veces** (*con frecuencia*) often; **pocas veces** seldom; **de** ~ **en cuando** from time to time; **7 veces 9** 7 times 9; **hacer las veces de** to stand in for; **tal** ~ perhaps; **¿lo viste alguna** ~? did you ever see it?; **¿cuántas veces?** how often?; **érase una** ~ once upon a time (there was)

v. g., v. gr. ABR (= *verbigracia*) viz

VHF SIGLA F (= *Very High Frequency*) VHF

vía ['bia] NF (*calle*) road; (*ruta*) track, route; (*Ferro*) line; (*fig*) way; (*Anat*) passage, tube ▶ PREP via, by way of; **por** ~ **bucal** orally; **por** ~ **judicial** by legal means; **por** ~ **oficial** through official channels; **por** ~ **de** by way of; **en vías de** in the process of; **un país en vías de desarrollo** a developing country; ~ **aérea** airway; **V~ Láctea** Milky Way; ~ **pública** public highway o thoroughfare; ~ **única** one-way street; **el tren está en la** ~ **8** the train is (standing) at platform 8

viable ['bjaβle] ADJ (*Com*) viable; (*plan etc*) feasible

viaducto [bja'ðukto] NM viaduct

viajante [bja'xante] NM commercial traveller, traveling salesman (*US*)

viajar [bja'xar] /**1a**/ VI to travel, journey

viaje ['bjaxe] NM journey; (*gira*) tour; (*Naut*) voyage; (*Com: carga*) load; **los viajes** travel *sg*;

estar de ~ to be on a journey; ~ **de ida y vuelta** round trip; ~ **de novios** honeymoon

viajero, -a [bja'xero, a] ADJ travelling (BRIT), traveling (US), (Zool) migratory ▸ NM/F (quien viaja) traveller; (pasajero) passenger

vial [bjal] ADJ road cpd, traffic cpd

vianda ['bjanda] NF (tb: **viandas**) food

viáticos ['bjatikos] NMPL (Com) travelling (BRIT) o traveling (US) expenses

víbora ['biβora] NF viper; (Am: venenoso) poisonous snake

vibración [biβra'θjon] NF vibration

vibrador [biβra'ðor] NM vibrator

vibrante [bi'βrante] ADJ vibrant, vibrating

vibrar [bi'βrar] /1a/ VT to vibrate ▸ VI to vibrate; (pulsar) to throb, beat, pulsate

vicario [bi'karjo] NM curate

vicecónsul [biθe'konsul] NM vice-consul

vicegerente [biθexe'rente] NMF assistant manager

vicepresidente [biθepresi'ðente] NMF vice president; (de comité etc) vice-chairman

viceversa [biθe'βersa] ADV vice versa

viciado, -a [bi'θjaðo, a] ADJ (corrompido) corrupt; (contaminado) foul, contaminated

viciar [bi'θjar] /1b/ VT (pervertir) to pervert; (adulterar) to adulterate; (falsificar) to falsify; (Jur) to nullify; (estropear) to spoil; (sentido) to twist; **viciarse** VR to become corrupted; (aire, agua) to be(come) polluted

vicio ['biθjo] NM (libertinaje) vice; (mala costumbre) bad habit; (mimo) spoiling; (alabeo) warp, warping; **de** o **por** ~ out of sheer habit

vicioso, -a [bi'θjoso, a] ADJ (muy malo) vicious; (corrompido) depraved; (mimado) spoiled ▸ NM/F depraved person; (adicto) addict

vicisitud [biθisi'tuð] NF vicissitude

víctima ['biktima] NF victim; (de accidente etc) casualty

victimario [bikti'marjo] NM (Am) killer, murderer

victoria [bik'torja] NF victory

victorioso, -a [bikto'rjoso, a] ADJ victorious

vicuña [bi'kuɲa] NF vicuna

vid [bið] NF vine

vida ['biða] NF life; (duración) lifetime; (modo de vivir) way of life; **¡~!, ¡~ mía!** (saludo cariñoso) my love!; **de por** ~ for life; **de ~ airada** o **libre** loose-living; **en la/mi** ~ never; **estar con** ~ to be still alive; **ganarse la** ~ to earn one's living; **¡esto es ~!** this is the life!; **le va la** ~ **en esto** his life depends on it

vidente [bi'ðente] NMF (adivino) clairvoyant; (no ciego) sighted person

vídeo ['biðeo] NM video; (aparato) video (recorder); **cinta de** ~ videotape; **película de** ~ videofilm; **grabar en** ~ to record, (video)tape; ~ **compuesto/inverso** (Inform) composite/reverse video

videocámara [biðeo'kamara] NF video camera; (pequeña) camcorder

videocasete, videocassette [biðeoka'set] NM video cassette

videoclip [biðeo'klip] NM (music) video

videoclub [biðeo'klub] NM video club; (tienda) video shop

videodatos [biðeo'ðatos] NMPL (Com) viewdata

videojuego [biðeo'xweɣo] NM video game

videojugador, -a [biðeoxuɣa'ðor, a] NM/F gamer

videollamada [biðeoʎa'maða] NF video call

videoteléfono [biðeote'lefono] NF videophone

videotex [biðeo'teks], **videotexto** [biðeo'tekso] NM Videotex®

vidriero, -a [bi'ðrjero, a] NM/F glazier ▸ NF (ventana) stained-glass window; (Am: de tienda) shop window; (puerta) glass door

vidrio ['biðrjo] NM glass; (Am) window; ~ **cilindrado/inastillable** plate/splinter-proof glass

vidrioso, -a [bi'ðrjoso, a] ADJ glassy; (frágil) fragile, brittle; (resbaladizo) slippery

vieira ['bjeira] NF scallop

viejo, -a ['bjexo, a] ADJ old ▸ NM/F old man/woman; **mi ~/vieja** (fam) my old man/woman; **hacerse** o **ponerse** ~ to grow o get old

Viena ['bjena] NF Vienna

viene etc ['bjene] VB ver **venir**

vienés, -esa [bje'nes, esa] ADJ, NM/F Viennese

viento ['bjento] NM wind; **hacer** ~ to be windy; **contra** ~ **y marea** at all costs; **ir** ~ **en popa** to go splendidly; (negocio) to prosper

vientre ['bjentre] NM belly; (matriz) womb; **vientres** NMPL bowels; **hacer de** ~ to have a bowel movement

vier. ABR (= viernes) Fri.

viernes ['bjernes] NM INV Friday; **V~ Santo** Good Friday; ver tb **Semana Santa**; **sábado**

vierta etc ['bjerta] VB ver **verter**

Vietnam [bjet'nam] NM: **el** ~ Vietnam

vietnamita [bjetna'mita] ADJ, NMF Vietnamese

viga ['biɣa] NF beam, rafter; (de metal) girder

vigencia [bi'xenθja] NF validity; (de contrato etc) term, life; **estar/entrar en** ~ to be in/come into effect o force

vigente [bi'xente] ADJ valid, in force; (imperante) prevailing

vigésimo, -a [bi'xesimo, a] NUM twentieth

vigía [bi'xia] NM look-out ▸ NF (atalaya) watchtower; (acción) watching

vigilancia [bixi'lanθja] NF vigilance; **tener a algn bajo** ~ to keep watch on sb

vigilante [bixi'lante] ADJ vigilant ▸ NM caretaker; (en cárcel) warder; (en almacén) shopwalker (BRIT), floor-walker (US);

V

401

~ jurado security guard (*licensed to carry a gun*); **~ nocturno** night watchman

vigilar [bixi'lar] /**1a**/ vt to watch over; (*cuidar*) to look after, keep an eye on ▶ vi to be vigilant; (*hacer guardia*) to keep watch; **~ por** to take care of

vigilia [vi'xilja] NF wakefulness; (*Rel*) vigil; (: *ayuno*) fast; **comer de ~** to fast

vigor [bi'ɣor] NM vigour, vitality; **en ~** in force; **entrar/poner en ~** to come/put into effect

vigoroso, -a [biɣo'roso, a] ADJ vigorous

VIH NM ABR (= *virus de inmunodeficiencia humana*) HIV; **~ negativo/positivo** HIV-negative/-positive

vil [bil] ADJ vile, low

vileza [bi'leθa] NF vileness; (*acto*) base deed

vilipendiar [bilipen'djar] /**1b**/ vt to vilify, revile

villa ['biʎa] NF (*casa*) villa; (*pueblo*) small town; (*municipalidad*) municipality; **la V~** (*Esp*) Madrid; **~ miseria** shanty town

villancico [biʎan'θiko] NM (Christmas) carol

villorrio [bi'ʎorrjo] NM one-horse town, dump; (*Am: barrio pobre*) shanty town

vilo ['bilo] **en ~** ADV in the air, suspended; (*fig*) on tenterhooks, in suspense; **estar** o **quedar en ~** to be left in suspense

vinagre [bi'naɣre] NM vinegar

vinagrera [bina'ɣrera] NF vinegar bottle; **vinagreras** NFPL cruet stand *sg*

vinagreta [bina'ɣreta] NF vinaigrette, French dressing

vinatería [binate'ria] NF wine shop

vinatero, -a [bina'tero, a] ADJ wine *cpd* ▶ NM wine merchant

vinculación [binkula'θjon] NF (*lazo*) link, bond; (*acción*) linking

vincular [binku'lar] /**1a**/ vt to link, bind

vínculo ['binkulo] NM link, bond

vindicar [bindi'kar] /**1g**/ vt to vindicate; (*vengar*) to avenge; (*Jur*) to claim

vine *etc* VB *ver* **venir**

vinícola [bi'nikola] ADJ (*industria*) wine *cpd*; (*región*) wine-growing *cpd*

vinicultor, -a [binikul'tor, a] NM/F wine grower

vinicultura [binikul'tura] NF wine growing

viniera *etc* VB *ver* **venir**

vino ['bino] VB *ver* **venir** ▶ NM wine; **~ de solera/seco/tinto** vintage/dry/red wine; **~ de Jerez** sherry; **~ de Oporto** port (wine)

viña ['biɲa] NF, **viñedo** [bi'ɲeðo] NM vineyard

viñeta [bi'ɲeta] NF (*en historieta*) cartoon

viola ['bjola] NF viola

violación [bjola'θjon] NF violation; (*Jur*) offence, infringement; (*estupro*): **~ (sexual)** rape; **~ de contrato** (*Com*) breach of contract

violar [bjo'lar] /**1a**/ vt to violate; (*Jur*) to infringe; (*cometer estupro*) to rape

violencia [bjo'lenθja] NF (*fuerza*) violence, force; (*embarazo*) embarrassment; (*acto injusto*) unjust act

violentar [bjolen'tar] /**1a**/ vt to force; (*casa*) to break into; (*agredir*) to assault; (*violar*) to violate

violento, -a [bjo'lento, a] ADJ violent; (*furioso*) furious; (*situación*) embarrassing; (*acto*) forced, unnatural; (*difícil*) awkward; **me es muy ~** it goes against the grain with me

violeta [bjo'leta] NF violet

violín [bjo'lin] NM violin

violón [bjo'lon] NM double bass

violoncelo [bjolon'θelo] NM cello

V.I.P. ['bip] SIGLA M (= *Very Important Person*) VIP

virador [bira'ðor] NM (*para fotocopiadora*) toner

viraje [bi'raxe] NM turn; (*de vehículo*) swerve; (*de carretera*) bend; (*fig*) change of direction

viral [bi'ral] ADJ viral

virar [bi'rar] /**1a**/ vi (*vehículo*) to turn; (: *con violencia*) to swerve; (*fig*) to change direction

virgen ['birxen] ADJ virgin; (*cinta*) blank ▶ NMF virgin; **la Santísima V~** (*Rel*) the Blessed Virgin

virginidad [birxini'ðað] NF virginity

Virgo ['birɣo] NM Virgo

viril [bi'ril] ADJ virile

virilidad [birili'ðað] NF virility

virrey [bi'rrei] NM viceroy

virtual [bir'twal] ADJ (*real*) virtual; (*en potencia*) potential

virtud [bir'tuð] NF virtue; **en ~ de** by virtue of

virtuoso, -a [bir'twoso, a] ADJ virtuous ▶ NM/F virtuoso

viruela [bi'rwela] NF smallpox; **viruelas** NFPL pockmarks; **viruelas locas** chickenpox *sg*

virulento, -a [biru'lento, a] ADJ virulent

virus ['birus] NM INV virus

viruta [bi'ruta] NF wood o metal shaving

vis [bis] NF: **~ cómica** sense of humour

visa ['bisa] NF (*Am*), **visado** [bi'saðo] NM (*Esp*) visa; **~ de permanencia** residence permit

visar [bi'sar] /**1a**/ vt (*pasaporte*) to visa; (*documento*) to endorse

víscera ['bisθera] NF internal organ; **vísceras** NFPL entrails

visceral [bisθe'ral] ADJ (*odio*) deep-rooted; **reacción ~** gut reaction

viscoso, -a [bis'koso, a] ADJ viscous

visera [bi'sera] NF visor

visibilidad [bisiβili'ðað] NF visibility

visible [bi'siβle] ADJ visible; (*fig*) obvious; **exportaciones/importaciones visibles** (*Com*) visible exports/imports

visillo [bi'siʎo] NM lace curtain

visión [bi'sjon] NF (*Anat*) vision, (eye)sight; (*fantasía*) vision, fantasy; (*panorama*) view;

ver visiones to see o be seeing things
visionario, -a [bisjo'narjo, a] ADJ (que prevé) visionary; (alucinado) deluded ▶ NM/F visionary; (chalado) lunatic
visita [bi'sita] NF call, visit; (persona) visitor; **horas/tarjeta de ~** visiting hours/card; **~ de cortesía/de cumplido/de despedida** courtesy/formal/farewell visit; **hacer una ~** to pay a visit; **ir de ~** to go visiting
visitante [bisi'tante] ADJ visiting ▶ NMF visitor
visitar [bisi'tar] /1a/ VT to visit, call on; (inspeccionar) to inspect
vislumbrar [bislum'brar] /1a/ VT to glimpse, catch a glimpse of
vislumbre [bis'lumbre] NF glimpse; (centelleo) gleam; (idea vaga) glimmer
viso ['biso] NM (de metal) glint, gleam; (de tela) sheen; (aspecto) appearance; **hay un ~ de verdad en esto** there is an element of truth in this
visón [bi'son] NM mink
visor [bi'sor] NM (Foto) viewfinder
víspera ['bispera] NF day before; **la ~ o en vísperas de** on the eve of
vista ['bista] NF sight, vision; (capacidad de ver) (eye)sight; (mirada) look(s); (Foto etc) view; (Jur) hearing ▶ NM customs officer; **a primera ~** at first glance; **~ general** overview; **fijar o clavar la ~ en** to stare at; **hacer la ~ gorda** to turn a blind eye; **volver la ~** to look back; **está a la ~ que** it's obvious that; **a la ~** (Com) at sight; **en ~ de** in view of; **en ~ de que** in view of the fact that; **¡hasta la ~!** so long!, see you!; **con vistas a** with a view to; ver tb **visto**
vistazo [bis'taθo] NM glance; **dar o echar un ~ a** to glance at
visto, -a ['bisto, a] VB ver **vestir** ▶ PP de **ver** ▶ ADJ seen; (considerado) considered ▶ NM: **~ bueno** approval; **"~ bueno"** "approved"; **por lo ~** apparently; **dar el ~ bueno a algo** to give sth the go-ahead; **está ~ que** it's clear that; **está bien/mal ~** it's acceptable/unacceptable; **está muy ~** it is very common; **estaba ~** it had to be; **~ que** conj since, considering that
vistoso, -a [bis'toso, a] ADJ colourful; (alegre) gay; (pey) gaudy
visual [bi'swal] ADJ visual
visualice etc [biswa'liθe] VB ver **visualizar**
visualizador [biswaliθa'ðor] NM (Inform) display screen, VDU
visualizar [biswali'θar] /1f/ VT (imaginarse) to visualize; (Inform) to display
vital [bi'tal] ADJ life cpd, living cpd; (fig) vital; (persona) lively, vivacious
vitalicio, -a [bita'liθjo, a] ADJ for life
vitalidad [bitali'ðað] NF vitality; (de persona, negocio) energy; (de ciudad) liveliness

vitamina [bita'mina] NF vitamin
vitaminado, -a [bitami'naðo, a] ADJ with added vitamins
vitamínico, -a [bita'miniko, a] ADJ vitamin cpd; **complejos vitamínicos** vitamin compounds
viticultor, a [bitikul'tor, a] NM/F vine grower
viticultura [bitikul'tura] NF vine growing
vitorear [bitore'ar] /1a/ VT to cheer, acclaim
vítores ['bitores] NMPL cheers
vitorano, -a [bito'rjano, a] ADJ of o from Vitoria ▶ NM/F native o inhabitant of Vitoria
vítreo, -a ['bitreo, a] ADJ vitreous
vitrina [bi'trina] NF glass case; (en casa) display cabinet; (AM) shop window
vituperar [bitupe'rar] /1a/ VT to condemn
vituperio [bitu'perjo] NM (condena) condemnation; (censura) censure; (insulto) insult
viudez [bju'ðeθ] NF widowhood
viudo, -a ['bjuðo, a] ADJ widowed ▶ NM widower ▶ NF widow
viva ['biβa] EXCL hurrah! ▶ NM cheer; **¡~ el rey!** long live the King!
vivacidad [biβaθi'ðað] NF (vigor) vigour; (vida) vivacity
vivamente [biβa'mente] ADV in lively fashion; (describir) vividly; (protestar) sharply; (emocionarse) acutely
vivaracho, -a [biβa'ratʃo, a] ADJ jaunty, lively; (ojos) bright, twinkling
vivaz [bi'βaθ] ADJ (que dura) enduring; (vigoroso) vigorous; (vivo) lively
vivencia [bi'βenθja] NF experience
víveres ['biβeres] NMPL provisions
vivero [bi'βero] NM (Horticultura) nursery; (para peces) fishpond; (: Com) fish farm; (fig) hotbed
viveza [bi'βeθa] NF liveliness; (agudeza: mental) sharpness
vividor, a [biβi'ðor, a] ADJ (pey) opportunistic ▶ NM (aprovechado) hustler
vivienda [bi'βjenda] NF (alojamiento) housing; (morada) dwelling; (casa) house; (piso) flat (BRIT), apartment (US); **viviendas protegidas o sociales** council housing sg (BRIT), public housing sg (US)
viviente [bi'βjente] ADJ living
vivificar [biβifi'kar] /1g/ VT to give life to
vivifique etc [biβi'fike] VB ver **vivificar**
vivir [bi'βir] /3a/ VT (experimentar) to live o go through ▶ VI (gen, Com): **~ (de)** to live (by, off, on) ▶ NM life, living; **¡viva!** hurray!; **¡viva el rey!** long live the king!
vivo, -a ['biβo, a] ADJ living, live, alive; (fig) vivid; (movimiento) quick; (color) bright; (protesta) strong; (persona: astuto) smart, clever; **en ~** (TV etc) live; **llegar a lo ~** to cut to the quick

vizcaíno, -a [biθka'ino, a] ADJ, NM/F Biscayan

Vizcaya [biθ'kaja] NF Biscay; **el Golfo de ~** the Bay of Biscay

V.O. ABR = **versión original**

V.°B.° ABR = **visto bueno**

vocablo [bo'kaβlo] NM (*palabra*) word; (*término*) term

vocabulario [bokaβu'larjo] NM vocabulary, word list

vocación [boka'θjon] NF vocation

vocacional [bokasjo'nal] NF (*Am*) ≈ technical college

vocal [bo'kal] ADJ vocal ▶ NMF member (of a committee *etc*) ▶ NM non-executive director ▶ NF vowel

vocalice *etc* [boka'liθe] VB *ver* **vocalizar**

vocalizar [bokali'θar] /1f/ VT to vocalize

voceador [bosea'ðor] NM (*Am*): **~ de periódicos** newspaper vendor *o* seller

vocear [boθe'ar] /1a/ VT (*para vender*) to cry; (*aclamar*) to acclaim; (*fig*) to proclaim ▶ VI to yell

vocerío [boθe'rio] NM shouting; (*escándalo*) hullabaloo

vocero, -a [bo'θero, a] NM/F (*Am*) spokesman/woman

voces ['boθes] NFPL *de* **voz**

vociferar [boθife'rar] /1a/ VT to shout; (*jactarse*) to proclaim boastfully ▶ VI to yell

vocinglero, -a [boθin'glero, a] ADJ vociferous; (*gárrulo*) garrulous; (*fig*) blatant

vodevil [boðe'βil] NM music hall, variety, vaudeville (*US*)

vodka ['boðka] NM vodka

vodú [bo'ðu] NM voodoo

vol. ABR = **volumen**

volado, -a [bo'laðo, a] ADJ: **estar ~** (*fam: inquieto*) to be worried; (: *loco*) to be crazy ▶ ADV (*Am*) in a rush, hastily

volador, a [bola'ðor, a] ADJ flying

voladura [bola'ðura] NF blowing up, demolition; (*Minería*) blasting

volandas [bo'landas] **en ~** ADV in *o* through the air; (*fig*) swiftly

volante [bo'lante] ADJ flying ▶ NM (*de máquina, coche*) steering wheel; (*de reloj*) balance; (*nota*) note; **ir al ~** to be at the wheel, be driving

volar [bo'lar] /1l/ VT (*demoler*) to blow up, demolish ▶ VI to fly; (*fig: correr*) to rush, hurry; (*fam: desaparecer*) to disappear; **voy volando** I must dash; **¡cómo vuela el tiempo!** how time flies!

volátil [bo'latil] ADJ volatile; (*fig*) changeable

volcán [bol'kan] NM volcano

volcánico, -a [bol'kaniko, a] ADJ volcanic

volcar [bol'kar] /1g, 1l/ VT to upset, overturn; (*tumbar, derribar*) to knock over; (*vaciar*) to empty out ▶ VI to overturn; **volcarse** VR to

tip over; (*barco*) to capsize

voleibol [bolei'βol] NM volleyball

voleo [bo'leo] NM volley; **a(l) ~** haphazardly; **de un ~** quickly

Volga ['bolɣa] NM Volga

volición [boli'θjon] NF volition

volqué [bol'ke], **volquemos** *etc* [bol'kemos] VB *ver* **volcar**

volquete [bol'kete] NM dumper, dump truck (*US*)

voltaje [bol'taxe] NM voltage

voltear [bolte'ar] /1a/ VT to turn over; (*volcar*) to knock over; (*doblar*) to peal ▶ VI to roll over; **voltearse** VR (*Am*) to turn round; **~ a hacer algo** (*Am*) to do sth again

voltereta [bolte'reta] NF somersault; **~ sobre las manos** handspring; **~ lateral** cartwheel

voltio ['boltjo] NM volt

voluble [bo'luβle] ADJ fickle

volumen [bo'lumen] NM volume; **~ monetario** money supply; **~ de negocios** turnover; **bajar el ~** to turn down the volume; **poner la radio a todo ~** to turn the radio up full

voluminoso, -a [bolumi'noso, a] ADJ voluminous; (*enorme*) massive

voluntad [bolun'tað] NF will, willpower; (*deseo*) desire, wish; (*afecto*) fondness; **a ~** at will; (*cantidad*) as much as one likes; **buena ~** goodwill; **mala ~** ill will, malice; **por causas ajenas a mi ~** for reasons beyond my control

voluntario, -a [bolun'tarjo, a] ADJ voluntary ▶ NM/F volunteer

voluntarioso, -a [bolunta'rjoso, a] ADJ headstrong

voluptuoso, -a [bolup'twoso, a] ADJ voluptuous

volver [bol'βer] /2h/ VT to turn; (*boca abajo*) to turn (over); (*voltear*) to turn round, turn upside down; (*poner del revés*) to turn inside out; (*devolver*) to return; (*transformar*) to change, transform; (*manga*) to roll up ▶ VI to return, go/come back; **volverse** VR to turn round; (*llegar a ser*) to become; **~ la espalda** to turn one's back; **~ bien por mal** to return good for evil; **~ a hacer** to do again; **~ en sí** to come to *o* round, regain consciousness; **~ la vista atrás** to look back; **~ triste** *etc* **a algn** to make sb sad *etc*; **~ loco a algn** to drive sb mad; **volverse loco** to go mad

vomitar [bomi'tar] /1a/ VT, VI to vomit

vómito ['bomito] NM (*acto*) vomiting; (*resultado*) vomit

voracidad [boraθi'ðað] NF voracity

vorágine [bo'raxine] NF whirlpool; (*fig*) maelstrom

voraz [bo'raθ] ADJ voracious; (*fig*) fierce

vórtice ['bortiθe] NM whirlpool; (*de aire*) whirlwind

VOS ABR = **versión original subtitulada**

vos [bos] PRON (*Am*) you

voseo [bo'seo] NM (*Am*) addressing a person as "vos" (*familiar usage*)

Vosgos ['bosɣos] NMPL Vosges

vosotros, -as [bo'sotros, as] PRON you *pl*; (*reflexivo*) yourselves; : **entre ~** among yourselves

votación [bota'θjon] NF (*acto*) voting; (*voto*) vote; ~ **a mano alzada** show of hands; **someter algo a ~** to put sth to the vote

votar [bo'tar] /**1a**/ VT (*Pol*: *partido etc*) to vote for; (: *proyecto*: *aprobar*) to pass; (*Rel*) to vow ▶ VI to vote

voto ['boto] NM vote; (*promesa*) vow; (*maldición*) oath, curse; **votos** NMPL (good) wishes; ~ **de bloque/de grupo** block/card vote; ~ **de censura/de (des)confianza/de gracias** vote of censure/(no) confidence/thanks; **dar su ~** to cast one's vote

voy [boi] VB *ver* **ir**

voz [boθ] NF voice; (*grito*) shout; (*chisme*) rumour; (*Ling*: *palabra*) word; (: *forma*) voice; **dar voces** to shout, yell; **llamar a algn a voces** to shout to sb; **llevar la ~ cantante** (*fig*) to be the boss; **tener la ~ tomada** to be hoarse; **tener ~ y voto** to have the right to speak; **en ~ baja** in a low voice; **a ~ en cuello** *o* **en grito** at the top of one's voice; **de viva ~** verbally; **en ~ alta** aloud; ~ **de mando** command

vozarrón [boθa'rron] NM booming voice

vra., vro. ABR = **vuestro**

Vto. ABR (*Com*) = **vencimiento**

vudú [bu'ðu] NM voodoo

vuelco *etc* ['bwelko] VB *ver* **volcar** ▶ NM spill, overturning; (*fig*) collapse; **mi corazón dio un ~** my heart missed a beat

vuelo ['bwelo] VB *ver* **volar** ▶ NM flight; (*encaje*) lace, frill; (*de falda etc*) loose part; (*fig*) importance; **de altos vuelos** (*fig*: *plan*) grandiose (: *persona*) ambitious; **alzar el ~** to take flight; (*fig*) to dash off; **coger al ~** to catch in flight; ~ **de bajo coste** low-cost flight; ~ **en picado** dive; ~ **libre** hang-gliding; ~ **regular** scheduled flight; **falda de mucho ~** full *o* wide skirt

vuelque *etc* ['bwelke] VB *ver* **volcar**

vuelta ['bwelta] NF turn; (*curva*) bend, curve; (*regreso*) return; (*revolución*) revolution; (*paseo*) stroll; (*circuito*) lap; (*de papel, tela*) reverse; (*de pantalón*) turn-up (*Brit*), cuff (*US*); (*cambio*) change; ~ **a empezar** back to square one; ~ **al mundo** world trip; ~ **ciclista** (*Deporte*) (cycle) tour; **V~ de Francia** Tour de France; ~ **cerrada** hairpin bend; **a la ~** (*Esp*) on one's return; **a la ~ de la esquina, a la ~** (*Am*) round the corner; **a ~ de correo** by return of post; **dar vueltas** to turn, revolve; (*cabeza*) to spin; **dar(se) la ~** (*volverse*) to turn round; **dar vueltas a una idea** to turn over an idea (in one's mind); **dar una ~** to go for a walk; (*en coche*) to go for a drive; **dar media ~** (*Auto*) to do a U-turn; (*fam*) to beat it; **estar de ~** (*fam*) to be back; **poner a algn de ~ y media** to heap abuse on sb; **no tiene ~ de hoja** there's no alternative

vueltita [bwel'tita] NF (*esp Am fam*) (little) walk; (: *en coche*) (little) drive

vuelto ['bwelto] PP *de* **volver** ▶ NM (*Am*: *moneda*) change

vuelvo *etc* ['bwelβo] VB *ver* **volver**

vuestro, -a ['bwestro, a] ADJ your; (*después de n*) of yours ▶ PRON: **el ~/la vuestra/los vuestros/las vuestras** yours; **lo ~** (what is) yours; **un amigo ~** a friend of yours; **una idea vuestra** an idea of yours

vulgar [bul'ɣar] ADJ (*ordinario*) vulgar; (*común*) common

vulgarice *etc* [bulɣa'riθe] VB *ver* **vulgarizar**

vulgaridad [bulɣari'ðað] NF commonness; (*acto*) vulgarity; (*expresión*) coarse expression; **vulgaridades** NFPL banalities

vulgarismo [bulɣa'rismo] NM popular form of a word

vulgarizar [bulɣari'θar] /**1f**/ VT to popularize

vulgo ['bulɣo] NM common people

vulnerable [bulne'raβle] ADJ vulnerable

vulnerar [bulne'rar] /**1a**/ VT (*Jur, Com*) to violate; (*derechos*) to violate, interfere with; (*reputación*) to harm, damage

vulva ['bulβa] NF vulva

V

Ww

W ABR (= *vatio(s)*) w

W, w ['uβe'doβle, (*Am*) 'doβleβe] NF (*letra*)
W, w; **W de Washington** W for William

walkie-talkie [walki'talki] NM
walkie-talkie

walkman® ['wal(k)man] NM Walkman®

WAP [wap] ADJ, NM WAP; **teléfono ~** WAP
phone

wáter ['bater] NM (*taza*) toilet; (*Am: lugar*)
toilet (*Brit*), rest room (*US*)

waterpolo [water'polo] NM waterpolo

web [web] NM O F (*página*) website; (*red*)
(World Wide) Web

webcam ['webkam] NF webcam

webmaster ['webmaster] NMF webmaster

web site ['websait] NM website

western ['western] (*pl* **westerns**) NM western

whisky ['wiski] NM whisky

widget [wi'tʃet] (*pl* **widgets** [wi'tʃets]) NM
(*Inform*) widget

wifi ['waifai] NM Wi-Fi

wiki ['wiki] NF wiki

Winchester ['wintʃester] NM (*Inform*): **disco ~**
Winchester disk

windsurf ['winsurf] NM windsurfing; **hacer
~** to go windsurfing

WWW NM O NF ABR (*Inform*: = *World Wide Web*)
WWW

Xx

X, x ['ekis] NF (*letra*) X, x; **X de xilófono**
X for Xmas
xenofobia [seno'foβja] NF xenophobia
xenófobo, -a [se'nofoβo, a] ADJ xenophobic
▸ NM/F xenophobe
xerografía [seroɣra'fia] NF xerography

xilófono [si'lofono] NM xylophone
xocoyote, -a [ksoko'jote, a] NM/F
(*AM*) baby of the family, youngest
child
Xunta ['ʃunta] NF (*tb*: **Xunta de Galicia**)
regional government of Galicia

Yy

Y, y [i'ɣrjeɣa] NF (letra) Y, y; **Y de Yegua** Y for Yellow (BRIT) o Yoke (US)

y [i] CONJ and; (AM fam: pues) well; (hora): **la una y cinco** five past one; **¿y eso?** why?, how so?; **¿y los demás?** what about the others?; **y bueno ...** (AM) well ...

ya [ja] ADV (gen) already; (ahora) now; (en seguida) at once; (pronto) soon ▸ EXCL all right!; (por supuesto) of course! ▸ CONJ (ahora que) now that; **ya no** not any more, no longer; **ya lo sé** I know; **ya dice que sí, ya dice que no** first he says yes, then he says no; **¡ya, ya!** yes, yes!; (con impaciencia) all right!, O.K.!; **¡ya está bien!** that's (quite) enough!; **¡ya voy!** (enfático: no se suele traducir) coming!; **ya que** since

yacer [ja'θer] /**2x**/ VI to lie

yacimiento [jaθi'mjento] NM bed, deposit; (arqueológico) site; **~ petrolífero** oilfield

Yakarta [ja'karta] NF Jakarta

yanqui ['janki] ADJ Yankee ▸ NMF Yank, Yankee

yate ['jate] NM yacht

yazco etc ['jaθko] VB ver **yacer**

yedra ['jeðra] NF ivy

yegua ['jeɣwa] NF mare

yema ['jema] NF (del huevo) yolk; (Bot) leaf bud; (fig) best part; **~ del dedo** fingertip

Yemen ['jemen] NM Yemen

yemení [jeme'ni] ADJ, NMF Yemeni

yendo ['jendo] VB ver **ir**

yerba ['jerβa] NF = **hierba**

yerbatero, -a [jerβa'tero, a] ADJ (AM) maté ▸ NM/F (AM) herbal healer

yerga etc ['jerɣa], **yergue** etc ['jerɣe] VB ver **erguir**

yermo, -a ['jermo, a] ADJ barren; (de gente) uninhabited ▸ NM waste land

yerno ['jerno] NM son-in-law

yerre etc ['jerre] VB ver **errar**

yerto, -a ['jerto, a] ADJ stiff

yesca ['jeska] NF tinder

yeso ['jeso] NM (Geo) gypsum; (Arq) plaster

yo [jo] PRON PERSONAL I; **soy yo** it's me, it is I; **yo que tú/usted** if I were you

yodo ['joðo] NM iodine

yoga ['joɣa] NM yoga

yogur(t) [jo'ɣur(t)] NM yogurt

yogurtera [joɣur'tera] NF yogurt maker

yuca ['juka] NF (Bot) yucca; (alimento) cassava, manioc root

yudo ['juðo] NM judo

yugo ['juɣo] NM yoke

Yugoslavia [juɣos'laβja] NF (Historia) Yugoslavia

yugoslavo, -a [juɣos'laβo, a] ADJ Yugoslavian ▸ NM/F Yugoslav

yugular [juɣu'lar] ADJ jugular

yunque ['junke] NM anvil

yunta ['junta] NF yoke

yuntero [jun'tero] NM ploughman

yute ['jute] NM jute

yuxtapondré etc [jukstapond're] VB ver **yuxtaponer**

yuxtaponer [jukstapo'ner] /**2q**/ VT to juxtapose

yuxtaponga etc [juksta'ponga] VB ver **yuxtaponer**

yuxtaposición [jukstaposi'θjon] NF juxtaposition

yuxtapuesto [juksta'pwesto], **yuxtapuse** etc [juksta'puse] VB ver **yuxtaponer**

yuyo ['jujo] NM (AM: mala hierba) weed

Zz

Z, z ['θeta, (*esp Am*) 'seta] NF (*letra*) Z, z; **Z de Zaragoza** Z for Zebra

zafar [θa'far] /**1a**/ VT (*soltar*) to untie; (*superficie*) to clear; **zafarse** VR (*escaparse*) to escape; (*ocultarse*) to hide o.s. away; (*Tec*) to slip off; **zafarse de** (*persona*) to get away from

zafio, -a ['θafjo, a] ADJ coarse

zafiro [θa'firo] NM sapphire

zaga ['θaɣa] NF rear; **a la ~** behind, in the rear

zagal [θa'ɣal] NM boy, lad

zagala [θa'ɣala] NF girl, lass

zaguán [θa'ɣwan] NM hallway

zaherir [θae'rir] /**3i**/ VT (*criticar*) to criticize; (*fig: herir*) to wound

zahiera *etc*, **zahiriendo** *etc* [θa'jera, θai'rjendo] VB *ver* **zaherir**

zahorí [θao'ri] NM clairvoyant

zaino, -a ['θaino, a] ADJ (*color de caballo*) chestnut; (*pérfido*) treacherous; (*animal*) vicious

zalamería [θalame'ria] NF flattery

zalamero, -a [θala'mero, a] ADJ flattering; (*relamido*) suave

zamarra [θa'marra] NF (*piel*) sheepskin; (*chaqueta*) sheepskin jacket

Zambeze [θam'beθe] NM Zambezi

zambo, -a ['θambo, a] ADJ knock-kneed ▶ NM/F (*Am*) mixed race (*of Black and Native American parentage*); (*mulato*) mulatto ▶ NF samba

zambullida [θambu'ʎiða] NF dive, plunge

zambullirse [θambu'ʎirse] /**3h**/ VR to dive; (*ocultarse*) to hide o.s.

zamorano, -a [θamo'rano, a] ADJ of *o* from Zamora ▶ NM/F native *o* inhabitant of Zamora

zampar [θam'par] /**1a**/ VT (*esconder*) to hide *o* put away (hurriedly); (*comer*) to gobble; (*arrojar*) to hurl ▶ VI to eat voraciously; **zamparse** VR (*chocar*) to bump; (*fig*) to gatecrash

zanahoria [θana'orja] NF carrot

zancada [θan'kaða] NF stride

zancadilla [θanka'ðiʎa] NF trip; (*fig*) stratagem; **echar la ~ a algn** to trip sb up

zancajo [θan'kaxo] NM (*Anat*) heel; (*fig*) dwarf

zanco ['θanko] NM stilt

zancudo, -a [θan'kuðo, a] ADJ long-legged ▶ NM (*Am*) mosquito

zángano ['θangano] NM drone; (*holgazán*) idler, slacker

zanja ['θanxa] NF (*fosa*) ditch; (*tumba*) grave

zanjar [θan'xar] /**1a**/ VT (*fosa*) to ditch, trench; (*problema*) to surmount; (*conflicto*) to resolve

zapapico [θapa'piko] NM pick, pickaxe

zapata [θa'pata] NF half-boot; (*Mecánica*) shoe

zapateado [θapate'aðo] NM (flamenco) tap dance

zapatear [θapate'ar] /**1a**/ VT (*tocar*) to tap with one's foot; (*patear*) to kick; (*fam*) to ill-treat ▶ VI to tap with one's feet

zapatería [θapate'ria] NF (*oficio*) shoemaking; (*tienda*) shoe-shop; (*fábrica*) shoe factory

zapatero, -a [θapa'tero, a] NM/F shoemaker; **~ remendón** cobbler

zapatilla [θapa'tiʎa] NF slipper; (*Tec*) washer; (*de deporte*) training shoe

zapato [θa'pato] NM shoe

zapear [θape'ar] /**1a**/ VI to flick through the channels

zapping ['θapin] NM channel-hopping; **hacer ~** to channel-hop, flick through the channels

zar [θar] NM tsar, czar

zarabanda [θara'βanda] NF saraband; (*fig*) whirl

Zaragoza [θara'ɣoθa] NF Saragossa

zaragozano, -a [θaraɣo'θano, a] ADJ of *o* from Saragossa ▶ NM/F native *o* inhabitant of Saragossa

zaranda [θa'randa] NF sieve

zarandear [θarande'ar] /**1a**/ VT to sieve; (*fam*) to shake vigorously

zarpa ['θarpa] NF (*garra*) claw, paw; **echar la ~ a** to claw at; (*fam*) to grab

zarpar [θar'par] /**1a**/ VI to weigh anchor

zarpazo [θar'paθo] NM: **dar un ~** to claw

zarza ['θarθa] NF (*Bot*) bramble

zarzal [θar'θal] NM (*matorral*) bramble patch

zarzamora [θarθa'mora] NF blackberry

zarzuela [θar'θwela] NF Spanish light opera; **la Z~** *home of the Spanish Royal Family*

zigzag [θiɣ'θaɣ] ADJ zigzag

zigzaguear [θiɣθaɣe'ar] /**1a**/ VI to zigzag

zinc [θink] NM zinc

zíper ['siper] NM (*Am*) zip, zipper (*US*)

zócalo ['θokalo] NM (*Arq*) plinth, base; (*de pared*) skirting board

zoclo ['θoklo] NM (*Am*) skirting board (*Brit*), baseboard (*US*)

zoco ['θoko] NM (Arab) market, souk

zodíaco [θo'ðiako] NM zodiac; **signo del ~** star sign

zona ['θona] NF area, zone; **~ cero** Ground Zero; **~ euro** Eurozone; **los países de la ~ euro** the Eurozone countries; **~ fronteriza** border area; **~ del dólar** (*Com*) dollar area; **~ de fomento** o **de desarrollo** development area; **~ roja** (*Am*) red-light district

zonzo, -a ['θonθo, a] (*Am*) ADJ silly ▶ NM/F fool

zoo ['θoo] NM zoo

zoología [θoolo'xia] NF zoology

zoológico, -a [θoo'loxiko, a] ADJ zoological ▶ NM (*tb*: **parque zoológico**) zoo

zoólogo, -a [θo'oloɣo, a] NM/F zoologist

zoom [θum] NM zoom lens

zopenco, -a [θo'penko, a] (*fam*) ADJ dull, stupid ▶ NM/F clot, nitwit

zopilote [θopi'lote] NM (*Am*) buzzard

zoquete [θo'kete] NM (*de madera*) block; (*de pan*) crust; (*fam*) blockhead

zorro, -a ['θorro, a] ADJ crafty ▶ NM/F fox/vixen ▶ NF (*fam*) whore, tart, hooker (*US*)

zote ['θote] (*fam*) ADJ dim, stupid ▶ NMF dimwit

zozobra [θo'θoβra] NF (*fig*) anxiety

zozobrar [θoθo'βrar] /**1a**/ VI (*hundirse*) to capsize; (*fig*) to fail

zueco ['θweko] NM clog

zulo ['θulo] NM (*de armas*) cache

zumbar [θum'bar] /**1a**/ VT (*burlar*) to tease; (*golpear*) to hit ▶ VI to buzz; (*fam*) to be very close; **zumbarse** VR: **zumbarse de** to tease; **me zumban los oídos** I have a buzzing o ringing in my ears

zumbido [θum'biðo] NM buzzing; (*fam*) punch; **~ de oídos** buzzing o ringing in the ears

zumo ['θumo] NM juice; (*ganancia*) profit; **~ de naranja** (fresh) orange juice

zurcir [θur'θir] /**3b**/ VT (*coser*) to darn; (*fig*) to put together; **¡que las zurzan!** to blazes with them!

zurdo, -a ['θurðo, a] ADJ (*mano*) left; (*persona*) left-handed

zurrar [θu'rrar] /**1a**/ VT (*Tec*) to dress; (*fam: pegar duro*) to wallop; (: *aplastar*) to flatten; (: *criticar*) to criticize harshly

zurriagazo [θurrja'ɣaθo] NM lash, stroke; (*desgracia*) stroke of bad luck

zurrón [θu'rron] NM pouch

zurza *etc* ['θurθa] VB *ver* **zurcir**

zutano, -a [θu'tano, a] NM/F so-and-so

Aa

A, a [eɪ] N (*letter*) A, a; (*Scol: mark*) ≈ sobresaliente; (*Mus*): **A** la *m*; **A for Andrew**, (*US*) **A for Able** A de Antonio; **A road** *n* (*Brit Aut*) ≈ carretera nacional

(KEYWORD)

a [ə] INDEF ART (*before vowel and silent h* **an**)
1 un(a); **a book** un libro; **an apple** una manzana; **she's a nurse** (ella) es enfermera; **I haven't got a car** no tengo coche
2 (*instead of the number "one"*) un(a); **a year ago** hace un año; **a hundred/thousand pounds** cien/mil libras
3 (*in expressing ratios, prices etc*): **three a day/week** tres al día/a la semana; **10 km an hour** 10 km por hora; **£5 a person** £5 por persona; **30p a kilo** 30p el kilo; **three times a month** tres veces al mes

a. ABBR = **acre**
A2 N (*Brit Scol*) *segunda parte de los "A levels"* (*módulos 4–6*)
AA N ABBR (*Brit*: = *Automobile Association*) ≈ RACE *m* (*Sp*); (= *Alcoholics Anonymous*) A.A.; (*US*: = *Associate in/of Arts*) *título universitario*; = **anti-aircraft**
AAA ['θriː'eɪz] N ABBR (= *American Automobile Association*) ≈ RACE *m* (*Sp*); (*Brit*: = *Amateur Athletics Association*) *asociación de atletismo amateur*
A & R N ABBR (*Mus*: = *artists and repertoire*) *nuevos artistas y canciones*; **~ man** *descubridor de jóvenes talentos*
AAUP N ABBR (= *American Association of University Professors*) *asociación de profesores universitarios*
AB ABBR (*Brit*) = **able-bodied seaman**; (*Canada*) = **Alberta**
aback [ə'bæk] ADV: **to be taken ~** quedar(se) desconcertado
abandon [ə'bændən] VT abandonar; (*renounce*) renunciar a ▶ N abandono; (*wild behaviour*): **with ~** con desenfreno; **to ~ ship** abandonar el barco

abandoned [ə'bændənd] ADJ (*child, house etc*) abandonado; (*unrestrained: manner*) desinhibido
abase [ə'beɪs] VT: **to ~ o.s. (so far as to do ...)** rebajarse (hasta el punto de hacer ...)
abashed [ə'bæʃt] ADJ avergonzado
abate [ə'beɪt] VI moderarse; (*lessen*) disminuir; (*calm down*) calmarse
abatement [ə'beɪtmənt] N (*of pollution, noise*) disminución *f*
abattoir ['æbətwɑːʳ] N (*Brit*) matadero
abbey ['æbɪ] N abadía
abbot ['æbət] N abad *m*
abbreviate [ə'briːvɪeɪt] VT abreviar
abbreviation [əbriːvɪ'eɪʃən] N (*short form*) abreviatura; (*act*) abreviación *f*
ABC N ABBR (= *American Broadcasting Company*) *cadena de televisión*
abdicate ['æbdɪkeɪt] VT, VI abdicar
abdication [æbdɪ'keɪʃən] N abdicación *f*
abdomen ['æbdəmən] N abdomen *m*
abdominal [æb'dɔmɪnl] ADJ abdominal
abduct [æb'dʌkt] VT raptar, secuestrar
abduction [æb'dʌkʃən] N rapto, secuestro
abductor [æb'dʌktəʳ] N raptor(a) *m/f*, secuestrador(a) *m/f*
Aberdonian [æbə'dəunɪən] ADJ de Aberdeen ▶ N nativo(-a) *or* habitante *mf* de Aberdeen
aberration [æbə'reɪʃən] N aberración *f*; **in a moment of mental ~** en un momento de enajenación mental
abet [ə'bɛt] VT *see* **aid**
abeyance [ə'beɪəns] N: **in ~** (*law*) en desuso; (*matter*) en suspenso
abhor [əb'hɔːʳ] VT aborrecer, abominar (de)
abhorrent [əb'hɔrənt] ADJ aborrecible, detestable
abide [ə'baɪd] VT: **I can't ~ it/him** no lo/le puedo ver *or* aguantar
▶ **abide by** VT FUS atenerse a
abiding [ə'baɪdɪŋ] ADJ (*memory etc*) perdurable
ability [ə'bɪlɪtɪ] N habilidad *f*, capacidad *f*; (*talent*) talento; **to the best of my ~** lo mejor que pueda *etc*

abject ['æbdʒɛkt] ADJ (poverty) sórdido; (apology) rastrero; (coward) vil

ablaze [ə'bleɪz] ADJ en llamas, ardiendo

able ['eɪbl] ADJ capaz; (skilled) hábil; **to be ~ to do sth** poder hacer algo

able-bodied ['eɪbl'bɔdɪd] ADJ sano; **~ seaman** marinero de primera

ably ['eɪblɪ] ADV hábilmente

ABM N ABBR = **anti-ballistic missile**

abnormal [æb'nɔːməl] ADJ anormal

abnormality [æbnɔː'mælɪtɪ] N (condition) anormalidad f; (instance) anomalía

aboard [ə'bɔːd] ADV a bordo ▶ PREP a bordo de; **~ the train** en el tren

abode [ə'bəud] N (old) morada; (Law) domicilio; **of no fixed ~** sin domicilio fijo

abolish [ə'bɔlɪʃ] VT suprimir, abolir

abolition [æbəu'lɪʃən] N supresión f, abolición f

abominable [ə'bɔmɪnəbl] ADJ abominable

aborigine [æbə'rɪdʒɪnɪ] N aborigen mf

abort [ə'bɔːt] VT abortar; (Comput) interrumpir ▶ VI (Comput) interrumpir el programa

abortion [ə'bɔːʃən] N aborto; **to have an ~** abortar

abortionist [ə'bɔːʃənɪst] N persona que practica abortos

abortive [ə'bɔːtɪv] ADJ fracasado

abound [ə'baund] VI: **to ~ (in or with)** abundar (de or en)

(KEYWORD)

about [ə'baut] ADV **1** (approximately) más o menos, aproximadamente; **about a hundred/thousand** etc unos(-as) or como cien/mil etc; **it takes about 10 hours** se tarda unas or más o menos 10 horas; **at about two o'clock** sobre las dos; **I've just about finished** casi he terminado

2 (referring to place) por todas partes; **to leave things lying about** dejar las cosas (tiradas) por ahí; **to run about** correr por todas partes; **to walk about** pasearse, ir y venir; **is Paul about?** ¿está por aquí Paul?; **it's the other way about** es al revés

3: **to be about to do sth** estar a punto de hacer algo; **I'm not about to do all that for nothing** no pienso hacer todo eso para nada ▶ PREP **1** (relating to) de, sobre, acerca de; **a book about London** un libro sobre or acerca de Londres; **what is it about?** (book, film) ¿de qué se trata?; **we talked about it** hablamos de eso or ello; **what** or **how about doing this?** ¿qué tal si hacemos esto?

2 (referring to place) por; **to walk about the town** caminar por la ciudad

about face, about turn N (Mil) media vuelta; (fig) cambio radical

above [ə'bʌv] ADV encima, por encima, arriba ▶ PREP encima de; (greater than: in number) más de; (: in rank) superior a; **mentioned ~** susodicho; **~ all** sobre todo; **he's not ~ a bit of blackmail** es capaz hasta de hacer chantaje

above board ADJ legítimo

above-mentioned [əbʌv'mɛnʃnd] ADJ susodicho

abrasion [ə'breɪʒən] N (on skin) abrasión f

abrasive [ə'breɪzɪv] ADJ abrasivo

abreast [ə'brɛst] ADV uno al lado de otro; **to keep ~ of** mantenerse al corriente de

abridge [ə'brɪdʒ] VT abreviar

abroad [ə'brɔːd] ADV (be) en el extranjero; (go) al extranjero; **there is a rumour ~ that ...** corre el rumor de que ...

abrupt [ə'brʌpt] ADJ (sudden: departure) repentino; (manner) brusco

abruptly [ə'brʌptlɪ] ADV (leave) repentinamente; (speak) bruscamente

abscess ['æbsɛs] N absceso

abscond [əb'skɔnd] VI fugarse

absence ['æbsəns] N ausencia; **in the ~ of** (person) en ausencia de; (thing) a falta de

absent ['æbsənt] ADJ ausente; **~ without leave (AWOL)** ausente sin permiso

absentee [æbsən'tiː] N ausente mf

absenteeism [æbsən'tiːɪzəm] N absentismo

absent-minded [æbsənt'maɪndɪd] ADJ distraído

absolute ['æbsəluːt] ADJ absoluto; **~ monopoly** monopolio total

absolutely [æbsə'luːtlɪ] ADV totalmente; **oh yes, ~!** ¡claro or por supuesto que sí!

absolution [æbsə'luːʃən] N (Rel) absolución f

absolve [əb'zɔlv] VT: **to ~ sb (from)** absolver a algn (de)

absorb [əb'zɔːb] VT absorber; **to be absorbed in a book** estar absorto en un libro

absorbent [əb'zɔːbənt] ADJ absorbente

absorbent cotton N (US) algodón m hidrófilo

absorbing [əb'zɔːbɪŋ] ADJ absorbente; (book etc) interesantísimo

absorption [əb'zɔːpʃən] N absorción f

abstain [əb'steɪn] VI: **to ~ (from)** abstenerse (de)

abstemious [əb'stiːmɪəs] ADJ abstemio

abstention [əb'stɛnʃən] N abstención f

abstinence ['æbstɪnəns] N abstinencia

abstract ['æbstrækt] ADJ abstracto

abstruse [æb'struːs] ADJ abstruso, oscuro

absurd [əb'səːd] ADJ absurdo

absurdity [əb'səːdɪtɪ] N absurdo

ABTA ['æbtə] N ABBR = **Association of British Travel Agents**

abundance [ə'bʌndəns] N abundancia

abundant [ə'bʌndənt] ADJ abundante

abuse [ə'bju:s] N (*insults*) insultos *mpl*, improperios *mpl*; (*misuse*) abuso ▶ VT [ə'bju:z] (*ill-treat*) maltratar; (*take advantage of*) abusar de; **open to ~** sujeto al abuso

abusive [ə'bju:sɪv] ADJ ofensivo

abysmal [ə'bɪzməl] ADJ pésimo; (*failure*) garrafal; (*ignorance*) supino

abyss [ə'bɪs] N abismo

AC ABBR (= *alternating current*) corriente *f* alterna ▶ N ABBR (*US*) = **athletic club**

a/c ABBR (*Banking etc*: = *account*) c/; (: = *account current*) c/c

academic [ækə'dɛmɪk] ADJ académico, universitario; (*pej: issue*) puramente teórico ▶ N estudioso(-a); (*lecturer*) profesor(a) *m/f* universitario(-a)

academic year N (*Univ*) año académico

academy [ə'kædəmɪ] N (*learned body*) academia; (*school*) instituto, colegio

academy of music N conservatorio

ACAS ['eɪkæs] N ABBR (*BRIT*: = *Advisory, Conciliation and Arbitration Service*) ≈ Instituto de Mediación, Arbitraje y Conciliación

accede [æk'si:d] VI: **to ~ to** acceder a

accelerate [æk'sɛləreɪt] VI acelerar

acceleration [æksɛlə'reɪʃən] N aceleración *f*

accelerator [æk'sɛləreɪtər] N (*BRIT*) acelerador *m*

accent ['æksɛnt] N acento; (*fig*) énfasis *m*

accentuate [æk'sɛntjueɪt] VT (*syllable*) acentuar; (*need, difference etc*) recalcar, subrayar

accept [ək'sɛpt] VT aceptar; (*approve*) aprobar; (*concede*) admitir

acceptable [ək'sɛptəbl] ADJ aceptable, admisible

acceptance [ək'sɛptəns] N aceptación *f*; aprobación *f*; **to meet with general ~** recibir la aprobación general

access ['æksɛs] N acceso ▶ VT (*Comput*) acceder a; **the burglars gained ~ through a window** los ladrones lograron entrar por una ventana; **to have ~ to** tener acceso a

accessible [æk'sɛsəbl] ADJ (*place, person*) accesible; (*knowledge etc*) asequible

accession [æk'sɛʃən] N (*of monarch*) subida, ascenso; (*addition*) adquisición *f*

accessory [æk'sɛsərɪ] N accesorio; (*Law*): **~ to** cómplice de; **toilet accessories** artículos *mpl* de tocador

access road N carretera de acceso; (*to motorway*) carril *m* de acceso

access time N (*Comput*) tiempo de acceso

accident ['æksɪdənt] N accidente *m*; (*chance*) casualidad *f*; **by ~** (*unintentionally*) sin querer; (*by coincidence*) por casualidad; **accidents at work** accidentes *mpl* de trabajo; **to meet with** *or* **to have an ~** tener *or* sufrir un accidente

accidental [æksɪ'dɛntl] ADJ accidental, fortuito

accidentally [æksɪ'dɛntəlɪ] ADV sin querer; por casualidad

Accident and Emergency Department N (*BRIT*) Urgencias *fpl*

accident insurance N seguro contra accidentes

accident-prone ['æksɪdənt'prəun] ADJ propenso a los accidentes

acclaim [ə'kleɪm] VT aclamar, aplaudir ▶ N aclamación *f*, aplausos *mpl*

acclamation [æklə'meɪʃən] N (*approval*) aclamación *f*; (*applause*) aplausos *mpl*; **by ~** por aclamación

acclimatize [ə'klaɪmətaɪz], (*US*) **acclimate** [ə'klaɪmət] VT: **to become acclimatized** aclimatarse

accolade ['ækəuleɪd] N (*prize*) premio; (*praise*) alabanzas *fpl*, homenaje *m*

accommodate [ə'kɔmədeɪt] VT alojar, hospedar; (*car, hotel etc*) tener cabida para; (*oblige, help*) complacer; **this car accommodates four people comfortably** en este coche caben cuatro personas cómodamente

accommodating [ə'kɔmədeɪtɪŋ] ADJ servicial, complaciente

accommodation N [əkɔmə'deɪʃən], (*US*) **accommodations** NPL alojamiento; **"~ to let"** "se alquilan habitaciones"; **seating ~** asientos *mpl*

accompaniment [ə'kʌmpənɪmənt] N acompañamiento

accompanist [ə'kʌmpənɪst] N (*Mus*) acompañante *mf*

accompany [ə'kʌmpənɪ] VT acompañar

accomplice [ə'kʌmplɪs] N cómplice *mf*

accomplish [ə'kʌmplɪʃ] VT (*finish*) concluir; (*aim*) realizar; (*task*) llevar a cabo

accomplished [ə'kʌmplɪʃt] ADJ experto, hábil

accomplishment [ə'kʌmplɪʃmənt] N (*ending*) conclusión *f*; (*bringing about*) realización *f*; (*skill*) talento

accord [ə'kɔ:d] N acuerdo ▶ VT conceder; **of his own ~** espontáneamente; **with one ~** de *or* por común acuerdo

accordance [ə'kɔ:dəns] N: **in ~ with** de acuerdo con

according [ə'kɔ:dɪŋ]: **~ to** *prep* según; (*in accordance with*) de acuerdo con; **it went ~ to plan** salió según lo previsto

accordingly [ə'kɔ:dɪŋlɪ] ADV (*thus*) por consiguiente, en consecuencia; (*appropriately*) de acuerdo con esto

accordion [ə'kɔ:dɪən] N acordeón *m*

accordionist [ə'kɔ:dɪənɪst] N acordeonista *mf*

accost [əˈkɔst] VT abordar, dirigirse a

account [əˈkaunt] N (Comm) cuenta, factura; (report) informe m; **accounts** NPL (Comm) cuentas fpl; **"~ payee only"** "únicamente en cuenta del beneficiario"; **your ~ is still outstanding** su cuenta está todavía pendiente; **of little ~** de poca importancia; **on ~** a crédito; **to buy sth on ~** comprar algo a crédito; **on no ~** bajo ningún concepto; **on ~ of** a causa de, por motivo de; **to take into ~, take ~ of** tener en cuenta; **to keep an ~ of** llevar la cuenta de; **to bring sb to ~ for sth/ for having done sth** pedirle cuentas a algn por algo/por haber hecho algo
  ▸ **account for** VT FUS (explain) explicar; **all the children were accounted for** no faltaba ningún niño

accountability [əkauntəˈbɪlɪtɪ] N responsabilidad f

accountable [əˈkauntəbl] ADJ: **~ (for)** responsable (de)

accountancy [əˈkauntənsɪ] N contabilidad f

accountant [əˈkauntənt] N contable mf, contador(a) m/f (LAM)

accounting [əˈkauntɪŋ] N contabilidad f

accounting period N período contable, ejercicio financiero

account number N (at bank etc) número de cuenta

account payable N cuenta por pagar

account receivable N cuenta por cobrar

accoutrements [əˈkuːtrəmənts] NPL equipo, pertrechos mpl

accredited [əˈkrɛdɪtɪd] ADJ (agent etc) autorizado, acreditado

accretion [əˈkriːʃən] N acumulación f

accrue [əˈkruː] VI (mount up) aumentar, incrementarse; (interest) acumularse; **to ~ to** corresponder a; **accrued charges** gastos mpl vencidos; **accrued interest** interés m acumulado

accumulate [əˈkjuːmjuleɪt] VT acumular ▸ VI acumularse

accumulation [əkjuːmjuˈleɪʃən] N acumulación f

accuracy [ˈækjurəsɪ] N (of total) exactitud f; (of description etc) precisión f

accurate [ˈækjurɪt] ADJ (number) exacto; (answer) acertado; (shot) certero

accurately [ˈækjurɪtlɪ] ADV (count, shoot, answer) con precisión

accursed [əˈkəːst] ADJ maldito

accusation [ækjuˈzeɪʃən] N acusación f

accusative [əˈkjuːzətɪv] N acusativo

accuse [əˈkjuːz] VT acusar; (blame) echar la culpa a; **to ~ sb (of sth)** acusar a algn (de algo)

accused [əˈkjuːzd] N acusado(-a)

accuser [əˈkjuːzəʳ] N acusador(a) m/f

accustom [əˈkʌstəm] VT acostumbrar; **to ~ o.s. to sth** acostumbrarse a algo

accustomed [əˈkʌstəmd] ADJ: **~ to** acostumbrado a

AC/DC ABBR (= alternating current/direct current) CA/CC

ACE [eɪs] N ABBR = **American Council on Education**

ace [eɪs] N as m

acerbic [əˈsəːbɪk] ADJ acerbo; (fig) mordaz

acetate [ˈæsɪteɪt] N acetato

ache [eɪk] N dolor m ▸ VI doler; (yearn): **to ~ to do sth** ansiar hacer algo; **I've got stomach ~** or (US) **a stomach ~** tengo dolor de estómago, me duele el estómago; **my head aches** me duele la cabeza

achieve [əˈtʃiːv] VT (reach) alcanzar; (realize) realizar; (victory, success) lograr, conseguir

achievement [əˈtʃiːvmənt] N (completion) realización f; (success) éxito

Achilles heel [əˈkɪliːz-] N talón m de Aquiles

acid [ˈæsɪd] ADJ ácido; (bitter) agrio ▸ N (Chem, inf: LSD) ácido

acidity [əˈsɪdɪtɪ] N acidez f; (Med) acedía

acid rain N lluvia ácida

acid test N (fig) prueba de fuego

acknowledge [əkˈnɔlɪdʒ] VT (letter: also: **acknowledge receipt of**) acusar recibo de; (fact) reconocer

acknowledgement [əkˈnɔlɪdʒmənt] N acuse m de recibo; reconocimiento; **acknowledgements** (in book) agradecimientos mpl

ACLU N ABBR (= American Civil Liberties Union) unión americana por libertades civiles

acme [ˈækmɪ] N súmmum m

acne [ˈæknɪ] N acné m

acorn [ˈeɪkɔːn] N bellota

acoustic [əˈkuːstɪk] ADJ acústico

acoustics [əˈkuːstɪks] N, NPL acústica sg

acquaint [əˈkweɪnt] VT: **to ~ sb with sth** (inform) poner a algn al corriente de algo; **to be acquainted with** (person) conocer; (fact) estar al corriente de

acquaintance [əˈkweɪntəns] N conocimiento; (person) conocido(-a); **to make sb's ~** conocer a algn

acquiesce [ækwɪˈɛs] VI (agree): **to ~ (in)** consentir (en), conformarse (con)

acquire [əˈkwaɪəʳ] VT adquirir

acquired [əˈkwaɪəd] ADJ adquirido; **it's an ~ taste** es algo a lo que uno se aficiona poco a poco

acquisition [ækwɪˈzɪʃən] N adquisición f

acquisitive [əˈkwɪzɪtɪv] ADJ codicioso

acquit [əˈkwɪt] VT absolver, exculpar; **to ~ o.s. well** salir con éxito

acquittal [əˈkwɪtl] N absolución f, exculpación f

acre ['eɪkə'] N acre m

acreage ['eɪkərɪdʒ] N extensión f

acrid ['ækrɪd] ADJ (smell) acre; (fig) mordaz, sarcástico

acrimonious [ækrɪ'məʊnɪəs] ADJ (remark) mordaz; (argument) reñido

acrobat ['ækrəbæt] N acróbata mf

acrobatic [ækrə'bætɪk] ADJ acrobático

acrobatics [ækrə'bætɪks] NPL acrobacia sg

acronym ['ækrənɪm] N siglas fpl

across [ə'krɔs] PREP (on the other side of) al otro lado de; (crosswise) a través de ▶ ADV de un lado a otro, de una parte a otra a través, al través; **to run/swim** ~ atravesar corriendo/nadando; ~ **from** enfrente de; **the lake is 12 km** ~ el lago tiene 12 km de ancho; **to get sth** ~ **to sb** (fig) hacer comprender algo a algn

acrylic [ə'krɪlɪk] ADJ acrílico

ACT N ABBR (= American College Test) prueba de aptitud estándar que por lo general hacen los estudiantes que quieren entrar a la universidad por primera vez

act [ækt] N acto, acción f; (Theat) acto; (in music-hall etc) número; (Law) decreto, ley f ▶ VI (behave) comportarse; (Theat) actuar; (pretend) fingir; (take action) tomar medidas ▶ VT (part) hacer, representar; ~ **of God** fuerza mayor; **it's only an** ~ es cuento; **to catch sb in the** ~ coger a algn in fraganti or con las manos en la masa; **to** ~ **Hamlet** hacer el papel de Hamlet; **to** ~ **as** actuar or hacer de; **acting in my capacity as chairman, I …** en mi calidad de presidente, yo …; **it acts as a deterrent** sirve para disuadir; **he's only acting** está fingiendo nada más

▶ **act on** VT: **to** ~ **on sth** actuar or obrar sobre algo

▶ **act out** VT (event) representar; (fantasies) realizar

▶ **act up** VI (inf: person) portarse mal

acting ['æktɪŋ] ADJ suplente ▶ N: **to do some** ~ hacer algo de teatro; **he is the** ~ **manager** es el gerente en funciones

action ['ækʃən] N acción f, acto; (Mil) acción f; (Law) proceso, demanda ▶ VT (Comm) llevar a cabo; **to put a plan into** ~ poner un plan en acción or en marcha; **killed in** ~ (Mil) muerto en acto de servicio or en combate; **out of** ~ (person) fuera de combate; (thing) averiado, estropeado; **to take** ~ tomar medidas; **to bring an** ~ **against sb** entablar or presentar demanda contra algn

action replay N (TV) repetición f

activate ['æktɪveɪt] VT activar

active ['æktɪv] ADJ activo, enérgico; (volcano) en actividad; **to play an** ~ **part in** colaborar activamente en

active duty N (US Mil) servicio activo

actively ['æktɪvlɪ] ADV (participate) activamente; (discourage, dislike) enérgicamente

active partner N (Comm) socio activo

activist ['æktɪvɪst] N activista mf

activity [æk'tɪvɪtɪ] N actividad f

activity holiday N vacaciones con actividades organizadas

actor ['æktə'] N actor m

actress ['æktrɪs] N actriz f

actual ['æktjuəl] ADJ verdadero, real

actually ['æktjuəlɪ] ADV realmente, en realidad

actuary ['æktjuərɪ] N (Comm) actuario(-a) (de seguros)

actuate ['æktjueɪt] VT mover, impulsar

acumen ['ækjumən] N perspicacia; **business** ~ talento para los negocios

acupuncture ['ækjupʌŋktʃə'] N acupuntura

acute [ə'kju:t] ADJ agudo

acutely [ə'kju:tlɪ] ADV profundamente, extremadamente

AD ADV ABBR (= Anno Domini) d.C. ▶ N ABBR (US Mil) = **active duty**

ad [æd] N ABBR = **advertisement**

adage ['ædɪdʒ] N refrán m, adagio

Adam ['ædəm] N Adán; ~**'s apple** n nuez f (de la garganta)

adamant ['ædəmənt] ADJ firme, inflexible

adapt [ə'dæpt] VT adaptar; (reconcile) acomodar ▶ VI: **to** ~ **(to)** adaptarse (a), ajustarse (a)

adaptability [ədæptə'bɪlɪtɪ] N (of person, device etc) adaptabilidad f

adaptable [ə'dæptəbl] ADJ (device) adaptable; (person) acomodadizo, que se adapta

adaptation [ædæp'teɪʃən] N adaptación f

adapter, adaptor [ə'dæptə'] N (Elec) adaptador m; (for several plugs) ladrón m

ADC N ABBR (Mil) = **aide-de-camp**; (US: = Aid to Dependent Children) ayuda para niños dependientes

add [æd] VT añadir, agregar (esp LAm); (figures: also: **add up**) sumar ▶ VI: **to** ~ **to** (increase) aumentar, acrecentar ▶ N (Internet): **thanks for the** ~ gracias por agregarme

▶ **add on** VT añadir

▶ **add up** VT (figures) sumar ▶ VI (fig): **it doesn't** ~ **up** no tiene sentido; **it doesn't** ~ **up to much** es poca cosa, no tiene gran or mucha importancia

addendum [ə'dɛndəm] N adenda m or f

adder ['ædə'] N víbora

addict ['ædɪkt] N (to drugs etc) adicto(-a); (enthusiast) aficionado(-a), entusiasta mf; **heroin** ~ heroinómano(-a)

addicted [ə'dɪktɪd] ADJ: **to be** ~ **to** ser adicto a; ser aficionado a

addiction [ə'dɪkʃən] N (to drugs etc) adicción f; (enthusiasm) afición f

addictive [əˈdɪktɪv] ADJ que causa adicción
adding machine [ˈædɪŋ-] N calculadora
Addis Ababa [ˈædɪsˈæbəbə] N Addis Abeba m
addition [əˈdɪʃən] N (adding up) adición f; (thing added) añadidura, añadido; **in ~** además, por añadidura; **in ~ to** además de
additional [əˈdɪʃənl] ADJ adicional
additive [ˈædɪtɪv] N aditivo
addled [ˈædld] ADJ (BRIT: rotten) podrido; (: fig) confuso
address [əˈdrɛs] N dirección f, señas fpl; (speech) discurso; (Comput) dirección f ▶ VT (letter) dirigir; (speak to) dirigirse a, dirigir la palabra a; **form of ~** tratamiento; **absolute/relative ~** (Comput) dirección f absoluta/relativa; **to ~ o.s. to sth** (issue, problem) abordar
address book N agenda (de direcciones)
addressee [ædrɛˈsiː] N destinatario(-a)
Aden [ˈeɪdn] N Adén m
adenoids [ˈædɪnɔɪdz] NPL vegetaciones fpl (adenoideas)
adept [ˈædɛpt] ADJ: **~ at** experto or ducho en
adequacy [ˈædɪkwəsɪ] N idoneidad f
adequate [ˈædɪkwɪt] ADJ (satisfactory) adecuado; (enough) suficiente; **to feel ~ to a task** sentirse con fuerzas para una tarea
adequately [ˈædɪkwɪtlɪ] ADV adecuadamente
adhere [ədˈhɪər] VI: **to ~ to** adherirse a; (fig: abide by) observar
adherent [ədˈhɪərənt] N partidario(-a)
adhesion [ədˈhiːʒən] N adherencia
adhesive [ədˈhiːzɪv] ADJ, N adhesivo
adhesive tape N (BRIT) cinta adhesiva; (US Med) esparadrapo
ad hoc [ædˈhɔk] ADJ (decision) ad hoc; (committee) formado con fines específicos ▶ ADV ad hoc
adieu [əˈdjuː] EXCL ¡vaya con Dios!
ad inf [ˈædˈɪnf] ADV hasta el infinito
adjacent [əˈdʒeɪsənt] ADJ: **~ to** contiguo a, inmediato a
adjective [ˈædʒɛktɪv] N adjetivo
adjoin [əˈdʒɔɪn] VT estar contiguo a; (land) lindar con
adjoining [əˈdʒɔɪnɪŋ] ADJ contiguo, vecino
adjourn [əˈdʒəːn] VT aplazar; (session) suspender, levantar; (US: end) terminar ▶ VI suspenderse; **the meeting has been adjourned till next week** se ha levantado la sesión hasta la semana que viene; **they adjourned to the pub** (inf) se trasladaron al bar
adjournment [əˈdʒəːnmənt] N (period) suspensión f; (postponement) aplazamiento
Adjt. ABBR (Mil) = **adjutant**
adjudicate [əˈdʒuːdɪkeɪt] VI sentenciar ▶ VT (contest) hacer de árbitro en, juzgar; (claim) decidir

adjudication [ədʒuːdɪˈkeɪʃən] N fallo
adjudicator [əˈdʒuːdɪkeɪtər] N juez m, árbitro f
adjust [əˈdʒʌst] VT (change) modificar; (arrange) arreglar; (machine) ajustar ▶ VI: **to ~ (to)** adaptarse (a)
adjustable [əˈdʒʌstəbl] ADJ ajustable
adjuster [əˈdʒʌstər] N see **loss adjuster**
adjustment [əˈdʒʌstmənt] N adaptación f; arreglo; (of prices, wages) ajuste m
adjutant [ˈædʒətənt] N ayudante m
ad-lib [ædˈlɪb] VT, VI improvisar ▶ ADV: **ad lib** a voluntad, a discreción
adman [ˈædmæn] N (irreg) (inf) publicista m
admin [ˈædmɪn] N ABBR (inf) = **administration**
administer [ədˈmɪnɪstər] VT proporcionar; (justice) administrar
administration [ædmɪnɪˈstreɪʃən] N administración f; (government) gobierno; **the A~** (US) la Administración
administrative [ədˈmɪnɪstrətɪv] ADJ administrativo
administrator [ədˈmɪnɪstreɪtər] N administrador(a) m/f
admirable [ˈædmərəbl] ADJ admirable
admiral [ˈædmərəl] N almirante m
Admiralty [ˈædmərəltɪ] N (BRIT) Ministerio de Marina, Almirantazgo
admiration [ædməˈreɪʃən] N admiración f
admire [ədˈmaɪər] VT admirar
admirer [ədˈmaɪərər] N admirador(a) m/f; (suitor) pretendiente m
admiring [ədˈmaɪərɪŋ] ADJ (expression) de admiración
admissible [ədˈmɪsəbl] ADJ admisible
admission [ədˈmɪʃən] N (to exhibition, nightclub) entrada; (enrolment) ingreso; (confession) confesión f; **"~ free"** "entrada gratis or libre"; **by his own ~** él mismo reconoce que
admit [ədˈmɪt] VT dejar entrar, dar entrada a; (permit) admitir; (acknowledge) reconocer; **"this ticket admits two"** "entrada para dos personas"; **children not admitted** se prohíbe la entrada a (los) menores de edad; **to be admitted to hospital** ingresar en el hospital; **I must ~ that ...** debo reconocer que ...
  ▶ **admit of** VT FUS admitir, permitir
  ▶ **admit to** VT FUS confesarse culpable de
admittance [ədˈmɪtəns] N entrada; **"no ~"** "se prohíbe la entrada", "prohibida la entrada"
admittedly [ədˈmɪtədlɪ] ADV es cierto que
admonish [ədˈmɔnɪʃ] VT amonestar; (advise) aconsejar
ad nauseam [ædˈnɔːsɪæm] ADV hasta la saciedad
ado [əˈduː] N: **without (any) more ~** sin más (ni más)
adolescence [ædəuˈlɛsns] N adolescencia

adolescent [ædəu'lɛsnt] ADJ, N adolescente *mf*

adopt [ə'dɔpt] VT adoptar

adopted [ə'dɔptɪd] ADJ adoptivo

adoption [ə'dɔpʃən] N adopción *f*

adoptive [ə'dɔptɪv] ADJ adoptivo

adorable [ə'dɔːrəbl] ADJ adorable

adoration [ædə'reɪʃən] N adoración *f*

adore [ə'dɔːʳ] VT adorar

adoring [ə'dɔːrɪŋ] ADJ: **to his ~ public** a un público que le adora *or* le adoraba *etc*

adorn [ə'dɔːn] VT adornar

adornment [ə'dɔːnmənt] N adorno

ADP N ABBR = **automatic data processing**

adrenalin [ə'drɛnəlɪn] N adrenalina

Adriatic [eɪdrɪ'ætɪk] N: **the ~ (Sea)** el (Mar) Adriático

adrift [ə'drɪft] ADV a la deriva; **to come ~** (*boat*) ir a la deriva, soltarse; (*wire, rope etc*) soltarse

adroit [ə'drɔɪt] ADJ diestro, hábil

ADSL N ABBR (= *asymmetric digital subscriber line*) ADSL *m*

ADT ABBR (*US*: = *Atlantic Daylight Time*) hora de verano de Nueva York

adulation [ædju'leɪʃən] N adulación *f*

adult ['ædʌlt] N adulto(-a) ▶ ADJ: **~ education** educación *f* para adultos

adulterate [ə'dʌltəreɪt] VT adulterar

adulterer [ə'dʌltərəʳ] N adúltero

adulteress [ə'dʌltrɪs] N adúltera

adultery [ə'dʌltərɪ] N adulterio

adulthood ['ædʌlthud] N edad *f* adulta

advance [əd'vɑːns] N adelanto, progreso; (*money*) anticipo; (*Mil*) avance *m* ▶ VT avanzar, adelantar; (*money*) anticipar ▶ VI avanzar, adelantarse; **in ~** por adelantado; (*book*) con antelación; **to make advances to sb** (*gen*) hacer una proposición a algn; (*amorously*) insinuarse a algn

advanced ADJ avanzado; (*Scol: studies*) adelantado; **~ in years** entrado en años

Advanced Higher N (*SCOTTISH Scol*) titulación que sigue al "*Higher*", ≈ Bachillerato

advancement [əd'vɑːnsmənt] N progreso; (*in rank*) ascenso

advance notice N previo aviso

advance payment N (*part sum*) anticipo

advantage [əd'vɑːntɪdʒ] N (*also Tennis*) ventaja; **to take ~ of** aprovecharse de; **it's to our ~** es ventajoso para nosotros

advantageous [ædvən'teɪdʒəs] ADJ ventajoso, provechoso

advent ['ædvənt] N advenimiento; **A~** Adviento

adventure [əd'vɛntʃəʳ] N aventura

adventure playground N parque *m* infantil

adventurous [əd'vɛntʃərəs] ADJ aventurero; (*bold*) arriesgado

adverb ['ædvəːb] N adverbio

adversary ['ædvəsərɪ] N adversario, contrario

adverse ['ædvəːs] ADJ adverso, contrario; **~ to** adverso a

adversity [əd'vəːsɪtɪ] N infortunio

advert ['ædvəːt] N ABBR (*BRIT*) = **advertisement**

advertise ['ædvətaɪz] VI hacer propaganda; (*in newspaper etc*) poner un anuncio, anunciarse ▶ VT anunciar; **to ~ for** (*staff*) buscar por medio de anuncios

advertisement [əd'vəːtɪsmənt] N anuncio

advertiser ['ædvətaɪzəʳ] N anunciante *mf*

advertising ['ædvətaɪzɪŋ] N publicidad *f*, propaganda; anuncios *mpl*; (*industry*) industria publicitaria

advertising agency N agencia de publicidad

advertising campaign N campaña de publicidad

advice [əd'vaɪs] N consejo, consejos *mpl*; (*notification*) aviso; **a piece of ~** un consejo; **to take legal ~** consultar a un abogado; **to ask (sb) for ~** pedir consejo (a algn)

advice note N (*BRIT*) nota de aviso

advisable [əd'vaɪzəbl] ADJ aconsejable, conveniente

advise [əd'vaɪz] VT aconsejar; **to ~ sb of sth** (*inform*) informar a algn de algo; **to ~ sb against sth/doing sth** desaconsejar algo a algn/aconsejar a algn que no haga algo; **you will be well/ill advised to go** deberías/no deberías ir

advisedly [əd'vaɪzɪdlɪ] ADV deliberadamente

adviser [əd'vaɪzəʳ] N consejero(-a); (*business adviser*) asesor(a) *m/f*

advisory [əd'vaɪzərɪ] ADJ consultivo; **in an ~ capacity** como asesor

advocate ['ædvəkeɪt] VT (*argue for*) abogar por; (*give support to*) ser partidario de ▶ N ['ædvəkɪt] abogado(-a); (*supporter*): **~ of** defensor(a) *m/f* de

advt. ABBR = **advertisement**

AEA N ABBR (*BRIT*: = *Atomic Energy Authority*) consejo de energía nuclear; (*BRIT Scol*: = *Advanced Extension Award*) titulación opcional para los alumnos mejor preparados de los "*A levels*"

AEC N ABBR (*US*: = *Atomic Energy Commission*) AEC *f*

Aegean [iː'dʒiːən] N: **the ~ (Sea)** el (Mar) Egeo

aegis ['iːdʒɪs] N: **under the ~ of** bajo la tutela de

aeon ['iːən] N eón *m*

aerial ['ɛərɪəl] N antena ▶ ADJ aéreo

aerie ['ɛərɪ] N (*US*) aguilera

aero- ['ɛərəu] PREF aero-

aerobatics [ɛərəu'bætɪks] NPL acrobacia aérea

aerobics [ɛəˈrəubɪks] NSG aerobic m, aerobismo (LAM)

aerodrome [ˈɛərədrəum] N (BRIT) aeródromo

aerodynamic [ɛərəudaɪˈnæmɪk] ADJ aerodinámico

aeronautics [ɛərəuˈnɔːtɪks] NSG aeronáutica

aeroplane [ˈɛərəpleɪn] N (BRIT) avión m

aerosol [ˈɛərəsɔl] N aerosol m

aerospace industry [ˈɛərəuspeɪs-] N industria aeroespacial

aesthetic [iːsˈθɛtɪk] ADJ estético

aesthetics [iːsˈθɛtɪks] NPL estética

afar [əˈfɑːʳ] ADV lejos; **from ~** desde lejos

AFB N ABBR (US) = **Air Force Base**

AFDC N ABBR (US) = Aid to Families with Dependent Children) ayuda a familias con hijos menores

affable [ˈæfəbl] ADJ afable

affair [əˈfɛəʳ] N asunto; (also: **love affair**) aventura f amorosa; **affairs** (business) asuntos mpl; **the Watergate ~** el asunto (de) Watergate

affect [əˈfɛkt] VT afectar, influir en; (move) conmover

affectation [æfɛkˈteɪʃən] N afectación f

affected [əˈfɛktɪd] ADJ afectado

affection [əˈfɛkʃən] N afecto, cariño

affectionate [əˈfɛkʃənɪt] ADJ afectuoso, cariñoso

affectionately [əˈfɛkʃənɪtlɪ] ADV afectuosamente

affidavit [æfɪˈdeɪvɪt] N (Law) declaración f jurada

affiliated [əˈfɪlieɪtɪd] ADJ afiliado; **~ company** empresa or compañía filial or subsidiaria

affinity [əˈfɪnɪtɪ] N afinidad f

affirm [əˈfəːm] VT afirmar

affirmation [æfəˈmeɪʃən] N afirmación f

affirmative [əˈfəːmətɪv] ADJ afirmativo

affix [əˈfɪks] VT (signature) estampar; (stamp) pegar

afflict [əˈflɪkt] VT afligir

affliction [əˈflɪkʃən] N enfermedad f, aflicción f

affluence [ˈæfluəns] N opulencia, riqueza

affluent [ˈæfluənt] ADJ acomodado; **the ~ society** la sociedad opulenta

afford [əˈfɔːd] VT poder permitirse; (provide) proporcionar; **can we ~ a car?** ¿podemos permitirnos el gasto de comprar un coche?

affordable [əˈfɔːdəbl] ADJ asequible

affray [əˈfreɪ] N refriega, reyerta

affront [əˈfrʌnt] N afrenta, ofensa

affronted [əˈfrʌntɪd] ADJ ofendido

Afghan [ˈæfɡæn] ADJ, N afgano(-a) m/f

Afghanistan [æfˈɡænɪstæn] N Afganistán m

afield [əˈfiːld] ADV: **far ~** muy lejos

AFL-CIO N ABBR (US: = American Federation of Labor and Congress of Industrial Organizations) confederación sindicalista

afloat [əˈfləut] ADV (floating) a flote; (at sea) en el mar

afoot [əˈfut] ADV: **there is something ~** algo se está tramando

aforesaid [əˈfɔːsɛd] ADJ susodicho; (Comm) mencionado anteriormente

afraid [əˈfreɪd] ADJ: **to be ~ of** (person) tener miedo a; (thing) tener miedo de; **to be ~ to** tener miedo de, temer; **I am ~ that** me temo que; **I'm ~ so** lo siento, pero es así, me temo que sí; **I'm ~ not** lo siento, pero no

afresh [əˈfrɛʃ] ADV de nuevo, otra vez

Africa [ˈæfrɪkə] N África

African [ˈæfrɪkən] ADJ, N africano(-a) m/f

African-American ADJ, N afroamericano(-a) m/f

Afrikaans [æfrɪˈkɑːns] N africaans m

Afrikaner [æfrɪˈkɑːnəʳ] N afrikáner mf

Afro-American [ˈæfrəuəˈmɛrɪkən] ADJ, N afroamericano(-a) m/f

AFT N ABBR (= American Federation of Teachers) sindicato de profesores

aft [ɑːft] ADV (be) en popa; (go) a popa

after [ˈɑːftəʳ] PREP (time) después de; (place, order) detrás de, tras ▸ ADV después ▸ CONJ después (de) que; **what/who are you ~?** ¿qué/a quién buscas?; **the police are ~ him** la policía le está buscando; **~ having done/he left** después de haber hecho/después de que se marchó; **~ dinner** después de cenar or comer; **the day ~ tomorrow** pasado mañana; **to ask ~ sb** preguntar por algn; **~ all** después de todo, al fin y al cabo; **~ you!** ¡pase usted!; **quarter ~ two** (US) las dos y cuarto

afterbirth [ˈɑːftəbəːθ] N placenta

aftercare [ˈɑːftəkɛəʳ] N (Med) asistencia postoperatoria

after-effects [ˈɑːftərɪfɛkts] NPL secuelas fpl, efectos mpl

afterlife [ˈɑːftəlaɪf] N vida después de la muerte

aftermath [ˈɑːftəmɑːθ] N consecuencias fpl, resultados mpl

afternoon [ɑːftəˈnuːn] N tarde f; **good ~!** ¡buenas tardes!

afterparty [ˈɑːftəpɑːtɪ] N fiesta f posterior

afters [ˈɑːftəz] N (inf: dessert) postre m

after-sales service [ɑːftəˈseɪlz-] N (BRIT Comm: for car, washing machine etc) servicio de asistencia pos-venta

after-shave [ˈɑːftəʃeɪv], **after-shave lotion** N loción f para después del afeitado, aftershave m

aftershock [ˈɑːftəʃɔk] N (of earthquake) pequeño temblor m posterior

aftersun [ˈɑːtəsʌn], **aftersun lotion** N
aftersun *m inv*

aftertaste [ˈɑːftəteɪst] N regusto

afterthought [ˈɑːftəθɔːt] N ocurrencia
(tardía)

afterwards [ˈɑːftəwədz] ADV después, más
tarde

again [əˈgen] ADV otra vez, de nuevo; **to do
sth ~** volver a hacer algo; **~ and ~** una y otra
vez; **now and ~** de vez en cuando

against [əˈgenst] PREP (*opposed*) en contra de;
(*close to*) contra, junto a; **I was leaning ~ the
desk** estaba apoyado en el escritorio; **(as) ~**
frente a

age [eɪdʒ] N edad *f*; (*old age*) vejez *f*; (*period*)
época ▸ VI envejecer(se) ▸ VT envejecer;
what ~ is he? ¿qué edad *or* cuántos años
tiene?; **he is 20 years of ~** tiene 20 años;
under ~ menor de edad; **to come of ~** llegar
a la mayoría de edad; **it's been ages since I
saw you** hace siglos que no te veo

aged [eɪdʒd] ADJ: **~ 10** de 10 años de edad
▸ NPL [ˈeɪdʒɪd]: **the ~** los ancianos

age group N: **to be in the same ~** tener la
misma edad; **the 40 to 50 ~** las personas de
40 a 50 años

ageing [ˈeɪdʒɪŋ] ADJ que envejece; (*pej*) en
declive ▸ N envejecimiento

ageless [ˈeɪdʒlɪs] ADJ (*eternal*) eterno; (*ever
young*) siempre joven

age limit N límite *m* de edad, edad *f* tope

agency [ˈeɪdʒənsɪ] N agencia; **through** *or* **by
the ~ of** por medio de

agenda [əˈdʒendə] N orden *m* del día; **on the
~** (*Comm*) en el orden del día

agent [ˈeɪdʒənt] N (*gen*) agente *mf*;
(*representative*) representante *mf* delegado(-a)

aggravate [ˈægrəveɪt] VT agravar; (*annoy*)
irritar, exasperar

aggravating [ˈægrəveɪtɪŋ] ADJ irritante,
molesto

aggravation [ægrəˈveɪʃən] N agravamiento

aggregate [ˈægrɪgeɪt] N conjunto

aggression [əˈgreʃən] N agresión *f*

aggressive [əˈgresɪv] ADJ agresivo; (*vigorous*)
enérgico

aggressiveness [əˈgresɪvnɪs] N agresividad *f*

aggressor [əˈgresər] N agresor(a) *m/f*

aggrieved [əˈgriːvd] ADJ ofendido, agraviado

aggro [ˈægrəu] N (*BRIT inf: physical violence*)
bronca; (: *bad feeling*) mal rollo; (: *hassle*) rollo,
movida

aghast [əˈgɑːst] ADJ horrorizado

agile [ˈædʒaɪl] ADJ ágil

agility [əˈdʒɪlɪtɪ] N agilidad *f*

agitate [ˈædʒɪteɪt] VT (*shake*) agitar; (*trouble*)
inquietar; **to ~ for** hacer campaña en pro de
or en favor de

agitated [ˈædʒɪteɪtɪd] ADJ agitado

agitator [ˈædʒɪteɪtər] N agitador(a) *m/f*

AGM N ABBR (= *annual general meeting*) junta *f*
general

agnostic [ægˈnɒstɪk] ADJ, N agnóstico(-a) *m/f*

ago [əˈgəu] ADV: **two days ~** hace dos días;
not long ~ hace poco; **how long ~?** ¿hace
cuánto tiempo?; **as long ~ as 1980** ya en
1980

agog [əˈgɒg] ADJ (*anxious*) ansioso; (*excited*):
(all) ~ (for) (todo) emocionado (por)

agonize [ˈægənaɪz] VI: **to ~ (over)**
atormentarse (por)

agonized [ˈægənaɪzd] ADJ angustioso

agonizing [ˈægənaɪzɪŋ] ADJ (*pain*) atroz;
(*suspense*) angustioso

agony [ˈægənɪ] N (*pain*) dolor *m* atroz; (*distress*)
angustia; **to be in ~** retorcerse de dolor

agony aunt N (*BRIT inf*) consejera
sentimental

agony column N consultorio sentimental

agree [əˈgriː] VT (*price*) acordar, quedar en ▸ VI
(*statements etc*) coincidir, concordar; **to ~
(with)** (*person*) estar de acuerdo (con),
ponerse de acuerdo (con); **to ~ to do** aceptar
hacer; **to ~ to sth** consentir en algo; **to ~
that** (*admit*) estar de acuerdo en que; **it was
agreed that ...** se acordó que ...; **garlic
doesn't ~ with me** el ajo no me sienta bien

agreeable [əˈgriːəbl] ADJ agradable; (*person*)
simpático; (*willing*) de acuerdo, conforme

agreeably [əˈgriːəblɪ] ADV agradablemente

agreed [əˈgriːd] ADJ (*time, place*) convenido

agreement [əˈgriːmənt] N acuerdo; (*Comm*)
contrato; **in ~** de acuerdo, conforme; **by
mutual ~** de común acuerdo

agricultural [ægrɪˈkʌltʃərəl] ADJ agrícola

agriculture [ˈægrɪkʌltʃər] N agricultura

aground [əˈgraund] ADV: **to run ~** encallar,
embarrancar

ahead [əˈhed] ADV delante; **~ of** delante de;
(*fig: schedule etc*) antes de; **~ of time** antes de
la hora; **to be ~ of sb** (*fig*) llevar ventaja *or* la
delantera a algn; **go right** *or* **straight ~** siga
adelante; **they were (right) ~ of us** iban
(justo) delante de nosotros

ahoy [əˈhɔɪ] EXCL ¡oiga!

AI N ABBR = **Amnesty International**; (*Comput*)
= **artificial intelligence**

AIB N ABBR (*BRIT*: = *Accident Investigation Bureau*)
oficina de investigación de accidentes

AID N ABBR (= *artificial insemination by donor*)
inseminación artificial por donante; (*US*:
= *Agency for International Development*) Agencia
Internacional para el Desarrollo

aid [eɪd] N ayuda, auxilio ▸ VT ayudar,
auxiliar; **in ~ of** a beneficio de; **with the ~
of** con la ayuda de; **to ~ and abet** (*Law*) ser
cómplice

aide [eɪd] N (*Pol*) ayudante *mf*

AIDS [eɪdz] N ABBR (= *acquired immune (or immuno-)deficiency syndrome*) SIDA *m*, sida *m*

AIH N ABBR (= *artificial insemination by husband*) inseminación artificial por esposo

ailing ['eɪlɪŋ] ADJ (*person, economy*) enfermizo

ailment ['eɪlmənt] N enfermedad *f*, achaque *m*

aim [eɪm] VT (*gun*) apuntar; (*missile, remark*) dirigir; (*blow*) asestar ▶ VI (*also*: **take aim**) apuntar ▶ N puntería; (*objective*) propósito, meta; **to ~ at** (*objective*) aspirar a, pretender; **to ~ to do** tener la intención de hacer, aspirar a hacer

aimless ['eɪmlɪs] ADJ sin propósito, sin objeto

aimlessly ['eɪmlɪslɪ] ADV sin rumbo fijo

ain't [eɪnt] (*inf*) = **are not**; **aren't**; **isn't**

air [ɛəʳ] N aire *m*; (*appearance*) aspecto ▶ VT (*room*) ventilar; (*clothes, bed, grievances, ideas*) airear; (*views*) hacer público ▶ CPD aéreo; **to throw sth into the ~** (*ball etc*) lanzar algo al aire; **by ~** (*travel*) en avión; **to be on the ~** (*Radio, TV: programme*) estarse emitiendo; (: *station*) estar en antena

airbag ['ɛəbæg] N airbag *m inv*

air base N (*Mil*) base *f* aérea

air bed N (*BRIT*) colchoneta inflable *or* neumática

airborne ['ɛəbɔːn] ADJ (*in the air*) en el aire; (*Mil*) aerotransportado; **as soon as the plane was ~** tan pronto como el avión estuvo en el aire

air cargo N carga aérea

air-conditioned ['ɛəkən'dɪʃənd] ADJ climatizado

air conditioning [-kən'dɪʃənɪŋ] N aire *m* acondicionado

air-cooled ['ɛəkuːld] ADJ refrigerado por aire

aircraft ['ɛəkrɑːft] N pl inv avión *m*

aircraft carrier N porta(a)viones *m inv*

air cushion N cojín *m* de aire; (*Aviat*) colchón *m* de aire

airdrome ['ɛədrəum] N (*US*) aeródromo

airfield ['ɛəfiːld] N campo de aviación

Air Force N fuerzas aéreas *fpl*, aviación *f*

air freight N flete *m* por avión

air freshener N ambientador *m*

air gun N escopeta de aire comprimido

air hostess (*BRIT*) N azafata, aeromoza (*LAM*)

airily ['ɛərɪlɪ] ADV muy a la ligera

airing ['ɛərɪŋ] N: **to give an ~ to** (*linen*) airear; (*room*) ventilar; (*fig: ideas etc*) airear, someter a discusión

airing cupboard N (*BRIT*) armario *m* para oreo

air letter N (*BRIT*) carta aérea

airlift ['ɛəlɪft] N puente *m* aéreo

airline ['ɛəlaɪn] N línea aérea

airliner ['ɛəlaɪnəʳ] N avión *m* de pasajeros

airlock ['ɛəlɔk] N (*in pipe*) esclusa de aire

airmail ['ɛəmeɪl] N: **by ~** por avión

air mattress N colchón *m* inflable *or* neumático

airplane ['ɛəpleɪn] N (*US*) avión *m*

air pocket N bolsa de aire

airport ['ɛəpɔːt] N aeropuerto

air rage N conducta agresiva de pasajeros a bordo de un avión

air raid N ataque *m* aéreo

air rifle N escopeta de aire comprimido

airsick ['ɛəsɪk] ADJ: **to be ~** marearse (en avión)

airspace N espacio aéreo

airspeed ['ɛəspiːd] N velocidad *f* de vuelo

airstrip ['ɛəstrɪp] N pista de aterrizaje

air terminal N terminal *f*

airtight ['ɛətaɪt] ADJ hermético

air time N (*Radio, TV*) tiempo en antena

air traffic control N control *m* de tráfico aéreo

air traffic controller N controlador(a) *m/f* aéreo(-a)

airway ['ɛəweɪ] N (*Aviat*) vía aérea; (*Anat*) vía respiratoria

airy ['ɛərɪ] ADJ (*room*) bien ventilado; (*manners*) desenfadado

aisle [aɪl] N (*of church*) nave *f* lateral; (*of theatre, plane*) pasillo

aisle seat N (*on plane*) asiento de pasillo

ajar [ə'dʒɑːʳ] ADJ entreabierto

AK ABBR (*US*) = **Alaska**

aka ABBR (= *also known as*) alias

akin [ə'kɪn] ADJ: **~ to** semejante a

AL ABBR (*US*) = **Alabama**

ALA N ABBR = **American Library Association**

Ala. ABBR (*US*) = **Alabama**

alabaster ['æləbɑːstəʳ] N alabastro

à la carte [ælæ'kɑːt] ADV a la carta

alacrity [ə'lækrɪtɪ] N: **with ~** con la mayor prontitud

alarm [ə'lɑːm] N alarma; (*anxiety*) inquietud *f* ▶ VT asustar, alarmar

alarm call N (*in hotel etc*) alarma

alarm clock N despertador *m*

alarmed [ə'lɑːmd] ADJ (*person*) alarmado, asustado; (*house, car etc*) con alarma

alarming [ə'lɑːmɪŋ] ADJ alarmante

alarmingly [ə'lɑːmɪŋlɪ] ADV de forma alarmante; **~ quickly** a una velocidad alarmante

alarmist [ə'lɑːmɪst] N alarmista *mf*

alas [ə'læs] ADV desgraciadamente ▶ EXCL ¡ay!

Alas. ABBR (*US*) = **Alaska**

Alaska [ə'læskə] N Alaska

Albania [æl'beɪnɪə] N Albania

Albanian [æl'beɪnɪən] ADJ albanés(-esa) ▶ N albanés(-esa) *m/f*; (*Ling*) albanés *m*

albatross ['ælbətrɔs] N albatros *m*

albeit [ɔːlˈbiːɪt] CONJ (*although*) aunque
album [ˈælbəm] N álbum *m*; (*L.P.*) elepé *m*
albumen [ˈælbjumɪn] N albúmina
alchemy [ˈælkɪmɪ] N alquimia
alcohol [ˈælkəhɔl] N alcohol *m*
alcohol-free [ˈælkəhɔlfriː] ADJ sin alcohol
alcoholic [ælkəˈhɔlɪk] ADJ, N alcohólico(-a) *m/f*
alcoholism [ˈælkəhɔlɪzəm] N alcoholismo
alcove [ˈælkəuv] N nicho, hueco
Ald. ABBR = **alderman**
alderman [ˈɔːldəmən] N (*irreg*) concejal *m*
ale [eɪl] N cerveza
alert [əˈləːt] ADJ alerta *inv*; (*sharp*) despierto, atento ▶ N alerta *m*, alarma ▶ VT poner sobre aviso; **to ~ sb (to sth)** poner sobre aviso *or* alertar a algn (de algo); **to ~ sb to the dangers of sth** poner sobre aviso *or* alertar a algn de los peligros de algo; **to be on the ~** estar alerta *or* sobre aviso
alertness [əˈləːtnɪs] N vigilancia
Aleutian Islands [əˈluːʃən-] NPL Islas *fpl* Aleutianas
A level N ABBR (*BRIT Scol*: = *Advanced level*) ≈ Bachillerato
Alexandria [ælɪɡˈzɑːndrɪə] N Alejandría
alfresco [ælˈfrɛskəu] ADJ, ADV al aire libre
algebra [ˈældʒɪbrə] N álgebra
Algeria [ælˈdʒɪərɪə] N Argelia
Algerian [ælˈdʒɪərɪən] ADJ, N argelino(-a) *m/f*
Algiers [ælˈdʒɪəz] N Argel *m*
algorithm [ˈælɡərɪðəm] N algoritmo
alias [ˈeɪlɪəs] ADV alias, conocido por ▶ N alias *m*; (*of criminal*) apodo; (*of writer*) seudónimo
alibi [ˈælɪbaɪ] N coartada
alien [ˈeɪlɪən] N (*foreigner*) extranjero(-a); (*extraterrestrial*) extraterrestre *mf* ▶ ADJ: **~ to** ajeno a
alienate [ˈeɪlɪəneɪt] VT enajenar, alejar
alienation [eɪlɪəˈneɪʃən] N alejamiento *m*
alight [əˈlaɪt] ADJ ardiendo ▶ VI apearse, bajar
align [əˈlaɪn] VT alinear
alignment [əˈlaɪnmənt] N alineación *f*; **the desks are out of ~** los pupitres no están bien alineados
alike [əˈlaɪk] ADJ semejantes, iguales ▶ ADV igualmente, del mismo modo; **to look ~** parecerse
alimony [ˈælɪmənɪ] N (*Law*) pensión *f* alimenticia
alive [əˈlaɪv] ADJ (*gen*) vivo; (*lively*) alegre
alkali [ˈælkəlaɪ] N álcali *m*

(KEYWORD)

all [ɔːl] ADJ todo(-a) *sg*, todos(-as) *pl*; **all day** todo el día; **all night** toda la noche; **all men** todos los hombres; **all five came** vinieron los cinco; **all the books** todos los libros; **all the time/his life** todo el tiempo/toda su vida; **for all their efforts** a pesar de todos sus esfuerzos
▶ PRON **1** todo; **I ate it all**, **I ate all of it** me lo comí todo; **all of them** todos (ellos); **all of us went** fuimos todos; **all the boys went** fueron todos los chicos; **is that all?** ¿eso es todo?, ¿algo más?; (*in shop*) ¿algo más?, ¿alguna cosa más?
2 (*in phrases*): **above all** sobre todo; por encima de todo; **after all** después de todo; **at all: anything at all** lo que sea; **not at all** (*in answer to question*) en absoluto; (*in answer to thanks*) ¡de nada!, ¡no hay de qué!; **I'm not at all tired** no estoy nada cansado(-a); **anything at all will do** cualquier cosa viene bien; **all in all** a fin de cuentas
▶ ADV: **all alone** completamente solo(-a); **to be/feel all in** estar rendido; **it's not as hard as all that** no es tan difícil como lo pintas; **all the more/the better** tanto más/mejor; **all but** casi; **the score is two all** están empatados a dos

Allah [ˈælə] N Alá *m*
all-around [ˈɔːləˈraund] ADJ (*US*) = **all-round**
allay [əˈleɪ] VT (*fears*) aquietar; (*pain*) aliviar
all clear N (*after attack etc*) fin *m* de la alerta; (*fig*) luz *f* verde
allegation [ælɪˈɡeɪʃən] N alegato
allege [əˈlɛdʒ] VT pretender; **he is alleged to have said ...** se afirma que él dijo ...
alleged [əˈlɛdʒd] ADJ supuesto, presunto
allegedly [əˈlɛdʒɪdlɪ] ADV supuestamente, según se afirma
allegiance [əˈliːdʒəns] N lealtad *f*
allegory [ˈælɪɡərɪ] N alegoría
all-embracing [ˈɔːləmˈbreɪsɪŋ] ADJ universal
allergic [əˈləːdʒɪk] ADJ: **~ to** alérgico a
allergy [ˈælədʒɪ] N alergia
alleviate [əˈliːvɪeɪt] VT aliviar
alleviation [əliːvɪˈeɪʃən] N alivio
alley [ˈælɪ] N (*street*) callejuela; (*in garden*) paseo
alleyway [ˈælɪweɪ] N callejón *m*
alliance [əˈlaɪəns] N alianza
allied [ˈælaɪd] ADJ aliado; (*related*) relacionado
alligator [ˈælɪɡeɪtər] N caimán *m*
all-important [ˈɔːlɪmˈpɔːtənt] ADJ de suma importancia
all-in [ˈɔːlɪn] ADJ, ADV (*BRIT: charge*) todo incluido
all-in wrestling N lucha libre
alliteration [əlɪtəˈreɪʃən] N aliteración *f*
all-night [ˈɔːlˈnaɪt] ADJ (*café*) abierto toda la noche; (*party*) que dura toda la noche
allocate [ˈæləkeɪt] VT (*share out*) repartir; (*devote*) asignar
allocation [æləˈkeɪʃən] N (*of money*) ración *f*, cuota; (*distribution*) reparto

allot [ə'lɔt] VT asignar; **in the allotted time** en el tiempo asignado

allotment [ə'lɔtmənt] N porción f; (*garden*) parcela

all-out ['ɔ:laut] ADJ (*effort etc*) supremo ▶ ADV: **all out** con todas las fuerzas, a fondo

allow [ə'lau] VT (*permit*) permitir, dejar; (*a claim*) admitir; (*sum to spend, time estimated*) dar, conceder; (*concede*): **to ~ that** reconocer que; **to ~ sb to do** permitir a algn hacer; **smoking is not allowed** prohibido or se prohíbe fumar; **he is allowed to …** se le permite …; **we must ~ three days for the journey** debemos dejar tres días para el viaje
▶ **allow for** VT FUS tener en cuenta

allowance [ə'lauəns] N concesión f; (*payment*) subvención f, pensión f; (*discount*) descuento, rebaja; (*tax allowance*) desgravación f; **to make allowances for** (*person*) disculpar a; (*thing: take into account*) tener en cuenta

alloy ['ælɔɪ] N aleación f

all right ADV (*feel, work*) bien; (*as answer*) ¡de acuerdo!, ¡está bien!

all-round ['ɔ:l'raund] ADJ completo o, (*view*) amplio

all-rounder ['ɔ:l'raundər] N: **to be a good ~** ser una persona que hace de todo

allspice ['ɔ:lspaɪs] N pimienta inglesa or de Jamaica

all-time ['ɔ:l'taɪm] ADJ (*record*) de todos los tiempos

allude [ə'lu:d] VI: **to ~ to** aludir a

alluring [ə'ljuərɪŋ] ADJ seductor(a), atractivo

allusion [ə'lu:ʒən] N referencia, alusión f

ally N ['ælaɪ] aliado(-a) ▶ VT [ə'laɪ]: **to ~ o.s. with** aliarse con

almanac ['ɔ:lmənæk] N almanaque m

almighty [ɔ:l'maɪtɪ] ADJ todopoderoso; (*row etc*) imponente

almond ['ɑ:mənd] N (*fruit*) almendra; (*tree*) almendro

almost ['ɔ:lməust] ADV casi; **he ~ fell** casi or por poco se cae

alms [ɑ:mz] NPL limosna sg

aloft [ə'lɔft] ADV arriba

alone [ə'ləun] ADJ solo ▶ ADV solo, solamente; **to leave sb ~** dejar a algn en paz; **to leave sth ~** no tocar algo; **let ~ …** y mucho menos …, y no digamos …

along [ə'lɔŋ] PREP a lo largo de, por ▶ ADV: **is he coming ~ with us?** ¿viene con nosotros?; **he was limping ~** iba cojeando; **~ with** junto con; **all ~** (*all the time*) desde el principio

alongside [ə'lɔŋ'saɪd] PREP al lado de ▶ ADV (*Naut*) de costado; **we brought our boat ~** atracamos nuestro barco

aloof [ə'lu:f] ADJ distante ▶ ADV: **to stand ~** mantenerse a distancia

aloud [ə'laud] ADV en voz alta

alphabet ['ælfəbɛt] N alfabeto

alphabetical [ælfə'bɛtɪkəl] ADJ alfabético; **in ~ order** por orden alfabético

alphanumeric [ælfənju:'mɛrɪk] ADJ alfanumérico

alpine ['ælpaɪn] ADJ alpino, alpestre

Alps [ælps] NPL: **the ~** los Alpes

already [ɔ:l'redɪ] ADV ya

alright ['ɔ:l'raɪt] ADV (*BRIT*) = **all right**

Alsatian [æl'seɪʃən] N (*dog*) pastor m alemán

also ['ɔ:lsəu] ADV también, además

Alta. ABBR (*CANADA*) = **Alberta**

altar ['ɔltər] N altar m

alter ['ɔltər] VT cambiar, modificar ▶ VI cambiar, modificarse

alteration [ɔltə'reɪʃən] N cambio, modificación f; **alterations** NPL (*Arch*) reformas fpl; (*Sewing*) arreglos mpl; **timetable subject to ~** el horario puede cambiar

altercation [ɔltə'keɪʃən] N altercado

alternate [ɔl'tə:nɪt] ADJ alterno ▶ VI ['ɔltəneɪt]: **to ~ (with)** alternar (con); **on ~ days** en días alternos

alternately [ɔl'tə:nɪtlɪ] ADV alternativamente, por turno

alternating ['ɔltəneɪtɪŋ] ADJ (*current*) alterno

alternative [ɔl'tə:nətɪv] ADJ alternativo ▶ N alternativa

alternatively [ɔl'tə:nətɪvlɪ] ADV: **~ one could …** por otra parte se podría …

alternative medicine N medicina alternativa

alternator ['ɔltəneɪtər] N (*Aut*) alternador m

although [ɔ:l'ðəu] CONJ aunque, si bien

altitude ['æltɪtju:d] N altitud f, altura

altitude sickness N mal m de altura, soroche m (*LAm*)

alto ['æltəu] N (*female*) contralto f; (*male*) alto

altogether [ɔ:ltə'gɛðər] ADV completamente, del todo; (*on the whole, in all*) en total, en conjunto; **how much is that ~?** ¿cuánto es todo or en total?

altruism ['æltruɪzəm] N altruismo

altruistic [æltru'ɪstɪk] ADJ altruista

aluminium [ælju'mɪnɪəm], (*US*) **aluminum** [ə'lu:mɪnəm] N aluminio

always ['ɔ:lweɪz] ADV siempre

Alzheimer's ['ælts haɪməz] N (*also:* **Alzheimer's disease**) (enfermedad f de) Alzheimer m

AM ABBR (= *amplitude modulation*) A.M. f ▶ N ABBR (*Pol: in Wales*) = **Assembly Member**

am [æm] VB *see* **be**

a.m. ADV ABBR (= *ante meridiem*) de la mañana

AMA N ABBR = **American Medical Association**

amalgam [ə'mælgəm] N amalgama

amalgamate [ə'mælgəmeɪt] VI amalgamarse ▸ VT amalgamar

amalgamation [əmælgə'meɪʃən] N (Comm) fusión f

amass [ə'mæs] VT amontonar, acumular

amateur ['æmətəʳ] N aficionado(-a), amateur mf; ~ **dramatics** dramas mpl presentados por aficionados, representación f de aficionados

amateurish ['æmətərɪʃ] ADJ (pej) torpe, inexperto

amaze [ə'meɪz] VT asombrar, pasmar

amazed ADJ [ə'meɪzd] asombrado; **to be ~ (at)** asombrarse (de)

amazement [ə'meɪzmənt] N asombro, sorpresa; **to my ~** para mi sorpresa

amazing [ə'meɪzɪŋ] ADJ extraordinario, asombroso; (bargain, offer) increíble

amazingly [ə'meɪzɪŋlɪ] ADV extraordinariamente

Amazon ['æməzən] N (Geo) Amazonas m; (Mythology) amazona ▸ CPD: **the ~ basin/ jungle** la cuenca/selva del Amazonas

Amazonian [æmə'zəʊniən] ADJ amazónico

ambassador [æm'bæsədəʳ] N embajador(a) m/f

amber ['æmbəʳ] N ámbar m; **at ~** (Brit Aut) en amarillo

ambidextrous [æmbɪ'dɛkstrəs] ADJ ambidextro

ambience ['æmbɪəns] N ambiente m

ambiguity [æmbɪ'gjuɪtɪ] N ambigüedad f; (of meaning) doble sentido

ambiguous [æm'bɪgjuəs] ADJ ambiguo

ambition [æm'bɪʃən] N ambición f; **to achieve one's ~** realizar su ambición

ambitious [æm'bɪʃəs] ADJ ambicioso; (plan) grandioso

ambivalent [æm'bɪvələnt] ADJ ambivalente; (pej) equívoco

amble ['æmbl] VI (gen: also: **amble along**) deambular, andar sin prisa

ambulance ['æmbjuləns] N ambulancia

ambulanceman ['æmbjulənsmən], **ambulancewoman** [-wumən] N (irreg) ambulanciero(-a)

ambush ['æmbuʃ] N emboscada ▸ VT tender una emboscada a; (fig) coger (Sp) or agarrar (Lam) por sorpresa

ameba [ə'mi:bə] N (US) = **amoeba**

ameliorate [ə'mi:lɪəreɪt] VT mejorar

amelioration [əmi:lɪə'reɪʃən] N mejora

amen [ɑː'mɛn] EXCL amén

amenable [ə'mi:nəbl] ADJ: ~ **to** (advice etc) sensible a

amend [ə'mɛnd] VT (law, text) enmendar; **to make amends** (apologize) enmendarlo, dar cumplida satisfacción

amendment [ə'mɛndmənt] N enmienda

amenity [ə'mi:nɪtɪ] N servicio; **amenities** NPL (facilities) servicios, instalaciones fpl

America [ə'mɛrɪkə] N América (del Norte); (USA) Estados mpl Unidos

American [ə'mɛrɪkən] ADJ, N (norte)americano(-a), estadounidense mf

American football N (Brit) fútbol m americano

Americanism [ə'mɛrɪkənɪzəm] N americanismo

americanize [ə'mɛrɪkənaɪz] VT americanizar

Amerindian [æmər'ɪndɪən] ADJ, N amerindio(-a) m/f

amethyst ['æmɪθɪst] N amatista

Amex ['æmɛks] N ABBR = **American Stock Exchange**

amiable ['eɪmɪəbl] ADJ (kind) amable, simpático

amicable ['æmɪkəbl] ADJ amistoso, amigable

amicably ['æmɪkəblɪ] ADV amigablemente; **to part ~** separarse amistosamente

amid [ə'mɪd], **amidst** [ə'mɪdst] PREP entre, en medio de

amiss [ə'mɪs] ADV: **to take sth ~** tomar algo a mal; **there's something ~** pasa algo

ammo ['æməʊ] N ABBR (inf) = **ammunition**

ammonia [ə'məʊnɪə] N amoníaco

ammunition [æmju'nɪʃən] N municiones fpl; (fig) argumentos mpl

ammunition dump N depósito de municiones

amnesia [æm'ni:zɪə] N amnesia

amnesty ['æmnɪstɪ] N amnistía; **to grant an ~ to** amnistiar (a); **A~ International** Amnistía Internacional

amoeba, (US) **ameba** [ə'mi:bə] N amiba

amok [ə'mɔk] ADV: **to run ~** enloquecerse, desbocarse

among [ə'mʌŋ], **amongst** [ə'mʌŋst] PREP entre, en medio de

amoral [æ'mɔrəl] ADJ amoral

amorous ['æmərəs] ADJ cariñoso

amorphous [ə'mɔ:fəs] ADJ amorfo

amortization [əmɔ:taɪ'zeɪʃən] N amortización f

amount [ə'maunt] N (gen) cantidad f; (of bill etc) suma, importe m ▸ VI: **to ~ to** (total) sumar; (be same as) equivaler a, significar; **this amounts to a refusal** esto equivale a una negativa; **the total ~** (of money) la suma total

amp [æmp], **ampère** ['æmpɛəʳ] N amperio; **a 13 ~ plug** un enchufe de 13 amperios

ampersand ['æmpəsænd] N signo &, "y" comercial

amphetamine [æm'fɛtəmi:n] N anfetamina

amphibian [æm'fɪbɪən] N anfibio

amphibious [æm'fɪbɪəs] ADJ anfibio
amphitheatre, (US) **amphitheater** ['æmfɪθɪətər] N anfiteatro
ample ['æmpl] ADJ (spacious) amplio; (abundant) abundante; **to have ~ time** tener tiempo de sobra
amplifier ['æmplɪfaɪər] N amplificador m
amplify ['æmplɪfaɪ] VT amplificar, aumentar; (explain) explicar
amply ['æmplɪ] ADV ampliamente
ampoule, (US) **ampule** ['æmpuːl] N (Med) ampolla
amputate ['æmpjuteɪt] VT amputar
amputee [æmpju'tiː] N persona que ha sufrido una amputación
Amsterdam ['æmstədæm] N Amsterdam m
amt ABBR = **amount**
Amtrak ['æmtræk] N (US) empresa nacional de ferrocarriles de los EE.UU.
amuck [ə'mʌk] ADV = **amok**
amuse [ə'mjuːz] VT divertir; (distract) distraer, entretener; **to ~ o.s. with sth/by doing sth** distraerse con algo/haciendo algo; **he was amused at the joke** le divirtió el chiste
amusement [ə'mjuːzmənt] N diversión f; (pastime) pasatiempo; (laughter) risa; **much to my ~** con gran regocijo mío
amusement arcade N salón m de juegos
amusement park N parque m de atracciones
amusing [ə'mjuːzɪŋ] ADJ divertido
an [æn, ən, n] INDEF ART see **a**
ANA N ABBR = **American Newspaper Association; American Nurses Association**
anachronism [ə'nækrənɪzəm] N anacronismo
anaemia [ə'niːmɪə] N anemia
anaemic [ə'niːmɪk] ADJ anémico; (fig) flojo
anaesthetic [ænɪs'θetɪk] N anestesia; **local/general ~** anestesia local/general
anaesthetist [æ'niːsθɪtɪst] N anestesista mf
anagram ['ænəgræm] N anagrama m
anal ['eɪnl] ADJ anal
analgesic [ænæl'dʒiːsɪk] ADJ, N analgésico
analogous [ə'næləgəs] ADJ: **~ to** or **with** análogo a
analogue, analog ADJ (watch) analógico
analogy [ə'nælədʒɪ] N analogía; **to draw an ~ between** señalar la analogía entre
analyse ['ænəlaɪz] VT (BRIT) analizar
analysis [ə'næləsɪs] (pl **analyses** [-siːz]) N análisis m inv
analyst ['ænəlɪst] N (political analyst, psychoanalyst) analista mf
analytic [ænə'lɪtɪk], **analytical** [ænə'lɪtɪkəl] ADJ analítico
analyze ['ænəlaɪz] VT (US) = **analyse**
anarchic [æ'nɑːkɪk] ADJ anárquico
anarchist ['ænəkɪst] ADJ, N anarquista mf

anarchy ['ænəkɪ] N anarquía, desorden m
anathema [ə'næθɪmə] N: **that is ~ to him** eso es pecado para él
anatomical [ænə'tɒmɪkəl] ADJ anatómico
anatomy [ə'nætəmɪ] N anatomía
ANC N ABBR = **African National Congress**
ancestor ['ænsɪstər] N antepasado
ancestral [æn'sɛstrəl] ADJ ancestral
ancestry ['ænsɪstrɪ] N ascendencia, abolengo
anchor ['æŋkər] N ancla, áncora ▶ VI (also: **to drop anchor**) anclar, echar el ancla ▶ VT (fig) sujetar, afianzar; **to weigh ~** levar anclas
anchorage ['æŋkərɪdʒ] N ancladero
anchor man, anchor woman N (irreg) (Radio, TV) presentador(a) m/f
anchovy ['æntʃəvɪ] N anchoa
ancient ['eɪnʃənt] ADJ antiguo; **~ monument** monumento histórico
ancillary [æn'sɪlərɪ] ADJ (worker, staff) auxiliar
and [ænd] CONJ y; (before i, hi) e; **~ so on** etcétera; **try ~ come** procura venir; **better ~ better** cada vez mejor
Andalusia [ændə'luːzɪə] N Andalucía
Andean ['ændɪən] ADJ andino(-a); **~ high plateau** altiplanicie f, altiplano (LAm)
Andes ['ændiːz] NPL: **the ~** los Andes
Andorra [æn'dɔːrə] N Andorra
anecdote ['ænɪkdəut] N anécdota
anemia [ə'niːmɪə] N (US) = **anaemia**
anemic [ə'niːmɪk] ADJ (US) = **anaemic**
anemone [ə'nɛmənɪ] N (Bot) anémone f; **sea ~** anémona
anesthetic [ænɪs'θetɪk] ADJ, N (US) = **anaesthetic**
anesthetist [æ'niːsθɪtɪst] N (US) = **anaesthetist**
anew [ə'njuː] ADV de nuevo, otra vez
angel ['eɪndʒəl] N ángel m
angel dust N polvo de ángel
angelic [æn'dʒelɪk] ADJ angélico
anger ['æŋgər] N ira, cólera, enojo (LAm) ▶ VT enojar, enfurecer
angina [æn'dʒaɪnə] N angina (del pecho)
angle ['æŋgl] N ángulo; **from their ~** desde su punto de vista
angler ['æŋglər] N pescador(a) m/f (de caña)
Anglican ['æŋglɪkən] ADJ, N anglicano(-a) m/f
anglicize ['æŋglɪsaɪz] VT anglicanizar
angling ['æŋglɪŋ] N pesca con caña
Anglo- ['æŋgləu] PREF anglo...
Angola [æŋ'gəulə] N Angola
Angolan [æŋ'gəulən] ADJ, N angoleño(-a) m/f
angrily ['æŋgrɪlɪ] ADV enojado, enfadado
angry ['æŋgrɪ] ADJ enfadado, enojado (esp LAm); **to be ~ with sb/at sth** estar enfadado con algn/por algo; **to get ~** enfadarse, enojarse (esp LAm)
anguish ['æŋgwɪʃ] N (physical) tormentos mpl; (mental) angustia

anguished ['æŋgwɪʃt] ADJ angustioso

angular ['æŋgjulər] ADJ (*shape*) angular; (*features*) anguloso

animal ['ænɪməl] ADJ, N animal *m*; (*pej: person*) bestia

animal rights [-raɪts] NPL derechos *mpl* de los animales

animate VT ['ænɪmeɪt] (*enliven*) animar; (*encourage*) estimular, alentar ▶ ADJ ['ænɪmɪt] vivo, animado

animated ['ænɪmeɪtɪd] ADJ vivo, animado

animation [ænɪ'meɪʃən] N animación *f*

animosity [ænɪ'mɔsɪtɪ] N animosidad *f*, rencor *m*

aniseed ['ænɪsiːd] N anís *m*

Ankara ['æŋkərə] N Ankara

ankle ['æŋkl] N tobillo *m*

ankle sock N calcetín *m*

annex N ['ænɛks] (BRIT: *also:* **annexe**: *building*) edificio anexo ▶ VT [æ'nɛks] (*territory*) anexionar

annihilate [ə'naɪəleɪt] VT aniquilar

annihilation [ənaɪə'leɪʃən] N aniquilación *f*

anniversary [ænɪ'vəːsərɪ] N aniversario

annotate ['ænəuteɪt] VT anotar

announce [ə'nauns] VT (*gen*) anunciar; (*inform*) comunicar; **he announced that he wasn't going** declaró que no iba

announcement [ə'naunsmənt] N (*gen*) anuncio; (*declaration*) declaración *f*; **I'd like to make an ~** quisiera anunciar algo

announcer [ə'naunsər] N (*Radio*) locutor(a) *m/f*; (*TV*) presentador(a) *m/f*

annoy [ə'nɔɪ] VT molestar, fastidiar, fregar (LAM), embromar (LAM); **to be annoyed (at sth/with sb)** estar enfadado *or* molesto (por algo/con algn); **don't get annoyed!** ¡no se enfade!

annoyance [ə'nɔɪəns] N enojo; (*thing*) molestia

annoying [ə'nɔɪɪŋ] ADJ molesto, fastidioso, fregado (LAM), embromado (LAM); (*person*) pesado

annual ['ænjuəl] ADJ anual ▶ N (*Bot*) anual *m*; (*book*) anuario

annual general meeting N junta general anual

annually ['ænjuəlɪ] ADV anualmente, cada año

annual report N informe *m or* memoria anual

annuity [ə'njuːɪtɪ] N renta *or* pensión *f* vitalicia

annul [ə'nʌl] VT anular; (*law*) revocar

annulment [ə'nʌlmənt] N anulación *f*

annum ['ænəm] N *see* **per annum**

Annunciation [ənʌnsɪ'eɪʃən] N Anunciación *f*

anode ['ænəud] N ánodo

anoint [ə'nɔɪnt] VT untar

anomalous [ə'nɔmələs] ADJ anómalo

anomaly [ə'nɔməlɪ] N anomalía

anon. [ə'nɔn] ABBR = **anonymous**

anonymity [ænə'nɪmɪtɪ] N anonimato

anonymous [ə'nɔnɪməs] ADJ anónimo; **to remain ~** quedar en el anonimato

anorak ['ænəræk] N anorak *m*

anorexia [ænə'rɛksɪə] N (*Med*) anorexia

anorexic [ænə'rɛksɪk] ADJ, N anoréxico(-a) *m/f*

another [ə'nʌðər] ADJ: **~ book** otro libro; **~ beer?** ¿(quieres) otra cerveza?; **in ~ five years** en cinco años más ▶ PRON otro; *see also* **one**

ANSI N ABBR (= *American National Standards Institution*) oficina de normalización de EE.UU.

answer ['ɑːnsər] N respuesta, contestación *f*; (*to problem*) solución *f* ▶ VI contestar, responder ▶ VT (*reply to*) contestar a, responder a; (*problem*) resolver; **in ~ to your letter** contestando *or* en contestación a su carta; **to ~ the phone** contestar el teléfono; **to ~ the bell** *or* **the door** abrir la puerta
▶ **answer back** VI replicar, ser respondón(-ona)
▶ **answer for** VT FUS responder de *or* por
▶ **answer to** VT FUS (*description*) corresponder a

answerable ['ɑːnsərəbl] ADJ: **~ to sb for sth** responsable ante algn de algo

answering machine ['ɑːnsərɪŋ-] N contestador *m* automático

answerphone ['ɑːnsəfəun] N (*esp BRIT*) contestador *m* (automático)

ant [ænt] N hormiga

ANTA N ABBR = **American National Theater and Academy**

antagonism [æn'tægənɪzəm] N antagonismo *m*

antagonist [æn'tægənɪst] N antagonista *mf*, adversario(-a)

antagonistic [æntægə'nɪstɪk] ADJ antagónico; (*opposed*) contrario, opuesto

antagonize [æn'tægənaɪz] VT provocar la enemistad de

Antarctic [ænt'ɑːktɪk] ADJ antártico ▶ N: **the ~ Antártico**

Antarctica [æn'tɑːktɪkə] N Antártida

Antarctic Circle N Círculo Polar Antártico

Antarctic Ocean N Océano Antártico

ante ['æntɪ] N: **to up the ~** subir la apuesta

ante... ['æntɪ] PREF ante...

anteater ['æntiːtər] N oso hormiguero

antecedent [æntɪ'siːdənt] N antecedente *m*

antechamber ['æntɪtʃeɪmbər] N antecámara

antelope ['æntɪləup] N antílope *m*

antenatal [æntɪ'neɪtl] ADJ prenatal

antenatal clinic N clínica prenatal

antenna [æn'tɛnə] (pl **antennae** [-ni:]) N
antena

anteroom ['æntɪrum] N antesala

anthem ['ænθəm] N: **national** ~ himno
nacional

anthology [æn'θɒlədʒɪ] N antología

anthrax ['ænθræks] N ántrax m

anthropologist [ænθrə'pɒlədʒɪst] N
antropólogo(-a)

anthropology [ænθrə'pɒlədʒɪ] N
antropología

anti... [æntɪ] PREF anti...

anti-aircraft ['æntɪ'eəkrɑ:ft] ADJ antiaéreo

antiballistic [æntɪbə'lɪstɪk] ADJ antibalístico

antibiotic [æntɪbaɪ'ɔtɪk] ADJ, N antibiótico

antibody ['æntɪbɒdɪ] N anticuerpo

anticipate [æn'tɪsɪpeɪt] VT (foresee) prever;
(expect) esperar, contar con; (forestall)
anticiparse a, adelantarse a; **this is worse
than I anticipated** esto es peor de lo que
esperaba; **as anticipated** según se esperaba

anticipation [æntɪsɪ'peɪʃən] N previsión f;
esperanza; anticipación f

anticlimax [æntɪ'klaɪmæks] N decepción f

anticlockwise [æntɪ'klɒkwaɪz] ADV en
dirección contraria a la de las agujas del
reloj

antics ['æntɪks] NPL gracias fpl

anticyclone [æntɪ'saɪkləun] N anticiclón m

antidepressant ['æntɪdɪ'presnt] N
antidepresivo

antidote ['æntɪdəut] N antídoto

antifreeze ['æntɪfri:z] N anticongelante m

anti-globalization ['æntɪgləubəlaɪ'zeɪʃən] N
antiglobalización f; ~ **protesters**
manifestantes mf antiglobalización

antihistamine [æntɪ'hɪstəmi:n] N
antihistamínico

Antilles [æn'tɪli:z] NPL: **the ~** las Antillas

antipathy [æn'tɪpəθɪ] N (between people)
antipatía; (to person, thing) aversión f

antiperspirant ['æntɪpə:spɪrənt] N
antitranspirante m

Antipodean [æntɪpə'di:ən] ADJ antípoda

Antipodes [æn'tɪpədi:z] NPL: **the ~** las
Antípodas

antiquarian [æntɪ'kwɛərɪən] N
anticuario(-a)

antiquated ['æntɪkweɪtɪd] ADJ anticuado

antique [æn'ti:k] N antigüedad f ▶ ADJ
antiguo

antique dealer N anticuario(-a)

antique shop N tienda de antigüedades

antiquity [æn'tɪkwɪtɪ] N antigüedad f

anti-Semitic ['æntɪsɪ'mɪtɪk] ADJ antisemita

anti-Semitism [æntɪ'sɛmɪtɪzəm] N
antisemitismo

antiseptic [æntɪ'sɛptɪk] ADJ, N antiséptico

antishake ['æntɪʃeɪk] ADJ estabilizador

antisocial [æntɪ'səuʃəl] ADJ antisocial

antitank [æntɪ'tæŋk] ADJ antitanque

antithesis [æn'tɪθɪsɪs] (pl **antitheses** [-si:z])
N antítesis f inv

antitrust [æntɪ'trʌst] ADJ: ~ **legislation**
legislación f antimonopolio

antiviral [æntɪ'vaɪrəl] ADJ (Med)
antivírico

antivirus [æntɪ'vaɪrəs] ADJ antivirus;
~ **software** antivirus m

antlers ['æntləz] NPL cornamenta

anus ['eɪnəs] N ano

anvil ['ænvɪl] N yunque m

anxiety [æŋ'zaɪətɪ] N (worry) inquietud f;
(eagerness) ansia, anhelo

anxious ['æŋkʃəs] ADJ (worried) inquieto;
(keen) deseoso; **to be ~ to do** tener muchas
ganas de hacer; **I'm very ~ about you** me
tienes muy preocupado

anxiously ['æŋkʃəslɪ] ADV con inquietud, de
manera angustiada

(KEYWORD)

any ['ɛnɪ] ADJ **1** (in questions etc) algún/alguna;
have you any butter/children? ¿tienes
mantequilla/hijos?; **if there are any
tickets left** si quedan billetes, si queda
algún billete

2 (with negative): **I haven't any money/books**
no tengo dinero/libros

3 (no matter which) cualquier; **any excuse will
do** valdrá or servirá cualquier excusa;
choose any book you like escoge el libro
que quieras; **any teacher you ask will tell
you** cualquier profesor al que preguntes te lo
dirá

4 (in phrases): **in any case** de todas formas, en
cualquier caso; **any day now** cualquier día
(de estos); **at any moment** en cualquier
momento, de un momento a otro; **at any
rate** en todo caso; **any time: come (at) any
time** ven cuando quieras; **he might come
(at) any time** podría llegar de un momento
a otro

▶ PRON **1** (in questions etc): **have you got any?**
¿tienes alguno/a?; **can any of you sing?**
¿sabe cantar alguno de vosotros/ustedes?

2 (with negative): **I haven't any (of them)** no
tengo ninguno

3 (no matter which one(s)): **take any of those
books (you like)** toma el libro que quieras
de ésos

▶ ADV **1** (in questions etc): **do you want any
more soup/sandwiches?** ¿quieres más
sopa/bocadillos?; **are you feeling any
better?** ¿te sientes algo mejor?

2 (with negative): **I can't hear him any more**
ya no le oigo; **don't wait any longer** no
esperes más

anybody ['ɛnɪbɔdɪ] PRON cualquiera, cualquier persona; (in interrogative sentences) alguien; (in negative sentences): **I don't see ~** no veo a nadie

anyhow ['ɛnɪhau] ADV de todos modos, de todas maneras; (carelessly) de cualquier manera; (haphazardly) de cualquier modo; **I shall go ~** iré de todas maneras

anyone ['ɛnɪwʌn] PRON = **anybody**

anyplace ['ɛnɪpleɪs] ADV (US) = **anywhere**

anything ['ɛnɪθɪŋ] PRON cualquier cosa; (in interrogative sentences) algo; (in negative sentences) nada; (everything) todo; **~ else?** ¿algo más?; **can you see ~?** ¿ves algo?; **he'll eat ~** come de todo or lo que sea; **it can cost ~ between £15 and £20** puede costar entre 15 y 20 libras

anytime ['ɛnɪtaɪm] ADV (at any moment) en cualquier momento, de un momento a otro; (whenever) no importa cuándo, cuando quiera

anyway ['ɛnɪweɪ] ADV (at any rate) de todos modos, de todas formas; (besides) además; **~, I couldn't come even if I wanted to** además, no podría venir aunque quisiera; **I shall go ~** iré de todos modos; **why are you phoning, ~?** ¿entonces, por qué llamas?, ¿por qué llamas, pues?

anywhere ['ɛnɪwɛəʳ] ADV dondequiera; (interrogative) en algún sitio; (negative sense) en ningún sitio; (everywhere) en or por todas partes; **I don't see him ~** no le veo en ningún sitio; **are you going ~?** ¿vas a algún sitio?; **~ in the world** en cualquier parte del mundo

Anzac ['ænzæk] N ABBR = **Australia-New Zealand Army Corps**

apace [ə'peɪs] ADV aprisa

apart [ə'pɑːt] ADV aparte, separadamente; **10 miles ~** separados por 10 millas; **to take ~** desmontar; **~ from** prep aparte de

apartheid [ə'pɑːteɪt] N apartheid m

apartment [ə'pɑːtmənt] N (US) piso, departamento (LAm), apartamento; (room) cuarto

apartment block, apartment building N (US) bloque m de apartamentos

apathetic [æpə'θɛtɪk] ADJ apático, indiferente

apathy ['æpəθɪ] N apatía, indiferencia

APB N ABBR (US: police expression: = all points bulletin) expresión usada por la policía que significa "descubrir y aprehender al sospechoso"

ape [eɪp] N mono ▶ VT imitar, remedar

Apennines ['æpənaɪnz] NPL: **the ~** los Apeninos mpl

aperitif [ə'pɛrɪtiːf] N aperitivo

aperture ['æpətʃuəʳ] N rendija, resquicio; (Phot) abertura

APEX ['eɪpɛks] N ABBR (Aviat: = advance purchase excursion) tarifa f APEX

apex ['eɪpɛks] N ápice m; (fig) cumbre f

aphid ['eɪfɪd] N pulgón m

aphorism ['æfərɪzəm] N aforismo

aphrodisiac [æfrəu'dɪzɪæk] ADJ, N afrodisíaco

API N ABBR = **American Press Institute**

apiece [ə'piːs] ADV cada uno

aplomb [ə'plɔm] N aplomo, confianza

APO N ABBR (US: = Army Post Office) servicio postal del ejército

Apocalypse [ə'pɔkəlɪps] N Apocalipsis m

apocryphal [ə'pɔkrɪfəl] ADJ apócrifo

apolitical [eɪpə'lɪtɪkl] ADJ apolítico

apologetic [əpɔlə'dʒɛtɪk] ADJ (look, remark) de disculpa

apologetically [əpɔlə'dʒɛtɪkəlɪ] ADV con aire de disculpa, excusándose, disculpándose

apologize [ə'pɔlədʒaɪz] VI: **to ~ (for sth to sb)** disculparse (con algn por algo)

apology [ə'pɔlədʒɪ] N disculpa, excusa; **please accept my apologies** le ruego me disculpe

apoplectic [æpə'plɛktɪk] ADJ (Med) apoplético; (inf): **~ with rage** furioso

apoplexy ['æpəplɛksɪ] N apoplejía

apostle [ə'pɔsl] N apóstol mf

apostrophe [ə'pɔstrəfɪ] N apóstrofo m

app ['æp] N ABBR (inf: Comput: = application) aplicación f

appal [ə'pɔːl] VT horrorizar, espantar

Appalachian Mountains [æpə'leɪʃən-] NPL: **the ~** los (Montes) Apalaches

appalling [ə'pɔːlɪŋ] ADJ espantoso; (awful) pésimo; **she's an ~ cook** es una cocinera malísima

apparatus [æpə'reɪtəs] N (equipment) equipo; (organization) aparato; (in gymnasium) aparatos mpl

apparel [ə'pærl] N (US) indumentaria

apparent [ə'pærənt] ADJ aparente; (obvious) manifiesto, evidente; **it is ~ that** está claro que

apparently [ə'pærəntlɪ] ADV por lo visto, al parecer, dizque (LAm)

apparition [æpə'rɪʃən] N aparición f

appeal [ə'piːl] VI (Law) apelar ▶ N (Law) apelación f; (request) llamamiento, llamado (LAm); (plea) petición f; (charm) atractivo, encanto; **to ~ for** solicitar; **to ~ to** (person) rogar a, suplicar a; (thing) atraer, interesar; **to ~ to sb for mercy** rogarle misericordia a algn; **it doesn't ~ to me** no me atrae, no me llama la atención; **right of ~** derecho de apelación

appealing [ə'piːlɪŋ] ADJ (nice) atractivo; (touching) conmovedor(a), emocionante

appear [ə'pɪər] vɪ aparecer, presentarse; (*Law*) comparecer; (*publication*) salir (a luz), publicarse; (*seem*) parecer; **to ~ on TV/in "Hamlet"** salir por la tele/hacer un papel en "Hamlet"; **it would ~ that** parecería que

appearance [ə'pɪərəns] N aparición f; (*look, aspect*) apariencia, aspecto; **to keep up appearances** salvar las apariencias; **to all appearances** al parecer

appease [ə'piːz] vᴛ (*pacify*) apaciguar; (*satisfy*) satisfacer

appeasement [ə'piːzmənt] N (*Pol*) apaciguamiento

append [ə'pɛnd] vᴛ (*Comput*) añadir (al final)

appendage [ə'pɛndɪdʒ] N añadidura

appendices [ə'pɛndɪsiːz] NPL *of* **appendix**

appendicitis [əpɛndɪ'saɪtɪs] N apendicitis f

appendix [ə'pɛndɪks] (*pl* **appendices** [-dɪsiːz]) N apéndice *m*; **to have one's ~ out** operarse de apendicitis

appetite ['æpɪtaɪt] N apetito; (*fig*) deseo, anhelo; **that walk has given me an ~** ese paseo me ha abierto el apetito

appetizer ['æpɪtaɪzər] N (*drink*) aperitivo; (*food*) tapas *fpl* (*Sᴘ*)

appetizing ['æpɪtaɪzɪŋ] ADJ apetitoso

applaud [ə'plɔːd] vᴛ, vɪ aplaudir

applause [ə'plɔːz] N aplausos *mpl*

apple ['æpl] N manzana

apple pie N pastel *m* de manzana, pay *m* de manzana (LAᴍ)

apple tree N manzano

appliance [ə'plaɪəns] N aparato; **electrical appliances** electrodomésticos *mpl*

applicable [ə'plɪkəbl] ADJ aplicable, pertinente; **the law is ~ from January** la ley es aplicable *or* se pone en vigor a partir de enero; **to be ~ to** referirse a

applicant ['æplɪkənt] N candidato(-a); solicitante *mf*

application [æplɪ'keɪʃən] N (*also Comput*) aplicación f; (*for a job, a grant etc*) solicitud f

application form N solicitud f

application program N (*Comput*) (programa *m* de) aplicación f

applications package N (*Comput*) paquete *m* de programas de aplicación

applied [ə'plaɪd] ADJ (*science, art*) aplicado

apply [ə'plaɪ] vᴛ: **to ~ (to)** aplicar (a); (*fig*) emplear (para) ▸ vɪ: **to ~ to** (*ask*) dirigirse a; (*be suitable for*) ser aplicable a; (*be relevant to*) tener que ver con; **to ~ for** (*permit, grant, job*) solicitar; **to ~ the brakes** echar el freno; **to ~ o.s. to** aplicarse a, dedicarse a

appoint [ə'pɔɪnt] vᴛ (*to post*) nombrar; (*date; place*) fijar, señalar

appointee [əpɔɪn'tiː] N persona nombrada

appointment [ə'pɔɪntmənt] N (*engagement*) cita; (*date*) compromiso; (*act*)

nombramiento; (*post*) puesto; **to make an ~ (with)** (*doctor*) pedir hora (con); (*friend*) citarse (con); **"appointments"** "ofertas de trabajo"; **by ~** mediante cita

apportion [ə'pɔːʃən] vᴛ repartir

appraisal [ə'preɪzl] N evaluación f

appraise [ə'preɪz] vᴛ (*value*) tasar, valorar; (*situation etc*) evaluar

appreciable [ə'priːʃəbl] ADJ sensible

appreciably [ə'priːʃəblɪ] ADV sensiblemente, de manera apreciable

appreciate [ə'priːʃɪeɪt] vᴛ (*like*) apreciar, tener en mucho; (*be grateful for*) agradecer; (*be aware of*) comprender ▸ vɪ (*Comm*) aumentar en valor; **I appreciated your help** agradecí tu ayuda

appreciation [əpriːʃɪ'eɪʃən] N apreciación f; (*gratitude*) reconocimiento, agradecimiento; (*Comm*) aumento en valor

appreciative [ə'priːʃɪətɪv] ADJ agradecido

apprehend [æprɪ'hɛnd] vᴛ percibir; (*arrest*) detener

apprehension [æprɪ'hɛnʃən] N (*fear*) aprensión f

apprehensive [æprɪ'hɛnsɪv] ADJ aprensivo

apprentice [ə'prɛntɪs] N aprendiz(a) *m/f* ▸ vᴛ: **to be apprenticed to** estar de aprendiz con

apprenticeship [ə'prɛntɪʃɪp] N aprendizaje *m*; **to serve one's ~** hacer el aprendizaje

appro. ['æprəʊ] ABBR (*Brɪᴛ Comm: inf*) *see* **approval**

approach [ə'prəʊtʃ] vɪ acercarse ▸ vᴛ acercarse a; (*be approximate*) aproximarse a; (*ask, apply to*) dirigirse a; (*problem*) abordar ▸ N acercamiento; aproximación f; (*access*) acceso; (*proposal*) proposición f; (*to problem etc*) enfoque *m*; **to ~ sb about sth** hablar con algn sobre algo

approachable [ə'prəʊtʃəbl] ADJ (*person*) abordable; (*place*) accesible

approach road N vía de acceso

approbation [æprə'beɪʃən] N aprobación f

appropriate [ə'prəʊprɪɪt] ADJ apropiado, conveniente ▸ vᴛ [-rɪeɪt] (*take*) apropiarse de; (*allot*): **to ~ sth for** destinar algo a; **~ for** *or* **to** apropiado para; **it would not be ~ for me to comment** no estaría bien *or* sería pertinente que yo diera mi opinión

appropriation [əprəʊprɪ'eɪʃən] N asignación f

approval [ə'pruːvəl] N aprobación f, visto bueno; **on ~** (*Comm*) a prueba; **to meet with sb's ~** obtener la aprobación de algn

approve [ə'pruːv] vᴛ aprobar ▸ **approve of** vᴛ ꜰᴜꜱ aprobar; **they don't ~ of her** (ella) no les parece bien

approved school [ə'pruːvɪd-] N (*Brɪᴛ*) correccional *m*

approx. ABBR (= *approximately*) aprox.

approximate [əˈprɒksɪmɪt] ADJ aproximado

approximately [əˈprɒksɪmɪtlɪ] ADV aproximadamente, más o menos

approximation [əprɒksɪˈmeɪʃən] N aproximación *f*

apr N ABBR (= *annual percentage rate*) tasa de interés anual

Apr. ABBR (= *April*) abr.

apricot [ˈeɪprɪkɒt] N albaricoque *m* (SP), damasco (LAM)

April [ˈeɪprəl] N abril *m*; *see also* **July**

April Fools' Day N ≈ día *m* de los (Santos) Inocentes; *ver nota*

El 1 de abril es *April Fools' Day* en la tradición anglosajona. Tal día se les gastan bromas a los más desprevenidos, quienes reciben la denominación de "*April Fool*" (= inocente), y tanto la prensa escrita como la televisión difunden alguna historia falsa con la que sumarse al espíritu del día.

apron [ˈeɪprən] N delantal *m*; (Aviat) pista

apse [æps] N (Arch) ábside *m*

APT N ABBR (BRIT) = **advanced passenger train**

apt [æpt] ADJ (*to the point*) acertado, oportuno; (*appropriate*) apropiado; **~ to do** (*likely*) propenso a hacer

Apt. ABBR = **apartment**

aptitude [ˈæptɪtjuːd] N aptitud *f*, capacidad *f*

aptitude test N prueba de aptitud

aptly [ˈæptlɪ] ADJ acertadamente

aqualung [ˈækwəlʌŋ] N escafandra autónoma

aquarium [əˈkwɛərɪəm] N acuario

Aquarius [əˈkwɛərɪəs] N Acuario

aquatic [əˈkwætɪk] ADJ acuático

aqueduct [ˈækwɪdʌkt] N acueducto

AR ABBR (US) = **Arkansas**

ARA N ABBR (BRIT) = **Associate of the Royal Academy**

Arab [ˈærəb] ADJ, N árabe *mf*

Arabia [əˈreɪbɪə] N Arabia

Arabian [əˈreɪbɪən] ADJ árabe, arábigo

Arabian Desert N Desierto de Arabia

Arabian Sea N Mar *m* de Omán

Arabic [ˈærəbɪk] ADJ (*language, manuscripts*) árabe, arábigo ▶ N árabe *m*; **~ numerals** numeración *f* arábiga

arable [ˈærəbl] ADJ cultivable

Aragon [ˈærəgən] N Aragón *m*

ARAM N ABBR (BRIT) = **Associate of the Royal Academy of Music**

arbiter [ˈɑːbɪtəʳ] N árbitro

arbitrary [ˈɑːbɪtrərɪ] ADJ arbitrario

arbitrate [ˈɑːbɪtreɪt] VI arbitrar

arbitration [ɑːbɪˈtreɪʃən] N arbitraje *m*; **the dispute went to ~** el conflicto laboral fue sometido al arbitraje

arbitrator [ˈɑːbɪtreɪtəʳ] N árbitro

ARC N ABBR = **American Red Cross**

arc [ɑːk] N arco

arcade [ɑːˈkeɪd] N (Arch) arcada; (*round a square*) soportales *mpl*; (*shopping arcade*) galería comercial

arch [ɑːtʃ] N arco; (*vault*) bóveda; (*of foot*) puente *m* ▶ VT arquear

archaeological [ɑːkɪəˈlɒdʒɪkl] ADJ arqueológico

archaeologist [ɑːkɪˈɒlədʒɪst] N arqueólogo(-a)

archaeology [ɑːkɪˈɒlədʒɪ] N arqueología

archaic [ɑːˈkeɪɪk] ADJ arcaico

archangel [ˈɑːkeɪndʒəl] N arcángel *m*

archbishop [ɑːtʃˈbɪʃəp] N arzobispo

arched [ɑːtʃt] ADJ abovedado

archenemy [ˈɑːtʃˈɛnəmɪ] N enemigo jurado

archeology *etc* [ɑːkɪˈɒlədʒɪ] (US) *see* **archaeology** *etc*

archer [ˈɑːtʃəʳ] N arquero(-a)

archery [ˈɑːtʃərɪ] N tiro al arco

archetypal [ˈɑːkɪtaɪpəl] ADJ arquetípico

archetype [ˈɑːkɪtaɪp] N arquetipo

archipelago [ɑːkɪˈpɛlɪgəu] N archipiélago

architect [ˈɑːkɪtɛkt] N arquitecto(-a)

architectural [ɑːkɪˈtɛktʃərəl] ADJ arquitectónico

architecture [ˈɑːkɪtɛktʃəʳ] N arquitectura

archive [ˈɑːkaɪv] N (*gen pl: also Comput*) archivo; **archives** NPL archivo *sg*

archive file N (Comput) fichero archivado

archivist [ˈɑːkɪvɪst] N archivero(-a)

archway [ˈɑːtʃweɪ] N arco, arcada

ARCM N ABBR (BRIT) = **Associate of the Royal College of Music**

Arctic [ˈɑːktɪk] ADJ ártico ▶ N: **the ~** el Ártico

Arctic Circle N Círculo Polar Ártico

Arctic Ocean N Océano (Glacial) Ártico

ARD N ABBR (US Med) = **acute respiratory disease**

ardent [ˈɑːdənt] ADJ (*desire*) ardiente; (*supporter, lover*) apasionado

ardour, (US) **ardor** [ˈɑːdəʳ] N ardor *m*, pasión *f*

arduous [ˈɑːdjuəs] ADJ (*gen*) arduo; (*journey*) penoso

are [ɑːʳ] VB *see* **be**

area [ˈɛərɪə] N área; (Math *etc*) superficie *f*, extensión *f*; (*zone*) región *f*, zona; (*of knowledge, experience*) campo; **the London ~** la zona de Londres

area code N (US Tel) prefijo

arena [əˈriːnə] N arena; (*of circus*) pista; (*for bullfight*) plaza, ruedo

aren't [ɑːnt] = **are not**

Argentina [ɑːdʒənˈtiːnə] N Argentina

Argentinian [ɑːdʒənˈtɪnɪən] ADJ, N argentino(-a) *m/f*

arguable [ˈɑːgjuəbl] ADJ: **it is ~ whether ...** es dudoso que + *subjun*

arguably [ˈɑːgjuəblɪ] ADV: **it is ~ ...** es discutiblemente ...

argue [ˈɑːgjuː] VT (*debate: case, matter*) mantener, argüir ▸ VI (*quarrel*) discutir; (*reason*) razonar, argumentar; **to ~ that** sostener que; **to ~ about sth (with sb)** pelearse (con algn) por algo

argument [ˈɑːgjumənt] N (*reasons*) argumento; (*quarrel*) discusión *f*; (*debate*) debate *m*; **~ for/against** argumento en pro/contra de

argumentative [ɑːgjuˈmɛntətɪv] ADJ discutidor(a)

aria [ˈɑːrɪə] N (*Mus*) aria

ARIBA N ABBR (*Brit*) = **Associate of the Royal Institute of British Architects**

arid [ˈærɪd] ADJ árido

aridity [əˈrɪdɪtɪ] N aridez *f*

Aries [ˈɛərɪz] N Aries *m*

arise [əˈraɪz] (*pt* **arose**, *pp* **arisen** [əˈrɪzn]) VI (*rise up*) levantarse, alzarse; (*emerge*) surgir, presentarse; **to ~ from** derivar de; **should the need ~** si fuera necesario

aristocracy [ærɪsˈtɔkrəsɪ] N aristocracia

aristocrat [ˈærɪstəkræt] N aristócrata *mf*

aristocratic [ərɪstəˈkrætɪk] ADJ aristocrático

arithmetic [əˈrɪθmətɪk] N aritmética

arithmetical [ærɪθˈmɛtɪkl] ADJ aritmético

Ariz. ABBR (*US*) = **Arizona**

Ark [ɑːk] N: **Noah's ~** el Arca *f* de Noé

Ark. ABBR (*US*) = **Arkansas**

arm [ɑːm] N (*Anat*) brazo ▸ VT armar; **~ in ~** cogidos del brazo; *see also* **arms**

armaments [ˈɑːməmənts] NPL (*weapons*) armamentos *mpl*

armchair [ˈɑːmtʃɛər] N sillón *m*, butaca

armed [ɑːmd] ADJ armado; **the ~ forces** las fuerzas armadas

armed robbery N robo a mano armada

Armenia [ɑːˈmiːnɪə] N Armenia

Armenian [ɑːˈmiːnɪən] ADJ armenio ▸ N armenio(-a); (*Ling*) armenio

armful [ˈɑːmful] N brazada

armistice [ˈɑːmɪstɪs] N armisticio

armour, (*US*) **armor** [ˈɑːmər] N armadura

armoured car, (*US*) **armored car** N coche *m* or carro (*Lam*) blindado

armoury, (*US*) **armory** [ˈɑːmərɪ] N arsenal *m*

armpit [ˈɑːmpɪt] N sobaco, axila

armrest [ˈɑːmrɛst] N reposabrazos *m inv*, brazo

arms [ɑːmz] NPL (*weapons*) armas *fpl*; (*Heraldry*) escudo *sg*

arms control N control *m* de armamentos

arms race N carrera de armamentos

army [ˈɑːmɪ] N ejército; (*fig*) multitud *f*

A road N (*Brit*) ≈ carretera *f* nacional

aroma [əˈrəumə] N aroma *m*, fragancia

aromatherapy [ərəuməˈθɛrəpɪ] N aromaterapia

aromatic [ærəˈmætɪk] ADJ aromático, fragante

arose [əˈrəuz] PT *of* **arise**

around [əˈraund] ADV alrededor; (*in the area*) a la redonda ▸ PREP alrededor de

arousal [əˈrauzəl] N (*sexual*) excitación *f*; (*of feelings, interest*) despertar *m*

arouse [əˈrauz] VT despertar; (*anger*) provocar

arrange [əˈreɪndʒ] VT arreglar, ordenar; (*programme*) organizar; (*appointment*) concertar ▸ VI: **we have arranged for a taxi to pick you up** hemos organizado todo para que le recoja un taxi; **to ~ to do sth** quedar en hacer algo; **it was arranged that ...** se quedó en que ...

arrangement [əˈreɪndʒmənt] N arreglo; (*agreement*) acuerdo; **arrangements** NPL (*plans*) planes *mpl*, medidas *fpl*; (*preparations*) preparativos *mpl*; **to come to an ~ (with sb)** llegar a un acuerdo (con algn); **by ~** a convenir; **I'll make arrangements for you to be met** haré los preparativos para que le estén esperando

arrant [ˈærənt] ADJ: **~ nonsense** una verdadera tontería

array [əˈreɪ] N (*Comput*) matriz *f*; **~ of** (*things*) serie *f* or colección *f* de; (*people*) conjunto de

arrears [əˈrɪəz] NPL atrasos *mpl*; **in ~** (*Comm*) en mora; **to be in ~ with one's rent** estar retrasado en el pago del alquiler

arrest [əˈrɛst] VT detener; (*sb's attention*) llamar ▸ N detención *f*; **under ~** detenido

arresting [əˈrɛstɪŋ] ADJ (*fig*) llamativo

arrival [əˈraɪvəl] N llegada, arribo (*Lam*); **new ~** recién llegado(-a)

arrive [əˈraɪv] VI llegar, arribar (*Lam*)
▸ **arrive at** VT FUS (*decision, solution*) llegar a

arrogance [ˈærəgəns] N arrogancia, prepotencia (*Lam*)

arrogant [ˈærəgənt] ADJ arrogante, prepotente (*Lam*)

arrow [ˈærəu] N flecha

arse [ɑːs] N (*Brit inf!*) culo, trasero

arsenal [ˈɑːsɪnl] N arsenal *m*

arsenic [ˈɑːsnɪk] N arsénico

arson [ˈɑːsn] N incendio provocado

art [ɑːt] N arte *m*; (*skill*) destreza; (*technique*) técnica; **Arts** NPL (*Scol*) Letras *fpl*; **work of ~** obra de arte

art and design N (*Brit Scol*) arte *m* y diseño, dibujo

art college N escuela *f* de Bellas Artes

artefact [ˈɑːtɪfækt] N artefacto

arterial [ɑːˈtɪərɪəl] ADJ (*Anat*) arterial; (*road etc*) principal

artery [ˈɑːtərɪ] N (*Med, road etc*) arteria

artful ['ɑːtful] ADJ (*cunning: person, trick*) mañoso

art gallery N pinacoteca, museo de pintura; (*Comm*) galería de arte

arthritis [ɑːˈθraɪtɪs] N artritis f

artichoke ['ɑːtɪtʃəuk] N alcachofa; **Jerusalem ~** aguaturma

article ['ɑːtɪkl] N artículo, objeto, cosa; (*in newspaper*) artículo; **articles** NPL (*BRIT Law: training*) contrato *sg* de aprendizaje; **articles of clothing** prendas *fpl* de vestir

articles of association NPL (*Comm*) estatutos *mpl* sociales, escritura social

articulate ADJ [ɑːˈtɪkjulɪt] (*speech*) claro; (*person*) que se expresa bien ▸ VI [ɑːˈtɪkjuleɪt] articular ▸ VT [ɑːˈtɪkjuleɪt] expresar

articulated lorry N (*BRIT*) trailer *m*

artifice ['ɑːtɪfɪs] N artificio, truco

artificial [ɑːtɪˈfɪʃəl] ADJ artificial; (*teeth etc*) postizo

artificial insemination N inseminación f artificial

artificial intelligence N inteligencia artificial

artificial respiration N respiración f artificial

artillery [ɑːˈtɪləri] N artillería

artisan ['ɑːtɪzæn] N artesano(-a)

artist ['ɑːtɪst] N artista *mf*; (*Mus*) intérprete *mf*

artistic [ɑːˈtɪstɪk] ADJ artístico

artistry ['ɑːtɪstrɪ] N arte *m*, habilidad f (artística)

artless ['ɑːtlɪs] ADJ (*innocent*) natural, sencillo; (*clumsy*) torpe

art school N escuela de bellas artes

artwork ['ɑːtwəːk] N material *m* gráfico

arty ['ɑːtɪ] ADJ artistoide

ARV N ABBR (= *American Revised Version*) traducción americana de la Biblia

AS N ABBR (*US Scol*) = **Associate in Science**

(KEYWORD)

as [æz] CONJ **1** (*referring to time: while*) mientras; (*: when*) cuando; **she wept as she told her story** lloraba mientras contaba lo que le ocurrió; **as the years go by** con el paso de los años, a medida que pasan los años; **he came in as I was leaving** entró cuando me marchaba; **as from tomorrow** a partir de *or* desde mañana

2 (*in comparisons*): **as big as** tan grande como; **twice as big as** el doble de grande que; **as much money/many books as** tanto dinero/ tantos libros como; **as soon as** en cuanto, no bien (*LAm*)

3 (*since, because*) como, ya que; **as I don't speak German I can't understand him** como no hablo alemán no le entiendo, no le entiendo ya que no hablo alemán

4 (*although*): **much as I like them, ...** aunque me gustan, ...

5 (*referring to manner, way*): **do as you wish** haz lo que quieras; **as she said** como dijo; **it's on the left as you go in** según se entra, a la izquierda

6 (*concerning*): **as for** *or* **to that** por *or* en lo que respecta a eso

7: **as if** *or* **though** como si; **he looked as if he was ill** parecía como si estuviera enfermo, tenía aspecto de enfermo; *see also* **long; such; well**

▸ PREP (*in the capacity of*): **he works as a barman** trabaja de barman; **as chairman of the company, he ...** como presidente de la compañía, ...; **he gave it to me as a present** me lo dio de regalo

ASA N ABBR (= *American Standards Association*) instituto de normalización; (*BRIT*: = *Advertising Standards Association*) departamento de control de la publicidad; (= *Amateur Swimming Association*) federación amateur de natación

a.s.a.p. ABBR (= *as soon as possible*) cuanto antes, lo más pronto posible

asbestos [æzˈbestəs] N asbesto, amianto

ascend [əˈsend] VT subir, ascender

ascendancy [əˈsendənsɪ] N ascendiente *m*, dominio

ascendant [əˈsendənt]: **to be in the ~** estar en auge, ir ganando predominio

Ascension [əˈsenʃən] N: **the ~** la Ascensión

Ascension Island N Isla Ascensión

ascent [əˈsent] N subida; (*slope*) cuesta, pendiente f; (*of plane*) ascenso

ascertain [æsəˈteɪn] VT averiguar

ascetic [əˈsetɪk] ADJ ascético

asceticism [əˈsetɪsɪzəm] N ascetismo

ASCII ['æskiː] N ABBR (= *American Standard Code for Information Interchange*) ASCII

ascribe [əˈskraɪb] VT: **to ~ sth to** atribuir algo a

ASCU N ABBR (*US*) = **Association of State Colleges and Universities**

ASE N ABBR = **American Stock Exchange**

ASH [æʃ] N ABBR (*BRIT*: = *Action on Smoking and Health*) organización anti-tabaco

ash [æʃ] N ceniza; (*tree*) fresno

ashamed [əˈʃeɪmd] ADJ avergonzado; **to be ~ of** avergonzarse de

ashcan ['æʃkæn] N (*US*) cubo *or* bote *m* (*LAm*) de la basura

ashen ['æʃn] ADJ pálido

ashore [əˈʃɔːr] ADV en tierra; (*swim etc*) a tierra

ashtray ['æʃtreɪ] N cenicero

Ash Wednesday N miércoles *m* de Ceniza

Asia ['eɪʃə] N Asia

Asian ['eɪʃən], **Asiatic** [eɪsɪˈætɪk] ADJ, N asiático(-a) *m/f*

aside [ə'saɪd] ADV a un lado ▶ N aparte *m*;
~ **from** *prep (as well as)* aparte *or* además de
ask [ɑːsk] VT *(question)* preguntar; *(demand)*
pedir; *(invite)* invitar ▶ VI: **to ~ about sth**
preguntar acerca de algo; **to ~ sb sth/to do**
sth preguntar algo a algn/pedir a algn que
haga algo; **to ~ sb about sth** preguntar algo
a algn; **to ~ (sb) a question** hacer una
pregunta (a algn); **to ~ sb the time**
preguntar la hora a algn; **to ~ sb out to**
dinner invitar a cenar a algn
▶ **ask after** VT FUS preguntar por
▶ **ask for** VT FUS pedir; **it's just asking for**
trouble *or* **for it** es buscarse problemas
askance [ə'skɑːns] ADV: **to look ~ at sb** mirar
con recelo a algn
askew [ə'skjuː] ADV sesgado, ladeado
asking price N *(Comm)* precio inicial
asleep [ə'sliːp] ADJ dormido; **to fall ~**
dormirse, quedarse dormido
ASLEF ['æzlɛf] N ABBR *(BRIT: = Associated Society*
of Locomotive Engineers and Firemen) sindicato de
ferroviarios
AS level N ABBR *(BRIT Scol: = Advanced Subsidiary*
level) título intermedio entre los "GCSEs" y los "A
levels"
asp [æsp] N áspid *m*
asparagus [əs'pærəgəs] N espárragos *mpl*
ASPCA N ABBR = **American Society for the**
Prevention of Cruelty to Animals
aspect ['æspɛkt] N aspecto, apariencia;
(direction in which a building etc faces)
orientación *f*
aspersions [əs'pə:ʃənz] NPL: **to cast ~ on**
difamar a, calumniar a
asphalt ['æsfælt] N asfalto
asphyxiate [æs'fɪksɪeɪt] VT asfixiar
asphyxiation [aesfɪksɪ'eɪʃən] N asfixia
aspirate ['æspəreɪt] VT aspirar ▶ ADJ
['æspərɪt] aspirado
aspirations [æspə'reɪʃənz] NPL aspiraciones
fpl; (ambition) ambición *f*
aspire [əs'paɪə^r] VI: **to ~ to** aspirar a,
ambicionar
aspirin ['æsprɪn] N aspirina
aspiring [əs'paɪərɪŋ] ADJ: **an ~ actor** un
aspirante a actor
ass [æs] N asno, burro; *(inf)* imbécil *mf; (US*
inf!) culo, trasero
assailant [ə'seɪlənt] N agresor(a) *m/f*
assassin [ə'sæsɪn] N asesino(-a)
assassinate [ə'sæsɪneɪt] VT asesinar
assassination [əsæsɪ'neɪʃən] N asesinato
assault [ə'sɔːlt] N *(gen: attack)* asalto; *(Law)*
agresión *f* ▶ VT asaltar, agredir; *(sexually)*
violar
assemble [ə'sɛmbl] VT reunir, juntar; *(Tech)*
montar ▶ VI reunirse, juntarse
assembly [ə'sɛmblɪ] N *(meeting)* reunión *f*,

asamblea; *(parliament)* parlamento;
(construction) montaje *m*
assembly language N *(Comput)* lenguaje *m*
ensamblador
assembly line N cadena de montaje
Assembly Member N *(in Wales)* miembro *mf*
de la Asamblea Nacional (de Gales)
assent [ə'sɛnt] N asentimiento, aprobación *f*
▶ VI consentir, asentir; **to ~ (to sth)**
consentir (en algo)
assert [ə'sə:t] VT afirmar; *(insist on)* hacer
valer; **to ~ o.s.** imponerse
assertion [ə'sə:ʃən] N afirmación *f*
assertive [ə'sə:tɪv] ADJ enérgico, agresivo,
perentorio
assess [ə'sɛs] VT valorar, calcular; *(tax,*
damages) fijar; *(property etc: for tax)* gravar
assessment [ə'sɛsmənt] N valoración *f*;
gravamen *m; (judgment)*: ~ **(of)** juicio (sobre)
assessor [ə'sɛsə^r] N asesor(a) *m/f; (of tax)*
tasador(a) *m/f*
asset ['æsɛt] N posesión *f; (quality)* ventaja;
assets NPL *(funds)* activo *sg*, fondos *mpl*
asset-stripping ['æsɛt'strɪpɪŋ] N *(Comm)*
acaparamiento de activos
assiduous [ə'sɪdjuəs] ADJ asiduo
assign [ə'saɪn] VT *(date)* fijar; *(task)* asignar;
(resources) destinar; *(property)* traspasar
assignment [ə'saɪnmənt] N asignación *f;*
(task) tarea
assimilate [ə'sɪmɪleɪt] VT asimilar
assimilation [əsɪmɪ'leɪʃən] N asimilación *f*
assist [ə'sɪst] VT ayudar
assistance [ə'sɪstəns] N ayuda, auxilio
assistant [ə'sɪstənt] N ayudante *mf; (BRIT:*
also: **shop assistant)** dependiente(-a) *m/f*
assistant manager N subdirector(a) *m/f*
assizes [ə'saɪzɪz] NPL sesión *f* de un tribunal
associate *[adj, n ə'səʊʃɪɪt, vt, vi ə'səʊʃɪeɪt]* ADJ
asociado ▶ N socio(-a), colega *mf; (in crime)*
cómplice *mf; (member)* miembro(-a) ▶ VT
asociar; *(ideas)* relacionar ▶ VI: **to ~ with sb**
tratar con algn; ~ **director** subdirector(a)
m/f; **associated company** compañía
afiliada
association [əsəʊsɪ'eɪʃən] N asociación *f;*
(Comm) sociedad *f;* **in ~ with** en asociación
con
association football N *(BRIT)* fútbol *m*
assorted [ə'sɔːtɪd] ADJ surtido, variado; **in ~**
sizes en distintos tamaños
assortment [ə'sɔːtmənt] N *(of shapes, colours)*
surtido; *(of books)* colección *f; (of people)*
mezcla
Asst. ABBR = **assistant**
assuage [ə'sweɪdʒ] VT mitigar
assume [ə'sjuːm] VT *(suppose)* suponer;
(responsibilities etc) asumir; *(attitude, name)*
adoptar, tomar

assumed name [ə'sju:md-] N nombre *m* falso

assumption [ə'sʌmpʃən] N (*supposition*) suposición *f*, presunción *f*; (*act*) asunción *f*; **on the ~ that** suponiendo que

assurance [ə'ʃuərəns] N garantía, promesa; (*confidence*) confianza, aplomo; (BRIT: *insurance*) seguro; **I can give you no assurances** no puedo hacerle ninguna promesa

assure [ə'ʃuər] VT asegurar

assured [ə'ʃuəd] ADJ seguro

assuredly [ə'ʃuərɪdlɪ] ADV indudablemente

AST ABBR (= *Atlantic Standard Time*) hora oficial del este del Canadá

asterisk ['æstərɪsk] N asterisco

astern [ə'stə:n] ADV a popa

asteroid ['æstərɔɪd] N asteroide *m*

asthma ['æsmə] N asma

asthmatic [æs'mætɪk] ADJ, N asmático(-a) *m/f*

astigmatism [ə'stɪgmətɪzəm] N astigmatismo

astir [ə'stə:r] ADV en acción

astonish [ə'stɒnɪʃ] VT asombrar, pasmar

astonished [ə'stɒnɪʃt] ADJ estupefacto, pasmado; **to be ~ (at)** asombrarse (de)

astonishing [ə'stɒnɪʃɪŋ] ADJ asombroso, pasmoso; **I find it ~ that ...** me asombra *or* pasma que ...

astonishingly [ə'stɒnɪʃɪŋlɪ] ADV increíblemente, asombrosamente

astonishment [ə'stɒnɪʃmənt] N asombro, sorpresa; **to my ~** con gran sorpresa mía

astound [ə'staund] VT asombrar, pasmar

astounding [ə'staundɪŋ] ADJ asombroso

astray [ə'streɪ] ADV: **to go ~** extraviarse; **to lead ~** llevar por mal camino; **to go ~ in one's calculations** equivocarse en sus cálculos

astride [ə'straɪd] PREP a caballo *or* horcajadas sobre

astringent [əs'trɪndʒənt] ADJ, N astringente *m*

astrologer [əs'trɒlədʒər] N astrólogo(-a)

astrology [əs'trɒlədʒɪ] N astrología

astronaut ['æstrənɔ:t] N astronauta *mf*

astronomer [əs'trɒnəmər] N astrónomo(-a)

astronomical [æstrə'nɒmɪkəl] ADJ astronómico

astronomy [əs'trɒnəmɪ] N astronomía

astrophysics ['æstrəu'fɪzɪks] N astrofísica

astute [əs'tju:t] ADJ astuto

asunder [ə'sʌndər] ADV: **to tear ~** hacer pedazos

ASV N ABBR (= *American Standard Version*) traducción de la Biblia

asylum [ə'saɪləm] N (*refuge*) asilo; (*hospital*) manicomio; **to seek political ~** pedir asilo político

asymmetric [eɪsɪ'mɛtrɪk], **asymmetrical** [eɪsɪ'mɛtrɪkl] ADJ asimétrico

(KEYWORD)

at [æt] PREP **1** (*referring to position*) en; (*direction*) a; **at the top** en lo alto; **at home/school** en casa/la escuela; **to look at sth/sb** mirar algo/a algn

2 (*referring to time*): **at four o'clock** a las cuatro; **at night** por la noche; **at Christmas** en Navidad; **at times** a veces

3 (*referring to rates, speed etc*): **at £1 a kilo** a una libra el kilo; **two at a time** de dos en dos; **at 50 km/h** a 50 km/h

4 (*referring to manner*): **at a stroke** de un golpe; **at peace** en paz

5 (*referring to activity*): **to be at work** estar trabajando; (*in office*) estar en el trabajo; **to play at cowboys** jugar a los vaqueros; **to be good at sth** ser bueno en algo

6 (*referring to cause*): **shocked/surprised/ annoyed at sth** asombrado/sorprendido/ fastidiado por algo; **I went at his suggestion** fui a instancias suyas

▸ N (*symbol @*) arroba

ate [ɛt, eɪt] PT *of* **eat**

atheism ['eɪθɪɪzəm] N ateísmo

atheist ['eɪθɪɪst] N ateo(-a)

Athenian [ə'θi:nɪən] ADJ, N ateniense *mf*

Athens ['æθɪnz] N Atenas *f*

athlete ['æθli:t] N atleta *mf*

athletic [æθ'lɛtɪk] ADJ atlético

athletics [æθ'lɛtɪks] N atletismo

Atlantic [ət'læntɪk] ADJ atlántico ▸ N: **the ~ (Ocean)** el (Océano) Atlántico

atlas ['ætləs] N atlas *m inv*

Atlas Mountains NPL: **the ~** el Atlas

A.T.M. N ABBR (= *Automated Telling Machine*) cajero automático

atmosphere ['ætməsfɪər] N (*air*) atmósfera; (*fig*) ambiente *m*

atom ['ætəm] N átomo N bomba atómica

atomic [ə'tɒmɪk] ADJ atómico

atomic power N energía atómica

atomizer ['ætəmaɪzər] N atomizador *m*

atone [ə'təun] VI: **to ~ for** expiar

atonement [ə'təunmənt] N expiación *f*

A to Z® N guía alfabética; (*map*) callejero

ATP N ABBR (= *Association of Tennis Professionals*) sindicato de jugadores de tenis profesionales

atrocious [ə'trəuʃəs] ADJ atroz; (*fig*) horrible, infame

atrocity [ə'trɒsɪtɪ] N atrocidad *f*

atrophy ['ætrəfɪ] N atrofia ▸ VI atrofiarse

attach [ə'tætʃ] VT sujetar; (*stick*) pegar; (*document, email, letter*) adjuntar; **to be attached to sb/sth** (*like*) tener cariño a algn/algo; **the attached letter** la carta adjunta

attaché [ə'tæʃeɪ] N agregado(-a)

attaché case N (BRIT) maletín m

attachment [ə'tætʃmənt] N (tool) accesorio; (Comput) archivo o documento adjunto; (love): ~ **(to)** apego (a), cariño (a)

attack [ə'tæk] VT (Mil) atacar; (criminal) agredir, asaltar; (criticize) criticar; (task etc) emprender ▶ N ataque m, asalto; (on sb's life) atentado; (fig: criticism) crítica; **heart ~** infarto (de miocardio)

attacker [ə'tækər] N agresor(a) m/f, asaltante mf

attain [ə'teɪn] VT (also: **attain to**) alcanzar; (achieve) lograr, conseguir

attainments [ə'teɪnmənts] NPL (skill) talento sg

attempt [ə'tɛmpt] N tentativa, intento; (attack) atentado ▶ VT intentar, tratar de; **he made no ~ to help** ni siquiera intentó ayudar

attempted [ə'tɛmptɪd] ADJ: ~ **murder/ burglary/suicide** tentativa or intento de asesinato/robo/suicidio

attend [ə'tɛnd] VT asistir a; (patient) atender ▶ **attend to** VT FUS (needs, affairs etc) ocuparse de; (speech etc) prestar atención a; (customer) atender a

attendance [ə'tɛndəns] N asistencia, presencia; (people present) concurrencia

attendant [ə'tɛndənt] N sirviente(-a) m/f, ayudante mf; (Theat) acomodador(a) m/f ▶ ADJ concomitante

attention [ə'tɛnʃən] N atención f ▶ EXCL (Mil) ¡firme(s)!; **for the ~ of ...** (Admin) a la atención de ...; **it has come to my ~ that ...** me he enterado de que ...

attentive [ə'tɛntɪv] ADJ atento; (polite) cortés

attenuate [ə'tɛnjueɪt] VT atenuar

attest [ə'tɛst] VI: **to ~ to** dar fe de

attic ['ætɪk] N desván m, altillo (LAM), entretecho (LAM)

attitude ['ætɪtjuːd] N (gen) actitud f; (disposition) disposición f

attorney [ə'təːnɪ] N (US: lawyer) abogado(-a); (having proxy) apoderado

Attorney General N (BRIT) ≈ fiscal mf general del Estado; (US) ≈ ministro(-a) de Justicia

attract [ə'trækt] VT atraer; (attention) llamar

attraction [ə'trækʃən] N (gen) encanto, atractivo; (Physics) atracción f; (towards sth) atracción f

attractive [ə'træktɪv] ADJ atractivo

attribute ['ætrɪbjuːt] N atributo ▶ VT [ə'trɪbjuːt]: **to ~ sth to** atribuir algo a; (accuse) achacar algo a

attrition [ə'trɪʃən] N: **war of ~** guerra de agotamiento or desgaste

Atty. Gen. ABBR = **Attorney General**

ATV N ABBR (= all terrain vehicle) vehículo todo terreno

atypical [eɪ'tɪpɪkl] ADJ atípico

AU N ABBR (= African Union) UA f (= Unión Africana)

aubergine ['əʊbəʒiːn] N (BRIT) berenjena; (colour) morado

auburn ['ɔːbən] ADJ color castaño rojizo

auction ['ɔːkʃən] N (also: **sale by auction**) subasta ▶ VT subastar

auctioneer [ɔːkʃə'nɪər] N subastador(a) m/f

auction room N sala de subastas

audacious [ɔː'deɪʃəs] ADJ (bold) audaz, osado; (impudent) atrevido, descarado

audacity [ɔː'dæsɪtɪ] N audacia, atrevimiento; (pej) descaro

audible ['ɔːdɪbl] ADJ audible, que se puede oír

audience ['ɔːdɪəns] N auditorio; (gathering) público; (Radio) radioescuchas mpl; (TV) telespectadores mpl; (interview) audiencia

audio-typist ['ɔːdɪəʊ'taɪpɪst] N mecanógrafo(-a) de dictáfono

audiovisual [ɔːdɪəʊ'vɪzjuəl] ADJ audiovisual

audiovisual aid N ayuda or medio audiovisual

audit ['ɔːdɪt] VT revisar, intervenir

audition [ɔː'dɪʃən] N audición f ▶ VI: **to ~ for the part of** hacer una audición para el papel de

auditor ['ɔːdɪtər] N interventor(a) m/f, censor(a) m/f de cuentas

auditorium [ɔːdɪ'tɔːrɪəm] N auditorio

Aug. ABBR (= August) ag.

augment [ɔːg'mɛnt] VT, VI aumentar

augur ['ɔːgər] VI: **it augurs well** es de buen agüero

August ['ɔːgəst] N agosto; see also **July**

august [ɔː'gʌst] ADJ augusto

aunt [ɑːnt] N tía

auntie, aunty ['ɑːntɪ] N DIMINUTIVE of **aunt**

au pair ['əʊ'pɛər] N (also: **au pair girl**) chica f au pair

aura ['ɔːrə] N aura; (atmosphere) ambiente m

auspices ['ɔːspɪsɪz] NPL: **under the ~ of** bajo los auspicios de

auspicious [ɔːs'pɪʃəs] ADJ propicio, de buen augurio

austere [ɔs'tɪər] ADJ austero; (manner) adusto

austerity [ɔ'stɛrɪtɪ] N austeridad f

Australasia [ɔːstrə'leɪzɪə] N Australasia

Australia [ɔs'treɪlɪə] N Australia

Australian [ɔs'treɪlɪən] ADJ, N australiano(-a) m/f

Austria ['ɔstrɪə] N Austria

Austrian ['ɔstrɪən] ADJ, N austríaco(-a) m/f

AUT N ABBR (BRIT: = Association of University Teachers) sindicato de profesores de universidad

authentic [ɔː'θɛntɪk] ADJ auténtico

authenticate [ɔ:'θentɪkeɪt] VT autentificar
authenticity [ɔ:θen'tɪsɪtɪ] N autenticidad f
author ['ɔ:θəʳ] N autor(a) m/f
authoritarian [ɔ:θɔrɪ'tɛərɪən] ADJ
autoritario
authoritative [ɔ:'θɔrɪtətɪv] ADJ autorizado;
(*manner*) autoritario
authority [ɔ:'θɔrɪtɪ] N autoridad f; **the
authorities** NPL las autoridades; **to have ~
to do sth** tener autoridad para hacer algo
authorization [ɔ:θəraɪ'zeɪʃən] N
autorización f
authorize ['ɔ:θəraɪz] VT autorizar
authorized capital N (*Comm*) capital m
autorizado or social
autistic [ɔ:'tɪstɪk] ADJ autista
auto ['ɔ:təu] N (*US*) coche m, carro (*LAM*), auto
(*LAM*), automóvil m
autobiographical [ɔ:təbaɪə'græfɪkəl] ADJ
autobiográfico
autobiography [ɔ:təbaɪ'ɔgrəfɪ] N
autobiografía
autocratic [ɔ:tə'krætɪk] ADJ autocrático
Autocue® ['ɔ:təukju:] N autocue m,
teleapuntador m
autograph ['ɔ:təgrɑ:f] N autógrafo ▶ VT
firmar; (*photo etc*) dedicar
autoimmune [ɔ:təuɪ'mju:n] ADJ
autoinmune
automat ['ɔ:təmæt] N (*US*) restaurante m de
autoservicio
automate ['ɔ:təmeɪt] VT automatizar
automated ['ɔ:təmeɪtɪd] ADJ automatizado
automatic [ɔ:tə'mætɪk] ADJ automático ▶ N
(*gun*) pistola automática; (*washing machine*)
lavadora
automatically [ɔ:tə'mætɪklɪ] ADV
automáticamente
automatic data processing N proceso
automático de datos
automation [ɔ:tə'meɪʃən] N
automatización f
automaton [ɔ:'tɔmətən] (*pl* **automata** [-tə])
N autómata
automobile ['ɔ:təməbi:l] N (*US*) coche m,
carro (*LAM*), auto (*LAM*), automóvil m
autonomous [ɔ:'tɔnəməs] ADJ autónomo
autonomy [ɔ:'tɔnəmɪ] N autonomía
autopsy ['ɔ:tɔpsɪ] N autopsia
autumn ['ɔ:təm] N otoño
auxiliary [ɔ:g'zɪlɪərɪ] ADJ auxiliar
AV N ABBR (= *Authorized Version*) *traducción inglesa
de la Biblia* ▶ ABBR = **audiovisual**
Av. ABBR (= *avenue*) Av., Avda
avail [ə'veɪl] VT: **to ~ o.s. of** aprovechar(se)
de, valerse de ▶ N: **to no ~** en vano, sin
resultado
availability [əveɪlə'bɪlɪtɪ] N disponibilidad f
available [ə'veɪləbl] ADJ disponible;

(*obtainable*) asequible; **to make sth ~ to sb**
poner algo a la disposición de algn; **is the
manager ~?** ¿está libre el gerente?
avalanche ['ævəlɑ:nʃ] N alud m, avalancha
avant-garde ['ævɑ̃'gɑ:d] ADJ de vanguardia
avarice ['ævərɪs] N avaricia
avaricious [ævə'rɪʃəs] ADJ avaricioso
avdp. ABBR = **avoirdupois**
Ave. ABBR (= *avenue*) Av., Avda
avenge [ə'vendʒ] VT vengar
avenue ['ævənju:] N avenida; (*fig*) camino, vía
average ['ævərɪdʒ] N promedio, media ▶ ADJ
(*mean*) medio; (*ordinary*) regular, corriente
▶ VT alcanzar un promedio de; **on ~** por
término medio
▶ **average out** VI: **to ~ out at** salir a un
promedio de
averse [ə'və:s] ADJ: **to be ~ to sth/doing** sentir
aversión or antipatía por algo/por hacer
aversion [ə'və:ʃən] N aversión f, repugnancia
avert [ə'və:t] VT prevenir; (*blow*) desviar;
(*one's eyes*) apartar
aviary ['eɪvɪərɪ] N pajarera
aviation [eɪvɪ'eɪʃən] N aviación f
aviator ['eɪvɪeɪtəʳ] N aviador(a) m/f
avid ['ævɪd] ADJ ávido, ansioso
avidly ['ævɪdlɪ] ADV ávidamente, con avidez
avocado [ævə'kɑ:dəu] N (*BRIT: also:* **avocado
pear**) aguacate m, palta (*LAM*)
avoid [ə'vɔɪd] VT evitar, eludir
avoidable [ə'vɔɪdəbl] ADJ evitable, eludible
avoidance [ə'vɔɪdəns] N evasión f
avow [ə'vau] VT prometer
avowal [ə'vauəl] N promesa, voto
avowed [ə'vaud] ADJ declarado
AVP N ABBR (*US*) = **assistant vice-president**
avuncular [ə'vʌŋkjuləʳ] ADJ paternal
AWACS ['eɪwæks] N ABBR (= *airborne warning
and control system*) AWACS m
await [ə'weɪt] VT esperar, aguardar; **long
awaited** largamente esperado
awake [ə'weɪk] (*pt* **awoke**, *pp* **awoken** or
awaked) ADJ despierto ▶ VT despertar ▶ VI
despertarse; **to be ~** estar despierto
awakening [ə'weɪknɪŋ] N despertar m
award [ə'wɔ:d] N (*prize*) premio; (*medal*)
condecoración f; (*Law*) fallo, sentencia; (*act*)
concesión f ▶ VT (*prize*) otorgar, conceder;
(*Law: damages*) adjudicar
aware [ə'wɛəʳ] ADJ consciente; (*awake*)
despierto; (*informed*) enterado; **to become ~
of** darse cuenta de, enterarse de; **I am fully
~ that** sé muy bien que
awareness [ə'wɛənɪs] N conciencia,
conocimiento
awash [ə'wɔʃ] ADJ inundado
away [ə'weɪ] ADV (*gen*) fuera; (*far away*) lejos;
two kilometres ~ a dos kilómetros (de
distancia); **two hours ~ by car** a dos horas

en coche; **the holiday was two weeks ~**
faltaban dos semanas para las vacaciones;
~ from lejos de, fuera de; **he's ~ for a week**
estará ausente una semana; **he's ~ in**
Barcelona está en Barcelona; **to take ~**
llevar(se); **to work/pedal ~** seguir
trabajando/pedaleando; **to fade ~**
desvanecerse; (*sound*) apagarse

away game N (*Sport*) partido de fuera

awe [ɔː] N respeto, admiración f respetuosa

awe-inspiring ['ɔːɪnspaɪərɪŋ] ADJ
imponente, pasmoso

awesome ['ɔːsəm] ADJ (*esp US: excellent*)
formidable

awestruck ['ɔːstrʌk] ADJ pasmado

awful ['ɔːfəl] ADJ terrible; **an ~ lot of** (*people,*
cars, dogs) la mar de, muchísimos

awfully ['ɔːfəlɪ] ADV (*very*) terriblemente

awhile [ə'waɪl] ADV (durante) un rato, algún
tiempo

awkward ['ɔːkwəd] ADJ (*clumsy*) desmañado,
torpe; (*shape, situation*) incómodo; (*difficult:*
question) difícil; (: *problem*) complicado

awkwardness ['ɔːkwədnɪs] N (*clumsiness*)
torpeza; (*of situation*) incomodidad f

awl [ɔːl] N lezna, subilla

awning ['ɔːnɪŋ] N (*of shop*) toldo; (*of window*
etc) marquesina

awoke [ə'wəuk] PT *of* **awake**

awoken [ə'wəukən] PP *of* **awake**

AWOL ['eɪwɔl] ABBR (*Mil etc*) = **absent**
without leave

awry [ə'raɪ] ADV: **to be ~** estar descolocado
or atravesado; **to go ~** salir mal, fracasar

axe, (*US*) **ax** [æks] N hacha ▸ VT (*employee*)
despedir; (*project etc*) cortar; (*jobs*) reducir;
to have an ~ to grind (*fig*) tener un interés
creado *or* algún fin interesado

axes ['æksiːz] NPL *of* **axis**

axiom ['æksɪəm] N axioma m

axiomatic [æksɪə'mætɪk] ADJ axiomático

axis ['æksɪs] (*pl* **axes** [-siːz]) N eje m

axle ['æksl] N eje m, árbol m

ay, aye [aɪ] EXCL (*yes*) sí; **the ayes** los que
votan a favor

AYH N ABBR = **American Youth Hostels**

AZ ABBR (*US*) = **Arizona**

azalea [ə'zeɪlɪə] N azalea

Azerbaijan [æzəbaɪ'dʒɑːn] N Azerbaiyán m

Azerbaijani [æzəbaɪ'dʒɑːnɪ], **Azeri** [ə'zɛərɪ]
ADJ, N azerbaiyano(-a), azerí mf

Azores [ə'zɔːz] NPL: **the ~** las (Islas)
Azores

AZT N ABBR (= *azidothymidine*) AZT m

Aztec ['æztɛk] ADJ, N azteca mf

azure ['eɪʒəʳ] ADJ celeste

Bb

B, b [bi:] N (*letter*) B, b *f*; (*Scol: mark*) N; (*Mus*):
B si *m*; **B for Benjamin**, (*US*) **B for Baker**
B de Barcelona; **B road** (*Brit Aut*) ≈ carretera
secundaria

b. ABBR = **born**

BA N ABBR = **British Academy**; (*Scol*)
= **Bachelor of Arts**; *see also* **bachelor's degree**

babble ['bæbl] VI farfullar

babe [beɪb] N criatura

baboon [bə'bu:n] N mandril *m*

baby ['beɪbɪ] N bebé *mf*; (*US inf: darling*) mi
amor

baby carriage N (*US*) cochecito

babyish ['beɪbɪɪʃ] ADJ infantil

baby-minder ['beɪbɪmaɪndər] N niñera *f*
(cualificada)

baby-sit ['beɪbɪsɪt] VI hacer de canguro

baby-sitter ['beɪbɪsɪtər] N canguro *mf*

baby wipe N toallita húmeda (*para bebés*)

bachelor ['bætʃələr] N soltero; **B~ of Arts/
Science (BA/BSc)** licenciado(-a) en Filosofía
y Letras/Ciencias

bachelor's degree N licenciatura; *ver nota*

> Se denomina *Bachelor's Degree* a la
> titulación que se recibe al finalizar el
> primer ciclo universitario, normalmente
> después de un período de estudio de tres
> o cuatro años. Las titulaciones más
> frecuentes son las de Letras, "*BA* (*Bachelor
> of Arts*)", Ciencias, "*BSc* (*Bachelor of Science*)",
> Educación, "*BEd* (*Bachelor of Education*)" y
> Derecho, "*LLB* (*Bachelor of Laws*)".

back [bæk] N (*of person*) espalda; (*of animal*)
lomo; (*of hand, page*) dorso; (*as opposed to front*)
parte *f* de atrás; (*of room*) fondo; (*of chair*)
respaldo; (*of page*) reverso; (*Football*) defensa
m ▶ VT (*candidate: also*: **back up**) respaldar,
apoyar; (*horse: at races*) apostar a; (*car*) dar
marcha atrás a *or* con ▶ VI (*car etc*) dar marcha
atrás ▶ ADJ (*in compounds: garden, room*) de atrás
▶ ADV (*not forward*) (hacia) atrás; **to have
one's ~ to the wall** (*fig*) estar entre la espada
y la pared; **to break the ~ of a job** hacer lo
más difícil de un trabajo; **~ to front** al revés;

**at the ~ of my mind was the thought that
…** en el fondo tenía la idea de que …; **he's ~**
(*returned*) ha vuelto; **~ seats/wheels** (*Aut*)
asientos *mpl* traseros, ruedas *fpl* traseras;
~ garden/room jardín *m*/habitación *f* de
atrás; **~ payments** pagos *mpl* con efecto
retroactivo; **~ rent** renta atrasada; **to take a
~ seat** (*fig*) pasar a segundo plano; **he ran ~**
volvió corriendo; **throw the ball ~**
(*restitution*) devuelve la pelota; **can I have it
~?** ¿me lo devuelve?; **he called ~** (*again*)
volvió a llamar; **~ and forth** de acá para allá;
as far ~ as the 13th century ya en el siglo
XIII; **when will you be ~?** ¿cuándo volverá?
▶ **back down** VI echarse atrás
▶ **back on to** VT FUS: **the house backs on to
the golf course** por atrás la casa da al campo
de golf
▶ **back out** VI (*of promise*) volverse atrás
▶ **back up** VT (*support: person*) apoyar,
respaldar; (: *theory*) defender; (: *car*) dar
marcha atrás a; (*Comput*) hacer una copia de
reserva de

backache ['bækeɪk] N dolor *m* de espalda

backbencher ['bæk'bentʃər] N (*Brit*) *diputado
sin cargo oficial en el gobierno o la oposición*

back benches NPL (*Brit*); *ver nota*

> Reciben el nombre genérico de *the back
> benches* los escaños más alejados del
> pasillo central en la Cámara de los
> Comunes del Parlamento británico, que
> son ocupados por los "*backbenchers*", los
> miembros de la cámara que no tienen
> cargo en el gobierno o en la oposición.

backbiting ['bækbaɪtɪŋ] N murmuración *f*

backbone ['bækbəʊn] N columna vertebral;
the ~ of the organization el pilar de la
organización

backchat ['bæktʃæt] N réplicas *fpl*

backcloth ['bækklɔθ] N telón *m* de fondo

backcomb ['bækkəʊm] VT cardar

backdate [bæk'deɪt] VT (*letter*) poner fecha
atrasada a; **backdated pay rise** aumento de
sueldo con efecto retroactivo

back door N puerta f trasera

backdrop ['bækdrɔp] N = **backcloth**

backer ['bækə^r] N partidario(-a); (*Comm*) promotor(a) *m/f*

backfire [bæk'faɪə^r] VI (*Aut*) petardear; (*plans*) fallar, salir mal

backgammon ['bækgæmən] N backgammon *m*

background ['bækgraund] N fondo; (*of events*) antecedentes *mpl*; (*basic knowledge*) bases *fpl*; (*experience*) conocimientos *mpl*, educación f ▶ CPD (*noise, music*) de fondo; (*Comput*) secundario; ~ **reading** lectura de preparación; **family** ~ origen *m*, antecedentes *mpl* familiares

backhand ['bækhænd] N (*Tennis: also:* **backhand stroke**) revés *m*

backhanded ['bæk'hændɪd] ADJ (*fig*) ambiguo, equívoco

backhander ['bæk'hændə^r] N (*Brit: bribe*) soborno

backing ['bækɪŋ] N (*fig*) apoyo, respaldo; (*Comm*) respaldo financiero; (*Mus*) acompañamiento

backlash ['bæklæʃ] N reacción f (en contra)

backlog ['bæklɔg] N: ~ **of work** trabajo atrasado

back number N (*of magazine etc*) número atrasado

backpack ['bækpæk] N mochila

backpacker ['bækpækə^r] N mochilero(-a)

back pay N atrasos *mpl*

backpedal ['bækpɛdl] VI (*fig*) volverse/ echarse atrás

backseat driver ['bæksiːt-] N *pasajero que se empeña en aconsejar al conductor*

backside ['bæksaɪd] N (*inf*) trasero

backslash ['bækslæʃ] N pleca, barra inversa

backslide ['bækslaɪd] VI reincidir, recaer

backspace ['bækspeɪs] VI (*in typing*) retroceder

backstage [bæk'steɪdʒ] ADV entre bastidores

back-street ['bækstriːt] ADJ de barrio; ~ **abortionist** *persona que practica abortos clandestinos*

backstroke ['bækstrəuk] N espalda

backtrack ['bæktræk] VI (*fig*) = **backpedal**

backup ['bækʌp] ADJ (*train, plane*) suplementario; (*Comput: disk, file*) de reserva ▶ N (*support*) apoyo; (*also:* **backup file**) copia de reserva; (*US: congestion*) embotellamiento, retención f

back-up lights NPL (*US*) luces *fpl* de marcha atrás

backward ['bækwəd] ADJ (*movement*) hacia atrás; (*person, country*) atrasado; (*shy*) tímido

backwardness ['bækwədnɪs] N atraso

backwards ['bækwədz] ADV (*move, go*) hacia atrás; (*read a list*) al revés; (*fall*) de espaldas;

to know sth ~ *or* (*US*) ~ **and forwards** (*inf*) saberse algo al dedillo

backwater ['bækwɔːtə^r] N (*fig*) lugar *m* atrasado *or* apartado

backyard [bæk'jɑːd] N patio trasero

bacon ['beɪkən] N tocino, bacón *m*, beicon *m*

bacteria [bæk'tɪərɪə] NPL bacterias *fpl*

bacteriology [bæktɪərɪ'ɔlədʒɪ] N bacteriología

bad [bæd] ADJ malo; (*serious*) grave; (*meat, food*) podrido, pasado; **to go** ~ pasarse; **to have a** ~ **time of it** pasarlo mal; **I feel** ~ **about it** (*guilty*) me siento culpable; ~ **debt** (*Comm*) cuenta incobrable; **in** ~ **faith** de mala fe

baddie, baddy ['bædɪ] N (*inf: Cine etc*) malo(-a)

bade [bæd, beɪd] PT *of* **bid**

badge [bædʒ] N insignia; (*metal badge*) chapa; (*of policeman*) placa; (*stick-on*) pegatina

badger ['bædʒə^r] N tejón *m*

badly ['bædlɪ] ADV (*work, dress etc*) mal; **to reflect** ~ **on sb** influir negativamente en la reputación de algn; ~ **wounded** gravemente herido; **he needs it** ~ le hace mucha falta; **to be** ~ **off (for money)** andar mal de dinero; **things are going** ~ las cosas van muy mal

bad-mannered ['bæd'mænəd] ADJ mal educado

badminton ['bædmɪntən] N bádminton *m*

bad-tempered ['bæd'tɛmpəd] ADJ de mal genio *or* carácter; (*temporarily*) de mal humor

baffle ['bæfl] VT desconcertar, confundir

baffling ['bæflɪŋ] ADJ incomprensible

bag [bæg] N bolsa; (*handbag*) bolso; (*satchel*) mochila; (*case*) maleta; (*of hunter*) caza ▶ VT (*inf: take*) coger (*SP*), agarrar (*LAM*), pescar; **bags of** (*inf: lots of*) un montón de; **to pack one's bags** hacer las maletas

bagful ['bægful] N saco (lleno)

baggage ['bægɪdʒ] N equipaje *m*

baggage allowance N límite *m* de equipaje

baggage claim, baggage reclaim N recogida de equipajes

baggy ['bægɪ] ADJ (*trousers*) ancho, holgado

Baghdad [bæg'dæd] N Bagdad *m*

bag lady N (*inf*) *mujer sin hogar cargada de bolsas*

bagpipes ['bægpaɪps] NPL gaita *sg*

bag-snatcher ['bægsnætʃə^r] N (*Brit*) ladrón(-ona) *m/f* de bolsos

bag-snatching ['bægsnætʃɪŋ] N (*Brit*) tirón *m* (de bolsos)

Bahamas [bə'hɑːməz] NPL: **the** ~ las (Islas) Bahama

Bahrain [bɑː'reɪn] N Bahrein *m*

bail [beɪl] N fianza ▶ VT (*prisoner: also:* **grant bail to**) poner en libertad bajo fianza; (*boat: also:* **bail out**) achicar; **on** ~ (*prisoner*) bajo fianza; **to be released on** ~ ser puesto en

libertad bajo fianza; **to ~ sb out** pagar la
fianza de algn; *see also* **bale**
bailiff ['beɪlɪf] N alguacil *m*
bailout ['beɪlaʊt] N rescate *m* (financiero)
bait [beɪt] N cebo ▶ VT poner el cebo en
bake [beɪk] VT cocer (al horno) ▶ VI (*cook*)
cocerse; (*be hot*) hacer un calor terrible
baked beans NPL judías *fpl* en salsa de
tomate
baked potato N patata al horno
baker ['beɪkə^r] N panadero(-a)
baker's dozen N docena del fraile
bakery ['beɪkərɪ] N (*for bread*) panadería; (*for
cakes*) pastelería
baking ['beɪkɪŋ] N (*act*) cocción *f*; (*batch*)
hornada
baking powder N levadura (en polvo)
baking tin N molde *m* (para horno)
balaclava [bælə'klɑːvə] N (*also:* **balaclava
helmet**) pasamontañas *m inv*
balance ['bæləns] N equilibrio; (*Comm: sum*)
balance *m*; (*remainder*) resto; (*scales*) balanza
▶ VT equilibrar; (*budget*) nivelar; (*account*)
saldar; (*compensate*) compensar; **~ of trade/
payments** balanza de comercio/pagos;
~ carried forward balance *m* pasado a
cuenta nueva; **~ brought forward** saldo de
hoja anterior; **to ~ the books** hacer el
balance
balanced ['bælənst] ADJ (*personality, diet*)
equilibrado; (*report*) objetivo
balance sheet N balance *m*
balcony ['bælkənɪ] N (*open*) balcón *m*; (*closed*)
galería; (*in theatre*) anfiteatro
bald [bɔːld] ADJ calvo; (*tyre*) liso
baldness ['bɔːldnɪs] N calvicie *f*
bale [beɪl] N (*Agr*) paca, fardo
▶ **bale out** VI (*of a plane*) lanzarse en
paracaídas ▶ VT (*Naut*) achicar; **to ~ sb out of
a difficulty** sacar a algn de un apuro
Balearic Islands [bælɪ'ærɪk-] NPL: **the ~** las
(Islas) Baleares
baleful ['beɪlful] ADJ (*look*) triste; (*sinister*)
funesto, siniestro
balk [bɔːk] VI: **to ~ (at)** resistirse (a); (*horse*)
plantarse (ante)
Balkan ['bɔːlkən] ADJ balcánico ▶ N: **the
Balkans** los Balcanes
ball [bɔːl] N (*sphere*) bola; (*football*) balón *m*; (*for
tennis, golf etc*) pelota; (*of wool, string*) ovillo;
(*dance*) baile *m*; **to be on the ~** (*fig: competent*)
ser un enterado (: *alert*) estar al tanto; **to
play ~ (with sb)** jugar a la pelota (con algn);
(*fig*) cooperar; **to start the ~ rolling** (*fig*)
empezar; **the ~ is in your court** (*fig*) le toca a
usted
ballad ['bæləd] N balada, romance *m*
ballast ['bæləst] N lastre *m*
ball bearing N cojinete *m* de bolas

ballcock ['bɔːlkɔk] N llave *f* de bola *or* de
flotador
ballerina [bælə'riːnə] N bailarina
ballet ['bæleɪ] N ballet *m*
ballet dancer N bailarín(-ina) *m/f* (de ballet)
ballistic [bə'lɪstɪk] ADJ balístico;
intercontinental ~ missile misil *m*
balístico intercontinental
ballistics [bə'lɪstɪks] N balística
balloon [bə'luːn] N globo; (*in comic strip*)
bocadillo ▶ VI dispararse
balloonist [bə'luːnɪst] N aeróstata *mf*
ballot ['bælət] N votación *f*
ballot box N urna (electoral)
ballot paper N papeleta
ballpark ['bɔːlpɑːk] N (*US*) estadio de béisbol
ball-point pen ['bɔːlpɔɪnt-] N bolígrafo
ballroom ['bɔːlrum] N salón *m* de baile
balm [bɑːm] N (*also fig*) bálsamo
balmy ['bɑːmɪ] ADJ (*breeze, air*) suave; (*inf*)
= **barmy**
BALPA ['bælpə] N ABBR (= *British Airline Pilots'
Association*) sindicato de pilotos de líneas aéreas
balsa ['bɔːlsə], **balsa wood** N (madera de)
balsa
Baltic ['bɔːltɪk] ADJ báltico ▶ N: **the ~ (Sea)** el
(Mar) Báltico
balustrade ['bæləstreɪd] N barandilla
bamboo [bæm'buː] N bambú *m*
bamboozle [bæm'buːzl] VT (*inf*) embaucar,
engatusar
ban [bæn] N prohibición *f* ▶ VT prohibir;
(*exclude*) excluir; **he was banned from
driving** le retiraron el carnet de conducir
banal [bə'nɑːl] ADJ banal, vulgar
banana [bə'nɑːnə] N plátano, banana (*LAm*)
band [bænd] N (*group*) banda; (*gang*) pandilla;
(*strip*) faja, tira; (*at a dance*) orquesta; (*Mil*)
banda; (*rock band*) grupo
▶ **band together** VI juntarse, asociarse
bandage ['bændɪdʒ] N venda, vendaje *m* ▶ VT
vendar
Band-Aid® ['bændeɪd] N (*US*) tirita, curita
(*LAm*)
B & B N ABBR = **bed and breakfast**
bandit ['bændɪt] N bandido; **one-armed ~**
máquina tragaperras
bandstand ['bændstænd] N quiosco de
música
bandwagon ['bændwægən] N: **to jump on
the ~** (*fig*) subirse al carro
bandy ['bændɪ] VT (*jokes, insults*) intercambiar
bandy-legged ['bændɪ'legd] ADJ patizambo
bane [beɪn] N: **it** (*or* **he** etc) **is the ~ of my life**
me amarga la vida
bang [bæŋ] N (*of gun, exhaust*) estallido; (*of
door*) portazo; (*blow*) golpe *m* ▶ VT (*door*) cerrar
de golpe; (*one's head*) golpear ▶ VI estallar
▶ ADV: **to be ~ on time** (*inf*) llegar en punto;

to ~ **the door** dar un portazo; **to ~ into sth** chocar con algo, golpearse contra algo; *see also* **bangs**

banger ['bæŋəʳ] N (*BRIT: car: also:* **old banger**) armatoste *m*, cacharro; (*inf: sausage*) salchicha; (*firework*) petardo

Bangkok [bæŋ'kɔk] N Bangkok *m*

Bangladesh [bæŋgləˈdɛʃ] N Bangladesh *f*

bangle ['bæŋgl] N brazalete *m*, ajorca

bangs [bæŋz] NPL (*US*) flequillo *sg*

banish ['bænɪʃ] VT desterrar

banister ['bænɪstəʳ] N, **banisters** ['bænɪstəz] NPL barandilla *f*, pasamanos *m inv*

banjo ['bændʒəu] (*pl* **banjoes** *or* **banjos**) N banjo

bank [bæŋk] N (*Comm*) banco; (*of river, lake*) ribera, orilla; (*of earth*) terraplén *m* ▸ VI (*Aviat*) ladearse; (*Comm*): **to ~ with** tener la cuenta en

▸ **bank on** VT FUS contar con

bank account N cuenta bancaria

bank balance N saldo

bank card N tarjeta bancaria

bank charges NPL comisión *fsg*

bank draft N letra de cambio

banker ['bæŋkəʳ] N banquero; **~'s card** (*BRIT*) tarjeta bancaria; **~'s order** orden *f* bancaria

bank giro N giro bancario

bank holiday N (*BRIT*) día *m* festivo *or* de fiesta; *ver nota*

El término *bank holiday* se aplica en el Reino Unido a todo día festivo oficial en el que cierran bancos y comercios. Los más destacados coinciden con Navidad, Semana Santa, finales de mayo y finales de agosto. Al contrario que en los países de tradición católica, no se celebran las festividades dedicadas a los santos.

banking ['bæŋkɪŋ] N banca

bank loan N préstamo bancario

bank manager N director(a) *m/f* (de sucursal) de banco

banknote ['bæŋknəut] N billete *m* de banco

bank rate N tipo de interés bancario

bankrupt ['bæŋkrʌpt] N quebrado(-a) ▸ ADJ quebrado, insolvente; **to go ~** quebrar, hacer bancarrota; **to be ~** estar en quiebra

bankruptcy ['bæŋkrʌptsɪ] N quiebra, bancarrota

bank statement N extracto de cuenta

banned substance ['bænd-] N (*Sport*) sustancia prohibida

banner ['bænəʳ] N bandera; (*in demonstration*) pancarta

bannister ['bænɪstəʳ] N, **bannisters** ['bænɪstəz] NPL = **banister**

banns [bænz] NPL amonestaciones *fpl*

banquet ['bæŋkwɪt] N banquete *m*

banter ['bæntəʳ] N guasa, bromas *fpl*

baptism ['bæptɪzəm] N bautismo; (*act*) bautizo

baptize [bæp'taɪz] VT bautizar

bar [baːʳ] N barra; (*on door*) tranca; (*of window, cage*) reja; (*of soap*) pastilla; (*of chocolate*) tableta; (*fig: hindrance*) obstáculo; (*prohibition*) prohibición *f*; (*pub*) bar *m*, cantina (*esp LAm*); (*counter: in pub*) barra, mostrador *m*; (*Mus*) barra ▸ VT (*road*) obstruir; (*window, door*) atrancar; (*person*) excluir; (*activity*) prohibir; **behind bars** entre rejas; **the B~** (*Law: profession*) la abogacía; (*: people*) el cuerpo de abogados; **~ none** sin excepción

Barbados [baː'beɪdɔs] N Barbados *m*

barbarian [baː'bɛərɪən] N bárbaro(-a)

barbaric [baː'bærɪk] ADJ bárbaro

barbarity [baː'bærɪtɪ] N barbaridad *f*

barbarous ['baːbərəs] ADJ bárbaro

barbecue ['baːbɪkjuː] N barbacoa, asado (*LAm*)

barbed wire ['baːbd-] N alambre *m* de espino

barber ['baːbəʳ] N peluquero, barbero

barber's (shop), (*US*) **barber (shop)** N peluquería

barbiturate [baː'bɪtjurɪt] N barbitúrico

Barcelona [baːsɪ'ləunə] N Barcelona

bar chart N gráfico de barras

bar code N código de barras

bare [bɛəʳ] ADJ desnudo; (*trees*) sin hojas; (*head*) descubierto ▸ VT desnudar; **to ~ one's teeth** enseñar los dientes

bareback ['bɛəbæk] ADV a pelo

barefaced ['bɛəfeɪst] ADJ descarado

barefoot ['bɛəfut] ADJ, ADV descalzo

bareheaded [bɛə'hɛdɪd] ADJ descubierto, sin sombrero

barely ['bɛəlɪ] ADV apenas

bareness ['bɛənɪs] N desnudez *f*

Barents Sea ['bærənts-] N: **the ~** el Mar de Barents

bargain ['baːgɪn] N pacto; (*transaction*) negocio; (*good buy*) ganga ▸ VI negociar; (*haggle*) regatear; **into the ~** además, por añadidura

▸ **bargain for** VT FUS (*inf*): **he got more than he bargained for** le resultó peor de lo que esperaba

bargaining ['baːgənɪŋ] N negociación *f*, regateo; **~ table** mesa de negociaciones

bargaining position N: **to be in a strong/weak ~** estar/no estar en una posición de fuerza para negociar

barge [baːdʒ] N barcaza

▸ **barge in** VI irrumpir; (*in conversation*) entrometerse

▸ **barge into** VT FUS dar contra

baritone ['bærɪtəun] N barítono

barium meal ['bɛərɪəm-] N (*Med*) sulfato de bario

bark [bɑːk] N (*of tree*) corteza; (*of dog*) ladrido
▶ VI ladrar

barley ['bɑːlɪ] N cebada

barley sugar N azúcar *m* cande

barmaid ['bɑːmeɪd] N camarera

barman ['bɑːmən] N (*irreg*) camarero,
barman *m*

barmy ['bɑːmɪ] ADJ (*inf*) chiflado, chalado

barn [bɑːn] N granero; (*for animals*) cuadra

barnacle ['bɑːnəkl] N percebe *m*

barn owl N lechuza

barometer [bə'rɔmɪtə'] N barómetro

baron ['bærən] N barón *m*; (*fig*) magnate *m*;
the press barons los magnates de la prensa

baroness ['bærənɪs] N baronesa

baroque [bə'rɔk] ADJ barroco

barrack ['bærək] VT (*BRIT*) abuchear

barracking ['bærəkɪŋ] N: **to give sb a ~** (*BRIT*)
abuchear a algn

barracks ['bærəks] NPL cuartel *msg*

barrage ['bærɑːʒ] N (*Mil*) cortina de fuego;
(*dam*) presa; (*fig: of criticism etc*) lluvia, aluvión
m; **a ~ of questions** una lluvia de preguntas

barrel ['bærəl] N barril *m*; (*of wine*) tonel *m*,
cuba; (*of gun*) cañón *m*

barren ['bærən] ADJ estéril

barrette [bə'rɛt] N (*US*) pasador *m*, broche *m*
(*MEX*)

barricade [bærɪ'keɪd] N barricada ▶ VT cerrar
con barricadas

barrier ['bærɪə'] N barrera; (*crash barrier*)
barrera

barrier cream N crema protectora

barring ['bɑːrɪŋ] PREP excepto, salvo

barrister ['bærɪstə'] N (*BRIT*) abogado(-a);
ver nota

En el sistema legal inglés *barrister* es el
abogado que se ocupa de defender los
casos de sus clientes en los tribunales
superiores. El equivalente escocés es
"*advocate*". Normalmente actúan según
instrucciones de un "*solicitor*", abogado de
despacho que no toma parte activa en los
juicios de dichos tribunales. El título de
barrister lo otorga el órgano colegiado
correspondiente, "*the Inns of Court*".

barrow ['bærəu] N (*cart*) carretilla

barstool ['bɑːstuːl] N taburete *m* (de bar)

Bart. ABBR (*BRIT*) = **baronet**

bartender ['bɑːtɛndə'] N (*US*) camarero,
barman *m*

barter ['bɑːtə'] VT: **to ~ sth for sth** trocar
algo por algo

base [beɪs] N base *f* ▶ VT: **to ~ sth on** basar *or*
fundar algo en ▶ ADJ bajo, infame; **to ~ at**
(*troops*) estacionar en; **I'm based in London**
(*work*) trabajo en Londres

baseball ['beɪsbɔːl] N béisbol *m*

baseball cap N gorra *f* de béisbol

base camp N campamento base

Basel ['bɑːzəl] N Basilea

baseless ['beɪslɪs] ADJ infundado

baseline ['beɪslaɪn] N (*Tennis*) línea de fondo

basement ['beɪsmənt] N sótano

base rate N tipo base

bases ['beɪsiːz] NPL *of* **basis**

bash [bæʃ] N: **I'll have a ~ (at it)** lo intentaré
▶ VT (*inf*) golpear

▶ **bash up** VT (*inf: car*) destrozar; (: *person*)
aporrear, vapulear

bashful ['bæʃful] ADJ tímido, vergonzoso

bashing ['bæʃɪŋ] N (*inf*) paliza; **to go Paki-/
queer-~** ir a dar una paliza a los
paquistaníes/a los maricas

BASIC ['beɪsɪk] N (*Comput*) BASIC *m*

basic ['beɪsɪk] ADJ (*salary etc*) básico;
(*elementary: principles*) fundamental

basically ['beɪsɪklɪ] ADV fundamentalmente,
en el fondo

basic rate N (*of tax*) base *f* mínima imponible

basics NPL: **the ~** los fundamentos

basil ['bæzl] N albahaca

basin ['beɪsn] N (*vessel*) cuenco, tazón *m*; (*Geo*)
cuenca; (*also*: **washbasin**) palangana,
jofaina; (: *in bathroom*) lavabo

basis ['beɪsɪs] N (*pl* **bases** [-siːz]) N base *f*; **on a
part-time/trial ~** a tiempo parcial/a prueba;
on the ~ of what you've said en base a lo
que has dicho

bask [bɑːsk] VI: **to ~ in the sun** tomar el sol

basket ['bɑːskɪt] N cesta, cesto

basketball ['bɑːskɪtbɔːl] N baloncesto

basketball player N jugador(a) *m/f* de
baloncesto

basketwork ['bɑːskɪtwəːk] N cestería

Basle [bɑːl] N Basilea

basmati rice [bəz'mætɪ-] N arroz *m* basmati

Basque [bæsk] ADJ, N vasco(-a) *m/f*

Basque Country N Euskadi *m*, País *m* Vasco

bass [beɪs] N (*Mus*) bajo

bass clef N clave *f* de fa

bassoon [bə'suːn] N fagot *m*

bastard ['bɑːstəd] N bastardo(-a); (*inf!*)
cabrón *m*, hijo de puta (!)

baste [beɪst] VT (*Culin*) rociar (con su salsa)

bastion ['bæstɪən] N bastión *m*, baluarte *m*

bat [bæt] N (*Zool*) murciélago; (*for ball games*)
palo; (*for cricket, baseball*) bate *m*; (*BRIT: for table
tennis*) pala ▶ VT: **he didn't ~ an eyelid** ni
pestañeó, ni se inmutó

batch [bætʃ] N lote *m*, remesa; (*of bread*)
hornada

bated ['beɪtɪd] ADJ: **with ~ breath** sin
respirar

bath [bɑːθ] N (*act*) baño; (*bathtub*) bañera,
tina (*esp LAM*) ▶ VT bañar; **to have a ~**
bañarse, darse un baño; *see also* **baths**

bath chair ['bɑːθtʃɛə'] N silla de ruedas

bathe [beɪð] VI bañarse; (US) darse un baño, bañarse ▸ VT (wound etc) lavar; (US) bañar, dar un baño a
bather ['beɪðə^r] N bañista mf
bathing ['beɪðɪŋ] N baño
bathing cap N gorro de baño
bathing costume, (US) **bathing suit** N bañador m, traje m de baño
bathing trunks NPL bañador msg
bathmat ['bɑːθmæt] N alfombrilla de baño
bathrobe ['bɑːθrəub] N albornoz m
bathroom ['bɑːθrum] N (cuarto de) baño
baths [bɑːðz] NPL piscina sg
bath towel N toalla de baño
bathtub ['bɑːθtʌb] N bañera
batman ['bætmən] N (irreg) (BRIT) ordenanza m
baton ['bætən] N (Mus) batuta; (weapon) porra
battalion [bə'tælɪən] N batallón m
batten ['bætn] N (Carpentry) listón m; (Naut) junquillo, sable m
   ▸ **batten down** VT (Naut): **to ~ down the hatches** atrancar las escotillas
batter ['bætə^r] VT maltratar; (wind, rain) azotar ▸ VI batido
battered ['bætəd] ADJ (hat, pan) estropeado
battery ['bætərɪ] N batería; (of torch) pila
battery charger N cargador m de baterías
battery farming N cría intensiva
battle ['bætl] N batalla; (fig) lucha ▸ VI luchar; **that's half the ~** (inf) ya hay medio camino andado; **to fight a losing ~** (fig) luchar por una causa perdida
battlefield ['bætlfiːld] N campo m de batalla
battlements ['bætlmənts] NPL almenas fpl
battleship ['bætlʃɪp] N acorazado
batty ['bætɪ] ADJ (inf: person) chiflado; (: idea) de chiflado
bauble ['bɔːbl] N chuchería
baud rate N (Comput) velocidad f (de transmisión) en baudios
bauxite ['bɔːksaɪt] N bauxita
Bavaria [bə'veərɪə] N Baviera
Bavarian [bə'veərɪən] ADJ, N bávaro(-a) m/f
bawdy ['bɔːdɪ] ADJ indecente; (joke) verde
bawl [bɔːl] VI chillar, gritar
bay [beɪ] N (Geo) bahía; (for parking) parking m, estacionamiento; (loading bay) patio de carga; (Bot) laurel m ▸ VI aullar; **to hold sb at ~** mantener a alguien a raya
bay leaf N (hoja de) laurel m
bayonet ['beɪənɪt] N bayoneta
bay window N ventana salediza
bazaar [bə'zɑː^r] N bazar m
bazooka [bə'zuːkə] N bazuca
BB N ABBR (BRIT: = Boys' Brigade) organización juvenil para chicos
BBB N ABBR (US: = Better Business Bureau) organismo para la defensa del consumidor

BBC N ABBR (= British Broadcasting Corporation) BBC f; ver nota

> La BBC es el organismo público británico de radio y televisión, autónomo en cuanto a su política de programas pero regulado por un estatuto ("BBC charter") que ha de aprobar el Parlamento. Además de cadenas nacionales de televisión y de radio, transmite también un servicio informativo mundial ("BBC World Service"). A no tener publicidad, se financia a través de operaciones comerciales paralelas y del cobro de una licencia anual obligatoria ("TV licence") para los que tienen aparato de televisión.

BC ADV ABBR (= before Christ) a. de J.C. ▸ ABBR (CANADA) = **British Columbia**
BCG N ABBR (= Bacillus Calmette-Guérin) vacuna de la tuberculosis
BD N ABBR (= Bachelor of Divinity) Licenciado/a en Teología
B/D ABBR = **bank draft**
BDS N ABBR (= Bachelor of Dental Surgery) título universitario

(KEYWORD)

be [biː] (pt **was, were,** pp **been**) AUX VB **1** (with present participle: forming continuous tenses): **what are you doing?** ¿qué estás haciendo?, ¿qué haces?; **they're coming tomorrow** vienen mañana; **I've been waiting for you for hours** llevo horas esperándote
2 (with pp: forming passives) ser (but often replaced by active or reflexive constructions); **to be murdered** ser asesinado; **the box had been opened** habían abierto la caja; **the thief was nowhere to be seen** no se veía al ladrón por ninguna parte
3 (in tag questions): **it was fun, wasn't it?** fue divertido, ¿no? or ¿verdad?; **he's good-looking, isn't he?** es guapo, ¿no te parece?; **she's back again, is she?** entonces, ¿ha vuelto?
4 (+ to + infin): **the house is to be sold** (necessity) hay que vender la casa; (future) van a vender la casa; **he's not to open it** no tiene que abrirlo; **he was to have come yesterday** debía de haber venido ayer; **am I to understand that ...?** ¿debo entender que ...?
> VB +COMPLEMENT **1** (with n or num complement) ser; **he's a doctor** es médico; **2 and 2 are 4** 2 y 2 son 4
2 (with adj complement: expressing permanent or inherent quality) ser; (: expressing state seen as temporary or reversible) estar; **I'm English** soy inglés(-esa); **she's tall/pretty** es alta/bonita; **he's young** es joven; **be careful/good/quiet** ten cuidado/pórtate bien/

cállate; **I'm tired** estoy cansado(-a); **I'm warm** tengo calor; **it's dirty** está sucio(-a) **3** (*of health*) estar; **how are you?** ¿cómo estás?; **he's very ill** está muy enfermo; **I'm better now** ya estoy mejor
4 (*of age*) tener; **how old are you?** ¿cuántos años tienes?; **I'm sixteen (years old)** tengo dieciséis años
5 (*cost*) costar; ser; **how much was the meal?** ¿cuánto fue *or* costó la comida?; **that'll be £5.75, please** son £5.75, por favor; **this shirt is £17** esta camisa cuesta £17
▶ VI **1** (*exist, occur etc*) existir, haber; **the best singer that ever was** el mejor cantante que existió jamás; **is there a God?** ¿hay un Dios?, ¿existe Dios?; **be that as it may** sea como sea; **so be it** así sea
2 (*referring to place*) estar; **I won't be here tomorrow** no estaré aquí mañana
3 (*referring to movement*): **where have you been?** ¿dónde has estado?
▶ IMPERS VB **1** (*referring to time*): **it's 5 o'clock** son las 5; **it's the 28th of April** estamos a 28 de abril
2 (*referring to distance*): **it's 10 km to the village** el pueblo está a 10 km
3 (*referring to the weather*): **it's too hot/cold** hace demasiado calor/frío; **it's windy today** hace viento hoy
4 (*emphatic*): **it's me** soy yo; **it was Maria who paid the bill** fue María la que pagó la cuenta

B/E ABBR = **bill of exchange**
beach [biːtʃ] N playa ▶ VT varar
beach buggy [-bʌɡɪ] N buggy *m*
beachcomber ['biːtʃkəumə^r] N raquero(-a)
beachwear ['biːtʃwɛə^r] N ropa de playa
beacon ['biːkən] N (*lighthouse*) faro; (*marker*) guía; (*radio beacon*) radiofaro
bead [biːd] N cuenta, abalorio; (*of dew, sweat*) gota; **beads** NPL (*necklace*) collar *m*
beady ['biːdɪ] ADJ (*eyes*) pequeño y brillante
beagle ['biːgl] N sabueso pequeño, beagle *m*
beak [biːk] N pico
beaker ['biːkə^r] N vaso
beam [biːm] N (*Arch*) viga; (*of light*) rayo, haz *m* de luz; (*Radio*) rayo ▶ VI brillar; (*smile*) sonreír; **to drive on full** *or* **main ~** conducir con las luces largas
beaming ['biːmɪŋ] ADJ (*sun, smile*) radiante
bean [biːn] N judía, fríjol/frijol *m* (*esp LAM*); **runner/broad ~** habichuela/haba; **coffee ~** grano de café
beanpole ['biːnpəul] N (*inf*) espárrago
bean sprouts ['biːnsprauts] NPL brotes *mpl* de soja
bear [bɛə^r] (*pt* **bore**, *pp* **borne**) N oso; (*Stock Exchange*) bajista *m* ▶ VT (*weight etc*) llevar;

(*cost*) pagar; (*responsibility*) tener; (*traces, signs*) mostrar; (*produce: fruit*) dar; (*Comm: interest*) devengar; (*person*) soportar, aguantar; (*stand up to*) resistir a; (*children*) tener, dar a luz; (*fruit*) dar ▶ VI: **to ~ right/left** torcer a la derecha/izquierda; **I can't ~ him** no le puedo ver, no lo soporto; **to bring pressure to ~ on sb** ejercer presión sobre algn
▶ **bear on** VT FUS tener que ver con, referirse a
▶ **bear out** VT FUS (*suspicions*) corroborar, confirmar; (*person*) confirmar lo dicho por
▶ **bear up** VI (*cheer up*) animarse; **he bore up well under the strain** resistió bien la presión
▶ **bear with** VT FUS (*sb's moods, temper*) tener paciencia con
bearable ['bɛərəbl] ADJ soportable, aguantable
beard [bɪəd] N barba
bearded ['bɪədɪd] ADJ con barba
bearer ['bɛərə^r] N (*of news, cheque*) portador(a) *m/f*; (*of passport*) titular *mf*
bearing ['bɛərɪŋ] N porte *m*; (*connection*) relación *f*; **(ball) bearings** NPL cojinetes *mpl* a bolas; **to take a ~** marcarse; **to find one's bearings** orientarse
bearskin ['bɛəskɪn] N (*Mil*) gorro militar (*de piel de oso*)
beast [biːst] N bestia; (*inf*) bruto, salvaje *m*
beastly ['biːstlɪ] ADJ bestial; (*awful*) horrible
beat [biːt] (*pt* **~**, **beaten** [ˈbiːtn]) N (*of heart*) latido; (*Mus*) ritmo, compás *m*; (*of policeman*) ronda ▶ VT (*hit*) golpear, pegar; (*eggs*) batir; (*defeat*) vencer, derrotar; (*better*) sobrepasar; (*drum*) redoblar; (*rhythm*) marcar ▶ VI (*heart*) latir; **off the beaten track** aislado; **to ~ about the bush** andarse con rodeos; **to ~ it** largarse; **that beats everything!** (*inf*) ¡eso es el colmo!; **to ~ on a door** dar golpes en una puerta
▶ **beat down** VT (*door*) derribar a golpes; (*price*) conseguir rebajar, regatear; (*seller*) hacer rebajar el precio ▶ VI (*rain*) llover a cántaros; (*sun*) caer de plomo
▶ **beat off** VT rechazar
▶ **beat up** VT (*inf: person*) dar una paliza a
beater ['biːtə^r] N (*for eggs, cream*) batidora
beating ['biːtɪŋ] N paliza, golpiza (*LAM*); **to take a ~** recibir una paliza
beat-up ['biːtˈʌp] ADJ (*inf*) destartalado
beautiful ['bjuːtɪful] ADJ hermoso, bello, lindo (*LAM*)
beautifully ['bjuːtɪfəlɪ] ADV de maravilla
beautify ['bjuːtɪfaɪ] VT embellecer
beauty ['bjuːtɪ] N belleza, hermosura; (*concept, person*) belleza; **the ~ of it is that ...** lo mejor de esto es que ...
beauty contest N concurso de belleza

beauty parlour, (US) **beauty parlor** N salón *m* de belleza

beauty queen N reina de la belleza

beauty salon N salón *m* de belleza

beauty sleep N: **to get one's** ~ *no perder horas de sueño*

beauty spot N lunar *m* postizo; (BRIT Tourism) lugar *m* pintoresco

beaver ['biːvəʳ] N castor *m*

becalmed [bɪ'kɑːmd] ADJ encalmado

became [bɪ'keɪm] PT of **become**

because [bɪ'kɔz] CONJ porque; ~ **of** prep debido a, a causa de

beck [bek] N: **to be at the** ~ **and call of** estar a disposición de

beckon ['bekən] VT (also: **beckon to**) llamar con señas

become [bɪ'kʌm] VI (irreg: like **come**) + noun hacerse, llegar a ser; + adj ponerse, volverse ▶ VT (suit) favorecer, sentar bien a; **to ~ fat** engordar; **to ~ angry** enfadarse; **it became known that ...** se descubrió que ...

becoming [bɪ'kʌmɪŋ] ADJ (behaviour) decoroso; (clothes) favorecedor(a)

becquerel [bekə'rel] N becquerelio

BECTU ['bektuː] N ABBR (BRIT) = **Broadcasting, Entertainment, Cinematograph and Theatre Union**

BEd N ABBR (= Bachelor of Education) título universitario; see also **bachelor's degree**

bed [bed] N cama; (of flowers) macizo; (of sea, lake) fondo; (of river) lecho; (of coal, clay) capa; **to go to** ~ acostarse
  ▶ **bed down** VI acostarse

bed and breakfast N ≈ pensión *f*; ver nota

> Se llama *Bed and Breakfast* a la casa de hospedaje particular, o granja si es en el campo, que ofrece cama y desayuno a tarifas inferiores a las de un hotel. El servicio se suele anunciar con carteles colocados en las ventanas del establecimiento, en el jardín o en la carretera y en ellos aparece a menudo únicamente el símbolo "B & B".

bedbug ['bedbʌg] N chinche *f*

bedclothes ['bedkləʊðz] NPL ropa de cama

bedding ['bedɪŋ] N ropa de cama

bedeck [bɪ'dek] VT engalanar, adornar

bedevil [bɪ'devl] VT (dog) acosar; (trouble) fastidiar

bedfellow ['bedfeləʊ] N: **they are strange bedfellows** (fig) hacen una pareja rara

bedlam ['bedləm] N confusión *f*

bed linen N (BRIT) ropa *f* de cama

bedpan ['bedpæn] N cuña

bedraggled [bɪ'drægld] ADJ desastrado

bedridden ['bedrɪdn] ADJ postrado (en cama)

bedrock ['bedrɔk] N (Geo) roca firme; (fig) pilar *m*

bedroom ['bedrum] N dormitorio, alcoba

Beds ABBR (BRIT) = **Bedfordshire**

bed settee N sofá-cama *m*

bedside ['bedsaɪd] N: **at sb's** ~ a la cabecera de alguien

bedside lamp N lámpara de noche

bedside table N mesilla de noche

bedsit ['bedsɪt], **bedsitter** ['bedsɪtəʳ] N (BRIT) estudio

bedspread ['bedspred] N cubrecama *m*, colcha

bedtime ['bedtaɪm] N hora de acostarse; **it's** ~ es hora de acostarse or de irse a la cama

bee [biː] N abeja; **to have a ~ in one's bonnet (about sth)** tener una idea fija (de algo)

beech [biːtʃ] N haya

beef [biːf] N carne *f* de vaca; **roast** ~ rosbif *m*
  ▶ **beef up** VT (inf) reforzar

beefburger ['biːfbəːgəʳ] N hamburguesa

beefeater ['biːfiːtəʳ] N alabardero de la Torre de Londres

beehive ['biːhaɪv] N colmena

bee-keeping ['biːkiːpɪŋ] N apicultura

beeline ['biːlaɪn] N: **to make a ~ for** ir derecho a

been [biːn] PP of **be**

beep [biːp] N pitido ▶ VI pitar

beeper ['biːpəʳ] N (of doctor etc) busca *m* inv

beer [bɪəʳ] N cerveza

beer belly N (inf) barriga (de bebedor de cerveza)

beer can N bote *m* or lata de cerveza

beer garden N (BRIT) terraza *f* de verano, jardín *m* (de un bar)

beet [biːt] N (US) remolacha

beetle ['biːtl] N escarabajo

beetroot ['biːtruːt] N (BRIT) remolacha

befall [bɪ'fɔːl] VI, VT (irreg: like **fall**) acontecer (a)

befit [bɪ'fɪt] VT convenir a, corresponder a

before [bɪ'fɔːʳ] PREP (of time) antes de; (of space) delante de ▶ CONJ antes (de) que ▶ ADV (time) antes; (space) delante, adelante; ~ **going** antes de marcharse; ~ **she goes** antes de que se vaya; **the week** ~ la semana anterior; **I've never seen it** ~ no lo he visto nunca

beforehand [bɪ'fɔːhænd] ADV de antemano, con anticipación

befriend [bɪ'frend] VT ofrecer amistad a

befuddled [bɪ'fʌdld] ADJ aturdido, atontado

beg [beg] VI pedir limosna, mendigar ▶ VT pedir, rogar; (entreat) suplicar; **to ~ sb to do sth** rogar a algn que haga algo; see also **pardon**

began [bɪ'gæn] PT of **begin**

beggar ['begəʳ] N mendigo(-a)

begin [bɪ'gɪn] (pt **began**, pp **begun**) VT, VI empezar, comenzar; **to ~ doing** or **to do sth** empezar a hacer algo; **I can't ~ to thank you** no encuentro palabras para agradecerle;

to ~ **with, I'd like to know ...** en primer lugar, quisiera saber ...; **beginning from Monday** a partir del lunes

beginner [bɪˈgɪnəʳ] N principiante *mf*

beginning [bɪˈgɪnɪŋ] N principio, comienzo; **right from the ~** desde el principio

begrudge [bɪˈgrʌdʒ] VT: **to ~ sb sth** tenerle envidia a alguien por algo

beguile [bɪˈgaɪl] VT (*enchant*) seducir

beguiling [bɪˈgaɪlɪŋ] ADJ seductor(a), atractivo

begun [bɪˈgʌn] PP *of* **begin**

behalf [bɪˈhɑːf] N: **on ~ of**, (*US*) **in ~ of** en nombre de, por; (*for benefit of*) en beneficio de; **on my/his ~** por mí/él

behave [bɪˈheɪv] VI (*person*) portarse, comportarse; (*thing*) funcionar; (*well: also:* **behave o.s.**) portarse bien

behaviour, (*US*) **behavior** [bɪˈheɪvjəʳ] N comportamiento, conducta

behead [bɪˈhed] VT decapitar

beheld [bɪˈheld] PT, PP *of* **behold**

behind [bɪˈhaɪnd] PREP detrás de ▶ ADV detrás, por detrás, atrás ▶ N trasero; **to be ~ (schedule)** ir retrasado; **~ the scenes** (*fig*) entre bastidores; **we're ~ them in technology** (*fig*) nos dejan atrás en tecnología; **to leave sth ~** olvidar *or* dejarse algo; **to be ~ with sth** estar atrasado en algo; **to be ~ with payments (on sth)** estar atrasado en el pago (de algo)

behold [bɪˈhəuld] VT (*irreg: like* **hold**) contemplar

beige [beɪʒ] ADJ (color) beige

Beijing [ˈbeɪˈdʒɪŋ] N Pekín *m*

being [ˈbiːɪŋ] N ser *m*; **to come into ~** nacer, aparecer

Beirut [beɪˈruːt] N Beirut *m*

Belarus [beləˈrus] N Bielorrusia

Belarussian [beləˈrʌʃən] ADJ, N bielorruso(-a) *m/f* ▶ N (*Ling*) bielorruso

belated [bɪˈleɪtɪd] ADJ atrasado, tardío

belch [beltʃ] VI eructar ▶ VT (*also:* **belch out**: *smoke etc*) vomitar, arrojar

beleaguered [bɪˈliːgəd] ADJ asediado

Belfast [ˈbelfɑːst] N Belfast *m*

belfry [ˈbelfrɪ] N campanario

Belgian [ˈbeldʒən] ADJ, N belga *mf*

Belgium [ˈbeldʒəm] N Bélgica

Belgrade [belˈgreɪd] N Belgrado

belie [bɪˈlaɪ] VT (*give false impression of*) desmentir, contradecir

belief [bɪˈliːf] N (*opinion*) opinión *f*; (*trust, faith*) fe *f*; (*acceptance as true*) creencia; **it's beyond ~** es increíble; **in the ~ that** creyendo que

believable [bɪˈliːvəbl] ADJ creíble

believe [bɪˈliːv] VT, VI creer; **to ~ (that)** creer (que); **to ~ in** (*God, ghosts*) creer en; (*method*) ser partidario de; **he is believed to be**

abroad se cree que está en el extranjero; **I don't ~ in corporal punishment** no soy partidario del castigo corporal

believer [bɪˈliːvəʳ] N (*in idea, activity*) partidario(-a); (*Rel*) creyente *mf*, fiel *mf*

belittle [bɪˈlɪtl] VT despreciar

Belize [beˈliːz] N Belice *f*

bell [bel] N campana; (*small*) campanilla; (*on door*) timbre *m*; (*animal's*) cencerro; (*on toy etc*) cascabel *m*; **that rings a ~** (*fig*) eso me suena

bellboy [ˈbelbɔɪ], (*US*) **bellhop** [ˈbelhɔp] N botones *m inv*

belligerent [bɪˈlɪdʒərənt] ADJ (*at war*) beligerante; (*fig*) agresivo

bellow [ˈbeləu] VI bramar; (*person*) rugir ▶ VT (*orders*) gritar

bellows [ˈbeləuz] NPL fuelle *msg*

bell pepper N (*esp US*) pimiento, pimentón *m* (*LAM*)

bell push N pulsador *m* de timbre

belly [ˈbelɪ] N barriga, panza

bellyache [ˈbelɪeɪk] N dolor *m* de barriga *or* de tripa ▶ VI (*inf*) gruñir

belly button (*inf*) N ombligo

bellyful [ˈbelɪful] N: **to have had a ~ of ...** (*inf*) estar más que harto de ...

belong [bɪˈlɔŋ] VI: **to ~ to** pertenecer a; (*club etc*) ser socio de; **this book belongs here** este libro va aquí

belongings [bɪˈlɔŋɪŋz] NPL (*also:* **personal belongings**) pertenencias *fpl*

Belorussia [beləuˈrʌʃə] N Bielorrusia

Belorussian [beləuˈrʌʃən] ADJ, N = **Belarussian**

beloved [bɪˈlʌvɪd] ADJ, N querido(-a) *m/f*, amado(-a) *m/f*

below [bɪˈləu] PREP bajo, debajo de; (*less than*) inferior a ▶ ADV abajo, (por) debajo; **see ~** véase más abajo

belt [belt] N cinturón *m*; (*Tech*) correa, cinta ▶ VT (*thrash*) pegar con correa; **industrial ~** cinturón industrial

▶ **belt out** VT (*song*) cantar a voz en grito *or* a grito pelado

▶ **belt up** VI (*Aut*) ponerse el cinturón de seguridad; (*fig, inf*) cerrar el pico

beltway [ˈbeltweɪ] N (*US Aut*) carretera de circunvalación

bemoan [bɪˈməun] VT lamentar

bemused [bɪˈmjuːzd] ADJ perplejo

bench [bentʃ] N banco; (*BRIT Pol*): **the Government/Opposition benches** (los asientos de) los miembros del Gobierno/de la Oposición; **the B~** (*Law*) la magistratura

bench mark N punto de referencia

bend [bend] (*pt, pp* **bent**) VT doblar; (*body, head*) inclinar ▶ VI inclinarse; (*road*) curvarse ▶ N (*in road, river*) recodo; (*in pipe*) codo; *see also* **bends**

▶ **bend down** VI inclinarse, doblarse

▶ **bend over** VI inclinarse

bends [bɛndz] NPL (*Med*) apoplejía por cambios bruscos de presión

beneath [bɪˈniːθ] PREP bajo, debajo de; (*unworthy of*) indigno de ▶ ADV abajo, (por) debajo

benefactor [ˈbɛnɪfæktəʳ] N bienhechor *m*

benefactress [ˈbɛnɪfæktrɪs] N bienhechora

beneficial [bɛnɪˈfɪʃəl] ADJ: **~ to** beneficioso para

beneficiary [bɛnɪˈfɪʃərɪ] N (*Law*) beneficiario(-a)

benefit [ˈbɛnɪfɪt] N beneficio, provecho; (*allowance of money*) subsidio ▶ VT beneficiar ▶ VI: **he'll ~ from it** le sacará provecho; **unemployment ~** subsidio de desempleo

Benelux [ˈbɛnɪlʌks] N Benelux *m*

benevolence [bɪˈnɛvələns] N benevolencia

benevolent [bɪˈnɛvələnt] ADJ benévolo

BEng N ABBR (= *Bachelor of Engineering*) título universitario

benign [bɪˈnaɪn] ADJ (*person*) benigno; (*Med*) benigno; (*smile*) afable

bent [bɛnt] PT, PP *of* **bend** ▶ N inclinación *f* ▶ ADJ (*wire, pipe*) doblado, torcido; **to be ~ on** estar empeñado en

bequeath [bɪˈkwiːð] VT legar

bequest [bɪˈkwɛst] N legado

bereaved [bɪˈriːvd] ADJ afligido ▶ N: **the ~** los allegados *mpl* del difunto

bereavement [bɪˈriːvmənt] N aflicción *f*

beret [ˈbɛreɪ] N boina

Bering Sea [ˈbɛərɪŋ-] N: **the ~** el Mar de Bering

berk [bəːk] N (*Brit inf*) capullo(-a) (*!*)

Berks ABBR (*Brit*) = **Berkshire**

Berlin [bəːˈlɪn] N Berlín *m*

berm [bəːm] N (*US Aut*) arcén *m*

Bermuda [bəːˈmjuːdə] N las (Islas) Bermudas

Bermuda shorts NPL bermudas *mf*

Bern [bəːn] N Berna

berry [ˈbɛrɪ] N baya

berserk [bəˈsəːk] ADJ: **to go ~** perder los estribos

berth [bəːθ] N (*bed*) litera; (*cabin*) camarote *m*; (*for ship*) amarradero ▶ VI atracar, amarrar; **to give sb a wide ~** (*fig*) evitar encontrarse con algn

beseech [bɪˈsiːtʃ] (*pt, pp* **besought** [-ˈsɔːt]) VT suplicar

beset [bɪˈsɛt] (*pt, pp* **~**) VT (*person*) acosar ▶ ADJ: **a policy ~ with dangers** una política rodeada de peligros

besetting [bɪˈsɛtɪŋ] ADJ: **his ~ sin** su principal falta

beside [bɪˈsaɪd] PREP junto a, al lado de; (*compared with*) comparado con; **to be ~ o.s. with anger** estar fuera de sí; **that's ~ the point** eso no tiene nada que ver

besides [bɪˈsaɪdz] ADV además ▶ PREP (*as well as*) además de; (*except*) excepto

besiege [bɪˈsiːdʒ] VT (*town*) sitiar; (*fig*) asediar

besmirch [bɪˈsməːtʃ] VT (*fig*) manchar, mancillar

besotted [bɪˈsɔtɪd] ADJ: **~ with** chiflado por

bespoke [bɪˈspəuk] ADJ (*garment*) hecho a la medida; **~ tailor** sastre *m* que confecciona a la medida

best [bɛst] ADJ (el/la) mejor ▶ ADV (lo) mejor; **the ~ part of** (*most*) la mayor parte de; **at ~** en el mejor de los casos; **to make the ~ of sth** sacar el mejor partido de algo; **to do one's ~** hacer todo lo posible; **to the ~ of my knowledge** que yo sepa; **to the ~ of my ability** como mejor puedo; **the ~ thing to do is …** lo mejor (que se puede hacer) es …; **he's not exactly patient at the ~ of times** no es que tenga mucha paciencia precisamente

best-before date N fecha de consumo preferente

bestial [ˈbɛstɪəl] ADJ bestial

best man N (*irreg*) padrino de boda

bestow [bɪˈstəu] VT otorgar; (*honour, praise*) dispensar; **~ to sth on sb** conceder *or* dar algo a algn

bestseller [ˈbɛstˈsɛləʳ] N éxito de ventas, best-seller *m*

bet [bɛt] N apuesta ▶ VT, VI (*pt, pp* **~** *or* **betted**): **to ~ (on)** apostar (a); **it's a safe ~** (*fig*) es cosa segura

Bethlehem [ˈbɛθlɪhɛm] N Belén *m*

betray [bɪˈtreɪ] VT traicionar; (*trust*) faltar a; (*inform on*) delatar

betrayal [bɪˈtreɪəl] N traición *f*

better [ˈbɛtəʳ] ADJ mejor ▶ ADV mejor ▶ VT mejorar; (*record etc*) superar ▶ N: **to get the ~ of sb** quedar por encima de algn; **you had ~ do it** más vale que lo hagas; **he thought ~ of it** cambió de parecer; **to get ~** mejorar(se); **that's ~!** ¡eso es!; **I had ~ go** tengo que irme; **a change for the ~** una mejora; **~ off** *adj* más acomodado

betting [ˈbɛtɪŋ] N juego, apuestas *fpl*

betting shop N (*Brit*) casa de apuestas

between [bɪˈtwiːn] PREP entre ▶ ADV (*also*: **in between**: *time*) mientras tanto; (: *place*) en medio; **the road ~ here and London** la carretera de aquí a Londres; **we only had 5 ~ us** teníamos sólo 5 entre todos

bevel [ˈbɛvəl] N (*also*: **bevel edge**) bisel *m*, chaflán *m*

beverage [ˈbɛvərɪdʒ] N bebida

bevy [ˈbɛvɪ] N: **a ~ of** una bandada de

bewail [bɪˈweɪl] VT lamentar

beware [bɪˈwɛəʳ] VI: **to ~ (of)** tener cuidado (con) ▶ EXCL ¡cuidado!; **"~ of the dog"** "perro peligroso"

bewildered [bɪ'wɪldəd] ADJ aturdido, perplejo

bewildering [bɪ'wɪldərɪŋ] ADJ desconcertante

bewitching [bɪ'wɪtʃɪŋ] ADJ hechicero, encantador(a)

beyond [bɪ'jɒnd] PREP más allá de; (past: understanding) fuera de; (after: date) después de, más allá de; (above) superior a ▶ ADV (in space) más allá; (in time) posteriormente; **~ doubt** fuera de toda duda; **~ repair** irreparable

b/f ABBR (= brought forward) saldo previo

BFPO N ABBR (= British Forces Post Office) servicio postal del ejército

bhp N ABBR (Aut: = brake horsepower) potencia al freno

bi ... [baɪ] PREF bi ...

biannual [baɪ'ænjuəl] ADJ semestral

bias ['baɪəs] N (prejudice) prejuicio; (preference) predisposición f

biased, biassed ['baɪəst] ADJ parcial; **to be ~ against** tener perjuicios contra

biathlon [baɪ'æθlən] N biatlón m

bib [bɪb] N babero

Bible ['baɪbl] N Biblia

biblical ['bɪblɪkəl] ADJ bíblico

bibliography [bɪblɪ'ɒgrəfɪ] N bibliografía

bicarbonate of soda [baɪ'kɑːbənɪt-] N bicarbonato sódico

bicentenary [baɪsɛn'tiːnərɪ], (US) **bicentennial** [baɪsɛn'tɛnɪəl] N bicentenario

biceps ['baɪsɛps] N bíceps m

bicker ['bɪkəʳ] VI reñir

bickering ['bɪkərɪŋ] N riñas fpl, altercados mpl

bicycle ['baɪsɪkl] N bicicleta

bicycle path N camino para ciclistas

bicycle pump N bomba de bicicleta

bid [bɪd] N (at auction) oferta, puja, postura; (attempt) tentativa, conato ▶ VI (pt, pp ~) hacer una oferta ▶ VT (pt **bade** [bæd], pp **bidden** ['bɪdn]) (offer) ofrecer; **to ~ sb good day** dar a algn los buenos días

bidder ['bɪdəʳ] N: **the highest ~** el mejor postor

bidding ['bɪdɪŋ] N (at auction) ofertas fpl, puja; (order) orden f, mandato

bide [baɪd] VT: **to ~ one's time** esperar el momento adecuado

bidet ['biːdeɪ] N bidet m

bidirectional ['baɪdɪ'rɛkʃənl] ADJ bidireccional

biennial [baɪ'ɛnɪəl] ADJ, N bienal f

bier [bɪəʳ] N féretro

bifocals [baɪ'fəuklz] NPL gafas fpl or anteojos mpl (LAM) bifocales

big [bɪg] ADJ grande; (brother, sister) mayor; **~ business** gran negocio; **to do things in a ~ way** hacer las cosas en grande

bigamy ['bɪgəmɪ] N bigamia

big dipper [-'dɪpəʳ] N montaña rusa

big end N (Aut) cabeza de biela

biggish ['bɪgɪʃ] ADJ más bien grande; (man) más bien alto

bigheaded ['bɪg'hɛdɪd] ADJ engreído

bigot ['bɪgət] N fanático(-a), intolerante mf

bigoted ['bɪgətɪd] ADJ fanático, intolerante

bigotry ['bɪgətrɪ] N fanatismo, intolerancia

big toe N dedo gordo (del pie)

big top N (circus) circo; (main tent) carpa principal

big wheel N (at fair) noria

bigwig ['bɪgwɪg] N (inf) pez m gordo

bike [baɪk] N bici f

bike lane N carril m de bicicleta, carril m bici

bikini [bɪ'kiːnɪ] N bikini m

bilateral [baɪ'lætərl] ADJ (agreement) bilateral

bile [baɪl] N bilis f

bilge [bɪldʒ] N (water) agua de sentina

bilingual [baɪ'lɪŋgwəl] ADJ bilingüe

bilious ['bɪlɪəs] ADJ bilioso (also fig)

bill [bɪl] N (gen) cuenta; (invoice) factura; (Pol) proyecto de ley; (US: banknote) billete m; (of bird) pico; (notice) cartel m; (Theat) programa m ▶ VT extender or pasar la factura a; **may I have the ~ please?** ¿puede traerme la cuenta, por favor?; **~ of exchange** letra de cambio; **~ of lading** conocimiento de embarque; **~ of sale** escritura de venta; **"post no bills"** "prohibido fijar carteles"; **to fit** or **fill the ~** (fig) cumplir con los requisitos

billboard ['bɪlbɔːd] N valla publicitaria

billet ['bɪlɪt] N alojamiento ▶ VT: **to ~ sb (on sb)** alojar a algn (con algn)

billfold ['bɪlfəuld] N (US) cartera

billiards ['bɪljədz] N billar m

billion ['bɪljən] N (BRIT) billón m; (US) mil millones mpl

billow ['bɪləu] N (of smoke) nube f; (of sail) ondulación f ▶ VI (smoke) salir en nubes; (sail) ondear, ondular

billy ['bɪlɪ] N (US) porra

billy goat N macho cabrío

bimbo ['bɪmbəu] N (inf) tía buena sin seso

bin [bɪn] N (gen) cubo or bote m (LAM) de la basura; (litterbin) papelera

binary ['baɪnərɪ] ADJ (Math) binario; **~ code** código binario

bind [baɪnd] (pt, pp **bound**) VT atar, liar; (wound) vendar; (book) encuadernar; (oblige) obligar ▶ N (inf: nuisance) lata
▶ **bind over** VT (Law) obligar por vía legal
▶ **bind up** VT (wound) vendar; **to be bound up in** (work, research etc) estar absorto en; **to be bound up with** (person) estar estrechamente ligado a

binder ['baɪndəʳ] N (*file*) archivador *m*
binding ['baɪndɪŋ] ADJ (*contract*) vinculante
binge [bɪndʒ] N borrachera, juerga; **to go on a ~** ir de juerga
bingo ['bɪŋgəu] N bingo *m*
bin-liner ['bɪnlaɪnəʳ] N bolsa de la basura
binoculars [bɪ'nɔkjuləz] NPL prismáticos *mpl*, gemelos *mpl*
bio [baɪə] ADJ (*inf*) biológico
biochemistry [baɪə'kɛmɪstrɪ] N bioquímica
biodegradable ['baɪəudɪ'greɪdəbl] ADJ biodegradable
biodiesel ['baɪəudi:zl] N biodiésel *m*
biodiversity ['baɪəudaɪ'və:sɪtɪ] N biodiversidad *f*
biofuel ['baɪəufjuəl] N biocombustible *m*, biocarburante *m*
biographer [baɪ'ɔgrəfəʳ] N biógrafo(-a)
biographical [baɪə'græfɪkəl] ADJ biográfico
biography [baɪ'ɔgrəfɪ] N biografía
biological [baɪə'lɔdʒɪkəl] ADJ biológico; (*products, foodstuffs etc*) orgánico(-a)
biological clock N reloj *m* biológico
biologist [baɪ'ɔlədʒɪst] N biólogo(-a)
biology [baɪ'ɔlədʒɪ] N biología
biometric [baɪə'mɛtrɪk] ADJ biométrico
biophysics ['baɪəu'fɪzɪks] NSG biofísica
biopic ['baɪəupɪk] N filme *m* biográfico
biopsy ['baɪɔpsɪ] N biopsia
biosphere ['baɪəsfɪəʳ] N biosfera
biotechnology ['baɪəutɛk'nɔlədʒɪ] N biotecnología
bioterrorism ['baɪəu'tɛrərɪzəm] N bioterrorismo
biped ['baɪpɛd] N bípedo
birch [bə:tʃ] N abedul *m*; (*cane*) vara
bird [bə:d] N ave *f*, pájaro; (BRIT *inf*: *girl*) chica
birdcage ['bə:dkeɪdʒ] N jaula
bird flu N gripe aviar
bird of prey N ave *f* de presa
bird's-eye view ['bə:dzaɪ-] N vista de pájaro
bird-watcher N ornitólogo(-a)
bird-watching N: **he likes to go ~ on Sundays** los domingos le gusta ir a ver pájaros
Biro® ['baɪrəu] N bolígrafo
birth [bə:θ] N nacimiento; (*Med*) parto; **to give ~ to** parir, dar a luz a; (*fig*) dar origen a
birth certificate N partida de nacimiento
birth control N control *m* de natalidad; (*methods*) métodos *mpl* anticonceptivos
birthday ['bə:θdeɪ] N cumpleaños *m inv*
birthday card N tarjeta de cumpleaños
birthmark N antojo, marca de nacimiento
birthplace ['bə:θpleɪs] N lugar *m* de nacimiento
birth rate N (tasa de) natalidad *f*
Biscay ['bɪskeɪ] N: **the Bay of ~** el Mar Cantábrico, el golfo de Vizcaya

biscuit ['bɪskɪt] N (BRIT) galleta
bisect [baɪ'sɛkt] VT (*also Math*) bisecar
bisexual ['baɪ'sɛksjuəl] ADJ, N bisexual *mf*
bishop ['bɪʃəp] N obispo; (*Chess*) alfil *m*
bistro ['bi:strəu] N café-bar *m*
bit [bɪt] PT *of* **bite** ▶ N trozo, pedazo, pedacito; (*Comput*) bit *m*; (*for horse*) freno, bocado; **a ~ of** un poco de; **a ~ mad** un poco loco; **~ by bit** poco a poco; **to come to bits** (*break*) hacerse pedazos; **to do one's ~** aportar su granito de arena; **bring all your bits and pieces** trae todas tus cosas
bitch [bɪtʃ] N (*dog*) perra; (*inf!: woman*) zorra (!)
bite [baɪt] VT, VI (*pt* **bit**, *pp* **bitten**) morder; (*insect etc*) picar ▶ N (*wound: of dog, snake etc*) mordedura; (: *of insect*) picadura; (*mouthful*) bocado; **to ~ one's nails** morderse las uñas; **let's have a ~ (to eat)** vamos a comer algo
biting ['baɪtɪŋ] ADJ (*wind*) que traspasa los huesos; (*criticism*) mordaz
bit part N (*Theat*) papel *m* sin importancia, papelito
bitten ['bɪtn] PP *of* **bite**
bitter ['bɪtəʳ] ADJ amargo; (*wind, criticism*) cortante, penetrante; (*icy: weather*) glacial; (: *battle*) encarnizado ▶ N (BRIT: *beer*) cerveza típica británica a base de lúpulos
bitterly ['bɪtəlɪ] ADV (*disappoint, complain, weep*) desconsoladamente; (*oppose, criticise*) implacablemente; (*jealous*) agriamente; **it's ~ cold** hace un frío glacial
bitterness ['bɪtənɪs] N amargura; (*anger*) rencor *m*
bitty ['bɪtɪ] ADJ deshilvanado
bitumen ['bɪtjumɪn] N betún *m*
bivouac ['bɪvuæk] N vivac *m*, vivaque *m*
bizarre [bɪ'zɑ:ʳ] ADJ raro, extraño
bk ABBR = **bank; book**
BL N ABBR = **Bachelor of Law(s)**; (= *Bachelor of Letters*) títulos universitarios; (US: = *Bachelor of Literature*) título universitario; *see also* **bachelor's degree**
B/L ABBR = **bill of lading**
blab [blæb] VI cantar ▶ VT (*also*: **blab out**) soltar, contar
black [blæk] ADJ (*colour*) negro; (*dark*) oscuro ▶ N (*colour*) color *m* negro; (*person*): **B~** negro(-a) ▶ VT (*shoes*) lustrar; (BRIT *Industry*) boicotear; **to give sb a ~ eye** ponerle a algn el ojo morado; **~ coffee** café *m* solo; **there it is in ~ and white** (*fig*) ahí está bien claro; **to be in the ~** (*in credit*) tener saldo positivo; **~ and blue** *adj* amoratado ▶ **black out** VI (*faint*) desmayarse
black belt N (*Sport*) cinturón *m* negro; (*US: area*) zona negra
blackberry ['blækbərɪ] N zarzamora
blackbird ['blækbə:d] N mirlo
blackboard ['blækbɔ:d] N pizarra

black box N (*Aviat*) caja negra

Black Country N (*Brit*): **the ~** región industrial del centro de Inglaterra

blackcurrant ['blæk'kʌrənt] N grosella negra

black economy N economía sumergida

blacken ['blækən] VT ennegrecer; (*fig*) denigrar

Black Forest N: **the ~** la Selva Negra

blackguard ['blæɡɑːd] N canalla *m*, pillo

black hole N (*Astro*) agujero negro

black ice N hielo invisible en la carretera

blackjack ['blækdʒæk] N (*US*) veintiuna

blackleg ['blæklɛɡ] N (*Brit*) esquirol *mf*

blacklist ['blæklɪst] N lista negra ▶ VT poner en la lista negra

blackmail ['blækmeɪl] N chantaje *m* ▶ VT chantajear

blackmailer ['blækmeɪlər] N chantajista *mf*

black market N mercado negro, estraperlo

blackness ['blæknɪs] N negrura

blackout ['blækaut] N (*Elec*) apagón *m*; (*TV*) bloqueo informativo; (*fainting*) desmayo, pérdida de conocimiento

black pepper N pimienta *f* negra

black pudding N morcilla

Black Sea N: **the ~** el Mar Negro

black sheep N oveja negra

blacksmith ['blæksmɪθ] N herrero

black spot N (*Aut*) punto negro

bladder ['blædər] N vejiga

blade [bleɪd] N hoja; (*cutting edge*) filo; **a ~ of grass** una brizna de hierba

Blairite ['blɛəraɪt] N, ADJ blairista *mf*

blame [bleɪm] N culpa ▶ VT: **to ~ sb for sth** echar a algn la culpa de algo; **to be to ~ (for)** tener la culpa (de); **I'm not to ~** yo no tengo la culpa; **and I don't ~ him** y lo comprendo perfectamente

blameless ['bleɪmlɪs] ADJ (*person*) inocente

blanch [blɑːntʃ] VI (*person*) palidecer; (*Culin*) escaldar

bland [blænd] ADJ suave; (*taste*) soso

blank [blæŋk] ADJ en blanco; (*shot*) de fogueo; (*look*) sin expresión ▶ N blanco, espacio en blanco; (*cartridge*) cartucho sin bala or de fogueo; **to draw a ~** (*fig*) no conseguir nada; **my mind is a ~** no puedo recordar nada

blank cheque, (*US*) **blank check** N cheque *m* en blanco

blanket ['blæŋkɪt] N manta, frazada (*Lam*), cobija (*Lam*); (*of snow*) capa; (*of fog*) manto ▶ ADJ (*statement, agreement*) comprensivo, general; **to give ~ cover** (*insurance policy*) dar póliza a todo riesgo

blankly ['blæŋklɪ] ADV: **she looked at me ~** me miró sin comprender

blare [blɛər] VI (*brass band, horns, radio*) resonar

blasé ['blɑːzeɪ] ADJ de vuelta de todo

blaspheme [blæs'fiːm] VI blasfemar

blasphemous ['blæsfɪməs] ADJ blasfemo

blasphemy ['blæsfɪmɪ] N blasfemia

blast [blɑːst] N (*of wind*) ráfaga, soplo; (*of whistle*) toque *m*; (*of explosive*) explosión *f*; (*force*) choque *m* ▶ VT (*blow up*) volar; (*blow open*) abrir con carga explosiva ▶ EXCL (*Brit inf*) ¡maldito sea!; **(at) full ~** (*also fig*) a toda marcha

▶ **blast off** VI (*spacecraft etc*) despegar

blast furnace N alto horno

blast-off ['blɑːstɒf] N (*Space*) lanzamiento

blatant ['bleɪtənt] ADJ descarado

blatantly ['bleɪtəntlɪ] ADV: **it's ~ obvious** está clarísimo

blather ['blæðər] VI decir tonterías

blaze [bleɪz] N (*fire*) fuego; (*flames*) llamarada; (*glow: of fire, sun etc*) resplandor *m*; (*fig*) arranque *m* ▶ VI (*fire*) arder en llamas; (*fig*) brillar ▶ VT: **to ~ a trail** (*fig*) abrir (un) camino; **in a ~ of publicity** bajo los focos de la publicidad

blazer ['bleɪzər] N *chaqueta de uniforme de colegial o de socio de club*

bleach [bliːtʃ] N (*also*: **household bleach**) lejía ▶ VT (*linen*) blanquear

bleached [bliːtʃt] ADJ (*hair*) de colorado; (*clothes*) blanqueado

bleachers ['bliːtʃəz] NPL (*US Sport*) gradas *fpl*

bleak [bliːk] ADJ (*countryside*) desierto; (*landscape*) desolado, desierto; (*weather*) desapacible; (*smile*) triste; (*prospect, future*) poco prometedor(a)

bleary-eyed ['blɪərɪ'aɪd] ADJ: **to be ~** tener ojos de cansado

bleat [bliːt] VI balar

bled [blɛd] PT, PP of **bleed**

bleed [bliːd] (*pt, pp* **bled**) VT sangrar; (*brakes, radiator*) desaguar ▶ VI sangrar; **my nose is bleeding** me está sangrando la nariz

bleeding ['bliːdɪŋ] ADJ sangrante

bleep [bliːp] N pitido ▶ VI pitar ▶ VT llamar por el busca

bleeper ['bliːpər] N (*of doctor etc*) busca *m*

blemish ['blɛmɪʃ] N marca, mancha; (*on reputation*) tacha

blench [blɛntʃ] VI (*shrink back*) acobardarse; (*grow pale*) palidecer

blend [blɛnd] N mezcla ▶ VT mezclar ▶ VI (*colours etc*) combinarse, mezclarse

blender ['blɛndər] N (*Culin*) batidora

bless [blɛs] (*pt, pp* **blessed** or **blest** [blɛst]) VT bendecir; **~ you!** (*after sneeze*) ¡Jesús!

blessed ['blɛsɪd] ADJ (*Rel: holy*) santo, bendito; (*: happy*) dichoso; **every ~ day** cada santo día

blessing ['blɛsɪŋ] N bendición *f*; (*advantage*) beneficio, ventaja; **to count one's blessings** agradecer lo que se tiene; **it was a ~ in disguise** no hay mal que por bien no venga

blew [blu:] PT of **blow**

blight [blaɪt] VT (hopes etc) frustrar, arruinar

blimey ['blaɪmɪ] EXCL (BRIT inf) ¡caray!

blind [blaɪnd] ADJ ciego ▶ N (for window) persiana ▶ VT cegar; (dazzle) deslumbrar; **to ~ sb to ...** (deceive) cegar a algn a ...; **the blind** NPL los ciegos

blind alley N callejón m sin salida

blind corner N (BRIT) esquina or curva sin visibilidad

blind date N cita a ciegas

blinders ['blaɪndəz] NPL (US) anteojeras fpl

blindfold ['blaɪndfəʊld] N venda ▶ ADJ, ADV con los ojos vendados ▶ VT vendar los ojos a

blinding ['blaɪndɪŋ] ADJ (flash, light) cegador; (pain) intenso

blindingly ['blaɪndɪŋlɪ] ADV: **it's ~ obvious** salta a la vista

blindly ['blaɪndlɪ] ADV a ciegas, ciegamente

blindness ['blaɪndnɪs] N ceguera

blind spot N (Aut) ángulo muerto; **to have a ~ about sth** estar ciego para algo

blink [blɪŋk] VI parpadear, pestañear; (light) oscilar; **to be on the ~** (inf) estar estropeado

blinkers ['blɪŋkəz] NPL (esp BRIT) anteojeras fpl

blinking ['blɪŋkɪŋ] ADJ (inf): **this ~ ...** este condenado ...

blip [blɪp] N señal f luminosa; (on graph) pequeña desviación f; (fig) pequeña anomalía

bliss [blɪs] N felicidad f

blissful ['blɪsful] ADJ dichoso; **in ~ ignorance** feliz en la ignorancia

blissfully ['blɪsfulɪ] ADV (sigh, smile) con felicidad; **~ happy** sumamente feliz

blister ['blɪstər] N (on skin, paint) ampolla ▶ VI ampollarse

blistering ['blɪstərɪŋ] ADJ (heat) abrasador(a)

BLit, BLitt N ABBR (= Bachelor of Literature) título universitario

blithely ['blaɪðlɪ] ADV alegremente, despreocupadamente

blithering ['blɪðərɪŋ] ADJ (inf): **this ~ idiot** este tonto perdido

blitz [blɪts] N bombardeo aéreo; **to have a ~ on sth** (fig) emprenderla con algo

blizzard ['blɪzəd] N ventisca

BLM N ABBR (US) = **Bureau of Land Management**

bloated ['bləʊtɪd] ADJ hinchado

blob [blɒb] N (drop) gota; (stain, spot) mancha

bloc [blɒk] N (Pol) bloque m

block [blɒk] N (also Comput) bloque m; (in pipes) obstáculo; (of buildings) manzana, cuadra (LAM) ▶ VT (gen) obstruir, cerrar; (progress) estorbar; (Comput) agrupar; **~ of flats** (BRIT) bloque m de pisos; **mental ~** bloqueo mental; **~ and tackle** (Tech) aparejo de polea;

3 blocks from here a 3 manzanas or cuadras (LAM) de aquí

▶ **block up** VT tapar, obstruir; (pipe) atascar

blockade [blɒ'keɪd] N bloqueo ▶ VT bloquear

blockage ['blɒkɪdʒ] N estorbo, obstrucción f

block booking N reserva en grupo

blockbuster ['blɒkbʌstər] N (book) best-seller m; (film) éxito de público

block capitals NPL mayúsculas fpl

block letters NPL mayúsculas fpl

block release N (BRIT) exención f por estudios

block vote N (BRIT) voto por delegación

blog [blɒg] (Comput) N blog m ▶ VI bloguear; **he blogs about politics** tiene un blog sobre política

blogger ['blɒgər] N (inf: person) bloguero(-a)

blogging ['blɒgɪŋ] N blogging m

blogosphere ['blɒgəsfɪər] N blogosfera

bloke [bləʊk] N (BRIT inf) tipo, tío

blond, blonde [blɒnd] ADJ, N rubio(-a) m/f

blood [blʌd] N sangre f; **new ~** (fig) gente f nueva

blood bank N banco de sangre

blood count N recuento de glóbulos rojos y blancos

blood donor N donante mf de sangre

blood group N grupo sanguíneo

bloodhound ['blʌdhaund] N sabueso

bloodless ['blʌdlɪs] ADJ (pale) exangüe; (revolt etc) sin derramamiento de sangre, incruento

bloodletting ['blʌdlɛtɪŋ] N (Med) sangría; (fig) sangría, carnicería

blood poisoning N septicemia, envenenamiento de la sangre

blood pressure N tensión f, presión f sanguínea; **to have high/low ~** tener la tensión alta/baja

bloodshed ['blʌdʃed] N baño de sangre

bloodshot ['blʌdʃɒt] ADJ inyectado en sangre

bloodstained ['blʌdsteɪnd] ADJ manchado de sangre

bloodstream ['blʌdstri:m] N corriente f sanguínea

blood test N análisis m de sangre

bloodthirsty ['blʌdθə:stɪ] ADJ sanguinario

blood transfusion N transfusión f de sangre

blood type N grupo sanguíneo

blood vessel N vaso sanguíneo

bloody ['blʌdɪ] ADJ sangriento; (BRIT inf!): **this ~ ...** este condenado or puñetero or fregado (LAM) (!) ... ▶ ADV (BRIT inf!): **~ strong/good** terriblemente fuerte/bueno

bloody-minded ['blʌdɪ'maɪndɪd] ADJ (BRIT inf) con malas pulgas

bloom [blu:m] N floración f; **in ~** en flor ▶ VI florecer

blooming ['blu:mɪŋ] ADJ (inf): **this ~ ...** este condenado ...

blossom ['blɔsəm] N flor f ▶ VI florecer; (fig) desarrollarse; **to ~ into** (fig) convertirse en

blot [blɔt] N borrón m ▶ VT (dry) secar; (stain) manchar; **to ~ out** vt (view) tapar; (memories) borrar; **to be a ~ on the landscape** estropear el paisaje; **to ~ one's copy book** (fig) manchar su reputación

blotchy ['blɔtʃɪ] ADJ (complexion) lleno de manchas

blotter ['blɔtər] N secante m

blotting paper ['blɔtɪŋ-] N papel m secante

blotto ['blɔtəʊ] ADJ (inf) mamado

blouse [blauz] N blusa

blow [bləʊ] (pt **blew**, pp **blown**) N golpe m ▶ VI soplar; (fuse) fundirse ▶ VT (glass) soplar; (fuse) quemar; (instrument) tocar; **to come to blows** llegar a golpes; **to ~ one's nose** sonarse
▶ **blow away** VT llevarse, arrancar
▶ **blow down** VT derribar
▶ **blow off** VT arrebatar
▶ **blow out** VT apagar ▶ VI apagarse; (tyre) reventar
▶ **blow over** VI amainar
▶ **blow up** VI estallar ▶ VT volar; (tyre) inflar; (Phot) ampliar

blow-dry ['bləʊdraɪ] N secado con secador de mano ▶ VT secar con secador de mano

blowlamp ['bləʊlæmp] N (BRIT) soplete m, lámpara de soldar

blown [bləʊn] PP of **blow**

blow-out ['bləʊaʊt] N (of tyre) pinchazo; (inf: big meal) banquete m, festín m

blowtorch ['bləʊtɔːtʃ] N = **blowlamp**

blow-up ['bləʊʌp] N (Phot) ampliación f

BLS N ABBR (US) = **Bureau of Labor Statistics**

blubber ['blʌbər] N grasa de ballena ▶ VI (pej) lloriquear

bludgeon ['blʌdʒən] VT: **to ~ sb into doing sth** coaccionar a algn a hacer algo

blue [bluː] ADJ azul; **~ film** película porno; **~ joke** chiste verde; **once in a ~ moon** de higos a brevas; **to come out of the ~** (fig) ser completamente inesperado; see also **blues**

blue baby N niño azul or cianótico

bluebell ['bluːbɛl] N campanilla, campánula azul

blueberry N arándano

blue-blooded [bluːˈblʌdɪd] ADJ de sangre azul

bluebottle ['bluːbɔtl] N moscarda, mosca azul

blue cheese N queso azul

blue-chip ['bluːtʃɪp] N: **~ investment** inversión f asegurada

blue-collar worker ['bluːkɔlər-] N obrero(-a)

blue jeans NPL tejanos mpl, vaqueros mpl

blueprint ['bluːprɪnt] N proyecto; **~ (for)** (fig) anteproyecto (de)

blues [bluːz] NPL: **the ~** (Mus) el blues; **to have the ~** estar triste

bluetit [bluːtɪt] N herrerillo m (común)

Bluetooth® ['bluːtuːθ] N Bluetooth® f; **~ technology** tecnología Bluetooth®

bluff [blʌf] VI tirarse un farol, farolear ▶ N bluff m, farol m; (Geo) precipicio, despeñadero; **to call sb's ~** coger a algn en un renuncio

bluish ['bluːɪʃ] ADJ azulado

blunder ['blʌndər] N patinazo, metedura de pata ▶ VI cometer un error, meter la pata; **to ~ into sb/sth** tropezar con algn/algo

blunt [blʌnt] ADJ (knife) desafilado; (person) franco, directo ▶ VT embotar, desafilar; **this pencil is ~** este lápiz está despuntado; **~ instrument** (Law) instrumento contundente

bluntly ['blʌntlɪ] ADV (speak) francamente, de modo terminante

bluntness ['blʌntnɪs] N (of person) franqueza, brusquedad f

blur [bləːr] N aspecto borroso; **to become a ~** hacerse borroso ▶ VT (vision) enturbiar; (memory) empañar

blurb [bləːb] N propaganda

blurred [bləːd] ADJ borroso

blurt [bləːt]: **to ~ out** vt (say) descolgarse con, dejar escapar

blush [blʌʃ] VI ruborizarse, ponerse colorado ▶ N rubor m

blusher ['blʌʃər] N colorete m

bluster ['blʌstər] N fanfarronada, bravata ▶ VI fanfarronear, echar bravatas

blustering ['blʌstərɪŋ] ADJ (person) fanfarrón(-ona)

blustery ['blʌstərɪ] ADJ (weather) tempestuoso, tormentoso

Blvd ABBR = **boulevard**

BM N ABBR = **British Museum**; (Univ: = Bachelor of Medicine) título universitario

BMA N ABBR = **British Medical Association**

BMJ N ABBR = **British Medical Journal**

BMus N ABBR (= Bachelor of Music) título universitario

BMX N ABBR (= bicycle motocross) BMX f; **~ bike** bici(cleta) f BMX

bn ABBR = **billion**

BO N ABBR (inf: = body odour) olor m a sudor; (US) = **box office**

boa ['bəʊə] N boa

boar [bɔːr] N verraco, cerdo

board [bɔːd] N tabla, tablero; (on wall) tablón m; (for chess etc) tablero; (committee) junta, consejo; (in firm) mesa or junta directiva; (Naut, Aviat): **on ~** a bordo ▶ VT (ship) embarcarse en; (train) subir a; **full ~** (BRIT) pensión f completa; **half ~** (BRIT) media pensión; **~ and lodging** alojamiento y

451

comida; **to go by the ~** (*fig*) irse por la borda;
above ~ (*fig*) sin tapujos; **across the ~** (*fig:
adv*) en todos los niveles (: *adj*) general
▶ **board up** VT (*door*) tapar, cegar

boarder ['bɔːdər] N huésped(a) *m/f*; (*Scol*)
interno(-a)

board game N juego de tablero

boarding card ['bɔːdɪŋ-] N (*BRIT Aviat, Naut*)
tarjeta de embarque

boarding house ['bɔːdɪŋ-] N casa de
huéspedes

boarding party ['bɔːdɪŋ-] N brigada de
inspección

boarding pass ['bɔːdɪŋ-] N (*US*) = **boarding
card**

boarding school ['bɔːdɪŋ-] N internado

board meeting N reunión *f* de la junta
directiva

board room N sala de juntas

boardwalk ['bɔːdwɔːk] N (*US*) paseo
entablado

boast [bəust] VI: **to ~ (about** *or* **of)** alardear
(de) ▶ VT ostentar ▶ N alarde *m*, baladronada

boastful ['bəustfəl] ADJ presumido,
jactancioso

boastfulness ['bəustfulnɪs] N fanfarronería,
jactancia

boat [bəut] N barco, buque *m*; (*small*) barca,
bote *m*; **to go by ~** ir en barco

boater ['bəutər] N (*hat*) canotié *m*

boating ['bəutɪŋ] N canotaje *m*

boatman ['bəutmən] N (*irreg*) barquero

boat people NPL *refugiados que huyen en barca*

boatswain ['bəusn] N contramaestre *m*

bob [bɔb] VI (*also*: **bob up and down**: *boat, cork
on water*) menearse, balancearse ▶ N (*BRIT inf*)
= **shilling**
▶ **bob up** VI (re)aparecer de repente

bobbin ['bɔbɪn] N (*of sewing machine*) carrete *m*,
bobina

bobby ['bɔbɪ] N (*BRIT inf*) poli *mf*

bobby pin N (*US*) horquilla

bobsleigh ['bɔbsleɪ] N bob *m*, trineo de
competición *f*

bode [bəud] VI: **to ~ well/ill (for)** ser de buen/
mal agüero (para)

bodice ['bɔdɪs] N corpiño

-bodied ['bɔdɪd] ADJ SUFF de cuerpo ...

bodily ['bɔdɪlɪ] ADJ (*comfort, needs*) corporal;
(*pain*) corpóreo ▶ ADV (*in person*) en persona;
(*carry*) corporalmente; (*lift*) en peso

body ['bɔdɪ] N cuerpo; (*corpse*) cadáver *m*; (*of
car*) caja, carrocería; (*also*: **body stocking**)
body *m*; (*fig: organization*) organización *f*;
(: *public body*) organismo; (*quantity*) masa; (*of
speech, document*) parte *f* principal; **ruling ~**
directiva; **in a ~** todos juntos, en masa

body blow N (*fig*) palo

body-building ['bɔdɪ'bɪldɪŋ] N culturismo

bodyguard ['bɔdɪgaːd] N guardaespaldas *m inv*

body language N lenguaje *m* gestual

body search N cacheo; **to carry out a ~ on
sb** registrar a algn; **to submit to** *or* **undergo
a ~** ser registrado

bodywork ['bɔdɪwəːk] N carrocería

boffin ['bɔfɪn] N (*BRIT*) científico(-a)

bog [bɔg] N pantano, ciénaga ▶ VT: **to get
bogged down** (*fig*) empantanarse, atascarse

boggle ['bɔgl] VI: **the mind boggles!** ¡no
puedo creerlo!

Bogotá [bəugə'taː] N Bogotá

bogus ['bəugəs] ADJ falso, fraudulento;
(*person*) fingido

Bohemia [bə'hiːmɪə] N Bohemia

Bohemian [bə'hiːmɪən] ADJ, N bohemio(-a) *m/f*

boil [bɔɪl] VT hervir; (*eggs*) pasar por agua ▶ VI
hervir; (*fig: with anger*) estar furioso ▶ N (*Med*)
furúnculo, divieso; **to bring to the ~**
calentar hasta que hierva; **to come to the ~**
(*BRIT*) *or* **a** (*US*) = comenzar a hervir; **boiled
egg** huevo pasado por agua; **boiled
potatoes** patatas *fpl* *or* papas *fpl* (*LAm*) cocidas
▶ **boil down** VI (*fig*): **to ~ down to** reducirse a
▶ **boil over** VI (*liquid*) salirse; (*anger, resentment*)
llegar al colmo

boiler ['bɔɪlər] N caldera

boiler suit N (*BRIT*) mono, overol *m* (*LAm*)

boiling ['bɔɪlɪŋ] ADJ: **I'm ~ (hot)** (*inf*) estoy asado

boiling point N punto de ebullición *f*

boil-in-the-bag [bɔɪlɪnðə'bæg] ADJ: **~ meals**
platos que se cuecen en su misma bolsa

boisterous ['bɔɪstərəs] ADJ (*noisy*) bullicioso;
(*excitable*) exuberante; (*crowd*) tumultuoso

bold [bəuld] ADJ (*brave*) valiente, audaz; (*pej*)
descarado; (*outline*) grueso; (*colour*)
llamativo; **~ type** (*Typ*) negrita

boldly ['bəuldlɪ] ADV audazmente

boldness ['bəuldnɪs] N valor *m*, audacia;
(*cheek*) descaro

Bolivia [bə'lɪvɪə] N Bolivia

Bolivian [bə'lɪvɪən] ADJ, N boliviano(-a) *m/f*

bollard ['bɔləd] N (*BRIT Aut*) poste *m*

Bollywood ['bɔlɪwud] N Bollywood *m*

bolshy ['bɔlʃɪ] ADJ (*BRIT inf*) protestón(-ona);
to be in a ~ mood tener el día protestón

bolster ['bəulstər] N travesero, cabezal *m*
▶ **bolster up** VT reforzar; (*fig*) alentar

bolt [bəult] N (*lock*) cerrojo; (*with nut*) perno,
tornillo ▶ ADV: **~ upright** rígido, erguido
▶ VT (*door*) echar el cerrojo a; (*food*) engullir
▶ VI fugarse; (*horse*) desbocarse

bomb [bɔm] N bomba ▶ VT bombardear

bombard [bɔm'baːd] VT bombardear; (*fig*)
asediar

bombardment [bɔm'baːdmənt] N
bombardeo

bombastic [bɔm'bæstɪk] ADJ rimbombante;
(*person*) pomposo

b

bomb disposal N desactivación f de explosivos

bomb disposal expert N artificiero(-a)

bomber ['bɒmə'] N (Aviat) bombardero; (terrorist) persona que pone bombas

bombing ['bɒmɪŋ] N bombardeo

bomb scare N amenaza de bomba

bombshell ['bɒmʃɛl] N obús m, granada; (fig) bomba

bomb site N lugar m donde estalló una bomba

bona fide ['bəunə'faɪdɪ] ADJ genuino, auténtico

bonanza [bə'nænzə] N bonanza

bond [bɒnd] N (binding promise) fianza; (Finance) bono; (link) vínculo, lazo; **in ~** (Comm) en depósito bajo fianza

bondage ['bɒndɪdʒ] N esclavitud f

bonded goods ['bɒndɪd-] NPL mercancías fpl en depósito de aduanas

bonded warehouse ['bɒndɪd-] N depósito de aduanas

bone [bəun] N hueso; (of fish) espina ▶ VT deshuesar; quitar las espinas a; **~ of contention** manzana de la discordia

bone china N porcelana fina

bone-dry ['bəun'draɪ] ADJ completamente seco

bone idle ADJ gandul

bone marrow N médula; **~ transplant** transplante m de médula

boner ['bəunə'] N (US inf) plancha, patochada

bonfire ['bɒnfaɪə'] N hoguera, fogata

bonk [bɒŋk] VT, VI (humorous, inf) chingar (!)

bonkers ['bɒŋkəz] ADJ (BRIT inf) majareta

Bonn [bɒn] N Bonn m

bonnet ['bɒnɪt] N gorra; (BRIT: of car) capó m

bonny ['bɒnɪ] ADJ (esp SCOTTISH) bonito, hermoso, lindo

bonus ['bəunəs] N (payment) paga extraordinaria, plus m; (fig) bendición f

bony ['bəunɪ] ADJ (arm, face) huesudo; (Med: tissue) huesudo; (: meat) lleno de huesos; (: fish) lleno de espinas; (thin: person) flaco, delgado

boo [bu:] EXCL ¡uh! ▶ VT abuchear

boob [bu:b] N (inf: mistake) disparate m, sandez f; (: breast) teta

booby prize ['bu:bɪ-] N premio de consolación (al último)

booby trap ['bu:bɪ-] N (Mil etc) trampa explosiva

book [buk] N libro; (notebook) libreta; (of stamps etc) librillo; **books** (Comm) cuentas fpl, contabilidad f ▶ VT (ticket, seat, room) reservar; (driver) fichar; (Football) amonestar; **to keep the books** llevar las cuentas or los libros; **by the ~** según las reglas; **to throw the ~ at sb** echar un rapapolvo a algn

▶ **book in** VI (at hotel) registrarse

▶ **book up** VT: **all seats are booked up** todas las plazas están reservadas; **the hotel is booked up** el hotel está completo

bookable ['bukəbl] ADJ: **seats are ~** los asientos se pueden reservar (de antemano)

bookcase ['bukkeɪs] N librería, estante m para libros

booking ['bukɪŋ] N reserva

booking office N (BRIT: Rail) despacho de billetes or boletos (LAM); (: Theat) taquilla, boletería (LAM)

book-keeping ['buk'ki:pɪŋ] N contabilidad f

booklet ['buklɪt] N folleto

bookmaker ['bukmeɪkə'] N corredor m de apuestas

bookmark ['bukmɑ:k] N (Comput) favorito, marcador m

bookseller ['buksɛlə'] N librero(-a)

bookshelf ['bukʃɛlf] N estante m

bookshop ['bukʃɒp] N librería

bookstall ['bukstɔ:l] N quiosco de libros

book store N = **bookshop**

book token N vale m para libros

book value N (Comm) valor m contable

bookworm ['bukwə:m] N (fig) ratón m de biblioteca

boom [bu:m] N (noise) trueno, estampido; (in prices etc) alza rápida; (Econ) boom m, auge m ▶ VI (cannon) hacer gran estruendo, retumbar; (Econ) estar en alza

boomerang ['bu:məræŋ] N bumerang m (also fig) ▶ VI: **to ~ on sb** (fig) ser contraproducente para algn

boom town N ciudad f de crecimiento rápido

boon [bu:n] N favor m, beneficio

boorish ['buərɪʃ] ADJ grosero

boost [bu:st] N estímulo, empuje m ▶ VT estimular, empujar; (increase: sales, production) aumentar; **to give a ~ to** (morale) levantar; **it gave a ~ to his confidence** le dio confianza en sí mismo

booster ['bu:stə'] N (Med) reinyección f; (TV) repetidor m; (Elec) elevador m de tensión; (also: **booster rocket**) cohete m

boot [bu:t] N bota; (ankle boot) botín m, borceguí m; (BRIT: of car) maleta, maletero, baúl m (LAM) ▶ VT dar un puntapié a; (Comput) arrancar; **to ~** (in addition) además, por añadidura; **to give sb the ~** (inf) despedir a algn, poner a algn en la calle

booth [bu:ð] N (at fair) barraca; (telephone booth, voting booth) cabina

bootleg ['bu:tlɛg] ADJ de contrabando; **~ record** disco pirata

booty ['bu:tɪ] N botín m

booze [bu:z] (inf) N bebida ▶ VI emborracharse

boozer ['bu:zə'] N (inf: person) bebedor(a) m/f; (: BRIT: pub) bar m

border ['bɔːdəʳ] N borde *m*, margen *m*; (*of a country*) frontera; (*for flowers*) arriate *m* ▸ ADJ fronterizo; **the Borders** *región fronteriza entre Escocia e Inglaterra*

▸ **border on** VT FUS lindar con; (*fig*) rayar en

borderline ['bɔːdəlaɪn] N (*fig*) frontera; **on the** ~ en el límite

bore [bɔːʳ] PT *of* **bear** ▸ VT (*hole*) hacer; (*person*) aburrir ▸ N (*person*) pelmazo, pesado; (*of gun*) calibre *m*

bored [bɔːd] ADJ aburrido; **he's ~ to tears** *or* **to death** *or* **stiff** está aburrido como una ostra, está muerto de aburrimiento

boredom ['bɔːdəm] N aburrimiento

boring ['bɔːrɪŋ] ADJ aburrido, pesado

born [bɔːn] ADJ: **to be** ~ nacer; **I was ~ in 1960** nací en 1960

born-again [bɔːnə'gɛn] ADJ: ~ **Christian** evangelista *mf*

borne [bɔːn] PP *of* **bear**

Borneo ['bɔːnɪəu] N Borneo

borough ['bʌrə] N municipio

borrow ['bɔrəu] VT: **to ~ sth (from sb)** tomar algo prestado (a alguien); **may I ~ your car?** ¿me prestas tu coche?

borrower ['bɔrəuəʳ] N prestatario(-a)

borrowing ['bɔrəuɪŋ] N préstamos *mpl*

borstal ['bɔːstl] N (BRIT) reformatorio (de menores)

Bosnia ['bɔznɪə] N Bosnia

Bosnia-Herzegovina, Bosnia-Hercegovina ['bɔːznɪəhɜːtsəgəu'viːnə] N Bosnia-Herzegovina

Bosnian ['bɔznɪən] ADJ, N bosnio(-a) *m/f*

bosom ['buzəm] N pecho; (*fig*) seno

bosom friend N amigo(-a) íntimo(-a) *or* del alma

boss [bɔs] N jefe(-a) *m/f*; (*employer*) patrón(-ona) *m/f*; (*political etc*) cacique *m* ▸ VT (*also:* **boss about** *or* **around**) mangonear; **stop bossing everyone about!** ¡deja de dar órdenes *or* de mangonear a todos!

bossy ['bɔsɪ] ADJ mandón(-ona)

bosun ['bəusn] N contramaestre *m*

botanical [bə'tænɪkl] ADJ botánico

botanist ['bɔtənɪst] N botanista *mf*

botany ['bɔtənɪ] N botánica

botch [bɔtʃ] VT (*also:* **botch up**) arruinar, estropear

both [bəuθ] ADJ, PRON ambos(-as), los/las dos; ~ **of us went**, **we ~ went** fuimos los dos, ambos fuimos ▸ ADV: ~ **A and B** tanto A como B

bother ['bɔðəʳ] VT (*worry*) preocupar; (*disturb*) molestar, fastidiar, fregar (LAM), embromar (LAM) ▸ VI (*gen*): **to ~ o.s.** molestarse ▸ N (*trouble*) dificultad *f*; (*nuisance*) molestia, lata; **what a ~!** ¡qué lata! ▸ EXCL ¡maldita sea!, ¡caramba!; **I'm sorry to ~ you** perdona que

te moleste; **to ~ doing** tomarse la molestia de hacer; **please don't** ~ no te molestes

Botswana [bɔt'swɑːnə] N Botswana

bottle ['bɔtl] N botella; (*small*) frasco; (*baby's*) biberón *m* ▸ VT embotellar; ~ **of wine/milk** botella de vino/de leche; **wine/milk** ~ botella de vino/de leche

▸ **bottle up** VT (*fig*) contener, reprimir

bottle bank N contenedor *m* de vidrio, iglú *m*

bottleneck ['bɔtlnɛk] N embotellamiento

bottle-opener ['bɔtləupnəʳ] N abrebotellas *m inv*

bottom ['bɔtəm] N (*of box, sea*) fondo; (*buttocks*) trasero, culo; (*of page, mountain, tree*) pie *m*; (*of list*) final *m* ▸ ADJ (*lowest*) más bajo; (*last*) último; **to get to the ~ of sth** (*fig*) llegar al fondo de algo

bottomless ['bɔtəmlɪs] ADJ sin fondo, insondable

bottom line N: **the ~** lo fundamental; **the ~ is he has to go** el caso es que tenemos que despedirle

botulism ['bɔtjulɪzəm] N botulismo

bough [bau] N rama

bought [bɔːt] PT, PP *of* **buy**

bouillon cube ['buːjɔn-] N (US) cubito de caldo

boulder ['bəuldəʳ] N canto rodado

boulevard ['buːləvɑːd] N bulevar

bounce [bauns] VI (*ball*) (re)botar; (*cheque*) ser rechazado ▸ VT hacer (re)botar ▸ N (*rebound*) (re)bote *m*; **he's got plenty of ~** (*fig*) tiene mucha energía

bouncer ['baunsəʳ] N (*inf*) forzudo, gorila *m*

bouncy castle® ['baunsɪ-] N castillo inflable

bound [baund] PT, PP *of* **bind** ▸ N (*leap*) salto; (*gen pl: limit*) límite *m* ▸ VI (*leap*) saltar ▸ ADJ: ~ **by** rodeado de; **to be ~ to do sth** (*obliged*) tener el deber de hacer algo; **he's ~ to come** es seguro que vendrá; **"out of bounds to the public"** "prohibido el paso"; ~ **for** con destino a

boundary ['baundrɪ] N límite *m*, lindero

boundless ['baundlɪs] ADJ ilimitado

bountiful ['bauntɪful] ADJ (*person*) liberal, generoso; (*God*) bondadoso; (*supply*) abundante

bounty ['bauntɪ] N (*generosity*) generosidad *f*; (*reward*) prima

bounty hunter N cazarrecompensas *m inv*

bouquet ['bukeɪ] N (*of flowers*) ramo, ramillete *m*; (*of wine*) aroma *m*

bourbon ['buəbən] N (US: *also:* **bourbon whiskey**) whisky *m* americano, bourbon *m*

bourgeois ['buəʒwɑː] ADJ, N burgués(-esa) *m/f*

bout [baut] N (*of malaria etc*) ataque *m*; (*Boxing etc*) combate *m*, encuentro

boutique [buː'tiːk] N boutique *f*, tienda de ropa

bow¹ [bəu] N (*knot*) lazo; (*weapon, Mus*) arco

bow² [bau] N (*of the head*) reverencia; (*Naut:* *also:* **bows**) proa ▸ VI inclinarse, hacer una reverencia; (yield): **to ~ to** or **before** ceder ante, someterse a; **to ~ to the inevitable** resignarse a lo inevitable

bowels ['bauəlz] NPL intestinos mpl, vientre m; (fig) entrañas fpl

bowl [bəul] N tazón m, cuenco; (for washing) palangana, jofaina; (ball) bola; (US: stadium) estadio ▶ VI (Cricket) arrojar la pelota; see also **bowls**

bow-legged ['bəu'lɛgɪd] ADJ estevado

bowler ['bəulər] N (Cricket) lanzador m (de la pelota); (BRIT: also: **bowler hat**) hongo, bombín m

bowling ['bəulɪŋ] N (game) bolos mpl, bochas fpl

bowling alley N bolera

bowling green N pista para bochas

bowls [bəulz] N juego de los bolos, bochas fpl

bow tie ['bəu-] N corbata de lazo, pajarita

box [bɔks] N (also: **cardboard box**) caja, cajón m; (for jewels) estuche m; (for money) cofre m; (crate) cofre m, arca; (Theat) palco ▶ VT encajonar ▶ VI (Sport) boxear

boxer ['bɔksər] N (person) boxeador m; (dog) bóxer m

boxer shorts ['bɔksəfɔːts] NPL bóxers; **a pair of ~** unos bóxers

box file N fichero

boxing ['bɔksɪŋ] N (Sport) boxeo, box m (LAM)

Boxing Day N (BRIT) día m de San Esteban; ver nota

El día después de Navidad es Boxing Day, fiesta en todo el Reino Unido, aunque si el 26 de diciembre cae en domingo el día de descanso se traslada al lunes. En dicho día solía ser tradición entregar "Christmas boxes" (aguinaldos) a empleados, proveedores a domicilio, carteros etc.

boxing gloves NPL guantes mpl de boxeo

boxing ring N ring m, cuadrilátero

box number N (for advertisements) apartado

box office N taquilla, boletería (LAM)

boxroom ['bɔksrum] N trastero

boy [bɔɪ] N (young) niño; (older) muchacho, chico; (son) hijo

boy band N boy band m (grupo musical de chicos)

boycott ['bɔɪkɔt] N boicot m ▶ VT boicotear

boyfriend ['bɔɪfrɛnd] N novio

boyish ['bɔɪɪʃ] ADJ de muchacho, inmaduro

boy scout N boy scout m

bp ABBR = **bishop**

Br. ABBR (Rel) = **brother**

bra [brɑː] N sostén m, sujetador m, corpiño (LAM)

brace [breɪs] N refuerzo, abrazadera; (BRIT: on teeth) corrector m, aparato; (tool) berbiquí m ▶ VT asegurar, reforzar; **to ~ o.s. (for)** (fig) prepararse (para); see also **braces**

bracelet ['breɪslɪt] N pulsera, brazalete m, pulso (LAM)

braces ['breɪsɪz] NPL (on teeth) corrector m; (BRIT: for trousers) tirantes mpl, suspensores mpl (LAM)

bracing ['breɪsɪŋ] ADJ vigorizante, tónico

bracken ['brækən] N helecho

bracket ['brækɪt] N (Tech) soporte m, puntal m; (group) clase f, categoría; (also: **brace bracket**) soporte m, abrazadera; (also: **round bracket**) paréntesis m inv ▶ VT (fig: also: **bracket together**) agrupar; **income ~** nivel m económico; **in brackets** entre paréntesis

brackish ['brækɪʃ] ADJ (water) salobre

brag [bræg] VI jactarse

braid [breɪd] N (trimming) galón m; (of hair) trenza

Braille [breɪl] N Braille m

brain [breɪn] N cerebro; **brains** NPL sesos mpl; **she's got brains** es muy lista

brainchild ['breɪntʃaɪld] N invención f

braindead ['breɪndɛd] ADJ (Med) clínicamente muerto; (inf) subnormal, tarado

brainfood ['breɪnfuːd] N alimentos pl para el cerebro

brainless ['breɪnlɪs] ADJ estúpido, insensato

brainstorm ['breɪnstɔːm] N (fig) ataque m de locura, frenesí m; (US: brainwave) idea luminosa or genial, inspiración f

brainstorming ['breɪnstɔːmɪŋ] N discusión intensa para solucionar problemas

brainwash ['breɪnwɔʃ] VT lavar el cerebro a

brainwave ['breɪnweɪv] N idea luminosa or genial, inspiración f

brainy ['breɪnɪ] ADJ muy listo or inteligente

braise [breɪz] VT cocer a fuego lento

brake [breɪk] N (on vehicle) freno ▶ VT, VI frenar

brake drum N tambor m de freno

brake fluid N líquido de frenos

brake light N luz f de frenado

brake pedal N pedal m de freno

bramble ['bræmbl] N (fruit) zarza

bran [bræn] N salvado

branch [brɑːntʃ] N rama; (fig) ramo; (Comm) sucursal f ▶ VI ramificarse; (fig) extenderse ▶ **branch off** VI: **a small road branches off to the right** hay una carretera pequeña que sale hacia la derecha ▶ **branch out** VI (fig) extenderse

branch line N (Rail) ramal m, línea secundaria

branch manager N director(a) m/f de sucursal

brand [brænd] N marca; (fig: type) tipo; (iron) hierro de marcar ▶ VT (cattle) marcar con hierro candente

brandish ['brændɪʃ] VT blandir

brand name N marca

brand-new ['brænd'njuː] ADJ flamante, completamente nuevo

brandy ['brændɪ] N coñac m, brandy m
brash [bræʃ] ADJ (rough) tosco; (cheeky) descarado
Brasilia [brə'zɪlɪə] N Brasilia
brass [brɑːs] N latón m; **the ~** (Mus) los cobres
brass band N banda de metal
brassière ['bræsɪəʳ] N sostén m, sujetador m, corpiño (LAM)
brass tacks NPL: **to get down to ~** ir al grano
brat [bræt] N (pej) mocoso(-a)
bravado [brə'vɑːdəu] N fanfarronería
brave [breɪv] ADJ valiente, valeroso ▶ N guerrero indio ▶ VT (challenge) desafiar; (resist) aguantar
bravely ['breɪvlɪ] ADV valientemente, con valor
bravery ['breɪvərɪ] N valor m, valentía
bravo [brɑː'vəu] EXCL ¡bravo!, ¡olé!
brawl [brɔːl] N pelea, reyerta ▶ VI pelearse
brawn [brɔːn] N fuerza muscular; (meat) carne f en gelatina
brawny ['brɔːnɪ] ADJ fornido, musculoso
bray [breɪ] N rebuzno ▶ VI rebuznar
brazen ['breɪzn] ADJ descarado, cínico ▶ VT: **to ~ it out** echarle cara al asunto
brazier ['breɪzɪəʳ] N brasero
Brazil [brə'zɪl] N (el) Brasil
Brazilian [brə'zɪlɪən] ADJ, N brasileño(-a) m/f
breach [briːtʃ] VT abrir brecha en ▶ N (gap) brecha; (estrangement) ruptura; (breaking): **~ of confidence** abuso de confianza; **~ of contract** infracción f de contrato; **in ~ of** por incumplimiento or infracción de; **~ of the peace** perturbación f del orden público
bread [brɛd] N pan m; (inf: money) pasta, lana (LAM); **~ and butter** n pan con mantequilla; (: fig) pan (de cada día); adj común y corriente; **to earn one's daily ~** ganarse el pan; **to know which side one's ~ is buttered (on)** saber dónde aprieta el zapato
breadbin ['brɛdbɪn] N panera
breadboard ['brɛdbɔːd] N (Comput) circuito experimental
breadbox ['brɛdbɔks] N (US) panera
breadcrumbs ['brɛdkrʌmz] NPL migajas fpl; (Culin) pan msg rallado
breadline ['brɛdlaɪn] N: **on the ~** en la miseria
breadth [brɛtθ] N anchura; (fig) amplitud f
breadwinner ['brɛdwɪnəʳ] N sostén m de la familia
break [breɪk] (pt **broke**, pp **broken**) VT (gen) romper; (promise) faltar a; (fall) amortiguar; (journey) interrumpir; (law) violar, infringir; (record) batir; (news) comunicar ▶ VI romperse, quebrarse; (storm) estallar; (weather) cambiar; (news etc) darse a conocer ▶ N (gap) abertura; (crack) grieta; (fracture) fractura; (in relations) ruptura; (rest) descanso; (time) intervalo; (: at school) (período de) recreo; (holiday) vacaciones fpl;

(chance) oportunidad f; (escape) evasión f, fuga; **to ~ with sb** (fig) romper con algn; **to ~ even** vi cubrir los gastos; **to ~ free** or **loose** vi escaparse; **lucky** ~ (inf) chiripa, racha de buena suerte; **to have** or **take a ~** (few minutes) descansar; **without a ~** sin descanso or descansar
▶ **break down** VT (door etc) echar abajo, derribar; (resistance) vencer, acabar con; (figures, data) analizar, descomponer; (undermine) acabar con ▶ VI estropearse; (Med) sufrir un colapso; (Aut) averiarse, descomponerse (LAM); (person) romper a llorar; (talks) fracasar
▶ **break in** VT (horse etc) domar ▶ VI (burglar) forzar una entrada
▶ **break into** VT FUS (house) forzar
▶ **break off** VI (speaker) pararse, detenerse; (branch) partir ▶ VT (talks) suspender; (engagement) romper
▶ **break open** VT (door etc) abrir por la fuerza, forzar
▶ **break out** VI estallar; (prisoner) escaparse; **to ~ out in spots** salir a algn granos
▶ **break through** VI: **the sun broke through** asomó el sol ▶ VT FUS (defences, barrier, crowd) abrirse paso por
▶ **break up** VI (marriage) deshacerse; (ship) hacerse pedazos; (crowd, meeting) disolverse; (Scol) terminar (el curso); (line) cortarse ▶ VT (rocks etc) partir; (journey) partir; (fight etc) acabar con; **the line's** or **you're breaking up** se corta
breakable ['breɪkəbl] ADJ quebradizo ▶ N: **breakables** cosas fpl frágiles
breakage ['breɪkɪdʒ] N rotura; **to pay for breakages** pagar por los objetos rotos
breakaway ['breɪkəweɪ] ADJ (group etc) disidente
break-dancing ['breɪkdɑːnsɪŋ] N break m
breakdown ['breɪkdaun] N (Aut) avería; (in communications) interrupción f; (Med: also: **nervous breakdown**) colapso, crisis f nerviosa; (of marriage, talks) fracaso; (of figures) desglose m
breakdown truck, breakdown van N (camión m) grúa
breaker ['breɪkəʳ] N rompiente m, ola grande
breakeven ['breɪk'iːvn] CPD: **~ chart** gráfico del punto de equilibrio; **~ point** punto de break-even or de equilibrio
breakfast ['brɛkfəst] N desayuno
breakfast cereal N cereales mpl para el desayuno
break-in ['breɪkɪn] N robo con allanamiento de morada
breaking and entering ['breɪkɪŋənd'ɛntərɪŋ] N (Law) violación f de domicilio, allanamiento de morada

breaking point ['breɪkɪŋ-] N punto de ruptura

breakthrough ['breɪkθruː] N ruptura; *(fig)* avance *m*, adelanto

break-up ['breɪkʌp] N *(of partnership, marriage)* disolución *f*

break-up value N *(Comm)* valor *m* de liquidación

breakwater ['breɪkwɔːtəʳ] N rompeolas *m inv*

breast [brest] N *(of woman)* pecho, seno; *(chest)* pecho; *(of bird)* pechuga

breast-feed ['brestfiːd] VT, VI *(irreg: like **feed**)* amamantar, dar el pecho

breaststroke ['breststrəʊk] N braza de pecho

breath [breθ] N aliento, respiración *f*; **to take a deep ~** respirar hondo; **out of ~** sin aliento, sofocado; **to go out for a ~ of air** salir a tomar el fresco

Breathalyser® ['breθəlaɪzəʳ] N *(BRIT)* alcoholímetro *m*; **~ test** *n* prueba de alcoholemia

breathe [briːð] VT, VI respirar; *(noisily)* resollar; **I won't ~ a word about it** no diré ni una palabra de ello
  ▸ **breathe in** VT, VI aspirar
  ▸ **breathe out** VT, VI espirar

breather ['briːðəʳ] N respiro, descanso

breathing ['briːðɪŋ] N respiración *f*

breathing space N *(fig)* respiro, pausa

breathless ['breθlɪs] ADJ sin aliento, jadeante; *(with excitement)* pasmado

breathtaking ['breθteɪkɪŋ] ADJ imponente, pasmoso

breath test N prueba de la alcoholemia

bred [bred] PT, PP of **breed**

-bred [bred] SUFF: **to be well/ill~** estar bien/ mal criado

breed [briːd] *(pt, pp* **bred** [bred]*)* VT criar; *(fig: hate, suspicion)* crear, engendrar ▸ VI reproducirse, procrear ▸ N raza, casta

breeder ['briːdəʳ] N *(person)* criador(a) *m/f*; *(Physics: also: **breeder reactor**)* reactor *m*

breeding ['briːdɪŋ] N *(of person)* educación *f*

breeze [briːz] N brisa

breezeblock ['briːzblɒk] N *(BRIT)* bovedilla

breezy ['briːzɪ] ADJ de mucho viento, ventoso; *(person)* despreocupado

Breton ['bretən] ADJ bretón(-ona) ▸ N bretón(-ona) *m/f*; *(Ling)* bretón *m*

brevity ['brevɪtɪ] N brevedad *f*

brew [bruː] VT *(tea)* hacer; *(beer)* elaborar; *(plot)* tramar ▸ VI hacerse; elaborarse; tramarse; *(fig: trouble)* prepararse; *(storm)* amenazar

brewer ['bruːəʳ] N cervecero, fabricante *m* de cerveza

brewery ['bruːərɪ] N fábrica de cerveza

briar ['braɪəʳ] N *(thorny bush)* zarza; *(wild rose)* escaramujo, rosa silvestre

bribe [braɪb] N soborno ▸ VT sobornar, cohechar; **to ~ sb to do sth** sobornar a algn para que haga algo

bribery ['braɪbərɪ] N soborno, cohecho

bric-a-brac ['brɪkəbræk] N INV baratijas *fpl*

brick [brɪk] N ladrillo

bricklayer ['brɪkleɪəʳ] N albañil *m*

brickwork ['brɪkwəːk] N enladrillado

brickworks ['brɪkwəːks] N ladrillar *m*

bridal ['braɪdl] ADJ nupcial

bride [braɪd] N novia

bridegroom ['braɪdgruːm] N novio

bridesmaid ['braɪdzmeɪd] N dama de honor

bridge [brɪdʒ] N puente *m*; *(Naut)* puente *m* de mando; *(of nose)* caballete *m*; *(Cards)* bridge *m* ▸ VT *(river)* tender un puente sobre; *(fig)*: **to ~ a gap** llenar un vacío

bridgehead ['brɪdʒhed] N cabeza de puente

bridging loan ['brɪdʒɪŋ-] N crédito provisional

bridle ['braɪdl] N brida, freno ▸ VT poner la brida a; *(fig)* reprimir, refrenar ▸ VI *(in anger etc)* picarse

bridle path N camino de herradura

brief [briːf] ADJ breve, corto ▸ N *(Law)* escrito ▸ VT *(inform)* informar; *(instruct)* dar instrucciones a; **in ~ ...** en resumen ...; **to ~ sb (about sth)** informar a algn (sobre algo)

briefcase ['briːfkeɪs] N cartera, portafolio(s) *m inv (LAM)*

briefing ['briːfɪŋ] N *(Press)* informe *m*

briefly ['briːflɪ] ADV *(smile, glance)* brevemente; *(explain, say)* brevemente, en pocas palabras

briefs [briːfs] NPL *(for men)* calzoncillos *mpl*; *(for women)* bragas *fpl*

Brig. ABBR = **brigadier**

brigade [brɪ'geɪd] N *(Mil)* brigada

brigadier [brɪgə'dɪəʳ] N general *m* de brigada

bright [braɪt] ADJ brillante; *(room)* luminoso; *(day)* de sol; *(person: clever)* listo, inteligente; *(: lively)* alegre, animado; *(colour)* vivo; *(future)* prometedor(a); **to look on the ~ side** mirar el lado bueno

brighten ['braɪtn], **brighten up** VT *(room)* hacer más alegre ▸ VI *(weather)* despejarse; *(person)* animarse, alegrarse

brill [brɪl] ADJ *(BRIT inf)* guay

brilliance ['brɪljəns] N brillo, brillantez *f*; *(fig: of person)* inteligencia

brilliant ['brɪljənt] ADJ *(light, idea, person, success)* brillante; *(clever)* genial

brilliantly ['brɪljəntlɪ] ADV brillantemente

brim [brɪm] N borde *m*; *(of hat)* ala

brimful ['brɪm'ful] ADJ lleno hasta el borde; *(fig)* rebosante

brine [braɪn] N *(Culin)* salmuera

bring [brɪŋ] *(pt, pp* **brought** [brɔːt]*)* VT *(thing)* traer; *(person)* conducir; **to ~ sth to an end** terminar con algo; **I can't ~ myself to sack**

him no soy capaz de echarle
▶ **bring about** VT ocasionar, producir
▶ **bring back** VT volver a traer; (*return*) devolver
▶ **bring down** VT (*government, plane*) derribar; (*price*) rebajar
▶ **bring forward** VT adelantar; (*Bookkeeping*) sumar y seguir
▶ **bring in** VT (*harvest*) recoger; (*person*) hacer entrar *or* pasar; (*object*) traer; (*Pol: bill, law*) presentar; (*Law: verdict*) pronunciar; (*produce: income*) producir, rendir
▶ **bring off** VT (*task, plan*) lograr, conseguir; (*deal*) cerrar
▶ **bring on** VT (*illness, attack*) producir, causar; (*player, substitute*) sacar (de la reserva), hacer salir
▶ **bring out** VT (*object*) sacar; (*new product*) sacar; (*book*) publicar
▶ **bring round** VT (*unconscious person*) hacer volver en sí; (*convince*) convencer
▶ **bring up** VT (*person*) educar, criar; (*carry up*) subir; (*question*) sacar a colación; (*food: vomit*) devolver, vomitar

brink [brɪŋk] N borde *m*; **on the ~ of doing sth** a punto de hacer algo; **she was on the ~ of tears** estaba al borde de las lágrimas
brisk [brɪsk] ADJ (*walk*) enérgico, vigoroso; (*speedy*) rápido; (*wind*) fresco; (*trade*) activo, animado; (*abrupt*) brusco; **business is ~** el negocio va bien *or* a paso activo
brisket ['brɪskɪt] N falda de vaca
bristle ['brɪsl] N cerda ▶ VI (*fur*) erizarse; **to ~ in anger** temblar de rabia
bristly ['brɪslɪ] ADJ (*beard, hair*) erizado; **to have a ~ chin** tener la barba crecida
Brit [brɪt] N ABBR (*inf: = British person*) británico(-a)
Britain ['brɪtən] N (*also:* **Great Britain**) Gran Bretaña
British ['brɪtɪʃ] ADJ británico; **the British** NPL los británicos
British Isles NPL: **the ~** las Islas Británicas
British Rail N = RENFE *f* (*SP*)
British Summer Time N hora de verano británica
Briton ['brɪtən] N británico(-a)
brittle ['brɪtl] ADJ quebradizo, frágil
Bro. ABBR (*Rel*) = **brother**
broach [brəutʃ] VT (*subject*) abordar
broad [brɔːd] ADJ ancho; (*range*) amplio; (*accent*) cerrado ▶ N (*US inf*) tía; **in ~ daylight** en pleno día; **the ~ outlines** las líneas generales
broadband ['brɔːdbænd] N banda ancha
broad bean N haba
broadcast ['brɔːdkɑːst] (*pt, pp ~*) N emisión *f* ▶ VT (*Radio*) emitir; (*TV*) transmitir ▶ VI emitir; transmitir

broadcaster ['brɔːdkɑːstəʳ] N locutor(a) *m/f*
broadcasting ['brɔːdkɑːstɪŋ] N radiodifusión *f*, difusión *f*
broadcasting station N emisora
broaden ['brɔːdn] VT ampliar ▶ VI ensancharse; **to ~ one's mind** hacer más tolerante a algn
broadly ['brɔːdlɪ] ADV en general
broad-minded ['brɔːd'maɪndɪd] ADJ tolerante, liberal
broadsheet ['brɔːdʃiːt] N (*BRIT*) periódico de gran formato (*no sensacionalista*); *see also* **quality press**
brocade [brə'keɪd] N brocado
broccoli ['brɔkəlɪ] N brécol *m*, bróculi *m*
brochure ['brəuʃjuəʳ] N folleto
brogue [brəug] N (*accent*) acento regional; (*shoe*) (*tipo de*) zapato de cuero grueso
broil [brɔɪl] VT (*US*) asar a la parrilla
broiler ['brɔɪləʳ] N (*grill*) parrilla; (*fowl*) pollo (para asar)
broke [brəuk] PT *of* **break** ▶ ADJ (*inf*) pelado, sin blanca; **to go ~** quebrar
broken ['brəukən] PP *of* **break** ▶ ADJ (*stick*) roto; (*fig: marriage*) deshecho; (: *promise, vow*) violado; **~ leg** pierna rota; **in ~ English** en un inglés chapurreado
broken-down ['brəukn'daun] ADJ (*car*) averiado; (*machine*) estropeado; (*house*) destartalado
broken-hearted ['brəukn'hɑːtɪd] ADJ con el corazón destrozado
broker ['brəukəʳ] N corredor(a) *m/f* de bolsa
brokerage ['brəukərɪdʒ] N corretaje *m*
brolly ['brɔlɪ] N (*BRIT inf*) paraguas *m inv*
bronchitis [brɔŋ'kaɪtɪs] N bronquitis *f*
bronze [brɔnz] N bronce *m*
bronzed [brɔnzd] ADJ bronceado
brooch [brəutʃ] N broche *m*
brood [bruːd] N camada, cría; (*children*) progenie *f* ▶ VI (*hen*) empollar; **to ~ over** dar vueltas a
broody ['bruːdɪ] ADJ (*fig*) triste, melancólico
brook [bruk] N arroyo
broom [brum] N escoba; (*Bot*) retama
broomstick ['brumstɪk] N palo de escoba
Bros. ABBR (*Comm*: = *Brothers*) Hnos
broth [brɔθ] N caldo
brothel ['brɔθl] N burdel *m*
brother ['brʌðəʳ] N hermano
brotherhood ['brʌðəhud] N hermandad *f*
brother-in-law ['brʌðərɪn'lɔː] N cuñado
brotherly ['brʌðəlɪ] ADJ fraternal
brought [brɔːt] PT, PP *of* **bring**
brow [brau] N (*forehead*) frente *f*; (*eyebrow*) ceja; (*of hill*) cumbre *f*
browbeat ['braubiːt] VT (*irreg: like* **beat**) intimidar
brown [braun] ADJ marrón; (*hair*) castaño;

(*tanned*) moreno ▸ N (*colour*) marrón *m* ▸ VT
(*tan*) poner moreno; (*Culin*) dorar; **to go ~**
(*person*) ponerse moreno; (*leaves*) dorarse
brown bread N pan *m* integral
Brownie ['braunɪ] N niña exploradora
brown paper N papel *m* de estraza
brown rice N arroz *m* integral
brown sugar N azúcar *m* moreno
browse [brauz] VI (*animal*) pacer; (*among
books*) hojear libros; **to ~ through a book**
hojear un libro
browser ['brauzəʳ] N (*Comput*) navegador *m*
bruise [bru:z] N (*on person*) cardenal *m*,
moretón *m* ▸ VT (*leg etc*) magullar; (*fig:
feelings*) herir
Brum [brʌm] N ABBR, **Brummagem**
['brʌmədʒəm] N (*inf*) = **Birmingham**
Brummie ['brʌmɪ] N (*inf*) habitante *mf* de
Birmingham
brunch [brʌntʃ] N desayuno-almuerzo
brunette [bru:'nɛt] N morena, morocha
(*LAM*)
brunt [brʌnt] N: **to bear the ~ of** llevar el
peso de
brush [brʌʃ] N cepillo, escobilla (*LAM*); (*large*)
escoba; (*for painting, shaving etc*) brocha;
(*artist's*) pincel *m*; (*Bot*) maleza ▸ VT (*sweep*)
barrer; (*groom*) cepillar; (*gen*): **to ~ past, ~
against** rozar al pasar; **to have a ~ with the
police** tener un roce con la policía
▸ **brush aside** VT rechazar, no hacer caso a
▸ **brush up** VT (*knowledge*) repasar, refrescar
brushed [brʌʃt] ADJ (*nylon, denim etc*) afelpado;
(*Tech: steel, chrome etc*) cepillado
brushwood ['brʌʃwud] N (*bushes*) maleza;
(*sticks*) leña
brusque [bru:sk] ADJ (*person, manner*) brusco;
(*tone*) áspero
Brussels ['brʌslz] N Bruselas
Brussels sprout N col *f* de Bruselas
brutal ['bru:tl] ADJ brutal
brutality [bru:'tælɪtɪ] N brutalidad *f*
brutalize ['bru:təlaɪz] VT (*harden*) embrutecer;
(*ill-treat*) tratar brutalmente a
brute [bru:t] N bruto; (*person*) bestia ▸ ADJ: **by
~ force** por la fuerza bruta
brutish ['bru:tɪʃ] ADJ brutal
BS N ABBR (*US*: = *Bachelor of Science*) título
universitario
bs ABBR = **bill of sale**
BSA N ABBR (*US*) = **Boy Scouts of America**
BSc ABBR (= *Bachelor of Science*) licenciado en
Ciencias
BSE N ABBR (= *bovine spongiform encephalopathy*)
encefalopatía espongiforme bovina
BSI N ABBR (= *British Standards Institution*)
institución británica de normalización
BST N ABBR (= *British Summer Time*) hora de verano
británica

Bt. ABBR (*BRIT*) = **baronet**
btu N ABBR (= *British thermal unit*) = 1054.2 julios
BTW ABBR (= *by the way*) por cierto
bubble ['bʌbl] N burbuja; (*in paint*) ampolla
▸ VI burbujear, borbotar
bubble bath N espuma para el baño
bubble gum N chicle *m* (de globo)
bubblejet printer ['bʌbldʒet-] N impresora
de inyección por burbujas
bubbly ['bʌblɪ] ADJ (*person*) vivaracho; (*liquid*)
con burbujas ▸ N (*inf*) champán *m*
Bucharest [bu:kə'rest] N Bucarest *m*
buck [bʌk] N (*rabbit*) macho; (*deer*) gamo; (*US
inf*) dólar *m* ▸ VI corcovear; **to pass the ~ (to
sb)** echar (a algn) el muerto
▸ **buck up** VI (*cheer up*) animarse, cobrar
ánimo ▸ VT: **to ~ one's ideas up** poner más
empeño
bucket ['bʌkɪt] N cubo, balde *m* (*esp LAM*) ▸ VI:
the rain is bucketing (down) (*inf*) está
lloviendo a cántaros
Buckingham Palace ['bʌkɪŋəm-] N el
Palacio de Buckingham; *ver nota*

Buckingham Palace es la residencia oficial
del monarca británico en Londres. Data
de 1703 y fue en principio el palacio del
Duque de Buckingham, para pasar a
manos de Jorge III en 1762. Fue
reconstruido en el siglo XIX y reformado
a principios del siglo pasado. Hoy en día
parte del palacio está abierto al público.

buckle ['bʌkl] N hebilla ▸ VT abrochar con
hebilla ▸ VI torcerse, combarse
▸ **buckle down** VI poner empeño
Bucks [bʌks] ABBR (*BRIT*) = **Buckinghamshire**
bud [bʌd] N (*of plant*) brote *m*, yema; (*of flower*)
capullo ▸ VI brotar, echar brotes
Budapest [bju:də'pɛst] N Budapest *m*
Buddhism ['budɪzm] N budismo
Buddhist ['budɪst] ADJ, N budista *mf*
budding ['bʌdɪŋ] ADJ en ciernes, en embrión
buddy ['bʌdɪ] N (*US*) compañero,
compinche *m*
budge [bʌdʒ] VT mover; (*fig*) hacer ceder ▸ VI
moverse
budgerigar ['bʌdʒərɪgɑ:ʳ] N periquito
budget ['bʌdʒɪt] N presupuesto ▸ VI: **to ~ for
sth** presupuestar algo; **I'm on a tight ~** no
puedo gastar mucho; **she works out her ~
every month** planea su presupuesto todos
los meses
budgie ['bʌdʒɪ] N = **budgerigar**
Buenos Aires ['bweinɔs'aiɾiz] N Buenos
Aires *m* ▸ ADJ bonaerense, porteño (*LAM*)
buff [bʌf] ADJ (*colour*) color de ante; (*inf: person:
well-muscled*) escultural ▸ N (*enthusiast*)
entusiasta *mf*
buffalo ['bʌfələu] (*pl* ~ *or* **buffaloes**) N (*BRIT*)
búfalo; (*US: bison*) bisonte *m*

buffer [ˈbʌfəʳ] N amortiguador m; (Rail) tope m; (Comput) memoria intermedia, buffer m ▶ VI (Comput) almacenar temporalmente

buffering [ˈbʌfərɪŋ] N (Comput) almacenamiento en memoria intermedia

buffer zone N zona (que sirve de) colchón

buffet [ˈbufeɪ] N (BRIT: bar) bar m, cafetería; (food) buffet m ▶ VT [ˈbʌfɪt] (strike) abofetear; (wind etc) golpear

buffet car N (BRIT Rail) coche-restaurante m

buffet lunch N buffet m (almuerzo)

buffoon [bəˈfuːn] N bufón m

bug [bʌɡ] N (insect) chinche m; (: gen) bicho, sabandija; (germ) microbio, bacilo; (spy device) micrófono oculto; (Comput) fallo, error m ▶ VT (annoy) fastidiar; (room) poner un micrófono oculto en; (phone) pinchar; **I've got the travel ~** (fig) me encanta viajar; **it really bugs me** me fastidia or molesta mucho

bugbear [ˈbʌɡbɛəʳ] N pesadilla

bugle [ˈbjuːɡl] N corneta, clarín m

build [bɪld] N (of person) talle m, tipo ▶ VT (pt, pp **built** [bɪlt]) construir, edificar

▶ **build on** VT FUS (fig) basar en

▶ **build up** VT (morale, forces, production) acrecentar; (Med) fortalecer; (stocks) acumular; (establish: business) fomentar, desarrollar; (: reputation) crear(se); (increase: production) aumentar; **don't ~ your hopes up too soon** no te hagas demasiadas ilusiones

builder [ˈbɪldəʳ] N constructor(a) m/f; (contractor) contratista mf

building [ˈbɪldɪŋ] N (act) construcción f; (habitation, offices) edificio

building contractor N contratista mf de obras

building industry N construcción f

building site N obra, solar m (SP)

building society N (BRIT) sociedad f de préstamo inmobiliario; ver nota

> En el Reino Unido existe un tipo de entidad financiera llamada building society de la que sus clientes son también propietarios y cuyos servicios son similares a los de los bancos, aunque se centran fundamentalmente en créditos hipotecarios y cuentas de ahorro. Son la entidad más utilizada por el público en general a la hora de pedir créditos para la compra de la vivienda.

building trade N = **building industry**

build-up [ˈbɪldʌp] N (publicity): **to give sb/sth a good ~** hacer mucha propaganda de algn/algo

built [bɪlt] PT, PP of **build**

built-in [ˈbɪltˈɪn] ADJ (cupboard) empotrado; (device) interior, incorporado; **~ obsolescence** caducidad f programada

built-up [ˈbɪltʌp] ADJ (area) urbanizado

bulb [bʌlb] N (Bot) bulbo; (Elec) bombilla, bombillo (LAM), foco (LAM)

bulbous [ˈbʌlbəs] ADJ bulboso

Bulgaria [bʌlˈɡɛərɪə] N Bulgaria

Bulgarian [bʌlˈɡɛərɪən] ADJ búlgaro ▶ N búlgaro(-a); (Ling) búlgaro

bulge [bʌldʒ] N bulto; (in birth rate, sales) alza, aumento ▶ VI bombearse, pandearse; (pocket etc) hacer bulto; **to ~ (with)** rebosar (de)

bulimia [bəˈlɪmɪə] N bulimia

bulimic [bjuːˈlɪmɪk] ADJ, N bulímico(-a) m/f

bulk [bʌlk] N (mass) bulto, volumen m; (major part) grueso; **in ~** (Comm) a granel; **the ~ of** la mayor parte de; **to buy in ~** comprar en grandes cantidades

bulk buying N compra a granel

bulk carrier N (buque m) granelero

bulkhead [ˈbʌlkhɛd] N mamparo

bulky [ˈbʌlkɪ] ADJ voluminoso, abultado

bull [bul] N toro; (Stock Exchange) alcista mf de bolsa; (Rel) bula

bulldog [ˈbuldɔɡ] N dogo

bulldoze [ˈbuldəuz] VT mover con excavadora; **I was bulldozed into doing it** (fig: inf) me obligaron a hacerlo

bulldozer [ˈbuldəuzəʳ] N bulldozer m, excavadora

bullet [ˈbulɪt] N bala; **~ wound** balazo

bulletin [ˈbulɪtɪn] N comunicado, parte m; (journal) boletín m

bulletin board N (US) tablón m de anuncios; (Comput) tablero de noticias

bulletproof [ˈbulɪtpruːf] ADJ a prueba de balas; **~ vest** chaleco antibalas

bullfight [ˈbulfaɪt] N corrida de toros

bullfighter [ˈbulfaɪtəʳ] N torero

bullfighting [ˈbulfaɪtɪŋ] N los toros mpl, el toreo; (art of bullfighting) tauromaquia

bullion [ˈbuljən] N oro or plata en barras

bullock [ˈbulək] N novillo

bullring [ˈbulrɪŋ] N plaza de toros

bull's-eye [ˈbulzaɪ] N blanco, diana

bullshit [ˈbulʃɪt] (inf!) EXCL chorradas ▶ N chorradas fpl ▶ VI decir chorradas ▶ VT: **to ~ sb** quedarse con algn

bully [ˈbulɪ] N valentón m, matón m ▶ VT intimidar, tiranizar

bullying [ˈbulɪɪŋ] N (at school) acoso escolar

bum [bʌm] N (inf: BRIT: backside) culo; (esp US: tramp) vagabundo; (: idler) holgazán(-ana) m/f, flojo(-a)

bumble [ˈbʌmbl] VI (walk unsteadily) andar de forma vacilante; (fig) farfullar, trastabillar

bumblebee [ˈbʌmblbiː] N abejorro

bumbling [ˈbʌmblɪŋ] N divagación f

bumf [bʌmf] N (inf: forms etc) papeleo

bump [bʌmp] N (blow) tope m, choque m; (jolt) sacudida; (noise) choque m, topetón m; (on road etc) bache m; (on head) chichón m ▶ VT (*strike*) chocar contra, topetar ▶ VI dar sacudidas

▶ **bump into** VT FUS chocar contra, tropezar con; (*person*) topar con; (*inf: meet*) tropezar con, toparse con

bumper ['bʌmpəʳ] N (*BRIT*) parachoques *m inv* ▶ ADJ: ~ **crop/harvest** cosecha abundante

bumper cars NPL (*US*) autos *or* coches *mpl* de choque

bumph [bʌmf] N = **bumf**

bumptious ['bʌmpʃəs] ADJ engreído, presuntuoso

bumpy ['bʌmpɪ] ADJ (*road*) lleno de baches; (*journey, flight*) agitado

bun [bʌn] N (*BRIT: cake*) pastel *m*; (*US: bread*) bollo; (*of hair*) moño

bunch [bʌntʃ] N (*of flowers*) ramo; (*of keys*) manojo; (*of bananas*) piña; (*of people*) grupo; (*pej*) pandilla; **bunches** NPL (*in hair*) coletas *fpl*

bundle ['bʌndl] N (*gen*) bulto, fardo; (*of sticks*) haz *m*; (*of papers*) legajo ▶ VT (*also: **bundle up***) atar, envolver; **to ~ sth/sb into** meter algo/a algn precipitadamente en

bun fight N (*BRIT inf: tea party*) merienda; (*: function*) fiesta oficial

bung [bʌŋ] N tapón *m*, bitoque *m* ▶ VT (*throw*) arrojar; (*also: **bung up***: *pipe, hole*) tapar; **my nose is bunged up** (*inf*) tengo la nariz atascada *or* taponada

bungalow ['bʌŋgələu] N bungalow *m*, chalé *m*

bungee jumping ['bʌndʒi:'dʒʌmpɪŋ] N puenting *m*, banyi *m*

bungle ['bʌŋgl] VT chapucear

bunion ['bʌnjən] N juanete *m*

bunk [bʌŋk] N litera; **~ beds** *npl* literas *fpl*

bunker ['bʌŋkəʳ] N (*coal store*) carbonera; (*Mil*) refugio; (*Golf*) búnker *m*

bunk off VI: **to ~ school** (*BRIT inf*) pirarse las clases; **I'll ~ at 3 this afternoon** me voy a pirar a las 3 esta tarde

bunny ['bʌnɪ] N (*also: **bunny rabbit***) conejito

Bunsen burner ['bʌnsn-] N mechero Bunsen

bunting ['bʌntɪŋ] N empavesada, banderas *fpl*

buoy [bɔɪ] N boya

▶ **buoy up** VT mantener a flote; (*fig*) animar

buoyancy ['bɔɪənsɪ] N (*of ship*) flotabilidad *f*

buoyant ['bɔɪənt] ADJ (*ship*) capaz de flotar; (*carefree*) boyante, optimista; (*Comm: market, prices etc*) sostenido; (*: economy*) boyante

BUPA ['bu:pə] N ABBR (= *British United Provident Association*) seguro médico privado

burden ['bə:dn] N carga ▶ VT cargar; **to be a ~ to sb** ser una carga para algn

bureau ['bjuərəu] (*pl* **bureaux** [-z]) N (*BRIT: writing desk*) escritorio, buró *m*; (*US: chest of drawers*) cómoda; (*office*) oficina, agencia

bureaucracy [bjuə'rɔkrəsɪ] N burocracia

bureaucrat ['bjuərəkræt] N burócrata *mf*

bureaucratic [bjuərə'krætɪk] ADJ burocrático

bureau de change [-də'ʃɑ:ʒ] (*pl* **bureaux de change**) N caja *f* de cambio

bureaux ['bjuərəuz] NPL *of* **bureau**

burgeon ['bə:dʒən] VI (*develop rapidly*) crecer, incrementarse; (*trade etc*) florecer

burger ['bə:gəʳ] N hamburguesa

burglar ['bə:gləʳ] N ladrón(-ona) *m/f*

burglar alarm N alarma *f* contra robo

burglarize ['bə:gləraɪz] VT (*US*) robar (con allanamiento)

burglary ['bə:glərɪ] N robo con allanamiento *or* fractura, robo de una casa

burgle ['bə:gl] VT robar (con allanamiento)

Burgundy ['bə:gəndɪ] N Borgoña

burial ['bɛrɪəl] N entierro

burial ground N cementerio

burlap ['bə:læp] N arpillera

burlesque [bə:'lɛsk] N parodia

burly ['bə:lɪ] ADJ fornido, membrudo

Burma ['bə:mə] N Birmania

Burmese [bə:'mi:z] ADJ birmano ▶ N *pl inv* birmano(-a); (*Ling*) birmano

burn [bə:n] (*pt, pp* **burned** *or* **burnt**) VT quemar; (*house*) incendiar ▶ VI quemarse, arder; (*sting*) escocer ▶ N (*Med*) quemadura; **the cigarette burnt a hole in her dress** se ha quemado el vestido con el cigarrillo; **I've burnt myself!** ¡me he quemado!

▶ **burn down** VT incendiar

▶ **burn out** VT (*writer etc*): **to ~ o.s. out** agotarse

burner ['bə:nəʳ] N (*gas*) quemador *m*

burning ['bə:nɪŋ] ADJ (*building, forest*) en llamas; (*hot: sand etc*) abrasador(a); (*ambition*) ardiente

Burns' Night [bə:nz-] N *ver nota*

Cada veinticinco de enero los escoceses celebran la llamada Burns' Night (noche de Burns), en honor al poeta escocés Robert Burns (1759-1796). Es tradición hacer una cena en la que, al son de la música de la gaita escocesa, se sirve *haggis*, plato tradicional de asadura de cordero cocida en el estómago del animal, acompañado de nabos y puré de patatas. Durante la misma se recitan poemas del autor y varios discursos conmemorativos de carácter festivo.

burnt [bə:nt] PT, PP *of* **burn**

burp [bə:p] (*inf*) N eructo ▶ VI eructar

burqa ['bə:kə] N burka *m*, burqa *m*

burrow ['bʌrəu] N madriguera ▶ VT hacer una madriguera

bursar ['bə:səʳ] N tesorero; (*BRIT: student*) becario(-a)

bursary ['bə:sərɪ] N (*BRIT*) beca

burst [bə:st] (*pt, pp* **~**) VT (*balloon, pipe*) reventar; (*banks etc*) romper ▶ VI reventarse; romperse; (*tyre*) pincharse ▶ N (*explosion*) estallido; (*also*: **burst pipe**) reventón *m*; **the river has ~ its banks** el río se ha desbordado; **to ~ into flames** estallar en llamas; **to ~ out laughing** soltar la carcajada; **to ~ into tears** deshacerse en lágrimas; **to be bursting with** reventar de; **a ~ of energy** una explosión de energía; **a ~ of applause** una salva de aplausos; **a ~ of speed** un acelerón; **to ~ open** abrirse de golpe
▶ **burst into** VT FUS (*room etc*) irrumpir en

bury [ˈbɛɪɪ] VT enterrar; (*body*) enterrar, sepultar; **to ~ the hatchet** enterrar el hacha (de guerra), echar pelillos a la mar

bus [bʌs] N autobús *m*, camión *m* (*LAM*)

bus boy N (*US*) ayudante *mf* de camarero

bus conductor N cobrador(a) *m/f*

bush [buʃ] N arbusto; (*scrub land*) monte *m* bajo; **to beat about the ~** andar(se) con rodeos

bushed [buʃt] ADJ (*inf*) molido

bushel [ˈbuʃl] N (*measure*: BRIT) = 36,36 *litros*; (: *US*) = 35,24 *litros*

bush fire N incendio en el monte

bushy [ˈbuʃɪ] ADJ (*beard, eyebrows*) poblado; (*hair*) espeso; (*fur*) tupido

busily [ˈbɪzɪlɪ] ADV afanosamente

business [ˈbɪznɪs] N (*matter, affair*) asunto; (*trading*) comercio, negocios *mpl*; (*firm*) empresa, casa; (*occupation*) oficio; **to be away on ~** estar en viaje de negocios; **it's my ~ to …** me toca *or* corresponde …; **it's none of my ~** no es asunto mío; **he means ~** habla en serio; **he's in the insurance ~** se dedica a los seguros; **I'm here on ~** estoy aquí por mi trabajo; **to do ~ with sb** hacer negocios con algn

business address N dirección *f* comercial

business card N tarjeta de visita

business class N (*Aviat*) clase *f* preferente

businesslike [ˈbɪznɪslaɪk] ADJ (*company*) serio; (*person*) eficiente

businessman [ˈbɪznɪsmən] N (*irreg*) hombre *m* de negocios

business trip N viaje *m* de negocios

businesswoman [ˈbɪznɪswumən] N (*irreg*) mujer *f* de negocios

busker [ˈbʌskəʳ] N (BRIT) músico(-a) ambulante

bus pass N bonobús

bus route N recorrido del autobús

bus shelter N parada cubierta

bus station N estación *f* or terminal *f* de autobuses

bus-stop [ˈbʌsstɔp] N parada de autobús, paradero (*LAM*)

bust [bʌst] N (*Anat*) pecho; (*sculpture*) busto ▶ ADJ (*inf: broken*) roto, estropeado ▶ VT (*inf:*

Police: arrest) detener; **to go ~** quebrar

bustle [ˈbʌsl] N bullicio, movimiento ▶ VI menearse, apresurarse

bustling [ˈbʌslɪŋ] ADJ (*town*) animado, bullicioso

bust-up [ˈbʌstʌp] N (*inf*) riña

busty [ˈbʌstɪ] ADJ (*inf*) pechugona, con buena delantera

busy [ˈbɪzɪ] ADJ ocupado, atareado; (*shop, street*) concurrido, animado ▶ VT: **to ~ o.s. with** ocuparse en; **he's a ~ man** (*normally*) es un hombre muy ocupado; (*temporarily*) está muy ocupado; **the line's ~** (*esp US*) está comunicando

busybody [ˈbɪzɪbɔdɪ] N entrometido(-a)

busy signal N (*US Tel*) señal *f* de comunicando

⬥ **(KEYWORD)**

but [bʌt] CONJ **1** pero; **he's not very bright, but he's hard-working** no es muy inteligente, pero es trabajador
2 (*in direct contradiction*) sino; **he's not English but French** no es inglés sino francés; **he didn't sing but he shouted** no cantó sino que gritó
3 (*showing disagreement, surprise etc*): **but that's far too expensive!** ¡pero eso es carísimo!; **but it does work!** ¡(pero) sí que funciona!
▶ PREP (*apart from, except*) menos, salvo; **we've had nothing but trouble** no hemos tenido más que problemas; **no-one but him can do it** nadie más que él puede hacerlo; **the last but one** el penúltimo; **who but a lunatic would do such a thing?** ¡sólo un loco haría una cosa así!; **but for you/your help** si no fuera por ti/tu ayuda; **anything but that** cualquier cosa menos eso
▶ ADV (*just, only*): **she's but a child** no es más que una niña; **had I but known** si lo hubiera sabido; **I can but try** al menos lo puedo intentar; **it's all but finished** está casi acabado

butane [ˈbjuːteɪn] N (*also*: **butane gas**) (gas *m*) butano

butch [butʃ] ADJ (*inf, pej: woman*) machirula, marimacho; (*man*) muy macho

butcher [ˈbutʃəʳ] N carnicero(-a) ▶ VT hacer una carnicería con; (*cattle etc for meat*) matar; **~'s (shop)** carnicería

butler [ˈbʌtləʳ] N mayordomo

butt [bʌt] N (*cask*) tonel *m*; (*for rain*) tina; (*thick end*) cabo, extremo; (*of gun*) culata; (*of cigarette*) colilla; (BRIT *fig: target*) blanco ▶ VT dar cabezadas contra, topetar
▶ **butt in** VI (*interrupt*) interrumpir

butter [ˈbʌtəʳ] N mantequilla, manteca (*LAM*) ▶ VT untar con mantequilla

butter bean N judía blanca

buttercup ['bʌtəkʌp] N ranúnculo
butterfingers ['bʌtəfɪŋɡəz] N (inf) torpe mf
butterfly ['bʌtəflaɪ] N mariposa; (Swimming: also: **butterfly stroke**) (braza de) mariposa
buttocks ['bʌtəks] NPL nalgas fpl
button ['bʌtn] N botón m ▶ VT (also: **button up**) abotonar, abrochar ▶ VI abrocharse
buttonhole ['bʌtnhəʊl] N ojal m; (flower) flor f que se lleva en el ojal ▶ VT obligar a escuchar
buttress ['bʌtrɪs] N contrafuerte m; (fig) apoyo, sostén m
buxom ['bʌksəm] ADJ (woman) frescachona, rolliza
buy [baɪ] (pt, pp **bought**) VT comprar ▶ N compra; **to ~ sb sth/sth from sb** comprarle algo a algn; **to ~ sb a drink** invitar a algn a tomar algo; **a good/bad ~** una buena/mala compra
  ▶ **buy back** VT volver a comprar
  ▶ **buy in** VT proveerse or abastecerse de
  ▶ **buy into** VT FUS comprar acciones en
  ▶ **buy off** VT (inf: bribe) sobornar
  ▶ **buy out** VT (partner) comprar la parte de
  ▶ **buy up** VT (property) acaparar; (stock) comprar todas las existencias de
buyer ['baɪər] N comprador(a) m/f; **~'s market** mercado favorable al comprador
buy-out ['baɪaʊt] N (Comm) adquisición f de (la totalidad de) las acciones
buzz [bʌz] N zumbido; (inf: phone call) llamada (telefónica) ▶ VT (call on intercom) llamar; (with buzzer) hacer sonar; (Aviat: plane, building) pasar rozando ▶ VI zumbar; **my head is buzzing** me zumba la cabeza
  ▶ **buzz off** VI (BRIT inf) largarse
buzzard ['bʌzəd] N (BRIT) águila ratonera; (US) buitre m, gallinazo (LAM)
buzzer ['bʌzər] N timbre m
buzz word N palabra que está de moda

(KEYWORD)

by [baɪ] PREP 1 (referring to cause, agent) por; de; **abandoned by his mother** abandonado por su madre; **surrounded by enemies** rodeados de enemigos; **a painting by Picasso** un cuadro de Picasso
2 (referring to method; manner: means): **by bus/car/train** en autobús/coche/tren; **to pay by cheque** pagar con cheque; **by moonlight/candlelight** a la luz de la luna/una vela; **by saving hard, he …** ahorrando, …
3 (via, through) por; **we came by Dover** vinimos por Dover
4 (close to, past): **the house by the river** la casa junto al río; **she rushed by me** pasó a mi lado como una exhalación; **I go by the post office every day** paso por delante de Correos todos los días
5 (time: not later than) para; (: during): **by**

daylight de día; **by 4 o'clock** para las cuatro; **by this time tomorrow** mañana a estas horas; **by the time I got here it was too late** cuando llegué ya era demasiado tarde
6 (amount): **by the metre/kilo** por metro/kilo; **paid by the hour** pagado por hora
7 (in measurements, sums): **to divide/multiply by 3** dividir/multiplicar por 3; **a room 3 metres by 4** una habitación de 3 metros por 4; **it's broader by a metre** es un metro más ancho; **the bus missed me by inches** no me pilló el autobús por un pelo
8 (according to) según, de acuerdo con; **it's 3 o'clock by my watch** según mi reloj, son las tres; **it's all right by me** por mí, está bien
9: **(all) by oneself** etc todo solo; **he did it (all) by himself** lo hizo él solo; **he was standing (all) by himself in a corner** estaba de pie solo en un rincón
10: **by the way** a propósito, por cierto; **this wasn't my idea, by the way** pues, no fue idea mía
  ▶ ADV 1 see **go**; **pass** etc
  2: **by and by** finalmente; **they'll come back by and by** acabarán volviendo; **by and large** en líneas generales, en general

bye(-bye) ['baɪ('baɪ)] EXCL adiós, hasta luego, chao (esp LAM)
bye-law ['baɪlɔ:] N see **by-law**
by-election ['baɪɪlɛkʃən] N (BRIT) elección f parcial; ver nota

> Se celebra una *by-election* en el Reino Unido y otros países de la *"Commonwealth"* cuando es necesario reemplazar a un parlamentario (*"Member of Parliament"*) cesado o fallecido durante una legislatura. Dichas elecciones tienen lugar únicamente en el área electoral representada por el citado parlamentario, su *"constituency"*.

Byelorussia [bjɛləʊ'rʌʃə] N Bielorrusia
Byelorussian [bjɛləʊ'rʌʃən] ADJ, N = **Belarussian**
bygone ['baɪɡɒn] ADJ pasado, del pasado ▶ N: **let bygones be bygones** lo pasado, pasado está
by-law ['baɪlɔ:] N ordenanza municipal
bypass ['baɪpɑ:s] N carretera de circunvalación; (Med) (operación f de) bypass m ▶ VT evitar
by-product ['baɪprɒdʌkt] N subproducto, derivado
bystander ['baɪstændər] N espectador(a) m/f
byte [baɪt] N (Comput) byte m, octeto
byway ['baɪweɪ] N camino poco frecuentado
byword ['baɪwə:d] N: **to be a ~ for** ser sinónimo de
by-your-leave ['baɪjɔ:'li:v] N: **without so much as a ~** sin decir nada, sin dar ningún tipo de explicación

Cc

C, c [siː] N (*letter*) C, c f; (*Mus*): **C** do m; **C for Charlie** C de Carmen
C ABBR (= *Celsius, centigrade*) C
c ABBR (= *century*) S.; (*US etc*) = **cent**; (= *circa*) hacia
CA N ABBR = **Central America**; (*BRIT*) = **chartered accountant**; (*US Post*) = **California**
ca. ABBR (= *circa*) C
c/a ABBR = **capital account**; **credit account**; **current account**
CAA N ABBR (*BRIT*: = *Civil Aviation Authority*) organismo de control y desarrollo de la aviación civil
CAB N ABBR (*BRIT*: = *Citizens' Advice Bureau*) ≈ Servicio de Información Ciudadana
cab [kæb] N taxi m; (*of truck*) cabina
cabaret ['kæbəreɪ] N cabaret m
cabbage ['kæbɪdʒ] N col f, berza
cabbie, cabby ['kæbɪ] N (*inf*) taxista mf
cab driver N taxista m
cabin ['kæbɪn] N cabaña; (*on ship*) camarote m
cabin crew N tripulación f de cabina
cabin cruiser N yate m de motor
cabinet ['kæbɪnɪt] N (*Pol*) consejo de ministros; (*furniture*) armario; (*also*: **display cabinet**) vitrina
cabinet-maker ['kæbɪnɪt'meɪkəʳ] N ebanista m
cabinet minister N ministro(-a) (del gabinete)
cable ['keɪbl] N cable m ▶ VT cablegrafiar
cable car N teleférico
cablegram ['keɪblgræm] N cablegrama m
cable television N televisión f por cable
cache [kæʃ] N (*of drugs*) alijo; (*of arms*) zulo
cackle ['kækl] VI cacarear
cactus ['kæktəs] (*pl* **cacti** [-taɪ]) N cacto
CAD ['kæd] N (= *computer-aided design*) DAO m
caddie, caddy ['kædɪ] N (*Golf*) cadi m
cadence ['keɪdəns] N ritmo; (*Mus*) cadencia
cadet [kə'dɛt] N (*Mil*) cadete m; **police ~** cadete m de policía
cadge [kædʒ] VT gorronear
cadger ['kædʒəʳ] N gorrón(-ona) m/f

cadre ['kædrɪ] N cuadro
Caesarean, (*US*) **Cesarean** [siː'zɛərɪən] ADJ: **~ (section)** cesárea
CAF ABBR (*BRIT*: = *cost and freight*) C y F
café ['kæfeɪ] N café m
cafeteria [kæfɪ'tɪərɪə] N cafetería (*con autoservicio para comer*)
caffeine ['kæfiːn] N cafeína
cage [keɪdʒ] N jaula ▶ VT enjaular
cagey ['keɪdʒɪ] ADJ (*inf*) cauteloso, reservado
cagoule [kə'guːl] N chubasquero
cahoots [kə'huːts] N: **to be in ~ (with sb)** estar conchabado (con algn)
Cairo ['kaɪərəu] N El Cairo
cajole [kə'dʒəul] VT engatusar
cake [keɪk] N (*large*) tarta; (*small*) pastel m; (*of soap*) pastilla; **he wants to have his ~ and eat it** (*fig*) quiere estar en misa y repicando; **it's a piece of ~** (*inf*) es pan comido
caked [keɪkt] ADJ: **~ with** cubierto de
cake shop N pastelería
Cal. ABBR (*US*) = **California**
calamine ['kæləmaɪn] N calamina
calamitous [kə'læmɪtəs] ADJ calamitoso
calamity [kə'læmɪtɪ] N calamidad f
calcium ['kælsɪəm] N calcio
calculate ['kælkjuleɪt] VT (*estimate: chances, effect*) calcular
▶ **calculate on** VT FUS: **to ~ on sth/on doing sth** contar con algo/con hacer algo
calculated ['kælkjuleɪtɪd] ADJ: **we took a ~ risk** calculamos el riesgo
calculating ['kælkjuleɪtɪŋ] ADJ (*scheming*) calculador(a)
calculation [kælkju'leɪʃən] N cálculo, cómputo
calculator ['kælkjuleɪtəʳ] N calculadora
calculus ['kælkjuləs] N cálculo
calendar ['kæləndəʳ] N calendario; **~ month/year** n mes m/año civil
calf [kɑːf] (*pl* **calves** [kɑːvz]) N (*of cow*) ternero, becerro; (*of other animals*) cría; (*also*: **calfskin**) piel f de becerro; (*Anat*) pantorrilla, canilla (*LAM*)

caliber ['kælɪbəʳ] N (US) = **calibre**
calibrate ['kælɪbreɪt] VT (gun etc) calibrar; (scale of measuring instrument) graduar
calibre, (US) **caliber** ['kælɪbəʳ] N calibre m
calico ['kælɪkəu] N calicó m
Calif. ABBR (US) = **California**
California [kælɪ'fɔːnɪə] N California
calipers ['kælɪpəz] NPL (US) = **callipers**
call [kɔːl] VT (gen) llamar; (Tel) llamar; (announce: flight) anunciar; (: meeting, strike) convocar ▶ VI (shout) llamar; (telephone) llamar (por teléfono), telefonear; (visit: also: **call in, call round**) hacer una visita ▶ N (shout) llamada, llamado (LAM); (Tel) llamada, llamado (LAM); (of bird) canto; (appeal) llamamiento, llamado (LAM); (summons: for flight etc) llamada; (fig: lure) llamada; **to be called** (person, object) llamarse; **to ~ sb names** poner verde a algn; **let's ~ it a day** (inf) ¡dejémoslo!, ¡ya está bien!; **who is calling?** ¿de parte de quién?; **London calling** (Radio) aquí Londres; **on ~** (nurse, doctor etc) de guardia; **please give me a ~ at seven** despiérteme or llámeme a las siete, por favor; **long-distance ~** conferencia (interurbana); **to make a ~** llamar por teléfono; **port of ~** puerto de escala; **to pay a ~ on sb** pasarse a ver a algn; **there's not much ~ for these items** estos artículos no tienen mucha demanda
▶ **call at** VT FUS (ship) hacer escala en, tocar en; (train) parar en
▶ **call back** VI (return) volver; (Tel) volver a llamar
▶ **call for** VT FUS (demand) pedir, exigir; (fetch) pasar a recoger
▶ **call in** VT (doctor, expert, police) llamar
▶ **call off** VT (cancel: meeting, race) cancelar; (: deal) anular; (: strike) desconvocar
▶ **call on** VT FUS (visit) ir a ver; (turn to) acudir a
▶ **call out** VI gritar, dar voces ▶ VT (doctor) llamar; (police, troops) hacer intervenir
▶ **call up** VT (Mil) llamar a filas
Callanetics® [kælə'netɪks] NSG gimnasia de repetición de pequeños ejercicios musculares
callbox ['kɔːlbɒks] N (BRIT) cabina telefónica
call centre N (BRIT) centro de atención al cliente
caller ['kɔːləʳ] N visita f; (Tel) usuario(-a); **hold the line, ~!** ¡no cuelgue!
call girl N prostituta
call-in ['kɔːlɪn] N (US) programa de línea abierta al público
calling ['kɔːlɪŋ] N vocación f; (profession) profesión f
calling card N tarjeta de visita
callipers, (US) **calipers** ['kælɪpəz] NPL (Med) aparato ortopédico; (Math) calibrador m

callous ['kæləs] ADJ insensible, cruel
callousness ['kæləsnɪs] N insensibilidad, crueldad f
callow ['kæləu] ADJ inexperto, novato
calm [kɑːm] ADJ tranquilo; (sea) tranquilo, en calma ▶ N calma, tranquilidad f ▶ VT calmar, tranquilizar
▶ **calm down** VI calmarse, tranquilizarse ▶ VT calmar, tranquilizar
calmly ['kɑːmlɪ] ADV tranquilamente, con calma
calmness ['kɑːmnɪs] N calma
Calor gas® ['kæləʳ-] N butano, camping gas® m inv
calorie ['kælərɪ] N caloría; **low-~ product** producto bajo en calorías
calve [kɑːv] VI parir
calves [kɑːvz] NPL of **calf**
CAM N ABBR (= computer-aided manufacturing) producción f asistida por ordenador
camber ['kæmbəʳ] N (of road) combadura
Cambodia [kæm'bəudjə] N Camboya
Cambodian [kæm'bəudjən] ADJ, N camboyano(-a) m/f
Cambs ABBR (BRIT) = **Cambridgeshire**
camcorder ['kæmkɔːdəʳ] N videocámara
came [keɪm] PT of **come**
camel ['kæməl] N camello
cameo ['kæmɪəu] N camafeo
camera ['kæmərə] N cámara or máquina fotográfica; (Cine, TV) cámara; (movie camera) cámara, tomavistas m inv; **in ~** (Law) a puerta cerrada
cameraman ['kæmərəmən] N (irreg) cámara m
camera phone N teléfono m con cámara
Cameroon, Cameroun [kæmə'ruːn] N Camerún m
camomile tea ['kæməmaɪl-] N manzanilla
camouflage ['kæməflɑːʒ] N camuflaje m ▶ VT camuflar
camp [kæmp] N campamento, camping m; (Mil) campamento; (for prisoners) campo; (fig: faction) bando ▶ VI acampar ▶ ADJ afectado, afeminado; **to go camping** ir de or hacer camping
campaign [kæm'peɪn] N (Mil, Pol etc) campaña ▶ VI: **to ~ (for/against)** hacer campaña (a favor de/en contra de)
campaigner [kæm'peɪnəʳ] N: **~ for** defensor(a) m/f de; **~ against** persona que hace campaña contra
campbed ['kæmpbed] N (BRIT) cama plegable
camper ['kæmpəʳ] N campista mf; (vehicle) caravana
campground ['kæmpgraund] N (US) camping m, campamento
camping ['kæmpɪŋ] N camping m
campsite ['kæmpsaɪt] N camping m

campus ['kæmpəs] N campus m
camshaft ['kæmʃɑːft] N árbol m de levas
can¹ [kæn] N (of oil, water) bidón m; (tin) lata, bote m ▶ VT enlatar; (preserve) conservar en lata; **a ~ of beer** una lata or un bote de cerveza; **to carry the ~** (inf) pagar el pato

(KEYWORD)

can² [kæn] (negative **cannot** or **can't**, pt, conditional **could**) AUX VB **1** (be able to) poder; **you can do it if you try** puedes hacerlo si lo intentas; **I can't see you** no te veo; **can you hear me?** (not translated) ¿me oyes?
2 (know how to) saber; **I can swim/play tennis/drive** sé nadar/jugar al tenis/conducir; **can you speak French?** ¿hablas or sabes hablar francés?
3 (may) poder; **can I use your phone?** ¿me dejas or puedo usar tu teléfono?; **could I have a word with you?** ¿podría hablar contigo un momento?
4 (expressing disbelief, puzzlement etc): **it can't be true!** ¡no puede ser (verdad)!; **what CAN he want?** ¿qué querrá?
5 (expressing possibility, suggestion etc): **he could be in the library** podría estar en la biblioteca; **she could have been delayed** puede que se haya retrasado

Canada ['kænədə] N Canadá m
Canadian [kə'neɪdɪən] ADJ, N canadiense mf
canal [kə'næl] N canal m
canary [kə'neərɪ] N canario
Canary Islands, Canaries [kə'neərɪz] NPL las (Islas) Canarias
Canberra ['kænbərə] N Canberra, Camberra
cancel ['kænsəl] VT cancelar; (train) suprimir; (appointment, cheque) anular; (cross out) tachar ▶ **cancel out** VT (Math) anular; (fig) contrarrestar; **they ~ each other out** se anulan mutuamente
cancellation [kænsə'leɪʃən] N cancelación f; supresión f
cancer ['kænsə^r] N cáncer m; **C~** (Astro) Cáncer m
cancerous ['kænsərəs] ADJ canceroso
cancer patient N enfermo(-a) m/f de cáncer
cancer research N investigación f del cáncer
C and F ABBR (= cost and freight) C y F
candid ['kændɪd] ADJ franco, abierto
candidacy ['kændɪdəsɪ] N candidatura
candidate ['kændɪdeɪt] N candidato(-a)
candidature ['kændɪdətʃə^r] N (BRIT) = **candidacy**
candidly ['kændɪdlɪ] ADV francamente, con franqueza
candle ['kændl] N vela; (in church) cirio
candle holder N see **candlestick**

candlelight ['kændllaɪt] N: **by ~** a la luz de una vela
candlestick ['kændlstɪk] N (single) candelero; (: low) palmatoria; (bigger, ornate) candelabro
candour, (US) candor ['kændə^r] N franqueza
C & W N ABBR = **country and western (music)**
candy ['kændɪ] N azúcar m cande; (US) caramelo ▶ VT (fruit) escarchar
candy bar (US) N barrita (dulce)
candyfloss ['kændɪflɒs] N (BRIT) algodón m (azucarado)
cane [keɪn] N (Bot) caña; (for baskets, chairs etc) mimbre m; (stick) vara, palmeta; (for walking) bastón m ▶ VT (BRIT Scol) castigar (con palmeta); **~ liquor** caña
canine ['kænaɪn] ADJ canino
canister ['kænɪstə^r] N bote m, lata
cannabis ['kænəbɪs] N canabis m
canned [kænd] ADJ en lata, de lata; (inf: music) grabado; (: drunk) mamado
cannibal ['kænɪbəl] N caníbal mf, antropófago(-a)
cannibalism ['kænɪbəlɪzəm] N canibalismo
cannon ['kænən] (pl ~ or **cannons**) N cañón m
cannonball ['kænənbɔːl] N bala (de cañón)
cannon fodder N carne f de cañón
cannot ['kænɒt] = **can not**
canny ['kænɪ] ADJ avispado
canoe [kə'nuː] N canoa; (Sport) piragua
canoeing [kə'nuːɪŋ] N (Sport) piragüismo
canoeist [kə'nuːɪst] N piragüista mf
canon ['kænən] N (clergyman) canónigo; (standard) canon m
canonize ['kænənaɪz] VT canonizar
can opener N abrelatas m inv
canopy ['kænəpɪ] N dosel m, toldo
can't [kɑːnt] = **can not**
Cantab. ABBR (BRIT: = cantabrigiensis) of Cambridge
cantankerous [kæn'tæŋkərəs] ADJ arisco, malhumorado
canteen [kæn'tiːn] N (eating place) comedor m; (BRIT: of cutlery) juego
canter ['kæntə^r] N medio galope ▶ VI ir a medio galope
cantilever ['kæntɪliːvə^r] N viga voladiza
canvas ['kænvəs] N (material) lona; (painting) lienzo; (Naut) velamen m; **under ~** (camping) en tienda de campaña
canvass ['kænvəs] VI (Pol): **to ~ for** solicitar votos por ▶ VT (Pol: district) hacer campaña (puerta a puerta) en; (: person) hacer campaña (puerta a puerta) a favor de; (Comm: district) sondear el mercado en; (: citizens, opinions) sondear
canvasser ['kænvəsə^r] N (Pol) representante mf electoral; (Comm) corredor(a) m/f
canyon ['kænjən] N cañón m
CAP N ABBR (= Common Agricultural Policy) PAC f

cap [kæp] N (*hat*) gorra; (*for swimming*) gorro; (*of pen*) capuchón *m*; (*of bottle*) tapón *m*, tapa; (: *metal*) chapa; (*BRIT: contraceptive*) diafragma *m* ▶ VT (*outdo*) superar; (*limit*) recortar; (*BRIT Sport*) seleccionar (para el equipo nacional); **and to ~ it all, he ...** y para colmo, él ...

capability [keɪpəˈbɪlɪtɪ] N capacidad *f*

capable [ˈkeɪpəbl] ADJ capaz

capacious [kəˈpeɪʃəs] ADJ amplio

capacity [kəˈpæsɪtɪ] N capacidad *f*; (*position*) calidad *f*; **filled to ~** lleno a reventar; **this work is beyond my ~** este trabajo es superior a mí; **in an advisory ~** como asesor

cape [keɪp] N capa; (*Geo*) cabo

Cape of Good Hope N Cabo de Buena Esperanza

caper [ˈkeɪpəʳ] N (*Culin: also:* **capers**) alcaparra; (*prank*) travesura

Cape Town N Ciudad *f* del Cabo

capital [ˈkæpɪtl] N (*also:* **capital city**) capital *f*; (*money*) capital *m*; (*also:* **capital letter**) mayúscula

capital account N cuenta de capital

capital allowance N desgravación *f* sobre bienes del capital

capital assets N activo fijo

capital expenditure N inversión *f* de capital

capital gains tax N impuesto sobre la plusvalía

capital goods NPL bienes *mpl* de capital

capital-intensive [kæpɪtlɪnˈtɛnsɪv] ADJ de utilización intensiva de capital

capital investment N inversión *f* de capital

capitalism [ˈkæpɪtəlɪzəm] N capitalismo

capitalist [ˈkæpɪtəlɪst] ADJ, N capitalista *mf*

capitalize [ˈkæpɪtəlaɪz] VT (*Comm: provide with capital*) capitalizar

▶ **capitalize on** VT FUS (*fig*) sacar provecho de, aprovechar

capital punishment N pena de muerte

capital transfer tax N impuesto sobre plusvalía de cesión

Capitol [ˈkæpɪtl] N: **the ~** el Capitolio

El Capitolio (*Capitol*) es el edificio en el que se reúne el Congreso de los Estados Unidos (*Congress*), situado en la ciudad de Washington. Por extensión, también se suele llamar así al edificio en el que tienen lugar las sesiones parlamentarias de la cámara de representantes de muchos de los estados.

capitulate [kəˈpɪtjuleɪt] VI capitular, rendirse

capitulation [kəpɪtjuˈleɪʃən] N capitulación *f*, rendición *f*

capricious [kəˈprɪʃəs] ADJ caprichoso

Capricorn [ˈkæprɪkɔːn] N Capricornio

caps [kæps] ABBR (= *capital letters*) may

capsize [kæpˈsaɪz] VT volcar, hacer zozobrar

▶ VI volcarse, zozobrar

capstan [ˈkæpstən] N cabrestante *m*

capsule [ˈkæpsjuːl] N cápsula

Capt. ABBR = **captain**

captain [ˈkæptɪn] N capitán *m* ▶ VT capitanear, ser el capitán de

caption [ˈkæpʃən] N (*heading*) título; (*to picture*) leyenda, pie *m*

captivate [ˈkæptɪveɪt] VT cautivar, encantar

captive [ˈkæptɪv] ADJ, N cautivo(-a) *m/f*

captivity [kæpˈtɪvɪtɪ] N cautiverio

captor [ˈkæptəʳ] N captor(a) *m/f*

capture [ˈkæptʃəʳ] VT capturar; (*place*) tomar; (*attention*) captar, llamar ▶ N captura; toma; (*Comput: also:* **data capture**) formulación *f* de datos

car [kɑːʳ] N coche *m*, carro (*LAM*), automóvil *m*, auto (*LAM*); (*US Rail*) vagón *m*; **by ~** en coche

Caracas [kəˈrækəs] N Caracas *m*

carafe [kəˈræf] N jarra

caramel [ˈkærəməl] N caramelo

carat [ˈkærət] N quilate *m*; **18-~ gold** oro de 18 quilates

caravan [ˈkærəvæn] N (*BRIT*) caravana, rulot *m*; (*of camels*) caravana

caravan site N (*BRIT*) camping *m* para caravanas

caraway [ˈkærəweɪ] N: **~ seed** carvi *m*

carb [kɑːb] N ABBR (*inf*: = *carbohydrate*) carbohidrato

carbohydrates [kɑːbəʊˈhaɪdreɪts] NPL (*foods*) hidratos *mpl* de carbono

carbolic [kɑːˈbɔlɪk] ADJ: **~ acid** ácido carbólico, fenol *m*

car bomb N coche-bomba *m*

carbon [ˈkɑːbən] N carbono

carbonated [ˈkɑːbəneɪtɪd] ADJ (*drink*) con gas

carbon copy N copia al carbón

carbon credit N bono *m* de carbono; crédito *m* (de emisión) de CO_2

carbon dioxide N dióxido de carbono, anhídrido carbónico

carbon footprint N huella de carbono

carbon monoxide N monóxido de carbono

carbon-neutral [kɑːbnˈnjuːtrəl] ADJ carbono neutral

carbon offset N compensación *f* de emisiones de carbono

carbon offsetting [-ˈɔfsɛtɪŋ] N compensación *f* de carbono

carbon paper N papel *m* carbón

carbon ribbon N cinta de carbón

car boot sale N mercadillo (*de objetos usados expuestos en el maletero del coche*)

carburettor, (*US*) **carburetor** [kɑːbjuˈrɛtəʳ] N carburador *m*

carcass [ˈkɑːkəs] N (*of animal*) res *f* muerta; (*dead body*) cadáver *m*

carcinogenic [kɑːsɪnəˈdʒɛnɪk] ADJ cancerígeno

card [kɑːd] N (*thin cardboard*) cartulina; (*playing card*) carta, naipe *m*; (*visiting card, greetings card etc*) tarjeta; (*index card*) ficha; **membership ~** carnet *m*; **to play cards** jugar a las cartas *or* los naipes

cardamom ['kɑːdəməm] N cardamomo

cardboard ['kɑːdbɔːd] N cartón *m*, cartulina

cardboard box N caja de cartón

cardboard city N zona de marginados sin hogar (*que se refugian entre cartones*)

card-carrying member ['kɑːdkærɪɪŋ-] N miembro con carnet

card game N juego de naipes *or* cartas

cardiac ['kɑːdɪæk] ADJ cardíaco

cardigan ['kɑːdɪɡən] N chaqueta (de punto), rebeca

cardinal ['kɑːdɪnl] ADJ cardinal; (*importance, principal*) esencial ▸ N cardenal *m*

cardinal number N número cardinal

card index N fichero

cardphone ['kɑːdfəʊn] N *cabina que funciona con tarjetas telefónicas*

cardsharp ['kɑːdʃɑːp] N fullero(-a)

card vote N voto por delegación

CARE [kɛəʳ] N ABBR (= *Cooperative for American Relief Everywhere*) *sociedad benéfica*

care [kɛəʳ] N cuidado; (*worry*) preocupación *f*; (*charge*) cargo, custodia ▸ VI: **to ~ about** preocuparse por; **~ of (c/o)** en casa de, al cuidado de; (*on letter*) para (entregar a); **in sb's ~** a cargo de algn; **the child has been taken into ~** pusieron al niño bajo custodia del gobierno; **"with ~"** "¡frágil!"; **to take ~ to** cuidarse de, tener cuidado de; **to take ~ of** vt cuidar; (*details, arrangements*) encargarse de; **I don't ~** no me importa; **I couldn't ~ less** me trae sin cuidado
▸ **care for** VT FUS cuidar; (*like*) querer

careen [kə'riːn] VI (*ship*) inclinarse, escorar ▸ VT carenar

career [kə'rɪəʳ] N carrera (profesional); (*occupation*) profesión *f* ▸ VI (*also:* **career along**) correr a toda velocidad

career girl N mujer *f* dedicada a su profesión

careers officer N consejero(-a) de orientación profesional

carefree ['kɛəfriː] ADJ despreocupado

careful ['kɛəful] ADJ cuidadoso; (*cautious*) cauteloso; (**be**) **~!** ¡(ten) cuidado!; **he's very ~ with his money** mira mucho el dinero; (*pej*) es muy tacaño

carefully ['kɛəfəlɪ] ADV con cuidado, cuidadosamente

caregiver ['kɛəɡɪvəʳ] N (*US: professional*) enfermero(-a); (*: unpaid*) persona que cuida a un pariente o vecino

careless ['kɛəlɪs] ADJ descuidado; (*heedless*) poco atento

carelessly ['kɛəlɪslɪ] ADV sin cuidado, a la ligera

carelessness ['kɛəlɪsnɪs] N descuido, falta de atención

carer ['kɛərəʳ] N (*professional*) enfermero(-a); (*unpaid*) persona que cuida a un pariente o vecino

caress [kə'res] N caricia ▸ VT acariciar

caretaker ['kɛəteɪkəʳ] N portero(-a), conserje *mf*

caretaker government N gobierno provisional

car-ferry ['kɑːfɛrɪ] N transbordador *m* para coches

cargo ['kɑːɡəʊ] (*pl* **cargoes**) N cargamento, carga

cargo boat N buque *m* de carga, carguero

cargo plane N avión *m* de carga

car hire N alquiler *m* de coches

Caribbean [kærɪ'biːən] ADJ caribe, caribeño; **the ~ (Sea)** el (Mar) Caribe

caricature ['kærɪkətjuəʳ] N caricatura

caring ['kɛərɪŋ] ADJ humanitario

carnage ['kɑːnɪdʒ] N matanza, carnicería

carnal ['kɑːnl] ADJ carnal

carnation [kɑː'neɪʃən] N clavel *m*

carnival ['kɑːnɪvəl] N carnaval *m*; (*US*) parque *m* de atracciones

carnivore ['kɑːnɪvɔːʳ] N carnívoro(-a)

carnivorous [kɑː'nɪvrəs] ADJ carnívoro

carol ['kærəl] N: (**Christmas**) **~** villancico

carouse [kə'rauz] VI estar de juerga

carousel [kærə'sel] N (*US*) tiovivo, caballitos *mpl*

carp [kɑːp] N (*fish*) carpa
▸ **carp at, carp about** VT FUS sacar faltas de

car park N (*BRIT*) aparcamiento, parking *m*, playa de estacionamiento (*LAM*)

carpenter ['kɑːpɪntəʳ] N carpintero(-a)

carpentry ['kɑːpɪntrɪ] N carpintería

carpet ['kɑːpɪt] N alfombra ▸ VT alfombrar; **fitted ~** moqueta

carpet bombing N bombardeo de arrasamiento

carpet slippers NPL zapatillas *fpl*

carpet sweeper [-'swiːpəʳ] N cepillo mecánico

car phone N teléfono de coche

carping ['kɑːpɪŋ] ADJ (*critical*) criticón(-ona)

car rental N (*US*) alquiler *m* de coches

carriage ['kærɪdʒ] N (*BRIT Rail*) vagón *m*; (*horse-drawn*) coche *m*; (*for goods*) transporte *m*; (*of typewriter*) carro; (*bearing*) porte *m*; **~ forward** porte *m* debido; **~ free** franco de porte; **~ paid** porte pagado; **~ inwards/outwards** gastos *mpl* de transporte a cargo del comprador/vendedor

carriage return N (*on typewriter etc*) tecla de regreso

carriageway ['kærɪdʒweɪ] N (*BRIT: part of road*) calzada; **dual ~** autovía

carrier ['kærɪəʳ] N transportista mf; (company) empresa de transportes; (Med) portador(a) m/f

carrier bag N (BRIT) bolsa de papel or plástico

carrier pigeon N paloma mensajera

carrion ['kærɪən] N carroña

carrot ['kærət] N zanahoria

carry ['kærɪ] VT (person) llevar; (transport) transportar; (a motion, bill) aprobar; (involve: responsibilities etc) entrañar, conllevar; (Comm: stock) tener en existencia; (: interest) llevar; (Math: figure) llevarse ▶ VI (sound) oírse; **to get carried away** (fig) entusiasmarse; **this loan carries 10% interest** este empréstito devenga un interés del 10 por ciento

▶ **carry forward** VT (Math, Comm) pasar a la página/columna siguiente

▶ **carry on** VI (continue) seguir (adelante), continuar; (inf: complain) montar el número ▶ VT seguir, continuar

▶ **carry out** VT (orders) cumplir; (investigation) llevar a cabo, realizar

carrycot ['kærɪkɒt] N (BRIT) cuna portátil, capazo

carry-on ['kærɪ'ɒn] N (inf) follón m

cart [kɑːt] N carro, carreta ▶ VT (inf: transport) cargar con

carte blanche ['kɑːt'blɒnʃ] N: **to give sb ~** dar carta blanca a algn

cartel [kɑː'tɛl] N (Comm) cartel m

cartilage ['kɑːtɪlɪdʒ] N cartílago

cartographer [kɑː'tɒgrəfəʳ] N cartógrafo(-a)

carton ['kɑːtən] N caja (de cartón); (of milk etc) bote m; (of cigarettes) cartón m

cartoon [kɑː'tuːn] N (Press) chiste m; (comic strip) historieta, tira cómica; (film) dibujos mpl animados

cartoonist [kɑː'tuːnɪst] N humorista mf gráfico

cartridge ['kɑːtrɪdʒ] N cartucho

cartwheel ['kɑːtwiːl] N: **to turn a ~** dar una voltereta lateral

carve [kɑːv] VT (meat) trinchar; (wood) tallar; (stone) cincelar, esculpir; (on tree) grabar

▶ **carve up** VT dividir, repartir; (meat) trinchar

carving ['kɑːvɪŋ] N (in wood etc) escultura; (design) talla

carving knife N trinchante m

car wash N túnel m de lavado

Casablanca [kæsə'blæŋkə] N Casablanca

cascade [kæs'keɪd] N salto de agua, cascada; (fig) chorro ▶ VI caer a chorros

case [keɪs] N (container) caja; (Med) caso; (for jewels etc) estuche m; (Law) causa, proceso; (BRIT: also: **suitcase**) maleta; **lower/upper ~** (Typ) caja baja/alta; **in ~ of** en caso de; **in any ~** en todo caso; **just in ~** por si acaso; **to have a good ~** tener buenas razones; **there's a**

strong ~ for reform hay razones sólidas para exigir una reforma

case history N (Med) historial m médico, historia clínica

case study N estudio de casos prácticos

cash [kæʃ] N (dinero en) efectivo; (inf: money) dinero ▶ VT cobrar, hacer efectivo; **to pay (in) ~** pagar al contado; **~ on delivery (COD)** entrega contra reembolso; **~ with order** paga al hacer el pedido; **to be short of ~** estar pelado, estar sin blanca

▶ **cash in** VT (insurance policy etc) cobrar ▶ VI: **to ~ in on sth** sacar partido or aprovecharse de algo

cash account N cuenta de caja

cash and carry N cash and carry m, autoservicio mayorista

cashback ['kæʃbæk] N (discount) devolución f; (at supermarket etc) retirada de dinero en efectivo de un establecimiento donde se ha pagado con tarjeta; también dinero retirado

cashbook ['kæʃbuk] N libro de caja

cash box N hucha

cash card N tarjeta f de(l) cajero (automático)

cash desk N (BRIT) caja

cash discount N descuento por pago al contado

cash dispenser N cajero automático

cashew [kæ'ʃuː] N (also: **cashew nut**) anacardo

cash flow N flujo de fondos, cash-flow m, movimiento de efectivo

cashier [kæ'ʃɪəʳ] N cajero(-a) ▶ VT (Mil) destituir, expulsar

cashmere ['kæʃmɪəʳ] N cachemir m, cachemira

cash payment N pago al contado

cash point N cajero automático

cash price N precio al contado

cash register N caja

cash reserves NPL reserva en efectivo

cash sale N venta al contado

casing ['keɪsɪŋ] N revestimiento

casino [kə'siːnəu] N casino

cask [kɑːsk] N tonel m, barril m

casket ['kɑːskɪt] N cofre m, estuche m; (US: coffin) ataúd m

Caspian Sea ['kæspɪən-] N: **the ~** el Mar Caspio

cassava [kə'sɑːvə] N mandioca

casserole ['kæsərəul] N (food, pot) cazuela

cassette [kæ'sɛt] N cas(s)et(t)e m or f

cassette deck N platina

cassette player, cassette recorder N cas(s)et(t)e m

cassock ['kæsək] N sotana

cast [kɑːst] (pt, pp ~) VT (throw) echar, arrojar, lanzar; (skin) mudar, perder; (metal) fundir; (Theat): **to ~ sb as Othello** dar a algn el papel de Otelo ▶ N (*Theat*) reparto; (*mould*) forma, molde *m*; (*also*: **plaster cast**) vaciado; **to ~ loose** soltar; **to ~ one's vote** votar

▶ **cast aside** VT (*reject*) descartar, desechar

▶ **cast away** VT desechar

▶ **cast down** VT derribar

▶ **cast off** VI (*Naut*) soltar amarras; (*Knitting*) cerrar los puntos ▶ VT (*Knitting*) cerrar; **to ~ sb off** abandonar a algn, desentenderse de algn

▶ **cast on** VT (*Knitting*) montar

castanets [kæstə'nɛts] NPL castañuelas *fpl*

castaway ['kɑːstəwəɪ] N náufrago(-a)

caste [kɑːst] N casta

caster sugar ['kɑːstə'-] N (*BRIT*) azúcar *m* extrafino

Castile [kæs'tiːl] N Castilla

Castilian [kæs'tɪlɪən] ADJ, N castellano(-a) *m/f* ▶ N (*Ling*) castellano

casting vote ['kɑːstɪŋ-] N (*BRIT*) voto decisivo

cast iron N hierro fundido *or* colado

cast-iron ['kɑːstaɪən] ADJ (*lit*) (hecho) de hierro fundido *or* colado; (*fig*: *alibi*) irrebatible; (*will*) férreo

castle ['kɑːsl] N castillo; (*Chess*) torre *f*

castor ['kɑːstə'] N (*wheel*) ruedecilla

castor oil N aceite *m* de ricino

castrate [kæs'treɪt] VT castrar

casual ['kæʒjul] ADJ (*by chance*) fortuito; (*irregular*: *work etc*) eventual, temporero; (*unconcerned*) despreocupado; (*informal*: *clothes*) de sport

casually ['kæʒjulɪ] ADV por casualidad; de manera despreocupada

casualty ['kæʒjultɪ] N víctima, herido; (*dead*) muerto; (*Mil*) baja; **heavy casualties** numerosas bajas *fpl*

casualty ward N urgencias *fpl*

cat [kæt] N gato

catacombs ['kætəkuːmz] NPL catacumbas *fpl*

Catalan ['kætəlæn] ADJ, N catalán(-ana) *m/f*

catalogue, (*US*) **catalog** ['kætələg] N catálogo ▶ VT catalogar

Catalonia [kætə'ləunɪə] N Cataluña

catalyst ['kætəlɪst] N catalizador *m*

catalytic converter [kætə'lɪtɪkkən'vəːtə'] N catalizador *m*

catapult ['kætəpʌlt] N tirachinas *m inv*

cataract ['kætərækt] N (*Med*) cataratas *fpl*

catarrh [kə'tɑː'] N catarro

catastrophe [kə'tæstrəfɪ] N catástrofe *f*

catastrophic [kætə'strɔfɪk] ADJ catastrófico

catcall ['kætkɔːl] N (*at meeting etc*) rechifla, silbido

catch [kætʃ] (*pt, pp* **caught**) VT coger (*SP*), agarrar (*LAm*); (*arrest*) atrapar, coger (*SP*); (*grasp*) asir; (*breath*) recobrar; (*person*: *by surprise*) pillar; (*attract*: *attention*) captar; (*Med*) pillar, coger; (*also*: **catch up**) alcanzar ▶ VI

(*fire*) encenderse; (*in branches etc*) engancharse ▶ N (*fish etc*) captura; (*act of catching*) cogida; (*trick*) trampa; (*of lock*) pestillo, cerradura; **to ~ fire** prenderse; (*house*) incendiarse; **to ~ sight of** divisar

▶ **catch on** VI (*understand*) caer en la cuenta; (*grow popular*) tener éxito, cuajar

▶ **catch out** VT (*fig*: *with trick question*) hundir

▶ **catch up** VI (*fig*) ponerse al día

catching ['kætʃɪŋ] ADJ (*Med*) contagioso

catchment area ['kætʃmənt-] N (*BRIT*) zona de captación

catch phrase N frase *f* de moda

catch-22 ['kætʃtwɛntɪ'tuː] N: **it's a ~ situation** es un callejón sin salida, es un círculo vicioso

catchy ['kætʃɪ] ADJ (*tune*) pegadizo

catechism ['kætɪkɪzəm] N (*Rel*) catecismo

categoric [kætɪ'gɔrɪk], **categorical** [kætɪ'gɔrɪkəl] ADJ categórico, terminante

categorically [kætɪ'gɔrɪkəlɪ] ADV categóricamente, terminantemente

categorize ['kætɪgəraɪz] VT clasificar

category ['kætɪgərɪ] N categoría

cater ['keɪtə'] VI: **to ~ for** (*BRIT*) abastecer a; (*needs*) atender a; (*consumers*) proveer a

caterer ['keɪtərə'] N abastecedor(a) *m/f*, proveedor(a) *m/f*

catering ['keɪtərɪŋ] N (*trade*) hostelería

caterpillar ['kætəpɪlə'] N oruga

caterpillar track N rodado de oruga

cat flap N gatera

cathedral [kə'θiːdrəl] N catedral *f*

cathode-ray tube ['kæθəudreɪ'tjuːb] N tubo de rayos catódicos

catholic ['kæθəlɪk] ADJ católico; **C~** *adj*, *n* (*Rel*) católico(-a) *m/f*

CAT scanner [kæt-] (*Med*) N ABBR (= *computerized axial tomography scanner*) escáner *m* TAC

Catseye® ['kætsaɪ] N (*BRIT Aut*) catadióptrico

catsup ['kætsəp] N (*US*) ketchup, catsup *m*

cattle ['kætl] NPL ganado *sg*

catty ['kætɪ] ADJ malicioso

catwalk ['kætwɔːk] N pasarela

Caucasian [kɔː'keɪzɪən] ADJ, N caucásico(-a) *m/f*

Caucasus ['kɔːkəsəs] N Cáucaso

caucus ['kɔːkəs] N (*Pol*: *local committee*) comité *m* local; (: *US*: *to elect candidates*) comité *m* electoral; (: *group*) camarilla política

caught [kɔːt] PT, PP *of* **catch**

cauliflower ['kɔlɪflauə'] N coliflor *f*

cause [kɔːz] N causa; (*reason*) motivo, razón *f* ▶ VT causar; (*provoke*) provocar; **to ~ sb to do sth** hacer que algn haga algo

causeway ['kɔːzweɪ] N (*road*) carretera elevada; (*embankment*) terraplén *m*

caustic ['kɔːstɪk] ADJ cáustico; (*fig*) mordaz

cauterize ['kɔ:təraɪz] VT cauterizar
caution ['kɔ:ʃən] N cautela, prudencia; (warning) advertencia, amonestación f ▶ VT amonestar
cautious ['kɔ:ʃəs] ADJ cauteloso, prudente, precavido
cautiously ['kɔ:ʃəslɪ] ADV con cautela
cautiousness ['kɔ:ʃəsnɪs] N cautela
cavalcade [kævəl'keɪd] N cabalgata
cavalier [kævə'lɪər] N (knight) caballero ▶ ADJ (pej: offhand: person, attitude) arrogante, desdeñoso
cavalry ['kævəlrɪ] N caballería
cave [keɪv] N cueva, caverna ▶ VI: **to go caving** ir en una expedición espeleológica ▶ **cave in** VI (roof etc) derrumbarse, hundirse
caveman ['keɪvmæn] N (irreg) cavernícola m
cavern ['kævən] N caverna
cavernous ['kævənəs] ADJ (cheeks, eyes) hundido
caviar, caviare ['kævɪɑ:r] N caviar m
cavity ['kævɪtɪ] N hueco, cavidad f
cavity wall insulation N aislamiento térmico
cavort [kə'vɔ:t] VI hacer cabrioladas
cayenne [keɪ'ɛn] N: **~ pepper** pimentón m picante
CB N ABBR (= Citizens' Band (Radio)) frecuencias de radio usadas para la comunicación privada; (BRIT: = Companion of (the Order of the Bath) título de nobleza
CBC N ABBR (= Canadian Broadcasting Corporation) cadena de radio y televisión
CBE N ABBR (BRIT: = Companion of (the Order of) the British Empire) título de nobleza
CBI N ABBR (= Confederation of British Industry) ≈ C.E.O.E. f (SP)
CBS N ABBR (US: = Columbia Broadcasting System) cadena de radio y televisión
CC ABBR (BRIT) = **county council**
cc ABBR (= cubic centimetres) cc, cm³; (on letter etc) = **carbon copy**
CCA N ABBR (US: = Circuit Court of Appeals) tribunal de apelación itinerante
CCTV N ABBR = **closed-circuit television**
CCTV camera N cámara de vigilancia, cámara de circuito cerrado de televisión
CCU N ABBR (esp US: = coronary care unit) unidad f de cuidados cardiológicos
CD N ABBR (= compact disc) CD m; (Mil: BRIT) = **Civil Defence (Corps)**; (: US: = Civil Defense) defensa civil ▶ ADJ (BRIT: = Corps Diplomatique) CD
CD burner N tostadora/grabadora f de CDs
CDC N ABBR (US) = **center for disease control**
CD player N reproductor m de CD
Cdr. ABBR = **commander**
CD-ROM ['si:di:'rɔm] N ABBR (= compact disc read-only memory) CD-ROM m

CDT N ABBR (US: = Central Daylight Time) hora de verano del centro; (BRIT Scol: = Craft, Design and Technology) artesanía, diseño y tecnología
CDW N ABBR = **collision damage waiver**
CD writer N grabadora f de CDs
cease [si:s] VT cesar
ceasefire ['si:sfaɪər] N alto m el fuego
ceaseless ['si:slɪs] ADJ incesante
ceaselessly ['si:slɪslɪ] ADV sin cesar
CED N ABBR (US) = **Committee for Economic Development**
cedar ['si:dər] N cedro
cede [si:d] VT ceder
CEEB N ABBR (US: = College Entrance Examination Board) tribunal para las pruebas de acceso a la universidad
ceilidh ['keɪlɪ] N baile con música y danzas tradicionales escocesas o irlandesas
ceiling ['si:lɪŋ] N techo; (fig: upper limit) límite m, tope m
celebrate ['sɛlɪbreɪt] VT celebrar; (have a party) festejar ▶ VI: **let's ~!** ¡vamos a celebrarlo!
celebrated ['sɛlɪbreɪtɪd] ADJ célebre
celebration [sɛlɪ'breɪʃən] N celebración f, festejo
celebrity [sɪ'lɛbrɪtɪ] N (person) famoso(-a)
celeriac [sə'lɛrɪæk] N apio-nabo
celery ['sɛlərɪ] N apio
celestial [sɪ'lɛstɪəl] ADJ (of the sky) celeste; (divine) celestial
celibacy ['sɛlɪbəsɪ] N celibato
cell [sɛl] N celda; (Biol) célula; (Elec) elemento
cellar ['sɛlər] N sótano; (for wine) bodega
cellist ['tʃɛlɪst] N violoncelista mf
cello ['tʃɛləu] N violoncelo
Cellophane® ['sɛləfeɪn] N celofán m
cellphone ['sɛlfəun] N móvil
cell tower N (US Tel) torre f de telefonía móvil, antena de telefonía móvil
cellular ['sɛljulər] ADJ celular
celluloid ['sɛljulɔɪd] N celuloide m
cellulose ['sɛljuləus] N celulosa
Celsius ['sɛlsɪəs] ADJ centígrado
Celt [kɛlt, sɛlt] N celta mf
Celtic ['kɛltɪk, 'sɛltɪk] ADJ celta, céltico ▶ N (Ling) celta m
cement [sə'mɛnt] N cemento ▶ VT cementar; (fig) cimentar
cement mixer N hormigonera
cemetery ['sɛmɪtrɪ] N cementerio
cenotaph ['sɛnətɑ:f] N cenotafio
censor ['sɛnsər] N censor(a) m/f ▶ VT (cut) censurar
censorship ['sɛnsəʃɪp] N censura
censure ['sɛnʃər] VT censurar
census ['sɛnsəs] N censo
cent [sɛnt] N (US: unit of dollar) centavo; (unit of euro) céntimo; see also **per**

centenary [sɛn'tiːnərɪ], (US) **centennial** [sɛn'tɛnɪəl] N centenario

center ['sɛntəʳ] N (US) = **centre**

centigrade ['sɛntɪgreɪd] ADJ centígrado

centilitre, (US) **centiliter** ['sɛntɪliːtəʳ] N centilitro

centimetre, (US) **centimeter** ['sɛntɪmiːtəʳ] N centímetro

centipede ['sɛntɪpiːd] N ciempiés m inv

central ['sɛntrəl] ADJ central; (house etc) céntrico

Central African Republic N República Centroafricana

Central America N Centroamérica

Central American ADJ, N centroamericano(-a) m/f

central heating N calefacción f central

centralize ['sɛntrəlaɪz] VT centralizar

central processing unit N (Comput) unidad f procesadora central, unidad f central de proceso

central reservation N (Brit Aut) mediana

centre, (US) **center** ['sɛntəʳ] N centro ▶ VT centrar; **to ~ (on)** (concentrate) concentrar (en)

centrefold, (US) **centerfold** ['sɛntəfəʊld] N página central plegable

centre-forward ['sɛntə'fɔːwəd] N (Sport) delantero centro

centre-half ['sɛntə'hɑːf] N (Sport) medio centro

centrepiece, (US) **centerpiece** ['sɛntəpiːs] N punto central

centre spread N (Brit) páginas fpl centrales

centre-stage ['sɛntəsteɪdʒ] N: **to take ~** pasar a primer plano

centrifuge ['sɛntrɪfjuːdʒ] N centrifugadora

century ['sɛntjurɪ] N siglo; **20th ~** siglo veinte; **in the twentieth ~** en el siglo veinte

CEO N ABBR = **chief executive officer**

ceramic [sɪ'ræmɪk] ADJ de cerámica

ceramics [sɪ'ræmɪks] N cerámica

cereal ['sɪrɪəl] N cereal m

cerebral ['sɛrɪbrəl] ADJ cerebral

ceremonial [sɛrɪ'məʊnɪəl] N ceremonial

ceremony ['sɛrɪmənɪ] N ceremonia; **to stand on ~** hacer ceremonias, andarse con cumplidos

cert [sə:t] N (Brit inf): **it's a dead ~** ¡es cosa segura!

certain ['sə:tən] ADJ seguro; (correct) cierto; (particular) cierto; **for ~** a ciencia cierta; **a ~ Mr Smith** un tal Sr. Smith

certainly ['sə:tənlɪ] ADV desde luego, por supuesto

certainty ['sə:təntɪ] N certeza, certidumbre f, seguridad f

certificate [sə'tɪfɪkɪt] N certificado

certified ['sə:tɪfaɪd] ADJ: **~ mail** (US) correo certificado

certified public accountant N (US) contable mf diplomado(-a)

certify ['sə:tɪfaɪ] VT certificar; (declare insane) declarar loco

cervical ['sə:vɪkl] ADJ: **~ cancer** cáncer m cervical; **~ smear** citología

cervix ['sə:vɪks] N cerviz f, cuello del útero

Cesarean [sɪ'zɛərɪən] ADJ, N (US) = **Caesarean**

cessation [sə'seɪʃən] N cese m, suspensión f

cesspit ['sɛspɪt] N pozo negro

CET N ABBR (= Central European Time) hora de Europa central

Ceylon [sɪ'lɔn] N Ceilán m

cf. ABBR (= compare) cfr.

c/f ABBR (Comm) = **carried forward**

CFC N ABBR (= chlorofluorocarbon) CFC m

CG N ABBR (US) = **coastguard**

cg ABBR (= centigram) cg

CH N ABBR (Brit: = Companion of Honour) título de nobleza

ch. ABBR (= chapter) cap.

Chad [tʃæd] N Chad m

chafe [tʃeɪf] VT (rub) rozar; (irritate) irritar; **to ~ (against)** (fig) irritarse or enojarse (con)

chaffinch ['tʃæfɪntʃ] N pinzón m (vulgar)

chagrin ['ʃægrɪn] N (annoyance) disgusto; (disappointment) desazón f

chain [tʃeɪn] N cadena; (of mountains) cordillera; (of events) sucesión f ▶ VT (also: **chain up**) encadenar

chain reaction N reacción f en cadena

chain-smoke ['tʃeɪnsməʊk] VI fumar un cigarrillo tras otro

chain store N tienda de una cadena, ≈ grandes almacenes mpl

chair [tʃɛəʳ] N silla; (armchair) sillón m; (of university) cátedra ▶ VT (meeting) presidir; **the ~** (US: electric chair) la silla eléctrica; **please take a ~** siéntese or tome asiento, por favor

chairlift ['tʃɛəlɪft] N telesilla m

chairman ['tʃɛəmən] N (irreg) presidente m

chairperson ['tʃɛəpə:sn] N presidente(-a) m/f

chairwoman ['tʃɛəwumən] N (irreg) presidenta

chalet ['ʃæleɪ] N chalet m (de madera)

chalice ['tʃælɪs] N cáliz m

chalk [tʃɔːk] N (Geo) creta; (for writing) tiza, gis m (Lam)
▶ **chalk up** VT apuntar; (fig: success, victory) apuntarse

chalkboard ['tʃɔːkbɔːd] (US) N pizarrón (Lam), pizarra (Sp)

challenge ['tʃælɪndʒ] N desafío, reto ▶ VT desafiar, retar; (statement, right) poner en duda; **to ~ sb to do sth** retar a algn a que haga algo

challenger ['tʃælɪndʒəʳ] N (Sport) contrincante mf

challenging ['tʃælɪndʒɪŋ] ADJ que supone un reto; (tone) de desafío

chamber ['tʃeɪmbəʳ] N cámara, sala

chambermaid ['tʃeɪmbəmeɪd] N camarera

chamber music N música de cámara

chamber of commerce N cámara de comercio

chamber pot ['tʃeɪmbəpɒt] N orinal m

chameleon [kə'miːlɪən] N camaleón m

chamois ['ʃæmwɑː] N gamuza

champagne [ʃæm'peɪn] N champaña m, champán m

champers ['ʃæmpəz] NSG (inf) champán m

champion ['tʃæmpɪən] N campeón(-ona) m/f; (of cause) defensor(a) m/f, paladín mf ▶ VT defender, apoyar

championship ['tʃæmpɪənʃɪp] N campeonato

chance [tʃɑːns] N (coincidence) casualidad f; (luck) suerte f; (fate) azar m; (opportunity) ocasión f, oportunidad f, chance m or f (LAM); (likelihood) posibilidad f; (risk) riesgo ▶ VT arriesgar, probar ▶ ADJ fortuito, casual; **to ~ it** arriesgarse, intentarlo; **to take a ~** arriesgarse; **by ~** por casualidad; **it's the ~ of a lifetime** es la oportunidad de su vida; **the chances are that ...** lo más probable es que ...; **to ~ to do sth** (happen) hacer algo por casualidad

▶ **chance (up)on** VT FUS tropezar(se) con

chancel ['tʃɑːnsəl] N coro y presbiterio

chancellor ['tʃɑːnsələʳ] N canciller m; **C~ of the Exchequer** (BRIT) Ministro de Economía y Hacienda; see also **Downing Street**

chancy ['tʃɑːnsɪ] ADJ (inf) arriesgado

chandelier [ʃændə'lɪəʳ] N araña (de luces)

change [tʃeɪndʒ] VT cambiar; (clothes, house) cambiarse de, mudarse de; (transform) transformar ▶ VI cambiar(se); (change trains) hacer transbordo; (be transformed): **to ~ into** transformarse en ▶ N cambio; (alteration) modificación f, transformación f; (coins) suelto; (money returned) vuelta, vuelto (LAM); **to ~ one's mind** cambiar de opinión or idea; **to ~ gear** (Aut) cambiar de marcha; **she changed into an old skirt** se puso una falda vieja; **for a ~** para variar; **can you give me ~ for £1?** ¿tiene cambio de una libra?; **keep the ~** quédese con la vuelta

▶ **change over** VI (from sth to sth) cambiar; (players etc) cambiar(se) ▶ VT cambiar

changeable ['tʃeɪndʒəbl] ADJ (weather) cambiable; (person) variable

changeless ['tʃeɪndʒlɪs] ADJ inmutable

change machine N máquina de cambio

changeover ['tʃeɪndʒəʊvəʳ] N (to new system) cambio

changing ['tʃeɪndʒɪŋ] ADJ cambiante

changing room N (BRIT) vestuario

channel ['tʃænl] N (TV) canal m; (of river) cauce m; (of sea) estrecho; (groove, fig: medium) conducto, medio ▶ VT (river etc) encauzar; **to ~ into** (fig: interest, energies) encauzar a, dirigir a; **the (English) C~** el Canal (de la Mancha); **the C~ Islands** las Islas Anglonormandas; **channels of communication** canales mpl de comunicación; **green/red ~** (Customs) pasillo verde/rojo

Channel Tunnel N: **the ~** el túnel del Canal de la Mancha, el Eurotúnel

chant [tʃɑːnt] N (also Rel) canto; (of crowd) gritos mpl ▶ VT cantar; (slogan, word) repetir a gritos; **the demonstrators chanted their disapproval** los manifestantes corearon su desaprobación

chaos ['keɪɒs] N caos m

chaos theory N teoría del caos

chaotic [keɪ'ɒtɪk] ADJ caótico

chap [tʃæp] N (BRIT inf: man) tío, tipo; **old ~** amigo (mío)

chapel ['tʃæpəl] N capilla

chaperone ['ʃæpərəʊn] N carabina

chaplain ['tʃæplɪn] N capellán m

chapped [tʃæpt] ADJ agrietado

chapter ['tʃæptəʳ] N capítulo

char [tʃɑːʳ] VT (burn) carbonizar, chamuscar ▶ N (BRIT) = **charlady**

character ['kærɪktəʳ] N carácter m, naturaleza, índole f; (in novel, film) personaje m; (role) papel m; (individuality) carácter m; (Comput) carácter m; **a person of good ~** una persona de buena reputación

character code N código de caracteres

characteristic [kærɪktə'rɪstɪk] ADJ característico ▶ N característica

characterize ['kærɪktəraɪz] VT caracterizar

charade [ʃə'rɑːd] N farsa, comedia; **charades** (game) charadas fpl

charcoal ['tʃɑːkəʊl] N carbón m vegetal; (Art) carboncillo

charge [tʃɑːdʒ] N (Law) carga, acusación f; (cost) precio, coste m; (responsibility) cargo; (task) encargo ▶ VT (Law): **to ~ (with)** acusar (de); (gun, battery) cargar; (Mil: enemy) cargar; (price) pedir; (customer) cobrar; (person: with task) encargar ▶ VI precipitarse; (make pay) cobrar; **charges** NPL: **bank charges** comisiones fpl bancarias; **extra ~** recargo, suplemento; **free of ~** gratis; **to reverse the charges** (BRIT Tel) llamar a cobro revertido; **to take ~ of** hacerse cargo de, encargarse de; **to be in ~ of** estar encargado de; **how much do you ~?** ¿cuánto cobra usted?; **to ~ an expense (up) to sb's account** cargar algo a cuenta de algn; **~ it to my account** póngalo or cárguelo a mi cuenta

charge account N (US) cuenta abierta or a crédito

charge card N tarjeta de cuenta

chargé d'affaires ['ʃɑːʒeɪdæ'feəʳ] N encargado de negocios

charge hand ['tʃɑːdʒhænd] N capataz m

charger ['tʃɑːdʒəʳ] N (*also*: **battery charger**) cargador m (de baterías)

chariot ['tʃærɪət] N carro

charisma [kæ'rɪzmə] N carisma m

charismatic [kærɪz'mætɪk] ADJ carismático

charitable ['tʃærɪtəbl] ADJ caritativo

charity ['tʃærɪtɪ] N (*gen*) caridad f; (*organization*) organización f benéfica; (*money, gifts*) limosnas fpl

charity shop N (BRIT) tienda de artículos de segunda mano que dedica su recaudación a causas benéficas

charlady ['tʃɑːleɪdɪ] N (BRIT) mujer f de la limpieza

charlatan ['ʃɑːlətən] N charlatán m

charm [tʃɑːm] N encanto, atractivo; (*spell*) hechizo; (*object*) amuleto; (*on bracelet*) dije m ▶ VT encantar; hechizar

charm bracelet N pulsera amuleto

charming ['tʃɑːmɪŋ] ADJ encantador(a); (*person*) simpático

chart [tʃɑːt] N (*table*) cuadro; (*graph*) gráfica; (*map*) carta de navegación; (*weather chart*) mapa m meteorológico ▶ VT (*course*) trazar; (*progress*) seguir; (*sales*) hacer una gráfica de; **to be in the charts** (*record, pop group*) estar en la lista de éxitos

charter ['tʃɑːtəʳ] VT (*bus*) alquilar; (*plane, ship*) fletar ▶ N (*document*) estatuto, carta; **on ~** en alquiler, alquilado

chartered accountant N (BRIT) contable mf diplomado(-a)

charter flight N vuelo chárter

charwoman ['tʃɑːwumən] N (*irreg*) = **charlady**

chase [tʃeɪs] VT (*pursue*) perseguir; (*hunt*) cazar ▶ N persecución f; caza; **to ~ after** correr tras ▶ **chase up** VT (*information*) tratar de conseguir; **to ~ sb up about sth** recordar algo a algn

chasm ['kæzəm] N abismo

chassis ['ʃæsɪ] N chasis m

chaste [tʃeɪst] ADJ casto

chastened ['tʃeɪsənd] ADJ escarmentado

chastening ['tʃeɪsnɪŋ] ADJ aleccionador(a)

chastity ['tʃæstɪtɪ] N castidad f

chat [tʃæt] VI (*also*: **have a chat**) charlar; (: *Internet*) chatear ▶ N charla; (*Internet*) chat m ▶ **chat up** VT (*inf: girl*) ligar con, enrollarse con

chatline ['tʃætlaɪn] N línea (telefónica) múltiple, party line f

chat room N (*Internet*) chat m, canal m de charla

chat show N (BRIT) programa m de entrevistas

chattel ['tʃætl] N bien m mueble

chatter ['tʃætəʳ] VI (*person*) charlar; (*teeth*) castañetear ▶ N (*of birds*) parloteo; (*of people*) charla, cháchara

chatterbox ['tʃætəbɒks] N parlanchín(-ina) m/f

chattering classes ['tʃætərɪŋ'klɑːsɪz] NPL (*inf, pej*): **the ~** los intelectualillos

chatty ['tʃætɪ] ADJ (*style*) informal; (*person*) hablador(a)

chauffeur ['ʃəufəʳ] N chófer m

chauvinist ['ʃəuvɪnɪst] N (*also*: **male chauvinist**) machista m; (*nationalist*) chovinista mf, patriotero(-a) m/f

ChE ABBR = **chemical engineer**

cheap [tʃiːp] ADJ barato; (*joke*) de mal gusto, chabacano; (*poor quality*) de mala calidad; (*reduced: ticket*) económico; (: *fare*) barato ▶ ADV barato

cheap day return N billete de ida y vuelta el mismo día

cheapen ['tʃiːpn] VT rebajar el precio de, abaratar

cheaply ['tʃiːplɪ] ADV barato, a bajo precio

cheat [tʃiːt] VI hacer trampa; (*in exam*) copiar ▶ VT estafar, timar ▶ N trampa; estafa; (*person*) tramposo(-a); **to ~ sb (out of sth)** estafar (algo) a algn ▶ **cheat on** VT FUS engañar; **he's been cheating on his wife** ha estado engañando a su esposa

cheating ['tʃiːtɪŋ] N trampa

Chechnya ['tʃetʃnɪə] N Chechenia

check [tʃɛk] VT (*examine*) controlar; (*facts*) comprobar; (*count*) contar; (*halt*) frenar; (*restrain*) refrenar, restringir ▶ VI: **to ~ with sb** consultar con algn; (*official etc*) informarse por ▶ N (*inspection*) control m, inspección f; (*curb*) freno; (*bill*) nota, cuenta; (*US*) = **cheque**; (*pattern: gen pl*) cuadro ▶ ADJ (*pattern, cloth: also*: **checked**) a cuadros; **to keep a ~ on sth/sb** controlar algo/a algn ▶ **check in** VI (*in hotel*) registrarse; (*at airport*) facturar ▶ VT (*luggage*) facturar ▶ **check off** VT (*esp US*: **check**) comprobar; (*cross off*) tachar ▶ **check out** VI (*of hotel*) desocupar la habitación ▶ VT (*investigate: story*) comprobar; (: *person*) informarse sobre ▶ **check up** VI: **to ~ up on sth** comprobar algo; **to ~ up on sb** investigar a algn

checkbook ['tʃɛkbuk] N (*US*) = **chequebook**

checked [tʃɛkt] ADJ a cuadros inv

checkered ['tʃɛkəd] ADJ (*US*) = **chequered**

checkers ['tʃɛkəz] N (*US*) damas fpl

check-in ['tʃɛkɪn] N (*also*: **check-in desk**: *at airport*) mostrador m de facturación

checking account ['tʃɛkɪŋ-] N (*US*) cuenta corriente
checklist ['tʃɛklɪst] N lista
checkmate ['tʃɛkmeɪt] N jaque *m* mate
checkout ['tʃɛkaut] N (*in supermarket*) caja
checkpoint ['tʃɛkpɔɪnt] N (punto de) control *m*, retén *m* (*LAM*)
checkroom ['tʃɛkrum] N (*US*) consigna
checkup ['tʃɛkʌp] N (*Med*) reconocimiento general; (*of machine*) revisión *f*
cheddar ['tʃɛdəʳ] N (*also*: **cheddar cheese**) queso *m* cheddar
cheek [tʃiːk] N mejilla; (*impudence*) descaro; **what a ~!** ¡qué cara!
cheekbone ['tʃiːkbəun] N pómulo
cheeky ['tʃiːkɪ] ADJ fresco, descarado
cheep [tʃiːp] N (*of bird*) pío ▸ VI piar
cheer [tʃɪəʳ] VT vitorear, ovacionar; (*gladden*) alegrar, animar ▸ VI dar vivas ▸ N viva *m*; **cheers** NPL vítores *mpl*; **cheers!** ¡salud!
▸ **cheer on** VT (*person etc*) animar con aplausos *or* gritos
▸ **cheer up** VI animarse ▸ VT alegrar, animar
cheerful ['tʃɪəful] ADJ alegre
cheerfulness ['tʃɪəfulnɪs] N alegría
cheering ['tʃɪərɪŋ] N ovaciones *fpl*, vítores *mpl*
cheerio [tʃɪərɪ'əu] EXCL (*BRIT*) ¡hasta luego!
cheerleader ['tʃɪəliːdəʳ] N animador(a) *m/f*
cheerless ['tʃɪəlɪs] ADJ triste, sombrío
cheese [tʃiːz] N queso
cheeseboard ['tʃiːzbɔːd] N tabla de quesos
cheeseburger ['tʃiːzbəːgəʳ] N hamburguesa con queso
cheesecake ['tʃiːzkeɪk] N pastel *m* de queso
cheetah ['tʃiːtə] N guepardo
chef [ʃɛf] N jefe(-a) *m/f* de cocina
chemical ['kɛmɪkəl] ADJ químico ▸ N producto químico
chemist ['kɛmɪst] N (*BRIT*: *pharmacist*) farmacéutico(-a); (*scientist*) químico(-a); **~'s (shop)** *n* (*BRIT*) farmacia
chemistry ['kɛmɪstrɪ] N química
chemotherapy [kiːməu'θɛrəpɪ] N quimioterapia
cheque, (*US*) **check** [tʃɛk] N cheque *m*; **to pay by ~** pagar con cheque
chequebook, (*US*) **checkbook** ['tʃɛkbuk] N talonario (de cheques), chequera (*LAM*)
cheque card N (*BRIT*) tarjeta de identificación bancaria
chequered, (*US*) **checkered** ['tʃɛkəd] ADJ (*fig*) accidentado; (*pattern*) de cuadros
cherish ['tʃɛrɪʃ] VT (*love*) querer, apreciar; (*protect*) cuidar; (*hope etc*) abrigar
cheroot [ʃə'ruːt] N puro (*cortado en los dos extremos*)
cherry ['tʃɛrɪ] N cereza; (*also*: **cherry tree**) cerezo
Ches ABBR (*BRIT*) = **Cheshire**

chess [tʃɛs] N ajedrez *m*
chessboard ['tʃɛsbɔːd] N tablero (de ajedrez)
chessman ['tʃɛsmən] N (*irreg*) pieza (de ajedrez)
chest [tʃɛst] N (*Anat*) pecho; (*box*) cofre *m*; **to get sth off one's ~** (*inf*) desahogarse; **~ of drawers** *n* cómoda
chest measurement N talla (*de chaqueta etc*)
chestnut ['tʃɛsnʌt] N castaña; (*also*: **chestnut tree**) castaño; (*colour*) castaño ▸ ADJ (color) castaño *inv*
chesty ['tʃɛstɪ] ADJ (*cough*) de bronquios, de pecho
chew [tʃuː] VT mascar, masticar
chewing gum ['tʃuːɪŋ-] N chicle *m*
chic [ʃiːk] ADJ elegante
chicanery [ʃɪ'keɪnərɪ] N embustes *mpl*, sofismas *mpl*
Chicano [tʃɪ'kaːnəu] ADJ, N chicano(-a) *m/f*
chick [tʃɪk] N pollito, polluelo; (*US inf*) chica
chicken ['tʃɪkɪn] N gallina, pollo; (*food*) pollo; (*inf*: *coward*) gallina *mf*
▸ **chicken out** VI (*inf*) rajarse; **to ~ out of doing sth** rajarse y no hacer algo
chickenpox ['tʃɪkɪnpɔks] N varicela
chickpea ['tʃɪkpiː] N garbanzo
chicory ['tʃɪkərɪ] N (*for coffee*) achicoria; (*salad*) escarola
chide [tʃaɪd] VT: **to ~ sb for sth** reprender a algn por algo
chief [tʃiːf] N jefe(-a) *m/f* ▸ ADJ principal, máximo (*esp LAM*); **C~ of Staff** (*esp Mil*) Jefe *m* del Estado mayor
chief executive, chief executive officer N director *m* general
chiefly ['tʃiːflɪ] ADV principalmente
chieftain ['tʃiːftən] N jefe *m*, cacique *m*
chiffon ['ʃɪfɔn] N gasa
chilblain ['tʃɪlbleɪn] N sabañón *m*
child [tʃaɪld] (*pl* **children** ['tʃɪldrən]) N niño(-a); (*offspring*) hijo(-a)
child abuse N (*with violence*) malos tratos *mpl* a niños; (*sexual*) abuso *m* sexual de niños
child benefit N (*BRIT*) subsidio por cada hijo pequeño
childbirth ['tʃaɪldbəːθ] N parto
childcare ['tʃaɪldkɛəʳ] N cuidado de los niños
childhood ['tʃaɪldhud] N niñez *f*, infancia
childish ['tʃaɪldɪʃ] ADJ pueril, infantil
childless ['tʃaɪldlɪs] ADJ sin hijos
childlike ['tʃaɪldlaɪk] ADJ de niño, infantil
child minder N (*BRIT*) niñera, madre *f* de día
child prodigy N niño(-a) prodigio *inv*
children ['tʃɪldrən] NPL *of* **child**
children's home N centro de acogida para niños
child's play N (*fig*): **this is ~** esto es coser y cantar
Chile ['tʃɪlɪ] N Chile *m*

C

Chilean ['tʃɪlɪən] ADJ, N chileno(-a) m/f
chill [tʃɪl] N frío; (Med) resfriado ▶ ADJ frío
▶ VT enfriar; (Culin) refrigerar
▶ **chill out** VI (esp US inf) tranquilizarse
N (BRIT) chile m, ají m (LAM)
chilling ['tʃɪlɪŋ] ADJ escalofriante
chilly ['tʃɪlɪ] ADJ frío
chime [tʃaɪm] N repique m, campanada ▶ VI
repicar, sonar
chimney ['tʃɪmnɪ] N chimenea
chimney sweep N deshollinador m
chimpanzee [tʃɪmpæn'ziː] N chimpancé m
chin [tʃɪn] N mentón m, barbilla
China ['tʃaɪnə] N China
china ['tʃaɪnə] N porcelana; (crockery) loza
Chinese [tʃaɪ'niːz] ADJ chino ▶ N pl inv
chino(-a); (Ling) chino
chink [tʃɪŋk] N (opening) rendija, hendedura;
(noise) tintineo
chintz [tʃɪnts] N cretona
chinwag ['tʃɪnwæg] N (BRIT inf): **to have a ~**
echar una parrafada
chip [tʃɪp] N (gen pl: Culin: BRIT) patata or (LAM)
papa frita; (: US: also: **potato chip**) patata or
(LAM) papa frita; (of wood) astilla; (stone)
lasca; (in gambling) ficha; (Comput) chip m
▶ VT (cup, plate) desconchar; **when the chips
are down** (fig) a la hora de la verdad
▶ **chip in** VI (inf: interrupt) interrumpir,
meterse; (: contribute) contribuir
chip and PIN N chip and PIN m (sistema de
tarjetas chip con número PIN); **~ machine** lector
m de tarjetas chip and PIN
chipboard ['tʃɪpbɔːd] N madera aglomerada
chipmunk ['tʃɪpmʌŋk] N ardilla listada
chip shop N ver nota

> Se denomina chip shop o fish-and-chip shop
> a un tipo de tienda popular de comida
> rápida en la que se despachan platos
> tradicionales británicos, principalmente
> filetes de pescado rebozado frito y
> patatas fritas.

chiropodist [kɪ'rɔpədɪst] N (BRIT)
podólogo(-a)
chiropody [kɪ'rɔpədɪ] N podología
chirp [tʃəːp] VI gorjear; (cricket) cantar ▶ N
(of cricket) canto
chirpy ['tʃəːpɪ] ADJ alegre, animado
chisel ['tʃɪzl] N (for wood) escoplo; (for stone)
cincel m
chit [tʃɪt] N nota
chitchat ['tʃɪttʃæt] N chismes mpl,
habladurías fpl
chivalrous ['ʃɪvəlrəs] ADJ caballeroso
chivalry ['ʃɪvlrɪ] N caballerosidad f
chives [tʃaɪvz] NPL cebollinos mpl
chloride ['klɔːraɪd] N cloruro
chlorinate ['klɔːrɪneɪt] VT clorar
chlorine ['klɔːriːn] N cloro

choc-ice ['tʃɔkaɪs] N (BRIT) helado m cubierto
de chocolate
chock-a-block ['tʃɔkə'blɔk], **chock-full**
[tʃɔk'ful] ADJ atestado
chocolate ['tʃɔklɪt] N chocolate m; (sweet)
bombón m
choice [tʃɔɪs] N elección f; (preference)
preferencia ▶ ADJ escogido; **I did it by** or
from ~ lo hice de buena gana; **a wide ~** un
gran surtido, una gran variedad
choir ['kwaɪə'] N coro
choirboy ['kwaɪəbɔɪ] N niño de coro
choke [tʃəuk] VI ahogarse; (on food)
atragantarse ▶ VT ahogar; (block) atascar ▶ N
(Aut) estárter m
choker ['tʃəukə'] N (necklace) gargantilla
cholera ['kɔlərə] N cólera m
cholesterol [kə'lɛstərəl] N colesterol m
chook [tʃuk] (AUSTRALIA, NEW ZEALAND inf) N
gallina; (as food) pollo
choose [tʃuːz] (pt **chose** [tʃəuz], pp **chosen**
[tʃəuzn]) VT escoger, elegir; (team)
seleccionar; **to ~ between** elegir or escoger
entre; **to ~ from** escoger entre; **to ~ to do
sth** optar por hacer algo
choosy ['tʃuːzɪ] ADJ remilgado
chop [tʃɔp] VT (wood) cortar, talar; (Culin: also:
chop up) picar ▶ N tajo, golpe m cortante;
(Culin) chuleta; **chops** NPL (jaws) boca sg; **to
get the ~** (inf: project) ser suprimido (: person:
be sacked) ser despedido
▶ **chop down** VT (tree) talar
▶ **chop off** VT cortar (de un tajo)
chopper ['tʃɔpə'] N (helicopter) helicóptero
choppy ['tʃɔpɪ] ADJ (sea) picado, agitado
chopsticks ['tʃɔpstɪks] NPL palillos mpl
choral ['kɔːrəl] ADJ coral
chord [kɔːd] N (Mus) acorde m
chore [tʃɔː'] N faena, tarea; (routine task)
trabajo rutinario
choreographer [kɔrɪ'ɔgrəfə'] N
coreógrafo(-a)
choreography [kɔrɪ'ɔgrəfɪ] N coreografía
chorister ['kɔrɪstə'] N corista mf; (US)
director(a) m/f de un coro
chortle ['tʃɔːtl] VI reírse satisfecho
chorus ['kɔːrəs] N coro; (repeated part of song)
estribillo
chose [tʃəuz] PT of **choose**
chosen ['tʃəuzn] PP of **choose**
chow [tʃau] N (dog) perro chino
chowder ['tʃaudə'] N (esp US) sopa de pescado
Christ [kraɪst] N Cristo
christen ['krɪsn] VT bautizar
christening ['krɪsnɪŋ] N bautizo
Christian ['krɪstɪən] ADJ, N cristiano(-a) m/f
Christianity [krɪstɪ'ænɪtɪ] N cristianismo
Christian name N nombre m de pila
Christmas ['krɪsməs] N Navidad f; **Merry ~!**

¡Felices Navidades!, ¡Felices Pascuas!

Christmas card N crismas *m inv*, tarjeta de Navidad

Christmas carol N villancico *m*

Christmas Day N día *m* de Navidad

Christmas Eve N Nochebuena

Christmas Island N Isla Christmas

Christmas pudding N *(esp BRIT)* pudín *m* de Navidad

Christmas tree N árbol *m* de Navidad

chrome [krəʊm] N = **chromium**

chromium ['krəʊmɪəm] N cromo; *(also:* **chromium plating**) cromado

chromosome ['krəʊməsəʊm] N cromosoma *m*

chronic ['krɒnɪk] ADJ crónico; *(fig: liar, smoker)* empedernido

chronicle ['krɒnɪkl] N crónica

chronological [krɒnə'lɒdʒɪkəl] ADJ cronológico

chrysalis ['krɪsəlɪs] N *(Biol)* crisálida

chrysanthemum [krɪ'sænθəməm] N crisantemo

chubby ['tʃʌbɪ] ADJ rechoncho

chuck [tʃʌk] *(inf)* VT lanzar, arrojar; *(BRIT: also:* **chuck in, chuck up**) abandonar
  ▶ **chuck out** VT *(person)* echar (fuera); *(rubbish etc)* tirar

chuckle ['tʃʌkl] VI reírse entre dientes

chuffed [tʃʌft] ADJ *(inf)*: **to be ~ (about sth)** estar encantado (con algo)

chug [tʃʌg] VI *(also:* **chug along**: *train)* ir despacio; *(: fig)* ir tirando

chum [tʃʌm] N amiguete(-a) *m/f*, coleguilla *mf*

chump [tʃʌmp] N *(inf)* tonto(-a), estúpido(-a)

chunk [tʃʌŋk] N pedazo, trozo

chunky ['tʃʌŋkɪ] ADJ *(furniture etc)* achaparrado; *(person)* fornido; *(knitwear)* de lana gorda, grueso

Chunnel [tʃʌnl] N = **Channel Tunnel**

church [tʃəːtʃ] N iglesia; **the C~ of England** la Iglesia Anglicana

churchyard ['tʃəːtʃjɑːd] N cementerio, camposanto

churlish ['tʃəːlɪʃ] ADJ grosero; *(mean)* arisco

churn [tʃəːn] N *(for butter)* mantequera; *(for milk)* lechera
  ▶ **churn out** VT producir en serie

chute [ʃuːt] N *(also:* **rubbish chute**) vertedero; *(BRIT: children's slide)* tobogán *m*

chutney ['tʃʌtnɪ] N *salsa picante de frutas y especias*

CIA N ABBR *(US:* = *Central Intelligence Agency)* CIA *f*, Agencia Central de Inteligencia

cicada [sɪ'kɑːdə] N cigarra

CID N ABBR *(BRIT:* = *Criminal Investigation Department)* ≈ B.I.C. *f (SP)*

cider ['saɪdə^r] N sidra

CIF ABBR *(= cost, insurance and freight)* c.s.f.

cigar [sɪ'gɑː^r] N puro

cigarette [sɪgə'ret] N cigarrillo, pitillo

cigarette case N pitillera

cigarette end N colilla

cigarette holder N boquilla

cigarette lighter N mechero

C-in-C ABBR *(= commander-in-chief)* comandante *mf* general

cinch [sɪntʃ] N: **it's a ~** está tirado

Cinderella [sɪndə'relə] N Cenicienta

cinders ['sɪndəz] NPL cenizas *fpl*

cine-camera ['sɪnɪ'kæmərə] N *(BRIT)* cámara cinematográfica

cine-film ['sɪnɪfɪlm] N *(BRIT)* película de cine

cinema ['sɪnəmə] N cine *m*

cinnamon ['sɪnəmən] N canela

cipher ['saɪfə^r] N clave *f*; *(fig)* cero; **in ~** en clave

circle ['səːkl] N círculo; *(in theatre)* anfiteatro
  ▶ VI dar vueltas ▶ VT *(surround)* rodear, cercar; *(move round)* dar la vuelta a

circuit ['səːkɪt] N circuito; *(track)* pista; *(lap)* vuelta

circuit board N tarjeta de circuitos

circuitous [səː'kjuːɪtəs] ADJ indirecto

circular ['səːkjulə^r] ADJ circular ▶ N circular *f*; *(as advertisement)* panfleto

circulate ['səːkjuleɪt] VI circular; *(person: socially)* alternar, circular ▶ VT poner en circulación

circulation [səːkju'leɪʃən] N circulación *f*; *(of newspaper etc)* tirada

circumcise ['səːkəmsaɪz] VT circuncidar

circumference [sə'kʌmfərəns] N circunferencia

circumscribe ['səːkəmskraɪb] VT circunscribir

circumspect ['səːkəmspekt] ADJ circunspecto, prudente

circumstances ['səːkəmstənsɪz] NPL circunstancias *fpl*; *(financial condition)* situación *f* económica; **in the ~** en *or* dadas las circunstancias; **under no ~** de ninguna manera, bajo ningún concepto

circumstantial [səːkəm'stænʃəl] ADJ detallado; **~ evidence** prueba indiciaria

circumvent ['səːkəmvent] VT *(rule etc)* burlar

circus ['səːkəs] N circo; *(also:* **Circus**: *in place names)* Plaza

cirrhosis [sɪ'rəʊsɪs] N *(also:* **cirrhosis of the liver**) cirrosis *f inv*

CIS N ABBR *(= Commonwealth of Independent States)* CEI *f*

cissy ['sɪsɪ] N = **sissy**

cistern ['sɪstən] N tanque *m*, depósito; *(in toilet)* cisterna

citation [saɪ'teɪʃən] N cita; *(Law)* citación *f*; *(Mil)* mención *f*

cite [saɪt] VT citar
citizen ['sɪtɪzn] N (Pol) ciudadano(-a); (of city) habitante mf, vecino(-a)
Citizens' Advice Bureau N (BRIT) organización voluntaria británica que aconseja especialmente en temas legales o financieros
citizenship ['sɪtɪznʃɪp] N ciudadanía; (BRIT Scol) civismo
citric ['sɪtrɪk] ADJ: ~ acid ácido cítrico
citrus fruits ['sɪtrəs-] NPL cítricos mpl
city ['sɪtɪ] N ciudad f; the C~ centro financiero de Londres
city centre N centro de la ciudad
City Hall N (US) ayuntamiento
City Technology College N (BRIT) ≈ Centro de formación profesional
civic ['sɪvɪk] ADJ cívico; (authorities) municipal
civic centre N (BRIT) centro de administración municipal
civil ['sɪvɪl] ADJ civil; (polite) atento, cortés; (well-bred) educado
civil defence N protección f civil
civil engineer N ingeniero(-a) de caminos
civil engineering N ingeniería de caminos
civilian [sɪ'vɪlɪən] ADJ civil; (clothes) de paisano ▶ N civil mf
civilization [sɪvɪlaɪ'zeɪʃən] N civilización f
civilized ['sɪvɪlaɪzd] ADJ civilizado
civil law N derecho civil
civil liberties NPL libertades fpl civiles
civil rights NPL derechos mpl civiles
civil servant N funcionario(-a) (del Estado)
Civil Service N administración f pública
civil war N guerra civil
civvies ['sɪvɪz] NPL (inf): **in ~** de paisano
CJD N ABBR (= Creutzfeldt-Jakob disease) enfermedad de Creutzfeldt-Jakob
cl ABBR (= centilitre) cl
clad [klæd] ADJ: ~ (in) vestido (de)
claim [kleɪm] VT exigir, reclamar; (rights etc) reivindicar; (assert) pretender ▶ VI (for insurance) reclamar ▶ N (for expenses) reclamación f; (Law) demanda; (pretension) pretensión f; **to put in a ~ for sth** presentar una demanda por algo
claimant ['kleɪmənt] N (Admin, Law) demandante mf
claim form N solicitud f
clairvoyant [kleə'vɔɪənt] N clarividente mf
clam [klæm] N almeja
▶ **clam up** VI (inf) cerrar el pico
clamber ['klæmbəʳ] VI trepar
clammy ['klæmɪ] ADJ (cold) frío y húmedo; (sticky) pegajoso
clamour, (US) **clamor** ['klæməʳ] N (noise) clamor m; (protest) protesta ▶ VI: **to ~ for sth** clamar por algo, pedir algo a voces
clamp [klæmp] N abrazadera; (laboratory clamp) grapa; (wheel clamp) cepo ▶ VT afianzar

(con abrazadera)
▶ **clamp down on** VT FUS (government, police) poner coto a
clampdown ['klæmpdaun] N restricción f; **there has been a ~ on terrorism** se ha puesto coto al terrorismo
clan [klæn] N clan m
clandestine [klæn'dɛstɪn] ADJ clandestino
clang [klæŋ] N estruendo ▶ VI sonar con estruendo
clanger [klæŋəʳ] N (BRIT inf): **to drop a ~** meter la pata
clansman ['klænzmən] N (irreg) miembro del clan
clap [klæp] VI aplaudir ▶ VT (hands) batir ▶ N (of hands) palmada; **to ~ one's hands** dar palmadas, batir las palmas; **a ~ of thunder** un trueno
clapping ['klæpɪŋ] N aplausos mpl
claptrap ['klæptræp] N (inf) gilipolleces fpl
claret ['klærət] N burdeos m inv
clarification [klærɪfɪ'keɪʃən] N aclaración f
clarify ['klærɪfaɪ] VT aclarar
clarinet [klærɪ'nɛt] N clarinete m
clarity ['klærɪtɪ] N claridad f
clash [klæʃ] N estruendo; (fig) choque m ▶ VI enfrentarse; (beliefs) chocar; (disagree) estar en desacuerdo; (colours) desentonar; (two events) coincidir
clasp [klɑːsp] N (hold) apretón m; (of necklace, bag) cierre m ▶ VT abrochar; (hand) apretar; (embrace) abrazar
class [klɑːs] N (gen) clase f; (group, category) clase f, categoría ▶ CPD de clase ▶ VT clasificar
class-conscious ['klɑːs'kɔnʃəs] ADJ clasista, con conciencia de clase
classic ['klæsɪk] ADJ clásico ▶ N (work) obra clásica, clásico; **classics** NPL (Univ) clásicas fpl
classical ['klæsɪkəl] ADJ clásico; **~ music** música clásica
classification [klæsɪfɪ'keɪʃən] N clasificación f
classified ['klæsɪfaɪd] ADJ (information) reservado
classified advertisement N anuncio por palabras
classify ['klæsɪfaɪ] VT clasificar
classless ['klɑːslɪs] ADJ: **~ society** sociedad f sin clases
classmate ['klɑːsmeɪt] N compañero(-a) de clase
classroom ['klɑːsrum] N aula
classroom assistant N profesor(a) m/f de apoyo
classy ['klɑːsɪ] ADJ (inf) elegante, con estilo
clatter ['klætəʳ] N ruido, estruendo; (of hooves) trápala ▶ VI hacer ruido or estruendo
clause [klɔːz] N cláusula; (Ling) oración f

claustrophobia [klɔːstrəˈfəubɪə] N claustrofobia

claustrophobic [klɔːstrəˈfəubɪk] ADJ claustrofóbico; **I feel ~** me entra claustrofobia

claw [klɔː] N (of cat) uña; (of bird of prey) garra; (of lobster) pinza; (Tech) garfio ▶ VI: **to ~ at** arañar; (tear) desgarrar

clay [kleɪ] N arcilla

clean [kliːn] ADJ limpio; (record, reputation) bueno, intachable; (joke) decente; (copy) en limpio; (lines) bien definido ▶ VT limpiar; (hands etc) lavar ▶ ADV: **he ~ forgot** lo olvidó por completo; **to come ~** (inf: admit guilt) confesarlo todo; **to have a ~ driving licence** tener el carnet de conducir sin sanciones; **to ~ one's teeth** lavarse los dientes

▶ **clean off** VT limpiar

▶ **clean out** VT limpiar (a fondo)

▶ **clean up** VT limpiar, asear ▶ VI (fig: make profit): **to ~ up on** sacar provecho de

clean-cut [ˈkliːnˈkʌt] ADJ bien definido; (outline) nítido; (person) de buen parecer

cleaner [ˈkliːnəʳ] N encargado(-a) m/f de la limpieza; (also: **dry cleaner**) tintorero(-a); (substance) producto para la limpieza

cleaning [ˈkliːnɪŋ] N limpieza

cleaning lady N señora de la limpieza, asistenta

cleanliness [ˈklɛnlɪnɪs] N limpieza

cleanse [klɛnz] VT limpiar

cleanser [ˈklɛnzəʳ] N detergente m; (cosmetic) loción f or crema limpiadora

clean-shaven [ˈkliːnˈʃeɪvn] ADJ bien afeitado

cleansing department [ˈklɛnzɪŋ-] N (BRIT) servicio municipal de limpieza

clean sweep N: **to make a ~** (Sport) arrasar, barrer

clean technology N tecnología limpia

clear [klɪəʳ] ADJ claro; (road, way) libre; (profit) neto; (majority) absoluto ▶ VT (space) despejar, limpiar; (Law: suspect) absolver; (obstacle) salvar, saltar por encima de; (debt) liquidar; (cheque) aceptar; (site, woodland) desmontar ▶ VI (fog etc) despejarse ▶ N: **to be in the ~** (out of debt) estar libre de deudas; (out of suspicion) estar fuera de toda sospecha; (out of danger) estar fuera de peligro ▶ ADV: **~ of** a distancia de; **to make o.s. ~** explicarse claramente; **to make it ~ to sb that ...** hacer entender a algn que ...; **I have a ~ day tomorrow** mañana tengo el día libre; **to keep ~ of sth/ sb** evitar algo/a algn; **to ~ a profit of ...** sacar una ganancia de ...; **to ~ the table** recoger or quitar la mesa

▶ **clear away** VT (things, clothes etc) quitar (de en medio); (dishes) retirar

▶ **clear off** VI (inf: leave) marcharse, mandarse mudar (LAM)

▶ **clear up** VT limpiar; (mystery) aclarar, resolver

clearance [ˈklɪərəns] N (removal) despeje m; (permission) acreditación f

clear-cut [ˈklɪəˈkʌt] ADJ bien definido, claro

clearing [ˈklɪərɪŋ] N (in wood) claro

clearing bank N (BRIT) banco central

clearing house N (Comm) cámara de compensación

clearly [ˈklɪəlɪ] ADV claramente; (evidently) sin duda

clearway [ˈklɪəweɪ] N (BRIT) carretera en la que no se puede estacionar

cleaver [ˈkliːvə] N cuchilla (de carnicero)

clef [klɛf] N (Mus) clave f

cleft [klɛft] N (in rock) grieta, hendedura

clemency [ˈklɛmənsɪ] N clemencia

clench [klɛntʃ] VT apretar, cerrar

clergy [ˈkləːdʒɪ] N clero

clergyman [ˈkləːdʒɪmən] N (irreg) clérigo

clerical [ˈklɛrɪkəl] ADJ de oficina; (Rel) clerical; (error) de copia

clerk [klɑːk, (US) kləːk] N oficinista mf; (US) dependiente(-a) m/f, vendedor(a) m/f; **C~ of the Court** secretario(-a) de juzgado

clever [ˈklɛvəʳ] ADJ (mentally) inteligente, listo; (skilful) hábil; (device, arrangement) ingenioso

cleverly [ˈklɛvəlɪ] ADV ingeniosamente

clew [kluː] N (US) = **clue**

cliché [ˈkliːʃeɪ] N cliché m, frase f hecha

click [klɪk] VT (tongue) chasquear ▶ VI (Comput) hacer clic; **to ~ one's heels** taconear; **to ~ on an icon** hacer clic en un icono

clickable [ˈklɪkəbl] ADJ (Comput) cliqueable

client [ˈklaɪənt] N cliente mf

clientele [kliːɑːnˈtɛl] N clientela

cliff [klɪf] N acantilado

cliffhanger [ˈklɪfhæŋəʳ] N: **it was a ~** estuvimos etc en ascuas hasta el final

climactic [klaɪˈmæktɪk] ADJ culminante

climate [ˈklaɪmɪt] N clima m; (fig) clima m, ambiente m

climate change N cambio climático

climax [ˈklaɪmæks] N (of battle, career) apogeo; (of film, book) punto culminante, clímax; (sexual) orgasmo

climb [klaɪm] VI subir, trepar; (plane) elevarse, remontar el vuelo ▶ VT (stairs) subir; (tree) trepar a; (mountain) escalar ▶ N subida, ascenso; **to ~ over a wall** saltar una tapia

▶ **climb down** VI (fig) volverse atrás

climbdown [ˈklaɪmdaun] N vuelta atrás

climber [ˈklaɪməʳ] N escalador(a) m/f

climbing [ˈklaɪmɪŋ] N escalada

clinch [klɪntʃ] VT (deal) cerrar; (argument) remachar

clincher [ˈklɪntʃəʳ] N (inf): **that was the ~ for me** eso me hizo decidir

cling [klɪŋ] (pt, pp **clung** [klʌŋ]) vi: **to ~ (to)** agarrarse (a); (clothes) pegarse (a)

clingfilm ['klɪŋfɪlm] N plástico adherente

clinic ['klɪnɪk] N clínica

clinical ['klɪnɪkl] ADJ clínico; (fig) frío, impasible

clink [klɪŋk] vi tintinear

clip [klɪp] N (for hair) horquilla; (also: **paper clip**) sujetapapeles m inv, clip m; (clamp) grapa ▶ vt (cut) cortar; (hedge) podar; (also: **clip together**) unir

clippers ['klɪpəz] NPL (for gardening) tijeras fpl de podar; (for hair) maquinilla sg; (for nails) cortauñas m inv

clipping ['klɪpɪŋ] N (from newspaper) recorte m

clique [kli:k] N camarilla

cloak [kləuk] N capa, manto ▶ vt (fig) encubrir, disimular

cloakroom ['kləukrum] N guardarropa m; (BRIT: WC) lavabo, aseos mpl, baño (esp LAM)

clobber ['klɔbər] N (inf) bártulos mpl, trastos mpl ▶ vt dar una paliza a

clock [klɔk] N reloj m; (in taxi) taxímetro; **to work against the ~** trabajar contra reloj; **around the ~** las veinticuatro horas; **to sleep round the ~** dormir un día entero; **30,000 on the ~** (Aut) treinta mil millas en el cuentakilómetros
▶ **clock in, clock on** vi fichar, picar
▶ **clock off, clock out** vi fichar or picar la salida
▶ **clock up** vt hacer

clockwise ['klɔkwaɪz] ADV en el sentido de las agujas del reloj

clockwork ['klɔkwə:k] N aparato de relojería ▶ ADJ (toy, train) de cuerda

clog [klɔg] N zueco, chanclo ▶ vt atascar ▶ vi (also: **clog up**) atascarse

cloister ['klɔɪstər] N claustro

clone [kləun] N clon m ▶ vt clonar

close [adj, adv kləus, vt, vi, n kləuz] ADJ cercano, próximo; (near): **~ (to)** cerca (de); (print, weave) tupido, compacto; (friend) íntimo; (connection) estrecho; (examination) detallado, minucioso; (weather) bochornoso; (atmosphere) sofocante; (room) mal ventilado ▶ ADV cerca; **~ to** prep cerca de ▶ vt cerrar; (end) concluir, terminar ▶ vi (shop etc) cerrar; (end) concluir(se), terminar(se) ▶ N (end) fin m, final m, conclusión f; **to have a ~ shave** (fig) escaparse por un pelo; **how ~ is Edinburgh to Glasgow?** ¿qué distancia hay de Edimburgo a Glasgow?; **~ by, ~ at hand** muy cerca; **at ~ quarters** de cerca; **to bring sth to a ~** terminar algo
▶ **close down** vi cerrar definitivamente
▶ **close in** vi (hunters) acercarse rodeando, rodear; (evening, night) caer; (fog) cerrarse; **to ~ in on sb** rodear or cercar a algn; **the days**

are closing in los días son cada vez más cortos
▶ **close off** vt (area) cerrar al tráfico or al público

closed [kləuzd] ADJ (shop etc) cerrado

closed-circuit ['kləuzd'sə:kɪt] ADJ: **~ television** televisión f por circuito cerrado

closed shop N empresa en la que todo el personal está afiliado a un sindicato

close-knit ['kləus'nɪt] ADJ (fig) muy unido

closely ['kləuslɪ] ADV (study) con detalle; (listen) con atención; (watch) de cerca; **we are ~ related** somos parientes cercanos; **a ~ guarded secret** un secreto rigurosamente guardado

close season [kləuz-] N (Football) temporada de descanso; (Hunting) veda

closet ['klɔzɪt] N (cupboard) armario, placar(d) m (LAM)

close-up ['kləusʌp] N primer plano

closing ['kləuzɪŋ] ADJ (stages, remarks) último, final; **~ price** (Stock Exchange) cotización f de cierre

closing time ['kləuzɪŋ-] N hora de cierre

closure ['kləuʒər] N cierre m

clot [klɔt] N (also: **blood clot**) coágulo; (inf: idiot) imbécil mf ▶ vi (blood) coagularse

cloth [klɔθ] N (material) tela, paño; (table cloth) mantel m; (rag) trapo

clothe [kləuð] vt vestir; (fig) revestir

clothes [kləuðz] NPL ropa sg; **to put one's ~ on** vestirse, ponerse la ropa; **to take one's ~ off** desvestirse, desnudarse

clothes brush N cepillo (para la ropa)

clothes line N cuerda (para tender la ropa)

clothes peg, (US) **clothes pin** N pinza

clothing ['kləuðɪŋ] N = **clothes**

clotted cream ['klɔtɪd-] N nata muy espesa

cloud [klaud] N nube f; (storm cloud) nubarrón m ▶ vt (liquid) enturbiar; **every ~ has a silver lining** no hay mal que por bien no venga; **to ~ the issue** empañar el problema
▶ **cloud over** vi (also fig) nublarse

cloudburst ['klaudbə:st] N chaparrón m

cloud computing N computación f en (la) nube

cloud-cuckoo-land ['klaud'kuku:'lænd] N Babia

cloudy ['klaudɪ] ADJ nublado; (liquid) turbio

clout [klaut] N (fig) influencia, peso ▶ vt dar un tortazo a

clove [kləuv] N clavo; **~ of garlic** diente m de ajo

clover ['kləuvər] N trébol m

clown [klaun] N payaso ▶ vi (also: **clown about, clown around**) hacer el payaso

cloying ['klɔɪɪŋ] ADJ (taste) empalagoso

club [klʌb] N (society) club m; (weapon) porra, cachiporra; (also: **golf club**) palo ▶ vt aporrear ▶ VI: **to ~ together** (join forces) unir fuerzas; **clubs** NPL (Cards) tréboles mpl

club car N (US Rail) coche m salón

club class N (Aviat) clase f preferente

clubhouse ['klʌbhaus] N local social, sobre todo en clubs deportivos

club soda N (US) soda

cluck [klʌk] VI cloquear

clue [klu:] N pista; (in crosswords) indicación f; **I haven't a ~** no tengo ni idea

clued up, (US) **clued in** [klu:d-] ADJ (inf) al tanto, al corriente

clueless ['klu:lɪs] ADJ (inf) desorientado

clump [klʌmp] N (of trees) grupo

clumsy ['klʌmzɪ] ADJ (person) torpe; (tool) difícil de manejar

clung [klʌŋ] PT, PP of **cling**

cluster ['klʌstə^r] N grupo; (Bot) racimo ▶ VI agruparse, apiñarse

clutch [klʌtʃ] N (Aut) embrague m; (pedal) (pedal m de) embrague m; **to fall into sb's clutches** caer en las garras de algn ▶ VT agarrar

clutter ['klʌtə^r] VT (also: **clutter up**) atestar, llenar desordenadamente ▶ N desorden m, confusión f

CM ABBR (US) = **North Mariana Islands**

cm ABBR (= centimetre) cm

CNAA N ABBR (BRIT: = Council for National Academic Awards) organismo no universitario que otorga diplomas

CND N ABBR (BRIT: = Campaign for Nuclear Disarmament) plataforma pro desarme nuclear

CO N ABBR = **commanding officer**; (BRIT) = **Commonwealth Office** ▶ ABBR (US) = **Colorado**

Co. ABBR = **county; company**

c/o ABBR (= care of) c/a, a/c

coach [kəutʃ] N (bus) autocar m (SP), autobús m; (horse-drawn) coche m; (ceremonial) carroza; (of train) vagón m, coche m; (Sport) entrenador(a) m/f, instructor(a) m/f ▶ VT (Sport) entrenar; (student) preparar, enseñar

coach station N (BRIT) estación f de autobuses etc

coach trip N excursión f en autocar

coagulate [kəu'æɡjuleɪt] VI coagularse

coal [kəul] N carbón m

coal face N frente m de carbón

coalfield ['kəulfi:ld] N yacimiento de carbón

coalition [kəuə'lɪʃən] N coalición f

coal man N (irreg) carbonero

coalmine ['kəulmaɪn] N mina de carbón

coalminer ['kəulmaɪnə^r] N minero (de carbón)

coalmining ['kəulmaɪnɪŋ] N minería (de carbón)

coarse [kɔːs] ADJ basto, burdo; (vulgar) grosero, ordinario

coast [kəust] N costa, litoral m ▶ VI (Aut) ir en punto muerto

coastal ['kəustl] ADJ costero

coaster ['kəustə^r] N buque m costero, barco de cabotaje

coastguard ['kəustɡɑːd] N guardacostas m inv

coastline ['kəustlaɪn] N litoral m

coat [kəut] N (jacket) chaqueta, saco (LAM); (overcoat) abrigo; (of animal) pelo, pelaje, lana; (of paint) mano f, capa ▶ VT cubrir, revestir

coat hanger N percha, gancho (LAM)

coating ['kəutɪŋ] N capa, baño

coat of arms N escudo de armas

co-author ['kəu'ɔ:θə^r] N coautor(a) m/f

coax [kəuks] VT engatusar

cob [kɔb] N see **corn**

cobbled ['kɔbld] ADJ: **~ street** calle f empedrada, calle f adoquinada

cobbler ['kɔblə^r] N zapatero (remendón)

cobbles ['kɔblz], **cobblestones** ['kɔblstəunz] NPL adoquines mpl

COBOL ['kəubɔl] N COBOL m

cobra ['kəubrə] N cobra

cobweb ['kɔbweb] N telaraña

cocaine [kə'keɪn] N cocaína

cock [kɔk] N (rooster) gallo; (male bird) macho ▶ VT (gun) amartillar

cock-a-hoop [kɔkə'hu:p] ADJ: **to be ~** estar más contento que unas pascuas

cockatoo [kɔkə'tu:] N cacatúa

cockerel ['kɔkərl] N gallito, gallo joven

cock-eyed ['kɔkaɪd] ADJ bizco; (fig: crooked) torcido; (: idea) disparatado

cockle ['kɔkl] N berberecho

cockney ['kɔknɪ] N habitante de ciertos barrios de Londres

cockpit ['kɔkpɪt] N (in aircraft) cabina

cockroach ['kɔkrəutʃ] N cucaracha

cocktail ['kɔkteɪl] N combinado, cóctel m; **prawn ~** cóctel m de gambas

cocktail cabinet N mueble-bar m

cocktail party N cóctel m

cocktail shaker [-ʃeɪkə^r] N coctelera

cocky ['kɔkɪ] ADJ farruco, flamenco

cocoa ['kəukəu] N cacao; (drink) chocolate m

coconut ['kəukənʌt] N coco

cocoon [kə'ku:n] N capullo

COD ABBR (BRIT: = cash on delivery; US: collect on delivery) C.A.E.

cod [kɔd] N bacalao

code [kəud] N código; (cipher) clave f; (Tel) prefijo; **~ of behaviour** código de conducta; **~ of practice** código profesional

codeine ['kəudi:n] N codeína

codger ['kɔdʒə^r] N (BRIT inf): **an old ~** un abuelo

codicil ['kɔdɪsɪl] N codicilo

codify ['kəudɪfaɪ] VT codificar

cod-liver oil ['kɒdlɪvər-] N aceite m de hígado de bacalao

co-driver ['kəu'draɪvər] N (in race) copiloto mf; (of lorry) segundo conductor m

co-ed ['kəuɛd] ADJ ABBR = **coeducational** ▶ N ABBR (US: = female student) alumna de una universidad mixta; (BRIT: school) colegio mixto

coeducational [kəuedju'keɪʃənl] ADJ mixto

coerce [kəu'əːs] VT forzar, coaccionar

coercion [kəu'əːʃən] N coacción f

coexistence ['kəuɪg'zɪstəns] N coexistencia

C. of C. N ABBR = **chamber of commerce**

C of E ABBR = **Church of England**

coffee ['kɒfɪ] N café m; **white ~**, (US) **~ with cream** café con leche

coffee bar N (BRIT) cafetería

coffee bean N grano de café

coffee break N descanso (para tomar café)

coffee cup N taza de café, pocillo (LAM)

coffee maker N máquina de hacer café, cafetera

coffeepot ['kɒfɪpɒt] N cafetera

coffee shop N café m

coffee table N mesita baja

coffin ['kɒfɪn] N ataúd m

C of I ABBR = **Church of Ireland**

C of S ABBR = **Church of Scotland**

cog [kɒg] N diente m

cogent ['kəudʒənt] ADJ lógico, convincente

cognac ['kɒnjæk] N coñac m

cognitive ['kɒgnɪtɪv] ADJ cognitivo(-a), cognoscitivo(-a)

cogwheel ['kɒgwiːl] N rueda dentada

cohabit [kəu'hæbɪt] VI (formal): **to ~ (with sb)** cohabitar (con algn)

coherent [kəu'hɪərənt] ADJ coherente

cohesion [kəu'hiːʒən] N cohesión f

cohesive [kəu'hiːsɪv] ADJ (fig) cohesivo, unido

COI N ABBR (BRIT: = Central Office of Information) servicio de información gubernamental

coil [kɔɪl] N rollo; (of rope) vuelta; (of smoke) espiral f; (Aut, Elec) bobina, carrete m; (contraceptive) DIU m ▶ VT enrollar

coin [kɔɪn] N moneda ▶ VT acuñar; (word) inventar, acuñar

coinage ['kɔɪnɪdʒ] N moneda

coin-box ['kɔɪnbɒks] N (BRIT) caja recaudadora

coincide [kəuɪn'saɪd] VI coincidir

coincidence [kəu'ɪnsɪdəns] N casualidad f, coincidencia

coin-operated ['kɔɪn'ɒpəreɪtɪd] ADJ (machine) que funciona con monedas

Coke® [kəuk] N Coca Cola® f

coke [kəuk] N (coal) coque m

Col. ABBR (= colonel) col; (US) = **Colorado**

COLA N ABBR (US: = cost-of-living adjustment) reajuste salarial de acuerdo con el coste de la vida

colander ['kɒləndər] N escurridor m

cold [kəuld] ADJ frío ▶ N frío; (Med) resfriado; **it's ~** hace frío; **to be ~** tener frío; **to catch a ~** resfriarse, acatarrarse, coger un catarro; **in ~ blood** a sangre fría; **the room's getting ~** está empezando a hacer frío en la habitación; **to give sb the ~ shoulder** tratar a algn con frialdad

cold-blooded ['kəuld'blʌdɪd] ADJ (Zool) de sangre fría

cold cream N crema

coldly ['kəuldlɪ] ADJ fríamente

cold sore N calentura, herpes m labial

cold sweat N: **to be in a ~ (about sth)** tener sudores fríos (por algo)

cold turkey N (inf) mono

Cold War N: **the ~** la guerra fría

coleslaw ['kəulslɔː] N ensalada de col con zanahoria

colic ['kɒlɪk] N cólico

colicky ['kɒlɪkɪ] ADJ: **to be ~** tener un cólico

collaborate [kə'læbəreɪt] VI colaborar

collaboration [kəlæbə'reɪʃən] N colaboración f; (Pol) colaboracionismo

collaborator [kə'læbəreɪtər] N colaborador(a) m/f; (Pol) colaboracionista mf

collage [kɔ'lɑːʒ] N collage m

collagen ['kɒlədʒən] N colágeno

collapse [kə'læps] VI (gen) hundirse, derrumbarse; (Med) sufrir un colapso ▶ N (gen) hundimiento, derrumbamiento; (Med) colapso; (of government) caída; (of plans, scheme) fracaso; (of business) ruina

collapsible [kə'læpsəbl] ADJ plegable

collar ['kɒlər] N (of coat, shirt) cuello; (for dog) collar m; (Tech) collar m ▶ VT (inf: person) agarrar; (: object) birlar

collarbone ['kɒləbəun] N clavícula

collate [kɔ'leɪt] VT cotejar

collateral [kɔ'lætərəl] N (Comm) garantía subsidiaria

collation [kə'leɪʃən] N colación f

colleague ['kɒliːg] N colega mf; (at work) compañero(-a) m/f

collect [kə'lɛkt] VT reunir; (as a hobby) coleccionar; (BRIT: call and pick up) recoger; (wages) cobrar; (debts) recaudar; (donations, subscriptions) colectar ▶ VI (crowd) reunirse ▶ ADV (US Tel): **to call ~** llamar a cobro revertido; **to ~ one's thoughts** reponerse, recobrar el dominio de sí mismo; **~ on delivery (COD)** (US) entrega contra reembolso

collection [kə'lɛkʃən] N colección f; (of fares, wages) cobro; (of post) recogida

collective [kə'lɛktɪv] ADJ colectivo

collective bargaining N negociación f del convenio colectivo

collector [kə'lɛktər] N coleccionista mf; (of taxes etc) recaudador(a) m/f; **~'s item** or **piece** pieza de coleccionista

college ['kɒlɪdʒ] N colegio; (of technology, agriculture etc) escuela

collide [kə'laɪd] VI chocar

collie ['kɒlɪ] N (dog) collie m, perro pastor escocés

colliery ['kɒlɪərɪ] N (BRIT) mina de carbón

collision [kə'lɪʒən] N choque m, colisión f; **to be on a ~ course** (also fig) ir rumbo al desastre

colloquial [kə'ləukwɪəl] ADJ coloquial

collusion [kə'luːʒən] N confabulación f, connivencia; **in ~ with** en connivencia con

Colo. ABBR (US) = **Colorado**

cologne [kə'ləun] N (also: **eau de cologne**) (agua de) colonia

Colombia [kə'lɒmbɪə] N Colombia

Colombian [kə'lɒmbɪən] ADJ, N colombiano(-a) m/f

colon ['kəulən] N (sign) dos puntos; (Med) colon m

colonel ['kɜːnl] N coronel m

colonial [kə'ləunɪəl] ADJ colonial

colonize ['kɒlənaɪz] VT colonizar

colonnade [kɒlə'neɪd] N columnata

colony ['kɒlənɪ] N colonia

color ['kʌləʳ] N (US) = **colour**

Colorado beetle [kɒlə'rɑːdəu-] N escarabajo de la patata

colossal [kə'lɒsl] ADJ colosal

colour, (US)**color** ['kʌləʳ] N color m ▶ VT colorear, pintar; (dye) teñir; (fig: account) adornar; (: judgement) distorsionar ▶ VI (blush) sonrojarse; **colours** NPL (of party, club) colores mpl

  ▶ **colour in** VT colorear

colour bar, (US)**color bar** N segregación f racial

colour-blind, (US)**color-blind** ['kʌləblaɪnd] ADJ daltónico

coloured, (US)**colored** ['kʌləd] ADJ de color; (photo) en color; (of race) de color

colour film, (US)**color film** N película en color

colourful, (US)**colorful** ['kʌləful] ADJ lleno de color; (person) pintoresco

colouring, (US)**coloring** ['kʌlərɪŋ] N colorido, color; (substance) colorante m

colourless, (US)**colorless** ['kʌləlɪs] ADJ incoloro, sin color

colour scheme, (US)**color scheme** N combinación f de colores

colour supplement N (BRIT Press) suplemento semanal or dominical

colour television, (US)**color television** N televisión f en color

colt [kəult] N potro

column ['kɒləm] N columna; (fashion column, sports column etc) sección f, columna; **the editorial ~** el editorial

columnist ['kɒləmnɪst] N columnista mf

coma ['kəumə] N coma m

comb [kəum] N peine m; (ornamental) peineta ▶ VT (hair) peinar; (area) registrar a fondo, peinar

combat ['kɒmbæt] N combate m ▶ VT combatir

combination [kɒmbɪ'neɪʃən] N (gen) combinación f

combination lock N cerradura de combinación

combine [kəm'baɪn] VT combinar; (qualities) reunir ▶ VI combinarse ▶ N ['kɒmbaɪn] (Econ) cartel m; (also: **combine harvester**) cosechadora; **a combined effort** un esfuerzo conjunto

combine harvester N cosechadora

combo ['kɒmbəu] N (jazz etc) conjunto

combustion [kəm'bʌstʃən] N combustión f

⎡KEYWORD⎤

come [kʌm] (pt **came**, pp **come**) VI
1 (movement towards) venir; **to come running** venir corriendo; **come with me** ven conmigo
2 (arrive) llegar; **he's come here to work** ha venido aquí para trabajar; **to come home** volver a casa; **we've just come from Seville** acabamos de llegar de Sevilla; **coming!** ¡voy!
3 (reach): **to come to** llegar a; **the bill came to £40** la cuenta ascendía a cuarenta libras
4 (occur): **an idea came to me** se me ocurrió una idea; **if it comes to it** llegado el caso
5 (be, become): **to come loose/undone** etc aflojarse/desabrocharse, desatarse etc; **I've come to like him** por fin ha llegado a gustarme

  ▶ **come about** VI suceder, ocurrir
  ▶ **come across** VT FUS (person) encontrarse con; (thing) encontrar ▶ VI: **to come across well/badly** causar buena/mala impresión
  ▶ **come along** VI (BRIT: progress) ir
  ▶ **come away** VI (leave) marcharse; (become detached) desprenderse
  ▶ **come back** VI (return) volver; (reply): **can I come back to you on that one?** volvamos sobre ese punto
  ▶ **come by** VT FUS (acquire) conseguir
  ▶ **come down** VI (price) bajar; (building) derrumbarse; (: be demolished) ser derribado
  ▶ **come forward** VI presentarse
  ▶ **come from** VT FUS (place, source) ser de
  ▶ **come in** VI (visitor) entrar; (train, report) llegar; (fashion) ponerse de moda; (on deal etc) entrar
  ▶ **come in for** VT FUS (criticism etc) recibir
  ▶ **come into** VT FUS (money) heredar; (be involved) tener que ver con; **to come into fashion** ponerse de moda

▶ **come off** VI (*button*) soltarse, desprenderse; (*attempt*) salir bien

▶ **come on** VI (*pupil, work, project*) marchar; (*lights*) encenderse; (*electricity*) volver; **come on!** ¡vamos!

▶ **come out** VI (*fact*) salir a la luz; (*book, sun*) salir; (*stain*) quitarse; **to come out (on strike)** declararse en huelga; **to come out for/against** declararse a favor/en contra de

▶ **come over** VT FUS: **I don't know what's come over him!** ¡no sé lo que le pasa!

▶ **come round** VI (*after faint, operation*) volver en sí

▶ **come through** VI (*survive*) sobrevivir; (*telephone call*): **the call came through** recibimos la llamada

▶ **come to** VI (*wake*) volver en sí; (*total*) sumar; **how much does it come to?** ¿cuánto es en total?, ¿a cuánto asciende?

▶ **come under** VT FUS (*heading*) entrar dentro de; (*influence*) estar bajo

▶ **come up** VI (*sun*) salir; (*problem*) surgir; (*event*) aproximarse; (*in conversation*) mencionarse

▶ **come up against** VT FUS (*resistance etc*) tropezar con

▶ **come upon** VT FUS (*find*) dar con

▶ **come up to** VT FUS llegar hasta; **the film didn't come up to our expectations** la película no fue tan buena como esperábamos

▶ **come up with** VT FUS (*idea*) sugerir; (*money*) conseguir

comeback ['kʌmbæk] N (*reaction*) reacción *f*; (*response*) réplica; **to make a ~** (*Theat*) volver a las tablas

comedian [kə'miːdɪən] N humorista *mf*

comedienne [kəmiːdɪ'ɛn] N humorista

comedown ['kʌmdaun] N revés *m*

comedy ['kɔmɪdɪ] N comedia

comet ['kɔmɪt] N cometa *m*

comeuppance [kʌm'ʌpəns] N: **to get one's ~** llevar su merecido

comfort ['kʌmfət] N comodidad *f*, confort *m*; (*well-being*) bienestar *m*; (*solace*) consuelo; (*relief*) alivio ▶ VT consolar; *see also* **comforts**

comfortable ['kʌmfətəbl] ADJ cómodo; (*income*) adecuado; (*majority*) suficiente; **I don't feel very ~ about it** la cosa me tiene algo preocupado

comfortably ['kʌmfətəblɪ] ADV (*sit*) cómodamente; (*live*) holgadamente

comforter ['kʌmfətə'] N (*US: pacifier*) chupete *m*; (: *bed cover*) colcha

comforts ['kʌmfəts] NPL comodidades *fpl*

comfort station N (*US*) servicios *mpl*

comic ['kɔmɪk] ADJ (*also:* **comical**) cómico, gracioso ▶ N (*comedian*) cómico; (*magazine*) tebeo; (*for adults*) cómic *m*

comic book N (*US*) libro *m* de cómics

comic strip N tira cómica

coming ['kʌmɪŋ] N venida, llegada ▶ ADJ que viene; (*next*) próximo; (*future*) venidero; **in the ~ weeks** en las próximas semanas

comings and goings NPL, **coming and going** N ir y venir *m*, ajetreo

Comintern ['kɔmɪntəːn] N Comintern *m*

comma ['kɔmə] N coma

command [kə'mɑːnd] N orden *f*, mandato; (*Mil: authority*) mando; (*mastery*) dominio; (*Comput*) orden *f*, comando ▶ VT (*troops*) mandar; (*give orders to*) mandar, ordenar; (*be able to get*) disponer de; (*deserve*) merecer; **to have at one's ~** (*money, resources etc*) disponer de; **to have/take ~ of** estar al/asumir el mando de

command economy N economía dirigida

commandeer [kɔmən'dɪə'] VT requisar

commander [kə'mɑːndə'] N (*Mil*) comandante *mf*, jefe(-a) *m/f*

commanding [kə'mɑːndɪŋ] ADJ (*appearance*) imponente; (*voice, tone*) imperativo; (*lead*) abrumador(-a); (*position*) dominante

commanding officer N comandante *m*

commandment [kə'mɑːndmənt] N (*Rel*) mandamiento

command module N módulo de mando

commando [kə'mɑːndəu] N comando

commemorate [kə'mɛməreɪt] VT conmemorar

commemoration [kəmɛmə'reɪʃən] N conmemoración *f*

commemorative [kə'mɛmərətɪv] ADJ conmemorativo

commence [kə'mɛns] VT, VI comenzar

commencement [kə'mɛnsmənt] N (*US Univ*) (ceremonia de) graduación *f*

commend [kə'mɛnd] VT (*praise*) elogiar, alabar; (*recommend*) recomendar; (*entrust*) encomendar

commendable [kə'mɛndəbl] ADJ encomiable

commendation [kɔmɛn'deɪʃən] N (*for bravery etc*) elogio, encomio

commensurate [kə'mɛnʃərɪt] ADJ: **~ with** en proporción a

comment ['kɔmɛnt] N comentario ▶ VT: **to ~ that** comentar *or* observar que ▶ VI: **to ~ (on)** comentar, hacer comentarios (sobre); **"no ~"** (*written*) "sin comentarios"; (*spoken*) "no tengo nada que decir"

commentary ['kɔməntərɪ] N comentario

commentator ['kɔmənteɪtə'] N comentarista *mf*

commerce ['kɔməːs] N comercio

commercial [kə'məːʃəl] ADJ comercial ▶ N (*TV*) anuncio

commercial bank N banco comercial

commercial break N intermedio para publicidad

commercialism [kə'məːʃəlɪzəm] N comercialismo

commercial television N televisión f comercial

commercial vehicle N vehículo comercial

commiserate [kə'mɪzəreɪt] VI: **to ~ with** compadecerse de, condolerse de

commission [kə'mɪʃən] N (*committee, fee, order for work of art etc*) comisión f; (*act*) perpetración f ▶ VT (*Mil*) nombrar; (*work of art*) encargar; **out of ~** (*machine*) fuera de servicio; **~ of inquiry** comisión f investigadora; **I get 10% ~** me dan el diez por ciento de comisión; **to ~ sb to do sth** encargar a algn que haga algo; **to ~ sth from sb** (*painting etc*) encargar algo a algn

commissionaire [kəmɪʃə'nɛəʳ] N (*BRIT*) portero, conserje m

commissioner [kə'mɪʃənəʳ] N comisario; (*Police*) comisario m de policía

commit [kə'mɪt] VT (*act*) cometer; (*resources*) dedicar; (*to sb's care*) entregar; **to ~ o.s. (to do)** comprometerse (a hacer); **to ~ suicide** suicidarse; **to ~ sb for trial** remitir a algn al tribunal

commitment [kə'mɪtmənt] N compromiso

committed [kə'mɪtɪd] ADJ (*writer, politician etc*) comprometido

committee [kə'mɪtɪ] N comité m; **to be on a ~** ser miembro(-a) de un comité

committee meeting N reunión f del comité

commodious [kə'məudɪəs] ADJ grande, espacioso

commodity [kə'mɔdɪtɪ] N mercancía

commodity exchange N bolsa de productos or de mercancías

commodity market N mercado de productos básicos

commodore [ˈkɔmədɔːʳ] N comodoro

common [ˈkɔmən] ADJ (*gen*) común; (*pej*) ordinario ▶ N campo común; **in ~** en común; **in ~ use** de uso corriente

common cold N: **the ~** el resfriado

common denominator N común denominador m

commoner [ˈkɔmənəʳ] N plebeyo(-a)

common land N campo comunal, ejido

common law N ley f consuetudinaria

common-law [ˈkɔmənlɔː] ADJ: **~ wife** esposa de hecho

commonly [ˈkɔmənlɪ] ADV comúnmente

Common Market N Mercado Común

commonplace [ˈkɔmənpleɪs] ADJ corriente

common room [ˈkɔmənrum] N sala de reunión

Commons [ˈkɔmənz] NPL (*BRIT Pol*): **the ~** (la Cámara de) los Comunes

common sense N sentido común

Commonwealth [ˈkɔmənwɛlθ] N: **the ~** la Comunidad (Británica) de Naciones, la Commonwealth; *ver nota*

La *Commonwealth* es la asociación de estados soberanos independientes y territorios asociados que formaban parte del antiguo Imperio Británico. Éste pasó a llamarse así después de la Segunda Guerra Mundial, aunque ya desde 1931 se le conocía como "*British Commonwealth of Nations*". Todos los estados miembros reconocen al monarca británico como "*Head of the Commonwealth*".

commotion [kə'məuʃən] N tumulto, confusión f

communal [ˈkɔmjuːnl] ADJ comunal; (*kitchen*) común

commune [ˈkɔmjuːn] N (*group*) comuna ▶ VI [kə'mjuːn]: **to ~ with** comunicarse con

communicate [kə'mjuːnɪkeɪt] VT comunicar ▶ VI: **to ~ (with)** comunicarse (con); (*in writing*) estar en contacto (con)

communication [kəmjuːnɪ'keɪʃən] N comunicación f

communication cord N (*BRIT*) timbre m de alarma

communications network N red f de comunicaciones

communications satellite N satélite m de comunicaciones

communicative [kə'mjuːnɪkətɪv] ADJ comunicativo

communion [kə'mjuːnɪən] N (*also*: **Holy Communion**) comunión f

communiqué [kə'mjuːnɪkeɪ] N comunicado, parte m

communism [ˈkɔmjunɪzəm] N comunismo

communist [ˈkɔmjunɪst] ADJ, N comunista mf

community [kə'mjuːnɪtɪ] N comunidad f; (*large group*) colectividad f; (*local*) vecindario

community centre N centro social

community chest N (*US*) fondo social

community health centre N centro médico, casa de salud

community service N trabajo m comunitario (*prestado en lugar de cumplir una pena de prisión*)

community spirit N civismo

commutation ticket [kɔmju'teɪʃən-] N (*US*) billete m de abono

commute [kə'mjuːt] VI *viajar a diario de casa al trabajo* ▶ VT conmutar

commuter [kə'mjuːtəʳ] N *persona que viaja a diario de casa al trabajo*

compact [kəm'pækt] ADJ compacto; (*style*) conciso; (*dense*) apretado ▶ N [ˈkɔmpækt] (*pact*) pacto; (*also*: **powder compact**) polvera

compact disc N compact disc *m*, disco compacto

compact disc player N lector *m or* reproductor *m* de discos compactos

companion [kəm'pænɪən] N compañero(-a)

companionship [kəm'pænjənʃɪp] N compañerismo

companionway [kəm'pænjənweɪ] N (*Naut*) escalerilla

company ['kʌmpənɪ] N (*gen*) compañía; (*Comm*) empresa, compañía; **to keep sb ~** acompañar a algn; **Smith and C~** Smith y Compañía

company car N coche *m* de la empresa

company director N director(a) *m/f* de empresa

company secretary N (*Brit*) administrador(a) *m/f* de empresa

comparable ['kɒmpərəbl] ADJ comparable

comparative [kəm'pærətɪv] ADJ (*freedom, luxury, cost*) relativo; (*study, linguistics*) comparado

comparatively [kəm'pærətɪvlɪ] ADV (*relatively*) relativamente

compare [kəm'pɛəʳ] VT comparar ▸ VI: **to ~ (with)** poder compararse (con); **compared with** *or* **to** comparado con *or* a; **how do the prices ~?** ¿cómo son los precios en comparación?

comparison [kəm'pærɪsn] N comparación *f*; **in ~ (with)** en comparación (con)

compartment [kəm'pɑːtmənt] N compartim(i)ento; (*Rail*) departamento, compartimiento

compass ['kʌmpəs] N brújula; **compasses** NPL compás *m*; **within the ~ of** al alcance de

compassion [kəm'pæʃən] N compasión *f*

compassionate [kəm'pæʃənɪt] ADJ compasivo; **on ~ grounds** por compasión

compassionate leave N permiso por asuntos familiares

compatibility [kəmpætɪ'bɪlɪtɪ] N compatibilidad *f*

compatible [kəm'pætɪbl] ADJ compatible

compel [kəm'pɛl] VT obligar

compelling [kəm'pɛlɪŋ] ADJ (*fig: argument*) convincente

compendium [kəm'pɛndɪəm] N compendio

compensate ['kɒmpənseɪt] VT compensar ▸ VI: **to ~ for** compensar

compensation [kɒmpən'seɪʃən] N (*for loss*) indemnización *f*

compère ['kɒmpɛəʳ] N presentador(a) *m/f*

compete [kəm'piːt] VI (*take part*) competir; (*vie with*) competir, hacer la competencia

competence ['kɒmpɪtəns] N capacidad *f*, aptitud *f*

competent ['kɒmpɪtənt] ADJ competente, capaz

competing [kəm'piːtɪŋ] ADJ (*rival*) competidor(-a); (*ideas*) contrapuesto

competition [kɒmpɪ'tɪʃən] N (*contest*) concurso; (*Sport*) competición *f*; (*Econ: rivalry*) competencia; **in ~ with** en competencia con

competitive [kəm'pɛtɪtɪv] ADJ (*Econ, Sport*) competitivo; (*spirit*) competidor(a), de competencia; (*selection*) por concurso

competitor [kəm'pɛtɪtəʳ] N (*rival*) competidor(a) *m/f*; (*participant*) concursante *mf*

compile [kəm'paɪl] VT recopilar

complacency [kəm'pleɪsnsɪ] N autosatisfacción *f*

complacent [kəm'pleɪsənt] ADJ autocomplaciente

complain [kəm'pleɪn] VI (*gen*) quejarse; (*Comm*) reclamar

complaint [kəm'pleɪnt] N (*gen*) queja; (*Comm*) reclamación *f*; (*Law*) demanda, querella; (*Med*) enfermedad *f*

complement ['kɒmplɪmənt] N complemento; (*esp ship's crew*) dotación *f* ▸ VT ['kɒmplɪment] (*enhance*) complementar

complementary [kɒmplɪ'mɛntərɪ] ADJ complementario

complete [kəm'pliːt] ADJ (*full*) completo; (*finished*) acabado ▸ VT (*fulfil*) completar; (*finish*) acabar; (*a form*) rellenar; **it's a ~ disaster** es un desastre total

completely [kəm'pliːtlɪ] ADV completamente

completion [kəm'pliːʃən] N (*gen*) conclusión *f*, terminación *f*; **to be nearing ~** estar a punto de terminarse; **on ~ of contract** cuando se realice el contrato

complex ['kɒmplɛks] ADJ complejo ▸ N (*gen*) complejo

complexion [kəm'plɛkʃən] N (*of face*) tez *f*, cutis *m*; (*fig*) aspecto

complexity [kəm'plɛksɪtɪ] N complejidad *f*

compliance [kəm'plaɪəns] N (*submission*) sumisión *f*; (*agreement*) conformidad *f*; **in ~ with** de acuerdo con

compliant [kəm'plaɪənt] ADJ sumiso; conforme

complicate ['kɒmplɪkeɪt] VT complicar

complicated ['kɒmplɪkeɪtɪd] ADJ complicado

complication [kɒmplɪ'keɪʃən] N complicación *f*

complicity [kəm'plɪsɪtɪ] N complicidad *f*

compliment ['kɒmplɪmənt] N (*formal*) cumplido; (*flirtation*) piropo ▸ VT felicitar; **compliments** NPL saludos *mpl*; **to pay sb a ~** (*formal*) hacer cumplidos a algn; (*flirt*) piropear, echar piropos a algn; **to ~ sb (on sth/on doing sth)** felicitar a algn (por algo/por haber hecho algo)

complimentary [kɒmplɪ'mɛntərɪ] ADJ

elogioso; (*copy*) de regalo; **~ ticket**
invitación f
compliments slip N saluda m
comply [kəm'plaɪ] VI: **to ~ with** acatar
component [kəm'pəʊnənt] ADJ componente
▶ N (*Tech*) pieza, componente m
compose [kəm'pəʊz] VT componer; **to be
composed of** componerse de, constar de; **to
~ o.s.** tranquilizarse
composed [kəm'pəʊzd] ADJ sosegado
composer [kəm'pəʊzə*] N (*Mus*)
compositor(a) m/f
composite ['kɔmpəzɪt] ADJ compuesto;
~ motion moción f compuesta
composition [kɔmpə'zɪʃən] N composición f
compositor [kəm'pɔzɪtə*] N (*Typ*) cajista mf
compos mentis ['kɔmpəs'mɛntɪs] ADJ: **to be
~** estar en su sano juicio
compost ['kɔmpɔst] N abono
compost heap N montón de basura orgánica
para abono
composure [kəm'pəʊʒə*] N serenidad f,
calma
compound ['kɔmpaʊnd] N (*Chem*)
compuesto; (*Ling*) término compuesto;
(*enclosure*) recinto ▶ ADJ (*gen*) compuesto;
(*fracture*) complicado ▶ VT [kəm'paʊnd] (*fig:
problem, difficulty*) agravar
comprehend [kɔmprɪ'hɛnd] VT comprender
comprehension [kɔmprɪ'hɛnʃən] N
comprensión f
comprehensive [kɔmprɪ'hɛnsɪv] ADJ (*broad*)
exhaustivo; (*general*) de conjunto; **~ (school)**
n centro estatal de enseñanza secundaria,
≈ Instituto Nacional de Bachillerato (SP);
ver nota

En los años 60 se creó un nuevo tipo
de centro educativo de enseñanza
secundaria (aproximadamente de los
once años en adelante) denominado
comprehensive school, abierto a todos los
alumnos independientemente de sus
capacidades, con el que se intentó poner
fin a la división tradicional entre centros
de enseñanzas teóricas para acceder a la
educación superior ("*grammar schools*")
y otros de enseñanzas básicamente
profesionales ("*secondary modern schools*").

comprehensive insurance policy N seguro
a todo riesgo
compress [kəm'prɛs] VT comprimir;
(*Comput*) comprimir ▶ N ['kɔmprɛs] (*Med*)
compresa
compression [kəm'prɛʃən] N compresión f
comprise [kəm'praɪz] VT (*also*: **be comprised
of**) comprender, constar de
compromise ['kɔmprəmaɪz] N solución f
intermedia; (*agreement*) arreglo ▶ VT
comprometer ▶ VI transigir, transar (*LAм*)

▶ CPD (*decision, solution*) de término medio
compulsion [kəm'pʌlʃən] N obligación f;
under ~ a la fuerza, por obligación
compulsive [kəm'pʌlsɪv] ADJ compulsivo;
(*viewing, reading*) obligado
compulsory [kəm'pʌlsərɪ] ADJ obligatorio
compulsory purchase N expropiación f
compunction [kəm'pʌŋkʃən] N escrúpulo;
to have no ~ about doing sth no tener
escrúpulos en hacer algo
computer [kəm'pju:tə*] N ordenador m,
computador m, computadora
computer game N juego de ordenador
computerize [kəm'pju:təraɪz] VT (*data*)
computerizar; (*system*) informatizar
computer language N lenguaje m de
ordenador *or* computadora
computer literate ADJ: **to be ~** tener
conocimientos de informática a nivel de
usuario
computer peripheral N periférico
computer program N programa m
informático *or* de ordenador
computer programmer N programador(a)
m/f
computer programming N programación f
computer science N informática
computer studies NPL informática fsg,
computación fsg (*LAM*)
computing [kəm'pju:tɪŋ] N (*activity*)
informática
comrade ['kɔmrɪd] N compañero(-a)
comradeship ['kɔmrɪdʃɪp] N camaradería,
compañerismo
comsat® ['kɔmsæt] N ABBR
= **communications satellite**
con [kɔn] VT timar, estafar ▶ N timo, estafa;
to ~ sb into doing sth (*inf*) engañar a algn
para que haga algo
concave ['kɔn'keɪv] ADJ cóncavo
conceal [kən'si:l] VT ocultar; (*thoughts etc*)
disimular
concede [kən'si:d] VT (*point, argument*)
reconocer; (*game*) darse por vencido en;
(*territory*) ceder; **to ~ (defeat)** darse por
vencido; **to ~ that** admitir que
conceit [kən'si:t] N orgullo, presunción f
conceited [kən'si:tɪd] ADJ orgulloso
conceivable [kən'si:vəbl] ADJ concebible;
it is ~ that ... es posible que ...
conceivably [kən'si:vəblɪ] ADV: **he may ~
be right** es posible que tenga razón
conceive [kən'si:v] VT, VI concebir; **to ~ of
sth/of doing sth** imaginar algo/imaginarse
haciendo algo
concentrate ['kɔnsəntreɪt] VI concentrarse
▶ VT concentrar
concentration [kɔnsən'treɪʃən] N
concentración f

concentration camp N campo de concentración

concentric [kən'sɛntrɪk] ADJ concéntrico

concept ['kɒnsɛpt] N concepto

conception [kən'sɛpʃən] N (*idea*) concepto, idea; (*Biol*) concepción f

concern [kən'sə:n] N (*matter*) asunto; (*Comm*) empresa; (*anxiety*) preocupación f ▶ VT (*worry*) preocupar; (*involve*) afectar; (*relate to*) tener que ver con; **to be concerned (about)** interesarse (por), preocuparse (por); **to be concerned with** tratar de; **"to whom it may ~"** "a quien corresponda"; **the department concerned** (*under discussion*) el departamento en cuestión; (*relevant*) el departamento competente; **as far as I am concerned** en cuanto a mí, por lo que a mí se refiere

concerning [kən'sə:nɪŋ] PREP sobre, acerca de

concert ['kɒnsət] N concierto

concerted [kən'sə:təd] ADJ (*efforts etc*) concertado

concert hall N sala de conciertos

concertina [kɒnsə'ti:nə] N concertina

concerto [kən'tʃə:təu] N concierto

concession [kən'sɛʃən] N concesión f; (*price concession*) descuento; **tax ~** privilegio fiscal

concessionaire [kənsɛʃə'nɛəʳ] N concesionario(-a)

concessionary [kən'sɛʃənərɪ] ADJ (*ticket, fare*) con descuento, a precio reducido

conciliation [kənsɪlɪ'eɪʃən] N conciliación f

conciliatory [kən'sɪlɪətrɪ] ADJ conciliador(a)

concise [kən'saɪs] ADJ conciso

conclave ['kɒnkleɪv] N cónclave m

conclude [kən'klu:d] VT (*finish*) concluir; (*treaty etc*) firmar; (*agreement*) llegar a; (*decide*): **to ~ that ...** llegar a la conclusión de que ... ▶ VI (*events*) concluir, terminar

concluding [kən'klu:dɪŋ] ADJ (*remarks etc*) final

conclusion [kən'klu:ʒən] N conclusión f; **to come to the ~ that** llegar a la conclusión de que

conclusive [kən'klu:sɪv] ADJ decisivo, concluyente

conclusively [kən'klu:sɪvlɪ] ADV concluyentemente

concoct [kən'kɒkt] VT (*food, drink*) preparar; (*story*) inventar; (*plot*) tramar

concoction [kən'kɒkʃən] N (*food*) mezcla; (*drink*) brebaje m

concord ['kɒnkɔ:d] N (*harmony*) concordia; (*treaty*) acuerdo

concourse ['kɒnkɔ:s] N (*hall*) vestíbulo

concrete ['kɒnkri:t] N hormigón m ▶ ADJ de hormigón; (*fig*) concreto

concrete mixer N hormigonera

concur [kən'kə:ʳ] VI estar de acuerdo

concurrently [kən'kʌrntlɪ] ADV al mismo tiempo

concussion [kən'kʌʃən] N conmoción f cerebral

condemn [kən'dɛm] VT condenar; (*building*) declarar en ruina

condemnation [kɒndɛm'neɪʃən] N (*gen*) condena; (*blame*) censura

condensation [kɒndɛn'seɪʃən] N condensación f

condense [kən'dɛns] VI condensarse ▶ VT condensar; (*text*) abreviar

condensed milk N leche f condensada

condescend [kɒndɪ'sɛnd] VI condescender; **to ~ to sb** tratar a algn con condescendencia; **to ~ to do sth** dignarse hacer algo

condescending [kɒndɪ'sɛndɪŋ] ADJ superior

condition [kən'dɪʃən] N condición f; (*of health*) estado; (*disease*) enfermedad f ▶ VT condicionar; **on ~ that** a condición (de) que; **weather conditions** condiciones atmosféricas; **in good/poor ~** en buenas/ malas condiciones, en buen/mal estado; **conditions of sale** condiciones de venta

conditional [kən'dɪʃənl] ADJ condicional

conditioned reflex [kən'dɪʃənd-] N reflejo condicionado

conditioner [kən'dɪʃənəʳ] N (*for hair*) suavizante m, acondicionador m

condo ['kɒndəu] N ABBR (*US inf*) = **condominium**

condolences [kən'dəulənsɪz] NPL pésame msg

condom ['kɒndəm] N condón m

condominium [kɒndə'mɪnɪəm] N (*US: building*) bloque m de pisos or apartamentos (*propiedad de quienes lo habitan*), condominio (*LAm*); (*: apartment*) piso or apartamento (en propiedad), condominio (*LAm*)

condone [kən'dəun] VT condonar

conducive [kən'dju:sɪv] ADJ: **~ to** conducente a

conduct ['kɒndʌkt] N conducta, comportamiento ▶ VT [kən'dʌkt] (*lead*) conducir; (*manage*) llevar, dirigir; (*Mus*) dirigir ▶ VI (*Mus*) llevar la batuta; **to ~ o.s.** comportarse

conducted tour N (*Brit*) visita con guía

conductor [kən'dʌktəʳ] N (*of orchestra*) director(a) m/f; (*US: on train*) revisor(a) m/f; (*on bus*) cobrador m; (*Elec*) conductor m

cone [kəun] N cono; (*pine cone*) piña; (*for ice cream*) cucurucho

confectioner [kən'fɛkʃənəʳ] N (*of cakes*) pastelero(-a); (*of sweets*) confitero(-a); **~'s (shop)** n pastelería; confitería

confectionery [kən'fɛkʃənrɪ] N pasteles mpl; dulces mpl

confederate [kən'fɛdrɪt] ADJ confederado
▶ N (*pej*) cómplice *mf*; (*US History*)
confederado(-a)
confederation [kənfɛdə'reɪʃən] N
confederación *f*
confer [kən'fəːʳ] VT: **to ~ (on)** otorgar (a) ▶ VI
conferenciar; **to ~ (with sb about sth)**
consultar (con algn sobre algo)
conference ['kɔnfərns] N (*meeting*) reunión *f*;
(*convention*) congreso; **to be in ~** estar en una
reunión
conference room N sala de conferencias
confess [kən'fɛs] VT confesar ▶ VI confesar;
(*Rel*) confesarse
confession [kən'fɛʃən] N confesión *f*
confessional [kən'fɛʃənl] VI confesionario
confessor [kən'fɛsəʳ] VI confesor *m*
confetti [kən'fɛtɪ] N confeti *m*
confide [kən'faɪd] VI: **to ~ in** confiar en
confidence ['kɔnfɪdns] N (*also:* **self-
confidence**) confianza; (*secret*) confidencia;
in ~ (*speak, write*) en confianza; **to have
(every) ~ that** estar seguro or confiado de
que; **motion of no ~** moción *f* de censura; **to
tell sb sth in strict ~** decir algo a algn de
manera confidencial
confidence trick N timo
confident ['kɔnfɪdənt] ADJ seguro de sí
mismo
confidential [kɔnfɪ'dɛnʃəl] ADJ confidencial;
(*secretary*) de confianza
confidentiality [kɔnfɪdɛnʃɪ'ælɪtɪ] N
confidencialidad *f*
configuration [kənfɪgju'reɪʃən] N (*Comput*)
configuración *f*
confine [kən'faɪn] VT (*limit*) limitar; (*shut up*)
encerrar; **to ~ o.s. to doing sth** limitarse a
hacer algo
confined [kən'faɪnd] ADJ (*space*) reducido
confinement [kən'faɪnmənt] N (*prison*)
reclusión *f*; (*Med*) parto; **in solitary ~**
incomunicado
confines ['kɔnfaɪnz] NPL confines *mpl*
confirm [kən'fəːm] VT confirmar
confirmation [kɔnfə'meɪʃən] N
confirmación *f*
confirmed [kən'fəːmd] ADJ empedernido
confiscate ['kɔnfɪskeɪt] VT confiscar
confiscation [kɔnfɪs'keɪʃən] N incautación *f*
conflagration [kɔnflə'greɪʃən] N
conflagración *f*
conflict ['kɔnflɪkt] N conflicto ▶ VI [kən'flɪkt]
(*opinions*) estar reñido; (*reports, evidence*)
contradecirse
conflicting [kən'flɪktɪŋ] ADJ (*reports, evidence,
opinions*) contradictorio
conform [kən'fɔːm] VI: **to ~ to** (*laws*)
someterse a; (*usages, mores*) amoldarse a;
(*standards*) ajustarse a

conformist [kən'fɔːmɪst] N conformista *mf*
confound [kən'faund] VT confundir; (*amaze*)
pasmar
confounded [kən'faundɪd] ADJ condenado
confront [kən'frʌnt] VT (*problems*) hacer
frente a; (*enemy, danger*) enfrentarse con
confrontation [kɔnfrən'teɪʃən] N
enfrentamiento, confrontación *f*
confrontational [kɔnfrən'teɪʃənəl] ADJ
conflictivo
confuse [kən'fjuːz] VT (*perplex*) desconcertar;
(*mix up*) confundir; (*complicate*) complicar
confused [kən'fjuːzd] ADJ confuso; (*person*)
desconcertado; **to get ~** desconcertarse;
(*muddled up*) hacerse un lío
confusing [kən'fjuːzɪŋ] ADJ confuso
confusion [kən'fjuːʒən] N confusión *f*
congeal [kən'dʒiːl] VI coagularse
congenial [kən'dʒiːnɪəl] ADJ agradable
congenital [kən'dʒɛnɪtl] ADJ congénito
congested [kən'dʒɛstɪd] ADJ (*gen*) atestado;
(*telephone lines*) saturado
congestion [kən'dʒɛstʃən] N congestión *f*
congestion charge N, **congestion charges**
NPL tasa por congestión
conglomerate [kən'glɔmərət] N (*Comm, Geo*)
conglomerado
conglomeration [kənglɔmə'reɪʃən] N
conglomeración *f*
Congo ['kɔŋgəu] N (*state*) Congo
congratulate [kən'grætjuleɪt] VT felicitar
congratulations [kəngrætju'leɪʃənz] NPL:
~ (on) felicitaciones *fpl* (por); **~!**
¡enhorabuena!, ¡felicidades!
congregate ['kɔŋgrɪgeɪt] VI congregarse
congregation [kɔŋgrɪ'geɪʃən] N (*in church*)
fieles *mpl*
congress ['kɔŋgrɛs] N congreso; (*US Pol*): **C~**
el Congreso (de los Estados Unidos); *ver nota*

En el Congreso de los Estados Unidos
(*Congress*) se elaboran y aprueban las leyes
federales. Consta de dos cámaras: la
Cámara de Representantes ("*House of
Representatives*"), cuyos 435 miembros son
elegidos cada dos años por voto popular
directo y en número proporcional a los
habitantes de cada estado, y el Senado
("*Senate*"), con 100 senadores ("*senators*"),
2 por estado, los que un tercio se elige
cada dos años y el resto cada seis.

congressman ['kɔŋgrɛsmən] N (*irreg*) (*US*)
diputado, miembro del Congreso
congresswoman ['kɔŋgrɛswumən] N (*irreg*)
(*US*) diputada, miembro *f* del Congreso
conical ['kɔnɪkl] ADJ cónico
conifer ['kɔnɪfəʳ] N conífera
coniferous [kə'nɪfərəs] ADJ (*forest*) conífero
conjecture [kən'dʒɛktʃəʳ] N conjetura
conjugal ['kɔndʒugl] ADJ conyugal

conjugate ['kɔndʒugeɪt] VT conjugar
conjugation [kɔndʒə'geɪʃən] N conjugación f
conjunction [kən'dʒʌŋkʃən] N conjunción f; **in ~ with** junto con
conjunctivitis [kəndʒʌŋktɪ'vaɪtɪs] N conjuntivitis f
conjure ['kʌndʒəʳ] VI hacer juegos de manos ▶ **conjure up** VT (*ghost, spirit*) hacer aparecer; (*memories*) evocar
conjurer ['kʌndʒərəʳ] N ilusionista mf
conjuring trick ['kʌndʒərɪŋ-] N juego de manos
conker ['kɔŋkəʳ] N (BRIT) castaño de Indias
conk out [kɔŋk-] VI (*inf*) estropearse, fastidiarse, descomponerse (LAM)
con man N (*irreg*) timador m
Conn. ABBR (*US*) = **Connecticut**
connect [kə'nɛkt] VT juntar, unir; (*Elec*) conectar; (*pipes*) empalmar; (*fig*) relacionar, asociar ▶ VI: **to ~ with** (*train*) enlazar con; **to be connected with** (*associated*) estar relacionado con; (*related*) estar emparentado con; **I am trying to ~ you** (*Tel*) estoy intentando ponerle al habla
connecting flight N vuelo m de enlace
connection [kə'nɛkʃən] N juntura, unión f; (*Elec*) conexión f; (*Tech*) empalme m; (*Rail*) enlace m; (*Tel*) comunicación f; (*fig*) relación f; **what is the ~ between them?** ¿qué relación hay entre ellos?; **in ~ with** con respecto a, en relación a; **she has many business connections** tiene muchos contactos profesionales; **to miss/make a ~** perder/coger el enlace
connive [kə'naɪv] VI: **to ~ at** hacer la vista gorda a
connoisseur [kɔnɪ'səːʳ] N experto(-a), entendido(-a)
connotation [kɔnə'teɪʃən] N connotación f
conquer ['kɔŋkəʳ] VT (*territory*) conquistar; (*enemy, feelings*) vencer
conqueror ['kɔŋkərəʳ] N conquistador(a) m/f
conquest ['kɔŋkwɛst] N conquista
cons [kɔnz] NPL *see* **mod cons**; **pro**
conscience ['kɔnʃəns] N conciencia; **in all ~** en conciencia
conscientious [kɔnʃɪ'ɛnʃəs] ADJ concienzudo; (*objection*) de conciencia
conscientious objector N objetor m de conciencia
conscious ['kɔnʃəs] ADJ consciente; (*deliberate: insult, error*) premeditado, intencionado; **to become ~ of sth/that** darse cuenta de algo/de que
consciousness ['kɔnʃəsnɪs] N conciencia; (*Med*) conocimiento
conscript ['kɔnskrɪpt] N recluta mf
conscription [kən'skrɪpʃən] N servicio militar (obligatorio)

consecrate ['kɔnsɪkreɪt] VT consagrar
consecutive [kən'sɛkjutɪv] ADJ consecutivo; **on 3 ~ occasions** en 3 ocasiones consecutivas
consensus [kən'sɛnsəs] N consenso; **the ~ of opinion** el consenso general
consent [kən'sɛnt] N consentimiento ▶ VI: **to ~ to** consentir en; **by common ~** de común acuerdo
consenting adults [kən'sɛntɪŋ-] NPL adultos con capacidad de consentir
consequence ['kɔnsɪkwəns] N consecuencia; **in ~** por consiguiente
consequently ['kɔnsɪkwəntlɪ] ADV por consiguiente
conservation [kɔnsə'veɪʃən] N conservación f; (*of nature*) conservación, protección f
conservationist [kɔnsə'veɪʃnɪst] N conservacionista mf
conservative [kən'səːvətɪv] ADJ conservador(a); (*cautious*) moderado; **C~** adj, n (BRIT Pol) conservador(a) m/f; **the C~ Party** el partido conservador (británico)
conservatory [kən'səːvətrɪ] N (*greenhouse*) invernadero
conserve [kən'səːv] VT conservar ▶ N conserva
consider [kən'sɪdəʳ] VT considerar; (*take into account*) tener en cuenta; (*study*) estudiar, examinar; **to ~ doing sth** pensar en (la posibilidad de) hacer algo; **all things considered** pensándolo bien; **~ yourself lucky** ¡date por satisfecho!
considerable [kən'sɪdərəbl] ADJ considerable
considerably [kən'sɪdərəblɪ] ADV bastante, considerablemente
considerate [kən'sɪdərɪt] ADJ considerado
consideration [kənsɪdə'reɪʃən] N consideración f; (*reward*) retribución f; **to be under ~** estar estudiándose; **my first ~ is my family** mi primera consideración es mi familia
considered [kən'sɪdəd] ADJ: **it's my ~ opinion that …** después de haber reflexionado mucho, pienso que …
considering [kən'sɪdərɪŋ] PREP: **~ (that)** teniendo en cuenta (que)
consign [kən'saɪn] VT consignar
consignee [kɔnsaɪ'niː] N consignatario(-a)
consignment [kən'saɪnmənt] N envío
consignment note N (*Comm*) talón m de expedición
consignor [kən'saɪnəʳ] N remitente mf
consist [kən'sɪst] VI: **to ~ of** consistir en
consistency [kən'sɪstənsɪ] N (*of person etc*) consecuencia, coherencia; (*thickness*) consistencia
consistent [kən'sɪstənt] ADJ (*person, argument*) consecuente, coherente; (*results*) constante
consolation [kɔnsə'leɪʃən] N consuelo

console [kən'səul] VT consolar ▶ N ['kɔnsəul] (*control panel*) consola

consolidate [kən'sɔlɪdeɪt] VT consolidar

consols ['kɔnsɔlz] NPL (*BRIT Stock Exchange*) valores *mpl* consolidados

consommé [kən'sɔmeɪ] N consomé *m*, caldo

consonant ['kɔnsənənt] N consonante *f*

consort ['kɔnsɔːt] N consorte *mf* ▶ VI [kən'sɔːt]: **to ~ with sb** (*often pej*) asociarse con algn; **prince ~** príncipe *m* consorte

consortium [kən'sɔːtɪəm] N consorcio

conspicuous [kən'spɪkjuəs] ADJ (*visible*) visible; (*garish etc*) llamativo; (*outstanding*) notable; **to make o.s. ~** llamar la atención

conspiracy [kən'spɪrəsɪ] N conjura, complot *m*

conspiratorial [kənspɪrə'tɔːrɪəl] ADJ de conspirador

conspire [kən'spaɪər] VI conspirar

constable ['kʌnstəbl] N (*BRIT*) agente *mf* (de policía); **chief ~** ≈ jefe *mf* de policía

constabulary [kən'stæbjulərɪ] N ≈ policía

constancy ['kɔnstənsɪ] N constancia; fidelidad *f*

constant ['kɔnstənt] ADJ (*gen*) constante; (*loyal*) leal, fiel

constantly ['kɔnstəntlɪ] ADV constantemente

constellation [kɔnstə'leɪʃən] N constelación *f*

consternation [kɔnstə'neɪʃən] N consternación *f*

constipated ['kɔnstɪpeɪtəd] ADJ estreñido

constipation [kɔnstɪ'peɪʃən] N estreñimiento

constituency [kən'stɪtjuənsɪ] N (*Pol*) distrito electoral; (*people*) electorado; *ver nota*

Constituency es la denominación que recibe un distrito o circunscripción electoral y el grupo de electores registrados en ella en el sistema electoral británico. Cada circunscripción elige a un diputado (*"Member of Parliament"*), el cual se halla disponible semanalmente para las consultas y peticiones de sus electores durante ciertas horas a la semana, tiempo al que se llama *"surgery"*.

constituency party N partido local

constituent [kən'stɪtjuənt] N (*Pol*) elector(a) *m/f*; (*part*) componente *m*

constitute ['kɔnstɪtjuːt] VT constituir

constitution [kɔnstɪ'tjuːʃən] N constitución *f*

constitutional [kɔnstɪ'tjuːʃənl] ADJ constitucional; **~ monarchy** monarquía constitucional

constrain [kən'streɪn] VT obligar

constrained [kən'streɪnd] ADJ: **to feel ~ to ...** sentirse obligado a ...

constraint [kən'streɪnt] N (*force*) fuerza; (*limit*) restricción *f*; (*restraint*) reserva; (*embarrassment*) cohibición *f*

constrict [kən'strɪkt] VT oprimir

constriction [kən'strɪkʃən] N constricción *f*, opresión *f*

construct [kən'strʌkt] VT construir

construction [kən'strʌkʃən] N construcción *f*; (*fig: interpretation*) interpretación *f*; **under ~** en construcción

construction industry N industria de la construcción

constructive [kən'strʌktɪv] ADJ constructivo

construe [kən'struː] VT interpretar

consul ['kɔnsl] N cónsul *mf*

consulate ['kɔnsjulɪt] N consulado

consult [kən'sʌlt] VT, VI consultar; **to ~ sb (about sth)** consultar a algn (sobre algo)

consultancy [kən'sʌltənsɪ] N (*Comm*) consultoría; (*Med*) puesto de especialista

consultant [kən'sʌltənt] N (*BRIT Med*) especialista *mf*; (*other specialist*) asesor(a) *m/f*, consultor(a) *m/f*

consultation [kɔnsəl'teɪʃən] N consulta; **in ~ with** en consulta con

consultative [kən'sʌltətɪv] ADJ consultivo

consulting room N (*BRIT*) consulta, consultorio

consume [kən'sjuːm] VT (*eat*) comerse; (*drink*) beberse; (*fire etc*) consumir; (*Comm*) consumir

consumer [kən'sjuːmər] N (*of electricity, gas etc*) consumidor(a) *m/f*

consumer association N asociación *f* de consumidores

consumer credit N crédito al consumidor

consumer durables NPL bienes *mpl* de consumo duraderos

consumer goods NPL bienes *mpl* de consumo

consumerism [kən'sjuːmərɪzəm] N consumismo

consumer society N sociedad *f* de consumo

consumer watchdog N organización *f* protectora del consumidor

consummate ['kɔnsʌmeɪt] VT consumar

consumption [kən'sʌmpʃən] N consumo; (*Med*) tisis *f*; **not fit for human ~** no apto para el consumo humano

cont. ABBR (= *continued*) sigue

contact ['kɔntækt] N contacto; (*person: pej*) enchufe *m* ▶ VT ponerse en contacto con; **~ lenses** npl lentes *fpl* de contacto; **to be in ~ with sb/sth** estar en contacto con algn/algo; **business contacts** relaciones *fpl* comerciales

contagious [kən'teɪdʒəs] ADJ contagioso

contain [kən'teɪn] VT contener; **to ~ o.s.** contenerse

container [kən'teɪnər] N recipiente *m*; (*for shipping etc*) contenedor *m*

491

containerize [kənˈteɪnəraɪz] VT transportar en contenedores

container ship N buque m contenedor, portacontenedores m inv

contaminate [kənˈtæmɪneɪt] VT contaminar

contamination [kəntæmɪˈneɪʃən] N contaminación f

cont'd ABBR (= continued) sigue

contemplate [ˈkɒntəmpleɪt] VT (gen) contemplar; (reflect upon) considerar; (intend) pensar

contemplation [kɒntəmˈpleɪʃən] N contemplación f

contemporary [kənˈtɛmpərərɪ] ADJ, N (of the same age) contemporáneo(-a) m/f

contempt [kənˈtɛmpt] N desprecio; ~ **of court** (Law) desacato (a los tribunales or a la justicia)

contemptible [kənˈtɛmptɪbl] ADJ despreciable, desdeñable

contemptuous [kənˈtɛmptjuəs] ADJ desdeñoso

contend [kənˈtɛnd] VT (argue) afirmar ▶ VI: **to ~ with/for** luchar contra/por; **he has a lot to ~ with** tiene que hacer frente a muchos problemas

contender [kənˈtɛndəʳ] N (Sport) contendiente mf

content ADJ [kənˈtɛnt] (happy) contento; (satisfied) satisfecho ▶ VT contentar; satisfacer ▶ N [ˈkɒntɛnt] contenido; **contents** NPL contenido msg; **(table of) contents** índice m de materias; (in magazine) sumario; **to be ~ with** conformarse con; **to ~ o.s. with sth/with doing sth** conformarse con algo/con hacer algo

contented [kənˈtɛntɪd] ADJ contento; satisfecho

contentedly [kənˈtɛntɪdlɪ] ADV con aire satisfecho

contention [kənˈtɛnʃən] N discusión f; (belief) argumento; **bone of ~** manzana de la discordia

contentious [kənˈtɛnʃəs] ADJ discutible

contentment [kənˈtɛntmənt] N satisfacción f

contest [ˈkɒntɛst] N contienda f; (competition) concurso ▶ VT [kənˈtɛst] (dispute) impugnar; (Law) disputar, litigar; (Pol: election, seat) presentarse como candidato(-a) a

contestant [kənˈtɛstənt] N concursante mf; (in fight) contendiente mf

context [ˈkɒntɛkst] N contexto; **in/out of ~** en/fuera de contexto

continent [ˈkɒntɪnənt] N continente m; **the C~** (Brit) el continente europeo, Europa; **on the C~** en el continente europeo, en Europa

continental [kɒntɪˈnɛntl] ADJ continental; (Brit: European) europeo

continental breakfast N desayuno estilo europeo

continental quilt N (Brit) edredón m

contingency [kənˈtɪndʒənsɪ] N contingencia

contingent [kənˈtɪndʒənt] N (group) representación f

continual [kənˈtɪnjuəl] ADJ continuo

continually [kənˈtɪnjuəlɪ] ADV continuamente

continuation [kəntɪnjuˈeɪʃən] N prolongación f; (after interruption) reanudación f; (of story, episode) continuación f

continue [kənˈtɪnjuː] VI, VT seguir, continuar; **continued on page 10** sigue en la página 10

continuing education [kənˈtɪnjuɪŋ-] N educación f continua de adultos

continuity [kɒntɪˈnjuɪtɪ] N (also Cine) continuidad f

continuity girl N (Cine) secretaria de continuidad

continuous [kənˈtɪnjuəs] ADJ continuo; **~ performance** (Cine) sesión f continua

continuous assessment N (Brit) evaluación f continua

continuously [kənˈtɪnjuəslɪ] ADV continuamente

contort [kənˈtɔːt] VT retorcer

contortion [kənˈtɔːʃən] N (movement) contorsión f

contortionist [kənˈtɔːʃənɪst] N contorsionista mf

contour [ˈkɒntuəʳ] N contorno; (also: **contour line**) curva de nivel

contraband [ˈkɒntrəbænd] N contrabando ▶ ADJ de contrabando

contraception [kɒntrəˈsɛpʃən] N contracepción f

contraceptive [kɒntrəˈsɛptɪv] ADJ, N anticonceptivo

contract [n ˈkɒntrækt, vi, vt kənˈtrækt] N contrato ▶ CPD [ˈkɒntrækt] (price, date) contratado, de contrato; (work) bajo contrato ▶ VI (Comm): **to ~ to do sth** comprometerse por contrato a hacer algo; (become smaller) contraerse, encogerse ▶ VT contraer; **to be under ~ to do sth** estar bajo contrato para hacer algo; **~ of employment** or **of service** contrato de trabajo

▶ **contract in** VI tomar parte

▶ **contract out** VI tomar parte (en); **to ~ out (of)** optar por no tomar parte (en); **to ~ out of a pension scheme** dejar de cotizar en un plan de jubilación

contraction [kənˈtrækʃən] N contracción f

contractor [kənˈtræktəʳ] N contratista mf

contractual [kənˈtræktjuəl] ADJ contractual

contradict [kɔntrə'dɪkt] vt (*declare to be wrong*) desmentir; (*be contrary to*) contradecir

contradiction [kɔntrə'dɪkʃən] n contradicción f; **to be in ~ with** contradecir

contradictory [kɔntrə'dɪktərɪ] adj (*statements*) contradictorio; **to be ~ to** contradecir

contralto [kən'træltəʊ] n contralto f

contraption [kən'træpʃən] n (*pej*) artilugio m

contrary[1] ['kɔntrərɪ] adj contrario ▶ n lo contrario; **on the ~** al contrario; **~ to what we thought** al contrario de lo que pensábamos; **unless you hear to the ~** a no ser que le digan lo contrario

contrary[2] [kən'trɛərɪ] adj (*perverse*) terco

contrast ['kɔntrɑːst] n contraste m ▶ vt [kən'trɑːst] contrastar; **in ~ to** or **with** a diferencia de

contrasting [kən'trɑːstɪŋ] adj (*opinion*) opuesto; (*colour*) que hace contraste

contravene [kɔntrə'viːn] vt contravenir

contravention [kɔntrə'vɛnʃən] n: **~ (of)** contravención f (de)

contribute [kən'trɪbjuːt] vi contribuir ▶ vt: **to ~ to** (*gen*) contribuir a; (*newspaper*) colaborar en; (*discussion*) intervenir en

contribution [kɔntrɪ'bjuːʃən] n (*money*) contribución f; (*to debate*) intervención f; (*to journal*) colaboración f

contributor [kən'trɪbjutər] n (*to newspaper*) colaborador(a) m/f

contributory [kən'trɪbjutərɪ] adj (*cause*) contribuyente; **it was a ~ factor in …** fue un factor que contribuyó en …

contributory pension scheme n plan m cotizable de jubilación

contrivance [kən'traɪvəns] n (*machine, device*) aparato, dispositivo

contrive [kən'traɪv] vt (*invent*) idear ▶ vi: **to ~ to do** lograr hacer; (*try*) procurar hacer

control [kən'trəʊl] vt controlar; (*traffic etc*) dirigir; (*machinery*) manejar; (*temper*) dominar; (*disease, fire*) dominar, controlar ▶ n (*command*) control m; (*of car*) conducción f; (*check*) freno; **controls** npl (*of vehicle*) instrumentos mpl de mando; (*of radio*) controles mpl; (*governmental*) medidas fpl de control; **to ~ o.s.** controlarse, dominarse; **everything is under ~** todo está bajo control; **to be in ~ of** estar al mando de; **the car went out of ~** perdió el control del coche

control group n (*Med, Psych etc*) grupo de control

control key n (*Comput*) tecla de control

controlled economy n economía dirigida

controller [kən'trəʊlər] n controlador(a) m/f

controlling interest [kən'trəʊlɪŋ-] n participación f mayoritaria

control panel n (*on aircraft, ship, TV etc*) tablero de instrumentos

control point n (puesto de) control m

control room n (*Naut, Mil*) sala de mandos; (*Radio, TV*) sala de control

control tower n (*Aviat*) torre f de control

control unit n (*Comput*) unidad f de control

controversial [kɔntrə'vəːʃl] adj polémico

controversy ['kɔntrəvəːsɪ] n polémica

conurbation [kɔnə'beɪʃən] n conurbación f

convalesce [kɔnvə'lɛs] vi convalecer

convalescence [kɔnvə'lɛsns] n convalecencia

convalescent [kɔnvə'lɛsnt] adj, n convaleciente mf

convector [kən'vɛktər] n calentador m de convección

convene [kən'viːn] vt (*meeting*) convocar ▶ vi reunirse

convenience [kən'viːnɪəns] n (*comfort*) comodidad f; (*advantage*) ventaja; **at your earliest ~** (*Comm*) tan pronto como le sea posible; **all modern conveniences** (*Brit*) todo confort

convenience foods npl platos mpl preparados

convenient [kən'viːnɪənt] adj (*useful*) útil; (*place*) conveniente; (*time*) oportuno; **if it is ~ for you** si le viene bien

conveniently [kən'viːnɪəntlɪ] adv (*happen*) oportunamente; (*situated*) convenientemente

convent ['kɔnvənt] n convento

convention [kən'vɛnʃən] n convención f; (*meeting*) asamblea

conventional [kən'vɛnʃənl] adj convencional

convent school n colegio de monjas

converge [kən'vəːdʒ] vi converger

conversant [kən'vəːsnt] adj: **to be ~ with** estar familiarizado con

conversation [kɔnvə'seɪʃən] n conversación f

conversational [kɔnvə'seɪʃənl] adj (*familiar*) familiar; (*talkative*) locuaz; **~ mode** (*Comput*) modo de conversación

converse ['kɔnvəːs] n inversa ▶ vi [kən'vəːs] conversar; **to ~ (with sb about sth)** conversar or platicar (*Lam*) (con algn de algo)

conversely [kɔn'vəːslɪ] adv a la inversa

conversion [kən'vəːʃən] n conversión f; (*house conversion*) reforma, remodelación f

conversion table n tabla de equivalencias

convert [kən'vəːt] vt (*Rel, Comm*) convertir; (*alter*) transformar ▶ n ['kɔnvəːt] converso(-a)

convertible [kən'vəːtəbl] adj convertible ▶ n descapotable m; **~ loan stock** obligaciones fpl convertibles

convex ['kɔn'vɛks] adj convexo

convey [kən'veɪ] vt transportar; (*thanks*) comunicar; (*idea*) expresar

conveyance [kən'veɪəns] N *(of goods)* transporte *m*; *(vehicle)* vehículo, medio de transporte

conveyancing [kən'veɪənsɪŋ] N *(Law)* preparación *f* de escrituras de traspaso

conveyor belt [kən'veɪəʳ-] N cinta transportadora

convict [kən'vɪkt] VT *(gen)* condenar; *(find guilty)* declarar culpable a ▶ N ['kɒnvɪkt] presidiario(-a)

conviction [kən'vɪkʃən] N condena; *(belief)* creencia, convicción *f*

convince [kən'vɪns] VT convencer; **to ~ sb (of sth/that)** convencer a algn (de algo/de que)

convinced [kən'vɪnst] ADJ: **~ of/that** convencido de/de que

convincing [kən'vɪnsɪŋ] ADJ convincente

convincingly [kən'vɪnsɪŋlɪ] ADV de modo convincente, convincentemente

convivial [kən'vɪvɪəl] ADJ *(person)* sociable; *(atmosphere)* alegre

convoluted ['kɒnvəluːtɪd] ADJ *(argument etc)* enrevesado; *(shape)* enrollado, enroscado

convoy ['kɒnvɔɪ] N convoy *m*

convulse [kən'vʌls] VT convulsionar; **to be convulsed with laughter** dislocarse de risa

convulsion [kən'vʌlʃən] N convulsión *f*

coo [kuː] VI arrullar

cook [kuk] VT cocinar; *(stew etc)* guisar; *(meal)* preparar ▶ VI hacerse; *(person)* cocinar ▶ N cocinero(-a)
  ▶ **cook up** VT *(inf: excuse, story)* inventar

cookbook ['kukbuk] N libro de cocina

cooker ['kukəʳ] N cocina

cookery ['kukərɪ] N cocina

cookery book N *(BRIT)* = **cookbook**

cookie ['kukɪ] N *(US)* galleta; *(Comput)* cookie *f*

cooking ['kukɪŋ] N cocina ▶ CPD *(apples)* para cocinar; *(utensils, salt, foil)* de cocina

cooking chocolate N chocolate *m* fondant *or* de hacer

cookout ['kukaut] N *(US)* comida al aire libre

cool [kuːl] ADJ fresco; *(not hot)* tibio; *(not afraid)* tranquilo; *(unfriendly)* frío ▶ VT enfriar ▶ VI enfriarse; **it is ~** *(weather)* hace fresco; **to keep sth ~** *or* **in a ~ place** conservar algo fresco *or* en un sitio fresco
  ▶ **cool down** VI enfriarse; *(fig: person, situation)* calmarse
  ▶ **cool off** VI *(become calmer)* calmarse, apaciguarse; *(lose enthusiasm)* perder (el) interés, enfriarse

coolant ['kuːlənt] N refrigerante *m*

cool box, *(US)* **cooler** ['kuːləʳ] N nevera portátil

cooling ['kuːlɪŋ] ADJ refrescante

cooling-off period [kuːlɪŋ'ɔf-] N *(Industry)* plazo de negociaciones

cooling tower N torre *f* de refrigeración

coolly ['kuːlɪ] ADV *(calmly)* con tranquilidad; *(audaciously)* descaradamente; *(unenthusiastically)* fríamente, con frialdad

coolness ['kuːlnɪs] N frescura; tranquilidad *f*; *(hostility)* frialdad *f*; *(indifference)* falta de entusiasmo

coop [kuːp] N gallinero ▶ VT: **to ~ up** *(fig)* encerrar

co-op ['kəuɒp] N ABBR (= *cooperative (society)*) cooperativa

cooperate [kəu'ɒpəreɪt] VI cooperar, colaborar; **will he ~?** ¿querrá cooperar?

cooperation [kəuɒpə'reɪʃən] N cooperación *f*, colaboración *f*

cooperative [kəu'ɒpərətɪv] ADJ cooperativo; *(person)* dispuesto a colaborar ▶ N cooperativa

co-opt [kəu'ɒpt] VT: **to ~ sb into sth** nombrar a algn para algo

coordinate [kəu'ɔːdɪneɪt] VT coordinar ▶ N [kəu'ɔːdɪnət] *(Math)* coordenada; **coordinates** NPL *(clothes)* coordinados *mpl*

coordination [kəuɔːdɪ'neɪʃən] N coordinación *f*

coot [kuːt] N focha *f* (común)

co-ownership [kəu'əunəʃɪp] N copropiedad *f*

cop [kɒp] N *(inf)* poli *m*

cope [kəup] VI: **to ~ with** poder con; *(problem)* hacer frente a

Copenhagen [kəupən'heɪgən] N Copenhague *m*

copier ['kɒpɪəʳ] N *(photocopier)* (foto)copiadora

co-pilot ['kəu'paɪlət] N copiloto *mf*

copious ['kəupɪəs] ADJ copioso, abundante

copper ['kɒpəʳ] N *(metal)* cobre *m*; *(inf: policeman)* poli *m*; **coppers** NPL perras *fpl*; *(small change)* calderilla

coppice ['kɒpɪs], **copse** [kɒps] N bosquecillo

copulate ['kɒpjuleɪt] VI copular

copulation [kɒpju'leɪʃən] N cópula

copy ['kɒpɪ] N copia; *(of book)* ejemplar *m*; *(of magazine)* número; *(material: for printing)* original *m* ▶ VT *(also Comput)* copiar; *(imitate)* copiar, imitar; **to make good ~** *(fig)* ser una noticia de interés; **rough ~** borrador *m*; **fair ~** copia en limpio
  ▶ **copy out** VT copiar

copycat ['kɒpɪkæt] N *(pej)* imitador(a) *m/f*

copyright ['kɒpɪraɪt] N derechos *mpl* de autor

copy typist N mecanógrafo(-a)

coral ['kɒrəl] N coral *m*

coral reef N arrecife *m* (de coral)

Coral Sea N: **the ~** el Mar del Coral

cord [kɔːd] N cuerda; *(Elec)* cable *m*; *(fabric)* pana; **cords** NPL *(trousers)* pantalones *mpl* de pana

cordial ['kɔːdɪəl] ADJ cordial ▶ N cordial *m*

cordless ['kɔːdlɪs] ADJ sin hilos; **~ telephone** teléfono inalámbrico

cordon ['kɔːdn] N cordón *m*

▶ **cordon off** VT acordonar

Cordova ['kɔ:dəvə] N Córdoba

corduroy ['kɔ:dərɔɪ] N pana

CORE [kɔ:ʳ] N ABBR (US) = **Congress of Racial Equality**

core [kɔ:ʳ] N (of earth, nuclear reactor) centro, núcleo; (of fruit) corazón m; (of problem etc) esencia, meollo ▶ VT quitar el corazón de

Corfu [kɔ:'fu] N Corfú m

coriander [kɔrɪ'ændəʳ] N culantro, cilantro

cork [kɔ:k] N corcho; (tree) alcornoque m

corkage ['kɔ:kɪdʒ] N precio que se cobra en un restaurante por una botella de vino traída de fuera

corked [kɔ:kt] ADJ (wine) con sabor a corcho

corkscrew ['kɔ:kskru:] N sacacorchos m inv

cormorant ['kɔ:mərənt] N cormorán m

Corn ABBR (BRIT) = **Cornwall**

corn [kɔ:n] N (BRIT: wheat) trigo; (US: maize) maíz m, choclo (LAM); (on foot) callo; ~ **on the cob** (Culin) maíz en la mazorca

cornea ['kɔ:nɪə] N córnea

corned beef ['kɔ:nd-] N carne f de vaca acecinada

corner ['kɔ:nəʳ] N (outside) esquina; (inside) rincón m; (in road) curva; (Football) córner m, saque m de esquina ▶ VT (trap) arrinconar; (Comm) acaparar ▶ VI (in car) tomar las curvas; **to cut corners** atajar

corner flag N (Football) banderola de esquina

corner kick N (Football) córner m, saque m de esquina

corner shop N (BRIT) tienda de la esquina

cornerstone ['kɔ:nəstəun] N piedra angular

cornet ['kɔ:nɪt] N (Mus) corneta; (BRIT: of ice cream) cucurucho

cornflakes ['kɔ:nfleɪks] NPL copos mpl de maíz, cornflakes mpl

cornflour ['kɔ:nflauəʳ] N (BRIT) harina de maíz

cornice ['kɔ:nɪs] N cornisa

Cornish ['kɔ:nɪʃ] ADJ de Cornualles

corn oil N aceite m de maíz

cornstarch ['kɔ:nstɑ:tʃ] N (US) = **cornflour**

cornucopia [kɔ:nju'kəupɪə] N cornucopia

Cornwall ['kɔ:nwəl] N Cornualles m

corny ['kɔ:nɪ] ADJ (inf) gastado

corollary [kə'rɔləri] N corolario

coronary ['kɔrənəri] N: ~ **(thrombosis)** infarto

coronation [kɔrə'neɪʃən] N coronación f

coroner ['kɔrənəʳ] N juez mf de instrucción

coronet ['kɔrənɪt] N corona

Corp. ABBR = **corporation**

corporal ['kɔ:pərl] N cabo ▶ ADJ: ~ **punishment** castigo corporal

corporate ['kɔ:pərɪt] ADJ (action, ownership) colectivo; (finance, image) corporativo

corporate hospitality N obsequios a los clientes por cortesía de la empresa

corporate identity, corporate image N (of organization) identidad f corporativa

corporation [kɔ:pə'reɪʃən] N (of town) ayuntamiento; (Comm) corporación f

corps [kɔ:ʳ] (pl ~ [kɔ:z]) N cuerpo; **press ~** gabinete m de prensa

corpse [kɔ:ps] N cadáver m

corpulent ['kɔ:pjulənt] ADJ corpulento(-a)

Corpus Christi ['kɔ:pəs'krɪstɪ] N Corpus m (Christi)

corpuscle ['kɔ:pʌsl] N corpúsculo

corral [kə'rɑ:l] N corral m

correct [kə'rɛkt] ADJ correcto; (accurate) exacto ▶ VT corregir; **you are ~** tiene razón

correction [kə'rɛkʃən] N (act) corrección f; (instance) rectificación f; (erasure) tachadura

correlate ['kɔrɪleɪt] VI: **to ~ with** tener correlación con

correlation [kɔrɪ'leɪʃən] N correlación f

correspond [kɔrɪs'pɔnd] VI: **to ~ (with)** (write) escribirse (con); (be in accordance) corresponder (con); **to ~ (to)** (be equivalent to) corresponder (a)

correspondence [kɔrɪs'pɔndəns] N correspondencia

correspondence course N curso por correspondencia

correspondent [kɔrɪs'pɔndənt] N corresponsal mf

corresponding [kɔrɪs'pɔndɪŋ] ADJ correspondiente

corridor ['kɔrɪdɔ:ʳ] N pasillo

corroborate [kə'rɔbəreɪt] VT corroborar

corroboration [kərɔbə'reɪʃən] N corroboración f, confirmación f

corrode [kə'rəud] VT corroer ▶ VI corroerse

corrosion [kə'rəuʒən] N corrosión f

corrosive [kə'rəusɪv] ADJ corrosivo

corrugated ['kɔrəgeɪtɪd] ADJ ondulado

corrugated cardboard N cartón m ondulado

corrugated iron N chapa ondulada

corrupt [kə'rʌpt] ADJ corrompido; (person) corrupto ▶ VT corromper; (bribe) sobornar; (Comput: data) degradar; ~ **practices** (dishonesty, bribery) corrupción f

corruption [kə'rʌpʃən] N corrupción f; (Comput: of data) alteración f

corset ['kɔ:sɪt] N faja; (old-style) corsé m

Corsica ['kɔ:sɪkə] N Córcega

Corsican ['kɔ:sɪkən] ADJ, N corso(-a) m/f

cortège [kɔ:'teɪʒ] N cortejo, comitiva

cortisone ['kɔ:tɪzəun] N cortisona

cosh [kɔʃ] N (BRIT) cachiporra

cosignatory ['kəu'sɪgnətəri] N cosignatario(-a)

cosine ['kəusaɪn] N coseno

cosiness ['kəuzinɪs] N comodidad f; (atmosphere) lo acogedor

cos lettuce [kɔs-] N lechuga romana

cosmetic [kɔz'mɛtɪk] N cosmético ▶ ADJ (*also* *fig*) cosmético

cosmetic surgery N cirugía f estética

cosmic ['kɔzmɪk] ADJ cósmico

cosmonaut ['kɔzmənɔːt] N cosmonauta mf

cosmopolitan [kɔzmə'pɔlɪtn] ADJ cosmopolita

cosmos ['kɔzmɔs] N cosmos m

cosset ['kɔsɪt] VT mimar

cost [kɔst] (*pt, pp* ~) N (*gen*) coste m, costo; (*price*) precio ▶ VI costar, valer ▶ VT preparar el presupuesto de; **costs** NPL (*Law*) costas fpl; **the ~ of living** el coste *or* costo de la vida; **how much does it ~?** ¿cuánto cuesta?, ¿cuánto vale?; **what will it ~ to have it repaired?** ¿cuánto costará repararlo?; **to ~ sb time/effort** costarle a algn tiempo/esfuerzo; **it ~ him his life** le costó la vida; **at all costs** cueste lo que cueste

cost accountant N contable m de costos

co-star ['kəustɑːʳ] N coprotagonista mf

Costa Rica ['kɔstə'riːkə] N Costa Rica

Costa Rican ['kɔstə'riːkən] ADJ, N costarriqueño(-a) m/f, costarricense mf

cost centre N centro (de determinación) de coste

cost control N control m de costes

cost-effective [kɔstɪ'fɛktɪv] ADJ (*Comm*) rentable

cost-effectiveness ['kɔstɪ'fɛktɪvnɪs] N relación f coste-rendimiento

costing ['kɔstɪŋ] N cálculo del coste

costly ['kɔstlɪ] ADJ (*expensive*) costoso

cost-of-living [kɔstəv'lɪvɪŋ] ADJ: **~ allowance** plus m de carestía de vida; **~ index** índice m del coste de vida

cost price N (BRIT) precio de coste

costume ['kɔstjuːm] N traje m; (BRIT: *also*: **swimming costume**) traje de baño

costume jewellery N bisutería

cosy, (US) **cozy** ['kəuzɪ] ADJ cómodo, a gusto; (*room, atmosphere*) acogedor(a)

cot [kɔt] N (BRIT: *child's*) cuna; (US: *folding bed*) cama plegable

cot death N muerte f en la cuna

Cotswolds ['kɔtswəuldz] NPL *región de colinas del suroeste inglés*

cottage ['kɔtɪdʒ] N casita de campo

cottage cheese N requesón m

cottage industry N industria artesanal

cottage pie N *pastel de carne cubierta de puré de patatas*

cotton ['kɔtn] N algodón m; (*thread*) hilo ▶ **cotton on** VI (*inf*): **to ~ on (to sth)** caer en la cuenta (de algo)

cotton bud N (BRIT) bastoncillo m de algodón

cotton candy N (US) algodón m (azucarado)

cotton wool N (BRIT) algodón m (hidrófilo)

couch [kautʃ] N sofá m; (*in doctor's surgery*) camilla; (*psychiatrist's*) diván m

couchette [kuː'ʃɛt] N litera

couch potato N (*inf*) *persona comodona que no se mueve en todo el día*

cough [kɔf] VI toser ▶ N tos f ▶ **cough up** VT escupir

cough drop N pastilla para la tos

cough mixture N jarabe m para la tos

could [kud] PT *of* **can²**

couldn't ['kudnt] = **could not**

council ['kaunsl] N consejo; **city** *or* **town ~** ayuntamiento, consejo municipal; **C~ of Europe** Consejo de Europa

council estate N (BRIT) barriada de viviendas sociales de alquiler

council house N (BRIT) vivienda social de alquiler

councillor ['kaunsləʳ] N concejal mf

council tax N (BRIT) contribución f municipal (*dependiente del valor de la vivienda*)

counsel ['kaunsl] N (*advice*) consejo; (*lawyer*) abogado(-a) ▶ VT aconsejar; **~ for the defence/the prosecution** abogado(-a) defensor(a)/fiscal; **to ~ sth/sb to do sth** aconsejar algo/a algn que haga algo

counselling, (US) **counseling** N (*Psych*) asistencia f psicológica

counsellor, (US) **counselor** ['kaunsləʳ] N consejero(-a); (US *Law*) abogado(-a)

count [kaunt] VT (*gen*) contar; (*include*) incluir ▶ VI contar ▶ N cuenta; (*of votes*) escrutinio; (*nobleman*) conde m; (*sum*) total m, suma; **to ~ the cost of** calcular el coste de; **not counting the children** niños aparte; **10 counting him** diez incluyéndolo a él, diez con él; **~ yourself lucky** date por satisfecho; **that doesn't ~!** ¡eso no vale!; **to ~ (up) to 10** contar hasta diez; **it counts for very little** cuenta poco; **to keep ~ of sth** llevar la cuenta de algo ▶ **count in** (*inf*) VT: **to ~ sb in on sth** contar con algn para algo ▶ **count on** VT FUS contar con; **to ~ on doing sth** contar con hacer algo ▶ **count up** VT contar

countdown ['kauntdaun] N cuenta atrás

countenance ['kauntɪnəns] N semblante m, rostro ▶ VT (*tolerate*) aprobar, consentir

counter ['kauntəʳ] N (*in shop*) mostrador m; (*position: in post office, bank*) ventanilla; (: *in games*) ficha; (*Tech*) contador m ▶ VT contrarrestar; (*blow*) parar; (*attack*) contestar a ▶ ADV: **~ to** contrario a; **to buy under the ~** (*fig*) comprar de estraperlo *or* bajo mano; **to ~ sth with sth/by doing sth** contestar algo con algo/haciendo algo

counteract ['kauntər'ækt] VT contrarrestar

counterattack ['kauntərə'tæk] N contraataque m ▶ VI contraatacar

counterbalance ['kauntə'bæləns] N contrapeso

counter-clockwise ['kauntə'klɔkwaɪz] ADV en sentido contrario al de las agujas del reloj

counter-espionage ['kauntər'ɛspɪənɑ:ʒ] N contraespionaje m

counterfeit ['kauntəfɪt] N falsificación f ▶ VT falsificar ▶ ADJ falso, falsificado

counterfoil ['kauntəfɔɪl] N (BRIT) matriz f, talón m

counterintelligence ['kauntərɪn'tɛlɪdʒəns] N contraespionaje m

countermand ['kauntəmɑ:nd] VT revocar

counter-measure ['kauntəmɛʒə'] N contramedida

counteroffensive ['kauntərə'fɛnsɪv] N contraofensiva

counterpane ['kauntəpeɪn] N colcha

counterpart ['kauntəpɑ:t] N (of person) homólogo(-a)

counter-productive [kauntəprə'dʌktɪv] ADJ contraproducente

counterproposal ['kauntəprə'pəuzl] N contrapropuesta

countersign ['kauntəsaɪn] VT ratificar, refrendar

counterterrorism [kauntə'tɛrərɪzəm] N antiterrorismo

countess ['kauntɪs] N condesa

countless ['kauntlɪs] ADJ innumerable

countrified ['kʌntrɪfaɪd] ADJ rústico

country ['kʌntrɪ] N país m; (native land) patria; (as opposed to town) campo; (region) región f, tierra; **in the ~** en el campo; **mountainous ~** región f montañosa

country and western, country and western music N música country

country dancing N (BRIT) baile m regional

country house N casa de campo

countryman ['kʌntrɪmən] N (irreg) (national) compatriota m; (rural) hombre m del campo

countryside ['kʌntrɪsaɪd] N campo

countrywide ['kʌntrɪ'waɪd] ADJ nacional ▶ ADV por todo el país

county ['kauntɪ] N condado; see also **district council**

county council N (BRIT) ≈ diputación f provincial

county town N cabeza de partido

coup [ku:] (pl **coups** [ku:z]) N golpe m; (triumph) éxito; (also: **coup d'état**) golpe de estado

coupé ['ku:peɪ] N cupé m

couple ['kʌpl] N (of things) par m; (of people) pareja; (married couple) matrimonio ▶ VT (ideas, names) unir, juntar; (machinery) acoplar; **a ~ of** un par de

couplet ['kʌplɪt] N pareado

coupling ['kʌplɪŋ] N (Rail) enganche m

coupon ['ku:pɔn] N cupón m; (voucher) valé m; (pools coupon) boleto (de quiniela)

courage ['kʌrɪdʒ] N valor m, valentía

courageous [kə'reɪdʒəs] ADJ valiente

courgette [kuə'ʒɛt] N (BRIT) calabacín m

courier ['kurɪə'] N mensajero(-a); (diplomatic) correo; (for tourists) guía mf (de turismo)

course [kɔ:s] N (direction) dirección f; (of river) curso; (Scol) curso; (of ship) rumbo; (fig) proceder m; (Golf) campo; (part of meal) plato; **of ~** adv desde luego, naturalmente; **of ~!** ¡claro!, ¡cómo no! (LAM); **(no) of ~ not!** ¡claro que no!, ¡por supuesto que no!; **in due ~** a su debido tiempo; **in the ~ of the next few days** durante los próximos días; **we have no other ~ but to ...** no tenemos más remedio que ...; **there are 2 courses open to us** se nos ofrecen dos posibilidades; **the best ~ would be to ...** lo mejor sería ...; **~ of treatment** (Med) tratamiento

court [kɔ:t] N (royal) corte f; (Law) tribunal m, juzgado; (Tennis) pista, cancha (LAM) ▶ VT (woman) cortejar; (fig: favour, popularity) solicitar, buscar; (: death, disaster, danger etc) buscar; **to take to ~** demandar; **~ of appeal** tribunal m de apelación

courteous ['kə:tɪəs] ADJ cortés

courtesan [kɔ:tɪ'zæn] N cortesana

courtesy ['kə:təsɪ] N cortesía; **by ~ of** (por) cortesía de

courtesy bus, courtesy coach N autobús m gratuito

courtesy light N (Aut) luz f interior

courthouse ['kɔ:thaus] N (US) palacio de justicia

courtier ['kɔ:tɪə'] N cortesano

court martial ['kɔ:t'mɑ:ʃəl] (pl **courts martial**) N consejo de guerra ▶ VT someter a consejo de guerra

courtroom ['kɔ:trum] N sala de justicia

court shoe N zapato de mujer de estilo clásico

courtyard ['kɔ:tjɑ:d] N patio

cousin ['kʌzn] N primo(-a); **first ~** primo(-a) carnal

cove [kəuv] N cala, ensenada

covenant ['kʌvənənt] N convenio ▶ VT: **to ~ £20 per year to a charity** concertar el pago de veinte libras anuales a una sociedad benéfica

Coventry ['kɔvəntrɪ] N: **to send sb to ~** (fig) hacer el vacío a algn

cover ['kʌvə'] VT cubrir; (with lid) tapar; (chairs etc) revestir; (distance) cubrir, recorrer; (include) abarcar; (protect) abrigar; (journalist) investigar; (issues) tratar ▶ N cubierta; (lid) tapa; (for chair etc) funda; (for bed: blanket) manta; (: sheet) sábana; (envelope) sobre m; (of magazine) portada; (shelter) abrigo; (insurance) cobertura; **to take ~** (shelter) protegerse,

497

resguardarse; **under ~** (*indoors*) bajo techo; **under ~ of darkness** al amparo de la oscuridad; **under separate ~** (*Comm*) por separado; **£10 will ~ everything** con diez libras cubriremos todos los gastos
▶ **cover up** VT (*child, object*) cubrir completamente, tapar; (*fig: hide: truth, facts*) ocultar ▶ VI: **to ~ up for sb** (*fig*) encubrir a algn
coverage ['kʌvərɪdʒ] N alcance m; (*in media*) cobertura informativa; (*Insurance*) cobertura
coveralls ['kʌvərɔːlz] NPL (*US*) mono sg
cover charge N precio del cubierto
covering ['kʌvərɪŋ] N cubierta, envoltura
covering letter, (*US*) **cover letter** N carta de explicación
cover note N (*Insurance*) póliza provisional
cover price N precio de cubierta
covert ['kʌuvət] ADJ (*secret*) secreto, encubierto; (*dissembled*) furtivo
cover-up ['kʌvərʌp] N encubrimiento
covet ['kʌvɪt] VT codiciar
covetous ['kʌvɪtəs] ADJ codicioso
cow [kau] N vaca ▶ VT intimidar
coward ['kauəd] N cobarde mf
cowardice ['kauədɪs] N cobardía
cowardly ['kauədlɪ] ADJ cobarde
cowboy ['kaubɔɪ] N vaquero
cower ['kauər] VI encogerse (de miedo)
co-worker ['kəuwəːkər] N colaborador(a) m/f
cowshed ['kauʃed] N establo
cowslip ['kauslɪp] N (*Bot*) primavera, prímula
cox ['kɔks], **coxswain** ['kɔksn] N timonel m
coy [kɔɪ] ADJ tímido
coyote [kɔɪ'əutɪ] N coyote m
cozy ['kəuzɪ] ADJ (*US*) = **cosy**
CP N ABBR (= *Communist Party*) PC m
cp. ABBR (= *compare*) cfr.
CPA N ABBR (*US*) = **certified public accountant**
CPI N ABBR (= *Consumer Price Index*) IPC m
Cpl. ABBR (*Mil*) = **corporal**
c.p.s. ABBR (= *characters per second*) c.p.s.
CPSA N ABBR (*BRIT*: = *Civil and Public Services Association*) sindicato de funcionarios
CPU N ABBR = **central processing unit**
cr. ABBR = **credit; creditor**
crab [kræb] N cangrejo
crab apple N manzana silvestre
crack [kræk] N grieta; (*noise*) crujido; (*: of whip*) chasquido; (*joke*) chiste m; (*inf: drug*) crack m; (*attempt*): **to have a ~ at sth** intentar algo ▶ VT agrietar, romper; (*nut*) cascar; (*safe*) forzar; (*whip etc*) chasquear; (*knuckles*) crujir; (*joke*) contar; (*case: solve*) resolver; (*code*) descifrar ▶ ADJ (*athlete*) de primera clase; **to ~ jokes** (*inf*) bromear
▶ **crack down on** VT FUS reprimir fuertemente, adoptar medidas severas contra
▶ **crack up** VI sufrir una crisis nerviosa

crackdown ['krækdaun] N: **~ (on)** (*on crime*) campaña (contra); (*on spending*) reducción f (en)
cracked [krækt] ADJ (*cup, window*) rajado; (*wall*) resquebrajado
cracker ['krækər] N (*biscuit*) galleta salada, crácker m; (*Christmas cracker*) petardo sorpresa
crackle ['krækl] VI crepitar
crackling ['kræklɪŋ] N (*on radio, telephone*) interferencia; (*of fire*) chisporroteo, crepitación f; (*of leaves etc*) crujido; (*of pork*) chicharrón m
crackpot ['krækpɔt] (*inf*) N pirado(-a) ▶ ADJ de pirado
cradle ['kreidl] N cuna ▶ VT (*child*) mecer, acunar; (*object*) abrazar
craft [krɑːft] N (*skill*) arte m; (*trade*) oficio; (*cunning*) astucia; (*boat*) embarcación f
craftsman ['krɑːftsmən] N (*irreg*) artesano
craftsmanship ['krɑːftsmənʃɪp] N destreza
crafty ['krɑːftɪ] ADJ astuto
crag [kræg] N peñasco
craggy ['krægɪ] ADJ escarpado
cram [kræm] VT (*fill*): **to ~ sth with** llenar algo (a reventar) de; (*put*): **to ~ sth into** meter algo a la fuerza en ▶ VI (*for exams*) empollar
crammed [kræmd] ADJ atestado
cramp [kræmp] N (*Med*) calambre m; (*Tech*) grapa ▶ VT (*limit*) poner trabas a
cramped [kræmpt] ADJ apretado; (*room*) minúsculo
crampon ['kræmpən] N crampón m
cranberry ['krænbərɪ] N arándano agrio
crane [kreɪn] N (*Tech*) grúa; (*bird*) grulla ▶ VT, VI: **to ~ forward, to ~ one's neck** estirar el cuello
cranium ['kreɪnɪəm] N cráneo
crank [kræŋk] N manivela; (*person*) chiflado(-a)
crankshaft ['kræŋkʃɑːft] N cigüeñal m
cranky ['kræŋkɪ] ADJ (*eccentric*) maniático; (*bad-tempered*) de mal genio
cranny ['krænɪ] N see **nook**
crap [kræp] N (*inf!*) mierda (!)
crappy ['kræpɪ] ADJ (*inf*) chungo
craps [kræps] N (*US*) dados mpl
crash [kræʃ] N (*noise*) estrépito; (*of cars, plane*) accidente m; (*of business*) quiebra; (*Stock Exchange*) crac m ▶ VT (*plane*) estrellar ▶ VI (*plane*) estrellarse; (*two cars*) chocar; (*fall noisily*) caer con estrépito; **he crashed the car into a wall** estrelló el coche contra una pared or tapia
▶ **crash out** VI (*inf: sleep*) quedarse frito; (*from competition*) quedar eliminado
crash barrier N (*Aut*) barrera de protección
crash course N curso acelerado
crash helmet N casco (protector)

crash landing N aterrizaje *m* forzoso
crass [kræs] ADJ grosero, maleducado
crate [kreɪt] N cajón *m* de embalaje; *(for bottles)* caja; *(inf)* armatoste *m*
crater ['kreɪtəʳ] N cráter *m*
cravat, cravate [krə'væt] N pañuelo
crave [kreɪv] VT, VI: **to ~ (for)** ansiar, anhelar
craving ['kreɪvɪŋ] N *(for food, cigarettes etc)* ansias *fpl*; *(during pregnancy)* antojo
crawl [krɔːl] VI *(drag o.s.)* arrastrarse; *(child)* andar a gatas, gatear; *(vehicle)* avanzar (lentamente); *(inf)*: **to ~ to sb** dar coba a algn, hacerle la pelota a algn ▶ N *(Swimming)* crol *m*
crawler lane [krɔːlə-] N *(BRIT Aut)* carril *m* para tráfico lento
crayfish ['kreɪfɪʃ] *(pl ~)* N INV *(freshwater)* cangrejo (de río); *(saltwater)* cigala
crayon ['kreɪən] N lápiz *m* de color
craze [kreɪz] N manía; *(fashion)* moda
crazed [kreɪzd] ADJ *(look, person)* loco, demente; *(pottery, glaze)* agrietado, cuarteado
crazy ['kreɪzɪ] ADJ *(person)* loco; *(idea)* disparatado; **to go ~** volverse loco; **to be ~ about sb/sth** *(inf)* estar loco por algn/algo
crazy paving N pavimento de baldosas irregulares
creak [kriːk] VI crujir; *(hinge etc)* chirriar, rechinar
cream [kriːm] N *(of milk)* nata, crema; *(lotion)* crema; *(fig)* flor *f* y nata ▶ ADJ *(colour)* color *m* crema; **whipped ~** nata batida
▶ **cream off** VT *(fig: best talents, part of profits)* separar lo mejor de
cream cake N pastel *m* de nata
cream cheese N queso blanco cremoso
creamery ['kriːmərɪ] N *(shop)* quesería; *(factory)* central *f* lechera
creamy ['kriːmɪ] ADJ cremoso
crease [kriːs] N *(fold)* pliegue *m*; *(in trousers)* raya; *(wrinkle)* arruga ▶ VT *(fold)* doblar, plegar; *(wrinkle)* arrugar ▶ VI *(wrinkle up)* arrugarse
crease-resistant ['kriːsrɪzɪstənt] ADJ inarrugable
create [kriː'eɪt] VT *(also Comput)* crear; *(impression)* dar; *(fuss, noise)* hacer
creation [kriː'eɪʃən] N creación *f*
creative [kriː'eɪtɪv] ADJ creativo
creativity [kriːeɪ'tɪvɪtɪ] N creatividad *f*
creator [kriː'eɪtəʳ] N creador(a) *m/f*
creature ['kriːtʃəʳ] N *(living thing)* criatura; *(animal)* animal *m*; *(insect)* bicho; *(person)* criatura
creature comforts NPL comodidades *fpl* materiales
crèche, creche [krɛʃ] N *(BRIT)* guardería (infantil)
credence ['kriːdəns] N: **to lend** *or* **give ~ to** creer en, dar crédito a

credentials [krɪ'dɛnʃlz] NPL credenciales *fpl*; *(letters of reference)* referencias *fpl*
credibility [krɛdɪ'bɪlɪtɪ] N credibilidad *f*
credible ['krɛdɪbl] ADJ creíble; *(witness, source)* fidedigno
credit ['krɛdɪt] N *(gen)* crédito; *(merit)* honor *m*, mérito ▶ VT *(Comm)* abonar; *(believe)* creer, dar crédito a ▶ ADJ crediticio; **to be in ~** *(person, bank account)* tener saldo a favor; **on ~** a crédito; *(inf)* al fiado; **he's a ~ to his family** hace honor a su familia; **to ~ sb with** *(fig)* reconocer a algn el mérito de; *see also* **credits**
creditable ['krɛdɪtəbl] ADJ estimable, digno de elogio
credit account N cuenta de crédito
credit agency N agencia de informes comerciales
credit balance N saldo acreedor
credit card N tarjeta de crédito
credit control N control *m* de créditos
credit crunch N crisis *f* crediticia
credit facilities NPL facilidades *fpl* de crédito
credit limit N límite *m* de crédito
credit note N nota de crédito
creditor ['krɛdɪtəʳ] N acreedor(a) *m/f*
credits ['krɛdɪts] NPL *(Cine)* títulos *mpl* or rótulos *mpl* de crédito, ficha técnica
credit transfer N transferencia de crédito
creditworthy ['krɛdɪtwəːðɪ] ADJ solvente
credulity [krɪ'djuːlɪtɪ] N credulidad *f*
creed [kriːd] N credo
creek [kriːk] N cala, ensenada; *(US)* riachuelo
creel [kriːl] N nasa
creep [kriːp] *(pt, pp crept* [krɛpt]*)* VI *(animal)* deslizarse; *(plant)* trepar; **to ~ up on sb** acercarse sigilosamente a algn; *(fig: old age etc)*: **to ~ up (on sb)** acercarse (a algn) ▶ N *(inf)*: **he's a ~** ¡qué lameculos es!; **it gives me the creeps** me da escalofríos
creeper ['kriːpəʳ] N enredadera
creepers ['kriːpəz] NPL *(US: for baby)* pelele *msg*
creepy ['kriːpɪ] ADJ *(frightening)* horripilante
creepy-crawly ['kriːpɪ'krɔːlɪ] N *(inf)* bicho
cremate [krɪ'meɪt] VT incinerar
cremation [krɪ'meɪʃən] N incineración *f*, cremación *f*
crematorium [krɛmə'tɔːrɪəm] *(pl* **crematoria** [krɛmə'tɔːrɪə]*)* N crematorio
creosote ['krɪəsəʊt] N creosota
crêpe [kreɪp] N *(fabric)* crespón *m*; *(also:* **crêpe rubber**) crep(é) *m*
crêpe bandage N *(BRIT)* venda elástica
crêpe paper N papel *m* crep(é)
crêpe sole N *(on shoes)* suela de crep(é)
crept [krɛpt] PT, PP *of* **creep**
crescent ['krɛsnt] N media luna; *(street)* calle *f (en forma de semicírculo)*
cress [krɛs] N berro

crest [krɛst] N (of bird) cresta; (of hill) cima, cumbre f; (of helmet) cimera; (of coat of arms) blasón m

crestfallen ['krɛstfɔːlən] ADJ alicaído

Crete [kriːt] N Creta

cretin ['krɛtɪn] N cretino(-a)

crevasse [krɪ'væs] N grieta

crevice ['krɛvɪs] N grieta, hendedura

crew [kruː] N (of ship etc) tripulación f; (Cine etc) equipo; (gang) pandilla, banda; (Mil) dotación f

crew-cut ['kruːkʌt] N corte m al rape

crew-neck ['kruːnɛk] N cuello a la caja

crib [krɪb] N cuna ▶ VT (inf) plagiar; (Scol) copiar

crick [krɪk] N: ~ **in the neck** tortícolis f inv

cricket ['krɪkɪt] N (insect) grillo; (game) críquet m

cricketer ['krɪkɪtəʳ] N jugador(a) m/f de críquet

crime [kraɪm] N crimen m; (less serious) delito

crime wave N ola de crímenes or delitos

criminal ['krɪmɪnl] N criminal mf, delincuente mf ▶ ADJ criminal; (law) penal

Criminal Investigation Department N ≈ Brigada de Investigación Criminal f (SP)

crimp [krɪmp] VT (hair) rizar

crimson ['krɪmzn] ADJ carmesí

cringe [krɪndʒ] VI encogerse

crinkle ['krɪŋkl] VT arrugar

crinkly ['krɪŋklɪ] ADJ (hair) rizado, crespo

cripple ['krɪpl] N lisiado(-a), cojo(-a) ▶ VT lisiar, mutilar; (ship, plane) inutilizar; (production, exports) paralizar; **crippled with arthritis** paralizado por la artritis

crippling ['krɪplɪŋ] ADJ (injury etc) debilitador(a); (prices, taxes) devastador(a)

crisis ['kraɪsɪs] (pl **crises** ['kraɪsiːz]) N crisis f

crisp [krɪsp] ADJ fresco; (toast, snow) crujiente; (manner) seco

crisps [krɪsps] NPL (BRIT) patatas fpl fritas (chips)

crispy ADJ crujiente

crisscross ['krɪskrɔs] ADJ entrelazado, entrecruzado ▶ VT entrecruzar(se)

criterion [kraɪ'tɪərɪən] (pl **criteria** [kraɪ'tɪərɪə]) N criterio

critic ['krɪtɪk] N crítico(-a)

critical ['krɪtɪkl] ADJ (gen) crítico; (illness) grave; **to be ~ of sb/sth** criticar a algn/algo

critically ['krɪtɪklɪ] ADV (speak etc) en tono crítico; (ill) gravemente

criticism ['krɪtɪsɪzm] N crítica

criticize ['krɪtɪsaɪz] VT criticar

critique [krɪ'tiːk] N crítica

croak [krəuk] VI (frog) croar; (raven) graznar ▶ N (of raven) graznido

Croat ['krəuæt] ADJ, N = **Croatian**

Croatia [krəu'eɪʃə] N Croacia

Croatian [krəu'eɪʃən] ADJ, N croata mf ▶ N (Ling) croata m

crochet ['krəuʃeɪ] N ganchillo

crock [krɔk] N cántaro; (inf: person: also: **old crock**) carcamal mf, vejestorio; (: car etc) cacharro

crockery ['krɔkərɪ] N (plates, cups etc) loza, vajilla

crocodile ['krɔkədaɪl] N cocodrilo

crocus ['krəukəs] N crocus m, croco

croft [krɔft] N granja pequeña

crofter ['krɔftəʳ] N pequeño granjero

croissant ['krwasã] N croissant m, medialuna (esp LAM)

crone [krəun] N arpía, bruja

crony ['krəunɪ] N compinche mf

crook [kruk] N (inf) ladrón(-ona) m/f; (of shepherd) cayado; (of arm) pliegue m

crooked ['krukɪd] ADJ torcido; (path) tortuoso; (inf) corrupto

crop [krɔp] N (produce) cultivo; (amount produced) cosecha; (riding crop) látigo de montar; (of bird) buche m ▶ VT cortar, recortar; (animals: grass) pacer
▶ **crop up** VI surgir, presentarse

crop spraying [-'spreɪɪŋ] N fumigación f de los cultivos

croquet ['krəukeɪ] N croquet m

croquette [krə'kɛt] N croqueta (de patata)

cross [krɔs] N cruz f ▶ VT (street etc) cruzar, atravesar; (thwart: person) contrariar, ir contra ▶ VI: **the boat crosses from Santander to Plymouth** el barco hace la travesía de Santander a Plymouth ▶ ADJ de mal humor, enojado; **it's a ~ between geography and sociology** es una mezcla de geografía y sociología; **to ~ o.s.** santiguarse; **they've got their lines crossed** (fig) hay un malentendido entre ellos; **to be/get ~ with sb (about sth)** estar enfadado/enfadarse con algn (por algo)
▶ **cross off** VT tachar
▶ **cross out** VT tachar
▶ **cross over** VI cruzar

crossbar ['krɔsbɑːʳ] N travesaño; (of bicycle) barra

crossbow ['krɔsbəu] N ballesta

cross-Channel ferry ['krɔs'tʃænl-] N transbordador m que cruza el Canal de la Mancha

cross-check ['krɔstʃɛk] N verificación f ▶ VT verificar

cross-country ['krɔs'kʌntrɪ], **cross-country race** N carrera a campo traviesa, cross m

cross-dressing [krɔs'drɛsɪŋ] N travestismo

cross-examination ['krɔsɪgzæmɪ'neɪʃən] N interrogatorio

cross-examine ['krɔsɪg'zæmɪn] VT interrogar

cross-eyed [ˈkrɔsaɪd] ADJ bizco
crossfire [ˈkrɔsfaɪəʳ] N fuego cruzado
crossing [ˈkrɔsɪŋ] N (on road) cruce m; (Rail) paso a nivel; (sea passage) travesía; (also: **pedestrian crossing**) paso de peatones
crossing guard N (US) persona encargada de ayudar a los niños a cruzar la calle
crossing point N paso; (at border) paso fronterizo
cross purposes NPL: **to be at ~ with sb** tener un malentendido con algn
cross-question [ˈkrɔsˈkwestʃən] VT interrogar
cross-reference [ˈkrɔsˈrɛfrəns] N remisión f
crossroads [ˈkrɔsrəudz] NSG cruce m; (fig) encrucijada
cross section N corte m transversal; (of population) muestra (representativa)
crosswalk [ˈkrɔswɔːk] N (US) paso de peatones
crosswind [ˈkrɔswɪnd] N viento de costado
crossword [ˈkrɔswəːd] N crucigrama m
crotch [krɔtʃ] N (of garment) entrepierna
crotchet [ˈkrɔtʃɪt] N (Brit Mus) negra
crotchety [ˈkrɔtʃɪtɪ] ADJ (person) arisco
crouch [krautʃ] VI agacharse, acurrucarse
croup [kruːp] N (Med) crup m
croupier [ˈkruːpɪə] N crupier mf
crouton [ˈkruːtɔn] N cubito de pan frito
crow [krəu] N (bird) cuervo; (of cock) canto, cacareo ▶ VI (cock) cantar; (fig) jactarse
crowbar [ˈkrəubaːʳ] N palanca
crowd [kraud] N muchedumbre f; (Sport) público; (common herd) vulgo ▶ VT (gather) amontonar; (fill) llenar ▶ VI (gather) reunirse; (pile up) amontonarse; **crowds of people** gran cantidad de gente
crowded [ˈkraudɪd] ADJ (full) atestado; (well-attended) concurrido; (densely populated) superpoblado
crowd scene N (Cine, Theat) escena con muchos comparsas
crowdsource [ˈkraudsɔːs] VT aplicar el crowdsourcing en, aplicar la tercerización masiva en
crowdsourcing [ˈkraudsɔːsɪŋ] N crowdsourcing m, tercerización f masiva
crown [kraun] N corona; (of head) coronilla; (of hat) copa; (of hill) cumbre f; (for tooth) funda ▶ VT (also tooth) coronar; **and to ~ it all …** (fig) y para colmo or remate …
crown court N (Law) tribunal m superior; ver nota

En el sistema legal inglés los delitos graves como asesinato, violación o atraco son juzgados por un jurado en un tribunal superior llamado *crown court* con sede en noventa ciudades. Los jueces de paz ("*Justice of the Peace*") juzgan delitos

menores e infracciones de la ley en juzgados llamados "*Magistrates' Courts*". Es el juez de paz quien decide remitir los casos pertinentes a la *crown court*, que en caso de recursos se remite al tribunal de apelación, "*Court of Appeal*".

crowning [ˈkraunɪŋ] ADJ (achievement, glory) máximo
crown jewels NPL joyas fpl reales
crown prince N príncipe m heredero
crow's feet [ˈkrəuziːt] NPL patas fpl de gallo
crucial [ˈkruːʃl] ADJ crucial, decisivo; **his approval is ~ to the success of the project** su aprobación es crucial para el éxito del proyecto
crucifix [ˈkruːsɪfɪks] N crucifijo
crucifixion [kruːsɪˈfɪkʃən] N crucifixión f
crucify [ˈkruːsɪfaɪ] VT crucificar; (fig) martirizar
crude [kruːd] ADJ (materials) bruto; (fig: basic) tosco; (: vulgar) ordinario ▶ N (also: **crude oil**) (petróleo) crudo
crude oil N petróleo crudo
cruel [ˈkruəl] ADJ cruel
cruelty [ˈkruəltɪ] N crueldad f
cruet [ˈkruːɪt] N vinagreras fpl
cruise [kruːz] N crucero ▶ VI (ship) navegar; (holidaymakers) hacer un crucero; (car) ir a velocidad constante
cruise missile N misil m de crucero
cruiser [ˈkruːzəʳ] N crucero
cruising speed [ˈkruːzɪŋ-] N velocidad f de crucero
crumb [krʌm] N miga, migaja
crumble [ˈkrʌmbl] VT desmenuzar ▶ VI (gen) desmenuzarse; (building) desmoronarse
crumbly [ˈkrʌmblɪ] ADJ desmenuzable
crummy [ˈkrʌmɪ] ADJ (inf: poor quality) pésimo, cutre (SP); (: unwell) fatal
crumpet [ˈkrʌmpɪt] N ≈ bollo para tostar
crumple [ˈkrʌmpl] VT (paper) estrujar; (material) arrugar
crunch [krʌntʃ] VT (with teeth) mascar; (underfoot) hacer crujir ▶ N (fig) hora de la verdad
crunchy [ˈkrʌntʃɪ] ADJ crujiente
crusade [kruːˈseɪd] N cruzada ▶ VI: **to ~ for/ against** (fig) hacer una campaña en pro de/ en contra de
crusader [kruːˈseɪdəʳ] N (fig) paladín mf
crush [krʌʃ] N (crowd) aglomeración f ▶ VT (gen) aplastar; (paper) estrujar; (cloth) arrugar; (grind, break up: garlic, ice) picar; (: fruit) exprimir; (: grapes) exprimir, prensar; (: opposition) aplastar; (: hopes) destruir; **to have a ~ on sb** estar enamorado de algn
crush barrier N barrera de seguridad
crushing [ˈkrʌʃɪŋ] ADJ aplastante; (burden) agobiante

501

crust [krʌst] N corteza
crustacean [krʌsˈteɪʃən] N crustáceo
crusty [ˈkrʌstɪ] ADJ (bread) crujiente; (person) de mal carácter; (remark) brusco
crutch [krʌtʃ] N (Med) muleta; (support) apoyo
crux [krʌks] N: **the ~** lo esencial, el quid
cry [kraɪ] VI llorar; (shout: also: **cry out**) gritar
▶ N grito; (of animal) aullido; (weep): **she had a good ~** lloró a lágrima viva; **what are you crying about?** ¿por qué lloras?; **to ~ for help** pedir socorro a voces; **it's a far ~ from …** (fig) dista mucho de …
▶ **cry off** VI retirarse
▶ **cry out** VI (call out, shout) lanzar un grito, echar un grito ▶ VT gritar
crypt [krɪpt] N cripta
cryptic [ˈkrɪptɪk] ADJ enigmático
crystal [ˈkrɪstl] N cristal m
crystal-clear [ˈkrɪstlˈklɪər] ADJ claro como el agua; (fig) cristalino
crystallize [ˈkrɪstəlaɪz] VT (fig) cristalizar ▶ VI cristalizarse; **crystallized fruits** frutas fpl escarchadas
CSA N ABBR = **Confederate States of America**; (= Child Support Agency) organismo que supervisa el pago de la pensión a hijos de padres separados
CSC N ABBR (= Civil Service Commission) comisión para la contratación de funcionarios
CS gas N (BRIT) gas m lacrimógeno
CST N ABBR (US: = Central Standard Time) huso horario
CT, Ct. ABBR (US) = **Connecticut**
ct ABBR = **cent**; **court**; **carat**
CTC N ABBR (BRIT: = city technology college) ≈ centro de formación profesional
cu. ABBR = **cubic**
cub [kʌb] N cachorro; (also: **cub scout**) niño explorador
Cuba [ˈkjuːbə] N Cuba
Cuban [ˈkjuːbən] ADJ, N cubano(-a) m/f
cubbyhole [ˈkʌbɪhəul] N cuchitril m
cube [kjuːb] N cubo; (of sugar) terrón m ▶ VT (Math) elevar al cubo
cube root N raíz f cúbica
cubic [ˈkjuːbɪk] ADJ cúbico; **~ capacity** (Aut) capacidad f cúbica
cubicle [ˈkjuːbɪkl] N (at pool) caseta; (for bed) cubículo
cubism [ˈkjuːbɪzəm] N cubismo
cuckoo [ˈkukuː] N cuco
cuckoo clock N reloj m de cuco
cucumber [ˈkjuːkʌmbər] N pepino
cuddle [ˈkʌdl] VT abrazar ▶ VI abrazarse
cuddly [ˈkʌdlɪ] ADJ mimoso; (toy) de peluche
cudgel [ˈkʌdʒəl] VT: **to ~ one's brains** devanarse los sesos
cue [kjuː] N (snooker cue) taco; (Theat etc) entrada

cuff [kʌf] N (BRIT: of shirt, coat etc) puño; (US: of trousers) vuelta; (blow) bofetada ▶ VT bofetear; **off the ~** adv improvisado
cufflinks [ˈkʌflɪŋks] NPL gemelos mpl
cu. ft. ABBR = **cubic feet**
cu. in. ABBR = **cubic inches**
cuisine [kwɪˈziːn] N cocina
cul-de-sac [ˈkʌldəsæk] N callejón m sin salida
culinary [ˈkʌlɪnərɪ] ADJ culinario
cull [kʌl] VT (select) entresacar; (kill selectively: animals) matar selectivamente ▶ N matanza selectiva; **seal ~** matanza selectiva de focas
culminate [ˈkʌlmɪneɪt] VI: **to ~ in** culminar en
culmination [kʌlmɪˈneɪʃən] N culminación f, colmo
culottes [kuːˈlɔts] NPL falda f pantalón
culpable [ˈkʌlpəbl] ADJ culpable
culprit [ˈkʌlprɪt] N culpable mf
cult [kʌlt] N culto; **a ~ figure** un ídolo
cultivate [ˈkʌltɪveɪt] VT (also fig) cultivar
cultivated [ˈkʌltɪveɪtɪd] ADJ culto
cultivation [kʌltɪˈveɪʃən] N cultivo; (fig) cultura
cultural [ˈkʌltʃərəl] ADJ cultural
culture [ˈkʌltʃər] N (also fig) cultura; (Biol) cultivo
cultured [ˈkʌltʃəd] ADJ culto
cumbersome [ˈkʌmbəsəm] ADJ voluminoso
cumin [ˈkʌmɪn] N (spice) comino
cummerbund [ˈkʌməbʌnd] N faja, fajín m
cumulative [ˈkjuːmjulətɪv] ADJ cumulativo
cunning [ˈkʌnɪŋ] N astucia ▶ ADJ astuto; (clever: device, idea) ingenioso
cunt [kʌnt] N (inf!) coño (!); (insult) mamonazo(-a) (!)
cup [kʌp] N taza; (prize, event) copa; **a ~ of tea** una taza de té
cupboard [ˈkʌbəd] N armario, placar(d) m (LAM); (in kitchen) alacena
cup final N (Football) final f de copa
cupful [ˈkʌpful] N taza
Cupid [ˈkjuːpɪd] N Cupido
cupola [ˈkjuːpələ] N cúpula
cuppa [ˈkʌpə] N (BRIT inf) (taza de) té m
cup-tie [ˈkʌptaɪ] N (BRIT) partido de copa
cur [kəːr] N perro de mala raza; (person) canalla m
curable [ˈkjuərəbl] ADJ curable
curate [ˈkjuərɪt] N coadjutor m
curator [kjuəˈreɪtər] N director(a) m/f
curb [kəːb] VT refrenar; (powers, spending) limitar ▶ N freno; (US: kerb) bordillo
curd cheese [kəːd-] N requesón m
curdle [ˈkəːdl] VI cuajarse
curds [kəːdz] NPL requesón msg
cure [kjuər] VT curar ▶ N cura, curación f; (fig: solution) remedio; **to be cured of sth** curarse de algo; **to take a ~** tomar un remedio

cure-all ['kjuərɔːl] N (*also fig*) panacea
curfew ['kəːfjuː] N toque *m* de queda
curio ['kjuərɪəu] N curiosidad *f*
curiosity [kjuərɪ'ɔsɪtɪ] N curiosidad *f*
curious ['kjuərɪəs] ADJ curioso; **I'm ~ about him** me intriga
curiously ['kjuərɪəslɪ] ADV curiosamente;
~ enough, ... aunque parezca extraño ...
curl [kəːl] N rizo; (*of smoke etc*) espiral *f*, voluta
  ▶ VT (*hair*) rizar; (*paper*) arrollar; (*lip*) fruncir
  ▶ VI rizarse; arrollarse
  ▶ **curl up** VI arrollarse; (*person*) hacerse un ovillo; (*inf*) morirse de risa
curler ['kəːləʳ] N bigudí *m*, rulo
curlew ['kəːluː] N zarapito
curling tongs, (US) **curling irons** ['kəːlɪŋ-] NPL tenacillas *fpl*
curly ['kəːlɪ] ADJ rizado
currant ['kʌrnt] N pasa; (*black, red*) grosella
currency ['kʌrnsɪ] N moneda; **to gain ~** (*fig*) difundirse
current ['kʌrnt] N corriente *f* ▶ ADJ actual; **direct/alternating ~** corriente directa/alterna; **the ~ issue of a magazine** el último número de una revista; **in ~ use** de uso corriente
current account N (BRIT) cuenta corriente
current affairs NPL (noticias *fpl* de) actualidad *f*
current assets NPL (*Comm*) activo disponible
current liabilities NPL (*Comm*) pasivo circulante
currently ['kʌrntlɪ] ADV actualmente
curriculum [kə'rɪkjuləm] (*pl* **curriculums** or **curricula** [kə'rɪkjulə]) N plan *m* de estudios
curriculum vitae [-'viːtaɪ] N currículum *m* (vitae)
curry ['kʌrɪ] N curry *m* ▶ VT: **to ~ favour with** buscar el favor de
curry powder N curry *m* en polvo
curse [kəːs] VI echar pestes, soltar palabrotas
  ▶ VT maldecir ▶ N maldición *f*; (*swearword*) palabrota, taco
cursor ['kəːsəʳ] N (*Comput*) cursor *m*
cursory ['kəːsərɪ] ADJ rápido, superficial
curt [kəːt] ADJ seco
curtail [kəː'teɪl] VT (*cut short*) acortar; (*restrict*) restringir
curtain ['kəːtn] N cortina; (*Theat*) telón *m*; **to draw the curtains** (*together*) cerrar las cortinas; (*apart*) abrir las cortinas
curtain call N (*Theat*) llamada a escena
curtain ring N anilla
curtsey, curtsy ['kəːtsɪ] N reverencia ▶ VI hacer una reverencia
curve [kəːv] N curva ▶ VI (*road*) hacer una curva; (*line etc*) curvarse
curved [kəːvd] ADJ curvo
cushion ['kuʃən] N cojín *m*; (*Snooker*) banda

  ▶ VT (*seat*) acolchar; (*shock*) amortiguar
cushy ['kuʃɪ] ADJ (*inf*): **a ~ job** un chollo; **to have a ~ time** tener la vida arreglada
custard ['kʌstəd] N (*for pouring*) natillas *fpl*
custard powder N polvos *mpl* para natillas
custodial sentence [kʌs'təudɪəl-] N pena de prisión
custodian [kʌs'təudɪən] N guardián(-ana) *m/f*; (*of museum etc*) conservador(a) *m/f*
custody ['kʌstədɪ] N custodia; **to take sb into ~** detener a algn; **in the ~ of** al cuidado *or* cargo de
custom ['kʌstəm] N costumbre *f*; (*Comm*) clientela; *see also* **customs**
customary ['kʌstəmərɪ] ADJ acostumbrado; **it is ~ to do** ... es la costumbre hacer ...
custom-built ['kʌstəm'bɪlt] ADJ = **custom-made**
customer ['kʌstəməʳ] N cliente *mf*; **he's an awkward ~** (*inf*) es un tipo difícil
customer profile N perfil *m* del cliente
customize ['kʌstəmaɪz] VT personalizar
customized ['kʌstəmaɪzd] ADJ (*car etc*) hecho a encargo
custom-made ['kʌstəm'meɪd] ADJ hecho a la medida
customs ['kʌstəmz] NPL aduana *sg*; **to go through (the) ~** pasar la aduana
Customs and Excise N (BRIT) Aduanas *fpl* y Arbitrios
customs officer N aduanero(-a), funcionario(-a) de aduanas
cut [kʌt] (*pt, pp* **~**) VT cortar; (*price*) rebajar; (*record*) grabar; (*reduce*) reducir; (*inf: avoid: class, lecture*) fumarse, faltar a ▶ VI cortar; (*intersect*) cruzarse ▶ N corte *m*; (*in skin*) corte, cortadura; (*with sword*) tajo; (*of knife*) cuchillada; (*in salary etc*) rebaja; (*in spending*) reducción *f*, recorte *m*; (*slice of meat*) tajada; **to ~ one's finger** cortarse un dedo; **to get one's hair ~** cortarse el pelo; **to ~ and paste** (*Comput*) cortar y pegar; **to ~ sb dead** negarle el saludo *or* cortarle (LAM) a algn; **it cuts both ways** (*fig*) tiene doble filo; **to ~ a tooth** echar un diente; **power ~** (BRIT) apagón *m*
  ▶ **cut back** VT (*plants*) podar; (*production, expenditure*) reducir
  ▶ **cut down** VT (*tree*) cortar, derribar; (*consumption, expenses*) reducir; **to ~ sb down to size** (*fig*) bajarle los humos a algn
  ▶ **cut in** VI: **to ~ in (on)** (*interrupt: conversation*) interrumpir, intervenir (en); (*Aut*) cerrar el paso (a)
  ▶ **cut off** VT cortar; (*fig*) aislar; (*troops*) cercar; **we've been ~ off** (*Tel*) nos han cortado la comunicación
  ▶ **cut out** VT (*shape*) recortar; (*delete*) suprimir
  ▶ **cut up** VT cortar (en pedazos); (*chop: food*) trinchar, cortar

cut-and-dried ['kʌtən'draɪd], **cut-and-dry** ['kʌtən'draɪ] ADJ arreglado de antemano, seguro

cutback ['kʌtbæk] N reducción f

cute [kjuːt] ADJ lindo, mono; (shrewd) listo

cuticle ['kjuːtɪkl] N cutícula

cutlery ['kʌtlərɪ] N cubiertos mpl

cutlet ['kʌtlɪt] N chuleta

cutoff ['kʌtɔf] N (also: **cutoff point**) límite m

cutout ['kʌtaut] N (cardboard cutout) recortable m

cut-price ['kʌt'praɪs], (US) **cut-rate** ['kʌt'reɪt] ADJ a precio reducido

cutthroat ['kʌtθrəut] N asesino(-a) ▸ ADJ feroz; ~ **competition** competencia encarnizada or despiadada

cutting ['kʌtɪŋ] ADJ (gen) cortante; (remark) mordaz ▸ N (BRIT: from newspaper) recorte m; (from plant) esqueje m; (BRIT Rail) desmonte m; (Cine) montaje m

cutting edge N (of knife) filo; (fig) vanguardia; **a country on** or **at the ~ of space technology** un país puntero en tecnología del espacio

cutting-edge [kʌtɪŋ'ɛdʒ] ADJ punta, de vanguardia

CV N ABBR = **curriculum vitae**

cwo ABBR (Comm) = **cash with order**

cwt. ABBR = **hundredweight**

cyanide ['saɪənaɪd] N cianuro

cyber attack ['saɪbərətæk] N ciberataque m

cyberbullying ['saɪbəbulɪŋ] N ciberacoso

cybercafé ['saɪbə͵kæfeɪ] N cibercafé m

cybernetics [saɪbə'nɛtɪks] NSG cibernética

cybersecurity [saɪbəsɪ'kjuərɪtɪ] N ciberseguridad f, seguridad f cibernética

cyberspace ['saɪbəspeɪs] N ciberespacio

cyberterrorism ['saɪbətɛrərɪzəm] N ciberterrorismo m

cyclamen ['sɪkləmən] N ciclamen m

cycle ['saɪkl] N ciclo; (bicycle) bicicleta ▸ VI ir en bicicleta

cycle hire N alquiler m de bicicletas

cycle lane N carril m de bicicleta, carril m bici

cycle path N carril-bici m

cycle race N carrera ciclista

cycle rack N soporte m para bicicletas

cycling ['saɪklɪŋ] N ciclismo

cycling holiday N vacaciones fpl en bicicleta

cyclist ['saɪklɪst] N ciclista mf

cyclone ['saɪkləun] N ciclón m

cygnet ['sɪgnɪt] N pollo de cisne

cylinder ['sɪlɪndəʳ] N cilindro

cylinder block N bloque m de cilindros

cylinder head N culata de cilindro

cylinder-head gasket N junta de culata

cymbals ['sɪmblz] NPL platillos mpl, címbalos mpl

cynic ['sɪnɪk] N cínico(-a)

cynical ['sɪnɪkl] ADJ cínico

cynicism ['sɪnɪsɪzəm] N cinismo

cypress ['saɪprɪs] N ciprés m

Cypriot ['sɪprɪət] ADJ, N chipriota mf

Cyprus ['saɪprəs] N Chipre f

cyst [sɪst] N quiste m

cystitis [sɪs'taɪtɪs] N cistitis f

CZ N ABBR (US: = Canal Zone) zona del Canal de Panamá

czar [zɑːʳ] N zar m

czarina [zɑː'riːnə] N zarina

Czech [tʃɛk] ADJ checo ▸ N checo(-a); (Ling) checo; **the ~ Republic** la República Checa

Czechoslovak [tʃɛkə'sləuvæk] ADJ, N (History) = **Czechoslovakian**

Czechoslovakia [tʃɛkəslə'vækɪə] N (History) Checoslovaquia

Czechoslovakian [tʃɛkəslə'vækɪən] ADJ, N (History) checoslovaco(-a) m/f

Dd

D, d [di:] N (*letter*) D, d; (*Mus*): **D** re *m*; **D for David**, (*US*) **D for Dog** D de Dolores

D ABBR (*US Pol*) = **democrat; democratic**

d ABBR (*BRIT old*) = **penny**

d. ABBR = **died**

DA N ABBR (*US*) = **district attorney**

dab [dæb] VT: **to ~ ointment onto a wound** aplicar pomada sobre una herida; **to ~ with paint** dar unos toques de pintura ▶ N (*light stroke*) toque *m*; (*small amount*) pizca

dabble ['dæbl] VI: **to ~ in** hacer por afición

Dacca ['dækə] N Dacca

dachshund ['dækshund] N perro tejonero

Dacron® ['deɪkrɒn] N (*US*) terylene *m*

dad [dæd], **daddy** ['dædɪ] N papá *m*

daddy-long-legs [dædɪ'lɒŋlɛgz] N típula

daffodil ['dæfədɪl] N narciso

daft [dɑ:ft] ADJ tonto

dagger ['dægəʳ] N puñal *m*, daga; **to look daggers at sb** fulminar a algn con la mirada

dahlia ['deɪljə] N dalia

daily ['deɪlɪ] ADJ diario, cotidiano ▶ N (*paper*) diario; (*domestic help*) asistenta ▶ ADV todos los días, cada día; **twice ~** dos veces al día

dainty ['deɪntɪ] ADJ delicado, (*tasteful*) elegante

dairy ['dɛərɪ] N (*shop*) lechería; (*on farm*) vaquería; (*products*) lácteos *pl* ▶ ADJ (*cow etc*) lechero

dairy cow N vaca lechera

dairy farm N vaquería

dairy produce N productos *mpl* lácteos

dais ['deɪɪs] N estrado

daisy ['deɪzɪ] N margarita

dale [deɪl] N valle *m*

dally ['dælɪ] VI entretenerse

Dalmatian [dæl'meɪʃən] N (*dog*) (perro) dálmata *m*

dam [dæm] N presa; (*reservoir*) embalse ▶ VT embalsar

damage ['dæmɪdʒ] N daño; (*fig*) perjuicio; (*to machine*) avería ▶ VT dañar; perjudicar; averiar; **~ to property** daños materiales; **damages** NPL (*Law*) daños y perjuicios;

to pay £5000 in damages pagar £5000 por daños y perjuicios

damaging ['dæmɪdʒɪŋ] ADJ: **~ (to)** perjudicial (a)

Damascus [də'mɑːskəs] N Damasco

dame [deɪm] N (*title*) dama; (*US inf*) tía; (*Theat*) vieja; *see also* **pantomime**

damn [dæm] VT condenar; (*curse*) maldecir ▶ N (*inf*): **I don't give a ~** me importa un pito ▶ ADJ (*inf: also*: **damned**) maldito, fregado (*LAM*); **~ (it)!** ¡maldito sea!

damnable ['dæmnəbl] ADJ (*inf: behaviour*) detestable; (*weather*) horrible

damnation [dæm'neɪʃən] N (*Rel*) condenación *f* ▶ EXCL (*inf*) ¡maldición!, ¡maldito sea!

damning ['dæmɪŋ] ADJ (*evidence*) irrecusable

damp [dæmp] ADJ húmedo, mojado ▶ N humedad *f* ▶ VT (*also*: **dampen**: *cloth, rag*) mojar; (: *enthusiasm*) enfriar

dampcourse ['dæmpkɔːs] N aislante *m* hidrófugo

damper ['dæmpəʳ] N (*Mus*) sordina; (*of fire*) regulador *m* de tiro; **to put a ~ on things** ser un jarro de agua fría

dampness ['dæmpnɪs] N humedad *f*

damson ['dæmzən] N ciruela damascena

dance [dɑːns] N baile *m* ▶ VI bailar; **to ~ about** saltar

dance floor N pista *f* de baile

dance hall N salón *m* de baile

dancer ['dɑːnsəʳ] N bailador(a) *m/f*; (*professional*) bailarín(-ina) *m/f*

dancing ['dɑːnsɪŋ] N baile *m*

D and C N ABBR (*Med*: = *dilation and curettage*) raspado

dandelion ['dændɪlaɪən] N diente *m* de león

dandruff ['dændrəf] N caspa

D & T (*BRIT Scol*) N ABBR (= *design and technology*) diseño y pretecnología

dandy ['dændɪ] N dandi *m* ▶ ADJ (*US inf*) estupendo

Dane [deɪn] N danés(-esa) *m/f*

danger ['deɪndʒə'] N peligro; (*risk*) riesgo; ~! (*on sign*) ¡peligro!; **to be in ~ of** correr riesgo de; **out of ~** fuera de peligro

danger list N (*Med*): **to be on the ~** estar grave

dangerous ['deɪndʒərəs] ADJ peligroso

dangerously ['deɪndʒərəslɪ] ADV peligrosamente; **~ ill** gravemente enfermo

danger zone N área *or* zona de peligro

dangle ['dæŋgl] VT colgar ▶ VI pender, estar colgado

Danish ['deɪnɪʃ] ADJ danés(-esa) ▶ N (*Ling*) danés *m*

Danish pastry N pastel *m* de almendra

dank [dæŋk] ADJ húmedo y malsano

dapper ['dæpə'] ADJ pulcro, apuesto

Dardanelles [dɑːdə'nɛlz] NPL Dardanelos *mpl*

dare [dɛə'] VT: **to ~ sb to do** desafiar a algn a hacer ▶ VI: **to ~ (to) do sth** atreverse a hacer algo; **I ~ say** (*I suppose*) puede ser, a lo mejor; **I ~ say he'll turn up** puede ser que *or* quizás venga; **I daren't tell him** no me atrevo a decírselo

daredevil ['dɛədɛvl] N temerario(-a), atrevido(-a)

Dar-es-Salaam ['dɑːrɛssə'lɑːm] N Dar es Salaam *m*

daring ['dɛərɪŋ] ADJ (*person*) osado; (*plan, escape*) atrevido ▶ N atrevimiento, osadía

dark [dɑːk] ADJ oscuro; (*hair, complexion*) moreno; (*fig: cheerless*) triste, sombrío ▶ N (*gen*) oscuridad *f*; (*night*) tinieblas *fpl*; **~ chocolate** chocolate *m* amargo; **in the ~** a oscuras; **it is/is getting ~** es de noche/está oscureciendo; **in the ~ about** (*fig*) ignorante de; **after ~** después del anochecer

darken ['dɑːkn] VT oscurecer; (*colour*) hacer más oscuro ▶ VI oscurecerse; (*cloud over*) nublarse

dark glasses NPL gafas *fpl* oscuras

dark horse N (*fig*) incógnita

darkly ['dɑːklɪ] ADV (*gloomily*) tristemente; (*sinisterly*) siniestramente

darkness ['dɑːknɪs] N (*in room*) oscuridad *f*; (*night*) tinieblas *fpl*

darkroom ['dɑːkrum] N cuarto oscuro

darling ['dɑːlɪŋ] ADJ, N querido(-a) *m/f*

darn [dɑːn] VT zurcir

dart [dɑːt] N dardo; (*in sewing*) pinza ▶ VI precipitarse; **to ~ away/along** salir/marchar disparado

dartboard ['dɑːtbɔːd] N diana

darts [dɑːts] N dardos *mpl*

dash [dæʃ] N (*small quantity: of liquid*) gota, chorrito; (*: of solid*) pizca; (*sign*) guión *m*; (*: long*) raya ▶ VT (*break*) romper, estrellar; (*hopes*) defraudar ▶ VI precipitarse, ir de prisa; **a ~ of soda** un poco *or* chorrito de sifón *or* soda

▶ **dash away, dash off** VI marcharse apresuradamente

dashboard ['dæʃbɔːd] N (*Aut*) salpicadero

dashing ['dæʃɪŋ] ADJ gallardo

dastardly ['dæstədlɪ] ADJ ruin, vil

DAT N ABBR (= *digital audio tape*) cas(s)et(t)e *m or f* digital

data ['deɪtə] NPL datos *mpl*

database ['deɪtəbeɪs] N base *f* de datos

data capture N recogida de datos

data link N enlace *m* de datos

data processing N proceso *or* procesamiento de datos

data transmission N transmisión *f* de datos

date [deɪt] N (*day*) fecha; (*with friend*) cita; (*fruit*) dátil *m* ▶ VT fechar; (*inf: girl etc*) salir con; **what's the ~ today?** ¿qué fecha es hoy?; **~ of birth** fecha de nacimiento; **closing ~** fecha tope; **to ~** *adv* hasta la fecha; **out of ~** pasado de moda; **up to ~** moderno; puesto al día; **to bring up to ~** (*correspondence, information*) poner al día; (*method*) actualizar; **to bring sb up to ~** poner a algn al corriente; **letter dated 5th July** *or* (*US*) **July 5th** carta fechada el 5 de julio

dated ['deɪtɪd] ADJ anticuado

date rape N *violación ocurrida durante una cita con un conocido*

date stamp N matasellos *m inv*; (*on fresh foods*) sello de fecha

dative ['deɪtɪv] N dativo

daub [dɔːb] VT embadurnar

daughter ['dɔːtə'] N hija

daughter-in-law ['dɔːtərɪnlɔː] N nuera, hija política

daunting ['dɔːntɪŋ] ADJ desalentador(-a)

davenport ['dævnpɔːt] N escritorio; (*US: sofa*) sofá *m*

dawdle ['dɔːdl] VI (*waste time*) perder el tiempo; (*go slowly*) andar muy despacio; **to ~ over one's work** trabajar muy despacio

dawn [dɔːn] N alba, amanecer *m*; (*fig*) nacimiento ▶ VI amanecer; (*fig*): **it dawned on him that ...** cayó en la cuenta de que ...; **at ~** al amanecer; **from ~ to dusk** de sol a sol

dawn chorus N canto de los pájaros al amanecer

day [deɪ] N día *m*; (*working day*) jornada; **the ~ before** el día anterior; **the ~ after tomorrow** pasado mañana; **the ~ before yesterday** anteayer, antes de ayer; **the ~ after, the following ~** el día siguiente; **by ~** de día; **~ by ~** día a día; **(on) the ~ that ...** el día que ...; **to work an eight-hour ~** trabajar ocho horas diarias *or* al día; **he works eight hours a ~** trabaja ocho horas al día; **paid by the ~** pagado por día; **these days, in the present ~** hoy en día

daybook ['deɪbuk] N (BRIT) diario or libro de entradas y salidas

daybreak ['deɪbreɪk] N amanecer m

day-care centre ['deɪkɛə-] N centro de día; (for children) guardería infantil

daydream ['deɪdri:m] N ensueño ▶ VI soñar despierto

daylight ['deɪlaɪt] N luz f (del día)

daylight robbery N: **it's ~!** (fig, inf) ¡es un robo descarado!

Daylight Saving Time N (US) hora de verano

day-release course [deɪrɪ'li:s-] N curso de formación de un día a la semana

day return, day return ticket N (BRIT) billete m de ida y vuelta (en un día)

day shift N turno de día

daytime ['deɪtaɪm] N día m

day-to-day ['deɪtə'deɪ] ADJ cotidiano, diario; (expenses) diario; **on a ~ basis** día por día

day trip N excursión f (de un día)

day tripper N excursionista mf

daze [deɪz] VT (stun) aturdir ▶ N: **in a ~** aturdido

dazed [deɪzd] ADJ aturdido

dazzle ['dæzl] VT deslumbrar

dazzling ['dæzlɪŋ] ADJ (light, smile) deslumbrante; (colour) fuerte

dB ABBR = **decibel**

DBS N ABBR (= direct broadcasting by satellite) transmisión vía satélite

DC ABBR (Elec) = **direct current**; (US) = **District of Columbia**

DCC® N ABBR (= digital compact cassette) cas(s)et(t)e m digital compacto

DD N ABBR (= Doctor of Divinity) título universitario ▶ ABBR = **direct debit**

dd. ABBR (Comm) = **delivered**

D-day ['di:deɪ] N (fig) día m clave

DDS N ABBR (US: = Doctor of Dental Science; Doctor of Dental Surgery) títulos universitarios

DDT N ABBR (= dichlorodiphenyl trichloroethane) DDT m

DE ABBR (US) = **Delaware**

DEA N ABBR (US: = Drug Enforcement Administration) brigada especial dedicada a la lucha contra el tráfico de estupefacientes

deacon ['di:kən] N diácono

dead [dɛd] ADJ muerto; (limb) dormido; (battery) agotado ▶ ADV (completely) totalmente; (exactly) justo; **he was ~ on arrival** ingresó cadáver; **to shoot sb ~** matar a algn a tiros; **~ tired** muerto (de cansancio); **to stop ~** parar en seco; **the line has gone ~** (Tel) se ha cortado la línea; **the ~** npl los muertos

dead beat ADJ: **to be ~** (inf) estar hecho polvo

deaden ['dɛdn] VT (blow, sound) amortiguar; (pain) calmar, aliviar

dead end N callejón m sin salida

dead-end ['dɛdɛnd] ADJ: **a ~ job** un trabajo sin porvenir

dead heat N (Sport) empate m

deadline ['dɛdlaɪn] N fecha tope; **to work to a ~** trabajar con una fecha tope

deadlock ['dɛdlɔk] N punto muerto

dead loss N (inf): **to be a ~** (person) ser un inútil; (thing) ser una birria

deadly ['dɛdlɪ] ADJ mortal, fatal; **~ dull** aburridísimo

deadly nightshade [-'naɪtʃeɪd] N belladona

deadpan ['dɛdpæn] ADJ sin expresión

Dead Sea N: **the ~** el Mar Muerto

dead season N (Tourism) temporada baja

deaf [dɛf] ADJ sordo; **to turn a ~ ear to sth** hacer oídos sordos a algo

deaf-aid ['dɛfeɪd] N audífono

deaf-and-dumb ['dɛfən'dʌm] ADJ (person) sordomudo; (alphabet) para sordomudos

deafen ['dɛfn] VT ensordecer

deafening ['dɛfnɪŋ] ADJ ensordecedor(-a)

deaf-mute ['dɛfmju:t] N sordomudo(-a)

deafness ['dɛfnɪs] N sordera

deal [di:l] N (agreement) pacto, convenio; (business) negocio, transacción f; (Cards) reparto ▶ VT (pt, pp **dealt**) (gen) dar; (card) repartir; **a great ~ (of)** bastante, mucho; **it's a ~!** (inf) ¡trato hecho!, ¡de acuerdo!; **to do a ~ with sb** hacer un trato con algn; **he got a bad/fair ~ from them** le trataron mal/bien
▶ **deal in** VT FUS tratar en, comerciar en
▶ **deal with** VT FUS (people) tratar con; (problem) ocuparse de; (subject) tratar de

dealer ['di:ləʳ] N comerciante mf; (Cards) mano f

dealership ['di:ləʃɪp] N concesionario

dealings ['di:lɪŋz] NPL (Comm) transacciones fpl; (relations) relaciones fpl

dealt [dɛlt] PT, PP of **deal**

dean [di:n] N (Rel) deán m; (Scol) decano(-a)

dear [dɪəʳ] ADJ querido; (expensive) caro ▶ N: **my ~** querido(-a); **~ me!** ¡Dios mío!; **D~ Sir/Madam** (in letter) Muy señor mío, Estimado señor/Estimada señora, De mi/nuestra (mayor) consideración (esp LAM); **D~ Mr/Mrs X** Estimado(-a) señor(a) X

dearly ['dɪəlɪ] ADV (love) mucho; (pay) caro

dearth [də:θ] N (of food, resources, money) escasez f

death [dɛθ] N muerte f

deathbed ['dɛθbɛd] N lecho de muerte

death certificate N partida de defunción

death duties NPL (BRIT) derechos mpl de sucesión

deathly ['dɛθlɪ] ADJ mortal; (silence) profundo

death penalty N pena de muerte

death rate N tasa de mortalidad

death row N: **to be on** ~ (US) estar condenado a muerte

death sentence N condena a muerte

death squad N escuadrón m de la muerte

death trap ['dɛθtræp] N lugar m (or vehículo etc) muy peligroso

deb [dɛb] N ABBR (inf) = **debutante**

debacle [deɪ'bɑːkl] N desastre m, catástrofe f

debar [dɪ'bɑːʳ] VT: **to ~ sb from doing** prohibir a algn hacer

debase [dɪ'beɪs] VT degradar

debatable [dɪ'beɪtəbl] ADJ discutible; **it is ~ whether ...** es discutible si ...

debate [dɪ'beɪt] N debate m ▶ VT discutir

debauched [dɪ'bɔːtʃt] ADJ vicioso

debauchery [dɪ'bɔːtʃərɪ] N libertinaje m

debenture [dɪ'bɛntʃəʳ] N (Comm) bono, obligación f

debenture capital N capital m hipotecario

debilitate [dɪ'bɪlɪteɪt] VT debilitar

debilitating [dɪ'bɪlɪteɪtɪŋ] ADJ (illness etc) debilitante

debit ['dɛbɪt] N debe m ▶ VT: **to ~ a sum to sb** or **to sb's account** cargar una suma en cuenta a algn

debit balance N saldo deudor or pasivo

debit card N tarjeta f de débito

debit note N nota de débito or cargo

debonair [dɛbə'nɛəʳ] ADJ jovial, cortés(-esa)

debrief [diː'briːf] VT hacer dar parte

debriefing [diː'briːfɪŋ] N relación f (de un informe)

debris ['dɛbriː] N escombros mpl

debt [dɛt] N deuda; **to be in ~** tener deudas; **debts of £5000** deudas de cinco mil libras; **bad ~** deuda incobrable

debt collector N cobrador(a) m/f de deudas

debtor ['dɛtəʳ] N deudor(a) m/f

debug ['diː'bʌg] VT (Comput) depurar, limpiar

debunk [diː'bʌŋk] VT (inf: theory) desprestigiar, desacreditar; (claim) desacreditar; (person, institution) desenmascarar

début ['deɪbjuː] N presentación f

debutante ['dɛbjutænt] N debutante f

Dec. ABBR (= December) dic.

decade ['dɛkeɪd] N década, decenio

decadence ['dɛkədəns] N decadencia

decadent ['dɛkədənt] ADJ decadente

de-caff ['diːkæf] N (inf) descafeinado

decaffeinated [dɪ'kæfɪneɪtɪd] ADJ descafeinado

decamp [dɪ'kæmp] VI (inf) escaparse, largarse, rajarse (LAm)

decant [dɪ'kænt] VT decantar

decanter [dɪ'kæntəʳ] N jarra, decantador m

decathlon [dɪ'kæθlən] N decatlón m

decay [dɪ'keɪ] N (fig) decadencia; (of building)

desmoronamiento; (of tooth) caries f inv ▶ VI (rot) pudrirse; (fig) decaer

decease [dɪ'siːs] N fallecimiento ▶ VI fallecer

deceased [dɪ'siːst] N: **the** ~ el (la) difunto(-a) ▶ ADJ difunto

deceit [dɪ'siːt] N engaño

deceitful [dɪ'siːtful] ADJ engañoso

deceive [dɪ'siːv] VT engañar

decelerate [diː'sɛləreɪt] VT moderar la marcha de ▶ VI decelerar

December [dɪ'sɛmbəʳ] N diciembre m; see also **July**

decency ['diːsənsɪ] N decencia

decent ['diːsənt] ADJ (proper) decente; (person) amable, bueno

decently ['diːsəntlɪ] ADV (respectably) decentemente; (kindly) amablemente

decentralization [diːsɛntrəlaɪ'zeɪʃən] N descentralización f

decentralize [diː'sɛntrəlaɪz] VT descentralizar

deception [dɪ'sɛpʃən] N engaño

deceptive [dɪ'sɛptɪv] ADJ engañoso

decibel ['dɛsɪbɛl] N decibel(io) m

decide [dɪ'saɪd] VT (person) decidir; (question, argument) resolver ▶ VI decidir; **to ~ to do/ that** decidir hacer/que; **to ~ on sth** tomar una decisión sobre algo; **to ~ against doing sth** decidir en contra de hacer algo

decided [dɪ'saɪdɪd] ADJ (resolute) decidido; (clear, definite) indudable

decidedly [dɪ'saɪdɪdlɪ] ADV decididamente

deciding [dɪ'saɪdɪŋ] ADJ decisivo

deciduous [dɪ'sɪdjuəs] ADJ de hoja caduca

decimal ['dɛsɪməl] ADJ decimal ▶ N decimal f; **to three ~ places** con tres cifras decimales

decimalize ['dɛsɪməlaɪz] VT convertir al sistema decimal

decimal point N coma decimal

decimal system N sistema m métrico decimal

decimate ['dɛsɪmeɪt] VT diezmar

decipher [dɪ'saɪfəʳ] VT descifrar

decision [dɪ'sɪʒən] N decisión f; **to make a ~** tomar una decisión

decisive [dɪ'saɪsɪv] ADJ (influence) decisivo; (manner, person) decidido; (reply) tajante

deck [dɛk] N (Naut) cubierta; (of bus) piso; (of cards) baraja; **record ~** platina; **to go up on ~** subir a (la) cubierta; **below ~** en la bodega

deckchair ['dɛktʃɛəʳ] N tumbona

deckhand ['dɛkhænd] N marinero de cubierta

declaration [dɛklə'reɪʃən] N declaración f

declare [dɪ'klɛəʳ] VT (gen) declarar

declassify [diː'klæsɪfaɪ] VT permitir que salga a la luz

decline [dɪ'klaɪn] N decaimiento, decadencia; (lessening) disminución f ▶ VT rehusar ▶ vɪ (*person, business*) decaer; (*strength*) disminuir; **~ in living standards** disminución *f* del nivel de vida; **to ~ to do sth** rehusar hacer algo

declutch [ˈdiːˈklʌtʃ] vɪ desembragar

decode [diːˈkəud] vт descifrar

decoder [diːˈkəudəʳ] ɴ (*Comput, TV*) de(s)codificador *m*

decompose [diːkəmˈpəuz] vɪ descomponerse

decomposition [diːkɔmpəˈzɪʃən] ɴ descomposición *f*

decompression [diːkəmˈpreʃən] ɴ descompresión *f*

decompression chamber ɴ cámara de descompresión

decongestant [diːkənˈdʒɛstənt] ɴ descongestionante *m*

decontaminate [diːkənˈtæmɪneɪt] vт descontaminar

decontrol [diːkənˈtrəul] vт (*trade*) quitar controles a; (*prices*) descongelar

décor [ˈdeɪkɔːʳ] ɴ decoración *f*; (*Theat*) decorado

decorate [ˈdɛkəreɪt] vт (*paint*) pintar; (*paper*) empapelar; (*adorn*): **to ~ (with)** adornar (de), decorar (de)

decoration [dɛkəˈreɪʃən] ɴ adorno; (*act*) decoración *f*; (*medal*) condecoración *f*

decorative [ˈdɛkərətɪv] ᴀᴅᴊ decorativo

decorator [ˈdɛkəreɪtəʳ] ɴ (*workman*) pintor *m* decorador

decorum [dɪˈkɔːrəm] ɴ decoro

decoy [ˈdiːkɔɪ] ɴ señuelo; **police ~** trampa *or* señuelo policial

decrease [ˈdiːkriːs] ɴ disminución *f* ▶ vт [diːˈkriːs] disminuir, reducir ▶ vɪ reducirse; **to be on the ~** ir disminuyendo

decreasing [diːˈkriːsɪŋ] ᴀᴅᴊ decreciente

decree [dɪˈkriː] ɴ decreto ▶ vт: **to ~ (that)** decretar (que); **~ absolute/nisi** sentencia absoluta/provisional de divorcio

decrepit [dɪˈkrepɪt] ᴀᴅᴊ (*person*) decrépito; (*building*) ruinoso

decry [dɪˈkraɪ] vт criticar, censurar

decrypt [diːˈkrɪpt] vт (*Comput, Tel*) descifrar

dedicate [ˈdɛdɪkeɪt] vт dedicar

dedicated [ˈdɛdɪkeɪtɪd] ᴀᴅᴊ dedicado; (*Comput*) especializado; **~ word processor** procesador *m* de textos especializado *or* dedicado

dedication [dɛdɪˈkeɪʃən] ɴ (*devotion*) dedicación *f*; (*in book*) dedicatoria

deduce [dɪˈdjuːs] vт deducir

deduct [dɪˈdʌkt] vт restar; (*from wage etc*) descontar, deducir

deduction [dɪˈdʌkʃən] ɴ (*amount deducted*) descuento; (*conclusion*) deducción *f*, conclusión *f*

deed [diːd] ɴ hecho, acto; (*feat*) hazaña;

(*Law*) escritura; **~ of covenant** escritura de contrato

deem [diːm] vт (*formal*) juzgar, considerar; **to ~ it wise to do** considerar prudente hacer

deep [diːp] ᴀᴅᴊ profundo; (*voice*) bajo; (*breath*) profundo, a pleno pulmón ▶ ᴀᴅᴠ: **the spectators stood 20 ~** los espectadores se formaron de 20 en fondo; **to be four metres ~** tener cuatro metros de profundidad

deepen [ˈdiːpn] vт ahondar, profundizar ▶ vɪ (*darkness*) intensificarse

deep-freeze [ˈdiːpˈfriːz] ɴ arcón *m* congelador

deep-fry [ˈdiːpˈfraɪ] vт freír en aceite abundante

deeply [ˈdiːplɪ] ᴀᴅᴠ (*breathe*) profundamente, a pleno pulmón; (*interested, moved, grateful*) profundamente, hondamente; **to regret sth ~** sentir algo profundamente

deep-rooted [ˈdiːpˈruːtɪd] ᴀᴅᴊ (*prejudice, habit*) profundamente arraigado; (*affection*) profundo

deep-sea [ˈdiːpˈsiː] ᴀᴅᴊ: **~ diver** buzo; **~ diving** buceo de altura

deep-seated [ˈdiːpˈsiːtɪd] ᴀᴅᴊ (*beliefs*) (profundamente) arraigado

deep-set [ˈdiːpsɛt] ᴀᴅᴊ (*eyes*) hundido

deep-vein thrombosis [ˈdiːpveɪn-] ɴ (*Med*) trombosis *f* venosa profunda

deer [dɪəʳ] (*pl* ~) ɴ ɪɴᴠ ciervo

deerstalker [ˈdɪəstɔːkəʳ] ɴ (*hat*) gorro de cazador

deface [dɪˈfeɪs] vт desfigurar, mutilar

defamation [dɛfəˈmeɪʃən] ɴ difamación *f*

defamatory [dɪˈfæmətrɪ] ᴀᴅᴊ difamatorio

default [dɪˈfɔːlt] vɪ faltar al pago; (*Sport*) no presentarse, no comparecer ▶ ɴ (*Comput*) defecto; **by ~** (*Law*) en rebeldía; (*Sport*) por incomparecencia; **to ~ on a debt** dejar de pagar una deuda

defaulter [dɪˈfɔːltəʳ] ɴ (*in debt*) moroso(-a)

default option ɴ (*Comput*) opción *f* por defecto

defeat [dɪˈfiːt] ɴ derrota ▶ vт derrotar, vencer; (*fig: efforts*) frustrar

defeatism [dɪˈfiːtɪzəm] ɴ derrotismo

defeatist [dɪˈfiːtɪst] ᴀᴅᴊ, ɴ derrotista *mf*

defecate [ˈdɛfəkeɪt] vɪ defecar

defect [ˈdiːfɛkt] ɴ defecto ▶ vɪ [dɪˈfɛkt]: **to ~ to the enemy** pasarse al enemigo; **physical ~** defecto físico; **mental ~** deficiencia mental

defective [dɪˈfɛktɪv] ᴀᴅᴊ (*gen*) defectuoso; (*person*) anormal

defector [dɪˈfɛktəʳ] ɴ tránsfuga *mf*

defence, (*US*) **defense** [dɪˈfɛns] ɴ defensa; **the Ministry of D~** el Ministerio de Defensa; **witness for the ~** testigo de descargo

defenceless [dɪˈfɛnslɪs] ADJ indefenso

defence spending N gasto militar

defend [dɪˈfɛnd] VT defender; *(decision, action)* defender; *(opinion)* mantener

defendant [dɪˈfɛndənt] N acusado(-a); *(in civil case)* demandado(-a)

defender [dɪˈfɛndəʳ] N defensor(a) *m/f*; *(Sport)* defensa *mf*

defending champion [dɪˈfɛndɪŋ-] N *(Sport)* defensor(-a) *m/f* del título

defending counsel N *(Law)* abogado defensor

defense [dɪˈfɛns] N *(US)* = **defence**

defensive [dɪˈfɛnsɪv] ADJ defensivo ▸ N defensiva; **on the ~** a la defensiva

defer [dɪˈfɜːʳ] VT *(postpone)* aplazar; **to ~ to** diferir a; *(submit)*: **to ~ to sb/sb's opinion** someterse a algn/a la opinión de algn

deference [ˈdɛfərəns] N deferencia, respeto; **out of** *or* **in ~ to** por respeto a

deferential [dɛfəˈrɛnʃəl] ADJ respetuoso

deferred [dɪˈfɜːd] ADJ: **~ creditor** acreedor *m* diferido

defiance [dɪˈfaɪəns] N desafío; **in ~ of** en contra de

defiant [dɪˈfaɪənt] ADJ *(insolent)* insolente; *(challenging)* retador(a), desafiante

defiantly [dɪˈfaɪəntlɪ] ADV con aire de desafío

deficiency [dɪˈfɪʃənsɪ] N *(lack)* falta; *(Comm)* déficit *m*; *(defect)* defecto

deficient [dɪˈfɪʃənt] ADJ *(lacking)* insuficiente; *(incomplete)* incompleto; *(defective)* defectuoso; *(mentally)* anormal; **~ in** deficiente en

deficit [ˈdɛfɪsɪt] N déficit *m*

defile [dɪˈfaɪl] VT manchar; *(violate)* violar

define [dɪˈfaɪn] VT *(Comput)* definir; *(limits etc)* determinar

definite [ˈdɛfɪnɪt] ADJ *(fixed)* determinado; *(clear, obvious)* claro; **he was ~ about it** no dejó lugar a dudas (sobre ello)

definitely [ˈdɛfɪnɪtlɪ] ADV: **he's ~ mad** no cabe duda de que está loco

definition [dɛfɪˈnɪʃən] N definición *f*

definitive [dɪˈfɪnɪtɪv] ADJ definitivo

deflate [diːˈfleɪt] VT *(gen)* desinflar; *(pompous person)* quitar *or* rebajar los humos a; *(Econ)* deflacionar

deflation [diːˈfleɪʃən] N *(Econ)* deflación *f*

deflationary [diːˈfleɪʃənrɪ] ADJ *(Econ)* deflacionario

deflect [dɪˈflɛkt] VT desviar

defog [diːˈfɔg] VT desempañar

defogger [diːˈfɔgəʳ] N *(US Aut)* dispositivo antivaho

deform [dɪˈfɔːm] VT deformar

deformed [dɪˈfɔːmd] ADJ deformado

deformity [dɪˈfɔːmɪtɪ] N deformación *f*

Defra N ABBR *(Brit)* = **Department for Environment, Food and Rural Affairs**

defraud [dɪˈfrɔːd] VT estafar; **to ~ sb of sth** estafar algo a algn

defray [dɪˈfreɪ] VT: **to ~ sb's expenses** reembolsar a algn los gastos

defriend [diːˈfrɛnd] VT *(Internet)* quitar de amigo a; **he has defriended her on Facebook** la ha quitado de amiga en Facebook

defrost [diːˈfrɔst] VT *(frozen food, fridge)* descongelar

defroster [diːˈfrɔstəʳ] N *(US)* eliminador *m* de vaho

deft [dɛft] ADJ diestro, hábil

defunct [dɪˈfʌŋkt] ADJ difunto; *(organization etc)* ya desaparecido

defuse [diːˈfjuːz] VT desarmar; *(situation)* calmar, apaciguar

defy [dɪˈfaɪ] VT *(resist)* oponerse a; *(challenge)* desafiar; *(order)* contravenir; **it defies description** resulta imposible describirlo

degenerate [dɪˈdʒɛnəreɪt] VI degenerar ▸ ADJ [dɪˈdʒɛnərɪt] degenerado

degradation [dɛgrəˈdeɪʃən] N degradación *f*

degrade [dɪˈgreɪd] VT degradar

degrading [dɪˈgreɪdɪŋ] ADJ degradante

degree [dɪˈgriː] N grado; *(Scol)* título; **10 degrees below freezing** 10 grados bajo cero; **to have a ~ in maths** ser licenciado(-a) en matemáticas; **by degrees** *(gradually)* poco a poco, por etapas; **to some ~, to a certain ~** hasta cierto punto; **a considerable ~ of risk** un gran índice de riesgo

dehydrated [diːhaɪˈdreɪtɪd] ADJ deshidratado; *(milk)* en polvo

dehydration [diːhaɪˈdreɪʃən] N deshidratación *f*

de-ice [diːˈaɪs] VT *(windscreen)* deshelar

de-icer [diːˈaɪsəʳ] N descongelador *m*

deign [deɪn] VI: **to ~ to do** dignarse hacer

deity [ˈdiːɪtɪ] N deidad *f*, divinidad *f*

déjà vu [deɪʒɑːˈvuː] N: **I had a sense of ~** sentía como si ya lo hubiera vivido

dejected [dɪˈdʒɛktɪd] ADJ abatido, desanimado

dejection [dɪˈdʒɛkʃən] N abatimiento

Del. ABBR *(US)* = **Delaware**

delay [dɪˈleɪ] VT demorar, aplazar; *(person)* entretener; *(train)* retrasar; *(payment)* aplazar ▸ VI tardar ▸ N demora, retraso; **without ~** en seguida, sin tardar

delayed-action [dɪleɪdˈækʃən] ADJ *(bomb etc)* de acción retardada

delectable [dɪˈlɛktəbl] ADJ *(person)* encantador(-a); *(food)* delicioso

delegate [ˈdɛlɪgɪt] N delegado(-a) ▸ VT [ˈdɛlɪgeɪt] *(person)* delegar en; *(task)* delegar; **to ~ sth to sb/sb to do sth** delegar algo en algn/en algn para hacer algo

delegation [dɛlɪ'geɪʃən] N (*of work etc*) delegación f

delete [dɪ'liːt] VT suprimir, tachar; (*Comput*) suprimir, borrar

Delhi ['dɛlɪ] N Delhi m

deli ['dɛlɪ] N = **delicatessen**

deliberate [dɪ'lɪbərɪt] ADJ (*intentional*) intencionado; (*slow*) pausado, lento ▶ VI [dɪ'lɪbəreɪt] deliberar

deliberately [dɪ'lɪbərɪtlɪ] ADV (*on purpose*) a propósito; (*slowly*) pausadamente

deliberation [dɪlɪbə'reɪʃən] N (*consideration*) reflexión f; (*discussion*) deliberación f, discusión f

delicacy ['dɛlɪkəsɪ] N delicadeza; (*choice food*) manjar m

delicate ['dɛlɪkɪt] ADJ (*gen*) delicado; (*fragile*) frágil

delicately ['dɛlɪkɪtlɪ] ADV con delicadeza, delicadamente; (*act, express*) con discreción

delicatessen [dɛlɪkə'tɛsn] N *tienda especializada en alimentos de calidad*

delicious [dɪ'lɪʃəs] ADJ delicioso, rico

delight [dɪ'laɪt] N (*feeling*) placer m, deleite m; (*object*) encanto, delicia ▶ VT encantar, deleitar; **to take ~ in** deleitarse en

delighted [dɪ'laɪtɪd] ADJ: **~ (at** or **with/to do)** encantado (con/de hacer); **to be ~ that** estar encantado de que; **I'd be ~** con mucho or todo gusto

delightful [dɪ'laɪtful] ADJ encantador(a), delicioso

delimit [diː'lɪmɪt] VT delimitar

delineate [dɪ'lɪnɪeɪt] VT delinear

delinquency [dɪ'lɪŋkwənsɪ] N delincuencia

delinquent [dɪ'lɪŋkwənt] ADJ, N delincuente mf

delirious [dɪ'lɪrɪəs] ADJ (*Med: fig*) delirante; **to be ~** delirar, desvariar

delirium [dɪ'lɪrɪəm] N delirio

deliver [dɪ'lɪvə^r] VT (*distribute*) repartir; (*hand over*) entregar; (*message*) comunicar; (*speech*) pronunciar; (*blow*) lanzar, dar; (*Med*) asistir al parto de

deliverance [dɪ'lɪvrəns] N liberación f

delivery [dɪ'lɪvərɪ] N reparto; entrega; (*of speaker*) modo de expresarse; (*Med*) parto, alumbramiento; **to take ~ of** recibir

delivery note N nota de entrega

delivery van N furgoneta de reparto

delta ['dɛltə] N delta m

delude [dɪ'luːd] VT engañar

deluge ['dɛljuːdʒ] N diluvio ▶ VT (*fig*): **to ~ (with)** inundar (de)

delusion [dɪ'luːʒən] N ilusión f, engaño

de luxe [də'lʌks] ADJ de lujo

delve [dɛlv] VI: **to ~ into** hurgar en

Dem. ABBR (*US Pol*) = **democrat; democratic**

demand [dɪ'mɑːnd] VT exigir; (*rights*) reclamar; (*need*) requerir ▶ N (*gen*) exigencia; (*claim*) reclamación f; (*Econ*) demanda; **to ~ sth (from** or **of sb)** exigir algo (a algn); **to be in ~** ser muy solicitado; **on ~** a solicitud

demanding [dɪ'mɑːndɪŋ] ADJ (*boss*) exigente; (*work*) absorbente

demarcation [diːmɑː'keɪʃən] N demarcación f

demarcation dispute N conflicto de definición or demarcación del trabajo

demean [dɪ'miːn] VT: **to ~ o.s.** rebajarse

demeanour, (*US*) **demeanor** [dɪ'miːnə^r] N porte m, conducta, comportamiento

demented [dɪ'mɛntɪd] ADJ demente

demi- ['dɛmɪ] PREF semi..., medio...

demilitarize [diː'mɪlɪtəraɪz] VT desmilitarizar; **demilitarized zone** zona desmilitarizada

demise [dɪ'maɪz] N (*death*) fallecimiento

demist [diː'mɪst] VT (*Aut*) eliminar el vaho de

demister [diː'mɪstə^r] N (*Aut*) eliminador m de vaho

demo ['dɛməu] N ABBR (*inf:* = *demonstration*) manifestación f

demobilization [diː'məubɪlaɪ'zeɪʃən] N desmovilización f

democracy [dɪ'mɔkrəsɪ] N democracia

democrat ['dɛməkræt] N demócrata mf

democratic [dɛmə'krætɪk] ADJ democrático; **the D~ Party** el partido demócrata (estadounidense)

demography [dɪ'mɔgrəfɪ] N demografía

demolish [dɪ'mɔlɪʃ] VT derribar, demoler; (*fig: argument*) destruir

demolition [dɛmə'lɪʃən] N derribo, demolición f

demon ['diːmən] N (*evil spirit*) demonio ▶ CPD temible

demonstrate ['dɛmənstreɪt] VT demostrar ▶ VI manifestarse; **to ~ (for/against)** manifestarse (a favor de/en contra de)

demonstration [dɛmən'streɪʃən] N (*Pol*) manifestación f; (*proof*) prueba, demostración f; **to hold a ~** (*Pol*) hacer una manifestación

demonstrative [dɪ'mɔnstrətɪv] ADJ (*person*) expresivo; (*Ling*) demostrativo

demonstrator ['dɛmənstreɪtə^r] N (*Pol*) manifestante mf

demoralize [dɪ'mɔrəlaɪz] VT desmoralizar

demote [dɪ'məut] VT degradar

demotion [dɪ'məuʃən] N degradación f; (*Comm*) descenso

demur [dɪ'mə^r] VI: **to ~ (at)** hacer objeciones (a), vacilar (ante) ▶ N: **without ~** sin objeción

demure [dɪ'mjuə^r] ADJ recatado

demurrage [dɪ'mʌrɪdʒ] N sobrestadía

den [dɛn] N (*of animal*) guarida; (*study*) estudio

d

denationalization [di:næʃnəlaɪ'zeɪʃən] N desnacionalización f

denationalize [di:'næʃnəlaɪz] VT desnacionalizar

denatured alcohol [di:'neɪtʃəd-] N (US) alcohol m desnaturalizado

denial [dɪ'naɪəl] N (refusal) denegación f; (of report etc) desmentido

denier ['dɛnɪəʳ] N denier m

denim ['dɛnɪm] N tela vaquera; see also **denims**

denim jacket N chaqueta vaquera, saco vaquero (LAm)

denims ['dɛnɪms] NPL vaqueros mpl

denizen ['dɛnɪzn] N (inhabitant) habitante mf; (foreigner) residente mf extranjero(-a)

Denmark ['dɛnmɑːk] N Dinamarca

denomination [dɪnɔmɪ'neɪʃən] N valor m; (Rel) confesión f

denominator [dɪ'nɔmɪneɪtəʳ] N denominador m

denote [dɪ'nəut] VT indicar, significar

denounce [dɪ'nauns] VT denunciar

dense [dɛns] ADJ (thick) espeso; (foliage etc) tupido; (stupid) torpe

densely [dɛnslɪ] ADV: ~ **populated** con una alta densidad de población

density ['dɛnsɪtɪ] N densidad f

dent [dɛnt] N abolladura ▶ VT (also: **make a dent in**) abollar

dental ['dɛntl] ADJ dental

dental floss [-flɔs] N seda dental

dental surgeon N odontólogo(-a)

dental surgery N clínica dental, consultorio dental

dentifrice ['dɛntɪfrɪs] N dentífrico

dentist ['dɛntɪst] N dentista mf; **~'s surgery** (BRIT) consultorio dental

dentistry ['dɛntɪstrɪ] N odontología

dentures ['dɛntʃəz] NPL dentadura sg (postiza)

denude [dɪ'njuːd] VT: **to ~ of** despojar de

denunciation [dɪnʌnsɪ'eɪʃən] N denuncia, denunciación f

deny [dɪ'naɪ] VT negar; (charge) rechazar; (report) desmentir; **to ~ o.s.** privarse (de); **he denies having said it** niega haberlo dicho

deodorant [di:'əudərənt] N desodorante m

depart [dɪ'pɑːt] VI irse, marcharse; (train) salir; **to ~ from** (fig: differ from) apartarse de

departed [dɪ'pɑːtɪd] ADJ (bygone: days, glory) pasado; (dead) difunto ▶ N: **the (dear) ~** el/la/los/las difunto/a/os/as

department [dɪ'pɑːtmənt] N (Comm) sección f; (Scol) departamento; (Pol) ministerio; **that's not my ~** (fig) no tiene que ver conmigo; **D~ of State** (US) Ministerio de Asuntos Exteriores

departmental [di:pɑːt'mɛntl] ADJ (dispute) departamental; (meeting) departamental, de departamento; **~ manager** jefe(-a) m/f de sección or de departamento or de servicio

department store N grandes almacenes mpl

departure [dɪ'pɑːtʃəʳ] N partida, ida; (of train) salida; **a new ~** un nuevo rumbo

departure lounge N (at airport) sala de embarque

depend [dɪ'pɛnd] VI: **to ~ (up)on** (be dependent upon) depender de; (rely on) contar con; **it depends** depende, según; **depending on the result** según el resultado

dependable [dɪ'pɛndəbl] ADJ (person) formal, serio

dependant [dɪ'pɛndənt] N dependiente mf

dependence [dɪ'pɛndəns] N dependencia

dependent [dɪ'pɛndənt] ADJ: **to be ~ (on)** depender (de) ▶ N = **dependant**

depict [dɪ'pɪkt] VT (in picture) pintar; (describe) representar

depilatory [dɪ'pɪlətrɪ] N (also: **depilatory cream**) depilatorio

depleted [dɪ'pliːtɪd] ADJ reducido

deplorable [dɪ'plɔːrəbl] ADJ deplorable

deplore [dɪ'plɔːʳ] VT deplorar

deploy [dɪ'plɔɪ] VT desplegar

depopulate [di:'pɔpjuleɪt] VT despoblar

depopulation ['di:pɔpju'leɪʃən] N despoblación f

deport [dɪ'pɔːt] VT deportar

deportation [di:pɔː'teɪʃən] N deportación f

deportation order N orden f de expulsión or deportación

deportee [di:pɔː'tiː] N deportado(-a)

deportment [dɪ'pɔːtmənt] N comportamiento

depose [dɪ'pəuz] VT deponer

deposit [dɪ'pɔzɪt] N depósito; (Chem) sedimento; (of ore, oil) yacimiento ▶ VT (gen) depositar; **to put down a ~ of £50** dejar un depósito de 50 libras

deposit account N (BRIT) cuenta de ahorros

depositor [dɪ'pɔzɪtəʳ] N depositante mf, cuentacorrentista mf

depository [dɪ'pɔzɪtərɪ] N almacén m depositario

depot ['dɛpəu] N (storehouse) depósito; (for vehicles) parque m

deprave [dɪ'preɪv] VT depravar

depraved [dɪ'preɪvd] ADJ depravado, vicioso

depravity [dɪ'prævɪtɪ] N depravación f, vicio

deprecate ['dɛprɪkeɪt] VT desaprobar, lamentar

deprecating ['dɛprɪkeɪtɪŋ] ADJ (disapproving) de desaprobación; (apologetic): **a ~ smile** una sonrisa de disculpa

depreciate [dɪ'priːʃɪeɪt] VI depreciarse, perder valor

depreciation [dɪpriːʃɪ'eɪʃən] N depreciación f

depress [dɪ'prɛs] VT deprimir; *(press down)* apretar

depressant [dɪ'prɛsnt] N *(Med)* calmante *m*, sedante *m*

depressed [dɪ'prɛst] ADJ deprimido; *(Comm: market, economy)* deprimido; *(: area)* deprimido (económicamente); **to get ~** deprimirse

depressing [dɪ'prɛsɪŋ] ADJ deprimente

depression [dɪ'prɛʃən] N depresión *f*; **the economy is in a state of ~** la economía está deprimida

deprivation [dɛprɪ'veɪʃən] N privación *f*; *(loss)* pérdida

deprive [dɪ'praɪv] VT: **to ~ sb of** privar a algn de

deprived [dɪ'praɪvd] ADJ necesitado

dept. ABBR (= *department*) dpto.

depth [dɛpθ] N profundidad *f*; **at a ~ of three metres** a tres metros de profundidad; **to be out of one's ~** *(swimmer)* perder pie; *(fig)* sentirse perdido; **to study sth in ~** estudiar algo a fondo; **in the depths of** en lo más hondo de

depth charge N carga de profundidad

deputation [dɛpju'teɪʃən] N delegación *f*

deputize ['dɛpjutaɪz] VI: **to ~ for sb** sustituir a algn

deputy ['dɛpjutɪ] ADJ: **~ head** subdirector(a) *m/f* ▶ N sustituto(-a), suplente *mf*; *(Pol)* diputado(-a); *(agent)* representante *mf*

deputy leader N vicepresidente(-a) *m/f*

derail [dɪ'reɪl] VT: **to be derailed** descarrilarse

derailment [dɪ'reɪlmənt] N descarrilamiento

deranged [dɪ'reɪndʒd] ADJ trastornado

derby ['dəːbɪ] N *(US)* hongo

deregulate [diː'rɛgjuleɪt] VT desreglamentar

deregulation [diːrɛgju'leɪʃən] N desreglamentación *f*

derelict ['dɛrɪlɪkt] ADJ abandonado

deride [dɪ'raɪd] VT ridiculizar, mofarse de

derision [dɪ'rɪʒən] N irrisión *f*, mofas *fpl*

derisive [dɪ'raɪsɪv] ADJ burlón(-ona)

derisory [dɪ'raɪzərɪ] ADJ *(sum)* irrisorio; *(laughter, person)* burlón(-ona), irónico

derivation [dɛrɪ'veɪʃən] N derivación *f*

derivative [dɪ'rɪvətɪv] N derivado ▶ ADJ *(work)* poco original

derive [dɪ'raɪv] VT derivar; *(benefit etc)* obtener ▶ VI: **to ~ from** derivarse de

derived [dɪ'raɪvd] ADJ derivado

dermatitis [dəːmə'taɪtɪs] N dermatitis *f*

dermatology [dəːmə'tɔlədʒɪ] N dermatología

derogatory [dɪ'rɔgətərɪ] ADJ despectivo

derrick ['dɛrɪk] N torre *f* de perforación

derv [dəːv] N *(BRIT)* gasoil *m*

descend [dɪ'sɛnd] VT, VI descender, bajar; **to ~ from** descender de; **in descending order of importance** de mayor a menor importancia

▶ **descend on** VT FUS *(enemy, angry person)* caer sobre; *(misfortune)* sobrevenir; *(gloom, silence)* invadir; **visitors descended on us** las visitas nos invadieron

descendant [dɪ'sɛndənt] N descendiente *mf*

descent [dɪ'sɛnt] N descenso; *(Geo)* pendiente *f*, declive *m*; *(origin)* descendencia

describe [dɪs'kraɪb] VT describir

description [dɪs'krɪpʃən] N descripción *f*; *(sort)* clase *f*, género; **of every ~** de toda clase

descriptive [dɪs'krɪptɪv] ADJ descriptivo

desecrate ['dɛsɪkreɪt] VT profanar

desegregation [diːsɛgrɪ'geɪʃən] N desegregación *f*

desert [*n* 'dɛzət, *vt, vi* dɪ'zəːt] N desierto ▶ VT abandonar, desamparar ▶ VI *(Mil)* desertar; *see also* **deserts**

deserted [dɪ'zəːtɪd] ADJ desierto

deserter [dɪ'zəːtər] N desertor(-a) *m/f*

desertion [dɪ'zəːʃən] N deserción *f*

desert island N isla desierta

deserts [dɪ'zəːts] NPL: **to get one's just ~** llevarse su merecido

deserve [dɪ'zəːv] VT merecer, ser digno de, ameritar *(LAM)*

deservedly [dɪ'zəːvɪdlɪ] ADV con razón

deserving [dɪ'zəːvɪŋ] ADJ *(person)* digno; *(action, cause)* meritorio

desiccated ['dɛsɪkeɪtɪd] ADJ desecado

design [dɪ'zaɪn] N *(sketch)* bosquejo; *(of dress, car)* diseño; *(pattern)* dibujo ▶ VT *(gen)* diseñar; **industrial ~** diseño industrial; **to have designs on sb** tener la(s) mira(s) puesta(s) en algn; **to be designed for sb/sth** estar hecho para algn/algo

design and technology N *(BRIT Scol)* diseño y tecnología

designate ['dɛzɪgneɪt] VT *(appoint)* nombrar; *(destine)* designar ▶ ADJ ['dɛzɪgnɪt] designado

designation [dɛzɪg'neɪʃən] N *(appointment)* nombramiento; *(name)* denominación *f*

designer [dɪ'zaɪnər] N diseñador(a) *m/f*

designer baby N bebé *m* de diseño

desirability [dɪzaɪərə'bɪlɪtɪ] N ventaja, atractivo

desirable [dɪ'zaɪərəbl] ADJ *(proper)* deseable; *(attractive)* atractivo; **it is ~ that** es conveniente que

desire [dɪ'zaɪər] N deseo ▶ VT desear; **to ~ sth/ to do sth/that** desear algo/hacer algo/que

desirous [dɪ'zaɪərəs] ADJ deseoso

desist [dɪ'zɪst] VI: **to ~ (from)** desistir (de)

desk [dɛsk] N *(in office)* escritorio; *(for pupil)* pupitre *m*; *(in hotel, at airport)* recepción *f*; *(BRIT: in shop, restaurant)* caja

desktop ['dɛsktɔp] N *(Comput)* escritorio

d

desktop computer N ordenador *m* de sobremesa

desktop publishing N autoedición *f*

desolate ['dɛsəlɪt] ADJ (*place*) desierto; (*person*) afligido

desolation [dɛsə'leɪʃən] N (*of place*) desolación *f*; (*of person*) aflicción *f*

despair [dɪs'pɛəʳ] N desesperación *f* ▶ VI: **to ~ of** desesperar de; **in ~** desesperado

despatch [dɪs'pætʃ] N, VT = **dispatch**

desperate ['dɛspərɪt] ADJ desesperado; (*fugitive*) peligroso; (*measures*) extremo; **we are getting ~** estamos al borde de desesperación; **to be ~ for sth/to do** necesitar urgentemente algo/hacer

desperately ['dɛspərɪtlɪ] ADV desesperadamente; (*very*) terriblemente, gravemente; **~ ill** gravemente enfermo

desperation [dɛspə'reɪʃən] N desesperación *f*; **in ~** desesperado

despicable [dɪs'pɪkəbl] ADJ vil, despreciable

despise [dɪs'paɪz] VT despreciar

despite [dɪs'paɪt] PREP a pesar de, pese a

despondent [dɪs'pɔndənt] ADJ deprimido, abatido

despot ['dɛspɔt] N déspota *mf*

dessert [dɪ'zəːt] N postre *m*

dessertspoon [dɪ'zəːtspuːn] N cuchara (de postre)

destabilize [diːˈsteɪbɪlaɪz] VT desestabilizar

destination [dɛstɪ'neɪʃən] N destino

destine ['dɛstɪn] VT destinar

destined ['dɛstɪnd] ADJ: **~ for London** con destino a Londres

destiny ['dɛstɪnɪ] N destino

destitute ['dɛstɪtjuːt] ADJ desamparado, indigente

destitution [dɛstɪ'tjuːʃən] N indigencia, miseria

destroy [dɪs'trɔɪ] VT destruir; (*finish*) acabar con

destroyer [dɪs'trɔɪəʳ] N (*Naut*) destructor *m*

destruction [dɪs'trʌkʃən] N destrucción *f*; (*fig*) ruina

destructive [dɪs'trʌktɪv] ADJ destructivo, destructor(a)

desultory ['dɛsəltərɪ] ADJ (*reading*) poco metódico; (*conversation*) inconexo; (*contact*) intermitente

detach [dɪ'tætʃ] VT separar; (*unstick*) despegar

detachable [dɪ'tætʃəbl] ADJ separable; (*Tech*) desmontable

detached [dɪ'tætʃt] ADJ (*attitude*) objetivo, imparcial

detached house N chalé *m*, chalet *m*

detachment [dɪ'tætʃmənt] N separación *f*; (*Mil*) destacamento; (*fig*) objetividad *f*, imparcialidad *f*

detail ['diːteɪl] N detalle *m*; (*Mil*)

destacamento ▶ VT detallar; (*Mil*) destacar; **in ~** detalladamente; **to go into ~(s)** entrar en detalles

detailed ['diːteɪld] ADJ detallado

detain [dɪ'teɪn] VT retener; (*in captivity*) detener

detainee [diːteɪ'niː] N detenido(-a)

detect [dɪ'tɛkt] VT (*discover*) descubrir; (*Med, Police*) identificar; (*Mil, Radar, Tech*) detectar; (*notice*) percibir

detection [dɪ'tɛkʃən] N descubrimiento; identificación *f*; **crime ~** investigación *f*; **to escape ~** (*criminal*) escaparse sin ser descubierto; (*mistake*) pasar inadvertido

detective [dɪ'tɛktɪv] N detective *m*

detective story N novela policíaca

detector [dɪ'tɛktəʳ] N detector *m*

détente [deɪ'tɑːnt] N distensión *f*, detente *f*

detention [dɪ'tɛnʃən] N detención *f*, arresto; (*Scol*) castigo

deter [dɪ'təːʳ] VT (*dissuade*) disuadir; (*prevent*) impedir; **to ~ sb from doing sth** disuadir a algn de que haga algo

detergent [dɪ'təːdʒənt] N detergente *m*

deteriorate [dɪ'tɪərɪəreɪt] VI deteriorarse

deterioration [dɪtɪərɪə'reɪʃən] N deterioro

determination [dɪtəːmɪ'neɪʃən] N resolución *f*

determine [dɪ'təːmɪn] VT determinar; **to ~ to do sth** decidir hacer algo

determined [dɪ'təːmɪnd] ADJ: **to be ~ to do sth** estar decidido *or* resuelto a hacer algo; **a ~ effort** un esfuerzo enérgico

deterrence [dɪ'tɛrns] N disuasión *f*

deterrent [dɪ'tɛrənt] N fuerza de disuasión; **to act as a ~** servir para prevenir

detest [dɪ'tɛst] VT aborrecer

detestable [dɪ'tɛstəbl] ADJ aborrecible

dethrone [diː'θrəun] VT destronar

detonate ['dɛtəneɪt] VI estallar ▶ VT hacer detonar

detonator ['dɛtəneɪtəʳ] N detonador *m*, fulminante *m*

detour ['diːtuəʳ] N (*gen, US Aut: diversion*) desvío ▶ VT (*US: traffic*) desviar; **to make a ~** dar un rodeo

detox ['diːtɔks] VI desintoxicarse ▶ N desintoxicación *f*

detoxification [diːtɔksɪfɪ'keɪʃən] N desintoxicación *f*

detoxify [diː'tɔksɪfaɪ] VI desintoxicarse

detract [dɪ'trækt] VT: **to ~ from** quitar mérito a, restar valor a

detractor [dɪ'træktəʳ] N detractor(-a) *m/f*

detriment ['dɛtrɪmənt] N: **to the ~ of** en perjuicio de; **without ~ to** sin detrimento de, sin perjuicio para

detrimental [dɛtrɪ'mɛntl] ADJ: **~ (to)** perjudicial (a)

deuce [djuːs] N (*Tennis*) cuarenta iguales

devaluation [diːvælju'eɪʃən] N devaluación *f*

devalue [dɪ'væljuː] VT devaluar

devastate ['dɛvəsteɪt] VT devastar; **he was devastated by the news** las noticias le dejaron desolado

devastating ['dɛvəsteɪtɪŋ] ADJ devastador(-a); (*fig*) arrollador(-a)

devastation [dɛvəs'teɪʃən] N devastación *f*, ruina

develop [dɪ'vɛləp] VT desarrollar; (*Phot*) revelar; (*disease*) contraer; (*habit*) adquirir ▶ VI desarrollarse; (*advance*) progresar; **this land is to be developed** se va a construir en este terreno; **to ~ a taste for sth** tomar gusto a algo; **to ~ into** transformarse *or* convertirse en

developer [dɪ'vɛləpər] N (*property developer*) promotor(-a) *m/f*

developing country N país *m* en (vías de) desarrollo

development [dɪ'vɛləpmənt] N desarrollo; (*advance*) progreso; (*of affair, case*) desenvolvimiento; (*of land*) urbanización *f*

development area N zona de fomento *or* desarrollo

deviant ['diːvɪənt] ADJ anómalo, pervertido

deviate ['diːvɪeɪt] VI: **to ~ (from)** desviarse (de)

deviation [diːvɪ'eɪʃən] N desviación *f*

device [dɪ'vaɪs] N (*scheme*) estratagema, recurso; (*apparatus*) aparato, mecanismo; (*explosive device*) artefacto explosivo

devil ['dɛvl] N diablo, demonio

devilish ['dɛvlɪʃ] ADJ diabólico

devil-may-care ['dɛvlmeɪ'kɛər] ADJ despreocupado

devil's advocate N: **to play (the) ~** hacer de abogado del diablo

devious ['diːvɪəs] ADJ intricado, enrevesado; (*person*) taimado

devise [dɪ'vaɪz] VT idear, inventar

devoid [dɪ'vɔɪd] ADJ: **~ of** desprovisto de

devolution [diːvə'luːʃən] N (*Pol*) descentralización *f*

devolve [dɪ'vɔlv] VI: **to ~ (up)on** recaer sobre

devote [dɪ'vəut] VT: **to ~ sth to** dedicar algo a

devoted [dɪ'vəutɪd] ADJ (*loyal*) leal, fiel; **to be ~ to sb** querer con devoción a algn; **the book is ~ to politics** el libro trata de política

devotee [dɛvəu'tiː] N devoto(-a)

devotion [dɪ'vəuʃən] N dedicación *f*; (*Rel*) devoción *f*

devour [dɪ'vauər] VT devorar

devout [dɪ'vaut] ADJ devoto

dew [djuː] N rocío

dexterity [dɛks'tɛrɪtɪ] N destreza

dexterous, dextrous ['dɛkstrəs] ADJ (*skilful*) diestro, hábil; (*movement*) ágil

DfE N ABBR (*BRIT*) = **Department for Education**

dg ABBR (= *decigram*) dg

diabetes [daɪə'biːtiːz] N diabetes *f*

diabetic [daɪə'bɛtɪk] N diabético(-a) ▶ ADJ diabético; (*chocolate, jam*) para diabéticos

diabolical [daɪə'bɔlɪkəl] ADJ diabólico; (*inf*: *dreadful*) horrendo, horroroso

diagnose ['daɪəgnəuz] VT diagnosticar

diagnosis [daɪəg'nəusɪs] (*pl* **diagnoses** [-siːz]) N diagnóstico

diagonal [daɪ'ægənl] ADJ diagonal ▶ N diagonal *f*

diagram ['daɪəgræm] N diagrama *m*, esquema *m*

dial ['daɪəl] N esfera; (*of radio*) dial *m*; (*tuner*) sintonizador *m*; (*of phone*) disco ▶ VT (*number*) marcar, discar (*LAM*); **to ~ a wrong number** equivocarse de número; **can I ~ London direct?** ¿puedo marcar un número de Londres directamente?

dial. ABBR = **dialect**

dial code N (*US*) prefijo

dialect ['daɪəlɛkt] N dialecto

dialling code ['daɪəlɪŋ-] N (*BRIT*) prefijo

dialling tone N (*BRIT*) señal *f or* tono de marcar

dialogue, (*US*) **dialog** ['daɪəlɔg] N diálogo

dial tone N (*US*) señal *f or* tono de marcar

dialysis [daɪ'ælɪsɪs] N diálisis *f*

diameter [daɪ'æmɪtər] N diámetro

diametrically [daɪə'mɛtrɪklɪ] ADV: **~ opposed (to)** diametralmente opuesto (a)

diamond ['daɪəmənd] N diamante *m*; **diamonds** NPL (*Cards*) diamantes *mpl*

diamond ring N anillo *or* sortija de diamantes

diaper ['daɪəpər] N (*US*) pañal *m*

diaphragm ['daɪəfræm] N diafragma *m*

diarrhoea, (*US*) **diarrhea** [daɪə'riːə] N diarrea

diary ['daɪərɪ] N (*daily account*) diario; (*book*) agenda; **to keep a ~** escribir un diario

diatribe ['daɪətraɪb] N: **~ (against)** diatriba (contra)

dice [daɪs] N *pl inv* dados *mpl* ▶ VT (*Culin*) cortar en cuadritos

dicey ['daɪsɪ] ADJ (*inf*): **it's a bit ~** (*risky*) es un poco arriesgado; (*doubtful*) es un poco dudoso

dichotomy [daɪ'kɔtəmɪ] N dicotomía

dickhead ['dɪkhɛd] N (*BRIT inf!*) gilipollas *m inv*

Dictaphone ® ['dɪktəfəun] N dictáfono®

dictate [dɪk'teɪt] VT dictar ▶ N ['dɪkteɪt] dictado

▶ **dictate to** VT FUS (*person*) dar órdenes a; **I won't be dictated to** no recibo órdenes de nadie

dictation [dɪk'teɪʃən] N (*to secretary etc*) dictado; **at ~ speed** para tomar al dictado
dictator [dɪk'teɪtə^r] N dictador *m*
dictatorship [dɪk'teɪtəʃɪp] N dictadura
diction ['dɪkʃən] N dicción *f*
dictionary ['dɪkʃənɪ] N diccionario
did [dɪd] PT *of* **do**
didactic [daɪ'dæktɪk] ADJ didáctico
diddle ['dɪdl] VT estafar, timar
didn't ['dɪdənt] = **did not**
die [daɪ] VI morir; **to ~ (of** *or* **from)** morirse (de); **to be dying** morirse, estar muriéndose; **to be dying for sth/to do sth** morirse por algo/de ganas de hacer algo
▶ **die away** VI (*sound, light*) desvanecerse
▶ **die down** VI (*gen*) apagarse; (*wind*) amainar
▶ **die out** VI desaparecer, extinguirse
diehard ['daɪhɑːd] N intransigente *mf*
diesel ['diːzl] N diesel *m*
diesel engine N motor *m* diesel
diesel fuel, diesel oil N gasoil *m*
diet ['daɪət] N dieta; (*restricted food*) régimen *m*
▶ VI (*also:* **be on a diet**) estar a dieta, hacer régimen; **to live on a ~ of** alimentarse de
dietician [daɪə'tɪʃən] N dietista *mf*
differ ['dɪfə^r] VI (*be different*) ser distinto, diferenciarse; (*disagree*) discrepar
difference ['dɪfrəns] N diferencia; (*quarrel*) desacuerdo; **it makes no ~ to me** me da igual *or* lo mismo; **to settle one's differences** arreglarse
different ['dɪfrənt] ADJ diferente, distinto
differential [dɪfə'renʃəl] N diferencial *f*
differentiate [dɪfə'renʃɪeɪt] VT distinguir
▶ VI diferenciarse; **to ~ between** distinguir entre
differently ['dɪfrəntlɪ] ADV de otro modo, en forma distinta
difficult ['dɪfɪkəlt] ADJ difícil; **~ to understand** difícil de entender
difficulty ['dɪfɪkəltɪ] N dificultad *f*; **to have difficulties with** (*police, landlord etc*) tener problemas con; **to be in ~** estar en apuros
diffidence ['dɪfɪdəns] N timidez *f*, falta de confianza en sí mismo
diffident ['dɪfɪdənt] ADJ tímido
diffuse [dɪ'fjuːs] ADJ difuso ▶ VT [dɪ'fjuːz] difundir
dig [dɪg] (*pt, pp* **dug** [dʌg]) VT (*hole*) cavar; (*ground*) remover; (*coal*) extraer; (*nails etc*) clavar ▶ N (*prod*) empujón *m*; (*archaeological*) excavación *f*; (*remark*) indirecta; **to ~ into** (*savings*) consumir; **to ~ into one's pockets for sth** hurgar en el bolsillo buscando algo; **to ~ one's nails into** clavar las uñas en; *see also* **digs**
▶ **dig in** VI (*also:* **dig o.s. in**: *Mil*) atrincherarse; (*inf: eat*) hincar los dientes ▶ VT (*compost*) añadir al suelo; (*knife, claw*) clavar; **to ~ in**

one's heels (*fig*) mantenerse en sus trece
▶ **dig out** VT (*hole*) excavar; (*survivors, car from snow*) sacar
▶ **dig up** VT desenterrar; (*plant*) desarraigar
digest [daɪ'dʒest] VT (*food*) digerir; (*facts*) asimilar ▶ N ['daɪdʒest] resumen *m*
digestible [daɪ'dʒestəbl] ADJ digerible
digestion [dɪ'dʒestʃən] N digestión *f*
digestive [daɪ'dʒestɪv] ADJ (*juices, system*) digestivo
digit ['dɪdʒɪt] N (*number*) dígito; (*finger*) dedo
digital ['dɪdʒɪtl] ADJ digital
digital camera N cámara digital
digital compact cassette N cas(s)et(t)e *m or f* digital compacto
digital TV N televisión *f* digital
dignified ['dɪgnɪfaɪd] ADJ grave, solemne; (*action*) decoroso
dignify ['dɪgnɪfaɪ] VT dignificar
dignitary ['dɪgnɪtərɪ] N dignatario(-a)
dignity ['dɪgnɪtɪ] N dignidad *f*
digress [daɪ'gres] VI: **to ~ from** apartarse de
digression [daɪ'greʃən] N digresión *f*
digs [dɪgz] NPL (BRIT *inf*) pensión *f*, alojamiento
dike [daɪk] N = **dyke**
dilapidated [dɪ'læpɪdeɪtɪd] ADJ desmoronado, ruinoso
dilate [daɪ'leɪt] VT dilatar ▶ VI dilatarse
dilatory ['dɪlətərɪ] ADJ (*person*) lento; (*action*) dilatorio
dilemma [daɪ'lemə] N dilema *m*; **to be in a ~** estar en un dilema
dilettante [dɪlɪ'tæntɪ] N diletante *mf*
diligence ['dɪlɪdʒəns] N diligencia
diligent ['dɪlɪdʒənt] ADJ diligente
dill [dɪl] N eneldo
dilly-dally ['dɪlɪ'dælɪ] VI (*hesitate*) vacilar; (*dawdle*) entretenerse
dilute [daɪ'luːt] VT diluir
dim [dɪm] ADJ (*light*) débil; (*sight*) turbio; (*outline*) borroso; (*stupid*) lerdo; (*room*) oscuro ▶ VT (*light*) bajar; **to take a ~ view of sth** tener una pobre opinión de algo
dime [daɪm] N (*US*) moneda de diez centavos
dimension [dɪ'menʃən] N dimensión *f*
-dimensional [dɪ'menʃənl] ADJ SUFF: **two~** de dos dimensiones
dimensions [dɪ'menʃənz] NPL dimensiones *fpl*
diminish [dɪ'mɪnɪʃ] VT, VI disminuir
diminished [dɪ'mɪnɪʃt] ADJ: **~ responsibility** (*Law*) responsabilidad *f* disminuida
diminutive [dɪ'mɪnjutɪv] ADJ diminuto ▶ N (*Ling*) diminutivo
dimly ['dɪmlɪ] ADV débilmente; (*not clearly*) vagamente
dimmer ['dɪmə^r] N (*also:* **dimmer switch**) regulador *m* (de intensidad); (*US Aut*) interruptor *m*

dimple ['dɪmpl] N hoyuelo

dimwitted ['dɪm'wɪtɪd] ADJ (*inf*) lerdo, de pocas luces

din [dɪn] N estruendo, estrépito ▶ VT: **to ~ sth into sb** (*inf*) meter algo en la cabeza a algn

dine [daɪn] VI cenar

diner ['daɪnə^r] N (*person: in restaurant*) comensal *mf*; (*US*) restaurante económico; (*BRIT Rail*) = **dining car**

dinghy ['dɪŋgɪ] N bote *m*; (*also*: **rubber dinghy**) lancha (neumática)

dingy ['dɪndʒɪ] ADJ (*room*) sombrío; (*dirty*) sucio; (*dull*) deslucido

dining car ['daɪnɪŋ-] N (*BRIT*) coche-restaurante *m*

dining room ['daɪnɪŋ-] N comedor *m*

dining table N mesa *f* de comedor

dinkum ['dɪŋkəm] ADJ (*AUSTRALIA, NEW ZEALAND inf: also*: **fair dinkum**) de verdad, auténtico; **to be fair ~ about sth** (*serious*) tomarse algo en serio; **fair ~?** ¿de verdad?

dinner ['dɪnə^r] N (*evening meal*) cena, comida (*LAM*); (*lunch*) comida; (*public*) cena, banquete *m*; **~'s ready!** ¡la cena está servida!

dinner jacket N smoking *m*

dinner party N cena

dinner time N (*evening*) hora de cenar; (*midday*) hora de comer

dinosaur ['daɪnəsɔː^r] N dinosaurio

dint [dɪnt] N: **by ~ of (doing) sth** a fuerza de (hacer) algo

diocese ['daɪəsɪs] N diócesis *f*

dioxide [daɪ'ɔksaɪd] N bióxido; **carbon ~** bióxido de carbono

dip [dɪp] N (*slope*) pendiente *f*; (*in sea*) chapuzón *m* ▶ VT (*in water*) mojar; (*ladle etc*) meter; (*BRIT Aut*): **to ~ one's lights** poner la luz de cruce ▶ VI descender, bajar

Dip. ABBR (*BRIT*) = **diploma**

diphtheria [dɪf'θɪərɪə] N difteria

diphthong ['dɪfθɔŋ] N diptongo

diploma [dɪ'pləumə] N diploma *m*

diplomacy [dɪ'pləuməsɪ] N diplomacia

diplomat ['dɪpləmæt] N diplomático(-a) *m/f*

diplomatic [dɪplə'mætɪk] ADJ diplomático; **to break off ~ relations** romper las relaciones diplomáticas

diplomatic corps N cuerpo diplomático

diplomatic immunity N inmunidad *f* diplomática

dipstick ['dɪpstɪk] N (*Aut*) varilla de nivel (del aceite)

dipswitch ['dɪpswɪtʃ] N (*BRIT Aut*) interruptor *m*

dire [daɪə^r] ADJ calamitoso

direct [daɪ'rɛkt] ADJ (*gen*) directo; (*manner, person*) franco ▶ VT dirigir; **can you ~ me to ...?** ¿puede indicarme dónde está ...?; **to ~ sb to do sth** mandar a algn hacer algo

direct cost N costo directo

direct current N corriente *f* continua

direct debit N domiciliación *f* bancaria de recibos; **to pay by ~** domiciliar el pago

direct dialling N servicio automático de llamadas

direction [dɪ'rɛkʃən] N dirección *f*; **sense of ~** sentido de la orientación; **directions** NPL (*advice*) órdenes *fpl*, instrucciones *fpl*; (*to a place*) señas *fpl*; **in the ~ of** hacia, en dirección a; **directions for use** modo de empleo; **to ask for directions** preguntar el camino

directional [dɪ'rɛkʃənl] ADJ direccional

directive [daɪ'rɛktɪv] N orden *f*, instrucción *f*; **a government ~** una orden del gobierno

direct labour N mano *f* de obra directa

directly [dɪ'rɛktlɪ] ADV (*in straight line*) directamente; (*at once*) en seguida

direct mail N correspondencia personalizada

direct mailshot N (*BRIT*) promoción *f* por correspondencia personalizada

directness [dɪ'rɛktnɪs] N (*of person, speech*) franqueza

director [dɪ'rɛktə^r] N director(a) *m/f*; **managing ~** director(a) *m/f* gerente

Director of Public Prosecutions N ≈ fiscal *mf* general del Estado

directory [dɪ'rɛktərɪ] N (*Tel*) guía (telefónica); (*street directory*) callejero; (*trade directory*) directorio de comercio; (*Comput*) directorio

directory enquiries, (*US*) **directory assistance** N (*service*) (servicio *m* de) información

dirt [dəːt] N suciedad *f*

dirt-cheap ['dəːt'tʃiːp] ADJ baratísimo

dirt road N (*US*) camino sin firme

dirty ['dəːtɪ] ADJ sucio; (*joke*) verde, colorado (*LAM*) ▶ VT ensuciar; (*stain*) manchar

dirty trick N mala jugada, truco sucio

disability [dɪsə'bɪlɪtɪ] N incapacidad *f*

disability allowance N pensión *f* de invalidez

disable [dɪs'eɪbl] VT (*illness, accident*) dejar incapacitado *or* inválido; (*tank, gun*) inutilizar; (*Law: disqualify*) incapacitar

disabled [dɪs'eɪbld] ADJ (*physically*) minusválido(-a); (*mentally*) deficiente mental

disabuse [dɪsə'bjuːz] VT desengañar

disadvantage [dɪsəd'vɑːntɪdʒ] N desventaja, inconveniente *m*

disadvantaged [dɪsəd'vɑːntɪdʒd] ADJ (*person*) desventajado

disadvantageous [dɪsædvən'teɪdʒəs] ADJ desventajoso

disaffected [dɪsə'fɛktɪd] ADJ descontento; **to be ~ (to or towards)** estar descontento (de)

517

disaffection [dɪsə'fɛkʃən] N desafecto, descontento

disagree [dɪsə'griː] VI (differ) discrepar; **to ~ (with)** no estar de acuerdo (con); **I ~ with you** no estoy de acuerdo contigo

disagreeable [dɪsə'grɪəbl] ADJ desagradable

disagreement [dɪsə'griːmənt] N (gen) desacuerdo; (quarrel) riña; **to have a ~ with sb** estar en desacuerdo con algn

disallow ['dɪsə'laʊ] VT (goal) anular; (claim) rechazar

disappear [dɪsə'pɪəʳ] VI desaparecer

disappearance [dɪsə'pɪərəns] N desaparición f

disappoint [dɪsə'pɔɪnt] VT decepcionar; (hopes) defraudar

disappointed [dɪsə'pɔɪntɪd] ADJ decepcionado

disappointing [dɪsə'pɔɪntɪŋ] ADJ decepcionante

disappointment [dɪsə'pɔɪntmənt] N decepción f

disapproval [dɪsə'pruːvəl] N desaprobación f

disapprove [dɪsə'pruːv] VI: **to ~ of** desaprobar

disapproving [dɪsə'pruːvɪŋ] ADJ de desaprobación, desaprobador(a)

disarm [dɪs'ɑːm] VT desarmar

disarmament [dɪs'ɑːməmənt] N desarme m

disarmament talks NPL conversaciones fpl de or sobre desarme

disarming [dɪs'ɑːmɪŋ] ADJ (smile) que desarma, encantador(a)

disarray [dɪsə'reɪ] N: **in ~** (troops) desorganizado; (thoughts) confuso; (hair, clothes) desarreglado; **to throw into ~** provocar el caos

disaster [dɪ'zɑːstəʳ] N desastre m

disaster area N zona catastrófica

disastrous [dɪ'zɑːstrəs] ADJ desastroso

disband [dɪs'bænd] VT disolver ▶ VI desbandarse

disbelief [dɪsbə'liːf] N incredulidad f; **in ~** con incredulidad

disbelieve ['dɪsbə'liːv] VT (person, story) poner en duda, no creer

disc [dɪsk] N disco; (Comput) = **disk**

disc. ABBR (Comm) = **discount**

discard [dɪs'kɑːd] VT tirar; (fig) descartar

discern [dɪ'sɜːn] VT percibir, discernir; (understand) comprender

discernible [dɪ'sɜːnəbl] ADJ perceptible

discerning [dɪ'sɜːnɪŋ] ADJ perspicaz

discharge [dɪs'tʃɑːdʒ] VT (task, duty) cumplir; (ship etc) descargar; (patient) dar de alta; (employee) despedir; (soldier) licenciar; (defendant) poner en libertad; (settle: debt) saldar ▶ N ['dɪstʃɑːdʒ] (Elec) descarga; (vaginal discharge) emisión f vaginal; (dismissal)

despedida; (of duty) desempeño; (of debt) pago, descargo; (of gas, chemicals) escape m; **discharged bankrupt** quebrado/a rehabilitado/a

disciple [dɪ'saɪpl] N discípulo(-a)

disciplinary ['dɪsɪplɪnərɪ] ADJ: **to take ~ action against sb** disciplinar a algn

discipline ['dɪsɪplɪn] N disciplina ▶ VT disciplinar; **to ~ o.s. to do sth** obligarse a hacer algo

disc jockey N pinchadiscos mf

disclaim [dɪs'kleɪm] VT negar tener

disclaimer [dɪs'kleɪməʳ] N rectificación f; **to issue a ~** hacer una rectificación

disclose [dɪs'kləʊz] VT revelar

disclosure [dɪs'kləʊʒəʳ] N revelación f

Discman® ['dɪskmən] N Discman® m

disco ['dɪskəʊ] N ABBR = **discothèque**

discolouration, (US) **discoloration** [dɪskʌlə'reɪʃən] N descoloramiento, decoloración f

discoloured, (US) **discolored** [dɪs'kʌləd] ADJ descolorido

discomfort [dɪs'kʌmfət] N incomodidad f; (unease) inquietud f; (physical) malestar m

disconcert [dɪskən'sɜːt] VT desconcertar

disconnect [dɪskə'nɛkt] VT (gen) separar; (Elec etc) desconectar; (supply) cortar (el suministro) a

disconsolate [dɪs'kɔnsəlɪt] ADJ desconsolado

discontent [dɪskən'tɛnt] N descontento

discontented [dɪskən'tɛntɪd] ADJ descontento

discontinue [dɪskən'tɪnjuː] VT interrumpir; (payments) suspender

discord ['dɪskɔːd] N discordia; (Mus) disonancia

discordant [dɪs'kɔːdənt] ADJ disonante

discothèque ['dɪskəʊtɛk] N discoteca

discount ['dɪskaʊnt] N descuento ▶ VT [dɪs'kaʊnt] descontar; (report etc) descartar; **at a ~** con descuento; **~ for cash** descuento por pago en efectivo; **to give sb a ~ on sth** hacer un descuento a algn en algo

discount house N (Finance) banco de descuento; (Comm: also: **discount store**) ≈ tienda de saldos

discount rate N (Comm) tipo de descuento

discount store N ≈ tienda de saldos

discourage [dɪs'kʌrɪdʒ] VT desalentar; (oppose) oponerse a; (dissuade, deter) desanimar, disuadir; **to ~ sb from doing** disuadir a algn de hacer

discouragement [dɪs'kʌrɪdʒmənt] N (dissuasion) disuasión f; (depression) desánimo, desaliento; **to act as a ~ to** servir para disuadir

discouraging [dɪs'kʌrɪdʒɪŋ] ADJ desalentador(a)

discourteous [dɪsˈkəːtɪəs] ADJ descortés
discover [dɪsˈkʌvəʳ] VT descubrir
discovery [dɪsˈkʌvərɪ] N descubrimiento
discredit [dɪsˈkrɛdɪt] VT desacreditar
discreet [dɪˈskriːt] ADJ (*tactful*) discreto;
(*careful*) circunspecto, prudente
discreetly [dɪˈskriːtlɪ] ADV discretamente
discrepancy [dɪˈskrɛpənsɪ] N (*difference*)
diferencia; (*disagreement*) discrepancia
discretion [dɪˈskrɛʃən] N (*tact*) discreción *f*;
(*care*) prudencia, circunspección *f*; **use your
own ~** haz lo que creas oportuno; **at the ~ of**
a criterio de
discretionary [dɪˈskrɛʃənrɪ] ADJ (*powers*)
discrecional
discriminate [dɪˈskrɪmɪneɪt] VI: **to ~
between** distinguir entre; **to ~ against**
discriminar contra
discriminating [dɪˈskrɪmɪneɪtɪŋ] ADJ
entendido
discrimination [dɪskrɪmɪˈneɪʃən] N
(*discernment*) perspicacia; (*bias*)
discriminación *f*; **racial/sexual ~**
discriminación racial/sexual
discus [ˈdɪskəs] N disco
discuss [dɪˈskʌs] VT (*gen*) discutir; (*a theme*)
tratar
discussion [dɪˈskʌʃən] N discusión *f*; **under ~**
en discusión
disdain [dɪsˈdeɪn] N desdén *m* ▶ VT desdeñar
disease [dɪˈziːz] N enfermedad *f*
diseased [dɪˈziːzd] ADJ enfermo
disembark [dɪsɪmˈbaːk] VT, VI desembarcar
disembarkation [dɪsɛmbaːˈkeɪʃən] N
desembarque *m*
disenchanted [dɪsɪnˈtʃaːntɪd] ADJ: **~ (with)**
desilusionado (con)
disenfranchise [ˈdɪsɪnˈfræntʃaɪz] VT privar
del derecho al voto; (*Comm*) privar de
franquicias
disengage [dɪsɪnˈgeɪdʒ] VT soltar; **to ~ the
clutch** (*Aut*) desembragar
disentangle [dɪsɪnˈtæŋgl] VT desenredar
disfavour, (*US*) **disfavor** [dɪsˈfeɪvəʳ] N
desaprobación *f*
disfigure [dɪsˈfɪgəʳ] VT desfigurar
disgorge [dɪsˈgɔːdʒ] VT verter
disgrace [dɪsˈgreɪs] N ignominia; (*downfall*)
caída; (*shame*) vergüenza, escándalo ▶ VT
deshonrar
disgraceful [dɪsˈgreɪsful] ADJ vergonzoso;
(*behaviour*) escandaloso
disgruntled [dɪsˈgrʌntld] ADJ disgustado,
descontento
disguise [dɪsˈgaɪz] N disfraz *m* ▶ VT disfrazar;
(*voice*) disimular; (*feelings etc*) ocultar; **in ~**
disfrazado; **to ~ o.s. as** disfrazarse de;
there's no disguising the fact that … no
puede ocultarse el hecho de que …

disgust [dɪsˈgʌst] N repugnancia ▶ VT
repugnar, dar asco a
disgusted [dɪsˈgʌstɪd] ADJ indignado
disgusting [dɪsˈgʌstɪŋ] ADJ repugnante,
asqueroso
dish [dɪʃ] N (*gen*) plato; **to do** *or* **wash the
dishes** fregar los platos
▶ **dish out** VT (*money, exam papers*) repartir;
(*food*) servir; (*advice*) dar
▶ **dish up** VT servir
dishcloth [ˈdɪʃklɔθ] N (*for washing*) bayeta;
(*for drying*) paño de cocina
dishearten [dɪsˈhaːtn] VT desalentar
dishevelled, (*US*) **disheveled** [dɪˈʃɛvəld] ADJ
(*hair*) despeinado; (*clothes, appearance*)
desarreglado
dishonest [dɪsˈɔnɪst] ADJ (*person*) poco
honrado, tramposo; (*means*) fraudulento
dishonesty [dɪsˈɔnɪstɪ] N falta de honradez
dishonour, (*US*) **dishonor** [dɪsˈɔnəʳ] N
deshonra
dishonourable, (*US*) **dishonorable**
[dɪsˈɔnərəbl] ADJ deshonroso
dish soap N (*US*) lavavajillas *m inv*
dishtowel [ˈdɪʃtauəl] N (*US*) bayeta
dishwasher [ˈdɪʃwɔʃəʳ] N lavaplatos *m inv*;
(*person*) friegaplatos *mf*
dishy [ˈdɪʃɪ] ADJ (*BRIT inf*) buenón(-ona)
disillusion [dɪsɪˈluːʒən] VT desilusionar;
to become disillusioned (with) quedar
desilusionado (con)
disillusionment [dɪsɪˈluːʒənmənt] N
desilusión *f*
disincentive [dɪsɪnˈsɛntɪv] N freno; **to act
as a ~ (to)** actuar de freno (a); **to be a ~ to** ser
un freno a
disinclined [ˈdɪsɪnˈklaɪnd] ADJ: **to be ~ to do
sth** estar poco dispuesto a hacer algo
disinfect [dɪsɪnˈfɛkt] VT desinfectar
disinfectant [dɪsɪnˈfɛktənt] N
desinfectante *m*
disinflation [dɪsɪnˈfleɪʃən] N desinflación *f*
disinformation [dɪsɪnfəˈmeɪʃən] N
desinformación *f*
disingenuous [dɪsɪnˈdʒɛnjuəs] ADJ poco
sincero, falso
disinherit [dɪsɪnˈhɛrɪt] VT desheredar
disintegrate [dɪsˈɪntɪgreɪt] VI disgregarse,
desintegrarse
disinterested [dɪsˈɪntrəstɪd] ADJ desinteresado
disjointed [dɪsˈdʒɔɪntɪd] ADJ inconexo
disk [dɪsk] N (*Comput*) disco, disquete *m*;
single-/double-sided ~ disco de una cara/
dos caras
disk drive N unidad *f* (de disco)
diskette [dɪsˈkɛt] N diskette *m*, disquete *m*,
disco flexible
disk operating system N sistema *m*
operativo de discos

dislike [dɪsˈlaɪk] N antipatía, aversión f ▸ VT tener antipatía a; **to take a ~ to sb/sth** cogerle or (LAM) agarrarle antipatía a algn/ algo; **I ~ the idea** no me gusta la idea

dislocate [ˈdɪsləkeɪt] VT dislocar; **he dislocated his shoulder** se dislocó el hombro

dislodge [dɪsˈlɔdʒ] VT sacar; (enemy) desalojar

disloyal [dɪsˈlɔɪəl] ADJ desleal

dismal [ˈdɪzml] ADJ (dark) sombrío; (depressing) triste; (very bad) fatal

dismantle [dɪsˈmæntl] VT desmontar, desarmar

dismay [dɪsˈmeɪ] N consternación f ▸ VT consternar; **much to my ~** para gran consternación mía

dismiss [dɪsˈmɪs] VT (worker) despedir; (official) destituir; (idea) rechazar; (Law) rechazar; (possibility) descartar ▸ VI (Mil) romper filas

dismissal [dɪsˈmɪsl] N despido; destitución f

dismount [dɪsˈmaunt] VI apearse; (rider) desmontar

disobedience [dɪsəˈbiːdɪəns] N desobediencia

disobedient [dɪsəˈbiːdɪənt] ADJ desobediente

disobey [dɪsəˈbeɪ] VT desobedecer; (rule) infringir

disorder [dɪsˈɔːdəʳ] N desorden m; (rioting) disturbio; (Med) trastorno; (disease) enfermedad f; **civil ~** desorden m civil

disorderly [dɪsˈɔːdəlɪ] ADJ (untidy) desordenado; (meeting) alborotado; **~ conduct** (Law) conducta escandalosa

disorganized [dɪsˈɔːɡənaɪzd] ADJ desorganizado

disorientated [dɪsˈɔːrɪɛnteɪtəd] ADJ desorientado

disown [dɪsˈəun] VT renegar de

disparaging [dɪsˈpærɪdʒɪŋ] ADJ despreciativo; **to be ~ about sth/sb** menospreciar algo/a algn

disparate [ˈdɪspərɪt] ADJ dispar

disparity [dɪsˈpærɪtɪ] N disparidad f

dispassionate [dɪsˈpæʃənɪt] ADJ (unbiased) imparcial; (unemotional) desapasionado

dispatch [dɪsˈpætʃ] VT enviar; (kill) despachar; (deal with: business) despachar ▸ N (sending) envío; (speed) prontitud f; (Press) informe m; (Mil) parte m

dispatch department N (Comm) departamento de envíos

dispatch rider N (Mil) correo

dispel [dɪsˈpɛl] VT disipar, dispersar

dispensary [dɪsˈpɛnsərɪ] N dispensario

dispensation [dɪspɛnˈseɪʃən] N (Rel) dispensa

dispense [dɪsˈpɛns] VT dispensar, repartir; (medicine) preparar

▸ **dispense with** VT FUS (make unnecessary) prescindir de

dispenser [dɪsˈpɛnsəʳ] N (container) distribuidor m automático

dispensing chemist [dɪsˈpɛnsɪŋ-] N (BRIT) farmacia

dispersal [dɪsˈpəːsl] N dispersión f

disperse [dɪsˈpəːs] VT dispersar ▸ VI dispersarse

dispirited [dɪsˈpɪrɪtɪd] ADJ desanimado, desalentado

displace [dɪsˈpleɪs] VT (person) desplazar; (replace) reemplazar

displaced person N (Pol) desplazado(-a)

displacement [dɪsˈpleɪsmənt] N cambio de sitio

display [dɪsˈpleɪ] N (in shop window) escaparate m; (exhibition) exposición f; (Comput) visualización f; (Mil) desfile m; (of feeling) manifestación f; (pej) aparato, pompa ▸ VT exponer; manifestar; (ostentatiously) lucir; **on ~** (exhibits) expuesto, exhibido; (goods) en el escaparate

display advertising N publicidad f gráfica

displease [dɪsˈpliːz] VT (offend) ofender; (annoy) fastidiar; **displeased with** disgustado con

displeasure [dɪsˈplɛʒəʳ] N disgusto

disposable [dɪsˈpəuzəbl] ADJ (not reusable) desechable; **~ personal income** ingresos mpl personales disponibles

disposable nappy N pañal m desechable

disposal [dɪsˈpəuzl] N (sale) venta; (of house) traspaso; (by giving away) donación f; (arrangement) colocación f; (of rubbish) destrucción f; **at one's ~** a la disposición de algn; **to put sth at sb's ~** poner algo a disposición de algn

dispose [dɪsˈpəuz] VI: **~ of** (time, money) disponer de; (unwanted goods) deshacerse de; (Comm: sell) traspasar, vender; (throw away) tirar

disposed [dɪsˈpəuzd] ADJ: **~ to do** dispuesto a hacer

disposition [dɪspəˈzɪʃən] N disposición f; (temperament) carácter m

dispossess [ˈdɪspəˈzɛs] VT: **to ~ sb (of)** desposeer a algn (de)

disproportion [dɪsprəˈpɔːʃən] N desproporción f

disproportionate [dɪsprəˈpɔːʃənət] ADJ desproporcionado

disprove [dɪsˈpruːv] VT refutar

dispute [dɪsˈpjuːt] N disputa; (verbal) discusión f; (also: **industrial dispute**) conflicto (laboral) ▸ VT (argue) disputar; (question) cuestionar; **to be in** or **under ~** (matter) discutirse; (territory) estar en disputa; (Law) estar en litigio

disqualification [dɪskwɔlɪfɪˈkeɪʃən] N inhabilitación f; (Sport) descalificación f; (from driving) descalificación f

disqualify [dɪsˈkwɔlɪfaɪ] VT (Sport) desclasificar; **to ~ sb for sth/from doing sth** incapacitar a algn para algo/para hacer algo

disquiet [dɪsˈkwaɪət] N preocupación f, inquietud f

disquieting [dɪsˈkwaɪətɪŋ] ADJ inquietante

disregard [dɪsrɪˈgɑːd] VT desatender; (ignore) no hacer caso de ▶ N (indifference: to feelings, danger, money): **~ (for)** indiferencia (a); **~ (of)** (non-observance: of law, rules) violación f (de)

disrepair [dɪsrɪˈpɛəʳ] N: **to fall into ~** (building) desmoronarse; (street) deteriorarse

disreputable [dɪsˈrɛpjutəbl] ADJ (person, area) de mala fama; (behaviour) vergonzoso

disrepute [ˈdɪsrɪˈpjuːt] N descrédito, ignominia; **to bring into ~** desacreditar

disrespectful [dɪsrɪˈspɛktful] ADJ irrespetuoso

disrupt [dɪsˈrʌpt] VT (plans) desbaratar, alternar, trastornar; (meeting, public transport, conversation) interrumpir

disruption [dɪsˈrʌpʃən] N desbaratamiento; trastorno; interrupción f

disruptive [dɪsˈrʌptɪv] ADJ (influence) disruptivo; (strike action) perjudicial

dissatisfaction [dɪssætɪsˈfækʃən] N disgusto, descontento

dissatisfied [dɪsˈsætɪsfaɪd] ADJ insatisfecho

dissect [dɪˈsɛkt] VT (also fig) disecar

disseminate [dɪˈsɛmɪneɪt] VT divulgar, difundir

dissent [dɪˈsɛnt] N disensión f

dissenter [dɪˈsɛntəʳ] N (Rel, Pol etc) disidente mf

dissertation [dɪsəˈteɪʃən] N (Univ) tesina; see also **master's degree**

disservice [dɪsˈsəːvɪs] N: **to do sb a ~** perjudicar a algn

dissident [ˈdɪsɪdnt] ADJ, N disidente mf

dissimilar [dɪˈsɪmɪləʳ] ADJ distinto

dissipate [ˈdɪsɪpeɪt] VT disipar; (waste) desperdiciar

dissipated [ˈdɪsɪpeɪtɪd] ADJ disoluto

dissipation [dɪsɪˈpeɪʃən] N disipación f (moral), libertinaje m, vicio; (waste) derroche m

dissociate [dɪˈsəuʃɪeɪt] VT disociar; **to ~ o.s. from** disociarse de

dissolute [ˈdɪsəluːt] ADJ disoluto

dissolution [dɪsəˈluːʃən] N disolución f

dissolve [dɪˈzɔlv] VT disolver ▶ VI disolverse

dissuade [dɪˈsweɪd] VT: **to ~ sb (from)** disuadir a algn (de)

distaff [ˈdɪstæf] N: **~ side** rama femenina

distance [ˈdɪstns] N distancia; **in the ~** a lo lejos; **what ~ is it to London?** ¿qué distancia hay de aquí a Londres?; **it's within walking ~** se puede ir andando

distant [ˈdɪstnt] ADJ lejano; (manner) reservado, frío

distaste [dɪsˈteɪst] N repugnancia

distasteful [dɪsˈteɪstful] ADJ repugnante, desagradable

Dist. Atty. ABBR (US) = **district attorney**

distemper [dɪsˈtɛmpəʳ] N (of dogs) moquillo

distend [dɪˈstɛnd] VT dilatar, hinchar ▶ VI dilatarse, hincharse

distended [dɪˈstɛndɪd] ADJ (stomach) hinchado

distil, (US) **distill** [dɪsˈtɪl] VT destilar

distillery [dɪsˈtɪlərɪ] N destilería

distinct [dɪsˈtɪŋkt] ADJ (different) distinto; (clear) claro; (unmistakeable) inequívoco; **as ~ from** a diferencia de

distinction [dɪsˈtɪŋkʃən] N distinción f; (in exam) sobresaliente m; **a writer of ~** un escritor destacado; **to draw a ~ between** hacer una distinción entre

distinctive [dɪsˈtɪŋktɪv] ADJ distintivo

distinctly [dɪsˈtɪŋktlɪ] ADV claramente

distinguish [dɪsˈtɪŋgwɪʃ] VT distinguir ▶ VI: **to ~ (between)** distinguir (entre)

distinguished [dɪsˈtɪŋgwɪʃt] ADJ (eminent) distinguido; (career) eminente; (refined) distinguido, de categoría

distinguishing [dɪsˈtɪŋgwɪʃɪŋ] ADJ (feature) distintivo

distort [dɪsˈtɔːt] VT deformar; (sound) distorsionar; (account, news) tergiversar

distortion [dɪsˈtɔːʃən] N deformación f; (of sound) distorsión f; (of truth etc) tergiversación f; (of facts) falseamiento

distract [dɪsˈtrækt] VT distraer

distracted [dɪsˈtræktɪd] ADJ distraído

distracting [dɪsˈtræktɪŋ] ADJ que distrae la atención, molesto

distraction [dɪsˈtrækʃən] N distracción f; (confusion) aturdimiento; (amusement) diversión f; **to drive sb to ~** (distress, anxiety) volver loco a algn

distraught [dɪsˈtrɔːt] ADJ turbado, enloquecido

distress [dɪsˈtrɛs] N (anguish) angustia; (want) miseria; (pain) dolor m; (danger) peligro ▶ VT afligir; (pain) doler; **in ~** (ship etc) en peligro

distressing [dɪsˈtrɛsɪŋ] ADJ angustioso; doloroso

distress signal N señal f de socorro

distribute [dɪsˈtrɪbjuːt] VT (gen) distribuir; (share out) repartir

distribution [dɪstrɪˈbjuːʃən] N distribución f

distribution cost N gastos mpl de distribución

d

distributor [dɪs'trɪbjutə^r] N (Aut)
distribuidor m; (Comm) distribuidora
district ['dɪstrɪkt] N (of country) zona, región f;
(of town) barrio; (Admin) distrito
district attorney N (US) fiscal mf
district council N ≈ municipio; ver nota

En Inglaterra y Gales, con la excepción de
Londres, la administración local corre a
cargo del *district council*, responsable de los
servicios municipales como vivienda,
urbanismo, recolección de basuras, salud
medioambiental etc. La mayoría de sus
miembros son elegidos a nivel local cada
cuatro años. Hay un total de 369 "*districts*"
(distritos), repartidos en 53 "*counties*"
(condados), que se financian a través de
los impuestos municipales y partidas
presupuestarias del Estado. Éste controla
sus gastos a través de una comisión
independiente.

district manager N representante mf
regional
district nurse N (Brit) enfermera que atiende a
pacientes a domicilio
distrust [dɪs'trʌst] N desconfianza ▸ VT
desconfiar de
distrustful [dɪs'trʌstful] ADJ desconfiado
disturb [dɪs'tə:b] VT (person: bother, interrupt)
molestar; (meeting) interrumpir; (disorganize)
desordenar; **sorry to ~ you** perdone la
molestia
disturbance [dɪs'tə:bəns] N (political etc)
disturbio; (violence) alboroto; (of mind)
trastorno; **to cause a ~** causar alboroto;
~ of the peace alteración f del orden
público
disturbed [dɪs'tə:bd] ADJ (worried, upset)
preocupado, angustiado; **to be
emotionally/mentally ~** tener problemas
emocionales/ser un trastornado mental
disturbing [dɪs'tə:bɪŋ] ADJ inquietante,
perturbador(a)
disuse [dɪs'ju:s] N: **to fall into ~** caer en
desuso
disused [dɪs'ju:zd] ADJ abandonado
ditch [dɪtʃ] N zanja; (irrigation ditch) acequia
▸ VT (inf: partner) deshacerse de; (: plan, car etc)
abandonar
dither ['dɪðə^r] VI vacilar
ditto ['dɪtəu] ADV ídem, lo mismo
divan [dɪ'væn] N diván m
divan bed N cama turca
dive [daɪv] N (from board) salto; (underwater)
buceo; (of submarine) inmersión f; (Aviat)
picada ▸ VI (swimmer: into water) saltar; (: under
water) zambullirse, bucear; (fish, submarine)
sumergirse; (bird) lanzarse en picado; **to ~
into** (bag etc) meter la mano en; (place)
meterse de prisa en

diver ['daɪvə^r] N (Sport) saltador(a) m/f;
(underwater) buzo
diverge [daɪ'və:dʒ] VI divergir
divergent [daɪ'və:dʒənt] ADJ divergente
diverse [daɪ'və:s] ADJ diversos(-as),
varios(-as)
diversification [daɪvə:sɪfɪ'keɪʃən] N
diversificación f
diversify [daɪ'və:sɪfaɪ] VT diversificar
diversion [daɪ'və:ʃən] N (Brit Aut) desviación
f; (distraction) diversión f; (Mil) diversión f
diversionary tactics [daɪ'və:ʃənrɪ-] NPL
tácticas fpl de diversión
diversity [daɪ'və:sɪtɪ] N diversidad f
divert [daɪ'və:t] VT (Brit: train, plane, traffic)
desviar; (amuse) divertir
divest [daɪ'vɛst] VT: **to ~ sb of sth** despojar a
algn de algo
divide [dɪ'vaɪd] VT dividir; (separate) separar
▸ VI dividirse; (road) bifurcarse; **to ~
(between or among)** repartir o dividir
(entre); **40 divided by 5** 40 dividido por 5
▸ **divide out** VT: **to ~ out (between or
among)** (sweets, tasks etc) repartir (entre)
divided [dɪ'vaɪdɪd] ADJ (country, couple)
dividido, separado; (opinions) en desacuerdo
divided highway N (US) carretera de doble
calzada
dividend ['dɪvɪdɛnd] N dividendo; (fig)
beneficio
dividend cover N cobertura de dividendo
dividers [dɪ'vaɪdəz] NPL compás msg de
puntas
divine [dɪ'vaɪn] ADJ divino ▸ VT (future)
vaticinar; (truth) alumbrar; (water, metal)
descubrir, detectar
diving ['daɪvɪŋ] N (Sport) salto; (underwater)
buceo
diving board N trampolín m
diving suit N escafandra
divinity [dɪ'vɪnɪtɪ] N divinidad f; (Scol)
teología
divisible [dɪ'vɪzɪbl] ADJ divisible
division [dɪ'vɪʒən] N (also Brit Football)
división f; (sharing out) reparto; (disagreement)
diferencias fpl; (Comm) sección f; (Brit Pol)
votación f; **~ of labour** división f del trabajo
divisive [dɪ'vaɪsɪv] ADJ divisivo
divorce [dɪ'vɔ:s] N divorcio ▸ VT divorciarse
de
divorced [dɪ'vɔ:st] ADJ divorciado
divorcee [dɪvɔ:'si:] N divorciado(-a)
divot ['dɪvət] N (Golf) chuleta
divulge [daɪ'vʌldʒ] VT divulgar, revelar
DIY ADJ, N ABBR (Brit) = **do-it-yourself**
dizziness ['dɪzɪnɪs] N vértigo
dizzy ['dɪzɪ] ADJ (person) mareado; (height)
vertiginoso; **to feel ~** marearse; **I feel ~**
estoy mareado

DJ N ABBR (= *disc jokey*) DJ *mf*

dj N ABBR = **dinner jacket**

Djakarta [dʒəˈkɑːtə] N Yakarta

DJIA N ABBR (*US Stock Exchange*) = **Dow-Jones Industrial Average**

dl ABBR (= *decilitre(s)*) dl

DLit, DLitt ABBR (= *Doctor of Literature, Doctor of Letters*) título universitario

dm ABBR (= *decimetre(s)*) dm

DMus ABBR (= *Doctor of Music*) título universitario

DMZ N ABBR (= *demilitarized zone*) zona desmilitarizada

DNA N ABBR (= *deoxyribonucleic acid*) ADN *m*

DNA test N prueba *f* del ADN

KEYWORD

do [duː] (*pt* **did**, *pp* **done**) N **1** (*inf: party etc*): **we're having a little do on Saturday** damos una fiestecita el sábado; **it was rather a grand do** fue un acontecimiento a lo grande

2: the dos and don'ts lo que se debe y no se debe hacer

▶ AUX VB **1** (*in negative constructions: not translated*): **I don't understand** no entiendo

2 (*to form questions: not translated*): **do you speak English?** ¿habla (usted) inglés?; **didn't you know?** ¿no lo sabías?; **what do you think?** ¿qué opinas?

3 (*for emphasis: in polite expressions*): **people do make mistakes sometimes** a veces sí se cometen errores; **she does seem rather late** a mí también me parece que se ha retrasado; **do sit down/help yourself** siéntate/sírvete por favor; **do take care!** ¡ten cuidado! ¿eh?; **I DO wish I could …** ojalá (que) pudiera …; **but I DO like it** pero, sí (que) me gusta

4 (*used to avoid repeating vb*): **she sings better than I do** canta mejor que yo; **do you agree?** — **yes, I do/no, I don't** ¿estás de acuerdo? — sí (lo estoy)/no (lo estoy); **she lives in Glasgow — so do I** vive en Glasgow — yo también; **he didn't like it and neither did we** no le gustó a nosotros tampoco; **who made this mess? — I did** ¿quién hizo esta chapuza? — yo; **he asked me to help him and I did** me pidió que le ayudara y lo hice

5 (*in question tags*): **you like him, don't you?** te gusta, ¿verdad? *or* ¿no?; **I don't know him, do I?** creo que no le conozco; **he laughed, didn't he?** se rió ¿no?

▶ VT **1** (*gen*): **what are you doing tonight?** ¿qué haces esta noche?; **what can I do for you?** (*in shop*) ¿en qué puedo servirle?; **what does he do for a living?** ¿a qué se dedica?; **I'll do all I can** haré todo lo que pueda; **what have you done with my slippers?** ¿qué has hecho con mis zapatillas?; **to do the**

washing-up/cooking fregar los platos/cocinar; **to do one's teeth/hair/nails** lavarse los dientes/arreglarse el pelo/arreglarse las uñas

2 (*Aut etc*): **the car was doing 100** el coche iba a 100; **we've done 200 km already** ya hemos hecho 200 km; **he can do 100 in that car** puede ir a 100 en ese coche

3 (*visit: city, museum*) visitar, recorrer

4 (*cook*): **a steak – well done please** un filete bien hecho, por favor

▶ VI **1** (*act, behave*) hacer; **do as I do** haz como yo

2 (*get on, fare*): **he's doing well/badly at school** va bien/mal en la escuela; **the firm is doing well** la empresa anda *or* va bien; **how do you do?** mucho gusto; (*less formal*) ¿qué tal?

3 (*suit*): **will it do?** ¿sirve?, ¿está *or* va bien?; **it doesn't do to upset her** cuidado en ofenderla

4 (*be sufficient*) bastar; **will £10 do?** ¿será bastante con £10?; **that'll do** así está bien; **that'll do!** (*in annoyance*) ¡ya está bien!, ¡basta ya!; **to make do (with)** arreglárselas (con)

▶ **do away with** VT FUS (*inf: kill*) eliminar; (*eradicate: disease*) eliminar; (*abolish: law etc*) abolir; (*withdraw*) retirar

▶ **do out of** VT FUS: **to do sb out of sth** pisar algo a algn

▶ **do up** VT (*laces*) atar; (*zip, dress, shirt*) abrochar; (*renovate: room, house*) renovar

▶ **do with** VT FUS (*need*): **I could do with a drink/some help** no me vendría mal un trago/un poco de ayuda; (*be connected with*) tener que ver con; **what has it got to do with you?** ¿qué tiene que ver contigo?

▶ **do without** VI: **if you're late for dinner then you'll do without** si llegas tarde tendrás que quedarte sin cenar ▶ VT FUS pasar sin; **I can do without a car** puedo pasar sin coche

do. ABBR = **ditto**

DOA ABBR = **dead on arrival**

d.o.b. ABBR = **date of birth**

doc [dɔk] N (*inf*) médico(-a)

docile [ˈdəʊsaɪl] ADJ dócil

dock [dɔk] N (*Naut: wharf*) dársena, muelle *m*; (*Law*) banquillo (de los acusados) ▶ VI (*enter dock*) atracar (en el muelle) ▶ VT (*pay etc*) descontar; **docks** NPL muelles *mpl*, puerto *sg*

dock dues NPL derechos *mpl* de muelle

docker [ˈdɔkəʳ] N trabajador *m* portuario, estibador *m*

docket [ˈdɔkɪt] N (*on parcel etc*) etiqueta

dockyard [ˈdɔkjɑːd] N astillero

doctor [ˈdɔktəʳ] N médico; (*PhD etc*) doctor(a) *m/f* ▶ VT (*fig*) arreglar, falsificar; (*drink etc*) adulterar

doctorate ['dɔktərɪt] N doctorado; *ver nota*

El grado más alto que conceden las universidades es el doctorado (*doctorate*), tras un período de estudio e investigación original no inferior a tres años que culmina con la presentación de una tesis ("*thesis*") en la que se exponen los resultados. El título más frecuente es el de "*PhD*" ("*Doctor of Philosophy*"), que se obtiene en Letras, Ciencias e Ingeniería, aunque también existen otros doctorados específicos en Música, Derecho etc.

Doctor of Philosophy N Doctor *m* (en Filosofía y Letras)

doctrinaire [dɔktrɪ'neər] ADJ doctrinario

doctrine ['dɔktrɪn] N doctrina

docudrama [dɔkju'drɑːmə] N (*TV*) docudrama *m*

document ['dɔkjumənt] N documento
▶ VT documentar

documentary [dɔkju'mentərɪ] ADJ documental ▶ N documental *m*

documentation [dɔkjumen'teɪʃən] N documentación *f*

DOD N ABBR (*US*: = *Department of Defense*) Ministerio de Defensa

doddering ['dɔdərɪŋ], **doddery** ['dɔdərɪ] ADJ vacilante

doddle ['dɔdl] N: **it's a ~** (*BRIT inf*) es pan comido

Dodecanese [dəudɪkə'niːz], **Dodecanese Islands** NPL Dodecaneso *sg*

dodge [dɔdʒ] N (*of body*) regate *m*; (*fig*) truco ▶ VT (*gen*) evadir; (*blow*) esquivar ▶ VI escabullirse; (*Sport*) hacer una finta; **to ~ out of the way** echarse a un lado; **to ~ through the traffic** esquivar el tráfico

Dodgems® ['dɔdʒəmz] NPL (*BRIT*) autos *or* coches *mpl* de choque

dodgy ['dɔdʒɪ] ADJ (*BRIT inf: uncertain*) dudoso; (: *shady*) sospechoso; (: *risky*) arriesgado

DOE N ABBR (*US*) = **Department of Energy**

doe [dəu] N (*deer*) cierva, gama; (*rabbit*) coneja

does [dʌz] VB *see* **do**

doesn't ['dʌznt] = **does not**

dog [dɔg] N perro ▶ VT seguir (de cerca); (*fig: memory etc*) perseguir; **to go to the dogs** (*person*) echarse a perder; (*nation etc*) ir a la ruina

dog biscuit N galleta de perro

dog collar N collar *m* de perro; (*fig*) alzacuello(s) *msg*

dog-eared ['dɔgɪəd] ADJ sobado; (*page*) con la esquina doblada

dogfish ['dɔgfɪʃ] N cazón *m*, perro marino

dog food N comida para perros

dogged ['dɔgɪd] ADJ tenaz, obstinado

doggy ['dɔgɪ] N (*inf*) perrito

doggy bag N bolsa para llevarse las sobras de la comida

dogma ['dɔgmə] N dogma *m*

dogmatic [dɔg'mætɪk] ADJ dogmático

do-gooder [duː'gudər] N (*inf, pej*): **to be a ~** ser una persona bien intencionada *or* un filantropista

dogsbody ['dɔgzbɔdɪ] N (*BRIT*) burro de carga

doily ['dɔɪlɪ] N pañito de adorno

doing ['duɪŋ] N: **this is your ~** esto es obra tuya; **doings** NPL (*events*) sucesos *mpl*; (*acts*) hechos *mpl*

do-it-yourself [duːɪtjɔː'sɛlf] N bricolaje *m*

doldrums ['dɔldrəmz] NPL: **to be in the ~** (*person*) estar abatido; (*business*) estar estancado

dole [dəul] N (*BRIT: payment*) subsidio de paro; **on the ~** parado
▶ **dole out** VT repartir

doleful ['dəulful] ADJ triste, lúgubre

doll [dɔl] N muñeca
▶ **doll up** VT: **to ~ o.s. up** ataviarse

dollar ['dɔlər] N dólar *m*

dollop ['dɔləp] N buena cucharada

dolphin ['dɔlfɪn] N delfín *m*

domain [də'meɪn] N (*fig*) campo, competencia; (*land*) dominios *mpl*

dome [dəum] N (*Arch*) cúpula; (*shape*) bóveda

domestic [də'mestɪk] ADJ (*animal, duty*) doméstico; (*flight, news, policy*) nacional

domestic appliance N aparato *m* doméstico, aparato *m* de uso doméstico

domesticated [də'mestɪkeɪtɪd] ADJ domesticado; (*person: home-loving*) casero, hogareño

domesticity [dəumes'tɪsɪtɪ] N vida casera

domestic servant N sirviente(-a) *m/f*

domicile ['dɔmɪsaɪl] N domicilio

dominant ['dɔmɪnənt] ADJ dominante

dominate ['dɔmɪneɪt] VT dominar

domination [dɔmɪ'neɪʃən] N dominación *f*

domineering [dɔmɪ'nɪərɪŋ] ADJ dominante

Dominican Republic [də'mɪnɪkən-] N República Dominicana

dominion [də'mɪnɪən] N dominio

domino ['dɔmɪnəu] (*pl* **dominoes**) N ficha de dominó

dominoes ['dɔmɪnəuz] N (*game*) dominó

don [dɔn] N (*BRIT*) profesor(a) *m/f* de universidad

donate [də'neɪt] VT donar

donation [də'neɪʃən] N donativo

done [dʌn] PP *of* **do**

dongle ['dɔŋgl] N (*Comput*) pincho

donkey ['dɔŋkɪ] N burro

donkey-work ['dɔŋkɪwəːk] N (*BRIT inf*) trabajo pesado

donor ['dəunər] N donante *mf*

donor card N carnet m de donante de órganos

don't [dəʊnt] = **do not**

donut ['dəʊnʌt] N (US) = **doughnut**

doodle ['du:dl] N garabato ▶ VI pintar dibujitos or garabatos

doom [du:m] N (fate) suerte f; (death) muerte f ▶ VT: **to be doomed to failure** estar condenado al fracaso

doomsday ['du:mzdeɪ] N día m del juicio final

door [dɔ:ʳ] N puerta; (of car) portezuela; (entry) entrada; **from ~ to ~** de puerta en puerta

doorbell ['dɔ:bɛl] N timbre m

door handle N tirador m; (of car) manija

doorknob N pomo m de la puerta, manilla f (LAM)

door knocker N aldaba

doorman ['dɔ:mən] N (irreg) (in hotel) portero

doormat ['dɔ:mæt] N felpudo, estera

doorstep ['dɔ:stɛp] N peldaño; **on your ~** en la puerta de casa; (fig) al lado de casa

door-to-door ['dɔ:tə'dɔ:ʳ] ADJ: **~ selling** venta a domicilio

doorway ['dɔ:weɪ] N entrada, puerta; **in the ~** en la puerta

dope [dəʊp] N (inf: illegal drug) droga; (: person) imbécil mf; (: information) información f, informes mpl ▶ VT (horse etc) drogar

dopey ['dəʊpɪ] ADJ atontado

dormant ['dɔ:mənt] ADJ inactivo; (latent) latente

dormer ['dɔ:məʳ] N (also: **dormer window**) buhardilla

dormitory ['dɔ:mɪtrɪ] N (BRIT) dormitorio; (US: hall of residence) residencia, colegio mayor

dormouse ['dɔ:maʊs] (pl **dormice** [-maɪs]) N lirón m

Dors ABBR (BRIT) = **Dorset**

DOS [dɔs] N ABBR = **disk operating system**

dosage ['dəʊsɪdʒ] N (on medicine bottle) dosis f inv, dosificación f

dose [dəʊs] N (of medicine) dosis f inv; **a ~ of flu** un ataque de gripe ▶ VT: **to ~ o.s. with** automedicarse con

dosser ['dɔsəʳ] N (BRIT inf) mendigo(-a); (lazy person) vago(-a)

doss house ['dɔs-] N (BRIT) pensión f de mala muerte

dossier ['dɔsɪeɪ] N: **~ (on)** expediente m (sobre)

DOT N ABBR (US: = Department of Transportation) ministerio de transporte

dot [dɔt] N punto ▶ VI: **dotted with** salpicado de; **on the ~** en punto

dotcom ['dɔtkɔm] N puntocom f

dot command N (Comput) instrucción f (precedida) de punto

dote [dəʊt]: **to ~ on** VT fus adorar, idolatrar

dot-matrix printer [dɔt'meɪtrɪks-] N impresora matricial or de matriz

dotted line ['dɔtɪd-] N línea de puntos; **to sign on the ~** firmar

dotty ['dɔtɪ] ADJ (inf) disparatado, chiflado

double ['dʌbl] ADJ doble ▶ ADV (twice): **to cost ~** costar el doble ▶ N (gen) doble m ▶ VT doblar; (efforts) redoblar ▶ VI doblarse; (have two uses etc): **to ~ as** hacer las veces de; **~ five two six (5526)** (Tel) cinco cinco dos seis; **spelt with a ~ "s"** escrito con dos "eses"; **on the ~**, (BRIT) **at the ~** corriendo
▶ **double back** VI (person) volver sobre sus pasos
▶ **double up** VI (bend over) doblarse; (share bedroom) compartir

double bass N contrabajo

double bed N cama de matrimonio

double-breasted ['dʌbl'brɛstɪd] ADJ cruzado

double-check ['dʌbltʃɛk] VT volver a revisar ▶ VI: **I'll ~** voy a revisarlo otra vez

double-click ['dʌbl'klɪk] (Comput) VI hacer doble clic

double cream N nata enriquecida

double-cross ['dʌbl'krɔs] VT (trick) engañar; (betray) traicionar

doubledecker ['dʌbl'dɛkəʳ] N autobús m de dos pisos

double glazing N (BRIT) doble acristalamiento

double indemnity N doble indemnización f

double-page ['dʌblpeɪdʒ] ADJ: **~ spread** doble página

double room N habitación f doble

doubles ['dʌblz] N (Tennis) juego de dobles

double time N tarifa doble

double whammy [-'wæmɪ] N (inf) palo doble

double yellow lines NPL (BRIT Aut) línea doble amarilla de prohibido aparcar, ≈ línea fsg amarilla continua

doubly ['dʌblɪ] ADV doblemente

doubt [daʊt] N duda ▶ VT dudar; (suspect) dudar de; **to ~ that** dudar que; **there is no ~ that** no cabe duda de que; **without (a) ~** sin duda (alguna); **beyond ~** fuera de duda; **I ~ it very much** lo dudo mucho

doubtful ['daʊtful] ADJ dudoso; (arousing suspicion: person) sospechoso; (unconvinced): **to be ~ about sth** tener dudas sobre algo; **I'm a bit ~** no estoy convencido

doubtless ['daʊtlɪs] ADV sin duda

dough [dəʊ] N masa, pasta; (inf: money) pasta, lana (LAM)

doughnut ['dəʊnʌt] N dónut m

douse [daʊs] VT (drench: with water) mojar; (extinguish: flames) apagar

dove [dʌv] N paloma

Dover ['dəʊvəʳ] N Dover

dovetail ['dʌvteɪl] VI (fig) encajar
dowager ['dauɪdʒə^r] N: ~ **duchess** duquesa viuda
dowdy ['daudɪ] ADJ desaliñado; (inelegant) poco elegante
Dow-Jones average ['daudʒəunz-] N (US) índice m Dow-Jones
Dow-Jones Index N (US) índice m Dow-Jones
down [daun] N (fluff) pelusa; (feathers) plumón m, flojel m; (hill) loma ▸ ADV (also: **downwards**) abajo, hacia abajo; (on the ground) por/en tierra ▸ PREP abajo ▸ VT (inf: drink) beberse, tragar(se); ~ **with X!** ¡abajo X!; ~ **there** allí abajo; ~ **here** aquí abajo; **I'll be** ~ **in a minute** ahora bajo; **England is two goals** ~ Inglaterra está perdiendo por dos tantos; **I've been** ~ **with flu** he estado con gripe; **the price of meat is** ~ ha bajado el precio de la carne; **I've got it** ~ **in my diary** lo he apuntado en mi agenda; **to pay £2** ~ dejar £2 de depósito; **he went** ~ **the hill** fue cuesta abajo; ~ **under** (in Australia etc) en Australia/Nueva Zelanda; **to** ~ **tools** (fig) declararse en huelga
down-and-out ['daunəndaut] N (tramp) vagabundo(-a)
down-at-heel ['daunət'hi:l] ADJ venido a menos; (appearance) desaliñado
downbeat ['daunbi:t] N (Mus) compás m ▸ ADJ (gloomy) pesimista
downcast ['daunkɑ:st] ADJ abatido
downer ['daunə^r] N (inf: drug) tranquilizante; **to be on a** ~ estar pasando un mal bache
downfall ['daunfɔ:l] N caída, ruina
downgrade [daun'greɪd] VT (job) degradar; (hotel) bajar de categoría
downhearted [daun'hɑ:tɪd] ADJ desanimado
downhill [daun'hɪl] ADV: **to go** ~ ir cuesta abajo; (business) estar en declive
Downing Street ['daunɪŋ-] N (BRIT) Downing Street f; ver nota

> Downing Street es la calle de Londres en la que tienen su residencia oficial tanto el Primer Ministro (Prime Minister) como el Ministro de Economía (Chancellor of the Exchequer). El primero vive en el n°10 y el segundo en el n°11. Es una calle cerrada al público que se encuentra en el barrio de Westminster, en el centro de Londres. Downing Street se usa también en lenguaje periodístico para referirse al jefe del gobierno británico.

download ['daunləud] VT (Comput) descargar, bajar
downloadable [daun'ləudəbl] ADJ (Comput) descargable
down-market [daun'mɑ:kɪt] ADJ de escasa calidad

down payment N entrada, pago al contado
downplay ['daunpleɪ] VT (US) quitar importancia a
downpour ['daunpɔ:^r] N aguacero
downright ['daunraɪt] ADJ (nonsense, lie) manifiesto; (refusal) terminante
downsize [daun'saɪz] VT reducir la plantilla de
Down's syndrome [daunz-] N síndrome m de Down
downstairs [daun'stɛəz] ADV (below) (en el piso de) abajo; (motion) escaleras abajo; **to come** (or **go**) ~ bajar la escalera
downstream [daun'stri:m] ADV aguas or río abajo
downtime ['dauntaɪm] N (Comm) tiempo inactivo
down-to-earth [dauntu'ə:θ] ADJ práctico
downtown [daun'taun] ADV en el centro de la ciudad
downtrodden ['dauntrɔdn] ADJ oprimido
down under ADV en Australia (or Nueva Zelanda)
downward ['daunwəd] ADV hacia abajo; **face** ~ (person) boca abajo; (object) cara abajo ▸ ADJ: **a** ~ **trend** una tendencia descendente
downwards ['daunwədz] ADV hacia abajo; **face** ~ (person) boca abajo; (object) cara abajo
dowry ['daurɪ] N dote f
doz. ABBR = **dozen**
doze [dəuz] VI dormitar ▸ **doze off** VI echar una cabezada
dozen ['dʌzn] N docena; **a** ~ **books** una docena de libros; **dozens of** cantidad de; **dozens of times** cantidad de veces; **80p a** ~ 80 peniques la docena
DPh, DPhil N ABBR (= Doctor of Philosophy) título universitario
DPP N ABBR (BRIT) = **Director of Public Prosecutions**
DPT N ABBR (Med: = diphtheria, pertussis, tetanus) vacuna trivalente
DPW N ABBR (US: = Department of Public Works) ministerio de obras públicas
Dr, Dr. ABBR (= doctor) Dr; (in street names) = **drive**
dr ABBR (Comm) = **debtor**
drab [dræb] ADJ gris, monótono
draft [drɑ:ft] N (first copy: of document, report) borrador m; (Comm) giro; (US: call-up) quinta ▸ VT (write roughly) hacer un borrador de; see also **draught**
draftsman etc ['drɑ:ftsmən] (US) = **draughtsman** etc
drag [dræg] VT arrastrar; (river) dragar, rastrear ▸ VI arrastrarse por el suelo ▸ N (Aviat: resistance) resistencia aerodinámica; (inf) lata; (women's clothing): **in** ~ vestido de mujer; **to** ~ **and drop** (Comput) arrastrar y soltar

▶ **drag away** VT: **to ~ away (from)** separar a rastras (de)

▶ **drag on** VI ser interminable

dragnet ['drægnɛt] N (*Naut*) rastra; (*fig*) emboscada

dragon ['drægən] N dragón *m*

dragonfly ['drægənflaɪ] N libélula

dragoon [drə'guːn] N (*cavalryman*) dragón *m*
▶ VT: **to ~ sb into doing sth** forzar a algn a hacer algo

drain [dreɪn] N desaguadero; (*in street*) sumidero; (*drain cover*) rejilla del sumidero
▶ VT (*land, marshes*) desecar; (*Med*) drenar; (*reservoir*) desecar; (*fig*) agotar ▶ VI escurrirse; **to be a ~ on** consumir, agotar; **to feel drained (of energy)** (*fig*) sentirse agotado

drainage ['dreɪnɪdʒ] N (*act*) desagüe *m*; (*Med, Agr*) drenaje *m*; (*sewage*) alcantarillado

draining board ['dreɪnɪŋ-], (*US*) **drainboard** ['dreɪnbɔːd] N escurridero, escurridor *m*

drainpipe ['dreɪnpaɪp] N tubo de desagüe

drake [dreɪk] N pato (macho)

dram [dræm] N (*drink*) traguito, copita

drama ['drɑːmə] N (*art*) teatro; (*play*) drama *m*

dramatic [drə'mætɪk] ADJ dramático; (*sudden, marked*) espectacular

dramatist ['dræmətɪst] N dramaturgo(-a)

dramatize ['dræmətaɪz] VT (*events etc*) dramatizar; (*adapt: novel: for TV, cinema*) adaptar

drank [dræŋk] PT *of* **drink**

drape [dreɪp] VT (*cloth*) colocar; (*flag*) colgar

draper ['dreɪpəʳ] N pañero, mercero

drapes [dreɪps] NPL (*US*) cortinas *fpl*

drastic ['dræstɪk] ADJ (*measure, reduction*) severo; (*change*) radical

draught, (*US*) **draft** [drɑːft] N (*of air*) corriente *f* de aire; (*drink*) trago; (*Naut*) calado; **on ~** (*beer*) de barril

draught beer N cerveza de barril

draughtboard ['drɑːftbɔːd] (*BRIT*) N tablero de damas

draughts [drɑːfts] N (*BRIT*) juego de damas

draughtsman, (*US*) **draftsman** ['drɑːftsmən] N (*irreg*) proyectista *m*, delineante *m*

draughtsmanship, (*US*) **draftsmanship** ['drɑːftsmənʃɪp] N (*drawing*) dibujo lineal; (*skill*) habilidad *f* para el dibujo

draw [drɔː] (*pt* **drew**, *pp* **drawn**) VT (*pull*) tirar; (*take out*) sacar; (*attract*) atraer; (*picture*) dibujar; (*money*) retirar; (*formulate: conclusion*): **to ~ (from)** sacar (de); (*comparison: distinction*): **to ~ (between)** hacer (entre) ▶ VI (*Sport*) empatar ▶ N (*Sport*) empate *m*; (*lottery*) sorteo; (*attraction*) atracción *f*; **to ~ near** acercarse
▶ **draw back** VI: **to ~ back (from)** echarse atrás (de)

▶ **draw in** VI (*car*) aparcar; (*train*) entrar en la estación

▶ **draw on** VT (*resources*) utilizar, servirse de; (*imagination, person*) recurrir a

▶ **draw out** VI (*lengthen*) alargarse

▶ **draw up** VI (*stop*) pararse ▶ VT (*document*) redactar; (*plan*) trazar

drawback ['drɔːbæk] N inconveniente *m*, desventaja

drawbridge ['drɔːbrɪdʒ] N puente *m* levadizo

drawee [drɔː'iː] N girado, librado

drawer [drɔːʳ] N cajón *m*; (*of cheque*) librador(a) *m/f*

drawing ['drɔːɪŋ] N dibujo

drawing board N tablero (de dibujante)

drawing pin N (*BRIT*) chincheta *m*

drawing room N salón *m*

drawl [drɔːl] N habla lenta y cansina

drawn [drɔːn] PP *of* **draw** ▶ ADJ (*haggard: with tiredness*) ojeroso; (: *with pain*) macilento

drawstring ['drɔːstrɪŋ] N cordón *m*

dread [drɛd] N pavor *m*, terror *m* ▶ VT temer, tener miedo *or* pavor a

dreadful ['drɛdful] ADJ espantoso; **I feel ~!** (*ill*) ¡me siento fatal *or* malísimo!; (*ashamed*) ¡qué vergüenza!

dream [driːm] N sueño ▶ VT, VI (*pt, pp* **dreamed** *or* **dreamt** [drɛmt]) soñar; **to have a ~ about sb/sth** soñar con algn/algo; **sweet dreams!** ¡que sueñes con los angelitos!
▶ **dream up** VT (*reason, excuse*) inventar; (*plan, idea*) idear

dreamer ['driːməʳ] N soñador(a) *m/f*

dreamt [drɛmt] PT, PP *of* **dream**

dream world N mundo imaginario *or* de ensueño

dreamy ['driːmɪ] ADJ (*person*) soñador(a), distraído; (*music*) de sueño

dreary ['drɪərɪ] ADJ monótono, aburrido

dredge [drɛdʒ] VT dragar
▶ **dredge up** VT sacar con draga; (*fig: unpleasant facts*) pescar, sacar a luz

dredger ['drɛdʒəʳ] N (*ship, machine*) draga; (*Culin*) tamiz *m*

dregs [drɛgz] NPL heces *fpl*

drench [drɛntʃ] VT empapar; **drenched to the skin** calado hasta los huesos

dress [drɛs] N vestido; (*clothing*) ropa ▶ VT vestir; (*wound*) vendar; (*Culin*) aliñar; (*shop window*) decorar, arreglar ▶ VI vestirse; **to ~ o.s., get dressed** vestirse; **she dresses very well** se viste muy bien
▶ **dress up** VI vestirse de etiqueta; (*in fancy dress*) disfrazarse

dress circle N (*BRIT*) principal *m*

dress designer N modisto(-a)

dresser ['drɛsəʳ] N (*furniture*) aparador *m*; (: *US*) tocador *m*; (*Theat*) camarero(-a)

dressing ['drɛsɪŋ] N (*Med*) vendaje *m*; (*Culin*) aliño

dressing gown N (*BRIT*) bata

dressing room N (*Theat*) camarín *m*; (*Sport*) vestuario

dressing table N tocador *m*

dressmaker ['drɛsmeɪkəʳ] N modista, costurera

dressmaking ['drɛsmeɪkɪŋ] N costura

dress rehearsal N ensayo general

dress shirt N camisa de frac

dressy ['drɛsɪ] ADJ (*inf*) elegante

drew [druː] PT *of* **draw**

dribble ['drɪbl] VI gotear, caer gota a gota; (*baby*) babear ▶ VT (*ball*) driblar, regatear

dried [draɪd] ADJ (*gen*) seco; (*fruit*) paso; (*milk*) en polvo

drier ['draɪəʳ] N = **dryer**

drift [drɪft] N (*of current etc*) flujo; (*of sand*) montón *m*; (*of snow*) ventisquero; (*meaning*) significado ▶ VI (*boat*) ir a la deriva; (*sand, snow*) amontonarse; **to catch sb's ~** cogerle el hilo a algn; **to let things ~** dejar las cosas como están; **to ~ apart** (*friends*) seguir su camino; (*lovers*) disgustarse, romper

drifter ['drɪftəʳ] N vagabundo(-a)

driftwood ['drɪftwud] N madera flotante

drill [drɪl] N taladro; (*bit*) broca; (*of dentist*) fresa; (*for mining etc*) perforadora, barrena; (*Mil*) instrucción *f* ▶ VT perforar, taladrar; (*soldiers*) ejercitar; (*pupils: in grammar*) hacer ejercicios con ▶ VI (*for oil*) perforar

drilling ['drɪlɪŋ] N (*for oil*) perforación *f*

drilling rig N (*on land*) torre *f* de perforación; (*at sea*) plataforma de perforación

drily ['draɪlɪ] ADV secamente

drink [drɪŋk] N bebida ▶ VT, VI (*pt* **drank**, *pp* **drunk**) beber, tomar (*LAM*); **to have a ~** tomar algo; tomar una copa *or* un trago; **a ~ of water** un trago de agua; **to invite sb for drinks** invitar a algn a tomar unas copas; **there's food and ~ in the kitchen** hay de comer y de beber en la cocina; **would you like something to ~?** ¿quieres beber *or* tomar algo?

▶ **drink in** VT (*person: fresh air*) respirar; (: *story, sight*) beberse

drinkable ['drɪŋkəbl] ADJ (*not poisonous*) potable; (*palatable*) aguantable

drink-driving [drɪŋk'draɪvɪŋ] N: **to be charged with ~** ser acusado de conducir borracho *or* en estado de embriaguez

drinker ['drɪŋkəʳ] N bebedor(a) *m/f*

drinking ['drɪŋkɪŋ] N (*drunkenness*) beber *m*

drinking fountain N fuente *f* de agua potable

drinking water N agua potable

drip [drɪp] N (*act*) goteo; (*one drip*) gota; (*Med*) gota a gota *m*; (*sound: of water etc*) goteo; (*inf:*

spineless person) soso(-a) ▶ VI gotear, caer gota a gota

drip-dry ['drɪp'draɪ] ADJ (*shirt*) de lava y pon

dripping ['drɪpɪŋ] N (*animal fat*) pringue *m* ▶ ADJ: **~ wet** calado

drive [draɪv] (*pt* **drove**, *pp* **driven**) N paseo (en coche); (*journey*) viaje *m* (en coche); (*also:* **driveway**) entrada; (*street*) calle; (*energy*) energía, vigor *m*; (*Psych*) impulso; (*Sport*) ataque *m*; (*Comput: also:* **disk drive**) unidad *f* (de disco) ▶ VT (*car*) conducir, manejar (*LAM*); (*nail*) clavar; (*push*) empujar; (*Tech: motor*) impulsar ▶ VI (*Aut: at controls*) conducir, manejar (*LAM*); (: *travel*) pasearse en coche; **to go for a ~** dar una vuelta en coche; **it's three hours' ~ from London** es un viaje de tres horas en coche desde Londres; **left-/right-hand ~** conducción *f* a la izquierda/derecha; **front-/rear-wheel ~** tracción *f* delantera/trasera; **sales ~** promoción *f* de ventas; **to ~ sb mad** volverle loco a algn; **to ~ sb to (do) sth** empujar a algn a (hacer) algo; **he drives a taxi** es taxista; **he drives a Mercedes** tiene un Mercedes; **can you ~?** ¿sabes conducir *or* (*LAM*) manejar?; **to ~ at 50 km an hour** ir a 50km por hora

▶ **drive at** VT FUS (*fig: intend, mean*) querer decir, insinuar

▶ **drive on** VI no parar, seguir adelante ▶ VT (*incite, encourage*) empujar

▶ **drive out** VT (*force out*) expulsar, echar

drive-by ['draɪvbaɪ] N: **~ shooting** tiroteo desde el coche

drive-in ['draɪvɪn] ADJ (*esp US*): **~ cinema** autocine *m*

drivel ['drɪvl] N (*inf*) tonterías *fpl*

driven ['drɪvn] PP *of* **drive**

driver ['draɪvəʳ] N conductor(a) *m/f*, chofer *m* (*LAM*); (*of taxi*) taxista *mf*

driver's license N (*US*) carnet *m* *or* permiso de conducir

driveway ['draɪvweɪ] N camino de entrada

driving ['draɪvɪŋ] N conducir *m*, manejar *m* (*LAM*) ▶ ADJ (*force*) impulsor(a)

driving instructor N instructor(a) *m/f* de autoescuela

driving lesson N clase *f* de conducir

driving licence N (*BRIT*) carnet *m* *or* permiso de conducir

driving school N autoescuela

driving test N examen *m* de conducir

drizzle ['drɪzl] N llovizna, garúa (*LAM*) ▶ VI lloviznar

droll [drəul] ADJ gracioso

dromedary ['drɔmɪdərɪ] N dromedario

drone [drəun] VI (*bee, aircraft, engine*) zumbar; (*also:* **drone on**) murmurar sin interrupción ▶ N zumbido; (*male bee*) zángano

drool [druːl] VI babear; **to ~ over sb/sth**

caérsele la baba por algn/algo

droop [druːp] vi (*flower*) marchitarse; (*shoulders*) encorvarse; (*head*) inclinarse; (*fig: spirits*) decaer, desanimarse

drop [drɔp] N (*of water*) gota; (*fall: in price*) bajada; (: *in salary*) disminución f ▶ vt (*allow to fall*) dejar caer; (*voice, eyes, price*) bajar; (*set down from car*) dejar ▶ vi (*object*) caer; (*price, temperature*) bajar; (*wind*) calmarse, amainar; (*numbers, attendance*) disminuir; **drops** NPL (*Med*) gotas fpl; **cough drops** pastillas fpl para la tos; **a ~ of 10%** una bajada del 10 por ciento; **to ~ anchor** echar el ancla; **to ~ sb a line** mandar unas líneas a algn

▶ **drop in** vi (*inf: visit*): **to ~ in (on)** pasar por casa (de)

▶ **drop off** vi (*sleep*) dormirse ▶ vt (*passenger*) bajar, dejar

▶ **drop out** vi (*withdraw*) retirarse

droplet ['drɔplɪt] N gotita

dropout ['drɔpaʊt] N (*from society*) marginado(-a); (*from university*) estudiante mf que ha abandonado los estudios

dropper ['drɔpəʳ] N (*Med*) cuentagotas m inv

droppings ['drɔpɪŋz] NPL excremento sg

dross [drɔs] N (*fig*) escoria

drought [draʊt] N sequía

drove [drəʊv] PT of **drive**

drown [draʊn] vt (*also:* **drown out**: *sound*) ahogar ▶ vi ahogarse

drowse [draʊz] vi estar medio dormido

drowsy ['draʊzɪ] ADJ soñoliento; **to be ~** tener sueño

drudge [drʌdʒ] N esclavo del trabajo

drudgery ['drʌdʒərɪ] N trabajo pesado or monótono

drug [drʌg] N (*Med*) medicamento, droga; (*narcotic*) droga ▶ vt drogar; **to be on drugs** drogarse; **he's on drugs** se droga

drug addict N drogadicto(-a)

drug dealer N traficante mf de drogas

drug-driving [drʌg'draɪvɪŋ] N conducción f bajo los efectos de las drogas

druggist ['drʌgɪst] N (*US*) farmacéutico(-a)

drug peddler N traficante mf de drogas

drugstore ['drʌgstɔːʳ] N (*US*) tienda (*de comestibles, periódicos y medicamentos*)

drug trafficker N narcotraficante mf

drum [drʌm] N tambor m; (*large*) bombo; (*for oil, petrol*) bidón m ▶ vi tocar el tambor; (*with fingers*) tamborilear ▶ vt: **to ~ one's fingers on the table** tamborilear con los dedos sobre la mesa; **drums** NPL batería sg

▶ **drum up** vt (*enthusiasm, support*) movilizar, fomentar

drummer ['drʌməʳ] N (*in military band*) tambor mf; (*in jazz/pop group*) batería mf

drumstick ['drʌmstɪk] N (*Mus*) palillo, baqueta; (*chicken leg*) muslo (de pollo)

drunk [drʌŋk] PP of **drink** ▶ ADJ borracho ▶ N (*also:* **drunkard**) borracho(-a); **to get ~** emborracharse

drunken ['drʌŋkən] ADJ borracho

drunkenness ['drʌŋkənnɪs] N embriaguez f

dry [draɪ] ADJ seco; (*day*) sin lluvia; (*climate*) árido, seco; (*humour*) agudo; (*uninteresting: lecture*) aburrido, pesado ▶ vt secar; (*tears*) enjugarse ▶ vi secarse; **on ~ land** en tierra firme; **to ~ one's hands/hair/eyes** secarse las manos/el pelo/las lágrimas

▶ **dry up** vi (*river*) secarse; (*supply, imagination etc*) agotarse; (*in speech*) atascarse

dry-clean ['draɪ'kliːn] vt limpiar or lavar en seco; **"~ only"** (*on label*) "limpieza or lavado en seco"

dry-cleaner's ['draɪ'kliːnəz] N tintorería

dry-cleaning ['draɪ'kliːnɪŋ] N lavado en seco

dry dock N (*Naut*) dique m seco

dryer ['draɪəʳ] N (*for hair*) secador m; (*for clothes*) secadora

dry goods NPL (*Comm*) mercería sg

dry goods store N (*US*) mercería

dry ice N nieve f carbónica, hielo seco

dryness ['draɪnɪs] N sequedad f

dry rot N putrefacción f

dry run N (*fig*) ensayo

dry ski slope N pista artificial de esquí

DSc N ABBR (= *Doctor of Science*) título universitario

DSS N ABBR (*Brit*) = **Department of Social Security**; *see* **social security**

DST N ABBR (*US:* = *Daylight Saving Time*) hora de verano

DT N ABBR (*Comput*) = **data transmission**

DTI N ABBR (*Brit*) = **Department of Trade and Industry**

DTP N ABBR = **desktop publishing**; (*Med: vaccination*) = **diphtheria, tetanus, pertussis**

DT's N ABBR (*inf:* = *delirium tremens*) delirium m tremens

dual ['djuəl] ADJ doble

dual carriageway N (*Brit*) ≈ autovía

dual-control ['djuəlkən'trəʊl] ADJ de doble mando

dual nationality N doble nacionalidad f

dual-purpose ['djuəl'pəːpəs] ADJ de doble uso

dubbed [dʌbd] ADJ (*Cine*) doblado

dubious ['djuːbɪəs] ADJ (*questionable: reputation*) dudoso; (: *character*) sospechoso; (*unsure*) indeciso; **I'm very ~ about it** tengo mis dudas sobre ello

Dublin ['dʌblɪn] N Dublín

Dubliner ['dʌblɪnəʳ] N dublinés(-esa) m/f

duchess ['dʌtʃɪs] N duquesa

duck [dʌk] N pato ▶ vi agacharse ▶ vt (*plunge in water*) zambullir

duckling ['dʌklɪŋ] N patito

duct [dʌkt] N conducto, canal m

dud [dʌd] N (*shell*) obús m que no estalla;

(*object, tool*): **it's a ~** es una filfa ▶ ADJ: **~ cheque** (*BRIT*) cheque *m* sin fondos

due [djuː] ADJ (*proper*) debido; (*fitting*) conveniente, oportuno ▶ ADV: **~ north** derecho al norte; **dues** NPL (*for club, union*) cuota *sg*; (*in harbour*) derechos *mpl*; **in ~ course** a su debido tiempo; **~ to** debido a; **to be ~ to** deberse a; **the train is ~ to arrive at 8.00** el tren tiene (prevista) la llegada a las ocho; **the rent's ~ on the 30th** hay que pagar el alquiler el día 30; **I am ~ six days' leave** me deben seis días de vacaciones; **she is ~ back tomorrow** ella debe volver mañana

due date N fecha de vencimiento
duel ['djuəl] N duelo
duet [djuːˈɛt] N dúo
duff [dʌf] ADJ sin valor
duffel bag ['dʌfl-] N macuto
duffel coat ['dʌfl-] N trenca
dug [dʌɡ] PT, PP of **dig**
dugout ['dʌɡaut] N (*canoe*) piragua (*hecha de un solo tronco*); (*Sport*) banquillo; (*Mil*) refugio subterráneo
duke [djuːk] N duque *m*
dull [dʌl] ADJ (*light*) apagado; (*stupid*) torpe; (*boring*) pesado; (*sound, pain*) sordo; (*weather, day*) gris ▶ VT (*pain, grief*) aliviar; (*mind, senses*) entorpecer
duly ['djuːlɪ] ADV debidamente; (*on time*) a su debido tiempo
dumb [dʌm] ADJ mudo; (*stupid*) estúpido; **to be struck ~** (*fig*) quedar boquiabierto
dumbbell ['dʌmbɛl] N (*Sport*) pesa
dumbfounded [dʌmˈfaundɪd] ADJ pasmado
dummy ['dʌmɪ] N (*tailor's model*) maniquí *m*; (*BRIT: for baby*) chupete *m* ▶ ADJ falso, postizo; **~ run** ensayo
dump [dʌmp] N (*heap*) montón *m* de basura; (*place*) basurero, vertedero; (: *inf*) tugurio; (*Mil*) depósito; (*Comput*) copia vaciada ▶ VT (*put down*) dejar; (*get rid of*) deshacerse de; (*Comput*) tirar (a la papelera); (*Comm: goods*) inundar el mercado de; **to be (down) in the dumps** (*inf*) tener murria, estar deprimido
dumping ['dʌmpɪŋ] N (*Econ*) dumping *m*; (*of rubbish*): **"no ~"** "prohibido verter basura"
dumpling ['dʌmplɪŋ] N bola de masa hervida
dumpy ['dʌmpɪ] ADJ regordete(-a)
dunce [dʌns] N zopenco
dune [djuːn] N duna
dung [dʌŋ] N estiércol *m*
dungarees [dʌŋɡəˈriːz] NPL mono *sg*, overol *msg* (*LAM*)
dungeon ['dʌndʒən] N calabozo
dunk [dʌŋk] VT mojar
duo ['djuːəu] N (*Mus*) dúo
duodenal [djuːəˈdiːnl] ADJ (*ulcer*) de duodeno
duodenum [djuːəˈdiːnəm] N duodeno

dupe [djuːp] N (*victim*) víctima ▶ VT engañar
duplex ['djuːplɛks] N (*US: also:* **duplex apartment**) dúplex *m*
duplicate ['djuːplɪkət] N duplicado; (*copy of letter etc*) copia ▶ ADJ (*copy*) duplicado ▶ VT ['djuːplɪkeɪt] duplicar; (*photocopy*) fotocopiar; (*repeat*) repetir; **in ~** por duplicado
duplicate key N duplicado de una llave
duplicating machine ['djuːplɪkeɪtɪŋ-], **duplicator** ['djuːplɪkeɪtəʳ] N multicopista *m*
duplicity [djuːˈplɪsɪtɪ] N doblez *f*, duplicidad *f*
Dur. ABBR (*BRIT*) = **Durham**
durability [djuərəˈbɪlɪtɪ] N durabilidad *f*
durable ['djuərəbl] ADJ duradero
duration [djuəˈreɪʃən] N duración *f*
duress [djuəˈrɛs] N: **under ~** por coacción
Durex® ['djuərɛks] N (*BRIT*) preservativo
during ['djuərɪŋ] PREP durante
dusk [dʌsk] N crepúsculo, anochecer *m*
dusky ['dʌskɪ] ADJ oscuro; (*complexion*) moreno
dust [dʌst] N polvo ▶ VT (*furniture*) desempolvar; (*cake etc*): **to ~ with** espolvorear de
▶ **dust off** VT (*also fig*) desempolvar, quitar el polvo de
dustbin ['dʌstbɪn] N (*BRIT*) cubo de la basura, balde *m* (*LAM*)
dustbin liner N bolsa de basura
duster ['dʌstəʳ] N paño, trapo; (*feather duster*) plumero
dust jacket N sobrecubierta
dustman ['dʌstmən] N (*irreg*) (*BRIT*) basurero
dustpan ['dʌstpæn] N cogedor *m*
dust storm N vendaval *m* de polvo
dusty ['dʌstɪ] ADJ polvoriento
Dutch [dʌtʃ] ADJ holandés(-esa) ▶ N (*Ling*) holandés *m* ▶ ADV: **to go ~** pagar a escote; **the Dutch** NPL los holandeses
Dutch auction N subasta a la rebaja
Dutchman ['dʌtʃmən], **Dutchwoman** ['dʌtʃwumən] N (*irreg*) holandés(-esa) *m/f*
dutiful ['djuːtɪful] ADJ (*child*) obediente; (*husband*) sumiso; (*employee*) cumplido
duty ['djuːtɪ] N deber *m*; (*tax*) derechos *mpl* de aduana; (*Med: in hospital*) servicio, guardia; **on ~** de servicio; (*at night etc*) de guardia; **off ~** libre (de servicio); **to make it one's ~ to do sth** encargarse de hacer algo sin falta; **to pay ~ on sth** pagar los derechos sobre algo
duty-free [djuːtɪˈfriː] ADJ libre de impuestos; **~ shop** tienda libre de impuestos
duty officer N (*Mil etc*) oficial *mf* de guardia
duvet ['duːveɪ] N (*BRIT*) edredón *m* (nórdico)
DV ABBR (= *Deo volente*) Dios mediante
DVD N ABBR (= *digital versatile or video disc*) DVD *m*
DVD player N lector *m* de DVD
DVD writer N grabadora de DVD
DVLA N ABBR (*BRIT*: = *Driver and Vehicle Licensing*

Agency) organismo encargado de la expedición de permisos de conducir y matriculación de vehículos

DVM N ABBR (*US:* = *Doctor of Veterinary Medicine*) título universitario

DVT N ABBR = **deep-vein thrombosis**

dwarf [dwɔːf] (*pl* **dwarves** [dwɔːvz]) N enano(-a) *m/f* ▶ VT empequeñecer

dwell [dwel] (*pt, pp* **dwelt** [dwelt]) VI morar ▶ **dwell on** VT FUS explayarse en

dweller ['dwelə*] N habitante *m*; **city ~** habitante *m* de la ciudad

dwelling ['dwelɪŋ] N vivienda

dwelt [dwelt] PT, PP *of* **dwell**

dwindle ['dwɪndl] VI menguar, disminuir

dwindling ['dwɪndlɪŋ] ADJ (*strength, interest*) menguante; (*resources, supplies*) en disminución

dye [daɪ] N tinte *m* ▶ VT teñir; **hair ~** tinte *m* para el pelo

dying ['daɪɪŋ] ADJ moribundo, agonizante; (*moments*) final; (*words*) último

dyke [daɪk] N (*barrier*) dique *m*; (*channel*) arroyo, acequia; (*causeway*) calzada

dynamic [daɪ'næmɪk] ADJ dinámico

dynamics [daɪ'næmɪks] N, NPL dinámica *sg*

dynamite ['daɪnəmaɪt] N dinamita ▶ VT dinamitar

dynamo ['daɪnəməu] N dinamo *f*, dinamo *m* (*LAm*)

dynasty ['dɪnəstɪ] N dinastía

dysentery ['dɪsɪntrɪ] N disentería

dyslexia [dɪs'leksɪə] N dislexia

dyslexic [dɪs'leksɪk] ADJ, N disléxico(-a) *m/f*

dyspepsia [dɪs'pepsɪə] N dispepsia

dystrophy ['dɪstrəfɪ] N distrofia; **muscular ~** distrofia muscular

d

Ee

E, e [iː] N (*letter*) E, e *f*; (*Mus*): **E** mi *m*; **E for Edward**, (*US*) **E for Easy** E de Enrique

E ABBR (= *east*) E ▶ N ABBR (= *ecstasy*) éxtasis *m*

E111 N ABBR (= *form E111*) impreso E111

ea. ABBR = **each**

E.A. ABBR (*US*: = *educational age*) nivel escolar

each [iːtʃ] ADJ cada *inv* ▶ PRON cada uno; **~ other** el uno al otro; **they hate ~ other** se odian (entre ellos *or* mutuamente); **~ day** cada día; **they have two books ~** tienen dos libros cada uno; **they cost £5 ~** cuestan cinco libras cada uno; **~ of us** cada uno de nosotros

eager ['iːɡər] ADJ (*gen*) impaciente; (*hopeful*) ilusionado; (*keen*) entusiasmado; (*pupil*) apasionado; **to be ~ to do sth** estar deseoso de hacer algo; **to be ~ for** tener muchas ganas de, ansiar

eagerly ['iːɡəlɪ] ADV con impaciencia; con ilusión; con entusiasmo

eagerness ['iːɡənɪs] N impaciencia; ilusión *f*; entusiasmo

eagle ['iːɡl] N águila

E & OE ABBR = **errors and omissions excepted**

ear [ɪər] N oreja; (*sense of hearing*) oído; (*of corn*) espiga; **up to the ears in debt** abrumado de deudas

earache ['ɪəreɪk] N dolor *m* de oídos

eardrum ['ɪədrʌm] N tímpano

earful ['ɪəful] N: **to give sb an ~** (*inf*) echar una bronca a algn

earl [əːl] N conde *m*

earlier ['əːlɪər] ADJ anterior ▶ ADV antes

early ['əːlɪ] ADV (*gen*) temprano; (*ahead of time*) con tiempo, con anticipación ▶ ADJ (*gen*) temprano; (*reply*) pronto; (*man*) primitivo; (*first: Christians, settlers*) primero; **to have an ~ night** acostarse temprano; **in the ~ or ~ in the spring/19th century** a principios de primavera/del siglo diecinueve; **you're ~!** ¡has llegado temprano *or* pronto!; **~ in the morning/afternoon** a primeras horas de la mañana/tarde; **she's in her ~ forties** tiene poco más de cuarenta años; **at your earliest convenience** (*Comm*) con la mayor brevedad posible; **I can't come any earlier** no puedo llegar antes

early retirement N jubilación *f* anticipada

early warning system N sistema *m* de alerta inmediata

earmark ['ɪəmɑːk] VT: **to ~ for** reservar para, destinar a

earn [əːn] VT (*gen*) ganar; (*salary*) percibir; (*interest*) devengar; (*praise*) ganarse; **to ~ one's living** ganarse la vida

earned income N renta del trabajo

earnest ['əːnɪst] ADJ (*wish*) fervoroso; (*person*) serio, formal ▶ N (*also*: **earnest money**) anticipo, señal *f*; **in ~** *adv* en serio

earnings ['əːnɪŋz] NPL (*personal*) ingresos *mpl*; (*of company etc*) ganancias *fpl*

earphones ['ɪəfəunz] NPL auriculares *mpl*

earplugs ['ɪəplʌgz] NPL tapones *mpl* para los oídos

earring ['ɪərɪŋ] N pendiente *m*, arete *m* (*LAM*)

earshot ['ɪəʃɔt] N: **out of/within ~** fuera del/al alcance del oído

earth [əːθ] N (*gen*) tierra; (*BRIT Elec*) toma de tierra ▶ VT (*BRIT Elec*) conectar a tierra

earthenware ['əːθnwɛər] N loza (de barro)

earthly ['əːθlɪ] ADJ terrenal, mundano; **~ paradise** paraíso terrenal; **there is no ~ reason to think ...** no existe razón para pensar ...

earthquake ['əːθkweɪk] N terremoto

earth-shattering ['əːθʃætərɪŋ] ADJ trascendental

earthworm ['əːθwəːm] N lombriz *f*

earthy ['əːθɪ] ADJ (*fig: uncomplicated*) sencillo; (*coarse*) grosero

earwig ['ɪəwɪg] N tijereta

ease [iːz] N facilidad *f*; (*comfort*) comodidad *f* ▶ VT (*task*) facilitar; (*problem*) mitigar; (*pain*) aliviar; (*loosen*) soltar; (*relieve: pressure, tension*) aflojar; (*weight*) aligerar; (*help pass*): **to ~ sth in/out** meter/sacar algo con cuidado ▶ VI (*situation*) relajarse; **with ~** con facilidad; **to**

feel at ~/ill at ~ sentirse a gusto/a disgusto; **at ~!** (*Mil*) ¡descansen!
▶ **ease off, ease up** VI (*work, business*) aflojar; (*person*) relajarse
easel ['i:zl] N caballete *m*
easily ['i:zɪlɪ] ADV fácilmente
easiness ['i:zɪnɪs] N facilidad *f*; (*of manners*) soltura
east [i:st] N este *m*, oriente *m* ▶ ADJ del este, oriental ▶ ADV al este, hacia el este; **the E~** el Oriente; (*Pol*) el Este
eastbound N en dirección al este
Easter ['i:stəʳ] N Pascua (de Resurrección)
Easter egg N huevo de Pascua
Easter holidays NPL Semana Santa *sg*
Easter Island N Isla de Pascua
easterly ['i:stəlɪ] ADJ (*to the east*) al este; (*from the east*) del este
Easter Monday N lunes *m* de Pascua
eastern ['i:stən] ADJ del este, oriental; **E~ Europe** Europa del Este; **the E~ bloc** (*Pol*) los países del Este
Easter Sunday N Domingo de Resurrección
East Germany N (*formerly*) Alemania Oriental *or* del Este
eastward ['i:stwəd], **eastwards** ['i:stwədz] ADV hacia el este
easy ['i:zɪ] ADJ fácil; (*life*) holgado, cómodo; (*relaxed*) natural ▶ ADV: **to take it** *or* **things ~** (*not worry*) no preocuparse; (*go slowly*) tomarlo con calma; (*rest*) descansar; **payment on ~ terms** (*Comm*) facilidades de pago; **I'm ~** (*inf*) me da igual, no me importa; **easier said than done** del dicho al hecho hay buen trecho
easy chair N butaca
easy-going ['i:zɪ'gəʊɪŋ] ADJ acomodadizo
easy touch [i:zɪ'tʌtʃ] N: **he's an ~** (*inf*) es fácil de convencer
eat [i:t] (*pt* **ate** [eɪt], *pp* **eaten** ['i:tn]) VT comer ▶ **eat away** VT (*sea*) desgastar; (*acid*) corroer
▶ **eat away at, eat into** VT FUS corroer
▶ **eat out** VI comer fuera
▶ **eat up** VT (*meal etc*) comerse; **it eats up electricity** devora la electricidad
eatable ['i:təbl] ADJ comestible
eau de Cologne [əʊdəkə'ləʊn] N (agua de) colonia
eaves [i:vz] NPL alero *sg*
eavesdrop ['i:vzdrɔp] VI: **to ~ (on sb)** escuchar a escondidas *or* con disimulo (a algn)
ebb [ɛb] N reflujo ▶ VI bajar; (*fig: also:* **ebb away**) decaer; **~ and flow** el flujo y reflujo; **to be at a low ~** (*fig: person*) estar de capa caída
ebb tide N marea menguante
ebony ['ɛbənɪ] N ébano
e-book ['i:buk] N libro electrónico, e-book *m*

ebullient [ɪ'bʌlɪənt] ADJ entusiasta, animado
e-business ['i:bɪznɪs] N (*commerce*) comercio electrónico; (*company*) negocio electrónico
EC N ABBR (= *European Community*) CE *f*
e-card ['i:kɑ:d] N tarjeta de felicitación electrónica, e-card *f*
ECB N ABBR (= *European Central Bank*) BCE *m*
eccentric [ɪk'sɛntrɪk] ADJ, N excéntrico(-a) *m/f*
ecclesiastical [ɪkli:zɪ'æstɪkəl] ADJ eclesiástico
ECG N ABBR (= *electrocardiogram*) E.C.G. *m*
echo ['ɛkəʊ] (*pl* **echoes**) N eco *m* ▶ VT (*sound*) repetir ▶ VI resonar, hacer eco
ECLA N ABBR (= *Economic Commission for Latin America*) CEPAL *f*
éclair ['eɪklɛəʳ] N petisú *m*
eclipse [ɪ'klɪps] N eclipse *m* ▶ VT eclipsar
ECM N ABBR (*US:* = *European Common Market*) MCE *m*
eco- ['i:kəʊ] PREF eco-
eco-friendly ['i:kəʊfrɛndlɪ] ADJ ecológico
ecological [i:kə'lɔdʒɪkl] ADJ ecológico
ecologist [ɪ'kɔlədʒɪst] N ecologista *mf*; (*scientist*) ecólogo(-a) *m/f*
ecology [ɪ'kɔlədʒɪ] N ecología
e-commerce ['i:kɔmə:s] N comercio electrónico
economic [i:kə'nɔmɪk] ADJ (*profitable: price*) económico; (*: business etc*) rentable
economical [i:kə'nɔmɪkl] ADJ económico
economically [i:kə'nɔmɪklɪ] ADV económicamente
economics [i:kə'nɔmɪks] N (*Scol*) economía ▶ NPL (*financial aspects*) finanzas *fpl*
economic warfare N guerra económica
economist [ɪ'kɔnəmɪst] N economista *mf*
economize [ɪ'kɔnəmaɪz] VI economizar, ahorrar
economy [ɪ'kɔnəmɪ] N economía; **economies of scale** economías *fpl* de escala
economy class N (*Aviat etc*) clase *f* turista
economy class syndrome N síndrome *m* de la clase turista
economy size N tamaño familiar
ecosystem ['i:kəʊsɪstəm] N ecosistema *m*
eco-tourism [i:kəʊ'tʊərɪzm] N turismo verde *or* ecológico
ECSC N ABBR (= *European Coal and Steel Community*) CECA *f*
ecstasy ['ɛkstəsɪ] N éxtasis *m inv*; (*drug*) éxtasis *m inv*
ecstatic [ɛks'tætɪk] ADJ extático, extasiado
ECT N ABBR = **electroconvulsive therapy**
Ecuador ['ɛkwədɔ:ʳ] N Ecuador *m*
Ecuadoran [ɛkwə'dɔ:rən], **Ecuadorian** [ɛkwə'dɔ:rɪən] ADJ, N ecuatoriano(-a) *m/f*
ecumenical [i:kju'mɛnɪkl] ADJ ecuménico
eczema ['ɛksɪmə] N eczema *m*

533

eddy ['ɛdɪ] N remolino

edge [ɛdʒ] N (of knife etc) filo; (of object) borde m; (of lake etc) orilla ▸ VT (Sewing) ribetear ▸ VI: **to ~ past** pasar con dificultad; **on ~** (fig) = **edgy**; **to ~ away from** alejarse poco a poco de; **to ~ forward** avanzar poco a poco; **to ~ up** subir lentamente

edgeways ['ɛdʒweɪz] ADV: **he couldn't get a word in ~** no pudo meter baza

edging ['ɛdʒɪŋ] N (Sewing) ribete m; (of path) borde m

edgy ['ɛdʒɪ] ADJ nervioso, inquieto

edible ['ɛdɪbl] ADJ comestible

edict ['i:dɪkt] N edicto

edifice ['ɛdɪfɪs] N edificio

edifying ['ɛdɪfaɪɪŋ] ADJ edificante

Edinburgh ['ɛdɪnbərə] N Edimburgo

edit ['ɛdɪt] VT (be editor of) dirigir; (re-write) redactar; (cut) cortar; (Comput) editar

edition [ɪ'dɪʃən] N (gen) edición f; (number printed) tirada

editor ['ɛdɪtəʳ] N (of newspaper) director(a) m/f; (of book) redactor(a) m/f; (also: **film editor**) montador(a) m/f

editorial [ɛdɪ'tɔ:rɪəl] ADJ editorial ▸ N editorial m; **~ staff** redacción f

EDP N ABBR (= electronic data processing) PED f

EDT N ABBR (US: = Eastern Daylight Time) hora de verano de Nueva York

educate ['ɛdjukeɪt] VT (gen) educar; (instruct) instruir

educated ['ɛdjukeɪtɪd] ADJ culto

educated guess ['ɛdjukeɪtɪd-] N hipótesis f sólida

education [ɛdju'keɪʃən] N educación f; (schooling) enseñanza; (Scol: subject etc) pedagogía; **primary/secondary ~** enseñanza primaria/secundaria

educational [ɛdju'keɪʃənl] ADJ (policy etc) de educación, educativo; (teaching) docente; (instructive) educativo; **~ technology** tecnología educacional

Edwardian [ɛd'wɔ:dɪən] ADJ eduardiano

EE ABBR = **electrical engineer**

EEG N ABBR = **electroencephalogram**

eel [i:l] N anguila

EENT N ABBR (US Med) = **eye, ear, nose and throat**

EEOC N ABBR (US: = Equal Employment Opportunity Commission) comisión que investiga discriminación racial o sexual en el empleo

eerie ['ɪərɪ] ADJ (sound, experience) espeluznante

EET N ABBR (= Eastern European Time) hora de Europa oriental

efface [ɪ'feɪs] VT borrar

effect [ɪ'fɛkt] N efecto ▸ VT efectuar, llevar a cabo; **effects** NPL (property) efectos mpl; **to take ~** (law) entrar en vigor or vigencia; (drug) surtir efecto; **in ~** en realidad; **to have an ~ on sb/sth** hacerle efecto a algn/afectar algo; **to put into ~** (plan) llevar a la práctica; **his letter is to the ~ that ...** su carta viene a decir que ...

effective [ɪ'fɛktɪv] ADJ (gen) eficaz; (striking: display, outfit) impresionante; (real) efectivo; **to become ~** (law) entrar en vigor; **~ date** fecha de vigencia

effectively [ɪ'fɛktɪvlɪ] ADV (efficiently) eficazmente; (strikingly) de manera impresionante; (in reality) de hecho

effectiveness [ɪ'fɛktɪvnɪs] N eficacia

effeminate [ɪ'fɛmɪnɪt] ADJ afeminado

effervescent [ɛfə'vɛsnt] ADJ efervescente

efficacy ['ɛfɪkəsɪ] N eficacia

efficiency [ɪ'fɪʃənsɪ] N (gen) eficiencia; (of machine) rendimiento

efficient [ɪ'fɪʃənt] ADJ eficiente; (remedy, product, system) eficaz; (machine, car) de buen rendimiento

efficiently [ɪ'fɪʃəntlɪ] ADV eficientemente, de manera eficiente

effigy ['ɛfɪdʒɪ] N efigie f

effluent ['ɛfluənt] N vertidos mpl

effort ['ɛfət] N esfuerzo; **to make an ~ to do sth** hacer un esfuerzo or esforzarse para hacer algo

effortless ['ɛfətlɪs] ADJ sin ningún esfuerzo

effrontery [ɪ'frʌntərɪ] N descaro

effusive [ɪ'fju:sɪv] ADJ efusivo

EFL N ABBR (Scol) = **English as a foreign language**

EFTA ['ɛftə] N ABBR (= European Free Trade Association) EFTA f

e.g. ADV ABBR (= exempli gratia) p.ej.

egg [ɛg] N huevo; **hard-boiled/soft-boiled/poached ~** huevo duro or (LAM) a la copa or (LAM) tibio/pasado por agua/escalfado; **scrambled eggs** huevos revueltos ▸ **egg on** VT incitar

eggcup ['ɛgkʌp] N huevera

eggnog [ɛg'nɔg] N ponche m de huevo

eggplant ['ɛgplɑ:nt] N (esp US) berenjena

eggshell ['ɛgʃɛl] N cáscara de huevo

egg-timer ['ɛgtaɪməʳ] N reloj m de arena (para cocer huevos)

egg white N clara de huevo

egg yolk N yema de huevo

ego ['i:gəu] N ego

egotism ['ɛgəutɪzəm] N egoísmo

egotist ['ɛgəutɪst] N egoísta mf

ego trip N: **to be on an ~** creerse el centro del mundo

Egypt ['i:dʒɪpt] N Egipto

Egyptian [ɪ'dʒɪpʃən] ADJ, N egipcio(-a) m/f

eiderdown ['aɪdədaun] N edredón m

eight [eɪt] NUM ocho

eighteen [eɪ'ti:n] NUM dieciocho

eighteenth ['eɪ'tiːnθ] ADJ decimoctavo; **the ~ floor** la planta dieciocho; **the ~ of August** el dieciocho de agosto

eighth [eɪtθ] ADJ octavo

eightieth ['eɪtɪɪθ] ADJ octogésimo

eighty ['eɪtɪ] NUM ochenta

Eire ['ɛərə] N Eire m

EIS N ABBR (= Educational Institute of Scotland) *sindicato de profesores escoceses*

either ['aɪðəʳ] ADJ cualquiera de los dos ...; (both, each) cada ▶ PRON: ~ (of them) cualquiera (de los dos) ▶ ADV tampoco ▶ CONJ: ~ yes or no o sí o no; on ~ side en ambos lados; I don't like ~ no me gusta ninguno de los dos; no, I don't ~ no, yo tampoco

eject [ɪ'dʒɛkt] VT echar; (tenant) desahuciar ▶ VI eyectarse

ejector seat [ɪ'dʒɛktə-] N asiento proyectable

eke out [iːk-] VT FUS (money) hacer que llegue

EKG N ABBR (US) see **electrocardiogram**

el [ɛl] N ABBR (US inf) = **elevated railroad**

elaborate ADJ [ɪ'læbərɪt] (design, pattern) complejo ▶ VT [ɪ'læbəreɪt] elaborar; (expand) ampliar; (refine) refinar ▶ VI explicarse con muchos detalles

elaborately [ɪ'læbərɪtlɪ] ADV de manera complicada; (decorated) profusamente

elaboration [ɪlæbə'reɪʃən] N elaboración f

elapse [ɪ'læps] VI transcurrir

elastic [ɪ'læstɪk] ADJ, N elástico

elastic band N (BRIT) gomita

elated [ɪ'leɪtɪd] ADJ: **to be ~** estar eufórico

elation [ɪ'leɪʃən] N euforia

elbow ['ɛlbəu] N codo ▶ VT: **to ~ one's way through the crowd** abrirse paso a codazos por la muchedumbre

elbow grease N (inf): **to use some** or **a bit of ~** menearse

elder ['ɛldəʳ] ADJ mayor ▶ N (tree) saúco; (person) mayor; (of tribe) anciano

elderly ['ɛldəlɪ] ADJ de edad, mayor ▶ NPL: **the ~** los mayores, los ancianos

elder statesman N (irreg) estadista m veterano; (fig) figura respetada

eldest ['ɛldɪst] ADJ, N el/la mayor

elect [ɪ'lɛkt] VT elegir; (choose): **to ~ to do** optar por hacer ▶ ADJ: **the president ~** el presidente electo

election [ɪ'lɛkʃən] N elección f; **to hold an ~** convocar elecciones

election campaign N campaña electoral

electioneering [ɪlɛkʃə'nɪərɪŋ] N campaña electoral

elector [ɪ'lɛktəʳ] N elector(a) m/f

electoral [ɪ'lɛktərəl] ADJ electoral

electoral college N colegio electoral

electoral roll N censo electoral

electorate [ɪ'lɛktərɪt] N electorado

electric [ɪ'lɛktrɪk] ADJ eléctrico

electrical [ɪ'lɛktrɪkl] ADJ eléctrico

electrical engineer N ingeniero(-a) electricista

electrical failure N fallo eléctrico

electric blanket N manta eléctrica

electric chair N silla eléctrica

electric cooker N cocina eléctrica

electric current N corriente f eléctrica

electric fire N estufa eléctrica

electrician [ɪlɛk'trɪʃən] N electricista mf

electricity [ɪlɛk'trɪsɪtɪ] N electricidad f; **to switch on/off the ~** conectar/desconectar la electricidad

electricity board N (BRIT) compañía eléctrica (estatal)

electric light N luz f eléctrica

electric shock N electrochoque m

electrification [ɪlɛktrɪfɪ'keɪʃən] N electrificación f

electrify [ɪ'lɛktrɪfaɪ] VT (Rail) electrificar; (fig: audience) electrizar

electro... [ɪ'lɛktrəu] PREF electro...

electrocardiogram [ɪ'lɛktrə'kɑːdɪəgræm] N electrocardiograma m

electrocardiograph [ɪ'lɛktrəu'kɑːdɪəgræf] N electrocardiógrafo

electro-convulsive therapy [ɪ'lɛktrəkən'vʌlsɪv-] N electroterapia

electrocute [ɪ'lɛktrəukjuːt] VT electrocutar

electrode [ɪ'lɛktrəud] N electrodo

electroencephalogram [ɪ'lɛktrəuen'sɛfələgræm] N electroencefalograma m

electrolysis [ɪlɛk'trɔlɪsɪs] N electrólisis f inv

electromagnetic [ɪ'lɛktrəmæg'nɛtɪk] ADJ electromagnético

electron [ɪ'lɛktrɔn] N electrón m

electronic [ɪlɛk'trɔnɪk] ADJ electrónico

electronic data processing N tratamiento or proceso electrónico de datos

electronic mail N correo electrónico

electronics [ɪlɛk'trɔnɪks] N electrónica

electron microscope N microscopio electrónico

electroplated [ɪ'lɛktrə'pleɪtɪd] ADJ galvanizado

electrotherapy [ɪ'lɛktrə'θɛrəpɪ] N electroterapia

elegance ['ɛlɪgəns] N elegancia

elegant ['ɛlɪgənt] ADJ elegante

elegy ['ɛlɪdʒɪ] N elegía

element ['ɛlɪmənt] N (gen) elemento; (of heater, kettle etc) resistencia

elementary [ɛlɪ'mɛntərɪ] ADJ elemental; (primitive) rudimentario; (school, education) primario

elementary school N (US) escuela de enseñanza primaria; *ver nota*

> En Estados Unidos y Canadá se llama *elementary school* al centro estatal en el que los niños reciben los primeros seis u ocho años de su educación, también llamado *"grade school"* o *"grammar school"*.

elephant ['ɛlɪfənt] N elefante m

elevate ['ɛlɪveɪt] VT (*gen*) elevar; (*in rank*) ascender

elevated railroad N (US) ferrocarril urbano elevado

elevation [ɛlɪ'veɪʃən] N elevación f; (*rank*) ascenso; (*height*) altitud f

elevator ['ɛlɪveɪtər] N (US) ascensor m, elevador m (LAM)

eleven [ɪ'lɛvn] NUM once

elevenses [ɪ'lɛvnzɪz] NPL (BRIT) ≈ café m de media mañana

eleventh [ɪ'lɛvnθ] ADJ undécimo; **at the ~ hour** (*fig*) a última hora

elf [ɛlf] (*pl* **elves** [ɛlvz]) N duende m

elicit [ɪ'lɪsɪt] VT: **to ~ sth (from sb)** obtener algo (de algn)

eligible ['ɛlɪdʒəbl] ADJ: **an ~ young man/woman** un buen partido; **to be ~ for sth** llenar los requisitos para algo; **to be ~ for a pension** tener derecho a una pensión

eliminate [ɪ'lɪmɪneɪt] VT eliminar; (*score out*) suprimir; (*a suspect, possibility*) descartar

elimination [ɪlɪmɪ'neɪʃən] N eliminación f; supresión f; **by process of ~** por eliminación

elite [eɪ'liːt] N élite f

elitist [eɪ'liːtɪst] ADJ (*pej*) elitista

elixir [ɪ'lɪksɪə'] N elixir m

Elizabethan [ɪlɪzə'biːθən] ADJ isabelino

elm [ɛlm] N olmo

elocution [ɛlə'kjuːʃən] N elocución f

elongated ['iːlɒŋgeɪtɪd] ADJ alargado

elope [ɪ'ləup] VI fugarse

elopement [ɪ'ləupmənt] N fuga

eloquence ['ɛləkwəns] N elocuencia

eloquent ['ɛləkwənt] ADJ elocuente

else [ɛls] ADV: **or ~** si no; **something ~** otra cosa o algo más; **somewhere ~** en otra parte; **everywhere ~** en todas partes menos aquí; **everyone ~** todos los demás; **nothing ~** nada más; **is there anything ~ I can do?** ¿puedo hacer algo más?; **where ~?** ¿dónde más?, ¿en qué otra parte?; **there was little ~ to do** apenas quedaba otra cosa que hacer; **nobody ~** nadie más

elsewhere [ɛls'wɛə'] ADV (*be*) en otra parte; (*go*) a otra parte

ELT N ABBR (Scol) = **English Language Teaching**

elucidate [ɪ'luːsɪdeɪt] VT esclarecer, elucidar

elude [ɪ'luːd] VT eludir; (*blow, pursuer*) esquivar

elusive [ɪ'luːsɪv] ADJ esquivo; (*answer*) difícil

de encontrar; **he is very ~** no es fácil encontrarlo

elves [ɛlvz] NPL of **elf**

emaciated [ɪ'meɪsɪeɪtɪd] ADJ escuálido

email ['iːmeɪl] N ABBR (= *electronic mail*) email m, correo electrónico ▸ VT: **to ~ sb** mandar un email or un correo electrónico a algn; **to ~ sb sth** mandar algo a algn por Internet, mandar algo a algn en un email or un correo electrónico

email account N cuenta de correo

email address N dirección f electrónica, email m

emanate ['ɛməneɪt] VI emanar, provenir

emancipate [ɪ'mænsɪpeɪt] VT emancipar

emancipated [ɪ'mænsɪpeɪtɪd] ADJ liberado

emancipation [ɪmænsɪ'peɪʃən] N emancipación f, liberación f

emasculate [ɪ'mæskjuleɪt] VT castrar; (*fig*) debilitar

embalm [ɪm'bɑːm] VT embalsamar

embankment [ɪm'bæŋkmənt] N (*of railway*) terraplén m; (*riverside*) dique m

embargo [ɪm'bɑːgəu] (*pl* **embargoes**) N prohibición f; (*Comm, Naut*) embargo; **to put an ~ on sth** poner un embargo en algo

embark [ɪm'bɑːk] VI embarcarse ▸ VT embarcar; **to ~ on** (*journey*) emprender, iniciar; (*fig*) emprender

embarkation [ɛmbɑː'keɪʃən] N (*of people*) embarco; (*of goods*) embarque m

embarrass [ɪm'bærəs] VT avergonzar, dar vergüenza a; (*financially etc*) poner en un aprieto

embarrassed [ɪm'bærəst] ADJ azorado, violento; **to be ~** sentirse azorado or violento

embarrassing [ɪm'bærəsɪŋ] ADJ (*situation*) violento; (*question*) embarazoso

embarrassment [ɪm'bærəsmənt] N vergüenza, azoramiento; (*financial*) apuros mpl

embassy ['ɛmbəsɪ] N embajada

embed [ɪm'bɛd] VT (*jewel*) empotrar; (*teeth etc*) clavar

embellish [ɪm'bɛlɪʃ] VT embellecer; (*fig: story, truth*) adornar

embers ['ɛmbəz] NPL rescoldo sg, ascuas

embezzle [ɪm'bɛzl] VT desfalcar, malversar

embezzlement [ɪm'bɛzlmənt] N desfalco, malversación f

embezzler [ɪm'bɛzlə'] N malversador(a) m/f

embitter [ɪm'bɪtə'] VT (*person*) amargar; (*relationship*) envenenar

embittered [ɪm'bɪtəd] ADJ resentido, amargado

emblem ['ɛmbləm] N emblema m

embody [ɪm'bɒdɪ] VT (*spirit*) encarnar; (*ideas*) expresar

embolden [ɪm'bəuldən] VT envalentonar

embolism ['ɛmbəlɪzəm] N embolia
emboss [ɪm'bɒs] VT estampar en relieve; (*metal, leather*) repujar
embossed [ɪm'bɒst] ADJ realzado; ~ **with …** con … en relieve
embrace [ɪm'breɪs] VT abrazar, dar un abrazo a; (*include*) abarcar; (*adopt: idea*) adherirse a ► VI abrazarse ► N abrazo
embroider [ɪm'brɔɪdər] VT bordar; (*fig: story*) adornar, embellecer
embroidery [ɪm'brɔɪdərɪ] N bordado
embroil [ɪm'brɔɪl] VT: **to become embroiled (in sth)** enredarse (en algo)
embryo ['ɛmbrɪəʊ] N (*also fig*) embrión m
emcee [ɛm'siː] N ABBR (*US: = master of ceremonies*) presentador(a) m/f
emend [ɪ'mɛnd] VT (*text*) enmendar
emerald ['ɛmərəld] N esmeralda
emerge [ɪ'məːdʒ] VI (*gen*) salir; (*arise*) surgir; **it emerges that** resulta que
emergence [ɪ'məːdʒəns] N (*of nation*) surgimiento
emergency [ɪ'məːdʒənsɪ] N (*event*) emergencia; (*crisis*) crisis f inv; **in an ~** en caso de urgencia; (**to declare a) state of ~** (declarar) estado de emergencia or de excepción
emergency brake N (*US*) freno de mano
emergency cord N (*US*) timbre m de alarma
emergency exit N salida de emergencia
emergency landing N aterrizaje m forzoso
emergency lane N (*US*) arcén m
emergency meeting N reunión f extraordinaria
emergency room(*US Med*) N sala f de urgencias
emergency service N servicio de urgencia
emergency stop N (*Aut*) parada en seco
emergent [ɪ'məːdʒənt] ADJ (*nation*) recientemente independizado
emery board ['ɛmərɪ-] N lima de uñas
emetic [ɪ'mɛtɪk] N vomitivo, emético
emigrant ['ɛmɪgrənt] N emigrante mf
emigrate ['ɛmɪgreɪt] VI emigrar
emigration [ɛmɪ'greɪʃən] N emigración f
émigré ['ɛmɪgreɪ] N emigrado(-a)
eminence ['ɛmɪnəns] N eminencia; **to gain** or **win ~** ganarse fama
eminent ['ɛmɪnənt] ADJ eminente
eminently ['ɛmɪnəntlɪ] ADV eminentemente
emirate ['ɛmɪrɪt] N emirato
emission [ɪ'mɪʃən] N emisión f
emit [ɪ'mɪt] VT emitir; (*smell, smoke*) despedir
emolument [ɪ'mɒljumənt] N (*gen pl: formal*) honorario, emolumento
emoticon [ɪ'məʊtɪkɒn] N emoticón m
emotion [ɪ'məʊʃən] N emoción f
emotional [ɪ'məʊʃənl] ADJ (*person*)

sentimental; (*scene*) conmovedor(a), emocionante
emotionally [ɪ'məʊʃnəlɪ] ADV (*behave, speak*) con emoción; (*be involved*) sentimentalmente
emotive [ɪ'məʊtɪv] ADJ emotivo
empathy ['ɛmpəθɪ] N empatía; **to feel ~ with sb** sentirse identificado con algn
emperor ['ɛmpərər] N emperador m
emphasis ['ɛmfəsɪs] (*pl* **emphases** [-siːz]) N énfasis m inv; **to lay** or **place ~ on sth** (*fig*) hacer hincapié en algo; **the ~ is on sport** se da mayor importancia al deporte
emphasize ['ɛmfəsaɪz] VT (*word, point*) subrayar, recalcar; (*feature*) hacer resaltar
emphatic [ɛm'fætɪk] ADJ (*condemnation*) enérgico; (*denial*) rotundo
emphatically [ɛm'fætɪklɪ] ADV con énfasis
emphysema [ɛmfɪ'siːmə] N (*Med*) enfisema m
empire ['ɛmpaɪər] N imperio
empirical [ɛm'pɪrɪkl] ADJ empírico
employ [ɪm'plɔɪ] VT (*give job to*) emplear; (*make use of: thing, method*) emplear, usar; **he's employed in a bank** está empleado en un banco
employee [ɪmplɔɪ'iː] N empleado(-a)
employer [ɪm'plɔɪər] N patrón(-ona) m/f; (*businessman*) empresario(-a)
employment [ɪm'plɔɪmənt] N empleo; **full ~** pleno empleo; **without ~** sin empleo; **to find ~** encontrar trabajo; **place of ~** lugar m de trabajo
employment agency N agencia de colocaciones or empleo
employment exchange N bolsa de trabajo
empower [ɪm'paʊər] VT: **to ~ sb to do sth** autorizar a algn para hacer algo
empress ['ɛmprɪs] N emperatriz f
emptiness ['ɛmptɪnɪs] N vacío
empty ['ɛmptɪ] ADJ vacío; (*street, area*) desierto; (*threat*) vano ► N (*bottle*) envase m ► VT vaciar; (*place*) dejar vacío ► VI vaciarse; (*house*) quedar(se) vacío or desocupado; (*place*) quedar(se) desierto; **to ~ into** (*river*) desembocar en
empty-handed ['ɛmptɪ'hændɪd] ADJ con las manos vacías
empty-headed ['ɛmptɪ'hɛdɪd] ADJ casquivano
EMS N ABBR (*= European Monetary System*) SME m
EMT N ABBR (*US*) = **emergency medical technician**
EMU N ABBR (*= Ecomomic and Monetary Union*; *European Monetary Union*) UME f
emulate ['ɛmjuleɪt] VT emular
emulsion [ɪ'mʌlʃən] N emulsión f
enable [ɪ'neɪbl] VT: **to ~ sb to do sth** (*allow*) permitir a algn hacer algo; (*prepare*) capacitar a algn para hacer algo

e

enact [ɪnˈækt] VT (*law*) promulgar; (*play, scene, role*) representar

enamel [ɪˈnæməl] N esmalte *m*

enamel paint N esmalte *m*

enamoured [ɪˈnæməd] ADJ: **to be ~ of** (*person*) estar enamorado de; (*activity etc*) tener gran afición a; (*idea*) aferrarse a

enc. ABBR (*on letters etc*: = *enclosed, enclosure*) adj

encampment [ɪnˈkæmpmənt] N campamento

encase [ɪnˈkeɪs] VT: **to ~ in** (*contain*) encajar; (*cover*) cubrir

encased [ɪnˈkeɪst] ADJ: **~ in** (*covered*) revestido de

enchant [ɪnˈtʃɑːnt] VT encantar

enchanting [ɪnˈtʃɑːntɪŋ] ADJ encantador(a)

encircle [ɪnˈsəːkl] VT (*gen*) rodear; (*waist*) ceñir

encl. ABBR (= *enclosed*) adj

enclave [ˈɛnkleɪv] N enclave *m*

enclose [ɪnˈkləʊz] VT (*land*) cercar; (*with letter etc*) adjuntar; (*in receptacle*): **to ~ (with)** encerrar (con); **please find enclosed** le mandamos adjunto

enclosure [ɪnˈkləʊʒəʳ] N cercado, recinto; (*Comm*) carta adjunta

encoder [ɪnˈkəʊdəʳ] N (*Comput*) codificador *m*

encompass [ɪnˈkʌmpəs] VT abarcar

encore [ɔŋˈkɔːʳ] EXCL ¡otra!, ¡bis! ▶ N bis *m*

encounter [ɪnˈkaʊntəʳ] N encuentro ▶ VT encontrar, encontrarse con; (*difficulty*) tropezar con

encourage [ɪnˈkʌrɪdʒ] VT alentar, animar; (*growth*) estimular; **to ~ sb (to do sth)** animar a algn (a hacer algo)

encouragement [ɪnˈkʌrɪdʒmənt] N estímulo; (*of industry*) fomento

encouraging [ɪnˈkʌrɪdʒɪŋ] ADJ alentador(a)

encroach [ɪnˈkrəʊtʃ] VI: **to ~ (up)on** (*gen*) invadir; (*time*) adueñarse de

encrust [ɪnˈkrʌst] VT incrustar

encrusted [ɪnˈkrʌstəd] ADJ: **~ with** recubierto de

encrypt [ɪnˈkrɪpt] VT (*Comput, Tel*) encriptar

encumber [ɪnˈkʌmbəʳ] VT: **to be encumbered with** (*carry*) estar cargado de; (*debts*) estar gravado de

encyclopaedia, encyclopedia [ɛnsaɪkləʊˈpiːdɪə] N enciclopedia

end [ɛnd] N fin *m*; (*of table*) extremo; (*of line, rope etc*) cabo; (*of pointed object*) punta; (*of town*) barrio; (*of street*) final *m*; (*Sport*) lado ▶ VT terminar, acabar; (*also*: **bring to an end, put an end to**) acabar con ▶ VI terminar, acabar; **to ~ (with)** terminar (con); **in the ~** al final; **to be at an ~** llegar a su fin; **at the ~ of the day** (*fig*) al fin y al cabo, a fin de cuentas; **to this ~, with this ~ in view** con este propósito;

from ~ to ~ de punta a punta; **on ~** (*object*) de punta, de cabeza; **to stand on ~** (*hair*) erizarse, ponerse de punta; **for hours on ~** hora tras hora

▶ **end up** VI: **to ~ up in** terminar en; (*place*) ir a parar a

endanger [ɪnˈdeɪndʒəʳ] VT poner en peligro; **an endangered species** (*of animal*) una especie en peligro de extinción

endear [ɪnˈdɪəʳ] VT: **to ~ o.s. to sb** ganarse la simpatía de algn

endearing [ɪnˈdɪərɪŋ] ADJ entrañable

endearment [ɪnˈdɪərmənt] N cariño, palabra cariñosa; **to whisper endearments** decir unas palabras cariñosas al oído; **term of ~** nombre *m* cariñoso

endeavour, (US) endeavor [ɪnˈdɛvəʳ] N esfuerzo; (*attempt*) tentativa ▶ VI: **to ~ to do** esforzarse por hacer; (*try*) procurar hacer

endemic [ɛnˈdɛmɪk] ADJ (*poverty, disease*) endémico

ending [ˈɛndɪŋ] N fin *m*, final *m*; (*of book*) desenlace *m*; (*Ling*) terminación *f*

endive [ˈɛndaɪv] N (*curly*) escarola; (*smooth, flat*) endibia

endless [ˈɛndlɪs] ADJ interminable, inacabable; (*possibilities*) infinito

endorse [ɪnˈdɔːs] VT (*cheque*) endosar; (*approve*) aprobar

endorsee [ɪndɔːˈsiː] N endosatario(-a)

endorsement [ɪnˈdɔːsmənt] N (*approval*) aprobación *f*; (*signature*) endoso; (BRIT: *on driving licence*) nota de sanción

endorser [ɪnˈdɔːsəʳ] N avalista *mf*

endow [ɪnˈdaʊ] VT (*provide with money*) dotar; (*found*) fundar; **to be endowed with** (*fig*) estar dotado de

endowment [ɪnˈdaʊmənt] ADJ (*amount*) donación *f*

endowment mortgage N hipoteca dotal

endowment policy N póliza dotal

end product N (*Industry*) producto final; (*fig*) resultado

end result N resultado

endurable [ɪnˈdjʊərəbl] ADJ soportable, tolerable

endurance [ɪnˈdjʊərəns] N resistencia

endurance test N prueba de resistencia

endure [ɪnˈdjʊəʳ] VT (*bear*) aguantar, soportar; (*resist*) resistir ▶ VI (*last*) perdurar; (*resist*) resistir

enduring [ɪnˈdjʊərɪŋ] ADJ duradero

end user N (*Comput*) usuario final

enema [ˈɛnɪmə] N (*Med*) enema *m*

enemy [ˈɛnəmɪ] ADJ, N enemigo(-a) *m/f*; **to make an ~ of sb** enemistarse con algn

energetic [ɛnəˈdʒɛtɪk] ADJ enérgico

energy [ˈɛnədʒɪ] N energía

energy crisis N crisis *f* energética

energy drink N bebida energética, bebida isotónica

energy-saving ['enədʒɪseɪvɪŋ] ADJ (*policy*) para ahorrar energía; (*device*) que ahorra energía ▶ N ahorro de energía

enervating ['enəveɪtɪŋ] ADJ deprimente

enforce [ɪn'fɔːs] VT (*law*) hacer cumplir

enforced [ɪn'fɔːst] ADJ forzoso, forzado

enfranchise [ɪn'fræntʃaɪz] VT (*give vote to*) conceder el derecho de voto a; (*set free*) emancipar

engage [ɪn'geɪdʒ] VT (*attention*) captar; (*in conversation*) abordar; (*worker, lawyer*) contratar ▶ VI (*Tech*) engranar; **to ~ in** dedicarse a, ocuparse en; **to ~ sb in conversation** entablar conversación con algn; **to ~ the clutch** embragar

engaged [ɪn'geɪdʒd] ADJ (*BRIT: busy, in use*) ocupado; (*betrothed*) prometido; **to get ~** prometerse; **he is ~ in research** se dedica a la investigación

engaged tone N (*BRIT Tel*) señal *f* de comunicando

engagement [ɪn'geɪdʒmənt] N (*appointment*) compromiso, cita; (*battle*) combate *m*; (*to marry*) compromiso; (*period*) noviazgo; **I have a previous ~** ya tengo un compromiso

engagement ring N anillo de pedida

engaging [ɪn'geɪdʒɪŋ] ADJ atractivo, simpático

engender [ɪn'dʒendə^r] VT engendrar

engine ['endʒɪn] N (*Aut*) motor *m*; (*Rail*) locomotora

engine driver N (*BRIT: of train*) maquinista *mf*

engineer [endʒɪ'nɪə^r] N ingeniero(-a); (*BRIT: for repairs*) técnico(-a); (*US Rail*) maquinista *mf*; **civil/mechanical ~** ingeniero(-a) de caminos, canales y puertos/industrial

engineering [endʒɪ'nɪərɪŋ] N ingeniería ▶ CPD (*works, factory*) de componentes mecánicos

engine failure, engine trouble N avería del motor

England ['ɪŋglənd] N Inglaterra

English ['ɪŋglɪʃ] ADJ inglés(-esa) ▶ N (*Ling*) el inglés; **the English** NPL los ingleses

English Channel N: **the ~** el Canal de la Mancha

Englishman ['ɪŋglɪʃmən], **Englishwoman** ['ɪŋglɪʃwumən] N (*irreg*) inglés(-esa) *m/f*

English-speaker ['ɪŋglɪʃspiːkə^r] N persona de habla inglesa

English-speaking ['ɪŋglɪʃspiːkɪŋ] ADJ de habla inglesa

engrave [ɪn'greɪv] VT grabar

engraving [ɪn'greɪvɪŋ] N grabado

engrossed [ɪn'grəust] ADJ: **~ in** absorto en

engulf [ɪn'gʌlf] VT sumergir, hundir; (*fire*) devorar

enhance [ɪn'hɑːns] VT (*gen*) aumentar; (*beauty*) realzar; (*position, reputation*) mejorar

enigma [ɪ'nɪgmə] N enigma *m*

enigmatic [ɛnɪg'mætɪk] ADJ enigmático

enjoy [ɪn'dʒɔɪ] VT (*have: health, fortune*) disfrutar de, gozar de; (: *food*) comer con gusto; **I ~ doing ...** me gusta hacer ...; **to ~ o.s.** divertirse, pasarlo bien

enjoyable [ɪn'dʒɔɪəbl] ADJ (*pleasant*) agradable; (*amusing*) divertido

enjoyment [ɪn'dʒɔɪmənt] N (*use*) disfrute *m*; (*joy*) placer *m*

enlarge [ɪn'lɑːdʒ] VT aumentar; (*broaden*) extender; (*Phot*) ampliar ▶ VI: **to ~ on** (*subject*) tratar con más detalles

enlarged [ɪn'lɑːdʒd] ADJ (*edition*) aumentado; (*Med: organ, gland*) dilatado

enlargement [ɪn'lɑːdʒmənt] N (*Phot*) ampliación *f*

enlighten [ɪn'laɪtn] VT informar, instruir

enlightened [ɪn'laɪtnd] ADJ iluminado; (*tolerant*) comprensivo

enlightening [ɪn'laɪtnɪŋ] ADJ informativo, instructivo

Enlightenment [ɪn'laɪtnmənt] N (*History*): **the ~** la Ilustración, el Siglo de las Luces

enlist [ɪn'lɪst] VT alistar; (*support*) conseguir ▶ VI alistarse; **enlisted man** (*US Mil*) soldado raso

enliven [ɪn'laɪvn] VT (*people*) animar; (*events*) avivar, animar

enmity ['enmɪtɪ] N enemistad *f*

ennoble [ɪ'nəubl] VT ennoblecer

enormity [ɪ'nɔːmɪtɪ] N enormidad *f*

enormous [ɪ'nɔːməs] ADJ enorme

enough [ɪ'nʌf] ADJ: **~ time/books** bastante tiempo/bastantes libros ▶ N: **have you got ~?** ¿tiene usted bastante? ▶ ADV: **big ~** bastante grande; **he has not worked ~** no ha trabajado bastante; (*that's*) **~!** ¡basta ya!, ¡ya está bien!; **that's ~, thanks** con eso basta, gracias; **will five be ~?** ¿bastará con cinco?; **I've had ~** estoy harto; **he was kind ~ to lend me the money** tuvo la bondad or amabilidad de prestarme el dinero; ... **which, funnily ~** ... ... lo que, por extraño que parezca ...

enquire [ɪn'kwaɪə^r] VT, VI = **inquire**

enrage [ɪn'reɪdʒ] VT enfurecer

enrich [ɪn'rɪtʃ] VT enriquecer

enrol, (*US*) **enroll** [ɪn'rəul] VT (*member*) inscribir; (*Scol*) matricular ▶ VI inscribirse; (*Scol*) matricularse

enrolment, (*US*) **enrollment** [ɪn'rəulmənt] N inscripción *f*; matriculación *f*

en route [ɔn'ruːt] ADV durante el viaje; **~ for/ from/to** camino de/de/a

ensconce [ɪn'skɔns] VT: **to ~ o.s.** instalarse cómodamente, acomodarse

ensemble [ɔnˈsɔmbl] N (*Mus*) conjunto

enshrine [ɪnˈʃraɪn] VT recoger

ensign [ˈɛnsaɪn] N (*flag*) bandera; (*Naut*) alférez *m*

enslave [ɪnˈsleɪv] VT esclavizar

ensue [ɪnˈsjuː] VI seguirse; (*result*) resultar

ensuing [ɪnˈsjuːɪŋ] ADJ subsiguiente

en suite [ɔnˈswiːt] ADJ: **with ~ bathroom** con baño

ensure [ɪnˈʃuəʳ] VT asegurar

ENT N ABBR (*Med*: = *ear, nose and throat*) otorrinolaringología

entail [ɪnˈteɪl] VT (*imply*) suponer; (*result in*) acarrear

entangle [ɪnˈtæŋgl] VT (*thread etc*) enredar, enmarañar; **to become entangled in sth** (*fig*) enredarse en algo

entanglement [ɪnˈtæŋglmənt] N enredo

enter [ˈɛntəʳ] VT (*room, profession*) entrar en; (*club*) hacerse socio de; (*army*) alistarse en; (*sb for a competition*) inscribir; (*write down*) anotar, apuntar; (*Comput*) introducir ▶ VI entrar

▶ **enter for** VT FUS presentarse a

▶ **enter into** VT FUS (*relations*) establecer; (*plans*) formar parte de; (*debate*) tomar parte en; (*negotiations*) entablar; (*agreement*) llegar a, firmar

▶ **enter (up)on** VT FUS (*career*) emprender

enteritis [ɛntəˈraɪtɪs] N enteritis *f*

enterprise [ˈɛntəpraɪz] N empresa; (*spirit*) iniciativa; **free ~** la libre empresa; **private ~** la iniciativa privada

enterprising [ˈɛntəpraɪzɪŋ] ADJ emprendedor(a)

entertain [ɛntəˈteɪn] VT (*amuse*) divertir; (*receive: guest*) recibir (en casa); (*idea*) abrigar

entertainer [ɛntəˈteɪnəʳ] N artista *mf*

entertaining [ɛntəˈteɪnɪŋ] ADJ divertido, entretenido ▶ N: **to do a lot of ~** dar muchas fiestas, tener muchos invitados

entertainment [ɛntəˈteɪnmənt] N (*amusement*) diversión *f*; (*show*) espectáculo; (*party*) fiesta

entertainment allowance N (*Comm*) gastos *mpl* de representación

enthral [ɪnˈθrɔːl] VT embelesar, cautivar

enthralled [ɪnˈθrɔːld] ADJ cautivado

enthralling [ɪnˈθrɔːlɪŋ] ADJ cautivador(a)

enthuse [ɪnˈθuːz] VI: **to ~ about** or **over** entusiasmarse por

enthusiasm [ɪnˈθuːzɪæzəm] N entusiasmo

enthusiast [ɪnˈθuːzɪæst] N entusiasta *mf*

enthusiastic [ɪnθuːzɪˈæstɪk] ADJ entusiasta; **to be ~ about sb/sth** estar entusiasmado con algn/algo

entice [ɪnˈtaɪs] VT tentar; (*seduce*) seducir

entire [ɪnˈtaɪəʳ] ADJ entero, todo

entirely [ɪnˈtaɪəlɪ] ADV totalmente

entirety [ɪnˈtaɪərətɪ] N: **in its ~** en su totalidad

entitle [ɪnˈtaɪtl] VT: **to ~ sb to sth** dar a algn derecho a algo

entitled [ɪnˈtaɪtld] ADJ (*book*) titulado; **to be ~ to sth/to do sth** tener derecho a algo/a hacer algo

entity [ˈɛntɪtɪ] N entidad *f*

entourage [ɔntuˈrɑːʒ] N séquito

entrails [ˈɛntreɪlz] NPL entrañas *fpl*; (*US: offal*) asadura *sg*, menudos *mpl*

entrance [ˈɛntrəns] N entrada ▶ VT [ɪnˈtrɑːns] encantar, hechizar; **to gain ~ to** (*university etc*) ingresar en

entrance examination N (*to school*) examen *m* de ingreso

entrance fee N (*to a show*) entrada; (*to a club*) cuota

entrance ramp N (*US Aut*) rampa de acceso

entrancing [ɪnˈtrɑːnsɪŋ] ADJ encantador(a)

entrant [ˈɛntrənt] N (*in race, competition*) participante *mf*; (*in exam*) candidato(-a)

entreat [ɛnˈtriːt] VT rogar, suplicar

entrenched [ɛnˈtrɛntʃd] ADJ: **~ interests** intereses *mpl* creados

entrepreneur [ɔntrəprəˈnəːʳ] N empresario(-a), capitalista *mf*

entrepreneurial [ɔntrəprəˈnəːrɪəl] ADJ empresarial

entrust [ɪnˈtrʌst] VT: **to ~ sth to sb** confiar algo a algn

entry [ˈɛntrɪ] N entrada; (*permission to enter*) acceso; (*in register, diary, ship's log*) apunte *m*; (*in account book, ledger, list*) partida; **no ~** prohibido el paso; (*Aut*) dirección prohibida; **single/double ~ book-keeping** contabilidad *f* simple/por partida doble

entry form N boletín *m* de inscripción

entry phone N (*Brit*) portero automático

E-number [ˈiːnʌmbəʳ] N número E

enumerate [ɪˈnjuːməreɪt] VT enumerar

enunciate [ɪˈnʌnsɪeɪt] VT pronunciar; (*principle etc*) enunciar

envelop [ɪnˈvɛləp] VT envolver

envelope [ˈɛnvələup] N sobre *m*

enviable [ˈɛnvɪəbl] ADJ envidiable

envious [ˈɛnvɪəs] ADJ envidioso; (*look*) de envidia

environment [ɪnˈvaɪərnmənt] N medio ambiente; (*surroundings*) entorno; **Department of the E~** ministerio del medio ambiente

environmental [ɪnvaɪərnˈmɛntl] ADJ (medio)ambiental; **~ studies** (*in school etc*) ecología *sg*

environmentalist [ɪnvaɪərnˈmɛntlɪst] N ecologista *mf*

environmentally [ɪnvaɪərnˈmɛntlɪ] ADV: **~ sound/friendly** ecológico

envisage [ɪn'vɪzɪdʒ] VT (*foresee*) prever; (*imagine*) concebir

envision [ɪn'vɪʒən] VT imaginar

envoy ['ɛnvɔɪ] N enviado(-a)

envy ['ɛnvɪ] N envidia ▶ VT tener envidia a; **to ~ sb sth** envidiar algo a algn

enzyme ['ɛnzaɪm] N enzima *m or f*

EPA N ABBR (*US: = Environmental Protection Agency*) *Agencia del Medio Ambiente*

ephemeral [ɪ'fɛmərl] ADJ efímero

epic ['ɛpɪk] N épica ▶ ADJ épico

epicentre, (*US*) **epicenter** ['ɛpɪsɛntə^r] N epicentro

epidemic [ɛpɪ'dɛmɪk] N epidemia

epigram ['ɛpɪɡræm] N epigrama *m*

epilepsy ['ɛpɪlɛpsɪ] N epilepsia

epileptic [ɛpɪ'lɛptɪk] ADJ, N epiléptico(-a) *m/f*

epileptic fit [ɛpɪ'lɛptɪk-] N ataque *m* de epilepsia, acceso *m* epiléptico

epilogue ['ɛpɪlɔɡ] N epílogo

episcopal [ɪ'pɪskəpl] ADJ episcopal

episode ['ɛpɪsəud] N episodio

epistle [ɪ'pɪsl] N epístola

epitaph ['ɛpɪtɑːf] N epitafio

epithet ['ɛpɪθɛt] N epíteto

epitome [ɪ'pɪtəmɪ] N arquetipo

epitomize [ɪ'pɪtəmaɪz] VT representar

epoch ['iːpɔk] N época

eponymous [ɪ'pɔnɪməs] ADJ epónimo

equable ['ɛkwəbl] ADJ (*climate*) estable; (*character*) ecuánime

equal ['iːkwl] ADJ (*gen*) igual; (*treatment*) equitativo ▶ N igual *mf* ▶ VT ser igual a; (*fig*) igualar; **to be ~ to** (*task*) estar a la altura de; **the E~ Opportunities Commission** (*BRIT*) *comisión para la igualdad de la mujer en el trabajo*

equality [iː'kwɔlɪtɪ] N igualdad *f*

equalize ['iːkwəlaɪz] VT, VI igualar; (*Sport*) empatar

equalizer ['iːkwəlaɪzə^r] N igualada

equally ['iːkwəlɪ] ADV igualmente; (*share etc*) a partes iguales; **they are ~ clever** son tan listos uno como otro

equals sign N signo igual

equanimity [ɛkwə'nɪmɪtɪ] N ecuanimidad *f*

equate [ɪ'kweɪt] VT: **to ~ sth with** equiparar algo con

equation [ɪ'kweɪʒən] N (*Math*) ecuación *f*

equator [ɪ'kweɪtə^r] N ecuador *m*

equatorial [ɛkwə'tɔːrɪəl] ADJ ecuatorial

Equatorial Guinea N Guinea Ecuatorial

equestrian [ɪ'kwɛstrɪən] ADJ ecuestre ▶ N jinete *mf*

equilibrium [iːkwɪ'lɪbrɪəm] N equilibrio

equinox ['iːkwɪnɔks] N equinoccio

equip [ɪ'kwɪp] VT (*gen*) equipar; (*person*) proveer; **equipped with** (*machinery etc*) provisto de; **to be well equipped** estar bien equipado; **he is well equipped for the job** está bien preparado para este puesto

equipment [ɪ'kwɪpmənt] N equipo

equitable ['ɛkwɪtəbl] ADJ equitativo

equities ['ɛkwɪtɪz] NPL (*BRIT Comm*) acciones *fpl* ordinarias

equity ['ɛkwɪtɪ] N (*fairness*) equidad *f*; (*Econ: of debtor*) valor *m* líquido

equity capital N capital *m* propio, patrimonio neto

equivalent [ɪ'kwɪvəlnt] ADJ, N equivalente *m*; **to be ~ to** equivaler a

equivocal [ɪ'kwɪvəkl] ADJ equívoco

equivocate [ɪ'kwɪvəkeɪt] VI andarse con ambigüedades

equivocation [ɪkwɪvə'keɪʃən] N ambigüedad *f*

ER ABBR (*BRIT*: = *Elizabeth Regina*) *la reina Isabel*; (*US Med*) = **emergency room**

er [əː] EXCL (*inf: in hesitation*) esto, este (*LAm*)

ERA N ABBR (*US Pol*: = *Equal Rights Amendment*) *enmienda sobre la igualdad de derechos de la mujer*

era ['ɪərə] N era, época

eradicate [ɪ'rædɪkeɪt] VT erradicar, extirpar

erase [ɪ'reɪz] VT (*Comput*) borrar

eraser [ɪ'reɪzə^r] N goma de borrar

e-reader, eReader ['iːriːdə^r] N lector *m* de libros electrónicos

erect [ɪ'rɛkt] ADJ erguido ▶ VT erigir, levantar; (*assemble*) montar

erection [ɪ'rɛkʃən] N (*of building*) construcción *f*; (*of machinery*) montaje *m*; (*structure*) edificio; (*Med*) erección *f*

ergonomics [əːɡə'nɔmɪks] N ergonomía

ERISA N ABBR (*US*: = *Employee Retirement Income Security Act*) *ley que regula las pensiones de jubilados*

Eritrea [ɛrɪ'treɪə] N Eritrea

ERM N ABBR (= *Exchange Rate Mechanism*) (mecanismo de cambios del) SME *m*

ermine ['əːmɪn] N armiño

ERNIE ['əːnɪ] N ABBR (*BRIT*: = *Electronic Random Number Indicator Equipment*) *ordenador que elige al azar los números ganadores de los bonos del Estado*

erode [ɪ'rəud] VT (*Geo*) erosionar; (*metal*) corroer, desgastar

erogenous zone [ɪ'rɔdʒənəs-] N zona erógena

erosion [ɪ'rəuʒən] N erosión *f*; desgaste *m*

erotic [ɪ'rɔtɪk] ADJ erótico

eroticism [ɪ'rɔtɪsɪzm] N erotismo

err [əː^r] VI errar; (*Rel*) pecar

errand ['ɛrnd] N recado, mandado (*LAm*); **to run errands** hacer recados; **~ of mercy** misión *f* de caridad

errand boy N recadero

erratic [ɪ'rætɪk] ADJ variable; (*results etc*) desigual, poco uniforme

erroneous [ɪ'rəunɪəs] ADJ erróneo

error ['ɛrə^r] N error *m*, equivocación *f*; **typing/spelling ~** error de mecanografía/

ortografía; **in ~** por equivocación; **errors and omissions excepted** salvo error u omisión

error message N (*Comput*) mensaje *m* de error

erstwhile ['ə:stwaɪl] ADJ antiguo, previo

erudite ['ɛrudaɪt] ADJ erudito

erudition [ɛru'dɪʃən] N erudición *f*

erupt [ɪ'rʌpt] VI entrar en erupción; (*Med*) hacer erupción; (*fig*) estallar

eruption [ɪ'rʌpʃən] N erupción *f*; (*fig: of anger, violence*) explosión *f*, estallido

ESA N ABBR (= *European Space Agency*) Agencia Espacial Europea

escalate ['ɛskəleɪt] VI extenderse, intensificarse; (*costs*) aumentar vertiginosamente

escalation clause [ɛskə'leɪʃən-] N cláusula de reajuste de los precios

escalator ['ɛskəleɪtəʳ] N escalera mecánica

escapade [ɛskə'peɪd] N aventura

escape [ɪ'skeɪp] N (*gen*) fuga; (*Tech*) escape *m*; (*from duties*) escapatoria; (*from chase*) evasión *f* ▶ VI (*gen*) escaparse; (*flee*) huir, evadirse ▶ VT evitar, eludir; (*consequences*) escapar a; **his name escapes me** no me sale su nombre; **to ~ from** (*place*) escaparse de; (*person*) huir de; (*clutches*) librarse de; **to ~ to** (*another place, freedom, safety*) huir a; **to ~ notice** pasar desapercibido

escape artist N artista *mf* de la evasión

escape clause N (*fig: in agreement*) cláusula de excepción

escapee [ɪskeɪ'pi:] N fugado(-a)

escape hatch N (*in submarine, space rocket*) escotilla de salvamento

escape key N (*Comput*) tecla de escape

escape route N (*from fire*) vía de escape

escapism [ɪ'skeɪpɪzəm] N escapismo, evasión *f*

escapist [ɪ'skeɪpɪst] ADJ escapista, de evasión ▶ N escapista *mf*

escapologist [ɛskə'pɔlədʒɪst] N (*Brit*) = **escape artist**

escarpment [ɪ'skɑ:pmənt] N escarpa

eschew [ɪs'tʃu:] VT evitar, abstenerse de

escort N ['ɛskɔ:t] acompañante *mf*; (*Mil*) escolta; (*Naut*) convoy *m* ▶ VT [ɪ'skɔ:t] acompañar; (*Mil, Naut*) escoltar

escort agency N agencia de acompañantes

Eskimo ['ɛskɪməu] ADJ esquimal ▶ N esquimal *mf*; (*Ling*) esquimal *m*

ESL N ABBR (*Scol*) = **English as a Second Language**

esophagus [i:'sɔfəgəs] N (*US*) = **oesophagus**

esoteric [ɛsəu'tɛrɪk] ADJ esotérico

ESP N ABBR = **extrasensory perception**; (*Scol*: = *English for Specific (or Special) Purposes*) inglés especializado

esp. ABBR = **especially**

especially [ɪ'spɛʃlɪ] ADV (*gen*) especialmente; (*above all*) sobre todo; (*particularly*) en especial

espionage ['ɛspɪənɑːʒ] N espionaje *m*

esplanade [ɛsplə'neɪd] N (*by sea*) paseo marítimo

espouse [ɪ'spauz] VT adherirse a

Esq. ABBR (= *Esquire*) D.

Esquire [ɪ'skwaɪəʳ] N: **J. Brown, ~** Sr. D. J. Brown

essay ['ɛseɪ] N (*Scol*) redacción *f*; (: *longer*) trabajo

essayist ['ɛseɪɪst] N ensayista *mf*

essence ['ɛsns] N esencia; **in ~** esencialmente; **speed is of the ~** es esencial hacerlo con la mayor prontitud

essential [ɪ'sɛnʃl] ADJ (*necessary*) imprescindible; (*basic*) esencial ▶ N (*gen pl*) lo esencial; **it is ~ that** es imprescindible que

essentially [ɪ'sɛnʃlɪ] ADV esencialmente

EST N ABBR (*US*: = *Eastern Standard Time*) hora de invierno de Nueva York

est. ABBR (= *established*) fundado; (= *estimated*) aprox.

establish [ɪ'stæblɪʃ] VT establecer; (*prove: fact*) comprobar, demostrar; (*identity*) verificar; (*relations*) entablar

established [ɪ'stæblɪʃt] ADJ (*business*) de buena reputación; (*staff*) de plantilla

establishment [ɪ'stæblɪʃmənt] N establecimiento; **the E~** la clase dirigente; **a teaching ~** un centro de enseñanza

estate [ɪ'steɪt] N (*land*) finca, hacienda; (*property*) propiedad *f*; (*inheritance*) herencia; (*Pol*) estado; **housing ~** (*Brit*) urbanización *f*; **industrial ~** polígono industrial

estate agency N (*Brit*) agencia inmobiliaria

estate agent N (*Brit*) agente *mf* inmobiliario(-a)

estate agent's N agencia inmobiliaria

estate car N (*Brit*) ranchera, coche *m* familiar

esteem [ɪ'sti:m] N: **to hold sb in high ~** estimar en mucho a algn ▶ VT estimar

esthetic [i:s'θɛtɪk] ADJ (*US*) = **aesthetic**

estimate ['ɛstɪmət] N estimación *f*; (*assessment*) tasa, cálculo; (*Comm*) presupuesto ▶ VT ['ɛstɪmeɪt] estimar; tasar, calcular; **to give sb an ~ of** presentar a algn un presupuesto de; **at a rough ~** haciendo un cálculo aproximado; **to ~ for** (*Comm*) hacer un presupuesto de, presupuestar

estimation [ɛstɪ'meɪʃən] N opinión *f*, juicio; (*esteem*) aprecio; **in my ~** a mi juicio

Estonia [ɛ'stəunɪə] N Estonia

Estonian [ɛ'stəunɪən] ADJ estonio ▶ N estonio(-a); (*Ling*) estonio

estranged [ɪ'streɪndʒd] ADJ separado

estrangement [ɪ'streɪndʒmənt] N

alejamiento, distanciamiento

estrogen ['i:trəudʒən] N (US) = **oestrogen**

estuary ['ɛstjuərɪ] N estuario, ría

ET N ABBR (BRIT: = Employment Training) plan estatal de formación para los desempleados ▸ ABBR (US) = **Eastern Time**

ETA N ABBR = **estimated time of arrival**

e-tailing ['i:teɪlɪŋ] N venta en línea, venta vía or por Internet

et al. ABBR (= et alii: and others) et al.

etc ABBR (= et cetera) etc

etch [ɛtʃ] VT grabar al aguafuerte

etching ['ɛtʃɪŋ] N aguafuerte m or f

ETD N ABBR = **estimated time of departure**

eternal [ɪ'tə:nl] ADJ eterno

eternity [ɪ'tə:nɪtɪ] N eternidad f

ether ['i:θəʳ] N éter m

ethereal [ɪ'θɪərɪəl] ADJ etéreo

ethical ['ɛθɪkl] ADJ ético; (honest) honrado

ethics ['ɛθɪks] N ética ▸ NPL moralidad f

Ethiopia [i:θɪ'əupɪə] N Etiopía

Ethiopian [i:θɪ'əupɪən] ADJ, N etíope mf

ethnic ['ɛθnɪk] ADJ étnico

ethnic cleansing [-klɛnzɪŋ] N limpieza étnica

ethnic minority N minoría étnica

ethos ['i:θɔs] N (of culture, group) sistema m de valores

e-ticket ['i:tɪkɪt] N billete electrónico, boleto electrónico (LAM)

etiquette ['ɛtɪkɛt] N etiqueta

ETV N ABBR (US: = Educational Television) televisión escolar

etymology [ɛtɪ'mɔlədʒɪ] N etimología

EU N ABBR (= European Union) UE f

eucalyptus [ju:kə'lɪptəs] N eucalipto

Eucharist ['ju:kərɪst] N Eucaristía

eulogy ['ju:lədʒɪ] N elogio, encomio

eunuch ['ju:nək] N eunuco

euphemism ['ju:fəmɪzm] N eufemismo

euphemistic [ju:fə'mɪstɪk] ADJ eufemístico

euphoria [ju:'fɔ:rɪə] N euforia

Eurasia [juə'reɪʒə] N Eurasia

Eurasian [juə'reɪʃən] ADJ, N eurasiático(-a) m/f

Euratom [juə'rætəm] N ABBR (= European Atomic Energy Commission) Euratom m

euro ['juərəu] N (currency) euro

Euro- PREF euro-

Eurocheque ['juərəutʃɛk] N Eurocheque m

Eurocrat ['juərəukræt] N eurócrata mf

Eurodollar ['juərəudɔləʳ] N eurodólar m

Euroland ['juərəulænd] N Eurolandia

Europe ['juərəp] N Europa

European [juərə'pi:ən] ADJ, N europeo(-a) m/f

European Community N Comunidad f Europea

European Court of Justice N Tribunal m de Justicia de las Comunidades Europeas

European Union N Unión f Europea

Euro-sceptic [juərəu'skɛptɪk] N euroescéptico(-a)

Eurostar® ['juərəustɑ:ʳ] N Eurostar® m

Eurozone ['juərəuzəun] N eurozona, zona euro

euthanasia [ju:θə'neɪzɪə] N eutanasia

evacuate [ɪ'vækjueɪt] VT evacuar; (place) desocupar

evacuation [ɪvækju'eɪʃən] N evacuación f

evacuee [ɪvækju'i:] N evacuado(-a)

evade [ɪ'veɪd] VT evadir, eludir

evaluate [ɪ'væljueɪt] VT evaluar; (value) tasar; (evidence) interpretar

evangelical [i:væn'dʒɛlɪkəl] ADJ evangélico

evangelist [ɪ'vændʒəlɪst] N evangelista m; (preacher) evangelizador(a) m/f

evaporate [ɪ'væpəreɪt] VI evaporarse; (fig) desvanecerse ▸ VT evaporar

evaporation [ɪvæpə'reɪʃən] N evaporación f

evasion [ɪ'veɪʒən] N evasión f

evasive [ɪ'veɪsɪv] ADJ evasivo

eve [i:v] N: **on the ~ of** en vísperas de

even ['i:vn] ADJ (level) llano; (smooth) liso; (speed, temperature) uniforme; (number) par; (Sport) igual(es) ▸ ADV hasta, incluso; **~ if**, **~ though** aunque + subjun, así + subjun (LAM); **~ more** aun más; **~ so** aun así; **not ~** ni siquiera; **~ he was there** hasta él estaba allí; **~ on Sundays** incluso los domingos; **~ faster** aún más rápido; **to break ~** cubrir los gastos; **to get ~ with sb** ajustar cuentas con algn; **to ~ out** vi nivelarse

even-handed [i:vn'hændɪd] ADJ imparcial

evening ['i:vnɪŋ] N tarde f; (dusk) atardecer m; (night) noche f; **in the ~** por la tarde; **this ~** esta tarde or noche; **tomorrow/yesterday ~** mañana/ayer por la tarde or noche

evening class N clase f nocturna

evening dress N (man's) traje m de etiqueta; (woman's) traje m de noche

evenly ['i:vnlɪ] ADV (distribute, space, spread) de modo uniforme; (divide) equitativamente

evensong ['i:vnsɔŋ] N vísperas fpl

event [ɪ'vɛnt] N suceso, acontecimiento; (Sport) prueba; **in the ~ of** en caso de; **in the ~ realidad; in the course of events** en el curso de los acontecimientos; **at all events**, **in any ~** en cualquier caso

eventful [ɪ'vɛntful] ADJ (life) azaroso; (day) ajetreado; (game) lleno de emoción; (journey) lleno de incidentes

eventing [ɪ'vɛntɪŋ] N (Horseriding) competición f

eventual [ɪ'vɛntʃuəl] ADJ final

eventuality [ɪvɛntʃu'ælɪtɪ] N eventualidad f

eventually [ɪ'vɛntʃuəlɪ] ADV (finally) por fin; (in time) con el tiempo

ever ['ɛvəʳ] ADV nunca, jamás; (at all times)

siempre ▸ CONJ después de que; **for ~** (para) siempre; **the best ~** lo nunca visto; **did you ~ meet him?** ¿llegaste a conocerle?; **have you ~ been there?** ¿has estado allí alguna vez?; **have you ~ seen it?** ¿lo has visto alguna vez?; **better than ~** mejor que nunca; **thank you ~ so much** muchísimas gracias; **yours ~** (in letters) un abrazo de; **~ since** adv desde entonces

Everest ['ɛvərɪst] N (also: **Mount Everest**) el Everest m

evergreen ['ɛvəgriːn] N árbol m de hoja perenne

everlasting [ɛvə'lɑːstɪŋ] ADJ eterno, perpetuo

(KEYWORD)

every ['ɛvrɪ] ADJ **1** (each) cada; **every one of them** (persons) todos ellos(-as); (objects) cada uno de ellos(-as); **every shop in the town was closed** todas las tiendas de la ciudad estaban cerradas
2 (all possible) todo(-a); **I gave you every assistance** te di toda la ayuda posible; **I have every confidence in him** tiene toda mi confianza; **we wish you every success** te deseamos toda suerte de éxitos
3 (showing recurrence) todo(-a); **every day/ week** todos los días/todas las semanas; **every other car had been broken into** habían forzado uno de cada dos coches; **she visits me every other/third day** me visita cada dos/tres días; **every now and then** de vez en cuando

everybody ['ɛvrɪbɒdɪ] PRON todos pron pl, todo el mundo; **~ knows about it** todo el mundo lo sabe; **~ else** todos los demás

everyday ['ɛvrɪdeɪ] ADJ (daily: use, occurrence, experience) diario, cotidiano; (usual: expression) corriente; (common) vulgar; (routine) rutinario

everyone ['ɛvrɪwʌn] PRON = **everybody**

everything ['ɛvrɪθɪŋ] PRON todo; **~ is ready** todo está dispuesto; **he did ~ possible** hizo todo lo posible

everywhere ['ɛvrɪwɛəʳ] ADV (be) en todas partes; (go) a or por todas partes; **~ you go you meet …** en todas partes encuentras …

evict [ɪ'vɪkt] VT desahuciar

eviction [ɪ'vɪkʃən] N desahucio

eviction notice N orden f de desahucio or desalojo (LAm)

evidence ['ɛvɪdəns] N (proof) prueba; (of witness) testimonio; (facts) datos mpl, hechos mpl; **to give ~** prestar declaración, dar testimonio

evident ['ɛvɪdənt] ADJ evidente, manifiesto

evidently ['ɛvɪdəntlɪ] ADV (obviously) obviamente, evidentemente; (apparently) por lo visto

evil ['iːvl] ADJ malo; (influence) funesto; (smell) horrible ▸ N mal m

evildoer ['iːvlduːəʳ] N malhechor(a) m/f

evince [ɪ'vɪns] VT mostrar, dar señales de

evocative [ɪ'vɒkətɪv] ADJ sugestivo, evocador(a)

evoke [ɪ'vəuk] VT evocar; (admiration) provocar

evolution [iːvə'luːʃən] N evolución f, desarrollo

evolve [ɪ'vɒlv] VT desarrollar ▸ VI evolucionar, desarrollarse

ewe [juː] N oveja

ex [ɛks] N (inf): **my ex** mi ex

ex- [ɛks] PREF (former: husband, president etc) ex-; (out of): **the price ~works** precio de fábrica

exacerbate [ɛk'sæsəbeɪt] VT exacerbar

exact [ɪg'zækt] ADJ exacto ▸ VT: **to ~ sth (from)** exigir algo (de)

exacting [ɪg'zæktɪŋ] ADJ exigente; (conditions) arduo

exactitude [ɪg'zæktɪtjuːd] N exactitud f

exactly [ɪg'zæktlɪ] ADV exactamente; (time) en punto; **~!** ¡exacto!

exactness [ɪg'zæktnɪs] N exactitud f

exaggerate [ɪg'zædʒəreɪt] VT, VI exagerar

exaggerated [ɪg'zædʒəreɪtɪd] ADJ exagerado

exaggeration [ɪgzædʒə'reɪʃən] N exageración f

exalt [ɪg'zɔːlt] VT (praise) ensalzar; (elevate) elevar

exalted [ɪg'zɔːltɪd] ADJ (position) elevado; (elated) enardecido

exam [ɪg'zæm] N ABBR (Scol) = **examination**

examination [ɪgzæmɪ'neɪʃən] N (gen) examen m; (Law) interrogación f; (Med) reconocimiento; (inquiry) investigación f; **to take** or **sit an ~** hacer un examen; **the matter is under ~** se está examinando el asunto

examine [ɪg'zæmɪn] VT (gen) examinar; (inspect: machine, premises) inspeccionar; (Scol, Law: person) interrogar; (at customs: luggage, passport) registrar; (Med) reconocer, examinar

examiner [ɪg'zæmɪnəʳ] N examinador(a) m/f

example [ɪg'zɑːmpl] N ejemplo; **for ~** por ejemplo; **to set a good/bad ~** dar buen/mal ejemplo

exasperate [ɪg'zɑːspəreɪt] VT exasperar, irritar; **exasperated by** or **at** or **with** exasperado por or con

exasperating [ɪg'zɑːspəreɪtɪŋ] ADJ irritante

exasperation [ɪgzɑːspə'reɪʃən] N exasperación f, irritación f

excavate ['ɛkskəveɪt] VT excavar

excavation [ɛkskə'veɪʃən] N excavación f

excavator ['ɛkskəveɪtəʳ] N excavadora

exceed [ɪk'siːd] VT exceder; (number) pasar de;

(*speed limit*) sobrepasar; (*limits*) rebasar; (*powers*) excederse en; (*hopes*) superar

exceedingly [ɪkˈsiːdɪŋlɪ] ADV sumamente, sobremanera

excel [ɪkˈsɛl] VI sobresalir; **to ~ o.s.** lucirse

excellence [ˈɛksələns] N excelencia

Excellency [ˈɛksələnsɪ] N: **His ~** Su Excelencia

excellent [ˈɛksələnt] ADJ excelente

except [ɪkˈsɛpt] PREP (*also:* **except for, excepting**) excepto, salvo ▶ VT exceptuar, excluir; **~ if/when** excepto si/cuando; **~ that** salvo que

exception [ɪkˈsɛpʃən] N excepción *f*; **to take ~ to** ofenderse por; **with the ~ of** a excepción de; **to make an ~** hacer una excepción

exceptional [ɪkˈsɛpʃənl] ADJ excepcional

exceptionally [ɪkˈsɛpʃənəlɪ] ADV excepcionalmente, extraordinariamente

excerpt [ˈɛksəːpt] N extracto

excess [ɪkˈsɛs] N exceso; **excesses** NPL excesos *mpl*; **in ~ of** superior a

excess baggage N exceso de equipaje

excess fare N suplemento

excessive [ɪkˈsɛsɪv] ADJ excesivo

excess supply N exceso de oferta

excess weight N exceso de peso

exchange [ɪksˈtʃeɪndʒ] N cambio; (*of prisoners*) canje *m*; (*of ideas*) intercambio; (*also:* **telephone exchange**) central *f* (telefónica) ▶ VT intercambiar; **to ~ (for)** cambiar (por); **in ~ for** a cambio de; **foreign ~** (*Comm*) divisas *fpl*

exchange control N control *m* de divisas

exchange rate N tipo de cambio

exchequer [ɪksˈtʃɛkəʳ] N: **the ~** (*Brit*) Hacienda

excisable [ɛkˈsaɪzəbl] ADJ sujeto al pago de impuestos sobre el consumo

excise [ˈɛksaɪz] N impuestos sobre el consumo interior

excitable [ɪkˈsaɪtəbl] ADJ excitable

excite [ɪkˈsaɪt] VT (*stimulate*) estimular; (*anger*) suscitar, provocar; (*move*) emocionar; **to get excited** emocionarse

excitement [ɪkˈsaɪtmənt] N emoción *f*

exciting [ɪkˈsaɪtɪŋ] ADJ emocionante

excl. ABBR = **excluding; exclusive (of)**

exclaim [ɪkˈskleɪm] VI exclamar

exclamation [ɛkskləˈmeɪʃən] N exclamación *f*

exclamation mark, (*US*) **exclamation point** N signo de admiración

exclude [ɪkˈskluːd] VT excluir; (*except*) exceptuar

excluding [ɪksˈkluːdɪŋ] PREP: **~ VAT** IVA no incluido

exclusion [ɪkˈskluːʒən] N exclusión *f*; **to the ~ of** con exclusión de

exclusion clause N cláusula de exclusión

exclusion zone N zona de exclusión

exclusive [ɪkˈskluːsɪv] ADJ exclusivo; (*club, district*) selecto; **~ of tax** excluyendo impuestos; **~ of postage/service** franqueo/servicio no incluido; **from 1st to 13th March** – del 1 al 13 de marzo exclusive

exclusively [ɪkˈskluːsɪvlɪ] ADV únicamente

excommunicate [ɛkskəˈmjuːnɪkeɪt] VT excomulgar

excrement [ˈɛkskrəmənt] N excremento

excrete [ɪkˈskriːt] VI excretar

excruciating [ɪkˈskruːʃɪeɪtɪŋ] ADJ (*pain*) agudísimo, atroz

excursion [ɪkˈskəːʃən] N excursión *f*

excursion ticket N billete *m* (especial) de excursión

excusable [ɪkˈskjuːsəbl] ADJ perdonable

excuse N [ɪkˈskjuːs] disculpa, excusa; (*evasion*) pretexto ▶ VT [ɪkˈskjuːz] disculpar, perdonar; (*justify*) justificar; **to make excuses for sb** presentar disculpas por algn; **to ~ sb from doing sth** dispensar a algn de hacer algo; **to ~ o.s. (for (doing) sth)** pedir disculpas a algn (por (hacer) algo); **~ me!** ¡perdone!; (*attracting attention*) ¡oiga (, por favor)!; **if you will ~ me** con su permiso

ex-directory [ˈɛksdɪˈrɛktərɪ] ADJ (*Brit*): **~ (phone) number** número que no figura en la guía (telefónica)

execrable [ˈɛksɪkrəbl] ADJ execrable, abominable; (*manners*) detestable

execute [ˈɛksɪkjuːt] VT (*plan*) realizar; (*order*) cumplir; (*person*) ajusticiar, ejecutar

execution [ɛksɪˈkjuːʃən] N realización *f*; cumplimiento; ejecución *f*

executioner [ɛksɪˈkjuːʃənəʳ] N verdugo

executive [ɪgˈzɛkjutɪv] N (*Comm*) ejecutivo(-a); (*Pol*) poder *m* ejecutivo ▶ ADJ ejecutivo; (*car, plane, position*) de ejecutivo; (*offices, suite*) de la dirección; (*secretary*) de dirección

executive director N director(a) *m/f* ejecutivo(-a)

executor [ɪgˈzɛkjutəʳ] N albacea *m*, testamentario

exemplary [ɪgˈzɛmplərɪ] ADJ ejemplar

exemplify [ɪgˈzɛmplɪfaɪ] VT ejemplificar

exempt [ɪgˈzɛmpt] ADJ: **~ from** exento de ▶ VT: **to ~ sb from** eximir a algn de

exemption [ɪgˈzɛmpʃən] N exención *f*; (*immunity*) inmunidad *f*

exercise [ˈɛksəsaɪz] N ejercicio ▶ VT ejercer; (*patience etc*) proceder con; (*dog*) sacar de paseo ▶ VI hacer ejercicio

exercise bike N bicicleta estática

exercise book N cuaderno de ejercicios

exert [ɪgˈzəːt] VT ejercer; (*strength, force*) emplear; **to ~ o.s.** esforzarse

exertion [ɪgˈzəːʃən] N esfuerzo

exfoliant [ɛks'fəʊlɪənt] N exfoliante *m*

ex gratia ['ɛks'greɪʃə] ADJ: ~ **payment** pago a título voluntario

exhale [ɛks'heɪl] VT despedir, exhalar ▸ VI espirar, exhalar

exhaust [ɪg'zɔːst] N (*pipe*) (tubo de) escape *m*; (*fumes*) gases *mpl* de escape ▸ VT agotar; **to ~ o.s.** agotarse

exhausted [ɪg'zɔːstɪd] ADJ agotado

exhausting [ɪg'zɔːstɪŋ] ADJ: **an ~ journey/ day** un viaje/día agotador

exhaustion [ɪg'zɔːstʃən] N agotamiento; **nervous ~** agotamiento nervioso

exhaustive [ɪg'zɔːstɪv] ADJ exhaustivo

exhibit [ɪg'zɪbɪt] N (*Art*) obra expuesta; (*Law*) objeto expuesto ▸ VT (*show: emotions*) manifestar; (: *courage, skill*) demostrar; (*paintings*) exponer

exhibition [ɛksɪ'bɪʃən] N exposición *f*

exhibitionist [ɛksɪ'bɪʃənɪst] N exhibicionista *mf*

exhibitor [ɪg'zɪbɪtə^r] N expositor(a) *m/f*

exhilarating [ɪg'zɪləreɪtɪŋ] ADJ estimulante, tónico

exhilaration [ɪgzɪlə'reɪʃən] N júbilo

exhort [ɪg'zɔːt] VT exhortar

exile ['ɛksaɪl] N exilio; (*person*) exiliado(-a) ▸ VT desterrar, exiliar

exist [ɪg'zɪst] VI existir

existence [ɪg'zɪstəns] N existencia

existentialism [ɛgzɪs'tɛnʃəlɪzəm] N existencialismo

existing [ɪg'zɪstɪŋ] ADJ existente, actual

exit ['ɛksɪt] N salida ▸ VI (*Theat*) hacer mutis; (*Comput*) salir (del sistema)

exit poll N encuesta a la salida de los colegios electorales

exit ramp N (*US Aut*) vía de acceso

exit visa N visado de salida

exodus ['ɛksədəs] N éxodo

ex officio ['ɛksə'fɪʃɪəʊ] ADJ de pleno derecho ▸ ADV ex oficio

exonerate [ɪg'zɒnəreɪt] VT: **to ~ from** exculpar de

exorbitant [ɪg'zɔːbɪtənt] ADJ (*price, demands*) exorbitante, excesivo

exorcize ['ɛksɔːsaɪz] VT exorcizar

exotic [ɪg'zɒtɪk] ADJ exótico

expand [ɪk'spænd] VT ampliar, extender; (*number*) aumentar ▸ VI (*trade etc*) ampliarse, expandirse; (*gas, metal*) dilatarse; **to ~ on** (*notes, story etc*) ampliar

expanse [ɪk'spæns] N extensión *f*

expansion [ɪk'spænʃən] N ampliación *f*; aumento; (*of trade*) expansión *f*

expansionism [ɪk'spænʃənɪzəm] N expansionismo

expansionist [ɪk'spænʃənɪst] ADJ expansionista

expatriate [ɛks'pætrɪət] N expatriado(-a)

expect [ɪk'spɛkt] VT (*gen*) esperar; (*count on*) contar con; (*suppose*) suponer ▸ VI: **to be expecting** estar encinta; **to ~ to do sth** esperar hacer algo; **as expected** como era de esperar; **I ~ so** supongo que sí

expectancy [ɪk'spɛktənsɪ] N (*anticipation*) expectación *f*; **life ~** esperanza de vida

expectantly [ɪk'spɛktəntlɪ] ADV (*look, listen*) con expectación

expectant mother [ɪk'spɛktənt-] N futura madre *f*

expectation [ɛkspɛk'teɪʃən] N (*hope*) esperanza; (*belief*) expectativa; **in ~ of** esperando; **against** or **contrary to all ~(s)** en contra de todas las previsiones; **to come** or **live up to sb's expectations** resultar tan bueno como se esperaba; **to fall short of sb's expectations** no cumplir las esperanzas de algn, decepcionar a algn

expedience [ɪk'spiːdɪəns], **expediency** [ɪk'spiːdɪənsɪ] N conveniencia

expedient [ɪk'spiːdɪənt] ADJ conveniente, oportuno ▸ N recurso, expediente *m*

expedite ['ɛkspɪdaɪt] VT (*speed up*) acelerar; (: *progress*) facilitar

expedition [ɛkspə'dɪʃən] N expedición *f*

expeditionary force [ɛkspə'dɪʃnrɪ-] N cuerpo expedicionario

expel [ɪk'spɛl] VT expulsar

expend [ɪk'spɛnd] VT gastar; (*use up*) consumir

expendable [ɪk'spɛndəbl] ADJ prescindible

expenditure [ɪk'spɛndɪtʃə^r] N gastos *mpl*, desembolso; (*of time, effort*) gasto

expense [ɪk'spɛns] N gasto, gastos *mpl*; (*high cost*) coste *m*; **expenses** NPL (*Comm*) gastos *mpl*; **at the ~ of** a costa de; **to meet the ~ of** hacer frente a los gastos de

expense account N cuenta de gastos (de representación)

expensive [ɪk'spɛnsɪv] ADJ caro, costoso

experience [ɪk'spɪərɪəns] N experiencia ▸ VT experimentar; (*suffer*) sufrir; **to learn by ~** aprender con la experiencia

experienced [ɪk'spɪərɪənst] ADJ experimentado

experiment [ɪk'spɛrɪmənt] N experimento ▸ VI hacer experimentos, experimentar; **to perform** or **carry out an ~** realizar un experimento; **as an ~** como experimento; **to ~ with a new vaccine** experimentar con una vacuna nueva

experimental [ɪkspɛrɪ'mɛntl] ADJ experimental; **the process is still at the ~ stage** el proceso está todavía en prueba

expert ['ɛkspəːt] ADJ experto, perito ▸ N experto(-a), perito(-a); (*specialist*) especialista *mf*; **~ witness** (*Law*) testigo pericial; **~ in** or **at**

doing sth experto *or* perito en hacer algo; **an ~ on sth** un experto en algo

expertise [ɛkspəːˈtiːz] N pericia

expiration [ɛkspɪˈreɪʃən] N *(gen)* expiración f, vencimiento

expire [ɪkˈspaɪəʳ] VI *(gen)* caducar, vencerse

expiry [ɪkˈspaɪərɪ] N caducidad f, vencimiento

expiry date N *(of medicine, food item)* fecha de caducidad

explain [ɪkˈspleɪn] VT explicar; *(mystery)* aclarar
▶ **explain away** VT justificar

explanation [ɛkspləˈneɪʃən] N explicación f; aclaración f; **to find an ~ for sth** encontrarle una explicación a algo

explanatory [ɪkˈsplænətrɪ] ADJ explicativo; aclaratorio

expletive [ɪkˈspliːtɪv] N imprecación f

explicable [ɪkˈsplɪkəbl] ADJ explicable

explicit [ɪkˈsplɪsɪt] ADJ explícito

explicitly [ɪkˈsplɪsɪtlɪ] ADV explícitamente

explode [ɪkˈspləud] VI estallar, explotar; *(with anger)* reventar ▶ VT hacer explotar; *(fig: theory, myth)* demoler

exploit [ˈɛksplɔɪt] N hazaña ▶ VT [ɪkˈsplɔɪt] explotar

exploitation [ɛksplɔɪˈteɪʃən] N explotación f

exploration [ɛkspləˈreɪʃən] N exploración f

exploratory [ɪkˈsplɔrətrɪ] ADJ *(fig: talks)* exploratorio, preliminar

explore [ɪkˈsplɔːʳ] VT explorar; *(fig)* examinar, sondear

explorer [ɪkˈsplɔːrəʳ] N explorador(a) m/f

explosion [ɪkˈspləuʒən] N explosión f

explosive [ɪkˈspləusɪv] ADJ, N explosivo

exponent [ɪkˈspəunənt] N partidario(-a); *(of skill, activity)* exponente mf

export VT [ɛkˈspɔːt] exportar ▶ N [ˈɛkspɔːt] exportación f ▶ CPD de exportación

exportation [ɛkspɔːˈteɪʃən] N exportación f

export drive N campaña de exportación

exporter [ɛkˈspɔːtəʳ] N exportador(a) m/f

export licence N licencia de exportación

export manager N gerente mf de exportación

export trade N comercio exterior

expose [ɪkˈspəuz] VT exponer; *(unmask)* desenmascarar

exposé [ɪkˈspəuzeɪ] N revelación f

exposed [ɪkˈspəuzd] ADJ expuesto; *(land, house)* desprotegido; *(Elec: wire)* al aire; *(pipe, beam)* al descubierto

exposition [ɛkspəˈzɪʃən] N exposición f

exposure [ɪkˈspəuʒəʳ] N exposición f; *(Phot: speed)* (tiempo m de) exposición f; *(: shot)* fotografía; **to die from ~** *(Med)* morir de frío

exposure meter N fotómetro

expound [ɪkˈspaund] VT exponer; *(theory, text)*

comentar; *(one's views)* explicar

express [ɪkˈspres] ADJ *(definite)* expreso, explícito; *(BRIT: letter etc)* urgente ▶ N *(train)* rápido ▶ ADV *(send)* por correo extraordinario ▶ VT expresar; *(squeeze)* exprimir; **to send sth ~** enviar algo por correo urgente; **to ~ o.s.** expresarse

expression [ɪkˈspreʃən] N expresión f

expressionism [ɪkˈspreʃənɪzm] N expresionismo

expressive [ɪkˈspresɪv] ADJ expresivo

expressly [ɪkˈspreslɪ] ADV expresamente

expressway [ɪkˈspresweɪ] N *(US: urban motorway)* autopista

expropriate [ɛksˈprəuprɪeɪt] VT expropiar

expulsion [ɪkˈspʌlʃən] N expulsión f

expurgate [ˈɛkspəgeɪt] VT expurgar

exquisite [ɛkˈskwɪzɪt] ADJ exquisito

exquisitely [ɛkˈskwɪzɪtlɪ] ADV exquisitamente

ex-serviceman [ˈɛksˈsəːvɪsmən] N *(irreg)* ex-combatiente m

ext. ABBR *(Tel)* = **extension**

extemporize [ɪkˈstempəraɪz] VI improvisar

extend [ɪkˈstend] VT *(visit, street)* prolongar; *(building)* ampliar; *(thanks, friendship etc)* extender; *(Comm: credit)* conceder; *(deadline)* prorrogar; *(invitation)* ofrecer ▶ VI *(land)* extenderse; **the contract extends to/for …** el contrato se prolonga hasta/por …

extension [ɪkˈstenʃən] N extensión f; *(building)* ampliación f; *(Tel: line)* extensión f; *(: telephone)* supletorio m; *(of deadline)* prórroga; **~ 3718** extensión 3718

extension cable N *(Elec)* alargador m

extensive [ɪkˈstensɪv] ADJ *(gen)* extenso; *(damage)* importante; *(knowledge)* amplio

extensively [ɪkˈstensɪvlɪ] ADV *(altered, damaged etc)* extensamente; **he's travelled ~** ha viajado por muchos países

extent [ɪkˈstent] N *(breadth)* extensión f; *(scope: of knowledge, activities)* alcance m; *(degree: of damage, loss)* grado; **to some ~** hasta cierto punto; **to a certain ~** hasta cierto punto; **to a large ~** en gran parte; **to the ~ of …** hasta el punto de …; **to such an ~ that …** hasta tal punto que …; **to what ~?** ¿hasta qué punto?; **debts to the ~ of £5000** deudas por la cantidad de £5000

extenuating [ɪkˈstenjueɪtɪŋ] ADJ: **~ circumstances** circunstancias fpl atenuantes

exterior [ɛkˈstɪərɪəʳ] ADJ exterior, externo ▶ N exterior m

exterminate [ɪkˈstəːmɪneɪt] VT exterminar

extermination [ɪkstəːmɪˈneɪʃən] N exterminio

external [ɛkˈstəːnl] ADJ externo, exterior ▶ N: **the externals** la apariencia exterior;

547

~ affairs asuntos *mpl* exteriores; **for ~ use only** (*Med*) para uso tópico

externally [ɛkˈstə:nəlɪ] ADV por fuera

extinct [ɪkˈstɪŋkt] ADJ (*volcano*) extinguido, apagado; (*race*) extinguido

extinction [ɪkˈstɪŋkʃən] N extinción *f*

extinguish [ɪkˈstɪŋgwɪʃ] VT extinguir, apagar

extinguisher [ɪkˈstɪŋgwɪʃəʳ] N extintor *m*

extol, (*US*) **extoll** [ɪkˈstəul] VT (*merits, virtues*) ensalzar, alabar; (*person*) alabar, elogiar

extort [ɪkˈstɔ:t] VT sacar a la fuerza; (*confession*) arrancar

extortion [ɪkˈstɔ:ʃən] N extorsión *f*

extortionate [ɪkˈstɔ:ʃnət] ADJ excesivo, exorbitante

extra [ˈɛkstrə] ADJ adicional ▶ ADV (*in addition*) más ▶ N (*addition*) extra *m*, suplemento; (*Theat*) extra *mf*, comparsa *mf*; (*newspaper*) edición *f* extraordinaria; **extras** NPL (*additional expense*) extras *mpl*; **wine will cost ~** el vino se paga aparte; **~ large sizes** tallas extragrandes

extra... [ˈɛkstrə] PREF extra...

extract VT [ɪkˈstrækt] sacar; (*tooth*) extraer; (*confession*) arrancar ▶ N [ˈɛkstrækt] fragmento; (*Culin*) extracto

extraction [ɪkˈstrækʃən] N extracción *f*; (*origin*) origen *m*

extractor fan [ɪkˈstræktə-] N extractor *m* de humos

extracurricular [ɛkstrəkəˈrɪkjuləʳ] ADJ (*Scol*) extraescolar

extradite [ˈɛkstrədaɪt] VT extraditar

extradition [ɛkstrəˈdɪʃən] N extradición *f*

extramarital [ɛkstrəˈmærɪtl] ADJ extramatrimonial

extramural [ɛkstrəˈmjuərl] ADJ extra-académico

extraneous [ɪkˈstreɪnɪəs] ADJ extraño, ajeno

extraordinary [ɪkˈstrɔ:dnrɪ] ADJ extraordinario; (*odd*) raro; **the ~ thing is that ...** lo más extraordinario es que ...

extraordinary general meeting N junta general extraordinaria

extrapolation [ɪkstræpəˈleɪʃən] N extrapolación *f*

extrasensory perception [ˈɛkstrəˈsɛnsərɪ-] N percepción *f* extrasensorial

extra time N (*Football*) prórroga

extravagance [ɪkˈstrævəgəns] N (*excessive spending*) derroche *m*; (*thing bought*) extravagancia

extravagant [ɪkˈstrævəgənt] ADJ (*wasteful*) derrochador(a); (*taste, gift*) excesivamente caro; (*price*) exorbitante; (*praise*) excesivo

extreme [ɪkˈstri:m] ADJ extremo; (*poverty etc*) extremado; (*case*) excepcional ▶ N extremo;

the ~ left/right (*Pol*) la extrema izquierda/ derecha; **extremes of temperature** temperaturas extremas

extremely [ɪkˈstri:mlɪ] ADV sumamente, extremadamente

extremist [ɪkˈstri:mɪst] ADJ, N extremista *mf*

extremity [ɪkˈstrɛmətɪ] N extremidad *f*, punta; (*need*) apuro, necesidad *f*; **extremities** NPL (*hands and feet*) extremidades *fpl*

extricate [ˈɛkstrɪkeɪt] VT: **to ~ o.s. from** librarse de

extrovert [ˈɛkstrəvə:t] N extrovertido(-a)

exuberance [ɪgˈzju:bərns] N exuberancia

exuberant [ɪgˈzju:bərnt] ADJ (*person*) eufórico; (*style*) exuberante

exude [ɪgˈzju:d] VT rezumar

exult [ɪgˈzʌlt] VI regocijarse

exultant [ɪgˈzʌltənt] ADJ (*person*) regocijado, jubiloso; (*shout, expression, smile*) de júbilo

exultation [ɛgzʌlˈteɪʃən] N regocijo, júbilo

eye [aɪ] N ojo ▶ VT mirar; **to keep an ~ on** vigilar; **as far as the ~ can see** hasta donde alcanza la vista; **with an ~ to doing sth** con vistas *or* miras a hacer algo; **to have an ~ for sth** tener mucha vista *or* buen ojo para algo; **there's more to this than meets the ~** esto tiene su miga

eyeball [ˈaɪbɔ:l] N globo ocular

eyebath [ˈaɪba:θ] N baño ocular, lavaojos *m inv*

eyebrow [ˈaɪbrau] N ceja

eyebrow pencil N lápiz *m* de cejas

eye-catching [ˈaɪkætʃɪŋ] ADJ llamativo

eye cup N (*US*) = **eyebath**

eyedrops [ˈaɪdrɔps] NPL gotas *fpl* para los ojos

eyeful [ˈaɪful] N (*inf*): **to get an ~ of sth** ver bien algo

eyelash [ˈaɪlæʃ] N pestaña

eyelet [ˈaɪlɪt] N ojete *m*

eye-level [ˈaɪlɛvl] ADJ a la altura de los ojos

eyelid [ˈaɪlɪd] N párpado

eyeliner [ˈaɪlaɪnəʳ] N lápiz *m* de ojos

eye-opener [ˈaɪəupnəʳ] N revelación *f*, gran sorpresa

eyeshadow [ˈaɪʃædəu] N sombra de ojos

eyesight [ˈaɪsaɪt] N vista

eyesore [ˈaɪsɔ:ʳ] N monstruosidad *f*

eyestrain [ˈaɪstreɪn] N: **to get ~** cansar la vista *or* los ojos

eyetooth [ˈaɪtu:θ] N (*pl* **eyeteeth** [-ti:θ]) N colmillo; **to give one's eyeteeth for sth/to do sth** (*inf, fig*) dar un ojo de la cara por algo/ por hacer algo

eyewash [ˈaɪwɔʃ] N (*fig*) disparates *mpl*, tonterías *fpl*

eye witness N testigo *mf* ocular

eyrie [ˈɪərɪ] N aguilera

Ff

F, f [ɛf] N (*letter*) F, f *f*; (*Mus*): **F** fa *m*; **F for Frederick**, (*US*) **F for Fox** F de Francia

F. ABBR = **Fahrenheit**

FA N ABBR (*BRIT*: = *Football Association*) ≈ AFE *f* (*SP*)

FAA N ABBR (*US*) = **Federal Aviation Administration**

fable ['feɪbl] N fábula

fabric ['fæbrɪk] N tejido, tela

fabricate ['fæbrɪkeɪt] VT fabricar; (*fig*) inventar

fabrication [fæbrɪ'keɪʃən] N fabricación *f*; (*fig*) invención *f*

fabric ribbon N (*for typewriter*) cinta de tela

fabulous ['fæbjuləs] ADJ fabuloso

façade [fə'saːd] N fachada

face [feɪs] N (*Anat*) cara, rostro; (*of clock*) esfera; (*side*) cara; (*surface*) superficie *f* ▸ VT (*direction*) estar de cara a; (*situation*) hacer frente a; (*facts*) aceptar; **~ down** (*person, card*) boca abajo; **to lose ~** desprestigiarse; **to save ~** salvar las apariencias; **to make** *or* **pull a ~** hacer muecas; **in the ~ of** (*difficulties etc*) en vista de, ante; **on the ~ of it** a primera vista; **~ to** cara a cara; **to ~ the fact that ...** reconocer que ...
  ▸ **face up to** VT FUS hacer frente a, enfrentarse a

Facebook® ['feɪsbuk] N Facebook® *m*

facebook® ['feɪsbuk] VT, VI enviar un mensaje por el Facebook®

face cloth N (*BRIT*) toallita

face cream N crema (de belleza)

faceless ['feɪslɪs] ADJ (*fig*) anónimo

face lift N lifting *m*, estirado facial

face pack N (*BRIT*) mascarilla

face powder N polvos *mpl* para la cara

face-saving ['feɪsseɪvɪŋ] ADJ para salvar las apariencias

facet ['fæsɪt] N faceta

facetious [fə'siːʃəs] ADJ chistoso

facetiously [fə'siːʃəslɪ] ADV chistosamente

face value N (*of stamp*) valor *m* nominal; **to take sth at ~** (*fig*) tomar algo en sentido literal, aceptar las apariencias de algo

facial ['feɪʃəl] ADJ de la cara ▸ N (*also*: **beauty facial**) tratamiento facial, limpieza

facile ['fæsaɪl] ADJ superficial

facilitate [fə'sɪlɪteɪt] VT facilitar

facility [fə'sɪlɪtɪ] N facilidad *f*; **facilities** NPL instalaciones *fpl*; **credit ~** facilidades de crédito

facing ['feɪsɪŋ] PREP frente a ▸ ADJ de enfrente

facsimile [fæk'sɪmɪlɪ] N facsímil(e) *m*

fact [fækt] N hecho; **in ~** en realidad; **to know for a ~ that ...** saber a ciencia cierta que ...

fact-finding ['fæktfaɪndɪŋ] ADJ: **a ~ tour/ mission** un viaje/una misión de reconocimiento

faction ['fækʃən] N facción *f*

factional ['fækʃənl] ADJ (*fighting*) entre distintas facciones

factor ['fæktəʳ] N factor *m*; (*Comm: person*) agente *mf* comisionado(-a) ▸ VI (*Comm*) comprar deudas; **safety ~** factor de seguridad

factory ['fæktərɪ] N fábrica

factory farming N cría industrial

factory floor N (*workers*) trabajadores *mpl*, mano *f* de obra directa; (*area*) talleres *mpl*

factory ship N buque *m* factoría

factual ['fæktjuəl] ADJ basado en los hechos

faculty ['fækltɪ] N facultad *f*; (*US: teaching staff*) personal *m* docente

fad [fæd] N novedad *f*, moda

fade [feɪd] VI descolorarse, desteñirse; (*sound, hope*) desvanecerse; (*light*) apagarse; (*flower*) marchitarse
  ▸ **fade away** VI (*sound*) apagarse
  ▸ **fade in** VT (*TV, Cine*) fundir; (*Radio: sound*) mezclar ▸ VI (*TV, Cine*) fundirse; (*Radio*) oírse por encima
  ▸ **fade out** VT (*TV, Cine*) fundir; (*Radio*) apagar, disminuir el volumen de ▸ VI (*TV, Cine*) desvanecerse; (*Radio*) apagarse, dejarse de oír

faded ['feɪdɪd] ADJ (*clothes, colour*) descolorido; (*flower*) marchito

faeces, (US) **feces** ['fiːsiːz] NPL excremento *sg*, heces *fpl*

fag [fæg] N (BRIT *inf: cigarette*) pitillo (SP), cigarro; (US *inf: homosexual*) maricón *m*

fag end N (BRIT *inf*) colilla

fagged [fægd] ADJ (BRIT *inf: exhausted*) rendido, agotado

Fahrenheit ['fɑːrənhaɪt] N Fahrenheit *m*

fail [feɪl] VT suspender; (*memory etc*) fallar a ▶ VI suspender; (*be unsuccessful*) fracasar; (*strength, brakes, engine*) fallar; **to ~ to do sth** (*neglect*) dejar de hacer algo; (*be unable*) no poder hacer algo; **without ~** sin falta; **words ~ me!** ¡no sé qué decir!

failing ['feɪlɪŋ] N falta, defecto ▶ PREP a falta de; **~ that** de no ser posible eso

failsafe ['feɪlseɪf] ADJ (*device etc*) de seguridad

failure ['feɪljə'] N fracaso; (*person*) fracasado(-a); (*mechanical etc*) fallo; (*in exam*) suspenso; (*of crops*) pérdida, destrucción *f*; **it was a complete ~** fue un fracaso total

faint [feɪnt] ADJ débil; (*smell, breeze, trace*) leve; (*recollection*) vago; (*mark*) apenas visible ▶ N desmayo ▶ VI desmayarse; **to feel ~** estar mareado, marearse

faintest ['feɪntɪst] ADJ: **I haven't the ~ idea** no tengo la más remota idea

faint-hearted ['feɪnt'hɑːtɪd] ADJ apocado

faintly ['feɪntlɪ] ADV débilmente; (*vaguely*) vagamente

faintness ['feɪntnɪs] N debilidad *f*; vaguedad *f*

fair [fɛə'] ADJ justo; (*hair, person*) rubio; (*weather*) bueno; (*good enough*) suficiente; (*sizeable*) considerable ▶ ADV: **to play ~** jugar limpio ▶ N feria; (BRIT: *funfair*) parque *m* de atracciones; **it's not ~!** ¡no es justo!, ¡no hay derecho!; **~ copy** copia en limpio; **~ play** juego limpio; **a ~ amount of** bastante; **~ wear and tear** desgaste *m* natural; **trade ~** feria de muestras

fair game N: **to be ~** ser blanco legítimo

fairground ['fɛəgraund] N recinto ferial

fair-haired [fɛə'hɛəd] ADJ (*person*) rubio

fairly ['fɛəlɪ] ADV (*justly*) con justicia; (*equally*) equitativamente; (*quite*) bastante; **I'm ~ sure** estoy bastante seguro

fairness ['fɛənɪs] N justicia; (*impartiality*) imparcialidad *f*; **in all ~** a decir verdad

fair trade N comercio justo

fairway ['fɛəweɪ] N (*Golf*) calle *f*

fairy ['fɛərɪ] N hada

fairy godmother N hada madrina

fairyland ['fɛərɪlænd] N el país de ensueño

fairy lights NPL bombillas *fpl* de colores

fairy tale N cuento de hadas

faith [feɪθ] N fe *f*; (*trust*) confianza; (*sect*)
religión *f*; **to have ~ in sb/sth** confiar en algn/algo

faithful ['feɪθful] ADJ (*loyal: troops etc*) leal; (*spouse*) fiel; (*account*) exacto

faithfully ['feɪθfulɪ] ADV fielmente; **yours ~** (BRIT: *in letters*) le saluda atentamente

faith healer N curador(a) *m/f* por fe

fake [feɪk] N (*painting etc*) falsificación *f*; (*person*) impostor(a) *m/f* ▶ ADJ falso ▶ VT fingir; (*painting etc*) falsificar

falcon ['fɔːlkən] N halcón *m*

Falkland Islands ['fɔːlklənd-] NPL Islas *fpl* Malvinas

fall [fɔːl] N caída; (US) otoño; (*decrease*) disminución *f* ▶ VI (*pt* **fell**, *pp* **fallen** ['fɔːlən]) caer; (*accidentally*) caerse; (*price*) bajar; **falls** NPL (*waterfall*) cataratas *fpl*, salto *sg* de agua; **a ~ of earth** un desprendimiento de tierra; **a ~ of snow** una nevada; **to ~ flat** VI (*on one's face*) caerse de bruces; (*joke, story*) no hacer gracia; **to ~ short of sb's expectations** decepcionar a algn; **to ~ in love (with sb/sth)** enamorarse (de algn/algo)
  ▶ **fall apart** VI deshacerse
  ▶ **fall back** VI retroceder
  ▶ **fall back on** VT FUS (*remedy etc*) recurrir a; **to have sth to ~ back on** tener algo a que recurrir
  ▶ **fall behind** VI quedarse atrás; (*fig: with payments*) retrasarse
  ▶ **fall down** VI (*person*) caerse; (*building*) derrumbarse
  ▶ **fall for** VT FUS (*trick*) tragar; (*person*) enamorarse de
  ▶ **fall in** VI (*roof*) hundirse; (*Mil*) alinearse
  ▶ **fall in with** VT FUS: **to ~ in with sb's plans** acomodarse con los planes de algn
  ▶ **fall off** VI caerse; (*diminish*) disminuir
  ▶ **fall out** VI (*friends etc*) reñir; (*hair, teeth*) caerse; (*Mil*) romper filas
  ▶ **fall over** VI caer(se)
  ▶ **fall through** VI (*plan, project*) fracasar

fallacy ['fæləsɪ] N error *m*

fallback position ['fɔːlbæk-] N posición *f* de repliegue

fallen ['fɔːlən] PP of **fall**

fallible ['fæləbl] ADJ falible

falling ['fɔːlɪŋ] ADJ: **~ market** mercado en baja

falling-off ['fɔːlɪŋ'ɔf] N (*reduction*) disminución *f*

Fallopian tube [fə'ləupɪən-] N (*Anat*) trompa de Falopio

fallout ['fɔːlaut] N lluvia radioactiva

fallout shelter N refugio antinuclear

fallow ['fæləu] ADJ (*land, field*) en barbecho

false [fɔːls] ADJ (*gen*) falso; (*teeth etc*) postizo; (*disloyal*) desleal, traidor(a); **under ~ pretences** con engaños

false alarm N falsa alarma
falsehood ['fɔ:lshud] N falsedad f
falsely ['fɔ:lslɪ] ADV falsamente
false teeth NPL (BRIT) dentadura sg postiza
falsify ['fɔ:lsɪfaɪ] VT falsificar
falter ['fɔ:ltər] VI vacilar
fame [feɪm] N fama
familiar [fə'mɪlɪər] ADJ familiar; (well-known)
conocido; (tone) de confianza; **to be ~ with**
(subject) conocer (bien); **to make o.s. ~ with**
familiarizarse con; **to be on ~ terms with**
sb tener confianza con algn
familiarity [fəmɪlɪ'ærɪtɪ] N familiaridad f
familiarize [fə'mɪlɪəraɪz] VT: **to ~ o.s. with**
familiarizarse con
family ['fæmɪlɪ] N familia
family business N negocio familiar
family credit N (BRIT) ≈ ayuda familiar
family doctor N médico(-a) de cabecera
family life N vida doméstica or familiar
family man N (irreg) (home-loving) hombre m
casero; (having family) padre m de familia
family planning N planificación f familiar
family planning clinic N clínica de
planificación familiar
family tree N árbol m genealógico
famine ['fæmɪn] N hambre f, hambruna
famished ['fæmɪʃt] ADJ hambriento; **I'm ~!**
(inf) ¡estoy muerto de hambre!, ¡tengo un
hambre canina!
famous ['feɪməs] ADJ famoso, célebre
famously ['feɪməslɪ] ADV (get on)
estupendamente
fan [fæn] N abanico; (Elec) ventilador m;
(person) aficionado(-a); (Sport) hincha mf; (of
pop star) fan mf ▶ VT abanicar; (fire, quarrel)
atizar
▶ **fan out** VI desplegarse
fanatic [fə'nætɪk] N fanático(-a)
fanatical [fə'nætɪkəl] ADJ fanático
fan belt N correa del ventilador
fancied ['fænsɪd] ADJ imaginario
fanciful ['fænsɪful] ADJ (gen) fantástico;
(imaginary) fantasioso; (design) rebuscado
fan club N club m de fans
fancy ['fænsɪ] N (whim) capricho, antojo;
(imagination) imaginación f ▶ ADJ (luxury) de
lujo; (price) desorbitado ▶ VT (feel like, want)
tener ganas de; (imagine) imaginarse,
figurarse; **to take a ~ to sb** tomar cariño a
algn; **when the ~ takes him** cuando se le
antoja; **it took** or **caught my ~** me cayó en
gracia; **to ~ that ...** imaginarse que ...; **he**
fancies her le gusta (ella) mucho
fancy dress N disfraz m
fancy-dress ball ['fænsɪdres-] N baile m de
disfraces
fancy goods N artículos mpl de fantasía
fanfare ['fænfɛər] N fanfarria (de trompeta)

fanfold paper ['fænfəuld-] N papel m
plegado en abanico or en acordeón
fang [fæŋ] N colmillo
fan heater N calefactor m de aire
fanlight ['fænlaɪt] N (montante m en)
abanico
fanny ['fænɪ] N (BRIT inf!) chocho (!); (US inf)
pompis m, culo (!)
fantasize ['fæntəsaɪz] VI fantasear, hacerse
ilusiones
fantastic [fæn'tæstɪk] ADJ fantástico
fantasy ['fæntəzɪ] N fantasía
fanzine ['fænziːn] N fanzine m
FAO N ABBR (= Food and Agriculture Organization)
OAA f, FAO f
FAQ ABBR (= free alongside quay) franco sobre
muelle
FAQs NPL ABBR (= frequently asked questions)
preguntas fpl frecuentes
far [fɑːr] ADJ (distant) lejano ▶ ADV lejos; **the ~**
left/right (Pol) la extrema izquierda/
derecha; **~ away, ~ off** (a lo) lejos; **~ better**
mucho mejor; **~ from** lejos de; **by ~** con
mucho; **it's by ~ the best** es con mucho el
mejor; **go as ~ as the farm** vaya hasta la
granja; **is it ~ to London?** ¿estamos lejos de
Londres?, ¿Londres queda lejos?; **it's not ~**
(from here) no está lejos (de aquí); **as ~ as I**
know que yo sepa; **how ~?** ¿hasta dónde?;
(fig) ¿hasta qué punto?; **how ~ have you got**
with your work? ¿hasta dónde has llegado
en tu trabajo?
faraway ['fɑːrəweɪ] ADJ remoto; (look)
ausente, perdido
farce [fɑːs] N farsa
farcical ['fɑːsɪkəl] ADJ absurdo
fare [fɛər] N (on trains, buses) precio (del
billete); (in taxi: cost) tarifa; (: passenger)
pasajero; (food) comida; **half/full ~** medio
billete m/billete m completo
Far East N: **the ~** el Extremo or Lejano
Oriente
farewell [fɛə'wel] EXCL, N adiós m
far-fetched [fɑː'fetʃt] ADJ inverosímil
farm [fɑːm] N granja, finca, estancia (LAM),
chacra (LAM) ▶ VT cultivar
▶ **farm out** VT (work): **to ~ out (to sb)** mandar
hacer fuera (a algn)
farmer ['fɑːmər] N granjero(-a),
estanciero(-a) (LAM)
farmhand ['fɑːmhænd] N peón m
farmhouse ['fɑːmhaus] N granja, casa de
hacienda (LAM)
farming ['fɑːmɪŋ] N (gen) agricultura; (tilling)
cultivo; **sheep ~** cría de ovejas
farm labourer N = **farmhand**
farmland ['fɑːmlænd] N tierra de cultivo
farm produce N productos mpl agrícolas
farm worker N = **farmhand**

farmyard ['fɑːmjɑːd] N corral m
Faroe Islands ['fɛərəu-], **Faroes** ['fɛərəuz] NPL: **the** ~ las Islas Feroe
far-reaching [fɑːˈriːtʃɪŋ] ADJ (reform, effect) de gran alcance
far-sighted [fɑːˈsaɪtɪd] ADJ previsor(a)
fart [fɑːt] (inf!) N pedo (!) ▶ VI tirarse un pedo (!)
farther ['fɑːðəʳ] ADV más lejos, más allá ▶ ADJ más lejano
farthest ['fɑːðɪst] SUPERLATIVE of **far**
FAS ABBR (BRIT: = free alongside ship) franco al costado del buque
fascinate ['fæsɪneɪt] VT fascinar
fascinated ['fæsɪneɪtəd] ADJ fascinado
fascinating ['fæsɪneɪtɪŋ] ADJ fascinante
fascination [fæsɪˈneɪʃən] N fascinación f
fascinator ['fæsɪneɪtəʳ] N (hat) tocado (de plumas, flores o cintas)
fascism ['fæʃɪzəm] N fascismo
fascist ['fæʃɪst] ADJ, N fascista mf
fashion ['fæʃən] N moda; (fashion industry) industria de la moda; (manner) manera ▶ VT formar; **in** ~ a la moda; **out of** ~ pasado de moda; **in the Greek** ~ a la griega, al estilo griego; **after a** ~ (finish, manage etc) en cierto modo
fashionable ['fæʃnəbl] ADJ de moda; (writer) de moda, popular; **it is** ~ **to do** ... está de moda hacer ...
fashion designer N diseñador(a) m/f de modas, modisto(-a)
fashionista [fæʃəˈnɪstə] N fashionista mf
fashion show N desfile m de modelos
fast [fɑːst] ADJ (also Phot: film) rápido; (dye, colour) sólido; (clock): **to be** ~ estar adelantado ▶ ADV rápidamente, de prisa; (stuck, held) firmemente ▶ N ayuno ▶ VI ayunar; ~ **asleep** profundamente dormido; **in the** ~ **lane** (Aut) en el carril de adelantamiento; **my watch is five minutes** ~ mi reloj está adelantado cinco minutos; **as** ~ **as I** etc **can** lo más rápido posible; **to make a boat** ~ amarrar una barca
fasten ['fɑːsn] VT asegurar, sujetar; (coat, belt) abrochar ▶ VI cerrarse
▶ **fasten (up)on** VT FUS (idea) aferrarse a
fastener ['fɑːsnəʳ] N cierre m; (of door etc) cerrojo; (BRIT: also: **zip fastener**) cremallera
fastening ['fɑːsnɪŋ] N = **fastener**
fast food N comida rápida, platos mpl preparados
fastidious [fæsˈtɪdɪəs] ADJ (fussy) delicado; (demanding) exigente
fat [fæt] ADJ gordo; (meat) con mucha grasa; (greasy) grasiento; (book) grueso; (profit) grande, pingüe ▶ N grasa; (on person) carnes fpl; (lard) manteca; **to live off the** ~ **of the land** vivir a cuerpo de rey

fatal ['feɪtl] ADJ (mistake) fatal; (injury) mortal; (consequence) funesto
fatalism ['feɪtəlɪzəm] N fatalismo
fatality [fəˈtælɪtɪ] N (road death etc) víctima f mortal
fatally ['feɪtəlɪ] ADV: ~ **injured** herido de muerte
fate [feɪt] N destino, sino
fated ['feɪtɪd] ADJ predestinado
fateful ['feɪtful] ADJ fatídico
fat-free ['fætfriː] ADJ sin grasa
father ['fɑːðəʳ] N padre m
Father Christmas N Papá m Noel
fatherhood ['fɑːðəhud] N paternidad f
father-in-law ['fɑːðərɪnlɔː] N suegro
fatherland ['fɑːðəlænd] N patria
fatherly ['fɑːðəlɪ] ADJ paternal
fathom ['fæðəm] N braza ▶ VT (unravel) desentrañar; (understand) explicarse
fatigue [fəˈtiːg] N fatiga, cansancio; **metal** ~ fatiga del metal
fatness ['fætnɪs] N gordura
fatten ['fætn] VT, VI engordar; **chocolate is fattening** el chocolate engorda
fatty ['fætɪ] ADJ (food) graso ▶ N (inf) gordito(-a), gordinflón(-ona) m/f
fatuous ['fætjuəs] ADJ fatuo, necio
faucet ['fɔːsɪt] N (US) grifo, llave f, canilla (LAm)
fault [fɔːlt] N (blame) culpa; (defect: in character) defecto; (: in manufacture) desperfecto; (Geo) falla ▶ VT criticar; **it's my** ~ es culpa mía; **to find** ~ **with** criticar, poner peros a; **at** ~ culpable
faultless ['fɔːltlɪs] ADJ (action) intachable; (person) sin defectos
faulty ['fɔːltɪ] ADJ defectuoso
fauna ['fɔːnə] N fauna
faux pas ['fəuˈpɑː] N desacierto
favour, (US) **favor** ['feɪvəʳ] N favor m; (approval) aprobación f ▶ VT (proposition) estar a favor de, aprobar; (person etc) preferir; (assist) favorecer; **to ask a** ~ **of** pedir un favor a; **to do sb a** ~ hacer un favor a algn; **to find** ~ **with sb** (person) caer en gracia a algn; (suggestion) tener buena acogida por parte de algn; **in** ~ **of** a favor de; **to be in** ~ **of sth/of doing sth** ser partidario or estar a favor de algo/de hacer algo
favourable, (US) **favorable** ['feɪvərəbl] ADJ favorable
favourably, (US) **favorably** ['feɪvərəblɪ] ADV favorablemente
favourite, (US) **favorite** ['feɪvərɪt] ADJ, N favorito(-a) m/f, preferido(-a) m/f
favouritism, (US) **favoritism** ['feɪvərɪtɪzəm] N favoritismo
fawn [fɔːn] N cervato ▶ ADJ (also: **fawn-coloured**) de color cervato, leonado ▶ VI: **to** ~ **(up)on** adular

fax [fæks] N fax *m* ▶ VT mandar *or* enviar por fax

FBI N ABBR (*US:* = *Federal Bureau of Investigation*) FBI *m*

FCC N ABBR (*US*) = **Federal Communications Commission**

FCO N ABBR (*BRIT:* = *Foreign and Commonwealth Office*) ≈ Min. de AA. EE.

FD N ABBR (*US*) = **fire department**

FDA N ABBR (*US:* = *Food and Drug Administration*) *oficina que se ocupa del control de los productos alimenticios y farmacéuticos*

FE N ABBR = **further education**

fear [fɪəʳ] N miedo, temor *m* ▶ VT temer; **for ~ of** por temor a; **~ of heights** vértigo; **to ~ for/that** temer por/que

fearful ['fɪəful] ADJ temeroso; (*awful*) espantoso; **to be ~ of** (*frightened*) tener miedo de

fearfully ['fɪəfulɪ] ADV (*timidly*) con miedo; (*inf: very*) terriblemente

fearless ['fɪəlɪs] ADJ (*gen*) sin miedo *or* temor; (*bold*) audaz

fearlessly ['fɪəlɪslɪ] ADV temerariamente

fearlessness ['fɪəlɪsnɪs] N temeridad *f*

fearsome ['fɪəsəm] ADJ (*opponent*) temible; (*sight*) espantoso

feasibility [fi:zə'bɪlɪtɪ] N factibilidad *f*, viabilidad *f*

feasibility study N estudio de viabilidad

feasible ['fi:zəbl] ADJ factible, viable

feast [fi:st] N banquete *m*; (*Rel: also:* **feast day**) fiesta ▶ VI festejar

feat [fi:t] N hazaña

feather ['fɛðəʳ] N pluma ▶ VT: **to ~ one's nest** (*fig*) hacer su agosto, sacar tajada ▶ CPD (*mattress, bed, pillow*) de plumas

feather-weight ['fɛðəweɪt] N (*Boxing*) peso pluma

feature ['fi:tʃəʳ] N (*gen*) característica; (*Anat*) rasgo; (*article*) reportaje *m* ▶ VT (*film*) presentar ▶ VI figurar; **features** NPL (*of face*) facciones *fpl*; **a (special) ~ on sth/sb** un reportaje (especial) sobre algo/algn; **it featured prominently in ...** tuvo un papel destacado en ...

feature film N largometraje *m*

Feb. ABBR (= *February*) feb.

February ['fɛbruərɪ] N febrero; *see also* **July**

feces ['fi:si:z] NPL (*US*) = **faeces**

feckless ['fɛklɪs] ADJ irresponsable, irreflexivo

Fed [fɛd] ABBR (*US*) = **federal**; **federation**

fed [fɛd] PT, PP *of* **feed**

Fed. [fɛd] N ABBR (*US inf*) = **Federal Reserve Board**

federal ['fɛdərəl] ADJ federal

Federal Republic of Germany N República Federal de Alemania

federation [fɛdə'reɪʃən] N federación *f*

fed up [fɛd'ʌp] ADJ: **to be ~ (with)** estar harto (de)

fee [fi:] N (*professional*) honorarios *mpl*; (*for examination*) derechos *mpl*; (*of school*) matrícula; (*also:* **membership fee**) cuota; (*also:* **entrance fee**) entrada; **for a small ~** por poco dinero

feeble ['fi:bl] ADJ débil

feeble-minded [fi:bl'maɪndɪd] ADJ imbécil

feed [fi:d] N (*gen*) comida; (*of animal*) pienso; (*on printer*) dispositivo de alimentación ▶ VT (*pt, pp* **fed**) (*gen*) alimentar; (*BRIT: breastfeed*) dar el pecho a; (*animal, baby*) dar de comer a ▶ VI (*baby, animal*) comer
 ▶ **feed back** VT (*results*) pasar
 ▶ **feed in** VT (*Comput*) introducir
 ▶ **feed into** VT (*data, information*) suministrar a; **to ~ sth into a machine** introducir algo en una máquina
 ▶ **feed on** VT FUS alimentarse de

feedback ['fi:dbæk] N (*from person*) reacción *f*; (*Tech*) realimentación *f*, feedback *m*

feeder ['fi:dəʳ] N (*bib*) babero

feeding bottle ['fi:dɪŋ-] N (*BRIT*) biberón *m*

feel [fi:l] N (*sensation*) sensación *f*; (*sense of touch*) tacto ▶ VT (*pt, pp* **felt**) tocar; (*cold, pain etc*) sentir; (*think, believe*) creer; **to get the ~ of sth** (*fig*) acostumbrarse a algo; **to ~ hungry/cold** tener hambre/frío; **to ~ lonely/better** sentirse solo/mejor; **I don't ~ well** no me siento bien; **it feels soft** es suave al tacto; **it feels colder out here** se siente más frío aquí fuera; **to ~ like** (*want*) tener ganas de; **I'm still feeling my way** (*fig*) todavía me estoy orientando; **I ~ that you ought to do it** creo que debes hacerlo
 ▶ **feel about, feel around** VI tantear

feeler ['fi:ləʳ] N (*of insect*) antena; **to put out feelers** (*fig*) tantear el terreno

feeling ['fi:lɪŋ] N (*physical*) sensación *f*; (*foreboding*) presentimiento; (*impression*) impresión *f*; (*emotion*) sentimiento; **what are your feelings about the matter?** ¿qué opinas tú del asunto?; **to hurt sb's feelings** herir los sentimientos de algn; **feelings ran high about it** causó mucha controversia; **I got the ~ that ...** me dio la impresión de que ...; **there was a general ~ that ...** la opinión general fue que ...

fee-paying school ['fi:peɪɪŋ-] N colegio de pago

feet [fi:t] NPL *of* **foot**

feign [feɪn] VT fingir

feigned [feɪnd] ADJ fingido

feline ['fi:laɪn] ADJ felino

fell [fɛl] PT *of* **fall** ▶ VT (*tree*) talar ▶ ADJ: **with one ~ blow** con un golpe feroz ▶ N (*BRIT: mountain*) montaña; (*moorland*) **the fells** los páramos; **at one ~ swoop** de un solo golpe

fellow ['fɛləu] N tipo, tío (SP); (of learned society) socio(-a); (Univ) miembro de la junta de gobierno de un colegio ▶ CPD: **~ students** compañeros(-as) mplfpl de curso

fellow citizen N conciudadano(-a)

fellow countryman N (irreg) compatriota m

fellow feeling N compañerismo

fellow men NPL semejantes mpl

fellowship ['fɛləuʃɪp] N compañerismo; (grant) beca

fellow traveller N compañero(-a) de viaje; (Pol: with communists) simpatizante mf

fellow worker N colega mf

felon ['fɛlən] N criminal mf

felony ['fɛlənɪ] N crimen m, delito mayor

felt [fɛlt] PT, PP of **feel** ▶ N fieltro

felt-tip pen ['fɛlttɪp-] N rotulador m

female ['fiːmeɪl] N (woman) mujer f; (Zool) hembra ▶ ADJ femenino

feminine ['fɛmɪnɪn] ADJ femenino

femininity [fɛmɪ'nɪnɪtɪ] N feminidad f

feminism ['fɛmɪnɪzəm] N feminismo

feminist ['fɛmɪnɪst] N feminista mf

fence [fɛns] N valla, cerca; (Racing) valla ▶ VT (also: **fence in**) cercar ▶ VI hacer esgrima; **to sit on the ~** (fig) nadar entre dos aguas
▶ **fence in** VT cercar
▶ **fence off** VT separar con cerca

fencing ['fɛnsɪŋ] N esgrima

fend [fɛnd] VI: **to ~ for o.s.** valerse por sí mismo
▶ **fend off** VT (attack, attacker) rechazar, repeler; (blow) desviar; (awkward question) esquivar

fender ['fɛndər] N pantalla; (US Aut) parachoques m inv; (Rail) trompa

fennel ['fɛnl] N hinojo

Fens [fɛnz] NPL (BRIT): **the ~** las tierras bajas de Norfolk (antiguamente zona de marismas)

ferment VI [fə'mɛnt] fermentar ▶ N ['fəːmɛnt] (fig) agitación f

fermentation [fəːmɛn'teɪʃən] N fermentación f

fern [fəːn] N helecho

ferocious [fə'rəuʃəs] ADJ feroz

ferociously [fə'rəuʃəslɪ] ADV ferozmente, con ferocidad

ferocity [fə'rɔsɪtɪ] N ferocidad f

ferret ['fɛrɪt] N hurón m
▶ **ferret about, ferret around** VI rebuscar
▶ **ferret out** VT (secret, truth) desentrañar

ferry ['fɛrɪ] N (small) barca de pasaje, balsa; (large: also: **ferryboat**) transbordador m, ferry m ▶ VT transportar; **to ~ sth/sb across** or **over** transportar algo/a algn a la otra orilla; **to ~ sb to and fro** llevar a algn de un lado para otro

ferryman ['fɛrɪmən] N (irreg) barquero

fertile ['fəːtaɪl] ADJ fértil; (Biol) fecundo

fertility [fə'tɪlɪtɪ] N fertilidad f; fecundidad f

fertility drug N medicamento contra la infertilidad

fertilization [fəːtɪlaɪ'zeɪʃən] N fertilización f; (Biol) fecundación f

fertilize ['fəːtɪlaɪz] VT fertilizar; (Biol) fecundar; (Agr) abonar

fertilizer ['fəːtɪlaɪzər] N abono, fertilizante m

fervent ['fəːvənt] ADJ ferviente

fervour, (US) **fervor** ['fəːvər] N fervor m, ardor m

fester ['fɛstər] VI supurar

festival ['fɛstɪvəl] N (Rel) fiesta; (Art, Mus) festival m

festive ['fɛstɪv] ADJ festivo; **the ~ season** (BRIT: Christmas) las Navidades

festivities [fɛs'tɪvɪtɪz] NPL festejos mpl

festoon [fɛs'tuːn] VT: **to ~ with** festonear or engalanar de

fetch [fɛtʃ] VT ir a buscar; (BRIT: sell for) venderse por; **how much did it ~?** ¿por cuánto se vendió?
▶ **fetch up** VI ir a parar

fetching ['fɛtʃɪŋ] ADJ atractivo

fête [feɪt] N fiesta

fetid ['fɛtɪd] ADJ fétido

fetish ['fɛtɪʃ] N fetiche m

fetter ['fɛtər] VT (person) encadenar, poner grillos a; (horse) trabar; (fig) poner trabas a

fetters ['fɛtəz] NPL grillos mpl

fettle ['fɛtl] N: **in fine ~** en buenas condiciones

fetus ['fiːtəs] N (US) = **foetus**

feud [fjuːd] N (hostility) enemistad f; (quarrel) disputa; **a family ~** una pelea familiar

feudal ['fjuːdl] ADJ feudal

feudalism ['fjuːdəlɪzəm] N feudalismo

fever ['fiːvər] N fiebre f; **he has a ~** tiene fiebre

feverish ['fiːvərɪʃ] ADJ febril

feverishly ['fiːvərɪʃlɪ] ADV febrilmente

few [fjuː] ADJ (not many) pocos; (some) algunos, unos ▶ PRON algunos; **a ~** adj unos pocos; **~ people** poca gente; **a good ~, quite a ~** bastantes; **in** or **over the next ~ days** en los próximos días; **every ~ weeks** cada dos o tres semanas; **a ~ more days** unos días más

fewer ['fjuːər] ADJ menos

fewest ['fjuːɪst] ADJ los/las menos

FFA N ABBR = **Future Farmers of America**

FH ABBR (BRIT) = **fire hydrant**

FHA N ABBR (US: = Federal Housing Administration) oficina federal de la vivienda

fiancé [fɪ'ɑ̃ːnseɪ] N novio, prometido

fiancée [fɪ'ɑ̃ːnseɪ] N novia, prometida

fiasco [fɪ'æskəu] N fiasco

fib [fɪb] N mentirijilla ▶ VI decir mentirijillas

fibre, (US) **fiber** ['faɪbər] N fibra

fibreboard, (US) **fiberboard** ['faɪbəbɔːd] N fibra vulcanizada

fibreglass, (US) **fiberglass** ['faɪbəglɑːs] N fibra de vidrio

fibrositis [faɪbrə'saɪtɪs] N fibrositis f inv

FICA N ABBR (US) = **Federal Insurance Contributions Act**

fickle ['fɪkl] ADJ inconstante

fiction ['fɪkʃən] N (gen) ficción f

fictional ['fɪkʃənl] ADJ novelesco

fictionalize ['fɪkʃənəlaɪz] VT novelar

fictitious [fɪk'tɪʃəs] ADJ ficticio

fiddle ['fɪdl] N (Mus) violín m; (cheating) trampa ▸ VT (BRIT: accounts) falsificar; **tax ~** evasión f fiscal; **to work a ~** hacer trampa
▸ **fiddle with** VT FUS juguetear con

fiddler ['fɪdlə'] N violinista mf

fiddly ['fɪdlɪ] ADJ (task) delicado, mañoso; (object) enrevesado

fidelity [fɪ'dɛlɪtɪ] N fidelidad f

fidget ['fɪdʒɪt] VI moverse (nerviosamente)

fidgety ['fɪdʒɪtɪ] ADJ nervioso

fiduciary [fɪ'duːʃɪərɪ] N fiduciario(-a)

field [fiːld] N (gen) campo; (Comput) campo; (fig) campo, esfera; (Sport) campo, cancha (LAm); (competitors) competidores mpl ▸ CPD:
to have a ~ day (fig) ponerse las botas; **to lead the ~** (Sport, Comm) llevar la delantera; **to give sth a year's trial in the ~** (fig) sacar algo al mercado a prueba por un año; **my particular ~** mi especialidad

field glasses NPL gemelos mpl

field hospital N hospital m de campaña

field marshal N mariscal m

fieldwork ['fiːldwəːk] N (Archeol, Geo) trabajo de campo

fiend [fiːnd] N demonio

fiendish ['fiːndɪʃ] ADJ diabólico

fierce [fɪəs] ADJ feroz; (wind, attack) violento; (heat) intenso; (fighting, enemy) encarnizado

fiercely ['fɪəslɪ] ADV con ferocidad; violentamente; intensamente; encarnizadamente

fierceness ['fɪəsnɪs] N ferocidad f; violencia; intensidad f; encarnizamiento

fiery ['faɪərɪ] ADJ (burning) ardiente; (temperament) apasionado

FIFA ['fiːfə] N ABBR (= Fédération Internationale de Football Association) FIFA f

fifteen [fɪf'tiːn] NUM quince

fifteenth [fɪf'tiːnθ] ADJ decimoquinto; **the ~ floor** la planta quince; **the ~ of August** el quince de agosto

fifth [fɪfθ] ADJ quinto

fiftieth ['fɪftɪɪθ] ADJ quincuagésimo

fifty ['fɪftɪ] NUM cincuenta; **the fifties** los años cincuenta; **to be in one's fifties** andar por los cincuenta

fifty-fifty ['fɪftɪ'fɪftɪ] ADJ (deal, split) a medias
▸ ADV: **to go ~ with sb** ir a medias con algn; **we have a ~ chance of success** tenemos

un cincuenta por ciento de posibilidades de tener éxito

fig [fɪg] N higo

fight [faɪt] (pt, pp **fought**) N (gen) pelea; (Mil) combate m; (struggle) lucha ▸ VT luchar contra; (cancer, alcoholism) combatir; (Law):
to ~ a case defenderse ▸ VI pelear, luchar; (quarrel): **to ~ (with sb)** pelear (con algn); (fig): **to ~ (for/against)** luchar (por/contra)
▸ **fight back** VI defenderse; (after illness) recuperarse ▸ VT (tears) contener
▸ **fight down** VT (anger, anxiety, urge) reprimir
▸ **fight off** VT (attack, attacker) rechazar; (disease, sleep, urge) luchar contra
▸ **fight out** VT: **to ~ it out** decidirlo en una pelea

fighter ['faɪtə'] N combatiente mf; (fig) luchador(a) m/f; (plane) caza m

fighter-bomber ['faɪtəbɔmə'] N cazabombardero

fighter pilot N piloto de caza

fighting ['faɪtɪŋ] N (gen) luchas fpl; (battle) combate m, pelea; (in streets) disturbios mpl

figment ['fɪgmənt] N: **a ~ of the imagination** un producto de la imaginación

figurative ['fɪgjurətɪv] ADJ (meaning) figurado; (Art) figurativo

figure ['fɪgə'] N (Drawing, Geom) figura, dibujo; (number, cipher) cifra; (person, outline) figura; (body shape) línea; (: attractive) tipo ▸ VT (esp US: think, calculate) calcular, imaginarse ▸ VI (appear) figurar; (esp US: make sense) ser lógico; **~ of speech** (Ling) figura retórica; **public ~** personaje m
▸ **figure on** VT FUS (US) contar con
▸ **figure out** VT (work out) resolver; (understand) comprender

figurehead ['fɪgəhɛd] N (fig) figura decorativa

figure skating N patinaje m artístico

Fiji ['fiːdʒiː], **Fiji Islands** NPL (Islas fpl) Fiji

filament ['fɪləmənt] N (Elec) filamento

filch [fɪltʃ] VT (inf: steal) birlar

file [faɪl] N (tool) lima; (for nails) lima de uñas; (dossier) expediente m; (folder) carpeta; (in cabinet) archivo; (Comput) fichero; (row) fila
▸ VT limar; (papers) clasificar; (Law: claim) presentar; (store) archivar; **to open/close a ~** (Comput) abrir/cerrar un fichero; **to ~ in/out** vi entrar/salir en fila; **to ~ a suit against sb** entablar pleito contra algn; **to ~ past** desfilar ante

file name N (Comput) nombre m de fichero

file sharing [-ʃɛərɪŋ] N (Comput) uso m compartido de archivos

filibuster ['fɪlɪbʌstə'] (esp US Pol) N obstruccionista mf, filibustero(-a) ▸ VI usar maniobras obstruccionistas

filing ['faɪlɪŋ] N: **to do the ~** llevar los archivos
filing cabinet N archivo
filing clerk N oficinista *mf*
Filipino [fɪlɪ'piːnəu] ADJ filipino ▶ N (*person*) filipino(-a); (*Ling*) tagalo
fill [fɪl] VT llenar; (*tooth*) empastar; (*vacancy*) cubrir ▶ N: **to eat one's ~** comer hasta hartarse; **we've already filled that vacancy** ya hemos cubierto esa vacante; **filled with admiration (for)** lleno de admiración (por)
▶ **fill in** VT rellenar; (*details, report*) completar; **to ~ sb in on sth** (*inf*) poner a algn al corriente *or* al día sobre algo
▶ **fill out** VT (*form, receipt*) rellenar
▶ **fill up** VT llenar (hasta el borde) ▶ VI (*Aut*) echar gasolina
fillet ['fɪlɪt] N filete *m*
fillet steak N filete *m* de ternera
filling ['fɪlɪŋ] N (*Culin*) relleno; (*for tooth*) empaste *m*
filling station N estación *f* de servicio
fillip ['fɪlɪp] N estímulo
filly ['fɪlɪ] N potra
film [fɪlm] N película ▶ VT (*scene*) filmar ▶ VI rodar
film script N guión *m*
film star N estrella de cine
filmstrip ['fɪlmstrɪp] N tira de diapositivas
film studio N estudio de cine
Filofax® ['faɪləufæks] N agenda (profesional)
filter ['fɪltəʳ] N filtro ▶ VT filtrar
▶ **filter in, filter through** VI filtrarse
filter coffee N café *m* (molido) para filtrar
filter lane N (BRIT) carril *m* de selección
filter-tipped ['fɪltətɪpt] ADJ con filtro
filth [fɪlθ] N suciedad *f*
filthy ['fɪlθɪ] ADJ sucio; (*language*) obsceno
fin [fɪn] N (*gen*) aleta
final ['faɪnl] ADJ (*last*) final, último; (*definitive*) definitivo ▶ N (*Sport*) final *f*; **finals** NPL (*Scol*) exámenes *mpl* finales
final demand N (*on invoice etc*) último aviso
final dividend N dividendo final
finale [fɪ'nɑːlɪ] N final *m*
finalist ['faɪnəlɪst] N (*Sport*) finalista *mf*
finality [faɪ'nælɪtɪ] N finalidad *f*; **with an air of ~** en tono resuelto, de modo terminante
finalize ['faɪnəlaɪz] VT ultimar
finally ['faɪnəlɪ] ADV (*lastly*) por último, finalmente; (*eventually*) por fin; (*irrevocably*) de modo definitivo; (*once and for all*) definitivamente
finance [faɪ'næns] N (*money, funds*) fondos *mpl* ▶ VT financiar; **finances** NPL finanzas *fpl*
financial [faɪ'nænʃəl] ADJ financiero
financially [faɪ'nænʃəlɪ] ADV económicamente

financial management N gestión *f* financiera
financial statement N estado financiero
financial year N ejercicio (financiero)
financier [faɪ'nænsɪəʳ] N financiero(-a)
find [faɪnd] VT (*pt, pp* **found** [faund]) (*gen*) encontrar, hallar; (*come upon*) descubrir ▶ N hallazgo; descubrimiento; **to ~ sb guilty** (*Law*) declarar culpable a algn; **I ~ it easy** me resulta fácil
▶ **find out** VT averiguar; (*truth, secret*) descubrir ▶ VI: **to ~ out about** enterarse de
findings ['faɪndɪŋz] NPL (*Law*) veredicto *sg*, fallo *sg*; (*of report*) recomendaciones *fpl*
fine [faɪn] ADJ (*delicate*) fino; (*beautiful*) hermoso ▶ ADV (*well*) bien ▶ N (*Law*) multa ▶ VT (*Law*) multar; **the weather is ~** hace buen tiempo; **he's ~** está muy bien; **you're doing ~** lo estás haciendo muy bien; **to cut it ~** (*of time, money*) calcular muy justo; **to get a ~ for (doing) sth** recibir una multa por (hacer) algo
fine arts NPL bellas artes *fpl*
finely ['faɪnlɪ] ADV (*splendidly*) con elegancia; (*chop*) en trozos pequeños, fino; (*adjust*) con precisión
fineness ['faɪnnɪs] N (*of cloth*) finura
fine print N: **the ~** la letra pequeña *or* menuda
finery ['faɪnərɪ] N galas *fpl*
finesse [fɪ'nɛs] N sutileza
fine-tooth comb ['faɪntuːθ-] N: **to go through sth with a ~** revisar algo a fondo
finger ['fɪŋɡəʳ] N dedo ▶ VT (*touch*) manosear; (*Mus*) puntear; **little/index ~** (dedo) meñique *m*/índice *m*
fingernail ['fɪŋɡəneɪl] N uña
fingerprint ['fɪŋɡəprɪnt] N huella dactilar
fingertip ['fɪŋɡətɪp] N yema del dedo; **to have sth at one's fingertips** saberse algo al dedillo
finicky ['fɪnɪkɪ] ADJ (*fussy*) delicado
finish ['fɪnɪʃ] N (*end*) fin *m*; (*Sport*) meta; (*polish etc*) acabado ▶ VT, VI acabar, terminar; **to ~ doing sth** acabar de hacer algo; **to ~ first/ second/third** (*Sport*) llegar el primero/ segundo/tercero; **I've finished with the paper** he terminado con el periódico; **she's finished with him** ha roto *or* acabado con él
▶ **finish off** VT acabar, terminar; (*kill*) rematar
▶ **finish up** VT acabar, terminar ▶ VI ir a parar, terminar
finished ['fɪnɪʃt] ADJ (*product*) acabado; (*performance*) pulido; (*inf: tired*) rendido, hecho polvo
finishing ['fɪnɪʃɪŋ] ADJ: **~ touches** toque *m* final
finishing line N línea de llegada *or* meta

finishing school N colegio para la educación social de señoritas

finite ['faɪnaɪt] ADJ finito

Finland ['fɪnlənd] N Finlandia

Finn [fɪn] N finlandés(-esa) m/f

Finnish ['fɪnɪʃ] ADJ finlandés(-esa) ▶ N (Ling) finlandés m

fiord [fjɔːd] N fiordo

fir [fəːʳ] N abeto

fire ['faɪəʳ] N fuego; (accidental, damaging) incendio; (heater) estufa ▶ VT (gun) disparar; (set fire to) incendiar; (excite) exaltar; (interest) despertar; (dismiss) despedir ▶ VI encenderse; (Aut: engine) encender; **electric/gas ~** estufa eléctrica/de gas; **on ~** ardiendo, en llamas; **to be on ~** estar ardiendo; **to catch ~** prenderse fuego; **to set ~ to sth, set sth on ~** prender fuego a algo; **insured against ~** asegurado contra incendios; **to be/come under ~** estar/caer bajo el fuego enemigo

fire alarm N alarma de incendios

firearm ['faɪərɑːm] N arma de fuego

fire brigade, (US) **fire department** N (cuerpo de) bomberos mpl

fire door N puerta contra incendios

fire drill N (ejercicio de) simulacro de incendio

fire engine N coche m de bomberos

fire escape N escalera de incendios

fire exit N salida de incendios

fire extinguisher N extintor m

fireguard ['faɪəgɑːd] N pantalla (guardallama)

fire hazard N = **fire risk**

fire hydrant N boca de incendios

fire insurance N seguro contra incendios

fireman ['faɪəmən] N (irreg) bombero

fireplace ['faɪəpleɪs] N chimenea

fireplug ['faɪəplʌg] N (US) boca de incendios

fire practice N = **fire drill**

fireproof ['faɪəpruːf] ADJ a prueba de fuego; (material) incombustible

fire regulations NPL reglamentos mpl contra incendios

fire risk N peligro de incendio

firescreen ['faɪəskriːn] N pantalla refractaria

fireside ['faɪəsaɪd] N: **by the ~** al lado de la chimenea

fire station N parque m de bomberos

firetruck N (US) = **fire engine**

firewall ['faɪəwɔːl] N (Internet) firewall m

firewood ['faɪəwud] N leña

fireworks ['faɪəwəːks] NPL fuegos mpl artificiales

firing ['faɪərɪŋ] N (Mil) disparos mpl, tiroteo

firing line N línea de fuego; **to be in the ~** (fig: liable to be criticised) estar en la línea de fuego

firing squad N pelotón m de ejecución

firm [fəːm] ADJ firme; (offer, decision) en firme ▶ N empresa; **to be a ~ believer in sth** ser un partidario convencido de algo; **to stand ~ or take a ~ stand on sth** (fig) mantenerse firme ante algo

firmly ['fəːmlɪ] ADV firmemente

firmness ['fəːmnɪs] N firmeza

first [fəːst] ADJ primero ▶ ADV (before others) primero; (when listing reasons etc) en primer lugar, primeramente ▶ N (person: in race) primero(-a); (Aut: also: **first gear**) primera; **at ~** al principio; **~ of all** ante todo; **the ~ of January** el uno or primero de enero; **in the ~ instance** en primer lugar; **I'll do it ~ thing tomorrow** lo haré mañana a primera hora; **for the ~ time** por primera vez; **head ~** de cabeza; **from the (very) ~** desde el principio

first aid N primeros auxilios mpl

first aid kit N botiquín m

first aid post, (US) **first aid station** N puesto de auxilio

first-class ['fəːstklɑːs] ADJ de primera clase; **~ ticket** (Rail etc) billete m or (LAm) boleto de primera clase; **~ mail** correo de primera clase

first-hand [fəːst'hænd] ADJ de primera mano

first lady N (esp US) primera dama

firstly ['fəːstlɪ] ADV en primer lugar

first name N nombre m de pila

first night N estreno

first-rate [fəːst'reɪt] ADJ de primera (clase)

first-time buyer [fəːsttaɪm-] N persona que compra su primera vivienda

fir tree N abeto

fiscal ['fɪskəl] ADJ fiscal; **~ year** año fiscal, ejercicio

fish [fɪʃ] N pl inv pez m; (food) pescado ▶ VT pescar en ▶ VI pescar; **to go fishing** ir de pesca; **~ and chips** pescado frito con patatas fritas

▶ **fish out** VT (from water, box etc) sacar

fish-and-chip shop N = **chip shop**

fishbone ['fɪʃbəun] N espina

fisherman ['fɪʃəmən] N (irreg) pescador m

fishery ['fɪʃərɪ] N pesquería

fish factory N fábrica de elaboración de pescado

fish farm N piscifactoría

fish fingers NPL (Brit) palitos mpl de pescado (empanado)

fishing boat ['fɪʃɪŋ-] N barca de pesca

fishing industry ['fɪʃɪŋ-] N industria pesquera

fishing line ['fɪʃɪŋ-] N sedal m

fishing net ['fɪʃɪŋ-] N red f de pesca

fishing rod ['fɪʃɪŋ-] N caña (de pescar)

fishing tackle ['fɪʃɪŋ-] N aparejo (de pescar)

fish market N mercado de pescado

fishmonger ['fɪʃmʌŋgəʳ] N (BRIT) pescadero(-a)

fishmonger's, fishmonger's shop N (BRIT) pescadería

fishseller ['fɪʃsɛləʳ] N (US) = **fishmonger**

fish slice N paleta para pescado

fish sticks NPL (US) = **fish fingers**

fishstore ['fɪʃstɔːʳ] N (US) = **fishmonger's**

fishy ['fɪʃɪ] ADJ (fig) sospechoso

fission ['fɪʃən] N fisión f; **atomic/nuclear ~** fisión f atómica/nuclear

fissure ['fɪʃəʳ] N fisura

fist [fɪst] N puño

fistfight ['fɪstfaɪt] N lucha a puñetazos

fit [fɪt] ADJ (Med, Sport) en (buena) forma; (proper) adecuado, apropiado ▶ VT (clothes) quedar bien a; (try on: clothes) probar; (instal) poner; (equip) proveer; (match: facts) cuadrar or corresponder or coincidir con; (: description) estar de acuerdo con; (accommodate) ajustar, adaptar ▶ VI (clothes) quedar bien; (in space, gap) caber; (facts) coincidir ▶ N (Med) ataque m; (outburst) arranque m; **~ to** apto para; **~ for** apropiado para; **do as you think** or **see ~** haz lo que te parezca mejor; **to keep ~** mantenerse en forma; **to be ~ for work** (after illness) estar en condiciones para trabajar; **~ of coughing** acceso de tos; **a ~ of anger/enthusiasm** un arranque de cólera/ entusiasmo; **to have** or **suffer a ~** tener un ataque or acceso; **this dress is a good ~** este vestido me queda bien; **by fits and starts** a rachas

▶ **fit in** VI encajar ▶ VT (object) acomodar; (fig: appointment, visitor) encontrar un hueco para; **to ~ in with sb's plans** acomodarse a los planes de algn

▶ **fit out**, (BRIT) **fit up** VT equipar

fitful ['fɪtful] ADJ espasmódico, intermitente

fitfully ['fɪtfəlɪ] ADV irregularmente; **to sleep ~** dormir a rachas

fitment ['fɪtmənt] N mueble m

fitness ['fɪtnɪs] N (Med) forma física; (of remark) conveniencia

fitness instructor N instructor(a) m/f de fitness

fitted ['fɪtɪd] ADJ (jacket, shirt) entallado; (sheet) de cuatro picos

fitted carpet ['fɪtɪd-] N moqueta

fitted cupboards ['fɪtɪd-] NPL armarios mpl empotrados

fitted kitchen ['fɪtɪd-] N cocina amueblada

fitter ['fɪtəʳ] N ajustador(a) m/f

fitting ['fɪtɪŋ] ADJ apropiado ▶ N (of dress) prueba; see also **fittings**

fitting room N (in shop) probador m

fittings ['fɪtɪŋz] NPL instalaciones fpl

five [faɪv] NUM cinco; **she is ~ (years old)** tiene cinco años (de edad); **it costs ~**

pounds cuesta cinco libras; **it's ~ (o'clock)** son las cinco

five-day week ['faɪvdeɪ] N semana inglesa

fiver ['faɪvəʳ] N (inf: BRIT) billete m de cinco libras; (: US) billete m de cinco dólares

fix [fɪks] VT (secure) fijar, asegurar; (mend) arreglar; (make ready: meal, drink) preparar
▶ N: **to be in a ~** estar en un aprieto; **to ~ sth in one's mind** fijar algo en la memoria; **the fight was a ~** (inf) la pelea estaba amañada
▶ **fix on** VT (decide on) fijar
▶ **fix up** VT (arrange: date, meeting) arreglar; **to ~ sb up with sth** conseguirle algo a algn

fixation [fɪkˈseɪʃən] N (Psych) fijación f

fixative ['fɪksətɪv] N fijador m

fixed [fɪkst] ADJ (prices etc) fijo; **how are you ~ for money?** (inf) ¿qué tal andas de dinero?

fixed assets NPL activo sg fijo

fixed charge N gasto fijo

fixture ['fɪkstʃəʳ] N (Sport) encuentro; **fixtures** NPL instalaciones fpl fijas

fizz [fɪz] VI burbujear

fizzle out ['fɪzl-] VI apagarse; (enthusiasm, interest) decaer; (plan) quedar en agua de borrajas

fizzy ['fɪzɪ] ADJ (drink) gaseoso

fjord [fjɔːd] N = **fiord**

FL, Fla. ABBR (US) = **Florida**

flabbergasted ['flæbəgɑːstɪd] ADJ pasmado

flabby ['flæbɪ] ADJ flojo (de carnes); (skin) fofo

flag [flæg] N bandera; (stone) losa ▶ VI decaer; **~ of convenience** pabellón m de conveniencia
▶ **flag down** VT: **to ~ sb down** hacer señas a algn para que se pare
▶ **flag up** VT recalcar

flagpole ['flægpəʊl] N asta de bandera

flagrant ['fleɪgrənt] ADJ flagrante

flagship ['flægʃɪp] N buque m insignia or almirante

flagstone ['flægstəʊn] N losa

flag stop N (US) parada discrecional

flair [flɛəʳ] N aptitud f especial

flak [flæk] N (Mil) fuego antiaéreo; (inf: criticism) lluvia de críticas

flake [fleɪk] N (of rust, paint) desconchón m; (of snow) copo; (of soap powder) escama ▶ VI (also: **flake off**: paint) desconcharse; (skin) descamarse

flaky ['fleɪkɪ] ADJ (paintwork) desconchado; (skin) escamoso

flaky pastry N (Culin) hojaldre m

flamboyant [flæmˈbɔɪənt] ADJ (dress) vistoso; (person) extravagante

flame [fleɪm] N llama; **to burst into flames** incendiarse; **old ~** (inf) antiguo amor mf

flamingo [fləˈmɪŋgəʊ] N flamenco

flammable ['flæməbl] ADJ inflamable

flan [flæn] N (BRIT) tarta

flank [flæŋk] N flanco; (of person) costado ▸ VT flanquear

flannel ['flænl] N (BRIT: also: **face flannel**) toallita; (fabric) franela; **flannels** NPL pantalones mpl de franela

flannelette [flænə'lɛt] N franela de algodón

flap [flæp] N (of pocket, envelope) solapa; (of table) hoja (plegadiza); (wing movement) aletazo; (Aviat) flap m ▸ VT (wings) batir ▸ VI (sail, flag) ondear

flapjack ['flæpdʒæk] N (US: pancake) torta, panqueque m (LAM)

flare [flɛəʳ] N llamarada; (Mil) bengala; (in skirt etc) vuelo; **flares** NPL (trousers) pantalones mpl de campana
▸ **flare up** VI encenderse; (fig: person) encolerizarse; (: revolt) estallar

flash [flæʃ] N relámpago; (also: **news flash**) noticias fpl de última hora; (Phot) flash m; (US: torch) linterna ▸ VT (light, headlights) lanzar destellos con; (torch) encender ▸ VI brillar; (hazard light etc) lanzar destellos; **in a ~** en un instante; **~ of inspiration** ráfaga de inspiración; **to ~ sth about** (fig, inf: flaunt) ostentar algo, presumir con algo; **he flashed by** or **past** pasó como un rayo

flashback ['flæʃbæk] N flashback m, escena retrospectiva

flashbulb ['flæʃbʌlb] N bombilla de flash

flash card N (Scol) tarjeta

flash drive N (Comput) memoria flash, flash drive m

flasher ['flæʃəʳ] N exhibicionista m

flashlight ['flæʃlaɪt] N (US: torch) linterna

flashpoint ['flæʃpɔɪnt] N punto de inflamación; (fig) punto de explosión

flashy ['flæʃɪ] ADJ (pej) ostentoso

flask [flɑːsk] N petaca; (also: **vacuum flask**) termo

flat [flæt] ADJ llano; (smooth) liso; (tyre) desinflado; (battery) descargado; (beer) sin gas; (Mus: instrument) desafinado ▸ N (BRIT: apartment) piso (SP), departamento (LAM), apartamento; (Aut) pinchazo; (Mus) bemol m; **(to work) ~ out** (trabajar) a tope; **~ rate of pay** sueldo fijo

flatfooted [flæt'futɪd] ADJ de pies planos

flatly ['flætlɪ] ADV rotundamente, de plano

flatmate ['flætmeɪt] N compañero(-a) de piso

flatness ['flætnɪs] N (of land) llanura, lo llano

flat pack N: **it comes in a ~** viene en un paquete plano para su automontaje

flat-pack ['flætpæk] ADJ: **~ furniture** muebles mpl automontables (embalados en paquetes planos)

flatscreen ['flætskriːn] ADJ pantalla plana

flatten ['flætn] VT (also: **flatten out**) allanar; (: smooth out) alisar; (house, city) arrasar

flatter ['flætəʳ] VT adular, halagar; (show to advantage) favorecer

flatterer ['flætərəʳ] N adulador(a) m/f

flattering ['flætərɪŋ] ADJ halagador(a); (clothes etc) que favorece, favorecedor(a)

flattery ['flætərɪ] N adulación f

flatulence ['flætjuləns] N flatulencia

flaunt [flɔːnt] VT ostentar, lucir

flavour, (US) flavor ['fleɪvəʳ] N sabor m, gusto ▸ VT sazonar, condimentar; **strawberry flavoured** con sabor a fresa

flavouring, (US) flavoring ['fleɪvərɪŋ] N (in product) aromatizante m

flaw [flɔː] N defecto

flawless ['flɔːlɪs] ADJ impecable

flax [flæks] N lino

flaxen ['flæksən] ADJ muy rubio

flea [fliː] N pulga

flea market N rastro, mercadillo

fleck [flɛk] N mota ▸ VT (with blood, mud etc) salpicar; **brown flecked with white** marrón con motas blancas

fledgeling, fledgling ['flɛdʒlɪŋ] N (fig) novato(-a), principiante mf

flee [fliː] (pt, pp **fled** [flɛd]) VT huir de, abandonar ▸ VI huir

fleece [fliːs] N (of sheep) vellón m; (wool) lana; (top) forro polar ▸ VT (inf) desplumar

fleecy ['fliːsɪ] ADJ (blanket) lanoso, lanudo; (cloud) aborregado

fleet [fliːt] N flota; (of cars, lorries etc) parque m

fleeting ['fliːtɪŋ] ADJ fugaz

Flemish ['flɛmɪʃ] ADJ flamenco ▸ N (Ling) flamenco; **the ~** los flamencos

flesh [flɛʃ] N carne f; (skin) piel f; (of fruit) pulpa; **of ~ and blood** de carne y hueso

flesh wound N herida superficial

flew [fluː] PT of **fly**

flex [flɛks] N cable m ▸ VT (muscles) tensar

flexibility [flɛksɪ'bɪlɪtɪ] N flexibilidad f

flexible ['flɛksəbl] ADJ flexible; **~ working hours** horario sg flexible

flexitime ['flɛksɪtaɪm] N horario flexible

flick [flɪk] N golpecito; (with finger) capirotazo; (BRIT inf: film) película ▸ VT dar un golpecito a
▸ **flick off** VT quitar con el dedo
▸ **flick through** VT FUS hojear

flicker ['flɪkəʳ] VI (light) parpadear; (flame) vacilar ▸ N parpadeo

flick knife N navaja de muelle

flier ['flaɪəʳ] N aviador(a) m/f

flies [flaɪz] NPL of **fly**

flight [flaɪt] N vuelo; (escape) huida, fuga; (also: **flight of steps**) tramo (de escaleras); **to take ~** huir, darse a la fuga; **to put to ~** ahuyentar; **how long does the ~ take?** ¿cuánto dura el vuelo?

flight attendant N (US) auxiliar mf de vuelo

flight deck N (Aviat) cabina de mandos

flight path N trayectoria de vuelo

flight recorder N registrador m de vuelo

flighty ['flaɪtɪ] ADJ caprichoso

flimsy ['flɪmzɪ] ADJ (thin) muy ligero; (excuse) flojo

flinch [flɪntʃ] VI encogerse; **to ~ from** retroceder ante

fling [flɪŋ] VT (pt, pp **flung** [flʌŋ]) arrojar ▶ N (love affair) aventura amorosa

flint [flɪnt] N pedernal m; (in lighter) piedra

flip [flɪp] VT: **to ~ a coin** echar a cara o cruz
  ▶ **flip over** VT dar la vuelta a
  ▶ **flip through** VT FUS (book) hojear; (records) ver de pasada

flip-flops ['flɪpflɒps] NPL (esp BRIT) chancletas fpl

flippancy ['flɪpənsɪ] N ligereza

flippant ['flɪpənt] ADJ poco serio

flipper ['flɪpəʳ] N aleta

flip side N (of record) cara B

flirt [flɜːt] VI coquetear, flirtear ▶ N coqueta f

flirtation [flɜːˈteɪʃən] N coqueteo, flirteo

flit [flɪt] VI revolotear

float [fləut] N flotador m; (in procession) carroza; (sum of money) reserva ▶ VI (Comm: currency) flotar; (swimmer) hacer la plancha
  ▶ VT (gen) hacer flotar; (company) lanzar; **to ~ an idea** plantear una idea

floating ['fləutɪŋ] ADJ: **~ vote** voto indeciso; **~ voter** votante mf indeciso(-a)

flock [flɒk] N (of sheep) rebaño; (of birds) bandada; (of people) multitud f ▶ VI: **to ~ to** acudir en tropel a

floe [fləu] N: **ice ~** témpano de hielo

flog [flɒg] VT azotar; (inf) vender

flood [flʌd] N inundación f; (of words, tears etc) torrente m; (of letters, imports etc) avalancha
  ▶ VT (Aut: carburettor) inundar ▶ VI (place) inundarse; (people): **to ~ into** inundar; **to ~ the market** (Comm) inundar el mercado

flooding ['flʌdɪŋ] N inundaciones fpl

floodlight ['flʌdlaɪt] N foco ▶ VT (irreg: like **light**) iluminar con focos

floodlit ['flʌdlɪt] PT, PP of **floodlight** ▶ ADJ iluminado

flood tide N pleamar f

floodwater ['flʌdwɔːtəʳ] N aguas fpl (de la inundación)

floor [flɔːʳ] N suelo, piso (LAM); (storey) piso; (of sea, valley) fondo; (dance floor) pista ▶ VT (with blow) derribar; (fig: baffle) dejar anonadado; **ground ~**, (US) **first ~** planta baja; **first ~**, (US) **second ~** primer piso; **top ~** último piso; **to have the ~** (speaker) tener la palabra

floorboard ['flɔːbɔːd] N tabla

flooring ['flɔːrɪŋ] N suelo; (material) solería

floor lamp N (US) lámpara de pie

floor show N cabaret m

floorwalker ['flɔːwɔːkəʳ] N (US Comm) supervisor(a) m/f

flop [flɒp] N fracaso ▶ VI (fail) fracasar

floppy ['flɒpɪ] ADJ flojo ▶ N (Comput: also: **floppy disk**) floppy m

flora ['flɔːrə] N flora

floral ['flɔːrl] ADJ floral; (pattern) floreado; (dress, wallpaper) de flores

Florence ['flɒrəns] N Florencia

Florentine ['flɒrəntaɪn] ADJ, N florentino(-a) m/f

florid ['flɒrɪd] ADJ (style) florido

florist ['flɒrɪst] N florista mf; **~'s (shop)** n floristería

flotation [fləuˈteɪʃən] N (of shares) emisión f; (of company) lanzamiento

flounce [flauns] N volante m
  ▶ **flounce in** VI entrar con gesto exagerado
  ▶ **flounce out** VI salir con gesto airado

flounder ['flaundəʳ] VI tropezar ▶ N (Zool) platija

flour ['flauəʳ] N harina

flourish ['flʌrɪʃ] VI florecer ▶ N ademán m, movimiento (ostentoso)

flourishing ['flʌrɪʃɪŋ] ADJ floreciente

flout [flaut] VT burlarse de; (order) no hacer caso de, hacer caso omiso de

flow [fləu] N (movement) flujo; (of traffic) circulación f; (direction) curso; (Elec) corriente f ▶ VI (river, blood) fluir; (traffic) circular

flow chart N organigrama m

flow diagram N organigrama m

flower ['flauəʳ] N flor f ▶ VI florecer; **in ~** en flor

flower bed N macizo

flowerpot ['flauəpɒt] N tiesto

flowery ['flauərɪ] ADJ florido; (perfume, pattern) de flores

flowing ['fləuɪŋ] ADJ (hair, clothes) suelto; (style) fluido

flown [fləun] PP of **fly**

fl. oz. ABBR = **fluid ounce**

flu [fluː] N gripe f; **to have the ~** tener la gripe

fluctuate ['flʌktjueɪt] VI fluctuar

fluctuation [flʌktjuˈeɪʃən] N fluctuación f

flue [fluː] N cañón m

fluency ['fluːənsɪ] N fluidez f, soltura

fluent ['fluːənt] ADJ (speech) elocuente; **he speaks ~ French, he's ~ in French** domina el francés

fluently ['fluːəntlɪ] ADV con soltura

fluff [flʌf] N pelusa

fluffy ['flʌfɪ] ADJ de pelo suave

fluid ['fluːɪd] ADJ (movement) fluido, líquido; (situation) inestable ▶ N fluido, líquido; (in diet) líquido

fluid ounce N onza f líquida

fluke [fluːk] N (inf) chiripa

flummox ['flʌməks] VT desconcertar

flung [flʌŋ] PT, PP *of* **fling**

flunky ['flʌŋkɪ] N lacayo

fluorescent [fluə'resnt] ADJ fluorescente

fluoride ['fluəraɪd] N fluoruro

fluoride toothpaste N pasta de dientes con flúor

flurry ['flʌrɪ] N (*of snow*) ventisca; (*haste*) agitación *f*; **~ of activity** frenesí *m* de actividad

flush [flʌʃ] N (*on face*) rubor *m*; (*fig: of youth, beauty*) resplandor *m* ▶ VT limpiar con agua; (*also*: **flush out**: *game, birds*) levantar; (: *fig: criminal*) poner al descubierto ▶ VI ruborizarse ▶ ADJ: **~ with** a ras de; **to ~ the toilet** tirar de la cadena (del wáter); **hot flushes** (*Med*) sofocos *mpl*

flushed [flʌʃt] ADJ ruborizado

fluster ['flʌstər] N aturdimiento ▶ VT aturdir

flustered ['flʌstəd] ADJ aturdido

flute [fluːt] N flauta travesera

flutter ['flʌtər] N (*of wings*) revoloteo, aleteo; (*inf: bet*) apuesta ▶ VI revolotear; **to be in a ~** estar nervioso

flux [flʌks] N flujo; **in a state of ~** cambiando continuamente

fly [flaɪ] (*pt* **flew**, *pp* **flown**) N (*insect*) mosca; (*on trousers*: *also*: **flies**) bragueta ▶ VT (*plane*) pilotar; (*cargo*) transportar (en avión); (*distance*) recorrer (en avión) ▶ VI volar; (*passenger*) ir en avión; (*escape*) evadirse; (*flag*) ondear
▶ **fly away** VI (*bird, insect*) irse volando
▶ **fly in** VI (*person*) llegar en avión; (*plane*) aterrizar; **he flew in from Bilbao** llegó en avión desde Bilbao
▶ **fly off** VI irse volando
▶ **fly out** VI irse en avión

fly-drive N: **~ holiday** vacaciones que incluyen vuelo y alquiler de coche

fly-fishing ['flaɪfɪʃɪŋ] N pesca con mosca

flying ['flaɪɪŋ] N (*activity*) (el) volar ▶ ADJ: **~ visit** visita relámpago; **with ~ colours** con lucimiento

flying buttress N arbotante *m*

flying picket N piquete *m* volante

flying saucer N platillo volante

flying squad N (*Police*) brigada móvil

flying start N: **to get off to a ~** empezar con buen pie

flyleaf ['flaɪliːf] (*pl* **flyleaves** [-liːvz]) N (hoja de) guarda

flyover ['flaɪəuvər] N (*BRIT: bridge*) paso elevado *or* (*LAM*) a desnivel

flypast ['flaɪpɑːst] N desfile *m* aéreo

flysheet ['flaɪʃiːt] N (*for tent*) doble techo

flyswatter ['flaɪswɔtər] N matamoscas *m inv*

flyweight ['flaɪweɪt] ADJ de peso mosca ▶ N peso mosca

flywheel ['flaɪwiːl] N volante *m* (de motor)

FM ABBR (*Radio*: = *frequency modulation*) FM; (*BRIT Mil*) = **field marshal**

FMB N ABBR (*US*) = **Federal Maritime Board**

FMCS N ABBR (*US*: = *Federal Mediation and Conciliation Services*) organismo de conciliación en conflictos laborales

FO N ABBR (*BRIT*: = *Foreign Office*) ≈ Min. de AA. EE. (= *Ministerio de Asuntos Exteriores*)

foal [fəul] N potro

foam [fəum] N espuma ▶ VI hacer espuma

foam rubber N goma espuma

FOB ABBR (= *free on board*) f.a.b.

fob [fɔb] N (*also*: **watch fob**) leontina ▶ VT: **to ~ sb off with sth** deshacerse de algn con algo

foc ABBR (*BRIT*: = *free of charge*) gratis

focal ['fəukəl] ADJ focal; **~ point** punto focal; (*fig*) centro de atención

focus ['fəukəs] (*pl* **focuses**) N foco; (*centre*) centro ▶ VT (*field glasses etc*) enfocar ▶ VI: **to ~ (on)** enfocar (a); (*issue etc*) centrarse en; **in/out of ~** enfocado/desenfocado

fodder ['fɔdər] N pienso

FOE N ABBR (= *Friends of the Earth*) Amigos *mpl* de la Tierra; (*US*: = *Fraternal Order of Eagles*) organización benéfica

foe [fəu] N enemigo

foetus, (*US*) **fetus** ['fiːtəs] N feto

fog [fɔg] N niebla

fogbound ['fɔgbaund] ADJ inmovilizado por la niebla

foggy ['fɔgɪ] ADJ: **it's ~** hay niebla

fog lamp, (*US*) **fog light** N (*Aut*) faro antiniebla

foible ['fɔɪbl] N manía

foil [fɔɪl] VT frustrar ▶ N hoja; (*also*: **kitchen foil**) papel *m* (de) aluminio; (*Fencing*) florete *m*

foist [fɔɪst] VT: **to ~ sth on sb** endilgarle algo a algn

fold [fəuld] N (*bend, crease*) pliegue *m*; (*Agr*) redil *m* ▶ VT doblar; **to ~ one's arms** cruzarse de brazos
▶ **fold up** VI plegarse, doblarse; (*business*) quebrar ▶ VT (*map etc*) plegar

folder ['fəuldər] N (*for papers*) carpeta; (*binder*) carpeta de anillas; (*brochure*) folleto; (*Comput*) directorio

folding ['fəuldɪŋ] ADJ (*chair, bed*) plegable

foliage ['fəulɪɪdʒ] N follaje *m*

folio ['fəulɪəu] N folio

folk [fəuk] NPL gente *f* ▶ ADJ popular, folklórico; **folks** NPL familia, parientes *mpl*

folklore ['fəuklɔːr] N folklore *m*

folk music N música folk

folk singer N cantante *mf* de música folk

folk song N canción *f* popular *or* folk

follow ['fɔləu] VT seguir ▶ VI seguir; (*result*) resultar; **he followed suit** hizo lo mismo;

561

to ~ **sb's advice** seguir el consejo de algn;
I don't quite ~ you no te comprendo muy
bien; **to ~ in sb's footsteps** seguir los pasos
de algn; **it doesn't ~ that** ... no se deduce
que ....

▸ **follow on** vi seguir; (continue): **to ~ on from**
ser la consecuencia lógica de

▸ **follow out** vt (implement: idea, plan) realizar,
llevar a cabo

▸ **follow through** vt llevar hasta el fin ▸ vi
(Sport) dar el remate

▸ **follow up** vt (letter, offer) responder a; (case)
investigar

follower ['fɔləuəʳ] n seguidor(a) m/f; (Pol)
partidario(-a)

following ['fɔləuɪŋ] adj siguiente ▸ n
seguidores mpl, afición f

follow-up ['fɔləuʌp] n continuación f

follow-up letter n carta recordatoria

folly ['fɔlɪ] n locura

fond [fɔnd] adj (loving) cariñoso; **to be ~ of sb**
tener cariño a algn; **she's ~ of swimming**
tiene afición a la natación, le gusta nadar

fondle ['fɔndl] vt acariciar

fondly ['fɔndlɪ] adv (lovingly) con cariño; **he ~
believed that** ... creía ingenuamente que ...

fondness ['fɔndnɪs] n (for things) afición f;
(for people) cariño

font [fɔnt] n pila bautismal

food [fuːd] n comida

food chain n cadena alimenticia

food mixer n batidora

food poisoning n intoxicación f alimentaria

food processor n robot m de cocina

food stamp n (US) vale m para comida

foodstuffs ['fuːdstʌfs] npl comestibles mpl

fool [fuːl] n tonto(-a); (Culin) puré m de frutas
con nata ▸ vt engañar; **to make a ~ of o.s.**
ponerse en ridículo; **you can't ~ me** a mí no
me engañas; see also **April Fools' Day**

▸ **fool about, fool around** vi hacer el tonto

foolhardy ['fuːlhɑːdɪ] adj temerario

foolish ['fuːlɪʃ] adj tonto; (careless)
imprudente

foolishly ['fuːlɪʃlɪ] adv tontamente,
neciamente

foolproof ['fuːlpruːf] adj (plan etc) infalible

foolscap ['fuːlskæp] n ≈ papel m tamaño folio

foot [fut] (pl **feet**) n (Anat) pie m; (of page, stairs,
mountain) pie m; (measure) pie m (= 304 mm); (of
animal, table) pata ▸ vt (bill) pagar; **on ~** a pie;
to find one's feet acostumbrarse; **to put
one's ~ down** (say no) plantarse; (Aut) pisar el
acelerador

footage ['futɪdʒ] n (Cine) imágenes fpl

foot-and-mouth [futənd'mauθ], **foot-and-
mouth disease** n fiebre f aftosa

football ['futbɔːl] n balón m; (game: Brit)
fútbol m; (: US) fútbol m americano

footballer ['futbɔːləʳ] n (Brit) = **football
player**

football match n partido de fútbol

football player n futbolista mf, jugador(a)
m/f de fútbol

footbrake ['futbreɪk] n freno de pie

footbridge ['futbrɪdʒ] n pasarela, puente m
para peatones

foothills ['futhɪlz] npl estribaciones fpl

foothold ['futhəuld] n pie m firme

footing ['futɪŋ] n (fig) nivel m; **to lose one's
~** perder pie; **on an equal ~** en pie de
igualdad

footlights ['futlaɪts] npl candilejas fpl

footman ['futmən] n (irreg) lacayo

footnote ['futnəut] n nota (de pie de página)

footpath ['futpɑːθ] n sendero

footprint ['futprɪnt] n huella, pisada

footrest ['futrest] n apoyapiés m inv

footsie ['futsɪ] n: **to play ~ with sb** (inf)
juguetear con los pies de algn

footsore ['futsɔːʳ] adj con los pies doloridos

footstep ['futstɛp] n paso

footwear ['futwɛəʳ] n calzado

FOR abbr (= free on rail) franco (puesto sobre)
vagón

(KEYWORD)

for [fɔː] prep **1** (indicating destination, intention)
para; **the train for London** el tren para
Londres; (in announcements) el tren con
destino a Londres; **he left for Rome** marchó
para Roma; **he went for the paper** fue por
el periódico; **is this for me?** ¿es esto para
mí?; **it's time for lunch** es la hora de comer
2 (indicating purpose) para; **what('s it) for?**
¿para qué (es)?; **what's this button for?**
¿para qué sirve este botón?; **to pray for
peace** rezar por la paz
3 (on behalf of, representing): **the MP for Hove**
el diputado por Hove; **he works for the
government/a local firm** trabaja para el
gobierno/en una empresa local; **I'll ask him
for you** se lo pediré por ti; **G for George** G de
Gerona
4 (because of) por esta razón; **for fear of being
criticized** por temor a ser criticado
5 (with regard to) para; **it's cold for July** hace
frío para julio; **he has a gift for languages**
tiene don de lenguas
6 (in exchange for) por; **I sold it for £5** lo vendí
por £5; **to pay 50 pence for a ticket** pagar
50 peniques por un billete
7 (in favour of): **are you for or against us?**
¿estás con nosotros o contra nosotros?; **I'm
all for it** estoy totalmente a favor; **vote for
X** vote (a) X
8 (referring to distance): **there are roadworks
for 5 km** hay obras en 5 km; **we walked for**

miles caminamos kilómetros y kilómetros
9 (*referring to time*): **he was away for two years** estuvo fuera (durante) dos años; **it hasn't rained for three weeks** no ha llovido durante *or* en tres semanas; **I have known her for years** la conozco desde hace años; **can you do it for tomorrow?** ¿lo podrás hacer para mañana?
10 (*with infinitive clauses*): **it is not for me to decide** la decisión no es cosa mía; **it would be best for you to leave** sería mejor que te fueras; **there is still time for you to do it** todavía te queda tiempo para hacerlo; **for this to be possible** ... para que esto sea posible ...
11 (*in spite of*) a pesar de; **for all his complaints** a pesar de sus quejas
▶ CONJ (*since, as: formal*) puesto que

forage ['fɔrɪdʒ] N forraje *m*
foray ['fɔreɪ] N incursión *f*
forbid [fə'bɪd] (*pt* **forbad(e)** [-'bæd], *pp* **forbidden** [-'bɪdn]) VT prohibir; **to ~ sb to do sth** prohibir a algn hacer algo
forbidden [fə'bɪdn] PT *of* **forbid** ▶ ADJ (*food, area*) prohibido; (*word, subject*) tabú
forbidding [fə'bɪdɪŋ] ADJ (*landscape*) inhóspito; (*severe*) severo
force [fɔːs] N fuerza ▶ VT obligar, forzar; **to ~ o.s. to do** hacer un esfuerzo por hacer; **the Forces** *npl* (*BRIT*) las Fuerzas Armadas; **sales ~** (*Comm*) personal *m* de ventas; **a ~ 5 wind** un viento fuerza 5; **to join forces** unir fuerzas; **in ~** (*law etc*) en vigor; **to ~ sb to do sth** obligar a algn a hacer algo
▶ **force back** VT (*crowd, enemy*) hacer retroceder; (*tears*) reprimir
▶ **force down** VT (*food*) tragar con esfuerzo
forced [fɔːst] ADJ (*smile*) forzado; (*landing*) forzoso
force-feed ['fɔːsfiːd] VT (*animal, prisoner*) alimentar a la fuerza
forceful ['fɔːsful] ADJ enérgico
forcemeat ['fɔːsmiːt] N (*Culin*) relleno
forceps ['fɔːseps] NPL fórceps *m inv*
forcible ['fɔːsəbl] ADJ (*violent*) a la fuerza; (*telling*) convincente
forcibly ['fɔːsəblɪ] ADV a la fuerza
ford [fɔːd] N vado ▶ VT vadear
fore [fɔːʳ] N: **to bring to the ~** sacar a la luz pública; **to come to the ~** empezar a destacar
forearm ['fɔːrɑːm] N antebrazo
forebear ['fɔːbɛəʳ] N antepasado
foreboding [fɔː'bəudɪŋ] N presentimiento
forecast ['fɔːkɑːst] N pronóstico ▶ VT (*irreg: like* **cast**) pronosticar; **weather ~** previsión *f* meteorológica
foreclose [fɔː'kləuz] VT (*Law: also:* **foreclose on**)

extinguir el derecho de redimir
foreclosure [fɔː'kləuʒəʳ] N apertura de un juicio hipotecario
forecourt ['fɔːkɔːt] N patio; (*of garage*) área de entrada
forefathers ['fɔːfɑːðəz] NPL antepasados *mpl*
forefinger ['fɔːfɪŋgəʳ] N (*dedo*) índice *m*
forefront ['fɔːfrʌnt] N: **in the ~ of** en la vanguardia de
forego [fɔː'gəu] VT (*irreg: like* **go**) = **forgo**
foregoing ['fɔːgəuɪŋ] ADJ anterior, precedente
foregone ['fɔːgɔn] PP *of* **forego** ▶ ADJ: **it's a ~ conclusion** es una conclusión inevitable
foreground ['fɔːgraund] N (*also Comput*) primer plano *m*
forehand ['fɔːhænd] N (*Tennis*) derechazo directo
forehead ['fɔrɪd] N frente *f*
foreign ['fɔrɪn] ADJ extranjero; (*trade*) exterior
foreign currency N divisas *fpl*
foreigner ['fɔrɪnəʳ] N extranjero(-a)
foreign exchange N (*system*) cambio de divisas; (*money*) divisas *fpl*, moneda extranjera
foreign investment N inversión *f* en el extranjero; (*money, stock*) inversiones *fpl* extranjeras
Foreign Minister N Ministro(-a) de Asuntos Exteriores, Canciller *m* (*LAm*)
Foreign Office N (*BRIT*) Ministerio de Asuntos Exteriores
Foreign Secretary N (*BRIT*) Ministro(-a) de Asuntos Exteriores, Canciller *m* (*LAm*)
foreleg ['fɔːleg] N pata delantera
foreman ['fɔːmən] N (*irreg*) capataz *m*; (*Law: of jury*) presidente *mf*
foremost ['fɔːməust] ADJ principal ▶ ADV: **first and ~** ante todo, antes que nada
forename ['fɔːneɪm] N nombre *m* (de pila)
forensic [fə'rɛnsɪk] ADJ forense; **~ scientist** forense *mf*
foreplay ['fɔːpleɪ] N preámbulos *mpl* (*de estimulación sexual*)
forerunner ['fɔːrʌnəʳ] N precursor(a) *m/f*
foresee [fɔː'siː] VT (*irreg: like* **see**) prever
foreseeable [fɔː'siːəbl] ADJ previsible
foreshadow [fɔː'ʃædəu] VT prefigurar, anunciar
foreshore ['fɔːʃɔːʳ] N playa
foreshorten [fɔː'ʃɔːtn] VT (*figure, scene*) escorzar
foresight ['fɔːsaɪt] N previsión *f*
foreskin ['fɔːskɪn] N (*Anat*) prepucio
forest ['fɔrɪst] N bosque *m*
forestall [fɔː'stɔːl] VT anticiparse a
forestry ['fɔrɪstrɪ] N silvicultura
foretaste ['fɔːteɪst] N anticipo

f

foretell [fɔːˈtɛl] (*pt, pp* **foretold** [-ˈtəuld]) ᴠᴛ predecir, pronosticar

forethought [ˈfɔːθɔːt] ɴ previsión *f*

forever [fəˈrɛvəʳ] ᴀᴅᴠ siempre; (*for good*) para siempre; (*endlessly*) constantemente

forewarn [fɔːˈwɔːn] ᴠᴛ avisar, advertir

forewent [fɔːˈwɛnt] ᴘᴛ *of* **forego**

foreword [ˈfɔːwəːd] ɴ prefacio

forfeit [ˈfɔːfɪt] ɴ (*in game*) prenda ▸ ᴠᴛ perder (derecho a)

forgave [fəˈgeɪv] ᴘᴛ *of* **forgive**

forge [fɔːdʒ] ɴ fragua; (*smithy*) herrería ▸ ᴠᴛ (*signature: Bʀɪᴛ: money*) falsificar; (*metal*) forjar ▸ **forge ahead** ᴠɪ avanzar mucho

forger [ˈfɔːdʒəʳ] ɴ falsificador(a) *m/f*

forgery [ˈfɔːdʒərɪ] ɴ falsificación *f*

forget [fəˈgɛt] (*pt* **forgot** [-ˈgɔt], *pp* **forgotten** [-ˈgɔtn]) ᴠᴛ olvidar, olvidarse de ▸ ᴠɪ olvidarse

forgetful [fəˈgɛtful] ᴀᴅᴊ olvidadizo, despistado

forget-me-not [fəˈgɛtmɪnɔt] ɴ nomeolvides *f inv*

forgive [fəˈgɪv] ᴠᴛ (*irreg: like* **give**) perdonar; **to ~ sb for sth/for doing sth** perdonar algo a algn/a algn por haber hecho algo

forgiveness [fəˈgɪvnɪs] ɴ perdón *m*

forgiving [fəˈgɪvɪŋ] ᴀᴅᴊ compasivo

forgo [fɔːˈgəu] ᴠᴛ (*irreg: like* **go**) (*give up*) renunciar a; (*go without*) privarse de

forgot [fəˈgɔt] ᴘᴛ *of* **forget**

forgotten [fəˈgɔtn] ᴘᴘ *of* **forget**

fork [fɔːk] ɴ (*for eating*) tenedor *m*; (*for gardening*) horca; (*of roads*) bifurcación *f*; (*in tree*) horcadura ▸ ᴠɪ (*road*) bifurcarse ▸ **fork out** ᴠᴛ (*inf: pay*) soltar

forked [fɔːkt] ᴀᴅᴊ (*lightning*) en zigzag

fork-lift truck [ˈfɔːklɪft-] ɴ máquina elevadora

forlorn [fəˈlɔːn] ᴀᴅᴊ (*person*) triste, melancólico; (*deserted: cottage*) abandonado; (*desperate: attempt*) desesperado

form [fɔːm] ɴ forma; (*Bʀɪᴛ Scol*) curso; (*document*) formulario, planilla (*LAm*) ▸ ᴠᴛ formar; **in the ~ of** en forma de; **in top ~** en plena forma; **to be in good ~** (*Sport: fig*) estar en plena forma; **to ~ part of sth** formar parte de algo; **to ~ a circle/a queue** hacer una curva/una cola

formal [ˈfɔːməl] ᴀᴅᴊ (*offer, receipt*) por escrito; (*person etc*) correcto; (*occasion, dinner*) ceremonioso; **~ dress** traje *m* de vestir; (*evening dress*) traje *m* de etiqueta

formalities [fɔːˈmælɪtɪz] ɴᴘʟ formalidades *fpl*

formality [fɔːˈmælɪtɪ] ɴ ceremonia

formalize [ˈfɔːməlaɪz] ᴠᴛ formalizar

formally [ˈfɔːməlɪ] ᴀᴅᴠ oficialmente

format [ˈfɔːmæt] ɴ formato ▸ ᴠᴛ (*Comput*) formatear

formation [fɔːˈmeɪʃən] ɴ formación *f*

formative [ˈfɔːmətɪv] ᴀᴅᴊ (*years*) de formación

former [ˈfɔːməʳ] ᴀᴅᴊ anterior; (*earlier*) antiguo; (*ex*) ex; **the ~ ... the latter ...** aquél ... éste ...; **the ~ president** el antiguo *or* ex presidente; **the ~ Yugoslavia/Soviet Union** la antigua *or* ex Yugoslavia/Unión Soviética

formerly [ˈfɔːməlɪ] ᴀᴅᴠ antes

form feed ɴ (*on printer*) salto de página

Formica® [fɔːˈmaɪkə] ɴ formica®

formidable [ˈfɔːmɪdəbl] ᴀᴅᴊ formidable

formula [ˈfɔːmjulə] ɴ fórmula; **F~ One** (*Aut*) Fórmula Uno

formulate [ˈfɔːmjuleɪt] ᴠᴛ formular

fornicate [ˈfɔːnɪkeɪt] ᴠɪ fornicar

forsake [fəˈseɪk] (*pt* **forsook** [-ˈsuk], *pp* **forsaken** [-ˈseɪkən]) ᴠᴛ (*gen*) abandonar; (*plan*) renunciar a

fort [fɔːt] ɴ fuerte *m*; **to hold the ~** (*fig*) quedarse a cargo

forte [ˈfɔːtɪ] ɴ fuerte *m*

forth [fɔːθ] ᴀᴅᴠ: **back and ~** de acá para allá; **and so ~** y así sucesivamente

forthcoming [fɔːθˈkʌmɪŋ] ᴀᴅᴊ próximo, venidero; (*character*) comunicativo

forthright [ˈfɔːθraɪt] ᴀᴅᴊ franco

forthwith [ˈfɔːθˈwɪθ] ᴀᴅᴠ en el acto, acto seguido

fortieth [ˈfɔːtɪɪθ] ᴀᴅᴊ cuadragésimo

fortification [fɔːtɪfɪˈkeɪʃən] ɴ fortificación *f*

fortified wine [ˈfɔːtɪfaɪd-] ɴ vino encabezado

fortify [ˈfɔːtɪfaɪ] ᴠᴛ fortalecer

fortitude [ˈfɔːtɪtjuːd] ɴ (*city*) fortificar; (*person*) fortalecer

fortnight [ˈfɔːtnaɪt] ɴ (*Bʀɪᴛ*) quincena; **it's a ~ since ...** hace quince días que ...

fortnightly [ˈfɔːtnaɪtlɪ] ᴀᴅᴊ quincenal ▸ ᴀᴅᴠ quincenalmente

FORTRAN [ˈfɔːtræn] ɴ FORTRAN *m*

fortress [ˈfɔːtrɪs] ɴ fortaleza

fortuitous [fɔːˈtjuːɪtəs] ᴀᴅᴊ fortuito

fortunate [ˈfɔːtʃənɪt] ᴀᴅᴊ: **it is ~ that ...** (es una) suerte que ...

fortunately [ˈfɔːtʃənɪtlɪ] ᴀᴅᴠ afortunadamente

fortune [ˈfɔːtʃən] ɴ suerte *f*; (*wealth*) fortuna; **to make a ~** hacer un dineral

fortune-teller [ˈfɔːtʃəntɛləʳ] ɴ adivino(-a)

forty [ˈfɔːtɪ] ɴᴜᴍ cuarenta

forum [ˈfɔːrəm] ɴ (*also fig*) foro

forward [ˈfɔːwəd] ᴀᴅᴊ (*position*) avanzado; (*movement*) hacia delante; (*front*) delantero; (*not shy*) atrevido ▸ ɴ (*Sport*) delantero ▸ ᴠᴛ (*letter*) remitir; (*career*) promocionar; **to move ~** avanzar; **"please ~"** "remítase al destinatario"

forward contract ɴ contrato a término

forward exchange ɴ cambio a término

forwarding address ɴ destinatario

forward planning N planificación f por anticipado

forward rate N tipo a término

forwards ['fɔːwədz] ADV (hacia) adelante

forward sales NPL ventas fpl a término

forward slash N barra diagonal

forwent [fɔː'wɛnt] PT of **forgo**

fossick ['fɔsɪk] VI (AUSTRALIA, NEW ZEALAND inf) buscar; **to ~ for sth** buscar algo

fossil ['fɔsl] N fósil m

fossil fuel N combustible m fósil

foster ['fɔstə^r] VT (child) acoger en familia; (idea) fomentar

foster brother N hermano de leche

foster child N (irreg) hijo(-a) adoptivo(-a)

foster mother N madre f adoptiva

foster sister N hermana de leche

fought [fɔːt] PT, PP of **fight**

foul [faul] ADJ (gen) sucio, puerco; (weather, smell etc) asqueroso; (language) grosero; (temper) malísimo ▶ N (Football) falta ▶ VT (dirty) ensuciar; (block) atascar; (entangle: anchor, propeller) atascar, enredarse en; (football player) cometer una falta contra

foul play N (Sport) mala jugada; (Law) muerte f violenta

found [faund] PT, PP of **find** ▶ VT (establish) fundar

foundation [faun'deɪʃən] N (act) fundación f; (basis) base f; (also: **foundation cream**) crema de base; **foundations** NPL (of building) cimientos mpl; **to lay the foundations** poner los cimientos

foundation stone N: **to lay the ~** poner la primera piedra

founder ['faundə^r] N fundador(a) m/f ▶ VI irse a pique

founding ['faundɪŋ] ADJ: **~ fathers** (esp US) fundadores mpl, próceres mpl; **~ member** miembro fundador

foundry ['faundrɪ] N fundición f

fountain ['fauntɪn] N fuente f

fountain pen N (pluma) estilográfica, plumafuente f (LAM)

four [fɔː^r] NUM cuatro; **on all fours** a gatas

four-by-four ['fɔːbaɪ'fɔː^r] N todoterreno, 4x4 m (cuatro por cuatro)

four-footed [fɔː'futɪd] ADJ cuadrúpedo

four-letter word ['fɔːlɛtə-] N taco

four-poster ['fɔː'pəustə^r] N (also: **four-poster bed**) cama de columnas

foursome ['fɔːsəm] N grupo de cuatro personas

fourteen ['fɔː'tiːn] NUM catorce

fourteenth [fɔː'tiːnθ] ADJ decimocuarto

fourth [fɔːθ] ADJ cuarto ▶ N (Aut: also: **fourth gear**) cuarta (velocidad)

four-wheel drive ['fɔːwiːl-] N tracción f a las cuatro ruedas

fowl [faul] N ave f (de corral)

fox [fɔks] N zorro ▶ VT confundir

fox fur N piel f de zorro

foxglove ['fɔksglʌv] N (Bot) dedalera

fox-hunting ['fɔkshʌntɪŋ] N caza de zorros

foxtrot ['fɔkstrɔt] N fox(trot) m

foyer ['fɔɪeɪ] N vestíbulo

FPA N ABBR (BRIT: = Family Planning Association) asociación de planificación familiar

Fr. ABBR (Rel: = father) P.; (= friar) Fr.

fracas ['frækɑː] N gresca, refriega

fraction ['frækʃən] N fracción f

fractionally ['frækʃnəlɪ] ADV ligeramente

fractious ['frækʃəs] ADJ (person, mood) irascible

fracture ['fræktʃə^r] N fractura ▶ VT fracturar

fragile ['frædʒaɪl] ADJ frágil

fragment ['frægmənt] N fragmento

fragmentary [fræg'mɛntərɪ] ADJ fragmentario

fragrance ['freɪgrəns] N fragancia

fragrant ['freɪgrənt] ADJ fragante, oloroso

frail [freɪl] ADJ (fragile) frágil, quebradizo; (weak) delicado

frame [freɪm] N (Tech) armazón f; (of picture, door etc) marco; (of spectacles: also: **frames**) montura ▶ VT encuadrar; (picture) enmarcar; (reply) formular; **to ~ sb** (inf) inculpar por engaños a algn

frame of mind N estado de ánimo

framework ['freɪmwəːk] N marco

France [frɑːns] N Francia

franchise ['fræntʃaɪz] N (Pol) derecho al voto, sufragio; (Comm) licencia, concesión f

franchisee [fræntʃaɪ'ziː] N concesionario(-a)

franchiser ['fræntʃaɪzə^r] N compañía concesionaria

frank [fræŋk] ADJ franco ▶ VT (BRIT: letter) franquear

frankfurter ['fræŋkfəːtə^r] N salchicha de Frankfurt

frankincense ['fræŋkɪnsɛns] N incienso

franking machine ['fræŋkɪŋ-] N máquina de franqueo

frankly ['fræŋklɪ] ADV francamente

frankness ['fræŋknɪs] N franqueza

frantic ['fræntɪk] ADJ (desperate: need, desire) desesperado; (: search) frenético; (: person) desquiciado

fraternal [frə'təːnl] ADJ fraterno

fraternity [frə'təːnɪtɪ] N (club) fraternidad f; (US) club m de estudiantes; (guild) gremio

fraternization [frætənaɪ'zeɪʃən] N fraternización f

fraternize ['frætənaɪz] VI confraternizar

fraud [frɔːd] N fraude m; (person) impostor(a) m/f

fraudulent ['frɔːdjulənt] ADJ fraudulento

fraught [frɔːt] ADJ (tense) tenso; **~ with** cargado de

fray [freɪ] N combate *m*, lucha, refriega ▸ VI deshilacharse; **tempers were frayed** el ambiente se ponía tenso

FRB N ABBR (*US*) = **Federal Reserve Board**

FRCM N ABBR (*BRIT*) = **Fellow of the Royal College of Music**

FRCO N ABBR (*BRIT*) = **Fellow of the Royal College of Organists**

FRCP N ABBR (*BRIT*) = **Fellow of the Royal College of Physicians**

FRCS N ABBR (*BRIT*) = **Fellow of the Royal College of Surgeons**

freak [fri:k] N (*person*) fenómeno; (*event*) suceso anormal; (*inf: enthusiast*) adicto(-a) ▸ ADJ (*storm, conditions*) anormal; **health** ~ (*inf*) maniático(-a) en cuestión de salud
▸ **freak out** VI (*inf: on drugs*) flipar

freakish ['fri:kɪʃ] ADJ (*result*) inesperado; (*appearance*) estrambótico; (*weather*) cambiadizo

freckle ['frɛkl] N peca

freckled ['frɛkld] ADJ pecoso, lleno de pecas

free [fri:] ADJ (*person: at liberty*) libre; (*not fixed*) suelto; (*gratis*) gratuito; (*unoccupied*) desocupado; (*liberal*) generoso ▸ VT (*prisoner etc*) poner en libertad; (*jammed object*) soltar; ~ **and easy** despreocupado; **to give sb a ~ hand** dar carta blanca a algn; **is this seat ~?** ¿está libre este asiento?; ~ **of tax** libre de impuestos; **admission** ~ entrada libre; ~ **(of charge)**, **for** ~ adv gratis

freebie ['fri:bɪ] N (*inf*): **it's a** ~ es gratis

freedom ['fri:dəm] N libertad *f*; ~ **of association** libertad de asociación

freedom fighter N luchador(a) *m/f* por la libertad

free enterprise N libre empresa

Freefone® ['fri:fəun] N (*BRIT*) número gratuito

free-for-all ['fri:fərɔ:l] N riña general

free gift N regalo

freehold ['fri:həuld] N propiedad *f* absoluta

free kick N tiro libre

freelance ['fri:lɑ:ns] ADJ independiente ▸ ADV por cuenta propia; **to do ~ work** trabajar por su cuenta

freely ['fri:lɪ] ADV libremente; (*liberally*) generosamente

free-market economy ['fri:'mɑ:kɪt-] N economía de libre mercado

freemason ['fri:meɪsn] N francmasón *m*

freemasonry ['fri:meɪsnrɪ] N (*franc*)masonería

Freepost® ['fri:pəust] N porte *m* pagado

free-range ['fri:'reɪndʒ] ADJ (*hen, egg*) de granja

free sample N muestra gratuita

freesia ['fri:ʒə] N fresia

free speech N libertad *f* de expresión

free trade N libre comercio

freeway ['fri:weɪ] N (*US*) autopista

freewheel [fri:'wi:l] VI ir en punto muerto

freewheeling [fri:'wi:lɪŋ] ADJ libre, espontáneo; (*careless*) irresponsable

free will N libre albedrío; **of one's own** ~ por su propia voluntad

freeze [fri:z] (*pt* **froze**, *pp* **frozen**) VI helarse, congelarse ▸ VT helar; (*prices, food, salaries*) congelar ▸ N helada; (*on arms, wages*) congelación *f*
▸ **freeze over** VI (*lake, river*) helarse, congelarse; (*window, windscreen*) cubrirse de escarcha
▸ **freeze up** VI helarse, congelarse

freeze-dried ['fri:zdraɪd] ADJ liofilizado

freezer ['fri:zəʳ] N congelador *m*, congeladora

freezing ['fri:zɪŋ] ADJ helado

freezing point N punto de congelación; **3 degrees below** ~ tres grados bajo cero

freight [freɪt] N (*goods*) carga; (*money charged*) flete *m*

freight car N vagón *m* de mercancías

freighter ['freɪtəʳ] N buque *m* de carga; (*Aviat*) avión *m* de transporte de mercancías

freight forward N contra reembolso del flete, flete por pagar

freight forwarder [-'fɔ:wədəʳ] N agente *m* expedidor

freight inward N flete sobre compras

freight train N (*US*) tren *m* de mercancías

French [frɛntʃ] ADJ francés(-esa) ▸ N (*Ling*) francés *m*; **the French** NPL los franceses

French bean N judía verde

French bread N pan *m* francés

French Canadian ADJ, N francocanadiense *mf*

French dressing N (*Culin*) vinagreta

French fried potatoes, (*US*) **French fries** NPL patatas *fpl* or (*LAm*) papas *fpl* fritas

French Guiana [-gaɪˈænə] N la Guayana Francesa

French loaf N barra de pan

Frenchman ['frɛntʃmən] N (*irreg*) francés *m*

French Riviera N: **the** ~ la Riviera, la Costa Azul

French stick N barra de pan

French window N puerta ventana

Frenchwoman ['frɛntʃwumən] N (*irreg*) francesa

frenetic [frə'nɛtɪk] ADJ frenético

frenzy ['frɛnzɪ] N frenesí *m*

frequency ['fri:kwənsɪ] N frecuencia

frequency modulation N frecuencia modulada

frequent ADJ ['fri:kwənt] frecuente ▸ VT [frɪ'kwɛnt] frecuentar

frequently ['fri:kwəntlɪ] ADV frecuentemente, a menudo

fresco ['freskəu] N fresco

fresh [freʃ] ADJ (gen) fresco; (bread) tierno; (new) nuevo; (water) dulce; **to make a ~ start** empezar de nuevo

freshen ['freʃən] VI (wind) arreciar; (air) refrescar
▶ **freshen up** VI (person) arreglarse

freshener ['freʃnəʳ] N: **air ~** ambientador m; **skin ~** tónico

fresher ['freʃəʳ] N (BRIT Scol: inf) estudiante mf de primer año

freshly ['freʃlɪ] ADV: **~ painted/arrived** recién pintado/llegado

freshman ['freʃmən] N (irreg) (US Scol) = **fresher**

freshness ['freʃnɪs] N frescura

freshwater ['freʃwɔːtəʳ] ADJ (fish) de agua dulce

fret [fret] VI inquietarse

fretful ['fretful] ADJ (child) quejumbroso

Freudian ['frɔɪdɪən] ADJ freudiano; **~ slip** lapsus m (freudiano)

FRG N ABBR (= Federal Republic of Germany) RFA f

Fri. ABBR (= Friday) vier.

friar ['fraɪəʳ] N fraile m; (before name) fray

friction ['frɪkʃən] N fricción f

friction feed N (on printer) avance m por fricción

Friday ['fraɪdɪ] N viernes m inv; see also **Tuesday**

fridge [frɪdʒ] N (BRIT) nevera, frigo, refrigeradora (LAM), heladera (LAM)

fridge-freezer ['frɪdʒ'friːzəʳ] N frigorífico-congelador m, combi m

fried [fraɪd] PT, PP of **fry** ▶ ADJ: **~ egg** huevo frito, huevo estrellado

friend [frend] N amigo(-a) ▶ VT (Internet) añadir como amigo a

friendliness ['frendlɪnɪs] N simpatía

friendly ['frendlɪ] ADJ simpático; (government) amigo; (place) acogedor(a); (match) amistoso

friendly fire N fuego amigo, disparos mpl del propio bando

friendly society N mutualidad f, montepío

friendship ['frendʃɪp] N amistad f

fries [fraɪz] NPL (esp US) = **French fried potatoes**

frieze [friːz] N friso

frigate ['frɪgɪt] N fragata

fright [fraɪt] N susto; **to take ~** asustarse

frighten ['fraɪtn] VT asustar
▶ **frighten away, frighten off** VT (birds, children etc) espantar, ahuyentar

frightened ['fraɪtnd] ADJ asustado

frightening ['fraɪtnɪŋ] ADJ: **it's ~** da miedo

frightful ['fraɪtful] ADJ espantoso, horrible

frightfully ['fraɪtfulɪ] ADV terriblemente; **I'm ~ sorry** lo siento muchísimo

frigid ['frɪdʒɪd] ADJ (Med) frígido

frigidity [frɪ'dʒɪdɪtɪ] N (Med) frigidez f

frill [frɪl] N volante m; **without frills** (fig) sin adornos

frilly ['frɪlɪ] ADJ con volantes

fringe [frɪndʒ] N (BRIT: of hair) flequillo; (edge: of forest etc) borde m, margen m

fringe benefits NPL ventajas fpl complementarias

fringe theatre N teatro experimental

Frisbee® ['frɪzbɪ] N frisbee® m

frisk [frɪsk] VT cachear, registrar

frisky ['frɪskɪ] ADJ juguetón(-ona)

fritter ['frɪtəʳ] N buñuelo
▶ **fritter away** VT desperdiciar

frivolity [frɪ'vɔlɪtɪ] N frivolidad f

frivolous ['frɪvələs] ADJ frívolo

frizzy ['frɪzɪ] ADJ crespo

fro [frəu] see **to**

frock [frɔk] N vestido

frog [frɔg] N rana; **to have a ~ in one's throat** tener carraspera

frogman ['frɔgmən] N (irreg) hombre-rana m

frogmarch ['frɔgmɑːtʃ] VT: **to ~ sb in/out** meter/sacar a algn a rastras

frolic ['frɔlɪk] VI juguetear

(KEYWORD)

from [frɔm] PREP **1** (indicating starting place) de, desde; **where do you come from?, where are you from?** ¿de dónde eres?; **where has he come from?** ¿de dónde ha venido?; **from London to Glasgow** de Londres a Glasgow; **to escape from sth/sb** escaparse de algo/algn

2 (indicating origin etc) de; **a letter/telephone call from my sister** una carta/llamada de mi hermana; **tell him from me that ...** dígale de mi parte que ...

3 (indicating time): **from one o'clock to** or **until** or **till nine** de la una a las nueve, desde la una hasta las nueve; **from January (on)** a partir de enero; **(as) from Friday** a partir del viernes

4 (indicating distance) de; **the hotel is 1 km from the beach** el hotel está a 1 km de la playa

5 (indicating price, number etc) de; **prices range from £10 to £50** los precios van desde £10 a or hasta £50; **the interest rate was increased from 9% to 10%** el tipo de interés fue incrementado de un 9% a un 10%

6 (indicating difference) de; **he can't tell red from green** no sabe distinguir el rojo del verde; **to be different from sb/sth** ser diferente a algn/algo

7 (because of, on the basis of): **from what he says** por lo que dice; **weak from hunger** debilitado por el hambre

frond [frɔnd] N fronda

front [frʌnt] N (foremost part) parte f delantera; (of house) fachada; (promenade: also: **sea front**) paseo marítimo; (Mil, Pol, Meteorology) frente m; (fig: appearances) apariencia ▸ ADJ (wheel, leg) delantero; (row, line) primero ▸ VI: **to ~ onto sth** dar a algo; **in ~ (of)** delante (de)

frontage ['frʌntɪdʒ] N (of building) fachada

frontal ['frʌntl] ADJ frontal

front bench N (BRIT Pol); ver nota

El término genérico front bench se usa para referirse a los escaños situados en primera fila a ambos lados del Presidente ("Speaker") de la Cámara de los Comunes ("House of Commons") del Parlamento británico. Dichos escaños son ocupados por los miembros del gobierno a un lado y los del gobierno en la oposición ("shadow cabinet") al otro. Por esta razón a todos ellos se les denomina "frontbenchers".

frontbencher ['frʌnt'bentʃər] N (BRIT) see **front bench**

front desk N (US) recepción f

front door N puerta principal

frontier ['frʌntɪər] N frontera

frontispiece ['frʌntɪspiːs] N frontispicio

front page N primera plana

front room N (BRIT) salón m, sala

front runner N favorito(-a)

front-wheel drive ['frʌntwiːl-] N tracción f delantera

frost [frɔst] N (gen) helada; (also: **hoarfrost**) escarcha ▸ VT (US Culin) escarchar

frostbite ['frɔstbaɪt] N congelación f

frosted ['frɔstɪd] ADJ (glass) esmerilado; (esp US: cake) glaseado

frosting ['frɔstɪŋ] N (esp US: icing) glaseado

frosty ['frɔsti] ADJ (weather) de helada; (surface) cubierto de escarcha; (welcome etc) glacial

froth [frɔθ] N espuma

frothy ['frɔθi] ADJ espumoso

frown [fraun] VI fruncir el ceño ▸ N: **with a ~** frunciendo el entrecejo
▸ **frown on** VT FUS desaprobar

froze [frəuz] PT of **freeze**

frozen ['frəuzn] PP of **freeze** ▸ ADJ (food) congelado; (Comm): **~ assets** activos mpl congelados or bloqueados

FRS N ABBR (BRIT: = Fellow of the Royal Society) miembro de la principal asociación de investigación científica; (US: = Federal Reserve System) banco central de los EE. UU.

frugal ['fruːgəl] ADJ (person) frugal

fruit [fruːt] N pl inv fruta

fruiterer ['fruːtərər] N frutero(-a); **~'s (shop)** frutería

fruit fly N mosca de la fruta

fruitful ['fruːtful] ADJ provechoso

fruition [fruːˈɪʃən] N: **to come to ~** realizarse

fruit juice N jugo or (SP) zumo de fruta

fruitless ['fruːtlɪs] ADJ (fig) infructuoso, inútil

fruit machine N (BRIT) máquina tragaperras

fruit salad N macedonia or (LAM) ensalada de frutas

frump [frʌmp] N espantajo, adefesio

frustrate [frʌsˈtreɪt] VT frustrar

frustrated [frʌsˈtreɪtɪd] ADJ frustrado

frustrating [frʌsˈtreɪtɪŋ] ADJ (job, day) frustrante

frustration [frʌsˈtreɪʃən] N frustración f

fry [fraɪ] (pt, pp **fried** [-d]) VT freír ▸ N: **small ~** gente f menuda

frying pan ['fraɪɪŋ-] N sartén f, sartén m (LAM)

FT N ABBR (BRIT: = Financial Times) periódico financiero; (= the FT index) el índice de valores del Financial Times

ft. ABBR = **foot**; **feet**

FTC N ABBR (US) = **Federal Trade Commission**

FTSE 100 Index N ABBR (= Financial Times Stock Exchange 100 Index) índice bursátil del Financial Times

fuchsia ['fjuːʃə] N fucsia

fuck [fʌk] (inf!) VT joder (SP !), coger (LAM !)
▸ VI joder (SP !), coger (LAM !); **~ off!** ¡vete a tomar por culo! (!)

fuddled ['fʌdld] ADJ (muddled) confuso, aturdido; (inf: tipsy) borracho

fuddy-duddy ['fʌdɪdʌdɪ] (pej) N carcamal m, carroza mf ▸ ADJ chapado a la antigua

fudge [fʌdʒ] N (Culin) caramelo blando ▸ VT (issue, problem) rehuir, esquivar

fuel [fjuəl] N (for heating) combustible m; (coal) carbón m; (wood) leña; (for engine) carburante m ▸ VT (furnace etc) alimentar; (aircraft, ship etc) aprovisionar de combustible

fuel oil N fueloil m

fuel poverty N pobreza energética

fuel pump N (Aut) surtidor m de gasolina

fuel tank N depósito de combustible

fug [fʌg] N aire m viciado

fugitive ['fjuːdʒɪtɪv] N (from prison) fugitivo(-a)

fulfil, (US) **fulfill** [ful'fɪl] VT (function) desempeñar; (condition) cumplir; (wish, desire) realizar

fulfilled [ful'fɪld] ADJ (person) realizado

fulfilment, (US) **fulfillment** [ful'fɪlmənt] N realización f; (of promise) cumplimiento

full [ful] ADJ lleno; (fig) pleno; (complete) completo; (maximum) máximo; (information) detallado; (price) íntegro, sin descuento
▸ ADV: **~ well** perfectamente; **we're ~ up for July** estamos completos para julio; **I'm ~ (up)** estoy lleno; **~ employment** pleno empleo; **~ name** nombre m completo; **a ~ two hours** dos horas enteras; **at ~ speed** a toda velocidad; **in ~** (reproduce, quote) íntegramente; **to write sth in ~** escribir

algo por extenso; **to pay in ~** pagar la deuda entera

fullback ['fulbæk] N (*Football*) defensa m; (*Rugby*) zaguero

full-blooded ['ful'blʌdɪd] ADJ (*vigorous: attack*) vigoroso; (*pure*) puro

full-cream ['ful'kri:m] ADJ: **~ milk** leche f entera

full driving licence N (*Brit Aut*) carnet m de conducir (*definitivo*); *see also* **L-plates**

full-fledged ['fulfledʒd] ADJ (*US*) = **fully-fledged**

full-grown ['ful'grəʊn] ADJ maduro

full-length ['ful'leŋθ] ADJ (*portrait*) de cuerpo entero; (*film*) de largometraje

full moon N luna llena, plenilunio

fullness ['fulnɪs] N plenitud f, amplitud f

full-scale ['fulskeɪl] ADJ (*attack, war, search, retreat*) en gran escala; (*plan, model*) de tamaño natural

full stop N punto

full-time ['fultaɪm] ADJ (*work*) de tiempo completo ▸ ADV: **to work ~** trabajar a tiempo completo

fully ['fulɪ] ADV completamente; (*at least*) al menos

fully-fledged ['fulɪ'fledʒd], (*US*) **full-fledged** ADJ (*teacher, barrister*) diplomado; (*bird*) con todas sus plumas, capaz de volar; (*fig*) de pleno derecho

fully-paid ['fulɪpeɪd] ADJ: **~ share** acción f liberada

fulsome ['fulsəm] ADJ (*pej: praise, gratitude*) excesivo, exagerado; (*manner*) obsequioso

fumble ['fʌmbl] VI: **to ~ with** manejar torpemente, manosear

fume [fju:m] VI estar furioso, echar humo

fumes [fju:mz] NPL humo sg, gases mpl

fumigate ['fju:mɪɡeɪt] VT fumigar

fun [fʌn] N (*amusement*) diversión f; (*joy*) alegría; **to have ~** divertirse; **for ~** por gusto; **to make ~ of** reírse de

function ['fʌŋkʃən] N función f ▸ VI funcionar; **to ~ as** hacer (las veces) de, fungir de (*Lam*)

functional ['fʌŋkʃənl] ADJ funcional

function key N (*Comput*) tecla de función

fund [fʌnd] N fondo; (*reserve*) reserva; **funds** NPL (*money*) fondos mpl

fundamental [fʌndə'mentl] ADJ fundamental; **fundamentals** NPL fundamentos mpl

fundamentalism [fʌndə'mentəlɪzəm] N fundamentalismo, integrismo

fundamentalist [fʌndə'mentəlɪst] N fundamentalista mf, integrista mf

fundamentally [fʌndə'mentəlɪ] ADV fundamentalmente

funding ['fʌndɪŋ] N financiación f

fund-raising ['fʌndreɪzɪŋ] N recaudación f de fondos

funeral ['fju:nərəl] N (*burial*) entierro; (*ceremony*) funerales mpl

funeral director N director(a) m/f de pompas fúnebres

funeral parlour N (*Brit*) funeraria

funeral service N misa de cuerpo presente

funereal [fju:'nɪərɪəl] ADJ fúnebre

funfair ['fʌnfeə^r] N (*Brit*) parque m de atracciones; (*travelling*) feria

fungus ['fʌŋɡəs] (*pl* **fungi** [-ɡaɪ]) N hongo; (*mould*) moho

funicular [fju:'nɪkjulə^r] N (*also:* **funicular railway**) funicular m

funky ['fʌŋkɪ] ADJ (*music*) funky; (*inf: good*) guay

funnel ['fʌnl] N embudo; (*of ship*) chimenea

funnily ['fʌnɪlɪ] ADV de modo divertido, graciosamente; (*oddly*) de una manera rara; **~ enough** aunque parezca extraño

funny ['fʌnɪ] ADJ gracioso, divertido; (*strange*) curioso, raro

funny bone N hueso de la alegría

fun run N maratón m popular

fur [fɜ:^r] N piel f; (*Brit: on tongue etc*) sarro

fur coat N abrigo de pieles

furious ['fjuərɪəs] ADJ furioso; (*effort, argument*) violento; **to be ~ with sb** estar furioso con algn

furiously ['fjuərɪəslɪ] ADV con furia

furl [fɜ:l] VT (*sail*) recoger

furlong ['fɜ:lɔŋ] N *octava parte de una milla*

furlough ['fɜ:ləʊ] N (*US Mil*) permiso

furnace ['fɜ:nɪs] N horno

furnish ['fɜ:nɪʃ] VT amueblar; (*supply*) proporcionar; (*information*) facilitar

furnished ['fɜ:nɪʃt] ADJ: **~ flat** or (*US*) **apartment** piso amueblado

furnishings ['fɜ:nɪʃɪŋz] NPL mobiliario sg

furniture ['fɜ:nɪtʃə^r] N muebles mpl; **piece of ~** mueble m

furniture polish N cera para muebles

furore [fjuə'rɔ:rɪ] N (*protests*) escándalo

furrier ['fʌrɪə^r] N peletero(-a)

furrow ['fʌrəʊ] N surco ▸ VT (*forehead*) arrugar

furry ['fɜ:rɪ] ADJ peludo; (*toy*) de peluche

further ['fɜ:ðə^r] ADJ (*new*) nuevo; (*place*) más lejano ▸ ADV más lejos; (*more*) más; (*moreover*) además ▸ VT hacer avanzar; **how much ~ is it?** ¿a qué distancia queda?; **~ to your letter of ...** (*Comm*) con referencia a su carta de ...; **to ~ one's interests** fomentar sus intereses

further education N educación f postescolar

furthermore [fɜ:ðə'mɔ:^r] ADV además

furthermost ['fɜ:ðəməʊst] ADJ más lejano

furthest ['fɜ:ðɪst] SUPERLATIVE *of* **far**

furtive ['fɜ:tɪv] ADJ furtivo

furtively ['fɜ:tɪvlɪ] ADV furtivamente, a escondidas

569

fury ['fjuərɪ] N furia

fuse, (US) **fuze** [fju:z] N fusible m; (for bomb etc) mecha ▶ VT (metal) fundir; (fig) fusionar ▶ VI fundirse; fusionarse; (BRIT Elec): **to ~ the lights** fundir los plomos; **a ~ has blown** se ha fundido un fusible

fuse box N caja de fusibles

fuselage ['fju:zəlɑ:ʒ] N fuselaje m

fuse wire N hilo fusible

fusillade [fju:zɪ'leɪd] N descarga cerrada; (fig) lluvia

fusion ['fju:ʒən] N fusión f

fuss [fʌs] N (excitement) conmoción f; (complaint) alboroto, protesta; (noise) bulla; (dispute) lío, jaleo ▶ VI preocuparse (por pequeñeces) ▶ VT (person) molestar; **to make a ~** armar jaleo
▶ **fuss over** VT FUS (person) contemplar, mimar

fusspot ['fʌspɔt] N (inf) quisquilloso(-a)

fussy ['fʌsɪ] ADJ (person) quisquilloso; **I'm not ~** (inf) me da igual

fusty ['fʌstɪ] ADJ (pej) rancio; **to smell ~** oler a cerrado

futile ['fju:taɪl] ADJ vano

futility [fju:'tɪlɪtɪ] N inutilidad f

futon ['fu:tɔn] N futón m

future ['fju:tʃəʳ] ADJ (gen) futuro; (coming) venidero ▶ N futuro, porvenir; **futures** NPL (Comm) operaciones fpl a término, futuros mpl; **in ~** de ahora en adelante

futuristic [fju:tʃə'rɪstɪk] ADJ futurista

fuze [fju:z] N, VB (US) = **fuse**

fuzzy ['fʌzɪ] ADJ (Phot) borroso; (hair) muy rizado

fwd. ABBR = **forward**

fwy ABBR (US) = **freeway**

FY ABBR = **fiscal year**

FYI ABBR = **for your information**

Gg

G, g [dʒiː] N (*letter*) G, g f; (*Mus*): **G** sol m; **G for George** G de Gerona

G N ABBR (*BRIT Scol: mark: = good*) N; (*US Cine: = general audience*) todos los públicos

g. ABBR (*= gram(s), gravity*) g

G8 N ABBR (*Pol: = Group of Eight*) G8 m

G20 N ABBR (*Pol: = Group of Twenty*) G20 m

GA ABBR (*US Post*) = **Georgia**

gab [gæb] N: **to have the gift of the ~** (*inf*) tener mucha labia

gabble ['gæbl] VI hablar atropelladamente; (*gossip*) cotorrear

gaberdine [gæbə'diːn] N gabardina

gable ['geɪbl] N aguilón m

Gabon [gə'bɒn] N Gabón m

gad about [gæd-] VI (*inf*) moverse mucho

gadget ['gædʒɪt] N aparato

gadgetry ['gædʒɪtrɪ] N chismes mpl

Gaelic ['geɪlɪk] ADJ, N (*Ling*) gaélico

gaffe [gæf] N plancha, patinazo, metedura de pata

gaffer ['gæfə'] N (*BRIT inf: boss*) jefe m; ((*old*) *man*) vejete m

gag [gæg] N (*on mouth*) mordaza; (*joke*) chiste m ▶ VT (*prisoner etc*) amordazar ▶ VI (*choke*) tener arcadas

gaga ['gɑːgɑː] ADJ: **to go ~** (*senile*) chochear; (*ecstatic*) caérsele a algn la baba

gage [geɪdʒ] N, VT (*US*) = **gauge**

gaiety ['geɪɪtɪ] N alegría

gaily ['geɪlɪ] ADV alegremente

gain [geɪn] N ganancia ▶ VT ganar ▶ VI (*watch*) adelantarse; **to ~ by sth** ganar con algo; **to ~ ground** ganar terreno; **to ~ 3 lbs (in weight)** engordar 3 libras
▶ **gain (up)on** VT FUS alcanzar

gainful ['geɪnful] ADJ (*employment*) remunerado

gainfully ['geɪnfulɪ] ADV: **to be ~ employed** tener un trabajo remunerado

gait [geɪt] N forma de andar, andares mpl

gal., gall. ABBR = **gallon**

gala ['gɑːlə] N gala; **swimming ~** certamen m de natación

Galapagos Islands [gə'læpəgəs-] NPL: **the ~** las Islas Galápagos

galaxy ['gæləksɪ] N galaxia

gale [geɪl] N (*wind*) vendaval m; **~ force 10** vendaval de fuerza 10

gall [gɔːl] N (*Anat*) bilis f, hiel f; (*fig: impudence*) descaro, caradura ▶ VT molestar

gallant ['gælənt] ADJ valeroso; (*towards ladies*) galante

gallantry ['gæləntrɪ] N valentía; (*courtesy*) galantería

gall bladder N vesícula biliar

galleon ['gælɪən] N galeón m

gallery ['gælərɪ] N (*Theat*) galería; (*for spectators*) tribuna; (*also:* **art gallery**: *state-owned*) pinacoteca or museo de arte; (*: private*) galería de arte

galley ['gælɪ] N (*ship's kitchen*) cocina; (*ship*) galera

galley proof N (*Typ*) prueba de galera, galerada

Gallic ['gælɪk] ADJ galo

gallon ['gæln] N galón m (*= 8 pintas; Brit = 4,546 litros; US = 3,785 litros*)

gallop ['gæləp] N galope m ▶ VI galopar; **galloping inflation** inflación f galopante

gallows ['gæləuz] N horca

gallstone ['gɔːlstəun] N cálculo biliar

Gallup poll ['gæləp-] N sondeo de opinión

galore [gə'lɔː'] ADV en cantidad, en abundancia

galvanize ['gælvənaɪz] VT (*metal*) galvanizar; (*fig*): **to ~ sb into action** mover or impulsar a algn a actuar

Gambia ['gæmbɪə] N Gambia

gambit ['gæmbɪt] N (*fig*): **opening ~** táctica inicial

gamble ['gæmbl] N (*risk*) jugada arriesgada; (*bet*) apuesta ▶ VT: **to ~ on** apostar a; (*fig*) contar con, confiar en que ▶ VI jugar; (*take a risk*) jugárselas; (*Comm*) especular; **to ~ on the Stock Exchange** jugar a la bolsa

gambler ['gæmblə'] N jugador(a) m/f

gambling ['gæmblɪŋ] N juego

gambol ['gæmbl] VI brincar, juguetear

game [geɪm] N (gen) juego; (match) partido; (of cards) partida; (Hunting) caza ▶ ADJ valiente; (ready): **to be ~ for anything** estar dispuesto a todo; **games** NPL (Scol) deportes mpl; **big ~** caza mayor

game bird N ave f de caza

gamekeeper ['geɪmkiːpəʳ] N guardabosque mf

gamely ['geɪmlɪ] ADV con decisión

game plan N (for game) plan m de juego; (gen) táctica

gamer ['geɪməʳ] N jugador(a) m/f de videojuegos, videojugador(a) m/f

game reserve N coto de caza

games console [geɪmz-] N consola de juegos

game show N programa m concurso inv, concurso

gamesmanship ['geɪmzmənʃɪp] N (uso de) artimañas fpl para ganar

gaming ['geɪmɪŋ] N (gambling) juego; (with video games) juegos mpl de ordenador or computadora

gammon ['gæmən] N (bacon) tocino ahumado; (ham) jamón m ahumado

gamut ['gæmət] N (Mus) gama; **to run the (whole) ~ of emotions** (fig) recorrer toda la gama de emociones

gander ['gændəʳ] N ganso

gang [gæŋ] N (of criminals etc) banda; (of kids) pandilla; (of colleagues) peña; (of workmen) brigada ▶ VI: **to ~ up on sb** conchabarse contra algn

Ganges ['gændʒiːz] N: **the ~** el Ganges

gangland ['gæŋglænd] ADJ: **~ bosses** cabecillas mafiosos; **~ killings** asesinatos entre bandas

gangling ['gæŋglɪŋ] ADJ larguirucho

gangly ['gæŋglɪ] ADJ desgarbado

gangplank ['gæŋplæŋk] N pasarela, plancha

gangrene ['gæŋgriːn] N gangrena

gangster ['gæŋstəʳ] N gángster m

gang warfare N guerra entre bandas

gangway ['gæŋweɪ] N (BRIT: in theatre, bus etc) pasillo; (on ship) pasarela

gantry ['gæntrɪ] N (for crane, railway signal) pórtico; (for rocket) torre f de lanzamiento

GAO N ABBR (US: = General Accounting Office) tribunal de cuentas

gaol [dʒeɪl] N, VT (BRIT) = **jail**

gap [gæp] N hueco; (in trees, traffic) claro; (in market, records) laguna; (in time) intervalo

gape [geɪp] VI mirar boquiabierto

gaping ['geɪpɪŋ] ADJ (hole) muy abierto

gap year N año sabático (antes de empezar a estudiar en la universidad)

garage ['gærɑːʒ] N garaje m; (for repairs) taller m

garage sale N venta de objetos usados (en el jardín de una casa particular)

garb [gɑːb] N atuendo

garbage ['gɑːbɪdʒ] N (US) basura; (nonsense) bobadas fpl; (fig: film, book etc) basura

garbage can N (US) cubo or balde m (LAM) or bote m (LAM) de la basura

garbage collector N (US) basurero(-a)

garbage disposal unit N triturador m (de basura)

garbage man N (irreg) basurero

garbage truck N (US) camión m de la basura

garbled ['gɑːbld] ADJ (account, explanation) confuso

garden ['gɑːdn] N jardín m; **gardens** NPL (public) parque m, jardines mpl; (private) huertos mpl

garden centre N (BRIT) centro de jardinería

garden city N (BRIT) ciudad f jardín

gardener ['gɑːdnəʳ] N jardinero(-a)

gardening ['gɑːdnɪŋ] N jardinería

garden party N recepción f al aire libre

gargle ['gɑːgl] VI hacer gárgaras, gargarear (LAM)

gargoyle ['gɑːgɔɪl] N gárgola

garish ['gɛərɪʃ] ADJ chillón(-ona)

garland ['gɑːlənd] N guirnalda

garlic ['gɑːlɪk] N ajo

garment ['gɑːmənt] N prenda (de vestir)

garner ['gɑːnəʳ] VT hacer acopio de

garnish ['gɑːnɪʃ] VT adornar; (Culin) aderezar

garret ['gærɪt] N desván m, buhardilla

garrison ['gærɪsn] N guarnición f ▶ VT guarnecer

garrulous ['gærjuləs] ADJ charlatán(-ana)

garter ['gɑːtəʳ] N (US) liga

garter belt N (US) liguero, portaligas m inv

gas [gæs] N gas m; (US: gasoline) gasolina ▶ VT asfixiar con gas; **Calor ~®** (gas m) butano

gas chamber N cámara de gas

Gascony ['gæskənɪ] N Gascuña

gas cooker N (BRIT) cocina de gas

gas cylinder N bombona de gas

gaseous ['gæsɪəs] ADJ gaseoso

gas fire N estufa de gas

gas-fired ['gæsfaɪəd] ADJ de gas

gash [gæʃ] N brecha, raja; (from knife) cuchillada ▶ VT rajar; (with knife) acuchillar

gasket ['gæskɪt] N (Aut) junta

gas mask N careta antigás

gas meter N contador m de gas

gasoline ['gæsəliːn] N (US) gasolina

gasp [gɑːsp] N grito sofocado ▶ VI (pant) jadear

▶ **gasp out** VT (say) decir jadeando

gas pedal N (esp US) acelerador m

gas ring N hornillo de gas

gas station N (US) gasolinera

gas stove N cocina de gas

gassy ['gæsɪ] ADJ con mucho gas

gas tank N (US Aut) depósito (de gasolina)

gas tap N llave f del gas

gastric ['gæstrɪk] ADJ gástrico

gastric band N banda gástrica

gastric ulcer N úlcera gástrica

gastroenteritis ['gæstrəʊɛntə'raɪtɪs] N gastroenteritis f

gasworks ['gæswəːks] NSG, NPL fábrica de gas

gate [geɪt] N (also at airport) puerta; (Rail: at level crossing) barrera; (metal) verja

gâteau ['gætəʊ] (pl **gâteaux** [-z]) N tarta

gatecrash ['geɪtkræʃ] VT colarse en

gatecrasher ['geɪtkræʃəʳ] N intruso(-a)

gated community ['geɪtɪd-] N urbanización f cerrada

gatehouse ['geɪthaʊs] N casa del guarda

gateway ['geɪtweɪ] N puerta

gather ['gæðəʳ] VT (flowers, fruit) coger (SP), recoger (LAM); (assemble) reunir; (pick up) recoger; (Sewing) fruncir; (understand) sacar en consecuencia ▶ VI (assemble) reunirse; (dust) acumularse; (clouds) cerrarse; **to ~ speed** ganar velocidad; **to ~ (from/that)** deducir (por/que); **as far as I can ~** por lo que tengo entendido

gathering ['gæðərɪŋ] N reunión f, asamblea

GATT [gæt] N ABBR (= General Agreement on Tariffs and Trade) GATT m

gauche [gəʊʃ] ADJ torpe

gaudy ['gɔːdɪ] ADJ chillón(-ona)

gauge, (US) gage [geɪdʒ] N calibre m; (Rail) ancho de vía, entrevía; (instrument) indicador m ▶ VT medir; (fig: sb's capabilities, character) juzgar, calibrar; **petrol ~** indicador m (del nivel) de gasolina; **to ~ the right moment** elegir el momento (oportuno)

gaunt [gɔːnt] ADJ descarnado; (fig) adusto

gauntlet ['gɔːntlɪt] N (fig): **to run the ~ of sth** exponerse a algo; **to throw down the ~** arrojar el guante

gauze [gɔːz] N gasa

gave [geɪv] PT of **give**

gawk [gɔːk] VI mirar pasmado

gawky ['gɔːkɪ] ADJ desgarbado

gay [geɪ] ADJ (homosexual) gay; (colour, person) alegre

gaze [geɪz] N mirada fija ▶ VI: **to ~ at sth** mirar algo fijamente

gazelle [gə'zɛl] N gacela

gazette [gə'zɛt] N (newspaper) gaceta; (official publication) boletín m oficial

gazetteer [gæzə'tɪəʳ] N índice geográfico

gazump [gə'zʌmp] VT, VI (BRIT) echarse atrás en la venta ya acordada de una casa por haber una oferta más alta

GB ABBR (= Great Britain) GB

GBH N ABBR (BRIT Law: inf) = **grievous bodily harm**

GC N ABBR (BRIT: = George Cross) distinción honorífica

GCE N ABBR (BRIT: = General Certificate of Education) ≈ certificado de bachillerato

GCHQ N ABBR (BRIT: = Government Communications Headquarters) centro de intercepción de las telecomunicaciones internacionales

GCSE N ABBR (BRIT: = General Certificate of Secondary Education) certificado del último ciclo de la enseñanza secundaria obligatoria

Gdns. ABBR (= gardens) jdns

GDP N ABBR (= gross domestic product) PIB m

GDR N ABBR (= German Democratic Republic) RDA f

gear [gɪəʳ] N equipo; (Tech) engranaje m; (Aut) velocidad f, marcha ▶ VT (fig: adapt): **to ~ sth to** adaptar or ajustar algo a; **top** or (US) **high/low ~** cuarta/primera; **in ~** con la marcha metida; **our service is geared to meet the needs of the disabled** nuestro servicio va enfocado a responder a las necesidades de los minusválidos
▶ **gear up** VI prepararse

gear box N caja de cambios

gear lever, (US) gear shift N palanca de cambio

gear stick N (BRIT) = **gear lever**

gear wheel N rueda dentada

GED N ABBR (US Scol) = **general educational development**

geese [giːs] NPL of **goose**

geezer ['giːzəʳ] N (BRIT inf) tipo, maromo (SP)

Geiger counter ['gaɪgə-] N contador m Geiger

gel [dʒɛl] N gel m

gelatin, gelatine ['dʒɛlətiːn] N gelatina

gelignite ['dʒɛlɪgnaɪt] N gelignita

gem [dʒɛm] N gema, piedra preciosa; (fig) joya

Gemini ['dʒɛmɪnaɪ] N Géminis m

gen [dʒɛn] N (BRIT inf): **to give sb the ~ on sth** poner a algn al tanto de algo

Gen. ABBR (Mil: = General) Gen., Gral

gen. ABBR (= general) grl.; = **generally**

gender ['dʒɛndəʳ] N género

gene [dʒiːn] N gen(e) m

genealogy [dʒiːnɪ'ælədʒɪ] N genealogía

general ['dʒɛnərl] N general m ▶ ADJ general; **in ~** en general; **~ audit** auditoría general; **the ~ public** el gran público

general anaesthetic, (US) general anesthetic N anestesia general

general delivery N (US) lista de correos

general election N elecciones fpl generales

generalization [dʒɛnrəlaɪ'zeɪʃən] N generalización f

generalize ['dʒɛnrəlaɪz] VI generalizar

generally ['dʒɛnrəlɪ] ADV generalmente, en general

573

general manager N director(a) *m/f* general
general practitioner N médico(-a) de
medicina general
general store N tienda *(que vende de todo)*
general strike N huelga general
generate ['dʒɛnəreɪt] VT generar
generation [dʒɛnə'reɪʃən] N generación *f*
generator ['dʒɛnəreɪtə'] N generador *m*
generic [dʒɪ'nɛrɪk] ADJ genérico
generosity [dʒɛnə'rɔsɪtɪ] N generosidad *f*
generous ['dʒɛnərəs] ADJ generoso; *(copious)*
abundante
generously ['dʒɛnərəslɪ] ADV
generosamente; abundantemente
genesis ['dʒɛnɪsɪs] N génesis *f*
genetic [dʒɪ'nɛtɪk] ADJ genético;
~ engineering ingeniería genética;
~ fingerprinting identificación *f* genética
genetically modified organism
[dʒɪ'nɛtɪkəlɪ-] N organismo genéticamente
modificado, organismo transgénico
genetic engineering N ingeniería genética
genetic fingerprinting [-'fɪŋɡəprɪntɪŋ] N
identificación *f* genética
genetics [dʒɪ'nɛtɪks] N genética
Geneva [dʒɪ'niːvə] N Ginebra
genial ['dʒiːnɪəl] ADJ afable
genitals ['dʒɛnɪtlz] NPL (órganos *mpl*)
genitales *mpl*
genitive ['dʒɛnɪtɪv] N genitivo
genius ['dʒiːnɪəs] N genio
Genoa ['dʒɛnəuə] N Génova
genocide ['dʒɛnəusaɪd] N genocidio
genome ['giːnəum] N genoma *m*
gent [dʒɛnt] N ABBR (BRIT *inf*) = **gentleman**
genteel [dʒɛn'tiːl] ADJ fino, distinguido
gentle ['dʒɛntl] ADJ *(sweet)* dulce; *(touch etc)*
ligero, suave
gentleman ['dʒɛntlmən] N *(irreg)* señor *m*;
(well-bred man) caballero; **~'s agreement**
acuerdo entre caballeros
gentlemanly ['dʒɛntlmənlɪ] ADJ caballeroso
gentleness ['dʒɛntlnɪs] N dulzura; *(of touch)*
suavidad *f*
gently ['dʒɛntlɪ] ADV suavemente
gentrification [dʒɛntrɪfɪ'keɪʃən] N
aburguesamiento
gentry ['dʒɛntrɪ] NPL pequeña nobleza *sg*
gents [dʒɛnts] N servicios *mpl* (de caballeros)
genuine ['dʒɛnjuɪn] ADJ auténtico; *(person)*
sincero
genuinely ['dʒɛnjuɪnlɪ] ADV sinceramente
geographer [dʒɪ'ɔɡrəfə'] N geógrafo(-a)
geographic [dʒɪə'ɡræfɪk], **geographical**
[dʒɪə'ɡræfɪkl] ADJ geográfico
geography [dʒɪ'ɔɡrəfɪ] N geografía
geological [dʒɪə'lɔdʒɪkl] ADJ geológico
geologist [dʒɪ'ɔlədʒɪst] N geólogo(-a)
geology [dʒɪ'ɔlədʒɪ] N geología

geometric [dʒɪə'mɛtrɪk], **geometrical**
[dʒɪə'mɛtrɪkl] ADJ geométrico
geometry [dʒɪ'ɔmətrɪ] N geometría
Geordie ['dʒɔːdɪ] N habitante *mf* de Tyneside
Georgia ['dʒɔːdʒə] N Georgia
Georgian ['dʒɔːdʒən] ADJ georgiano ▶ N
georgiano(-a); *(Ling)* georgiano
geranium [dʒɪ'reɪnjəm] N geranio
gerbil ['dʒɜːbɪl] N gerbo
geriatric [dʒɛrɪ'ætrɪk] ADJ, N geriátrico(-a)
m/f
germ [dʒɜːm] N *(microbe)* microbio, bacteria;
(seed) germen *m*
German ['dʒɜːmən] ADJ alemán(-ana) ▶ N
alemán(-ana) *m/f*; *(Ling)* alemán *m*
German Democratic Republic N República
Democrática Alemana
germane [dʒə'meɪn] ADJ: **~ (to)** pertinente
(a)
German measles N rubéola, rubéola
German Shepherd N *(dog)* pastor *m* alemán
Germany ['dʒɜːmənɪ] N Alemania; **East/
West ~** *(History)* Alemania Oriental *or*
Democrática/Occidental *or* Federal
germination [dʒɜːmɪ'neɪʃən] N
germinación *f*
germ warfare N guerra bacteriológica
gesticulate [dʒɛs'tɪkjuleɪt] VI gesticular
gesticulation [dʒɛstɪkju'leɪʃən] N
gesticulación *f*
gesture ['dʒɛstjə'] N gesto; **as a ~ of
friendship** en señal de amistad

(KEYWORD)

get [ɡɛt] *(pt, pp* **got,** US *pp* **gotten)** VI **1** *(become,
be)* ponerse, volverse; **to get old/tired**
envejecer/cansarse; **to get drunk**
emborracharse; **to get dirty** ensuciarse; **to
get ready/washed** prepararse/lavarse; **to
get married** casarse; **when do I get paid?**
¿cuándo me pagan *or* se me paga?; **it's
getting late** se está haciendo tarde
2 *(go)*: **to get to/from** llegar a/de; **to get
home** llegar a casa; **he got under the fence**
pasó por debajo de la barrera
3 *(begin)* empezar a; **to get to know sb** (llegar
a) conocer a algn; **I'm getting to like him**
me está empezando a gustar; **let's get
going** *or* **started** ¡vamos (a empezar)!
4 *(modal aux vb)*: **you've got to do it** tienes
que hacerlo
▶ VT **1**: **to get sth done** *(finish)* hacer algo;
(have done) mandar hacer algo; **to get one's
hair cut** cortarse el pelo; **to get the car
going** *or* **to go** arrancar el coche; **to get sb to
do sth** conseguir *or* hacer que algn haga
algo; **to get sth/sb ready** preparar algo/a
algn
2 *(obtain: money, permission, results)* conseguir;

(find: *job, flat*) encontrar; (fetch: *person, doctor*) buscar; (: *object*) ir a buscar, traer; **to get sth for sb** conseguir algo para algn; **get me Mr Jones, please** (*Tel*) póngame *or* (*LAm*) comuníqueme con el Sr. Jones, por favor; **can I get you a drink?** ¿quieres algo de beber?

3 (receive: *present, letter*) recibir; (acquire: *reputation*) alcanzar; (: *prize*) ganar; **what did you get for your birthday?** ¿qué te regalaron por tu cumpleaños?; **how much did you get for the painting?** ¿cuánto sacaste por el cuadro?

4 (*catch* (SP), agarrar (LAm); (hit: *target etc*) dar en; **to get sb by the arm/throat** coger *or* agarrar a algn por el brazo/cuello; **get him!** ¡cógelo! (SP), ¡atrápalo! (LAm); **the bullet got him in the leg** la bala le dio en la pierna

5 (take, move) llevar; **to get sth to sb** hacer llegar algo a algn; **do you think we'll get it through the door?** ¿crees que lo podremos meter por la puerta?

6 (catch, take: *plane, bus etc*) coger (SP), tomar (LAm); **where do I get the train for Birmingham?** ¿dónde se coge *or* se toma el tren para Birmingham?

7 (understand) entender; (hear) oír; **I've got it!** ¡ya lo tengo!, ¡eureka!; **I don't get your meaning** no te entiendo; **I'm sorry, I didn't get your name** lo siento, no me he enterado de tu nombre

8 (have, possess): **to have got** tener

9 (inf: annoy) molestar; (: *thrill*) chiflar

▸ **get about** VI salir mucho; (news) divulgarse

▸ **get across** VT (message, meaning) lograr comunicar ▸ VI: **to get across to sb** hacer que algn comprenda

▸ **get along** VI (agree) llevarse bien; (depart) marcharse; (manage) = **get by**

▸ **get at** VT FUS (attack) meterse con; (reach) alcanzar; (the truth) descubrir; **what are you getting at?** ¿qué insinúas?

▸ **get away** VI marcharse; (escape) escaparse

▸ **get away with** VT FUS hacer impunemente

▸ **get back** VI (return) volver ▸ VT recobrar

▸ **get back at** VT FUS (inf): **to get back at sb (for sth)** vengarse de algn (por algo)

▸ **get by** VI (pass) (lograr) pasar; (manage) arreglárselas; **I can get by in Dutch** me defiendo en holandés

▸ **get down** VI bajar(se) ▸ VT FUS bajar ▸ VT bajar; (depress) deprimir

▸ **get down to** VT FUS (work) ponerse a

▸ **get in** VI entrar; (train) llegar; (arrive home) volver a casa, regresar; (political party) salir ▸ VT (bring in: *harvest*) recoger; (: *coal, shopping, supplies*) comprar, traer; (insert) meter

▸ **get into** VT FUS entrar en; (vehicle) subir a; **to get into a rage** enfadarse

▸ **get off** VI (from train etc) bajar(se); (depart: *person, car*) marcharse ▸ VT (remove) quitar; (send off) mandar; (have as leave: *day, time*) tener libre ▸ VT FUS (train, bus) bajar(se) de; **to get off to a good start** (fig) empezar muy bien *or* con buen pie

▸ **get on** VI (at exam etc): **how are you getting on?** ¿cómo te va?; **to get on (with)** (agree) llevarse bien (con) ▸ VT FUS subir(se) a

▸ **get on to** VT FUS (deal with) ocuparse de; (inf: contact on phone etc) hablar con

▸ **get out** VI salir; (of vehicle) bajar(se); (news) saberse ▸ VT sacar

▸ **get out of** VT FUS salir de; (duty etc) escaparse de; (gain from: *pleasure, benefit*) sacar de

▸ **get over** VT FUS (illness) recobrarse de

▸ **get round** VT FUS rodear; (fig: *person*) engatusar a ▸ VI: **to get round to doing sth** encontrar tiempo para hacer algo

▸ **get through** VT FUS (finish) acabar ▸ VI (Tel) (lograr) comunicar

▸ **get through to** VT FUS (Tel) comunicar con

▸ **get together** VI reunirse ▸ VT reunir, juntar

▸ **get up** VI (rise) levantarse ▸ VT FUS subir; **to get up enthusiasm for sth** cobrar entusiasmo por algo

▸ **get up to** VT FUS (reach) llegar a; (prank) hacer

getaway ['gɛtəweɪ] N fuga

getaway car N: **the thieves'** ~ el coche en que huyeron los ladrones

get-together ['gɛttəgɛðəʳ] N reunión f; (party) fiesta

get-up ['gɛtʌp] N (BRIT inf: *outfit*) atavío, atuendo

get-well card [gɛt'wɛl-] N tarjeta en la que se desea a un enfermo que se mejore

geyser ['giːzəʳ] N (water heater) calentador m de agua; (Geo) géiser m

Ghana ['gɑːnə] N Ghana

Ghanaian [gɑːˈneɪən] ADJ, N ghanés(-esa) *m/f*

ghastly ['gɑːstlɪ] ADJ horrible; (pale) pálido

gherkin ['gɜːkɪn] N pepinillo

ghetto ['gɛtəu] N gueto

ghetto blaster [-ˈblɑːstəʳ] N radiocas(s)et(t)e m portátil (de gran tamaño)

ghost [gəust] N fantasma m ▸ VT (book) escribir por otro

ghostly ['gəustlɪ] ADJ fantasmal

ghost story N cuento de fantasmas

ghostwriter ['gəustraɪtəʳ] N negro(-a)

ghoul [guːl] N espíritu m necrófago

GHQ N ABBR (Mil: = *general headquarters*) cuartel m general

GI N ABBR (*US inf*: = *government issue*) soldado del ejército norteamericano

giant ['dʒaɪənt] N gigante *mf* ▶ ADJ gigantesco, gigante; ~ **(size) packet** paquete *m* (de tamaño) gigante *or* familiar

giant killer N (*Sport*) matagigantes *m inv*

gibber ['dʒɪbər] VI farfullar

gibberish ['dʒɪbərɪʃ] N galimatías *m*

gibe [dʒaɪb] N pulla

giblets ['dʒɪblɪts] NPL menudillos *mpl*

Gibraltar [dʒɪ'brɔːltər] N Gibraltar *m*

giddiness ['gɪdɪnɪs] N mareo

giddy ['gɪdɪ] ADJ (*dizzy*) mareado; (*height, speed*) vertiginoso; **it makes me ~** me marea; **I feel ~** me siento mareado

gift [gɪft] N (*gen*) regalo; (*Comm: also*: **free gift**) obsequio; (*ability*) don *m*; **to have a ~ for sth** tener dotes para algo

gifted ['gɪftɪd] ADJ dotado

gift shop, (*US*) **gift store** N tienda de regalos

gift token, gift voucher N vale-regalo *m*

gig[1] [gɪg] N (*inf: concert*) actuación *f*

gig[2] [gɪg] N ABBR (*inf:* = *gigabyte*) giga *m*

gigabyte ['gɪgəbaɪt] N gigabyte *m*

gigantic [dʒaɪ'gæntɪk] ADJ gigantesco

giggle ['gɪgl] VI reírse tontamente ▶ N risilla

GIGO ['gaɪgəu] ABBR (*Comput: inf*) = **garbage in, garbage out**

gill [dʒɪl] N (*measure*) 0.25 pintas (Brit = 0,148 litros; US = 0,118 litros.)

gills [gɪlz] NPL (*of fish*) branquias *fpl*, agallas *fpl*

gilt [gɪlt] ADJ, N dorado

gilt-edged ['gɪltedʒd] ADJ (*Comm: stocks, securities*) de máxima garantía

gimlet ['gɪmlɪt] N barrena de mano

gimmick ['gɪmɪk] N reclamo; **sales ~** reclamo promocional

gimmicky ['gɪmɪkɪ] ADJ de reclamo

gin [dʒɪn] N (*liquor*) ginebra

ginger ['dʒɪndʒər] N jengibre *m*

ginger ale N ginger ale *m*

ginger beer N refresco *m* de jengibre

gingerbread ['dʒɪndʒəbred] N pan *m* de jengibre

ginger-haired [dʒɪndʒə'hɛəd] ADJ pelirrojo

gingerly ['dʒɪndʒəlɪ] ADV con pies de plomo

ginseng ['dʒɪnsɛŋ] N ginseng *m*

gipsy ['dʒɪpsɪ] N gitano(-a)

giraffe [dʒɪ'rɑːf] N jirafa

girder ['gəːdər] N viga

girdle ['gəːdl] N (*corset*) faja ▶ VT ceñir

girl [gəːl] N (*small*) niña; (*young woman*) chica, joven *f*, muchacha; **an English ~** una (chica) inglesa

girl band N girl band *m* (*grupo musical de chicas*)

girlfriend ['gəːlfrɛnd] N (*of girl*) amiga; (*of boy*) novia

Girl Guide N exploradora

girlish ['gəːlɪʃ] ADJ de niña

Girl Scout N (*US*) = **Girl Guide**

giro ['dʒaɪrəu] N (*BRIT: bank giro*) giro bancario; (: *post office giro*) giro postal

girth [gəːθ] N circunferencia; (*of saddle*) cincha

gist [dʒɪst] N lo esencial

give [gɪv] (*pt* **gave** [geɪv], *pp* **given** ['gɪvn]) VT dar; (*deliver*) entregar; (*as gift*) regalar ▶ VI (*break*) romperse; (*stretch: fabric*) dar de sí; **to ~ sb sth, ~ sth to sb** dar algo a algn; **how much did you ~ for it?** ¿cuánto pagaste por él?; **12 o'clock, ~ or take a few minutes** más o menos las doce; **~ them my regards** dales recuerdos de mi parte; **I can ~ you 10 minutes** le puedo conceder 10 minutos; **to ~ way** (*BRIT Aut*) ceder el paso; **to ~ way to despair** ceder a la desesperación

▶ **give away** VT (*give free*) regalar; (*betray*) traicionar; (*disclose*) revelar

▶ **give back** VT devolver

▶ **give in** VI ceder ▶ VT entregar

▶ **give off** VT despedir

▶ **give out** VT distribuir ▶ VI (*be exhausted: supplies*) agotarse; (*fail: engine*) averiarse; (: *strength*) fallar

▶ **give up** VI rendirse, darse por vencido ▶ VT renunciar a; **to ~ up smoking** dejar de fumar; **to ~ o.s. up** entregarse

give-and-take ['gɪvənd'teɪk] N (*inf*) toma y daca *m*

giveaway ['gɪvəweɪ] N (*inf*): **her expression was a ~** su expresión la delataba ▶ CPD: **~ prices** precios *mpl* de regalo; **the exam was a ~!** ¡el examen estaba tirado!

given ['gɪvn] PP *of* **give** ▶ ADJ (*fixed: time, amount*) determinado ▶ CONJ: ~ **(that)** ... dado (que) ...; ~ **the circumstances** ... dadas las circunstancias ...

glacial ['gleɪsɪəl] ADJ glacial

glacier ['glæsɪər] N glaciar *m*

glad [glæd] ADJ contento; **to be ~ about sth/ that** alegrarse de algo/de que; **I was ~ of his help** agradecí su ayuda

gladden ['glædn] VT alegrar

glade [gleɪd] N claro

gladiator ['glædɪeɪtər] N gladiador *m*

gladioli [glædɪ'əulaɪ] NPL gladiolos *mpl*

gladly ['glædlɪ] ADV con mucho gusto

glamorous ['glæmərəs] ADJ con glamour, glam(o)uroso

glamour, (*US*) **glamor** ['glæmər] N encanto, atractivo

glance [glɑːns] N ojeada, mirada ▶ VI: **to ~ at** echar una ojeada a

▶ **glance off** VT FUS (*bullet*) rebotar en

glancing ['glɑːnsɪŋ] ADJ (*blow*) oblicuo

gland [glænd] N glándula

glandular ['glændjulər] ADJ: ~ **fever** mononucleosis *f* infecciosa

glare [glεə^r] N deslumbramiento, brillo
▶ VI deslumbrar; **to ~ at** mirar con odio
glaring ['glεərɪŋ] ADJ (*mistake*) manifiesto
glass [glɑ:s] N vidrio, cristal *m*; (*for drinking*)
vaso; (*with stem*) copa; (*also:* **looking glass**)
espejo
glass-blowing ['glɑ:sbləʊɪŋ] N soplado de
vidrio
glass ceiling N (*fig*) techo *or* barrera invisible
(*que impide ascender profesionalmente a las mujeres o*
miembros de minorías étnicas)
glasses ['glɑ:səs] NPL gafas *fpl*, anteojos *mpl*
(*LAm*)
glass fibre, (*US*) **glass fiber** N fibra de vidrio
glasshouse ['glɑ:shaus] N invernadero
glassware ['glɑ:swεə^r] N cristalería
glassy ['glɑ:sɪ] ADJ (*eyes*) vidrioso
Glaswegian [glæs'wi:dʒən] ADJ de Glasgow
▶ N nativo(-a) *or* habitante *m/f* de Glasgow
glaze [gleɪz] VT (*window*) acristalar; (*pottery*)
vidriar; (*Culin*) glasear ▶ N barniz *m*; (*Culin*)
glaseado
glazed [gleɪzd] ADJ (*eye*) vidrioso; (*pottery*)
vidriado
glazier ['gleɪzɪə^r] N vidriero(-a)
gleam [gli:m] N destello ▶ VI relucir;
a ~ of hope un rayo de esperanza
gleaming ['gli:mɪŋ] ADJ reluciente
glean [gli:n] VT (*gather: information*) recoger
glee [gli:] N alegría, regocijo
gleeful ['gli:ful] ADJ alegre
glen [glεn] N cañada
glib [glɪb] ADJ (*person*) de mucha labia;
(*comment*) fácil
glibly ['glɪblɪ] ADV (*explain*) con mucha labia
glide [glaɪd] VI deslizarse; (*Aviat: bird*) planear
glider ['glaɪdə^r] N (*Aviat*) planeador *m*
gliding ['glaɪdɪŋ] N (*Aviat*) vuelo sin motor
glimmer ['glɪmə^r] N luz *f* tenue; (*of hope*) rayo
glimpse [glɪmps] N vislumbre *m* ▶ VT
vislumbrar, entrever; **to catch a ~ of**
vislumbrar
glint [glɪnt] N destello; (*in the eye*) chispa
▶ VI centellear
glisten ['glɪsn] VI relucir, brillar
glitter ['glɪtə^r] VI relucir, brillar ▶ N brillo
glittering ['glɪtərɪŋ] ADJ reluciente, brillante
glitz [glɪts] N (*inf*) vistosidad *f*
gloat [gləut] VI: **to ~ over** regodearse con
global ['gləubl] ADJ (*world-wide*) mundial;
(*comprehensive*) global
globalization ['gləubəlaɪzeɪʃən] N
globalización *f*, mundialización *f*
global warming [-'wɔ:mɪŋ] N
(re)calentamiento global *or* de la tierra
globe [gləub] N globo, esfera; (*model*) bola del
mundo; globo terráqueo
globetrotter ['gləubtrɔtə^r] N trotamundos
m inv

globule ['glɔbju:l] N glóbulo
gloom [glu:m] N penumbra; (*sadness*)
desaliento, melancolía
gloomily ['glu:mɪlɪ] ADV tristemente; de
modo pesimista
gloomy ['glu:mɪ] ADJ (*dark*) oscuro; (*sad*)
triste; (*pessimistic*) pesimista; **to feel ~**
sentirse pesimista
glorification [glɔ:rɪfɪ'keɪʃən] N
glorificación *f*
glorify ['glɔ:rɪfaɪ] VT glorificar
glorious ['glɔ:rɪəs] ADJ glorioso; (*weather,*
sunshine) espléndido
glory ['glɔ:rɪ] N gloria
Glos ABBR (*BRIT*) = **Gloucestershire**
gloss [glɔs] N (*shine*) brillo; (*also:* **gloss paint**)
(pintura) esmalte *m*
▶ **gloss over** VT FUS restar importancia a;
(*omit*) pasar por alto
glossary ['glɔsərɪ] N glosario
glossy ['glɔsɪ] ADJ lustroso; (*hair*) brillante;
(*photograph*) con brillo; (*magazine*) de papel
satinado *or* cuché
glove [glʌv] N guante *m*
glove compartment N (*Aut*) guantera
glow [gləu] VI (*shine*) brillar ▶ N brillo
glower ['glauə^r] VI: **to ~ at** mirar con ceño
glowing ['gləuɪŋ] ADJ (*fire*) vivo; (*complexion*)
encendido; (*fig: report, description*) entusiasta
glow-worm ['gləuwə:m] N luciérnaga
glucose ['glu:kəus] N glucosa
glue [glu:] N pegamento, cemento (*LAm*) ▶ VT
pegar
glue-sniffing ['glu:snɪfɪŋ] N inhalación *f* de
pegamento *or* (*LAm*) cemento
glum [glʌm] ADJ (*mood*) abatido; (*person, tone*)
melancólico
glut [glʌt] N superabundancia
glutinous ['glu:tɪnəs] ADJ glutinoso,
pegajoso
glutton ['glʌtn] N glotón(-ona) *m/f*; **~ for**
punishment masoquista *mf*
gluttony ['glʌtənɪ] N gula, glotonería
glycerin, glycerine ['glɪsəri:n] N glicerina
GM ADJ ABBR (= *genetically-modified*) transgénico
gm ABBR (= *gram*) g
GMAT N ABBR (*US:* = *Graduate Management*
Admissions Test) examen de admisión al segundo
ciclo de la enseñanza superior
GMB N ABBR (*BRIT*) = **General, Municipal, and**
Boilermakers (Union)
GM crop N cultivo transgénico
GM foods N alimentos *mpl* transgénicos
GMO N ABBR (= *genetically modified organism*)
organismo transgénico, OGM *m*
GMT ABBR (= *Greenwich Mean Time*) GMT
gnarled [nɑ:ld] ADJ nudoso
gnash [næʃ] VT: **to ~ one's teeth** hacer
rechinar los dientes

g

gnat [næt] N mosquito
gnaw [nɔː] VT roer
gnome [nəum] N gnomo
GNP N ABBR (= *gross national product*) PNB *m*
GNVQ N ABBR (BRIT: = *general national vocational qualification*) título general de formación profesional
go [gəu] (*pt* **went**, *pp* **gone**) VI ir; (*travel*) viajar; (*depart*) irse, marcharse; (*work*) funcionar, marchar; (*be sold*) venderse; (*time*) pasar; (*become*) ponerse; (*break etc*) estropearse, romperse ▶ N (*pl* **goes**): **to have a go (at)** probar suerte (con); **to be on the go** no parar; **whose go is it?** ¿a quién le toca?; **to go by car/on foot** ir en coche/a pie; **he's going to do it** va a hacerlo; **to go for a walk** ir a dar un paseo; **to go dancing** ir a bailar; **to go looking for sth/sb** ir a buscar algo/a algn; **to make sth go, get sth going** poner algo en marcha; **my voice has gone** he perdido la voz; **the cake is all gone** se acabó la tarta; **the money will go towards our holiday** el dinero es para (ayuda de) nuestras vacaciones; **how did it go?** ¿qué tal salió *or* resultó?, ¿cómo ha ido?; **the meeting went well** la reunión salió bien; **to go and see sb** ir a ver a algn; **to go to sleep** dormirse; **I'll take whatever is going** acepto lo que haya; **... to go** (US: *food*) ... para llevar
▶ **go about** VI (*rumour*) propagarse; (*also*: **go round**: *wander about*) andar (de un sitio para otro) ▶ VT FUS: **how do I go about this?** ¿cómo me las arreglo para hacer esto?; **to go about one's business** ocuparse de sus asuntos
▶ **go after** VT FUS (*pursue*) perseguir; (*job, record etc*) andar tras
▶ **go against** VT FUS (*be unfavourable to: results*) ir en contra de; (*be contrary to: principles*) ser contrario a
▶ **go ahead** VI seguir adelante
▶ **go along** VI ir ▶ VT FUS bordear; **as you go along** sobre la marcha
▶ **go along with** VT FUS (*accompany*) acompañar; (*agree with: idea*) estar de acuerdo con
▶ **go around** VI = **go round**
▶ **go away** VI irse, marcharse
▶ **go back** VI volver
▶ **go back on** VT FUS (*promise*) faltar a
▶ **go by** VI (*years, time*) pasar ▶ VT FUS guiarse por
▶ **go down** VI bajar; (*ship*) hundirse; (*sun*) ponerse ▶ VT FUS bajar por; **that should go down well with him** eso le va a gustar; **he's gone down with flu** ha cogido la gripe
▶ **go for** VT FUS (*fetch*) ir por; (*like*) gustar; (*attack*) atacar
▶ **go in** VI entrar

▶ **go in for** VT FUS (*competition*) presentarse a
▶ **go into** VT FUS entrar en; (*investigate*) investigar; (*embark on*) dedicarse a
▶ **go off** VI irse, marcharse; (*food*) pasarse; (*lights etc*) apagarse; (*explode*) estallar; (*event*) realizarse ▶ VT FUS perder el interés por; **I'm going off him/the idea** ya no me gusta tanto él/la idea; **the party went off well** la fiesta salió bien
▶ **go on** VI (*continue*) seguir, continuar; (*lights*) encenderse; (*happen*) pasar, ocurrir; (*be guided by: evidence etc*) partir de; **to go on doing sth** seguir haciendo algo; **what's going on here?** ¿qué pasa aquí?
▶ **go on at** VT FUS (*nag*) soltarle el rollo a
▶ **go out** VI salir; (*fire, light*) apagarse; (*ebb: tide*) bajar, menguar; **to go out with sb** salir con algn
▶ **go over** VI (*ship*) zozobrar ▶ VT FUS (*check*) revisar; **to go over sth in one's mind** repasar algo mentalmente
▶ **go past** VI, VT FUS pasar
▶ **go round** VI (*circulate: news, rumour*) correr; (*suffice*) alcanzar, bastar; (*revolve*) girar, dar vueltas; (*make a detour*): **to go round (by)** dar la vuelta (por); (*visit*): **to go round (to sb's)** pasar a ver (a algn) ▶ VT FUS: **to go round the back** pasar por detrás
▶ **go through** VT FUS (*town etc*) atravesar; (*search through*) revisar; (*perform: ceremony*) realizar; (*examine: list, book*) repasar
▶ **go through with** VT FUS (*plan, crime*) llevar a cabo; **I couldn't go through with it** no pude llevarlo a cabo
▶ **go together** VI entenderse
▶ **go under** VI (*sink: ship, person*) hundirse; (*fig: business, firm*) quebrar
▶ **go up** VI subir; **to go up in flames** estallar en llamas
▶ **go with** VT FUS (*accompany*) ir con; (*fit, suit*) hacer juego con, acompañar a
▶ **go without** VT FUS pasarse sin
goad [gəud] VT aguijonear
go-ahead [ˈgəuəhɛd] ADJ emprendedor(a)
▶ N luz *f* verde; **to give sth/sb the ~** dar luz verde a algo/algn
goal [gəul] N meta, arco (LAM); (*score*) gol *m*
goal difference N diferencia por goles
goalie [ˈgəulɪ] N (*inf*) = **goalkeeper**
goalkeeper [ˈgəulkiːpəʳ] N portero, guardameta *mf*, arquero (LAM)
goal post N poste *m* (de la portería)
goat [gəut] N cabra *f*
gobble [ˈgɔbl] VT (*also*: **gobble down**, **gobble up**) engullir
go-between [ˈgəubɪtwiːn] N intermediario(-a)
Gobi Desert [ˈgəubɪ-] N Desierto de Gobi
goblet [ˈgɔblɪt] N copa

goblin ['gɔblɪn] N duende m
go-cart ['gəʊkɑːt] N = **go-kart**
god [gɔd] N dios m; **G~** Dios m
god-awful [gɔd'ɔːfəl] ADJ (inf) de puta pena
godchild ['gɔdtʃaɪld] N (irreg) ahijado(-a)
goddamn ['gɔddæm] ADJ (inf: also:
goddamned) maldito, puñetero ▶ EXCL: **~!**
¡cagüen diez!
goddaughter ['gɔddɔːtəʳ] N ahijada
goddess ['gɔdɪs] N diosa
godfather ['gɔdfɑːðəʳ] N padrino
god-fearing ['gɔdfɪərɪŋ] ADJ temeroso de
Dios
god-forsaken ['gɔdfəseɪkən] ADJ dejado de la
mano de Dios
godmother ['gɔdmʌðəʳ] N madrina
godparents ['gɔdpɛərənts] NPL: **the ~** los
padrinos
godsend ['gɔdsɛnd] N: **to be a ~** venir como
llovido del cielo
godson ['gɔdsʌn] N ahijado
goes [gəʊz] VB see **go**
gofer ['gəʊfəʳ] N (inf) chico(-a) para todo
go-getter ['gəʊgɛtəʳ] N ambicioso(-a)
goggle ['gɔgl] VI: **to ~ (at)** mirar con ojos
desorbitados
goggles ['gɔglz] NPL (Aut) gafas fpl, anteojos
mpl (LAm); (diver's) gafas fpl submarinas
going ['gəʊɪŋ] N (conditions) cosas fpl ▶ ADJ:
the ~ rate la tarifa corriente or en vigor;
it was slow ~ las cosas iban lentas
going-over [gəʊɪŋ'əʊvəʳ] N (inf) revisión f;
(beating) paliza
goings-on ['gəʊɪŋz'ɔn] NPL (inf) tejemanejes
mpl
go-kart ['gəʊkɑːt] N kart m
gold [gəʊld] N oro ▶ ADJ (reserves) de oro
golden ['gəʊldn] ADJ (made of gold) de oro;
(colour) dorado
Golden Age N Siglo de Oro
golden handshake N cuantiosa gratificación
por los servicios prestados
golden rule N regla de oro
goldfish ['gəʊldfɪʃ] N pez m de colores
gold leaf N pan m de oro
gold medal N (Sport) medalla de oro
goldmine ['gəʊldmaɪn] N mina de oro
gold-plated ['gəʊld'pleɪtɪd] ADJ chapado en
oro
goldsmith ['gəʊldsmɪθ] N orfebre mf
gold standard N patrón m oro
golf [gɔlf] N golf m
golf ball N (for game) pelota de golf; (on
typewriter) esfera impresora
golf club N club m de golf; (stick) palo (de golf)
golf course N campo de golf
golfer ['gɔlfəʳ] N jugador(a) m/f de golf,
golfista mf
golfing ['gɔlfɪŋ] N: **to go ~** jugar al golf

gondola ['gɔndələ] N góndola
gondolier [gɔndə'lɪəʳ] N gondolero
gone [gɔn] PP of **go**
goner ['gɔnəʳ] N (inf): **to be a ~** estar en las
últimas
gong [gɔŋ] N gong m
gonorrhea [gɔnə'rɪə] N gonorrea
good [gʊd] ADJ bueno; (before m sg n) buen;
(well-behaved) educado ▶ N bien m; **~!** ¡qué
bien!; **he's ~ at it** se le da bien; **to be ~ for**
servir para; **it's ~ for you** te hace bien;
would you be ~ enough to ...? ¿podría
hacerme el favor de ...?, ¿sería tan amable de
...?; **that's very ~ of you** es usted muy
amable; **to feel ~** sentirse bien; **it's ~ to see
you** me alegro de verte; **a ~ deal (of)** mucho;
a ~ many muchos; **to make ~** reparar; **it's
no ~ complaining** no sirve de nada quejarse;
is this any ~? (will it do?) ¿sirve esto?; (what's it
like?) ¿qué tal es esto?; **it's a ~ thing you
were there** menos mal que estabas allí;
for ~ (for ever) para siempre, definitivamente;
~ morning/afternoon ¡buenos días/buenas
tardes!; **~ evening!** ¡buenas noches!;
~ night! ¡buenas noches!; **he's up to no ~**
está tramando algo; **for the common ~** para
el bien común; see also **goods**
goodbye [gʊd'baɪ] EXCL ¡adiós!; **to say ~ (to)**
(person) despedirse (de)
good faith N buena fe f
good-for-nothing ['gʊdfənʌθɪŋ] N inútil mf
Good Friday N Viernes m Santo
good-humoured ['gʊd'hjuːməd] ADJ (person)
afable, de buen humor; (remark, joke) bien
intencionado
good-looking ['gʊd'lʊkɪŋ] ADJ guapo
good-natured ['gʊd'neɪtʃəd] ADJ (person) de
buen carácter; (discussion) cordial
goodness ['gʊdnɪs] N (of person) bondad f; **for
~ sake!** ¡por Dios!; **~ gracious!** ¡madre mía!
goods [gʊdz] NPL bienes mpl; (Comm etc)
géneros mpl, mercancías fpl, artículos mpl;
all his ~ and chattels todos sus bienes
goods train N (BRIT) tren m de mercancías
goodwill [gʊd'wɪl] N buena voluntad f;
(Comm) fondo de comercio; (customer
connections) clientela
goody-goody ['gʊdɪgʊdɪ] N (pej)
santurrón(-ona) m/f
gooey ['guːɪ] ADJ (inf) pegajoso; (cake,
behaviour) empalagoso
Google® ['guːgl] N Google m® ▶ VT: **to ~**
buscar en Google®
goose [guːs] N (pl **geese** [giːs]) N ganso, oca
gooseberry ['gʊzbərɪ] N grosella espinosa or
silvestre; **to play ~** hacer de carabina
gooseflesh ['guːsfleʃ] N, **goosepimples**
['guːspɪmplz] NPL carne f de gallina
goose step N (Mil) paso de la oca

GOP N ABBR (*US Pol: inf:* = *Grand Old Party*) Partido Republicano

gopher ['gəufə^r] N = **gofer**

gore [gɔː^r] VT dar una cornada a, cornear ▸ N sangre f

gorge [gɔːdʒ] N garganta ▸ VR: **to ~ o.s. (on)** atracarse (de)

gorgeous ['gɔːdʒəs] ADJ precioso; (*weather*) estupendo; (*person*) guapísimo

gorilla [gə'rɪlə] N gorila m

gormless ['gɔːmlɪs] ADJ (*inf*) ceporro, zoquete

gorse [gɔːs] N tojo

gory ['gɔːrɪ] ADJ sangriento

gosh [gɔʃ] (*inf*) EXCL ¡cielos!

go-slow ['gəu'sləu] N (*BRIT*) huelga de celo

gospel ['gɔspl] N evangelio

gossamer ['gɔsəmə^r] N gasa

gossip ['gɔsɪp] N cotilleo; (*person*) cotilla mf ▸ VI cotillear, comadrear (*LAM*); **a piece of ~** un cotilleo

gossip column N ecos mpl de sociedad

got [gɔt] PT, PP *of* **get**

Gothic ['gɔθɪk] ADJ gótico

gotten ['gɔtn] (*US*) PP *of* **get**

gouge [gaudʒ] VT (*also:* **gouge out**: *hole etc*) excavar; (*initials*) grabar; **to ~ sb's eyes out** sacar los ojos a algn

goulash ['guːlæʃ] N g(o)ulash m

gourd [guəd] N calabaza

gourmet ['guəmeɪ] N gastrónomo(-a) m/f

gout [gaut] N gota

govern ['gʌvən] VT (*gen*) gobernar; (*event, conduct*) regir

governess ['gʌvənɪs] N institutriz f

governing ['gʌvənɪŋ] ADJ (*Pol*) de gobierno, gubernamental; **~ body** organismo de gobierno

government ['gʌvnmənt] N gobierno; **local ~** administración f municipal

governmental [gʌvn'mentl] ADJ gubernamental

government stock N papel m del Estado

governor ['gʌvənə^r] N gobernador(a) m/f; (*of school etc*) miembro del consejo; (*of jail*) director(a) m/f

Govt ABBR (= *Government*) gobno.

gown [gaun] N vestido; (*of teacher, judge*) toga

GP N ABBR (*Med*) = **general practitioner**

GPMU N ABBR (*BRIT*: = *Graphical, Paper and Media Union*) *sindicato de trabajadores del sector editorial*

GPO N ABBR (*BRIT*: *old*) = **General Post Office**; (*US*) = **Government Printing Office**

GPS N ABBR (= *global positioning system*) GPS m

gr. ABBR (*Comm*: = *gross*) bto.

grab [græb] VT agarrar, coger (*SP*); **to ~ at** intentar agarrar

grace [greɪs] N (*Rel*) gracia; (*gracefulness*) elegancia, gracia; (*graciousness*) cortesía, gracia ▸ VT (*favour*) honrar; (*adorn*) adornar;

5 days' ~ un plazo de 5 días; **to say** ~ bendecir la mesa; **his sense of humour is his saving** ~ lo que le salva es su sentido del humor

graceful ['greɪsful] ADJ grácil, ágil; (*style, shape*) elegante, gracioso

gracious ['greɪʃəs] ADJ amable ▸ EXCL: **good ~!** ¡Dios mío!

grade [greɪd] N (*quality*) clase f, calidad f; (*in hierarchy*) grado; (*Scol: mark*) nota; (*US: Scol*) curso; (*: gradient*) pendiente f, cuesta ▸ VT clasificar; **to make the ~** (*fig*) dar el nivel; *see also* **high school**

grade crossing N (*US*) paso a nivel

grade school N (*US*) escuela primaria; *see also* **elementary school**

gradient ['greɪdɪənt] N pendiente f

gradual ['grædjuəl] ADJ gradual

gradually ['grædjuəlɪ] ADV gradualmente

graduate N ['grædjuɪt] licenciado(-a), graduado(-a), egresado(-a) (*LAM*); (*US Scol*) bachiller mf ▸ VI ['grædjueɪt] licenciarse, graduarse, recibirse (*LAM*); (*US*) obtener el título de bachillerato

graduated pension ['grædjueɪtɪd-] N pensión f escalonada

graduation [grædju'eɪʃən] N graduación f; (*US Scol*) entrega de los títulos de bachillerato

graffiti [grə'fiːtɪ] NPL pintadas fpl

graft [grɑːft] N (*Agr, Med*) injerto; (*bribery*) corrupción f ▸ VT injertar; **hard ~** (*inf*) trabajo duro

grain [greɪn] N (*single particle*) grano; (*no pl: cereals*) cereales mpl; (*US: corn*) trigo; (*in wood*) veta

gram [græm] N gramo

grammar ['græmə^r] N gramática

grammar school N (*BRIT*) ≈ instituto (de segunda enseñanza); (*US*) escuela primaria; *see also* **comprehensive (school)**

grammatical [grə'mætɪkl] ADJ gramatical

gramme [græm] N = **gram**

gramophone ['græməfəun] N (*BRIT*) gramófono

gran [græn] (*inf*) N (*BRIT*) abuelita

granary ['grænərɪ] N granero

grand [grænd] ADJ magnífico, imponente; (*wonderful*) estupendo; (*gesture etc*) grandioso ▸ N (*US inf*) mil dólares mpl

grandad ['grændæd] (*inf*) N = **granddad**

grandchild ['græntʃaɪld] (*pl* **grandchildren**) N (*irreg*) nieto(-a)

granddad ['grændæd] N yayo, abuelito

granddaughter ['grændɔːtə^r] N nieta

grandeur ['grændjə^r] N grandiosidad f

grandfather ['grænfɑːðə^r] N abuelo

grandiose ['grændɪəuz] ADJ grandioso; (*pej*) pomposo

grand jury N (*US*) jurado de acusación

grandma ['grænmɑː] N yaya, abuelita

grandmother ['grænmʌðəʳ] N abuela
grandpa ['grænpɑ:] N = **granddad**
grandparents ['grændpɛərənts] NPL
abuelos *mpl*
grand piano N piano de cola
Grand Prix ['grɑ:'pri:] N (*Aut*) gran premio,
Grand Prix *m*
grandson ['grænsʌn] N nieto
grandstand ['grændstænd] N (*Sport*) tribuna
grand total N suma total, total *m*
granite ['grænɪt] N granito
granny ['grænɪ] N abuelita, yaya
grant [grɑ:nt] VT (*concede*) conceder; (*admit*):
to ~ (that) reconocer (que) ▶ N (*Scol*) beca; **to
take sth for granted** dar algo por sentado
granulated sugar ['grænjuleɪtɪd-] N (*Brit*)
azúcar *m* granulado
granule ['grænju:l] N gránulo
grape [greɪp] N uva; **sour grapes** (*fig*)
envidia *sg*; **a bunch of grapes** un racimo de
uvas
grapefruit ['greɪpfru:t] N pomelo, toronja
(*Lam*)
grape juice N jugo *or* (*Sp*) zumo de uva
grapevine ['greɪpvaɪn] N vid *f*, parra; **I heard
it on the ~** (*fig*) me enteré, me lo contaron
graph [grɑ:f] N gráfica
graphic ['græfɪk] ADJ gráfico
graphic designer N diseñador(a) *m/f*
gráfico(-a)
graphic equalizer N ecualizador *m* gráfico
graphics ['græfɪks] N (*art, process*) artes *fpl*
gráficas ▶ NPL (*drawings: Comput*) gráficos *mpl*
graphite ['græfaɪt] N grafito
graph paper N papel *m* cuadriculado
grapple ['græpl] VI (*also*: **to grapple with a
problem**) enfrentarse a un problema
grappling iron ['græplɪŋ-] N (*Naut*) rezón *m*
grasp [grɑ:sp] VT agarrar, asir; (*understand*)
comprender ▶ N (*grip*) asimiento; (*reach*)
alcance *m*; (*understanding*) comprensión *f*;
to have a good ~ of (*subject*) dominar
▶ **grasp at** VT FUS (*rope etc*) tratar de agarrar;
(*fig: opportunity*) aprovechar
grasping ['grɑ:spɪŋ] ADJ avaro
grass [grɑ:s] N hierba; (*lawn*) césped *m*;
(*pasture*) pasto; (*inf: informer*) soplón(-ona) *m/f*
grasshopper ['grɑ:shɔpəʳ] N saltamontes
m inv
grassland ['grɑ:slænd] N pradera, pampa
(*Lam*)
grass roots ADJ de base ▶ NPL (*Pol*) bases *fpl*
grass snake N culebra
grassy ['grɑ:sɪ] ADJ cubierto de hierba
grate [greɪt] N parrilla ▶ VI chirriar, rechinar
▶ VT (*Culin*) rallar
grateful ['greɪtful] ADJ agradecido
gratefully ['greɪtfəlɪ] ADV con
agradecimiento

grater ['greɪtəʳ] N rallador *m*
gratification [grætɪfɪ'keɪʃən] N satisfacción *f*
gratify ['grætɪfaɪ] VT complacer; (*whim*)
satisfacer
gratifying ['grætɪfaɪɪŋ] ADJ gratificante
grating ['greɪtɪŋ] N (*iron bars*) rejilla ▶ ADJ
(*noise*) chirriante
gratitude ['grætɪtju:d] N agradecimiento
gratuitous [grə'tju:ɪtəs] ADJ gratuito
gratuity [grə'tju:ɪtɪ] N gratificación *f*
grave [greɪv] N tumba ▶ ADJ serio, grave
gravedigger ['greɪvdɪgəʳ] N sepulturero(-a)
gravel ['grævl] N grava
gravely ['greɪvlɪ] ADV seriamente; **~ ill** muy
grave
gravestone ['greɪvstəun] N lápida
graveyard ['greɪvjɑ:d] N cementerio,
camposanto
gravitate ['grævɪteɪt] VI gravitar
gravitation [grævɪ'teɪʃən] N gravitación *f*
gravity ['grævɪtɪ] N gravedad *f*; (*seriousness*)
seriedad *f*
gravy ['greɪvɪ] N salsa de carne
gravy boat N salsera
gravy train N (*esp US inf*): **to get on the ~**
coger un chollo
gray [greɪ] ADJ (*US*) = **grey**
graze [greɪz] VI pacer ▶ VT (*touch lightly, scrape*)
rozar ▶ N (*Med*) rozadura
grazing ['greɪzɪŋ] N (*for livestock*) pastoreo
grease [gri:s] N (*fat*) grasa; (*lubricant*)
lubricante *m* ▶ VT engrasar; **to ~ the skids**
(*US fig*) engrasar el mecanismo
grease gun N pistola engrasadora
greasepaint ['gri:speɪnt] N maquillaje *m*
greaseproof ['gri:spru:f] ADJ a prueba de
grasa; (*Brit: paper*) de grasa
greasy ['gri:sɪ] ADJ (*hands, clothes*) grasiento;
(*road, surface*) resbaladizo
great [greɪt] ADJ grande; (*before n sing*) gran;
(*inf*) estupendo, macanudo (*Lam*), regio (*Lam*);
(*pain, heat*) intenso; **we had a ~ time** nos lo
pasamos muy bien; **they're ~ friends** son
íntimos or muy amigos; **the ~ thing is that
…** lo bueno es que …; **it was ~!** ¡fue
estupendo!
Great Barrier Reef N Gran Barrera de Coral
Great Britain N Gran Bretaña
greater ['greɪtəʳ] ADJ mayor; **G~ London** el
área metropolitana de Londres
greatest ['greɪtɪst] ADJ (el/la) mayor
great-grandchild [greɪt'grændtʃaɪld] (*pl*
-children [-'tʃɪldrən]) N (*irreg*) bisnieto(-a)
great-grandfather [greɪt'grændfɑ:ðəʳ] N
bisabuelo
great-grandmother [greɪt'grændmʌðəʳ] N
bisabuela
Great Lakes NPL: **the ~** los Grandes Lagos
greatly ['greɪtlɪ] ADV muy; (*with verb*) mucho

g

greatness ['greɪtnɪs] N grandeza
Greece [gri:s] N Grecia
greed [gri:d] N (also: **greediness**) codicia; (for food) gula; (for power etc) avidez f
greedily ['gri:dɪlɪ] ADV con avidez
greedy ['gri:dɪ] ADJ codicioso; (for food) glotón(-ona)
Greek [gri:k] ADJ griego ▶ N griego(-a); (Ling) griego; **ancient/modern** ~ griego antiguo/moderno
green [gri:n] ADJ verde; (inexperienced) novato ▶ N verde m; (stretch of grass) césped m; (of golf course) campo, green m; **the G~ party** (Pol) el partido verde; **greens** NPL verduras fpl; **to have ~ fingers** (fig) tener buena mano para las plantas
green belt N cinturón m verde
green card N (Aut) carta verde; (US: work permit) permiso de trabajo para los extranjeros en EE. UU.
greenery ['gri:nərɪ] N vegetación f
greenfly ['gri:nflaɪ] N pulgón m
greengage ['gri:ngeɪdʒ] N (ciruela) claudia
greengrocer ['gri:ngrəusəʳ] N (BRIT) frutero(-a), verdulero(-a)
greenhouse ['gri:nhaus] N invernadero
greenhouse effect N efecto invernadero
greenhouse gas N gas m que produce el efecto invernadero
greenish ['gri:nɪʃ] ADJ verdoso
Greenland ['gri:nlənd] N Groenlandia
Greenlander ['gri:nləndəʳ] N groenlandés(-esa) m/f
green light N luz f verde
green pepper N pimiento verde
green salad N ensalada f (de lechuga, pepino, pimiento verde etc)
green tax N impuesto ambiental
greet [gri:t] VT saludar; (news) recibir
greeting ['gri:tɪŋ] N (gen) saludo; (welcome) bienvenida; **greetings** saludos mpl; **season's greetings** Felices Pascuas
greetings card N tarjeta de felicitación
gregarious [grə'gɛərɪəs] ADJ gregario
grenade [grə'neɪd] N (also: **hand grenade**) granada
grew [gru:] PT of **grow**
grey [greɪ] ADJ gris; **to go ~** salirle canas
grey-haired [greɪ'hɛəd] ADJ canoso
greyhound ['greɪhaund] N galgo
grey vote N voto de la tercera edad
grid [grɪd] N rejilla; (Elec) red f; **off-~** sin conexión a la red
griddle ['grɪdl] N (esp US) plancha
gridiron ['grɪdaɪən] N (Culin) parrilla
gridlock ['grɪdlɔk] N (esp US) retención f
grief [gri:f] N dolor m, pena; **to come to ~** (plan) fracasar, ir al traste; (person) acabar mal, desgraciarse

grievance ['gri:vəns] N (cause for complaint) motivo de queja, agravio
grieve [gri:v] VI afligirse, acongojarse ▶ VT afligir, apenar; **to ~ for** llorar por; **to ~ for sb** (dead person) llorar la pérdida de algn
grievous ['gri:vəs] ADJ grave; (loss) cruel; **~ bodily harm** (Law) daños mpl corporales graves
grill [grɪl] N (on cooker) parrilla ▶ VT (BRIT) asar a la parrilla; (question) interrogar; **grilled meat** (BRIT) carne f (asada) a la parrilla or plancha
grille [grɪl] N rejilla
grim [grɪm] ADJ (place) lúgubre; (person) adusto
grimace [grɪ'meɪs] N mueca ▶ VI hacer muecas
grime [graɪm] N mugre f
grimly ['grɪmlɪ] ADV (say) sombríamente
grimy ['graɪmɪ] ADJ mugriento
grin [grɪn] N sonrisa abierta ▶ VI: **to ~ (at)** sonreír abiertamente (a)
grind [graɪnd] (pt, pp **ground**) VT (coffee, pepper etc) moler; (US: meat) picar; (make sharp) afilar; (polish: gem, lens) esmerilar ▶ VI (car gears) rechinar ▶ N: **the daily ~** (inf) la rutina diaria; **to ~ one's teeth** hacer rechinar los dientes; **to ~ to a halt** (vehicle) pararse con gran estruendo de frenos; (fig: talks, scheme) interrumpirse; (work, production) paralizarse
grinder ['graɪndəʳ] N (machine: for coffee) molinillo
grindstone ['graɪndstəun] N: **to keep one's nose to the ~** trabajar sin descanso
grip [grɪp] N (hold) asimiento; (of hands) apretón m; (handle) asidero; (of racquet etc) mango; (understanding) comprensión f ▶ VT agarrar; **to get to grips with** enfrentarse con; **to lose one's ~** (fig) perder el control; **he lost his ~ of the situation** la situación se le fue de las manos
gripe [graɪp] N (inf: complaint) queja ▶ VI (inf: complain): **to ~ (about)** quejarse (de); **gripes** NPL retortijones mpl
gripping ['grɪpɪŋ] ADJ absorbente
grisly ['grɪzlɪ] ADJ horripilante, horrible
gristle ['grɪsl] N cartílago
grit [grɪt] N gravilla; (courage) valor m ▶ VT (road) poner gravilla en; **I've got a piece of ~ in my eye** tengo una arenilla en el ojo; **to ~ one's teeth** apretar los dientes
grits [grɪts] NPL (US) maíz msg a medio moler
grizzle ['grɪzl] VI (cry) lloriquear
grizzly ['grɪzlɪ] N (also: **grizzly bear**) oso pardo
groan [grəun] N gemido, quejido ▶ VI gemir, quejarse
grocer ['grəusəʳ] N tendero (de ultramarinos); **~'s (shop)** n tienda de ultramarinos or (LAm) de abarrotes

groceries ['grəʊsərɪz] NPL comestibles *mpl*
grocery ['grəʊsərɪ] N (*shop*) tienda de ultramarinos
grog [grɔg] N (BRIT) grog *m*
groggy ['grɔgɪ] ADJ atontado
groin [grɔɪn] N ingle *f*
groom [gru:m] N mozo(-a) de cuadra; (*also*: **bridegroom**) novio ▶ VT (*horse*) almohazar; (*fig*): **to ~ sb for** preparar a algn para; **well-groomed** acicalado
groove [gru:v] N ranura; (*of record*) surco
grope [grəʊp] VI ir a tientas; **to ~ for** buscar a tientas
gross [grəʊs] ADJ (*neglect, injustice*) grave; (*vulgar: behaviour*) grosero; (: *appearance*) de mal gusto; (*Comm*) bruto ▶ VT (*Comm*) recaudar en bruto
gross domestic product N producto interior bruto
gross income N ingresos *mpl* brutos
grossly ['grəʊslɪ] ADV (*greatly*) enormemente
gross national product N producto nacional bruto
gross profit N beneficios *mpl* brutos
gross sales NPL ventas *fpl* brutas
grotesque [grə'tɛsk] ADJ grotesco
grotto ['grɔtəʊ] N gruta
grotty ['grɔtɪ] ADJ asqueroso
grouch [graʊtʃ] VI (*inf*) refunfuñar ▶ N (*inf: person*) refunfuñón(-ona) *m/f*
ground [graʊnd] PT, PP *of* **grind** ▶ N suelo, tierra; (*Sport*) campo, terreno; (*reason: gen pl*) motivo, razón *f*; (*US: also*: **ground wire**) tierra ▶ VT (*plane*) mantener en tierra; (*US Elec*) conectar con tierra ▶ VI (*ship*) varar, encallar ▶ ADJ (*coffee etc*) molido; **grounds** NPL (*of coffee etc*) poso *sg*; (*gardens etc*) jardines *mpl*, parque *m*; **on the ~** en el suelo; **common ~** terreno común; **to gain/lose ~** ganar/perder terreno; **to the ~** al suelo; **below ~** bajo tierra; **he covered a lot of ~ in his lecture** abarcó mucho en la clase
ground cloth N (*US*) = **groundsheet**
ground control N control *m* desde tierra
ground floor N (BRIT) planta baja
grounding ['graʊndɪŋ] N (*in education*) conocimientos *mpl* básicos
groundkeeper ['graʊndki:pəʳ] N = **groundsman**
groundless ['graʊndlɪs] ADJ infundado, sin fundamento
groundnut ['graʊndnʌt] N cacahuete *m*
ground rent N alquiler *m* del terreno
ground rules NPL normas básicas
groundsheet ['graʊndʃi:t] (BRIT) N tela impermeable
groundsman ['graʊndzmən] (*irreg*), (*US*)
groundskeeper ['graʊndzki:pəʳ] N (*Sport*) encargado de pista de deportes

ground staff N personal *m* de tierra
ground swell N mar *m* or *f* de fondo; (*fig*) ola
ground-to-air ['graʊntə'ɛəʳ] ADJ tierra-aire
ground-to-ground ['graʊntə'graʊnd] ADJ tierra-tierra
groundwork ['graʊndwə:k] N trabajo preliminar
Ground Zero N zona cero
group [gru:p] N grupo; (*Mus: pop group*) conjunto, grupo ▶ VT (*also*: **group together**) agrupar ▶ VI agruparse
groupie ['gru:pɪ] N groupie *f*
group therapy N terapia de grupo
grouse [graʊs] N *pl inv* (*bird*) urogallo ▶ VI (*complain*) quejarse
grove [grəʊv] N arboleda
grovel ['grɔvl] VI (*fig*) arrastrarse
grow [grəʊ] (*pt* **grew** [gru:], *pp* **grown** [grəʊn]) VI crecer; (*increase*) aumentar; (*expand*) desarrollarse; (*become*) volverse ▶ VT cultivar; (*hair, beard*) dejar crecer; **to ~ rich/weak** enriquecerse/debilitarse; **to ~ tired of waiting** cansarse de esperar
▶ **grow apart** VI (*fig*) alejarse uno del otro
▶ **grow away from** VT FUS (*fig*) alejarse de
▶ **grow on** VT FUS: **that painting is growing on me** ese cuadro me gusta cada vez más
▶ **grow out of** VT FUS (*habit*) perder; (*clothes*): **I've grown out of this shirt** esta camisa se me ha quedado pequeña
▶ **grow up** VI crecer, hacerse hombre/mujer
grower ['grəʊəʳ] N (*Agr*) cultivador(a) *m/f*, productor(a) *m/f*
growing ['grəʊɪŋ] ADJ creciente; **~ pains** (*also fig*) problemas *mpl* de crecimiento
growl [graʊl] VI gruñir
grown [grəʊn] PP *of* **grow**
grown-up [grəʊn'ʌp] N adulto(-a), mayor *mf*
growth [grəʊθ] N crecimiento, desarrollo; (*what has grown*) brote *m*; (*Med*) tumor *m*
growth rate N tasa de crecimiento
grub [grʌb] N gusano; (*inf: food*) comida
grubby ['grʌbɪ] ADJ sucio, mugriento, mugroso (LAM)
grudge [grʌdʒ] N rencor ▶ VT: **to ~ sb sth** dar algo a algn de mala gana; **to bear sb a ~** guardar rencor a algn; **he grudges (giving) the money** da el dinero de mala gana
grudgingly ['grʌdʒɪŋlɪ] ADV de mala gana
gruelling, (*US*) **grueling** ['gruəlɪŋ] ADJ agotador
gruesome ['gru:səm] ADJ horrible
gruff [grʌf] ADJ (*voice*) ronco; (*manner*) brusco
grumble ['grʌmbl] VI refunfuñar, quejarse
grumpy ['grʌmpɪ] ADJ gruñón(-ona)
grunge [grʌndʒ] N (*Mus: fashion*) grunge *m*
grunt [grʌnt] VI gruñir ▶ N gruñido
G-string ['dʒi:strɪŋ] N tanga *m*

g

GSUSA N ABBR = **Girl Scouts of the United States of America**

GT ABBR (Aut: = gran turismo) GT

GU ABBR (US Post) = **Guam**

guarantee [gærən'tiː] N garantía ▸ VT garantizar; **he can't ~ (that) he'll come** no está seguro de poder venir

guarantor [gærən'tɔːʳ] N garante mf, fiador(a) m/f

guard [gɑːd] N guardia; (person) guarda mf; (BRIT Rail) jefe m de tren; (safety device: on machine) cubierta de protección; (protection) protección f; (fireguard) pantalla; (mudguard) guardabarros m inv ▸ VT guardar; **to ~ (against or from)** proteger (de); **to be on one's ~** (fig) estar en guardia
▸ **guard against** VI: **to ~ against doing sth** guardarse de hacer algo

guard dog N perro guardián

guarded ['gɑːdɪd] ADJ (fig) cauteloso

guardian ['gɑːdɪən] N guardián(-ana) m/f; (of minor) tutor(a) m/f

guardrail ['gɑːdreɪl] N pretil m

guard's van N (BRIT Rail) furgón m del jefe de tren

Guatemala [gwɑːtə'mɑːlə] N Guatemala

Guatemalan [gwɑːtə'mɑːlən] ADJ, N guatemalteco(-a) m/f

Guernsey ['gəːnzɪ] N Guernsey m

guerrilla [gə'rɪlə] N guerrillero(-a)

guerrilla warfare N guerra de guerrillas

guess [gɛs] VI, VT (gen) adivinar; (suppose) suponer ▸ N suposición f, conjetura; **I ~ you're right** (esp US) supongo que tienes razón; **to keep sb guessing** mantener a algn a la expectativa; **to take or have a ~** tratar de adivinar; **my ~ is that …** yo creo que …

guesstimate ['gɛstɪmɪt] N cálculo aproximado

guesswork ['gɛswəːk] N conjeturas fpl; **I got the answer by ~** acerté a ojo de buen cubero

guest [gɛst] N invitado(-a); (in hotel) huésped(a) m/f; **be my ~** (inf) estás en tu casa

guest-house ['gɛsthaʊs] N casa de huéspedes, pensión f

guest room N cuarto de huéspedes

guff [gʌf] N (inf) bobadas fpl

guffaw [gʌ'fɔː] N carcajada ▸ VI reírse a carcajadas

guidance ['gaɪdəns] N (gen) dirección f; (advice) consejos mpl; **marriage/vocational ~** orientación f matrimonial/profesional

guide [gaɪd] N (person) guía mf; (book, fig) guía f; (also: **girl guide**) exploradora ▸ VT guiar; **to be guided by sb/sth** dejarse guiar por algn/algo

guidebook ['gaɪdbʊk] N guía

guided missile ['gaɪdɪd-] N misil m teledirigido

guide dog N perro guía

guided tour N visita f con guía

guidelines ['gaɪdlaɪnz] NPL (fig) directrices fpl

guild [gɪld] N gremio

guildhall ['gɪldhɔːl] N (BRIT: town hall) ayuntamiento

guile [gaɪl] N astucia

guileless ['gaɪllɪs] ADJ cándido

guillotine ['gɪlətiːn] N guillotina

guilt [gɪlt] N culpabilidad f

guilty ['gɪltɪ] ADJ culpable; **to feel ~ (about)** sentirse culpable (de); **to plead ~/not ~** declararse culpable/inocente

Guinea ['gɪnɪ] N: **Republic of ~** República de Guinea

guinea ['gɪnɪ] N (BRIT old) guinea (21 chelines: en la actualidad ya no se usa esta moneda)

guinea pig N cobaya; (fig) conejillo de Indias

guise [gaɪz] N: **in or under the ~ of** bajo la apariencia de

guitar [gɪ'tɑːʳ] N guitarra

guitarist [gɪ'tɑːrɪst] N guitarrista mf

gulch [gʌltʃ] N (US) barranco

gulf [gʌlf] N golfo; (abyss) abismo; **the G~** el Golfo (Pérsico)

Gulf States NPL: **the ~** los países del Golfo

Gulf Stream N: **the ~** la Corriente del Golfo

gull [gʌl] N gaviota

gullet ['gʌlɪt] N esófago

gullibility [gʌlɪ'bɪlɪtɪ] N credulidad f

gullible ['gʌlɪbl] ADJ crédulo

gully ['gʌlɪ] N barranco

gulp [gʌlp] VI tragar saliva ▸ VT (also: **gulp down**) tragarse ▸ N (of liquid) trago; (of food) bocado; **in or at one ~** de un trago

gum [gʌm] N (Anat) encía; (glue) goma, cemento (LAm); (sweet) gominola; (also: **chewing-gum**) chicle m ▸ VT pegar con goma
▸ **gum up** VT: **to ~ up the works** (inf) entorpecerlo todo

gumboots ['gʌmbuːts] NPL (BRIT) botas fpl de goma

gumption ['gʌmpʃən] N (inf) iniciativa

gum tree N árbol m gomero

gun [gʌn] N (small) pistola; (shotgun) escopeta; (rifle) fusil m; (cannon) cañón m ▸ VT (also: **gun down**) abatir a tiros; **to stick to one's guns** (fig) mantenerse firme or en sus trece

gunboat ['gʌnbəʊt] N cañonero

gun dog N perro de caza

gunfire ['gʌnfaɪəʳ] N disparos mpl

gung-ho [gʌŋ'həʊ] ADJ (inf) patriotero

gunk [gʌŋk] N (inf) masa viscosa

gunman ['gʌnmən] N (irreg) pistolero

gunner ['gʌnəʳ] N artillero

gunpoint ['gʌnpɔɪnt] N: **at ~** a mano armada

gunpowder ['gʌnpaʊdəʳ] N pólvora

gunrunner [ˈgʌnrʌnəʳ] N traficante *mf* de armas

gunrunning [ˈgʌnrʌnɪŋ] N tráfico de armas

gunshot [ˈgʌnʃɔt] N disparo

gunsmith [ˈgʌnsmɪθ] N armero

gurgle [ˈgəːgl] VI gorgotear

guru [ˈguːruː] N gurú *m*

gush [gʌʃ] VI chorrear, salir a raudales; (*fig*) deshacerse en efusiones

gushing [ˈgʌʃɪŋ] ADJ efusivo

gusset [ˈgʌsɪt] N (*in tights, pants*) escudete *m*

gust [gʌst] N (*of wind*) ráfaga

gusto [ˈgʌstəu] N entusiasmo

gusty [ˈgʌstɪ] ADJ racheado

gut [gʌt] N intestino; (*Mus etc*) cuerda de tripa ▶ VT (*poultry, fish*) destripar; (*building*): **the blaze gutted the entire building** el fuego destruyó el edificio entero

gut reaction N reacción *f* instintiva

guts [gʌts] NPL (*courage*) agallas *fpl*, valor *m*; (*inf: innards: of people, animals*) tripas *fpl*; **to hate sb's ~** odiar a algn (a muerte)

gutsy [ˈgʌtsɪ] ADJ: **to be ~** (*inf*) tener agallas

gutted [ˈgʌtɪd] ADJ (*inf: disappointed*): **I was ~** me quedé hecho polvo

gutter [ˈgʌtəʳ] N (*of roof*) canalón *m*; (*in street*) cuneta; **the ~** (*fig*) el arroyo

gutter press N (*inf*): **the ~** la prensa sensacionalista *or* amarilla; *see also* **tabloid press**

guttural [ˈgʌtərl] ADJ gutural

guy [gaɪ] N (*also*: **guyrope**) viento, cuerda; (*inf: man*) tío (SP), tipo

Guyana [gaɪˈænə] N Guayana

Guy Fawkes Night [gaɪˈfɔːks-] N *ver nota*

La noche del cinco de noviembre, *Guy Fawkes Night*, se celebra el fracaso de la conspiración de la pólvora (*Gunpowder Plot*), el intento fallido de volar el parlamento de Jaime 1 en 1605. Esa noche se lanzan fuegos artificiales y se queman en muchas hogueras muñecos de trapo que representan a *Guy Fawkes*, uno de los cabecillas. Días antes los niños tienen por costumbre pedir a los viandantes *a penny for the guy*, dinero para comprar los cohetes.

guzzle [ˈgʌzl] VI tragar ▶ VT engullir

gym [dʒɪm] N (*also*: **gymnasium**) gimnasio; (*also*: **gymnastics**) gimnasia

gymkhana [dʒɪmˈkɑːnə] N gincana

gymnasium [dʒɪmˈneɪzɪəm] N gimnasio

gymnast [ˈdʒɪmnæst] N gimnasta *mf*

gymnastics [dʒɪmˈnæstɪks] N gimnasia

gym shoes NPL zapatillas *fpl* de gimnasia

gym slip N (BRIT) pichi *m*

gynaecologist, (US) **gynecologist** [gaɪnɪˈkɔlədʒɪst] N ginecólogo(-a)

gynaecology, (US) **gynecology** [gaɪnəˈkɔlədʒɪ] N ginecología

gypsy [ˈdʒɪpsɪ] N = **gipsy**

gyrate [dʒaɪˈreɪt] VI girar

gyroscope [ˈdʒaɪrəskəup] N giroscopio

585

Hh

H, h [eɪtʃ] N (*letter*) H, h *f*; **H for Harry**, (*US*) **H for How** H de Historia

habeas corpus ['heɪbɪəs'kɔːpəs] N (*Law*) hábeas corpus *m*

haberdashery ['hæbə'dæʃərɪ] N (*Brit*) mercería; (*US: men's clothing*) prendas *fpl* de caballero

habit ['hæbɪt] N hábito, costumbre *f*; (*drug habit*) adicción *f*; **to get out of/into the ~ of doing sth** perder la costumbre de/ acostumbrarse a hacer algo

habitable ['hæbɪtəbl] ADJ habitable

habitat ['hæbɪtæt] N hábitat *m*

habitation [hæbɪ'teɪʃən] N habitación *f*

habitual [hə'bɪtjuəl] ADJ acostumbrado, habitual; (*drinker, liar*) empedernido

habitually [hə'bɪtjuəlɪ] ADV por costumbre

hack [hæk] VT (*cut*) cortar; (*slice*) tajar ▶ N corte *m*; (*axe blow*) hachazo; (*pej: writer*) escritor(a) *m/f* a sueldo; (*old horse*) jamelgo

hacker ['hækəʳ] N (*Comput*) pirata *m* informático

hackles ['hæklz] NPL: **to make sb's ~ rise** (*fig*) poner furioso a algn

hackney cab ['hæknɪ-] N coche *m* de alquiler

hackneyed ['hæknɪd] ADJ trillado, gastado

hacksaw ['hæksɔː] N sierra para metales

had [hæd] PT, PP *of* **have**

haddock ['hædək] N (*pl ~ or* **haddocks**) *especie de merluza*

hadn't ['hædnt] = **had not**

haematology, (*US*) **hematology** ['hiːmə'tɔlədʒɪ] N hematología

haemoglobin, (*US*) **hemoglobin** ['hiːmə'gləubɪn] N hemoglobina

haemophilia, (*US*) **hemophilia** ['hiːmə'fɪlɪə] N hemofilia

haemorrhage, (*US*) **hemorrhage** ['hɛmərɪdʒ] N hemorragia

haemorrhoids, (*US*) **hemorrhoids** ['hɛmərɔɪdz] NPL hemorroides *fpl*, almorranas *fpl*

hag [hæg] N (*ugly*) vieja fea, tarasca; (*nasty*) bruja; (*witch*) hechicera

haggard ['hægəd] ADJ ojeroso

haggis ['hægɪs] N (*Scottish*) *asadura de cordero cocida; see also* **Burns' Night**

haggle ['hægl] VI (*argue*) discutir; (*bargain*) regatear

haggling ['hæglɪŋ] N regateo

Hague [heɪg] N: **The ~** La Haya

hail [heɪl] N (*weather*) granizo ▶ VT saludar; (*call*) llamar a ▶ VI granizar; **to ~ (as)** aclamar (como), celebrar (como); **he hails from Scotland** es natural de Escocia

hailstone ['heɪlstəun] N (piedra de) granizo

hailstorm ['heɪlstɔːm] N granizada

hair [hɛəʳ] N (*gen*) pelo, cabellos *mpl*; (*one hair*) pelo, cabello; (*head of hair*) pelo, cabellera; (*on legs etc*) vello; **to do one's ~** arreglarse el pelo; **grey ~** canas *fpl*

hairband ['hɛəbænd] N cinta

hairbrush ['hɛəbrʌʃ] N cepillo (para el pelo)

haircut ['hɛəkʌt] N corte *m* de pelo

hairdo ['hɛəduː] N peinado

hairdresser ['hɛədrɛsəʳ] N peluquero(-a); **~'s** peluquería

hairdryer ['hɛədraɪəʳ] N secador *m* (de pelo)

-haired [hɛəd] ADJ SUFF: **fair/long~** (de pelo) rubio *or* (*Lam*) güero/de pelo largo

hair gel N fijador

hairgrip ['hɛəgrɪp] N horquilla

hairline ['hɛəlaɪn] N nacimiento del pelo

hairline fracture N fractura muy fina

hairnet ['hɛənɛt] N redecilla

hair oil N brillantina

hairpiece ['hɛəpiːs] N trenza postiza

hairpin ['hɛəpɪn] N horquilla

hairpin bend, (*US*) **hairpin curve** N curva muy cerrada

hair-raising ['hɛəreɪzɪŋ] ADJ espeluznante

hair remover N depilatorio

hair's breadth N: **by a ~** por un pelo

hair spray N laca

hairstyle ['hɛəstaɪl] N peinado

hairy ['hɛərɪ] ADJ peludo, velludo; (*inf: frightening*) espeluznante

Haiti ['heɪtɪ] N Haití *m*

haka ['hɑːkə] N (New Zealand) haka m or f
hake [heɪk] N merluza
halcyon ['hælsɪən] ADJ feliz
hale [heɪl] ADJ: **~ and hearty** sano y fuerte
half [hɑːf] (pl **halves** [hɑːvz]) N mitad f; (Sport: of match) tiempo, parte f; (: of ground) campo; (of beer) ≈ caña (Sp); media pinta; (Rail) billete m de niño ► ADV medio, a medias; **~-an-hour** media hora; **two and a ~** dos y media; **~ a dozen** media docena; **~ a pound** media libra, ≈ 250 gr; **to cut sth in ~** cortar algo por la mitad; **to go halves (with sb)** ir a medias (con algn); **~ empty/closed** medio vacío/entreabierto; **~ asleep** medio dormido; **~ past 3** las 3 y media
half-back ['hɑːfbæk] N (Sport) medio
half-baked ['hɑːfbeɪkt] ADJ (inf: idea, scheme) mal concebido or pensado
half board N (Brit: in hotel) media pensión
half-breed ['hɑːfbriːd] N = **half-caste**
half-brother ['hɑːfbrʌðəʳ] N hermanastro
half-caste ['hɑːfkɑːst] N mestizo(-a)
half day N medio día m, media jornada
half fare N medio pasaje m
half-hearted ['hɑːfhɑːtɪd] ADJ indiferente, poco entusiasta
half-hour [hɑːf'auəʳ] N media hora
half-mast ['hɑːfmɑːst] N: **at ~** (flag) a media asta
halfpenny ['heɪpnɪ] N medio penique m
half-price ['hɑːf'praɪs] ADJ a mitad de precio
half term N (Brit Scol) vacaciones de mediados del trimestre
half-time [hɑːf'taɪm] N descanso
halfway ['hɑːf'weɪ] ADV a medio camino; **to meet sb ~** (fig) llegar a un acuerdo con algn
halfway house N centro de readaptación de antiguos presos; (fig) solución f intermedia
half-wit ['hɑːfwɪt] N (inf) zoquete m
half-yearly [hɑːf'jɪəlɪ] ADV semestralmente ► ADJ semestral
halibut ['hælɪbət] N pl inv halibut m
halitosis [hælɪ'təʊsɪs] N halitosis f
hall [hɔːl] N (for concerts) sala; (entrance way) entrada, vestíbulo
hallmark ['hɔːlmɑːk] N (mark) rasgo distintivo; (seal) sello
hallo [hə'ləʊ] EXCL = **hello**
hall of residence N (Brit) colegio mayor, residencia universitaria
Hallowe'en [hæləʊ'iːn] N víspera de Todos los Santos; ver nota

La tradición anglosajona dice que en la noche del 31 de octubre, Hallowe'en, víspera de Todos los Santos, es fácil ver a brujas y fantasmas. Es una ocasión festiva en la que los niños se disfrazan y van de puerta en puerta llevando un farol hecho con una calabaza en forma de cabeza humana. Cuando se les abre la puerta gritan "trick or treat" para indicar que gastarán una broma a quien no les dé un pequeño regalo (como golosinas o dinero).

hallucination [həluːsɪ'neɪʃən] N alucinación f
hallucinogenic [həluːsɪnəʊ'dʒɛnɪk] ADJ alucinógeno
hallway ['hɔːlweɪ] N vestíbulo
halo ['heɪləʊ] N (of saint) aureola, halo
halt [hɔːlt] N (stop) alto, parada; (Rail) apeadero ► VT parar ► VI pararse; (process) interrumpirse; **to call a ~ (to sth)** (fig) poner fin (a algo)
halter ['hɔːltəʳ] N (for horse) cabestro
halterneck ['hɔːltənɛk] ADJ de espalda escotada
halve [hɑːv] VT partir por la mitad
halves [hɑːvz] PL of **half**
ham [hæm] N jamón m (cocido); (inf: also: **radio ham**) radioaficionado(-a) m/f; (also: **ham actor**) comicastro
hamburger ['hæmbəgəʳ] N hamburguesa
ham-fisted ['hæm'fɪstɪd] ADJ torpe, desmañado
hamlet ['hæmlɪt] N aldea
hammer ['hæməʳ] N martillo ► VT (nail) clavar; **to ~ a point home to sb** remacharle un punto a algn
► **hammer out** VT (metal) forjar a martillo; (fig: solution, agreement) elaborar (trabajosamente)
hammock ['hæmək] N hamaca
hamper ['hæmpəʳ] VT estorbar ► N cesto
hamster ['hæmstəʳ] N hámster m
hamstring ['hæmstrɪŋ] N (Anat) tendón m de la corva
hand [hænd] N mano f; (of clock) aguja, manecilla; (writing) letra; (worker) obrero; (measurement: of horse) palmo ► VT (give) dar, pasar; (deliver) entregar; **to give sb a ~** echar una mano a algn, ayudar a algn; **to force sb's ~** forzarle la mano a algn; **at ~** a mano; **in ~** entre manos; **we have the matter in ~** tenemos el asunto entre manos; **to have in one's ~** (knife, victory) tener en la mano; **to have a free ~** tener carta blanca; **on ~** (person, services) a mano, al alcance; **to ~** (information etc) a mano; **on the one ~ ..., on the other ~ ...** por una parte ... por otra (parte) ...
► **hand down** VT pasar, bajar; (tradition) transmitir; (heirloom) dejar en herencia; (US: sentence, verdict) imponer
► **hand in** VT entregar
► **hand out** VT (leaflets, advice) repartir, distribuir
► **hand over** VT (deliver) entregar; (surrender) ceder

587

▶ **hand round** VT (BRIT: *information, papers*) pasar (de mano en mano); (: *chocolates etc*) ofrecer

handbag ['hændbæg] N bolso, cartera (LAM)

hand baggage N = **hand luggage**

handball ['hændbɔːl] N balonmano

handbasin ['hændbeɪsn] N lavabo

handbook ['hændbʊk] N manual *m*

handbrake ['hændbreɪk] N freno de mano

h & c ABBR (BRIT) = **hot and cold (water)**

hand cream N crema para las manos

handcuffs ['hændkʌfs] NPL esposas *fpl*

handful ['hændful] N puñado

hand-held ['hænd'held] ADJ de mano

handicap ['hændɪkæp] N desventaja; (*Sport*) hándicap *m* ▶ VT estorbar

handicapped ['hændɪkæpt] ADJ: **to be mentally ~** ser discapacitado(-a) mental; **to be physically ~** ser minusválido(-a)

handicraft ['hændɪkrɑːft] N artesanía

handiwork ['hændɪwəːk] N manualidad(es) *f(pl)*; (*fig*) obra; **this looks like his ~** (*pej*) es obra de él, parece

handkerchief ['hæŋkətʃɪf] N pañuelo

handle ['hændl] N (*of door etc*) pomo, tirador *m*; (*of cup etc*) asa; (*of knife etc*) mango; (*for winding*) manivela ▶ VT (*touch*) tocar; (*deal with*) encargarse de; (*treat: people*) manejar; **"~ with care"** "(manéjese) con cuidado"; **to fly off the ~** perder los estribos

handlebar ['hændlbɑːʳ] N, **handlebars** ['hændlbɑːz] NPL manillar *msg*

handling ['hændlɪŋ] N (*Aut*) conducción *f*; **his ~ of the matter** su forma de llevar el asunto

handling charges NPL gastos *mpl* de tramitación

hand luggage N equipaje *m* de mano

handmade ['hændmeɪd] ADJ hecho a mano

handout ['hændaut] N (*distribution*) repartición *f*; (*charity*) limosna; (*leaflet*) folleto, octavilla; (*press handout*) nota

hand-picked ['hænd'pɪkt] ADJ (*produce*) escogido a mano; (*staff etc*) seleccionado cuidadosamente

handrail ['hændreɪl] N (*on staircase etc*) pasamanos *m inv*, barandilla

handset ['hændset] N (*Tel*) auricular *m*

hands-free ['hændzfriː] ADJ (*Tel: telephone*) manos libres; **~ kit** manos libres *m inv*

handshake ['hændʃeɪk] N apretón *m* de manos; (*Comput*) coloquio

handsome ['hænsəm] ADJ guapo

hands-on ['hændz'ɔn] ADJ práctico; **she has a very ~ approach** le gusta tomar parte activa; **~ experience** (*Comput*) experiencia práctica

handstand ['hændstænd] N voltereta, salto mortal

hand-to-mouth ['hændtə'mauθ] ADJ (*existence*) precario

handwriting ['hændraɪtɪŋ] N letra

handwritten ['hændrɪtn] ADJ escrito a mano, manuscrito

handy ['hændɪ] ADJ (*close at hand*) a mano; (*useful: machine, tool etc*) práctico; (*skilful*) hábil, diestro; **to come in ~** venir bien

handyman ['hændɪmæn] N (*irreg*) manitas *m inv*

hang [hæŋ] (*pt, pp* **hung** [hʌŋ]) VT colgar; (*head*) bajar; (*pt, pp* **hanged**: *criminal*) ahorcar ▶ N **to get the ~ of sth** (*inf*) coger el tranquillo a algo

▶ **hang about, hang around** VI haraganear

▶ **hang back** VI (*hesitate*): **to ~ back (from doing)** vacilar (en hacer)

▶ **hang down** VI colgar, pender

▶ **hang on** VI (*wait*) esperar ▶ VT FUS (*depend on: decision etc*) depender de; **to ~ on to** (*keep*) guardar, quedarse con

▶ **hang out** VT (*washing*) tender, colgar ▶ VI (*inf: live*) vivir; (: *often be found*) moverse; **to ~ out of sth** colgar fuera de algo

▶ **hang round** VI = **hang about**

▶ **hang together** VI (*cohere: argument etc*) sostenerse

▶ **hang up** VT (*coat*) colgar ▶ VI (*Tel*) colgar; **to ~ up on sb** colgarle a algn

hangar ['hæŋəʳ] N hangar *m*

hangdog ['hæŋdɔg] ADJ (*guilty: look, expression*) avergonzado

hanger ['hæŋəʳ] N percha

hanger-on [hæŋər'ɔn] N parásito

hang-glider ['hæŋglaɪdəʳ] N ala delta

hang-gliding ['hæŋglaɪdɪŋ] N vuelo con ala delta

hanging ['hæŋɪŋ] N (*execution*) ejecución *f* (en la horca)

hangman ['hæŋmən] N (*irreg*) verdugo

hangover ['hæŋəuvəʳ] N (*after drinking*) resaca

hang-up ['hæŋʌp] N complejo

hanker ['hæŋkəʳ] VI: **to ~ after** (*miss*) echar de menos; (*long for*) añorar

hankie, hanky ['hæŋkɪ] N ABBR = **handkerchief**

Hansard ['hænsɑːd] N actas oficiales de las sesiones del parlamento británico

Hants ABBR (BRIT) = **Hampshire**

haphazard [hæp'hæzəd] ADJ fortuito

hapless ['hæplɪs] ADJ desventurado

happen ['hæpən] VI suceder, ocurrir; (*take place*) tener lugar, realizarse; (*chance*): **he happened to hear/see** dio la casualidad de que oyó/vio; **as it happens** da la casualidad de que; **what's happening?** ¿qué pasa?

▶ **happen (up)on** VT FUS tropezar *or* dar con

happening ['hæpnɪŋ] N suceso, acontecimiento

happily ['hæpɪlɪ] ADV (luckily) afortunadamente; (cheerfully) alegremente

happiness ['hæpɪnɪs] N (contentment) felicidad f; (joy) alegría

happy ['hæpɪ] ADJ feliz; (cheerful) alegre; **to be ~ (with)** estar contento (con); **yes, I'd be ~ to** sí, con mucho gusto; **H~ Christmas!** ¡Feliz Navidad!; **H~ New Year!** ¡Feliz Año Nuevo!; **~ birthday!** ¡feliz cumpleaños!

happy-go-lucky ['hæpɪgəu'lʌkɪ] ADJ despreocupado

happy hour N horas en las que la bebida es más barata en un bar

harangue [hə'ræŋ] VT arengar

harass ['hærəs] VT acosar, hostigar

harassed ['hærəst] ADJ agobiado, presionado

harassment ['hærəsmənt] N persecución f, acoso; (worry) preocupación f

harbour, (US) **harbor** ['hɑ:bər] N puerto ▶ VT (fugitive) dar abrigo a; (hope etc) abrigar; (hide) dar abrigo a; (retain: grudge etc) guardar

harbour dues, (US) **harbor dues** NPL derechos mpl portuarios

hard [hɑ:d] ADJ duro; (difficult) difícil; (work) arduo; (person) severo ▶ ADV (work) mucho, duro; (think) profundamente; **to look ~ at sb/sth** clavar los ojos en algn/algo; **to try ~** esforzarse; **no ~ feelings!** ¡sin rencor(es)!; **to be ~ of hearing** ser duro de oído; **to be ~ done by** ser tratado injustamente; **to be ~ on sb** ser muy duro con algn; **I find it ~ to believe that ...** me cuesta trabajo creer que ...

hard-and-fast ['hɑ:dən'fɑ:st] ADJ rígido, definitivo

hardback ['hɑ:dbæk] N libro de tapa dura

hardboard ['hɑ:dbɔ:d] N aglomerado m (de madera)

hard cash N dinero en efectivo

hard copy N (Comput) copia impresa

hard-core ['hɑ:d'kɔ:r] ADJ (pornography) duro; (supporters) incondicional

hard court N (Tennis) pista or cancha (de tenis) de cemento

hard disk N (Comput) disco duro

hard drive N (Comput) unidad f de disco duro

harden ['hɑ:dn] VT endurecer; (steel) templar; (fig) curtir; (: determination) fortalecer ▶ VI (substance) endurecerse; (fig) curtirse

hardened ['hɑ:dnd] ADJ (criminal) habitual; **to be ~ to sth** estar acostumbrado a algo

hard-headed ['hɑ:d'hedɪd] ADJ poco sentimental, realista

hard-hearted ['hɑ:d'hɑ:tɪd] ADJ insensible

hard-hitting ['hɑ:d'hɪtɪŋ] ADJ (speech, article) contundente

hard labour N trabajos mpl forzados

hardliner [hɑ:d'laɪnər] N partidario(-a) de la línea dura

hard-luck story ['hɑ:dlʌk-] N dramón m

hardly ['hɑ:dlɪ] ADV (scarcely) apenas; **that can ~ be true** eso difícilmente puede ser cierto; **~ ever** casi nunca; **I can ~ believe it** apenas me lo puedo creer

hardness ['hɑ:dnɪs] N dureza

hard-nosed ['hɑ:d'nəuzd] ADJ duro, sin contemplaciones

hard-pressed ['hɑ:d'prest] ADJ en apuros

hard sell N publicidad f agresiva; **~ techniques** técnicas fpl agresivas de venta

hardship ['hɑ:dʃɪp] N (troubles) penas fpl; (financial) apuro

hard shoulder N (Aut) arcén m

hard-up [hɑ:d'ʌp] ADJ (inf) sin un duro (SP), sin plata (LAm)

hardware ['hɑ:dwɛər] N ferretería; (Comput) hardware m

hardware shop, (US) **hardware store** N ferretería

hard-wearing [hɑ:d'wɛərɪŋ] ADJ resistente, duradero; (shoes) resistente

hard-won ['hɑ:d'wʌn] ADJ ganado con esfuerzo

hard-working [hɑ:d'wə:kɪŋ] ADJ trabajador(a)

hardy ['hɑ:dɪ] ADJ fuerte; (plant) resistente

hare [hɛər] N liebre f

hare-brained ['hɛəbreɪnd] ADJ atolondrado

harelip ['hɛəlɪp] N labio leporino

harem [hɑ:'ri:m] N harén m

haricot ['hærɪkəu], **haricot bean** N alubia

hark back [hɑ:k-] VI: **to ~ to** (former days, earlier occasion) recordar

harm [hɑ:m] N daño, mal m ▶ VT (person) hacer daño a; (health, interests) perjudicar; (thing) dañar; **out of ~'s way** a salvo; **there's no ~ in trying** no se pierde nada con intentar

harmful ['hɑ:mful] ADJ (gen) dañino; (reputation) perjudicial

harmless ['hɑ:mlɪs] ADJ (person) inofensivo; (drug) inocuo; (joke etc) inocente

harmonica [hɑ:'mɔnɪkə] N armónica

harmonious [hɑ:'məunɪəs] ADJ armonioso

harmonize ['hɑ:mənaɪz] VT, VI armonizar

harmony ['hɑ:mənɪ] N armonía

harness ['hɑ:nɪs] N arreos mpl ▶ VT (horse) enjaezar; (resources) aprovechar

harp [hɑ:p] N arpa ▶ VI: **to ~ on (about)** machacar (con)

harpoon [hɑ:'pu:n] N arpón m

harrow ['hærəu] N grada ▶ VT gradar

harrowing ['hærəuɪŋ] ADJ angustioso

harry ['hærɪ] VT (Mil) acosar; (person) hostigar

harsh [hɑ:ʃ] ADJ (cruel) duro, cruel; (severe) severo; (words) hosco; (colour) chillón(-ona); (contrast) violento

harshly ['hɑ:ʃlɪ] ADV (say) con aspereza; (treat) con mucha dureza

harshness ['hɑːʃnɪs] N dureza

harvest ['hɑːvɪst] N (*harvest time*) siega; (*of cereals etc*) cosecha; (*of grapes*) vendimia ▸ VT, VI cosechar

harvester ['hɑːvɪstəʳ] N (*machine*) cosechadora; (*person*) segador(a) *m/f*; **combine ~** segadora trilladora

has [hæz] VB *see* **have**

has-been ['hæzbiːn] N (*inf: person*) persona acabada; (: *thing*) vieja gloria

hash [hæʃ] N (*Culin*) picadillo; (*fig: mess*) lío; (*symbol*) almohadilla

hashish ['hæʃɪʃ] N hachís *m*

hashtag ['hæʃtæg] N (*on Twitter*) hashtag *m*

hasn't ['hæznt] = **has not**

hassle ['hæsl] N (*inf*) lío, rollo ▸ VT incordiar

haste [heɪst] N prisa

hasten ['heɪsn] VT acelerar ▸ VI darse prisa; **I ~ to add that ...** me apresuro a añadir que ...

hastily ['heɪstɪlɪ] ADV de prisa

hasty ['heɪstɪ] ADJ apresurado

hat [hæt] N sombrero

hatbox ['hætbɒks] N sombrerera

hatch [hætʃ] N (*Naut: also:* **hatchway**) escotilla ▸ VI salir del cascarón ▸ VT incubar; (*fig: scheme, plot*) idear, tramar; **5 eggs have hatched** han salido 5 pollos

hatchback ['hætʃbæk] N (*Aut*) tres *or* cinco puertas *m*

hatchet ['hætʃɪt] N hacha

hatchet job N (*inf*) varapalo

hatchet man N (*irreg*) (*inf*) ejecutor de faenas desagradables por cuenta de otro

hate [heɪt] VT odiar, aborrecer ▸ N odio; **I ~ to trouble you, but ...** siento *or* lamento molestarle, pero ...

hateful ['heɪtful] ADJ odioso

hater ['heɪtəʳ] N: **cop-~** *persona que siente aversión a la policía;* **woman-~** misógino

hatred ['heɪtrɪd] N odio

hat trick N: **to score a ~** (*Brit Sport*) marcar tres tantos (*or* triunfos) seguidos

haughtily ['hɔːtɪlɪ] ADV con arrogancia

haughty ['hɔːtɪ] ADJ altanero, arrogante

haul [hɔːl] VT tirar, jalar (*LAm*); (*by lorry*) transportar ▸ N (*of fish*) redada; (*of stolen goods etc*) botín *m*

haulage ['hɔːlɪdʒ] N (*Brit*) transporte *m*; (*costs*) gastos *mpl* de transporte

haulage contractor N (*firm*) empresa de transportes; (*person*) transportista *mf*

haulier ['hɔːlɪəʳ], (US) **hauler** ['hɔːləʳ] N transportista *mf*

haunch [hɔːntʃ] N anca; (*of meat*) pierna

haunt [hɔːnt] VT (*ghost*) aparecer en; (*frequent*) frecuentar; (*obsess*) obsesionar ▸ N guarida

haunted ['hɔːntɪd] ADJ (*castle etc*) embrujado; (*look*) de angustia

haunting ['hɔːntɪŋ] ADJ (*sight, music*) evocativo

Havana [hə'vɑːnə] N La Habana

KEYWORD

have [hæv] (*pt, pp* **had**) AUX VB **1** (*gen*) haber; **to have arrived/eaten** haber llegado/comido; **having finished** *or* **when he had finished, he left** cuando hubo acabado, se fue

2 (*in tag questions*): **you've done it, haven't you?** lo has hecho, ¿verdad? *or* ¿no?

3 (*in short answers and questions*): **I haven't** no; **so I have** pues, es verdad; **we haven't paid — yes we have!** no hemos pagado — ¡sí que hemos pagado!; **I've been there before, have you?** he estado allí antes, ¿y tú?

▸ MODAL AUX VB (*be obliged*): **to have (got) to do sth** tener que hacer algo; **you haven't to tell her** no hay que *or* no debes decírselo

▸ VT **1** (*possess*) tener; **he has (got) blue eyes/dark hair** tiene los ojos azules/el pelo negro

2 (*referring to meals etc*): **to have breakfast/lunch/dinner** desayunar/comer/cenar; **to have a drink/a cigarette** tomar algo/fumar un cigarrillo

3 (*receive*) recibir; (: *obtain*) obtener; **may I have your address?** ¿puedes darme tu dirección?; **you can have it for £5** te lo puedes quedar por £5; **I must have it by tomorrow** lo necesito para mañana; **to have a baby** tener un niño *or* bebé

4 (*maintain, allow*): **I won't have it!** ¡no lo permitiré!; **I won't have this nonsense!** ¡no permitiré estas tonterías!; **we can't have that** no podemos permitir eso

5: **to have sth done** hacer *or* mandar hacer algo; **to have one's hair cut** cortarse el pelo; **to have sb do sth** hacer que algn haga algo

6 (*experience, suffer*): **to have a cold/flu** tener un resfriado/la gripe; **she had her bag stolen/her arm broken** le robaron el bolso/se rompió un brazo; **to have an operation** operarse

7 (*+ noun*): **to have a swim/walk/bath/rest** nadar/dar un paseo/darse un baño/descansar; **let's have a look** vamos a ver; **to have a meeting/party** celebrar una reunión/una fiesta; **let me have a try** déjame intentarlo

▸ **have in** VT: **to have it in for sb** (*inf*) tenerla tomada con algn

▸ **have on** VT: **have you anything on tomorrow?** ¿vas a hacer algo mañana?; **I don't have any money on me** no llevo dinero (encima); **to have sb on** (*Brit inf*) tomarle el pelo a algn

▸ **have out** VT: **to have it out with sb** (*settle a problem etc*) dejar las cosas en claro con algn

haven ['heɪvn] N puerto; (*fig*) refugio

haven't ['hævnt] = **have not**

haversack ['hævəsæk] N macuto

haves [hævz] NPL: **the ~ and the have-nots** los ricos y los pobres

havoc ['hævək] N estragos *mpl*; **to play ~ with sth** hacer estragos en algo

Hawaii [hə'waiiː] N (Islas *fpl*) Hawai *m*

Hawaiian [hə'waijən] ADJ, N hawaiano(-a) *m/f*

hawk [hɔːk] N halcón *m* ▶ VT (*goods for sale*) pregonar

hawkish ['hɔːkiʃ] ADJ beligerante

hawthorn ['hɔːθɔːn] N espino

hay [hei] N heno

hay fever N fiebre *f* del heno

haystack ['heistæk] N almiar *m*

haywire ['heiwaiəʳ] ADJ (*inf*): **to go ~** (*person*) volverse loco; (*plan*) irse al garete

hazard ['hæzəd] N riesgo; (*danger*) peligro ▶ VT (*remark*) aventurar; (*one's life*) arriesgar; **to be a health ~** ser un peligro para la salud; **to ~ a guess** aventurar una respuesta or hipótesis

hazardous ['hæzədəs] ADJ (*dangerous*) peligroso; (*risky*) arriesgado

hazard warning lights NPL (*Aut*) señales *fpl* de emergencia

haze [heiz] N neblina

hazel ['heizl] N (*tree*) avellano ▶ ADJ (*eyes*) color *m* de avellana

hazelnut ['heizlnʌt] N avellana

hazy ['heizi] ADJ brumoso; (*idea*) vago

H-bomb ['eitʃbɔm] N bomba H

HD ABBR (= *high definition*) HD *m*

HDTV ABBR (= *high definition television*) HDTV *f*

HE ABBR = **high explosive**; (*Rel, Diplomacy*: = *His (or Her) Excellency*) S. Excª

he [hiː] PRON él; **he who …** aquél que …, quien …

head [hɛd] N cabeza; (*leader*) jefe(-a) *m/f* ▶ VT (*list*) encabezar; (*group*) capitanear; **heads (or tails)** cara (o cruz); **~ first** de cabeza; **~ over heels** patas arriba; **~ over heels in love** perdidamente enamorado; **on your ~ be it!** ¡allá tú!; **they went over my ~ to the manager** fueron directamente al gerente sin hacerme caso; **it was above** or **over their heads** no alcanzaron a entenderlo; **to come to a ~** (*fig: situation etc*) llegar a un punto crítico; **to have a ~ for business** tener talento para los negocios; **to have no ~ for heights** no resistir las alturas; **to lose/keep one's ~** perder la cabeza/mantener la calma; **to sit at the ~ of the table** sentarse a la cabecera de la mesa; **to ~ the ball** cabecear (el balón)

▶ **head for** VT FUS dirigirse a; (*disaster*) ir camino de

▶ **head off** VT (*threat, danger*) evitar

headache ['hɛdeik] N dolor *m* de cabeza; **to have a ~** tener dolor de cabeza

headband ['hɛdbænd] N cinta (para la cabeza), vincha (*LAm*)

headboard ['hɛdbɔːd] N cabecera

headdress ['hɛddrɛs] N (*of bride, Indian*) tocado

headed notepaper ['hɛdid-] N papel *m* con membrete

header ['hɛdəʳ] N (*Brit inf: Football*) cabezazo; (: *fall*) caída de cabeza

headfirst [hɛd'fəːst] ADV de cabeza

headhunt ['hɛdhʌnt] VT: **to be headhunted** ser seleccionado por un cazatalentos

headhunter ['hɛdhʌntəʳ] N (*fig*) cazaejecutivos *m inv*

heading ['hɛdiŋ] N título

headlamp ['hɛdlæmp] N (*Brit*) = **headlight**

headland ['hɛdlənd] N promontorio

headlight ['hɛdlait] N faro

headline ['hɛdlain] N titular *m*

headlong ['hɛdlɔŋ] ADV (*fall*) de cabeza; (*rush*) precipitadamente

headmaster/mistress [hɛd'mɑːstəʳ/mistris] N director(a) *m/f* (de escuela)

head office N oficina central, central *f*

head-on [hɛd'ɔn] ADJ (*collision*) de frente

headphones ['hɛdfəunz] NPL auriculares *mpl*

headquarters ['hɛdkwɔːtəz] NPL sede *f* central; (*Mil*) cuartel *m* general

head-rest ['hɛdrɛst] N reposa-cabezas *m inv*

headroom ['hɛdrum] N (*in car*) altura interior; (*under bridge*) (límite *m* de) altura

headscarf ['hɛdskɑːf] N pañuelo

headset ['hɛdsɛt] N cascos *mpl*

headstone ['hɛdstəun] N lápida

headstrong ['hɛdstrɔŋ] ADJ testarudo

head teacher N director(a)

head waiter N maître *m*

headway ['hɛdwei] N: **to make ~** (*fig*) hacer progresos

headwind ['hɛdwind] N viento contrario

heady ['hɛdi] ADJ (*experience, period*) apasionante; (*wine*) fuerte

heal [hiːl] VT curar ▶ VI cicatrizar

health [hɛlθ] N salud *f*

health care N asistencia sanitaria

health centre N ambulatorio, centro médico

health food N, **health foods** NPL alimentos *mpl* orgánicos

health hazard N riesgo para la salud

Health Service N (*Brit*) servicio de salud pública, ≈ Insalud *m* (*Sp*)

healthy ['hɛlθi] ADJ (*gen*) sano; (*economy, bank balance*) saludable

heap [hiːp] N montón *m* ▶ VT amontonar; (*plate*) colmar; **heaps of** (*inf: lots*) montones de; **to ~ favours/praise/gifts** *etc* **on sb** colmar a algn de favores/elogios/regalos *etc*

hear [hiəʳ] (*pt, pp* **heard** [həːd]) VT oír; (*news*)

h

saber; (*perceive*) sentir; (*listen to*) escuchar; (*lecture*) asistir a; (*Law: case*) ver ▸ VI oír; **to ~ about** oír hablar de; **to ~ from sb** tener noticias de algn; **I've never heard of that book** nunca he oído hablar de ese libro ▸ **hear out** VT: **to ~ sb out** dejar que algn termine de hablar

heard [həːd] PT, PP of **hear**

hearing ['hɪərɪŋ] N (*sense*) oído; (*Law*) vista; **to give sb a ~** dar a algn la oportunidad de hablar, escuchar a algn

hearing aid N audífono

hearsay ['hɪəseɪ] N rumores *mpl*, habladurías *fpl*

hearse [həːs] N coche *m* fúnebre

heart [hɑːt] N corazón *m*; (*fig*) valor *m*; (*of lettuce*) cogollo; **hearts** NPL (*Cards*) corazones *mpl*; **at ~** en el fondo; **by ~** (*learn, know*) de memoria; **to have a weak ~** tener el corazón débil; **to set one's ~ on sth/on doing sth** anhelar algo/hacer algo; **I did not have the ~ to tell her** no tuve valor para decírselo; **to take ~** cobrar ánimos; **the ~ of the matter** lo esencial or el meollo del asunto

heartache ['hɑːteɪk] N angustia

heart attack N infarto (de miocardio)

heartbeat ['hɑːtbiːt] N latido (del corazón)

heartbreak ['hɑːtbreɪk] N angustia, congoja

heartbreaking ['hɑːtbreɪkɪŋ] ADJ desgarrador(a)

heartbroken ['hɑːtbrəukən] ADJ: **she was ~ about it** eso le partió el corazón

heartburn ['hɑːtbəːn] N acedía

heart disease N enfermedad *f* cardíaca

-hearted ['hɑːtɪd] ADJ SUFF: **a kind~ person** una persona bondadosa

heartening ['hɑːtnɪŋ] ADJ alentador(a)

heart failure N (*Med*) paro cardíaco

heartfelt ['hɑːtfɛlt] ADJ (*cordial*) cordial; (*deeply felt*) sincero

hearth [hɑːθ] N (*gen*) hogar *m*; (*fireplace*) chimenea

heartily ['hɑːtɪlɪ] ADV sinceramente, cordialmente; (*laugh*) a carcajadas; (*eat*) con buen apetito; **to be ~ sick of** estar completamente harto de

heartland ['hɑːtlænd] N zona interior or central; (*fig*) corazón *m*

heartless ['hɑːtlɪs] ADJ despiadado

heartstrings ['hɑːtstrɪŋz] NPL: **to tug (at) sb's ~** tocar la fibra sensible de algn

heart-throb ['hɑːtθrɔb] N ídolo

heart-to-heart ['hɑːttə'hɑːt] N (*also*: **heart-to-heart talk**) conversación *f* íntima

heart transplant N transplante *m* de corazón

hearty ['hɑːtɪ] ADJ (*person*) campechano; (*laugh*) sano; (*dislike, support*) absoluto

heat [hiːt] N (*gen*) calor *m*; (*Sport: also:* **qualifying heat**) prueba eliminatoria ▸ VT calentar ▸ **heat up** VI (*gen*) calentarse ▸ VT calentar

heated ['hiːtɪd] ADJ caliente; (*fig*) acalorado

heater ['hiːtər] N calentador *m*, estufa

heath [hiːθ] N (*BRIT*) brezal *m*

heathen ['hiːðn] ADJ, N pagano(-a) *m/f*

heather ['hɛðər] N brezo

heating ['hiːtɪŋ] N calefacción *f*

heat-resistant ['hiːtrɪzɪstənt] ADJ refractario

heat-seeking ['hiːtsiːkɪŋ] ADJ guiado por infrarrojos, termoguiado

heatstroke ['hiːtstrəuk] N insolación *f*

heatwave ['hiːtweɪv] N ola de calor

heave [hiːv] VT (*pull*) tirar; (*push*) empujar con esfuerzo; (*lift*) levantar (con esfuerzo) ▸ VI (*water*) subir y bajar ▸ N tirón *m*; empujón *m*; (*effort*) esfuerzo; (*throw*) echada; **to ~ a sigh** dar or echar un suspiro, suspirar ▸ **heave to** VI (*Naut*) ponerse al pairo

heaven ['hɛvn] N cielo; (*Rel*) paraíso; **thank ~!** ¡gracias a Dios!; **for ~'s sake!** (*pleading*) ¡por el amor de Dios!, ¡por lo que más quiera!; (*protesting*) ¡por Dios!

heavenly ['hɛvnlɪ] ADJ celestial; (*Rel*) divino

heavenly body N cuerpo celeste

heavily ['hɛvɪlɪ] ADV pesadamente; (*drink, smoke*) en exceso; (*sleep, sigh*) profundamente

heavy ['hɛvɪ] ADJ pesado; (*work*) duro; (*sea, rain, meal*) fuerte; (*drinker, smoker*) empedernido; (*eater*) comilón(-ona); (*responsibility*) grave; (*schedule*) ocupado; (*weather*) bochornoso

heavy-duty ['hɛvɪ'djuːtɪ] ADJ resistente

heavy goods vehicle N (*BRIT*) vehículo pesado

heavy-handed ['hɛvɪ'hændɪd] ADJ (*clumsy, tactless*) torpe

heavy industry N industria pesada

heavy metal N (*Mus*) heavy *m* (metal)

heavy-set [hɛvɪ'sɛt] ADJ (*esp US*) corpulento, fornido

heavy user N consumidor *m* intensivo

heavyweight ['hɛvɪweɪt] N (*Sport*) peso pesado

Hebrew ['hiːbruː] ADJ, N (*Ling*) hebreo

Hebrides ['hɛbrɪdiːz] NPL: **the ~** las Hébridas

heck [hɛk] N (*inf*): **why the ~ ...?** ¿por qué porras ...?; **a ~ of a lot of** cantidad de

heckle ['hɛkl] VT interrumpir

heckler ['hɛklər] N el/la que interrumpe a un orador

hectare ['hɛktɑːr] N (*BRIT*) hectárea

hectic ['hɛktɪk] ADJ agitado; (*busy*) ocupado

hector ['hɛktər] VT intimidar con bravatas

he'd [hiːd] = **he would**; **he had**

hedge [hɛdʒ] N seto ▸ VT cercar (con un seto) ▸ VI contestar con evasivas; **as a ~ against**

inflation como protección contra la
inflación; **to ~ one's bets** (fig) cubrirse
hedgehog ['hɛdʒhɒg] N erizo
hedgerow ['hɛdʒrəʊ] N seto vivo
hedonism ['hi:dənɪzəm] N hedonismo
heed [hi:d] VT (also: **take heed of**: pay attention)
hacer caso de; (: bear in mind) tener en cuenta;
to pay (no) ~ to, take (no) ~ of (no) hacer
caso a, (no) tener en cuenta
heedless ['hi:dlɪs] ADJ desatento
heel [hi:l] N talón m; (of shoe) tacón m ▶ VT
(shoe) poner tacón a; **to take to one's heels**
(inf) poner pies en polvorosa; **to bring to ~**
meter en cintura; see also **dig**
hefty ['hɛftɪ] ADJ (person) fornido; (piece)
grande; (price) alto
heifer ['hɛfər] N novilla, ternera
height [haɪt] N (of person) talla, estatura; (of
building) altura; (high ground) cerro; (altitude)
altitud f; **what ~ are you?** ¿cuánto mides?;
of average ~ de estatura mediana; **to be
afraid of heights** tener miedo a las alturas;
at the ~ of summer en los días más
calurosos del verano; **it's the ~ of fashion**
es el último grito en moda
heighten ['haɪtn] VT elevar; (fig) aumentar
heinous ['heɪnəs] ADJ atroz, nefasto
heir [ɛər] N heredero
heir apparent N presunto heredero
heiress ['ɛərɛs] N heredera
heirloom ['ɛəluːm] N reliquia de familia
heist [haɪst] N (inf: hold-up) atraco a mano
armada
held [hɛld] PT, PP of **hold**
helicopter ['hɛlɪkɒptər] N helicóptero
heliport ['hɛlɪpɔːt] N (Aviat) helipuerto
helium ['hiːlɪəm] N helio
hell [hɛl] N infierno; **oh ~!** (inf) ¡demonios!,
¡caramba!
he'll [hiːl] = **he will; he shall**
hellbent ['hɛl'bɛnt] ADJ (inf): **he was ~ on
going** se le metió entre ceja y ceja ir
hellish ['hɛlɪʃ] ADJ infernal; (inf) horrible
hello [hə'ləʊ] EXCL ¡hola!; (to attract attention)
¡oiga!; (surprise) ¡caramba!; (Tel) ¡dígame! (esp
SP), ¡aló! (LAM)
helm [hɛlm] N (Naut) timón m
helmet ['hɛlmɪt] N casco
helmsman ['hɛlmzmən] N (irreg) timonel m
help [hɛlp] N ayuda; (cleaner etc) criada,
asistenta ▶ VT ayudar; **~!** ¡socorro!; **with the
~ of** con la ayuda de; **can I ~ you?** (in shop)
¿qué desea?; **to be of ~ to sb** servir a algn; **to
~ sb (to) do sth** echarle una mano or ayudar
a algn a hacer algo; **~ yourself** sírvete; **he
can't ~ it** no lo puede evitar
▶ **help out** VI ayudar, echar una mano ▶ VT:
to ~ sb out ayudar a algn, echar una mano a
algn

help desk N (esp Comput) centro de asistencia
helper ['hɛlpər] N ayudante mf
helpful ['hɛlpful] ADJ útil; (person) servicial
helping ['hɛlpɪŋ] N ración f
helping hand N: **to give sb a ~** echar una
mano a algn
helpless ['hɛlplɪs] ADJ (incapable) incapaz;
(defenceless) indefenso
helpline ['hɛlplaɪn] N teléfono de asistencia
al público
Helsinki ['hɛlsɪŋkɪ] N Helsinki m
helter-skelter ['hɛltə'skɛltər] N (in funfair)
tobogán m
hem [hɛm] N dobladillo ▶ VT poner or coser el
dobladillo a
▶ **hem in** VT cercar; **to feel hemmed in**
(fig) sentirse acosado
he-man ['hiːmæn] N (irreg) macho
hematology [hiːmə'tɒlədʒɪ] N (US)
= **haematology**
hemisphere ['hɛmɪsfɪər] N hemisferio
hemline ['hɛmlaɪn] N bajo (del vestido)
hemlock ['hɛmlɒk] N cicuta
hemoglobin [hiːmə'gləʊbɪn] N (US)
= **haemoglobin**
hemophilia [hiːmə'fɪlɪə] N (US)
= **haemophilia**
hemorrhage ['hɛmərɪdʒ] N (US)
= **haemorrhage**
hemorrhoids ['hɛmərɔɪdz] NPL (US)
= **haemorrhoids**
hemp [hɛmp] N cáñamo
hen [hɛn] N gallina; (female bird) hembra
hence [hɛns] ADV (therefore) por lo tanto;
two years ~ de aquí a dos años
henceforth [hɛns'fɔːθ] ADV de hoy en adelante
henchman ['hɛntʃmən] N (irreg) (pej) secuaz m
henna ['hɛnə] N alheña
hen night N (inf) despedida de soltera
hen party N (inf) reunión f de mujeres
henpecked ['hɛnpɛkt] ADJ: **to be ~** ser un
calzonazos
hepatitis [hɛpə'taɪtɪs] N hepatitis f inv
her [həːr] PRON (direct) la; (indirect) le; (stressed,
after prep) ella ▶ ADJ su; see also **me; my**
herald ['hɛrəld] N (forerunner) precursor(a) m/f
▶ VT anunciar
heraldic [hɛ'rældɪk] ADJ heráldico
heraldry ['hɛrəldrɪ] N heráldica
herb [həːb] N hierba
herbaceous [həː'beɪʃəs] ADJ herbáceo
herbal ['həːbl] ADJ de hierbas
herbal tea N infusión f de hierbas
herbicide ['həːbɪsaɪd] N herbicida m
herd [həːd] N rebaño; (of wild animals, swine)
piara ▶ VT (drive, gather: animals) llevar en
manada; (: people) reunir
▶ **herd together** VT agrupar, reunir ▶ VI
apiñarse, agruparse

here [hɪəʳ] ADV aquí; **~!** (present) ¡presente!; **~ is/are** aquí está/están; **~ she is** aquí está; **come ~!** ¡ven aquí or acá!; **~ and there** aquí y allá

hereabouts ['hɪərə'bauts] ADV por aquí (cerca)

hereafter [hɪər'ɑːftəʳ] ADV en el futuro ▸ N: **the ~** el más allá

hereby [hɪə'baɪ] ADV (in letter) por la presente

hereditary [hɪ'rɛdɪtrɪ] ADJ hereditario

heredity [hɪ'rɛdɪtɪ] N herencia

heresy ['hɛrəsɪ] N herejía

heretic ['hɛrətɪk] N hereje mf

heretical [hɪ'rɛtɪkəl] ADJ herético

herewith [hɪə'wɪð] ADV: **I send you ~ ...** le mando adjunto ...

heritage ['hɛrɪtɪdʒ] N (gen) herencia; (fig) patrimonio; **our national ~** nuestro patrimonio nacional

hermetically [hə:'mɛtɪkəlɪ] ADV: **~ sealed** herméticamente cerrado

hermit ['hə:mɪt] N ermitaño(-a)

hernia ['hə:nɪə] N hernia

hero ['hɪərəu] (pl **heroes**) N héroe m; (in book, film) protagonista m

heroic [hɪ'rəuɪk] ADJ heroico

heroin ['hɛrəuɪn] N heroína

heroin addict N heroinómano(-a), adicto(-a) a la heroína

heroine ['hɛrəuɪn] N heroína; (in book, film) protagonista

heroism ['hɛrəuɪzm] N heroísmo

heron ['hɛrən] N garza

hero worship N veneración f

herring ['hɛrɪŋ] pl inv N arenque m

hers [hə:z] PRON (el) suyo/(la) suya etc; **a friend of ~** un amigo suyo; **this is ~** esto es suyo or de ella; see also **mine**

herself [hə:'sɛlf] PRON (reflexive) se; (emphatic) ella misma; (after prep) sí (misma); see also **oneself**

Herts ABBR (BRIT) = **Hertfordshire**

he's [hi:z] = **he is; he has**

hesitant ['hɛzɪtənt] ADJ indeciso; **to be ~ about doing sth** no decidirse a hacer algo

hesitate ['hɛzɪteɪt] VI dudar, vacilar; (in speech) titubear; (be unwilling) resistirse a; **don't ~ to ask (me)** no dudes en pedírmelo

hesitation [hɛzɪ'teɪʃən] N indecisión f; **I have no ~ in saying (that) ...** no tengo el menor reparo en afirmar que ...

hessian ['hɛsɪən] N arpillera

heterogeneous ['hɛtərə'dʒi:nɪəs] ADJ heterogéneo

heterosexual [hɛtərəu'sɛksjuəl] ADJ, N heterosexual mf

het up [hɛt'ʌp] ADJ (inf) agitado, nervioso

HEW N ABBR (US: = Department of Health, Education, and Welfare) ministerio de sanidad, educación y bienestar público

hew [hju:] VT cortar

hex [hɛks] (US) N maleficio, mal m de ojo ▸ VT embrujar

hexagon ['hɛksəgən] N hexágono

hexagonal [hɛk'sægənl] ADJ hexagonal

hey [heɪ] EXCL ¡oye!, ¡oiga!

heyday ['heɪdeɪ] N: **the ~ of** el apogeo de

HF N ABBR = **high frequency**

HGV N ABBR = **heavy goods vehicle**

HI ABBR (US) = **Hawaii**

hi [haɪ] EXCL ¡hola!

hiatus [haɪ'eɪtəs] N vacío, interrupción f; (Ling) hiato

hibernate ['haɪbəneɪt] VI invernar

hibernation [haɪbə'neɪʃən] N hibernación f

hiccough, hiccup ['hɪkʌp] VI hipar; **hiccoughs** NPL hipo sg

hick [hɪk] N (US inf) paleto(-a)

hid [hɪd] PT of **hide**

hidden ['hɪdn] PP of **hide** ▸ ADJ: **there are no ~ extras** no hay suplementos ocultos; **~ agenda** plan m encubierto

hide [haɪd] (pt **hid**, pp **hidden**) N (skin) piel f ▸ VT esconder, ocultar; (feelings, truth) encubrir, ocultar ▸ VI: **to ~ (from sb)** esconderse or ocultarse (de algn)

hide-and-seek ['haɪdn'si:k] N escondite m

hideaway ['haɪdəweɪ] N escondite m

hideous ['hɪdɪəs] ADJ horrible

hideously ['hɪdɪəslɪ] ADV horriblemente

hide-out ['haɪdaut] N escondite m, refugio

hiding ['haɪdɪŋ] N (beating) paliza; **to be in ~** (concealed) estar escondido

hiding place N escondrijo

hierarchy ['haɪərɑ:kɪ] N jerarquía

hieroglyphic [haɪərə'glɪfɪk] ADJ jeroglífico ▸ N: **hieroglyphics** jeroglíficos mpl

hi-fi ['haɪfaɪ] ABBR = **high fidelity** ▸ N estéreo, hifi m ▸ ADJ de alta fidelidad

higgledy-piggledy ['hɪgldɪ'pɪgldɪ] ADV en desorden, de cualquier modo

high [haɪ] ADJ alto; (speed, number) grande, alto; (price) elevado; (wind) fuerte; (voice) agudo; (inf: on drugs) colocado; (: on drink) borracho; (Culin: meat, game) pasado; (: spoilt) estropeado ▸ ADV alto, a gran altura ▸ N: **exports have reached a new ~** las exportaciones han alcanzado niveles inusitados; **it is 20 m ~** tiene 20 m de altura; **~ in the air** en las alturas; **to pay a ~ price for sth** pagar algo muy caro

highball ['haɪbɔ:l] N (US: drink) whisky m soda, highball m (LAM), jaibol m (LAM)

highboy ['haɪbɔɪ] N (US) cómoda alta

highbrow ['haɪbrau] ADJ culto

highchair ['haɪtʃɛəʳ] N silla alta (para niños)

high-class ['haɪ'klɑ:s] ADJ (neighbourhood) de alta sociedad; (hotel) de lujo; (person) distinguido, de categoría; (food) de alta categoría

High Court N (*Law*) tribunal *m* supremo; *ver nota*

> En el sistema legal de Inglaterra y Gales *High Court* es la forma abreviada de "*High Court of Justice*", tribunal superior que junto con el de apelación ("*Court of Appeal*") forma el Tribunal Supremo ("*Supreme Court of Judicature*"). En el sistema legal escocés es la forma abreviada de "*High Court of Justiciary*", tribunal con jurado que juzga los delitos más serios, que pueden dar lugar a una pena de gran severidad.

higher ['haɪə'] ADJ (*form of life, study etc*) superior ▶ ADV más alto ▶ N (SCOTTISH *Scol*): **H~** *cada una de las asignaturas que se estudian entre los 16 y los 17 años generalmente, así como el certificado de haberlas probado*

higher education N educación *f* or enseñanza superior

high explosive N explosivo de gran potencia

highfalutin [haɪfə'luːtɪn] ADJ (*inf*) de altos vuelos, encopetado

high finance N altas finanzas *fpl*

high-flier, high-flyer [haɪ'flaɪə'] N ambicioso(-a)

high-handed [haɪ'hændɪd] ADJ despótico

high-heeled [haɪ'hiːld] ADJ de tacón alto

high heels NPL (*heels*) tacones *mpl* altos; (*shoes*) zapatos *mpl* de tacón

highjack ['haɪdʒæk] VB, N = **hijack**

high jump N (*Sport*) salto de altura

highlands ['haɪləndz] NPL tierras *fpl* altas; **the H~** (*in Scotland*) las Tierras Altas de Escocia

high-level ['haɪlɛvl] ADJ (*talks etc*) de alto nivel

highlight ['haɪlaɪt] N (*fig: of event*) punto culminante ▶ VT subrayar; **highlights** NPL (*in hair*) reflejos *mpl*

highlighter N rotulador

highly ['haɪlɪ] ADV sumamente; **~ paid** muy bien pagado; **to speak ~ of** hablar muy bien de; **~ strung** muy excitable

High Mass N misa mayor

highness ['haɪnɪs] N altura; **Her** or **His H~** Su Alteza

high-pitched [haɪ'pɪtʃt] ADJ agudo

high point N: **the ~** el punto culminante

high-powered ['haɪpauəd] ADJ (*engine*) de gran potencia; (*fig: person*) importante

high-pressure ['haɪprɛʃə'] ADJ de alta presión; (*fig: salesman etc*) enérgico

high-rise ['haɪraɪz] N (*also:* **high-rise block**, **high-rise building**) torre *f* de pisos

high school N centro de enseñanza secundaria, ≈ Instituto Nacional de Bachillerato (SP), liceo (LAM); *ver nota*

> El término *high school* se aplica en Estados Unidos a dos tipos de centros de educación secundaria: "*Junior High Schools*", en los que se imparten normalmente del 7° al 9° curso (llamado "*grade*") y "*Senior High Schools*", que abarcan los cursos 10°, 11° y 12° y en ocasiones el 9°. Aquí pueden estudiarse asignaturas tanto de contenido académico como profesional. En Gran Bretaña también se llaman *high school* algunos centros de enseñanza secundaria.

high season N (BRIT) temporada alta

high-speed ['haɪspiːd] ADJ de alta velocidad

high-spirited [haɪ'spɪrɪtɪd] ADJ animado

high spirits NPL ánimos *mpl*

high street N (BRIT) calle *f* mayor

high-tech (*inf*) ADJ al-tec (*inf*), de alta tecnología

high tide N marea alta

highway ['haɪweɪ] N carretera; (US) autopista

Highway Code N (BRIT) código de la circulación

highwayman ['haɪweɪmən] N (*irreg*) salteador *m* de caminos

hijack ['haɪdʒæk] VT secuestrar ▶ N (*also:* **hijacking**) secuestro

hijacker ['haɪdʒækə'] N secuestrador(a) *m/f*

hike [haɪk] VI (*go walking*) ir de excursión (a pie); (*tramp*) caminar ▶ N caminata; (*inf: in prices etc*) aumento
▶ **hike up** VT (*raise*) aumentar

hiker ['haɪkə'] N excursionista *mf*

hiking ['haɪkɪŋ] N senderismo

hilarious [hɪ'lɛərɪəs] ADJ divertidísimo

hilarity [hɪ'lærɪtɪ] N (*laughter*) risas *fpl*, carcajadas *fpl*

hill [hɪl] N colina; (*high*) montaña; (*slope*) cuesta

hillbilly ['hɪlbɪlɪ] N (US) rústico(-a) montañés(-esa); (*pej*) palurdo(-a)

hillock ['hɪlək] N montecillo, altozano

hillside ['hɪlsaɪd] N ladera

hilltop ['hɪltɔp] N cumbre *f*

hill walking N senderismo (de montaña)

hilly ['hɪlɪ] ADJ montañoso; (*uneven*) accidentado

hilt [hɪlt] N (*of sword*) empuñadura; **to the ~** (*fig: support*) incondicionalmente; **to be in debt up to the ~** estar hasta el cuello de deudas

him [hɪm] PRON (*direct*) le, lo; (*indirect*) le; (*stressed, after prep*) él; *see also* **me**

Himalayas [hɪmə'leɪəz] NPL: **the ~** el Himalaya

himself [hɪm'sɛlf] PRON (*reflexive*) se; (*emphatic*) él mismo; (*after prep*) sí (mismo); *see also* **oneself**

hind [haɪnd] ADJ posterior ▸ N cierva
hinder ['hɪndəʳ] VT estorbar, impedir
hindquarters ['haɪndkwɔːtəz] NPL (Zool) cuartos mpl traseros
hindrance ['hɪndrəns] N estorbo, obstáculo
hindsight ['haɪndsaɪt] N percepción f tardía or retrospectiva; **with ~** en retrospectiva; **with the benefit of ~** con la perspectiva del tiempo transcurrido
Hindu ['hɪnduː] N hindú mf
Hinduism ['hɪnduːɪzm] N (Rel) hinduismo
hinge [hɪndʒ] N bisagra, gozne m ▸ VI (fig): **to ~ on** depender de
hint [hɪnt] N indirecta; (advice) consejo ▸ VT: **to ~ that** insinuar que ▸ VI: **to ~ at** aludir a; **to drop a ~** soltar or tirar una indirecta; **give me a ~** dame una pista
hip [hɪp] N cadera; (Bot) escaramujo
hip flask N petaca
hip-hop ['hɪphɔp] N hip hop m
hippie ['hɪpɪ] N hippie mf, jipi mf
hippo ['hɪpəu] (pl **hippos**) N hipopótamo
hip pocket N bolsillo de atrás
hippopotamus [hɪpə'pɔtəməs] (pl **hippopotamuses** or **hippopotami** [-'pɔtəmaɪ]) N hipopótamo
hippy ['hɪpɪ] N = **hippie**
hire ['haɪəʳ] VT (BRIT: car, equipment) alquilar; (worker) contratar ▸ N alquiler m; **for ~** se alquila; (taxi) libre; **on ~** de alquiler
▸ **hire out** VT alquilar, arrendar
hire car, hired car N (BRIT) coche m de alquiler
hire purchase N (BRIT) compra a plazos; **to buy sth on ~** comprar algo a plazos
his [hɪz] PRON (el) suyo/(la) suya etc ▸ ADJ su; **this is ~** esto es suyo or de él; see also **my**; **mine**
Hispanic [hɪs'pænɪk] ADJ hispánico
hiss [hɪs] VI sisear; (in protest) silbar ▸ N siseo; silbido
histogram ['hɪstəgræm] N histograma m
historian [hɪ'stɔːrɪən] N historiador(a) m/f
historic [hɪ'stɔrɪk], **historical** [hɪ'stɔrɪkl] ADJ histórico
history ['hɪstərɪ] N historia; **there's a long ~ of that illness in his family** esa enfermedad corre en su familia
histrionics [hɪstrɪ'ɔnɪks] NPL histrionismo
hit [hɪt] VT (pt, pp ~) (strike) golpear, pegar; (reach: target) alcanzar; (collide with: car) chocar contra; (fig: affect) afectar ▸ N golpe m; (success) éxito; (on website) visita; (in web search) correspondencia; **to ~ the headlines** salir en primera plana; **to ~ the road** (inf) largarse; **to ~ it off with sb** llevarse bien con algn
▸ **hit back** VI defenderse; (fig) devolver golpe por golpe
▸ **hit out at** VT FUS asestar un golpe a; (fig) atacar
▸ **hit (up)on** VT FUS (answer) dar con; (solution) hallar, encontrar
hit and miss ADJ: **it's very ~**, **it's a ~ affair** es cuestión de suerte
hit-and-run driver ['hɪtən'rʌn-] N conductor que tras atropellar a algn se da a la fuga
hitch [hɪtʃ] VT (fasten) atar, amarrar; (also: **hitch up**) arremangarse ▸ N (difficulty) problema, pega; **to ~ a lift** hacer autostop; **technical ~** problema m técnico
▸ **hitch up** VT (horse, cart) enganchar, uncir
hitch-hike ['hɪtʃhaɪk] VI hacer autostop
hitch-hiker ['hɪtʃhaɪkəʳ] N autostopista mf
hitch-hiking ['hɪtʃhaɪkɪŋ] N autostop m
hi-tech [haɪ'tɛk] ADJ de alta tecnología
hitherto ['hɪðə'tuː] ADV hasta ahora, hasta aquí
hit list N lista negra
hitman ['hɪtmæn] N (irreg) asesino a sueldo
hit or miss ['hɪtə'mɪs] ADJ = **hit and miss**
hit parade N: **the ~** los cuarenta principales
HIV N ABBR (= human immunodeficiency virus) VIH m; **~-negative** VIH negativo; **~-positive** VIH positivo, seropositivo
hive [haɪv] N colmena; **the shop was a ~ of activity** (fig) la tienda era una colmena humana
▸ **hive off** VT (inf: separate) separar; (: privatize) privatizar
hl ABBR (= hectolitre) hl
HM ABBR (= His (or Her) Majesty) S.M.
HMG ABBR (BRIT) = **Her/His Majesty's Government**
HMI N ABBR (BRIT Scol) = **Her/His Majesty's Inspector**
HMO N ABBR (US: = Health Maintenance Organization) seguro médico global
HMS ABBR = **Her/His Majesty's Ship**
HMSO N ABBR (BRIT: = Her/His Majesty's Stationery Office) distribuidor oficial de las publicaciones del gobierno del Reino Unido
HNC N ABBR (BRIT: = Higher National Certificate) título académico
HND N ABBR (BRIT: = Higher National Diploma) título académico
hoard [hɔːd] N (treasure) tesoro; (stockpile) provisión f ▸ VT acumular
hoarding ['hɔːdɪŋ] N (for posters) valla publicitaria
hoarfrost ['hɔːfrɔst] N escarcha
hoarse [hɔːs] ADJ ronco
hoax [həuks] N engaño
hob [hɔb] N quemador m
hobble ['hɔbl] VI cojear
hobby ['hɔbɪ] N pasatiempo, afición f
hobby-horse ['hɔbɪhɔːs] N (fig) tema preferido
hobnob ['hɔbnɔb] VI: **to ~ (with)** alternar (con)

hobo ['həubəu] N (US) vagabundo

hock [hɔk] N corvejón m; (inf): **to be in ~** (person) estar empeñado or endeudado; (object) estar empeñado

hockey ['hɔkɪ] N hockey m

hockey stick N palo m de hockey

hocus-pocus [həukəs'pəukəs] N (trickery) engañifa; (words: of magician) abracadabra m

hod [hɔd] N capacho

hodge-podge ['hɔdʒpɔdʒ] N (US) = hotchpotch

hoe [həu] N azadón m ▶ VT azadonar

hog [hɔg] N cerdo, puerco ▶ VT (fig) acaparar; **to go the whole ~** echar el todo por el todo

Hogmanay [hɔgmə'neɪ] N (SCOTTISH) Nochevieja; ver nota

> La Nochevieja o New Year's Eve se conoce como Hogmanay en Escocia, donde se festeje de forma especial. La familia y los amigos se suelen juntar para oír las campanadas del reloj y luego se hace el first-footing, costumbre que consiste en visitar a los amigos y vecinos llevando algo de beber (generalmente whisky) y un trozo de carbón que se supone que traerá buena suerte para el año entrante.

hoist [hɔɪst] N (crane) grúa ▶ VT levantar, alzar

hoity-toity [hɔɪtɪ'tɔɪtɪ] ADJ (inf): **to be ~** darse humos

hold [həuld] (pt, pp **held**) VT sostener; (contain) contener; (have: power, qualification) tener; (keep back) retener; (believe) sostener; (take hold of) coger (SP), agarrar (LAM); (bear: weight) soportar; (: meeting) celebrar ▶ VI (withstand: pressure) resistir; (be valid) ser válido; (stick) pegarse ▶ N (grasp) asimiento; (fig) dominio; (Wrestling) presa; (Naut) bodega; **~ the line!** (Tel) ¡no cuelgue!; **to ~ one's own** (fig) defenderse; **to ~ office** (Pol) ocupar un cargo; **to ~ firm** or **fast** mantenerse firme; **he holds the view that ...** opina or es su opinión que ...; **to ~ sb responsible for sth** culpar or echarle la culpa a algn de algo; **where can I get ~ of ...?** ¿dónde puedo encontrar (a) ...?; **to catch** or **get (a) ~ of** agarrarse o asirse de

▶ **hold back** VT retener; (secret) ocultar; **to ~ sb back from doing sth** impedir a algn hacer algo, impedir que algn haga algo

▶ **hold down** VT (person) sujetar; (job) mantener

▶ **hold forth** VI perorar

▶ **hold off** VT (enemy) rechazar ▶ VI: **if the rain holds off** si no llueve

▶ **hold on** VI agarrarse bien; (wait) esperar; **~ on!** (Tel) ¡(espere) un momento!

▶ **hold on to** VT FUS agarrarse a; (keep) guardar

▶ **hold out** VT ofrecer ▶ VI (resist) resistir; **to ~ out (against)** resistir (a), sobrevivir

▶ **hold over** VT (meeting etc) aplazar

▶ **hold up** VT (raise) levantar; (support) apoyar; (delay) retrasar; (: traffic) demorar; (rob: bank) asaltar, atracar

holdall ['həuldɔːl] N (BRIT) bolsa

holder ['həuldər] N (of ticket, record) poseedor(a) m/f; (of passport, post, office, title etc) titular mf

holding ['həuldɪŋ] N (share) participación f

holding company N holding m

holdup ['həuldʌp] N (robbery) atraco; (delay) retraso; (BRIT: in traffic) embotellamiento

hole [həul] N agujero ▶ VT agujerear; **~ in the heart** (Med) boquete m en el corazón; **to pick holes in** (fig) encontrar defectos en; **the ship was holed** se abrió una vía de agua en el barco

▶ **hole up** VI esconderse

holiday ['hɔlədɪ] N vacaciones fpl; (day off) (día m de) fiesta, día m festivo or feriado (LAM); **on ~** de vacaciones; **to be on ~** estar de vacaciones

holiday camp N (BRIT) colonia or centro vacacional; (for children) colonia veraniega infantil

holiday home N residencia vacacional

holiday job N (BRIT) trabajo para las vacaciones

holidaymaker ['hɔlədɪmeɪkər] N (BRIT) turista mf

holiday pay N paga de las vacaciones

holiday resort N centro turístico

holiday season N temporada de vacaciones

holiness ['həulɪnɪs] N santidad f

holistic [həu'lɪstɪk] ADJ holístico

Holland ['hɔlənd] N Holanda

holler ['hɔlər] VI (inf) gritar, vocear

hollow ['hɔləu] ADJ hueco; (fig) vacío; (eyes) hundido; (sound) sordo ▶ N (gen) hueco; (in ground) hoyo ▶ VT: **to ~ out** ahuecar

holly ['hɔlɪ] N acebo

hollyhock ['hɔlɪhɔk] N malva loca

Hollywood ['hɔlɪwud] N Hollywood m

holocaust ['hɔləkɔːst] N holocausto

hologram ['hɔləgræm] N holograma m

holster ['həulstər] N pistolera

holy ['həulɪ] ADJ (gen) santo, sagrado; (water) bendito; **the H~ Father** el Santo Padre

Holy Communion N Sagrada Comunión f

Holy Ghost, Holy Spirit N Espíritu m Santo

homage ['hɔmɪdʒ] N homenaje m; **to pay ~ to** rendir homenaje a

home [həum] N casa; (country) patria; (institution) asilo; (Comput) punto inicial or de partida ▶ ADJ (domestic) casero, de casa; (Econ, Pol) nacional; (Sport: team) de casa; (: match, win) en casa ▶ ADV (direction) a casa;

h

597

at ~ en casa; **to go/come** ~ ir/volver a casa; **make yourself at** ~ ¡estás en tu casa!; **it's near my** ~ está cerca de mi casa
▶ **home in on** VT FUS (*missile*) dirigirse hacia
home address N domicilio
home-brew [həum'bru:] N cerveza *etc* casera
homecoming ['həumkʌmɪŋ] N regreso (al hogar)
home computer N ordenador *m* doméstico
Home Counties NPL *condados que rodean Londres*
home economics N economía doméstica
home ground N: **to be on** ~ estar en su *etc* terreno
home-grown ['həumɡrəun] ADJ de cosecha propia
home help N (BRIT) trabajador(a) *m/f* del servicio de atención domiciliaria
homeland ['həumlænd] N tierra natal
homeless ['həumlɪs] ADJ sin hogar, sin casa
▶ NPL: **the** ~ las personas sin hogar
home loan N préstamo para la vivienda
homely ['həumlɪ] ADJ (*domestic*) casero; (*simple*) sencillo
home-made [həum'meɪd] ADJ casero
home match N partido en casa
Home Office N (BRIT) Ministerio del Interior
homeopathy *etc* [həumɪ'ɔpθɪ] (US) = **homoeopathy** *etc*
home owner N propietario(-a) de una casa
home page N (*Comput*) página de inicio
home rule N autonomía
Home Secretary N (BRIT) Ministro del Interior
homesick ['həumsɪk] ADJ: **to be** ~ tener morriña *or* nostalgia
homestead ['həumstɛd] N hacienda
home town N ciudad *f* natal
home truth N: **to tell sb a few home truths** decir cuatro verdades a algn
homeward ['həumwəd] ADJ (*journey*) de vuelta ▶ ADV hacia casa
homewards ['həumwədz] ADV hacia casa
homework ['həumwə:k] N deberes *mpl*
homicidal [hɔmɪ'saɪdl] ADJ homicida
homicide ['hɔmɪsaɪd] N (US) homicidio
homily ['hɔmɪlɪ] N homilía
homing ['həumɪŋ] ADJ (*device, missile*) buscador(a); ~ **pigeon** paloma mensajera
homoeopath, (US) **homeopath** ['həumɪəupæθ] N homeópata *mf*
homoeopathic, (US) **homeopathic** [həumɪəu'pæθɪk] ADJ homeopático
homoeopathy, (US) **homeopathy** [həumɪ'ɔpθɪ] N homeopatía
homogeneous [hɔmə'dʒi:nɪəs] ADJ homogéneo
homogenize [hə'mɔdʒənaɪz] VT homogeneizar

homosexual [hɔməu'sɛksjuəl] ADJ, N homosexual *mf*
Hon ABBR (= *honourable, honorary*) *en títulos*
Honduras [hɔn'djuərəs] N Honduras *fpl*
hone [həun] VT (*sharpen*) afilar; (*fig*) perfeccionar
honest ['ɔnɪst] ADJ honrado; (*sincere*) franco, sincero; **to be quite** ~ **with you** ... para serte franco ...
honestly ['ɔnɪstlɪ] ADV honradamente; francamente, de verdad
honesty ['ɔnɪstɪ] N honradez *f*
honey ['hʌnɪ] N miel *f*; (*US inf*) cariño; (: *to strangers*) guapo, linda
honeycomb ['hʌnɪkəum] N panal *m*; (*fig*) laberinto
honeymoon ['hʌnɪmu:n] N luna de miel
honeysuckle ['hʌnɪsʌkl] N madreselva
Hong Kong ['hɔŋ'kɔŋ] N Hong-Kong *m*
honk [hɔŋk] VI (*Aut*) tocar la bocina
Honolulu [hɔnə'lu:lu:] N Honolulú *m*
honorary ['ɔnərərɪ] ADJ no remunerado; (*duty, title*) honorífico; ~ **degree** doctorado honoris causa
honour, (US) **honor** ['ɔnəʳ] VT honrar; (*commitment, promise*) cumplir con ▶ N honor *m*, honra; **in** ~ **of** en honor de; **it's a great** ~ es un gran honor
honourable, (US) **honorable** ['ɔnərəbl] ADJ honrado, honorable
honour-bound, (US) **honor-bound** ['ɔnə'baund] ADJ moralmente obligado
honours degree N (*Univ*) licenciatura superior; *ver nota*

Tras un período de estudios de tres años normalmente (cuatro en Escocia), los universitarios obtienen una licenciatura llamada *honours degree*. La calificación global que se recibe, en una escala de mayor a menor es la siguiente: "*first class*" (I), "*upper-second class*" (II:1), "*lower-second class*" (II:2) y "*third class*" (III). El licenciado puede añadir las letras "*Hons*" al título obtenido tras su nombre y apellidos, por ejemplo "BA Hons".

honours list N (BRIT) lista de distinciones honoríficas que entrega la reina; *ver nota*

A la lista con los títulos honoríficos y condecoraciones que el monarca británico otorga en Año Nuevo y en el día de su cumpleaños se la conoce con el nombre de *honours list*. Las personas que reciben dichas distinciones suelen ser miembros destacados de la vida pública (ámbito empresarial, ejército, deportes, espectáculos), aunque últimamente también se reconoce con ellas el trabajo abnegado y anónimo de la gente de la calle.

Hons. [ɔnz] ABBR (*Univ*) = **honours degree**
hood [hud] N capucha; (*Brit Aut*) capota; (*US Aut*) capó m; (*US inf*) matón m; (*of cooker*) campana de humos
hooded ['hudɪd] ADJ (*robber*) encapuchado
hoodie ['hudɪ] N (*pullover*) sudadera f con capucha; (*young person*) capuchero(-a) m/f
hoodlum ['hu:dləm] N matón m
hoodwink ['hudwɪŋk] VT (*Brit*) timar, engañar
hoof [hu:f] (*pl* **hoofs** *or* **hooves** [hu:vz]) N pezuña
hook [huk] N gancho; (*on dress*) corchete m, broche m; (*for fishing*) anzuelo ▶ VT enganchar; **hooks and eyes** corchetes mpl, macho y hembra m; **by ~ or by crook** por las buenas o por las malas, cueste lo que cueste; **to be hooked on** (*inf*) estar enganchado a ▶ **hook up** VT (*Radio, TV*) transmitir en cadena
hooligan ['hu:lɪgən] N gamberro
hooliganism ['hu:lɪgənɪzəm] N gamberrismo
hoop [hu:p] N aro
hooray [hu:'reɪ] EXCL = **hurrah**
hoot [hu:t] VI (*Brit Aut*) tocar la bocina; (*siren*) sonar; (*owl*) ulular ▶ N bocinazo, toque m de sirena; **to ~ with laughter** morirse de risa
hooter ['hu:tər] N (*Brit Aut*) bocina; (*of ship, factory*) sirena
hoover® ['hu:vər] (*Brit*) N aspiradora ▶ VT pasar la aspiradora por
hooves [hu:vz] PL *of* **hoof**
hop [hɔp] VI saltar, brincar; (*on one foot*) saltar con un pie ▶ N salto, brinco; *see also* **hops**
hope [həup] VT, VI esperar ▶ N esperanza; **I ~ so/not** espero que sí/no
hopeful ['həupful] ADJ (*person*) optimista; (*situation*) prometedor(a); **I'm ~ that she'll manage to come** confío en que podrá venir
hopefully ['həupfulɪ] ADV con optimismo, con esperanza; **~ he will recover** esperamos que se recupere
hopeless ['həuplɪs] ADJ desesperado
hopelessly ['həuplɪslɪ] ADV (*live etc*) sin esperanzas; **I'm ~ confused/lost** estoy totalmente despistado/perdido
hopper ['hɔpər] N (*chute*) tolva
hops [hɔps] NPL lúpulo sg
horde [hɔ:d] N horda
horizon [hə'raɪzn] N horizonte m
horizontal [hɔrɪ'zɔntl] ADJ horizontal
hormone ['hɔ:məun] N hormona
hormone replacement therapy N terapia hormonal sustitutiva
horn [hɔ:n] N cuerno, cacho (*Lam*); (*Mus: also:* **French horn**) trompa; (*Aut*) bocina, claxon m
horned [hɔ:nd] ADJ con cuernos
hornet ['hɔ:nɪt] N avispón m

horny ['hɔ:nɪ] ADJ (*material*) córneo; (*hands*) calloso; (*US inf*) cachondo
horoscope ['hɔrəskəup] N horóscopo
horrendous [hɔ'rɛndəs] ADJ horrendo
horrible ['hɔrɪbl] ADJ horrible
horribly ['hɔrɪblɪ] ADV horriblemente
horrid ['hɔrɪd] ADJ horrible, horroroso
horridly ['hɔrɪdlɪ] ADV (*behave*) tremendamente mal
horrific [hɔ'rɪfɪk] ADJ (*accident*) horroroso; (*film*) horripilante
horrify ['hɔrɪfaɪ] VT horrorizar
horrifying ['hɔrɪfaɪɪŋ] ADJ horroroso
horror ['hɔrər] N horror m
horror film N película de terror *or* miedo
horror-struck ['hɔrəstrʌk], **horror-stricken** ['hɔrəstrɪkn] ADJ horrorizado
hors d'œuvre [ɔ:'də:vrə] N entremeses mpl
horse [hɔ:s] N caballo
horseback ['hɔ:sbæk] N: **on ~** a caballo
horsebox ['hɔ:sbɔks] N remolque m para transportar caballos
horse chestnut N (*tree*) castaño de Indias; (*nut*) castaña de Indias
horsedrawn ['hɔ:sdrɔ:n] ADJ de tracción animal
horsefly ['hɔ:sflaɪ] N tábano
horseman ['hɔ:smən] N (*irreg*) jinete m
horsemanship ['hɔ:smənʃɪp] N equitación f, manejo del caballo
horseplay ['hɔ:spleɪ] N pelea amistosa
horsepower ['hɔ:spauər] N caballo (de fuerza), potencia en caballos
horse-racing ['hɔ:sreɪsɪŋ] N carreras fpl de caballos
horseradish ['hɔ:srædɪʃ] N rábano picante
horse riding N (*Brit*) equitación f
horseshoe ['hɔ:sʃu:] N herradura
horse show N concurso hípico
horse-trader ['hɔ:streɪdər] N chalán(-ana) m/f
horse trials NPL = **horse show**
horsewhip ['hɔ:swɪp] VT azotar
horsewoman ['hɔ:swumən] N (*irreg*) amazona
horsey ['hɔ:sɪ] ADJ (*inf: person*) aficionado a los caballos
horticulture ['hɔ:tɪkʌltʃər] N horticultura
hose [həuz] N (*also:* **hosepipe**) manguera ▶ **hose down** VT limpiar con manguera
hosiery ['həuzɪərɪ] N calcetería
hospice ['hɔspɪs] N hospicio
hospitable ['hɔspɪtəbl] ADJ hospitalario
hospital ['hɔspɪtl] N hospital m
hospitality [hɔspɪ'tælɪtɪ] N hospitalidad f
hospitalize ['hɔspɪtəlaɪz] VT hospitalizar
host [həust] N anfitrión m; (*TV, Radio*) presentador(a) m/f; (*of inn etc*) mesonero; (*Rel*) hostia; (*large number*): **a ~ of** multitud de

599

hostage ['hɔstɪdʒ] N rehén m
hostel ['hɔstl] N hostal m; (for students, nurses etc) residencia; (for homeless people) albergue; **(youth)** ~ albergue m juvenil
hostelling ['hɔstlɪŋ] N: **to go (youth)** ~ hospedarse en albergues
hostess ['həustɪs] N anfitriona; (BRIT: air hostess) azafata; (TV, Radio) presentadora; (in night-club) señorita de compañía
hostile ['hɔstaɪl] ADJ hostil
hostility [hɔ'stɪlɪtɪ] N hostilidad f
hot [hɔt] ADJ caliente; (weather) caluroso, de calor; (as opposed to only warm) muy caliente; (spicy) picante; (fig) ardiente, acalorado; **to be** ~ (person) tener calor; (object) estar caliente; (weather) hacer calor
▶ **hot up** VI (inf: situation) ponerse difícil or apurado; (: party) animarse ▶ VT (inf: pace) apretar; (: engine) aumentar la potencia de
hot air N (inf) palabras fpl huecas
hot-air balloon [hɔt'eə-] N (Aviat) globo aerostático or de aire caliente
hotbed ['hɔtbɛd] N (fig) semillero
hot-blooded [hɔt'blʌdɪd] ADJ impetuoso
hotchpotch ['hɔtʃpɔtʃ] N mezcolanza, baturrillo
hot dog N perrito caliente
hotel [həu'tɛl] N hotel m
hotelier [həu'tɛlɪə'] N hotelero
hotel industry N industria hotelera
hotel room N habitación f de hotel
hot flush N (BRIT) sofoco
hotfoot ['hɔtfut] ADV a toda prisa
hothead ['hɔthɛd] N (fig) exaltado(-a)
hot-headed [hɔt'hɛdɪd] ADJ exaltado
hothouse ['hɔthaus] N invernadero
hot line N (Pol) teléfono rojo, línea directa
hotly ['hɔtlɪ] ADV con pasión, apasionadamente
hotplate ['hɔtpleɪt] N (on cooker) hornillo
hotpot ['hɔtpɔt] N (BRIT Culin) estofado
hot potato N (BRIT inf) asunto espinoso; **to drop sth/sb like a** ~ no querer saber ya nada de algo/algn
hot seat N primera fila
hotspot ['hɔtspɔt] N (Comput: also: **wireless hotspot**) punto de acceso inalámbrico
hot spot N (trouble spot) punto caliente; (night club etc) lugar m popular
hot-tempered ['hɔt'tɛmpəd] ADJ de mal genio or carácter
hot-water bottle [hɔt'wɔːtə-] N bolsa de agua caliente
hot-wire ['hɔtwaɪə'] VT (inf: car) hacer el puente en
hound [haund] VT acosar ▶ N perro de caza
hour ['auə'] N hora; **at 30 miles an** ~ a 30 millas por hora; **lunch** ~ la hora del almuerzo or de comer; **to pay sb by the** ~ pagar a algn por horas
hourly ['auəlɪ] ADJ (de) cada hora; (rate) por hora ▶ ADV cada hora
house [haus] (pl **houses** ['hauzɪz]) N casa; (Pol) cámara; (Theat) sala ▶ VT [hauz] (person) alojar; **at/to my** ~ en/a mi casa; **the H~ of Commons/Lords** (BRIT) la Cámara de los Comunes/Lores; **the H~ of Representatives** (US) la Cámara de Representantes; **it's on the** ~ (fig) la casa invita
house arrest N arresto domiciliario
houseboat ['hausbəut] N casa flotante
housebound ['hausbaund] ADJ confinado en casa
housebreaking ['hausbreɪkɪŋ] N allanamiento de morada
house-broken ['hausbrəukən] ADJ (US) = **house-trained**
housecoat ['hauskəut] N bata
household ['haushəuld] N familia
householder ['haushəuldə'] N propietario(-a); (head of house) cabeza de familia
househunting ['haushʌntɪŋ] N: **to go** ~ ir en busca de vivienda
housekeeper ['hauski:pə'] N ama de llaves
housekeeping ['hauski:pɪŋ] N (work) trabajos mpl domésticos; (Comput) gestión f interna; (also: **housekeeping money**) dinero para gastos domésticos
houseman ['hausmən] N (irreg) (BRIT Med) médico residente
house-owner ['hausəunə'] N propietario(a) de una vivienda
house plant N planta de interior
house-proud ['hauspraud] ADJ preocupado por el embellecimiento de la casa
house-to-house ['haustə'haus] ADJ (search) casa por casa; (collection) de casa en casa
house-train ['haustreɪn] VT (pet) enseñar (a hacer sus necesidades en el sitio apropiado)
house-trained ['haustreɪnd] ADJ (BRIT: animal) enseñado
house-warming ['hauswɔːmɪŋ] N (also: **house-warming party**) fiesta de estreno de una casa
housewife ['hauswaɪf] N (irreg) ama de casa
house wine N vino m de la casa
housework ['hauswəːk] N faenas fpl (de la casa)
housing ['hauzɪŋ] N (act) alojamiento; (houses) viviendas fpl ▶ CPD (problem, shortage) de (la) vivienda
housing association N asociación f de la vivienda
housing benefit N (BRIT) subsidio por alojamiento
housing conditions NPL condiciones fpl de habitabilidad

housing development, (Brit) **housing estate** N urbanización *f*

hovel ['hɔvl] N casucha

hover ['hɔvər] VI flotar (en el aire); *(helicopter)* cernerse; **to ~ on the brink of disaster** estar al borde mismo del desastre

hovercraft ['hɔvəkrɑːft] N aerodeslizador *m*, hovercraft *m*

hoverport ['hɔvəpɔːt] N puerto de aerodeslizadores

how [hau] ADV cómo; **~ are you?** ¿cómo estás?; *(formal)* ¿cómo está usted?; **~ do you do?** encantado, mucho gusto; **~ far is it to ...?** ¿qué distancia hay de aquí a ...?; **~ long have you been here?** ¿cuánto (tiempo) hace que estás aquí?, ¿cuánto (tiempo) llevas aquí?; **~ lovely!** ¡qué bonito!; **~ many/ much?** ¿cuántos/cuánto?; **~ much does it cost?** ¿cuánto cuesta?; **~ old are you?** ¿cuántos años tienes?; **~ is school?** ¿qué tal la escuela?; **~ was the film?** ¿qué tal la película?; **~ about a drink?** ¿te gustaría algo de beber?, ¿qué te parece una copa?

however [hau'ɛvər] ADV de cualquier manera; *(+ adjective)* por muy ... que; *(in questions)* cómo ▶ CONJ sin embargo, no obstante; **~ I do it** lo haga como lo haga; **~ cold it is** por mucho frío que haga; **~ did you do it?** ¿cómo lo hiciste?

howitzer ['hauɪtsər] N *(Mil)* obús *m*

howl [haul] N aullido ▶ VI aullar; *(person)* dar alaridos; *(wind)* ulular

howler ['haulər] N plancha, falta garrafal

howling ['haulɪŋ] ADJ *(wind)* huracanado

HP N ABBR *(Brit)* = **hire purchase**

hp ABBR *(Aut)* = **horsepower**

HQ N ABBR = **headquarters**

HR N ABBR = **human resources**; *(US)* = **House of Representatives**

hr, hrs ABBR *(= hour(s))* h

HRH ABBR *(= His (or Her) Royal Highness)* S.A.R.

HRT N ABBR = **hormone replacement therapy**

HS ABBR *(US)* = **high school**

HST ABBR *(US: = Hawaiian Standard Time)* hora de Hawai

HT ABBR = **high tension**

HTML N ABBR *(Comput: = hypertext markup language)* HTML *m*

hub [hʌb] N *(of wheel)* cubo; *(fig)* centro

hubbub ['hʌbʌb] N barahúnda, barullo

hubcap ['hʌbkæp] N tapacubos *m inv*

HUD N ABBR *(US: = Department of Housing and Urban Development)* ministerio de la vivienda y urbanismo

huddle ['hʌdl] VI: **to ~ together** amontonarse

hue [hjuː] N color *m*, matiz *m*; **~ and cry** n protesta

huff [hʌf] N: **in a ~** enojado

huffy ['hʌfɪ] ADJ *(inf)* mosqueado

hug [hʌg] VT abrazar ▶ N abrazo

huge [hjuːdʒ] ADJ enorme

hulk [hʌlk] N *(ship)* barco viejo; *(person, building etc)* mole *f*

hulking ['hʌlkɪŋ] ADJ pesado

hull [hʌl] N *(of ship)* casco

hullabaloo ['hʌləbəluː] N *(inf: noise)* algarabía, jaleo

hullo [hə'ləu] EXCL = **hello**

hum [hʌm] VT tararear, canturrear ▶ VI tararear, canturrear; *(insect)* zumbar ▶ N *(Elec)* zumbido; *(of traffic, machines)* zumbido, ronroneo; *(of voices etc)* murmullo

human ['hjuːmən] ADJ humano ▶ N *(also:* **human being***)* ser *m* humano

humane [hjuː'meɪn] ADJ humano, humanitario

humanism ['hjuːmənɪzəm] N humanismo

humanitarian [hjuːmænɪ'tɛərɪən] ADJ humanitario

humanity [hjuː'mænɪtɪ] N humanidad *f*

humanly ['hjuːmənlɪ] ADV humanamente

humanoid ['hjuːmənɔɪd] ADJ, N humanoide *mf*

human relations NPL relaciones *fpl* humanas

human rights NPL derechos *mpl* humanos

humble ['hʌmbl] ADJ humilde ▶ VT humillar

humbly ['hʌmblɪ] ADV humildemente

humbug ['hʌmbʌg] N patrañas *fpl*; *(Brit: sweet)* caramelo de menta

humdrum ['hʌmdrʌm] ADJ *(boring)* monótono, aburrido; *(routine)* rutinario

humid ['hjuːmɪd] ADJ húmedo

humidifier [hjuː'mɪdɪfaɪər] N humectador *m*

humidity [hjuː'mɪdɪtɪ] N humedad *f*

humiliate [hjuː'mɪlɪeɪt] VT humillar

humiliating [hjuː'mɪlɪeɪtɪŋ] ADJ humillante, vergonzoso

humiliation [hjuːmɪlɪ'eɪʃən] N humillación *f*

humility [hjuː'mɪlɪtɪ] N humildad *f*

hummus ['huməs] N humus *m*

humorist ['hjuːmərɪst] N humorista *mf*

humorous ['hjuːmərəs] ADJ gracioso, divertido

humour, *(US)* **humor** ['hjuːmər] N humorismo, sentido del humor; *(mood)* humor *m* ▶ VT *(person)* complacer; **sense of ~** sentido del humor; **to be in a good/bad ~** estar de buen/mal humor

humourless, *(US)* **humorless** ['hjuːmərlɪs] ADJ serio

hump [hʌmp] N *(in ground)* montículo; *(camel's)* giba

humus ['hjuːməs] N *(Biol)* humus *m*

hunch [hʌntʃ] N *(premonition)* presentimiento; **I have a ~ that** tengo la corazonada or el presentimiento de que

hunchback ['hʌntʃbæk] N jorobado(-a)
hunched [hʌntʃt] ADJ jorobado
hundred ['hʌndrəd] NUM ciento; (*before n*) cien; **about a ~ people** unas cien personas, alrededor de cien personas; **hundreds of** centenares de; **hundreds of people** centenares de personas; **I'm a ~ per cent sure** estoy completamente seguro
hundredth ['hʌndrɪdθ] ADJ centésimo
hundredweight ['hʌndrədweɪt] N (BRIT) = 50.8 kg; 112 lb; (US) = 45.3 kg; 100 lb
hung [hʌŋ] PT, PP of **hang**
Hungarian [hʌŋ'gɛərɪən] ADJ húngaro ▸ N húngaro(-a) *m/f*; (*Ling*) húngaro
Hungary ['hʌŋgərɪ] N Hungría
hunger ['hʌŋgəʳ] N hambre *f* ▸ VI: **to ~ for** (*fig*) tener hambre de, anhelar
hunger strike N huelga de hambre
hungover [hʌŋ'əuvəʳ] ADJ (*inf*): **to be ~** tener resaca
hungrily ['hʌŋgrəlɪ] ADV ávidamente, con ganas
hungry ['hʌŋgrɪ] ADJ hambriento; **to be ~** tener hambre; **~ for** (*fig*) sediento de
hunk [hʌŋk] N (*of bread etc*) trozo, pedazo
hunt [hʌnt] VT (*seek*) buscar; (*Sport*) cazar ▸ VI (*search*): **to ~ (for)** buscar; (*Sport*) cazar ▸ N caza, cacería
 ▸ **hunt down** VT acorralar, seguir la pista a
hunter ['hʌntəʳ] N cazador(a) *m/f*; (*horse*) caballo de caza
hunting ['hʌntɪŋ] N caza
hurdle ['hə:dl] N (*Sport*) valla; (*fig*) obstáculo
hurl [hə:l] VT lanzar, arrojar
hurling ['hə:lɪŋ] N (*Sport*) juego irlandés semejante al hockey
hurly-burly ['hə:lɪ'bə:lɪ] N jaleo, follón *m*
hurrah [hu'rɑ:], **hurray** [hu'reɪ] N ¡viva!, ¡hurra!
hurricane ['hʌrɪkən] N huracán *m*
hurried ['hʌrɪd] ADJ (*fast*) apresurado; (*rushed*) hecho de prisa
hurriedly ['hʌrɪdlɪ] ADV con prisa, apresuradamente
hurry ['hʌrɪ] N prisa ▸ VI apresurarse, darse prisa, apurarse (LAM) ▸ VT (*person*) dar prisa a; (*work*) apresurar, hacer de prisa; **to be in a ~** tener prisa, tener apuro (LAM), estar apurado (LAM); **to ~ back/home** darse prisa en volver/ volver a casa
 ▸ **hurry along** VI pasar de prisa
 ▸ **hurry away, hurry off** VI irse corriendo
 ▸ **hurry on** VI: **to ~ on to say** apresurarse a decir
 ▸ **hurry up** VI darse prisa, apurarse (LAM)
hurt [hə:t] (*pt, pp* ~) VT hacer daño a; (*business, interests etc*) perjudicar ▸ VI doler ▸ ADJ lastimado; **I ~ my arm** me lastimé el brazo; **where does it ~?** ¿dónde te duele?

hurtful ['hə:tful] ADJ (*remark etc*) hiriente, dañino
hurtle ['hə:tl] VI: **to ~ past** pasar como un rayo
husband ['hʌzbənd] N marido
hush [hʌʃ] N silencio ▸ VT hacer callar; (*cover up*) encubrir; **~!** ¡chitón!, ¡cállate!
 ▸ **hush up** VT (*fact*) encubrir, callar
hushed [hʌʃt] ADJ (*voice*) bajo
hush-hush [hʌʃ'hʌʃ] ADJ (*inf*) muy secreto
husk [hʌsk] N (*of wheat*) cáscara
husky ['hʌskɪ] ADJ ronco; (*burly*) fornido ▸ N perro esquimal
hustings ['hʌstɪŋz] NPL (*Pol*) mitin *msg* preelectoral
hustle ['hʌsl] VT (*push*) empujar; (*hurry*) dar prisa a ▸ N bullicio, actividad *f* febril; **~ and bustle** ajetreo
hut [hʌt] N cabaña; (*shed*) cobertizo
hutch [hʌtʃ] N conejera
hyacinth ['haɪəsɪnθ] N jacinto
hybrid ['haɪbrɪd] ADJ, N híbrido; **~ car** coche híbrido; **~ engine** motor híbrido
hydrangea [haɪ'dreɪnʒə] N hortensia
hydrant ['haɪdrənt] N (*also*: **fire hydrant**) boca de incendios
hydraulic [haɪ'drɔ:lɪk] ADJ hidráulico
hydraulics [haɪ'drɔ:lɪks] N hidráulica
hydrochloric ['haɪdrəu'klɔrɪk] ADJ: **~ acid** ácido clorhídrico
hydroelectric [haɪdrəuɪ'lɛktrɪk] ADJ hidroeléctrico
hydrofoil ['haɪdrəfɔɪl] N aerodeslizador *m*
hydrogen ['haɪdrədʒən] N hidrógeno
hydrogen bomb N bomba de hidrógeno
hydrophobia [haɪdrə'fəubɪə] N hidrofobia
hydroplane ['haɪdrəpleɪn] N hidroavión *m*, hidroavioneta
hyena [haɪ'i:nə] N hiena
hygiene ['haɪdʒi:n] N higiene *f*
hygienic [haɪ'dʒi:nɪk] ADJ higiénico
hymn [hɪm] N himno
hype [haɪp] N (*inf*) bombo
hyperactive [haɪpər'æktɪv] ADJ hiperactivo
hyperlink ['haɪpəlɪŋk] N hiperenlace *m*
hypermarket ['haɪpəmɑ:kɪt] N hipermercado
hypertension ['haɪpə'tɛnʃən] N hipertensión *f*
hypertext ['haɪpə'tɛkst] N (*Comput*) hipertexto *m*
hyphen ['haɪfn] N guión *m*
hypnosis [hɪp'nəusɪs] N hipnosis *f*
hypnotic [hɪp'nɔtɪk] ADJ hipnótico
hypnotism ['hɪpnətɪzəm] N hipnotismo
hypnotist ['hɪpnətɪst] N hipnotista *mf*
hypnotize ['hɪpnətaɪz] VT hipnotizar
hypoallergenic ['haɪpəuælə'dʒɛnɪk] ADJ hipoalergénico

hypochondriac [haɪpəuˈkɔndriæk] N
 hipocondríaco(-a)
hypocrisy [hɪˈpɔkrɪsɪ] N hipocresía
hypocrite [ˈhɪpəkrɪt] N hipócrita *mf*
hypocritical [hɪpəˈkrɪtɪkl] ADJ hipócrita
hypodermic [haɪpəˈdəːmɪk] ADJ
 hipodérmico ▶ N (*syringe*) aguja hipodérmica
hypotenuse [haɪˈpɔtɪnjuːz] N hipotenusa
hypothermia [haɪpəuˈθəːmɪə] N hipotermia
hypothesis [haɪˈpɔθɪsɪs] (*pl* **hypotheses**

[-siːz]) N hipótesis *f inv*
hypothetical [haɪpəˈθɛtɪkl] ADJ hipotético
hysterectomy [hɪstəˈrɛktəmɪ] N
 histerectomía
hysteria [hɪˈstɪərɪə] N histeria
hysterical [hɪˈstɛrɪkl] ADJ histérico
hysterics [hɪˈstɛrɪks] NPL histeria *sg*,
 histerismo *sg*; **to have ~** ponerse histérico;
 to be in ~ (*fig*) morirse de risa
Hz ABBR (= *Hertz*) Hz

I i

I, i [aɪ] N (*letter*) I, i *f*; **I for Isaac**, (US) **I for Item** I de Inés, I de Israel

I [aɪ] PRON yo ▶ ABBR = **island; isle**

IA, Ia. ABBR (US) = **Iowa**

IAEA N ABBR = **International Atomic Energy Agency**

ib., ibid. ABBR (= *ibidem: from the same source*) ibídem

IBA N ABBR (BRIT: = *Independent Broadcasting Authority*) *see* **ITV**

Iberian [aɪ'bɪərɪən] ADJ ibero, ibérico

Iberian Peninsula N: **the ~** la Península Ibérica

IBEW N ABBR (US: = *International Brotherhood of Electrical Workers*) sindicato internacional de electricistas

i/c ABBR (BRIT) = **in charge**

ICBM N ABBR (= *intercontinental ballistic missile*) misil *m* balístico intercontinental

ICC N ABBR (= *International Chamber of Commerce*) CCI *f*; (US) = **Interstate Commerce Commission**

ice [aɪs] N hielo ▶ VT (*cake*) alcorzar ▶ VI (*also:* **ice over, ice up**) helarse; **to keep sth on ~** (*fig: plan, project*) tener algo en reserva

ice age N período glaciar

ice axe N piqueta (de alpinista)

iceberg ['aɪsbə:g] N iceberg *m*; **the tip of the ~** la punta del iceberg

icebox ['aɪsbɔks] N (BRIT) congelador *m*; (US) nevera, refrigeradora (LAM)

icebreaker ['aɪsbreɪkə'] N rompehielos *m inv*

ice bucket N cubo para el hielo

icecap ['aɪskæp] N casquete *m* polar

ice-cold [aɪs'kəuld] ADJ helado

ice cream N helado

ice-cream soda N soda mezclada con helado

ice cube N cubito de hielo

iced [aɪst] ADJ (*drink*) con hielo; (*cake*) escarchado

ice hockey N hockey *m* sobre hielo

Iceland ['aɪslənd] N Islandia

Icelander ['aɪsləndə'] N islandés(-esa) *m/f*

Icelandic [aɪs'lændɪk] ADJ islandés(-esa) ▶ N

(*Ling*) islandés *m*

ice lolly N (BRIT) polo

ice pick N piolet *m*

ice rink N pista de hielo

ice-skate ['aɪsskeɪt] N patín *m* de hielo ▶ VI patinar sobre hielo

ice-skating ['aɪsskeɪtɪŋ] N patinaje *m* sobre hielo

icicle ['aɪsɪkl] N carámbano

icing ['aɪsɪŋ] N (*Culin*) alcorza; (*Aviat etc*) formación *f* de hielo

icing sugar N (BRIT) azúcar *m* glas(eado)

ICJ N ABBR = **International Court of Justice**

icon ['aɪkɔn] N (*gen*) icono; (*Comput*) icono

ICR N ABBR (US) = **Institute for Cancer Research**

ICT N ABBR (= *Information and Communication(s) Technology*) TIC *f*, tecnología de la información; (BRIT Scol) informática

ICU N ABBR (= *intensive care unit*) UVI *f*

icy ['aɪsɪ] ADJ (*road*) helado; (*fig*) glacial

I'd [aɪd] = **I would; I had**

Ida. ABBR (US Post) = **Idaho**

ID card N (*identity card*) DNI *m*

IDD N ABBR (BRIT Tel: = *international direct dialling*) servicio automático internacional

idea [aɪ'dɪə] N idea; **good ~!** ¡buena idea!; **to have an ~ that ...** tener la impresión de que ...; **I haven't the least ~** no tengo ni (la más remota) idea

ideal [aɪ'dɪəl] N ideal *m* ▶ ADJ ideal

idealism [aɪ'dɪəlɪzəm] N idealismo

idealist [aɪ'dɪəlɪst] N idealista *mf*

ideally [aɪ'dɪəlɪ] ADV: **~, the book should have ...** lo ideal sería que el libro tuviera ...

identical [aɪ'dɛntɪkl] ADJ idéntico

identification [aɪdɛntɪfɪ'keɪʃən] N identificación *f*; **means of ~** documentos *mpl* personales

identify [aɪ'dɛntɪfaɪ] VT identificar ▶ VI: **to ~ with** identificarse con

Identikit® [aɪ'dɛntɪkɪt] N: **~ (picture)** retrato-robot *m*

identity [aɪ'dɛntɪtɪ] N identidad f
identity card N carnet m de identidad, cédula (de identidad) (LAm)
identity papers NPL documentos mpl (de identidad), documentación fsg
identity parade N identificación f de acusados
identity theft N robo de identidad
ideological [aɪdɪə'lɔdʒɪkəl] ADJ ideológico
ideology [aɪdɪ'ɔlədʒɪ] N ideología
idiocy ['ɪdɪəsɪ] N idiotez f; (stupid act) estupidez f
idiom ['ɪdɪəm] N modismo; (style of speaking) lenguaje m
idiomatic [ɪdɪə'mætɪk] ADJ idiomático
idiosyncrasy [ɪdɪəu'sɪŋkrəsɪ] N idiosincrasia
idiot ['ɪdɪət] N (gen) idiota mf; (fool) tonto(-a)
idiotic [ɪdɪ'ɔtɪk] ADJ idiota; tonto
idle ['aɪdl] ADJ (inactive) ocioso; (lazy) holgazán(-ana); (unemployed) parado, desocupado; (talk) frívolo ▶ VI (machine) funcionar or marchar en vacío; ~ **capacity** (Comm) capacidad f sin utilizar; ~ **money** (Comm) capital m improductivo; ~ **time** (Comm) tiempo de paro
   ▶ **idle away** VT: **to ~ away one's time** malgastar or desperdiciar el tiempo
idleness ['aɪdlnɪs] N holgazanería; paro, desocupación f
idler ['aɪdlə'] N holgazán(-ana) m/f, vago(-a)
idol ['aɪdl] N ídolo
idolize ['aɪdəlaɪz] VT idolatrar
idyllic [ɪ'dɪlɪk] ADJ idílico
i.e. ABBR (= id est) es decir
IED [aɪiː'diː] N (= Improvised Explosive Device) artefacto explosivo improvisado, bomba caminera
if [ɪf] CONJ si ▶ N: **there are a lot of ifs and buts** hay muchas dudas sin resolver; (even) **if** aunque, si bien; **I'd be pleased if you could do it** yo estaría contento si pudieras hacerlo; **if necessary** si resultase necesario; **if I were you** yo en tu lugar; **if only** si solamente; **as if** como si
iffy ['ɪfɪ] ADJ (inf) dudoso
igloo ['ɪgluː] N iglú m
ignite [ɪg'naɪt] VT (set fire to) encender ▶ VI encenderse
ignition [ɪg'nɪʃən] N (Aut: process) ignición f; (: mechanism) encendido; **to switch on/off the ~** arrancar/apagar el motor
ignition key N (Aut) llave f de contacto
ignoble [ɪg'nəubl] ADJ innoble, vil
ignominious [ɪgnə'mɪnɪəs] ADJ ignominioso, vergonzoso
ignoramus [ɪgnə'reɪməs] N ignorante mf, inculto(-a)
ignorance ['ɪgnərəns] N ignorancia; **to keep sb in ~ of sth** ocultarle algo a algn

ignorant ['ɪgnərənt] ADJ ignorante; **to be ~ of** (subject) desconocer; (events) ignorar
ignore [ɪg'nɔː'] VT (person) no hacer caso de; (fact) pasar por alto
ikon ['aɪkɔn] N = **icon**
IL ABBR (US Post) = **Illinois**
ILA N ABBR (US: = International Longshoremen's Association) sindicato internacional de trabajadores portuarios
ill [ɪl] ADJ enfermo, malo ▶ N mal m; (fig) infortunio ▶ ADV mal; **to take** or **be taken ~** caer or ponerse enfermo; **to feel ~ (with)** encontrarse mal (de); **to speak/think ~ of sb** hablar/pensar mal de algn; see also **ills**
Ill. ABBR (US Post) = **Illinois**
I'll [aɪl] = **I will**; **I shall**
ill-advised [ɪləd'vaɪzd] ADJ poco recomendable; **he was ~ to go** se equivocaba al ir
ill-at-ease [ɪlət'iːz] ADJ incómodo
ill-considered [ɪlkən'sɪdəd] ADJ (plan) poco pensado
ill-disposed [ɪldɪs'pəuzd] ADJ: **to be ~ towards sb/sth** estar maldispuesto hacia algn/algo
illegal [ɪ'liːgl] ADJ ilegal
illegible [ɪ'lɛdʒɪbl] ADJ ilegible
illegitimate [ɪlɪ'dʒɪtɪmət] ADJ ilegítimo
ill-fated [ɪl'feɪtɪd] ADJ malogrado
ill-favoured, (US) **ill-favored** [ɪl'feɪvəd] ADJ poco agraciado
ill feeling N rencor m
ill-gotten ['ɪlgɔtn] ADJ (gains etc) mal adquirido
ill health N mala salud f; **to be in ~** estar mal de salud
illicit [ɪ'lɪsɪt] ADJ ilícito
ill-informed [ɪlɪn'fɔːmd] ADJ (judgement) erróneo; (person) mal informado
illiterate [ɪ'lɪtərət] ADJ analfabeto
ill-mannered [ɪl'mænəd] ADJ mal educado
illness ['ɪlnɪs] N enfermedad f
illogical [ɪ'lɔdʒɪkl] ADJ ilógico
ills [ɪlz] NPL males mpl
ill-suited [ɪl'suːtɪd] ADJ (couple) incompatible; **he is ~ to the job** no es la persona indicada para el trabajo
ill-timed [ɪl'taɪmd] ADJ inoportuno
ill-treat [ɪl'triːt] VT maltratar
ill-treatment [ɪl'triːtmənt] N malos tratos mpl
illuminate [ɪ'luːmɪneɪt] VT (room, street) iluminar, alumbrar; (subject) aclarar; **illuminated sign** letrero luminoso
illuminating [ɪ'luːmɪneɪtɪŋ] ADJ revelador(a)
illumination [ɪluːmɪ'neɪʃən] N alumbrado; **illuminations** NPL luminarias fpl, luces fpl
illusion [ɪ'luːʒən] N ilusión f; **to be under the ~ that ...** estar convencido de que ...

illusive [ɪˈluːsɪv], **illusory** [ɪˈluːsərɪ] ADJ ilusorio

illustrate [ˈɪləstreɪt] VT ilustrar

illustration [ɪləˈstreɪʃən] N (*example*) ejemplo, ilustración f; (*in book*) lámina, ilustración f

illustrator [ˈɪləstreɪtər] N ilustrador(a) *m/f*

illustrious [ɪˈlʌstrɪəs] ADJ ilustre

ill will N rencor *m*

ILO N ABBR (= *International Labour Organization*) OIT f

IM N ABBR (= *instant messaging*) IM f ▸ VT enviar un mensaje instantáneo

I'm [aɪm] = **I am**

image [ˈɪmɪdʒ] N imagen f

imagery [ˈɪmɪdʒərɪ] N imágenes fpl

imaginable [ɪˈmædʒɪnəbl] ADJ imaginable

imaginary [ɪˈmædʒɪnərɪ] ADJ imaginario

imagination [ɪmædʒɪˈneɪʃən] N imaginación f; (*inventiveness*) inventiva; (*illusion*) fantasía

imaginative [ɪˈmædʒɪnətɪv] ADJ imaginativo

imagine [ɪˈmædʒɪn] VT imaginarse; (*suppose*) suponer

imbalance [ɪmˈbæləns] N desequilibrio

imbecile [ˈɪmbəsiːl] N imbécil *mf*

imbue [ɪmˈbjuː] VT: **to ~ sth with** imbuir algo de

IMF N ABBR (= *International Monetary Fund*) FMI *m*

imitate [ˈɪmɪteɪt] VT imitar

imitation [ɪmɪˈteɪʃən] N imitación f; (*copy*) copia; (*pej*) remedo

imitator [ˈɪmɪteɪtər] N imitador(a) *m/f*

immaculate [ɪˈmækjulət] ADJ limpísimo, inmaculado; (*Rel*) inmaculado

immaterial [ɪməˈtɪərɪəl] ADJ incorpóreo; **it is ~ whether ...** no importa si ...

immature [ɪməˈtjuər] ADJ (*person*) inmaduro; (*of one's youth*) joven

immaturity [ɪməˈtjuərɪtɪ] N inmadurez f

immeasurable [ɪˈmeʒrəbl] ADJ inconmensurable

immediacy [ɪˈmiːdɪəsɪ] N urgencia, proximidad f

immediate [ɪˈmiːdɪət] ADJ inmediato; (*pressing*) urgente, apremiante; (*nearest*: *family*) próximo; (: *neighbourhood*) inmediato; **in the ~ future** en un futuro próximo

immediately [ɪˈmiːdɪətlɪ] ADV (*at once*) en seguida; (*directly*) inmediatamente; **~ next to** justo al lado de

immense [ɪˈmens] ADJ inmenso, enorme

immensely [ɪˈmenslɪ] ADV enormemente

immensity [ɪˈmensɪtɪ] N (*of size, difference*) inmensidad f; (*of problem*) enormidad f

immerse [ɪˈmɜːs] VT (*submerge*) sumergir; **to be immersed in** (*fig*) estar absorto en

immersion heater [ɪˈmɜːʃən-] N (*BRIT*) calentador *m* de inmersión

immigrant [ˈɪmɪgrənt] N inmigrante *mf*

immigrate [ˈɪmɪgreɪt] VI inmigrar

immigration [ɪmɪˈgreɪʃən] N inmigración f

immigration authorities NPL servicio *sg* de inmigración

immigration laws NPL leyes fpl de inmigración

imminent [ˈɪmɪnənt] ADJ inminente

immobile [ɪˈməubaɪl] ADJ inmóvil

immobilize [ɪˈməubɪlaɪz] VT inmovilizar

immoderate [ɪˈmɒdərɪt] ADJ (*person*) desmesurado; (*opinion, reaction, demand*) excesivo

immodest [ɪˈmɒdɪst] ADJ (*indecent*) desvergonzado, impúdico; (*boasting*) jactancioso

immoral [ɪˈmɒrl] ADJ inmoral

immorality [ɪmɒˈrælɪtɪ] N inmoralidad f

immortal [ɪˈmɔːtl] ADJ inmortal

immortality [ɪmɔːˈtælɪtɪ] N inmortalidad f

immortalize [ɪˈmɔːtlaɪz] VT inmortalizar

immovable [ɪˈmuːvəbl] ADJ (*object*) imposible de mover; (*person*) inconmovible

immune [ɪˈmjuːn] ADJ: **~ (to)** inmune (a)

immune system N sistema *m* inmunitario

immunity [ɪˈmjuːnɪtɪ] N (*Med*: *of diplomat*) inmunidad f; (*Comm*) exención f

immunization [ɪmjunaɪˈzeɪʃən] N inmunización f

immunize [ˈɪmjunaɪz] VT inmunizar

imp [ɪmp] N (*small devil, child*) diablillo

impact [ˈɪmpækt] N (*gen*) impacto

impair [ɪmˈpɛər] VT perjudicar

-impaired [ɪmˈpɛəd] SUFF: **visually~** con defectos de visión

impale [ɪmˈpeɪl] VT (*with sword*) atravesar

impart [ɪmˈpɑːt] VT comunicar; (*make known*) participar; (*bestow*) otorgar

impartial [ɪmˈpɑːʃl] ADJ imparcial

impartiality [ɪmpɑːʃɪˈælɪtɪ] N imparcialidad f

impassable [ɪmˈpɑːsəbl] ADJ (*barrier*) infranqueable; (*road*) intransitable

impasse [ɪmˈpɑːs] N callejón *m* sin salida; **to reach an ~** llegar a un punto muerto

impassioned [ɪmˈpæʃənd] ADJ apasionado, exaltado

impassive [ɪmˈpæsɪv] ADJ impasible

impatience [ɪmˈpeɪʃəns] N impaciencia

impatient [ɪmˈpeɪʃənt] ADJ impaciente; **to get *or* grow ~** impacientarse

impatiently [ɪmˈpeɪʃəntlɪ] ADV con impaciencia

impeachment [ɪmˈpiːtʃmənt] N denuncia, acusación f

impeccable [ɪmˈpɛkəbl] ADJ impecable

impecunious [ɪmpɪˈkjuːnɪəs] ADJ sin dinero

impede [ɪmˈpiːd] VT estorbar, dificultar

impediment [ɪmˈpɛdɪmənt] N obstáculo,

estorbo; (also: **speech impediment**) defecto (del habla)

impel [ɪm'pɛl] VT (force): **to ~ sb (to do sth)** obligar a algn (a hacer algo)

impending [ɪm'pɛndɪŋ] ADJ inminente

impenetrable [ɪm'pɛnɪtrəbl] ADJ (jungle, fortress) impenetrable; (unfathomable) insondable

imperative [ɪm'pɛrətɪv] ADJ (tone) imperioso; (necessary) imprescindible ▶ N (Ling) imperativo

imperceptible [ɪmpə'sɛptɪbl] ADJ imperceptible

imperfect [ɪm'pə:fɪkt] ADJ imperfecto; (goods etc) defectuoso ▶ N (Ling: also: **imperfect tense**) imperfecto

imperfection [ɪmpə'fɛkʃən] N (blemish) desperfecto; (fault, flaw) defecto

imperial [ɪm'pɪərɪəl] ADJ imperial

imperialism [ɪm'pɪərɪəlɪzəm] N imperialismo

imperil [ɪm'pɛrɪl] VT poner en peligro

imperious [ɪm'pɪərɪəs] ADJ señorial, apremiante

impersonal [ɪm'pə:sənl] ADJ impersonal

impersonate [ɪm'pə:səneɪt] VT hacerse pasar por

impersonation [ɪmpə:sə'neɪʃən] N imitación f

impersonator [ɪm'pə:səneɪtəʳ] N (Theat etc) imitador(a) m/f

impertinence [ɪm'pə:tɪnəns] N impertinencia, insolencia

impertinent [ɪm'pə:tɪnənt] ADJ impertinente, insolente

imperturbable [ɪmpə'tə:bəbl] ADJ imperturbable, impasible

impervious [ɪm'pə:vɪəs] ADJ impermeable; (fig): **~ to** insensible a

impetuous [ɪm'pɛtjuəs] ADJ impetuoso

impetus ['ɪmpətəs] N ímpetu m; (fig) impulso

impinge [ɪm'pɪndʒ]: **to ~ on** vt fus (affect) afectar a

impish ['ɪmpɪʃ] ADJ travieso

implacable [ɪm'plækəbl] ADJ implacable

implant [ɪm'plɑ:nt] VT (Med) injertar, implantar; (fig: idea, principle) inculcar

implausible [ɪm'plɔ:zɪbl] ADJ inverosímil

implement N ['ɪmplɪmənt] instrumento, herramienta ▶ VT ['ɪmplɪmɛnt] hacer efectivo; (carry out) realizar

implicate ['ɪmplɪkeɪt] VT (compromise) comprometer; (involve) enredar; **to ~ sb in sth** comprometer a algn en algo

implication [ɪmplɪ'keɪʃən] N consecuencia; **by ~** indirectamente

implicit [ɪm'plɪsɪt] ADJ (gen) implícito; (complete) absoluto

implicitly [ɪm'plɪsɪtlɪ] ADV implícitamente

implore [ɪm'plɔ:ʳ] VT (person) suplicar

imploring [ɪm'plɔ:rɪŋ] ADJ de súplica

imply [ɪm'plaɪ] VT (involve) implicar, suponer; (hint) insinuar

impolite [ɪmpə'laɪt] ADJ mal educado

impolitic [ɪm'pɒlɪtɪk] ADJ poco diplomático

imponderable [ɪm'pɒndərəbl] ADJ imponderable

import VT [ɪm'pɔ:t] importar ▶ N ['ɪmpɔ:t] (Comm) importación f; (: article) producto importado; (meaning) significado, sentido ▶ CPD (duty, licence etc) de importación

importance [ɪm'pɔ:təns] N importancia; **to be of great/little ~** tener mucha/poca importancia

important [ɪm'pɔ:tənt] ADJ importante; **it's not ~** no importa, no tiene importancia; **it is ~ that** es importante que

importantly [ɪm'pɔ:təntlɪ] ADV (pej) dándose importancia; **but, more ~ ...** pero, lo que es aún más importante ...

import duty N derechos mpl de importación

imported [ɪm'pɔ:tɪd] ADJ importado

importer [ɪm'pɔ:təʳ] N importador(a) m/f

import licence, (US) **import license** N licencia de importación

impose [ɪm'pəuz] VT imponer ▶ VI: **to ~ on sb** abusar de algn

imposing [ɪm'pəuzɪŋ] ADJ imponente, impresionante

imposition [ɪmpə'zɪʃən] N (of tax etc) imposición f; **to be an ~** (on person) molestar

impossibility [ɪmpɒsə'bɪlɪtɪ] N imposibilidad f

impossible [ɪm'pɒsɪbl] ADJ imposible; (person) insoportable; **it is ~ for me to leave now** me es imposible salir ahora

impossibly [ɪm'pɒsɪblɪ] ADV imposiblemente

impostor [ɪm'pɒstəʳ] N impostor(a) m/f

impotence ['ɪmpətəns] N impotencia

impotent ['ɪmpətənt] ADJ impotente

impound [ɪm'paund] VT embargar

impoverished [ɪm'pɒvərɪʃt] ADJ necesitado; (land) agotado

impracticable [ɪm'præktɪkəbl] ADJ no factible, irrealizable

impractical [ɪm'præktɪkl] ADJ (person) poco práctico

imprecise [ɪmprɪ'saɪs] ADJ impreciso

impregnable [ɪm'prɛgnəbl] ADJ invulnerable; (castle) inexpugnable

impregnate ['ɪmprɛgneɪt] VT (gen) impregnar; (soak) empapar; (fertilize) fecundar

impresario [ɪmprɪ'sɑ:rɪəu] N empresario(-a)

impress [ɪm'prɛs] VT impresionar; (mark) estampar ▶ VI causar buena impresión; **to ~ sth on sb** convencer a algn de la importancia de algo

impression [ɪm'prɛʃən] N impresión f; (*footprint etc*) huella; (*print run*) edición f; **to be under the ~ that** tener la impresión de que; **to make a good/bad ~ on sb** causar buena/mala impresión a algn

impressionable [ɪm'prɛʃnəbl] ADJ impresionable

impressionist [ɪm'prɛʃənɪst] N impresionista *mf*

impressive [ɪm'prɛsɪv] ADJ impresionante

imprint ['ɪmprɪnt] N (*Publishing*) pie *m* de imprenta; (*fig*) sello

imprison [ɪm'prɪzn] VT encarcelar

imprisonment [ɪm'prɪznmənt] N encarcelamiento; (*term of imprisonment*) cárcel f; **life ~** cadena perpetua

improbable [ɪm'prɒbəbl] ADJ improbable, inverosímil

impromptu [ɪm'prɒmptju:] ADJ improvisado ▸ ADV de improviso

improper [ɪm'prɒpəʳ] ADJ (*incorrect*) impropio; (*unseemly*) indecoroso; (*indecent*) indecente; (*dishonest: activities*) deshonesto

impropriety [ɪmprə'praɪətɪ] N falta de decoro; (*indecency*) indecencia; (*of language*) impropiedad f

improve [ɪm'pru:v] VT mejorar; (*foreign language*) perfeccionar ▸ VI mejorar
▸ **improve (up)on** VT FUS (*offer*) mejorar

improvement [ɪm'pru:vmənt] N mejora; perfeccionamiento; **to make improvements to** mejorar

improvise ['ɪmprəvaɪz] VT, VI improvisar

imprudence [ɪm'pru:dns] N imprudencia

imprudent [ɪm'pru:dnt] ADJ imprudente

impudent ['ɪmpjudnt] ADJ descarado, insolente

impugn [ɪm'pju:n] VT impugnar

impulse ['ɪmpʌls] N impulso; **to act on ~** actuar sin reflexionar, dejarse llevar por el impulso

impulse buying N compra impulsiva

impulsive [ɪm'pʌlsɪv] ADJ irreflexivo, impulsivo

impunity [ɪm'pju:nɪtɪ] N: **with ~** impunemente

impure [ɪm'pjuəʳ] ADJ (*adulterated*) adulterado; (*morally*) impuro

impurity [ɪm'pjuərɪtɪ] N impureza

IN ABBR (*US Post*) = **Indiana**

(KEYWORD)

in [ɪn] PREP **1** (*indicating place, position, with place names*) en; **in the house/garden** en (la) casa/el jardín; **in here/there** aquí/ahí or allí dentro; **in London/England** en Londres/Inglaterra; **in town** en el centro (de la ciudad)

2 (*indicating time*) en; **in spring** en (la) primavera; **in 1988/May** en 1988/mayo; **in the afternoon** por la tarde; **at four o'clock in the afternoon** a las cuatro de la tarde; **I did it in three hours/days** lo hice en tres horas/días; **I'll see you in two weeks** *or* **in two weeks' time** te veré dentro de dos semanas; **once in a hundred years** una vez cada cien años

3 (*indicating manner etc*) en; **in a loud/soft voice** en voz alta/baja; **in pencil/ink** a lápiz/bolígrafo; **the boy in the blue shirt** el chico de la camisa azul; **in writing** por escrito; **to pay in dollars** pagar en dólares

4 (*indicating circumstances*): **in the sun/shade** al sol/a la sombra; **in the rain** bajo la lluvia; **a change in policy** un cambio de política; **a rise in prices** un aumento de precios

5 (*indicating mood: state*): **in tears** llorando; **in anger/despair** enfadado/desesperado; **to live in luxury** vivir lujosamente; **in that** *conj* ya que

6 (*with ratios: numbers*): **1 in 10 households**, **1 household in 10** una de cada 10 familias; **20 pence in the pound** 20 peniques por libra; **they lined up in twos** se alinearon de dos en dos; **in hundreds** a *or* por centenares

7 (*referring to people, works*) en; entre; **the disease is common in children** la enfermedad es común entre los niños; **in (the works of) Dickens** en (las obras de) Dickens

8 (*indicating profession etc*): **to be in teaching** dedicarse a la enseñanza

9 (*after superlative*) de; **the best pupil in the class** el/la mejor alumno(-a) de la clase

10 (*with present participle*): **in saying this** al decir esto

▸ ADV: **to be in** (*person: at home*) estar en casa; (: *at work*) estar; (*train, ship, plane*) haber llegado; (*in fashion*) estar de moda; **she'll be in later today** llegará más tarde hoy; **to ask sb in** hacer pasar a algn; **to run/limp** *etc* **in** entrar corriendo/cojeando *etc*

▸ N: **the ins and outs** (*of proposal, situation etc*) los detalles

in., ins ABBR = **inch; inches**

inability [ɪnə'bɪlɪtɪ] N: **~ (to do)** incapacidad f (de hacer); **~ to pay** insolvencia en el pago

inaccessible [ɪnæk'sɛsɪbl] ADJ inaccesible

inaccuracy [ɪn'ækjurəsɪ] N inexactitud f

inaccurate [ɪn'ækjurət] ADJ inexacto, incorrecto

inaction [ɪn'ækʃən] N inacción f

inactive [ɪn'æktɪv] ADJ inactivo

inactivity [ɪnæk'tɪvɪtɪ] N inactividad f

inadequacy [ɪn'ædɪkwəsɪ] N insuficiencia; incapacidad f

inadequate [ɪn'ædɪkwət] ADJ (*insufficient*)

insuficiente; (*unsuitable*) inadecuado; (*person*) incapaz

inadmissible [ɪnəd'mɪsəbl] ADJ improcedente, inadmisible

inadvertent [ɪnəd'vəːtənt] ADJ descuidado, involuntario

inadvertently [ɪnəd'vəːtntlɪ] ADV por descuido

inadvisable [ɪnəd'vaɪzəbl] ADJ poco aconsejable

inane [ɪ'neɪn] ADJ necio, fatuo

inanimate [ɪn'ænɪmət] ADJ inanimado

inapplicable [ɪn'æplɪkəbl] ADJ inaplicable

inappropriate [ɪnə'prəuprɪət] ADJ inadecuado

inapt [ɪn'æpt] ADJ impropio

inaptitude [ɪn'æptɪtjuːd] N incapacidad *f*

inarticulate [ɪnɑː'tɪkjulət] ADJ (*person*) incapaz de expresarse; (*speech*) mal pronunciado

inartistic [ɪnɑː'tɪstɪk] ADJ antiestético

inasmuch as [ɪnəz'mʌtʃ-] ADV en la medida en que

inattention [ɪnə'tɛnʃən] N desatención *f*

inattentive [ɪnə'tɛntɪv] ADJ distraído

inaudible [ɪn'ɔːdɪbl] ADJ inaudible

inaugural [ɪ'nɔːgjurəl] ADJ inaugural; (*speech*) de apertura

inaugurate [ɪ'nɔːgjureɪt] VT inaugurar; (*president, official*) investir

inauguration [ɪnɔːgju'reɪʃən] N inauguración *f*; (*of official*) investidura; (*of event*) ceremonia de apertura

inauspicious [ɪnɔːs'pɪʃəs] ADJ poco propicio, inoportuno

in-between [ɪnbɪ'twiːn] ADJ intermedio

inborn [ɪn'bɔːn] ADJ (*feeling*) innato

inbox ['ɪnbɒks] N (*Comput*) buzón *m* de entrada; (*US: in-tray*) bandeja de entrada

inbred [ɪn'brɛd] ADJ innato; (*family*) consanguíneo

inbreeding [ɪn'briːdɪŋ] N endogamia

Inc. ABBR = **incorporated**

Inca ['ɪŋkə] ADJ (*also*: **Incan**) inca, de los incas ▶ N inca *mf*

incalculable [ɪn'kælkjuləbl] ADJ incalculable

incapability [ɪnkeɪpə'bɪlɪtɪ] N incapacidad *f*

incapable [ɪn'keɪpəbl] ADJ: ~ **(of doing sth)** incapaz (de hacer algo)

incapacitate [ɪnkə'pæsɪteɪt] VT: **to ~ sb** incapacitar a algn

incapacitated [ɪnkə'pæsɪteɪtɪd] ADJ incapacitado

incapacity [ɪnkə'pæsɪtɪ] N (*inability*) incapacidad *f*

incarcerate [ɪn'kɑːsəreɪt] VT encarcelar

incarnate ADJ [ɪn'kɑːnɪt] en persona ▶ VT ['ɪnkɑːneɪt] encarnar

incarnation [ɪnkɑː'neɪʃən] N encarnación *f*

incendiary [ɪn'sɛndɪərɪ] ADJ incendiario ▶ N (*bomb*) bomba incendiaria

incense N ['ɪnsɛns] incienso ▶ VT [ɪn'sɛns] (*anger*) indignar, encolerizar

incentive [ɪn'sɛntɪv] N incentivo, estímulo

incentive bonus N prima

incentive scheme N plan *m* de incentivos

inception [ɪn'sɛpʃən] N comienzo, principio

incessant [ɪn'sɛsnt] ADJ incesante, continuo

incessantly [ɪn'sɛsəntlɪ] ADV constantemente

incest ['ɪnsɛst] N incesto

inch [ɪntʃ] N pulgada; **to be within an ~ of** estar a dos dedos de; **he didn't give an ~** no hizo la más mínima concesión; **a few inches** unas pulgadas
▶ **inch forward** VI avanzar palmo a palmo

incidence ['ɪnsɪdns] N (*of crime, disease*) incidencia

incident ['ɪnsɪdnt] N incidente *m*; (*in book*) episodio

incidental [ɪnsɪ'dɛntl] ADJ circunstancial, accesorio; (*unplanned*) fortuito; ~ **to** relacionado con; ~ **expenses** (*gastos mpl*) imprevistos *mpl*

incidentally [ɪnsɪ'dɛntəlɪ] ADV (*by the way*) por cierto

incidental music N música de fondo

incident room N (*Police*) centro de coordinación

incinerate [ɪn'sɪnəreɪt] VT incinerar, quemar

incinerator [ɪn'sɪnəreɪtər] N incinerador *m*, incineradora

incipient [ɪn'sɪpɪənt] ADJ incipiente

incision [ɪn'sɪʒən] N incisión *f*

incisive [ɪn'saɪsɪv] ADJ (*mind*) penetrante; (*remark etc*) incisivo

incisor [ɪn'saɪzər] N incisivo

incite [ɪn'saɪt] VT provocar, incitar

incl. ABBR = **including**; **inclusive (of)**

inclement [ɪn'klɛmənt] ADJ inclemente

inclination [ɪnklɪ'neɪʃən] N (*tendency*) tendencia, inclinación *f*

incline [*n* 'ɪnklaɪn, *vt, vi* ɪn'klaɪn] N pendiente *f*, cuesta ▶ VT (*slope*) inclinar; (*head*) poner de lado ▶ VI inclinarse; **to be inclined to** (*tend*) ser propenso a; (*be willing*) estar dispuesto a

include [ɪn'kluːd] VT incluir, comprender; (*in letter*) adjuntar; **the tip is/is not included** la propina está/no está incluida

including [ɪn'kluːdɪŋ] PREP incluso, inclusive; ~ **tip** propina incluida

inclusion [ɪn'kluːʒən] N inclusión *f*

inclusive [ɪn'kluːsɪv] ADJ inclusivo ▶ ADV inclusive; ~ **of tax** incluidos los impuestos; **$50, ~ of all surcharges** 50 dólares, incluidos todos los recargos

incognito [ɪnkɒg'niːtəu] ADV de incógnito

incoherent [ɪnkəu'hɪərənt] ADJ incoherente

income ['ɪnkʌm] N (*personal*) ingresos *mpl*; (*from property etc*) renta; (*profit*) rédito; **gross/ net** ~ ingresos *mpl* brutos/netos; **~ and expenditure account** cuenta de gastos e ingresos

income bracket N categoría económica

income support N (BRIT) ≈ ayuda familiar

income tax N impuesto sobre la renta

income tax inspector N inspector(a) *m/f* de Hacienda

income tax return N declaración *f* de ingresos

incoming ['ɪnkʌmɪŋ] ADJ (*passengers, flight*) de llegada; (*government*) entrante; (*tenant*) nuevo

incommunicado ['ɪnkəmjuːnɪ'kɑːdəʊ] ADJ: **to hold sb** ~ mantener incomunicado a algn

incomparable [ɪn'kɒmpərəbl] ADJ incomparable, sin par

incompatible [ɪnkəm'pætɪbl] ADJ incompatible

incompetence [ɪn'kɒmpɪtəns] N incompetencia

incompetent [ɪn'kɒmpɪtənt] ADJ incompetente

incomplete [ɪnkəm'pliːt] ADJ incompleto; (*unfinished*) sin terminar

incomprehensible [ɪnkɒmprɪ'hensɪbl] ADJ incomprensible

inconceivable [ɪnkən'siːvəbl] ADJ inconcebible

inconclusive [ɪnkən'kluːsɪv] ADJ sin resultado (definitivo); (*argument*) poco convincente

incongruity [ɪnkɒŋ'gruːɪtɪ] N incongruencia

incongruous [ɪn'kɒŋgruəs] ADJ discordante

inconsequential [ɪnkɒnsɪ'kwenʃl] ADJ intranscendente

inconsiderable [ɪnkən'sɪdərəbl] ADJ insignificante

inconsiderate [ɪnkən'sɪdərət] ADJ desconsiderado; **how ~ of him!** ¡qué falta de consideración (de su parte)!

inconsistency [ɪnkən'sɪstənsɪ] N inconsecuencia; (*of actions etc*) falta de lógica; (*of work*) carácter *m* desigual, inconsistencia; (*of statement etc*) contradicción *f*

inconsistent [ɪnkən'sɪstnt] ADJ inconsecuente; (*contradictory*) incongruente; **~ with** que no concuerda con

inconsolable [ɪnkən'səʊləbl] ADJ inconsolable

inconspicuous [ɪnkən'spɪkjuəs] ADJ (*discreet*) discreto; (*person*) que llama poco la atención

inconstancy [ɪn'kɒnstənsɪ] N inconstancia

inconstant [ɪn'kɒnstənt] ADJ inconstante

incontinence [ɪn'kɒntɪnəns] N incontinencia

incontinent [ɪn'kɒntɪnənt] ADJ incontinente

incontrovertible [ɪnkɒntrə'vɜːtəbl] ADJ incontrovertible

inconvenience [ɪnkən'viːnjəns] N (*gen*) inconvenientes *mpl*; (*trouble*) molestia ▶ VT incomodar; **to put sb to great** ~ causar mucha molestia a algn; **don't ~ yourself** no se moleste

inconvenient [ɪnkən'viːnjənt] ADJ incómodo, poco práctico; (*time, place*) inoportuno; **that time is very ~ for me** esa hora me es muy inconveniente

incorporate [ɪn'kɔːpəreɪt] VT incorporar; (*contain*) comprender; (*add*) agregar

incorporated [ɪn'kɔːpəreɪtɪd] ADJ: **~ company** (US) ≈ Sociedad *f* Anónima (S.A.)

incorrect [ɪnkə'rekt] ADJ incorrecto

incorrigible [ɪn'kɒrɪdʒəbl] ADJ incorregible

incorruptible [ɪnkə'rʌptɪbl] ADJ incorruptible

increase [N 'ɪnkriːs, vi, vt ɪn'kriːs] N aumento ▶ VI aumentar; (*grow*) crecer; (*price*) subir ▶ VT aumentar; (*price*) subir; **an ~ of 5%** un aumento de 5%; **to be on the ~** ir en aumento

increasing [ɪn'kriːsɪŋ] ADJ (*number*) creciente, que va en aumento

increasingly [ɪn'kriːsɪŋlɪ] ADV cada vez más

incredible [ɪn'kredɪbl] ADJ increíble

incredibly [ɪn'kredɪblɪ] ADV increíblemente

incredulity [ɪnkrɪ'djuːlɪtɪ] N incredulidad *f*

incredulous [ɪn'kredjuləs] ADJ incrédulo

increment ['ɪnkrɪmənt] N aumento, incremento

incriminate [ɪn'krɪmɪneɪt] VT incriminar

incriminating [ɪn'krɪmɪneɪtɪŋ] ADJ incriminatorio

incrust [ɪn'krʌst] VT = **encrust**

incubate ['ɪnkjubeɪt] VT (*egg*) incubar, empollar ▶ VI (*egg, disease*) incubar

incubation [ɪnkju'beɪʃən] N incubación *f*

incubation period N período de incubación

incubator ['ɪnkjubeɪtər] N incubadora

inculcate ['ɪnkʌlkeɪt] VT: **to ~ sth in sb** inculcar algo en algn

incumbent [ɪn'kʌmbənt] N ocupante *mf* ▶ ADJ: **it is ~ on him to ...** le incumbe ...

incur [ɪn'kɜːr] VT (*expenses*) incurrir en; (*loss*) sufrir; (*anger, disapproval*) provocar

incurable [ɪn'kjuərəbl] ADJ incurable

incursion [ɪn'kɜːʃən] N incursión *f*

Ind. ABBR (US) = **Indiana**

indebted [ɪn'detɪd] ADJ: **to be ~ to sb** estar agradecido a algn

indecency [ɪn'diːsnsɪ] N indecencia

indecent [ɪn'diːsnt] ADJ indecente

indecent assault N (BRIT) atentado contra el pudor

indecent exposure N exhibicionismo

indecipherable [ɪndɪ'saɪfərəbl] ADJ indescifrable

indecision [ɪndɪ'sɪʒən] N indecisión *f*

indecisive [ɪndɪˈsaɪsɪv] ADJ indeciso; (*discussion*) no resuelto, inconcluyente

indeed [ɪnˈdiːd] ADV efectivamente, en realidad; (*in fact*) en efecto; (*furthermore*) es más; **yes ~!** ¡claro que sí!

indefatigable [ɪndɪˈfætɪgəbl] ADJ incansable, infatigable

indefensible [ɪndɪˈfɛnsəbl] ADJ (*conduct*) injustificable

indefinable [ɪndɪˈfaɪnəbl] ADJ indefinible

indefinite [ɪnˈdɛfɪnɪt] ADJ indefinido; (*uncertain*) incierto

indefinitely [ɪnˈdɛfɪnɪtlɪ] ADV (*wait*) indefinidamente

indelible [ɪnˈdɛlɪbl] ADJ imborrable

indelicate [ɪnˈdɛlɪkɪt] ADJ (*tactless*) indiscreto, inoportuno; (*not polite*) poco delicado

indemnify [ɪnˈdɛmnɪfaɪ] VT indemnizar, resarcir

indemnity [ɪnˈdɛmnɪtɪ] N (*insurance*) indemnidad *f*; (*compensation*) indemnización *f*

indent [ɪnˈdɛnt] VT (*text*) sangrar

indentation [ɪndɛnˈteɪʃən] N mella; (*Typ*) sangría

indenture [ɪnˈdɛntʃəʳ] N escritura, instrumento

independence [ɪndɪˈpɛndns] N independencia

Independence Day N Día *m* de la Independencia

> El cuatro de julio es la fiesta nacional de los Estados Unidos, *Independence Day*, en conmemoración de la Declaración de Independencia escrita por Thomas Jefferson y adoptada en 1776. En ella se proclamaba la ruptura total con Gran Bretaña de las trece colonias americanas que fueron el origen de los Estados Unidos de América.

independent [ɪndɪˈpɛndənt] ADJ independiente; **to become ~** independizarse

independent school N (*Brit*) escuela *f* privada, colegio *m* privado

in-depth [ˈɪndɛpθ] ADJ en profundidad, a fondo

indescribable [ɪndɪˈskraɪbəbl] ADJ indescriptible

indestructible [ɪndɪsˈtrʌktəbl] ADJ indestructible

indeterminate [ɪndɪˈtəːmɪnɪt] ADJ indeterminado

index [ˈɪndɛks] N (*pl* **indexes**) (*in book*) índice *m*; (*in library etc*) catálogo; (*pl* **indices** [ˈɪndɪsiːz]: *ratio, sign*) exponente *m*

index card N ficha

index finger N índice *m*

index-linked [ˈɪndɛksˈlɪŋkt], (*US*) **indexed** [ˈɪndɛkst] ADJ indexado

India [ˈɪndɪə] N la India

Indian [ˈɪndɪən] ADJ, N indio(-a) *m/f*; (*also:* **American Indian**) indio(-a) *m/f* de América, amerindio(-a) *m/f*; (*pej*) **Red ~** piel roja *mf*

Indian Ocean N: **the ~** el Océano Índico, el Mar de las Indias

Indian summer N (*fig*) veranillo de San Martín

india rubber N caucho

indicate [ˈɪndɪkeɪt] VT indicar ▶ VI (*Brit Aut*): **to ~ left/right** indicar a la izquierda/a la derecha

indication [ɪndɪˈkeɪʃən] N indicio, señal *f*

indicative [ɪnˈdɪkətɪv] ADJ: **to be ~ of sth** indicar algo ▶ N (*Ling*) indicativo

indicator [ˈɪndɪkeɪtəʳ] N (*gen*) indicador *m*; (*Aut*) intermitente *m*, direccional *m* (*LAM*)

indices [ˈɪndɪsiːz] NPL *of* **index**

indict [ɪnˈdaɪt] VT acusar

indictable [ɪnˈdaɪtəbl] ADJ: **~ offence** delito procesable

indictment [ɪnˈdaɪtmənt] N acusación *f*

indifference [ɪnˈdɪfrəns] N indiferencia

indifferent [ɪnˈdɪfrənt] ADJ indiferente; (*poor*) regular

indigenous [ɪnˈdɪdʒɪnəs] ADJ indígena

indigestible [ɪndɪˈdʒɛstɪbl] ADJ indigesto

indigestion [ɪndɪˈdʒɛstʃən] N indigestión *f*

indignant [ɪnˈdɪgnənt] ADJ: **to be ~ about sth** indignarse por algo

indignation [ɪndɪgˈneɪʃən] N indignación *f*

indignity [ɪnˈdɪgnɪtɪ] N indignidad *f*

indigo [ˈɪndɪgəu] ADJ (*colour*) (de color) añil ▶ N añil *m*

indirect [ɪndɪˈrɛkt] ADJ indirecto

indirectly [ɪndɪˈrɛktlɪ] ADV indirectamente

indiscernible [ɪndɪˈsəːnəbl] ADJ imperceptible

indiscreet [ɪndɪˈskriːt] ADJ indiscreto, imprudente

indiscretion [ɪndɪˈskrɛʃən] N indiscreción *f*, imprudencia

indiscriminate [ɪndɪˈskrɪmɪnət] ADJ indiscriminado

indispensable [ɪndɪˈspɛnsəbl] ADJ indispensable, imprescindible

indisposed [ɪndɪˈspəuzd] ADJ (*unwell*) indispuesto

indisposition [ɪndɪspəˈzɪʃən] N indisposición *f*

indisputable [ɪndɪˈspjuːtəbl] ADJ incontestable

indistinct [ɪndɪˈstɪŋkt] ADJ indistinto

indistinguishable [ɪndɪˈstɪŋgwɪʃəbl] ADJ indistinguible

individual [ɪndɪˈvɪdjuəl] N individuo ▶ ADJ individual; (*personal*) personal; (*particular*) particular

individualist [ˌɪndɪˈvɪdjuəlɪst] N
individualista *mf*

individuality [ˌɪndɪvɪdjuˈælɪtɪ] N
individualidad *f*

individually [ˌɪndɪˈvɪdjuəlɪ] ADV
individualmente; particularmente

indivisible [ˌɪndɪˈvɪzəbl] ADJ indivisible

Indo-China [ˈɪndəʊˈtʃaɪnə] N Indochina

indoctrinate [ɪnˈdɔktrɪneɪt] VT adoctrinar

indoctrination [ɪndɔktrɪˈneɪʃən] N
adoctrinamiento

indolence [ˈɪndələns] N indolencia

indolent [ˈɪndələnt] ADJ indolente, perezoso

Indonesia [ɪndəˈniːzɪə] N Indonesia

Indonesian [ɪndəˈniːzɪən] ADJ indonesio ▶ N
indonesio(-a); (*Ling*) indonesio

indoor [ˈɪndɔːʳ] ADJ (*swimming pool*) cubierto;
(*plant*) de interior; (*sport*) bajo cubierta

indoors [ɪnˈdɔːz] ADV dentro; (*at home*) en
casa

indubitable [ɪnˈdjuːbɪtəbl] ADJ indudable

indubitably [ɪnˈdjuːbɪtəblɪ] ADV
indudablemente

induce [ɪnˈdjuːs] VT inducir, persuadir; (*bring
about*) producir; **to ~ sb to do sth** persuadir a
algn a que haga algo

inducement [ɪnˈdjuːsmənt] N (*incentive*)
incentivo, aliciente *m*

induct [ɪnˈdʌkt] VT iniciar; (*in job, rank,
position*) instalar

induction [ɪnˈdʌkʃən] N (*Med: of birth*)
inducción *f*

induction course N (*Brit*) cursillo
introductorio *or* de iniciación

indulge [ɪnˈdʌldʒ] VT (*whim*) satisfacer;
(*person*) complacer; (*child*) mimar ▶ VI: **to ~ in**
darse el gusto de

indulgence [ɪnˈdʌldʒəns] N vicio

indulgent [ɪnˈdʌldʒənt] ADJ indulgente

industrial [ɪnˈdʌstrɪəl] ADJ industrial

industrial action N huelga

industrial estate N (*Brit*) polígono *or* (*Lam*)
zona industrial

industrial goods NPL bienes *mpl* de
producción

industrialist [ɪnˈdʌstrɪəlɪst] N industrial *mf*

industrialize [ɪnˈdʌstrɪəlaɪz] VT
industrializar

industrial park N (*US*) = **industrial estate**

industrial relations NPL relaciones *fpl*
empresariales

industrial tribunal N magistratura de
trabajo, tribunal *m* laboral

industrial unrest N (*Brit*) agitación *f* obrera

industrious [ɪnˈdʌstrɪəs] ADJ (*gen*)
trabajador(a); (*student*) aplicado

industry [ˈɪndəstrɪ] N industria; (*diligence*)
aplicación *f*

inebriated [ɪˈniːbrɪeɪtɪd] ADJ borracho

inedible [ɪnˈɛdɪbl] ADJ incomible; (*plant etc*)
no comestible

ineffective [ɪnɪˈfɛktɪv], **ineffectual**
[ɪnɪˈfɛktʃuəl] ADJ ineficaz, inútil

inefficiency [ɪnɪˈfɪʃənsɪ] N ineficacia

inefficient [ɪnɪˈfɪʃənt] ADJ ineficaz,
ineficiente

inelegant [ɪnˈɛlɪgənt] ADJ poco elegante

ineligible [ɪnˈɛlɪdʒɪbl] ADJ inelegible

inept [ɪˈnɛpt] ADJ incompetente, incapaz

ineptitude [ɪˈnɛptɪtjuːd] N incapacidad *f*,
ineptitud *f*

inequality [ɪnɪˈkwɔlɪtɪ] N desigualdad *f*

inequitable [ɪnˈɛkwɪtəbl] ADJ injusto

ineradicable [ɪnɪˈrædɪkəbl] ADJ inextirpable

inert [ɪˈnəːt] ADJ inerte, inactivo; (*immobile*)
inmóvil

inertia [ɪˈnəːʃə] N inercia; (*laziness*) pereza

inertia-reel seat-belt [ɪˈnəːʃəˈriːl-] N
cinturón *m* de seguridad retráctil

inescapable [ɪnɪˈskeɪpəbl] ADJ ineludible,
inevitable

inessential [ɪnɪˈsɛnʃl] ADJ no esencial

inestimable [ɪnˈɛstɪməbl] ADJ inestimable

inevitability [ɪnevɪtəˈbɪlɪtɪ] N
inevitabilidad *f*

inevitable [ɪnˈevɪtəbl] ADJ inevitable;
(*necessary*) forzoso

inevitably [ɪnˈevɪtəblɪ] ADV inevitablemente;
as ~ happens ... como siempre pasa ...

inexact [ɪnɪgˈzækt] ADJ inexacto

inexcusable [ɪnɪksˈkjuːzəbl] ADJ
imperdonable

inexhaustible [ɪnɪgˈzɔːstɪbl] ADJ inagotable

inexorable [ɪnˈɛksərəbl] ADJ inexorable,
implacable

inexpensive [ɪnɪkˈspɛnsɪv] ADJ económico

inexperience [ɪnɪkˈspɪərɪəns] N falta de
experiencia

inexperienced [ɪnɪkˈspɪərɪənst] ADJ
inexperto; **to be ~ in sth** no tener
experiencia en algo

inexplicable [ɪnɪkˈsplɪkəbl] ADJ inexplicable

inexpressible [ɪnɪkˈsprɛsəbl] ADJ
inexpresable

inextricable [ɪnɪksˈtrɪkəbl] ADJ inseparable

inextricably [ɪnɪksˈtrɪkəblɪ] ADV
indisolublemente

infallibility [ɪnfæləˈbɪlɪtɪ] N infalibilidad *f*

infallible [ɪnˈfælɪbl] ADJ infalible

infamous [ˈɪnfəməs] ADJ infame

infamy [ˈɪnfəmɪ] N infamia

infancy [ˈɪnfənsɪ] N infancia

infant [ˈɪnfənt] N niño(-a); (*baby*) niño(-a)
pequeño(-a), bebé *mf*

infantile [ˈɪnfəntaɪl] ADJ infantil; (*pej*)
aniñado

infant mortality N mortalidad *f* infantil

infantry [ˈɪnfəntrɪ] N infantería

infantryman ['ɪnfəntrɪmən] N (irreg) soldado de infantería
infant school N (BRIT) escuela infantil; see also **primary school**
infatuated [ɪn'fætjʊeɪtɪd] ADJ: ~ **with** (in love) loco por; **to become ~ (with sb)** enamoriscarse (de algn), encapricharse (con algn)
infatuation [ɪnfætjʊ'eɪʃən] N enamoramiento
infect [ɪn'fɛkt] VT (wound) infectar; (food) contaminar; (person, animal) contagiar; (fig: pej) corromper; **infected with** (illness) contagiado de; **to become infected** (wound) infectarse
infection [ɪn'fɛkʃən] N infección f; (fig) contagio
infectious [ɪn'fɛkʃəs] ADJ contagioso; (fig) infeccioso
infer [ɪn'fəːʳ] VT deducir, inferir; **to ~ (from)** inferir (de), deducir (de)
inference ['ɪnfərəns] N deducción f, inferencia
inferior [ɪn'fɪərɪəʳ] ADJ, N inferior mf; **to feel ~** sentirse inferior
inferiority [ɪnfɪərɪ'ɔrətɪ] N inferioridad f
inferiority complex N complejo de inferioridad
infernal [ɪn'fəːnl] ADJ infernal
inferno [ɪn'fəːnəʊ] N infierno; (fig) hoguera
infertile [ɪn'fəːtaɪl] ADJ estéril; (person) infecundo
infertility [ɪnfəː'tɪlɪtɪ] N esterilidad f; infecundidad f
infest [ɪn'fɛst] VT infestar
infested [ɪn'fɛstɪd] ADJ: ~ **(with)** plagado (de)
infidel ['ɪnfɪdəl] N infiel mf
infidelity [ɪnfɪ'dɛlɪtɪ] N infidelidad f
in-fighting ['ɪnfaɪtɪŋ] N (fig) lucha(s) f(pl) interna(s)
infiltrate ['ɪnfɪltreɪt] VT (troops etc) infiltrarse en ► VI infiltrarse
infinite ['ɪnfɪnɪt] ADJ infinito; **an ~ amount of money/time** un sinfín de dinero/tiempo
infinitely ['ɪnfɪnɪtlɪ] ADV infinitamente
infinitesimal [ɪnfɪnɪ'tɛsɪməl] ADJ infinitésimo
infinitive [ɪn'fɪnɪtɪv] N infinitivo
infinity [ɪn'fɪnɪtɪ] N (Math) infinito; **an ~** infinidad f
infirm [ɪn'fəːm] ADJ enfermizo, débil
infirmary [ɪn'fəːmərɪ] N hospital m
infirmity [ɪn'fəːmɪtɪ] N debilidad f; (illness) enfermedad f, achaque m
inflame [ɪn'fleɪm] VT inflamar
inflamed [ɪn'fleɪmd] ADJ: **to become ~** inflamarse
inflammable [ɪn'flæməbl] ADJ inflamable; (situation etc) explosivo

inflammation [ɪnflə'meɪʃən] N inflamación f
inflammatory [ɪn'flæmətərɪ] ADJ (speech) incendiario
inflatable [ɪn'fleɪtəbl] ADJ inflable
inflate [ɪn'fleɪt] VT (tyre) inflar; (fig) hinchar
inflated [ɪn'fleɪtɪd] ADJ (tyre etc) inflado; (price, self-esteem etc) exagerado
inflation [ɪn'fleɪʃən] N (Econ) inflación f
inflationary [ɪn'fleɪʃnərɪ] ADJ inflacionario
inflationary spiral N espiral f inflacionista
inflexible [ɪn'flɛksɪbl] ADJ inflexible
inflict [ɪn'flɪkt] VT: **to ~ on** infligir en; (tax etc) imponer a
in-flight ['ɪnflaɪt] ADJ durante el vuelo
inflow ['ɪnfləʊ] N afluencia
influence ['ɪnfluəns] N influencia ► VT influir en, influenciar; **under the ~ of alcohol** en estado de embriaguez
influential [ɪnflu'ɛnʃl] ADJ influyente
influenza [ɪnflu'ɛnzə] N gripe f
influx ['ɪnflʌks] N afluencia
info ['ɪnfəʊ] N (inf) = **information**
inform [ɪn'fɔːm] VT: **to ~ sb of sth** informar a algn sobre or de algo; (warn) avisar a algn de algo; (communicate) comunicar algo a algn ► VI: **to ~ on sb** delatar a algn
informal [ɪn'fɔːml] ADJ (manner, tone) desenfadado; (dress, occasion) informal; (visit, meeting) extraoficial
informality [ɪnfɔː'mælɪtɪ] N falta de ceremonia; (intimacy) intimidad f; (familiarity) familiaridad f; (ease) afabilidad f
informally [ɪn'fɔːməlɪ] ADV sin ceremonia; (invite) informalmente
informant [ɪn'fɔːmənt] N informante mf
informatics [ɪnfɔː'mætɪks] N informática
information [ɪnfə'meɪʃən] N información f; (news) noticias fpl; (knowledge) conocimientos mpl; (Law) delación f; **a piece of ~** un dato; **for your ~** para su información; **~ and communication(s) technology** (gen) tecnología de la información y de las comunicaciones; (BRIT Scol) informática
information bureau N oficina de información
information office N información f
information processing N procesamiento de datos
information retrieval N recuperación f de información
information science N gestión f de la información
information technology N informática
informative [ɪn'fɔːmətɪv] ADJ informativo
informed [ɪn'fɔːmd] ADJ (observer) informado, al corriente; **an ~ guess** una opinión bien fundamentada
informer [ɪn'fɔːməʳ] N delator(a) m/f; (also: **police informer**) soplón(-ona) m/f

infra dig ['ɪnfrə'dɪg] ADJ ABBR (inf: = infra dignitatem: = beneath one's dignity) denigrante

infra-red [ɪnfrə'red] ADJ infrarrojo

infrastructure ['ɪnfrəstrʌktʃəʳ] N infraestructura

infrequent [ɪn'fri:kwənt] ADJ infrecuente

infringe [ɪn'frɪndʒ] VT infringir, violar ▸ VI: **to ~ on** invadir

infringement [ɪn'frɪndʒmənt] N infracción f; (of rights) usurpación f; (Sport) falta

infuriate [ɪn'fjuərɪet] VT: **to become infuriated** ponerse furioso

infuriating [ɪn'fjuərɪeɪtɪŋ] ADJ (habit, noise) enloquecedor(a); **I find it ~** me saca de quicio

infuse [ɪn'fju:z] VT (with courage, enthusiasm): **to ~ sb with sth** infundir algo a algn

infusion [ɪn'fju:ʒən] N (tea etc) infusión f

ingenious [ɪn'dʒi:njəs] ADJ ingenioso

ingenuity [ɪndʒɪ'nju:ɪtɪ] N ingeniosidad f

ingenuous [ɪn'dʒɛnjuəs] ADJ ingenuo

ingot ['ɪŋgət] N lingote m, barra

ingrained [ɪn'greɪnd] ADJ arraigado

ingratiate [ɪn'greɪʃɪeɪt] VT: **to ~ o.s. with** congraciarse con

ingratiating [ɪn'greɪʃɪeɪtɪŋ] ADJ (smile, speech) insinuante; (person) zalamero, congraciador(a)

ingratitude [ɪn'grætɪtju:d] N ingratitud f

ingredient [ɪn'gri:dɪənt] N ingrediente m

ingrowing ['ɪngrəʊɪŋ] ADJ: **~ (toe)nail** uña encarnada

inhabit [ɪn'hæbɪt] VT vivir en; (occupy) ocupar

inhabitable [ɪn'hæbɪtəbl] ADJ habitable

inhabitant [ɪn'hæbɪtənt] N habitante mf

inhale [ɪn'heɪl] VT inhalar ▸ VI (breathe in) aspirar; (in smoking) tragar

inhaler [ɪn'heɪləʳ] N inhalador m

inherent [ɪn'hɪərənt] ADJ: **~ in or to** inherente a

inherently [ɪn'hɪərəntlɪ] ADV intrínsecamente

inherit [ɪn'hɛrɪt] VT heredar

inheritance [ɪn'hɛrɪtəns] N herencia; (fig) patrimonio

inhibit [ɪn'hɪbɪt] VT inhibir, impedir; **to ~ sb from doing sth** impedir a algn hacer algo

inhibited [ɪn'hɪbɪtɪd] ADJ (person) cohibido

inhibition [ɪnhɪ'bɪʃən] N cohibición f

inhospitable [ɪnhɔs'pɪtəbl] ADJ (person) inhospitalario; (place) inhóspito

in-house ['ɪnhaʊs] ADJ dentro de la empresa

inhuman [ɪn'hju:mən] ADJ inhumano

inhumane [ɪnhju:'meɪn] ADJ inhumano

inimitable [ɪ'nɪmɪtəbl] ADJ inimitable

iniquity [ɪ'nɪkwɪtɪ] N iniquidad f; (injustice) injusticia

initial [ɪ'nɪʃl] ADJ inicial; (first) primero ▸ N inicial f ▸ VT firmar con las iniciales; **initials** NPL iniciales fpl; (abbreviation) siglas fpl

initialize [ɪ'nɪʃəlaɪz] VT (Comput) inicializar

initially [ɪ'nɪʃlɪ] ADV en un principio

initiate [ɪ'nɪʃɪeɪt] VT (start) iniciar; **to ~ sb into a secret** iniciar a algn en un secreto; **to ~ proceedings against sb** (Law) poner una demanda contra algn

initiation [ɪnɪʃɪ'eɪʃən] N (into secret etc) iniciación f; (beginning) comienzo

initiative [ɪ'nɪʃətɪv] N iniciativa; **to take the ~** tomar la iniciativa

inject [ɪn'dʒɛkt] VT inyectar; (money, enthusiasm) aportar

injection [ɪn'dʒɛkʃən] N inyección f; **to have an ~** ponerse una inyección

injudicious [ɪndʒu'dɪʃəs] ADJ imprudente, indiscreto

injunction [ɪn'dʒʌŋkʃən] N entredicho, interdicto

injure ['ɪndʒəʳ] VT herir; (hurt) lastimar; (fig: reputation etc) perjudicar; (feelings) herir; **to ~ o.s.** hacerse daño, lastimarse

injured ['ɪndʒəd] ADJ (also fig) herido; **~ party** (Law) parte f perjudicada

injurious [ɪn'dʒuərɪəs] ADJ: **~ (to)** perjudicial (para)

injury ['ɪndʒərɪ] N herida, lesión f; (wrong) perjuicio, daño; **to escape without ~** salir ileso

injury time N (Sport) descuento

injustice [ɪn'dʒʌstɪs] N injusticia; **you do me an ~** usted es injusto conmigo

ink [ɪŋk] N tinta

ink-jet printer ['ɪŋkdʒɛt-] N impresora de chorro de tinta

inkling ['ɪŋklɪŋ] N sospecha; (idea) idea

inkpad ['ɪŋkpæd] N almohadilla

inlaid ['ɪnleɪd] ADJ (wood) taraceado; (tiles) entarimado

inland ADJ ['ɪnlənd] interior; (town) del interior ▸ ADV [ɪn'lænd] tierra adentro

Inland Revenue N (BRIT) ≈ Hacienda, ≈ Agencia Tributaria

in-laws ['ɪnlɔ:z] NPL suegros mpl

inlet ['ɪnlɛt] N (Geo) ensenada, cala; (Tech) admisión f, entrada

inmate ['ɪnmeɪt] N (in prison) preso(-a), presidiario(-a); (in asylum) internado(-a)

inmost ['ɪnməʊst] ADJ más íntimo, más secreto

inn [ɪn] N posada, mesón m

innards ['ɪnədz] NPL (inf) tripas fpl

innate [ɪ'neɪt] ADJ innato

inner ['ɪnəʳ] ADJ interior, interno; (feelings) íntimo

inner city N barrios deprimidos del centro de una ciudad

inner-city ADJ (schools, problems) de las zonas céntricas pobres, de los barrios céntricos pobres

innermost ['ɪnəməust] ADJ más íntimo, más secreto

inner tube N (of tyre) cámara, llanta (LAM)

inning ['ɪnɪŋ] N (US Baseball) inning m, entrada; **innings** (Cricket) entrada, turno

innocence ['ɪnəsns] N inocencia

innocent ['ɪnəsnt] ADJ inocente

innocuous [ɪ'nɔkjuəs] ADJ inocuo

innovation [ɪnəu'veɪʃən] N novedad f

innovative ['ɪnəuvətɪv] ADJ innovador

innuendo [ɪnju'ɛndəu] (pl **innuendoes** [-əuz]) N indirecta

innumerable [ɪ'nju:mrəbl] ADJ innumerable

inoculate [ɪ'nɔkjuleɪt] VT: **to ~ sb with sth/against sth** inocular or vacunar a algn con algo/contra algo

inoculation [ɪnɔkju'leɪʃən] N inoculación f

inoffensive [ɪnə'fɛnsɪv] ADJ inofensivo

inopportune [ɪn'ɔpətju:n] ADJ inoportuno

inordinate [ɪ'nɔ:dɪnət] ADJ excesivo, desmesurado

inordinately [ɪ'nɔ:dɪnətlɪ] ADV excesivamente, desmesuradamente

inorganic [ɪnɔ:'gaenɪk] ADJ inorgánico

in-patient ['ɪnpeɪʃənt] N (paciente mf) interno(-a)

input ['ɪnput] N (Elec) entrada; (of resources) inversión f; (Comput) entrada de datos ▶ VT (Comput) introducir, entrar

inquest ['ɪnkwɛst] N (coroner's) investigación f post-mortem

inquire [ɪn'kwaɪər] VI preguntar ▶ VT: **to ~ when/where/whether** preguntar cuándo/dónde/si; **to ~ about** (person) preguntar por; (fact) informarse de
▶ **inquire into** VT FUS: **to ~ into sth** investigar or indagar algo

inquiring [ɪn'kwaɪərɪŋ] ADJ (mind) inquieto; (look) interrogante

inquiry [ɪn'kwaɪərɪ] N pregunta; (Law) investigación f, pesquisa; (commission) comisión f investigadora; **to hold an ~ into sth** emprender una investigación sobre algo; **"Inquiries"** "Información"

inquiry desk N mesa de información

inquiry office N (BRIT) oficina de información

inquisition [ɪnkwɪ'zɪʃən] N inquisición f

inquisitive [ɪn'kwɪzɪtɪv] ADJ (mind) inquisitivo; (person) fisgón(-ona)

inroad ['ɪnrəud] N incursión f; (fig) invasión f; **to make inroads into** (time) ocupar parte de; (savings, supplies) agotar parte de

insane [ɪn'seɪn] ADJ loco; (Med) demente

insanitary [ɪn'sænɪtərɪ] ADJ insalubre

insanity [ɪn'sænɪtɪ] N demencia, locura

insatiable [ɪn'seɪʃəbl] ADJ insaciable

inscribe [ɪn'skraɪb] VT inscribir; (book etc): **to ~ (to sb)** dedicar (a algn)

inscription [ɪn'skrɪpʃən] N (gen) inscripción f; (in book) dedicatoria

inscrutable [ɪn'skru:təbl] ADJ inescrutable, insondable

inseam measurement ['ɪnsi:m-] N (US) = **inside leg measurement**

insect ['ɪnsɛkt] N insecto

insect bite N picadura

insecticide [ɪn'sɛktɪsaɪd] N insecticida m

insect repellent N loción f contra los insectos

insecure [ɪnsɪ'kjuər] ADJ inseguro

insecurity [ɪnsɪ'kjuərɪtɪ] N inseguridad f

insemination [ɪnsɛmɪ'neɪʃən] N: **artificial ~** inseminación f artificial

insensible [ɪn'sɛnsɪbl] ADJ inconsciente; (unconscious) sin conocimiento

insensitive [ɪn'sɛnsɪtɪv] ADJ insensible

insensitivity [ɪnsɛnsɪ'tɪvɪtɪ] N insensibilidad f

inseparable [ɪn'sɛprəbl] ADJ inseparable; **they were ~ friends** los unía una estrecha amistad

insert VT [ɪn'sə:t] (into sth) introducir; (Comput) insertar ▶ N ['ɪnsə:t] encarte m

insertion [ɪn'sə:ʃən] N inserción f

in-service [ɪn'sə:vɪs] ADJ (training, course) en el trabajo, a cargo de la empresa

inshore [ɪn'ʃɔ:r] ADJ: **~ fishing** pesca f costera ▶ ADV (fish) a lo largo de la costa; (move) hacia la orilla

inside ['ɪn'saɪd] N interior m; (lining) forro; (of road: BRIT) izquierdo; (: in US, Europe etc) derecho ▶ ADJ interior, interno ▶ ADV (within) (por) dentro, adentro (esp LAM); (with movement) hacia dentro; (inf: in prison) en chirona ▶ PREP dentro de; (of time): **~ 10 minutes** en menos de 10 minutos; **insides** NPL (inf) tripas fpl; **~ out** adv (turn) al revés; (know) a fondo

inside forward N (Sport) interior m

inside information N información f confidencial

inside lane N (Aut: BRIT) carril m izquierdo; (: in US, Europe etc) carril m derecho

inside leg measurement N medida de pernera

insider [ɪn'saɪdər] N enterado(-a)

insider dealing, insider trading N (Stock Exchange) abuso de información privilegiada

inside story N historia íntima

insidious [ɪn'sɪdɪəs] ADJ insidioso

insight ['ɪnsaɪt] N perspicacia, percepción f; **to gain** or **get an ~ into sth** comprender algo mejor

insignia [ɪn'sɪgnɪə] NPL insignias fpl

insignificant [ɪnsɪg'nɪfɪknt] ADJ insignificante

insincere [ɪnsɪn'sɪər] ADJ poco sincero

insincerity [ɪnsɪn'sɛrɪtɪ] N falta de sinceridad, doblez f

insinuate [ɪn'sɪnjueɪt] VT insinuar

insinuation [ɪnsɪnju'eɪʃən] N insinuación f

insipid [ɪn'sɪpɪd] ADJ soso, insulso

insist [ɪn'sɪst] VI insistir; **to ~ on doing** empeñarse en hacer; **to ~ that** insistir en que; (claim) exigir que

insistence [ɪn'sɪstəns] N insistencia; (stubbornness) empeño

insistent [ɪn'sɪstənt] ADJ insistente; (noise, action) persistente

insofar as [ɪnsəu'fɑ:-] CONJ en la medida en que, en tanto que

insole ['ɪnsəul] N plantilla

insolence ['ɪnsələns] N insolencia, descaro

insolent ['ɪnsələnt] ADJ insolente, descarado

insoluble [ɪn'sɔljubl] ADJ insoluble

insolvency [ɪn'sɔlvənsɪ] N insolvencia

insolvent [ɪn'sɔlvənt] ADJ insolvente

insomnia [ɪn'sɔmnɪə] N insomnio

insomniac [ɪn'sɔmnɪæk] N insomne mf

inspect [ɪn'spɛkt] VT inspeccionar, examinar; (troops) pasar revista a

inspection [ɪn'spɛkʃən] N inspección f, examen m; (of troops) revista

inspector [ɪn'spɛktə^r] N inspector(a) m/f; (BRIT: on buses, trains) revisor(a) m/f

inspiration [ɪnspə'reɪʃən] N inspiración f

inspire [ɪn'spaɪə^r] VT inspirar; **to ~ sb (to do sth)** alentar a algn (a hacer algo)

inspired [ɪn'spaɪəd] ADJ (writer, book etc) inspirado, genial, iluminado; **in an ~ moment** en un momento de inspiración

inspiring [ɪn'spaɪərɪŋ] ADJ inspirador(a)

inst. [ɪnst] ABBR (BRIT Comm: = instant, of the present month) cte.

instability [ɪnstə'bɪlɪtɪ] N inestabilidad f

install, (US) **instal** [ɪn'stɔ:l] VT instalar

installation [ɪnstə'leɪʃən] N instalación f

installment plan N (US) compra a plazos

instalment, (US) **installment** [ɪn'stɔ:lmənt] N plazo; (of story) entrega; (of TV serial etc) capítulo; **in instalments** (pay, receive) a plazos; **to pay in instalments** pagar a plazos or por abonos

instance ['ɪnstəns] N ejemplo, caso; **for ~** por ejemplo; **in the first ~** en primer lugar; **in that ~** en ese caso

instant ['ɪnstənt] N instante m, momento ▸ ADJ inmediato; (coffee) instantáneo

instantaneous [ɪnstən'teɪnɪəs] ADJ instantáneo

instantly ['ɪnstəntlɪ] ADV en seguida, al instante

instant message N mensaje m instantáneo

instant messaging [-'mɛsədʒɪŋ] N mensajería instantánea

instant replay N (US TV) repetición f de la jugada

instead [ɪn'stɛd] ADV en cambio; **~ of** en lugar de, en vez de

instep ['ɪnstɛp] N empeine m

instigate ['ɪnstɪgeɪt] VT (rebellion, strike, crime) instigar; (new ideas etc) fomentar

instigation [ɪnstɪ'geɪʃən] N instigación f; **at sb's ~** a instigación de algn

instil [ɪn'stɪl] VT: **to ~ into** inculcar a

instinct ['ɪnstɪŋkt] N instinto

instinctive [ɪn'stɪŋktɪv] ADJ instintivo

instinctively [ɪn'stɪŋktɪvlɪ] ADV por instinto

institute ['ɪnstɪtju:t] N instituto; (professional body) colegio ▸ VT (begin) iniciar, empezar; (proceedings) entablar

institution [ɪnstɪ'tju:ʃən] N institución f; (beginning) iniciación f; (Med: home) asilo; (: asylum) manicomio; (: custom) costumbre f arraigada

institutional [ɪnstɪ'tju:ʃənl] ADJ institucional

instruct [ɪn'strʌkt] VT: **to ~ sb in sth** instruir a algn en or sobre algo; **to ~ sb to do sth** dar instrucciones a algn de or mandar a algn hacer algo

instruction [ɪn'strʌkʃən] N (teaching) instrucción f; **instructions** NPL órdenes fpl; **instructions (for use)** modo sg de empleo

instruction book N manual m

instructive [ɪn'strʌktɪv] ADJ instructivo

instructor [ɪn'strʌktə^r] N instructor(a) m/f

instrument ['ɪnstrəmənt] N instrumento

instrumental [ɪnstrə'mɛntl] ADJ (Mus) instrumental; **to be ~ in** ser el artífice de; **to be ~ in sth/in doing sth** ser responsable de algo/de hacer algo

instrumentalist [ɪnstrə'mɛntəlɪst] N instrumentista mf

instrument panel N tablero (de instrumentos)

insubordinate [ɪnsə'bɔ:dənɪt] ADJ insubordinado

insubordination [ɪnsəbɔ:də'neɪʃən] N insubordinación f

insufferable [ɪn'sʌfrəbl] ADJ insoportable

insufficient [ɪnsə'fɪʃənt] ADJ insuficiente

insufficiently [ɪnsə'fɪʃəntlɪ] ADV insuficientemente

insular ['ɪnsjulə^r] ADJ insular; (outlook) estrecho de miras

insularity [ɪnsju'lærɪtɪ] N insularidad f

insulate ['ɪnsjuleɪt] VT aislar

insulating tape ['ɪnsjuleɪtɪŋ-] N cinta aislante

insulation [ɪnsju'leɪʃən] N aislamiento

insulator ['ɪnsjuleɪtə^r] N aislante m

insulin ['ɪnsjulɪn] N insulina

insult N ['ɪnsʌlt] insulto; (offence) ofensa ▸ VT [ɪn'sʌlt] insultar; ofender

insulting [ɪnˈsʌltɪŋ] ADJ insultante; ofensivo

insuperable [ɪnˈsjuːprəbl] ADJ insuperable

insurance [ɪnˈʃʊərəns] N seguro; **fire/life ~** seguro contra incendios/de vida; **to take out ~ (against)** hacerse un seguro (contra)

insurance agent N agente *mf* de seguros

insurance broker N corredor(a) *m/f* or agente *mf* de seguros

insurance company N compañía *f* de seguros

insurance policy N póliza (de seguros)

insurance premium N prima de seguros

insure [ɪnˈʃʊər] VT asegurar; **to ~ sb** or **sb's life** hacer un seguro de vida a algn; **to ~ (against)** asegurar (contra); **to be insured for £5000** tener un seguro de 5000 libras

insured [ɪnˈʃʊəd] N: **the ~** el asegurado(-a)

insurer [ɪnˈʃʊərər] N asegurador(a)

insurgent [ɪnˈsɜːdʒənt] ADJ, N insurgente *mf*, insurrecto(-a) *m/f*

insurmountable [ɪnsəˈmauntəbl] ADJ insuperable

insurrection [ɪnsəˈrɛkʃən] N insurrección *f*

intact [ɪnˈtækt] ADJ íntegro; (*untouched*) intacto

intake [ˈɪnteɪk] N (*Tech*) entrada, toma; (*: pipe*) tubo de admisión; (*of food*) ingestión *f*; (*Brit Scol*): **an ~ of 200 a year** 200 matriculados al año

intangible [ɪnˈtændʒɪbl] ADJ intangible

integer [ˈɪntɪdʒər] N (número) entero

integral [ˈɪntɪɡrəl] ADJ (*whole*) íntegro; (*part*) integrante

integrate [ˈɪntɪɡreɪt] VT integrar ▶ VI integrarse

integrated circuit [ˈɪntɪɡreɪtɪd-] N (*Comput*) circuito integrado

integration [ɪntɪˈɡreɪʃən] N integración *f*; **racial ~** integración de razas

integrity [ɪnˈtɛɡrɪtɪ] N honradez *f*, rectitud *f*; (*Comput*) integridad *f*

intellect [ˈɪntəlɛkt] N intelecto

intellectual [ɪntəˈlɛktjuəl] ADJ, N intelectual *mf*

intelligence [ɪnˈtɛlɪdʒəns] N inteligencia

intelligence quotient N coeficiente *m* intelectual

Intelligence Service N Servicio de Inteligencia

intelligence test N prueba de inteligencia

intelligent [ɪnˈtɛlɪdʒənt] ADJ inteligente

intelligently [ɪnˈtɛlɪdʒəntlɪ] ADV inteligentemente

intelligentsia [ɪntɛlɪˈdʒɛntsɪə] N intelectualidad *f*

intelligible [ɪnˈtɛlɪdʒɪbl] ADJ inteligible, comprensible

intemperate [ɪnˈtɛmpərət] ADJ inmoderado

intend [ɪnˈtɛnd] VT (*gift etc*): **to ~ sth for** destinar algo a; **to ~ to do sth** tener intención de or pensar hacer algo

intended [ɪnˈtɛndɪd] ADJ (*effect*) deseado

intense [ɪnˈtɛns] ADJ intenso; **to be ~** (*person*) tomárselo todo muy en serio

intensely [ɪnˈtɛnslɪ] ADV intensamente; (*very*) sumamente

intensify [ɪnˈtɛnsɪfaɪ] VT intensificar; (*increase*) aumentar

intensity [ɪnˈtɛnsɪtɪ] N (*gen*) intensidad *f*

intensive [ɪnˈtɛnsɪv] ADJ intensivo

intensive care N: **to be in ~** estar bajo cuidados intensivos; **~ unit** unidad *f* de vigilancia intensiva

intensively [ɪnˈtɛnsɪvlɪ] ADV intensivamente

intent [ɪnˈtɛnt] N propósito; (*Law*) premeditación *f* ▶ ADJ (*absorbed*) absorto; (*attentive*) atento; **to all intents and purposes** a efectos prácticos; **to be ~ on doing sth** estar resuelto or decidido a hacer algo

intention [ɪnˈtɛnʃən] N intención *f*, propósito

intentional [ɪnˈtɛnʃənl] ADJ deliberado

intentionally [ɪnˈtɛnʃnəlɪ] ADV a propósito

intently [ɪnˈtɛntlɪ] ADV atentamente, fijamente

inter [ɪnˈtɜːr] VT enterrar, sepultar

inter- [ˈɪntər] PREF inter-

interact [ɪntərˈækt] VI (*substances*) influirse mutuamente; (*people*) relacionarse

interaction [ɪntərˈækʃən] N interacción *f*, acción *f* recíproca

interactive [ɪntərˈæktɪv] ADJ (*Comput*) interactivo

intercede [ɪntəˈsiːd] VI interceder; **to ~ with sb/on behalf of sb** interceder con algn/en nombre de algn

intercept [ɪntəˈsɛpt] VT interceptar; (*stop*) detener

interception [ɪntəˈsɛpʃən] N interceptación *f*; detención *f*

interchange N [ˈɪntətʃeɪndʒ] intercambio; (*on motorway*) intersección *f* ▶ VT [ɪntəˈtʃeɪndʒ] intercambiar

interchangeable [ɪntəˈtʃeɪndʒəbl] ADJ intercambiable

intercity [ɪntəˈsɪtɪ] ADJ: **~ (train)** (tren *m*) intercity *m*

intercom [ˈɪntəkɒm] N interfono

interconnect [ɪntəkəˈnɛkt] VI (*rooms*) comunicar(se)

intercontinental [ˈɪntəkɒntɪˈnɛntl] ADJ intercontinental

intercourse [ˈɪntəkɔːs] N (*also*: **sexual intercourse**) relaciones *fpl* sexuales, contacto sexual; (*social*) trato

interdependence [ɪntədɪˈpɛndəns] N interdependencia

617

interdependent [ɪntədɪ'pɛndənt] ADJ interdependiente

interest ['ɪntrɪst] N (Comm) interés m ▶ VT interesar; **compound/simple ~** interés compuesto/simple; **business interests** negocios mpl; **British interests in the Middle East** los intereses británicos en el Medio Oriente

interested ['ɪntrɪstɪd] ADJ interesado; **to be ~ in** interesarse por

interest-free ['ɪntrɪst'fri:] ADJ libre de interés

interesting ['ɪntrɪstɪŋ] ADJ interesante

interest rate N tipo de interés

interface ['ɪntəfeɪs] N (Comput) junción f, interface m

interfere [ɪntə'fɪər] VI: **to ~ in** (quarrel, other people's business) entrometerse en; **to ~ with** (hinder) estorbar; (damage) estropear; (Radio) interferir con

interference [ɪntə'fɪərəns] N (gen) intromisión f; (Radio, TV) interferencia

interfering [ɪntə'fɪərɪŋ] ADJ entrometido

interim ['ɪntərɪm] ADJ provisional ▶ N: **in the ~** en el ínterin; **~ dividend** dividendo parcial

interior [ɪn'tɪərɪər] N interior m ▶ ADJ interior

interior decorator, interior designer N interiorista mf, diseñador(a) m/f de interiores

interior design N interiorismo, decoración f de interiores

interjection [ɪntə'dʒɛkʃən] N interrupción f

interlock [ɪntə'lɔk] VI entrelazarse; (wheels etc) endentarse

interloper ['ɪntələupər] N intruso(-a)

interlude ['ɪntəlu:d] N intervalo; (rest) descanso; (Theat) intermedio

intermarriage [ɪntə'mærɪdʒ] N endogamia

intermarry [ɪntə'mærɪ] VI casarse (entre parientes)

intermediary [ɪntə'mi:dɪərɪ] N intermediario(-a)

intermediate [ɪntə'mi:dɪət] ADJ intermedio

interminable [ɪn'tə:mɪnəbl] ADJ inacabable

intermission [ɪntə'mɪʃən] N (Theat) descanso

intermittent [ɪntə'mɪtnt] ADJ intermitente

intermittently [ɪntə'mɪtntlɪ] ADV intermitentemente

intern VT [ɪn'tə:n] internar; (enclose) encerrar ▶ N ['ɪntə:n] (esp US: doctor) médico(-a) interno(-a); (: on work placement) becario(-a)

internal [ɪn'tə:nl] ADJ interno, interior; (injury, structure, memo) interno; **~ injuries** heridas fpl or lesiones fpl internas

internally [ɪn'tə:nəlɪ] ADV interiormente; **"not to be taken ~"** "uso externo"

Internal Revenue Service N (US) ≈ Hacienda, ≈ Agencia Tributaria

international [ɪntə'næʃənl] ADJ internacional; **~ (game)** partido internacional; **~ (player)** jugador(a) m/f internacional

International Atomic Energy Agency N Organismo Internacional de Energía Atómica

International Chamber of Commerce N Cámara de Comercio Internacional

International Court of Justice N Corte f Internacional de Justicia

international date line N línea de cambio de fecha

internationally [ɪntə'næʃnəlɪ] ADV internacionalmente

International Monetary Fund N Fondo Monetario Internacional

internecine [ɪntə'ni:saɪn] ADJ de aniquilación mutua

internee [ɪntə:'ni:] N interno(-a), recluso(-a)

internet, Internet ['ɪntənɛt] N: **the ~** (el or la) Internet

internet café N cibercafé m

Internet Service Provider N proveedor m de (acceso a) Internet

internet user N internauta mf

internment [ɪn'tə:nmənt] N internamiento

interplanetary [ɪntə'plænɪtərɪ] ADJ interplanetario

interplay ['ɪntəpleɪ] N interacción f

Interpol ['ɪntəpɔl] N Interpol f

interpret [ɪn'tə:prɪt] VT interpretar; (translate) traducir; (understand) entender ▶ VI hacer de intérprete

interpretation [ɪntə:prɪ'teɪʃən] N interpretación f; traducción f

interpreter [ɪn'tə:prɪtər] N intérprete mf

interrelated [ɪntərɪ'leɪtɪd] ADJ interrelacionado

interrogate [ɪn'tɛrəugeɪt] VT interrogar

interrogation [ɪntɛrəu'geɪʃən] N interrogatorio

interrogative [ɪntə'rɔgətɪv] ADJ interrogativo

interrupt [ɪntə'rʌpt] VT, VI interrumpir

interruption [ɪntə'rʌpʃən] N interrupción f

intersect [ɪntə'sɛkt] VT cruzar ▶ VI (roads) cruzarse

intersection [ɪntə'sɛkʃən] N intersección f; (of roads) cruce m

intersperse [ɪntə'spə:s] VT: **to ~ with** salpicar de

interstate ['ɪntərsteɪt] N (US) carretera interestatal

intertwine [ɪntə'twaɪn] VT entrelazar ▶ VI entrelazarse

interval ['ɪntəvl] N intervalo; (BRIT Theat, Sport) descanso; (Scol) recreo; **at intervals** a ratos, de vez en cuando; **sunny intervals** (Meteorology) claros mpl

intervene [ɪntəˈviːn] VI intervenir; (*take part*) participar; (*occur*) sobrevenir
intervening [ɪntəˈviːnɪŋ] ADJ intermedio
intervention [ɪntəˈvɛnʃən] N intervención *f*
interview [ˈɪntəvjuː] N (*Radio, TV etc*) entrevista ▸ VT entrevistar a
interviewee [ɪntəvjuːˈiː] N entrevistado(-a)
interviewer [ˈɪntəvjuːəʳ] N entrevistador(a) *m/f*
intestate [ɪnˈtɛsteɪt] ADJ intestado
intestinal [ɪnˈtɛstɪnl] ADJ intestinal
intestine [ɪnˈtɛstɪn] N: **large/small ~** intestino grueso/delgado
intimacy [ˈɪntɪməsɪ] N intimidad *f*; (*relations*) relaciones *fpl* íntimas
intimate ADJ [ˈɪntɪmət] íntimo; (*friendship*) estrecho; (*knowledge*) profundo ▸ VT [ˈɪntɪmeɪt] (*announce*) dar a entender
intimately [ˈɪntɪmətlɪ] ADV íntimamente
intimidate [ɪnˈtɪmɪdeɪt] VT intimidar, amedrentar
intimidating [ɪnˈtɪmɪdeɪtɪŋ] ADJ amedrentador, intimidante
intimidation [ɪntɪmɪˈdeɪʃən] N intimidación *f*
into [ˈɪntuː] PREP (*gen*) en; (*towards*) a; (*inside*) hacia el interior de; **~ three pieces/French** en tres pedazos/al francés; **to change pounds ~ euros** cambiar libras por euros
intolerable [ɪnˈtɔlərəbl] ADJ intolerable, insoportable
intolerance [ɪnˈtɔlərəns] N intolerancia
intolerant [ɪnˈtɔlərənt] ADJ: **~ (of)** intolerante (con)
intonation [ɪntəuˈneɪʃən] N entonación *f*
intoxicate [ɪnˈtɔksɪkeɪt] VT embriagar
intoxicated [ɪnˈtɔksɪkeɪtɪd] ADJ embriagado
intoxication [ɪntɔksɪˈkeɪʃən] N embriaguez *f*
intractable [ɪnˈtræktəbl] ADJ (*person*) intratable; (*problem*) irresoluble; (*illness*) incurable
intranet [ˈɪntrənet] N intranet *f*
intransigence [ɪnˈtrænsɪdʒəns] N intransigencia
intransigent [ɪnˈtrænsɪdʒənt] ADJ intransigente
intransitive [ɪnˈtrænsɪtɪv] ADJ intransitivo
intravenous [ɪntrəˈviːnəs] ADJ intravenoso
in-tray [ˈɪntreɪ] N bandeja de entrada
intrepid [ɪnˈtrɛpɪd] ADJ intrépido
intricacy [ˈɪntrɪkəsɪ] N complejidad *f*
intricate [ˈɪntrɪkət] ADJ (*design, pattern*) intrincado; (*plot, problem*) complejo
intrigue [ɪnˈtriːg] N intriga ▸ VT fascinar ▸ VI andar en intrigas
intriguing [ɪnˈtriːgɪŋ] ADJ fascinante
intrinsic [ɪnˈtrɪnsɪk] ADJ intrínseco
introduce [ɪntrəˈdjuːs] VT introducir, meter; (*speaker, TV show etc*) presentar; **to ~ sb (to sb)** presentar algn (a algn); **to ~ sb to** (*pastime,*

technique) introducir a algn a; **may I ~ ...?** permítame presentarle a ...
introduction [ɪntrəˈdʌkʃən] N introducción *f*; (*of person*) presentación *f*; **a letter of ~** una carta de recomendación
introductory [ɪntrəˈdʌktərɪ] ADJ introductorio; **an ~ offer** una oferta introductoria; **~ remarks** comentarios *mpl* preliminares
introspection [ɪntrəuˈspɛkʃən] N introspección *f*
introspective [ɪntrəuˈspɛktɪv] ADJ introspectivo
introvert [ˈɪntrəuvəːt], N introvertido(-a) *m/f*
intrude [ɪnˈtruːd] VI (*person*) entrometerse; **to ~ on** estorbar
intruder [ɪnˈtruːdəʳ] N intruso(-a)
intrusion [ɪnˈtruːʒən] N invasión *f*
intrusive [ɪnˈtruːsɪv] ADJ intruso
intuition [ɪntjuːˈɪʃən] N intuición *f*
intuitive [ɪnˈtjuːɪtɪv] ADJ intuitivo
intuitively [ɪnˈtjuːɪtɪvlɪ] ADV por intuición, intuitivamente
inundate [ˈɪnʌndeɪt] VT: **to ~ with** inundar de
inure [ɪnˈjuəʳ] VT: **to ~ (to)** acostumbrar or habituar (a)
invade [ɪnˈveɪd] VT invadir
invader [ɪnˈveɪdəʳ] N invasor(a) *m/f*
invalid N [ˈɪnvəlɪd] minusválido(-a) ▸ ADJ [ɪnˈvælɪd] (*not valid*) inválido, nulo
invalidate [ɪnˈvælɪdeɪt] VT invalidar, anular
invalid chair N silla de ruedas
invaluable [ɪnˈvæljuəbl] ADJ inestimable
invariable [ɪnˈvɛərɪəbl] ADJ invariable
invariably [ɪnˈvɛərɪəblɪ] ADV sin excepción, siempre; **she is ~ late** siempre llega tarde
invasion [ɪnˈveɪʒən] N invasión *f*
invective [ɪnˈvɛktɪv] N invectiva
inveigle [ɪnˈviːgl] VT: **to ~ sb into (doing) sth** embaucar or engatusar a algn para (que haga) algo
invent [ɪnˈvɛnt] VT inventar
invention [ɪnˈvɛnʃən] N invento; (*inventiveness*) inventiva; (*lie*) invención *f*
inventive [ɪnˈvɛntɪv] ADJ inventivo
inventiveness [ɪnˈvɛntɪvnɪs] N ingenio, inventiva
inventor [ɪnˈvɛntəʳ] N inventor(a) *m/f*
inventory [ˈɪnvəntrɪ] N inventario
inventory control N control *m* de existencias
inverse [ɪnˈvəːs] ADJ, N inverso; **in ~ proportion (to)** en proporción inversa (a)
inversely [ɪnˈvəːslɪ] ADV a la inversa
invert [ɪnˈvəːt] VT invertir
invertebrate [ɪnˈvəːtɪbrət] N invertebrado
inverted commas [ɪnˈvəːtɪd-] NPL (*BRIT*) comillas *fpl*

invest [ɪn'vɛst] vt invertir; (fig: time, effort) dedicar ▶ vi: **to ~ in** (company etc) invertir dinero en; (fig: sth useful) comprar; **to ~ sb with sth** conferir algo a algn

investigate [ɪn'vɛstɪgeɪt] vt investigar; (study) estudiar, examinar

investigation [ɪnvɛstɪ'geɪʃən] N investigación f, pesquisa; examen m

investigative journalism [ɪn'vɛstɪgətɪv-] N periodismo de investigación

investigator [ɪn'vɛstɪgeɪtər] N investigador(a) m/f; **private ~** investigador(a) m/f privado(-a)

investiture [ɪn'vɛstɪtʃər] N investidura

investment [ɪn'vɛstmənt] N inversión f

investment grant N subvención f para la inversión

investment income N ingresos mpl procedentes de inversiones

investment portfolio N cartera de inversiones

investment trust N compañía inversionista, sociedad f de cartera

investor [ɪn'vɛstər] N inversor(a) m/f

inveterate [ɪn'vɛtərət] ADJ empedernido

invidious [ɪn'vɪdɪəs] ADJ odioso

invigilate [ɪn'vɪdʒɪleɪt] vt, vi (in exam) vigilar

invigilator [ɪn'vɪdʒɪleɪtər] N celador(a) m/f

invigorating [ɪn'vɪgəreɪtɪŋ] ADJ vigorizante

invincible [ɪn'vɪnsɪbl] ADJ invencible

inviolate [ɪn'vaɪələt] ADJ inviolado

invisible [ɪn'vɪzɪbl] ADJ invisible

invisible assets NPL activo invisible

invisible ink N tinta simpática

invisible mending N puntada invisible

invitation [ɪnvɪ'teɪʃən] N invitación f; **at sb's ~** a invitación de algn; **by ~ only** solamente por invitación

invite [ɪn'vaɪt] vt invitar; (opinions etc) solicitar, pedir; (trouble) buscarse; **to ~ sb (to do)** invitar a algn (a hacer); **to ~ sb to dinner** invitar a algn a cenar
  ▶ **invite out** vt invitar a salir
  ▶ **invite over** vt invitar a casa

inviting [ɪn'vaɪtɪŋ] ADJ atractivo; (look) provocativo; (food) apetitoso

invoice ['ɪnvɔɪs] N factura ▶ vt facturar; **to ~ sb for goods** facturar a algn las mercancías

invoicing ['ɪnvɔɪsɪŋ] N facturación f

invoke [ɪn'vəuk] vt invocar; (aid) pedir; (law) recurrir a

involuntary [ɪn'vɒləntrɪ] ADJ involuntario

involve [ɪn'vɒlv] vt (entail) suponer, implicar, tener que ver con; (concern, affect) corresponder a; **to ~ sb (in sth)** involucrar a algn (en algo), comprometer a algn (con algo)

involved [ɪn'vɒlvd] ADJ complicado; **to be ~ in sth** (take part) estar involucrado en algo; (engrossed in) estar muy metido

involvement [ɪn'vɒlvmənt] N participación f, dedicación f; (obligation) compromiso; (difficulty) apuro

invulnerable [ɪn'vʌlnərəbl] ADJ invulnerable

inward ['ɪnwəd] ADJ (movement) interior, interno; (thought, feeling) íntimo ▶ ADV hacia dentro

inwardly ['ɪnwədlɪ] ADV (feel, think etc) para sí, para dentro

inwards ['ɪnwədz] ADV hacia dentro

I/O ABBR (Comput: = input/output) E/S; **~ error** error m de E/S

IOC N ABBR (= International Olympic Committee) COI m

iodine ['aɪəudi:n] N yodo

IOM ABBR (BRIT) = **Isle of Man**

ion ['aɪən] N ion m

Ionian Sea [aɪ'əunɪən-] N: **the ~** el Mar Jónico

ioniser ['aɪənaɪzər] N ionizador m

iota [aɪ'əutə] N (fig) jota, ápice m

IOU N ABBR (= I owe you) pagaré m

IOW ABBR (BRIT) = **Isle of Wight**

IPA N ABBR (= International Phonetic Alphabet) AFI m

iPad® ['aɪpæd] N iPad® m, tableta (digital)

iPhone® ['aɪfəun] N iPhone® m, teléfono inteligente

iPod® ['aɪpɒd] N iPod® m

IQ N ABBR (= intelligence quotient) C.I. m

IRA N ABBR (= Irish Republican Army) IRA m; (US) = **individual retirement account**

Iran [ɪ'rɑːn] N Irán m

Iranian [ɪ'reɪnɪən] ADJ iraní ▶ N iraní mf; (Ling) iraní m

Iraq [ɪ'rɑːk] N Irak m

Iraqi [ɪ'rɑːkɪ] ADJ, N irakí mf

irascible [ɪ'ræsɪbl] ADJ irascible

irate [aɪ'reɪt] ADJ enojado, airado

Ireland ['aɪələnd] N Irlanda; **Republic of ~** República de Irlanda

iris ['aɪrɪs] (pl **irises** [-ɪz]) N (Anat) iris m; (Bot) lirio

Irish ['aɪrɪʃ] ADJ irlandés(-esa) ▶ N (Ling) irlandés m; **the ~** npl los irlandeses

Irishman ['aɪrɪʃmən] N (irreg) irlandés m

Irish Sea N: **the ~** el Mar de Irlanda

Irishwoman ['aɪrɪʃwumən] N (irreg) irlandesa f

irk [ə:k] vt fastidiar

irksome ['ə:ksəm] ADJ fastidioso

IRN N ABBR (= Independent Radio News) servicio de noticias en las cadenas de radio privadas

IRO N ABBR (US) = **International Refugee Organization**

iron ['aɪən] N hierro; (for clothes) plancha ▶ ADJ de hierro ▶ vt (clothes) planchar; **irons** NPL (chains) grilletes mpl
  ▶ **iron out** vt (crease) quitar; (fig) allanar, resolver

Iron Curtain N: **the ~** el Telón de Acero

iron foundry N fundición f, fundidora
ironic [aɪˈrɒnɪk], **ironical** [aɪˈrɒnɪkl] ADJ
irónico
ironically [aɪˈrɒnɪklɪ] ADV irónicamente
ironing [ˈaɪənɪŋ] N (act) planchado; (ironed clothes) ropa planchada; (clothes to be ironed) ropa por planchar
ironing board N tabla de planchar
iron lung N (Med) pulmón m de acero
ironmonger [ˈaɪənmʌŋɡəʳ] N (BRIT) ferretero(-a); **~'s (shop)** ferretería
iron ore N mineral m de hierro
ironworks [ˈaɪənwəːks] N fundición f
irony [ˈaɪrənɪ] N ironía; **the ~ of it is that ...** lo irónico del caso es que ...
irrational [ɪˈræʃənl] ADJ irracional
irreconcilable [ɪrɛkənˈsaɪləbl] ADJ inconciliable; (enemies) irreconciliable
irredeemable [ɪrɪˈdiːməbl] ADJ irredimible
irrefutable [ɪrɪˈfjuːtəbl] ADJ irrefutable
irregular [ɪˈrɛɡjʊləʳ] ADJ irregular; (surface) desigual; (action, event) anómalo; (behaviour) poco ortodoxo
irregularity [ɪrɛɡjuˈlærɪtɪ] N irregularidad f; desigualdad f
irrelevance [ɪˈrɛləvəns] N irrelevancia
irrelevant [ɪˈrɛləvənt] ADJ irrelevante; **to be ~** estar fuera de lugar, no venir al caso
irreligious [ɪrɪˈlɪdʒəs] ADJ irreligioso
irreparable [ɪˈrɛprəbl] ADJ irreparable
irreplaceable [ɪrɪˈpleɪsəbl] ADJ irreemplazable
irrepressible [ɪrɪˈprɛsəbl] ADJ incontenible
irreproachable [ɪrɪˈprəutʃəbl] ADJ irreprochable
irresistible [ɪrɪˈzɪstɪbl] ADJ irresistible
irresolute [ɪˈrɛzəluːt] ADJ indeciso
irrespective [ɪrɪˈspɛktɪv]: **~ of** prep sin tener en cuenta, no importa
irresponsibility [ɪrɪspɒnsɪˈbɪlɪtɪ] N irresponsabilidad f
irresponsible [ɪrɪˈspɒnsɪbl] ADJ (act) irresponsable; (person) poco serio
irretrievable [ɪrɪˈtriːvəbl] ADJ (object) irrecuperable; (loss, damage) irremediable, irreparable
irretrievably [ɪrɪˈtriːvəblɪ] ADV irremisiblemente
irreverence [ɪˈrɛvərns] N irreverencia
irreverent [ɪˈrɛvərnt] ADJ irreverente, irrespetuoso
irrevocable [ɪˈrɛvəkəbl] ADJ irrevocable
irrigate [ˈɪrɪɡeɪt] VT regar
irrigation [ɪrɪˈɡeɪʃən] N riego
irritability [ɪrɪtəˈbɪlɪtɪ] N irritabilidad f
irritable [ˈɪrɪtəbl] ADJ (person: temperament) irritable; (: mood) de mal humor
irritant [ˈɪrɪtənt] N agente m irritante
irritate [ˈɪrɪteɪt] VT fastidiar; (Med) picar

irritating [ˈɪrɪteɪtɪŋ] ADJ fastidioso
irritation [ɪrɪˈteɪʃən] N fastidio; picazón f, picor m
IRS N ABBR (US) = **Internal Revenue Service**
is [ɪz] VB see **be**
ISA [ˈaɪsə] N ABBR (BRIT: = individual savings account) plan de ahorro personal para pequeños inversores con fiscalidad cero
ISBN N ABBR (= International Standard Book Number) ISBN m
ISDN N ABBR (= Integrated Services Digital Network) RDSI f
Islam [ˈɪzlɑːm] N Islam m
Islamic [ɪzˈlæmɪk] ADJ islámico
island [ˈaɪlənd] N isla; (also: **traffic island**) isleta
islander [ˈaɪləndəʳ] N isleño(-a)
isle [aɪl] N isla
isn't [ˈɪznt] = **is not**
isobar [ˈaɪsəubɑːʳ] N isobara
isolate [ˈaɪsəleɪt] VT aislar
isolated [ˈaɪsəleɪtɪd] ADJ aislado
isolation [aɪsəˈleɪʃən] N aislamiento
isolationism [aɪsəˈleɪʃənɪzəm] N aislacionismo
isolation ward N pabellón m de aislamiento
isotope [ˈaɪsəutəup] N isótopo
ISP N ABBR = **Internet Service Provider**
Israel [ˈɪzreɪl] N Israel m
Israeli [ɪzˈreɪlɪ] N, ADJ israelí mf
issue [ˈɪsjuː] N cuestión f, asunto; (outcome) resultado; (of banknotes etc) emisión f; (of newspaper etc) número; (offspring) sucesión f, descendencia ▸ VT (rations, equipment) distribuir, repartir; (orders) dar; (certificate, passport) expedir; (decree) promulgar; (magazine) publicar; (cheque) extender; (banknotes, stamp) emitir ▸ VI: **to ~ (from)** derivar (de), brotar (de); **at ~** en cuestión; **to take ~ with sb (over)** disentir con algn (en); **to avoid the ~** andarse con rodeos; **to confuse** or **obscure the ~** confundir las cosas; **to make an ~ of sth** dar a algo más importancia de lo necesario; **to ~ sth to sb**, **~ sb with sth** entregar algo a algn
Istanbul [ɪstænˈbuːl] N Estambul m
isthmus [ˈɪsməs] N istmo
IT N ABBR = **information technology**

(KEYWORD)

it [ɪt] PRON **1** (specific subject: not generally translated) él (ella); (direct object) lo (la); (indirect object) le; (after prep) él (ella); (abstract concept) ello; **it's on the table** está en la mesa; **I can't find it** no lo (or la) encuentro; **give it to me** dámelo (or dámela); **I spoke to him about it** le hablé del asunto; **what did you learn from it?** ¿qué aprendiste de él (or ella)?; **did you go to it?** (party, concert etc) ¿fuiste?

2 (*impersonal*): **it's raining** llueve, está lloviendo; **it's 6 o'clock/the 10th of August** son las 6/es el 10 de agosto; **how far is it?** — **it's 10 miles/2 hours on the train** ¿a qué distancia está? — a 10 millas/2 horas en tren; **who is it?** — **it's me** ¿quién es? — soy yo

ITA N ABBR (*Brit:* = *initial teaching alphabet*) alfabeto parcialmente fonético, ayuda para enseñar a leer

Italian [ɪ'tæljən] ADJ italiano ▸ N italiano(-a); (*Ling*) italiano

italic [ɪ'tælɪk] ADJ cursivo; **italics** NPL cursiva *sg*

Italy ['ɪtəlɪ] N Italia

ITC N ABBR (*Brit*) = **Independent Television Commission**

itch [ɪtʃ] N picazón *f*; (*fig*) prurito ▸ VI (*person*) sentir *or* tener comezón; (*part of body*) picar; **to be itching to do sth** rabiar por *or* morirse de ganas de hacer algo

itching ['ɪtʃɪŋ] N picazón *f*, comezón *f*

itchy ['ɪtʃɪ] ADJ: **to be ~** picar; **my hand is ~** me pica la mano

it'd ['ɪtd] = **it would; it had**

item ['aɪtəm] N artículo; (*on agenda*) asunto (a tratar); (*in programme*) número; (*also:* **news item**) noticia; **items of clothing** prendas *fpl* de vestir

itemize ['aɪtəmaɪz] VT detallar

itemized bill ['aɪtəmaɪzd-] N recibo detallado

itinerant [ɪ'tɪnərənt] ADJ ambulante

itinerary [aɪ'tɪnərərɪ] N itinerario

it'll ['ɪtl] = **it will; it shall**

ITN N ABBR (*Brit*) = **Independent Television News**

its [ɪts] ADJ su

it's [ɪts] = **it is; it has**

itself [ɪt'sɛlf] PRON (*reflexive*) sí mismo(-a); (*emphatic*) él mismo(-a)

ITV N ABBR (*Brit:* = *Independent Television*) cadena de televisión comercial; *ver nota*

En el Reino Unido la ITV ("*Independent Television*") es una cadena de emisoras comerciales regionales con licencia exclusiva para emitir en su región. Suelen producir sus propios programas, se financian con publicidad y están bajo el control del organismo oficial independiente "*Independent Broadcasting Authority*" ("*IBA*"). El servicio de noticias nacionales e internacionales, "*ITN*" ("*Independent Television News*"), funciona como una compañía productora para toda la cadena.

IUD N ABBR (= *intra-uterine device*) DIU *m*

I've [aɪv] = **I have**

ivory ['aɪvərɪ] N marfil *m*

Ivory Coast N: **the ~** la Costa de Marfil

ivory tower N (*fig*) torre *f* de marfil

ivy ['aɪvɪ] N hiedra

Ivy League N (*US*); *ver nota*

Las ocho universidades más prestigiosas del nordeste de los Estados Unidos reciben el nombre colectivo de *Ivy League*, por sus muros cubiertos de hiedra. Son: Brown, Columbia, Cornell, Dartmouth College, Harvard, Princeton, la universidad de Pennsylvania y Yale. También se llaman así las competiciones deportivas que celebran entre ellas.

Jj

J, j [dʒeɪ] N (letter) J, j f; **J for Jack**, (US) **J for Jig** J de José

JA N ABBR = **judge advocate**

J/A ABBR = **joint account**

jab [dʒæb] N codazo; golpe m (rápido); (Med inf) pinchazo ▶ VT (elbow) dar un codazo a; (punch) dar un golpe rápido a; **to ~ sth into sth** clavar algo en algo ▶ VI: **to ~ at** intentar golpear a

jabber ['dʒæbə'] VT, VI farfullar

jack [dʒæk] N (Aut) gato; (Bowls) boliche m; (Cards) sota
  ▶**jack in** VT (inf) dejar
  ▶**jack up** VT (Aut) levantar con el gato

jackal ['dʒækl] N (Zool) chacal m

jackass ['dʒækæs] N (also fig) asno, burro

jackdaw ['dʒækdɔ:] N grajo(-a), chova

jacket ['dʒækɪt] N chaqueta, americana, saco (LAm); (of boiler etc) camisa; (of book) sobrecubierta

jacket potato N patata asada (con piel)

jack-in-the-box ['dʒækɪnðəbɔks] N caja sorpresa, caja de resorte

jack-knife ['dʒæknaɪf] VI colear

jack-of-all-trades ['dʒækəv'ɔ:ltreɪdz] N aprendiz m de todo

jack plug N (Elec) enchufe m de clavija

jackpot ['dʒækpɔt] N premio gordo

Jacuzzi® [dʒə'ku:zɪ] N jacuzzi® m

jade [dʒeɪd] N (stone) jade m

jaded ['dʒeɪdɪd] ADJ (tired) cansado; (fed up) hastiado

jagged ['dʒægɪd] ADJ dentado

jaguar ['dʒægjuə'] N jaguar m

jail [dʒeɪl] N cárcel f ▶ VT encarcelar

jailbird ['dʒeɪlbə:d] N preso(-a) reincidente

jailbreak ['dʒeɪlbreɪk] N fuga or evasión f (de la cárcel)

jailer ['dʒeɪlə'] N carcelero(-a)

jail sentence N pena f de cárcel

jalopy [dʒə'lɔpɪ] N (inf) cacharro, armatoste m

jam [dʒæm] N mermelada; (also: **traffic jam**) atasco, embotellamiento; (difficulty) apuro
  ▶ VT (passage etc) obstruir; (mechanism, drawer etc) atascar; (Radio) interferir ▶ VI atascarse, trabarse; **to get sb out of a ~** sacar a algn del paso or de un apuro; **to ~ sth into sth** meter algo a la fuerza en algo; **the telephone lines are jammed** las líneas están saturadas

Jamaica [dʒə'meɪkə] N Jamaica

Jamaican [dʒə'meɪkən] ADJ, N jamaicano(-a) m/f

jamb [dʒæm] N jamba

jamboree [dʒæmbə'ri:] N congreso de niños exploradores

jammed [dʒæmd] ADJ atascado

jam-packed [dʒæm'pækt] ADJ: **~ (with)** atestado (de)

jam session N concierto improvisado de jazz/rock etc

Jan. ABBR (= January) ene.

jangle ['dʒæŋgl] VI sonar (de manera) discordante

janitor ['dʒænɪtə'] N (caretaker) portero, conserje m

January ['dʒænjuərɪ] N enero; see also **July**

Japan [dʒə'pæn] N (el) Japón

Japanese [dʒæpə'ni:z] ADJ japonés(-esa)
  ▶ N pl inv japonés(-esa) m/f; (Ling) japonés m

jar [dʒɑ:'] N (glass: large) jarra; (: small) tarro
  ▶ VI (sound) chirriar; (colours) desentonar

jargon ['dʒɑ:gən] N jerga

jarring ['dʒɑ:rɪŋ] ADJ (sound) discordante, desafinado; (colour) chocante

Jas. ABBR = **James**

jasmine, jasmin ['dʒæzmɪn] N jazmín m

jaundice ['dʒɔ:ndɪs] N ictericia

jaundiced ['dʒɔ:ndɪst] ADJ (fig: embittered) amargado; (: disillusioned) desilusionado

jaunt [dʒɔ:nt] N excursión f

jaunty ['dʒɔ:ntɪ] ADJ alegre; (relaxed) desenvuelto

Java ['dʒɑ:və] N Java

javelin ['dʒævlɪn] N jabalina

jaw [dʒɔ:] N mandíbula; **jaws** NPL (Tech: of vice etc) mordaza sg

jawbone ['dʒɔ:bəun] N mandíbula, quijada

jay [dʒeɪ] N (Zool) arrendajo
jaywalker ['dʒeɪwɔːkəʳ] N peatón(-ona) m/f imprudente
jazz [dʒæz] N jazz m
▶ **jazz up** VT (liven up) animar
jazz band N orquesta de jazz
jazzy ['dʒæzɪ] ADJ de colores llamativos
JCB® N ABBR excavadora
JCS N ABBR (US) = **Joint Chiefs of Staff**
JD N ABBR (US: = Doctor of Laws) título universitario; (= Justice Department) Ministerio de Justicia
jealous ['dʒɛləs] ADJ (gen) celoso; (envious) envidioso; **to be ~** tener celos
jealously ['dʒɛləslɪ] ADV (enviously) envidiosamente; (watchfully) celosamente
jealousy ['dʒɛləsɪ] N celos mpl; envidia
jeans [dʒiːnz] NPL (pantalones mpl) vaqueros mpl or tejanos mpl, bluejean m inv (LAM)
Jeep® [dʒiːp] N jeep m
jeer [dʒɪəʳ] VI: **to ~ (at)** (boo) abuchear; (mock) mofarse (de)
jeering ['dʒɪərɪŋ] ADJ (crowd) insolente, ofensivo ▶ N protestas fpl; (mockery) burlas fpl
Jello® ['dʒɛləu] N (US) gelatina
jelly ['dʒɛlɪ] N (jam) jalea; (dessert etc) gelatina
jellyfish ['dʒɛlɪfɪʃ] N medusa
jemmy ['dʒɛmɪ] N palanqueta
jeopardize ['dʒɛpədaɪz] VT arriesgar, poner en peligro
jeopardy ['dʒɛpədɪ] N: **to be in ~** estar en peligro
jerk [dʒəːk] N (jolt) sacudida; (wrench) tirón m; (US inf) imbécil mf, pendejo(-a) (LAM) ▶ VT dar una sacudida a; tirar bruscamente de ▶ VI (vehicle) dar una sacudida
jerkin ['dʒəːkɪn] N chaleco
jerky ['dʒəːkɪ] ADJ espasmódico
jerry-built ['dʒɛrɪbɪlt] ADJ mal construido
jerry can ['dʒɛrɪ-] N bidón m
Jersey ['dʒəːzɪ] N Jersey m
jersey ['dʒəːzɪ] N jersey m; (fabric) tejido de punto
Jerusalem [dʒəˈruːsləm] N Jerusalén m
jest [dʒɛst] N broma
jester ['dʒɛstəʳ] N bufón m
Jesus ['dʒiːzəs] N Jesús m; **~ Christ** Jesucristo
jet [dʒɛt] N (of gas, liquid) chorro; (Aviat) avión m a reacción
jet-black ['dʒɛt'blæk] ADJ negro como el azabache
jet engine N motor m a reacción
jet lag N desorientación f por desfase horario
jetsam ['dʒɛtsəm] N echazón f
jet-setter ['dʒɛtsɛtəʳ] N personaje m de la jet
jet-ski ['dʒɛtskiː] VI practicar el motociclismo acuático
jettison ['dʒɛtɪsn] VT desechar

jetty ['dʒɛtɪ] N muelle m, embarcadero
Jew [dʒuː] N judío(-a)
jewel ['dʒuːəl] N joya; (in watch) rubí m
jeweller, (US) **jeweler** ['dʒuːələʳ] N joyero(-a); **~'s (shop)** joyería
jewellery, (US) **jewelry** ['dʒuːəlrɪ] N joyas fpl, alhajas fpl
Jewess ['dʒuːɪs] N judía
Jewish ['dʒuːɪʃ] ADJ judío
JFK N ABBR (US) = **John Fitzgerald Kennedy International Airport**
jib [dʒɪb] N (horse) plantarse; **to ~ at doing sth** resistirse a hacer algo
jibe [dʒaɪb] N mofa
jiffy ['dʒɪfɪ] N (inf): **in a ~** en un santiamén
jig [dʒɪg] N (dance, tune) giga
jigsaw ['dʒɪgsɔː] N (also: **jigsaw puzzle**) rompecabezas m inv, puzle m; (tool) sierra de vaivén
jilt [dʒɪlt] VT dejar plantado a
jingle ['dʒɪŋgl] N (advert) musiquilla ▶ VI tintinear
jingoism ['dʒɪŋgəuɪzəm] N patriotería, jingoísmo
jinx [dʒɪŋks] N (inf): **there's a ~ on it** está gafado
jitters ['dʒɪtəz] NPL (inf): **to get the ~** ponerse nervioso
jittery ['dʒɪtərɪ] ADJ (inf) agitado
jiujitsu [dʒuːˈdʒɪtsuː] N jiujitsu m
job [dʒɔb] N trabajo; (task) tarea; (duty) deber m; (post) empleo; (inf: difficulty) dificultad f; **it's a good ~ that ...** menos mal que ...; **just the ~!** ¡justo lo que necesito!; **a part-time/full-time ~** un trabajo a tiempo parcial/tiempo completo; **that's not my ~** eso no me incumbe or toca a mí; **he's only doing his ~** está cumpliendo nada más
job centre N (BRIT) oficina de empleo
job creation scheme N plan m de creación de puestos de trabajo
job description N descripción f del puesto de trabajo
jobless ['dʒɔblɪs] ADJ sin trabajo ▶ NPL: **the ~** los parados
job lot N lote m de mercancías, saldo
job satisfaction N satisfacción f en el trabajo
job security N garantía de trabajo
job specification N especificación f del trabajo, profesiograma m
Jock N (inf: Scotsman) escocés m
jockey ['dʒɔkɪ] N jockey mf ▶ VI: **to ~ for position** maniobrar para sacar delantera
jockey box N (US Aut) guantera
jockstrap ['dʒɔkstræp] N suspensorio
jocular ['dʒɔkjuləʳ] ADJ (humorous) gracioso; (merry) alegre
jodhpurs ['dʒɔdpəːz] NPL pantalón msg de montar

jog [dʒɔg] VT empujar (ligeramente) ▶ VI (run) hacer footing; **to ~ along** (fig) ir tirando; **to ~ sb's memory** refrescar la memoria a algn
jogger ['dʒɔgəʳ] N corredor(a) m/f
jogging ['dʒɔgɪŋ] N footing m
john [dʒɔn] N (US inf) wáter m
join [dʒɔɪn] VT (things) unir, juntar; (become member of: club) hacerse socio de; (Pol: party) afiliarse a; (meet: people) reunirse con; (fig) unirse a ▶ VI (roads) empalmar; (rivers) confluir ▶ N juntura; **will you ~ us for dinner?** ¿quieres cenar con nosotros?; **I'll ~ you later** me reuniré contigo luego; **to ~ forces (with)** aliarse (con)
  ▶ **join in** VI tomar parte, participar ▶ VT FUS tomar parte or participar en
  ▶ **join up** VI unirse; (Mil) alistarse
joiner ['dʒɔɪnəʳ] N carpintero(-a)
joinery ['dʒɔɪnərɪ] N carpintería
joint [dʒɔɪnt] N (Tech) juntura, unión f; (Anat) articulación f; (BRIT Culin) pieza de carne (para asar); (inf: place) garito; (of cannabis) porro ▶ ADJ (common) común; (combined) conjunto; (responsibility) compartido; (committee) mixto
joint account N (with bank etc) cuenta común
jointly ['dʒɔɪntlɪ] ADV (gen) en común; (together) conjuntamente
joint owners NPL copropietarios mpl
joint ownership N copropiedad f, propiedad f común
joint-stock bank ['dʒɔɪntstɔk-] N banco por acciones
joint-stock company ['dʒɔɪntstɔk-] N sociedad f anónima
joint venture N empresa conjunta
joist [dʒɔɪst] N viga
joke [dʒəuk] N chiste m; (also: **practical joke**) broma ▶ VI bromear; **to play a ~ on** gastar una broma a
joker ['dʒəukəʳ] N chistoso(-a), bromista mf; (Cards) comodín m
joking ['dʒəukɪŋ] N bromas fpl
jokingly ['dʒəukɪŋlɪ] ADV en broma
jollity ['dʒɔlɪtɪ] N alegría
jolly ['dʒɔlɪ] ADJ (merry) alegre; (enjoyable) divertido ▶ ADV (inf) muy, la mar de ▶ VT: **to ~ sb along** animar or darle ánimos a algn; **~ good!** ¡estupendo!
jolt [dʒəult] N (shake) sacudida; (blow) golpe m; (shock) susto ▶ VT (physically) sacudir; (emotionally) asustar
Jordan ['dʒɔːdən] N (country) Jordania; (river) Jordán m
joss stick [dʒɔs-] N barrita de incienso, pebete m
jostle ['dʒɔsl] VT dar empujones or empellones a
jot [dʒɔt] N: **not one ~** ni pizca, ni un ápice
  ▶ **jot down** VT apuntar

jotter ['dʒɔtəʳ] N (BRIT) bloc m
journal ['dʒəːnl] N (paper) periódico; (magazine) revista; (diary) diario
journalese [dʒəːnə'liːz] N (pej) lenguaje m periodístico
journalism ['dʒəːnəlɪzəm] N periodismo
journalist ['dʒəːnəlɪst] N periodista mf
journey ['dʒəːnɪ] N viaje m; (distance covered) trayecto ▶ VI viajar; **return ~** viaje de regreso; **a five-hour ~** un viaje de cinco horas
jovial ['dʒəuvɪəl] ADJ risueño, alegre
jowl [dʒaul] N quijada
joy [dʒɔɪ] N alegría
joyful ['dʒɔɪful] ADJ alegre
joyfully ['dʒɔɪfulɪ] ADV alegremente
joyous ['dʒɔɪəs] ADJ alegre
joyride ['dʒɔɪraɪd] N: **to go for a ~** darse una vuelta en un coche robado
joyrider ['dʒɔɪraɪdəʳ] N persona que se da una vuelta en un coche robado
joystick ['dʒɔɪstɪk] N (Aviat) palanca de mando; (Comput) palanca de control
JP N ABBR = **Justice of the Peace**
Jr ABBR = **junior**
JTPA N ABBR (US: = Job Training Partnership Act) programa gubernamental de formación profesional
jubilant ['dʒuːbɪlnt] ADJ jubiloso
jubilation [dʒuːbɪ'leɪʃən] N júbilo
jubilee ['dʒuːbɪliː] N aniversario; **silver ~** vigésimo quinto aniversario
judge [dʒʌdʒ] N juez mf ▶ VT juzgar; (competition) actuar de or ser juez en; (estimate) considerar; (: weight, size etc) calcular ▶ VI: **judging** or **to ~ by his expression** a juzgar por su expresión; **as far as I can ~** por lo que puedo entender, a mi entender; **I judged it necessary to inform him** consideré necesario informarle
judge advocate N (Mil) auditor m de guerra
judgment, judgement ['dʒʌdʒmənt] N juicio; (punishment) sentencia, fallo; **to pass ~ (on)** (Law) pronunciar or dictar sentencia (sobre); (fig) emitir un juicio crítico or dictaminar (sobre); **in my ~** a mi juicio
judicial [dʒuː'dɪʃl] ADJ judicial
judiciary [dʒuː'dɪʃɪərɪ] N poder m judicial, magistratura
judicious [dʒuː'dɪʃəs] ADJ juicioso
judo ['dʒuːdəu] N judo
jug [dʒʌg] N jarra
jugged hare [dʒʌgd-] N (BRIT) estofado de liebre
juggernaut ['dʒʌgənɔːt] N (BRIT: huge truck) camión m de carga pesada
juggle ['dʒʌgl] VI hacer juegos malabares
juggler ['dʒʌgləʳ] N malabarista mf
Jugoslav etc ['juːgəuslaːv] = **Yugoslav** etc
jugular ['dʒʌgjuləʳ] ADJ: **~ vein** (vena) yugular f

juice [dʒuːs] N jugo, zumo (SP); (of meat) jugo; (inf: petrol): **we've run out of ~** se nos acabó la gasolina

juiciness ['dʒuːsɪnɪs] N jugosidad f

juicy ['dʒuːsɪ] ADJ jugoso

jujitsu [dʒuː'dʒɪtsuː] N jujitsu m

jukebox ['dʒuːkbɒks] N máquina de discos

Jul. ABBR (= July) jul.

July [dʒuː'laɪ] N julio; **the first of ~** el uno or primero de julio; **during ~** en el mes de julio; **in ~ of next year** en julio del año que viene

jumble ['dʒʌmbl] N revoltijo ▶ VT (also: **jumble together, jumble up**: mix up) revolver; (: disarrange) mezclar

jumble sale N (BRIT) mercadillo; ver nota

En cada jumble sale pueden comprarse todo tipo de objetos baratos de segunda mano, especialmente ropa, juguetes, libros, vajillas y muebles. Suelen organizarse en los locales de un colegio, iglesia, ayuntamiento o similar, con fines benéficos, bien en ayuda de una organización benéfica conocida o para solucionar problemas más concretos de la comunidad.

jumbo ['dʒʌmbəʊ], **jumbo jet** N jumbo

jump [dʒʌmp] VI saltar, dar saltos; (start) sobresaltarse; (increase) aumentar ▶ VT saltar ▶ N salto; (fence) obstáculo; (increase) aumento; **to ~ the queue** (BRIT) colarse
  ▶ **jump about** VI dar saltos, brincar
  ▶ **jump at** VT FUS (fig) apresurarse a aprovechar; **he jumped at the offer** se apresuró a aceptar la oferta
  ▶ **jump down** VI bajar de un salto, saltar a tierra
  ▶ **jump up** VI levantarse de un salto

jumped-up ['dʒʌmptʌp] ADJ (pej) engreído

jumper ['dʒʌmpər] N (BRIT: pullover) jersey m, suéter m; (US: dress) pichi m; (Sport) saltador(a) m/f

jump leads, (US) **jumper cables** NPL cables mpl puente de batería

jump-start ['dʒʌmpstɑːt] VT (car) arrancar con ayuda de otra batería or empujando; (fig: economy) reactivar

jump suit N mono

jumpy ['dʒʌmpɪ] ADJ nervioso

Jun. ABBR = **junior**; (= June) jun.

junction ['dʒʌŋkʃən] N (BRIT: of roads) cruce m; (Rail) empalme m

juncture ['dʒʌŋktʃər] N: **at this ~** en este momento, en esta coyuntura

June [dʒuːn] N junio; see also **July**

jungle ['dʒʌŋgl] N selva, jungla

junior ['dʒuːnɪər] ADJ (in age) menor, más joven; (competition) juvenil; (position) subalterno ▶ N menor mf, joven mf;

he's ~ to me es menor que yo

junior executive N ejecutivo(-a) subalterno(-a)

junior high school N (US) centro de educación secundaria; see also **high school**

junior school N (BRIT) escuela primaria; see also **primary school**

junk [dʒʌŋk] N (cheap goods) baratijas fpl; (lumber) trastos mpl viejos; (rubbish) basura; (ship) junco ▶ VT (esp US) deshacerse de

junk bond N (Comm) obligación f basura inv

junk dealer N vendedor(a) m/f de objetos usados

junket ['dʒʌŋkɪt] N (Culin) dulce de leche cuajada; (BRIT inf): **to go on a ~, go junketing** viajar a costa ajena or del erario público

junk food N comida basura or de plástico

junkie ['dʒʌŋkɪ] N (inf) yonqui mf, heroinómano(-a)

junk mail N propaganda (buzoneada), correo m basura inv

junk room N trastero

junk shop N tienda de objetos usados

junta ['dʒʌntə] N junta militar

Jupiter ['dʒuːpɪtər] N (Mythology, Astro) Júpiter m

jurisdiction [dʒuərɪs'dɪkʃən] N jurisdicción f; **it falls** or **comes within/outside our ~** es/ no es de nuestra competencia

jurisprudence [dʒuərɪs'pruːdəns] N jurisprudencia

juror ['dʒuərər] N jurado

jury ['dʒuərɪ] N jurado

jury box N tribuna del jurado

juryman ['dʒuərɪmən] N (irreg) miembro del jurado

just [dʒʌst] ADJ justo ▶ ADV (exactly) exactamente; (only) sólo, solamente, no más (LAm); **he's ~ done it/left** acaba de hacerlo/ irse; **I've ~ seen him** acabo de verle; **~ right** perfecto; **~ two o'clock** las dos en punto; **she's ~ as clever as you** es tan lista como tú; **~ as well that ...** menos mal que ...; **it's ~ as well you didn't go** menos mal que no fuiste; **it's ~ as good (as)** es igual (que), es tan bueno (como); **~ as he was leaving** en el momento en que se marchaba; **we were ~ going** ya nos íbamos; **I was ~ about to phone** estaba a punto de llamar; **~ before/ enough** justo antes/lo suficiente; **~ here** aquí mismo; **he ~ missed** falló por poco; **~ listen to this** escucha esto un momento; **~ ask someone the way** simplemente pregúntale a alguien por dónde se va; **not ~ now** ahora no

justice ['dʒʌstɪs] N justicia; (US: judge) juez mf; **to do ~ to** (fig) hacer justicia a; **this photo doesn't do you ~** esta foto no te favorece

Justice of the Peace N juez *mf* de paz; *see also* **crown court**

justifiable [dʒʌstɪˈfaɪəbl] ADJ justificable, justificado

justifiably [dʒʌstɪˈfaɪəblɪ] ADV justificadamente, con razón

justification [dʒʌstɪfɪˈkeɪʃən] N justificación *f*

justify [ˈdʒʌstɪfaɪ] VT justificar; (*text*) alinear, justificar; **to be justified in doing sth** tener motivo para *or* razón al hacer algo

justly [ˈdʒʌstlɪ] ADV (*gen*) justamente; (*with reason*) con razón

justness [ˈdʒʌstnɪs] N justicia

jut [dʒʌt] VI (*also*: **jut out**) sobresalir

jute [dʒuːt] N yute *m*

juvenile [ˈdʒuːvənaɪl] ADJ juvenil; (*humour, mentality*) infantil; (*court*) de menores ▶ N joven *mf*, menor *mf* de edad

juvenile delinquency N delincuencia juvenil

juvenile delinquent N delincuente *mf* juvenil

juxtapose [dʒʌkstəpəuz] VT yuxtaponer

juxtaposition [dʒʌkstəpəˈzɪʃən] N yuxtaposición *f*

j

Kk

K, k [keɪ] N (letter) K, k f; **K for King** K de Kilo
K ABBR (= one thousand) mil; (BRIT: = Knight)
  título; (= kilobyte) K
kaftan ['kæftæn] N caftán m
Kalahari Desert [kælə'hɑːrɪ-] N desierto de
  Kalahari
kale [keɪl] N col f rizada
kaleidoscope [kə'laɪdəskəup] N calidoscopio
kamikaze [kæmɪ'kɑːzɪ] ADJ kamikaze
Kampala [kæm'pɑːlə] N Kampala
Kampuchea [kæmpu'tʃɪə] N Kampuchea
kangaroo [kæŋgə'ruː] N canguro
Kans. ABBR (US) = **Kansas**
kaput [kə'put] ADJ (inf) roto, estropeado
karaoke [kɑːrə'əukɪ] N karaoke
karate [kə'rɑːtɪ] N karate m
Kashmir [kæʃ'mɪər] N Cachemira
kayak ['kaɪæk] N kayak m
Kazakhstan [kæzæk'stɑːn] N Kazajstán m
KC N ABBR (BRIT Law: = King's Counsel) título
  concedido a determinados abogados
kebab [kə'bæb] N pincho moruno, brocheta
keel [kiːl] N quilla; **on an even ~** (fig) en
  equilibrio
  ▶ **keel over** VI (Naut) zozobrar, volcarse;
  (person) desplomarse
keen [kiːn] ADJ (interest, desire) grande, vivo;
  (eye, intelligence) agudo; (competition) reñido;
  (edge) afilado; (BRIT: eager) entusiasta; **to be ~
  to do** or **on doing sth** tener muchas ganas
  de hacer algo; **to be ~ on sth/sb** interesarse
  por algo/algn; **I'm not ~ on going** no tengo
  ganas de ir
keenly ['kiːnlɪ] ADV (enthusiastically) con
  entusiasmo; (acutely) vivamente; (intensely)
  intensamente
keenness ['kiːnnɪs] N (eagerness) entusiasmo,
  interés m
keep [kiːp] (pt, pp **kept**) VT (retain, preserve)
  guardar; (hold back) quedarse con; (shop) ser
  propietario de; (feed: family etc) mantener;
  (promise) cumplir; (chickens, bees etc) criar ▶ VI
  (food) conservarse; (remain) seguir, continuar
  ▶ N (of castle) torreón m; (food etc) comida,

sustento; **to ~ doing sth** seguir haciendo
algo; **to ~ sb from doing sth** impedir a algn
hacer algo; **to ~ sth from happening**
impedir que algo ocurra; **to ~ sb happy**
tener a algn contento; **to ~ sb waiting** hacer
esperar a algn; **to ~ a place tidy** mantener
un lugar limpio; **to ~ sth to o.s.** no decirle
algo a nadie; **to ~ time** (clock) mantener la
hora exacta; **~ the change** quédese con la
vuelta; **to ~ an appointment** acudir a una
cita; **to ~ a record** or **note of sth** tomar nota
de or apuntar algo; see also **keeps**
  ▶ **keep away** VT: **to ~ sth/sb away from sb**
mantener algo/a algn apartado de algn
  ▶ VI: **to ~ away (from)** mantenerse
apartado (de)
  ▶ **keep back** VT (crowd, tears) contener;
(money) quedarse con; (conceal: information):
to ~ sth back from sb ocultar algo a algn
  ▶ VI hacerse a un lado
  ▶ **keep down** VT (control: prices, spending)
controlar; (retain: food) retener ▶ VI seguir
agachado, no levantar la cabeza
  ▶ **keep in** VT (invalid, child) impedir que salga,
no dejar salir; (Scol) castigar (a quedarse en
el colegio) ▶ VI (inf): **to ~ in with sb** mantener
la relación con algn
  ▶ **keep off** VT (dog, person) mantener a
distancia ▶ VI evitar; **~ your hands off!** ¡no
toques!; **"~ off the grass"** "prohibido pisar
el césped"
  ▶ **keep on** VI seguir, continuar; **to ~ on
doing** seguir or continuar haciendo; **to ~ on
(about sth)** no parar de hablar (de algo)
  ▶ **keep out** VI (stay out) permanecer fuera;
"~ out" "prohibida la entrada"
  ▶ **keep up** VT mantener, conservar ▶ VI no
rezagarse; (fig: in comprehension) seguir (el
hilo); **to ~ up with** (pace) ir al paso de; (level)
mantenerse a la altura de; **to ~ up with sb**
seguir el ritmo a algn; (fig) seguir a algn
keeper ['kiːpər] N guarda mf
keep-fit [kiːp'fɪt] N gimnasia (de
mantenimiento)

keeping ['ki:pɪŋ] N (*care*) cuidado; **in ~ with** de acuerdo con

keeps [ki:ps] N: **for ~** (*inf*) para siempre

keepsake ['ki:pseɪk] N recuerdo

keg [kɛg] N barrilete *m*, barril *m*

Ken. ABBR (*US*) = **Kentucky**

kennel ['kɛnl] N perrera; **kennels** NPL residencia canina

Kenya ['kɛnjə] N Kenia

Kenyan ['kɛnjən] ADJ, N keniata *mf*, keniano(-a) *m/f*

kept [kɛpt] PT, PP of **keep**

kerb [kə:b] N (*BRIT*) bordillo

kerb crawler [-krɔ:lə^r] N *conductor en busca de prostitutas desde su coche*

kernel ['kə:nl] N (*nut*) fruta; (*fig*) meollo

kerosene ['kɛrəsi:n] N keroseno

kestrel ['kɛstrəl] N cernícalo

ketchup ['kɛtʃəp] N salsa de tomate, ketchup *m*

kettle ['kɛtl] N hervidor *m*

kettle drum N (*Mus*) timbal *m*

kettling ['kɛtəlɪŋ] N (*BRIT inf*) acorralamiento *m* (mediante cordón) policial

key [ki:] N (*gen*) llave *f*; (*Mus*) tono; (*of piano, typewriter*) tecla; (*on map*) clave *f* ▶ CPD (*vital: position, issue, industry etc*) clave ▶ VT (*also*: **key in**) teclear

keyboard ['ki:bɔ:d] N teclado ▶ VT (*text*) teclear

keyboarder ['ki:bɔ:də^r] N teclista *mf*

keyed up [ki:d-] ADJ (*person*) nervioso; **to be (all) ~** estar nervioso or emocionado

keyhole ['ki:həul] N ojo (de la cerradura)

keyhole surgery N cirugía cerrada or no invasiva

key man N (*irreg*) hombre *m* clave

keynote ['ki:nəut] N (*Mus*) tónica; (*fig*) idea fundamental

keynote speech N discurso de apertura

keypad ['ki:pæd] N teclado numérico

keyring ['ki:rɪŋ] N llavero

keystone ['ki:stəun] N piedra clave

keystroke ['ki:strəuk] N pulsación *f* (de una tecla)

kg ABBR (= *kilogram*) kg

KGB N ABBR KGB *m*

khaki ['kɑ:kɪ] N caqui

kibbutz [kɪ'buts] (*pl* **kibbutzim** [-ɪm]) N kibutz *m*

kick [kɪk] VT (*person*) dar una patada a; (*ball*) dar un puntapié a; (*inf: habit*) quitarse de ▶ VI (*horse*) dar coces ▶ N patada; puntapié *m*, tiro; (*of rifle*) culetazo; (*inf: thrill*): **he does it for kicks** lo hace por pura diversión
▶ **kick around** VT (*idea*) dar vueltas a; (*person*) tratar a patadas a
▶ **kick off** VI (*Sport*) hacer el saque inicial

kick-off ['kɪkɔf] N saque inicial; **the ~ is at 10 o'clock** el partido empieza a las diez

kick-start ['kɪkstɑ:t] N (*also*: **kick-starter**) (pedal *m* de) arranque *m*

kid [kɪd] N (*inf: child*) niño(-a), chiquillo(-a); (*animal*) cabrito; (*leather*) cabritilla ▶ VI (*inf*) bromear

kid gloves NPL: **to treat sb with ~** andarse con pies de plomo con algn

kidnap ['kɪdnæp] VT secuestrar

kidnapper ['kɪdnæpə^r] N secuestrador(a) *m/f*

kidnapping ['kɪdnæpɪŋ] N secuestro

kidney ['kɪdnɪ] N riñón *m*

kidney bean N judía, alubia

kidney machine N riñón *m* artificial

kill [kɪl] VT matar; (*murder*) asesinar; (*fig: rumour, conversation*) acabar con ▶ N matanza; **to ~ time** matar el tiempo
▶ **kill off** VT exterminar, terminar con; (*fig*) echar por tierra

killer ['kɪlə^r] N asesino(-a)

killer app N ABBR (*inf*: = *killer application*) aplicación *f* rompedora, aplicación *f* de excelente rendimiento

killer instinct N: **to have the ~** ir a por todas

killing ['kɪlɪŋ] N (*one*) asesinato; (*several*) matanza; **to make a ~** (*Comm*) hacer su agosto

killjoy ['kɪldʒɔɪ] N (*BRIT*) aguafiestas *mf*

kiln [kɪln] N horno

kilo ['ki:ləu] N ABBR (= *kilogram(me)*) kilo

kilobyte ['kɪləubaɪt] N (*Comput*) kilobyte *m*

kilogram, kilogramme ['kɪləugræm] N kilogramo

kilometre, (US) kilometer ['kɪləmi:tə^r] N kilómetro

kilowatt ['kɪləuwɔt] N kilovatio

kilt [kɪlt] N falda escocesa

kilter ['kɪltə^r] N: **out of ~** desbaratado

kimono [kɪ'məunəu] N quimono

kin [kɪn] N parientes *mpl*

kind [kaɪnd] ADJ (*treatment*) bueno, cariñoso; (*person, act, word*) amable, atento ▶ N clase *f*, especie *f*; (*species*) género; **in ~** (*Comm*) en especie; **a ~ of** una especie de; **to be two of a ~** ser tal para cual; **would you be ~ enough to …?, would you be so ~ as to …?** ¿me hace el favor de …?; **it's very ~ of you (to do)** le agradezco mucho (el que haya hecho)

kindergarten ['kɪndəgɑ:tn] N jardín *m* de infancia

kind-hearted [kaɪnd'hɑ:tɪd] ADJ bondadoso, de buen corazón

Kindle® ['kɪndl] N Kindle® *m*, libro electrónico

kindle ['kɪndl] VT encender

kindliness ['kaɪndlɪnəs] N bondad *f*, amabilidad *f*

kindling ['kɪndlɪŋ] N leña (menuda)

kindly ['kaɪndlɪ] ADJ bondadoso; (gentle) cariñoso ▶ ADV bondadosamente, amablemente; **will you ~ ...** sería usted tan amable de ...

kindness ['kaɪndnɪs] N bondad f, amabilidad f; (act) favor m

kindred ['kɪndrɪd] N familia, parientes mpl ▶ ADJ: **~ spirits** almas fpl gemelas

kinetic [kɪ'netɪk] ADJ cinético

king [kɪŋ] N rey m

kingdom ['kɪŋdəm] N reino

kingfisher ['kɪŋfɪʃəʳ] N martín m pescador

kingpin ['kɪŋpɪn] N (Tech) perno real or pinzote; (fig) persona clave

king-size ['kɪŋsaɪz], **king-sized** ['kɪŋsaɪzd] ADJ de tamaño gigante; (cigarette) extra largo; **~ bed** cama de matrimonio extragrande

kink [kɪŋk] N (in rope etc) enroscadura; (in hair) rizo; (fig: emotional, psychological) manía

kinky ['kɪŋkɪ] ADJ (pej) perverso

kinship ['kɪnʃɪp] N parentesco; (fig) afinidad f

kinsman ['kɪnzmən] N (irreg) pariente m

kinswoman ['kɪnzwumən] N (irreg) parienta f

kiosk ['kiːɔsk] N quiosco; (BRIT Tel) cabina; **newspaper ~** quiosco, kiosco

kipper ['kɪpəʳ] N arenque m ahumado

Kirghizia [kəˈgɪzɪə] N Kirguizistán m

kiss [kɪs] N beso ▶ VT besar; **~ of life** (artificial respiration) respiración f boca a boca; **to ~ sb goodbye** dar un beso de despedida a algn; **to ~ (each other)** besarse

kissagram ['kɪsəgræm] N servicio de felicitaciones mediante el que se envía a una persona vestida de manera sugerente para besar a algn

kit [kɪt] N equipo; (set of tools etc) (caja de) herramientas fpl; (assembly kit) juego de armar; **tool ~** juego or estuche m de herramientas
▶ **kit out** VT equipar

kitbag ['kɪtbæg] N (Mil) macuto

kitchen ['kɪtʃɪn] N cocina

kitchen garden N huerto

kitchen sink N fregadero

kitchen unit N módulo de cocina

kitchenware ['kɪtʃɪnwɛəʳ] N batería de cocina

kite [kaɪt] N (toy) cometa

kith [kɪθ] N: **~ and kin** parientes mpl y allegados

kitten ['kɪtn] N gatito(-a)

kitty ['kɪtɪ] N (pool of money) fondo común; (Cards) bote m

kiwi ['kiːwiː] N (also: **kiwi fruit**) kiwi m; **K~** (inf: New Zealander) neozelandés(-esa) m/f

KKK N ABBR (US) = **Ku Klux Klan**

kleptomaniac [klɛptəu'meɪnɪæk] N cleptómano(-a)

km ABBR (= kilometre) km

km/h ABBR (= kilometres per hour) km/h

knack [næk] N: **to have the ~ of doing sth** tener facilidad para hacer algo

knackered ['nækəd] ADJ (inf) hecho polvo

knapsack ['næpsæk] N mochila

knead [niːd] VT amasar

knee [niː] N rodilla

kneecap ['niːkæp] VT destrozar a tiros la rótula de ▶ N rótula

knee-deep ['niːdiːp] ADJ: **the water was ~** el agua llegaba hasta la rodilla

kneel [niːl] (pt, pp **knelt** [nɛlt]) VI (also: **kneel down**) arrodillarse

kneepad ['niːpæd] N rodillera

knell [nɛl] N toque m de difuntos

knelt [nɛlt] PT, PP of **kneel**

knew [njuː] PT of **know**

knickers ['nɪkəz] NPL (BRIT) bragas fpl, calzones mpl (LAM)

knick-knack ['nɪknæk] N chuchería, baratija

knife [naɪf] (pl **knives**) N cuchillo ▶ VT acuchillar; **~, fork and spoon** cubiertos mpl

knife edge N: **to be on a ~** estar en la cuerda floja

knight [naɪt] N caballero; (Chess) caballo

knighthood ['naɪthud] N (title): **to get a ~** recibir el título de Sir

knit [nɪt] VT tejer, tricotar; (brows) fruncir; (fig): **to ~ together** unir, juntar ▶ VI hacer punto, tejer, tricotar; (bones) soldarse

knitted ['nɪtɪd] ADJ de punto

knitting ['nɪtɪŋ] N labor f de punto

knitting machine N máquina de tricotar

knitting needle, (US) **knit pin** N aguja de hacer punto or tejer

knitting pattern N patrón m para tricotar

knitwear ['nɪtwɛəʳ] N prendas fpl de punto

knives [naɪvz] PL of **knife**

knob [nɔb] N (of door) pomo; (of stick) puño; (on radio, TV) botón m; (lump) bulto; **a ~ of butter** (BRIT) un pedazo de mantequilla

knobbly ['nɔblɪ], (US) **knobby** ['nɔbɪ] ADJ (wood, surface) nudoso; (knee) huesudo

knock [nɔk] VT (strike) golpear; (bump into) chocar contra; (fig: inf) criticar ▶ VI (at door etc): **to ~ at/on** llamar a ▶ N golpe m; (on door) llamada; **he knocked at the door** llamó a la puerta
▶ **knock down** VT (pedestrian) atropellar; (price) rebajar
▶ **knock off** VI (inf: finish) salir del trabajo ▶ VT (inf: steal) birlar; (strike off) quitar; (fig: from price: record): **to ~ off £10** rebajar en £10
▶ **knock out** VT dejar sin sentido; (Boxing) poner fuera de combate, dejar K.O.; (in competition) eliminar; (stop) estropear, dejar fuera de servicio
▶ **knock over** VT (object) derribar, tirar; (pedestrian) atropellar

knockdown ['nɔkdaun] ADJ (price) de saldo

knocker ['nɔkəʳ] N (*on door*) aldaba
knocking ['nɔkɪŋ] N golpes *mpl*, golpeteo
knock-kneed [nɔk'niːd] ADJ patizambo
knockout ['nɔkaut] N (*Boxing*) K.O. *m*,
knockout *m*
knock-up ['nɔkʌp] N (*Tennis*) peloteo
knot [nɔt] N (*gen*) nudo ▸ VT anudar; **to tie a**
~ hacer un nudo
knotted ['nɔtɪd] ADJ anudado
knotty ['nɔtɪ] ADJ (*fig*) complicado
know [nəu] (*pt* **knew** [njuː], *pp* **known** [nəun])
VT (*gen*) saber; (*person, author, place*) conocer;
(*recognize*) reconocer ▸ VI: **as far as I ~** ... que
yo sepa ...; **yes, I ~** sí, ya lo sé; **I don't ~** no lo
sé; **to ~ how to do** saber hacer; **to ~ how to**
swim saber nadar; **to ~ about** *or* **of sb/sth**
saber de algn/algo; **to get to ~ sth** enterarse
de algo; **I ~ nothing about it** no sé nada de
eso; **I don't ~ him** no lo *or* le conozco; **to ~**
right from wrong saber distinguir el bien
del mal
know-all ['nəuɔːl] N (*BRIT pej*) sabelotodo *mf*,
sabihondo(-a)
know-how ['nəuhau] N conocimientos *mpl*
knowing ['nəuɪŋ] ADJ (*look etc*) de
complicidad
knowingly ['nəuɪŋlɪ] ADV (*purposely*) a
sabiendas; (*smile, look*) con complicidad
know-it-all ['nəuɪtɔːl] N (*US*) = **know-all**
knowledge ['nɔlɪdʒ] N (*gen*) conocimiento;
(*learning*) saber *m*, conocimientos *mpl*; **to**
have no ~ of no saber nada de; **with my ~**
con mis conocimientos, sabiéndolo; **to (the**
best of) my ~ a mi entender, que yo sepa;
not to my ~ que yo sepa, no; **it is common ~**
that ... es del dominio público que ...;
it has come to my ~ that ... me he enterado
de que ...; **to have a working ~ of Spanish**
defenderse con el español
knowledgeable ['nɔlɪdʒəbl] ADJ entendido,
erudito
known [nəun] PP *of* **know** ▸ ADJ (*thief, facts*)
conocido; (*expert*) reconocido
knuckle ['nʌkl] N nudillo
▸ **knuckle down** VI (*inf*) ponerse a trabajar en
serio
▸ **knuckle under** VI someterse
knuckleduster ['nʌkldʌstəʳ] N puño de
hierro
KO ABBR (= *knock out*) K.O. *m* ▸ VT (*knock out*)
dejar K.O.
koala [kəu'ɑːlə] N (*also:* **koala bear**) koala *m*
kook [kuːk] N (*US inf*) chiflado(-a) *m/f*,
majareta *mf*
Koran [kɔ'rɑːn] N Corán *m*
Korea [kə'rɪə] N Corea; **North/South ~** Corea
del Norte/Sur
Korean [kə'rɪən] ADJ, N coreano(-a) *m/f*
kosher ['kəuʃəʳ] ADJ autorizado por la ley
judía
Kosovar ['kɔsəvɑːʳ], **Kosovan** ['kɔsəvən] ADJ
kosovar
Kosovo ['kɔsəvəu] N Kosovo *m*
kowtow ['kau'tau] VI: **to ~ to sb** humillarse
ante algn
Kremlin ['kremlɪn] N: **the ~** el Kremlin
KS ABBR (*US*) = **Kansas**
Kt ABBR (*BRIT*: = *Knight*) caballero de una orden
Kuala Lumpur ['kwɑːlə'lumpuəʳ] N Kuala
Lumpur *m*
kudos ['kjuːdɔs] N gloria, prestigio
Kurd [kəːd] N kurdo(-a)
Kuwait [ku'weɪt] N Kuwait *m*
Kuwaiti [ku'weɪtɪ] ADJ, N Kuwaití *mf*
kW ABBR (= *kilowatt*) Kv
KY, Ky. ABBR (*US*) = **Kentucky**

k

Ll

L, l [ɛl] N (letter) L, l f; **L for Lucy**, (US) **L for Love** L de Lorenzo

L ABBR (on maps etc) = **lake**; (size) = **large**; (= left) izq.; (BRIT Aut: = learner) L

l ABBR = **litre**

LA N ABBR (US) = **Los Angeles** ▶ ABBR (US) = **Louisiana**

La. ABBR (US) = **Louisiana**

lab [læb] N ABBR = **laboratory**

Lab. ABBR (CANADA) = **Labrador**

label ['leɪbl] N etiqueta; (brand: of record) sello (discográfico) ▶ VT poner una etiqueta a, etiquetar

labor ['leɪbəʳ] N, VB (US) = **labour**

laboratory [ləˈbɔrətərɪ] N laboratorio

Labor Day N (US) día m de los trabajadores (primer lunes de septiembre)

laborious [ləˈbɔːrɪəs] ADJ penoso

laboriously [ləˈbɔːrɪəslɪ] ADV penosamente

labor union N (US) sindicato

labor unrest N (US) conflictividad f laboral

Labour ['leɪbəʳ] N (BRIT Pol: also: **the Labour Party**) el partido laborista, los laboristas

labour, (US) **labor** ['leɪbəʳ] N (task) trabajo; (also: **labour force**) mano f de obra; (workers) trabajadores mpl; (Med) (dolores mpl de) parto ▶ VI: **to ~ (at)** trabajar (en) ▶ VT: **to ~ a point** insistir en un punto; **hard ~** trabajos mpl forzados; **to be in ~** (Med) estar de parto; **the L~ party** (BRIT) el partido laborista, los laboristas mpl

labour cost, (US) **labor cost** N costo de la mano de obra

labour dispute, (US) **labor dispute** N conflicto laboral

laboured, (US) **labored** ['leɪbəd] ADJ (breathing) fatigoso; (style) forzado, pesado

labourer, (US) **laborer** ['leɪbərəʳ] N peón m; (on farm) peón m, obrero; (day labourer) jornalero

labour force, (US) **labor force** N mano f de obra

labour-intensive, (US) **labor-intensive** [leɪbərɪn'tɛnsɪv] ADJ que necesita mucha mano de obra

labour relations, (US) **labor relations** NPL relaciones fpl laborales

labour-saving, (US) **labor-saving** ['leɪbəseɪvɪŋ] ADJ que ahorra trabajo

laburnum [ləˈbəːnəm] N codeso

labyrinth ['læbɪrɪnθ] N laberinto

lace [leɪs] N encaje m; (of shoe etc) cordón m ▶ VT (shoes: also: **lace up**) atarse; (drink: fortify with spirits) echar licor a

lacemaking ['leɪsmeɪkɪŋ] N obra de encaje

lacerate ['læsəreɪt] VT lacerar

laceration [læsəˈreɪʃən] N laceración f

lace-up ['leɪsʌp] ADJ (shoes etc) con cordones

lack [læk] N (absence) falta, carencia; (scarcity) escasez f ▶ VT faltarle a algn, carecer de; **through** or **for ~ of** por falta de; **to be lacking** faltar, no haber; **to be lacking in sth** faltarle a algn algo

lackadaisical [lækəˈdeɪzɪkl] ADJ (careless) descuidado; (indifferent) indiferente

lackey ['lækɪ] N (also fig) lacayo

lacklustre, (US) **lackluster** ['læklʌstəʳ] ADJ (surface) deslustrado, deslucido; (style) inexpresivo; (eyes) apagado

laconic [ləˈkɔnɪk] ADJ lacónico

lacquer ['lækəʳ] N laca; **hair ~** laca para el pelo

lacrosse [ləˈkrɔs] N lacrosse f

lacy ['leɪsɪ] ADJ (like lace) como de encaje

lad [læd] N muchacho, chico; (in stable etc) mozo

ladder ['lædəʳ] N escalera (de mano); (BRIT: in tights) carrera ▶ VT (BRIT: tights) hacer una carrera en

laden ['leɪdn] ADJ: **~ (with)** cargado (de); **fully ~** (truck, ship) cargado hasta el tope

ladle ['leɪdl] N cucharón m

lady ['leɪdɪ] N señora; (distinguished, noble) dama; **young ~** señorita; **the ladies' (room)** los servicios de señoras; **"ladies and gentlemen ..."** "señoras y caballeros ..."

ladybird ['leɪdɪbəːd], (US) **ladybug** ['leɪdɪbʌg] N mariquita

lady doctor N médica, doctora
lady-in-waiting ['leɪdɪɪn'weɪtɪŋ] N dama de honor
ladykiller ['leɪdɪkɪləʳ] N robacorazones *m inv*
ladylike ['leɪdɪlaɪk] ADJ fino
Ladyship ['leɪdɪʃɪp] N: **your ~** su Señoría
LAFTA N ABBR (= *Latin American Free Trade Association*) ALALC *f*
lag [læg] VI (*also*: **lag behind**) retrasarse, quedarse atrás ▶ VT (*pipes*) revestir
lager ['lɑ:gəʳ] N cerveza (rubia)
lager lout VI (*BRIT inf*) gamberro borracho
lagging ['lægɪŋ] N revestimiento
lagoon [lə'gu:n] N laguna
Lagos ['leɪgɔs] N Lagos *m*
laid [leɪd] PT, PP *of* **lay**
laid-back [leɪd'bæk] ADJ (*inf*) tranquilo, relajado
laid up ADJ: **to be ~** (*person*) tener que guardar cama
lain [leɪn] PP *of* **lie**
lair [lɛəʳ] N guarida
laissez-faire [lɛseɪ'fɛəʳ] N laissez-faire *m*
laity ['leɪtɪ] N laicado
lake [leɪk] N lago
Lake District N (*BRIT*): **the ~** la Región de los Lagos
lamb [læm] N cordero; (*meat*) carne *f* de cordero
lamb chop N chuleta de cordero
lambswool ['læmzwul] N lana de cordero
lame [leɪm] ADJ cojo, rengo (*LAM*); (*weak*) débil; (*excuse*) poco convincente; **~ duck** (*fig*: *person*) inútil *mf* (: *firm*) empresa en quiebra
lamely ['leɪmlɪ] ADV (*fig*) sin convicción
lament [lə'mɛnt] N lamento ▶ VT lamentarse de
lamentable ['læməntəbl] ADJ lamentable
lamentation [læmən'teɪʃən] N lamento
laminated ['læmɪneɪtɪd] ADJ laminado
lamp [læmp] N lámpara
lamplight ['læmplaɪt] N: **by ~** a la luz de la lámpara
lampoon [læm'pu:n] VT satirizar
lamppost ['læmppəust] N (*BRIT*) farola
lampshade ['læmpʃeɪd] N pantalla
lance [lɑ:ns] N lanza ▶ VT (*Med*) abrir con lanceta
lance corporal N (*BRIT*) soldado de primera clase
lancet ['lɑ:nsɪt] N (*Med*) lanceta
Lancs [læŋks] ABBR (*BRIT*) = **Lancashire**
land [lænd] N tierra; (*country*) país *m*; (*piece of land*) terreno; (*estate*) tierras *fpl*, finca; (*Agr*) campo ▶ VI (*from ship*) desembarcar; (*Aviat*) aterrizar; (*fig*: *fall*) caer ▶ VT (*obtain*) conseguir; (*passengers, goods*) desembarcar; **to go/travel by ~** ir/viajar por tierra; **to own ~** ser dueño de tierras; **to ~ on one's feet** caer

de pie; (*fig*: *to be lucky*) salir bien parado; **to ~ sb with sth** (*inf*) hacer cargar a algn con algo
▶ **land up** VI: **to ~ up in/at** ir a parar a/en
landed ['lændɪd] ADJ: **~ gentry** terratenientes *mpl*
landfill site ['lændfɪl-] N vertedero
landing ['lændɪŋ] N desembarco; aterrizaje *m*; (*of staircase*) rellano
landing card N tarjeta de desembarque
landing craft N lancha de desembarco
landing gear N (*Aviat*) tren *m* de aterrizaje
landing stage N (*BRIT*) desembarcadero
landing strip N pista de aterrizaje
landlady ['lændleɪdɪ] N (*owner*) dueña; (*of boarding house*) patrona
landline ['lændlaɪn] N (*teléfono*) fijo; **can I ring you on your ~?** ¿te puedo llamar al fijo?
landlocked ['lændlɔkt] ADJ cercado de tierra
landlord ['lændlɔ:d] N propietario; (*of pub etc*) patrón *m*
landlubber ['lændlʌbəʳ] N marinero de agua dulce
landmark ['lændmɑ:k] N lugar *m* conocido; **to be a ~** (*fig*) hacer época
landowner ['lændəunəʳ] N terrateniente *mf*
landscape ['lænskeɪp] N paisaje *m*
landscape architecture N arquitectura paisajista
landscaped ['lænskeɪpt] ADJ reformado artísticamente
landscape gardener N diseñador(a) *m/f* de paisajes
landscape gardening N jardinería paisajista
landscape painting N (*Art*) paisaje *m*
landslide ['lændslaɪd] N (*Geo*) corrimiento de tierras; (*fig, Pol*) victoria arrolladora
lane [leɪn] N (*in country*) camino; (*in town*) callejón *m*; (*Aut*) carril *m*; (*in race*) calle *f*; (*for air or sea traffic*) ruta; **shipping ~** ruta marina
language ['læŋgwɪdʒ] N lenguaje *m*; (*national tongue*) idioma *m*, lengua; **bad ~** palabrotas *fpl*
language laboratory N laboratorio de idiomas
language school N academia de idiomas
language studies NPL estudios *mpl* filológicos
languid ['læŋgwɪd] ADJ lánguido
languish ['læŋgwɪʃ] VI languidecer
languor ['læŋgəʳ] N languidez *f*
languorous ['læŋgərəs] ADJ lánguido
lank [læŋk] ADJ (*hair*) lacio
lanky ['læŋkɪ] ADJ larguirucho
lanolin, lanoline ['lænəlɪn] N lanolina
lantern ['læntn] N linterna, farol *m*
lanyard ['lænjed] N acollador *m*
Laos [laus] N Laos *m*
lap [læp] N (*of track*) vuelta; (*of body*) regazo
▶ VI (*waves*) chapotear; **to sit on sb's ~**

sentarse en las rodillas de algn
▶ **lap up** VT beber a lengüetadas or con la lengua; (fig: compliments, attention) disfrutar; (: lies etc) tragarse
La Paz [læ'pæz] N La Paz
lapdog ['læpdɔg] N perro faldero
lapel [lə'pɛl] N solapa
Lapland ['læplænd] N Laponia
Laplander ['læplændəʳ] N lapón(-ona) m/f
lapse [læps] N (fault) error m, fallo; (moral) desliz m ▶ VI (expire) caducar; (morally) cometer un desliz; (time) pasar, transcurrir; **to ~ into bad habits** volver a las andadas; **~ of time** lapso, intervalo; **a ~ of memory** un lapsus de memoria
laptop ['læptɔp] N (also: **laptop computer**) (ordenador m) portátil m
larceny ['lɑːsənɪ] N latrocinio
lard [lɑːd] N manteca (de cerdo)
larder ['lɑːdəʳ] N despensa
large [lɑːdʒ] ADJ grande ▶ ADV: **by and ~** en general, en términos generales; **at ~** (free) en libertad; (generally) en general; **to make ~(r)** hacer mayor or más extenso; **a ~ number of people** una gran cantidad de personas; **on a ~ scale** a gran escala
largely ['lɑːdʒlɪ] ADV (mostly) en su mayor parte; (introducing reason) en gran parte
large-scale ['lɑːdʒ'skeɪl] ADJ (map, drawing) a gran escala; (reforms, business activities) importante
largesse [lɑː'ʒɛs] N generosidad f
lark [lɑːk] N (bird) alondra; (joke) broma
▶ **lark about** VI bromear, hacer el tonto
larrikin ['lærɪkɪn] N (AUSTRALIA, NEW ZEALAND inf) gamberro(-a)
larva ['lɑːvə] (pl **larvae** [-iː]) N larva
laryngitis [lærɪn'dʒaɪtɪs] N laringitis f
larynx ['lærɪŋks] N laringe f
lasagne [lə'zænjə] N lasaña
lascivious [lə'sɪvɪəs] ADJ lascivo
laser ['leɪzəʳ] N láser m
laser beam N rayo láser
laser printer N impresora láser
lash [læʃ] N latigazo; (punishment) azote m; (also: **eyelash**) pestaña ▶ VT azotar; (tie) atar
▶ **lash down** VT sujetar con cuerdas ▶ VI (rain) caer a trombas
▶ **lash out** VI (inf: spend) gastar a la loca; **to ~ out (at sb)** (hit) arremeter (contra algn); **to ~ out against sb** lanzar invectivas contra algn
lashing ['læʃɪŋ] N (beating) azotaina, flagelación f; **lashings of** (inf) montones mpl de
lass [læs] N chica
lassitude ['læsɪtjuːd] N lasitud f
lasso [læ'suː] N lazo ▶ VT coger con lazo
last [lɑːst] ADJ (gen) último, final; (final) último, final ▶ ADV (finally) por último ▶ VI (endure)

durar; (continue) continuar, seguir; **~ night** anoche; **~ week** la semana pasada; **at ~** por fin; **~ but one** penúltimo; **~ time** la última vez; **it lasts (for) two hours** dura dos horas
last-ditch ['lɑːst'dɪtʃ] ADJ (attempt) de último recurso, último, desesperado
lasting ['lɑːstɪŋ] ADJ duradero
lastly ['lɑːstlɪ] ADV por último, finalmente
last-minute ['lɑːstmɪnɪt] ADJ de última hora
latch [lætʃ] N picaporte m, pestillo
▶ **latch on to** VT FUS (cling to: person) pegarse a; (: idea) aferrarse a
latchkey ['lætʃkiː] N llavín m
latchkey child N (irreg) niño cuyos padres trabajan
late [leɪt] ADJ (not on time) tarde, atrasado; (towards end of period, life) tardío; (hour) avanzado; (deceased) fallecido ▶ ADV tarde; (behind time, schedule) con retraso; **to be (10 minutes) ~** llegar con (10 minutos de) retraso; **to be ~ with** estar atrasado con; **~ delivery** entrega tardía; **~ in life** a una edad avanzada; **of ~** últimamente; **~ at night** a última hora de la noche; **in ~ May** hacia fines de mayo; **the ~ Mr X** el difunto Sr. X; **to work ~** trabajar hasta tarde
latecomer ['leɪtkʌməʳ] N recién llegado(-a)
lately ['leɪtlɪ] ADV últimamente
lateness ['leɪtnɪs] N (of person) demora; (of event) tardanza
latent ['leɪtnt] ADJ latente; **~ defect** defecto latente
later ['leɪtəʳ] ADJ (date etc) posterior; (version etc) más reciente ▶ ADV más tarde, después; **~ on today** hoy más tarde
lateral ['lætərl] ADJ lateral
latest ['leɪtɪst] ADJ último; **at the ~** a más tardar
latex ['leɪtɛks] N látex m
lathe [leɪð] N torno
lather ['lɑːðəʳ] N espuma (de jabón) ▶ VT enjabonar
Latin ['lætɪn] N latín m ▶ ADJ latino
Latin America N América Latina, Latinoamérica
Latin American ADJ, N latinoamericano(-a) m/f
Latino [læ'tiːnəu] ADJ, N latino(-a) m/f
latitude ['lætɪtjuːd] N latitud f; (fig: freedom) libertad f
latrine [lə'triːn] N letrina
latter ['lætəʳ] ADJ último; (of two) segundo ▶ N: **the ~** el último, éste
latter-day ['lætədeɪ] ADJ moderno
latterly ['lætəlɪ] ADV últimamente
lattice ['lætɪs] N enrejado
lattice window N ventana enrejada or de celosía
lattice work N enrejado

Latvia ['lætvɪə] N Letonia
Latvian ['lætvɪən] ADJ letón(-ona) ▶ N letón(-ona) m/f; (Ling) letón m
laudable ['lɔ:dəbl] ADJ loable
laugh [lɑ:f] N risa; (loud) carcajada ▶ VI reírse, reír; reírse a carcajadas; **(to do sth) for a ~** (hacer algo) en broma
▶ **laugh at** VT FUS reírse de
▶ **laugh off** VT tomar a risa
laughable ['lɑ:fəbl] ADJ ridículo
laughing ['lɑ:fɪŋ] ADJ risueño ▶ N: **it's no ~ matter** no es cosa de risa
laughing gas N gas m hilarante
laughing stock N: **to be the ~ of the town** ser el hazmerreír de la ciudad
laughter ['lɑ:ftər] N risa
launch [lɔ:ntʃ] N (boat) lancha; see also **launching** ▶ VT (ship) botar; (rocket, plan) lanzar; (fig) comenzar
▶ **launch forth** VI: **to ~ forth (into)** lanzarse a or en, emprender
▶ **launch into** VT FUS lanzarse a
▶ **launch out** VI = **launch forth**
launching ['lɔ:ntʃɪŋ] N (of rocket etc) lanzamiento; (inauguration) estreno
launching pad, launch pad N plataforma de lanzamiento
launder ['lɔ:ndər] VT lavar
Launderette® [lɔ:n'drɛt], (US) **Laundromat®** ['lɔ:ndrəmæt] N lavandería (automática)
laundry ['lɔ:ndrɪ] N lavandería; (clothes: dirty) ropa sucia; (: clean) colada; **to do the ~** hacer la colada
laureate ['lɔ:rɪət] ADJ see **poet laureate**
laurel ['lɔrl] N laurel m; **to rest on one's laurels** dormirse en or sobre los laureles
lava ['lɑ:və] N lava
lavatory ['lævətərɪ] N wáter m; **lavatories** NPL servicios mpl, aseos mpl, sanitarios mpl (LAM)
lavatory paper N papel m higiénico
lavender ['lævəndər] N lavanda
lavish ['lævɪʃ] ADJ abundante; (giving freely): **~ with** pródigo en ▶ VT: **to ~ sth on sb** colmar a algn de algo
lavishly ['lævɪʃlɪ] ADV (give, spend) generosamente; (furnished) lujosamente
law [lɔ:] N ley f; (study) derecho; (of game) regla; **against the ~** contra la ley; **to study ~** estudiar derecho; **to go to ~** recurrir a la justicia
law-abiding ['lɔ:əbaɪdɪŋ] ADJ respetuoso con la ley
law and order N orden m público
lawbreaker ['lɔ:breɪkər] N infractor(a) m/f de la ley
law court N tribunal m (de justicia)
lawful ['lɔ:ful] ADJ legítimo, lícito

lawfully ['lɔ:fulɪ] ADV legalmente
lawless ['lɔ:lɪs] ADJ (act) ilegal; (person) rebelde; (country) ingobernable
Law Lord N (BRIT) miembro de la Cámara de los Lores y del más alto tribunal de apelación
lawmaker ['lɔ:meɪkər] N legislador(a) m/f
lawn [lɔ:n] N césped m
lawnmower ['lɔ:nməuər] N cortacésped m
lawn tennis N tenis m sobre hierba
law school N (US) facultad f de derecho
law student N estudiante mf de derecho
lawsuit ['lɔ:su:t] N pleito; **to bring a ~ against** entablar un pleito contra
lawyer ['lɔ:jər] N abogado(-a); (for sales, wills etc) notario(-a)
lax [læks] ADJ (discipline) relajado; (person) negligente
laxative ['læksətɪv] N laxante m
laxity ['læksɪtɪ] N flojedad f; (moral) relajamiento; (negligence) negligencia
lay [leɪ] PT of **lie** ▶ ADJ laico; (not expert) lego ▶ VT (pt, pp **laid** [leɪd]) (place) colocar; (eggs, table) poner; (trap) tender; (carpet) extender; **to ~ the facts/one's proposals before sb** presentar los hechos/sus propuestas a algn
▶ **lay aside, lay by** VT dejar a un lado
▶ **lay down** VT (pen etc) dejar; (arms) rendir; (policy) trazar; (rules etc) establecer; **to ~ down the law** imponer las normas
▶ **lay in** VT abastecerse de
▶ **lay into** VT FUS (inf: attack, scold) arremeter contra
▶ **lay off** VT (workers) despedir
▶ **lay on** VT (water, gas) instalar; (meal, facilities) proveer
▶ **lay out** VT (plan) trazar; (display) exponer; (spend) gastar
▶ **lay up** VT (store) guardar; (ship) desarmar; (illness) obligar a guardar cama
layabout ['leɪəbaut] N vago(-a)
lay-by ['leɪbaɪ] N (BRIT Aut) área de descanso
lay days NPL días mpl de inactividad
layer ['leɪər] N capa
layette [leɪ'ɛt] N ajuar m (de niño)
layman ['leɪmən] N (irreg) lego
lay-off ['leɪɔf] N despido, paro forzoso
layout ['leɪaut] N (design) plan m, trazado; (disposition) disposición f; (Press) composición f
laze [leɪz] VI no hacer nada; (pej) holgazanear
lazily ['leɪzɪlɪ] ADV perezosamente
laziness ['leɪzɪnɪs] N pereza
lazy ['leɪzɪ] ADJ perezoso, vago, flojo (LAM)
LB ABBR (CANADA) = **Labrador**
lb. ABBR (weight) = **pound**
lbw ABBR (Cricket) = **leg before wicket**
LC N ABBR (US) = **Library of Congress**
lc ABBR (Typ: = lower case) min.
L/C ABBR = **letter of credit**

635

LCD N ABBR = **liquid crystal display**

Ld ABBR (*Brit*: = *Lord*) *título de nobleza*

LDS N ABBR (= *Licentiate in Dental Surgery*) *diploma universitario*; (= *Latter-day Saints*) Iglesia de Jesucristo de los Santos del último día

LEA N ABBR (*Brit*: = *local education authority*) *organismo local encargado de la enseñanza*

lead¹ [liːd] (*pt, pp* **led** [lɛd]) N (*front position*) delantera; (*distance, time ahead*) ventaja; (*clue*) pista; (*Elec*) cable *m*; (*for dog*) correa; (*Theat*) papel *m* principal ▸ VT conducir; (*life*) llevar; (*be leader of*) dirigir; (*Sport*) ir en cabeza de; (*orchestra*: *Brit*) ser el primer violín en; (: *US*) dirigir ▸ VI ir primero; **to be in the ~** (*Sport*) llevar la delantera; (*fig*) ir a la cabeza; **to take the ~** (*Sport*) tomar la delantera; (*fig*) tomar la iniciativa; **to ~ sb to believe that ...** hacer creer a algn que ...; **to ~ sb to do sth** llevar a algn a hacer algo
  ▸ **lead astray** VT llevar por mal camino
  ▸ **lead away** VT llevar
  ▸ **lead back** VT hacer volver
  ▸ **lead off** VT llevar ▸ VI (*in game*) abrir
  ▸ **lead on** VT (*tease*) engañar; **to ~ sb on to** (*induce*) incitar a algn a
  ▸ **lead to** VT FUS producir, provocar
  ▸ **lead up to** VT FUS (*events*) conducir a; (*in conversation*) preparar el terreno para

lead² [lɛd] N (*metal*) plomo; (*in pencil*) mina

leaded [ˈlɛdɪd] ADJ: **~ windows** ventanas *fpl* emplomadas

leaden [ˈlɛdn] ADJ (*sky, sea*) plomizo; (*heavy*: *footsteps*) pesado

leader [ˈliːdəʳ] N jefe(-a) *m/f*, líder *m*; (*of union etc*) dirigente *mf*; (*guide*) guía *mf*; (*of newspaper*) editorial *m*; **they are leaders in their field** (*fig*) llevan la delantera en su especialidad

leadership [ˈliːdəʃɪp] N dirección *f*; **qualities of ~** iniciativa *sg*; **under the ~ of ...** bajo la dirección de ..., al mando de ...

lead-free [ˈlɛdfriː] ADJ sin plomo

leading [ˈliːdɪŋ] ADJ (*main*) principal; (*outstanding*) destacado; (*first*) primero; (*front*) delantero; **a ~ question** una pregunta tendenciosa

leading lady N (*Theat*) primera actriz *f*

leading light N (*fig*: *person*) figura principal

leading man N (*irreg*) (*Theat*) primer actor *m*

leading role N papel *m* principal

lead pencil N lápiz *m*

lead poisoning N envenenamiento plúmbico

lead singer [liːd-] N cantante *mf*

lead time N (*Comm*) plazo de entrega

lead-up [ˈliːdʌp] N: **in the ~ to the election** cuando falta *etc* poco para las elecciones

lead weight N peso de plomo

leaf [liːf] (*pl* **leaves** [liːvz]) N hoja; **to turn over a new ~** (*fig*) hacer borrón y cuenta nueva; **to take a ~ out of sb's book** (*fig*) seguir el ejemplo de algn
  ▸ **leaf through** VT FUS (*book*) hojear

leaflet [ˈliːflɪt] N folleto

leafy [ˈliːfɪ] ADJ frondoso

league [liːg] N sociedad *f*; (*Football*) liga; **to be in ~ with** estar confabulado con

league table N clasificación *f*

leak [liːk] N (*of liquid, gas*) escape *m*, fuga; (*in pipe*) agujero; (*in roof*) gotera; (*fig*: *of information, in security*) filtración *f* ▸ VI (*ship*) hacer agua; (*shoes*) tener un agujero; (*pipe*) tener un escape; (*roof*) tener goteras; (*liquid, gas*: *also*: **leak out**) escaparse, salirse; (*fig*: *news*) trascender, divulgarse ▸ VT (*gen*) dejar escapar; (*fig*: *information*) filtrar

leakage [ˈliːkɪdʒ] N (*of water, gas etc*) escape *m*, fuga

leaky [ˈliːkɪ] ADJ (*roof*) con goteras; (*bucket, shoe*) con agujeros; (*pipe*) con un escape; (*boat*) que hace agua

lean [liːn] (*pt, pp* **leaned** *or* **leant** [lɛnt]) ADJ (*thin*) flaco; (*meat*) magro ▸ VT: **to ~ sth on sth** apoyar algo en algo ▸ VI (*slope*) inclinarse; (*rest*): **to ~ against** apoyarse contra; **to ~ on** apoyarse en
  ▸ **lean back** VI inclinarse hacia atrás
  ▸ **lean forward** VI inclinarse hacia adelante
  ▸ **lean out** VI: **to ~ out (of)** asomarse (a)
  ▸ **lean over** VI inclinarse

leaning [ˈliːnɪŋ] ADJ inclinado ▸ N: **~ (towards)** inclinación *f* (hacia); **the L~ Tower of Pisa** la Torre Inclinada de Pisa

leant [lɛnt] PT, PP *of* **lean**

lean-to [ˈliːntuː] N (*roof*) tejado de una sola agua; (*building*) cobertizo

leap [liːp] N salto ▸ VI (*pt, pp* **leaped** *or* **leapt** [lɛpt]) saltar; **to ~ at an offer** apresurarse a aceptar una oferta
  ▸ **leap up** VI (*person*) saltar

leapfrog [ˈliːpfrɔg] N pídola ▸ VI: **to ~ over sb/sth** saltar por encima de algn/algo

leapt [lɛpt] PT, PP *of* **leap**

leap year N año bisiesto

learn [ləːn] (*pt, pp* **learned**, **learnt** [ləːnt]) VT (*gen*) aprender; (*come to know of*) enterarse de ▸ VI aprender; **to ~ how to do sth** aprender a hacer algo; **to ~ that ...** enterarse *or* informarse de que ...; **to ~ about sth** (*Scol*) aprender algo; (*hear*) enterarse *or* informarse de algo; **we were sorry to ~ that ...** nos dio tristeza saber que ...

learned [ˈləːnɪd] ADJ erudito

learner [ˈləːnəʳ] N principiante *mf*; (*Brit*: *also*: **learner driver**) conductor(a) *m/f* en prácticas; *see also* **L-plates**

learning [ˈləːnɪŋ] N saber *m*, conocimientos *mpl*

learnt [ləːnt] PP *of* **learn**

lease [liːs] N arriendo ▶ VT arrendar; **on ~** en arriendo
▶ **lease back** VT subarrendar

leaseback ['liːsbæk] N subarriendo

leasehold ['liːshəʊld] N (*contract*) derechos *mpl* de arrendamiento ▶ ADJ arrendado

leash [liːʃ] N correa

least [liːst] ADJ (*slightest*) menor, más pequeño; (*smallest amount of*) mínimo ▶ ADV menos ▶ N: **the ~** lo menos; **the ~ expensive car** el coche menos caro; **at ~** por lo menos, al menos; **you could at ~ have phoned** por lo menos podías haber llamado; **not in the ~** en absoluto

leather ['lɛðəʳ] N cuero ▶ CPD: **~ goods** artículos *mpl* de cuero *or* piel

leathery ['lɛðərɪ] (*skin*) curtido

leave [liːv] (*pt, pp* **left**) VT dejar; (*go away from*) abandonar ▶ VI irse; (*train*) salir ▶ N permiso; **to ~ school** dejar la escuela *or* el colegio; **~ it to me!** ¡yo me encargo!; **he's already left for the airport** ya se ha marchado al aeropuerto; **to be left** quedar, sobrar; **there's some milk left over** sobra *or* queda algo de leche; **on ~** de permiso; **to take one's ~ of** despedirse de
▶ **leave behind** VT (*on purpose*) dejar (atrás); (*accidentally*) olvidar
▶ **leave off** VT (*lid*) no poner; (*switch*) no encender; (*inf: stop*): **to ~ off doing sth** dejar de hacer algo
▶ **leave on** VT (*lid*) dejar puesto; (*light, fire, cooker*) dejar encendido
▶ **leave out** VT omitir
▶ **leave over** VT (*postpone*) dejar, aplazar

leave of absence N excedencia

leaves [liːvz] PL *of* **leaf**

leavetaking ['liːvteɪkɪŋ] N despedida

Lebanon ['lɛbənən] N: **the ~** el Líbano

lecherous ['lɛtʃərəs] ADJ lascivo

lectern ['lɛktɜːn] N atril *m*

lecture ['lɛktʃəʳ] N conferencia; (*Scol*) clase *f* ▶ VI dar clase(s) ▶ VT (*scold*) sermonear; (*reprove*) echar una reprimenda a; **to give a ~ on** dar una conferencia sobre

lecture hall N sala de conferencias; (*Univ*) aula

lecturer ['lɛktʃərəʳ] N conferenciante *mf*; (*Brit: at university*) profesor(a) *m/f*

lecture theatre N = **lecture hall**

LED N ABBR (*Elec*: = *light-emitting diode*) LED *m*

led [lɛd] PT, PP *of* **lead¹**

ledge [lɛdʒ] N (*on wall*) repisa; (*of window*) alféizar *m*; (*of mountain*) saliente *m*

ledger ['lɛdʒəʳ] N libro mayor

lee [liː] N sotavento; **in the ~ of** al abrigo de

leech [liːtʃ] N sanguijuela

leek [liːk] N puerro

leer [lɪəʳ] VI: **to ~ at sb** mirar de manera lasciva a algn

leeway ['liːweɪ] N (*fig*): **to have some ~** tener cierta libertad de acción

left [lɛft] PT, PP *of* **leave** ▶ ADJ izquierdo; (*remaining*): **there are two ~** quedan dos ▶ N izquierda ▶ ADV a la izquierda; **on** *or* **to the ~** a la izquierda; **the L~** (*Pol*) la izquierda

left-click ['lɛftklɪk] VI clicar con el botón izquierdo del ratón ▶ VT: **to ~ an icon** clicar en un icono con el botón izquierdo del ratón

left-hand ['lɛfthænd] ADJ: **the ~ side** la izquierda

left-hand drive N conducción *f* por la izquierda

left-handed [lɛft'hændɪd] ADJ zurdo; **~ scissors** tijeras *fpl* zurdas *or* para zurdos

left-hand side ['lɛfthænd-] N izquierda

leftie ['lɛftɪ] N = **lefty**

leftist ['lɛftɪst] ADJ (*Pol*) izquierdista

left-luggage [lɛft'lʌgɪdʒ], **left-luggage office** N (*Brit*) consigna

left-luggage locker N (*Brit*) consigna *f* automática

left-overs ['lɛftəʊvəz] NPL sobras *fpl*

left-wing ['lɛft'wɪŋ] ADJ (*Pol*) de izquierda(s), izquierdista

left-winger ['lɛft'wɪŋəʳ] N (*Pol*) izquierdista *mf*

lefty ['lɛftɪ] N (*inf: Pol*) rojillo(-a)

leg [lɛg] N pierna; (*of animal, chair*) pata; (*Culin: of meat*) pierna; (: *of chicken*) pata; (*of journey*) etapa; **1st/2nd ~** (*Sport*) partido de ida/de vuelta; **to pull sb's ~** tomar el pelo a algn; **to stretch one's legs** dar una vuelta

legacy ['lɛgəsɪ] N herencia; (*fig*) herencia, legado

legal ['liːgl] ADJ (*permitted by law*) lícito; (*of law*) legal; (*inquiry etc*) jurídico; **to take ~ action** *or* **proceedings against sb** entablar *or* levantar un pleito contra algn

legal adviser N asesor(a) *m/f* jurídico(-a)

legal holiday N (*US*) fiesta oficial

legality [lɪ'gælɪtɪ] N legalidad *f*

legalize ['liːgəlaɪz] VT legalizar

legally ['liːgəlɪ] ADV legalmente; **~ binding** con fuerza legal

legal tender N moneda de curso legal

legend ['lɛdʒənd] N leyenda

legendary ['lɛdʒəndərɪ] ADJ legendario

-legged ['lɛgɪd] SUFF: **two~** (*table etc*) de dos patas

leggings ['lɛgɪŋz] NPL mallas *fpl*, leggins *mpl*

leggy ['lɛgɪ] ADJ de piernas largas

legibility [lɛdʒɪ'bɪlɪtɪ] N legibilidad *f*

legible ['lɛdʒəbl] ADJ legible

legibly ['lɛdʒəblɪ] ADV legiblemente

legion ['liːdʒən] N legión *f*

legionnaire [liːdʒə'nɛəʳ] N legionario

legionnaire's disease N enfermedad *f* del legionario

637

legislation [ledʒɪs'leɪʃən] N legislación f;
a piece of ~ (bill) un proyecto de ley; (act)
una ley

legislative ['ledʒɪslətɪv] ADJ legislativo

legislator ['ledʒɪsleɪtəʳ] N legislador(a) m/f

legislature ['ledʒɪslətʃəʳ] N cuerpo
legislativo

legitimacy [lɪ'dʒɪtɪməsɪ] N legitimidad f

legitimate [lɪ'dʒɪtɪmət] ADJ legítimo

legitimize [lɪ'dʒɪtɪmaɪz] VT legitimar

legless ['leglɪs] ADJ (BRIT inf) mamado

leg-room ['legruːm] N espacio para las
piernas

Leics ABBR (BRIT) = **Leicestershire**

leisure ['leʒəʳ] N ocio, tiempo libre; **at ~**
con tranquilidad

leisure centre N polideportivo

leisurely ['leʒəlɪ] ADJ sin prisa; lento

leisure suit N conjunto tipo chandal

lemon ['lemən] N limón m

lemonade [lemə'neɪd] N (fruit juice)
limonada; (fizzy) gaseosa

lemon cheese, lemon curd N queso de
limón

lemon juice N zumo de limón

lemon tea N té m con limón

lend [lend] (pt, pp **lent** [lent]) VT: **to ~ sth to
sb** prestar algo a algn

lender ['lendəʳ] N prestamista mf

lending library ['lendɪŋ-] N biblioteca de
préstamo

length [leŋθ] N (size) largo, longitud f; (section:
of road, pipe) tramo; (: of rope etc) largo; (of wood,
string) trozo; (amount of time) duración f;
at ~ (at last) por fin, finalmente; (lengthily)
largamente; **it is two metres in ~** tiene dos
metros de largo; **what ~ is it?** ¿cuánto tiene
de largo?; **to fall full ~** caer de bruces; **to go
to any ~(s) to do sth** ser capaz de hacer
cualquier cosa para hacer algo

lengthen ['leŋθn] VT alargar ▶ VI alargarse

lengthways ['leŋθweɪz] ADV a lo largo

lengthy ['leŋθɪ] ADJ largo, extenso; (meeting)
prolongado

lenient ['liːnɪənt] ADJ indulgente

lens [lenz] N (of spectacles) lente f; (of camera)
objetivo

Lent [lent] N Cuaresma

lent [lent] PT, PP of **lend**

lentil ['lentl] N lenteja

Leo ['liːəʊ] N Leo

leopard ['lepəd] N leopardo

leotard ['liːətɑːd] N malla

leper ['lepəʳ] N leproso(-a)

leper colony N colonia de leprosos

leprosy ['leprəsɪ] N lepra

lesbian ['lezbɪən] ADJ lesbiano ▶ N lesbiana

lesion ['liːʒən] N (Med) lesión f

Lesotho [lɪ'suːtuː] N Lesotho

less [les] ADJ (in size, degree etc) menor; (in
quantity) menos ▶ PRON, ADV menos; **~ than
half** menos de la mitad; **~ than £1/a kilo/
3 metres** menos de una libra/un kilo/3 metros;
~ than ever menos que nunca; **~ 5%** menos
el cinco por ciento; **~ and ~** cada vez menos;
the ~ he works ... cuanto menos trabaja ...

lessee [le'siː] N inquilino(-a), arrendatario(-a)

lessen ['lesn] VI disminuir, reducirse ▶ VT
disminuir, reducir

lesser ['lesəʳ] ADJ menor; **to a ~ extent** or
degree en menor grado

lesson ['lesn] N clase f; **a maths ~** una clase
de matemáticas; **to give lessons in** dar
clases de; **it taught him a ~** (fig) le sirvió de
lección

lessor ['lesɔːʳ, le'sɔːʳ] N arrendador(a) m/f

lest [lest] CONJ: **~ it happen** para que no pase

let [let] (pt, pp **~**) VT (allow) dejar, permitir;
(BRIT: lease) alquilar; **to ~ sb do sth** dejar que
algn haga algo; **to ~ sb have sth** dar algo a
algn; **to ~ sb know sth** comunicar algo a
algn; **~'s go** ¡vamos!; **~ him come** que
venga; **"to ~"** "se alquila"
  ▶ **let down** VT (lower) bajar; (dress) alargar;
(tyre) desinflar; (hair) soltar; (disappoint)
defraudar
  ▶ **let go** VI soltar; (fig) dejarse ir ▶ VT soltar
  ▶ **let in** VT dejar entrar; (visitor etc) hacer
pasar; **what have you ~ yourself in for?** ¿en
qué te has metido?
  ▶ **let off** VT dejar escapar; (firework etc)
disparar; (bomb) accionar; (passenger) dejar,
bajar; **to ~ off steam** (fig, inf) desahogarse,
desfogarse
  ▶ **let on** VI: **to ~ on that ...** revelar que ...
  ▶ **let out** VT dejar salir; (dress) ensanchar;
(rent out) alquilar
  ▶ **let up** VI disminuir; (rain etc) amainar

let-down ['letdaʊn] N (disappointment)
decepción f

lethal ['liːθl] ADJ (weapon) mortífero; (poison,
wound) mortal

lethargic [le'θɑːdʒɪk] ADJ aletargado

lethargy ['leθədʒɪ] N letargo

letter ['letəʳ] N (of alphabet) letra;
(correspondence) carta; **letters** NPL (literature,
learning) letras fpl; **small/capital ~**
minúscula/mayúscula; **covering ~** carta
adjunta

letter bomb N carta-bomba

letterbox ['letəbɒks] N (BRIT) buzón m

letterhead ['letəhed] N membrete m,
encabezamiento

lettering ['letərɪŋ] N letras fpl

letter of credit N carta de crédito;
documentary ~ carta de crédito
documentaria; **irrevocable ~** carta de
crédito irrevocable

letter-opener ['lɛtərəʊpnəʳ] N abrecartas *m inv*

letterpress ['lɛtəprɛs] N (*method*) prensa de copiar; (*printed page*) impresión *f* tipográfica

letter quality N calidad *f* de correspondencia

letters patent NPL letra *sg* de patente

lettuce ['lɛtɪs] N lechuga

let-up ['lɛtʌp] N descanso, tregua

leukaemia, (*US*) **leukemia** [luː'kiːmɪə] N leucemia

level ['lɛvl] ADJ (*flat*) llano; (*flattened*) nivelado; (*uniform*) igual ▶ ADV a nivel ▶ N nivel *m*; (*height*) altura ▶ VT nivelar, allanar; (*destroy: building*) derribar; (*gun*) apuntar; (*accusation*): **to ~ (against)** levantar (contra) ▶ VI (*inf*): **to ~ with sb** ser franco con algn; **to be ~ with** estar a nivel de; **a ~ spoonful** (*Culin*) una cucharada rasa; **to draw ~ with** (*team*) igualar; (*runner, car*) alcanzar a; **A levels** (*BRIT*) ≈ exámenes *mpl* de bachillerato superior; **O levels** *npl* (*BRIT: formerly*) ≈ bachillerato *sg* elemental, octavo *sg* de Básica; **on the ~** (*fig: honest*) en serio; **talks at ministerial ~** charlas *fpl* a nivel ministerial ▶ **level off, level out** VI (*prices etc*) estabilizarse; (*ground*) nivelarse; (*aircraft*) ponerse en una trayectoria horizontal

level crossing N (*BRIT*) paso a nivel

level-headed [lɛvl'hɛdɪd] ADJ sensato

levelling, (*US*) **leveling** ['lɛvlɪŋ] ADJ (*process, effect*) de nivelación ▶ N igualación *f*, allanamiento

level playing field N situación *f* de igualdad; **to compete on a ~** competir en igualdad de condiciones

lever ['liːvəʳ] N palanca ▶ VT: **to ~ up** levantar con palanca

leverage ['liːvərɪdʒ] N (*fig: influence*) influencia

levity ['lɛvɪtɪ] N frivolidad *f*, informalidad *f*

levy ['lɛvɪ] N impuesto ▶ VT exigir, recaudar

lewd [luːd] ADJ lascivo, obsceno, colorado (*LAM*)

lexicographer [lɛksɪ'kɔgrəfəʳ] N lexicógrafo(-a) *m/f*

lexicography [lɛksɪ'kɔgrəfɪ] N lexicografía

LGBT ABBR (= *lesbian, gay, bisexual and/or transgender*) LGTB

LGV N ABBR (= *Large Goods Vehicle*) vehículo pesado

LI ABBR (*US*) = **Long Island**

liabilities [laɪə'bɪlətɪz] NPL obligaciones *fpl*; pasivo *sg*

liability [laɪə'bɪlətɪ] N (*pej: person, thing*) estorbo, lastre *m*; (*Law: responsibility*) responsabilidad *f*; (*handicap*) desventaja

liable ['laɪəbl] ADJ (*subject*): **~ to** sujeto a; (*responsible*): **~ for** responsable de; (*likely*): **~ to do** propenso a hacer; **to be ~ to a fine** exponerse a una multa

liaise [liː'eɪz] VI: **to ~ (with)** colaborar (con); **to ~ with sb** mantener informado a algn

liaison [liː'eɪzɔn] N (*coordination*) enlace *m*; (*affair*) relación *f*

liar ['laɪəʳ] N mentiroso(-a)

libel ['laɪbl] N calumnia ▶ VT calumniar

libellous ['laɪbləs] ADJ difamatorio, calumnioso

liberal ['lɪbərl] ADJ (*gen*) liberal; (*generous*): **~ with** generoso con ▶ N: **L~** (*Pol*) liberal *mf*

Liberal Democrat N (*BRIT*) demócrata *mf* liberal

liberality [lɪbə'rælɪtɪ] N (*generosity*) liberalidad *f*, generosidad *f*

liberalize ['lɪbərəlaɪz] VT liberalizar

liberally ['lɪbərəlɪ] ADV liberalmente

liberal-minded ['lɪbərl'maɪndɪd] ADJ de miras anchas, liberal

liberate ['lɪbəreɪt] VT (*people: from poverty etc*) librar; (*prisoner*) libertar; (*country*) liberar

liberation [lɪbə'reɪʃən] N liberación *f*

liberation theology N teología de la liberación

Liberia [laɪ'bɪərɪə] N Liberia

Liberian [laɪ'bɪərɪən] ADJ, N liberiano(-a) *m/f*

liberty ['lɪbətɪ] N libertad *f*; **to be at ~** (*criminal*) estar en libertad; **to be at ~ to do** estar libre para hacer; **to take the ~ of doing sth** tomarse la libertad de hacer algo

libido [lɪ'biːdəʊ] N libido

Libra ['liːbrə] N Libra

librarian [laɪ'brɛərɪən] N bibliotecario(-a)

library ['laɪbrərɪ] N biblioteca

library book N libro de la biblioteca

libretto [lɪ'brɛtəʊ] N libreto

Libya ['lɪbɪə] N Libia

Libyan ['lɪbɪən] ADJ, N libio(-a) *m/f*

lice [laɪs] PL *of* **louse**

licence, (*US*) **license** ['laɪsns] N licencia; (*permit*) permiso; (*also*: **driving licence**, (*US*) **driver's license**) carnet *m* de conducir, permiso de manejar (*LAM*); (*excessive freedom*) libertad *f*; **import ~** licencia or permiso de importación; **produced under ~** elaborado bajo licencia

licence number N (número de) matrícula

licence plate N (placa de) matrícula

license ['laɪsns] N (*US*) = **licence** ▶ VT autorizar, dar permiso a; (*car*) sacar la matrícula de *or* (*LAM*) la patente de

licensed ['laɪsnst] ADJ (*for alcohol*) autorizado para vender bebidas alcohólicas

licensed trade N comercio *or* negocio autorizado

licensee [laɪsən'siː] N (*in a pub*) concesionario(-a), dueño(-a) de un bar

license plate N (*US*) placa (de matrícula)

licensing hours NPL (*BRIT*) horas durante las cuales se permite la venta y consumo de alcohol (en un bar etc)

licentious [laɪ'sɛnʃəs] ADJ licencioso
lichen ['laɪkən] N liquen m
lick [lɪk] VT lamer; (inf: defeat) dar una paliza a ▶ N lamedura; **a ~ of paint** una mano de pintura; **to ~ one's lips** relamerse
licorice ['lɪkərɪs] N = **liquorice**
lid [lɪd] N (of box, case, pan) tapa, tapadera; **to take the ~ off sth** (fig) exponer algo a la luz pública
lido ['laɪdəu] N (BRIT) piscina, alberca (LAM)
lie [laɪ] N mentira ▶ VI mentir; (pt **lay** [leɪ], pp **lain** [leɪn]) (rest) estar echado, estar acostado; (be situated: object) estar, encontrarse; **to tell lies** mentir; **to ~ low** (fig) mantenerse a escondidas
  ▶ **lie about, lie around** VI (things) estar tirado; (BRIT: people) estar acostado or tumbado
  ▶ **lie back** VI recostarse
  ▶ **lie down** VI echarse, tumbarse
  ▶ **lie up** VI (hide) esconderse
Liechtenstein ['lɪktənstaɪn] N Liechtenstein m
lie detector N detector m de mentiras
lie-down ['laɪdaun] N (BRIT): **to have a ~** echarse (una siesta)
lie-in ['laɪɪn] N (BRIT): **to have a ~** quedarse en la cama
lieu [lu:]: **in ~ of** prep en lugar de
Lieut. ABBR = **lieutenant**
lieutenant [lɛf'tɛnənt, (US) lu:'tɛnənt] N (Mil) teniente m
lieutenant colonel N teniente m coronel
life [laɪf] (pl **lives** [laɪvz]) N vida; (of licence etc) vigencia; **to be sent to prison for ~** ser condenado a cadena perpetua; **country/city ~** la vida en el campo/en la ciudad; **true to ~** fiel a la realidad; **to paint from ~** pintar del natural; **to put** or **breathe new ~ into** (person) reanimar; (project, area etc) infundir nueva vida a
life assurance N (BRIT) seguro de vida
lifebelt ['laɪfbɛlt] N (BRIT) cinturón m salvavidas
lifeblood ['laɪfblʌd] N (fig) alma, nervio
lifeboat ['laɪfbəut] N lancha de socorro
life-buoy ['laɪfbɔɪ] N boya or guindola salvavidas
life coach N profesional encargado de mejorar la situación laboral y personal de sus clientes
life expectancy N esperanza de vida
lifeguard ['laɪfgɑːd] N vigilante mf, socorrista mf
life imprisonment N cadena perpetua
life insurance N = **life assurance**
life jacket N chaleco salvavidas
lifeless ['laɪflɪs] ADJ sin vida; (dull) soso
lifelike ['laɪflaɪk] ADJ natural
lifeline ['laɪflaɪn] N (fig) cordón m umbilical
lifelong ['laɪflɔŋ] ADJ de toda la vida

life preserver N (US) = **lifebelt**
lifer ['laɪfə'] N (inf) condenado(-a) m/f a cadena perpetua
life-saver ['laɪfseɪvə'] N socorrista mf
life sentence N cadena perpetua
life-sized ['laɪfsaɪzd] ADJ de tamaño natural
life span N vida
lifestyle ['laɪfstaɪl] N estilo de vida
life support system N (Med) sistema m de respiración asistida
lifetime ['laɪftaɪm] N: **in his ~** durante su vida; **once in a ~** una vez en la vida; **the chance of a ~** una oportunidad única
lift [lɪft] VT levantar; (copy) plagiar ▶ VI (fog) disiparse ▶ N (BRIT: elevator) ascensor m, elevador m (LAM); **to give sb a ~** (BRIT) llevar a algn en coche
  ▶ **lift off** VT levantar, quitar ▶ VI (rocket, helicopter) despegar
  ▶ **lift out** VT sacar; (troops, evacuees etc) evacuar
  ▶ **lift up** VT levantar
lift-off ['lɪftɔf] N despegue m
ligament ['lɪgəmənt] N ligamento
light [laɪt] N luz f; (flame) lumbre f; (lamp) luz f, lámpara; (daylight) luz f del día; (headlight) faro; (rear light) luz f trasera; (for cigarette etc): **have you got a ~?** ¿tienes fuego? ▶ VT (pt, pp **lighted** or **lit** [lɪt]) (candle, cigarette, fire) encender; (room) alumbrar ▶ ADJ (colour) claro; (room) con mucha luz ▶ ADV (travel) con poco equipaje; **lights** NPL (traffic lights) semáforos mpl; **to turn the ~ on/off** encender/apagar la luz; **in the ~ of** a la luz de; **to come to ~** salir a la luz; **to cast** or **shed** or **throw ~ on** arrojar luz sobre; **to make ~ of sth** (fig) no dar importancia a algo
  ▶ **light up** VI (smoke) encender un cigarrillo; (face) iluminarse ▶ VT (illuminate) iluminar, alumbrar; (set fire to) encender
light bulb N bombilla, bombillo (LAM), foco (LAM)
lighten ['laɪtn] VI (grow light) clearear ▶ VT (give light to) iluminar; (make lighter) aclarar; (make less heavy) aligerar
lighter ['laɪtə'] N (also: **cigarette lighter**) encendedor m (LAM), mechero
light-fingered [laɪt'fɪŋgəd] ADJ de manos largas
light-headed [laɪt'hɛdɪd] ADJ (dizzy) mareado; (excited) exaltado; (by nature) atolondrado
light-hearted [laɪt'hɑːtɪd] ADJ (person) alegre; (remark etc) divertido
lighthouse ['laɪthaus] N faro
lighting ['laɪtɪŋ] N (act) iluminación f; (system) alumbrado
lighting-up time [laɪtɪŋ'ʌp-] N (BRIT) hora de encendido del alumbrado

lightly ['laɪtlɪ] ADV ligeramente; (*not seriously*) con poca seriedad; **to get off ~** ser castigado con poca severidad

light meter N (*Phot*) fotómetro

lightness ['laɪtnɪs] N claridad *f*; (*in weight*) ligereza

lightning ['laɪtnɪŋ] N relámpago, rayo

lightning conductor, (*US*) **lightning rod** N pararrayos *m inv*

lightning strike N huelga relámpago

lightweight ['laɪtweɪt] ADJ (*suit*) ligero ▶ N (*Boxing*) peso ligero

light year N año luz

like [laɪk] VT (*person*) querer a; (*thing*) **I ~ swimming/apples** me gusta nadar/me gustan las manzanas ▶ PREP como ▶ ADJ parecido, semejante ▶ N: **did you ever see the ~ (of it)?** ¿has visto cosa igual?; **his likes and dislikes** sus gustos y aversiones; **the likes of him** personas como él; **I would ~,** **I'd ~** me gustaría; (*for purchase*) quisiera; **would you ~ a coffee?** ¿te apetece un café?; **I ~ swimming** me gusta nadar; **to be** *or* **look ~ sb/sth** parecerse a algn/algo; **that's just ~ him** es muy de él, es típico de él; **do it ~ this** hazlo así; **it is nothing ~ ...** no tiene parecido alguno con ...; **what's he ~?** ¿cómo es (él)?; **what's the weather ~?** ¿qué tiempo hace?; **something ~ that** algo así *or* por el estilo; **I feel ~ a drink** me apetece algo de beber; **if you ~** si quieres

likeable ['laɪkəbl] ADJ simpático, agradable

likelihood ['laɪklɪhud] N probabilidad *f*; **in all ~** según todas las probabilidades

likely ['laɪklɪ] ADJ probable, capaz (*LAM*); **he's ~ to leave** es probable *or* (*LAM*) capaz que se vaya; **not ~!** ¡ni hablar!

like-minded [laɪk'maɪndɪd] ADJ de la misma opinión

liken ['laɪkən] VT: **to ~ to** comparar con

likeness ['laɪknɪs] N (*similarity*) semejanza, parecido

likewise ['laɪkwaɪz] ADV igualmente; **to do ~** hacer lo mismo

liking ['laɪkɪŋ] N: **~ (for)** (*person*) cariño (a); (*thing*) afición (a); **to take a ~ to sb** tomar cariño a algn; **to be to sb's ~** ser del gusto de algn

lilac ['laɪlək] N (*tree*) lilo; (*flower*) lila ▶ ADJ (*colour*) de color lila

Lilo® ['laɪləu] N colchoneta inflable

lilt [lɪlt] N deje *m*

lilting ['lɪltɪŋ] ADJ melodioso

lily ['lɪlɪ] N lirio, azucena

Lima ['liːmə] N Lima

limb [lɪm] N miembro; (*of tree*) rama; **to be out on a ~** (*fig*) estar aislado

limber up ['lɪmbəʳ-] VI (*fig*) entrenarse; (*Sport*) hacer (ejercicios de) precalentamiento

limbo ['lɪmbəu] N: **to be in ~** (*fig*) quedar a la expectativa

lime [laɪm] N (*tree*) limero; (*fruit*) lima; (*Geo*) cal *f*

lime juice N zumo (*SP*) *or* jugo de lima

limelight ['laɪmlaɪt] N: **to be in the ~** (*fig*) ser el centro de atención

limerick ['lɪmərɪk] N quintilla humorística

limestone ['laɪmstəun] N piedra caliza

limit ['lɪmɪt] N límite *m* ▶ VT limitar; **weight/ speed ~** peso máximo/velocidad *f* máxima; **within limits** entre límites

limitation [lɪmɪ'teɪʃən] N limitación *f*

limited ['lɪmɪtɪd] ADJ limitado; **to be ~ to** limitarse a; **~ edition** edición limitada

limited company, limited liability company N (*BRIT*) sociedad *f* anónima

limitless ['lɪmɪtlɪs] ADJ sin límites

limousine ['lɪməziːn] N limusina

limp [lɪmp] N: **to have a ~** tener cojera ▶ VI cojear, renguear (*LAM*) ▶ ADJ flojo

limpet ['lɪmpɪt] N lapa

limpid ['lɪmpɪd] ADJ (*poetic*) límpido, cristalino

limply ['lɪmplɪ] ADV desmayadamente; **to say ~** decir débilmente

linchpin ['lɪntʃpɪn] N pezonera; (*fig*) eje *m*

Lincs [lɪŋks] ABBR (*BRIT*) = **Lincolnshire**

line [laɪn] N (*Comm*) línea; (*straight line*) raya; (*rope*) cuerda; (*for fishing*) sedal *m*; (*wire*) hilo; (*row, series*) fila, hilera; (*of writing*) renglón *m*; (*on face*) arruga; (*Rail*) vía; (*speciality*) rama ▶ VT (*Sewing*): **to ~ (with)** forrar (de); **to ~ the streets** ocupar las aceras; **in ~ with** de acuerdo con; **she's in ~ for promotion** (*fig*) tiene muchas posibilidades de que la asciendan; **to bring sth into ~ with sth** poner algo de acuerdo con algo; **~ of research/business** campo de investigación/ comercio; **to take the ~ that ...** ser de la opinión que ...; **hold the ~ please** (*Tel*) no cuelgue usted, por favor; **to draw the ~ at doing sth** negarse a hacer algo; no permitir que se haga algo; **on the right lines** por buen camino; **a new ~ in cosmetics** una nueva línea en cosméticos; *see also* **lines** ▶ **line up** VI hacer cola ▶ VT alinear, poner en fila; **to have sth lined up** tener algo arreglado

linear ['lɪnɪəʳ] ADJ lineal

lined [laɪnd] ADJ (*face*) arrugado; (*paper*) rayado; (*clothes*) forrado

line editing N (*Comput*) corrección *f* por líneas

line feed N (*Comput*) avance *m* de línea

lineman ['laɪnmən] N (*irreg: US*) técnico de las líneas; (*Football*) delantero

linen ['lɪnɪn] N ropa blanca; (*cloth*) lino

line printer N impresora de línea

liner ['laɪnəʳ] N vapor *m* de línea transatlántico; **dustbin ~** bolsa de la basura

lines [laɪnz] NPL (Rail) vía sg, raíles mpl
linesman ['laɪnzmən] N (irreg) (Sport) juez m de línea
line-up ['laɪnʌp] N (US: queue) cola; (Sport) alineación f
linger ['lɪŋgəʳ] VI retrasarse, tardar en marcharse; (smell, tradition) persistir
lingerie ['lænʒəri:] N ropa interior (de mujer), lencería
lingering ['lɪŋgərɪŋ] ADJ persistente; (death) lento
lingo ['lɪŋgəu] (pl **lingoes** [-gəuz]) N (pej) jerga
linguist ['lɪŋgwɪst] N lingüista mf
linguistic [lɪŋ'gwɪstɪk] ADJ lingüístico
linguistics [lɪŋ'gwɪstɪks] N lingüística
liniment ['lɪnɪmənt] N linimento
lining ['laɪnɪŋ] N forro; (Tech) revestimiento; (of brake) guarnición f
link [lɪŋk] N (of chain) eslabón m; (connection) conexión f; (relationship) relación f; (bond) vínculo, lazo; (Internet) enlace m ▶ VT vincular, unir; (associate): **to ~ with** or **to** relacionar con; **links** NPL (Golf) campo sg de golf; **rail** ~ línea de ferrocarril, servicio de trenes
▶ **link up** VT acoplar ▶ VI unirse
link-up ['lɪŋkʌp] N (gen) unión f; (meeting) encuentro, reunión f; (of roads) empalme m; (of spaceships) acoplamiento; (Radio, TV) enlace m
lino ['laɪnəu], **linoleum** [lɪ'nəuliəm] N linóleo
linseed oil ['lɪnsi:d-] N aceite m de linaza
lint [lɪnt] N gasa
lintel ['lɪntl] N dintel m
lion ['laɪən] N león m
lioness ['laɪənɪs] N leona
lip [lɪp] N labio; (of jug) pico; (of cup etc) borde m
liposuction ['lɪpəusʌkʃən] N liposucción f
lip-read ['lɪpri:d] VI leer los labios
lip salve N crema protectora para labios
lip service N: **to pay ~ to sth** alabar algo pero sin hacer nada
lipstick ['lɪpstɪk] N lápiz m or barra de labios, carmín m
liquefy ['lɪkwɪfaɪ] VT licuar ▶ VI licuarse
liqueur [lɪ'kjuəʳ] N licor m
liquid ['lɪkwɪd] ADJ, N líquido
liquidate ['lɪkwɪdeɪt] VT liquidar
liquidation [lɪkwɪ'deɪʃən] N liquidación f; **to go into** ~ entrar en liquidación
liquid crystal display N pantalla de cristal líquido
liquidity [lɪ'kwɪdɪtɪ] N (Comm) liquidez f
liquidize ['lɪkwɪdaɪz] VT (Culin) licuar
liquidizer ['lɪkwɪdaɪzəʳ] N (Culin) licuadora
liquor ['lɪkəʳ] N licor m, bebidas fpl alcohólicas
liquorice ['lɪkərɪs] N regaliz m

liquor store N (US) bodega, tienda de vinos y bebidas alcohólicas
Lisbon ['lɪzbən] N Lisboa
lisp [lɪsp] N ceceo ▶ VI cecear
lissom ['lɪsəm] ADJ ágil
list [lɪst] N lista; (of ship) inclinación f ▶ VT (write down) hacer una lista de; (mention) enumerar; (Comput) hacer un listado de ▶ VI (ship) inclinarse; **shopping** ~ lista de las compras; see also **lists**
listed building ['lɪstɪd-] N (Arch) edificio de interés histórico-artístico
listed company ['lɪstɪd-] N compañía cotizable
listen ['lɪsn] VI escuchar, oír; (pay attention) atender
listener ['lɪsnəʳ] N oyente mf
listeria [lɪs'tɪərɪə] N listeria
listing ['lɪstɪŋ] N (Comput) listado
listless ['lɪstlɪs] ADJ apático, indiferente
listlessly ['lɪstlɪslɪ] ADV con indiferencia
listlessness ['lɪstlɪsnɪs] N indiferencia, apatía
list price N precio de catálogo
lists [lɪsts] NPL (History) liza sg; **to enter the ~ (against sb/sth)** salir a la palestra (contra algn/algo)
lit [lɪt] PT, PP of **light**
litany ['lɪtənɪ] N letanía
liter ['li:təʳ] N (US) = **litre**
literacy ['lɪtərəsɪ] N capacidad f de leer y escribir
literacy campaign N campaña de alfabetización
literal ['lɪtərl] ADJ literal
literally ['lɪtrəlɪ] ADV literalmente
literary ['lɪtərərɪ] ADJ literario
literate ['lɪtərət] ADJ que sabe leer y escribir; (educated) culto
literature ['lɪtərɪtʃəʳ] N literatura; (brochures etc) folletos mpl
lithe [laɪð] ADJ ágil
lithography [lɪ'θɔgrəfɪ] N litografía
Lithuania [lɪθju'eɪnɪə] N Lituania
Lithuanian [lɪθju'eɪnɪən] ADJ lituano ▶ N lituano(-a); (Ling) lituano
litigate ['lɪtɪgeɪt] VI litigar
litigation [lɪtɪ'geɪʃən] N litigio
litmus paper ['lɪtməs-] N papel m de tornasol
litre, (US) liter ['li:təʳ] N litro
litter ['lɪtəʳ] N (rubbish) basura; (paper) papeles mpl (tirados); (young animals) camada, cría
litter bin N (Brit) papelera
littered ['lɪtəd] ADJ: ~ **with** lleno de
litter lout, (US) litterbug ['lɪtəbʌg] N persona que tira papeles usados en la vía pública
little ['lɪtl] ADJ (small) pequeño, chico (LAm); (not much) poco; (diminutive): ~ **house** casita ▶ ADV poco; **a** ~ un poco (de); **a** ~ **bit** un

poquito; **~ by ~** poco a poco; **~ finger** (dedo)
meñique *m*; **for a ~ while** (durante) un rato;
with ~ difficulty sin problema or dificultad;
as ~ as possible lo menos posible
little-known ['lɪtl'nəʊn] ADJ poco conocido
liturgy ['lɪtədʒɪ] N liturgia
live¹ [laɪv] ADJ (*animal*) vivo; (*wire*) conectado;
(*broadcast*; (*issue*) de actualidad;
(*unexploded*) sin explotar
live² [lɪv] VI vivir ▶ VT (*a life*) llevar; (*experience*)
vivir; **to ~ in London** vivir en Londres; **to ~
together** vivir juntos
▶ **live down** VT hacer olvidar
▶ **live off** VT FUS (*land, fish etc*) vivir de; (*pej:
parents etc*) vivir a costa de
▶ **live on** VT FUS (*food*) vivir de, alimentarse
de; **to ~ on £50 a week** vivir con 50 libras
semanales or a la semana
▶ **live out** VI (*student*) ser externo ▶ VT: **to ~
out one's days** or **life** pasar el resto de la
vida
▶ **live up** VT: **to ~ it up** (*inf*) tirarse la gran
vida
▶ **live up to** VT FUS (*fulfil*) cumplir con; (*justify*)
justificar
live-in ['lɪvɪn] ADJ: **~ partner** pareja,
compañero(-a) sentimental; **~ maid**
asistenta interna
livelihood ['laɪvlɪhʊd] N sustento
liveliness ['laɪvlɪnɪs] N viveza
lively ['laɪvlɪ] ADJ (*gen*) vivo; (*interesting: place,
book etc*) animado; (*pace*) rápido; (*party, tune*)
alegre
liven up ['laɪvn-] VT (*discussion, evening*) animar
▶ VI animarse
liver ['lɪvəʳ] N hígado
liverish ['lɪvərɪʃ] ADJ: **to feel ~** sentirse or
encontrarse mal, no estar muy católico
Liverpudlian [lɪvə'pʌdlɪən] ADJ de Liverpool
▶ N nativo(-a) or habitante *m/f* de Liverpool
livery ['lɪvərɪ] N librea
lives [laɪvz] NPL of **life**
livestock ['laɪvstɔk] N ganado
live wire [laɪv-] N (*fig, inf*): **he's a real ~!** ¡tiene
una marcha!
livid ['lɪvɪd] ADJ lívido; (*furious*) furioso
living ['lɪvɪŋ] ADJ (*alive*) vivo ▶ N: **to earn** or
make a ~ ganarse la vida; **cost of ~** coste *m*
de la vida; **in ~ memory** que se recuerde or
recuerda
living conditions NPL condiciones *fpl* de vida
living expenses NPL gastos *mpl* de
mantenimiento
living room N sala (de estar), living *m* (LAM)
living standards NPL nivel *msg* de vida
living wage N sueldo suficiente para vivir
living will N testamento vital
lizard ['lɪzəd] N lagartija
llama ['lɑːmə] N llama

LLB N ABBR (= *Bachelor of Laws*) Ldo.(-a.) en
Dcho.; *see also* **bachelor's degree**
LLD N ABBR (= *Doctor of Laws*) Dr(a). en Dcho.
LMT N ABBR (*US*: = *Local Mean Time*) hora local
load [ləʊd] N (*gen*) carga; (*weight*) peso ▶ VT
(*also Comput*) cargar; **a ~ of, loads of** (*fig*)
(gran) cantidad de, montones de; **to ~ (up)
with** cargar con or de
loaded ['ləʊdɪd] ADJ (*dice*) cargado; (*question*)
intencionado; (*inf: rich*) forrado (de dinero)
loading ['ləʊdɪŋ] N (*Comm*) sobreprima
loading bay N área de carga y descarga
loaf [ləʊf] (*pl* **loaves** [ləʊvz]) N (barra de) pan *m*
▶ VI (*also*: **loaf about, loaf around**) holgazanear
loam [ləʊm] N marga
loan [ləʊn] N préstamo; (*Comm*) empréstito
▶ VT prestar; **on ~** (*book, painting*) prestado;
to raise a ~ (*money*) procurar un empréstito
loan account N cuenta de crédito
loan capital N empréstito
loan shark N (*inf, pej*) prestamista *mf* sin
escrúpulos
loath [ləʊθ] ADJ: **to be ~ to do sth** ser reacio
a hacer algo
loathe [ləʊð] VT aborrecer; (*person*) odiar
loathing ['ləʊðɪŋ] N aversión *f*; odio
loathsome ['ləʊðsəm] ADJ asqueroso,
repugnante; (*person*) odioso
loaves [ləʊvz] PL of **loaf**
lob [lɔb] VT (*ball*) volear por alto
lobby ['lɔbɪ] N vestíbulo, sala de espera; (*Pol:
pressure group*) grupo de presión ▶ VT presionar
lobbyist ['lɔbɪɪst] N cabildero(-a)
lobe [ləʊb] N lóbulo
lobster ['lɔbstəʳ] N langosta
lobster pot N nasa, langostera
local ['ləʊkl] ADJ local ▶ N (*pub*) bar *m*; **the
locals** NPL los vecinos, los del lugar
local anaesthetic, (*US*) **local anesthetic** N
(*Med*) anestesia local
local authority N municipio, ayuntamiento
(*Sp*)
local call N (*Tel*) llamada local
local government N gobierno municipal
locality [ləʊ'kælɪtɪ] N localidad *f*
localize ['ləʊkəlaɪz] VT localizar
locally ['ləʊkəlɪ] ADV en la vecindad
locate [ləʊ'keɪt] VT (*find*) localizar; (*situate*):
to be located in estar situado en
location [ləʊ'keɪʃən] N situación *f*; **on ~** (*Cine*)
en exteriores, fuera del estudio
loch [lɔx] N lago
lock [lɔk] N (*of door, box*) cerradura, chapa
(LAM); (*of canal*) esclusa; (*of hair*) mechón *m*
▶ VT (*with key*) cerrar con llave; (*immobilize*)
inmovilizar ▶ VI (*door etc*) cerrarse con llave;
(*wheels*) trabarse; **~ stock and barrel** (*fig*) por
completo or entero; **on full ~** (*Aut*) con el
volante girado al máximo

▶ **lock away** VT (*valuables*) guardar bajo llave; (*criminal*) encerrar

▶ **lock in** VT encerrar

▶ **lock out** VT (*person*) cerrar la puerta a; **the workers were locked out** los trabajadores tuvieron que enfrentarse con un cierre patronal

▶ **lock up** VT (*criminal*) meter en la cárcel; (*mental patient*) encerrar; (*house*) cerrar (con llave) ▶ VI echar la llave

locker ['lɔkər] N casillero

locker-room ['lɔkərum] N (*US Sport*) vestuario

locket ['lɔkɪt] N medallón *m*

lockout ['lɔkaut] N (*Industry*) paro *or* cierre *m* patronal, lockout *m*

locksmith ['lɔksmɪθ] N cerrajero(-a)

lock-up ['lɔkʌp] N (*prison*) cárcel *f*; (*cell*) jaula; (*also*: **lock-up garage**) jaula, cochera

locomotive [ləukə'məutɪv] N locomotora

locum ['ləukəm] N (*Med*) (médico(-a)) suplente *m/f*

locust ['ləukəst] N langosta

lodge [lɔdʒ] N casa del guarda; (*porter's*) portería; (*Freemasonry*) logia ▶ VI (*person*): **to ~ (with)** alojarse (en casa de) ▶ VT (*complaint*) presentar

lodger ['lɔdʒər] N huésped *mf*

lodging ['lɔdʒɪŋ] N alojamiento, hospedaje *m*

lodging house ['lɔdʒɪŋ-] N pensión *f*, casa de huéspedes

lodgings ['lɔdʒɪŋz] NPL alojamiento *sg*; (*house*) casa *sg* de huéspedes

loft [lɔft] N desván *m*

lofty ['lɔftɪ] ADJ alto; (*haughty*) altivo, arrogante; (*sentiments, aims*) elevado, noble

log [lɔg] N (*of wood*) leño, tronco; (*written account*) diario; (*book*) = **logbook** ▶ N ABBR (= *logarithm*) log ▶ VT anotar, registrar

▶ **log in, log on** VI (*Comput*) iniciar la sesión

▶ **log off, log out** VI (*Comput*) finalizar la sesión

logarithm ['lɔgərɪðəm] N logaritmo

logbook ['lɔgbuk] N (*Naut*) diario de a bordo; (*Aviat*) libro de vuelo; (*of car*) documentación *f* (del coche)

log cabin N cabaña de troncos

log fire N fuego de leña

logger ['lɔgər] N leñador(a) *m/f*

loggerheads ['lɔgəhɛdz] NPL: **at ~ (with)** de pique (con)

logic ['lɔdʒɪk] N lógica

logical ['lɔdʒɪkl] ADJ lógico

logically ['lɔdʒɪkəlɪ] ADV lógicamente

login ['lɔgɪn] N (*Comput*) login *m*

logistics [lɔ'dʒɪstɪks] N logística

log jam N: **to break the ~** poner fin al estancamiento

logo ['ləugəu] N logotipo

loin [lɔɪn] N (*Culin*) lomo, solomillo; **loins** NPL lomos *mpl*

loin cloth N taparrabos *m inv*

loiter ['lɔɪtər] VI vagar; (*pej*) merodear

LOL ABBR (*inf*: = *laughing out loud*) LOL, qué risa

loll [lɔl] VI (*also*: **loll about**) repantigarse

lollipop ['lɔlɪpɔp] N pirulí *m*; (*iced*) polo

lollipop lady N (BRIT) *ver nota*

lollipop man, lollipop lady N (*irreg*) (BRIT) *persona encargada de ayudar a los niños a cruzar la calle; ver nota*

> Se llama *lollipop man* o *lollipop lady* a la persona encargada de parar el tráfico en las carreteras cercanas a los colegios británicos para que los niños las crucen sin peligro. Suelen ser personas ya jubiladas, vestidas con un abrigo de color luminoso y llevando una señal de stop en un poste portátil, la cual recuerda por su forma a un chupachups, de ahí su nombre.

lollop ['lɔləp] VI (BRIT) moverse desgarbadamente

lolly ['lɔlɪ] N (*inf*: *ice cream*) polo; (: *lollipop*) piruleta; (: *money*) guita

London ['lʌndən] N Londres *m*

Londoner ['lʌndənər] N londinense *mf*

lone [ləun] ADJ solitario

loneliness ['ləunlɪnɪs] N soledad *f*, aislamiento

lonely ['ləunlɪ] ADJ (*situation*) solitario; (*person*) solo; (*place*) aislado

lonely hearts ADJ: **~ ad** anuncio de la sección de contactos; **~ column** sección *f* de contactos

lone parent family N familia monoparental

loner ['ləunər] N solitario(-a)

lonesome ['ləunsəm] ADJ (*esp US*) = **lonely**

long [lɔŋ] ADJ largo ▶ ADV mucho tiempo, largamente ▶ VI: **to ~ for sth** anhelar algo ▶ N: **the ~ and the short of it is that …** (*fig*) en resumidas cuentas …; **in the ~ run** a la larga; **so** *or* **as ~ as** mientras, con tal de que; **don't be ~!** ¡no tardes!, ¡vuelve pronto!; **how ~ is the street?** ¿cuánto tiene la calle de largo?; **how ~ is the lesson?** ¿cuánto dura la clase?; **six metres ~** que mide seis metros, de seis metros de largo; **six months ~** que dura seis meses, de seis meses de duración; **all night ~** toda la noche; **~ ago** hace mucho (tiempo); **he no longer comes** ya no viene; **~ before** mucho antes; **before ~** (+ *future*) dentro de poco; (+ *past*) poco tiempo después; **at ~ last** al fin, por fin; **I shan't be ~** termino pronto

long-distance [lɔŋ'dɪstəns] ADJ (*race*) de larga distancia; (*call*) interurbano

longevity [lɔn'dʒɛvɪtɪ] N longevidad *f*

long-haired ['lɔŋ'hɛəd] ADJ de pelo largo

longhand ['lɔŋhænd] N escritura (corriente)

long-haul ['lɔŋhɔːl] ADJ (*flight*) de larga distancia

longing ['lɔŋɪŋ] N anhelo, ansia; (*nostalgia*) nostalgia ▶ ADJ anhelante

longingly ['lɔŋɪŋlɪ] ADV con ansia

longitude ['lɔŋgɪtjuːd] N longitud f

long jump N salto de longitud

long-life ['lɔŋlaɪf] ADJ (*batteries*) de larga duración; (*milk*) uperizado

long-lost ['lɔŋlɔst] ADJ desaparecido hace mucho tiempo

long-playing record ['lɔŋpleɪɪŋ-] N elepé m, disco de larga duración

long-range ['lɔŋ'reɪndʒ] ADJ de gran alcance; (*weather forecast*) a largo plazo

longshoreman ['lɔŋ'ʃɔːmən] N (*irreg*) (*US*) estibador m

long-sighted ['lɔŋ'saɪtɪd] ADJ (*BRIT*) présbita

long-standing ['lɔŋ'stændɪŋ] ADJ de mucho tiempo

long-suffering [lɔŋ'sʌfərɪŋ] ADJ sufrido

long-term ['lɔŋtəːm] ADJ a largo plazo

long wave N onda larga

long-winded [lɔŋ'wɪndɪd] ADJ prolijo

loo [luː] N (*BRIT inf*) wáter m

loofah ['luːfə] N esponja de lufa

look [luk] VI mirar; (*seem*) parecer; (*building etc*): **to ~ south/on to the sea** dar al sur/al mar ▶ N mirada; (*glance*) vistazo; (*appearance*) aire m, aspecto; **looks** NPL físico *sg*, belleza *sg*; **to ~ ahead** mirar hacia delante; **it looks about four metres long** yo calculo que tiene unos cuatro metros de largo; **it looks all right to me** a mí me parece que está bien; **to have a ~ at sth** echar un vistazo a algo; **to have a ~ for sth** buscar algo; **~ (here)!** (*expressing annoyance etc*) ¡oye!; **~!** (*expressing surprise*) ¡mira!

▶ **look after** VT FUS (*care for*) cuidar a; (*deal with*) encargarse de

▶ **look around** VI echar una mirada alrededor

▶ **look at** VT FUS mirar; (*consider*) considerar

▶ **look back** VI mirar hacia atrás; **to ~ back at sb/sth** mirar hacia atrás algo/a algn; **to ~ back on** (*event, period*) recordar

▶ **look down on** VT FUS (*fig*) despreciar, mirar con desprecio

▶ **look for** VT FUS buscar

▶ **look forward to** VT FUS esperar con ilusión; (*in letters*): **we ~ forward to hearing from you** quedamos a la espera de su respuesta *or* contestación; **I'm not looking forward to it** no tengo ganas de eso, no me hace ilusión

▶ **look in** VI: **to ~ in on sb** (*visit*) pasar por casa de algn

▶ **look into** VT FUS investigar

▶ **look on** VI mirar (como espectador)

▶ **look out** VI (*beware*): **to ~ out (for)** tener cuidado (de)

▶ **look out for** VT FUS (*seek*) buscar; (*await*) esperar

▶ **look over** VT (*essay*) revisar; (*town, building*) inspeccionar, registrar; (*person*) examinar

▶ **look round** VI (*turn*) volver la cabeza; **to ~ round for sth** buscar algo

▶ **look through** VT FUS (*papers, book*) hojear; (*briefly*) echar un vistazo a; (*telescope*) mirar por

▶ **look to** VT FUS ocuparse de; (*rely on*) contar con

▶ **look up** VI mirar hacia arriba; (*improve*) mejorar ▶ VT (*word*) buscar; (*friend*) visitar

▶ **look up to** VT FUS admirar

look-out ['lukaut] N (*tower etc*) puesto de observación; (*person*) vigía mf; **to be on the ~ for sth** estar al acecho de algo

look-up table ['lukʌp-] N (*Comput*) tabla de consulta

loom [luːm] N telar m ▶ VI: **~ (up)** (*threaten*) surgir, amenazar; (*event: approach*) aproximarse

loony ['luːnɪ] ADJ, N (*inf*) loco(-a) m/f

loop [luːp] N lazo; (*bend*) vuelta, recodo; (*Comput*) bucle m

loophole ['luːphəul] N laguna

loose [luːs] ADJ (*gen*) suelto; (*not tight*) flojo; (*wobbly etc*) movedizo; (*clothes*) ancho; (*morals, discipline*) relajado ▶ VT (*free*) soltar; (*slacken*) aflojar; (*also*: **loose off**: *arrow*) disparar, soltar; **~ connection** (*Elec*) hilo desempalmado; **to be at a ~ end** *or* (*US*) **at ~ ends** no saber qué hacer; **to tie up ~ ends** (*fig*) no dejar ningún cabo suelto, atar cabos

loose change N cambio

loose chippings [-'tʃɪpɪŋz] NPL (*on road*) gravilla *sg* suelta

loose-fitting ['luːsfɪtɪŋ] ADJ suelto

loose-leaf ['luːsliːf] ADJ: **~ binder** *or* **folder** carpeta de anillas

loose-limbed ['luːslɪmd] ADJ ágil, suelto

loosely ['luːslɪ] ADV libremente, aproximadamente

loosely-knit [-nɪt] ADJ de estructura abierta

loosen ['luːsn] VT (*free*) soltar; (*untie*) desatar; (*slacken*) aflojar

▶ **loosen up** VI (*before game*) hacer (ejercicios de) precalentamiento; (*inf: relax*) soltarse, relajarse

looseness ['luːsnɪs] N soltura; flojedad f

loot [luːt] N botín m ▶ VT saquear

looter ['luːtər] N saqueador(a) m/f

looting ['luːtɪŋ] N pillaje m

lop [lɔp]: **to ~ off** VT cortar; (*branches*) podar

lop-sided ['lɔp'saɪdɪd] ADJ torcido; (*fig*) desequilibrado

lord [lɔːd] N señor m; **L~ Smith** Lord Smith; **the L~** el Señor; **the (House of) Lords** (BRIT) la Cámara de los Lores

lordly ['lɔːdlɪ] ADJ señorial

Lordship ['lɔːdʃɪp] N: **your** ~ su Señoría

lore [lɔːʳ] N saber m popular, tradiciones fpl

lorry ['lɔrɪ] N (BRIT) camión m

lorry driver N camionero(-a)

lorry load N carga

lose [luːz] (pt, pp **lost** [lɔst]) VT perder ▸ VI perder, ser vencido; **to ~ (time)** (clock) atrasarse; **to ~ no time (in doing sth)** no tardar (en hacer algo); **to get lost** (object) extraviarse; (person) perderse ▸ **lose out** VI salir perdiendo

loser ['luːzəʳ] N perdedor(a) m/f; **to be a bad ~** no saber perder

losing ['luːzɪŋ] ADJ (team etc) vencido, perdedor(a)

loss [lɔs] N pérdida; **heavy losses** (Mil) grandes pérdidas fpl; **to be at a ~** no saber qué hacer; **to be a dead ~** ser completamente inútil; **to make a ~** sufrir pérdidas; **to cut one's losses** reducir las pérdidas; **to sell sth at a ~** vender algo perdiendo dinero

loss adjuster N (Insurance) perito(-a) m/f or tasador(-a) mf de pérdidas

loss leader N (Comm) artículo de promoción

lost [lɔst] PT, PP of **lose** ▸ ADJ perdido; ~ **in thought** absorto, ensimismado

lost and found N (US) objetos mpl perdidos

lost cause N causa perdida

lost property N (BRIT) objetos mpl perdidos

lost property office, lost property department N (BRIT) departamento de objetos perdidos

lot [lɔt] N (at auction) lote m; (destiny) suerte f; **the ~** el todo, todos mpl, todas fpl; **a ~** mucho, bastante; **a ~ of, lots of** muchos(-as); (with singular noun) mucho(-a); **I read a ~** leo bastante; **to draw lots (for sth)** echar suertes (para decidir algo)

lotion ['ləuʃən] N loción f

lottery ['lɔtərɪ] N lotería

loud [laud] ADJ (voice, sound) fuerte; (laugh, shout) estrepitoso; (gaudy) chillón(-ona) ▸ ADV (speak etc) fuerte; **out ~** en voz alta

loudhailer [laud'heɪləʳ] N (BRIT) megáfono

loudly ['laudlɪ] ADV (noisily) fuerte; (aloud) en alta voz

loudness ['laudnɪs] N (of sound etc) fuerza

loudspeaker [laud'spiːkəʳ] N altavoz m

lounge [laundʒ] N salón m, sala de estar; (of hotel) salón m; (of airport) sala de embarque ▸ VI (also: **lounge about, lounge around**) holgazanear, no hacer nada; see also **pub**

lounge bar N salón m

lounge suit N (BRIT) traje m de calle

louse [laus] (pl **lice** [laɪs]) N piojo ▸ **louse up** VT (inf) echar a perder

lousy ['lauzɪ] ADJ (fig) vil, asqueroso; (ill) fatal

lout [laut] N gamberro(-a)

louvre, (US) **louver** ['luːvəʳ] ADJ: ~ **door** puerta de rejilla; ~ **window** ventana de libro

lovable ['lʌvəbl] ADJ amable, simpático

love [lʌv] N (romantic, sexual) amor m; (kind, caring) cariño ▸ VT amar, querer; **to send one's ~ to sb** dar sus recuerdos a algn; ~ **from Anne** (in letter) con cariño de Anne; **I ~ to read** me encanta leer; **to be in ~ with** estar enamorado de; **to make ~** hacer el amor; **I ~ you** te quiero; **for the ~ of** por amor a; **"15 ~ "** (Tennis) "15 a cero"; **I ~ paella** me encanta la paella; **I'd ~ to come** me gustaría muchísimo venir

love affair N aventura sentimental or amorosa

love child N (irreg) hijo(-a) natural

loved ones ['lʌvdwʌnz] NPL seres mpl queridos

love-hate relationship ['lʌvheɪt-] N relación f de amor y odio

love letter N carta de amor

love life N vida sentimental

lovely ['lʌvlɪ] ADJ (delightful) precioso, encantador(a), lindo (esp LAM); (beautiful) precioso, lindo (esp LAM); **we had a ~ time** lo pasamos estupendo

lovemaking ['lʌvmeɪkɪŋ] N relaciones fpl sexuales

lover ['lʌvəʳ] N amante mf; (amateur): **a ~ of** un(a) aficionado(-a) or un(a) amante de

lovesick ['lʌvsɪk] ADJ enfermo de amor, amartelado

love song ['lʌvsɔŋ] N canción f de amor

loving ['lʌvɪŋ] ADJ amoroso, cariñoso

lovingly ['lʌvɪŋlɪ] ADV amorosamente, cariñosamente

low [ləu] ADJ, ADV bajo ▸ N (Meteorology) área de baja presión ▸ VI (cow) mugir; **to feel ~** sentirse deprimido; **to turn (down) ~** bajar; **to reach a new** or **an all-time ~** llegar a su punto más bajo

low-alcohol [ləu'ælkəhɔl] ADJ bajo en alcohol

lowbrow ['ləubrau] ADJ (person) de poca cultura

low-calorie ['ləu'kælərɪ] ADJ bajo en calorías

low-carb [ləu'kɑːb] ADJ (inf) bajo(-a) en carbohidratos

low-cut ['ləukʌt] ADJ (dress) escotado

low-down ['ləudaun] N (inf): **he gave me the ~ on it** me puso al corriente ▸ ADJ (mean) vil, bajo

lower ['ləuəʳ] ADJ más bajo; (less important) menos importante ▸ VT bajar; (reduce: price)

reducir, rebajar; (: *resistance*) debilitar; **to ~ o.s. to** (*fig*) rebajarse a ▸ vɪ ['ləuəʳ]: **to ~ (at sb)** fulminar (a algn) con la mirada
lower case N (*Typ*) minúscula
Lower House N (*Pol*): **the ~** la Cámara baja
lowering ['lauərɪŋ] ADJ (*sky*) amenazador(a)
low-fat ['ləu'fæt] ADJ (*milk, yoghurt*) desnatado; (*diet*) bajo en calorías
low-key ['ləu'ki:] ADJ de mínima intensidad; (*operation*) de poco perfil
lowland ['ləulənd] N tierra baja
low-level ['ləulɛvl] ADJ de bajo nivel; (*flying*) a poca altura
low-loader ['ləuləudəʳ] N camión *m* de caja a bajo nivel
lowly ['ləulɪ] ADJ humilde
low-lying [ləu'laɪɪŋ] ADJ bajo
low-rise ['ləuraɪz] ADJ bajo
low-tech ['ləutɛk] ADJ de baja tecnología, tradicional
loyal ['lɔɪəl] ADJ leal
loyalist ['lɔɪəlɪst] N legitimista *mf*
loyally ['lɔɪəlɪ] ADV lealmente
loyalty ['lɔɪəltɪ] N lealtad *f*
loyalty card N (*BRIT*) tarjeta cliente
lozenge ['lɔzɪndʒ] N (*Med*) pastilla
LP N ABBR (= *long-playing record*) elepé *m*
LPG N ABBR (= *liquefied petroleum gas*) GLP *m* (= *Gas Licuado de Petróleo*)
L-plates ['ɛlpleɪts] NPL (*BRIT*) (placas *fpl* de) la L; *ver nota*

En el Reino Unido las personas que están aprendiendo a conducir han de llevar indicativos blancos con una L en rojo llamados normalmente *L-plates* (de *learner*) en la parte delantera y trasera de los automóviles que conducen. No tienen que ir a clases teóricas, sino que desde el principio se les entrega un carnet de conducir provisional (*provisional driving licence*) para que realicen sus prácticas, que han de estar supervisadas por un conductor con carnet definitivo (*full driving licence*). Tampoco se les permite hacer prácticas en autopistas aunque vayan acompañados.

LPN N ABBR (*US*: = *Licensed Practical Nurse*) enfermero(-a) practicante
LRAM N ABBR (*BRIT*) = **Licentiate of the Royal Academy of Music**
LSAT N ABBR (*US*) = **Law School Admissions Test**
LSD N ABBR (= *lysergic acid diethylamide*) LSD *m*; (*BRIT*: = *pounds, shillings and pence*) sistema monetario usado en Gran Bretaña hasta 1971
LSE N ABBR = **London School of Economics**
LT ABBR (*Elec*) = **low tension**
Lt. ABBR (= *lieutenant*) Tte.
Ltd ABBR (*Comm*: = *limited company*) S.A.

lubricant ['lu:brɪkənt] N lubricante *m*
lubricate ['lu:brɪkeɪt] VT lubricar, engrasar
lubrication [lu:brɪ'keɪʃən] N lubricación *f*
lucid ['lu:sɪd] ADJ lúcido
lucidity [lu:'sɪdɪtɪ] N lucidez *f*
lucidly ['lu:sɪdlɪ] ADV lúcidamente
luck [lʌk] N suerte *f*; **good/bad** ~ buena/mala suerte; **good ~!** ¡(que tengas) suerte!; **to be in** ~ estar de suerte; **to be out of** ~ tener mala suerte; **bad** *or* **hard** *or* **tough ~!** ¡qué pena!
luckily ['lʌkɪlɪ] ADV afortunadamente
luckless ['lʌklɪs] ADJ desafortunado
lucky ['lʌkɪ] ADJ afortunado; (*at cards etc*) con suerte; (*object*) que trae suerte
lucrative ['lu:krətɪv] ADJ lucrativo
ludicrous ['lu:dɪkrəs] ADJ absurdo
ludo ['lu:dəu] N parchís *m*
lug [lʌg] VT (*drag*) arrastrar
luggage ['lʌgɪdʒ] N equipaje *m*
luggage rack N (*in train*) rejilla, redecilla; (*on car*) baca, portaequipajes *m inv*
luggage van N furgón *m or* vagón *m* de equipaje
lugubrious [lu'gu:brɪəs] ADJ lúgubre
lukewarm ['lu:kwɔ:m] ADJ tibio, templado
lull [lʌl] N tregua ▸ VT (*child*) acunar; (*person, fear*) calmar; **to ~ sb to sleep** arrullar a algn; **to ~ sb into a false sense of security** dar a algn una falsa sensación de seguridad
lullaby ['lʌləbaɪ] N nana
lumbago [lʌm'beɪgəu] N lumbago
lumber ['lʌmbəʳ] N (*junk*) trastos *mpl* viejos; (*wood*) maderos *mpl* ▸ VT (*BRIT inf*): **to ~ sb with sth/sb** hacer que algn cargue con algo/algn ▸ VI (*also*: **lumber about, lumber along**) moverse pesadamente
lumberjack ['lʌmbədʒæk] N maderero
lumber room N (*BRIT*) cuarto trastero
lumber yard N (*US*) almacén *m* de madera
luminous ['lu:mɪnəs] ADJ luminoso
lump [lʌmp] N terrón *m*; (*fragment*) trozo; (*in sauce*) grumo; (*in throat*) nudo; (*swelling*) bulto ▸ VT (*also*: **lump together**) juntar; (: *persons*) poner juntos
lump sum N suma global
lumpy ['lʌmpɪ] ADJ (*sauce*) lleno de grumos
lunacy ['lu:nəsɪ] N locura
lunar ['lu:nəʳ] ADJ lunar
lunatic ['lu:nətɪk] ADJ, N loco(-a) *m/f*
lunatic asylum N manicomio
lunch [lʌntʃ] N almuerzo, comida ▸ VI almorzar; **to invite sb to** *or* **for** ~ invitar a algn a almorzar
lunch break, lunch hour N hora del almuerzo
luncheon ['lʌntʃən] N almuerzo
luncheon meat N *tipo de fiambre*
luncheon voucher N vale *m* de comida

lunchtime ['lʌntʃtaɪm] N hora del almuerzo or de comer

lung [lʌŋ] N pulmón m

lung cancer N cáncer m del pulmón

lunge [lʌndʒ] VI (also: **lunge forward**) abalanzarse; **to ~ at** arremeter contra

lupin ['luːpɪn] N altramuz m

lurch [ləːtʃ] VI dar sacudidas ▶ N sacudida; **to leave sb in the ~** dejar a algn plantado

lure [luəʳ] N (bait) cebo; (decoy) señuelo; (attraction) atracción f ▶ VT convencer con engaños

lurid ['luərɪd] ADJ (colour) chillón(-ona); (account) sensacional; (detail) horripilante

lurk [ləːk] VI (hide) esconderse; (wait) estar al acecho; (fig) acechar

luscious ['lʌʃəs] ADJ delicioso

lush [lʌʃ] ADJ exuberante

lust [lʌst] N lujuria; (greed) codicia ▶ **lust after** VT FUS codiciar

lustful ['lʌstful] ADJ lascivo, lujurioso

lustre, (US) **luster** ['lʌstəʳ] N lustre m, brillo

lustrous ['lʌstrəs] ADJ brillante

lusty ['lʌstɪ] ADJ robusto, fuerte

lute [luːt] N laúd m

Luxembourg ['lʌksəmbəːg] N Luxemburgo

luxuriant [lʌg'zjuərɪənt] ADJ exuberante

luxurious [lʌg'zjuərɪəs] ADJ lujoso

luxury ['lʌkʃərɪ] N lujo ▶ CPD de lujo

luxury tax N impuesto de lujo

LV N ABBR (BRIT) = **luncheon voucher**

LW ABBR (Radio) = **long wave**

Lycra® ['laɪkrə] N licra®

lying ['laɪɪŋ] N mentiras fpl ▶ ADJ (statement, story) falso; (person) mentiroso

lynch [lɪntʃ] VT linchar

lynx [lɪŋks] N lince m

Lyons ['laɪənz] N Lyón m

lyre ['laɪəʳ] N lira

lyric ['lɪrɪk] ADJ lírico; **lyrics** NPL (of song) letra sg

lyrical ['lɪrɪkl] ADJ lírico

Mm

M, m [ɛm] N (*letter*) M, m *f*; **M for Mary**, (*US*)
  M for Mike M de Madrid
M N ABBR (*BRIT*): = **motorway the M8** ≈ la A8
  ▶ ABBR (= *medium*) M
m ABBR (= *metre*) m.; = **mile**; **million**
MA N ABBR (*Scol*) = **Master of Arts**; (*US*)
  = **Military Academy** ▶ ABBR (*US*)
  = **Massachusetts**
ma [mɑ:] (*inf*) N mamá
mac [mæk] N (*BRIT*) impermeable *m*
macabre [mə'kɑ:brə] ADJ macabro
macaroni [mækə'rəʊnɪ] N macarrones *mpl*
macaroon [mækə'ru:n] N macarrón *m*,
  mostachón *m*
mace [meɪs] N (*weapon, ceremonial*) maza;
  (*spice*) macis *f*
Macedonia [mæsɪ'dəʊnɪə] N Macedonia
Macedonian [mæsɪ'dəʊnɪən] ADJ
  macedonio ▶ N macedonio(-a); (*Ling*)
  macedonio
machinations [mæʃɪ'neɪʃənz] NPL intrigas
  fpl, maquinaciones *fpl*
machine [mə'ʃi:n] N máquina ▶ VT (*dress etc*)
  coser a máquina; (*Tech*) trabajar a máquina
machine code N (*Comput*) código máquina
machine gun N ametralladora
machine language N (*Comput*) lenguaje *m*
  máquina
machine readable ADJ (*Comput*) legible por
  máquina
machinery [mə'ʃi:nərɪ] N maquinaria; (*fig*)
  mecanismo
machine shop N taller *m* de máquinas
machine tool N máquina herramienta
machine translation N traducción *f*
  automática
machine washable ADJ lavable a máquina
machinist [mə'ʃi:nɪst] N operario(-a) *m/f* (de
  máquina)
macho ['mætʃəʊ] ADJ macho
mackerel ['mækrl] N *pl inv* caballa
mackintosh ['mækɪntɔʃ] N (*BRIT*)
  impermeable *m*
macro ... ['mækrəʊ] PREF macro...

macro-economics ['mækrəʊi:kə'nɔmɪks] N
  macroeconomía
mad [mæd] ADJ loco; (*idea*) disparatado;
  (*angry*) furioso, enojado (*LAM*); ~ **(at** or **with**
  sb) furioso (con algn); **to be ~ (keen) about**
  or **on sth** estar loco por algo; **to go ~** volverse
  loco, enloquecer(se)
madam ['mædəm] N señora; **can I help you,**
  ~? ¿le puedo ayudar, señora?; **M~ Chairman**
  Señora Presidenta
madcap ['mædkæp] ADJ (*inf*) alocado,
  disparatado
mad cow disease N encefalopatía
  espongiforme bovina
madden ['mædn] VT volver loco
maddening ['mædnɪŋ] ADJ enloquecedor(a)
made [meɪd] PT, PP of **make**
Madeira [mə'dɪərə] N (*Geo*) Madeira; (*wine*)
  madeira *m*
made-to-measure ['meɪdtəmɛʒəʳ] ADJ (*BRIT*)
  hecho a la medida
made-up ['meɪdʌp] ADJ (*story*) ficticio
madhouse ['mædhaʊs] N (*also fig*) manicomio
madly ['mædlɪ] ADV locamente
madman ['mædmən] N (*irreg*) loco
madness ['mædnɪs] N locura
Madonna [mə'dɔnə] N Virgen *f*
Madrid [mə'drɪd] N Madrid *m*
madrigal ['mædrɪgəl] N madrigal *m*
Mafia ['mæfɪə] N Mafia
mag [mæg] N ABBR (*BRIT inf*) = **magazine**
magazine [mægə'zi:n] N revista; (*Mil: store*)
  almacén *m*; (*of firearm*) recámara
maggot ['mægət] N gusano
magic ['mædʒɪk] N magia ▶ ADJ mágico
magical ['mædʒɪkəl] ADJ mágico
magician [mə'dʒɪʃən] N mago(-a)
magistrate ['mædʒɪstreɪt] N juez *mf*
  (municipal); **Magistrates' Court** (*BRIT*) *see*
  crown court
magnanimity [mægnə'nɪmɪtɪ] N
  magnanimidad *f*
magnanimous [mæg'nænɪməs] ADJ
  magnánimo

magnate ['mægneɪt] N magnate mf
magnesium [mæg'niːzɪəm] N magnesio
magnet ['mægnɪt] N imán m
magnetic [mæg'nɛtɪk] ADJ magnético
magnetic disk N (*Comput*) disco magnético
magnetic tape N cinta magnética
magnetism ['mægnɪtɪzəm] N magnetismo
magnification [mægnɪfɪ'keɪʃən] N aumento
magnificence [mæg'nɪfɪsns] N
  magnificencia
magnificent [mæg'nɪfɪsnt] ADJ magnífico
magnificently [mæg'nɪfɪsntlɪ] ADV
  magníficamente
magnify ['mægnɪfaɪ] VT (*object*) ampliar;
  (*sound*) aumentar; (*fig*) exagerar
magnifying glass ['mægnɪfaɪɪŋ-] N lupa
magnitude ['mægnɪtjuːd] N magnitud f
magnolia [mæg'nəʊlɪə] N magnolia
magpie ['mægpaɪ] N urraca
maharajah [mɑːhə'rɑːdʒə] N maharajá m
mahogany [mə'hɒgənɪ] N caoba ▶ CPD de
  caoba
maid [meɪd] N criada; **old ~** (*pej*) solterona
maiden ['meɪdn] N doncella ▶ ADJ (*aunt etc*)
  solterona; (*speech, voyage*) inaugural
maiden name N apellido de soltera
mail [meɪl] N correo; (*letters*) cartas fpl ▶ VT
  (*post*) echar al correo; (*send*) mandar por
  correo; **by ~** por correo
mailbox ['meɪlbɒks] N (*Comput, US: for letters
  etc*) buzón m
mailing list ['meɪlɪŋ-] N lista de direcciones
mailman ['meɪlmæn] N (*irreg*) (*US*) cartero
mail-order ['meɪlɔːdəʳ] N pedido postal;
  (*business*) venta por correo ▶ ADJ: **~ firm** or
  house casa de venta por correo
mailshot ['meɪlʃɒt] N mailing m inv
mailtrain ['meɪltreɪn] N tren m correo
mail van, (*US*) **mail truck** N (*Aut*) camioneta
  de correos or de reparto
maim [meɪm] VT mutilar, lisiar
main [meɪn] ADJ principal, mayor ▶ N (*pipe*)
  cañería principal or maestra; (*US*) red f
  eléctrica; **the mains** (*Brit Elec*) la red
  eléctrica; **in the ~** en general
main course N (*Culin*) plato principal
mainframe ['meɪnfreɪm] N (*also*: **mainframe
  computer**) ordenador m or computadora
  central
mainland ['meɪnlənd] N continente m
main line N línea principal
mainly ['meɪnlɪ] ADV principalmente, en su
  mayoría
main road N carretera principal
mainstay ['meɪnsteɪ] N (*fig*) pilar m
mainstream ['meɪnstriːm] N (*fig*) corriente f
  principal
main street N calle f mayor
maintain [meɪn'teɪn] VT mantener;

(*affirm*) sostener; **to ~ that ...** mantener or
  sostener que ...
maintenance ['meɪntənəns] N
  mantenimiento; (*alimony*) pensión f
  alimenticia
maintenance contract N contrato de
  mantenimiento
maintenance order N (*Law*) obligación f de
  pagar una pensión alimenticia al cónyuge
maisonette [meɪzə'nɛt] N dúplex m
maize [meɪz] N (*Brit*) maíz m, choclo (*Lam*)
Maj. ABBR (*Mil*) = **major**
majestic [mə'dʒɛstɪk] ADJ majestuoso
majesty ['mædʒɪstɪ] N majestad f; **Your M~**
  Su Majestad
major ['meɪdʒəʳ] N (*Mil*) comandante m
  ▶ ADJ principal; (*Mus*) mayor ▶ VI (*US Univ*):
  to ~ in especializarse en; **a ~ operation**
  una operación or intervención de gran
  importancia
Majorca [mə'jɔːkə] N Mallorca
major general N (*Mil*) general m de división
majority [mə'dʒɒrɪtɪ] N mayoría ▶ CPD
  (*verdict*) mayoritario
majority holding N (*Comm*): **to have a ~**
  tener un interés mayoritario
make [meɪk] (*pt, pp* **made** [meɪd]) VT hacer;
  (*manufacture*) hacer, fabricar; (*mistake*)
  cometer; (*speech*) pronunciar; (*cause to be*):
  to ~ sb sad poner triste or entristecer a algn;
  (*force*): **to ~ sb do sth** obligar a algn a hacer
  algo; (*equal*): **2 and 2 ~ 4** 2 y 2 son 4 ▶ N marca;
  to ~ a fool of sb poner a algn en ridículo;
  to ~ a profit/loss obtener ganancias/sufrir
  pérdidas; **to ~ a profit of £500** sacar una
  ganancia de 500 libras; **to ~ it** (*arrive*) llegar;
  (*achieve sth*) tener éxito; **what time do you ~
  it?** ¿qué hora tienes?; **to ~ do with**
  contentarse con
  ▶ **make for** VT FUS (*place*) dirigirse a
  ▶ **make off** VI largarse
  ▶ **make out** VT (*decipher*) descifrar;
  (*understand*) entender; (*see*) distinguir; (*write:
  cheque*) extender; **to ~ out (that)** (*claim, imply*)
  dar a entender (que); **to ~ out a case for sth**
  dar buenas razones en favor de algo
  ▶ **make over** VT (*assign*): **to ~ over (to)** ceder
  or traspasar (a)
  ▶ **make up** VT (*invent*) inventar; (*parcel*) hacer
  ▶ VI reconciliarse; (*with cosmetics*) maquillarse;
  to be made up of estar compuesto de
  ▶ **make up for** VT FUS compensar
make-believe ['meɪkbɪliːv] N ficción f,
  fantasía
makeover ['meɪkəʊvəʳ] N cambio de
  imagen; **to give sb a ~** hacerle a algn un
  cambio de imagen
maker ['meɪkəʳ] N fabricante mf; (*of film,
  programme*) autor(a) m/f

makeshift ['meɪkʃɪft] ADJ improvisado
make-up ['meɪkʌp] N maquillaje *m*
make-up bag N bolsita del maquillaje *or* de los cosméticos
make-up remover N desmaquillador *m*
making ['meɪkɪŋ] N (*fig*): **in the ~** en vías de formación; **to have the makings of** (*person*) tener madera de
maladjusted [mælə'dʒʌstɪd] ADJ inadaptado
maladroit [mælə'drɔɪt] ADJ torpe
malaise [mæ'leɪz] N malestar *m*
malaria [mə'lɛərɪə] N malaria
Malawi [mə'lɑːwɪ] N Malawi *m*
Malay [mə'leɪ] ADJ malayo ▶ N malayo(-a); (*Ling*) malayo
Malaya [mə'leɪə] N Malaya, Malaca
Malayan [mə'leɪən] ADJ, N = **Malay**
Malaysia [mə'leɪzɪə] N Malaisia, Malaysia
Malaysian [mə'leɪzɪən] ADJ, N malaisio(-a) *m/f*, malasio(-a) *m/f*
Maldive Islands ['mɔːldiːv-], **Maldives** ['mɔːldiːvz] NPL: **the ~** las Maldivas
male [meɪl] N (*Biol, Elec*) macho ▶ ADJ (*sex, attitude*) masculino; (*child etc*) varón
male chauvinist, male chauvinist pig N machista *m*
male nurse N enfermero
malevolence [mə'lɛvələns] N malevolencia
malevolent [mə'lɛvələnt] ADJ malévolo
malfunction [mæl'fʌŋkʃən] N mal funcionamiento
malice ['mælɪs] N (*ill will*) malicia; (*rancour*) rencor *m*
malicious [mə'lɪʃəs] ADJ malicioso; rencoroso
maliciously [mə'lɪʃəslɪ] ADV con malevolencia, con malicia; rencorosamente
malign [mə'laɪn] VT difamar, calumniar ▶ ADJ maligno
malignant [mə'lɪgnənt] ADJ (*Med*) maligno
malinger [mə'lɪŋgəʳ] VI fingirse enfermo
malingerer [mə'lɪŋgərəʳ] N enfermo(-a) fingido(-a)
mall [mɔːl] N (*US: also*: **shopping mall**) centro comercial
malleable ['mælɪəbl] ADJ maleable
mallet ['mælɪt] N mazo
malnutrition [mælnjuː'trɪʃən] N desnutrición *f*
malpractice [mæl'præktɪs] N negligencia profesional
malt [mɔːlt] N malta; (*whisky*) whisky *m* de malta
Malta ['mɔːltə] N Malta
Maltese [mɔːl'tiːz] ADJ maltés(-esa) ▶ N *pl inv* maltés(-esa) *m/f*; (*Ling*) maltés *m*
maltreat [mæl'triːt] VT maltratar
malware ['mælwɛəʳ] N (*Comput*) malware *m*, software *m* malicioso

mammal ['mæml] N mamífero
mammoth ['mæməθ] N mamut *m* ▶ ADJ gigantesco
man [mæn] (*pl* **men** [mɛn]) N hombre *m*; (*mankind*) el hombre; (*Chess*) pieza ▶ VT (*Naut*) tripular; (*Mil*) defender; (*operate: machine*) manejar; **an old ~** un viejo; **~ and wife** marido y mujer
Man. ABBR (*CANADA*) = **Manitoba**
manacle ['mænəkl] N esposa, manilla; **manacles** NPL grillos *mpl*
manage ['mænɪdʒ] VI arreglárselas ▶ VT (*be in charge of*) dirigir; (*person etc*) manejar; **to ~ to do sth** conseguir hacer algo; **to ~ without sth/sb** poder prescindir de algo/algn
manageable ['mænɪdʒəbl] ADJ manejable
management ['mænɪdʒmənt] N dirección *f*, administración *f*; **"under new ~"** "bajo nueva dirección"
management accounting N contabilidad *f* de gestión
management buyout N adquisición *f* por parte de la dirección
management consultant N consultor(a) *m/f* en dirección de empresas
manager ['mænɪdʒəʳ] N director(a) *m/f*; (*of pop star*) mánager *mf*; (*Sport*) entrenador(a) *m/f*; **sales ~** jefe(-a) *m/f* de ventas
manageress ['mænɪdʒərɛs] N directora; (*Sport*) entrenadora
managerial [mænə'dʒɪərɪəl] ADJ directivo
managing director ['mænɪdʒɪŋ-] N director(a) *m/f* general
Mancunian [mæŋ'kjuːnɪən] ADJ de Manchester ▶ N nativo(-a) *or* habitante *m/f* de Manchester
mandarin ['mændərɪn] N (*also*: **mandarin orange**) mandarina; (*person*) mandarín *m*
mandate ['mændeɪt] N mandato
mandatory ['mændətərɪ] ADJ obligatorio
mandolin, mandoline ['mændəlɪn] N mandolina
mane [meɪn] N (*of horse*) crin *f*; (*of lion*) melena
maneuver [mə'nuːvəʳ] VB, N (*US*) = **manoeuvre**
manful ['mænful] ADJ resuelto
manfully ['mænfəlɪ] ADV resueltamente
mangetout [mɔnʒ'tuː] N tirabeque *m*
mangle ['mæŋgl] VT mutilar, destrozar ▶ N escurridor *m*
mango ['mæŋgəu] (*pl* **mangoes**) N mango
mangrove ['mæŋgrəuv] N mangle *m*
mangy ['meɪndʒɪ] ADJ roñoso; (*Med*) sarnoso
manhandle ['mænhændl] VT maltratar; (*move by hand: goods*) manipular
manhole ['mænhəul] N boca de alcantarilla
manhood ['mænhud] N edad *f* viril; (*manliness*) virilidad *f*
man-hour ['mæn'auəʳ] N hora-hombre *f*

manhunt ['mænhʌnt] N caza de hombre
mania ['meɪnɪə] N manía
maniac ['meɪnɪæk] N maníaco(-a); (fig) maniático
manic ['mænɪk] ADJ (behaviour, activity) frenético
manic-depressive ['mænɪkdɪ'presɪv] ADJ, N maniacodepresivo(-a) m/f
manicure ['mænɪkjuəʳ] N manicura
manicure set N estuche m de manicura
manifest ['mænɪfest] VT manifestar, mostrar ▶ ADJ manifiesto ▶ N manifiesto
manifestation [mænɪfes'teɪʃən] N manifestación f
manifestly ['mænɪfestlɪ] ADV evidentemente
manifesto [mænɪ'festəu] N manifiesto
manifold ['mænɪfəuld] ADJ múltiples ▶ N (Aut etc): **exhaust ~** colector m de escape
Manila [mə'nɪlə] N Manila
manila, manilla [mə'nɪlə] N (paper, envelope) manila
manipulate [mə'nɪpjuleɪt] VT manipular
manipulation [mənɪpju'leɪʃən] N manipulación f, manejo
mankind [mæn'kaɪnd] N humanidad f, género humano
manliness ['mænlɪnɪs] N virilidad f, hombría
manly ['mænlɪ] ADJ varonil
man-made ['mæn'meɪd] ADJ artificial
manna ['mænə] N maná m
mannequin ['mænɪkɪn] N (dummy) maniquí m; (fashion model) maniquí mf
manner ['mænəʳ] N manera, modo; (behaviour) conducta, manera de ser; (type) clase f; **manners** NPL modales mpl, educación fsg; **(good) manners** (buena) educación fsg, (buenos) modales mpl; **bad manners** falta sg de educación, malos modales mpl; **all ~ of** toda clase or suerte de
mannerism ['mænərɪzəm] N gesto típico
mannerly ['mænəlɪ] ADJ bien educado, formal
manoeuvrable, (US) maneuverable [mə'nu:vrəbl] ADJ (car etc) manejable
manoeuvre, (US) maneuver [mə'nu:vəʳ] VT, VI maniobrar ▶ N maniobra; **to ~ sb into doing sth** manipular a algn para que haga algo
manor ['mænəʳ] N (also: **manor house**) casa solariega
manpower ['mænpauəʳ] N mano f de obra
Manpower Services Commission N (BRIT) comisión para el aprovechamiento de los recursos humanos
manservant ['mænsə:vənt] N criado
mansion ['mænʃən] N mansión f
manslaughter ['mænslɔ:təʳ] N homicidio involuntario

mantelpiece ['mæntlpi:s] N repisa de la chimenea
mantle ['mæntl] N manto
man-to-man ['mæntə'mæn] ADJ de hombre a hombre
manual ['mænjuəl] ADJ manual ▶ N manual m; **~ worker** obrero(-a), trabajador(a) m/f manual
manufacture [mænju'fæktʃəʳ] VT fabricar ▶ N fabricación f
manufactured goods [mænju'fæktʃəd-] NPL manufacturas fpl, bienes mpl manufacturados
manufacturer [mænju'fæktʃərəʳ] N fabricante mf
manufacturing industries [mænju'fæktʃrɪŋ-] NPL industrias fpl manufactureras
manure [mə'njuəʳ] N estiércol m, abono
manuscript ['mænjuskrɪpt] N manuscrito
Manx [mæŋks] ADJ de la Isla de Man
many ['menɪ] ADJ muchos(-as) ▶ PRON muchos(-as); **a great ~** muchísimos, un buen número de; **~ a time** muchas veces; **too ~ difficulties** demasiadas dificultades; **twice as ~** el doble; **how ~?** ¿cuántos?
Maori ['mauri] ADJ, N maorí mf
map [mæp] N mapa m ▶ VT trazar el mapa de ▶ **map out** VT (fig: career, holiday, essay) proyectar, planear
maple ['meɪpl] N arce m, maple m (LAM)
mar [mɑ:ʳ] VT estropear
Mar. ABBR (= March) mar.
marathon ['mærəθən] N maratón m ▶ ADJ: **a ~ session** una sesión maratoniana
marathon runner N corredor(a) m/f de maratones
marauder [mə'rɔ:dəʳ] N merodeador(a) m/f
marble ['mɑ:bl] N mármol m; (toy) canica
March [mɑ:tʃ] N marzo; see also **July**
march [mɑ:tʃ] VI (Mil) marchar; (demonstrators) manifestarse; (fig) caminar con resolución ▶ N marcha; (demonstration) manifestación f
marcher ['mɑ:tʃəʳ] N manifestante mf
marching ['mɑ:tʃɪŋ] N: **to give sb his ~ orders** (fig) mandar a paseo a algn; (employee) poner de patitas en la calle a algn
march-past ['mɑ:tʃpɑ:st] N desfile m
mare [mɛəʳ] N yegua
margarine [mɑ:dʒə'ri:n] N margarina
marge, marg [mɑ:dʒ] N ABBR (inf) = **margarine**
margin ['mɑ:dʒɪn] N margen m; (Comm: profit margin) margen m de beneficios
marginal ['mɑ:dʒɪnl] ADJ marginal
marginally ['mɑ:dʒɪnəlɪ] ADV ligeramente
marginal seat N (Pol) circunscripción f políticamente no definida

marigold ['mærɪɡəʊld] N caléndula

marijuana [mærɪ'wɑːnə] N marihuana

marina [mə'riːnə] N puerto deportivo

marinade [mærɪ'neɪd] N adobo

marinate ['mærɪneɪt] VT adobar

marine [mə'riːn] ADJ marino ▶ N soldado de infantería de marina

marine insurance N seguro marítimo

mariner ['mærɪnəʳ] N marinero, marino

marionette [mærɪə'nɛt] N marioneta, títere m

marital ['mærɪtl] ADJ matrimonial; **~ status** estado civil

maritime ['mærɪtaɪm] ADJ marítimo

marjoram ['mɑːdʒərəm] N mejorana

mark [mɑːk] N marca, señal f; (in snow, mud etc) huella; (stain) mancha; (Brit Scol) nota; (currency) marco ▶ VT (Sport: player) marcar; (stain) manchar; (Brit Scol) calificar, corregir; **punctuation marks** signos mpl de puntuación; **to be quick off the ~** (fig) ser listo; **up to the ~** (in efficiency) a la altura de las circunstancias; **to ~ time** marcar el paso; (fig) marcar(se) un ritmo

▶ **mark down** VT (reduce: prices, goods) rebajar

▶ **mark off** VT (tick) indicar, señalar

▶ **mark out** VT trazar

▶ **mark up** VT (price) aumentar

marked [mɑːkt] ADJ marcado, acusado

markedly ['mɑːkɪdlɪ] ADV marcadamente, apreciablemente

marker ['mɑːkəʳ] N (sign) marcador m; (bookmark) registro

market ['mɑːkɪt] N mercado ▶ VT (Comm) comercializar; (promote) publicitar; **open ~** mercado libre; **to be on the ~** estar en venta; **to play the ~** jugar a la bolsa

marketable ['mɑːkɪtəbl] ADJ comerciable

market analysis N análisis m del mercado

market day N día m de mercado

market demand N demanda de mercado

market economy N economía de mercado

market forces NPL tendencias fpl del mercado

market garden N (Brit) huerto

marketing ['mɑːkɪtɪŋ] N marketing m, mercadotecnia

marketing manager N director m de marketing

market leader N líder m de ventas

marketplace ['mɑːkɪtpleɪs] N mercado

market price N precio de mercado

market research N (Comm) estudios mpl de mercado

market value N valor m en el mercado

marking ['mɑːkɪŋ] N (on animal) pinta; (on road) señal f

marking ink N tinta indeleble or de marcar

marksman ['mɑːksmən] N (irreg) tirador m

marksmanship ['mɑːksmənʃɪp] N puntería

mark-up ['mɑːkʌp] N (Comm: margin) margen m de beneficio; (: increase) aumento

marmalade ['mɑːməleɪd] N mermelada de naranja

maroon [mə'ruːn] VT: **to be marooned** (shipwrecked) quedar aislado; (fig) quedar abandonado ▶ N (colour) granate m ▶ ADJ (colour) granate inv

marquee [mɑː'kiː] N carpa, entoldado

marquess, marquis ['mɑːkwɪs] N marqués m

Marrakech, Marrakesh [mærə'kɛʃ] N Marrakech m

marriage ['mærɪdʒ] N (state) matrimonio; (wedding) boda; (act) casamiento

marriage bureau N agencia matrimonial

marriage certificate N partida de casamiento

marriage guidance, (US) marriage counseling N orientación f matrimonial

marriage of convenience N matrimonio de conveniencia

married ['mærɪd] ADJ casado; (life, love) conyugal

marrow ['mærəʊ] N médula; (vegetable) calabacín m

marry ['mærɪ] VT casarse con; (father, priest etc) casar ▶ VI (also: **get married**) casarse

Mars [mɑːz] N Marte m

Marseilles [mɑː'seɪ] N Marsella

marsh [mɑːʃ] N pantano; (salt marsh) marisma

marshal ['mɑːʃl] N (Mil) mariscal m; (at sports meeting, demonstration etc) oficial m; (US: of police, fire department) jefe(-a) m/f ▶ VT (facts) ordenar; (soldiers) formar

marshalling yard ['mɑːʃəlɪŋ-] N (Rail) estación f clasificadora

marshmallow ['mɑːʃmæləʊ] N (Bot) malvavisco; (sweet) nube f, dulce m de merengue blando

marshy ['mɑːʃɪ] ADJ pantanoso

marsupial [mɑː'suːpɪəl] ADJ, N marsupial m

martial ['mɑːʃl] ADJ marcial

martial arts NPL artes fpl marciales

martial law N ley f marcial

martin ['mɑːtɪn] N (also: **house martin**) avión m

martyr ['mɑːtəʳ] N mártir mf ▶ VT martirizar

martyrdom ['mɑːtədəm] N martirio

marvel ['mɑːvl] N maravilla, prodigio ▶ VI: **to ~ (at)** maravillarse (de)

marvellous, (US) marvelous ['mɑːvləs] ADJ maravilloso

marvellously, (US) marvelously ['mɑːvləslɪ] ADV maravillosamente

Marxism ['mɑːksɪzəm] N marxismo

Marxist ['mɑːksɪst] ADJ, N marxista mf

653

marzipan ['mɑːzɪpæn] N mazapán m
mascara [mæs'kɑːrə] N rímel m
mascot ['mæskət] N mascota
masculine ['mæskjulɪn] ADJ masculino
masculinity [mæskju'lɪnɪtɪ] N
masculinidad f
MASH [mæʃ] N ABBR (US Mil) = **mobile army surgical hospital**
mash [mæʃ] VT machacar ▶ N (mix) mezcla; (Culin) puré m; (pulp) amasijo
mashed potatoes [mæʃt-] NPL puré m de patatas or (LAm) papas
mask [mɑːsk] N máscara ▶ VT (hide: feelings) esconder; **to ~ one's face** (cover) ocultarse la cara
masochism ['mæsəkɪzəm] N masoquismo
masochist ['mæsəukɪst] N masoquista mf
mason ['meɪsn] N (also: **stonemason**) albañil m; (also: **freemason**) masón m
masonic [mə'sɔnɪk] ADJ masónico
masonry ['meɪsnrɪ] N masonería; (in building) mampostería
masquerade [mæskə'reɪd] N baile m de máscaras; (fig) mascarada ▶ VI: **to ~ as** disfrazarse de, hacerse pasar por
mass [mæs] N (people) muchedumbre f; (Physics) masa; (Rel) misa; (great quantity) montón m ▶ VI reunirse; (Mil) concentrarse; **the masses** las masas; **to go to ~** ir a or oír misa
Mass. ABBR (US) = **Massachusetts**
massacre ['mæsəkər] N masacre f ▶ VT masacrar
massage ['mæsɑːʒ] N masaje m ▶ VT dar masajes or un masaje a
masseur [mæ'sər] N masajista m
masseuse [mæ'səːz] N masajista f
massive ['mæsɪv] ADJ enorme; (support, intervention) masivo
mass media NPL medios mpl de comunicación de masas
mass meeting N (of everyone concerned) reunión f en masa; (huge) mitin m
mass-produce ['mæsprə'djuːs] VT fabricar en serie
mass-production ['mæsprə'dʌkʃən] N fabricación f or producción f en serie
mast [mɑːst] N (Naut) mástil m; (Radio etc) torre f, antena
mastectomy [mæs'tɛktəmɪ] N mastectomía
master ['mɑːstər] N (of servant, animal) amo; (fig: of situation) dueño; (Art, Mus) maestro; (in secondary school) profesor m; (title for boys): **M~ X** Señorito X ▶ VT dominar
master disk N (Comput) disco maestro
masterful ['mɑːstəful] ADJ magistral, dominante
master key N llave f maestra
masterly ['mɑːstəlɪ] ADJ magistral

mastermind ['mɑːstəmaɪnd] N inteligencia superior ▶ VT dirigir, planear
Master of Arts N licenciatura superior en Letras; see also **master's degree**
Master of Ceremonies N encargado de protocolo
Master of Science N licenciatura superior en Ciencias; see also **master's degree**
masterpiece ['mɑːstəpiːs] N obra maestra
master plan N plan m rector
master's degree N máster m

> Los estudios de postgrado británicos que llevan a la obtención de un *master's degree* consisten generalmente en una combinación de curso(s) académico(s) y tesina (*dissertation*) sobre un tema original, o bien únicamente la redacción de una tesina. El primer caso es el más frecuente para los títulos de *MA* (*Master of Arts*) y *MSc* (*Master of Science*), mientras que los de *MLitt* (*Master of Letters*) o *MPhil* (*Master of Philosophy*) se obtienen normalmente mediante tesina. En algunas universidades, como las escocesas, el título de *master's degree* no es de postgrado, sino que corresponde a la licenciatura.

master stroke N golpe m maestro
mastery ['mɑːstərɪ] N maestría
mastiff ['mæstɪf] N mastín m
masturbate ['mæstəbeɪt] VI masturbarse
masturbation [mæstə'beɪʃən] N masturbación f
MAT N ABBR (= machine-assisted translation) TAO
mat [mæt] N alfombrilla; (also: **doormat**) felpudo ▶ ADJ = **matt**
match [mætʃ] N cerilla, fósforo; (game) partido; (fig) igual mf ▶ VT emparejar; (go well with) hacer juego con; (equal) igualar; (correspond to) corresponderse con; (pair: also: **match up**) casar con ▶ VI hacer juego; **to be a good ~** hacer buena pareja
matchbox ['mætʃbɔks] N caja de cerillas
matching ['mætʃɪŋ] ADJ que hace juego
matchless ['mætʃlɪs] ADJ sin par, incomparable
matchmaker ['mætʃmeɪkər] N casamentero
mate [meɪt] N (workmate) compañero(-a), colega mf; (inf: friend) amigo(-a), compadre mf (LAm); (animal) macho (hembra); (in merchant navy) primer oficial m, segundo de a bordo ▶ VI acoplarse, aparearse ▶ VT acoplar, aparear
maté ['mɑːteɪ] N mate m (cocido), yerba mate
material [mə'tɪərɪəl] N (substance) materia; (equipment) material m; (cloth) tela, tejido ▶ ADJ material; (important) esencial; **materials** NPL materiales mpl; (equipment etc) artículos mpl

materialistic [mətɪərɪə'lɪstɪk] ADJ materialista

materialize [mə'tɪərɪəlaɪz] VI materializarse

materially [mə'tɪərɪəlɪ] ADV materialmente

maternal [mə'tə:nl] ADJ maternal; **~ grandmother** abuela materna

maternity [mə'tə:nɪtɪ] N maternidad *f*

maternity benefit N subsidio por maternidad

maternity dress N vestido premamá

maternity hospital N hospital *m* de maternidad

maternity leave N baja por maternidad

math [mæθ] N ABBR (*US*: = *mathematics*) matemáticas *fpl*

mathematical [mæθə'mætɪkl] ADJ matemático

mathematically [mæθɪ'mætɪklɪ] ADV matemáticamente

mathematician [mæθəmə'tɪʃən] N matemático(-a) *m/f*

mathematics [mæθə'mætɪks] N matemáticas *fpl*

maths [mæθs] N ABBR (*BRIT*: = *mathematics*) matemáticas *fpl*

matinée ['mætɪneɪ] N sesión *f* de tarde, vermut *m* (*LAM*)

mating ['meɪtɪŋ] N aparejamiento

mating call N llamada del macho

mating season N época de celo

matins ['mætɪnz] N maitines *mpl*

matriarchal [meɪtrɪ'ɑ:kl] ADJ matriarcal

matrices ['meɪtrɪsi:z] PL of **matrix**

matriculation [mətrɪkju'leɪʃən] N matriculación *f*, matrícula

matrimonial [mætrɪ'məunɪəl] ADJ matrimonial

matrimony ['mætrɪmənɪ] N matrimonio

matrix ['meɪtrɪks] (*pl* **matrices** ['meɪtrɪsi:z]) N matriz *f*

matron ['meɪtrən] N (*in hospital*) enfermera jefe; (*in school*) ama de llaves

matronly ['meɪtrənlɪ] ADJ de matrona; (*fig: figure*) corpulento

matt [mæt] ADJ mate

matted ['mætɪd] ADJ enmarañado

matter ['mætəʳ] N cuestión *f*, asunto; (*Physics*) sustancia, materia; (*content*) contenido; (*Med: pus*) pus *m* ▶ VI importar; **it doesn't ~** no importa; **what's the ~?** ¿qué pasa?; **no ~ what** pase lo que pase; **as a ~ of course** por rutina; **as a ~ of fact** en realidad; **printed ~** impresos *mpl*; **reading ~** material *m* de lectura, lecturas *fpl*

matter-of-fact ['mætərəv'fækt] ADJ (*style*) prosaico; (*person*) práctico; (*voice*) neutro

mattress ['mætrɪs] N colchón *m*

mature [mə'tjuəʳ] ADJ maduro ▶ VI madurar

mature student N *estudiante de más de 21 años*

maturity [mə'tjuərɪtɪ] N madurez *f*

maudlin ['mɔ:dlɪn] ADJ llorón(-ona)

maul [mɔ:l] VT magullar

Mauritania [mɔ:rɪ'teɪnɪə] N Mauritania

Mauritius [mə'rɪʃəs] N Mauricio

mausoleum [mɔ:sə'lɪəm] N mausoleo

mauve [məuv] ADJ de color malva

maverick ['mævrɪk] N (*fig*) inconformista *mf*, persona independiente

mawkish ['mɔ:kɪʃ] ADJ sensiblero, empalagoso

max ABBR = **maximum**

maxim ['mæksɪm] N máxima

maxima ['mæksɪmə] PL of **maximum**

maximize ['mæksɪmaɪz] VT (*profits etc*) llevar al máximo; (*chances*) maximizar

maximum ['mæksɪməm] ADJ máximo ▶ N (*pl* **maxima** ['mæksɪmə]) máximo

May [meɪ] N mayo; *see also* **July**

may [meɪ] VI (*conditional* **might**) (*indicating possibility*): **he ~ come** puede que venga; (*be allowed to*): **~ I smoke?** ¿puedo fumar?; (*wishes*): **~ God bless you!** ¡que Dios le bendiga!; **~ I sit here?** ¿me puedo sentar aquí?

maybe ['meɪbi:] ADV quizá(s); **~ not** quizá(s) no

mayday ['meɪdeɪ] N señal *f* de socorro

May Day N el primero de Mayo

mayhem ['meɪhɛm] N caos *m* total

mayonnaise [meɪə'neɪz] N mayonesa

mayor [mɛəʳ] N alcalde *m*

mayoress ['mɛərɛs] N alcaldesa

maypole ['meɪpəul] N mayo

maze [meɪz] N laberinto

MB ABBR (*Comput*) = **megabyte**; (*CANADA*) = **Manitoba**

MBA N ABBR (= *Master of Business Administration*) máster *m* en administración de empresas

MBBS, MBChB N ABBR (*BRIT*: = *Bachelor of Medicine and Surgery*) título universitario

MBE N ABBR (*BRIT*: = *Member of the Order of the British Empire*) título ceremonial

MBO N ABBR *see* **management buyout**

MC N ABBR (= *master of ceremonies*) e.p.; (*US*: = *Member of Congress*) diputado del Congreso de los Estados Unidos

MCAT N ABBR (*US*: = *Medical College Admissions Test*) examen de ingreso en los estudios superiores de Medicina

MD N ABBR (= *Doctor of Medicine*) título universitario; (*Comm*) = **managing director**; (= *MiniDisc®*) MiniDisc® *m*, minidisc *m* ▶ ABBR (*US*) = **Maryland**

Md. ABBR (*US*) = **Maryland**

MD player N MiniDisc *m*, minidisc *m*

MDT N ABBR (*US*: = *Mountain Daylight Time*) hora de verano de las Montañas Rocosas

ME ABBR (*US Post*) = **Maine** ▶ N ABBR (*US Med*) = **medical examiner**; (*Med*: = *myalgic encephalomyelitis*) encefalomielitis *f* miálgica

m

me [miː] PRON (direct) me; (stressed, after pronoun) mí; **can you hear me?** ¿me oyes?; **he heard ME!** me oyó a mí; **it's me** soy yo; **give them to me** dámelos; **with/without me** conmigo/sin mí; **it's for me** es para mí

meadow ['mɛdəu] N prado, pradera

meagre, (US) **meager** ['miːgəʳ] ADJ escaso, pobre

meal [miːl] N comida; (flour) harina; **to go out for a ~** salir a comer

meals on wheels NSG (BRIT) servicio de alimentación a domicilio para necesitados y tercera edad

mealtime ['miːltaɪm] N hora de comer

mealy-mouthed ['miːlɪmauðd] ADJ: **to be ~** no decir nunca las cosas claras

mean [miːn] ADJ (with money) tacaño; (unkind) mezquino, malo; (average) medio; (US: vicious: animal) resabiado; (: person) malicioso ▶ VT (pt, pp **meant** [mɛnt]) (signify) querer decir, significar; (intend): **to ~ to do sth** tener la intención de or pensar hacer algo ▶ N medio, término medio; **do you ~ it?** ¿lo dices en serio?; **what do you ~?** ¿qué quieres decir?; **to be meant for sb/sth** ser para algn/algo; see also **means**

meander [mɪ'ændəʳ] VI (river) serpentear; (person) vagar

meaning ['miːnɪŋ] N significado, sentido

meaningful ['miːnɪŋful] ADJ significativo

meaningless ['miːnɪŋlɪs] ADJ sin sentido

meanness ['miːnnɪs] N (with money) tacañería; (unkindness) maldad f, mezquindad f

means [miːnz] NPL medio sg, manera sg; (resource) recursos mpl, medios mpl; **by ~ of** mediante, por medio de; **by all ~!** ¡naturalmente!, ¡claro que sí!

means test N control m de los recursos económicos

meant [mɛnt] PT, PP of **mean**

meantime ['miːntaɪm], **meanwhile** ['miːnwaɪl] ADV (also: **in the meantime**) mientras tanto

measles ['miːzlz] N sarampión m

measly ['miːzlɪ] ADJ (inf) miserable

measurable ['mɛʒərəbl] ADJ mensurable, que se puede medir

measure ['mɛʒəʳ] VT medir; (for clothes etc) tomar las medidas a ▶ VI medir ▶ N medida; (ruler) cinta métrica, metro; **a litre ~** una medida de un litro; **some ~ of success** cierto éxito; **to take measures to do sth** tomar medidas para hacer algo
▶ **measure up** VI: **to ~ up (to)** estar a la altura (de)

measured ['mɛʒəd] ADJ moderado; (tone) mesurado

measurement ['mɛʒəmənt] N (measure) medida; (act) medición f; **to take sb's measurements** tomar las medidas a algn

meat [miːt] N carne f; **cold meats** fiambres mpl; **crab ~** carne f de cangrejo

meatball ['miːtbɔːl] N albóndiga

meat pie N pastel m de carne

meaty ['miːtɪ] ADJ (person) fuerte, corpulento; (role) sustancioso; **a ~ meal** una comida con bastante carne

Mecca ['mɛkə] N (city) la Meca; (fig) meca

mechanic [mɪ'kænɪk] N mecánico(-a)

mechanical [mɪ'kænɪkl] ADJ mecánico

mechanical engineering N (science) ingeniería mecánica; (industry) construcción f mecánica

mechanics [mə'kænɪks] N mecánica ▶ NPL mecanismo sg

mechanism ['mɛkənɪzəm] N mecanismo

mechanization [mɛkənaɪ'zeɪʃən] N mecanización f

mechanize ['mɛkənaɪz] VT mecanizar; (factory etc) automatizar

MEd N ABBR (= Master of Education) título universitario

medal ['mɛdl] N medalla

medallion [mɪ'dælɪən] N medallón m

medallist, (US) **medalist** ['mɛdlɪst] N (Sport) medallista mf

meddle ['mɛdl] VI: **to ~ in** entrometerse en; **to ~ with sth** manosear algo

meddlesome ['mɛdlsəm], **meddling** ['mɛdlɪŋ] ADJ (interfering) entrometido; (touching things) curioso

media ['miːdɪə] NPL medios mpl de comunicación

media circus N circo mediático

mediaeval [mɛdɪ'iːvl] ADJ = **medieval**

median ['miːdɪən] N (US: also: **median strip**) mediana

media research N estudio de los medios de publicidad

mediate ['miːdɪeɪt] VI mediar

mediation [miːdɪ'eɪʃən] N mediación f

mediator ['miːdɪeɪtəʳ] N mediador(a) m/f

Medicaid ['mɛdɪkeɪd] N (US) programa de ayuda médica

medical ['mɛdɪkl] ADJ médico ▶ N (also: **medical examination**) reconocimiento médico

medical certificate N certificado médico

Medicare ['mɛdɪkɛəʳ] N (US) seguro médico del Estado

medicated ['mɛdɪkeɪtɪd] ADJ medicinal

medication [mɛdɪ'keɪʃən] N (drugs etc) medicación f

medicinal [mɛ'dɪsɪnl] ADJ medicinal

medicine ['mɛdsɪn] N medicina; (drug) medicamento

medicine chest N botiquín m

medicine man N (*irreg*) hechicero
medieval, mediaeval [mɛdɪ'iːvl] ADJ medieval
mediocre [miːdɪ'əʊkə'] ADJ mediocre
mediocrity [miːdɪ'ɔkrɪtɪ] N mediocridad f
meditate ['mɛdɪteɪt] VI meditar
meditation [mɛdɪ'teɪʃən] N meditación f
Mediterranean [mɛdɪtə'reɪnɪən] ADJ mediterráneo; **the ~ (Sea)** el (mar m) Mediterráneo
medium ['miːdɪəm] ADJ mediano; (*level, height*) medio ▸ N (*pl* **media**) (*means*) medio; (*pl* **mediums**) (*person*) médium mf; **happy ~** punto justo
medium-dry ['miːdɪəm'draɪ] ADJ semiseco
medium-sized ['miːdɪəm'saɪzd] ADJ de tamaño mediano; (*clothes*) de (la) talla mediana
medium wave N onda media
medley ['mɛdlɪ] N mezcla; (*Mus*) popurrí m
meek [miːk] ADJ manso, sumiso
meekly ['miːklɪ] ADV mansamente, dócilmente
meet [miːt] (*pt, pp* **met**) VT encontrar; (*accidentally*) encontrarse con; (*by arrangement*) reunirse con; (*for the first time*) conocer; (*go and fetch*) ir a buscar; (*opponent*) enfrentarse con; (*obligations*) cumplir; (*bill, expenses*) pagar, costear ▸ VI encontrarse; (*in session*) reunirse; (*join: objects*) unirse; (*get to know*) conocerse ▸ N (*BRIT Hunting*) cacería; (*US Sport*) encuentro; **pleased to ~ you!** ¡encantado (de conocerle)!, ¡mucho gusto!
▸ **meet up** VI: **to ~ up with sb** reunirse con algn
▸ **meet with** VT FUS reunirse con; (*difficulty*) tropezar con
meeting ['miːtɪŋ] N (*also Sport: rally*) encuentro; (*arranged*) cita, compromiso (*LAm*); (*formal session, business meeting*) reunión f; (*Pol*) mitin m; **to call a ~** convocar una reunión
meeting place N lugar m de reunión or encuentro
meg [mɛg] N ABBR (*inf: = megabyte*) megabyte m
megabyte ['mɛgə'baɪt] N (*Comput*) megabyte m, megaocteto
megalomaniac [mɛgələʊ'meɪnɪæk] ADJ, N megalómano(-a) m/f
megaphone ['mɛgəfəʊn] N megáfono
megapixel ['mɛgəpɪksl] N megapíxel m
megawatt ['mɛgəwɔt] N megavatio
meh [mɛ] EXCL ¡bah!
melancholy ['mɛlənkəlɪ] N melancolía ▸ ADJ melancólico
melee ['mɛleɪ] N refriega
mellow ['mɛləʊ] ADJ (*wine*) añejo; (*sound, colour*) suave; (*fruit*) maduro ▸ VI (*person*) madurar

melodious [mɪ'ləʊdɪəs] ADJ melodioso
melodrama ['mɛləʊdrɑːmə] N melodrama m
melodramatic [mɛləʊdrə'mætɪk] ADJ melodramático
melody ['mɛlədɪ] N melodía
melon ['mɛlən] N melón m
melt [mɛlt] VI (*metal*) fundirse; (*snow*) derretirse; (*fig*) ablandarse ▸ VT (*also:* **melt down**) fundir; **melted butter** mantequilla derretida
▸ **melt away** VI desvanecerse
meltdown ['mɛltdaʊn] N (*in nuclear reactor*) fusión f (de un reactor nuclear)
melting point ['mɛltɪŋ-] N punto de fusión
melting pot ['mɛltɪŋ-] N (*fig*) crisol m; **to be in the ~** estar sobre el tapete
member ['mɛmbə'] N (*of political party*) miembro; (*of club*) socio(-a); **M~ of Parliament** (*BRIT*) diputado(-a); **M~ of the European Parliament** (*BRIT*) eurodiputado(-a); **M~ of Congress** (*US*) miembro del Congreso; **M~ of the House of Representatives** (*US*) miembro mf de la Cámara de Representantes; **M~ of the Scottish Parliament** (*BRIT*) diputado(-a) del Parlamento escocés
membership ['mɛmbəʃɪp] N (*members*) miembros mpl; socios mpl; (*numbers*) número de miembros or socios; **to seek ~ of** pedir el ingreso a
membership card N carnet m de socio
membrane ['mɛmbreɪn] N membrana
memento [mə'mɛntəʊ] N recuerdo
memo ['mɛməʊ] N apunte m, nota
memoirs ['mɛmwɑːz] NPL memorias fpl
memo pad N bloc m de notas
memorable ['mɛmərəbl] ADJ memorable
memorandum [mɛmə'rændəm] (*pl* **memoranda** [-də]) N nota (de servicio); (*Pol*) memorándum m
memorial [mɪ'mɔːrɪəl] N monumento conmemorativo ▸ ADJ conmemorativo
Memorial Day N (*US*) *día de conmemoración de los caídos en la guerra*
memorize ['mɛmərɑɪz] VT aprender de memoria
memory ['mɛmərɪ] N memoria; (*recollection*) recuerdo; (*Comput*) memoria; **to have a good/bad ~** tener buena/mala memoria; **loss of ~** pérdida de memoria
memory card N tarjeta de memoria
memory stick N (*Comput*) llave f de memoria
men [mɛn] PL *of* **man**
menace ['mɛnəs] N amenaza; (*inf: nuisance*) lata ▸ VT amenazar; **a public ~** un peligro público
menacing ['mɛnɪsɪŋ] ADJ amenazador(-a)
menacingly ['mɛnɪsɪŋlɪ] ADV amenazadoramente

m

menagerie [mɪ'nædʒərɪ] N casa de fieras
mend [mɛnd] VT reparar, arreglar; (*darn*) zurcir ▸ VI reponerse ▸ N (*gen*) remiendo; (*darn*) zurcido; **to be on the ~** ir mejorando; **to ~ one's ways** enmendarse
mending ['mɛndɪŋ] N arreglo, reparación *f*; (*clothes*) ropa por remendar
menial ['miːnɪəl] ADJ (*pej*) bajo, servil
meningitis [mɛnɪn'dʒaɪtɪs] N meningitis *f*
menopause ['mɛnəʊpɔːz] N menopausia
men's room N (*US*): **the ~** el servicio de caballeros
menstrual ['mɛnstruəl] ADJ menstrual
menstruate ['mɛnstrueɪt] VI menstruar
menstruation [mɛnstru'eɪʃən] N menstruación *f*
menswear ['mɛnzwɛəʳ] N confección *f* de caballero
mental ['mɛntl] ADJ mental; **~ illness** enfermedad *f* mental
mental hospital N (hospital *m*) psiquiátrico
mentality [mɛn'tælɪtɪ] N mentalidad *f*
mentally ['mɛntlɪ] ADV: **to be ~ ill** tener una enfermedad mental
menthol ['mɛnθɒl] N mentol *m*
mention ['mɛnʃən] N mención *f* ▸ VT mencionar; (*speak of*) hablar de; **don't ~ it!** ¡de nada!; **I need hardly ~ that ...** huelga decir que ...; **not to ~, without mentioning** sin contar
mentor ['mɛntɔːʳ] N mentor *m*
menu ['mɛnjuː] N (*set menu*) menú *m*; (*printed*) carta; (*Comput*) menú *m*
menu-driven ['mɛnjuːdrɪvn] ADJ (*Comput*) guiado por menú
MEP N ABBR = **Member of the European Parliament**
mercantile ['məːkəntaɪl] ADJ mercantil
mercenary ['məːsɪnərɪ] ADJ, N mercenario(-a) *m/f*
merchandise ['məːtʃəndaɪz] N mercancías *fpl*
merchandiser ['məːtʃəndaɪzəʳ] N comerciante *mf*, tratante *m*
merchant ['məːtʃənt] N comerciante *mf*
merchant bank N (*BRIT*) banco comercial
merchantman ['məːtʃəntmən] N (*irreg*) buque *m* mercante
merchant navy, (*US*) merchant marine N marina mercante
merciful ['məːsɪful] ADJ compasivo
mercifully ['məːsɪfulɪ] ADV con compasión; (*fortunately*) afortunadamente
merciless ['məːsɪlɪs] ADJ despiadado
mercilessly ['məːsɪlɪslɪ] ADV despiadadamente, sin piedad
mercurial [məːˈkjuərɪəl] ADJ veleidoso, voluble
mercury ['məːkjurɪ] N mercurio

mercy ['məːsɪ] N compasión *f*; (*Rel*) misericordia; **at the ~ of** a la merced de
mercy killing N eutanasia
mere [mɪəʳ] ADJ simple, mero
merely ['mɪəlɪ] ADV simplemente, sólo
merge [məːdʒ] VT (*join*) unir; (*mix*) mezclar; (*fuse*) fundir; (*Comput: files, text*) fusionar ▸ VI unirse; (*Comm*) fusionarse
merger ['məːdʒəʳ] N (*Comm*) fusión *f*
meridian [mə'rɪdɪən] N meridiano
meringue [mə'ræŋ] N merengue *m*
merit ['mɛrɪt] N mérito ▸ VT merecer
meritocracy [mɛrɪ'tɔkrəsɪ] N meritocracia
mermaid ['məːmeɪd] N sirena
merrily ['mɛrɪlɪ] ADV alegremente
merriment ['mɛrɪmənt] N alegría
merry ['mɛrɪ] ADJ alegre; **M~ Christmas!** ¡Felices Pascuas!
merry-go-round ['mɛrɪgəʊraund] N tiovivo
mesh [mɛʃ] N malla; (*Tech*) engranaje *m* ▸ VI (*gears*) engranar; **wire ~** tela metálica
mesmerize ['mɛzməraɪz] VT hipnotizar
mess [mɛs] N confusión *f*; (*of objects*) revoltijo; (*dirt*) porquería; (*tangle*) lío; (*Mil*) comedor *m*; **to be (in) a ~** (*room*) estar revuelto; **to be/get o.s. in a ~** estar/meterse en un lío
  ▸ **mess about, mess around** VI (*inf*) perder el tiempo; (*pass the time*) pasar el rato
  ▸ **mess about with, mess around with** VT FUS (*inf: play with*) divertirse con; (*handle*) manosear
  ▸ **mess up** VT (*inf: disarrange*) desordenar; (*spoil*) estropear; (*dirty*) ensuciar
  ▸ **mess with** VT FUS (*inf: challenge, confront*) meterse con (*inf*); (*interfere with*) interferir con
message ['mɛsɪdʒ] N mensaje *m*, recado ▸ VT (*inf: person*) mandar un mensaje a; (*: comment*) mandar; **to get the ~** (*fig, inf*) enterarse
message board N (*Internet*) foro de debate
message switching N (*Comput*) conmutación *f* de mensajes
messenger ['mɛsɪndʒəʳ] N mensajero(-a)
Messiah [mɪ'saɪə] N Mesías *m*
Messrs, Messrs. ABBR (*on letters: = Messieurs*) Sres.
messy ['mɛsɪ] ADJ (*dirty*) sucio; (*untidy*) desordenado; (*confused: situation etc*) confuso
Met [mɛt] N ABBR (*US*) = **Metropolitan Opera**
met [mɛt] PT, PP *of* **meet** ▸ ADJ ABBR = **meteorological**
metabolism [mɛ'tæbəlɪzəm] N metabolismo
metal ['mɛtl] N metal *m*
metallic [mɛ'tælɪk] ADJ metálico
metallurgy [mɛ'tælədʒɪ] N metalurgia
metalwork ['mɛtlwəːk] N (*craft*) metalistería
metamorphosis [mɛtə'mɔːfəsɪs] (*pl* **metamorphoses** [-siːz]) N metamorfosis *f* inv
metaphor ['mɛtəfəʳ] N metáfora

metaphorical [mɛtə'fɔrɪkl] ADJ metafórico
metaphysics [mɛtə'fɪzɪks] N metafísica
mete [mi:t]: **to ~ out** vt (*punishment*) imponer
meteor ['mi:tɪəʳ] N meteoro
meteoric [mi:tɪ'ɒrɪk] ADJ (*fig*) meteórico
meteorite ['mi:tɪəraɪt] N meteorito
meteorological [mi:tɪərə'lɒdʒɪkl] ADJ
meteorológico
meteorology [mi:tɪə'rɒlədʒɪ] N meteorología
meter ['mi:təʳ] N (*instrument*) contador *m*;
(*US: unit*) = **metre** ▶ VT (*US Post*) franquear;
parking ~ parquímetro
methane ['mi:θeɪn] N metano
method ['mɛθəd] N método; **~ of payment**
método de pago
methodical [mɪ'θɒdɪkl] ADJ metódico
Methodist ['mɛθədɪst] ADJ, N metodista *mf*
methodology [mɛθə'dɒlədʒɪ] N metodología
meths [mɛθs] N (*BRIT*) = **methylated spirit**
methylated spirit ['mɛθɪleɪtɪd-] N (*BRIT*)
alcohol *m* metilado *or* desnaturalizado
meticulous [mɛ'tɪkjuləs] ADJ meticuloso
metre, (*US*) **meter** ['mi:təʳ] N metro
metric ['mɛtrɪk] ADJ métrico; **to go ~** pasar al
sistema métrico
metrication [mɛtrɪ'keɪʃən] N conversión *f* al
sistema métrico
metric system N sistema *m* métrico
metric ton N tonelada métrica
metronome ['mɛtrənəum] N metrónomo
metropolis [mɪ'trɔpəlɪs] N metrópoli(s) *f*
metropolitan [mɛtrə'pɔlɪtən] ADJ
metropolitano
Metropolitan Police N (*BRIT*): **the ~** la
policía londinense
mettle ['mɛtl] N valor *m*, ánimo
mew [mju:] VI (*cat*) maullar
mews [mju:z] (*BRIT*) N: **~ cottage** *casa
acondicionada en antiguos establos o cocheras*;
~ flat *piso en antiguos establos o cocheras*
Mexican ['mɛksɪkən] ADJ, N mexicano(-a)
m/f, mejicano(-a) *m/f*
Mexico ['mɛksɪkəu] N México, Méjico
Mexico City N Ciudad *f* de México *or* Méjico
mezzanine ['mɛtsəni:n] N entresuelo
MFA N ABBR (*US: = Master of Fine Arts*) *título
universitario*
mfr ABBR (*= manufacturer*) fab.; **= manufacture**
mg ABBR (*= milligram*) mg
Mgr ABBR (*= Monseigneur, Monsignor*) Mons;
(*Comm*) = **manager**
mgr ABBR = **manager**
MHR N ABBR (*US*) = **Member of the House of
Representatives**
MHz ABBR (*= megahertz*) MHz
MI ABBR (*US*) = **Michigan**
MI5 N ABBR (*BRIT*: = *Military Intelligence, section
five*) *servicio de contraespionaje del gobierno
británico*

MI6 N ABBR (*BRIT*: = *Military Intelligence,
section six*) *servicio de inteligencia del gobierno
británico*
MIA ABBR (*Mil*: = *missing in action*) desaparecido
miaow [mi:'au] VI maullar
mice [maɪs] PL *of* **mouse**
Mich. ABBR (*US*) = **Michigan**
mickey ['mɪkɪ] N: **to take the ~ out of sb**
tomar el pelo a algn
micro ['maɪkrəu] N = **microcomputer**
micro... [maɪkrəu] PREF micro...
microbe ['maɪkrəub] N microbio
microbiology [maɪkrəubaɪ'ɔlədʒɪ] N
microbiología
microblog ['maɪkrəublɒg] N microblog *m*
microchip ['maɪkrəutʃɪp] N microchip *m*,
microplaqueta
microcomputer ['maɪkrəukəm'pju:təʳ] N
microordenador *m*, microcomputador *m*
(*LAm*)
microcosm ['maɪkrəukɔzəm] N microcosmo
microeconomics ['maɪkrəui:kə'nɔmɪks] N
microeconomía
microfiche ['maɪkrəufi:ʃ] N microficha
microfilm ['maɪkrəufɪlm] N microfilm *m*
microlight ['maɪkrəulaɪt] N ultraligero
micrometer [maɪ'krɔmɪtəʳ] N micrómetro
microphone ['maɪkrəfəun] N micrófono
microprocessor ['maɪkrəu'prəusɛsəʳ] N
microprocesador *m*
microscope ['maɪkrəskəup] N microscopio;
under the ~ al microscopio
microscopic [maɪkrə'skɔpɪk] ADJ
microscópico
microwave ['maɪkrəuweɪv] N (*also:*
microwave oven) horno microondas
mid [mɪd] ADJ: **in ~ May** a mediados de mayo;
in ~ afternoon a media tarde; **in ~ air** en el
aire; **he's in his ~ thirties** tiene unos
treinta y cinco años
midday [mɪd'deɪ] N mediodía *m*
middle ['mɪdl] N centro; (*half-way point*)
medio; (*waist*) cintura ▶ ADJ de en medio;
in the ~ of the night en plena noche;
I'm in the ~ of reading it lo estoy leyendo
ahora mismo
middle-aged [mɪdl'eɪdʒd] ADJ de mediana
edad
Middle Ages NPL: **the ~** la Edad Media
middle class N: **the ~(es)** la clase media
▶ ADJ: **middle-class** de clase media
Middle East N Oriente *m* Medio
middleman ['mɪdlmæn] N (*irreg*)
intermediario
middle management N dirección *f* de nivel
medio
middle name N segundo nombre *m*
middle-of-the-road ['mɪdləvðə'rəud] ADJ
moderado

m

659

middle school N (US) *colegio para niños de doce a catorce años*; (BRIT) *colegio para niños de ocho o nueve a doce o trece años*

middleweight ['mɪdlweɪt] N (*Boxing*) peso medio

middling ['mɪdlɪŋ] ADJ mediano

Middx ABBR (BRIT) = **Middlesex**

midge [mɪdʒ] N mosquito

midget ['mɪdʒɪt] N enano(-a)

midi system N minicadena

Midlands ['mɪdləndz] NPL *región central de Inglaterra*

midnight ['mɪdnaɪt] N medianoche f; **at ~** a medianoche

midriff ['mɪdrɪf] N diafragma m

midst [mɪdst] N: **in the ~ of** entre, en medio de; (*situation, action*) en mitad de

midsummer [mɪd'sʌmər] N: **a ~ day** un día de pleno verano

Midsummer's Day N Día m de San Juan

midway [mɪd'weɪ] ADJ, ADV: **~ (between)** a medio camino (entre); **~ through** a la mitad (de)

midweek [mɪd'wiːk] ADV entre semana

midwife ['mɪdwaɪf] (*pl* **midwives** [-waɪvz]) N matrona, comadrona

midwifery ['mɪdwɪfərɪ] N tocología

midwinter [mɪd'wɪntər] N: **in ~** en pleno invierno

miffed [mɪft] ADJ (*inf*) mosqueado

might [maɪt] VB *see* **may** ▸ N fuerza, poder m; **he ~ be there** puede que esté allí, a lo mejor está allí; **I ~ as well go** más vale que vaya; **you ~ like to try** podría intentar

mightily ['maɪtɪlɪ] ADV fuertemente, poderosamente; **I was ~ surprised** me sorprendí enormemente

mightn't ['maɪtnt] = **might not**

mighty ['maɪtɪ] ADJ fuerte, poderoso

migraine ['miːgreɪn] N jaqueca

migrant ['maɪgrənt] ADJ migratorio; (*worker*) emigrante ▸ N (*bird*) ave f migratoria; (*worker*) emigrante mf

migrate [maɪ'greɪt] VI emigrar

migration [maɪ'greɪʃən] N emigración f

mike [maɪk] N ABBR (= *microphone*) micro

Milan [mɪ'læn] N Milán m

mild [maɪld] ADJ (*person*) apacible; (*climate*) templado; (*slight*) ligero; (*taste*) suave; (*illness*) leve

mildew ['mɪldjuː] N moho

mildly ['maɪldlɪ] ADV ligeramente; suavemente; **to put it ~** por no decir algo peor

mildness ['maɪldnɪs] N suavidad f; (*of illness*) levedad f

mile [maɪl] N milla; **to do 20 miles per gallon** hacer 20 millas por galón

mileage ['maɪlɪdʒ] N número de millas; (*Aut*) kilometraje m

mileage allowance N ≈ asignación f por kilometraje

mileometer [maɪ'lɔmɪtər] N (BRIT) = **milometer**

milestone ['maɪlstəun] N mojón m; (*fig*) hito

milieu ['miːljəː] N (medio) ambiente m, entorno

militant ['mɪlɪtnt] ADJ, N militante mf

militarism ['mɪlɪtərɪzəm] N militarismo

militaristic [mɪlɪtə'rɪstɪk] ADJ militarista

military ['mɪlɪtərɪ] ADJ militar

military service N servicio militar

militate ['mɪlɪteɪt] VI: **to ~ against** militar en contra de

militia [mɪ'lɪʃə] N milicia

milk [mɪlk] N leche f ▸ VT (*cow*) ordeñar; (*fig*) chupar

milk chocolate N chocolate m con leche

milk float N (BRIT) furgoneta de la leche

milking ['mɪlkɪŋ] N ordeño

milkman ['mɪlkmən] N (*irreg*) lechero, repartidor m de la leche

milk shake N batido, malteada (LAM)

milk tooth N diente m de leche

milk truck N (US) = **milk float**

milky ['mɪlkɪ] ADJ lechoso

Milky Way N Vía Láctea

mill [mɪl] N (*windmill etc*) molino; (*coffee mill*) molinillo; (*factory*) fábrica; (*spinning mill*) hilandería ▸ VT moler ▸ VI (*also*: **mill about**) arremolinarse

milled [mɪld] ADJ (*grain*) molido; (*coin, edge*) acordonado

millennium [mɪ'lɛnɪəm] (*pl* **millenniums** *or* **millennia** [-'lɛnɪə]) N milenio

millennium bug N (*Comput*): **the ~** el (problema del) efecto 2000

miller ['mɪlər] N molinero

millet ['mɪlɪt] N mijo

milli... ['mɪlɪ] PREF mili...

milligram, milligramme ['mɪlɪgraem] N miligramo

millilitre, (US) milliliter ['mɪlɪliːtər] N mililitro

millimetre, (US) millimeter ['mɪlɪmiːtər] N milímetro

milliner ['mɪlɪnər] N sombrerero(-a)

millinery ['mɪlɪnərɪ] N sombrerería

million ['mɪljən] N millón m; **a ~ times** un millón de veces

millionaire [mɪljə'nɛər] N millonario(-a)

millionth ['mɪljənθ] ADJ millonésimo

millipede ['mɪlɪpiːd] N milpiés m inv

millstone ['mɪlstəun] N piedra de molino

millwheel ['mɪlwiːl] N rueda de molino

milometer [maɪ'lɔmɪtər] N (BRIT) cuentakilómetros m inv

mime [maɪm] N mímica; (*actor*) mimo(-a) ▸ VT remedar ▸ VI actuar de mimo

mimic ['mɪmɪk] N imitador(a) m/f ▶ ADJ mímico ▶ VT remedar, imitar

mimicry ['mɪmɪkrɪ] N imitación f

Min ABBR (BRIT Pol: = Ministry) Min

min. ABBR (= minute(s)) m.; = **minimum**

minaret [mɪnə'rɛt] N alminar m, minarete m

mince [mɪns] VT picar ▶ VI (in walking) andar con pasos menudos ▶ N (BRIT Culin) carne f picada, picadillo

mincemeat ['mɪnsmiːt] N conserva de fruta picada; (US: meat) carne f picada

mince pie N pastelillo relleno de fruta picada

mincer ['mɪnsə'] N picadora de carne

mincing ['mɪnsɪŋ] ADJ afectado

mind [maɪnd] N (gen) mente f; (contrasted with matter) espíritu m ▶ VT (attend to, look after) ocuparse de, cuidar; (be careful of) tener cuidado con; (object to): **I don't ~ the noise** no me molesta el ruido; **it is on my ~** me preocupa; **to my ~** a mi parecer or juicio; **to change one's ~** cambiar de idea or de parecer; **to bring** or **call sth to ~** recordar algo; **to have sth/sb in ~** tener algo/a algn en mente; **to be out of one's ~** haber perdido el juicio; **to bear sth in ~** tomar or tener algo en cuenta; **to make up one's ~** decidirse; **it went right out of my ~** se me fue por completo (de la cabeza); **to be in two minds about sth** estar indeciso or dudar ante algo; **I don't ~** me es igual; **~ you, ...** te advierto que ...; **never ~!** ¡es igual!, ¡no importa!; (don't worry) ¡no te preocupes!; **"~ the step"** "cuidado con el escalón"

mind-boggling ['maɪndbɔglɪŋ] ADJ (inf) alucinante, increíble

-minded [-maɪndɪd] ADJ: **fair~** imparcial; **an industrially~ nation** una nación orientada a la industria

minder ['maɪndə'] N guardaespaldas m inv

mindful ['maɪndful] ADJ: **~ of** consciente de

mindless ['maɪndlɪs] ADJ (violence, crime) sin sentido; (work) de autómata

mine [maɪn] PRON (el) mío/(la) mía etc ▶ ADJ: **this book is ~** este libro es mío ▶ N mina ▶ VT (coal) extraer; (ship, beach) minar

mine detector N detector m de minas

minefield ['maɪnfiːld] N campo de minas

miner ['maɪnə'] N minero(-a)

mineral ['mɪnərəl] ADJ mineral ▶ N mineral m; **minerals** NPL (BRIT: soft drinks) refrescos mpl con gas

mineral water N agua mineral

minesweeper ['maɪnswiːpə'] N dragaminas m inv

mingle ['mɪŋgl] VI: **to ~ with** mezclarse con

mingy ['mɪndʒɪ] ADJ (inf) tacaño

mini ... ['mɪnɪ] PREF mini..., micro...

miniature ['mɪnətʃə'] ADJ (en) miniatura ▶ N miniatura

minibar ['mɪnɪbɑː'] N minibar m

minibus ['mɪnɪbʌs] N microbús m

minicab ['mɪnɪkæb] N taxi m (que sólo puede pedirse por teléfono)

minicomputer ['mɪnɪkəm'pjuːtə'] N miniordenador m, minicomputador m (LAm)

MiniDisc® ['mɪnɪdɪsk] N MiniDisc® m

minim ['mɪnɪm] N (BRIT Mus) blanca

minimal ['mɪnɪml] ADJ mínimo

minimalist ['mɪnɪməlɪst] ADJ, N minimalista mf

minimize ['mɪnɪmaɪz] VT minimizar; (play down) empequeñecer

minimum ['mɪnɪməm] N (pl **minima** ['mɪnɪmə]) mínimo ▶ ADJ mínimo; **to reduce to a ~** reducir algo al mínimo; **~ wage** salario mínimo

minimum lending rate N tipo de interés mínimo

mining ['maɪnɪŋ] N minería ▶ ADJ minero

minion ['mɪnjən] N secuaz m

mini-series ['mɪnɪsɪərɪz] N miniserie f

miniskirt ['mɪnɪskəːt] N minifalda

minister ['mɪnɪstə'] N (BRIT Pol) ministro(-a); (: junior) secretario(-a) de Estado; (Rel) pastor m ▶ VI: **to ~ to** atender a

ministerial [mɪnɪs'tɪərɪəl] ADJ (BRIT Pol) ministerial

ministry ['mɪnɪstrɪ] N (BRIT Pol) ministerio; (Rel) sacerdocio; **M~ of Defence** Ministerio de Defensa

mink [mɪŋk] N visón m

mink coat N abrigo de visón

Minn. ABBR (US) = **Minnesota**

minnow ['mɪnəu] N pececillo (de agua dulce)

minor ['maɪnə'] ADJ (repairs, injuries) leve; (poet, planet) menor; (unimportant) secundario; (Mus) menor ▶ N (Law) menor mf de edad

Minorca [mɪ'nɔːkə] N Menorca

minority [maɪ'nɔrɪtɪ] N minoría; **to be in a ~** estar en or ser minoría

minority interest N participación f minoritaria

minster ['mɪnstə'] N catedral f

minstrel ['mɪnstrəl] N juglar m

mint [mɪnt] N (plant) menta, hierbabuena; (sweet) caramelo de menta ▶ VT (coins) acuñar; **the (Royal) M~**, (US) **the (US) M~** la Casa de la Moneda; **in ~ condition** en perfecto estado

mint sauce N salsa de menta

minuet ['mɪnju'et] N minué m

minus ['maɪnəs] N (also: **minus sign**) signo menos ▶ PREP menos; **12 - 6 equals 6** 12 menos 6 son 6; **~ 24°C** 24°C bajo cero

minuscule ['mɪnəskjuːl] ADJ minúsculo

minute¹ ['mɪnɪt] N minuto; (fig) momento; **minutes** NPL (of meeting) actas fpl; **it is 5 minutes past 3** son las 3 y 5 (minutos);

at the last ~ a última hora; **wait a ~!** ¡espera un momento!; **up to the** ~ de última hora

minute² [maɪˈnjuːt] ADJ diminuto; (*search*) minucioso; **in ~ detail** con todo detalle

minute book N libro de actas

minute hand N minutero

minutely [maɪˈnjuːtlɪ] ADV (*by a small amount*) por muy poco; (*in detail*) detalladamente, minuciosamente

minutiae [mɪˈnjuːʃiː] NPL minucias *fpl*

miracle [ˈmɪrəkl] N milagro

miracle play N auto, milagro

miraculous [mɪˈrækjuləs] ADJ milagroso

miraculously [mɪˈrækjuləslɪ] ADV milagrosamente

mirage [ˈmɪrɑːʒ] N espejismo

mire [maɪəʳ] N fango, lodo

mirror [ˈmɪrəʳ] N espejo; (*in car*) retrovisor *m*
▶ VT reflejar

mirror image N reflejo inverso

mirth [məːθ] N alegría; (*laughter*) risa, risas *fpl*

misadventure [mɪsədˈvɛntʃəʳ] N desventura; **death by ~** muerte *f* accidental

misanthropist [mɪˈzænθrəpɪst] N misántropo(-a)

misapply [mɪsəˈplaɪ] VT emplear mal

misapprehension [ˈmɪsæprɪˈhɛnʃən] N equivocación *f*

misappropriate [mɪsəˈprəuprɪeɪt] VT (*funds*) malversar

misappropriation [ˈmɪsəprəuprɪˈeɪʃən] N malversación *f*, desfalco

misbehave [mɪsbɪˈheɪv] VI portarse mal

misbehaviour, (US) **misbehavior** [mɪsbɪˈheɪvjəʳ] N mala conducta

misc. ABBR = **miscellaneous**

miscalculate [mɪsˈkælkjuleɪt] VT calcular mal

miscalculation [mɪskælkjuˈleɪʃən] N error *m* (de cálculo)

miscarriage [ˈmɪskærɪdʒ] N (*Med*) aborto (no provocado); **~ of justice** error *m* judicial

miscarry [mɪsˈkærɪ] VI (*Med*) abortar (de forma natural); (*fail: plans*) fracasar, malograrse

miscellaneous [mɪsɪˈleɪnɪəs] ADJ varios(-as), diversos(-as); **~ expenses** gastos diversos

miscellany [mɪˈsɛlənɪ] N miscelánea

mischance [mɪsˈtʃɑːns] N desgracia, mala suerte *f*; **by (some)** ~ por (alguna) desgracia

mischief [ˈmɪstʃɪf] N (*naughtiness*) travesura; (*harm*) mal *m*, daño; (*maliciousness*) malicia

mischievous [ˈmɪstʃɪvəs] ADJ travieso; dañino; (*playful*) malicioso

mischievously [ˈmɪstʃɪvəslɪ] ADV por travesura; maliciosamente

misconception [ˈmɪskənˈsɛpʃən] N idea equivocada; equivocación *f*

misconduct [mɪsˈkɔndʌkt] N mala conducta; **professional** ~ falta profesional

misconstrue [mɪskənˈstruː] VT interpretar mal

miscount [mɪsˈkaunt] VT, VI contar mal

misdeed [mɪsˈdiːd] N (*old*) fechoría, delito

misdemeanour, (US) **misdemeanor** [mɪsdɪˈmiːnəʳ] N delito, ofensa

misdirect [mɪsdɪˈrɛkt] VT (*person*) informar mal; (*letter*) poner señas incorrectas en

miser [ˈmaɪzəʳ] N avaro(-a)

miserable [ˈmɪzərəbl] ADJ (*unhappy*) triste, desgraciado; (*wretched*) miserable; **to feel** ~ sentirse triste

miserably [ˈmɪzərəblɪ] ADV (*smile, answer*) tristemente; (*fail*) rotundamente; **to pay** ~ pagar una miseria

miserly [ˈmaɪzəlɪ] ADJ avariento, tacaño

misery [ˈmɪzərɪ] N (*unhappiness*) tristeza; (*wretchedness*) miseria, desdicha

misfire [mɪsˈfaɪəʳ] VI fallar

misfit [ˈmɪsfɪt] N (*person*) inadaptado(-a)

misfortune [mɪsˈfɔːtʃən] N desgracia

misgiving [mɪsˈgɪvɪŋ] N, **misgivings** [mɪsˈgɪvɪŋz] NPL (*mistrust*) recelo; (*apprehension*) presentimiento; **to have misgivings about sth** tener dudas sobre algo

misguided [mɪsˈgaɪdɪd] ADJ equivocado

mishandle [mɪsˈhændl] VT (*treat roughly*) maltratar; (*mismanage*) manejar mal

mishap [ˈmɪshæp] N desgracia, contratiempo

mishear [mɪsˈhɪəʳ] VT, VI (*irreg: like* **hear**) oír mal

mishmash [ˈmɪʃmæʃ] N (*inf*) revoltijo

misinform [mɪsɪnˈfɔːm] VT informar mal

misinterpret [mɪsɪnˈtəːprɪt] VT interpretar mal

misinterpretation [ˈmɪsɪntəːprɪˈteɪʃən] N mala interpretación *f*

misjudge [mɪsˈdʒʌdʒ] VT juzgar mal

mislay [mɪsˈleɪ] VT (*irreg: like* **lay**) extraviar, perder

mislead [mɪsˈliːd] VT (*irreg: like* **lead¹**) llevar a conclusiones erróneas; (*deliberately*) engañar

misleading [mɪsˈliːdɪŋ] ADJ engañoso

misled [mɪsˈlɛd] PT, PP *of* **mislead**

mismanage [mɪsˈmænɪdʒ] VT administrar mal

mismanagement [mɪsˈmænɪdʒmənt] N mala administración *f*

misnomer [mɪsˈnəuməʳ] N término inapropiado *or* equivocado

misogynist [mɪˈsɔdʒɪnɪst] N misógino

misplace [mɪsˈpleɪs] VT (*lose*) extraviar; **misplaced** (*trust etc*) inmerecido

misprint [ˈmɪsprɪnt] N errata, error *m* de imprenta

mispronounce [mɪsprə'nauns] VT pronunciar mal

misquote ['mɪs'kwəut] VT citar incorrectamente

misread [mɪs'riːd] VT (irreg: like **read**) leer mal

misrepresent [mɪsreprɪ'zɛnt] VT falsificar

misrepresentation [mɪsreprɪzɛn'teɪʃən] N (Law) falsa declaración f

Miss [mɪs] N Señorita; **Dear ~ Smith** Estimada Señorita Smith

miss [mɪs] VT (train etc) perder; (target) errar; (appointment, class) faltar a; (escape, avoid) evitar; (notice loss of: money etc) notar la falta de, echar en falta; (regret the absence of): **I ~ him** le echo de menos ▶ VI fallar ▶ N (shot) tiro fallido; **the bus just missed the wall** faltó poco para que el autobús se estrella contra el muro; **you're missing the point** no has entendido la idea

▶ **miss out** VT (BRIT) omitir

▶ **miss out on** VT FUS (fun, party, opportunity) perderse

Miss. ABBR (US) = **Mississippi**

missal ['mɪsl] N misal m

misshapen [mɪs'ʃeɪpən] ADJ deforme

missile ['mɪsaɪl] N (Aviat) misil m; (object thrown) proyectil m

missile base N base f de misiles

missile launcher N lanzamisiles m inv

missing ['mɪsɪŋ] ADJ (pupil) ausente, que falta; (thing) perdido; **to be ~** faltar; **~ person** desaparecido(-a); **~ in action** desaparecido en combate

mission ['mɪʃən] N misión f; **on a ~ for sb** en una misión para algn

missionary ['mɪʃənrɪ] N misionero(-a)

misspell [mɪs'spɛl] VT (irreg: like **spell**) escribir mal

misspent ['mɪs'spɛnt] ADJ: **his ~ youth** su juventud disipada

mist [mɪst] N (light) neblina; (heavy) niebla; (at sea) bruma ▶ VI (also: **mist over, mist up**: weather) nublarse; (: BRIT: windows) empañarse

mistake [mɪs'teɪk] N error m ▶ VT (irreg: like **take**) entender mal; **by ~** por equivocación; **to make a ~** (about sb/sth) equivocarse; (in writing, calculating etc) cometer un error; **to ~ A for B** confundir A con B

mistaken [mɪs'teɪkən] PP of **mistake** ▶ ADJ (idea etc) equivocado; **to be ~** equivocarse, engañarse; **~ identity** identificación f errónea

mistakenly [mɪs'teɪkənlɪ] ADV erróneamente

mister ['mɪstər] N (inf) señor m; see also **Mr**

mistletoe ['mɪsltəu] N muérdago

mistook [mɪs'tuk] PT of **mistake**

mistranslation [mɪstræns'leɪʃən] N mala traducción f

mistreat [mɪs'triːt] VT maltratar, tratar mal

mistress ['mɪstrɪs] N (lover) amante f; (of house) señora (de la casa); (BRIT: in primary school) maestra; (: in secondary school) profesora; see also **Mrs**

mistrust [mɪs'trʌst] VT desconfiar de ▶ N: **~ (of)** desconfianza (de)

mistrustful [mɪs'trʌstful] ADJ: **~ (of)** desconfiado (de), receloso (de)

misty ['mɪstɪ] ADJ nebuloso, brumoso; (day) de niebla; (glasses) empañado

misty-eyed ['mɪstɪ'aɪd] ADJ sentimental

misunderstand [mɪsʌndə'stænd] VT, VI (irreg: like **understand**) entender mal

misunderstanding [mɪsʌndə'stændɪŋ] N malentendido

misunderstood [mɪsʌndə'stud] PT, PP of **misunderstand** ▶ ADJ (person) incomprendido

misuse N [mɪs'juːs] mal uso; (of power) abuso; (of funds) malversación f ▶ VT [mɪs'juːz] abusar de; (funds) malversar

MIT N ABBR (US) = **Massachusetts Institute of Technology**

mite [maɪt] N (small quantity) pizca; **poor ~!** ¡pobrecito!

mitigate ['mɪtɪgeɪt] VT mitigar; **mitigating circumstances** circunstancias fpl atenuantes

mitigation [mɪtɪ'geɪʃən] N mitigación f, alivio

mitre, (US) miter ['maɪtər] N mitra

mitt ['mɪt], **mitten** ['mɪtn] N manopla

mix [mɪks] VT (gen) mezclar; (combine) unir ▶ VI mezclarse; (people) llevarse bien ▶ N mezcla; **to ~ sth with sth** mezclar algo con algo; **to ~ business with pleasure** combinar los negocios con el placer; **cake ~** preparado para pastel

▶ **mix in** VT (eggs etc) añadir

▶ **mix up** VT mezclar; (confuse) confundir; **to be mixed up in sth** estar metido en algo

mixed [mɪkst] ADJ (assorted) variado, surtido; (school, marriage etc) mixto; (feelings etc) encontrado

mixed-ability ['mɪkstə'bɪlɪtɪ] ADJ (class etc) de alumnos de distintas capacidades

mixed blessing N: **it's a ~** tiene su lado bueno y su lado malo

mixed doubles N (Sport) dobles mpl mixtos

mixed economy N economía mixta

mixed grill N (BRIT) parrillada mixta

mixed salad N ensalada mixta

mixed-up [mɪkst'ʌp] ADJ (confused) confuso, revuelto

mixer ['mɪksər] N (for food) batidora; (person): **he's a good ~** tiene don de gentes

mixer tap N (grifo) monomando

mixture ['mɪkstʃər] N mezcla

mix-up ['mɪksʌp] N confusión f

Mk ABBR (BRIT Tech: = mark) Mk

mkt ABBR = **market**

ml ABBR (= *millilitre(s)*) ml

MLA N ABBR (*BRIT Pol: Northern Ireland*: = *Member of the Legislative Assembly*) miembro de la asamblea legislativa

MLitt N ABBR = **Master of Literature**; (= *Master of Letters*) título universitario de *postgrado; see also* **master's degree**

MLR N ABBR (*BRIT*) = **minimum lending rate**

mm ABBR (= *millimetre*) mm

MMR vaccine N (*against measles, mumps, rubella*) vacuna triple vírica

MMS N ABBR (= *multimedia messaging service*) MMS *m*

MN ABBR (*BRIT*) = **Merchant Navy**; (*US*) = **Minnesota**

MO N ABBR (*Med*) = **medical officer**; (*US inf*) = **modus operandi** ▶ ABBR (*US*) = **Missouri**

Mo. ABBR (*US*) = **Missouri**

m.o. ABBR (= *money order*) g/

moan [məun] N gemido ▶ VI gemir; (*inf: complain*): **to ~ (about)** quejarse (de)

moaning ['məunɪŋ] N gemidos *mpl*; quejas *fpl*

moat [məut] N foso

mob [mɔb] N multitud *f*; (*pej*): **the ~** el populacho ▶ VT acosar

mobile ['məubaɪl] ADJ móvil ▶ N móvil *m*

mobile home N caravana

mobile phone N teléfono móvil

mobile phone mast N (*BRIT Tel*) torre *f* de telefonía móvil, antena de telefonía móvil

mobility [məu'bɪlɪtɪ] N movilidad *f*; **~ of labour** *or* (*US*) **labor** movilidad *f* de la mano de obra

mobilize ['məubɪlaɪz] VT movilizar

moccasin ['mɔkəsɪn] N mocasín *m*

mock [mɔk] VT (*make ridiculous*) ridiculizar; (*laugh at*) burlarse de ▶ ADJ fingido; **~ exams** (*BRIT Scol*) exámenes *mpl* de prueba

mockery ['mɔkərɪ] N burla; **to make a ~ of** desprestigiar

mocking ['mɔkɪŋ] ADJ (*tone*) burlón(-ona)

mockingbird ['mɔkɪŋbə:d] N sinsonte *m* (*LAM*), zenzontle *m* (*LAM*)

mock-up ['mɔkʌp] N maqueta

MOD N ABBR (*BRIT*) = **Ministry of Defence**; *see* **defence**

mod cons ['mɔd'kɔnz] NPL ABBR (= *modern conveniences*) *see* **convenience**

mode [məud] N modo; (*of transport*) medio; (*Comput*) modo, modalidad *f*

model ['mɔdl] N (*gen*) modelo; (*Arch*) maqueta; (*person: for fashion, art*) modelo *mf* ▶ ADJ modelo *inv* ▶ VT modelar; **to ~ o.s. on** tomar como modelo a ▶ VI ser modelo; **~ railway** ferrocarril *m* de juguete; **to ~ clothes** pasar modelos, ser modelo; **to ~ on** crear a imitación de

modelling, (*US*) **modeling** ['mɔdlɪŋ] N (*modelmaking*) modelado

modem ['məudəm] N módem *m*

moderate ADJ, N ['mɔdərət] moderado(-a) *m/f* ▶ VI ['mɔdəreit] moderarse, calmarse ▶ VT ['mɔdəreit] moderar

moderately ['mɔdərətlɪ] ADV (*act*) con moderación; (*expensive, difficult*) medianamente; (*pleased, happy*) bastante

moderation [mɔdə'reɪʃən] N moderación *f*; **in ~** con moderación

moderator ['mɔdəreitəʳ] N (*mediator*) moderador(a) *m/f*

modern ['mɔdən] ADJ moderno; **~ languages** lenguas *fpl* modernas

modernity [mə'də:nɪtɪ] N modernidad *f*

modernization [mɔdənaɪ'zeɪʃən] N modernización *f*

modernize ['mɔdənaɪz] VT modernizar

modest ['mɔdɪst] ADJ modesto; (*small*) módico

modestly ['mɔdɪstlɪ] ADV modestamente

modesty ['mɔdɪstɪ] N modestia

modicum ['mɔdɪkəm] N: **a ~ of** un mínimo de

modification [mɔdɪfɪ'keɪʃən] N modificación *f*; **to make modifications** hacer cambios *or* modificaciones

modify ['mɔdɪfaɪ] VT modificar

modish ['məudɪʃ] ADJ de moda

Mods [mɔdz] N ABBR (*BRIT*: = *Honour Moderations*) examen de licenciatura de la universidad de Oxford

modular ['mɔdjuləʳ] ADJ (*filing, unit*) modular

modulate ['mɔdjuleit] VT modular

modulation [mɔdju'leɪʃən] N modulación *f*

module ['mɔdju:l] N módulo

modus operandi ['məudəsɔpə'rændi:] N manera de actuar

Mogadishu [mɔgə'dɪʃu:] N Mogadiscio

mogul ['məugəl] N (*fig*) magnate *m*

MOH N ABBR (*BRIT*) = **Medical Officer of Health**

mohair ['məuhɛəʳ] N mohair *m*

Mohammed [mə'hæmɛd] N Mahoma *m*

moist [mɔɪst] ADJ húmedo

moisten ['mɔɪsn] VT humedecer

moisture ['mɔɪstʃəʳ] N humedad *f*

moisturize ['mɔɪstʃəraɪz] VT (*skin*) hidratar

moisturizer ['mɔɪstʃəraɪzəʳ] N crema hidratante

molar ['məuləʳ] N muela

molasses [məu'læsɪz] N melaza

mold [məuld] N, VT (*US*) = **mould**

Moldavia [mɔl'deɪvɪə], **Moldova** [mɔl'dəuvə] N Moldavia, Moldova

Moldavian [mɔl'deɪvɪən], **Moldovan** [mɔl'dəuvən] ADJ, N moldavo(-a) *m/f*

mole [məul] N (*animal*) topo; (*spot*) lunar *m*

molecular [məˈlɛkjuləʳ] ADJ molecular
molecule [ˈmɒlɪkjuːl] N molécula
molest [məuˈlɛst] VT importunar; (*sexually*) abusar sexualmente de
moll [mɒl] N (*inf*) amiga
mollusc, (US) mollusk [ˈmɒləsk] N molusco
mollycoddle [ˈmɒlɪkɒdl] VT mimar
Molotov cocktail [ˈmɒlətɒf-] N cóctel *m* Molotov
molt [məult] VI (*US*) = **moult**
molten [ˈməultən] ADJ fundido; (*lava*) líquido
mom [mɒm] N (*US*) = **mum**
moment [ˈməumənt] N momento; **at** *or* **for the ~** de momento, por el momento, por ahora; **in a ~** dentro de un momento
momentarily [ˈməuməntrɪlɪ] ADV momentáneamente; (*US: very soon*) de un momento a otro
momentary [ˈməuməntərɪ] ADJ momentáneo
momentous [məuˈmɛntəs] ADJ trascendental, importante
momentum [məuˈmɛntəm] N momento; (*fig*) ímpetu *m*; **to gather ~** cobrar velocidad; (*fig*) cobrar fuerza
mommy [ˈmɒmɪ] N (*US*) = **mummy**
Mon. ABBR (= *Monday*) lun.
Monaco [ˈmɒnəkəu] N Mónaco
monarch [ˈmɒnək] N monarca *mf*
monarchist [ˈmɒnəkɪst] N monárquico(-a)
monarchy [ˈmɒnəkɪ] N monarquía
monastery [ˈmɒnəstərɪ] N monasterio
monastic [məˈnæstɪk] ADJ monástico
Monday [ˈmʌndɪ] N lunes *m inv*; *see also* **Tuesday**
Monegasque [mɒnɪˈgæsk] ADJ, N monegasco(-a) *m/f*
monetarist [ˈmʌnɪtərɪst] N monetarista *mf*
monetary [ˈmʌnɪtərɪ] ADJ monetario
monetary policy N política monetaria
money [ˈmʌnɪ] N dinero, plata (*LAm*); **to make ~** ganar dinero; **I've got no ~ left** no me queda dinero
money belt N riñonera
moneyed [ˈmʌnɪd] ADJ adinerado
moneylender [ˈmʌnɪlɛndəʳ] N prestamista *mf*
moneymaker [ˈmʌnɪmeɪkəʳ] N (*BRIT inf: business*) filón *m*
moneymaking [ˈmʌnɪmeɪkɪŋ] ADJ rentable
money market N mercado monetario
money order N giro
money-spinner [ˈmʌnɪspɪnəʳ] N (*inf: person, idea, business*) filón *m*
money supply N oferta monetaria, medio circulante, volumen *m* monetario
Mongol [ˈmɒŋgəl] N mongol(a) *m/f*; (*Ling*) mongol *m*
mongol [ˈmɒŋgəl] ADJ, N (*Med*) mongólico

Mongolia [mɒŋˈgəulɪə] N Mongolia
Mongolian [mɒŋˈgəulɪən] ADJ mongol(a) ▸ N mongol(a) *m/f*; (*Ling*) mongol *m*
mongoose [ˈmɒŋguːs] N mangosta
mongrel [ˈmʌŋgrəl] N (*dog*) perro cruzado
monitor [ˈmɒnɪtəʳ] N (*Scol*) monitor *m*; (*also:* **television monitor**) receptor *m* de control; (*of computer*) monitor *m* ▸ VT controlar; (*foreign station*) escuchar
monk [mʌŋk] N monje *m*
monkey [ˈmʌŋkɪ] N mono
monkey business N, **monkey tricks** NPL tejemanejes *mpl*
monkey nut N (*BRIT*) cacahuete *m*, maní *m* (*LAm*)
monkey wrench N llave *f* inglesa
mono [ˈmɒnəu] ADJ (*broadcast etc*) mono *inv*
mono... [mɒnəu] PREF mono ...
monochrome [ˈmɒnəukrəum] ADJ monocromo
monocle [ˈmɒnəkl] N monóculo
monogamous [məˈnɒgəməs] ADJ monógamo
monogram [ˈmɒnəgræm] N monograma *m*
monolith [ˈmɒnəlɪθ] N monolito
monolithic [mɒnəˈlɪθɪk] ADJ monolítico
monologue [ˈmɒnəlɒg] N monólogo
monoplane [ˈmɒnəpleɪn] N monoplano
monopolist [məˈnɒpəlɪst] N monopolista *mf*
monopolize [məˈnɒpəlaɪz] VT monopolizar
monopoly [məˈnɒpəlɪ] N monopolio;
Monopolies and Mergers Commission (*BRIT*) *comisión reguladora de monopolios y fusiones*
monorail [ˈmɒnəureɪl] N monocarril *m*, monorraíl *m*
monosodium glutamate [mɒnəˈsəudɪəmˈgluːtəmeɪt] N glutamato monosódico
monosyllabic [mɒnəsɪˈlæbɪk] ADJ monosílabo
monosyllable [ˈmɒnəsɪləbl] N monosílabo
monotone [ˈmɒnətəun] N voz *f* (*or* tono) monocorde
monotonous [məˈnɒtənəs] ADJ monótono
monotony [məˈnɒtənɪ] N monotonía
monoxide [məˈnɒksaɪd] N: **carbon ~** monóxido de carbono
monseigneur [mɒnsɛnˈjəːʳ], **monsignor** [mɒnˈsiːnjəʳ] N monseñor *m*
monsoon [mɒnˈsuːn] N monzón *m*
monster [ˈmɒnstəʳ] N monstruo
monstrosity [mɒnsˈtrɒsɪtɪ] N monstruosidad *f*
monstrous [ˈmɒnstrəs] ADJ (*huge*) enorme; (*atrocious*) monstruoso
Mont. ABBR (*US*) = **Montana**
montage [mɒnˈtɑːʒ] N montaje *m*
Mont Blanc [mɔ̃ˈblɑ̃] N Mont Blanc *m*
month [mʌnθ] N mes *m*; **300 dollars a ~** 300 dólares al mes; **every ~** cada mes

m

monthly ['mʌnθlɪ] ADJ mensual ▶ ADV mensualmente ▶ N (*magazine*) revista mensual; **twice** ~ dos veces al mes; ~ **instalment** mensualidad *f*
monument ['mɔnjumənt] N monumento
monumental [mɔnju'mɛntl] ADJ monumental
moo [muː] VI mugir
mood [muːd] N humor *m*; **to be in a good/bad** ~ estar de buen/mal humor
moodily ['muːdɪlɪ] ADV malhumoradamente
moodiness ['muːdɪnɪs] N humor *m* cambiante; (*bad mood*) mal humor *m*
moody ['muːdɪ] ADJ (*changeable*) de humor variable; (*sullen*) malhumorado
moon [muːn] N luna
moonbeam ['muːnbiːm] N rayo de luna
moon landing N alunizaje *m*
moonless ['muːnlɪs] ADJ sin luna
moonlight ['muːnlaɪt] N luz *f* de la luna ▶ VI hacer pluriempleo
moonlighting ['muːnlaɪtɪŋ] N pluriempleo
moonlit ['muːnlɪt] ADJ: **a** ~ **night** una noche de luna
moonshot ['muːnʃɔt] N lanzamiento de una astronave a la luna
moonstruck ['muːnstrʌk] ADJ chiflado
moony ['muːnɪ] ADJ: **to have** ~ **eyes** estar soñando despierto, estar pensando en las musarañas
Moor [muəʳ] N moro(-a)
moor [muəʳ] N páramo ▶ VT (*ship*) amarrar ▶ VI echar las amarras
moorings ['muərɪŋz] NPL (*chains*) amarras *fpl*; (*place*) amarradero *sg*
Moorish ['muərɪʃ] ADJ moro; (*architecture*) árabe
moorland ['muələnd] N páramo, brezal *m*
moose [muːs] N *pl inv* alce *m*
moot [muːt] VT proponer para la discusión, sugerir ▶ ADJ: ~ **point** punto discutible
mop [mɔp] N fregona; (*of hair*) melena ▶ VT fregar ▶ **mop up** VT limpiar
mope [məup] VI estar deprimido ▶ **mope about, mope around** VI andar abatido
moped ['məupɛd] N ciclomotor *m*
moquette [mɔ'kɛt] N moqueta
MOR ADJ ABBR (*Mus*: = *middle-of-the-road*) para el gran público
moral ['mɔrl] ADJ moral ▶ N moraleja; **morals** NPL moralidad *f*, moral *f*
morale [mɔ'rɑːl] N moral *f*
morality [mə'rælɪtɪ] N moralidad *f*
moralize ['mɔrəlaɪz] VI: **to** ~ **(about)** moralizar (sobre)
morally ['mɔrəlɪ] ADV moralmente
moral victory N victoria moral

morass [mə'ræs] N pantano
moratorium [mɔrə'tɔːrɪəm] N moratoria
morbid ['mɔːbɪd] ADJ (*interest*) morboso; (*Med*) mórbido

KEYWORD

more [mɔːʳ] ADJ **1** (*greater in number etc*) más; **more people/work than before** más gente/trabajo que antes
2 (*additional*) más; **do you want (some) more tea?** ¿quieres más té?; **is there any more wine?** ¿queda vino?; **it'll take a few more weeks** tardará unas semanas más; **it's 2 kms more to the house** faltan 2 km para la casa; **more time/letters than we expected** más tiempo del que/más cartas de las que esperábamos; **I have no more money, I don't have any more money** (ya) no tengo más dinero
▶ PRON (*greater amount, additional amount*) más; **more than 10** más de 10; **it cost more than the other one/than we expected** costó más que el otro/más de lo que esperábamos; **is there any more?** ¿hay más?; **I want more** quiero más; **and what's more ...** y además ...; **many/much more** muchos(-as) más, mucho(-a) más
▶ ADV más; **more dangerous/easily (than)** más peligroso/fácilmente (que); **more and more expensive** cada vez más caro; **more or less** más o menos; **more than ever** más que nunca; **she doesn't live here any more** ya no vive aquí

moreover [mɔː'rəuvəʳ] ADV además, por otra parte
morgue [mɔːg] N depósito de cadáveres
MORI ['mɔːrɪ] N ABBR (*BRIT*) = **Market and Opinion Research Institute**
moribund ['mɔrɪbʌnd] ADJ moribundo
Mormon ['mɔːmən] N mormón(-ona) *m/f*
morning ['mɔːnɪŋ] N (*gen*) mañana; (*early morning*) madrugada; **in the** ~ por la mañana; **7 o'clock in the** ~ las 7 de la mañana; **this** ~ esta mañana
morning-after pill ['mɔːnɪŋ'ɑːftə-] N píldora del día después
morning sickness N (*Med*) náuseas *fpl* del embarazo
Moroccan [mə'rɔkən] ADJ, N marroquí *mf*
Morocco [mə'rɔkəu] N Marruecos *m*
moron ['mɔːrɔn] N imbécil *mf*
morose [mə'rəus] ADJ hosco, malhumorado
morphine ['mɔːfiːn] N morfina
morris dancing ['mɔrɪs] N (*BRIT*) *baile tradicional inglés en el que se llevan cascabeles en la ropa*
Morse [mɔːs] N (*also:* **Morse code**) (código) morse *m*

morsel ['mɔːsl] N (of food) bocado

mortal ['mɔːtl] ADJ, N mortal m

mortality [mɔː'tælɪtɪ] N mortalidad f

mortality rate N tasa de mortalidad

mortally ['mɔːtəlɪ] ADV mortalmente

mortar ['mɔːtəʳ] N argamasa; (implement) mortero

mortgage ['mɔːgɪdʒ] N hipoteca ▶ VT hipotecar; **to take out a ~** sacar una hipoteca

mortgage company N (US) ≈ banco hipotecario

mortgagee [mɔːgə'dʒiː] N acreedor(a) m/f hipotecario(-a)

mortgager ['mɔːgədʒəʳ] N deudor(a) m/f hipotecario(-a)

mortice ['mɔːtɪs] = **mortise**

mortician [mɔː'tɪʃən] N (US) director(a) m/f de pompas fúnebres

mortification ['mɔːtɪfɪ'keɪʃən] N mortificación f, humillación f

mortified ['mɔːtɪfaɪd] ADJ: **I was ~** me dio muchísima vergüenza

mortise ['mɔːtɪs], **mortise lock** N cerradura de muesca

mortuary ['mɔːtjuərɪ] N depósito de cadáveres

mosaic [məu'zeɪɪk] N mosaico

Moscow ['mɔskəu] N Moscú m

Moslem ['mɔzləm] ADJ, N = **Muslim**

mosque [mɔsk] N mezquita

mosquito [mɔs'kiːtəu] (pl **mosquitoes**) N mosquito, zancudo (LAM)

moss [mɔs] N musgo

mossy ['mɔsɪ] ADJ musgoso, cubierto de musgo

most [məust] ADJ la mayor parte de, la mayoría de ▶ PRON la mayor parte, la mayoría ▶ ADV el más; (very) muy; **the ~** (also: + adjective) el más; **~ of them** la mayor parte de ellos; **I saw the ~** yo fui el que más vi; **at the (very) ~** a lo sumo, todo lo más; **to make the ~ of** aprovechar (al máximo); **a ~ interesting book** un libro interesantísimo

mostly ['məustlɪ] ADV en su mayor parte, principalmente

MOT N ABBR (BRIT: = Ministry of Transport): **the ~ (test)** ≈ la ITV

motel [məu'tɛl] N motel m

moth [mɔθ] N mariposa nocturna; (clothes moth) polilla

mothball ['mɔθbɔːl] N bola de naftalina

moth-eaten ['mɔθiːtn] ADJ apolillado

mother ['mʌðəʳ] N madre f ▶ ADJ materno ▶ VT (care for) cuidar (como una madre)

mother board N (Comput) placa madre

motherhood ['mʌðəhud] N maternidad f

mother-in-law ['mʌðərɪnlɔː] N suegra

motherly ['mʌðəlɪ] ADJ maternal

mother-of-pearl ['mʌðərəv'pəːl] N nácar m

Mother's Day N Día m de la Madre

mother's help N niñera

mother-to-be ['mʌðətə'biː] N futura madre

mother tongue N lengua materna

mothproof ['mɔθpruːf] ADJ a prueba de polillas

motif [məu'tiːf] N motivo; (theme) tema m

motion ['məuʃən] N movimiento; (gesture) ademán m, señal f; (at meeting) moción f; (BRIT: also: **bowel motion**) evacuación f intestinal ▶ VT, VI: **to ~ (to) sb to do sth** hacer señas a algn para que haga algo; **to be in ~** (vehicle) estar en movimiento; **to set in ~** poner en marcha; **to go through the motions of doing sth** (fig) hacer algo mecánicamente or sin convicción

motionless ['məuʃənlɪs] ADJ inmóvil

motion picture N película

motivate ['məutɪveɪt] VT motivar

motivated ['məutɪveɪtɪd] ADJ motivado

motivation [məutɪ'veɪʃən] N motivación f

motivational research [məutɪ'veɪʃənl-] N estudios mpl de motivación

motive ['məutɪv] N motivo; **from the best motives** con las mejores intenciones

motley ['mɔtlɪ] ADJ variopinto

motor ['məutəʳ] N motor m; (BRIT inf: vehicle) coche m, carro (LAM), automóvil m, auto m (LAM) ▶ ADJ motor(a), motriz

motorbike ['məutəbaɪk] N moto f

motorboat ['məutəbəut] N lancha motora

motorcade ['məutəkeɪd] N desfile m de automóviles

motorcar ['məutəkaːʳ] N (BRIT) coche m, carro (LAM), automóvil m, auto m (LAM)

motorcoach ['məutəkəutʃ] N autocar m, autobús m, camión m (LAM)

motorcycle ['məutəsaɪkl] N motocicleta

motorcycle racing N motociclismo

motorcyclist ['məutəsaɪklɪst] N motociclista mf

motoring ['məutərɪŋ] N (BRIT) automovilismo ▶ ADJ (accident, offence) de tráfico or tránsito

motorist ['məutərɪst] N conductor(a) m/f, automovilista mf

motorize ['məutəraɪz] VT motorizar

motor oil N aceite m para motores

motor racing N (BRIT) carreras fpl de coches, automovilismo

motor scooter N vespa®

motor vehicle N automóvil m

motorway ['məutəweɪ] N (BRIT) autopista

mottled ['mɔtld] ADJ moteado

motto ['mɔtəu] (pl **mottoes**) N lema m; (watchword) consigna

mould, (US) mold [məuld] N molde m; (mildew) moho ▶ VT moldear; (fig) formar

moulder, (US) **molder** ['məuldə^r] vi (decay) decaer

moulding, (US) **molding** ['məuldɪŋ] N (Arch) moldura

mouldy, (US) **moldy** ['məuldɪ] ADJ enmohecido

moult, (US) **molt** [məult] vi mudar la piel; (bird) mudar las plumas

mound [maund] N montón m, montículo

mount [maunt] N monte m; (horse) montura; (for jewel etc) engarce m; (for picture) marco ▶ vt montar en, subir a; (stairs) subir; (exhibition) montar; (attack) lanzar; (stamp) pegar, fijar; (picture) enmarcar ▶ vi (also: **mount up**: increase) aumentar; (on horse) montar

mountain ['mauntɪn] N montaña ▶ cpd de montaña; **to make a ~ out of a molehill** hacer una montaña de un grano de arena

mountain bike N bicicleta de montaña

mountaineer [mauntɪ'nɪə^r] N montañero(-a), alpinista mf, andinista mf (LAm)

mountaineering [mauntɪ'nɪərɪŋ] N montañismo, alpinismo, andinismo (LAm)

mountainous ['mauntɪnəs] ADJ montañoso

mountain range N sierra

mountain rescue team N equipo de rescate de montaña

mountainside ['mauntɪnsaɪd] N ladera de la montaña

mounted ['mauntɪd] ADJ montado

Mount Everest N Monte m Everest

mourn [mɔ:n] vt llorar, lamentar ▶ vi: **to ~ for** llorar la muerte de, lamentarse por

mourner ['mɔ:nə^r] N doliente mf

mournful ['mɔ:nful] ADJ triste, lúgubre

mourning ['mɔ:nɪŋ] N luto ▶ cpd (dress) de luto; **in ~** de luto

mouse [maus] (pl **mice** [maɪs]) N (also Comput) ratón m

mouse mat, mouse pad N (Comput) alfombrilla, almohadilla

mousetrap ['maustræp] N ratonera

mousse [mu:s] N (Culin) mousse f; (for hair) espuma (moldeadora)

moustache [məs'ta:ʃ], (US) **mustache** ['mʌstæʃ] N bigote m

mousy ['mausɪ] ADJ (person) tímido; (hair) pardusco

mouth [mauθ] (pl **mouths** [-ðz]) N boca; (of river) desembocadura

mouthful ['mauθful] N bocado

mouth organ N armónica

mouthpiece ['mauθpi:s] N (of musical instrument) boquilla; (Tel) micrófono; (spokesman) portavoz mf

mouth-to-mouth ['mauθtə'mauθ] ADJ (also: **mouth-to-mouth resuscitation**) boca a boca m

mouthwash ['mauθwɔʃ] N enjuague m bucal

mouth-watering ['mauθwɔ:tərɪŋ] ADJ apetitoso

movable ['mu:vəbl] ADJ movible

move [mu:v] N (movement) movimiento; (in game) jugada; (: turn to play) turno; (change of house) mudanza ▶ vt mover; (emotionally) conmover; (Pol: resolution etc) proponer ▶ vi (gen) moverse; (traffic) circular; (Brit: also: **move house**) trasladarse, mudarse; **to get a ~ on** darse prisa; **to ~ sb to do sth** mover a algn a hacer algo; **to be moved** estar conmovido

▶ **move about, move around** vi moverse; (travel) viajar

▶ **move along** vi (stop loitering) circular; (along seat etc) correrse

▶ **move away** vi (leave) marcharse

▶ **move back** vi (return) volver

▶ **move down** vt (demote) degradar

▶ **move forward** vi avanzar ▶ vt adelantar

▶ **move in** vi (to a house) instalarse

▶ **move off** vi ponerse en camino

▶ **move on** vi seguir viaje ▶ vt (onlookers) hacer circular

▶ **move out** vi (of house) mudarse

▶ **move over** vi hacerse a un lado, correrse

▶ **move up** vi subir; (employee) ascender

movement ['mu:vmənt] N movimiento; (Tech) mecanismo; **~ (of the bowels)** (Med) evacuación f

mover ['mu:və^r] N proponente mf

movie ['mu:vɪ] N película; **to go to the movies** ir al cine

movie camera N cámara cinematográfica

moviegoer ['mu:vɪgəuə^r] N (US) aficionado(-a) al cine

movie theater N (US) cine m

moving ['mu:vɪŋ] ADJ (emotional) conmovedor(a); (that moves) móvil; (instigating) motor(a)

mow [məu] (pt **mowed**, pp **mowed** or **mown** [məun]) vt (grass) cortar; (corn) segar; (also: **mow down**: shoot) acribillar

mower ['məuə^r] N (also: **lawnmower**) cortacésped m

Mozambique [məuzæm'bi:k] N Mozambique m

MP N ABBR (= Military Police) PM; (Brit) = **Member of Parliament**; (Canada) = **Mounted Police**

mpg N ABBR (= miles per gallon) 30 mpg = 9.4 l. per 100 km

mph ABBR (= miles per hour) 60 mph = 96 km/h

MPhil N ABBR (= Master of Philosophy) título universitario de postgrado; see also **master's degree**

MPS N ABBR (Brit) = **Member of the Pharmaceutical Society**

MP3 ['ɛmpiːˈθriː] N MP3 m

MP3 player N reproductor m MP3

Mr, Mr. ['mɪstəʳ] N: **Mr Smith** (el) Sr. Smith

MRC N ABBR (*BRIT*: = *Medical Research Council*) *departamento estatal que controla la investigación médica*

MRCP N ABBR (*BRIT*) = **Member of the Royal College of Physicians**

MRCS N ABBR (*BRIT*) = **Member of the Royal College of Surgeons**

MRCVS N ABBR (*BRIT*) = **Member of the Royal College of Veterinary Surgeons**

Mrs, Mrs. ['mɪsɪz] N: ~ **Smith** (la) Sra. de Smith

MS N ABBR (= *manuscript*) MS; = **multiple sclerosis**; (*US*: = *Master of Science*) título universitario ▶ ABBR (*US*) = **Mississippi**

Ms, Ms. [mɪz] N (*Miss or Mrs*) abreviatura con la que se evita hacer expreso el estado civil de una mujer; **Ms Smith** (la) Sra. Smith

MSA N ABBR (*US*: = *Master of Science in Agriculture*) título universitario

MSc ABBR *see* **Master of Science**

MSG N ABBR = **monosodium glutamate**

MSP N ABBR (*BRIT*) = **Member of the Scottish Parliament**

MST ABBR (*US*: = *Mountain Standard Time*) hora de invierno de las Montañas Rocosas

MSW N ABBR (*US*: = *Master of Social Work*) título universitario

MT ABBR (*US*) = **Montana** ▶ N ABBR = **machine translation**

Mt ABBR (*Geo*: = *mount*) m.

mth ABBR (= *month*) m

MTV N ABBR = **music television**

much [mʌtʃ] ADJ mucho ▶ ADV, N, PRON mucho; (*before pp*) muy; **how ~ is it?** ¿cuánto es?, ¿cuánto cuesta?; **too ~** demasiado; **so ~** tanto; **it's not ~** no es mucho; **as ~ as** tanto como; **however ~ he tries** por mucho que se esfuerce; **I like it very/so ~** me gusta mucho/tanto; **thank you very ~** muchas gracias, muy agradecido

muck [mʌk] N (*dirt*) suciedad f; (*fig*) porquería ▶ **muck about, muck around** VI (*inf*) perder el tiempo; (*enjoy o.s.*) entretenerse; (*tinker*) manosear

▶ **muck in** VI (*inf*) arrimar el hombro

▶ **muck out** VT (*stable*) limpiar

▶ **muck up** VT (*inf: dirty*) ensuciar; (*spoil*) echar a perder; (*ruin*) estropear

muckraking ['mʌkreɪkɪŋ] (*fig: inf*) N amarillismo ▶ ADJ especializado en escándalos

mucky ['mʌkɪ] ADJ (*dirty*) sucio

mucus ['mjuːkəs] N mucosidad f, moco

mud [mʌd] N barro, lodo

muddle ['mʌdl] N desorden m, confusión f; (*mix-up*) embrollo, lío ▶ VT (*also*: **muddle up**) embrollar, confundir

▶ **muddle along, muddle on** VI arreglárselas de alguna manera

▶ **muddle through** VI salir del paso

muddle-headed [mʌdl'hɛdɪd] ADJ (*person*) despistado, confuso

muddy ['mʌdɪ] ADJ fangoso, cubierto de lodo

mudguard ['mʌdgɑːd] N guardabarros m inv

mudpack ['mʌdpæk] N mascarilla

mudslide ['mʌdslaɪd] N desprendimiento de tierra

mud-slinging ['mʌdslɪŋɪŋ] N injurias fpl, difamación f

muesli ['mjuːzlɪ] N muesli m

muff [mʌf] N manguito ▶ VT (*chance*) desperdiciar; (*lines*) estropear; (*shot, catch etc*) fallar; **to ~ it** fracasar

muffin ['mʌfɪn] N bollo, ≈ magdalena

muffle ['mʌfl] VT (*sound*) amortiguar; (*against cold*) abrigar

muffled ['mʌfld] ADJ sordo, apagado; (*noise etc*) amortiguado

muffler ['mʌfləʳ] N (*scarf*) bufanda; (*US: Aut*) silenciador m; (: *on motorbike*) silenciador m, mofle m

mufti ['mʌftɪ] N: **in ~** (vestido) de paisano

mug [mʌg] N (*cup*) taza alta; (*for beer*) jarra; (*inf: face*) jeta; (: *fool*) bobo ▶ VT (*assault*) atracar; **it's a ~'s game** es cosa de bobos ▶ **mug up** VT (*inf: also*: **mug up on**) empollar

mugger ['mʌgəʳ] N atracador(a) m/f

mugging ['mʌgɪŋ] N atraco callejero

muggins ['mʌgɪnz] NSG (*inf*) tonto(-a) del bote

muggy ['mʌgɪ] ADJ bochornoso

mug shot N (*inf*) foto f (para la ficha policial)

mulatto [mjuːˈlætəu] (*pl* **mulattoes**) N mulato(-a)

mulberry ['mʌlbrɪ] N (*fruit*) mora; (*tree*) morera, moral m

mule [mjuːl] N mula

mull [mʌl]: **to ~ over** vt meditar sobre

mulled [mʌld] ADJ: ~ **wine** vino caliente (*con especias*)

mullioned ['mʌlɪənd] ADJ (*window*) dividido por parteluces

multi... [mʌltɪ] PREF multi...

multi-access ['mʌltɪ'ækses] ADJ (*Comput*) multiacceso, de acceso múltiple

multicoloured, (*US*) **multicolored** ['mʌltɪkʌləd] ADJ multicolor

multifarious [mʌltɪˈfɛərɪəs] ADJ múltiple, vario

multilateral [mʌltɪˈlætərl] ADJ (*Pol*) multilateral

multi-level [mʌltɪˈlɛvl] ADJ (*US*) = **multistorey**

multimedia ['mʌltɪˈmiːdɪə] ADJ multimedia inv

multimillionaire [mʌltɪmɪljəˈnɛəʳ] N multimillonario(-a)

multinational [mʌltɪ'næʃənl] N
multinacional f ▸ ADJ multinacional
multiple ['mʌltɪpl] ADJ múltiple ▸ N
múltiplo; (BRIT: also: **multiple store**) (cadena
de) grandes almacenes mpl
multiple choice N (also: **multiple choice
test**) examen m de tipo test
multiple crash N colisión f en cadena
multiple sclerosis [-sklɪ'rəʊsɪs] N esclerosis
f múltiple
multiplex ['mʌltɪplɛks] N (also: **multiplex
cinema**) multicines m inv
multiplication [mʌltɪplɪ'keɪʃən] N
multiplicación f
multiplication table N tabla de multiplicar
multiplicity [mʌltɪ'plɪsɪtɪ] N multiplicidad f
multiply ['mʌltɪplaɪ] VT multiplicar ▸ VI
multiplicarse
multiracial [mʌltɪ'reɪʃl] ADJ multirracial
multistorey [mʌltɪ'stɔːrɪ] ADJ (BRIT: building,
car park) de muchos pisos
multi-tasking ['mʌltɪtɑːskɪŋ] N (Comput)
ejecución f de tareas múltiples, multitarea
multitude ['mʌltɪtjuːd] N multitud f
mum [mʌm] N (BRIT) mamá f ▸ ADJ: **to keep ~
(about sth)** no decir ni mu (de algo)
mumble ['mʌmbl] VT decir entre dientes ▸ VI
hablar entre dientes, musitar
mumbo jumbo ['mʌmbəʊ-] N (inf)
galimatías m inv
mummify ['mʌmɪfaɪ] VT momificar
mummy ['mʌmɪ] N (BRIT: mother) mamá f;
(embalmed) momia
mumps [mʌmps] N paperas fpl
munch [mʌntʃ] VT, VI mascar
mundane [mʌn'deɪn] ADJ mundano
municipal [mju:'nɪsɪpl] ADJ municipal
municipality [mju:nɪsɪ'pælɪtɪ] N municipio
munificence [mu:'nɪfɪsns] N munificencia
munitions [mju:'nɪʃənz] NPL municiones fpl
mural ['mjuərl] N (pintura) mural m
murder ['mə:dər] N asesinato; (in law)
homicidio ▸ VT asesinar, matar; **to commit
~** cometer un asesinato or homicidio
murderer ['mə:dərər] N asesino
murderess ['mə:dərɪs] N asesina
murderous ['mə:dərəs] ADJ homicida
murk [mə:k] N oscuridad f, tinieblas fpl
murky ['mə:kɪ] ADJ (water, past) turbio; (room)
sombrío
murmur ['mə:mər] N murmullo ▸ VT, VI
murmurar; **heart ~** soplo cardíaco
MusB, MusBac N ABBR (= Bachelor of Music)
título universitario
muscle ['mʌsl] N músculo; (fig: strength)
garra, fuerza
▸ **muscle in** VI entrometerse
muscular ['mʌskjʊlər] ADJ muscular; (person)
musculoso

muscular dystrophy N distrofia muscular
MusD, MusDoc N ABBR (= Doctor of Music)
título universitario
muse [mju:z] VI meditar ▸ N musa
museum [mju:'zɪəm] N museo
mush [mʌʃ] N gachas fpl
mushroom ['mʌʃrum] N (gen) seta, hongo;
(small) champiñón m ▸ VI (fig) crecer de la
noche a la mañana
mushy ['mʌʃɪ] ADJ (vegetables) casi hecho puré;
(story) sentimentaloide
music ['mju:zɪk] N música
musical ['mju:zɪkl] ADJ musical; (sound)
melodioso; (person) con talento musical ▸ N
(show) (comedia) musical m
musical box N = **music box**
musical chairs N juego de las sillas; (fig): **to
play ~** cambiar de puesto continuamente
musical instrument N instrumento
musical
musically ['mju:zɪklɪ] ADV melodiosamente,
armoniosamente
music box N caja de música
music centre N equipo de música
music hall N teatro de variedades
musician [mju:'zɪʃən] N músico(-a)
music stand N atril m
musk [mʌsk] N (perfume m de) almizcle m
musket ['mʌskɪt] N mosquete m
musk rat N ratón m almizclero
musk rose N (Bot) rosa almizcleña
Muslim ['mʌzlɪm] ADJ, N musulmán(-ana) m/f
muslin ['mʌzlɪn] N muselina
musquash ['mʌskwɒʃ] N (fur) piel f del ratón
almizclero
muss [mʌs] VT (inf: hair) despeinar; (: dress)
arrugar
mussel ['mʌsl] N mejillón m
must [mʌst] AUX VB (obligation): **I ~ do it** debo
hacerlo, tengo que hacerlo; (probability): **he ~
be there by now** ya debe (de) estar allí ▸ N:
it's a ~ es imprescindible
mustache ['mʌstæʃ] N (US) = **moustache**
mustard ['mʌstəd] N mostaza
mustard gas N gas m mostaza
muster ['mʌstər] VT juntar, reunir; (also:
muster up) reunir; (: courage) armarse de
mustiness ['mʌstɪnɪs] N olor m a cerrado
mustn't ['mʌsnt] = **must not**
musty ['mʌstɪ] ADJ mohoso, que huele a
humedad
mutant ['mju:tənt] ADJ, N mutante m
mutate [mju:'teɪt] VI sufrir mutación,
transformarse
mutation [mju:'teɪʃən] N mutación f
mute [mju:t] ADJ, N mudo(-a) m/f
muted ['mju:tɪd] ADJ (noise) sordo; (criticism)
callado
mutilate ['mju:tɪleɪt] VT mutilar

mutilation [mjuːtɪˈleɪʃən] N mutilación f
mutinous [ˈmjuːtɪnəs] ADJ (*troops*) amotinado; (*attitude*) rebelde
mutiny [ˈmjuːtɪnɪ] N motín m ▸ VI amotinarse
mutter [ˈmʌtəʳ] VT, VI murmurar
mutton [ˈmʌtn] N (carne f de) cordero
mutual [ˈmjuːtʃuəl] ADJ mutuo; (*friend*) común
mutually [ˈmjuːtʃuəlɪ] ADV mutuamente
Muzak® [ˈmjuːzæk] N hilo musical
muzzle [ˈmʌzl] N hocico; (*protective device*) bozal m; (*of gun*) boca ▸ VT amordazar; (*dog*) poner un bozal a
MV ABBR = **motor vessel**
MVP N ABBR (*US Sport*) = **most valuable player**
MW ABBR (*Radio*: = *medium wave*) onda media
my [maɪ] ADJ mi(s); **my house/brother** mi casa/hermano; **my sisters** mis hermanas; **I've washed my hair/cut my finger** me he lavado el pelo/cortado un dedo; **is this my pen or yours?** ¿este bolígrafo es mío o tuyo?
Myanmar [ˈmaɪænmɑːʳ] N Myanmar m

myopic [maɪˈɔpɪk] ADJ miope
myriad [ˈmɪrɪəd] N (*of people, things*) miríada
myrrh [məːʳ] N mirra
myself [maɪˈsɛlf] PRON (*reflexive*) me; (*emphatic*) yo mismo; (*after prep*) mí (mismo); *see also* **oneself**
mysterious [mɪsˈtɪərɪəs] ADJ misterioso
mysteriously [mɪsˈtɪərɪəslɪ] ADV misteriosamente
mystery [ˈmɪstərɪ] N misterio
mystery play N auto, misterio
mystic [ˈmɪstɪk] ADJ, N místico(-a) m/f
mystical [ˈmɪstɪkl] ADJ místico
mysticism [ˈmɪstɪsɪzəm] N misticismo
mystification [mɪstɪfɪˈkeɪʃən] N perplejidad f; desconcierto
mystify [ˈmɪstɪfaɪ] VT (*perplex*) dejar perplejo; (*disconcert*) desconcertar
mystique [mɪsˈtiːk] N misterio
myth [mɪθ] N mito
mythical [ˈmɪθɪkl] ADJ mítico
mythological [mɪθəˈlɔdʒɪkl] ADJ mitológico
mythology [mɪˈθɔlədʒɪ] N mitología

m

Nn

N, n [ɛn] N (*letter*) N, n *f*; **N for Nellie**, (*US*) **N for Nan** N de Navarra

N ABBR (= *North*) N

NA N ABBR (*US*: = *Narcotics Anonymous*) organización de ayuda a los drogadictos; (*US*) = **National Academy**

n/a ABBR (= *not applicable*) no interesa; (*Comm etc*) = **no account**

NAACP N ABBR (*US*) = **National Association for the Advancement of Colored People**

NAAFI ['næfɪ] N ABBR (*BRIT*: = *Navy, Army & Air Force Institutes*) servicio de cantinas etc para las fuerzas armadas

naan [nɑːn] N = **nan bread**

nab [næb] VT (*inf: grab*) coger (*SP*), agarrar (*LAM*); (: *catch out*) pillar

NACU N ABBR (*US*) = **National Association of Colleges and Universities**

nadir ['neɪdɪəʳ] N (*Astro*) nadir *m*; (*fig*) punto más bajo

NAFTA ['næftə] N ABBR (= *North Atlantic Free Trade Agreement*) TLC *m*

nag [næg] N (*pej: horse*) rocín *m* ▸ VT (*scold*) regañar; (*annoy*) fastidiar

nagging ['nægɪŋ] ADJ (*doubt*) persistente; (*pain*) continuo ▸ N quejas *fpl*

nail [neɪl] N (*human*) uña; (*metal*) clavo ▸ VT clavar; (*fig: catch*) coger (*SP*), pillar; **to pay cash on the ~** pagar a tocateja; **to ~ sb down to a date/price** hacer que algn se comprometa a una fecha/un precio

nailbrush ['neɪlbrʌʃ] N cepillo para las uñas

nailfile ['neɪlfaɪl] N lima para las uñas

nail polish N esmalte *m or* laca para las uñas

nail polish remover N quitaesmalte *m*

nail scissors NPL tijeras *fpl* para las uñas

nail varnish N (*BRIT*) = **nail polish**

Nairobi [naɪˈrəʊbɪ] N Nairobi *m*

naïve [naɪˈiːv] ADJ ingenuo

naïvely [naɪˈiːvlɪ] ADV ingenuamente

naïveté [nɑːiːˈvteɪ], **naivety** [naɪˈiːvɪtɪ] N ingenuidad *f*, candidez *f*

naked ['neɪkɪd] ADJ (*nude*) desnudo; (*flame*) expuesto al aire; **with the ~ eye** a simple vista

NAM N ABBR (*US*) = **National Association of Manufacturers**

name [neɪm] N (*gen*) nombre *m*; (*surname*) apellido; (*reputation*) fama, renombre *m* ▸ VT (*child*) poner nombre a; (*criminal*) identificar; (*price, date etc*) fijar; (*appoint*) nombrar; **by ~** de nombre; **in the ~ of** en nombre de; **what's your ~?** ¿cómo se llama usted?; **my ~ is Peter** me llamo Peter; **to give one's ~ and address** dar sus señas; **to take sb's ~ and address** apuntar las señas de algn; **to make a ~ for o.s.** hacerse famoso; **to get (o.s.) a bad ~** forjarse una mala reputación

name-drop ['neɪmdrɒp] VI: **he's always name-dropping** siempre está presumiendo de la gente que conoce

nameless ['neɪmlɪs] ADJ anónimo, sin nombre

namely ['neɪmlɪ] ADV a saber

nameplate ['neɪmpleɪt] N (*on door etc*) placa

namesake ['neɪmseɪk] N tocayo(-a)

nan bread [nɑːn-] N pan indio sin apenas levadura

nanny ['nænɪ] N niñera

nap [næp] N (*sleep*) sueñecito, siesta; **they were caught napping** les pilló desprevenidos

NAPA N ABBR (*US*: = *National Association of Performing Artists*) sindicato de trabajadores del espectáculo

napalm ['neɪpɑːm] N napalm *m*

nape [neɪp] N: **~ of the neck** nuca, cogote *m*

napkin ['næpkɪn] N (*also*: **table napkin**) servilleta

Naples ['neɪplz] N Nápoles *m*

nappy ['næpɪ] N (*BRIT*) pañal *m*

nappy liner N gasa

nappy rash N prurito

narcissism [nɑːˈsɪsɪzəm] N narcisismo

narcissus [nɑːˈsɪsəs] (*pl* **narcissi** [-saɪ]) N narciso

narcotic [nɑːˈkɒtɪk] ADJ, N narcótico;

narcotics NPL estupefacientes *mpl*, narcóticos *mpl*

narrate [nə'reɪt] VT narrar, contar

narration [nə'reɪʃən] N narración *f*, relato

narrative ['nærətɪv] N narrativa ▸ ADJ narrativo

narrator [nə'reɪtə'] N narrador(a) *m/f*

narrow ['nærəu] ADJ estrecho; (*resources, means*) escaso ▸ VI estrecharse; (*diminish*) reducirse; **to have a ~ escape** escaparse por los pelos
▸ **narrow down** VT (*search, investigation, possibilities*) restringir, limitar; (*list*) reducir

narrow gauge ADJ (*Rail*) de vía estrecha

narrowly ['nærəlɪ] ADV (*miss*) por poco

narrow-minded [nærəu'maɪndɪd] ADJ de miras estrechas

narrow-mindedness ['nærəu'maɪndɪdnɪs] N estrechez *f* de miras

NAS N ABBR (*US*) = **National Academy of Sciences**

NASA ['næsə] N ABBR (*US*: = *National Aeronautics and Space Administration*) NASA *f*

nasal ['neɪzl] ADJ nasal

Nassau ['næsɔː] N (*in Bahamas*) Nassau *m*

nastily ['nɑːstɪlɪ] ADV (*unpleasantly*) de mala manera; (*spitefully*) con rencor

nastiness ['nɑːstɪnɪs] N (*malice*) malevolencia; (*rudeness*) grosería; (*of person, remark*) maldad *f*; (*spitefulness*) rencor *m*

nasturtium [nəs'təːʃəm] N capuchina

nasty ['nɑːstɪ] ADJ (*remark*) feo; (*person*) antipático; (*revolting: taste, smell*) asqueroso; (*wound, disease etc*) peligroso, grave; **to turn ~** (*situation*) ponerse feo; (*weather*) empeorar; (*person*) ponerse negro

NAS/UWT N ABBR (*BRIT*: = *National Association of Schoolmasters/Union of Women Teachers*) sindicato de profesores

nation ['neɪʃən] N nación *f*

national ['næʃənl] ADJ nacional ▸ N súbdito(-a)

national anthem N himno nacional

National Curriculum N (*BRIT*) plan *m* general de estudios (*en Inglaterra y Gales*)

national debt N deuda pública

national dress N traje *m* típico del país

National Guard N (*US*) Guardia Nacional

National Health Service N (*BRIT*) servicio nacional de salud, ≈ INSALUD *m* (*SP*)

National Insurance N (*BRIT*) seguro social nacional, ≈ Seguridad *f* Social

nationalism ['næʃnəlɪzəm] N nacionalismo

nationalist ['næʃnəlɪst] ADJ, N nacionalista *mf*

nationality [næʃə'nælɪtɪ] N nacionalidad *f*

nationalization [næʃnəlaɪ'zeɪʃən] N nacionalización *f*

nationalize ['næʃnəlaɪz] VT nacionalizar;

nationalized industry industria nacionalizada

nationally ['næʃnəlɪ] ADV (*nationwide*) a escala nacional; (*as a nation*) como nación

national press N prensa nacional

national service N (*Mil*) servicio militar

National Trust N (*BRIT*) organización encargada de preservar el patrimonio histórico británico

nationwide ['neɪʃənwaɪd] ADJ a escala nacional

native ['neɪtɪv] N (*local inhabitant*) natural *mf*; (*in colonies*) indígena *mf*, nativo(-a) ▸ ADJ (*indigenous*) indígena; (*country*) natal; (*innate*) natural, innato; **a ~ of Russia** un(a) natural de Rusia; **~ language** lengua materna; **a ~ speaker of French** un hablante nativo de francés

Native American ADJ, N americano(-a) indígena *m/f*, amerindio(-a) *m/f*

native speaker N hablante *mf* nativo(-a)

Nativity [nə'tɪvɪtɪ] N: **the ~** Navidad *f*

nativity play N auto del nacimiento

NATO ['neɪtəu] N ABBR (= *North Atlantic Treaty Organization*) OTAN *f*

natter ['nætə'] VI (*BRIT*) charlar ▸ N: **to have a ~** charlar

natural ['nætʃrəl] ADJ natural; **death from ~ causes** (*Law*) muerte *f* por causas naturales

natural childbirth N parto natural

natural gas N gas *m* natural

natural history N historia natural

naturalist ['nætʃrəlɪst] N naturalista *mf*

naturalization [nætʃrəlaɪ'zeɪʃən] N naturalización *f*

naturalize ['nætʃrəlaɪz] VT: **to become naturalized** (*person*) naturalizarse; (*plant*) aclimatarse

naturally ['nætʃrəlɪ] ADV (*speak etc*) naturalmente; (*of course*) desde luego, por supuesto, ¡cómo no! (*LAM*); (*instinctively*) por naturaleza

naturalness ['nætʃrəlnɪs] N naturalidad *f*

natural resources NPL recursos *mpl* naturales

natural selection N selección *f* natural

natural wastage N (*Industry*) desgaste *m* natural

nature ['neɪtʃə'] N naturaleza; (*group, sort*) género, clase *f*; (*character*) modo de ser, carácter *m*; **by ~** por naturaleza; **documents of a confidential ~** documentos *mpl* de tipo confidencial

-natured ['neɪtʃəd] SUFF: **ill~** malhumorado

nature reserve N reserva natural

nature trail N camino forestal educativo

naturist ['neɪtʃərɪst] N naturista *mf*

naught [nɔːt] N = **nought**

naughtily ['nɔːtɪlɪ] ADV (*behave*) mal; (*say*) con malicia

naughtiness ['nɔ:tınıs] N travesuras *fpl*

naughty ['nɔ:tı] ADJ (*child*) travieso; (*story, film*) picante, escabroso, colorado (*LAm*)

nausea ['nɔ:sıə] N náusea

nauseate ['nɔ:sıeıt] VT dar náuseas a; (*fig*) dar asco a

nauseating ['nɔ:sıeıtıŋ] ADJ nauseabundo; (*fig*) asqueroso, repugnante

nauseous ['nɔ:sıəs] ADJ nauseabundo; **to feel ~** sentir náuseas

nautical ['nɔ:tıkl] ADJ náutico, marítimo; **~ mile** milla marina

naval ['neıvl] ADJ naval, de marina

naval officer N oficial *mf* de marina

nave [neıv] N nave *f*

navel ['neıvl] N ombligo

navigable ['nævıgəbl] ADJ navegable

navigate ['nævıgeıt] VT (*ship*) gobernar; (*river etc*) navegar por ▶ VI navegar; (*Aut*) ir de copiloto

navigation [nævı'geıʃən] N (*action*) navegación *f*; (*science*) náutica

navigator ['nævıgeıtəʳ] N navegante *mf*

navvy ['nævı] N (*BRIT*) peón *m* caminero

navy ['neıvı] N marina de guerra; (*ships*) armada, flota ▶ ADJ azul marino

navy-blue ['neıvı'blu:] ADJ azul marino

Nazareth ['næzərıθ] N Nazaret *m*

Nazi ['nɑ:tsı] ADJ, N nazi *mf*

NB ABBR (= *nota bene*) nótese; (*CANADA*) = **New Brunswick**

NBA N ABBR (*US*) = **National Basketball Association; National Boxing Association**

NBC N ABBR (*US*: = *National Broadcasting Company*) cadena de televisión

NBS N ABBR (*US*: = *National Bureau of Standards*) ≈ Oficina Nacional de Normalización

NC ABBR (*Comm etc*) = **no charge**; (*US*) = **North Carolina**

NCC N ABBR (*BRIT*: = *Nature Conservancy Council*) ≈ ICONA *m*; (*US*) = **National Council of Churches**

NCCL N ABBR (*BRIT*: = *National Council for Civil Liberties*) *asociación para la defensa de las libertades públicas*

NCO N ABBR = **non-commissioned officer**

ND, N. Dak. ABBR (*US*) = **North Dakota**

NE ABBR (*US*) = **Nebraska; New England**

NEA N ABBR (*US*) = **National Education Association**

Neapolitan [nıə'pɔlıtən] ADJ, N napolitano(-a) *m/f*

neap tide [ni:p-] N marea muerta

near [nıəʳ] ADJ (*place, relation*) cercano; (*time*) próximo ▶ ADV cerca ▶ PREP (*also*: **near to**: *space*) cerca de, junto a; (: *time*) cerca de ▶ VT acercarse a, aproximarse a; **~ here/there** cerca de aquí/de allí; **£25,000 or nearest offer** 25,000 libras o precio a discutir;

in the ~ future en fecha próxima; **the building is nearing completion** el edificio está casi terminado

nearby [nıə'baı] ADJ cercano, próximo ▶ ADV cerca

nearly ['nıəlı] ADV casi, por poco; **I ~ fell** por poco me caigo; **not ~** ni mucho menos, ni con mucho

near miss N (*shot*) tiro casi en el blanco; (*Aviat*) accidente evitado por muy poco

nearness ['nıənıs] N cercanía, proximidad *f*

nearside ['nıəsaıd] N (*Aut*: *right-hand drive*) lado izquierdo; (: *left-hand drive*) lado derecho

near-sighted [nıə'saıtıd] ADJ miope, corto de vista

neat [ni:t] ADJ (*place*) ordenado, bien cuidado; (*person*) pulcro; (*plan*) ingenioso; (*spirits*) solo

neatly ['ni:tlı] ADV (*tidily*) con esmero; (*skilfully*) ingeniosamente

neatness ['ni:tnıs] N (*tidiness*) orden *m*; (*skilfulness*) destreza, habilidad *f*

Nebr. ABBR (*US*) = **Nebraska**

nebulous ['nebjuləs] ADJ (*fig*) vago, confuso

necessarily ['nesısrılı] ADV necesariamente; **not ~** no necesariamente

necessary ['nesısrı] ADJ necesario, preciso; **he did all that was ~** hizo todo lo necesario; **if ~** si es necesario

necessitate [nı'sesıteıt] VT necesitar, precisar

necessity [nı'sesıtı] N necesidad *f*; **necessities** NPL artículos *mpl* de primera necesidad; **in case of ~** en caso de urgencia

neck [nɛk] N (*Anat*) cuello; (*of animal*) pescuezo ▶ VI besuquearse; **~ and ~** parejos; **to stick one's ~ out** (*inf*) arriesgarse

necklace ['nɛklıs] N collar *m*

neckline ['nɛklaın] N escote *m*

necktie ['nɛktaı] N (*US*) corbata

nectar ['nɛktəʳ] N néctar *m*

nectarine ['nɛktərın] N nectarina

née [neı] ADJ: **~ Scott** de soltera Scott

need [ni:d] N (*lack*) escasez *f*, falta; (*necessity*) necesidad *f* ▶ VT (*require*) necesitar; **in case of ~** en caso de necesidad; **there's no ~ for ...** no hace(n) falta ...; **to be in ~ of, have ~ of** necesitar; **10 will meet my immediate needs** 10 satisfarán mis necesidades más apremiantes; **the needs of industry** las necesidades de la industria; **I ~ it** lo necesito; **a signature is needed** se requiere una firma; **I ~ to do it** tengo que hacerlo; **you don't ~ to go** no hace falta que vayas

needle ['ni:dl] N aguja ▶ VT (*fig: inf*) picar, fastidiar

needless ['ni:dlıs] ADJ innecesario, inútil; **~ to say** huelga decir que

needlessly ['ni:dlıslı] ADV innecesariamente, inútilmente

needlework ['ni:dlwə:k] N (*activity*) costura, labor f de aguja

needn't ['ni:dnt] = **need not**

needy ['ni:dɪ] ADJ necesitado

negation [nɪ'geɪʃən] N negación f

negative ['nɛgətɪv] N (*Phot*) negativo; (*answer*) negativa; (*Ling*) negación f ▶ ADJ negativo

negative cash flow N flujo negativo de efectivo

negative equity N *situación en la que el valor de la vivienda es menor que el de la hipoteca que pesa sobre ella*

neglect [nɪ'glɛkt] VT (*one's duty*) faltar a, no cumplir con; (*child*) descuidar, desatender ▶ N (*state*) abandono; (*personal*) dejadez f; (*of child*) desatención f; (*of duty*) incumplimiento; **to ~ to do sth** olvidarse de hacer algo

neglected [nɪ'glɛktɪd] ADJ abandonado

neglectful [nɪ'glɛktful] ADJ negligente; **to be ~ of sth/sb** desatender algo/a algn

negligee ['nɛglɪʒeɪ] N (*nightdress*) salto de cama

negligence ['nɛglɪdʒəns] N negligencia

negligent ['nɛglɪdʒənt] ADJ negligente; (*casual*) descuidado

negligently ['nɛglɪdʒəntlɪ] ADV negligentemente; (*casually*) con descuido

negligible ['nɛglɪdʒɪbl] ADJ insignificante, despreciable

negotiable [nɪ'gəʊʃɪəbl] ADJ: **not ~** (*cheque*) no trasferible

negotiate [nɪ'gəʊʃɪeɪt] VT (*treaty, loan*) negociar; (*obstacle*) franquear; (*bend in road*) tomar ▶ VI: **to ~ (with)** negociar (con); **to ~ with sb for sth** tratar or negociar con algn por algo

negotiating table [nɪ'gəʊʃɪeɪtɪŋ-] N mesa de negociaciones

negotiation [nɪgəʊʃɪ'eɪʃən] N negociación f, gestión f; **negotiations** NPL negociaciones; **to enter into negotiations with sb** entrar en negociaciones con algn

negotiator [nɪ'gəʊʃɪeɪtə'] N negociador(a) m/f

neigh [neɪ] N relincho ▶ VI relinchar

neighbour, (*US*) **neighbor** ['neɪbə'] N vecino(-a)

neighbourhood, (*US*) **neighborhood** ['neɪbəhud] N (*place*) vecindad f, barrio; (*people*) vecindario

neighbourhood watch N (*Brit: also:* **neighbourhood watch scheme**) vigilancia del barrio por los propios vecinos

neighbouring, (*US*) **neighboring** ['neɪbərɪŋ] ADJ vecino

neighbourly, (*US*) **neighborly** ['neɪbəlɪ] ADJ amigable, sociable

neither ['naɪðə'] ADJ ni ▶ CONJ: **I didn't move and ~ did John** no me he movido, ni Juan tampoco ▶ PRON ninguno ▶ ADV: **~ good nor bad** ni bueno ni malo

neo ... [ni:əu] PREF neo...

Neolithic [ni:əu'lɪθɪk] ADJ neolítico

neologism [nɪ'ɔlədʒɪzəm] N neologismo

neon ['ni:ɔn] N neón m

neon light N lámpara de neón

Nepal [nɪ'pɔ:l] N Nepal m

nephew ['nɛvju:] N sobrino

nepotism ['nɛpətɪzəm] N nepotismo

nerd [nə:d] N (*inf*) primo(-a)

nerve [nə:v] N (*Anat*) nervio; (*courage*) valor m; (*impudence*) descaro, frescura; **nerves** (*nervousness*) nerviosismo msg, nervios mpl; **a fit of nerves** un ataque de nervios; **to lose one's ~** (*self-confidence*) perder el valor

nerve centre N (*Anat*) centro nervioso; (*fig*) punto neurálgico

nerve gas N gas m nervioso

nerve-racking ['nə:vrækɪŋ] ADJ angustioso

nervous ['nə:vəs] ADJ (*anxious*) nervioso; (*Anat*) nervioso; (*timid*) tímido, miedoso

nervous breakdown N crisis f nerviosa

nervously ['nə:vəslɪ] ADV nerviosamente; tímidamente

nervousness ['nə:vəsnɪs] N nerviosismo; timidez f

nervous wreck N (*inf*): **to be a ~** estar de los nervios

nervy ['nə:vɪ] ADJ: **to be ~** estar nervioso

nest [nɛst] N (*of bird*) nido ▶ VI anidar

nest egg N (*fig*) ahorros mpl

nestle ['nɛsl] VI: **to ~ down** acurrucarse

nestling ['nɛstlɪŋ] N pajarito

Net [nɛt] N: **the ~** (*Internet*) la Red

net [nɛt] N (*gen*) red f; (*fabric*) tul m ▶ ADJ (*Comm*) neto, líquido; (*weight, price, salary*) neto ▶ VT coger (*Sp*) or agarrar (*Lam*) con red; (*money: person*) cobrar; (*: deal, sale*) conseguir; (*Sport*) marcar; **~ of tax** neto; **he earns £10,000 ~ per year** gana 10,000 libras netas por año

netball ['nɛtbɔ:l] N balonred m

net curtain N visillo

Netherlands ['nɛðələndz] NPL: **the ~** los Países Bajos

net income N renta neta

netiquette ['nɛtɪkɛt] N netiqueta

net loss N pérdida neta

net profit N beneficio neto

nett [nɛt] ADJ = **net**

netting ['nɛtɪŋ] N red f, redes fpl

nettle ['nɛtl] N ortiga

network ['nɛtwə:k] N red f ▶ VT (*Radio, TV*) difundir por la red de emisores; **local area ~** red local; **there's no ~ coverage here** (*Tel*) aquí no hay cobertura

n

neuralgia [njuəˈrældʒə] N neuralgia
neurological [njuərəˈlɒdʒɪkl] ADJ
neurológico
neurosis [njuəˈrəusɪs] (pl **neuroses** [-siːz]) N
neurosis f inv
neurotic [njuəˈrɒtɪk] ADJ, N neurótico(-a) m/f
neuter [ˈnjuːtər] ADJ (Ling) neutro ▸ VT
castrar, capar
neutral [ˈnjuːtrəl] ADJ (person) neutral; (colour
etc) neutro; (Elec) neutro ▸ N (Aut) punto
muerto
neutrality [njuːˈtrælɪtɪ] N neutralidad f
neutralize [ˈnjuːtrəlaɪz] VT neutralizar
neutron [ˈnjuːtrɒn] N neutrón m
neutron bomb N bomba de neutrones
Nev. ABBR (US) = **Nevada**
never [ˈnɛvər] ADV nunca, jamás; **I ~ went** no
fui nunca; **~ in my life** jamás en la vida; see
also **mind**
never-ending [nɛvərˈɛndɪŋ] ADJ
interminable, sin fin
nevertheless [nɛvəðəˈlɛs] ADV sin embargo,
no obstante
new [njuː] ADJ nuevo; (recent) reciente;
as good as ~ como nuevo
New Age N Nueva era
newbie [ˈnjuːbɪ] N recién llegado(-a) m/f
newborn [ˈnjuːbɔːn] ADJ recién nacido
newcomer [ˈnjuːkʌmər] N recién venido or
llegado
new-fangled [ˈnjuːfæŋgld] ADJ (pej)
modernísimo
new-found [ˈnjuːfaund] ADJ (friend) nuevo;
(enthusiasm) recién adquirido
New Guinea N Nueva Guinea
newly [ˈnjuːlɪ] ADV recién
newly-weds [ˈnjuːlɪwɛdz] NPL recién casados
new moon N luna nueva
newness [ˈnjuːnɪs] N novedad f; (fig)
inexperiencia
news [njuːz] N noticias fpl; **a piece of ~**
una noticia; **the ~** (Radio, TV) las noticias fpl,
el telediario; **good/bad ~** buenas/malas
noticias fpl; **financial ~** noticias fpl
financieras
news agency N agencia de noticias
newsagent [ˈnjuːzeɪdʒənt] N (Brit)
vendedor(a) m/f de periódicos
news bulletin N (Radio, TV) noticiario
newscaster [ˈnjuːzkɑːstər] N presentador(a)
m/f, locutor(a) m/f
news dealer N (US) = **newsagent**
news flash N noticia de última hora
newsletter [ˈnjuːzlɛtər] N hoja informativa,
boletín m
newspaper [ˈnjuːzpeɪpər] N periódico, diario;
daily ~ diario; **weekly ~** periódico semanal
newsprint [ˈnjuːzprɪnt] N papel m de
periódico

newsreader [ˈnjuːzriːdər] N = **newscaster**
newsreel [ˈnjuːzriːl] N noticiario
newsroom [ˈnjuːzruːm] N (Press, Radio, TV)
sala de redacción
news stand N quiosco or puesto de periódicos
newsworthy [ˈnjuːzwəːðɪ] ADJ: **to be ~** ser de
interés periodístico
newt [njuːt] N tritón m
new town N (Brit) ciudad f nueva (construida
con subsidios estatales)
New Year N Año Nuevo; **Happy ~!** ¡Feliz Año
Nuevo!; **to wish sb a happy ~** desear a algn
un feliz Año Nuevo
New Year's Day N Día m de Año Nuevo
New Year's Eve N Nochevieja
New York [-ˈjɔːk] N Nueva York
New Zealand [ˈziːlənd] N Nueva Zelanda
(Sp), Nueva Zelandia (Lam) ▸ ADJ
neozelandés(-esa)
New Zealander [-ˈziːləndər] N
neozelandés(-esa) m/f
next [nɛkst] ADJ (house, room) vecino, de al
lado; (meeting) próximo; (page) siguiente
▸ ADV después; **the ~ day** el día siguiente;
~ time la próxima vez; **~ year** el año próximo
or que viene; **~ month** el mes que viene or
entrante; **the week after ~** no la semana
que viene sino la otra; **"turn to the ~ page"**
"vuelva a la página siguiente"; **you're ~** le
toca; **~ to** prep junto a, al lado de; **~ to**
nothing casi nada
next door ADV en la casa de al lado ▸ ADJ
vecino, de al lado
next-of-kin [ˈnɛkstəvˈkɪn] N pariente(s) m(pl)
más cercano(s)
NF N ABBR (Brit Pol: = National Front) partido
político de la extrema derecha ▸ ABBR (Canada)
= **Newfoundland**
NFL N ABBR (US) = **National Football League**
Nfld. ABBR (Canada) = **Newfoundland**
NG ABBR (US) = **National Guard**
NGO N ABBR (= non-governmental organization)
ONG f
NH ABBR (US) = **New Hampshire**
NHL N ABBR (US) = **National Hockey League**
NHS N ABBR (Brit) = **National Health Service**
NI ABBR = **Northern Ireland**; (Brit) = **National**
Insurance
nib [nɪb] N plumilla
nibble [ˈnɪbl] VT mordisquear
Nicaragua [nɪkəˈrægjuə] N Nicaragua
Nicaraguan [nɪkəˈrægjuən] ADJ, N
nicaragüense mf
Nice [niːs] N Niza
nice [naɪs] ADJ (likeable) simpático, majo;
(kind) amable; (pleasant) agradable; (attractive)
bonito, mono; (distinction) fino; (taste, smell,
meal) rico
nice-looking [ˈnaɪslukɪŋ] ADJ guapo

nicely ['naɪslɪ] ADV amablemente; (of health etc) bien; **that will do ~** perfecto
niceties ['naɪsɪtɪz] NPL detalles mpl
niche [niːʃ] N (Arch) nicho, hornacina
nick [nɪk] N (wound) rasguño; (cut, indentation) mella, muesca ▸ VT (cut) cortar; (inf) birlar, mangar; (: arrest) pillar; **in the ~ of time** justo a tiempo; **in good ~** en buen estado; **to ~ o.s.** cortarse
nickel ['nɪkl] N níquel m; (US) moneda de 5 centavos
nickname ['nɪkneɪm] N apodo, mote m ▸ VT apodar
Nicosia [nɪkə'siːə] N Nicosia
nicotine ['nɪkətiːn] N nicotina
nicotine patch N parche m de nicotina
niece [niːs] N sobrina
nifty ['nɪftɪ] ADJ (inf: car, jacket) elegante, chulo; (: gadget, tool) ingenioso
Niger ['naɪdʒəʳ] N (country, river) Níger m
Nigeria [naɪ'dʒɪərɪə] N Nigeria
Nigerian [naɪ'dʒɪərɪən] ADJ, N nigeriano(-a) m/f
niggardly ['nɪgədlɪ] ADJ (person) avaro, tacaño, avariento; (allowance, amount) miserable
nigger ['nɪgəʳ] N (inf!: highly offensive) negro(-a)
niggle ['nɪgl] VT preocupar ▸ VI (complain) quejarse; (fuss) preocuparse por minucias
niggling ['nɪglɪŋ] ADJ (detail: trifling) nimio, insignificante; (: annoying) molesto; (doubt, pain) constante
night [naɪt] N (gen) noche f; (evening) tarde f; **last ~** anoche; **the ~ before last** anteanoche, antes de ayer por la noche; **at ~**, **by ~** de noche, por la noche; **in the ~**, **during the ~** durante la noche, por la noche
night-bird ['naɪtbəːd] N (fig) trasnochador(a) m/f, madrugador(a) m/f (LAM)
nightcap ['naɪtkæp] N (drink) bebida que se toma antes de acostarse
night club N club nocturno, discoteca
nightdress ['naɪtdrɛs] N (BRIT) camisón m
nightfall ['naɪtfɔːl] N anochecer m
nightgown ['naɪtgaun], (BRIT) **nightie** ['naɪtɪ] N = **nightdress**
nightingale ['naɪtɪŋgeɪl] N ruiseñor m
night life N vida nocturna
nightly ['naɪtlɪ] ADJ de todas las noches ▸ ADV todas las noches, cada noche
nightmare ['naɪtmɛəʳ] N pesadilla
night porter N guardián m nocturno
night safe N caja fuerte
night school N clase(s) f(pl) nocturna(s)
nightshade ['naɪtʃeɪd] N: **deadly ~** (Bot) belladona
night shift N turno nocturno or de noche
night-time ['naɪttaɪm] N noche f
night watchman N (irreg) vigilante m nocturno, sereno

nihilism ['naɪɪlɪzəm] N nihilismo
nil [nɪl] N (BRIT Sport) cero, nada
Nile [naɪl] N: **the ~** el Nilo
nimble ['nɪmbl] ADJ (agile) ágil, ligero; (skilful) diestro
nimbly ['nɪmblɪ] ADV ágilmente; con destreza
nine [naɪn] NUM nueve
9-11, Nine-Eleven [naɪn'lɛvn] N 11-S m
nineteen ['naɪn'tiːn] NUM diecinueve
nineteenth [naɪn'tiːnθ] ADJ decimonoveno, decimonono
ninetieth ['naɪntɪɪθ] ADJ nonagésimo
ninety ['naɪntɪ] NUM noventa
ninth [naɪnθ] ADJ noveno
nip [nɪp] VT (pinch) pellizcar; (bite) morder ▸ VI (BRIT inf): **to ~ out/down/up** salir/bajar/subir un momento ▸ N (drink) trago
nipple ['nɪpl] N (Anat) pezón m; (of bottle) tetilla; (Tech) boquilla, manguito
nippy ['nɪpɪ] ADJ (BRIT: person) rápido; (US: taste) picante; **it's a very ~ car** es un coche muy potente para el tamaño que tiene
nit [nɪt] N (of louse) liendre f; (inf: idiot) imbécil mf
nit-pick ['nɪtpɪk] VI (inf) sacar punta a todo
nitrogen ['naɪtrədʒən] N nitrógeno
nitroglycerin, nitroglycerine ['naɪtrəu'glɪsəriːn] N nitroglicerina
nitty-gritty ['nɪtɪ'grɪtɪ] N (inf): **to get down to the ~** ir al grano
nitwit ['nɪtwɪt] N cretino(-a)
NJ ABBR (US) = **New Jersey**
NLF N ABBR (= National Liberation Front) FLN m
NLRB N ABBR (US: = National Labor Relations Board) organismo de protección al trabajador
NM, N. Mex. ABBR (US) = **New Mexico**

(KEYWORD)

no [nəu] ADV (opposite of "yes") no; **are you coming? — no (I'm not)** ¿vienes? — no; **would you like some more? — no thank you** ¿quieres más? — no gracias
▸ ADJ **1** (not any): **I have no money/time/ books** no tengo dinero/tiempo/libros; **no other man would have done it** ningún otro lo hubiera hecho
2: **"no entry"** "prohibido el paso"; **"no smoking"** "prohibido fumar"
▸ N (pl **noes**) no m

no. ABBR (= number) nº, núm.
nobble ['nɔbl] VT (BRIT inf: bribe) sobornar; (catch) pescar; (Racing) drogar
Nobel prize [nəu'bɛl-] N premio Nobel
nobility [nəu'bɪlɪtɪ] N nobleza
noble ['nəubl] ADJ (person) noble; (title) de nobleza
nobleman ['nəublmən] N (irreg) noble m

nobly ['nəublɪ] ADV (*selflessly*) noblemente
nobody ['nəubədɪ] PRON nadie
no-claims bonus ['nəukleɪmz-] N bonificación *f* por carencia de reclamaciones
nocturnal [nɔk'tə:nl] ADJ nocturno
nod [nɔd] VI saludar con la cabeza; (*in agreement*) asentir con la cabeza ▶ VT: **to ~ one's head** inclinar la cabeza ▶ N inclinación *f* de cabeza; **they nodded their agreement** asintieron con la cabeza ▶ **nod off** VI cabecear
no-fly zone [nəu'flaɪ-] N zona de exclusión aérea
noise [nɔɪz] N ruido; (*din*) escándalo, estrépito
noisily ['nɔɪzɪlɪ] ADV ruidosamente, estrepitosamente
noisy ['nɔɪzɪ] ADJ (*gen*) ruidoso; (*child*) escandaloso
nomad ['nəumæd] N nómada *mf*
nomadic [nəu'mædɪk] ADJ nómada
no man's land N tierra de nadie
nominal ['nɔmɪnl] ADJ nominal
nominate ['nɔmɪneɪt] VT (*propose*) proponer; (*appoint*) nombrar
nomination [nɔmɪ'neɪʃən] N propuesta; nombramiento
nominee [nɔmɪ'ni:] N candidato(-a)
non... [nɔn] PREF no, des..., in...
nonalcoholic [nɔnælkə'hɔlɪk] ADJ sin alcohol
nonaligned [nɔnə'laɪnd] ADJ no alineado
nonarrival [nɔnə'raɪvl] N falta de llegada
nonce word [nɔns-] N hápax *m*
nonchalant ['nɔnʃələnt] ADJ indiferente
noncommissioned [nɔnkə'mɪʃənd] ADJ: **~ officer** suboficial *mf*
noncommittal ['nɔnkə'mɪtl] ADJ (*reserved*) reservado; (*uncommitted*) evasivo
nonconformist [nɔnkən'fɔ:mɪst] ADJ inconformista ▶ N inconformista *mf*; (BRIT Rel) no conformista *mf*
noncontributory [nɔnkən'trɪbjutərɪ] ADJ: **~ pension scheme** *or* (US) **plan** fondo de pensiones no contributivo
noncooperation ['nɔnkəuɔpə'reɪʃən] N no cooperación *f*
nondescript ['nɔndɪskrɪpt] ADJ anodino, soso
none [nʌn] PRON ninguno(-a) ▶ ADV de ninguna manera; **~ of you** ninguno de vosotros; **I've ~ left** no me queda ninguno(-a); **he's ~ the worse for it** no le ha perjudicado; **I have ~** no tengo ninguno; **~ at all** (*not one*) ni uno
nonentity [nɔ'nentɪtɪ] N cero a la izquierda, nulidad *f*
nonessential [nɔnɪ'senʃl] ADJ no esencial ▶ N: **nonessentials** cosas *fpl* secundarias *or* sin importancia

nonetheless [nʌnðə'lɛs] ADV sin embargo, no obstante, aún así
non-EU [nɔni'ju:] ADJ (*citizen, passport*) no comunitario; (*imports*) de fuera de la Unión Europea
non-event [nɔnɪ'vɛnt] N acontecimiento sin importancia; **it was a ~** no pasó absolutamente nada
nonexecutive [nɔnɪg'zɛkjutɪv] ADJ: **~ director** director *m* no ejecutivo
nonexistent [nɔnɪg'zɪstənt] ADJ inexistente
non-fiction [nɔn'fɪkʃən] N no ficción *f*
nonintervention [nɔnɪntə'vɛnʃən] N no intervención *f*
no-no ['nəunəu] N (*inf*): **it's a ~** de eso ni hablar
non obst. ABBR (= *non obstante*: *notwithstanding*) no obstante
no-nonsense [nəu'nɔnsəns] ADJ sensato
nonpayment [nɔn'peɪmənt] N falta de pago
nonplussed [nɔn'plʌst] ADJ perplejo
non-profit-making [nɔn'prɔfɪtmeɪkɪŋ] ADJ no lucrativo
nonsense ['nɔnsəns] N tonterías *fpl*, disparates *fpl*; **~!** ¡qué tonterías!; **it is ~ to say that ...** es absurdo decir que ...
nonsensical [nɔn'sɛnsɪkl] ADJ disparatado, absurdo
nonshrink [nɔn'ʃrɪŋk] ADJ que no encoge
nonskid [nɔn'skɪd] ADJ antideslizante
non-smoker ['nɔn'sməukəʳ] N no fumador(a) *m/f*
non-smoking ['nɔn'sməukɪŋ] ADJ (de) no fumador
nonstarter [nɔn'stɑ:təʳ] N: **it's a ~** no tiene futuro
non-stick ['nɔn'stɪk] ADJ (*pan, surface*) antiadherente
nonstop ['nɔn'stɔp] ADJ continuo; (*Rail*) directo ▶ ADV sin parar
nontaxable [nɔn'tæksəbl] ADJ: **~ income** renta no imponible
non-U ['nɔnju:] ADJ ABBR (BRIT *inf*: = *non-upper class*) que no pertenece a la clase alta
nonvolatile [nɔn'vɔlətaɪl] ADJ: **~ memory** (*Comput*) memoria permanente
nonvoting [nɔn'vəutɪŋ] ADJ: **~ shares** acciones *fpl* sin derecho a voto
non-White ['nɔn'waɪt] ADJ de color ▶ N (*person*) persona de color
noodles ['nu:dlz] NPL tallarines *mpl*
nook [nuk] N rincón *m*; **nooks and crannies** escondrijos *mpl*
noon [nu:n] N mediodía *m*
no-one ['nəuwʌn] PRON = **nobody**
noose [nu:s] N lazo corredizo
nor [nɔ:ʳ] CONJ = **neither** ▶ ADV *see* **neither**
Norf ABBR (BRIT) = **Norfolk**
norm [nɔ:m] N norma

normal ['nɔ:ml] ADJ normal; **to return to ~** volver a la normalidad

normality [nɔ:'mælɪtɪ] N normalidad f

normally ['nɔ:məlɪ] ADV normalmente

Normandy ['nɔ:məndɪ] N Normandía

north [nɔ:θ] N norte m ▶ ADJ (del) norte ▶ ADV al or hacia el norte

North Africa N África del Norte

North African ADJ, N norteafricano(-a) m/f

North America N América del Norte

North American ADJ, N norteamericano(-a) m/f

Northants [nɔ:'θænts] ABBR (BRIT) = **Northamptonshire**

northbound ['nɔ:θbaund] ADJ en dirección al norte

Northd ABBR (BRIT) = **Northumberland**

north-east [nɔ:θ'i:st] N nor(d)este m

northeastern [nɔ:θ'i:stən] ADJ nor(d)este, del nor(d)este

northerly ['nɔ:ðəlɪ] ADJ (point, direction) hacia el norte, septentrional; (wind) del norte

northern ['nɔ:ðən] ADJ norteño, del norte

Northern Ireland N Irlanda del Norte

North Korea N Corea del Norte

North Pole N: **the ~** el Polo Norte

North Sea N: **the ~** el mar del Norte

North Sea oil N petróleo del Mar del Norte

northward ['nɔ:θwəd], **northwards** ['nɔ:θwədz] ADV hacia el norte

north-west [nɔ:θ'west] N noroeste m

northwestern [nɔ:θ'westən] ADJ noroeste, del noroeste

Norway ['nɔ:weɪ] N Noruega

Norwegian [nɔ:'wi:dʒən] ADJ noruego(-a) ▶ N noruego(-a); (Ling) noruego

nos. ABBR (= numbers) núms.

nose [nəuz] N (Anat) nariz f; (Zool) hocico; (sense of smell) olfato ▶ VI (also: **nose one's way**) avanzar con cautela; **to pay through the ~ (for sth)** (inf) pagar un dineral (por algo)

▶ **nose about, nose around** VI curiosear

nosebleed ['nəuzbli:d] N hemorragia nasal

nose-dive ['nəuzdaɪv] N picado vertical

nose drops NPL gotas fpl para la nariz

nosey ['nəuzɪ] ADJ curioso, fisgón(-ona)

nostalgia [nɔs'tældʒɪə] N nostalgia

nostalgic [nɔs'tældʒɪk] ADJ nostálgico

nostril ['nɔstrɪl] N ventana or orificio de la nariz

nosy ['nəuzɪ] ADJ = **nosey**

not [nɔt] ADV no; **~ at all** no ... en absoluto; **~ that ...** no es que ...; **it's too late, isn't it?** es demasiado tarde, ¿verdad?; **~ yet** todavía no; **~ now** ahora no; **why ~?** ¿por qué no?; **I hope ~** espero que no; **~ at all** no ... nada; (after thanks) de nada

notable ['nəutəbl] ADJ notable

notably ['nəutəblɪ] ADV especialmente; (in particular) sobre todo

notary ['nəutərɪ] N (also: **notary public**) notario(-a)

notation [nəu'teɪʃən] N notación f

notch [nɔtʃ] N muesca, corte m

▶ **notch up** VT (score, victory) apuntarse

note [nəut] N (Mus: record, letter) nota; (banknote) billete m; (tone) tono ▶ VT (observe) notar, observar; (write down) apuntar, anotar; **delivery ~** nota de entrega; **to compare notes** (fig) cambiar impresiones; **of ~** conocido, destacado; **to take ~** prestar atención a; **just a quick ~ to let you know that ...** sólo unas líneas para informarte que ...

notebook ['nəutbuk] N libreta, cuaderno; (for shorthand) libreta

notecase ['nəutkeɪs] N (BRIT) cartera, billetero

noted ['nəutɪd] ADJ célebre, conocido

notepad ['nəutpæd] N bloc m

notepaper ['nəutpeɪpə] N papel m para cartas

noteworthy ['nəutwə:ðɪ] ADJ notable, digno de atención

nothing ['nʌθɪŋ] N nada; (zero) cero; **he does ~** no hace nada; **~ new** nada nuevo; **~ much** no mucho; **for ~** (free) gratis; (in vain) en balde; **~ at all** nada en absoluto

notice ['nəutɪs] N (announcement) anuncio; (warning) aviso; (dismissal) despido; (resignation) dimisión f; (review: of play etc) reseña ▶ VT (observe) notar, observar; **to bring sth to sb's ~** (attention) llamar la atención de algn sobre algo; **to take ~ of** hacer caso de, prestar atención a; **at short ~** con poca antelación; **without ~** sin previo aviso; **advance ~** previo aviso; **until further ~** hasta nuevo aviso; **to give sb ~ of sth** avisar a algn de algo; **to hand in one's ~**, **give ~** dimitir, renunciar; **it has come to my ~ that ...** he llegado a saber que ...; **to escape or avoid ~** pasar inadvertido

noticeable ['nəutɪsəbl] ADJ evidente, obvio

notice board N (BRIT) tablón m de anuncios

notification [nəutɪfɪ'keɪʃən] N aviso; (announcement) anuncio

notify ['nəutɪfaɪ] VT: **to ~ sb (of sth)** comunicar (algo) a algn

notion ['nəuʃən] N noción f, idea; (opinion) opinión f

notions ['nəuʃənz] NPL (US) mercería

notoriety [nəutə'raɪətɪ] N notoriedad f, mala fama

notorious [nəu'tɔ:rɪəs] ADJ notorio, tristemente célebre

notoriously [nəu'tɔ:rɪəslɪ] ADV notoriamente

Notts [nɔts] ABBR (BRIT) = **Nottinghamshire**
notwithstanding [nɔtwɪθ'stændɪŋ] ADV no obstante, sin embargo; **~ this** a pesar de esto
nougat ['nuːgɑː] N turrón m
nought [nɔːt] N cero
noun [naun] N nombre m, sustantivo
nourish ['nʌrɪʃ] VT nutrir; (fig) alimentar
nourishing ['nʌrɪʃɪŋ] ADJ nutritivo, rico
nourishment ['nʌrɪʃmənt] N alimento, sustento
Nov. ABBR (= November) nov.
novel ['nɔvl] N novela ▶ ADJ (new) nuevo, original; (unexpected) insólito
novelist ['nɔvəlɪst] N novelista mf
novelty ['nɔvəltɪ] N novedad f
November [nəu'vɛmbəʳ] N noviembre m; see also **July**
novice ['nɔvɪs] N principiante mf, novato(-a); (Rel) novicio(-a)
NOW [nau] N ABBR (US) = **National Organization for Women**
now [nau] ADV (at the present time) ahora; (these days) actualmente, hoy día ▶ CONJ: **~ (that)** ya que, ahora que; **right ~** ahora mismo; **by ~** ya; **I'll do it just ~** ahora mismo lo hago; **~ and then, ~ and again** de vez en cuando; **from ~ on** de ahora en adelante; **between ~ and Monday** entre hoy y el lunes; **in 3 days from ~** de hoy en 3 días; **that's all for ~** eso es todo por ahora
nowadays ['nauədeɪz] ADV hoy (en) día, actualmente
nowhere ['nəuwɛəʳ] ADV (direction) a ninguna parte; (location) en ninguna parte; **~ else** en or a ninguna otra parte
no-win situation [nəu'wɪn-] N: **I'm in a ~** haga lo que haga, llevo las de perder
noxious ['nɔkʃəs] ADJ nocivo
nozzle ['nɔzl] N boquilla
NP N ABBR = **notary public**
nr ABBR (BRIT) = **near**
NS ABBR (CANADA) = **Nova Scotia**
NSC N ABBR (US) = **National Security Council**
NSF N ABBR (US) = **National Science Foundation**
NSPCC N ABBR (BRIT) = **National Society for the Prevention of Cruelty to Children**
NSW ABBR (AUSTRALIA) = **New South Wales**
NT N ABBR = **New Testament** ▶ ABBR (CANADA) = **Northwest Territories**
nth [ɛnθ] ADJ: **for the ~ time** (inf) por enésima vez
nuance ['njuːɑːns] N matiz m
nubile ['njuːbaɪl] ADJ núbil
nuclear ['njuːklɪəʳ] ADJ nuclear
nuclear disarmament N desarme m nuclear
nuclear family N familia nuclear
nuclear-free zone ['njuːklɪə'friː-] N zona desnuclearizada

nucleus ['njuːklɪəs] (pl **nuclei** ['njuːklaɪ]) N núcleo
NUCPS N ABBR (BRIT: = National Union of Civil and Public Servants) sindicato de funcionarios
nude [njuːd] ADJ, N desnudo m; **in the ~** desnudo
nudge [nʌdʒ] VT dar un codazo a
nudist ['njuːdɪst] N nudista mf
nudist colony N colonia nudista
nudity ['njuːdɪtɪ] N desnudez f
nugget ['nʌgɪt] N pepita
nuisance ['njuːsns] N molestia, fastidio; (person) pesado, latoso; **what a ~!** ¡qué lata!
NUJ N ABBR (BRIT: = National Union of Journalists) sindicato de periodistas
nuke [njuːk] (inf) N bomba atómica ▶ VT atacar con arma nuclear
null [nʌl] ADJ: **~ and void** nulo y sin efecto
nullify ['nʌlɪfaɪ] VT anular, invalidar
NUM N ABBR (BRIT: = National Union of Mineworkers) sindicato de mineros
numb [nʌm] ADJ entumecido; (fig) insensible ▶ VT quitar la sensación a, entumecer, entorpecer; **to be ~ with cold** estar entumecido de frío; **~ with fear/grief** paralizado de miedo/dolor
number ['nʌmbəʳ] N número; (numeral) número, cifra; (quantity) cantidad f ▶ VT (pages etc) numerar, poner número a; (amount to) sumar, ascender a; **reference ~** número de referencia; **telephone ~** número de teléfono; **wrong ~** (Tel) número equivocado; **opposite ~** (person) homólogo(-a); **to be numbered among** figurar entre; **a ~ of** varios, algunos; **they were ten in ~** eran diez
number plate N (BRIT) matrícula, placa
Number Ten N (BRIT: 10 Downing Street) residencia del primer ministro
numbness ['nʌmnɪs] N insensibilidad f, parálisis f inv; (due to cold) entumecimiento
numbskull ['nʌmskʌl] N (inf) papanatas mf
numeral ['njuːmərəl] N número, cifra
numerate ['njuːmərɪt] ADJ competente en aritmética
numerical [njuː'mɛrɪkl] ADJ numérico
numerous ['njuːmərəs] ADJ numeroso, muchos
nun [nʌn] N monja, religiosa
nunnery ['nʌnərɪ] N convento de monjas
nuptial ['nʌpʃəl] ADJ nupcial
nurse [nəːs] N enfermero(-a); (nanny) niñera ▶ VT (patient) cuidar, atender; (baby: BRIT) mecer; (: US) criar, amamantar; **male ~** enfermero
nursery ['nəːsərɪ] N (institution) guardería infantil; (room) cuarto de los niños; (for plants) criadero, semillero
nursery rhyme N canción f infantil

nursery school N escuela infantil

nursery slope N (BRIT Ski) cuesta para principiantes

nursing ['nəːsɪŋ] N (profession) profesión f de enfermera; (care) asistencia, cuidado ▶ ADJ (mother) lactante

nursing home N clínica de reposo

nurture ['nəːtʃəʳ] VT (child, plant) alimentar, nutrir

NUS N ABBR (BRIT: = National Union of Students) sindicato de estudiantes

NUT N ABBR (BRIT: = National Union of Teachers) sindicato de profesores

nut [nʌt] N (Tech) tuerca; (Bot) nuez f ▶ ADJ (chocolate etc) con nueces; **nuts** (Culin) frutos secos

nutcrackers ['nʌtkrækəz] NPL cascanueces m inv

nutmeg ['nʌtmɛg] N nuez f moscada

nutrient ['njuːtrɪənt] ADJ nutritivo ▶ N elemento nutritivo

nutrition [njuːˈtrɪʃən] N nutrición f, alimentación f

nutritionist [njuːˈtrɪʃənɪst] N dietista mf

nutritious [njuːˈtrɪʃəs] ADJ nutritivo

nuts [nʌts] ADJ (inf) chiflado

nutshell ['nʌtʃɛl] N cáscara de nuez; **in a ~** en resumidas cuentas

nutty ['nʌtɪ] ADJ (flavour) a frutos secos; (inf: foolish) chalado

nuzzle ['nʌzl] VI: **to ~ up to** arrimarse a

NV ABBR (US) = **Nevada**

NVQ N ABBR (BRIT: = national vocational qualification) título de formación profesional

NWT ABBR (CANADA) = **Northwest Territories**

NY ABBR (US) = **New York**

NYC ABBR (US) = **New York City**

nylon ['naɪlɔn] N nilón m ▶ ADJ de nilón

nymph [nɪmf] N ninfa

nymphomaniac ['nɪmfəuˈmeɪnɪæk] ADJ, N ninfómana

NYSE N ABBR (US) = **New York Stock Exchange**

O, o [əu] N (*letter*) O, o f; **O for Oliver,** (*US*) **O for Oboe** O de Oviedo

oaf [əuf] N zoquete *mf*

oak [əuk] N roble *m* ▶ ADJ de roble

O & M N ABBR = **organization and method**

OAP N ABBR (*BRIT*) = **old-age pensioner**

oar [ɔːʳ] N remo; **to put** *or* **shove one's ~ in** (*fig, inf*) entrometerse

oarsman ['ɔːzmən] N (*irreg*) remero

OAS N ABBR (= *Organization of American States*) OEA f

oasis [əu'eɪsɪs] (*pl* **oases** [əu'eɪsiːz]) N oasis *m inv*

oath [əuθ] N juramento; (*swear word*) palabrota; **on** (*BRIT*) *or* **under ~** bajo juramento

oatmeal ['əutmiːl] N harina de avena

oats [əuts] NPL avena

OAU N ABBR (= *Organization of African Unity*) OUA f

obdurate ['ɔbdjurɪt] ADJ (*stubborn*) terco, obstinado; (*sinner*) empedernido; (*unyielding*) inflexible, firme

OBE N ABBR (*BRIT*: = *Order of the British Empire*) título ceremonial

obedience [ə'biːdɪəns] N obediencia; **in ~ to** de acuerdo con

obedient [ə'biːdɪənt] ADJ obediente

obelisk ['ɔbɪlɪsk] N obelisco

obese [əu'biːs] ADJ obeso

obesity [əu'biːsɪtɪ] N obesidad f

obey [ə'beɪ] VT obedecer; (*instructions*) cumplir

obituary [ə'bɪtjuərɪ] N necrología

object N ['ɔbdʒɪkt] (*gen*) objeto; (*purpose*) objeto, propósito; (*Ling*) objeto, complemento ▶ VI [əb'dʒɛkt]: **to ~ to** (*attitude*) estar en contra de; (*proposal*) oponerse a; **to ~ that** objetar que; **expense is no ~** no importa lo que cueste; **I ~!** ¡protesto!; **to ~ that** objetar que

objection [əb'dʒɛkʃən] N objeción f; **I have no ~ to ...** no tengo inconveniente en que ...

objectionable [əb'dʒɛkʃənəbl] ADJ (*gen*) desagradable; (*conduct*) censurable

objective [əb'dʒɛktɪv] ADJ, N objetivo

objectively [əb'dʒɛktɪvlɪ] ADV objetivamente

objectivity [ɔbdʒɪk'tɪvɪtɪ] N objetividad f

object lesson N (*fig*) (buen) ejemplo

objector [əb'dʒɛktəʳ] N objetor(a) *m/f*

obligation [ɔblɪ'geɪʃən] N obligación f; (*debt*) deber *m*; "**without ~**" "sin compromiso"; **to be under an ~ to sb/to do sth** estar comprometido con algn/a hacer algo

obligatory [ə'blɪgətərɪ] ADJ obligatorio

oblige [ə'blaɪdʒ] VT (*do a favour for*) complacer, hacer un favor a; **to ~ sb to do sth** obligar a algn a hacer algo; **to be obliged to sb for sth** estarle agradecido a algn por algo; **anything to ~!** ¡todo sea por complacerte!

obliging [ə'blaɪdʒɪŋ] ADJ servicial, atento

oblique [ə'bliːk] ADJ oblicuo; (*allusion*) indirecto ▶ N (*Typ*) barra

obliterate [ə'blɪtəreɪt] VT arrasar; (*memory*) borrar

oblivion [ə'blɪvɪən] N olvido

oblivious [ə'blɪvɪəs] ADJ: **~ of** inconsciente de

oblong ['ɔblɔŋ] ADJ rectangular ▶ N rectángulo

obnoxious [əb'nɔkʃəs] ADJ odioso, detestable; (*smell*) nauseabundo

o.b.o. ABBR (*US*: = *or best offer*: *in classified ads*) abierto a ofertas

oboe ['əubəu] N oboe *m*

obscene [əb'siːn] ADJ obsceno

obscenity [əb'senɪtɪ] N obscenidad f

obscure [əb'skjuəʳ] ADJ oscuro ▶ VT oscurecer; (*hide: sun*) ocultar

obscurity [əb'skjuərɪtɪ] N oscuridad f; (*obscure point*) punto oscuro; **to rise from ~** salir de la nada

obsequious [əb'siːkwɪəs] ADJ servil

observable [əb'zəːvəbl] ADJ observable, perceptible

observance [əb'zəːvns] N observancia, cumplimiento; (*ritual*) práctica; **religious observances** prácticas *fpl* religiosas

observant [əb'zəːvnt] ADJ observador(a)

observation [ɔbzə'veɪʃən] N (*Med*) observación f; (*by police etc*) vigilancia

observation post N (*Mil*) puesto de observación

observatory [əb'zə:vətrɪ] N observatorio

observe [əb'zə:v] VT (*gen*) observar; (*rule*) cumplir

observer [əb'zə:vəʳ] N observador(a) *m/f*

obsess [əb'sɛs] VT obsesionar; **to be obsessed by** or **with sb/sth** estar obsesionado con algn/algo

obsession [əb'sɛʃən] N obsesión *f*

obsessive [əb'sɛsɪv] ADJ obsesivo

obsolescence [ɔbsə'lɛsns] N obsolescencia

obsolescent [ɔbsə'lɛsnt] ADJ que está cayendo en desuso

obsolete ['ɔbsəli:t] ADJ obsoleto

obstacle ['ɔbstəkl] N obstáculo; (*nuisance*) estorbo

obstacle race N carrera de obstáculos

obstetrician [ɔbstə'trɪʃən] N obstetra *mf*

obstetrics [ɔb'stɛtrɪks] N obstetricia

obstinacy ['ɔbstɪnəsɪ] N terquedad *f*, obstinación *f*; tenacidad *f*

obstinate ['ɔbstɪnɪt] ADJ terco, obstinado; (*determined*) tenaz

obstinately ['ɔbstɪnɪtlɪ] ADV tercamente, obstinadamente

obstreperous [əb'strɛpərəs] ADJ ruidoso; (*unruly*) revoltoso

obstruct [əb'strʌkt] VT (*block*) obstruir; (*hinder*) estorbar, obstaculizar

obstruction [əb'strʌkʃən] N obstrucción *f*; (*object*) estorbo, obstáculo

obstructive [əb'strʌktɪv] ADJ obstruccionista; **stop being ~!** ¡deja de poner peros!

obtain [əb'teɪn] VT (*get*) obtener; (*achieve*) conseguir; **to ~ sth (for o.s.)** conseguir or adquirir algo

obtainable [əb'teɪnəbl] ADJ asequible

obtrusive [əb'tru:sɪv] ADJ (*person*) importuno; (: *interfering*) entrometido; (*building etc*) demasiado visible

obtuse [əb'tju:s] ADJ obtuso

obverse ['ɔbvə:s] N (*of medal*) anverso; (*fig*) complemento

obviate ['ɔbvɪeɪt] VT obviar, evitar

obvious ['ɔbvɪəs] ADJ (*clear*) obvio, evidente; (*unsubtle*) poco sutil; **it's ~ that ...** está claro que ..., es evidente que ...

obviously ['ɔbvɪəslɪ] ADV obviamente, evidentemente; **~ not!** ¡por supuesto que no!; **he was ~ not drunk** era evidente que no estaba borracho; **he was not ~ drunk** no se le notaba que estaba borracho

OCAS N ABBR (= *Organization of Central American States*) ODECA *f*

occasion [ə'keɪʒən] N oportunidad *f*, ocasión *f*; (*event*) acontecimiento ▶ VT ocasionar, causar; **on that ~** esa vez, en aquella ocasión; **to rise to the ~** ponerse a la altura de las circunstancias

occasional [ə'keɪʒənl] ADJ poco frecuente, ocasional

occasionally [ə'keɪʒənlɪ] ADV de vez en cuando; **very ~** muy de tarde en tarde, en muy contadas ocasiones

occasional table N mesita

occult [ɔ'kʌlt] ADJ (*gen*) oculto

occupancy ['ɔkjupənsɪ] N ocupación *f*

occupant ['ɔkjupənt] N (*of house*) inquilino(-a); (*of boat, car*) ocupante *mf*

occupation [ɔkju'peɪʃən] N (*of house*) tenencia; (*job*) trabajo; (*pastime*) ocupaciones *fpl*; (*calling*) oficio

occupational accident [ɔkju'peɪʃənl-] N accidente *m* laboral

occupational guidance N orientación *f* profesional

occupational hazard N gajes *mpl* del oficio

occupational pension scheme N plan *m* profesional de jubilación

occupational therapy N terapia ocupacional

occupier ['ɔkjupaɪəʳ] N inquilino(-a)

occupy ['ɔkjupaɪ] VT (*seat, post, time*) ocupar; (*house*) habitar; **to ~ o.s. with** or **by doing** (*as job*) dedicarse a hacer; (*to pass time*) entretenerse haciendo; **to be occupied with sth/in doing sth** estar ocupado con algo/haciendo algo

occur [ə'kə:ʳ] VI ocurrir, suceder; **to ~ to sb** ocurrírsele a algn

occurrence [ə'kʌrəns] N suceso

ocean ['əuʃən] N océano; **oceans of** (*inf*) la mar de

ocean bed N fondo del océano

ocean-going ['əuʃəngəuɪŋ] ADJ de alta mar

Oceania [əuʃɪ'eɪə:nɪə] N Oceanía

ocean liner N buque *m* transoceánico

ochre, (*US*) **ocher** ['əukəʳ] N ocre *m*

o'clock [ə'klɔk] ADV: **it is five ~** son las cinco

OCR N ABBR = **optical character recognition/ reader**

Oct. ABBR (= *October*) oct.

octagonal [ɔk'tægənl] ADJ octagonal

octane ['ɔkteɪn] N octano; **high ~ petrol** or (*US*) **gas** gasolina de alto octanaje

octave ['ɔktɪv] N octava

October [ɔk'təubəʳ] N octubre *m*; *see also* **July**

octogenarian ['ɔktəudʒɪ'nɛərɪən] N octogenario(-a)

octopus ['ɔktəpəs] N pulpo

oculist ['ɔkjulɪst] N oculista *mf*

odd [ɔd] ADJ (*strange*) extraño, raro; (*number*) impar; (*sock, shoe etc*) suelto; **60~** 60 y pico; **at ~ times** de vez en cuando; **to be the ~ one out** estar de más; **if you have the ~ minute** si tienes unos minutos libres; *see also* **odds**

oddball [ˈɔdbɔːl] N (inf) bicho raro
oddity [ˈɔdɪtɪ] N rareza; (person) excéntrico(-a)
odd-job man [ɔdˈdʒɔb-] N (irreg) hombre m que hace chapuzas
odd jobs NPL chapuzas fpl
oddly [ˈɔdlɪ] ADV extrañamente
oddments [ˈɔdmənts] NPL (BRIT Comm) restos mpl
odds [ɔdz] NPL (in betting) puntos mpl de ventaja; **it makes no ~** da lo mismo; **at ~** reñidos(-as); **to succeed against all the ~** tener éxito contra todo pronóstico; **~ and ends** cachivaches mpl
odds-on [ɔdzˈɔn] ADJ (inf): **the ~ favourite** el máximo favorito; **it's ~ he'll come** seguro que viene
ode [əud] N oda
odious [ˈəudɪəs] ADJ odioso
odometer [ɔˈdɔmɪtəʳ] N (US) cuentakilómetros m inv
odour, (US) **odor** [ˈəudəʳ] N olor m; (unpleasant) hedor m; (perfume) perfume m
odourless, (US) **odorless** [ˈəudəlɪs] ADJ sin olor
OECD N ABBR (= Organization for Economic Cooperation and Development) OCDE f
oesophagus, (US) **esophagus** [iːˈsɔfəgəs] N esófago
oestrogen, (US) **estrogen** [ˈiːstrədʒən] N estrógeno

(KEYWORD)

of [ɔv, əv] PREP **1** (gen) de; **a friend of ours** un amigo nuestro; **a boy of 10** un chico de 10 años; **that was kind of you** eso fue muy amable de tu parte
2 (expressing quantity, amount, dates etc) de; **a kilo of flour** un kilo de harina; **there were three of them** había tres; **three of us went** tres de nosotros fuimos; **the 5th of July** el 5 de julio; **a quarter of four** (US) las cuatro menos cuarto
3 (from, out of) de; **made of wood** (hecho) de madera

Ofcom [ˈɔfkɔm] N ABBR (BRIT) = **Office of Communications**

off [ɔf] ADJ, ADV (engine, light) apagado; (tap) cerrado; (BRIT: food: bad) pasado, malo; (: milk) cortado; (cancelled) suspendido; (removed): **the lid was ~** no estaba puesta la tapadera ► PREP de; **to be ~** (leave) irse, marcharse; **to be ~ sick** estar enfermo or de baja; **a day ~** un día libre; **to have an ~ day** tener un mal día; **he had his coat ~** se había quitado el abrigo; **10% ~** (Comm) (con el) 10% de descuento; **it's a long way ~** está muy lejos; **5 km ~ (the road)** a 5 km (de la carretera); **~ the coast**

frente a la costa; **I'm ~ meat** (no longer eat/like it) paso de la carne; **on the ~ chance** por si acaso; **~ and on, on and ~** de vez en cuando; **I must be ~** tengo que irme; **to be well/badly ~** andar bien/mal de dinero; **I'm afraid the chicken is ~** desgraciadamente ya no queda pollo; **that's a bit ~, isn't it?** (fig, inf) ¡eso no se hace!

offal [ˈɔfl] N (BRIT Culin) menudillos mpl, asaduras fpl
off-centre, (US) **off-center** [ɔfˈsɛntəʳ] ADJ descentrado, ladeado
off-colour [ˈɔfˈkʌləʳ] ADJ (BRIT: ill) indispuesto; **to feel ~** sentirse or estar mal
offence, (US) **offense** [əˈfɛns] N (crime) delito; (insult) ofensa; **to take ~ at** ofenderse por; **to commit an ~** cometer un delito
offend [əˈfɛnd] VT (person) ofender ► VI: **to ~ against** (law, rule) infringir
offender [əˈfɛndəʳ] N delincuente mf; (against regulations) infractor(a) m/f
offending [əˈfɛndɪŋ] ADJ culpable; (object) molesto; (word) problemático
offense [əˈfɛns] N (US) = **offence**
offensive [əˈfɛnsɪv] ADJ ofensivo; (smell etc) repugnante ► N (Mil) ofensiva
offer [ˈɔfəʳ] N (gen) oferta, ofrecimiento; (proposal) propuesta ► VT ofrecer; **"on ~"** (Comm) "en oferta"; **to make an ~ for sth** hacer una oferta por algo; **to ~ sth to sb,** **~ sb sth** ofrecer algo a algn; **to ~ to do sth** ofrecerse a hacer algo
offering [ˈɔfərɪŋ] N (Rel) ofrenda
offer price N precio de oferta
offertory [ˈɔfətrɪ] N (Rel) ofertorio
offhand [ɔfˈhænd] ADJ informal; (brusque) desconsiderado ► ADV de improviso, sin pensarlo; **I can't tell you ~** no te lo puedo decir así de improviso or (LAM) así nomás
office [ˈɔfɪs] N (place) oficina; (room) despacho; (position) cargo, oficio; **doctor's ~** (US) consultorio; **to take ~** entrar en funciones; **through his good offices** gracias a sus buenos oficios; **O~ of Fair Trading** (BRIT) oficina que regula normas comerciales
office automation N ofimática, buromática
office bearer N (of club etc) titular mf (de una cartera)
office block, (US) **office building** N bloque m de oficinas
office boy N ordenanza m
office hours NPL horas fpl de oficina; (US Med) horas fpl de consulta
office manager N jefe(-a) m/f de oficina
officer [ˈɔfɪsəʳ] N (Mil etc) oficial mf; (of organization) director(a) m/f; (also: **police officer**) agente mf de policía
office work N trabajo de oficina

office worker N oficinista *mf*
official [ə'fɪʃl] ADJ (*authorized*) oficial, autorizado; (*strike*) oficial ▸ N funcionario(-a)
officialdom [ə'fɪʃldəm] N burocracia
officially [ə'fɪʃəlɪ] ADV oficialmente
official receiver N síndico
officiate [ə'fɪʃɪeɪt] VI (*Rel*) oficiar; **to ~ as Mayor** ejercer las funciones de alcalde; **to ~ at a marriage** celebrar una boda
officious [ə'fɪʃəs] ADJ oficioso
offing ['ɔfɪŋ] N: **in the ~** (*fig*) en perspectiva
off-key [ɔf'kiː] ADJ desafinado ▸ ADV desafinadamente
off-licence ['ɔflaɪsns] N (*Brit: shop*) tienda de bebidas alcohólicas; *ver nota*

> En el Reino Unido una *off-licence* es una tienda especializada en la venta de bebidas alcohólicas para el consumo fuera del establecimiento. De ahí su nombre, pues se necesita un permiso especial para tal venta, que está estrictamente regulada. Suelen vender además bebidas sin alcohol, tabaco, chocolate, patatas fritas etc y a menudo son parte de grandes cadenas nacionales.

off-limits [ɔf'lɪmɪts] ADJ (*US Mil*) prohibido al personal militar
off line ADJ, ADV (*Comput*) fuera de línea; (*switched off*) desconectado
off-load ['ɔfləud] VT descargar, desembarcar
off-peak ['ɔf'piːk] ADJ (*holiday*) de temporada baja; (*electricity*) de banda económica; (*ticket*) billete de precio reducido para viajar fuera de las horas punta
off-putting ['ɔfputɪŋ] ADJ (*Brit: person*) poco amable, difícil; (*behaviour*) chocante; (*remark*) desalentador(a)
off-season ['ɔf'siːzn] ADJ, ADV fuera de temporada
offset ['ɔfsɛt] VT (*irreg: like* **set**) (*counteract*) contrarrestar, compensar ▸ N (*also:* **offset printing**) offset *m*
offshoot ['ɔfʃuːt] N (*Bot*) vástago; (*fig*) ramificación *f*
offshore [ɔf'ʃɔːʳ] ADJ (*breeze, island*) costero; (*fishing*) de bajura; **~ oilfield** campo petrolífero submarino
offside ['ɔf'saɪd] N (*Aut: with right-hand drive*) lado derecho; (: *with left-hand drive*) lado izquierdo ▸ ADJ (*Sport*) fuera de juego; (*Aut: in UK*) del lado derecho; (: *in US, Europe etc*) del lado izquierdo
offspring ['ɔfsprɪŋ] N descendencia
offstage [ɔf'steɪdʒ] ADV entre bastidores
off-the-cuff [ɔfðə'kʌf] ADJ espontáneo
off-the-job [ɔfðə'dʒɔb] ADJ: **~ training** formación *f* fuera del trabajo
off-the-peg [ɔfðə'pɛg], (*US*) **off-the-rack** [ɔfðə'ræk] ADV confeccionado

off-the-record ['ɔfðə'rɛkɔːd] ADJ extraoficial, confidencial ▸ ADV extraoficialmente, confidencialmente
off-white ['ɔfwaɪt] ADJ blanco grisáceo
Ofgas ['ɔfgæs] N ABBR (*Brit: = Office of Gas Supply*) organismo que controla a las empresas del gas en Gran Bretaña
Ofgem ['ɔfdʒɛm] N ABBR (*Brit*) = **Office of Gas and Electricity Markets**
Oftel ['ɔftɛl] N ABBR (*Brit: = Office of Telecommunications*) organismo que controla las telecomunicaciones británicas
often ['ɔfn] ADV a menudo, con frecuencia, seguido (*Lam*); **how ~ do you go?** ¿cada cuánto vas?
Ofwat ['ɔfwɔt] N ABBR (*Brit: = Office of Water Services*) organismo que controla a las empresas suministradoras del agua en Inglaterra y Gales
ogle ['əugl] VT comerse con los ojos a
ogre ['əugəʳ] N ogro
OH ABBR (*US*) = **Ohio**
oh [əu] EXCL ¡ah!
OHMS ABBR (*Brit*) = **On Her/His Majesty's Service**
oil [ɔɪl] N aceite *m*; (*petroleum*) petróleo ▸ VT (*machine*) engrasar; **fried in ~** frito en aceite
oilcan ['ɔɪlkæn] N lata de aceite
oilfield ['ɔɪlfiːld] N campo petrolífero
oil filter N (*Aut*) filtro de aceite
oil-fired ['ɔɪlfaɪəd] ADJ de fueloil
oil gauge N indicador *m* del aceite
oil industry N industria petrolífera
oil level N nivel *m* del aceite
oil painting N pintura al óleo
oil refinery N refinería de petróleo
oil rig N torre *f* de perforación
oilskins ['ɔɪlskɪnz] NPL impermeable *msg*, chubasquero *sg*
oil slick N marea negra
oil tanker N petrolero; (*truck*) camión *m* cisterna
oil well N pozo (de petróleo)
oily ['ɔɪlɪ] ADJ aceitoso; (*food*) grasiento
ointment ['ɔɪntmənt] N ungüento
OK ABBR (*US*) = **Oklahoma**
O.K., okay ['əu'keɪ] EXCL O.K., ¡está bien!, ¡vale! ▸ ADJ bien ▸ N: **to give sth one's O.K.** dar el visto bueno a or aprobar algo ▸ VT dar el visto bueno a; **it's O.K. with** or **by me** estoy de acuerdo, me parece bien; **are you O.K. for money?** ¿andas or vas bien de dinero?
Okla. ABBR (*US*) = **Oklahoma**
old [əuld] ADJ viejo; (*former*) antiguo; **how ~ are you?** ¿cuántos años tienes?, ¿qué edad tienes?; **he's 10 years ~** tiene 10 años; **older brother** hermano mayor; **any ~ thing will do** sirve cualquier cosa
old age N vejez *f*

O

old-age pension ['əuldeidʒ-] N (BRIT)
jubilación f, pensión f
old-age pensioner ['əuldeidʒ-] N (BRIT)
jubilado(-a)
olden ['əuldən] ADJ antiguo
old-fashioned ['əuld'fæʃənd] ADJ anticuado,
pasado de moda
old maid N solterona
old people's home N (esp BRIT) residencia de
ancianos
old-style ['əuldstail] ADJ tradicional,
chapado a la antigua
old-time ['əuld'taim] ADJ antiguo, de antaño
old-timer [əuld'taimər] N veterano(-a); (old
person) anciano(-a)
old wives' tale N cuento de viejas, patraña
olive ['ɔliv] N (fruit) aceituna; (tree) olivo ▶ ADJ
(also: **olive-green**) verde oliva inv
olive branch N (fig): **to offer an ~ to sb**
ofrecer hacer las paces con algn
olive oil N aceite m de oliva
Olympic [əu'limpik] ADJ olímpico; **the ~
Games, the Olympics** npl los Juegos
Olímpicos, las Olimpiadas
OM N ABBR (BRIT: = Order of Merit) título
ceremonial
Oman [əu'mɑːn] N Omán m
OMB N ABBR (US: = Office of Management and
Budget) servicio que asesora al presidente en
materia presupuestaria
omelette, omelet ['ɔmlit] N tortilla, tortilla
de huevo (LAM)
omen ['əumən] N presagio
OMG ABBR (inf: = Oh my God!) Dios mío, cielos
ominous ['ɔminəs] ADJ de mal agüero,
amenazador(a)
omission [əu'miʃən] N omisión f; (error)
descuido
omit [əu'mit] VT omitir; (by mistake) olvidar,
descuidar; **to ~ to do sth** olvidarse or dejar
de hacer algo
omnivorous [ɔm'nivərəs] ADJ omnívoro
ON ABBR (CANADA) = **Ontario**

KEYWORD

on [ɔn] PREP **1** (indicating position) en; sobre; **on
the wall** en la pared; **it's on the table** está
sobre or en la mesa; **on the left** a la
izquierda; **I haven't got any money on me**
no llevo dinero encima
2 (indicating means: method: condition etc): **on
foot** a pie; **on the train/plane** (go) en tren/
avión; (be) en el tren/el avión; **on the radio/
television** por or en la radio/televisión; **on
the telephone** al teléfono; **to be on drugs**
drogarse; (Med) estar a tratamiento; **to be
on holiday/business** estar de vacaciones/en
viaje de negocios; **we're on irregular verbs**
estamos con los verbos irregulares

3 (referring to time): **on Friday** el viernes; **on
Fridays** los viernes; **on June 20th** el 20 de
junio; **a week on Friday** del viernes en una
semana; **on arrival** al llegar; **on seeing
this** al ver esto
4 (about, concerning) sobre, acerca de; **a book
on physics** un libro de or sobre física
5 (at the expense of): **this round's on me** esta
ronda la pago yo, invito yo a esta ronda;
(earning): **he's on sixteen thousand pounds
a year** gana dieciséis mil libras al año
▶ ADV **1** (referring to dress): **to have one's coat
on** tener or llevar el abrigo puesto; **she put
her gloves on** se puso los guantes
2 (referring to covering): **"screw the lid on
tightly"** "cerrar bien la tapa"
3 (further, continuously): **to walk/run** etc **on**
seguir caminando/corriendo etc; **from that
day on** desde aquel día; **it was well on in
the evening** estaba ya entrada la tarde
4 (in phrases): **I'm on to sth** creo haber
encontrado algo; **my father's always on at
me to get a job** (inf) mi padre siempre me
está dando la lata para que me ponga a
trabajar
▶ ADJ **1** (functioning, in operation: machine, radio,
TV, light) encendido (SP), prendido (LAM);
(: tap) abierto; (: brakes) echado, puesto;
is the meeting still on? (in progress) ¿todavía
continúa la reunión?; (not cancelled) ¿va a
haber reunión al fin?; **there's a good film
on at the cinema** ponen una buena película
en el cine
2: **that's not on!** (inf: not possible) ¡eso ni
hablar!; (: not acceptable) ¡eso no se hace!

ONC N ABBR (BRIT: = Ordinary National Certificate)
título escolar
once [wʌns] ADV una vez; (formerly)
antiguamente ▶ CONJ una vez que; **~ he had
left/it was done** una vez que se había
marchado/se hizo; **at ~** en seguida,
inmediatamente; (simultaneously) a la vez; **~ a
week** una vez a la semana; **~ more** otra vez; **~
and for all** de una vez por todas; **~ upon a
time** érase una vez; **I knew him ~** le conocía
hace tiempo
oncoming ['ɔnkʌmiŋ] ADJ (traffic) que viene
de frente
OND N ABBR (BRIT: = Ordinary National Diploma)
título escolar

KEYWORD

one [wʌn] NUM un/una; **one hundred and
fifty** ciento cincuenta; **one by one** uno a
uno; **it's one (o'clock)** es la una
▶ ADJ **1** (sole) único; **the one book which**
el único libro que; **the one man who** el
único que

2 (*same*) mismo(-a); **they came in the one car** vinieron en un solo coche
▶ PRON **1: this one** este, éste; **that one** ese, ése; (*more remote*) aquel, aquél; **I've already got (a red) one** ya tengo uno(-a) (rojo(-a)); **one by one** uno(-a) por uno(-a); **to be one up on sb** llevar ventaja a algn; **to be at one (with sb)** estar completamente de acuerdo (con algn)
2: one another (*us*) nos; (*you*) os (*SP*); (*you: formal, them*) se; (*them*) se; **do you two ever see one another?** ¿os veis alguna vez? (*SP*), ¿se ven alguna vez?; **the two boys didn't dare**
look at one another los dos chicos no se atrevieron a mirarse (el uno al otro); **they all kissed one another** se besaron unos a otros
3 *impers*: **one never knows** nunca se sabe; **to cut one's finger** cortarse el dedo; **one needs to eat** hay que comer

one-armed bandit ['wʌnɑːmd-] N máquina tragaperras
one-day excursion ['wʌndeɪ-] N (*US*) billete *m* de ida y vuelta en un día
One-hundred share index ['wʌnhʌndrəd-] N índice *m* bursátil (*del Financial Times*)
one-man ['wʌn'mæn] ADJ (*business*) individual
one-man band N hombre-orquesta *m*
one-off [wʌn'ɔf] N (*BRIT inf: object*) artículo único; (: *event*) caso especial
one-parent family ['wʌnpɛərənt-] N familia monoparental
one-piece ['wʌnpiːs] ADJ (*bathing suit*) de una pieza
onerous ['ɔnərəs] ADJ (*task, duty*) pesado; (*responsibility*) oneroso
oneself [wʌn'sɛlf] PRON (*reflexive*) se; (*after prep*) sí; (*emphatic*) uno(-a) mismo(-a); **to hurt ~** hacerse daño; **to keep sth for ~** guardarse algo; **to talk to ~** hablar solo
one-shot [wʌn'ʃɔt] N (*US*) = **one-off**
one-sided [wʌn'saɪdɪd] ADJ (*argument*) parcial; (*decision, view*) unilateral; (*game, contest*) desigual
one-time ['wʌntaɪm] ADJ antiguo, ex-
one-to-one ['wʌntəwʌn] ADJ (*relationship*) individualizado
one-upmanship [wʌn'ʌpmənʃɪp] N: **the art of ~** el arte de quedar siempre por encima
one-way ['wʌnweɪ] ADJ (*street, traffic*) de dirección única; (*ticket*) sencillo
ongoing ['ɔngəʊɪŋ] ADJ continuo
onion ['ʌnjən] N cebolla
online [ɔn'laɪn] ADJ, ADV (*Comput*) en línea; (*switched on*) conectado
onlooker ['ɔnlʊkəʳ] N espectador(a) *m/f*

only ['əʊnlɪ] ADV solamente, solo, sólo (*to avoid confusion with adj*), nomás (*LAM*) ▶ ADJ único, solo ▶ CONJ solamente que, pero; **an ~ child** un hijo único; **not ~ ... but also ...** no sólo ... sino también ...; **I'd be ~ too pleased to help** encantado de ayudarles; **I saw her ~ yesterday** le vi ayer mismo; **I would come, ~ I'm very busy** iría, sólo que estoy muy atareado
ono ABBR (= *or nearest offer: in classified ads*) abierto ofertas
on-screen [ɔn'skriːn] ADJ (*Comput etc*) en pantalla; (*romance, kiss*) cinematográfico
onset ['ɔnsɛt] N comienzo
onshore ['ɔnʃɔːʳ] ADJ (*wind*) que sopla del mar hacia la tierra
onslaught ['ɔnslɔːt] N ataque *m*, embestida
Ont. ABBR (*CANADA*) = **Ontario**
on-the-job ['ɔnðə'dʒɔb] ADJ: **~ training** formación *f* en el trabajo *or* sobre la práctica
onto ['ɔntu] PREP = **on to**
onus ['əʊnəs] N responsabilidad *f*; **the ~ is upon him to prove it** le incumbe a él demostrarlo
onward ['ɔnwəd], **onwards** ['ɔnwədz] ADV (*move*) (hacia) (hacia) adelante; **from that time ~** desde entonces en adelante
onyx ['ɔnɪks] N ónice *m*, ónix *m*
oops [ups] EXCL (*also*: **oops-a-daisy!**) ¡huy!
ooze [uːz] VI rezumar
opal ['əʊpl] N ópalo
opaque [əu'peɪk] ADJ opaco
OPEC ['əʊpɛk] N ABBR (= *Organization of Petroleum-Exporting Countries*) OPEP *f*
open ['əʊpn] ADJ abierto; (*car*) descubierto; (*road, view*) despejado; (*meeting*) público; (*admiration*) manifiesto ▶ VT abrir ▶ VI (*flower, eyes, door, debate*) abrirse; (*book etc: commence*) comenzar; **in the ~ (air)** al aire libre; **~ verdict** veredicto inconcluso; **~ ticket** billete *m* abierto; **~ ground** (*among trees*) claro; (*waste ground*) solar *m*; **to have an ~ mind (on sth)** estar sin decidirse aún (sobre algo); **to ~ a bank account** abrir una cuenta en el banco
▶ **open on to** VT FUS (*room, door*) dar a
▶ **open out** VT abrir ▶ VI (*person*) abrirse
▶ **open up** VT abrir; (*blocked road*) despejar ▶ VI abrirse
open-and-shut ['əʊpənən'ʃʌt] ADJ: **~ case** caso claro *or* evidente
open day N (*BRIT*) jornada de puertas abiertas *or* acceso público
open-ended [əupn'ɛndɪd] ADJ (*fig*) indefinido, sin definir
opener ['əupnəʳ] N (*also*: **can opener, tin opener**) abrelatas *m inv*
open-heart surgery [əupn'hɑːt-] N cirugía a corazón abierto

opening ['əupnıŋ] N abertura; (*beginning*) comienzo; (*opportunity*) oportunidad f; (*job*) puesto vacante, vacante f

opening hours NPL horario de apertura

opening night N estreno

open learning N *enseñanza flexible a tiempo parcial*

openly ['əupnlı] ADV abiertamente

open-minded [əupn'maındıd] ADJ de amplias miras, sin prejuicios

open-necked ['əupnnɛkt] ADJ sin corbata

openness ['əupnnıs] N (*frankness*) franqueza

open-plan ['əupn'plæn] ADJ diáfano, sin tabiques

open prison N centro penitenciario de régimen abierto

open return N vuelta con fecha abierta

open shop N *empresa que contrata a mano de obra no afiliada a ningún sindicato*

Open University N (*BRIT*) ≈ Universidad f Nacional de Enseñanza a Distancia, UNED f; *ver nota*

> La *Open University*, fundada en 1969, está especializada en impartir cursos a distancia y a tiempo parcial con sus propios materiales de apoyo diseñados para tal fin, entre ellos programas de radio y televisión emitidos por la BBC. Los trabajos se envían por correo y se complementan con la asistencia obligatoria a cursos de verano. Para obtener la licenciatura es necesario estudiar un mínimo de módulos y alcanzar un determinado número de créditos.

opera ['ɔpərə] N ópera

opera glasses NPL gemelos *mpl*

opera house N teatro de la ópera

opera singer N cantante *mf* de ópera

operate ['ɔpəreɪt] VT (*machine*) hacer funcionar; (*company*) dirigir ▸ VI funcionar; (*drug*) hacer efecto; **to ~ on sb** (*Med*) operar a algn

operatic [ɔpə'rætɪk] ADJ de ópera

operating costs ['ɔpəreɪtɪŋ-] NPL gastos *mpl* operacionales

operating profit N beneficio de explotación

operating room N (*US*) quirófano, sala de operaciones

operating table N mesa de operaciones

operating theatre N quirófano, sala de operaciones

operation [ɔpə'reɪʃən] N (*gen*) operación f; (*of machine*) funcionamiento; **to be in ~** estar funcionando *or* en funcionamiento; **to have an ~** (*Med*) ser operado; **to have an ~ for** operarse de; **the company's operations during the year** las actividades de la compañía durante el año

operational [ɔpə'reɪʃənl] ADJ operacional, en buen estado; (*Comm*) en condiciones de servicio; (*ready for use or action*) en condiciones de funcionar; **when the service is fully ~** cuando el servicio esté en pleno funcionamiento

operative ['ɔpərətɪv] ADJ (*measure*) en vigor; **the ~ word** la palabra clave

operator ['ɔpəreɪtəʳ] N (*of machine*) operario(-a), maquinista *mf*; (*Tel*) operador(a) *m/f*, telefonista *mf*

operetta [ɔpə'rɛtə] N opereta

ophthalmic [ɔf'θælmɪk] ADJ oftálmico

ophthalmologist [ɔfθæl'mɔlədʒɪst] N oftalmólogo(-a)

opinion [ə'pɪnjən] N (*gen*) opinión f; **in my ~** en mi opinión, a mi juicio; **to seek a second ~** pedir una segunda opinión

opinionated [ə'pɪnjəneɪtɪd] ADJ testarudo

opinion poll N encuesta, sondeo

opium ['əupɪəm] N opio

opponent [ə'pəunənt] N adversario(-a), contrincante *mf*

opportune ['ɔpətju:n] ADJ oportuno

opportunism [ɔpə'tju:nɪzm] N oportunismo

opportunist [ɔpə'tju:nɪst] N oportunista *mf*

opportunity [ɔpə'tju:nɪtɪ] N oportunidad f, chance *m or f* (*LAM*); **to take the ~ to do** *or* **of doing** aprovechar la ocasión para hacer

oppose [ə'pəuz] VT oponerse a; **to be opposed to sth** oponerse a algo; **as opposed to** en vez de; (*unlike*) a diferencia de

opposing [ə'pəuzıŋ] ADJ (*side*) opuesto, contrario

opposite ['ɔpəzɪt] ADJ opuesto, contrario; (*house etc*) de enfrente ▸ ADV en frente ▸ PREP en frente de, frente a ▸ N lo contrario; **the ~ sex** el otro sexo, el sexo opuesto

opposite number N (*BRIT*) homólogo(-a)

opposition [ɔpə'zɪʃən] N oposición f

oppress [ə'prɛs] VT oprimir

oppression [ə'prɛʃən] N opresión f

oppressive [ə'prɛsɪv] ADJ opresivo

opprobrium [ə'prəubrɪəm] N (*formal*) oprobio

opt [ɔpt] VI: **to ~ for** optar por; **to ~ to do** optar por hacer

▸ **opt out** VI: **to ~ out of** optar por no hacer

optical ['ɔptɪkl] ADJ óptico

optical character reader N lector *m* óptico de caracteres

optical character recognition N reconocimiento *m* óptico de caracteres

optical fibre N fibra óptica

optician [ɔp'tɪʃən] N óptico(-a)

optics ['ɔptɪks] N óptica

optimism ['ɔptɪmɪzəm] N optimismo

optimist ['ɔptɪmɪst] N optimista *mf*

optimistic [ɔptɪ'mɪstɪk] ADJ optimista

optimum ['ɔptɪməm] ADJ óptimo

option ['ɔpʃən] N opción f; **to keep one's options open** (fig) mantener las opciones abiertas; **I have no ~** no tengo más or otro remedio

optional ['ɔpʃənl] ADJ opcional; (course) optativo; **~ extras** opciones fpl extras

opulence ['ɔpjuləns] N opulencia

opulent ['ɔpjulənt] ADJ opulento

OR ABBR (US) = **Oregon**

or [ɔːʳ] CONJ o; (before o, ho) u; (with negative): **he hasn't seen or heard anything** no ha visto ni oído nada; **or else** si no; **let me go or I'll scream!** ¡suéltame, o me pongo a gritar!

oracle ['ɔrəkl] N oráculo

oral ['ɔːrəl] ADJ oral ► N examen m oral

orange ['ɔrɪndʒ] N (fruit) naranja ► ADJ (de color) naranja inv

orangeade [ɔrɪndʒ'eɪd] N naranjada, refresco de naranja

orange juice N jugo m de naranja, zumo m de naranja (Sp)

orange squash N bebida de naranja

orang-outang, orang-utan [ɔ'ræŋuː'tæn] N orangután m

oration [ɔː'reɪʃən] N discurso solemne; **funeral ~** oración f fúnebre

orator ['ɔrətəʳ] N orador(a) m/f

oratorio [ɔrə'tɔːrɪəu] N oratorio

orbit ['ɔːbɪt] N órbita ► VT, VI orbitar; **to be in/go into ~ (round)** estar en/entrar en órbita (alrededor de)

orbital ['ɔːbɪtl] N (also: **orbital motorway**) autopista de circunvalación

orchard ['ɔːtʃəd] N huerto; **apple ~** manzanar m, manzanal m

orchestra ['ɔːkɪstrə] N orquesta; (US: seating) platea

orchestral [ɔː'kɛstrəl] ADJ de orquesta

orchestrate ['ɔːkɪstreɪt] VT orquestar

orchid ['ɔːkɪd] N orquídea

ordain [ɔː'deɪn] VT (Rel) ordenar

ordeal [ɔː'diːl] N experiencia terrible

order ['ɔːdəʳ] N orden m; (command) orden f; (type, kind) clase f; (state) estado; (Comm) pedido, encargo ► VT (also: **put in order**) ordenar, poner en orden; (Comm) encargar, pedir; (command) mandar, ordenar; **in ~** (gen) en orden; (of document) en regla; **in (working) ~** en funcionamiento; **a machine in working ~** una máquina en funcionamiento; **to be out of ~** estar desordenado; (not working) no funcionar; **in ~ to do** para hacer; **in ~ that** para que + subjun; **on ~** (Comm) pedido; **to be on ~** estar pedido; **we are under orders to do it** tenemos orden de hacerlo; **a point of ~** una cuestión de procedimiento; **to place an ~ for sth with sb** hacer un pedido de algo a algn; **made to ~** hecho a la medida; **his income is**

of the ~ of £24,000 per year sus ingresos son del orden de 24 mil libras al año; **to the ~ of** (Banking) a la orden de; **to ~ sb to do sth** mandar a algn hacer algo

order book N cartera de pedidos

order form N hoja de pedido

orderly ['ɔːdəlɪ] N (Mil) ordenanza m; (Med) auxiliar mf (de hospital) ► ADJ ordenado

orderly officer N (Mil) oficial m del día

order number N número de pedido

ordinal ['ɔːdɪnl] ADJ ordinal

ordinarily ['ɔːdnrɪlɪ] ADV por lo común

ordinary ['ɔːdnrɪ] ADJ corriente, normal; (pej) común y corriente; **out of the ~** fuera de lo común, extraordinario

ordinary degree N (Brit) diploma m; ver nota

> Después de tres años de estudios, algunos universitarios obtienen la titulación de *ordinary degree*. Esto ocurre en el caso poco frecuente de que no aprueben los exámenes que conducen al título de "honours degree" pero sus examinadores consideren que a lo largo de la carrera han logrado unos resultados mínimos satisfactorios. También es una opción que tienen los estudiantes de las universidades escocesas no interesados en estudiar en la universidad más de tres años.

ordinary seaman N (irreg) (Brit) marinero

ordinary shares NPL acciones fpl ordinarias

ordination [ɔːdɪ'neɪʃən] N ordenación f

ordnance ['ɔːdnəns] N (Mil: unit) artillería

ordnance factory N fábrica de artillería

Ordnance Survey N (Brit) servicio oficial de topografía y cartografía

ore [ɔːʳ] N mineral m

Ore., Oreg. ABBR (US) = **Oregon**

oregano [ɔrɪ'gɑːnəu] N orégano

organ ['ɔːgən] N órgano

organic [ɔː'gænɪk] ADJ orgánico; (vegetables, produce) biológico

organism ['ɔːgənɪzəm] N organismo

organist ['ɔːgənɪst] N organista mf

organization [ɔːgənaɪ'zeɪʃən] N organización f

organization chart N organigrama m

organize ['ɔːgənaɪz] VT organizar

organized ['ɔːgənaɪzd] ADJ organizado; **to get ~** organizarse

organized crime N crimen m organizado

organizer ['ɔːgənaɪzəʳ] N organizador(a) m/f

orgasm ['ɔːgæzəm] N orgasmo

orgy ['ɔːdʒɪ] N orgía

Orient ['ɔːrɪənt] N Oriente m

oriental [ɔːrɪ'ɛntl] ADJ oriental

orientate ['ɔːrɪənteɪt] VT orientar

orientation [ɔːrɪen'teɪʃən] N orientación f

origin ['ɒrɪdʒɪn] N origen m; (point of departure) procedencia

original [əˈrɪdʒɪnl] ADJ original; (first) primero; (earlier) primitivo ▶ N original m

originality [ərɪdʒɪˈnælɪtɪ] N originalidad f

originally [əˈrɪdʒɪnəlɪ] ADV (at first) al principio; (with originality) con originalidad

originate [əˈrɪdʒɪneɪt] VI: **to ~ from, to ~ in** surgir de, tener su origen en

originator [əˈrɪdʒɪneɪtəʳ] N inventor(a) m/f, autor(a) m/f

Orkneys ['ɔːknɪz] NPL: **the ~** (also: **the Orkney Islands**) las Orcadas

ornament ['ɔːnəmənt] N adorno; (trinket) chuchería

ornamental [ɔːnəˈmɛntl] ADJ decorativo, de adorno

ornamentation [ɔːnəmɛnˈteɪʃən] N ornamentación f

ornate [ɔːˈneɪt] ADJ recargado

ornithologist [ɔːnɪˈθɒlədʒɪst] N ornitólogo(-a)

ornithology [ɔːnɪˈθɒlədʒɪ] N ornitología

orphan ['ɔːfn] N huérfano(-a) ▶ VT: **to be orphaned** quedar huérfano(-a)

orphanage ['ɔːfənɪdʒ] N orfanato

orthodox ['ɔːθədɒks] ADJ ortodoxo

orthodoxy ['ɔːθədɒksɪ] N ortodoxia

orthopaedic, (US) **orthopedic** [ɔːθəˈpiːdɪk] ADJ ortopédico

orthopaedics, (US) **orthopedics** [ɔːθəˈpiːdɪks] N ortopedia

OS ABBR (BRIT: = Ordnance Survey) servicio oficial de topografía y cartografía; (: Naut) = **ordinary seaman**; (: Dress) = **outsize**

O.S. ABBR = **out of stock**

Oscar ['ɒskəʳ] N óscar m

oscillate ['ɒsɪleɪt] VI oscilar; (person) vacilar

oscillation [ɒsɪˈleɪʃən] N oscilación f; (of prices) fluctuación f

OSHA N ABBR (US: = Occupational Safety and Health Administration) oficina de la higiene y la seguridad en el trabajo

Oslo ['ɒzləu] N Oslo

ostensible [ɒsˈtɛnsɪbl] ADJ aparente

ostensibly [ɒsˈtɛnsɪblɪ] ADV aparentemente

ostentatious [ɒstɛnˈteɪʃəs] ADJ pretencioso, aparatoso; (person) ostentativo

osteopath ['ɒstɪəpæθ] N osteópata mf

ostracize ['ɒstrəsaɪz] VT hacer el vacío a

ostrich ['ɒstrɪtʃ] N avestruz m

OT N ABBR (= Old Testament) A.T.

OTB N ABBR (US: = off-track betting) apuestas hechas fuera del hipódromo

OTE ABBR (= on-target earnings) beneficios según objetivos

other ['ʌðəʳ] ADJ otro ▶ PRON: **the ~ one** el (la) otro(-a); **others** (other people) otros; **~ than** (apart from) aparte de; **the ~ day** el otro día;

some **~ people have still to arrive** quedan por llegar otros; **some actor or ~** un actor cualquiera; **somebody or ~** alguien, alguno; **it was no ~ than the bishop** no era otro que el obispo

otherwise ['ʌðəwaɪz] ADV, CONJ de otra manera; (if not) si no; **an ~ good piece of work** un trabajo que, quitando eso, es bueno

OTT ABBR (inf) = **over the top**; see **top**

otter ['ɒtəʳ] N nutria

OU N ABBR (BRIT) = **Open University**

ouch [autʃ] EXCL ¡ay!

ought [ɔːt] AUX VB: **I ~ to do it** debería hacerlo; **this ~ to have been corrected** esto debiera de haberse corregido; **he ~ to win** (probability) debiera ganar; **you ~ to go and see it** vale la pena ir a verlo

ounce [auns] N onza (=28.35g: 16oz = 1lb)

our ['auəʳ] ADJ nuestro; see also **my**

ours ['auəz] PRON (el) nuestro/(la) nuestra etc; see also **mine**

ourselves [auəˈsɛlvz] PRON PL (reflexive, after prep) nosotros(-as); (emphatic) nosotros(-as) mismos(-as); **we did it (all) by ~** lo hicimos nosotros solos; see also **oneself**

oust [aust] VT desalojar

out [aut] ADV fuera, afuera; (not at home) fuera (de casa); (light, fire) apagado; (on strike) en huelga ▶ VT: **to ~ sb** revelar públicamente la homosexualidad de algn; **~ there** allí (fuera); **he's ~** (absent) no está, ha salido; **to be ~ in one's calculations** equivocarse (en sus cálculos); **to run ~** salir corriendo; **~ loud** en alta voz; **~ of** prep (outside) fuera de; (because of: anger etc) por; **to look ~ of the window** mirar por la ventana; **to drink ~ of a cup** beber de una taza; **made ~ of wood** de madera; **~ of petrol** sin gasolina; **"~ of order"** "no funciona"; **it's ~ of stock** (Comm) está agotado; **to be ~ and about again** estar repuesto y levantado; **the journey ~** el viaje de ida; **the boat was 10 km ~** el barco estaba a 10 kilómetros de la costa; **before the week was ~** antes del fin de la semana; **he's ~ for all he can get** busca sus propios fines, anda detrás de lo suyo

out-and-out ['autəndaut] ADJ (liar, thief etc) redomado, empedernido

outback ['autbæk] N interior m

outbid [autˈbɪd] VT pujar más alto que, sobrepujar

outboard ['autbɔːd] ADJ: **~ motor** (motor m) fuera borda m

outbound ['autbaund] ADJ (flight) de salida; (flight: not return) de ida; **~ from/for** con salida de/hacia

outbox ['autbɒks] N (Comput) buzón m de salida; (US: out-tray) bandeja de salida

outbreak ['autbreɪk] N (*of war*) comienzo; (*of disease*) epidemia; (*of violence etc*) ola
outbuilding ['autbɪldɪŋ] N dependencia; (*shed*) cobertizo
outburst ['autbə:st] N explosión *f*, arranque *m*
outcast ['autkɑ:st] N paria *mf*
outclass [aut'klɑ:s] VT aventajar, superar
outcome ['autkʌm] N resultado
outcrop ['autkrɒp] N (*of rock*) afloramiento
outcry ['autkraɪ] N protestas *fpl*
outdated [aut'deɪtɪd] ADJ anticuado
outdistance [aut'dɪstəns] VT dejar atrás
outdo [aut'du:] VT (*irreg: like* **do**) superar
outdoor [aut'dɔ:ʳ] ADJ al aire libre; (*clothes*) de calle
outdoors [aut'dɔ:z] ADV al aire libre
outer ['autəʳ] ADJ exterior, externo
outer space N espacio exterior
outfit ['autfɪt] N equipo; (*clothes*) traje *m*; (*inf: organization*) grupo, organización *f*
outfitter's ['autfɪtəz] N (BRIT) sastrería
outgoing ['autgəuɪŋ] ADJ (*president, tenant*) saliente; (*means of transport*) que sale; (*character*) extrovertido
outgoings ['autgəuɪŋz] NPL (BRIT) gastos *mpl*
outgrow [aut'grəu] VT (*irreg: like* **grow**): **he has outgrown his clothes** su ropa le queda pequeña ya
outhouse ['authaus] N dependencia
outing ['autɪŋ] N excursión *f*, paseo
outlandish [aut'lændɪʃ] ADJ estrafalario
outlast [aut'lɑ:st] VT durar más tiempo que, sobrevivir a
outlaw ['autlɔ:] N proscrito(-a) ▸ VT (*person*) declarar fuera de la ley; (*practice*) declarar ilegal
outlay ['autleɪ] N inversión *f*
outlet ['autlet] N salida; (*of pipe*) desagüe *m*; (*US Elec*) toma de corriente; (*for emotion*) desahogo; (*also*: **retail outlet**) punto de venta
outline ['autlaɪn] N (*shape*) contorno, perfil *m*; (*sketch, plan*) esbozo ▸ VT (*plan etc*) esbozar; **in ~** (*fig*) a grandes rasgos
outlive [aut'lɪv] VT sobrevivir a
outlook ['autluk] N (*fig: prospects*) perspectivas *fpl*; (: *for weather*) pronóstico; (: *opinion*) punto de vista
outlying ['autlaɪɪŋ] ADJ remoto, aislado
outmanoeuvre, (US) **outmaneuver** [autmə'nu:vəʳ] VT (*Mil: fig*) superar en la estrategia
outmoded [aut'məudɪd] ADJ anticuado, pasado de moda
outnumber [aut'nʌmbəʳ] VT exceder *or* superar en número
out of bounds [autəv'baundz] ADJ: **it's ~** está prohibido el paso
out-of-court [autəv'kɔ:t] ADJ, ADV sin ir a juicio

out-of-date [autəv'deɪt] ADJ (*passport*) caducado, vencido; (*theory, idea*) anticuado; (*clothes, customs*) pasado de moda
out-of-doors [autəv'dɔ:z] ADV al aire libre
out-of-the-way [autəvðə'weɪ] ADJ (*remote*) apartado; (*unusual*) poco común *or* corriente
out-of-touch [autəv'tʌtʃ] ADJ: **to be ~** estar desconectado
out-of-town [autəv'taun] ADJ (*shopping centre etc*) en las afueras
outpatient ['autpeɪʃənt] N paciente *mf* externo(-a)
outpost ['autpəust] N puesto avanzado
outpouring ['autpɔ:rɪŋ] N (*fig*) efusión *f*
output ['autput] N (volumen *m* de) producción *f*, rendimiento; (*Comput*) salida ▸ VT (*Comput: to power*) imprimir
outrage ['autreɪdʒ] N (*scandal*) escándalo; (*atrocity*) atrocidad *f* ▸ VT ultrajar
outrageous [aut'reɪdʒəs] ADJ (*clothes*) extravagante; (*behaviour*) escandaloso
outright ADV [aut'raɪt] (*ask, deny*) francamente; (*refuse*) rotundamente; (*win*) de manera absoluta; (*be killed*) en el acto; (*completely*) completamente ▸ ADJ ['autraɪt] completo; (*winner*) absoluto; (*refusal*) rotundo
outrun [aut'rʌn] VT (*irreg: like* **run**) correr más que, dejar atrás
outset ['autset] N principio
outshine [aut'ʃaɪn] VT (*irreg: like* **shine**) (*fig*) eclipsar, brillar más que
outside [aut'saɪd] N exterior *m* ▸ ADJ exterior, externo ▸ ADV fuera, afuera (LAM) ▸ PREP fuera de; (*beyond*) más allá de; **at the ~** (*fig*) a lo sumo; **an ~ chance** una posibilidad remota; **~ left/right** (*esp Football*) extremo izquierdo/derecho
outside broadcast N (*Radio, TV*) emisión *f* exterior
outside contractor N contratista *mf* independiente
outside lane N (*Aut: in Britain*) carril *m* de la derecha; (: *in US, Europe etc*) carril *m* de la izquierda
outside line N (*Tel*) línea (exterior)
outsider [aut'saɪdəʳ] N (*stranger*) forastero(-a)
outsize ['autsaɪz] ADJ (*clothes*) de talla grande
outskirts ['autskə:ts] NPL alrededores *mpl*, afueras *fpl*
outsmart [aut'smɑ:t] VT ser más listo que
outspoken [aut'spəukən] ADJ muy franco
outspread [aut'spred] ADJ extendido; (*wings*) desplegada
outstanding [aut'stændɪŋ] ADJ excepcional, destacado; (*unfinished*) pendiente
outstay [aut'steɪ] VT: **to ~ one's welcome** quedarse más de la cuenta
outstretched [aut'stretʃt] ADJ (*arm*) extendido

o

outstrip [aut'strɪp] VT (*competitors, demand*: *also fig*) dejar atrás, aventajar

out-tray ['auttreɪ] N bandeja de salida

outvote [aut'vəut] VT: **it was outvoted (by …)** fue rechazado en el voto (por …)

outward ['autwəd] ADJ (*sign, appearances*) externo; (*journey*) de ida

outwardly ['autwədlɪ] ADV por fuera

outwards [autwədz] ADJ (*esp* BRIT) = **outward**

outweigh [aut'weɪ] VT pesar más que

outwit [aut'wɪt] VT ser más listo que

outworn [aut'wɔːn] ADJ (*expression*) cansado

oval ['əuvl] ADJ ovalado ▶ N óvalo

ovarian [əu'vɛərɪən] ADJ ovárico; (*cancer*) de ovario

ovary ['əuvərɪ] N ovario

ovation [əu'veɪʃən] N ovación f

oven ['ʌvn] N horno

oven glove N guante m para el horno, manopla para el horno

ovenproof ['ʌvnpruːf] ADJ refractario, resistente al horno

oven-ready ['ʌvnrɛdɪ] ADJ listo para el horno

ovenware ['ʌvnwɛəʳ] N artículos mpl para el horno

over ['əuvəʳ] ADV encima, por encima ▶ ADJ (*finished*) terminado; (*surplus*) de sobra; (*excessively*) demasiado ▶ PREP (por) encima de; (*above*) sobre; (*on the other side of*) al otro lado de; (*more than*) más de; (*during*) durante; (*about, concerning*): **they fell out ~ money** riñeron por una cuestión de dinero; **~ here** (por) aquí; **~ there** (por) allí *or* allá; **all ~** (*everywhere*) por todas partes; **~ and ~ (again)** una y otra vez; **~ and above** además de; **to ask sb ~** invitar a algn a casa; **to bend ~** inclinarse; **now ~ to our Paris correspondent** damos la palabra a nuestro corresponsal de París; **the world ~** en todo el mundo, en el mundo entero; **she's not ~ intelligent** no es muy lista que digamos

over... [əuvəʳ] PREF sobre..., super...

overact [əuvər'ækt] VI (*Theat*) exagerar el papel

overall ['əuvərɔːl] ADJ (*length*) total; (*study*) de conjunto ▶ ADV [əuvər'ɔːl] en conjunto ▶ N (BRIT) guardapolvo; **overalls** NPL mono *sg*, overol *msg* (LAM)

overall majority N mayoría absoluta

overanxious [əuvər'æŋkʃəs] ADJ demasiado preocupado *or* ansioso

overawe [əuvər'ɔː] VT intimidar

overbalance [əuvə'bæləns] VI perder el equilibrio

overbearing [əuvə'bɛərɪŋ] ADJ autoritario, imperioso

overboard ['əuvəbɔːd] ADV (*Naut*) por la borda; **to go ~ for sth** (*fig*) enloquecer por algo

overbook [əuvə'buk] VT sobrerreservar, reservar con exceso

overcame [əuvə'keɪm] PT *of* **overcome**

overcapitalize [əuvə'kæpɪtəlaɪz] VI sobrecapitalizar

overcast ['əuvəkɑːst] ADJ encapotado

overcharge [əuvə'tʃɑːdʒ] VT: **to ~ sb** cobrar un precio excesivo a algn

overcoat ['əuvəkəut] N abrigo

overcome [əuvə'kʌm] VT (*irreg: like* **come**) (*gen*) vencer; (*difficulty*) superar; **she was quite ~ by the occasion** la ocasión le conmovió mucho

overconfident [əuvə'kɔnfɪdənt] ADJ demasiado confiado

overcrowded [əuvə'kraudɪd] ADJ atestado de gente; (*city, country*) superpoblado

overcrowding [əuvə'kraudɪŋ] N (*in town, country*) superpoblación f; (*in bus etc*) hacinamiento, apiñamiento

overdo [əuvə'duː] VT (*irreg: like* **do**) exagerar; (*overcook*) cocer demasiado; **to ~ it** (*work etc*) pasarse

overdone [əuvə'dʌn] ADJ (*vegetables*) recocido; (*steak*) demasiado hecho

overdose ['əuvədəus] N sobredosis f *inv*

overdraft ['əuvədrɑːft] N saldo deudor

overdrawn [əuvə'drɔːn] ADJ (*account*) en descubierto

overdrive ['əuvədraɪv] N (*Aut*) sobremarcha, superdirecta

overdue [əuvə'djuː] ADJ retrasado; (*recognition*) tardío; (*bill*) vencido y no pagado; **that change was long ~** ese cambio tenía que haberse hecho hace tiempo

overemphasis [əuvər'ɛmfəsɪs] N: **to put an ~ on** poner énfasis excesivo en

overenthusiastic ['əuvərənθuːzɪ'æstɪk] ADJ demasiado entusiasta

overestimate [əuvər'ɛstɪmeɪt] VT sobreestimar

overexcited [əuvərɪk'saɪtɪd] ADJ sobreexcitado

overexertion [əuvərɪg'zəːʃən] N agotamiento, fatiga

overexpose [əuvərɪk'spəuz] VT (*Phot*) sobreexponer

overflow [əuvə'fləu] VI desbordarse ▶ N ['əuvəfləu] (*excess*) exceso; (*of river*) desbordamiento; (*also:* **overflow pipe**) (cañería de) desagüe m

overfly [əuvə'flaɪ] VT (*irreg: like* **fly**) sobrevolar

overgenerous [əuvə'dʒɛnərəs] ADJ demasiado generoso

overgrown [əuvə'grəun] ADJ (*garden*) cubierto de hierba; **he's just an ~ schoolboy** es un niño en grande

overhang [əuvə'hæŋ] VT (*irreg: like* **hang**) sobresalir por encima de ▶ VI sobresalir

overhaul VT [əuvə'hɔːl] revisar, repasar ▶ N ['əuvəhɔːl] revisión f

overhead ADV [əuvə'hɛd] por arriba or encima ▶ ADJ ['əuvəhɛd] (cable) aéreo; (railway) elevado, aéreo ▶ N ['əuvəhɛd] (US) = **overheads**

overhead projector N retroproyector

overheads ['əuvəhɛdz] NPL (BRIT) gastos mpl generales

overhear [əuvə'hɪər] VT (irreg: like **hear**) oír por casualidad

overheat [əuvə'hiːt] VI (engine) recalentarse

overjoyed [əuvə'dʒɔɪd] ADJ encantado, lleno de alegría

overkill ['əuvəkɪl] N (Mil) capacidad f excesiva de destrucción; (fig) exceso

overland ['əuvəlænd] ADJ, ADV por tierra

overlap VI [əuvə'læp] superponerse ▶ N ['əuvəlæp] superposición f

overleaf [əuvə'liːf] ADV al dorso

overload [əuvə'ləud] VT sobrecargar

overlook [əuvə'luk] VT (have view of) dar a, tener vistas a; (miss) pasar por alto; (excuse) perdonar

overlord ['əuvəlɔːd] N señor m

overmanning [əuvə'mænɪŋ] N exceso de mano de obra; (in organization) exceso de personal

overnight [əuvə'naɪt] ADV durante la noche; (fig) de la noche a la mañana ▶ ADJ de noche; **to stay ~** pasar la noche

overnight bag N neceser m de viaje

overnight stay N estancia de una noche

overpass ['əuvəpɑːs] N (US) paso elevado or a desnivel

overpay [əuvə'peɪ] VT: **to ~ sb by £50** pagar 50 libras de más a algn

overplay [əuvə'pleɪ] VT exagerar; **to ~ one's hand** desmedirse

overpower [əuvə'pauər] VT dominar; (fig) embargar

overpowering [əuvə'pauərɪŋ] ADJ (heat) agobiante; (smell) penetrante

overproduction [əuvəprə'dʌkʃən] N superproducción f

overrate [əuvə'reɪt] VT sobrevalorar

overreach [əuvə'riːtʃ] VT: **to ~ o.s.** ir demasiado lejos, pasarse

overreact [əuvərɪ'ækt] VI reaccionar de manera exagerada

override [əuvə'raɪd] VT (irreg: like **ride**) (order, objection) no hacer caso de

overriding [əuvə'raɪdɪŋ] ADJ predominante

overrule [əuvə'ruːl] VT (decision) anular; (claim) denegar

overrun [əuvə'rʌn] VT (irreg: like **run**) (Mil: country) invadir; (: time limit) rebasar, exceder ▶ VI rebasar el límite previsto; **the town is ~**

with tourists el pueblo está inundado de turistas

overseas [əuvə'siːz] ADV en ultramar; (abroad) en el extranjero ▶ ADJ (trade) exterior; (visitor) extranjero

oversee [əuvə'siː] VT (irreg: like **see**) supervisar

overseer ['əuvəsɪər] N (in factory) supervisor(a) m/f; (foreman) capataz m

overshadow [əuvə'ʃædəu] VT (fig) eclipsar; **to be overshadowed by** estar a la sombra de

overshoot [əuvə'ʃuːt] VT (irreg: like **shoot**) excederse

oversight ['əuvəsaɪt] N descuido; **due to an ~** a causa de un descuido or una equivocación

oversimplify [əuvə'sɪmplɪfaɪ] VT simplificar demasiado

oversleep [əuvə'sliːp] VI (irreg: like **sleep**) dormir más de la cuenta, no despertarse a tiempo

overspend [əuvə'spɛnd] VI (irreg: like **spend**) gastar más de la cuenta; **we have overspent by five dollars** hemos excedido el presupuesto en cinco dólares

overspill ['əuvəspɪl] N exceso de población

overstaffed [əuvə'stɑːft] ADJ: **to be ~** tener exceso de plantilla

overstate [əuvə'steɪt] VT exagerar

overstatement ['əuvəsteɪtmənt] N exageración f

overstay [əuvə'steɪ] VT: **to ~ one's time** or **welcome** quedarse más de lo conveniente

overstep [əuvə'stɛp] VT: **to ~ the mark** or **the limits** pasarse de la raya

overstock [əuvə'stɔk] VT abarrotar

overstretched [əuvə'strɛtʃt] ADJ utilizado por encima de su capacidad

overstrike N ['əuvəstraɪk] (on printer) superposición f ▶ VT (irreg: like **strike**) superponer

oversubscribed [əuvəsəb'skraɪbd] ADJ suscrito en exceso

overt [əu'vəːt] ADJ abierto

overtake [əuvə'teɪk] VT (irreg: like **take**) sobrepasar; (BRIT Aut) adelantar

overtax [əuvə'tæks] VT (Econ) exigir contribuciones fpl excesivas or impuestos mpl excesivos a; (fig: strength) poner a prueba; (patience) agotar, abusar de; **to ~ o.s.** fatigarse demasiado

overthrow [əuvə'θrəu] VT (irreg: like **throw**) (government) derrocar

overtime ['əuvətaɪm] N horas fpl extraordinarias; **to do** or **work ~** hacer or trabajar horas extraordinarias or extras

overtime ban N prohibición f de (hacer) horas extraordinarias

overtone ['əuvətəun] N (fig) tono

overtook [əuvə'tuk] PT of **overtake**

overture ['əʊvətʃʊəʳ] N (*Mus*) obertura; (*fig*) propuesta

overturn [əʊvə'tə:n] VT volcar; (*fig: plan*) desbaratar; (: *government*) derrocar ▶ VI volcar

overview ['əʊvəvju:] N visión f de conjunto

overweight [əʊvə'weɪt] ADJ demasiado gordo *or* pesado

overwhelm [əʊvə'wɛlm] VT aplastar

overwhelming [əʊvə'wɛlmɪŋ] ADJ (*victory, defeat*) arrollador(a); (*desire*) irresistible; **one's ~ impression is of heat** lo que más impresiona es el calor

overwhelmingly [əʊvə'wɛlmɪŋlɪ] ADV abrumadoramente

overwork [əʊvə'wə:k] N trabajo excesivo ▶ VT hacer trabajar demasiado ▶ VI trabajar demasiado

overwrite [əʊvə'raɪt] VT (*irreg: like* **write**) (*Comput: file, disk*) sobre(e)scribir

overwrought [əʊvə'rɔ:t] ADJ sobreexcitado

ovulation [ɔvju'leɪʃən] N ovulación f

owe [əʊ] VT deber; **to ~ sb sth**, **to ~ sth to sb** deber algo a algn

owing to ['əʊɪŋtu:] PREP debido a, por causa de

owl [aʊl] N (*also*: **long-eared owl**) búho; (*also*: **barn owl**) lechuza

own [əʊn] VT tener, poseer ▶ VI: **to ~ to sth/ to having done sth** confesar *or* reconocer algo/haber hecho algo ▶ ADJ propio; **a room of my ~** mi propia habitación; **to get one's back** tomarse la revancha; **on one's ~** solo, a solas; **can I have it for my (very) ~?** ¿puedo quedarme con él?; **to come into one's ~** llegar a realizarse
▶ **own up** VI confesar

own brand N (*Comm*) marca propia

owner ['əʊnəʳ] N dueño(-a)

owner-occupier ['əʊnər'ɔkjupaɪəʳ] N ocupante propietario(-a) *m/f*

ownership ['əʊnəʃɪp] N posesión f; **it's under new ~** está bajo nueva dirección

own goal N (*Sport*) autogol *m*; **to score an ~** marcar un gol en propia puerta, marcar un autogol

ox [ɔks] (*pl* **oxen** ['ɔksn]) N buey *m*

Oxbridge ['ɔksbrɪdʒ] N *universidades de Oxford y Cambridge*; *ver nota*

> El término *Oxbridge* es una fusión de Ox(ford) y (Cam)bridge, las dos universidades británicas más antiguas y con mayor prestigio académico y social. Muchos miembros destacados de la clase dirigente del país son antiguos alumnos de una de las dos. El mismo término suele aplicarse a todo lo que ambas representan en cuestión de prestigio y privilegios sociales.

oxen ['ɔksən] NPL *of* **ox**

Oxfam ['ɔksfæm] N ABBR (*BRIT*: = *Oxford Committee for Famine Relief*) OXFAM

oxide ['ɔksaɪd] N óxido

Oxon. ['ɔksn] ABBR (*BRIT*) = **Oxoniensis**; **of Oxford (University)**

oxtail ['ɔksteɪl] N: **~ soup** sopa de rabo de buey

oxyacetylene ['ɔksɪə'sɛtɪli:n] ADJ oxiacetilénico; **~ burner**, **~ torch** soplete *m* oxiacetilénico

oxygen ['ɔksɪdʒən] N oxígeno

oxygen mask N máscara de oxígeno

oxygen tent N tienda de oxígeno

oyster ['ɔɪstəʳ] N ostra

oz. ABBR = **ounce**

ozone ['əʊzəʊn] N ozono

ozone-friendly ADJ que no daña la capa de ozono

ozone layer N capa de ozono

Pp

P, p [piː] N (letter) P, p f; **P for Peter** P de París
P ABBR = **president; prince**
p ABBR (= page) pág.; (BRIT) = **penny; pence**
PA N ABBR = **personal assistant; public
  address system** ▶ ABBR (US) = **Pennsylvania**
pa [pɑː] N (inf) papá m
p.a. ABBR = **per annum**
PAC N ABBR (US) = **political action committee**
pace [peɪs] N paso; (rhythm) ritmo ▶ VI: **to ~
  up and down** pasearse de un lado a otro;
  to keep ~ with llevar el mismo paso que;
  (events) mantenerse a la altura de or al
  corriente de; (fig) marcar la pauta; **to put sb
  through his paces** (fig) poner a algn a
  prueba
pacemaker ['peɪsmeɪkər] N (Med)
  marcapasos m inv; (Sport: also: **pacesetter**)
  liebre f
pacific [pəˈsɪfɪk] ADJ pacífico ▶ N: **the P~
  (Ocean)** el (océano) Pacífico
pacification [pæsɪfɪˈkeɪʃən] N pacificación f
pacifier ['pæsɪfaɪər] N (US: dummy) chupete m
pacifism ['pæsɪfɪzəm] N pacifismo
pacifist ['pæsɪfɪst] N pacifista mf
pacify ['pæsɪfaɪ] VT (soothe) apaciguar;
  (country) pacificar
pack [pæk] N (packet) paquete m; (Comm)
  embalaje m; (of hounds) jauría; (of people)
  manada; (of thieves etc) banda; (of cards)
  baraja; (bundle) fardo; (US: of cigarettes)
  paquete m, cajetilla ▶ VT (wrap) empaquetar;
  (fill) llenar; (in suitcase etc) meter, poner;
  (cram) llenar, atestar; (fig: meeting etc) llenar
  de partidarios; (Comput) comprimir; **to ~
  (one's bags)** hacer las maletas; **to ~ sb off**
  (inf) despachar a algn; **the place was
  packed** el local estaba (lleno) hasta los topes;
  to send sb packing (inf) echar a algn con
  cajas destempladas
  ▶ **pack in** VI (inf: break down) estropearse ▶ VT
  (inf) dejar; **~ it in!** ¡para!, ¡basta ya!
  ▶ **pack up** VI (inf: machine) estropearse;
  (person) irse ▶ VT (belongings, clothes) recoger;
  (goods, presents) empaquetar, envolver
package ['pækɪdʒ] N paquete m; (bulky) bulto;
  (Comput) paquete m (de software); (also:
  package deal) acuerdo global ▶ VT (Comm:
  goods) envasar, embalar
package holiday N viaje m organizado (con
  todo incluido)
package tour N viaje m organizado
packaging ['pækɪdʒɪŋ] N envase m
packed [pækt] ADJ abarrotado
packed lunch [pækt-] N almuerzo frío
packer ['pækər] N (person) empacador(a) m/f
packet ['pækɪt] N paquete m
packet switching [-'swɪtʃɪŋ] N (Comput)
  conmutación f por paquetes
packhorse ['pækhɔːs] N caballo de carga
pack ice N banco de hielo
packing ['pækɪŋ] N embalaje m
packing case N cajón m de embalaje
pact [pækt] N pacto
pad [pæd] N (of paper) bloc m; (cushion) cojinete
  m; (launching pad) plataforma (de
  lanzamiento); (inf: flat) casa ▶ VT rellenar
padded [pædɪd] ADJ (jacket) acolchado; (bra)
  reforzado
padded cell N celda acolchada
padding ['pædɪŋ] N relleno; (fig) paja
paddle ['pædl] N (oar) canalete m, pala; (US:
  for table tennis) pala ▶ VT remar ▶ VI (with feet)
  chapotear
paddle steamer N vapor m de ruedas
paddling pool ['pædlɪŋ-] N (BRIT) piscina
  para niños
paddock ['pædək] N (field) potrero
paddy field ['pædɪ-] N arrozal m
padlock ['pædlɔk] N candado ▶ VT cerrar con
  candado
padre ['pɑːdrɪ] N capellán m
paediatrician, (US) **pediatrician**
  [piːdɪəˈtrɪʃən] N pediatra mf
paediatrics, (US) **pediatrics** [piːdɪˈætrɪks] N
  pediatría
paedophile, (US) **pedophile** ['piːdəufaɪl] ADJ
  de pedófilos ▶ N pedófilo(-a)

P

pagan ['peɪɡən] ADJ, N pagano(-a) m/f
page [peɪdʒ] N página; (also: **page boy**) paje m ▶ VT (in hotel etc) llamar por altavoz a
pageant ['pædʒənt] N (procession) desfile m; (show) espectáculo
pageantry ['pædʒəntrɪ] N pompa
page break N límite m de la página
pager ['peɪdʒəʳ] N busca m
paginate ['pædʒɪneɪt] VT paginar
pagination [pædʒɪ'neɪʃən] N paginación f
pagoda [pə'ɡəudə] N pagoda
paid [peɪd] PT, PP of **pay** ▶ ADJ (work) remunerado; (holiday) pagado; (official) a sueldo; **to put ~ to** (BRIT) acabar con
paid-up ['peɪdʌp], (US) **paid-in** ['peɪdɪn] ADJ (member) con sus cuotas pagadas o al día; (share) liberado; **~ capital** capital m desembolsado
pail [peɪl] N cubo, balde m
pain [peɪn] N dolor m; **to be in ~** sufrir; **on ~ of death** so or bajo pena de muerte; see also **pains**
pained [peɪnd] ADJ (expression) afligido
painful ['peɪnful] ADJ doloroso; (difficult) penoso; (disagreeable) desagradable
painfully ['peɪnfəlɪ] ADV (fig: very) terriblemente
painkiller ['peɪnkɪləʳ] N analgésico
painless ['peɪnlɪs] ADJ sin dolor; (method) fácil
pains [peɪnz] NPL (efforts) esfuerzos mpl; **to take ~ to do sth** tomarse el trabajo de hacer algo
painstaking ['peɪnzteɪkɪŋ] ADJ (person) concienzudo, esmerado
paint [peɪnt] N pintura ▶ VT pintar; **a tin of ~** un bote de pintura; **to ~ the door blue** pintar la puerta de azul
paintbox ['peɪntbɔks] N caja de pinturas
paintbrush ['peɪntbrʌʃ] N (artist's) pincel m; (decorator's) brocha
painter ['peɪntəʳ] N pintor(a) m/f
painting ['peɪntɪŋ] N pintura
paintwork ['peɪntwəːk] N pintura
pair [peəʳ] N (of shoes, gloves etc) par m; (of people) pareja; **a ~ of scissors** unas tijeras; **a ~ of trousers** unos pantalones, un pantalón ▶ **pair off** VI: **to ~ off (with sb)** hacer pareja (con algn)
pajamas [pɪ'dʒɑːməz] NPL (US) pijama msg, piyama msg (LAM)
Pakistan [pɑːkɪ'stɑːn] N Paquistán m
Pakistani [pɑːkɪ'stɑːnɪ] ADJ, N paquistaní mf
PAL [pæl] N ABBR (TV) = **phase alternation line**
pal [pæl] N (inf) amiguete(-a) m/f, colega mf
palace ['pæləs] N palacio
palatable ['pælɪtəbl] ADJ sabroso; (acceptable) aceptable
palate ['pælɪt] N paladar m

palatial [pə'leɪʃəl] ADJ (surroundings, residence) suntuoso, espléndido
palaver [pə'lɑːvəʳ] N (fuss) lío
pale [peɪl] ADJ (gen) pálido; (colour) claro ▶ N: **to be beyond the ~** pasarse de la raya ▶ VI palidecer; **to grow** or **turn ~** palidecer; **to ~ into insignificance (beside)** no poderse comparar (con)
paleness ['peɪlnɪs] N palidez f
Palestine ['pælɪstaɪn] N Palestina
Palestinian [pælɪs'tɪnɪən] ADJ, N palestino(-a) m/f
palette ['pælɪt] N paleta
paling ['peɪlɪŋ] N (stake) estaca; (fence) valla
palisade [pælɪ'seɪd] N palizada
pall [pɔːl] N (of smoke) cortina ▶ VI cansar
pallbearer ['pɔːlbɛərəʳ] N portador m del féretro
pallet ['pælɪt] N (for goods) pallet m
palletization [pælɪtaɪ'zeɪʃən] N paletización f
palliative ['pælɪətɪv] N paliativo
pallid ['pælɪd] ADJ pálido
pallor ['pæləʳ] N palidez f
pally ['pælɪ] ADJ (inf): **to be very ~ with sb** ser muy amiguete de algn
palm [pɑːm] N (Anat) palma; (also: **palm tree**) palmera, palma ▶ VT: **to ~ sth off on sb** (BRIT inf) endosarle algo a algn
palmist ['pɑːmɪst] N quiromántico(-a), palmista mf
Palm Sunday N Domingo de Ramos
palpable ['pælpəbl] ADJ palpable
palpably ['pælpəblɪ] ADV obviamente
palpitation [pælpɪ'teɪʃən] N palpitación f; **to have palpitations** tener palpitaciones
paltry ['pɔːltrɪ] ADJ (amount etc) miserable; (insignificant: person) insignificante
pamper ['pæmpəʳ] VT mimar
pamphlet ['pæmflət] N folleto; (political: handed out in street) panfleto
pan [pæn] N (also: **saucepan**) cacerola, cazuela, olla; (also: **frying pan**) sartén f; (of lavatory) taza ▶ VI (Cine) tomar panorámicas; **to ~ for gold** cribar oro
pan- [pæn] PREF pan-
panacea [pænə'sɪə] N panacea
panache [pə'næʃ] N gracia, garbo
Panama ['pænəmɑː] N Panamá m
Panama Canal N Canal m de Panamá
pancake ['pænkeɪk] N crepe f, panqueque m (LAM)
Pancake Day N martes m de carnaval
pancake roll N rollito de primavera
pancreas ['pæŋkrɪəs] N páncreas m
panda ['pændə] N panda m
panda car N (BRIT) coche m de la policía
pandemic [pæn'dɛmɪk] N pandemia; **flu ~** pandemia de gripe

pandemonium [pændɪˈməunɪəm] N (*mess*) caos *m*; (*noise*): **there was ~** se armó un tremendo jaleo

pander [ˈpændə^r] VI: **to ~ to** complacer a

p & h ABBR (*US*: = *postage and handling*) gastos de envío

P & L ABBR = **profit and loss**

p & p ABBR (*BRIT*: = *postage and packing*) gastos de envío

pane [peɪn] N cristal *m*

panel [ˈpænl] N (*of wood*) panel *m*; (*of cloth*) paño; (*Radio, TV*) panel *m* de invitados

panel game N (*TV*) programa *m* concurso para equipos

panelling, (*US*) **paneling** [ˈpænəlɪŋ] N paneles *mpl*

panellist, (*US*) **panelist** [ˈpænəlɪst] N miembro del jurado

pang [pæŋ] N: **pangs of conscience** remordimientos *mpl*; **pangs of hunger** dolores *mpl* del hambre

panhandler [ˈpænhændlə^r] N (*US inf*) mendigo(-a)

panic [ˈpænɪk] N pánico ▶ VI dejarse llevar por el pánico

panic buying [-baɪɪŋ] N compras masivas por miedo a futura escasez

panicky [ˈpænɪkɪ] ADJ (*person*) asustadizo

panic-stricken [ˈpænɪkstrɪkən] ADJ preso del pánico

pannier [ˈpænɪə^r] N (*on bicycle*) cartera; (*on mule etc*) alforja

panorama [pænəˈrɑːmə] N panorama *m*

panoramic [pænəˈræmɪk] ADJ panorámico

pansy [ˈpænzɪ] N (*Bot*) pensamiento; (*inf, pej*) maricón *m*

pant [pænt] VI jadear

panther [ˈpænθə^r] N pantera

panties [ˈpæntɪz] NPL bragas *fpl*

pantihose [ˈpæntɪhəuz] N (*US*) medias *fpl*, pantis *mpl*

panto [ˈpæntəu] N (*BRIT inf*) = **pantomime**

pantomime [ˈpæntəmaɪm] N (*BRIT*) representación *f* musical navideña; *ver nota*

En época navideña los teatros británicos ponen en escena representaciones llamadas *pantomimes*, versiones libres de cuentos tradicionales como Aladino o El gato con botas. En ella nunca faltan personajes como la dama (*dame*), papel que siempre interpreta un actor; el protagonista joven (*principal boy*), normalmente interpretado por una actriz, y el malvado (*villain*). Es un espectáculo familiar dirigido a los niños pero con grandes dosis de humor para adultos en el que se alienta la participación del público.

pantry [ˈpæntrɪ] N despensa

pants [pænts] NPL (*BRIT*: *underwear*: *woman's*) bragas *fpl*; (: *man's*) calzoncillos *mpl*; (*US*: *trousers*) pantalones *mpl*

pantsuit [ˈpæntsjuːt] N (*US*) traje *m* de chaqueta y pantalón

papal [ˈpeɪpəl] ADJ papal

paparazzi [pæpəˈrætsɪ] NPL paparazzi *mpl*

paper [ˈpeɪpə^r] N papel *m*; (*also*: **newspaper**) periódico, diario; (*study, article*) artículo; (*exam*) examen *m* ▶ ADJ de papel ▶ VT empapelar; (**identity**) **papers** *npl* papeles *mpl*, documentos *mpl*; **a piece of ~** un papel; **to put sth down on ~** poner algo por escrito

paper advance N (*on printer*) avance *m* de papel

paperback [ˈpeɪpəbæk] N libro de bolsillo

paper bag N bolsa de papel

paperboy [ˈpeɪpəbɔɪ] N (*selling*) vendedor *m* de periódicos; (*delivering*) repartidor *m* de periódicos

paper clip N clip *m*

paper hankie N pañuelo de papel

paper money N papel *m* moneda

paper profit N beneficio no realizado

paper shop N (*BRIT*) tienda de periódicos

paperweight [ˈpeɪpəweɪt] N pisapapeles *m inv*

paperwork [ˈpeɪpəwəːk] N trabajo administrativo; (*pej*) papeleo

papier-mâché [ˈpæpɪeɪˈmæʃeɪ] N cartón *m* piedra

paprika [ˈpæprɪkə] N pimentón *m*

Pap test [ˈpæp-] N (*Med*) frotis *m* (cervical)

papyrus [pəˈpaɪərəs] N papiro

par [pɑː^r] N par *f*; (*Golf*) par *m* ▶ ADJ a la par; **to be on a ~ with** estar a la par con; **at ~** a la par; **to be above/below ~** estar sobre/bajo par; **to feel under ~** sentirse en baja forma

parable [ˈpærəbl] N parábola

paracetamol [pærəˈsiːtəmɔl] N (*BRIT*) paracetamol *m*

parachute [ˈpærəʃuːt] N paracaídas *m inv* ▶ VI lanzarse en paracaídas

parachutist [ˈpærəʃuːtɪst] N paracaidista *mf*

parade [pəˈreɪd] N desfile *m* ▶ VT (*gen*) recorrer, desfilar por; (*show off*) hacer alarde de ▶ VI desfilar; (*Mil*) pasar revista; **a fashion ~** un desfile de modelos

parade ground N plaza de armas

paradise [ˈpærədaɪs] N paraíso

paradox [ˈpærədɔks] N paradoja

paradoxical [pærəˈdɔksɪkl] ADJ paradójico

paradoxically [pærəˈdɔksɪklɪ] ADV paradójicamente

paraffin [ˈpærəfɪn] N (*BRIT*): **~ (oil)** parafina

paraffin heater N estufa de parafina

paraffin lamp N quinqué *m*

paragon [ˈpærəgən] N modelo

paragraph ['pærəgrɑːf] N párrafo, acápite *m* (*LAm*); **new ~** punto y aparte, punto acápite (*LAm*)

Paraguay ['pærəgwaɪ] N Paraguay *m*

Paraguayan [pærə'gwaɪən] ADJ, N paraguayo(-a) *m/f*, paraguayano(-a) *m/f*

parallel ['pærəlɛl] ADJ: **~ (with/to)** en paralelo (con/a); (*fig*) semejante (a) ▶ N (*line*) paralela; (*fig*) paralelo; (*Geo*) paralelo

paralysis [pə'rælɪsɪs] N parálisis *f inv*

paralytic [pærə'lɪtɪk] ADJ paralítico

paralyze ['pærəlaɪz] VT paralizar; **paralyzed** paralizado

paramedic [pærə'mɛdɪk] N auxiliar *mf* sanitario(-a)

parameter [pə'ræmɪtər] N parámetro

paramilitary [pærə'mɪlɪtərɪ] ADJ (*organization, operations*) paramilitar

paramount ['pærəmaunt] ADJ: **of ~ importance** de suma importancia

paranoia [pærə'nɔɪə] N paranoia

paranoid ['pærənɔɪd] ADJ (*person, feeling*) paranoico

paranormal [pærə'nɔːml] ADJ paranormal

parapet ['pærəpɪt] N parapeto

paraphernalia [pærəfə'neɪlɪə] N parafernalia

paraphrase ['pærəfreɪz] VT parafrasear

paraplegic [pærə'pliːdʒɪk] N parapléjico(-a)

parapsychology [pærəsaɪ'kɔlədʒɪ] N parapsicología

parasite ['pærəsaɪt] N parásito(-a)

parasol ['pærəsɔl] N sombrilla, quitasol *m*

paratrooper ['pærətruːpər] N paracaidista *mf*

parcel ['pɑːsl] N paquete *m* ▶ VT (*also*: **parcel up**) empaquetar, embalar; **to be part and ~ of** ser parte integrante de
▶ **parcel out** VT parcelar, repartir

parcel bomb N paquete *m* bomba

parcel post N servicio de paquetes postales

parch [pɑːtʃ] VT secar, resecar

parched [pɑːtʃt] ADJ (*person*) muerto de sed

parchment ['pɑːtʃmənt] N pergamino

pardon ['pɑːdn] N perdón *m*; (*Law*) indulto
▶ VT perdonar; indultar; **~ me!, I beg your ~!** ¡perdone usted!; **(I beg your) ~?**, (*US*) **~ me?** ¿cómo (dice)?

pare [pɛər] VT (*nails*) cortar; (*fruit etc*) pelar

parent ['pɛərənt] N (*mother*) madre *f*; (*father*) padre *m*; **parents** NPL padres *mpl*

parentage ['pɛərəntɪdʒ] N familia, linaje *m*; **of unknown ~** de padres desconocidos

parental [pə'rɛntl] ADJ paternal/maternal

parent company N casa matriz

parenthesis [pə'rɛnθɪsɪs] N (*pl* **parentheses** [-θɪsiːz]) N paréntesis *m inv*; **in parentheses** entre paréntesis

parenthood ['pɛərənthud] N el ser padres

parent ship N buque *m* nodriza

Paris ['pærɪs] N París *m*

parish ['pærɪʃ] N parroquia

parish council N consejo parroquial

parishioner [pə'rɪʃənər] N feligrés(-esa) *m/f*

Parisian [pə'rɪzɪən] ADJ, N parisino(-a) *m/f*, parisiense *mf*

parity ['pærɪtɪ] N paridad *f*, igualdad *f*

park [pɑːk] N parque *m*, jardín *m* público
▶ VT, VI aparcar, estacionar

parka ['pɑːkə] N parka

park and ride N aparcamiento disuasorio

parking ['pɑːkɪŋ] N aparcamiento, estacionamiento; **"no ~"** "prohibido aparcar *or* estacionarse"

parking lights NPL luces *fpl* de estacionamiento

parking lot N (*US*) parking *m*, aparcamiento, playa *f* de estacionamiento (*LAm*)

parking meter N parquímetro

parking offence, (*US*) **parking violation** N ofensa por aparcamiento indebido

parking place N sitio para aparcar, aparcamiento

parking ticket N multa de aparcamiento

Parkinson's N (*also*: **Parkinson's disease**) (enfermedad *f* de) Parkinson *m*

parkway ['pɑːkweɪ] N (*US*) alameda

parlance ['pɑːləns] N lenguaje *m*; **in common/modern ~** en lenguaje corriente/moderno

parliament ['pɑːləmənt] N parlamento; (*Spanish*) las Cortes *fpl*; *ver nota*

> El Parlamento británico (*Parliament*) tiene como sede el palacio de Westminster, también llamado *Houses of Parliament*. Consta de dos cámaras; la Cámara de los Comunes (*House of Commons*) está formada por 650 diputados (*Members of Parliament*) que acceden a ella tras ser elegidos por sufragio universal en su respectiva área o circunscripción electoral (*constituency*). Se reúne 175 días al año y sus sesiones son presididas y moderadas por el Presidente de la Cámara (*Speaker*). La cámara alta es la Cámara de los Lores (*House of Lords*) y sus miembros son nombrados por el monarca o bien han heredado su escaño. Su poder es limitado, aunque actúa como tribunal supremo de apelación, excepto en Escocia.

parliamentary [pɑːlə'mɛntərɪ] ADJ parlamentario

parlour, (*US*) **parlor** ['pɑːlər] N salón *m*, living *m* (*LAm*)

parlous ['pɑːləs] ADJ peligroso, alarmante

Parmesan [pɑːmɪ'zæn] N (*also*: **Parmesan cheese**) queso parmesano

parochial [pə'rəukɪəl] ADJ parroquial; (*pej*) de miras estrechas

parody ['pærədɪ] N parodia ▶ VT parodiar

parole [pə'rəul] N: **on ~** en libertad condicional

paroxysm ['pærəksɪzəm] N (*Med*) paroxismo, ataque *m*; (*of anger, laughter, coughing*) ataque *m*; (*of grief*) crisis *f*

parquet ['pɑːkeɪ] N: **~ floor(ing)** parquet *m*

parrot ['pærət] N loro, papagayo

parrot fashion ADV como un loro

parry ['pærɪ] VT parar

parsimonious [pɑːsɪ'məunɪəs] ADJ tacaño

parsley ['pɑːslɪ] N perejil *m*

parsnip ['pɑːsnɪp] N chirivía

parson ['pɑːsn] N cura *m*

part [pɑːt] N (*gen*) parte *f*; (*Mus*) parte *f*; (*bit*) trozo; (*of machine*) pieza; (*Theat etc*) papel *m*; (*of serial*) entrega; (*US: in hair*) raya **= partly** ▶ VT separar; (*break*) partir ▶ VI (*people*) separarse; (*roads*) bifurcarse; (*crowd*) apartarse; (*break*) romperse; **to take ~ in** participar *or* tomar parte en; **to take sb's ~** tomar partido por algn; **for my ~** por mi parte; **for the most ~** en su mayor parte; (*people*) en su mayoría; **for the better ~ of the day** durante la mayor parte del día; **~ of speech** (*Ling*) categoría gramatical, parte *f* de la oración; **to take sth in good/bad ~** aceptar algo bien/tomarse algo a mal ▶ **part with** VT FUS ceder, entregar; (*money*) pagar; (*get rid of*) deshacerse de

partake [pɑː'teɪk] VI (*irreg: like* **take**) (*formal*): **to ~ of sth** (*food*) comer algo; (*drink*) tomar *or* beber algo

part exchange N (*BRIT*): **in ~** como parte del pago

partial ['pɑːʃl] ADJ parcial; **to be ~ to** (*like*) ser aficionado a

partially ['pɑːʃəlɪ] ADV en parte, parcialmente

participant [pɑː'tɪsɪpənt] N (*in competition*) concursante *mf*

participate [pɑː'tɪsɪpeɪt] VI: **to ~ in** participar en

participation [pɑːtɪsɪ'peɪʃən] N participación *f*

participle ['pɑːtɪsɪpl] N participio

particle ['pɑːtɪkl] N partícula; (*of dust*) mota; (*fig*) pizca

particular [pə'tɪkjulə*r*] ADJ (*special*) particular; (*concrete*) concreto; (*given*) determinado; (*detailed*) detallado, minucioso; (*fussy*) quisquilloso; (*demanding*) exigente; **particulars** NPL (*information*) datos *mpl*, detalles *mpl*; (*details*) pormenores *mpl*; **in ~ en particular**; **to be very ~ about** ser muy exigente en cuanto a; **I'm not ~** me es *or* da igual

particularly [pə'tɪkjulalɪ] ADV (*in particular*) sobre todo; (*difficult, good etc*) especialmente

parting ['pɑːtɪŋ] N (*act of*) separación *f*; (*farewell*) despedida; (*BRIT: in hair*) raya ▶ ADJ de despedida; **~ shot** (*fig*) golpe *m* final

partisan [pɑːtɪ'zæn] ADJ partidista ▶ N partidario(-a); (*fighter*) partisano(-a)

partition [pɑː'tɪʃən] N (*Pol*) división *f*; (*wall*) tabique *m* ▶ VT dividir; dividir con tabique

partly ['pɑːtlɪ] ADV en parte

partner ['pɑːtnə*r*] N (*Comm*) socio(-a); (*Sport*) pareja; (*at dance*) pareja; (*spouse*) cónyuge *mf*; (*friend etc*) compañero(-a) ▶ VT acompañar

partnership ['pɑːtnəʃɪp] N (*gen*) asociación *f*; (*Comm*) sociedad *f*; **to go into** *or* **(with), form a ~ (with)** asociarse (con)

part payment N pago parcial

partridge ['pɑːtrɪdʒ] N perdiz *f*

part-time ['pɑːt'taɪm] ADJ, ADV a tiempo parcial

part-timer [pɑːt'taɪmə*r*] N trabajador(a) *m/f* a tiempo parcial

party ['pɑːtɪ] N (*Pol*) partido; (*celebration*) fiesta; (*group*) grupo; (*Law*) parte *f*, interesado ▶ ADJ (*Pol*) de partido; (*dress etc*) de fiesta, de gala; **to have** *or* **give** *or* **throw a ~** organizar una fiesta; **dinner ~** cena; **to be a ~ to a crime** ser cómplice *mf* de un crimen

party line N (*Pol*) línea política del partido; (*Tel*) línea compartida

party piece N: **to do one's ~** hacer su numerito (de fiesta)

party political broadcast N ≈ espacio electoral

pass [pɑːs] VT (*time, object*) pasar; (*place*) pasar por; (*exam, law*) aprobar; (*overtake, surpass*) rebasar; (*approve*) aprobar ▶ VI pasar; (*Scol*) aprobar ▶ N (*permit*) permiso, pase *m*; (*membership card*) carnet *m*; (*in mountains*) puerto; (*Sport*) pase *m*; (*Scol: also*: **pass mark**) aprobado; **to ~ sth through sth** pasar algo por algo; **to ~ the time of day with sb** pasar el rato con algn; **things have come to a pretty ~!** ¡hasta dónde hemos llegado!; **to make a ~ at sb** (*inf*) insinuársele a algn
▶ **pass away** VI fallecer
▶ **pass by** VI pasar ▶ VT (*ignore*) pasar por alto
▶ **pass down** VT (*customs, inheritance*) pasar, transmitir
▶ **pass for** VT FUS pasar por; **she could ~ for 25** se podría creer que sólo tiene 25 años
▶ **pass on** VI (*die*) fallecer, morir ▶ VT (*hand on*): **to ~ on (to)** transmitir (a); (*cold, illness*) pegar (a); (*benefits*) dar (a); (*price rises*) pasar (a)
▶ **pass out** VI desmayarse; (*Mil*) graduarse
▶ **pass over** VI (*die*) fallecer ▶ VT omitir, pasar por alto
▶ **pass up** VT (*opportunity*) dejar pasar, no aprovechar

passable ['pɑːsəbl] ADJ (*road*) transitable; (*tolerable*) pasable

passably ['pɑːsəblɪ] ADV pasablemente

passage ['pæsɪdʒ] N pasillo; (*act of passing*) tránsito; (*fare, in book*) pasaje *m*; (*by boat*) travesía

passageway ['pæsɪdʒweɪ] N (*in house*) pasillo, corredor *m*; (*between buildings etc*) pasaje *m*, pasadizo

passenger ['pæsɪndʒəʳ] N pasajero(-a), viajero(-a)

passer-by ['pɑːsə'baɪ] N transeúnte *mf*

passing ['pɑːsɪŋ] ADJ (*fleeting*) pasajero; **in ~** de paso

passing place N (*Aut*) apartadero

passion ['pæʃən] N pasión *f*

passionate ['pæʃənɪt] ADJ apasionado

passionately ['pæʃənɪtlɪ] ADV apasionadamente, con pasión

passion fruit N fruta de la pasión, granadilla

passion play N drama *m* de la Pasión

passive ['pæsɪv] ADJ (*also Ling*) pasivo

passive smoking N *efectos del tabaco en fumadores pasivos*

passkey ['pɑːskiː] N llave *f* maestra

Passover ['pɑːsəuvəʳ] N Pascua (de los judíos)

passport ['pɑːspɔːt] N pasaporte *m*

passport control N control *m* de pasaporte

passport office N oficina de pasaportes

password ['pɑːswəːd] N (*also Comput*) contraseña

past [pɑːst] PREP (*further than*) más allá de; (*later than*) después de ▶ ADJ pasado; (*president etc*) antiguo ▶ N (*time*) pasado; (*of person*) antecedentes *mpl*; **quarter/half ~ four** las cuatro y cuarto/media; **he's ~ forty** tiene más de cuarenta años; **I'm ~ caring** ya no me importa; **to be ~ it** (*inf: person*) estar acabado; **for the ~ few/three days** durante los últimos días/últimos tres días; **to run ~** pasar corriendo; **in the ~** en el pasado, antes

pasta ['pæstə] N pasta

paste [peɪst] N (*gen*) pasta; (*glue*) engrudo ▶ VT (*stick*) pegar; (*glue*) engomar; **tomato ~** tomate concentrado

pastel ['pæstl] ADJ pastel; (*painting*) al pastel

pasteurized ['pæstəraɪzd] ADJ pasteurizado

pastille ['pæstl] N pastilla

pastime ['pɑːstaɪm] N pasatiempo

past master N: **to be a ~ at** ser un maestro en

pastor ['pɑːstəʳ] N pastor *m*

pastoral ['pɑːstərl] ADJ pastoral

past participle [-'pɑːtɪsɪpl] N (*Ling*) participio *m* (de) pasado *or* (de) pretérito *or* pasivo

pastry ['peɪstrɪ] N (*dough*) pasta; (*cake*) pastel *m*

pasture ['pɑːstʃəʳ] N (*grass*) pasto

pasty N ['pæstɪ] empanada ▶ ADJ ['peɪstɪ] pastoso; (*complexion*) pálido

pat [pæt] VT dar una palmadita a; (*dog etc*) acariciar ▶ N (*of butter*) porción *f* ▶ ADJ: **he knows it (off) ~** se lo sabe de memoria *or* al dedillo; **to give sb/o.s. a ~ on the back** (*fig*) felicitar a algn/felicitarse

patch [pætʃ] N (*of material*) parche *m*; (*mended part*) remiendo; (*of land*) terreno; (*Comput*) ajuste *m* ▶ VT (*clothes*) remendar; **(to go through) a bad ~** (pasar por) una mala racha ▶ **patch up** VT (*mend temporarily*) reparar; **to ~ up a quarrel** hacer las paces

patchwork ['pætʃwəːk] N labor *f* de retales

patchy ['pætʃɪ] ADJ desigual

pate [peɪt] N: **bald ~** calva

pâté ['pæteɪ] N paté *m*

patent ['peɪtnt] N patente *f* ▶ VT patentar ▶ ADJ patente, evidente

patent leather N charol *m*

patently ['peɪtntlɪ] ADV evidentemente

patent medicine N específico

patent office N oficina de patentes y marcas

patent rights NPL derechos *mpl* de patente

paternal [pə'təːnl] ADJ paternal; (*relation*) paterno

paternalistic [pətəːnə'lɪstɪk] ADJ paternalista

paternity [pə'təːnɪtɪ] N paternidad *f*

paternity leave N permiso *m* por paternidad, licencia por paternidad

paternity suit N (*Law*) caso de paternidad

path [pɑːθ] N camino, sendero; (*trail, track*) pista; (*of missile*) trayectoria

pathetic [pə'θetɪk] ADJ (*pitiful*) penoso, patético; (*very bad*) malísimo; (*moving*) conmovedor(a)

pathetically [pə'θetɪklɪ] ADV penosamente, patéticamente; (*very badly*) malísimamente mal, de pena

pathname ['pɑːθneɪm] N (*Comput*) nombre *m* del directorio

pathological [pæθə'lɒdʒɪkəl] ADJ patológico

pathologist [pə'θɒlədʒɪst] N patólogo(-a)

pathology [pə'θɒlədʒɪ] N patología

pathos ['peɪθɒs] N patetismo

pathway ['pɑːθweɪ] N sendero, vereda

patience ['peɪʃns] N paciencia; (*BRIT Cards*) solitario; **to lose one's ~** perder la paciencia

patient ['peɪʃnt] N paciente *mf* ▶ ADJ paciente, sufrido; **to be ~ with sb** tener paciencia con algn

patiently ['peɪʃəntlɪ] ADV pacientemente, con paciencia

patio ['pætɪəu] N patio

patriot ['peɪtrɪət] N patriota *mf*

patriotic [pætrɪ'ɒtɪk] ADJ patriótico

patriotism ['pætrɪətɪzəm] N patriotismo

patrol [pə'trəul] N patrulla ▶ VT patrullar por; **to be on ~** patrullar, estar de patrulla

patrol boat N patrullero, patrullera

patrol car N coche m patrulla

patrolman [pə'trəulmən] N (irreg) (US) policía m

patron ['peitrən] N (in shop) cliente mf; (of charity) patrocinador(a) m/f; **~ of the arts** mecenas m inv

patronage ['pætrənidʒ] N patrocinio, protección f

patronize ['pætrənaiz] VT (shop) ser cliente de; (look down on) tratar con condescendencia a

patronizing ['pætrənaiziŋ] ADJ condescendiente

patron saint N santo(-a) patrón(-ona)

patter ['pætər] N golpeteo; (sales talk) labia ▶ VI (rain) tamborilear

pattern ['pætən] N (Sewing) patrón m; (design) dibujo; (behaviour, events) esquema m; **~ of events** curso de los hechos; **behaviour patterns** modelos mpl de comportamiento

patterned ['pætənd] ADJ (material) estampado

paucity ['pɔ:siti] N escasez f

paunch [pɔ:ntʃ] N panza, barriga

pauper ['pɔ:pər] N pobre mf

pause [pɔ:z] N pausa; (interval) intervalo ▶ VI hacer una pausa; **to ~ for breath** detenerse para tomar aliento

pave [peiv] VT pavimentar; **to ~ the way for** preparar el terreno para

pavement ['peivmənt] N (BRIT) acera, vereda (LAM), andén m (LAM), banqueta (LAM); (US) calzada, pavimento

pavilion [pə'viliən] N pabellón m; (Sport) vestuarios mpl

paving ['peiviŋ] N pavimento, enlosado

paving stone N losa

paw [pɔ:] N pata; (claw) garra ▶ VT (animal) tocar con la pata; (pej: touch) tocar, manosear

pawn [pɔ:n] N (Chess) peón m; (fig) instrumento ▶ VT empeñar

pawnbroker ['pɔ:nbrəukər] N prestamista mf

pawnshop ['pɔ:nʃɔp] N casa de empeños

pay [pei] (pt, pp **paid**) N paga; (wage etc) sueldo, salario ▶ VT (visit) hacer; (respect) ofrecer ▶ VI pagar; (be profitable) rendir, compensar, ser rentable; **to be in sb's ~** estar al servicio de algn; **to ~ attention (to)** prestar atención (a); **I paid £5 for that record** pagué 5 libras por ese disco; **how much did you ~ for it?** ¿cuánto pagaste por él?; **to ~ one's way** (contribute one's share) pagar su parte; (remain solvent: company) ser solvente; **to ~ dividends** (Comm) pagar dividendos; (fig) compensar; **it won't ~ you to do that** no te merece la pena hacer eso; **to put paid to** (plan, person) acabar con
▶ **pay back** VT (money) devolver, reembolsar; (person) pagar

▶ **pay for** VT FUS pagar

▶ **pay in** VT ingresar

▶ **pay off** VT liquidar; (person) pagar; (debts) liquidar, saldar; (creditor) cancelar, redimir; (workers) despedir; (mortgage) cancelar, redimir ▶ VI (scheme, decision) dar resultado; **to ~ sth off in instalments** pagar algo a plazos

▶ **pay out** VT (rope) ir dando; (money) gastar, desembolsar

▶ **pay up** VT pagar

payable ['peiəbl] ADJ pagadero; **to make a cheque ~ to sb** extender un cheque a favor de algn

pay-as-you-go [peiəzjə'gəu] ADJ (mobile phone) (de) prepago

pay award N aumento de sueldo

pay day N día m de paga

PAYE N ABBR (BRIT: = pay as you earn) sistema de retención fiscal en la fuente de ingresos

payee [pei'i:] N portador(a) m/f

pay envelope N (US) = **pay packet**

paying ['peiiŋ] ADJ: **~ guest** huésped(a) m/f de pago

payload ['peiləud] N carga útil

payment ['peimənt] N pago; **advance ~** (part sum) anticipo, adelanto; (total sum) saldo; **monthly ~** mensualidad f; **deferred ~, ~ by instalments** pago a plazos or diferido; **on ~ of £5** mediante pago de or pagando £5; **in ~ for** en pago de

payout ['peijaut] N pago; (in competition) premio en metálico

pay packet N (BRIT) sobre m (de la paga)

pay-phone ['peifəun] N teléfono público

payroll ['peirəul] N plantilla, nómina; **to be on a firm's ~** estar en la plantilla or nómina de una empresa

pay slip N nómina, hoja del sueldo

pay station N (US) teléfono público

pay television N televisión f de pago

paywall ['peiwɔ:l] N (Comput) barrera de pago

PBS N ABBR (US: = Public Broadcasting Service) agrupación de ayuda a la realización de emisiones para la TV pública

PBX ABBR (Tel) = **private branch exchange**

PC N ABBR (= personal computer) PC m; (BRIT) = **police constable** ▶ ABBR (BRIT) = **Privy Councillor** ▶ ADJ ABBR = **politically correct**

pc ABBR (= per cent) = **postcard**

p/c ABBR = **petty cash**

PCB N ABBR (= printed circuit board) TCI f

pcm ABBR = **per calendar month**

PD N ABBR (US) = **police department**

pd ABBR = **paid**

PDA N ABBR (= personal digital assistant) agenda electrónica

PDSA N ABBR (BRIT) = **People's Dispensary for Sick Animals**

P

PDT N ABBR (US: = *Pacific Daylight Time*) hora de verano del Pacífico

PE N ABBR (= *physical education*) ed. física ▶ ABBR (CANADA) = **Prince Edward Island**

pea [piː] N guisante *m*, chícharo (LAM), arveja (LAM)

peace [piːs] N paz *f*; (*calm*) paz *f*, tranquilidad *f*; **to be at ~ with sb/sth** estar en paz con algn/algo; **to keep the ~** (*policeman*) mantener el orden; (*citizen*) guardar el orden

peaceable ['piːsəbl] ADJ pacífico

peaceably [pɪˈsəblɪ] ADV pacíficamente

peaceful ['piːsful] ADJ (*gentle*) pacífico; (*calm*) tranquilo, sosegado

peacekeeping ['piːskiːpɪŋ] ADJ de pacificación ▶ N pacificación *f*

peacekeeping force N fuerza de pacificación

peace offering N (*fig*) prenda de paz

peacetime ['piːstaɪm] N: **in ~** en tiempo de paz

peach [piːtʃ] N melocotón *m*, durazno (LAM)

peacock ['piːkɔk] N pavo real

peak [piːk] N (*of mountain: top*) cumbre *f*, cima; (: *point*) pico; (*of cap*) visera; (*fig*) cumbre *f*

peak-hour ['piːkauəʳ] ADJ (*traffic etc*) de horas punta

peak hours NPL, **peak period** N horas *fpl* punta

peak rate N tarifa máxima

peaky ['piːkɪ] ADJ (BRIT *inf*) pálido, paliducho; **I'm feeling a bit ~** estoy malucho, no me encuentro bien

peal [piːl] N (*of bells*) repique *m*; **~ of laughter** carcajada

peanut ['piːnʌt] N cacahuete *m*, maní *m* (LAM)

peanut butter N mantequilla de cacahuete

pear [pɛəʳ] N pera

pearl [pəːl] N perla

peasant ['peznt] N campesino(-a)

peat [piːt] N turba

pebble ['pɛbl] N guijarro

peck [pɛk] VT (*also*: **peck at**) picotear; (: *food*) comer sin ganas ▶ N picotazo; (*kiss*) besito

pecking order ['pɛkɪŋ-] N orden *m* de jerarquía

peckish ['pɛkɪʃ] ADJ (BRIT *inf*): **I feel ~** tengo ganas de picar algo

peculiar [pɪˈkjuːlɪəʳ] ADJ (*odd*) extraño, raro; (*typical*) propio, característico; (*particular: importance, qualities*) particular; **~ to** propio de

peculiarity [pɪkjuːlɪˈærɪtɪ] N peculiaridad *f*, característica

peculiarly [pɪˈkjuːlɪəlɪ] ADV extrañamente; particularmente

pedal ['pɛdl] N pedal *m* ▶ VI pedalear

pedal bin N cubo de la basura con pedal

pedalo ['pɛdələu] N patín *m* a pedal

pedant ['pɛdənt] N pedante *mf*

pedantic [pɪˈdæntɪk] ADJ pedante

pedantry ['pɛdəntrɪ] N pedantería

peddle ['pɛdl] VT (*goods*) ir vendiendo *or* vender de puerta en puerta; (*drugs*) traficar con; (*gossip*) divulgar

peddler ['pɛdləʳ] N vendedor(a) *m/f* ambulante

pedestal ['pɛdəstl] N pedestal *m*

pedestrian [pɪˈdɛstrɪən] N peatón *m* ▶ ADJ pedestre

pedestrian crossing N (BRIT) paso de peatones

pedestrianized ADJ: **a ~ street** una calle peatonal

pedestrian precinct, (US) **pedestrian zone** N zona peatonal

pediatrics [piːdɪˈætrɪks] N (US) = **paediatrics**

pedigree ['pɛdɪɡriː] N genealogía; (*of animal*) pedigrí *m* ▶ CPD (*animal*) de raza, de casta

pedlar ['pɛdləʳ] N (BRIT) = **peddler**

pedophile ['piːdəufaɪl] N (US) = **paedophile**

pee [piː] VI (*inf*) mear

peek [piːk] VI mirar a hurtadillas; (*Comput*) inspeccionar

peel [piːl] N piel *f*; (*of orange, lemon*) cáscara; (: *removed*) peladuras *fpl* ▶ VT pelar ▶ VI (*paint etc*) desconcharse; (*wallpaper*) despegarse, desprenderse; (*skin*) pelar
▶ **peel back** VT pelar

peeler ['piːləʳ] N: **potato ~** mondador *m or* pelador *m* de patatas, pelapatatas *m inv*

peep [piːp] N (*look*) mirada furtiva; (*sound*) pío ▶ VI (*look*) mirar furtivamente
▶ **peep out** VI asomar la cabeza

peephole ['piːphəul] N mirilla

peer [pɪəʳ] VI: **to ~ at** escudriñar ▶ N (*noble*) par *m*; (*equal*) igual *m*; (*contemporary*) contemporáneo(-a)

peerage ['pɪərɪdʒ] N nobleza

peerless ['pɪəlɪs] ADJ sin par, incomparable, sin igual

peeved [piːvd] ADJ enojado

peevish ['piːvɪʃ] ADJ malhumorado

peevishness ['piːvɪʃnɪs] N mal humor *m*

peg [pɛɡ] N clavija; (*for coat etc*) gancho, colgador *m*; (BRIT: *also*: **clothes peg**) pinza; (*also*: **tent peg**) estaca ▶ VT (*clothes*) tender; (*groundsheet*) fijar con estacas; (*fig: wages, prices*) fijar

pejorative [pɪˈdʒɔrətɪv] ADJ peyorativo

Pekin [piːˈkɪn], **Peking** [piːˈkɪŋ] N Pekín *m*

pekinese [piːkɪˈniːz] N pequinés(-esa) *m/f*

pelican ['pɛlɪkən] N pelícano

pelican crossing N (BRIT Aut) paso de peatones señalizado

pellet ['pɛlɪt] N bolita; (*bullet*) perdigón *m*

pell-mell ['pɛl'mɛl] ADV en tropel

pelmet ['pɛlmɪt] N galería

pelt [pɛlt] VT: **to ~ sb with sth** arrojarle algo a algn ▶ VI (*rain: also*: **pelt down**) llover a cántaros; (*inf: run*) correr ▶ N pellejo

pelvis ['pɛlvɪs] N pelvis *f*

pen [pɛn] N (*also*: **ballpoint pen**) bolígrafo; (*also*: **fountain pen**) pluma; (*for sheep*) redil *m*; (*US inf: prison*) cárcel *f*, chirona; **to put ~ to paper** tomar la pluma

penal ['pi:nl] ADJ penal; **~ servitude** trabajos *mpl* forzados

penalize ['pi:nəlaɪz] VT (*punish*) castigar; (*Sport*) sancionar, penalizar

penalty ['pɛnltɪ] N (*gen*) pena; (*fine*) multa; (*Sport*) sanción *f*; (*also*: **penalty kick**: *Football*) penalty *m*

penalty area N (*BRIT Sport*) área de castigo

penalty clause N cláusula de penalización

penalty shoot-out [-'ʃu:taut] N (*Football*) tanda de penaltis

penance ['pɛnəns] N penitencia

pence [pɛns] PL *of* **penny**

penchant ['pɒŋʃɒŋ] N predilección *f*, inclinación *f*

pencil ['pɛnsl] N lápiz *m*, lapicero (*LAM*) ▶ VT (*also*: **pencil in**) escribir con lápiz; (: *fig*) apuntar con carácter provisional

pencil case N estuche *m*

pencil sharpener N sacapuntas *m inv*

pendant ['pɛndnt] N pendiente *m*

pending ['pɛndɪŋ] PREP antes de ▶ ADJ pendiente; **~ the arrival of ...** hasta que llegue ..., hasta llegar ...

pendulum ['pɛndjuləm] N péndulo

penetrate ['pɛnɪtreɪt] VT penetrar

penetrating ['pɛnɪtreɪtɪŋ] ADJ penetrante

penetration [pɛnɪ'treɪʃən] N penetración *f*

penfriend ['pɛnfrɛnd] N (*BRIT*) amigo(-a) por correspondencia

penguin ['pɛŋgwɪn] N pingüino

penicillin [pɛnɪ'sɪlɪn] N penicilina

peninsula [pə'nɪnsjulə] N península

penis ['pi:nɪs] N pene *m*

penitence ['pɛnɪtns] N penitencia

penitent ['pɛnɪtnt] ADJ arrepentido; (*Rel*) penitente

penitentiary [pɛnɪ'tɛnʃərɪ] N (*US*) cárcel *f*, presidio

penknife ['pɛnnaɪf] N navaja

Penn., Penna. ABBR (*US*) = **Pennsylvania**

pen name N seudónimo

pennant ['pɛnənt] N banderola; banderín *m*

penniless ['pɛnɪlɪs] ADJ sin dinero

Pennines ['pɛnaɪnz] NPL (Montes *mpl*) Peninos *mpl*

penny ['pɛnɪ] (*pl* **pennies** ['pɛnɪz] *or* (*BRIT*) **pence** [pɛns]) N (*BRIT*) penique *m*; (*US*) centavo

penpal ['pɛnpæl] N amigo(-a) por correspondencia

penpusher ['pɛnpuʃər] N (*pej*) chupatintas *mf*

pension ['pɛnʃən] N (*allowance, state payment*) pensión *f*; (*old-age*) jubilación *f* ▶ **pension off** VT jubilar

pensioner ['pɛnʃənər] N (*BRIT*) jubilado(-a)

pension fund N fondo de pensiones

pensive ['pɛnsɪv] ADJ pensativo; (*withdrawn*) preocupado

pentagon ['pɛntəgən] N pentágono; **the P~** (*US Pol*) el Pentágono

> Se conoce como el Pentágono (*the Pentagon*) al edificio de planta pentagonal que acoge las dependencias del Ministerio de Defensa estadounidense (*Department of Defense*) en Arlington, Virginia. En lenguaje periodístico se aplica también a la dirección militar del país.

Pentecost ['pɛntɪkɒst] N Pentecostés *m*

penthouse ['pɛnthaus] N ático (de lujo)

pent-up ['pɛntʌp] ADJ (*feelings*) reprimido

penultimate [pɛ'nʌltɪmət] ADJ penúltimo

penury ['pɛnjurɪ] N miseria, pobreza

people ['pi:pl] NPL gente *f*; (*citizens*) pueblo *sg*, ciudadanos *mpl*; (*Pol*): **the ~** el pueblo ▶ N (*nation, race*) pueblo, nación *f* ▶ VT poblar; **several ~ came** vinieron varias personas; **~ say that ...** dice la gente que ...; **old/young ~** los ancianos/jóvenes; **~ at large** la gente en general; **a man of the ~** un hombre del pueblo

PEP [pɛp] N ABBR (= *personal equity plan*) plan personal de inversión con desgravación fiscal

pep [pɛp] N (*inf*) energía ▶ **pep up** VT animar

pepper ['pɛpər] N (*spice*) pimienta; (*vegetable*) pimiento, ají *m* (*LAM*), chile *m* (*LAM*) ▶ VT: **to ~ with** (*fig*) salpicar de

peppermint ['pɛpəmɪnt] N menta; (*sweet*) pastilla de menta

pepperoni [pɛpə'rəunɪ] N ≈ salchichón *m* picante

pepper pot ['pɛpəpɒt] N pimentero

pep talk ['pɛptɔ:k] N (*inf*): **to give sb a ~** darle a algn una inyección de ánimo

per [pə:r] PREP por; **~ day/person** por día/persona; **~ annum** al año; **as ~ your instructions** de acuerdo con sus instrucciones

per capita ADJ, ADV per cápita

perceive [pə'si:v] VT percibir; (*realize*) darse cuenta de

per cent, (*US*) **percent** [pə'sɛnt] N por ciento; **a 20 ~ discount** un descuento del 20 por ciento

percentage [pə'sɛntɪdʒ] N porcentaje *m*; **to get a ~ on all sales** percibir un tanto por ciento sobre todas las ventas; **on a ~ basis** a porcentaje

percentage point N punto (porcentual)

perceptible [pə'sɛptəbl] ADJ perceptible; (*notable*) sensible

p

perception [pə'sɛpʃən] N percepción f; (insight) perspicacia

perceptive [pə'sɛptɪv] ADJ perspicaz

perch [pə:tʃ] N (fish) perca; (for bird) percha ▶ vɪ: **to ~ (on)** (bird) posarse (en); (person) encaramarse (en)

percolate ['pə:kəleɪt] VT (coffee) filtrar ▶ vɪ (coffee) filtrarse; (fig) filtrarse

percolator ['pə:kəleɪtəʳ] N cafetera de filtro

percussion [pə'kʌʃən] N percusión f

percussionist [pə'kʌʃənɪst] N percusionista mf

peremptory [pə'rɛmptərɪ] ADJ perentorio

perennial [pə'rɛnɪəl] ADJ perenne

perfect ADJ ['pə:fɪkt] perfecto ▶ N (also: **perfect tense**) perfecto ▶ VT [pə'fɛkt] perfeccionar; **he's a ~ stranger to me** no le conozco de nada, me es completamente desconocido

perfection [pə'fɛkʃən] N perfección f

perfectionist [pə'fɛkʃənɪst] N perfeccionista mf

perfectly ['pə:fɪktlɪ] ADV perfectamente; **I'm ~ happy with the situation** estoy muy contento con la situación; **you know ~ well** lo sabes muy bien or perfectamente

perforate ['pə:fəreɪt] VT perforar

perforated ulcer N úlcera perforada

perforation [pə:fə'reɪʃən] N perforación f

perform [pə'fɔ:m] VT (carry out) realizar, llevar a cabo; (Theat) representar; (piece of music) interpretar ▶ vɪ (Theat) actuar; (Tech) funcionar

performance [pə'fɔ:məns] N (of task) realización f; (of a play) representación f; (of player etc) actuación f; (of engine) rendimiento; (of car) prestaciones fpl; (of function) desempeño; **the team put up a good ~** el equipo se defendió bien

performer [pə'fɔ:məʳ] N (actor) actor m, actriz f; (Mus) intérprete mf

performing [pə'fɔ:mɪŋ] ADJ (animal) amaestrado

performing arts NPL: **the ~** las artes teatrales

perfume ['pə:fju:m] N perfume m

perfunctory [pə'fʌŋktərɪ] ADJ superficial

perhaps [pə'hæps] ADV quizá(s), tal vez; **~ so/not** puede que sí/no

peril ['pɛrɪl] N peligro, riesgo

perilous ['pɛrɪləs] ADJ peligroso

perilously ['pɛrɪləslɪ] ADV: **they came ~ close to being caught** por poco les cogen or agarran

perimeter [pə'rɪmɪtəʳ] N perímetro

period ['pɪərɪəd] N período, periodo; (History) época; (Scol) clase f; (full stop) punto; (Med) regla, periodo; (US Sport) tiempo ▶ ADJ (costume, furniture) de época; **for a ~ of three**

weeks durante (un período de) tres semanas; **the holiday ~** el período de vacaciones

periodic [pɪərɪ'ɔdɪk] ADJ periódico

periodical [pɪərɪ'ɔdɪkl] ADJ periódico ▶ N revista, publicación f periódica

periodically [pɪərɪ'ɔdɪklɪ] ADV de vez en cuando, cada cierto tiempo

period pains NPL dolores mpl de la regla or la menstruación

peripatetic [pɛrɪpə'tɛtɪk] ADJ (salesman) ambulante; (teacher) con trabajo en varios colegios

peripheral [pə'rɪfərəl] ADJ periférico ▶ N (Comput) periférico, unidad f periférica

periphery [pə'rɪfərɪ] N periferia

periscope ['pɛrɪskəup] N periscopio

perish ['pɛrɪʃ] vɪ perecer; (decay) echarse a perder

perishable ['pɛrɪʃəbl] ADJ perecedero

perishables ['pɛrɪʃəblz] NPL productos mpl perecederos

peritonitis [pɛrɪtə'naɪtɪs] N peritonitis f

perjure ['pə:dʒəʳ] VT: **to ~ o.s.** perjurar

perjury ['pə:dʒərɪ] N (Law) perjurio

perk [pə:k] N beneficio, extra m ▶ **perk up** vɪ (cheer up) animarse

perky ['pə:kɪ] ADJ alegre, animado

perm [pə:m] N permanente f ▶ VT: **to have one's hair permed** hacerse una permanente

permanence ['pə:mənəns] N permanencia

permanent ['pə:mənənt] ADJ permanente; (job, position) fijo; (dye, ink) indeleble; **~ address** domicilio permanente; **I'm not ~ here** no estoy fijo aquí

permanently ['pə:mənəntlɪ] ADV (lastingly) para siempre, de modo definitivo; (all the time) permanentemente

permeate ['pə:mɪeɪt] vɪ penetrar, trascender ▶ VT penetrar, trascender a

permissible [pə'mɪsɪbl] ADJ permisible, lícito

permission [pə'mɪʃən] N permiso; **to give sb ~ to do sth** autorizar a algn para que haga algo; **with your ~** con su permiso

permissive [pə'mɪsɪv] ADJ permisivo

permit N ['pə:mɪt] permiso, licencia; (entrance pass) pase m ▶ VT [pə'mɪt] permitir; (accept) tolerar ▶ vɪ [pə'mɪt]: **weather permitting** si el tiempo lo permite; **fishing ~** permiso de pesca; **building/export ~** licencia or permiso de construcción/ exportación

permutation [pə:mju'teɪʃən] N permutación f

pernicious [pə:'nɪʃəs] ADJ nocivo; (Med) pernicioso

pernickety [pə'nɪkɪtɪ] ADJ (inf: person) quisquilloso; (task) delicado

perpendicular [pə:pənˈdɪkjuləʳ] ADJ perpendicular

perpetrate [ˈpə:pɪtreɪt] VT cometer

perpetual [pəˈpɛtjuəl] ADJ perpetuo

perpetually [pəˈpɛtjuəlɪ] ADV (*eternally*) perpetuamente; (*continuously*) constantemente, continuamente

perpetuate [pəˈpɛtjueɪt] VT perpetuar

perpetuity [pə:pɪˈtjuːɪtɪ] N: **in ~** a perpetuidad

perplex [pəˈplɛks] VT dejar perplejo

perplexed [pəˈplɛkst] ADJ perplejo, confuso

perplexing [pəˈplɛksɪŋ] ADJ que causa perplejidad

perplexity [pəˈplɛksɪtɪ] N perplejidad *f*, confusión *f*

perquisites [ˈpə:kwɪzɪts] NPL (*also*: **perks**) beneficios *mpl*

persecute [ˈpə:sɪkjuːt] VT (*pursue*) perseguir; (*harass*) acosar

persecution [pə:sɪˈkjuːʃən] N persecución *f*

perseverance [pə:sɪˈvɪərəns] N perseverancia

persevere [pə:sɪˈvɪəʳ] VI perseverar

Persia [ˈpə:ʃə] N Persia

Persian [ˈpə:ʃən] ADJ, N persa *mf* ▶ N (*Ling*) persa *m*; **the ~ Gulf** el Golfo Pérsico

Persian cat N gato persa

persist [pəˈsɪst] VI persistir; **to ~ in doing sth** empeñarse en hacer algo

persistence [pəˈsɪstəns] N empeño

persistent [pəˈsɪstənt] ADJ (*lateness, rain*) persistente; (*determined*) porfiado; (*continuing*) constante; **~ offender** (*Law*) multirreincidente *mf*

persistently [pəˈsɪstəntlɪ] ADV persistentemente; (*continually*) constantemente

persnickety [pəˈsnɪkətɪ] ADJ (*US inf*) = **pernickety**

person [ˈpə:sn] N persona; **in ~** en persona; **on** *or* **about one's ~** encima; **a ~ to ~ call** una llamada (de) persona a persona

personable [ˈpə:snəbl] ADJ atractivo

personal [ˈpə:snl] ADJ personal, individual; (*visit*) en persona; (*Brit Tel*) (de) persona a persona

personal allowance N desgravación *f* personal

personal assistant N ayudante *mf* personal

personal belongings NPL efectos *mpl* personales

personal column N anuncios *mpl* personales

personal computer N ordenador *m* personal

personal effects NPL efectos *mpl* personales

personal identification number N número personal de identificación

personality [pə:səˈnælɪtɪ] N personalidad *f*

personally [ˈpə:snəlɪ] ADV personalmente;

(*in person*) en persona; **to take sth ~** tomarse algo a mal

personal organizer N agenda; (*electronic*) agenda electrónica

personal property N bienes *mpl* muebles

personal, social and health education N (*Brit Scol*) formación social y sanitaria para la vida adulta

personal stereo N walkman® *m*

personification [pə:sɔnɪfɪˈkeɪʃən] N personificación *f*

personify [pə:ˈsɔnɪfaɪ] VT encarnar, personificar

personnel [pə:səˈnɛl] N personal *m*

personnel department N departamento de personal

personnel management N gestión *f* de personal

personnel manager N jefe *m* de personal

perspective [pəˈspɛktɪv] N perspectiva; **to get sth into ~** ver algo en perspectiva *or* como es

Perspex® [ˈpə:spɛks] N (*Brit*) vidrio acrílico, plexiglás® *m*

perspiration [pə:spɪˈreɪʃən] N transpiración *f*, sudor *m*

perspire [pəˈspaɪəʳ] VI transpirar, sudar

persuade [pəˈsweɪd] VT: **to ~ sb to do sth** persuadir a algn para que haga algo; **to ~ sb of sth/that** persuadir *or* convencer a algn de algo/de que; **I am persuaded that …** estoy convencido de que …

persuasion [pəˈsweɪʒən] N persuasión *f*; (*persuasiveness*) persuasiva; (*creed*) creencia

persuasive [pəˈsweɪsɪv] ADJ persuasivo

persuasively [pəˈsweɪsɪvlɪ] ADV de modo persuasivo

pert [pə:t] ADJ impertinente, fresco, atrevido

pertaining [pə:ˈteɪnɪŋ]: **~ to** *prep* relacionado con

pertinent [ˈpə:tɪnənt] ADJ pertinente, a propósito

perturb [pəˈtə:b] VT perturbar

perturbing [pəˈtə:bɪŋ] ADJ inquietante, perturbador(a)

Peru [pəˈruː] N el Perú

perusal [pəˈruːzəl] N (*quick*) lectura somera; (*careful*) examen *m*

peruse [pəˈruːz] VT (*examine*) leer con detención, examinar; (*glance at*) mirar por encima

Peruvian [pəˈruːvɪən] ADJ, N peruano(-a) *m/f*

pervade [pəˈveɪd] VT impregnar; (*influence, ideas*) extenderse por

pervasive [pəˈveɪsɪv] ADJ (*smell*) penetrante; (*influence*) muy extendido; (*gloom, feelings, ideas*) reinante

perverse [pəˈvə:s] ADJ perverso; (*stubborn*) terco; (*wayward*) travieso

perversely [pə'vəːslɪ] ADV perversamente; tercamente; traviesamente

perverseness [pə'vəːsnɪs] N perversidad f; terquedad f; travesura

perversion [pə'vəːʃən] N perversión f

pervert N ['pəːvəːt] pervertido(-a) ▶ VT [pə'vəːt] pervertir

pessary ['pɛsərɪ] N pesario

pessimism ['pɛsɪmɪzəm] N pesimismo

pessimist ['pɛsɪmɪst] N pesimista mf

pessimistic [pɛsɪ'mɪstɪk] ADJ pesimista

pest [pɛst] N (insect) insecto nocivo; (fig) lata, molestia; **pests** NPL plaga

pest control N control m de plagas

pester ['pɛstə'] VT molestar, acosar

pesticide ['pɛstɪsaɪd] N pesticida m

pestilence ['pɛstɪləns] N pestilencia

pestle ['pɛsl] N mano f de mortero or de almirez

pet [pɛt] N animal m doméstico; (favourite) favorito(-a) ▶ VT acariciar ▶ VI (inf) besuquearse ▶ CPD: **teacher's ~** favorito(-a) (del profesor); **~ hate** manía

petal ['pɛtl] N pétalo

peter ['piːtə']: **to ~ out** VI agotarse, acabarse

petite [pə'tiːt] ADJ menuda, chiquita

petition [pə'tɪʃən] N petición f ▶ VT presentar una petición a ▶ VI: **to ~ for divorce** pedir el divorcio

pet name N nombre m cariñoso, apodo

petrified ['pɛtrɪfaɪd] ADJ (fig) pasmado, horrorizado

petrochemical [pɛtrə'kɛmɪkl] ADJ petroquímico

petrodollars ['pɛtrəudɔləz] NPL petrodólares mpl

petrol ['pɛtrəl] N (BRIT) gasolina; (for lighter) bencina; **two/four-star ~** gasolina normal/súper

petrol bomb N cóctel m Molotov

petrol can N bidón m de gasolina

petrol engine N (BRIT) motor m de gasolina

petroleum [pə'trəulɪəm] N petróleo

petroleum jelly N vaselina

petrol pump N (BRIT: in car) bomba de gasolina; (: in garage) surtidor m de gasolina

petrol station N (BRIT) gasolinera

petrol tank N (BRIT) depósito (de gasolina)

petticoat ['pɛtɪkəut] N combinación f, enagua(s) f(pl) (LAM)

pettifogging ['pɛtɪfɔgɪŋ] ADJ quisquilloso

pettiness ['pɛtɪnɪs] N mezquindad f

petty ['pɛtɪ] ADJ (mean) mezquino; (unimportant) insignificante

petty cash N dinero para gastos menores

petty cash book N libro de caja auxiliar

petty officer N contramaestre m

petulant ['pɛtjulənt] ADJ malhumorado

pew [pjuː] N banco

pewter ['pjuːtə'] N peltre m

Pfc ABBR (US Mil) = **private first class**

PG N ABBR (Cine) = **parental guidance**

PG 13 ABBR (US Cine: = Parental Guidance 13) no apto para menores de 13 años

PGA N ABBR = **Professional Golfers' Association**

PH N ABBR (US Mil: = Purple Heart) decoración otorgada a los heridos de guerra

pH N ABBR (= pH value) pH

PHA N ABBR (US) = **Public Housing Administration**

phallic ['fælɪk] ADJ fálico

phantom ['fæntəm] N fantasma m

Pharaoh ['fɛərəu] N faraón m

pharmaceutical [fɑːmə'sjuːtɪkl] ADJ farmacéutico

pharmacist ['fɑːməsɪst] N farmacéutico(-a)

pharmacy ['fɑːməsɪ] N (US) farmacia

phase [feɪz] N fase f ▶ VT: **phased withdrawal** retirada progresiva

▶ **phase in** VT introducir progresivamente

▶ **phase out** VT (machinery, product) retirar progresivamente; (job, subsidy) eliminar por etapas

PhD ABBR = **Doctor of Philosophy**

pheasant ['fɛznt] N faisán m

phenomena [fə'nɔmɪnə] NPL of **phenomenon**

phenomenal [fɪ'nɔmɪnl] ADJ fenomenal, extraordinario

phenomenally [fɪ'nɔmɪnlɪ] ADV extraordinariamente

phenomenon [fə'nɔmɪnən] (pl **phenomena** [-nə]) N fenómeno

phial ['faɪəl] N ampolla

philanderer [fɪ'lændərə'] N donjuán m, don Juan m

philanthropic [fɪlən'θrɔpɪk] ADJ filantrópico

philanthropist [fɪ'lænθrəpɪst] N filántropo(-a)

philatelist [fɪ'lætəlɪst] N filatelista mf

philately [fɪ'lætəlɪ] N filatelia

Philippines ['fɪlɪpiːnz] NPL: **the ~** (las Islas) Filipinas

philosopher [fɪ'lɔsəfə'] N filósofo(-a)

philosophical [fɪlə'sɔfɪkl] ADJ filosófico

philosophy [fɪ'lɔsəfɪ] N filosofía

phishing ['fɪʃɪŋ] N phishing m, método de estafa a través de Internet

phlegm [flɛm] N flema

phlegmatic [flɛg'mætɪk] ADJ flemático

phobia ['fəubjə] N fobia

phone [fəun] N teléfono ▶ VT telefonear, llamar por teléfono; **to be on the ~** tener teléfono; (be calling) estar hablando por teléfono

▶ **phone back** VT, VI volver a llamar

▶ **phone up** VT, VI llamar por teléfono

phone book N guía telefónica
phone box, phone booth N cabina telefónica
phone call N llamada (telefónica)
phonecard ['fəʊnkɑːd] N tarjeta telefónica
phone-in ['fəʊnɪn] N (*Brit Radio, TV*) programa de radio o televisión con las líneas abiertas al público
phone number N número de teléfono
phone tapping [-tæpɪŋ] N escuchas telefónicas
phonetics [fə'nɛtɪks] N fonética
phoney ['fəʊnɪ] ADJ = **phony**
phonograph ['fəʊnəgræf] N (*US*) fonógrafo, tocadiscos *m inv*
phonology [fəʊ'nɔlədʒɪ] N fonología
phony ['fəʊnɪ] ADJ falso ▶ N (*person*) farsante *mf*
phosphate ['fɔsfeɪt] N fosfato
phosphorus ['fɔsfərəs] N fósforo
photo ['fəʊtəʊ] N foto *f*
photo... ['fəʊtəʊ] PREF foto...
photo album N álbum *m* de fotos
photocall ['fəʊtəʊkɔːl] N sesión *f* fotográfica para la prensa
photocopier ['fəʊtəʊkɔpɪəʳ] N fotocopiadora
photocopy ['fəʊtəʊkɔpɪ] N fotocopia ▶ VT fotocopiar
photoelectric [fəʊtəʊ'lɛktrɪk] ADJ: **~ cell** célula fotoeléctrica
photo finish N resultado comprobado por fotocontrol
Photofit® ['fəʊtəʊfɪt] N (*also:* **Photofit picture**) retrato robot
photogenic [fəʊtəʊ'dʒɛnɪk] ADJ fotogénico
photograph ['fəʊtəgræf] N fotografía ▶ VT fotografiar; **to take a ~ of sb** sacar una foto de algn
photographer [fə'tɔgrəfəʳ] N fotógrafo(-a)
photographic [fəʊtə'græfɪk] ADJ fotográfico
photography [fə'tɔgrəfɪ] N fotografía
photo opportunity N oportunidad de salir en la foto
Photoshop® ['fəʊtəʊʃɔp] N Photoshop® *m* ▶ VT editar en Photoshop
Photostat® ['fəʊtəʊstæt] N fotostato
photosynthesis [fəʊtəʊ'sɪnθəsɪs] N fotosíntesis *f*
phrase [freɪz] N frase *f* ▶ VT (*letter*) expresar, redactar
phrase book N libro de frases
physical ['fɪzɪkl] ADJ físico; **~ examination** reconocimiento médico; **~ exercises** ejercicios *mpl* físicos
physical education N educación *f* física
physically ['fɪsɪklɪ] ADV físicamente
physical training N gimnasia
physician [fɪ'zɪʃən] N médico(-a)
physicist ['fɪzɪsɪst] N físico(-a)
physics ['fɪzɪks] N física

physiological [fɪzɪə'lɔdʒɪkl] ADJ fisiológico
physiology [fɪzɪ'ɔlədʒɪ] N fisiología
physiotherapist [fɪzɪəʊ'θɛrəpɪst] N fisioterapeuta *mf*
physiotherapy [fɪzɪəʊ'θɛrəpɪ] N fisioterapia
physique [fɪ'ziːk] N físico
pianist ['pɪənɪst] N pianista *mf*
piano [pɪ'ænəʊ] N piano
piano accordion N (*Brit*) acordeón-piano *m*
piccolo ['pɪkələʊ] N (*Mus*) flautín *m*
pick [pɪk] N (*tool: also:* **pickaxe**) pico, piqueta ▶ VT (*select*) elegir, escoger; (*gather*) coger (*Sp*), recoger (*Lam*); (*lock*) abrir con ganzúa; (*scab, spot*) rascar ▶ VI: **to ~ and choose** ser muy exigente; **take your ~** escoja lo que quiera; **the ~ of** lo mejor de; **to ~ one's nose/teeth** hurgarse la nariz/escarbarse los dientes; **to ~ pockets** ratear, ser carterista; **to ~ one's way through** andar a tientas, abrirse camino; **to ~ a fight/quarrel with sb** buscar pelea/camorra con algn; **to ~ sb's brains** aprovecharse de los conocimientos de algn
▶ **pick at** VT FUS: **to ~ at one's food** comer con poco apetito
▶ **pick off** VT (*kill*) matar de un tiro
▶ **pick on** VT FUS (*person*) meterse con
▶ **pick out** VT escoger; (*distinguish*) identificar
▶ **pick up** VI (*improve: sales*) ir mejor; (*: patient*) reponerse; (*: Finance*) recobrarse ▶ VT (*from floor*) recoger; (*buy*) comprar; (*find*) encontrar; (*learn*) aprender; (*Police: arrest*) detener; (*Radio, TV, Tel*) captar; **to ~ up speed** acelerarse; **to ~ o.s. up** levantarse; **to ~ up where one left off** volver a empezar algo donde lo había dejado
pickaxe, (*US*) **pickax** ['pɪkæks] N pico, zapapico
picket ['pɪkɪt] N (*in strike*) piquete *m* ▶ VT hacer un piquete en, piquetear; **to be on ~ duty** estar de piquete
picketing ['pɪkɪtɪŋ] N organización *f* de piquetes
picket line N piquete *m*
pickings ['pɪkɪŋz] NPL (*pilferings*): **there are good ~ to be had here** se pueden sacar buenas ganancias de aquí
pickle ['pɪkl] N (*also:* **pickles**: *as condiment*) escabeche *m*; (*fig: mess*) apuro ▶ VT conservar en escabeche; (*in vinegar*) conservar en vinagre; **in a ~** en un lío, en apuros
pick-me-up ['pɪkmɪʌp] N reconstituyente *m*
pickpocket ['pɪkpɔkɪt] N carterista *mf*
pickup ['pɪkʌp] N (*also:* **pickup truck**, **pickup van**) furgoneta, camioneta
picnic ['pɪknɪk] N picnic *m*, merienda ▶ VI hacer un picnic
picnic area N zona de picnic; (*Aut*) área de descanso

p

pictorial [pɪk'tɔːrɪəl] ADJ pictórico; (*magazine etc*) ilustrado

picture ['pɪktʃəʳ] N cuadro; (*painting*) pintura; (*photograph*) fotografía; (*film*) película; (*TV*) imagen *f*; (*fig: description*) descripción *f*; (: *situation*) situación *f* ▶ VT pintar; (*imagine*) imaginar; **the pictures** (BRIT) el cine; **we get a good ~ here** captamos bien la imagen aquí; **to take a ~ of sb/sth** hacer *or* sacar una foto a algn/de algo; **the garden is a ~ in June** el jardín es una preciosidad en junio; **the overall ~** la impresión general; **to put sb in the ~** poner a algn al corriente *or* al tanto

picture book N libro de dibujos

picture frame N marco

picture message N mensaje *m* con foto

picture messaging N (envío de) mensajes *mpl* con imágenes

picturesque [pɪktʃə'rɛsk] ADJ pintoresco

piddling ['pɪdlɪŋ] ADJ insignificante

pidgin ['pɪdʒɪn] ADJ: **~ English** lengua franca basada en el inglés

pie [paɪ] N (*of meat etc: large*) pastel *m*; (: *small*) empanada; (*sweet*) tarta

piebald ['paɪbɔːld] ADJ pío

piece [piːs] N pedazo, trozo; (*of cake*) trozo; (*Draughts etc*) ficha; (*Chess*) pieza; (*part of a set*) pieza; (*item*): **a ~ of furniture/advice** un mueble/un consejo ▶ VT: **to ~ together** juntar; (*Tech*) armar; **to take to pieces** desmontar; **a ~ of news** una noticia; **a 10p ~** una moneda de 10 peniques; **a six-~ band** un conjunto de seis (músicos); **in one ~** (*object*) de una sola pieza; **~ by ~** pieza por *or* a pieza; **to say one's ~** decir su parecer

piecemeal ['piːsmiːl] ADV poco a poco

piece rate N tarifa a destajo

piecework ['piːswəːk] N trabajo a destajo

pie chart N gráfico de sectores *or* de tarta

pier [pɪəʳ] N muelle *m*, embarcadero

pierce [pɪəs] VT penetrar en, perforar; **to have one's ears pierced** hacerse los agujeros de las orejas

piercing ['pɪəsɪŋ] ADJ (*cry*) penetrante ▶ N (*body art*) piercing *m*

piety ['paɪətɪ] N piedad *f*

pig [pɪg] N cerdo, puerco, chancho (LAm); (*person: greedy*) tragón(-ona) *m/f*, comilón(-ona) *m/f*; (: *nasty*) cerdo(-a)

pigeon ['pɪdʒən] N paloma; (*as food*) pichón *m*

pigeonhole ['pɪdʒənhəul] N casilla

piggy bank ['pɪgɪbæŋk] N hucha (*en forma de cerdito*)

pigheaded ['pɪg'hɛdɪd] ADJ terco, testarudo

piglet ['pɪglɪt] N cerdito, cochinillo

pigment ['pɪgmənt] N pigmento

pigmentation [pɪgmən'teɪʃən] N pigmentación *f*

pigmy ['pɪgmɪ] N = **pygmy**

pigskin ['pɪgskɪn] N piel *f* de cerdo

pigsty ['pɪgstaɪ] N pocilga

pigtail ['pɪgteɪl] N (*girl's*) trenza; (*Chinese*) coleta; (*Taur*) coleta

pike [paɪk] N (*spear*) pica; (*fish*) lucio

pilchard ['pɪltʃəd] N sardina

pile [paɪl] N (*heap*) montón *m*; (*of carpet*) pelo ▶ VI: **to ~ into** (*car*) meterse en; **in a ~** en un montón
  ▶ **pile on** VT: **to ~ it on** (*inf*) exagerar
  ▶ **pile up** VI (*accumulate: work*) amontonarse, acumularse ▶ VT (*put in a heap: books, clothes*) apilar, amontonar; (*accumulate*) acumular

piles [paɪlz] NPL (*Med*) almorranas *fpl*, hemorroides *mpl*

pile-up ['paɪlʌp] N (*Aut*) accidente *m* múltiple

pilfer ['pɪlfəʳ] VT, VI ratear, robar, sisar

pilfering ['pɪlfərɪŋ] N ratería

pilgrim ['pɪlgrɪm] N peregrino(-a); **the P~ Fathers** *or* **Pilgrims** los primeros colonos norteamericanos; *see also* **Thanksgiving (Day)**

pilgrimage ['pɪlgrɪmɪdʒ] N peregrinación *f*, romería

pill [pɪl] N píldora; **the ~** la píldora; **to be on the ~** tomar la píldora (anticonceptiva)

pillage ['pɪlɪdʒ] VT pillar, saquear

pillar ['pɪləʳ] N pilar *m*, columna

pillar box N (BRIT) buzón *m*

pillion ['pɪljən] N (*of motorcycle*) asiento trasero; **to ride** ~ ir en el asiento trasero

pillion passenger N pasajero que va detrás

pillory ['pɪlərɪ] VT poner en ridículo

pillow ['pɪləu] N almohada

pillowcase ['pɪləukeɪs], **pillowslip** ['pɪləuslɪp] N funda (de almohada)

pilot ['paɪlət] N piloto *mf* ▶ ADJ (*scheme etc*) piloto *inv* ▶ VT pilotar; (*fig*) guiar, conducir

pilot light N piloto

pimento [pɪ'mɛntəu] N pimiento morrón

pimp [pɪmp] N chulo, cafiche *m* (LAm)

pimple ['pɪmpl] N grano

pimply ['pɪmplɪ] ADJ lleno de granos

PIN N ABBR (= *personal identification number*) PIN *m*

pin [pɪn] N alfiler *m*; (*Elec: of plug*) clavija; (*Tech*) perno; (: *wooden*) clavija; (*drawing pin*) chincheta; (*in grenade*) percutor *m* ▶ VT prender con (alfiler); sujetar con perno; **pins and needles** hormigueo *sg*; **to ~ sth on sb** (*fig*) cargar a algn con la culpa de algo
  ▶ **pin down** VT (*fig*): **there's something strange here, but I can't quite ~ it down** aquí hay algo raro pero no puedo precisar qué es; **to ~ sb down** hacer que algn concrete

pinafore ['pɪnəfɔːʳ] N delantal *m*

pinafore dress N (BRIT) pichi *m*

pinball ['pɪnbɔːl] N (*also*: **pinball machine**) millón *m*, flipper *m*

pincers ['pɪnsəz] NPL pinzas fpl, tenazas fpl

pinch [pɪntʃ] N pellizco; (of salt etc) pizca ▶ VT pellizcar; (inf: steal) birlar ▶ VI (shoe) apretar; **at a ~** en caso de apuro; **to feel the ~** (fig) pasar apuros or estrecheces

pinched [pɪntʃt] ADJ (drawn) cansado; **~ with cold** transido de frío; **~ for money/space** mal or falto de dinero/espacio or sitio

pincushion ['pɪnkuʃən] N acerico

pine [paɪn] N (also: **pine tree**) pino ▶ VI: **to ~ for** suspirar por
▶ **pine away** VI morirse de pena

pineapple ['paɪnæpl] N piña, ananá(s) m (LAM)

pine cone N piña

pine needle N aguja de pino

ping [pɪŋ] N (noise) sonido agudo

Ping-Pong® ['pɪŋpɔŋ] N ping-pong m

pink [pɪŋk] ADJ (de color) rosa inv ▶ N (colour) rosa m; (Bot) clavel m

pinking shears ['pɪŋkɪŋ-] NPL tijeras fpl dentadas

pin money N dinero para gastos extra

pinnacle ['pɪnəkl] N cumbre f

pinpoint ['pɪnpɔɪnt] VT precisar

pinstripe ['pɪnstraɪp] ADJ: **~ suit** traje m a rayas

pint [paɪnt] N pinta (Brit = 0,57 l, US = 0,47 l); (BRIT inf: of beer) pinta de cerveza, ≈ jarra (SP)

pin-up ['pɪnʌp] N (picture) fotografía de mujer u hombre medio desnudos; **~ (girl)** ≈ chica de calendario

pioneer [paɪə'nɪər] N pionero(-a) ▶ VT promover

pious ['paɪəs] ADJ piadoso, devoto

pip [pɪp] N (seed) pepita; **the pips** (BRIT Tel) la señal

pipe [paɪp] N tubería, cañería; (for smoking) pipa, cachimba (LAM), cachimbo (LAM) ▶ VT conducir en cañerías; **(bag)pipes** npl gaita sg
▶ **pipe down** VI (inf) callarse

pipe cleaner N limpiapipas m inv

piped music [paɪpt-] N música ambiental

pipe dream N sueño imposible

pipeline ['paɪplaɪn] N tubería, cañería; (for oil) oleoducto; (for natural gas) gaseoducto; **it is in the ~** (fig) está en trámite

piper ['paɪpər] N (gen) flautista mf; (with bagpipes) gaitero(-a)

pipe tobacco N tabaco de pipa

piping ['paɪpɪŋ] ADV: **to be ~ hot** estar calentito

piquant ['pi:kənt] ADJ picante

pique [pi:k] N pique m, resentimiento

pirate ['paɪərət] N pirata mf ▶ VT (record, video, book) hacer una copia pirata de, piratear

pirated ['paɪərətɪd] ADJ (book, record etc) pirata inv

pirate radio N (BRIT) emisora pirata

pirouette [pɪru'ɛt] N pirueta ▶ VI piruetear

Pisces ['paɪsi:z] N Piscis m

piss [pɪs] VI (inf) mear

pissed [pɪst] ADJ (inf: drunk) mamado, pedo

pistol ['pɪstl] N pistola

piston ['pɪstən] N pistón m, émbolo

pit [pɪt] N hoyo; (also: **coal pit**) mina; (in garage) foso de inspección; (also: **orchestra pit**) foso de la orquesta; (quarry) cantera ▶ VT (chickenpox) picar; (rust) comer; **to ~ A against B** oponer A a B; **pits** NPL (Aut) box msg; **pitted with** (chickenpox) picado de; **to ~ one's wits against sb** medir fuerzas con algn

pitapat ['pɪtə'pæt] ADV: **to go ~** (heart) latir rápidamente; (rain) golpetear

pitch [pɪtʃ] N (throw) lanzamiento; (Mus) tono; (BRIT Sport) campo, terreno; (tar) brea; (in market etc) puesto; (fig: degree) nivel m, grado ▶ VT (throw) arrojar, lanzar ▶ VI (fall) caer(se); (Naut) cabecear; **I can't keep working at this ~** no puedo seguir trabajando a este ritmo; **at its (highest) ~** en su punto máximo; **his anger reached such a ~ that ...** su ira or cólera llegó a tal extremo que ...; **to ~ a tent** montar una tienda (de campaña); **to ~ one's aspirations too high** tener ambiciones desmesuradas

pitch-black ['pɪtʃ'blæk] ADJ negro como boca de lobo

pitched battle [pɪtʃt-] N batalla campal

pitcher ['pɪtʃər] N cántaro, jarro

pitchfork ['pɪtʃfɔ:k] N horca

piteous ['pɪtɪəs] ADJ lastimoso

pitfall ['pɪtfɔ:l] N riesgo

pith [pɪθ] N (of orange) piel f blanca; (fig) meollo

pithead ['pɪthed] N (BRIT) bocamina

pithy ['pɪθɪ] ADJ jugoso

pitiful ['pɪtɪful] ADJ (touching) lastimoso, conmovedor(a); (contemptible) lamentable

pitifully ['pɪtɪfəlɪ] ADV: **it's ~ obvious** es tan evidente que da pena

pitiless ['pɪtɪlɪs] ADJ despiadado, implacable

pitilessly ['pɪtɪlɪslɪ] ADV despiadadamente, implacablemente

pittance ['pɪtns] N miseria

pity ['pɪtɪ] N (compassion) compasión f, piedad f; (shame) lástima ▶ VT compadecer(se de); **to have** or **take ~ on sb** compadecerse de algn; **what a ~!** ¡qué pena!; **it is a ~ that you can't come** ¡qué pena que no puedas venir!

pitying ['pɪtɪɪŋ] ADJ compasivo, de lástima

pivot ['pɪvət] N eje m ▶ VI: **to ~ on** girar sobre; (fig) depender de

pixel ['pɪksl] N (Comput) píxel m

pixie ['pɪksɪ] N duendecillo

pizza ['pi:tsə] N pizza

placard ['plækɑ:d] N (in march etc) pancarta

p

placate [pləˈkeɪt] VT apaciguar
place [pleɪs] N lugar *m*, sitio; (*rank*) rango; (*seat*) plaza, asiento; (*post*) puesto; (*in street names*) plaza; (*home*): **at/to his** ~ en/a su casa ▶ VT (*object*) poner, colocar; (*identify*) reconocer; (*find a post for*) dar un puesto a, colocar; (*goods*) vender; **to take** ~ tener lugar; **to be placed** (*in race, exam*) colocarse; **out of** ~ (*not suitable*) fuera de lugar; **in the first** ~ (*first of all*) en primer lugar; **to change places with sb** cambiarse de sitio con algn; ~ **of birth** lugar *m* de nacimiento; **from** ~ **to** ~ de un sitio a or para otro; **all over the** ~ por todas partes; **he's going places** (*fig, inf*) llegará lejos; **I feel rather out of** ~ **here** me encuentro algo desplazado; **to put sb in his** ~ (*fig*) poner a algn en su lugar; **it is not my** ~ **to do it** no me incumbe a mí hacerlo; **to** ~ **an order with sb (for)** hacer un pedido a algn (de); **we are better placed than a month ago** estamos en mejor posición que hace un mes
placebo [pləˈsiːbəʊ] N placebo
place mat N (*wooden etc*) salvamanteles *m inv*; (*in linen etc*) mantel *m* individual
placement [ˈpleɪsmənt] N colocación *f*; (*at work*) emplazamiento
place name N topónimo
placid [ˈplæsɪd] ADJ apacible, plácido
placidity [plæˈsɪdɪtɪ] N placidez *f*
plagiarism [ˈpleɪdʒərɪzm] N plagio
plagiarist [ˈpleɪdʒərɪst] N plagiario(-a)
plagiarize [ˈpleɪdʒəraɪz] VT plagiar
plague [pleɪg] N plaga; (*Med*) peste *f* ▶ VT (*fig*) acosar, atormentar; **to** ~ **sb with questions** acribillar a algn a preguntas
plaice [pleɪs] N pl inv platija
plaid [plæd] N (*material*) tela de cuadros
plain [pleɪn] ADJ (*clear*) claro, evidente; (*simple*) sencillo; (*frank*) franco, abierto; (*not handsome*) poco atractivo; (*pure*) natural, puro ▶ ADV claramente ▶ N llano, llanura; **in** ~ **clothes** (*police*) vestido de paisano; **to make sth** ~ **to sb** dejar algo en claro a algn
plain chocolate N chocolate *m* oscuro or amargo
plainly [ˈpleɪnlɪ] ADV claramente, evidentemente; (*frankly*) francamente
plainness [ˈpleɪnnɪs] N (*clarity*) claridad *f*; (*simplicity*) sencillez *f*; (*of face*) falta de atractivo
plain speaking N: **there has been some** ~ se ha hablado claro
plaintiff [ˈpleɪntɪf] N demandante *mf*
plaintive [ˈpleɪntɪv] ADJ (*cry, voice*) lastimero, quejumbroso; (*look*) que da lástima
plait [plæt] N trenza ▶ VT trenzar
plan [plæn] N (*drawing*) plano; (*scheme*) plan *m*, proyecto ▶ VT (*think*) pensar; (*prepare*) proyectar, planear; (*intend*) pensar, tener la intención de ▶ VI hacer proyectos; **have you any plans for today?** ¿piensas hacer algo hoy?; **to** ~ **to do** pensar hacer; **how long do you** ~ **to stay?** ¿cuánto tiempo piensas quedarte?; **to** ~ **(for)** planear, proyectar ▶ **plan out** VT planear detalladamente
plane [pleɪn] N (*Aviat*) avión *m*; (*tree*) plátano; (*tool*) cepillo; (*Math*) plano
planet [ˈplænɪt] N planeta *m*
planetarium [plænɪˈtɛərɪəm] N planetario
planetary [ˈplænɪtərɪ] ADJ planetario
plank [plæŋk] N tabla
plankton [ˈplæŋktən] N plancton *m*
planned economy [plænd-] N economía planificada
planner [ˈplænəʳ] N planificador(-a) *m/f*; (*chart*) diagrama *m* de planificación; **town** ~ urbanista *mf*
planning [ˈplænɪŋ] N (*Pol, Econ*) planificación *f*; **family** ~ planificación familiar
planning committee N (*in local government*) comité *m* de planificación
planning permission N licencia de obras
plant [plɑːnt] N planta; (*machinery*) maquinaria; (*factory*) fábrica ▶ VT plantar; (*field*) sembrar; (*bomb*) colocar
plantain [ˈplænteɪn] N llantén *m*
plantation [plænˈteɪʃən] N plantación *f*; (*estate*) hacienda
planter [ˈplɑːntəʳ] N hacendado
plant pot N maceta, tiesto
plaque [plæk] N placa
plasma [ˈplæzmə] N plasma *m*
plasma screen N pantalla de plasma
plaster [ˈplɑːstəʳ] N (*for walls*) yeso; (*also*: **plaster of Paris**) yeso mate; (*Med: for broken leg etc*) escayola; (*BRIT: also*: **sticking plaster**) tirita, esparadrapo ▶ VT enyesar; (*cover*): **to** ~ **with** llenar or cubrir de; **to be plastered with mud** estar cubierto de barro
plasterboard [ˈplɑːstəbɔːd] N cartón *m* yeso
plaster cast N (*Med*) escayola; (*model, statue*) vaciado de yeso
plastered [ˈplɑːstəd] ADJ (*inf*) borracho
plasterer [ˈplɑːstərəʳ] N yesero
plastic [ˈplæstɪk] N plástico ▶ ADJ de plástico
plastic bag N bolsa de plástico
plastic bullet N bala de goma
plastic explosive N explosivo plástico
plasticine® [ˈplæstɪsiːn] N (*BRIT*) plastilina®
plastic surgery N cirugía plástica
plastinate [ˈplæstɪneɪt] VT plastinar
plate [pleɪt] N (*dish*) plato; (*metal, in book*) lámina; (*Phot*) placa; (*on door*) placa; (*Aut: also*: **number plate**) matrícula; (*dental plate*) placa de dentadura postiza
plateau (*pl* **plateaus** or **plateaux** [ˈplætəʊz]) N meseta, altiplanicie *f*

plateful ['pleɪtful] N plato
plate glass N vidrio or cristal m cilindrado
platen ['plætən] N (on typewriter, printer) rodillo
plate rack N escurreplatos m inv
platform ['plætfɔːm] N (Rail) andén m; (stage) plataforma; (at meeting) tribuna; (Pol) programa m (electoral); **the train leaves from ~ seven** el tren sale del andén número siete
platform ticket N (BRIT) billete m de andén
platinum ['plætɪnəm] N platino
platitude ['plætɪtjuːd] N tópico, lugar m común
platonic [plə'tɒnɪk] ADJ platónico
platoon [plə'tuːn] N pelotón m
platter ['plætəʳ] N fuente f
plaudits ['plɔːdɪts] NPL aplausos mpl
plausibility [plɔːzɪ'bɪlɪtɪ] N verosimilitud f, credibilidad f
plausible ['plɔːzɪbl] ADJ verosímil; (person) convincente
play [pleɪ] N (gen) juego; (Theat) obra ▶ VT (game) jugar; (football, tennis, cards) jugar a; (compete against) jugar contra; (instrument) tocar; (Theat: part) hacer el papel de; representar; (fig) desempeñar ▶ VI jugar; (band) tocar; (tape, record) sonar; (frolic) juguetear; **to ~ safe** ir a lo seguro; **to bring** or **call into ~** poner en juego; **to ~ a trick on sb** gastar una broma a algn; **they're playing at soldiers** están jugando a (los) soldados; **to ~ for time** (fig) tratar de ganar tiempo; **to ~ into sb's hands** (fig) hacerle el juego a algn; **a smile played on his lips** una sonrisa le bailaba en los labios
▶ **play about, play around** VI (person) hacer el tonto; **to ~ about** or **around with** (fiddle with) juguetear con; (idea) darle vueltas a
▶ **play along** VI: **to ~ along with** seguirle el juego a ▶ VT: **to ~ sb along** (fig) jugar con algn
▶ **play back** VT (tape) poner
▶ **play down** VT quitar importancia a
▶ **play on** VT FUS (sb's feelings, credulity) aprovecharse de; **to ~ on sb's nerves** atacarle los nervios a algn
▶ **play up** VI (cause trouble) dar guerra
playact ['pleɪækt] VI (fig) hacer comedia or teatro
play-acting ['pleɪæktɪŋ] N teatro
playboy ['pleɪbɔɪ] N playboy m
player ['pleɪəʳ] N jugador(a) m/f; (Theat) actor m, actriz f; (Mus) músico(-a) m/f
playful ['pleɪful] ADJ juguetón(-ona)
playground ['pleɪɡraʊnd] N (in school) patio de recreo; (in park) parque m infantil
playgroup ['pleɪɡruːp] N jardín m de infancia
playing card ['pleɪɪŋ-] N naipe m, carta
playing field N campo de deportes

playmaker ['pleɪmeɪkəʳ] N (Sport) creador(a) m/f de juego
playmate ['pleɪmeɪt] N compañero(-a) de juego
play-off ['pleɪɒf] N (Sport) (partido de) desempate m
playpen ['pleɪpɛn] N corral m
playroom ['pleɪruːm] N cuarto de juego
playschool ['pleɪskuːl] N = **playgroup**
plaything ['pleɪθɪŋ] N juguete m
playtime ['pleɪtaɪm] N (Scol) (hora de) recreo
playwright ['pleɪraɪt] N dramaturgo(-a)
plc ABBR (BRIT: = public limited company) S.A.
plea [pliː] N (request) súplica, petición f; (excuse) pretexto, disculpa; (Law) alegato, defensa
plea bargaining N (Law) acuerdo entre fiscal y defensor para agilizar los trámites judiciales
plead [pliːd] VT (give as excuse) poner como pretexto; (Law): **to ~ sb's case** defender a algn ▶ VI (Law) declararse; (beg): **to ~ with sb** suplicar or rogar a algn; **to ~ guilty/not guilty** (defendant) declararse culpable/inocente; **to ~ for sth** (beg for) suplicar algo
pleasant ['plɛznt] ADJ agradable
pleasantly ['plɛzntlɪ] ADV agradablemente
pleasantries ['plɛzntrɪz] NPL (polite remarks) cortesías fpl; **to exchange ~** conversar amablemente
please [pliːz] EXCL ¡por favor! ▶ VT (give pleasure to) dar gusto a, agradar ▶ VI (think fit): **do as you ~** haz lo que quieras or lo que te dé la gana; **to ~ o.s.** hacer lo que le parezca; **~!** ¡por favor!; **~ yourself!** ¡haz lo que quieras!, ¡como quieras!; **~ don't cry!** ¡no llores! te lo ruego
pleased [pliːzd] ADJ (happy) alegre, contento; (satisfied): **~ (with)** satisfecho (de); **~ to meet you** ¡encantado!, ¡tanto or mucho gusto!; **to be ~ (about sth)** alegrarse (de algo); **we are ~ to inform you that ...** tenemos el gusto de comunicarle que ...
pleasing ['pliːzɪŋ] ADJ agradable, grato
pleasurable ['plɛʒərəbl] ADJ agradable, grato
pleasurably ['plɛʒərəblɪ] ADV agradablemente, gratamente
pleasure ['plɛʒəʳ] N placer m, gusto; (will) voluntad f ▶ CPD de recreo; **"it's a ~"** "el gusto es mío"; **it's a ~ to see him** da gusto verle; **I have much ~ in informing you that ...** tengo el gran placer de comunicarles que ...; **with ~** con mucho or todo gusto; **is this trip for business or ~?** ¿este viaje es de negocios o de placer?
pleasure cruise N crucero de placer
pleasure ground N parque m de atracciones
pleasure-seeking ['plɛʒəsiːkɪŋ] ADJ hedonista
pleat [pliːt] N pliegue m

pleb [plɛb] N: **the plebs** la gente baja, la plebe

plebeian [plɪ'biːən] N plebeyo(-a) ▸ ADJ plebeyo; (*pej*) ordinario

plebiscite ['plɛbɪsɪt] N plebiscito

plectrum ['plɛktrəm] N plectro

pledge [plɛdʒ] N (*object*) prenda; (*promise*) promesa, voto ▸ VT (*pawn*) empeñar; (*promise*) prometer; **to ~ support for sb** prometer su apoyo a algn; **to ~ sb to secrecy** hacer jurar a algn que guardará el secreto

plenary ['pliːnərɪ] ADJ: **in ~ session** en sesión plenaria

plentiful ['plɛntɪful] ADJ copioso, abundante

plenty ['plɛntɪ] N abundancia; **~ of** mucho(s)(-a(s)); **we've got ~ of time to get there** tenemos tiempo de sobra para llegar

plethora ['plɛθərə] N plétora

pleurisy ['pluərɪsɪ] N pleuresía

pliability [plaɪə'bɪlɪtɪ] N flexibilidad f

pliable ['plaɪəbl] ADJ flexible

pliers ['plaɪəz] NPL alicates *mpl*, tenazas *fpl*

plight [plaɪt] N condición f or situación f difícil

plimsolls ['plɪmsəlz] NPL (BRIT) zapatillas *fpl* de tenis

plinth [plɪnθ] N plinto

PLO N ABBR (= *Palestine Liberation Organization*) OLP f

plod [plɒd] VI caminar con paso pesado; (*fig*) trabajar laboriosamente

plodder ['plɒdəʳ] N trabajador(a) diligente pero lento/a

plodding ['plɒdɪŋ] ADJ (*student*) empollón(-ona); (*worker*) más aplicado que brillante

plonk [plɒŋk] (*inf*) N (BRIT: *wine*) vino peleón ▸ VT: **to ~ sth down** dejar caer algo

plot [plɒt] N (*scheme*) complot *m*, conjura; (*of story, play*) argumento; (*of land*) terreno, parcela ▸ VT (*mark out*) trazar; (*conspire*) tramar, urdir ▸ VI conspirar; **a vegetable ~** un cuadro de hortalizas

plotter ['plɒtəʳ] N (*instrument*) trazador *m* (de gráficos)

plotting ['plɒtɪŋ] N conspiración f, intrigas *fpl*

plough, (US) **plow** [plau] N arado ▸ VT (*earth*) arar

▸ **plough back** VT (*Comm*) reinvertir

▸ **plough through** VT FUS (*crowd*) abrirse paso a la fuerza por

ploughing ['plauɪŋ] N labranza

ploughman ['plaumən] N (*irreg*): **~'s lunch** pan *m* con queso y cebolla

plow [plau] N, VB (US) = **plough**

ploy [plɔɪ] N truco, estratagema

pluck [plʌk] VT (*fruit*) coger (SP), recoger (LAM); (*musical instrument*) puntear; (*bird*) desplumar ▸ N valor *m*, ánimo; **to ~ up courage** hacer de tripas corazón; **to ~ one's eyebrows** depilarse las cejas

plucky ['plʌkɪ] ADJ valiente

plug [plʌg] N tapón *m*; (*Elec*) enchufe *m*, clavija; (*Aut: also*: **spark(ing) plug**) bujía ▸ VT (*hole*) tapar; (*inf*: *advertise*) dar publicidad a; **to give sb/sth a ~** dar publicidad a algn/ algo; **to ~ a lead into a socket** enchufar un hilo en una toma

▸ **plug in** VT, VI (*Elec*) enchufar

plughole ['plʌghəul] N desagüe *m*

plug-in ['plʌgɪn] N (*Comput*) plug-in *m*

plum [plʌm] N (*fruit*) ciruela; (*also*: **plum job**) chollo

plumage ['pluːmɪdʒ] N plumaje *m*

plumb [plʌm] ADJ vertical ▸ N plomo ▸ ADV (*exactly*) exactamente, en punto ▸ VT sondar; (*fig*) sondear

▸ **plumb in** VT (*washing machine*) conectar

plumber ['plʌməʳ] N fontanero(-a), plomero(-a) (LAM)

plumbing ['plʌmɪŋ] N (*trade*) fontanería, plomería (LAM); (*piping*) cañerías

plume [pluːm] N (*gen*) pluma; (*on helmet*) penacho

plummet ['plʌmɪt] VI: **to ~ (down)** caer a plomo

plump [plʌmp] ADJ rechoncho, rollizo ▸ VT: **to ~ sth (down) on** dejar caer algo en

▸ **plump for** VT FUS (*inf*: *choose*) optar por

▸ **plump up** VT ahuecar

plumpness ['plʌmpnɪs] N gordura

plunder ['plʌndəʳ] N pillaje *m*; (*loot*) botín *m* ▸ VT saquear, pillar

plunge [plʌndʒ] N zambullida ▸ VT sumergir, hundir ▸ VI (*fall*) caer; (*dive*) saltar; (*person*) arrojarse; (*sink*) hundirse; **to take the ~** lanzarse; **to ~ a room into darkness** sumir una habitación en la oscuridad

plunger ['plʌndʒəʳ] N émbolo; (*for drain*) desatascador *m*

plunging ['plʌndʒɪŋ] ADJ (*neckline*) escotado

pluperfect [pluː'pəːfɪkt] N pluscuamperfecto

plural ['pluərl] ADJ plural ▸ N plural *m*

plus [plʌs] N (*also*: **plus sign**) signo más; (*fig*) punto a favor ▸ ADJ: **a ~ factor** (*fig*) un factor *m* a favor ▸ PREP más, y, además de; **ten/ twenty ~** más de diez/veinte

plush [plʌʃ] ADJ de felpa

plus-one ['plʌs'wʌn] N (*inf*) acompañante *mf*

plutonium [pluː'təunɪəm] N plutonio

ply [plaɪ] VT (*a trade*) ejercer ▸ VI (*ship*) ir y venir; (*for hire*) ofrecerse (para alquilar); **three ~** (*wool*) de tres cabos; **to ~ sb with drink** no dejar de ofrecer copas a algn

plywood ['plaɪwud] N madera contrachapada

PM N ABBR (BRIT) = **Prime Minister**

p.m. ADV ABBR (= *post meridiem*) de la tarde or noche

PMS N ABBR (= *premenstrual syndrome*) SPM *m*

PMT N ABBR (= *premenstrual tension*) SPM *m*

pneumatic [nju:'mætɪk] ADJ neumático

pneumatic drill N taladradora neumática

pneumonia [nju:'məunɪə] N pulmonía, neumonía

PO N ABBR (= *Post Office*) Correos *mpl*; (*Naut*) = **petty officer**

po ABBR = **postal order**

POA N ABBR (*Brit*) = **Prison Officers' Association**

poach [pəutʃ] VT (*cook*) escalfar; (*steal*) cazar/pescar en vedado ▶ VI cazar/pescar en vedado

poached [pəutʃt] ADJ (*egg*) escalfado

poacher ['pəutʃər] N cazador(a) *m/f* furtivo(-a)

poaching ['pəutʃɪŋ] N caza/pesca furtiva

PO Box N ABBR (= *Post Office Box*) apdo., aptdo.

pocket ['pɔkɪt] N bolsillo; (*of air, Geo, fig*) bolsa; (*Billiards*) tronera ▶ VT meter en el bolsillo; (*steal*) embolsarse; (*Billiards*) entronerar; **breast ~** bolsillo de pecho; **~ of resistance** foco de resistencia; **~ of warm air** bolsa de aire caliente; **to be out of ~** salir perdiendo; **to be £5 in/out of ~** salir ganando/perdiendo 5 libras

pocketbook ['pɔkɪtbuk] N (*US: wallet*) cartera; (: *handbag*) bolso

pocketful ['pɔkɪtful] N bolsillo lleno

pocket knife N navaja

pocket money N asignación *f*

pockmarked ['pɔkmɑ:kt] ADJ (*face*) picado de viruelas

pod [pɔd] N vaina

podcast ['pɔdkɑ:st] N podcast *m* ▶ VI podcastear

podcasting ['pɔdkɑ:stɪŋ] N podcasting *m*

podgy ['pɔdʒɪ] ADJ gordinflón(-ona)

podiatrist [pɔ'di:ətrɪst] N (*US*) podólogo(-a)

podiatry [pɔ'di:ətrɪ] N (*US*) podología

podium ['pəudɪəm] N podio

POE N ABBR = **port of embarkation**; **port of entry**

poem ['pəuɪm] N poema *m*

poet ['pəuɪt] N poeta *mf*

poetic [pəu'ɛtɪk] ADJ poético

poet laureate [-'lɔ:rɪɪt] N poeta *m* laureado; *ver nota*

> El poeta de la corte, denominado *Poet Laureate*, ocupa como tal un puesto vitalicio al servicio de la Casa Real británica. Era tradición que escribiera poemas conmemorativos para ocasiones oficiales, aunque hoy día esto es poco frecuente. El primer poeta así distinguido fue Ben Jonson, en 1616.

poetry ['pəuɪtrɪ] N poesía

poignant ['pɔɪnjənt] ADJ conmovedor(a)

poignantly ['pɔɪnjəntlɪ] ADV de modo conmovedor

point [pɔɪnt] N punto; (*tip*) punta; (*purpose*) fin *m*, propósito; (*Brit Elec*: *also*: **power point**) toma de corriente, enchufe *m*; (*use*) utilidad *f*; (*significant part*) lo esencial; (*place*) punto, lugar *m*; (*also*: **decimal point**): **2 – 3 (2.3)** dos coma tres (2,3) ▶ VT (*gun etc*): **to ~ at sb** apuntar con algo a algn ▶ VI: **to ~ at** señalar; **points** NPL (*Aut*) contactos *mpl*; (*Rail*) agujas *fpl*; **to be on the ~ of doing sth** estar a punto de hacer algo; **to make a ~ of doing sth** poner empeño en hacer algo; **to get the ~** comprender; **to come to the ~** ir al meollo; **there's no ~ (in doing)** no tiene sentido (hacer); **~ of departure** (*also fig*) punto de partida; **~ of order** cuestión *f* de procedimiento; **~ of sale** (*Comm*) punto de venta; **~-of-sale advertising** publicidad *f* en el punto de venta; **the train stops at Carlisle and all points south** el tren para en Carlisle, y en todas las estaciones al sur; **when it comes to the ~** a la hora de la verdad; **in ~ fact** en realidad; **that's the whole ~!** ¡de eso se trata!; **to be beside the ~** no venir al caso; **you've got a ~ there!** ¡tienes razón!

▶ **point out** VT señalar

▶ **point to** VT FUS indicar con el dedo; (*fig*) indicar, señalar

point-blank ['pɔɪnt'blæŋk] ADV (*say, refuse*) sin más hablar; (*also*: **at point-blank range**) a quemarropa

point duty N (*Brit*) control *m* de circulación

pointed ['pɔɪntɪd] ADJ (*shape*) puntiagudo, afilado; (*remark*) intencionado

pointedly ['pɔɪntɪdlɪ] ADV intencionadamente

pointer ['pɔɪntər] N (*stick*) puntero; (*needle*) aguja, indicador *m*; (*clue*) indicación *f*, pista; (*advice*) consejo

pointless ['pɔɪntlɪs] ADJ sin sentido

pointlessly ['pɔɪntlɪslɪ] ADV inútilmente, sin motivo

point of view N punto de vista

poise [pɔɪz] N (*of head, body*) porte *m*; (*calmness*) aplomo

poised [pɔɪzd] ADJ (*in temperament*) sereno

poison ['pɔɪzn] N veneno ▶ VT envenenar

poisoning ['pɔɪznɪŋ] N envenenamiento

poisonous ['pɔɪznəs] ADJ venenoso; (*fumes etc*) tóxico; (*fig*: *ideas, literature*) pernicioso; (: *rumours, individual*) nefasto

poke [pəuk] VT (*fire*) hurgar, atizar; (*jab with finger, stick etc*) empujar; (*Comput*) almacenar; (*put*): **to ~ sth in(to)** introducir algo en ▶ N (*jab*) empujoncito; (*with elbow*) codazo; **to ~ one's head out of the window** asomar la cabeza por la ventana; **to ~ fun at sb**

713

ridiculizar a algn; **to give the fire a ~** atizar el fuego
▸ **poke about** VI fisgonear
▸ **poke out** VI (*stick out*) salir
poker ['pəukər] N atizador m; (*Cards*) póker m
poker-faced ['pəukə'feɪst] ADJ con cara de póker
poky ['pəukɪ] ADJ estrecho
Poland ['pəulənd] N Polonia
polar ['pəulər] ADJ polar
polar bear N oso polar
polarization [pəulərɑɪ'zeɪʃən] N polarización f
polarize ['pəulərɑɪz] VT polarizar
Pole [pəul] N polaco(-a)
pole [pəul] N palo; (*Geo*) polo; (*Tel*) poste m; (*flagpole*) asta; (*tent pole*) mástil m
poleaxe ['pəulæks] VT (*fig*) desnucar
pole bean N (*US*) judía trepadora
polecat ['pəulkæt] N (*BRIT*) turón m; (*US*) mofeta
Pol. Econ. ['pɔlɪkən] N ABBR = **political economy**
polemic [pɔ'lɛmɪk] N polémica
polemicist [pɔ'lɛmɪsɪst] N polemista mf
pole star N estrella polar
pole vault N salto con pértiga
police [pə'liːs] N policía ▸ VT (*streets, city, frontier*) vigilar
police car N coche-patrulla m
police constable N (*BRIT*) guardia m, policía m
police department N (*US*) policía
police force N cuerpo de policía
policeman [pə'liːsmən] N (*irreg*) guardia m, policía m, agente m (*LAM*)
police officer N guardia mf, policía mf
police record N: **to have a ~** tener antecedentes penales
police state N estado policial
police station N comisaría
policewoman [pə'liːswumən] N (*irreg*) (mujer f) policía
policy ['pɔlɪsɪ] N política; (*also:* **insurance policy**) póliza; (*of newspaper, company*) política; **it is our ~ to do that** tenemos por norma hacer eso; **to take out a ~** sacar una póliza, hacerse un seguro
policy holder N asegurado(-a)
policy-making ['pɔlɪsɪmeɪkɪŋ] N elaboración f de directrices generales
policy-making body N organismo encargado de elaborar las directrices generales
polio ['pəulɪəu] N polio f
Polish ['pəulɪʃ] ADJ polaco ▸ N (*Ling*) polaco
polish ['pɔlɪʃ] N (*for shoes*) betún m; (*for floor*) cera (de lustrar); (*for nails*) esmalte m; (*shine*) brillo, lustre m; (*fig: refinement*) refinamiento ▸ VT (*shoes*) limpiar; (*make shiny*) pulir, sacar

brillo a; (*fig: improve*) perfeccionar, refinar
▸ **polish off** VT (*work*) terminar; (*food*) despachar
▸ **polish up** VT (*shoes, furniture etc*) limpiar, sacar brillo a; (*fig: language*) perfeccionar
polished ['pɔlɪʃt] ADJ (*fig: person*) refinado
polite [pə'laɪt] ADJ cortés, atento; (*formal*) correcto; **it's not ~ to do that** es de mala educación hacer eso
politely [pə'laɪtlɪ] ADV cortésmente
politeness [pə'laɪtnɪs] N cortesía
politic ['pɔlɪtɪk] ADJ prudente
political [pə'lɪtɪkl] ADJ político
political asylum N asilo político
politically [pə'lɪtɪkəlɪ] ADV políticamente
politically correct ADJ políticamente correcto
politician [pɔlɪ'tɪʃən] N político(-a)
politics ['pɔlɪtɪks] N política
polka ['pɔlkə] N polca
polka dot N lunar m
poll [pəul] N (*votes*) votación f, votos mpl; (*also:* **opinion poll**) sondeo, encuesta ▸ VT (*votes*) obtener; (*in opinion poll*) encuestar; **to go to the polls** (*voters*) votar; (*government*) acudir a las urnas
pollen ['pɔlən] N polen m
pollen count N índice m de polen
pollination [pɔlɪ'neɪʃən] N polinización f
polling ['pəulɪŋ] N (*Pol*) votación f; (*Tel*) interrogación f
polling booth N cabina de votar
polling day N día m de elecciones
polling station N centro electoral
pollster ['pəulstər] N (*person*) encuestador(a) m/f; (*organization*) empresa de encuestas or sondeos
poll tax N (*BRIT*) contribución f municipal (*no progresiva*)
pollutant [pə'luːtənt] N (*agente m*) contaminante m
pollute [pə'luːt] VT contaminar
pollution [pə'luːʃən] N contaminación f
polo ['pəuləu] N (*sport*) polo
polo-neck ['pəuləunek] ADJ de cuello vuelto ▸ N (*sweater*) suéter m de cuello vuelto
polo shirt N polo, niqui m
poly ['pɔlɪ] N ABBR (*BRIT*) = **polytechnic**
poly... [pɔlɪ] PREF poli...
poly bag N (*BRIT inf*) bolsa de plástico
polyester [pɔlɪ'estər] N poliéster m
polyethylene [pɔlɪ'eθɪliːn] N (*US*) polietileno
polygamy [pə'lɪgəmɪ] N poligamia
polygraph ['pɔlɪgrɑːf] N polígrafo
Polynesia [pɔlɪ'niːzɪə] N Polinesia
Polynesian [pɔlɪ'niːzɪən] ADJ, N polinesio(-a) m/f
polyp ['pɔlɪp] N (*Med*) pólipo
polystyrene [pɔlɪ'staɪriːn] N poliestireno

polytechnic [pɒlɪ'tɛknɪk] N escuela politécnica

polythene [pɒlɪθi:n] N (BRIT) polietileno

polythene bag N bolsa de plástico

polyurethane [pɒlɪ'juərɪθeɪn] N poliuretano

pomegranate ['pɒmɪgrænɪt] N granada

pommel ['pɒml] N pomo ▸ VT = **pummel**

pomp [pɒmp] N pompa

pompom ['pɒmpɒm] N borla

pompous ['pɒmpəs] ADJ pomposo; (person) presumido

pond [pɒnd] N (natural) charca; (artificial) estanque m

ponder ['pɒndə^r] VT meditar

ponderous ['pɒndərəs] ADJ pesado

pong [pɒŋ] N (BRIT inf) peste f ▸ VI (BRIT inf) apestar

pontiff ['pɒntɪf] N pontífice m

pontificate [pɒn'tɪfɪkeɪt] VI (fig): **to ~ (about)** pontificar (sobre)

pontoon [pɒn'tu:n] N pontón m; (BRIT: card game) veintiuna

pony ['pəʊnɪ] N poney m, potro

ponytail ['pəʊnɪteɪl] N coleta, cola de caballo

pony trekking N (BRIT) excursión f a caballo

poodle ['pu:dl] N caniche m

pool [pu:l] N (natural) charca; (pond) estanque m; (also: **swimming pool**) piscina, alberca (LAM); (billiards) billar m americano; (Comm: consortium) consorcio; (US: monopoly trust) trust m ▸ VT juntar; **typing ~** servicio de mecanografía; (**football**) **pools** npl quinielas fpl

poor [puə^r] ADJ pobre; (bad) malo ▸ NPL: **the ~** los pobres

poorly ['puəlɪ] ADJ mal, enfermo ▸ ADV mal

pop [pɒp] N ¡pum!; (sound) ruido seco; (Mus) (música) pop m; (US inf: father) papá m; (inf: drink) gaseosa ▸ VT (burst) hacer reventar ▸ VI reventar; (cork) saltar; **she popped her head out (of the window)** sacó de repente la cabeza (por la ventana)

▸ **pop in** VI entrar un momento

▸ **pop out** VI salir un momento

▸ **pop up** VI aparecer inesperadamente

pop concert N concierto pop

popcorn ['pɒpkɔ:n] N palomitas fpl (de maíz)

pope [pəʊp] N papa m

poplar ['pɒplə^r] N álamo

poplin ['pɒplɪn] N popelina

popper ['pɒpə^r] N corchete m, botón m automático

poppy ['pɒpɪ] N amapola; see also **Remembrance Day**

poppycock ['pɒpɪkɒk] N (inf) tonterías fpl

Popsicle® ['pɒpsɪkl] N (US) polo

pop star N estrella del pop

populace ['pɒpjʊləs] N pueblo

popular ['pɒpjʊlə^r] ADJ popular; **a ~ song** una canción popular; **to be ~ (with)** (person) caer bien (a); (decision) ser popular (entre)

popularity [pɒpjʊ'lærɪtɪ] N popularidad f

popularize ['pɒpjʊləraɪz] VT popularizar; (disseminate) vulgarizar

populate ['pɒpjʊleɪt] VT poblar

population [pɒpjʊ'leɪʃən] N población f

population explosion N explosión f demográfica

populous ['pɒpjʊləs] ADJ populoso

pop-up ['pɒpʌp] ADJ desplegable, pop-up inv ▸ N desplegable m

pop-up book N libro desplegable

pop-up menu N (Comput) menú m desplegable

porcelain ['pɔ:slɪn] N porcelana

porch [pɔ:tʃ] N pórtico, entrada; (US) veranda

porcupine ['pɔ:kjupaɪn] N puerco m espín

pore [pɔ:^r] N poro ▸ VI: **to ~ over** enfrascarse en

pork [pɔ:k] N (carne f de) cerdo or chancho (LAM)

pork chop N chuleta de cerdo

pork pie N (BRIT Culin) empanada de carne de cerdo

porn [pɔ:n] ADJ (inf) porno inv ▸ N porno

pornographic [pɔ:nə'græfɪk] ADJ pornográfico

pornography [pɔ:'nɒgrəfɪ] N pornografía

porous ['pɔ:rəs] ADJ poroso

porpoise ['pɔ:pəs] N marsopa

porridge ['pɒrɪdʒ] N gachas fpl de avena

port [pɔ:t] N (harbour) puerto; (Naut: left side) babor m; (wine) oporto; (Comput) puerta, puerto, port m; **~ of call** puerto de escala

portable ['pɔ:təbl] ADJ portátil

portal ['pɔ:tl] N puerta (grande), portalón m

port authorities NPL autoridades fpl portuarias

portcullis [pɔ:t'kʌlɪs] N rastrillo

portend [pɔ:'tɛnd] VT presagiar, anunciar

portent ['pɔ:tɛnt] N presagio, augurio

porter ['pɔ:tə^r] N (for luggage) maletero; (doorkeeper) portero(-a), conserje mf; (US Rail) mozo de los coches-cama

portfolio [pɔ:t'fəʊlɪəʊ] N (case, of artist) cartera, carpeta; (Pol, Finance) cartera

porthole ['pɔ:thəʊl] N portilla

portico ['pɔ:tɪkəʊ] N pórtico

portion ['pɔ:ʃən] N porción f; (helping) ración f

portly ['pɔ:tlɪ] ADJ corpulento

portrait ['pɔ:treɪt] N retrato

portray [pɔ:'treɪ] VT retratar; (in writing) representar

portrayal [pɔ:'treɪəl] N representación f

Portugal ['pɔ:tjʊgl] N Portugal m

Portuguese [pɔ:tjʊ'gi:z] ADJ portugués(-esa) ▸ N pl inv portugués(-esa) m/f; (Ling) portugués m

P

715

Portuguese man-of-war [-mænəu'wɔ:ʳ] N (*jellyfish*) *especie de medusa*

pose [pəuz] N postura, actitud *f*; (*pej*) afectación *f*, pose *f* ▶ VI posar; (*pretend*): **to ~ as** hacerse pasar por ▶ VT (*question*) plantear; **to ~ for** posar para; **to strike a ~** tomar *or* adoptar una pose *or* actitud

poser ['pəuzəʳ] N problema *m*/pregunta difícil; (*person*) = **poseur**

poseur [pəu'zə:ʳ] N presumido(-a), persona afectada

posh [pɔʃ] ADJ (*inf*) elegante, de lujo ▶ ADV (*inf*): **to talk ~** hablar con acento afectado

position [pə'zɪʃən] N posición *f*; (*job*) puesto ▶ VT colocar; **to be in a ~ to do sth** estar en condiciones de hacer algo

positive ['pɔzɪtɪv] ADJ positivo; (*certain*) seguro; (*definite*) definitivo; **we look forward to a ~ reply** (*Comm*) esperamos que pueda darnos una respuesta en firme; **he's a ~ nuisance** es un auténtico pelmazo; **~ cash flow** (*Comm*) flujo positivo de efectivo

positively ['pɔzɪtɪvlɪ] ADV (*affirmatively, enthusiastically*) de forma positiva; (*inf: really*) absolutamente

posse ['pɔsɪ] N (*US*) pelotón *m*

possess [pə'zɛs] VT poseer; **like one possessed** como un poseído; **whatever can have possessed you?** ¿cómo se te ocurrió?

possessed [pə'zɛst] ADJ poseso, poseído

possession [pə'zɛʃən] N posesión *f*; **possessions** NPL (*belongings*) pertenencias *fpl*; **to take ~ of sth** tomar posesión de algo

possessive [pə'zɛsɪv] ADJ posesivo

possessiveness [pə'zɛsɪvnɪs] N posesividad *f*

possessor [pə'zɛsəʳ] N poseedor(a) *m/f*, dueño(-a)

possibility [pɔsɪ'bɪlɪtɪ] N posibilidad *f*; **he's a ~ for the part** es uno de los posibles para el papel

possible ['pɔsɪbl] ADJ posible; **as big as ~** lo más grande posible; **it is ~ to do it** es posible hacerlo; **as far as ~** en la medida de lo posible; **a ~ candidate** un(a) posible candidato(-a)

possibly ['pɔsɪblɪ] ADV (*perhaps*) posiblemente, tal vez; **I cannot ~ come** me es imposible venir; **could you ~ ...?** ¿podrías ...?

post [pəust] N (*Brit: system*) correos *mpl*; (: *letters, delivery*) correo; (*job, situation*) puesto; (*trading post*) factoría; (*pole*) poste *m*; (*on blog, social network*) post *m* ▶ VT (*Brit: send by post*) mandar por correo; (: *put in mailbox*) echar al correo; (*on blog, social network*) publicar; (*Mil*) apostar; (*bills*) fijar, pegar; (*Brit: appoint*) **to ~ to** destinar a; **by ~** por correo; **by return of ~** a vuelta de correo; **to keep sb posted** tener a algn al corriente

post ... [pəust] PREF post..., pos...; **post 1950** pos(t) 1950

postage ['pəustɪdʒ] N porte *m*, franqueo

postage stamp N sello (de correo)

postal ['pəustl] ADJ postal, de correos

postal order N giro postal

postbag ['pəustbæg] N (*Brit*) correspondencia, cartas *fpl*

postbox ['pəustbɔks] N (*Brit*) buzón *m*

postcard ['pəustkɑ:d] N (tarjeta) postal *f*

postcode ['pəustkəud] N (*Brit*) código postal

postdate [pəust'deɪt] VT (*cheque*) poner fecha adelantada a

poster ['pəustəʳ] N cartel *m*, afiche *m* (*Lam*)

poste restante [pəust'rɛstɔnt] N (*Brit*) lista de correos

posterior [pɔs'tɪərɪəʳ] N (*inf*) trasero

posterity [pɔs'tɛrɪtɪ] N posteridad *f*

poster paint N pintura al agua

post-free [pəust'fri:] ADJ (con) porte pagado

postgraduate ['pəust'grædjuɪt] N posgraduado(-a)

posthumous ['pɔstjuməs] ADJ póstumo

posthumously ['pɔstjuməslɪ] ADV póstumamente, con carácter póstumo

posting ['pəustɪŋ] N destino

postman ['pəustmən] N (*irreg: like* **man**) (*Brit*) cartero

postmark ['pəustmɑ:k] N matasellos *m inv*

postmaster ['pəustmɑ:stəʳ] N administrador *m* de correos

Postmaster General N director *m* general de correos

postmistress ['pəustmɪstrɪs] N administradora de correos

post-mortem [pəust'mɔ:təm] N autopsia

postnatal ['pəust'neɪtl] ADJ postnatal, posparto

post office N (*building*) (oficina de) correos *m*; (*organization*): **the Post Office** Dirección *f* General de Correos

Post Office Box N apartado postal, casilla de correos (*Lam*)

post-paid ['pəust'peɪd] ADJ porte pagado

postpone [pəs'pəun] VT aplazar, postergar (*Lam*)

postponement [pəs'pəunmənt] N aplazamiento

postscript ['pəustskrɪpt] N posdata

postulate ['pɔstjuleɪt] VT postular

posture ['pɔstʃəʳ] N postura, actitud *f*

post-war [pəust'wɔ:ʳ] ADJ de la posguerra

postwoman ['pəustwumən] N (*irreg: like* **woman**) (*Brit*) cartera

posy ['pəuzɪ] N ramillete *m* (de flores)

pot [pɔt] N (*for cooking*) olla; (*teapot*) tetera; (*coffeepot*) cafetera; (*for flowers*) maceta; (*for jam*) tarro, pote *m* (*Lam*); (*piece of pottery*) cacharro; (*inf: marijuana*) costo, chocolate *m*

▶ VT (*plant*) poner en tiesto; (*conserve*) conservar (en tarros); **pots of** (*inf*) montones de; **to go to ~** (*inf: work, performance*) irse al traste

potash ['pɒtæʃ] N potasa

potassium [pə'tæsɪəm] N potasio

potato [pə'teɪtəu] (*pl* **potatoes**) N patata, papa (*LAm*)

potato crisps, (*US*) **potato chips** NPL patatas *fpl* fritas, papas *fpl* fritas (*LAm*)

potato peeler N pelapatatas *m inv*

potbellied ['pɒtbelɪd] ADJ (*from overeating*) barrigón(-ona); (*from malnutrition*) con el vientre hinchado

potency ['pəutnsɪ] N potencia

potent ['pəutnt] ADJ potente, poderoso; (*drink*) fuerte

potentate ['pəutnteɪt] N potentado

potential [pə'tenʃl] ADJ potencial, posible ▶ N potencial *m*; **to have ~** prometer

potentially [pə'tenʃəlɪ] ADV en potencia

pothole ['pɒthəul] N (*in road*) bache *m*; (*BRIT: underground*) gruta

potholer ['pɒthəulə'] N (*BRIT*) espeleólogo(-a)

potholing ['pɒthəulɪŋ] N (*BRIT*): **to go ~** dedicarse a la espeleología

potion ['pəuʃən] N poción *f*, pócima

potluck [pɒt'lʌk] N: **to take ~** conformarse con lo que haya

pot plant N planta de interior

pot roast N carne *f* asada

potshot ['pɒtʃɒt] N: **to take a ~ at sth** tirar a algo sin apuntar

potted ['pɒtɪd] ADJ (*food*) en conserva; (*plant*) en tiesto or maceta; (*fig: shortened*) resumido

potter ['pɒtə'] N alfarero(-a) ▶ VI: **to ~ around**, **~ about** entretenerse haciendo cosillas; **to ~ round the house** estar en casa haciendo cosillas; **~'s wheel** torno de alfarero

pottery ['pɒtərɪ] N cerámica; (*factory*) alfarería; **a piece of ~** un objeto de cerámica

potty ['pɒtɪ] ADJ (*inf: mad*) chiflado ▶ N orinal *m* de niño

potty-trained ['pɒtɪtreɪnd] ADJ que ya no necesita pañales

pouch [pautʃ] N (*Zool*) bolsa; (*for tobacco*) petaca

pouf, pouffe [pu:f] N (*stool*) puf *m*

poultry ['pəultrɪ] N aves *fpl* de corral; (*meat*) pollo

poultry farm N granja avícola

poultry farmer N avicultor(-a) *m/f*

pounce [pauns] VI: **to ~ on** precipitarse sobre ▶ N salto, ataque *m*

pound [paund] N libra; (*for dogs*) perrera; (*for cars*) depósito ▶ VT (*beat*) golpear; (*crush*) machacar ▶ VI (*beat*) dar golpes; **half a ~** media libra; **a one ~ note** un billete de una libra

pounding ['paundɪŋ] N: **to take a ~** (*team*) recibir una paliza

pound sterling N libra esterlina

pour [pɔː'] VT echar; (*tea*) servir ▶ VI correr, fluir; (*rain*) llover a cántaros; **to ~ sb a drink** servirle a algn una copa
  ▶ **pour away, pour off** VT vaciar, verter
  ▶ **pour in** VI (*people*) entrar en tropel; **to come pouring in** (*water*) entrar a raudales; (*letters*) llegar a montones; (*cars, people*) llegar en tropel
  ▶ **pour out** VI (*people*) salir en tropel ▶ VT (*drink*) echar, servir; (*fig*): **to ~ out one's feelings** desahogarse

pouring ['pɔːrɪŋ] ADJ: **~ rain** lluvia torrencial

pout [paut] VI hacer pucheros

poverty ['pɒvətɪ] N pobreza, miseria; (*fig*) falta, escasez *f*

poverty line N: **below the ~** por debajo del umbral de pobreza

poverty-stricken ['pɒvətɪstrɪkn] ADJ necesitado

poverty trap N trampa de la pobreza

POW N ABBR = **prisoner of war**

powder ['paudə'] N polvo; (*also:* **face powder**) polvos *mpl*; (*also:* **gun powder**) pólvora ▶ VT empolvar; **to ~ one's face** empolvarse la cara; **to ~ one's nose** empolvarse la nariz, ponerse polvos; (*euphemism*) ir al baño

powder compact N polvera

powdered milk ['paudəd-] N leche *f* en polvo

powder keg N (*fig*) polvorín *m*

powder puff N borla (para empolvarse)

powder room N aseos *mpl*

powdery ['paudərɪ] ADJ polvoriento

power ['pauə'] N poder *m*; (*strength*) fuerza; (*nation*) potencia; (*drive*) empuje *m*; (*Tech*) potencia; (*Elec*) energía ▶ VT impulsar; **to be in ~** (*Pol*) estar en el poder; **to do all in one's ~ to help sb** hacer todo lo posible por ayudar a algn; **the world powers** las potencias mundiales

powerboat ['pauəbəut] N lancha a motor

power cut N (*BRIT*) apagón *m*

powered ['pauəd] ADJ: **~ by** impulsado por; **nuclear-~ submarine** submarino nuclear

power failure N = **power cut**

powerful ['pauəful] ADJ poderoso; (*engine*) potente; (*strong*) fuerte; (*play, speech*) convincente

powerhouse ['pauəhaus] N (*fig: person*) fuerza motriz; **a ~ of ideas** una cantera de ideas

powerless ['pauəlɪs] ADJ impotente

power line N línea de conducción eléctrica

power of attorney N poder *m*, procuración *f*

power point N (*BRIT*) enchufe *m*

power station N central *f* eléctrica

power steering N (*Aut*) dirección *f* asistida

P

powwow ['pauwau] N conferencia ▶ vi conferenciar

pp ABBR (= *per procurationem*: *by proxy*) p.p.; = **pages**

PPE N ABBR (*Brit Scol*) = **philosophy, politics and economics**

PPS N ABBR (= *post postscriptum*) posdata adicional; (*Brit*: = *Parliamentary Private Secretary*) ayudante de un ministro

PQ ABBR (*Canada*) = **Province of Quebec**

PR N ABBR *see* **proportional representation** (= *public relations*) relaciones *fpl* públicas
▶ ABBR (*US*) = **Puerto Rico**

Pr. ABBR (= *prince*) P

practicability [præktɪkə'bɪlɪtɪ] N factibilidad *f*

practicable ['præktɪkəbl] ADJ (*scheme*) factible

practical ['præktɪkl] ADJ práctico

practicality [præktɪ'kælɪtɪ] N (*of situation etc*) aspecto práctico

practical joke N broma pesada

practically ['præktɪklɪ] ADV (*almost*) casi, prácticamente

practice ['præktɪs] N (*habit*) costumbre *f*; (*exercise*), (*training*) adiestramiento; (*Med: of profession*) práctica, ejercicio; (*Med, Law: business*) consulta ▶ vt, vi (*US*) = **practise**; **in ~** (*in reality*) en la práctica; **out of ~** desentrenado; **to put sth into ~** poner algo en práctica; **it's common ~** es bastante corriente; **target ~** práctica de tiro; **he has a small ~** (*doctor*) tiene pocos pacientes; **to set up in ~ as** establecerse como

practise, (*US*) **practice** ['præktɪs] vt (*carry out*) practicar; (*profession*) ejercer; (*train at*) practicar ▶ vi ejercer; (*train*) practicar

practised, (*US*) **practiced** ['præktɪst] ADJ (*person*) experto; (*performance*) bien ensayado; (*liar*) consumado; **with a ~ eye** con ojo experto

practising, (*US*) **practicing** ['præktɪsɪŋ] ADJ (*Christian etc*) practicante; (*lawyer*) en ejercicio; (*homosexual*) activo

practitioner [præk'tɪʃənəʳ] N practicante *mf*; (*Med*) médico(-a)

pragmatic [præg'mætɪk] ADJ pragmático

pragmatism ['prægmətɪzəm] N pragmatismo

pragmatist ['prægmətɪst] N pragmatista *mf*

Prague [prɑːg] N Praga

prairie ['prɛərɪ] N (*US*) pradera

praise [preɪz] N alabanza(s) *f(pl)*, elogio(s) *m(pl)* ▶ vt alabar, elogiar

praiseworthy ['preɪzwəːðɪ] ADJ loable

pram [præm] N (*Brit*) cochecito de niño

prance [prɑːns] vi (*horse*) hacer cabriolas

prank [præŋk] N travesura

prat [præt] N (*Brit inf*) imbécil *mf*

prattle ['prætl] vi parlotear; (*child*) balbucear

prawn [prɔːn] N gamba

prawn cocktail N cóctel *m* de gambas

pray [preɪ] vi rezar; **to ~ for forgiveness** pedir perdón

prayer [prɛəʳ] N oración *f*, rezo; (*entreaty*) ruego, súplica

prayer book N devocionario, misal *m*

pre- ['priː] PREF pre..., ante-; **~1970** pre 1970

preach [priːtʃ] vi predicar

preacher ['priːtʃəʳ] N predicador(a) *m/f*; (*US: minister*) pastor(a) *m/f*

preamble [prɪ'æmbl] N preámbulo

prearrange [priːə'reɪndʒ] vt organizar *or* acordar de antemano

prearrangement [priːə'reɪndʒmənt] N: **by ~** por previo acuerdo

precarious [prɪ'kɛərɪəs] ADJ precario

precariously [prɪ'kɛərɪəslɪ] ADV precariamente

precaution [prɪ'kɔːʃən] N precaución *f*

precautionary [prɪ'kɔːʃənrɪ] ADJ (*measure*) de precaución

precede [prɪ'siːd] vt, vi preceder

precedence ['presɪdəns] N precedencia; (*priority*) preferencia

precedent ['presɪdənt] N precedente *m*; **to establish** *or* **set a ~** sentar un precedente

preceding [prɪ'siːdɪŋ] ADJ precedente

precept ['priːsept] N precepto

precinct [prɪ'sɪŋkt] N recinto; (*US: district*) distrito, barrio; **precincts** NPL recinto; **pedestrian ~** (*Brit*) zona peatonal; **shopping ~** (*Brit*) zona comercial

precious ['preʃəs] ADJ precioso; (*treasured*) querido; (*stylized*) afectado ▶ ADV (*inf*): **~ little/few** muy poco/pocos; **your ~ dog** (*ironic*) tu querido perro

precipice ['presɪpɪs] N precipicio

precipitate ADJ [prɪ'sɪpɪtɪt] (*hasty*) precipitado ▶ vt [prɪ'sɪpɪteɪt] precipitar

precipitation [prɪsɪpɪ'teɪʃən] N precipitación *f*

precipitous [prɪ'sɪpɪtəs] ADJ (*steep*) escarpado; (*hasty*) precipitado

précis ['preɪsiː] N resumen *m*

precise [prɪ'saɪs] ADJ preciso, exacto; (*person*) escrupuloso

precisely [prɪ'saɪslɪ] ADV exactamente, precisamente

precision [prɪ'sɪʒən] N precisión *f*

preclude [prɪ'kluːd] vt excluir

precocious [prɪ'kəuʃəs] ADJ precoz

preconceived [priːkən'siːvd] ADJ (*idea*) preconcebido

preconception [priːkən'sepʃən] N (*idea*) idea preconcebida

precondition [priːkən'dɪʃən] N condición *f* previa

precursor [priːˈkəːsəʳ] N precursor(a) *m/f*
predate [ˈpriːˈdeɪt] VT (*precede*) preceder
predator [ˈprɛdətəʳ] N depredador *m*
predatory [ˈprɛdətərɪ] ADJ depredador(a)
predecessor [ˈpriːdɪsɛsəʳ] N antecesor(a) *m/f*
predestination [priːdɛstɪˈneɪʃən] N
   predestinación *f*
predestine [priːˈdɛstɪn] VT predestinar
predetermine [priːdɪˈtəːmɪn] VT
   predeterminar
predicament [prɪˈdɪkəmənt] N apuro
predicate [ˈprɛdɪkɪt] N predicado
predict [prɪˈdɪkt] VT predecir, pronosticar
predictable [prɪˈdɪktəbl] ADJ previsible
predictably [prɪˈdɪktəblɪ] ADV (*behave, react*)
   de forma previsible; **~ she didn't arrive**
   como era de prever, no llegó
prediction [prɪˈdɪkʃən] N pronóstico,
   predicción *f*
predispose [ˈpriːdɪsˈpəuz] VT predisponer
predominance [prɪˈdɔmɪnəns] N
   predominio
predominant [prɪˈdɔmɪnənt] ADJ
   predominante
predominantly [prɪˈdɔmɪnəntlɪ] ADV en su
   mayoría
predominate [prɪˈdɔmɪneɪt] VI predominar
pre-eminent [priːˈɛmɪnənt] ADJ
   preeminente
pre-empt [priːˈɛmt] VT (*BRIT*) adelantarse a
pre-emptive [priːˈɛmtɪv] ADJ: **~ strike**
   ataque *m* preventivo
preen [priːn] VT: **to ~ itself** (*bird*) limpiarse
   las plumas; **to ~ o.s.** pavonearse
prefab [ˈpriːfæb] N casa prefabricada
prefabricated [priːˈfæbrɪkeɪtɪd] ADJ
   prefabricado
preface [ˈprɛfəs] N prefacio
prefect [ˈpriːfɛkt] N (*BRIT: in school*) monitor(a)
   m/f
prefer [prɪˈfəːʳ] VT preferir; (*Law: charges,
   complaint*) presentar; (*: action*) entablar; **to ~
   coffee to tea** preferir el café al té
preferable [ˈprɛfrəbl] ADJ preferible
preferably [ˈprɛfrəblɪ] ADV preferentemente,
   más bien
preference [ˈprɛfrəns] N preferencia; (*priority*)
   prioridad *f*; **in ~ to sth** antes que algo
preference shares NPL acciones *fpl*
   privilegiadas
preferential [prɛfəˈrɛnʃəl] ADJ preferente
prefix [ˈpriːfɪks] N prefijo
pregnancy [ˈprɛɡnənsɪ] N (*of woman*)
   embarazo; (*of animal*) preñez *f*
pregnancy test N prueba del embarazo
pregnant [ˈprɛɡnənt] ADJ (*woman*)
   embarazada; (*animal*) preñada; **3 months ~**
   embarazada de tres meses; **~ with meaning**
   cargado de significado

prehistoric [ˈpriːhɪsˈtɔrɪk] ADJ prehistórico
prehistory [priːˈhɪstərɪ] N prehistoria
prejudge [priːˈdʒʌdʒ] VT prejuzgar
prejudice [ˈprɛdʒudɪs] N (*bias*) prejuicio;
   (*harm*) perjuicio ▶ VT (*bias*) predisponer;
   (*harm*) perjudicar; **to ~ sb in favour of/
   against** (*bias*) predisponer a algn a favor de/
   en contra de
prejudiced [ˈprɛdʒudɪst] ADJ (*person*)
   predispuesto; (*view*) parcial, interesado; **to
   be ~ against sb/sth** estar predispuesto en
   contra de algn/algo
prelate [ˈprɛlət] N prelado
preliminaries [prɪˈlɪmɪnərɪz] NPL
   preliminares *mpl*, preparativos *mpl*
preliminary [prɪˈlɪmɪnərɪ] ADJ preliminar
prelude [ˈprɛljuːd] N preludio
premarital [ˈpriːˈmærɪtl] ADJ
   prematrimonial, premarital
premature [ˈprɛmətʃuəʳ] ADJ (*arrival etc*)
   prematuro; **you are being a little ~** te has
   adelantado
prematurely [prɛməˈtʃuəlɪ] ADV
   prematuramente, antes de tiempo
premeditate [priːˈmɛdɪteɪt] VT premeditar
premeditated [priːˈmɛdɪteɪtɪd] ADJ
   premeditado
premeditation [priːmɛdɪˈteɪʃən] N
   premeditación *f*
premenstrual [priːˈmɛnstruəl] ADJ
   premenstrual
premenstrual tension N (*Med*) tensión *f*
   premenstrual
premier [ˈprɛmɪəʳ] ADJ primero, principal
   ▶ N (*Pol*) primer(a) ministro(-a)
première [ˈprɛmɪɛəʳ] N estreno
Premier League [prɛmɪəˈliːɡ] N primera
   división
premise [ˈprɛmɪs] N premisa
premises [ˈprɛmɪsɪs] NPL local *msg*; **on the ~**
   en el lugar mismo; **business ~** locales *mpl*
   comerciales
premium [ˈpriːmɪəm] N premio; (*insurance*)
   prima; **to be at a ~** estar muy solicitado;
   to sell at a ~ (*shares*) vender caro
premium bond N (*BRIT*) *bono del estado que
   participa en una lotería nacional; ver nota*

> Se conoce como *Premium Bonds* o *Premium
> Savings Bonds* a los bonos emitidos por el
> Ministerio de Economía británico
> (*Treasury*) en los que se pueden invertir los
> ahorros. No producen intereses, pero dan
> acceso a un sorteo mensual de premios en
> metálico.

premium deal N (*Comm*) oferta
   extraordinaria
premium gasoline N (*US*) (gasolina) súper *m*
premonition [prɛməˈnɪʃən] N
   presentimiento

preoccupation [priːɔkjuˈpeɪʃən] N preocupación f

preoccupied [priːˈɔkjupaɪd] ADJ (worried) preocupado; (absorbed) ensimismado

pre-owned [priːˈəund] ADJ usado, de segunda mano

prep [prɛp] ADJ ABBR: ~ **school** = **preparatory school** ▶ N ABBR (Scol: = preparation) deberes mpl

prepaid [priːˈpeɪd] ADJ porte pagado; ~ **envelope** sobre m de porte pagado

preparation [prɛpəˈreɪʃən] N preparación f; **preparations** NPL preparativos mpl; **in ~ for sth** en preparación para algo

preparatory [prɪˈpærətərɪ] ADJ preparatorio, preliminar; ~ **to sth/to doing sth** como preparación para algo/para hacer algo

preparatory school N (BRIT) colegio privado de enseñanza primaria; (US) colegio privado de enseñanza secundaria; see also **public school**

prepare [prɪˈpɛər] VT preparar, disponer; (Culin) preparar ▶ VI: **to ~ for** (action) prepararse or disponerse para; (event) hacer preparativos para

prepared [prɪˈpɛəd] ADJ (willing): **to be ~ to help sb** estar dispuesto a ayudar a algn; ~ **for** listo para

preponderance [prɪˈpɔndərns] N preponderancia, predominio

preposition [prɛpəˈzɪʃən] N preposición f

prepossessing [priːpəˈzɛsɪŋ] ADJ agradable, atractivo

preposterous [prɪˈpɔstərəs] ADJ absurdo, ridículo

prep school [prɛp-] N = **preparatory school**

prerecorded [ˈpriːrɪˈkɔːdɪd] ADJ: ~ **broadcast** programa m grabado de antemano

prerequisite [priːˈrɛkwɪzɪt] N requisito previo

prerogative [prɪˈrɔɡətɪv] N prerrogativa

Presbyterian [prɛzbɪˈtɪərɪən] ADJ, N presbiteriano(-a) m/f

presbytery [ˈprɛzbɪtərɪ] N casa parroquial

preschool [ˈpriːˈskuːl] ADJ (child, age) preescolar

prescribe [prɪˈskraɪb] VT prescribir; (Med) recetar; **prescribed books** (BRIT Scol) libros mpl del curso

prescription [prɪˈskrɪpʃən] N (Med) receta; **to make up a ~**, (US) **fill a ~** preparar una receta; **only available on ~** se vende solamente con receta (médica)

prescription charges NPL (BRIT) precio sg de las recetas

prescriptive [prɪˈskrɪptɪv] ADJ normativo

presence [ˈprɛzns] N presencia; (attendance) asistencia; **in sb's ~** en presencia de algn; ~ **of mind** aplomo

presence of mind N aplomo

present ADJ [ˈprɛznt] (in attendance) presente; (current) actual ▶ N [ˈprɛznt] (gift) regalo; (actuality): **the ~** la actualidad, el presente ▶ VT [prɪˈzɛnt] (introduce) presentar; (expound) exponer; (give) presentar, dar, ofrecer; (Theat) representar; **to be ~ at** asistir a, estar presente en; **those ~** los presentes; **to give sb a ~, make sb a ~ of sth** regalar algo a algn; **at ~** actualmente; **to ~ o.s. for an interview** presentarse a una entrevista; **may I ~ Miss Clark** permítame presentarle or le presento a la Srta Clark

presentable [prɪˈzɛntəbl] ADJ: **to make o.s. ~** arreglarse

presentation [prɛznˈteɪʃən] N presentación f; (gift) obsequio; (of case) exposición f; (Theat) representación f; **on ~ of the voucher** al presentar el vale

present-day [ˈprɛzntdeɪ] ADJ actual

presenter [prɪˈzɛntər] N (Radio, TV) locutor(a) m/f

presently [ˈprɛzntlɪ] ADV (soon) dentro de poco; (US: now) ahora

present participle N participio (de) presente

present tense N (tiempo) presente m

preservation [prɛzəˈveɪʃən] N conservación f

preservative [prɪˈzəːvətɪv] N conservante m

preserve [prɪˈzəːv] VT (keep safe) preservar, proteger; (maintain) mantener; (food) conservar; (in salt) salar ▶ N (for game) coto, vedado; (often pl: jam) confitura

preshrunk [ˈpriːˈʃrʌŋk] ADJ inencogible

preside [prɪˈzaɪd] VI presidir

presidency [ˈprɛzɪdənsɪ] N presidencia

president [ˈprɛzɪdənt] N presidente mf; (US: of company) director(a) m/f

presidential [prɛzɪˈdɛnʃl] ADJ presidencial

press [prɛs] N (tool, machine, newspapers) prensa; (printer's) imprenta; (of hand) apretón m ▶ VT (push) empujar; (: button) apretar; (grapes) pisar; (iron: clothes) planchar; (pressure) presionar; (doorbell) apretar, pulsar, tocar; (insist): **to ~ sth on sb** insistir en que algn acepte algo ▶ VI (squeeze) apretar; (pressurize) ejercer presión; **to go to ~** (newspaper) entrar en prensa; **to be in the ~** (being printed) estar en prensa; (in the newspapers) aparecer en la prensa; **we are pressed for time** tenemos poco tiempo; **to ~ sb to do** or **into doing sth** (urge, entreat) presionar a algn para que haga algo; **to ~ sb for an answer** insistir a algn para que conteste; **to ~ charges against sb** (Law) demandar a algn
▶ **press ahead** VI seguir adelante
▶ **press on** VI avanzar; (hurry) apretar el paso

press agency N agencia de prensa

press clipping N = **press cutting**

press conference N rueda de prensa

press cutting N recorte m (de periódico)

pressing [ˈprɛsɪŋ] ADJ apremiante

pressman [ˈprɛsmæn] N (irreg) periodista m
press officer N jefe(-a) m/f de prensa
press release N comunicado de prensa
press stud N (BRIT) botón m de presión
press-up [ˈprɛsʌp] N (BRIT) flexión f
pressure [ˈprɛʃəʳ] N presión f; (urgency) apremio, urgencia; (influence) influencia; **high/low ~** alta/baja presión; **to put ~ on sb** presionar a algn, hacer presión sobre algn
pressure cooker N olla a presión
pressure gauge N manómetro
pressure group N grupo de presión
pressurize [ˈprɛʃəraɪz] VT presurizar; **to ~ sb (into doing sth)** presionar a algn (para que haga algo)
pressurized [ˈprɛʃəraɪzd] ADJ (container) a presión
Prestel® [ˈprɛstel] N videotex m
prestige [prɛsˈtiːʒ] N prestigio
prestigious [prɛsˈtɪdʒəs] ADJ prestigioso
presumably [prɪˈzjuːməblɪ] ADV es de suponer que, cabe presumir que; **~ he did it** es de suponer que lo hizo él
presume [prɪˈzjuːm] VT: **to ~ (that)** presumir (que), suponer (que); **to ~ to do** (dare) atreverse a hacer
presumption [prɪˈzʌmpʃən] N suposición f; (pretension) presunción f
presumptuous [prɪˈzʌmptjuəs] ADJ presumido
presuppose [priːsəˈpəuz] VT presuponer
presupposition [priːsʌpəˈzɪʃən] N presuposición f
pre-tax [priːˈtæks] ADJ anterior al impuesto
pretence, (US) **pretense** [prɪˈtɛns] N (claim) pretensión f; (pretext) pretexto; (make-believe) fingimiento; **on** or **under the ~ of doing sth** bajo or con el pretexto de hacer algo; **she is devoid of all ~** no es pretenciosa; **under false pretences** con engaños
pretend [prɪˈtɛnd] VT (feign) fingir ▶ VI (feign) fingir; (claim): **to ~ to sth** pretender a algo
pretense [prɪˈtɛns] N (US) = pretence
pretension [prɪˈtɛnʃən] N (claim) pretensión f; **to have no pretensions to sth/to being sth** no engañarse en cuanto a algo/a ser algo
pretentious [prɪˈtɛnʃəs] ADJ pretencioso; (ostentatious) ostentoso, aparatoso
pretext [ˈpriːtɛkst] N pretexto; **on** or **under the ~ of doing sth** con el pretexto de hacer algo
prettily [ˈprɪtɪlɪ] ADV encantadoramente, con gracia
pretty [ˈprɪtɪ] ADJ (gen) bonito, lindo (LAM) ▶ ADV bastante
prevail [prɪˈveɪl] VI (gain mastery) prevalecer; (be current) predominar; (persuade): **to ~ (up)on sb to do sth** persuadir a algn para que haga algo

prevailing [prɪˈveɪlɪŋ] ADJ (dominant) predominante
prevalent [ˈprɛvələnt] ADJ (dominant) dominante; (widespread) extendido; (fashionable) de moda
prevarication [prɪværɪˈkeɪʃən] N evasivas fpl
prevent [prɪˈvɛnt] VT: **to ~ (sb) from doing sth** impedir (a algn) hacer algo; **to ~ sth from happening** evitar que ocurra algo
preventable [prɪˈvɛntəbl] ADJ evitable
preventative [prɪˈvɛntətɪv] ADJ preventivo
prevention [prɪˈvɛnʃən] N prevención f
preventive [prɪˈvɛntɪv] ADJ preventivo
preview [ˈpriːvjuː] N (of film) preestreno
previous [ˈpriːvɪəs] ADJ previo, anterior; **he has no ~ experience in that field** no tiene experiencia previa en ese campo; **I have a ~ engagement** tengo un compromiso anterior
previously [ˈpriːvɪəslɪ] ADV antes
prewar [priːˈwɔːʳ] ADJ antes de la guerra
prey [preɪ] N presa ▶ VI: **to ~ on** vivir a costa de; (feed on) alimentarse de; **it was preying on his mind** le obsesionaba
price [praɪs] N precio; (Betting: odds) puntos mpl de ventaja ▶ VT (goods) fijar el precio de; **to go up** or **rise in ~** subir de precio; **what is the ~ of ...?** ¿qué precio tiene ...?; **to put a ~ on sth** poner precio a algo; **what ~ his promises now?** ¿para qué sirven ahora sus promesas?; **he regained his freedom, but at a ~** recobró su libertad, pero le había costado caro; **to be priced out of the market** (article) no encontrar comprador por ese precio; (nation) no ser competitivo
price control N control m de precios
price-cutting [ˈpraɪskʌtɪŋ] N reducción f de precios
priceless [ˈpraɪslɪs] ADJ que no tiene precio; (inf: amusing) divertidísimo
price list N tarifa
price range N gama de precios; **it's within my ~** está al alcance de mi bolsillo
price tag N etiqueta
price war N guerra de precios
pricey [ˈpraɪsɪ] ADJ (BRIT inf) caro
prick [prɪk] N pinchazo; (with pin) alfilerazo; (sting) picadura ▶ VT pinchar; (hurt) picar; **to ~ up one's ears** aguzar el oído
prickle [ˈprɪkl] N (sensation) picor m; (Bot) espina; (Zool) púa
prickly [ˈprɪklɪ] ADJ espinoso; (fig: person) enojadizo
prickly heat N sarpullido causado por exceso de calor
prickly pear N higo chumbo
pride [praɪd] N orgullo; (pej) soberbia ▶ VT: **to ~ o.s. on** enorgullecerse de; **to take (a) ~ in** enorgullecerse de; **her ~ and joy** su orgullo; **to have ~ of place** tener prioridad

P

priest [pri:st] N sacerdote m
priestess ['pri:stɪs] N sacerdotisa
priesthood ['pri:sthud] N (practice) sacerdocio; (priests) clero
prig [prɪg] N gazmoño(-a)
prim [prɪm] ADJ (demure) remilgado; (prudish) gazmoño
primacy ['praɪməsɪ] N primacía
prima donna ['pri:mə'dɒnə] N primadonna, diva
prima facie ['praɪmə'feɪʃɪ] ADJ: **to have a ~ case** (Law) tener razón a primera vista
primal ['praɪməl] ADJ original; (important) principal
primarily ['praɪmərɪlɪ] ADV (above all) ante todo, primordialmente
primary ['praɪmərɪ] ADJ primario; (first in importance) principal ▶ N (US: also: **primary election**) (elección f) primaria; ver nota

> Las elecciones primarias (primaries) sirven para preseleccionar a los candidatos de los partidos Demócrata ("Democratic") y Republicano ("Republican") durante la campaña que precede a las elecciones a presidente de los Estados Unidos. Se inician en New Hampshire y tienen lugar en 35 estados de febrero a junio. El número de votos obtenidos por cada candidato determina el número de delegados que votarán en el congreso general ("National Convention") de julio y agosto, cuando se decide el candidato definitivo de cada partido.

primary colour, (US) **primary color** N color m primario
primary education N enseñanza primaria
primary school N (BRIT) escuela primaria; ver nota

> En el Reino Unido la escuela a la que van los niños entre cinco y once años se llama primary school, a menudo dividida en "infant school" (entre cinco y siete años de edad) y "junior school" (entre siete y once).

primate N ['praɪmɪt] (Rel) primado ▶ N ['praɪmeɪt] (Zool) primate m
prime [praɪm] ADJ primero, principal; (basic) fundamental; (excellent) selecto, de primera clase ▶ N: **in the ~ of life** en la flor de la vida ▶ VT (gun, pump) cebar; (wood: also fig) preparar; **~ example** ejemplo típico
Prime Minister N primer(a) ministro(-a); see also **Downing Street**
primer ['praɪmə'] N (book) texto elemental; (paint) capa preparatoria
prime time N (Radio, TV) horas fpl de mayor audiencia
primeval [praɪ'mi:vəl] ADJ primitivo
primitive ['prɪmɪtɪv] ADJ primitivo; (crude) rudimentario; (uncivilized) inculto

primly ['prɪmlɪ] ADV remilgadamente; con gazmoñería
primrose ['prɪmrəuz] N primavera, prímula
primus® ['praɪməs], **primus stove** N (BRIT) hornillo de camping
prince [prɪns] N príncipe m
prince charming N príncipe m azul
princess [prɪn'ses] N princesa
principal ['prɪnsɪpl] ADJ principal ▶ N director(a) m/f; (in play) protagonista principal mf; (Comm) capital m, principal m; see also **pantomime**
principality [prɪnsɪ'pælɪtɪ] N principado
principally ['prɪnsɪplɪ] ADV principalmente
principle ['prɪnsɪpl] N principio; **in ~** en principio; **on ~** por principio
print [prɪnt] N (impression) marca, impresión f; (footprint) huella; (fingerprint) huella dactilar; (letters) letra de molde; (fabric) estampado; (Art) grabado; (Phot) impresión f ▶ VT (gen) imprimir; (on mind) grabar; (write in capitals) escribir en letras de molde; **out of ~** agotado ▶ **print out** VT (Comput) imprimir
printed circuit ['prɪntɪd-] N circuito impreso
printed circuit board N tarjeta de circuito impreso
printed matter N impresos mpl
printer ['prɪntə'] N (person) impresor(a) m/f; (machine) impresora
printhead ['prɪnthed] N cabeza impresora
printing ['prɪntɪŋ] N (art) imprenta; (act) impresión f; (quantity) tirada
printing press N prensa
printout ['prɪntaut] N (Comput) copia impresa
print wheel N rueda impresora
prior ['praɪə'] ADJ anterior, previo; (more important) más importante ▶ N prior m; **~ to doing** antes de or hasta hacer; **without ~ notice** sin previo aviso; **to have a ~ claim to sth** tener prioridad en algo
prioress [praɪə'res] N priora
priority [praɪ'ɒrɪtɪ] N prioridad f; **to have** or **take ~ over sth** tener prioridad sobre algo
priory ['praɪərɪ] N priorato
prise, (US) **prize** [praɪz] VT: **to ~ open** abrir con palanca
prism ['prɪzəm] N prisma m
prison ['prɪzn] N cárcel f, prisión f ▶ CPD carcelario
prison camp N campo de prisioneros
prisoner ['prɪznə'] N (in prison) preso(-a); (captured person) prisionero(-a); (under arrest) detenido(-a); (in dock) acusado(-a); **the ~ at the bar** el acusado(-a); **to take sb ~** hacer or tomar prisionero a algn
prisoner of war N prisionero(-a) or preso(-a) de guerra
prissy ['prɪsɪ] ADJ remilgado

pristine ['prɪstiːn] ADJ prístino
privacy ['prɪvəsɪ] N (*seclusion*) soledad *f*; (*intimacy*) intimidad *f*; **in the strictest ~** con el mayor secreto
private ['praɪvɪt] ADJ (*personal*) particular; (*confidential*) secreto, confidencial; (*property, industry, discussion etc*) privado; (*person*) reservado; (*place*) tranquilo; (*sitting etc*) a puerta cerrada ▶ N soldado raso; **"~"** (*on envelope*) "confidencial"; (*on door*) "privado"; **in ~** en privado; **in (his) ~ life** en su vida privada; **to be in ~ practice** tener consulta particular
private enterprise N la empresa privada
private eye N detective *mf* privado(-a)
private hearing N (*Law*) vista a puerta cerrada
private limited company N (BRIT) sociedad *f* de responsabilidad limitada
privately ['praɪvɪtlɪ] ADV en privado; (*in o.s.*) en secreto
private parts NPL partes *fpl* pudendas
private property N propiedad *f* privada
private school N colegio privado
privation [praɪ'veɪʃən] N (*state*) privación *f*; (*hardship*) privaciones *fpl*, estrecheces *fpl*
privatize ['praɪvɪtaɪz] VT privatizar
privet ['prɪvɪt] N alheña
privilege ['prɪvɪlɪdʒ] N privilegio; (*prerogative*) prerrogativa
privileged ['prɪvɪlɪdʒd] ADJ privilegiado; **to be ~ to do sth** gozar del privilegio de hacer algo
privy ['prɪvɪ] ADJ: **to be ~ to** estar enterado de
Privy Council N consejo privado (de la Corona); *ver nota*

> El consejo de asesores de la Corona conocido como *Privy Council* tuvo su origen en la época de los normandos, y fue adquiriendo mayor importancia hasta ser substituido en 1688 por el actual Consejo de Ministros ("*Cabinet*"). Hoy día sigue existiendo con un carácter fundamentalmente honorífico y los ministros del gobierno y otras personalidades políticas, eclesiásticas y jurídicas adquieren el rango de "*Privy Councillors*" de manera automática.

prize [praɪz] N premio ▶ ADJ (*first class*) de primera clase ▶ VT apreciar, estimar; (*US*) **= prise**
prize fighter N boxeador *m* profesional
prize fighting N boxeo *m* profesional
prize-giving ['praɪzgɪvɪŋ] N distribución *f* de premios
prize money N (*Sport*) bolsa
prizewinner ['praɪzwɪnəʳ] N premiado(-a)
prizewinning ['praɪzwɪnɪŋ] ADJ (*novel, essay*) premiado

PRO N ABBR = **public relations officer**
pro [prəu] N (*Sport*) profesional *mf*; **the pros and cons** los pros y los contras
pro- [prəu] PREF (*in favour of*) pro, en pro de; **~Soviet** pro-soviético
proactive [prəu'æktɪv] ADJ: **to be ~** impulsar la actividad
probability [prɔbə'bɪlɪtɪ] N probabilidad *f*; **in all ~** lo más probable
probable ['prɔbəbl] ADJ probable; **it is ~/ hardly ~ that** es probable/poco probable que
probably ['prɔbəblɪ] ADV probablemente
probate ['prəubeɪt] N (*Law*) legalización *f* de un testamento
probation [prə'beɪʃən] N: **on ~** (*employee*) a prueba; (*Law*) en libertad condicional
probationary [prə'beɪʃənrɪ] ADJ: **~ period** período de prueba
probationer [prə'beɪʃənəʳ] N (*Law*) persona en libertad condicional; (*nurse*) ≈ ATS *mf* (SP) *or* enfermero(-a) en prácticas
probation officer N *persona a cargo de los presos en libertad condicional*
probe [prəub] N (*Med, Space*) sonda; (*enquiry*) investigación *f* ▶ VT sondar; (*investigate*) investigar
probity ['prəubɪtɪ] N probidad *f*
problem ['prɔbləm] N problema *m*; **what's the ~?** ¿cuál es el problema?, ¿qué pasa?; **no ~!** ¡por supuesto!; **to have problems with the car** tener problemas con el coche
problematic [prɔblə'mætɪk], **problematical** [prɔblə'mætɪkl] ADJ problemático
problem-solving [prɔbləm'sɔlvɪŋ] N resolución *f* de problemas; **~ skills** técnicas de resolución de problemas
procedural [prəu'siːdʒərəl] ADJ de procedimiento; (*Law*) procesal
procedure [prə'siːdʒəʳ] N procedimiento; (*bureaucratic*) trámites *mpl*; **cashing a cheque is a simple ~** cobrar un cheque es un trámite sencillo
proceed [prə'siːd] VI proceder; (*continue*): **to ~ (with)** continuar (con); **to ~ against sb** (*Law*) proceder contra algn; **I am not sure how to ~** no sé cómo proceder; *see also* **proceeds**
proceedings [prə'siːdɪŋz] NPL acto(s) *m(pl)*; (*Law*) proceso *sg*; (*meeting*) función *fsg*; (*records*) actas *fpl*
proceeds ['prəusiːdz] NPL ganancias *fpl*, ingresos *mpl*
process ['prəusɛs] N proceso; (*method*) método, sistema *m*; (*proceeding*) procedimiento ▶ VT tratar, elaborar ▶ VI [prə'sɛs] (BRIT formal: *go in procession*) desfilar; **in ~** en curso; **we are in the ~ of moving to …** estamos en vías de mudarnos a …

p

processed cheese ['prəusɛst-], (US) **process cheese** N queso fundido
processing ['prəusɛsɪŋ] N elaboración f
procession [prə'sɛʃən] N desfile m; **funeral ~** cortejo fúnebre
pro-choice [prəu'tʃɔɪs] ADJ en favor del derecho de elegir de la madre
proclaim [prə'kleɪm] VT proclamar; (announce) anunciar
proclamation [prɔklə'meɪʃən] N proclamación f; (written) proclama
proclivity [prə'klɪvɪtɪ] N propensión f, inclinación f
procrastinate [prəu'kræstɪneɪt] VI demorarse
procrastination [prəukræstɪ'neɪʃən] N dilación f
procreation [prəukrɪ'eɪʃən] N procreación f
Procurator Fiscal ['prɔkjureɪtə-] N (SCOTTISH) fiscal mf
procure [prə'kjuər] VT conseguir, obtener
procurement [prə'kjuəmənt] N obtención f
prod [prɔd] VT (push) empujar; (with elbow) dar un codazo a ▶ N empujoncito; codazo
prodigal ['prɔdɪgl] ADJ pródigo
prodigious [prə'dɪdʒəs] ADJ prodigioso
prodigy ['prɔdɪdʒɪ] N prodigio
produce N ['prɔdjuːs] (Agr) productos mpl agrícolas ▶ VT [prə'djuːs] producir; (yield) rendir; (bring) sacar; (show) presentar, mostrar; (proof of identity) enseñar, presentar; (Theat) presentar, poner en escena; (offspring) dar a luz
produce dealer N (US) verdulero(-a)
producer [prə'djuːsər] N (Theat) director(a) m/f; (Agr, Cine) productor(a) m/f
product ['prɔdʌkt] N producto
production [prə'dʌkʃən] N (act) producción f; (Theat) representación f, montaje m; **to put into ~** lanzar a la producción
production agreement N (US) acuerdo de productividad
production line N línea de producción
production manager N jefe(-a) m/f de producción
productive [prə'dʌktɪv] ADJ productivo
productivity [prɔdʌk'tɪvɪtɪ] N productividad f
productivity agreement N (BRIT) acuerdo de productividad
productivity bonus N bono de productividad
Prof. [prɔf] ABBR (= professor) Prof
profane [prə'feɪn] ADJ profano
profess [prə'fɛs] VT profesar; **I do not ~ to be an expert** no pretendo ser experto
professed [prə'fɛst] ADJ (self-declared) declarado
profession [prə'fɛʃən] N profesión f

professional [prə'fɛʃnl] N profesional mf; (skilled person) perito ▶ ADJ profesional; (by profession) de profesión; **to take ~ advice** buscar un consejo profesional
professionalism [prə'fɛʃnəlɪzm] N profesionalismo
professionally [prə'fɛʃnəlɪ] ADV: **I only know him ~** sólo le conozco por nuestra relación de trabajo
professor [prə'fɛsər] N (BRIT) catedrático(-a); (US: teacher) profesor(a) m/f
professorship [prə'fɛsəʃɪp] N cátedra
proffer ['prɔfər] VT ofrecer
proficiency [prə'fɪʃənsɪ] N capacidad f, habilidad f
proficiency test N prueba de capacitación
proficient [prə'fɪʃənt] ADJ experto, hábil
profile ['prəufaɪl] N perfil m; **to keep a high/low ~** tratar de llamar la atención/pasar inadvertido
profit ['prɔfɪt] N (Comm) ganancia; (fig) provecho ▶ VI: **to ~ by or from** aprovechar or sacar provecho de; **~ and loss account** cuenta de ganancias y pérdidas; **with profits endowment assurance** seguro dotal con beneficios; **to sell sth at a ~** vender algo con ganancia
profitability [prɔfɪtə'bɪlɪtɪ] N rentabilidad f
profitable ['prɔfɪtəbl] ADJ (Econ) rentable; (beneficial) provechoso, útil
profitably ['prɔfɪtəblɪ] ADV rentablemente; provechosamente
profit centre, (US) **profit center** N centro de beneficios
profiteering [prɔfɪ'tɪərɪŋ] N (pej) explotación f
profit-making ['prɔfɪtmeɪkɪŋ] ADJ rentable
profit margin N margen m de ganancia
profit-sharing ['prɔfɪtʃɛərɪŋ] N participación f de empleados en los beneficios
profits tax N impuesto sobre los beneficios
profligate ['prɔflɪgɪt] ADJ (dissolute: behaviour, act) disoluto; (: person) libertino; (extravagant): **he's very ~ with his money** es muy derrochador
pro forma ['prəu'fɔːmə] ADJ: **~ invoice** factura pro-forma
profound [prə'faund] ADJ profundo
profoundly [prə'faundlɪ] ADV profundamente
profusely [prə'fjuːslɪ] ADV profusamente
profusion [prə'fjuːʒən] N profusión f, abundancia
progeny ['prɔdʒɪnɪ] N progenie f
programme, (US, Comput) **program** ['prəugræm] N programa m ▶ VT programar
programmer, (US) **programer** ['prəugræmər] N programador(a) m/f
programming, (US) **programing** ['prəugræmɪŋ] N programación f

programming language, (US) **programing language** N lenguaje m de programación

progress N ['prəugrɛs] progreso; (*development*) desarrollo ▸ VI [prə'grɛs] progresar, avanzar; desarrollarse; **in** ~ (*meeting, work etc*) en curso; **as the match progressed** a medida que avanzaba el partido

progression [prə'grɛʃən] N progresión f

progressive [prə'grɛsɪv] ADJ progresivo; (*person*) progresista

progressively [prə'grɛsɪvlɪ] ADV progresivamente, poco a poco

progress report N (*Med*) informe m sobre el estado del paciente; (*Admin*) informe m sobre la marcha del trabajo

prohibit [prə'hɪbɪt] VT prohibir; **to ~ sb from doing sth** prohibir a algn hacer algo; **"smoking prohibited"** "prohibido fumar"

prohibition [prəuɪ'bɪʃən] N (US) prohibicionismo

prohibitive [prə'hɪbɪtɪv] ADJ (*price etc*) prohibitivo

project N ['prɔdʒɛkt] proyecto; (*Scol, Univ: research*) trabajo, proyecto ▸ VT [prə'dʒɛkt] proyectar ▸ VI (*stick out*) salir, sobresalir

projectile [prə'dʒɛktaɪl] N proyectil m

projection [prə'dʒɛkʃən] N proyección f; (*overhang*) saliente m

projectionist [prə'dʒɛkʃənɪst] N (*Cine*) operador(a) m/f de cine

projection room N (*Cine*) cabina de proyección

projector [prə'dʒɛktəʳ] N proyector m

proletarian [prəulɪ'tɛərɪən] ADJ proletario

proletariat [prəulɪ'tɛərɪət] N proletariado

pro-life [prəu'laɪf] ADJ pro-vida

proliferate [prə'lɪfəreɪt] VI proliferar, multiplicarse

proliferation [prəlɪfə'reɪʃən] N proliferación f

prolific [prə'lɪfɪk] ADJ prolífico

prologue, (US) **prolog** ['prəulɔg] N prólogo

prolong [prə'lɔŋ] VT prolongar, extender

prom [prɔm] N ABBR (BRIT) = **promenade**; **promenade concert**; (*US: ball*) baile m de gala; *ver nota*

Los conciertos de música clásica más conocidos en Inglaterra son los llamados *Proms* (o *promenade concerts*), que tienen lugar en el *Royal Albert Hall* de Londres, aunque también se llama así a cualquier concierto de esas características. Su nombre se debe al hecho de que en un principio el público paseaba durante las actuaciones; en la actualidad parte de la gente que acude a ellos permanece de pie. En Estados Unidos se llama *prom* a un baile de gala en un colegio o universidad.

promenade [prɔmə'nɑːd] N (*by sea*) paseo marítimo ▸ VI (*stroll*) pasearse

promenade concert N concierto (*en que parte del público permanece de pie*)

promenade deck N cubierta de paseo

prominence ['prɔmɪnəns] N (*fig*) importancia

prominent ['prɔmɪnənt] ADJ (*standing out*) saliente; (*important*) eminente, importante; **he is ~ in the field of ...** destaca en el campo de ...

prominently ['prɔmɪnəntlɪ] ADV (*display, set*) muy a la vista; **he figured ~ in the case** desempeñó un papel destacado en el juicio

promiscuity [prɔmɪs'kjuːɪtɪ] N promiscuidad f

promiscuous [prə'mɪskjuəs] ADJ (*sexually*) promiscuo

promise ['prɔmɪs] N promesa ▸ VT, VI prometer; **to make sb a ~** prometer algo a algn; **a young man of ~** un joven con futuro; **to ~ (sb) to do sth** prometer (a algn) hacer algo; **to ~ well** ser muy prometedor

promising ['prɔmɪsɪŋ] ADJ prometedor(a)

promissory note ['prɔmɪsərɪ-] N pagaré m

promontory ['prɔməntrɪ] N promontorio

promote [prə'məut] VT promover; (*new product*) dar publicidad a, lanzar; (*Mil*) ascender; (*employee*) ascender; (*ideas*) fomentar; **the team was promoted to the second division** (BRIT *Football*) el equipo ascendió a la segunda división

promoter [prə'məutəʳ] N (*of sporting event*) promotor(a) m/f; (*of company, business*) patrocinador(a) m/f

promotion [prə'məuʃən] N (*gen*) promoción f; (*Mil*) ascenso

prompt [prɔmpt] ADJ pronto ▸ ADV: **at six o'clock ~** a las seis en punto ▸ N (*Comput*) aviso, guía ▸ VT (*urge*) mover, incitar; (*when talking*) instar; (*Theat*) apuntar; **to ~ sb to do sth** instar a algn a hacer algo; **to be ~ to do sth** no tardar en hacer algo; **they're very ~** (*punctual*) son muy puntuales

prompter ['prɔmptəʳ] N (*Theat*) apuntador(a) m/f

promptly ['prɔmptlɪ] ADV (*punctually*) puntualmente; (*rapidly*) rápidamente

promptness ['prɔmptnɪs] N puntualidad f; rapidez f

promulgate ['prɔməlgeɪt] VT promulgar

prone [prəun] ADJ (*lying*) postrado; ~ **to** propenso a

prong [prɔŋ] N diente m, punta

pronoun ['prəunaun] N pronombre m

pronounce [prə'nauns] VT pronunciar; (*declare*) declarar ▸ VI: **to ~ (up)on** pronunciarse sobre; **they pronounced him unfit to plead** le declararon incapaz de defenderse

pronounced [prə'naunst] ADJ (*marked*) marcado

P

pronouncement [prəˈnaunsmənt] N declaración f

pronunciation [prənʌnsɪˈeɪʃən] N pronunciación f

proof [pruːf] N prueba; **70°** ~ graduación f del 70 por 100 ▶ ADJ: ~ **against** a prueba de ▶ VT (tent, anorak) impermeabilizar

proofreader [ˈpruːfriːdəʳ] N corrector(a) m/f de pruebas

prop [prɔp] N apoyo; (fig) sostén m ▶ VT (lean): **to ~ sth against** apoyar algo contra; **props** NPL accesorios mpl, at(t)rezzo msg ▶ **prop up** VT (roof, structure) apuntalar; (economy) respaldar

Prop. ABBR (Comm) = **proprietor**

propaganda [prɔpəˈgændə] N propaganda

propagate [ˈprɔpəgeɪt] VT propagar

propagation [prɔpəˈgeɪʃən] N propagación f

propel [prəˈpel] VT impulsar, propulsar

propeller [prəˈpeləʳ] N hélice f

propelling pencil [prəˈpelɪŋ-] N (BRIT) portaminas m inv

propensity [prəˈpensɪtɪ] N propensión f

proper [ˈprɔpəʳ] ADJ (suited, right) propio; (exact) justo; (apt) apropiado, conveniente; (timely) oportuno; (seemly) correcto, decente; (authentic) verdadero; (inf: real) auténtico; **to go through the ~ channels** (Admin) ir por la vía oficial

properly [ˈprɔpəlɪ] ADV (adequately) correctamente; (decently) decentemente

proper noun N nombre m propio

property [ˈprɔpətɪ] N propiedad f; (estate) finca; **properties** NPL (Theat) accesorios mpl, at(t)rezzo msg; **lost ~** objetos mpl perdidos; **personal ~** bienes mpl muebles

property developer N promotor(a) m/f de construcciones

property owner N dueño(-a) de propiedades

property tax N impuesto sobre la propiedad

prophecy [ˈprɔfɪsɪ] N profecía

prophesy [ˈprɔfɪsaɪ] VT profetizar; (fig) predecir

prophet [ˈprɔfɪt] N profeta mf

prophetic [prəˈfetɪk] ADJ profético

proportion [prəˈpɔːʃən] N proporción f; (share) parte f; **proportions** NPL (size) dimensiones fpl; **to be in/out of ~ to or with sth** estar en/no guardar proporción con algo; **to see sth in ~** (fig) ver algo en su justa medida

proportional [prəˈpɔːʃənl] ADJ proporcional; ~ **(to)** en proporción (con)

proportionally [prəpɔːˈʃnəlɪ] ADV proporcionalmente, en proporción

proportional representation N (Pol) representación f proporcional

proportional spacing N (on printer) espaciado proporcional

proportionate [prəˈpɔːʃənɪt] ADJ proporcionado

proportionately [prəˈpɔːʃnɪtlɪ] ADV proporcionadamente, en proporción

proportioned [prəˈpɔːʃənd] ADJ proporcionado

proposal [prəˈpəuzl] N propuesta; (offer of marriage) oferta de matrimonio; (plan) proyecto; (suggestion) sugerencia

propose [prəˈpəuz] VT proponer; (have in mind): **to ~ sth/to do** or **doing sth** proponer algo/proponerse hacer algo ▶ VI declararse; **to ~ to do** tener intención de hacer

proposer [prəˈpəuzəʳ] N (of motion) proponente mf

proposition [prɔpəˈzɪʃən] N propuesta, proposición f; **to make sb a ~** proponer algo a algn

propound [prəˈpaund] VT (theory) exponer

proprietary [prəˈpraɪətərɪ] ADJ (Comm): ~ **article** artículo de marca; ~ **brand** marca comercial

proprietor [prəˈpraɪətəʳ] N propietario(-a), dueño(-a)

propriety [prəˈpraɪətɪ] N decoro

propulsion [prəˈpʌlʃən] N propulsión f

pro rata [prəuˈrɑːtə] ADV a prorrata

prosaic [prəuˈzeɪɪk] ADJ prosaico

Pros. Atty. ABBR (US) = **prosecuting attorney**

proscribe [prəuˈskraɪb] VT proscribir

prose [prəuz] N prosa; (Scol) traducción f inversa

prosecute [ˈprɔsɪkjuːt] VT (Law) procesar; **"trespassers will be prosecuted"** (Law) "se procesará a los intrusos"

prosecution [prɔsɪˈkjuːʃən] N proceso, causa; (accusing side) acusación f

prosecutor [ˈprɔsɪkjuːtəʳ] N acusador(a) m/f; (also: **public prosecutor**) fiscal mf

prospect N [ˈprɔspekt] (chance) posibilidad f; (outlook) perspectiva; (hope) esperanza ▶ VT [prəˈspekt] explorar ▶ VI [prəˈspekt] buscar; **prospects** NPL (for work etc) perspectivas fpl; **to be faced with the ~ of** tener que enfrentarse a la posibilidad de que ...; **we were faced with the ~ of leaving early** se nos planteó la posibilidad de marcharnos pronto; **there is every ~ of an early victory** hay buenas perspectivas de una pronta victoria

prospecting [prəˈspektɪŋ] N prospección f

prospective [prəˈspektɪv] ADJ (possible) probable, eventual; (certain) futuro; (buyer) presunto; (legislation, son-in-law) futuro

prospector [prəˈspektəʳ] N explorador(a) m/f; **gold ~** buscador m de oro

prospectus [prəˈspektəs] N prospecto

prosper [ˈprɔspəʳ] VI prosperar

prosperity [prɔˈsperɪtɪ] N prosperidad f

prosperous ['prɒspərəs] ADJ próspero

prostate ['prɒsteɪt] N (*also*: **prostate gland**) próstata

prostitute ['prɒstɪtjuːt] N prostituta; **male ~** prostituto

prostitution [prɒstɪ'tjuːʃən] N prostitución f

prostrate ['prɒstreɪt] ADJ postrado; (*fig*) abatido ▶ VT: **to ~ o.s.** postrarse

protagonist [prə'tægənɪst] N protagonista mf

protect [prə'tɛkt] VT proteger

protection [prə'tɛkʃən] N protección f; **to be under sb's ~** estar amparado por algn

protectionism [prə'tɛkʃənɪzəm] N proteccionismo

protection racket N chantaje m

protective [prə'tɛktɪv] ADJ protector(a); **~ custody** (*Law*) detención f preventiva

protector [prə'tɛktər] N protector(a) m/f

protégé ['prəutɛʒeɪ] N protegido(-a)

protein ['prəutiːn] N proteína

pro tem [prəu'tɛm] ADV ABBR (= *pro tempore*: *for the time being*) provisionalmente

protest N ['prəutɛst] protesta ▶ VI [prə'tɛst]: **to ~ about** *or* **at/against** protestar de/contra ▶ VT (*affirm*) afirmar, declarar; (*insist*): **to ~ (that)** insistir en (que); **to do sth under ~** hacer algo bajo protesta; **to ~ against/ about** protestar en contra de/por

Protestant ['prɒtɪstənt] ADJ, N protestante mf

protester, protestor [prə'tɛstər] N (*in demonstration*) manifestante mf

protest march N manifestación f *or* marcha (de protesta)

protocol ['prəutəkɒl] N protocolo

prototype ['prəutətaɪp] N prototipo

protracted [prə'træktɪd] ADJ prolongado

protractor [prə'træktər] N (*Geom*) transportador m

protrude [prə'truːd] VI salir, sobresalir

protuberance [prə'tjuːbərəns] N protuberancia

proud [praud] ADJ orgulloso; (*pej*) soberbio, altanero ▶ ADV: **to do sb ~** tratar a algn a cuerpo de rey; **to do o.s. ~** no privarse de nada; **to be ~ to do sth** estar orgulloso de hacer algo

proudly ['praudlɪ] ADV orgullosamente, con orgullo; (*pej*) con soberbia, con altanería

prove [pruːv] VT probar; (*verify*) comprobar; (*show*) demostrar ▶ VI: **to ~ correct** resultar correcto; **to ~ o.s.** ponerse a prueba; **he was proved right in the end** al final se vio que tenía razón

proverb ['prɒvəːb] N refrán m

proverbial [prə'vəːbɪəl] ADJ proverbial

proverbially [prə'vəːbɪəlɪ] ADV proverbialmente

provide [prə'vaɪd] VT proporcionar, dar; **to ~ sb with sth** proveer a algn de algo; **to be provided with** ser provisto de
▶ **provide for** VT FUS (*person*) mantener a; (*problem etc*) tener en cuenta

provided [prə'vaɪdɪd] CONJ: **~ (that)** con tal de que, a condición de que

Providence ['prɒvɪdəns] N Divina Providencia

providing [prə'vaɪdɪŋ] CONJ: **~ (that)** a condición de que, con tal de que

province ['prɒvɪns] N provincia; (*fig*) esfera

provincial [prə'vɪnʃəl] ADJ provincial; (*pej*) provinciano

provision [prə'vɪʒən] N provisión f; (*supply*) suministro, abastecimiento; **provisions** NPL provisiones fpl, víveres mpl; **to make ~ for** (*one's family, future*) atender las necesidades de

provisional [prə'vɪʒənl] ADJ provisional, provisorio (*LAm*); (*temporary*) interino ▶ N: **P~** (*IRELAND Pol*) Provisional m (*miembro de la tendencia activista del IRA*)

provisional driving licence N (*BRIT Aut*) carnet m de conducir provisional; *see also* **L-plates**

proviso [prə'vaɪzəu] N condición f, estipulación f; **with the ~ that** a condición de que

Provo ['prɒvəu] N ABBR (*inf*) = **Provisional**

provocation [prɒvə'keɪʃən] N provocación f

provocative [prə'vɒkətɪv] ADJ provocativo

provoke [prə'vəuk] VT (*arouse*) provocar, incitar; (*cause*) causar, producir; (*anger*) enojar; **to ~ sb to sth/to do** *or* **into doing sth** provocar a algn a algo/a hacer algo

provoking [prə'vəukɪŋ] ADJ provocador(a)

provost ['prɒvəst] N (*BRIT: of university*) rector(a) m/f; (*SCOTTISH*) alcalde(-esa) m/f

prow [prau] N proa

prowess ['praus] N (*skill*) destreza, habilidad f; (*courage*) valor m; **his ~ as a footballer** (*skill*) su habilidad como futbolista

prowl [praul] VI (*also*: **prowl about, prowl around**) merodear ▶ N: **on the ~** de merodeo, merodeando

prowler ['praulər] N merodeador(a) m/f

proximity [prɒk'sɪmɪtɪ] N proximidad f

proxy ['prɒksɪ] N poder m; (*person*) apoderado(-a); **by ~** por poderes

PRP N ABBR (= *performance related pay*) retribución en función del rendimiento en el trabajo

prude [pruːd] N gazmoño(-a), mojigato(-a)

prudence ['pruːdns] N prudencia

prudent ['pruːdnt] ADJ prudente

prudently ['pruːdntlɪ] ADV prudentemente, con prudencia

prudish ['pruːdɪʃ] ADJ gazmoño

prudishness [pruːdɪʃnɪs] N gazmoñería

prune [pruːn] N ciruela pasa ▶ VT podar

p

pry [praɪ] VI: **to ~ into** entrometerse en

PS ABBR (= *postscript*) P.D.

psalm [sɑːm] N salmo

PSAT N ABBR (*US*) = **Preliminary Scholastic Aptitude Test**

PSBR N ABBR (*BRIT*: = *public sector borrowing requirement*) necesidades de endeudamiento del sector público

pseud [sjuːd] N (*BRIT inf*: *intellectually*) farsante *mf*; (: *socially*) pretencioso(-a)

pseudo... [sjuːdəu] PREF seudo...

pseudonym ['sjuːdənɪm] N seudónimo

PSHE N ABBR (*BRIT Scol*: = *personal, social and health education*) formación social y sanitaria para la vida adulta

PST N ABBR (*US*: = *Pacific Standard Time*) hora de invierno del Pacífico

PSV N ABBR (*BRIT*) = **public service vehicle**

psyche ['saɪkɪ] N psique *f*

psychiatric [saɪkɪˈætrɪk] ADJ psiquiátrico

psychiatrist [saɪˈkaɪətrɪst] N psiquiatra *mf*

psychiatry [saɪˈkaɪətrɪ] N psiquiatría

psychic ['saɪkɪk] ADJ (*also*: **psychical**) psíquico

psycho ['saɪkəu] N (*inf*) psicópata *mf*, pirado(-a)

psychoanalyse, psychoanalyze [saɪkəuˈænəlaɪz] VT psicoanalizar

psychoanalysis [saɪkəuəˈnælɪsɪs] (*pl* **psychoanalyses** [-siːz]) N psicoanálisis *m inv*

psychoanalyst [saɪkəuˈænəlɪst] N psicoanalista *mf*

psychological [saɪkəˈlɔdʒɪkl] ADJ psicológico

psychologically [saɪkəˈlɔdʒɪklɪ] ADV psicológicamente

psychologist [saɪˈkɔlədʒɪst] N psicólogo(-a)

psychology [saɪˈkɔlədʒɪ] N psicología

psychopath ['saɪkəupæθ] N psicópata *mf*

psychosis [saɪˈkəusɪs] (*pl* **psychoses** [-siːz]) N psicosis *f inv*

psychosomatic ['saɪkəusəˈmætɪk] ADJ psicosomático

psychotherapy [saɪkəuˈθɛrəpɪ] N psicoterapia

psychotic [saɪˈkɔtɪk] ADJ, N psicótico(-a) *m/f*

PT N ABBR (*BRIT*: = *physical training*) Ed. Fís.

pt ABBR = **pint; point**

Pt. ABBR (*Geo: in place names*: = *Point*) Pta

PTA N ABBR (*BRIT*: = *Parent-Teacher Association*) ≈ Asociación *f* de Padres de Alumnos

Pte. ABBR (*BRIT Mil*) = **private**

PTO ABBR (= *please turn over*) sigue

PTV N ABBR (*US*) = **pay television; public television**

pub [pʌb] N ABBR (= *public house*) pub *m*, bar *m*; *ver nota*

> En un *pub* (o *public house*) se pueden consumir fundamentalmente bebidas alcohólicas, aunque en la actualidad también se sirven platos ligeros durante el almuerzo. Es, además, un lugar de encuentro donde se juega a los dardos o al billar, entre otras actividades. La estricta regulación sobre la venta de alcohol controla las horas de apertura, aunque éstas son más flexibles desde hace unos años. No se puede servir alcohol a los menores de 18 años.

pub crawl N (*inf*): **to go on a ~** ir a recorrer bares

puberty ['pjuːbətɪ] N pubertad *f*

pubic ['pjuːbɪk] ADJ púbico

public ['pʌblɪk] ADJ público ▶ N: **the ~** el público; **in ~** en público; **to make sth ~** revelar *or* hacer público algo; **to be ~ knowledge** ser del dominio público; **to go ~** (*Comm*) proceder a la venta pública de acciones

public address system N megafonía, sistema *m* de altavoces

publican ['pʌblɪkən] N dueño(-a) *or* encargado(-a) de un bar

publication [pʌblɪˈkeɪʃən] N publicación *f*

public company N sociedad *f* anónima

public convenience N (*BRIT*) aseos *mpl* públicos, sanitarios *mpl* (*LAM*)

public holiday N día *m* de fiesta, (día) feriado (*LAM*)

public house N (*BRIT*) pub *m*, bar *m*

publicity [pʌbˈlɪsɪtɪ] N publicidad *f*

publicize ['pʌblɪsaɪz] VT publicitar; (*advertise*) hacer propaganda para

public limited company N sociedad *f* anónima

publicly ['pʌblɪklɪ] ADV públicamente, en público

public opinion N opinión *f* pública

public ownership N propiedad *f* pública; **to be taken into ~** ser nacionalizado

Public Prosecutor N Fiscal *mf* del Estado

public relations N relaciones *fpl* públicas

public relations officer N encargado(-a) de relaciones públicas

public school N (*BRIT*) colegio privado; (*US*) instituto; *ver nota*

> En Inglaterra el término *public school* se usa para referirse a un colegio privado de pago, generalmente de alto prestigio social y en régimen de internado. Algunos de los más conocidos son Eton o Harrow. Muchos de sus alumnos estudian previamente hasta los 13 años en un centro privado de pago llamado "*prep(aratory) school*" y al terminar el bachiller pasan a estudiar en las universidades de Oxford y Cambridge. En otros lugares como Estados Unidos el mismo término se refiere a una escuela pública de enseñanza gratuita administrada por el Estado.

public sector N sector m público

public service vehicle N vehículo de servicio público

public-spirited [ˌpʌblɪkˈspɪrɪtɪd] ADJ cívico

public transport, (US) **public transportation** N transporte m público

public utility N servicio público

public works NPL obras fpl públicas

publish [ˈpʌblɪʃ] VT publicar

publisher [ˈpʌblɪʃəʳ] N (person) editor(a) m/f; (firm) editorial f

publishing [ˈpʌblɪʃɪŋ] N (industry) industria del libro

publishing company N (casa) editorial f

pub lunch N almuerzo que se sirve en un pub; **to go for a ~** almorzar o comer en un pub

puce [pjuːs] ADJ de color pardo rojizo

puck [pʌk] N (Ice Hockey) puck m

pucker [ˈpʌkəʳ] VT (pleat) arrugar; (brow etc) fruncir

pudding [ˈpudɪŋ] N pudín m; (BRIT: sweet) postre m; **black ~** morcilla; **rice ~** arroz m con leche

puddle [ˈpʌdl] N charco

puerile [ˈpjuəraɪl] ADJ pueril

Puerto Rican [ˈpwɛːtəuˈriːkən] ADJ, N puertorriqueño(-a) m/f

Puerto Rico [-ˈriːkəu] N Puerto Rico

puff [pʌf] N soplo; (of smoke) bocanada; (of breathing, engine) resoplido; (also: **powder puff**) borla ▶ VT: **to ~ one's pipe** dar chupadas a la pipa; (also: **puff out**: sails, cheeks) hinchar, inflar ▶ VI (gen) soplar; (pant) jadear; **to ~ out smoke** echar humo

puffed [pʌft] ADJ (inf: out of breath) sin aliento

puffin [ˈpʌfɪn] N frailecillo

puff pastry, (US) **puff paste** N hojaldre m

puffy [ˈpʌfɪ] ADJ hinchado

pull [pul] N (fig: advantage) ventaja; (: influence) influencia ▶ VT tirar de, jalar (LAM); (haul) tirar, jalar (LAM), arrastrar ▶ VI tirar, jalar (LAM); **to give sth a ~** (tug) dar un tirón a algo; **to ~ a muscle** sufrir un tirón; **to ~ to pieces** hacer pedazos; **to ~ one's punches** andarse con bromas; **to ~ one's weight** hacer su parte; **to ~ o.s. together** tranquilizarse, sobreponerse; **to ~ sb's leg** tomar el pelo a algn; **to ~ strings (for sb)** enchufar (a algn)

▶ **pull about** VT (handle roughly: object) manosear; (: person) maltratar

▶ **pull apart** VT (take apart) desmontar; (break) romper

▶ **pull away** VI (vehicle: move off) salir, arrancar; (draw back) apartarse bruscamente

▶ **pull back** VT (lever etc) tirar hacia sí; (curtains) descorrer ▶ VI (refrain) contenerse; (Mil: withdraw) retirarse

▶ **pull down** VT (house) derribar

▶ **pull in** VI (Aut: at the kerb) parar (junto a la acera); (Rail) llegar

▶ **pull off** VT (deal etc) cerrar

▶ **pull out** VI irse, marcharse; (car, train etc) salir ▶ VT sacar, arrancar

▶ **pull over** VI (Aut) hacerse a un lado

▶ **pull round, pull through** VI salvarse; (Med) recobrar la salud

▶ **pull up** VI (stop) parar ▶ VT (uproot) arrancar, desarraigar; (stop) parar

pulley [ˈpulɪ] N polea

pull-out [ˈpulaut] N suplemento ▶ CPD (pages, magazine) separable

pullover [ˈpuləuvəʳ] N jersey m, suéter m

pulp [pʌlp] N (of fruit) pulpa; (for paper) pasta; (pej: also: **pulp magazines** etc) prensa amarilla; **to reduce sth to ~** hacer algo papilla

pulpit [ˈpulpɪt] N púlpito

pulsate [pʌlˈseɪt] VI pulsar, latir

pulse [pʌls] N (Anat) pulso; (of music, engine) pulsación f; (Bot) legumbre f; **pulses** NPL legumbres; **to feel** or **take sb's ~** tomar el pulso a algn

pulverize [ˈpʌlvəraɪz] VT pulverizar; (fig) hacer polvo

puma [ˈpjuːmə] N puma m

pumice [ˈpʌmɪs], **pumice stone** N piedra pómez

pummel [ˈpʌml] VT aporrear

pump [pʌmp] N bomba; (shoe) zapatilla de tenis ▶ VT sacar con una bomba; (fig: inf) (son)sacar; **to ~ sb for information** (son)sacarle información a algn

▶ **pump up** VT inflar

pumpkin [ˈpʌmpkɪn] N calabaza

pun [pʌn] N juego de palabras

punch [pʌntʃ] N (blow) golpe m, puñetazo; (tool) punzón m; (for paper) perforadora; (for tickets) taladro; (drink) ponche m ▶ VT (make a hole in) punzar; perforar; **to ~ sb/sth** (hit) dar un puñetazo or golpear a algn/algo

punch card, punched card [pʌntʃt-] N tarjeta perforada

punch-drunk [ˈpʌntʃdrʌŋk] ADJ (BRIT) grogui, sonado

punch line N (of joke) remate m

punch-up [ˈpʌntʃʌp] N (BRIT inf) riña

punctual [ˈpʌŋktjuəl] ADJ puntual

punctuality [pʌŋktjuˈælɪtɪ] N puntualidad f

punctually [ˈpʌŋktjuəlɪ] ADV: **it will start ~ at six** empezará a las seis en punto

punctuate [ˈpʌŋktjueɪt] VT puntuar; (fig) interrumpir

punctuation [pʌŋktjuˈeɪʃən] N puntuación f

punctuation mark N signo de puntuación

puncture [ˈpʌŋktʃəʳ] (BRIT) N pinchazo ▶ VT pinchar; **to have a ~** tener un pinchazo

pundit [ˈpʌndɪt] N experto(-a)

pungent ['pʌndʒənt] ADJ acre
punish ['pʌnɪʃ] VT castigar; **to ~ sb for sth/
for doing sth** castigar a algn por algo/por
haber hecho algo
punishable ['pʌnɪʃəbl] ADJ punible, castigable
punishing ['pʌnɪʃɪŋ] ADJ (fig: exhausting)
agotador(a)
punishment ['pʌnɪʃmənt] N castigo; (fig: inf):
to take a lot of ~ (boxer) recibir una paliza;
(car) ser maltratado
punitive ['pju:nɪtɪv] ADJ punitivo
punk [pʌŋk] N (also: **punk rocker**) punki mf;
(also: **punk rock**) música punk; (US inf:
hoodlum) matón m
punt [pʌnt] N (boat) batea; (IRELAND) libra
irlandesa ▶ VI (bet) apostar
punter ['pʌntəʳ] N (gambler) jugador(a) m/f
puny ['pju:nɪ] ADJ enclenque
pup [pʌp] N cachorro
pupil ['pju:pl] N alumno(-a); (of eye) pupila
puppet ['pʌpɪt] N títere m
puppet government N gobierno títere
puppy ['pʌpɪ] N cachorro, perrito
purchase ['pə:tʃɪs] N compra; (grip) agarre m,
asidero ▶ VT comprar
purchase order N orden f de compra
purchase price N precio de compra
purchaser ['pə:tʃɪsəʳ] N comprador(a) m/f
purchase tax N (BRIT) impuesto sobre la
venta
purchasing power ['pə:tʃɪsɪŋ-] N poder m
adquisitivo
pure [pjuəʳ] ADJ puro; **a ~ wool jumper** un
jersey de pura lana; **it's laziness, ~ and
simple** es pura vagancia
purebred ['pjuəbred] ADJ de pura sangre
purée ['pjuəreɪ] N puré m
purely ['pjuəlɪ] ADV puramente
purgatory ['pə:gətərɪ] N purgatorio
purge [pə:dʒ] N (Med, Pol) purga ▶ VT purgar
purification [pjuərɪfɪ'keɪʃən] N purificación
f, depuración f
purify ['pjuərɪfaɪ] VT purificar, depurar
purist ['pjuərɪst] N purista mf
puritan ['pjuərɪtən] N puritano(-a)
puritanical [pjuərɪ'tænɪkl] ADJ puritano
purity ['pjuərɪtɪ] N pureza
purl [pə:l] N punto del revés
purloin [pə:'lɔɪn] VT hurtar, robar
purple ['pə:pl] ADJ morado
purport [pə:'pɔ:t] VI: **to ~ to be/do** dar a
entender que es/hace
purpose ['pə:pəs] N propósito; **on ~** a
propósito, adrede; **to no ~** para nada, en
vano; **for teaching purposes** con fines
pedagógicos; **for the purposes of this
meeting** para los fines de esta reunión
purpose-built ['pə:pəs'bɪlt] ADJ (BRIT)
construido especialmente

purposeful ['pə:pəsful] ADJ resuelto,
determinado
purposely ['pə:pəslɪ] ADV a propósito, adrede
purr [pə:ʳ] N ronroneo ▶ VI ronronear
purse [pə:s] N monedero; (US: handbag) bolso,
cartera (LAM) ▶ VT fruncir
purser ['pə:səʳ] N (Naut) comisario(-a)
purse snatcher [-snætʃəʳ] N (US) persona que
roba por el procedimiento del tirón
pursue [pə'sju:] VT seguir; (harass) perseguir;
(profession) ejercer; (pleasures) buscar; (inquiry,
matter) seguir
pursuer [pə'sju:əʳ] N perseguidor(a) m/f
pursuit [pə'sju:t] N (chase) caza; (of pleasure etc)
busca; (occupation) actividad f; **in (the) ~ of
sth** en busca de algo
purveyor [pə'veɪəʳ] N proveedor(a) m/f
pus [pʌs] N pus m
push [puʃ] N empujón m; (Mil) ataque m;
(drive) empuje m ▶ VT empujar; (button)
apretar; (promote) promover; (fig: press,
advance: views) fomentar; (thrust): **to ~ sth
(into)** meter algo a la fuerza (en) ▶ VI
empujar; (fig) hacer esfuerzos; **at a ~** (inf) a
duras penas; **she is pushing 50** (inf) raya en
los 50; **to be pushed for time/money** andar
justo de tiempo/escaso de dinero; **to ~ a
door open/shut** abrir/cerrar una puerta
empujándola; **to ~ for** (better pay, conditions)
reivindicar; **"~"** (on door) "empujar"; (on bell)
"pulse"
▶ **push aside** VT apartar con la mano
▶ **push in** VI colarse
▶ **push off** VI (inf) largarse
▶ **push on** VI (continue) seguir adelante
▶ **push over** VT (cause to fall) hacer caer,
derribar; (knock over) volcar
▶ **push through** VI (crowd) abrirse paso a
empujones ▶ VT (measure) despachar
▶ **push up** VT (total, prices) hacer subir
push-bike ['puʃbaɪk] N (BRIT) bicicleta
push-button ['puʃbʌtn] ADJ con botón de
mando
pushchair ['puʃtʃɛəʳ] N (BRIT) silla de niño
pusher ['puʃəʳ] N (also: **drug pusher**)
traficante mf de drogas
pushover ['puʃəuvəʳ] N (inf): **it's a ~** está
tirado
push-up ['puʃʌp] N (US) flexión f
pushy ['puʃɪ] ADJ (pej) agresivo
puss [pus], **pussy** ['pusɪ], **pussy-cat**
['pusɪkæt] N minino
put (pt, pp ~) [put] VT (place) poner, colocar;
(put into) meter; (express, say) expresar; (a
question) hacer; (estimate) calcular; (cause to
be): **to ~ sb in a good/bad mood** poner a algn
de buen/mal humor; **to ~ a lot of time into
sth** dedicar mucho tiempo a algo; **to ~
money on a horse** apostar dinero en un

caballo; **to ~ money into a company** invertir dinero en una compañía; **to ~ sb to a lot of trouble** causar mucha molestia a algn; **we ~ the children to bed** acostamos a los niños; **how shall I ~ it?** ¿cómo puedo explicarlo or decirlo?; **I ~ it to you that ...** le sugiero que ...; **to stay ~** no moverse

▸ **put about** VI (*Naut*) virar ▸ VT (*rumour*) hacer correr

▸ **put across** VT (*ideas etc*) comunicar

▸ **put aside** VT (*lay down: book etc*) dejar or poner a un lado; (*save*) ahorrar; (*in shop*) guardar

▸ **put away** VT (*store*) guardar

▸ **put back** VT (*replace*) devolver a su lugar; (*postpone*) aplazar; (*set back: watch, clock*) retrasar; **this will ~ us back 10 years** esto nos retrasará 10 años

▸ **put by** VT (*money*) guardar

▸ **put down** VT (*on ground*) poner en el suelo; (*animal*) sacrificar; (*in writing*) apuntar; (*suppress: revolt etc*) sofocar; (*attribute*) atribuir; **~ me down for £15** apúntame por 15 libras; **~ it down on my account** (*Comm*) póngalo en mi cuenta

▸ **put forward** VT (*ideas*) presentar, proponer; (*date*) adelantar

▸ **put in** VT (*application, complaint*) presentar; (*time*) dedicar

▸ **put in for** VT FUS (*job*) solicitar; (*promotion*) pedir

▸ **put off** VT (*postpone*) aplazar; (*discourage*) desanimar, quitar las ganas a

▸ **put on** VT (*clothes, lipstick etc*) ponerse; (*light etc*) encender; (*play etc*) presentar; (*brake*) echar; (*record, kettle etc*) poner; (*assume: accent, manner*) afectar, fingir; (*: airs*) adoptar, darse; (*concert, exhibition etc*) montar; (*extra bus, train etc*) poner; (*inf: kid, have on: esp US*) tomar el pelo a; (*inform, indicate*): **to ~ sb on to sb/sth** informar a algn de algn/algo; **to ~ on weight** engordar

▸ **put out** VT (*fire, light*) apagar; (*rubbish etc*) sacar; (*cat etc*) echar; (*one's hand*) alargar; (*news, rumour*) hacer circular; (*tongue etc*) sacar; (*inconvenience: person*) molestar, fastidiar; (*dislocate: shoulder, vertebra, knee*) dislocar(se) ▸ VI (*Naut*): **to ~ out to sea** hacerse a la mar; **to ~ out from Plymouth** salir de Plymouth

▸ **put through** VT (*call*) poner; (*plan etc*) hacer aprobar; **~ me through to Mr Low** póngame or comuníqueme (*LAm*) con el Señor Low

▸ **put together** VT unir, reunir; (*assemble: furniture*) armar, montar; (*meal*) preparar

▸ **put up** VT (*raise*) levantar, alzar; (*hang*) colgar; (*build*) construir; (*increase*) aumentar; (*accommodate*) alojar; (*incite*): **to ~ sb up to doing sth** instar or incitar a algn a hacer algo; **to ~ sth up for sale** poner algo a la venta

▸ **put upon** VT FUS: **to be ~ upon** (*imposed upon*) dejarse explotar

▸ **put up with** VT FUS aguantar

putrid ['pjuːtrɪd] ADJ podrido

putsch [putʃ] N golpe *m* de estado

putt [pʌt] VT hacer un putt ▸ N putt *m*

putter ['pʌtə^r] N putter *m*

putting green ['pʌtɪŋ-] N green *m*, minigolf *m*

putty ['pʌtɪ] N masilla

put-up ['putʌp] ADJ: **~ job** (*BRIT*) estafa

puzzle ['pʌzl] N (*riddle*) acertijo; (*jigsaw*) rompecabezas *m inv*; (*also:* **crossword puzzle**) crucigrama *m*; (*mystery*) misterio ▸ VT dejar perplejo, confundir ▸ VI: **to ~ about** quebrar la cabeza por; **to ~ over** (*sb's actions*) quebrarse la cabeza por; (*mystery, problem*) devanarse los sesos sobre; **to be puzzled about sth** no llegar a entender algo

puzzling ['pʌzlɪŋ] ADJ (*question*) misterioso, extraño; (*attitude, instructions*) extraño

PVC N ABBR (= *polyvinyl chloride*) P.V.C. *m*

Pvt. ABBR (*US Mil*) = **private**

PW N ABBR (*US*) = **prisoner of war**

pw ABBR (= *per week*) por semana

PX N ABBR (*US Mil*: = *post exchange*) economato militar

pygmy ['pɪgmɪ] N pigmeo(-a)

pyjamas, (*US*) **pajamas** [pɪ'dʒɑːməz] NPL pijama *msg*, piyama *msg* (*LAm*); **a pair of ~** un pijama

pylon ['paɪlən] N torre *f* de conducción eléctrica

pyramid ['pɪrəmɪd] N pirámide *f*

Pyrenean [pɪrə'niːən] ADJ pirenaico

Pyrenees [pɪrə'niːz] NPL: **the ~** los Pirineos

Pyrex® ['paɪreks] N pírex *m* ▸ CPD: **~ casserole** cazuela de pírex

python ['paɪθən] N pitón *m*

731

Qq

Q, q [kju:] N (letter) Q, q f; **Q for Queen** Q de Quebec

Qatar [kæ'tɑ:] N Qatar m

QC N ABBR (BRIT: = Queen's Counsel) título concedido a determinados abogados

QCA N ABBR (BRIT: = Qualifications and Curriculum Authority) organismo que se encarga del currículum educativo en Inglaterra

QED ABBR (= quod erat demonstrandum) Q.E.D.

QM N ABBR see **quartermaster**

q.t. N ABBR (inf) = **quiet**; **on the q.t.** a hurtadillas

qty ABBR (= quantity) cantidad

quack [kwæk] N (of duck) graznido; (pej: doctor) curandero(-a), matasanos m inv ▶ vi graznar

quad [kwɔd] ABBR = **quadrangle**; **quadruple**; **quadruplet**

quadrangle ['kwɔdræŋgl] N (BRIT: courtyard: abbr: quad) patio

quadruple [kwɔ'dru:pl] VT, vi cuadruplicar

quadruplet [kwɔ'dru:plɪt] N cuatrillizo

quagmire ['kwægmaɪə'] N lodazal m, cenagal m

quail [kweɪl] N (bird) codorniz f ▶ vi amedrentarse

quaint [kweɪnt] ADJ extraño; (picturesque) pintoresco

quaintly ['kweɪntlɪ] ADV extrañamente; pintorescamente

quaintness ['kweɪntnɪs] N lo pintoresco, tipismo

quake [kweɪk] vi temblar ▶ N ABBR = **earthquake**

Quaker ['kweɪkə'] N cuáquero(-a)

qualification [kwɔlɪfɪ'keɪʃən] N (ability) capacidad f; (often pl: diploma etc) título; (reservation) salvedad f; (modification) modificación f; (act) calificación f; **what are your qualifications?** ¿qué títulos tienes?

qualified ['kwɔlɪfaɪd] ADJ (trained) cualificado; (fit) capacitado; (limited) limitado; (professionally) titulado; **~ for/to do sth** capacitado para/para hacer algo; **he's not ~ for the job** no está capacitado para ese

trabajo; **it was a ~ success** fue un éxito relativo

qualify ['kwɔlɪfaɪ] VT (Ling) calificar a; (capacitate) capacitar; (modify) matizar; (limit) moderar ▶ vi: **to ~ (for)** (in competition) calificarse (para); (be eligible) reunir los requisitos (para); **to ~ (as)** (pass examination) calificarse (de), graduarse (en), recibirse (de) (LAM); **to ~ as an engineer** sacar el título de ingeniero

qualifying ['kwɔlɪfaɪɪŋ] ADJ (exam, round) eliminatorio

qualitative ['kwɔlɪtətɪv] ADJ cualitativo

quality ['kwɔlɪtɪ] N calidad f; (moral) cualidad f; **of good/poor ~** de buena or alta/poca calidad

quality control N control m de calidad

quality of life N calidad f de vida

quality press N prensa seria; ver nota

> La expresión *quality press* se refiere los periódicos que dan un tratamiento serio de las noticias, ofreciendo información detallada sobre un amplio espectro de temas y análisis en profundidad de la actualidad. Por su tamaño, considerablemente mayor que el de los periódicos sensacionalistas, se les llama también "*broadsheets*".

qualm [kwɑ:m] N escrúpulo; **to have qualms about sth** sentir escrúpulos por algo

quandary ['kwɔndrɪ] N: **to be in a ~** verse en un dilema

quango ['kwæŋgəu] N ABBR (BRIT: = quasi-autonomous non-governmental organization) organismo semiautónomo de subvención estatal

quantifiable [kwɔntɪ'faɪəbl] ADJ cuantificable

quantify ['kwɔntɪfaɪ] VT cuantificar

quantitative ['kwɔntɪtətɪv] ADJ cuantitativo

quantity ['kwɔntɪtɪ] N cantidad f; **in ~** en grandes cantidades

quantity surveyor N aparejador(a) m/f

quantum leap ['kwɔntəm-] N (fig) avance m espectacular

quarantine ['kwɔrntiːn] N cuarentena

quark [kwɑːk] N cuark m

quarrel ['kwɔrl] N riña, pelea ▶ VI reñir, pelearse; **to have a ~ with sb** reñir or pelearse con algn; **I can't ~ with that** no le veo pegas

quarrelsome ['kwɔrəlsəm] ADJ pendenciero

quarry ['kwɔrɪ] N (for stone) cantera; (animal) presa

quart [kwɔːt] N cuarto de galón (= 1.136 l)

quarter ['kwɔːtə'] N cuarto, cuarta parte f; (US: coin) moneda de 25 centavos; (of year) trimestre m; (district) barrio ▶ VT dividir en cuartos; (Mil: lodge) alojar; **quarters** NPL (barracks) cuartel msg; (living quarters) alojamiento sg; **a ~ of an hour** un cuarto de hora; **to pay by the ~** pagar trimestralmente or cada tres meses; **it's a ~ to** or (US) **of three** son las tres menos cuarto; **it's a ~ past** or (US) **after three** son las tres y cuarto; **from all quarters** de todas partes; **at close quarters** de cerca

quarterback ['kwɔːtəbæk] N (US: football) mariscal m de campo

quarter-deck ['kwɔːtədɛk] N (Naut) alcázar m

quarter final N cuarto de final

quarterly ['kwɔːtəlɪ] ADJ trimestral ▶ ADV cada 3 meses, trimestralmente

quartermaster ['kwɔːtəmɑːstə'] N (Mil) comisario, intendente m militar

quartet, quartette [kwɔːˈtɛt] N cuarteto

quarto ['kwɔːtəu] N tamaño holandés ▶ ADJ de tamaño holandés

quartz [kwɔːts] N cuarzo

quash [kwɔʃ] VT (verdict) anular, invalidar

quasi- ['kweɪzaɪ] PREF cuasi

quaver ['kweɪvə'] N (Brit Mus) corchea ▶ VI temblar

quay [kiː] N (also: **quayside**) muelle m

Que. ABBR (Canada) = **Quebec**

queasiness ['kwiːzɪnɪs] N malestar m, náuseas fpl

queasy ['kwiːzɪ] ADJ: **to feel ~** tener náuseas

Quebec [kwɪˈbɛk] N Quebec m

queen [kwiːn] N reina; (Cards etc) dama

queen mother N reina madre

Queen's Speech [kwiːnz-] N ver nota

Se llama Queen's Speech (o "King's Speech") al discurso que pronuncia el monarca durante la sesión de apertura del Parlamento británico, en el que se expresan las líneas generales de la política del gobierno para la nueva legislatura. El Primer Ministro se encarga de redactarlo con la ayuda del Consejo de Ministros y es leído en la Cámara de los Lores ("House of Lords") ante los miembros de ambas cámaras.

queer [kwɪə'] ADJ (odd) raro, extraño ▶ N (pej, inf!) marica m (!)

quell [kwɛl] VT calmar; (put down) sofocar

quench [kwɛntʃ] VT (flames) apagar; **to ~ one's thirst** apagar la sed

querulous ['kwɛruləs] ADJ (person, voice) quejumbroso

query ['kwɪərɪ] N (question) pregunta; (doubt) duda ▶ VT preguntar; (disagree with, dispute) no estar conforme con, dudar de

quest [kwɛst] N busca, búsqueda

question ['kwɛstʃən] N pregunta; (matter) asunto, cuestión f ▶ VT (doubt) dudar de; (interrogate) interrogar, hacer preguntas a; **to ask sb a ~**, **put a ~ to sb** hacerle una pregunta a algn; **the ~ is ...** el asunto es ...; **to bring** or **call sth into ~** poner algo en (tela de) duda; **beyond ~** fuera de toda duda; **out of the ~** imposible, ni hablar

questionable ['kwɛstʃənəbl] ADJ discutible; (doubtful) dudoso

questioner ['kwɛstʃənə'] N interrogador(a) m/f

questioning ['kwɛstʃənɪŋ] ADJ inquisitivo ▶ N preguntas fpl; (by police etc) interrogatorio

question mark N punto de interrogación

questionnaire [kwɛstʃəˈnɛə'] N cuestionario

queue [kjuː] (Brit) N cola ▶ VI hacer cola; **to jump the ~** colarse

quibble ['kwɪbl] VI andarse con sutilezas

quiche [kiːʃ] N quiche m

quick [kwɪk] ADJ rápido; (temper) vivo; (agile) ágil; (mind) listo; (eye) agudo; (ear) fino ▶ N: **cut to the ~** (fig) herido en lo más vivo; **be ~!** ¡date prisa!; **to be ~ to act** obrar con prontitud; **she was ~ to see that** se dio cuenta de eso en seguida

quicken ['kwɪkən] VT apresurar ▶ VI apresurarse, darse prisa

quick-fire ['kwɪkfaɪə'] ADJ (questions etc) rápido, (hecho) a quemarropa

quick fix N (pej) parche m

quickly ['kwɪklɪ] ADV rápidamente, de prisa; **we must act ~** tenemos que actuar cuanto antes

quickness ['kwɪknɪs] N rapidez f; (of temper) viveza; (agility) agilidad f; (of mind, eye etc) agudeza

quicksand ['kwɪksænd] N arenas fpl movedizas

quickstep ['kwɪkstɛp] N baile de ritmo rápido

quick-tempered [kwɪkˈtɛmpəd] ADJ de genio vivo

quick-witted [kwɪkˈwɪtɪd] ADJ listo, despabilado

quid [kwɪd] N pl inv (Brit inf) libra

quid pro quo ['kwɪdprəu'kwəu] N quid pro quo m, compensación f

quiet ['kwaɪət] ADJ (voice, music etc) bajo;

(*person, place*) tranquilo; (*silent*) callado; (*reserved*) reservado; (*discreet*) discreto; (*not noisy: engine*) silencioso ▸ N silencio; (*calm*) tranquilidad f ▸ VT, VI (*US*) = **quieten**; **keep ~!** ¡cállate!, ¡silencio!; **business is ~ at this time of year** hay poco movimiento en esta época

quieten ['kwaɪətn], **quieten down** VI (*grow calm*) calmarse; (*grow silent*) callarse ▸ VT calmar; hacer callar

quietly ['kwaɪətlɪ] ADV tranquilamente; (*silently*) silenciosamente

quietness ['kwaɪətnɪs] N (*silence*) silencio; (*calm*) tranquilidad f

quill [kwɪl] N (*of porcupine*) púa; (*pen*) pluma

quilt [kwɪlt] N (*BRIT*) edredón m

quin [kwɪn] N ABBR = **quintuplet**

quince [kwɪns] N membrillo

quinine [kwɪ'niːn] N quinina

quintet, quintette [kwɪn'tɛt] N quinteto

quintuplet [kwɪn'tjuːplɪt] N quintillizo

quip [kwɪp] N ocurrencia ▸ VI decir con ironía

quire ['kwaɪəʳ] N mano f de papel

quirk [kwəːk] N peculiaridad f; **by some ~ of fate** por algún capricho del destino

quirky ['kwɜːkɪ] ADJ raro, estrafalario

quit [kwɪt] (*pt ~, pp ~ or* **quitted**) VT dejar, abandonar; (*premises*) desocupar; (*Comput*) abandonar ▸ VI (*give up*) renunciar; (*go away*) irse; (*resign*) dimitir; **~ stalling!** (*US inf*) ¡déjate de evasivas!

quite [kwaɪt] ADV (*rather*) bastante; (*entirely*) completamente; **~ a few of them** un buen

número de ellos; **~ (so)!** ¡así es!, ¡exactamente!; **~ new** bastante nuevo; **that's not ~ right** eso no está del todo bien; **not ~ as many as last time** no tantos como la última vez; **she's ~ pretty** es bastante guapa

Quito ['kiːtəu] N Quito

quits [kwɪts] ADJ: **~ (with)** en paz (con); **let's call it ~** quedamos en paz

quiver ['kwɪvəʳ] VI estremecerse ▸ N (*for arrows*) carcaj m

quiz [kwɪz] N (*game*) concurso; (: *TV, Radio*) programa-concurso; (*questioning*) interrogatorio ▸ VT interrogar

quizzical ['kwɪzɪkl] ADJ burlón(-ona)

quoits [kwɔɪts] NPL juego de aros

quorum ['kwɔːrəm] N quórum m

quota ['kwəutə] N cuota

quotation [kwəu'teɪʃən] N cita; (*estimate*) presupuesto

quotation marks NPL comillas fpl

quote [kwəut] N cita ▸ VT (*sentence*) citar; (*Comm: sum, figure*) cotizar ▸ VI: **to ~ from** citar de; **quotes** NPL (*inverted commas*) comillas fpl; **in quotes** entre comillas; **the figure quoted for the repairs** el presupuesto dado para las reparaciones; **~ ... unquote** (*in dictation*) comillas iniciales ... finales

quotient ['kwəuʃənt] N cociente m

qv N ABBR (= *quod vide: which see*) q.v.

qwerty keyboard ['kwəːtɪ-] N teclado QWERTY

Rr

R, r [ɑːʳ] N (letter) R, r f; **R for Robert**, (US) **R for Roger** R de Ramón

R ABBR (= right) dcha.; (US Cine: = restricted) sólo mayores; (US Pol) = **republican**; (BRIT: = Rex, Regina) R; (= river) R.; (= Réaumur (scale)) R

RA ABBR = **rear admiral** ▶ N ABBR (BRIT) = **Royal Academy; Royal Academician**

RAAF N ABBR = **Royal Australian Air Force**

Rabat [rəˈbɑːt] N Rabat m

rabbi [ˈræbaɪ] N rabino

rabbit [ˈræbɪt] N conejo ▶ VI: **to ~ (on)** (BRIT inf) hablar sin ton ni son

rabbit hutch N conejera

rabble [ˈræbl] N (pej) chusma, populacho

rabies [ˈreɪbiːz] N rabia

RAC N ABBR (BRIT: = Royal Automobile Club) ≈ RACE m (SP)

raccoon, racoon [rəˈkuːn] N mapache m

race [reɪs] N carrera; (species) raza ▶ VT (horse) hacer correr; (person) competir contra; (engine) acelerar ▶ VI (compete) competir; (run) correr; (pulse) latir a ritmo acelerado; **the arms ~** la carrera armamentista; **the human ~** el género humano; **he raced across the road** cruzó corriendo la carretera; **to ~ in/out** entrar/salir corriendo

race car N (US) = **racing car**

race car driver N (US) = **racing driver**

racecourse [ˈreɪskɔːs] N hipódromo

racehorse [ˈreɪshɔːs] N caballo de carreras

race meeting N concurso hípico

race relations NPL relaciones fpl raciales

racetrack [ˈreɪstræk] N hipódromo; (for cars) circuito de carreras

racial [ˈreɪʃl] ADJ racial

racial discrimination N discriminación f racial

racial integration N integración f racial

racialism [ˈreɪʃəlɪzəm] N racismo

racialist [ˈreɪʃəlɪst] ADJ, N racista mf

racing [ˈreɪsɪŋ] N carreras fpl

racing car N (BRIT) coche m de carreras

racing driver N (BRIT) piloto mf de carreras

racism [ˈreɪsɪzəm] N racismo

racist [ˈreɪsɪst] ADJ, N racista mf

rack [ræk] N (also: **luggage rack**) rejilla (portaequipajes); (shelf) estante m; (also: **roof rack**) baca; (also: **clothes rack**) perchero ▶ VT (cause pain to) atormentar; **to go to ~ and ruin** venirse abajo; **to ~ one's brains** devanarse los sesos

▶ **rack up** VT conseguir, ganar

racket [ˈrækɪt] N (for tennis) raqueta; (inf: noise) ruido, estrépito; (: swindle) estafa, timo

racketeer [rækɪˈtɪəʳ] N (esp US) estafador(a) m/f

racquet [ˈrækɪt] N raqueta

racy [ˈreɪsɪ] ADJ picante, subido

RADA [ˈrɑːdə] N ABBR (BRIT) = **Royal Academy of Dramatic Art**

radar [ˈreɪdɑːʳ] N radar m

radar trap N trampa radar

radial [ˈreɪdɪəl] ADJ (tyre: also: **radial-ply**) radial

radiance [ˈreɪdɪəns] N brillantez f, resplandor m

radiant [ˈreɪdɪənt] ADJ brillante, resplandeciente

radiate [ˈreɪdɪeɪt] VT (heat) radiar, irradiar ▶ VI (lines) extenderse

radiation [reɪdɪˈeɪʃən] N radiación f

radiation sickness N enfermedad f de radiación

radiator [ˈreɪdɪeɪtəʳ] N (Aut) radiador m

radiator cap N tapón m del radiador

radiator grill N (Aut) rejilla del radiador

radical [ˈrædɪkl] ADJ radical

radically [ˈrædɪkəlɪ] ADV radicalmente

radii [ˈreɪdɪaɪ] NPL of **radius**

radio [ˈreɪdɪəu] N radio f ▶ VI: **to ~ to sb** mandar un mensaje por radio a algn ▶ VT (information) radiar, transmitir por radio; (one's position) indicar por radio; (person) llamar por radio; **on the ~** en or por la radio

radioactive [reɪdɪəuˈæktɪv] ADJ radi(o)activo

radioactivity [reɪdɪəuækˈtɪvɪtɪ] N radi(o)actividad f

radio announcer N locutor(a) m/f de radio

radio-controlled [ˈreɪdɪəukənˈtrəuld] ADJ teledirigido

radiographer [reɪdɪˈɔɡrəfəʳ] N radiógrafo(-a)

radiography [reɪdɪˈɔɡrəfɪ] N radiografía

radiology [reɪdɪˈɔlədʒɪ] N radiología

radio station N emisora

radio taxi N radio taxi *m*

radiotelephone [reɪdɪəuˈtɛlɪfəun] N radioteléfono

radio telescope [reɪdɪəuˈtɛlɪskəup] N radiotelescopio

radiotherapist [reɪdɪəuˈθɛrəpɪst] N radioterapeuta *mf*

radiotherapy [ˈreɪdɪəuθɛrəpɪ] N radioterapia

radish [ˈrædɪʃ] N rábano

radium [ˈreɪdɪəm] N radio

radius [ˈreɪdɪəs] (*pl* **radii** [-ɪaɪ]) N radio; **within a ~ of 50 miles** en un radio de 50 millas

RAF N ABBR (*BRIT*) = **Royal Air Force**

raffia [ˈræfɪə] N rafia

raffle [ˈræfl] N rifa, sorteo ▶ VT (*object*) rifar

raft [rɑːft] N (*craft*) balsa; (*also:* **life raft**) balsa salvavidas

rafter [ˈrɑːftəʳ] N viga

rag [ræɡ] N (*piece of cloth*) trapo; (*torn cloth*) harapo; (*pej: newspaper*) periodicucho; (*for charity*) actividades estudiantiles benéficas ▶ VT (*BRIT*) tomar el pelo a; **rags** NPL harapos *mpl*; **in rags** en harapos, hecho jirones

rag-and-bone man [ræɡənˈbəunmæn] N (*irreg*) (*BRIT*) trapero

rag doll N muñeca de trapo

rage [reɪdʒ] N (*fury*) rabia, furor *m* ▶ VI (*person*) rabiar, estar furioso; (*storm*) bramar; **to fly into a ~** montar en cólera; **it's all the ~** es lo último; (*very fashionable*) está muy de moda

ragged [ˈræɡɪd] ADJ (*edge*) desigual, mellado; (*cuff*) roto; (*appearance*) andrajoso, harapiento; **~ left/right** (*text*) margen *m* izquierdo/derecho irregular

raging [ˈreɪdʒɪŋ] ADJ furioso; **in a ~ temper** de un humor de mil demonios

rag trade N: **the ~** (*inf*) el ramo de la confección

rag week N *ver nota*

En la universidad los estudiantes suelen organizar cada año lo que llaman *rag week*. Consiste en una serie de actos festivos y de participación general como teatro en la calle, marchas patrocinadas etc, para hacer colectas con fines benéficos. En ocasiones hacen también una revista ("*rag mag*"), que consiste básicamente en chistes más bien picantes para vender a los transeúntes, e incluso un baile de gala ("*rag ball*").

raid [reɪd] N (*Mil*) incursión *f*; (*criminal*) asalto; (*by police*) redada, allanamiento (*LAm*) ▶ VT invadir, atacar; asaltar

raider [ˈreɪdəʳ] N invasor(a) *m/f*

rail [reɪl] N (*on stair*) barandilla, pasamanos *m inv*; (*on bridge*) pretil *m*; (*of balcony, ship*) barandilla; (*for train*) riel *m*, carril *m*; **rails** NPL vía *sg*; **by ~** por ferrocarril, en tren

railcard [ˈreɪlkɑːd] N (*BRIT*) tarjeta para obtener descuentos en el tren; **Young Person's R~** ≈ Tarjeta joven (*SP*)

railing [ˈreɪlɪŋ] N, **railings** [ˈreɪlɪŋz] NPL verja *sg*

railway [ˈreɪlweɪ], (*US*) **railroad** [ˈreɪlrəud] N ferrocarril *m*, vía férrea

railway engine N (máquina) locomotora

railway line N (*BRIT*) línea (de ferrocarril)

railwayman [ˈreɪlweɪmən] N (*irreg*) (*BRIT*) ferroviario

railway station N (*BRIT*) estación *f* de ferrocarril

rain [reɪn] N lluvia ▶ VI llover; **in the ~** bajo la lluvia; **it's raining** llueve, está lloviendo; **it's raining cats and dogs** está lloviendo a cántaros *or* a mares

rainbow [ˈreɪnbəu] N arco iris

raincoat [ˈreɪnkəut] N impermeable *m*

raindrop [ˈreɪndrɔp] N gota de lluvia

rainfall [ˈreɪnfɔːl] N lluvia

rainforest [ˈreɪnfɔrɪst] N selva tropical

rainproof [ˈreɪnpruːf] ADJ impermeable, a prueba de lluvia

rainstorm [ˈreɪnstɔːm] N temporal *m* (de lluvia)

rainwater [ˈreɪnwɔːtəʳ] N agua de lluvia

rainy [ˈreɪnɪ] ADJ lluvioso

raise [reɪz] N aumento ▶ VT (*lift*) levantar; (*build*) erigir, edificar; (*increase*) aumentar; (*improve: morale*) subir; (*: standards*) mejorar; (*doubts*) suscitar; (*a question*) plantear; (*cattle, family*) criar; (*crop*) cultivar; (*army*) reclutar; (*funds*) reunir; (*loan*) obtener; (*end: embargo*) levantar; **to ~ one's voice** alzar la voz; **to ~ one's glass to sb/sth** brindar por algn/algo; **to ~ a laugh/a smile** provocar risa/una sonrisa; **to ~ sb's hopes** dar esperanzas a algn

raisin [ˈreɪzn] N pasa de Corinto

rake [reɪk] N (*tool*) rastrillo; (*person*) libertino ▶ VT (*garden*) rastrillar; (*fire*) hurgar; (*with machine gun*) barrer
  ▶ **rake in, rake together** VT sacar

rake-off [ˈreɪkɔf] N (*inf*) comisión *f*, tajada

rakish [ˈreɪkɪʃ] ADJ (*dissolute*) libertino; **at a ~ angle** (*hat*) echado a un lado, de lado

rally [ˈrælɪ] N reunión *f*; (*Pol*) mitin *m*; (*Aut*) rally *m*; (*Tennis*) peloteo ▶ VT reunir ▶ VI reunirse; (*sick person*) recuperarse; (*Stock Exchange*) recuperarse

▶ **rally round** VT FUS (*fig*) dar apoyo a

rallying point ['rælɪɪŋ-] N (*Pol, Mil*) punto de reunión

RAM [ræm] N ABBR (*Comput: = random access memory*) RAM *f*

ram [ræm] N carnero; (*Tech*) pisón *m*; (*also:* **battering ram**) ariete *m* ▶ VT (*crash into*) dar contra, chocar con; (*push: fist etc*) empujar con fuerza; (*tread down*) apisonar

Ramadan ['ræmədæn] N Ramadán *m*

ramble ['ræmbl] N caminata, excursión *f* en el campo ▶ VI (*pej: also:* **ramble on**) divagar

rambler ['ræmbləʳ] N excursionista *mf*; (*Bot*) trepadora

rambling ['ræmblɪŋ] ADJ (*speech*) inconexo; (*Bot*) trepador(a); (*house*) laberíntico

rambunctious [ræm'bʌŋkʃəs] ADJ (*US*) = **rumbustious**

RAMC N ABBR (*Brit*) = **Royal Army Medical Corps**

ramification [ræmɪfɪ'keɪʃən] N ramificación *f*

ramp [ræmp] N rampa; **on/off ~ n** (*US Aut*) vía de acceso/salida; **"~"** (*Aut*) "rampa"

rampage [ræm'peɪdʒ] N: **to be on the ~** desmandarse ▶ VI: **they went rampaging through the town** recorrieron la ciudad armando alboroto

rampant ['ræmpənt] ADJ (*disease etc*): **to be ~** estar muy extendido

rampart ['ræmpɑːt] N terraplén *m*; (*wall*) muralla

ram raid VT atracar (*rompiendo el escaparate con un coche*)

ramshackle ['ræmʃækl] ADJ destartalado

RAN N ABBR = **Royal Australian Navy**

ran [ræn] PT of **run**

ranch [rɑːntʃ] N (*US*) hacienda, estancia

rancher ['rɑːntʃəʳ] N ganadero

rancid ['rænsɪd] ADJ rancio

rancour, (*US*) **rancor** ['ræŋkəʳ] N rencor *m*

R & B N ABBR = **rhythm and blues**

R & D N ABBR (*= research and development*) I + D

random ['rændəm] ADJ fortuito, sin orden; (*Comput, Math*) aleatorio ▶ N: **at ~** al azar

random access N (*Comput*) acceso aleatorio

R & R N ABBR (*also US Mil*) = **rest and recreation**

randy ['rændɪ] ADJ (*Brit inf*) cachondo, caliente

rang [ræŋ] PT of **ring**

range [reɪndʒ] N (*of mountains*) cadena de montañas, cordillera; (*of missile*) alcance *m*; (*of voice*) registro; (*series*) serie *f*; (*of products*) surtido; (*Mil: also:* **shooting range**) campo de tiro; (*also:* **kitchen range**) fogón *m* ▶ VT (*place*) colocar; (*arrange*) arreglar ▶ VI: **to ~ over** (*wander*) recorrer; (*extend*) extenderse por; **within (firing) ~** a tiro; **do you have**

anything else in this price ~? ¿tiene algo más de esta gama de precios?; **intermediate-/short-~ missile** proyectil *m* de medio/corto alcance; **to ~ from ... to ...** oscilar entre ... y ...; **ranged left/right** (*text*) alineado a la izquierda/derecha

ranger [reɪndʒəʳ] N guardabosques *m inv*

Rangoon [ræŋ'guːn] N Rangún *m*

rangy ['reɪndʒɪ] ADJ alto y delgado

rank [ræŋk] N (*row*) fila; (*Mil*) rango; (*status*) categoría; (*Brit: also:* **taxi rank**) parada ▶ VI: **to ~ among** figurar entre ▶ ADJ (*stinking*) fétido, rancio; (*hypocrisy, injustice etc*) manifiesto; **the ~ and file** (*fig*) las bases; **to close ranks** (*Mil*) cerrar filas; (*fig*) hacer un frente común; **~ outsider** participante *mf* sin probabilidades de vencer; **I ~ him sixth** yo le pongo en sexto lugar

rankle ['ræŋkl] VI (*insult*) doler

ransack ['rænsæk] VT (*search*) registrar; (*plunder*) saquear

ransom ['rænsəm] N rescate *m*; **to hold sb to ~** (*fig*) poner a algn entre la espada y la pared

rant [rænt] VI despotricar

ranting ['ræntɪŋ] N desvaríos *mpl*

rap [ræp] VT golpear, dar un golpecito en ▶ N (*music*) rap *m*

rape [reɪp] N violación *f*; (*Bot*) colza ▶ VT violar

rape oil, rapeseed oil ['reɪpsiː-] N aceite *m* de colza

rapid ['ræpɪd] ADJ rápido

rapidity [rə'pɪdɪtɪ] N rapidez *f*

rapidly ['ræpɪdlɪ] ADV rápidamente

rapids ['ræpɪdz] NPL (*Geo*) rápidos *mpl*

rapier ['reɪpɪəʳ] N estoque *m*

rapist ['reɪpɪst] N violador *m*

rapport [ræ'pɔː] N entendimiento

rapprochement [ræ'prɔʃmãːŋ] N acercamiento

rapt [ræpt] ADJ (*attention*) profundo; **to be ~ in contemplation** estar ensimismado

rapture ['ræptʃəʳ] N éxtasis *m*

rapturous ['ræptʃərəs] ADJ extático; (*applause*) entusiasta

rare [rɛəʳ] ADJ raro, poco común; (*Culin: steak*) poco hecho; **it is ~ to find that ...** es raro descubrir que ...

rarefied ['rɛərɪfaɪd] ADJ (*air, atmosphere*) enrarecido

rarely ['rɛəlɪ] ADV rara vez, pocas veces

raring ['rɛərɪŋ] ADJ: **to be ~ to go** (*inf*) tener muchas ganas de empezar

rarity ['rɛərɪtɪ] N rareza

rascal ['rɑːskl] N pillo(-a), pícaro(-a)

rash [ræʃ] ADJ imprudente, precipitado ▶ N (*Med*) sarpullido, erupción *f* (*cutánea*); **to come out in a ~** salir salpullidos

rasher ['ræʃəʳ] N loncha

r

rashly ['ræʃlɪ] ADV imprudentemente, precipitadamente

rashness ['ræʃnɪs] N imprudencia, precipitación f

rasp [rɑːsp] N (tool) escofina ▸ VT (speak: also: **rasp out**) decir con voz áspera

raspberry ['rɑːzbərɪ] N frambuesa

rasping ['rɑːspɪŋ] ADJ: **a ~ noise** un ruido áspero

Rastafarian [ræstə'fɛərɪən] ADJ, N rastafari mf

rat [ræt] N rata

ratchet ['rætʃɪt] N (Tech) trinquete m

rate [reɪt] N (ratio) razón f; (percentage) tanto por ciento; (price) precio; (: of hotel) tarifa; (of interest) tipo; (speed) velocidad f ▸ VT (value) tasar; (estimate) estimar; **to ~ as** ser considerado como; **rates** NPL (BRIT) impuesto sg municipal; (fees) tarifa sg; **failure ~** porcentaje m de fallos; **pulse ~** pulsaciones fpl por minuto; **~ of pay** tipos mpl de sueldo; **at a ~ of 60 kph** a una velocidad de 60 kph; **~ of growth** ritmo de crecimiento; **~ of return** (Comm) tasa de rendimiento; **bank ~** tipo or tasa de interés bancario; **at any ~** en todo caso; **to ~ sb/sth highly** tener a algn/algo en alta estima; **the house is rated at £84 per annum** (BRIT) la casa está tasada en 84 libras al año

rateable value ['reɪtəbl-] N (BRIT) valor m impuesto

rate-capping ['reɪtkæpɪŋ] N (BRIT) fijación f de las contribuciones

ratepayer ['reɪtpeɪər] N (BRIT) contribuyente mf

rather ['rɑːðər] ADV antes, más bien; (somewhat) algo, un poco; (quite) bastante; **it's ~ expensive** es algo caro; (too much) es demasiado caro; **there's ~ a lot** hay bastante; **I would** or **I'd ~ go** preferiría ir; **I'd ~ not** prefiero que no; **I ~ think he won't come** me inclino a creer que no vendrá; **or ~** (more accurately) o mejor dicho

ratification [rætɪfɪ'keɪʃən] N ratificación f

ratify ['rætɪfaɪ] VT ratificar

rating ['reɪtɪŋ] N (valuation) tasación f; (standing) posición f; (BRIT Naut: sailor) marinero; **ratings** NPL (Radio, TV) niveles mpl de audiencia

ratio ['reɪʃɪəu] N razón f; **in the ~ of 100 to 1** a razón de or en la proporción de 100 a 1

ration ['ræʃən] N ración f ▸ VT racionar; **rations** NPL víveres mpl

rational ['ræʃənl] ADJ racional; (solution, reasoning) lógico, razonable; (person) cuerdo, sensato

rationale [ræʃə'nɑːl] N razón f fundamental

rationalism ['ræʃnəlɪzəm] N racionalismo

rationalization [ræʃnəlaɪ'zeɪʃən] N racionalización f

rationalize ['ræʃnəlaɪz] VT (reorganize: industry) racionalizar

rationally ['ræʃnəlɪ] ADV racionalmente; (logically) lógicamente

rationing ['ræʃnɪŋ] N racionamiento

ratpack ['rætpæk] N (BRIT inf) periodistas que persiguen a los famosos

rat race N lucha incesante por la supervivencia

rattan [ræ'tæn] N rota, caña de Indias

rattle ['rætl] N golpeteo; (of train etc) traqueteo; (object: of baby) sonaja, sonajero; (: of sports fan) matraca ▸ VI (small objects) castañetear; (car, bus): **to ~ along** traquetear ▸ VT hacer sonar agitando; (inf: disconcert) poner nervioso a

rattlesnake ['rætlsneɪk] N serpiente f de cascabel

ratty ['rætɪ] ADJ (inf) furioso; **to get ~** mosquearse

raucous ['rɔːkəs] ADJ estridente, ronco

raucously ['rɔːkəslɪ] ADV de modo estridente, roncamente

raunchy ['rɔːntʃɪ] ADJ (inf) lascivo

ravage ['rævɪdʒ] VT hacer estragos en, destrozar; **ravages** NPL estragos mpl

rave [reɪv] VI (in anger) encolerizarse; (with enthusiasm) entusiasmarse; (Med) delirar, desvariar ▸ CPD: **~ review** reseña entusiasta; **a ~ (party)** una macrofiesta con música máquina ▸ N (inf: party) rave m; **~ music** música máquina

raven ['reɪvən] N cuervo

ravenous ['rævənəs] ADJ: **to be ~** tener un hambre canina

ravine [rə'viːn] N barranco

raving ['reɪvɪŋ] ADJ: **~ lunatic** loco de atar

ravings ['reɪvɪŋz] NPL desvaríos mpl

ravioli [rævɪ'əulɪ] N ravioles mpl, ravioli mpl

ravish ['rævɪʃ] VT (charm) encantar, embelesar; (rape) violar

ravishing ['rævɪʃɪŋ] ADJ encantador(a)

raw [rɔː] ADJ (uncooked) crudo; (not processed) bruto; (sore) vivo; (inexperienced) novato, inexperto; **~ materials** materias primas

Rawalpindi [rɔːl'pɪndɪ] N Rawalpindi m

raw data N (Comput) datos mpl en bruto

raw deal N (inf: bad deal) mala pasada or jugada; (: harsh treatment) injusticia

raw material N materia prima

ray [reɪ] N rayo; **~ of hope** (rayo de) esperanza

rayon ['reɪɔn] N rayón m

raze [reɪz] VT (also: **raze to the ground**) arrasar, asolar

razor ['reɪzər] N (open) navaja; (safety razor) máquina de afeitar; (electric razor) máquina (eléctrica) de afeitar

razor blade N hoja de afeitar

razzle ['ræzl], **razzle-dazzle** ['ræzl'dæzl] N (BRIT inf): **to be/go on the ~** estar/irse de juerga

razzmatazz ['ræzmə'tæz] N (inf) animación f, bullicio

RC ABBR = **Roman Catholic**

RCAF N ABBR = **Royal Canadian Air Force**

RCMP N ABBR = **Royal Canadian Mounted Police**

RCN N ABBR = **Royal Canadian Navy**

RD ABBR (US Post) = **rural delivery**

Rd ABBR = **road**

RDC N ABBR (BRIT) = **rural district council**

RE N ABBR (BRIT Scol) = **religious education**; (BRIT Mil) = **Royal Engineers**

re [riː] PREP con referencia a

re... [riː] PREF re...

reach [riːtʃ] N alcance m; (Boxing) envergadura; (of river etc) extensión f entre dos recodos ▶ VT alcanzar, llegar a; (achieve) lograr ▶ VI extenderse; (stretch out hand: also: **reach down**, **reach over**, **reach across** etc) tender la mano; **within ~** al alcance (de la mano); **out of ~** fuera del alcance; **can I ~ you at your hotel?** ¿puedo localizarte en tu hotel?; **to ~ sb by phone** comunicarse con algn por teléfono
▶ **reach out** VT (hand) tender ▶ VI: **to ~ out for sth** alargar or tender la mano para tomar algo

react [riː'ækt] VI reaccionar

reaction [riː'ækʃən] N reacción f

reactionary [riː'ækʃənrɪ] ADJ, N reaccionario(-a) m/f

reactor [riː'æktər] N (also: **nuclear reactor**) reactor m (nuclear)

read [riːd] (pt, pp ~ [red]) VI leer ▶ VT leer; (understand) entender; (study) estudiar; **to take sth as ~** (fig) dar algo por sentado; **do you ~ me?** (Tel) ¿me escucha?; **to ~ between the lines** leer entre líneas
▶ **read out** VT leer en alta voz
▶ **read over** VT repasar
▶ **read through** VT (quickly) leer rápidamente, echar un vistazo a; (thoroughly) leer con cuidado or detenidamente
▶ **read up**, **read up on** VT FUS documentarse sobre

readable ['riːdəbl] ADJ (writing) legible; (book) que merece la pena leer

reader ['riːdər] N lector(a) m/f; (book) libro de lecturas; (BRIT: at university) profesor(a) m/f

readership ['riːdəʃɪp] N (of paper etc) número de lectores

readily ['redɪlɪ] ADV (willingly) de buena gana; (easily) fácilmente; (quickly) en seguida

readiness ['redɪnɪs] N buena voluntad; (preparedness) preparación f; **in ~** (prepared) listo, preparado

reading ['riːdɪŋ] N lectura; (understanding) comprensión f; (on instrument) indicación f

reading lamp N lámpara portátil

reading matter N lectura

reading room N sala de lectura

readjust [riːə'dʒʌst] VT reajustar ▶ VI (person): **to ~ to** reajustarse a

readjustment [riːə'dʒʌstmənt] N reajuste m

ready ['redɪ] ADJ listo, preparado; (willing) dispuesto; (available) disponible ▶ ADV: **~-cooked** listo para comer ▶ N: **at the ~** (Mil) listo para tirar ▶ VT preparar; **~ for use** listo para usar; **to be ~ to do sth** estar listo para hacer algo; **to get ~** vi prepararse

ready cash N efectivo

ready-made ['redɪ'meɪd] ADJ confeccionado

ready money N dinero contante

ready reckoner N tabla de cálculos hechos

ready-to-wear ['redɪtə'weər] ADJ confeccionado

reaffirm [riːə'fəːm] VT reafirmar

reagent [riː'eɪdʒənt] N reactivo

real [rɪəl] ADJ verdadero, auténtico; **in ~ terms** en términos reales; **in ~ life** en la vida real, en la realidad

real ale N cerveza elaborada tradicionalmente

real estate N bienes mpl raíces

real estate agency N = **estate agency**

realism ['rɪəlɪzəm] N (also Art) realismo

realist ['rɪəlɪst] N realista mf

realistic [rɪə'lɪstɪk] ADJ realista

realistically [rɪə'lɪstɪklɪ] ADV de modo realista

reality [riː'ælɪtɪ] N realidad f; **in ~** en realidad

reality TV N telerrealidad f

realization [rɪəlaɪ'zeɪʃən] N comprensión f; (of a project) realización f; (Comm: of assets) realización f

realize ['rɪəlaɪz] VT (understand) darse cuenta de; (a project) realizar; (Comm: asset) realizar; **I ~ that ...** comprendo or entiendo que ...

really ['rɪəlɪ] ADV realmente; (for emphasis) verdaderamente; **what ~ happened** (actually) lo que pasó en realidad; **~?** ¿de veras?; **~!** (annoyance) ¡vamos!, ¡por favor!

realm [relm] N reino; (fig) esfera

real time N (also Comput) tiempo real

realtor ['rɪəltɔːr] N (US) corredor(a) m/f de bienes raíces

ream [riːm] N resma; **reams** (fig, inf) montones mpl

reap [riːp] VT segar; (fig) cosechar, recoger

reaper ['riːpər] N segador(a) m/f

reappear [riːə'pɪər] VI reaparecer

reappearance [riːə'pɪərəns] N reaparición f

reapply [riːə'plaɪ] VI volver a presentarse, hacer or presentar una nueva solicitud

reappoint [riːə'pɔɪnt] VT volver a nombrar

reappraisal [ˌriːəˈpreɪzl] N revaluación f

rear [rɪəʳ] ADJ trasero ▸ N parte f trasera ▸ VT (*cattle, family*) criar ▸ VI (*also:* **rear up:** *animal*) encabritarse

rear-engined [ˈrɪərˈɛndʒɪnd] ADJ (*Aut*) con motor trasero

rearguard [ˈrɪəgɑːd] N retaguardia

rearm [riːˈɑːm] VT rearmar ▸ VI rearmarse

rearmament [riːˈɑːməmənt] N rearme m

rearrange [riːəˈreɪndʒ] VT ordenar *or* arreglar de nuevo

rear-view mirror [ˈrɪəvjuː] N (*Aut*) espejo retrovisor

rear-wheel drive N tracción f trasera

reason [ˈriːzn] N razón f ▸ VI: **to ~ with sb** tratar de que algn entre en razón; **it stands to ~ that …** es lógico que …; **the ~ for/why** la causa de/la razón por la cual; **she claims with good ~ that she's underpaid** dice con razón que está mal pagada; **all the more ~ why you should not sell it** razón de más para que no lo vendas

reasonable [ˈriːznəbl] ADJ razonable; (*sensible*) sensato

reasonably [ˈriːznəblɪ] ADV razonablemente; **a ~ accurate report** un informe bastante exacto

reasoned [ˈriːznd] ADJ (*argument*) razonado

reasoning [ˈriːznɪŋ] N razonamiento, argumentos mpl

reassemble [riːəˈsɛmbl] VT volver a reunir; (*machine*) montar de nuevo ▸ VI volver a reunirse

reassert [riːəˈsəːt] VT reafirmar, reiterar

reassurance [riːəˈʃuərəns] N consuelo

reassure [riːəˈʃuəʳ] VT tranquilizar; **to ~ sb that** tranquilizar a algn asegurándole que

reassuring [riːəˈʃuərɪŋ] ADJ tranquilizador(a)

reawakening [riːəˈweɪknɪŋ] N despertar m

rebate [ˈriːbeɪt] N (*on product*) rebaja; (*on tax etc*) desgravación f; (*repayment*) reembolso

rebel N [ˈrɛbl] rebelde mf ▸ VI [rɪˈbɛl] rebelarse, sublevarse

rebellion [rɪˈbɛljən] N rebelión f, sublevación f

rebellious [rɪˈbɛljəs] ADJ rebelde; (*child*) revoltoso

rebirth [riːˈbəːθ] N renacimiento

rebound [rɪˈbaʊnd] VI (*ball*) rebotar ▸ N [ˈriːbaʊnd] rebote m

rebuff [rɪˈbʌf] N desaire m, rechazo ▸ VT rechazar

rebuild [riːˈbɪld] VT (*irreg: like* **build**) reconstruir

rebuilding [riːˈbɪldɪŋ] N reconstrucción f

rebuke [rɪˈbjuːk] N reprimenda ▸ VT reprender

rebut [rɪˈbʌt] VT rebatir

recalcitrant [rɪˈkælsɪtrənt] ADJ reacio

recall [rɪˈkɔːl] VT (*remember*) recordar; (*ambassador etc*) retirar; (*Comput*) volver a llamar ▸ N recuerdo

recant [rɪˈkænt] VI retractarse

recap [ˈriːkæp] VT, VI recapitular

recapitulate [riːkəˈpɪtjuleɪt] VT, VI = **recap**

recapture [riːˈkæptʃəʳ] VT (*town*) reconquistar; (*atmosphere*) hacer revivir

recd., rec'd ABBR (= *received*) recibido

recede [rɪˈsiːd] VI retroceder

receding [rɪˈsiːdɪŋ] ADJ (*forehead, chin*) hundido; **~ hairline** entradas fpl

receipt [rɪˈsiːt] N (*document*) recibo; (*act of receiving*) recepción f; **receipts** NPL (*Comm*) ingresos mpl; **to acknowledge ~ of** acusar recibo de; **we are in ~ of …** obra en nuestro poder …

receivable [rɪˈsiːvəbl] ADJ (*Comm*) a cobrar

receive [rɪˈsiːv] VT recibir; (*guest*) acoger; (*wound*) sufrir; **"received with thanks"** "recibí"

Received Pronunciation [rɪˈsiːvd-] N *see* **RP**

receiver [rɪˈsiːvəʳ] N (*Tel*) auricular m; (*Radio*) receptor m; (*of stolen goods*) perista mf; (*Law*) administrador m jurídico

receivership [rɪˈsiːvəʃɪp] N: **to go into ~** entrar en liquidación

recent [ˈriːsnt] ADJ reciente; **in ~ years** en los últimos años

recently [ˈriːsntlɪ] ADV recientemente, recién (*LAm*); **~ arrived** recién llegado; **until ~** hasta hace poco

receptacle [rɪˈsɛptɪkl] N receptáculo

reception [rɪˈsɛpʃən] N (*in building, office etc*) recepción f; (*welcome*) acogida

reception centre N (*Brit*) centro de recepción

reception desk N recepción f

receptionist [rɪˈsɛpʃənɪst] N recepcionista mf

receptive [rɪˈsɛptɪv] ADJ receptivo

recess [rɪˈsɛs] N (*in room*) hueco; (*for bed*) nicho; (*secret place*) escondrijo; (*Pol etc: holiday*) período vacacional; (*US Law: short break*) descanso; (*Scol: esp US*) recreo

recession [rɪˈsɛʃən] N recesión f, depresión f

recessionista [rɪsɛʃəˈnɪstə] N recesionista mf

recharge [riːˈtʃɑːdʒ] VT (*battery*) recargar

rechargeable [riːˈtʃɑːdʒəbl] ADJ recargable

recipe [ˈrɛsɪpɪ] N receta; (*for disaster, success*) fórmula

recipient [rɪˈsɪpɪənt] N recibidor(a) m/f; (*of letter*) destinatario(-a)

reciprocal [rɪˈsɪprəkl] ADJ recíproco

reciprocate [rɪˈsɪprəkeɪt] VT devolver, corresponder a ▸ VI corresponder

recital [rɪˈsaɪtl] N (*Mus*) recital m

recitation [rɛsɪˈteɪʃən] N (*of poetry*) recitado; (*of complaints etc*) enumeración f, relación f

recite [rɪˈsaɪt] VT (*poem*) recitar; (*complaints etc*) enumerar

reckless ['rɛkləs] ADJ temerario, imprudente; (*speed*) peligroso

recklessly ['rɛkləslɪ] ADV imprudentemente; de modo peligroso

recklessness ['rɛkləsnɪs] N temeridad *f*, imprudencia

reckon ['rɛkən] VT (*calculate*) calcular; (*consider*) considerar ▶ VI: **to ~ without sb/ sth** dejar de contar con algn/algo; **he is somebody to be reckoned with** no se le puede descartar; **I ~ that ...** me parece que ..., creo que ...
  ▶ **reckon on** VT FUS contar con

reckoning ['rɛkənɪŋ] N (*calculation*) cálculo

reclaim [rɪ'kleɪm] VT (*land*) recuperar; (: *from sea*) rescatar; (*demand back*) reclamar

reclamation [rɛklə'meɪʃən] N recuperación *f*; rescate *m*

recline [rɪ'klaɪn] VI reclinarse

reclining [rɪ'klaɪnɪŋ] ADJ (*seat*) reclinable

recluse [rɪ'kluːs] N recluso(-a)

recognition [rɛkəg'nɪʃən] N reconocimiento; **transformed beyond ~** irreconocible; **in ~ of** en reconocimiento de

recognizable ['rɛkəgnaɪzəbl] ADJ: **~ (by)** reconocible (por)

recognize ['rɛkəgnaɪz] VT reconocer, conocer; **to ~ (by/as)** reconocer (por/como)

recoil [rɪ'kɔɪl] VI (*person*): **to ~ from doing sth** retraerse de hacer algo ▶ N (*of gun*) retroceso

recollect [rɛkə'lɛkt] VT recordar, acordarse de

recollection [rɛkə'lɛkʃən] N recuerdo; **to the best of my ~** que yo recuerde

recommend [rɛkə'mɛnd] VT recomendar; **she has a lot to ~ her** tiene mucho a su favor

recommendation [rɛkəmɛn'deɪʃən] N recomendación *f*

recommended retail price N (BRIT) precio (recomendado) de venta al público

recompense ['rɛkəmpɛns] VT recompensar ▶ N recompensa

reconcilable ['rɛkənsaɪləbl] ADJ (re)conciliable

reconcile ['rɛkənsaɪl] VT (*two people*) reconciliar; (*two facts*) conciliar; **to ~ o.s. to sth** resignarse *or* conformarse a algo

reconciliation [rɛkənsɪlɪ'eɪʃən] N reconciliación *f*

recondite [rɪ'kɔndaɪt] ADJ recóndito

recondition [riː kən'dɪʃən] VT (*machine*) reparar, reponer

reconditioned [riː kən'dɪʃənd] ADJ renovado, reparado

reconnaissance [rɪ'kɔnɪsns] N (*Mil*) reconocimiento

reconnoitre, (US) **reconnoiter** [rɛkə'nɔɪtəʳ] VT, VI (*Mil*) reconocer

reconsider [riː kən'sɪdəʳ] VT repensar

reconstitute [riː'kɔnstɪtjuːt] VT reconstituir

reconstruct [riː kən'strʌkt] VT reconstruir

reconstruction [riː kən'strʌkʃən] N reconstrucción *f*

reconvene [riː kən'viːn] VT volver a convocar ▶ VI volver a reunirse

record N ['rɛkɔːd] (*Mus*) disco; (*of meeting etc*) acta; (*register*) registro, partida; (*file*) archivo; (*also*: **police** *or* **criminal record**) antecedentes *mpl* penales; (*written*) expediente *m*; (*Sport*) récord *m*; (*Comput*) registro ▶ VT [rɪ'kɔːd] (*set down*) registrar; (*Comput*) registrar; (*relate*) hacer constar; (*Mus: song etc*) grabar; **in ~ time** en un tiempo récord; **public records** archivos *mpl* nacionales; **he is on ~ as saying that ...** hay pruebas de que ha dicho públicamente que ...; **Spain's excellent ~** el excelente historial de España; **off the ~** *adj* no oficial; *adv* confidencialmente

record card N (*in file*) ficha

recorded delivery [rɪ'kɔːdɪd-] N (BRIT Post) entrega con acuse de recibo

recorded music N música grabada

recorder [rɪ'kɔːdəʳ] N (*Mus*) flauta de pico; (*Tech*) contador *m*

record holder N (*Sport*) actual poseedor(a) *m/f* del récord

recording [rɪ'kɔːdɪŋ] N (*Mus*) grabación *f*

recording studio N estudio de grabación

record library N discoteca

record player N tocadiscos *m inv*

recount VT [rɪ'kaunt] contar

re-count ['riːkaunt] N (*Pol: of votes*) segundo escrutinio, recuento ▶ VT [riː'kaunt] volver a contar

recoup [rɪ'kuːp] VT: **to ~ one's losses** recuperar las pérdidas

recourse [rɪ'kɔːs] N recurso; **to have ~ to** recurrir a

recover [rɪ'kʌvəʳ] VT recuperar; (*rescue*) rescatar ▶ VI recuperarse

recovery [rɪ'kʌvərɪ] N recuperación *f*; rescate *m*; (*Med*): **to make a ~** restablecerse

recreate [riːkrɪ'eɪt] VT recrear

recreation [rɛkrɪ'eɪʃən] N recreación *f*; (*amusement*) recreo

recreational [rɛkrɪ'eɪʃnl] ADJ recreativo

recreational drug N droga recreativa

recreational vehicle N (US) caravana *or* roulotte *f* pequeña

recrimination [rɪkrɪmɪ'neɪʃən] N recriminación *f*

recruit [rɪ'kruːt] N recluta *mf* ▶ VT reclutar; (*staff*) contratar

recruiting office [rɪ'kruːtɪŋ-] N caja de reclutas

recruitment [rɪ'kruːtmənt] N reclutamiento

rectangle ['rɛktæŋgl] N rectángulo

rectangular [rɛk'tæŋgjuləʳ] ADJ rectangular

741

rectify ['rɛktɪfaɪ] VT rectificar
rector ['rɛktəʳ] N (Rel) párroco; (Scol) rector(a) m/f
rectory ['rɛktərɪ] N casa del párroco
rectum ['rɛktəm] N (Anat) recto
recuperate [rɪ'kuːpəreɪt] VI reponerse, restablecerse
recur [rɪ'kəːʳ] VI repetirse; (pain, illness) producirse de nuevo
recurrence [rɪ'kəːrns] N repetición f
recurrent [rɪ'kəːrnt] ADJ repetido
recurring [rɪ'kəːrɪŋ] ADJ (problem) repetido, constante
recyclable [riː'saɪkləbl] ADJ reciclable
recycle [riː'saɪkl] VT reciclar
recycling [riː'saɪklɪŋ] N reciclaje m
red [rɛd] N rojo ▶ ADJ rojo; (hair) pelirrojo; (wine) tinto; **to be in the ~** (account) estar en números rojos; (business) tener un saldo negativo; **to give sb the ~ carpet treatment** recibir a algn con todos los honores
red alert N alerta roja
red-blooded ['rɛd'blʌdɪd] ADJ (inf) viril
redbrick university ['rɛdbrɪk-] N ver nota

> El término *redbrick university* se aplica a las universidades construidas en los grandes centros urbanos industriales como Birmingham, Liverpool o Manchester a finales del siglo XIX o principios del XX. Deben su nombre a que sus edificios son normalmente de ladrillo, a diferencia de las universidades tradicionales de Oxford y Cambridge, cuyos edificios suelen ser de piedra.

Red Cross N Cruz f Roja
redcurrant ['rɛdkʌrənt] N grosella roja
redden ['rɛdn] VT enrojecer ▶ VI enrojecerse
reddish ['rɛdɪʃ] ADJ (hair) rojizo
redecorate [riː'dɛkəreɪt] VT pintar de nuevo; volver a decorar
redecoration [riː'dɛkə'reɪʃən] N renovación f
redeem [rɪ'diːm] VT redimir; (promises) cumplir; (sth in pawn) desempeñar; (Rel: fig) rescatar
redeemable [rɪ'diːməbl] ADJ canjeable
redeeming [rɪ'diːmɪŋ] ADJ: **~ feature** punto bueno or favorable
redefine [riːdɪ'faɪn] VT redefinir
redemption [rɪ'dɛmpʃən] N (Rel) redención f; **to be past** or **beyond ~** no tener remedio
redeploy [riːdɪ'plɔɪ] VT disponer de nuevo
redeployment [riːdɪ'plɔɪmənt] N redistribución f
redevelop [riːdɪ'vɛləp] VT reorganizar
redevelopment [riːdɪ'vɛləpmənt] N reorganización f

red-handed [rɛd'hændɪd] ADJ: **he was caught ~** le pillaron con las manos en la masa
redhead ['rɛdhɛd] N pelirrojo(-a)
red herring N (fig) pista falsa
red-hot [rɛd'hɔt] ADJ candente
redirect [riːdaɪ'rɛkt] VT (mail) reexpedir
rediscover [riːdɪs'kʌvəʳ] VT redescubrir
rediscovery [riːdɪs'kʌvərɪ] N redescubrimiento
redistribute [riːdɪs'trɪbjuːt] VT redistribuir, hacer una nueva distribución de
red-letter day [rɛd'lɛtə-] N día m señalado, día m especial
red light N: **to go through** or **jump a ~** (Aut) saltarse un semáforo
red-light district N barrio chino, zona de tolerancia
red meat N carne f roja
redness ['rɛdnɪs] N rojez f
redo [riː'duː] VT (irreg: like **do**) rehacer
redolent ['rɛdələnt] ADJ: **~ of** (smell) con fragancia a; **to be ~ of** (fig) evocar
redouble [riː'dʌbl] VT: **to ~ one's efforts** redoblar los esfuerzos
redraft [riː'drɑːft] VT volver a redactar
redress [rɪ'drɛs] N reparación f ▶ VT reparar, corregir; **to ~ the balance** restablecer el equilibrio
Red Sea N: **the ~** el mar Rojo
redskin ['rɛdskɪn] N piel roja mf
red tape N (fig) trámites mpl, papeleo (inf)
reduce [rɪ'djuːs] VT reducir; (lower) rebajar; **to ~ sth by/to** reducir algo en/a; **to ~ sb to silence/despair/tears** hacer callar/ desesperarse/llorar a algn; **"~ speed now"** (Aut) "reduzca la velocidad"
reduced [rɪ'djuːst] ADJ (decreased) reducido, rebajado; **at a ~ price** con rebaja or descuento; **"greatly ~ prices"** "grandes rebajas"
reduction [rɪ'dʌkʃən] N reducción f; (of price) rebaja; (discount) descuento
redundancy [rɪ'dʌndənsɪ] N despido; (unemployment) desempleo; **voluntary ~** baja voluntaria
redundancy payment N indemnización f por desempleo
redundant [rɪ'dʌndənt] ADJ (Brit: worker) parado, sin trabajo; (detail, object) superfluo; **to be made ~** (Brit) quedar(se) sin trabajo, perder el empleo
reed [riːd] N (Bot) junco, caña; (Mus: of clarinet etc) lengüeta
re-educate [riː'ɛdjukeɪt] VT reeducar
reedy ['riːdɪ] ADJ (voice, instrument) aflautado
reef [riːf] N (at sea) arrecife m
reek [riːk] VI: **to ~ (of)** oler or apestar (a)
reel [riːl] N carrete m, bobina; (of film) rollo

▶ VT (*Tech*) devanar; (*also*: **reel in**) sacar ▶ VI (*sway*) tambalear(se); **my head is reeling** me da vueltas la cabeza
▶ **reel off** VT recitar de memoria
re-election [riː'ılɛkʃən] N reelección *f*
re-engage [riːɪn'geɪdʒ] VT contratar de nuevo
re-enter [riː'ɛntə^r] VT reingresar en, volver a entrar en
re-entry [riː'ɛntrɪ] N reingreso, reentrada
re-examine [riːɪg'zæmɪn] VT reexaminar
re-export VT ['riːɪks'pɔːt] reexportar ▶ N [riː'ɛkspɔːt] reexportación *f*
ref [rɛf] N ABBR (*inf*) = **referee**
ref. ABBR (*Comm*: = *with reference to*) Ref
refectory [rɪ'fɛktərɪ] N comedor *m*
refer [rɪ'fəː^r] VT (*send*: *patient*) referir; (: *matter*) remitir; (*ascribe*) referir a, relacionar con ▶ VI: **to ~ to** (*allude to*) referirse a, aludir a; (*apply to*) relacionarse con; (*consult*) remitirse a; **he referred me to the manager** me envió al gerente
referee [rɛfə'riː] N árbitro; (*BRIT*: *for job application*): **to be a ~ for sb** proporcionar referencias a algn ▶ VT (*match*) arbitrar en
reference ['rɛfrəns] N (*mention*: *in book*) referencia; (*sending*) remisión *f*; (*relevance*) relación *f*; (*for job application*: *letter*) carta de recomendación; **with ~ to** con referencia a; (*Comm*: *in letter*) me remito a
reference book N libro de consulta
reference library N biblioteca de consulta
reference number N número de referencia
referendum [rɛfə'rɛndəm] (*pl* **referenda** [-də]) N referéndum *m*
referral [rɪ'fəːrəl] N remisión *f*
refill VT [riː'fɪl] rellenar ▶ N ['riːfɪl] repuesto, recambio
refine [rɪ'faɪn] VT (*sugar, oil*) refinar
refined [rɪ'faɪnd] ADJ (*person, taste*) refinado, fino
refinement [rɪ'faɪnmənt] N (*of person*) cultura, educación *f*
refinery [rɪ'faɪnərɪ] N refinería
refit (*also Naut*) N ['riːfɪt] reparación *f* ▶ VT [riː'fɪt] reparar
reflate [riː'fleɪt] VT (*economy*) reflacionar
reflation [riː'fleɪʃən] N reflación *f*
reflationary [riː'fleɪʃənrɪ] ADJ reflacionario
reflect [rɪ'flɛkt] VT (*light, image*) reflejar ▶ VI (*think*) reflexionar, pensar; **it reflects badly/well on him** lo perjudica/le hace honor
reflection [rɪ'flɛkʃən] N (*act*) reflexión *f*; (*image*) reflejo; (*discredit*) crítica; **on ~** pensándolo bien
reflector [rɪ'flɛktə^r] N (*Aut*) cataforos *m inv*; (*telescope*) reflector *m*
reflex ['riːflɛks] ADJ, N reflejo
reflexive [rɪ'flɛksɪv] ADJ (*Ling*) reflexivo

reform [rɪ'fɔːm] N reforma ▶ VT reformar
reformat [riː'fɔːmæt] VT (*Comput*) volver a formatear
Reformation [rɛfə'meɪʃən] N: **the ~** la Reforma
reformatory [rɪ'fɔːmətərɪ] N (*US*) reformatorio
reformer [rɪ'fɔːmə^r] N reformador(a) *m/f*
refrain [rɪ'freɪn] VI: **to ~ from doing** abstenerse de hacer ▶ N (*Mus etc*) estribillo
refresh [rɪ'frɛʃ] VT refrescar
refresher course [rɪ'frɛʃə-] N (*BRIT*) curso de repaso
refreshing [rɪ'frɛʃɪŋ] ADJ (*drink*) refrescante; (*sleep*) reparador; (*change etc*) estimulante; (*idea, point of view*) estimulante, interesante
refreshments [rɪ'frɛʃmənts] NPL (*drinks*) refrescos *mpl*
refrigeration [rɪfrɪdʒə'reɪʃən] N refrigeración *f*
refrigerator [rɪ'frɪdʒəreɪtə^r] N frigorífico, refrigeradora (*LAM*), heladera (*LAM*)
refuel [riː'fjuəl] VI repostar (combustible)
refuelling, (*US*) **refueling** [riː'fjuəlɪŋ] N reabastecimiento de combustible
refuge ['rɛfjuːdʒ] N refugio, asilo; **to take ~ in** refugiarse en
refugee [rɛfju'dʒiː] N refugiado(-a)
refugee camp N campamento para refugiados
refund N ['riːfʌnd] reembolso ▶ VT [rɪ'fʌnd] devolver, reembolsar
refurbish [riː'fəːbɪʃ] VT restaurar, renovar
refurnish [riː'fəːnɪʃ] VT amueblar de nuevo
refusal [rɪ'fjuːzəl] N negativa; **first ~** primera opción; **to have first ~ on sth** tener la primera opción a algo
refuse¹ ['rɛfjuːs] N basura
refuse² [rɪ'fjuːz] VT (*reject*) rechazar; (*invitation*) declinar; (*permission*) denegar; (*say no to*) negarse a ▶ VI negarse; (*horse*) rehusar; **to ~ to do sth** negarse a *or* rehusar hacer algo
refuse bin N cubo *or* bote *m* (*LAM*) *or* balde *m* (*LAM*) de la basura
refuse collection N recogida de basuras
refuse disposal N eliminación *f* de basuras
refusenik [rɪ'fjuːznɪk] N *judío/a que tenía prohibido emigrar de la ex Unión Soviética*
refuse tip N vertedero
refute [rɪ'fjuːt] VT refutar, rebatir
regain [rɪ'geɪn] VT recobrar, recuperar
regal ['riːgl] ADJ regio, real
regale [rɪ'geɪl] VT agasajar, entretener
regalia [rɪ'geɪlɪə] N galas *fpl*
regard [rɪ'gɑːd] N (*gaze*) mirada; (*aspect*) respecto; (*esteem*) respeto; (*attention*) consideración *f* ▶ VT (*consider*) considerar; (*look at*) mirar; **to give one's regards to**

r

743

saludar de su parte a; **"(kind) regards"** "muy atentamente"; **"with kindest regards"** "con muchos recuerdos"; **regards to María, please give my regards to María** recuerdos a María, dele recuerdos a María de mi parte; **as regards, with ~ to** con respecto a, en cuanto a

regarding [rɪ'gɑːdɪŋ] PREP con respecto a, en cuanto a

regardless [rɪ'gɑːdlɪs] ADV a pesar de todo; **~ of** sin reparar en

regatta [rɪ'gætə] N regata

regency ['riːdʒənsɪ] N regencia

regenerate [rɪ'dʒɛnəreɪt] VT regenerar

regent ['riːdʒənt] N regente *mf*

reggae ['rɛgeɪ] N reggae *m*

régime [reɪ'ʒiːm] N régimen *m*

regiment ['rɛdʒɪmənt] N regimiento ▶ VT ['rɛdʒɪmɛnt] reglamentar

regimental [rɛdʒɪ'mɛntl] ADJ militar

regimentation [rɛdʒɪmɛn'teɪʃən] N regimentación *f*

region ['riːdʒən] N región *f*; **in the ~ of** (*fig*) alrededor de

regional ['riːdʒənl] ADJ regional

regional development N desarrollo, regional

register ['rɛdʒɪstəʳ] N registro ▶ VT registrar; (*birth*) declarar; (*car*) matricular; (*letter*) certificar; (*instrument*) marcar, indicar ▶ VI (*at hotel*) registrarse; (*as student*) matricularse; (*sign on*) inscribirse; (*make impression*) producir impresión; **to ~ a protest** presentar una queja; **to ~ for a course** matricularse *or* inscribirse en un curso

registered ['rɛdʒɪstəd] ADJ (*design*) registrado; (*BRIT: letter*) certificado; (*student*) matriculado; (*voter*) registrado

registered company N sociedad *f* legalmente constituida

registered nurse N (*US*) enfermero(-a) titulado(-a)

registered office N domicilio social

registered trademark N marca registrada

registrar ['rɛdʒɪstrɑːʳ] N secretario(-a) (del registro civil)

registration [rɛdʒɪs'treɪʃən] N (*act*) declaración *f*; (*Aut: also:* **registration number**) matrícula

registry ['rɛdʒɪstrɪ] N registro

registry office N (*BRIT*) registro civil; **to get married in a ~** casarse por lo civil

regret [rɪ'grɛt] N sentimiento, pesar *m*; (*remorse*) remordimiento ▶ VT sentir, lamentar; (*repent of*) arrepentirse de; **we ~ to inform you that ...** sentimos informarle que ...

regretful [rɪ'grɛtful] ADJ pesaroso, arrepentido

regretfully [rɪ'grɛtfəlɪ] ADV con pesar, sentidamente

regrettable [rɪ'grɛtəbl] ADJ lamentable; (*loss*) sensible

regrettably [rɪ'grɛtəblɪ] ADV desgraciadamente

regroup [riː'gruːp] VT reagrupar ▶ VI reagruparse

regt ABBR = **regiment**

regular ['rɛgjuləʳ] ADJ regular; (*soldier*) profesional; (*inf: intensive*) verdadero; (*listener, reader*) asiduo; (*usual*) habitual ▶ N (*client etc*) cliente(-a) *m/f* habitual

regularity [rɛgju'lærɪtɪ] N regularidad *f*

regularly ['rɛgjuləlɪ] ADV con regularidad

regulate ['rɛgjuleɪt] VT (*gen*) controlar; (*Tech*) regular, ajustar

regulation [rɛgju'leɪʃən] N (*rule*) regla, reglamento; (*adjustment*) regulación *f*

rehabilitate [riːə'bɪlɪteɪt] VT rehabilitar

rehabilitation ['riːəbɪlɪ'teɪʃən] N rehabilitación *f*

rehash [riː'hæʃ] VT (*inf*) hacer un refrito de

rehearsal [rɪ'həːsəl] N ensayo; **dress ~** ensayo general *or* final

rehearse [rɪ'həːs] VT ensayar

rehouse [riː'hauz] VT dar nueva vivienda a

reign [reɪn] N reinado; (*fig*) predominio ▶ VI reinar; (*fig*) imperar

reigning ['reɪnɪŋ] ADJ (*monarch*) reinante, actual; (*predominant*) imperante

reiki ['reɪkɪ] N reiki *m*

reimburse [riːɪm'bəːs] VT reembolsar

rein [reɪn] N (*for horse*) rienda; **to give sb free ~** dar rienda suelta a algn

reincarnation [riːɪnkɑː'neɪʃən] N reencarnación *f*

reindeer ['reɪndɪəʳ] N *pl inv* reno

reinforce [riːɪn'fɔːs] VT reforzar

reinforced concrete [riːɪn'fɔːst-] N hormigón *m* armado

reinforcement [riːɪn'fɔːsmənt] N (*action*) refuerzo; **reinforcements** NPL (*Mil*) refuerzos *mpl*

reinstate [riːɪn'steɪt] VT (*worker*) reintegrar (a su puesto); (*tax, law*) reinstaurar

reinstatement [riːɪn'steɪtmənt] N reintegración *f*

reissue [riː'ɪʃuː] VT (*record, book*) reeditar

reiterate [riː'ɪtəreɪt] VT reiterar, repetir

reject N ['riːdʒɛkt] (*thing*) desecho ▶ VT [rɪ'dʒɛkt] rechazar; (*proposition, offer etc*) descartar

rejection [rɪ'dʒɛkʃən] N rechazo

rejoice [rɪ'dʒɔɪs] VI: **to ~ at** *or* **over** regocijarse *or* alegrarse de

rejoinder [rɪ'dʒɔɪndəʳ] N (*retort*) réplica

rejuvenate [rɪ'dʒuːvəneɪt] VT rejuvenecer

rekindle [riː'kɪndl] VT volver a encender; (*fig*) despertar

relapse [rɪ'læps] N (*Med*) recaída; (*into crime*) reincidencia

relate [rɪ'leɪt] VT (*tell*) contar, relatar; (*connect*) relacionar ▶ VI relacionarse; **to ~ to** (*connect*) relacionarse *or* tener que ver con

related [rɪ'leɪtɪd] ADJ afín; (*person*) emparentado; **to be ~ to** (*connected*) guardar relación con; (*by family*) ser pariente de

relating [rɪ'leɪtɪŋ]: **~ to** *prep* referente a

relation [rɪ'leɪʃən] N (*person*) pariente *mf*; (*link*) relación *f*; **in ~ to** en relación con, en lo que se refiere a; **relations** NPL (*relatives*) familiares *mpl*; **to bear a ~ to** guardar relación con; **diplomatic relations** relaciones *fpl* diplomáticas

relationship [rɪ'leɪʃənʃɪp] N relación *f*; (*personal*) relaciones *fpl*; (*also*: **family relationship**) parentesco

relative ['rɛlətɪv] N pariente *mf*, familiar *mf* ▶ ADJ relativo

relatively ['rɛlətɪvlɪ] ADV (*fairly, rather*) relativamente

relative pronoun N pronombre *m* relativo

relax [rɪ'læks] VI descansar; (*quieten down*) relajarse ▶ VT relajar; (*grip*) aflojar; **~!** (*calm down*) ¡tranquilo!

relaxation [riːlæk'seɪʃən] N (*rest*) descanso; (*easing*) relajación *f*, relajamiento *m*; (*amusement*) recreo; (*entertainment*) diversión *f*

relaxed [rɪ'lækst] ADJ relajado; (*tranquil*) tranquilo

relaxing [rɪ'læksɪŋ] ADJ relajante

relay N ['riːleɪ] (*race*) carrera de relevos ▶ VT [rɪ'leɪ] (*Radio, TV*) retransmitir; (*pass on*) retransmitir

release [rɪ'liːs] N (*liberation*) liberación *f*; (*discharge*) puesta en libertad; (*of gas etc*) escape *m*; (*of film etc*) estreno; (*of record*) lanzamiento ▶ VT (*prisoner*) poner en libertad; (*film*) estrenar; (*book*) publicar; (*piece of news*) difundir; (*gas etc*) despedir, arrojar; (*free: from wreckage etc*) liberar; (*Tech: catch, spring etc*) desenganchar; (*let go*) soltar, aflojar

relegate ['rɛləgeɪt] VT relegar; (*Sport*): **to be relegated to** bajar a

relent [rɪ'lɛnt] VI ceder, ablandarse; (*let up*) descansar

relentless [rɪ'lɛntlɪs] ADJ implacable

relentlessly [rɪ'lɛntlɪslɪ] ADV implacablemente

relevance ['rɛləvəns] N relación *f*

relevant ['rɛləvənt] ADJ (*fact*) pertinente; **~ to** relacionado con

reliability [rɪlaɪə'bɪlɪtɪ] N fiabilidad *f*; seguridad *f*; veracidad *f*

reliable [rɪ'laɪəbl] ADJ (*person, firm*) de confianza, de fiar; (*method, machine*) seguro; (*source*) fidedigno

reliably [rɪ'laɪəblɪ] ADV: **to be ~ informed that ...** saber de fuente fidedigna que ...

reliance [rɪ'laɪəns] N: **~ (on)** dependencia (de)

reliant [rɪ'laɪənt] ADJ: **to be ~ on sth/sb** depender de algo/algn

relic ['rɛlɪk] N (*Rel*) reliquia; (*of the past*) vestigio

relief [rɪ'liːf] N (*from pain, anxiety*) alivio, desahogo; (*help, supplies*) socorro, ayuda; (*Art, Geo*) relieve *m*; **by way of light ~** a modo de diversión

relief road N carretera de descongestionamiento

relieve [rɪ'liːv] VT (*pain, patient*) aliviar; (*bring help to*) ayudar, socorrer; (*burden*) aligerar; (*take over from: gen*) sustituir a; (*: guard*) relevar; **to ~ sb of sth** quitar algo a algn; **to ~ sb of his command** (*Mil*) relevar a algn de su mando; **to ~ o.s.** hacer sus necesidades

relieved [rɪ'liːvd] ADJ: **to be ~** sentir un gran alivio

religion [rɪ'lɪdʒən] N religión *f*

religious [rɪ'lɪdʒəs] ADJ religioso

religious education N educación *f* religiosa

religiously [rɪ'lɪdʒəslɪ] ADV religiosamente

relinquish [rɪ'lɪŋkwɪʃ] VT abandonar; (*plan, habit*) renunciar a

relish ['rɛlɪʃ] N (*Culin*) salsa; (*enjoyment*) entusiasmo; (*flavour*) sabor *m*, gusto ▶ VT (*food, challenge etc*) saborear; **to ~ doing** gozar haciendo

relive [riː'lɪv] VT vivir de nuevo, volver a vivir

relocate [riːləu'keɪt] VT trasladar ▶ VI trasladarse

reluctance [rɪ'lʌktəns] N desgana, renuencia

reluctant [rɪ'lʌktənt] ADJ reacio; **to be ~ to do sth** resistirse a hacer algo

reluctantly [rɪ'lʌktəntlɪ] ADV de mala gana

rely [rɪ'laɪ]: **to ~ on** *vt fus* confiar en, fiarse de; (*be dependent on*) depender de; **you can ~ on my discretion** puedes contar con mi discreción

remain [rɪ'meɪn] VI (*survive*) quedar; (*be left*) sobrar; (*continue*) quedar(se), permanecer; **to ~ silent** permanecer callado; **I ~, yours faithfully** (*in letters*) le saluda atentamente

remainder [rɪ'meɪndə^r] N resto

remaining [rɪ'meɪnɪŋ] ADJ restante, que queda(n)

remains [rɪ'meɪnz] NPL restos *mpl*

remand [rɪ'mɑːnd] N: **on ~** detenido (bajo custodia) ▶ VT: **to ~ in custody** mantener bajo custodia

remand home N (*BRIT*) reformatorio

remark [rɪ'mɑːk] N comentario ▶ VT comentar; **to ~ on sth** hacer observaciones sobre algo

remarkable [rɪ'mɑːkəbl] ADJ notable; (*outstanding*) extraordinario

r

remarkably [rɪˈmɑːkəblɪ] ADV extraordinariamente

remarry [riːˈmærɪ] VI casarse por segunda vez, volver a casarse

remedial [rɪˈmiːdɪəl] ADJ: **~ education** educación f de los niños atrasados

remedy [ˈrɛmədɪ] N remedio ▶ VT remediar, curar

remember [rɪˈmɛmbəʳ] VT recordar, acordarse de; (*bear in mind*) tener presente; **I ~ seeing it, I ~ having seen it** recuerdo haberlo visto; **she remembered doing it** se acordó de hacerlo; **~ me to your wife and children!** ¡dele recuerdos a su familia!

remembrance [rɪˈmɛmbrəns] N (*memory, souvenir*) recuerdo; **in ~ of** en conmemoración de

Remembrance Day, Remembrance Sunday N (*BRIT*) *ver nota*

> En el Reino Unido el domingo más cercano al 11 de noviembre es *Remembrance Day* o *Remembrance Sunday*, aniversario de la firma del armisticio de 1918 que puso fin a la Primera Guerra Mundial. Tal día se recuerda a todos aquellos que murieron en las dos guerras mundiales con dos minutos de silencio a las once de la mañana (hora en que se firmó el armisticio), durante los actos de conmemoración celebrados en los monumentos a los caídos. Allí se colocan coronas de amapolas, flor que también se suele llevar prendida en el pecho tras pagar un donativo para los inválidos de guerra.

remind [rɪˈmaɪnd] VT: **to ~ sb to do sth** recordar a algn que haga algo; **to ~ sb of sth** recordar algo a algn; **she reminds me of her mother** me recuerda a su madre; **that reminds me!** ¡a propósito!

reminder [rɪˈmaɪndəʳ] N notificación f; (*memento*) recuerdo

reminisce [rɛmɪˈnɪs] VI recordar (viejas historias)

reminiscences [rɛmɪˈnɪsnsɪz] NPL reminiscencias fpl, recuerdos mpl

reminiscent [rɛmɪˈnɪsnt] ADJ: **to be ~ of sth** recordar algo

remiss [rɪˈmɪs] ADJ descuidado; **it was ~ of me** fue un descuido de mi parte

remission [rɪˈmɪʃən] N remisión f; (*of sentence*) reducción f de la pena

remit [rɪˈmɪt] VT (*send: money*) remitir, enviar

remittance [rɪˈmɪtns] N remesa, envío

remnant [ˈrɛmnənt] N resto; (*of cloth*) retal m, retazo; **remnants** NPL (*Comm*) restos de serie

remonstrate [ˈrɛmənstreɪt] VI protestar

remorse [rɪˈmɔːs] N remordimientos mpl

remorseful [rɪˈmɔːsful] ADJ arrepentido

remorseless [rɪˈmɔːslɪs] ADJ (*fig*) implacable, inexorable

remorselessly [rɪˈmɔːslɪslɪ] ADV implacablemente, inexorablemente

remote [rɪˈməut] ADJ remoto; (*distant*) lejano; (*person*) distante; **there is a ~ possibility that ...** hay una posibilidad remota de que ...

remote control N mando a distancia

remote-controlled [rɪˈməutkən'trəuld] ADJ teledirigido, con mando a distancia

remotely [rɪˈməutlɪ] ADV remotamente; (*slightly*) levemente

remoteness [rɪˈməutnɪs] N alejamiento; distancia

remould [ˈriːməuld] N (*BRIT: tyre*) neumático or llanta (*LAm*) recauchutado(-a)

removable [rɪˈmuːvəbl] ADJ (*detachable*) separable

removal [rɪˈmuːvəl] N (*taking away*) (el) quitar; (*BRIT: from house*) mudanza; (*from office: dismissal*) destitución f; (*Med*) extirpación f

removal man N (*irreg*) (*BRIT*) mozo de mudanzas

removal van N (*BRIT*) camión m de mudanzas

remove [rɪˈmuːv] VT quitar; (*employee*) destituir; (*name: from list*) tachar, borrar; (*doubt*) disipar; (*Tech*) retirar, separar; (*Med*) extirpar; **first cousin once removed** (*parent's cousin*) tío(-a) segundo(-a); (*cousin's child*) sobrino(-a) segundo(-a)

remover [rɪˈmuːvəʳ] N: **make-up ~** desmaquilladora

remunerate [rɪˈmjuːnəreɪt] VT remunerar

remuneration [rɪmjuːnəˈreɪʃən] N remuneración f

Renaissance [rɪˈneɪsɔ̃s] N: **the ~** el Renacimiento

rename [riːˈneɪm] VT poner nuevo nombre a

render [ˈrɛndəʳ] VT (*thanks*) dar; (*aid*) proporcionar; (*honour*) dar, conceder; (*assistance*) dar, prestar; **to ~ sth + adj** volver algo + adj; **to ~ sth useless** hacer algo inútil

rendering [ˈrɛndərɪŋ] N (*Mus etc*) interpretación f

rendez-vous [ˈrɔndɪvuː] N cita ▶ VI reunirse, encontrarse; (*spaceship*) efectuar una reunión espacial

rendition [rɛnˈdɪʃən] N (*Mus*) interpretación f

renegade [ˈrɛnɪgeɪd] N renegado(-a)

renew [rɪˈnjuː] VT renovar; (*resume*) reanudar; (*extend date*) prorrogar; (*negotiations*) volver a

renewable [rɪˈnjuːəbl] ADJ renovable; **~ energy, renewables** energías renovables

renewal [rɪˈnjuːəl] N renovación f; reanudación f; prórroga

renounce [rɪˈnauns] VT renunciar a; (*right, inheritance*) renunciar

renovate [ˈrɛnəveɪt] VT renovar

renovation [rɛnəˈveɪʃən] N renovación f

renown [rɪ'naun] N renombre *m*
renowned [rɪ'naund] ADJ renombrado
rent [rɛnt] N alquiler *m*; *(for house)* arriendo, renta ▶ VT *(also: **rent out**)* alquilar
rental ['rɛntl] N *(for television, car)* alquiler *m*
rent boy N *(BRIT inf)* chapero
renunciation [rɪnʌnsɪ'eɪʃən] N renuncia
reopen [ri:'əupən] VT volver a abrir, reabrir
reorder [ri:'ɔ:dər] VT volver a pedir, repetir el pedido de; *(rearrange)* volver a ordenar *or* arreglar
reorganization [ri:ɔ:gənaɪ'zeɪʃən] N reorganización *f*
reorganize [ri:'ɔ:gənaɪz] VT reorganizar
Rep ABBR *(US Pol)* = **representative**; **republican**
rep [rɛp] N ABBR *(Comm)* = **representative**; *(Theat)* = **repertory**
repair [rɪ'pɛər] N reparación *f*, arreglo; *(patch)* remiendo ▶ VT reparar, arreglar; **in good/ bad** ~ en buen/mal estado; **under** ~ en obras
repair kit N caja de herramientas
repair man N *(irreg)* mecánico
repair shop N taller *m* de reparaciones
repartee [rɛpɑ:'ti:] N réplicas *fpl* agudas
repast [rɪ'pɑ:st] N *(formal)* comida
repatriate [ri:'pætrɪeɪt] VT repatriar
repay [ri:'peɪ] VT *(irreg: like **pay**)* *(money)* devolver, reembolsar; *(person)* pagar; *(debt)* liquidar; *(sb's efforts)* devolver, corresponder a
repayment [ri:'peɪmənt] N reembolso, devolución *f*; *(sum of money)* recompensa
repeal [rɪ'pi:l] N revocación *f* ▶ VT revocar
repeat [rɪ'pi:t] N *(Radio, TV)* reposición *f* ▶ VT repetir ▶ VI repetirse
repeatedly [rɪ'pi:tɪdlɪ] ADV repetidas veces
repeat order N *(Comm)*: **to place a ~ for** renovar un pedido de
repeat prescription N *(BRIT)* receta renovada
repel [rɪ'pɛl] VT repugnar
repellent [rɪ'pɛlənt] ADJ repugnante ▶ N: **insect ~** crema/loción *f* anti-insectos
repent [rɪ'pɛnt] VI: **to ~ (of)** arrepentirse (de)
repentance [rɪ'pɛntəns] N arrepentimiento
repercussion [ri:pə'kʌʃən] N *(consequence)* repercusión *f*; **to have repercussions** repercutir
repertoire ['rɛpətwɑ:r] N repertorio
repertory ['rɛpətərɪ] N *(also: **repertory theatre**)* teatro de repertorio
repertory company N compañía de repertorio
repetition [rɛpɪ'tɪʃən] N repetición *f*
repetitious [rɛpɪ'tɪʃəs] ADJ repetidor(a), que se repite
repetitive [rɪ'pɛtɪtɪv] ADJ *(movement, work)* repetitivo, reiterativo; *(speech)* lleno de repeticiones

rephrase [ri:'freɪz] VT decir *or* formular de otro modo
replace [rɪ'pleɪs] VT *(put back)* devolver a su sitio; *(take the place of)* reemplazar, sustituir
replacement [rɪ'pleɪsmənt] N reemplazo; *(act)* reposición *f*; *(thing)* recambio; *(person)* suplente *mf*
replacement cost N costo de sustitución
replacement part N repuesto
replacement value N valor *m* de sustitución
replay ['ri:pleɪ] N *(Sport)* partido de desempate; *(TV: playback)* repetición *f*
replenish [rɪ'plɛnɪʃ] VT *(tank etc)* rellenar; *(stock etc)* reponer; *(with fuel)* repostar
replete [rɪ'pli:t] ADJ repleto, lleno
replica ['rɛplɪkə] N réplica, reproducción *f*
reply [rɪ'plaɪ] N respuesta, contestación *f* ▶ VI contestar, responder; **in** ~ en respuesta; **there's no** ~ *(Tel)* no contestan
reply coupon N cupón-respuesta *m*
reply-paid [rɪ'plaɪ'peɪd] ADJ: ~ **postcard** tarjeta postal con respuesta pagada
report [rɪ'pɔ:t] N informe *m*; *(Press etc)* reportaje *m*; *(BRIT: also: **school report**)* informe *m* escolar; *(of gun)* detonación *f* ▶ VT informar sobre; *(Press etc)* hacer un reportaje sobre; *(notify: accident, culprit)* denunciar ▶ VI *(make a report)* presentar un informe; *(present o.s.)*: **to ~ (to sb)** presentarse (ante algn); **annual ~** *(Comm)* informe *m* anual; **to ~ (on)** hacer un informe (sobre); **it is reported from Berlin that …** se informa desde Berlín que …
report card N *(US, SCOTTISH)* cartilla escolar
reportedly [rɪ'pɔ:tɪdlɪ] ADV según se dice, según se informa
reporter [rɪ'pɔ:tər] N *(Press)* periodista *mf*, reportero(-a); *(Radio, TV)* locutor(a) *m/f*
repose [rɪ'pəuz] N: **in** ~ *(face, mouth)* en reposo
repossess [ri:pə'zɛs] VT recuperar
repossession order [ri:pə'zɛʃən-] N orden de devolución de la vivienda por el impago de la hipoteca
reprehensible [rɛprɪ'hɛnsɪbl] ADJ reprensible, censurable
represent [rɛprɪ'zɛnt] VT representar; *(Comm)* ser agente de
representation [rɛprɪzɛn'teɪʃən] N representación *f*; *(petition)* petición *f*; **representations** NPL *(protest)* quejas *fpl*
representative [rɛprɪ'zɛntətɪv] N *(US Pol)* representante *mf*, diputado(-a); *(Comm)* representante *mf* ▶ ADJ: ~ **(of)** representativo (de)
repress [rɪ'prɛs] VT reprimir
repression [rɪ'prɛʃən] N represión *f*
repressive [rɪ'prɛsɪv] ADJ represivo
reprieve [rɪ'pri:v] N *(Law)* indulto; *(fig)* alivio ▶ VT indultar; *(fig)* salvar

r

747

reprimand ['rɛprɪmɑːnd] N reprimenda ▸ VT reprender

reprint ['riːprɪnt] N reimpresión f ▸ VT [riː'prɪnt] reimprimir

reprisal [rɪ'praɪzl] N represalia; **to take reprisals** tomar represalias

reproach [rɪ'prəʊtʃ] N reproche m ▸ VT: **to ~ sb with sth** reprochar algo a algn; **beyond ~** intachable

reproachful [rɪ'prəʊtʃful] ADJ de reproche, de acusación

reproduce [riːprə'djuːs] VT reproducir ▸ VI reproducirse

reproduction [riːprə'dʌkʃən] N reproducción f

reproductive [riːprə'dʌktɪv] ADJ reproductor(a)

reproof [rɪ'pruːf] N reproche m

reprove [rɪ'pruːv] VT: **to ~ sb for sth** reprochar algo a algn

reptile ['rɛptaɪl] N reptil m

Repub. ABBR (US Pol) = **republican**

republic [rɪ'pʌblɪk] N república

republican [rɪ'pʌblɪkən] ADJ, N republicano(-a) m/f

repudiate [rɪ'pjuːdɪeɪt] VT (accusation) rechazar; (obligation) negarse a reconocer

repudiation [rɪpjuːdɪ'eɪʃən] N incumplimiento

repugnance [rɪ'pʌgnəns] N repugnancia

repugnant [rɪ'pʌgnənt] ADJ repugnante

repulse [rɪ'pʌls] VT rechazar

repulsion [rɪ'pʌlʃən] N repulsión f, repugnancia

repulsive [rɪ'pʌlsɪv] ADJ repulsivo

repurchase [riː'pəːtʃəs] VT volver a comprar, readquirir

reputable ['rɛpjutəbl] ADJ (make etc) de renombre

reputation [rɛpju'teɪʃən] N reputación f; **he has a ~ for being awkward** tiene fama de difícil

repute [rɪ'pjuːt] N reputación f, fama

reputed [rɪ'pjuːtɪd] ADJ supuesto; **to be ~ to be rich/intelligent** etc tener fama de rico/inteligente etc

reputedly [rɪ'pjuːtɪdlɪ] ADV según dicen or se dice

request [rɪ'kwɛst] N solicitud f, petición f ▸ VT: **to ~ sth of** or **from sb** solicitar algo a algn; **at the ~ of** a petición de; **"you are requested not to smoke"** "se ruega no fumar"

request stop N (BRIT) parada discrecional

requiem ['rɛkwɪəm] N réquiem m

require [rɪ'kwaɪəʳ] VT (need: person) necesitar, tener necesidad de; (: thing, situation) exigir, requerir; (want) pedir; (demand) insistir en que; **to ~ sb to do sth/sth of sb** exigir que

algn haga algo; **what qualifications are required?** ¿qué títulos se requieren?; **required by law** requerido por la ley

requirement [rɪ'kwaɪəmənt] N requisito; (need) necesidad f

requisite ['rɛkwɪzɪt] N requisito ▸ ADJ necesario, requerido

requisition [rɛkwɪ'zɪʃən] N solicitud f; (Mil) requisa ▸ VT (Mil) requisar

reroute [riː'ruːt] VT desviar

resale ['riːseɪl] N reventa

resale price maintenance N mantenimiento del precio de venta

resat [riː'sæt] PT, PP of **resit**

rescind [rɪ'sɪnd] VT (Law) abrogar; (contract) rescindir; (order etc) anular

rescue ['rɛskjuː] N rescate m ▸ VT rescatar; **to come/go to sb's ~** ir en auxilio de uno, socorrer a algn; **to ~ from** librar de

rescue party N equipo de salvamento

rescuer ['rɛskjuəʳ] N salvador(a) m/f

research [rɪ'səːtʃ] N investigaciones fpl ▸ VT investigar; **a piece of ~** un trabajo de investigación; **to ~ (into sth)** investigar (algo)

research and development N investigación f y desarrollo

researcher [rɪ'səːtʃəʳ] N investigador(a) m/f

research work N investigación f

resell [riː'sɛl] (pt, pp **resold** [-'səuld]) VT revender

resemblance [rɪ'zɛmbləns] N parecido; **to bear a strong ~ to** parecerse mucho a

resemble [rɪ'zɛmbl] VT parecerse a

resent [rɪ'zɛnt] VT resentirse por, ofenderse por; **he resents my being here** le molesta que esté aquí

resentful [rɪ'zɛntful] ADJ resentido

resentment [rɪ'zɛntmənt] N resentimiento

reservation [rɛzə'veɪʃən] N reserva; (BRIT: also: **central reservation**) mediana; **with reservations** con reservas

reservation desk N (US: in hotel) recepción f

reserve [rɪ'zəːv] N reserva; (Sport) suplente mf ▸ VT (seats etc) reservar; **reserves** NPL (Mil) reserva sg; **in ~** en reserva

reserve currency N divisa de reserva

reserved [rɪ'zəːvd] ADJ reservado

reserve price N (BRIT) precio mínimo

reserve team N (Sport) equipo reserva

reservist [rɪ'zəːvɪst] N (Mil) reservista m

reservoir ['rɛzəvwɑːʳ] N (artificial lake) embalse m, represa; (tank) depósito

reset [riː'sɛt] (pt, pp **~**) VT (Comput) reinicializar

reshape [riː'ʃeɪp] VT (policy) reformar, rehacer

reshuffle [riː'ʃʌfl] N: **Cabinet ~** (Pol) remodelación f del gabinete

reside [rɪ'zaɪd] VI residir

residence ['rɛzɪdəns] N residencia; *(formal: home)* domicilio; *(length of stay)* permanencia; **in ~** *(doctor)* residente; **to take up ~** instalarse

residence permit N (BRIT) permiso de residencia

resident ['rɛzɪdənt] N vecino(-a); *(in hotel)* huésped(a) *m/f* ▶ ADJ residente; *(population)* permanente

residential [rɛzɪ'dɛnʃəl] ADJ residencial

residue ['rɛzɪdjuː] N resto, residuo

resign [rɪ'zaɪn] VT *(gen)* renunciar a ▶ VI: **to ~ (from)** dimitir (de), renunciar (a); **to ~ o.s. to** *(endure)* resignarse a

resignation [rɛzɪg'neɪʃən] N dimisión *f*; *(state of mind)* resignación *f*; **to tender one's ~** presentar la dimisión

resigned [rɪ'zaɪnd] ADJ resignado

resilience [rɪ'zɪlɪəns] N *(of material)* elasticidad *f*; *(of person)* resistencia

resilient [rɪ'zɪlɪənt] ADJ *(person)* resistente

resin ['rɛzɪn] N resina

resist [rɪ'zɪst] VT resistirse a; *(temptation, damage)* resistir

resistance [rɪ'zɪstəns] N resistencia

resistant [rɪ'zɪstənt] ADJ: **~ (to)** resistente (a)

resit [riː'sɪt] *(pt, pp resat* [-'sæt]*)* VT (BRIT: *exam)* volver a presentarse a; *(: subject)* recuperar, volver a examinarse de (SP)

resolute ['rɛzəluːt] ADJ resuelto

resolutely ['rɛzəluːtlɪ] ADV resueltamente

resolution [rɛzə'luːʃən] N *(gen, Comput)* resolución *f*; *(purpose)* propósito; **to make a ~** tomar una resolución

resolve [rɪ'zɔlv] N *(determination)* resolución *f*; *(purpose)* propósito ▶ VT resolver ▶ VI resolverse; **to ~ to do** resolver hacer

resolved [rɪ'zɔlvd] ADJ resuelto

resonance ['rɛzənəns] N resonancia

resonant ['rɛzənənt] ADJ resonante

resort [rɪ'zɔːt] N *(town)* centro turístico; *(recourse)* recurso ▶ VI: **to ~ to** recurrir a; **in the last ~** como último recurso; **seaside ~** playa, estación *f* balnearia; **winter sports ~** centro de deportes de invierno

resound [rɪ'zaund] VI: **to ~ (with)** resonar (con)

resounding [rɪ'zaundɪŋ] ADJ sonoro; *(fig)* clamoroso

resource [rɪ'sɔːs] N recurso; **resources** NPL recursos *mpl*; **natural resources** recursos *mpl* naturales; **to leave sb to his/her own resources** *(fig)* abandonar a algn/a sus propios recursos

resourceful [rɪ'sɔːsful] ADJ ingenioso

resourcefulness [rɪ'sɔːsfulnɪs] N inventiva, iniciativa

respect [rɪs'pɛkt] N *(consideration)* respeto; *(relation)* respecto ▶ VT respetar; **respects** NPL recuerdos *mpl*, saludos *mpl*; **with ~ to** con respecto a; **in this ~** en cuanto a eso; **to have** *or* **show ~ for** tener *or* mostrar respeto a; **out of ~ for** por respeto a; **in some respects** en algunos aspectos; **with due ~ I still think you're wrong** con el respeto debido, sigo creyendo que está equivocado

respectability [rɪspɛktə'bɪlɪtɪ] N respetabilidad *f*

respectable [rɪs'pɛktəbl] ADJ respetable; *(quite big: amount etc)* apreciable; *(passable)* tolerable; *(quite good: player, result etc)* bastante bueno

respected [rɪs'pɛktɪd] ADJ respetado, estimado

respectful [rɪs'pɛktful] ADJ respetuoso

respectfully [rɪs'pɛktfulɪ] ADV respetuosamente; **Yours ~** Le saluda atentamente

respecting [rɪs'pɛktɪŋ] PREP (con) respecto a, en cuanto a

respective [rɪs'pɛktɪv] ADJ respectivo

respectively [rɪs'pɛktɪvlɪ] ADV respectivamente

respiration [rɛspɪ'reɪʃən] N respiración *f*

respiratory [rɛs'pɪrətərɪ] ADJ respiratorio

respite ['rɛspaɪt] N respiro; *(Law)* prórroga

resplendent [rɪs'plɛndənt] ADJ resplandeciente

respond [rɪs'pɔnd] VI responder; *(react)* reaccionar

respondent [rɪs'pɔndənt] N *(Law)* demandado(-a)

response [rɪs'pɔns] N respuesta; *(reaction)* reacción *f*; **in ~ to** como respuesta a

responsibility [rɪspɔnsɪ'bɪlɪtɪ] N responsabilidad *f*; **to take ~ for sth/sb** admitir responsabilidad por algo/uno

responsible [rɪs'pɔnsɪbl] ADJ *(liable)*: **~ (for)** responsable (de); *(character)* serio, formal; *(job)* de responsabilidad; **to be ~ to sb (for sth)** ser responsable ante algn (de algo)

responsibly [rɪs'pɔnsɪblɪ] ADV con seriedad

responsive [rɪs'pɔnsɪv] ADJ sensible

rest [rɛst] N descanso, reposo; *(Mus)* pausa, silencio; *(support)* apoyo; *(remainder)* resto ▶ VI descansar; *(be supported)*: **to ~ on** apoyarse en ▶ VT *(lean)*: **to ~ sth on/against** apoyar algo en *or* sobre/contra; **the ~ of them** *(people, objects)* los demás; **to set sb's mind at ~** tranquilizar a algn; **to ~ one's eyes** *or* **gaze on** fijar la mirada en; **it rests with him** depende de él; **~ assured that …** tenga por seguro que …

restaurant ['rɛstərɒŋ] N restaurante *m*

restaurant car N (BRIT) coche-comedor *m*

restaurant owner N dueño(-a) *or* propietario(-a) de un restaurante

rest cure N cura de reposo

restful ['rɛstful] ADJ descansado, tranquilo

rest home N residencia de ancianos

restitution [rɛstɪ'tjuːʃən] N: **to make ~ to sb for sth** restituir algo a algn; (*paying*) indemnizar a algn por algo

restive ['rɛstɪv] ADJ inquieto; (*horse*) rebelón(-ona)

restless ['rɛstlɪs] ADJ inquieto; **to get ~** impacientarse

restlessly ['rɛstlɪslɪ] ADV inquietamente, con inquietud f

restlessness ['rɛstlɪsnɪs] N inquietud f

restock [riː'stɔk] VT reaprovisionar

restoration [rɛstə'reɪʃən] N restauración f; (*giving back*) devolución f, restitución f

restorative [rɪ'stɔːrətɪv] ADJ reconstituyente, fortalecedor(a) ▶ N reconstituyente m

restore [rɪ'stɔːʳ] VT (*building*) restaurar; (*sth stolen*) devolver, restituir; (*health*) restablecer

restorer [rɪ'stɔːrəʳ] N (*Art etc*) restaurador(a) m/f

restrain [rɪs'treɪn] VT (*feeling*) contener, refrenar; (*person*): **to ~ (from doing)** disuadir (de hacer)

restrained [rɪs'treɪnd] ADJ (*style*) reservado

restraint [rɪs'treɪnt] N (*restriction*) freno, control m; (*moderation*) moderación f; (*of style*) reserva; **wage ~** control m de los salarios

restrict [rɪs'trɪkt] VT restringir, limitar

restricted [rɪs'trɪktɪd] ADJ restringido, limitado

restriction [rɪs'trɪkʃən] N restricción f, limitación f

restrictive [rɪs'trɪktɪv] ADJ restrictivo

restrictive practices NPL (*Industry*) prácticas fpl restrictivas

rest room N (*US*) aseos mpl

restructure [riː'strʌktʃəʳ] VT reestructurar

result [rɪ'zʌlt] N resultado ▶ VI: **to ~ in** terminar en, tener por resultado; **as a ~ of** a or como consecuencia de; **to ~ (from)** resultar (de)

resultant [rɪ'zʌltənt] ADJ resultante

resume [rɪ'zjuːm] VT (*work, journey*) reanudar; (*sum up*) resumir ▶ VI (*meeting*) continuar

résumé ['reɪzjuːmeɪ] N resumen m

resumption [rɪ'zʌmpʃən] N reanudación f

resurgence [rɪ'səːdʒəns] N resurgimiento

resurrection [rɛzə'rɛkʃən] N resurrección f

resuscitate [rɪ'sʌsɪteɪt] VT (*Med*) resucitar

resuscitation [rɪsʌsɪ'teɪʃn] N resucitación f

retail ['riːteɪl] N venta al por menor ▶ CPD al por menor ▶ VT vender al por menor or al detalle ▶ VI: **to ~ at** (*Comm*) tener precio de venta al público de

retailer ['riːteɪləʳ] N minorista mf, detallista mf

retail outlet N punto de venta

retail price N precio de venta al público, precio al detalle or al por menor

retail price index N índice m de precios al por menor

retain [rɪ'teɪn] VT (*keep*) retener, conservar; (*employ*) contratar

retainer [rɪ'teɪnəʳ] N (*servant*) criado; (*fee*) anticipo

retaliate [rɪ'tælɪeɪt] VI: **to ~ (against)** tomar represalias (contra)

retaliation [rɪtælɪ'eɪʃən] N represalias fpl; **in ~ for** como represalia por

retaliatory [rɪ'tælɪətərɪ] ADJ de represalia

retarded [rɪ'tɑːdɪd] ADJ retrasado

retch [rɛtʃ] VI darle a algn arcadas

retentive [rɪ'tentɪv] ADJ (*memory*) retentivo

rethink [riː'θɪŋk] VT repensar

reticence ['rɛtɪsns] N reticencia, reserva

reticent ['rɛtɪsnt] ADJ reticente, reservado

retina ['rɛtɪnə] N retina

retinue ['rɛtɪnjuː] N séquito, comitiva

retire [rɪ'taɪəʳ] VI (*give up work*) jubilarse; (*withdraw*) retirarse; (*go to bed*) acostarse

retired [rɪ'taɪəd] ADJ (*person*) jubilado

retirement [rɪ'taɪəmənt] N jubilación f; **early ~** jubilación f anticipada

retiring [rɪ'taɪərɪŋ] ADJ (*departing: chairman*) saliente; (*shy*) retraído

retort [rɪ'tɔːt] N (*reply*) réplica ▶ VI replicar

retrace [riː'treɪs] VT: **to ~ one's steps** volver sobre sus pasos, desandar lo andado

retract [rɪ'trækt] VT (*statement*) retirar; (*claws*) retraer; (*undercarriage, aerial*) replegar ▶ VI retractarse

retractable [rɪ'træktəbl] ADJ replegable

retrain [riː'treɪn] VT reciclar

retraining [riː'treɪnɪŋ] N reciclaje m, readaptación f profesional

retread ['riːtrɛd] N neumático or llanta (*LAm*) recauchutado(-a)

retreat [rɪ'triːt] N (*place*) retiro; (*Mil*) retirada ▶ VI retirarse; (*flood*) bajar; **to beat a hasty ~** (*fig*) retirarse en desbandada

retrial ['riːtraɪəl] N nuevo proceso

retribution [rɛtrɪ'bjuːʃən] N desquite m

retrieval [rɪ'triːvəl] N recuperación f; **information ~** recuperación f de datos

retrieve [rɪ'triːv] VT recobrar; (*situation, honour*) salvar; (*Comput*) recuperar; (*error*) reparar

retriever [rɪ'triːvəʳ] N perro cobrador

retroactive [rɛtrəʊˈæktɪv] ADJ retroactivo

retrograde ['rɛtrəgreɪd] ADJ retrógrado

retrospect ['rɛtrəspɛkt] N: **in ~** retrospectivamente

retrospective [rɛtrə'spɛktɪv] ADJ retrospectivo; (*law*) retroactivo ▶ N exposición f retrospectiva

return [rɪ'təːn] N (*going or coming back*) vuelta, regreso; (*of sth stolen etc*) devolución *f*; (*recompense*) recompensa; (*Finance: from land, shares*) ganancia, ingresos *mpl*; (*Comm: of merchandise*) devolución *f* ▸ CPD (*journey*) de regreso; (*BRIT: ticket*) de ida y vuelta; (*match*) de vuelta ▸ VI (*person etc: come or go back*) volver, regresar; (*symptoms etc*) reaparecer ▸ VT devolver; (*favour, love etc*) corresponder a; (*verdict*) pronunciar; (*Pol: candidate*) elegir; **returns** NPL (*Comm*) ingresos *mpl*; **tax ~** declaración *f* de la renta; **in ~ (for)** a cambio (de); **by ~ of post** a vuelta de correo; **many happy returns (of the day)!** ¡feliz cumpleaños!

returnable [rɪ'təːnəbl] ADJ: **~ bottle** envase *m* retornable

returner [rɪ'təːnəʳ] N *mujer que vuelve a trabajar tras un tiempo dedicada a la familia*

returning officer [rɪ'təːnɪŋ-] N (*BRIT Pol*) escrutador(a) *m/f*

return key N (*Comput*) tecla de retorno

return ticket N (*esp BRIT*) billete *m* (*SP*) or boleto *m* (*LAM*) de ida y vuelta, billete *m* redondo (*MEX*)

retweet [riː'twiːt] VT (*on Twitter*) retuitear ▸ N retuit *m*

reunion [riː'juːnɪən] N (*of family*) reunión *f*; (*of two people, school*) reencuentro

reunite [riːjuː'naɪt] VT reunir; (*reconcile*) reconciliar

rev [rɛv] N ABBR (*Aut: = revolution*) revolución *f* ▸ VT (*also: rev up*) acelerar

Rev., Revd. ABBR (*= reverend*) R., Rvdo

revaluation [riːvæljuː'eɪʃən] N revalorización *f*

revamp [riː'væmp] VT renovar

reveal [rɪ'viːl] VT (*make known*) revelar

revealing [rɪ'viːlɪŋ] ADJ revelador(a)

reveille [rɪ'vælɪ] N (*Mil*) diana

revel ['rɛvl] VI: **to ~ in sth/in doing sth** gozar de algo/haciendo algo

revelation [rɛvə'leɪʃən] N revelación *f*

reveller, (US) reveler ['rɛvləʳ] N jaranero, juerguista *mf*

revelry ['rɛvlrɪ] N jarana, juerga

revenge [rɪ'vɛndʒ] N venganza; (*in sport*) revancha; **to take ~ on** vengarse de; **to get one's ~ (for sth)** vengarse (de algo)

revengeful [rɪ'vɛndʒful] ADJ vengativo

revenue ['rɛvənjuː] N ingresos *mpl*, rentas *fpl*

revenue account N cuenta de ingresos presupuestarios

revenue expenditure N gasto corriente

reverberate [rɪ'vəːbəreɪt] VI (*sound*) resonar, retumbar

reverberation [rɪvəːbə'reɪʃən] N resonancia

revere [rɪ'vɪəʳ] VT reverenciar, venerar

reverence ['rɛvərəns] N reverencia

Reverend ['rɛvərənd] ADJ (*in titles*): **the ~ John Smith** (*Anglican*) el Reverendo John Smith; (*Catholic*) el Padre John Smith; (*Protestant*) el Pastor John Smith

reverent ['rɛvərənt] ADJ reverente

reverie ['rɛvərɪ] N ensueño

reversal [rɪ'vəːsl] N (*of order*) inversión *f*; (*of policy*) cambio de rumbo; (*of decision*) revocación *f*

reverse [rɪ'vəːs] N (*opposite*) contrario; (*back: of cloth*) revés *m*; (: *of coin*) reverso; (: *of paper*) dorso; (*Aut: also:* **reverse gear**) marcha atrás ▸ ADJ (*order*) inverso; (*direction*) contrario ▸ VT (*decision*) dar marcha atrás a; (*Aut*) dar marcha atrás a; (*position, function*) invertir ▸ VI (*BRIT Aut*) poner en marcha atrás; **in ~ order** en orden inverso; **the ~** lo contrario; **to go into ~** dar marcha atrás

reverse-charge call [rɪ'vəːstʃɑː'dʒ-] N (*BRIT*) llamada a cobro revertido

reverse video N vídeo inverso

reversible [rɪ'vəːsəbl] ADJ (*garment, procedure*) reversible

reversing lights [rɪ'vəːsɪŋ-] NPL (*BRIT Aut*) luces *fpl* de marcha atrás

revert [rɪ'vəːt] VI: **to ~ to** volver or revertir a

review [rɪ'vjuː] N (*magazine: also Mil*) revista; (*of book, film*) reseña; (*US: examination*) repaso, examen *m* ▸ VT repasar, examinar; (*Mil*) pasar revista a; (*book, film*) reseñar; **to come under ~** ser examinado

reviewer [rɪ'vjuːəʳ] N crítico(-a)

revile [rɪ'vaɪl] VT injuriar, vilipendiar

revise [rɪ'vaɪz] VT (*manuscript*) corregir; (*opinion*) modificar; (*price, procedure*) revisar; (*BRIT: study: subject*) repasar; (*look over*) revisar; **revised edition** edición *f* corregida

revision [rɪ'vɪʒən] N corrección *f*; modificación *f*; (*of subject*) repaso; (*revised version*) revisión *f*

revisit [riː'vɪzɪt] VT volver a visitar

revitalize [riː'vaɪtəlaɪz] VT revivificar

revival [rɪ'vaɪvəl] N (*recovery*) reanimación *f*; (*Pol*) resurgimiento; (*of interest*) renacimiento; (*Theat*) reestreno; (*of faith*) despertar *m*

revive [rɪ'vaɪv] VT resucitar; (*custom*) restablecer; (*hope, courage*) reanimar; (*play*) reestrenar ▸ VI (*person*) volver en sí; (*from tiredness*) reponerse; (*business*) reactivarse

revoke [rɪ'vəuk] VT revocar

revolt [rɪ'vəult] N rebelión *f* ▸ VI rebelarse, sublevarse ▸ VT dar asco a, repugnar; **to ~ (against sb/sth)** rebelarse (contra algn/algo)

revolting [rɪ'vəultɪŋ] ADJ asqueroso, repugnante

revolution [rɛvə'luːʃən] N revolución *f*

revolutionary [rɛvə'luːʃənrɪ] ADJ, N revolucionario(-a) *m/f*

r

revolutionize [rɛvəˈluːʃənaɪz] VT revolucionar

revolve [rɪˈvɔlv] VI dar vueltas, girar; **to ~ (a)round** girar en torno a

revolver [rɪˈvɔlvəʳ] N revólver *m*

revolving [rɪˈvɔlvɪŋ] ADJ (*chair, door etc*) giratorio

revue [rɪˈvjuː] N (*Theat*) revista

revulsion [rɪˈvʌlʃən] N asco, repugnancia

reward [rɪˈwɔːd] N premio, recompensa ▸ VT: **to ~ (for)** recompensar *or* premiar (por)

rewarding [rɪˈwɔːdɪŋ] ADJ (*fig*) gratificante; **financially ~** económicamente provechoso

rewind [riːˈwaɪnd] (*pt, pp* **rewound** [-ˈwaund]) VT (*tape*) rebobinar; (*watch*) dar cuerda a; (*wool etc*) devanar

rewire [riːˈwaɪəʳ] VT (*house*) renovar la instalación eléctrica de

reword [riːˈwəːd] VT expresar en otras palabras

rewritable [riːˈraɪtəbl] ADJ reescribible

rewrite [riːˈraɪt] VT (*irreg: like* **write**) reescribir

Reykjavik [ˈreɪkjəviːk] N Reykjavik *m*

RFD ABBR (*US Post*) = **rural free delivery**

RGN N ABBR (*BRIT*) = **Registered General Nurse**

Rh ABBR (= *rhesus*) Rh *m*

rhapsody [ˈræpsədɪ] N (*Mus*) rapsodia; (*fig*): **to go into rhapsodies over** extasiarse por

rhesus negative [ˈriːsəs-] ADJ (*Med*) Rh negativo

rhesus positive ADJ (*Med*) Rh positivo

rhetoric [ˈrɛtərɪk] N retórica

rhetorical [rɪˈtɔrɪkl] ADJ retórico

rheumatic [ruːˈmætɪk] ADJ reumático

rheumatism [ˈruːmətɪzəm] N reumatismo, reúma

rheumatoid arthritis [ˈruːmətɔɪd-] N reúma *m* articular

Rhine [raɪn] N: **the ~** el (río) Rin

rhinestone [ˈraɪnstəun] N diamante *m* de imitación

rhinoceros [raɪˈnɔsərəs] N rinoceronte *m*

Rhodes [rəudz] N Rodas *f*

rhododendron [rəudəˈdɛndrn] N rododendro

Rhone [rəun] N: **the ~** el (río) Ródano

rhubarb [ˈruːbɑːb] N ruibarbo

rhyme [raɪm] N rima; (*verse*) poesía ▸ VI: **to ~ (with)** rimar (con); **without ~ or reason** sin ton ni son

rhythm [ˈrɪðm] N ritmo

rhythmic [ˈrɪðmɪk], **rhythmical** [ˈrɪðmɪkl] ADJ rítmico

rhythmically [ˈrɪðmɪklɪ] ADV rítmicamente

rhythm method N método (de) Ogino

RI N ABBR (*BRIT*: = *religious instruction*) ed. religiosa ▸ ABBR (*US Post*) = **Rhode Island**

rib [rɪb] N (*Anat*) costilla ▸ VT (*mock*) tomar el pelo a

ribald [ˈrɪbəld] ADJ escabroso

ribbon [ˈrɪbən] N cinta; **in ribbons** (*torn*) hecho trizas

rice [raɪs] N arroz *m*

ricefield [ˈraɪsfiːld] N arrozal *m*

rice pudding N arroz *m* con leche

rich [rɪtʃ] ADJ rico; (*soil*) fértil; (*food*) pesado; (*: sweet*) empalagoso; **the rich** NPL los ricos; **riches** NPL riqueza *sg*; **to be ~ in sth** abundar en algo

richly [ˈrɪtʃlɪ] ADV ricamente

richness [ˈrɪtʃnɪs] N riqueza; (*of soil*) fertilidad *f*

rickets [ˈrɪkɪts] N raquitismo

rickety [ˈrɪkɪtɪ] ADJ (*old*) desvencijado; (*shaky*) tambaleante

rickshaw [ˈrɪkʃɔː] N carro de culí

ricochet [ˈrɪkəʃeɪ] N rebote *m* ▸ VI rebotar

rid [rɪd] (*pt, pp* **~**) VT: **to ~ sb of sth** librar a algn de algo; **to get ~ of** deshacerse *or* desembarazarse de

riddance [ˈrɪdns] N: **good ~!** ¡y adiós muy buenas!

ridden [ˈrɪdn] PP *of* **ride**

-ridden [ˈrɪdn] SUFF: **disease~** plagado de enfermedades; **inflation~** minado por la inflación

riddle [ˈrɪdl] N (*conundrum*) acertijo; (*mystery*) enigma *m*, misterio ▸ VT: **to be riddled with** ser lleno *or* plagado de

ride [raɪd] (*pt* **rode**, *pp* **ridden**) N paseo; (*distance covered*) viaje *m*, recorrido ▸ VI (*on horse: as sport*) montar; (*go somewhere: on horse, bicycle*) dar un paseo, pasearse; (*journey: on bicycle, motor cycle, bus*) viajar ▸ VT (*a horse*) montar a; (*distance*) recorrer; **to ~ a bicycle** andar en bicicleta; **to ~ at anchor** (*Naut*) estar fondeado; **can you ~ a bike?** ¿sabes montar en bici(cleta)?; **to go for a ~** dar un paseo; **to take sb for a ~** (*fig*) tomar el pelo a algn

▸ **ride out** VT: **to ~ out the storm** (*fig*) capear el temporal

rider [ˈraɪdəʳ] N (*on horse*) jinete *m*; (*on bicycle*) ciclista *mf*; (*on motorcycle*) motociclista *mf*

ridge [rɪdʒ] N (*of hill*) cresta; (*of roof*) caballete *m*; (*wrinkle*) arruga

ridicule [ˈrɪdɪkjuːl] N irrisión *f*, burla ▸ VT poner en ridículo a, burlarse de; **to hold sth/sb up to ~** poner algo/a algn en ridículo

ridiculous [rɪˈdɪkjuləs] ADJ ridículo

ridiculously [rɪˈdɪkjuləslɪ] ADV ridículamente, de modo ridículo

riding [ˈraɪdɪŋ] N equitación *f*; **I like ~** me gusta montar a caballo

riding habit N traje *m* de montar

riding school N escuela de equitación

rife [raɪf] ADJ: **to be ~** ser muy común; **to be ~ with** abundar en

riffraff ['rɪfræf] N chusma, gentuza

rifle ['raɪfl] N rifle m, fusil m ▶ VT saquear
▶ **rifle through** VT FUS saquear

rifle range N campo de tiro; (at fair) tiro al blanco

rift [rɪft] N (fig: between friends) desavenencia; (: in party) escisión f

rig [rɪg] N (also: **oil rig**: on land) torre f de perforación; (: at sea) plataforma petrolera ▶ VT (election etc) amañar los resultados de
▶ **rig out** VT (BRIT) ataviar
▶ **rig up** VT improvisar

rigging ['rɪgɪŋ] N (Naut) aparejo

right [raɪt] ADJ (true, correct) correcto, exacto; (suitable) indicado, debido; (proper) apropiado, propio; (just) justo; (morally good) bueno; (not left) derecho ▶ N (title, claim) derecho; (not left) derecha ▶ ADV (correctly) bien, correctamente; (straight) derecho, directamente; (not on the left) a la derecha; (to the right) hacia la derecha ▶ VT (put straight) enderezar; (correct) corregir ▶ EXCL ¡bueno!, ¡está bien!; **to be ~** (person) tener razón; (answer) ser correcto; **to get sth ~** corregir en algo; **you did the ~ thing** hiciste bien; **let's get it ~ this time!** ¡a ver si esta vez nos sale bien!; **to put a mistake ~** corregir un error; **the ~ time** la hora exacta; (fig) el momento oportuno; **by rights** en justicia; **~ and wrong** el bien y el mal; **film rights** derechos mpl de la película; **on the ~** a la derecha; **to be in the ~** tener razón; **~ now** ahora mismo; **~ before/after** inmediatamente antes/después; **~ in the middle** exactamente en el centro; **~ away** en seguida; **to go ~ to the end of sth** llegar hasta el final de algo; **~, who's next?** bueno, ¿quién sigue?; **all ~!** ¡vale!; **I'm/I feel all ~ now** ya estoy bien

right angle N ángulo recto

right-click ['raɪtklɪk] VI clicar con el botón derecho del ratón ▶ VT: **to ~ an icon** clicar en un icono con el botón derecho del ratón

righteous ['raɪtʃəs] ADJ justo, honrado; (anger) justificado

righteousness ['raɪtʃəsnɪs] N justicia

rightful ['raɪtful] ADJ (heir) legítimo

right-hand ['raɪthænd] ADJ: **~ drive** conducción f por la derecha; **the ~ side** derecha

right-handed [raɪt'hændɪd] ADJ (person) que usa la mano derecha, diestro

right-hand man N (irreg) brazo derecho

right-hand side N derecha

rightly ['raɪtlɪ] ADV correctamente, debidamente; (with reason) con razón; **if I remember ~** si recuerdo bien

right-minded ['raɪt'maɪndɪd] ADJ (sensible)

sensato; (decent) honrado

right of way N (on path etc) derecho de paso; (Aut) prioridad f de paso

right-wing [raɪt'wɪŋ] ADJ (Pol) de derechas, derechista

right-winger [raɪt'wɪŋəʳ] N (Pol) persona de derechas, derechista mf; (Sport) extremo derecha

rigid ['rɪdʒɪd] ADJ rígido; (person, ideas) inflexible

rigidity [rɪ'dʒɪdɪtɪ] N rigidez f; inflexibilidad f

rigidly ['rɪdʒɪdlɪ] ADV rígidamente; (inflexibly) inflexiblemente

rigmarole ['rɪgmərəul] N galimatías m inv

rigor mortis ['rɪgə'mɔːtɪs] N rigidez f cadavérica

rigorous ['rɪgərəs] ADJ riguroso

rigorously ['rɪgərəslɪ] ADV rigurosamente

rigour, (US) **rigor** ['rɪgəʳ] N rigor m, severidad f

rile [raɪl] VT irritar

rim [rɪm] N borde m; (of spectacles) montura, aro; (of wheel) llanta

rimless ['rɪmlɪs] ADJ (spectacles) sin aros

rimmed [rɪmd] ADJ: **~ with** con un borde de, bordeado de

rind [raɪnd] N (of bacon, cheese) corteza; (of lemon etc) cáscara

ring [rɪŋ] (pt **rang**, pp **rung**) N (of metal) aro; (on finger) anillo; (of people) corro; (of objects) círculo; (gang) banda; (for boxing) cuadrilátero; (of circus) pista; (bull ring) ruedo, plaza; (sound of bell) toque m; (telephone call) llamada ▶ VI (on telephone) llamar por teléfono; (large bell) repicar; (doorbell, phone) sonar; (also: **ring out**: voice, words) sonar; (ears) zumbar ▶ VT (BRIT Tel: also: **ring up**) llamar; (bell etc) hacer sonar; (doorbell) tocar; **that has the ~ of truth about it** eso suena a verdad; **to give sb a ~** (BRIT Tel) llamar a algn, dar un telefonazo a algn; **the name doesn't ~ a bell (with me)** el nombre no me suena; **to ~ sb (up)** llamar a algn
▶ **ring back** VT, VI (Tel) devolver la llamada
▶ **ring off** VI (BRIT Tel) colgar, cortar la comunicación
▶ **ring up** VT (BRIT Tel) llamar, telefonear

ring binder N carpeta de anillas

ring-fence [rɪŋ'fɛns] VT proteger, blindar

ring finger N (dedo) anular m

ringing ['rɪŋɪŋ] N (of bell) toque m, tañido; (of large bell) repique m; (in ears) zumbido

ringing tone N (Tel) tono de llamada

ringleader ['rɪŋliːdəʳ] N cabecilla mf

ringlets ['rɪŋlɪts] NPL tirabuzones mpl, bucles mpl

ring road N (BRIT) carretera periférica or de circunvalación

r

ringtone ['rɪŋtəun] N tono de llamada
rink [rɪŋk] N (also: **ice rink**) pista de hielo; (for roller-skating) pista de patinaje
rinse [rɪns] N (of dishes) enjuague m; (of clothes) aclarado; (hair colouring) reflejo ▶ VT enjuagar, aclarar; (hair) dar reflejos a
Rio ['riːəu], **Rio de Janeiro** ['riːəudəʒə'nɪərəu] N Río de Janeiro
riot ['raɪət] N motín m, disturbio ▶ VI amotinarse; **to run** ~ desmandarse
rioter ['raɪətər] N amotinado(-a)
riot gear N uniforme m antidisturbios inv
riotous ['raɪətəs] ADJ alborotado; (party) bullicioso; (uncontrolled) desenfrenado
riotously ['raɪətəslɪ] ADV bulliciosamente
riot police N policía antidisturbios
RIP ABBR (= requiescat or requiescant in pace: rest in peace) q.e.p.d.
rip [rɪp] N rasgón m, desgarrón m ▶ VT rasgar, desgarrar ▶ VI rasgarse
  ▶ **rip off** VT (inf: cheat) estafar
  ▶ **rip up** VT hacer pedazos
ripcord ['rɪpkɔːd] N cabo de desgarre
ripe [raɪp] ADJ (fruit) maduro
ripen ['raɪpən] VT, VI madurar
ripeness ['raɪpnɪs] N madurez f
rip-off ['rɪpɔf] N (inf): **it's a ~!** ¡es una estafa!, ¡es un timo!
riposte [rɪ'pɔst] N respuesta aguda, réplica
ripple ['rɪpl] N onda, rizo; (sound) murmullo ▶ VI rizarse ▶ VT rizar
rise [raɪz] (pt **rose** [rəuz], pp **risen** ['rɪzn]) N (slope) cuesta, pendiente f; (hill) altura; (increase: in wages: BRIT) aumento; (: in prices, temperature) subida, alza; (fig: to power etc) ascenso; (: ascendancy) auge m ▶ VI (gen) elevarse; (prices) subir; (waters) crecer; (river) nacer; (sun) salir; (person: from bed etc) levantarse; (also: **rise up**: rebel) sublevarse; (in rank) ascender; ~ **to power** ascenso al poder; **to give ~ to** dar lugar or origen a; **to ~ to the occasion** ponerse a la altura de las circunstancias
risen ['rɪzn] PP of **rise**
rising ['raɪzɪŋ] ADJ (increasing: number) creciente; (: prices) en aumento or alza; (tide) creciente; (sun, moon) naciente ▶ N (uprising) sublevación f
rising damp N humedad f de paredes
rising star N (fig) figura en alza
risk [rɪsk] N riesgo, peligro ▶ VT (gen) arriesgar; (dare) atreverse a; **to take** or **run the ~ of doing** correr el riesgo de hacer; **at ~** en peligro; **at one's own ~** bajo su propia responsabilidad; **fire/health/security ~** peligro de incendio/para la salud/para la seguridad
risk capital N capital m de riesgo
risky ['rɪskɪ] ADJ arriesgado, peligroso

risqué ['riːskeɪ] ADJ (joke) subido de color
rissole ['rɪsəul] N croqueta
rite [raɪt] N rito; **last rites** últimos sacramentos mpl
ritual ['rɪtjuəl] ADJ ritual ▶ N ritual m, rito
rival ['raɪvl] N rival mf; (in business) competidor(a) m/f ▶ ADJ rival, opuesto ▶ VT competir con
rivalry ['raɪvlrɪ] N rivalidad f, competencia
river ['rɪvər] N río ▶ CPD (port, traffic) de río, del río; **up/down** ~ río arriba/abajo
riverbank ['rɪvəbæŋk] N orilla (del río)
riverbed ['rɪvəbed] N lecho, cauce m
rivet ['rɪvɪt] N roblón m, remache m ▶ VT remachar; (fig) fascinar
riveting ['rɪvɪtɪŋ] ADJ (fig) fascinante
Riviera [rɪvɪ'ɛərə] N: **the (French)** ~ la Costa Azul, la Riviera (francesa); **the Italian** ~ la Riviera italiana
Riyadh [rɪ'jɑːd] N Riyadh m
RMT N ABBR (= National Union of Rail, Maritime and Transport Workers) sindicato de transportes
RN N ABBR (BRIT) = **Royal Navy**; (US) = **registered nurse**
RNA N ABBR (= ribonucleic acid) ARN m, RNA m
RNLI N ABBR (BRIT: = Royal National Lifeboat Institution) organización benéfica que proporciona un servicio de lanchas de socorro
RNZAF N ABBR = **Royal New Zealand Air Force**
RNZN N ABBR = **Royal New Zealand Navy**
road [rəud] N (gen) camino; (motorway etc) carretera; (in town) calle f; **major/minor** ~ carretera general/secundaria; **main** ~ carretera; **it takes four hours by** ~ se tarda cuatro horas por carretera; **on the ~ to success** camino del éxito
roadblock ['rəudblɔk] N barricada, control m, retén m (LAM)
road haulage N transporte m por carretera
road hog ['rəudhɔg] N loco(-a) del volante
road map N mapa m de carreteras
road rage N conducta agresiva de los conductores
road safety N seguridad f vial
roadside ['rəudsaɪd] N borde m (del camino) ▶ CPD al lado de la carretera; **by the** ~ al borde del camino
roadsign ['rəudsaɪn] N señal f de tráfico
roadsweeper ['rəudswiːpər] N (BRIT: person) barrendero(-a)
road tax N (BRIT) impuesto de rodaje
road user N usuario(-a) de la vía pública
roadway ['rəudweɪ] N calzada
roadworks ['rəudwəːks] NPL obras fpl
roadworthy ['rəudwəːðɪ] ADJ (car) en buen estado para circular
roam [rəum] VI vagar ▶ VT vagar por
roar [rɔːr] N (of animal) rugido, bramido; (of crowd) clamor m, rugido; (of vehicle, storm)

estruendo; (*of laughter*) carcajada ▶ vi rugir, bramar; hacer estruendo; **to ~ with laughter** reírse a carcajadas

roaring ['rɔːrɪŋ] ADJ: **a ~ success** un tremendo éxito; **to do a ~ trade** hacer buen negocio

roast [rəust] N carne *f* asada, asado ▶ vt (*meat*) asar; (*coffee*) tostar

roast beef N rosbif *m*

roasting ['rəustɪŋ] N: **to give sb a ~** (*inf*) echar una buena bronca a algn

rob [rɔb] vt robar; **to ~ sb of sth** robar algo a algn; (*fig: deprive*) quitar algo a algn

robber ['rɔbəʳ] N ladrón(-ona) *m/f*

robbery ['rɔbərɪ] N robo

robe [rəub] N (*for ceremony etc*) toga; (*also*: **bath robe**) bata, albornoz *m*

robin ['rɔbɪn] N petirrojo

robot ['rəubɔt] N robot *m*

robotics [rəu'bɔtɪks] N robótica

robust [rəu'bʌst] ADJ robusto, fuerte

rock [rɔk] N (*gen*) roca; (*boulder*) peña, peñasco; (*BRIT: sweet*) ≈ pirulí *m* ▶ vt (*swing gently*) mecer; (*shake*) sacudir ▶ vi mecerse, balancearse; sacudirse; **on the rocks** (*drink*) con hielo; **their marriage is on the rocks** su matrimonio se está yendo a pique; **to ~ the boat** (*fig*) crear problemas

rock and roll N rock and roll *m*, rocanrol *m*

rock-bottom ['rɔk'bɔtəm] ADJ (*fig*) por los suelos; **to reach** *or* **touch ~** (*price*) estar por los suelos; (*person*) tocar fondo

rock cake N (*BRIT*) *bollito de pasas con superficie rugosa*

rock climber N escalador(a) *m/f*

rock climbing N (*Sport*) escalada

rockery ['rɔkərɪ] N cuadro alpino

rocket ['rɔkɪt] N cohete *m* ▶ vi (*prices*) dispararse, ponerse por las nubes

rocket launcher N lanzacohetes *m inv*

rock face N pared *f* de roca

rocking chair ['rɔkɪŋ-] N mecedora

rocking horse N caballo de balancín

rocky ['rɔkɪ] ADJ (*gen*) rocoso; (*unsteady: table*) inestable

Rocky Mountains NPL: **the ~** las Montañas Rocosas

rococo [rə'kəukəu] ADJ rococó *inv* ▶ N rococó

rod [rɔd] N vara, varilla; (*Tech*) barra; (*also*: **fishing rod**) caña

rode [rəud] PT *of* **ride**

rodent ['rəudnt] N roedor *m*

rodeo ['rəudɪəu] N rodeo

roe [rəu] N (*species: also*: **roe deer**) corzo; (*of fish*): **hard/soft ~** hueva/lecha

rogue [rəug] N pícaro, pillo

roguish ['rəugɪʃ] ADJ (*child*) travieso; (*smile etc*) pícaro

role [rəul] N papel *m*, rol *m*

role-model ['rəulmɔdl] N modelo a imitar

role play N (*also*: **role playing**) juego de papeles *or* roles

roll [rəul] N rollo; (*of bank notes*) fajo; (*also*: **bread roll**) panecillo; (*register*) lista, nómina; (*sound: of drums etc*) redoble *m*; (*movement: of ship*) balanceo ▶ vt hacer rodar; (*also*: **roll up**: *string*) enrollar; (: *sleeves*) arremangar; (*cigarettes*) liar; (*also*: **roll out**: *pastry*) aplanar ▶ vi (*gen*) rodar; (*drum*) redoblar; (*in walking*) bambolearse; (*ship*) balancearse; **cheese ~** panecillo de queso
  ▶ **roll about, roll around** vi (*person*) revolcarse
  ▶ **roll by** vi (*time*) pasar
  ▶ **roll in** vi (*mail, cash*) entrar a raudales
  ▶ **roll over** vi dar una vuelta
  ▶ **roll up** vi (*inf: arrive*) presentarse, aparecer
  ▶ vt (*carpet, cloth, map*) arrollar; (*sleeves*) arremangar; **to ~ o.s. up into a ball** acurrucarse, hacerse un ovillo

roll call N: **to take a ~** pasar lista

rolled [rəuld] ADJ (*umbrella*) plegado

roller ['rəuləʳ] N rodillo; (*wheel*) rueda; (*for road*) apisonadora; (*for hair*) rulo

Rollerblades® ['rəuləbleɪdz] NPL patines *mpl* en línea

roller blind N (*BRIT*) persiana (enrollable)

roller coaster N montaña rusa

roller skates NPL patines *mpl* de rueda

roller-skating ['rəuləskeɪtɪŋ] N patinaje sobre ruedas; **to go ~** ir a patinar (*sobre ruedas*)

rollicking ['rɔlɪkɪŋ] ADJ: **we had a ~ time** nos divertimos una barbaridad

rolling ['rəulɪŋ] ADJ (*landscape*) ondulado

rolling mill N taller *m* de laminación

rolling pin N rodillo (de cocina)

rolling stock N (*Rail*) material *m* rodante

ROM [rɔm] N ABBR (*Comput*: = *read-only memory*) (memoria) ROM *f*

Roman ['rəumən] ADJ, N romano(-a) *m/f*

Roman Catholic ADJ, N católico(-a) *m/f* (romano(-a))

romance [rə'mæns] N (*love affair*) amor *m*, idilio; (*charm*) lo romántico; (*novel*) novela de amor

Romanesque [rəumə'nɛsk] ADJ románico

Romania [ru:'meɪnɪə] N = **Rumania**

Romanian [ru:'meɪnɪən] ADJ, N = **Rumanian**

Roman numeral N número romano

romantic [rə'mæntɪk] ADJ romántico

romanticism [rə'mæntɪsɪzəm] N romanticismo

Romany ['rəumənɪ] ADJ gitano ▶ N (*person*) gitano(-a); (*Ling*) lengua gitana, caló (*SP*)

Rome [rəum] N Roma

romp [rɔmp] N retozo, jugueteo ▶ vi (*also*: **romp about**) juguetear; **to ~ home** (*horse*) ganar fácilmente

rompers ['rɔmpəz] NPL pelele *m*

r

roof [ru:f] N (gen) techo; (of house) tejado ▸ VT techar, poner techo a; **~ of the mouth** paladar m

roofing ['ru:fɪŋ] N techumbre f

roof rack N (Aut) baca, portaequipajes msg

rook [ruk] N (bird) graja; (Chess) torre f

rookie ['rukɪ] N (inf) novato(-a); (Mil) chivo

room [ru:m] N (in house) cuarto, habitación f, pieza (esp LAm); (also: **bedroom**) dormitorio; (in school etc) sala; (space) sitio; **rooms** NPL (lodging) alojamiento sg; **"rooms to let"**, (US) **"rooms for rent"** "se alquilan pisos or cuartos"; **single/double ~** habitación individual/doble or para dos personas; **is there ~ for this?** ¿cabe esto?; **to make ~ for sb** hacer sitio para algn; **there is ~ for improvement** podría mejorarse

roominess ['ru:mɪnɪs] N amplitud f, espaciosidad f

rooming house ['ru:mɪŋ-] N (US) pensión f

roommate ['ru:mmeɪt] N compañero(-a) de cuarto

room service N servicio de habitaciones

room temperature N temperatura ambiente

roomy ['ru:mɪ] ADJ espacioso

roost [ru:st] N percha ▸ VI pasar la noche

rooster ['ru:stər] N gallo

root [ru:t] N (Bot, Math) raíz f ▸ VI (plant, belief) arraigar(se); **to take ~** (plant) echar raíces; (idea) arraigar(se); **the ~ of the problem is that ...** la raíz del problema es que ...
  ▸ **root about** VI (fig) rebuscar
  ▸ **root for** VT FUS apoyar a
  ▸ **root out** VT desarraigar

root beer N (US) refresco sin alcohol de extractos de hierbas

rooted ['ru:tɪd] ADJ enraizado; (opinions etc) arraigado

rope [rəup] N cuerda; (Naut) cable m ▸ VT (box) atar or amarrar con (una) cuerda; (climbers: also: **rope together**) encordarse; (an area: also: **rope off**) acordonar; **to ~ sb in** (fig) persuadir a algn a tomar parte; **to know the ropes** (fig) conocer los trucos (del oficio)

rope ladder N escala de cuerda

ropey ['rəupɪ] ADJ (inf) chungo

rort [rɔ:t] (Australia, New Zealand inf) N estafa ▸ VT estafar

rosary ['rəuzərɪ] N rosario

rose [rəuz] PT of **rise** ▸ N rosa; (also: **rosebush**) rosal m; (on watering can) roseta ▸ ADJ color de rosa

rosé ['rəuzeɪ] N vino rosado, clarete m

rosebed ['rəuzbɛd] N rosaleda

rosebud ['rəuzbʌd] N capullo de rosa

rosebush ['rəuzbʊʃ] N rosal m

rosemary ['rəuzmərɪ] N romero

rosette [rəu'zɛt] N rosetón m

ROSPA ['rɔspə] N ABBR (Brit) = **Royal Society for the Prevention of Accidents**

roster ['rɔstər] N: **duty ~** lista de tareas

rostrum ['rɔstrəm] N tribuna

rosy ['rəuzɪ] ADJ rosado, sonrosado; **the future looks ~** el futuro parece prometedor

rot [rɔt] N (decay) putrefacción f, podredumbre f; (fig: pej) tonterías fpl ▸ VT pudrir, corromper ▸ VI pudrirse, corromperse; **it has rotted** está podrido; **to stop the ~** (fig) poner fin a las pérdidas

rota ['rəutə] N lista (de tareas)

rotary ['rəutərɪ] ADJ rotativo

rotate [rəu'teɪt] VT (revolve) hacer girar, dar vueltas a; (change round: crops) cultivar en rotación; (: jobs) alternar ▸ VI (revolve) girar, dar vueltas

rotating [rəu'teɪtɪŋ] ADJ (movement) rotativo

rotation [rəu'teɪʃən] N rotación f; **in ~** por turno

rote [rəut] N: **by ~** de memoria

rotor ['rəutər] N rotor m

rotten ['rɔtn] ADJ (decayed) podrido; (: wood) carcomido; (fig) corrompido; (inf: bad) pésimo; **to feel ~** (ill) sentirse fatal; **~ to the core** completamente podrido

rotund [rəu'tʌnd] ADJ rotundo

rouble, (US) **ruble** ['ru:bl] N rublo

rouge [ru:ʒ] N colorete m

rough [rʌf] ADJ (skin, surface) áspero; (terrain) accidentado; (road) desigual; (voice) bronco; (person, manner: coarse) tosco, grosero; (weather) borrascoso; (treatment) brutal; (sea) embravecido; (town, area) peligroso; (cloth) basto; (plan) preliminar; (guess) aproximado; (violent) violento ▸ N (Golf): **in the ~** en las hierbas altas; **to ~ it** vivir sin comodidades; **to sleep ~** (Brit) pasar la noche al raso; **the sea is ~ today** el mar está agitado hoy; **to have a ~ time (of it)** pasar una mala racha; **~ estimate** cálculo aproximado

roughage ['rʌfɪdʒ] N fibra(s) f(pl), forraje m

rough-and-ready ['rʌfən'rɛdɪ] ADJ improvisado, tosco

rough-and-tumble ['rʌfən'tʌmbl] N pelea

roughcast ['rʌfkɑ:st] N mezcla gruesa

rough copy, rough draft N borrador m

roughen ['rʌfn] VT (a surface) poner áspero

roughly ['rʌflɪ] ADV (handle) torpemente; (make) toscamente; (approximately) aproximadamente; **~ speaking** más o menos

roughness ['rʌfnɪs] N aspereza; tosquedad f; brutalidad f

roughshod ['rʌfʃɔd] ADV: **to ride ~ over** (person) pisotear a; (objections) hacer caso omiso de

rough work N (Scol etc) borrador m

roulette [ru:'lɛt] N ruleta

Roumania [ruːˈmeɪnɪə] N = **Rumania**

round [raund] ADJ redondo ▶ N círculo; (of policeman) ronda; (of milkman) recorrido; (of doctor) visitas fpl; (game: in competition, cards) partida; (of ammunition) cartucho; (Boxing) asalto; (of talks) ronda ▶ VT (corner) doblar ▶ PREP alrededor de; (surrounding): ~ **his neck/ the table** en su cuello/alrededor de la mesa; (in a circular movement): **to move ~ the room/ sail ~ the world** dar una vuelta a la habitación/circunnavegar el mundo; (in various directions): **to move ~ a room/house** moverse por toda la habitación/casa ▶ ADV: **all ~** por todos lados; **all the year ~** durante todo el año; **the long way ~** por el camino menos directo; **it's just ~ the corner** (fig) está a la vuelta de la esquina; **to ask sb ~** invitar a algn a casa; **I'll be ~ at six o'clock** llegaré a eso de las seis; **she arrived ~ (about) noon** llegó alrededor del mediodía; **~ the clock** adv las 24 horas; **to go ~ to sb's (house)** ir a casa de algn; **to go ~ the back** pasar por atrás; **enough to go ~** bastante (para todos); **in ~ figures** en números redondos; **to go the rounds** (story) divulgarse; **a ~ of applause** una salva de aplausos; **a ~ of drinks/sandwiches** una ronda de bebidas/bocadillos; **a ~ of toast** (BRIT) una tostada; **the daily ~** la rutina cotidiana

▶ **round off** VT (speech etc) acabar, poner término a

▶ **round up** VT (cattle) acorralar; (people) reunir; (prices) redondear

roundabout [ˈraundəbaut] N (BRIT: Aut) glorieta, rotonda; (: at fair) tiovivo ▶ ADJ (route, means) indirecto

rounded [ˈraundɪd] ADJ redondeado, redondo

rounders [ˈraundəz] N (BRIT: game) juego similar al béisbol

roundly [ˈraundlɪ] ADV (fig) rotundamente

round-robin [ˈraundrɔbɪn] N (Sport: also: **round-robin tournament**) liguilla

round-shouldered [ˈraundˈʃəuldəd] ADJ cargado de espaldas

round trip N viaje m de ida y vuelta

roundup [ˈraundʌp] N rodeo; (of criminals) redada; **a ~ of the latest news** un resumen de las últimas noticias

rouse [rauz] VT (wake up) despertar; (stir up) suscitar

rousing [ˈrauzɪŋ] ADJ (applause) caluroso; (speech) conmovedor(a)

rout [raut] N (Mil) derrota; (flight) desbandada ▶ VT derrotar

route [ruːt] N ruta, camino; (of bus) recorrido; (of shipping) rumbo, derrota; **the best ~ to London** el mejor camino or la mejor ruta para ir a Londres; **en ~ from ... to** en el viaje de ... a; **en ~ for** rumbo a, con destino en

route map N (BRIT: for journey) mapa m de carreteras

routine [ruːˈtiːn] ADJ (work) rutinario ▶ N rutina; (Theat) número; (Comput) rutina; **~ procedure** trámite m rutinario

rover [ˈrəuvər] N vagabundo(-a)

roving [ˈrəuvɪŋ] ADJ (wandering) errante; (salesman) ambulante; (reporter) volante

row[1] [rəu] N (line) fila, hilera; (Knitting) vuelta ▶ VI (in boat) remar ▶ VT (boat) conducir remando; **four days in a ~** cuatro días seguidos

row[2] [rau] N (noise) escándalo; (dispute) bronca, pelea; (fuss) jaleo; (scolding) reprimenda ▶ VI reñir(se); **to have a ~** armar un lío; **to have a ~** pelearse, reñir

rowboat [ˈrəubəut] N (US) bote m de remos

rowdy [ˈraudɪ] ADJ (person: noisy) ruidoso; (: quarrelsome) pendenciero; (occasion) alborotado ▶ N pendenciero

rowdyism [ˈraudɪɪzəm] N gamberrismo

row houses NPL (US) casas fpl adosadas

rowing [ˈrəuɪŋ] N remo

rowing boat N (BRIT) bote m or barco de remos

rowlock [ˈrɔlək] N (BRIT) chumacera

royal [ˈrɔɪəl] ADJ real

Royal Academy, Royal Academy of Arts N (BRIT) la Real Academia (de Bellas Artes); ver nota

> La *Royal Academy* (of Arts), fundada en 1768 durante el reinado de Jorge III, es una institución dedicada al fomento de la pintura, escultura y arquitectura en el Reino Unido. Además de dar cursos de arte, presenta una exposición anual de artistas contemporáneos en su sede de Burlington House, en el centro de Londres. No existe una institución equivalente a la Real Academia de la Lengua.

Royal Air Force N Fuerzas fpl Aéreas Británicas

royal blue N azul m marino

royalist [ˈrɔɪəlɪst] ADJ, N monárquico(-a) m/f

Royal Navy N (BRIT) Marina Británica

royalty [ˈrɔɪəltɪ] N (royal persons) (miembros mpl de la) familia real; (payment to author) derechos mpl de autor

RP N ABBR (BRIT: = Received Pronunciation) ver nota

> El acento con el que suelen hablar las clases medias y altas de Inglaterra se denomina RP (o *Received Pronunciation*). Es el acento estándar, sin variaciones regionales, que aún usan los locutores en los informativos nacionales de la "BBC". También suele tomarse como norma en la enseñanza del inglés británico como lengua extranjera. Todavía conserva un

r

gran prestigio, aunque la gran mayoría de la población habla con el acento de su región, que puede ser más o menos fuerte según su educación o clase social.

rpm ABBR (= *revolutions per minute*) r.p.m.

RR ABBR (*US*) = **railway**

RRP N ABBR (*BRIT*: = *recommended retail price*) PVP *m*

RSA N ABBR (*BRIT*) = **Royal Society of Arts**; **Royal Scottish Academy**

RSI N ABBR (*Med*: = *repetitive strain injury*) lesión *f* por esfuerzo repetitivo

RSPB N ABBR (*BRIT*) = **Royal Society for the Protection of Birds**

RSPCA N ABBR (*BRIT*) = **Royal Society for the Prevention of Cruelty to Animals**

RSVP ABBR (= *répondez s'il vous plaît*) SRC

RTA N ABBR (= *road traffic accident*) accidente *m* de carretera

Rt. Hon. ABBR (*BRIT*: = *Right Honourable*) tratamiento honorífico de diputado

Rt. Rev. ABBR (= *Right Reverend*) Rvdo.

rub [rʌb] VT (*gen*) frotar; (*hard*) restregar ▸ N (*gen*) frotamiento; (*touch*) roce *m*; **to give sth a ~** frotar algo; **to ~ sb up** *or* (*US*) **~ sb the wrong way** sacar de quicio a algn
▸ **rub down** VT (*body*) secar frotando; (*horse*) almohazar
▸ **rub in** VT (*ointment*) frotar
▸ **rub off** VT borrarse ▸ VI quitarse (frotando); **to ~ off on sb** influir en algn, pegársele a algn
▸ **rub out** VT borrar ▸ VI borrarse

rubber [ˈrʌbəʳ] N caucho, goma; (*BRIT*: *eraser*) goma de borrar

rubber band N goma, gomita

rubber bullet N bala de goma

rubber gloves NPL guantes *mpl* de goma

rubber plant N ficus *m*

rubber ring N (*for swimming*) flotador *m*

rubber stamp N sello (de caucho) ▸ VT: **rubber-stamp** (*fig*) aprobar maquinalmente

rubbery [ˈrʌbərɪ] ADJ (*como*) de goma

rubbish [ˈrʌbɪʃ] (*BRIT*) N (*from household*) basura; (*waste*) desperdicios *mpl*; (*fig*: *pej*) tonterías *fpl*; (*trash*) basura, porquería ▸ VT (*inf*) poner por los suelos; **what you've just said is ~** lo que acabas de decir es una tontería

rubbish bin N cubo *or* bote *m* (*LAM*) de la basura

rubbish dump N (*in town*) vertedero, basurero

rubbishy [ˈrʌbɪʃɪ] ADJ de mala calidad, de pacotilla

rubble [ˈrʌbl] N escombros *mpl*

ruby [ˈruːbɪ] N rubí *m*

RUC N ABBR (= *Royal Ulster Constabulary*) fuerza de policía en Irlanda del Norte

rucksack [ˈrʌksæk] N mochila

ructions [ˈrʌkʃənz] NPL: **there will be ~** se va a armar la gorda

rudder [ˈrʌdəʳ] N timón *m*

ruddy [ˈrʌdɪ] ADJ (*face*) rubicundo; (*inf*: *damned*) condenado

rude [ruːd] ADJ (*impolite*: *person*) grosero, maleducado; (: *word*, *manners*) rudo, grosero; (*indecent*) indecente; **to be ~ to sb** ser grosero con algn

rudeness [ˈruːdnɪs] N grosería, tosquedad *f*

rudiment [ˈruːdɪmənt] N rudimento

rudimentary [ruːdɪˈmɛntərɪ] ADJ rudimentario

rue [ruː] VT arrepentirse de

rueful [ˈruːful] ADJ arrepentido

ruffian [ˈrʌfɪən] N matón *m*, criminal *m*

ruffle [ˈrʌfl] VT (*hair*) despeinar; (*clothes*) arrugar; (*fig*: *person*) agitar

rug [rʌg] N alfombra; (*BRIT*: *for knees*) manta

rugby [ˈrʌgbɪ] N (*also*: **rugby football**) rugby *m*

rugged [ˈrʌgɪd] ADJ (*landscape*) accidentado; (*features*) robusto

rugger [ˈrʌgəʳ] N (*BRIT inf*) rugby *m*

ruin [ˈruːɪn] N ruina ▸ VT arruinar; (*spoil*) estropear; **ruins** NPL ruinas *fpl*, restos *mpl*; **in ruins** en ruinas

ruinous [ˈruːɪnəs] ADJ ruinoso

rule [ruːl] N (*norm*) norma, costumbre *f*; (*regulation*, *ruler*) regla; (*government*) dominio; (*dominion etc*): **under British ~** bajo el dominio británico ▸ VT (*country*, *person*) gobernar; (*decide*) disponer; (*draw lines*) trazar ▸ VI gobernar; (*Law*) fallar; **to ~ against/in favour of/on** fallar en contra de/a favor de/ sobre; **to ~ that ...** (*umpire*, *judge*) fallar que ...; **it's against the rules** está prohibido; **as a ~** por regla general, generalmente; **by ~ of thumb** por experiencia; **majority ~** (*Pol*) gobierno mayoritario
▸ **rule out** VT excluir

ruled [ruːld] ADJ (*paper*) rayado

ruler [ˈruːləʳ] N (*sovereign*) soberano; (*for measuring*) regla

ruling [ˈruːlɪŋ] ADJ (*party*) gobernante; (*class*) dirigente ▸ N (*Law*) fallo, decisión *f*

rum [rʌm] N ron *m*

Rumania [ruːˈmeɪnɪə] N Rumanía

Rumanian [ruːˈmeɪnɪən] ADJ, N rumano(-a) *m/f*

rumble [ˈrʌmbl] N ruido sordo; (*of thunder*) redoble *m* ▸ VI retumbar, hacer un ruido sordo; (*stomach*, *pipe*) sonar

rumbustious [rʌmˈbʌstʃəs] ADJ (*person*) bullicioso

rummage [ˈrʌmɪdʒ] VI revolverlo todo

rumour, (*US*) **rumor** [ˈruːməʳ] N rumor *m* ▸ VT: **it is rumoured that ...** se rumorea que ...; **~ has it that ...** corre la voz de que ...

rump [rʌmp] N (*of animal*) ancas *fpl*, grupa

rumple ['rʌmpl] vt (clothes) arrugar; (hair) despeinar

rump steak N filete m de lomo

rumpus ['rʌmpəs] N (inf) lío, jaleo; (quarrel) pelea, riña; **to kick up a ~** armar un follón or armar bronca

run [rʌn] (pt **ran**, pp **~**) N (Sport) carrera; (outing) paseo, excursión f; (distance travelled) trayecto; (series) serie f; (Theat) temporada; (Ski) pista; (in tights, stockings) carrera ▶ vt (operate: business) dirigir; (: competition, course) organizar; (: hotel, house) administrar, llevar; (Comput: program) ejecutar; (to pass: hand) pasar; (Press: feature) publicar ▶ vi (gen) correr; (work: machine) funcionar, marchar; (bus, train: operate) circular, ir; (: travel) ir; (continue: play) seguir en cartel; (: contract) ser válido; (flow: river, bath) fluir; (colours, washing) desteñirse; (in election) ser candidato; **to go for a ~** ir a correr; **to make a ~ for it** echar(se) a correr, escapar(se), huir; **to have the ~ of sb's house** tener el libre uso de la casa de algn; **a ~ of luck** una racha de suerte; **there was a ~ on** (meat, tickets) hubo mucha demanda de; **in the long ~** a la larga; **on the ~** en fuga; **I'll ~ you to the station** te llevaré a la estación en coche; **to ~ a risk** correr un riesgo; **to ~ a bath** llenar la bañera; **to ~ errands** hacer recados; **it's very cheap to ~** es muy económico; **to be ~ off one's feet** estar ocupadísimo; **to ~ for the bus** correr tras el autobús; **we shall have to ~ for it** tendremos que escapar; **the train runs between Gatwick and Victoria** el tren circula entre Gatwick y Victoria; **the bus runs every 20 minutes** el autobús pasa cada 20 minutos; **to ~ on petrol/on diesel/off batteries** funcionar con gasolina/gasoil/baterías; **my salary won't ~ to a car** mi sueldo no me da para comprarme un coche; **the car ran into the lamppost** el coche chocó contra el farol

▶ **run about, run around** vi (children) correr por todos lados

▶ **run across** vt fus (find) dar or topar con

▶ **run after** vt fus (to catch up) correr tras; (chase) perseguir

▶ **run away** vi huir

▶ **run down** vi (clock) pararse ▶ vt (reduce: production) ir reduciendo; (factory) restringir la producción de; (Aut) atropellar; (criticize) criticar; **to be ~ down** (person: tired) encontrarse agotado

▶ **run in** vt (Brit: car) rodar

▶ **run into** vt fus (meet: person, trouble) tropezar con; (collide with) chocar con; **to ~ into debt** contraer deudas, endeudarse

▶ **run off** vt (water) dejar correr ▶ vi huir corriendo

▶ **run out** vi (person) salir corriendo; (liquid) irse; (lease) caducar, vencer; (money) acabarse

▶ **run out of** vt fus quedar sin; **I've ~ out of petrol** se me acabó la gasolina

▶ **run over** vt (Aut) atropellar ▶ vt fus (revise) repasar

▶ **run through** vt fus (instructions) repasar

▶ **run up** vt (debt) incurrir en; **to ~ up against** (difficulties) tropezar con

run-around ['rʌnəraund] N: **to give sb the ~** traer a algn al retortero

runaway ['rʌnəwei] adj (horse) desbocado; (truck) sin frenos; (person) fugitivo

rundown ['rʌndaun] N (Brit: of industry etc) cierre m gradual

rung [rʌŋ] pp of **ring** ▶ N (of ladder) escalón m, peldaño

run-in ['rʌnin] N (inf) altercado

runner ['rʌnər] N (in race: person) corredor(a) m/f; (: horse) caballo; (on sledge) patín m; (wheel) ruedecilla

runner bean N (Brit) judía verde

runner-up [rʌnər'ʌp] N subcampeón(-ona) m/f

running ['rʌnɪŋ] N (sport) atletismo; (race) carrera ▶ adj (costs, water) corriente; (commentary) en directo; **to be in/out of the ~ for sth** tener/no tener posibilidades de ganar algo; **6 days** ~ 6 días seguidos

running costs NPL (of business) gastos mpl corrientes; (of car) gastos mpl de mantenimiento

running head N (Typ) encabezamiento normal

running mate N (US Pol) candidato(-a) a la vicepresidencia

runny ['rʌni] adj líquido; (eyes) lloroso; **to have a ~ nose** tener mocos

run-off ['rʌnɔf] N (in contest, election) desempate m; (extra race) carrera de desempate

run-of-the-mill ['rʌnəvðə'mil] adj común y corriente

runt [rʌnt] N (also pej) enano

run-up ['rʌnʌp] N: **~ to** (election etc) período previo a

runway ['rʌnwei] N (Aviat) pista (de aterrizaje)

rupee [ru:'pi:] N rupia

rupture ['rʌptʃər] N (Med) hernia ▶ vt: **to ~ o.s.** causarse una hernia

rural ['ruərl] adj rural

ruse [ru:z] N ardid m

rush [rʌʃ] N ímpetu m; (hurry) prisa, apuro (LAm); (Comm) demanda repentina; (Bot) junco; (current) corriente f fuerte, ráfaga; (of feeling) torrente m ▶ vt apresurar; (work) hacer de prisa; (attack: town etc) asaltar ▶ vi correr, precipitarse; **gold** ~ fiebre f del oro; **we've had a ~ of orders** ha habido una gran

demanda; **I'm in a ~ (to do)** tengo prisa or apuro (LAM) (por hacer); **is there any ~ for this?** ¿te corre prisa esto?; **to ~ sth off** hacer algo de prisa y corriendo
▶ **rush through** VT FUS (*meal*) comer de prisa; (*book*) leer de prisa; (*work*) hacer de prisa; (*town*) atravesar a toda velocidad ▶ VT SEP (*Comm: order*) despachar rápidamente

rush hour N hora *f* punta
rush job N (*urgent*) trabajo urgente
rusk [rʌsk] N bizcocho tostado
Russia ['rʌʃə] N Rusia
Russian ['rʌʃən] ADJ ruso ▶ N ruso(-a); (*Ling*) ruso

rust [rʌst] N herrumbre *f*, moho ▶ VI oxidarse
rustic ['rʌstɪk] ADJ rústico
rustle ['rʌsl] VI susurrar ▶ VT (*paper*) hacer crujir; (*US: cattle*) hurtar, robar
rustproof ['rʌstpruːf] ADJ inoxidable
rusty ['rʌstɪ] ADJ oxidado
rut [rʌt] N surco; (*Zool*) celo; **to be in a ~** ser esclavo de la rutina
ruthless ['ruːθlɪs] ADJ despiadado
RV ABBR (= *revised version*) traducción inglesa de la Biblia de 1855 ▶ N ABBR (*US*) = **recreational vehicle**
rye [raɪ] N centeno
rye bread N pan de centeno

Ss

S, s [ɛs] N (letter) S, s f; **S for Sugar** S de sábado
S ABBR (= Saint) Sto.(-a.); (US Scol: mark:
= satisfactory) suficiente; (on clothes) = **small**;
(= south) S
SA N ABBR = **South Africa; South America**
Sabbath ['sæbəθ] N domingo; (Jewish) sábado
sabbatical [sə'bætɪkl] ADJ: ~ **year** año
sabático
sabotage ['sæbətɑːʒ] N sabotaje m ▶ VT
sabotear
sabre, (US) **saber** ['seɪbəʳ] N sable m
saccharin, saccharine ['sækərɪn] N
sacarina
sachet ['sæʃeɪ] N sobrecito
sack [sæk] N (bag) saco, costal m ▶ VT (dismiss)
despedir, echar; (plunder) saquear; **to get the
~** ser despedido; **to give sb the ~** despedir or
echar a algn
sackful ['sækful] N saco
sacking ['sækɪŋ] N (material) arpillera
sacrament ['sækrəmənt] N sacramento
sacred ['seɪkrɪd] ADJ sagrado, santo
sacred cow N (fig) vaca sagrada
sacrifice ['sækrɪfaɪs] N sacrificio ▶ VT
sacrificar; **to make sacrifices (for sb)**
sacrificarse (por algn)
sacrilege ['sækrɪlɪdʒ] N sacrilegio
sacrosanct ['sækrəusæŋkt] ADJ sacrosanto
sad [sæd] ADJ (unhappy) triste; (deplorable)
lamentable
sadden ['sædn] VT entristecer
saddle ['sædl] N silla (de montar); (of cycle)
sillín m ▶ VT (horse) ensillar; **to ~ sb with sth**
(inf: task, bill, name) cargar a algn con algo;
(responsibility) gravar a algn con algo; **to be
saddled with sth** (inf) quedar cargado con
algo
saddlebag ['sædlbæg] N alforja
sadism ['seɪdɪzm] N sadismo
sadist ['seɪdɪst] N sádico(-a)
sadistic [sə'dɪstɪk] ADJ sádico
sadly ['sædlɪ] ADV tristemente; (regrettably)
desgraciadamente; **~ lacking (in)** muy
deficiente (en)

sadness ['sædnɪs] N tristeza
sado-masochism [seɪdəu'mæsəkɪzm] N
sadomasoquismo
sae ABBR (BRIT: = stamped addressed envelope)
sobre con las propias señas de uno y con sello
safari [sə'fɑːrɪ] N safari m
safari park N safari m
safe [seɪf] ADJ (out of danger) fuera de peligro;
(not dangerous, sure) seguro; (unharmed) ileso;
(trustworthy) digno de confianza ▶ N caja de
caudales, caja fuerte; **~ and sound** sano y
salvo; **(just) to be on the ~ side** para mayor
seguridad; **~ journey!** ¡buen viaje!; **it is ~
to say that …** se puede decir con confianza
que …
safe bet N apuesta segura; **it's a ~ she'll
turn up** seguro que viene
safe-breaker ['seɪfbreɪkəʳ] N (BRIT)
ladrón(-ona) m/f de cajas fuertes
safe-conduct [seɪf'kɔndʌkt] N
salvoconducto
safe-cracker ['seɪfkrækəʳ] N (US) = **safe-
breaker**
safe-deposit ['seɪfdɪpɔzɪt] N (vault) cámara
acorazada; (box) caja de seguridad or de
caudales
safeguard ['seɪfgɑːd] N protección f, garantía
▶ VT proteger, defender
safe haven N refugio
safekeeping ['seɪf'kiːpɪŋ] N custodia
safely ['seɪflɪ] ADV seguramente, con
seguridad; (without mishap) sin peligro;
I can ~ say puedo decir or afirmar con toda
seguridad; **to arrive ~** llegar bien
safeness ['seɪfnɪs] N seguridad f
safe passage N garantías fpl para marcharse
en libertad
safe sex N sexo seguro or sin riesgo
safety ['seɪftɪ] N seguridad f ▶ CPD de
seguridad; **road ~** seguridad f en carretera;
~ first! ¡precaución!
safety belt N cinturón m (de seguridad)
safety catch N seguro
safety net N red f (de seguridad)

safety pin N imperdible *m*, seguro (LAM)
safety valve N válvula de seguridad *or* de escape
saffron ['sæfrən] N azafrán *m*
sag [sæg] VI aflojarse
saga ['sɑːgə] N (History) saga; (fig) epopeya
sage [seɪdʒ] N (herb) salvia; (man) sabio
Sagittarius [sædʒɪ'tɛərɪəs] N Sagitario
sago ['seɪgəu] N sagú *m*
Sahara [sə'hɑːrə] N: **the ~ (Desert)** el (desierto del) Sáhara
Sahel [sæ'hɛl] N Sahel *m*
said [sɛd] PT, PP *of* **say**
Saigon [saɪ'gɔn] N Saigón *m*
sail [seɪl] N (on boat) vela ▸ VT (boat) gobernar ▸ VI (travel: ship) navegar; (: passenger) pasear en barco; (Sport) hacer vela; (set off: also: **to set sail**) zarpar; **to go for a ~** dar un paseo en barco; **they sailed into Copenhagen** arribaron a Copenhague
  ▸ **sail through** VT FUS (exam) aprobar fácilmente
sailboat ['seɪlbəut] N (US) velero, barco de vela
sailing ['seɪlɪŋ] N (Sport) vela; **to go ~** hacer vela
sailing boat N velero, barco de vela
sailing ship N barco de vela
sailor ['seɪləʳ] N marinero, marino
saint [seɪnt] N santo; **S~ John** San Juan
saintliness ['seɪntlɪnɪs] N santidad *f*
saintly ['seɪntlɪ] ADJ santo
sake [seɪk] N: **for the ~ of** por; **for the ~ of argument** digamos, es un decir; **art for art's ~** el arte por el arte
salad ['sæləd] N ensalada; **tomato ~** ensalada de tomate
salad bowl N ensaladera
salad cream N (BRIT) mayonesa
salad dressing N aliño
salad oil N aceite *m* para ensalada
salami [sə'lɑːmɪ] N salami *m*, salchichón *m*
salaried ['sælərɪd] ADJ asalariado
salary ['sælərɪ] N sueldo
salary earner N asalariado(-a)
salary scale N escala salarial
sale [seɪl] N venta; (at reduced prices) liquidación *f*, saldo; (auction) subasta; **sales** NPL (total amount sold) ventas *fpl*, facturación *f*; **"for ~"** "se vende"; **on ~** en venta; **on ~ or return** (goods) venta por reposición; **closing-down** *or* (US) **liquidation ~** liquidación *f*; **~ and lease back** venta y arrendamiento al vendedor
saleroom ['seɪlruːm] N sala de subastas
sales assistant N (BRIT) dependiente(-a) *m/f*
sales campaign N campaña de venta
sales clerk N (US) dependiente(-a) *m/f*
sales conference N conferencia de ventas

sales drive N promoción *f* de ventas
sales figures NPL cifras *fpl* de ventas
sales force N personal *m* de ventas
salesman ['seɪlzmən] N (irreg) vendedor *m*; (in shop) dependiente *m*; (representative) viajante *m*
sales manager N gerente *mf* de ventas
salesmanship ['seɪlzmənʃɪp] N arte *m* de vender
sales meeting N reunión *f* de ventas
salesperson ['seɪlzpəːsən] N vendedor(a) *m/f*, dependiente(-a) *mf*
sales rep N representante *mf*, agente *mf* comercial
sales tax N (US) = **purchase tax**
saleswoman ['seɪlzwumən] N (irreg) vendedora; (in shop) dependienta; (representative) viajante *f*
salient ['seɪlɪənt] ADJ (features, points) sobresaliente
saline ['seɪlaɪn] ADJ salino
saliva [sə'laɪvə] N saliva
sallow ['sæləu] ADJ cetrino
sally forth, sally out ['sælɪ-] VI salir, ponerse en marcha
salmon ['sæmən] N *pl inv* salmón *m*
salon ['sælɔn] N (hairdressing salon, beauty salon) salón *m*
saloon [sə'luːn] N (US) bar *m*, taberna; (BRIT Aut) (coche *m* de) turismo; (ship's lounge) cámara, salón *m*
SALT [sɔːlt] N ABBR (= Strategic Arms Limitation Talks/Treaty) tratado SALT
salt [sɔːlt] N sal *f* ▸ VT salar; (put salt on) poner sal en; **an old ~** un lobo de mar
  ▸ **salt away** VT (inf: money) ahorrar
salt cellar N salero
salt mine N mina de sal
saltwater ['sɔːltwɔːtəʳ] ADJ (fish etc) de agua salada, de mar
salty ['sɔːltɪ] ADJ salado
salubrious [sə'luːbrɪəs] ADJ sano; (fig: district etc) atractivo
salutary ['sæljutərɪ] ADJ saludable
salute [sə'luːt] N saludo; (of guns) salva ▸ VT saludar
salvage ['sælvɪdʒ] N (saving) salvamento, recuperación *f*; (things saved) objetos *mpl* salvados ▸ VT salvar
salvage vessel N buque *m* de salvamento
salvation [sæl'veɪʃən] N salvación *f*
Salvation Army N Ejército de Salvación
salve [sælv] N (cream etc) ungüento, bálsamo
salvo ['sælvəu] N (Mil) salva
Samaritan [sə'mærɪtən] N: **to call the Samaritans** llamar al teléfono de la esperanza
same [seɪm] ADJ mismo ▸ PRON: **the ~** el mismo (la misma); **the ~ book as** el mismo

libro que; **on the ~ day** el mismo día; **at the ~ time** (*at the same moment*) al mismo tiempo; (*yet*) sin embargo; **all** *or* **just the ~** sin embargo, aun así; **they're one and the ~** (*person*) son la misma persona; (*thing*) son iguales; **to do the ~ (as sb)** hacer lo mismo (que otro); **and the ~ to you!** ¡igualmente!; **~ here!** ¡yo también!; **the ~ again** (*in bar etc*) otro igual

sampan ['sæmpæn] N sampán m

sample ['saːmpl] N muestra ▸ VT (*food, wine*) probar; **to take a ~** tomar una muestra; **free ~** muestra gratuita

sanatorium [sænə'tɔːrɪəm] (*pl* **sanatoria** [-rɪə]) N (*BRIT*) sanatorio

sanctify ['sæŋktɪfaɪ] VT santificar

sanctimonious [sæŋktɪ'məʊnɪəs] ADJ santurrón(-ona)

sanction ['sæŋkʃən] N sanción f ▸ VT sancionar; **sanctions** NPL (*Pol*) sanciones fpl; **to impose economic sanctions on** *or* **against** imponer sanciones económicas a *or* contra

sanctity ['sæŋktɪtɪ] N (*gen*) santidad f; (*inviolability*) inviolabilidad f

sanctuary ['sæŋktjʊərɪ] N (*gen*) santuario; (*refuge*) asilo, refugio; (*for wildlife*) reserva

sand [sænd] N arena; (*beach*) playa; **sands** NPL playa sg de arena ▸ VT (*also*: **sand down**: *wood etc*) lijar

sandal ['sændl] N sandalia

sandalwood ['sændlwʊd] N sándalo

sandbag ['sændbæg] N saco de arena

sandblast ['sændblaːst] VT limpiar con chorro de arena

sandbox ['sændbɒks] N (*US*) = **sandpit**

sandcastle ['sændkaːsl] N castillo de arena

sand dune N duna

sander ['sændər] N pulidora

sandpaper ['sændpeɪpər] N papel m de lija

sandpit ['sændpɪt] N (*for children*) cajón m de arena

sandstone ['sændstəʊn] N piedra arenisca

sandstorm ['sændstɔːm] N tormenta de arena

sandwich ['sændwɪtʃ] N bocadillo (*SP*), sandwich m (*LAM*) ▸ VT (*also*: **sandwich in**) intercalar; **to be sandwiched between** estar apretujado entre; **cheese/ham ~** sandwich de queso/jamón

sandwich board N cartelón m

sandwich course N (*BRIT*) *programa que intercala períodos de estudio con prácticas profesionales*

sandy ['sændɪ] ADJ arenoso; (*colour*) rojizo

sane [seɪn] ADJ cuerdo, sensato

sang [sæŋ] PT *of* **sing**

sanitarium [sænɪ'tɛərɪəm] N (*US*) = **sanatorium**

sanitary ['sænɪtərɪ] ADJ (*system, arrangements*) sanitario; (*clean*) higiénico

sanitary towel, (*US*) **sanitary napkin** N paño higiénico, compresa

sanitation [sænɪ'teɪʃən] N (*in house*) servicios mpl higiénicos; (*in town*) servicio de desinfección

sanitation department N (*US*) departamento de limpieza y recogida de basuras

sanity ['sænɪtɪ] N cordura; (*of judgment*) sensatez f

sank [sæŋk] PT *of* **sink**

San Marino ['sænmə'riːnəʊ] N San Marino

Santa Claus [sæntə'klɔːz] N San Nicolás m, Papá Noel m

Santiago [sæntɪ'aːgəʊ] N (*also*: **Santiago de Chile**) Santiago (de Chile)

sap [sæp] N (*of plants*) savia ▸ VT (*strength*) minar, agotar

sapling ['sæplɪŋ] N árbol nuevo *or* joven

sapphire ['sæfaɪər] N zafiro

Saragossa [særə'gɒsə] N Zaragoza

sarcasm ['saːkæzm] N sarcasmo

sarcastic [saː'kæstɪk] ADJ sarcástico; **to be ~** ser sarcástico

sarcophagus [saː'kɒfəgəs] (*pl* **sarcophagi** [-gaɪ]) N sarcófago

sardine [saː'diːn] N sardina

Sardinia [saː'dɪnɪə] N Cerdeña

Sardinian [saː'dɪnɪən] ADJ, N sardo(-a) m/f

sardonic [saː'dɒnɪk] ADJ sardónico

sari ['saːrɪ] N sari m

SARS ['saːz] N ABBR (= *severe acute respiratory syndrome*) neumonía asiática, SARS m

SAS N ABBR (*BRIT Mil*: = *Special Air Service*) *cuerpo del ejército británico encargado de misiones clandestinas*

SASE N ABBR (*US*: = *self-addressed stamped envelope*) *sobre con las propias señas de uno y con sello*

sash [sæʃ] N faja

Sask. ABBR (*CANADA*) = **Saskatchewan**

SAT N ABBR (*US*) = **Scholastic Aptitude Test**

sat [sæt] PT, PP *of* **sit**

Sat. ABBR (= *Saturday*) sáb.

Satan ['seɪtn] N Satanás m

satanic [sə'tænɪk] ADJ satánico

satchel ['sætʃl] N bolsa; (*child's*) cartera, mochila (*LAM*)

sated ['seɪtɪd] ADJ (*appetite, person*) saciado

satellite ['sætəlaɪt] N satélite m

satellite dish N (antena) parabólica

satellite navigation system N sistema m de navegación por satélite

satellite television N televisión f por satélite

satiate ['seɪʃɪeɪt] VT saciar, hartar

satin ['sætɪn] N raso ▸ ADJ de raso; **with a ~ finish** satinado

S

satire ['sætaɪə^r] N sátira
satirical [sə'tɪrɪkl] ADJ satírico
satirist ['sætɪrɪst] N (writer etc) escritor(a) m/f satírico(-a); (cartoonist) caricaturista mf
satirize ['sætɪraɪz] VT satirizar
satisfaction [sætɪs'fækʃən] N satisfacción f; **it gives me great ~** es para mí una gran satisfacción; **has it been done to your ~?** ¿se ha hecho a su satisfacción?
satisfactorily [sætɪs'fæktərɪlɪ] ADV satisfactoriamente, de modo satisfactorio
satisfactory [sætɪs'fæktərɪ] ADJ satisfactorio
satisfied ['sætɪsfaɪd] ADJ satisfecho; **to be ~ (with sth)** estar satisfecho (de algo)
satisfy ['sætɪsfaɪ] VT satisfacer; (pay) liquidar; (convince) convencer; **to ~ the requirements** llenar los requisitos; **to ~ sb that** convencer a algn de que; **to ~ o.s. of sth** convencerse de algo
satisfying ['sætɪsfaɪɪŋ] ADJ satisfactorio
satnav ['sætnæv] N ABBR (= satellite navigation) navegador m (GPS)
satsuma [sæt'suːmə] N satsuma
saturate ['sætʃəreɪt] VT: **to ~ (with)** empapar or saturar (de)
saturated fat [sætʃəreɪtɪd-] N grasa saturada
saturation [sætʃə'reɪʃən] N saturación f
Saturday ['sætədɪ] N sábado; see also **Tuesday**
sauce [sɔːs] N salsa; (sweet) crema; (fig: cheek) frescura
saucepan ['sɔːspən] N cacerola, olla
saucer ['sɔːsə^r] N platillo
saucily ['sɔːsɪlɪ] ADV con frescura, descaradamente
sauciness ['sɔːsɪnɪs] N frescura, descaro
saucy ['sɔːsɪ] ADJ fresco, descarado
Saudi, Saudi Arabian ['saudɪ-] ADJ, N saudí mf, saudita mf
Saudi Arabia N Arabia Saudí or Saudita
sauna ['sɔːnə] N sauna
saunter ['sɔːntə^r] VI deambular
sausage ['sɔsɪdʒ] N salchicha; (salami etc) salchichón m
sausage roll N empanadilla de salchicha
sauté ['səuteɪ] ADJ (Culin: potatoes) salteado; (: onions) dorado, rehogado ▶ VT saltear; dorar
sautéed ['səuteɪd] ADJ salteado
savage ['sævɪdʒ] ADJ (cruel, fierce) feroz, furioso; (primitive) salvaje ▶ N salvaje mf ▶ VT (attack) embestir
savagely ['sævɪdʒlɪ] ADV con ferocidad, furiosamente; de modo salvaje
savagery ['sævɪdʒrɪ] N ferocidad f; salvajismo
save [seɪv] VT (rescue) salvar, rescatar; (money, time) ahorrar; (put by) guardar; (Comput) salvar, guardar; (avoid: trouble) evitar; (Sport)

parar ▶ VI (also: **save up**) ahorrar ▶ N (Sport) parada ▶ PREP salvo, excepto; **to ~ face** salvar las apariencias; **God ~ the Queen!** ¡Dios guarde a la Reina!, ¡Viva la Reina!; **I saved you a piece of cake** te he guardado un trozo de tarta; **it will ~ me an hour** con ello ganaré una hora
saving ['seɪvɪŋ] N (on price etc) economía ▶ ADJ: **the ~ grace of** el único mérito de; **savings** NPL ahorros mpl; **to make savings** economizar
savings account N cuenta de ahorros
savings and loan association N (US) sociedad f de ahorro y préstamo
savings bank N caja de ahorros
saviour, (US) **savior** ['seɪvjə^r] N salvador(a) m/f
savoir-faire ['sævwɑː'fɛə^r] N don m de gentes
savour, (US) **savor** ['seɪvə^r] N sabor m, gusto ▶ VT saborear
savoury, (US) **savory** ['seɪvərɪ] ADJ sabroso; (dish: not sweet) salado
savvy ['sævɪ] N (inf) conocimiento, experiencia
saw [sɔː] PT of **see** ▶ N (tool) sierra ▶ VT (pt **sawed,** pp **sawed** or **sawn** [sɔːn]) serrar; **to ~ sth up** (a)serrar algo
sawdust ['sɔːdʌst] N (a)serrín m
sawmill ['sɔːmɪl] N aserradero
sawn [sɔːn] PP of **saw**
sawn-off ['sɔːnɔf], (US) **sawed-off** ['sɔːdɔf] ADJ: **~ shotgun** escopeta de cañones recortados
saxophone ['sæksəfəun] N saxófono
say [seɪ] (pt, pp **said** [sɛd]) N: **to have one's ~** expresar su opinión ▶ VT, VI decir; **to have a** or **some ~ in sth** tener voz y voto en algo; **to ~ yes/no** decir que sí/no; **my watch says 3 o'clock** mi reloj marca las tres; **that is to ~** es decir; **that goes without saying** ni que decir tiene; **she said (that) I was to give you this** me pidió que te diera esto; **I should ~ it's worth about £100** yo diría que vale unas 100 libras; **~ after me** repite lo que yo diga; **shall we ~ Tuesday?** ¿quedamos, por ejemplo, el martes?; **that doesn't ~ much for him** eso no dice nada a su favor; **when all is said and done** al fin y al cabo, a fin de cuentas; **there is something** or **a lot to be said for it** hay algo or mucho que decir a su favor
saying ['seɪɪŋ] N dicho, refrán m
say-so ['seɪsəu] N (inf) autorización f
SBA N ABBR (US) = **Small Business Administration**
SC N ABBR (US) = **Supreme Court** ▶ ABBR (US) = **South Carolina**
s/c ABBR = **self-contained**
scab [skæb] N costra; (pej) esquirol(a) m/f

scaffold ['skæfəld] N (for execution) cadalso
scaffolding ['skæfəldɪŋ] N andamio, andamiaje m
scald [skɔːld] N escaldadura ▸ VT escaldar
scalding ['skɔːldɪŋ] ADJ (also: **scalding hot**) hirviendo, que arde
scale [skeɪl] N (gen) escala; (Mus) escala; (of fish) escama; (of salaries, fees etc) escalafón m ▸ VT (mountain) escalar; (tree) trepar; **scales** NPL (small) balanza sg; (large) báscula sg; **on a large ~** a gran escala; **~ of charges** tarifa, lista de precios; **pay ~** escala salarial; **to draw sth to ~** dibujar algo a escala
▸ **scale down** VT reducir
scaled-down [skeɪld'daun] ADJ reducido proporcionalmente
scale model N modelo a escala
scallion ['skæljən] N (US) cebolleta
scallop ['skɔləp] N (Zool) venera; (Sewing) festón m
scalp [skælp] N cabellera ▸ VT escalpar
scalpel ['skælpl] N bisturí m
scam [skæm] N (inf) estafa, timo
scamper ['skæmpər] VI **to ~ away, ~ off** escabullirse
scampi ['skæmpɪ] NPL gambas fpl
scan [skæn] VT (examine) escudriñar; (glance at quickly) dar un vistazo a; (TV, Radar) explorar, registrar; (Comput) escanear ▸ N (Med) examen m ultrasónico; **to have a ~** pasar por el escáner
scandal ['skændl] N escándalo; (gossip) chismes mpl
scandalize ['skændəlaɪz] VT escandalizar
scandalous ['skændələs] ADJ escandaloso
Scandinavia [skændɪ'neɪvɪə] N Escandinavia
Scandinavian [skændɪ'neɪvɪən] ADJ, N escandinavo(-a) m/f
scanner ['skænər] N (Radar, Med, Comput) escáner m
scant [skænt] ADJ escaso
scantily ['skæntɪlɪ] ADV: **~ clad** or **dressed** ligero de ropa
scantiness ['skæntɪnɪs] N escasez f, insuficiencia
scanty ['skæntɪ] ADJ (meal) insuficiente; (clothes) ligero
scapegoat ['skeɪpgəut] N cabeza de turco, chivo expiatorio
scar [skɑː] N cicatriz f ▸ VT marcar con una cicatriz ▸ VI cicatrizarse
scarce [skɛəs] ADJ escaso; **to make o.s. ~** (inf) esfumarse
scarcely ['skɛəslɪ] ADV apenas; **~ anybody** casi nadie; **I can ~ believe it** casi no puedo creerlo
scarceness ['skɛəsnɪs], **scarcity** ['skɛəsɪtɪ] N escasez f

scarcity value N valor m de escasez
scare [skɛər] N susto, sobresalto; (panic) pánico ▸ VT asustar, espantar; **to ~ sb stiff** dar a algn un susto de muerte; **bomb ~** amenaza de bomba
▸ **scare away, scare off** VT espantar, ahuyentar
scarecrow ['skɛəkrəu] N espantapájaros m inv
scared [skɛəd] ADJ: **to be ~** asustarse, estar asustado
scaremonger ['skɛəmʌŋgər] N alarmista mf
scarf [skɑːf] (pl **scarves** [skɑːvz]) N (long) bufanda; (square) pañuelo
scarlet ['skɑːlɪt] ADJ escarlata
scarlet fever N escarlatina
scarper ['skɑːpər] VI (BRIT inf) largarse
scarred [skɑːd] ADJ lleno de cicatrices
scarves [skɑːvz] NPL of **scarf**
scary ['skɛərɪ] ADJ (inf) de miedo; **it's ~** da miedo
scathing ['skeɪðɪŋ] ADJ mordaz; **to be ~ about sth** criticar algo duramente
scatter ['skætər] VT (spread) esparcir, desparramar; (put to flight) dispersar ▸ VI desparramarse; dispersarse
scatterbrained ['skætəbreɪnd] ADJ ligero de cascos
scavenge ['skævɪndʒ] VI: **to ~ (for)** (person) revolver entre la basura (para encontrar); **to ~ for food** (hyenas etc) nutrirse de carroña
scavenger ['skævɪndʒər] N (person) mendigo/a que rebusca en la basura; (Zool: animal) animal m de carroña; (: bird) ave f de carroña
SCE N ABBR = **Scottish Certificate of Education**
scenario [sɪ'nɑːrɪəu] N (Theat) argumento; (Cine) guión m; (fig) escenario
scene [siːn] N (Theat) escena; (of crime, accident) escenario; (sight, view) vista, panorama; (fuss) escándalo; **the political ~ in Spain** el panorama político español; **behind the scenes** (also fig) entre bastidores; **to appear** or **come on the ~** (also fig) aparecer, presentarse; **to make a ~** (inf: fuss) armar un escándalo
scenery ['siːnərɪ] N (Theat) decorado; (landscape) paisaje m
scenic ['siːnɪk] ADJ (picturesque) pintoresco
scent [sɛnt] N perfume m, olor m; (fig: track) rastro, pista; (sense of smell) olfato ▸ VT perfumar; (suspect) presentir; **to put** or **throw sb off the ~** (fig) despistar a algn
sceptic, (US) **skeptic** ['skɛptɪk] N escéptico(-a)
sceptical, (US) **skeptical** ['skɛptɪkl] ADJ escéptico
scepticism, (US) **skepticism** ['skɛptɪsɪzm] N escepticismo

S

sceptre, (US) **scepter** ['sɛptə'] N cetro
schedule ['ʃɛdjuːl, (US) 'skɛdjuːl] N (of trains) horario; (of events) programa m; (list) lista ▸ vT (timetable) establecer el horario de; (list) catalogar; (visit) fijar la hora de; **on ~ a la** hora, sin retraso; **to be ahead of/behind ~** ir adelantado/retrasado; **we are working to a very tight ~** tenemos un programa de trabajo muy apretado; **everything went according to ~** todo salió según lo previsto; **the meeting is scheduled for seven** or **to begin at seven** la reunión está fijada para las siete
scheduled ['ʃɛdjuːld, 'skɛdjuːld] (US) ADJ (date, time) fijado; (visit, event, bus, train) programado; (stop) previsto; **~ flight** vuelo regular
schematic [skɪ'mætɪk] ADJ (diagram etc) esquemático
scheme [skiːm] N (plan) plan m, proyecto; (method) esquema m; (plot) intriga; (trick) ardid m; (arrangement) disposición f; (pension scheme etc) sistema m ▸ vT proyectar ▸ vI (plan) hacer proyectos; (intrigue) intrigar; **colour ~** combinación f de colores
scheming ['skiːmɪŋ] ADJ intrigante
schism ['skɪzəm] N cisma m
schizophrenia [skɪtsəʊ'friːnɪə] N esquizofrenia
schizophrenic [skɪtsə'frɛnɪk] ADJ esquizofrénico
scholar ['skɒlə'] N (pupil) alumno(-a), estudiante mf; (learned person) sabio(-a), erudito(-a)
scholarly ['skɒləlɪ] ADJ erudito
scholarship ['skɒləʃɪp] N erudición f; (grant) beca
school [skuːl] N (gen) escuela, colegio; (in university) facultad f; (of fish) banco ▸ vT (animal) amaestrar; **to be at** or **go to ~** ir al colegio or a la escuela
school age N edad f escolar
schoolbook ['skuːlbuk] N libro de texto
schoolboy ['skuːlbɔɪ] N alumno
schoolchild ['skuːltʃaɪld] N (irreg) alumno(-a)
schooldays ['skuːldeɪz] NPL años mpl del colegio
schoolgirl ['skuːlgəːl] N alumna
schooling ['skuːlɪŋ] N enseñanza
school-leaver ['skuːlliːvə'] N (Brit) joven que ha terminado la educación secundaria
schoolmaster ['skuːlmɑːstə'] N (primary) maestro; (secondary) profesor m
schoolmistress ['skuːlmɪstrɪs] N (primary) maestra; (secondary) profesora
schoolroom ['skuːlrum] N clase f
schoolteacher ['skuːltiːtʃə'] N (primary) maestro(-a); (secondary) profesor(a) m/f

schoolyard ['skuːljɑːd] N (US) patio del colegio
schooner ['skuːnə'] N (ship) goleta
sciatica [saɪ'ætɪkə] N ciática
science ['saɪəns] N ciencia; **the sciences** las ciencias
science fiction N ciencia-ficción f
scientific [saɪən'tɪfɪk] ADJ científico
scientist ['saɪəntɪst] N científico(-a)
sci-fi ['saɪfaɪ] N ABBR (inf) = **science fiction**
Scilly Isles ['sɪlɪ-], **Scillies** ['sɪlɪz] NPL: **the ~** las Islas Sorlingas
scintillating ['sɪntɪleɪtɪŋ] ADJ (wit, conversation, company) brillante, chispeante, ingenioso
scissors ['sɪzəz] NPL tijeras fpl; **a pair of ~** unas tijeras
scoff [skɒf] vT (Brit inf: eat) engullir ▸ vI: **to ~ (at)** (mock) mofarse (de)
scold [skəʊld] vT regañar
scolding ['skəʊldɪŋ] N riña, reprimenda
scone [skɒn] N pastel de pan
scoop [skuːp] N cucharón m; (for flour etc) pala; (Press) exclusiva ▸ vT (Comm: market) adelantarse a; (: profit) sacar; (Comm, Press: competitors) adelantarse a
▸ **scoop out** vT excavar
▸ **scoop up** vT recoger
scooter ['skuːtə'] N (motor cycle) Vespa®; (toy) patinete m
scope [skəʊp] N (of plan, undertaking) ámbito; (reach) alcance m; (of person) competencia; (opportunity) libertad f (de acción); **there is plenty of ~ for improvement** hay bastante campo para efectuar mejoras
scorch [skɔːtʃ] vT (clothes) chamuscar; (earth, grass) quemar, secar
scorcher ['skɔːtʃə'] N (inf: hot day) día m abrasador
scorching ['skɔːtʃɪŋ] ADJ abrasador(a)
score [skɔː'] N (points etc) puntuación f; (Mus) partitura; (reckoning) cuenta; (twenty) veintena ▸ vT (goal, point) ganar; (mark, cut) rayar ▸ vI marcar un tanto; (Football) marcar un gol; (keep score) llevar el tanteo; **to keep (the) ~** llevar la cuenta; **to have an old ~ to settle with sb** (fig) tener cuentas pendientes con algn; **on that ~** en lo que se refiere a eso; **scores of people** (fig) muchísima gente, cantidad de gente; **to ~ 6 out of 10** obtener una puntuación de 6 sobre 10
▸ **score out** vT tachar
scoreboard ['skɔːbɔːd] N marcador m
scoreline ['skɔːlaɪn] N (Sport) resultado final
scorer ['skɔːrə'] N marcador(a) m/f; (keeping score) encargado(-a) del marcador
scorn [skɔːn] N desprecio ▸ vT despreciar
scornful ['skɔːnful] ADJ desdeñoso, despreciativo

scornfully ['skɔːnfʊlɪ] ADV desdeñosamente, con desprecio

Scorpio ['skɔːpɪəʊ] N Escorpión *m*

scorpion ['skɔːpɪən] N alacrán *m*, escorpión *m*

Scot [skɔt] N escocés(-esa) *m/f*

Scotch [skɔtʃ] N whisky *m* escocés

scotch [skɔtʃ] VT (*rumour*) desmentir; (*plan*) frustrar

Scotch tape® N (*US*) cinta adhesiva, celo, scotch® *m*

scot-free [skɔt'friː] ADV: **to get off ~** (*unpunished*) salir impune; (*unhurt*) salir ileso

Scotland ['skɔtlənd] N Escocia

Scots [skɔts] ADJ escocés(-esa)

Scotsman ['skɔtsmən] N (*irreg*) escocés *m*

Scotswoman ['skɔtswʊmən] N (*irreg*) escocesa

Scottish ['skɔtɪʃ] ADJ escocés(-esa); **the ~ National Party** partido político independista escocés; **the ~ Parliament** el Parlamento escocés

scoundrel ['skaʊndrəl] N canalla *mf*, sinvergüenza *mf*

scour ['skaʊə^r] VT (*clean*) fregar, estregar; (*search*) recorrer, registrar

scourer ['skaʊərə^r] N (*pad*) estropajo; (*powder*) limpiador *m*

scourge [skəːdʒ] N azote *m*

scout [skaʊt] N explorador *m*; **girl ~** (*US*) niña exploradora
▶ **scout around** VI reconocer el terreno

scowl [skaʊl] VI fruncir el ceño; **to ~ at sb** mirar con ceño a algn

scrabble ['skræbl] VI (*claw*): **to ~ (at)** arañar
▶ N: **S-**® Scrabble® *m*, Intelect® *m*; **to ~ around for sth** revolver todo buscando algo

scraggy ['skrægɪ] ADJ flaco, delgaducho

scram [skræm] VI (*inf*) largarse

scramble ['skræmbl] N (*climb*) subida (difícil); (*struggle*) pelea ▶ VI: **to ~ out/ through** salir/abrirse paso con dificultad; **to ~ for** pelear por; **to go scrambling** (*Sport*) hacer motocross

scrambled eggs ['skræmbld-] NPL huevos *mpl* revueltos

scrap [skræp] N (*bit*) pedacito; (*fig*) pizca; (*fight*) riña, bronca; (*also:* **scrap iron**) chatarra, hierro viejo ▶ VT (*discard*) desechar, descartar ▶ VI reñir, armar (una) bronca; **scraps** NPL (*waste*) sobras *fpl*, desperdicios *mpl*; **to sell sth for ~** vender algo como chatarra

scrapbook ['skræpbʊk] N álbum *m* de recortes

scrap dealer N chatarrero(-a)

scrape [skreɪp] N (*fig*) lío, apuro ▶ VT raspar; (*skin etc*) rasguñar; (*also:* **scrape against**) rozar; **to get into a ~** meterse en un lío
▶ **scrape through** VI (*succeed*) salvarse por los pelos; (*in exam*) aprobar por los pelos

scraper ['skreɪpə^r] N raspador *m*

scrap heap N (*fig*): **on the ~** desperdiciado; **to throw sth on the ~** desechar *or* descartar algo

scrap iron N chatarra

scrap merchant N (*BRIT*) chatarrero(-a)

scrap metal N chatarra, desecho de metal

scrap paper N pedazos *mpl* de papel

scrappy ['skræpɪ] ADJ (*essay etc*) deshilvanado; (*education*) incompleto

scrap yard N depósito de chatarra; (*for cars*) cementerio de coches

scratch [skrætʃ] N rasguño; (*from claw*) arañazo ▶ ADJ: **~ team** equipo improvisado ▶ VT (*paint, car*) rayar; (*with claw, nail*) rasguñar, arañar; (*Comput*) borrar ▶ VI rascarse; **to start from ~** partir de cero; **to be up to ~** cumplir con los requisitos

scratch card N (*BRIT*) tarjeta *f* de "rasque y gane"

scratchpad ['skrætʃpæd] N (*US*) bloc *m* de notas

scrawl [skrɔːl] N garabatos *mpl* ▶ VI hacer garabatos

scrawny ['skrɔːnɪ] ADJ (*person, neck*) flaco

scream [skriːm] N chillido ▶ VI chillar; **it was a ~** (*fig, inf*) fue para morirse de risa *or* muy divertido; **he's a ~** (*fig, inf*) es muy divertido *or* de lo más gracioso; **to ~ at sb (to do sth)** gritarle a algn (para que haga algo)

scree [skriː] N cono de desmoronamiento

screech [skriːtʃ] VI chirriar

screen [skriːn] N (*Cine, TV*) pantalla; (*movable*) biombo; (*wall*) tabique *m*; (*also:* **windscreen**) parabrisas *m inv* ▶ VT (*conceal*) tapar; (*from the wind etc*) proteger; (*film*) proyectar; (*fig: person: for security*) investigar; (: *for illness*) hacer una exploración a

screen editing N (*Comput*) corrección *f* en pantalla

screenful ['skriːnfʊl] N pantalla

screening ['skriːnɪŋ] N (*of film*) proyección *f*; (*for security*) investigación *f*; (*Med*) exploración *f*

screen memory N (*Comput*) memoria de la pantalla

screenplay ['skriːnpleɪ] N guión *m*

screen saver [-seɪvə^r] N (*Comput*) salvapantallas *m inv*

screenshot ['skriːnʃɔt] N (*Comput*) pantallazo, captura de pantalla

screen test N prueba de pantalla

screw [skruː] N tornillo; (*propeller*) hélice *f* ▶ VT atornillar; **to ~ sth to the wall** fijar algo a la pared con tornillos
▶ **screw up** VT (*paper, material etc*) arrugar; (*inf: ruin*) fastidiar; **to ~ up one's eyes** arrugar el entrecejo; **to ~ up one's face** torcer *or* arrugar la cara

S

screwdriver ['skru:draɪvəʳ] N destornillador m

screwed-up ['skru:d'ʌp] ADJ (inf): **she's totally ~** está trastornada

screwy ['skru:ɪ] ADJ (inf) chiflado

scribble ['skrɪbl] N garabatos mpl ▶ VI garabatear ▶ VT escribir con prisa; **to ~ sth down** garabatear algo

script [skrɪpt] N (Cine etc) guión m; (writing) escritura, letra

scripted ['skrɪptɪd] ADJ (Radio, TV) escrito

Scripture ['skrɪptʃəʳ] N Sagrada Escritura

scriptwriter ['skrɪptraɪtəʳ] N guionista mf

scroll [skrəul] N rollo ▶ VT (Comput) desplazar

scrotum ['skrəutəm] N escroto

scrounge [skraundʒ] (inf) VT: **to ~ sth off** or **from sb** gorronear algo a algn ▶ VI: **to ~ on sb** vivir a costa de algn

scrounger ['skraundʒəʳ] N gorrón(-ona) m/f

scrub [skrʌb] N (clean) fregado; (land) maleza ▶ VT fregar, restregar; (reject) cancelar, anular

scrubbing brush ['skrʌbɪŋ-] N cepillo de fregar

scruff [skrʌf] N: **by the ~ of the neck** por el pescuezo

scruffy ['skrʌfɪ] ADJ desaliñado, desaseado

scrum ['skrʌm], **scrummage** ['skrʌmɪdʒ] N (Rugby) melé f

scruple ['skru:pl] N escrúpulo; **to have no scruples about doing sth** no tener reparos en or escrúpulos para hacer algo

scrupulous ['skru:pjuləs] ADJ escrupuloso

scrupulously ['skru:pjuləslɪ] ADV escrupulosamente; **to be ~ fair/honest** ser sumamente justo/honesto

scrutinize ['skru:tɪnaɪz] VT escudriñar; (votes) escrutar

scrutiny ['skru:tɪnɪ] N escrutinio, examen m; **under the ~ of sb** bajo la mirada or el escrutinio de algn

scuba ['sku:bə] N escafandra autónoma

scuba diving ['sku:bə'daɪvɪŋ] N submarinismo

scuff [skʌf] VT (shoes, floor) rayar

scuffle ['skʌfl] N refriega

scullery ['skʌlərɪ] N trascocina

sculptor ['skʌlptəʳ] N escultor(a) m/f

sculpture ['skʌlptʃəʳ] N escultura

scum [skʌm] N (on liquid) espuma; (pej: people) escoria

scupper ['skʌpəʳ] VT (boat) hundir; (BRIT fig: plans etc) acabar con

scurrilous ['skʌrɪləs] ADJ difamatorio, calumnioso

scurry ['skʌrɪ] VI: **to ~ off** escabullirse

scurvy ['skə:vɪ] N escorbuto

scuttle ['skʌtl] N (also: **coal scuttle**) cubo, carbonera ▶ VT (ship) barrenar ▶ VI (scamper): **to ~ away, ~ off** escabullirse

scythe [saɪð] N guadaña

SD, S. Dak. ABBR (US) = **South Dakota**

SDI N ABBR (= Strategic Defense Initiative) IDE f

SDLP N ABBR (BRIT Pol) = **Social Democratic and Labour Party**

sea [si:] N mar m or f; **by ~ (travel)** en barco; **on the ~ (boat)** en el mar; (town) junto al mar; **to be all at ~ (fig)** estar despistado; **out to** or **at ~** en alta mar; **to go by ~** ir en barco; **heavy** or **rough seas** marejada; **by** or **beside the ~ (holiday)** en la playa; (village) a orillas del mar; **a ~ of faces** una multitud de caras

sea bed N fondo del mar

sea bird N ave f marina

seaboard ['si:bɔ:d] N litoral m

sea breeze N brisa de mar

seadog ['si:dɔg] N lobo de mar

seafarer ['si:fɛərəʳ] N marinero

seafaring ['si:fɛərɪŋ] ADJ (community) marinero; (life) de marinero

seafood ['si:fu:d] N mariscos mpl

sea front N (beach) playa; (prom) paseo marítimo

seagoing ['si:gəuɪŋ] ADJ (ship) de alta mar

seagull ['si:gʌl] N gaviota

seal [si:l] N (animal) foca; (stamp) sello ▶ VT (close) cerrar; (: with seal) sellar; (decide: sb's fate) decidir; (: bargain) cerrar; **~ of approval** sello de aprobación
▶ **seal off** VT obturar

seal cull N matanza de crías de foca

sea level N nivel m del mar

sealing wax ['si:lɪŋ-] N lacre m

sea lion N león m marino

sealskin ['si:lskɪn] N piel f de foca

seam [si:m] N costura; (of metal) juntura; (of coal) veta, filón m; **the hall was bursting at the seams** la sala rebosaba de gente

seaman ['si:mən] N (irreg) marinero

seamanship ['si:mənʃɪp] N náutica

seamy ['si:mɪ] ADJ sórdido

seance ['seɪɔns] N sesión f de espiritismo

seaplane ['si:pleɪn] N hidroavión m

seaport ['si:pɔ:t] N puerto de mar

search [sə:tʃ] N (for person, thing) busca, búsqueda; (of drawer, pockets) registro; (inspection) reconocimiento ▶ VT (look in) buscar en; (examine) examinar; (person, place) registrar; (Comput) buscar ▶ VI: **to ~ for** buscar; **in ~ of** en busca de; **"~ and replace"** (Comput) "buscar y reemplazar"
▶ **search through** VT FUS registrar

search engine N (Internet) buscador m

searcher ['sə:tʃəʳ] N buscador(a) m/f

searching ['sə:tʃɪŋ] ADJ (question) penetrante

searchlight ['sə:tʃlaɪt] N reflector m

search party N equipo de salvamento

search warrant N mandamiento judicial

searing ['sɪərɪŋ] ADJ (heat) abrasador(a); (pain) agudo

seashore ['si:ʃɔ:] N playa, orilla del mar;
on the ~ a la orilla del mar

seasick ['si:sɪk] ADJ mareado; **to be ~**
marearse

seaside ['si:saɪd] N playa, orilla del mar;
to go to the ~ ir a la playa

seaside resort N centro turístico costero

season ['si:zn] N (of year) estación f; (sporting
etc) temporada; (gen) época, período ▶ VT
(food) sazonar; **to be in/out of ~** estar en
sazón/fuera de temporada; **the busy ~** (for
shops, hotels etc) la temporada alta; **the open
~** (Hunting) la temporada de caza or de pesca

seasonal ['si:znl] ADJ estacional

seasoned ['si:znd] ADJ (wood) curado; (fig:
worker, actor) experimentado; (troops) curtido;
~ campaigner veterano(-a)

seasoning ['si:znɪŋ] N condimento

season ticket N abono

seat [si:t] N (in bus, train: place) asiento; (chair)
silla; (Parliament) escaño; (buttocks) trasero;
(centre: of government etc) sede f ▶ VT sentar;
(have room for) tener cabida para; **are there
any seats left?** ¿quedan plazas?; **to take
one's ~** sentarse, tomar asiento; **to be
seated** estar sentado, sentarse

seat belt N cinturón m de seguridad

seating ['si:tɪŋ] N asientos mpl

seating arrangements NPL distribución fsg
de los asientos

seating capacity N número de asientos,
aforo

SEATO ['si:təu] N ABBR (= Southeast Asia Treaty
Organization) OTASE f

sea water N agua m del mar

seaweed ['si:wi:d] N alga marina

seaworthy ['si:wə:ðɪ] ADJ en condiciones
de navegar

SEC N ABBR (US: = Securities and Exchange
Commission) comisión de operaciones bursátiles

sec. ABBR = **second**

secateurs [sɛkə'tə:z] NPL podadera sg

secede [sɪ'si:d] VI: **to ~ (from)** separarse (de)

secluded [sɪ'klu:dɪd] ADJ retirado

seclusion [sɪ'klu:ʒən] N retiro

second ['sɛkənd] ADV (in race
etc) en segundo lugar ▶ N (gen) segundo; (Aut:
also: **second gear**) segunda; (Comm) artículo
con algún desperfecto; (Brit Scol: degree)
título universitario de segunda clase ▶ VT
(motion) apoyar; [sɪ'kɔnd] (employee) trasladar
temporalmente; **~ floor** (Brit) segundo piso;
(US) primer piso; **Charles the S~** Carlos
Segundo; **to ask for a ~ opinion** (Med) pedir
una segunda opinión; **just a ~!** ¡un
momento!; **to have ~ thoughts** cambiar de
opinión; **on ~ thoughts** or (US) **thought**
pensándolo bien; **~ mortgage** segunda
hipoteca

secondary ['sɛkəndərɪ] ADJ secundario

secondary education N enseñanza
secundaria

secondary school N escuela secundaria

second-best [sɛkənd'bɛst] N segundo

second-class ['sɛkənd'klɑ:s] ADJ de segunda
clase ▶ ADV: **to send sth ~** enviar algo por
correo de segunda clase; **to travel ~** viajar
en segunda; **~ citizen** ciudadano(-a) de
segunda (clase)

second cousin N primo(-a) segundo(-a)

seconder ['sɛkəndər] N el (la) que apoya una
moción

second-guess ['sɛkənd'gɛs] VT (evaluate)
juzgar (a posteriori); (anticipate): **to ~ sth/sb**
(intentar) adivinar algo/lo que va a hacer
algn

secondhand ['sɛkənd'hænd] ADJ de segunda
mano, usado ▶ ADV: **to buy sth ~** comprar
algo de segunda mano; **to hear sth ~** oír
algo indirectamente

second hand N (on clock) segundero

second-in-command ['sɛkəndɪnkə'mɑ:nd]
N (Mil) segundo en el mando; (Admin)
segundo(-a), ayudante mf

secondly ['sɛkəndlɪ] ADV en segundo lugar

secondment [sɪ'kɔndmənt] N (Brit) traslado
temporal

second-rate ['sɛkənd'reɪt] ADJ de segunda
categoría

secrecy ['si:krəsɪ] N secreto

secret ['si:krɪt] ADJ, N secreto; **in ~** adv en
secreto; **to keep sth ~ (from sb)** ocultarle
algo (a algn); **to make no ~ of sth** no ocultar
algo

secret agent N agente mf secreto(-a), espía mf

secretarial [sɛkrɪ'tɛərɪəl] ADJ (course) de
secretariado; (staff) de secretaría; (work,
duties) de secretaria

secretariat [sɛkrɪ'tɛərɪət] N secretaría

secretary ['sɛkrətərɪ] N secretario(-a); **S~ of
State** (Brit Pol) Ministro (con cartera)

secretary-general ['sɛkrətərɪ'dʒɛnərl] N
secretario(-a) general

secretary pool N (US) = **typing pool**

secrete [sɪ'kri:t] VT (Med, Anat, Biol) secretar;
(hide) ocultar, esconder

secretion [sɪ'kri:ʃən] N secreción f

secretive ['si:krətɪv] ADJ reservado, sigiloso

secretly ['si:krɪtlɪ] ADV en secreto

secret police N policía secreta

secret service N servicio secreto

sect [sɛkt] N secta

sectarian [sɛk'tɛərɪən] ADJ sectario

section ['sɛkʃən] N sección f; (part) parte f;
(of document) artículo; (of opinion) sector m;
business ~ (Press) sección f de economía

sectional ['sɛkʃənl] ADJ (regional) regional,
local

sector ['sɛktər] N sector m
secular ['sɛkjulər] ADJ secular, seglar
secure [sɪ'kjuər] ADJ (free from anxiety) seguro; (firmly fixed) firme, fijo ▶ VT (fix) asegurar, afianzar; (get) conseguir; (Comm: loan) garantizar; **to make sth ~** afianzar algo; **to ~ sth for sb** conseguir algo para algn
secured creditor [sɪ'kjuəd-] N acreedor(a) m/f con garantía
securely [sɪ'kjuəlɪ] ADV firmemente; **it is ~ fastened** está bien sujeto
security [sɪ'kjuərɪtɪ] N seguridad f; (for loan) fianza; (: object) prenda; **securities** NPL (Comm) valores mpl, títulos mpl; **~ of tenure** tenencia asegurada; **to increase/tighten ~** aumentar/estrechar las medidas de seguridad; **job ~** seguridad f en el empleo
Security Council N: **the ~** el Consejo de Seguridad
security forces NPL fuerzas fpl de seguridad
security guard N guardia mf de seguridad
security risk N riesgo para la seguridad
secy. ABBR (= secretary) Sec.
sedan [sɪ'dæn] N (US Aut) sedán m
sedate [sɪ'deɪt] ADJ tranquilo ▶ VT administrar sedantes a, sedar
sedation [sɪ'deɪʃən] N (Med) sedación f; **to be under ~** estar bajo sedación
sedative ['sɛdɪtɪv] N sedante m, calmante m
sedentary ['sɛdntrɪ] ADJ sedentario
sediment ['sɛdɪmənt] N sedimento
sedimentary [sɛdɪ'mɛntərɪ] ADJ (Geo) sedimentario
sedition [sɪ'dɪʃən] N sedición f
seduce [sɪ'djuːs] VT (gen) seducir
seduction [sɪ'dʌkʃən] N seducción f
seductive [sɪ'dʌktɪv] ADJ seductor(-a)
see [siː] (pt **saw**, pp **seen**) VT (gen) ver; (understand) ver, comprender; (look at) mirar ▶ VI ver ▶ N sede f; **to ~ sb to the door** acompañar a algn a la puerta; **to ~ that** (ensure) asegurarse de que; **~ you soon/later/tomorrow!** ¡hasta pronto/luego/mañana!; **as far as I can ~** por lo visto or por lo que veo; **there was nobody to be seen** no se veía a nadie; **let me ~** (show me) a ver; (let me think) vamos a ver; **to go and ~ sb** ir a ver a algn; **~ for yourself** compruébalo tú mismo; **I don't know what she sees in him** no sé qué le encuentra
▶ **see about** VT FUS atender a, encargarse de
▶ **see off** VT despedir
▶ **see out** VT (take to the door) acompañar hasta la puerta
▶ **see through** VT FUS calar ▶ VT llevar a cabo
▶ **see to** VT FUS atender a, encargarse de
seed [siːd] N semilla; (in fruit) pepita; (fig) germen m; (Tennis) preseleccionado(-a); **to go to ~** (plant) granar; (fig) descuidarse

seedless ['siːdlɪs] ADJ sin semillas or pepitas
seedling ['siːdlɪŋ] N planta de semillero
seedy ['siːdɪ] ADJ (person) desaseado; (place) sórdido
seeing ['siːɪŋ] CONJ: **~ (that)** visto que, en vista de que
seek [siːk] (pt, pp **sought** [sɔːt]) VT (gen) buscar; (post) solicitar; **to ~ advice/help from sb** pedir consejos/solicitar ayuda a algn
▶ **seek out** VT (person) buscar
seem [siːm] VI parecer; **there seems to be … ** parece que hay …; **it seems (that) …** parece que …; **what seems to be the trouble?** ¿qué pasa?; **I did what seemed best** hice lo que parecía mejor
seemingly ['siːmɪŋlɪ] ADV aparentemente, según parece
seen [siːn] PP of **see**
seep [siːp] VI filtrarse
seer [sɪər] N vidente mf, profeta mf
seersucker ['sɪə'sʌkər] N sirsaca
seesaw ['siːsɔː] N balancín m, subibaja m
seethe [siːð] VI hervir; **to ~ with anger** enfurecerse
see-through ['siːθruː] ADJ transparente
segment ['sɛgmənt] N segmento; (of citrus fruit) gajo
segregate ['sɛgrɪgeɪt] VT segregar
segregation [sɛgrɪ'geɪʃən] N segregación f
Seine [seɪn] N Sena m
seismic ['saɪzmɪk] ADJ sísmico
seize [siːz] VT (grasp) agarrar, asir; (take possession of) secuestrar; (: territory) apoderarse de; (opportunity) aprovecharse de
▶ **seize up** VI (Tech) agarrotarse
▶ **seize (up)on** VT FUS valerse de
seizure ['siːʒər] N (Med) ataque m; (Law) incautación f
seldom ['sɛldəm] ADV rara vez
select [sɪ'lɛkt] ADJ selecto, escogido; (hotel, restaurant, clubs) exclusivo ▶ VT escoger, elegir; (Sport) seleccionar; **a ~ few** una minoría selecta
selection [sɪ'lɛkʃən] N selección f, elección f; (Comm) surtido
selection committee N comisión f de nombramiento
selective [sɪ'lɛktɪv] ADJ selectivo
self [sɛlf] N (pl **selves** [sɛlvz]) uno mismo
▶ PREF auto…; **the ~** el yo
self-addressed ['sɛlfə'drɛst] ADJ: **~ envelope** sobre m con la dirección propia
self-adhesive [sɛlfəd'hiːzɪv] ADJ autoadhesivo, autoadherente
self-appointed [sɛlfə'pɔɪntɪd] ADJ autonombrado
self-assurance [sɛlfə'ʃuərəns] N confianza en sí mismo

self-assured [sɛlfə'ʃuəd] ADJ seguro de sí mismo

self-catering [sɛlf'keɪtərɪŋ] ADJ (BRIT) sin pensión or servicio de comida; **~ apartment** apartamento con cocina propia

self-centred, (US) **self-centered** [sɛlf'sɛntəd] ADJ egocéntrico

self-cleaning [sɛlf'kli:nɪŋ] ADJ autolimpiador

self-confessed [sɛlfkən'fɛst] ADJ (alcoholic etc) confeso

self-confidence [sɛlf'kɒnfɪdns] N confianza en sí mismo

self-confident [sɛlf'kɒnfɪdnt] ADJ seguro de sí (mismo), lleno de confianza en sí mismo

self-conscious [sɛlf'kɒnʃəs] ADJ cohibido

self-contained [sɛlfkən'teɪnd] ADJ (gen) independiente; (BRIT: flat) con entrada particular

self-control [sɛlfkən'trəul] N autodominio

self-defeating [sɛlfdɪ'fi:tɪŋ] ADJ contraproducente

self-defence, (US) **self-defense** [sɛlfdɪ'fɛns] N defensa propia

self-discipline [sɛlf'dɪsɪplɪn] N autodisciplina

self-employed [sɛlfɪm'plɔɪd] ADJ que trabaja por cuenta propia, autónomo

self-esteem [sɛlfɪ'sti:m] N amor m propio

self-evident [sɛlf'ɛvɪdnt] ADJ patente

self-explanatory [sɛlfɪks'plænətərɪ] ADJ que no necesita explicación

self-financing [sɛlffaɪ'nænsɪŋ] ADJ autofinanciado

self-governing [sɛlf'ɡʌvənɪŋ] ADJ autónomo

self-harm [sɛlf'hɑ:m] VI autolesionarse ▶ N autolesión f

self-help [sɛlf'hɛlp] N autosuficiencia, ayuda propia

self-importance [sɛlfɪm'pɔ:tns] N presunción f, vanidad f

self-important [sɛlfɪm'pɔ:tnt] ADJ vanidoso

self-indulgent [sɛlfɪn'dʌldʒənt] ADJ indulgente consigo mismo

self-inflicted [sɛlfɪn'flɪktɪd] ADJ infligido a sí mismo

self-interest [sɛlf'ɪntrɪst] N egoísmo

selfish ['sɛlfɪʃ] ADJ egoísta

selfishly ['sɛlfɪʃlɪ] ADV con egoísmo, de modo egoísta

selfishness ['sɛlfɪʃnɪs] N egoísmo

selfless ['sɛlflɪs] ADJ desinteresado

selflessly ['sɛlflɪslɪ] ADV desinteresadamente

self-made man ['sɛlfmeɪd-] N (irreg) hombre m hecho a sí mismo

self-pity [sɛlf'pɪtɪ] N lástima de sí mismo

self-portrait [sɛlf'pɔ:treɪt] N autorretrato

self-possessed [sɛlfpə'zɛst] ADJ sereno, dueño de sí mismo

self-preservation ['sɛlfprɛzə'veɪʃən] N propia conservación f

self-propelled [sɛlfprə'pɛld] ADJ autopropulsado, automotor(-triz)

self-raising [sɛlf'reɪzɪŋ], (US) **self-rising** [sɛlf'raɪzɪŋ] ADJ: **~ flour** harina con levadura

self-reliant [sɛlfrɪ'laɪənt] ADJ independiente, autosuficiente

self-respect [sɛlfrɪ'spɛkt] N amor m propio

self-respecting [sɛlfrɪ'spɛktɪŋ] ADJ que tiene amor propio

self-righteous [sɛlf'raɪtʃəs] ADJ santurrón(-ona)

self-rising [sɛlf'raɪzɪŋ] ADJ (US) = **self-raising**

self-sacrifice [sɛlf'sækrɪfaɪs] N abnegación f

self-same [sɛlfseɪm] ADJ mismo, mismísimo

self-satisfied [sɛlf'sætɪsfaɪd] ADJ satisfecho de sí mismo

self-service [sɛlf'sə:vɪs] ADJ de autoservicio

self-styled ['sɛlfstaɪld] ADJ supuesto, sedicente

self-sufficient [sɛlfsə'fɪʃənt] ADJ autosuficiente

self-supporting [sɛlfsə'pɔ:tɪŋ] ADJ económicamente independiente

self-tanning [sɛlf'tænɪŋ] ADJ autobronceador

self-taught [sɛlf'tɔ:t] ADJ autodidacta

self-test ['sɛlftɛst] N (Comput) autocomprobación f

sell [sɛl] (pt, pp **sold** [səuld]) VT vender ▶ VI venderse; **to ~ at** or **for £10** venderse a 10 libras; **to ~ sb an idea** (fig) convencer a algn de una idea
  ▶ **sell off** VT liquidar
  ▶ **sell out** VI transigir, transar (LAM); **to ~ out (to sb/sth)** (Comm) vender su negocio (a algn/algo) ▶ VT agotar las existencias de, venderlo todo; **the tickets are all sold out** las entradas están agotadas
  ▶ **sell up** VI (Comm) liquidarse

sell-by date ['sɛlbaɪ-] N fecha de caducidad

seller ['sɛləʳ] N vendedor(a) m/f; **~'s market** mercado de demanda

selling price ['sɛlɪŋ-] N precio de venta

Sellotape® ['sɛləuteɪp] N (BRIT) cinta adhesiva, celo, scotch® m

sellout ['sɛlaut] N traición f; **it was a ~** (Theat etc) fue un éxito de taquilla

selves [sɛlvz] NPL of **self**

semantic [sɪ'mæntɪk] ADJ semántico

semaphore ['sɛməfɔ:ʳ] N semáforo

semblance ['sɛmbləns] N apariencia

semen ['si:mən] N semen m

semester [sɪ'mɛstəʳ] N (US) semestre m

semi ['sɛmɪ] N = **semidetached**

semi... [sɛmɪ] PREF semi..., medio...

semicircle ['sɛmɪsə:kl] N semicírculo

semicircular ['sɛmɪ'sə:kjuləʳ] ADJ semicircular

S

semicolon [ˈsɛmɪˈkəʊlən] N punto y coma
semiconductor [ˈsɛmɪkənˈdʌktəʳ] N semiconductor *m*
semiconscious [ˈsɛmɪˈkɒnʃəs] ADJ semiconsciente
semidetached [ˈsɛmɪdɪˈtætʃt], **semidetached house** N casa adosada
semi-final [ˈsɛmɪˈfaɪnl] N semifinal *f*
seminar [ˈsɛmɪnɑːʳ] N seminario
seminary [ˈsɛmɪnərɪ] N (Rel) seminario
semiprecious stone [ˈsɛmɪˈprɛʃəs-] N piedra semipreciosa
semiquaver [ˈsɛmɪkweɪvəʳ] N (BRIT) semicorchea
semiskilled [ˈsɛmɪskɪld] ADJ (work, worker) semicualificado
semi-skimmed [ˈsɛmɪˈskɪmd] ADJ semidesnatado
semi-skimmed (milk) N leche semidesnatada
semitone [ˈsɛmɪtəʊn] N semitono
semolina [ˌsɛməˈliːnə] N sémola
Sen., sen. ABBR = **senator**; **senior**
senate [ˈsɛnɪt] N senado; *see also* **Congress**
senator [ˈsɛnɪtəʳ] N senador(a) *m/f*
send [sɛnd] (pt, pp **sent** [sɛnt]) VT mandar, enviar; **to ~ by post** mandar por correo; **to ~ sb for sth** mandar a algn a buscar algo; **to ~ word that ...** avisar *or* mandar aviso de que ...; **she sends (you) her love** te manda *or* envía cariñosos recuerdos; **to ~ sb to sleep/into fits of laughter** dormir/hacer reír a algn; **to ~ sb flying** echar a algn; **to ~ sth flying** tirar algo
▸ **send away** VT (letter, goods) despachar
▸ **send away for** VT FUS pedir
▸ **send back** VT devolver
▸ **send for** VT FUS mandar traer; (by post) escribir pidiendo algo
▸ **send in** VT (report, application, resignation) mandar
▸ **send off** VT (goods) despachar; (BRIT Sport: player) expulsar
▸ **send on** VT (letter, luggage) remitir
▸ **send out** VT (invitation) mandar; (emit: light, heat) emitir, difundir; (: signal) emitir
▸ **send round** VT (letter, document etc) hacer circular
▸ **send up** VT (person, price) hacer subir; (BRIT: parody) parodiar
sender [ˈsɛndəʳ] N remitente *mf*
send-off [ˈsɛndɔf] N: **a good ~** una buena despedida
send-up [ˈsɛndʌp] N (inf) parodia, sátira
Senegal [sɛnɪˈɡɔːl] N Senegal *m*
Senegalese [sɛnɪɡəˈliːz] ADJ, N senegalés(-esa) *m/f*
senile [ˈsiːnaɪl] ADJ senil
senility [sɪˈnɪlɪtɪ] N senilidad *f*

senior [ˈsiːnɪəʳ] ADJ (older) mayor, más viejo; (on staff) de más antigüedad; (of higher rank) superior ▸ N mayor *m*; **P. Jones ~** P. Jones padre
senior citizen N persona de la tercera edad
senior high school N (US) ≈ instituto de enseñanza media; *see also* **high school**
seniority [siːnɪˈɒrɪtɪ] N antigüedad *f*; (in rank) rango superior
sensation [sɛnˈseɪʃən] N (physical feeling, impression) sensación *f*
sensational [sɛnˈseɪʃənl] ADJ sensacional
sense [sɛns] N (faculty, meaning) sentido; (feeling) sensación *f*; (good sense) sentido común, juicio ▸ VT sentir, percibir; **~ of humour** sentido del humor; **it makes ~** tiene sentido; **there is no ~ in (doing) that** no tiene sentido (hacer) eso; **to come to one's senses** (regain consciousness) volver en sí, recobrar el sentido; **to take leave of one's senses** perder el juicio
senseless [ˈsɛnslɪs] ADJ estúpido, insensato; (unconscious) sin conocimiento
senselessly [ˈsɛnslɪslɪ] ADV estúpidamente, insensatamente
sense of humour N (BRIT) sentido del humor
sensibility [sɛnsɪˈbɪlɪtɪ] N sensibilidad *f*; **sensibilities** NPL delicadeza *sg*
sensible [ˈsɛnsɪbl] ADJ sensato; (reasonable) razonable, lógico
sensibly [ˈsɛnsɪblɪ] ADV sensatamente; razonablemente, de modo lógico
sensitive [ˈsɛnsɪtɪv] ADJ sensible; (touchy) susceptible; **he is very ~ about it** es muy susceptible acerca de eso
sensitivity [sɛnsɪˈtɪvɪtɪ] N sensibilidad *f*; susceptibilidad *f*
sensual [ˈsɛnsjuəl] ADJ sensual
sensuous [ˈsɛnsjuəs] ADJ sensual
sent [sɛnt] PT, PP of **send**
sentence [ˈsɛntəns] N (Ling) frase *f*, oración *f*; (Law) sentencia, fallo ▸ VT: **to ~ sb to death/ to five years** condenar a algn a muerte/a cinco años de cárcel; **to pass ~ on sb** (also fig) sentenciar *or* condenar a algn
sentiment [ˈsɛntɪmənt] N sentimiento; (opinion) opinión *f*
sentimental [sɛntɪˈmɛntl] ADJ sentimental
sentimentality [sɛntɪmɛnˈtælɪtɪ] N sentimentalismo, sensiblería
sentinel [ˈsɛntɪnl] N centinela *m*
sentry [ˈsɛntrɪ] N centinela *m*
sentry duty N: **to be on ~** estar de guardia, hacer guardia
Seoul [səʊl] N Seúl *m*
Sep. ABBR (= September) sep., set.
separable [ˈsɛpərəbl] ADJ separable
separate ADJ [ˈsɛprɪt] separado; (distinct) distinto; **separates** NPL (clothes) coordinados *mpl* ▸ VT [ˈsɛpəreɪt] separar; (part) dividir

▸ VI ['sɛpəreɪt] separarse; **~ from** separado *or* distinto de; **under ~ cover** (*Comm*) por separado; **to ~ into** dividir *or* separar en; **he is separated from his wife, but not divorced** está separado de su mujer, pero no (está) divorciado

separately ['sɛprɪtlɪ] ADV por separado

separation [sɛpə'reɪʃən] N separación *f*

sepia ['siːpɪə] ADJ color sepia *inv*

Sept. ABBR (= *September*) sep.

September [sɛp'tɛmbəʳ] N se(p)tiembre *m*; *see also* **July**

septic ['sɛptɪk] ADJ séptico; **to go ~** ponerse séptico

septicaemia, (*US*) **septicemia** [sɛptɪ'siːmɪə] N septicemia

septic tank N fosa séptica

sequel ['siːkwl] N consecuencia, resultado; (*of story*) continuación *f*

sequence ['siːkwəns] N sucesión *f*, serie *f*; (*Cine*) secuencia; **in ~** en orden *or* serie

sequential [sɪ'kwɛnʃəl] ADJ: **~ access** (*Comput*) acceso en serie

sequin ['siːkwɪn] N lentejuela .

Serb [səːb] ADJ, N = **Serbian**

Serbia ['səːbɪə] N Serbia

Serbian ['səːbɪən] ADJ serbio ▸ N serbio(-a); (*Ling*) serbio

Serbo-Croat ['səːbəu'krəuæt] N (*Ling*) serbocroata *m*

serenade [sɛrə'neɪd] N serenata ▸ VT dar serenata a

serene [sɪ'riːn] ADJ sereno, tranquilo

serenely [sɪ'riːnlɪ] ADV serenamente, tranquilamente

serenity [sə'rɛnɪtɪ] N serenidad *f*, tranquilidad *f*

sergeant ['sɑːdʒənt] N sargento

sergeant major N sargento mayor

serial ['sɪərɪəl] N novela por entregas; (*TV*) serie *f*

serial access N (*Comput*) acceso en serie

serial interface N (*Comput*) interface *m* en serie

serialize ['sɪərɪəlaɪz] VT publicar/televisar por entregas

serial killer N asesino(-a) en serie

serial number N número de serie

series ['sɪəriːz] N *pl inv* serie *f*

serious ['sɪərɪəs] ADJ serio; (*grave*) grave; **are you ~ (about it)?** ¿lo dices en serio?

seriously ['sɪərɪəslɪ] ADV en serio; (*ill, wounded etc*) gravemente; (*inf: extremely*) de verdad; **to take sth/sb ~** tomar algo/a algn en serio; **he's ~ rich** es una pasada de rico

seriousness ['sɪərɪəsnɪs] N seriedad *f*; gravedad *f*

sermon ['səːmən] N sermón *m*

serpent ['səːpənt] N serpiente *f*

serrated [sɪ'reɪtɪd] ADJ serrado, dentellado

serum ['sɪərəm] N suero

servant ['səːvənt] N (*gen*) servidor(a) *m/f*; (*also:* **house servant**) criado(-a) *m/f*

serve [səːv] VT servir; (*customer*) atender; (*train*) tener parada en; (*apprenticeship*) hacer; (*prison term*) cumplir ▸ VI (*servant, soldier etc*) servir; (*Tennis*) sacar ▸ N (*Tennis*) saque *m*; **it serves him right** se lo merece, se lo tiene merecido; **to ~ a summons on sb** entregar una citación a algn; **it serves my purpose** me sirve para lo que quiero; **are you being served?** ¿le atienden?; **the power station serves the entire region** la central eléctrica abastece a toda la región; **to ~ as/for/to do** servir de/para/para hacer; **to ~ on a committee/a jury** ser miembro de una comisión/un jurado
▸ **serve out, serve up** VT (*food*) servir

server N (*Comput*) servidor *m*

service ['səːvɪs] N (*gen*) servicio; (*Rel: Catholic*) misa; (: *other*) oficio (religioso); (*Aut*) mantenimiento; (*of dishes*) juego ▸ VT (*car, washing machine*) revisar; (: *repair*) reparar; **services** NPL (*Econ: tertiary sector*) sector *m* terciario *or* (de) servicios; (*Brit: on motorway*) área de servicio; **the Services** las fuerzas armadas; **funeral ~** exequias *fpl*; **to hold a ~** celebrar un oficio religioso; **the essential services** los servicios esenciales; **medical/social services** servicios *mpl* médicos/sociales; **the train ~ to London** los trenes a Londres; **to be of ~ to sb** ser útil a algn; **~ included/not included** servicio incluido/no incluido

serviceable ['səːvɪsəbl] ADJ servible, utilizable

service area N (*on motorway*) área de servicio

service charge N (*Brit*) servicio

service industries NPL industrias *fpl* de servicios

serviceman ['səːvɪsmən] N (*irreg*) militar *m*

service station N estación *f* de servicio

servicing ['səːvɪsɪŋ] N (*of car*) revisión *f*; (*of washing machine etc*) servicio de reparaciones

serviette [səːvɪ'ɛt] N (*Brit*) servilleta

servile ['səːvaɪl] ADJ servil

session ['sɛʃən] N (*sitting*) sesión *f*; **to be in ~** estar en sesión

session musician N músico *mf* de estudio

set [sɛt] (*pt, pp ~*) N juego; (*Radio*) aparato; (*TV*) televisor *m*; (*of utensils*) batería; (*of cutlery*) cubierto; (*of books*) colección *f*; (*Tennis*) set *m*; (*group of people*) grupo; (*Cine*) plató *m*; (*Theat*) decorado; (*Hairdressing*) marcado ▸ ADJ (*fixed*) fijo; (*ready*) listo; (*resolved*) resuelto, decidido ▸ VT (*place*) poner, colocar; (*fix*) fijar; (*adjust*) ajustar, arreglar; (*decide: rules etc*) establecer, decidir; (*assign: task*) asignar;

773

(: *homework*) poner ▸ vi (*sun*) ponerse; (*jam, jelly*) cuajarse; (*concrete*) fraguar; **a ~ of false teeth** una dentadura postiza; **a ~ of dining-room furniture** muebles *mpl* de comedor; **~ in one's ways** con costumbres arraigadas; **a ~ phrase** una frase hecha; **to be all ~ to do sth** estar listo para hacer algo; **to be ~ on doing sth** estar empeñado en hacer algo; **a novel ~ in Valencia** una novela ambientada en Valencia; **to ~ to music** poner música a; **to ~ on fire** incendiar, prender fuego a; **to ~ free** poner en libertad; **to ~ sth going** poner algo en marcha; **to ~ sail** zarpar, hacerse a la mar
▸ **set about** vt fus: **to ~ about doing sth** ponerse a hacer algo
▸ **set aside** vt poner aparte, dejar de lado
▸ **set back** vt (*progress*): **to ~ back (by)** retrasar (por); **a house ~ back from the road** una casa apartada de la carretera
▸ **set down** vt (*bus, train*) dejar; (*record*) poner por escrito
▸ **set in** vi (*infection*) declararse; (*complications*) comenzar; **the rain has ~ in for the day** parece que va a llover todo el día
▸ **set off** vi partir ▸ vt (*bomb*) hacer estallar; (*cause to start*) poner en marcha; (*show up well*) hacer resaltar
▸ **set out** vi partir ▸ vt (*arrange*) disponer; (*state*) exponer; **to ~ out to do sth** proponerse hacer algo; **to ~ out (from)** salir (de)
▸ **set up** vt (*organization*) establecer
setback ['sɛtbæk] N (*hitch*) revés *m*, contratiempo; (*in health*) recaída
set menu N menú *m*
set phrase N frase *f* hecha
set square N cartabón *m*
settee [sɛ'ti:] N sofá *m*
setting ['sɛtɪŋ] N (*scenery*) marco *m*; (*of jewel*) engaste *m*, montadura
setting lotion N fijador *m* (para el pelo)
settle ['sɛtl] vt (*argument, matter*) resolver; (*pay: bill, accounts*) pagar, liquidar; (*colonize: land*) colonizar; (*Med: calm*) calmar, sosegar
▸ vi (*dust etc*) depositarse; (*weather*) estabilizarse; **to ~ for sth** convenir en aceptar algo; **to ~ on sth** decidirse por algo; **that's settled then** bueno, está arreglado; **to ~ one's stomach** asentar el estómago
▸ **settle down** vi (*get comfortable*) ponerse cómodo, acomodarse; (*calm down*) calmarse, tranquilizarse; (*live quietly*) echar raíces
▸ **settle in** vi instalarse
▸ **settle up** vi: **to ~ up with sb** ajustar cuentas con algn
settlement ['sɛtlmənt] N (*payment*) liquidación *f*; (*agreement*) acuerdo, convenio; (*village etc*) poblado; **in ~ of our account**

(*Comm*) en pago *or* liquidación de nuestra cuenta
settler ['sɛtlər] N colono(-a), colonizador(a) *m/f*
setup ['sɛtʌp] N sistema *m*
seven ['sɛvn] NUM siete
seventeen [sɛvn'ti:n] NUM diecisiete
seventeenth [sɛvn'ti:nθ] ADJ decimoséptimo
seventh ['sɛvnθ] ADJ séptimo
seventieth ['sɛvntɪθ] ADJ septuagésimo
seventy ['sɛvntɪ] NUM setenta
sever ['sɛvər] vt cortar; (*relations*) romper
several ['sɛvərl] ADJ, PRON varios(-as) *m/fpl*, algunos(-as) *m/fpl*; **~ of us** varios de nosotros; **~ times** varias veces
severance ['sɛvərəns] N (*of relations*) ruptura
severance pay N indemnización *f* por despido
severe [sɪ'vɪər] ADJ severo; (*serious*) grave; (*hard*) duro; (*pain*) intenso
severely [sɪ'vɪəlɪ] ADV severamente; (*wounded, ill*) de gravedad, gravemente
severity [sɪ'vɛrɪtɪ] N severidad *f*; gravedad *f*; intensidad *f*
Seville [sə'vɪl] N Sevilla
sew [səu] (*pt* **sewed** [səud], *pp* **sewn** [səun]) vt, vi coser
▸ **sew up** vt coser
sewage ['su:ɪdʒ] N (*effluence*) aguas *fpl* residuales; (*system*) alcantarillado
sewage works N estación *f* depuradora (de aguas residuales)
sewer ['su:ər] N alcantarilla, cloaca
sewing ['səuɪŋ] N costura
sewing machine N máquina de coser
sewn [səun] PP *of* **sew**
sex [sɛks] N sexo; **the opposite ~** el sexo opuesto; **to have ~** hacer el amor
sex act N acto sexual, coito
sex appeal N sex-appeal *m*, gancho
sex education N educación *f* sexual
sexism ['sɛksɪzəm] N sexismo
sexist ['sɛksɪst] ADJ, N sexista *mf*
sex life N vida sexual
sex object N objeto sexual
sextant ['sɛkstənt] N sextante *m*
sextet [sɛks'tɛt] N sexteto
sexual ['sɛksjuəl] ADJ sexual; **~ assault** atentado contra el pudor; **~ harassment** acoso sexual; **~ intercourse** relaciones *fpl* sexuales
sexuality [sɛksju'ælɪtɪ] N sexualidad *f*
sexually ['sɛksjuəlɪ] ADV sexualmente
sexy ['sɛksɪ] ADJ sexy
Seychelles [seɪ'ʃɛlz] NPL: **the ~** las Seychelles
SF N ABBR = **science fiction**
SG N ABBR (*US*: = *Surgeon General*) jefe del servicio federal de sanidad

Sgt. ABBR (= *sergeant*) Sgto.

shabbily ['ʃæbɪlɪ] ADV (*treat*) injustamente; (*dressed*) pobremente

shabbiness ['ʃæbɪnɪs] N (*of dress, person*) aspecto desharrapado; (*of building*) mal estado

shabby ['ʃæbɪ] ADJ (*person*) desharrapado; (*clothes*) raído, gastado

shack [ʃæk] N choza, chabola

shackle ['ʃækl] VT encadenar; (*fig*): **to be shackled by sth** verse obstaculizado por algo

shackles ['ʃæklz] NPL grillos *mpl*, grilletes *mpl*

shade [ʃeɪd] N sombra; (*for lamp*) pantalla; (*for eyes*) visera; (*of colour*) tono *m*, tonalidad *f*; (*US: window shade*) persiana ▶ VT dar sombra a; **shades** NPL (*US: sunglasses*) gafas *fpl* de sol; **in the ~** a la sombra; **a ~ more** (*small quantity*) un poquito más; **a ~ smaller** un poquito más pequeño

shadow ['ʃædəu] N sombra ▶ VT (*follow*) seguir y vigilar; **without** *or* **beyond a ~ of doubt** sin lugar a dudas

shadow cabinet N (BRIT Pol) gobierno en la oposición

shadowy ['ʃædəuɪ] ADJ oscuro; (*dim*) indistinto

shady ['ʃeɪdɪ] ADJ sombreado; (*fig: dishonest*) sospechoso; (*deal*) turbio

shaft [ʃɑːft] N (*of arrow, spear*) astil *m*; (Aut, Tech) eje *m*, árbol *m*; (*of mine*) pozo; (*of lift*) hueco, caja; (*of light*) rayo; **ventilator ~** chimenea de ventilación

shaggy ['ʃægɪ] ADJ peludo

shake [ʃeɪk] (*pt* **shook**, *pp* **shaken** ['ʃeɪkn]) VT sacudir; (*building*) hacer temblar; (*perturb*) inquietar, perturbar; (*weaken*) debilitar; (*alarm*) trastornar ▶ VI estremecerse; (*tremble*) temblar ▶ N (*movement*) sacudida; **to ~ one's head** (*in refusal*) negar con la cabeza; (*in dismay*) mover *or* menear la cabeza, incrédulo; **to ~ hands with sb** estrechar la mano a algn; **to ~ in one's shoes** (*fig*) temblar de miedo

▶ **shake off** VT sacudirse; (*fig*) deshacerse de

▶ **shake up** VT agitar

shake-up ['ʃeɪkʌp] N reorganización *f*

shakily ['ʃeɪkɪlɪ] ADV (*reply*) con voz temblorosa *or* trémula; (*walk*) con paso vacilante; (*write*) con mano temblorosa

shaky ['ʃeɪkɪ] ADJ (*unstable*) inestable, poco firme; (*trembling*) tembloroso; (*health*) delicado; (*memory*) defectuoso; (*person: from illness*) temblando; (*premise etc*) incierto

shale [ʃeɪl] N esquisto

shall [ʃæl] AUX VB: **I ~ go** iré; **~ I help you?** ¿quieres que te ayude?; **I'll buy three, ~ I?** compro tres, ¿no te parece?

shallot [ʃə'lɔt] N (BRIT) cebollita, chalote *m*

shallow ['ʃæləu] ADJ poco profundo; (*fig*) superficial

shallows ['ʃæləuz] NPL bajío *sg*, bajos *mpl*

sham [ʃæm] N fraude *m*, engaño ▶ ADJ falso, fingido ▶ VT fingir, simular

shambles ['ʃæmblz] N desorden *m*, confusión *f*; **the economy is (in) a complete ~** la economía está en un estado desastroso

shambolic [ʃæm'bɔlɪk] ADJ (*inf*) caótico

shame [ʃeɪm] N vergüenza; (*pity*) lástima, pena ▶ VT avergonzar; **it is a ~ that/to do** es una lástima *or* pena que/hacer; **what a ~!** ¡qué lástima *or* pena!; **to put sth/sb to ~** (*fig*) ridiculizar algo/a algn

shamefaced ['ʃeɪmfeɪst] ADJ avergonzado

shameful ['ʃeɪmful] ADJ vergonzoso

shamefully ['ʃeɪmfulɪ] ADV vergonzosamente

shameless ['ʃeɪmlɪs] ADJ descarado

shampoo [ʃæm'puː] N champú *m* ▶ VT lavar con champú

shampoo and set N lavado y marcado

shamrock ['ʃæmrɔk] N trébol *m*

shandy ['ʃændɪ], (US) **shandygaff** ['ʃændɪgæf] N clara, cerveza con gaseosa

shan't [ʃɑːnt] = **shall not**

shanty town ['ʃæntɪ-] N barrio de chabolas

SHAPE [ʃeɪp] N ABBR (= *Supreme Headquarters Allied Powers, Europe*) cuartel general de las fuerzas aliadas en Europa

shape [ʃeɪp] N forma ▶ VT formar, dar forma a; (*clay*) modelar; (*stone*) labrar; (*sb's ideas*) formar; (*sb's life*) determinar ▶ VI (*also:* **shape up**: *events*) desarrollarse; (*person*) formarse; **to take ~** tomar forma; **to get o.s. into ~** ponerse en forma *or* en condiciones; **in the ~ of a heart** en forma de corazón; **I can't bear gardening in any ~ or form** no aguanto la jardinería de ningún modo

-shaped SUFF: **heart~** en forma de corazón

shapeless ['ʃeɪplɪs] ADJ informe, sin forma definida

shapely ['ʃeɪplɪ] ADJ bien formado *or* proporcionado

share [ʃeəʳ] N (*part*) parte *f*, porción *f*; (*contribution*) cuota; (Comm) acción *f* ▶ VT dividir; (*fig: have in common*) compartir; **to have a ~ in the profits** tener una proporción de las ganancias; **he has a 50% ~ in a new business venture** tiene una participación del 50% en un nuevo negocio; **to ~ in** participar en; **to ~ out (among** *or* **between)** repartir (entre)

share capital N (Comm) capital *m* social en acciones

share certificate N certificado *or* título de una acción

shareholder ['ʃeəhəuldəʳ] N (BRIT) accionista *mf*

S

share index N (Comm) índice m de la bolsa
share issue N emisión f de acciones
share price N (Comm) cotización f
shark [ʃɑːk] N tiburón m
sharp [ʃɑːp] ADJ (razor, knife) afilado; (point)
puntiagudo; (outline) definido; (pain)
intenso; (Mus) desafinado; (contrast)
marcado; (voice) agudo; (curve, bend) cerrado;
(person: quick-witted) avispado; (: dishonest) poco
escrupuloso ▶ N (Mus) sostenido ▶ ADV: **at
two o'clock ~** a las dos en punto; **to be ~
with sb** hablar a algn de forma brusca y
tajante; **turn ~ left** tuerce del todo a la
izquierda
sharpen [ˈʃɑːpn] VT afilar; (pencil) sacar punta
a; (fig) agudizar
sharpener [ˈʃɑːpnər] N (gen) afilador m; (also:
pencil sharpener) sacapuntas m inv
sharp-eyed [ʃɑːpˈaɪd] ADJ de vista aguda
sharpish [ˈʃɑːpɪʃ] ADV (BRIT inf: quickly)
prontito, bien pronto
sharply [ˈʃɑːplɪ] ADV (abruptly) bruscamente;
(clearly) claramente; (harshly) severamente
sharp-tempered [ʃɑːpˈtempəd] ADJ de genio
arisco
sharp-witted [ʃɑːpˈwɪtɪd] ADJ listo,
despabilado
shatter [ˈʃætər] VT hacer añicos or pedazos;
(fig: ruin) destruir, acabar con ▶ VI hacerse
añicos
shattered [ˈʃætəd] ADJ (grief-stricken)
destrozado, deshecho; (exhausted) agotado,
hecho polvo
shattering [ˈʃætərɪŋ] ADJ (experience)
devastador(a), anonadante
shatterproof [ˈʃætəpruːf] ADJ inastillable
shave [ʃeɪv] VT afeitar, rasurar ▶ VI afeitarse
▶ N: **to have a ~** afeitarse
shaven [ˈʃeɪvn] ADJ (head) rapado
shaver [ˈʃeɪvər] N (also: **electric shaver**)
máquina de afeitar (eléctrica)
shaving [ˈʃeɪvɪŋ] N (action) afeitado; **shavings**
NPL (of wood etc) virutas fpl
shaving brush N brocha (de afeitar)
shaving cream N crema (de afeitar)
shaving foam N espuma de afeitar
shaving point N enchufe m para máquinas
de afeitar
shaving soap N jabón m de afeitar
shawl [ʃɔːl] N chal m
she [ʃiː] PRON ella; **there ~ is** allí está; **~-cat**
gata
sheaf [ʃiːf] (pl **sheaves** [ʃiːvz]) N (of corn)
gavilla; (of arrows) haz m; (of papers) fajo
shear [ʃɪər] VT (pt **sheared**, pp **sheared** or
shorn [ʃɔːn]) (sheep) esquilar, trasquilar
▶ **shear off** VI romperse
shears [ʃɪəz] NPL (for hedge) tijeras fpl de
jardín

sheath [ʃiːθ] N vaina; (contraceptive)
preservativo
sheath knife N cuchillo de monte
sheaves [ʃiːvz] NPL of **sheaf**
shed (pt, pp ~) [ʃed] N cobertizo; (Industry, Rail)
nave f ▶ VT (skin) mudar; (tears) derramar;
(workers) despedir; **to ~ light on** (problem,
mystery) aclarar, arrojar luz sobre
she'd [ʃiːd] = **she had**; **she would**
sheen [ʃiːn] N brillo, lustre m
sheep [ʃiːp] N pl inv oveja
sheepdog [ˈʃiːpdɔɡ] N perro pastor
sheep farmer N ganadero (de ovejas)
sheepish [ˈʃiːpɪʃ] ADJ tímido, vergonzoso
sheepskin [ˈʃiːpskɪn] N piel f de carnero
sheepskin jacket N zamarra
sheer [ʃɪər] ADJ (utter) puro, completo; (steep)
escarpado; (material) diáfano ▶ ADV
verticalmente; **by ~ chance** de pura
casualidad
sheet [ʃiːt] N (on bed) sábana; (of paper) hoja;
(of glass, metal) lámina
sheet feed N (on printer) alimentador m de
papel
sheet lightning N relámpago (difuso)
sheet metal N metal m en lámina
sheet music N hojas fpl de partitura
sheik, sheikh [ʃeɪk] N jeque m
shelf [ʃelf] (pl **shelves** [ʃelvz]) N estante m
shelf life N (Comm) periodo de conservación
antes de la venta
shell [ʃel] N (on beach) concha, caracol m (LAm);
(of egg, nut etc) cáscara; (explosive) proyectil m,
obús m; (of building) armazón m ▶ VT (peas)
desenvainar; (Mil) bombardear
▶ **shell out** VI (inf): **to ~ out (for)** soltar el
dinero (para), desembolsar (para)
she'll [ʃiːl] = **she will**; **she shall**
shellfish [ˈʃelfɪʃ] N pl inv crustáceo; (pl: as food)
mariscos mpl
shellsuit [ˈʃelsuːt] N chándal m (de Tactel®)
shelter [ˈʃeltər] N abrigo, refugio ▶ VT (aid)
amparar, proteger; (give lodging to) abrigar;
(hide) esconder ▶ VI abrigarse, refugiarse;
to take ~ (from) refugiarse or asilarse (de);
bus ~ marquesina
sheltered [ˈʃeltəd] ADJ (life) protegido; (spot)
abrigado
shelve [ʃelv] VT (fig) dar carpetazo a
shelves [ʃelvz] NPL of **shelf**
shelving [ˈʃelvɪŋ] N estantería
shepherd [ˈʃepəd] N pastor m ▶ VT (guide)
guiar, conducir
shepherdess [ˈʃepədɪs] N pastora
shepherd's pie N pastel de carne y puré de
patatas
sherbet [ˈʃəːbət] N (BRIT: powder) polvos mpl
azucarados; (US: water ice) sorbete m
sheriff [ˈʃerɪf] N (US) sheriff m

sherry [ˈʃɛrɪ] N jerez m
she's [ʃiːz] = **she is; she has**
Shetland [ˈʃɛtlənd] N (also: **the Shetlands, the Shetland Isles**) las Islas fpl Shetland
Shetland pony N pony m de Shetland
shield [ʃiːld] N escudo; (Tech) blindaje m ▶ VT: **to ~ (from)** proteger (de)
shift [ʃɪft] N (change) cambio; (at work) turno ▶ VT trasladar; (remove) quitar ▶ VI moverse; (change place) cambiar de sitio; **the wind has shifted to the south** el viento ha virado al sur; **a ~ in demand** (Comm) un desplazamiento de la demanda
shift key N (on typewriter) tecla de mayúsculas
shiftless [ˈʃɪftlɪs] ADJ (person) vago
shift work N (BRIT) trabajo por turnos; **to do ~** trabajar por turnos
shifty [ˈʃɪftɪ] ADJ tramposo; (eyes) furtivo
Shiite [ˈʃiːaɪt] ADJ, N chiita mf
shilling [ˈʃɪlɪŋ] N (BRIT: formerly) chelín m (= 12 peniques antiguos; una libra tenía 20 chelines)
shilly-shally [ˈʃɪlɪʃælɪ] VI titubear, vacilar
shimmer [ˈʃɪmər] N reflejo trémulo ▶ VI relucir
shimmering [ˈʃɪmərɪŋ] ADJ reluciente; (haze) trémulo; (satin etc) lustroso
shin [ʃɪn] N espinilla ▶ VI: **to ~ down/up a tree** bajar de/trepar un árbol
shindig [ˈʃɪndɪɡ] N (inf) fiesta, juerga
shine [ʃaɪn] N (pt, pp **shone**) N brillo, lustre m ▶ VI brillar, relucir ▶ VT (shoes) lustrar, sacar brillo a; **to ~ a torch on sth** dirigir una linterna hacia algo
shingle [ˈʃɪŋɡl] N (on beach) guijarras fpl
shingles [ˈʃɪŋɡlz] N (Med) herpes msg
shining [ˈʃaɪnɪŋ] ADJ (surface, hair) lustroso; (light) brillante
shiny [ˈʃaɪnɪ] ADJ brillante, lustroso
ship [ʃɪp] N buque m, barco ▶ VT (goods) embarcar; (oars) desarmar; (send) transportar or enviar por vía marítima; **~'s manifest** manifiesto del buque; **on board ~** a bordo
shipbuilder [ˈʃɪpbɪldər] N constructor(a) m/f naval
shipbuilding [ˈʃɪpbɪldɪŋ] N construcción f naval
ship canal N canal m de navegación
ship chandler [-ˈtʃɑːndlər] N proveedor m de efectos navales
shipment [ˈʃɪpmənt] N (act) embarque m; (goods) envío
shipowner [ˈʃɪpəunər] N naviero, armador m
shipper [ˈʃɪpər] N compañía naviera
shipping [ˈʃɪpɪŋ] N (act) embarque m; (traffic) buques mpl
shipping agent N agente mf marítimo(-a)
shipping company N compañía naviera
shipping lane N ruta de navegación

shipping line N = **shipping company**
shipshape [ˈʃɪpʃeɪp] ADJ en buen orden
shipwreck [ˈʃɪprɛk] N naufragio ▶ VT: **to be shipwrecked** naufragar
shipyard [ˈʃɪpjɑːd] N astillero
shire [ˈʃaɪər] N (BRIT) condado
shirk [ʃəːk] VT eludir, esquivar; (obligations) faltar a
shirt [ʃəːt] N camisa; **in ~ sleeves** en mangas de camisa
shirty [ˈʃəːtɪ] ADJ (BRIT inf): **to be ~** estar de malas pulgas
shit [ʃɪt] (inf!) N mierda (!); (nonsense) chorradas fpl ▶ EXCL ¡mierda! (!); **tough ~!** ¡te jodes! (!)
shiver [ˈʃɪvər] N escalofrío ▶ VI temblar, estremecerse; (with cold) tiritar
shoal [ʃəul] N (of fish) banco
shock [ʃɔk] N (impact) choque m; (Elec) descarga (eléctrica); (emotional) conmoción f; (start) sobresalto, susto; (Med) postración f nerviosa ▶ VT dar un susto a; (offend) escandalizar; **to get a ~** (Elec) sentir una sacudida eléctrica; **to give sb a ~** dar un susto a algn; **to be suffering from ~** padecer una postración nerviosa; **it came as a ~ to hear that ...** me etc asombró descubrir que ...
shock absorber [-əbsɔːbər] N amortiguador m
shocker [ˈʃɔkər] N (inf): **it was a real ~** fue muy fuerte
shocking [ˈʃɔkɪŋ] ADJ (awful: weather, handwriting) espantoso, horrible; (improper) escandaloso; (result) inesperado
shock therapy, shock treatment N (Med) terapia de choque
shock wave N onda expansiva or de choque
shod [ʃɔd] PT, PP of **shoe** ▶ ADJ calzado
shoddiness [ˈʃɔdɪnɪs] N baja calidad f
shoddy [ˈʃɔdɪ] ADJ de pacotilla
shoe [ʃuː] N (pt, pp **shod** [ʃɔd]) N zapato; (for horse) herradura; (brake shoe) zapata ▶ VT (horse) herrar
shoebrush [ˈʃuːbrʌʃ] N cepillo para zapatos
shoehorn [ˈʃuːhɔːn] N calzador m
shoelace [ˈʃuːleɪs] N cordón m
shoemaker [ˈʃuːmeɪkər] N zapatero(-a)
shoe polish N betún m
shoeshop [ˈʃuːʃɔp] N zapatería
shoestring [ˈʃuːstrɪŋ] N (shoelace) cordón m; (fig): **on a ~** con muy poco dinero, a lo barato
shone [ʃɔn] PT, PP of **shine**
shonky [ˈʃɔŋkɪ] ADJ (AUSTRALIA, NEW ZEALAND inf) chapucero
shoo [ʃuː] EXCL ¡fuera!; (to animals) ¡zape! ▶ VT (also: **shoo away, shoo off**) ahuyentar
shook [ʃuk] PT of **shake**
shoot [ʃuːt] N (pt, pp **shot**) N (on branch, seedling)

S

retoño, vástago; (*shooting party*) cacería; (*competition*) concurso de tiro; (*preserve*) coto de caza ▸ vt disparar; (*kill*) matar a tiros; (*execute*) fusilar; (*Cine: film, scene*) rodar, filmar ▸ vi (*Football*) chutar; **to ~ (at)** tirar (a); **to ~ past** pasar como un rayo; **to ~ in/out** vi entrar corriendo/salir disparado
▸ **shoot down** vt (*plane*) derribar
▸ **shoot up** vi (*prices*) dispararse

shooting ['ʃuːtɪŋ] N (*shots*) tiros *mpl*, tiroteo; (*Hunting*) caza con escopeta; (*act, murder*) asesinato (a tiros); (*Cine*) rodaje *m*

shooting star N estrella fugaz

shop [ʃɒp] N tienda; (*workshop*) taller *m* ▸ vi (*also:* **go shopping**) ir de compras; **to talk ~** (*fig*) hablar del trabajo; **repair ~** taller *m* de reparaciones
▸ **shop around** vi comparar precios

shopaholic ['ʃɒpə'hɒlɪk] N (*inf*) adicto(-a) a las compras

shop assistant N (*Brit*) dependiente(-a) *m/f*

shop floor N (*Brit fig*) taller *m*, fábrica

shopkeeper ['ʃɒpkiːpər] N (*Brit*) tendero(-a)

shoplift ['ʃɒplɪft] vi robar en las tiendas

shoplifter ['ʃɒplɪftər] N ratero(-a)

shoplifting ['ʃɒplɪftɪŋ] N ratería, robo (en las tiendas)

shopper ['ʃɒpər] N comprador(a) *m/f*

shopping ['ʃɒpɪŋ] N (*goods*) compras *fpl*

shopping bag N bolsa (de compras)

shopping cart N (*US also Comput*) carrito de la compra

shopping centre, (*US*) **shopping center** N centro comercial

shopping mall N centro comercial

shopping trolley N (*Brit*) carrito de la compra

shop-soiled ['ʃɒpsɔɪld] ADJ (*Brit*) usado

shop steward N (*Brit Industry*) enlace *mf* sindical

shop window N escaparate *m*, vidriera (*LAM*)

shopworn ['ʃɒpwɔːn] ADJ (*US*) usado

shore [ʃɔːr] N (*of sea, lake*) orilla ▸ vt: **to ~ (up)** reforzar; **on ~** en tierra

shore leave N (*Naut*) permiso para bajar a tierra

shorn [ʃɔːn] PP *of* **shear**

short [ʃɔːt] ADJ (*not long*) corto; (*in time*) breve, de corta duración; (*person*) bajo; (*curt*) brusco, seco ▸ vi (*Elec*) ponerse en cortocircuito ▸ N (*also:* **short film**) cortometraje *m*; (**a pair of**) **shorts** (unos) pantalones *mpl* cortos; **to be ~ of sth** estar falto de algo; **in ~** en pocas palabras; **a ~ time ago** hace poco (tiempo); **in the ~ term** a corto plazo; **to be in ~ supply** escasear, haber escasez de; **I'm ~ of time** me falta tiempo; **~ of doing ...** a menos que hagamos *etc* ...; **everything ~ of ...** todo menos ...; **it is ~ for** es la forma

abreviada de; **to cut ~** (*speech, visit*) interrumpir, terminar inesperadamente; **to fall ~ of** no alcanzar; **to run ~ of sth** acabársele algo; **to stop ~** parar en seco; **to stop ~ of** detenerse antes de

shortage ['ʃɔːtɪdʒ] N escasez *f*, falta

shortbread ['ʃɔːtbrɛd] N galleta de mantequilla, *especie de mantecada*

short-change [ʃɔːt'tʃeɪndʒ] vt: **to ~ sb** no dar el cambio completo a algn

short-circuit [ʃɔːt'səːkɪt] N cortocircuito ▸ vt poner en cortocircuito ▸ vi ponerse en cortocircuito

shortcoming ['ʃɔːtkʌmɪŋ] N defecto, deficiencia

N (*Brit*) pasta quebradiza

shortcut ['ʃɔːtkʌt] N atajo

shorten ['ʃɔːtn] vt acortar; (*visit*) interrumpir

shortfall ['ʃɔːtfɔːl] N déficit *m*, deficiencia

shorthand ['ʃɔːthænd] N (*Brit*) taquigrafía; **to take sth down in ~** taquigrafiar algo

shorthand notebook N cuaderno de taquigrafía

shorthand typist N (*Brit*) taquimecanógrafo(-a)

short list N (*Brit: for job*) lista de candidatos pre-seleccionados

short-lived ['ʃɔːt'lɪvd] ADJ efímero

shortly ['ʃɔːtlɪ] ADV en breve, dentro de poco

shortness N (*of distance*) cortedad *f*; (*of time*) brevedad *f*; (*manner*) brusquedad *f*

short-sighted [ʃɔːt'saɪtɪd] ADJ (*Brit*) miope, corto de vista; (*fig*) imprudente

short-sightedness [ʃɔːt'saɪtɪdnɪs] N miopía; (*fig*) falta de previsión, imprudencia

short-sleeved ADJ de manga corta

short-staffed [ʃɔːt'stɑːft] ADJ falto de personal

short story N cuento

short-tempered [ʃɔːt'tɛmpəd] ADJ enojadizo

short-term ['ʃɔːttəːm] ADJ (*effect*) a corto plazo

short time N: **to work ~, be on ~** (*Industry*) trabajar con sistema de horario reducido

short-time working ['ʃɔːttaɪm-] N trabajo de horario reducido

short wave N (*Radio*) onda corta

shot [ʃɒt] PT, PP *of* **shoot** ▸ N (*sound*) tiro, disparo; (*person*) tirador(a) *m/f*; (*try*) tentativa; (*injection*) inyección *f*; (*Phot*) toma, fotografía; (*shotgun pellets*) perdigones *mpl*; **to fire a ~ at sb/sth** tirar *or* disparar contra algn/algo; **to have a ~ at (doing) sth** probar suerte con algo; **like a ~** (*without any delay*) como un rayo; **a big ~** (*inf*) un pez gordo; **to get ~ of sth/sb** (*inf*) deshacerse de algo/algn, quitarse algo/a algn de encima

shotgun ['ʃɒtɡʌn] N escopeta

should [ʃud] AUX VB: **I ~ go now** debo irme

ahora; **he ~ be there now** debe de haber llegado (ya); **I ~ go if I were you** yo en tu lugar me iría; **I ~ like to** me gustaría; **~ he phone ...** si llamara ..., en caso de que llamase ...

shoulder [ˈʃəʊldəʳ] N hombro; (BRIT: of road): **hard ~** arcén m ▶ VT (fig) cargar con; **to look over one's ~** mirar hacia atrás; **to rub shoulders with sb** (fig) codearse con algn; **to give sb the cold ~** (fig) dar de lado a algn

shoulder bag N bolso de bandolera

shoulder blade N omóplato

shoulder strap N tirante m

shouldn't [ˈʃʊdnt] = **should not**

shout [ʃaʊt] N grito ▶ VT gritar ▶ VI gritar, dar voces
▶ **shout down** VT hundir a gritos

shouting [ˈʃaʊtɪŋ] N griterío

shouting match N (inf) discusión f a voz en grito

shove [ʃʌv] N empujón m ▶ VT empujar; (inf: put): **to ~ sth in** meter algo a empellones; **he shoved me out of the way** me quitó de en medio de un empujón
▶ **shove off** VI (Naut) alejarse del muelle; (fig: inf) largarse

shovel [ˈʃʌvl] N pala; (mechanical) excavadora ▶ VT mover con pala

show [ʃəʊ] (pt **showed**, pp **shown**) N (of emotion) demostración f; (semblance) apariencia; (Comm, Tech: exhibition) exhibición f, exposición f; (Theat) función f, espectáculo; (organization) negocio, empresa ▶ VT mostrar, enseñar; (courage etc) mostrar, manifestar; (exhibit) exponer; (film) proyectar ▶ VI mostrarse; (appear) aparecer; **on ~** (exhibits etc) expuesto; **to be on ~** estar expuesto; **it's just for ~** es sólo para impresionar; **to ask for a ~ of hands** pedir una votación a mano alzada; **who's running the ~ here?** ¿quién manda aquí?; **to ~ a profit/loss** (Comm) arrojar un saldo positivo/negativo; **I have nothing to ~ for it** no saqué ningún provecho (de ello); **to ~ sb to his seat/to the door** acompañar a algn a su asiento/a la puerta; **as shown in the illustration** como se ve en el grabado; **it just goes to ~ that ...** queda demostrado que ...; **it doesn't ~** no se ve or nota
▶ **show in** VT (person) hacer pasar
▶ **show off** VI (pej) presumir ▶ VT (display) lucir; (pej) hacer alarde de
▶ **show out** VT: **to ~ sb out** acompañar a algn a la puerta
▶ **show up** VI (stand out) destacar; (inf: turn up) presentarse ▶ VT descubrir; (unmask) desenmascarar

showbiz [ˈʃəʊbɪz] N (inf) = **show business**

show business N el mundo del espectáculo

showcase [ˈʃəʊkeɪs] N vitrina; (fig) escaparate m

showdown [ˈʃəʊdaʊn] N crisis f, momento decisivo

shower [ˈʃaʊəʳ] N (rain) chaparrón m, chubasco; (of stones etc) lluvia; (also: **shower bath**) ducha ▶ VI llover ▶ VT: **to ~ sb with sth** colmar a algn de algo; **to have** or **take a ~** ducharse

shower cap N gorro de baño

shower gel N gel de ducha

showerproof [ˈʃaʊəpruːf] ADJ impermeable

showery [ˈʃaʊərɪ] ADJ (weather) lluvioso

showground [ˈʃəʊgraʊnd] N ferial m, real m (de la feria)

showing [ˈʃəʊɪŋ] N (of film) proyección f

show jumping N hípica

showman [ˈʃəʊmən] N (irreg) (at fair, circus) empresario (de espectáculos); (fig) actor m consumado

showmanship [ˈʃəʊmənʃɪp] N dotes fpl teatrales

shown [ʃəʊn] PP of **show**

show-off [ˈʃəʊɒf] N (inf: person) fanfarrón(-ona) m/f

showpiece [ˈʃəʊpiːs] N (of exhibition etc) objeto más valioso, joya; **that hospital is a ~** ese hospital es un modelo del género

showroom [ˈʃəʊruːm] N sala de muestras

show trial N juicio propagandístico

showy [ˈʃəʊɪ] ADJ ostentoso

shrank [ʃræŋk] PT of **shrink**

shrapnel [ˈʃræpnl] N metralla

shred [ʃrɛd] N (gen pl) triza, jirón m; (fig: of truth, evidence) pizca, chispa ▶ VT hacer trizas; (documents) triturar; (Culin) desmenuzar

shredder [ˈʃrɛdəʳ] N (vegetable shredder) picadora; (document shredder) trituradora (de papel)

shrewd [ʃruːd] ADJ astuto

shrewdly [ˈʃruːdlɪ] ADV astutamente

shrewdness [ˈʃruːdnɪs] N astucia

shriek [ʃriːk] N chillido ▶ VT, VI chillar

shrill [ʃrɪl] ADJ agudo, estridente

shrimp [ʃrɪmp] N camarón m

shrine [ʃraɪn] N santuario, sepulcro

shrink [ʃrɪŋk] (pt **shrank** [ʃræŋk], pp **shrunk** [ʃrʌŋk]) VI encogerse; (be reduced) reducirse ▶ VT encoger ▶ N (inf, pej) loquero(-a); **to ~ from (doing) sth** no atreverse a hacer algo
▶ **shrink away** VI retroceder, retirarse

shrinkage [ˈʃrɪŋkɪdʒ] N encogimiento; reducción f; (Comm: in shops) pérdidas fpl

shrink-wrap [ˈʃrɪŋkræp] VT empaquetar en envase termorretráctil

shrivel [ˈʃrɪvl], **shrivel up** VT (dry) secar; (crease) arrugar ▶ VI secarse; arrugarse

shroud [ʃraʊd] N sudario ▶ VT: **shrouded in mystery** envuelto en el misterio

Shrove Tuesday ['ʃrəuv-] N martes m de carnaval

shrub [ʃrʌb] N arbusto

shrubbery ['ʃrʌbərɪ] N arbustos mpl

shrug [ʃrʌg] N encogimiento de hombros
▸ VT, VI: **to ~ (one's shoulders)** encogerse de hombros
▸ **shrug off** VT negar importancia a; (cold, illness) deshacerse de

shrunk [ʃrʌŋk] PP of **shrink**

shrunken ['ʃrʌŋkn] ADJ encogido

shudder ['ʃʌdəʳ] N estremecimiento, escalofrío ▸ VI estremecerse

shuffle ['ʃʌfl] VT (cards) barajar; **to ~ (one's feet)** arrastrar los pies

shun [ʃʌn] VT rehuir, esquivar

shunt [ʃʌnt] VT (Rail) maniobrar

shunting yard ['ʃʌntɪŋ-] N estación f de maniobras

shut [ʃʌt] (pt, pp ~) VT cerrar ▸ VI cerrarse
▸ **shut down** VT, VI cerrar; (machine) parar
▸ **shut off** VT (stop: power, water supply etc) interrumpir, cortar; (: engine) parar
▸ **shut out** VT (person) excluir, dejar fuera; (noise, cold) no dejar entrar; (block: view) tapar; (: memory) tratar de olvidar
▸ **shut up** VI (inf: keep quiet) callarse ▸ VT (close) cerrar; (silence) callar

shutdown ['ʃʌtdaun] N cierre m

shutter ['ʃʌtəʳ] N contraventana; (Phot) obturador m

shuttle ['ʃʌtl] N lanzadera; (also: **shuttle service**: Aviat) puente m aéreo ▸ VI (vehicle, person) ir y venir ▸ VT (passengers) transportar, trasladar

shuttlecock ['ʃʌtlkɔk] N volante m

shuttle diplomacy N viajes mpl diplomáticos

shy [ʃaɪ] ADJ tímido ▸ VI: **to ~ away from doing sth** (fig) rehusar hacer algo; **to be ~ of doing sth** esquivar hacer algo

shyly ['ʃaɪlɪ] ADV tímidamente

shyness ['ʃaɪnɪs] N timidez f

Siam [saɪ'æm] N Siam m

Siamese [saɪə'miːz] ADJ siamés(-esa) ▸ N (person) siamés(-esa) m/f; (Ling) siamés m; **~ cat** gato siamés; **~ twins** gemelos(-as) mpl/fpl siameses(-esas)

Siberia [saɪ'bɪərɪə] N Siberia

sibling ['sɪblɪŋ] N (formal) hermano(-a)

Sicilian [sɪ'sɪlɪən] ADJ, N siciliano(-a) m/f

Sicily ['sɪsɪlɪ] N Sicilia

sick [sɪk] ADJ (ill) enfermo; (nauseated) mareado; (humour) morboso; **to be ~** (BRIT) vomitar; **to feel ~** tener náuseas; **to be ~ of** (fig) estar harto de; **a ~ person** un(a) enfermo(-a); **to be (off) ~** estar ausente por enfermedad; **to fall** or **take ~** ponerse enfermo

sickbag ['sɪkbæg] N bolsa para el mareo

sick bay N enfermería

sickbed ['sɪkbɛd] N lecho de enfermo

sick building syndrome N enfermedad causada por falta de ventilación y luz natural en un edificio

sicken ['sɪkn] VT dar asco a ▸ VI enfermar; **to be sickening for** (cold, flu etc) mostrar síntomas de

sickening ['sɪknɪŋ] ADJ (fig) asqueroso

sickle ['sɪkl] N hoz f

sick leave N baja por enfermedad

sickle-cell anaemia ['sɪklsɛl-] N anemia de células falciformes, drepanocitosis f

sick list N: **to be on the ~** estar de baja

sickly ['sɪklɪ] ADJ enfermizo; (taste) empalagoso

sickness ['sɪknɪs] N enfermedad f, mal m; (vomiting) náuseas fpl

sickness benefit N subsidio de enfermedad

sick pay N prestación por enfermedad pagada por la empresa

sickroom ['sɪkruːm] N cuarto del enfermo

side [saɪd] N (gen) lado; (face, surface) cara; (of paper) cara; (slice of bread) rebanada; (of body) costado; (of animal) ijar m, ijada; (of lake) orilla; (part) lado; (aspect) aspecto; (team: Sport) equipo; (: Pol etc) partido; (of hill) ladera ▸ ADJ (door, entrance) lateral ▸ VI: **to ~ with sb** tomar partido por algn; **by the ~ of** al lado de; **~ by ~** juntos(-as); **from all sides** de todos lados; **to take sides (with)** tomar partido (por); **~ of beef** flanco de vaca; **the right/wrong ~** el derecho/revés; **from ~ to ~** de un lado a otro

sideboard ['saɪdbɔːd] N aparador m

sideboards ['saɪdbɔːdz], (BRIT) **sideburns** ['saɪdbəːnz] NPL patillas fpl

sidecar ['saɪdkɑːʳ] N sidecar m

side dish N entremés m

side drum N (Mus) tamboril m

side effect N efecto secundario

sidekick ['saɪdkɪk] N compinche m

sidelight ['saɪdlaɪt] N (Aut) luz f lateral

sideline ['saɪdlaɪn] N (Sport) línea de banda; (fig) empleo suplementario

sidelong ['saɪdlɔŋ] ADJ de soslayo; **to give a ~ glance at sth** mirar algo de reojo

side plate N platito

side road N (BRIT) calle f lateral

side-saddle ['saɪdsædl] ADV a la amazona

side show N (stall) caseta; (fig) atracción f secundaria

sidestep ['saɪdstɛp] VT (question) eludir; (problem) esquivar ▸ VI (Boxing etc) dar un quiebro

side street N calle f lateral

sidetrack ['saɪdtræk] VT (fig) desviar (de su propósito)

sidewalk ['saɪdwɔ:k] N (US) acera, vereda (LAM), andén m (LAM), banqueta (LAM)
sideways ['saɪdweɪz] ADV de lado
siding ['saɪdɪŋ] N (Rail) apartadero, vía muerta
sidle ['saɪdl] VI: **to ~ up (to)** acercarse furtivamente (a)
SIDS [sɪdz] N ABBR (= sudden infant death syndrome) (síndrome m de la) muerte f súbita
siege [si:dʒ] N cerco, sitio; **to lay ~ to** cercar, sitiar
siege economy N economía de sitio or de asedio
Sierra Leone [sɪ'ɛrəlɪ'əun] N Sierra Leona
siesta [sɪ'ɛstə] N siesta
sieve [sɪv] N colador m ▶ VT cribar
sift [sɪft] VT cribar ▶ VI: **to ~ through** (information) examinar cuidadosamente
sigh [saɪ] N suspiro ▶ VI suspirar
sight [saɪt] N (faculty) vista; (spectacle) espectáculo; (on gun) mira, alza ▶ VT ver, divisar; **in ~** a la vista; **out of ~** fuera de (la) vista; **at ~** a la vista; **at first ~** a primera vista; **to lose ~ of sth/sb** perder algo/a algn de vista; **to catch ~ of sth/sb** divisar algo/a algn; **I know her by ~** la conozco de vista; **to set one's sights on (doing) sth** aspirar a or ambicionar (hacer) algo
sighted ['saɪtɪd] ADJ vidente, de vista normal; **partially ~** de vista limitada
sightseeing ['saɪtsi:ɪŋ] N turismo; **to go ~** hacer turismo
sightseer ['saɪtsi:əʳ] N turista mf
sign [saɪn] N (with hand) señal f, seña; (trace) huella, rastro; (notice) letrero; (written) signo; (also: **road sign**) indicador m; (: with instructions) señal f de tráfico ▶ VT firmar; (Sport) fichar; **as a ~ of** en señal de; **it's a good/bad ~** es buena/mala señal; **plus/minus ~** signo de más/de menos; **to ~ one's name** firmar
▶ **sign away** VT (rights etc) ceder
▶ **sign in** VI firmar el registro (al entrar)
▶ **sign off** VI (Radio, TV) cerrar el programa
▶ **sign on** VI (Mil) alistarse; (as unemployed) apuntarse al paro; (employee) firmar un contrato ▶ VT (Mil) alistar; (employee) contratar; **to ~ on for a course** matricularse en un curso
▶ **sign out** VI firmar el registro (al salir)
▶ **sign over** VT: **to ~ sth over to sb** traspasar algo a algn
▶ **sign up** VI (Mil) alistarse; (for course) inscribirse ▶ VT (player) fichar; (contract) contratar
signal ['sɪgnl] N señal f ▶ VI (Aut) señalizar ▶ VT (person) hacer señas a; (message) transmitir; **the engaged ~** (Tel) la señal de comunicando; **the ~ is very weak** (TV) no

captamos bien el canal; **to ~ a left/right turn** (Aut) indicar que se va a doblar a la izquierda/derecha; **to ~ to sb (to do sth)** hacer señas a algn (para que haga algo)
signal box N (Rail) garita de señales
signalman ['sɪgnlmən] N (irreg) (Rail) guardavía m
signatory ['sɪgnətərɪ] N firmante mf
signature ['sɪgnətʃəʳ] N firma
signature tune N sintonía
signet ring ['sɪgnət-] N (anillo de) sello
significance [sɪg'nɪfɪkəns] N significado; (importance) trascendencia; **that is of no ~** eso no tiene importancia
significant [sɪg'nɪfɪkənt] ADJ significativo; (important) trascendente; **it is ~ that …** es significativo que …
significantly [sɪg'nɪfɪkəntlɪ] ADV (smile) expresivamente; (improve, increase) sensiblemente; **and, ~ …** y debe notarse que …
signify ['sɪgnɪfaɪ] VT significar
sign language N mímica, lenguaje m por or de señas
signpost ['saɪnpəust] N indicador m
Sikh [si:k] ADJ, N sij mf
silage ['saɪlɪdʒ] N ensilaje m
silence ['saɪlns] N silencio ▶ VT hacer callar, acallar; (guns) reducir al silencio
silencer ['saɪlnsəʳ] N silenciador m
silent ['saɪlnt] ADJ (gen) silencioso; (not speaking) callado; (film) mudo; **to keep** or **remain ~** guardar silencio
silently ['saɪlntlɪ] ADV silenciosamente, en silencio
silent partner N (Comm) socio(-a) comanditario(-a)
silhouette [sɪlu:'ɛt] N silueta; **silhouetted against** destacado sobre or contra
silicon ['sɪlɪkən] N silicio
silicon chip N chip m, plaqueta de silicio
silicone ['sɪlɪkəun] N silicona
silk [sɪlk] N seda ▶ CPD de seda
silky ['sɪlkɪ] ADJ sedoso
sill [sɪl] N (also: **windowsill**) alféizar m; (Aut) umbral m
silliness ['sɪlɪnɪs] N (of person) necedad f; (of idea) lo absurdo
silly ['sɪlɪ] ADJ (person) tonto; (idea) absurdo; **to do sth ~** hacer una tontería
silo ['saɪləu] N silo
silt [sɪlt] N sedimento
silver ['sɪlvəʳ] N plata; (money) moneda suelta ▶ ADJ de plata
silver foil, (BRIT) **silver paper** N papel m de plata
silver plate N vajilla de plata
silver-plated [sɪlvə'pleɪtɪd] ADJ plateado
silversmith ['sɪlvəsmɪθ] N platero(-a)

silverware ['sɪlvəwɛəʳ] N plata
silver wedding, silver wedding anniversary N (BRIT) bodas fpl de plata
silvery ['sɪlvrɪ] ADJ plateado
SIM card ['sɪm-] N (Tel) SIM card m or f, tarjeta SIM
similar ['sɪmɪləʳ] ADJ: ~ **to** parecido or semejante a
similarity [sɪmɪ'lærɪtɪ] N parecido, semejanza
similarly ['sɪmɪləlɪ] ADV del mismo modo; (in a similar way) de manera parecida; (equally) igualmente
simile ['sɪmɪlɪ] N símil m
simmer ['sɪməʳ] VI hervir a fuego lento
▶ **simmer down** VI (fig, inf) calmarse, tranquilizarse
simpering ['sɪmpərɪŋ] ADJ afectado; (foolish) bobo
simple ['sɪmpl] ADJ (easy) sencillo; (foolish) simple; (Comm) simple; **the ~ truth** la pura verdad
simple interest N (Comm) interés m simple
simple-minded [sɪmpl'maɪndɪd] ADJ simple, ingenuo
simpleton ['sɪmpltən] N inocentón(-ona) m/f
simplicity [sɪm'plɪsɪtɪ] N sencillez f; (foolishness) ingenuidad f
simplification [sɪmplɪfɪ'keɪʃən] N simplificación f
simplify ['sɪmplɪfaɪ] VT simplificar
simply ['sɪmplɪ] ADV (in a simple way: live, talk) sencillamente; (just, merely) sólo
simulate ['sɪmjuleɪt] VT simular
simulation [sɪmju'leɪʃən] N simulación f
simultaneous [sɪməl'teɪnɪəs] ADJ simultáneo
simultaneously [sɪməl'teɪnɪəslɪ] ADV simultáneamente, a la vez
sin [sɪn] N pecado ▶ VI pecar
since [sɪns] ADV desde entonces ▶ PREP desde
▶ CONJ (time) desde que; (because) ya que, puesto que; ~ **then**, **ever ~** desde entonces; ~ **Monday** desde el lunes; (**ever**) ~ **I arrived** desde que llegué
sincere [sɪn'sɪəʳ] ADJ sincero
sincerely [sɪn'sɪəlɪ] ADV sinceramente; **yours ~** (in letters) le saluda (afectuosamente); ~ **yours** (US: in letters) le saluda atentamente
sincerity [sɪn'serɪtɪ] N sinceridad f
sinecure ['saɪnɪkjuəʳ] N chollo
sinew ['sɪnjuː] N tendón m
sinful ['sɪnful] ADJ (thought) pecaminoso; (person) pecador(a)
sing [sɪŋ] (pt **sang** [sæŋ], pp **sung** [sʌŋ]) VT cantar ▶ VI (gen) cantar; (bird) trinar; (ears) zumbar
Singapore [sɪŋə'pɔːʳ] N Singapur m

singe [sɪndʒ] VT chamuscar
singer ['sɪŋəʳ] N cantante mf
Singhalese [sɪŋə'liːz] ADJ = **Sinhalese**
singing ['sɪŋɪŋ] N (of person, bird) canto; (songs) canciones fpl; (in the ears) zumbido; (of kettle) silbido
single ['sɪŋgl] ADJ único, solo; (unmarried) soltero; (not double) individual, sencillo ▶ N (BRIT: also: **single ticket**) billete m sencillo; (record) sencillo, single m; **singles** NPL (Tennis) individuales mpl; **not a ~ one was left** no quedaba ni uno; **every ~ day** todos los días (sin excepción)
▶ **single out** VT (choose) escoger; (point out) singularizar
single bed N cama individual
single-breasted [sɪŋgl'brestɪd] ADJ (jacket, suit) recto, sin cruzar
single-entry book-keeping ['sɪŋglentrɪ-] N contabilidad f por partida simple
Single European Market N: **the ~** el Mercado Único Europeo
single file N: **in ~** en fila de uno
single-handed [sɪŋgl'hændɪd] ADV sin ayuda
single-minded [sɪŋgl'maɪndɪd] ADJ resuelto, firme
single parent N (mother) madre f soltera; (father) padre m soltero; **single-parent family** familia monoparental
single-parent family ['sɪŋglpɛərənt-] N familia monoparental
single room N habitación f individual
singles bar N (esp US) bar m para solteros
single-sex school ['sɪŋglseks-] N escuela no mixta
single-sided [sɪŋgl'saɪdɪd] ADJ (Comput: disk) de una cara
single spacing N (Typ): **in ~** a un espacio
singlet ['sɪŋglɪt] N camiseta
singly ['sɪŋglɪ] ADV uno por uno
singsong ['sɪŋsɔŋ] ADJ (tone) cantarín(-ina)
▶ N (songs): **to have a ~** tener un concierto improvisado
singular ['sɪŋgjuləʳ] ADJ singular, extraordinario, raro, extraño; (outstanding) excepcional; (Ling) singular ▶ N (Ling) singular m; **in the feminine ~** en femenino singular
singularly ['sɪŋgjuləlɪ] ADV singularmente, extraordinariamente
Sinhalese [sɪnhə'liːz] ADJ cingalés
sinister ['sɪnɪstəʳ] ADJ siniestro
sink [sɪŋk] (pt **sank**, pp **sunk**) N fregadero ▶ VT (ship) hundir, echar a pique; (foundations) excavar; (piles etc): **to ~ sth into** hundir algo en ▶ VI (gen) hundirse; **he sank into a chair/ the mud** se dejó caer en una silla/se hundió en el barro; **the shares** or **share prices have**

sunk to three dollars las acciones han bajado a tres dólares
▶ **sink in** VI (*fig*) penetrar, calar; **the news took a long time to ~ in** la noticia tardó mucho en hacer mella en él (*or* mí *etc*)
sinking ['sɪŋkɪŋ] ADJ: **that ~ feeling** la sensación esa de desmoralización
sinking fund N fondo de amortización
sink unit N fregadero
sinner ['sɪnər] N pecador(a) *m/f*
Sinn Féin [ʃɪn'feɪn] N partido político republicano de Irlanda del Norte
sinuous ['sɪnjuəs] ADJ sinuoso
sinus ['saɪnəs] N (*Anat*) seno
sip [sɪp] N sorbo ▶ VT sorber, beber a sorbitos
siphon ['saɪfən] N sifón *m* ▶ VT (*also:* **siphon off:** *funds*) desviar
sir [sə:r] N señor *m*; **S~ John Smith** Sir John Smith; **yes ~** sí, señor; **Dear S~** (*in letter*) Muy señor mío, Estimado Señor; **Dear Sirs** Muy señores nuestros, Estimados Señores
siren ['saɪərn] N sirena
sirloin ['sə:lɔɪn] N solomillo
sirloin steak N filete *m* de solomillo
sisal ['saɪsəl] N pita, henequén *m* (*LAM*)
sissy ['sɪsɪ] (*inf*) marica *m*
sister ['sɪstər] N hermana; (*BRIT: nurse*) enfermera jefe
sister-in-law ['sɪstərɪnlɔː] N cuñada
sister organization N organización *f* hermana
sister ship N barco gemelo
sit [sɪt] (*pt, pp* **sat** [sæt]) VI sentarse; (*be sitting*) estar sentado; (*assembly*) reunirse; (*dress etc*) caer, sentar; (*for painter*) posar ▶ VT (*exam*) presentarse a; **that jacket sits well** esa chaqueta sienta bien; **to ~ on a committee** ser miembro de una comisión *or* un comité
▶ **sit about, sit around** VI holgazanear
▶ **sit back** VI (*in seat*) recostarse
▶ **sit down** VI sentarse; **to be sitting down** estar sentado
▶ **sit in on** VT FUS: **to ~ in on a discussion** asistir a una discusión
▶ **sit on** VT FUS (*jury, committee*) ser miembro de, formar parte de
▶ **sit up** VI incorporarse; (*not go to bed*) no acostarse
sitcom ['sɪtkɔm] N ABBR (*TV:* = *situation comedy*) comedia de situación, telecomedia
sit-down ['sɪtdaun] ADJ: **~ strike** huelga de brazos caídos; **a ~ meal** una comida sentada
site [saɪt] N sitio; (*also:* **building site**) solar *m* ▶ VT situar
sit-in ['sɪtɪn] N (*demonstration*) sentada *f*
siting ['saɪtɪŋ] N (*location*) situación *f*, emplazamiento
sitter ['sɪtər] N (*Art*) modelo *mf*; (*babysitter*) canguro *mf*

sitting ['sɪtɪŋ] N (*of assembly etc*) sesión *f*; (*in canteen*) turno
sitting member N (*Pol*) titular *mf* de un escaño
sitting room N sala de estar
sitting tenant N inquilino con derechos de estancia en una vivienda
situate ['sɪtjueɪt] VT situar, ubicar (*LAM*)
situated ['sɪtjueɪtɪd] ADJ situado, ubicado (*LAM*)
situation [sɪtju'eɪʃən] N situación *f*; **"situations vacant"** (*BRIT*) "ofertas de trabajo"
situation comedy N (*TV, Radio*) comedia de situación, telecomedia
six [sɪks] NUM seis
six-pack ['sɪkspæk] N (*esp US*) paquete *m* de seis cervezas
sixteen [sɪks'ti:n] NUM dieciséis
sixteenth [sɪks'ti:nθ] ADJ decimosexto
sixth [sɪksθ] ADJ sexto; **the upper/lower ~** (*Scol*) el séptimo/sexto año
sixth form N (*BRIT*) clase *f* de alumnos del sexto año (*de 16 a 18 años de edad*)
sixth-form college N instituto *m* para alumnos de 16 a 18 años
sixtieth ['sɪkstɪɪθ] ADJ sexagésimo
sixty ['sɪkstɪ] NUM sesenta
size [saɪz] N (*gen*) tamaño; (*extent*) extensión *f*; (*of clothing*) talla; (*of shoes*) número; **I take ~ 5 shoes** calzo el número cinco; **I take ~ 14** mi talla es la 42; **I'd like the small/large ~** (*of soap powder etc*) quisiera el tamaño pequeño/grande
▶ **size up** VT formarse una idea de
sizeable ['saɪzəbl] ADJ importante, considerable
sizzle ['sɪzl] VI crepitar
SK ABBR (*CANADA*) = **Saskatchewan**
skate [skeɪt] N patín *m*; (*fish: pl inv*) raya ▶ VI patinar
▶ **skate over, skate round** VT FUS (*problem, issue*) pasar por alto
skateboard ['skeɪtbɔːd] N monopatín *m*
skateboarding N monopatín *m*
skater ['skeɪtər] N patinador(a) *m/f*
skating ['skeɪtɪŋ] N patinaje *m*; **figure ~** patinaje *m* artístico
skating rink N pista de patinaje
skeleton ['skɛlɪtn] N esqueleto; (*Tech*) armazón *m*; (*outline*) esquema *m*
skeleton key N llave *f* maestra
skeleton staff N personal *m* reducido
skeptic *etc* ['skɛptɪk] (*US*) = **sceptic** *etc*
sketch [skɛtʃ] N (*drawing*) dibujo; (*outline*) esbozo, bosquejo; (*Theat*) pieza corta, sketch *m* ▶ VT dibujar; (*plan etc: also:* **sketch out**) esbozar
sketch book N bloc *m* de dibujo

S

sketching ['skɛtʃɪŋ] N dibujo
sketch pad N bloc *m* de dibujo
sketchy ['skɛtʃɪ] ADJ incompleto
skewer ['skju:əʳ] N brocheta
ski [ski:] N esquí *m* ▶ VI esquiar
ski boot N bota de esquí
skid [skɪd] N patinazo ▶ VI patinar; **to go into a ~** comenzar a patinar
skid mark N señal *f* de patinazo
skier ['ski:əʳ] N esquiador(a) *m/f*
skiing ['ski:ɪŋ] N esquí *m*; **to go ~** practicar el esquí, (ir a) esquiar
ski instructor N instructor(a) *m/f* de esquí
ski jump N pista para salto de esquí
skilful, (US) **skillful** ['skɪlful] ADJ diestro, experto
skilfully, (US) **skillfully** ['skɪlfulɪ] ADV hábilmente, con destreza
ski lift N telesilla *m*, telesquí *m*
skill [skɪl] N destreza, pericia; (*technique*) arte *m*, técnica; **there's a certain ~ to doing it** se necesita cierta habilidad para hacerlo
skilled [skɪld] ADJ hábil, diestro; (*worker*) cualificado
skillet ['skɪlɪt] N sartén *f* pequeña
skillful ['skɪlful] (US) = **skilful**
skim [skɪm] VT (*milk*) desnatar; (*glide over*) rozar, rasar ▶ VI: **to ~ through** (*book*) hojear
skimmed milk [skɪmd-] N leche *f* desnatada *or* descremada
skimp [skɪmp] VT (*work*) chapucear; (*cloth etc*) escatimar; **to ~ on** (*material etc*) economizar; (*work*) escatimar
skimpy ['skɪmpɪ] ADJ (*meagre*) escaso; (*skirt*) muy corto
skin [skɪn] N (*gen*) piel *f*; (*complexion*) cutis *m*; (*of fruit, vegetable*) piel *f*, cáscara; (*crust: on pudding, paint*) nata ▶ VT (*fruit etc*) pelar; (*animal*) despellejar; **wet** *or* **soaked to the ~** calado hasta los huesos
skin cancer N cáncer *m* de piel
skin-deep ['skɪn'di:p] ADJ superficial
skin diver N buceador(a) *m/f*
skin diving N buceo
skinflint ['skɪnflɪnt] N tacaño(-a), roñoso(-a)
skinhead ['skɪnhɛd] N cabeza *mf* rapada, skin(head) *mf*
skinny ['skɪnɪ] ADJ flaco, magro
skintight ['skɪntaɪt] ADJ (*dress etc*) muy ajustado
skip [skɪp] N brinco, salto; (*container*) contenedor *m* ▶ VI brincar; (*with rope*) saltar a la comba ▶ VT (*pass over*) omitir, saltarse
ski pants NPL pantalones *mpl* de esquí
ski pass N forfait *m* (de esquí)
ski pole N bastón *m* de esquiar
skipper ['skɪpəʳ] N (*Naut, Sport*) capitán *m*
skipping rope ['skɪpɪŋ-] N (*Brit*) comba, cuerda (de saltar)

ski resort N estación *f* de esquí
skirmish ['skə:mɪʃ] N escaramuza
skirt [skə:t] N falda, pollera (*Lam*) ▶ VT (*surround*) ceñir, rodear; (*go round*) ladear
skirting board ['skə:tɪŋ-] N (*Brit*) rodapié *m*
ski run N pista de esquí
ski slope N pista de esquí
ski suit N traje *m* de esquiar
skit [skɪt] N sátira, parodia
ski tow N arrastre *m* (de esquí)
skittle ['skɪtl] N bolo; **skittles** (*game*) boliche *m*
skive [skaɪv] VI (*Brit inf*) gandulear
skulk [skʌlk] VI esconderse
skull [skʌl] N calavera; (*Anat*) cráneo
skullcap ['skʌlkæp] N (*worn by Jews*) casquete *m*; (*worn by Pope*) solideo
skunk [skʌŋk] N mofeta
sky [skaɪ] N cielo; **to praise sb to the skies** poner a algn por las nubes
sky-blue [skaɪ'blu:] ADJ (azul) celeste
skydiving ['skaɪdaɪvɪŋ] N paracaidismo acrobático
sky-high ['skaɪ'haɪ] ADJ (*inf*) por las nubes ▶ ADV (*throw*) muy alto; **prices have gone ~** (*inf*) los precios están por las nubes
skylark ['skaɪlɑ:k] N (*bird*) alondra
skylight ['skaɪlaɪt] N tragaluz *m*, claraboya
skyline ['skaɪlaɪn] N (*horizon*) horizonte *m*; (*of city*) perfil *m*
Skype® [skaɪp] (*Internet, Tel*) N Skype® *m* ▶ VT hablar con algn a través de Skype
skyscraper ['skaɪskreɪpəʳ] N rascacielos *m inv*
slab [slæb] N (*stone*) bloque *m*; (*of wood*) tabla, plancha; (*flat*) losa; (*of cake*) trozo; (*of meat, cheese*) tajada, trozo
slack [slæk] ADJ (*loose*) flojo; (*slow*) de poca actividad; (*careless*) descuidado; (*Comm: market*) poco activo; (: *demand*) débil; (*period*) bajo; **business is ~** hay poco movimiento en el negocio
slacken ['slækn] VI (*also*: **slacken off**) aflojarse ▶ VT aflojar; (*speed*) disminuir
slackness ['slæknɪs] N flojedad *f*; negligencia
slacks [slæks] NPL pantalones *mpl*
slag [slæg] N escoria, escombros *mpl*
slag heap N escorial *m*, escombrera
slain [sleɪn] PP *of* **slay**
slake [sleɪk] VT (*one's thirst*) apagar
slalom ['slɑ:ləm] N eslálom *m*
slam [slæm] VT (*door*) cerrar de golpe; (*throw*) arrojar (violentamente); (*criticize*) vapulear, vituperar ▶ VI cerrarse de golpe; **to ~ the door** dar un portazo
slammer ['slæməʳ] N (*inf*): **the ~** la trena, el talego
slander ['slɑ:ndəʳ] N calumnia, difamación *f* ▶ VT calumniar, difamar

slanderous ['slɑːndərəs] ADJ calumnioso, difamatorio

slang [slæŋ] N argot m; (jargon) jerga

slanging match ['slæŋɪŋ-] N (BRIT inf) bronca gorda

slant [slɑːnt] N sesgo, inclinación f; (fig) punto de vista, interpretación f; **to get a new ~ on sth** obtener un nuevo punto de vista sobre algo

slanted ['slɑːntɪd], **slanting** ['slɑːntɪŋ] ADJ inclinado

slap [slæp] N palmada; (in face) bofetada ▶ VT dar una palmada/bofetada a; (paint etc): **to ~ sth on sth** embadurnar algo con algo ▶ ADV (directly) de lleno

slapdash ['slæpdæʃ] ADJ chapucero

slaphead ['slæphɛd] N (inf) colgado(-a)

slapstick ['slæpstɪk] N: **~ comedy** comedia de payasadas

slap-up ['slæpʌp] ADJ: **a ~ meal** (BRIT) un banquetazo, una comilona

slash [slæʃ] VT acuchillar; (fig: prices) fulminar

slat [slæt] N (of wood, plastic) tablilla, listón m

slate [sleɪt] N pizarra ▶ VT (BRIT fig: criticize) vapulear

slaughter ['slɔːtə'] N (of animals) matanza; (of people) carnicería ▶ VT matar

slaughterhouse ['slɔːtəhaus] N matadero

Slav [slɑːv] ADJ eslavo

slave [sleɪv] N esclavo(-a) ▶ VI (also: **slave away**) trabajar como un negro; **to ~ (away) at sth** trabajar como un negro en algo

slave driver N (inf, pej) tirano(-a)

slave labour, (US) **slave labor** N trabajo de esclavos

slaver ['slævə'] VI (dribble) babear

slavery ['sleɪvərɪ] N esclavitud f

slavish ['sleɪvɪʃ] ADJ (devotion) de esclavo; (imitation) servil

slay [sleɪ] (pt **slew** [sluː], pp **slain** [sleɪn]) VT (literary) matar

sleazy ['sliːzɪ] ADJ (fig: place) sórdido

sledge [slɛdʒ], (US) **sled** [slɛd] N trineo

sledgehammer ['slɛdʒhæmə'] N mazo

sleek [sliːk] ADJ (shiny) lustroso

sleep [sliːp] (pt, pp **slept**) N sueño ▶ VI dormir ▶ VT: **we can ~ 4** podemos alojar a 4, tenemos cabida para 4; **to go to ~** dormirse; **to have a good night's ~** dormir toda la noche; **to put to ~** (patient) dormir; (animal: euphemism: kill) sacrificar; **to ~ lightly** tener el sueño ligero; **to ~ with sb** (euphemism) acostarse con algn ▶ **sleep in** VI (oversleep) quedarse dormido

sleeper ['sliːpə'] N (person) durmiente mf; (BRIT Rail: on track) traviesa; (: train) coche-cama m

sleepiness ['sliːpɪnɪs] N somnolencia

sleeping bag ['sliːpɪŋ-] N saco de dormir

sleeping car N coche-cama m

sleeping partner N (Comm) socio(-a) comanditario(-a)

sleeping pill N somnífero

sleeping sickness N enfermedad f del sueño

sleepless ['sliːplɪs] ADJ: **a ~ night** una noche en blanco

sleeplessness ['sliːplɪsnɪs] N insomnio

sleepover ['sliːpəuvə'] N: **we're having a ~ at Fiona's** nos quedamos a dormir en casa de Fiona

sleepwalk ['sliːpwɔːk] VI caminar dormido; (habitually) ser sonámbulo

sleepwalker ['sliːpwɔːkə'] N sonámbulo(-a)

sleepy ['sliːpɪ] ADJ soñoliento; (place) soporífero; **to be** or **feel ~** tener sueño

sleet [sliːt] N aguanieve f

sleeve [sliːv] N manga; (Tech) manguito; (of record) funda

sleeveless ['sliːvlɪs] ADJ (garment) sin mangas

sleigh [sleɪ] N trineo

sleight [slaɪt] N: **~ of hand** prestidigitación f

slender ['slɛndə'] ADJ delgado; (means) escaso

slept [slɛpt] PT, PP of **sleep**

sleuth [sluːθ] N (inf) detective mf

slew [sluː] VI (veer) torcerse ▶ PT of **slay**

slice [slaɪs] N (of meat) tajada; (of bread) rebanada; (of lemon) rodaja; (utensil) paleta ▶ VT cortar, tajar; rebanar; **sliced bread** pan m de molde

slick [slɪk] ADJ (skilful) hábil, diestro; (clever) astuto ▶ N (also: **oil slick**) marea negra

slid [slɪd] PT, PP of **slide**

slide [slaɪd] (pt, pp **slid**) N (in playground) tobogán m; (Phot) diapositiva; (microscope slide) portaobjetos m inv, plaquilla de vidrio; (BRIT: also: **hair slide**) pasador m ▶ VT correr, deslizar ▶ VI (slip) resbalarse; (glide) deslizarse; **to let things ~** (fig) dejar que ruede la bola

slide projector N (Phot) proyector m de diapositivas

slide rule N regla de cálculo

slide show N (Comput) pase m de diapositivas

sliding ['slaɪdɪŋ] ADJ (door) corredizo; **~ roof** (Aut) techo de corredera

sliding scale N escala móvil

slight [slaɪt] ADJ (slim) delgado; (frail) delicado; (pain etc) leve; (trifling) insignificante; (small) pequeño ▶ N desaire m ▶ VT (offend) ofender, desairar; **a ~ improvement** una ligera mejora; **not in the slightest** en absoluto; **there's not the slightest possibility** no hay la menor or más mínima posibilidad

slightly ['slaɪtlɪ] ADV ligeramente, un poco; **~ built** delgado

slim [slɪm] ADJ delgado, esbelto ▶ VI adelgazar

slime [slaɪm] N limo, cieno

slimming ['slɪmɪŋ] N adelgazamiento ▶ ADJ (*diet, pills*) adelgazante

slimness ['slɪmnɪs] N delgadez *f*

slimy ['slaɪmɪ] ADJ cenagoso; (*covered with mud*) fangoso; (*also fig: person*) adulón, zalamero

sling [slɪŋ] (*pt, pp* **slung** [slʌŋ]) N (*Med*) cabestrillo; (*weapon*) honda ▶ VT tirar, arrojar; **to have one's arm in a ~** llevar el brazo en cabestrillo

slink [slɪŋk] (*pt, pp* **slunk** [slʌŋk]) VI: **to ~ away, ~ off** escabullirse

slinky ['slɪŋkɪ] ADJ (*clothing*) pegado al cuerpo, superajustado

slip [slɪp] N (*slide*) resbalón *m*; (*mistake*) descuido; (*underskirt*) combinación *f*; (*of paper*) papelito ▶ VT (*slide*) deslizar ▶ VI (*slide*) deslizarse; (*stumble*) resbalar(se); (*decline*) decaer; (*move smoothly*): **to ~ into/out of** (*room etc*) colarse en/salirse de; **to let a chance ~ by** dejar escapar la oportunidad; **to ~ sth on/off** ponerse/quitarse algo; **to ~ on a jumper** ponerse un jersey *or* un suéter; **it slipped from her hand** se la cayó de la mano; **to give sb the ~** dar esquinazo a algn; **wages ~** (*BRIT*) hoja del sueldo; **a ~ of the tongue** un lapsus
  ▶ **slip away** VI escabullirse
  ▶ **slip in** VT meter ▶ VI meterse, colarse
  ▶ **slip out** VI (*go out*) salir (un momento)
  ▶ **slip up** VI (*make mistake*) equivocarse; meter la pata

slip-on ['slɪpɔn] ADJ de quita y pon; (*shoes*) sin cordones

slipped disc [slɪpt-] N vértebra dislocada

slipper ['slɪpəʳ] N zapatilla, pantufla

slippery ['slɪpərɪ] ADJ resbaladizo

slip road N (*BRIT*) carretera de acceso

slipshod ['slɪpʃɔd] ADJ descuidado, chapucero

slipstream ['slɪpstriːm] N viento de la hélice

slip-up ['slɪpʌp] N (*error*) desliz *m*

slipway ['slɪpweɪ] N grada, gradas *fpl*

slit [slɪt] (*pt, pp* **~**) N raja; (*cut*) corte *m* ▶ VT rajar, cortar; **to ~ sb's throat** cortarle el pescuezo a algn

slither ['slɪðəʳ] VI deslizarse

sliver ['slɪvəʳ] N (*of glass, wood*) astilla; (*of cheese, sausage*) lonja, loncha

slob [slɔb] N (*inf*) patán(-ana) *m/f*, palurdo(-a) *m/f*

slog [slɔg] (*BRIT*) VI sudar tinta ▶ N: **it was a ~** costó trabajo (hacerlo)

slogan ['sləʊgən] N eslogan *m*, lema *m*

slop [slɔp] VI (*also*: **slop over**) derramarse, desbordarse ▶ VT derramar, verter

slope [sləʊp] N (*up*) cuesta, pendiente *f*; (*down*) declive *m*; (*side of mountain*) falda, vertiente *f* ▶ VI: **to ~ down** estar en declive; **to ~ up** subir (en pendiente)

sloping ['sləʊpɪŋ] ADJ en pendiente; en declive

sloppily ['slɔpɪlɪ] ADV descuidadamente; con descuido *or* desaliño

sloppiness ['slɔpɪnɪs] N descuido; desaliño

sloppy ['slɔpɪ] ADJ (*work*) descuidado; (*appearance*) desaliñado

slosh [slɔʃ] VI: **to ~ about** *or* **around** chapotear

sloshed [slɔʃt] ADJ (*inf: drunk*): **to get ~** agarrar una trompa

slot [slɔt] N ranura; (*fig: in timetable*) hueco; (*Radio, TV*) espacio ▶ VT: **to ~ into** encajar en

sloth [sləʊθ] N (*vice*) pereza; (*Zool*) oso perezoso

slot machine N (*BRIT: vending machine*) máquina expendedora; (*for gambling*) máquina tragaperras

slot meter N contador *m*

slouch [slaʊtʃ] VI: **to ~ about, ~ around** (*laze*) gandulear

Slovak ['sləʊvæk] ADJ eslovaco ▶ N eslovaco(-a); (*Ling*) eslovaco; **the ~ Republic** Eslovaquia

Slovakia [sləʊ'vækɪə] N Eslovaquia

Slovakian [sləʊ'vækɪən] ADJ, N = **Slovak**

Slovene [sləʊ'viːn] ADJ esloveno ▶ N esloveno(-a); (*Ling*) esloveno

Slovenia [sləʊ'viːnɪə] N Eslovenia

Slovenian [sləʊ'viːnɪən] ADJ, N = **Slovene**

slovenly ['slʌvənlɪ] ADJ (*dirty*) desaliñado, desaseado; (*careless*) descuidado

slow [sləʊ] ADJ lento; (*watch*): **to be ~** ir atrasado ▶ ADV lentamente, despacio ▶ VT (*also*: **slow down, slow up**) retardar; (: *engine, machine*) reducir la marcha de ▶ VI (*also*: **slow down, slow up**) ir más despacio; **"~"** (*road sign*) "disminuir la velocidad"; **at a ~ speed** a una velocidad lenta; **the ~ lane** el carril derecho; **business is ~** (*Comm*) hay poca actividad; **my watch is 20 minutes ~** mi reloj lleva 20 minutos de retraso; **bake for two hours in a ~ oven** cocer *or* asar dos horas en el horno a fuego lento; **to be ~ to act/decide** tardar en obrar/decidir; **to go ~** (*driver*) conducir despacio; (*in industrial dispute*) trabajar a ritmo lento

slow-acting [sləʊ'æktɪŋ] ADJ de efecto retardado

slowcoach ['sləʊkəʊtʃ] N (*BRIT inf*) tortuga

slowdown ['sləʊdaʊn] N (*US*) huelga de celo

slowly ['sləʊlɪ] ADV lentamente, despacio; **to drive ~** conducir despacio; **~ but surely** lento pero seguro

slow motion N: **in ~** a cámara lenta

slow-moving ['sləʊ'muːvɪŋ] ADJ lento

slowpoke ['sləʊpəʊk] N (*US inf*) = **slowcoach**

sludge [slʌdʒ] N lodo, fango

slug [slʌg] N babosa; (*bullet*) posta

sluggish ['slʌgɪʃ] ADJ (slow) lento; (lazy) perezoso; (business, market, sales) inactivo

sluggishly ['slʌgɪʃlɪ] ADV lentamente

sluggishness ['slʌgɪʃnɪs] N lentitud f

sluice [sluːs] N (gate) esclusa; (channel) canal m ▶ VT: **to ~ down** or **out** regar

slum [slʌm] N (area) barrios mpl bajos; (house) casucha

slumber ['slʌmbə'] N sueño

slum clearance, slum clearance programme N (programa m de) deschabolización f

slump [slʌmp] N (economic) depresión f ▶ VI hundirse; (prices) caer en picado; **the ~ in the price of copper** la baja repentina del precio del cobre; **he was slumped over the wheel** se había desplomado encima del volante

slung [slʌŋ] PT, PP of **sling**

slunk [slʌŋk] PT, PP of **slink**

slur [sləː'] N calumnia ▶ VT calumniar, difamar; (word) pronunciar mal; **to cast a ~ on sb** manchar la reputación de algn, difamar a algn

slurp [sləːp] VT, VI sorber ruidosamente

slurred [sləːd] ADJ (pronunciation) poco claro

slush [slʌʃ] N nieve f a medio derretir

slush fund N fondos mpl para sobornar

slushy ['slʌʃɪ] ADJ (inf: poetry etc) sentimentaloide

slut [slʌt] N marrana

sly [slaɪ] ADJ (clever) astuto; (nasty) malicioso

slyly ['slaɪlɪ] ADV astutamente; taimadamente

slyness ['slaɪnɪs] N astucia

SM N ABBR = **sado-masochism**

smack [smæk] N (slap) bofetada; (blow) golpe m ▶ VT dar una manotada a; golpear con la mano ▶ VI: **to ~ of** saber a, oler a ▶ ADV: **it fell ~ in the middle** (inf) cayó justo en medio

smacker ['smækə'] N (inf: kiss) besazo; (: BRIT: pound note) billete m de una libra; (: US: dollar bill) billete m de un dólar

small [smɔːl] ADJ pequeño, chico (LAM); (in height) bajo, chaparro (LAM); (letter) en minúscula ▶ N: **~ of the back** región f lumbar; **~ shopkeeper** pequeño(-a) comerciante m/f; **to get** or **grow smaller** (stain, town) empequeñecer; (debt, organization, numbers) reducir, disminuir; **to make smaller** (amount, income) reducir; (garden, object, garment) achicar

small ads NPL (BRIT) anuncios mpl por palabras

small arms NPL armas fpl cortas

small business N pequeño negocio; **small businesses** la pequeña empresa

small change N suelto, cambio

smallholder ['smɔːlhəʊldə'] N (BRIT) granjero(-a), parcelero(-a)

smallholding ['smɔːlhəʊldɪŋ] N parcela, minifundio

small hours NPL: **in the ~** a altas horas de la noche

smallish ['smɔːlɪʃ] ADJ más bien pequeño

small-minded [smɔːl'maɪndɪd] ADJ mezquino, de miras estrechas

smallness ['smɔːlnɪs] N pequeñez f

smallpox ['smɔːlpɒks] N viruela

small print N letra pequeña or menuda

small-scale ['smɔːlskeɪl] ADJ (map, model) a escala reducida; (business, farming) en pequeña escala

small talk N cháchara

small-time ['smɔːltaɪm] ADJ (inf) de poca categoría or monta; **a ~ thief** un(a) ratero(-a)

small-town ['smɔːltəʊn] ADJ de provincias

smarmy ['smɑːmɪ] ADJ (BRIT pej) pelotillero (inf)

smart [smɑːt] ADJ elegante; (clever) listo, inteligente; (quick) rápido, vivo; (weapon) inteligente ▶ VI escocer, picar; **the ~ set** la gente de buen tono; **to look ~** estar elegante; **my eyes are smarting** me pican los ojos

smartcard ['smɑːtkɑːd] N tarjeta inteligente

smarten up ['smɑːtn-] VI arreglarse ▶ VT arreglar

smartness ['smɑːtnɪs] N elegancia; (cleverness) inteligencia

smart phone N smartphone m

smash [smæʃ] N (also: **smash-up**) choque m; (sound) estrépito ▶ VT (break) hacer pedazos; (car etc) estrellar; (Sport: record) batir ▶ VI hacerse pedazos; (against wall etc) estrellarse ▶ **smash up** VT (car) hacer pedazos; (room) destrozar

smash hit N exitazo

smashing ['smæʃɪŋ] ADJ (inf) estupendo

smattering ['smætərɪŋ] N: **a ~ of Spanish** algo de español

smear [smɪə'] N mancha; (Med) frotis m inv (cervical); (insult) calumnia ▶ VT untar; (fig) calumniar, difamar; **his hands were smeared with oil/ink** tenía las manos manchadas de aceite/tinta

smear campaign N campaña de calumnias

smear test N (Med) citología, frotis m inv (cervical)

smell [smɛl] (pt, pp **smelt** or **smelled**) N olor m; (sense) olfato ▶ VT, VI oler; **it smells good/of garlic** huele bien/a ajo

smelly ['smɛlɪ] ADJ maloliente

smelt [smɛlt] VT (ore) fundir ▶ PT, PP of **smell**

smile [smaɪl] N sonrisa ▶ VI sonreír

smiley ['smaɪlɪ] N (in email etc) smiley m, emoticón m

smiling ['smaɪlɪŋ] ADJ sonriente, risueño

smirk [sməːk] N sonrisa falsa or afectada

smith [smɪθ] N herrero

smitten ['smɪtn] ADJ: **he's really ~ with her** está totalmente loco por ella

smock [smɔk] N blusón; (*children's*) babi *m*; (*US: overall*) guardapolvo, bata

smog [smɔg] N smog *m*

smoke [sməʊk] N humo ▶ VI fumar; (*chimney*) echar humo ▶ VT (*cigarettes*) fumar; **to go up in ~** quemarse; (*fig*) quedar en agua de borrajas

smoke alarm N detector *m* de humo, alarma contra incendios

smoked [sməʊkt] ADJ (*bacon, glass*) ahumado

smokeless fuel ['sməʊklɪs-] N combustible *m* sin humo

smokeless zone ['sməʊklɪs-] N zona libre de humo

smoker ['sməʊkə'] N fumador(a) *m/f*

smoke screen N cortina de humo

smoke shop N (*US*) estanco, tabaquería

smoking ['sməʊkɪŋ] N: **"no ~"** "prohibido fumar"; **he's given up ~** ha dejado de fumar

smoking compartment, (*US*) **smoking car** N departamento de fumadores

smoky ['sməʊkɪ] ADJ (*room*) lleno de humo

smolder ['sməʊldə'] VI (*US*) = **smoulder**

smoochy ['smu:tʃɪ] ADJ (*inf*) blandengue

smooth [smu:ð] ADJ liso; (*sea*) tranquilo; (*flavour, movement*) suave; (*person: pej*) meloso ▶ VT alisar; (*also*: **smooth out**: *creases*) alisar; (: *difficulties*) allanar

▶ **smooth over** VT: **to ~ things over** (*fig*) limar las asperezas

smoothly ['smu:ðlɪ] ADV (*easily*) fácilmente; **everything went ~** todo fue sobre ruedas

smoothness ['smu:ðnɪs] N (*of skin, cloth*) tersura; (*of surface, flavour, movement*) suavidad *f*

smother ['smʌðə'] VT sofocar; (*repress*) contener

smoulder, (*US*) **smolder** ['sməʊldə'] VI arder sin llama

SMS N ABBR (= *short message service*) SMS *m*

SMS message N (mensaje *m*) SMS *m*

smudge [smʌdʒ] N mancha ▶ VT manchar

smug [smʌg] ADJ engreído

smuggle ['smʌgl] VT pasar de contrabando; **to ~ in/out** (*goods etc*) meter/sacar de contrabando

smuggler ['smʌglə'] N contrabandista *mf*

smuggling ['smʌglɪŋ] N contrabando

smugly ['smʌglɪ] ADV con suficiencia

smugness ['smʌgnɪs] N suficiencia

smut [smʌt] N (*grain of soot*) carbonilla, hollín *m*; (*mark*) tizne *m*; (*in conversation etc*) obscenidades *fpl*

smutty ['smʌtɪ] ADJ (*fig*) verde, obsceno

snack [snæk] N bocado, tentempié *m*; **to have a ~** tomar un bocado

snack bar N cafetería

snag [snæg] N problema *m*; **to run into** or **hit a ~** encontrar inconvenientes, dar con un obstáculo

snail [sneɪl] N caracol *m*

snake [sneɪk] N (*gen*) serpiente *f*; (*harmless*) culebra; (*poisonous*) víbora

snap [snæp] N (*sound*) chasquido; golpe *m* seco; (*photograph*) foto *f* ▶ ADJ (*decision*) instantáneo ▶ VT (*fingers etc*) castañetear; (*break*) partir, quebrar; (*photograph*) tomar una foto de ▶ VI (*break*) partirse, quebrarse; (*fig: person*) contestar bruscamente; **to ~ shut** cerrarse de golpe; **a cold ~** (*of weather*) una ola de frío

▶ **snap at** VT FUS: **to ~ (at sb)** (*person*) hablar con brusquedad (a algn); (*dog*) intentar morder (a algn); **to ~ one's fingers at sth/ sb** (*fig*) burlarse de algo/uno

▶ **snap off** VI (*break*) partirse

▶ **snap up** VT agarrar

snap fastener N (*US*) botón *m* de presión

snappy ['snæpɪ] ADJ (*answer*) instantáneo; (*slogan*) conciso; **make it ~!** (*inf: hurry up*) ¡date prisa!

snapshot ['snæpʃɔt] N foto *f* (instántanea)

snare [snɛə'] N trampa ▶ VT cazar con trampa; (*fig*) engañar

snarl [snɑ:l] N gruñido ▶ VI gruñir; **to get snarled up** (*wool, plans*) enmarañarse, enredarse; (*traffic*) quedar atascado

snatch [snætʃ] N (*small piece*) fragmento; (*fig*) robo; **snatches of** trocitos *mpl* de ▶ VT (*snatch away*) arrebatar; (*grasp*) coger (*SP*), agarrar; **snatches of conversation** fragmentos *mpl* de conversación; **to ~ a sandwich** comer un bocadillo aprisa; **to ~ some sleep** buscar tiempo para dormir; **don't ~!** ¡no me lo quites!

▶ **snatch up** VT agarrar

snazzy ['snæzɪ] ADJ (*inf*) guapo

sneak [sni:k] VI: **to ~ in/out** entrar/salir a hurtadillas ▶ VT: **to ~ a look at sth** mirar algo de reojo ▶ N (*inf*) soplón(-ona) *m/f*; **to ~ up on sb** aparecérsele de improviso a algn

sneakers ['sni:kəz] NPL (*US*) zapatos *mpl* de lona, zapatillas *fpl*

sneaking ['sni:kɪŋ] ADJ: **to have a ~ feeling/ suspicion that ...** tener la sensación/ sospecha de que ...

sneaky ['sni:kɪ] ADJ furtivo

sneer [snɪə'] N sonrisa de desprecio ▶ VI sonreír con desprecio; **to ~ at sth/sb** burlarse or mofarse de algo/algn

sneeze [sni:z] N estornudo ▶ VI estornudar

snide [snaɪd] ADJ (*inf: sarcastic*) sarcástico

sniff [snɪf] VI sorber (por la nariz) ▶ VT husmear, oler; (*glue, drug*) esnifar

▶ **sniff at** VT FUS: **it's not to be sniffed at** no es de despreciar

sniffer dog ['snɪfə-] N (*for drugs*) perro antidroga; (*for explosives*) perro antiexplosivos

snigger ['snɪgər] N risa disimulada ▶ VI reírse con disimulo

snip [snɪp] N (*piece*) recorte *m*; (*bargain*) ganga ▶ VT tijeretear

sniper ['snaɪpər] N francotirador(a) *m/f*

snippet ['snɪpɪt] N retazo

snivelling, (*US*) **sniveling** ['snɪvlɪŋ] ADJ llorón(-ona)

snob [snɔb] N (e)snob *mf*

snobbery ['snɔbərɪ] N (e)snobismo

snobbish ['snɔbɪʃ] ADJ (e)snob

snobbishness ['snɔbɪʃnɪs] N (e)snobismo

snog [snɔg] VI (*BRIT inf*) besuquearse, morrear; **to ~ sb** besuquear a algn

snooker ['snuːkər] N snooker *m*, billar *m* inglés

snoop [snuːp] VI: **to ~ about** fisgonear

snooper ['snuːpər] N fisgón(-ona) *m/f*

snooty ['snuːtɪ] ADJ (e)snob

snooze [snuːz] N siesta ▶ VI echar una siesta

snore [snɔːʳ] VI roncar ▶ N ronquido

snoring ['snɔːrɪŋ] N ronquidos *mpl*

snorkel ['snɔːkl] N tubo de respiración

snort [snɔːt] N bufido ▶ VI bufar ▶ VT (*inf: drugs*) esnifar

snotty ['snɔtɪ] ADJ (*inf*) creído

snout [snaut] N hocico, morro

snow [snəu] N nieve *f* ▶ VI nevar ▶ VT: **to be snowed under with work** estar agobiado de trabajo

snowball ['snəubɔːl] N bola de nieve ▶ VI ir aumentando

snow-blind ['snəublaɪnd] ADJ cegado por la nieve

snowboarding ['snəubɔːdɪŋ] N snowboard *m*

snowbound ['snəubaund] ADJ bloqueado por la nieve

snow-capped ['snəukæpt] ADJ (*peak*) cubierto de nieve, nevado

snowdrift ['snəudrɪft] N ventisquero

snowdrop ['snəudrɔp] N campanilla

snowfall ['snəufɔːl] N nevada

snowflake ['snəufleɪk] N copo de nieve

snowline ['snəulaɪn] N límite *m* de las nieves perpetuas

snowman ['snəumæn] N (*irreg*) figura de nieve

snowplough, (*US*) **snowplow** ['snəuplau] N quitanieves *m inv*

snowshoe ['snəuʃuː] N raqueta (de nieve)

snowstorm ['snəustɔːm] N tormenta de nieve, nevasca

Snow White N Blancanieves *f*

snowy ['snəuɪ] ADJ de (mucha) nieve

SNP N ABBR (*BRIT Pol*) = **Scottish National Party**

snub [snʌb] VT: **to ~ sb** desairar a algn ▶ N desaire *m*, repulsa

snub-nosed [snʌb'nəuzd] ADJ chato

snuff [snʌf] N rapé *m* ▶ VT (*also:* **snuff out**: *candle*) apagar

snuffbox ['snʌfbɔks] N caja de rapé

snuff movie N (*inf*) película porno (*que acaba con un asesinato real*)

snug [snʌg] ADJ (*cosy*) cómodo; (*fitted*) ajustado

snuggle ['snʌgl] VI: **to ~ down in bed** hacerse un ovillo *or* acurrucarse en la cama; **to ~ up to sb** acurrucarse junto a algn

snugly ['snʌglɪ] ADV cómodamente; **it fits ~** (*object in pocket etc*) cabe perfectamente; (*garment*) ajusta perfectamente

SO ABBR (*Banking*) = **standing order**

(KEYWORD)

so [səu] ADV **1** (*thus, likewise*) así, de este modo; **if so** de ser así; **I like swimming — so do I** a mí me gusta nadar — a mí también; **I've got work to do — so has Paul** tengo trabajo que hacer — Paul también; **it's five o'clock — so it is!** son las cinco — ¡pues es verdad!; **I hope/think so** espero/creo que sí; **so far** hasta ahora; (*in past*) hasta este momento; **so to speak** por decirlo así

2 (*in comparisons etc: to such a degree*) tan; **so quickly (that)** tan rápido (que); **so big (that)** tan grande (que); **she's not so clever as her brother** no es tan lista como su hermano; **we were so worried** estábamos preocupadísimos

3: **so much** *adj* tanto(-a); *adv* tanto; **so many** tantos(-as)

4 (*phrases*): **10 or so** unos 10, 10 o así; **so long!** (*inf: goodbye*) ¡hasta luego!; **she didn't so much as send me a birthday card** no me mandó ni una tarjeta siquiera por mi cumpleaños; **so (what)?** (*inf*) ¿y qué?

▶ CONJ **1** (*expressing purpose*): **so as to do** para hacer; **so (that)** para que + *subjun*; **we hurried so (that) we wouldn't be late** nos dimos prisa para no llegar tarde

2 (*expressing result*) así que; **so you see, I could have gone** así que ya ves, (yo) podría haber ido; **so that's the reason!** ¡así que es por eso *or* por eso es!

soak [səuk] VT (*drench*) empapar; (*put in water*) remojar ▶ VI remojarse, estar a remojo

▶ **soak in** VI penetrar

▶ **soak up** VT absorber

soaking ['səukɪŋ] ADJ (*also:* **soaking wet**) calado *or* empapado (hasta los huesos *or* el tuétano)

so-and-so ['səuənsəu] N (*somebody*) fulano(-a) de tal

soap [səup] N jabón *m*

soapbox ['səupbɔks] N tribuna improvisada

S

soapflakes ['səupfleɪks] NPL jabón *msg* en escamas

soap opera N (*TV*) telenovela; (*Radio*) radionovela

soap powder N jabón *m* en polvo

soapsuds ['səupsʌdz] NPL espuma *sg*

soapy ['səupɪ] ADJ jabonoso

soar [sɔːʳ] VI (*on wings*) remontarse; (*building etc*) elevarse; (*price*) dispararse; (*morale*) elevarse

soaring ['sɔːrɪŋ] ADJ (*flight*) por lo alto; (*prices*) en alza *or* aumento; **~ inflation** inflación *f* altísima *or* en aumento

sob [sɔb] N sollozo ▶ VI sollozar

s.o.b. N ABBR (*US: inf!: = son of a bitch*) hijo de puta (!)

sober ['səubəʳ] ADJ (*moderate*) moderado; (*serious*) serio; (*not drunk*) sobrio; (*colour, style*) discreto

▶ **sober up** VI pasársele a algn la borrachera

soberly ['səubəlɪ] ADV sobriamente

sobriety [sə'braɪətɪ] N (*not being drunk*) sobriedad *f*; (*seriousness, sedateness*) seriedad *f*, sensatez *f*

sob story N (*inf, pej*) dramón *m*

Soc. ABBR (= *society*) S

so-called ['səu'kɔːld] ADJ llamado

soccer ['sɔkəʳ] N fútbol *m*

soccer pitch N campo *or* cancha (*LAм*) de fútbol

soccer player N jugador(a) *m/f* de fútbol

sociability [səuʃə'bɪlɪtɪ] N sociabilidad *f*

sociable ['səuʃəbl] ADJ sociable

social ['səuʃl] ADJ social ▶ N velada, fiesta

social class N clase *f* social

social climber N arribista *mf*

social club N club *m*

Social Democrat N socialdemócrata *mf*

social insurance N (*US*) seguro social

socialism ['səuʃəlɪzəm] N socialismo

socialist ['səuʃəlɪst] ADJ, N socialista *mf*

socialite ['səuʃəlaɪt] N *persona que alterna con la buena sociedad*

socialize ['səuʃəlaɪz] VI hacer vida social; **to ~ with** (*colleagues*) salir con

social life N vida social

socially ['səuʃəlɪ] ADV socialmente

social media NPL medios sociales

social networking [-'nɛtwə:kɪŋ] N interacción *f* social a través de la red

social networking site N red *f* social

social science N, **social sciences** NPL ciencias *fpl* sociales

social security N seguridad *f* social

social services NPL servicios *mpl* sociales

social welfare N asistencia social

social work N asistencia social

social worker N asistente(-a) *m/f* social

society [sə'saɪətɪ] N sociedad *f*; (*club*) asociación *f*; (*also*: **high society**) alta sociedad ▶ CPD (*party, column*) social, de sociedad

socio-economic ['səusɪəui:kə'nɔmɪk] ADJ socioeconómico

sociological [səusɪə'lɔdʒɪkəl] ADJ sociológico

sociologist [səusɪ'ɔlədʒɪst] N sociólogo(-a)

sociology [səusɪ'ɔlədʒɪ] N sociología

sock [sɔk] N calcetín *m*, media (*LAм*); **to pull one's socks up** (*fig*) hacer esfuerzos, despabilarse

socket ['sɔkɪt] N (*Elec*) enchufe *m*

sod [sɔd] N (*of earth*) césped *m*; (*inf!*) cabrón(-ona) *m/f* (!) ▶ EXCL: **~ off!** (*inf!*) ¡vete a la porra!

soda ['səudə] N (*Chem*) sosa; (*also*: **soda water**) soda; (*US: also*: **soda pop**) gaseosa

sodden ['sɔdn] ADJ empapado

sodium ['səudɪəm] N sodio

sodium chloride N cloruro sódico *or* de sodio

sofa ['səufə] N sofá *m*

sofa bed N sofá-cama *m*

Sofia ['səufɪə] N Sofía

soft [sɔft] ADJ (*teacher, parent*) blando; (*gentle, not loud*) suave; (*stupid*) bobo; **~ currency** divisa blanda *or* débil

soft-boiled ['sɔftbɔɪld] ADJ (*egg*) pasado por agua

soft copy N (*Comput*) copia transitoria

soft drink N bebida no alcohólica

soft drugs NPL drogas *fpl* blandas

soften ['sɔfn] VT ablandar; suavizar ▶ VI ablandarse; suavizarse

softener ['sɔfnəʳ] N suavizante *m*

soft fruit N bayas *fpl*

soft furnishings NPL tejidos *mpl* para el hogar

soft-hearted [sɔft'hɑːtɪd] ADJ bondadoso

softly ['sɔftlɪ] ADV suavemente; (*gently*) delicadamente, con delicadeza

softness ['sɔftnɪs] N blandura; suavidad *f*

soft option N alternativa fácil

soft sell N venta persuasiva

soft target N blanco *or* objetivo fácil

soft toy N juguete *m* de peluche

software ['sɔftwɛəʳ] N (*Comput*) software *m*

soft water N agua blanda

soggy ['sɔgɪ] ADJ empapado

soil [sɔɪl] N (*earth*) tierra, suelo ▶ VT ensuciar

soiled [sɔɪld] ADJ sucio, manchado

sojourn ['sɔdʒəːn] N (*formal*) estancia

solace ['sɔlɪs] N consuelo

solar ['səuləʳ] ADJ solar

solarium [sə'lɛərɪəm] (*pl* **solaria** [-rɪə]) N solario

solar panel N panel *m* solar

solar plexus [-'plɛksəs] N (*Anat*) plexo solar

solar power N energía solar

solar system N sistema m solar
sold [səuld] PT, PP of **sell**
solder ['səuldə^r] VT soldar ▶ N soldadura
soldier ['səuldʒə^r] N (gen) soldado; (army man) militar m ▶ VI: **to ~ on** seguir adelante; **toy ~** soldadito de plomo
sold out ADJ (Comm) agotado
sole [səul] N (of foot) planta; (of shoe) suela; (fish: pl inv) lenguado ▶ ADJ único; **the ~ reason** la única razón
solely ['səullɪ] ADV únicamente, sólo, solamente; **I will hold you ~ responsible** le consideraré el único responsable
solemn ['sɔləm] ADJ solemne
sole trader N (Comm) comerciante mf exclusivo(-a)
solicit [sə'lɪsɪt] VT (request) solicitar ▶ VI (prostitute) abordar clientes
solicitor [sə'lɪsɪtə^r] N (BRIT: for wills etc) ≈ notario(-a); (in court) ≈ abogado(-a); see also **barrister**
solid ['sɔlɪd] ADJ sólido; (gold etc) macizo; (line) continuo; (vote) unánime ▶ N sólido; **we waited two ~ hours** esperamos dos horas enteras; **to be on ~ ground** estar en tierra firme; (fig) estar seguro
solidarity [sɔlɪ'dærɪtɪ] N solidaridad f
solid fuel N combustible m sólido
solidify [sə'lɪdɪfaɪ] VI solidificarse
solidity [sə'lɪdɪtɪ] N solidez f
solidly ['sɔlɪdlɪ] ADV sólidamente; (fig) unánimemente
solid-state ['sɔlɪdsteɪt] ADJ (Elec) estado sólido
soliloquy [sə'lɪləkwɪ] N soliloquio
solitaire [sɔlɪ'tɛə^r] N (game, gem) solitario
solitary ['sɔlɪtərɪ] ADJ solitario, solo; (isolated) apartado, aislado; (only) único
solitary confinement N incomunicación f; **to be in ~** estar incomunicado
solitude ['sɔlɪtjuːd] N soledad f
solo ['səuləu] N solo ▶ ADV (fly) en solitario
soloist ['səuləuɪst] N solista mf
Solomon Islands ['sɔləmən-] NPL: **the ~** las Islas Salomón
solstice ['sɔlstɪs] N solsticio
soluble ['sɔljubl] ADJ soluble
solution [sə'luːʃən] N solución f
solve [sɔlv] VT resolver, solucionar
solvency ['sɔlvənsɪ] N (Comm) solvencia
solvent ['sɔlvənt] ADJ (Comm) solvente ▶ N (Chem) solvente m
solvent abuse N uso indebido de disolventes
Som. ABBR (BRIT) = **Somerset**
Somali [sə'mɑːlɪ] ADJ, N somalí mf
Somalia [sə'mɑːlɪə] N Somalia
Somaliland [sə'mɑːlɪlænd] N Somaliland f
sombre, (US) **somber** ['sɔmbə^r] ADJ sombrío

(KEYWORD)

some [sʌm] ADJ **1** (a certain amount or number of): **some tea/water/biscuits** té/agua/(unas) galletas; **have some tea** tómese un té; **there's some milk in the fridge** hay leche en el frigo; **there were some people outside** había algunas personas fuera; **I've got some money, but not much** tengo algo de dinero, pero no mucho
2 (certain: in contrasts) algunos(-as); **some people say that …** hay quien dice que …; **some films were excellent, but most were mediocre** hubo películas excelentes, pero la mayoría fueron mediocres
3 (unspecified): **some woman was asking for you** una mujer estuvo preguntando por ti; **some day** algún día; **some day next week** un día de la semana que viene; **he was asking for some book (or other)** pedía no se qué libro; **in some way or other** de alguna que otra manera
4 (considerable amount of) bastante; **some days ago** hace unos cuantos días; **after some time** pasado algún tiempo; **at some length** con mucho detalle
5 (inf: intensive): **that was some party!** ¡menuda fiesta!
▶ PRON **1** (a certain number): **I've got some** (books etc) tengo algunos(-as)
2 (a certain amount) algo; **I've got some** (money, milk) tengo algo; **would you like some?** (coffee etc) ¿quiere un poco?; (books etc) ¿quiere alguno?; **could I have some of that cheese?** ¿me puede dar un poco de ese queso?; **I've read some of the book** he leído parte del libro
▶ ADV: **some 10 people** unas 10 personas, una decena de personas

somebody ['sʌmbədɪ] PRON alguien; **~ or other** alguien
someday ['sʌmdeɪ] ADV algún día
somehow ['sʌmhau] ADV de alguna manera; (for some reason) por una u otra razón
someone ['sʌmwʌn] PRON = **somebody**
someplace ['sʌmpleɪs] ADV (US) = **somewhere**
somersault ['sʌməsɔːlt] N (deliberate) salto mortal; (accidental) vuelco ▶ VI dar un salto mortal; dar vuelcos
something ['sʌmθɪŋ] PRON algo ▶ ADV: **he's ~ like me** es un poco como yo; **~ to do** algo que hacer; **it's ~ of a problem** es bastante problemático; **would you like ~ to eat/drink?** ¿te gustaría cenar/tomar algo?
sometime ['sʌmtaɪm] ADV (in future) algún día, en algún momento; **~ last month** durante el mes pasado; **I'll finish it ~** lo terminaré un día de éstos

S

sometimes ['sʌmtaɪmz] ADV a veces

somewhat ['sʌmwɔt] ADV algo

somewhere ['sʌmwɛər] ADV (be) en alguna parte; (go) a alguna parte; **~ else** (be) en otra parte; (go) a otra parte

son [sʌn] N hijo

sonar ['səʊnɑːr] N sonar m

sonata [sə'nɑːtə] N sonata

song [sɒŋ] N canción f

songwriter ['sɒŋraɪtər] N compositor(a) m/f de canciones

sonic ['sɒnɪk] ADJ (boom) sónico

son-in-law ['sʌnɪnlɔː] N yerno

sonnet ['sɒnɪt] N soneto

sonny ['sʌnɪ] N (inf) hijo

soon [suːn] ADV pronto, dentro de poco; **~ afterwards** poco después; **very/quite ~** muy/bastante pronto; **how ~ can you be ready?** ¿cuánto tardas en prepararte?; **it's too ~ to tell** es demasiado pronto para saber; **see you ~!** ¡hasta pronto!; see also **as**

sooner ['suːnər] ADV (time) antes, más temprano; **I would ~ do that** preferiría hacer eso; **~ or later** tarde o temprano; **no ~ said than done** dicho y hecho; **the ~ the better** cuanto antes mejor; **no ~ had we left than ...** apenas nos habíamos marchado cuando ...

soot [sʊt] N hollín m

soothe [suːð] VT tranquilizar; (pain) aliviar

soothing ['suːðɪŋ] ADJ (ointment etc) sedante; (tone, words etc) calmante, tranquilizante

SOP N ABBR = **standard operating procedure**

sophisticated [sə'fɪstɪkeɪtɪd] ADJ sofisticado

sophistication [səfɪstɪ'keɪʃən] N sofisticación f

sophomore ['sɒfəmɔːr] N (US) estudiante mf de segundo año

soporific [sɒpə'rɪfɪk] ADJ soporífero

sopping ['sɒpɪŋ] ADJ: **~ (wet)** empapado

soppy ['sɒpɪ] ADJ (pej) bobo, tonto

soprano [sə'prɑːnəʊ] N soprano f

sorbet ['sɔːbeɪ] N sorbete m

sorcerer ['sɔːsərər] N hechicero

sordid ['sɔːdɪd] ADJ (place etc) sórdido; (motive etc) mezquino

sore [sɔːr] ADJ (painful) doloroso, que duele; (offended) resentido ▶ N llaga; **~ throat** dolor m de garganta; **my eyes are ~, I have ~ eyes** me duelen los ojos; **it's a ~ point** es un asunto delicado or espinoso

sorely ADV: **I am ~ tempted to (do it)** estoy muy tentado a (hacerlo)

soreness ['sɔːnɪs] N dolor m

sorrel ['sɒrəl] N (Bot) acedera

sorrow ['sɒrəʊ] N pena, dolor m

sorrowful ['sɒrəʊful] ADJ afligido, triste

sorrowfully ['sɒrəʊfulɪ] ADV tristemente

sorry ['sɒrɪ] ADJ (regretful) arrepentido; (condition, excuse) lastimoso; (sight, failure) triste; **~!** ¡perdón!, ¡perdone!; **~?** ¿cómo?; **I am ~** lo siento; **I feel ~ for him** me da lástima or pena; **I'm ~ to hear that ...** siento saber que ...; **to be ~ about sth** lamentar algo

sort [sɔːt] N clase f, género, tipo; (make: of coffee, car etc) marca ▶ VT (also: **sort out**: papers) clasificar; (: organize) ordenar, organizar; (: resolve: problem, situation etc) arreglar, solucionar; (: Comput) clasificar; **what ~ do you want?** (make) ¿qué marca quieres?; **what ~ of car?** ¿qué tipo de coche?; **I shall do nothing of the ~** no pienso hacer nada parecido; **it's ~ of awkward** (inf) es bastante difícil

sortie ['sɔːtɪ] N salida

sorting office ['sɔːtɪŋ-] N oficina de clasificación del correo

SOS N SOS m

so-so ['səʊsəʊ] ADV regular, así así

soufflé ['suːfleɪ] N suflé m

sought [sɔːt] PT, PP of **seek**

sought-after ['sɔːtɑːftər] ADJ solicitado, codiciado

soul [səʊl] N alma f; **God rest his ~** Dios le reciba en su seno or en su gloria; **I didn't see a ~** no vi a nadie; **the poor ~ had nowhere to sleep** el pobre no tenía dónde dormir

soul-destroying ['səʊldɪstrɔɪɪŋ] ADJ (work) deprimente

soulful ['səʊlful] ADJ lleno de sentimiento

soulmate ['səʊlmeɪt] N compañero(-a) del alma

soul-searching ['səʊlsɜːtʃɪŋ] N: **after much ~** después de pensarlo mucho, después de darle muchas vueltas

sound [saʊnd] ADJ (healthy) sano; (safe, not damaged) en buen estado; (valid: argument, policy, claim) válido; (: move) acertado; (dependable: person) de fiar; (sensible) sensato, razonable ▶ ADV: **~ asleep** profundamente dormido ▶ N (noise) sonido, ruido; (volume: on TV etc) volumen m; (Geo) estrecho ▶ VT (alarm) sonar; (also: **sound out**: opinions) consultar, sondear ▶ VI sonar, resonar; (fig: seem) parecer; **to ~ like** sonar a; **to be of ~ mind** estar en su sano juicio; **I don't like the ~ of it** no me gusta nada; **it sounds as if ...** parece que ...
▶ **sound off** VI (inf): **to ~ off (about)** (give one's opinions) despotricar (contra)

sound barrier N barrera del sonido

sound bite N cita jugosa

sound effects NPL efectos mpl sonoros

sound engineer N ingeniero(-a) de sonido

sounding ['saʊndɪŋ] N (Naut etc) sondeo

sounding board N caja de resonancia

soundly ['saʊndlɪ] ADV (sleep) profundamente; (beat) completamente

soundproof ['saundpru:f] ADJ insonorizado
sound system N equipo de sonido
soundtrack ['saundtræk] N (of film) banda sonora
sound wave N (Physics) onda sonora
soup [su:p] N (thick) sopa; (thin) caldo; **in the ~** (fig) en apuros
soup kitchen N comedor m de beneficencia
soup plate N plato sopero
soupspoon ['su:pspu:n] N cuchara sopera
sour ['sauə^r] ADJ agrio; (milk) cortado; **it's just ~ grapes!** (fig) ¡pura envidia!, ¡están verdes!; **to go** or **turn ~** (milk) cortarse; (wine) agriarse; (fig: relationship) agriarse; (: plans) irse a pique
source [sɔ:s] N fuente f; **I have it from a reliable ~ that …** sé de fuente fidedigna que …
source language N (Comput) lenguaje m fuente or de origen
south [sauθ] N sur m ▶ ADJ del sur ▶ ADV al sur, hacia el sur; **(to the) ~ of** al sur de; **the S~ of France** el Sur de Francia; **to travel ~** viajar hacia el sur
South Africa N Sudáfrica
South African ADJ, N sudafricano(-a) m/f
South America N América del Sur, Sudamérica
South American ADJ, N sudamericano(-a) m/f
southbound ['sauθbaund] ADJ en dirección al sur
south-east [sauθ'i:st] N sudeste m, sureste m ▶ ADJ (counties etc) (del) sudeste, (del) sureste
Southeast Asia N Sudeste m asiático
southeastern [sauθ'i:stən] ADJ (del) sudeste, (del) sureste
southerly ['sʌðəlɪ] ADJ sur; (from the south) del sur
southern ['sʌðən] ADJ del sur, meridional; **the ~ hemisphere** el hemisferio sur
South Korea N Corea del Sur
South Pole N Polo Sur
South Sea Islands NPL: **the ~** Oceanía
South Seas NPL: **the ~** los Mares del Sur
South Vietnam N Vietnam m del Sur
southward ['sauθwəd], **southwards** ['sauθwədz] ADV hacia el sur
south-west [sauθ'wɛst] N suroeste m
southwestern [sauθ'wɛstən] ADJ suroeste
souvenir [su:və'nɪə^r] N recuerdo
sovereign ['sɔvrɪn] ADJ, N soberano(-a) m/f
sovereignty ['sɔvrɪntɪ] N soberanía
soviet ['səuvɪət] ADJ soviético
Soviet Union N: **the ~** la Unión Soviética
sow¹ [sau] N cerda, puerca
sow² [səu] (pt **sowed**, pp **sown** [səun]) VT sembrar
soya ['sɔɪə], (US) **soy** [sɔɪ] N soja
soya bean, (US) **soy bean** N semilla de soja

soya sauce, (US) **soy sauce** N salsa de soja
sozzled ['sɔzld] ADJ (BRIT inf) mamado
spa [spɑ:] N balneario
space [speɪs] N espacio; (room) sitio ▶ VT (also: **space out**) espaciar; **to clear a ~ for sth** hacer sitio para algo; **in a confined ~** en un espacio restringido; **in a short ~ of time** en poco or un corto espacio de tiempo; **(with)in the ~ of an hour/three generations** en el espacio de una hora/tres generaciones
space bar N (on typewriter) barra espaciadora
spacecraft ['speɪskrɑ:ft] N nave f espacial, astronave f
spaceman ['speɪsmæn] N (irreg) astronauta m, cosmonauta m
spaceship ['speɪsʃɪp] N = **spacecraft**
space shuttle N transportador m espacial
spacesuit ['speɪssu:t] N traje m espacial
spacewoman ['speɪswumən] N (irreg) astronauta, cosmonauta
spacing ['speɪsɪŋ] N espacio
spacious ['speɪʃəs] ADJ amplio
spade [speɪd] N (tool) pala; **spades** NPL (Cards: British) picas fpl; (: Spanish) espadas fpl
spadework ['speɪdwə:k] N (fig) trabajo preliminar
spaghetti [spə'gɛtɪ] N espaguetis mpl
Spain [speɪn] N España
spam [spæm] N (junk email) correo basura
span [spæn] N (of bird, plane) envergadura; (of hand) palmo; (of arch) luz f; (in time) lapso ▶ VT extenderse sobre, cruzar; (fig) abarcar
Spaniard ['spænjəd] N español(a) m/f
spaniel ['spænjəl] N perro de aguas
Spanish ['spænɪʃ] ADJ español(a) ▶ N (Ling) español m, castellano; **the Spanish** NPL (people) los españoles; **~ omelette** tortilla española or de patata
spank [spæŋk] VT zurrar, dar unos azotes a
spanner ['spænə^r] N (BRIT) llave f inglesa
spar [spɑ:^r] N palo, verga ▶ VI (Boxing) entrenarse (en el boxeo)
spare [spɛə^r] ADJ de reserva; (surplus) sobrante, de más ▶ N (part) pieza de repuesto ▶ VT (do without) pasarse sin; (afford to give) tener de sobra; (refrain from hurting) perdonar; (details etc) ahorrar; **to ~** (surplus) sobrante, de sobra; **there are two going ~** sobran or quedan dos; **to ~ no expense** no escatimar gastos; **can you ~ (me) £10?** ¿puedes prestarme or darme 10 libras?; **can you ~ the time?** ¿tienes tiempo?; **I've a few minutes to ~** tengo unos minutos libres; **there is no time to ~** no hay tiempo que perder
spare part N pieza de repuesto
spare room N cuarto de los invitados
spare time N ratos mpl de ocio, tiempo libre
spare tyre, (US) **spare tire** N (Aut) neumático or llanta (LAM) de recambio

S

793

spare wheel N (*Aut*) rueda de recambio
sparing ['spɛərɪŋ] ADJ: **to be ~ with** ser parco en
sparingly ['spɛərɪŋlɪ] ADV escasamente
spark [spɑːk] N chispa; (*fig*) chispazo
sparking plug ['spɑːk(ɪŋ)-] N = **spark plug**
sparkle ['spɑːkl] N centelleo, destello ▶ VI centellear; (*shine*) relucir, brillar
sparkler ['spɑːklə^r] N bengala
sparkling ['spɑːklɪŋ] ADJ centelleante; (*wine*) espumoso
spark plug N bujía
sparring partner ['spɑːrɪŋ-] N spárring *m*; (*fig*) contrincante *mf*
sparrow ['spærəu] N gorrión *m*
sparse [spɑːs] ADJ esparcido, escaso
sparsely ['spɑːslɪ] ADV escasamente; **a ~ furnished room** un cuarto con pocos muebles
spartan ['spɑːtən] ADJ (*fig*) espartano
spasm ['spæzəm] N (*Med*) espasmo; (*fig*) arranque *m*, ataque *m*
spasmodic [spæz'mɔdɪk] ADJ espasmódico
spastic ['spæstɪk] N espástico(-a)
spat [spæt] PT, PP of **spit** ▶ N (*US*) riña
spate [speɪt] N (*fig*): **~ of** torrente *m* de; **in ~** (*river*) crecido
spatial ['speɪʃl] ADJ espacial
spatter ['spætə^r] VT: **to ~ with** salpicar de
spatula ['spætjulə] N espátula
spawn [spɔːn] VT (*pej*) engendrar ▶ VI desovar, frezar ▶ N huevas *fpl*
SPCA N ABBR (*US*) = **Society for the Prevention of Cruelty to Animals**
SPCC N ABBR (*US*) = **Society for the Prevention of Cruelty to Children**
speak [spiːk] (*pt* **spoke** [spəuk], *pp* **spoken** ['spəukn]) VT (*language*) hablar; (*truth*) decir ▶ VI hablar; (*make a speech*) intervenir; **to ~ one's mind** hablar claro or con franqueza; **to ~ to sb/of** or **about sth** hablar con algn/de or sobre algo; **to ~ at a conference/in a debate** hablar en un congreso/un debate; **he has no money to ~ of** no tiene mucho dinero que digamos; **speaking!** ¡al habla!; **~ up!** ¡habla más alto!
▶ **speak for** VT FUS: **to ~ for sb** hablar por or en nombre de algn; **that picture is already spoken for** (*in shop*) ese cuadro está reservado
speaker ['spiːkə^r] N (*in public*) orador(a) *m/f*; (*also:* **loudspeaker**) altavoz *m*; (: *for stereo etc*) bafle *m*; **the S~** (*Pol: Brit*) el Presidente de la Cámara de los Comunes; (*US*) el Presidente del Congreso; **are you a Welsh ~?** ¿habla Vd galés?
speaking ['spiːkɪŋ] ADJ hablante
-speaking ['spiːkɪŋ] SUFF -hablante; **Spanish~ people** los hispanohablantes

spear [spɪə^r] N lanza; (*for fishing*) arpón *m*
▶ VT alancear; arponear
spearhead ['spɪəhɛd] VT (*attack etc*) encabezar ▶ N punta de lanza, vanguardia
spearmint ['spɪəmɪnt] N menta verde
spec [spɛk] N (*inf*): **on ~** por si acaso; **to buy on ~** arriesgarse a comprar
special ['spɛʃl] ADJ especial; (*edition etc*) extraordinario; (*delivery*) urgente ▶ N (*train*) tren *m* especial; **nothing ~** nada de particular, nada extraordinario
special agent N agente *mf* especial
special correspondent N corresponsal *mf* especial
special delivery N (*Post*): **by ~** por entrega urgente
special effects NPL (*Cine*) efectos *mpl* especiales
specialist ['spɛʃəlɪst] N especialista *mf*; **a heart ~** (*Med*) un(-a) especialista del corazón
speciality [spɛʃɪ'ælɪtɪ], (*US*) **specialty** ['spɛʃəltɪ] N especialidad *f*
specialize ['spɛʃəlaɪz] VI: **to ~ (in)** especializarse (en)
specially ['spɛʃlɪ] ADV especialmente
special offer N (*Comm*) oferta especial
special school N (*Brit*) colegio *m* de educación especial
special train N tren *m* especial
specialty ['spɛʃəltɪ] N (*US*) = **speciality**
species ['spiːʃiːz] N especie *f*
specific [spə'sɪfɪk] ADJ específico
specifically [spə'sɪfɪklɪ] ADV (*explicitly: state, warn*) específicamente, expresamente; (*especially: design, intend*) especialmente
specification [spɛsɪfɪ'keɪʃən] N especificación *f*; **specifications** NPL (*plan*) presupuesto *sg*; (*of car, machine*) descripción *f* técnica; (*for building*) plan *msg* detallado
specify ['spɛsɪfaɪ] VT, VI especificar, precisar; **unless otherwise specified** salvo indicaciones contrarias
specimen ['spɛsɪmən] N ejemplar *m*; (*Med: of urine*) espécimen *m*; (: *of blood*) muestra
specimen copy N ejemplar *m* de muestra
specimen signature N muestra de firma
speck [spɛk] N grano, mota
speckled ['spɛkld] ADJ moteado
specs [spɛks] NPL (*inf*) gafas *fpl* (*Sp*), anteojos *mpl*
spectacle ['spɛktəkl] N espectáculo; **spectacles** NPL (*Brit: glasses*) gafas *fpl* (*Sp*), anteojos *mpl*
spectacle case N estuche *m* or funda (de gafas)
spectacular [spɛk'tækjulə^r] ADJ espectacular; (*success*) impresionante
spectator [spɛk'teɪtə^r] N espectador(a) *m/f*
spectator sport N deporte *m* espectáculo

spectra ['spɛktrə] N PL of **spectrum**

spectre, (US) **specter** ['spɛktər] N espectro, fantasma m

spectrum ['spɛktrəm] (pl **spectra** [-trə]) N espectro

speculate ['spɛkjuleɪt] VI especular; (try to guess): **to ~ about** especular sobre

speculation [spɛkju'leɪʃən] N especulación f

speculative ['spɛkjulətɪv] ADJ especulativo

speculator ['spɛkjuleɪtər] N especulador(a) m/f

sped [spɛd] PT, PP of **speed**

speech [spiːtʃ] N (faculty) habla; (formal talk) discurso; (words) palabras fpl; (manner of speaking) forma de hablar; (language) idioma m, lenguaje m

speech day N (BRIT Scol) ≈ día de reparto de premios

speech impediment N defecto del habla

speechless ['spiːtʃlɪs] ADJ mudo, estupefacto

speech therapy N logopedia

speed [spiːd] (pt, pp **sped** [spɛd]) N (also Aut, Tech: gear) velocidad f; (: haste) prisa; (: promptness) rapidez f; ▶ VI (Aut: exceed speed limit) conducir con exceso de velocidad; **at full** or **top ~** a máxima velocidad; **at a ~ of 70 km/h** a una velocidad de 70 km por hora; **at ~** a gran velocidad; **a five-~ gearbox** una caja de cambios de cinco velocidades; **shorthand/typing ~** rapidez f en taquigrafía/mecanografía; **the years sped by** los años pasaron volando
  ▶ **speed up** VI acelerarse ▶ VT acelerar

speedboat ['spiːdbəut] N lancha motora

speed camera N cámara de control de velocidad

speedily ['spiːdɪlɪ] ADV rápido, rápidamente

speeding ['spiːdɪŋ] N (Aut) exceso de velocidad

speed limit N límite m de velocidad, velocidad f máxima

speedometer [spɪ'dɔmɪtər] N velocímetro

speed trap N (Aut) control m de velocidad

speedway ['spiːdweɪ] N (Sport) pista de carrera

speedy ['spiːdɪ] ADJ (fast) veloz, rápido; (prompt) pronto

spell [spɛl] N (also: **magic spell**) encanto, hechizo; (period of time) rato, período; (turn) turno ▶ VT (pt, pp **spelt** [spɛlt] or **spelled** [spɛld]) deletrear; (fig) anunciar, presagiar; **to cast a ~ on sb** hechizar a algn; **he can't ~** no sabe escribir bien, comete faltas de ortografía; **can you ~ it for me?** ¿cómo se deletrea or se escribe?; **how do you ~ your name?** ¿cómo se escribe tu nombre?
  ▶ **spell out** VT (explain): **to ~ sth out for sb** explicar algo a algn en detalle

spellbound ['spɛlbaund] ADJ embelesado, hechizado

spellchecker N (Comput) corrector m (ortográfico)

spelling ['spɛlɪŋ] N ortografía

spelling mistake N falta de ortografía

spelt [spɛlt] PT, PP of **spell**

spend [spɛnd] (pt, pp **spent** [spɛnt]) VT (money) gastar; (time) pasar; (life) dedicar; **to ~ time/money/effort on sth** gastar tiempo/dinero/energías en algo

spending ['spɛndɪŋ] N: **government ~** gastos mpl del gobierno

spending money N dinero para gastos

spending power N poder m adquisitivo

spendthrift ['spɛndθrɪft] N derrochador(a) m/f manirroto(-a)

spent [spɛnt] PT, PP of **spend** ▶ ADJ (cartridge, bullets, match) usado

sperm [spəːm] N esperma

sperm bank N banco de esperma

sperm whale N cachalote m

spew [spjuː] VT vomitar, arrojar

sphere [sfɪər] N esfera

spherical ['sfɛrɪkl] ADJ esférico

sphinx [sfɪŋks] N esfinge f

spice [spaɪs] N especia ▶ VT especiar

spiciness ['spaɪsɪnɪs] N lo picante

spick-and-span ['spɪkən'spæn] ADJ impecable

spicy ['spaɪsɪ] ADJ picante

spider ['spaɪdər] N araña

spider's web N telaraña

spiel [ʃpiːl] N (inf) rollo

spike [spaɪk] N (point) punta; (Zool) pincho, púa; (Bot) espiga; (Elec) pico parásito ▶ VT: **to ~ a quote** cancelar una cita; **spikes** N PL (Sport) zapatillas fpl con clavos

spiky ['spaɪkɪ] ADJ (bush, branch) cubierto de púas; (animal) erizado

spill [spɪl] (pt, pp **spilt** [spɪlt] or **spilled** [spɪld]) VT derramar, verter; (blood) derramar ▶ VI derramarse; **to ~ the beans** (inf) descubrir el pastel
  ▶ **spill out** VI derramarse, desparramarse
  ▶ **spill over** VI desbordarse

spillage ['spɪlɪdʒ] N (event) derrame m; (substance) vertidos

spin [spɪn] (pt, pp **spun**) N (revolution of wheel) vuelta, revolución f; (Aviat) barrena; (trip in car) paseo (en coche) ▶ VT (wool etc) hilar; (wheel) girar ▶ VI girar, dar vueltas; **the car spun out of control** el coche se descontroló y empezó a dar vueltas
  ▶ **spin out** VT alargar, prolongar

spina bifida ['spaɪnə'bɪfɪdə] N espina f bífida

spinach ['spɪnɪtʃ] N espinacas fpl

spinal ['spaɪnl] ADJ espinal

spinal column N columna vertebral

spinal cord N médula espinal

spin class N (Sport) clase f de spinning

S

spindly ['spɪndlɪ] ADJ (*leg*) zanquivano
spin doctor N (*inf*) informador(a) parcial al servicio de un partido político
spin-dry ['spɪn'draɪ] VT centrifugar
spin-dryer [spɪn'draɪəʳ] N (*BRIT*) secadora centrífuga
spine [spaɪn] N espinazo, columna vertebral; (*thorn*) espina
spine-chilling ['spaɪntʃɪlɪŋ] ADJ terrorífico
spineless ['spaɪnlɪs] ADJ (*fig*) débil, flojo
spinet [spɪ'nɛt] N espineta
spinning ['spɪnɪŋ] N (*of thread*) hilado; (*art*) hilandería; (*Sport*) spinning m
spinning top N peonza
spinning wheel N rueca, torno de hilar
spin-off ['spɪnɔf] N derivado, producto secundario
spinster ['spɪnstəʳ] N soltera; (*pej*) solterona
spiral ['spaɪərl] N espiral f ▶ ADJ en espiral ▶ VI (*prices*) dispararse; **the inflationary ~** la espiral inflacionista
spiral staircase N escalera de caracol
spire ['spaɪəʳ] N aguja, chapitel m
spirit ['spɪrɪt] N (*soul*) alma f; (*ghost*) fantasma m; (*attitude*) espíritu m; (*courage*) valor m, ánimo; **spirits** NPL (*drink*) alcohol msg, bebidas fpl alcohólicas; **in good spirits** alegre, de buen ánimo; **Holy S~** Espíritu m Santo; **community ~, public ~** civismo
spirit duplicator N copiadora al alcohol
spirited ['spɪrɪtɪd] ADJ enérgico, vigoroso
spirit level N nivel m de aire
spiritual ['spɪrɪtjuəl] ADJ espiritual ▶ N (*also:* **Negro spiritual**) canción f religiosa, espiritual m
spiritualism ['spɪrɪtjuəlɪzəm] N espiritualismo
spit [spɪt] (*pt, pp* **spat** [spæt]) N (*for roasting*) asador m, espetón m; (*spittle*) esputo, escupitajo; (*saliva*) saliva ▶ VI escupir; (*sound*) chisporrotear
spite [spaɪt] N rencor m, ojeriza ▶ VT fastidiar; **in ~ of** a pesar de, pese a
spiteful ['spaɪtful] ADJ rencoroso, malévolo
spitting ['spɪtɪŋ] N: **"~ prohibited"** "se prohíbe escupir" ▶ ADJ: **to be the ~ image of sb** ser la viva imagen de algn
spittle ['spɪtl] N saliva, baba
splash [splæʃ] N (*sound*) chapoteo; (*of colour*) mancha ▶ VT salpicar ▶ VI (*also:* **splash about**) chapotear; **to ~ paint on the floor** manchar el suelo de pintura
▶ **splash out** VI (*BRIT inf*) derrochar dinero
splashdown ['splæʃdaun] N amaraje m, amerizaje m
spleen [spli:n] N (*Anat*) bazo
splendid ['splɛndɪd] ADJ espléndido
splendidly ['splɛndɪdlɪ] ADV espléndidamente; **everything went ~** todo

fue a las mil maravillas
splendour, (US**) splendor** ['splɛndəʳ] N esplendor m; (*fig*) brillo, gloria
splice [splaɪs] VT empalmar
splint [splɪnt] N tablilla
splinter ['splɪntəʳ] N astilla; (*in finger*) espigón m ▶ VI astillarse, hacer astillas
splinter group N grupo disidente, facción f
split [splɪt] (*pt, pp* **~**) N hendedura, raja; (*fig*) división f; (*Pol*) escisión f ▶ VT partir, rajar; (*party*) dividir; (*work, profits*) repartir ▶ VI (*divide*) dividirse, escindirse; **to ~ the difference** partir la diferencia; **to do the splits** hacer el spagat; **to ~ sth down the middle** (*also fig*) dividir algo en dos
▶ **split up** VI (*couple*) separarse, romper; (*meeting*) acabarse
split-level ['splɪtlɛvl] ADJ (*house*) dúplex
split peas NPL guisantes mpl secos
split personality N doble personalidad f
split second N fracción f de segundo
splitting ['splɪtɪŋ] ADJ (*headache*) horrible
splutter ['splʌtəʳ] VI chisporrotear; (*person*) balbucear
spoil [spɔɪl] (*pt, pp* **spoilt** [spɔɪlt] or **spoiled** [spɔɪld]) VT (*damage*) dañar; (*ruin*) estropear, echar a perder; (*child*) mimar, consentir; (*ballot paper*) invalidar ▶ VI: **to be spoiling for a fight** estar con ganas de lucha, andar con ganas de pelea
spoiled [spɔɪld] ADJ (*US: food: bad*) pasado, malo; (: *milk*) cortado
spoils [spɔɪlz] NPL despojo sg, botín msg
spoilsport ['spɔɪlspɔ:t] N aguafiestas m inv
spoilt [spɔɪlt] PT, PP of **spoil** ▶ ADJ (*child*) mimado, consentido; (*ballot paper*) invalidado
spoke [spəuk] PT of **speak** ▶ N rayo, radio
spoken ['spəukn] PP of **speak**
spokesman ['spəuksmən] N (*irreg*) portavoz m, vocero (*LAm*)
spokesperson ['spəukspə:sn] N portavoz mf, vocero(-a) (*LAm*)
spokeswoman ['spəukswumən] N (*irreg*) portavoz f, vocera (*LAm*)
sponge [spʌndʒ] N esponja; (*Culin: also:* **sponge cake**) bizcocho ▶ VT (*wash*) lavar con esponja ▶ VI: **to ~ on** or (*US*) **off sb** vivir a costa de algn
sponge bag N (*BRIT*) neceser m
sponge cake N bizcocho, pastel m
sponger ['spʌndʒəʳ] N gorrón(-ona) m/f
spongy ['spʌndʒɪ] ADJ esponjoso
sponsor ['spɔnsəʳ] N (*Radio, TV*) patrocinador(a) m/f; (*for membership*) padrino (madrina); (*Comm*) fiador(a) m/f, avalador(a) m/f ▶ VT patrocinar; apadrinar; (*parliamentary bill*) apoyar, respaldar; (*idea etc*) presentar, promover; **I sponsored him at 3p a mile** (*in*

fund-raising race) me apunté para darle 3 peniques la milla

sponsorship ['spɔnsəʃɪp] N patrocinio

spontaneity [spɔntə'neɪɪtɪ] N espontaneidad f

spontaneous [spɔn'teɪnɪəs] ADJ espontáneo

spontaneously [spɔn'teɪnɪəslɪ] ADV espontáneamente

spooky ['spu:kɪ] ADJ *(inf: place, atmosphere)* espeluznante, horripilante

spool [spu:l] N carrete m; *(of sewing machine)* canilla

spoon [spu:n] N cuchara

spoon-feed ['spu:nfi:d] VT dar de comer con cuchara a; *(fig)* dárselo todo mascado a

spoonful ['spu:nful] N cucharada

sporadic [spə'rædɪk] ADJ esporádico

sport [spɔ:t] N deporte m; *(amusement)* juego, diversión f; **to be a good ~** *(person)* ser muy majo; **indoor/outdoor sports** deportes mpl en pista cubierta/al aire libre; **to say sth in ~** decir algo en broma

sport coat N *(US)* = **sports jacket**

sporting ['spɔ:tɪŋ] ADJ deportivo; **to give sb a ~ chance** darle a algn su oportunidad

sport jacket N *(US)* = **sports jacket**

sports car N coche m sport

sports centre N *(BRIT)* polideportivo

sports coat N *(US)* = **sports jacket**

sports drink N bebida energética, bebida isotónica

sports ground N campo de deportes, centro deportivo

sports jacket, *(US)* **sport jacket** N chaqueta deportiva

sportsman ['spɔ:tsmən] N *(irreg)* deportista m

sportsmanship ['spɔ:tsmənʃɪp] N deportividad f

sports pages NPL páginas fpl deportivas

sports utility vehicle N SUV m, todoterreno m inv

sportswear ['spɔ:tswɛəᵊ] N ropa de deporte

sportswoman ['spɔ:tswumən] N *(irreg)* deportista

sporty ['spɔ:tɪ] ADJ deportivo

spot [spɔt] N sitio, lugar m; *(dot: on pattern)* punto, mancha; *(pimple)* grano; *(also:* **advertising spot**) spot m ▶ VT *(notice)* notar, observar ▶ ADJ *(Comm)* inmediatamente efectivo; **on the ~** en el acto; *(in difficulty)* en un aprieto; **to do sth on the ~** hacer algo en el acto; **to put sb on the ~** poner a algn en un apuro

spot check N reconocimiento rápido

spotless ['spɔtlɪs] ADJ *(clean)* inmaculado; *(reputation)* intachable

spotlessly ['spɔtlɪslɪ] ADV: **~ clean** limpísimo

spotlight ['spɔtlaɪt] N foco, reflector m; *(Aut)* faro auxiliar

spot-on [spɔt'ɔn] ADJ *(BRIT inf)* exacto

spot price N precio de entrega inmediata

spotted ['spɔtɪd] ADJ *(pattern)* de puntos

spotty ['spɔtɪ] ADJ *(face)* con granos

spouse [spauz] N cónyuge mf

spout [spaut] N *(of jug)* pico; *(pipe)* caño ▶ VI chorrear

sprain [spreɪn] N torcedura, esguince m ▶ VT: **to ~ one's ankle** torcerse el tobillo

sprang [spræŋ] PT of **spring**

sprawl [sprɔ:l] VI tumbarse ▶ N: **urban ~** crecimiento urbano descontrolado; **to send sb sprawling** tirar a algn al suelo

sprawling ['sprɔ:lɪŋ] ADJ *(town)* desparramado

spray [spreɪ] N rociada; *(of sea)* espuma; *(container)* atomizador m; *(of paint)* pistola rociadora; *(of flowers)* ramita ▶ VT rociar; *(crops)* regar ▶ CPD *(deodorant)* en atomizador

spread [sprɛd] *(pt, pp ~)* N extensión f; *(of idea)* diseminación f; *(inf: food)* comilona; *(Press, Typ: two pages)* plana ▶ VT extender; diseminar; *(butter)* untar; *(wings, sails)* desplegar; *(scatter)* esparcir ▶ VI *(also:* **spread out**: *stain)* extenderse; *(news)* diseminarse; **middle-age ~** gordura de la mediana edad; **repayments will be ~ over 18 months** los pagos se harán a lo largo de 18 meses
▶ **spread out** VI *(move apart)* separarse

spread-eagled ['sprɛdi:gld] ADJ: **to be ~** estar despatarrado

spreadsheet ['sprɛdʃi:t] N *(Comput)* hoja de cálculo

spree [spri:] N: **to go on a ~** ir de juerga or farra *(LAM)*

sprightly ['spraɪtlɪ] ADJ vivo, enérgico

spring [sprɪŋ] *(pt* **sprang**, *pp* **sprung**) N *(season)* primavera; *(leap)* salto, brinco; *(coiled metal)* resorte m; *(of water)* fuente f, manantial m; *(bounciness)* elasticidad f ▶ VI *(arise)* brotar, nacer; *(leap)* saltar, brincar ▶ VT: **to ~ a leak** *(pipe etc)* empezar a hacer agua; **he sprang the news on me** de repente me soltó la noticia; **in (the) ~** en (la) primavera; **to walk with a ~ in one's step** andar dando saltos or brincos; **to ~ into action** lanzarse a la acción
▶ **spring up** VI *(thing: appear)* aparecer; *(problem)* surgir

springboard ['sprɪŋbɔ:d] N trampolín m

spring-clean [sprɪŋ'kli:n] N *(also:* **spring-cleaning**) limpieza general

spring onion N cebolleta

spring roll N rollito de primavera

springtime ['sprɪŋtaɪm] N primavera

springy ['sprɪŋɪ] ADJ elástico; *(grass)* mullido

sprinkle ['sprɪŋkl] VT *(pour: liquid)* rociar; *(: salt, sugar)* espolvorear; **to ~ water etc on, ~ with water etc** rociar or salpicar de agua etc

sprinkler ['sprɪŋklə^r] N (for lawn) aspersor m; (to put out fire) aparato de rociadura automática

sprinkling ['sprɪŋklɪŋ] N (of water) rociada; (of salt, sugar) un poco de

sprint [sprɪnt] N (e)sprint m ▸ VI (gen) correr a toda velocidad; (Sport) esprintar; **the 200 metres** ~ los 200 metros lisos

sprinter ['sprɪntə^r] N velocista mf

spritzer ['sprɪtsə^r] N vino blanco con soda

sprocket ['sprɔkɪt] N (on printer etc) rueda dentada

sprocket feed N avance m por rueda dentada

sprout [spraut] VI brotar, retoñar ▸ N: **(Brussels) sprouts** npl coles fpl de Bruselas

spruce [spru:s] N (Bot) pícea ▸ ADJ aseado, pulcro
▸ **spruce up** VT (tidy) arreglar, acicalar; (smarten up: room etc) ordenar; **to ~ o.s. up** arreglarse

sprung [sprʌŋ] PP of **spring**

spry [spraɪ] ADJ ágil, activo

SPUC N ABBR (= Society for the Protection of Unborn Children) ≈ Federación f Española de Asociaciones Provida

spun [spʌn] PT, PP of **spin**

spur [spə:^r] N espuela; (fig) estímulo, aguijón m ▸ VT (also: **spur on**) estimular, incitar; **on the ~ of the moment** de improviso

spurious ['spjuəriəs] ADJ falso

spurn [spə:n] VT desdeñar, rechazar

spurt [spə:t] N chorro; (of energy) arrebato ▸ VI chorrear; **to put in** or **on a ~** (runner) acelerar; (fig: in work etc) hacer un gran esfuerzo

sputter ['spʌtə^r] VI = **splutter**

spy [spaɪ] N espía mf ▸ VI: **to ~ on** espiar a ▸ VT (see) divisar, lograr ver ▸ CPD (film, story) de espionaje

spying ['spaɪɪŋ] N espionaje m

spyware ['spaɪweə^r] N (Comput) spyware m

Sq. ABBR (in address: = Square) Pl.

sq. ABBR (Math etc) = **square**

squabble ['skwɔbl] N riña, pelea ▸ VI reñir, pelear

squad [skwɔd] N (Mil) pelotón m; (Police) brigada; (Sport) equipo; **flying ~** (Police) brigada móvil

squad car N (Police) coche-patrulla m

squaddie ['skwɔdɪ] N (Mil: inf) chivo

squadron ['skwɔdrn] N (Mil) escuadrón m; (Aviat, Naut) escuadra

squalid ['skwɔlɪd] ADJ miserable

squall [skwɔ:l] N (storm) chubasco; (wind) ráfaga

squalor ['skwɔlə^r] N miseria

squander ['skwɔndə^r] VT (money) derrochar, despilfarrar; (chances) desperdiciar

square [skweə^r] N cuadro; (in town) plaza; (US: block of houses) manzana, cuadra (LAm); (inf: person) carca mf ▸ ADJ cuadrado; (inf: ideas, tastes) trasnochado ▸ VT (arrange) arreglar; (Math) cuadrar; (reconcile) compaginar ▸ VI cuadrar, conformarse; **all** ~ igual(es); **a ~ meal** una comida decente; **two metres** ~ dos metros por dos; **one ~ metre** un metro cuadrado; **to get one's accounts** ~ dejar las cuentas claras; **I'll ~ it with him** (inf) yo lo arreglo con él; **can you ~ it with your conscience?** ¿cómo se justifica ante sí mismo?; **we're back to ~ one** (fig) hemos vuelto al punto de partida
▸ **square up** VI (settle): **to ~ up (with sb)** ajustar cuentas (con algn)

square bracket N (Typ) corchete m

squarely ['skweəlɪ] ADV (fully) de lleno; (honestly, fairly) justamente, justamente

square root N raíz f cuadrada

squash [skwɔʃ] N (vegetable) calabaza; (Sport) squash m; (BRIT: drink): **lemon/orange** ~ zumo (SP) or jugo (LAm) de limón/naranja ▸ VT aplastar

squat [skwɔt] ADJ achaparrado ▸ VI agacharse, sentarse en cuclillas; (on property) ocupar ilegalmente

squatter ['skwɔtə^r] N ocupante mf ilegal, okupa mf

squawk [skwɔ:k] VI graznar

squeak [skwi:k] VI (hinge, wheel) chirriar, rechinar; (shoe, wood) crujir; (mouse) chillar ▸ N (of hinge, wheel etc) chirrido, rechinamiento; (of shoes) crujir m; (of mouse etc) chillido

squeaky ['skwi:kɪ] ADJ que cruje; **to be ~ clean** (fig) ser superhonrado

squeal [skwi:l] VI chillar, dar gritos agudos

squeamish ['skwi:mɪʃ] ADJ delicado, remilgado

squeeze [skwi:z] N presión f; (of hand) apretón m; (Comm: credit squeeze) restricción f ▸ VT (lemon etc) exprimir; (hand, arm) apretar; **a ~ of lemon** unas gotas de limón; **to ~ past/ under sth** colarse al lado de/por debajo de algo
▸ **squeeze out** VT exprimir; (fig) excluir
▸ **squeeze through** VI abrirse paso con esfuerzos

squelch [skwɛltʃ] VI chapotear

squid [skwɪd] N pl inv calamar m

squiggle ['skwɪgl] N garabato

squint [skwɪnt] VI bizquear, ser bizco ▸ N (Med) estrabismo; **to ~ at sth** mirar algo entornando los ojos

squire ['skwaɪə^r] N (BRIT) terrateniente m

squirm [skwə:m] VI retorcerse, revolverse

squirrel ['skwɪrəl] N ardilla

squirt [skwə:t] VI salir a chorros ▸ VT chiscar

Sr ABBR = **senior**; (Rel) = **sister**

SRC N ABBR (BRIT: = Students' Representative Council) consejo de estudiantes

Sri Lanka [srɪ'læŋkə] N Sri Lanka m

SRO ABBR (US) = **standing room only**
SS ABBR (= steamship) M.V.
SSA N ABBR (US: = Social Security Administration) ≈ Seguro Social
SST N ABBR (US) = **supersonic transport**
ST ABBR (US: = Standard Time) hora oficial
St ABBR (= saint) Sto.(-a.); (= street) c/
stab [stæb] N (with knife etc) puñalada; (of pain) pinchazo; **to have a ~ at (doing) sth** (inf) probar (a hacer) algo ▶ VT apuñalar; **to ~ sb to death** matar a algn a puñaladas
stabbing ['stæbɪŋ] N: **there's been a ~** han apuñalado a alguien ▶ ADJ (pain) punzante
stability [stə'bɪlɪtɪ] N estabilidad f
stabilization [steɪbəlaɪ'zeɪʃən] N estabilización f
stabilize ['steɪbəlaɪz] VT estabilizar ▶ VI estabilizarse
stabilizer ['steɪbəlaɪzə'] N (Aviat, Naut) estabilizador m
stable ['steɪbl] ADJ estable ▶ N cuadra, caballeriza; **riding stables** escuela hípica
staccato [stə'kɑːtəʊ] ADJ, ADV staccato
stack [stæk] N montón m, pila; (inf) mar f ▶ VT amontonar, apilar; **there's stacks of time to finish it** hay cantidad de tiempo para acabarlo
stacker ['stækə'] N (for printer) apiladora
stadium ['steɪdɪəm] N estadio
staff [stɑːf] N (work force) personal m, plantilla; (BRIT Scol: also: **teaching staff**) cuerpo docente; (stick) bastón m ▶ VT proveer de personal; **to be staffed by Asians/women** tener una plantilla asiática/femenina
staffroom ['stɑːfruːm] N sala de profesores
Staffs ABBR (BRIT) = **Staffordshire**
stag [stæg] N ciervo, venado; (BRIT Stock Exchange) especulador m con nuevas emisiones
stage [steɪdʒ] N escena; (point) etapa; (platform) plataforma; **the ~** el escenario, el teatro ▶ VT (play) poner en escena, representar; (organize) montar, organizar; (fig: perform: recovery etc) efectuar; **in stages** por etapas; **in the early/final stages** en las primeras/últimas etapas; **to go through a difficult ~** pasar una fase or etapa mala
stagecoach ['steɪdʒkəʊtʃ] N diligencia
stage door N entrada de artistas
stagehand ['steɪdʒhænd] N tramoyista mf
stage-manage ['steɪdʒmænɪdʒ] VT (fig) manipular
stage manager N director(a) m/f de escena
stagger ['stægə'] VI tambalear ▶ VT (amaze) asombrar; (hours, holidays) escalonar
staggering ['stægərɪŋ] ADJ (amazing) asombroso, pasmoso
staging post ['steɪdʒɪŋ-] N escala

stagnant ['stægnənt] ADJ estancado
stagnate [stæg'neɪt] VI estancarse; (fig: economy, mind) quedarse estancado
stagnation [stæg'neɪʃən] N estancamiento
stag night, stag party N despedida de soltero
staid [steɪd] ADJ (clothes) serio, formal
stain [steɪn] N mancha; (colouring) tintura ▶ VT manchar; (wood) teñir
stained glass N vidrio m de color
stained glass window [steɪnd-] N vidriera de colores
stainless ['steɪnlɪs] ADJ (steel) inoxidable
stainless steel N acero inoxidable
stain remover N quitamanchas m inv
stair [stɛə'] N (step) peldaño, escalón m; **stairs** NPL escaleras fpl
staircase ['stɛəkeɪs], **stairway** ['stɛəweɪ] N escalera
stairwell ['stɛəwɛl] N hueco or caja de la escalera
stake [steɪk] N estaca, poste m; (Comm) interés m; (Betting) apuesta ▶ VT (bet) apostar; (also: **stake out**: area) cercar con estacas; **to be at ~** estar en juego; **to have a ~ in sth** tener interés en algo; **to ~ a claim to (sth)** presentar reclamación por or reclamar (algo)
stake-out ['steɪkaʊt] N vigilancia; **to be on a ~** estar de vigilancia
stalactite ['stæləktaɪt] N estalactita
stalagmite ['stæləgmaɪt] N estalagmita
stale [steɪl] ADJ (bread) duro; (food) pasado; (smell) rancio; (beer) agrio
stalemate ['steɪlmeɪt] N tablas fpl; **to reach ~** (fig) estancarse, alcanzar un punto muerto
stalk [stɔːk] N tallo, caña ▶ VT acechar, cazar al acecho; **to ~ off** irse airado
stall [stɔːl] N (in market) puesto; (in stable) casilla (de establo) ▶ VT (Aut) parar, calar; (fig) dar largas a ▶ VI (Aut) pararse, calarse; (fig) buscar evasivas; **stalls** NPL (BRIT: in cinema, theatre) butacas fpl; **a newspaper ~** un quiosco (de periódicos); **a flower ~** un puesto de flores
stallholder ['stɔːlhəʊldə'] N dueño(-a) de un puesto
stallion ['stælɪən] N semental m, garañón m
stalwart ['stɔːlwət] N partidario(-a) incondicional
stamen ['steɪmɛn] N estambre m
stamina ['stæmɪnə] N resistencia
stammer ['stæmə'] N tartamudeo, balbuceo ▶ VI tartamudear, balbucir
stamp [stæmp] N sello, estampilla (LAm); (mark) marca, huella; (on document) timbre m ▶ VI (also: **stamp one's foot**) patear ▶ VT patear, golpear con el pie; (letter) poner sellos en, franquear; (with rubber stamp) marcar con sello; **stamped addressed envelope (sae)**

S

sobre m franqueado con la dirección propia
▶ **stamp out** VT (*fire*) apagar con el pie; (*crime, opposition*) acabar con

stamp album N álbum m para sellos

stamp collecting N filatelia

stamp duty N (BRIT) derecho de timbre

stampede [stæm'piːd] N (*of cattle*) estampida

stamp machine N máquina (expendedora) de sellos

stance [stæns] N postura

stand [stænd] (*pt, pp* **stood**) N (*attitude*) posición f, postura; (*for taxis*) parada; (*also:* **music stand**) atril m; (*Sport*) tribuna; (*at exhibition*) stand m ▶ VI (*be*) estar, encontrarse; (*be on foot*) estar de pie; (*rise*) levantarse; (*remain*) quedar en pie ▶ VT (*place*) poner, colocar; (*tolerate, withstand*) aguantar, soportar; **to make a ~** (*fig*) resistir, mantener una postura firme; **to take a ~ on an issue** adoptar una actitud hacia una cuestión; **to ~ for parliament** (BRIT) presentarse (como candidato) a las elecciones; **nothing stands in our way** nada nos lo impide; **to ~ still** quedarse inmóvil; **to let sth ~ as it is** dejar algo como está; **as things ~** tal como están las cosas; **to ~ sb a drink/meal** invitar a algn a una copa/a comer; **the company will have to ~ the loss** la empresa tendrá que hacer frente a las pérdidas; **I can't ~ him** no le aguanto, no le puedo ver; **to ~ guard** or **watch** (*Mil*) hacer guardia

▶ **stand aside** VI apartarse, mantenerse aparte

▶ **stand back** VI retirarse

▶ **stand by** VI (*be ready*) estar listo ▶ VT FUS (*opinion*) mantener

▶ **stand down** VI (*withdraw*) ceder el puesto; (*Mil, Law*) retirarse

▶ **stand for** VT FUS (*signify*) significar; (*tolerate*) aguantar, permitir

▶ **stand in for** VT FUS suplir a

▶ **stand out** VI (*be prominent*) destacarse

▶ **stand up** VI (*rise*) levantarse, ponerse de pie

▶ **stand up for** VT FUS defender

▶ **stand up to** VT FUS hacer frente a

stand-alone ['stændəlaun] ADJ (*Comput*) autónomo

standard ['stændəd] N patrón m, norma; (*flag*) estandarte m ▶ ADJ (*size etc*) normal, corriente, estándar; **standards** NPL (*morals*) valores mpl morales; **the gold ~** (*Comm*) el patrón oro; **high/low ~** de alto/bajo nivel; **below** or **not up to ~** (*work*) de calidad inferior; **to be** or **come up to ~** satisfacer los requisitos; **to apply a double ~** aplicar un doble criterio

Standard Grade N (SCOTTISH *Scol*) certificado del último ciclo de la enseñanza secundaria obligatoria

standardization [stændədaɪ'zeɪʃən] N normalización f

standardize ['stændədaɪz] VT estandarizar

standard lamp N (BRIT) lámpara de pie

standard model N modelo estándar

standard of living N nivel m de vida

standard practice N norma, práctica común

standard rate N tasa de imposición

standard time N hora oficial

stand-by ['stændbaɪ] N (*alert*) alerta, aviso; (*also:* **stand-by ticket**: *Theat*) entrada reducida de última hora; (: *Aviat*) billete m standby; **to be on ~** estar preparado; (*doctor*) estar listo para acudir; (*Aviat*) estar en la lista de espera

stand-by generator N generador m de reserva

stand-by passenger N (*Aviat*) pasajero(-a) en lista de espera

stand-by ticket N (*Aviat*) (billete m) standby m

stand-in ['stændɪn] N suplente mf; (*Cine*) doble mf

standing ['stændɪŋ] ADJ (*upright*) derecho; (*on foot*) de pie, en pie; (*permanent*: *committee*) permanente; (: *rule*) fijo; (: *army*) permanente, regular; (*grievance*) constante, viejo ▶ N reputación f; (*duration*): **of six months' ~** que lleva seis meses; **of many years' ~** que lleva muchos años; **he was given a ~ ovation** le dieron una calurosa ovación de pie; **~ joke** motivo constante de broma; **a man of some ~** un hombre de cierta posición or categoría

standing order N (BRIT: *at bank*) giro bancario; **standing orders** npl (*Mil*) reglamento sg general

standing room N sitio para estar de pie

stand-off ['stændɔf] N punto muerto

stand-offish [stænd'ɔfɪʃ] ADJ distante

standpipe ['stændpaɪp] N tubo vertical

standpoint ['stændpɔɪnt] N punto de vista

standstill ['stændstɪl] N: **at a ~** (*industry, traffic*) paralizado, en un punto muerto; **to come to a ~** pararse, quedar paralizado

stank [stæŋk] PT *of* **stink**

staple ['steɪpl] N (*for papers*) grapa; (*product*) producto or artículo de primeva necesidad ▶ ADJ (*crop, industry, food etc*) básico ▶ VT grapar

stapler ['steɪplər] N grapadora

star [stɑːr] N estrella; (*celebrity*) estrella, astro ▶ VI: **to ~ in** ser la estrella de ▶ VT (*Theat, Cine*) ser el/la protagonista de; **the stars** NPL (*Astrology*) el horóscopo; **4-~ petrol** gasolina extra; **four-~ hotel** hotel m de cuatro estrellas

star attraction N atracción f principal

starboard ['stɑːbəd] N estribor m

starch [stɑːtʃ] N almidón m

starchy ['stɑːtʃɪ] ADJ (*food*) feculento

stardom ['stɑ:dəm] N estrellato
stare [stɛəʳ] N mirada fija ▶ VI: **to ~ at** mirar fijo
starfish ['stɑ:fɪʃ] N estrella de mar
stark [stɑ:k] ADJ (*bleak*) severo, escueto; (*simplicity, colour*) austero; (*reality, truth*) puro; (*poverty*) absoluto ▶ ADV: **~ naked** en cueros
starkers ['stɑ:kəz] ADJ (BRIT *inf*): **to be ~** estar en cueros
starlet ['stɑ:lɪt] N (*Cine*) actriz *f* principiante
starling ['stɑ:lɪŋ] N estornino
starry ['stɑ:rɪ] ADJ estrellado
starry-eyed [stɑ:rɪ'aɪd] ADJ (*gullible, innocent*) inocentón(-ona), ingenuo; (*idealistic*) idealista; (*from wonder*) asombrado; (*from love*) enamoradísimo
Stars and Stripes NPL: **the ~** las barras y las estrellas, la bandera de EE.UU.
star sign N signo del zodíaco
star-studded ['stɑ:stʌdɪd] ADJ: **a ~ cast** un elenco estelar
start [stɑ:t] N (*beginning*) principio, comienzo; (*departure*) salida; (*sudden movement*) sobresalto; (*advantage*) ventaja ▶ VT empezar, comenzar; (*cause*) causar; (*found: business, newspaper*) establecer, fundar; (*engine*) poner en marcha ▶ VI (*begin*) comenzar, empezar; (*with fright*) asustarse, sobresaltarse; (*train etc*) salir; **to give sb a ~** dar un susto a algn; **at the ~** al principio; **for a ~** en primer lugar; **to make an early ~** ponerse en camino temprano; **the thieves had three hours' ~** los ladrones llevaban tres horas de ventaja; **to ~ a fire** provocar un incendio; **to ~ doing** *or* **to do sth** empezar a hacer algo; **to ~ (off) with …** (*firstly*) para empezar; (*at the beginning*) al principio
▶ **start off** VI empezar, comenzar; (*leave*) salir, ponerse en camino
▶ **start out** VI (*begin*) empezar; (*set out*) partir, salir
▶ **start over** VI (US) volver a empezar
▶ **start up** VI comenzar; (*car*) ponerse en marcha ▶ VT comenzar; (*car*) poner en marcha
starter ['stɑ:təʳ] N (*Aut*) botón *m* de arranque; (*Sport: official*) juez *mf* de salida; (: *runner*) corredor(a) *m/f*; (BRIT *Culin*) entrada, entrante *m*
starting point ['stɑ:tɪŋ-] N punto de partida
starting price N (*Comm*) precio inicial
startle ['stɑ:tl] VT sobresaltar
startling ['stɑ:tlɪŋ] ADJ alarmante
star turn N (BRIT) atracción *f* principal
starvation [stɑ:'veɪʃən] N hambre *f*, hambruna (LAM); (*Med*) inanición *f*
starvation wages NPL sueldo *sg* de hambre
starve [stɑ:v] VI pasar hambre; (*to death*) morir de hambre ▶ VT hacer pasar hambre;

(*fig*) privar; **I'm starving** estoy muerto de hambre
stash [stæʃ] VT: **to ~ sth away** (*inf*) poner algo a buen recaudo
state [steɪt] N estado; (*pomp*): **in ~** con mucha ceremonia ▶ VT (*say, declare*) afirmar; (*a case*) presentar, exponer; **~ of emergency** estado de excepción o emergencia; **~ of mind** estado de ánimo; **to lie in ~** (*corpse*) estar de cuerpo presente; **to be in a ~** estar agitado; **the States** los Estados Unidos
State Department N (US) Ministerio de Asuntos Exteriores
state education N (BRIT) enseñanza pública
stateless ['steɪtlɪs] ADJ desnacionalizado
stately ['steɪtlɪ] ADJ majestuoso, imponente
statement ['steɪtmənt] N afirmación *f*; (*Law*) declaración *f*; (*Comm*) estado; **official ~** informe *m* oficial; **~ of account, bank ~** estado de cuenta
state-of-the-art ['steɪtəvðɪ'ɑ:t] ADJ (*technology etc*) puntero
state-owned ['steɪtəund] ADJ estatal, del estado
States [steɪts] NPL: **the ~** los Estados Unidos
state school N escuela *or* colegio estatal
statesman ['steɪtsmən] N (*irreg*) estadista *m*
statesmanship ['steɪtsmənʃɪp] N habilidad *f* política, arte *m* de gobernar
static ['stætɪk] N (*Radio*) parásitos *mpl* ▶ ADJ estático
static electricity N electricidad *f* estática
station ['steɪʃən] N (*gen*) estación *f*; (*place*) puesto, sitio; (*Radio*) emisora; (*rank*) posición *f* social ▶ VT colocar, situar; (*Mil*) apostar; **action stations!** ¡a los puestos de combate!; **to be stationed in** (*Mil*) estar estacionado en
stationary ['steɪʃnərɪ] ADJ estacionario, fijo
stationer ['steɪʃənəʳ] N papelero(-a)
stationer's, stationer's shop N (BRIT) papelería
stationery ['steɪʃənərɪ] N (*writing paper*) papel *m* de escribir; (*writing materials*) artículos *mpl* de escritorio
station master N (*Rail*) jefe *m* de estación
station wagon N (US) ranchera
statistic [stə'tɪstɪk] N estadística
statistical [stə'tɪstɪkl] ADJ estadístico
statistics [stə'tɪstɪks] N (*science*) estadística
statue ['stætju:] N estatua
statuette [stætju'et] N figurilla
stature ['stætʃəʳ] N estatura; (*fig*) talla
status ['steɪtəs] N condición *f*, estado; (*reputation*) reputación *f*, estatus *m*
status line N (*Comput*) línea de situación *or* de estado
status quo N (e)statu quo *m*
status symbol N símbolo de prestigio
statute ['stætju:t] N estatuto, ley *f*

S

statute book N código de leyes
statutory ['stætjutri] ADJ estatutario;
~ **meeting** junta ordinaria
staunch [stɔːntʃ] ADJ leal, incondicional
▶ VT (flow, blood) restañar
stave [steɪv] VT: **to ~ off** (attack) rechazar;
(threat) evitar
stay [steɪ] N (period of time) estancia; (Law):
~ **of execution** aplazamiento de una
sentencia ▶ VI (remain) quedar(se); (as guest)
hospedarse; **to ~ put** seguir en el mismo
sitio; **to ~ the night/5 days** pasar la noche/
estar or quedarse 5 días
▶ **stay away** VI (from person, building) no
acercarse; (from event) no acudir
▶ **stay behind** VI quedar atrás
▶ **stay in** VI (at home) quedarse en casa
▶ **stay on** VI quedarse
▶ **stay out** VI (of house) no volver a casa;
(strikers) no volver al trabajo
▶ **stay up** VI (at night) velar, no acostarse
staycation [steɪˈkeɪʃən] N (inf) vacaciones fpl
en casa
staying power ['steɪɪŋ-] N resistencia,
aguante m
STD N ABBR (= sexually transmitted disease) ETS f;
(BRIT: = subscriber trunk dialling) servicio de
conferencias automáticas
stead [sted] N: **in sb's ~** en lugar de algn;
to stand sb in good ~ ser muy útil a algn
steadfast ['stedfɑːst] ADJ firme, resuelto
steadily ['stedɪlɪ] ADV (firmly) firmemente;
(unceasingly) sin parar; (fixedly) fijamente;
(drive) a velocidad constante
steady ['stedɪ] ADJ (fixed) firme, fijo; (regular)
regular; (boyfriend etc) formal, fijo; (person,
character) sensato, juicioso ▶ VT (hold)
mantener firme; (stabilize) estabilizar;
(nerves) calmar; **to ~ o.s. on** or **against sth**
afirmarse en algo
steak [steɪk] N (gen) filete m; (beef) bistec m
steal [stiːl] (pt **stole** [stəul], pp **stolen**
['stəuln]) VT, VI robar
▶ **steal away, steal off** VI marcharse
furtivamente, escabullirse
stealth [stelθ] N: **by ~** a escondidas,
sigilosamente
stealthy ['stelθɪ] ADJ cauteloso, sigiloso
steam [stiːm] N vapor m; (mist) vaho, humo
▶ VT (Culin) cocer al vapor ▶ VI echar vapor;
(ship): **to ~ along** avanzar, ir avanzando;
under one's own ~ (fig) por sus propios
medios or propias fuerzas; **to run out of ~**
(fig: person) quedar(se) agotado, quemarse;
to let off ~ (fig) desahogarse
▶ **steam up** VI (window) empañarse; **to get
steamed up about sth** (fig) ponerse negro
por algo
steam engine N máquina de vapor

steamer ['stiːmər] N (buque m de) vapor m;
(Culin) recipiente para cocinar al vapor
steam iron N plancha de vapor
steamroller ['stiːmrəulər] N apisonadora
steamship ['stiːmʃɪp] N = **steamer**
steamy ['stiːmɪ] ADJ (room) lleno de vapor;
(window) empañado; (heat, atmosphere)
bochornoso
steel [stiːl] N acero ▶ ADJ de acero
steel band N banda de percusión del Caribe
steel industry N industria siderúrgica
steel mill N fábrica de acero
steelworks ['stiːlwəːks] N acería, fundición f
de acero
steely ['stiːlɪ] ADJ (determination) inflexible;
(gaze) duro; (eyes) penetrante; ~ **grey** gris m
metálico
steelyard ['stiːljɑːd] N romana
steep [stiːp] ADJ escarpado, abrupto; (stair)
empinado; (price) exorbitante, excesivo ▶ VT
empapar, remojar
steeple ['stiːpl] N aguja, campanario
steeplechase ['stiːpltʃeɪs] N carrera de
obstáculos
steeplejack ['stiːpldʒæk] N reparador(a) m/f
de chimeneas or de campanarios
steer [stɪər] VT (car) conducir (SP), manejar
(LAM); (person) dirigir, guiar ▶ VI conducir
(SP), manejar (LAM); **to ~ clear of sb/sth** (fig)
esquivar a algn/evadir algo
steering ['stɪərɪŋ] N (Aut) dirección f
steering committee N comisión f directiva
steering wheel N volante m
stellar ['stelər] ADJ estelar
stem [stem] N (of plant) tallo; (of glass) pie m;
(of pipe) cañón m ▶ VT detener; (blood)
restañar
▶ **stem from** VT FUS ser consecuencia de
stem cell N célula madre
stench [stentʃ] N hedor m
stencil ['stensl] N (typed) cliché m, clisé m;
(lettering) plantilla ▶ VT hacer un cliché de
stenographer [steˈnɔgrəfər] N (US)
taquígrafo(-a)
step [step] N paso; (sound) paso, pisada; (stair)
peldaño, escalón m ▶ VI: **to ~ forward** dar un
paso adelante; **steps** NPL (BRIT) = **stepladder**;
~ **by** ~ paso a paso; (fig) poco a poco; **to keep
in ~ (with)** llevar el paso de; (fig) llevar el
paso de, estar de acuerdo con; **to be in/out
of ~ with** estar acorde con/estar en
disonancia con; **to take steps to solve a
problem** tomar medidas para resolver un
problema
▶ **step down** VI (fig) retirarse
▶ **step in** VI entrar; (fig) intervenir
▶ **step off** VT FUS bajar de
▶ **step on** VT FUS pisar
▶ **step over** VT FUS pasar por encima de

▶ **step up** VT (*increase*) aumentar

step aerobics NPL step *m*

stepbrother ['stɛpbrʌðə^r] N
hermanastro

stepchild ['stɛptʃaɪld] N (*irreg*) hijastro(-a)

stepdaughter ['stɛpdɔ:tə^r] N hijastra

stepfather ['stɛpfɑ:ðə^r] N padrastro

stepladder ['stɛplædə^r] N escalera doble *or* de
tijera

stepmother ['stɛpmʌðə^r] N madrastra

stepping stone ['stɛpɪŋ-] N pasadera

step Reebok® [-'ri:bɔk] N step *m*

stepsister ['stɛpsɪstə^r] N hermanastra

stepson ['stɛpsʌn] N hijastro

stereo ['stɛrɪəu] N estéreo ▶ ADJ (*also:*
stereophonic) estéreo, estereofónico;
in ~ en estéreo

stereotype ['stɪərɪətaɪp] N estereotipo
▶ VT estereotipar

sterile ['stɛraɪl] ADJ estéril

sterilization [stɛrɪlaɪ'zeɪʃən] N
esterilización *f*

sterilize ['stɛrɪlaɪz] VT esterilizar

sterling ['stə:lɪŋ] ADJ (*silver*) de ley ▶ N (*Econ*)
libras *fpl* esterlinas; **a pound ~** una libra
esterlina; **he is of ~ character** tiene un
carácter excelente

stern [stə:n] ADJ severo, austero ▶ N (*Naut*)
popa

sternum ['stə:nəm] N esternón *m*

steroid ['stɪərɔɪd] N esteroide *m*

stethoscope ['stɛθəskəup] N estetoscopio

stevedore ['sti:vədɔ:^r] N estibador *m*

stew [stju:] N cocido, estofado, guisado (*LAm*)
▶ VT, VI estofar, guisar; (*fruit*) cocer; **stewed
fruit** compota de fruta

steward ['stju:əd] N (*gen*) camarero; (*shop
steward*) enlace *mf* sindical

stewardess ['stju:ədəs] N azafata

stewardship ['stju:ədʃɪp] N tutela

stewing steak ['stju:ɪŋ-], (*US*) **stew meat** N
carne *f* de vaca

St. Ex. ABBR = **stock exchange**

stick [stɪk] (*pt, pp* **stuck**) N palo; (*as weapon*)
porra; (*also:* **walking stick**) bastón *m* ▶ VT
(*glue*) pegar; (*inf: put*) meter; (: *tolerate*)
aguantar, soportar ▶ VI pegarse; (*come to a
stop*) quedarse parado; (*get jammed*: *door, lift*)
atascarse; **to get hold of the wrong end
of the ~** entender al revés; **to ~ to** (*word,
principles*) atenerse a, ser fiel a; (*promise*)
cumplir; **it stuck in my mind** se me quedó
grabado; **to ~ sth into** clavar *or* hincar
algo en

▶ **stick around** VI (*inf*) quedarse

▶ **stick out** VI sobresalir ▶ VT: **to ~ it out** (*inf*)
aguantar

▶ **stick up** VI sobresalir

▶ **stick up for** VT FUS defender

sticker ['stɪkə^r] N (*label*) etiqueta adhesiva;
(*with slogan*) pegatina

sticking plaster ['stɪkɪŋ-] N (*Brit*)
esparadrapo

sticking point N (*fig*) punto de fricción

stick insect N insecto palo

stickler ['stɪklə^r] N: **to be a ~ for** insistir
mucho en

stick shift N (*US Aut*) palanca de cambios

stick-up ['stɪkʌp] N asalto, atraco

sticky ['stɪkɪ] ADJ pegajoso; (*label*) adhesivo;
(*fig*) difícil

stiff [stɪf] ADJ rígido, tieso; (*hard*) duro;
(*difficult*) difícil; (*person*) inflexible; (*price*)
exorbitante ▶ ADV: **scared/bored ~** muerto
de miedo/aburrimiento; **to have a ~ neck/
back** tener tortícolis/dolor de espalda; **the
door's ~** la puerta está atrancada

stiffen ['stɪfn] VT hacer más rígido; (*limb*)
entumecer ▶ VI endurecerse; (*grow stronger*)
fortalecerse

stiffness ['stɪfnɪs] N rigidez *f*

stifle ['staɪfl] VT ahogar, sofocar

stifling ['staɪflɪŋ] ADJ (*heat*) sofocante,
bochornoso

stigma ['stɪgmə] N (*Bot, Med, Rel pl* **stigmata**
[stɪg'mɑ:tə], *fig pl* **stigmas**) estigma *m*

stile [staɪl] N escalera (*para pasar una cerca*)

stiletto [stɪ'lɛtəu] N (*Brit: also:* **stiletto heel**)
tacón *m* de aguja

still [stɪl] ADJ inmóvil, quieto; (*orange juice etc*)
sin gas ▶ ADV (*up to this time*) todavía; (*even*)
aún; (*nonetheless*) sin embargo, aun así ▶ N
(*Cine*) foto *f* fija; **keep ~!** ¡estate quieto!, ¡no te
muevas!; **he ~ hasn't arrived** todavía no ha
llegado

stillborn ['stɪlbɔ:n] ADJ nacido muerto

still life N naturaleza muerta

stilt [stɪlt] N zanco; (*pile*) pilar *m*, soporte *m*

stilted ['stɪltɪd] ADJ afectado, artificial

stimulant ['stɪmjulənt] N estimulante *m*

stimulate ['stɪmjuleɪt] VT estimular

stimulating ['stɪmjuleɪtɪŋ] ADJ estimulante

stimulation [stɪmju'leɪʃən] N estímulo

stimulus ['stɪmjuləs] (*pl* **stimuli** [-laɪ]) N
estímulo, incentivo

sting [stɪŋ] (*pt, pp* **stung**) N (*wound*) picadura;
(*pain*) escozor *m*, picazón *m*; (*organ*) aguijón *m*;
(*inf: confidence trick*) timo ▶ VT picar ▶ VI picar,
escocer; **my eyes are stinging** me pican *or*
escuecen los ojos

stingy ['stɪndʒɪ] ADJ tacaño

stink [stɪŋk] (*pt* **stank** [stæŋk], *pp* **stunk**
[stʌŋk]) N hedor *m*, tufo ▶ VI heder, apestar

stinking ['stɪŋkɪŋ] ADJ hediondo, fétido;
(*fig: inf*) horrible

stint [stɪnt] N tarea, destajo; **to do one's
~ (at sth)** hacer su parte (de algo), hacer lo que
corresponde (de algo) ▶ VI: **to ~ on** escatimar

S

stipend ['staɪpɛnd] N salario, remuneración f
stipendiary [staɪ'pɛndɪərɪ] ADJ:
~ **magistrate** magistrado(-a)
estipendiario(-a)
stipulate ['stɪpjuleɪt] VT estipular
stipulation [stɪpju'leɪʃən] N estipulación f
stir [stə:ʳ] N (fig: agitation) conmoción f ▶ VT
(tea etc) remover; (fire) atizar; (move) agitar;
(fig: emotions) provocar ▶ VI moverse; **to give
sth a ~** remover algo; **to cause a ~** causar
conmoción or sensación
▶ **stir up** VT excitar; (trouble) fomentar
stir-fry ['stə:fraɪ] VT sofreír removiendo
▶ N plato preparado sofriendo y removiendo los
ingredientes
stirrup ['stɪrəp] N estribo
stitch [stɪtʃ] N (Sewing) puntada; (Knitting)
punto; (Med) punto (de sutura); (pain)
punzada ▶ VT coser; (Med) suturar
stoat [stəut] N armiño
stock [stɔk] N (Comm: reserves) existencias fpl,
stock m; (: selection) surtido; (Agr) ganado,
ganadería; (Culin) caldo; (fig: lineage) estirpe f,
cepa; (Finance) capital m; (: shares) acciones fpl;
(Rail: rolling stock) material m rodante ▶ ADJ
(Comm: goods, size) normal, de serie; (fig: reply
etc) clásico, trillado; (: greeting) acostumbrado
▶ VT (have in stock) tener existencias de;
(: supply) proveer, abastecer; **stocks** NPL
(History: punishment) cepo sg; **stocks and
shares** acciones y valores; **in ~** en existencia
or almacén; **to have sth in ~** tener
existencias de algo; **out of ~** agotado; **to
take ~ of** (fig) considerar, examinar;
government ~ papel m del Estado
▶ **stock up with** VT FUS abastecerse de
stockbroker ['stɔkbrəukəʳ] N agente mf or
corredor(a) m/f de bolsa
stock control N (Comm) control m de
existencias
stock cube N pastilla or cubito de caldo
stock exchange N bolsa
stockholder ['stɔkhəuldəʳ] N (US) accionista
mf
Stockholm ['stɔkhəum] N Estocolmo
stocking ['stɔkɪŋ] N media
stock-in-trade ['stɔkɪn'treɪd] N (tools etc)
herramientas fpl; (stock) existencia de
mercancías; (fig): **it's his ~** es su
especialidad
stockist ['stɔkɪst] N (BRIT) distribuidor(a) m/f
stock market N bolsa (de valores)
stock phrase N vieja frase f
stockpile ['stɔkpaɪl] N reserva ▶ VT
acumular, almacenar
stockroom ['stɔkru:m] N almacén m,
depósito
stocktaking ['stɔkteɪkɪŋ] N (BRIT Comm)
inventario, balance m

stocky ['stɔkɪ] ADJ (strong) robusto; (short)
achaparrado
stodgy ['stɔdʒɪ] ADJ indigesto, pesado
stoical ['stəuɪkəl] ADJ estoico
stoke [stəuk] VT atizar
stole [stəul] PT of **steal** ▶ N estola
stolen ['stəuln] PP of **steal**
stolid ['stɔlɪd] ADJ (person) imperturbable,
impasible
stomach ['stʌmək] N (Anat) estómago; (belly)
vientre m ▶ VT tragar, aguantar
stomachache N dolor m de estómago
stomach pump N bomba gástrica
stomach ulcer N úlcera de estómago
stomp [stɔmp] VI: **to ~ in/out** entrar/salir
con pasos ruidosos
stone [stəun] N piedra; (in fruit) hueso; (BRIT:
weight) = 6.348 kg; 14lb ▶ ADJ de piedra ▶ VT
apedrear; (fruit) deshuesar; **within a ~'s
throw of the station** a tiro de piedra or a dos
pasos de la estación
Stone Age N: **the ~** la Edad de Piedra
stone-cold ['stəun'kəuld] ADJ helado
stoned [stəund] ADJ (inf: drunk) trompa,
borracho, colocado
stone-deaf ['stəun'dɛf] ADJ sordo como una
tapia
stonemason ['stəunmeɪsən] N albañil m
stonewall [stəun'wɔ:l] VI alargar la cosa
innecesariamente ▶ VT dar largas a
stonework ['stəunwə:k] N (art) cantería
stony ['stəunɪ] ADJ pedregoso; (glance) glacial
stood [stud] PT, PP of **stand**
stooge [stu:dʒ] N (inf) hombre m de paja
stool [stu:l] N taburete m
stoop [stu:p] VI (also: **stoop down**) doblarse,
agacharse; (also: **have a stoop**) ser cargado
de espaldas; (bend) inclinarse, encorvarse;
to ~ to (doing) sth rebajarse a (hacer) algo
stop [stɔp] N parada, alto; (in punctuation)
punto ▶ VT parar, detener; (break off)
suspender; (block: pay) suspender; (: cheque)
invalidar; (prevent) impedir; (also: **put a stop
to**) poner término a ▶ VI pararse, detenerse;
(end) acabarse; **to ~ doing sth** dejar de hacer
algo; **to ~ sb (from) doing sth** impedir a
algn hacer algo; **to ~ dead** pararse en seco;
~ **it!** ¡basta ya!, ¡párate!
▶ **stop by** VI pasar por
▶ **stop off** VI interrumpir el viaje
▶ **stop up** VT (hole) tapar
stopcock ['stɔpkɔk] N llave f de paso
stopgap ['stɔpgæp] N interino; (person)
sustituto(-a); (measure) medida provisional
▶ CPD (situation) provisional
stoplights ['stɔplaɪts] NPL (Aut) luces fpl de
detención
stopover ['stɔpəuvəʳ] N parada intermedia;
(Aviat) escala

stoppage ['stɔpɪdʒ] N (*strike*) paro; (*temporary stop*) interrupción f; (*of pay*) suspensión f; (*blockage*) obstrucción f

stopper ['stɔpər] N tapón m

stop press N noticias fpl de última hora

stopwatch ['stɔpwɔtʃ] N cronómetro

storage ['stɔːrɪdʒ] N almacenaje m; (*Comput*) almacenamiento

storage capacity N capacidad f de almacenaje

storage heater N acumulador m de calor

store [stɔːr] N (*stock*) provisión f; (*depot*) almacén m; (*Brit: large shop*) almacén m; (*US*) tienda; (*reserve*) reserva, repuesto ▶ VT (*gen*) almacenar; (*Comput*) almacenar; (*keep*) guardar; (*in filing system*) archivar; **stores** NPL víveres mpl; **who knows what is in ~ for us** quién sabe lo que nos espera; **to set great/little ~ by sth** dar mucha/poca importancia a algo, valorar mucho/poco algo
▶ **store up** VT acumular

storehouse ['stɔːhaus] N almacén m, depósito

storekeeper ['stɔːkiːpər] N (*US*) tendero(-a)

storeroom ['stɔːruːm] N despensa

storey, (*US*) **story** ['stɔːrɪ] N piso

stork [stɔːk] N cigüeña

storm [stɔːm] N tormenta; (*wind*) vendaval m; (*fig: of applause*) salva; (*: of criticism*) nube f
▶ VI (*fig*) rabiar ▶ VT tomar por asalto, asaltar; **to take a town by ~** (*Mil*) tomar una ciudad por asalto

storm cloud N nubarrón m

storm door N contrapuerta

stormy ['stɔːmɪ] ADJ tempestuoso

story ['stɔːrɪ] N historia; (*Press*) artículo; (*joke*) cuento, chiste m; (*plot*) argumento; (*lie*) cuento; (*US*) = **storey**

storybook ['stɔːrɪbuk] N libro de cuentos

storyteller ['stɔːrɪtelər] N cuentista mf

stout [staut] ADJ (*strong*) sólido; (*fat*) gordo, corpulento ▶ N cerveza negra

stove [stəuv] N (*for cooking*) cocina; (*for heating*) estufa; **gas/electric ~** cocina de gas/eléctrica

stow [stəu] VT meter, poner; (*Naut*) estibar

stowaway ['stəuəwei] N polizón(-ona) m/f

straddle ['strædl] VT montar a horcajadas

straggle ['strægl] VI (*wander*) vagar en desorden; (*lag behind*) rezagarse

straggler ['stræglər] N rezagado(-a)

straggling ['stræglɪŋ], **straggly** ['stræglɪ] ADJ (*hair*) desordenado

straight [streit] ADJ (*direct*) recto, derecho; (*plain, uncomplicated*) sencillo; (*frank*) franco, directo; (*in order*) en orden; (*continuous*) continuo; (*Theat: part, play*) serio; (*: person: conventional*) recto, convencional; (*: heterosexual*) heterosexual ▶ ADV derecho,

directamente; (*drink*) solo; **to put** or **get sth ~** dejar algo en claro; **10 ~ wins** 10 victorias seguidas; **to be (all) ~** (*tidy*) estar en orden; (*clarified*) estar claro; **I went ~ home** (me) fui directamente a casa; **~ away, ~ off** (*at once*) en seguida

straighten ['streitn] VT (*also:* **straighten out**) enderezar, poner derecho ▶ VI (*also:* **straighten up**) enderezarse, ponerse derecho; **to ~ things out** poner las cosas en orden

straighteners ['streitnəz] NPL (*for hair*) plancha de pelo

straight-faced [streit'feist] ADJ serio ▶ ADV sin mostrar emoción, impávido

straightforward [streit'fɔːwəd] ADJ (*simple*) sencillo; (*honest*) sincero

strain [strein] N (*gen*) tensión f; (*Tech*) presión f; (*Med*) distensión f, torcedura; (*breed*) raza; (*lineage*) linaje m; (*of virus*) variedad f ▶ VT (*back etc*) distender, torcerse; (*resources*) agotar; (*tire*) cansar; (*stretch*) estirar; (*filter*) filtrar; (*meaning*) tergiversar ▶ VI esforzarse; **strains** NPL (*Mus*) son msg; **she's under a lot of ~** está bajo mucha tensión

strained [streind] ADJ (*muscle*) torcido; (*laugh*) forzado; (*relations*) tenso

strainer ['streinər] N colador m

strait [streit] N (*Geo*) estrecho; **to be in dire straits** (*fig*) estar en un gran aprieto

straitjacket ['streitdʒækit] N camisa de fuerza

strait-laced [streit'leist] ADJ mojigato, gazmoño

strand [strænd] N (*of thread*) hebra; (*of rope*) ramal m; **a ~ of hair** un pelo

stranded ['strændid] ADJ (*person: without money*) desamparado; (*: without transport*) colgado

strange [streindʒ] ADJ (*not known*) desconocido; (*odd*) extraño, raro

strangely ADV de un modo raro; *see also* **enough**

stranger ['streindʒər] N desconocido(-a); (*from another area*) forastero(-a); **I'm a ~ here** no soy de aquí

strangle ['stræŋgl] VT estrangular

stranglehold ['stræŋglhəuld] N (*fig*) dominio completo

strangulation [stræŋgju'leiʃən] N estrangulación f

strap [stræp] N correa; (*of slip, dress*) tirante m ▶ VT atar con correa

straphanging ['stræphæŋɪŋ] N viajar m de pie or parado (*LAm*)

strapless ['stræplis] ADJ (*bra, dress*) sin tirantes

strapped [stræpt] ADJ: **to be ~ for cash** (*inf*) andar mal de dinero

S

strapping ['stræpɪŋ] ADJ robusto, fornido
Strasbourg ['stræzbə:g] N Estrasburgo
strata ['strɑ:tə] NPL of **stratum**
stratagem ['strætɪdʒəm] N estratagema
strategic [strə'ti:dʒɪk] ADJ estratégico
strategy ['strætɪdʒɪ] N estrategia
stratum ['strɑ:təm] (pl **strata** ['strɑ:tə]) N
 estrato
straw [strɔ:] N paja; (also: **drinking straw**)
 caña, pajita; **that's the last ~!** ¡eso es el
 colmo!
strawberry ['strɔ:bərɪ] N fresa, frutilla (LAm)
stray [streɪ] ADJ (animal) extraviado; (bullet)
 perdido; (scattered) disperso ▶ VI extraviarse,
 perderse; (wander: walker) vagar, ir sin rumbo
 fijo; (: speaker) desvariar
streak [stri:k] N raya; (fig: of madness etc) vena
 ▶ VT rayar ▶ VI: **to ~ past** pasar como un rayo;
 to have streaks in one's hair tener vetas en
 el pelo; **a winning/losing ~** una racha de
 buena/mala suerte
streaker ['stri:kər] N corredor(a) m/f
 desnudo(-a)
streaky ['stri:kɪ] ADJ rayado
stream [stri:m] N riachuelo, arroyo; (jet)
 chorro; (flow) corriente f; (of people) oleada
 ▶ VT (Scol) dividir en grupos por habilidad
 ▶ VI correr, fluir; **to ~ in/out** (people) entrar/
 salir en tropel; **against the ~** a
 contracorriente; **on ~** (new power plant etc) en
 funcionamiento
streamer ['stri:mər] N serpentina
stream feed N (on photocopier etc)
 alimentación f continua
streamline ['stri:mlaɪn] VT aerodinamizar;
 (fig) racionalizar
streamlined ['stri:mlaɪnd] ADJ aerodinámico
street [stri:t] N calle f ▶ ADJ callejero; **the
 back streets** las callejuelas; **to be on the
 streets** (homeless) estar sin vivienda; (as
 prostitute) hacer la calle
streetcar ['stri:tkɑ:] N (US) tranvía m
street cred [-krɛd] N (inf) imagen de estar en
 la onda
street lamp N farol m
street light N farol m (LAm), farola (Sp)
street lighting N alumbrado público
street map N plano (de la ciudad)
street market N mercado callejero
street plan N plano callejero
streetwise ['stri:twaɪz] ADJ (inf) pícaro
strength [strɛŋθ] N fuerza; (of girder, knot etc)
 resistencia; (of chemical solution) potencia;
 (of wine) graduación f de alcohol; (fig: power)
 poder m; **on the ~ of** a base de, en base a; **to
 be at full/below ~** tener/no tener completo
 el cupo
strengthen ['strɛŋθn] VT fortalecer, reforzar
strenuous ['strɛnjuəs] ADJ (tough) arduo;

(energetic) enérgico; (opposition) firme, tenaz;
 (efforts) intensivo
stress [strɛs] N (force, pressure) presión f;
 (mental strain) estrés m, tensión f; (accent,
 emphasis) énfasis m, acento; (Ling, Poetry)
 acento; (Tech) tensión f, carga ▶ VT subrayar,
 recalcar; **to be under ~** estar estresado; **to
 lay great ~ on sth** hacer hincapié en algo
stressed [strɛst] ADJ (tense) estresado,
 agobiado; (syllable) acentuado
stressful ['strɛsful] ADJ (job) estresante
stretch [strɛtʃ] N (of sand etc) trecho; (of road)
 tramo; (of time) período, tiempo ▶ VI
 estirarse; (extend): **to ~ to** or **as far as**
 extenderse hasta; (be enough: money, food):
 to ~ to alcanzar para, dar de sí para ▶ VT
 extender, estirar; (make demands of) exigir el
 máximo esfuerzo a; **to ~ one's legs** estirar
 las piernas
 ▶ **stretch out** VI tenderse ▶ VT (arm etc)
 extender; (spread) estirar
stretcher ['strɛtʃər] N camilla
stretcher-bearer ['strɛtʃəbɛərər] N
 camillero(-a)
stretch marks NPL estrías fpl
strewn [stru:n] ADJ: **~ with** cubierto or
 sembrado de
stricken ['strɪkən] ADJ (person) herido; (city,
 industry etc) condenado; (~ with (arthritis,
 disease) afligido por; **grief-~** destrozado por
 el dolor
strict [strɪkt] ADJ (order, rule etc) estricto;
 (discipline, ban) severo; **in ~ confidence** en la
 más absoluta confianza
strictly ['strɪktlɪ] ADV estrictamente; (totally)
 terminantemente; **~ confidential**
 estrictamente confidencial; **~ speaking** en
 (el) sentido estricto (de la palabra);
 ~ between ourselves ... entre nosotros ...
stridden ['strɪdn] PP of **stride**
stride [straɪd] (pt **strode** [strəud], pp **stridden**
 ['strɪdn]) N zancada, tranco ▶ VI dar
 zancadas, andar a trancos; **to take in one's
 ~** (fig: changes etc) tomar con calma
strident ['straɪdnt] ADJ estridente; (colour)
 chillón(-ona)
strife [straɪf] N lucha
strike [straɪk] (pt, pp **struck**) N huelga; (of oil
 etc) descubrimiento; (attack) ataque m; (Sport)
 golpe m ▶ VT golpear, pegar; (oil etc)
 descubrir; (obstacle) topar con; (produce: coin,
 medal) acuñar; (: agreement, deal) alcanzar ▶ VI
 declarar la huelga; (attack: Mil etc) atacar;
 (clock) dar la hora; **on ~** (workers) en huelga;
 to call a ~ declarar una huelga; **to go on** or
 come out on ~ ponerse or declararse en
 huelga; **to ~ a match** encender una cerilla;
 to ~ a balance (fig) encontrar un equilibrio;
 to ~ a bargain cerrar un trato; **the clock**

struck nine o'clock el reloj dio las nueve
▶ **strike back** VI (Mil) contraatacar; (fig) devolver el golpe
▶ **strike down** VT derribar
▶ **strike off** VT (from list) tachar; (doctor etc) suspender
▶ **strike out** VT borrar, tachar
▶ **strike up** VT (Mus) empezar a tocar; (conversation) entablar; (friendship) trabar

strikebreaker ['straɪkbreɪkə'] N rompehuelgas mf, esquirol mf

striker ['straɪkə'] N huelguista mf; (Sport) delantero

striking ['straɪkɪŋ] ADJ (colour) llamativo; (obvious) notorio

Strimmer® ['strɪmə'] N cortacéspedes m inv (especial para los bordes)

string [strɪŋ] (pt, pp **strung** [strʌŋ]) N (gen) cuerda; (row) hilera; (Comput) cadena ▶ VT: **to ~ together** ensartar; **to ~ out** extenderse; **the strings** NPL (Mus) los instrumentos de cuerda; **to pull strings** (fig) mover palancas; **to get a job by pulling strings** conseguir un trabajo por enchufe; **with no strings attached** (fig) sin compromiso

string bean N judía verde, habichuela

stringed instrument [strɪŋd-], **string instrument** N (Mus) instrumento de cuerda

stringent ['strɪndʒənt] ADJ riguroso, severo

string quartet N cuarteto de cuerdas

strip [strɪp] N tira; (of land) franja; (of metal) cinta, lámina ▶ VT desnudar; (also: **strip down**: machine) desmontar ▶ VI desnudarse
▶ **strip off** VT (paint etc) quitar ▶ VI (person) desnudarse

strip cartoon N tira cómica, historieta (LAm)

stripe [straɪp] N raya; (Mil) galón m; **white with green stripes** blanco con rayas verdes

striped [straɪpt] ADJ a rayas, rayado

strip lighting N alumbrado fluorescente

stripper ['strɪpə'] N artista mf de striptease

strip-search ['strɪpsə:tʃ] VT: **to ~ sb** desnudar y registrar a algn

striptease ['strɪpti:z] N striptease m

strive [straɪv] (pt **strove** [strəuv], pp **striven** ['strɪvn]) VI: **to ~ to do sth** esforzarse or luchar por hacer algo

strobe [strəub] N (also: **strobe light**) luz f estroboscópica

strode [strəud] PT of **stride**

stroke [strəuk] N (blow) golpe m; (Swimming) brazada; (Med) apoplejía; (caress) caricia; (of pen) trazo; (Swimming: style) estilo; (of piston) carrera ▶ VT acariciar; **at a ~** de golpe; **a ~ of luck** un golpe de suerte; **two-~ engine** motor m de dos tiempos

stroll [strəul] N paseo, vuelta ▶ VI dar un paseo or una vuelta; **to go for a ~**, **have** or **take a ~** dar un paseo

stroller ['strəulə'] N (US: pushchair) cochecito

strong [strɔŋ] ADJ fuerte; (bleach, acid) concentrado ▶ ADV: **to be going ~** (company) marchar bien; (person) conservarse bien; **they are 50 ~** son 50

strong-arm ['strɔŋɑ:m] ADJ (tactics, methods) represivo

strongbox ['strɔŋbɔks] N caja fuerte

strong drink N bebida cargada or fuerte

stronghold ['strɔŋhəuld] N fortaleza; (fig) baluarte m

strong language N lenguaje m fuerte

strongly ['strɔŋlɪ] ADV fuertemente, con fuerza; (believe) firmemente; **to feel ~ about sth** tener una opinión firme sobre algo

strongman ['strɔŋmæn] N (irreg) forzudo; (fig) hombre m robusto

strongroom ['strɔŋru:m] N cámara acorazada

stroppy ['strɔpɪ] ADJ (BRIT inf) borde; **to get ~** ponerse borde

strove [strəuv] PT of **strive**

struck [strʌk] PT, PP of **strike**

structural ['strʌktʃərəl] ADJ estructural

structure ['strʌktʃə'] N estructura; (building) construcción f

struggle ['strʌgl] N lucha ▶ VI luchar; **to have a ~ to do sth** esforzarse por hacer algo

strum [strʌm] VT (guitar) rasguear

strung [strʌŋ] PT, PP of **string**

strut [strʌt] N puntal m ▶ VI pavonearse

strychnine ['strɪkni:n] N estricnina

stub [stʌb] N (of ticket etc) matriz f; (of cigarette) colilla ▶ VT: **to ~ one's toe on sth** dar con el dedo del pie contra algo
▶ **stub out** VT (cigarette) apagar

stubble ['stʌbl] N rastrojo; (on chin) barba (incipiente)

stubborn ['stʌbən] ADJ terco, testarudo

stucco ['stʌkəu] N estuco

stuck [stʌk] PT, PP of **stick** ▶ ADJ (jammed) atascado

stuck-up [stʌk'ʌp] ADJ engreído, presumido

stud [stʌd] N (shirt stud) corchete m; (of boot) taco; (earring) pendiente m (de bolita); (also: **stud farm**) caballeriza; (also: **stud horse**) caballo semental ▶ VT (fig): **studded with** salpicado de

student ['stju:dənt] N estudiante mf ▶ ADJ estudiantil; **a law/medical ~** un(a) estudiante de derecho/medicina

student driver N (US Aut) aprendiz(a) m/f de conductor

students' union N (BRIT: association) sindicato de estudiantes; (: building) centro de estudiantes

studio ['stju:dɪəu] N estudio; (artist's) taller m

studio flat, (US) **studio apartment** N estudio

S

studious ['stju:dɪəs] ADJ estudioso; (studied) calculado

studiously ['stju:dɪəslɪ] ADV (carefully) con esmero

study ['stʌdɪ] N estudio ▸ VT estudiar; (examine) examinar, investigar ▸ VI estudiar; **to make a ~ of sth** realizar una investigación de algo; **to ~ for an exam** preparar un examen

stuff [stʌf] N materia; (cloth) tela; (substance) material m, sustancia; (things, belongings) cosas fpl ▸ VT llenar; (Culin) rellenar; (animal: for exhibition) disecar; **my nose is stuffed up** tengo la nariz tapada; **stuffed toy** juguete m or muñeco de trapo

stuffing ['stʌfɪŋ] N relleno

stuffy ['stʌfɪ] ADJ (room) mal ventilado; (person) de miras estrechas

stumble ['stʌmbl] VI tropezar, dar un traspié ▸ **stumble across** VT FUS (fig) tropezar con

stumbling block ['stʌmblɪŋ-] N tropiezo, obstáculo

stump [stʌmp] N (of tree) tocón m; (of limb) muñón m ▸ VT: **to be stumped** quedarse perplejo; **to be stumped for an answer** quedarse sin saber qué contestar

stun [stʌn] VT aturdir

stung [stʌŋ] PT, PP of **sting**

stunk [stʌŋk] PP of **stink**

stunned [stʌnd] ADJ (dazed) aturdido, atontado; (amazed) pasmado; (shocked) anonadado

stunning ['stʌnɪŋ] ADJ (fig: news) pasmoso; (: outfit etc) sensacional

stunt [stʌnt] N (Aviat) vuelo acrobático; (in film) escena peligrosa; (also: **publicity stunt**) truco publicitario

stunted ['stʌntɪd] ADJ enano, achaparrado

stuntman ['stʌntmæn] N (irreg) especialista m

stupefaction [stju:pɪ'fækʃən] N estupefacción f

stupefy ['stju:pɪfaɪ] VT dejar estupefacto

stupendous [stju:'pɛndəs] ADJ estupendo, asombroso

stupid ['stju:pɪd] ADJ estúpido, tonto

stupidity [stju:'pɪdɪtɪ] N estupidez f

stupor ['stju:pə'] N estupor m

sturdy ['stə:dɪ] ADJ robusto, fuerte

stutter ['stʌtə'] N tartamudeo ▸ VI tartamudear

sty [staɪ] N (for pigs) pocilga

stye [staɪ] N (Med) orzuelo

style [staɪl] N estilo; (fashion) moda; (of dress etc) hechura; (hair style) corte m; **in the latest ~** en el último modelo

stylish ['staɪlɪʃ] ADJ elegante, a la moda

stylist ['staɪlɪst] N (hair stylist) peluquero(-a)

stylus ['staɪləs] (pl **styli** or **styluses** [-laɪ]) N (of record player) aguja

Styrofoam® ['staɪrəfəum] N (US) poliestireno ▸ ADJ (cup) de poliestireno

suave [swɑ:v] ADJ cortés, fino

sub [sʌb] N ABBR = **submarine**; **subscription**

sub... [sʌb] PREF sub...

subcommittee ['sʌbkəmɪtɪ] N subcomisión f

subconscious [sʌb'kɔnʃəs] ADJ subconsciente ▸ N subconsciente m

subcontinent [sʌb'kɔntɪnənt] N: **the Indian ~** el subcontinente de la India

subcontract N ['sʌb'kɔntrækt] subcontrato ▸ VT ['sʌbkən'trækt] subcontratar

subcontractor ['sʌbkən'træktə'] N subcontratista mf

subdivide [sʌbdɪ'vaɪd] VT subdividir

subdue [səb'dju:] VT sojuzgar; (passions) dominar

subdued [səb'dju:d] ADJ (light) tenue; (person) sumiso, manso

sub-editor ['sʌb'ɛdɪtə'] N (BRIT) redactor(a) m/f

subject N ['sʌbdʒɪkt] súbdito; (Scol) tema m, materia; (Grammar) sujeto ▸ VT [səb'dʒɛkt]: **to ~ sb to sth** someter a algn a algo ▸ ADJ ['sʌbdʒɪkt]: **to be ~ to** (law) estar sujeto a; (person) ser propenso a; **to change the ~** cambiar de tema; **~ to confirmation in writing** sujeto a confirmación por escrito

subjective [səb'dʒɛktɪv] ADJ subjetivo

subject matter N materia; (content) contenido

sub judice [sʌb'dju:dɪsɪ] ADJ (Law) pendiente de resolución

subjugate ['sʌbdʒugeɪt] VT subyugar, sojuzgar

subjunctive [səb'dʒʌŋktɪv] ADJ, N subjuntivo

sublet [sʌb'lɛt] VT, VI subarrendar, realquilar

sublime [sə'blaɪm] ADJ sublime

subliminal [sʌb'lɪmɪnl] ADJ subliminal

submachine gun ['sʌbmə'ʃi:n-] N metralleta

submarine [sʌbmə'ri:n] N submarino

submerge [səb'mə:dʒ] VT sumergir; (flood) inundar ▸ VI sumergirse

submersion [səb'mə:ʃən] N sumersión f

submission [səb'mɪʃən] N sumisión f; (to committee etc) ponencia

submissive [səb'mɪsɪv] ADJ sumiso

submit [səb'mɪt] VT someter; (proposal, claim) presentar ▸ VI someterse; **I ~ that ...** me permito sugerir que ...

subnormal [sʌb'nɔ:məl] ADJ subnormal

subordinate [sə'bɔ:dɪnət] ADJ, N subordinado(-a) m/f

subpoena [səb'pi:nə] (Law) N citación f ▸ VT citar

subprime ['sʌbpraɪm] ADJ de alto riesgo; **~ mortgage** (Finance) hipoteca de alto riesgo

subroutine [sʌbru:'ti:n] N (Comput) subrutina

subscribe [səb'skraɪb] vɪ suscribir; **to ~ to** (*fund, opinion*) suscribir, aprobar; (*opinion*) estar de acuerdo con; (*newspaper*) suscribirse a

subscribed capital [səb'skraɪbd-] N capital *m* suscrito

subscriber [səb'skraɪbə^r] N (*to periodical*) suscriptor(a) *m/f*; (*to telephone*) abonado(-a)

subscript ['sʌbskrɪpt] N (*Typ*) subíndice *m*

subscription [səb'skrɪpʃən] N (*to club*) abono; (*to magazine*) suscripción *f*; **to take out a ~ to** suscribirse a

subsequent ['sʌbsɪkwənt] ADJ subsiguiente, posterior; **~ to** posterior a

subsequently ['sʌbsɪkwəntlɪ] ADV posteriormente, más tarde

subservient [səb'sə:vɪənt] ADJ: **~ (to)** servil (a)

subside [səb'saɪd] vɪ hundirse; (*flood*) bajar; (*wind*) amainar

subsidence [səb'saɪdns] N hundimiento; (*in road*) socavón *m*

subsidiarity [səbsɪdɪ'ærɪtɪ] N (*Pol*) subsidiariedad *f*

subsidiary [səb'sɪdɪərɪ] N sucursal *f*, filial *f* ▶ ADJ (*Univ: subject*) secundario

subsidize ['sʌbsɪdaɪz] vᴛ subvencionar

subsidy ['sʌbsɪdɪ] N subvención *f*

subsist [səb'sɪst] vɪ: **to ~ on sth** subsistir a base de algo, sustentarse con algo

subsistence [səb'sɪstəns] N subsistencia

subsistence allowance N dietas *fpl*

subsistence level N nivel *m* de subsistencia

subsistence wage N sueldo de subsistencia

substance ['sʌbstəns] N sustancia; (*fig*) esencia; **to lack ~** (*argument*) ser poco convincente; (*accusation*) no tener fundamento; (*film, book*) tener poca profundidad

substance abuse N uso indebido de sustancias tóxicas

substandard [sʌb'stændəd] ADJ (*goods*) inferior; (*housing*) deficiente

substantial [səb'stænʃl] ADJ sustancial, sustancioso; (*fig*) importante

substantially [səb'stænʃəlɪ] ADV sustancialmente; **~ bigger** bastante más grande

substantiate [səb'stænʃɪeɪt] vᴛ comprobar

substitute ['sʌbstɪtjuːt] N (*person*) suplente *mf*; (*thing*) sustituto ▶ vᴛ: **to ~ A for B** sustituir B por A, reemplazar A por B

substitution [sʌbstɪ'tjuːʃən] N sustitución *f*

subterfuge ['sʌbtəfjuːdʒ] N subterfugio

subterranean [sʌbtə'reɪnɪən] ADJ subterráneo

subtitle ['sʌbtaɪtl] N subtítulo

subtle ['sʌtl] ADJ sutil

subtlety ['sʌtltɪ] N sutileza

subtly ['sʌtlɪ] ADV sutilmente

subtotal [sʌb'təʊtl] N subtotal *m*

subtract [səb'trækt] vᴛ restar; sustraer

subtraction [səb'trækʃən] N resta; sustracción *f*

suburb ['sʌbəːb] N barrio residencial; **the suburbs** las afueras (de la ciudad)

suburban [sə'bəːbən] ADJ suburbano; (*train etc*) de cercanías

suburbia [sə'bəːbɪə] N barrios *mpl* residenciales

subversion [sʌb'vəːʃən] N subversión *f*

subversive [sʌb'vəːsɪv] ADJ subversivo

subway ['sʌbweɪ] N (*Brɪt*) paso subterráneo or inferior; (*US*) metro

sub-zero [sʌb'zɪərəʊ] ADJ: **~ temperatures** temperaturas *fpl* bajo cero

succeed [sək'siːd] vɪ (*person*) tener éxito; (*plan*) salir bien ▶ vᴛ suceder a; **to ~ in doing** lograr hacer

succeeding [sək'siːdɪŋ] ADJ (*following*) sucesivo; **~ generations** generaciones *fpl* futuras

success [sək'sɛs] N éxito; (*gain*) triunfo

successful [sək'sɛsful] ADJ (*venture*) de éxito, exitoso (*esp Lᴀᴍ*); **to be ~ (in doing)** lograr (hacer)

successfully [sək'sɛsfulɪ] ADV con éxito

succession [sək'sɛʃən] N (*series*) sucesión *f*, serie *f*; (*descendants*) descendencia; **in ~** sucesivamente

successive [sək'sɛsɪv] ADJ sucesivo, consecutivo; **on three ~ days** tres días seguidos

successor [sək'sɛsə^r] N sucesor(a) *m/f*

succinct [sək'sɪŋkt] ADJ sucinto

succulent ['sʌkjulənt] ADJ suculento; **succulents** NPL (*Bot*) plantas *fpl* carnosas

succumb [sə'kʌm] vɪ sucumbir

such [sʌtʃ] ADJ tal, semejante; (*of that kind*): **~ a book** tal libro; **~ books** tales libros; (*so much*): **~ courage** tanto valor ▶ ADV tan; **~ a long trip** un viaje tan largo; **~ a lot of** tanto; **~ as** (*like*) tal como; **a noise ~ as to** un ruido tal que; **~ books as I have** cuantos libros tengo; **I said no ~ thing** no dije tal cosa; **it's ~ a long time since we saw each other** hace tanto tiempo que no nos vemos; **~ a long time ago** hace tantísimo tiempo; **as ~** adv como tal

such-and-such ['sʌtʃənsʌtʃ] ADJ tal o cual

suchlike ['sʌtʃlaɪk] PRON (*inf*): **and ~** y cosas por el estilo

suck [sʌk] vᴛ chupar; (*bottle*) sorber; (*breast*) mamar; (*pump, machine*) aspirar

sucker ['sʌkə^r] N (*Bot*) serpollo; (*Zool*) ventosa; (*inf*) bobo, primo

sucrose ['suːkrəuz] N sacarosa

suction ['sʌkʃən] N succión *f*

suction pump N bomba aspirante or de succión

S

Sudan [suˈdæn] N Sudán m
Sudanese [suːdəˈniːz] ADJ, N sudanés(-esa) m/f
sudden [ˈsʌdn] ADJ (rapid) repentino, súbito; (unexpected) imprevisto; **all of a ~** de repente
sudden-death [sʌdnˈdɛθ] N (also: **sudden-death play off**) muerte f súbita
suddenly [ˈsʌdnlɪ] ADV de repente
sudoku [suˈdəuku:] N sudoku m
suds [sʌdz] NPL espuma sg de jabón
sue [suː] VT demandar; **to ~ (for)** demandar (por); **to ~ for divorce** solicitar or pedir el divorcio; **to ~ for damages** demandar por daños y perjuicios
suede [sweɪd] N ante m, gamuza (LAM)
suet [ˈsuɪt] N sebo
Suez Canal [ˈsuːɪz-] N Canal m de Suez
Suff. ABBR (BRIT) = **Suffolk**
suffer [ˈsʌfəʳ] VT sufrir, padecer; (tolerate) aguantar, soportar; (undergo: loss, setback) experimentar ▶ VI sufrir, padecer; **to ~ from** padecer, sufrir; **to ~ from the effects of alcohol/a fall** sufrir los efectos del alcohol/resentirse de una caída
sufferance [ˈsʌfərns] N: **he was only there on ~** estuvo allí sólo porque se lo toleraron
sufferer [ˈsʌfərəʳ] N víctima f; (Med): **~ from** enfermo(-a) de
suffering [ˈsʌfərɪŋ] N (hardship, deprivation) sufrimiento; (pain) dolor m
suffice [səˈfaɪs] VI bastar, ser suficiente
sufficient [səˈfɪʃənt] ADJ suficiente, bastante
sufficiently [səˈfɪʃəntlɪ] ADV suficientemente, bastante
suffix [ˈsʌfɪks] N sufijo
suffocate [ˈsʌfəkeɪt] VI ahogarse, asfixiarse
suffocation [sʌfəˈkeɪʃən] N sofocación f, asfixia
suffrage [ˈsʌfrɪdʒ] N sufragio
suffuse [səˈfjuːz] VT: **to ~ (with)** (colour) bañar (de); **her face was suffused with joy** su cara estaba llena de alegría
sugar [ˈʃugəʳ] N azúcar m ▶ VT echar azúcar a, azucarar
sugar basin N (BRIT) = **sugar bowl**
sugar beet N remolacha
sugar bowl N azucarero
sugar cane N caña de azúcar
sugar-coated [ˈʃugəˈkəutɪd] ADJ azucarado
sugar lump N terrón m de azúcar
sugar refinery N refinería de azúcar
sugary [ˈʃugərɪ] ADJ azucarado
suggest [səˈdʒɛst] VT sugerir; (recommend) aconsejar; **what do you ~ I do?** ¿qué sugieres que haga?; **this suggests that ...** esto hace pensar que ...
suggestion [səˈdʒɛstʃən] N sugerencia; **there's no ~ of ...** no hay indicación or evidencia de ...

suggestive [səˈdʒɛstɪv] ADJ sugestivo; (pej: indecent) indecente
suicidal [suɪˈsaɪdl] ADJ suicida
suicide [ˈsuɪsaɪd] N suicidio; (person) suicida mf; **to commit ~** suicidarse
suicide attack N atentado suicida
suicide attempt, suicide bid N intento de suicidio
suicide bomber N terrorista mf suicida
suicide bombing N atentado m suicida
suit [suːt] N traje m; (Law) pleito; (Cards) palo ▶ VT convenir; (clothes) sentar bien a, ir bien a; (adapt): **to ~ sth to** adaptar or ajustar algo a; **to be suited to sth** (suitable for) ser apto para algo; **well suited** (couple) hechos el uno para el otro; **to bring a ~ against sb** entablar demanda contra algn; **to follow ~** (Cards) seguir el palo; (fig) seguir el ejemplo (de algn); **that suits me** me va bien
suitable [ˈsuːtəbl] ADJ conveniente; (apt) indicado
suitably [ˈsuːtəblɪ] ADV convenientemente; (appropriately) en forma debida
suitcase [ˈsuːtkeɪs] N maleta, valija (LAM)
suite [swiːt] N (of rooms) suite f; (Mus) suite f; (furniture): **bedroom/dining room ~** (juego de) dormitorio/comedor m; **a three-piece ~** un tresillo
suitor [ˈsuːtəʳ] N pretendiente m
sulfate [ˈsʌlfeɪt] N (US) = **sulphate**
sulfur [ˈsʌlfəʳ] N (US) = **sulphur**
sulk [sʌlk] VI estar de mal humor
sulky [ˈsʌlkɪ] ADJ malhumorado
sullen [ˈsʌlən] ADJ hosco, malhumorado
sulphate, (US) sulfate [ˈsʌlfeɪt] N sulfato; **copper ~** sulfato de cobre
sulphur, (US) sulfur [ˈsʌlfəʳ] N azufre m
sulphur dioxide N dióxido de azufre
sultan [ˈsʌltən] N sultán m
sultana [sʌlˈtɑːnə] N (fruit) pasa de Esmirna
sultry [ˈsʌltrɪ] ADJ (weather) bochornoso; (seductive) seductor(a)
sum [sʌm] N suma; (total) total m ▶ **sum up** VT resumir; (evaluate rapidly) evaluar ▶ VI hacer un resumen
Sumatra [suˈmɑːtrə] N Sumatra
summarize [ˈsʌməraɪz] VT resumir
summary [ˈsʌmərɪ] N resumen m ▶ ADJ (justice) sumario
summer [ˈsʌməʳ] N verano ▶ ADJ de verano; **in (the) ~** en (el) verano
summer holidays NPL vacaciones fpl de verano
summerhouse [ˈsʌməhaus] N (in garden) cenador m, glorieta
summertime [ˈsʌmətaɪm] N (season) verano
summer time N (by clock) hora de verano
summery [ˈsʌmərɪ] ADJ veraniego
summing-up [sʌmɪŋˈʌp] N (Law) resumen m

summit ['sʌmɪt] N cima, cumbre f; (also: **summit conference**) (conferencia) cumbre f
summit conference N (conferencia en la) cumbre f
summon ['sʌmən] VT (person) llamar; (meeting) convocar; **to ~ a witness** citar a un testigo
▶ **summon up** VT (courage) armarse de
summons ['sʌmənz] N llamamiento, llamada ▶ VT citar, emplazar; **to serve a ~ on sb** citar a algn ante el juicio
sumo ['su:məu] N (also: **sumo wrestling**) sumo
sump [sʌmp] N (BRIT Aut) cárter m
sumptuous ['sʌmptjuəs] ADJ suntuoso
sun [sʌn] N sol m; **they have everything under the ~** no les falta nada, tienen de todo
Sun. ABBR (= Sunday) dom.
sunbathe ['sʌnbeɪð] VI tomar el sol
sunbeam ['sʌnbi:m] N rayo de sol
sunbed ['sʌnbed] N cama solar
sunblock ['sʌnblɔk] N filtro solar
sunburn ['sʌnbə:n] N (painful) quemadura del sol; (tan) bronceado
sunburnt ['sʌnbə:nt], **sunburned** ['sʌnbə:nd] ADJ (tanned) bronceado; (painfully) quemado por el sol
sundae ['sʌndeɪ] N helado con frutas y nueces
Sunday ['sʌndɪ] N domingo; see also **Tuesday**
Sunday paper N (periódico) dominical m
Sunday school N catequesis f
sundial ['sʌndaɪəl] N reloj m de sol
sundown ['sʌndaun] N anochecer m, puesta de sol
sundries ['sʌndrɪz] NPL géneros mpl diversos
sundry ['sʌndrɪ] ADJ varios, diversos; **all and ~** todos sin excepción
sunflower ['sʌnflauə'] N girasol m
sung [sʌŋ] PP of **sing**
sunglasses ['sʌnglɑ:sɪz] NPL gafas fpl de sol
sunk [sʌŋk] PP of **sink**
sunken ['sʌŋkn] ADJ (bath) hundido
sunlamp ['sʌnlæmp] N lámpara solar ultravioleta
sunlight ['sʌnlaɪt] N luz f del sol
sunlit ['sʌnlɪt] ADJ iluminado por el sol
sun lounger N tumbona, perezosa (LAM)
sunny ['sʌnɪ] ADJ soleado; (day) de sol; (fig) alegre; **it is ~** hace sol
sunrise ['sʌnraɪz] N salida del sol
sun roof N (Aut) techo corredizo or solar; (on building) azotea, terraza
sunscreen ['sʌnskri:n] N filtro solar
sunset ['sʌnset] N puesta del sol
sunshade ['sʌnʃeɪd] N (over table) sombrilla
sunshine ['sʌnʃaɪn] N sol m
sunstroke ['sʌnstrəuk] N insolación f
suntan ['sʌntæn] N bronceado
suntan lotion N bronceador m

suntanned ['sʌntænd] ADJ bronceado
suntan oil N aceite m bronceador
super ['su:pə'] ADJ (inf) genial
superannuation [su:pərænju'eɪʃən] N jubilación f, pensión f
superb [su:'pə:b] ADJ magnífico, espléndido
Super Bowl N (US Sport) super copa de fútbol americano
supercilious [su:pə'sɪlɪəs] ADJ (disdainful) desdeñoso; (haughty) altanero
superconductor [su:pəkən'dʌktə'] N superconductor m
superficial [su:pə'fɪʃəl] ADJ superficial
superfluous [su'pə:fluəs] ADJ superfluo, de sobra
superglue ['su:pəglu:] N cola de contacto, supercola
superhighway ['su:pəhaɪweɪ] N (US) superautopista; **the information ~** la superautopista de la información
superhuman [su:pə'hju:mən] ADJ sobrehumano
superimpose ['su:pərɪm'pəuz] VT sobreponer
superintend [su:pərɪn'tend] VT supervisar
superintendent [su:pərɪn'tendənt] N director(a) m/f; (also: **police superintendent**) subjefe(-a) m/f
superior [su'pɪərɪə'] ADJ superior; (smug: person) altivo, desdeñoso; (: smile, air) de suficiencia; (: remark) desdeñoso ▶ N superior m; **Mother S~** (Rel) madre f superiora
superiority [supɪərɪ'ɔrɪtɪ] N superioridad f; desdén m
superlative [su'pə:lətɪv] ADJ, N superlativo
superman ['su:pəmæn] N (irreg) superhombre m
supermarket ['su:pəmɑ:kɪt] N supermercado
supermodel ['su:pəmɔdl] N top model f, supermodelo f
supernatural [su:pə'nætʃərəl] ADJ sobrenatural ▶ N: **the ~** lo sobrenatural
supernova [su:pə'nəuvə] N supernova
superpower ['su:pəpauə'] N (Pol) superpotencia
supersede [su:pə'si:d] VT suplantar
supersonic ['su:pə'sɔnɪk] ADJ supersónico
superstar ['su:pəstɑ:'] N superestrella ▶ ADJ de superestrella
superstition [su:pə'stɪʃən] N superstición f
superstitious [su:pə'stɪʃəs] ADJ supersticioso
superstore ['su:pəstɔ:'] N (BRIT) hipermercado
supertanker ['su:pətæŋkə'] N superpetrolero
supertax ['su:pətæks] N sobretasa, sobreimpuesto
supervise ['su:pəvaɪz] VT supervisar

S

supervision [suːpəˈvɪʒən] N supervisión f

supervisor [ˈsuːpəvaɪzəʳ] N supervisor(a) m/f

supervisory [ˈsuːpəvaɪzərɪ] ADJ de supervisión

supper [ˈsʌpəʳ] N cena; **to have ~** cenar

supplant [səˈplɑːnt] VT suplantar, reemplazar

supple [ˈsʌpl] ADJ flexible

supplement N [ˈsʌplɪmənt] suplemento ▶ VT [sʌplɪˈmɛnt] suplir

supplementary [sʌplɪˈmɛntərɪ] ADJ suplementario

supplementary benefit N (BRIT) subsidio adicional de la seguridad social

supplier [səˈplaɪəʳ] N suministrador(a) m/f; (Comm) distribuidor(a) m/f

supply [səˈplaɪ] VT (provide) suministrar; (information) facilitar; (fill: need, want) suplir, satisfacer; (equip): **to ~ (with)** proveer (de) ▶ N provisión f; (of gas, water etc) suministro ▶ ADJ (BRIT: teacher etc) suplente; **supplies** NPL (food) víveres mpl; (Mil) pertrechos mpl; **office supplies** materiales mpl para oficina; **to be in short ~** escasear, haber escasez de; **the electricity/water/gas ~** el suministro de electricidad/agua/gas; **~ and demand** la oferta y la demanda

support [səˈpɔːt] N (moral, financial etc) apoyo; (Tech) soporte m ▶ VT apoyar; (financially) mantener; (uphold) sostener; (Sport: team) seguir, ser hincha de; **they stopped work in ~ (of)** pararon de trabajar en apoyo (de); **to ~ o.s.** (financially) ganarse la vida

support buying [-ˈbaɪɪŋ] N compra proteccionista

supporter [səˈpɔːtəʳ] N (Pol etc) partidario(-a); (Sport) aficionado(-a); (Football) hincha mf

supporting [səˈpɔːtɪŋ] ADJ (wall) de apoyo; **~ role** papel m secundario; **~ actor/actress** actor mf secundario(-a)

supportive [səˈpɔːtɪv] ADJ de apoyo; **I have a ~ family/wife** mi familia/mujer me apoya

suppose [səˈpəuz] VT, VI suponer; (imagine) imaginarse; **to be supposed to do sth** deber hacer algo; **I don't ~ she'll come** no creo que venga; **he's supposed to be an expert** se le supone un experto

supposedly [səˈpəuzɪdlɪ] ADV según cabe suponer

supposing [səˈpəuzɪŋ] CONJ en caso de que; **always ~ (that) he comes** suponiendo que venga

supposition [sʌpəˈzɪʃən] N suposición f

suppository [səˈpɔzɪtrɪ] N supositorio

suppress [səˈprɛs] VT suprimir; (yawn) ahogar

suppression [səˈprɛʃən] N represión f

supremacy [suˈprɛməsɪ] N supremacía

supreme [suˈpriːm] ADJ supremo

Supreme Court N (US) Tribunal m Supremo, Corte f Suprema

supremo [suˈpriːməu] N autoridad f máxima

Supt. ABBR (Police) = **superintendent**

surcharge [ˈsəːtʃɑːdʒ] N sobretasa, recargo

sure [ʃuəʳ] ADJ seguro; (definite, convinced) cierto; (aim) certero ▶ ADV: **that ~ is pretty, that's ~ pretty** (US) ¡qué bonito es! **to be ~ of sth** estar seguro de algo; **to be ~ of o.s.** estar seguro de sí mismo; **to make ~ of sth/ that** asegurarse de algo/asegurar que; **I'm not ~ how/why/when** no estoy seguro de cómo/por qué/cuándo; **~!** (of course) ¡claro!, ¡por supuesto!; **~ enough** efectivamente

sure-fire [ˈʃuəfaɪəʳ] ADJ (inf) infalible

sure-footed [ʃuəˈfutɪd] ADJ de pie firme

surely [ˈʃuəlɪ] ADV (certainly) seguramente; **~ you don't mean that!** ¡no lo dices en serio!

surety [ˈʃuərətɪ] N fianza; (person) fiador(a) m/f; **to go** or **stand ~ for sb** ser fiador de algn, salir garante por algn

surf [səːf] N olas fpl ▶ VT hacer surf ▶ VT (Internet): **to ~ the Net** navegar por Internet

surface [ˈsəːfɪs] N superficie f ▶ VT (road) revestir ▶ VI salir a la superficie ▶ CPD (Mil, Naut) de (la) superficie; **on the ~ it seems that ...** (fig) a primera vista parece que ...

surface area N área de la superficie

surface mail N vía terrestre

surface-to-air [ˈsəːfɪstəˈɛəʳ] ADJ (Mil) tierra-aire

surface-to-surface [ˈsəːfɪstəˈsəːfɪs] ADJ (Mil) tierra-tierra

surfboard [ˈsəːfbɔːd] N tabla (de surf)

surfeit [ˈsəːfɪt] N: **a ~ of** un exceso de

surfer [ˈsəːfəʳ] N surfista mf; **web** or **net ~** internauta mf

surfing [ˈsəːfɪŋ] N surf m

surge [səːdʒ] N oleada, oleaje m; (Elec) sobretensión f transitoria ▶ VI (wave) romper; (people) avanzar a tropel; **to ~ forward** avanzar rápidamente

surgeon [ˈsəːdʒən] N cirujano(-a)

surgery [ˈsəːdʒərɪ] N cirugía; (BRIT: room) consultorio; (: Pol) horas en las que los electores pueden reunirse personalmente con su diputado; **to undergo ~** operarse; see also **constituency**

surgery hours NPL (BRIT) horas fpl de consulta

surgical [ˈsəːdʒɪkl] ADJ quirúrgico

surgical spirit N (BRIT) alcohol m

surly [ˈsəːlɪ] ADJ hosco, malhumorado

surmount [səːˈmaunt] VT superar, vencer

surname [ˈsəːneɪm] N apellido

surpass [səːˈpɑːs] VT superar, exceder

surplus [ˈsəːpləs] N excedente m; (Comm) superávit m ▶ ADJ (Comm) excedente, sobrante; **to have a ~ of sth** tener un excedente de algo; **it is ~ to our requirements** nos sobra; **~ stock** saldos mpl

surprise [sə'praɪz] N sorpresa ▶ VT
sorprender; **to take by ~** (person) coger
desprevenido or por sorpresa a, sorprender a;
(Mil: town, fort) atacar por sorpresa
surprised [sə'praɪzd] ADJ (look, smile) de
sorpresa; **to be ~** sorprenderse
surprising [sə'praɪzɪŋ] ADJ sorprendente
surprisingly [sə'praɪzɪŋlɪ] ADV (easy, helpful)
de modo sorprendente; **(somewhat) ~**,
he agreed para sorpresa de todos, aceptó
surrealism [sə'rɪəlɪzəm] N surrealismo
surrender [sə'rɛndər] N rendición f, entrega
▶ VI rendirse, entregarse ▶ VT renunciar
surrender value N valor m de rescate
surreptitious [sʌrəp'tɪʃəs] ADJ subrepticio
surrogate ['sʌrəgɪt] N (BRIT) sustituto(-a)
surrogate mother N madre f de alquiler
surround [sə'raund] VT rodear, circundar;
(Mil etc) cercar
surrounding [sə'raundɪŋ] ADJ circundante
surroundings [sə'raundɪŋz] NPL alrededores
mpl, cercanías fpl
surtax ['sə:tæks] N sobretasa, sobreimpuesto
surveillance [sə:'veɪləns] N vigilancia
survey N ['sə:veɪ] inspección f
reconocimiento, (inquiry) encuesta;
(comprehensive view: of situation etc) vista de
conjunto ▶ VT [sə:'veɪ] examinar,
inspeccionar; (Surveying: building)
inspeccionar; (: land) hacer un
reconocimiento de, reconocer; (look at)
mirar, contemplar; (make inquiries about)
hacer una encuesta de; **to carry out a ~ of**
inspeccionar, examinar
surveyor [sə'veɪər] N (BRIT: of building) perito
mf; (of land) agrimensor(a) m/f
survival [sə'vaɪvl] N supervivencia
survival course N curso de supervivencia
survival kit N equipo de emergencia
survive [sə'vaɪv] VI sobrevivir; (custom etc)
perdurar ▶ VT sobrevivir a
survivor [sə'vaɪvər] N superviviente mf
susceptibility [səsɛptə'bɪlɪtɪ] N (to illness)
propensión f
susceptible [sə'sɛptəbl] ADJ (easily influenced)
influenciable; (to disease, illness): **~ to**
propenso a
sushi ['suːʃɪ] N sushi m
suspect ADJ, N ['sʌspɛkt] sospechoso(-a) m/f
▶ VT [səs'pɛkt] sospechar
suspected [səs'pɛktɪd] ADJ presunto; **to
have a ~ fracture** tener una posible fractura
suspend [səs'pɛnd] VT suspender
suspended animation [səs'pɛndəd-] N:
in a state of ~ en (estado de) hibernación
suspended sentence N (Law) libertad f
condicional
suspender belt [səs'pɛndər-] N (BRIT) liguero,
portaligas m inv (LAM)

suspenders [səs'pɛndəz] NPL (BRIT) ligas fpl;
(US) tirantes mpl
suspense [səs'pɛns] N incertidumbre f,
duda; (in film etc) suspense m; **to keep sb in ~**
mantener a algn en suspense
suspension [səs'pɛnʃən] N (gen) suspensión f;
(of driving licence) privación f
suspension bridge N puente m colgante
suspension file N archivador m colgante
suspicion [səs'pɪʃən] N sospecha; (distrust)
recelo; (trace) traza; **to be under ~** estar bajo
sospecha; **arrested on ~ of murder**
detenido bajo sospecha de asesinato
suspicious [səs'pɪʃəs] ADJ (suspecting) receloso;
(causing suspicion) sospechoso; **to be ~ of** or
about sb/sth tener sospechas de algn/algo
suss out [sʌs-] VT (BRIT inf) calar
sustain [səs'teɪn] VT sostener, apoyar; (suffer)
sufrir, padecer
sustainable [səs'teɪnəbl] ADJ sostenible;
~ development desarrollo sostenible
sustained [səs'teɪnd] ADJ (effort) sostenido
sustenance ['sʌstɪnəns] N sustento
suture ['suːtʃər] N sutura
SUV ['ɛs'juː'viː] N ABBR (= sports utility vehicle)
SUV m, todoterreno m inv
SVQ N ABBR (= Scottish Vocational Qualification)
titulación de formación profesional en Escocia
SW ABBR = **short wave**
swab [swɔb] N (Med) algodón m, frotis m inv
▶ VT (Naut: also: **swab down**) limpiar, fregar
swagger ['swægər] VI pavonearse
swallow ['swɔləu] N (bird) golondrina; (of
food) bocado; (of drink) trago ▶ VT tragar
▶ **swallow up** VT (savings etc) consumir
swam [swæm] PT of **swim**
swamp [swɔmp] N pantano, ciénaga ▶ VT
abrumar, agobiar
swampy ['swɔmpɪ] ADJ pantanoso
swan [swɔn] N cisne m
swank [swæŋk] (inf) N (vanity, boastfulness)
fanfarronada ▶ VI fanfarronear, presumir
swan song N (fig) canto del cisne
swap [swɔp] N canje m, trueque m ▶ VT:
to ~ (for) canjear (por), cambiar (por)
SWAPO ['swɑːpəu] N ABBR (= South-West Africa
People's Organization) SWAPO f
swarm [swɔːm] N (of bees) enjambre m; (fig)
multitud f ▶ VI (bees) formar un enjambre;
(fig) hormiguear, pulular
swarthy ['swɔːðɪ] ADJ moreno
swashbuckling ['swɔʃbʌklɪŋ] ADJ (person)
aventurero; (film) de capa y espada
swastika ['swɔstɪkə] N esvástica, cruz f
gamada
SWAT [swɔt] N ABBR (US: = Special Weapons and
Tactics) unidad especial de la policía
swat [swɔt] VT aplastar ▶ N (also: **fly swat**)
matamoscas m inv

swathe [sweɪð] VT: **to ~ in** (blankets) envolver en; (bandages) vendar en

sway [sweɪ] VI mecerse, balancearse ▶ VT (influence) mover, influir en ▶ N (rule, power): **~ (over)** dominio (sobre); **to hold ~ over sb** dominar a algn, mantener el dominio sobre algn

Swaziland ['swɑːzɪlænd] N Swazilandia

swear [sweəʳ] (pt **swore** [swɔːʳ], pp **sworn** [swɔːn]) VI jurar; (with swearwords) decir tacos ▶ VT: **to ~ an oath** prestar juramento, jurar; **to ~ to sth** declarar algo bajo juramento ▶ **swear in** VT tomar juramento (a); **to be sworn in** prestar juramento

swearword ['sweəwəːd] N taco, palabrota

sweat [swɛt] N sudor m ▶ VI sudar

sweatband ['swɛtbænd] N (Sport: on head) banda; (: on wrist) muñequera

sweater ['swɛtəʳ] N suéter m

sweatshirt ['swɛtʃəːt] N sudadera

sweatshop ['swɛtʃɔp] N fábrica donde se explota al obrero

sweaty ['swɛtɪ] ADJ sudoroso

Swede [swiːd] N sueco(-a)

swede [swiːd] N (BRIT) nabo

Sweden ['swiːdn] N Suecia

Swedish ['swiːdɪʃ] ADJ, N (Ling) sueco

sweep [swiːp] (pt, pp **swept**) N (act) barrida; (of arm) manotazo m; (curve) curva, alcance m; (also: **chimney sweep**) deshollinador(a) m/f ▶ VT barrer; (with arm) empujar; (current) arrastrar; (disease, fashion) recorrer ▶ VI barrer ▶ **sweep away** VT barrer; (rub out) borrar ▶ **sweep past** VI pasar rápidamente; (brush by) rozar ▶ **sweep up** VI barrer

sweeper ['swiːpəʳ] N (person) barrendero(-a); (machine) barredora; (Football) líbero, libre m

sweeping ['swiːpɪŋ] ADJ (gesture) dramático; (generalized) generalizado; (changes, reforms) radical

sweepstake ['swiːpsteɪk] N lotería

sweet [swiːt] N (BRIT: candy) dulce m, caramelo; (: pudding) postre m ▶ ADJ dulce; (sugary) azucarado; (charming: person) encantador(a); (: smile, character) dulce, amable, agradable ▶ ADV: **to smell/taste ~** oler/saber dulce

sweet and sour ADJ agridulce

sweetcorn ['swiːtkɔːn] N maíz m (dulce)

sweeten ['swiːtn] VT (person) endulzar; (add sugar to) poner azúcar a

sweetener ['swiːtnəʳ] N (Culin) edulcorante m

sweetheart ['swiːthɑːt] N amor m, novio(-a); (in speech) amor, cariño

sweetness ['swiːtnɪs] N (gen) dulzura

sweet pea N guisante m de olor

sweet potato N batata, camote m (LAM)

sweetshop ['swiːtʃɔp] N (BRIT) confitería, bombonería

swell [swɛl] (pt **swelled**, pp **swollen** or **swelled**) N (of sea) marejada, oleaje m ▶ ADJ (US inf: excellent) estupendo, fenomenal ▶ VT hinchar, inflar ▶ VI (also: **swell up**) hincharse; (numbers) aumentar; (sound, feeling) ir aumentando

swelling ['swɛlɪŋ] N (Med) hinchazón f

sweltering ['swɛltərɪŋ] ADJ sofocante, de mucho calor

swept [swɛpt] PT, PP of **sweep**

swerve [swəːv] N regate m; (in car) desvío brusco ▶ VI desviarse bruscamente

swift [swɪft] N (bird) vencejo ▶ ADJ rápido, veloz

swiftly ['swɪftlɪ] ADV rápidamente

swiftness ['swɪftnɪs] N rapidez f, velocidad f

swig [swɪɡ] N (inf: drink) trago

swill [swɪl] N bazofia ▶ VT (also: **swill out**, **swill down**) lavar, limpiar con agua

swim [swɪm] (pt **swam**, pp **swum**) N: **to go for a ~** ir a nadar or a bañarse ▶ VI nadar; (head, room) dar vueltas ▶ VT pasar a nado; **to go swimming** ir a nadar; **to ~ a length** nadar or hacer un largo

swimmer ['swɪməʳ] N nadador(a) m/f

swimming ['swɪmɪŋ] N natación f

swimming cap N gorro de baño

swimming costume N bañador m, traje m de baño

swimmingly ['swɪmɪŋlɪ] ADV: **to go ~** (wonderfully) ir como una seda or sobre ruedas

swimming pool N piscina, alberca (LAM)

swimming trunks NPL bañador msg

swimsuit ['swɪmsuːt] N = **swimming costume**

swindle ['swɪndl] N estafa ▶ VT estafar

swine [swaɪn] N pl inv cerdo, puerco; (inf!) canalla m (!)

swine flu [swaɪn-] N gripe f porcina

swing [swɪŋ] (pt, pp **swung**) N (in playground) columpio; (movement) balanceo, vaivén m; (change of direction) viraje m; (rhythm) ritmo; (Pol: in votes etc): **there has been a ~ towards/ away from Labour** ha habido un viraje en favor/en contra del Partido Laborista ▶ VT balancear; (on a swing) columpiar; (also: **swing round**) voltear, girar ▶ VI balancearse, columpiarse; (also: **swing round**) dar media vuelta; **a ~ to the left** un movimiento hacia la izquierda; **to be in full ~** estar en plena marcha; **to get into the ~ of things** meterse en situación; **the road swings south** la carretera gira hacia al sur

swing bridge N puente m giratorio

swing door, (US) swinging door ['swɪŋɪŋ-] N puerta giratoria

swingeing ['swɪndʒɪŋ] ADJ (BRIT) abrumador(a)

swipe [swaɪp] N golpe m fuerte ▸ VT (*hit*) golpear fuerte; (*inf: steal*) guindar; (*credit card etc*) pasar

swipe card [swaɪp-] N tarjeta magnética deslizante, tarjeta swipe

swirl [swə:l] VI arremolinarse

swish [swɪʃ] N (*sound: of whip*) chasquido; (*: of skirts*) frufrú m; (*: of grass*) crujido ▸ ADJ (*inf: smart*) elegante ▸ VI chasquear

Swiss [swɪs] ADJ, N pl inv suizo(-a) m/f

switch [swɪtʃ] N (*for light, radio etc*) interruptor m; (*change*) cambio ▸ VT (*change*) cambiar de; (*invert: also:* **switch round**, **switch over**) intercambiar

▸ **switch off** VT apagar; (*engine*) parar

▸ **switch on** VT (*Aut: ignition*) encender, prender (LAM); (*engine, machine*) arrancar; (*water supply*) conectar

switchboard ['swɪtʃbɔːd] N (*Tel*) centralita (de teléfonos), conmutador m (LAM)

Switzerland ['swɪtsələnd] N Suiza

swivel ['swɪvl] VI (*also:* **swivel round**) girar

swollen ['swəʊlən] PP of **swell**

swoon [swuːn] VI desmayarse

swoop [swuːp] N (*by police etc*) redada; (*of bird etc*) descenso en picado, calada ▸ VI (*also:* **swoop down**) caer en picado

swop [swɔp] N, VB = **swap**

sword [sɔːd] N espada

swordfish ['sɔːdfɪʃ] N pez m espada

swore [swɔːʳ] PT of **swear**

sworn [swɔːn] PP of **swear** ▸ ADJ (*statement*) bajo juramento; (*enemy*) implacable

swot [swɔt] (BRIT) VT, VI empollar ▸ N empollón(-ona) m/f

swum [swʌm] PP of **swim**

swung [swʌŋ] PT, PP of **swing**

sycamore ['sɪkəmɔːʳ] N sicomoro

sycophant ['sɪkəfænt] N adulador(a) m/f, pelotillero(-a) m/f

Sydney ['sɪdnɪ] N Sídney m

syllable ['sɪləbl] N sílaba

syllabus ['sɪləbəs] N programa m de estudios; **on the ~** en el programa de estudios

symbol ['sɪmbl] N símbolo

symbolic [sɪm'bɔlɪk], **symbolical** [sɪm'bɔlɪkl] ADJ simbólico; **to be ~ of sth** simbolizar algo

symbolism ['sɪmbəlɪzəm] N simbolismo

symbolize ['sɪmbəlaɪz] VT simbolizar

symmetrical [sɪ'metrɪkl] ADJ simétrico

symmetry ['sɪmɪtrɪ] N simetría

sympathetic [sɪmpə'θetɪk] ADJ compasivo; (*understanding*) comprensivo; **to be ~ to a**

cause (*well-disposed*) apoyar una causa; **to be ~ towards** (*person*) ser comprensivo con

sympathize ['sɪmpəθaɪz] VI: **to ~ with** (*person*) compadecerse de; (*feelings*) comprender; (*cause*) apoyar

sympathizer ['sɪmpəθaɪzəʳ] N (*Pol*) simpatizante mf

sympathy ['sɪmpəθɪ] N (*pity*) compasión f; (*understanding*) comprensión f; **a letter of ~** un pésame; **with our deepest ~** nuestro más sentido pésame

symphony ['sɪmfənɪ] N sinfonía

symposium [sɪm'pəuzɪəm] N simposio

symptom ['sɪmptəm] N síntoma m, indicio

symptomatic [sɪmptə'mætɪk] ADJ: **~ (of)** sintomático (de)

synagogue ['sɪnəgɔg] N sinagoga

sync [sɪŋk] N (*inf*): **to be in/out of ~ (with)** ir/no ir al mismo ritmo (que); (*fig: people*) conectar/no conectar con

synchromesh ['sɪŋkrəumeʃ] N cambio sincronizado de velocidades

synchronize ['sɪŋkrənaɪz] VT sincronizar ▸ VI: **to ~ with** sincronizarse con

synchronized swimming ['sɪŋkrənaɪzd-] N natación f sincronizada

syncopated ['sɪŋkəpeɪtɪd] ADJ sincopado

syndicate ['sɪndɪkɪt] N (*gen*) sindicato; (*Press*) agencia (de noticias)

syndrome ['sɪndrəum] N síndrome m

synonym ['sɪnənɪm] N sinónimo

synonymous [sɪ'nɔnɪməs] ADJ: **~ (with)** sinónimo (de)

synopsis [sɪ'nɔpsɪs] (pl **synopses** [-siːz]) N sinopsis f inv

syntax ['sɪntæks] N sintaxis f

syntax error N (*Comput*) error m sintáctico

synthesis ['sɪnθəsɪs] (pl **syntheses** [-siːz]) N síntesis f inv

synthesizer ['sɪnθəsaɪzəʳ] N sintetizador m

synthetic [sɪn'θetɪk] ADJ sintético ▸ N sintético

syphilis ['sɪfɪlɪs] N sífilis f

syphon ['saɪfən] N, VB = **siphon**

Syria ['sɪrɪə] N Siria

Syrian ['sɪrɪən] ADJ, N sirio(-a) m/f

syringe [sɪ'rɪndʒ] N jeringa

syrup ['sɪrəp] N jarabe m, almíbar m

system ['sɪstəm] N sistema m; (*Anat*) organismo; **it was quite a shock to his ~** fue un golpe para él

systematic [sɪstə'mætɪk] ADJ sistemático; metódico

system disk N (*Comput*) disco del sistema

systems analyst N analista mf de sistemas

S

Tt

T, t [tiː] N (letter) T, t f; **T for Tommy** T de Tarragona

TA N ABBR (BRIT) = **Territorial Army**

ta [tɑː] EXCL (BRIT inf) ¡gracias!

tab [tæb] N ABBR = **tabulator** ▶ N lengüeta; (label) etiqueta; **to keep tabs on** (fig) vigilar

tabby ['tæbɪ] N (also: **tabby cat**) gato atigrado

tabernacle ['tæbənækl] N tabernáculo

table ['teɪbl] N mesa; (chart: of statistics etc) cuadro, tabla ▶ VT (BRIT: motion etc) presentar; **to lay** or **set the ~** poner la mesa; **to clear the ~** quitar or levantar la mesa; **league ~** (Football, Rugby) clasificación f del campeonato; **~ of contents** índice m de materias

tablecloth ['teɪblklɔθ] N mantel m

table d'hôte [tɑːbl'dəʊt] N menú m

table lamp N lámpara de mesa

tablemat ['teɪblmæt] N (for plate) posaplatos m inv; (for hot dish) salvamanteles m inv

tablespoon ['teɪblspuːn] N cuchara grande; (also: **tablespoonful:** as measurement) cucharada grande

tablet ['tæblɪt] N (Med) pastilla, comprimido; (for writing) bloc m; (of stone) lápida; **~ of soap** pastilla de jabón

table talk N conversación f de sobremesa

table tennis N ping-pong m, tenis m de mesa

table wine N vino de mesa

tabloid ['tæblɔɪd] N (newspaper) periódico popular sensacionalista

tabloid press N ver nota

> El término genérico tabloid press o tabloids se usa para referirse a los periódicos populares británicos, por su tamaño reducido. A diferencia de la llamada "quality press", estos periódicos se caracterizan por su lenguaje sencillo, presentación llamativa y contenido a menudo sensacionalista, con gran énfasis en noticias sobre escándalos financieros y sexuales de los famosos, por lo que también reciben el nombre peyorativo de "gutter press".

taboo [tə'buː] ADJ, N tabú m

tabulate ['tæbjuleɪt] VT disponer en tablas

tabulator ['tæbjuleɪtəʳ] N tabulador m

tachograph ['tækəɡrɑːf] N tacógrafo

tachometer [tæ'kɔmɪtəʳ] N taquímetro

tacit ['tæsɪt] ADJ tácito

tacitly ['tæsɪtlɪ] ADV tácitamente

taciturn ['tæsɪtəːn] ADJ taciturno

tack [tæk] N (nail) tachuela; (stitch) hilván m; (Naut) bordada ▶ VT (nail) clavar con tachuelas; (stitch) hilvanar ▶ VI virar; **to ~ sth on to (the end of) sth** (of letter, book) añadir algo a (l final de) algo

tackle ['tækl] N (gear) equipo; (fishing tackle, for lifting) aparejo; (Football) entrada, tackle m; (Rugby) placaje m ▶ VT (difficulty) enfrentarse a, abordar; (challenge: person) hacer frente a; (grapple with) agarrar; (Football) entrar a; (Rugby) placar

tacky ['tækɪ] ADJ pegajoso; (inf) hortera inv, de mal gusto

tact [tækt] N tacto, discreción f

tactful ['tæktful] ADJ discreto, diplomático; **to be ~** tener tacto, actuar discretamente

tactfully ['tæktfulɪ] ADV diplomáticamente, con tacto

tactical ['tæktɪkl] ADJ táctico

tactical voting N voto útil

tactician [tæk'tɪʃən] N táctico(-a)

tactics ['tæktɪks] NPL táctica sg

tactless ['tæktlɪs] ADJ indiscreto

tactlessly ['tæktlɪslɪ] ADV indiscretamente, sin tacto

tadpole ['tædpəʊl] N renacuajo

taffy ['tæfɪ] N (US) melcocha

tag [tæɡ] N (label) etiqueta; **price/name ~** etiqueta del precio/con el nombre ▶ **tag along** VI: **to ~ along with sb** engancharse a algn

tag question N pregunta coletilla

Tahiti [tɑː'hiːtɪ] N Tahití m

tail [teɪl] N cola; (Zool) rabo; (of shirt, coat) faldón m ▶ VT (follow) vigilar a; **tails** NPL (formal suit) levita; **heads or tails** cara o cruz;

to turn ~ volver la espalda
▶ **tail away, tail off** vi (*in size, quality etc*) ir disminuyendo
tailback ['teɪlbæk] N (*Brit Aut*) cola
tail coat N frac m
tail end N cola, parte f final
tailgate ['teɪlɡeɪt] N (*Aut*) puerta trasera
tail light N (*Aut*) luz f trasera
tailor ['teɪlə^r] N sastre m ▶ vt: **to ~ sth (to)** confeccionar algo a medida (para); **~'s (shop)** sastrería
tailoring ['teɪlərɪŋ] N (*cut*) corte m; (*craft*) sastrería
tailor-made ['teɪlə'meɪd] ADJ (*also fig*) hecho a (la) medida
tailwind ['teɪlwɪnd] N viento de cola
taint [teɪnt] vt (*meat, food*) contaminar; (*fig: reputation*) manchar, tachar (*Lam*)
tainted ['teɪntɪd] ADJ (*water, air*) contaminado; (*fig*) manchado
Taiwan [taɪ'wɑːn] N Taiwán m
Taiwanese [taɪwə'niːz] ADJ, N taiwanés(-esa) m/f
Tajikistan [tɑːdʒɪkɪ'stɑːn] N Tayikistán m
take [teɪk] (*pt* **took**, *pp* **taken**) vt tomar; (*grab*) coger (*Sp*), agarrar (*Lam*); (*gain: prize*) ganar; (*require: effort, courage*) exigir; (*support weight of*) aguantar; (*hold: passengers etc*) tener cabida para; (*accompany, bring, carry*) llevar; (*exam*) presentarse a; (*conduct: meeting*) presidir ▶ vi (*fire*) prender; (*dye*) coger (*Sp*), agarrar, tomar ▶ N (*Cine*) toma; **to ~ sth from** (*drawer etc*) sacar algo de; (*person*) quitar algo a, coger algo a (*Sp*); **to ~ sb's hand** tomar de la mano a algn; **to ~ notes** tomar apuntes; **to be taken ill** ponerse enfermo; **~ the first on the left** toma la primera a la izquierda; **I only took Russian for one year** sólo estudié ruso un año; **I took him for a doctor** le tenía por médico; **it won't ~ long** durará poco; **it will ~ at least five litres** tiene cabida por lo menos para cinco litros; **to be taken with sb/sth** (*attracted*) tomarle cariño a algn/tomarle gusto a algo; **I ~ it that ...** supongo que ...
▶ **take after** vt fus parecerse a
▶ **take apart** vt desmontar
▶ **take away** vt (*remove*) quitar; (*carry off*) llevar ▶ vi: **to ~ away from** quitar mérito a
▶ **take back** vt (*return*) devolver; (*one's words*) retractar
▶ **take down** vt (*building*) derribar; (*dismantle: scaffolding*) desmantelar; (*message etc*) apuntar, tomar nota de
▶ **take in** vt (*deceive*) engañar; (*understand*) entender; (*include*) abarcar; (*lodger*) acoger, recibir; (*orphan, stray dog*) recoger; (*Sewing*) achicar
▶ **take off** vi (*Aviat*) despegar, decolar (*Lam*)

▶ vt (*remove*) quitar; (*imitate*) imitar, remedar
▶ **take on** vt (*work*) emprender; (*employee*) contratar; (*opponent*) desafiar
▶ **take out** vt sacar; (*remove*) quitar; **don't ~ it out on me!** ¡no te desquites conmigo!
▶ **take over** vt (*business*) tomar posesión de ▶ vi: **to ~ over from sb** reemplazar a algn
▶ **take to** vt fus (*person*) coger cariño a (*Sp*), encariñarse con (*Lam*); (*activity*) aficionarse a; **to ~ to doing sth** aficionarse a (hacer) algo
▶ **take up** vt (*a dress*) acortar; (*occupy: time, space*) ocupar; (*engage in: hobby etc*) dedicarse a; (*absorb: liquids*) absorber; (*accept: offer, challenge*) aceptar ▶ vi: **to ~ up with sb** hacerse amigo de algn; **to ~ sb up on** aceptar algo de algn
▶ **take upon** vt: **to ~ it upon o.s. to do sth** encargarse de hacer algo
takeaway ['teɪkəweɪ] ADJ (*Brit: food*) para llevar ▶ N tienda *or* restaurante m de comida para llevar
take-home pay ['teɪkhəum-] N salario neto
taken ['teɪkən] PP *of* **take**
takeoff ['teɪkɔf] N (*Aviat*) despegue m, decolaje m (*Lam*)
takeover ['teɪkəuvə^r] N (*Comm*) absorción f
takeover bid N oferta pública de adquisición
takings ['teɪkɪŋz] NPL (*Comm*) ingresos mpl
talc [tælk] N (*also:* **talcum powder**) talco
tale [teɪl] N (*story*) cuento; (*account*) relación f; **to tell tales** (*fig*) contar chismes
talent ['tælnt] N talento
talented ['tæləntɪd] ADJ talentoso, de talento
talisman ['tælɪzmən] N talismán m
talk [tɔːk] N charla; (*gossip*) habladurías fpl, chismes mpl; (*conversation*) conversación f ▶ vi (*speak*) hablar; (*chatter*) charlar; **talks** NPL (*Pol etc*) conversaciones fpl; **to give a ~** dar una charla *or* conferencia; **to ~ about** hablar de; **to ~ sb into doing sth** convencer a algn para que haga algo; **to ~ sb out of doing sth** disuadir a algn de que haga algo; **to ~ shop** hablar del trabajo; **talking of films, have you seen ...?** hablando de películas, ¿has visto ...?
▶ **talk over** vt discutir
talkative ['tɔːkətɪv] ADJ hablador(a)
talker ['tɔːkə^r] N hablador(a) m/f
talking point ['tɔːkɪŋ-] N tema m de conversación
talking-to ['tɔːkɪŋtuː] N: **to give sb a good ~** echar una buena bronca a algn
talk show N programa m magazine
tall [tɔːl] ADJ alto; (*tree*) grande; **to be 6 feet ~** ≈ medir 1 metro 80, tener 1 metro 80 de alto; **how ~ are you?** ¿cuánto mides?
tallboy ['tɔːlbɔɪ] N (*Brit*) cómoda alta
tallness ['tɔːlnɪs] N altura
tall story N cuento chino

tally ['tælɪ] N cuenta ▶ VI: **to ~ (with)** concordar (con), cuadrar (con); **to keep a ~ of sth** llevar la cuenta de algo

talon ['tælən] N garra

tambourine [tæmbə'riːn] N pandereta

tame [teɪm] ADJ (mild) manso; (tamed) domesticado; (fig: story, style, person) soso, anodino

tameness ['teɪmnɪs] N mansedumbre f

Tamil ['tæmɪl] ADJ tamil ▶ N tamil mf; (Ling) tamil m

tamper ['tæmpər] VI: **to ~ with** (lock etc) intentar forzar; (papers) falsificar

tampon ['tæmpən] N tampón m

tan [tæn] N (also: **suntan**) bronceado ▶ VT broncear ▶ VI ponerse moreno ▶ ADJ (colour) marrón; **to get a ~** broncearse, ponerse moreno

tandem ['tændəm] N tándem m

tandoori [tæn'duərɪ] ADJ, N tandoori m (asado a la manera hindú, en horno de barro)

tang [tæŋ] N sabor m fuerte

tangent ['tændʒənt] N (Math) tangente f; **to go off at a ~** (fig) salirse por la tangente

tangerine [tændʒə'riːn] N mandarina

tangible ['tændʒəbl] ADJ tangible; **~ assets** bienes mpl tangibles

Tangier [tæn'dʒɪər] N Tánger m

tangle ['tæŋgl] N enredo; **to get in(to) a ~** enredarse

tango ['tæŋgəu] N tango

tank [tæŋk] N (also: **water tank**) depósito, tanque m; (for fish) acuario; (Mil) tanque m

tankard ['tæŋkəd] N bock m

tanker ['tæŋkər] N (ship) petrolero; (truck) camión m cisterna

tankful ['tæŋkful] N: **to get a ~ of petrol** llenar el depósito de gasolina

tankini [tæŋ'kiːnɪ] N tankini m

tanned [tænd] ADJ (skin) moreno, bronceado

tannin ['tænɪn] N tanino

tanning ['tænɪŋ] N (of leather) curtido

tannoy® ['tænɔɪ] N: **over the ~** por el altavoz

tantalizing ['tæntəlaɪzɪŋ] ADJ tentador(a)

tantamount ['tæntəmaunt] ADJ: **~ to** equivalente a

tantrum ['tæntrəm] N rabieta; **to throw a ~** coger una rabieta

Tanzania [tænzə'nɪə] N Tanzania

Tanzanian [tænzə'nɪən] ADJ, N tanzano(-a) m/f

tap [tæp] N (Brit: on sink etc) grifo, canilla (LAm); (gentle blow) golpecito; (gas tap) llave f ▶ VT (table etc) tamborilear; (shoulder etc) dar palmaditas en; (resources) utilizar, explotar; (telephone conversation) intervenir, pinchar; **on ~** (fig: resources) a mano; **beer on ~** cerveza de barril

tap dancing ['tæpdɑːnsɪŋ] N claqué m

tape [teɪp] N cinta; (also: **magnetic tape**) cinta magnética; (sticky tape) cinta adhesiva ▶ VT (record) grabar (en cinta); **on ~** (song etc) grabado (en cinta)

tape deck N pletina

tape measure N cinta métrica, metro

taper ['teɪpər] N cirio ▶ VI afilarse

tape-record ['teɪprɪkɔːd] VT grabar (en cinta)

tape recorder N grabadora

tape recording N grabación f

tapered ['teɪpəd], **tapering** ['teɪpərɪŋ] ADJ terminado en punta

tapestry ['tæpɪstrɪ] N (object) tapiz m; (art) tapicería

tape-worm ['teɪpwəːm] N solitaria, tenia

tapioca [tæpɪ'əukə] N tapioca

tappet ['tæpɪt] N excéntrica

tar [tɑːr] N alquitrán m, brea; **low/middle ~ cigarettes** cigarrillos con contenido bajo/medio de alquitrán

tarantula [tə'ræntjulə] N tarántula

tardy ['tɑːdɪ] ADJ (late) tardío; (slow) lento

tare [tɛər] N (Comm) tara

target ['tɑːgɪt] N (gen) blanco; **to be on ~** (project) seguir el curso previsto

target audience N público al que va destinado un programa etc

target market N (Comm) mercado al que va destinado un producto etc

target practice N tiro al blanco

tariff ['tærɪf] N (on goods) arancel m; (Brit: in hotels etc) tarifa

tariff barrier N (Comm) barrera arancelaria

tarmac ['tɑːmæk] N (Brit: on road) asfalto; (Aviat) pista (de aterrizaje)

tarn [tɑːn] N lago pequeño de montaña

tarnish ['tɑːnɪʃ] VT deslustrar

tarot ['tærəu] N tarot m

tarpaulin [tɑː'pɔːlɪn] N lona (impermeabilizada)

tarragon ['tærəgən] N estragón m

tarry ['tærɪ] VI entretenerse, quedarse atrás

tart [tɑːt] N (Culin) tarta; (Brit inf, pej: woman) fulana ▶ ADJ (flavour) agrio, ácido ▶ **tart up** VT (room, building) dar tono a

tartan ['tɑːtn] N tartán m, tela escocesa ▶ ADJ de tartán

tartar ['tɑːtər] N (on teeth) sarro

tartar sauce, tartare sauce N salsa tártara

tartly ['tɑːtlɪ] ADV (answer) ásperamente

task [tɑːsk] N tarea; **to take to ~** reprender

task force N (Mil, Police) grupo de operaciones

taskmaster ['tɑːskmɑːstər] N: **he's a hard ~** es muy exigente

tassel ['tæsl] N borla

taste [teɪst] N sabor m, gusto; (also: **aftertaste**) dejo; (sip) sorbo; (fig: glimpse, idea) muestra, idea ▶ VT probar ▶ VI: **to ~ of** or **like** (fish etc) saber a; **you can ~ the garlic (in it)**

se nota el sabor a ajo; **can I have a ~ of this wine?** ¿puedo probar este vino?; **to have a ~ for sth** ser aficionado a algo; **in good/bad ~** de buen/mal gusto; **to be in bad** or **poor ~** ser de mal gusto

taste bud N papila gustativa or del gusto
tasteful ['teɪstful] ADJ de buen gusto
tastefully ['teɪstfulɪ] ADV elegantemente, con buen gusto
tasteless ['teɪstlɪs] ADJ (food) soso; (remark) de mal gusto
tastelessly ['teɪstlɪslɪ] ADV con mal gusto
tastily ['teɪstɪlɪ] ADV sabrosamente
tastiness ['teɪstɪnɪs] N (buen) sabor m, lo sabroso
tasty ['teɪstɪ] ADJ sabroso, rico
ta-ta ['tæ'taː] EXCL (BRIT inf) hasta luego, adiós
tatters ['tætəz] NPL: **in ~** (also: **tattered**) hecho jirones
tattoo [tə'tuː] N tatuaje m; (spectacle) espectáculo militar ▶ VT tatuar
tatty ['tætɪ] ADJ (BRIT inf) cochambroso
taught [tɔːt] PT, PP of **teach**
taunt [tɔːnt] N pulla ▶ VT lanzar pullas a
Taurus ['tɔːrəs] N Tauro
taut [tɔːt] ADJ tirante, tenso
tavern ['tævən] N (old) posada, fonda
tawdry ['tɔːdrɪ] ADJ de mal gusto
tawny ['tɔːnɪ] ADJ leonado
tax [tæks] N impuesto ▶ VT gravar (con un impuesto); (fig: test) poner a prueba; (: patience) agotar; **before/after ~** impuestos excluidos/incluidos; **free of ~** libre de impuestos
taxable ['tæksəbl] ADJ (income) imponible, sujeto a impuestos
tax allowance N desgravación f fiscal
taxation [tæk'seɪʃən] N impuestos mpl; **system of ~** sistema m tributario
tax avoidance N evasión f de impuestos
tax collector N recaudador(a) m/f
tax disc N (BRIT Aut) pegatina del impuesto de circulación
tax evasion N evasión f fiscal
tax exemption N exención f de impuestos
tax-free ['tæksfriː] ADJ libre de impuestos
tax haven N paraíso fiscal
taxi ['tæksɪ] N taxi m ▶ VI (Aviat) rodar por la pista
taxidermist ['tæksɪdəːmɪst] N taxidermista mf
taxi driver N taxista mf
tax inspector N inspector(a) m/f de Hacienda
taxi rank, (US) **taxi stand** N parada de taxis
tax payer N contribuyente mf
tax rebate N devolución f de impuestos, reembolso fiscal
tax relief N desgravación f fiscal
tax return N declaración f de la renta

tax shelter N protección f fiscal
tax year N año fiscal
TB N ABBR = **tuberculosis**
tbc ABBR (= to be confirmed) por confirmar
TD N ABBR (US) = **Treasury Department**; (Football) = **touchdown**
tea [tiː] N té m; (BRIT: snack) ≈ merienda; **high ~** ≈ merienda-cena
tea bag N bolsita de té
tea break N (BRIT) descanso para el té
teacake ['tiːkeɪk] N bollito, queque m (LAM)
teach [tiːtʃ] (pt, pp **taught** [tɔːt]) VT: **to ~ sb sth**, **~ sth to sb** enseñar algo a algn ▶ VI enseñar; (be a teacher) ser profesor(a); **it taught him a lesson** (eso) le sirvió de escarmiento
teacher ['tiːtʃər] N (in secondary school) profesor(a) m/f; (in primary school) maestro(-a); **Spanish ~** profesor(a) m/f de español
teacher training college N (for primary schools) escuela normal; (for secondary schools) centro de formación del profesorado
teach-in ['tiːtʃɪn] N seminario
teaching ['tiːtʃɪŋ] N enseñanza
teaching aids NPL materiales mpl pedagógicos
teaching hospital N hospital universitario
tea cloth N (BRIT) paño de cocina, trapo de cocina (LAM)
tea cosy N cubretetera m
teacup ['tiːkʌp] N taza de té
teak [tiːk] N (madera de) teca
tea leaves NPL hojas fpl de té
team [tiːm] N equipo; (of animals) pareja ▶ **team up** VI asociarse
team spirit N espíritu m de equipo
teamwork ['tiːmwəːk] N trabajo en equipo
tea party N té m
teapot ['tiːpɔt] N tetera
tear¹ [tɪər] N lágrima; **in tears** llorando; **to burst into tears** deshacerse en lágrimas
tear² [tɛər] (pt **tore**, pp **torn**) N rasgón m, desgarrón m ▶ VT romper, rasgar ▶ VI rasgarse; **to ~ to pieces** or **to bits** or **to shreds** (also fig) hacer pedazos, destrozar
▶ **tear along** VI (rush) precipitarse
▶ **tear apart** VT (also fig) hacer pedazos
▶ **tear away** VT: **to ~ o.s. away (from sth)** alejarse (de algo)
▶ **tear down** VT (building, statue) derribar; (poster, flag) arrancar
▶ **tear off** VT (sheet of paper etc) arrancar; (one's clothes) quitarse a tirones
▶ **tear out** VT (sheet of paper, cheque) arrancar
▶ **tear up** VT (sheet of paper etc) romper
tearaway ['tɛərəweɪ] N (inf) gamberro(-a)
teardrop ['tɪədrɔp] N lágrima
tearful ['tɪəful] ADJ lloroso
tear gas N gas m lacrimógeno

t

819

tearing ['tɛərɪŋ] ADJ: **to be in a ~ hurry** tener muchísima prisa

tearoom ['tiːruːm] N salón m de té

tease [tiːz] N bromista mf ▶ VT tomar el pelo a

tea set N servicio de té

teashop ['tiːʃɔp] N café m, cafetería

Teasmaid® ['tiːzmeɪd] N tetera automática

teaspoon ['tiːspuːn] N cucharita; (also: **teaspoonful**: as measurement) cucharadita

tea strainer N colador m de té

teat [tiːt] N (of bottle) boquilla, tetilla

teatime ['tiːtaɪm] N hora del té

tea towel N (BRIT) paño de cocina

tea urn N tetera grande

tech [tɛk] N ABBR (inf) = **technology**; **technical college**

technical ['tɛknɪkl] ADJ técnico

technical college N centro de formación profesional

technicality [tɛknɪ'kælɪtɪ] N detalle m técnico; **on a legal ~** por una cuestión formal

technically ['tɛknɪklɪ] ADV técnicamente

technician [tɛk'nɪʃn] N técnico(-a)

technique [tɛk'niːk] N técnica

techno ['tɛknəu] N (Mus) (música) tecno

technocrat ['tɛknəkræt] N tecnócrata mf

technological [tɛknə'lɔdʒɪkl] ADJ tecnológico

technologist [tɛk'nɔlədʒɪst] N tecnólogo(-a)

technology [tɛk'nɔlədʒɪ] N tecnología

teddy ['tɛdɪ], **teddy bear** N osito de peluche

tedious ['tiːdɪəs] ADJ pesado, aburrido

tedium ['tiːdɪəm] N tedio

tee [tiː] N (Golf) tee m

teem [tiːm] VI: **to ~ with** rebosar de; **it is teeming (with rain)** llueve a mares

teen [tiːn] ADJ = **teenage** ▶ N (US) = **teenager**

teenage ['tiːneɪdʒ] ADJ (fashions etc) juvenil

teenager ['tiːneɪdʒəʳ] N adolescente mf, quinceañero(-a)

teens [tiːnz] NPL: **to be in one's ~** ser adolescente

tee-shirt ['tiːʃəːt] N = **T-shirt**

teeter ['tiːtəʳ] VI balancearse

teeth [tiːθ] NPL of **tooth**

teethe [tiːð] VI echar los dientes

teething ring ['tiːðɪŋ-] N mordedor m

teething troubles ['tiːðɪŋ-] NPL (fig) dificultades fpl iniciales

teetotal ['tiː'təutl] ADJ (person) abstemio

teetotaller, (US) **teetotaler** ['tiː'təutləʳ] N (person) abstemio(-a)

TEFL ['tɛfl] N ABBR = **Teaching of English as a Foreign Language**; **~ qualification** título para la enseñanza del inglés como lengua extranjera

Teflon® ['tɛflɔn] N teflón® m

Teheran [tɛə'rɑːn] N Teherán m

tel. ABBR (= telephone) tel.

Tel Aviv ['tɛlə'viːv] N Tel Aviv m

telecast ['tɛlɪkɑːst] VT, VI transmitir por televisión

telecommunications ['tɛlɪkəmjuːnɪ'keɪʃənz] N telecomunicaciones fpl

teleconferencing ['tɛlɪkɒnfərənsɪŋ] N teleconferencias fpl

telefax ['tɛlɪfæks] N telefax m

telegram ['tɛlɪgræm] N telegrama m

telegraph ['tɛlɪgrɑːf] N telégrafo

telegraphic [tɛlɪ'græfɪk] ADJ telegráfico

telegraph pole N poste m telegráfico

telegraph wire N hilo telegráfico

telepathic [tɛlɪ'pæθɪk] ADJ telepático

telepathy [tə'lɛpəθɪ] N telepatía

telephone ['tɛlɪfəun] N teléfono ▶ VT llamar por teléfono, telefonear; **to be on the ~** (subscriber) tener teléfono; (be speaking) estar hablando por teléfono

telephone book N guía f telefónica

telephone booth, (BRIT) **telephone box** N cabina telefónica

telephone call N llamada telefónica

telephone directory N guía telefónica

telephone exchange N central f telefónica

telephone number N número de teléfono

telephonist [tə'lɛfənɪst] N (BRIT) telefonista mf

telephoto ['tɛlɪ'fəutəu] ADJ: **~ lens** teleobjetivo

teleprinter ['tɛlɪprɪntəʳ] N teletipo, teleimpresora

teleprompter® ['tɛlɪprɔmptəʳ] N teleapuntador m

telesales ['tɛlɪseɪlz] NPL televentas fpl

telescope ['tɛlɪskəup] N telescopio

telescopic [tɛlɪ'skɒpɪk] ADJ telescópico; (umbrella) plegable

Teletext® ['tɛlɪtɛkst] N teletexto m

telethon ['tɛlɪθɔn] N telemaratón m, maratón m televisivo (con fines benéficos)

televise ['tɛlɪvaɪz] VT televisar

television ['tɛlɪvɪʒən] N televisión f; **to watch ~** mirar or ver la televisión

television licence N licencia que se paga por el uso del televisor, destinada a financiar la BBC

television programme N programa m de televisión

television set N televisor m

teleworking ['tɛlɪ,wɜːkɪŋ] N teletrabajo

telex ['tɛlɛks] N télex m ▶ VT (message) enviar por télex; (person) enviar un télex a ▶ VI enviar un télex

tell [tɛl] (pt, pp **told** [təuld]) VT decir; (relate: story) contar; (distinguish): **to ~ sth from** distinguir algo de ▶ VI (talk): **to ~ (of)** contar; (have effect) tener efecto; **to ~ sb to do sth**

decir a algn que haga algo; **to ~ sb about
sth** contar algo a algn; **to ~ the time** dar or
decir la hora; **can you ~ me the time?** ¿me
puedes decir la hora?; **(I) ~ you what …**
fíjate …; **I couldn't ~ them apart** no podía
distinguirlos
▶ **tell off** VT: **to ~ sb off** regañar a algn
▶ **tell on** VT FUS: **to ~ on sb** chivarse de algn
teller ['tɛlər] N (*in bank*) cajero(-a)
telling ['tɛlɪŋ] ADJ (*remark, detail*) revelador(a)
telltale ['tɛlteɪl] ADJ (*sign*) indicador(a)
telly ['tɛlɪ] N (BRIT *inf*) tele *f*
temerity [tə'mɛrɪtɪ] N temeridad *f*
temp [tɛmp] N ABBR (BRIT: = *temporary office
worker*) empleado(-a) eventual ▶ VI trabajar
como empleado(-a) eventual
temper ['tɛmpər] N (*mood*) humor *m*; (*bad
temper*) (mal) genio; (*fit of anger*) ira; (*of child*)
rabieta ▶ VT (*moderate*) moderar; **to be in a ~**
estar furioso; **to lose one's ~** enfadarse,
enojarse (LAM); **to keep one's ~** contenerse,
no alterarse
temperament ['tɛmprəmənt] N (*nature*)
temperamento
temperamental [tɛmprə'mɛntl] ADJ
temperamental
temperance ['tɛmpərns] N moderación *f*;
(*in drinking*) sobriedad *f*
temperate ['tɛmprət] ADJ moderado;
(*climate*) templado
temperature ['tɛmprətʃər] N temperatura;
to have or **run a ~** tener fiebre
tempered ['tɛmpəd] ADJ (*steel*) templado
tempest ['tɛmpɪst] N tempestad *f*
tempestuous [tɛm'pɛstjuəs] ADJ (*relationship,
meeting*) tempestuoso
tempi ['tɛmpi:] NPL *of* **tempo**
template ['tɛmplɪt] N plantilla
temple ['tɛmpl] N (*building*) templo; (*Anat*)
sien *f*
templet ['tɛmplɪt] N = **template**
tempo ['tɛmpəu] (*pl* **tempos** *or* **tempi**
['tɛmpi:]) N tempo; (*fig: of life etc*) ritmo
temporal ['tɛmpərl] ADJ temporal
temporarily ['tɛmpərərɪlɪ] ADV
temporalmente
temporary ['tɛmpərərɪ] ADJ provisional,
temporal; (*passing*) transitorio; (*worker*)
eventual; (*job*) temporal; **~ teacher**
maestro(-a) interino(-a)
tempt [tɛmpt] VT tentar; **to ~ sb into doing
sth** tentar or inducir a algn a hacer algo;
to be tempted to do sth (*person*) sentirse
tentado de hacer algo
temptation [tɛmp'teɪʃən] N tentación *f*
tempting ['tɛmptɪŋ] ADJ tentador(a);
(*food*) apetitoso
ten [tɛn] NUM diez; **tens of thousands**
decenas *fpl* de miles

tenable ['tɛnəbl] ADJ sostenible
tenacious [tə'neɪʃəs] ADJ tenaz
tenaciously [tə'neɪʃəslɪ] ADV tenazmente
tenacity [tə'næsɪtɪ] N tenacidad *f*
tenancy ['tɛnənsɪ] N alquiler *m*
tenant ['tɛnənt] N (*rent-payer*) inquilino(-a);
(*occupant*) habitante *mf*
tend [tɛnd] VT (*sick etc*) cuidar, atender;
(*cattle, machine*) vigilar, cuidar ▶ VI: **to ~ to do
sth** tener tendencia a hacer algo
tendency ['tɛndənsɪ] N tendencia
tender ['tɛndər] ADJ tierno, blando; (*delicate*)
delicado; (*meat*) tierno; (*sore*) sensible;
(*affectionate*) tierno, cariñoso ▶ N (*Comm: offer*)
oferta; (*money*): **legal ~** moneda de curso
legal ▶ VT ofrecer; **to put in a ~ (for)** hacer
una oferta (para); **to put work out to ~**
ofrecer un trabajo a contrata; **to ~ one's
resignation** presentar la dimisión
tenderize ['tɛndəraɪz] VT (*Culin*) ablandar
tenderly ['tɛndəlɪ] ADV tiernamente
tenderness ['tɛndənɪs] N ternura; (*of meat*)
blandura
tendon ['tɛndən] N tendón *m*
tendril ['tɛndrɪl] N zarcillo
tenement ['tɛnəmənt] N casa *or* bloque *m* de
pisos *or* vecinos (LAM)
Tenerife [tɛnə'ri:f] N Tenerife *m*
tenet ['tɛnət] N principio
Tenn. ABBR (US) = **Tennessee**
tenner ['tɛnər] N (billete *m* de) diez libras *fpl*
tennis ['tɛnɪs] N tenis *m*
tennis ball N pelota de tenis
tennis club N club *m* de tenis
tennis court N cancha de tenis
tennis elbow N (*Med*) codo de tenista,
sinovitis *f* del codo
tennis match N partido de tenis
tennis player N tenista *mf*
tennis racket N raqueta de tenis
tennis shoes NPL zapatillas *fpl* de tenis
tenor ['tɛnər] N (*Mus*) tenor *m*
tenpin bowling ['tɛnpɪn-] N bolos *mpl*
tense [tɛns] ADJ tenso; (*stretched*) tirante;
(*stiff*) rígido, tieso; (*person*) nervioso ▶ N (*Ling*)
tiempo ▶ VT (*tighten: muscles*) tensar
tensely ['tɛnslɪ] ADV: **they waited ~**
esperaban tensos
tenseness ['tɛnsnɪs] N tirantez *f*, tensión *f*
tension ['tɛnʃən] N tensión *f*
tent [tɛnt] N tienda (de campaña), carpa
(LAM)
tentacle ['tɛntəkl] N tentáculo
tentative ['tɛntətɪv] ADJ (*person*) indeciso;
(*provisional*) provisional
tentatively ['tɛntətɪvlɪ] ADV con indecisión;
(*provisionally*) provisionalmente
tenterhooks ['tɛntəhuks] NPL: **on ~** sobre
ascuas

t

821

tenth [tɛnθ] ADJ décimo
tent peg N clavija, estaca
tent pole N mástil m
tenuous ['tɛnjuəs] ADJ tenue
tenure ['tɛnjuəʳ] N posesión f, tenencia; **to have** ~ tener posesión or título de propiedad
tepid ['tɛpɪd] ADJ tibio
Ter. ABBR = **terrace**
term [tə:m] N (limit) límite m; (Comm) plazo; (word) término; (period) período; (Scol) trimestre m ▶ VT llamar, calificar de; **terms** NPL (conditions) condiciones fpl; (Comm) precio, tarifa; **in the short/long** ~ a corto/largo plazo; **during his** ~ **of office** bajo su mandato; **to be on good terms with sb** llevarse bien con algn; **to come to terms with** (problem) aceptar; **in terms of ...** en cuanto a ..., en términos de ...
terminal ['tə:mɪnl] ADJ (disease) mortal; (patient) terminal ▶ N (Elec) borne m; (Comput) terminal m; (also: **air terminal**) terminal f; (BRIT: also: **coach terminal**) (estación f) terminal f
terminate ['tə:mɪneɪt] VT poner término a; (pregnancy) interrumpir ▶ VI: **to** ~ **in** acabar en
termination [tə:mɪ'neɪʃən] N fin m; (of contract) terminación f; ~ **of pregnancy** interrupción f del embarazo
termini ['tə:mɪnaɪ] NPL of **terminus**
terminology [tə:mɪ'nɔlədʒɪ] N terminología
terminus ['tə:mɪnəs] (pl **termini** ['tə:mɪnaɪ]) N término, (estación f) terminal f
termite ['tə:maɪt] N termita, comején m
term paper N (US Univ) trabajo escrito trimestral or semestral
Terr. ABBR = **terrace**
terrace ['tɛrəs] N terraza; (BRIT: row of houses) hilera de casas adosadas; **the terraces** (BRIT Sport) las gradas fpl
terraced ['tɛrəst] ADJ (garden) escalonado; (house) adosado
terracotta ['tɛrə'kɔtə] N terracota
terrain [tɛ'reɪn] N terreno
terrestrial [tɪ'rɛstrɪəl] ADJ (life) terrestre; (BRIT: channel) de transmisión (por) vía terrestre
terrible ['tɛrɪbl] ADJ terrible, horrible; (inf) malísimo
terribly ['tɛrɪblɪ] ADV terriblemente; (very badly) malísimamente
terrier ['tɛrɪəʳ] N terrier m
terrific [tə'rɪfɪk] ADJ fantástico, fenomenal, macanudo (LAM); (wonderful) maravilloso
terrify ['tɛrɪfaɪ] VT aterrorizar; **to be terrified** estar aterrado or aterrorizado
terrifying ['tɛrɪfaɪɪŋ] ADJ aterrador(a)
territorial [tɛrɪ'tɔ:rɪəl] ADJ territorial
territorial waters NPL aguas fpl jurisdiccionales

territory ['tɛrɪtərɪ] N territorio
terror ['tɛrəʳ] N terror m
terror attack N atentado (terrorista)
terrorism ['tɛrərɪzəm] N terrorismo
terrorist ['tɛrərɪst] N terrorista mf
terrorist attack N atentado (terrorista)
terrorize ['tɛrəraɪz] VT aterrorizar
terse [tə:s] ADJ (style) conciso; (reply) brusco
tertiary ['tə:ʃərɪ] ADJ terciario; ~ **education** enseñanza superior
Terylene® ['tɛrəli:n] N (BRIT) terylene® m
TESL [tɛsl] N ABBR = **Teaching of English as a Second Language**
TESSA ['tɛsə] N ABBR (BRIT: = Tax Exempt Special Savings Account) plan de ahorro por el que se invierte a largo plazo a cambio de intereses libres de impuestos
test [tɛst] N (trial, check) prueba, ensayo; (: of goods in factory) control m; (of courage etc) prueba; (Chem, Med) prueba; (of blood, urine) análisis m inv; (exam) examen m, test m; (also: **driving test**) examen m de conducir ▶ VT probar, poner a prueba; (Med) examinar; (: blood) analizar; **to put sth to the** ~ someter algo a prueba; **to** ~ **sth for sth** analizar algo en busca de algo
testament ['tɛstəmənt] N testamento; **the Old/New T**~ el Antiguo/Nuevo Testamento
test ban N (also: **nuclear test ban**) suspensión f de pruebas nucleares
test card N (TV) carta de ajuste
test case N juicio que sienta precedente
testes ['tɛsti:z] NPL testes mpl
test flight N vuelo de ensayo
testicle ['tɛstɪkl] N testículo
testify ['tɛstɪfaɪ] VI (Law) prestar declaración; **to** ~ **to sth** atestiguar algo
testimonial [tɛstɪ'məunɪəl] N (of character) (carta de) recomendación f
testimony ['tɛstɪmənɪ] N (Law) testimonio, declaración f
testing ['tɛstɪŋ] ADJ (difficult: time) duro
test match N partido internacional
testosterone [tɛs'tɔstərəun] N testosterona
test paper N examen m, test m
test pilot N piloto mf de pruebas
test tube N probeta
test-tube baby N bebé m probeta inv
testy ['tɛstɪ] ADJ irritable
tetanus ['tɛtənəs] N tétano
tetchy ['tɛtʃɪ] ADJ irritable
tether ['tɛðəʳ] VT atar ▶ N: **to be at the end of one's** ~ no aguantar más
Tex. ABBR (US) = **Texas**
text [tɛkst] N texto; (on mobile) mensaje m de texto ▶ VT: **to** ~ **sb** enviar un mensaje (de texto) a algn
textbook ['tɛkstbuk] N libro de texto
textiles ['tɛkstaɪlz] NPL tejidos mpl

text message N mensaje *m* de texto
text messaging [-'mɛsɪdʒɪŋ] N (envío de) mensajes *mpl* de texto
textual ['tɛkstjuəl] ADJ del texto, textual
texture ['tɛkstʃəʳ] N textura
TGIF ABBR (*inf*) = **thank God it's Friday**
TGWU N ABBR (BRIT: = *Transport and General Workers' Union*) sindicato de transportistas
Thai [taɪ] ADJ, N tailandés(-esa) *m/f*
Thailand ['taɪlænd] N Tailandia
thalidomide® [θə'lɪdəmaɪd] N talidomida®
Thames [tɛmz] N: **the** ~ el (río) Támesis
than [ðæn, ðən] CONJ que; (*with numerals*): **more** ~ **10/once** más de 10/una vez; **I have more/less** ~ **you** tengo más/menos que tú; **it is better to phone** ~ **to write** es mejor llamar por teléfono que escribir; **no sooner did he leave** ~ **the phone rang** en cuanto se marchó, sonó el teléfono
thank [θæŋk] VT dar las gracias a, agradecer; ~ **you (very much)** (muchas) gracias; ~ **heavens**, ~ **God!** ¡gracias a Dios!, ¡menos mal!; *see also* **thanks**
thankful ['θæŋkful] ADJ: ~ **for** agradecido (por)
thankfully ['θæŋkfəlɪ] ADV (*gratefully*) con agradecimiento; (*with relief*) por suerte; ~ **there were few victims** afortunadamente hubo pocas víctimas
thankless ['θæŋklɪs] ADJ ingrato
thanks [θæŋks] NPL gracias *fpl* ▶ EXCL ¡gracias!; **many** ~, ~ **a lot** ¡muchas gracias!; ~ **to** prep gracias a
Thanksgiving (Day) ['θæŋksɡɪvɪŋ-] N día *m* de Acción de Gracias; *ver nota*

En Estados Unidos el cuarto jueves de noviembre es *Thanksgiving Day*, fiesta oficial en la que se conmemora la celebración que tuvieron los primeros colonos norteamericanos (*Pilgrims* o *Pilgrim Fathers*) tras la estupenda cosecha de 1621, por la que se dan gracias a Dios. En Canadá se celebra una fiesta semejante el segundo lunes de octubre, aunque no está relacionada con dicha fecha histórica.

(KEYWORD)

that [ðæt] (*pl* **those**) ADJ (*demonstrative*) ese(-a); (*: more remote*) aquel (aquella); **leave that book on the table** deja ese libro sobre la mesa; **that one** ese (esa), ése (ésa); (*more remote*) aquel (aquella), aquél (aquélla) (*to avoid confusion with adj*); **that one over there** ese (esa) de ahí, ése (ésa) de ahí; aquel (aquella) de allí, aquél (aquélla) de allí; *see also* **those**

▶ PRON **1** (*demonstrative*) ese(-a), ése(-a) (*to avoid confusion with adj*), eso (*neuter*); (*: more remote*) aquel (aquella), aquél (aquélla) (*to avoid confusion with adj*), aquello (*neuter*); **what's that?** ¿qué es eso (*or* aquello)?; **who's that?** ¿quién es?; (*pointing etc*) ¿quién es ese/a?; **is that you?** ¿eres tú?; **will you eat all that?** ¿vas a comer todo eso?; **that's my house** esa es mi casa; **that's what he said** eso es lo que dijo; **that is (to say)** es decir; **at** *or* **with that she …** en eso, ella …; **do it like that** hazlo así; *see also* **those**
2 (*relative: subject, object*) que; (*: with preposition*) (el (la)) que, el (la) cual; **the book (that) I read** el libro que leí; **the books that are in the library** los libros que están en la biblioteca; **all (that) I have** todo lo que tengo; **the box (that) I put it in** la caja en la que *or* donde lo puse; **the people (that) I spoke to** la gente con la que hablé; **not that I know of** que yo sepa, no
3 (*relative: of time*) que; **the day (that) he came** el día (en) que vino
▶ CONJ que; **he thought that I was ill** creyó que yo estaba enfermo
▶ ADV (*demonstrative*): **I can't work that much** no puedo trabajar tanto; **I didn't realize it was that bad** no creí que fuera tan malo; **that high** así de alto

thatched [θætʃt] ADJ (*roof*) de paja; ~ **cottage** casita con tejado de paja
Thatcherism ['θætʃərɪzəm] N thatcherismo
thaw [θɔ:] N deshielo ▶ VI (*ice*) derretirse; (*food*) descongelarse ▶ VT descongelar

(KEYWORD)

the [ði:, ðə] DEF ART **1** (*gen*) el *m*, la *f*, los *mpl*, las *fpl* (NB = **el** *immediately before feminine noun beginning with stressed* (h)a; **a** + **el** = **al**; **de** + **el** = **del**); **the boy/girl** el chico/la chica; **the books/flowers** los libros/las flores; **to the postman** al cartero; **from the drawer** del cajón; **I haven't the time/money** no tengo tiempo/dinero; **1.10 euros to the dollar** 1,10 euros por dólar; **paid by the hour** pagado por hora
2 (+ *adj to form noun*) los; lo; **the rich and the poor** los ricos y los pobres; **to attempt the impossible** intentar lo imposible
3 (*in titles, surnames*): **Elizabeth the First** Isabel Primera; **Peter the Great** Pedro el Grande; **do you know the Smiths?** ¿conoce a los Smith?
4 (*in comparisons*): **the more he works the more he earns** cuanto más trabaja más gana

theatre, (*US*) **theater** ['θɪətəʳ] N teatro; (*also*: **lecture theatre**) aula; (*Med: also*: **operating theatre**) quirófano

823

theatre-goer, *(US)* **theater-goer** ['θɪətəgəuəʳ] N aficionado(-a) al teatro

theatrical [θɪ'ætrɪkl] ADJ teatral

theft [θɛft] N robo

their [ðɛəʳ] ADJ su

theirs [ðɛəz] PRON (el) suyo/(la) suya *etc; see also* **my; mine**

them [ðɛm, ðəm] PRON *(direct)* los (las); *(indirect)* les; *(stressed, after prep)* ellos (ellas); **I see ~** los veo; **both of ~** ambos(-as), los (las) dos; **give me a few of ~** dame algunos(-as); *see also* **me**

theme [θiːm] N tema *m*

theme park N parque *m* temático

theme song N tema *m* (musical)

themselves [ðəm'sɛlvz] PRON PL *(subject)* ellos mismos (ellas mismas); *(complement)* se; *(after prep)* sí (mismos(-as)); *see also* **oneself**

then [ðɛn] ADV *(at that time)* entonces; *(next)* pues; *(later)* luego, después; *(and also)* además ▶ CONJ *(therefore)* en ese caso, entonces ▶ ADJ: **the ~ president** el entonces presidente; **from ~ on** desde entonces; **until ~** hasta entonces; **and ~ what?** y luego, ¿qué?; **what do you want me to do, ~?** ¿entonces, qué quiere me haga?

theologian [θɪə'ləudʒən] N teólogo(-a)

theological [θɪə'lɔdʒɪkl] ADJ teológico

theology [θɪ'ɔlədʒɪ] N teología

theorem ['θɪərəm] N teorema *m*

theoretical [θɪə'rɛtɪkl] ADJ teórico

theoretically [θɪə'rɛtɪklɪ] ADV teóricamente, en teoría

theorize ['θɪəraɪz] VI teorizar

theory ['θɪərɪ] N teoría

therapeutic [θɛrə'pjuːtɪk], **therapeutical** [θɛrə'pjuːtɪkl] ADJ terapéutico

therapist ['θɛrəpɪst] N terapeuta *mf*

therapy ['θɛrəpɪ] N terapia

(KEYWORD)

there ['ðɛəʳ] ADV **1: there is, there are** hay; **there is no-one here** no hay nadie aquí; **there is no bread left** no queda pan; **there has been an accident** ha habido un accidente

2 *(referring to place)* ahí; *(: distant)* allí; **it's there** está ahí; **put it in/on/up/down there** ponlo ahí dentro/encima/arriba/abajo; **I want that book there** quiero ese libro de ahí; **there he is!** ¡ahí está!; **there's the bus** ahí *or* ya viene el autobús; **back/down there** allí atrás/abajo; **over there, through there** por allí

3: there, there *(esp to child)* venga, venga, bueno

thereabouts ['ðɛərə'bauts] ADV por ahí

thereafter [ðɛər'ɑːftəʳ] ADV después

thereby ['ðɛəbaɪ] ADV así, de ese modo

therefore ['ðɛəfɔːʳ] ADV por lo tanto

there's [ðɛəz] = **there is; there has**

thereupon [ðɛərə'pɔn] ADV *(at that point)* en eso, en seguida

thermal ['θəːml] ADJ termal; *(paper)* térmico

thermal paper N papel *m* térmico

thermal printer N termoimpresora

thermodynamics ['θəːmədaɪnæmɪks] N termodinámica

thermometer [θə'mɔmɪtəʳ] N termómetro

thermonuclear [θə:məu'njuːklɪəʳ] ADJ termonuclear

Thermos® ['θəːməs] N *(also:* **Thermos flask***)* termo

thermostat ['θəːməustæt] N termostato

thesaurus [θɪ'sɔːrəs] N tesoro, diccionario de sinónimos

these [ðiːz] ADJ PL estos(-as) ▶ PRON PL estos(-as), éstos(-as) *(to avoid confusion with adj)*; **~ children/flowers** estos chicos/estas flores; *see also* **this**

thesis ['θiːsɪs] *(pl* **theses** [-siːz]*)* N tesis *f inv*; *see also* **doctorate**

they [ðeɪ] PRON PL ellos (ellas); **~ say that …** *(it is said that)* se dice que …

they'd [ðeɪd] = **they had; they would**

they'll [ðeɪl] = **they will; they shall**

they're [ðɛəʳ] = **they are**

they've [ðeɪv] = **they have**

thick [θɪk] ADJ *(wall, slice)* grueso; *(dense: liquid, smoke etc)* espeso; *(: vegetation, beard)* tupido; *(stupid)* ▶ N: **in the ~ of the battle** en lo más reñido de la batalla; **it's 20 cm ~** tiene 20 cm de espesor

thicken ['θɪkn] VI espesarse ▶ VT *(sauce etc)* espesar

thicket ['θɪkɪt] N espesura

thickly ['θɪklɪ] ADV *(spread)* en capa espesa; *(cut)* en rebanada gruesa; *(populated)* densamente

thickness ['θɪknɪs] N espesor *m*, grueso

thickset [θɪk'sɛt] ADJ fornido

thick-skinned [θɪk'skɪnd] ADJ *(fig)* insensible

thief [θiːf] *(pl* **thieves** [θiːvz]*)* N ladrón(-ona) *m/f*

thieving ['θiːvɪŋ] N robo, hurto ▶ ADJ ladrón(-ona)

thigh [θaɪ] N muslo

thighbone ['θaɪbəun] N fémur *m*

thimble ['θɪmbl] N dedal *m*

thin [θɪn] ADJ delgado; *(wall, layer)* fino; *(watery)* aguado; *(light)* tenue; *(hair)* escaso; *(fog)* ligero; *(crowd)* disperso ▶ VT: **to ~** *(down)* *(sauce, paint)* diluir ▶ VI *(fog)* aclararse; *(also:* **thin out***: crowd)* dispersarse; **his hair is thinning** se está quedando calvo

thing [θɪŋ] N cosa; *(object)* objeto, artículo; *(contraption)* chisme *m*; *(mania)* manía; **things**

NPL (*belongings*) cosas *fpl*; **the best ~ would be to ...** lo mejor sería ...; **the main ~ is ...** lo principal es ...; **first ~ (in the morning)** a primera hora (de la mañana); **last ~ (at night)** a última hora (de la noche); **the ~ is ...** lo que pasa es que ...; **how are things?** ¿qué tal van las cosas?; **she's got a ~ about mice** le dan no sé qué los ratones; **poor ~!** ¡pobre! *mf*, ¡pobrecito(-a)!

think [θɪŋk] (*pl* **thought** [θɔːt]) VI pensar ▶ VT pensar, creer; (*imagine*) imaginar; **what did you ~ of it?** ¿qué te pareció?; **what did you ~ of them?** ¿qué te parecieron?; **to ~ about sth/sb** pensar en algo/algn; **I'll ~ about it** lo pensaré; **to ~ of doing sth** pensar en hacer algo; **I ~ so/not** creo que sí/no; **~ again!** ¡piénsalo bien!; **to ~ aloud** pensar en voz alta; **to ~ well of sb** tener buen concepto de algn
▶ **think out** VT (*plan*) elaborar, tramar; (*solution*) encontrar
▶ **think over** VT reflexionar sobre, meditar; **I'd like to ~ things over** me gustaría pensármelo
▶ **think through** VT pensar bien
▶ **think up** VT imaginar

thinking [ˈθɪŋkɪŋ] N: **to my (way of) ~** a mi parecer

think tank N grupo de expertos

thinly [ˈθɪnlɪ] ADV (*cut*) en lonchas finas; (*spread*) en una capa fina

thinness [ˈθɪnnɪs] N delgadez *f*

third [θəːd] ADJ (*before n*) tercer(a); (*following n*) tercero(-a) ▶ N tercero(-a); (*fraction*) tercio; (BRIT: *degree*) título universitario de tercera clase

third degree ADJ (*burns*) de tercer grado

thirdly [ˈθəːdlɪ] ADV en tercer lugar

third party insurance N (BRIT) seguro a terceros

third-rate [ˈθəːdˈreɪt] ADJ de poca calidad

Third World N: **the ~** el Tercer Mundo ▶ CPD tercermundista

thirst [θəːst] N sed *f*

thirsty [ˈθəːstɪ] ADJ (*person*) sediento; **to be ~** tener sed

thirteen [θəːˈtiːn] NUM trece

thirteenth [θəːˈtiːnθ] ADJ decimotercero ▶ N (*in series*) decimotercero(-a); (*fraction*) decimotercio

thirtieth [ˈθəːtɪəθ] ADJ trigésimo ▶ N (*in series*) trigésimo(-a); (*fraction*) treintavo

thirty [ˈθəːtɪ] NUM treinta

(KEYWORD)

this [ðɪs] (*pl* **these**) ADJ (*demonstrative*) este(-a); **this man/woman** este hombre/esta mujer; **this way** por aquí; **this time last year** hoy hace un año; **this one (here)** este(-a), éste(-a), esto (de aquí); *see also* **these**
▶ PRON (*demonstrative*) este(-a), éste(-a) (*to avoid confusion with adj*), esto *neuter*; **who is this?** ¿quién es este (esta)?; **what is this?** ¿qué es esto?; **this is where I live** aquí vivo; **this is what he said** esto es lo que dijo; **this is Mr Brown** (*in introductions*) le presento al Sr. Brown; (*photo*) este es el Sr. Brown; (*on telephone*) habla el Sr. Brown; **they were talking of this and that** hablaban de esto y lo otro; *see also* **these**
▶ ADV (*demonstrative*): **this high/long** así de alto/largo; **this far** hasta aquí

thistle [ˈθɪsl] N cardo

thong [θɔŋ] N correa

thorn [θɔːn] N espina

thorny [ˈθɔːnɪ] ADJ espinoso

thorough [ˈθʌrə] ADJ (*search*) minucioso; (*knowledge*) profundo; (*research*) a fondo

thoroughbred [ˈθʌrəbred] ADJ (*horse*) de pura sangre

thoroughfare [ˈθʌrəfɛəʳ] N calle *f*; **"no ~"** "prohibido el paso"

thoroughgoing [ˈθʌrəgəʊɪŋ] ADJ a fondo

thoroughly [ˈθʌrəlɪ] ADV (*search*) minuciosamente; (*study*) profundamente; (*wash*) a fondo; (*utterly: bad, wet etc*) completamente, totalmente

thoroughness [ˈθʌrənɪs] N minuciosidad *f*

those [ðəʊz] ADJ PL esos (esas); (*more remote*) aquellos(-as) ▶ PRON PL esos (esas), ésos (ésas) (*to avoid confusion with adj*); (*more remote*) aquellos(-as), aquéllos(-as) (*to avoid confusion with adj*); **leave ~ books on the table** deja esos libros sobre la mesa

though [ðəʊ] CONJ aunque ▶ ADV sin embargo, aún así; **even ~** aunque; **it's not so easy, ~** sin embargo no es tan fácil

thought [θɔːt] PT, PP of **think** ▶ N pensamiento; (*opinion*) opinión *f*; (*intention*) intención *f*; **to give sth some ~** pensar algo detenidamente; **after much ~** después de pensarlo bien; **I've just had a ~** se me acaba de ocurrir una idea

thoughtful [ˈθɔːtful] ADJ pensativo; (*considerate*) atento

thoughtfully [ˈθɔːtfəlɪ] ADV pensativamente; atentamente

thoughtless [ˈθɔːtlɪs] ADJ desconsiderado

thoughtlessly [ˈθɔːtlɪslɪ] ADV insensatamente

thought-provoking [ˈθɔːtprəvəʊkɪŋ] ADJ estimulante

thousand [ˈθaʊzənd] NUM mil; **two ~** dos mil; **thousands of** miles de

thousandth [ˈθaʊzəntθ] NUM milésimo

thrash [θræʃ] VT dar una paliza a
▶ **thrash about** VI revolverse
▶ **thrash out** VT discutir a fondo

825

thrashing ['θræʃɪŋ] N: **to give sb a ~** dar una paliza a algn

thread [θrɛd] N hilo; (of screw) rosca ▶ VT (needle) enhebrar

threadbare ['θrɛdbɛəʳ] ADJ raído

threat [θrɛt] N amenaza; **to be under ~ of** estar amenazado de

threaten ['θrɛtn] VI amenazar ▶ VT: **to ~ sb with sth/to do** amenazar a algn con algo/con hacer

threatening ['θrɛtnɪŋ] ADJ amenazador(a), amenazante

three [θriː] NUM tres

three-dimensional [θriːdɪ'mɛnʃənl] ADJ tridimensional

threefold ['θriːfəuld] ADV: **to increase ~** triplicar

three-piece ['θriːpiːs] CPD: **~ suit** traje m de tres piezas; **~ suite** tresillo

three-ply [θriː'plaɪ] ADJ (wood) de tres capas; (wool) triple

three-quarter [θriː'kwɔːtəʳ] ADJ: **~ length sleeves** mangas fpl tres cuartos

three-quarters [θriː'kwɔːtəz] NPL tres cuartas partes; **~ full** tres cuartas partes lleno

three-wheeler [θriː'wiːləʳ] N (car) coche m cabina

thresh [θrɛʃ] VT (Agr) trillar

threshing machine ['θrɛʃɪŋ-] N trilladora

threshold ['θrɛʃhəuld] N umbral m; **to be on the ~ of** (fig) estar al borde de

threshold agreement N convenio de nivel crítico

threw [θruː] PT of **throw**

thrift [θrɪft] N economía

thrifty ['θrɪftɪ] ADJ económico

thrill [θrɪl] N (excitement) emoción f ▶ VT emocionar; **to be thrilled** (with gift etc) estar encantado

thriller ['θrɪləʳ] N película/novela de suspense

thrilling ['θrɪlɪŋ] ADJ emocionante

thrive [θraɪv] (pt **thrived** or **throve** [θrəuv], pp **thrived** or **thriven** ['θrɪvn]) VI (grow) crecer; (do well) prosperar

thriving ['θraɪvɪŋ] ADJ próspero

throat [θrəut] N garganta; **I have a sore ~** me duele la garganta

throb [θrɔb] N (of heart) latido; (of engine) vibración f ▶ VI latir; vibrar; (with pain) dar punzadas; **my head is throbbing** la cabeza me da punzadas

throes [θrəuz] NPL: **in the ~ of** en medio de

thrombosis [θrɔm'bəusɪs] N trombosis f

throne [θrəun] N trono

throng [θrɔŋ] N multitud f, muchedumbre f ▶ VT, VI apiñarse, agolparse

throttle ['θrɔtl] N (Aut) acelerador m ▶ VT estrangular

through [θruː] PREP por, a través de; (time) durante; (by means of) por medio de, mediante; (owing to) gracias a ▶ ADJ (ticket, train) directo ▶ ADV completamente, de parte a parte; de principio a fin; **(from) Monday ~ Friday** (US) de lunes a viernes; **to go ~ sb's papers** mirar entre los papeles de algn; **I am halfway ~ the book** voy por la mitad del libro; **the soldiers didn't let us ~** los soldados no nos dejaron pasar; **to put sb ~ to sb** (Tel) poner or pasar a algn con algn; **to be ~** (Tel) tener comunicación; (have finished) haber terminado; **"no ~ road"** (BRIT) "calle sin salida"

throughout [θruː'aut] PREP (place) por todas partes de, por todo; (time) durante todo ▶ ADV por or en todas partes

throughput ['θruːput] N (of goods, materials) producción f; (Comput) capacidad f de procesamiento

throve [θrəuv] PT of **thrive**

throw [θrəu] (pt **threw** [θruː], pp **thrown** [θrəun]) N tiro; (Sport) lanzamiento ▶ VT tirar, echar, botar (LAM); (Sport) lanzar; (rider) derribar; (fig) desconcertar; **to ~ a party** dar una fiesta

▶ **throw about, throw around** VT (litter etc) tirar, esparcir

▶ **throw away** VT tirar

▶ **throw in** VT (Sport: ball) sacar; (include) incluir

▶ **throw off** VT deshacerse de

▶ **throw open** VT (doors, windows) abrir de par en par; (house, gardens etc) abrir al público; (competition, race) abrir a todos

▶ **throw out** VT tirar, botar (LAM)

▶ **throw together** VT (clothes) amontonar; (meal) preparar a la carrera; (essay) hacer sin cuidado

▶ **throw up** VI vomitar, devolver

throwaway ['θrəuəweɪ] ADJ para tirar, desechable

throwback ['θrəubæk] N: **it's a ~ to** (fig) eso nos lleva de nuevo a

throw-in ['θrəuɪn] N (Sport) saque m de banda

thrown [θrəun] PP of **throw**

thru [θruː] PREP, ADJ, ADV (US) = **through**

thrush [θrʌʃ] N zorzal m, tordo; (Med) candidiasis f

thrust [θrʌst] (pt, pp ~) N (Tech) empuje m ▶ VT empujar; (push in) introducir

thrusting ['θrʌstɪŋ] ADJ (person) dinámico, con empuje

thud [θʌd] N golpe m sordo

thug [θʌg] N gamberro(-a)

thumb [θʌm] N (Anat) pulgar m ▶ VT: **to ~ a lift** hacer dedo; **to give sth/sb the thumbs up/down** aprobar/desaprobar algo/a algn

▶ **thumb through** VT FUS (book) hojear

thumb index N uñero, índice m recortado
thumbnail ['θʌmneɪl] N uña del pulgar
thumbnail sketch N esbozo
thumbtack ['θʌmtæk] N (US) chincheta, chinche f (LAM)
thump [θʌmp] N golpe m; (sound) ruido seco or sordo ▶ VT, VI golpear
thumping ['θʌmpɪŋ] ADJ (inf: huge) descomunal
thunder ['θʌndər] N trueno; (of applause etc) estruendo ▶ VI tronar; (train etc): to ~ past pasar como un trueno
thunderbolt ['θʌndəbəult] N rayo
thunderclap ['θʌndəklæp] N trueno
thunderous ['θʌndərəs] ADJ ensordecedor(a), estruendoso
thunderstorm ['θʌndəstɔːm] N tormenta
thunderstruck ['θʌndəstrʌk] ADJ pasmado
thundery ['θʌndərɪ] ADJ tormentoso
ABBR (= Thursday) juev.
Thursday ['θɜːzdɪ] N jueves m inv; see also **Tuesday**
thus [ðʌs] ADV así, de este modo
thwart [θwɔːt] VT frustrar
thyme [taɪm] N tomillo
thyroid ['θaɪrɔɪd] N tiroides m inv
tiara [tɪ'ɑːrə] N tiara, diadema
Tiber ['taɪbər] N Tíber m
Tibet [tɪ'bɛt] N el Tibet
Tibetan [tɪ'bɛtən] ADJ tibetano ▶ N tibetano(-a); (Ling) tibetano
tibia ['tɪbɪə] N tibia
tic [tɪk] N tic m
tick [tɪk] N (sound: of clock) tictac m; (mark) señal f (de visto bueno), palomita (LAM); (Zool) garrapata; (BRIT inf): in a ~ en un instante; (BRIT inf: credit): to buy sth on ~ comprar algo a crédito ▶ VI hacer tictac ▶ VT marcar, señalar; to put a ~ against sth poner una señal en algo
▶ **tick off** VT marcar; (person) reñir
▶ **tick over** VI (BRIT: engine) girar en marcha lenta; (: fig) ir tirando
ticker tape ['tɪkə-] N cinta perforada
ticket ['tɪkɪt] N billete m, tique m, boleto (LAM); (for cinema etc) entrada, boleto (LAM); (in shop: on goods) etiqueta; (for library) tarjeta; (US Pol) lista (de candidatos); to get a parking ~ (Aut) ser multado por estacionamiento ilegal
ticket agency N (Theat) agencia de venta de entradas
ticket barrier N (BRIT Rail) barrera más allá de la cual se necesita billete/boleto
ticket collector N revisor(a) m/f
ticket holder N poseedor(a) m/f de billete or entrada
ticket inspector N revisor(a) m/f, inspector(a) m/f de boletos (LAM)

ticket machine N máquina de billetes (SP) or boletos (LAM)
ticket office N (Theat) taquilla, boletería (LAM); (Rail) despacho de billetes or boletos (LAM)
ticking-off ['tɪkɪŋ'ɔf] N (inf): to give sb a ~ echarle una bronca a algn
tickle ['tɪkl] N: to give sb a ~ hacer cosquillas a algn ▶ VT hacer cosquillas a ▶ VI hacer cosquillas
ticklish ['tɪklɪʃ] ADJ (which tickles: blanket) que pica; (: cough) irritante; (fig: problem) delicado; to be ~ tener cosquillas
tidal ['taɪdl] ADJ de marea
tidal wave N maremoto
tidbit ['tɪdbɪt] N (US) = **titbit**
tiddlywinks ['tɪdlɪwɪŋks] N juego de la pulga
tide [taɪd] N marea; (fig: of events) curso, marcha ▶ VT: to ~ sb over or through (until) sacar a algn del apuro (hasta); high/low ~ marea alta/baja; the ~ of public opinion la tendencia de la opinión pública
tidily ['taɪdɪlɪ] ADV bien, ordenadamente; to arrange ~ ordenar; to dress ~ vestir bien
tidiness ['taɪdɪnɪs] N (order) orden m; (cleanliness) aseo
tidy ['taɪdɪ] ADJ (room) ordenado; (drawing, work) limpio; (person) (bien) arreglado; (: in character) metódico; (mind) claro, metódico ▶ VT (also: **tidy up**) ordenar, poner en orden
tie [taɪ] N (string etc) atadura; (BRIT: necktie) corbata; (fig: link) vínculo, lazo; (Sport: draw) empate m ▶ VT atar ▶ VI (Sport) empatar; family ties obligaciones fpl familiares; cup ~ (Sport: match) partido de copa; to ~ in a bow hacer un lazo; to ~ a knot in sth hacer un nudo en algo
▶ **tie down** VT atar; (fig): to ~ sb down to obligar a algn a
▶ **tie in** VI: to ~ in (with) (correspond) concordar (con)
▶ **tie on** VT (BRIT: label etc) atar
▶ **tie up** VT (parcel) envolver; (dog) atar; (boat) amarrar; (arrangements) concluir; to be tied up (busy) estar ocupado
tie-break ['taɪbreɪk], **tie-breaker** ['taɪbreɪkər] N (Tennis) tiebreak m, muerte f súbita; (in quiz) punto decisivo
tie-on ['taɪɔn] ADJ (BRIT: label) para atar
tie-pin ['taɪpɪn] N (BRIT) alfiler m de corbata
tier [tɪər] N grada; (of cake) piso
tie tack N (US) alfiler m de corbata
tiff [tɪf] N (inf) pelea, riña
tiger ['taɪgər] N tigre m
tight [taɪt] ADJ (rope) tirante; (money) escaso; (clothes, budget) ajustado; (programme) apretado; (budget) ajustado; (security) estricto; (inf: drunk) borracho ▶ ADV (squeeze) muy fuerte; (shut) herméticamente; to be

packed ~ (*suitcase*) estar completamente lleno; (*people*) estar apretados; **everybody hold ~!** ¡agárrense bien!

tighten ['taɪtn] VT (*rope*) tensar, estirar; (*screw*) apretar ▶ VI estirarse; apretarse

tight-fisted ['taɪt'fɪstɪd] ADJ tacaño

tight-lipped ['taɪt'lɪpt] ADJ: **to be ~** (*silent*) rehusar hablar; (*angry*) apretar los labios

tightly ['taɪtlɪ] ADV (*grasp*) muy fuerte

tightness ['taɪtnɪs] N (*of rope*) tirantez *f*; (*of clothes*) estrechez *f*; (*of budget*) lo ajustado

tightrope ['taɪtrəup] N cuerda floja

tightrope walker N equilibrista *mf*, funambulista *mf*

tights [taɪts] NPL (*BRIT*) medias *fpl*, pantis *mpl*

tigress ['taɪgrɪs] N tigresa

tilde ['tɪldə] N tilde *f*

tile [taɪl] N (*on roof*) teja; (*on floor*) baldosa; (*on wall*) azulejo ▶ VT (*floor*) poner baldosas en; (*wall*) alicatar

tiled [taɪld] ADJ (*floor*) embaldosado; (*wall, bathroom*) alicatado; (*roof*) con tejas

till [tɪl] N caja (registradora) ▶ VT (*land*) cultivar ▶ PREP, CONJ = **until**

tiller ['tɪlər] N (*Naut*) caña del timón

tilt [tɪlt] VT inclinar ▶ VI inclinarse ▶ N (*slope*) inclinación *f*; **to wear one's hat at a ~** llevar el sombrero echado a un lado *or* terciado; (**at**) **full ~** a toda velocidad *or* carrera

timber ['tɪmbər] N (*material*) madera; (*trees*) árboles *mpl*

time [taɪm] N tiempo; (*epoch: often pl*) época; (*by clock*) hora; (*moment*) momento; (*occasion*) vez *f*; (*Mus*) compás *m* ▶ VT calcular *or* medir el tiempo de; (*race*) cronometrar; (*remark etc*) elegir el momento para; **a long ~** mucho tiempo; **four at a ~** cuatro a la vez; **for the ~ being** de momento, por ahora; **at times** a veces, a ratos; **~ after ~, ~ and again** repetidas veces, una y otra vez; **from ~ to ~** de vez en cuando; **in ~** (*soon enough*) a tiempo; (*after some time*) con el tiempo; (*Mus*) al compás; **in a week's ~** dentro de una semana; **in no ~** en un abrir y cerrar de ojos; **any ~** cuando sea; **on ~** a la hora; **to be 30 minutes behind/ahead of ~** llevar media hora de retraso/adelanto; **to take one's ~** tomárselo con calma; **he'll do it in his own ~** (*without being hurried*) lo hará sin prisa; (*out of working hours*) lo hará en su tiempo libre; **by the ~ he arrived** cuando llegó; **5 times 5** 5 por 5; **what ~ is it?** ¿qué hora es?; **what ~ do you make it?** ¿qué hora es *or* tiene?; **to be behind the times** estar atrasado; **to carry three boxes at a ~** llevar tres cajas a la vez; **to keep ~** llevar el ritmo *or* el compás; **to have a good ~** pasarlo bien, divertirse; **to ~ sth well/badly** elegir un buen/mal momento para algo; **the bomb was timed to explode five minutes later** la bomba estaba programada para explotar cinco minutos más tarde

time-and-motion expert ['taɪmənd'məuʃən-] N experto(-a) en la ciencia de la producción

time-and-motion study ['taɪmənd'məuʃən-] N estudio de desplazamientos y tiempos

time bomb N bomba de relojería

time card N tarjeta de registro horario

time clock N reloj *m* registrador

time-consuming ['taɪmkənsju:mɪŋ] ADJ que requiere mucho tiempo

time frame N plazo

time-honoured, (*US*) **time-honored** ['taɪmɒnəd] ADJ consagrado

timekeeper ['taɪmki:pər] N (*Sport*) cronómetro

time lag N desfase *m*

timeless ['taɪmlɪs] ADJ eterno

time limit N (*gen*) límite *m* de tiempo; (*Comm*) plazo

timeline ['taɪmlaɪn] N línea de tiempo

timely ['taɪmlɪ] ADJ oportuno

time off N tiempo libre

timer ['taɪmər] N (*also:* **timer switch**) interruptor *m*; (*in kitchen*) temporizador *m*; (*Tech*) temporizador *m*

time-saving ['taɪmseɪvɪŋ] ADJ que ahorra tiempo

time scale N escala de tiempo

time sharing N (*Comput*) tiempo compartido

time sheet N = **time card**

time signal N señal *f* horaria

time switch N (*BRIT*) interruptor *m* (horario)

timetable ['taɪmteɪbl] N horario; (*programme of events etc*) programa *m*

time zone N huso horario

timid ['tɪmɪd] ADJ tímido

timidity [tɪ'mɪdɪtɪ] N timidez *f*

timidly ['tɪmɪdlɪ] ADV tímidamente

timing ['taɪmɪŋ] N (*Sport*) cronometraje *m*; **the ~ of his resignation** el momento que eligió para dimitir

timpani ['tɪmpənɪ] NPL tímpanos *mpl*

tin [tɪn] N estaño; (*also:* **tin plate**) hojalata; (*BRIT: can*) lata

tinfoil ['tɪnfɔɪl] N papel *m* de estaño

tinge [tɪndʒ] N matiz *m* ▶ VT: **tinged with** teñido de

tingle ['tɪŋgl] N hormigueo ▶ VI (*cheeks, skin: from cold*) sentir comezón; (: *from bad circulation*) sentir hormigueo; **to ~ with** estremecerse de

tinker ['tɪŋkər] N calderero(-a); (*gipsy*) gitano(-a) ▶ **tinker with** VT FUS jugar con, tocar

tinkle ['tɪŋkl] VI tintinear

tin mine N mina de estaño

tinned [tɪnd] ADJ (*BRIT: food*) en lata, en conserva

tinnitus ['tɪnɪtəs] N (*Med*) acúfeno
tinny ['tɪnɪ] ADJ (*sound, taste*) metálico; (*pej: car*) poco sólido, de pacotilla
tin opener [-əupnəʳ] N (*BRIT*) abrelatas *m inv*
tinsel ['tɪnsl] N oropel *m*
tint [tɪnt] N matiz *m*; (*for hair*) tinte *m* ▶ VT (*hair*) teñir
tinted ['tɪntɪd] ADJ (*hair*) teñido; (*glass, spectacles*) ahumado
tiny ['taɪnɪ] ADJ minúsculo, pequeñito
tip [tɪp] N (*end*) punta; (*gratuity*) propina; (*BRIT: for rubbish*) vertedero; (*advice*) consejo ▶ VT (*waiter*) dar una propina a; (*tilt*) inclinar; (*empty: also: **tip out***) vaciar, echar; (*predict: winner*) pronosticar; (*: horse*) recomendar; **he tipped out the contents of the box** volcó el contenido de la caja
  ▶ **tip off** VT avisar, poner sobre aviso a
  ▶ **tip over** VT volcar ▶ VI volcarse
tip-off ['tɪpɔf] N (*hint*) advertencia
tipped [tɪpt] ADJ (*BRIT: cigarette*) con filtro
Tipp-Ex® ['tɪpɛks] N Tipp-Ex® *m*
tipple ['tɪpl] N (*BRIT*): **his ~ is Cointreau** bebe Cointreau
tipster ['tɪpstəʳ] N (*Racing*) pronosticador(a) *m/f*
tipsy ['tɪpsɪ] ADJ alegre, achispado
tiptoe ['tɪptəu] N (*BRIT*): **on ~** de puntillas
tiptop ['tɪptɔp] ADJ: **in ~ condition** en perfectas condiciones
tirade [taɪ'reɪd] N diatriba
tire ['taɪəʳ] N (*US*) = **tyre** ▶ VT cansar ▶ VI (*gen*) cansarse; (*become bored*) aburrirse
  ▶ **tire out** VT agotar, rendir
tired ['taɪəd] ADJ cansado; **to be ~ of sth** estar harto de algo; **to be/feel/look ~** estar/sentirse/parecer cansado
tiredness ['taɪədnɪs] N cansancio
tireless ['taɪəlɪs] ADJ incansable
tirelessly ['taɪəlɪslɪ] ADV incansablemente
tire pressure N (*US*) = **tyre pressure**
tiresome ['taɪəsəm] ADJ aburrido
tiring ['taɪrɪŋ] ADJ cansado
tissue ['tɪʃuː] N tejido; (*paper handkerchief*) pañuelo de papel, kleenex® *m*
tissue paper N papel *m* de seda
tit [tɪt] N (*bird*) herrerillo común; **to give ~ for tat** dar ojo por ojo
titbit ['tɪtbɪt], (*US*) **tidbit** ['tɪdbɪt] N (*food*) golosina; (*news*) pedazo
titillate ['tɪtɪleɪt] VT estimular, excitar
titillation [tɪtɪ'leɪʃən] N estimulación *f*, excitación *f*
titivate ['tɪtɪveɪt] VT emperejilar
title ['taɪtl] N título; (*Law: right*): **~ (to)** derecho (a)
title deed N (*Law*) título de propiedad
title page N portada
title role N papel *m* principal

titter ['tɪtəʳ] VI reírse entre dientes
tittle-tattle ['tɪtltætl] N chismes *mpl*
titular ['tɪtjuləʳ] ADJ (*in name only*) nominal
T-junction ['tiːdʒʌŋkʃən] N cruce *m* en T
TM ABBR (= *trademark*) marca de fábrica; = **transcendental meditation**
TN ABBR (*US*) = **Tennessee**
TNT N ABBR (= *trinitrotuluene*) TNT *m*

(KEYWORD)

to [tuː, tə] PREP **1** (*direction*) a; **to go to France/London/school/the station** ir a Francia/Londres/al colegio/a la estación; **to go to Claude's/the doctor's** ir a casa de Claude/al médico; **the road to Edinburgh** la carretera de Edimburgo; **to the left/right** a la izquierda/derecha
2 (*as far as*) hasta, a; **from here to London** de aquí a *or* hasta Londres; **to count to 10** contar hasta 10; **from 40 to 50 people** entre 40 y 50 personas
3 (*with expressions of time*): **a quarter/twenty to five** las cinco menos cuarto/veinte
4 (*for, of*): **the key to the front door** la llave de la puerta principal; **she is secretary to the director** es la secretaria del director; **a letter to his wife** una carta a *or* para su mujer
5 (*expressing indirect object*) a; **to give sth to sb** darle algo a algn; **give it to me** dámelo; **to talk to sb** hablar con algn; **to be a danger to sb** ser un peligro para algn; **to carry out repairs to sth** hacer reparaciones en algo
6 (*in relation to*): **3 goals to 2** 3 goles a 2; **30 miles to the gallon** ≈ 9,4 litros a los cien (kilómetros); **8 apples to the kilo** 8 manzanas por kilo
7 (*purpose, result*): **to come to sb's aid** venir en auxilio *or* ayuda de algn; **to sentence sb to death** condenar a algn a muerte; **to my great surprise** con gran sorpresa mía
  ▶ INFIN PARTICLE **1** (*simple infin*): **to go/eat** ir/comer
2 (*following another vb; see also relevant vb*): **to want/try/start to do** querer/intentar/empezar a hacer
3 (*with vb omitted*): **I don't want to** no quiero
4 (*purpose, result*) para; **I did it to help you** lo hice para ayudarte; **he came to see you** vino a verte
5 (*equivalent to relative clause*): **I have things to do** tengo cosas que hacer; **the main thing is to try** lo principal es intentarlo
6 (*after adj etc*): **ready to go** listo para irse; **too old to ...** demasiado viejo (como) para ...
  ▶ ADV: **pull/push the door to** tirar de/empujar la puerta; **to go to and fro** ir y venir

t

toad [təud] N sapo

toadstool ['təudstu:l] N seta venenosa

toady ['təudɪ] N pelota mf ▸ vɪ: **to ~ to sb** hacer la pelota or dar coba a algn

toast [təust] N (Culin: also: **piece of toast**) tostada; (drink, speech) brindis m inv ▸ vᴛ (Culin) tostar; (drink to) brindar por

toaster ['təustəʳ] N tostador m

toastmaster ['təustmɑ:stəʳ] N persona que propone brindis y anuncia a los oradores en un banquete

toast rack N rejilla para tostadas

tobacco [tə'bækəu] N tabaco; **pipe ~** tabaco de pipa

tobacconist [tə'bækənɪst] N estanquero(-a), tabaquero(-a) (LAM); **~'s (shop)** (BRIT) estanco, tabaquería (LAM)

tobacco plantation N plantación f de tabaco, tabacal m

Tobago [tə'beɪgəu] N see **Trinidad and Tobago**

toboggan [tə'bɔgən] N tobogán m

today [tə'deɪ] ADV, N (also fig) hoy m; **what day is it ~?** ¿qué día es hoy?; **what date is it ~?** ¿a qué fecha estamos hoy?; **~ is the 4th of March** hoy es el 4 de marzo; **~'s paper** el periódico de hoy; **a fortnight ~** de hoy en 15 días, dentro de 15 días

toddle ['tɔdl] vɪ empezar a andar, dar los primeros pasos

toddler ['tɔdləʳ] N niño(-a) (que empieza a andar)

toddy ['tɔdɪ] N ponche m

to-do [tə'du:] N (fuss) lío

toe [təu] N dedo (del pie); (of shoe) punta ▸ vᴛ: **to ~ the line** (fig) acatar las normas; **big/little ~** dedo gordo/pequeño del pie

TOEFL ['təufl] N ABBR = **Test(ing) of English as a Foreign Language**

toehold ['təuhəuld] N punto de apoyo (para el pie)

toenail ['təuneɪl] N uña del pie

toffee ['tɔfɪ] N caramelo

toffee apple N (BRIT) manzana de caramelo

tofu ['təufu:] N tofu m

toga ['təugə] N toga

together [tə'gɛðəʳ] ADV juntos; (at same time) al mismo tiempo, a la vez; **~ with** junto con

togetherness [tə'gɛðənɪs] N compañerismo

toggle switch ['tɔgl-] N (Comput) conmutador m de palanca

Togo ['təugəu] N Togo

togs [tɔgz] NPL (inf: clothes) atuendo, ropa

toil [tɔɪl] N trabajo duro, labor f ▸ vɪ esforzarse

toilet ['tɔɪlət] N (BRIT: lavatory) servicios mpl, baño ▸ CPD (bag, soap etc) de aseo; **to go to the ~** ir al baño; see also **toilets**

toilet bag N neceser m, bolsa de aseo

toilet bowl N taza (de retrete)

toilet paper N papel m higiénico

toiletries ['tɔɪlətrɪz] NPL artículos mpl de aseo; (make-up etc) artículos mpl de tocador

toilet roll N rollo de papel higiénico

toilets ['tɔɪləts] NPL (BRIT) servicios mpl

toilet soap N jabón m de tocador

toilet water N (agua de) colonia

to-ing and fro-ing ['tuɪŋən'frəuɪŋ] N vaivén m

token ['təukən] N (sign) señal f, muestra; (souvenir) recuerdo; (voucher) vale m; (disc) ficha ▸ CPD (fee, strike) nominal, simbólico; **book/record ~** (BRIT) vale m para comprar libros/discos; **by the same ~** (fig) por la misma razón

tokenism ['təukənɪzəm] N (Pol) política simbólica or de fachada

Tokyo ['təukjəu] N Tokio

told [təuld] PT, PP of **tell**

tolerable ['tɔlərəbl] ADJ (bearable) soportable; (fairly good) pasable

tolerably ['tɔlərəblɪ] ADV (good, comfortable) medianamente

tolerance ['tɔlərns] N (also Tech) tolerancia

tolerant ['tɔlərnt] ADJ: **~ of** tolerante con

tolerantly ['tɔlərntlɪ] ADV con tolerancia

tolerate ['tɔləreɪt] vᴛ tolerar

toleration [tɔlə'reɪʃən] N tolerancia

toll [təul] N (of casualties) número de víctimas; (tax, charge) peaje m ▸ vɪ (bell) doblar

toll bridge N puente m de peaje

toll call N (US Tel) conferencia, llamada interurbana

toll-free ['tɔl'fri:] ADJ, ADV (US) gratis

toll road N carretera de peaje

tomato [tə'mɑ:təu] (pl **tomatoes**) N tomate m

tomato puree N puré m de tomate

tomato sauce N salsa de tomate

tomb [tu:m] N tumba

tombola [tɔm'bəulə] N tómbola

tomboy ['tɔmbɔɪ] N marimacho

tombstone ['tu:mstəun] N lápida

tomcat ['tɔmkæt] N gato

tomorrow [tə'mɔrəu] ADV, N (also fig) mañana; **the day after ~** pasado mañana; **~ morning** mañana por la mañana; **a week ~** de mañana en ocho (días)

ton [tʌn] N tonelada; **tons of** (inf) montones de

tonal ['təunl] ADJ tonal

tone [təun] N tono ▸ vɪ armonizar; **dialling ~** (Tel) señal f para marcar

▸ **tone down** vᴛ (criticism) suavizar; (colour) atenuar

▸ **tone up** vᴛ (muscles) tonificar

tone-deaf [təun'dɛf] ADJ sin oído musical

toner ['təunəʳ] N (for photocopier) virador m

Tonga ['tɔŋə] N Islas fpl Tonga

tongs [tɒŋz] N PL (for coal) tenazas fpl; (for hair) tenacillas fpl

tongue [tʌŋ] N lengua; **~ in cheek** en broma

tongue-tied ['tʌŋtaɪd] ADJ (fig) mudo

tongue-twister ['tʌŋtwɪstər] N trabalenguas m inv

tonic ['tɒnɪk] N (Med) tónico; (Mus) tónica; (also: **tonic water**) (agua) tónica

tonight [tə'naɪt] ADV, N esta noche; **I'll see you ~** nos vemos esta noche

tonnage ['tʌnɪdʒ] N (Naut) tonelaje m

tonsil ['tɒnsl] N amígdala; **to have one's tonsils out** sacarse las amígdalas or anginas

tonsillitis [tɒnsɪ'laɪtɪs] N amigdalitis f

too [tu:] ADV, ADJ (excessively) demasiado; (very) muy; (also) también; **it's ~ sweet** está demasiado dulce; **I'm not ~ sure about that** no estoy muy seguro de eso; **I went ~** yo también fui; **~ much** adv, adj demasiado; **~ many** adj demasiados(-as); **~ bad!** ¡mala suerte!

took [tuk] PT of **take**

tool [tu:l] N herramienta; (fig: person) instrumento

toolbar ['tu:lbɑːr] N barra de herramientas

tool box N caja de herramientas

tool kit N juego de herramientas

tool shed N cobertizo (para herramientas)

toot [tu:t] N (of horn) bocinazo; (of whistle) silbido ▸ VI (with car horn) tocar la bocina

tooth [tu:θ] (pl **teeth** [ti:θ]) N (Anat, Tech) diente m; (molar) muela; **to clean one's teeth** lavarse los dientes; **to have a ~ out** sacarse una muela; **by the skin of one's teeth** por un pelo

toothache ['tu:θeɪk] N dolor m de muelas

toothbrush ['tu:θbrʌʃ] N cepillo de dientes

toothpaste ['tu:θpeɪst] N pasta de dientes

toothpick ['tu:θpɪk] N palillo

tooth powder N polvos mpl dentífricos

top [tɒp] N (of mountain) cumbre f, cima; (of head) coronilla; (of ladder) alto; (of cupboard, table) superficie f; (lid: of box, jar) tapa; (: of bottle) tapón m; (of list, table, queue, page) cabeza; (toy) peonza; (Dress: blouse) blusa; (: T-shirt) camiseta; (: of pyjamas) chaqueta ▸ ADJ de arriba; (in rank) principal, primero; (best) mejor ▸ VT (exceed) exceder; (be first in) encabezar; **on ~ of** sobre, encima de; **from ~ to bottom** de pies a cabeza; **the ~ of the milk** la nata; **at the ~ of the stairs** en lo alto de la escalera; **at the ~ of the street** al final de la calle; **at the ~ of one's voice** (fig) a voz en grito; **over the ~** (inf) excesivo, desmesurado; **to go over the ~** pasarse; **at ~ speed** a máxima velocidad; **a ~ surgeon** un cirujano eminente

▸ **top off** (US) VT volver a llenar

▸ **top up** VT volver a llenar; (mobile phone) recargar el saldo de

topaz ['təupæz] N topacio

top-class ['tɒp'klɑːs] ADJ de primera clase

topcoat ['tɒpkəut] N sobretodo, abrigo

topflight ['tɒpflaɪt] ADJ de primera (categoría or clase)

top floor N último piso

top hat N sombrero de copa

top-heavy [tɒp'hɛvɪ] ADJ (object) con más peso en la parte superior

topic ['tɒpɪk] N tema m

topical ['tɒpɪkl] ADJ actual

topless ['tɒplɪs] ADJ (bather etc) topless inv

top-level ['tɒplɛvl] ADJ (talks) al más alto nivel

topmost ['tɒpməust] ADJ más alto

top-notch ['tɒp'nɒtʃ] ADJ (inf) de primerísima categoría

topography [tə'pɒgrəfɪ] N topografía

topping ['tɒpɪŋ] N (Culin): **with a ~ of cream** con nata por encima

topple ['tɒpl] VT volcar, derribar ▸ VI caerse

top-ranking ['tɒpræŋkɪŋ] ADJ de alto rango

top-secret [tɒp'si:krɪt] ADJ de alto secreto

top-security ['tɒpsɪ'kjuərɪtɪ] ADJ (BRIT) de máxima seguridad

topsy-turvy ['tɒpsɪ'tə:vɪ] ADJ, ADV patas arriba

top-up ['tɒpʌp] N: **would you like a ~?** ¿quiere que se lo vuelva a llenar?

top-up card N (for mobile phone) tarjeta prepago

top-up loan N (BRIT) préstamo complementario

torch [tɔːtʃ] N antorcha; (BRIT: electric) linterna

tore [tɔːr] PT of **tear**¹

torment N ['tɔːmɛnt] tormento ▸ VT [tɔː'mɛnt] atormentar; (fig: annoy) fastidiar

torn [tɔːn] PP of **tear**¹

tornado [tɔː'neɪdəu] (pl **tornadoes**) N tornado

torpedo [tɔː'piːdəu] (pl **torpedoes**) N torpedo

torpedo boat N torpedero, lancha torpedera

torpor ['tɔːpər] N letargo

torrent ['tɒrnt] N torrente m

torrential [tɔː'rɛnʃl] ADJ torrencial

torrid ['tɒrɪd] ADJ tórrido; (fig) apasionado

torso ['tɔːsəu] N torso

tortoise ['tɔːtəs] N tortuga

tortoiseshell ['tɔːtəʃɛl] ADJ de carey

tortuous ['tɔːtjuəs] ADJ tortuoso

torture ['tɔːtʃər] N tortura ▸ VT torturar; (fig) atormentar

torturer ['tɔːtʃərər] N torturador(a) m/f

Tory ['tɔːrɪ] ADJ, N (BRIT Pol) conservador(a) m/f

toss [tɒs] VT tirar, echar; (head) sacudir ▸ N (movement: of head etc) sacudida; (: of coin) tirada, echada (LAM); **to ~ a coin** echar a cara o cruz; **to ~ up for sth** jugar algo a cara o cruz; **to ~ and turn** (*in bed*) dar vueltas (en la cama); **to win/lose the ~** (*also Sport*) ganar/perder (a cara o cruz)

tot [tɔt] N (*BRIT: drink*) copita; (*child*) nene(-a) *m/f*
  ▶ **tot up** VT sumar

total ['təʊtl] ADJ total, entero; (*emphatic: failure etc*) completo, total ▶ N total *m*, suma ▶ VT (*add up*) sumar; (*amount to*) ascender a; **grand ~** cantidad *f* total; (*cost*) importe *m* total; **in ~** en total, en suma

totalitarian [təʊtælɪ'tɛərɪən] ADJ totalitario

totality [təʊ'tælɪtɪ] N totalidad *f*

total loss N siniestro total

totally ['təʊtəlɪ] ADV totalmente

tote [təʊt] VT (*inf*) acarrear, cargar con

tote bag N bolsa

totem pole ['təʊtəm-] N poste *m* totémico

totter ['tɔtəʳ] VI tambalearse

touch [tʌtʃ] N (*sense*) tacto; (*contact*) contacto; (*Football*) lateral *m* ▶ VT tocar; (*emotionally*) conmover; **a ~ of** (*fig*) una pizca *or* un poquito de; **to get in ~ with sb** ponerse en contacto con algn; **I'll be in ~** le llamaré/escribiré; **to lose ~** (*friends*) perder contacto; **to be out of ~ with events** no estar al corriente (de los acontecimientos); **the personal ~** el toque personal; **to put the finishing touches to sth** dar el último toque a algo; **no artist in the country can ~ him** no hay artista en todo el país que le iguale
  ▶ **touch down** VI (*on land*) aterrizar
  ▶ **touch on** VT FUS (*topic*) aludir (brevemente) a
  ▶ **touch up** VT (*paint*) retocar

touch-and-go ['tʌtʃən'gəʊ] ADJ arriesgado

touchdown ['tʌtʃdaʊn] N aterrizaje *m*; (*US Football*) ensayo

touched [tʌtʃt] ADJ conmovido; (*inf*) chiflado

touchiness ['tʌtʃɪnɪs] N susceptibilidad *f*

touching ['tʌtʃɪŋ] ADJ conmovedor(a)

touchline ['tʌtʃlaɪn] N (*Sport*) línea de banda

touch screen N (*Tech*) pantalla táctil; **~ mobile** móvil *m* con pantalla táctil; **~ technology** tecnología táctil

touch-sensitive ['tʌtʃ'sɛnsɪtɪv] ADJ táctil, sensible al tacto

touch-type ['tʌtʃtaɪp] VI mecanografiar al tacto

touchy ['tʌtʃɪ] ADJ (*person*) quisquilloso

tough [tʌf] ADJ (*meat*) duro; (*journey*) penoso; (*task, problem, situation*) difícil; (*resistant*) resistente; (*person*) fuerte; (*: pej*) bruto ▶ N (*gangster etc*) gorila *m*; **they got ~ with the workers** se pusieron muy duros con los trabajadores

toughen ['tʌfn] VT endurecer

toughness ['tʌfnɪs] N dureza; (*resistance*) resistencia; (*strictness*) inflexibilidad *f*

toupée ['tu:peɪ] N peluquín *m*

tour ['tʊəʳ] N viaje *m*; (*also*: **package tour**) viaje *m* con todo incluido; (*of town, museum*) visita ▶ VT viajar por; **to go on a ~ of** (*region, country*) ir de viaje por; (*museum, castle*) visitar; **to go on ~** partir *or* ir de gira

tour guide N guía *mf* turístico(-a)

touring ['tʊərɪŋ] N viajes *mpl* turísticos, turismo

tourism ['tʊərɪzm] N turismo

tourist ['tʊərɪst] N turista *mf* ▶ CPD turístico; **the ~ trade** el turismo

tourist class N (*Aviat*) clase *f* turista

tourist office N oficina de turismo

tournament ['tʊənəmənt] N torneo

tourniquet ['tʊənɪkeɪ] N (*Med*) torniquete *m*

tour operator N touroperador(a) *m/f*, operador(a) *m/f* turístico(-a)

tousled ['taʊzld] ADJ (*hair*) despeinado

tout [taʊt] VI: **to ~ for business** solicitar clientes ▶ N: **ticket ~** revendedor(a) *m/f*

tow [təʊ] N: **to give sb a ~** (*Aut*) remolcar a algn ▶ VT remolcar; **"on** *or* (*US*) **in ~"** (*Aut*) "a remolque"
  ▶ **tow away** VT llevarse a remolque

toward [tə'wɔːd], **towards** [tə'wɔːdz] PREP hacia; (*of attitude*) respecto a, con; (*of purpose*) para; **~ noon** alrededor de mediodía; **~ the end of the year** hacia finales de año; **to feel friendly ~ sb** sentir amistad hacia algn

towel ['taʊəl] N toalla; **to throw in the ~** (*fig*) darse por vencido, renunciar

towelling ['taʊəlɪŋ] N (*fabric*) felpa

towel rail, (*US*) **towel rack** N toallero

tower ['taʊəʳ] N torre *f* ▶ VI (*building, mountain*) elevarse; **to ~ above** *or* **over sth/sb** dominar algo/destacarse sobre algn

tower block N (*BRIT*) bloque *m* de pisos

towering ['taʊərɪŋ] ADJ muy alto, imponente

town [taʊn] N ciudad *f*; **to go to ~** ir a la ciudad; (*fig*) tirar la casa por la ventana; **in the ~** en la ciudad; **to be out of ~** estar fuera de la ciudad

town centre N centro de la ciudad

town clerk N secretario(-a) del Ayuntamiento

town council N Ayuntamiento, consejo municipal

town crier [-kraɪəʳ] N (*BRIT*) pregonero

town hall N ayuntamiento

townie ['taʊnɪ] N (*BRIT inf*) urbanita *mf*, persona de la ciudad

town plan N plano de la ciudad

town planner N urbanista *mf*

town planning N urbanismo

township ['taʊnʃɪp] N *municipio habitado sólo por negros en Sudáfrica*

townspeople ['taʊnzpiːpl] NPL gente *f* de ciudad

towpath ['təupɑːθ] N camino de sirga
towrope ['təurəup] N cable m de remolque
tow truck N (US) camión m grúa
toxic ['tɔksɪk] ADJ tóxico
toxic asset N (Econ) activo tóxico
toxic bank N (Econ) banco malo
toxin ['tɔksɪn] N toxina
toy [tɔɪ] N juguete m
  ▶ **toy with** VT FUS jugar con; (idea) acariciar
toyshop ['tɔɪʃɔp] N juguetería
toy train N tren m de juguete
trace [treɪs] N rastro ▶ VT (draw) trazar,
  delinear; (locate) encontrar; **there was no ~
  of it** no había ningún indicio de ello
trace element N oligoelemento
trachea [trə'kɪə] N (Anat) tráquea
tracing paper ['treɪsɪŋ-] N papel m de calco
track [træk] N (mark) huella, pista; (path: gen)
  camino, senda; (: of bullet etc) trayectoria;
  (: of suspect, animal) pista, rastro; (Rail) vía;
  (Comput, Sport) pista; (on album) canción f ▶ VT
  seguir la pista de; **to keep ~ of** mantenerse
  al tanto de, seguir; **a four-~ tape** una cinta
  de cuatro pistas; **the first ~ on the record/
  tape** la primera canción en el disco/la cinta;
  to be on the right ~ (fig) ir por buen camino
  ▶ **track down** VT (person) localizar; (sth lost)
  encontrar
tracker dog ['trækə^r-] N (BRIT) perro
  rastreador
track events NPL (Sport) pruebas fpl en pista
tracking station ['trækɪŋ-] N (Space)
  estación f de seguimiento
track meet N (US) concurso de carreras y
  saltos
track record N: **to have a good ~** (fig) tener
  un buen historial
tracksuit ['træksuːt] N chandal m
tract [trækt] N (Geo) región f; (pamphlet) folleto
traction ['trækʃən] N (Aut: power) tracción f;
  in ~ (Med) en tracción
traction engine N locomotora de tracción
tractor ['træktə^r] N tractor m
trade [treɪd] N comercio, negocio; (skill, job)
  oficio, empleo; (industry) industria ▶ VI
  negociar, comerciar; **foreign ~** comercio
  exterior ▶ VT (exchange): **to ~ sth (for sth)**
  cambiar algo (por algo)
  ▶ **trade in** VT (old car etc) ofrecer como parte
  del pago
trade barrier N barrera comercial
trade deficit N déficit m comercial
Trade Descriptions Act N (BRIT) ley sobre
  descripciones comerciales
trade discount N descuento comercial
trade fair N feria de muestras
trade-in ['treɪdɪn] ADJ: **~ price/value** precio/
  valor de un artículo usado que se descuenta del
  precio de otro nuevo

trademark ['treɪdmɑːk] N marca de fábrica
trade mission N misión f comercial
trade name N marca registrada
trade-off ['treɪdɔf] N: **a ~ (between)** un
  equilibrio (entre)
trade price N precio al detallista
trader ['treɪdə^r] N comerciante mf
trade reference N referencia comercial
trade secret N secreto profesional
tradesman ['treɪdzmən] N (irreg) (shopkeeper)
  comerciante mf
trade union N sindicato
trade unionist [-'juːnjənɪst] N sindicalista
  mf
trade wind N viento alisio
trading ['treɪdɪŋ] N comercio
trading account N cuenta de compraventa
trading estate N (BRIT) polígono industrial
trading stamp N cupón m, sello de prima
tradition [trə'dɪʃən] N tradición f
traditional [trə'dɪʃənl] ADJ tradicional
traditionally [trə'dɪʃənlɪ] ADV
  tradicionalmente
traffic ['træfɪk] N tráfico, circulación f,
  tránsito ▶ VI: **to ~ in** (pej: liquor, drugs) traficar
  en; **air ~** tráfico aéreo
traffic calming [-'kɑːmɪŋ] N reducción f de
  la velocidad de la circulación
traffic circle N (US) rotonda, glorieta
traffic island N refugio, isleta
traffic jam N embotellamiento, atasco
trafficker ['træfɪkə^r] N traficante mf
traffic lights NPL semáforo sg
traffic offence, (US) **traffic violation** N
  infracción f de tráfico
traffic warden N guardia mf de tráfico
tragedy ['trædʒədɪ] N tragedia
tragic ['trædʒɪk] ADJ trágico
tragically ['trædʒɪkəlɪ] ADV trágicamente
trail [treɪl] N (tracks) rastro, pista; (path)
  camino, sendero; (dust, smoke) estela ▶ VT
  (drag) arrastrar; (follow) seguir la pista de;
  (follow closely) vigilar ▶ VI arrastrarse; (in
  contest etc) ir perdiendo; **to be on sb's ~**
  seguir la pista de algn
  ▶ **trail away, trail off** VI (sound) desvanecerse;
  (interest, voice) desaparecer
  ▶ **trail behind** VI quedar a la zaga
trailer ['treɪlə^r] N (Aut) remolque m; (caravan)
  caravana; (Cine) trailer m, avance m
trailer truck N (US) camión articulado
train [treɪn] N tren m; (of dress) cola; (series):
  ~ of events curso de los acontecimientos
  ▶ VT (educate) formar; (teach skills to) adiestrar;
  (sportsman) entrenar; (dog) adiestrar,
  amaestrar; (point: gun etc): **to ~ on** apuntar a
  ▶ VI (Sport) entrenarse; (be educated, learn a skill)
  formarse; **to go by ~** ir en tren; **to ~ as a
  teacher** etc estudiar para profesor etc; **one's**

t

~ **of thought** el razonamiento de algn; **to ~ sb to do sth** enseñar a algn a hacer algo

train attendant N (*US Rail*) empleado(-a) de coches-cama

trained [treɪnd] ADJ (*worker*) cualificado; (*animal*) amaestrado

trainee [treɪˈniː] N trabajador(a) *m/f* en prácticas ▸ CPD: **he's a ~ teacher** (*primary*) es estudiante de magisterio; (*secondary*) está haciendo las prácticas del I.C.E.

trainer [ˈtreɪnəʳ] N (*Sport*) entrenador(a) *m/f*; (*of animals*) domador(a) *m/f*; **trainers** NPL (*shoes*) zapatillas *fpl* (de deporte)

training [ˈtreɪnɪŋ] N formación *f*; entrenamiento; **to be in ~** (*Sport*) estar entrenando

training college N (*gen*) colegio de formación profesional; (*for teachers*) escuela normal

training course N curso de formación

training shoes NPL zapatillas *fpl* (de deporte)

train wreck N (*fig*) destrozo; **he's a complete ~** está completamente destrozado

traipse [treɪps] VI andar penosamente

trait [treɪt] N rasgo

traitor [ˈtreɪtəʳ] N traidor(a) *m/f*

trajectory [trəˈdʒɛktəri] N trayectoria, curso

tram [træm] N (*BRIT: also:* **tramcar**) tranvía *m*

tramline [ˈtræmlaɪn] N carril *m* de tranvía

tramp [træmp] N (*person*) vagabundo(-a); (*inf, pej: woman*) puta ▸ VI andar con pasos pesados

trample [ˈtræmpl] VT: **to ~ (underfoot)** pisotear

trampoline [ˈtræmpəliːn] N trampolín *m*

trance [trɑːns] N trance *m*; **to go into a ~** entrar en trance

tranquil [ˈtræŋkwɪl] ADJ tranquilo

tranquillity, (*US*) **tranquility** [træŋˈkwɪlɪti] N tranquilidad *f*

tranquillizer, (*US*) **tranquilizer** [ˈtræŋkwɪlaɪzəʳ] N (*Med*) tranquilizante *m*

trans- [trænz] PREF trans-, tras-

transact [trænˈzækt] VT (*business*) tramitar

transaction [trænˈzækʃən] N transacción *f*, operación *f*; **cash transactions** transacciones al contado

transatlantic [ˈtrænzətˈlæntɪk] ADJ transatlántico

transcend [trænˈsɛnd] VT rebasar

transcendent [trænˈsɛndənt] ADJ trascendente

transcendental [trænsɛnˈdɛntl] ADJ: **~ meditation** meditación *f* transcendental

transcribe [trænˈskraɪb] VT transcribir, copiar

transcript [ˈtrænskrɪpt] N copia

transcription [trænˈskrɪpʃən] N transcripción *f*

transept [ˈtrænsɛpt] N crucero

transfer N [ˈtrænsfəʳ] transferencia; (*Sport*) traspaso; (*picture, design*) calcomanía ▸ VT [trænsˈfəːʳ] trasladar, pasar; **to ~ the charges** (*BRIT Tel*) llamar a cobro revertido; **by bank ~** por transferencia bancaria *or* giro bancario; **to ~ money from one account to another** transferir dinero de una cuenta a otra; **to ~ sth to sb's name** transferir algo al nombre de algn

transferable [trænsˈfəːrəbl] ADJ: **not ~** intransferible

transfix [trænsˈfɪks] VT traspasar; (*fig*): **transfixed with fear** paralizado por el miedo

transform [trænsˈfɔːm] VT transformar

transformation [trænsfəˈmeɪʃən] N transformación *f*

transformer [trænsˈfɔːməʳ] N (*Elec*) transformador *m*

transfusion [trænsˈfjuːʒən] N transfusión *f*

transgress [trænsˈɡrɛs] VT (*go beyond*) traspasar; (*violate*) violar, infringir

tranship [trænˈʃɪp] VT trasbordar

transient [ˈtrænzɪənt] ADJ transitorio

transistor [trænˈzɪstəʳ] N (*Elec*) transistor *m*

transistorized [trænˈzɪstəraɪzd] ADJ (*circuit*) transistorizado

transistor radio N transistor *m*

transit [ˈtrænzɪt] N: **in ~** en tránsito

transit camp N campamento de tránsito

transition [trænˈzɪʃən] N transición *f*

transitional [trænˈzɪʃənl] ADJ transitorio

transition period N período de transición

transitive [ˈtrænzɪtɪv] ADJ (*Ling*) transitivo

transitively [ˈtrænzɪtɪvli] ADV transitivamente

transitory [ˈtrænzɪtəri] ADJ transitorio

transit visa N visado de tránsito

translate [trænzˈleɪt] VT: **to ~ (from/into)** traducir (de/a)

translation [trænzˈleɪʃən] N traducción *f*

translator [trænzˈleɪtəʳ] N traductor(a) *m/f*

translucent [trænzˈluːsnt] ADJ traslúcido

transmission [trænzˈmɪʃən] N transmisión *f*

transmit [trænzˈmɪt] VT transmitir

transmitter [trænzˈmɪtəʳ] N transmisor *m*; (*station*) emisora

transparency [trænsˈpɛərnsi] N (*BRIT Phot*) diapositiva

transparent [trænsˈpærnt] ADJ transparente

transpire [trænsˈpaɪəʳ] VI (*turn out*) resultar (ser); (*happen*) ocurrir, suceder; (*become known*): **it finally transpired that ...** por fin se supo que ...

transplant VT [trænsˈplɑːnt] transplantar ▸ N [ˈtrænsplɑːnt] (*Med*) transplante *m*; **to have a heart ~** hacerse un transplante de corazón

transport N [ˈtrænspɔːt] transporte *m* ▸ VT [trænsˈpɔːt] transportar; **public ~** transporte *m* público

transportable [træns'pɔ:təbl] ADJ transportable

transportation [trænspɔ:'teɪʃən] N transporte m; (of prisoners) deportación f

transport café N (BRIT) bar-restaurante m de carretera

transpose [træns'pəuz] VT transponer

transsexual [trænz'sɛksjuəl] ADJ, N transexual mf

transverse ['trænzvə:s] ADJ transverso, transversal

transvestite [trænz'vɛstaɪt] N travesti mf

trap [træp] N (snare, trick) trampa; (carriage) cabriolé m ▶ VT coger (SP) or agarrar (LAM) en una trampa; (trick) engañar; (confine) atrapar; (immobilize) bloquear; (jam) atascar; **to set** or **lay a ~ (for sb)** poner(le) una trampa (a algn); **to ~ one's finger in the door** pillarse el dedo en la puerta

trap door N escotilla

trapeze [trə'pi:z] N trapecio

trapper ['træpə'] N trampero, cazador m

trappings ['træpɪŋz] NPL adornos mpl

trash [træʃ] N basura; (inf: nonsense) tonterías fpl; **the book/film is ~** el libro/la película no vale nada

trash can N (US) cubo, balde m (LAM) or bote m (LAM) de la basura

trash can liner N (US) bolsa de basura

trashy ['træʃɪ] ADJ (inf) chungo

trauma ['trɔ:mə] N trauma m

traumatic [trɔ:'mætɪk] ADJ traumático

travel ['trævl] N viaje m ▶ VI viajar ▶ VT (distance) recorrer; **this wine doesn't ~ well** este vino pierde con los viajes

travel agency N agencia de viajes

travel agent N agente mf de viajes

travel brochure N folleto turístico

travel insurance N seguro de viaje

traveller, (US) **traveler** ['trævlə'] N viajero(-a); (Comm) viajante mf

traveller's cheque, (US) **traveler's check** N cheque m de viaje

travelling, (US) **traveling** ['trævlɪŋ] N los viajes, el viajar ▶ ADJ (circus, exhibition) ambulante ▶ CPD (bag, clock) de viaje

travelling expenses, (US) **traveling expenses** NPL dietas fpl

travelling salesman, (US) **traveling salesman** N (irreg) viajante m

travelogue ['trævəlɔg] N (book) relación f de viajes; (film) documental m de viajes; (talk) recuento de viajes

travel-sick ['trævəlsɪk] ADJ: **to get ~** marearse al viajar

travel sickness N mareo

traverse ['trævəs] VT atravesar

travesty ['trævəstɪ] N parodia

trawler ['trɔ:lə'] N pesquero de arrastre

tray [treɪ] N (for carrying) bandeja; (on desk) cajón m

treacherous ['trɛtʃərəs] ADJ traidor(a); **road conditions are ~** el estado de las carreteras es peligroso

treachery ['trɛtʃərɪ] N traición f

treacle ['tri:kl] N (BRIT) melaza

tread [trɛd] (pt **trod** [trɔd], pp **trodden** ['trɔdn]) N paso, pisada; (of tyre) banda de rodadura ▶ VI pisar
▶ **tread on** VT FUS pisar

treas. ABBR = **treasurer**

treason ['tri:zn] N traición f

treasure ['trɛʒə'] N tesoro ▶ VT (value) apreciar, valorar

treasure hunt N caza del tesoro

treasurer ['trɛʒərə'] N tesorero(-a)

treasury ['trɛʒərɪ] N: **the T~**, (US) **the T~ Department** ≈ el Ministerio de Economía y de Hacienda

treasury bill N bono del Tesoro

treat [tri:t] N (present) regalo; (pleasure) placer m ▶ VT tratar; (consider) considerar; **to give sb a ~** hacer un regalo a algn; **to ~ sb to sth** invitar a algn a algo; **to ~ sth as a joke** tomar algo a broma

treatise ['tri:tɪz] N tratado

treatment ['tri:tmənt] N tratamiento; **to have ~ for sth** recibir tratamiento por algo

treaty ['tri:tɪ] N tratado

treble ['trɛbl] ADJ triple ▶ VT triplicar ▶ VI triplicarse

treble clef N (Mus) clave f de sol

tree [tri:] N árbol m

tree-lined ['tri:laɪnd] ADJ bordeado de árboles

tree trunk N tronco de árbol

trek [trɛk] N (long journey) expedición f; (tiring walk) caminata

trellis ['trɛlɪs] N enrejado

tremble ['trɛmbl] VI temblar

trembling ['trɛmblɪŋ] N temblor m ▶ ADJ tembloroso

tremendous [trɪ'mɛndəs] ADJ tremendo; (enormous) enorme; (excellent) estupendo

tremendously [trɪ'mɛndəslɪ] ADV enormemente, sobremanera; **he enjoyed it ~** lo disfrutó de lo lindo

tremor ['trɛmə'] N temblor m; (also: **earth tremor**) temblor m de tierra

trench [trɛntʃ] N zanja; (Mil) trinchera

trench coat N trinchera

trench warfare N guerra de trincheras

trend [trɛnd] N (tendency) tendencia; (of events) curso; (fashion) moda; **~ towards/ away from sth** tendencia hacia/en contra de algo; **to set the ~** marcar la pauta

trendy ['trɛndɪ] ADJ de moda

trepidation [trɛpɪ'deɪʃən] N inquietud f

trespass ['trɛspəs] VI: **to ~ on** entrar sin permiso en; **"no trespassing"** "prohibido el paso"

trespasser ['trɛspəsə^r] N intruso(-a) m/f; **"trespassers will be prosecuted"** "se procesará a los intrusos"

tress [trɛs] N guedeja

trestle ['trɛsl] N caballete m

trestle table N mesa de caballete

tri- [traɪ] PREF tri-

trial ['traɪəl] N (Law) juicio, proceso; (test: of machine etc) prueba; (hardship) desgracia; **trials** NPL (Athletics) pruebas fpl; (of horses) pruebas fpl; **to bring sb to ~ (for a crime)** llevar a algn a juicio (por un delito); **~ by jury** juicio ante jurado; **to be sent for ~** ser remitido al tribunal; **by ~ and error** a fuerza de probar

trial balance N balance m de comprobación

trial basis N: **on a ~** a modo de prueba

trial offer N oferta de prueba

trial period N periodo de prueba

trial run N prueba

triangle ['traɪæŋgl] N (Math, Mus) triángulo

triangular [traɪˈæŋgjulə^r] ADJ triangular

triathlon [traɪˈæθlən] N triatlón m

tribal ['traɪbəl] ADJ tribal

tribe [traɪb] N tribu f

tribesman ['traɪbzmən] N (irreg) miembro de una tribu

tribulation [trɪbjuˈleɪʃən] N tribulación f

tribunal [traɪˈbjuːnl] N tribunal m

tributary ['trɪbjuːtərɪ] N (river) afluente m

tribute ['trɪbjuːt] N homenaje m, tributo; **to pay ~ to** rendir homenaje a

trice [traɪs] N: **in a ~** en un santiamén

trick [trɪk] N trampa; (conjuring trick, deceit) truco; (joke) broma; (Cards) baza ▶ VT engañar; **it's a ~ of the light** es una ilusión óptica; **to play a ~ on sb** gastar una broma a algn; **that should do the ~** eso servirá; **to ~ sb out of sth** quitarle algo a algn con engaños; **to ~ sb into doing sth** hacer que algn haga algo con engaños

trickery ['trɪkərɪ] N engaño

trickle ['trɪkl] N (of water etc) hilo ▶ VI gotear

trick question N pregunta capciosa

trickster ['trɪkstə^r] N estafador(a) m/f

tricky ['trɪkɪ] ADJ difícil; (problem) delicado

tricycle ['traɪsɪkl] N triciclo

tried [traɪd] ADJ probado

trifle ['traɪfl] N bagatela; (Culin) dulce de bizcocho, gelatina, fruta y natillas ▶ ADV: **a ~ long** un pelín largo ▶ VI: **to ~ with** jugar con

trifling ['traɪflɪŋ] ADJ insignificante

trigger ['trɪgə^r] N (of gun) gatillo
▶ **trigger off** VT desencadenar

trigonometry [trɪgəˈnɒmətrɪ] N trigonometría

trilby ['trɪlbɪ] N (also: **trilby hat**) sombrero flexible or tirolés

trill [trɪl] N (of bird) gorjeo; (Mus) trino

trilogy ['trɪlədʒɪ] N trilogía

trim [trɪm] ADJ (elegant) aseado; (house, garden) en buen estado; (figure): **to be ~** tener buen talle ▶ N (haircut etc) recorte m ▶ VT (neaten) arreglar; (cut) recortar; (decorate) adornar; (Naut: a sail) orientar; **to keep in (good) ~** mantener en buen estado

trimmings ['trɪmɪŋz] NPL (extras) accesorios mpl; (cuttings) recortes mpl

Trinidad and Tobago ['trɪnɪdæd-] N Trinidad f y Tobago

Trinity ['trɪnɪtɪ] N: **the ~** la Trinidad

trinket ['trɪŋkɪt] N chuchería, baratija

trio ['triːəu] N trío

trip [trɪp] N viaje m; (excursion) excursión f; (stumble) traspié m ▶ VI (stumble) tropezar; (go lightly) andar a paso ligero; **on a ~** de viaje
▶ **trip over** VT FUS tropezar con
▶ **trip up** VI tropezar, caerse ▶ VT hacer tropezar or caer

tripartite [traɪˈpɑːtaɪt] ADJ (agreement, talks) tripartito

tripe [traɪp] N (Culin) callos mpl; (pej: rubbish) bobadas fpl

triple ['trɪpl] ADJ triple ▶ ADV: **~ the distance/ the speed** 3 veces la distancia/la velocidad

triple jump N triple salto

triplets ['trɪplɪts] NPL trillizos(-as) mpl(pl)

triplicate ['trɪplɪkət] N: **in ~** por triplicado

tripod ['traɪpɒd] N trípode m

Tripoli ['trɪpəlɪ] N Trípoli m

tripper ['trɪpə^r] N turista mf, excursionista mf

tripwire ['trɪpwaɪə^r] N cable m de trampa

trite [traɪt] ADJ trillado

triumph ['traɪʌmf] N triunfo ▶ VI: **to ~ (over)** vencer

triumphal [traɪˈʌmfl] ADJ triunfal

triumphant [traɪˈʌmfənt] ADJ triunfante

triumphantly [traɪˈʌmfəntlɪ] ADV triunfalmente, en tono triunfal

trivia ['trɪvɪə] NPL trivialidades fpl

trivial ['trɪvɪəl] ADJ insignificante, trivial

triviality [trɪvɪˈælɪtɪ] N insignificancia, trivialidad f

trivialize ['trɪvɪəlaɪz] VT trivializar

trod [trɒd] PT of **tread**

trodden ['trɒdn] PP of **tread**

troll [trɒl] N (Comput) troll m

trolley ['trɒlɪ] N carrito; (in hospital) camilla

trolley bus N trolebús m

trombone [trɒmˈbəun] N trombón m

troop [truːp] N grupo, banda; **troops** NPL (Mil) tropas fpl
▶ **troop in** VI entrar en tropel
▶ **troop out** VI salir en tropel

troop carrier N (*plane*) transporte *m* (militar); (*Naut*) buque *m* de) transporte *m*

trooper ['tru:pəʳ] N (*Mil*) soldado (de caballería); (*US: policeman*) policía *mf* montado(-a)

trooping the colour ['tru:pɪŋ-] N (*ceremony*) presentación *f* de la bandera

troopship ['tru:pʃɪp] N (buque *m* de) transporte *m*

trophy ['trəufɪ] N trofeo

tropic ['trɒpɪk] N trópico; **the tropics** los trópicos, la zona tropical; **T~ of Cancer/Capricorn** trópico de Cáncer/Capricornio

tropical ['trɒpɪkl] ADJ tropical

trot [trɒt] N trote *m* ▸ VI trotar; **on the ~** (*BRIT fig*) seguidos(-as)
  ▸ **trot out** VT (*excuse, reason*) volver a usar; (*names, facts*) sacar a relucir

trouble ['trʌbl] N problema *m*, dificultad *f*; (*worry*) preocupación *f*; (*bother, effort*) molestia, esfuerzo; (*unrest*) inquietud *f*; (*with machine etc*) fallo, avería; (*Med*): **stomach ~** problemas *mpl* gástricos ▸ VT molestar; (*worry*) preocupar, inquietar ▸ VI: **to ~ to do sth** molestarse en hacer algo; **troubles** NPL (*Pol etc*) conflictos *mpl*; **to be in ~** estar en un apuro; (*for doing wrong*) tener problemas; **to have ~ doing sth** tener dificultad en *or* para hacer algo; **to go to the ~ of doing sth** tomarse la molestia de hacer algo; **it's no ~!** ¡no es molestia (ninguna)!; **what's the ~?** ¿qué pasa?; **the ~ is …** el problema es …, lo que pasa es …; **please don't ~ yourself** por favor no se moleste

troubled ['trʌbld] ADJ (*person*) preocupado; (*epoch, life*) agitado

trouble-free ['trʌblfri:] ADJ sin problemas *or* dificultades

troublemaker ['trʌblmeɪkəʳ] N agitador(a) *m/f*

troubleshooter ['trʌblʃu:təʳ] N (*in conflict*) mediador(a) *m/f*

troublesome ['trʌblsəm] ADJ molesto, inoportuno

trouble spot N centro de fricción, punto caliente

troubling ['trʌblɪŋ] ADJ (*thought*) preocupante; **these are ~ times** son malos tiempos

trough [trɒf] N (*also*: **drinking trough**) abrevadero; (*also*: **feeding trough**) comedero; (*channel*) canal *m*

trounce [trauns] VT dar una paliza a

troupe [tru:p] N grupo

trouser press N prensa para pantalones

trousers ['trauzəz] NPL pantalones *mpl*; **short ~** pantalones *mpl* cortos

trouser suit N traje *m* de chaqueta y pantalón

trousseau ['tru:səu] (*pl* **trousseaux** *or* **trousseaus** [-z]) N ajuar *m*

trout [traut] N *pl inv* trucha

trowel ['trauəl] N paleta

truant ['truənt] N: **to play ~** (*BRIT*) hacer novillos

truce [tru:s] N tregua

truck [trʌk] N (*US*) camión *m*; (*Rail*) vagón *m*

truck driver N camionero(-a)

trucker ['trʌkəʳ] N (*esp US*) camionero(-a)

truck farm N (*US*) huerto de hortalizas

trucking ['trʌkɪŋ] N (*esp US*) transporte *m* en camión

trucking company N (*US*) compañía de transporte por carretera

truckload ['trʌkləud] N camión *m* lleno

truculent ['trʌkjulənt] ADJ agresivo

trudge [trʌdʒ] VI caminar penosamente

true [tru:] ADJ verdadero; (*accurate*) exacto; (*genuine*) auténtico; (*faithful*) fiel; (*wheel*) centrado; (*wall*) a plomo; (*beam*) alineado; **~ to life** verídico; **to come ~** realizarse, cumplirse

truffle ['trʌfl] N trufa

truly ['tru:lɪ] ADV realmente; (*faithfully*) fielmente; **yours ~** (*in letter-writing*) atentamente

trump [trʌmp] N (*Cards*) triunfo; **to turn up trumps** (*fig*) salir *or* resultar bien

trump card N triunfo; (*fig*) baza

trumped-up ['trʌmptʌp] ADJ inventado

trumpet ['trʌmpɪt] N trompeta

truncated [trʌŋ'keɪtɪd] ADJ truncado

truncheon ['trʌntʃən] N (*BRIT*) porra

trundle ['trʌndl] VT, VI: **to ~ along** rodar haciendo ruido

trunk [trʌŋk] N (*of tree, person*) tronco; (*of elephant*) trompa; (*case*) baúl *m*; (*US Aut*) maletero, baúl *m* (*LAM*)

trunk call N (*BRIT Tel*) llamada interurbana

trunk road N carretera principal

trunks [trʌŋks] NPL (*also*: **swimming trunks**) bañador *m*

truss [trʌs] N (*Med*) braguero ▸ VT: **to ~ (up)** atar

trust [trʌst] N confianza; (*Comm*) trust *m*; (*Law*) fideicomiso ▸ VT (*rely on*) tener confianza en; **to ~ sth to sb** (*entrust*) confiar algo a algn; **to ~ (that)** (*hope*) esperar (que); **in ~** en fideicomiso; **you'll have to take it on ~** tienes que aceptarlo a ojos cerrados

trust company N banco fideicomisario

trusted ['trʌstɪd] ADJ de confianza, fiable, de fiar

trustee [trʌs'ti:] N (*Law*) fideicomisario

trustful ['trʌstful] ADJ confiado

trust fund N fondo fiduciario *or* de fideicomiso

trusting ['trʌstɪŋ] ADJ confiado

trustworthy ['trʌstwə:ðɪ] ADJ digno de confianza, fiable, de fiar

trusty ['trʌstɪ] ADJ fiel

truth [tru:θ] (pl **truths** [tru:ðz]) N verdad f

truthful ['tru:θfəl] ADJ (person) sincero; (account) fidedigno

truthfully ['tru:θfulɪ] ADV (answer) con sinceridad

truthfulness ['tru:θfulnıs] N (of account) verdad f; (of person) sinceridad f

try [traɪ] N tentativa, intento; (Rugby) ensayo ▶ VT (Law) juzgar, procesar; (test: sth new) probar, someter a prueba; (attempt) intentar; (strain: patience) hacer perder ▶ VI probar; **to give sth a ~** intentar hacer algo; **to ~ one's (very) best** or **hardest** poner todo su empeño, esmerarse; **to ~ to do sth** intentar hacer algo; **~ again!** ¡vuelve a probar!; **~ harder!** ¡esfuérzate más!; **well, I tried** al menos lo intenté

▶ **try on** VT (clothes) probarse

▶ **try out** VT probar, poner a prueba

trying ['traɪɪŋ] ADJ cansado; (person) pesado

tsar [zɑ:ʳ] N zar m

T-shirt ['ti:ʃə:t] N camiseta

TSO N ABBR (BRIT) = **The Stationery Office**

T-square ['ti:skwɛəʳ] N regla en T

tsunami [tsʊ'nɑ:mɪ] N tsunami m

TT ADJ ABBR (BRIT inf) = **teetotal** ▶ ABBR (US) = **Trust Territory**

tub [tʌb] N cubo (SP), balde m (LAM); (bath) bañera, tina (LAM)

tuba ['tju:bə] N tuba

tubby ['tʌbɪ] ADJ regordete

tube [tju:b] N tubo; (BRIT: underground) metro; (US inf: television) tele f

tubeless ['tju:blɪs] ADJ (tyre) sin cámara

tuber ['tju:bəʳ] N (Bot) tubérculo

tuberculosis [tjubə:kju'ləusɪs] N tuberculosis f inv

tube station N (BRIT) estación f de metro

tubing ['tju:bɪŋ] N tubería (SP), cañería; **a piece of ~** un trozo de tubo

tubular ['tju:bjuləʳ] ADJ tubular

TUC N ABBR (BRIT: = Trades Union Congress) federación nacional de sindicatos

tuck [tʌk] N (Sewing) pliegue m ▶ VT (put) poner

▶ **tuck away** VT esconder

▶ **tuck in** VT meter; (child) arropar ▶ VI (eat) comer con apetito

▶ **tuck up** VT (child) arropar

tucker ['tʌkəʳ] N (AUSTRALIA, NEW ZEALAND inf) papeo

tuck shop N (Scol) tienda de golosinas

Tue., Tues. ABBR (= Tuesday) mart.

Tuesday ['tju:zdɪ] N martes m inv; **on ~** el martes; **on Tuesdays** los martes; **every ~** todos los martes; **every other ~** cada dos

martes, un martes sí y otro no; **last/next ~** el martes pasado/próximo; **a week/fortnight on ~, ~ week/fortnight** del martes en 8/15 días, del martes en una semana/dos semanas

tuft [tʌft] N mechón m; (of grass etc) manojo

tug [tʌg] N (ship) remolcador m ▶ VT remolcar

tug-of-love [tʌgəv'lʌv] N: **~ children** hijos envueltos en el litigio de los padres por su custodia

tug-of-war [tʌgəv'wɔ:ʳ] N juego de la cuerda

tuition [tju:'ɪʃən] N (BRIT) enseñanza; (: private tuition) clases fpl particulares; (US: school fees) matrícula

tulip ['tju:lɪp] N tulipán m

tumble ['tʌmbl] N (fall) caída ▶ VI caerse, tropezar; **to ~ to sth** (inf) caer en la cuenta de algo

tumbledown ['tʌmbldaun] ADJ ruinoso

tumble dryer N (BRIT) secadora

tumbler ['tʌmbləʳ] N vaso

tummy ['tʌmɪ] N (inf) barriga, vientre m

tumour, (US) **tumor** ['tju:məʳ] N tumor m

tumult ['tju:mʌlt] N tumulto

tumultuous [tju:'mʌltjuəs] ADJ tumultuoso

tuna ['tju:nə] N pl inv (also: **tuna fish**) atún m

tundra ['tʌndrə] N tundra

tune [tju:n] N (melody) melodía ▶ VT (Mus) afinar; (Radio, TV, Aut) sintonizar; **to be in/out of ~** (instrument) estar afinado/ desafinado; (singer) afinar/desafinar; **to be in/out of ~ with** (fig) armonizar/desentonar con; **to the ~ of** (fig: amount) por (la) cantidad de

▶ **tune in** VI (Radio, TV): **to ~ in (to)** sintonizar (con)

▶ **tune up** VI (musician) afinar (su instrumento)

tuneful ['tju:nful] ADJ melodioso

tuner ['tju:nəʳ] N (radio set) sintonizador m; **piano ~** afinador(a) m/f de pianos

tungsten ['tʌŋstn] N tungsteno

tunic ['tju:nɪk] N túnica

tuning ['tju:nɪŋ] N sintonización f; (Mus) afinación f

tuning fork N diapasón m

Tunis ['tju:nɪs] N Túnez m

Tunisia [tju:'nɪzɪə] N Túnez m

Tunisian [tju:'nɪzɪən] ADJ, N tunecino(-a) m/f

tunnel ['tʌnl] N túnel m; (in mine) galería ▶ VI construir un túnel/una galería

tunnel vision N (Med) visión f periférica restringida; (fig) estrechez f de miras

tunny ['tʌnɪ] N atún m

turban ['tə:bən] N turbante m

turbid ['tə:bɪd] ADJ turbio

turbine ['tə:baɪn] N turbina

turbo ['tə:bəu] N turbo

turboprop ['tə:bəuprɔp] N turbohélice m

turbot ['tə:bət] N pl inv rodaballo

turbulence ['tə:bjuləns] N (*Aviat*) turbulencia

turbulent ['tə:bjulənt] ADJ turbulento

tureen [tə'ri:n] N sopera

turf [tə:f] N césped *m*; (*clod*) tepe *m* ▶ VT cubrir con césped

▶ **turf out** VT (*inf*) echar a la calle

turf accountant N corredor(a) *m/f* de apuestas

turgid ['tə:dʒɪd] ADJ (*prose*) pesado

Turin [tjuə'rɪn] N Turín *m*

Turk [tə:k] N turco(-a)

Turkey ['tə:kɪ] N Turquía

turkey ['tə:kɪ] N pavo

Turkish ['tə:kɪʃ] ADJ turco ▶ N (*Ling*) turco

Turkish bath N baño turco

turmeric ['tə:mərɪk] N cúrcuma

turmoil ['tə:mɔɪl] N desorden *m*, alboroto; **in ~** revuelto

turn [tə:n] N turno; (*in road*) curva; (*Theat*) número; (*Med*) ataque *m* ▶ VT girar, volver, voltear (*LAм*); (*collar, steak*) dar la vuelta a; (*shape: wood, metal*) tornear; (*change*): **to ~ sth into** convertir algo en ▶ VI volver, voltearse (*LAм*); (*person: look back*) volverse; (*reverse direction*) dar la vuelta, voltear (*LAм*); (*milk*) cortarse; (*change*) cambiar; (*become*): **to ~ into sth** convertirse or transformarse en algo; **a good ~** un favor; **it gave me quite a ~** me dio un susto; **"no left ~"** (*Aut*) "prohibido girar a la izquierda"; **it's your ~** te toca a ti; **in ~** por turnos; **to take turns** turnarse; **at the ~ of the year/century** a fin de año/a finales de siglo; **to take a ~ for the worse** (*situation, patient*) empeorar; **they turned him against us** le pusieron en contra nuestra; **the car turned the corner** el coche dobló la esquina; **to ~ left** (*Aut*) torcer or girar a la izquierda; **she has no-one to ~ to** no tiene a quién recurrir

▶ **turn around** VI (*person*) volverse, darse la vuelta ▶ VT (*object*) dar la vuelta a, voltear (*LAм*)

▶ **turn away** VI apartar la vista ▶ VT (*reject: person, business*) rechazar

▶ **turn back** VI volverse atrás ▶ VT hacer retroceder; (*clock*) retrasar

▶ **turn down** VT (*refuse*) rechazar; (*reduce*) bajar; (*fold*) doblar

▶ **turn in** VI (*inf: go to bed*) acostarse ▶ VT (*fold*) doblar hacia dentro

▶ **turn off** VI (*from road*) desviarse ▶ VT (*light, radio etc*) apagar; (*engine*) parar

▶ **turn on** VT (*light, radio etc*) encender, prender (*LAм*); (*engine*) poner en marcha

▶ **turn out** VT (*light, gas*) apagar; (*produce: goods, novel etc*) producir ▶ VI (*attend: troops*) presentarse; (*: doctor*) atender; **to ~ out to be ...** resultar ser ...

▶ **turn over** VI (*person*) volverse ▶ VT (*mattress, card*) dar la vuelta a; (*page*) volver

▶ **turn round** VI volverse; (*rotate*) girar

▶ **turn to** VT FUS: **to ~ to sb** acudir a algn

▶ **turn up** VI (*person*) llegar, presentarse; (*lost object*) aparecer ▶ VT (*radio*) subir, poner más alto; (*heat, gas*) poner más fuerte

turnabout ['tə:nəbaut], **turnaround** ['tə:nəraund] N (*fig*) giro total

turncoat ['tə:nkəut] N renegado(-a)

turned-up ['tə:ndʌp] ADJ (*nose*) respingón(-ona)

turning ['tə:nɪŋ] N (*side road*) bocacalle *f*; (*bend*) curva; **the first ~ on the right** la primera bocacalle a la derecha

turning point N (*fig*) momento decisivo

turnip ['tə:nɪp] N nabo

turnkey system ['tə:nki:-] N (*Comput*) sistema *m* de seguridad

turnout ['tə:naut] N (*attendance*) asistencia; (*number of people attending*) número de asistentes; (*spectators*) público

turnover ['tə:nəuvə'] N (*Comm: amount of money*) facturación *f*; (*of goods*) movimiento; **there is a rapid ~ in staff** hay mucho movimiento de personal

turnpike ['tə:npaik] N (*US*) autopista de peaje

turnstile ['tə:nstail] N torniquete *m*

turntable ['tə:nteibl] N plato

turn-up ['tə:nʌp] N (*Brit: on trousers*) vuelta

turpentine ['tə:pəntain] N (*also*: **turps**) trementina

turquoise ['tə:kwɔiz] N (*stone*) turquesa ▶ ADJ color turquesa *inv*

turret ['tʌrɪt] N torreón *m*

turtle ['tə:tl] N tortuga (marina)

turtleneck ['tə:tlnɛk], **turtleneck sweater** N (jersey *m* de) cuello cisne

Tuscany ['tʌskənɪ] N Toscana

tusk [tʌsk] N colmillo

tussle ['tʌsl] N lucha, pelea

tutor ['tju:tə'] N profesor(a) *m/f*

tutorial [tju:'tɔ:rɪəl] N (*Scol*) seminario

tuxedo [tʌk'si:dəu] N (*US*) smoking *m*, esmoquin *m*

TV [ti:'vi:] N ABBR (= *television*) televisión *f*

TV dinner N cena precocinada

TV licence N *licencia que se paga por el uso del televisor, destinada a financiar la BBC*

twaddle ['twɔdl] N (*inf*) tonterías *fpl*

twang [twæŋ] N (*of instrument*) tañido; (*of voice*) timbre *m* nasal

tweak [twi:k] VT (*nose, ear*) pellizcar; (*hair*) tirar

tweed [twi:d] N tweed *m*

tweet [twi:t] N (*on Twitter*) tweet *m*, tuit *m* ▶ VT, VI (*on Twitter*) tuitear

tweezers ['twi:zəz] NPL pinzas *fpl* (de depilar)

twelfth [twɛlfθ] NUM duodécimo

t

Twelfth Night N (Día m de) Reyes mpl

twelve [twɛlv] NUM doce; **at ~ o'clock** (midday) a mediodía; (midnight) a medianoche

twentieth [ˈtwɛntɪɪθ] NUM vigésimo

twenty [ˈtwɛntɪ] NUM veinte; **in ~ fourteen** en dos mil catorce

twerp [twəːp] N (inf) idiota mf

twice [twaɪs] ADV dos veces; **~ as much** dos veces más, el doble; **she is ~ your age** ella te dobla edad; **~ a week** dos veces a la or por semana

twiddle [ˈtwɪdl] VT, VI: **to ~ (with) sth** dar vueltas a algo; **to ~ one's thumbs** (fig) estar de brazos cruzados

twig [twɪg] N ramita ▶ VI (inf) caer en la cuenta

twilight [ˈtwaɪlaɪt] N crepúsculo; (morning) madrugada; **in the ~** en la media luz

twill [twɪl] N sarga, estameña

twin [twɪn] ADJ, N gemelo(-a) m/f ▶ VT hermanar

twin-bedded room [ˈtwɪnˈbɛdɪd-] N = **twin room**

twin beds NPL camas fpl gemelas

twin-carburettor [ˈtwɪnkɑːbjuˈrɛtəʳ] ADJ de dos carburadores

twine [twaɪn] N bramante m ▶ VI (plant) enroscarse

twin-engined [twɪnˈendʒɪnd] ADJ bimotor; **~ aircraft** avión m bimotor

twinge [twɪndʒ] N (of pain) punzada; (of conscience) remordimiento

twinkle [ˈtwɪŋkl] N centelleo ▶ VI centellear; (eyes) parpadear

twin room N habitación f con dos camas

twin town N ciudad f hermanada or gemela

twirl [twəːl] N giro ▶ VT dar vueltas a ▶ VI piruetear

twist [twɪst] N (action) torsión f; (in road, coil) vuelta; (in wire, flex) doblez f; (in story) giro ▶ VT torcer, retorcer; (roll around) enrollar; (fig) deformar ▶ VI serpentear; **to ~ one's ankle/wrist** (Med) torcerse el tobillo/la muñeca

twisted [ˈtwɪstɪd] ADJ (wire, rope) trenzado, enroscado; (ankle, wrist) torcido; (fig: logic, mind) retorcido

twit [twɪt] N (inf) tonto

twitch [twɪtʃ] N sacudida; (nervous) tic m nervioso ▶ VI moverse nerviosamente

Twitter® [ˈtwɪtəʳ] N Twitter® m ▶ VI conectarse a Twitter

two [tuː] NUM dos; **~ by ~, in twos** de dos en dos; **to put ~ and ~ together** (fig) atar cabos

two-bit [tuːˈbɪt] ADJ (esp US inf, pej) de poca monta, de tres al cuarto

two-door [tuːˈdɔːʳ] ADJ (Aut) de dos puertas

two-faced [tuːˈfeɪst] ADJ (pej: person) falso, hipócrita

twofold [ˈtuːfəuld] ADV: **to increase ~** duplicarse ▶ ADJ (increase) doble; (reply) en dos partes

two-piece [tuːˈpiːs] N (also: **two-piece suit**) traje m de dos piezas; (also: **two-piece swimsuit**) dos piezas m inv, bikini m

two-seater [tuːˈsiːtəʳ] N (plane, car) avión m/ coche m de dos plazas, biplaza m

twosome [ˈtuːsəm] N (people) pareja

two-stroke [ˈtuːstrəuk] N (also: **two-stroke engine**) motor m de dos tiempos ▶ ADJ de dos tiempos

two-tone [ˈtuːtəun] ADJ (colour) bicolor, de dos tonos

two-way [ˈtuːweɪ] ADJ: **~ traffic** circulación f de dos sentidos; **~ radio** radio f emisora y receptora

TX ABBR (US) = **Texas**

tycoon [taɪˈkuːn] N: **(business) ~** magnate mf

type [taɪp] N (category) tipo, género; (model) modelo; (Typ) tipo, letra ▶ VT (letter etc) escribir a máquina; **what ~ do you want?** ¿qué tipo quieres?; **in bold/italic ~** en negrita/cursiva

type-cast [ˈtaɪpkɑːst] ADJ (actor) encasillado

typeface [ˈtaɪpfeɪs] N tipo de letra

typescript [ˈtaɪpskrɪpt] N texto mecanografiado

typeset [ˈtaɪpsɛt] VT (irreg: like **set**) componer

typesetter [ˈtaɪpsɛtəʳ] N cajista mf

typewriter [ˈtaɪpraɪtəʳ] N máquina de escribir

typewritten [ˈtaɪprɪtn] ADJ mecanografiado

typhoid [ˈtaɪfɔɪd] N (fiebre f) tifoidea

typhoon [taɪˈfuːn] N tifón m

typhus [ˈtaɪfəs] N tifus m

typical [ˈtɪpɪkl] ADJ típico

typically [ˈtɪpɪklɪ] ADV típicamente

typify [ˈtɪpɪfaɪ] VT tipificar

typing [ˈtaɪpɪŋ] N mecanografía

typing pool N (BRIT) servicio de mecanógrafos

typist [ˈtaɪpɪst] N mecanógrafo(-a)

typography [taɪˈpɔgrəfɪ] N tipografía

tyranny [ˈtɪrənɪ] N tiranía

tyrant [ˈtaɪərənt] N tirano(-a)

tyre, (US) **tire** [ˈtaɪəʳ] N neumático, llanta (LAM)

tyre pressure N presión f de los neumáticos

Tyrol [tɪˈrəul] N Tirol m

Tyrolean [tɪrəˈlɪən], **Tyrolese** [tɪrəˈliːz] ADJ tirolés(-esa)

Tyrrhenian Sea [tɪˈriːnɪən-] N Mar m Tirreno

tzar [zɑːʳ] N = **tsar**

Uu

U, u [juː] N (*letter*) U, u f; **U for Uncle** U de Uruguay

U N ABBR (*BRIT Cine*: = *universal*) todos los públicos

UAW N ABBR (*US*) = **United Automobile Workers**

UB40 N ABBR (*BRIT*: = *unemployment benefit form 40*) número de referencia en la solicitud de inscripción en la lista de parados; por extensión, la tarjeta del paro o su beneficiario

U-bend ['juːbɛnd] N recodo

ubiquitous [juːˈbɪkwɪtəs] ADJ omnipresente, ubicuo

UCAS ['juːkæs] N ABBR (*BRIT*) = **Universities and Colleges Admissions Service**

UDA N ABBR (*BRIT*: = *Ulster Defence Association*) organización paramilitar protestante de Irlanda del Norte

UDC N ABBR (*BRIT*) = **Urban District Council**

udder ['ʌdər] N ubre f

UDI N ABBR (*BRIT Pol*) = **unilateral declaration of independence**

UDR N ABBR (*BRIT*: = *Ulster Defence Regiment*) fuerza de seguridad de Irlanda del Norte

UEFA [juːˈeɪfə] N ABBR (= *Union of European Football Associations*) UEFA f

UFO ['juːfəu] N ABBR (= *unidentified flying object*) OVNI m

Uganda [juːˈgændə] N Uganda

Ugandan [juːˈgændən] ADJ, N ugandés(-esa) m/f

UGC N ABBR (*BRIT*: = *University Grants Committee*) entidad gubernamental que controla las finanzas de las universidades

ugh [əːh] EXCL ¡uf!

ugliness ['ʌglɪnɪs] N fealdad f

ugly ['ʌglɪ] ADJ feo; (*dangerous*) peligroso

UHF ABBR (= *ultra-high frequency*) UHF f

UHT ADJ ABBR = **ultra heat treated**; **~ milk** leche f uperizada

UK N ABBR (= *United Kingdom*) Reino Unido, R.U.

Ukraine [juːˈkreɪn] N Ucrania

Ukrainian [juːˈkreɪnɪən] ADJ ucraniano ▸ N ucraniano(-a); (*Ling*) ucraniano

ulcer ['ʌlsər] N úlcera; **mouth ~** llaga bucal

Ulster ['ʌlstər] N Ulster m

ulterior [ʌlˈtɪərɪər] ADJ ulterior; **~ motive** segundas intenciones fpl

ultimate ['ʌltɪmət] ADJ último, final; (*greatest*) mayor ▸ N: **the ~ in luxury** el colmo del lujo

ultimately ['ʌltɪmətlɪ] ADV (*in the end*) por último, al final; (*fundamentally*) a fin de cuentas

ultimatum [ʌltɪˈmeɪtəm] (*pl* **ultimatums** or **ultimata** [-tə]) N ultimátum m

ultra- ['ʌltrə] PREF ultra-

ultrasonic [ʌltrəˈsɔnɪk] ADJ ultrasónico

ultrasound ['ʌltrəsaund] N (*Med*) ultrasonido

ultraviolet [ʌltrəˈvaɪəlɪt] ADJ ultravioleta

um [ʌm] EXCL (*inf: in hesitation*) esto, este (*LAM*)

umbilical cord [ʌmbɪˈlaɪkl-] N cordón m umbilical

umbrage ['ʌmbrɪdʒ] N: **to take ~ (at)** ofenderse (por)

umbrella [ʌmˈbrɛlə] N paraguas m inv; **under the ~ of** (*fig*) bajo la protección de

umlaut ['umlaut] N diéresis f inv

umpire ['ʌmpaɪər] N árbitro ▸ VT arbitrar

umpteen [ʌmpˈtiːn] NUM enésimos(-as); **for the umpteenth time** por enésima vez

UMW N ABBR (= *United Mineworkers of America*) sindicato de mineros

UN N ABBR (= *United Nations*) ONU f

un- [ʌn] PREF in-; des-; no ...; poco ...; nada ...

unabashed [ʌnəˈbæʃt] ADJ nada avergonzado

unabated [ʌnəˈbeɪtɪd] ADJ: **to continue ~** seguir con la misma intensidad

unable [ʌnˈeɪbl] ADJ: **to be ~ to do sth** no poder hacer algo; (*not know how to*) ser incapaz de hacer algo, no saber hacer algo

unabridged [ʌnəˈbrɪdʒd] ADJ íntegro

unacceptable [ʌnəkˈsɛptəbl] ADJ (*proposal, behaviour, price*) inaceptable; **it's ~ that** no se puede aceptar que

unaccompanied [ʌnəˈkʌmpənɪd] ADJ no acompañado; (*singing, song*) sin acompañamiento

u

unaccountably [ʌnə'kauntəblɪ] ADV inexplicablemente

unaccounted [ʌnə'kauntɪd] ADJ: **two passengers are ~ for** faltan dos pasajeros

unaccustomed [ʌnə'kʌstəmd] ADJ: **to be ~ to** no estar acostumbrado a

unacquainted [ʌnə'kweɪntɪd] ADJ: **to be ~ with** (facts) desconocer, ignorar

unadulterated [ʌnə'dʌltəreɪtɪd] ADJ (gen) puro; (wine) sin mezcla

unaffected [ʌnə'fɛktɪd] ADJ (person, behaviour) sin afectación, sencillo; (emotionally): **to be ~ by** no estar afectado por

unafraid [ʌnə'freɪd] ADJ: **to be ~** no tener miedo

unaided [ʌn'eɪdɪd] ADJ sin ayuda, por sí solo

unanimity [juːnə'nɪmɪtɪ] N unanimidad f

unanimous [juː'nænɪməs] ADJ unánime

unanimously [juːˈnænɪməslɪ] ADV unánimemente

unanswered [ʌn'ɑːnsəd] ADJ (question, letter) sin contestar; (criticism) incontestado

unappetizing [ʌn'æpɪtaɪzɪŋ] ADJ poco apetitoso

unappreciative [ʌnə'priːʃɪətɪv] ADJ desagradecido

unarmed [ʌn'ɑːmd] ADJ (person) desarmado; (combat) sin armas

unashamed [ʌnə'ʃeɪmd] ADJ desvergonzado

unassisted [ʌnə'sɪstɪd] ADJ, ADV sin ayuda

unassuming [ʌnə'sjuːmɪŋ] ADJ modesto, sin pretensiones

unattached [ʌnə'tætʃt] ADJ (person) soltero; (part etc) suelto

unattended [ʌnə'tɛndɪd] ADJ (car, luggage) desatendido

unattractive [ʌnə'træktɪv] ADJ poco atractivo

unauthorized [ʌn'ɔːθəraɪzd] ADJ no autorizado

unavailable [ʌnə'veɪləbl] ADJ (article, room, book) no disponible; (person) ocupado

unavoidable [ʌnə'vɔɪdəbl] ADJ inevitable

unavoidably [ʌnə'vɔɪdəblɪ] ADV (detained) por causas ajenas a su voluntad

unaware [ʌnə'wɛəʳ] ADJ: **to be ~ of** ignorar

unawares [ʌnə'wɛəz] ADV: **to catch sb ~** pillar a algn desprevenido

unbalanced [ʌn'bælənst] ADJ desequilibrado; (mentally) trastornado

unbearable [ʌn'bɛərəbl] ADJ insoportable

unbeatable [ʌn'biːtəbl] ADJ (gen) invencible; (price) inmejorable

unbeaten [ʌn'biːtn] ADJ (team) imbatido; (army) invicto; (record) no batido

unbecoming [ʌnbɪ'kʌmɪŋ] ADJ (unseemly: language, behaviour) indecoroso, impropio; (unflattering: garment) poco favorecedor(a)

unbeknown [ʌnbɪ'nəun], **unbeknownst** [ʌnbɪ'nəunst] ADV: **~(st) to me** sin saberlo yo

unbelief [ʌnbɪ'liːf] N incredulidad f

unbelievable [ʌnbɪ'liːvəbl] ADJ increíble

unbelievingly [ʌnbɪ'liːvɪŋlɪ] ADV sin creer

unbend [ʌn'bɛnd] VI (irreg: like **bend**) (fig: person) relajarse ▸ VT (wire) enderezar

unbending [ʌn'bɛndɪŋ] ADJ (fig) inflexible

unbiased, unbiassed [ʌn'baɪəst] ADJ imparcial

unblemished [ʌn'blɛmɪʃt] ADJ sin mancha

unblock [ʌn'blɔk] VT (pipe) desatascar; (road) despejar

unborn [ʌn'bɔːn] ADJ que va a nacer

unbounded [ʌn'baundɪd] ADJ ilimitado, sin límite

unbreakable [ʌn'breɪkəbl] ADJ irrompible

unbridled [ʌn'braɪdld] ADJ (fig) desenfrenado

unbroken [ʌn'brəukən] ADJ (seal) intacto; (series) continuo, ininterrumpido; (record) no batido; (spirit) indómito

unbuckle [ʌn'bʌkl] VT desabrochar

unburden [ʌn'bəːdn] VT: **to ~ o.s.** desahogarse

unbusinesslike [ʌn'bɪznɪslaɪk] ADJ (trader) poco profesional; (transaction) incorrecto; (fig: person) poco práctico; (: without method) desorganizado

unbutton [ʌn'bʌtn] VT desabrochar

uncalled-for [ʌn'kɔːldfɔːʳ] ADJ gratuito, inmerecido

uncanny [ʌn'kænɪ] ADJ extraño, extraordinario

unceasing [ʌn'siːsɪŋ] ADJ incesante

unceremonious ['ʌnsɛrɪ'məunɪəs] ADJ (abrupt, rude) brusco, hosco

uncertain [ʌn'səːtn] ADJ incierto; (indecisive) indeciso; **it's ~ whether** no se sabe si; **in no ~ terms** sin dejar lugar a dudas

uncertainty [ʌn'səːtntɪ] N incertidumbre f

unchallenged [ʌn'tʃælɪndʒd] ADJ (Law etc) incontestado; **to go ~** no encontrar respuesta

unchanged [ʌn'tʃeɪndʒd] ADJ sin cambiar or alterar

uncharitable [ʌn'tʃærɪtəbl] ADJ (remark, behaviour) demasiado duro

uncharted [ʌn'tʃɑːtɪd] ADJ inexplorado

unchecked [ʌn'tʃɛkt] ADJ desenfrenado

uncivil [ʌn'sɪvɪl] ADJ descortés, grosero

uncivilized [ʌn'sɪvɪlaɪzd] ADJ (gen) inculto, poco civilizado; (fig: behaviour etc) bárbaro

uncle ['ʌŋkl] N tío

unclear [ʌn'klɪəʳ] ADJ poco claro; **I'm still ~ about what I'm supposed to do** todavía no tengo muy claro lo que tengo que hacer

uncoil [ʌn'kɔɪl] VT desenrollar ▸ VI desenrollarse

uncomfortable [ʌn'kʌmfətəbl] ADJ incómodo; (uneasy) inquieto

uncomfortably [ʌnˈkʌmfətəblɪ] ADV (*uneasily: say*) con inquietud; (: *think*) con remordimiento *or* nerviosismo

uncommitted [ʌnkəˈmɪtɪd] ADJ (*attitude, country*) no comprometido; **to remain ~ to** (*policy, party*) no comprometerse a

uncommon [ʌnˈkɔmən] ADJ poco común, raro

uncommunicative [ʌnkəˈmjuːnɪkətɪv] ADJ poco comunicativo, reservado

uncomplicated [ʌnˈkɔmplɪkeɪtɪd] ADJ sin complicaciones

uncompromising [ʌnˈkɔmprəmaɪzɪŋ] ADJ intransigente

unconcerned [ʌnkənˈsəːnd] ADJ indiferente; **to be ~ about** ser indiferente a, no preocuparse de

unconditional [ʌnkənˈdɪʃənl] ADJ incondicional

uncongenial [ʌnkənˈdʒiːnɪəl] ADJ desagradable

unconnected [ʌnkəˈnɛktɪd] ADJ (*unrelated*): **to be ~ with** no estar relacionado con

unconscious [ʌnˈkɔnʃəs] ADJ sin sentido; (*unaware*) inconsciente ▶ N: **the ~** el inconsciente; **to knock sb ~** dejar a algn sin sentido

unconsciously [ʌnˈkɔnʃəslɪ] ADV inconscientemente

unconsciousness [ʌnˈkɔnʃəsnɪs] N inconsciencia

unconstitutional [ʌnkɔnstɪˈtjuːʃənl] ADJ anticonstitucional

uncontested [ʌnkənˈtɛstɪd] ADJ (*champion*) incontestado; (*Parliament: seat*) ganado sin oposición

uncontrollable [ʌnkənˈtrəʊləbl] ADJ (*temper*) indomable; (*laughter*) incontenible

uncontrolled [ʌnkənˈtrəʊld] ADJ (*child, dog, emotion*) incontrolado; (*inflation, price rises*) desenfrenado

unconventional [ʌnkənˈvɛnʃənl] ADJ poco convencional

unconvinced [ʌnkənˈvɪnst] ADJ: **to be** *or* **remain ~** seguir sin convencerse

unconvincing [ʌnkənˈvɪnsɪŋ] ADJ poco convincente

uncork [ʌnˈkɔːk] VT descorchar

uncorroborated [ʌnkəˈrɔbəreɪtɪd] ADJ no confirmado

uncouth [ʌnˈkuːθ] ADJ grosero, inculto

uncover [ʌnˈkʌvəʳ] VT (*gen*) descubrir; (*take lid off*) destapar

undamaged [ʌnˈdæmɪdʒd] ADJ (*goods*) en buen estado; (*fig: reputation*) intacto

undaunted [ʌnˈdɔːntɪd] ADJ: **~ by** sin dejarse desanimar por

undecided [ʌndɪˈsaɪdɪd] ADJ (*person*) indeciso; (*question*) no resuelto, pendiente

undelivered [ʌndɪˈlɪvəd] ADJ no entregado al destinatario; **if ~ return to sender** en caso de no llegar a su destino devolver al remitente

undeniable [ʌndɪˈnaɪəbl] ADJ innegable

undeniably [ʌndɪˈnaɪəblɪ] ADV innegablemente

under [ˈʌndəʳ] PREP debajo de; (*less than*) menos de; (*according to*) según, de acuerdo con ▶ ADV debajo, abajo; **~ there** ahí debajo; **~ construction** en construcción, en obras; **~ the circumstances** dadas las circunstancias; **in ~ two hours** en menos de dos horas; **~ anaesthetic** bajo los efectos de la anestesia; **~ discussion** en discusión, sobre el tapete

under... [ʌndəʳ] PREF sub...

under-age [ʌndərˈeɪdʒ] ADJ menor de edad

underarm [ˈʌndərɑːm] N axila, sobaco ▶ CPD: **~ deodorant** desodorante *m* corporal

undercapitalised [ʌndəˈkæpɪtəlaɪzd] ADJ descapitalizado

undercarriage [ˈʌndəkærɪdʒ] N (BRIT *Aviat*) tren *m* de aterrizaje

undercharge [ʌndəˈtʃɑːdʒ] VT cobrar de menos

underclass [ˈʌndəklɑːs] N clase *f* marginada

underclothes [ˈʌndəkləʊðz] NPL ropa *sg* interior *or* íntima (LAM)

undercoat [ˈʌndəkəʊt] N (*paint*) primera mano

undercover [ʌndəˈkʌvəʳ] ADJ clandestino

undercurrent [ˈʌndəkʌrnt] N corriente *f* submarina; (*fig*) tendencia oculta

undercut [ˈʌndəkʌt] VT (*irreg: like* **cut**) vender más barato que; fijar un precio más barato que

underdeveloped [ʌndədɪˈvɛləpt] ADJ subdesarrollado

underdog [ˈʌndədɔg] N desvalido(-a)

underdone [ʌndəˈdʌn] ADJ (*Culin*) poco hecho

underemployment [ʌndərɪmˈplɔɪmənt] N subempleo

underestimate [ʌndərˈɛstɪmeɪt] VT subestimar

underexposed [ʌndərɪksˈpəʊzd] ADJ (*Phot*) subexpuesto

underfed [ʌndəˈfɛd] ADJ subalimentado

underfoot [ʌndəˈfut] ADV: **it's wet ~** el suelo está mojado

underfunded [ʌndəˈfʌndɪd] ADJ infradotado (económicamente)

undergo [ʌndəˈgəʊ] VT (*irreg: like* **go**) sufrir; (*treatment*) recibir, someterse a; **the car is undergoing repairs** están reparando el coche

undergraduate [ˈʌndəˈgrædjuət] N estudiante *mf* ▶ CPD: **~ courses** cursos *mpl* de licenciatura

u

843

underground [ˈʌndəgraund] N (BRIT: railway) metro; (Pol) movimiento clandestino ▸ ADJ subterráneo ▸ ADV (work) en la clandestinidad

undergrowth [ˈʌndəgrəuθ] N maleza

underhand [ʌndəˈhænd], **underhanded** [ʌndəˈhændɪd] ADJ (fig) poco limpio

underinsured [ʌndərɪnˈʃuəd] ADJ insuficientemente asegurado

underlie [ʌndəˈlaɪ] VT (irreg: like **lie**) (fig) ser la razón fundamental de; **the underlying cause** la causa fundamental

underline [ʌndəˈlaɪn] VT subrayar

underling [ˈʌndəlɪŋ] N (pej) subalterno(-a)

undermanning [ʌndəˈmænɪŋ] N falta de personal

undermentioned [ʌndəˈmɛnʃənd] ADJ abajo citado

undermine [ʌndəˈmaɪn] VT socavar, minar

underneath [ʌndəˈniːθ] ADV debajo ▸ PREP debajo de, bajo

undernourished [ʌndəˈnʌrɪʃt] ADJ desnutrido

underpaid [ʌndəˈpeɪd] ADJ mal pagado

underpants [ˈʌndəpænts] NPL calzoncillos mpl

underpass [ˈʌndəpɑːs] N (BRIT) paso subterráneo

underpin [ʌndəˈpɪn] VT (argument, case) secundar, sostener

underplay [ʌndəˈpleɪ] VT (BRIT) minimizar

underpopulated [ʌndəˈpɔpjuleɪtɪd] ADJ poco poblado

underprice [ʌndəˈpraɪs] VT vender demasiado barato

underpriced [ʌndəˈpraɪst] ADJ con precio demasiado bajo

underprivileged [ʌndəˈprɪvɪlɪdʒd] ADJ desposeído

underrate [ʌndəˈreɪt] VT infravalorar, subestimar

underscore [ˈʌndəskɔːr] VT subrayar, sostener

underseal [ʌndəˈsiːl] VT (Aut) proteger contra la corrosión

undersecretary [ʌndəˈsɛkrətrɪ] N subsecretario(-a)

undersell [ʌndəˈsɛl] (pt, pp **undersold** [-ˈsəuld]) VT (competitors) vender más barato que

undershirt [ˈʌndəʃəːt] N (US) camiseta

undershorts [ˈʌndəʃɔːts] NPL (US) calzoncillos mpl

underside [ˈʌndəsaɪd] N parte f inferior, revés m

undersigned [ˈʌndəsaɪnd] ADJ, N: **the ~** el/la etc abajo firmante

underskirt [ˈʌndəskəːt] N (BRIT) enaguas fpl

understaffed [ʌndəˈstɑːft] ADJ falto de personal

understand [ʌndəˈstænd] VT, VI (irreg: like **stand**) entender, comprender; (assume) tener entendido; **to make o.s. understood** hacerse entender; **I ~ you have been absent** tengo entendido que (usted) ha estado ausente

understandable [ʌndəˈstændəbl] ADJ comprensible

understanding [ʌndəˈstændɪŋ] ADJ comprensivo ▸ N comprensión f, entendimiento; (agreement) acuerdo; **to come to an ~ with sb** llegar a un acuerdo con algn; **on the ~ that** a condición de que + subjun

understate [ʌndəˈsteɪt] VT minimizar

understatement [ʌndəˈsteɪtmənt] N subestimación f; (modesty) modestia (excesiva); **to say it was good is quite an ~** decir que estuvo bien es quedarse corto

understood [ʌndəˈstud] PT, PP of **understand** ▸ ADJ entendido; (implied): **it is ~ that** se sobreentiende que

understudy [ˈʌndəstʌdɪ] N suplente mf

undertake [ʌndəˈteɪk] VT (irreg: like **take**) emprender; **to ~ to do sth** comprometerse a hacer algo

undertaker [ˈʌndəteɪkər] N director(a) m/f de pompas fúnebres

undertaking [ˈʌndəteɪkɪŋ] N empresa; (promise) promesa

undertone [ˈʌndətəun] N (of criticism) connotación f; (low voice): **in an ~** en voz baja

undervalue [ʌndəˈvæljuː] VT (fig) subestimar, infravalorar; (Comm etc) valorizar por debajo de su precio

underwater [ʌndəˈwɔːtər] ADV bajo el agua ▸ ADJ submarino

underway [ʌndəˈweɪ] ADJ: **to be ~** (meeting) estar en marcha; (investigation) estar llevándose a cabo

underwear [ˈʌndəwɛər] N ropa interior or íntima (LAm)

underweight [ʌndəˈweɪt] ADJ de peso insuficiente; (person) demasiado delgado

underwent [ʌndəˈwɛnt] VB see **undergo**

underworld [ˈʌndəwəːld] N (of crime) hampa, inframundo

underwrite [ʌndəˈraɪt] VT (irreg: like **write**) (Comm) suscribir; (Insurance) asegurar (contra riesgos)

underwriter [ˈʌndəraɪtər] N (Insurance) asegurador(a) m/f

undeserving [ʌndɪˈzəːvɪŋ] ADJ: **to be ~ of** no ser digno de

undesirable [ʌndɪˈzaɪərəbl] ADJ indeseable

undeveloped [ʌndɪˈvɛləpt] ADJ (land, resources) sin explotar

undies [ˈʌndɪz] NPL (inf) paños mpl menores

undiluted [ʌndaɪˈluːtɪd] ADJ (concentrate) concentrado

undiplomatic [ʌndɪplə'mætɪk] ADJ poco diplomático

undischarged [ʌndɪs'tʃɑːdʒd] ADJ: **~ bankrupt** quebrado(-a) no rehabilitado(-a)

undisciplined [ʌn'dɪsɪplɪnd] ADJ indisciplinado

undiscovered [ʌndɪs'kʌvəd] ADJ no descubierto; (*unknown*) desconocido

undisguised [ʌndɪs'gaɪzd] ADJ franco, abierto

undisputed [ʌndɪ'spjuːtɪd] ADJ incontestable

undistinguished [ʌndɪs'tɪŋgwɪʃt] ADJ mediocre

undisturbed [ʌndɪs'təːbd] ADJ (*sleep*) ininterrumpido; **to leave sth ~** dejar algo tranquilo *or* como está

undivided [ʌndɪ'vaɪdɪd] ADJ: **I want your ~ attention** quiero su completa atención

undo [ʌn'duː] VT (*irreg: like* **do**) (*laces*) desatar; (*button etc*) desabrochar; (*spoil*) deshacer

undoing [ʌn'duːɪŋ] N ruina, perdición f

undone [ʌn'dʌn] PP *of* **undo** ▸ ADJ: **to come ~** (*clothes*) desabrocharse; (*parcel*) desatarse

undoubted [ʌn'dautɪd] ADJ indudable

undoubtedly [ʌn'dautɪdlɪ] ADV indudablemente, sin duda

undress [ʌn'drɛs] VI desnudarse, desvestirse (*esp LAM*)

undrinkable [ʌn'drɪŋkəbl] ADJ (*unpalatable*) imbebible; (*poisonous*) no potable

undue [ʌn'djuː] ADJ indebido, excesivo

undulating ['ʌndjuleɪtɪŋ] ADJ ondulante

unduly [ʌn'djuːlɪ] ADV excesivamente, demasiado

undying [ʌn'daɪɪŋ] ADJ eterno

unearned [ʌn'əːnd] ADJ (*praise, respect*) inmerecido; **~ income** ingresos *mpl* no ganados, renta no ganada *or* salarial

unearth [ʌn'əːθ] VT desenterrar

unearthly [ʌn'əːθlɪ] ADJ: **~ hour** (*inf*) hora intempestiva

unease [ʌn'iːz] N malestar *m*

uneasy [ʌn'iːzɪ] ADJ intranquilo; (*worried*) preocupado; **to feel ~ about doing sth** sentirse incómodo con la idea de hacer algo

uneconomic ['ʌniːkə'nɔmɪk], **uneconomical** ['ʌniːkə'nɔmɪkl] ADJ no económico

uneducated [ʌn'ɛdjukeɪtɪd] ADJ ignorante, inculto

unemployed [ʌnɪm'plɔɪd] ADJ parado, sin trabajo ▸ N: **the ~** los parados

unemployment [ʌnɪm'plɔɪmənt] N paro, desempleo, cesantía (*LAM*)

unemployment benefit N (*BRIT*) subsidio de desempleo *or* paro

unending [ʌn'ɛndɪŋ] ADJ interminable

unenviable [ʌn'ɛnvɪəbl] ADJ poco envidiable

unequal [ʌn'iːkwəl] ADJ (*length, objects etc*) desigual; (*amounts*) distinto; (*division of labour*) poco justo

unequalled, (*US*) **unequaled** [ʌn'iːkwəld] ADJ inigualado, sin par

unequivocal [ʌnɪ'kwɪvəkəl] ADJ (*answer*) inequívoco, claro; (*person*) claro

unerring [ʌn'əːrɪŋ] ADJ infalible

UNESCO [juː'nɛskəu] N ABBR (= *United Nations Educational, Scientific and Cultural Organization*) UNESCO f

unethical [ʌn'ɛθɪkəl] ADJ (*methods*) inmoral; (*doctor's behaviour*) que infringe la ética profesional

uneven [ʌn'iːvn] ADJ desigual; (*road etc*) con baches

uneventful [ʌnɪ'vɛntful] ADJ sin incidentes

unexceptional [ʌnɪk'sɛpʃənl] ADJ sin nada de extraordinario, corriente

unexciting [ʌnɪk'saɪtɪŋ] ADJ (*news*) sin interés; (*film, evening*) aburrido

unexpected [ʌnɪk'spɛktɪd] ADJ inesperado

unexpectedly [ʌnɪk'spɛktɪdlɪ] ADV inesperadamente

unexplained [ʌnɪks'pleɪnd] ADJ inexplicado

unexploded [ʌnɪks'pləudɪd] ADJ sin explotar

unfailing [ʌn'feɪlɪŋ] ADJ (*support*) indefectible; (*energy*) inagotable

unfair [ʌn'fɛəʳ] ADJ: **~ (to sb)** injusto (con algn); **it's ~ that ...** es injusto que ..., no es justo que ...

unfair dismissal N despido improcedente

unfairly [ʌn'fɛəlɪ] ADV injustamente

unfaithful [ʌn'feɪθful] ADJ infiel

unfamiliar [ʌnfə'mɪlɪəʳ] ADJ extraño, desconocido; **to be ~ with sth** desconocer *or* ignorar algo

unfashionable [ʌn'fæʃnəbl] ADJ (*clothes*) pasado *or* fuera de moda; (*district*) poco elegante

unfasten [ʌn'fɑːsn] VT desatar

unfathomable [ʌn'fæðəməbl] ADJ insondable

unfavourable, (*US*) **unfavorable** [ʌn'feɪvərəbl] ADJ desfavorable

unfavourably, (*US*) **unfavorably** [ʌn'feɪvrəblɪ] ADV: **to look ~ upon** ser adverso a

unfeeling [ʌn'fiːlɪŋ] ADJ insensible

unfinished [ʌn'fɪnɪʃt] ADJ inacabado, sin terminar

unfit [ʌn'fɪt] ADJ en baja forma; (*incompetent*) incapaz; **~ for work** no apto para trabajar

unflagging [ʌn'flægɪŋ] ADJ incansable

unflappable [ʌn'flæpəbl] ADJ imperturbable

unflattering [ʌn'flætərɪŋ] ADJ (*dress, hairstyle*) poco favorecedor

unflinching [ʌn'flɪntʃɪŋ] ADJ impávido

unfold [ʌn'fəuld] VT desdoblar; (*fig*) revelar ▸ VI abrirse; revelarse

u

845

unforeseeable [ʌnfɔːˈsiːəbl] ADJ imprevisible
unforeseen [ˈʌnfɔːˈsiːn] ADJ imprevisto
unforgettable [ʌnfəˈɡetəbl] ADJ inolvidable
unforgivable [ʌnfəˈɡɪvəbl] ADJ imperdonable
unformatted [ʌnˈfɔːmætɪd] ADJ (disk, text) sin formatear
unfortunate [ʌnˈfɔːtʃnət] ADJ desgraciado; (event, remark) inoportuno
unfortunately [ʌnˈfɔːtʃnətlɪ] ADV desgraciadamente, por desgracia
unfounded [ʌnˈfaʊndɪd] ADJ infundado
unfriend [ʌnˈfrend] VT (Internet) quitar de amigo a; **he has unfriended her on Facebook** la ha quitado de amiga en Facebook
unfriendly [ʌnˈfrendlɪ] ADJ antipático; (behaviour, remark) hostil, poco amigable
unfulfilled [ʌnfʊlˈfɪld] ADJ (ambition) sin realizar; (prophecy, promise, terms of contract) incumplido; (desire, person) insatisfecho
unfurl [ʌnˈfɜːl] VT desplegar
unfurnished [ʌnˈfɜːnɪʃt] ADJ sin amueblar
ungainly [ʌnˈɡeɪnlɪ] ADJ (walk) desgarbado
ungodly [ʌnˈɡɒdlɪ] ADJ: **at an ~ hour** a una hora intempestiva
ungrateful [ʌnˈɡreɪtful] ADJ ingrato
unguarded [ʌnˈɡɑːdɪd] ADJ (moment) de descuido
unhappily [ʌnˈhæpɪlɪ] ADV (unfortunately) desgraciadamente
unhappiness [ʌnˈhæpɪnɪs] N tristeza
unhappy [ʌnˈhæpɪ] ADJ (sad) triste; (unfortunate) desgraciado; (childhood) infeliz; ~ **with** (arrangements etc) poco contento con, descontento de
unharmed [ʌnˈhɑːmd] ADJ (person) ileso
UNHCR N ABBR (= United Nations High Commission for Refugees) ACNUR m
unhealthy [ʌnˈhelθɪ] ADJ (gen) malsano, insalubre; (person) enfermizo; (interest) morboso
unheard-of [ʌnˈhɜːdɒv] ADJ inaudito, sin precedente
unhelpful [ʌnˈhelpful] ADJ (person) poco servicial; (advice) inútil
unhesitating [ʌnˈhezɪteɪtɪŋ] ADJ (loyalty) automático; (reply, offer) inmediato; (person) resuelto
unholy [ʌnˈhəʊlɪ] ADJ: **an ~ alliance** una alianza nefasta; **he returned at an ~ hour** volvió a una hora intempestiva
unhook [ʌnˈhʊk] VT desenganchar; (from wall) descolgar; (undo) desabrochar
unhurt [ʌnˈhɜːt] ADJ ileso
unhygienic [ʌnhaɪˈdʒiːnɪk] ADJ antihigiénico
UNICEF [ˈjuːnɪsef] N ABBR (= United Nations International Children's Emergency Fund) UNICEF f

unidentified [ʌnaɪˈdentɪfaɪd] ADJ no identificado; ~ **flying object** objeto volante no identificado
unification [juːnɪfɪˈkeɪʃən] N unificación f
uniform [ˈjuːnɪfɔːm] N uniforme m ▶ ADJ uniforme
uniformity [juːnɪˈfɔːmɪtɪ] N uniformidad f
unify [ˈjuːnɪfaɪ] VT unificar, unir
unilateral [juːnɪˈlætərəl] ADJ unilateral
unimaginable [ʌnɪˈmædʒɪnəbl] ADJ inconcebible, inimaginable
unimaginative [ʌnɪˈmædʒɪnətɪv] ADJ falto de imaginación
unimpaired [ʌnɪmˈpɛəd] ADJ (unharmed) intacto; (not lessened) no disminuido; (unaltered) inalterado
unimportant [ʌnɪmˈpɔːtənt] ADJ sin importancia
unimpressed [ʌnɪmˈprest] ADJ poco impresionado
uninhabited [ʌnɪnˈhæbɪtɪd] ADJ desierto; (country) despoblado; (house) deshabitado, desocupado
uninhibited [ʌnɪnˈhɪbɪtɪd] ADJ nada cohibido, desinhibido
uninjured [ʌnˈɪndʒəd] ADJ (person) ileso
uninspiring [ʌnɪnˈspaɪərɪŋ] ADJ anodino
uninstall [ˈʌnɪnstɔːl] VT (Comput) desinstalar
unintelligent [ʌnɪnˈtelɪdʒənt] ADJ poco inteligente
unintentional [ʌnɪnˈtenʃənəl] ADJ involuntario
unintentionally [ʌnɪnˈtenʃnəlɪ] ADV sin querer
uninvited [ʌnɪnˈvaɪtɪd] ADJ (guest) sin invitación
uninviting [ʌnɪnˈvaɪtɪŋ] ADJ (place, offer) poco atractivo; (food) poco apetecible
union [ˈjuːnjən] N unión f; (also: **trade union**) sindicato ▶ CPD sindical; **the U~** (US) la Unión
union card N carnet m de sindicato
unionize [ˈjuːnjənaɪz] VT sindicalizar
Union Jack N bandera del Reino Unido
Union of Soviet Socialist Republics N Unión f de Repúblicas Socialistas Soviéticas
union shop N (US) empresa de afiliación sindical obligatoria
unique [juːˈniːk] ADJ único
unisex [ˈjuːnɪseks] ADJ unisex
Unison [ˈjuːnɪsn] N (trade union) gran sindicato de funcionarios
unison [ˈjuːnɪsn] N: **in ~** en armonía
unissued capital [ʌnˈɪʃuːd-] N capital m no emitido
unit [ˈjuːnɪt] N unidad f; (team, squad) grupo; **kitchen ~** módulo de cocina; **production ~** taller m de fabricación; **sink ~** fregadero
unit cost N costo unitario

unite [juːˈnaɪt] VT unir ▸ VI unirse
united [juːˈnaɪtɪd] ADJ unido
United Arab Emirates NPL Emiratos mpl Árabes Unidos
United Kingdom N Reino Unido
United Nations, United Nations Organization N Naciones Unidas fpl
United States, United States of America N Estados Unidos mpl (de América)
unit price N precio unitario
unit trust N (BRIT) bono fiduciario
unity [ˈjuːnɪtɪ] N unidad f
Univ. ABBR = **university**
universal [juːnɪˈvəːsl] ADJ universal
universally [juːnɪˈvəːsəlɪ] ADV universalmente
universe [ˈjuːnɪvəːs] N universo
university [juːnɪˈvəːsɪtɪ] N universidad f ▸ CPD (student, professor, education, degree) universitario; (year) académico; **to be at/go to ~** estudiar en/ir a la universidad
unjust [ʌnˈdʒʌst] ADJ injusto
unjustifiable [ʌndʒʌstɪˈfaɪəbl] ADJ injustificable
unjustified [ʌnˈdʒʌstɪfaɪd] ADJ (text) no alineado or justificado
unkempt [ʌnˈkɛmpt] ADJ descuidado; (hair) despeinado
unkind [ʌnˈkaɪnd] ADJ poco amable; (comment etc) cruel
unkindly [ʌnˈkaɪndlɪ] ADV (speak) severamente; (treat) cruelmente, mal
unknown [ʌnˈnəun] ADJ desconocido ▸ ADV: **~ to me** sin saberlo yo; **~ quantity** incógnita
unladen [ʌnˈleɪdən] ADJ (weight) vacío, sin cargamento
unlawful [ʌnˈlɔːful] ADJ ilegal, ilícito
unleaded [ʌnˈlɛdɪd] N (also: **unleaded petrol**) gasolina sin plomo
unleash [ʌnˈliːʃ] VT desatar
unleavened [ʌnˈlɛvənd] ADJ ácimo, sin levadura
unless [ʌnˈlɛs] CONJ a menos que; **~ he comes** a menos que venga; **~ otherwise stated** salvo indicación contraria; **~ I am mistaken** si no mi equivoco
unlicensed [ʌnˈlaɪsənst] ADJ (BRIT: to sell alcohol) no autorizado
unlike [ʌnˈlaɪk] ADJ distinto ▸ PREP a diferencia de
unlikelihood [ʌnˈlaɪklɪhud] N improbabilidad f
unlikely [ʌnˈlaɪklɪ] ADJ improbable
unlimited [ʌnˈlɪmɪtɪd] ADJ ilimitado; **~ liability** responsabilidad f ilimitada
unlisted [ʌnˈlɪstɪd] ADJ (US Tel) que no figura en la guía; **~ company** empresa sin cotización en bolsa
unlit [ʌnˈlɪt] ADJ (room) oscuro, sin luz

unload [ʌnˈləud] VT descargar
unlock [ʌnˈlɔk] VT abrir (con llave)
unlucky [ʌnˈlʌkɪ] ADJ desgraciado; (object, number) que da mala suerte; **to be ~** (person) tener mala suerte
unmanageable [ʌnˈmænɪdʒəbl] ADJ (unwieldy: tool, vehicle) difícil de manejar; (: situation) incontrolable
unmanned [ʌnˈmænd] ADJ (spacecraft) sin tripulación
unmannerly [ʌnˈmænəlɪ] ADJ mal educado, descortés
unmarked [ʌnˈmɑːkt] ADJ (unstained) sin mancha; **~ police car** vehículo policial camuflado
unmarried [ʌnˈmærɪd] ADJ soltero
unmask [ʌnˈmɑːsk] VT desenmascarar
unmatched [ʌnˈmætʃt] ADJ incomparable
unmentionable [ʌnˈmɛnʃnəbl] ADJ (topic, vice) indecible; (word) que no se debe decir
unmerciful [ʌnˈməːsiful] ADJ despiadado
unmistakable [ʌnmɪsˈteɪkəbl] ADJ inconfundible
unmistakably [ʌnmɪsˈteɪkəblɪ] ADV de modo inconfundible
unmitigated [ʌnˈmɪtɪgeɪtɪd] ADJ rematado, absoluto
unnamed [ʌnˈneɪmd] ADJ (nameless) sin nombre; (anonymous) anónimo
unnatural [ʌnˈnætʃrəl] ADJ (gen) antinatural; (manner) afectado; (habit) perverso
unnecessary [ʌnˈnɛsəsərɪ] ADJ innecesario, inútil
unnerve [ʌnˈnəːv] VT (accident) poner nervioso; (hostile attitude) acobardar; (long wait, interview) intimidar
unnoticed [ʌnˈnəutɪst] ADJ: **to go** or **pass ~** pasar desapercibido
UNO [ˈjuːnəu] N ABBR (= United Nations Organization) ONU f
unobservant [ʌnəbˈzəːvnt] ADJ: **to be ~** ser poco observador, ser distraído
unobtainable [ʌnəbˈteɪnəbl] ADJ inasequible; (Tel) inexistente
unobtrusive [ʌnəbˈtruːsɪv] ADJ discreto
unoccupied [ʌnˈɔkjupaɪd] ADJ (house etc) libre, desocupado
unofficial [ʌnəˈfɪʃl] ADJ no oficial; **~ strike** huelga no oficial
unopened [ʌnˈəupənd] ADJ (letter, present) sin abrir
unopposed [ʌnəˈpəuzd] ADV (enter, be elected) sin oposición
unorthodox [ʌnˈɔːθədɔks] ADJ poco ortodoxo
unpack [ʌnˈpæk] VI deshacer las maletas, desempacar (LAM) ▸ VT deshacer
unpaid [ʌnˈpeɪd] ADJ (bill, debt) sin pagar, impagado; (Comm) pendiente; (holiday) sin sueldo; (work) sin pago, voluntario

unpalatable [ʌnˈpælətəbl] ADJ (truth) desagradable

unparalleled [ʌnˈpærəleld] ADJ (unequalled) sin par; (unique) sin precedentes

unpatriotic [ʌnpætrɪˈɔtɪk] ADJ (person) poco patriota; (speech, attitude) antipatriótico

unplanned [ʌnˈplænd] ADJ (visit) imprevisto; (baby) no planeado

unpleasant [ʌnˈplɛznt] ADJ (disagreeable) desagradable; (person, manner) antipático

unplug [ʌnˈplʌg] VT desenchufar, desconectar

unpolluted [ʌnpəˈluːtɪd] ADJ impoluto, no contaminado

unpopular [ʌnˈpɔpjuləʳ] ADJ poco popular; **to be ~ with sb** (person, law) no ser popular con algn; **to make o.s. ~ (with)** hacerse impopular (con)

unprecedented [ʌnˈprɛsɪdəntɪd] ADJ sin precedentes

unpredictable [ʌnprɪˈdɪktəbl] ADJ imprevisible

unprejudiced [ʌnˈprɛdʒudɪst] ADJ (not biased) imparcial; (having no prejudices) sin prejuicio

unprepared [ʌnprɪˈpɛəd] ADJ (person) desprevenido; (speech) improvisado

unprepossessing [ʌnpriːpəˈzɛsɪŋ] ADJ poco atractivo

unprincipled [ʌnˈprɪnsɪpld] ADJ sin escrúpulos

unproductive [ʌnprəˈdʌktɪv] ADJ improductivo; (discussion) infructuoso

unprofessional [ʌnprəˈfɛʃənl] ADJ poco profesional; **~ conduct** negligencia

unprofitable [ʌnˈprɔfɪtəbl] ADJ poco provechoso, no rentable

UNPROFOR N ABBR (= United Nations Protection Force) FORPRONU f, Unprofor f

unprotected [ˈʌnprəˈtɛktɪd] ADJ (sex) sin protección

unprovoked [ʌnprəˈvəukt] ADJ no provocado

unpunished [ʌnˈpʌnɪʃt] ADJ: **to go ~** quedar sin castigo, salir impune

unqualified [ʌnˈkwɔlɪfaɪd] ADJ sin título, no cualificado; (success) total, incondicional

unquestionably [ʌnˈkwɛstʃənəblɪ] ADV indiscutiblemente

unquestioning [ʌnˈkwɛstʃənɪŋ] ADJ (obedience, acceptance) incondicional

unravel [ʌnˈrævl] VT desenmarañar

unreal [ʌnˈrɪəl] ADJ irreal

unrealistic [ʌnrɪəˈlɪstɪk] ADJ poco realista

unreasonable [ʌnˈriːznəbl] ADJ irrazonable; **to make ~ demands on sb** hacer demandas excesivas a algn

unrecognizable [ʌnˈrɛkəgnaɪzəbl] ADJ irreconocible

unrecognized [ʌnˈrɛkəgnaɪzd] ADJ (talent, genius) ignorado; (Pol: regime) no reconocido

unrecorded [ʌnrɪˈkɔːdɪd] ADJ no registrado

unrefined [ʌnrɪˈfaɪnd] ADJ (sugar, petroleum) sin refinar

unrehearsed [ʌnrɪˈhəːst] ADJ (Theat etc) improvisado; (spontaneous) espontáneo

unrelated [ʌnrɪˈleɪtɪd] ADJ sin relación; (family) no emparentado

unrelenting [ʌnrɪˈlɛntɪŋ] ADJ implacable

unreliable [ʌnrɪˈlaɪəbl] ADJ (person) informal; (machine) poco fiable

unrelieved [ʌnrɪˈliːvd] ADJ (monotony) constante

unremitting [ʌnrɪˈmɪtɪŋ] ADJ incesante

unrepeatable [ʌnrɪˈpiːtəbl] ADJ irrepetible

unrepentant [ʌnrɪˈpɛntənt] ADJ (smoker, sinner) impenitente; **to be ~ about sth** no arrepentirse de algo

unrepresentative [ʌnrɛprɪˈzɛntətɪv] ADJ (untypical) poco representativo

unreserved [ʌnrɪˈzəːvd] ADJ (seat) no reservado; (approval, admiration) total

unreservedly [ʌnrɪˈzəːvɪdlɪ] ADV sin reserva

unresponsive [ʌnrɪˈspɔnsɪv] ADJ insensible

unrest [ʌnˈrɛst] N inquietud f, malestar m; (Pol) disturbios mpl

unrestricted [ʌnrɪˈstrɪktɪd] ADJ (power, time) sin restricción; (access) libre

unrewarded [ʌnrɪˈwɔːdɪd] ADJ sin recompensa

unripe [ʌnˈraɪp] ADJ verde, inmaduro

unrivalled, (US) **unrivaled** [ʌnˈraɪvəld] ADJ incomparable, sin par

unroll [ʌnˈrəul] VT desenrollar

unruffled [ʌnˈrʌfld] ADJ (person) imperturbable; (hair) liso

unruly [ʌnˈruːlɪ] ADJ indisciplinado

unsafe [ʌnˈseɪf] ADJ (journey) peligroso; (car etc) inseguro; (method) arriesgado; **~ to drink/eat** no apto para el consumo humano

unsaid [ʌnˈsɛd] ADJ: **to leave sth ~** dejar algo sin decir

unsaleable, (US) **unsalable** [ʌnˈseɪləbl] ADJ invendible

unsatisfactory [ˈʌnsætɪsˈfæktərɪ] ADJ poco satisfactorio

unsatisfied [ʌnˈsætɪsfaɪd] ADJ (desire, need etc) insatisfecho

unsavoury, (US) **unsavory** [ʌnˈseɪvərɪ] ADJ (fig) repugnante

unscathed [ʌnˈskeɪðd] ADJ ileso

unscientific [ʌnsaɪənˈtɪfɪk] ADJ poco científico

unscrew [ʌnˈskruː] VT destornillar

unscrupulous [ʌnˈskruːpjuləs] ADJ sin escrúpulos

unseat [ʌnˈsiːt] VT (rider) hacer caerse de la silla a; (fig: official) hacer perder su escaño a

unsecured [ʌnsɪˈkjuəd] ADJ: **~ creditor** acreedor(a) m/f común

unseeded [ʌnˈsiːdɪd] ADJ (Sport) no preseleccionado

unseen [ʌnˈsiːn] ADJ (person, danger) oculto

unselfish [ʌnˈsɛlfɪʃ] ADJ generoso, poco egoísta; (act) desinteresado

unsettled [ʌnˈsɛtld] ADJ inquieto; (situation) inestable; (weather) variable

unsettling [ʌnˈsɛtlɪŋ] ADJ perturbador(a), inquietante

unshakable, unshakeable [ʌnˈʃeɪkəbl] ADJ inquebrantable

unshaven [ʌnˈʃeɪvn] ADJ sin afeitar

unsightly [ʌnˈsaɪtlɪ] ADJ desagradable

unskilled [ʌnˈskɪld] ADJ: ~ **workers** mano f de obra no cualificada

unsociable [ʌnˈsəʊʃəbl] ADJ insociable

unsocial [ʌnˈsəʊʃl] ADJ: ~ **hours** horario nocturno

unsold [ʌnˈsəʊld] ADJ sin vender

unsolicited [ʌnsəˈlɪsɪtɪd] ADJ no solicitado

unsophisticated [ʌnsəˈfɪstɪkeɪtɪd] ADJ (person) sencillo, ingenuo; (method) poco sofisticado

unsound [ʌnˈsaʊnd] ADJ (health) malo; (in construction: floor, foundations) defectuoso; (: policy, advice, judgment) erróneo; (: investment) poco seguro

unspeakable [ʌnˈspiːkəbl] ADJ indecible; (awful) incalificable

unspoiled [ˈʌnˈspɔɪld], **unspoilt** [ˈʌnˈspɔɪlt] ADJ (place) que no ha perdido su belleza natural

unspoken [ʌnˈspəʊkn] ADJ (words) sobreentendido; (agreement, approval) tácito

unstable [ʌnˈsteɪbl] ADJ inestable

unsteady [ʌnˈstɛdɪ] ADJ inestable

unstinting [ʌnˈstɪntɪŋ] ADJ (support etc) pródigo

unstuck [ʌnˈstʌk] ADJ: **to come ~** despegarse; (fig) fracasar

unsubscribe [ʌnsəbˈskraɪb] VT (Internet) borrarse

unsubstantiated [ʌnsəbˈstænʃɪeɪtɪd] ADJ (rumour, accusation) no comprobado

unsuccessful [ʌnsəkˈsɛsful] ADJ (attempt) infructuoso; (writer, proposal) sin éxito; **to be ~** (in attempting sth) no tener éxito, fracasar

unsuccessfully [ʌnsəkˈsɛsfulɪ] ADV en vano, sin éxito

unsuitable [ʌnˈsuːtəbl] ADJ inconveniente, inapropiado; (time) inoportuno

unsuited [ʌnˈsuːtɪd] ADJ: **to be ~ for** or **to** no ser apropiado para

unsung [ˈʌnsʌŋ] ADJ: **an ~ hero** un héroe desconocido

unsupported [ʌnsəˈpɔːtɪd] ADJ (claim) sin fundamento; (theory) sin base firme

unsure [ʌnˈʃuəʳ] ADJ inseguro, poco seguro; **to be ~ of o.s.** estar poco seguro de sí mismo

unsuspecting [ʌnsəˈspɛktɪŋ] ADJ confiado

unsweetened [ʌnˈswiːtnd] ADJ sin azúcar

unsympathetic [ʌnsɪmpəˈθɛtɪk] ADJ (attitude) poco comprensivo; (person) sin compasión; ~ **(to)** indiferente (a)

untangle [ʌnˈtæŋgl] VT desenredar

untapped [ʌnˈtæpt] ADJ (resources) sin explotar

untaxed [ʌnˈtækst] ADJ (goods) libre de impuestos; (income) antes de impuestos

unthinkable [ʌnˈθɪŋkəbl] ADJ inconcebible, impensable

unthinkingly [ʌnˈθɪŋkɪŋlɪ] ADV irreflexivamente

untidy [ʌnˈtaɪdɪ] ADJ (room) desordenado, en desorden; (appearance) desaliñado

untie [ʌnˈtaɪ] VT desatar

until [ənˈtɪl] PREP hasta ▶ CONJ hasta que; ~ **he comes** hasta que venga; ~ **now** hasta ahora; ~ **then** hasta entonces; **from morning ~ night** de la mañana a la noche

untimely [ʌnˈtaɪmlɪ] ADJ inoportuno; (death) prematuro

untold [ʌnˈtəʊld] ADJ (story) nunca contado; (suffering) indecible; (wealth) incalculable

untouched [ʌnˈtʌtʃt] ADJ (not used etc) intacto, sin tocar; (safe: person) indemne, ileso; (unaffected): ~ **by** insensible a

untoward [ʌntəˈwɔːd] ADJ (behaviour) impropio; (event) adverso

untrained [ʌnˈtreɪnd] ADJ (worker) sin formación; (troops) no entrenado; **to the ~ eye** para los no entendidos

untrammelled, (US) untrammeled [ʌnˈtræməld] ADJ ilimitado

untranslatable [ʌntrænzˈleɪtəbl] ADJ intraducible

untried [ʌnˈtraɪd] ADJ (plan) no probado

untrue [ʌnˈtruː] ADJ (statement) falso

untrustworthy [ʌnˈtrʌstwəːðɪ] ADJ (person) poco fiable

unusable [ʌnˈjuːzəbl] ADJ inservible

unused [ʌnˈjuːzd] ADJ sin usar, nuevo; **to be ~ to (doing) sth** no estar acostumbrado a (hacer) algo

unusual [ʌnˈjuːʒʊəl] ADJ insólito, poco común

unusually [ʌnˈjuːʒʊəlɪ] ADV: **he arrived ~ early** llegó más temprano que de costumbre

unveil [ʌnˈveɪl] VT (statue) descubrir

unwanted [ʌnˈwɒntɪd] ADJ (person, effect) no deseado

unwarranted [ʌnˈwɒrəntɪd] ADJ injustificado

unwary [ʌnˈwɛərɪ] ADJ imprudente, incauto

unwavering [ʌnˈweɪvərɪŋ] ADJ inquebrantable

unwelcome [ʌnˈwɛlkəm] ADJ (at a bad time) inoportuno, molesto; **to feel ~** sentirse incómodo

u

unwell [ʌn'wɛl] ADJ: **to feel ~** estar indispuesto, sentirse mal

unwieldy [ʌn'wiːldɪ] ADJ difícil de manejar

unwilling [ʌn'wɪlɪŋ] ADJ: **to be ~ to do sth** estar poco dispuesto a hacer algo

unwillingly [ʌn'wɪlɪŋlɪ] ADV de mala gana

unwind [ʌn'waɪnd] VT (irreg: like **wind²**) desenvolver ▶ VI (relax) relajarse

unwise [ʌn'waɪz] ADJ imprudente

unwitting [ʌn'wɪtɪŋ] ADJ inconsciente

unwittingly [ʌn'wɪtɪŋlɪ] ADV inconscientemente, sin darse cuenta

unworkable [ʌn'wə:kəbl] ADJ (plan) impracticable

unworthy [ʌn'wə:ðɪ] ADJ indigno; **to be ~ of sth/to do sth** ser indigno de algo/de hacer algo

unwrap [ʌn'ræp] VT desenvolver

unwritten [ʌn'rɪtn] ADJ (agreement) tácito; (rules, law) no escrito

unzip [ʌn'zɪp] VT abrir la cremallera de; (Comput) descomprimir

(KEYWORD)

up [ʌp] PREP: **to go/be up sth** subir/estar subido en algo; **he went up the stairs/the hill** subió las escaleras/la colina; **we walked/climbed up the hill** subimos la colina; **they live further up the street** viven más arriba en la calle; **go up that road and turn left** sigue por esa calle y gira a la izquierda

▶ ADV **1** (upwards, higher) más arriba; **up in the mountains** en lo alto (de la montaña); **put it a bit higher up** ponlo un poco más arriba or alto; **to stop halfway up** pararse a la mitad del camino or de la subida; **up there** ahí or allí arriba; **up above** en lo alto, por encima, arriba; **"this side up"** "este lado hacia arriba"; **to live/go up North** vivir en el norte/ir al norte

2: **to be up** (out of bed) estar levantado; (prices, level) haber subido; (building) estar construido; (tent) estar montado; (curtains, paper etc) estar puesto; **time's up** se acabó el tiempo; **when the year was up** al terminarse el año; **he's well up in** or **on politics** (BRIT: knowledgeable) está muy al día en política; **what's up?** (wrong) ¿qué pasa?; **what's up with him?** ¿qué le pasa?; **prices are up on last year** los precios han subido desde el año pasado

3: **up to** (as far as) hasta; **up to now** hasta ahora or la fecha

4: **to be up to** (depending on): **it's up to you** depende de ti; **he's not up to it** (job, task etc) no es capaz de hacerlo; **I don't feel up to it** no me encuentro con ánimos para ello; **his work is not up to the required standard** su trabajo no da la talla; **what is he up to?** (inf: doing) ¿qué estará tramando?

▶ VI (inf): **she upped and left** se levantó y se marchó

▶ VT (inf: price) subir

▶ N: **ups and downs** altibajos mpl

up-and-coming [ʌpənd'kʌmɪŋ] ADJ prometedor(a)

upbeat ['ʌpbiːt] N (Mus) tiempo no acentuado; (in economy, prosperity) aumento ▶ ADJ (inf) optimista, animado

upbraid [ʌp'breɪd] VT censurar, reprender

upbringing ['ʌpbrɪŋɪŋ] N educación f

upcoming ['ʌpkʌmɪŋ] ADJ próximo

update [ʌp'deɪt] VT poner al día

upend [ʌp'end] VT poner vertical

upfront [ʌp'frʌnt] ADJ claro, directo ▶ ADV a las claras; (pay) por adelantado; **to be ~ about sth** admitir algo claramente

upgrade [ʌp'greɪd] VT ascender; (Comput) actualizar

upheaval [ʌp'hiːvl] N trastornos mpl; (Pol) agitación f

uphill [ʌp'hɪl] ADJ cuesta arriba; (fig: task) penoso, difícil ▶ ADV: **to go ~** ir cuesta arriba

uphold [ʌp'həʊld] VT (irreg: like **hold**) sostener

upholstery [ʌp'həʊlstərɪ] N tapicería

upkeep ['ʌpkiːp] N mantenimiento

upload ['ʌpləʊd] VT (Comput) subir

upmarket [ʌp'mɑːkɪt] ADJ (product) de categoría

upon [ə'pɒn] PREP sobre

upper ['ʌpəʳ] ADJ superior, de arriba ▶ N (of shoe: also: **uppers**) pala

upper case N (Typ) mayúsculas fpl

upper-class [ʌpə'klɑːs] ADJ (district, people, accent) de clase alta; (attitude) altivo

uppercut ['ʌpəkʌt] N uppercut m, gancho a la cara

upper hand N: **to have the ~** tener la sartén por el mango

Upper House N (Pol): **the ~** la Cámara alta

uppermost ['ʌpəməʊst] ADJ el más alto; **what was ~ in my mind** lo que me preocupaba más

Upper Volta [-'vɒltə] N Alto Volta m

upright ['ʌpraɪt] ADJ vertical; (fig) honrado

uprising ['ʌpraɪzɪŋ] N sublevación f

uproar ['ʌprɔːʳ] N tumulto, escándalo

uproarious [ʌp'rɔːrɪəs] ADJ escandaloso; (hilarious) graciosísimo

uproot [ʌp'ruːt] VT desarraigar

upset N ['ʌpset] (to plan etc) revés m, contratiempo; (Med) trastorno ▶ VT [ʌp'set] (irreg: like **set**) (glass etc) volcar; (spill) derramar; (plan) alterar; (person) molestar, perturbar ▶ ADJ [ʌp'set] preocupado, perturbado; (stomach) revuelto; **to have a**

stomach ~ (BRIT) tener el estómago revuelto; **to get** ~ molestarse, llevarse un disgusto

upset price N (US, SCOTTISH) precio mínimo or de reserva

upsetting [ʌpˈsɛtɪŋ] ADJ (worrying) inquietante; (offending) ofensivo; (annoying) molesto

upshot [ˈʌpʃɒt] N resultado

upside-down [ˈʌpsaɪdˈdaun] ADV al revés; **to turn a place** ~ (fig) revolverlo todo

upstage [ˈʌpˈsteɪdʒ] VT robar protagonismo a

upstairs [ʌpˈstɛəz] ADV arriba ▶ ADJ (room) de arriba ▶ N el piso superior

upstart [ˈʌpstɑːt] N advenedizo

upstream [ʌpˈstriːm] ADV río arriba

upsurge [ˈʌpsəːdʒ] N (of enthusiasm etc) arrebato

uptake [ˈʌpteɪk] N: **he is quick/slow on the** ~ es muy listo/torpe

uptight [ʌpˈtaɪt] ADJ tenso, nervioso

up-to-date [ˈʌptəˈdeɪt] ADJ actual, moderno; **to bring sb** ~ **(on sth)** poner a algn al corriente/tanto (de algo)

uptown [ˈʌptaun] ADV (US) hacia las afueras ▶ ADJ exterior, de las afueras

upturn [ˈʌptəːn] N (in luck) mejora; (Comm: in market) resurgimiento económico; (: in value of currency) aumento

upturned [ˈʌptəːnd] ADJ: ~ **nose** nariz f respingona

upward, upwards [ˈʌpwəd(z)] ADV hacia arriba; (more than): ~ **of** más de

upwardly-mobile [ˈʌpwədlɪˈməubaɪl] ADJ: **to be** ~ mejorar socialmente

URA N ABBR (US) = **Urban Renewal Administration**

Ural Mountains [ˈjuərəl-] NPL: **the** ~ (also: **the Urals**) los Montes Urales

uranium [juəˈreɪnɪəm] N uranio

Uranus [juəˈreɪnəs] N (Astro) Urano

urban [ˈəːbən] ADJ urbano

urbane [əːˈbeɪn] ADJ cortés, urbano

urbanization [ˈəːbənaɪˈzeɪʃən] N urbanización f

urchin [ˈəːtʃɪn] N pilluelo, golfillo

Urdu [ˈuəduː] N urdu m

urge [əːdʒ] N (force) impulso; (desire) deseo ▶ VT: **to** ~ **sb to do sth** animar a algn a hacer algo
▶ **urge on** VT animar

urgency [ˈəːdʒənsɪ] N urgencia

urgent [ˈəːdʒənt] ADJ (earnest, persistent: plea) insistente; (: tone) urgente

urgently [ˈəːdʒəntlɪ] ADV con urgencia, urgentemente

urinal [ˈjuərɪnl] N (building) urinario; (vessel) orinal m

urinate [ˈjuərɪneɪt] VI orinar

urine [ˈjuərɪn] N orina

URL N ABBR (= uniform resource locator) URL m

urn [əːn] N urna; (also: **tea urn**) tetera (grande)

Uruguay [ˈjuərəgwaɪ] N el Uruguay

Uruguayan [juərəˈgwaɪən] ADJ, N uruguayo(-a) m/f

US N ABBR (= United States) EE.UU.

us [ʌs] PRON nos; (after prep) nosotros(-as); (inf: me): **give us a kiss** dame un beso; see also **me**

USA N ABBR = **United States of America**; (Mil) = **United States Army**

usable [ˈjuːzəbl] ADJ utilizable

USAF N ABBR = **United States Air Force**

usage [ˈjuːzɪdʒ] N (Ling) uso; (utilization) utilización f

USB ABBR (= universal serial bus) USB m

USB key N llave f USB, memoria f USB

USB stick N memoria USB, llave f de memoria

USCG N ABBR = **United States Coast Guard**

USDA N ABBR = **United States Department of Agriculture**

USDAW [ˈʌzdɔː] N ABBR (BRIT: = Union of Shop, Distributive and Allied Workers) sindicato de empleados de comercio

USDI N ABBR = **United States Department of the Interior**

use N [juːs] uso, empleo; (usefulness) utilidad f ▶ VT [juːz] usar, emplear; **in** ~ en uso; **out of** ~ en desuso; **to be of** ~ servir; **ready for** ~ listo (para usar); **to make** ~ **of sth** aprovecharse or servirse de algo; **it's no** ~ (pointless) es inútil; (not useful) no sirve; **what's this used for?** ¿para qué sirve esto?; **to be used to** estar acostumbrado a (SP), acostumbrar; **to get used to** acostumbrarse a; **she used to do it** (ella) solía or acostumbraba hacerlo
▶ **use up** VT (food) consumir; (money) gastar

used [juːzd] ADJ (car) usado

useful [ˈjuːsful] ADJ útil; **to come in** ~ ser útil

usefulness [ˈjuːsfəlnɪs] N utilidad f

useless [ˈjuːslɪs] ADJ inútil; (unusable: object) inservible

uselessly [ˈjuːslɪslɪ] ADV inútilmente, en vano

uselessness [ˈjuːslɪsnɪs] N inutilidad f

user [ˈjuːzəʳ] N usuario(-a); (of petrol, gas etc) consumidor(a) m/f

user-friendly [ˈjuːzəˈfrɛndlɪ] ADJ (Comput) fácil de utilizar

username [ˈjuːzəneɪm] N (Comput) nombre m de usuario

USES N ABBR = **United States Employment Service**

usher [ˈʌʃəʳ] N (at wedding) ujier m; (in cinema etc) acomodador m ▶ VT: **to** ~ **sb in** (into room) hacer pasar a algn; **it ushered in a new era** (fig) inició una nueva era

usherette [ʌʃəˈrɛt] N (*in cinema*) acomodadora

USIA N ABBR = **United States Information Agency**

USM N ABBR = **United States Mail; United States Mint**

USN N ABBR = **United States Navy**

USP N ABBR = **unique selling point; unique selling proposition**

USPHS N ABBR = **United States Public Health Service**

USPO N ABBR = **United States Post Office**

USS ABBR = **United States Ship; United States Steamer**

USSR N ABBR (*History*) = **Union of Soviet Socialist Republics; the (former)** ~ la (antigua) U.R.S.S. (= *Unión de Repúblicas Socialistas Soviéticas*)

usu. ABBR = **usually**

usual [ˈjuːʒuəl] ADJ normal, corriente; **as** ~ como de costumbre, como siempre

usually [ˈjuːʒuəlɪ] ADV normalmente

usurer [ˈjuːʒərəʳ] N usurero

usurp [juːˈzəːp] VT usurpar

usury [ˈjuːʒərɪ] N usura

UT ABBR (*US*) = **Utah**

ute [juːt] N ABBR (*AUSTRALIA, NEW ZEALAND: inf:* = *utility truck*) camioneta

utensil [juːˈtɛnsl] N utensilio; **kitchen utensils** batería de cocina

uterus [ˈjuːtərəs] N útero

utilitarian [juːtɪlɪˈtɛərɪən] ADJ utilitario

utility [juːˈtɪlɪtɪ] N utilidad *f*; (*public utility*) (empresa de) servicio público

utility room N trascocina

utilization [juːtɪlaɪˈzeɪʃən] N utilización *f*

utilize [ˈjuːtɪlaɪz] VT utilizar

utmost [ˈʌtməust] ADJ mayor ▶ N: **to do one's** ~ hacer todo lo posible; **it is of the ~ importance that …** es de la mayor importancia que …

utter [ˈʌtəʳ] ADJ total, completo ▶ VT pronunciar, proferir

utterance [ˈʌtərns] N palabras *fpl*, declaración *f*

utterly [ˈʌtəlɪ] ADV completamente, totalmente

U-turn [ˈjuːˈtəːn] N cambio de sentido; (*fig*) giro de 180 grados

Uzbekistan [ʌzbɛkɪˈstɑːn] N Uzbekistán *m*

Vv

V, v [viː] N (letter) V, v f; **V for Victor** V de Valencia

v. ABBR (= verse) vers.°; (= see) V, vid., vide; (= versus) vs.; = **volt**

VA, Va. ABBR (US) = **Virginia**

vac [væk] N ABBR (BRIT inf) = **vacation**

vacancy ['veɪkənsɪ] N (job) vacante f; (room) cuarto libro; **have you any vacancies?** ¿tiene or hay alguna habitación or algún cuarto libre?; **"no vacancies"** "completo"

vacant ['veɪkənt] ADJ desocupado, libre; (expression) distraído

vacant lot N (US) solar m

vacate [vəˈkeɪt] VT (house) desocupar; (job) dejar (vacante)

vacation [vəˈkeɪʃən] N vacaciones fpl; **on ~** de vacaciones; **to take a ~** (esp US) tomarse unas vacaciones

vacation course N curso de vacaciones

vacationer [vəˈkeɪʃənər], **vacationist** [vəˈkeɪʃənɪst] N (US) turista mf

vaccinate ['væksɪneɪt] VT vacunar

vaccination [væksɪˈneɪʃən] N vacunación f

vaccine ['væksiːn] N vacuna

vacuum ['vækjum] N vacío

vacuum bottle N (US) = **vacuum flask**

vacuum cleaner N aspiradora

vacuum flask N (BRIT) termo

vacuum-packed ['vækjum'pækt] ADJ envasado al vacío

vagabond ['vægəbɒnd] N vagabundo(-a)

vagary ['veɪgərɪ] N capricho

vagina [vəˈdʒaɪnə] N vagina

vagrancy ['veɪgrənsɪ] N vagabundeo

vagrant ['veɪgrənt] N vagabundo(-a)

vague [veɪg] ADJ vago; (blurred: memory) borroso; (uncertain) incierto; (ambiguous) impreciso; (person: absent-minded) distraído; (: evasive): **to be ~** no decir las cosas claramente; **I haven't the vaguest idea** no tengo la más remota idea

vaguely ['veɪglɪ] ADV vagamente

vagueness ['veɪgnɪs] N vaguedad f; imprecisión f; (absent-mindedness) despiste m

vain [veɪn] ADJ (conceited) presumido; (useless) vano, inútil; **in ~** en vano

vainly ['veɪnlɪ] ADV (to no effect) en vano; (conceitedly) vanidosamente

valance ['væləns] N (for bed) volante alrededor de la colcha o sábana que cuelga hasta el suelo

valedictory [vælɪˈdɪktərɪ] ADJ de despedida

valentine ['væləntaɪn] N (also: **valentine card**) tarjeta del Día de los Enamorados

Valentine's Day N día de los enamorados (el 14 de febrero, día de San Valentín)

valet ['væleɪ] N ayuda m de cámara

valet service N (for clothes) planchado

valiant ['væljənt] ADJ valiente

valiantly ['væljəntlɪ] ADV valientemente, con valor

valid ['vælɪd] ADJ válido; (ticket) valedero; (law) vigente

validate ['vælɪdeɪt] VT (contract, document) convalidar; (argument, claim) dar validez a

validity [vəˈlɪdɪtɪ] N validez f; vigencia

valise [vəˈliːz] N maletín m

valley ['vælɪ] N valle m

valour, (US) valor ['vælər] N valor m, valentía

valuable ['væljuəbl] ADJ (jewel) de valor; (time) valioso; **valuables** NPL objetos mpl de valor

valuation [væljuˈeɪʃən] N tasación f, valuación f

value ['væljuː] N valor m; (importance) importancia ▶ VT (fix price of) tasar, valorar; (esteem) apreciar; **values** NPL (moral) valores mpl morales; **to lose (in) ~** (currency) bajar; (property) desvalorizarse; **to gain (in) ~** (currency) subir; (property) revalorizarse; **you get good ~ (for money) in that shop** la relación calidad-precio es muy buena en esa tienda; **to be of great ~ to sb** ser de gran valor para algn; **it is valued at £8** está valorado en ocho libras

value added tax N (BRIT) impuesto sobre el valor añadido or agregado (LAM)

valued ['væljuːd] ADJ (appreciated) apreciado

valueless ['væljuːlɪs] ADJ sin valor

valuer ['væljuːər] N tasador(a) m/f

valve [vælv] N (Anat, Tech) válvula
vampire ['væmpaɪə^r] N vampiro
van [væn] N (Aut) furgoneta, camioneta (LAm); (Brit Rail) furgón m (de equipajes)
V and A N ABBR (Brit) = **Victoria and Albert Museum**
vandal ['vændl] N vándalo(-a)
vandalism ['vændəlɪzəm] N vandalismo
vandalize ['vændəlaɪz] VT dañar, destruir, destrozar
vanguard ['vænɡɑːd] N vanguardia
vanilla [və'nɪlə] N vainilla
vanish ['vænɪʃ] VI desaparecer, esfumarse
vanity ['vænɪtɪ] N vanidad f
vanity case N neceser m
vantage point ['vɑːntɪdʒ-] N posición f ventajosa
vaporize ['veɪpəraɪz] VT vaporizar ▶ VI vaporizarse
vapour, (US) **vapor** ['veɪpə^r] N vapor m; (on breath, window) vaho
vapour trail, (US) **vapor trail** N (Aviat) estela
variable ['vɛərɪəbl] ADJ variable ▶ N variable f
variance ['vɛərɪəns] N: **to be at ~ (with)** estar en desacuerdo (con), no cuadrar (con)
variant ['vɛərɪənt] N variante f
variation [vɛərɪ'eɪʃən] N variación f
varicose ['værɪkəʊs] ADJ: **~ veins** varices fpl
varied ['vɛərɪd] ADJ variado
variety [və'raɪətɪ] N variedad f, diversidad f; (quantity) surtido; **for a ~ of reasons** por varias or diversas razones
variety show N espectáculo de variedades
various ['vɛərɪəs] ADJ varios(-as), diversos(-as); **at ~ times** (different) en distintos momentos; (several) varias veces
varnish ['vɑːnɪʃ] N (gen) barniz m; (also: **nail varnish**) esmalte m ▶ VT (gen) barnizar; (nails) pintar (con esmalte)
vary ['vɛərɪ] VT variar; (change) cambiar ▶ VI variar; (disagree) discrepar; **to ~ with** or **according to** variar según or de acuerdo con
varying ['vɛərɪɪŋ] ADJ diversos(-as)
vase [vɑːz] N florero, jarrón m
vasectomy [və'sɛktəmɪ] N vasectomía
Vaseline® ['væsɪliːn] N vaselina®
vast [vɑːst] ADJ enorme; (success) abrumador(a), arrollador(a)
vastly ['vɑːstlɪ] ADV enormemente
vastness ['vɑːstnɪs] N inmensidad f
VAT [væt] N ABBR (Brit: = value added tax) IVA m
vat [væt] N tina, tinaja
Vatican ['vætɪkən] N: **the ~** el Vaticano
vatman ['vætmæn] N (irreg) (Brit inf) inspector m or recaudador m del IVA; **"how to avoid the ~"** "cómo evitar pagar el IVA"
vaudeville ['vəʊdəvɪl] N (US) vodevil m
vault [vɔːlt] N (of roof) bóveda; (tomb) panteón m; (in bank) cámara acorazada ▶ VT (also:

vault over) saltar (por encima de)
vaunted ['vɔːntɪd] ADJ: **much ~** cacareado
VC N ABBR = **vice-chairman**; = **vice-chancellor** (Brit: = Victoria Cross) condecoración militar
VCR N ABBR = **video cassette recorder**
VD N ABBR = **venereal disease**
VDU N ABBR (= visual display unit) UPV f
veal [viːl] N ternera
veer [vɪə^r] VI (vehicle) virar; (wind) girar
veg. [vɛdʒ] N ABBR (Brit inf) = **vegetable**
vegan ['viːɡən] N vegano(-a)
vegeburger, veggieburger ['vɛdʒɪbəːɡə^r] N hamburguesa vegetal
vegetable ['vɛdʒtəbl] N (Bot) vegetal m; (edible plant) legumbre f, hortaliza ▶ ADJ vegetal; **vegetables** NPL (cooked) verduras fpl
vegetable garden N huerta, huerto
vegetarian [vɛdʒɪ'tɛərɪən] ADJ, N vegetariano(-a) m/f
vegetate ['vɛdʒɪteɪt] VI vegetar
vegetation [vɛdʒɪ'teɪʃən] N vegetación f
vegetative ['vɛdʒɪtətɪv] ADJ vegetativo; (Bot) vegetal
vehemence ['viːɪməns] N vehemencia; violencia
vehement ['viːɪmənt] ADJ vehemente, apasionado; (dislike, hatred) violento
vehicle ['viːɪkl] N vehículo; (fig) vehículo, medio
vehicular [vɪ'hɪkjʊlə^r] ADJ: **~ traffic** circulación f rodada
veil [veɪl] N velo ▶ VT velar; **under a ~ of secrecy** (fig) en el mayor secreto
veiled [veɪld] ADJ (also fig) disimulado, velado
vein [veɪn] N vena; (of ore etc) veta
Velcro® ['vɛlkrəʊ] N velcro® m
vellum ['vɛləm] N (writing paper) papel m vitela
velocity [vɪ'lɒsɪtɪ] N velocidad f
velour [və'lʊə^r] N terciopelo
velvet ['vɛlvɪt] N terciopelo ▶ ADJ aterciopelado
vendetta [vɛn'dɛtə] N vendetta
vending machine ['vɛndɪŋ-] N máquina expendedora, expendedor m
vendor ['vɛndə^r] N vendedor(a) m/f; **street ~** vendedor(a) m/f callejero(-a)
veneer [və'nɪə^r] N chapa, enchapado; (fig) barniz m
venereal [vɪ'nɪərɪəl] ADJ: **~ disease** enfermedad f venérea
Venetian blind [vɪ'niːʃən-] N persiana
Venezuela [vɛnɛ'zweɪlə] N Venezuela
Venezuelan [vɛnɛ'zweɪlən] ADJ, N venezolano(-a) m/f
vengeance ['vɛndʒəns] N venganza; **with a ~** (fig) con creces
vengeful ['vɛndʒfʊl] ADJ vengativo
Venice ['vɛnɪs] N Venecia
venison ['vɛnɪsn] N carne f de venado

venom ['vɛnəm] N veneno
venomous ['vɛnəməs] ADJ venenoso
venomously ['vɛnəməslɪ] ADV con odio
vent [vɛnt] N (*opening*) abertura; (*air-hole*) respiradero; (*in wall*) rejilla (de ventilación) ▶ VT (*fig: feelings*) desahogar
ventilate ['vɛntɪleɪt] VT ventilar
ventilation [vɛntɪ'leɪʃən] N ventilación f
ventilation shaft N pozo de ventilación
ventilator ['vɛntɪleɪtə'] N ventilador m
ventriloquist [vɛn'trɪləkwɪst] N ventrílocuo(-a)
venture ['vɛntʃə'] N empresa ▶ VT arriesgar; (*opinion*) ofrecer ▶ VI arriesgarse, lanzarse; **a business ~** una empresa comercial; **to ~ to do sth** aventurarse a hacer algo
venture capital N capital m de riesgo
venue ['vɛnjuː] N (*meeting place*) lugar m de reunión; (*for concert*) local m
Venus ['viːnəs] N (*Astro*) Venus m
veracity [və'ræsɪtɪ] N veracidad f
veranda, verandah [və'rændə] N terraza; (*with glass*) galería
verb [vəːb] N verbo
verbal ['vəːbl] ADJ verbal
verbally ['vəːbəlɪ] ADV verbalmente, de palabra
verbatim [vəː'beɪtɪm] ADJ, ADV al pie de la letra, palabra por palabra
verbose [vəː'bəus] ADJ prolijo
verdict ['vəːdɪkt] N veredicto, fallo; (*fig: opinion*) opinión f, juicio; **~ of guilty/not guilty** veredicto de culpabilidad/inocencia
verge [vəːdʒ] N (*BRIT*) borde m; **to be on the ~ of doing sth** estar a punto de hacer algo ▶ **verge on** VT FUS rayar en
verger ['vəːdʒə'] N sacristán m
verification [vɛrɪfɪ'keɪʃən] N comprobación f, verificación f
verify ['vɛrɪfaɪ] VT comprobar, verificar; (*prove the truth of*) confirmar
veritable ['vɛrɪtəbl] ADJ verdadero, auténtico
vermin ['vəːmɪn] NPL (*animals*) bichos mpl; (*insects*) sabandijas fpl; (*fig*) sabandijas fpl
vermouth ['vəːməθ] N vermut m
vernacular [və'nækjulə'] N lengua vernácula
versatile ['vəːsətaɪl] ADJ (*person*) polifacético; (*machine, tool etc*) versátil
versatility [vəːsə'tɪlɪtɪ] N versatilidad f
verse [vəːs] N versos mpl, poesía; (*stanza*) estrofa; (*in bible*) versículo; **in ~** en verso
versed [vəːst] ADJ: (**well-**)**~ in** versado en
version ['vəːʃən] N versión f
versus ['vəːsəs] PREP contra
vertebra ['vəːtɪbrə] (*pl* **vertebrae** [briː]) N vértebra
vertebrate ['vəːtɪbrɪt] N vertebrado
vertical ['vəːtɪkl] ADJ vertical

vertically ['vəːtɪkəlɪ] ADV verticalmente
vertigo ['vəːtɪgəu] N vértigo; **to suffer from ~** tener vértigo
verve [vəːv] N brío
very ['vɛrɪ] ADV muy ▶ ADJ: **the ~ book which** el mismo libro que; **the ~ last** el último (de todos); **at the ~ least** al menos; **~ much** muchísimo; **~ well/little** muy bien/poco; **~ high frequency** (*Radio*) frecuencia muy alta; **it's ~ cold** hace mucho frío; **the ~ thought (of it) alarms me** con sólo pensarlo me entra miedo
vespers ['vɛspəz] NPL vísperas fpl
vessel ['vɛsl] N (*Anat*) vaso; (*ship*) barco; (*container*) vasija
vest [vɛst] N (*BRIT*) camiseta; (*US: waistcoat*) chaleco
vested interests ['vɛstɪd-] NPL (*Comm*) intereses mpl creados
vestibule ['vɛstɪbjuːl] N vestíbulo
vestige ['vɛstɪdʒ] N vestigio, rastro
vestry ['vɛstrɪ] N sacristía
Vesuvius [vɪ'suːvɪəs] N Vesubio
vet [vɛt] N ABBR = **veterinary surgeon**; (*US inf*) = **veteran** ▶ VT revisar; **to ~ sb for a job** someter a investigación a algn para un trabajo
veteran ['vɛtərn] N veterano(-a) ▶ ADJ: **she is a ~ campaigner for ...** es una veterana de la campaña de ...
veteran car N coche m antiguo
veterinarian [vɛtrɪ'nɛərɪən] N (*US*) = **veterinary surgeon**
veterinary ['vɛtrɪnərɪ] ADJ veterinario
veterinary surgeon N (*BRIT*) veterinario(-a)
veto ['viːtəu] N (*pl* **vetoes**) veto ▶ VT prohibir, vedar; **to put a ~ on** vetar
vetting ['vɛtɪŋ] N: **positive ~** investigación gubernamental de los futuros altos cargos de la Administración
vex [vɛks] VT (*irritate*) fastidiar; (*make impatient*) impacientar
vexed [vɛkst] ADJ (*question*) controvertido
vexing ['vɛksɪŋ] ADJ molesto, engorroso
VFD N ABBR (*US*) = **voluntary fire department**
VG N ABBR (*BRIT Scol etc* = *very good*) S (= *sobresaliente*)
VHF ABBR (= *very high frequency*) VHF f
VI ABBR (*US*) = **Virgin Islands**
via ['vaɪə] PREP por, por vía de
viability [vaɪə'bɪlɪtɪ] N viabilidad f
viable ['vaɪəbl] ADJ viable
viaduct ['vaɪədʌkt] N viaducto
vial ['vaɪəl] N frasco pequeño
vibes [vaɪbz] NPL (*inf*): **I got good/bad ~** me dio buen/mal rollo
vibrant ['vaɪbrənt] ADJ (*lively, bright*) vivo; (*full of emotion: voice*) vibrante; (*: colour*) fuerte
vibraphone ['vaɪbrəfəun] N vibráfono

V

855

vibrate [vaɪˈbreɪt] VI vibrar
vibration [vaɪˈbreɪʃən] N vibración f
vibrator [vaɪˈbreɪtəʳ] N vibrador m
vicar [ˈvɪkəʳ] N párroco
vicarage [ˈvɪkərɪdʒ] N parroquia
vicarious [vɪˈkɛərɪəs] ADJ indirecto; (responsibility) delegado
vice [vaɪs] N (evil) vicio; (Tech) torno de banco
vice- [vaɪs] PREF vice...
vice-chairman [ˈvaɪsˈtʃɛəmən] N (irreg) vicepresidente m
vice-chancellor [vaɪsˈtʃɑːnsələʳ] N (BRIT Univ) rector(a) m/f
vice-president [vaɪsˈprɛzɪdənt] N vicepresidente(-a) m/f
viceroy [ˈvaɪsrɔɪ] N virrey m
vice versa [ˈvaɪsɪˈvəːsə] ADV viceversa
vicinity [vɪˈsɪnɪtɪ] N (area) vecindad f; (nearness) proximidad f; **in the ~ (of)** cercano (a)
vicious [ˈvɪʃəs] ADJ (remark) malicioso; (blow) brutal; (dog, horse) resabido; **a ~ circle** un círculo vicioso
viciousness [ˈvɪʃəsnɪs] N brutalidad f
vicissitudes [vɪˈsɪsɪtjuːdz] NPL vicisitudes fpl, peripecias fpl
victim [ˈvɪktɪm] N víctima; **to be the ~ of** ser víctima de
victimization [vɪktɪmaɪˈzeɪʃən] N persecución f; (of striker etc) represalias fpl
victimize [ˈvɪktɪmaɪz] VT (strikers etc) tomar represalias contra
victor [ˈvɪktəʳ] N vencedor(a) m/f
Victorian [vɪkˈtɔːrɪən] ADJ victoriano
victorious [vɪkˈtɔːrɪəs] ADJ vencedor(a)
victory [ˈvɪktərɪ] N victoria; **to win a ~ over sb** obtener una victoria sobre algn
video [ˈvɪdɪəu] CPD de vídeo ▶ N vídeo ▶ VT grabar (en vídeo)
video call N videollamada
video camera N videocámara, cámara de vídeo
video cassette N videocassette f
video cassette recorder N = **video recorder**
videodisk [ˈvɪdɪəudɪsk] N videodisco
video game N videojuego
video nasty N vídeo de violencia y/o porno duro
videophone [ˈvɪdɪəufəun] N videoteléfono, videófono
video recorder N vídeo, videocassette f
video recording N videograbación f
video tape N cinta de vídeo
vie [vaɪ] VI: **to ~ with** competir con
Vienna [vɪˈɛnə] N Viena
Viennese [vɪəˈniːz] ADJ, N vienés(-esa) m/f
Vietnam, Viet Nam [vjɛtˈnæm] N Vietnam m
Vietnamese [vjɛtnəˈmiːz] ADJ vietnamita

▶ N pl inv vietnamita mf; (Ling) vietnamita m
view [vjuː] N vista; (landscape) paisaje m; (opinion) opinión f, criterio ▶ VT (look at) mirar; (examine) examinar; **on ~** (in museum etc) expuesto; **in full ~ of sb** a la vista de algn; **to be within ~ (of sth)** estar a la vista (de algo); **an overall ~ of the situation** una visión de conjunto de la situación; **in ~ of the fact that** en vista de que; **to take** or **hold the ~ that ...** opinar or pensar que ...; **with a ~ to doing sth** con miras or vistas a hacer algo
viewdata [ˈvjuːdeɪtə] N (BRIT) videodatos mpl
viewer [ˈvjuːəʳ] N (small projector) visionadora; (TV) televidente mf, telespectador(a) m/f
viewfinder [ˈvjuːfaɪndəʳ] N visor m de imagen
viewpoint [ˈvjuːpɔɪnt] N punto de vista
vigil [ˈvɪdʒɪl] N vigilia; **to keep ~** velar
vigilance [ˈvɪdʒɪləns] N vigilancia
vigilance committee N (US) comité m de autodefensa
vigilant [ˈvɪdʒɪlənt] ADJ vigilante
vigilante [vɪdʒɪˈlæntɪ] N vecino/a que se toma la justicia por su mano
vigorous [ˈvɪgərəs] ADJ enérgico, vigoroso
vigorously [ˈvɪgərəslɪ] ADV enérgicamente, vigorosamente
vigour, (US) vigor [ˈvɪgəʳ] N energía, vigor m
vile [vaɪl] ADJ (action) vil, infame; (smell) repugnante; (temper) endemoniado
vilify [ˈvɪlɪfaɪ] VT denigrar, vilipendiar
villa [ˈvɪlə] N (country house) casa de campo; (suburban house) chalet m
village [ˈvɪlɪdʒ] N aldea
villager [ˈvɪlɪdʒəʳ] N aldeano(-a)
villain [ˈvɪlən] N (scoundrel) malvado(-a); (criminal) maleante mf; see also **pantomime**
VIN N ABBR (US) = **vehicle identification number**
vinaigrette [vɪneɪˈgrɛt] N vinagreta
vindicate [ˈvɪndɪkeɪt] VT vindicar, justificar
vindication [vɪndɪˈkeɪʃən] N: **in ~ of** en justificación de
vindictive [vɪnˈdɪktɪv] ADJ vengativo
vine [vaɪn] N vid f
vinegar [ˈvɪnɪgəʳ] N vinagre m
vine-growing [ˈvaɪngrəuɪŋ] ADJ (region) viticultor(a)
vineyard [ˈvɪnjɑːd] N viña, viñedo
vintage [ˈvɪntɪdʒ] N (year) vendimia, cosecha; **the 1970 ~** la cosecha de 1970
vintage car N coche m antiguo or de época
vintage wine N vino añejo
vintage year N: **it's been a ~ for plays** ha sido un año destacado en lo que a teatro se refiere
vinyl [ˈvaɪnl] N vinilo
viola [vɪˈəulə] N (Mus) viola

violate ['vaɪəleɪt] VT violar

violation [vaɪə'leɪʃən] N violación f; **in ~ of sth** en violación de algo

violence ['vaɪələns] N violencia; **acts of ~** actos mpl de violencia

violent ['vaɪələnt] ADJ (gen) violento; (pain) intenso; **a ~ dislike of sb/sth** una profunda antipatía or manía a algn/algo

violently ['vaɪələntlɪ] ADV (severely: ill, angry) muy

violet ['vaɪələt] ADJ violado, violeta inv ▶ N (plant) violeta

violin [vaɪə'lɪn] N violín m

violinist [vaɪə'lɪnɪst] N violinista mf

VIP N ABBR (= very important person) VIP mf

viper ['vaɪpər] N víbora

viral ['vaɪərəl] ADJ (Med) vírico; (Comput) viral; **~ marketing** márketing m viral; **to go ~** difundirse de forma viral

virgin ['vɜːdʒɪn] N virgen mf ▶ ADJ virgen; **the Blessed V~** la Santísima Virgen

virginity [vɜː'dʒɪnɪtɪ] N virginidad f

Virgo ['vɜːgəu] N Virgo

virile ['vɪraɪl] ADJ viril

virility [vɪ'rɪlɪtɪ] N virilidad f

virtual ['vɜːtjuəl] ADJ (also Comput, Physics) virtual

virtually ['vɜːtjuəlɪ] ADV (almost) prácticamente, virtualmente; **it is ~ impossible** es prácticamente imposible

virtual reality N (Comput) realidad f virtual

virtue ['vɜːtjuː] N virtud f; **by ~ of** en virtud de

virtuosity [vɜːtju'ɔsɪtɪ] N virtuosismo

virtuoso [vɜːtju'əusəu] N virtuoso

virtuous ['vɜːtjuəs] ADJ virtuoso

virulence ['vɪruləns] N virulencia

virulent ['vɪrulənt] ADJ virulento, violento

virus ['vaɪərəs] N virus m inv

visa ['viːzə] N visado, visa (LAm)

vis-à-vis [viːzə'viː] PREP con respecto a

viscount ['vaɪkaunt] N vizconde m

viscous ['vɪskəs] ADJ viscoso

vise [vaɪs] N (US Tech) = **vice**

visibility [vɪzɪ'bɪlɪtɪ] N visibilidad f

visible ['vɪzəbl] ADJ visible; **~ exports/ imports** exportaciones fpl/importaciones fpl visibles

visibly ['vɪzɪblɪ] ADV visiblemente

vision ['vɪʒən] N (sight) vista; (foresight, in dream) visión f

visionary ['vɪʒənrɪ] N visionario(-a)

visit ['vɪzɪt] N visita ▶ VT (person) visitar, hacer una visita a; (place) ir a, (ir a) conocer; **to pay a ~ to** (person) visitar a; **on a private/official ~** en visita privada/oficial

visiting ['vɪzɪtɪŋ] ADJ (speaker, professor) invitado; (team) visitante

visiting card N tarjeta de visita

visiting hours NPL (in hospital etc) horas fpl de visita

visitor [vɪzɪtər] N (gen) visitante mf; (to one's house) visita; (tourist) turista mf; (tripper) excursionista mf; **to have visitors** (at home) tener visita

visitor centre, (US) **visitor center** N centro m de información

visitors' book N libro de visitas

visor ['vaɪzər] N visera

VISTA ['vɪstə] N ABBR (= Volunteers In Service to America) programa de ayuda voluntaria a los necesitados

vista ['vɪstə] N vista, panorama

visual ['vɪzjuəl] ADJ visual

visual aid N medio visual

visual arts NPL artes fpl plásticas

visual display unit N unidad f de despliegue visual, monitor m

visualize ['vɪzjuəlaɪz] VT imaginarse; (foresee) prever

visually ['vɪzjuəlɪ] ADV: **~ handicapped** con visión deficiente

vital ['vaɪtl] ADJ (essential) esencial, imprescindible; (crucial) crítico; (person) enérgico, vivo; (organ) vital; **of ~ importance (to sb/sth)** de suma importancia (para algn/algo)

vitality [vaɪ'tælɪtɪ] N energía, vitalidad f

vitally ['vaɪtəlɪ] ADV: **~ important** de suma importancia

vital statistics NPL (of population) estadísticas fpl demográficas; (inf: of woman) medidas fpl (corporales)

vitamin ['vɪtəmɪn] N vitamina

vitamin pill N pastilla de vitaminas

vitreous ['vɪtrɪəs] ADJ (china, enamel) vítreo

vitriolic [vɪtrɪ'ɔlɪk] ADJ mordaz

viva ['vaɪvə] N (also: **viva voce**) examen m oral

vivacious [vɪ'veɪʃəs] ADJ vivaz, alegre

vivacity [vɪ'væsɪtɪ] N vivacidad f

vivid ['vɪvɪd] ADJ (account) gráfico; (light) intenso; (imagination) vivo

vividly ['vɪvɪdlɪ] ADV (describe) gráficamente; (remember) como si fuera hoy

vivisection [vɪvɪ'sɛkʃən] N vivisección f

vixen ['vɪksn] N (Zool) zorra, raposa; (pej: woman) arpía, bruja

viz ABBR (= videlicet: namely) v. gr.

VLF ABBR = **very low frequency**

V-neck ['viːnɛk] N cuello de pico

VOA N ABBR (= Voice of America) Voz f de América

vocabulary [vəu'kæbjulərɪ] N vocabulario

vocal ['vəukl] ADJ vocal; (articulate) elocuente

vocal cords NPL cuerdas fpl vocales

vocalist ['vəukəlɪst] N cantante mf

vocation [vəu'keɪʃən] N vocación f

V

vocational [vəʊˈkeɪʃənl] ADJ profesional;
  ~ guidance orientación f profesional;
  ~ training formación f profesional
vociferous [vəˈsɪfərəs] ADJ vociferante
vociferously [vəˈsɪfərəslɪ] ADV a gritos
vodka [ˈvɒdkə] N vodka m
vogue [vəʊg] N boga, moda; **to be in ~**, **be
  the ~** estar de moda or en boga
voice [vɔɪs] N voz f ▶ VT (opinion) expresar; **in
  a loud/soft ~** en voz alta/baja; **to give ~ to**
  expresar
voice mail N (Tel) correo de voz, buzón m de
  voz
voice-over [ˈvɔɪsəʊvəʳ] N voz f en off
void [vɔɪd] N vacío; (hole) hueco ▶ ADJ (invalid)
  nulo, inválido; (empty): **~ of** carente or
  desprovisto de
voile [vɔɪl] N gasa
vol. ABBR (= volume) t
volatile [ˈvɒlətaɪl] ADJ (situation) inestable;
  (person) voluble; (liquid) volátil; (Comput:
  memory) no permanente
volcanic [vɒlˈkænɪk] ADJ volcánico
volcano [vɒlˈkeɪnəʊ] (pl **volcanoes**) N
  volcán m
volition [vəˈlɪʃən] N: **of one's own ~** por su
  propia voluntad
volley [ˈvɒlɪ] N (of gunfire) descarga; (of stones
  etc) lluvia; (Tennis etc) volea
volleyball [ˈvɒlɪbɔːl] N voleibol m,
  balonvolea m
volt [vəʊlt] N voltio
voltage [ˈvəʊltɪdʒ] N voltaje m; **high/low ~**
  alto/bajo voltaje, alta/baja tensión
volte-face [ˈvɒltˈfɑːs] N viraje m
voluble [ˈvɒljʊbl] ADJ locuaz, hablador(a)
volume [ˈvɒljuːm] N (of tank) volumen m;
  (book) tomo; **~ one/two** (of book) tomo
  primero/segundo; **volumes** NPL (great
  quantities) cantidad fsg; **his expression
  spoke volumes** su expresión (lo) decía todo
volume control N (Radio, TV) (botón m del)
  volumen m
volume discount N (Comm) descuento por
  volumen de compras
voluminous [vəˈluːmɪnəs] ADJ (large)
  voluminoso; (prolific) prolífico
voluntarily [ˈvɒləntrɪlɪ] ADV libremente,
  voluntariamente
voluntary [ˈvɒləntərɪ] ADJ voluntario,
  espontáneo

voluntary liquidation N (Comm) liquidación
  f voluntaria
voluntary redundancy N (BRIT) despido
  voluntario
volunteer [vɒlənˈtɪəʳ] N voluntario(-a) ▶ VT
  (information) ofrecer ▶ VI ofrecerse (de
  voluntario); **to ~ to do** ofrecerse a hacer
voluptuous [vəˈlʌptjuəs] ADJ voluptuoso
vomit [ˈvɒmɪt] N vómito ▶ VT, VI vomitar
voracious [vəˈreɪʃəs] ADJ voraz; (reader) ávido
vote [vəʊt] N voto; (votes cast) votación f; (right
  to vote) derecho a votar; (franchise) sufragio
  ▶ VT (chairman) elegir ▶ VI votar, ir a votar;
  ~ of thanks voto de gracias; **to put sth to
  the ~**, **to take a ~ on sth** someter algo a
  votación; **~ for or in favour of/against** voto a
  favor de/en contra de; **to ~ to do sth** votar
  por hacer algo; **he was voted secretary** fue
  elegido secretario por votación; **to pass a ~
  of confidence/no confidence** aprobar un
  voto de confianza/de censura
voter [ˈvəʊtəʳ] N votante mf
voting [ˈvəʊtɪŋ] N votación f
voting paper N (BRIT) papeleta de votación
voting right N derecho a voto
vouch [vautʃ]: **to ~ for** vt fus garantizar,
  responder de
voucher [ˈvautʃəʳ] N (for meal, petrol) vale m;
  luncheon/travel ~ vale m de comida/de
  viaje
vow [vau] N voto ▶ VI hacer voto ▶ VT: **to ~ to
  do/that** jurar hacer/que; **to take or make a
  ~ to do sth** jurar hacer algo, comprometerse
  a hacer algo
vowel [ˈvauəl] N vocal f
voyage [ˈvɔɪɪdʒ] N (journey) viaje m; (crossing)
  travesía
voyeur [vwɑːˈjəːʳ] N voyeur mf, mirón(-ona) m/f
VP N ABBR (= vice-president) V.P.
vs ABBR (= versus) vs.
VSO N ABBR (BRIT: = Voluntary Service Overseas)
  organización que envía jóvenes voluntarios a
  trabajar y enseñar en los países del Tercer Mundo
VT, Vt. ABBR (US) = **Vermont**
vulgar [ˈvʌlgəʳ] ADJ (rude) ordinario, grosero;
  (in bad taste) de mal gusto
vulgarity [vʌlˈgærɪtɪ] N grosería; mal gusto
vulnerability [vʌlnərəˈbɪlɪtɪ] N
  vulnerabilidad f
vulnerable [ˈvʌlnərəbl] ADJ vulnerable
vulture [ˈvʌltʃəʳ] N buitre m, gallinazo (LAM)

Ww

W, w ['dʌblju:] N (*letter*) W, w *f*; **W for William** W de Washington

W ABBR (= *west*) O; (*Elec*: = *watt*) v

WA ABBR (*US*) = **Washington**

wad [wɔd] N (*of cotton wool, paper*) bolita; (*of banknotes etc*) fajo

wadding ['wɔdɪŋ] N relleno

waddle ['wɔdl] vi andar como un pato

wade [weɪd] vi : **to ~ through** (*fig: a book*) leer con dificultad; **to ~ through the water** caminar por el agua

wading pool ['weɪdɪŋ-] N (*US*) piscina para niños

wafer ['weɪfə'] N (*biscuit*) barquillo; (*Rel*) oblea; (: *consecrated*) hostia; (*Comput*) oblea, microplaqueta

wafer-thin ['weɪfə'θɪn] ADJ finísimo

waffle ['wɔfl] N (*Culin*) gofre *m* ▶ vi meter el rollo

waffle iron N molde *m* para hacer gofres

waft [wɔft] vt llevar por el aire ▶ vi flotar

wag [wæg] vt menear, agitar ▶ vi moverse, menearse; **the dog wagged its tail** el perro meneó la cola

wage [weɪdʒ] N (*also*: **wages**) sueldo, salario ▶ vt: **to ~ war** hacer la guerra; **a day's ~** el sueldo de un día

wage claim N reivindicación *f* salarial

wage differential N diferencia salarial

wage earner N asalariado(-a)

wage freeze N congelación *f* de salarios

wage packet N sobre *m* de la paga

wager ['weɪdʒə'] N apuesta ▶ vt apostar

waggle ['wægl] vt menear, mover N (*horse-drawn*) carro; (*BRIT Rail*) vagón *m*

wail [weɪl] N gemido ▶ vi gemir

waist [weɪst] N cintura, talle *m*

waistcoat ['weɪstkəut] N (*BRIT*) chaleco

waistline ['weɪstlaɪn] N talle *m*

wait [weɪt] N espera; (*interval*) pausa ▶ vi esperar; **to lie in ~ for** acechar a; **I can't ~ to** (*fig*) estoy deseando; **to ~ for** esperar (a); **to keep sb waiting** hacer esperar a algn; **~ a moment!** ¡un momento!, ¡un momentito!; **"repairs while you ~"** "reparaciones en el acto"

▶ **wait behind** vi quedarse

▶ **wait on** vt fus servir a

▶ **wait up** vi esperar levantado

waiter ['weɪtə'] N camarero

waiting ['weɪtɪŋ] N: **"no ~"** (*BRIT Aut*) "prohibido estacionar"

waiting list N lista de espera

waiting room N sala de espera

waitress ['weɪtrɪs] N camarera

waive [weɪv] vt suspender

waiver ['weɪvə'] N renuncia

wake [weɪk] (*pt* **woke** or **waked**, *pp* **woken** or **waked**) vt (*also*: **wake up**) despertar ▶ vi (*also*: **wake up**) despertarse ▶ N (*for dead person*) velatorio; (*Naut*) estela; **to ~ up to sth** (*fig*) darse cuenta de algo; **in the ~ of** tras, después de; **to follow in sb's ~** (*fig*) seguir las huellas de algn

waken ['weɪkn] vt, vi = **wake**

Wales [weɪlz] N País *m* de Gales

walk [wɔ:k] N (*stroll*) paseo; (*hike*) excursión *f* a pie, caminata; (*gait*) paso, andar *m*; (*in park etc*) paseo ▶ vi andar, caminar; (*for pleasure, exercise*) pasearse ▶ vt (*distance*) recorrer a pie, andar; (*dog*) (sacar a) pasear; **to go for a ~** ir a dar un paseo; **10 minutes' ~ from here** a 10 minutos de aquí andando; **people from all walks of life** gente de todas las esferas; **to ~ in one's sleep** ser sonámbulo(-a); **I'll ~ you home** te acompañaré a casa

▶ **walk out** vi (*go out*) salir; (*as protest*) marcharse, salirse; (*strike*) declararse en huelga; **to ~ out on sb** abandonar a algn

walkabout ['wɔ:kəbaut] N: **to go (on a) ~** darse un baño de multitudes

walker ['wɔ:kə'] N (*person*) paseante *mf*, caminante *mf*

walkie-talkie ['wɔ:kɪ'tɔ:kɪ] N walkie-talkie *m*

walking ['wɔ:kɪŋ] N (el) andar; **it's within ~ distance** se puede ir andando or a pie

walking shoes NPL zapatos *mpl* para andar

walking stick N bastón *m*

Walkman® ['wɔːkmən] N walkman® m
walk-on ['wɔːkɔn] ADJ (Theat: part) de comparsa
walkout ['wɔːkaut] N (of workers) huelga
walkover ['wɔːkəuvəʳ] N (inf) pan m comido
walkway ['wɔːkweɪ] N paseo
wall [wɔːl] N pared f; (exterior) muro; (city wall etc) muralla; **to go to the ~** (fig: firm etc) quebrar, ir a la bancarrota
▶ **wall in** VT (garden etc) cercar con una tapia
walled [wɔːld] ADJ (city) amurallado; (garden) con tapia
wallet ['wɔlɪt] N cartera, billetera (esp LAM)
wallflower ['wɔːlflauəʳ] N alhelí m; **to be a ~** (fig) comer pavo
wall hanging N tapiz m
wallop ['wɔləp] VT (inf) zurrar
wallow ['wɔləu] VI revolcarse; **to ~ in one's grief** sumirse en su pena
wallpaper ['wɔːlpeɪpəʳ] N (for walls) papel m pintado; (Comput) fondo de escritorio ▶ VT empapelar
wall-to-wall ['wɔːltə'wɔːl] ADJ: **~ carpeting** moqueta
wally ['wɔlɪ] N (inf) majadero(-a)
walnut ['wɔːlnʌt] N nuez f; (tree) nogal m
walrus ['wɔːlrəs] (pl **~ or walruses**) N morsa
waltz [wɔːlts] N vals m ▶ VI bailar el vals
wan [wɔn] ADJ pálido
wand [wɔnd] N (also: **magic wand**) varita (mágica)
wander ['wɔndəʳ] VI (person) vagar; deambular; (thoughts) divagar; (get lost) extraviarse ▶ VT recorrer, vagar por
wanderer ['wɔndərəʳ] N vagabundo(-a)
wandering ['wɔndərɪŋ] ADJ (tribe) nómada; (minstrel, actor) ambulante; (path, river) sinuoso; (glance, mind) distraído
wane [weɪn] VI menguar
wangle ['wæŋgl] (BRIT inf) VT: **to ~ sth** agenciarse or conseguir algo ▶ N chanchullo
wanker ['wæŋkəʳ] N (inf!) pajero(-a) (!); (as insult) mamón(-ona) (!) mf
want [wɔnt] VT (wish for) querer, desear; (need) necesitar; (lack) carecer de ▶ N (poverty) pobreza; **for ~ of** por falta de; **wants** NPL (needs) necesidades fpl; **to ~ to do** querer hacer; **to ~ sb to do sth** querer que algn haga algo; **you're wanted on the phone** te llaman al teléfono; **to be in ~** estar necesitado
want ads NPL (US) anuncios mpl por palabras
wanted ['wɔntɪd] ADJ (criminal) buscado; **"~"** (in advertisements) "se busca"
wanting ['wɔntɪŋ] ADJ: **to be ~ (in)** estar falto (de); **to be found ~** no estar a la altura de las circunstancias
wanton ['wɔntn] ADJ (licentious) lascivo

WAP [wæp] N ABBR (= wireless application protocol) WAP m
WAP phone N teléfono WAP
war [wɔːʳ] N guerra; **to make ~** hacer la guerra; **the First/Second World W~** la Primera/Segunda Guerra Mundial
warble ['wɔːbl] N (of bird) trino, gorjeo ▶ VI (bird) trinar
war cry N grito de guerra
ward [wɔːd] N (in hospital) sala; (Pol) distrito electoral; (Law: child: also: **ward of court**) pupilo(-a)
▶ **ward off** VT desviar, parar; (attack) rechazar
warden ['wɔːdn] N (BRIT: of institution) director(a) m/f; (of park, game reserve) guardián(-ana) m/f; (BRIT: also: **traffic warden**) guardia mf
warder ['wɔːdəʳ] N (BRIT) guardián(-ana) m/f, carcelero(-a) m/f
wardrobe ['wɔːdrəub] N armario, guardarropa, ropero, clóset/closet m (LAM)
warehouse ['wɛəhaus] N almacén m, depósito
wares [wɛəz] NPL mercancías fpl
warfare ['wɔːfɛəʳ] N guerra
war game N juego de estrategia militar
warhead ['wɔːhɛd] N cabeza armada; **nuclear warheads** cabezas fpl nucleares
warily ['wɛərɪlɪ] ADV con cautela, cautelosamente
warlike ['wɔːlaɪk] ADJ guerrero
warm [wɔːm] ADJ caliente; (person, greeting, heart) afectuoso, cariñoso; (supporter) entusiasta; (thanks, congratulations, apologies) efusivo; (clothes etc) que abriga; (welcome, day) caluroso; **it's ~** hace calor; **I'm ~** tengo calor; **to keep sth ~** mantener algo caliente
▶ **warm up** VI (room) calentarse; (person) entrar en calor; (athlete) hacer ejercicios de calentamiento; (discussion) acalorarse ▶ VT calentar
warm-blooded ['wɔːm'blʌdɪd] ADJ de sangre caliente
war memorial N monumento a los caídos
warm-hearted [wɔːm'hɑːtɪd] ADJ afectuoso
warmly ['wɔːmlɪ] ADV afectuosamente
warmonger ['wɔːmʌŋgəʳ] N belicista mf
warmongering ['wɔːmʌŋgrɪŋ] N belicismo
warmth [wɔːmθ] N calor m
warm-up ['wɔːmʌp] N (Sport) ejercicios mpl de calentamiento
warn [wɔːn] VT avisar, advertir; **to ~ sb not to do sth** or **against doing sth** aconsejar a algn que no haga algo
warning ['wɔːnɪŋ] N aviso, advertencia; **gale ~** (Meteorology) aviso de vendaval; **without (any) ~** sin aviso or avisar
warning light N luz f de advertencia

warning triangle N (*Aut*) triángulo señalizador

warp [wɔːp] VI (*wood*) combarse

warpath ['wɔːpɑːθ] N: **to be on the ~** (*fig*) estar en pie de guerra

warped [wɔːpt] ADJ (*wood*) alabeado; (*fig: character, sense of humour etc*) pervertido

warrant ['wɔrnt] N (*Law: to arrest*) orden *f* de detención; (*: to search*) mandamiento de registro ▶ VT (*justify, merit*) merecer

warrant officer N (*Mil*) brigada *m*; (*Naut*) contramaestre *m*

warranty ['wɔrənti] N garantía; **under ~** (*Comm*) bajo garantía

warren ['wɔrən] N (*of rabbits*) madriguera; (*fig*) laberinto

warring ['wɔːrɪŋ] ADJ (*interests etc*) opuesto; (*nations*) en guerra

warrior ['wɔrɪəʳ] N guerrero(-a)

Warsaw ['wɔːsɔː] N Varsovia

warship ['wɔːʃɪp] N buque *m* or barco de guerra

wart [wɔːt] N verruga

wartime ['wɔːtaɪm] N: **in ~** en tiempos de guerra, en la guerra

wary ['wɛərɪ] ADJ cauteloso; **to be ~ about** or **of doing sth** tener cuidado con hacer algo

was [wɔz] PT of **be**

wash [wɔʃ] VT lavar; (*sweep, carry: sea etc*) llevar ▶ VI lavarse ▶ N (*clothes etc*) lavado; (*bath*) baño; (*of ship*) estela; **he was washed overboard** fue arrastrado del barco por las olas; **to have a ~** lavarse
  ▶ **wash away** VT (*stain*) quitar lavando; (*river etc*) llevarse; (*fig*) limpiar
  ▶ **wash down** VT lavar
  ▶ **wash off** VT quitar lavando
  ▶ **wash up** VI (*Brit*) fregar los platos; (*US: have a wash*) lavarse

Wash. ABBR (*US*) = **Washington**

washable ['wɔʃəbl] ADJ lavable

washbasin ['wɔʃbeɪsn], (*US*) **washbowl** ['wɔʃbəul] N lavabo

washcloth ['wɔʃklɔθ] N (*US*) manopla

washer ['wɔʃəʳ] N (*Tech*) arandela

washing ['wɔʃɪŋ] N (*dirty*) ropa sucia; (*clean*) colada

washing line N cuerda de (colgar) la ropa

washing machine N lavadora

washing powder N (*Brit*) detergente *m* (en polvo)

Washington ['wɔʃɪŋtən] N (*city, state*) Washington *m*

washing-up [wɔʃɪŋ'ʌp] N fregado; (*dishes*) platos *mpl* (para fregar); **to do the ~** fregar los platos

washing-up liquid N lavavajillas *m inv*

wash leather N gamuza

wash-out ['wɔʃaut] N (*inf*) fracaso

washroom ['wɔʃrum] N servicios *mpl*

wasn't ['wɔznt] = **was not**

WASP, Wasp [wɔsp] N ABBR (*US: inf*: = *White Anglo-Saxon Protestant*) sobrenombre, en general peyorativo, que se da a los americanos de origen anglosajón, acomodados y de tendencia conservadora

wasp [wɔsp] N avispa

waspish ['wɔspɪʃ] ADJ (*character*) irascible; (*comment*) mordaz, punzante

wastage ['weɪstɪdʒ] N desgaste *m*; (*loss*) pérdida; **natural ~** desgaste natural

waste [weɪst] N derroche *m*, despilfarro; (*misuse*) desgaste *m*; (*of time*) pérdida; (*food*) sobras *fpl*; (*rubbish*) basura, desperdicios *mpl* ▶ ADJ (*material*) de desecho; (*left over*) sobrante; (*energy, heat*) desperdiciado; (*land, ground*: in city) sin construir; (*: in country*) baldío ▶ VT (*squander*) malgastar, derrochar; (*time*) perder; (*opportunity*) desperdiciar; **wastes** NPL (*area of land*) tierras *fpl* baldías; **to lay ~** devastar, arrasar; **it's a ~ of money** es tirar el dinero; **to go to ~** desperdiciarse
  ▶ **waste away** VI consumirse

wastebasket ['weɪstbɑːskɪt] N (*esp US*) = **wastepaper basket**

waste disposal, waste disposal unit N (*Brit*) triturador *m* de basura

wasteful ['weɪstful] ADJ derrochador(a); (*process*) antieconómico

wastefully ['weɪstfulɪ] ADV: **to spend money ~** derrochar dinero

waste ground N (*Brit*) terreno baldío

wasteland ['weɪstlænd] N (*urban*) descampados *mpl*

wastepaper basket ['weɪstpeɪpə-] N papelera; (*Comput*) papelera de reciclaje

waste pipe N tubo de desagüe

waste products NPL (*Industry*) residuos *mpl*

waster ['weɪstəʳ] N (*inf*) gandul *mf*

watch [wɔtʃ] N reloj *m*; (*vigil*) vigilia; (*vigilance*) vigilancia; (*Mil: guard*) centinela *m*; (*Naut: spell of duty*) guardia ▶ VT (*look at*) mirar, observar; (*: match, programme*) ver; (*spy on, guard*) vigilar; (*be careful of*) cuidar, tener cuidado de ▶ VI ver, mirar; (*keep guard*) montar guardia; **to keep a close ~ on sth/ sb** vigilar algo/a algn de cerca; **~ how you drive/what you're doing** ten cuidado al conducir/con lo que haces
  ▶ **watch out** VI cuidarse, tener cuidado

watch band N (*US*) pulsera (de reloj)

watchdog ['wɔtʃdɔg] N perro guardián; (*fig*) organismo de control

watchful ['wɔtʃful] ADJ vigilante, sobre aviso

watchfully ['wɔtʃfulɪ] ADV: **to stand ~** permanecer vigilante

watchmaker ['wɔtʃmeɪkəʳ] N relojero(-a)

W

watchman ['wɒtʃmən] N (*irreg: like* **man**) guardián *m*; (*also*: **night watchman**) sereno, vigilante *m*; (: *in factory*) vigilante *m* nocturno
watch stem N (*US*) cuerda
watch strap N pulsera (de reloj)
watchword ['wɒtʃwɜːd] N consigna, contraseña
water ['wɔːtəʳ] N agua ▸ VT (*plant*) regar ▸ VI (*eyes*) llorar; **I'd like a drink of ~** quisiera un vaso de agua; **in British waters** en aguas británicas; **to pass ~** orinar; **his mouth watered** se le hizo la boca agua
▸ **water down** VT (*milk etc*) aguar; (*fig: story*) dulcificar, diluir
water closet N wáter *m*
watercolour, (*US*) **watercolor** ['wɔːtəklʌəʳ] N acuarela
water-cooled ['wɔːtəkuːld] ADJ refrigerado (por agua)
watercress ['wɔːtəkrɛs] N berro
waterfall ['wɔːtəfɔːl] N cascada, salto de agua
waterfront ['wɔːtəfrʌnt] N (*seafront*) parte *f* que da al mar; (*at docks*) muelles *mpl*
water heater N calentador *m* de agua
water hole N abrevadero
watering can ['wɔːtərɪŋ-] N regadera
water level N nivel *m* del agua
water lily N nenúfar *m*
waterline ['wɔːtəlaɪn] N (*Naut*) línea de flotación
waterlogged ['wɔːtəlɒgd] ADJ (*boat*) anegado; (*ground*) inundado
water main N cañería del agua
watermark ['wɔːtəmɑːk] N (*on paper*) filigrana
watermelon ['wɔːtəmɛlən] N sandía
water polo N waterpolo, polo acuático
waterproof ['wɔːtəpruːf] ADJ impermeable
water-repellent ['wɔːtərɪˈpɛlənt] ADJ hidrófugo
watershed ['wɔːtəʃɛd] N (*Geo*) cuenca; (*fig*) momento crítico
water-skiing ['wɔːtəskiːɪŋ] N esquí *m* acuático
water softener N ablandador *m* de agua
water tank N depósito de agua
watertight ['wɔːtətaɪt] ADJ hermético
water vapour, (*US*) **water vapor** N vapor *m* de agua
waterway ['wɔːtəweɪ] N vía fluvial *or* navegable
waterworks ['wɔːtəwəːks] NPL central *fsg* depuradora
watery ['wɔːtərɪ] ADJ (*colour*) desvaído; (*coffee*) aguado; (*eyes*) lloroso
watt [wɒt] N vatio
wattage ['wɒtɪdʒ] N potencia en vatios
wattle ['wɒtl] N zarzo

wave [weɪv] N ola; (*of hand*) señal *f* con la mano; (*Radio*) onda; (*in hair*) onda; (*fig: of enthusiasm, strikes*) oleada ▸ VI agitar la mano; (*flag*) ondear ▸ VT (*handkerchief, gun*) agitar; **short/medium/long ~** (*Radio*) onda corta/media/larga; **the new ~** (*Cine, Mus*) la nueva ola; **to ~ goodbye to sb** decir adiós a algn con la mano; **he waved us over to his table** nos hizo señas (con la mano) para que nos acercásemos a su mesa
▸ **wave aside, wave away** VT (*person*): **to ~ sb aside** apartar a algn con la mano; (*fig: suggestion, objection*) rechazar; (*doubts*) desechar
waveband ['weɪvbænd] N banda de ondas
wavelength ['weɪvlɛŋθ] N longitud *f* de onda
waver ['weɪvəʳ] VI oscilar; (*confidence*) disminuir; (*faith*) flaquear
wavy ['weɪvɪ] ADJ ondulado
wax [wæks] N cera ▸ VT encerar ▸ VI (*moon*) crecer
waxen ['wæksn] ADJ (*fig: pale*) blanco como la cera
waxworks ['wæksˈwəːks] NPL museo *sg* de cera
way [weɪ] N camino; (*distance*) trayecto, recorrido; (*direction*) dirección *f*, sentido; (*manner*) modo, manera; (*habit*) costumbre *f*; **which ~? — this ~** ¿por dónde? *or* ¿en qué dirección? — por aquí; **on the ~** (*en route*) en (el) camino; (*expected*) en camino; **to be on one's ~** estar en camino; **you pass it on your ~ home** está de camino a tu casa; **to be in the ~** bloquear el camino; (*fig*) estorbar; **to keep out of sb's ~** esquivar a algn; **to make ~ (for sb/sth)** dejar paso (a algn/algo); (*fig*) abrir camino (a algn/algo); **to go out of one's ~ to do sth** desvivirse por hacer algo; **to lose one's ~** perderse, extraviarse; **to be the wrong ~ round** estar del *or* al revés; **in a ~** en cierto modo *or* sentido; **by the ~** a propósito; **by ~ of** (*via*) pasando por; (*as a sort of*) como, a modo de; **"~ in"** (*Brit*) "entrada"; **"~ out"** (*Brit*) "salida"; **the ~ back** el camino de vuelta; **the village is rather out of the ~** el pueblo está un poco apartado *or* retirado; **it's a long ~ away** está muy lejos; **to get one's own ~** salirse con la suya; **"give ~"** (*Brit Aut*) "ceda el paso"; **no ~!** (*inf*) ¡ni pensarlo!; **put it the right ~ up** ponlo boca arriba; **he's in a bad ~** está grave; **to be under ~** (*work, project*) estar en marcha
waybill ['weɪbɪl] N (*Comm*) hoja de ruta, carta de porte
waylay ['weɪleɪ] VT (*irreg: like* **lay**) atacar
wayside ['weɪsaɪd] N borde *m* del camino; **to fall by the ~** (*fig*) fracasar
way station N (*US Rail*) apeadero
wayward ['weɪwəd] ADJ díscolo, caprichoso

WC ['dʌblju:'si:] N ABBR (BRIT: = *water closet*) wáter *m*

WCC N ABBR = **World Council of Churches**

we [wi:] PRON PL nosotros(-as); **we understand** (nosotros) entendemos; **here we are** aquí estamos

weak [wi:k] ADJ débil, flojo; (*tea, coffee*) flojo, aguado; **to grow ~(er)** debilitarse

weaken ['wi:kən] VI debilitarse; (*give way*) ceder ▸ VT debilitar

weak-kneed [wi:k'ni:d] ADJ (*fig*) sin voluntad *or* carácter

weakling ['wi:klɪŋ] N debilucho(-a)

weakly ['wi:klɪ] ADJ enfermizo, débil ▸ ADV débilmente

weakness ['wi:knɪs] N debilidad *f*; (*fault*) punto débil; **to have a ~ for** tener debilidad por

wealth [wɛlθ] N (*money, resources*) riqueza; (*of details*) abundancia

wealth tax N impuesto sobre el patrimonio

wealthy ['wɛlθɪ] ADJ rico

wean [wi:n] VT destetar

weapon ['wɛpən] N arma; **weapons of mass destruction** armas de destrucción masiva

wear [wɛəʳ] (*pt* **wore**, *pp* **worn**) N (*use*) uso; (*deterioration through use*) desgaste *m*; (*clothing*): **sports/babywear** ropa de deportes/de niños ▸ VT (*clothes, beard*) llevar; (*shoes*) calzar; (*look, smile*) tener; (*damage: through use*) gastar, usar ▸ VI (*last*) durar; (*rub through etc*) desgastarse; **evening ~** (*man's*) traje *m* de etiqueta; (*woman's*) traje *m* de noche; **to ~ a hole in sth** hacer un agujero en algo

▸ **wear away** VT gastar ▸ VI desgastarse

▸ **wear down** VT gastar; (*strength*) agotar

▸ **wear off** VI (*pain, excitement etc*) pasar, desaparecer

▸ **wear out** VT desgastar; (*person, strength*) agotar

wearable ['wɛərəbl] ADJ que se puede llevar, ponible

wear and tear N desgaste *m*

wearer ['wɛərəʳ] N: **the ~ of this jacket** el/la que lleva puesta esta chaqueta

wearily ['wɪərɪlɪ] ADV con cansancio

weariness ['wɪərɪnɪs] N cansancio; abatimiento

wearisome ['wɪərɪsəm] ADJ (*tiring*) cansado, pesado; (*boring*) aburrido

weary ['wɪərɪ] ADJ (*tired*) cansado; (*dispirited*) abatido ▸ VT cansar ▸ VI: **to ~ of** cansarse de, aburrirse de

weasel ['wi:zl] N (*Zool*) comadreja

weather ['wɛðəʳ] N tiempo ▸ VT (*storm, crisis*) hacer frente a; **under the ~** (*fig: ill*) mal, pachucho; **what's the ~ like?** ¿qué tiempo hace?, ¿cómo hace?

weather-beaten ['wɛðəbi:tn] ADJ curtido

weathercock ['wɛðəkɔk] N veleta

weather forecast N boletín *m* meteorológico

weatherman ['wɛðəmæn] N (*irreg*) hombre *m* del tiempo

weatherproof ['wɛðəpru:f] ADJ (*garment*) impermeable

weather report N parte *m* meteorológico

weather vane N = **weathercock**

weave [wi:v] (*pt* **wove** [wəuv], *pp* **woven** ['wəuvn]) VT (*cloth*) tejer; (*fig*) entretejer ▸ VI (*pt, pp* **weaved**) (*fig: move in and out*) zigzaguear

weaver ['wi:vəʳ] N tejedor(a) *m/f*

weaving ['wi:vɪŋ] N tejeduría

web [wɛb] N (*of spider*) telaraña; (*on foot*) membrana; (*Comput: network*) red *f*; **the W~** la Red

web address N dirección *f* de página web

webbed [wɛbd] ADJ (*foot*) palmeado

webbing ['wɛbɪŋ] N (*on chair*) cinchas *fpl*

webcam ['wɛbkæm] N webcam *f*

webinar ['wɛbɪnɑːʳ] N (*Comput*) seminario web, webinar *m*

weblog ['wɛblɔg] N weblog *m*

webmail ['wɛbmeɪl] N (*Comput*) correo web, webmail *m*

web page N página web

website ['wɛbsaɪt] N sitio web

wed [wɛd] (*pt, pp* **wedded**) VT casar ▸ VI casarse ▸ N: **the newly-weds** los recién casados

Wed. ABBR (= *Wednesday*) miérc.

we'd [wi:d] = **we had**; **we would**

wedded ['wɛdɪd] PT, PP *of* **wed**

wedding ['wɛdɪŋ] N boda, casamiento

wedding anniversary N aniversario de boda; **silver/golden ~** bodas *fpl* de plata/ de oro

wedding day N día *m* de la boda

wedding dress N traje *m* de novia

wedding present N regalo de boda

wedding ring N alianza

wedge [wɛdʒ] N (*of wood etc*) cuña; (*of cake*) trozo ▸ VT acuñar; (*push*) apretar

wedge-heeled ['wɛdʒ'hi:ld] ADJ con suela de cuña

wedlock ['wɛdlɔk] N matrimonio

Wednesday ['wɛdnzdɪ] N miércoles *m inv*; *see also* **Tuesday**

wee [wi:] ADJ (SCOTTISH) pequeñito

weed [wi:d] N mala hierba, maleza ▸ VT escardar, desherbar

▸ **weed out** VT eliminar

weedkiller ['wi:dkɪləʳ] N herbicida *m*

weedy ['wi:dɪ] ADJ (*person*) debilucho

week [wi:k] N semana; **a ~ today** de hoy en ocho días; **Tuesday ~**, **a ~ on Tuesday** del martes en una semana; **once/twice a ~** una vez/dos veces a la semana; **this ~** esta semana;

W

in two weeks' time dentro de dos semanas; **every other ~** cada dos semanas

weekday ['wi:kdeɪ] N día m laborable; **on weekdays** entre semana, en días laborables

weekend [wi:k'ɛnd] N fin m de semana

weekend case N neceser m

weekly ['wi:klɪ] ADV semanalmente, cada semana ▶ ADJ semanal ▶ N semanario; **~ newspaper** semanario

weep [wi:p] (pt, pp **wept** [wɛpt]) VI, VT llorar; (Med: wound etc) supurar

weeping willow ['wi:pɪŋ-] N sauce m llorón

weepy ['wi:pɪ] N (inf: film) película lacrimógena; (: story) historia lacrimógena

weft [wɛft] N (Textiles) trama

weigh [weɪ] VT, VI pesar; **to ~ anchor** levar anclas; **to ~ the pros and cons** pesar los pros y los contras
 ▶ **weigh down** VT sobrecargar; (fig: with worry) agobiar
 ▶ **weigh out** VT (goods) pesar
 ▶ **weigh up** VT sopesar

weighbridge ['weɪbrɪdʒ] N báscula para camiones

weighing machine ['weɪɪŋ-] N báscula, peso

weight [weɪt] N peso; (on scale) pesa; **to lose/put on ~** adelgazar/engordar; **weights and measures** pesas y medidas

weighting ['weɪtɪŋ] N (allowance): (**London) ~** dietas (por residir en Londres)

weightlessness ['weɪtlɪsnɪs] N ingravidez f

weight lifter N levantador(a) m/f de pesas

weightlifting ['weɪtlɪftɪŋ] N levantamiento de pesas

weight limit N límite m de peso

weight training N musculación f (con pesas)

weighty ['weɪtɪ] ADJ pesado

weir [wɪəʳ] N presa

weird [wɪəd] ADJ raro, extraño

weirdo ['wɪədəu] N (inf) tío(-a) raro(-a)

welcome ['wɛlkəm] ADJ bienvenido ▶ N bienvenida ▶ VT dar la bienvenida a; (be glad of) alegrarse de; **to make sb ~** recibir or acoger bien a algn; **thank you — you're ~** gracias — de nada; **you're ~ to try** puede intentar cuando quiera; **we ~ this step** celebramos esta medida

weld [wɛld] N soldadura ▶ VT soldar

welding ['wɛldɪŋ] N soldadura

welfare ['wɛlfɛəʳ] N bienestar m; (social aid) asistencia social; **W~** (US) subsidio de paro; **to look after sb's ~** cuidar del bienestar de algn

welfare state N estado del bienestar

welfare work N asistencia social

well [wɛl] N pozo ▶ ADV bien ▶ ADJ: **to be ~** estar bien (de salud) ▶ EXCL ¡vaya!, ¡bueno!; **as ~** (in addition) además, también; **as ~ as** además de; **you might as ~ tell me** más vale

que me lo digas; **it would be as ~ to ask** más valdría preguntar; **~ done!** ¡bien hecho!; **get ~ soon!** ¡que te mejores pronto!; **to do ~** (business) ir bien; **I did ~ in my exams** me han salido bien los exámenes; **they are doing ~ now** les va bien ahora; **to think ~ of sb** pensar bien de algn; **I don't feel ~** no me encuentro or siento bien; **~, as I was saying ...** bueno, como decía ...
 ▶ **well up** VI brotar

we'll [wi:l] = **we will**; **we shall**

well-behaved ['wɛlbɪ'heɪvd] ADJ: **to be ~** portarse bien

well-being ['wɛl'bi:ɪŋ] N bienestar m

well-bred ['wɛl'brɛd] ADJ bien educado

well-built ['wɛl'bɪlt] ADJ (person) fornido

well-chosen ['wɛl'tʃəuzn] ADJ (remarks, words) acertado

well-deserved ['wɛldɪ'zə:vd] ADJ merecido

well-developed ['wɛldɪ'vɛləpt] ADJ (arm, muscle etc) bien desarrollado; (sense) agudo, fino

well-disposed ['wɛldɪs'pəuzd] ADJ: **~ to(wards)** bien dispuesto a

well-dressed ['wɛl'drɛst] ADJ bien vestido

well-earned ['wɛl'ə:nd] ADJ (rest) merecido

well-groomed ['wɛl'gru:md] ADJ de apariencia cuidada

well-heeled ['wɛl'hi:ld] ADJ (inf: wealthy) rico

wellies ['wɛlɪz] NPL (BRIT inf) botas de goma

well-informed ['wɛlɪn'fɔ:md] ADJ (having knowledge of sth) enterado, al corriente

Wellington ['wɛlɪŋtən] N Wellington m

wellingtons ['wɛlɪŋtənz] NPL (also: **Wellington boots**) botas fpl de goma

well-kept ['wɛl'kɛpt] ADJ (secret) bien guardado; (hair, hands, house, grounds) bien cuidado

well-known ['wɛl'nəun] ADJ (person) conocido

well-mannered ['wɛl'mænəd] ADJ educado

well-meaning ['wɛl'mi:nɪŋ] ADJ bienintencionado

well-nigh ['wɛl'naɪ] ADV: **~ impossible** casi imposible

well-off ['wɛl'ɔf] ADJ acomodado

well-paid [wɛl'peɪd] ADJ bien pagado, bien retribuido

well-read ['wɛl'rɛd] ADJ culto

well-spoken ['wɛl'spəukən] ADJ bienhablado

well-stocked ['wɛl'stɔkt] ADJ (shop, larder) bien surtido

well-timed ['wɛl'taɪmd] ADJ oportuno

well-to-do ['wɛltə'du:] ADJ acomodado

well-wisher ['wɛlwɪʃəʳ] N admirador(a) m/f

well-woman clinic ['wɛlwumən-] N centro de prevención médica para mujeres

Welsh [wɛlʃ] ADJ galés(-esa) ▶ N (Ling) galés m; **the Welsh** NPL los galeses; **the ~ Assembly** el Parlamento galés

Welshman ['wɛlʃmən] N (irreg) galés m

Welsh rarebit [-'rɛəbɪt] N pan m con queso tostado

Welshwoman ['wɛlʃwumən] N (irreg) galesa

welter ['wɛltər] N mescolanza, revoltijo

went [wɛnt] PT of **go**

wept [wɛpt] PT, PP of **weep**

were [wəːr] PT of **be**

we're [wɪər] = **we are**

weren't [wəːnt] = **were not**

werewolf ['wɪəwulf] (pl **werewolves** [-wulvz]) N hombre m lobo

west [wɛst] N oeste m ▶ ADJ occidental, del oeste ▶ ADV al or hacia el oeste; **the W~** Occidente m

westbound ['wɛstbaund] ADJ (traffic, carriageway) en dirección al oeste

West Country N: **the ~** el suroeste de Inglaterra

westerly ['wɛstəlɪ] ADJ (wind) del oeste

western ['wɛstən] ADJ occidental ▶ N (Cine) película del oeste

westerner ['wɛstənər] N (Pol) occidental mf

westernized ['wɛstənaɪzd] ADJ occidentalizado

West German (formerly) ADJ de Alemania Occidental ▶ N alemán(-ana) m/f (de Alemania Occidental)

West Germany N (formerly) Alemania Occidental

West Indian ADJ, N antillano(-a) m/f

West Indies [-'ɪndɪz] NPL: **the ~** las Antillas

Westminster ['wɛstmɪnstər] N el parlamento británico, Westminster m

westward ['wɛstwəd], **westwards** ['wɛstwədz] ADV hacia el oeste

wet [wɛt] ADJ (damp) húmedo; (wet through) mojado; (rainy) lluvioso ▶ VT: **to ~ one's pants** or **o.s.** mearse; **to get ~** mojarse; **"~ paint"** "recién pintado"

wet blanket N: **to be a ~** (fig) ser un (una) aguafiestas

wetness ['wɛtnɪs] N humedad f

wet rot N putrefacción f por humedad

wetsuit ['wɛtsuːt] N traje m de buzo

we've [wiːv] = **we have**

whack [wæk] VT dar un buen golpe a

whale [weɪl] N (Zool) ballena

whaler ['weɪlər] N (ship) ballenero

whaling ['weɪlɪŋ] N pesca de ballenas

wharf [wɔːf] (pl **wharves** [wɔːvz]) N muelle m

(KEYWORD)

what [wɔt] ADJ **1** (in direct/indirect questions) qué; **what size is he?** ¿qué talla usa?; **what colour/shape is it?** ¿de qué color/forma es?; **what books do you need?** ¿qué libros necesitas?

2 (in exclamations): **what a mess!** ¡qué desastre!;

what a fool I am! ¡qué tonto soy!

▶ PRON **1** (interrogative) qué; **what are you doing?** ¿qué haces or estás haciendo?; **what is happening?** ¿qué pasa or está pasando?; **what is it called?** ¿cómo se llama?; **what about me?** ¿y yo qué?; **what about doing ...?** ¿qué tal si hacemos ...?; **what is his address?** ¿cuáles son sus señas?; **what will it cost?** ¿cuánto costará?

2 (relative) lo que; **I saw what you did/was on the table** vi lo que hiciste/había en la mesa; **what I want is a cup of tea** lo que quiero es una taza de té; **I don't know what to do** no sé qué hacer; **tell me what you're thinking about** dime en qué estás pensando

3 (reported questions): **she asked me what I wanted** me preguntó qué quería

▶ EXCL (disbelieving) ¡cómo!; **what, no coffee!** ¡que no hay café!

---

whatever [wɔt'ɛvər] ADJ: **~ book you choose** cualquier libro que elijas ▶ PRON: **do ~ is necessary** haga lo que sea necesario; **no reason ~** ninguna razón en absoluto; **nothing ~** nada en absoluto; **~ it costs** cueste lo que cueste

whatsoever [wɔtsəu'ɛvər] ADJ see **whatever**

wheat [wiːt] N trigo

wheatgerm ['wiːtdʒəːm] N germen m de trigo

wheatmeal ['wiːtmiːl] N harina de trigo

wheedle ['wiːdl] VT: **to ~ sb into doing sth** engatusar a algn para que haga algo; **to ~ sth out of sb** sonsacar algo a algn

wheel [wiːl] N rueda; (Aut: also: **steering wheel**) volante m; (Naut) timón m ▶ VT (pram etc) empujar ▶ VI (also: **wheel round**) dar la vuelta, girar; **four-/rear-~ drive** tracción f en las cuatro ruedas; **front-/rear-~ drive** tracción f delantera/trasera

wheelbarrow ['wiːlbærəu] N carretilla

wheelbase ['wiːlbeɪs] N batalla

wheelchair ['wiːltʃɛər] N silla de ruedas

wheel clamp N (Aut) cepo

wheeler-dealer ['wiːlə'diːlər] N chanchullero(-a)

wheelie-bin ['wiːlɪbɪn] N (BRIT) contenedor m de basura

wheeling ['wiːlɪŋ] N: **~ and dealing** (inf) chanchullos mpl

wheeze [wiːz] VI resollar

wheezy ['wiːzɪ] ADJ silbante

(KEYWORD)

when [wɛn] ADV cuando; **when did it happen?** ¿cuándo ocurrió?; **I know when it happened** sé cuándo ocurrió

▶ CONJ **1** (at, during, after the time that) cuando; **be careful when you cross the road** ten

W

cuidado al cruzar la calle; **that was when I needed you** entonces era cuando te necesitaba; **I'll buy you a car when you're 18** te compraré un coche cuando cumplas 18 años

2 (*on, at which*): **on the day when I met him** el día en qué le conocí

3 (*whereas*) cuando; **you said I was wrong when in fact I was right** dijiste que no tenía razón, cuando en realidad sí la tenía

whenever [wɛnˈɛvəʳ] CONJ cuando; (*every time*) cada vez que; **I go ~ I can** voy siempre or todas las veces que puedo

where [wɛəʳ] ADV dónde ▶ CONJ donde; **this is ~** aquí es donde; **~ possible** donde sea posible; **~ are you from?** ¿de dónde es usted?

whereabouts [ˈwɛərəbauts] ADV dónde ▶ N: **nobody knows his ~** nadie conoce su paradero

whereas [wɛərˈæz] CONJ mientras

whereby [wɛəˈbai] ADV mediante el (la) cual *etc*, por lo (la) cual *etc*

whereupon [wɛərəˈpɔn] CONJ con lo cual, después de lo cual

wherever [wɛərˈɛvəʳ] ADV dondequiera que; (*interrogative*) dónde; **sit ~ you like** siéntese donde quiera

wherewithal [ˈwɛəwɪðɔːl] N recursos *mpl*; **the ~ (to do sth)** los medios económicos (para hacer algo)

whet [wɛt] VT estimular; (*appetite*) abrir

whether [ˈwɛðəʳ] CONJ si; **I don't know ~ to accept or not** no sé si aceptar o no; **~ you go or not** vayas o no vayas

whey [wei] N suero

(KEYWORD)

which [wɪtʃ] ADJ **1** (*interrogative: direct, indirect*) qué; **which picture(s) do you want?** ¿qué cuadro(s) quieres?; **which one?** ¿cuál?; **which one of you?** ¿cuál de vosotros?; **tell me which one you want** dime cuál (es el que) quieres

2: **in which case** en cuyo caso; **we got there at eight pm, by which time the cinema was full** llegamos allí a las ocho, cuando el cine estaba lleno

▶ PRON **1** (*interrogative*) cual; **I don't mind which** el (la) que sea; **which do you want?** ¿cuál quieres?

2 (*relative: replacing noun*) que; (: *replacing clause*) lo que; (: *after preposition*) (el (la)) que, el (la) cual; **the apple which you ate/which is on the table** la manzana que comiste/que está en la mesa; **the chair on which you are sitting** la silla en la que estás sentado; **he didn't believe it, which upset me** no se lo creyó, lo cual or lo que me disgustó; **after which** después de lo cual

whichever [wɪtʃˈɛvəʳ] ADJ: **take ~ book you prefer** coja el libro que prefiera; **~ book you take** cualquier libro que coja

whiff [wɪf] N bocanada; **to catch a ~ of sth** oler algo

while [wail] N rato, momento ▶ CONJ durante; (*whereas*) mientras; (*although*) aunque ▶ VT: **to ~ away the time** pasar el rato; **for a ~** durante algún tiempo; **in a ~** dentro de poco; **all the ~** todo el tiempo; **we'll make it worth your ~** te compensaremos generosamente

whilst [wailst] CONJ = **while**

whim [wɪm] N capricho

whimper [ˈwɪmpəʳ] N (*weeping*) lloriqueo; (*moan*) quejido ▶ VI lloriquear; quejarse

whimsical [ˈwɪmzɪkl] ADJ (*person*) caprichoso

whine [wain] N (*of pain*) gemido; (*of engine*) zumbido ▶ VI gemir; zumbar; (*fig: complain*) gimotear

whip [wɪp] N látigo; (*BRIT Pol*) *diputado encargado de la disciplina del partido en el parlamento* ▶ VT azotar; (*snatch*) arrebatar; *US Culin* batir

▶ **whip up** VT (*cream etc*) batir (rápidamente); (*inf: meal*) preparar rápidamente; (: *stir up: support, feeling*) avivar; *ver nota*

En el Parlamento británico la disciplina de partido (en concreto de voto y de asistencia a la Cámara de los Comunes) está a cargo de un grupo de parlamentarios llamados **whips**, encabezados por el "*Chief Whip*". Por lo general todos ellos tienen también altos cargos en la Administración del Estado si pertenecen al partido en el poder.

whiplash [ˈwɪplæʃ] N (*Med: also*: **whiplash injury**) latigazo

whipped cream [wɪpt-] N nata montada

whipping boy [ˈwɪpɪŋ-] N (*fig*) cabeza de turco

whip-round [ˈwɪpraund] N (*BRIT*) colecta

whirl [wəːl] N remolino ▶ VT hacer girar, dar vueltas a ▶ VI (*dancers*) girar, dar vueltas; (*leaves, dust, water etc*) arremolinarse

whirlpool [ˈwəːlpuːl] N remolino

whirlwind [ˈwəːlwɪnd] N torbellino

whirr [wəːʳ] VI zumbar

whisk [wɪsk] N (*BRIT Culin*) batidor *m* ▶ VT (*BRIT Culin*) batir; **to ~ sb away** or **off** llevarse volando a algn

whiskers [ˈwɪskəz] NPL (*of animal*) bigotes *mpl*; (*of man*) patillas *fpl*

whisky, (*US, IRELAND*) **whiskey** [ˈwɪskɪ] N whisky *m*

whisper [ˈwɪspəʳ] N cuchicheo; (*rumour*)

rumor *m*; (*fig*) susurro, murmullo ▶ VI
cuchichear, hablar bajo; (*fig*) susurrar ▶ VT
susurrar; **to ~ sth to sb** decirle algo al oído a
algn

whispering ['wɪspərɪŋ] N cuchicheo

whist [wɪst] N (BRIT) whist *m*

whistle ['wɪsl] N (*sound*) silbido; (*object*)
silbato ▶ VI silbar; **to ~ a tune** silbar una
melodía

whistle-stop ['wɪslstɔp] ADJ: **~ tour** (US Pol)
gira electoral rápida; (*fig*) recorrido rápido

Whit [wɪt] N Pentecostés *m*

white [waɪt] ADJ blanco; (*pale*) pálido ▶ N
blanco; (*of egg*) clara; **to turn** or **go ~** (*person*)
palidecer, ponerse blanco; (*hair*) encanecer;
the whites (*washing*) la ropa blanca; **tennis
whites** ropa *f* de tenis

whitebait ['waɪtbeɪt] N chanquetes *mpl*

whiteboard ['waɪtbɔːd] N pizarra blanca;
interactive ~ pizarra interactiva

white coffee N (BRIT) café *m* con leche

white-collar worker ['waɪtkɔlə-] N
oficinista *mf*

white elephant N (*fig*) maula

white goods NPL (*appliances*)
electrodomésticos *mpl* de línea blanca;
(*linen etc*) ropa blanca

white-hot [waɪt'hɔt] ADJ (*metal*) candente,
calentado al (rojo) blanco

White House N (US) Casa Blanca

white lie N mentirijilla

whiteness ['waɪtnɪs] N blancura

white noise N sonido blanco

whiteout ['waɪtaut] N resplandor *m* sin
sombras; (*fig*) masa confusa

white paper N (Pol) libro blanco

whitewash ['waɪtwɔʃ] N (*paint*) cal *f*,
jalbegue *m* ▶ VT encalar, blanquear;
(*fig*) encubrir

whiting ['waɪtɪŋ] N *pl inv* (*fish*) pescadilla

Whit Monday N lunes *m* de Pentecostés

Whitsun ['wɪtsn] N (BRIT) Pentecostés *m*

whittle ['wɪtl] VT: **to ~ away, ~ down** ir
reduciendo

whizz [wɪz] VI: **to ~ past** or **by** pasar a toda
velocidad

whizz kid N (*inf*) prodigio(-a)

WHO N ABBR (= World Health Organization)
OMS *f*

who [huː] PRON **1** (*interrogative*) quién; **who is
it?, who's there?** ¿quién es?; **who are you
looking for?** ¿a quién buscas?; **I told her
who I was** le dije quién era yo
2 (*relative*) que; **the man/woman who spoke
to me** el hombre/la mujer que habló
conmigo; **those who can swim** los que
saben or sepan nadar

whodunit, whodunnit [huː'dʌnɪt] N (*inf*)
novela policíaca

whoever [huː'ɛvəʳ] PRON: **~ finds it**
cualquiera or quienquiera que lo encuentre;
ask ~ you like pregunta a quien quieras;
~ he marries se case con quien se case

whole [həul] ADJ (*complete*) todo, entero;
(*not broken*) intacto ▶ N (*total*) total *m*; (*sum*)
conjunto; **~ villages were destroyed**
pueblos enteros fueron destruidos; **the ~ of
the town** toda la ciudad, la ciudad entera;
on the ~, as a ~ en general

wholefood ['həulfuːd] N, **wholefoods**
['həulfuːdz] NPL alimento(s) *m(pl)* integral(es)

wholehearted [həul'hɑːtɪd] ADJ (*support,
approval*) total; (*sympathy*) todo

wholeheartedly [həul'hɑːtɪdlɪ] ADV con
entusiasmo

wholemeal ['həulmiːl] ADJ (BRIT: *flour, bread*)
integral

wholesale ['həulseɪl] N venta al por mayor
▶ ADJ al por mayor; (*destruction*) sistemático

wholesaler ['həulseɪləʳ] N mayorista *mf*

wholesome ['həulsəm] ADJ sano

wholewheat ['həulwiːt] ADJ = **wholemeal**

wholly ['həulɪ] ADV totalmente, enteramente

whom [huːm] PRON **1** (*interrogative*): **whom
did you see?** ¿a quién viste?; **to whom did
you give it?** ¿a quién se lo diste?; **tell me
from whom you received it** dígame de
quién lo recibió
2 (*relative*) que; **to whom** a quien(es); **of
whom** de quien(es), del/de la que; **the man
whom I saw** el hombre que vi; **the man to
whom I wrote** el hombre a quien escribí;
the lady about whom I was talking la
señora de (la) que hablaba; **the lady with
whom I was talking** la señora con quien or
(la) que hablaba

whooping cough ['huːpɪŋ-] N tos *f* ferina

whoops [wuːps] EXCL (*also*: **whoops-a-daisy!**)
¡huy!

whoosh [wuʃ] N: **it came out with a ~** (*sauce
etc*) salió todo de repente; (*air*) salió con
mucho ruido

whopper ['wɔpəʳ] N (*inf*: *lie*) embuste *m*;
(*large thing*): **a ~** uno(-a) enorme

whopping ['wɔpɪŋ] ADJ (*inf*) enorme

whore [hɔːʳ] N (*inf, pej*) puta

whose [huːz] ADJ **1** (*possessive: interrogative*) de
quién; **whose book is this?, whose is this
book?** ¿de quién es este libro?; **whose pencil
have you taken?** ¿de quién es el lápiz que
has cogido?; **whose daughter are you?**

¿de quién eres hija?

2 (*possessive: relative*) cuyo(-a) *m/f*, cuyos(-as) *mpl/fpl*; **the man whose son they rescued** el hombre cuyo hijo rescataron; **the girl whose sister he was speaking to** la chica con cuya hermana estaba hablando; **those whose passports I have** aquellas personas cuyos pasaportes tengo; **the woman whose car was stolen** la mujer a quien le robaron el coche

▶ PRON de quién; **whose is this?** ¿de quién es esto?; **I know whose it is** sé de quién es

(KEYWORD)

why [waɪ] ADV por qué; **why not?** ¿por qué no?; **why not do it now?** ¿por qué no lo haces (*or* hacemos) ahora?

▶ CONJ: **I wonder why he said that** me pregunto por qué dijo eso; **that's not why I'm here** no es por eso (por lo) que estoy aquí; **the reason why** la razón por la que

▶ EXCL (*expressing surprise, shock, annoyance*) ¡hombre!, ¡vaya!; (*explaining*): **why, it's you!** ¡hombre, eres tú!; **why, that's impossible** ¡pero si eso es imposible!

whyever [waɪˈɛvəʳ] ADV por qué

WI N ABBR (*BRIT* = *Women's Institute*) asociación de amas de casa ▶ ABBR (*Geo*) = **West Indies**; (*US*) = **Wisconsin**

wick [wɪk] N mecha

wicked ['wɪkɪd] ADJ malvado, cruel

wickedness ['wɪkɪdnɪs] N maldad *f*, crueldad *f*

wicker ['wɪkəʳ] N mimbre *m*

wickerwork ['wɪkəwəːk] N artículos *mpl* de mimbre

wicket ['wɪkɪt] N (*Cricket*) palos *mpl*

wicket keeper N guardameta *m*

wide [waɪd] ADJ ancho; (*area, knowledge*) vasto, grande; (*choice*) amplio ▶ ADV: **to open ~** abrir de par en par; **to shoot ~** errar el tiro; **it is three metres ~** tiene tres metros de ancho

wide-angle lens ['waɪdæŋgl-] N (objetivo) gran angular *m*

wide-awake [waɪdəˈweɪk] ADJ bien despierto

wide-eyed [waɪdˈaɪd] ADJ con los ojos muy abiertos; (*fig*) ingenuo

widely ['waɪdlɪ] ADV (*differing*) muy; **it is ~ believed that …** existe la creencia generalizada de que …; **to be ~ read** (*author*) ser muy leído; (*reader*) haber leído mucho

widen ['waɪdn] VT ensanchar; (*experience*) ampliar ▶ VI ensancharse

wideness ['waɪdnɪs] N anchura; amplitud *f*

wide open ADJ abierto de par en par

wide-ranging [waɪdˈreɪndʒɪŋ] ADJ (*survey, report*) de gran alcance; (*interests*) muy diversos

widespread ['waɪdsprɛd] ADJ (*belief etc*) extendido, general

widget ['wɪdʒɪt] N (*Comput*) mini aplicación *f*, widget *m*

widow ['wɪdəu] N viuda

widowed ['wɪdəud] ADJ viudo

widower ['wɪdəuəʳ] N viudo

width [wɪdθ] N anchura; (*of cloth*) ancho; **it's seven metres in ~** tiene siete metros de ancho

widthways ['wɪdθweɪz] ADV a lo ancho

wield [wiːld] VT (*sword*) blandir; (*power*) ejercer

wife [waɪf] (*pl* **wives** [waɪvz]) N mujer *f*, esposa

Wi-Fi ['waɪfaɪ] N ABBR (= *wireless fidelity*) wi-fi *m* ▶ ADJ (*hot spot, network etc*) wi-fi

wig [wɪg] N peluca

wigging ['wɪgɪŋ] N (*BRIT inf*) rapapolvo, bronca

wiggle ['wɪgl] VT menear ▶ VI menearse

wiggly ['wɪglɪ] ADJ (*line*) ondulado

wigwam ['wɪgwæm] N tipi *m*, tienda india

wiki ['wiːkiː] N (*Comput*) wiki *f*

wild [waɪld] ADJ (*animal*) salvaje; (*plant*) silvestre; (*idea*) descabellado; (*rough: sea*) bravo; (*: land*) agreste; (*: weather*) muy revuelto; (*inf: angry*) furioso ▶ N: **the ~** la naturaleza; **wilds** NPL regiones *fpl* salvajes, tierras *fpl* vírgenes; **to be ~ about** (*enthusiastic*) estar *or* andar loco por; **in its ~ state** en estado salvaje

wild card N (*Comput*) comodín *m*

wildcat ['waɪldkæt] N gato montés

wildcat strike N huelga salvaje

wilderness ['wɪldənɪs] N desierto; (*jungle*) jungla

wildfire ['waɪldfaɪəʳ] N: **to spread like ~** correr como un reguero de pólvora

wild-goose chase [waɪldˈguːs-] N (*fig*) búsqueda inútil

wildlife ['waɪldlaɪf] N fauna

wildly ['waɪldlɪ] ADV (*roughly*) violentamente; (*foolishly*) locamente; (*rashly*) descabelladamente; (*lash out*) a diestro y siniestro; (*guess*) a lo loco; (*happy*) a más no poder

wiles [waɪlz] NPL artimañas *fpl*, ardides *mpl*

wilful, (*US*) **willful** ['wɪlful] ADJ (*action*) deliberado; (*obstinate*) testarudo

(KEYWORD)

will [wɪl] AUX VB **1** (*forming future tense*): **I will finish it tomorrow** lo terminaré *or* voy a terminar mañana; **I will have finished it by tomorrow** lo habré terminado para mañana; **will you do it? — yes I will/no I won't** ¿lo harás? — sí/no; **you won't lose it, will you?** no lo vayas a perder *or* no lo perderás ¿verdad?

2 (*in conjectures: predictions*): **he will** *or* **he'll be there by now** ya habrá llegado, ya debe (de) haber llegado; **that will be the postman** será el cartero, debe ser el cartero
3 (*in commands, requests, offers*): **will you be quiet!** ¿quieres callarte?; **will you help me?** ¿quieres ayudarme?; **will you have a cup of tea?** ¿te apetece un té?; **I won't put up with it!** ¡no lo soporto!
4 (*habits, persistence*): **the car won't start** el coche no arranca; **accidents will happen** son cosas que pasan
▸ VT (*pt, pp* **willed**): **to will sb to do sth** desear que algn haga algo; **he willed himself to go on** con gran fuerza de voluntad, continuó
▸ N **1** (*desire*) voluntad *f*; **against sb's will** contra la voluntad de algn; **he did it of his own free will** lo hizo por su propia voluntad
2 (*Law*) testamento; **to make a** *or* **one's will** hacer su testamento

willful ['wɪful] ADJ (*US*) = **wilful**
willing ['wɪlɪŋ] ADJ (*with goodwill*) de buena voluntad; (*enthusiastic*) entusiasta; **he's ~ to do it** está dispuesto a hacerlo; **to show ~** mostrarse dispuesto
willingly ['wɪlɪŋlɪ] ADV con mucho gusto
willingness ['wɪlɪŋnɪs] N buena voluntad
will-o'-the-wisp ['wɪləðə'wɪsp] N fuego fatuo; (*fig*) quimera
willow ['wɪləu] N sauce *m*
willpower ['wɪlpauə'] N fuerza de voluntad
willy-nilly [wɪlɪ'nɪlɪ] ADV quiérase o no
wilt [wɪlt] VI marchitarse
Wilts ABBR (*BRIT*) = **Wiltshire**
wily ['waɪlɪ] ADJ astuto
wimp [wɪmp] N (*inf*) enclenque *mf*; (*character*) calzonazos *m inv*
win [wɪn] (*pt, pp* **won**) N (*in sports etc*) victoria, triunfo ▸ VT ganar; (*obtain: contract etc*) conseguir, lograr ▸ VI ganar
▸ **win over**, (*BRIT*) **win round** VT convencer a
wince [wɪns] VI encogerse
winch [wɪntʃ] N torno
Winchester disk® ['wɪntʃɪstə-] N (*Comput*) disco Winchester®
wind[1] [wɪnd] N viento; (*Med*) gases *mpl*; (*breath*) aliento ▸ VT (*take breath away from*) dejar sin aliento a; **into** *or* **against the ~** contra el viento; **to get ~ of sth** enterarse de algo; **to break ~** ventosear
wind[2] [waɪnd] (*pt, pp* **wound** [waund]) VT enrollar; (*wrap*) envolver; (*clock, toy*) dar cuerda a ▸ VI (*road, river*) serpentear
▸ **wind down** VT (*car window*) bajar; (*fig: production, business*) disminuir
▸ **wind up** VT (*clock*) dar cuerda a; (*debate*) concluir, terminar

windbreak ['wɪndbreɪk] N barrera contra el viento
windcheater ['wɪndtʃiːtə'], (*US*)
windbreaker ['wɪndbreɪkə'] N cazadora
winder ['waɪndə'] N (*on watch*) cuerda
wind erosion N erosión *f* del viento
windfall ['wɪndfɔːl] N golpe *m* de suerte
wind farm N parque *m* eólico
winding ['waɪndɪŋ] ADJ (*road*) tortuoso
wind instrument N (*Mus*) instrumento de viento
windmill ['wɪndmɪl] N molino de viento
window ['wɪndəu] N ventana; (*in car, train*) ventana; (*in shop etc*) escaparate *m*, vitrina (*LAm*), vidriera (*LAm*); (*Comput*) ventana
window box N jardinera (de ventana)
window cleaner N (*person*) limpiacristales *m inv*
window dressing N decoración *f* de escaparates
window envelope N sobre *m* de ventanilla
window frame N marco de ventana
window ledge N alféizar *m*, repisa
window pane N cristal *m*
window seat N asiento junto a la ventana
window-shopping [wɪndəu'ʃɔpɪŋ] N: **to go ~** ir a ver *or* mirar escaparates
windowsill ['wɪndəusɪl] N alféizar *m*, repisa
windpipe ['wɪndpaɪp] N tráquea
wind power N energía eólica
windscreen ['wɪndskriːn], (*US*) **windshield** ['wɪndʃiːld] N parabrisas *m inv*
windscreen washer, (*US*) **windshield washer** N lavaparabrisas *m inv*
windscreen wiper, (*US*) **windshield wiper** N limpiaparabrisas *m inv*
windsurfing ['wɪndsəːfɪŋ] N windsurf *m*
windswept ['wɪndswɛpt] ADJ azotado por el viento
wind tunnel N túnel *m* aerodinámico
wind turbine ['wɪndtəːbaɪn] N aerogenerador *m*
windy ['wɪndɪ] ADJ de mucho viento; **it's ~** hace viento
wine [waɪn] N vino ▸ VT: **to ~ and dine sb** agasajar *or* festejar a algn
wine bar N bar especializado en vinos
wine cellar N bodega
wine glass N copa (de *or* para vino)
wine-growing ['waɪngrəuɪŋ] ADJ viticultor(a)
wine list N lista de vinos
wine merchant N vinatero
wine tasting N degustación *f* de vinos
wine waiter N escanciador *m*
wing [wɪŋ] N ala; (*BRIT Aut*) aleta; **wings** NPL (*Theat*) bastidores *mpl*
winger ['wɪŋə'] N (*Sport*) extremo
wing mirror N (espejo) retrovisor *m*

W

wing nut N tuerca (de) mariposa

wingspan ['wɪŋspaen], **wingspread** ['wɪŋspred] N envergadura

wink [wɪŋk] N guiño; (*blink*) pestañeo ▸ vi guiñar; (*blink*) pestañear; (*light etc*) parpadear

winkle ['wɪŋkl] N bígaro, bigarro

winner ['wɪnə^r] N ganador(a) *m/f*

winning ['wɪnɪŋ] ADJ (*team*) ganador(a); (*goal*) decisivo; (*charming*) encantador(a)

winning post N meta

winnings ['wɪnɪŋz] NPL ganancias *fpl*

winter ['wɪntə^r] N invierno ▸ vi invernar

winter sports NPL deportes *mpl* de invierno

wintertime ['wɪntətaɪm] N invierno

wintry ['wɪntrɪ] ADJ invernal

wipe [waɪp] N: **to give sth a ~** pasar un trapo sobre algo ▸ vt limpiar; (*tape*) borrar; **to ~ one's nose** limpiarse la nariz
  ▸ **wipe off** vt limpiar con un trapo
  ▸ **wipe out** vt (*debt*) liquidar; (*memory*) borrar; (*destroy*) destruir
  ▸ **wipe up** vt limpiar

wire ['waɪə^r] N alambre *m*; (*Elec*) cable *m* (eléctrico); (*Tel*) telegrama *m* ▸ vt (*house*) poner la instalación eléctrica en; (*also*: **wire up**) conectar

wire cutters NPL cortaalambres *msg inv*

wireless ['waɪəlɪs] N (*BRIT*) radio *f* ▸ ADJ inalámbrico

wireless technology N tecnología inalámbrica

wire mesh, wire netting N tela metálica

wire service N (*US*) agencia de noticias

wire-tapping ['waɪə'tæpɪŋ] N intervención *f* telefónica

wiring ['waɪərɪŋ] N instalación *f* eléctrica

wiry ['waɪərɪ] ADJ enjuto y fuerte

Wis., Wisc. ABBR (*US*) = **Wisconsin**

wisdom ['wɪzdəm] N sabiduría, saber *m*; (*good sense*) cordura

wisdom tooth N muela del juicio

wise [waɪz] ADJ sabio; (*sensible*) juicioso; **I'm none the wiser** sigo sin entender
  ▸ **wise up** vi (*inf*): **to ~ up (to sth)** enterarse (de algo)

...wise [waɪz] SUFF: **timewise** en cuanto a *or* respecto al tiempo

wisecrack ['waɪzkræk] N broma

wish [wɪʃ] N (*desire*) deseo ▸ vt desear; (*want*) querer; **best wishes** (*on birthday etc*) felicidades *fpl*; **with best wishes** (*in letter*) saludos *mpl*, recuerdos *mpl*; **he wished me well** me deseó mucha suerte; **to ~ sth on sb** imponer algo a algn; **to ~ to do/sb to do sth** querer hacer/que algn haga algo; **to ~ for** desear

wishbone ['wɪʃbəun] N espoleta (*de la que tiran dos personas; quien se quede con el hueso más largo pide un deseo*)

wishful ['wɪʃful] ADJ: **it's ~ thinking** eso es hacerse ilusiones

wishy-washy ['wɪʃɪwɔʃɪ] ADJ (*inf*: *colour*) desvaído; (: *ideas, thinking*) flojo

wisp [wɪsp] N mechón *m*; (*of smoke*) voluta

wistful ['wɪstful] ADJ pensativo; (*nostalgic*) nostálgico

wit [wɪt] N (*wittiness*) ingenio, gracia; (*intelligence: also*: **wits**) inteligencia; (: *person*) chistoso(-a); **to have** *or* **keep one's wits about one** no perder la cabeza

witch [wɪtʃ] N bruja

witchcraft ['wɪtʃkrɑːft] N brujería

witch doctor N hechicero

witch-hunt ['wɪtʃhʌnt] N (*Pol*) caza de brujas

(KEYWORD)

with [wɪð, wɪθ] PREP **1** (*accompanying, in the company of*) con (*con +mí, ti, sí = conmigo, contigo, consigo*); **I was with him** estaba con él; **we stayed with friends** nos quedamos en casa de unos amigos

2 (*descriptive, indicating manner etc*) con, de; **a room with a view** una habitación con vistas; **the man with the grey hat/blue eyes** el hombre del sombrero gris/de los ojos azules; **red with anger** rojo de ira; **to shake with fear** temblar de miedo; **to fill sth with water** llenar algo de agua

3: **I'm with you/I'm not with you** (*understand*) ya te entiendo/no te entiendo; **to be with it** (*inf*: *person: up-to-date*) estar al tanto; (: *alert*) ser despabilado; **I'm not really with it today** no doy pie con bola hoy

withdraw [wɪð'drɔː] vt (*irreg: like* **draw**) retirar ▸ vi retirarse; (*go back on promise*) retractarse; **to ~ money (from the bank)** retirar fondos (del banco); **to ~ into o.s.** ensimismarse

withdrawal [wɪð'drɔːəl] N retirada; (*of money*) reintegro

withdrawal symptoms NPL síndrome *m* de abstinencia

withdrawn [wɪð'drɔːn] ADJ (*person*) reservado, introvertido ▸ PP *of* **withdraw**

withdrew [wɪð'druː] PT *of* **withdraw**

wither ['wɪðə^r] vi marchitarse

withered ['wɪðəd] ADJ marchito, seco

withhold [wɪð'həuld] vt (*irreg: like* **hold**) (*money*) retener; (*decision*) aplazar; (*permission*) negar; (*information*) ocultar

within [wɪð'ɪn] PREP dentro de ▸ ADV dentro; **~ reach** al alcance de la mano; **~ sight of** a la vista de; **~ the week** antes de que acabe la semana; **to be ~ the law** atenerse a la legalidad; **~ an hour from now** dentro de una hora; **~ a mile (of)** a menos de una milla (de)

without [wɪð'aut] PREP sin; **to go** or **do ~ sth** prescindir de algo; **~ anybody knowing** sin saberlo nadie

withstand [wɪθ'stænd] VT (irreg: like **stand**) resistir a

witness ['wɪtnɪs] N (person) testigo mf; (evidence) testimonio ▶ VT (event) presenciar, ser testigo de; (document) atestiguar la veracidad de; **~ for the prosecution/defence** testigo de cargo/descargo; **to ~ to (having seen) sth** dar testimonio de (haber visto) algo; **to bear ~ to** (fig) ser testimonio de

witness box, (US) **witness stand** N tribuna de los testigos

witticism ['wɪtɪsɪzm] N dicho ingenioso

wittily ['wɪtɪlɪ] ADV ingeniosamente

witty ['wɪtɪ] ADJ ingenioso

wives [waɪvz] NPL of **wife**

wizard ['wɪzəd] N hechicero

wizened ['wɪznd] ADJ arrugado, marchito

wk ABBR = **week**

Wm. ABBR = **William**

WMD N ABBR = **weapons of mass destruction**

WO N ABBR = **warrant officer**

wobble ['wɔbl] VI tambalearse

wobbly ['wɔblɪ] ADJ (hand, voice) tembloroso; (table, chair) tambaleante, cojo

woe [wəu] N desgracia

woeful ['wəuful] ADJ (bad) lamentable; (sad) apesadumbrado

wok [wɔk] N wok m

woke [wəuk] PT of **wake**

woken ['wəukn] PP of **wake**

wolf [wulf] (pl **wolves** [wulvz]) N lobo

woman ['wumən] (pl **women** ['wɪmɪn]) N mujer f; **young ~** (mujer f) joven f; **women's page** (Press) sección f de la mujer

woman doctor N doctora

woman friend N amiga

womanize ['wumənaɪz] VI ser un mujeriego

womanly ['wumənlɪ] ADJ femenino

womb [wu:m] N (Anat) matriz f, útero

women ['wɪmɪn] NPL of **woman**

Women's Liberation Movement, Women's Movement N (also: **women's lib**) Movimiento de liberación de la mujer

won [wʌn] PT, PP of **win**

wonder ['wʌndəʳ] N maravilla, prodigio; (feeling) asombro ▶ VI: **to ~ whether** preguntarse si; **to ~ at** asombrarse de; **to ~ about** pensar sobre or en; **it's no ~ that** no es de extrañar que

wonderful ['wʌndəful] ADJ maravilloso

wonderfully ['wʌndəfəlɪ] ADV maravillosamente, estupendamente

wonky ['wɔŋkɪ] ADJ (BRIT: inf: unsteady) poco seguro, cojo; (: broken down) estropeado

wont [wɔnt] N: **as is his/her ~** como tiene por costumbre

won't [wəunt] = **will not**

woo [wu:] VT (woman) cortejar

wood [wud] N (timber) madera; (forest) bosque m ▶ CPD de madera

wood alcohol N (US) alcohol m desnaturalizado

wood carving N tallado en madera

wooded ['wudɪd] ADJ arbolado

wooden ['wudn] ADJ de madera; (fig) inexpresivo

woodland ['wudlənd] N bosque m

woodpecker ['wudpɛkəʳ] N pájaro carpintero

wood pigeon N paloma torcaz

woodwind ['wudwɪnd] N (Mus) instrumentos mpl de viento de madera

woodwork ['wudwə:k] N carpintería

woodworm ['wudwə:m] N carcoma

woof [wuf] N (of dog) ladrido ▶ VI ladrar; **~, ~!** ¡guau, guau!

wool [wul] N lana; **knitting ~** lana (de hacer punto); **to pull the ~ over sb's eyes** (fig) dar a algn gato por liebre

woollen, (US) **woolen** ['wulən] ADJ de lana ▶ N: **woollens** géneros mpl de lana

woolly, (US) **wooly** ['wulɪ] ADJ de lana; (fig: ideas) confuso

woozy ['wu:zɪ] ADJ (inf) mareado

word [wə:d] N palabra; (news) noticia; (promise) palabra (de honor) ▶ VT redactar; **~ for ~** palabra por palabra; **what's the ~ for "pen" in Spanish?** ¿cómo se dice "pen" en español?; **to put sth into words** expresar algo en palabras; **to have a ~ with sb** hablar (dos palabras) con algn; **in other words** en otras palabras; **to break/keep one's ~** faltar a la palabra/cumplir la promesa; **to leave ~ (with/for sb) that ...** dejar recado (con/para algn) de que ...; **to have words with sb** (quarrel with) discutir or reñir con algn

wording ['wə:dɪŋ] N redacción f

word-of-mouth [wə:dəv'mauθ] N: **by** or **through ~** de palabra, boca a boca

word-perfect ['wə:d'pə:fɪkt] ADJ (speech etc) sin faltas de expresión

word processing N procesamiento or tratamiento de textos

word processor [-'prəusɛsəʳ] N procesador m de textos

word wrapping ['wə:dræp] N (Comput) salto de línea automático

wordy ['wə:dɪ] ADJ verboso, prolijo

wore [wɔ:ʳ] PT of **wear**

work [wə:k] N trabajo; (job) empleo, trabajo; (Art, Lit) obra ▶ VI trabajar; (mechanism) funcionar, marchar; (medicine) ser eficaz, surtir efecto ▶ VT (shape) trabajar; (stone etc) tallar; (mine etc) explotar; (machine) manejar, hacer funcionar; (cause) producir; **to go to ~**

W

ir a trabajar *or* al trabajo; **to be at ~ (on sth)** estar trabajando (en algo); **to set to ~, start ~** ponerse a trabajar; **to be out of ~** estar parado, no tener trabajo; **his life's ~** el trabajo de su vida; **to ~ hard** trabajar mucho *or* duro; **to ~ to rule** (*Industry*) hacer una huelga de celo; **to ~ loose** (*part*) desprenderse; (*knot*) aflojarse; *see also* **works**
▶ **work off** VT: **to ~ off one's feelings** desahogarse
▶ **work on** VT FUS trabajar en, dedicarse a; (*principle*) basarse en; **he's working on the car** está reparando el coche
▶ **work out** VI (*plans etc*) salir bien, funcionar; (*Sport*) hacer ejercicios ▶ VT (*problem*) resolver; (*plan*) elaborar; **it works out at £100** asciende a 100 libras
▶ **work up** VT: **he worked his way up in the company** ascendió en la compañía mediante sus propios esfuerzos

workable ['wə:kəbl] ADJ (*solution*) práctico, factible
workaholic [wə:kə'hɔlɪk] N adicto(-a) al trabajo
workbench ['wə:kbentʃ] N banco *or* mesa de trabajo
worked up [wə:kt-] ADJ: **to get ~** excitarse
worker ['wə:kər] N trabajador(a) *m/f*, obrero(-a) *m/f*; **office ~** oficinista *mf*
work experience N: **I'm going to do my ~ in a factory** voy a hacer las prácticas en una fábrica
work force N mano *f* de obra
work-in ['wə:kɪn] N (*Brit*) ocupación *f* (de la empresa sin interrupción del trabajo)
working ['wə:kɪŋ] ADJ (*day, week*) laborable; (*tools, conditions, clothes*) de trabajo; (*wife*) que trabaja; (*partner*) activo
working capital N (*Comm*) capital *m* circulante
working class N clase *f* obrera ▶ ADJ: **working-class** obrero
working knowledge N conocimientos *mpl* básicos
working man N (*irreg*) obrero
working order N: **in ~** en funcionamiento
working party N comisión *f* de investigación, grupo de trabajo
working week N semana laboral
work-in-progress ['wə:kɪn'prəugrɛs] N (*Comm*) trabajo en curso
workload ['wə:kləud] N cantidad *f* de trabajo
workman ['wə:kmən] N (*irreg*) obrero
workmanship ['wə:kmənʃɪp] N (*art*) hechura; (*skill*) habilidad *f*
workmate ['wə:kmeɪt] N compañero(-a) de trabajo
work of art N obra de arte
workout ['wə:kaut] N (*Sport*) sesión *f* de ejercicios

work permit N permiso de trabajo
workplace ['wə:kpleɪs] N lugar *m* de trabajo
works [wə:ks] NSG (*Brit: factory*) fábrica ▶ NPL (*of clock, machine*) mecanismo; **road ~** obras *fpl*
works council N comité *m* de empresa
worksheet ['wə:kʃi:t] N (*Comput*) hoja de trabajo; (*Scol*) hoja de ejercicios
workshop ['wə:kʃɔp] N taller *m*
work station N estación *f* de trabajo
work study N estudio del trabajo
work surface N encimera
worktop ['wə:ktɔp] N encimera
work-to-rule ['wə:ktə'ru:l] N (*Brit*) huelga de celo
world [wə:ld] N mundo ▶ CPD (*champion*) del mundo; (*power, war*) mundial; **all over the ~** por todo el mundo, en el mundo entero; **the business ~** el mundo de los negocios; **what in the ~ is he doing?** ¿qué diablos está haciendo?; **to think the ~ of sb** (*fig*) tener un concepto muy alto de algn; **to do sb a ~ of good** sentar muy bien a algn; **W~ War One/Two** la Primera/Segunda Guerra Mundial
World Cup N (*Football*): **the ~** el Mundial, los Mundiales
world-famous [wə:ld'feɪməs] ADJ de fama mundial, mundialmente famoso
worldly ['wə:ldlɪ] ADJ mundano
world music N música étnica
World Series N: **the ~** (*US Baseball*) el campeonato nacional de béisbol de EE.UU.
World Service N *see* **BBC**
world-wide ['wə:ldwaɪd] ADJ mundial, universal
World-Wide Web N: **the ~** la World Wide Web
worm [wə:m] N gusano; (*earthworm*) lombriz *f*
worn [wɔ:n] PP *of* **wear** ▶ ADJ usado
worn-out ['wɔ:naut] ADJ (*object*) gastado; (*person*) rendido, agotado
worried ['wʌrɪd] ADJ preocupado; **to be ~ about sth** estar preocupado por algo
worrisome ['wʌrɪsəm] ADJ preocupante, inquietante
worry ['wʌrɪ] N preocupación *f* ▶ VT preocupar, inquietar ▶ VI preocuparse; **to ~ about *or* over sth/sb** preocuparse por algo/algn
worrying ['wʌrɪɪŋ] ADJ inquietante
worse [wə:s] ADJ, ADV peor ▶ N el peor, lo peor; **a change for the ~** un empeoramiento; **so much the ~ for you** tanto peor para ti; **he is none the ~ for it** se ha quedado tan fresco *or* tan tranquilo; **to get ~, to grow ~** empeorar
worsen ['wə:sn] VT, VI empeorar
worse off ADJ (*financially*): **to be ~** tener menos dinero; (*fig*) **you'll be ~ this way** de esta forma estarás peor que antes

worship ['wəːʃɪp] N (*organized worship*) culto; (*act*) adoración f ▶ VT adorar; **Your W~** (BRIT: *to mayor*) su Ilustrísima (: *to judge*) su señoría

worshipper, (US) **worshiper** ['wəːʃɪpəʳ] N devoto(-a)

worst [wəːst] ADJ (el/la) peor ▶ ADV peor ▶ N lo peor; **at ~** en el peor de los casos; **to come off ~** llevar la peor parte; **if the ~ comes to the ~** en el peor de los casos

worst-case ['wəːstkeɪs] ADJ: **the ~ scenario** el peor de los casos

worsted ['wustɪd] N: (**wool**) **~** estambre m

worth [wəːθ] N valor m ▶ ADJ: **to be ~** valer; **how much is it ~?** ¿cuánto vale?; **it's ~ it** vale or merece la pena; **to be ~ one's while (to do)** merecer la pena (hacer); **it's not ~ the trouble** no vale or merece la pena

worthless ['wəːθlɪs] ADJ sin valor; (*useless*) inútil

worthwhile ['wəːθwaɪl] ADJ (*activity*) que merece la pena; (*cause*) loable

worthy ['wəːðɪ] ADJ (*person*) respetable; (*motive*) honesto; **~ of** digno de

(KEYWORD)

would [wud] AUX VB **1** (*conditional tense*): **if you asked him he would do it** si se lo pidieras, lo haría; **if you had asked him he would have done it** si se lo hubieras pedido, lo habría or hubiera hecho

2 (*in offers: invitations: requests*): **would you like a biscuit?** ¿quieres una galleta?; (*formal*) ¿querría una galleta?; **would you ask him to come in?** ¿quiere hacerle pasar?; **would you open the window please?** ¿quiere or podría abrir la ventana, por favor?

3 (*in indirect speech*): **I said I would do it** dije que lo haría

4 (*emphatic*): **it WOULD have to snow today!** ¡tenía que nevar precisamente hoy!

5 (*insistence*): **she wouldn't behave** no quiso comportarse bien

6 (*conjecture*): **it would have been midnight** sería medianoche; **it would seem so** parece ser que sí

7 (*indicating habit*): **he would go there on Mondays** iba allí los lunes

would-be ['wudbiː] ADJ (*pej*) presunto
wouldn't ['wudnt] = **would not**
wound¹ [wuːnd] N herida ▶ VT herir
wound² [waund] PT, PP of **wind²**
wove [wəuv] PT of **weave**
woven ['wəuvən] PP of **weave**
WP N ABBR = **word processing; word processor** ▶ ABBR (BRIT: *inf*: = *weather permitting*) si lo permite el tiempo
WPC N ABBR (BRIT) = **woman police constable**
wpm ABBR (= *words per minute*) p.p.m.

WRAC N ABBR (BRIT: = *Women's Royal Army Corps*) *cuerpo auxiliar femenino del ejército de tierra*

WRAF N ABBR (BRIT: = *Women's Royal Air Force*) *cuerpo auxiliar femenino del ejército del aire*

wrangle ['ræŋgl] N riña ▶ VI reñir

wrap [ræp] N (*stole*) chal m ▶ VT (*also*: **wrap up**) envolver; (: *gift*) envolver, abrigar ▶ VI (*dress warmly*) abrigarse; **under wraps** (*fig*: *plan, scheme*) oculto, tapado

wrapper ['ræpəʳ] N (BRIT: *of book*) sobrecubierta; (*on chocolate etc*) envoltura

wrapping paper ['ræpɪŋ-] N papel m de envolver

wrath [rɔθ] N cólera

wreak [riːk] VT (*destruction*) causar; **to ~ havoc (on)** hacer or causar estragos (en); **to ~ vengeance (on)** vengarse (en)

wreath [riːθ] (*pl* **wreaths** [riːðz]) N (*also*: **funeral wreath**) corona; (*of flowers*) guirnalda

wreck [rɛk] N (*ship*: *destruction*) naufragio; (: *remains*) restos mpl del barco; (*pej*: *person*) ruina ▶ VT destrozar; (*chances*) arruinar; **to be wrecked** (*Naut*) naufragar

wreckage ['rɛkɪdʒ] N (*remains*) restos mpl; (*of building*) escombros mpl

wrecker ['rɛkəʳ] N (US: *breakdown van*) camión-grúa m

WREN [rɛn] N ABBR (BRIT) *miembro del WRNS*

wren [rɛn] N (*Zool*) reyezuelo

wrench [rɛntʃ] N (*Tech*) llave f inglesa; (*tug*) tirón m ▶ VT arrancar; **to ~ sth from sb** arrebatar algo violentamente a algn

wrest [rɛst] VT: **to ~ sth from sb** arrebatar or arrancar algo a algn

wrestle ['rɛsl] VI: **to ~ (with sb)** luchar (con or contra algn)

wrestler ['rɛsləʳ] N luchador(a) m/f (de lucha libre)

wrestling ['rɛslɪŋ] N lucha libre

wrestling match N combate m de lucha libre

wretch [rɛtʃ] N desgraciado(-a), miserable mf; **little ~!** (*often humorous*) ¡granuja!

wretched ['rɛtʃɪd] ADJ miserable

wriggle ['rɪgl] VI serpentear; (*also*: **wriggle about**) menearse, retorcerse

wring [rɪŋ] (*pt, pp* **wrung** [rʌŋ]) VT torcer, retorcer; (*wet clothes*) escurrir; (*fig*): **to ~ sth out of sb** sacar algo por la fuerza a algn

wringer ['rɪŋəʳ] N escurridor m

wringing ['rɪŋɪŋ] ADJ (*also*: **wringing wet**) empapado

wrinkle ['rɪŋkl] N arruga ▶ VT arrugar ▶ VI arrugarse

wrinkled ['rɪŋkld], **wrinkly** ['rɪŋklɪ] ADJ (*fabric, paper etc*) arrugado

wrist [rɪst] N muñeca

wristband ['rɪstbænd] N (BRIT: *of shirt*) puño; (: *of watch*) correa

wrist watch N reloj m de pulsera

W

873

writ [rɪt] N mandato judicial; **to serve a ~ on sb** notificar un mandato judicial a algn

writable ['raɪtəbl] ADJ (CD, DVD) escribible

write [raɪt] (pt **wrote** [rəut], pp **written** ['rɪtn]) VT escribir; (cheque) extender ▶ VI escribir; **to ~ sb a letter** escribir una carta a algn

▶ **write away** VI: **to ~ away for** (information, goods) pedir por escrito or carta

▶ **write down** VT escribir; (note) apuntar

▶ **write off** VT (debt) borrar (como incobrable); (fig) desechar por inútil; (smash up: car) destrozar

▶ **write out** VT escribir

▶ **write up** VT redactar

write-off ['raɪtɔf] N siniestro total; **the car is a ~** el coche es pura chatarra

write-protect ['raɪtprə'tekt] VT (Comput) proteger contra escritura

writer ['raɪtəʳ] N escritor(a) m/f

write-up ['raɪtʌp] N (review) crítica, reseña

writhe [raɪð] VI retorcerse

writing ['raɪtɪŋ] N escritura; (handwriting) letra; (of author) obras fpl; **in ~** por escrito; **to put sth in ~** poner algo por escrito; **in my own ~** escrito por mí; see also **writings**

writing case N estuche m de papel de escribir

writing desk N escritorio

writing paper N papel m de escribir

writings ['raɪtɪŋz] NPL obras fpl

written ['rɪtn] PP of **write**

WRNS N ABBR (BRIT: = Women's Royal Naval Service) cuerpo auxiliar femenino de la armada

wrong [rɔŋ] ADJ (wicked) malo; (unfair) injusto; (incorrect) equivocado, incorrecto; (not suitable) inoportuno, inconveniente

▶ ADV mal ▶ N mal m; (injustice) injusticia

▶ VT ser injusto con; (hurt) agraviar; **to be ~** (answer) estar equivocado; (in doing, saying) equivocarse; **it's ~ to steal, stealing is ~** robar está mal; **you are ~ to do it** haces mal en hacerlo; **you are ~ about that, you've got it ~** en eso estás equivocado; **to be in the ~** no tener razón; (guilty) tener la culpa; **what's ~?** ¿qué pasa?; **what's ~ with the car?** ¿qué le pasa al coche?; **there's nothing ~** no pasa nada; **you have the ~ number** (Tel) se ha equivocado de número; **to go ~** (person) equivocarse; (plan) salir mal; (machine) estropearse

wrongdoer ['rɔŋduəʳ] N malhechor(a) m/f

wrong-foot [rɔŋ'fut] VT (Sport) hacer perder el equilibrio a; (fig) poner en un aprieto a

wrongful ['rɔŋful] ADJ injusto; **~ dismissal** (Industry) despido improcedente

wrongly ['rɔŋli] ADV (answer, do, count) incorrectamente; (treat) injustamente

wrong number N (Tel): **you've got the ~** se ha equivocado de número

wrote [rəut] PT of **write**

wrought [rɔːt] ADJ: **~ iron** hierro forjado

wrung [rʌŋ] PT, PP of **wring**

WRVS N ABBR (BRIT: = Women's Royal Voluntary Service) cuerpo de voluntarias al servicio de la comunidad

wry [raɪ] ADJ irónico

wt. ABBR = **weight**

WV, W.Va. ABBR (US) = **West Virginia**

WWW N ABBR (= World Wide Web) WWW m or f

WY, Wyo. ABBR (US) = **Wyoming**

WYSIWYG ['wɪziwɪg] ABBR (Comput: = what you see is what you get) tipo de presentación en un procesador de textos

Xx

X, x [εks] N (*letter*) X, x *f*; (*BRIT Cine: formerly*) no apto para menores de 18 años; **X for Xmas** X de Xiquena; **if you earn X dollars a year** si ganas X dólares al año

X-certificate ['εkssə'tɪfɪkɪt] ADJ (*BRIT: film: formerly*) no apto para menores de 18 años

Xerox® ['zɪərɔks] N (*also*: **Xerox machine**) fotocopiadora; (*photocopy*) fotocopia ▶ VT fotocopiar

XL ABBR = **extra large**

Xmas ['εksməs] N ABBR = **Christmas**

X-rated ['εks'reɪtɪd] ADJ (*US: film*) no apto para menores de 18 años

X-ray [εks'reɪ] N radiografía ▶ VT radiografiar; **X-rays** NPL rayos *mpl* X

xylophone ['zaɪləfəun] N xilófono

Y y

Y, y [waɪ] N (*letter*) Y, y f; **Y for Yellow**, (*US*) **Y for Yoke** Y de Yegua

Y2K [ˌwaɪtuːˈkeɪ] ABBR = **Year 2000; the ~ problem** (*Comput*) el efecto 2000

yacht [jɔt] N yate m

yachting [ˈjɔtɪŋ] N (*sport*) balandrismo

yachtsman [ˈjɔtsmən] N (*irreg*) balandrista m

yachtswoman [ˈjɔtswumən] N (*irreg*) balandrista

yakka [ˈjækə] N (*Australia, New Zealand inf*) curro

yam [jæm] N ñame m; (*sweet potato*) batata, camote m (*LAM*)

Yank [jæŋk], **Yankee** [ˈjæŋkɪ] N (*pej*) yanqui mf

yank [jæŋk] VT tirar de, jalar de (*LAM*) ▶ N tirón m

yap [jæp] VI (*dog*) aullar

yard [jɑːd] N patio; (*US: garden*) jardín m; (*measure*) yarda; **builder's ~** almacén m

yard sale N (*US*) venta de objetos usados (*en el jardín de una casa particular*)

yardstick [ˈjɑːdstɪk] N (*fig*) criterio, norma

yarn [jɑːn] N hilo; (*tale*) cuento (chino), historia

yawn [jɔːn] N bostezo ▶ VI bostezar

yawning [ˈjɔːnɪŋ] ADJ (*gap*) muy abierto

yd. ABBR (= *yard*) yda

yeah [jɛə] ADV (*inf*) sí

year [jɪəʳ] N año; (*Scol, Univ*) curso; **this ~** este año; **~ in, ~ out** año tras año; **a** or **per ~** al año; **to be eight years old** tener ocho años; **she's three years old** tiene tres años; **an eight-~-old child** un niño de ocho años (de edad)

yearbook [ˈjɪəbuk] N anuario

yearling [ˈjɪəlɪŋ] N (*racehorse*) potro de un año

yearly [ˈjɪəlɪ] ADJ anual ▶ ADV anualmente, cada año; **twice ~** dos veces al año

yearn [jəːn] VI: **to ~ for sth** añorar algo, suspirar por algo

yearning [ˈjəːnɪŋ] N ansia; (*longing*) añoranza

yeast [jiːst] N levadura

yell [jɛl] N grito, alarido ▶ VI gritar

yellow [ˈjɛləu] ADJ, N amarillo

yellow fever N fiebre f amarilla

yellowish [ˈjɛləuɪʃ] ADJ amarillento

Yellow Pages® NPL páginas fpl amarillas

Yellow Sea N: **the ~** el Mar Amarillo

yelp [jɛlp] N aullido ▶ VI aullar

Yemen [ˈjɛmən] N Yemen m

Yemeni [ˈjɛmənɪ] ADJ, N yemení mf, yemenita mf

yen [jɛn] N (*currency*) yen m

yeoman [ˈjəumən] N (*irreg*): **Y~ of the Guard** alabardero de la Casa Real

yes [jɛs] ADV, N sí m; **to say/answer ~** decir/ contestar que sí; **to say ~ (to)** decir que sí (a), conformarse (con)

yes man N (*irreg*) pelotillero

yesterday [ˈjɛstədɪ] ADV, N ayer m; **~ morning/evening** ayer por la mañana/ tarde; **all day ~** todo el día de ayer; **the day before ~** antes de ayer, anteayer

yet [jɛt] ADV todavía ▶ CONJ sin embargo, a pesar de todo; **~ again** de nuevo; **it is not finished ~** todavía no está acabado; **the best ~** el/la mejor hasta ahora; **as ~** hasta ahora, todavía

yew [juː] N tejo

Y-fronts® [ˈwaɪfrʌnts] NPL (*Brit*) calzoncillos mpl, eslip msg tradicional

YHA N ABBR (*Brit*: = *Youth Hostel Association*) ≈ Red f Española de Albergues Juveniles

Yiddish [ˈjɪdɪʃ] N yídish m, judeoalemán m

yield [jiːld] N producción f; (*Agr*) cosecha; (*Comm*) rendimiento ▶ VT producir, dar; (*profit*) rendir ▶ VI rendirse, ceder; (*US Aut*) ceder el paso; **a ~ of 5%** un rédito del 5 por ciento

YMCA N ABBR (= *Young Men's Christian Association*) Asociación f de Jóvenes Cristianos

yob [ˈjɔb], **yobbo** [ˈjɔbbəu] N (*Brit inf*) gamberro

yodel [ˈjəudl] VI cantar a la tirolesa

yoga [ˈjəugə] N yoga m

yoghurt, yogurt [ˈjəugət] N yogur m

yoke [jəuk] N (*of oxen*) yunta; (*on shoulders*) balancín *m*; (*fig*) yugo ▸ VT (*also*: **yoke together**: *oxen*) uncir

yolk [jəuk] N yema (de huevo)

yonder ['jɔndəʳ] ADV allá (a lo lejos)

yonks [jɔŋks] NPL (*inf*): **I haven't seen him for** ~ hace siglos que no lo veo

Yorks [jɔːks] ABBR (*BRIT*) = **Yorkshire**

(KEYWORD)

you [juː] PRON **1** (*subject*: *familiar*: *singular*) tú; (: *plural*) vosotros(-as) *pl* (*SP*), ustedes *pl* (*LAM*); (: *polite*) usted *sg*, ustedes *pl*; **you are very kind** eres/es *etc* muy amable; **you French enjoy your food** a vosotros (*or* ustedes) los franceses os (*or* les) gusta la comida; **you and I will go** iremos tú y yo
2 (*object*: *direct*: *familiar*: *singular*) te; (: *plural*) os (*SP*), les (*LAM*); (: *polite*: *singular masc*) lo *or* le; (: *plural masc*) los *or* les; (: *singular fem*) la; (: *plural fem*) las; **I know you** te/le *etc* conozco
3 (*object*: *indirect*: *familiar*: *singular*) te; (: *plural*) os (*SP*), les (*LAM*); (: *polite*) le *sg*, les *pl*; **I gave the letter to you yesterday** te/os *etc* di la carta ayer
4 (*stressed*): **I told YOU to do it** te dije a ti que lo hicieras, es a ti a quien dije que lo hicieras
5 (*after prep*: NB: con + ti = contigo: *familiar*: *singular*) ti; (: *plural*) vosotros(-as) (*SP*), ustedes (*LAM*); (: *polite*) usted, ustedes *pl*; **it's for you** es para ti/vosotros *etc*
6 (*comparisons*: *familiar*: *singular*) tú; (: *plural*) vosotros/as (*SP*), ustedes (*LAM*); (: *polite*) usted, ustedes *pl*; **she's younger than you** es más joven que tú/vosotros *etc*
7 (*impersonal*: *one*): **fresh air does you good** el aire puro (te) hace bien; **you never know** nunca se sabe; **you can't do that!** ¡eso no se hace!

you'd [juːd] = **you had; you would**
you'll [juːl] = **you will; you shall**
young [jʌŋ] ADJ joven ▸ NPL (*of animal*) cría; (*people*): **the** ~ los jóvenes, la juventud; **a ~ man/lady** un(a) joven; **my younger brother** mi hermano menor *or* pequeño; **the younger generation** la nueva generación

youngster ['jʌŋstəʳ] N joven *mf*

your [jɔːʳ] ADJ tu, vuestro *pl*; (*formal*) su; ~ **house** tu *etc* casa; *see also* **my**

you're [juəʳ] = **you are**

yours [jɔːz] PRON tuyo, vuestro *pl*; (*formal*) suyo; **a friend of** ~ un amigo tuyo *etc*; *see also* **faithfully; mine; sincerely**

yourself [jɔːˈsɛlf] PRON (*reflexive*) tú mismo; (*complement*) te; (*after prep*) ti (mismo); (*formal*) usted mismo; (: *complement*) se; (: *after prep*) sí (mismo); **you ~ told me** me lo dijiste tú mismo; **(all) by** ~ sin ayuda de nadie, solo; *see also* **oneself**

yourselves [jɔːˈsɛlvz] PRON PL vosotros mismos; (*after prep*) vosotros (mismos); (*formal*) ustedes (mismos); (: *complement*) se; (: *after prep*) sí mismos

youth [juːθ] N juventud *f*; (*pl* **youths** [juːðz]: *young man*) joven *m*; **in my** ~ en mi juventud

youth club N club *m* juvenil

youthful ['juːθful] ADJ juvenil

youthfulness ['juːθfəlnɪs] N juventud *f*

youth hostel N albergue *m* juvenil

youth movement N movimiento juvenil

you've [juːv] = **you have**

yowl [jaul] N (*of animal, person*) aullido ▸ VI aullar

yr ABBR (= *year*) a

YT ABBR (*CANADA*) = **Yukon Territory**

Yugoslav ['juːgəuslɑːv] ADJ, N yugoslavo(-a) *m/f*

Yugoslavia [juːgəuˈslɑːvɪə] N Yugoslavia

Yugoslavian [juːgəuˈslɑːvɪən] ADJ yugoslavo(-a)

yuppie ['jʌpɪ] (*inf*) ADJ, N yuppie *mf*

YWCA N ABBR (= *Young Women's Christian Association*) Asociación *f* de Jóvenes Cristianas

877

Zz

Z, z [zɛd, (US) ziː] N (letter) Z, z f; **Z for Zebra** Z de Zaragoza

Zaire [zɑːˈiːəʳ] N Zaire m

Zambia [ˈzæmbɪə] N Zambia

Zambian [ˈzæmbɪən] ADJ, N zambiano(-a) m/f

zany [ˈzeɪnɪ] ADJ estrafalario

zap [zæp] VT (Comput) borrar

zeal [ziːl] N celo, entusiasmo

zealot [ˈzɛlət] N fanático(-a)

zealous [ˈzɛləs] ADJ celoso, entusiasta

zebra [ˈziːbrə] N cebra

zebra crossing N (BRIT) paso de peatones

zenith [ˈzɛnɪθ] N (Astro) cénit m; (fig) apogeo

zero [ˈzɪərəu] N cero; **5 degrees below ~** 5 grados bajo cero

zero hour N hora cero

zero option N (Pol) opción f cero

zero-rated [ˈzɪərəureɪtɪd] ADJ (BRIT) de tasa cero

zest [zɛst] N ánimo, vivacidad f; (of orange) piel f; **~ for living** brío

zigzag [ˈzɪgzæg] N zigzag m ▶ VI zigzaguear

Zimbabwe [zɪmˈbɑːbwɪ] N Zimbabwe m

Zimbabwean [zɪmˈbɑːbwɪən] ADJ, N zimbabuense mf

Zimmer® [ˈzɪməʳ] N (also: **Zimmer frame**) andador m, andaderas fpl

zinc [zɪŋk] N cinc m, zinc m

Zionism [ˈzaɪənɪzm] N sionismo

Zionist [ˈzaɪənɪst] ADJ, N sionista mf

zip [zɪp] N (also: **zip fastener**, (US) **zipper**) cremallera, cierre m relámpago (LAM); (energy) energía, vigor m ▶ VT (Comput) comprimir; (also: **zip up**) cerrar la cremallera de ▶ VI: **to ~ along to the shops** ir de compras volando

zip code N (US) código postal

zip file N (Comput) archivo m comprimido

zipper [ˈzɪpəʳ] N (US) cremallera

zit [zɪt] N grano

zither [ˈzɪðəʳ] N cítara

zodiac [ˈzəudɪæk] N zodíaco

zombie [ˈzɔmbɪ] N zombi m

zone [zəun] N zona

zonked [zɔŋkt] ADJ (inf) hecho polvo

zoo [zuː] N zoo, (parque m) zoológico

zoological [zuːəˈlɔdʒɪkəl] ADJ zoológico

zoologist [zuːˈɔlədʒɪst] N zoólogo(-a)

zoology [zuːˈɔlədʒɪ] N zoología

zoom [zuːm] VI: **to ~ past** pasar zumbando; **to ~ in (on sth/sb)** (Phot, Cine) enfocar (algo/a algn) con el zoom

zoom lens N zoom m

zucchini [zuːˈkiːnɪ] N, PL (US) calabacín(-ines) m(pl)

Gramm
Gramátic

Using the grammar

The Grammar section deals systematically and comprehensively with all the information you will need in order to communicate accurately in Spanish. The user-friendly layout explains the grammar point on a left hand page, leaving the facing page free for illustrative examples. The circled numbers, → ● etc, direct you to the relevant example in every case. Another strong point of the Grammar section is its comprehensive treatment of verbs. Regular verbs are fully explained, and 80 major irregular verbs are conjugated in their simple tenses. The irregular verbs are given in alphabetical order and laid out in tables, making them easy and efficient to consult. In addition, a verb index lists every Spanish verb in this dictionary each cross-referred to the appropriate conjugation model.

The Grammar section also provides invaluable guidance on the danger of translating English structures by identical structures in Spanish. Use of Numbers and Punctuation are important areas covered towards the end of the section. Finally, the index lists the main words and grammatical terms in both English and Spanish.

Abbreviations

cond.	conditional
fem.	feminine
masc.	masculine
plur.	plural
sing.	singular
subj	subjunctive
algn	alguien
sb	somebody
sth	something

Contents

Verbs

Simple Tenses: Formation

In Spanish the simple tenses are:

- Present → ①
- Imperfect → ②
- Future → ③
- Conditional → ④
- Preterite → ⑤
- Present Subjunctive → ⑥
- Imperfect Subjunctive → ⑦

They are formed by adding endings to a verb stem. The endings show the number and person of the subject of the verb → ⑧

The stem and endings of regular verbs are totally predictable. The following sections show all the patterns for regular verbs. For irregular verbs see page 80 onwards.

Regular Verbs

There are three regular verb patterns (called conjugations), each identifiable by the ending of the infinitive:

First conjugation verbs end in **-ar** e.g. **hablar** to speak.

Second conjugation verbs end in **-er** e.g. **comer** to eat.

Third conjugation verbs end in -ir e.g. **vivir** to live.

These three conjugations are treated in order on the following pages. The subject pronouns will appear in brackets because they are not always necessary in Spanish (see page 230).

Examples

1 (yo) hablo

I speak
I am speaking
I do speak

2 (yo) hablaba

I spoke
I was speaking
I used to speak

3 (yo) hablaré

I shall speak
I shall be speaking

4 (yo) hablaría

I should/would speak
I should/would be speaking

5 (yo) hablé

I spoke

6 (que) (yo) hable

(that) I speak

7 (que) (yo) hablara *or* hablase

(that) I spoke

8 (yo) hablo
(nosotros) hablamos
(yo) hablaría
(nosotros) hablaríamos

I speak
we speak
I would speak
we would speak

Simple Tenses: First Conjugation

The stem is formed as follows:

TENSE	FORMATION	EXAMPLE
Present		
Imperfect		
Preterite	infinitive minus -ar	habl-
Present Subjunctive	For irregular verbs see page 80	
Imperfect Subjunctive		
Future	infinitive	hablar-
Conditional		

To the appropriate stem add the following endings:

		① PRESENT	② IMPERFECT	③ PRETERITE
sing.	1st person	-o	-aba	-é
	2nd person	-as	-abas	-aste
	3rd person	-a	-aba	-ó
plur.	1st person	-amos	-ábamos	-amos
	2nd person	-áis	-abais	-asteis
	3rd person	-an	-aban	-aron

		④ PRESENT SUBJUNCTIVE	⑤ IMPERFECT SUBJUNCTIVE
sing.	1st person	-e	-ara or -ase
	2nd person	-es	-aras or -ases
	3rd person	-e	-ara or -ase
plur.	1st person	-emos	-áramos or -ásemos
	2nd person	-éis	-arais or -aseis
	3rd person	-en	-aran or -asen

		⑥ FUTURE	⑦ CONDITIONAL
sing.	1st person	-é	-ía
	2nd person	-ás	-ías
	3rd person	-á	-ía
plur.	1st person	-emos	-íamos
	2nd person	-éis	-íais
	3rd person	-án	-ían

1 PRESENT

(yo)	hablo
(tú)	hablas
(él/ella/Vd)	habla
(nosotros/as)	hablamos
(vosotros/as)	habláis
(ellos/as/Vds)	hablan

2 IMPERFECT

hablaba
hablabas
hablaba
hablábamos
hablabais
hablaban

3 PRETERITE

hablé
hablaste
habló
hablamos
hablasteis
hablaron

4 PRESENT SUBJUNCTIVE

(yo)	hable
(tú)	hables
(él/ella/Vd)	hable
(nosotros/as)	hablemos
(vosotros/as)	habléis
(ellos/as/Vds)	hablen

5 IMPERFECT SUBJUNCTIVE

hablara *or* hablase
hablaras *or* hablases
hablara *or* hablase
habláramos *or* hablásemos
hablarais *or* hablaseis
hablaran *or* hablasen

6 FUTURE

(yo)	hablaré
(tú)	hablarás
(él/ella/Vd)	hablará
(nosotros/as)	hablaremos
(vosotros/as)	hablaréis
(ellos/as/Vds)	hablarán

7 CONDITIONAL

hablaría
hablarías
hablaría
hablaríamos
hablaríais
hablarían

9

Simple Tenses: Second Conjugation

The stem is formed as follows:

TENSE	FORMATION	EXAMPLE
Present		
Imperfect		
Preterite	infinitive minus -er	com-
Present Subjunctive	For irregular verbs see page 80	
Imperfect Subjunctive		
Future	infinitive	comer-
Conditional		

To the appropriate stem add the following endings:

		① PRESENT	② IMPERFECT	③ PRETERITE
	1st person	-o	-ía	-í
sing.	2nd person	-es	-ías	-iste
	3rd person	-e	-ía	-ió
	1st person	-emos	-íamos	-imos
plur.	2nd person	-éis	-íais	-isteis
	3rd person	-en	-ían	-ieron

		④ PRESENT SUBJUNCTIVE	⑤ IMPERFECT SUBJUNCTIVE
	1st person	-a	-iera or -iese
sing.	2nd person	-as	-ieras or -ieses
	3rd person	-a	-iera or -iese
	1st person	-amos	-iéramos or -iésemos
plur.	2nd person	-áis	-ierais or -ieseis
	3rd person	-an	-ieran or -iesen

		⑥ FUTURE	⑦ CONDITIONAL
	1st person	-é	-ía
sing.	2nd person	-ás	-ías
	3rd person	-á	-ía
	1st person	-emos	-íamos
plur.	2nd person	-éis	-íais
	3rd person	-án	-ían

1 PRESENT

(yo)	como
(tú)	comes
(él/ella/Vd)	come
(nosotros/as)	comemos
(vosotros/as)	coméis
(ellos/as/Vds)	comen

2 IMPERFECT

comía
comías
comía
comíamos
comíais
comían

3 PRETERITE

comí
comiste
comió
comimos
comisteis
comieron

4 PRESENT SUBJUNCTIVE

(yo)	coma
(tú)	comas
(él/ella/Vd)	coma
(nosotros/as)	comamos
(vosotros/as)	comáis
(ellos/as/Vds)	coman

5 IMPERFECT SUBJUNCTIVE

comiera or comiese
comieras or comieses
comiera or comiese
comiéramos or comiésemos
comierais or comieseis
comieran or comiesen

6 FUTURE

(yo)	comeré
(tú)	comerás
(él/ella/Vd)	comerá
(nosotros/as)	comeremos
(vosotros/as)	comeréis
(ellos/as/Vds)	comerán

7 CONDITIONAL

comería
comerías
comería
comeríamos
comeríais
comerían

Simple Tenses: Third Conjugation

The stem is formed as follows:

TENSE	FORMATION	EXAMPLE
Present		
Imperfect		
Preterite	infinitive minus -ir	viv-
Present Subjunctive	For irregular verbs see page 80	
Imperfect Subjunctive		
Future	infinitive	vivir-
Conditional		

To the appropriate stem add the following endings:

		① PRESENT	② IMPERFECT	③ PRETERITE
	1st person	-o	-ía	-í
sing.	2nd person	-es	-ías	-iste
	3rd person	-e	-ía	-ió
	1st person	-imos	-íamos	-imos
plur.	2nd person	-ís	-íais	-isteis
	3rd person	-en	-ían	-ieron

		④ PRESENT SUBJUNCTIVE	⑤ IMPERFECT SUBJUNCTIVE
	1st person	-a	-iera or -iese
sing.	2nd person	-as	-ieras or -ieses
	3rd person	-a	-iera or -iese
	1st person	-amos	-iéramos or -iésemos
plur.	2nd person	-áis	-ierais or -ieseis
	3rd person	-an	-ieran or -iesen

		⑥ FUTURE	⑦ CONDITIONAL
	1st person	-é	-ía
sing.	2nd person	-ás	-ías
	3rd person	-á	-ía
	1st person	-emos	-íamos
plur.	2nd person	-éis	-íais
	3rd person	-án	-ían

Examples

① PRESENT

(yo)	vivo
(tú)	vives
(él/ella/Vd)	vive
(nosotros/as)	vivimos
(vosotros/as)	vivís
(ellos/as/Vds)	viven

② IMPERFECT

vivía
vivías
vivía
vivíamos
vivíais
vivían

③ PRETERITE

viví
viviste
vivió
vivimos
vivisteis
vivieron

④ PRESENT SUBJUNCTIVE

(yo)	viva
(tú)	vivas
(él/ella/Vd)	viva
(nosotros/as)	vivamos
(vosotros/as)	viváis
(ellos/as/Vds)	vivan

⑤ IMPERFECT SUBJUNCTIVE

viviera *or* viviese
vivieras *or* vivieses
viviera *or* viviese
viviéramos *or* viviésemos
vivierais *or* vivieseis
vivieran *or* viviesen

⑥ FUTURE

(yo)	viviré
(tú)	vivirás
(él/ella/Vd)	vivirá
(nosotros/as)	viviremos
(vosotros/as)	viviréis
(ellos/as/Vds)	vivirán

⑦ CONDITIONAL

viviría
vivirías
viviría
viviríamos
viviríais
vivirían

13

The Imperative

The imperative is the form of the verb used to give commands or orders. It can be used politely, as in English 'Shut the door, please'.

In *positive* commands, the imperative forms for Vd, Vds and nosotros are the same as the subjunctive. The other forms are as follows:

tú (same as 3rd person singular present indicative)
vosotros (final -r of infinitive changes to -d) → ❶

(tú)	**habla** speak	**come** eat	**vive** live
(Vd)	**hable** speak	**coma** eat	**viva** live
(nosotros)	**hablemos**	**comamos**	**vivamos**
	let's speak	let's eat	let's live
(vosotros)	**hablad** speak	**comed** eat	**vivid** live
(Vds)	**hablen** speak	**coman** eat	**vivan** live

In *negative* commands, all the imperative forms are exactly the same as the present subjunctive.

The imperative of irregular verbs is given in the verb tables, pages 82 to 160.

Position of object pronouns with the imperative:
- in *positive* commands: they follow the verb and are attached to it. An accent is needed to show the correct position for stress (see page 296) → ❷
- in *negative* commands: they precede the verb and are not attached to it → ❸

For the order of object pronouns, see page 236.

❶ cantar — to sing
cantad — sing

❷ Perdóneme — Excuse me
Enviémoselos — Let's send them to him/her/them

Elíjanos — Choose us
Explíquemelo — Explain it to me

Esperémosla — Let's wait for her/it
Devuélvaselo — Give it back to him/her/them

❸ No me molestes — Don't disturb me
No se la devolvamos — Let's not give it back to him/her/them

No les castiguemos — Let's not punish them
No me lo mandes — Don't send it to me
No las conteste — Don't answer them
No nos lo hagan — Don't do it to us

The Imperative *continued*

For reflexive verbs – e.g. levantarse to get up – the object pronoun is the reflexive pronoun. It should be noted that the imperative forms need an accent to show the correct position for stress (see page 296). The forms nosotros and vosotros also drop the final -s and -d respectively before the pronoun → ①

> BUT: idos (vosotros) go

① Note: For general instructions, the infinitive is used instead of the imperative → ②, but when it is preceded by vamos a it often translates *let's* … → ③

1 Levántate — Get up
No te levantes — Don't get up
Levántese (Vd) — Get up
No se levante (Vd) — Don't get up
Levantémonos — Let's get up
No nos levantemos — Let's not get up
Levantaos — Get up
No os levantéis — Don't get up
Levántense (Vds) — Get up
No se levanten (Vds) — Don't get up

2 Ver pág ... — See page
No pasar — Do not pass ...

3 Vamos a ver — Let's see
Vamos a empezar — Let's start

Compound Tenses: formation

In Spanish the compound tenses are:

Perfect → ①
Pluperfect → ②
Future Perfect → ③
Conditional Perfect → ④
Past Anterior → ⑤
Perfect Subjunctive → ⑥
Pluperfect Subjunctive → ⑦

They consist of the past participle of the verb together with the auxiliary verb **haber**.

Compound tenses are formed in exactly the same way for both regular and irregular verbs, the only difference being that irregular verbs may have an irregular past participle.

The Past Participle

For all compound tenses you need to know how to form the past participle of the verb. For regular verbs this is as follows:

First conjugation: replace the **-ar** of the infinitive by **-ado** → ⑧

Second conjugation: replace the **-er** of the infinitive by **-ido** → ⑨

Third conjugation: replace the **-ir** of the infinitive by **-ido** → ⑩

Examples

① (yo) he hablado   I have spoken

② (yo) había hablado   I had spoken

③ (yo) habré hablado   I shall have spoken

④ (yo) habría hablado   I should/would have spoken

⑤ (yo) hube hablado   I had spoken

⑥ (que) (yo) haya hablado   (that) I spoke, have spoken

⑦ (que) (yo) hubiera/hubiese hablado   (that) I had spoken

⑧ cantar to sing → cantado sung

⑨ comer to eat → comido eaten

⑩ vivir to live → vivido lived

Compound Tenses: formation *continued*

PERFECT TENSE
The present tense of haber plus the past participle → ❶

PLUPERFECT TENSE
The imperfect tense of haber plus the past participle → ❷

FUTURE PERFECT
The future tense of haber plus the past participle → ❸

CONDITIONAL PERFECT
The conditional of haber plus the past participle → ❹

① PERFECT

(yo)	**he** habl**ado**
(tú)	**has** habl**ado**
(él/ella/Vd)	**ha** habl**ado**
(nosotros/as)	**hemos** habl**ado**
(vosotros/as)	**habéis** habl**ado**
(ellos/as/Vds)	**han** habl**ado**

② PLUPERFECT

(yo)	**había** habl**ado**
(tú)	**habías** habl**ado**
(él/ella/Vd)	**había** habl**ado**
(nosotros/as)	**habíamos** habl**ado**
(vosotros/as)	**habíais** habl**ado**
(ellos/as/Vds)	**habían** habl**ado**

③ FUTURE PERFECT

(yo)	**habré** habl**ado**
(tú)	**habrás** habl**ado**
(él/ella/Vd)	**habrá** habl**ado**
(nosotros/as)	**habremos** habl**ado**
(vosotros/as)	**habréis** habl**ado**
(ellos/as/Vds)	**habrán** habl**ado**

④ CONDITIONAL PERFECT

(yo)	**habría** habl**ado**
(tú)	**habrías** habl**ado**
(él/ella/Vd)	**habría** habl**ado**
(nosotros/as)	**habríamos** habl**ado**
(vosotros/as)	**habríais** habl**ado**
(ellos/as/Vds)	**habrían** habl**ado**

Compound Tenses: Formation *continued*

PAST ANTERIOR
The preterite of haber plus the past participle → ❶

PERFECT SUBJUNCTIVE
The present subjunctive of haber plus the past participle → ❷

PLUPERFECT SUBJUNCTIVE
The imperfect subjunctive of haber plus the past participle → ❸

For how to form the past participle of regular verbs see page 18.
The past participle of irregular verbs is given for each verb in the verb
tables, pages 82 to 160.

Examples

①　PAST ANTERIOR

(yo)	**hube** hablado
(tú)	**hubiste** hablado
(él/ella/Vd)	**hubo** hablado
(nosotros/as)	**hubimos** hablado
(vosotros/as)	**hubisteis** hablado
(ellos/as/Vds)	**hubieron** hablado

②　PERFECT SUBJUNCTIVE

(yo)	**haya** hablado
(tú)	**hayas** hablado
(él/ella/Vd)	**haya** hablado
(nosotros/as)	**hayamos** hablado
(vosotros/as)	**hayáis** hablado
(ellos/as/Vds)	**hayan** hablado

③　PLUPERFECT SUBJUNCTIVE

(yo)	**hubiera** or **hubiese** hablado
(tú)	**hubieras** or **hubieses** hablado
(él/ella/Vd)	**hubiera** or **hubiese** hablado
(nosotros/as)	**hubiéramos** or **hubiésemos** hablado
(vosotros/as)	**hubierais** or **hubieseis** hablado
(ellos/as/Vds)	**hubieran** or **hubiesen** hablado

Reflexive Verbs

A reflexive verb is one accompanied by a reflexive pronoun. The infinitive of a reflexive verb ends with the pronoun se, which is added to the verb form e.g.
levantarse to get up; lavarse to wash (oneself)
The reflexive pronouns are:

	SINGULAR	PLURAL
1st person	me	nos
2nd person	te	os
3rd person	se	se

The reflexive pronoun 'reflects back' to the subject, but it is not always translated in English → ①

> The plural pronouns are sometimes translated as 'one another', 'each other' (the *reciprocal* meaning) → ②

> The reciprocal meaning may be emphasized by el uno al otro/ la una a la otra (los unos a los otros/las unas a las otras) → ③

Both simple and compound tenses of reflexive verbs are conjugated in exactly the same way as those of non-reflexive verbs, except that the reflexive pronoun is always used.

The only irregularity is in the 1st and 2nd person plural of the affirmative imperative (see page 16). A sample reflexive verb is conjugated in full on pages 28 to 31.

Position of reflexive pronouns

Except with the infinitive, gerund and positive commands, the pronoun comes before the verb → ④

In the infinitive, gerund and positive commands, the pronoun follows the verb and is attached to it (but see also page 232) → ⑤

Examples

1. Me visto — I'm dressing (myself)
   Nos lavamos — We're washing (ourselves)
   Se levanta — He gets up

2. Nos queremos — We love each other
   Se parecen — They resemble one another

3. Se miraban el uno al otro — They were looking at each other

4. Me acuesto temprano — I go to bed early
   ¿Cómo se llama Vd? — What is your name?
   No se ha despertado — He hasn't woken up
   No te levantes — Don't get up

5. Quiero irme — I want to go away
   Estoy levantándome — I am getting up
   Siéntense — Sit down
   Vámonos — Let's go

Reflexive Verbs *continued*

Some verbs have both a reflexive and non-reflexive form. When used reflexively, they have a different but closely related meaning, as shown in the following examples.

NON-REFLEXIVE	REFLEXIVE
acostar to put to bed	acostarse to go to bed
casar to marry (off)	casarse to get married
detener to stop	detenerse to come to a halt
dormir to sleep	dormirse to go to sleep
enfadar to annoy	enfadarse to get annoyed
hacer to make	hacerse to become
ir to go	irse to leave, go away
lavar to wash	lavarse to get washed
levantar to raise	levantarse to get up
llamar to call	llamarse to be called
poner to put	ponerse to put on (clothing), to become
sentir to feel (something)	sentirse to feel (sick, tired, *etc*)
vestir to dress (someone)	vestirse to get dressed
volver to return	volverse to turn round

Some other verbs exist only in the reflexive:

arrepentirse to repent	jactarse to boast
atreverse to dare	quejarse to complain

Some verbs acquire a different nuance when used reflexively:

caer to fall → ❶   caerse to fall down (by accident) → ❷

morir to die, be killed (by accident or on purpose) → ❸   morirse to die (from natural causes) → ❹

Often a reflexive verb can be used:

- to avoid the passive (see page 32) → ❺
- in impersonal expressions (see page 40) → ❻

1. El agua caía desde las rocas — Water fell from the rocks

2. Me caí y me rompí el brazo — I fell and broke my arm

3. Tres personas han muerto en un accidente/atentado terrorista — Three people were killed in an accident/a terrorist attack

4. Mi abuelo se murió a los ochenta años — My grandfather died at the age of eighty

5. Se perdió la batalla — The battle was lost
   No se veían las casas — The houses could not be seen

6. Se dice que ... — (It is said that) People say that ...
   No se puede entrar — You/One can't go in
   No se permite — It is not allowed

Reflexive Verbs *continued*

Conjugation of: **lavarse** to wash oneself

1 SIMPLE TENSES

PRESENT

(yo)	**me** lav**o**
(tú)	**te** lav**as**
(él/ella/Vd)	**se** lav**a**
(nosotros/as)	**nos** lav**amos**
(vosotros/as)	**os** lav**áis**
(ellos/as/Vds)	**se** lav**an**

IMPERFECT

(yo)	**me** lav**aba**
(tú)	**te** lav**abas**
(él/ella/Vd)	**se** lav**aba**
(nosotros/as)	**nos** lav**ábamos**
(vosotros/as)	**os** lav**abais**
(ellos/as/Vds)	**se** lav**aban**

FUTURE

(yo)	**me** lavar**é**
(tú)	**te** lavar**ás**
(él/ella/Vd)	**se** lavar**á**
(nosotros/as)	**nos** lavar**emos**
(vosotros/as)	**os** lavar**éis**
(ellos/as/Vds)	**se** lavar**án**

CONDITIONAL

(yo)	**me** lavar**ía**
(tú)	**te** lavar**ías**
(él/ella/Vd)	**se** lavar**ía**
(nosotros/as)	**nos** lavar**íamos**
(vosotros/as)	**os** lavar**íais**
(ellos/as/Vds)	**se** lavar**ían**

Reflexive Verbs *continued*

Conjugation of: lavarse to wash oneself

1 SIMPLE TENSES

PRETERITE

(yo)	**me** lav**é**
(tú)	**te** lav**aste**
(él/ella/Vd)	**se** lav**ó**
(nosotros/as)	**nos** lav**amos**
(vosotros/as)	**os** lav**asteis**
(ellos/as/Vds)	**se** lav**aron**

PRESENT SUBJUNCTIVE

(yo)	**me** lav**e**
(tú)	**te** lav**es**
(él/ella/Vd)	**se** lav**e**
(nosotros/as)	**nos** lav**emos**
(vosotros/as)	**os** lav**éis**
(ellos/as/Vds)	**se** lav**en**

IMPERFECT SUBJUNCTIVE

(yo)	**me** lav**ara** *or* lav**ase**
(tú)	**te** lav**aras** *or* lav**ases**
(él/ella/Vd)	**se** lav**ara** *or* lav**ase**
(nosotros/as)	**nos** lav**áramos** *or* lav**ásemos**
(vosotros/as)	**os** lav**arais** *or* lav**aseis**
(ellos/as/Vds)	**se** lav**aran** *or* lav**asen**

Reflexive Verbs *continued*

Conjugation of: **lavarse** to wash oneself

2 COMPOUND TENSES

PERFECT

(yo)	**me he** lavado
(tú)	**te has** lavado
(él/ella/Vd)	**se ha** lavado
(nosotros/as)	**nos hemos** lavado
(vosotros/as)	**os habéis** lavado
(ellos/as/Vds)	**se han** lavado

PLUPERFECT

(yo)	**me había** lavado
(tú)	**te habías** lavado
(él/ella/Vd)	**se había** lavado
(nosotros/as)	**nos habíamos** lavado
(vosotros/as)	**os habíais** lavado
(ellos/as/Vds)	**se habían** lavado

FUTURE PERFECT

(yo)	**me habré** lavado
(tú)	**te habrás** lavado
(él/ella/Vd)	**se habrá** lavado
(nosotros/as)	**nos habremos** lavado
(vosotros/as)	**os habréis** lavado
(ellos/as/Vds)	**se habrán** lavado

Reflexive Verbs *continued*

Conjugation of: **lavarse** to wash oneself

2 COMPOUND TENSES

PAST ANTERIOR

(yo)	**me hube** lavado
(tú)	**te hubiste** lavado
(él/ella/Vd)	**se hubo** lavado
(nosotros/as)	**nos hubimos** lavado
(vosotros/as)	**os hubisteis** lavado
(ellos/as/Vds)	**se hubieron** lavado

PERFECT SUBJUNCTIVE

(yo)	**me haya** lavado
(tú)	**te hayas** lavado
(él/ella/Vd)	**se haya** lavado
(nosotros/as)	**nos hayamos** lavado
(vosotros/as)	**os hayáis** lavado
(ellos/as/Vds)	**se hayan** lavado

PLUPERFECT SUBJUNCTIVE

(yo)	**me hubiera** *or* **hubiese** lavado
(tú)	**te hubieras** *or* **hubieses** lavado
(él/ella/Vd)	**se hubiera** *or* **hubiese** lavado
(nosotros/as)	**nos hubiéramos** *or* **hubiésemos** lavado
(vosotros/as)	**os hubierais** *or* **hubieseis** lavado
(ellos/as/Vds)	**se hubieran** *or* **hubiesen** lavado

The Passive

In active sentences, the subject of a verb carries out the action of that verb, but in passive sentences the subject receives the action. Compare the following:

> The car hit Jane (*subject*: the car)
> Jane was hit by the car (*subject*: Jane)

English uses the verb 'to be' with the past participle to form passive sentences. Spanish forms them in the same way, i.e.:
> a tense of ser + *past participle*.

The past participle agrees in number and gender with the subject → ❶

A sample verb is conjugated in the passive voice on pages 36 to 39.

In English, the word 'by' usually introduces the agent through which the action of a passive sentence is performed. In Spanish this agent is preceded by por → ❷

The passive voice is used much less frequently in Spanish than English. It is, however, often used in expressions where the identity of the agent is unknown or unimportant → ❸

Examples

1 Pablo ha sido despedido
Su madre era muy admirada
El palacio será vendido
Las puertas habían sido cerradas

Paul has been sacked
His mother was greatly admired
The palace will be sold
The doors had been closed

2 La casa fue diseñada por mi
hermano

The house was designed by my
brother

3 La ciudad fue conquistada tras
un largo asedio
Ha sido declarado el estado de
excepción

The city was conquered after a
long siege
A state of emergency has been
declared

The Passive *continued*

In English the indirect object in an active sentence can become the subject of the related passive sentence, e.g.

> 'His mother gave him the book' (*indirect object*: him)
> He was given the book by his mother

This is not possible in Spanish. The indirect object remains as such, while the object of the active sentence becomes the subject of the passive sentence → ❶

Other ways to express a passive meaning

Since modern Spanish tends to avoid the passive, it uses various other constructions to replace it:

If the agent (person or object performing the action) is known, the active is often preferred where English might prefer the passive → ❷

The 3rd person plural of the active voice can be used. The meaning is equivalent to 'they' + *verb* → ❸

When the action of the sentence is performed on a person, the reflexive form of the verb can be used in the 3rd person singular, and the person becomes the object → ❹

When the action is performed on a thing, this becomes the subject of the sentence and the verb is made reflexive, agreeing in number with the subject → ❺

Examples

1. Su madre le regaló el libro
   BECOMES:
   El libro le fue regalado por su
   madre

   His mother gave him the book

   The book was given to him by
   his mother

2. La policía interrogó al
   sospechoso
   RATHER THAN:
   El sospechoso fue interrogado
   por la policía

   The police questioned the
   suspect

3. Usan demasiada publicidad en
   la televisión

   Too much advertising is used
   on television

4. Últimamente no se le/les ha
   visto mucho en público

   He has/they have not been seen
   much in public recently

5. Esta palabra ya no se usa
   Todos los libros se han vendido

   This word is no longer used
   All the books have been sold

35

The Passive *continued*

Conjugation of: ser amado to be loved

PRESENT

(yo)	soy amado(a)
(tú)	eres amado(a)
(él/ella/Vd)	es amado(a)
(nosotros/as)	somos amado(a)s
(vosotros/as)	sois amado(a)s
(ellos/as/Vds)	son amado(a)s

IMPERFECT

(yo)	era amado(a)
(tú)	eras amado(a)
(él/ella/Vd)	era amado(a)
(nosotros/as)	éramos amado(a)s
(vosotros/as)	erais amado(a)s
(ellos/as/Vds)	eran amado(a)s

FUTURE

(yo)	seré amado(a)
(tú)	serás amado(a)
(él/ella/Vd)	será amado(a)
(nosotros/as)	seremos amado(a)s
(vosotros/as)	seréis amado(a)s
(ellos/as/Vds)	serán amado(a)s

CONDITIONAL

(yo)	sería amado(a)
(tú)	serías amado(a)
(él/ella/Vd)	sería amado(a)
(nosotros/as)	seríamos amado(a)s
(vosotros/as)	seríais amado(a)s
(ellos/as/Vds)	serían amado(a)s

The Passive *continued*

Conjugation of: ser amado to be loved

PRETERITE

(yo)	**fui** amado(a)
(tú)	**fuiste** amado(a)
(él/ella/Vd)	**fue** amado(a)
(nosotros/as)	**fuimos** amado(a)s
(vosotros/as)	**fuisteis** amado(a)s
(ellos/as/Vds)	**fueron** amado(a)s

PRESENT SUBJUNCTIVE

(yo)	**sea** amado(a)
(tú)	**seas** amado(a)
(él/ella/Vd)	**sea** amado(a)
(nosotros/as)	**seamos** amado(a)s
(vosotros/as)	**seáis** amado(a)s
(ellos/as/Vds)	**sean** amado(a)s

IMPERFECT SUBJUNCTIVE

(yo)	**fuera** *or* **fuese** amado(a)
(tú)	**fueras** *or* **fueses** amado(a)
(él/ella/Vd)	**fuera** *or* **fuese** amado(a)
(nosotros/as)	**fuéramos** *or* **fuésemos** amado(a)s
(vosotros/as)	**fuerais** *or* **fueseis** amado(a)s
(ellos/as/Vds)	**fueran** *or* **fuesen** amado(a)s

The Passive *continued*

Conjugation of: **ser amado** to be loved

PERFECT

(yo)	**he sido** amado(a)
(tú)	**has sido** amado(a)
(él/ella/Vd)	**ha sido** amado(a)
(nosotros/as)	**hemos sido** amado(a)s
(vosotros/as)	**habéis sido** amado(a)s
(ellos/as/Vds)	**han sido** amado(a)s

PLUPERFECT

(yo)	**había sido** amado(a)
(tú)	**habías sido** amado(a)
(él/ella/Vd)	**había sido** amado(a)
(nosotros/as)	**habíamos sido** amado(a)s
(vosotros/as)	**habíais sido** amado(a)s
(ellos/as/Vds)	**habían sido** amado(a)s

FUTURE PERFECT

(yo)	**habré sido** amado(a)
(tú)	**habrás sido** amado(a)
(él/ella/Vd)	**habrá sido** amado(a)
(nosotros/as)	**habremos sido** amado(a)s
(vosotros/as)	**habréis sido** amado(a)s
(ellos/as/Vds)	**habrán sido** amado(a)s

CONDITIONAL PERFECT

(yo)	**habría sido** amado(a)
(tú)	**habrías sido** amado(a)
(él/ella/Vd)	**habría sido** amado(a)
(nosotros/as)	**habríamos sido** amado(a)s
(vosotros/as)	**habríais sido** amado(a)s
(ellos/as/Vds)	**habrían sido** amado(a)s

The Passive *continued*

Conjugation of: **ser amado** to be loved

PAST ANTERIOR

(yo)	**hube sido** amado(a)
(tú)	**hubiste sido** amado(a)
(él/ella/Vd)	**hubo sido** amado(a)
(nosotros/as)	**hubimos sido** amado(a)s
(vosotros/as)	**hubisteis sido** amado(a)s
(ellos/as/Vds)	**hubieron sido** amado(a)s

PERFECT SUBJUNCTIVE

(yo)	**haya sido** amado(a)
(tú)	**hayas sido** amado(a)
(él/ella/Vd)	**haya sido** amado(a)
(nosotros/as)	**hayamos sido** amado(a)s
(vosotros/as)	**hayáis sido** amado(a)s
(ellos/as/Vds)	**hayan sido** amado(a)s

PLUPERFECT SUBJUNCTIVE

(yo)	**hubiera/-se sido** amado(a)
(tú)	**hubieras/-ses sido** amado(a)
(él/ella/Vd)	**hubiera/-se sido** amado(a)
(nosotros/as)	**hubiéramos/-semos sido** amado(a)s
(vosotros/as)	**hubierais/-seis sido** amado(a)s
(ellos/as/Vds)	**hubieran/-sen sido** amado(a)s

Impersonal Verbs

Impersonal verbs are used only in the infinitive, the gerund, and in the 3rd person (usually singular); unlike English, Spanish does not use the subject pronoun with impersonal verbs, e.g.

> **llueve** it's raining
> **es fácil decir que ...** it's easy to say that ...

The most common impersonal verbs are:

INFINITIVE	CONSTRUCTION
amanecer	amanece/está amaneciendo
	it's daybreak
anochecer	anochece/está anocheciendo
	it's getting dark
granizar	graniza/está granizando
	it's hailing
llover	llueve/está lloviendo
	it's raining → ①
lloviznar	llovizna/está lloviznando
	it's drizzling
nevar	nieva/está nevando
	it's snowing → ①
tronar	truena/está tronando
	it's thundering

Some reflexive verbs are also used impersonally.
The most common are:

INFINITIVE	CONSTRUCTION
creerse	se cree que* + *indicative* → ②
	it is thought that; people think that
decirse	se dice que* + *indicative* → ③
	it is said that; people say that

1. Llovía a cántaros — It was raining cats and dogs
   Estaba nevando cuando salieron — It was snowing when they left

2. Se cree que llegarán mañana — It is thought they will arrive tomorrow

3. Se dice que ha sido el peor invierno en 50 años — People say it's been the worst winter in 50 years

Impersonal Verbs *continued*

INFINITIVE	CONSTRUCTION
poderse	se puede + *infinitive* → ① one/people can, it is possible to
tratarse de	se trata de + *noun* → ② it's a question/matter of something it's about something
	se trata de + *infinitive* → ③ it's a question/matter of doing; somebody must do
venderse	se vende* + *noun* → ④ to be sold; for sale

*This impersonal construction conveys the same meaning as the 3rd person plural of these verbs; creen que, dicen que, venden

The following verbs are also commonly used in impersonal constructions:

INFINITIVE	CONSTRUCTION
bastar	basta con + *infinitive* → ⑤ it is enough to do basta con + *noun* → ⑥ something is enough, it only takes something
faltar	falta + *infinitive* → ⑦ we still have to/one still has to
haber	hay + *noun* → ⑧ there is/are hay que + *infinitive* → ⑨ one has to/we have to
hacer	hace + *noun/adjective depicting weather/dark/light etc* → ⑩ it is hace + *time expression* + que + *indicative* → ⑪ somebody has done *or* been doing something since ... hace + *time expression* + que + *negative indicative* → ⑫ it is ... since

1. Aquí se puede aparcar — One can park here

2. No se trata de dinero — It isn't a question/matter of money

3. Se trata de poner fin al asunto — We must put an end to the matter

4. Se vende coche — Car for sale

5. Basta con telefonear para reservar un asiento — You need only phone to reserve a seat

6. Basta con un error para que todo se estropee — One single error is enough to ruin everything

7. Aún falta cerrar las maletas — We/One still have/has to close the suitcases

8. Hay una habitación libre — There is one spare room
   No había cartas esta mañana — There were no letters this morning

9. Hay que cerrar las puertas — We have/One has to shut the doors

10. Hace calor/viento/sol — It is hot/windy/sunny
    Mañana hará bueno — It'll be nice (weather) tomorrow

11. Hace seis meses que vivo/vivimos aquí — I/We have lived or been living here for six months

12. Hace tres años que no le veo — It is three years since I last saw him

Impersonal Verbs *continued*

INFINITIVE	CONSTRUCTION
hacer falta	hace falta + *noun object* (+ *indirect object*) → ❶
	(somebody) needs something; something is necessary (to somebody)
	hace falta + *infinitive* (+ *indirect object*) → ❷
	it is necessary to do
	hace falta que + *subjunctive* → ❸
	it is necessary to do, somebody must do
parecer	parece que (+ *indirect object*) + *indicative* → ❹
	it seems/appears that
ser	es/son + *time expression* → ❺
	it is
	es + de día/noche → ❻
	it is
	es + *adjective* + *infinitive* → ❼
	it is
ser mejor	es mejor + *infinitive* → ❽
	it's better to do
	es mejor que + *subjunctive* → ❾
	it's better if/that
valer más	más vale + *infinitive* → ❿
	it's better to do
	más vale que + *subjunctive* → ⓫
	it's better to do/that somebody does

Examples

1. Hace falta valor para hacer eso — One needs courage to do that/ Courage is needed to do that

   Me hace falta otro vaso más — I need an extra glass

2. Hace falta volver — It is necessary to return/ We/I/You must return*

   Me hacía falta volver — I had to return

3. Hace falta que Vd se vaya — You have to/must leave

4. (Me) parece que estás equivocado — It seems (to me) you are wrong

5. Son las tres y media — It is half past three
   Ya es primavera — It is spring now

6. Era de noche cuando llegamos — It was night when we arrived

7. Era inútil protestar — It was useless to complain

8. Es mejor no decir nada — It's better to keep quiet

9. Es mejor que lo pongas aquí — It's better if/that you put it here

10. Más vale prevenir que curar — Prevention is better than cure

11. Más valdría que no fuéramos — It would be better if we didn't go/ We'd better not go

* The translation here obviously depends on context

The Infinitive

The infinitive is the form of the verb found in dictionary entries meaning 'to ...', e.g. hablar to speak, vivir to live.

The infinitive is used in the following ways:

After a preposition → ①

As a verbal noun → ②
In this use the article may precede the infinitive, especially when the infinitive is the subject and begins the sentence → ③

As a dependent infinitive, in the following verbal constructions:
- with no linking preposition → ④
- with the linking preposition a → ⑤
  (see also page 66)
- with the linking preposition de → ⑥
  (see also page 66)
- with the linking preposition en → ⑦
  (see also page 66)
- with the linking preposition con → ⑧
  (see also page 66)
- with the linking preposition por → ⑨
  (see also page 66)

The following construction should also be noted:
indefinite pronoun + que + *infinitive* → ⑩

The object pronouns generally follow the infinitive and are attached to it. For exceptions see page 232.

Examples

1 Después de acabar el desayuno, salió de casa
After finishing her breakfast she went out

Al enterarse de lo ocurrido se puso furiosa
When she found out what had happened she was furious

Me hizo daño sin saberlo
She hurt me without her knowing

2 Su deporte preferido es montar a caballo
Her favourite sport is horse riding

Ver es creer
Seeing is believing

3 El viajar tanto me resulta cansado
I find so much travelling tiring

4 ¿Quiere Vd esperar?
Would you like to wait?

5 Aprenderán pronto a nadar
They will soon learn to swim

6 Pronto dejará de llover
It'll stop raining soon

7 La comida tarda en hacerse
The meal takes a long time to cook

8 Amenazó con denunciarles
He threatened to report them (to the police)

9 Comience Vd por decirme su nombre
Please start by giving me your name

10 Tengo algo que decirte
I have something to tell you

The Infinitive *continued*

The verbs set out below are followed by the infinitive with no linking preposition.

deber, poder, saber, querer and tener que (hay que in impersonal constructions) → ①

valer más, hacer falta: see Impersonal Verbs, page 44.

verbs of seeing or hearing, e.g. ver to see, oír to hear → ②

hacer → ③

dejar to let, allow → ③

The following common verbs:

. aconsejar to advise → ④
conseguir to manage to → ⑤
decidir to decide
desear to wish, want → ⑥
esperar to hope → ⑦
evitar to avoid → ⑧
impedir to prevent → ⑨
intentar to try → ⑩
lograr to manage to → ⑤

necesitar to need → ⑪
odiar to hate
olvidar to forget → ⑫
pensar to think → ⑬
preferir to prefer → ⑭
procurar to try → ⑩
prohibir to forbid → ⑮
prometer to promise → ⑯
proponer to propose → ⑰

1. ¿Quiere Vd esperar?
   No puede venir

   Would you like to wait?
   She can't come

2. Nos ha visto llegar
   Se les oye cantar

   She saw us arriving
   You can hear them singing

3. No me hagas reír
   Déjeme pasar

   Don't make me laugh
   Let me past

4. Le aconsejamos dejarlo para
   mañana

   We advise you to leave it until
   tomorrow

5. Aún no he conseguido/logrado
   entenderlo

   I still haven't managed to
   understand it

6. No desea tener más hijos

   She doesn't want to have any
   more children

7. Esperamos ir de vacaciones
   este verano

   We are hoping to go on holiday
   this summer

8. Evite beber cuando conduzca

   Avoid drinking and driving

9. No pudo impedirle hablar

   He couldn't prevent him from
   speaking

10. Intentamos/procuramos pasar
    desapercibidos

    We tried not to be noticed

11. Necesitaba salir a la calle

    I/he/she needed to go out

12. Olvidó dejar su dirección

    He/she forgot to leave his/
    her address

13. ¿Piensan venir por Navidad?

    Are you thinking of coming for
    Christmas?

14. Preferiría elegirlo yo mismo

    I'd rather choose it myself

15. Prohibió fumar a los alumnos

    He forbade the pupils to smoke

16. Prometieron volver pronto

    They promised to come back soon

17. Propongo salir cuanto antes

    I propose to leave as soon as
    possible

49

The Infinitive: Set Expressions

The following are set in Spanish with the meaning shown:

> dejar caer to drop → ①
> hacer entrar to show in → ②
> hacer saber to let know, make known → ③
> hacer salir to let out → ④
> hacer venir to send for → ⑤
> ir(se) a buscar to go for, go and get → ⑥
> mandar hacer to order → ⑦
> mandar llamar to send for → ⑧
> oír decir que to hear it said that → ⑨
> oír hablar de to hear of/about → ⑩
> querer decir to mean → ⑪

The Perfect Infinitive

The perfect infinitive is formed using the auxiliary verb haber with the past participle of the verb → ⑫

The perfect infinitive is found:
- following certain prepositions, especially después de after → ⑬
- following certain verbal constructions → ⑭

Examples

1	Al verlo, dejó caer lo que llevaba en las manos	When he saw him he dropped what he was carrying
2	Haz entrar a nuestros invitados	Show our guests in
3	Quiero hacerles saber que no serán bien recibidos	I want to let them know that they won't be welcome
4	Hágale salir, por favor	Please let him out
5	Le he hecho venir a Vd porque ...	I sent for you because ...
6	Vete a buscar los guantes	Go and get your gloves
7	Me he mandado hacer un traje	I have ordered a suit
8	Mandaron llamar al médico	They sent for the doctor
9	He oído decir que está enfermo	I've heard it said that he's ill
10	No he oído hablar más de él	I haven't heard anything more (said) of him
11	¿Qué quiere decir eso?	What does that mean?
12	haber terminado haberse vestido	to have finished to have got dressed
13	Después de haber comprado el regalo, volvió a casa Después de haber madrugado tanto, el taxi se retrasó	After buying/having bought the present, he went back home After she got up so early, the taxi arrived late
14	perdonar a alguien por haber hecho dar las gracias a alguien por haber hecho pedir perdón por haber hecho	to forgive somebody for doing/having done to thank somebody for doing/having done to be sorry for doing/having done

The Gerund

Formation

First conjugation:
- replace the -ar of the infinitive by -ando → ❶

Second conjugation:
- replace the -er of the infinitive by -iendo → ❷

Third conjugation:
- replace the -ir of the infinitive by -iendo → ❸

For irregular gerunds, see irregular verbs, page 80 onwards.

Uses

After the verb estar, to form the continuous tenses → ❹

After the verbs seguir and continuar *to continue*, and ir when meaning to *happen gradually* → ❺

In time constructions, after llevar → ❻

When the action in the main clause needs to be complemented by another action → ❼

The position of object pronouns is the same as for the infinitive (see page 46).

The gerund is invariable and strictly verbal in sense.

The Present Participle

It is formed by replacing the -ar of the infinitive of 1st conjugation verbs by -ante, and the -er and -ir of the 2nd and 3rd conjugations by -iente → ❽

A very limited number of verbs have a present participle used either as an adjective or a noun → ❾/❿

1. cantar **to sing** → cantando **singing**

2. temer **to fear** → temiendo **fearing**

3. partir **to leave** → partiendo **leaving**

4. Estoy escribiendo una carta **I am writing a letter**
   Estaban esperándonos **They were waiting for us**

5. Sigue viniendo todos los días **He/she is still coming every day**
   Continuarán subiendo los precios **Prices will continue to go up**
   El ejército iba avanzando poco **The army was gradually**
    a poco **advancing**

6. Lleva dos años estudiando inglés **He/she has been studying**
    English for two years

7. Pasamos el día tomando el sol **We spent the day sunbathing**
    en la playa **on the beach**
   Iba cojeando **He/she/I was limping**
   Salieron corriendo **They ran out**

8. cantar **to sing** → cantante **singing/singer**
   pender **to hang** → pendiente **hanging**
   seguir **to follow** → siguiente **following**

9. agua corriente **running water**

10. un estudiante **a student**

Use of Tenses

The Present

Unlike English, Spanish often uses the same verb form for the simple present (e.g. I smoke, he reads, we live) and the continuous present (e.g. I am smoking, he is reading, we are living) → ①

Normally, however, the continuous present is used to translate the Spanish:
   estar haciendo to be doing → ②

Spanish uses the present tense where English uses the perfect in the following cases:
   • with certain prepositions of time – notably desde for/since – when an action begun in the past is continued in the present → ③
     ⓘ Note: The perfect can be used as in English when the verb is negative → ④
   • in the construction acabar de hacer to have just done → ⑤

Like English, Spanish often uses the present where a future action is implied → ⑥

The Future

The future is generally used as in English → ⑦, but note the following:

   Immediate future time is often expressed by means of the present tense of ir + a + infinitive → ⑧

   When 'will' or 'shall' mean 'wish to', 'are willing to', querer is used → ⑨

The Future Perfect

Used as in English shall/will have done → ⑩

It can also express conjecture, usually about things in the recent past → ⑪

1. Fumo I smoke *or* I am smoking
   Lee He reads *or* He is reading
   Vivimos We live *or* We are living

2. Está fumando

   He is smoking

3. Linda estudia español desde
   hace seis meses
   Estoy de pie desde las siete
   ¿Hace mucho que esperan?
   Ya hace dos semanas que
   estamos aquí

   Linda's been learning Spanish for
   six months (and still is)
   I've been up since seven
   Have you been waiting long?
   That's two weeks we've been
   here (now)

4. No se han visto desde hace
   meses

   They haven't seen each other for
   months

5. Isabel acaba de salir

   Isabel has just left

6. Mañana voy a Madrid

   I am going to Madrid tomorrow

7. Lo haré mañana

   I'll do it tomorrow

8. Te vas a caer si no tienes cuidado
   Va a perder el tren
   Va a llevar una media hora

   You'll fall if you're not careful
   He's going to miss the train
   It'll take about half an hour

9. ¿Me quieres esperar un
   momento, por favor?

   Will you wait for me a second,
   please?

10. Lo habré acabado para mañana

    I will have finished it for
    tomorrow

11. Ya habrán llegado a casa

    They must have arrived home by
    now

Use of Tenses *continued*

The Imperfect

The imperfect describes:
- an action or state in the past without definite limits in time → ①
- habitual action(s) in the past (often expressed in English by means of would or used to) → ②

Spanish uses the imperfect tense where English uses the pluperfect in the following cases:
- with certain prepositions of time – notably desde for/since – when an action begun in the remoter past was continued in the more recent past → ③
  - ⓘ Note: The pluperfect is used as in English when the verb is negative or the action has been completed → ④
- in the construction acabar de hacer to have just done → ⑤

Both the continuous and simple forms in English can be translated by the Spanish simple imperfect, but the continuous imperfect is used when the emphasis is on the fact that an action was going on at a precise moment in the past → ⑥

The Perfect

The perfect is generally used as in English → ⑦

The Preterite

The preterite generally corresponds to the English simple past in both written and spoken Spanish → ⑧

However, while English can use the simple past to describe habitual actions or settings, Spanish uses the imperfect (see above) → ⑨

The Past Anterior

This tense is only ever used in written, literary Spanish, to replace the pluperfect in time clauses where the verb in the main clause is in the preterite → ⑩

Examples

1. Todos mirábamos en silencio — We were all watching in silence
   Nuestras habitaciones daban a la playa — Our rooms overlooked the beach

2. En su juventud se levantaba de madrugada — In his youth he got up at dawn
   Hablábamos sin parar durante horas — We would talk non-stop for hours on end
   Mi hermano siempre me tomaba el pelo — My brother always used to tease me

3. Hacía dos años que vivíamos en Irlanda — We had been living in Ireland for two years
   Estaba enfermo desde 2012 — He had been ill since 2012
   Hacía mucho tiempo que salían juntos — They had been going out together for a long time

4. Hacía un año que no le había visto — I hadn't seen him for a year
   Hacía una hora que había llegado — She had arrived an hour before

5. Acababa de encontrármelos — I had just met them

6. Cuando llegué, todos estaban fumando — When I arrived, they were all smoking

7. Todavía no han salido — They haven't come out yet

8. Me desperté y salté de la cama — I woke up and jumped out of bed

9. Siempre iban en coche al trabajo — They always travelled to work by car

10. Apenas hubo acabado, se oyeron unos golpes en la puerta — She had scarcely finished when there was a knock at the door

The Subjunctive: when to use it

For how to form the subjunctive see page 6 onwards.

After verbs of:

- 'wishing'

  querer que ⎤
  desear que ⎦   to wish that, want → ①

- 'emotion' (e.g. regret, surprise, shame, pleasure, etc)

  sentir que   to be sorry that → ②
  sorprender que   to be surprised that → ③
  alegrarse de que   to be pleased that → ④

- 'asking' and 'advising'

  pedir que   to ask that → ⑤
  aconsejar que   to advise that → ⑥

In all the above constructions, when the subject of the verbs in the main and subordinate clause is the same, the infinitive is used, and the conjunction que omitted → ⑦

- 'ordering', 'forbidding', 'allowing'

  mandar que* ⎤
  ordenar que ⎦   to order that → ⑧

  permitir que* ⎤
  dejar que* ⎦   to allow that → ⑨

  prohibir que*   to forbid that → ⑩
  impedir que*   to prevent that → ⑪

  * With these verbs either the subjunctive or the infinitive is used when
  the object of the main verb is the subject of the subordinate verb → ⑫

Always after verbs expressing doubt or uncertainty, and verbs of opinion used negatively.

  dudar que   to doubt that → ⑬

  no creer que ⎤
  no pensar que ⎦   not to think that → ⑭

Examples

1. Queremos que esté contenta

   We want her to be happy
   (*literally*: We want that she is happy)

   ¿Desea Vd que lo haga yo?

   Do you want me to do it?

2. Sentí mucho que no vinieran

   I was very sorry that they didn't come

3. Nos sorprendió que no les vieran Vds

   We were surprised you didn't see them

4. Me alegro de que te gusten

   I'm pleased that you like them

5. Sólo les pedimos que tengan cuidado

   We're only asking you to take care

6. Le aconsejé que no llegara tarde

   I advised him not to be late

7. Quiero que lo termines pronto
   BUT:
   Quiero terminarlo pronto

   I want you to finish it soon

   I want to finish it soon

8. Ha mandado que vuelvan
   Ordenó que fueran castigados

   He has ordered them to come back
   He ordered them to be punished

9. No permitas que te tomen el pelo
   No me dejó que la llevara a casa

   Don't let them pull your leg
   She didn't allow me to take her home

10. Te prohíbo que digas eso

    I forbid you to say that

11. No les impido que vengan

    I am not preventing them from coming

12. Les ordenó que salieran
    or Les ordenó salir

    She ordered them to go out

13. Dudo que lo sepan hacer

    I doubt they can do it

14. No creo que sean tan listos

    I don't think they are as clever as that

59

The Subjunctive: when to use it *continued*

In impersonal constructions which express necessity, possibility, etc:

hace falta que es necesario que	it is necessary that → ①
es posible que	it is possible that → ②
más vale que	it is better that → ③
es una lástima que	it is a pity that → ④

ⓘ Note: In impersonal constructions which state a fact or express certainty the indicative is used when the impersonal verb is affirmative. When it is negative, the subjunctive is used → ⑤

After certain conjunctions:

para que a fin de que*	so that → ⑥
como si	as if → ⑦
sin que*	without → ⑧
a condición de que* con tal (de) que* siempre que	provided that, on condition that → ⑨
a menos que a no ser que	unless → ⑩
antes (de) que*	before → ⑪
no sea que	lest/in case → ⑫
mientras (que) siempre que	as long as → ⑬
(el) que	the fact that → ⑭

*When the subject of both verbs is the same, the infinitive is used, and the final que is omitted → ⑧

1. ¿Hace falta que vaya Jaime? — Does James have to go?

2. Es posible que tengan razón — It's possible that they are right

3. Más vale que se quede Vd en su casa — It's better that you stay at home

4. Es una lástima que haya perdido su perrito — It's a shame/pity that she has lost her puppy

5. Es verdad que va a venir — It's true that he's coming
   BUT:
   No es verdad que vayan a hacerlo — It's not true that they are going to do it

6. Átalas bien para que no se caigan — Tie them up tightly so that they won't fall

7. Hablaba como si no creyera en sus propias palabras — He talked as if he didn't believe in his own words

8. Salimos sin que nos vieran — We left without them seeing us
   BUT:
   Me fui sin esperarla — I went without waiting for her

9. Lo haré con tal de que me cuentes todo lo que pasó — I'll do it provided you tell me all that happened

10. Saldremos de paseo a menos que esté lloviendo — We'll go for a walk unless it's raining

11. Avísale antes de que sea demasiado tarde — Warn him before it's too late

12. Habla en voz baja, no sea que alguien nos oiga — Speak softly in case anyone hears us

13. Eso no pasará mientras yo sea el jefe aquí — That won't happen as long as I am the boss here

14. El que no me escribiera no me importaba demasiado — The fact that he didn't write didn't matter to me too much

The Subjunctive: when to use it *continued*

After the conjunctions:
> de modo que
> de forma que   so that (*indicating a purpose*) → ❶
> de manera que

> ⓘ Note: When these conjunctions introduce a result and not a
> purpose the subjunctive is not used → ❷

In relative clauses with an antecedent which is:
- negative → ❸
- indefinite → ❹
- non-specific → ❺

In main clauses, to express a wish or exhortation. The verb may be
preceded by expressions like ojalá or que → ❻

In the si clause of conditions where the English sentence contains a
conditional tense → ❼

In set expressions → ❽

In the following constructions which translate however:
- por + *adjective* + *subjunctive* → ❾
- por + *adverb* + *subjunctive* → ❿
- por + mucho + *subjunctive* → ⓫

Examples

1. Vuélvanse de manera que les vea bien

   Turn round so that I can see you properly

2. No quieren hacerlo, de manera que tendré que hacerlo yo

   They won't do it, so I'll have to do it myself

3. No he encontrado a nadie que la conociera

   I haven't met anyone who knows her

   No dijo nada que no supiéramos ya

   He/she didn't say anything we didn't already know

4. Necesito alguien que sepa conducir

   I need someone who can drive

   Busco algo que me distraiga

   I'm looking for something to take my mind off it

5. Busca una casa que tenga calefacción central

   He/she's looking for a house which has central heating
   (*subjunctive used since such a house may or may not exist*)

   El que lo haya visto tiene que decírmelo

   Anyone who has seen it must tell me
   (*subjunctive used since it is not known who has seen it*)

6. ¡Ojalá haga buen tiempo!

   Let's hope the weather will be good!

   ¡Que te diviertas!

   Have a good time!

7. Si fuéramos en coche llegaríamos a tiempo

   If we went by car we'd be there in time

8. Diga lo que diga ...

   Whatever he may say ...

   Sea lo que sea ...

   Be that as it may ...

   Pase lo que pase ...

   Come what may ...

   Sea como sea ...

   One way or another ...

9. Por cansado que esté, seguirá trabajando

   No matter how/however tired he may be, he'll go on working

10. Por lejos que viva, iremos a buscarle

    No matter how/however far away he lives, we'll go and look for him

11. Por mucho que lo intente, nunca lo conseguirá

    No matter how/however hard he tries, he'll never succeed

The Subjunctive: when to use it *continued*

Clauses taking either a subjunctive or an indicative

In certain constructions, a subjunctive is needed when the action refers to future events or hypothetical situations, whereas an indicative is used when stating a fact or experience → ①

The commonest of these are:

The conjunctions:

cuando	when → ①
en cuanto	as soon as → ②
tan pronto como	
después (de) que*	after → ③
hasta que	until → ④
mientras	while → ⑤
siempre que	whenever → ⑥
aunque	even though → ⑦

All conjunctions and pronouns ending in -quiera (-*ever*) → ⑧

* ⓘ Note: If the subject of both verbs is the same, the subjunctive introduced by después (de) que may be replaced by después de + *infinitive* → ⑨

Sequence of tenses in Subordinate Clauses

If the verb in the main clause is in the present, future or imperative, the verb in the dependent clause will be in the present or perfect subjunctive → ⑩

If the verb in the main clause is in the conditional or any past tense, the verb in the dependent clause will be in the imperfect or pluperfect subjunctive → ⑪

1 Le aconsejé que oyera música cuando estuviera nervioso

I advised him to listen to music when he felt nervous

Me gusta nadar cuando hace calor

I like to swim when it is warm

2 Te devolveré el libro tan pronto como lo haya leído

I'll give you back the book as soon as I have read it

3 Te lo diré después de que te hayas sentado

I'll tell you after you've sat down

4 Quédate aquí hasta que volvamos

Stay here until we come back

5 No hablen en voz alta mientras estén ellos aquí

Don't speak loudly while they are here

6 Vuelvan por aquí siempre que quieran

Come back whenever you wish to

7 No le creeré aunque diga la verdad

I won't believe him even if he tells the truth

8 La encontraré dondequiera que esté

I will find her wherever she might be

9 Después de cenar nos fuimos al cine

After dinner we went to the cinema

Quiero que lo hagas (*pres + pres subj*)

I want you to do it

Temo que no haya venido (*pres + perf subj*)

I fear he hasn't come (might not have come)

Iremos por aquí para que no nos vean (*future + pres subj*)

We'll go this way so that they won't see us

Me gustaría que llegaras temprano (*cond + imperf subj*)

I'd like you to arrive early

Les pedí que me esperaran (*preterite + imperf subj*)

I asked them to wait for me

Sentiría mucho que hubiese muerto (*cond + pluperf subj*)

I would be very sorry if he were dead

Verbs governing a, de, con, en, por and para

The following lists (pages 66 to 73) contain common verbal constructions using the prepositions a, de, con, en, por and para.

Note the following abbreviations:

infin.	*infinitive*
perf. infin.	*perfect infinitive**
algn	alguien
sb	somebody
sth	something

* For information see page 50.

aburrirse de + *infin.*	to get bored with doing → ❶
acabar con algo/algn	to put an end to sth/finish with sb → ❷
acabar de* + *infin.*	to have just done → ❸
acabar por + *infin.*	to end up doing → ❹
acercarse a algo/algn	to approach sth/sb
acordarse de algo/algn/de + *infin.*	to remember sth/sb/doing → ❺
acostumbrarse a algo/algn/a + *infin.*	to get used to sth/sb/to doing → ❻
acusar a algn de algo/de + *perf. infin*	to accuse sb of sth/of doing, having done. → ❼
advertir a algn de algo	to notify, warn sb about sth → ❽
aficionarse a algo/a + *infin.*	to grow fond of sth/of doing → ❾
alegrarse de algo/de + *perf. infin.*	to be glad about sth/of doing, having done → ❿
alejarse de algn/algo	to move away from sb/sth
amenazar a algn con algo/con + *infin.*	to threaten sb with sth/to do → ⓫
animar a algn a + *infin.*	to encourage sb to do
apresurarse a + *infin.*	to hurry to do → ⓬

* See also Use of Tenses, pages 54 and 56

1. Me aburría de no poder salir de casa

   I used to get bored with not being able to leave the house

2. Quiso acabar con su vida

   He wanted to put an end to his life

3. Acababan de llegar cuando ...

   They had just arrived when ...

4. El acusado acabó por confesarlo todo

   The accused ended up by confessing everything

5. Nos acordamos muy bien de aquellas vacaciones

   We remember that holiday very well

6. Me he acostumbrado a levantarme temprano

   I've got used to getting up early

7. Le acusó de haber mentido

   She accused him of lying

8. Advertí a mi amigo del peligro que corría

   I warned my friend about the danger he was in

9. Nos hemos aficionado a la música clásica

   We've grown fond of classical music

10. Me alegro de haberle conocido

    I'm glad I met him

11. Amenazó con denunciarles

    He threatened to report them

12. Se apresuraron a coger sitio

    They hurried to find a seat

Verbs governing a, de, con, en, por and para *continued*

aprender a + *infin*.	to learn to do → ①
aprovecharse de algo/algn	to take advantage of sth/sb
aproximarse a algn/algo	to approach sb/sth
asistir a algo	to attend sth, be at sth
asomarse a/por	to lean out of → ②
asombrarse de + *infin*.	to be surprised at doing → ③
atreverse a + *infin*.	to dare to do
avergonzarse de algo/algn/de + *perf. infin*.	to be ashamed of sth/sb/of doing, having done → ④
ayudar a algn a + *infin*.	to help sb to do → ⑤
bajarse de (+ *place/vehicle*)	to get off/out of → ⑥
burlarse de algn	to make fun of sb
cansarse de algo/algn/de + *infin*.	to tire of sth/sb/of doing
carecer de algo	to lack sth → ⑦
cargar de algo	to load with sth → ⑧
casarse con algn	to get married to sb → ⑨
cesar de + *infin*.	to stop doing
chocar con algo	to crash/bump into sth → ⑩
comenzar a + *infin*.	to begin to do
comparar con algn/algo	to compare with sb/sth
consentir en + *infin*.	to agree to do
consistir en + *infin*.	to consist of doing → ⑪
constar de algo	to consist of sth → ⑫
contar con algn/algo	to rely on sb/sth → ⑬
convenir en + *infin*.	to agree to do → ⑭
darse cuenta de algo	to realize sth
dejar de + *infin*.	to stop doing → ⑮
depender de algo/algn	to depend on sth/sb → ⑯
despedirse de algn	to say goodbye to sb
dirigirse a algn/+ place	to address sb/head for
disponerse a + *infin*.	to get ready to do
empezar a + *infin*.	to begin to do
empezar por + *infin*.	to begin by doing → ⑰

①	Me gustaría aprender a nadar	I'd like to learn to swim
②	No te asomes a la ventana	Don't lean out of the window
③	Nos asombramos mucho de verles ahí	We were very surprised at seeing them there
④	No me avergüenzo de haberlo hecho	I'm not ashamed of having done it
⑤	Ayúdeme a llevar estas maletas	Help me to carry these cases
⑥	Se bajó del coche	He got out of the car
⑦	La casa carecía de jardín	The house lacked (did not have) a garden
⑧	El carro iba cargado de paja	The cart was loaded with straw
⑨	Se casó con Andrés	She married Andrés
⑩	Enciende la luz, o chocarás con la puerta	Turn the light on, or you'll bump into the door
⑪	Mi plan consistía en vigilarles de cerca	My plan consisted of keeping a close eye on them
⑫	El examen consta de tres partes	The exam consists of three parts
⑬	Cuento contigo para que me ayudes a hacerlo	I rely on you to help me do it
⑭	Convinieron en reunirse al día siguiente	They agreed to meet the following day
⑮	¿Quieres dejar de hablar?	Will you stop talking?
⑯	No depende de mí	It doesn't depend on me
⑰	Empieza por enterarte de lo que se trata	Begin by finding out what it is about

Verbs governing a, de, con, en, por **and** para *continued*

encontrarse con algn	to meet sb (by chance) → ❶
enfadarse con algn	to get annoyed with sb
enseñar a algn a + *infin.*	to teach sb to → ❷
enterarse de algo	to find out about sth → ❸
entrar en (+ *place*)	to enter, go into
esperar a + *infin.*	to wait until → ❹
estar de acuerdo con algn/algo	to agree with sb/sth
fiarse de algn/algo	to trust sb/sth
fijarse en algo/algn	to notice sth/sb → ❺
hablar con algn	to talk to sb → ❻
hacer caso a algn	to pay attention to sb
hartarse de algo/algn/de + *infin.*	to get fed up with sth/sb/with doing → ❼
interesarse por algo/algn	to be interested in sth/sb → ❽
invitar a algn a + *infin.*	to invite sb to do
jugar a (+ sports, games)	to play
luchar por algo/por + *infin.*	to fight, strive for/to do → ❾
llegar a + *infin./*(place)	to manage to do/to reach → ❿
llenar de algo	to fill with sth
negarse a + *infin.*	to refuse to do → ⓫
obligar a algn a + *infin.*	to make sb do → ⓬
ocuparse de algn/algo	to take care of sb/attend to sth
oler a algo	to smell of sth → ⓭
olvidarse de algo/algn/de + *infin.*	to forget sth/sb/to do → ⓮
oponerse a algo/a + *infin.*	to be opposed to sth/to doing
parecerse a algn/algo	to resemble sb/sth
pensar en algo/algn/en + *infin.*	to think about sth/sb/about doing → ⓯
preguntar por algn	to ask for/about sb
preocuparse de *or* por algo/algn	to worry about sth/sb → ⓰

Examples

1. Me encontré con ella al entrar en el banco

   I met her as I was entering the bank

2. Le estoy enseñando a nadar

   I am teaching him to swim

3. ¿Te has enterado del sitio adonde hay que ir?

   Have you found out where we have to go?

4. Espera a saber lo que quiere antes de comprar el regalo

   Wait until you know what he wants before buying the present

5. Me fijé en él cuando subía a su coche

   I noticed him when he was getting into his car

6. ¿Puedo hablar con Vd un momento?

   May I talk to you for a moment?

7. Me he hartado de escribirle

   I've got fed up with writing to him

8. Me interesaba mucho por la arqueología

   I was very interested in archaeology

9. Hay que luchar por mantener la paz

   One must strive to preserve peace

10. Lo intenté sin llegar a conseguirlo

    I tried without managing to do it

11. Se negó a hacerlo

    He refused to do it

12. Le obligó a sentarse

    He made him sit down

13. Este perfume huele a jazmín

    This perfume smells of jasmine

14. Siempre me olvido de cerrar la puerta

    I always forget to shut the door

15. No quiero pensar en eso

    I don't want to think about that

16. Se preocupa mucho de/por su apariencia

    He worries a lot about his appearance

Verbs governing a, de, con, en, por **and** para *continued*

prepararse a + *infin.*	to prepare to do
probar a + *infin.*	to try to do
quedar en + *infin.*	to agree to do → ❶
quedar por + *infin.*	to remain to be done → ❷
quejarse de algo	to complain of sth
referirse a algo	to refer to sth
reírse de algo/algn	to laugh at sth/sb
rodear de	to surround with → ❸
romper a + *infin.*	to (suddenly) start to do → ❹
salir de (+ *place*)	to leave
sentarse a (+ *table etc*)	to sit down at
subir(se) a (+ *vehicle/place*)	to get on, into/to climb → ❺
servir de algo a algn	to be useful to/serve sb as sth → ❻
servir para algo/para + *infin.*	to be good as sth/for doing → ❼
servirse de algo	to use sth → ❽
soñar con algn/algo/con + *infin.*	to dream about/of sb/sth/of doing
sorprenderse de algo	to be surprised at sth
tardar en + *infin.*	to take time to do → ❾
tener ganas de algo/de + *infin.*	to want sth/to do → ❿
tener miedo de algo	to be afraid of sth → ⓫
tener miedo a algn	to be afraid of sb → ⓬
terminar por + *infin.*	to end by doing
tirar de algo/algn	to pull sth/sb
trabajar de (+ *occupation*)	to work as → ⓭
trabajar en (+ *place of work*)	to work at/in → ⓮
traducir a (+ *language*)	to translate into
tratar de + *infin.*	to try to do → ⓯
tratarse de algo/algn/de + *infin.*	to be a question of sth/about sb/about doing → ⓰
vacilar en + *infin.*	to hesitate to do → ⓱
volver a + *infin.*	to do again → ⓲

1. Habíamos quedado en encontrarnos a las 8

   We had agreed to meet at 8

2. Queda por averiguar dónde se ocultan

   It remains to be discovered where they are hiding

3. Habían rodeado el jardín de un seto de cipreses

   They had surrounded the garden with a hedge of cypress trees

4. Al apagarse la luz, el niño rompió a llorar

   When the lights went out, the little boy suddenly started to cry

5. ¡De prisa, sube al coche!

   Get into the car, quick!

6. Esto me servirá de bastón

   This will serve me as a walking stick

7. No sirvo para (ser) jardinero

   I'm no good as a gardener

8. Se sirvió de un destornillador para abrirlo

   She used a screwdriver to open it

9. Tardaron mucho en salir

   They took a long time to come out

10. Tengo ganas de volver a España

    I want to go back to Spain

11. Mi hija tiene miedo de la oscuridad

    My daughter is afraid of the dark

12. Nunca tuvieron miedo a su padre

    They were never afraid of their father

13. Pedro trabaja de camarero en Londres

    Pedro works as a waiter in London

14. Trabajaba en una oficina

    I used to work in an office

15. No trates de engañarme

    Don't try to fool me

16. Se trata de nuestro nuevo vecino

    It's about our new neighbour

17. Nunca vacilaban en pedir dinero

    They never hesitated to borrow money

18. No vuelvas a hacerlo nunca más

    Don't ever do it again

Ser **and** Estar

Spanish has two verbs – ser and estar – for 'to be'.

They are not interchangeable and each one is used in defined contexts.

ser is used:
- with an adjective, to express a permanent or inherent quality → ①
- to express occupation or nationality → ②
- to express possession → ③
- to express origin or the material from which something is made → ④
- with a noun, pronoun or infinitive following the verb → ⑤
- to express the time and date → ⑥
- to form the passive, with the past participle (see page 32).

  ⓘ Note: This use emphasizes the action of the verb. If, however, the resultant state or condition needs to be emphasized, estar is used. The past participle then functions as an adjective (see page 208) and has to agree in gender and in number with the noun → ⑦

estar is used:
- always, to indicate place or location → ⑧
- with an adjective or adjectival phrase, to express a quality or state seen by the speaker as subject to change or different from expected → ⑨
- when speaking of a person's state of health → ⑩
- to form the continuous tenses, used with the gerund (see page 52) → ⑪
- with de + *noun*, to indicate a temporary occupation → ⑫

1. Mi hermano es alto — My brother is tall
   María es inteligente — María is intelligent

2. Javier es aviador — Javier is an airman
   Sus padres son italianos — His parents are Italian

3. La casa es de Miguel — The house belongs to Miguel

4. Mi hermana es de Granada — My sister is from Granada
   Las paredes son de ladrillo — The walls are made of brick

5. Andrés es un niño travieso — Andrés is a naughty boy
   Soy yo, Enrique — It's me, Enrique
   Todo es proponérselo — It's all a question of putting your mind to it

6. Son las tres y media — It's half past three
   Mañana es sábado — Tomorrow is Saturday

7. Las puertas eran cerradas sigilosamente — The doors were being silently closed
   Las puertas estaban cerradas — The doors were closed (resultant action)

8. La comida está en la mesa — The meal is on the table

9. Su amigo está enfermo — Her friend is ill
   El lavabo está ocupado — The toilet is engaged
   Hoy estoy de mal humor — I'm in a bad mood today
   Las tiendas están cerradas — The shops are closed

10. ¿Cómo están Vds? — How are you?
    Estamos todos bien — We are all well

11. Estamos aprendiendo mucho — We are learning a great deal

12. Mi primo está de médico en un pueblo — My cousin works as a doctor in a village

Ser and Estar *continued*

With certain adjectives, both ser and estar can be used, although they are not interchangeable when used in this way:
- ser will express a permanent or inherent quality → ❶
- estar will express a temporary state or quality → ❷

Both ser and estar may also be used in set expressions.

The commonest of these are:

With ser

Sea como sea	Be that as it may
Es igual/Es lo mismo	It's all the same
llegar a ser	to become
¿Cómo fue eso?	How did that happen?
¿Qué ha sido de él?	What has become of him?
ser para (*with the idea of purpose*)	to be for → ❸

With estar

estar de pie/de rodillas	to be standing/kneeling
estar de viaje	to be travelling
estar de vacaciones	to be on holiday
estar de vuelta	to be back
estar de moda	to be in fashion
Está bien	It's all right
estar para	to be about to do sth/to be in a mood for → ❹
estar por	to be inclined to/to be (all) for → ❺
estar a punto de	to be just about to do sth → ❻

1. Su hermana es muy joven/vieja — His sister is very young/old
   Son muy ricos/pobres — They are very rich/poor
   Su amigo era un enfermo — His friend was an invalid
   Es un borracho — He is a drunkard
   Mi hijo es bueno/malo — My son is good/naughty
   Viajar es cansado — Travelling is tiring

2. Está muy joven/vieja con ese vestido — She looks very young/old in that dress
   Ahora están muy ricos/pobres — They have become very rich/poor lately
   Estaba enfermo — He was ill
   Está borracho — He is drunk
   Está bueno/malo — He is well/ill
   Hoy estoy cansada — I am tired today

3. Este paquete es para Vd — This parcel is for you
   Esta caja es para guardar semillas — This box is for keeping seeds in

4. Están para llegar — They're about to arrive

5. Estoy por irme a vivir a España — I'm inclined to go and live in Spain

6. Las rosas están a punto de salir — The roses are about to come out

Verbal Idioms

Special Intransitive Verbs

With the following verbs the Spanish construction is the opposite of the English. The subject in English becomes the indirect object of the Spanish verb, while the object in English becomes the subject of the Spanish verb. Compare the following:

> I like that house (subject: I, object: that house)
> Esa casa me gusta (subject: esa casa, indirect object: me)

The commonest of these verbs are:

gustar	to like → ①
gustar más	to prefer → ②
encantar	(colloquial) to love → ③
faltar	to need/to be short of/to have missing → ④
quedar	to be/have left → ⑤
doler	to have a pain in/to hurt, ache → ⑥
interesar	to be interested in → ⑦
importar	to mind → ⑧

①	Me gusta este vestido	I like this dress (This dress pleases me)
②	Me gustan más éstas	I prefer these
③	Nos encanta hacer deporte	We love sport
④	Me faltaban 100 euros	I was short of 100 euros
	Sólo le falta el toque final	It just needs the finishing touch
	Le faltaban tres dientes	He/she had three teeth missing
⑤	Sólo nos quedan dos kilómetros	We only have two kilometres (left) to go
⑥	Me duele la cabeza	I have a headache
⑦	Nos interesa mucho la política	We are very interested in politics
⑧	No me importa la lluvia	I don't mind the rain

Irregular Verbs

The verbs listed opposite and conjugated on pages 82 to 160 provide the main patterns for irregular verbs. The verbs are grouped opposite according to their infinitive ending and are shown in the following tables in alphabetical order.

In the tables, the most important irregular verbs are given in their most common simple tenses, together with the imperative and the gerund.

The past participle is also shown for each verb, to enable you to form all the compound tenses, as on pages 18 to 23.

The pronouns ella and Vd take the same verb endings as él, while ellas and Vds take the same endings as ellos.

All the verbs included in the tables differ from the three conjugations set out on pages 8 to 13. Many – e.g. contar – serve as models for groups of verbs, while others – e.g. ir – are unique. On pages 161–190 you will find every verb in this dictionary listed alphabetically and cross-referred either to the relevant basic conjugation or to the appropriate model in the verb tables.

Imperfect Subjunctive of Irregular Verbs

For verbs with an irregular root form in the preterite tense – e.g. andar → anduvieron – the imperfect subjunctive is formed by using the root form of the 3rd person plural of the preterite tense, and adding the imperfect subjunctive endings -iera/-iese etc where the verb has an 'i' in the preterite ending – e.g. anduvieron → anduviera/iese. Where the verb has no 'i' in the preterite ending, add -era/-ese etc – e.g. produjeron → produjera/ese.

'-ar':			
	actuar		saber
	almorzar		satisfacer
	andar		ser
	aullar		tener
	avergonzar		torcer
	averiguar		traer
	contar		valer
	cruzar		vencer
	dar		ver
	empezar		volver
	enviar		
	errar	'-ir':	abolir
	estar		abrir
	jugar		adquirir
	negar		bendecir
	pagar		conducir
	pensar		construir
	rehusar		decir
	rogar		dirigir
	sacar		distinguir
	volcar		dormir
			elegir
'-er':	caber		erguir
	caer		escribir
	cocer		freír
	coger		gruñir
	crecer		ir
	entender		lucir
	haber		morir
	hacer		oír
	hay		pedir
	leer		prohibir
	llover		reír
	mover		reñir
	nacer		reunir
	oler		salir
	poder		seguir
	poner		sentir
	querer		venir
	resolver		zurcir
	romper		

abolir (to abolish)

	PRESENT*		**IMPERFECT**
nosotros	abol**imos**	yo	abol**ía**
vosotros	abol**ís**	tú	abol**ías**
		él	abol**ía**

* Present tense only used in persons shown

		nosotros	abol**íamos**
		vosotros	abol**íais**
		ellos	abol**ían**

	FUTURE		**CONDITIONAL**
yo	abolir**é**	yo	abolir**ía**
tú	abolir**ás**	tú	abolir**ías**
él	abolir**á**	él	abolir**ía**
nosotros	abolir**emos**	nosotros	abolir**íamos**
vosotros	abolir**éis**	vosotros	abolir**íais**
ellos	abolir**án**	ellos	abolir**ían**

PRESENT SUBJUNCTIVE		**PRETERITE**
not used	yo	abol**í**
	tú	abol**iste**
	él	abol**ió**
	nosotros	abol**imos**
	vosotros	abol**isteis**
	ellos	abol**ieron**

PAST PARTICIPLE	**IMPERATIVE**
abol**ido**	abol**id**

GERUND
abol**iendo**

abrir (to open)

	PRESENT		**IMPERFECT**
yo	abro	yo	abría
tú	abres	tú	abrías
él	abre	él	abría
nosotros	abrimos	nosotros	abríamos
vosotros	abrís	vosotros	abríais
ellos	abren	ellos	abrían

	FUTURE		**CONDITIONAL**
yo	abriré	yo	abriría
tú	abrirás	tú	abrirías
él	abrirá	él	abriría
nosotros	abriremos	nosotros	abriríamos
vosotros	abriréis	vosotros	abriríais
ellos	abrirán	ellos	abrirían

	PRESENT SUBJUNCTIVE		**PRETERITE**
yo	abra	yo	abrí
tú	abras	tú	abriste
él	abra	él	abrió
nosotros	abramos	nosotros	abrimos
vosotros	abráis	vosotros	abristeis
ellos	abran	ellos	abrieron

PAST PARTICIPLE	**IMPERATIVE**
abierto	abre
	abrid

GERUND
abriendo

actuar (to act)

	PRESENT		IMPERFECT
yo	actúo	yo	actuaba
tú	actúas	tú	actuabas
él	actúa	él	actuaba
nosotros	actuamos	nosotros	actuábamos
vosotros	actuáis	vosotros	actuabais
ellos	actúan	ellos	actuaban

	FUTURE		CONDITIONAL
yo	actuaré	yo	actuaría
tú	actuarás	tú	actuarías
él	actuará	él	actuaría
nosotros	actuaremos	nosotros	actuaríamos
vosotros	actuaréis	vosotros	actuaríais
ellos	actuarán	ellos	actuarían

	PRESENT SUBJUNCTIVE		PRETERITE
yo	actúe	yo	actué
tú	actúes	tú	actuaste
él	actúe	él	actuó
nosotros	actuemos	nosotros	actuamos
vosotros	actuéis	vosotros	actuasteis
ellos	actúen	ellos	actuaron

PAST PARTICIPLE	IMPERATIVE
actuado	actúa
	actuad

GERUND

actuando

adquirir (to acquire)

	PRESENT		IMPERFECT
yo	**adquiero**	yo	adquir**ía**
tú	**adquieres**	tú	adquir**ías**
él	**adquiere**	él	adquir**ía**
nosotros	adquir**imos**	nosotros	adquir**íamos**
vosotros	adquir**ís**	vosotros	adquir**íais**
ellos	**adquieren**	ellos	adquir**ían**

	FUTURE		CONDITIONAL
yo	adquirir**é**	yo	adquirir**ía**
tú	adquirir**ás**	tú	adquirir**ías**
él	adquirir**á**	él	adquirir**ía**
nosotros	adquirir**emos**	nosotros	adquirir**íamos**
vosotros	adquirir**éis**	vosotros	adquirir**íais**
ellos	adquirir**án**	ellos	adquirir**ían**

	PRESENT SUBJUNCTIVE		PRETERITE
yo	**adquiera**	yo	adquir**í**
tú	**adquieras**	tú	adquir**iste**
él	**adquiera**	él	adquir**ió**
nosotros	adquir**amos**	nosotros	adquir**imos**
vosotros	adquir**áis**	vosotros	adquir**isteis**
ellos	**adquieran**	ellos	adquir**ieron**

PAST PARTICIPLE	IMPERATIVE
adquir**ido**	**adquiere**
	adquir**id**

GERUND

adquir**iendo**

almorzar (to have lunch)

	PRESENT		IMPERFECT
yo	almuerzo	yo	almorzaba
tú	almuerzas	tú	almorzabas
él	almuerza	él	almorzaba
nosotros	almorzamos	nosotros	almorzábamos
vosotros	almorzáis	vosotros	almorzabais
ellos	almuerzan	ellos	almorzaban

	FUTURE		CONDITIONAL
yo	almorzaré	yo	almorzaría
tú	almorzarás	tú	almorzarías
él	almorzará	él	almorzaría
nosotros	almorzaremos	nosotros	almorzaríamos
vosotros	almorzaréis	vosotros	almorzaríais
ellos	almorzarán	ellos	almorzarían

	PRESENT SUBJUNCTIVE		PRETERITE
yo	almuerce	yo	almorcé
tú	almuerces	tú	almorzaste
él	almuerce	él	almorzó
nosotros	almorcemos	nosotros	almorzamos
vosotros	almorcéis	vosotros	almorzasteis
ellos	almuercen	ellos	almorzaron

PAST PARTICIPLE	IMPERATIVE
almorzado	almuerza
	almorzad

GERUND

almorzando

andar (to walk)

	PRESENT		IMPERFECT
yo	ando	yo	andaba
tú	andas	tú	andabas
él	anda	él	andaba
nosotros	andamos	nosotros	andábamos
vosotros	andáis	vosotros	andabais
ellos	andan	ellos	andaban

	FUTURE		CONDITIONAL
yo	andaré	yo	andaría
tú	andarás	tú	andarías
él	andará	él	andaría
nosotros	andaremos	nosotros	andaríamos
vosotros	andaréis	vosotros	andaríais
ellos	andarán	ellos	andarían

	PRESENT SUBJUNCTIVE		PRETERITE
yo	ande	yo	anduve
tú	andes	tú	anduviste
él	ande	él	anduvo
nosotros	andemos	nosotros	anduvimos
vosotros	andéis	vosotros	anduvisteis
ellos	anden	ellos	anduvieron

PAST PARTICIPLE	IMPERATIVE
andado	anda
	andad

GERUND
andando

aullar (to howl)

	PRESENT		IMPERFECT
yo	aúllo	yo	aullaba
tú	aúllas	tú	aullabas
él	aúlla	él	aullaba
nosotros	aullamos	nosotros	aullábamos
vosotros	aulláis	vosotros	aullabais
ellos	aúllan	ellos	aullaban

	FUTURE		CONDITIONAL
yo	aullaré	yo	aullaría
tú	aullarás	tú	aullarías
él	aullará	él	aullaría
nosotros	aullaremos	nosotros	aullaríamos
vosotros	aullaréis	vosotros	aullaríais
ellos	aullarán	ellos	aullarían

	PRESENT SUBJUNCTIVE		PRETERITE
yo	aúlle	yo	aullé
tú	aúlles	tú	aullaste
él	aúlle	él	aulló
nosotros	aullemos	nosotros	aullamos
vosotros	aulléis	vosotros	aullasteis
ellos	aúllen	ellos	aullaron

PAST PARTICIPLE	IMPERATIVE
aullado	aúlla
	aullad

GERUND

aullando

avergonzar (to shame)

	PRESENT		IMPERFECT
yo	avergüenzo	yo	avergonzaba
tú	avergüenzas	tú	avergonzabas
él	avergüenza	él	avergonzaba
nosotros	avergonzamos	nosotros	avergonzábamos
vosotros	avergonzáis	vosotros	avergonzabais
ellos	avergüenzan	ellos	avergonzaban

	FUTURE		CONDITIONAL
yo	avergonzaré	yo	avergonzaría
tú	avergonzarás	tú	avergonzarías
él	avergonzará	él	avergonzaría
nosotros	avergonzaremos	nosotros	avergonzaríamos
vosotros	avergonzaréis	vosotros	avergonzaríais
ellos	avergonzarán	ellos	avergonzarían

	PRESENT SUBJUNCTIVE		PRETERITE
yo	avergüence	yo	avergoncé
tú	avergüences	tú	avergonzaste
él	avergüence	él	avergonzó
nosotros	avergoncemos	nosotros	avergonzamos
vosotros	avergoncéis	vosotros	avergonzasteis
ellos	avergüencen	ellos	avergonzaron

PAST PARTICIPLE	IMPERATIVE
avergonzado	avergüenza
	avergonzad

GERUND

avergonzando

averiguar (to find out)

	PRESENT		IMPERFECT
yo	averiguo	yo	averiguaba
tú	averiguas	tú	averiguabas
él	averigua	él	averiguaba
nosotros	averiguamos	nosotros	averiguábamos
vosotros	averiguáis	vosotros	averiguabais
ellos	averiguan	ellos	averiguaban

	FUTURE		CONDITIONAL
yo	averiguaré	yo	averiguaría
tú	averiguarás	tú	averiguarías
él	averiguará	él	averiguaría
nosotros	averiguaremos	nosotros	averiguaríamos
vosotros	averiguaréis	vosotros	averiguaríais
ellos	averiguarán	ellos	averiguarían

	PRESENT SUBJUNCTIVE		PRETERITE
yo	averigüe	yo	averigüé
tú	averigües	tú	averiguaste
él	averigüe	él	averiguó
nosotros	averigüemos	nosotros	averiguamos
vosotros	averigüéis	vosotros	averiguasteis
ellos	averigüen	ellos	averiguaron

PAST PARTICIPLE	IMPERATIVE
averiguado	averigua
	averiguad

GERUND
averiguando

bendecir (to bless)

	PRESENT		IMPERFECT
yo	bendigo	yo	bendecía
tú	bendices	tú	bendecías
él	bendice	él	bendecía
nosotros	bendecimos	nosotros	bendecíamos
vosotros	bendecís	vosotros	bendecíais
ellos	bendicen	ellos	bendecían

	FUTURE		CONDITIONAL
yo	bendeciré	yo	bendeciría
tú	bendecirás	tú	bendecirías
él	bendecirá	él	bendeciría
nosotros	bendeciremos	nosotros	bendeciríamos
vosotros	bendeciréis	vosotros	bendeciríais
ellos	bendecirán	ellos	bendecirían

	PRESENT SUBJUNCTIVE		PRETERITE
yo	bendiga	yo	bendije
tú	bendigas	tú	bendijiste
él	bendiga	él	bendijo
nosotros	bendigamos	nosotros	bendijimos
vosotros	bendigáis	vosotros	bendijisteis
ellos	bendigan	ellos	bendijeron

PAST PARTICIPLE	IMPERATIVE
bendecido	bendice
	bendecid

GERUND
bendiciendo

caber (to fit)

	PRESENT		IMPERFECT
yo	quepo	yo	cabía
tú	cabes	tú	cabías
él	cabe	él	cabía
nosotros	cabemos	nosotros	cabíamos
vosotros	cabéis	vosotros	cabíais
ellos	caben	ellos	cabían

	FUTURE		CONDITIONAL
yo	cabré	yo	cabría
tú	cabrás	tú	cabrías
él	cabrá	él	cabría
nosotros	cabremos	nosotros	cabríamos
vosotros	cabréis	vosotros	cabríais
ellos	cabrán	ellos	cabrían

	PRESENT SUBJUNCTIVE		PRETERITE
yo	quepa	yo	cupe
tú	quepas	tú	cupiste
él	quepa	él	cupo
nosotros	quepamos	nosotros	cupimos
vosotros	quepáis	vosotros	cupisteis
ellos	quepan	ellos	cupieron

PAST PARTICIPLE	IMPERATIVE
cabido	cabe
	cabed

GERUND
cabiendo

caer (to fall)

	PRESENT			IMPERFECT
yo	caigo		yo	caía
tú	caes		tú	caías
él	cae		él	caía
nosotros	caemos		nosotros	caíamos
vosotros	caéis		vosotros	caíais
ellos	caen		ellos	caían

	FUTURE			CONDITIONAL
yo	caeré		yo	caería
tú	caerás		tú	caerías
él	caerá		él	caería
nosotros	caeremos		nosotros	caeríamos
vosotros	caeréis		vosotros	caeríais
ellos	caerán		ellos	caerían

	PRESENT SUBJUNCTIVE			PRETERITE
yo	caiga		yo	caí
tú	caigas		tú	caíste
él	caiga		él	cayó
nosotros	caigamos		nosotros	caímos
vosotros	caigáis		vosotros	caísteis
ellos	caigan		ellos	cayeron

PAST PARTICIPLE	IMPERATIVE
caído	cae
	caed

GERUND

cayendo

cocer (to boil)

	PRESENT		IMPERFECT
yo	cuezo	yo	cocía
tú	cueces	tú	cocías
él	cuece	él	cocía
nosotros	cocemos	nosotros	cocíamos
vosotros	cocéis	vosotros	cocíais
ellos	cuecen	ellos	cocían

	FUTURE		CONDITIONAL
yo	coceré	yo	cocería
tú	cocerás	tú	cocerías
él	cocerá	él	cocería
nosotros	coceremos	nosotros	coceríamos
vosotros	coceréis	vosotros	coceríais
ellos	cocerán	ellos	cocerían

	PRESENT SUBJUNCTIVE		PRETERITE
yo	cueza	yo	cocí
tú	cuezas	tú	cociste
él	cueza	él	coció
nosotros	cozamos	nosotros	cocimos
vosotros	cozáis	vosotros	cocisteis
ellos	cuezan	ellos	cocieron

PAST PARTICIPLE	IMPERATIVE
cocido	cuece
	coced

GERUND
cociendo

coger (to take)

	PRESENT		IMPERFECT
yo	cojo	yo	cogía
tú	coges	tú	cogías
él	coge	él	cogía
nosotros	cogemos	nosotros	cogíamos
vosotros	cogéis	vosotros	cogíais
ellos	cogen	ellos	cogían

	FUTURE		CONDITIONAL
yo	cogeré	yo	cogería
tú	cogerás	tú	cogerías
él	cogerá	él	cogería
nosotros	cogeremos	nosotros	cogeríamos
vosotros	cogeréis	vosotros	cogeríais
ellos	cogerán	ellos	cogerían

	PRESENT SUBJUNCTIVE		PRETERITE
yo	coja	yo	cogí
tú	cojas	tú	cogiste
él	coja	él	cogió
nosotros	cojamos	nosotros	cogimos
vosotros	cojáis	vosotros	cogisteis
ellos	cojan	ellos	cogieron

PAST PARTICIPLE	IMPERATIVE
cogido	coge
	coged

GERUND
cogiendo

conducir (to drive, to lead)

	PRESENT		IMPERFECT
yo	conduzco	yo	conducía
tú	conduces	tú	conducías
él	conduce	él	conducía
nosotros	conducimos	nosotros	conducíamos
vosotros	conducís	vosotros	conducíais
ellos	conducen	ellos	conducían

	FUTURE		CONDITIONAL
yo	conduciré	yo	conduciría
tú	conducirás	tú	conducirías
él	conducirá	él	conduciría
nosotros	conduciremos	nosotros	conduciríamos
vosotros	conduciréis	vosotros	conduciríais
ellos	conducirán	ellos	conducirían

	PRESENT SUBJUNCTIVE		PRETERITE
yo	conduzca	yo	conduje
tú	conduzcas	tú	condujiste
él	conduzca	él	condujo
nosotros	conduzcamos	nosotros	condujimos
vosotros	conduzcáis	vosotros	condujisteis
ellos	conduzcan	ellos	condujeron

PAST PARTICIPLE	IMPERATIVE
conducido	conduce
	conducid

GERUND
conduciendo

construir (to build)

	PRESENT		IMPERFECT
yo	**construyo**	yo	construía
tú	**construyes**	tú	construías
él	**construye**	él	construía
nosotros	constru**imos**	nosotros	construíamos
vosotros	constru**ís**	vosotros	construíais
ellos	**construyen**	ellos	construían

	FUTURE		CONDITIONAL
yo	construir**é**	yo	construir**ía**
tú	construir**ás**	tú	construir**ías**
él	construir**á**	él	construir**ía**
nosotros	construir**emos**	nosotros	construir**íamos**
vosotros	construir**éis**	vosotros	construir**íais**
ellos	construir**án**	ellos	construir**ían**

	PRESENT SUBJUNCTIVE		PRETERITE
yo	**construya**	yo	constru**í**
tú	**construyas**	tú	constru**iste**
él	**construya**	él	**construyó**
nosotros	**construyamos**	nosotros	constru**imos**
vosotros	**construyáis**	vosotros	constru**isteis**
ellos	**construyan**	ellos	**construyeron**

PAST PARTICIPLE
constru**ido**

IMPERATIVE
construye
constru**id**

GERUND
construyendo

contar (to tell, to count)

	PRESENT		IMPERFECT
yo	cuento	yo	contaba
tú	cuentas	tú	contabas
él	cuenta	él	contaba
nosotros	contamos	nosotros	contábamos
vosotros	contáis	vosotros	contabais
ellos	cuentan	ellos	contaban

	FUTURE		CONDITIONAL
yo	contaré	yo	contaría
tú	contarás	tú	contarías
él	contará	él	contaría
nosotros	contaremos	nosotros	contaríamos
vosotros	contaréis	vosotros	contaríais
ellos	contarán	ellos	contarían

	PRESENT SUBJUNCTIVE		PRETERITE
yo	cuente	yo	conté
tú	cuentes	tú	contaste
él	cuente	él	contó
nosotros	contemos	nosotros	contamos
vosotros	contéis	vosotros	contasteis
ellos	cuenten	ellos	contaron

PAST PARTICIPLE	IMPERATIVE
contado	cuenta
	contad

GERUND

contando

crecer (to grow)

	PRESENT		IMPERFECT
yo	crezco	yo	crecía
tú	creces	tú	crecías
él	crece	él	crecía
nosotros	crecemos	nosotros	crecíamos
vosotros	crecéis	vosotros	crecíais
ellos	crecen	ellos	crecían

	FUTURE		CONDITIONAL
yo	creceré	yo	crecería
tú	crecerás	tú	crecerías
él	crecerá	él	crecería
nosotros	creceremos	nosotros	creceríamos
vosotros	creceréis	vosotros	creceríais
ellos	crecerán	ellos	crecerían

	PRESENT SUBJUNCTIVE		PRETERITE
yo	crezca	yo	crecí
tú	crezcas	tú	creciste
él	crezca	él	creció
nosotros	crezcamos	nosotros	crecimos
vosotros	crezcáis	vosotros	crecisteis
ellos	crezcan	ellos	crecieron

PAST PARTICIPLE	IMPERATIVE
crecido	crece
	creced

GERUND
creciendo

cruzar (to cross)

	PRESENT		IMPERFECT
yo	cruzo	yo	cruzaba
tú	cruzas	tú	cruzabas
él	cruza	él	cruzaba
nosotros	cruzamos	nosotros	cruzábamos
vosotros	cruzáis	vosotros	cruzabais
ellos	cruzan	ellos	cruzaban

	FUTURE		CONDITIONAL
yo	cruzaré	yo	cruzaría
tú	cruzarás	tú	cruzarías
él	cruzará	él	cruzaría
nosotros	cruzaremos	nosotros	cruzaríamos
vosotros	cruzaréis	vosotros	cruzaríais
ellos	cruzarán	ellos	cruzarían

	PRESENT SUBJUNCTIVE		PRETERITE
yo	cruce	yo	crucé
tú	cruces	tú	cruzaste
él	cruce	él	cruzó
nosotros	crucemos	nosotros	cruzamos
vosotros	crucéis	vosotros	cruzasteis
ellos	crucen	ellos	cruzaron

PAST PARTICIPLE	IMPERATIVE
cruzado	cruza
	cruzad

GERUND

cruzando

dar (to give)

	PRESENT		IMPERFECT
yo	doy	yo	daba
tú	das	tú	dabas
él	da	él	daba
nosotros	damos	nosotros	dábamos
vosotros	dais	vosotros	dabais
ellos	dan	ellos	daban

	FUTURE		CONDITIONAL
yo	daré	yo	daría
tú	darás	tú	darías
él	dará	él	daría
nosotros	daremos	nosotros	daríamos
vosotros	daréis	vosotros	daríais
ellos	darán	ellos	darían

	PRESENT SUBJUNCTIVE		PRETERITE
yo	dé	yo	di
tú	des	tú	diste
él	dé	él	dio
nosotros	demos	nosotros	dimos
vosotros	deis	vosotros	disteis
ellos	den	ellos	dieron

PAST PARTICIPLE
dado

IMPERATIVE
da
dad

GERUND
dando

decir (to say)

	PRESENT		IMPERFECT
yo	digo	yo	decía
tú	dices	tú	decías
él	dice	él	decía
nosotros	decimos	nosotros	decíamos
vosotros	decís	vosotros	decíais
ellos	dicen	ellos	decían

	FUTURE		CONDITIONAL
yo	diré	yo	diría
tú	dirás	tú	dirías
él	dirá	él	diría
nosotros	diremos	nosotros	diríamos
vosotros	diréis	vosotros	diríais
ellos	dirán	ellos	dirían

	PRESENT SUBJUNCTIVE		PRETERITE
yo	diga	yo	dije
tú	digas	tú	dijiste
él	diga	él	dijo
nosotros	digamos	nosotros	dijimos
vosotros	digáis	vosotros	dijisteis
ellos	digan	ellos	dijeron

PAST PARTICIPLE
dicho

IMPERATIVE
di
decid

GERUND
diciendo

dirigir (to direct)

	PRESENT		**IMPERFECT**
yo	**diri**jo	yo	dirig**ía**
tú	dirig**es**	tú	dirig**ías**
él	dirig**e**	él	dirig**ía**
nosotros	dirig**imos**	nosotros	dirig**íamos**
vosotros	dirig**ís**	vosotros	dirig**íais**
ellos	dirig**en**	ellos	dirig**ían**

	FUTURE		**CONDITIONAL**
yo	dirigir**é**	yo	dirigir**ía**
tú	dirigir**ás**	tú	dirigir**ías**
él	dirigir**á**	él	dirigir**ía**
nosotros	dirigir**emos**	nosotros	dirigir**íamos**
vosotros	dirigir**éis**	vosotros	dirigir**íais**
ellos	dirigir**án**	ellos	dirigir**ían**

	PRESENT SUBJUNCTIVE		**PRETERITE**
yo	**dirija**	yo	dirig**í**
tú	**dirijas**	tú	dirig**iste**
él	**dirija**	él	dirig**ió**
nosotros	**dirijamos**	nosotros	dirig**imos**
vosotros	**dirijáis**	vosotros	dirig**isteis**
ellos	**dirijan**	ellos	dirig**ieron**

PAST PARTICIPLE
dirig**ido**

IMPERATIVE
dirig**e**
dirig**id**

GERUND
dirig**iendo**

distinguir (to distinguish)

	PRESENT		IMPERFECT
yo	distingo	yo	distinguía
tú	distingues	tú	distinguías
él	distingue	él	distinguía
nosotros	distinguimos	nosotros	distinguíamos
vosotros	distinguís	vosotros	distinguíais
ellos	distinguen	ellos	distinguían

	FUTURE		CONDITIONAL
yo	distinguiré	yo	distinguiría
tú	distinguirás	tú	distinguirías
él	distinguirá	él	distinguiría
nosotros	distinguiremos	nosotros	distinguiríamos
vosotros	distinguiréis	vosotros	distinguiríais
ellos	distinguirán	ellos	distinguirían

	PRESENT SUBJUNCTIVE		PRETERITE
yo	distinga	yo	distinguí
tú	distingas	tú	distinguiste
él	distinga	él	distinguió
nosotros	distingamos	nosotros	distinguimos
vosotros	distingáis	vosotros	distinguisteis
ellos	distingan	ellos	distinguieron

PAST PARTICIPLE	IMPERATIVE
distinguido	distingue
	distinguid

GERUND

distinguiendo

dormir (to sleep)

	PRESENT		IMPERFECT
yo	duermo	yo	dormía
tú	duermes	tú	dormías
él	duerme	él	dormía
nosotros	dormimos	nosotros	dormíamos
vosotros	dormís	vosotros	dormíais
ellos	duermen	ellos	dormían

	FUTURE		CONDITIONAL
yo	dormiré	yo	dormiría
tú	dormirás	tú	dormirías
él	dormirá	él	dormiría
nosotros	dormiremos	nosotros	dormiríamos
vosotros	dormiréis	vosotros	dormiríais
ellos	dormirán	ellos	dormirían

	PRESENT SUBJUNCTIVE		PRETERITE
yo	duerma	yo	dormí
tú	duermas	tú	dormiste
él	duerma	él	durmió
nosotros	durmamos	nosotros	dormimos
vosotros	durmáis	vosotros	dormisteis
ellos	duerman	ellos	durmieron

PAST PARTICIPLE
dormido

IMPERATIVE
duerme
dormid

GERUND
durmiendo

elegir (to choose)

	PRESENT		IMPERFECT
yo	elijo	yo	elegía
tú	eliges	tú	elegías
él	elige	él	elegía
nosotros	elegimos	nosotros	elegíamos
vosotros	elegís	vosotros	elegíais
ellos	eligen	ellos	elegían

	FUTURE		CONDITIONAL
yo	elegiré	yo	elegiría
tú	elegirás	tú	elegirías
él	elegirá	él	elegiría
nosotros	elegiremos	nosotros	elegiríamos
vosotros	elegiréis	vosotros	elegiríais
ellos	elegirán	ellos	elegirían

	PRESENT SUBJUNCTIVE		PRETERITE
yo	elija	yo	elegí
tú	elijas	tú	elegiste
él	elija	él	eligió
nosotros	elijamos	nosotros	elegimos
vosotros	elijáis	vosotros	elegisteis
ellos	elijan	ellos	eligieron

PAST PARTICIPLE	IMPERATIVE
elegido	elige
	elegid

GERUND

eligiendo

empezar (to begin)

	PRESENT		**IMPERFECT**
yo	empiezo	yo	empezaba
tú	empiezas	tú	empezabas
él	empieza	él	empezaba
nosotros	empezamos	nosotros	empezábamos
vosotros	empezáis	vosotros	empezabais
ellos	empiezan	ellos	empezaban

	FUTURE		**CONDITIONAL**
yo	empezaré	yo	empezaría
tú	empezarás	tú	empezarías
él	empezará	él	empezaría
nosotros	empezaremos	nosotros	empezaríamos
vosotros	empezaréis	vosotros	empezaríais
ellos	empezarán	ellos	empezarían

	PRESENT SUBJUNCTIVE		**PRETERITE**
yo	empiece	yo	empecé
tú	empieces	tú	empezaste
él	empiece	él	empezó
nosotros	empecemos	nosotros	empezamos
vosotros	empecéis	vosotros	empezasteis
ellos	empiecen	ellos	empezaron

PAST PARTICIPLE
empezado

IMPERATIVE
empieza
empezad

GERUND
empezando

entender (to understand)

	PRESENT		IMPERFECT
yo	entiendo	yo	entendía
tú	entiendes	tú	entendías
él	entiende	él	entendía
nosotros	entendemos	nosotros	entendíamos
vosotros	entendéis	vosotros	entendíais
ellos	entienden	ellos	entendían

	FUTURE		CONDITIONAL
yo	entenderé	yo	entendería
tú	entenderás	tú	entenderías
él	entenderá	él	entendería
nosotros	entenderemos	nosotros	entenderíamos
vosotros	entenderéis	vosotros	entenderíais
ellos	entenderán	ellos	entenderían

	PRESENT SUBJUNCTIVE		PRETERITE
yo	entienda	yo	entendí
tú	entiendas	tú	entendiste
él	entienda	él	entendió
nosotros	entendamos	nosotros	entendimos
vosotros	entendáis	vosotros	entendisteis
ellos	entiendan	ellos	entendieron

PAST PARTICIPLE	IMPERATIVE
entendido	entiende
	entended

GERUND
entendiendo

enviar (to send)

	PRESENT		IMPERFECT
yo	envío	yo	enviaba
tú	envías	tú	enviabas
él	envía	él	enviaba
nosotros	enviamos	nosotros	enviábamos
vosotros	enviáis	vosotros	enviabais
ellos	envían	ellos	enviaban

	FUTURE		CONDITIONAL
yo	enviaré	yo	enviaría
tú	enviarás	tú	enviarías
él	enviará	él	enviaría
nosotros	enviaremos	nosotros	enviaríamos
vosotros	enviaréis	vosotros	enviaríais
ellos	enviarán	ellos	enviarían

	PRESENT SUBJUNCTIVE		PRETERITE
yo	envíe	yo	envié
tú	envíes	tú	enviaste
él	envíe	él	envió
nosotros	enviemos	nosotros	enviamos
vosotros	enviéis	vosotros	enviasteis
ellos	envíen	ellos	enviaron

PAST PARTICIPLE	IMPERATIVE
enviado	envía
	enviad

GERUND

enviando

erguir (to erect)

	PRESENT		IMPERFECT
yo	yergo	yo	erguía
tú	yergues	tú	erguías
él	yergue	él	erguía
nosotros	erguimos	nosotros	erguíamos
vosotros	erguís	vosotros	erguíais
ellos	yerguen	ellos	erguían

	FUTURE		CONDITIONAL
yo	erguiré	yo	erguiría
tú	erguirás	tú	erguirías
él	erguirá	él	erguiría
nosotros	erguiremos	nosotros	erguiríamos
vosotros	erguiréis	vosotros	erguiríais
ellos	erguirán	ellos	erguirían

	PRESENT SUBJUNCTIVE		PRETERITE
yo	yerga	yo	erguí
tú	yergas	tú	erguiste
él	yerga	él	irguió
nosotros	irgamos	nosotros	erguimos
vosotros	irgáis	vosotros	erguisteis
ellos	yergan	ellos	irguieron

PAST PARTICIPLE	IMPERATIVE
erguido	yergue
	erguid

GERUND
irguiendo

errar (to err)

	PRESENT		IMPERFECT
yo	yerro	yo	erraba
tú	yerras	tú	errabas
él	yerra	él	erraba
nosotros	erramos	nosotros	errábamos
vosotros	erráis	vosotros	errabais
ellos	yerran	ellos	erraban

	FUTURE		CONDITIONAL
yo	erraré	yo	erraría
tú	errarás	tú	errarías
él	errará	él	erraría
nosotros	erraremos	nosotros	erraríamos
vosotros	erraréis	vosotros	erraríais
ellos	errarán	ellos	errarían

	PRESENT SUBJUNCTIVE		PRETERITE
yo	yerre	yo	erré
tú	yerres	tú	erraste
él	yerre	él	erró
nosotros	erremos	nosotros	erramos
vosotros	erréis	vosotros	errasteis
ellos	yerren	ellos	erraron

PAST PARTICIPLE
errado

IMPERATIVE
yerra
errad

GERUND
errando

escribir (to write)

	PRESENT			IMPERFECT
yo	escribo		yo	escribía
tú	escribes		tú	escribías
él	escribe		él	escribía
nosotros	escribimos		nosotros	escribíamos
vosotros	escribís		vosotros	escribíais
ellos	escriben		ellos	escribían

	FUTURE			CONDITIONAL
yo	escribiré		yo	escribiría
tú	escribirás		tú	escribirías
él	escribirá		él	escribiría
nosotros	escribiremos		nosotros	escribiríamos
vosotros	escribiréis		vosotros	escribiríais
ellos	escribirán		ellos	escribirían

	PRESENT SUBJUNCTIVE			PRETERITE
yo	escriba		yo	escribí
tú	escribas		tú	escribiste
él	escriba		él	escribió
nosotros	escribamos		nosotros	escribimos
vosotros	escribáis		vosotros	escribisteis
ellos	escriban		ellos	escribieron

PAST PARTICIPLE
escrito

IMPERATIVE
escribe
escribid

GERUND
escribiendo

estar (to be)

	PRESENT		IMPERFECT
yo	estoy	yo	estaba
tú	estás	tú	estabas
él	está	él	estaba
nosotros	estamos	nosotros	estábamos
vosotros	estáis	vosotros	estabais
ellos	están	ellos	estaban

	FUTURE		CONDITIONAL
yo	estaré	yo	estaría
tú	estarás	tú	estarías
él	estará	él	estaría
nosotros	estaremos	nosotros	estaríamos
vosotros	estaréis	vosotros	estaríais
ellos	estarán	ellos	estarían

	PRESENT SUBJUNCTIVE		PRETERITE
yo	esté	yo	estuve
tú	estés	tú	estuviste
él	esté	él	estuvo
nosotros	estemos	nosotros	estuvimos
vosotros	estéis	vosotros	estuvisteis
ellos	estén	ellos	estuvieron

PAST PARTICIPLE	IMPERATIVE
estado	está
	estad

GERUND
estando

freír (to fry)

	PRESENT			IMPERFECT
yo	frío		yo	freía
tú	fríes		tú	freías
él	fríe		él	freía
nosotros	freímos		nosotros	freíamos
vosotros	freís		vosotros	freíais
ellos	fríen		ellos	freían

	FUTURE			CONDITIONAL
yo	freiré		yo	freiría
tú	freirás		tú	freirías
él	freirá		él	freiría
nosotros	freiremos		nosotros	freiríamos
vosotros	freiréis		vosotros	freiríais
ellos	freirán		ellos	freirían

	PRESENT SUBJUNCTIVE			PRETERITE
yo	fría		yo	freí
tú	frías		tú	freíste
él	fría		él	frió
nosotros	friamos		nosotros	freímos
vosotros	friáis		vosotros	freísteis
ellos	frían		ellos	frieron

PAST PARTICIPLE	IMPERATIVE
frito	fríe
	freíd

GERUND
friendo

gruñir (to grunt)

	PRESENT			IMPERFECT
yo	gruño		yo	gruñía
tú	gruñes		tú	gruñías
él	gruñe		él	gruñía
nosotros	gruñimos		nosotros	gruñíamos
vosotros	gruñís		vosotros	gruñíais
ellos	gruñen		ellos	gruñían

	FUTURE			CONDITIONAL
yo	gruñiré		yo	gruñiría
tú	gruñirás		tú	gruñirías
él	gruñirá		él	gruñiría
nosotros	gruñiremos		nosotros	gruñiríamos
vosotros	gruñiréis		vosotros	gruñiríais
ellos	gruñirán		ellos	gruñirían

	PRESENT SUBJUNCTIVE			PRETERITE
yo	gruña		yo	gruñí
tú	gruñas		tú	gruñíste
él	gruña		él	gruñó
nosotros	gruñamos		nosotros	gruñimos
vosotros	gruñáis		vosotros	gruñisteis
ellos	gruñan		ellos	gruñeron

PAST PARTICIPLE
gruñido

IMPERATIVE
gruñe
gruñid

GERUND
gruñendo

haber (to have, *auxiliary*)

	PRESENT		IMPERFECT
yo	he	yo	había
tú	has	tú	habías
él	ha	él	había
nosotros	hemos	nosotros	habíamos
vosotros	habéis	vosotros	habíais
ellos	han	ellos	habían

	FUTURE		CONDITIONAL
yo	habré	yo	habría
tú	habrás	tú	habrías
él	habrá	él	habría
nosotros	habremos	nosotros	habríamos
vosotros	habréis	vosotros	habríais
ellos	habrán	ellos	habrían

	PRESENT SUBJUNCTIVE		PRETERITE
yo	haya	yo	hube
tú	hayas	tú	hubiste
él	haya	él	hubo
nosotros	hayamos	nosotros	hubimos
vosotros	hayáis	vosotros	hubisteis
ellos	hayan	ellos	hubieron

PAST PARTICIPLE	IMPERATIVE
habido	*not used*

GERUND
habiendo

hacer (to do, to make)

	PRESENT		**IMPERFECT**
yo	hago	yo	hacía
tú	haces	tú	hacías
él	hace	él	hacía
nosotros	hacemos	nosotros	hacíamos
vosotros	hacéis	vosotros	hacíais
ellos	hacen	ellos	hacían

	FUTURE		**CONDITIONAL**
yo	haré	yo	haría
tú	harás	tú	harías
él	hará	él	haría
nosotros	haremos	nosotros	haríamos
vosotros	haréis	vosotros	haríais
ellos	harán	ellos	harían

	PRESENT SUBJUNCTIVE		**PRETERITE**
yo	haga	yo	hice
tú	hagas	tú	hiciste
él	haga	él	hizo
nosotros	hagamos	nosotros	hicimos
vosotros	hagáis	vosotros	hicisteis
ellos	hagan	ellos	hicieron

PAST PARTICIPLE
hecho

IMPERATIVE
haz
haced

GERUND
haciendo

hay (there is, there are)

PRESENT
hay

IMPERFECT
hab**í**a

FUTURE
habrá

CONDITIONAL
habría

PRESENT SUBJUNCTIVE
haya

PRETERITE
hubo

PAST PARTICIPLE
hab**ido**

IMPERATIVE
not used

GERUND
hab**iendo**

ir (to go)

	PRESENT		IMPERFECT
yo	voy	yo	iba
tú	vas	tú	ibas
él	va	él	iba
nosotros	vamos	nosotros	íbamos
vosotros	vais	vosotros	ibais
ellos	van	ellos	iban

	FUTURE		CONDITIONAL
yo	iré	yo	iría
tú	irás	tú	irías
él	irá	él	iría
nosotros	iremos	nosotros	iríamos
vosotros	iréis	vosotros	iríais
ellos	irán	ellos	irían

	PRESENT SUBJUNCTIVE		PRETERITE
yo	vaya	yo	fui
tú	vayas	tú	fuiste
él	vaya	él	fue
nosotros	vayamos	nosotros	fuimos
vosotros	vayáis	vosotros	fuisteis
ellos	vayan	ellos	fueron

PAST PARTICIPLE	IMPERATIVE
ido	ve
	id

GERUND

yendo

jugar (to play)

	PRESENT		IMPERFECT
yo	juego	yo	jugaba
tú	juegas	tú	jugabas
él	juega	él	jugaba
nosotros	jugamos	nosotros	jugábamos
vosotros	jugáis	vosotros	jugabais
ellos	juegan	ellos	jugaban

	FUTURE		CONDITIONAL
yo	jugaré	yo	jugaría
tú	jugarás	tú	jugarías
él	jugará	él	jugaría
nosotros	jugaremos	nosotros	jugaríamos
vosotros	jugaréis	vosotros	jugaríais
ellos	jugarán	ellos	jugarían

	PRESENT SUBJUNCTIVE		PRETERITE
yo	juegue	yo	jugué
tú	juegues	tú	jugaste
él	juegue	él	jugó
nosotros	juguemos	nosotros	jugamos
vosotros	juguéis	vosotros	jugasteis
ellos	jueguen	ellos	jugaron

PAST PARTICIPLE	IMPERATIVE
jugado	juega
	jugad

GERUND
jugando

leer (to read)

	PRESENT		IMPERFECT
yo	leo	yo	leía
tú	lees	tú	leías
él	lee	él	leía
nosotros	leemos	nosotros	leíamos
vosotros	leéis	vosotros	leíais
ellos	leen	ellos	leían

	FUTURE		CONDITIONAL
yo	leeré	yo	leería
tú	leerás	tú	leerías
él	leerá	él	leería
nosotros	leeremos	nosotros	leeríamos
vosotros	leeréis	vosotros	leeríais
ellos	leerán	ellos	leerían

	PRESENT SUBJUNCTIVE		PRETERITE
yo	lea	yo	leí
tú	leas	tú	leíste
él	lea	él	leyó
nosotros	leamos	nosotros	leímos
vosotros	leáis	vosotros	leísteis
ellos	lean	ellos	leyeron

PAST PARTICIPLE
leído

IMPERATIVE
lee
leed

GERUND
leyendo

121

lucir (to shine)

	PRESENT			IMPERFECT
yo	luzco		yo	lucía
tú	luces		tú	lucías
él	luce		él	lucía
nosotros	lucimos		nosotros	lucíamos
vosotros	lucís		vosotros	lucíais
ellos	lucen		ellos	lucían

	FUTURE			CONDITIONAL
yo	luciré		yo	luciría
tú	lucirás		tú	lucirías
él	lucirá		él	luciría
nosotros	luciremos		nosotros	luciríamos
vosotros	luciréis		vosotros	luciríais
ellos	lucirán		ellos	lucirían

	PRESENT SUBJUNCTIVE			PRETERITE
yo	luzca		yo	lucí
tú	luzcas		tú	luciste
él	luzca		él	lució
nosotros	luzcamos		nosotros	lucimos
vosotros	luzcáis		vosotros	lucisteis
ellos	luzcan		ellos	lucieron

PAST PARTICIPLE	IMPERATIVE
lucido	luce
	lucid

GERUND
luciendo

llover (to rain)

PRESENT
llueve

IMPERFECT
llovía

FUTURE
lloverá

CONDITIONAL
llovería

PRESENT SUBJUNCTIVE
llueva

PRETERITE
llovió

PAST PARTICIPLE
llovido

IMPERATIVE
not used

GERUND
lloviendo

morir (to die)

	PRESENT		IMPERFECT
yo	muero	yo	moría
tú	mueres	tú	morías
él	muere	él	moría
nosotros	morimos	nosotros	moríamos
vosotros	morís	vosotros	moríais
ellos	mueren	ellos	morían

	FUTURE		CONDITIONAL
yo	moriré	yo	moriría
tú	morirás	tú	morirías
él	morirá	él	moriría
nosotros	moriremos	nosotros	moriríamos
vosotros	moriréis	vosotros	moriríais
ellos	morirán	ellos	morirían

	PRESENT SUBJUNCTIVE		PRETERITE
yo	muera	yo	morí
tú	mueras	tú	moriste
él	muera	él	murió
nosotros	muramos	nosotros	morimos
vosotros	muráis	vosotros	moristeis
ellos	mueran	ellos	murieron

PAST PARTICIPLE
muerto

IMPERATIVE
muere
morid

GERUND
muriendo

mover (to move)

	PRESENT		IMPERFECT
yo	muevo	yo	movía
tú	mueves	tú	movías
él	mueve	él	movía
nosotros	movemos	nosotros	movíamos
vosotros	movéis	vosotros	movíais
ellos	mueven	ellos	movían

	FUTURE		CONDITIONAL
yo	moveré	yo	movería
tú	moverás	tú	moverías
él	moverá	él	movería
nosotros	moveremos	nosotros	moveríamos
vosotros	moveréis	vosotros	moveríais
ellos	moverán	ellos	moverían

	PRESENT SUBJUNCTIVE		PRETERITE
yo	mueva	yo	moví
tú	muevas	tú	moviste
él	mueva	él	movió
nosotros	movamos	nosotros	movimos
vosotros	mováis	vosotros	movisteis
ellos	muevan	ellos	movieron

PAST PARTICIPLE	IMPERATIVE
movido	mueve
	moved

GERUND
moviendo

nacer (to be born)

	PRESENT		IMPERFECT
yo	nazco	yo	nacía
tú	naces	tú	nacías
él	nace	él	nacía
nosotros	nacemos	nosotros	nacíamos
vosotros	nacéis	vosotros	nacíais
ellos	nacen	ellos	nacían

	FUTURE		CONDITIONAL
yo	naceré	yo	nacería
tú	nacerás	tú	nacerías
él	nacerá	él	nacería
nosotros	naceremos	nosotros	naceríamos
vosotros	naceréis	vosotros	naceríais
ellos	nacerán	ellos	nacerían

	PRESENT SUBJUNCTIVE		PRETERITE
yo	nazca	yo	nací
tú	nazcas	tú	naciste
él	nazca	él	nació
nosotros	nazcamos	nosotros	nacimos
vosotros	nazcáis	vosotros	nacisteis
ellos	nazcan	ellos	nacieron

PAST PARTICIPLE	IMPERATIVE
nacido	nace
	naced

GERUND

naciendo

negar (to deny)

	PRESENT		IMPERFECT
yo	niego	yo	negaba
tú	niegas	tú	negabas
él	niega	él	negaba
nosotros	negamos	nosotros	negábamos
vosotros	negáis	vosotros	negabais
ellos	niegan	ellos	negaban

	FUTURE		CONDITIONAL
yo	negaré	yo	negaría
tú	negarás	tú	negarías
él	negará	él	negaría
nosotros	negaremos	nosotros	negaríamos
vosotros	negaréis	vosotros	negaríais
ellos	negarán	ellos	negarían

	PRESENT SUBJUNCTIVE		PRETERITE
yo	niegue	yo	negué
tú	niegues	tú	negaste
él	niegue	él	negó
nosotros	neguemos	nosotros	negamos
vosotros	neguéis	vosotros	negasteis
ellos	nieguen	ellos	negaron

PAST PARTICIPLE	IMPERATIVE
negado	niega
	negad

GERUND
negando

Oír (to hear)

	PRESENT		IMPERFECT
yo	oigo	yo	oía
tú	oyes	tú	oías
él	oye	él	oía
nosotros	oímos	nosotros	oíamos
vosotros	oís	vosotros	oíais
ellos	oyen	ellos	oían

	FUTURE		CONDITIONAL
yo	oiré	yo	oiría
tú	oirás	tú	oirías
él	oirá	él	oiría
nosotros	oiremos	nosotros	oiríamos
vosotros	oiréis	vosotros	oiríais
ellos	oirán	ellos	oirían

	PRESENT SUBJUNCTIVE		PRETERITE
yo	oiga	yo	oí
tú	oigas	tú	oíste
él	oiga	él	oyó
nosotros	oigamos	nosotros	oímos
vosotros	oigáis	vosotros	oísteis
ellos	oigan	ellos	oyeron

PAST PARTICIPLE	IMPERATIVE
oído	oye
	oíd

GERUND
oyendo

oler (to smell)

	PRESENT		IMPERFECT
yo	huelo	yo	olía
tú	hueles	tú	olías
él	huele	él	olía
nosotros	olemos	nosotros	olíamos
vosotros	oléis	vosotros	olíais
ellos	huelen	ellos	olían

	FUTURE		CONDITIONAL
yo	oleré	yo	olería
tú	olerás	tú	olerías
él	olerá	él	olería
nosotros	oleremos	nosotros	oleríamos
vosotros	oleréis	vosotros	oleríais
ellos	olerán	ellos	olerían

	PRESENT SUBJUNCTIVE		PRETERITE
yo	huela	yo	olí
tú	huelas	tú	oliste
él	huela	él	olió
nosotros	olamos	nosotros	olimos
vosotros	oláis	vosotros	olisteis
ellos	huelan	ellos	olieron

PAST PARTICIPLE
olido

IMPERATIVE
huele
oled

GERUND
oliendo

pagar (to pay)

	PRESENT		IMPERFECT
yo	pago	yo	pagaba
tú	pagas	tú	pagabas
él	paga	él	pagaba
nosotros	pagamos	nosotros	pagábamos
vosotros	pagáis	vosotros	pagabais
ellos	pagan	ellos	pagaban

	FUTURE		CONDITIONAL
yo	pagaré	yo	pagaría
tú	pagarás	tú	pagarías
él	pagará	él	pagaría
nosotros	pagaremos	nosotros	pagaríamos
vosotros	pagaréis	vosotros	pagaríais
ellos	pagarán	ellos	pagarían

	PRESENT SUBJUNCTIVE		PRETERITE
yo	pague	yo	pagué
tú	pagues	tú	pagaste
él	pague	él	pagó
nosotros	paguemos	nosotros	pagamos
vosotros	paguéis	vosotros	pagasteis
ellos	paguen	ellos	pagaron

PAST PARTICIPLE	IMPERATIVE
pagado	paga
	pagad

GERUND
pagando

pedir (to ask for)

	PRESENT		IMPERFECT
yo	pido	yo	pedía
tú	pides	tú	pedías
él	pide	él	pedía
nosotros	pedimos	nosotros	pedíamos
vosotros	pedís	vosotros	pedíais
ellos	piden	ellos	pedían

	FUTURE		CONDITIONAL
yo	pediré	yo	pediría
tú	pedirás	tú	pedirías
él	pedirá	él	pediría
nosotros	pediremos	nosotros	pediríamos
vosotros	pediréis	vosotros	pediríais
ellos	pedirán	ellos	pedirían

	PRESENT SUBJUNCTIVE		PRETERITE
yo	pida	yo	pedí
tú	pidas	tú	pediste
él	pida	él	pidió
nosotros	pidamos	nosotros	pedimos
vosotros	pidáis	vosotros	pedisteis
ellos	pidan	ellos	pidieron

PAST PARTICIPLE
pedido

IMPERATIVE
pide
pedid

GERUND
pidiendo

pensar (to think)

	PRESENT		IMPERFECT
yo	pienso	yo	pensaba
tú	piensas	tú	pensabas
él	piensa	él	pensaba
nosotros	pensamos	nosotros	pensábamos
vosotros	pensáis	vosotros	pensabais
ellos	piensan	ellos	pensaban

	FUTURE		CONDITIONAL
yo	pensaré	yo	pensaría
tú	pensarás	tú	pensarías
él	pensará	él	pensaría
nosotros	pensaremos	nosotros	pensaríamos
vosotros	pensaréis	vosotros	pensaríais
ellos	pensarán	ellos	pensarían

	PRESENT SUBJUNCTIVE		PRETERITE
yo	piense	yo	pensé
tú	pienses	tú	pensaste
él	piense	él	pensó
nosotros	pensemos	nosotros	pensamos
vosotros	penséis	vosotros	pensasteis
ellos	piensen	ellos	pensaron

PAST PARTICIPLE
pensado

IMPERATIVE
piensa
pensad

GERUND
pensando

poder (to be able)

	PRESENT		**IMPERFECT**
yo	puedo	yo	podía
tú	puedes	tú	podías
él	puede	él	podía
nosotros	podemos	nosotros	podíamos
vosotros	podéis	vosotros	podíais
ellos	pueden	ellos	podían

	FUTURE		**CONDITIONAL**
yo	podré	yo	podría
tú	podrás	tú	podrías
él	podrá	él	podría
nosotros	podremos	nosotros	podríamos
vosotros	podréis	vosotros	podríais
ellos	podrán	ellos	podrían

	PRESENT SUBJUNCTIVE		**PRETERITE**
yo	pueda	yo	pude
tú	puedas	tú	pudiste
él	pueda	él	pudo
nosotros	podamos	nosotros	pudimos
vosotros	podáis	vosotros	pudisteis
ellos	puedan	ellos	pudieron

PAST PARTICIPLE
podido

IMPERATIVE
puede
poded

GERUND
pudiendo

poner (to put)

	PRESENT		IMPERFECT
yo	pongo	yo	ponía
tú	pones	tú	ponías
él	pone	él	ponía
nosotros	ponemos	nosotros	poníamos
vosotros	ponéis	vosotros	poníais
ellos	ponen	ellos	ponían

	FUTURE		CONDITIONAL
yo	pondré	yo	pondría
tú	pondrás	tú	pondrías
él	pondrá	él	pondría
nosotros	pondremos	nosotros	pondríamos
vosotros	pondréis	vosotros	pondríais
ellos	pondrán	ellos	pondrían

	PRESENT SUBJUNCTIVE		PRETERITE
yo	ponga	yo	puse
tú	pongas	tú	pusiste
él	ponga	él	puso
nosotros	pongamos	nosotros	pusimos
vosotros	pongáis	vosotros	pusisteis
ellos	pongan	ellos	pusieron

PAST PARTICIPLE
puesto

IMPERATIVE
pon
poned

GERUND
poniendo

prohibir (to forbid)

PRESENT

yo	prohíbo
tú	prohíbes
él	prohíbe
nosotros	prohibimos
vosotros	prohibís
ellos	prohíben

IMPERFECT

yo	prohibía
tú	prohibías
él	prohibía
nosotros	prohibíamos
vosotros	prohibíais
ellos	prohibían

FUTURE

yo	prohibiré
tú	prohibirás
él	prohibirá
nosotros	prohibiremos
vosotros	prohibiréis
ellos	prohibirán

CONDITIONAL

yo	prohibiría
tú	prohibirías
él	prohibiría
nosotros	prohibiríamos
vosotros	prohibiríais
ellos	prohibirían

PRESENT SUBJUNCTIVE

yo	prohíba
tú	prohíbas
él	prohíba
nosotros	prohibamos
vosotros	prohibáis
ellos	prohíban

PRETERITE

yo	prohibí
tú	prohibiste
él	prohibió
nosotros	prohibimos
vosotros	prohibisteis
ellos	prohibieron

PAST PARTICIPLE
prohibido

IMPERATIVE
prohíbe
prohibid

GERUND
prohibiendo

querer (to want)

	PRESENT		IMPERFECT
yo	quiero	yo	quería
tú	quieres	tú	querías
él	quiere	él	quería
nosotros	queremos	nosotros	queríamos
vosotros	queréis	vosotros	queríais
ellos	quieren	ellos	querían

	FUTURE		CONDITIONAL
yo	querré	yo	querría
tú	querrás	tú	querrías
él	querrá	él	querría
nosotros	querremos	nosotros	querríamos
vosotros	querréis	vosotros	querríais
ellos	querrán	ellos	querrían

	PRESENT SUBJUNCTIVE		PRETERITE
yo	quiera	yo	quise
tú	quieras	tú	quisiste
él	quiera	él	quiso
nosotros	queramos	nosotros	quisimos
vosotros	queráis	vosotros	quisisteis
ellos	quieran	ellos	quisieron

PAST PARTICIPLE	IMPERATIVE
querido	quiere
	quered

GERUND

queriendo

rehusar (to refuse)

	PRESENT		IMPERFECT
yo	rehúso	yo	rehusaba
tú	rehúsas	tú	rehusabas
él	rehúsa	él	rehusaba
nosotros	rehusamos	nosotros	rehusábamos
vosotros	rehusáis	vosotros	rehusabais
ellos	rehúsan	ellos	rehusaban

	FUTURE		CONDITIONAL
yo	rehusaré	yo	rehusaría
tú	rehusarás	tú	rehusarías
él	rehusará	él	rehusaría
nosotros	rehusaremos	nosotros	rehusaríamos
vosotros	rehusaréis	vosotros	rehusaríais
ellos	rehusarán	ellos	rehusarían

	PRESENT SUBJUNCTIVE		PRETERITE
yo	rehúse	yo	rehusé
tú	rehúses	tú	rehusaste
él	rehúse	él	rehusó
nosotros	rehusemos	nosotros	rehusamos
vosotros	rehuséis	vosotros	rehusasteis
ellos	rehúsen	ellos	rehusaron

PAST PARTICIPLE	IMPERATIVE
rehusado	rehúsa
	rehusad

GERUND

rehusando

reír (to laugh)

	PRESENT		IMPERFECT
yo	río	yo	reía
tú	ríes	tú	reías
él	ríe	él	reía
nosotros	reímos	nosotros	reíamos
vosotros	reís	vosotros	reíais
ellos	ríen	ellos	reían

	FUTURE		CONDITIONAL
yo	reiré	yo	reiría
tú	reirás	tú	reirías
él	reirá	él	reiría
nosotros	reiremos	nosotros	reiríamos
vosotros	reiréis	vosotros	reiríais
ellos	reirán	ellos	reirían

	PRESENT SUBJUNCTIVE		PRETERITE
yo	ría	yo	reí
tú	rías	tú	reíste
él	ría	él	rió
nosotros	riamos	nosotros	reímos
vosotros	riáis	vosotros	reísteis
ellos	rían	ellos	rieron

PAST PARTICIPLE
reído

IMPERATIVE
ríe
reíd

GERUND
riendo

reñir (to scold)

	PRESENT		IMPERFECT
yo	riño	yo	reñía
tú	riñes	tú	reñías
él	riñe	él	reñía
nosotros	reñimos	nosotros	reñíamos
vosotros	reñís	vosotros	reñíais
ellos	riñen	ellos	reñían

	FUTURE		CONDITIONAL
yo	reñiré	yo	reñiría
tú	reñirás	tú	reñirías
él	reñirá	él	reñiría
nosotros	reñiremos	nosotros	reñiríamos
vosotros	reñiréis	vosotros	reñiríais
ellos	reñirán	ellos	reñirían

	PRESENT SUBJUNCTIVE		PRETERITE
yo	riña	yo	reñí
tú	riñas	tú	reñiste
él	riña	él	riñó
nosotros	riñamos	nosotros	reñimos
vosotros	riñáis	vosotros	reñisteis
ellos	riñan	ellos	riñeron

PAST PARTICIPLE
reñido

IMPERATIVE
ríñe
reñid

GERUND
riñendo

resolver (to solve)

	PRESENT		IMPERFECT
yo	resuelvo	yo	resolvía
tú	resuelves	tú	resolvías
él	resuelve	él	resolvía
nosotros	resolvemos	nosotros	resolvíamos
vosotros	resolvéis	vosotros	resolvíais
ellos	resuelven	ellos	resolvían

	FUTURE		CONDITIONAL
yo	resolveré	yo	resolvería
tú	resolverás	tú	resolverías
él	resolverá	él	resolvería
nosotros	resolveremos	nosotros	resolveríamos
vosotros	resolveréis	vosotros	resolveríais
ellos	resolverán	ellos	resolverían

	PRESENT SUBJUNCTIVE		PRETERITE
yo	resuelva	yo	resolví
tú	resuelvas	tú	resolviste
él	resuelva	él	resolvió
nosotros	resolvamos	nosotros	resolvimos
vosotros	resolváis	vosotros	resolvisteis
ellos	resuelvan	ellos	resolvieron

PAST PARTICIPLE	IMPERATIVE
resuelto	resuelve
	resolved

GERUND
resolviendo

reunir (to put together, to gather)

	PRESENT		IMPERFECT
yo	reúno	yo	reunía
tú	reúnes	tú	reunías
él	reúne	él	reunía
nosotros	reunimos	nosotros	reuníamos
vosotros	reunís	vosotros	reuníais
ellos	reúnen	ellos	reunían

	FUTURE		CONDITIONAL
yo	reuniré	yo	reuniría
tú	reunirás	tú	reunirías
él	reunirá	él	reuniría
nosotros	reuniremos	nosotros	reuniríamos
vosotros	reuniréis	vosotros	reuniríais
ellos	reunirán	ellos	reunirían

	PRESENT SUBJUNCTIVE		PRETERITE
yo	reúna	yo	reuní
tú	reúnas	tú	reuniste
él	reúna	él	reunió
nosotros	reunamos	nosotros	reunimos
vosotros	reunáis	vosotros	reunisteis
ellos	reúnan	ellos	reunieron

PAST PARTICIPLE	IMPERATIVE
reunido	reúne
	reunid

GERUND
reuniendo

rogar (to beg)

	PRESENT		IMPERFECT
yo	ruego	yo	rogaba
tú	ruegas	tú	rogabas
él	ruega	él	rogaba
nosotros	rogamos	nosotros	rogábamos
vosotros	rogáis	vosotros	rogabais
ellos	ruegan	ellos	rogaban

	FUTURE		CONDITIONAL
yo	rogaré	yo	rogaría
tú	rogarás	tú	rogarías
él	rogará	él	rogaría
nosotros	rogaremos	nosotros	rogaríamos
vosotros	rogaréis	vosotros	rogaríais
ellos	rogarán	ellos	rogarían

	PRESENT SUBJUNCTIVE		PRETERITE
yo	ruegue	yo	rogué
tú	ruegues	tú	rogaste
él	ruegue	él	rogó
nosotros	roguemos	nosotros	rogamos
vosotros	roguéis	vosotros	rogasteis
ellos	rueguen	ellos	rogaron

PAST PARTICIPLE	IMPERATIVE
rogado	ruega
	rogad

GERUND
rogando

romper (to break)

	PRESENT		IMPERFECT
yo	rompo	yo	rompía
tú	rompes	tú	rompías
él	rompe	él	rompía
nosotros	rompemos	nosotros	rompíamos
vosotros	rompéis	vosotros	rompíais
ellos	rompen	ellos	rompían

	FUTURE		CONDITIONAL
yo	romperé	yo	rompería
tú	romperás	tú	romperías
él	romperá	él	rompería
nosotros	romperemos	nosotros	romperíamos
vosotros	romperéis	vosotros	romperíais
ellos	romperán	ellos	romperían

	PRESENT SUBJUNCTIVE		PRETERITE
yo	rompa	yo	rompí
tú	rompas	tú	rompiste
él	rompa	él	rompió
nosotros	rompamos	nosotros	rompimos
vosotros	rompáis	vosotros	rompisteis
ellos	rompan	ellos	rompieron

PAST PARTICIPLE	IMPERATIVE
roto	rompe
	romped

GERUND
rompiendo

saber (to know)

	PRESENT		IMPERFECT
yo	sé	yo	sabía
tú	sabes	tú	sabías
él	sabe	él	sabía
nosotros	sabemos	nosotros	sabíamos
vosotros	sabéis	vosotros	sabíais
ellos	saben	ellos	sabían

	FUTURE		CONDITIONAL
yo	sabré	yo	sabría
tú	sabrás	tú	sabrías
él	sabrá	él	sabría
nosotros	sabremos	nosotros	sabríamos
vosotros	sabréis	vosotros	sabríais
ellos	sabrán	ellos	sabrían

	PRESENT SUBJUNCTIVE		PRETERITE
yo	sepa	yo	supe
tú	sepas	tú	supiste
él	sepa	él	supo
nosotros	sepamos	nosotros	supimos
vosotros	sepáis	vosotros	supisteis
ellos	sepan	ellos	supieron

PAST PARTICIPLE	IMPERATIVE
sabido	sabe
	sabed

GERUND
sabiendo

sacar (to take out)

	PRESENT		IMPERFECT
yo	saco	yo	sacaba
tú	sacas	tú	sacabas
él	saca	él	sacaba
nosotros	sacamos	nosotros	sacábamos
vosotros	sacáis	vosotros	sacabais
ellos	sacan	ellos	sacaban

	FUTURE		CONDITIONAL
yo	sacaré	yo	sacaría
tú	sacarás	tú	sacarías
él	sacará	él	sacaría
nosotros	sacaremos	nosotros	sacaríamos
vosotros	sacaréis	vosotros	sacaríais
ellos	sacarán	ellos	sacarían

	PRESENT SUBJUNCTIVE		PRETERITE
yo	saque	yo	saqué
tú	saques	tú	sacaste
él	saque	él	sacó
nosotros	saquemos	nosotros	sacamos
vosotros	saquéis	vosotros	sacasteis
ellos	saquen	ellos	sacaron

PAST PARTICIPLE
sacado

IMPERATIVE
saca
sacad

GERUND
sacando

salir (to go out)

	PRESENT		IMPERFECT
yo	salgo	yo	salía
tú	sales	tú	salías
él	sale	él	salía
nosotros	salimos	nosotros	salíamos
vosotros	salís	vosotros	salíais
ellos	salen	ellos	salían

	FUTURE		CONDITIONAL
yo	saldré	yo	saldría
tú	saldrás	tú	saldrías
él	saldrá	él	saldría
nosotros	saldremos	nosotros	saldríamos
vosotros	saldréis	vosotros	saldríais
ellos	saldrán	ellos	saldrían

	PRESENT SUBJUNCTIVE		PRETERITE
yo	salga	yo	salí
tú	salgas	tú	saliste
él	salga	él	salió
nosotros	salgamos	nosotros	salimos
vosotros	salgáis	vosotros	salisteis
ellos	salgan	ellos	salieron

PAST PARTICIPLE
salido

IMPERATIVE
sal
salid

GERUND
saliendo

satisfacer (to satisfy)

	PRESENT		IMPERFECT
yo	satisfago	yo	satisfacía
tú	satisfaces	tú	satisfacías
él	satisface	él	satisfacía
nosotros	satisfacemos	nosotros	satisfacíamos
vosotros	satisfacéis	vosotros	satisfacíais
ellos	satisfacen	ellos	satisfacían

	FUTURE		CONDITIONAL
yo	satisfaré	yo	satisfaría
tú	satisfarás	tú	satisfarías
él	satisfará	él	satisfaría
nosotros	satisfaremos	nosotros	satisfaríamos
vosotros	satisfaréis	vosotros	satisfaríais
ellos	satisfarán	ellos	satisfarían

	PRESENT SUBJUNCTIVE		PRETERITE
yo	satisfaga	yo	satisfice
tú	satisfagas	tú	satisficiste
él	satisfaga	él	satisfizo
nosotros	satisfagamos	nosotros	satisficimos
vosotros	satisfagáis	vosotros	satisficisteis
ellos	satisfagan	ellos	satisficieron

PAST PARTICIPLE
satisfecho

IMPERATIVE
satisfaz/satisface
satisfaced

GERUND
satisfaciendo

seguir (to follow)

	PRESENT		IMPERFECT
yo	sigo	yo	seguía
tú	sigues	tú	seguías
él	sigue	él	seguía
nosotros	seguimos	nosotros	seguíamos
vosotros	seguís	vosotros	seguíais
ellos	siguen	ellos	seguían

	FUTURE		CONDITIONAL
yo	seguiré	yo	seguiría
tú	seguirás	tú	seguirías
él	seguirá	él	seguiría
nosotros	seguiremos	nosotros	seguiríamos
vosotros	seguiréis	vosotros	seguiríais
ellos	seguirán	ellos	seguirían

	PRESENT SUBJUNCTIVE		PRETERITE
yo	siga	yo	seguí
tú	sigas	tú	seguiste
él	siga	él	siguió
nosotros	sigamos	nosotros	seguimos
vosotros	sigáis	vosotros	seguisteis
ellos	sigan	ellos	siguieron

PAST PARTICIPLE
seguido

IMPERATIVE
sigue
seguid

GERUND
siguiendo

sentir (to feel)

	PRESENT		IMPERFECT
yo	siento	yo	sentía
tú	sientes	tú	sentías
él	siente	él	sentía
nosotros	sentimos	nosotros	sentíamos
vosotros	sentís	vosotros	sentíais
ellos	sienten	ellos	sentían

	FUTURE		CONDITIONAL
yo	sentiré	yo	sentiría
tú	sentirás	tú	sentirías
él	sentirá	él	sentiría
nosotros	sentiremos	nosotros	sentiríamos
vosotros	sentiréis	vosotros	sentiríais
ellos	sentirán	ellos	sentirían

	PRESENT SUBJUNCTIVE		PRETERITE
yo	sienta	yo	sentí
tú	sientas	tú	sentiste
él	sienta	él	sintió
nosotros	sintamos	nosotros	sentimos
vosotros	sintáis	vosotros	sentisteis
ellos	sientan	ellos	sintieron

PAST PARTICIPLE
sentido

IMPERATIVE
siente
sentid

GERUND
sintiendo

ser (to be)

	PRESENT		IMPERFECT
yo	soy	yo	era
tú	eres	tú	eras
él	es	él	era
nosotros	somos	nosotros	éramos
vosotros	sois	vosotros	erais
ellos	son	ellos	eran

	FUTURE		CONDITIONAL
yo	seré	yo	sería
tú	serás	tú	serías
él	será	él	sería
nosotros	seremos	nosotros	seríamos
vosotros	seréis	vosotros	seríais
ellos	serán	ellos	serían

	PRESENT SUBJUNCTIVE		PRETERITE
yo	sea	yo	fui
tú	seas	tú	fuiste
él	sea	él	fue
nosotros	seamos	nosotros	fuimos
vosotros	seáis	vosotros	fuisteis
ellos	sean	ellos	fueron

PAST PARTICIPLE	IMPERATIVE
sido	sé
	sed

GERUND

siendo

tener (to have)

	PRESENT		IMPERFECT
yo	**tengo**	yo	tenía
tú	**tienes**	tú	tenías
él	**tiene**	él	tenía
nosotros	ten**emos**	nosotros	teníamos
vosotros	ten**éis**	vosotros	teníais
ellos	**tienen**	ellos	tenían

	FUTURE		CONDITIONAL
yo	**tendré**	yo	**tendría**
tú	**tendrás**	tú	**tendrías**
él	**tendrá**	él	**tendría**
nosotros	**tendremos**	nosotros	**tendríamos**
vosotros	**tendréis**	vosotros	**tendríais**
ellos	**tendrán**	ellos	**tendrían**

	PRESENT SUBJUNCTIVE		PRETERITE
yo	**tenga**	yo	**tuve**
tú	**tengas**	tú	**tuviste**
él	**tenga**	él	**tuvo**
nosotros	**tengamos**	nosotros	**tuvimos**
vosotros	**tengáis**	vosotros	**tuvisteis**
ellos	**tengan**	ellos	**tuvieron**

PAST PARTICIPLE	IMPERATIVE
ten**ido**	**ten**
	tene**d**

GERUND

ten**iendo**

torcer (to twist)

	PRESENT		**IMPERFECT**
yo	**tuerzo**	yo	torcía
tú	**tuerces**	tú	torcías
él	**tuerce**	él	torcía
nosotros	torc**emos**	nosotros	torcíamos
vosotros	torc**éis**	vosotros	torcíais
ellos	**tuercen**	ellos	torcían

	FUTURE		**CONDITIONAL**
yo	torcer**é**	yo	torcería
tú	torcer**ás**	tú	torcerías
él	torcer**á**	él	torcería
nosotros	torcer**emos**	nosotros	torceríamos
vosotros	torcer**éis**	vosotros	torceríais
ellos	torcer**án**	ellos	torcerían

	PRESENT SUBJUNCTIVE		**PRETERITE**
yo	**tuerza**	yo	torc**í**
tú	**tuerzas**	tú	torc**iste**
él	**tuerza**	él	torc**ió**
nosotros	**torzamos**	nosotros	torc**imos**
vosotros	**torzáis**	vosotros	torc**isteis**
ellos	**tuerzan**	ellos	torc**ieron**

PAST PARTICIPLE
torc**ido**

IMPERATIVE
tuerce
torc**ed**

GERUND
torc**iendo**

traer (to bring)

	PRESENT		IMPERFECT
yo	traigo	yo	traía
tú	traes	tú	traías
él	trae	él	traía
nosotros	traemos	nosotros	traíamos
vosotros	traéis	vosotros	traíais
ellos	traen	ellos	traían

	FUTURE		CONDITIONAL
yo	traeré	yo	traería
tú	traerás	tú	traerías
él	traerá	él	traería
nosotros	traeremos	nosotros	traeríamos
vosotros	traeréis	vosotros	traeríais
ellos	traerán	ellos	traerían

	PRESENT SUBJUNCTIVE		PRETERITE
yo	traiga	yo	traje
tú	traigas	tú	trajiste
él	traiga	él	trajo
nosotros	traigamos	nosotros	trajimos
vosotros	traigáis	vosotros	trajisteis
ellos	traigan	ellos	trajeron

PAST PARTICIPLE
traído

IMPERATIVE
trae
traed

GERUND
trayendo

valer (to be worth)

	PRESENT		IMPERFECT
yo	valgo	yo	valía
tú	vales	tú	valías
él	vale	él	valía
nosotros	valemos	nosotros	valíamos
vosotros	valéis	vosotros	valíais
ellos	valen	ellos	valían

	FUTURE		CONDITIONAL
yo	valdré	yo	valdría
tú	valdrás	tú	valdrías
él	valdrá	él	valdría
nosotros	valdremos	nosotros	valdríamos
vosotros	valdréis	vosotros	valdríais
ellos	valdrán	ellos	valdrían

	PRESENT SUBJUNCTIVE		PRETERITE
yo	valga	yo	valí
tú	valgas	tú	valiste
él	valga	él	valió
nosotros	valgamos	nosotros	valimos
vosotros	valgáis	vosotros	valisteis
ellos	valgan	ellos	valieron

PAST PARTICIPLE	IMPERATIVE
valido	vale
	valed

GERUND

valiendo

vencer (to win)

	PRESENT		IMPERFECT
yo	**venzo**	yo	venc**ía**
tú	venc**es**	tú	venc**ías**
él	venc**e**	él	venc**ía**
nosotros	venc**emos**	nosotros	venc**íamos**
vosotros	venc**éis**	vosotros	venc**íais**
ellos	venc**en**	ellos	venc**ían**

	FUTURE		CONDITIONAL
yo	vencer**é**	yo	vencer**ía**
tú	vencer**ás**	tú	vencer**ías**
él	vencer**á**	él	vencer**ía**
nosotros	vencer**emos**	nosotros	vencer**íamos**
vosotros	vencer**éis**	vosotros	vencer**íais**
ellos	vencer**án**	ellos	vencer**ían**

	PRESENT SUBJUNCTIVE		PRETERITE
yo	**venza**	yo	venc**í**
tú	**venzas**	tú	venc**iste**
él	**venza**	él	venc**ió**
nosotros	**venzamos**	nosotros	venc**imos**
vosotros	**venzáis**	vosotros	venc**isteis**
ellos	**venzan**	ellos	venc**ieron**

PAST PARTICIPLE
venc**ido**

IMPERATIVE
venc**e**
venc**ed**

GERUND
venc**iendo**

venir (to come)

	PRESENT		IMPERFECT
yo	vengo	yo	venía
tú	vienes	tú	venías
él	viene	él	venía
nosotros	venimos	nosotros	veníamos
vosotros	venís	vosotros	veníais
ellos	vienen	ellos	venían

	FUTURE		CONDITIONAL
yo	vendré	yo	vendría
tú	vendrás	tú	vendrías
él	vendrá	él	vendría
nosotros	vendremos	nosotros	vendríamos
vosotros	vendréis	vosotros	vendríais
ellos	vendrán	ellos	vendrían

	PRESENT SUBJUNCTIVE		PRETERITE
yo	venga	yo	vine
tú	vengas	tú	viniste
él	venga	él	vino
nosotros	vengamos	nosotros	vinimos
vosotros	vengáis	vosotros	vinisteis
ellos	vengan	ellos	vinieron

PAST PARTICIPLE	IMPERATIVE
venido	ven
	venid

GERUND

viniendo

ver (to see)

	PRESENT		IMPERFECT
yo	**veo**	yo	**veía**
tú	ve**s**	tú	**veías**
él	ve	él	**veía**
nosotros	ve**mos**	nosotros	**veíamos**
vosotros	ve**is**	vosotros	**veíais**
ellos	ve**n**	ellos	**veían**

	FUTURE		CONDITIONAL
yo	ver**é**	yo	ver**ía**
tú	ver**ás**	tú	ver**ías**
él	ver**á**	él	ver**ía**
nosotros	ver**emos**	nosotros	ver**íamos**
vosotros	ver**éis**	vosotros	ver**íais**
ellos	ver**án**	ellos	ver**ían**

	PRESENT SUBJUNCTIVE		PRETERITE
yo	**vea**	yo	v**i**
tú	**veas**	tú	v**iste**
él	**vea**	él	v**io**
nosotros	**veamos**	nosotros	v**imos**
vosotros	**veáis**	vosotros	v**isteis**
ellos	**vean**	ellos	v**ieron**

PAST PARTICIPLE	IMPERATIVE
v**isto**	ve
	ve**d**

GERUND
v**iendo**

volcar (to overturn)

	PRESENT		IMPERFECT
yo	vuelco	yo	volcaba
tú	vuelcas	tú	volcabas
él	vuelca	él	volcaba
nosotros	volcamos	nosotros	volcábamos
vosotros	volcáis	vosotros	volcabais
ellos	vuelcan	ellos	volcaban

	FUTURE		CONDITIONAL
yo	volcaré	yo	volcaría
tú	volcarás	tú	volcarías
él	volcará	él	volcaría
nosotros	volcaremos	nosotros	volcaríamos
vosotros	volcaréis	vosotros	volcaríais
ellos	volcarán	ellos	volcarían

	PRESENT SUBJUNCTIVE		PRETERITE
yo	vuelque	yo	volqué
tú	vuelques	tú	volcaste
él	vuelque	él	volcó
nosotros	volquemos	nosotros	volcamos
vosotros	volquéis	vosotros	volcasteis
ellos	vuelquen	ellos	volcaron

PAST PARTICIPLE	IMPERATIVE
volcado	vuelca
	volcad

GERUND
volcando

volver (to return)

	PRESENT			IMPERFECT
yo	**vuelvo**		yo	volvía
tú	**vuelves**		tú	volvías
él	**vuelve**		él	volvía
nosotros	volv**emos**		nosotros	volvíamos
vosotros	volv**éis**		vosotros	volvíais
ellos	**vuelven**		ellos	volvían

	FUTURE			CONDITIONAL
yo	volver**é**		yo	volvería
tú	volver**ás**		tú	volverías
él	volver**á**		él	volvería
nosotros	volver**emos**		nosotros	volveríamos
vosotros	volver**éis**		vosotros	volveríais
ellos	volver**án**		ellos	volverían

	PRESENT SUBJUNCTIVE			PRETERITE
yo	**vuelva**		yo	volví
tú	**vuelvas**		tú	volviste
él	**vuelva**		él	volvió
nosotros	volv**amos**		nosotros	volvimos
vosotros	volv**áis**		vosotros	volvisteis
ellos	**vuelvan**		ellos	volvieron

PAST PARTICIPLE	IMPERATIVE
vuelto	**vuelve**
	volved

GERUND
volviendo

zurcir (to darn)

	PRESENT		IMPERFECT
yo	zurzo	yo	zurcía
tú	zurces	tú	zurcías
él	zurce	él	zurcía
nosotros	zurcimos	nosotros	zurcíamos
vosotros	zurcís	vosotros	zurcíais
ellos	zurcen	ellos	zurcían

	FUTURE		CONDITIONAL
yo	zurciré	yo	zurciría
tú	zurcirás	tú	zurcirías
él	zurcirá	él	zurciría
nosotros	zurciremos	nosotros	zurciríamos
vosotros	zurciréis	vosotros	zurciríais
ellos	zurcirán	ellos	zurcirían

	PRESENT SUBJUNCTIVE		PRETERITE
yo	zurza	yo	zurcí
tú	zurzas	tú	zurciste
él	zurza	él	zurció
nosotros	zurzamos	nosotros	zurcimos
vosotros	zurzáis	vosotros	zurcisteis
ellos	zurzan	ellos	zurcieron

PAST PARTICIPLE	IMPERATIVE
zurcido	zurce
	zurcid

GERUND
zurciendo

The following pages, 162 to 190, contain an index of all the Spanish verbs in this dictionary cross-referred to the appropriate conjugation model:

- Regular verbs belonging to the first, second and third conjugation are numbered 1, 2 and 3 respectively. For the regular conjugations see pages 6 to 13.

- Irregular verbs are numerically cross-referred to the appropriate model as conjugated on pages 82 to 160. Thus, alzar is cross-referred to page 100 where cruzar, the model for this verb group, is conjugated.

- Verbs which are most commonly used in the reflexive form – e.g. amodorrarse – have been cross-referred to the appropriate non-reflexive model. For the full conjugation of a reflexive verb, see pages 28 to 31.

- Verbs printed in bold – e.g. abrir – are themselves models.

- Superior numbers refer you to notes on page 191 which indicate how the verb differs from its model.

Verb Index

Verb Index

Verb Index

Verb Index

Verb Index

Verb Index

Verb Index

Verb index

Verb Index

freír	114	gotear	1	heredar	1
frenar	1	gozar	100	herir	149
frotar	1	grabar	1	hermanar	1
fruncir	160	graduar	84	herniarse	1
frustrar	1	granar	1	hervir	149
fugarse	1	granizar¹	100	hibernar	1
fulminar	1	granjear	1	hidratar	1
fumar	1	gratificar	145	hilar	1
fumigar	130	gratinar	1	hilvanar	1
funcionar	1	gravar	1	hincar	145
fundamentar	1	gravitar	1	hinchar	1
fundar	1	graznar	1	hipar	1
fundir	3	gritar	1	hipnotizar	100
fungir	103	**gruñir**	115	hipotecar	145
fusilar	1	guadañar	1	hojear	1
fusionar	1	guardar	1	holgar	142
gafar	1	guarecer	99	holgazanear	1
galantear	1	guarnecer	99	hollar	98
galardonar	1	guerrear	1	homologar	130
galopar	1	guiar	109	honrar	1
galvanizar	100	guindar	1	horadar	1
ganar	1	guiñar	1	horripilar	1
garabatear	1	guisar	1	horrorizar	100
garantizar	100	gustar	1	hospedar	1
gastar	1	**haber**	116	hospitalizar	100
gatear	1	habilitar	1	hostigar	130
gemir	131	habitar	1	huir	97
generalizar	100	habituar	84	humanizar	100
generar	1	hablar	1	humedecer	99
germinar	1	**hacer**	117	humillar	1
gesticular	1	hacinar	1	hundir	3
gestionar	1	halagar	130	hurgar	130
gimotear	1	hallar	1	hurgonear	1
girar	1	haraganear	1	hurtar	1
glorificar	145	hartar	1	husmear	1
glosar	1	hastiar	109	idealizar	100
gobernar	132	hechizar	100	idear	1
golear	1	heder	108	identificar	145
golpear	1	helar¹	132	idolatrar	1
gorjear	1	henchir	131	ignorar	1
gorronear	1	hender	108	igualar	1

Verb Index

Verb Index

malvender	2	medicar	145	molestar	1
malversar	1	medir	131	mondar	1
mamar	1	meditar	1	monopolizar	100
manar	1	medrar	1	montar	1
manchar	1	mejorar	1	moralizar	100
mancillar	1	memorizar	100	morar	1
mancomunar	1	mencionar	1	morder	125
mandar	1	mendigar	130	mordisquear	1
manejar	1	menear	1	**morir**	124
mangar	130	menguar	90	mortificar	145
mangonear	1	menoscabar	1	mosquear	1
maniatar	1	menospreciar	1	mostrar	98
manifestar	132	menstruar	84	motivar	1
maniobrar	1	mentalizar	100	**mover**	125
manipular	1	mentar	132	movilizar	100
manosear	1	mentir	149	mudar	1
mantener	151	menudear	1	mugir	103
maquillar	1	merecer	99	multar	1
maquinar	1	merendar	132	multiplicar	145
maravillar	1	mermar	1	murmurar	1
marcar	145	merodear	1	musitar	1
marchar	1	mesarse	1	mutilar	1
marchitar	1	mesurar	1	nacer	126
marear	1	metamorfosear	1	nacionalizar	100
marginar	1	meter	2	nadar	1
mariposear	1	mezclar	1	narcotizar	100
martillear	1	militar	1	narrar	1
martirizar	100	mimar	1	naturalizarse	100
masacrar	1	minar	1	naufragar	130
mascar	145	minimizar	100	navegar	130
mascullar	1	mirar	1	necesitar	1
masticar	145	mitigar	130	**negar**	127
masturbarse	1	modelar	1	negociar	1
matar	1	moderar	1	neutralizar	100
matizar	100	modernizar	100	nevar[1]	132
matricular	1	modificar	145	niquelar	1
maullar	1	mofarse	1	nivelar	1
mear	1	mojar	1	nombrar	1
mecanizar	100	molar	1	nominar	1
mecer	155	moldear	1	normalizar	100
mediar	1	moler	125	notar	1

Verb Index

Notes

The notes below indicate special peculiarities of individual verbs.
When only some forms of a given tense are affected, all these are shown.
When all forms of the tense are affected, only the 1st and 2nd persons are
shown, followed by *etc*.

1 Gerund 2 Past Participle 3 Present 4 Preterite 5 Present Subjunctive
6 Imperfect Subjunctive

1 **acaecer, acontecer, amanecer, anochecer, competer, deshelar,
   escampar, granizar, helar, nevar, nublar, relampaguear, tronar,
   verdear**: used almost exclusively in infinitive and 3rd person singular
2 **asir** 3 asgo 5 asga, asgar *etc*
3 **atañer, -tañer** 1 atañendo 4 atañó: see also 1 above
4 **balbucir** 3 balbuceo 5 balbucee, balbucees *etc*
5 **concernir** 3 concierne, conciernen 5 concierna, conciernan:
   only used in 3rd person
6 **degollar** 3 degüello, degüellas, degüella, degüellan 5 degüelle,
   degüelles, degüellen
7 **delinquir** 3 delinco 5 delinca, delincas *etc*
8 **desasir** 3 desasgo 5 desasga, desasgas *etc*
9 **discernir** 3 discierno, disciernes, discierne, disciernen 5 discierna,
   disciernas, disciernan
10 **enraizar** 3 enraízo, enraízas, enraíza, enraízan 5 enraíce, enraíces,
   enraícen
11 **pudrir** 2 podrido
12 **rehuir** 3 rehúyo, rehúyes, rehúye, rehúyen 5 rehúya, rehúyas,
   rehúyan
13 **roer** 4 royó, royeron 6 royera, royeras *etc*
14 **soler**: used only in present and imperfect indicative
15 **yacer** 3 yazgo *or* yazco *or* yago 5 yazga *etc* or yazca *etc or* yaga *etc*

The Gender of Nouns

In Spanish, all nouns are either masculine or feminine, whether denoting people, animals or things. Gender is largely unpredictable and has to be learnt for each noun. However, the following guidelines will help you determine the gender for certain types of nouns:

Nouns denoting male people and animals are usually – but not always – masculine, e.g.

un hombre a man
un toro a bull
un enfermero a (*male*) nurse
un semental a stallion

Nouns denoting female people and animals are usually – but not always – feminine, e.g.

una niña a girl
una vaca a cow
una enfermera a nurse
una yegua a mare

Some nouns are masculine *or* feminine depending on the sex of the person to whom they refer, e.g.

un camarada a (*male*) comrade
una camarada a (*female*) comrade
un belga a Belgian (*man*)
una belga a Belgian (*woman*)
un marroquí a Moroccan (*man*)
una marroquí a Moroccan (*woman*)

Other nouns referring to either men *or* women have only one gender which applies to both, e.g.

una persona a person
una visita a visitor
una víctima a victim
una estrella a star

Often the ending of a noun indicates its gender. Shown opposite are some of the most important to guide you.

Nouns

Often the ending of the noun indicates its gender. Shown below are some of the most important to guide you:

Masculine endings

-o	un clavo a nail, un plátano a banana EXCEPTIONS: mano hand, foto photograph, moto(cicleta) motorbike
-l	un tonel a barrel, un hotel a hotel EXCEPTIONS: cal lime, cárcel prison, catedral cathedral, col cabbage, miel honey, piel skin, sal salt, señal sign
-r	un tractor a tractor, el altar the altar EXCEPTIONS: coliflor cauliflower, flor flower, labor task
-y	el rey the king, un buey an ox EXCEPTION: ley law

Feminine endings

-a	una casa a house, la cara the face EXCEPTIONS: día day, mapa map, planeta planet, tranvía tram, and most words ending in -ma (tema subject, problema problem, *etc*)
-ión	una canción a song, una procesión a procession EXCEPTIONS: most nouns not ending in -ción or -sión, e.g. avión aeroplane, camión lorry, gorrión sparrow
-dad, -tad, -tud	una ciudad a town, la libertad freedom una multitud a crowd
-ed	una pared a wall, la sed thirst EXCEPTION: césped lawn
-itis	una faringitis pharyngitis, la celulitis cellulitis
-iz	una perdiz a partridge, una matriz a matrix EXCEPTIONS: lápiz pencil, maíz corn, tapiz tapestry
-sis	una tesis a thesis, una dosis a dose EXCEPTIONS: análisis analysis, énfasis emphasis, paréntesis parenthesis
-umbre	la podredumbre rot, la muchedumbre crowd

The Gender of Nouns *continued*

Some nouns change meaning according to gender. The most common are set out below:

	MASCULINE	FEMININE
capital	capital (*money*)	capital (*city*) → ①
clave	harpsichord	clue
cólera	cholera	anger → ②
cometa	comet	kite
corriente	current month	current
corte	cut	court (*royal*) → ③
coma	coma	comma → ④
cura	priest	cure → ⑤
frente	front (*in war*)	forehead → ⑥
guardia	guard(sman)	guard → ⑦
guía	guide (*person*)	guide(book) → ⑧
moral	mulberry tree	morals
orden	order (*arrangement*)	order (*command*) → ⑨
ordenanza	office boy	ordinance
papa	Pope	potato
parte	dispatch	part → ⑩
pendiente	earring	slope
pez	fish	pitch
policía	policeman	police
radio	radius, radium	radio

1. Invirtieron mucho capital — They invested a lot of capital
   La capital es muy fea — The capital city is very ugly

2. Es difícil luchar contra el cólera — Cholera is difficult to combat
   Montó en cólera — He got angry

3. Me encanta tu corte de pelo — I love your haircut
   Se trasladó la corte a Madrid — The court was moved to Madrid

4. Entró en un coma profundo — He went into a deep coma
   Aquí hace falta una coma — You need to put a comma here

5. ¿Quién es? – El cura — Who is it? – The priest
   No tiene cura — It's hopeless

6. Han mandado a su hijo al frente — Her son has been sent to the front
   Tiene la frente muy ancha — She has a very broad forehead

7. Vino un guardia de tráfico — A traffic policeman came
   Están relevando la guardia ahora — They're changing the guard now

8. Nuestro guía nos hizo reír a carcajadas — Our guide had us falling about laughing
   Busco una guía turística — I'm looking for a guidebook

9. Están en orden alfabético — They're in alphabetical order
   No hemos recibido la orden de pago — We haven't had the payment order

10. Le mandó un parte al general — He sent a dispatch to the general
    En alguna parte debe estar — It must be somewhere or other

Gender: the Formation of Feminines

As in English, male and female are sometimes differentiated by the use of two quite separate words, e.g.

mi marido my husband
mi mujer my wife
un toro a bull
una vaca a cow

There are, however, some words in Spanish which show this distinction by the form of their ending:

Nouns ending in -o change to -a to form the feminine → ①

If the masculine singular form already ends in -a, no further -a is added to the feminine → ②

If the last letter of the masculine singular form is a consonant, an -a is normally added in the feminine* → ③

Feminine forms to note

MASCULINE	FEMININE	
el abad	la abadesa	abbot/abbess
un actor	una actriz	actor/actress
el alcalde	la alcaldesa	mayor/mayoress
el conde	la condesa	count/countess
el duque	la duquesa	duke/duchess
el emperador	la emperatriz	emperor/empress
un poeta	una poetisa	poet/poetess
el príncipe	la princesa	prince/princess
el rey	la reina	king/queen
un sacerdote	una sacerdotisa	priest/priestess
un tigre	una tigresa	tiger/tigress
el zar	la zarina	tzar/tzarina

* If the last syllable has an accent, it disappears in the feminine (see page 296) → ④

Examples

1 un amigo a (*male*) friend   una amiga a (*female*) friend
un empleado a (*male*) employee   una empleada a (*female*) employee
un gato a cat   una gata a (*female*) cat

2 un deportista a sportsman   una deportista a sportswoman
un colega a (*male*) colleague   una colega a (*female*) colleague
un camarada a (*male*) comrade   una camarada a (*female*) comrade

3 un español a Spaniard,   una española a Spanish woman
   a Spanish man
un vendedor a salesman   una vendedora a saleswoman
un jugador a (*male*) player   una jugadora a (*female*) player

4 un lapón a Laplander (*man*)   una lapona a Laplander (*woman*)
un león a lion   una leona a lioness
un neocelandés   una neocelandesa
   a New Zealander (*man*)   a New Zealander (*woman*)

The Formation of Plurals

Nouns ending in an unstressed vowel add -s to the singular form → ❶

Nouns ending in a consonant or a stressed vowel add -es to the singular form → ❷

    ⓘ BUT: café coffee shop (*plural*: cafés)
              mamá mummy (*plural*: mamás)
              papá daddy (*plural*: papás)
              pie foot (*plural*: pies)
              sofá sofa (*plural*: sofás)
              té tea (*plural*: tes)

and words of foreign origin ending in a consonant, e.g.:

              coñac brandy (*plural*: coñacs)
              jersey jumper (*plural*: jerseys)

    ⓘ Note:

- nouns ending in -n or -s with an accent on the last syllable drop this accent in the plural (see page 296) → ❸
- nouns ending in -n with the stress on the second-last syllable in the singular add an accent to that syllable in the plural in order to show the correct position for stress (see page 296) → ❹
- nouns ending in -z change this to c in the plural → ❺

Nouns with an unstressed final syllable ending in -s do not change in the plural → ❻

1. la casa **the house**
   el libro **the book**

   las casas **the houses**
   los libros **the books**

2. un rumor **a rumour**
   un jabalí **a boar**

   unos rumores **(some) rumours**
   unos jabalíes **(some) boars**

3. la canción **the song**
   el autobús **the bus**

   las canciones **the songs**
   los autobuses **the buses**

4. un examen **an exam**
   un crimen **a crime**

   unos exámenes **(some) exams**
   unos crímenes **(some) crimes**

5. la luz **the light**

   las luces **the lights**

6. un paraguas **an umbrella**
   la dosis **the dose**
   el lunes **Monday**

   unos paraguas **(some) umbrellas**
   las dosis **the doses**
   los lunes **Mondays**

The Definite Article

	WITH MASC. NOUN	WITH FEM. NOUN	
SING.	el	la	the
PLUR.	los	las	the

The gender and number of the noun determine the form of the article → ❶

> ⓘ Note: However, if the article comes directly before a feminine singular noun which starts with a stressed a- or ha-, the masculine form el is used instead of the feminine la → ❷

For uses of the definite article see page 203.

a + el becomes al → ❸

de + el becomes del → ❹

1. el tren **the train**　　　　　la estación **the station**
   el actor **the actor**　　　　　la actriz **the actress**
   los hoteles **the hotels**　　　las escuelas **the schools**
   los profesores **the teachers**　las mujeres **the women**

2. el agua　　　　　　　　　　　the water
   BUT:
   la misma agua　　　　　　　　the same water

   el hacha　　　　　　　　　　　the axe
   BUT:
   la mejor hacha　　　　　　　　the best axe

3. al cine　　　　　　　　　　　to the cinema
   al empleado　　　　　　　　　to the employee
   al hospital　　　　　　　　　　to the hospital

4. del departamento　　　　　　from/of the department
   del autor　　　　　　　　　　from/of the author
   del presidente　　　　　　　　from/of the president

Uses of the Definite Article

While the definite article is used in much the same way in Spanish as it is in English, its use is more widespread in Spanish. Unlike English the definite article is also used:

> with abstract nouns, except when following certain prepositions → ①
>
> in generalizations, especially with plural or uncountable* nouns → ②
>
> with parts of the body → ③
> 'Ownership' is often indicated by an indirect object pronoun or a reflexive pronoun → ④
>
> with titles/ranks/professions followed by a proper name → ⑤
> EXCEPTIONS: with Don/Doña, San/Santo(a) → ⑥
>
> before nouns of official, academic and religious buildings, and names of meals and games → ⑦
>
> The definite article is *not* used with nouns in apposition unless those nouns are individualized → ⑧

* An uncountable noun is one which cannot be used in the plural or with an indefinite article, e.g. el acero steel; la leche milk.

1

Los precios suben	Prices are rising
El tiempo es oro	Time is money

BUT:

con pasión	with passion
sin esperanza	without hope

2

No me gusta el café	I don't like coffee
Los niños necesitan ser queridos	Children need to be loved

3

Vuelva la cabeza hacia la izquierda	Turn your head to the left
No puedo mover las piernas	I can't move my legs

4

La cabeza me da vueltas	My head is spinning
Lávate las manos	Wash your hands

5

El rey Jorge III	King George III
el capitán Menéndez	Captain Menéndez
el doctor Ochoa	Doctor Ochoa
el señor Ramírez	Mr Ramírez

6

Don Arturo Ruiz	Mr Arturo Ruiz
Santa Teresa	Saint Teresa

7

en la cárcel	in prison
en la universidad	at university
en la iglesia	at church
la cena	dinner
el tenis	tennis
el ajedrez	chess

8

Madrid, capital de España, es la ciudad que ...	Madrid, the capital of Spain, is the city which ...

BUT:

Maria Callas, la famosa cantante de ópera ...	Maria Callas, the famous opera singer ...

The Indefinite Article

	WITH MASC. NOUN	WITH FEM. NOUN	
SING.	un	una	a
PLUR.	unos	unas	some

The indefinite article is used in Spanish largely as it is in English.

BUT:

There is no article when a person's profession is being stated → ①

The article is used, however, when the profession is qualified by an adjective → ②

The article is not used with the following words:

otro	another	→ ③
cierto	certain	→ ④
semejante	such (a)	→ ⑤
tal	such (a)	→ ⑥
cien	a hundred	→ ⑦
mil	a thousand	→ ⑧
sin	without	→ ⑨
qué	what a	→ ⑩

There is no article with a noun in apposition → ⑪. When an abstract noun is qualified by an adjective, the indefinite article is used, but is not translated in English → ⑫

Examples

1. Es profesor — He's a teacher
   Mi madre es enfermera — My mother is a nurse

2. Es un buen médico — He's a good doctor
   Se hizo una escritora célebre — She became a famous writer

3. otro libro — another book

4. cierta calle — a certain street

5. semejante ruido — such a noise

6. tal mentira — such a lie

7. cien soldados — a hundred soldiers

8. mil años — a thousand years

9. sin casa — without a house

10. ¡Qué sorpresa! — What a surprise!

11. Baroja, gran escritor de la Generación del 98 — Baroja, a great writer of the 'Generación del 98'

12. con una gran sabiduría/un valor admirable — with great wisdom/admirable courage
    Dieron pruebas de una sangre fría increíble — They showed incredible coolness
    una película de un mal gusto espantoso — a film in appallingly bad taste

Articles

The Article 'lo'

This is never used with a noun. Instead, it is used in the following ways:

as an intensifier before an adjective or adverb in the construction

lo + adjective/adverb + que → ❶

ⓘ Note: The adjective agrees with the noun it refers to → ❷

With an adjective or participle to form an abstract noun → ❸

In the phrase lo de to refer to a subject of which speaker and listener are already aware. It can often be translated as *the business/affair of/about …* → ❹

In set expressions, the commonest of which are:

a lo mejor	maybe, perhaps	→ ❺
a lo lejos	in the distance	→ ❻
a lo largo de	along, through	→ ❼
por lo menos	at least	→ ❽
por lo tanto	therefore, so	→ ❾
por lo visto	apparently	→ ❿

Examples

1. No sabíamos lo pequeña que era la casa

   We didn't know how small the house was

   Sé lo mucho que te gusta la música

   I know how much you like music

2. No te imaginas lo simpáticos que son

   You can't imagine how nice they are

   Ya sabes lo buenas que son estas manzanas

   You already know how good these apples are

3. Lo bueno de eso es que ...

   The good thing about it is that ...

   Sentimos mucho lo ocurrido

   We are very sorry about what happened

4. Lo de ayer es mejor que lo olvides

   It's better if you forget what happened yesterday

   Lo de tu hermano me preocupa mucho

   The business about your brother worries me very much

5. A lo mejor ha salido

   Perhaps he's gone out

6. A lo lejos se veían unas casas

   Some houses could be seen in the distance

7. A lo largo de su vida

   Throughout his life

   A lo largo de la carretera

   Along the road

8. Hubo por lo menos cincuenta heridos

   At least fifty people were injured

9. No hemos recibido ninguna instrucción al respecto, y por lo tanto no podemos ...

   We have not received any instructions about it, therefore we cannot ...

10. Por lo visto, no viene

    Apparently he's not coming *or:* He's not coming, it seems

Adjectives

Most adjectives agree in number and in gender with the noun or pronoun.

> ⓘ Note that:

- if the adjective refers to two or more singular nouns of the same gender, a plural ending of that gender is required → ❶
- if the adjective refers to two or more singular nouns of different genders, a masculine plural ending is required → ❷

The formation of feminines

Adjectives ending in -o change to -a → ❸

Some groups of adjectives add -a:
- adjectives of nationality or geographical origin → ❹
- adjectives ending in -or (except irregular comparatives: see page 214), -án, -ón, -ín → ❺

> ⓘ Note: When there is an accent on the last syllable, it disappears in the feminine (see page 296).

Other adjectives do not change → ❻

The formation of plurals

Adjectives ending in an unstressed vowel add -s → ❼

Adjectives ending in a stressed vowel or a consonant add -es → ❽

> ⓘ Note:

- if there is an accent on the last syllable of a word ending in a consonant, it will disappear in the plural (see page 296) → ❾
- if the last letter is a z it will become a c in the plural → ❿

1 la lengua y la literatura
     españolas

(the) Spanish language and
     literature

2 Nunca había visto árboles y
     flores tan raros

I had never seen such strange
     trees and flowers

3 mi hermano pequeño
     mi hermana pequeña

my little brother
my little sister

4 un chico español
     una chica española
     el equipo barcelonés
     la vida barcelonesa

a Spanish boy
a Spanish girl
the team from Barcelona
the Barcelona way of life

5 un niño encantador
     una niña encantadora
     un hombre holgazán
     una mujer holgazana
     un gesto burlón
     una sonrisa burlona
     un chico cantarín
     una chica cantarina

a charming little boy
a charming little girl
an idle man
an idle woman
a mocking gesture
a mocking smile
a boy fond of singing
a girl fond of singing

6 un final feliz
     una infancia feliz
     mi amigo belga
     mi amiga belga
     el vestido verde
     la blusa verde

a happy ending
a happy childhood
my Belgian (*male*) friend
my Belgian (*female*) friend
the green dress
the green blouse

7 el último tren
     los últimos trenes
     una casa vieja
     unas casas viejas

the last train
the last trains
an old house
(some) old houses

8 un médico iraní
     unos médicos iraníes
     un examen fácil
     unos exámenes fáciles

an Iranian doctor
(some) Iranian doctors
an easy exam
(some) easy exams

9 un río francés
     unos ríos franceses

a French river
(some) French rivers

10 un día feliz
      unos días felices

a happy day
 (some) happy days

Adjectives

Invariable Adjectives

Some adjectives and other parts of speech when used adjectivally never change in the feminine or plural.

The commonest of these are:
- nouns denoting colour → ①
- compound adjectives → ②
- nouns used as adjectives → ③

Shortening of adjectives

The following drop the final -o before a masculine singular noun:

bueno good → ④
malo bad
alguno* some → ⑤
ninguno* none
uno one → ⑥
primero first → ⑦
tercero third
postrero last → ⑧

* ⓘ Note: An accent is required to show the correct position for stress.

Grande *big*, *great* is usually shortened to **gran** before a masculine *or* feminine singular noun → ⑨

Santo *Saint* changes to **San** except with saints' names beginning with **Do-** *or* **To-** → ⑩

Ciento *a hundred* is shortened to **cien** before a masculine *or* feminine plural noun → ⑪

Cualquiera drops the final -a before a masculine *or* feminine singular noun → ⑫

①	los vestidos naranja	the orange dresses
②	las chaquetas azul marino	the navy blue jackets
③	bebés probeta	test-tube babies
	mujeres soldado	women soldiers
④	un buen libro	a good book
⑤	algún libro	some book
⑥	cuarenta y un años	forty-one years
⑦	el primer hijo	the first child
⑧	un postrer deseo	a last wish
⑨	un gran actor	a great actor
	una gran decepción	a great disappointment
⑩	San Antonio	Saint Anthony
	Santo Tomás	Saint Thomas
⑪	cien años	a hundred years
	cien millones	a hundred million
⑫	cualquier día	any day
	a cualquier hora	any time

Comparatives and Superlatives

Comparatives

These are formed using the following constructions:

> más ... (que) more ... (than) → ①
> menos ... (que) less ... (than) → ②
> tanto ... como as ... as → ③
> tan ... como as ... as → ④
> tan ... que so ... that → ⑤
> demasiado ... ⌉ too ... ⌉
> bastante ... ⎟ para enough ... ⎟ to → ⑥
> suficiente ... ⌋ enough ... ⌋

'Than' followed by a clause is translated by de lo que → ⑦

Superlatives

These are formed using the following constructions:

> el/la/los/las más ... (que) the most ... (that) → ⑧
> el/la/los/las menos ... (que) the least ... (that) → ⑨

> After a superlative the preposition de is often translated as 'in' → ⑩

> The absolute superlative (*very, most, extremely + adjective*) is expressed in Spanish by muy + adjective, or by adding -ísimo/a/os/as to the adjective when it ends in a consonant, or to its stem (adjective minus final vowel) when it ends in a vowel → ⑪

> ⓘ Note: It is sometimes necessary to change the spelling of the adjective when -ísimo is added, in order to maintain the same sound (see page 300) → ⑫

Examples

1   una razón más seria   a more serious reason
     Es más alto que mi hermano   He's taller than my brother

2   una película menos conocida   a less well known film
     Luis es menos tímido que tú   Luis is less shy than you

3   Pablo tenía tanto miedo como yo   Pablo was as frightened as I was

4   No es tan grande como creía   It isn't as big as I thought

5   El examen era tan difícil que   The exam was so difficult that
       nadie aprobó   nobody passed

6   No tengo suficiente dinero para   I haven't got enough money to
       comprarlo   buy it

7   Está más cansada de lo que parece   She is more tired than she seems

8   el caballo más veloz   the fastest horse
     la casa más pequeña   the smallest house
     los días más lluviosos   the wettest days
     las manzanas más maduras   the ripest apples

9   el hombre menos simpático   the least likeable man
     la niña menos habladora   the least talkative girl
     los cuadros menos bonitos   the least attractive paintings
     las camisas menos viejas   the least old shirts

10   la estación más ruidosa de Londres   the noisiest station in London

11   Este libro es muy interesante   This book is very interesting

12   Tienen un coche rapidísimo   They have an extremely fast car
     Era facilísimo de hacer   It was very easy to make
     Mi tío era muy rico   My uncle was very rich
     Se hizo riquísimo   He became extremely rich
     un león muy feroz   a very ferocious lion
     un tigre ferocísimo   an extremely ferocious tiger

Comparatives and Superlatives *continued*

Adjectives with irregular comparatives/superlatives

ADJECTIVE	COMPARATIVE	SUPERLATIVE
bueno	mejor	el mejor
good	better	the best
malo	peor	el peor
bad	worse	the worst
grande	mayor *or* más grande	el más grande
big	bigger; older	the biggest; the oldest
pequeño	menor *or* más pequeño	el más pequeño
small	smaller; younger;	the smallest; the youngest;
	lesser	the least

The irregular comparative and superlative forms of grande and pequeño are used mainly to express:
- age, in which case they come after the noun → ❶
- abstract size and degrees of importance, in which case they come before the noun → ❷

The regular forms are used mainly to express physical size → ❸

Irregular comparatives and superlatives have one form for both masculine and feminine, but always agree in number with the noun → ❶

Examples

1 mis hermanos mayores — my older brothers
la hija menor — the youngest daughter

2 el menor ruido — the slightest sound
las mayores dificultades — the biggest difficulties

3 Este plato es más grande que aquél — This plate is bigger than that one
Mi casa es más pequeña que la tuya — My house is smaller than yours

Demonstrative Adjectives

	MASCULINE	FEMININE	
SING.	este	esta	this
	ese	esa	that
	aquel	aquella	
PLUR.	estos	estas	these
	esos	esas	those
	aquellos	aquellas	

Demonstrative adjectives normally precede the noun and always agree in number and in gender → ①

The forms ese/a/os/as are used:
- to indicate distance from the speaker but proximity to the person addressed → ②
- to indicate a not too remote distance → ③

The forms aquel/la/los/las are used to indicate distance, in space or time → ④

1 Este bolígrafo no escribe — This pen is not working

Esa revista es muy mala — That is a very bad magazine

Aquella montaña es muy alta — That mountain (over there) is very high

¿Conoces a esos señores? — Do you know those gentlemen?

Siga Vd hasta aquellos edificios — Carry on until you come to those buildings

¿Ves aquellas personas? — Can you see those people (over there)?

2 Ese papel en donde escribes ... — That paper you are writing on ...

3 No me gustan esos cuadros — I don't like those pictures

4 Aquella calle parece muy ancha — That street (over there) looks very wide

Aquellos años sí que fueron felices — Those were really happy years

Interrogative Adjectives

	MASCULINE	FEMININE	
SING.	¿qué?	¿qué?	what?, which?
	¿cuánto?	¿cuánta?	how much?, how many?
PLUR.	¿qué?	¿qué?	what?, which?
	¿cuántos?	¿cuántas?	how much?, how many?

Interrogative adjectives, when not invariable, agree in number and gender with the noun →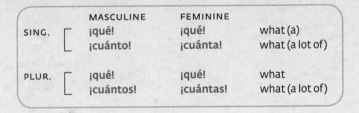

The forms shown above are also used in indirect questions → ❷

Exclamatory Adjectives

	MASCULINE	FEMININE	
SING.	¡qué!	¡qué!	what (a)
	¡cuánto!	¡cuánta!	what (a lot of)
PLUR.	¡qué!	¡qué!	what
	¡cuántos!	¡cuántas!	what (a lot of)

Exclamatory adjectives, when not invariable, agree in number and gender with the noun → ❸

1 ¿Qué libro te gustó más? — Which book did you like most?
¿Qué clase de hombre es? — What type of man is he?
¿Qué instrumentos toca Vd? — What instruments do you play?
¿Qué ofertas ha recibido Vd? — What offers have you received?
¿Cuánto dinero te queda? — How much money have you got left?

¿Cuánta lluvia ha caído? — How much rain have we had?
¿Cuántos vestidos quieres comprar? — How many dresses do you want to buy?
¿Cuántas personas van a venir? — How many people are coming?

2 No sé a qué hora llegó — I don't know at what time she arrived

Dígame cuántas postales quiere — Tell me how many postcards you'd like

3 ¡Qué pena! — What a pity!
¡Qué tiempo tan/más malo! — What lousy weather!
¡Cuánto tiempo! — What a long time!
¡Cuánta pobreza! — What poverty!
¡Cuántos autobuses! — What a lot of buses!
¡Cuántas mentiras! — What a lot of lies!

Possessive Adjectives

Weak forms

WITH SING. NOUN		WITH PLUR. NOUN		
MASC.	FEM.	MASC.	FEM.	
mi	mi	mis	mis	my
tu	tu	tus	tus	your
su	su	sus	sus	his; her; its; your (of Vd)
nuestro	nuestra	nuestros	nuestras	our
vuestro	vuestra	vuestros	vuestras	your
su	su	sus	sus	their; your (of Vds)

All possessive adjectives agree in number and (when applicable) in gender with the noun, not with the owner → ❶
The weak forms always precede the noun → ❶

Since the form su(s) can mean his, her, your (of Vd, Vds) or their, clarification is often needed. This is done by adding de él, de ella, de Vds etc to the noun, and usually (but not always) changing the possessive to a definite article → ❷

Examples

1 Pilar no ha traído nuestros libros — Pilar hasn't brought our books

Antonio irá a vuestra casa — Antonio will go to your house

¿Han vendido su coche tus vecinos? — Have your neighbours sold their car?

Mi hermano y tu primo no se llevan bien — My brother and your cousin don't get on

2 su casa → la casa de él — his house

sus amigos → los amigos de Vd — your friends

sus coches → los coches de ellos — their cars

su abrigo → el abrigo de ella — her coat

Possessive Adjectives *continued*

Strong forms

WITH SING. NOUN		WITH PLUR. NOUN		
MASC.	FEM.	MASC.	FEM.	
mío	mía	míos	mías	my
tuyo	tuya	tuyos	tuyas	your
suyo	suya	suyos	suyas	his; her; its; your (of Vd)
nuestro	nuestra	nuestros	nuestras	our
vuestro	vuestra	vuestros	vuestras	your
suyo	suya	suyos	suyas	their; your (of Vds)

The strong forms agree in the same way as the weak forms (see page 220)

The strong forms always follow the noun, and they are used:
- to translate the English *of mine*, *of yours*, etc → ❶
- to address people → ❷

Examples

1 Es un capricho suyo   It's a whim of hers
       un amigo nuestro   a friend of ours
       una revista tuya   a magazine of yours

2 Muy señor mío **(in letters)**   Dear Sir
       hija mía   my daughter
       ¡Dios mío!   My God!
       Amor mío   Darling/My love

Indefinite Adjectives

alguno(a)s	some
ambos(as)	both
cada	each; every
cierto(a)s	certain; definite
cualquiera plural cualesquiera	some; any
los (las) demás	the others; the remainder
mismo(a)s	same; -self
mucho(a)s	many; much
ningún, ninguna plural ningunos, ningunas	any; no
otro(a)s	other; another
poco(a)s	few; little
tal(es)	such (a)
tanto(a)s	so much; so many
todo(a)s	all; every
varios(as)	several; various

Unless invariable, all indefinite adjectives agree in number and gender with the noun → ❶

alguno
Before a masculine singular noun, this drops the final -o and adds an accent to show the correct position for stress → ❷ (see also page 296)

ambos
This is usually only used in written Spanish. The spoken language prefers the form los dos/las dos → ❸

cierto and mismo
These change their meaning according to their position in relation to the noun (see also Position of Adjectives, page 228) → ❹

cualquiera
This drops the final -a before a masculine or feminine noun → ❺

1 el mismo día   the same day
   las mismas películas   the same films
   mucha/poca gente   many/few people
   mucho/poco dinero   much/little money

2 algún día   some day
   alguna razón   some reason

3 Me gustan los dos cuadros   I like both pictures
   ¿Conoces a las dos enfermeras?   Do you know both nurses?

4 cierto tiempo   a certain time
   BUT:
   éxito cierto   sure success
   el mismo color   the same colour
   BUT:
   en la iglesia misma   in the church itself

5 cualquier casa   any house
   BUT:
   una revista cualquiera   any magazine

Indefinite Adjectives *continued*

ningún is only used in negative sentences or phrases → ①

otro is never preceded by an indefinite article → ②

tal is never followed by an indefinite article → ③

todo can be followed by a definite article, a demonstrative or possessive adjective or a place name → ④

> EXCEPTIONS:
> - when **todo** in the singular means any, every, or each → ⑤
> - in some set expressions → ⑥

\

1 No es ninguna tonta   She's no fool
  ¿No tienes parientes?   Haven't you any relatives?
  — No, ninguno   — No, none

2 ¿Me das otra manzana?   Will you give me another apple?
  Prefiero estos otros zapatos   I prefer these other shoes

3 Nunca dije tal cosa   I never said such a thing

4 Estudian durante toda la noche   They study all night
  Ha llovido toda esta semana   It has rained all this week
  Pondré en orden todos mis libros   I'll sort out all my books
  Lo sabe todo Madrid   All Madrid knows it

5 Podrá entrar toda persona que   Any person who wishes to enter
    lo desee   may do so
  BUT:
  Vienen todos los días   They come every day

6 de todos modos   anyway
  a toda velocidad   at full/top speed
  por todas partes ⎤
  por todos lados
  a/en todas partes   everywhere
  a/en todos lados ⎦

Position of Adjectives

Spanish adjectives usually follow the noun → ① , ②

Note that when used figuratively or to express a quality already inherent in the noun, adjectives can precede the noun → ③

As in English, demonstrative, possessive (weak forms), numerical, interrogative and exclamatory adjectives precede the noun → ④

Indefinite adjectives also usually precede the noun → ⑤

ⓘ Note: **alguno** *some* in negative expressions follows the noun → ⑥

Some adjectives can precede or follow the noun, but their meaning varies according to their position:

	BEFORE NOUN	AFTER NOUN
antiguo	former	old, ancient → ⑦
diferente	various	different → ⑧
grande	great	big → ⑨
medio	half	average → ⑩
mismo	same	-self, very/precisely → ⑪
nuevo	new, another, fresh	brand new → ⑫
pobre	poor (wretched)	poor (not rich) → ⑬
puro	sheer, mere	pure (clear) → ⑭
varios	**several**	various, different → ⑮
viejo	old (long known, etc)	old (aged) → ⑯

Adjectives following the noun are linked by y → ⑰

Examples

1. la página siguiente — the following page
   la hora exacta — the right time

2. una corbata azul — a blue tie
   una palabra española — a Spanish word

3. un dulce sueño — a sweet dream
   un terrible desastre — a terrible disaster
   (all disasters are terrible)

4. este sombrero — this hat
   mi padre — my father
   ¿qué hombre? — what man?

5. cada día — every day
   otra vez — another time
   poco dinero — little money

6. sin duda alguna — without any doubt

7. un antiguo colega — a former colleague
   la historia antigua — ancient history

8. diferentes capítulos — various chapters
   personas diferentes — different people

9. un gran pintor — a great painter
   una casa grande — a big house

10. medio melón — half a melon
    velocidad media — average speed

11. la misma respuesta — the same answer
    yo mismo — myself
    eso mismo — precisely that

12. mi nuevo coche — my new car
    unos zapatos nuevos — (some) brand new shoes

13. esa pobre mujer — that poor woman
    un país pobre — a poor country

14. la pura verdad — the plain truth
    aire puro — fresh air

15. varios caminos — several ways/paths
    artículos varios — various items

16. un viejo amigo — an old friend
    esas toallas viejas — those old towels

17. una acción cobarde y falsa — a cowardly, deceitful act

Personal Pronouns

SUBJECT PRONOUNS			
	SINGULAR	PLURAL	
1st person	yo I	nosotros we	*(masc./masc. + fem.)*
		nosotras we	*(all fem.)*
2nd person	tú you	vosotros you	*(masc./masc. + fem.)*
		vosotras you	*(all fem.)*
3rd person	él he; it	ellos they	*(masc./masc. + fem.)*
	ella she; it	ellas they	*(all fem.)*
	usted (Vd) you	ustedes (Vds) you	

Subject pronouns have a limited usage in Spanish. Normally they are only used:
- for emphasis → ❶
- for clarity → ❷

BUT: **Vd** and **Vds** should always be used for politeness, whether they are otherwise needed or not → ❸

It as subject and *they*, referring to things, are never translated into Spanish → ❹

tú/usted
As a general rule, you should use **tú** (or **vosotros**, if plural) when addressing a friend, a child, a relative, someone you know well, or when invited to do so. In all other cases, use **usted** (or **ustedes**).

nosotros/as; vosotros/as; él/ella; ellos/ellas
All these forms reflect the number and gender of the noun(s) they replace. **Nosotros**, **vosotros** and **ellos** also replace a combination of masculine and feminine nouns.

Examples

1 Ellos sí que llegaron tarde
    They really did arrive late

    Tú no tienes por qué venir
    There is no reason for you to come

    Ella jamás creería eso
    She would never believe that

2 Yo estudio español pero él estudia francés
    I study Spanish but he studies French

    Ella era muy deportista pero él prefería jugar a las cartas
    She was a sporty type but he preferred to play cards

    Vosotros saldréis primero y nosotros os seguiremos
    You leave first and we will follow you

3 Pase Vd por aquí
    Please come this way

    ¿Habían estado Vds antes en esta ciudad?
    Had you been to this town before?

4 ¿Qué es? — Es una sorpresa
    What is it? — It's a surprise

    ¿Qué son? — Son abrelatas
    What are they? — They are tin-openers

Personal Pronouns *continued*

	DIRECT OBJECT PRONOUNS	
	SINGULAR	PLURAL
1st person	me me	nos us
2nd person	te you	os you
3rd person (*masc.*)	lo him; it; you (of Vd)	los them; you (of Vds)
(*fem.*)	la her; it; you (of Vd)	las them; you (of Vds)

lo sometimes functions as a 'neuter' pronoun, referring to an idea or information contained in a previous statement or question. It is often not translated → ①

Position of direct object pronouns

In constructions other than the imperative affirmative, infinitive or gerund, the pronoun always comes before the verb → ②

In the imperative affirmative, infinitive and gerund, the pronoun follows the verb and is attached to it. An accent is needed in certain cases to show the correct position for stress (see also page 296) → ③

Where an infinitive or gerund depends on a previous verb, the pronoun may be used either after the infinitive or gerund, or before the main verb → ④

ⓘ Note: see how this applies to reflexive verbs → ④

For further information, see Order of Object Pronouns, page 236.

Reflexive Pronouns

These are dealt with under reflexive verbs, page 24.

Examples

❶ ¿Va a venir María? — No lo sé   Is Maria coming? — I don't know

Hay que regar las plantas   The plants need watering
    — Yo lo haré   — I'll do it

Habían comido ya pero no nos   They had already eaten, but they
    lo dijeron   didn't tell us

Yo conduzco de prisa pero él lo   I drive fast but he drives slowly
    hace despacio

❷ Te quiero   I love you

¿Las ve Vd?   Can you see them?

¿No me oyen Vds?   Can't you hear me?

Tu hija no nos conoce   Your daughter doesn't know us

No los toques   Don't touch them

❸ Ayúdame   Help me

Acompáñenos   Come with us

Quiero decirte algo   I want to tell you something

Estaban persiguiéndonos   They were coming after us

❹ Lo está comiendo *or*   She is eating it
Está comiéndolo

Nos vienen a ver *or*   They are coming to see us
Vienen a vernos

No quería levantarse *or*   He didn't want to get up
No se quería levantar

Estoy afeitándome *or*   I'm shaving
Me estoy afeitando

Personal Pronouns *continued*

	INDIRECT OBJECT PRONOUNS	
	SINGULAR	PLURAL
1st person	me	nos
2nd person	te	os
3rd person	le	les

The pronouns shown in the above table replace the preposition a + noun → ❶

Position of indirect object pronouns

In constructions other than the imperative affirmative, the infinitive or the gerund, the pronoun comes before the verb → ❷

> In the imperative affirmative, infinitive and gerund, the pronoun follows the verb and is attached to it. An accent is needed in certain cases to show the correct position for stress (see also page 296) → ❸

Where an infinitive or gerund depends on a previous verb, the pronoun may be used either after the infinitive or gerund, or before the main verb → ❹

For further information, see Order of Object Pronouns, page 236.

Reflexive Pronouns

These are dealt with under reflexive verbs, page 24.

① Estoy escribiendo a Teresa I am writing to Teresa
 Le estoy escribiendo   I am writing to her
 Da de comer al gato   Give the cat some food
 Dale de comer   Give it some food

② Sofía os ha escrito   Sofía has written to you
 ¿Os ha escrito Sofía?   Has Sofía written to you?
 Carlos no nos habla   Carlos doesn't speak to us
 ¿Qué te pedían?   What were they asking you for?
 No les haga caso Vd   Don't take any notice of them

③ Respóndame Vd   Answer me
 Díganos Vd la respuesta Tell us the answer
 No quería darte la noticia I didn't want to tell you the news
  todavía   yet
 Llegaron diciéndome que ... They came telling me that ...

④ Estoy escribiéndole *or* I am writing to him/her
 Le estoy escribiendo
 Les voy a hablar *or*   I'm going to talk to them
 Voy a hablarles

Personal Pronouns *continued*

Order of object pronouns

When two object pronouns of different persons are combined, the order is: indirect before direct, i.e.

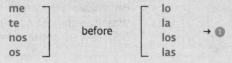

> ⓘ Note: When two 3rd person object pronouns are combined, the first (i.e. the indirect object pronoun) becomes se → ②

Points to note on object pronouns

As le/les can refer to either gender, and se to either gender, singular or plural, sometimes clarification is needed. This is done by adding a él *to him*, a ella *to her*, a Vd *to you* etc to the phrase, usually after the verb → ③

When a noun object precedes the verb, the corresponding object pronoun must be used too → ④

Indirect object pronouns are often used instead of possessive adjectives with parts of the body or clothing to indicate 'ownership', and also in certain common constructions involving reflexive verbs (see also The Indefinite Article, page 202) → ⑤

Le and les are often used in Spanish instead of lo and los when referring to people. Equally la is sometimes used instead of le when referring to a feminine person or animal, although this usage is considered incorrect by some speakers of Spanish → ⑥

Examples

1 Paloma os lo mandará mañana

Paloma is sending it to you tomorrow

¿Te los ha enseñado mi hermana?

Has my sister shown them to you?

No me lo digas

Don't tell me (that)

Todos estaban pidiéndotelo

They were all asking you for it

No quiere prestárnosla

He won't lend it to us

2 Se lo di ayer

I gave it to him/her/them yesterday

3 Le escriben mucho a ella

They write to her often

Se lo van a mandar pronto a ellos

They will be sending it to them soon

4 A tu hermano lo conozco bien

I know your brother well

A María la vemos algunas veces

We sometimes see Maria

5 La chaqueta le estaba ancha

His jacket was too loose

Me duele el tobillo

My ankle is aching

Se me ha perdido el bolígrafo

I have lost my pen

6 Le/lo encontraron en el cine

They met him at the cinema

Les/los oímos llegar

We heard them coming

Le/la escribimos una carta

We wrote a letter to her

Personal Pronouns *continued*

Pronouns after prepositions

These are the same as the subject pronouns, except for the forms
mí me, ti you (*singular*), and the reflexive sí himself, herself, themselves,
yourselves → ①

Con with combines with mí, ti and sí to form

conmigo	with me → ②
contigo	with you
consigo	with himself/herself *etc*

The following prepositions always take a subject pronoun:

entre	between, among → ③
hasta incluso	} even, including → ④
salvo menos	} except → ⑤
según	according to → ⑥

These pronouns are used for emphasis, especially where contrast is
involved → ⑦

Ello it, that is used after a preposition when referring to an idea already
mentioned, but never to a concrete noun → ⑦

A él, de él never contract → ⑨

① Pienso en ti — I think about you
¿Son para mí? — Are they for me?
Es para ella — This is for her
Iban hacia ellos — They were going towards them
Volveréis sin nosotros — You'll come back without us
Volaban sobre vosotros — They were flying above you
Hablaba para sí — He was talking to himself

② Venid conmigo — Come with me
Lo trajeron consigo — They brought it/him with them
BUT:
¿Hablaron con vosotros? — Did they talk to you?

③ entre tú y ella — between you and her

④ Hasta yo puedo hacerlo — Even I can do it

⑤ todos menos yo — everybody except me

⑥ según tú — according to you

⑦ ¿A ti no te escriben? — Don't they write to you?
Me lo manda a mí, no a ti — She is sending it to me, not to you

⑧ Nunca pensaba en ello — He never thought about it
Por todo ello me parece que … — For all those reasons it seems to me that …

⑨ A él no lo conozco — I don't know him
No he sabido nada de él — I haven't heard from him

Indefinite Pronouns

algo	something, anything → ①
alguien	somebody, anybody → ②
alguno/a/os/as	some, a few → ③
cada uno/a	each (one) → ④
	everybody
cualquiera	anybody; any → ⑤
los/las demás	the others
	the rest → ⑥
mucho/a/os/as	many; much → ⑦
nada	nothing → ⑧
nadie	nobody → ⑨
ninguno/a	none, not any → ⑩
poco/a/os/as	few; little → ⑪
tanto/a/os/as	so much; so many → ⑫
todo/a/os/as	all; everything → ⑬
uno ... (el) otro	(the) one ... the other
una ... (la) otra	
unos ... (los) otros	→ ⑭
unas ... (las) otras	some ... (the) others
varios/as	several → ⑮

algo, alguien, alguno

They can never be used after a negative. The appropriate negative
pronouns are used instead: nada, nadie, ninguno (see also negatives,
page 276) → ⑯

Examples

1. Tengo algo para ti
   ¿Viste algo?

   I have something for you
   Did you see anything?

2. Alguien me lo ha dicho
   ¿Has visto a alguien?

   Somebody said it to me
   Have you seen anybody?

3. Algunos de los niños ya sabían
   leer

   Some of the children could read
   already

4. Le dio una manzana a cada uno
   ¡Cada uno a su casa!

   She gave each of them an apple
   Everybody go home!

5. Cualquiera puede hacerlo
   Cualquiera de las explicaciones
   vale

   Anybody can do it
   Any of the explanations is a valid
   one

6. Yo me fui, los demás se quedaron

   I went, the others stayed

7. Muchas de las casas no tenían
   jardín

   Many of the houses didn't have a
   garden

8. ¿Qué tienes en la mano?
   — Nada

   What have you got in your hand?
   — Nothing

9. ¡A quién ves? — A nadie

   Who can you see? — Nobody

10. ¿Cuántas tienes? — Ninguna

    How many have you got? — None

11. Había muchos cuadros,
    pero vi pocos que me gustaran

    There were many pictures,
    but I saw few I liked

12. ¿Se oía mucho ruido? — No tanto

    Was it very noisy? — Not so very

13. Lo ha estropeado todo
    Todo va bien

    He has spoiled everything
    All is going well

14. Unos cuestan 30 euros,
    los otros 40 euros

    Some cost 30 euros, the
    others 40 euros

15. Varios de ellos me gustaron mucho

    I liked several of them very much

16. Veo a alguien
    No veo a nadie
    Tengo algo que hacer
    No tengo nada que hacer

    I can see somebody
    I can't see anybody
    I have something to do
    I don't have anything to do

Relative Pronouns

<table>
<tr><td colspan="2">PEOPLE</td><td></td></tr>
<tr><td>SINGULAR</td><td>PLURAL</td><td></td></tr>
<tr><td>que</td><td>que</td><td>who, that (subject) → ❶</td></tr>
<tr><td>que</td><td>que</td><td rowspan="2">who(m), that (direct object) → ❷</td></tr>
<tr><td>a quien</td><td>a quienes</td></tr>
<tr><td>a quien</td><td>a quienes</td><td>to whom, that → ❸</td></tr>
<tr><td>de que</td><td>de que</td><td rowspan="2">of whom, that → ❹</td></tr>
<tr><td>de quien</td><td>de quienes</td></tr>
<tr><td>cuyo/a</td><td>cuyos/as</td><td>whose → ❺</td></tr>
</table>

THINGS	
SINGULAR AND PLURAL	
que	which, that (*subject*) → ❻
que	which, that (*direct object*) → ❼
a que	to which, that → ❽
de que	of which, that → ❾
cuyo	whose → ❿

ⓘ Note: These forms can also refer to people.

cuyo agrees with the noun it accompanies, not with the owner → ❺/❿

You cannot omit the relative pronoun in Spanish as you can in English → ❷/❼

Examples

1. Mi hermano, que tiene veinte años, es el más joven

   My brother, who is twenty, is the youngest

2. Los amigos que más quiero son ...

   The friends (that) I like best are ...

   María, a quien Daniel admira tanto, es ...

   Maria, whom Daniel admires so much, is ...

3. Mis abogados, a quienes he escrito hace poco, están ...

   My lawyers, to whom I wrote recently, are ...

4. La chica de que te hablé llega mañana

   The girl (that) I told you about is coming tomorrow

   los niños de quienes se ocupa Vd

   the children (that) you look after

5. Vendrá la mujer cuyo hijo está enfermo

   The woman whose son is ill will be coming

6. Hay una escalera que lleva a la buhardilla

   There's a staircase which leads to the loft

7. La casa que hemos comprado tiene ...

   The house (which) we've bought has ...

   Este es el regalo que me ha mandado mi amiga

   This is the present (that) my friend has sent to me

8. la tienda a que siempre va

   the shop (which) she always goes to

9. las injusticias de que se quejan

   the injustices (that) they're complaining about

10. la ventana cuyas cortinas están corridas

    the window whose curtains are drawn

Relative Pronouns *continued*

el cual, el que

These are used when the relative is separated from the word it refers to, or when it would otherwise be unclear which word it referred to. The pronouns always agree in number and gender with the noun → ①

> **El cual** may also be used when the verb in the relative clause is separated from the relative pronoun → ②

lo que, lo cual

The neuter form **lo** is normally used when referring to an idea, statement or abstract noun. In certain expressions, the form **lo cual** may also be used as the subject of the relative clause → ③

Relative pronouns after prepositions

Que and **quienes** are generally used after the prepositions:

a	to	→	④
con	with	→	⑤
de	from, about, of	→	⑥
en	in, on, into	→	⑦

It should be noted that **en que** can sometimes be translated by:
- *where*. In this case it can also be replaced by **en donde** or **donde** → ⑧
- *when*. Sometimes here it can be replaced by **cuando** → ⑨

El que or **el cual** are used after other prepositions, and they always agree → ⑩

Examples

1 El padre de Elena, el cual tiene
mucho dinero, es ...
  (el cual is used here since que *or* quien *might equally refer to Elena)*

    Elena's father, who has a lot of
    money, is ...

Su hermana, a la cual/la que
hacía mucho que no veía,
estaba también allí

    His sister, whom I hadn't seen
    for a long time, was also there

2 Vieron a su tío, el cual, después
de levantarse, salió

    They saw their uncle, who, after
    having got up, went out

3 No sabe lo que hace

    He doesn't know what he is
    doing

Lo que dijiste fue una tontería
Todo estaba en silencio, lo que
(*or* lo cual) me pareció muy raro

    What you said was foolish
    All was silent, which I thought
    most odd

4 las tiendas a (las) que íbamos

    the shops we used to go to

5 la chica con quien (or la que) sale

    the girl he's going out with

6 el libro de(l) que te hablé

    the book I told you about

7 el lío en (el) que te has metido

    the trouble you've got yourself
    into

8 el sitio en que (en donde/donde)
se escondía

    the place where he/she was
    hiding

9 el año en que naciste

    the year (when) you were born

10 el puente debajo del que/cual
pasa el río
las obras por las cuales/que es
famosa

    the bridge under which the
    river flows
    the plays for which she is famous

Relative Pronouns *continued*

el que, la que; los que, las que
These mean *the one(s) who/which, those who* → ❶

> ⓘ Note: **quien(es)** can replace **el que** *etc* when used in a general
> sense → ❷

todos los que, todas las que
These mean *all who, all those/the ones which* → ❸

todo lo que
This translates *all that, everything that* → ❹

el de, la de; los de, las de
These can mean:
- *the one(s) of, that/those of* → ❺
- *the one(s) with* → ❻

① Esa película es la que quiero ver
    That film is the one I want to see

¿Te acuerdas de ese amigo?
    Do you remember that friend?

  El que te presenté ayer
      The one I introduced you to yesterday

Los que quieran entrar tendrán que pagar
    Those who want to go in will have to pay

② Quien (*or* el que) llegue antes ganará el premio
    He who arrives first will win the prize

③ Todos los que salían iban de negro
    All those who were coming out were dressed in black

¿Qué autobuses puedo tomar?
    Which buses can I take?

  – Todos los que pasen por aquí
      – Any (All those) that come this way

④ Quiero saber todo lo que ha pasado
    I want to know all that has happened

⑤ Trae la foto de tu novio y la de tu hermano
    Bring the photo of your boyfriend and the one of your brother

Viajamos en mi coche y en el de María
    We travelled in my car and Maria's

Te doy estos libros y también los de mi hermana
    I'll give you these books and my sister's too

⑥ Tu amigo, el de las gafas, me lo contó
    Your friend, the one with glasses, told me

Interrogative Pronouns

¿qué? what?; which?
¿cuál(es)? which?; what?
¿quién(es)? who?

qué

It always translates *what* → ①

ⓘ Note: por + qué is normally translated by *why* → ②

cuál

It normally implies a choice, and translates *which* → ③

ⓘ EXCEPT: when no choice is implied or more specific information is required → ④

ⓘ Note: Whilst the pronoun qué can also work as an adjective, cuál only works as a pronoun → ⑤

quién

SUBJECT *or* AFTER PREPOSITION	quién(es)	who → ⑥
OBJECT	a quién(es)	whom → ⑦
	de quién(es)	whose → ⑧

All the forms shown above are also used in indirect questions → ⑨

Examples

① ¿Qué estan haciendo? — What are they doing?
¿Qué dices? — What are you saying?
¿Para qué lo quieres? — What do you want it for?

② ¿Por qué no llegaron Vds antes? — Why didn't you arrive earlier?

③ ¿Cuál de estos vestidos te gusta más? — Which of these dresses do you like best?
¿Cuáles viste? — Which ones did you see?

④ ¿Cuál es la capital de España? — What is the capital of Spain?
¿Cuál es tu consejo? — What is your advice?
¿Cuál es su fecha de nacimiento? — What is your date of birth?

⑤ ¿Qué libro es más interesante? — Which book is more interesting?
¿Cuál (de estos libros) es más interesante? — Which (of these books) is more interesting?

⑥ ¿Quién ganó la carrera? — Who won the race?
¿Con quiénes los viste? — Who did you see them with?

⑦ ¿A quiénes ayudaste? — Who(m) did you help?
¿A quién se lo diste? — Who did you give it to?

⑧ ¿De quién es este libro? — Whose is this book?

⑨ Le pregunté para qué lo quería — I asked him/her what he/she wanted it for

No me dijeron cuáles preferían — They didn't tell me which ones they preferred

No sabía a quién acudir — I didn't know who to turn to

Possessive Pronouns

These are the same as the strong forms of the possessive adjectives, but they are always accompanied by the definite article.

Singular:

MASCULINE	FEMININE	
el mío	la mía	mine
el tuyo	la tuya	yours (of tú)
el suyo	la suya	his; hers; its; yours (of Vd)
el nuestro	la nuestra	ours
el vuestro	la vuestra	yours (of vosotros)
el suyo	la suya	theirs; yours (of Vds)

Plural:

MASCULINE	FEMININE	
los míos	las mías	mine
los tuyos	las tuyas	yours (of tú)
los suyos	las suyas	his; hers; its; yours (of Vd)
los nuestros	las nuestras	ours
los vuestros	las vuestras	yours (of vosotros)
los suyos	las suyas	theirs; yours (of Vds)

The pronoun agrees in number and gender with the noun it replaces, not with the owner → ①

Alternative translations are 'my own', 'your own' etc → ②

After the prepositions a and de the article el is contracted in the normal way (see page 200):

a + el mío → al mío → ③

de + el mío → del mío → ④

Examples

❶ Pregunta a Cristina si este bolígrafo es el suyo

Ask Cristina if this pen is hers

¿Qué equipo ha ganado, el suyo o el nuestro?

Which team won – theirs or ours?

Mi perro es más joven que el tuyo

My dog is younger than yours

Daniel pensó que esos libros eran los suyos

Daniel thought those books were his

Si no tienes discos, te prestaré los míos

If you don't have any records, I'll lend you mine

Las habitaciones son menos amplias que las vuestras

The rooms are smaller than yours

❷ ¿Es su familia tan grande como la tuya?

Is his/her/their family as big as your own?

Sus precios son más bajos que los nuestros

Their prices are lower than our own

❸ ¿Por qué prefieres este sombrero al mío?

Why do you prefer this hat to mine?

Su coche se parece al vuestro

His/her/their car looks like yours

❹ Mi libro está encima del tuyo

My book is on top of yours

Su padre vive cerca del nuestro

His/her/their father lives near ours

Demonstrative Pronouns

	MASCULINE	FEMININE	NEUTER	
SING.	éste	ésta	esto	this
	ése	ésa	eso	that
	aquél	aquélla	aquello	
PLUR.	éstos	éstas		these
	ésos	ésas		those
	aquéllos	aquéllas		

The pronoun agrees in number and gender with the noun it replaces → ➊

The difference in meaning between the forms ése and aquél is the same as between the corresponding adjectives (see page 216).

The masculine and feminine forms have an accent, which is the only thing that differentiates them from the corresponding adjectives.

The neuter forms always refer to an idea or a statement or to an object when we want to identify it, etc, but never to specified nouns → ➋

An additional meaning of aquél is *the former*, and of éste *the latter* → ➌

Examples

① ¿Qué abrigo te gusta más?
— Éste de aquí
Aquella casa era más grande
que ésta
estos libros y aquéllos

Quiero estas sandalias y ésas

Which coat do you like best?
— This one here
That house was bigger than
this one
these books and those (over
there)
I'd like these sandals and those
ones

② No puedo creer que esto me
esté pasando a mí
Eso de madrugar es algo que
no le gusta

Aquello sí que me gustó
Esto es una bicicleta

I can't believe this is really
happening to me
(This business of) getting up
early is something she doesn't
like
I really did like that
This is a bicycle

③ Hablaban Jaime y Andrés, éste a
voces y aquél casi en un susurro

Jaime and Andrés were talking,
the latter in a loud voice and
the former almost in a whisper

Adverbs

Formation

Most adverbs are formed by adding -mente to the feminine form of
the adjective. Accents on the adjective are not affected since the suffix
-mente is stressed independently → ①

   ⓘ Note: -mente is omitted:
- in the first of two or more of these adverbs when joined by a
  conjunction → ②
- in recientemente *recently* when immediately preceding a past
  participle → ③
  An accent is then needed on the last syllable (see page 296)

The following adverbs are formed in an irregular way:

bueno →	bien
good	well
malo →	mal
bad	badly

Adjectives used as adverbs

Certain adjectives are used adverbially. These include:
alto, bajo, barato, caro, claro, derecho, fuerte and rápido → ④

   ⓘ Note: Other adjectives used as adverbs agree with the subject,
and can normally be replaced by the adverb ending in -mente or
an adverbial phrase → ⑤

Position of adverbs

When the adverb accompanies a verb, it may either immediately follow
it or precede it for emphasis → ⑥

   ⓘ Note: The adverb can never be placed between haber and the
past participle in compound tenses → ⑦

When the adverb accompanies an adjective or another adverb, it generally
precedes the adjective or adverb → ⑧

1 FEM ADJECTIVE	ADVERB
lenta slow	lentamente slowly
franca frank	francamente frankly
feliz happy	felizmente happily
fácil easy	fácilmente easily

2 Lo hicieron lenta pero eficazmente | They did it slowly but efficiently

3 El pan estaba recién hecho | The bread had just been baked

4 hablar alto/bajo | to speak loudly/softly
cortar derecho | to cut (in a) straight (line)
costar barato/caro | to be cheap/expensive
Habla muy fuerte | He talks very loudly
ver claro | to see clearly
correr rápido | to run fast

5 Esperaban impacientes | They were waiting impatiently
(*or* impacientemente/ |
con impaciencia) |
Vivieron muy felices (*or* muy | They lived very happily
felizmente) |

6 No conocemos aún al nuevo | We still haven't met the new
médico | doctor
Aún estoy esperando | I'm still waiting
Han hablado muy bien | They have spoken very well
Siempre le regalaban flores | They always gave her flowers

7 Lo he hecho ya | I've already done it
No ha estado nunca en Italia | She's never been to Italy

8 un sombrero muy bonito | a very nice hat
hablar demasiado alto | to talk too loud
mañana temprano | early tomorrow
hoy mismo | today

Comparatives and Superlatives

Comparatives

These are formed using the following constructions:

más ... (que) more ... (than) → ❶
menos ... (que) less ... (than) → ❷
tanto como as much as → ❸
tan ... como as ... as → ❹
tan ... que so ... that → ❺
demasiado ... para too ... to → ❻
(lo) bastante ... ⎫
(lo) suficientemente ... ⎭ para enough to → ❼
cada vez más/menos more and more/less and less → ❽

Superlatives

These are formed by placing más/menos *the most/the least* before the adverb → ❾

lo is added before a superlative which is qualified → ❿

The absolute superlative (*very, most, extremely* + adverb) is formed by placing muy before the adverb. The form -ísimo (see also page 296) is also occasionally found → ⓫

Adverbs with irregular comparatives/superlatives

ADVERB	COMPARATIVE	SUPERLATIVE
bien well	mejor* better	(lo) mejor (the) best
mal badly	peor worse	(lo) peor (the) worst
mucho a lot	más more	(lo) más (the) most
poco little	menos less	(lo) menos (the) least

* más bien also exists, meaning *rather* → ⓬

1. más deprisa — more quickly
   más abiertamente — more openly
   Mi hermana canta más fuerte que yo — My sister sings louder than me

2. menos fácilmente — less easily
   menos a menudo — less often
   Nos vemos menos frecuentemente que antes — We see each other less frequently than before

3. Daniel no lee tanto como Andrés — Daniel doesn't read as much as Andrés

4. Hágalo tan rápido como le sea posible — Do it as quickly as you can
   Ganan tan poco como nosotros — They earn as little as we do

5. Llegaron tan pronto que tuvieron que esperarnos — They arrived so early that they had to wait for us

6. Es demasiado tarde para ir al cine — It's too late to go to the cinema

7. Eres (lo) bastante grande para hacerlo solo — You're old enough to do it by yourself

8. Me gusta el campo cada vez más — I like the countryside more and more

9. María es la que corre más rápido — María is the one who runs fastest
   El que llegó menos tarde fue Miguel — Miguel was the one to arrive the least late

10. Lo hice lo más de prisa que pude — I did it as quickly as I could

11. muy lentamente — very slowly
    tempranísimo — extremely early
    muchísimo — very much

12. Era un hombre más bien bajito — He was a rather short man
    Estaba más bien inquieta que impaciente — I was restless rather than impatient

257

Common Adverbs and their Usage

Some common adverbs:

bastante	enough; quite → ❶
bien	well → ❷
cómo	how → ❸
cuánto	how much → ❹
demasiado	too much; too → ❺
más	more → ❻
menos	less → ❼
mucho	a lot; much → ❽
poco	little, not much; not very → ❾
siempre	always → ❿
también	also, too → ⓫
tan	as → ⓬
tanto	as much → ⓭
todavía/aún	still; yet; even → ⓮
ya	already → ⓯

bastante, cuánto, demasiado, mucho, poco and **tanto** are also used as adjectives that agree with the noun they qualify (see indefinite adjectives, page 224 and interrogative adjectives, page 218)

1	Es bastante tarde	It's quite late
2	¡Bien hecho!	Well done!
3	¡Cómo me ha gustado!	How I liked it!
4	¿Cuánto cuesta este libro?	How much is this book?
5	He comido demasiado	I've eaten too much
	Es demasiado caro	It's too expensive
6	Mi hermano trabaja más ahora	My brother works more now
	Es más tímida que Sofía	She is shyer than Sofía
7	Se debe beber menos	One must drink less
	Estoy menos sorprendida que tú	I'm less surprised than you are
8	¿Lees mucho?	Do you read a lot?
	¿Está mucho más lejos?	Is it much further?
9	Comen poco	They don't eat (very) much
	María es poco decidida	Maria is not very daring
10	Siempre dicen lo mismo	They always say the same (thing)
11	A mí también me gusta	I like it too
12	Ana es tan alta como yo	Ana is as tall as I am
13	Nos aburrimos tanto como vosotros	We got as bored as you did
14	Todavía/aún tengo dos	I've still got two
	Todavía/aún no han llegado	They haven't arrived yet
	Mejor aún/todavía	Even better
15	Ya lo he hecho	I've done it already

Prepositions

On the following pages you will find some of the most frequent uses of prepositions in Spanish. Particular attention is paid to cases where usage differs markedly from English. It is often difficult to give an English equivalent for Spanish prepositions, since usage *does* vary so much between the two languages. In the list below, the broad meaning of the preposition is given on the left, with examples of usage following. Prepositions are dealt with in alphabetical order, except a, de, en and por which are shown first.

a

at	echar algo a algn	to throw sth at sb
	a 50 euros el kilo	(at) 50 euros a kilo
	a 100 km por hora	at 100 km per hour
	sentarse a la mesa	to sit down at the table
in	al sol	in the sun
	a la sombra	in the shade
onto	cayeron al suelo	they fell onto the floor
	pegar una foto al álbum	to stick a photo into the album
to	ir al cine	to go to the cinema
	dar algo a algn	to give sth to sb
	venir a hacer	to come to do
from	quitarle algo a algn	to take sth from sb
	robarle algo a algn	to steal sth from sb
	arrebatarle algo a algn	to snatch sth from sb
	comprarle algo a algn	to buy sth from/for sb*
	esconderle algo a algn	to hide sth from sb
means	a mano	by hand
	a caballo	on horseback
	(*but note other forms of transport used with* en *and* por)	
	a pie	on foot

* The translation here obviously depends on the context.

manner	a la inglesa in the English manner
	a pasos lentos with slow steps
	poco a poco little by little
	a ciegas blindly
time, date:	a medianoche at midnight
at, on	a las dos y cuarto at quarter past two
	a tiempo on time
	a final/fines de mes at the end of the month
	a veces at times
distance	a 8 km de aquí (at a distance of) 8 kms from here
	a dos pasos de mi casa just a step from my house
	a lo lejos in the distance
with el + *infin.*	al levantarse on getting up
	al abrir la puerta on opening the door
after certain adjectives	dispuesto a todo ready for anything
	parecido a esto similar to this
	obligado a ello obliged to (do) that
after certain verbs	see page 66

Personal a

When the direct object of a verb is a person or pet animal, a must always be placed immediately before it.

EXAMPLES: querían mucho a sus hijos
     they loved their children dearly
   el niño miraba a su perro con asombro
     the boy kept looking at his dog in astonishment

EXCEPTIONS: tener
     to have
   tienen dos hijos
     they have two children

Prepositions

de

from	**venir de Londres** to come from London **un médico de Valencia** a doctor from Valencia **de la mañana a la noche** from morning till night **de 10 a 15** from 10 to 15
belonging to, of	**el sombrero de mi padre** my father's hat **las lluvias de abril** April showers
contents, composition, material	**una caja de cerillas** a box of matches **una taza de té** a cup of tea; a tea-cup **un vestido de seda** a silk dress
destined for	**una silla de cocina** a kitchen chair **un traje de noche** an evening dress
descriptive	**la mujer del sombrero verde** the woman with the green hat **el vecino de al lado** the next door neighbour
manner	**de manera irregular** in an irregular way **de una puñalada** by stabbing
quality	**una mujer de edad** an aged lady **objetos de valor** valuable items
comparative + *a number*	**había más/menos de 100 personas** there were more/fewer than 100 people
in (*after superlatives*)	**la ciudad más/menos bonita del mundo** the most/least beautiful city in the world
after certain adjectives	**contento de ver** pleased to see **fácil/difícil de entender** easy/difficult to understand **capaz de hacer** capable of doing
after certain verbs	see page 66

Prepositions

en

in, at	**en el campo** in the country
	en Londres in London
	en la cama in bed
	con un libro en la mano with a book in his hand
	en voz baja in a low voice
	en la escuela in/at school
into	**entra en la casa** go into the house
	metió la mano en su bolso she put her hand into her handbag
on	**un cuadro en la pared** a picture on the wall
	sentado en una silla sitting on a chair
	en la planta baja on the ground floor
time, dates, months: at, in	**en este momento** at this moment
	en 2012 in 2012
	en enero in January
transport: by	**en coche** by car
	en avión by plane
	en tren by train (but see also **por**)
language	**en español** in Spanish
duration	**lo haré en una semana** I'll do it in one week
after certain adjectives	**es muy buena/mala en geografía** she is very good/bad at geography
	fueron los primeros/últimos/únicos en + *infin.* they were the first/last/only ones + *infin.*
after certain verbs	see page 66

Prepositions

por

motion: along, through, around	vaya por ese camino go along that path
	por el túnel through the tunnel
	pasear por el campo to walk around the countryside
vague location	tiene que estar por aquí it's got to be somewhere around here
	le busqué por todas partes I looked for him everywhere
vague time	por la tarde in the afternoon
	por aquellos días in those days
rate	90 km por hora 90 km per hour
	un cinco por ciento five per cent
	ganaron por 3 a 0 they won by 3 to 0
by (*agent of passive*)	descubierto por unos niños discovered by some children
	odiado por sus enemigos hated by his enemies
by (*means of*)	por barco by boat
	por tren by train (freight)
	por correo aéreo by airmail
	llamar por teléfono to telephone
cause, reason: for, because	¿por qué? why?, for what reason?
	por todo eso because of all that
	por lo que he oído judging by what I've heard
+ *infinitive*: to	libros por leer books to be read
	cuentas por pagar bills to be paid
equivalence	¿me tienes por tonto? do you think I'm stupid?
+ *adjective*/+ *adverb* + que: however	por buenos que sean however good they are
	por mucho que lo quieras however much you want it

Prepositions

for

¿cuanto me darán por este libro?
how much will they give me for this book?
te lo cambio por éste I'll swap you this one for it
no siento nada por ti I feel nothing for you
si no fuera por ti if it weren't for you
¡Por Dios! For God's sake!

for the benefit of

lo hago por ellos I do it for their benefit

on behalf of

firma por mí sign on my behalf

por also combines with other prepositions to form double prepositions usually conveying the idea of movement. The commonest of these are:

over

saltó por encima de la mesa
she jumped over the table

under

nadamos por debajo del puente
we swam under the bridge

past

pasaron por delante de Correos
they went past the post office

behind

por detrás de la puerta behind the door

through

la luz entraba por entre las cortinas
light was coming in through the curtains

+ donde

¿por dónde has venido? which way did you come?

ante

faced with, before

lo hicieron ante mis propios ojos
they did it before my very eyes
ante eso no se puede hacer nada
one can't do anything when faced with that

preference

la salud ante todo health above all things

antes de

before (*time*)

antes de las 5 before 5 o'clock

Prepositions

bajo/debajo de

These are usually equivalent, although bajo is used more frequently in a figurative sense and with temperatures.

under	**bajo/debajo de la cama** under the bed
	bajo el dominio romano under Roman rule
below	**un grado bajo cero** one degree below zero

con

with	**vino con su amigo** she came with her friend
after certain adjectives	**enfadado con ellos** angry with them
	magnánimo con sus súbditos
	magnanimous with his subjects

contra

against	**no tengo nada contra ti** I've nothing against you
	apoyado contra la pared leaning against the wall

delante de

in front of	**iba delante de mí** she was walking in front of me

desde

from	**desde aquí se puede ver** you can see it from here
	llamaban desde España
	they were phoning from Spain
	desde otro punto de vista
	from a different point of view
	desde la 1 hasta las 6 from 1 till 6
	desde entonces from then onwards
since	**desde que volvieron** since they returned

Prepositions

| for | **viven en esa casa desde hace 3 años**
they've been living in that house for 3 years
(*note tense*) |

detrás de

| behind | **están detrás de la puerta** they are behind the door |

durante

| during | **durante la guerra** during the war |
| for | **anduvieron durante 3 días** they walked for 3 days |

entre
.

between	**entre 8 y 10** between 8 and 10
among	**María y Elena, entre otras** Maria and Elena, among others
reciprocal	**ayudarse entre sí** to help each other

excepto

| except (for) | **todos excepto tú** everybody except you |

hacia

| towards | **van hacia ese edificio**
they're going towards that building |
| around (*time*) | **hacia las 3** at around 3 (o'clock)
hacia fines de enero around the end of January |

Prepositions

Hacia can also combine with some adverbs to convey a sense of motion in a particular direction:

> hacia arriba upwards
> hacia abajo downwards
> hacia adelante forwards
> hacia atrás backwards
> hacia adentro inwards
> hacia afuera outwards

hasta

until	**hasta la noche** until night
as far as	**viajaron hasta Sevilla** they travelled as far as Seville
up to	**conté hasta 300 ovejas** I counted up to 300 lambs **hasta ahora no los había visto** up to now I hadn't seen them
even	**hasta un tonto lo entendería** even an imbecile would understand that

para

for	**es para ti** it's for you
	es para mañana it's for tomorrow
	una habitación para dos noches
	  a room for two nights
	para ser un niño, lo hace muy bien
	  for a child he is very good at it
	salen para Cádiz they are leaving for Cádiz
	se conserva muy bien para sus años
	  he keeps very well for his age

+ *infinitive*: (in order) to	**es demasiado torpe para comprenderlo** he's too stupid to understand
+ sí: to oneself	**hablar para sí** to talk to oneself **reír para sí** to laugh to oneself
with time	**todavía tengo para 1 hora** I'll be another hour (at it) yet

Prepositions

salvo

except (for)	**todos salvo él** all except him
	salvo cuando llueve except when it's raining
barring	**salvo imprevistos** barring the unexpected
	salvo contraorden unless you hear to the contrary

según

according to	**según su consejo** according to her advice
	según lo que me dijiste according to what you told me

sin

without	**sin agua/dinero** without water/money
	sin mi marido without my husband
+ *infinitive*	**sin contar a los otros** without counting the others

sobre

on	**sobre la cama** on the bed
	sobre el armario on (top of) the wardrobe
on (to)	**póngalo sobre la mesa** put it on the table
about, on	**un libro sobre Eva Perón** a book about Eva Perón
above, over	**volábamos sobre el mar** we were flying over the sea
	la nube sobre aquella montaña
	the cloud above that mountain
approximately	**vendré sobre las 4** I'll come about 4 o'clock
about	**Madrid tiene sobre 4 millones de habitantes**
	Madrid has about 4 million inhabitants

tras

behind	**está tras el asiento** it's behind the seat
after	**uno tras otro** one after another
	día tras día day after day
	corrieron tras el ladrón they ran after the thief

Conjunctions

There are conjunctions which introduce a main clause, such as **y** (*and*), **pero** (*but*), **si** (*if*), **o** (*or*) etc, and those which introduce subordinate clauses like **porque** (*because*), **mientras que** (*while*), **después de que** (*after*) etc. They are all used in much the same way as in English, but the following points are of note:

Some conjunctions in Spanish require a following subjunctive, see pages 60 to 63.

Some conjunctions are 'split' in Spanish like 'both ... and', 'either ... or' in English:

tanto ... como both ... and → ①
ni ... ni neither ... nor → ②
o (bien) ... o (bien) either ... or (else) → ③
sea ... sea either ... or, whether ... or → ④

y
- Before words beginning with **i-** or **hi-** + consonant it becomes **e** → ⑤

o
- Before words beginning with **o-** or **ho-** it becomes **u** → ⑥
- Between numerals it becomes **ó** → ⑦

que
- meaning *that* → ⑧
- in comparisons, meaning *than* → ⑨
- followed by the subjunctive, see page 58.

porque (Not to be confused with **por qué** *why*)
- **como** should be used instead at the beginning of a sentence → ⑩

pero, sino
- **pero** normally translates *but* → ⑪
- **sino** is used when there is a direct contrast after a negative → ⑫

Examples

1. Estas flores crecen tanto en verano como en invierno
   These flowers grow in both summer and winter

2. Ni él ni ella vinieron
   Neither he nor she came
   No tengo ni dinero ni comida
   I have neither money nor food

3. Debe de ser o ingenua o tonta
   She must be either naïve or stupid
   O bien me huyen o bien no me reconocen
   Either they're avoiding me or else they don't recognize me

4. Sea en verano, sea en invierno, siempre me gusta andar
   I always like walking, whether in summer or in winter

5. Diana e Isabel
   Diana and Isabel
   madre e hija
   mother and daughter
   BUT:
   árboles y hierba
   trees and grass

6. diez u once
   ten or eleven
   minutos u horas
   minutes or hours

7. 37 ó 38
   37 or 38

8. Dicen que te han visto
   They say (that) they've seen you
   ¿Sabías que estábamos allí?
   Did you know that we were there?

9. Le gustan más que nunca
   He likes them more than ever
   María es menos guapa que su hermana
   Maria is less attractive than her sister

10. Como estaba lloviendo no pudimos salir
    Because/As it was raining we couldn't go out
    (*Compare with*: No pudimos salir porque estaba lloviendo)

11. Me gustaría ir, pero estoy muy cansada
    I'd like to go, but I am very tired

12. No es escocesa sino irlandesa
    She is not Scottish but Irish

Augmentative, Diminutive and Pejorative Suffixes

These can be used after nouns, adjectives and some adverbs. They are attached to the end of the word after any final vowel has been removed:

> e.g.   puerta → puertita
> doctor → doctorcito

ⓘ Note: Further changes sometimes take place (see page 300).

Augmentatives

These are used mainly to imply largeness, but they can also suggest clumsiness, ugliness or grotesqueness. The commonest augmentatives are:
ón/ona → ❶
azo/a → ❷
ote/a → ❸

Diminutives

These are used mainly to suggest smallness or to express a feeling of affection. Occasionally they can be used to express ridicule or contempt. The commonest diminutives are:
ito/a → ❹
(e)cito/a → ❺
(ec)illo/a → ❻
(z)uelo/a → ❼

Pejoratives

These are used to convey the idea that something is unpleasant or to express contempt. The commonest suffixes are:
ucho/a → ❽
acho/a → ❾
uzo/a → ❿
uco/a → ⓫
astro/a → ⓬

ORIGINAL WORD	DERIVED FORM
1 un hombre **a man**	un hombrón **a big man**
2 bueno **good**	buenazo **(person) easily imposed on**
un perro **a dog**	un perrazo **a really big dog**
gripe **flu**	un gripazo **a really bad bout of flu**
3 grande **big**	grandote **huge**
palabra **word**	palabrota **swear word**
amigo **friend**	amigote **old pal**
4 una casa **a house**	una casita **a cottage**
un poco **a little**	un poquito **a little bit**
un rato **a while**	un ratito **a little while**
mi hija **my daughter**	mi hijita **my dear sweet daughter**
despacio **slowly**	despacito **nice and slowly**
5 un viejo **an old man**	un viejecito **a little old man**
un pueblo **a village**	un pueblecito **a small village**
una voz **a voice**	una vocecita **a sweet little voice**
6 una ventana **a window**	una ventanilla **a small window** *(car, train etc)*
un chico **a boy**	un chiquillo **a small boy**
una campana **a bell**	una campanilla **a small bell**
un palo **a stick**	un palillo **a toothpick**
un médico **a doctor**	un mediquillo **a quack** *(doctor)*
7 los pollos **the chickens**	los polluelos **the little chicks**
hoyos **hollows**	hoyuelos **dimples**
un ladrón **a thief**	un ladronzuelo **a petty thief**
una mujer **a woman**	una mujerzuela **a whore**
8 un animal **an animal**	un animalucho **a wretched animal**
un cuarto **a room**	un cuartucho **a poky little room**
una casa **a house**	una casucha **a shack**
9 rico **rich**	ricacho **nouveau riche**
10 gente **people**	gentuza **scum**
11 una ventana **a window**	un ventanuco **a miserable little window**
12 un político **a politician**	un politicastro **a third-rate politician**

Sentence structure

Word Order

Word order in Spanish is much more flexible than in English. You can often find the subject placed after the verb or the object before the verb, either for emphasis or for stylistic reasons → **1**

There are some cases, however, where the order is always different from English. Most of these have already been dealt with under the appropriate part of speech, but are summarized here along with other instances not covered elsewhere.

Object pronouns nearly always come before the verb → **2**
For details, see pages 232 to 235.

Qualifying adjectives nearly always come after the noun → **3**
For details, see page 228.

Following direct speech the subject always follows the verb → **4**

For word order in negative sentences, see page 276.

For word order in interrogative sentences, see page 280 → **1**

Examples

1. Ese libro te lo di yo   I gave you that book
   No nos vio nadie   Nobody saw us

2. Ya los veo   I can see them now
   Me lo dieron ayer   They gave it to me yesterday

3. Ya los veo   I can see them now
   Me lo dieron ayer   They gave it to me yesterday

4. una ciudad española   a Spanish town
   vino tinto   red wine

5. – Pienso que sí – dijo María   'I think so,' said Maria
   – No importa – replicó Daniel   'It doesn't matter,' Daniel replied

Negatives

A sentence is made negative by adding no between the subject and the verb (and any preceding object pronouns) → ❶

There are, however, some points to note:
- in phrases like *not her*, *not now*, etc the Spanish no usually comes after the word it qualifies → ❷
- with verbs of saying, hoping, thinking etc *not* is translated by que no → ❸

Double negatives

The following are the most common negative pairs:

no ... nada nothing (*not ... anything*)
no ... nadie nobody (*not ... anybody*)
no ... más no longer (*not ... any more*)
no ... nunca never (*not ... ever*)
no ... jamás never (stronger) (*not ... ever*)
no ... más que only (*not ... more than*)
no ... ningún(o)(a) no (*not any*)
no ... tampoco not ... either
no ... ni ... ni neither ... nor
no ... ni siquiera not even

Word order

No precedes the verb (and any object pronouns) in both simple and compound tenses, and the second element follows the verb → ❹

Sometimes the above negatives are placed before the verb (with the exception of más and más que), and no is then dropped → ❺

For use of nada, nadie and ninguno as pronouns, see page 240.

Examples

AFFIRMATIVE		NEGATIVE
1 El coche es suyo	→	El coche no es suyo
The car is his		**The car is not his**
Yo me lo pondré	→	Yo no me lo pondré
I will put it on		**I will not put it on**

2 ¿Quién lo ha hecho? — Ella no
¿Quieres un cigarrillo?
  — Ahora no
Dame ese libro, el que está a tu
  lado no, el otro

Who did it? — Not her
Do you want a cigarette?
  — Not now
Give me that book, not the one
  near you, the other one

3 Opino que no
Dijeron que no

I think not
They said not

4 No dicen nada
No han visto a nadie
No me veréis más
No te olvidaré nunca/jamás
No habían recorrido más que
  40 kms cuando ...
No se me ha ocurrido ninguna idea
No les estaban esperando ni mi
  hijo ni mi hija
No ha venido ni siquiera Juan

They don't say anything
They haven't seen anybody
You won't see me any more
I'll never forget you
They hadn't travelled more than
  40 kms when ...
I haven't had any ideas
Neither my son nor my daughter
  were waiting for them
Even Juan hasn't come

5 Nadie ha venido hoy
Nunca me han gustado
Ni mi hermano ni mi hermana
  fuman

Nobody came today
I've never liked them
Neither my brother nor my sister
  smokes

Negatives *continued*

Negatives in short replies

No *no* is the usual negative response to a question → ❶

> ⓘ Note: It is often translated as 'not' → ❷
> (see also page 276)

Nearly all the other negatives listed on page 276 may be used without a verb in a short reply → ❸

Combination of negatives

These are the most common combinations of negative particles:

> no ... nunca más → ❹
> no ... nunca a nadie → ❺
> no ... nunca nada/nada nunca → ❻
> no ... nunca más que → ❼
> no ... ni ... nunca ... → ❽

Examples

1	¿Quieres venir con nosotros? — No	Do you want to come with us? — No
2	¿Vienes o no?	Are you coming or not?
3	¿Ha venido alguien? — ¡Nadie! ¿Has ido al Japón alguna vez? — Nunca	Has anyone come? — Nobody! Have you ever been to Japan? — Never
4	No lo haré nunca más	I'll never do it again
5	No se ve nunca a nadie por allí	You never see anybody around there
6	No cambiaron nada nunca	They never changed anything
7	No he hablado nunca más que con su mujer	I've only ever spoken to his wife
8	No me ha escrito ni llamado por teléfono nunca	He/she has never written to me or phoned me

Question Forms

Direct

There are two ways of forming direct questions in Spanish:

> by inverting the normal word order so that
> *subject + verb* → *verb + subject* → ❶

> by maintaining the word order *subject + verb*, but by using a rising
> intonation at the end of the sentence → ❷

> ⓘ Note: In compound tenses the auxiliary may never be
> separated from the past participle, as happens in English → ❸

Indirect

An indirect question is one that is 'reported', e.g. he asked me 'what the
time was', tell me 'which way to go'. Word order in indirect questions can
adopt one of the two following patterns:

> *interrogative word + subject + verb* → ❹

> *interrogative word + verb + subject* → ❺

¿verdad?, ¿no?

These are used wherever English would use 'isn't it?', 'don't they?', 'weren't
we?', 'is it?' etc tagged on to the end of a sentence → ❻

sí

Sí is the word for 'yes' in answer to a question put either in the affirmative
or in the negative → ❼

Examples

1 ¿Vendrá tu madre? Will your mother come?
  ¿Lo trajo Vd? Did you bring it?
  ¿Es posible eso? Is it possible?
  ¿Cuándo volverán Vds? When will you come back?

2 El gato, ¿se bebió toda la leche? Did the cat drink up all his milk?
  Andrés, ¿va a venir? Is Andrés coming?

3 ¿Lo ha terminado Vd? Have you finished it?
  ¿Había llegado tu amigo? Had your friend arrived?

4 Dime qué autobuses pasan por aquí Tell me which buses come this way
  No sé cuántas personas vendrán I don't know how many people will turn up

5 Me preguntó dónde trabajaba mi hermano He asked me where my brother worked
  No sabemos a qué hora empieza la película We don't know what time the film starts

6 Hace calor, ¿verdad? It's warm, isn't it?
  No se olvidará Vd, ¿verdad? You won't forget, will you?
  Estaréis cansados, ¿no? You will be tired, won't you?
  Te lo dijo María, ¿no? Maria told you, didn't she?

7 ¿Lo has hecho? — Sí Have you done it? — Yes (I have)
  ¿No lo has hecho? — Sí Haven't you done it? — Yes (I have)

Translation problems

Beware of translating word by word. While on occasions this is possible, quite often it is not. The need for caution is illustrated by the following:

English phrasal verbs (i.e. verbs followed by a preposition), e.g. 'to run away', 'to fall down', are often translated by one word in Spanish → ❶

English verbal constructions often contain a preposition where none exists in Spanish, or vice versa → ❷

Two or more prepositions in English may have a single rendering in Spanish → ❸

A word which is singular in English may be plural in Spanish, or vice versa → ❹

Spanish has no equivalent of the possessive construction denoted by ...'s/...s' → ❺

Problems

-ing

This is translated in a variety of ways in Spanish:

'to be ... -ing' can sometimes be translated by a simple tense (see also pages 54 to 56) → ❻
But, when a physical position is denoted, a past participle is used → ❼

in the construction 'to see/hear sb ... -ing', use an infinitive → ❽
'-ing' can also be translated by:
- an infinitive, see page 46 → ❾
- a perfect infinitive, see page 50 → ❿
- a gerund, see page 52 → ⓫
- a noun → ⓬

Examples

❶ huir — to run away
caerse — to fall down
ceder — to give in

❷ pagar — to pay for
mirar — to look at
escuchar — to listen to
encontrarse con — to meet
fijarse en — to notice
servirse de — to use

❸ extrañarse de — to be surprised at
harto de — fed up with
soñar con — to dream of
contar con — to count on

❹ unas vacaciones — a holiday
sus cabellos — his/her hair
la gente — people
mi pantalón — my trousers

❺ el coche de mi hermano — my brother's car
(*literally*: ... of my brother)

el cuarto de las niñas — the children's bedroom
(*literally*: ... of the children)

❻ Se va mañana — He/she is leaving tomorrow
¿Qué haces? — What are you doing?

❼ Está sentado ahí — He is sitting over there
Estaba tendida en el suelo — She was lying on the ground

❽ Les veo venir — I can see them coming
La he oído cantar — I've heard her singing

❾ Me gusta ir al cine — I like going to the cinema

❿ ¡Deja de hablar! — Stop talking!
En vez de contestar — Instead of answering
Antes de salir — Before leaving
Después de haber abierto la caja, María ... — After opening the box, Maria ...

⓫ Pasamos la tarde fumando y charlando — We spent the afternoon smoking and chatting

⓬ El esquí me mantiene en forma — Skiing keeps me fit

283

to be (*See also Verbal Idioms*, pages 74 to 76)

In set expressions, describing physical and emotional conditions, tener is used:

> tener calor/frío to be warm/cold
> tener hambre/sed to be hungry/thirsty
> tener miedo to be afraid
> tener razón to be right

Describing the weather, e.g. 'what's the weather like?', 'it's windy/sunny', use hacer → ①

For ages, e.g. 'he is 6', use tener (see also page 310) → ②

there is/there are

Both are translated by hay → ③

can, be able

Physical ability is expressed by poder → ④

If the meaning is 'to know how to', use saber → ⑤

'Can' + a 'verb of hearing or seeing etc' in English is not translated in Spanish → ⑥

to

Generally translated by a → ⑦

In time expressions, e.g. 10 to 6, use menos → ⑧

When the meaning is 'in order to', use para → ⑨

Following a verb, as in 'to try to do', 'to like to do', see pages 46 and 48.

'easy/difficult/impossible' etc 'to do' are translated by fácil/difícil/imposible etc de hacer → ⑩

Examples

1. ¿Qué tiempo hace?
Hace bueno/malo/viento

   What's the weather like?
   It's lovely/miserable/windy

2. ¿Cuántos años tienes?
Tengo quince (años)

   How old are you?
   I'm fifteen

3. Hay un señor en la puerta
Hay cinco libros en la mesa

   There's a gentleman at the door
   There are five books on the table

4. No puedo salir contigo

   I can't go out with you

5. ¿Sabes nadar?

   Can you swim?

6. No veo nada
¿Es que no me oyes?

   I can't see anything
   Can't you hear me?

7. Dale el libro a Isabel

   Give the book to Isabel

8. las diez menos cinco
a las siete menos cuarto

   five to ten
   at a quarter to seven

9. Lo hice para ayudaros
Se inclinó para atarse el cordón
de zapato

   I did it to help you
   He bent down to tie his
   shoe-lace

10. Este libro es fácil/difícil de leer

    This book is easy/difficult to read

must

When *must* expresses an assumption, **deber de** is often used → ①

> ⓘ Note: This meaning is also often expressed by **deber** directly followed by the infinitive → ②

When it expresses obligation, there are three possible translations:
- **tener que** → ③
- **deber** → ④
- **hay que** (impersonal) → ⑤

may

If *may* expresses possibility, it can be translated by:
- **poder** → ⑥
- **puede (ser) que** + *subjunctive*

To express permission, use **poder** → ⑦

will

If *will* expresses willingness or desire rather than the future, the present tense of **querer** is used → ⑧

would

If *would* expresses willingness, use the preterite or imperfect of **querer** → ⑨

When a repeated or habitual action in the past is referred to, use
- the imperfect → ⑩
- the imperfect of **soler** + *infinitive* → ⑪

1 Ha debido de mentir — He must have lied

Debe de gustarle — She must like it

2 Debe estar por aquí cerca — It must be near here

Debo haberlo dejado en el tren — I must have left it on the train

3 Tenemos que salir temprano mañana — We must leave early tomorrow

Tengo que irme — I must go

4 Debo visitarles — I must visit them

Debéis escuchar lo que se os dice — You must listen to what is said to you

5 Hay que entrar por ese lado — One (We etc) must get in that way

6 Todavía puede cambiar de opinión — He may still change his mind

Creo que puede llover esta tarde — I think it may rain this afternoon

Puede (ser) que no lo sepa — She may not know

7 ¿Puedo irme? — May I go?

Puede sentarse — You may sit down

8 Quiere Vd esperar un momento, por favor? — Will you wait a moment, please?

No quiere ayudarme — He won't help me

9 No quisieron venir — They wouldn't come

10 Las miraba hora tras hora — She would watch them for hours on end

11 Últimamente solía comer muy poco — Latterly he would eat very little

Pronunciation of Vowels

Spanish vowels are always clearly pronounced and not relaxed in unstressed syllables as happens in English.

	EXAMPLES	HINTS ON PRONUNCIATION
[a]	casa	Between English *a* as in *hat* and *u* as in *hut*
[e]	pensar	Similar to English *e* in *pet*
[i]	filo	Between English *i* as in *pin* and *ee* as in *been*
[o]	loco	Similar to English *o* in *hot*
[u]	luna	Between English *ew* as in *few* and *u* as in *put*

Pronunciation of Diphthongs

All these diphthongs are shorter than similar English diphthongs.

[ai]	baile hay	Like *i* in *side*
[au]	causa	Like *ou* in *sound*
[ei]	peine rey	Like *ey* in *grey*
[eu]	deuda	Like the vowel sounds in English *may you*, but without the sound of the *y*
[oi]	boina voy	Like *oy* in *boy*

Semi-consonants

[j]	hacia ya tiene yeso labio yo	i following a consonant and preceding a vowel, and y preceding a vowel are pronounced as y inEnglish yet
[w]	agua bueno arduo ruido	u following a consonant and preceding a vowel is pronounced as w in English walk

EXCEPTIONS: gue, gui (see page 290)

Pronunciation of Consonants

Some consonants are pronounced almost exactly as in English:
[l, m, n, f, k, and in some cases g].

Others, listed below, are similar to English, but differences should be
noted.

	EXAMPLES	HINTS ON PRONUNCIATION
[p]	padre	They are not aspirated, unlike
[k]	coco	English pot, cook and ten.
[t]	tan	
[t]	todo tú	Pronounced with the tip of the
[d]	doy balde	tongue touching the upper front teeth and not the roof of the mouth as in English.

The following consonants are not heard in English:

[β]	labio	This is pronounced between upper and lower lips, which do not touch, unlike English b as in bend.
[ɣ]	haga	Similar to English g as in gate, but tongue does not touch the soft palate.
[ɲ]	año	Similar to ni in onion
[x]	jota	Like the guttural ch in loch
[ɾ]	pera	A single trill with the tip of the tongue against the teeth ridge.
[rr]	rojo perro	A multiple trill with the tip of the tongue against the teeth ridge.

Pronunciation

From Spelling to Sounds

Note the pronunciation of the following (groups of) letters.

LETTER	PRONOUNCED	EXAMPLES
b,v	[b]	These letters have the same value. At the start of a breath group, and after written m and n, the sound is similar to English boy → ①
	[β]	in all other positions, the sound is unknown in English (see page 289) → ②
c	[k]	Before a, o, u or a consonant, like English keep, but not aspirated → ③
	[θ/s]	Before e, i like English thin, or, in Latin America and parts of Spain, like English same → ④
ch	[tʃ]	Like English church → ⑤
d	[d]	At the start of the breath group and after l or n, it is pronounced similar to English deep (see page 289) → ⑥
	[ð]	Between vowels and after consonants (except l or n), it is pronounced very like English though → ⑦
	[(ð)]	At the end of words, and in the verb ending -ado, it is often not pronounced → ⑧
g	[x]	Before e, i, pronounced gutturally, similar to English loch → ⑨
	[g]	At the start of the breath group and after n, it is pronounced like English get → ⑩
	[ɣ]	In other positions the sound is unknown in English → ⑪
gue	[ge/ɣe]	The u is silent → ⑫
gui	[gi/ɣi]	
güe	[gwe/ɣwe]	The u is pronounced like English
güi	[gwi/ɣwi]	walk → ⑬

1. bomba ['bomba]   voy [boi]   vicio ['biθjo]

2. hubo ['uβo]   de veras [de 'βeras]   lavar [la'βar]

3. casa ['kasa]   coco ['koko]   cumbre ['kumbre]

4. cero ['θero/'sero]   cinco ['θiŋko/'siŋko]

5. mucho ['mutʃo]   chuchería [tʃutʃe'ria]

6. doy [doi]   balde ['balde]   bondad [bon'dað]

7. modo ['moðo]   ideal [iðe'al]

8. Madrid [ma'ðri(ð)]   comprado [kom'pra(ð)o]

9. gente ['xente]   giro ['xiro]   general [xene'ral]

10. ganar [ga'nar]   pongo ['poŋgo]

11. agua ['aɣwa]   agrícola [a'ɣrikola]

12. guija ['gixa]   guerra ['gerra]   pague ['paɣe]

13. agüero [a 'ɣwero]   argüir [ar'ɣwir]

From Spelling to Sounds *continued*

LETTER	PRONOUNCED	EXAMPLES
h	[-]	This is always silent → ①
j	[x]	Like the guttural sound in English lo*ch*, but often aspirated at the end of a word → ②
ll	[ʎ]	Similar to English -*ll*- in mi*ll*ion → ③
	[j/ʒ]	In some parts of Spain and in Latin America, like English *y*et or pleasure → ④
-nv-	[mb]	This combination of letters is pronounced as in English *imb*ibe → ⑤
ñ	[ɲ]	As in English o*ni*on → ⑥
q	[k]	Always followed by silent letter u, and pronounced as in English *k*eep, but not aspirated → ⑦
s	[s]	Except where mentioned below, like English *s*ing → ⑧
	[z]	When followed by b, d, g, l, m, n like English *z*oo → ⑨
w	[w]	Like English *v*, *w* → ⑩
x	[ks]	Between vowels, often like English e*x*it → ⑪
	[s]	Before a consonant, and, increasingly, even between vowels, like English *s*end → ⑫
y	[j]	Like English *y*es → ⑬
	[ʒ]	In some parts of Latin America, like English lei*s*ure → ⑭
z	[θ]	Like English *th*in → ⑮
	[s]	In some parts of Spain and in Latin America, like English *s*end → ⑯

Examples

1. hombre ['ombre] hoja ['oxa] ahorrar [ao'rrar]

2. jota ['xota] tejer [te'xer] reloj [re'lo(h)]

3. calle ['kaʎe] llamar [ʎa'mar]

4. pillar [pi'jar/pi'ʒar] olla ['oja/'oʒa]

5. enviar [em'bjar] sin valor ['sim ba'lor]

6. uña ['uɲa] bañar [ba'ɲar]

7. aquel [a'kel] querer [ke'rer]

8. está [es'ta] serio ['serjo]

9. desde ['dezðe] mismo ['mizmo] asno ['azno]

10. wáter ['bater] Walkman® [wak'man]

11. éxito ['eksito] máximo ['maksimo]

12. extra ['estra] sexto ['sesto]

13. yo [jo] yedra ['jeðra]

14. yeso ['ʒeso] yerno ['ʒerno]

15. zapato [θa'pato] zona ['θona] luz [luθ]

16. zaguán [sa'ʎwan] zueco ['sweko] pez [pes]

Normal Word Stress

There are simple rules to establish which syllable in a Spanish word is stressed. When an exception to these rules occurs an acute accent (stress-mark) is needed (see page 296). These rules are as follows:

- words ending in a vowel or combination of vowels, or with the consonants -s or -n are stressed on the next to last syllable. The great majority of Spanish words fall into this category → ①
- words ending in a consonant other than -s or -n bear the stress on the last syllable → ②
- a minority of words bear the stress on the second to last syllable, and these always need an accent → ③
- some nouns change their stress from singular to plural → ④

Stress in Diphthongs

In the case of diphthongs there are rules to establish which of the vowels is stressed (see page 288 for pronunciation). These rules are as follows:

- diphthongs formed by the combination of a 'weak' vowel (i, u) and a 'strong' vowel (a, e or o) bear the stress on the strong vowel → ⑤
- diphthongs formed by the combination of two 'weak' vowels bear the stress on the second vowel → ⑥

ⓘ Note: Two 'strong' vowels don't form a diphthong but are pronounced as two separate vowels. In these cases stress follows the normal rules → ⑦

Examples

1. casa house
   corre he runs
   palabra word
   crisis crisis

   casas houses
   corren they run
   palabras words
   crisis crises

2. reloj watch
   verdad truth
   batidor beater

3. murciélago bat
   pájaro bird

4. carácter character
   régimen regime

   caracteres characters
   regímenes regimes

5. baile dance
   boina beret
   peine comb
   causa cause
   reina queen

6. fui I went
   viudo widower

7. me mareo I feel dizzy
   caer to fall
   caos chaos
   correa leash

The Acute Accent (´)

This is used in writing to show that a word is stressed contrary to the normal rules for stress (see page 294) → ❶

The following points should be noted:

The same syllable is stressed in the plural form of adjectives and nouns as in the singular. To show this, it is necessary to
- add an accent in the case of unaccented nouns and adjectives ending in -n → ❷
- drop the accent from nouns and adjectives ending in -n or -s which have an accent on the last syllable → ❸

The feminine form of accented nouns or adjectives does not have an accent → ❹

When object pronouns are added to certain verb forms an accent is required to show that the syllable stressed in the verb form does not change. These verb forms are:
- the gerund → ❺
- the infinitive, when followed by two pronouns → ❻
- imperative forms, except for the 2nd person plural → ❼

The absolute superlative forms of adjectives are always accented → ❽

Accents on adjectives are not affected by the addition of the adverbial suffix -mente → ❾

Examples

1 autobús
bus
relámpago
lightning

revolución
revolution
árboles
trees

2 orden → órdenes
order **orders**
examen → exámenes
examination **examinations**
joven → jóvenes
young **young**

3 revolución → revoluciones
revolution **revolutions**
autobús → autobuses
bus **buses**
parlanchín → parlanchines
chatty **chatty**

4 marqués → marquesa
marquis **marchioness**
francés → francesa
French (_masc_**)** **French (**_fem_**)**

5 comprando → comprándo(se)lo
buying **buying it (for him/her/them)**

6 vender → vendérselas
to sell **to sell them to him/her/them**

7 compra → cómpralo
buy **buy it**
hagan → háganselo
do **do it for him/her/them**

8 viejo → viejísimo
old **ancient**
caro → carísimo
expensive **very expensive**

9 fácil → fácilmente
easy **easily**

The Acute Accent *continued*

It is also used to distinguish between the written forms of words which are pronounced the same but have a different meaning or function. These are as follows:

Possessive adjectives/personal pronouns → ❶

Demonstrative adjectives/demonstrative pronouns → ❷

Interrogative and exclamatory forms of adverbs, pronouns and adjectives → ❸

ⓘ Note: The accent is used in indirect as well as direct questions and exclamations → ❹

The pronoun él and the article el → ❺

A small group of words which could otherwise be confused. These are:

de	of, from	dé	give (*pres. subj.*)
mas	but	más	more
si	if	sí	yes; himself etc → ❻
solo/a	alone	sólo	only → ❼
te	you	té	tea

The Dieresis (¨)

This is used only in the combinations güi or güe to show that the u is pronounced as a semi-consonant (see page 288) → ❽

Examples

① Han robado mi coche — They've stolen my car
A mí no me vio — He didn't see me
¿Te gusta tu trabajo? — Do you like your job?
Tú, ¿que opinas? — What do you think?

② Me gusta esta casa — I like this house
Me quedo con ésta — I'll take this one
¿Ves aquellos edificios? — Can you see those buildings?
Aquéllos son más bonitos — Those are prettier

③ El chico con quien viajé — The boy I travelled with
¿Con quién viajaste? — Who did you travel with?
Donde quieras — Wherever you want
¿Dónde encontraste eso? — Where did you find that?

④ ¿Cómo se abre? — How does it open?
No sé cómo se abre — I don't know how it opens

⑤ El puerto queda cerca — The harbour's nearby
Él no quiso hacerlo — *He* refused to do it

⑥ si no viene — if he doesn't come
Sí que lo sabe — Yes he *does* know

⑦ Vino solo — He came by himself
Sólo lo sabe él — Only he knows

⑧ ¡Qué vergüenza! — How shocking!
En seguida averigüé dónde estaba — I found out straight away where it was

Regular Spelling Changes

The consonants c, g and z are modified by the addition of certain verb or plural endings and by some suffixes. Most of the cases where this occurs have already been dealt with under the appropriate part of speech, but are summarized here along with other instances not covered elsewhere.

Verbs

The changes set out below occur so that the consonant of the verb stem is always pronounced the same as in the infinitive. For verbs affected by these changes see the list of verbs on page 81.

INFINITIVE	CHANGE			TENSES AFFECTED	
-car	c + e	→	-que	Present subj, pret →	❶
-cer, -cir	c + a, o	→	-za, -zo	Present, pres subj →	❷
-gar	g + e, i	→	-gue	Present subj, pret →	❸
-guar	gu + e	→	-güe	Present subj, pret →	❹
-ger, -gir	g + a, o	→	-ja, -jo	Present, pres subj →	❺
-guir	gu + a, o	→	-ga, -go	Present, pres subj →	❻
-zar	z + e	→	-ce	Present subj, pret →	❼

Noun and adjective plurals

SINGULAR		PLURAL	
vowel + z	→	-ces →	❽

Nouns and adjectives + suffixes

ENDING	SUFFIX	NEW ENDING	
vowel + z +	-cito	-cecito →	❾
-go, -ga +	-ito, -illo	-guito/a, -guillo/a →	❿
-co, -ca +	-ito, -illo	-quito/a, -quillo/a →	⓫

Adjective absolute superlatives

ENDING	SUPERLATVE	
-co	-quísimo →	⓬
-go	-guísimo →	⓭
vowel + z	-císimo →	⓮

1 Es inútil que lo busques aquí — It's no good looking for it here

Saqué dos entradas — I got two tickets

2 Hace falta que venzas tu miedo — You must overcome your fear

3 No creo que lleguemos antes — I don't think we'll be there any sooner

Ya le pagué — I've already paid her

4 Averigüé dónde estaba la casa — I found out where the house was

5 Cojo el autobús, es más barato — I take the bus, it's cheaper

6 ¿Sigo? — Shall I go on?

7 No permiten que se cruce la frontera — They don't allow people to cross the border

Nunca simpaticé mucho con él — I never got on very well with him

8
voz	→	voces	luz	→	luces
voice		voices	light		lights
veloz	→	veloces	capaz	→	capaces
quick			capable		

9 luz → lucecita

light — little light

10 amigo → amiguito

friend — chum

11 chico → chiquillo

boy — little boy

12 rico → riquísimo

rich — extremely rich

13 largo → larguísimo

long — very, very long

14 feroz → ferocísimo

fierce — extremely fierce

The Alphabet

A, a [a]	J, j ['xota]	R, r ['erre]
B, b [be]	K, k [ka]	S, s ['ese]
C, c [θe]	L, l ['ele]	T, t [te]
Ch, ch [tʃe]	Ll, ll ['eʎe]	U, u [u]
D, d [de]	M, m ['eme]	V, v ['uβe]
E, e [e]	N, n ['ene]	W, w ['uβe'doble]
F, f ['efe]	Ñ, ñ ['eɲe]	X, x ['ekis]
G, g [xe]	O, o [o]	Y, y [i'ɣrjeɣa]
H, h ['atʃe]	P, p [pe]	Z, z ['θeta]
I, i [i]	Q, q [ku]	

The letters are feminine and you therefore talk of **una a**, or **la a**.

Capital letters are used as in English except for the following:

> adjectives of nationality:
> e.g. **una ciudad alemana** a German town
> **un autor español** a Spanish author

> languages:
> e.g. **¿Habla Vd inglés?** Do you speak English?
> **Hablan español e italiano** They speak Spanish and Italian

> days of the week:
> | | |
> |---|---|
> | **lunes** Monday | **viernes** Friday |
> | **martes** Tuesday | **sábado** Saturday |
> | **miércoles** Wednesday | **domingo** Sunday |
> | **jueves** Thursday | |

> months of the year:
> | | |
> |---|---|
> | **enero** January | **julio** July |
> | **febrero** February | **agosto** August |
> | **marzo** March | **se(p)tiembre** September |
> | **abril** April | **octubre** October |
> | **mayo** May | **noviembre** November |
> | **junio** June | **diciembre** December |

Punctuation

Spanish punctuation differs from English in the following ways:

Question marks

There are inverted question marks and exclamation marks at the beginning of a question or exclamation, as well as upright ones at the end.

Indications of dialogue

Dashes are used to indicate dialogue, and are equivalent to the English inverted commas:

> – ¿Vendrás conmigo? – le preguntó María
> 'Will you come with me?' Maria asked him

ⓘ Note: When no expression of saying, replying etc follows, only one dash is used at the beginning:
> – Sí. 'Yes.'

Letter headings

At the beginning of a letter, a colon is used instead of the English comma:

> Querida Cristina: **Dear Cristina,** Muy Sr. mío: **Dear Sir,**

Punctuation terms in Spanish

.	**punto**	!	**se cierra admiración**
,	**coma**	" "	**comillas** (used as '...')
;	**punto y coma**	"	**se abren comillas**
:	**dos puntos**	"	**se cierran comillas**
...	**puntos suspensivos**	( )	**paréntesis**
¿?	**interrogación**	(	**se abre paréntesis**
¿	**se abre interrogación**	)	**se cierra paréntesis**
?	**se cierra interrogación**	–	**guión**
¡!	**admiración**		
¡	**se abre admiración**	**punto y aparte**	**new paragraph**
		punto final	**last full stop**

Numbers

Cardinal (one, two, three *etc*)

cero	0	setenta	70
uno (un, una)	1	ochenta	80
dos	2	noventa	90
tres	3	cien (ciento)	100
cuatro	4	ciento uno(una)	101
cinco	5	ciento dos	102
seis	6	ciento diez	110
siete	7	ciento cuarenta y dos	142
ocho	8	doscientos(as)	200
nueve	9	doscientos(as) uno(una)	201
diez	10	doscientos(as) dos	202
once	11	trescientos(as)	300
doce	12	cuatrocientos(as)	400
trece	13	quinientos(as)	500
catorce	14	seiscientos(as)	600
quince	15	setecientos(as)	700
dieciséis	16	ochocientos(as)	800
diecisiete	17	novecientos(as)	900
dieciocho	18	mil	1.000
diecinueve	19	mil uno(una)	1.001
veinte	20	mil dos	1.002
veintiuno	21	mil doscientos veinte	1.220
veintidós	22	dos mil	2.000
treinta	30	cien mil	100.000
treinta y uno	31	doscientos(as) mil	200.000
cuarenta	40	un millón	1.000.000
cincuenta	50	dos millones	2.000.000
sesenta	60	un billón	1.000.000.000.000

Fractions

un medio; medio(a)	½
un tercio	⅓
dos tercios	⅔
un cuarto	¼
tres cuartos	¾
un quinto	⅕
cinco y tres cuartos	5¾

Others

cero coma cinco	0,5
uno coma tres	1,3
(el, un) diez por ciento	10%
dos más/y dos	2 + 2
dos menos dos	2 − 2
dos por dos	2 × 2
dos dividido por dos	2 ÷ 2

Points to note on cardinals

uno drops the o before masculine nouns, and the same applies when in compound numerals:
- un libro 1 book, treinta y un niños 31 children

1, 21, 31 etc and 200, 300, 400 etc have feminine forms:
- cuarenta y una euros 41 euros, quinientas libras £500

ciento is used before numbers smaller than 100, otherwise cien is used:
- ciento cuatro 104 but cien euros 100 euros, cien mil 100,000 (see also page 210)

millón takes de before a noun:
- un millón de personas 1,000,000 people

mil is only found in the plural when meaning thousands of:
- miles de solicitantes thousands of applicants

cardinals normally precede ordinals:
- los tres primeros pisos the first three floors

ⓘ Note: The full stop is used with numbers over one thousand and the comma with decimals i.e. the opposite of English usage.

Ordinal Numbers (first, second, third *etc*)

primero (primer, primera)	1°,1ª	undécimo(a)	11°,11ª
segundo(a)	2°,2ª	duodécimo(a)	12°,12ª
tercero (tercer, tercera)	3°,3ª	decimotercer(o)(a)	13°,13ª
cuarto(a)	4°,4ª	decimocuarto(a)	14°,14ª
quinto(a)	5°,5ª	decimoquinto(a)	15°,15ª
sexto(a)	6°,6ª	decimosexto(a)	16°,16ª
séptimo(a)	7°,7ª	decimoséptimo(a)	17°,17ª
octavo(a)	8°,8ª	decimoctavo(a)	18°,18ª
noveno(a)	9°,9ª	decimonoveno(a)	19°,19ª
décimo(a)	10°,10ª	vigésimo(a)	20°,20ª

Points to note on ordinals

They agree in gender and in number with the noun, which they normally precede, except with royal titles:

> la primera vez the first time
> Felipe segundo Philip ll

primero and tercero drop the o before a masculine singular noun:

> el primer premio the first prize
> el tercer día the third day

Beyond décimo ordinal numbers are rarely used, and they are replaced by the cardinal number placed immediately after the noun:

> el siglo diecisiete the seventeenth century
> Alfonso doce Alfonso XII
> en el piso trece on the 13th floor

> BUT: vigésimo(a) 20th
> (but not with royal titles or centuries)
> centésimo(a) 100th
> milésimo(a) 1,000th
> millonésimo(a) 1,000,000th

Other Uses

collective numbers:

un par	2, a couple
una decena (de personas)	about 10 (people)
una docena (de niños)	(about) a dozen (children)
una quincena (de hombres)	about fifteen (men)
una veintena* (de coches)	about twenty (cars)
un centenar, una centena (de casas)	about a hundred (houses)
cientos/centenares de personas	hundreds of people
un millar (de soldados)	about a thousand (soldiers)
miles/millares de moscas	thousands of flies

* 20, 30, 40, 50 can also be converted in the same way.

measurements:

veinte metros cuadrados	20 square metres
veinte metros cúbicos	20 cubic metres
un puente de cuarenta metros de largo/longitud	a bridge 40 metres long

distance:

De aquí a Madrid hay 400 km	Madrid is 400 km away
a siete km de aquí	7 km from here

Telephone numbers

Póngame con Madrid, el cuatro, cincuenta y ocho, veintidós, noventa y tres
  I would like Madrid 458 22 93
Me da Valencia, el veinte, cincuenta y uno, setenta y tres
  Could you get me Valencia 20 51 73
Extensión tres, tres, cinco/trescientos treinta y cinco
  Extension number 335

ⓘ Note: In Spanish telephone numbers may be read out individually, but more frequently they are broken down into groups of two. They are written in groups of two or three numbers (never four).

The Time

¿Qué hora es? *What time is it?*
Es ... *(1 o'clock, midnight, noon)* ⎤ It's ...
Son las ... *(other times)* ⎦
Es la una y cuarto   It's 1.15
Son las diez menos cinco   It's 9.55

00.00	**medianoche; las doce (de la noche)** midnight, twelve o'clock
00.10	**las doce y diez (de la noche)**
00.15	**las doce y cuarto**
00.30	**las doce y media**
00.45	**la una menos cuarto**
01.00	**la una (de la madrugada)** one a.m., one o'clock in the morning
01.10	**la una y diez (de la madrugada)**
02.45	**las tres menos cuarto**
07.00	**las siete (de la mañana)**
07.50	**las ocho menos diez**
12.00	**mediodía; las doce (de la mañana)** noon, twelve o'clock
13.00	**la una (de la tarde)** one p.m., one o'clock in the afternoon
19.00	**las siete (de la tarde)** seven p.m., seven o'clock in the evening
21.00	**las nueve (de la noche)** nine p.m., nine o'clock at night

ⓘ Note: When referring to a timetable, the 24 hour clock is used:

las dieciséis cuarenta y cinco   16.45
las veintiuna quince   21.15

Examples

¿A qué hora vas a venir?	What time are you coming?
— A las siete	— At seven o'clock
Las oficinas cierran de dos a cuatro	The offices are closed from two until four
Vendré a eso de/hacia las siete y media	I'll come at around 7.30
a las seis y pico	just after 6 o'clock
a las cinco en punto	at 5 o'clock sharp
entre las ocho y las nueve	between 8 and 9 o'clock
Son más de las tres y media	It's after half past three
Hay que estar allí lo más tarde a las diez	You have to be there by ten o'clock at the latest
Tiene para media hora	He'll be half an hour (at it)
Estuvo sin conocimiento durante un cuarto de hora	She was unconscious for a quarter of an hour
Les estoy esperando desde hace una hora/desde las dos	I've been waiting for them for an hour/since two o'clock
Se fueron hace unos minutos	They left a few minutes ago
Lo hice en veinte minutos	I did it in twenty minutes
El tren llega dentro de una hora	The train arrives in an hour('s time)
¿Cuánto (tiempo) dura la película?	How long does the film last?
por la mañana/tarde/noche	in the morning/afternoon or evening/at night
mañana por la mañana	tomorrow morning
ayer por la tarde	yesterday afternoon or evening
anoche	last night
anteayer	the day before yesterday
pasado mañana	the day after tomorrow

Dates

¿Qué día es hoy?	What's the date today?
¿A qué día estamos?	
Es (el) ...	It's the ...
Estamos a ...	
uno/primero de mayo	1st of May
dos de mayo	2nd of May
veintiocho de mayo	28th of May
lunes tres de octubre	Monday the 3rd of October
Vienen el siete de marzo	They're coming on the 7th of March

ⓘ Note: Use cardinal numbers for dates. Only for the first of the month can the ordinal number sometimes be used.

Years

Nací en 1990	I was born in 1990
el veinte de enero de mil novecientos noventa	(on) 20th January 1990

Other expressions

en los años cincuenta	during the fifties
en el siglo veinte	in the twentieth century
en mayo	in May
lunes (quince)	Monday (the 15th)
el quince de marzo	on March the 15th
el/los lunes	on Monday/Mondays
dentro de diez días	in 10 days' time
hace diez días	10 days ago

Age

¿Qué edad tiene?	How old is he/she?
¿Cuántos años tiene?	
Tiene 23 (años)	He/She is 23
Tiene unos 40 años	He/She is around 40
A los 21 años	At the age of 21

Index

The following index lists comprehensively both grammatical terms and key words in English and Spanish.

Index

Index

Index

Index

Index

Index

Index